RIA Federal Tax Handbook Quick Reference Card
2013 Income, Estate and Gift Tax Rates

Single Taxpayers

Taxable income	Amount of tax
Not over $ 8,925	10% of taxable income
Over $ 8,925 but not over $ 36,250	$ 892.50 plus 15% of the amount over $ 8,925
Over $ 36,250 but not over $ 87,850	$ 4,991.25 plus 25% of the amount over $ 36,250
Over $ 87,850 but not over $ 183,250	$ 17,891.25 plus 28% of the amount over $ 87,850
Over $ 183,250 but not over $ 398,350	$ 44,603.25 plus 33% of the amount over $ 183,250
Over $ 398,350 but not over $400,000	$ 115,586.25 plus 35% of the amount over $ 398,350
Over $ 400,000	$ 116,163.75 plus 39.6% of the amount over $ 400,000

Married Taxpayers Filing Separate Returns

Taxable income	Amount of tax
Not over $ 8,925	10% of taxable income
Over $ 8,925 but not over $ 36,250	$ 892.50 plus 15% of the amount over $ 8,925
Over $ 36,250 but not over $ 73,200	$ 4,991.25 plus 25% of the amount over $ 36,250
Over $ 73,200 but not over $ 111,525	$ 14,228.75 plus 28% of the amount over $ 73,200
Over $ 111,525 but not over $ 199,175	$ 24,959.75 plus 33% of the amount over $ 111,525
Over $ 199,175 but not over $225,000	$ 53,884.25 plus 35% of the amount over $ 199,175
Over $ 225,000	$ 62,923 plus 39.6% of the amount over $ 225,000

Estates and Trusts

Taxable income	Amount of tax
Not over $ 2,450	15% of taxable income
Over $ 2,450 but not over $ 5,700	$ 367.50 plus 25% of the amount over $ 2,450
Over $ 5,700 but not over $ 8,750	$ 1,180 plus 28% of the amount over $ 5,700
Over $ 8,750 but not over $ 11,950	$ 2,034 plus 33% of the amount over $ 8,750
Over $ 11,950	$ 3,090 plus 39.6% of the amount over $ 11,950

Bankruptcy estates use the rate schedules for married taxpayers filing separate returns.

Standard Deductions

Basic*

Single or married filing separate	$ 6,100
Married filing joint and surviving spouses	$ 12,200
Head of household	$ 8,950

Additional (for 65 or over and/or blind)

Unmarried (including head of household)	$ 1,500
Married or surviving spouse (whether or not joint return)	$ 1,200

* Limited to greater of $ 1,000 or the sum of $ 350 plus earned income for individuals who can be claimed as a dependent by another taxpayer.

Married Taxpayers Filing Joint Returns and Qualifying Widows and Widowers

Taxable income	Amount of tax
Not over $ 17,850	10% of taxable income
Over $ 17,850 but not over $ 72,500	$ 1,785 plus 15% of the amount over $ 17,850
Over $ 72,500 but not over $ 146,400	$ 9,982.50 plus 25% of the amount over $ 72,500
Over $ 146,400 but not over $ 223,050	$ 28,457.50 plus 28% of the amount over $ 146,400
Over $ 223,050 but not over $ 398,350	$ 49,919.50 plus 33% of the amount over $ 223,050
Over $ 398,350 but not over $450,000	$ 107,768.50 plus 35% of the amount over $ 398,350
Over $ 450,000	$ 125,846 plus 39.6% of the amount over $ 450,000

Heads Of Household

Taxable income	Amount of tax
Not over $ 12,750	10% of taxable income
Over $ 12,750 but not over $ 48,600	$ 1,275 plus 15% of the amount over $ 12,750
Over $ 48,600 but not over $ 125,450	$ 6,652.50 plus 25% of the amount over $ 48,600
Over $ 125,450 but not over $ 203,150	$ 25,865 plus 28% of the amount over $ 125,450
Over $ 203,150 but not over $ 398,350	$ 47,621 plus 33% of the amount over $ 203,150
Over $ 398,350 but not over $ 425,000	$ 112,037 plus 35% of the amount over $ 398,350
Over $ 425,000	$ 121,364.50 plus 39.6% of the amount over $ 425,000

Capital gains and qualified dividend income*— Individuals, Estates & Trusts

Net short-term (held one year or less) capital gain is taxed at: Ordinary income rates

Long-term (held more than one year) **capital gain** and **qualified dividend income*** are taxed at:

0% (for gain otherwise taxable at 10% or 15% rate); 15% (for gain otherwise taxable at 25%, 28%, 33% or 35% rates); 20% (for gain otherwise taxable at 39.6% rate)

Except the maximum tax on:

Unrecaptured section 1250 gain (attributable to real estate depreciation) is:	25%
Collectibles gain (on works of art, rugs, antiques, etc.) is:	28%
Section 1202 gain (from the sale of small business stock eligible for partial exclusion from gross income) is:	28%

* Dividends from domestic corporations and qualified foreign corporations that meet specified holding period requirements. Exclusions may apply.

Standard Mileage Rates

Business use of auto	56.5¢ a mile
Charitable	14¢
Medical	24¢
Moving expenses	24¢

RIA Federal Tax Handbook Quick Reference Card
2013 Income, Estate and Gift Tax Rates

Itemized Deductions Percentage Limitations

Medical expenses	10% of adjusted gross income (AGI)—floor*
Personal interest	0%
Net nonbusiness casualty losses	10% of AGI (after $100 per casualty limitation) — floor
Charitable contributions	50%** of AGI—ceiling on deductible amount
Miscellaneous itemized deductions	2% of AGI—floor

* 7.5% if taxpayer or spouse attained age 65 by year end.

** Other limits apply depending on type of gift and/or recipient.

Personal Exemption

Exemption amount $3,900

Alternative Minimum Tax

AMT rates (on taxable excess — i.e., alternative minimum taxable income less exemption amount):

Individual, estate, trust:*	26% of taxable excess that doesn't exceed $179,500 ($89,750 for married filing separately)
	28% of taxable excess that exceeds $179,500 ($89,750 for married filing separately)
Corporation (other than an exempt small corporation):	20% of taxable excess

*Tax rate on net capital gain is the same as for regular tax.

AMT Exemption Amounts		Phaseout range
Single*	$51,900	$115,400 – 323,000
Married filing separate**	40,400	76,950 – 238,550
Joint filers or surviving spouse	80,800	153,900 – 477,100
Estate, trust	23,100	76,950 – 169,350
Corporation	40,000	150,000 – 310,000

* Special calculations apply to child subject to the kiddie tax.

** Must also add to AMTI the lesser of $40,400 or 25% of the excess of AMTI (without regard to the exemption reduction) over $238,550.

2013 Social Security Tax

FICA	Tax base	Rate	Maximum tax
Social Security			
Employer's share	$ 113,700	6.2%	$ 7,049.40
Employee's share	$ 113,700	6.2%	$ 7,049.40
Medicare			
Employers	no limit	1.45%	no limit
Employees	no limit*	1.45%/2.35%*	no limit*

* Employees pay 1.45% on the first $200,000 of wages ($250,000 of combined wages on a joint return; $125,000 on a separate return), and 2.35% (1.45% plus 0.9%) on wages in excess of these amounts.

2013 Self-Employment Tax

FICA	Tax base	Rate	Maximum tax
Social Security	$ 113,700	12.4%	$ 14,098.80
Medicare	no limit*	2.9%/3.8%*	no limit*

* Self-employeds pay 2.9% on the first $200,000 of self-employment (SE) income ($125,000 on a separate return, $250,000 of combined SE income on a joint return), and 3.8% (2.9% plus 0.9%) on SE income in excess of these amounts.

Corporations

Taxable income	Amount of tax
Not over $ 50,000	15% of taxable income
Over $ 50,000 but not over $ 75,000	$ 7,500 plus 25% of the amount over $ 50,000
Over $ 75,000 but not over $ 100,000	$ 13,750 plus 34% of the amount over $ 75,000
Over $ 100,000 but not over $ 335,000	$ 22,250 plus 39% of the amount over $ 100,000
Over $ 335,000 but not over $ 10,000,000	$ 113,900 plus 34% of the amount over $ 335,000
Over $ 10,000,000 but not over $ 15,000,000	$ 3,400,000 plus 35% of the amount over $ 10,000,000
Over $ 15,000,000 but not over $ 18,333,333	$ 5,150,000 plus 38% of the amount over $ 15,000,000
Over $ 18,333,333	35% of taxable income

Capital gains are taxable at regular corporate rates. The tax on qualified personal service corporations is 35% of taxable income.

Estate and Gift Tax Rates

For 2013, the estate tax and gift tax rates are as listed below, and a $5,250,000 exemption applies for both taxes:

If the amount with respect to which the tentative tax to be computed is:	The tentative tax is
Not over $ 10,000	18% of such amount
Over $ 10,000 but not over $ 20,000	$ 1,800, plus 20% of the excess over $ 10,000
Over $ 20,000 but not over $ 40,000	$ 3,800, plus 22% of the excess over $ 20,000
Over $ 40,000 but not over $ 60,000	$ 8,200, plus 24% of the excess over $ 40,000
Over $ 60,000 but not over $ 80,000	$ 13,000, plus 26% of the excess over $ 60,000
Over $ 80,000 but not over $ 100,000	$ 18,200, plus 28% of the excess over $ 80,000
Over $ 100,000 but not over $ 150,000	$ 23,800, plus 30% of the excess over $ 100,000
Over $ 150,000 but not over $ 250,000	$ 38,800, plus 32% of the excess over $ 150,000
Over $ 250,000 but not over $ 500,000	$ 70,800, plus 34% of the excess over $ 250,000
Over $ 500,000 but not over $750,000	$ 155,800, plus 37% of the excess over $ 500,000
Over $ 750,000 but not over $1,000,000	$ 248,300, plus 39% of the excess over $ 750,000
Over $ 1,000,000	$345,800, plus 40% of the excess over $1,000,000

3.8% Tax on Individuals' Net Investment Income

Individuals with modified AGI (MAGI) over $200,000 ($250,000 for joint filers or surviving spouses; $125,000 for married separate filers) must pay the Net Investment Income Tax (not withheld), which is 3.8% of the lesser of: (1) "net investment income" (interest, dividends, etc.), or (2) MAGI over these thresholds.

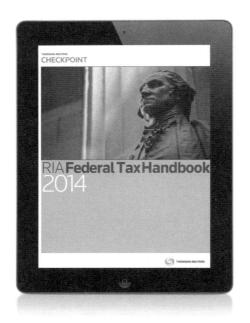

RIA® Book-Based Self-Study

Presented in Partnership with PPC

Expert coverage of tax and accounting issues from Thomson Reuters

For more than 70 years, RIA has delivered accurate, insightful and accessible research and productivity-enhancing solutions to tax, accounting and corporate finance professionals.

Visit tax.thomsonreuters.com/store to learn more about additional products available such as the 2014 RIA FEDERAL TAX HANDBOOK, the premier source for today's federal tax law.

Rely on RIA's must-have Federal Tax Review

RIA Federal Tax Review Course 2014

The RIA *Federal Tax Review 2014* CPE Course is comprised of three modules: Individual Taxes (8 CPE), Business Taxes (10 CPE), and Special Situations (9 CPE). A general refresher in federal taxation, this course will reinforce basic tax law interpretations to keep you up to date on the latest and most important changes for both the 2013 and 2014 tax years.

Grading fee of $95 for each module, with discounts available if you complete two or all three modules—see website for details.

Immediate RIA course access plus Online Grading

Download PDF version of this course at no charge!
At cl.thomsonreuters.com, click on the "Find a CPE Course" link in the top menu and type "RIA" under Keywords.

> **RIA self-study grading fees are included with the Premier and Premier Plus CPE Packages! Details on reverse.**

Online Grading for immediate results!
The Checkpoint Learning Online Grading Center provides convenient access to self-study course exams, with real-time test results as soon as you complete your courses. Print CPE certificates with a simple mouse click—the Online Grading Center retains all of your certificates and exam results for retrieval at any time!

For more CPE information and to access the PDF download of this course or the online grading tool for this course, visit cl.thomsonreuters.com.

RFBB013

CHECKPOINT LEARNING

Checkpoint Learning

1-800-231-1860 | cl.thomsonreuters.com

ONLINE LEARNING

Checkpoint Learning Platform
Checkpoint Learning provides reporting, learning reminders and prompts, CPE compliance tracking, and much more—including the ability to purchase and complete hundreds of courses directly from Checkpoint Learning.

Checkpoint Learning CPE Packages
Our single-price comprehensive subscriptions are an industry first, bringing all of your CPE needs together: online and print-based self-study courses; webinars; CPE tracking and compliance monitoring; plus huge discounts on live seminars and conferences! Visit website for details on the Premier, Premier Plus, Compliance, and Professional CPE Packages.

MicroMash
A trusted provider of technology-based CPE and training for over 20 years. Choose from over 200 courses on hot topics that will help you stay on top of your field.

PASS Online
A CPE provider since 1990, PASS Online offers more than 140 interactive courses covering a variety of accounting and tax topics, including industry-leading state and specialty ethics training courses.

Checkpoint Learning Webinars
You'll find webinars (with live streaming video) on the latest developments in tax, accounting, auditing, finance and more!

SELF-STUDY COURSES

Gear Up Self-Study
Standalone and seminar-based self-study courses.

PPC Self-Study
Convenient self-study courses are available on a variety of accounting & auditing and tax topics , related to PPC Guides.

Quickfinder Self-Study
Quickfinder's trusted content combined with Gear Up's expertise in tax & accounting professional education.

IN-HOUSE TRAINING

PPC In-House Seminars
On-site customized training on over 50 topics related to accounting and tax professions. This learning experience is custom-tailored to meet your needs, taught by highly rated instructors, and features current, relevant course content. For more information call 1-800-387-1120.

Practitioners Monthly Video Digest
A convenient and cost-effective way for firms to provide timely, leading-edge in-house training, with monthly training modules (excluding February and March) that contain DVD instructor's guide and participant materials.

AuditWatch
AuditWatch has an intense focus on serving the audit and accounting profession with leading experts to train and consult with firms that provide auditing services. Call 1-800-775-9866 for more information.

LIVE SEMINARS & CONFERENCES

Gear Up Live Seminars & Conferences
A leading provider of tax and accounting education for more than 40 years, with nationwide combining seminars and exciting conferences! Week-long conferences take place throughout the year in Chicago, Las Vegas, and Orlando.

AuditWatch Live Seminars
Staff training programs in 15 locations nationwide, including AuditWatch University, Yellow Book University, and TaxWatch University.

For more CPE information on all of these solutions and products, visit cl.thomsonreuters.com.

THOMSON REUTERS
CHECKPOINT™

RIA Federal Tax Handbook

Information Products Staff

James F. Fegen, Jr.
Senior Vice President,
Product Operations

Cornell R. Fuerst
(J.D., NY Bar)
Director, Federal Taxes

Christine Carr
Director, Data
Management

Mark Sheiner
Senior Product
Manager

Laurie Asch
(LL.M., NY Bar)
Managing Editor

Kersten Behrens
(J.D., NY, NJ Bar)
Managing Editor

John G. Clark
(LL.M., NY Bar)
Managing Editor

Thomas Long
(LL.M., NY, NJ Bar)
Managing Editor

Dennis P. McMahon
(LL.M., NY,
MA Bar)
Managing Editor

Richard S. Nadler
(LL.M., NY Bar)
Managing Editor

Jeffrey N. Pretsfelder
(J.D., C.P.A., NJ, NY Bar)
Managing Editor

Suzanne Baillie Schmitt
(LL.M., NY Bar)
Managing Editor

David Freid
(J.D., NY Bar)
Senior Editor

Elyce Friedfeld
(LL.M., NY Bar)
Senior Editor

Lesli S. Laffie
(LL.M., NY, NJ Bar)
Senior Editor

Carla M. Martin
(LL.M., AL, FL Bar)
Senior Editor

Marian Rosenberg
(LL.M., NY Bar)
Senior Editor

Simon Schneebalg
(LL.M., NY Bar)
Senior Editor

Richard H. Sternberg
(LL.M., NY Bar)
Senior Editor

Scott E. Weiner
(J.D., NY Bar)
Senior Editor

Stanley V. Baginski
(LL.M., NY Bar)
Senior Project Editor

E.H. Rubinsky
(LL.M., NY Bar)
Senior Project Editor

Rosemary Saldan-Pawson
(J.D., NY, KS Bar)
Senior Project Editor

Harris Abrams
(LL.M., PA Bar)

Wendy C. Bicovny
(LL.M., C.P.A.,
NY, CA Bar)

Mary-Agnes Bornhoeft
(J.D., NY Bar)

Gary S. Bronstein
(LL.M., CA,
MA Bar)

Steve Brylski
(LL.M., NY Bar)

Gregory J. Evanella
(J.D., NJ Bar)

Elizabeth A. Feeley
(LL.M., NY Bar)

Rachel Glatt
(J.D., NY Bar)

Catherine Graf
(J.D., C.P.A.,
NY Bar)

Rex J. Iacurci
(LL.M., C.P.A., CT Bar)

Min Soo Kim
(LL.M., NY Bar)

Kevin Ledig
(J.D., NY, NJ Bar)

Michael A. Levin
(J.D., NY Bar)

Gwenn Lukas
(LL.M., IL, WI Bar)

Elizabeth McLeod
(J.D., NY Bar)

Shilpa Mirchandani
(LL.M., FL Bar)

Sean Mitts
(J.D., NY Bar)

Catherine E. Murray
(LL.M., NY Bar)

Cara O'Brien
(LL.M., NY Bar)

Richard O'Donnell
(LL.M., NJ Bar (Retired))

Peter Ogrodnik
(LL.M., NJ Bar)

Michael E. Overton
(LL.M., NY,
VA Bar)

Tola Ozim
(J.D., NY Bar)

Karen A. Rennie
(LL.M., NY Bar)

Karen E. Rodrigues
(LL.M., TX Bar)

Julie S. Rose
(J.D., CT Bar)

Robert Rywick
(J.D., NY Bar)

James Seidel
(LL.M., NY Bar)

Ralph M. Silberman
(J.D., VA, DC Bar)

David Simonetti
(LL.M., NY Bar)

Debrah M. Smith
(LL.M., NY,
NJ, PA Bar)

Kristina G. Smith
(J.D., NY, DC,
WY Bar)

Michael A. Sonnenblick
(LL.M., NY Bar)

Nicholas Stevens
(LL.M., NY, CA Bar)

Natalie Tal
(LL.M., NY Bar)

Robert Trinz
(M.A., M.S. (Tax))

Jabari M. Vaughn
(LL.M., NY Bar)

Anne Wagenbrenner
(LL.M., NY,
CT Bar)

Sidney Weinman
(J.D., NY, NJ Bar)

James M. Wilson
(LL.M., NY, GA Bar)

Elizabeth V. Zanet
(LL.M., NY Bar)

Data Management

Kurt Coffman,
Manager

Taji Mabra,
Manager

Ajeya Kumar B N,
Assistant Manager

June Babb,
Supervisor

Dino Colacito
Michael Gonzalez
Neville Lewin
Angel Morales
Brian Spach
Norine Wright

Ruby Charles,
Supervisor

Akinsheye Babb
Jon Benson
Lourdes Chin
Nancy Golden
Kathleen Griffin
Vijay Jagdeo
Henry Rodgers

Judy Cosme,
Supervisor

Deborah Aznar
Christopher Barbieri
Lisa Crater
Geneva Gittens
Robert Gleason
Andrew Pascual
Xiomara Tejeda

Dan Danquah,
Supervisor

Charlene Brown
Craig Clark
Lenar Clark
Anthony Kibort
Luke Sims
Lisa Zolesi

Gregg Reed Harris,
Supervisor

Michelle Bell
Natalie Carrero
Anissa Esquina
Ron Gittens
Anthony Guglielmo
Marcia Sam
Dominic Smith

Deepika Jaiwala,
Team Lead

Ravi Prasad Chari
Anuradha Kadari
Chirag Ravrani
Maneesha Sheshgir
Santosh Tiruvakour
Roja Prasanna Y
Narenreddy Yedla

Sri Rekha Lakkaraju,
Team Lead

Somrita Ganchoudhuri
Srikanth Kukunoor
Akifuddin Mohammed
Chandil Ponnu
Rahul Manudhanya
Varun Jain

Partha Sarathi Maitra,
Team Lead

Khaja Fareeduddin
Naga Laxmi Mantri
Sarveshwar Suluganti
Prashanth Reddy T

Helen McFarlane,
Supervisor

Melissa Acquafredda
Oksana Artemenko
Marie Rivera
Carol Watson
Brett Whitmoyer

Sue Ellen Sobel,
Supervisor

Alexis Brown
Frank Callan
Adel Faltas
Jennifer Huber
Stefan Kunar
Amelia Massiah

Tushar Shetty,
Supervisor

Raymond AuYeung
Ruth Garcia
Michelle Harmon
Cindy Sotero

Christopher Stryshak,
Supervisor

John Harrison
Mimoza Osmanaj

Senior Data
Support Coordinators

Joan Baselice
Andrew Glicklin
Lisa Sarracino
Jonathan Thayer
Melanie Thomas

Data Analysts

Lisa Alcock
Denise Dockery

Paralegals

Joann Casanova
Catherine Daleo
Monica Grier
Danny Wang

Legal Resource Center & Indexing

Peter Durham,
Manager

Tom Adewolu
Bernie Bayless
Pierre Calixte
Andrea Leal
Patricia Link
Theresa Scherne

To order additional copies of this publication, please call Toll Free 1-800-950-1216, ext. 1, or visit our Product Store at tax.thomsonreuters.com/store.

2014 RIA Federal Tax Handbook

The 2014 edition of the RIA Federal Tax Handbook is designed to answer the tax questions and resolve the tax problems that arise in everyday business and personal transactions. It helps in preparing 2013 federal income tax returns, and provides specific guidance to tax consequences of transactions occurring in 2014. It is prepared by the professional staff that prepares the comprehensive federal tax service, RIA's Federal Tax Coordinator 2d, and the complete income tax service, RIA's Analysis of Federal Taxes: Income, and is derived from these tax services and RIA's Tax Desk and Tax Guide.

The 2014 RIA Federal Tax Handbook reflects all federal tax legislation passed by Congress to date of publication. It also reflects other key developments (such as new regulations, rulings, and revenue procedures) affecting the 2013 return and the 2014 tax year.

✏️caution: For highlights of later-enacted tax laws that affect the 2014 edition, consult the homepage dedicated to Handbook users (tax.thomsonreuters.com/federaltaxhandbookupdates).

The Handbook discusses and explains common tax problems in clear, concise, nontechnical language. And, where appropriate, the Handbook includes:

✏️illustration: To clarify the tax rules and problems discussed, with simple, easy-to-follow illustrations.

✏️caution: To warn of dangers that arise in particular tax situations and, where appropriate, to indicate what should be done.

✏️recommendation: To provide specific, carefully studied guides to action which will keep taxes at a legal minimum.

✏️observation: For professional analysis or commentary that is not part of cited authorities.

Forms to use: The Handbook explains which IRS forms to use to report transactions, pay taxes, make elections, etc. For a complete list of all official forms discussed, with references to the paragraph where they are discussed, see the "Forms" entry in the Topic Index.

References: The Handbook uses the following references:

. . . "Code Sec." references are to sections of the Internal Revenue Code.

. . . "Reg § " references are to sections of the federal tax regulations. "Prop Reg § " references are to proposed regulations, which are only cited in the text where IRS has indicated that "Taxpayers may rely" on them.

. . . Footnote references beginning with a single letter are to paragraphs in RIA's Federal Tax Coordinator 2d and RIA's Analysis of Federal Taxes: Income. However, RIA's Analysis of Federal Taxes: Income doesn't include coverage of estate, gift and excise taxes. Accordingly, references to ¶Q-1000 *et seq.* (gift tax), ¶R-1000 *et seq.* (estate tax), and ¶W-1000 *et seq.* (excise taxes) are only to paragraphs in RIA's Federal Tax Coordinator 2d. References beginning with numbers are to paragraphs in RIA's United States Tax Reporter. References beginning with the letters "TD" are to paragraphs in RIA's Tax Desk.

¶ 101. Highlights of the 2014 Edition.

The 2014 RIA Federal Tax Handbook reflects federal tax laws enacted since publication of the 2013 edition in November of 2012—most notably, the American Taxpayer Relief Act of 2012 (P.L. 112-240, 1/2/2013). It also includes: the Supreme Court's landmark *Windsor* decision, which struck down a key section of the Defense of Marriage Act that had required same-sex spouses to be treated as unmarried for federal law purposes; IRS's post-*Windsor* guidance; the long-awaited capitalization vs. repair regulations; the most recent guidance on the newly effective 0.9% payroll tax on wages and self-employment income and 3.8% surtax on net investment income; and other key developments (such as new regulations, rulings and revenue procedures) affecting the 2013 return and the 2014 tax year.

What's new in the 2014 Edition. The 2014 RIA Federal Tax Handbook reflects the new tax developments listed below.

- "What's new on the 2013 IRS Form 1040." (¶105)
- 2013 and 2014 income tax rates for individuals, trusts and estates. (¶1100)
- 2013 and 2014 wage bases and rates for Social Security and Medicare taxes, for employers, employees and self-employed taxpayers. (¶1109).
- Draft tax tables for individuals. (¶1111 *et seq.*)
- 2013 and 2014 gift and estate tax rates. (¶1114)
- EGTRRA and JGTRRA sunsets are eliminated.
- Incentive to health care professionals and hospitals for using electronic records is income to recipients. (¶1206)
- IRS has delayed to 2014 implementing FICA guidance on employers treatment of tips and service charges. (¶1211)
- The maximum fair market value (FMV) for 2013 for which the fleet-average valuation method can be used is $21,200 for a passenger auto and $22,300 for a truck or van. (¶1233)
- The maximum FMV for 2013 for which the cents-per-mile valuation method can be used is $16,000 for passenger autos and $17,000 for a truck or van. (¶1236)
- For 2013, an employee may exclude up to $245 a month of employer-provided qualified parking, transit, and vanpooling benefits. For 2014, an employee can exclude up to $250 a month of employer-provided qualified parking benefits, and $130 for the combined value of transit passes and transportation in a commuter highway vehicle. (¶1247)
- For 2013, the maximum exclusion for employer-provided adoption assistance is $12,970 ($13,190 for 2014). (¶1254)
- IRS modified "use-or-lose" rule for health FSAs to allow employees to carry over up to $500 of unused amounts remaining at year-end. (¶1269)
- IRS provides guidance on the $2,500 limit on health FSAs that applies in 2013 and 2014. (¶1269)
- For 2013, top dividend rate rises to 20% for certain higher-income taxpayers. (¶1286)
- IRS has provided a safe harbor accounting method for calculating OID on a pool of credit card receivables (¶1313)
- Regs provide that Treasury TIPS issued with more than a de minimis amount of premium are subject to the coupon bond method. (¶1333)
- IRS provides the 2013 and 2014 income threshold ($115,000) for the definition of a "highly compensated employee." (¶1353)
- The per-diem dollar threshold in computing the limits for the exclusion of benefits from long-term care insurance is $320 for 2013 ($330 for 2014). (¶1376)
- Regs issued on elective deferral of COD income from reacquisition of debt instruments. (¶1394)

- New reliance regs provide definitions, exceptions, etc. regarding the $500,000 limit for certain remuneration paid by health insurers. (¶1519)

- Inflation-indexed definition of a high deductible health plan and limit on contributions for 2013 and 2014 for Archer MSA (¶1528) and HSA (¶1529) purposes are provided.

- The standard mileage rate for business travel is 56.5¢ for 2013. (¶1560)

- The simplified (high-low) per diem rates for post-Sept. 30, 2013 travel are reflected. (¶1581)

- Puerto Rico is treated as included in the U.S. for purposes of calculating domestic production gross receipts (DPGR) through 2013. (¶1616)

- An optional safe harbor method of calculating a home office deduction is available starting with the 2013 tax year. (¶1644)

- Taxpayers using their car to travel to a new location because of a change their work location may claim a 24¢ per-mile moving expense deduction for 2013. (¶1648)

- Final regs issued under Code Sec. 162(a) and Code Sec. 263(a) for amounts paid to acquire, produce, or improve tangible property, covering: deductible repairs and maintenance costs at ¶1656; timing rules for deducting materials and supplies at ¶1658; how to handle the cost of rotable, temporary and standby emergency spare parts at ¶1658; general capitalization rules at ¶1659; amounts paid to acquire property at ¶1660; and amounts paid to improve property at ¶1661.

- The treatment of mortgage insurance premiums as qualified residence interest is extended through 2013. (¶1736)

- IRS issues final regs on allocation of prepaid qualified mortgage insurance premiums. (¶1736)

- The election under Code Sec. 164 to deduct state and local sales taxes instead of state and local income taxes is extended through 2013. (¶1756)

- A co-op stockholder may be entitled to a casualty loss deduction for damage to the co-op's premises if the taxpayer has a sufficient property interest under state law. (¶1792)

- Temporary regs provide that taxpayers can deduct amounts paid for repairs and maintenance to tangible property if the amounts paid do not otherwise have to be capitalized. (¶1793)

- Beginning during 2013, proposed reliance regs provide a regrouping "fresh start" under the passive activity rules for certain taxpayers subject to the 3.8% surtax on unearned income. (¶1824)

- Proposed reliance regs would modify rules for determining what transactions are dispositions of MACRS assets. (¶1906)

- Proposed reliance regs would modify rules for accounting for MACRS depreciation using general asset accounts. (¶1909)

- 7-year MACRS depreciation for motorsports entertainment complexes is extended through 2013. (¶1916)

- 15-year MACRS depreciation for qualified leasehold improvement property, qualified restaurant property and qualified retail improvement property is extended through 2013. (¶1918)

- Open-air parking garages are characterized under MACRS as 39-year nonresidential real property. (¶1920)

- Hotel and a residential condominium are treated as a single building for MACRS purposes. (¶1920)

- Faster MACRS depreciation for qualified Indian reservation property is extended through 2013. (¶1924)

- 50% bonus depreciation is extended to apply to property placed in service before 2014 (before 2015 for certain long-production-period property and aircraft). (¶1933)

- Another round of trading bonus and accelerated depreciation for certain otherwise-deferred credits is provided for property placed in service before 2014 (before 2015 for certain long-production-period property and aircraft). (¶1939)
- Federal sequester imposes limit on the amounts refundable for trading bonus and accelerated depreciation for certain otherwise-deferred credits. (¶1939)
- 50% bonus depreciation for certain property used in biofuel production is extended through 2013 and expanded. (¶1940)
- Code Sec. 179 expensing limit is set at $500,000, and the investment-based phase-out level for the expensing is set at $2,000,000, for tax years beginning in 2012 and 2013. (¶1941)
- S corporations aren't subject to Code Sec. 179 limitations that apply to consolidated groups. (¶1941)
- Right to revoke or alter a Code Sec. 179 expensing election without IRS consent is extended to cover tax years beginning before 2014. ¶1941)
- Up to $250,000 of qualified real property is made eligible for Code Sec. 179 expensing for tax years beginning in 2012 and 2013. (¶1944)
- Eligibility of off-the-shelf computer software for Code Sec. 179 expensing is extended to cover tax years beginning before 2014. (¶1944)
- Enhanced Code Sec. 179 expensing for qualified zone property is extended generally through 2013. (¶1944)
- Autos, trucks and vans placed in service in 2013 are subject to revised auto depreciation and expensing dollar caps; vehicles eligible for bonus depreciation are subject to higher auto depreciation and expensing dollar caps. (¶1952, ¶1953)
- Autos, trucks and vans leased in 2013 are subject to revised income inclusion amounts. (¶1957)
- 50% expensing for qualified advanced mine safety equipment applies through 2013. (¶1964)
- Expensing for certain film and TV production costs applies through 2013. (¶1964)
- Deductible amounts for insubstantial benefit to donors of charitable contributions increase. (¶2104)
- Above-basis deduction rules retroactively extended for charitable contributions of food inventory by both non-corporate taxpayers (¶2107) and C corporations made before 2014. (¶2108)
- No qualified easement in property subject to mortgage unless mortgagee timely subordinates rights to those of charitable donee. (¶2114)
- No qualified easement if property can be substituted for property originally transferred subject to easement. (¶2114)
- Increased charitable deduction for qualified conservation easements contributed by individuals (including ranchers and farmers) retroactively extended for contributions made before 2014. (¶2123)
- Increased charitable deduction for qualified conservation easements contributed by corporate ranchers and farmers retroactively extended for contributions made before 2014. (¶2131)
- Maximum premiums paid for a qualified long-term care insurance contract, deductible as a medical expense, increase. (¶2145)
- Mileage rate for use of a car for qualified medical transportation is set at 24¢ a mile for expenses paid or incurred in 2013. (¶2148)
- The American Opportunity Tax Credit for higher education expenses is extended

through 2017. (¶2202)

- For 2013 and 2014, the Lifetime Learning credit phases out over higher levels of modified AGI. (¶2203)
- For Coverdell education savings accounts (CESAs), $2,000 contribution limit, higher phase-out ranges, and other enhancements are made permanent. (¶2207)
- Exclusion for employer-provided education assistance (including assistance for graduate-level courses) is made permanent. (¶2215)
- Exclusion for awards received under the National Health Service Corps and Armed Services Health Professions scholarship programs is made permanent. (¶2218)
- For student loan interest deduction, removal of 60-month limit and increased phase-out ranges are made permanent. (¶2223)
- Phaseout ranges are provided for the deduction for interest paid on qualified higher education loans in 2013 and 2014. (¶2223)
- Up-to-$250 above-the-line deduction for teachers out-of-pocket classroom-related expenses applies through 2013. (¶2229)
- Above-the-line deduction for qualified tuition and related expenses applies through 2013. ¶2230)
- The railroad track maintenance credit is retroactively extended for two years through 2013. (¶2302)
- The mine rescue team training credit is retroactively extended for two years through 2013. (¶2302)
- The work opportunity tax credit is retroactively extended for two years through 2013. (¶2316)
- The cellulosic biofuel producer credit is modified and extended for one year through 2013. (¶2318)
- The research credit is modified and retroactively extended for two years through 2013. (¶2319)
- Current low-income housing credit percentages are provided. The minimum low-income tax credit rate for nonfederally subsidized new buildings is extended for allocations before 2014. (¶2320)
- The production credit for Indian coal facilities is extended for one year through 2013. (¶2324)
- A facility using wind to produce electricity will be a qualified facility if it is placed in service before 2014. The credits for facilities producing energy from certain renewable resources are modified to include facilities, the construction of which begins before 2014. (¶2324)
- The Indian employment tax credit is retroactively extended for two years through 2013. (¶2326)
- The new markets tax credits is retroactively extended for two years through 2013. (¶2329)
- Sequester reduces tax-exempt employer's small business health care credit. (¶2332)
- The credit for biodiesel and renewable diesel is retroactively extended for two years through 2013. (¶2333)
- The credit for energy-efficient new homes is retroactively extended for two years through 2013. (¶2334)
- The credit for energy-efficient appliances is retroactively extended for two years through 2013. (¶2335)
- The employer wage credit for employees who are active duty members of the uniformed services is retroactively extended for two years through 2013. (¶2336)

- Nonrefundable personal credits can offset alternative minimum tax and regular tax. (¶2338)
- Earned income tax credit changes relating to higher amounts for eligible taxpayers with three or more children, and increases in threshold phaseout amounts for singles, surviving spouses, and heads of households are extended for five years through 2017. (¶2339 *et seq.*)
- The maximum amount of the earned income credit (EIC) and AGI-based phaseout thresholds increase for 2013. (¶2339)
- The maximum amount of disqualified income that can be received for EIC purposes increases for 2013 to $3,300 ($3,350 for 2014). (¶2342)
- Final regs explain "affordability" of employer-sponsored coverage for health care premium tax credit. (¶2345)
- The adoption credit rules (but not refundability provisions) are made permanent. (¶2354)
- Eased rules in qualifying for the refundable child credit are extended for five years through 2017. (¶2355)
- The nonbusiness energy property credit is retroactively extended for two years through 2013. (¶2358)
- The alternative fuel vehicle refueling property credit (nonhydrogen property) is retroactively extended for two years through 2013. (¶2361)
- The credit for 2- or 3-wheeled plug-in electric vehicles is modified and retroactively extended for two years through 2013. (¶2362)
- The AGI amounts used in computing the "saver's" credit for elective deferrals and IRA contributions increase for 2013 and 2014. (¶2363)
- Qualified zone academy bonds are retroactively extended for two years through 2013. (¶2366)
- Sequester reduces direct payment of refundable tax credit bonds. (¶2366)
- The American Samoa economic development credit is modified and extended through 2014. (¶2367)
- The Supreme Court held that a U.K. windfall tax qualified for the foreign tax credit. (¶2369)
- Tax-free exchange of life insurance contract or annuities applies to beneficiaries after death of owner. (¶2417)
- State treatment of property as real or personal not determinative for like-kind exchange purposes. (¶2419)
- Depreciation part of standard mileage rate remains at 23¢ for 2013. (¶2476)
- Maximum tax rate on long-term capital gains of higher income noncorporate taxpayers increased to 20% in tax years beginning after 2012. (¶2603)
- 100% gain exclusion for qualified small business stock is retroactively restored and extended through 2013. (¶2648)
- An obligation under a debt instrument may be a position in personal property that is part of a straddle. (¶2654)
- Temporary regs provide rules for determining when to take unrealized gain or loss into account on mixed straddles established after Aug. 1, 2013. (¶2658)
- IRS provides guidance for allocating gain on the sale of qualified real property for which a Code Sec. 179 election was made between Code Sec. 1245 property and Code Sec. 1250 property. (¶2695)
- Automatic change in accounting procedures will apply for repair/capitalization regs under Code Sec. 162 and Code Sec. 263. (¶2845)
- Worker providing services in multiple roles can be both an employee and an independent contractor, when working on two projects for the same company. (¶3003)

- IRS released a revised Form 8952 to apply for the misclassified worker settlement program. (¶3003)
- Settlement payment for age discrimination treated as wages for FICA purposes. (¶3004)
- Circuit split exists on FICA tax treatment of severance pay. (¶3004)
- IRS provided proposed reliance regs explaining the additional Medicare tax. (¶3004)
- Beginning in 2013, the voluntary withholding rates on specified federal payments permanently remain at 7%, 10%, 15% or 25%. (¶3009)
- Beginning in 2013, the voluntary withholding rate on unemployment benefits permanently remains at 10%. (¶3009)
- Beginning in 2013, the optional flat rate for supplemental wage payments totaling $1 million or less for a calendar year permanently remains at 25%. (¶3011)
- Beginning in 2013, the mandatory flat rate for supplemental wage payments totaling more than $1 million for a calendar year is increased to 39.6% (from 35%). (¶3011)
- IRS provided guidance on whether an employee may ask for additional withholding on supplemental wages. (¶3011)
- For 2014, an employee who can be claimed as a dependent on someone else's return can't claim an exemption from withholding if his income exceeds $1,000 and includes more than $350 of unearned income. (¶3017)
- IRS has provided optional procedures for employers to adjust the employment taxes of same-sex spouses. (¶3020)
- Threshold amount for cash payments to domestic service employees (e.g., nannies) to be subject to FICA is $1,800 for 2013 ($1,900 for 2014). (¶3030)
- Beginning in 2013, the withholding rate on gambling rates permanently remains at 25%. (¶3033)
- Beginning in 2013, the backup withholding rate on reportable payments permanently remains at 28%. (¶3044)
- For 2013 and later years, the above-the-line deduction for self-employment tax is 50% of all self-employment tax. (¶3102)
- The standard deduction amounts for 2013 and 2014 are listed. (¶3112)
- For 2013 and later years, the overall limitation on itemized deductions (the "Pease" limitation) is restored. For 2013, it applies when AGI exceeds $300,000 for joint returns, $275,000 for heads of household, $250,000 for single filers, and $150,000 for married individuals filing separately. The 2014 thresholds are also listed. (¶3114)
- For 2013, the personal exemption amount is $3,900 ($3,950 for 2014). (¶3115)
- For 2013 and later years, the personal exemption phaseout (PEP) applies. For 2013, it applies when AGI exceeds $300,000 for joint returns, $275,000 for heads of household, $250,000 for single filers, and $150,000 for married individuals filing separately. The 2014 thresholds are also listed. (¶3117)
- The tax rates on individuals' incomes for 2013 and later years include a seventh, higher, tax bracket: the tax rates are 10%, 15%, 25%, 28%, 33%, 35%, and 39.6%. (¶3130)
- Under the kiddie tax, the parents' highest tax rate applies to a child's unearned income over $2,000 for 2013 and 2014. (¶3135)
- For 2013, the dollar thresholds for the optional methods of computing net earnings from self-employment are $4,640 and $6,960 ($4,800 and $7,200 for 2014). (¶3149)
- Proposed reliance regs clarify application of the post-2012 3.8% net investment income tax. (¶3150 *et seq.*)
- The $175,000 statutory amount used to determine tentative minimum tax is adjusted for inflation for any tax year beginning in 2013 and thereafter. The inflation-adjusted amount for 2013 is $179,500; the amount for 2014 is also listed. (¶3201)

- The individual AMT exemption amounts for tax years beginning in 2013 and thereafter are increased. The 2013 amounts are: $51,900 for unmarried individuals, $80,800 for married individuals filing jointly, and $40,400 (50% of the joint filing amount) for married individuals filing separately. The 2014 amounts are also listed. (¶3203)

- The AMT exemption amount for estates and trusts for tax years beginning in 2013 is $23,100. The 2014 amount is also listed. (¶3203)

- The AMT exemption amounts and phase-out of exemption amounts are adjusted for inflation for any tax year beginning in 2013 and thereafter. (¶3203)

- The AMT exemption amounts for 2013 and 2014 for a child subject to the kiddie tax are provided. (¶3204) \

- Accumulated earnings tax rate increases to 20% for tax years beginning in 2013 and thereafter. (¶3316)

- Personal holding company penalty tax rate increases to 20% for tax years beginning in 2013 and thereafter. (¶3320)

- IRS provides new simplified methods for taxpayers to request relief for late S corporation and related elections. (¶3358)

- IRS privately rules that a membership interest can satisfy the requirement for tax-free distribution that a distribution be made "with respect to its stock." (¶3360)

- Reduced 5-year recognition period for S corporation's built-in gains applies for tax years beginning in 2011, 2012, and 2013. (¶3362)

- A Court of Appeal has held that if a shareholder fails to claim a suspended loss deduction and is later time-barred from doing so, he can't claim a corresponding reduction in basis. (¶3369)

- IRS issues final regs barring use of controlled corporations to avoid related corporation redemption rules. (¶3533)

- Rule treating ordinary income from disposition of Section 306 stock as qualified dividend income is made permanent. (¶3536)

- Long-term exempt rates for Code Sec. 382 limitation are updated. (¶3569)

- IRS issues final regs on deemed asset sale treatment for certain transactions under Code Sec. 336(e). (¶3587)

- IRS issues final regs on outbound stock transfers from a U.S. person to a foreign corporation. (¶3588)

- Rule treating ordinary income from disposition of Section 306 stock as qualified dividend income is made permanent. (¶3536)

- Long-term exempt rates for Code Sec. 382 limitation are updated. (¶3569)

- Collapsible corporation rules are permanently repealed.

- ESBTs taxed at a flat rate of 39.6% on some income. (¶3910)

- New treatment of the 3.8% surtax on unearned income of estates and trusts. (¶3956)

- Court denied debtor NOLs carryovers of terminated bankruptcy estate. (¶3979)

- IRS issues guidance for Type III supporting organizations. (¶4125)

- For 2013, unrelated business taxable income excludes annual dues of up to $155 ($158 for 2014) per member received by agricultural or horticultural organizations. (¶4122)

- For 2013 and 2014, the limit on 401(k) plan elective deferrals is $17,500. (¶4317)

- For 2013 and 2014, compensation for "highly compensated employee" status is $115,000. (¶4326)

- For 2013, the limit on annual additions to a defined compensation plan is $51,000 ($52,000 for 2014). (¶4328)

- For 2013, the maximum annual benefit from a defined benefit plan is $205,000 ($210,000 for 2014). (¶4328)

- The rule allowing up to $100,000 in required minimum distributions from IRAs to be contributed tax-free to charity applies through 2013. (¶4357)

- Final regs have been issued providing additional guidance on withholding on payments to foreign financial institutions and others (FATCA withholding). (¶4672)

- IRS postpones implementation dates in FATCA regs, with withholding being implemented in phases beginning on July 1, 2014. (¶4672)

- Individual return filing thresholds are increased for 2013 and 2014. (¶4701)

- For joint return purposes, an individual is married to a person of the same sex if the individuals are lawfully married under state law. IRS recognizes a marriage of same-sex individuals that was validly entered into under state law ("state of celebration"), even if the married couple is domiciled in a state that does not recognize the validity of same-sex marriages. (¶4705)

- New guidelines for taxpayers requesting equitable relief from income tax liability under the innocent spouse rules apply to requests filed (or pending) after Sept. 15, 2013. (¶4711)

- Income tax return filing threshold for a bankruptcy estate of an individual is increased for 2013 and 2014. (¶4736)

- For covered securities acquired after 2013, brokers have to report bond premiums or acquisition premiums. (¶4741)

- For less complex debt instruments acquired after 2013, brokers have to report information relating to the basis of the debt instrument and character of any gain. For more complex debt instruments, brokers don't have to report the information until after 2015. (¶4746)

- Applicable large employers and insurers don't have to report information about an employee's insurance coverage for periods beginning after 2014. (¶4746)

- A district court has enjoined IRS from enforcing its regulatory scheme for registered tax return preparers. (¶4750)

- Information return preparers can use truncated TINs (TTINs) on certain paper payee statements. (¶4752)

- In fiscal year 2012, IRS audited 1.0% of individual returns filed in the previous year. (¶4803)

- Guidance clarifies treatment of statutory deficiency notices issued pursuant to a civil examination for tax periods also covered by a restitution order and restitution-based assessments. (¶4827)

- Overpayment (¶4853) and underpayment (¶4866) interest rates for all four quarters of 2013 were the same as the rates that applied for the fourth quarter of 2012.

- Proposed reliance regs clarify material advisor penalty and allow for 20-day discretionary extension. (¶4890)

- Proposed reliance regs provide guidance regarding terms relevant to the employer's shared responsibility mandate and provide general operating rules and transition relief associated with its implementation. (¶4896)

- IRS provides penalty relief for good faith, but incorrect, information reporting under Code Sec. 6050W for payments in 2012 and 2013 on returns filed in 2013 and 2014. (¶4897)

- The basic exclusion amount for gifts and estates, and the exemption amount for the generation-skipping transfer (GST) tax, is $5,250,000 for 2013 ($5,340,000 for 2014). (¶5000)

- The maximum 2013 and 2014 estate, gift and GST tax rates are 40%. (¶5000)

- New Schedule PC-Protective Claim for Refund preserves estate's right to a refund of estate taxes paid when a claim or expense that is the subject of unresolved controversy at the time of filing the return later becomes deductible. (¶5018)

- Finding Section 3 of the Defense of Marriage Act to be unconstitutional, the Supreme Court allows a marital deduction for property left to the decedent's same-sex spouse. (¶5021)

- For decedents dying in 2013, the basic exclusion amount is $5,250,000 and the applicable credit amount is $2,045,800. Amounts for 2014 are also provided. (¶5028)

- Code Sec. 2010(c)(4) is amended, conforming to the regs, replacing basic exclusion amount with applicable exclusion amount. (¶5029)

- Regs flesh out portability election for decedents dying after 2010. (¶5029)

- Forms 706 and 709 include a new section and schedule, respectively, for portability. (¶5029)

- An executor must file an estate tax return if the decedent's gross estate at death exceeds the basic exclusion amount ($5,250,000 for estates of individuals dying in 2013; $5,340,000 for estates of individuals dying in 2014). (¶5034)

- The Ninth Circuit finds that an executor's reliance on an accountant, which caused a delay in filing the estate tax return, was not reasonable. ¶5035)

- Gift tax exemption is $5,250,000 for 2013 ($5,340,000 for 2014) (¶5038)

- Fixed-dollar gifts of limited liability company (LLC) interests aren't void as against public policy. (¶5044)

- Gift tax annual exclusion is $14,000 for 2013 and 2014. (¶5046)

- For 2013, $143,000 ($145,000 for 2014) may be transferred to a noncitizen spouse free of gift tax. (¶5046)

- The unified credit amount is increased to $2,045,800 (the tax otherwise imposed on $5,250,000) in 2013 ($2,081,800 in 2014). (¶5050)

- The GST exemption is increased to $5,250,000 in 2013 ($5,340,000 in 2014). (¶5058)

- GST tax is computed. (¶5059)

¶ 105. What's New on the 2013 Form 1040?

Here are the changes with the greatest impact on the preparation of 2013 individual returns, cross-referenced to where they are discussed in the Handbook, and referenced to the appropriate lines on the Form 1040 and related Schedules.

☑️ observation: The instructions to the Form 1040 for 2013 carry a section titled "What's New." This section includes most, but not all, of the many tax return changes highlighted below.

FORM 1040—U.S. INDIVIDUAL INCOME TAX RETURN—FILING STATUS

Same sex couples. Same sex spouses who legally married on or before Dec. 31, 2013 in a state that recognizes same-sex marriage must file as married filed jointly or married filing separately even if they now live in a state that does not recognize same-sex marriage. For this purpose, "state" means any domestic or foreign jurisdiction having the legal authority to sanction marriages. Individuals who have entered into a registered domestic partnership, civil union, or other similar relationship that is not considered a marriage under state law are not considered married for federal tax purposes.

FORM 1040—U.S. INDIVIDUAL INCOME TAX RETURN—GROSS INCOME

Adoption exclusion. For 2013, the maximum exclusion for employer-provided adoption assistance is $12,970 per eligible child. (¶1254)

ADJUSTED GROSS INCOME

Line 26. Moving expenses. The 2013 standard mileage rate for moving expenses is 24¢ per mile. (¶1648)

Line 32. IRA deduction. In general, an individual who isn't an active participant in certain employer-sponsored retirement plans, and whose spouse isn't an active participant, may make an annual deductible cash contribution to an IRA up to the lesser of: (1) a statutory dollar limit, or (2) 100% of the compensation that's includible in his gross income for that year. For 2013, the statutory dollar limit is $5,500 (increased from $5,000, for 2012), plus an additional $1,000 for those age 50 or older. If the individual (or his spouse) is an active plan participant, the deduction phases out over a specified dollar range of modified AGI (MAGI). For 2013, a taxpayer may be able to take an IRA deduction if he was covered by a retirement plan and his 2013 MAGI is less than $69,000 ($115,000 if married filing jointly or qualifying widow(er)). If the taxpayer's spouse was covered by a retirement plan, but the taxpayer was not, he may be able to take an IRA deduction if his 2013 MAGI is less than $188,000. (¶4352)

TAX AND CREDITS

Line 40. Itemized deductions or standard deduction. For 2013, the standard deduction is $6,100 for single filers and for married persons filing separately, $12,200 for joint filers and qualifying widow(er)s, and $8,950 for heads of household. (¶3112)

Line 42. Exemptions. The amount for each exemption for 2013 is $3,900. (¶3115)

Line 45. Alternative minimum tax. Under Code Sec. 55(d), the AMT exemption amount for 2013 is $51,900 ($80,800 if married filing jointly or a qualifying widow(er); $40,400 if married filing separately). (¶3203)

Line 53. Other credits. For 2013, the maximum adoption credit is $12,970 per eligible child for both non-special needs adoptions and special needs adoptions. (¶2354)

OTHER TAXES

Line 56. Self-employment tax. Maximum amount of self-employment income subject to FICA tax is $113,700; no ceiling on Medicare wage base.

The self-employment tax rate is 15.3%. (¶1109)

An individual may use the farm optional method only if (a) his gross farm income was not more than $6,980 or (b) his net farm profits were less than $5,024. Using this method, farm self-employment earnings equals the smaller of (1) two-thirds of gross farm income, or (2) $4,640. (¶3149)

An individual may use the nonfarm optional method only if (a) his net nonfarm profits were less than $5,024 and also less than 72.189% of his gross nonfarm income and (b) he had net earnings from self-employment of at least $400 in 2 of the prior 3 years. Individuals may compute their self-employment earnings as the smaller of two-thirds of gross nonfarm income or $4,640(¶3149)

A self-employed individual with both farm and nonfarm incomes is allowed to use both optional computation methods if the farm income qualifies for the farm optional method and the nonfarm income qualifies for the nonfarm optional method. If both optional methods are used to compute net earnings from self-employment, the maximum combined total net earnings from self-employment for any tax year can't be more than $4,640. (¶3149)

Line 60. Additional Medicare tax. For tax years beginning after 2012, a 0.9% additional Medicare tax applies to a taxpayer's Medicare wages, Railroad Retirement Tax Act (RRTA) compensation, and self-employment income above a threshold amount ($250,000 for joint returns, $125,000 for married persons filing separately, and $200,000 for all others). Use Form 8959, Additional Medicare Tax, to figure this tax.

Line 60. 3.8% surtax on unearned income. For tax years beginning after Dec. 31, 2012, individuals are subject to a surtax of 3.8% of the lesser of: (1) net investment income, or (2) the excess of modified adjusted gross income (MAGI) over an unindexed threshold amount ($250,000 for joint filers or surviving spouses, $125,000 for a married individual filing a separate return, and $200,000 in any other case). Net investment income may include rental and royalty income, income from partnerships, S corporations and trusts, and income from other passive activities reported on a taxpayer's Schedule E. Use Form 8960, Net Investment Income Tax—Individuals, Estates, and Trusts, to figure this tax.

PAYMENTS

Line 64. Earned income credit (EIC). The maximum credit is higher, and the AGI-based phaseout figures are revised. (¶2339)

Line 69. Excess social security and RRTA tax withheld. Maximum Social Security (OASDI) tax for 2013 is $7,049.40 (computed on the first $113,700 of wages) for purposes of credit for excess tax withheld. (¶1108)

FORM 1040—SCHEDULE A, ITEMIZED DEDUCTIONS

Line 1. Medical and dental expenses. The 2013 standard mileage rate for medically-related use of an auto is 24¢ per mile. (¶2148)

Line 3. Medical and dental expenses. Beginning Jan. 1, 2013, a taxpayer can deduct only the part of his or her medical and dental expenses that exceeds 10% of the taxpayer's AGI (7.5% if either the taxpayer or the taxpayer's spouse is age 65 or older).

Line 20. Casualty and theft losses. There is a new Section C on Form 4684, Casualties and Thefts, for Ponzi-type investment schemes. A taxpayer must complete Section C if the taxpayer is claiming a theft loss deduction due to a Ponzi-type investment scheme and is using Revenue Procedure 2009-20, as modified by Revenue Procedure 2011-58.

Line 21. Unreimbursed employee expenses. The 2013 standard mileage rate for business travel is 56.5¢ per mile. (¶1560)

Line 29. Limit on itemized deductions. Beginning Jan. 1, 2013, itemized deductions for taxpayers with adjusted gross incomes in excess of the "applicable amount" ($300,000 for joint filers or a surviving spouse, $275,000 for a head of household, $250,000 for a single individual who isn't a surviving spouse, and $150,000 for marrieds filing separately) may be reduced. (¶3114)

FORM 1040—SCHEDULE B, INTEREST AND ORDINARY DIVIDENDS

Line 1. Interest. Accrued interest on Series EE U.S. savings bonds issued in '83 is taxable. (¶1334)

Line 3. Excludable interest on Series EE or Series I U.S. savings bonds. The exclusion for education related savings bond interest phases out at higher income levels. For 2013, the phaseout begins at modified AGI above $74,700 ($112,050 on a joint return). (¶2220)

FORM 1040—SCHEDULE C, PROFIT OR LOSS FROM BUSINESS

No separate payment card reporting requirements. Gross receipts received via payment card (credit and debit cards) and third-party network payments are not separately reported on Schedule C.

Part II. Expenses. Line 9. Car and truck expenses. The 2013 standard mileage rate for business travel is 56.5¢ per mile. (¶1560)

Part II. Expenses. Line 13. Depreciation and section 179 expense. See entries for Form 4562, see below.

FORM 4562, DEPRECIATION AND AMORTIZATION

Part I. Election to expense certain tangible property under Sec. 179. For tax years beginning in 2013, the maximum section 179 expense deduction is $500,000 ($535,000 for enterprise zone property). This limit is reduced by the amount by which the cost of section 179 property placed in service during the tax year exceeds $2 million. (¶1941)

Part II. Special depreciation allowance. For qualified property acquired and placed in service after 2011 and before 2014 (before 2015 for aircraft and certain long-production period property), a 50% bonus first-year depreciation allowance applies under Code Sec. 168(k). (¶1933)

Part V. Listed property. First-year luxury auto limits for vehicles first placed in service in 2013 are $11,160 for autos and $11,360 for light trucks or vans (if bonus depreciation rules apply) and $3,160 and $3,360, respectively (if bonus depreciation rules don't apply). (¶1953)

FORM 1040—SCHEDULE D, CAPITAL GAINS AND LOSSES

Full small business stock exclusion. The exclusion of 100% of gain on certain small business stock under Code Sec. 1202(a)(4) applies for qualified stock acquired after Sep. 27, 2010 and before Jan. 1, 2014. (¶2648)

Form 1040—SCHEDULE E, SUPPLEMENTAL INCOME AND LOSS

3.8% surtax on unearned income. For tax years beginning after Dec. 31, 2012, individuals are subject to a surtax of 3.8% of the lesser of: (1) net investment income, or (2) the excess of modified adjusted gross income (MAGI) over an unindexed threshold amount ($250,000 for joint filers or surviving spouses, $125,000 for a married individual filing a separate return, and $200,000 in any other case). Net investment income may include rental and royalty income, income from partnerships, S corporations and trusts, and income from other passive activities reported on a taxpayer's Schedule E. Use Form 8960, Net Investment Income Tax—Individuals, Estates, and Trusts, to figure this tax.

Standard mileage rate. The standard mileage rate for miles driven in connection with the taxpayer's rental activities is 56.5¢ per mile. (¶1560)

FORM 1040—SCHEDULE F, PROFIT OR LOSS FROM FARMING

Part II. Farm Expenses—Cash and Accrual Method. Line 10. Car and truck expenses. The 2013 standard mileage rate for business travel is 56.5¢ per mile. (¶1560)

¶1000. Tax Calendar—2014 Due Dates.

Here are the principal 2014 tax due dates. The effect of Saturdays, Sundays, and federal (but not State) holidays has been taken into account.

January 15, 2014

Individuals.

Make a payment of your estimated tax for 2013, if you didn't pay your income tax for the year through withholding (or didn't pay in enough tax that way). Use Form 1040-ES or pay by credit card or by EFTPS. This is the final installment date for 2013 estimated tax. However, you don't have to make this payment if you file your 2013 return (Form 1040) and pay any tax due by Jan. 31, 2014.

Farmers and fishermen.

Pay your estimated tax for 2013 using Form 1040-ES or pay by credit card or by EFTPS. You can then file your 2013 income tax return (Form 1040) by Apr. 15. If you don't pay at this time, file your 2013 return and pay any tax due by Mar. 3, 2014, to avoid an estimated tax penalty.

January 31, 2014

All employers.

Give your employees their copies of Form W-2 for 2013.

All businesses.

Give an annual information statement to recipients of certain payments you made during 2013. (You can use a copy of the appropriate Form 1099.)

Individuals.

File your income tax return (Form 1040) for 2013 if you didn't pay your last installment of estimated tax by Jan. 15. Filing your return now prevents any penalty for late payment of the last installment.

February 18, 2014

Individuals.

If you claimed exemption from income tax withholding for 2013 on the Form W-4 you gave your employer, you must file a new Form W-4 by this date to continue your exemption for another year.

All businesses.

Give an annual information statement to recipients of certain payments (e.g., proceeds from broker and barter transactions) you made during 2013. (You can use a copy of the appropriate Form 1099.)

February 28, 2014

All businesses.

File an information return (Form 1099) with IRS for certain payments you made during 2013. There are different versions of Form 1099 for different types of payments. Use a separate Form 1096 to summarize and transmit each separate version. For a 30-day extension of time to file, use Form 8809. The due date for electronic filers is Mar. 31, 2014.

All employers.

File Form W-3 along with Copy A of all the Form W-2s you issued for 2013. The due date for electronic filers is Mar. 31, 2014.

Large food and beverage establishment employers.

File Form 8027 to report tip income and allocated tips. Use Form 8027-T to summarize and transmit Form 8027 if you have more than one establishment. The due date for electronic filers is Mar. 31, 2014.

March 3, 2014

Farmers and fishermen.

File your 2013 income tax return (Form 1040) and pay any tax due. However, you have until Apr. 15, if you paid your 2013 estimated tax by Jan. 15, 2014.

March 17, 2014

C corporations and S corporations.

File a 2013 calendar year income tax return (Form 1120 or Form 1120S) and pay any tax still due. If you want an automatic 6-month extension, file Form 7004 and deposit what you estimate you owe.

S elections.

File Form 2553 to choose to be treated as an S corporation, beginning with calendar year 2014. If Form 2553 is filed late, S treatment will begin with calendar year 2015 (unless the taxpayer qualifies for late election relief).

Electing large partnerships.

Provide each partner with a copy of Schedule K-1 of Form 1065-B.

March 31, 2014

Electronic filers of information returns.

File information returns listed under Feb. 28 (e.g., Form 1099s, Form W-2s, etc.), which is the due date for non-electronic filers.

April 15, 2014

Individuals.

File an income tax return for 2013 (Form 1040, Form 1040A, or Form 1040EZ), and pay any tax due. Taxpayers who can't make payments should request (on Form 9465) an agreement to pay in installments. If you want an automatic 6-month extension to file, file Form 4868 and estimate your tax or pay by credit card. Then file Form 1040 or Form 1040A by Oct. 15.

If you paid cash wages of $1,800 or more in 2013 to a household employee, you must file Schedule H with your income tax return (Form 1040) and report any employment taxes and withheld income taxes for those employees.

Contributions to an IRA for 2013 must be made by this date.

If you aren't paying your 2014 income tax through withholding (or won't pay in enough tax during the year that way), pay the first installment of your 2014 estimated tax by this date. Use Form 1040-ES or pay by credit card or by EFTPS.

Partnerships.

File a 2013 calendar year return (Form 1065) and provide each partner with a copy of Schedule K-1. If you want an automatic 5-month extension to file the return and provide Schedule K-1 or a substitute Schedule K-1, file Form 7004. Then file Form 1065 by Sept. 15.

Electing large partnerships.

File a 2013 calendar year return (Form 1065-B). If you want an automatic 6-month extension to file the return and provide Schedule K-1 or a substitute Schedule K-1, file Form 7004. Then file Form 1065-B by Oct. 15.

Corporations.

Deposit the first installment of estimated income tax for 2014.

June 16, 2014

Individuals.

If you are a U.S. citizen or resident alien living and working (or on military duty) outside the U.S. and Puerto Rico, file your 2013 Form 1040 and pay any tax, interest and penalties due. Otherwise, see Apr. 15, above. However, if you are a participant in a combat zone, you may be able to further extend the filing deadline.

Make the second installment payment of your 2014 estimated tax, if you aren't paying your income tax for the year through withholding (or won't pay in enough tax that way). Use Form 1040-ES or pay by credit card or by EFTPS.

Corporations.

Deposit the second installment of estimated income tax for 2014.

July 31, 2014

All employers.

If you maintain an employee benefit plan, such as a pension, profit-sharing, or stock bonus plan, file Form 5500 or Form 5500-EZ for calendar year 2013. If you use a fiscal year as your plan year, file the form by the last day of the seventh month after the plan year ends.

September 15, 2014

Individuals.

Make the third installment payment of your 2014 estimated tax, if you aren't paying your income tax for the year through withholding (or won't pay in enough tax that way). Use Form 1040-ES or pay by credit card or by EFTPS.

C corporations and S corporations.

File a 2013 calendar year income tax return (Form 1120 or Form 1120S) and pay any tax due if you were given an automatic 6-month extension.

Corporations.

Deposit the third installment of estimated income tax for 2014.

Partnerships.

File a 2013 calendar year return (Form 1065) if you were given an automatic 5-month extension.

October 15, 2014

Individuals.

If you have an automatic 6-month extension to file your income tax return for 2013, file Form 1040 and pay any tax, interest, and penalties due.

Electing large partnerships.

File a 2013 calendar year return (Form 1065-B) if you were given an automatic 6-month extension.

During November, 2014

All employers.

Request employees whose withholding exemptions will be different in 2015 to fill out a new Form W-4.

December 15, 2014

Corporations.

Deposit the fourth installment of estimated income tax for 2014.

2014 RIA FEDERAL TAX HANDBOOK

Contents

Highlights of the 2014 Edition . . . . ¶101

What's New on the 2013 Form 1040? . . . . ¶105

Tax Calendar—2014 Due Dates . . . . ¶1000

	Paragraph No.
Chapter 1. Tax Rates and Tables	¶1100
Chapter 2. Income—Taxable and Exempt	¶1200
Chapter 3. Deductions—Expenses of a Business	¶1500
Chapter 4. Interest Expense—Taxes—Losses—Bad Debts	¶1700
Chapter 5. Depreciation, Amortization, Property Expensing and Depletion	¶1900
Chapter 6. Charitable Contributions—Medical Expenses—Alimony—Other Nonbusiness Deductions	¶2100
Chapter 7. Education—Tax Credits, Exclusions, Deductions	¶2200
Chapter 8. Tax Credits	¶2300
Chapter 9. Sales and Exchanges—Tax-Free Exchanges—Basis	¶2400
Chapter 10. Capital Gains and Losses—Section 1231—Depreciation Recapture	¶2600
Chapter 11. Tax Accounting—Inventories	¶2800
Chapter 12. Withholding Tax on Wages and Other Income Payments	¶3000
Chapter 13. Individual's Tax Computation—Kiddie Tax—Self-Employment Tax—3.8% Surtax—Estimated Tax	¶3100
Chapter 14. Alternative Minimum Tax	¶3200
Chapter 15. Corporations—Accumulated Earnings Tax—Personal Holding Companies—Consolidated Returns—Estimated Tax—S Corporations	¶3300
Chapter 16. Corporate Transactions—Organization—Distributions—Reorganization—Acquisitions—Liquidations	¶3510
Chapter 17. Partnerships	¶3700
Chapter 18. Trusts—Estates—Decedents	¶3900
Chapter 19. Exempt Organizations	¶4100
Chapter 20. RICs (Mutual Funds), REITs, REMICs, Banks and Other Special Corporations	¶4200
Chapter 21. Pension and Profit-Sharing Plans—401(k) Plans—Roth 401(k) Plans—IRAs—Roth IRAs—SEPs—SIMPLE Plans	¶4310
Chapter 22. Farmers	¶4500
Chapter 23. Foreign Income—Foreign Taxpayers—Foreign Currency Transactions	¶4610
Chapter 24. Returns and Payment of Tax	¶4700
Chapter 25. Deficiencies—Refunds—Penalties	¶4800
Chapter 26. Estate, Gift and Generation-Skipping Transfer Taxes	¶5000

Table of Contents—Main Topics

Chapter 1. Tax Rates and Tables

    Tax Rates and Tables. . . . .   ¶1100

    Applicable Federal Rates. . . . .   ¶1116

    MACRS Tables. . . . .   ¶1117

    Income Inclusion Amounts for Autos, Trucks and Vans. . . . .   ¶1118

Chapter 2. Income—Taxable and Exempt

    Gross Income. . . . .   ¶1200

    Compensation Income. . . . .   ¶1208

    Fringe Benefits. . . . .   ¶1228

    Time for Reporting Compensation. . . . .   ¶1271

    Social Security, Unemployment and Certain Disability Payments. . . . .   ¶1278

    Dividends. . . . .   ¶1285

    Interest Income. . . . .   ¶1301

    Rents and Royalties. . . . .   ¶1338

    Life Insurance Proceeds. . . . .   ¶1346

    Taxation of Annuity Payments. . . . .   ¶1354

    Gifts and Inheritances. . . . .   ¶1370

    Prizes and Awards. . . . .   ¶1372

    Accident and Health Insurance Benefits. . . . .   ¶1374

    Damages. . . . .   ¶1380

    Income Realized on Discharge or Cancellation of Indebtedness. . . . .   ¶1385

Chapter 3. Deductions—Expenses of a Business

    Start-Up Expenditures. . . . .   ¶1500

    Ordinary and Necessary Business Expenses. . . . .   ¶1506

    Compensation Deduction. . . . .   ¶1515

    Travel Expenses. . . . .   ¶1541

    Transportation Expenses. . . . .   ¶1554

    Entertainment Expenses. . . . .   ¶1561

    Expense Reimbursements. . . . .   ¶1573

    Substantiating T&E and "Listed Property" Expenses. . . . .   ¶1579

    Business Gifts and Employee Awards. . . . .   ¶1589

    Rent Expense. . . . .   ¶1593

    Research and Experimental Expenditures. . . . .   ¶1601

    Legal and Accounting Expenses. . . . .   ¶1603

    Insurance Premiums. . . . .   ¶1606

    Bribes, Kickbacks, Fines and Penalties. . . . .   ¶1610

    Domestic Production Activities Deduction. . . . .   ¶1614

    Miscellaneous Business Expenses. . . . .   ¶1617

    Employee Business Expenses. . . . .   ¶1631

    Residence Used in Part for Business—Home Office Deduction. . . . .   ¶1638

    Moving Expenses. . . . .   ¶1646

    Deduction vs Capitalization of Tangible Property Costs. . . . .   ¶1655

    Capitalization Rules for Intangible Assets. . . . .   ¶1663

    Uniform Capitalization (UNICAP) Rules . . . .   ¶1666

Chapter 4. Interest Expense—Taxes—Losses—Bad Debts

Deduction for Interest. . . . . ¶1700

Investment Interest Deduction Limitations. . . . . ¶1726

Qualified Residence Interest. . . . . ¶1730

Allocation Rules for Interest and Debt. . . . . ¶1737

When Interest May Be Deducted. . . . . ¶1743

Deduction for Taxes. . . . . ¶1754

Deduction for Losses. . . . . ¶1773

Casualty, Disaster, and Theft Losses. . . . . ¶1792

At-Risk Limitations. . . . . ¶1803

"Passive Activity" Losses and Credits. . . . . ¶1810

Net Operating Losses (NOLs). . . . . ¶1839

Deduction for Bad Debts. . . . . ¶1848

Chapter 5. Depreciation, Amortization, Property Expensing and Depletion

The Depreciation Allowance. . . . . ¶1900

The Modified Accelerated Cost Recovery System (MACRS). . . . . ¶1907

Sec. 179 Expense Election—Form 4562. . . . . ¶1941

"Luxury" Automobiles and "Listed Property." . . . . ¶1946

Depreciation Deduction Under the Income Forecast Method. . . . . ¶1959

Depreciation Deduction Under the "Useful-Life" Rules. . . . . ¶1960

Special Expensing and Amortization Provisions. . . . . ¶1964

Amortization of Intangibles. . . . . ¶1973

Depletion Deduction. . . . . ¶1976

Chapter 6. Charitable Contributions—Medical Expenses—Alimony—Other Nonbusiness Deductions

Charitable Contribution Deduction. . . . . ¶2100

Specialized Rules for Claiming Charitable Contributions. . . . . ¶2134

Medical Expenses. . . . . ¶2140

Alimony or Separate Maintenance. . . . . ¶2152

"Nonbusiness" Expenses. . . . . ¶2163

Bond Premium Amortization. . . . . ¶2169

Chapter 7. Education—Tax Credits, Exclusions, Deductions

Education—Tax Credits, Exclusions, Deductions. . . . . ¶2200

Tax Credits for Higher Education. . . . . ¶2201

Coverdell Education Savings Accounts (CESAs). . . . . ¶2205

Qualified Tuition Programs (QTPs)—529 Plans. . . . . ¶2209

Employer-Provided Educational Benefits; Scholarships and Fellowships. . . . ¶2213

Higher Education Exclusion for Savings Bond Income. . . . . ¶2219

Deduction for Interest Paid on Qualified Education Loans. . . . . ¶2222

Education Expenses Related to Business or Employment. . . . . ¶2225

Above-the-Line Deduction for Higher Education Expenses. . . . . ¶2230

Chapter 8. Tax Credits

Tax Credits. . . . . ¶2300

Business Incentive Credits. . . . . ¶2301

Personal (Refundable and Nonrefundable) Credits. . . . . ¶2338

Foreign Tax Credit. . . . . ¶2367

Chapter 9. Sales and Exchanges—Tax-Free Exchanges—Basis

Gain or Loss on Sales or Exchanges. ¶2400
Nontaxable Exchanges. ¶2413
"Like-Kind" (Code Sec. 1031) Exchanges. ¶2418
Rollover of Gain from Certain Sales. ¶2426
Involuntary Conversions—Form 4797. ¶2430
Exclusion of Gain on Principal Residence. ¶2442
Sales and Exchanges Between Related Taxpayers. ¶2446
Installment Sales and Other Deferred Payment Sales. ¶2452
Wash Sales. ¶2461
Basis of Property. ¶2463
Property Acquired in Nontaxable Exchanges. ¶2482
Property Acquired by Gift, from a Decedent, or from a Spouse. ¶2507

Chapter 10. Capital Gains and Losses—Section 1231—Depreciation Recapture

Capital Gains and Losses. ¶2600
Assets to Which Capital Gain and Loss Rules Apply. ¶2616
Constructive Sales of Appreciated Financial Positions. ¶2637
Short Sales. ¶2639
Section 1244 ("Small Business Corporation") Stock. ¶2644
Exclusion of Gain from Qualified Small Business Stock (QSBS). ¶2648
Tax-Free Capital Gains for Investment in Renewal Communities and DC Zone Assets. ¶2650
Tax Straddles and Section 1256 Contracts. ¶2653
Securities Futures Contracts. ¶2661
Conversion and Constructive Ownership Transactions. ¶2664
Holding Period. ¶2667
Sales and Exchanges. ¶2676
Capital Gain—Ordinary Loss Rule. ¶2684
Sale of Depreciable Property to Related Parties. ¶2690
Depreciation Recapture. ¶2692

Chapter 11. Tax Accounting—Inventories

Accounting Periods. ¶2800
Accounting Methods. ¶2816
The Cash Method of Accounting. ¶2819
The Accrual Method of Accounting. ¶2824
Changes of Accounting Methods. ¶2837
Reserves for Expenses. ¶2846
Long-Term Contracts. ¶2848
Reconstruction of Income by IRS. ¶2857
Reallocations of Income by IRS. ¶2858
Previously Reported Income Repayments. ¶2860
Inventories. ¶2863

Chapter 12. Withholding Tax on Wages and Other Income Payments

Withholding on Wages. ¶3000
Payment of Domestic Service Employment Tax ("Nanny Tax"). ¶3029
Nonpayroll Withheld Taxes. ¶3031
Pension, Annuity and Other Withholding. ¶3034
Backup Withholding. ¶3043

Chapter 13. Individual's Tax Computation—Kiddie Tax—Self-Employment Tax—3.8% Surtax—Estimated Tax

How Income Tax on Individuals Is Computed. . . . . ¶3100
Tax on Unearned Income of Children—Kiddie Tax. . . . . ¶3135
Self-Employment Tax. . . . . ¶3140
3.8% Surtax on Unearned Income. . . . . ¶3150
Individual Estimated Tax. . . . . ¶3154

Chapter 14. Alternative Minimum Tax
Alternative Minimum Tax. . . . . ¶3200

Chapter 15. Corporations—Accumulated Earnings Tax—Personal Holding Companies—Consolidated Returns—Estimated Tax—S Corporations

Taxation of Corporations. . . . . ¶3300
How C Corporations Are Taxed. . . . . ¶3303
Dividends-Received Deduction. . . . . ¶3306
Accumulated Earnings Tax. . . . . ¶3316
Personal Holding Company (PHC) Tax. . . . . ¶3320
Qualified Personal Service Corporations (PSCs). . . . . ¶3329
Dividend Distributions to Cut Special Taxes on Corporations. . . . . ¶3330
Limitation on Tax Benefits for Members of "Controlled Groups." . . . . ¶3337
Consolidated Returns by Affiliated Groups. . . . . ¶3338
Dual Consolidated Losses. . . . . ¶3342
Corporate Estimated Tax. . . . . ¶3343
S Corporations. . . . . ¶3350

Chapter 16. Corporate Transactions—Organization—Distributions—Reorganization—Acquisitions—Liquidations

Incorporations and Transfers to Controlled Corporations—Code Sec. 351. . . . . ¶3510
Corporate Distributions; Earnings and Profits (E&P). . . . . ¶3521
Stock Redemptions. . . . . ¶3526
Section 306 Stock. . . . . ¶3535
Nonliquidating Property Distributions. . . . . ¶3538
Corporate Reorganizations. . . . . ¶3541
Spin-Offs, Split-Offs and Split-Ups. . . . . ¶3559
Carryovers of Tax Items. . . . . ¶3563
Tax Avoidance Acquisition Bar to Tax Benefits. ¶3565
Limits on Use of Built-in Gains of One Corporation to Offset Losses of Another. . . . . . . ¶3566
Trafficking in Net Operating Losses (NOLs) and Other Carryovers—Code Sec. 382 Limitation. . . . . ¶3567
Corporate Liquidations. . . . . ¶3574
Code Sec. 338 Election to Treat a Stock Purchase as an Asset Purchase. . . . . . ¶3581
Transfers to Foreign Corporations—Code Sec. 367 Transfers. . . . . ¶3588

Chapter 17. Partnerships
Partnerships. . . . . ¶3700
Treatment of Contributions to a Partnership. . . . . ¶3709
Partnership Income and Deductions. . . . . ¶3715
Partnership Allocations. . . . . ¶3724
Partner's Dealings with Partnership. . . . . ¶3728
Limitations on a Partner's Deductible Loss. . . . . ¶3734
Basis of Partnership Interest. . . . . ¶3738
Distributions to a Partner. . . . . ¶3742
Disproportionate Distributions. . . . . ¶3754

	Paragraph No.
Liabilities of Partnerships and Partners.	¶3759
Transfer and Liquidation of Partnership Interest.	¶3763
Payments After Partner's Death or Retirement.	¶3768
Special Basis Adjustments to Partnership Property.	¶3775
Terminations.	¶3781

Chapter 18. Trusts—Estates—Decedents

Trust and Estate Income Tax Rules.	¶3900
Decedent's Income and Deductions.	¶3965
Bankruptcy Estate for Bankrupt Individual.	¶3973

Chapter 19. Exempt Organizations

Tax-Exempt Organizations.	¶4100
Private Foundations and Donor Advised Funds.	¶4125

Chapter 20. RICs (Mutual Funds), REITs, REMICs, Banks and Other Special Corporations

Special Corporations and Other Entities.	¶4200

Chapter 21. Pension and Profit-Sharing Plans—401(k) Plans—Roth 401(k) Plans—IRAs—Roth IRAs—SEPs—SIMPLE Plans

Employee Benefit Plans.	¶4310
Retirement Savings Plans for Individuals (IRAs).	¶4351
Roth IRAs.	¶4367
Designated Roth (Roth 401(k)) Accounts.	¶4375
Deemed IRAs.	¶4376
Simplified Employee Pensions (SEPs).	¶4377
"SIMPLE" Retirement Plans.	¶4382
Tax-Sheltered 403(b) Annuities.	¶4388

Chapter 22. Farmers

Farmers.	¶4500

Chapter 23. Foreign Income—Foreign Taxpayers—Foreign Currency Transactions

Foreign Income of U.S. Taxpayers.	¶4610
Resident Aliens Taxed as U.S. Persons.	¶4633
Taxation of Nonresident Aliens and Foreign Corporations.	¶4637
Returns Relating to Foreign Taxpayers.	¶4656
Tax Withholding on Payments to Foreign Taxpayers.	¶4662
Foreign Currency Rules.	¶4674
Reporting Gifts from Foreign Persons.	¶4677

Chapter 24. Returns and Payment of Tax

Returns and Payment of Tax.	¶4700

Chapter 25. Deficiencies—Refunds—Penalties

Tax Audits, Deficiencies and Assessments.	¶4800
Unified Audit and Review for Partnerships.	¶4840
Refunds; Tax Litigation.	¶4846
Interest and Penalties.	¶4864
Tax Collection.	¶4902

Chapter 26. Estate, Gift and Generation-Skipping Transfer Taxes

Estate Tax.	¶5000
Gift Tax.	¶5038
Generation-Skipping Transfer (GST) Tax.	¶5056
Index	

Chapter 1   Tax Rates and Tables

¶ 1100   Tax Rates and Tables.

Federal tax rates for income, gift, excise and other taxes are set forth in this Chapter. Also included are current income tax tables.

¶ 1101   Income tax rates for individuals.

Different rates apply to:

. . . single taxpayers (¶1102);

. . . married persons filing joint returns (see ¶4705) and qualified widows and widowers (¶1103);

. . . married persons filing separate returns (¶1104); and

. . . heads of households (¶1105).

Bankruptcy estates of individuals compute their tax using the same rate schedule as married individuals filing separate tax returns.

Individuals with taxable income under a ceiling amount ($100,000) may compute their tax using tax tables (Code Sec. 3); see ¶1111.

For the 3.8% surtax on "unearned income," see ¶1107.

For capital gains rates, see ¶2600 *et seq.*

¶ 1102   Single individuals.

Taxpayers who aren't married *at year's end* and who don't qualify as surviving spouses or heads of household, and certain married taxpayers living apart compute their tax under the following tax rates for single persons if they can't use the tax tables.

The rates for 2013 are:

If taxable income is:	The tax is:
Not over $8,925	10% of the taxable income
Over $8,925 but not over $36,250	$892.50 plus 15% of the excess over $8,925
Over $36,250 but not over $87,850	$4,991.25 plus 25% of the excess over $36,250
Over $87,850 but not over $183,250	$17,891.25 plus 28% of the excess over $87,850
Over $183,250 but not over $398,350	$44,603.25 plus 33% of the excess over $183,250
Over $398,350 not over $400,000	$115,586.25 plus 35% of the excess over $398,350
Over $400,000	$116,163.75 plus 39.6% of the excess over $400,000

The rates for 2014 are:

If taxable income is:	The tax is:
Not over $9,075	10% of taxable income
Over $9,075 but not over $36,900	$907.50 plus 15% of the excess over $9,075
Over $36,900 but not over $89,350	$5,081.25 plus 25% of the excess over $36,900
Over $89,350 but not over $186,350	$18,193.75 plus 28% of the excess over $89,350

References beginning with a single letter are to paragraphs in RIA's Federal Tax Coordinator 2d and RIA's Analysis of Federal Taxes: Income. Those beginning with numbers are to paragraphs in RIA's United States Tax Reporter. Those beginning with TD are to paragraphs in RIA's Tax Desk.

23

Over $186,350 but not over $405,100	$45,353.75 plus 33% of the excess over $186,350
Over $405,100 but not over $406,750	$117,541.25 plus 35% of the excess over $405,100
Over $406,750	$118,118.75 plus 39.6% of the excess over $406,750

¶ 1103 Married filing joint returns and surviving spouses.

Married taxpayers filing joint returns (see ¶4705) and surviving spouses who can't use the tax tables compute their tax on the basis of the rates indicated below.

The rates for 2013 are:

If taxable income is:	The tax is:
Not over $17,850	10% of the taxable income
Over $17,850 but not over $72,500	$1,785 plus 15% of the excess over $17,850
Over $72,500 but not over $146,400	$9,982.50 plus 25% of the excess over $72,500
Over $146,400 but not over $223,050	$28,457.50 plus 28% of the excess over $146,400
Over $223,050 but not over $398,350	$49,919.50 plus 33% of the excess over $223,050
Over $398,350 but not over $450,000	$107,768.50 plus 35% of the excess over $398,350
Over $450,000	$125,846 plus 39.6% of the excess over $450,000

The rates for 2014 are:

If taxable income is:	The tax is:
Not over $18,150	10% of taxable income
Over $18,150 but not over $73,800	$1,815.00 plus 15% of the excess over $18,150
Over $73,800 but not over $148,850	$10,162.50 plus 25% of the excess over $73,800
Over $148,850 but not over $226,850	$28,925.00 plus 28% of the excess over $148,850
Over $226,850 but not over $405,100	$50,765.00 plus 33% of the excess over $226,850
Over $405,100 but not over $457,600	$109,587.50 plus 35% of the excess over $405,100
Over $457,600	$127,962.50 plus 39.6% of the excess over $457,600

¶ 1104 Married filing separate returns.

Married taxpayers filing separate returns who can't use the tax tables compute their tax on the basis of the rates indicated below.

The rates for 2013 are:

If taxable income is:	The tax is:
Not over $8,925	10% of the taxable income
Over $8,925 but not over $36,250	$892.50 plus 15% of the excess over $8,925
Over $36,250 but not over $73,200	$4,991.25 plus 25% of the excess over $36,250

Over $73,200 but not over $111,525	$14,228.75 plus 28% of the excess over $73,200
Over $111,525 but not over $199,175	$24,959.75 plus 33% of the excess over $111,525
Over $199,175 not over $225,000	$53,884.25 plus 35% of the excess over $199,175
Over $225,000	$62,923 plus 39.6% of the excess over $225,000

The rates for 2014 are:

If taxable income is:	The tax is:
Not over $9,075	10% of taxable income
Over $9,075 but not over $36,900	$907.50 plus 15% of the excess over $9,075
Over $36,900 but not over $74,425	$5,081.25 plus 25% of the excess over $36,900
Over $74,425 but not over $113,425	$14,462.50 plus 28% of the excess over $74,425
Over $113,425 but not over $202,550	$25,382.50 plus 33% of the excess over $113,425
Over $202,550 but not over $228,800	$54,793.75 plus 35% of the excess over $202,550
Over $228,800	$63,981.25 plus 39.6% of the excess over $228,800

¶ 1105 Head of household.

Unmarried persons maintaining households who can't use the tax tables compute their tax on the basis of the rates indicated below.

The rates for 2013 are:

If taxable income is:	The tax is:
Not over $12,750	10% of the taxable income
Over $12,750 but not over $48,600	$1,275 plus 15% of the excess over $12,750
Over $48,600 but not over $125,450	$6,652.50 plus 25% of the excess over $48,600
Over $125,450 but not over $203,150	$25,865 plus 28% of the excess over $125,450
Over $203,150 but not over $398,350	$47,621 plus 33% of the excess over $203,150
Over $398,350 not over $425,000	$112,037 plus 35% of the excess over $398,350
Over $425,000	$121,364.50 plus 39.6% of the excess over $425,000

The rates for 2014 are:

If taxable income is:	The tax is:
Not over $12,950	10% of taxable income
Over $12,950 but not over $49,400	$1,295.00 plus 15% of the excess over $12,950
Over $49,400 but not over $127,550	$6,762.50 plus 25% of the excess over $49,400
Over $127,550 but not over $206,600	$26,300.00 plus 28% of the excess over $127,550
Over $206,600 but not over $405,100	$48,434.00 plus 33% of the excess over $206,600
Over $405,100 but not over $432,200	$113,939.00 plus 35% of the excess over $405,100

Over $432,200 . . . . $123,424.00 plus 39.6% of the excess over
$432,200

¶ 1106   Income tax rates for trusts and estates.

The income tax on trusts and decedent's estates is imposed at graduated rates on their taxable income. (Code Sec. 1(e)) For capital gains rates, see ¶2600.

The rates for 2013 are:

If taxable income is:	The tax is:
Not over $2,450	15% of the taxable income
Over $2,450 but not over $5,700	$367.50 plus 25% of the excess over $2,450
Over $5,700 but not over $8,750	$1,180 plus 28% of the excess over $5,700
Over $8,750 but not over $11,950	$2,034 plus 33% of the excess over $8,750
Over $11,950	$3,090 plus 39.6% of the excess over $11,950

The rates for 2014 are:

If taxable income is:	The tax is:
Not over $2,500	15% of taxable income
Over $2,500 but not over $5,800	$375.00 plus 25% of the excess over $2,500
Over $5,800 but not over $8,900	$1,200.00 plus 28% of the excess over $5,800
Over $8,900 but not over $12,150	$2,068.00 plus 33% of the excess over $8,900
Over $12,150	$3,140.50 plus 39.6% of the excess over $12,150

¶ 1107   3.8% surtax on "unearned income."

For tax years beginning after 2012, certain unearned income of individuals, trusts, and estates is subject to a surtax (i.e., it's payable on top of any other tax payable on that income). For individuals, the surtax is 3.8% of the lesser of (1) "net investment income" or (2) the excess of modified adjusted gross income (MAGI) over the threshold amount ($250,000 for joint filers or surviving spouses, $125,000 for a married individual filing a separate return, and $200,000 in any other case). Special computations apply to estates and trusts. (Code Sec. 1411(a)(1), Code Sec. 1411(b))[1] For details, see ¶3150 *et seq.*

¶ 1108   FICA (Social Security and Medicare) tax.

For 2013, an employer pays a 7.65% FICA tax, consisting of:

(1) 6.20% Social Security tax on the first $113,700 of an employee's wages (maximum tax is $7,049.40 [6.20% of $113,700]), plus

(2) 1.45% Medicare tax on the employee's total wages (no ceiling). (Code Sec. 3101(a), Code Sec. 3101(b), Code Sec. 3111(a), Code Sec. 3111(b))

For 2013, an employee pays:

(1) 6.20% Social Security tax on the first $113,700 of wages (maximum tax is $7,049.40 [6.20% of $113,700]), plus

(2) 1.45% Medicare tax on the first $200,000 of wages ($250,000 for joint returns; $125,000 for married taxpayers filing a separate return), plus

(3) 2.35% Medicare tax (regular 1.45% Medicare tax + 0.9% additional Medicare tax) on all wages in excess of $200,000 ($250,000 for joint returns; $125,000 for married taxpayers filing a separate return). (Code Sec. 3101(b)(2))

1. ¶A-6361; ¶14,114.01; TD ¶576,301

For 2014, an employer pays a 7.65% FICA tax, consisting of:

(a) 6.20% Social Security tax on the first $117,000 of an employee's wages (maximum tax is $7,254 [6.20% of $117,000]), plus

(b) 1.45% Medicare tax on the employee's total wages (no ceiling).

For 2014, an employee pays:

(a) 6.20% Social Security tax on the first $117,000 of wages (maximum tax is $7,254 [6.20% of $117,000]), plus

(b) 1.45% Medicare tax on the first $200,000 of wages ($250,000 for joint returns; $125,000 for married taxpayers filing a separate return), plus

(c) 2.35% Medicare tax (regular 1.45% Medicare tax + 0.9% additional Medicare tax) on all wages in excess of $200,000 ($250,000 for joint returns; $125,000 for married taxpayers filing a separate return). (Code Sec. 3101(b)(2))

The 0.9% additional Medicare tax applies only to employees, not employers. Employers must begin withholding the additional Medicare tax once an employee's wages exceed $200,000, even if the employee may not ultimately be liable for the additional tax (e.g., employee earns $210,000, his spouse earns $25,000, and they file a joint return). Any excess additional Medicare tax withheld will be credited against the total tax liability shown on the employee's income tax return. Conversely, the 0.9% additional Medicare tax may be owed on the employee's income tax return where there was no withholding for it (e.g., employee earns $175,000 and her spouse earns $150,000).[2]

¶ 1109   Self-employment tax.

For 2013, the self-employment tax imposed on self-employed people is:

* 12.40% OASDI on the first $113,700 of self-employment income, for a maximum tax of $14,098.80 (12.40% of $113,700); plus

* 2.90% Medicare tax on the first $200,000 of self-employment income ($250,000 of combined self-employment income on a joint return, $125,000 on a separate return), (Code Sec. 1401(a), Code Sec. 1401(b)); plus

* 3.8% (2.90% regular Medicare tax + 0.9% additional Medicare tax) on all self-employment income in excess of $200,000 ($250,000 of combined self-employment income on a joint return, $125,000 for married taxpayers filing a separate return). (Code Sec. 1401(b)(2))

For 2014, the self-employment tax imposed on self-employed people is:

* 12.40% OASDI on the first $117,000 of self-employment income, for a maximum tax of $14,508 (12.40% of $117,000); plus

* 2.90% Medicare tax on the first $200,000 of self-employment income ($250,000 of combined self-employment income on a joint return, $125,000 on a separate return), (Code Sec. 1401(a), Code Sec. 1401(b)); plus

* 3.8% (2.90% regular Medicare tax + 0.9% additional Medicare tax) on all self-employment income in excess of $200,000 ($250,000 of combined self-employment income on a joint return, $125,000 for married taxpayers filing a separate return). (Code Sec. 1401(b)(2))

The above $250,000, $125,000, and $200,000 thresholds are reduced (but not below zero) by the amount of wages taken into account in determining the additional 0.9% HI tax on wages (see ¶1108). (Code Sec. 1401(b)(2)(B))[3]

---

2. ¶H-4687; ¶35,014.07; TD ¶541,002   3. ¶A-6100.2; ¶14,014; TD ¶575,501

observation: Sole proprietors and partners are subject to Medicare tax on their entire self-employment income even if the income isn't distributed (unlike shareholders in an S corporation, who aren't subject to the self-employment tax on their share of the corporation's net income whether distributed or not, see ¶3143).

observation: Amounts subject to self-employment tax are excluded from "investment income" for purposes of the post-2012 3.8% net investment income tax (¶1107).

¶ 1110   Federal unemployment tax (FUTA).

Employers pay a 6.0% (Code Sec. 3301) tax on the first $7,000 paid each employee as wages during the calendar year. (Code Sec. 3306(b)) This tax may be offset by a credit of up to 5.4% for contributions paid into state unemployment funds, effectively reducing the net FUTA tax rate for the majority of employers to 0.6% (i.e., 6.0% – 5.4%). However, the amount of the 5.4% credit can be reduced for employers in states that borrowed funds from the federal government to pay unemployment benefits and defaulted on repayment of the loan.

¶ 1111   Tax Table for Individuals.

2013
Tax Table

See the instructions for line 44 to see if you must use the Tax Table below to figure your tax.

Example. Mr. and Mrs. Brown are filing a joint return. Their taxable income on Form 1040, line 43, is $25,300. First, they find the $25,300-$25,350 taxable income line. Next, they find the column for married filing jointly and read down the column. The amount shown where the taxable income line and filing status column meet is $2,906. This is the tax amount they should enter on Form 1040, line 44.

Sample Table

At Least	But Less Than	Single	Married filing jointly *	Married filing separately	Head of a household
			Your tax is—		
25,200	25,250	3,338	2,891	3,338	3,146
25,250	25,300	3,345	2,899	3,345	3,154
25,300	25,350	3,353	2,906	3,353	3,161
25,350	25,400	3,360	2,914	3,360	3,169

If line 43 (taxable income) is— At least	But less than	And you are— Single	Married filing jointly *	Married filing separately	Head of a house-hold
			Your tax is—		
0	5	0	0	0	0
5	15	1	1	1	1
15	25	2	2	2	2
25	50	4	4	4	4
50	75	6	6	6	6
75	100	9	9	9	9
100	125	11	11	11	11
125	150	14	14	14	14
150	175	16	16	16	16
175	200	19	19	19	19
200	225	21	21	21	21
225	250	24	24	24	24
250	275	26	26	26	26
275	300	29	29	29	29
300	325	31	31	31	31
325	350	34	34	34	34
350	375	36	36	36	36
375	400	39	39	39	39
400	425	41	41	41	41
425	450	44	44	44	44
450	475	46	46	46	46
475	500	49	49	49	49
500	525	51	51	51	51
525	550	54	54	54	54
550	575	56	56	56	56
575	600	59	59	59	59
600	625	61	61	61	61
625	650	64	64	64	64
650	675	66	66	66	66
675	700	69	69	69	69
700	725	71	71	71	71
725	750	74	74	74	74
750	775	76	76	76	76
775	800	79	79	79	79
800	825	81	81	81	81
825	850	84	84	84	84
850	875	86	86	86	86
875	900	89	89	89	89
900	925	91	91	91	91
925	950	94	94	94	94
950	975	96	96	96	96
975	1,000	99	99	99	99

1,000

If line 43 (taxable income) is— At least	But less than	And you are— Single	Married filing jointly *	Married filing separately	Head of a house-hold
			Your tax is—		
1,000	1,025	101	101	101	101
1,025	1,050	104	104	104	104
1,050	1,075	106	106	106	106
1,075	1,100	109	109	109	109
1,100	1,125	111	111	111	111
1,125	1,150	114	114	114	114
1,150	1,175	116	116	116	116
1,175	1,200	119	119	119	119
1,200	1,225	121	121	121	121
1,225	1,250	124	124	124	124
1,250	1,275	126	126	126	126
1,275	1,300	129	129	129	129
1,300	1,325	131	131	131	131
1,325	1,350	134	134	134	134
1,350	1,375	136	136	136	136
1,375	1,400	139	139	139	139
1,400	1,425	141	141	141	141
1,425	1,450	144	144	144	144
1,450	1,475	146	146	146	146
1,475	1,500	149	149	149	149
1,500	1,525	151	151	151	151
1,525	1,550	154	154	154	154
1,550	1,575	156	156	156	156
1,575	1,600	159	159	159	159
1,600	1,625	161	161	161	161
1,625	1,650	164	164	164	164
1,650	1,675	166	166	166	166
1,675	1,700	169	169	169	169
1,700	1,725	171	171	171	171
1,725	1,750	174	174	174	174
1,750	1,775	176	176	176	176
1,775	1,800	179	179	179	179
1,800	1,825	181	181	181	181
1,825	1,850	184	184	184	184
1,850	1,875	186	186	186	186
1,875	1,900	189	189	189	189
1,900	1,925	191	191	191	191
1,925	1,950	194	194	194	194
1,950	1,975	196	196	196	196
1,975	2,000	199	199	199	199

2,000

If line 43 (taxable income) is— At least	But less than	And you are— Single	Married filing jointly *	Married filing separately	Head of a house-hold
			Your tax is—		
2,000	2,025	201	201	201	201
2,025	2,050	204	204	204	204
2,050	2,075	206	206	206	206
2,075	2,100	209	209	209	209
2,100	2,125	211	211	211	211
2,125	2,150	214	214	214	214
2,150	2,175	216	216	216	216
2,175	2,200	219	219	219	219
2,200	2,225	221	221	221	221
2,225	2,250	224	224	224	224
2,250	2,275	226	226	226	226
2,275	2,300	229	229	229	229
2,300	2,325	231	231	231	231
2,325	2,350	234	234	234	234
2,350	2,375	236	236	236	236
2,375	2,400	239	239	239	239
2,400	2,425	241	241	241	241
2,425	2,450	244	244	244	244
2,450	2,475	246	246	246	246
2,475	2,500	249	249	249	249
2,500	2,525	251	251	251	251
2,525	2,550	254	254	254	254
2,550	2,575	256	256	256	256
2,575	2,600	259	259	259	259
2,600	2,625	261	261	261	261
2,625	2,650	264	264	264	264
2,650	2,675	266	266	266	266
2,675	2,700	269	269	269	269
2,700	2,725	271	271	271	271
2,725	2,750	274	274	274	274
2,750	2,775	276	276	276	276
2,775	2,800	279	279	279	279
2,800	2,825	281	281	281	281
2,825	2,850	284	284	284	284
2,850	2,875	286	286	286	286
2,875	2,900	289	289	289	289
2,900	2,925	291	291	291	291
2,925	2,950	294	294	294	294
2,950	2,975	296	296	296	296
2,975	3,000	299	299	299	299

* This column must also be used by a qualifying widow(er).

(Continued)

NOTE: DRAFT AS OF SEPTEMBER 16, 2013.

2013 Tax Table—*Continued*

At least	But less than	Single	Married filing jointly *	Married filing separately	Head of a household
3,000					
3,000	3,050	303	303	303	303
3,050	3,100	308	308	308	308
3,100	3,150	313	313	313	313
3,150	3,200	318	318	318	318
3,200	3,250	323	323	323	323
3,250	3,300	328	328	328	328
3,300	3,350	333	333	333	333
3,350	3,400	338	338	338	338
3,400	3,450	343	343	343	343
3,450	3,500	348	348	348	348
3,500	3,550	353	353	353	353
3,550	3,600	358	358	358	358
3,600	3,650	363	363	363	363
3,650	3,700	368	368	368	368
3,700	3,750	373	373	373	373
3,750	3,800	378	378	378	378
3,800	3,850	383	383	383	383
3,850	3,900	388	388	388	388
3,900	3,950	393	393	393	393
3,950	4,000	398	398	398	398
4,000					
4,000	4,050	403	403	403	403
4,050	4,100	408	408	408	408
4,100	4,150	413	413	413	413
4,150	4,200	418	418	418	418
4,200	4,250	423	423	423	423
4,250	4,300	428	428	428	428
4,300	4,350	433	433	433	433
4,350	4,400	438	438	438	438
4,400	4,450	443	443	443	443
4,450	4,500	448	448	448	448
4,500	4,550	453	453	453	453
4,550	4,600	458	458	458	458
4,600	4,650	463	463	463	463
4,650	4,700	468	468	468	468
4,700	4,750	473	473	473	473
4,750	4,800	478	478	478	478
4,800	4,850	483	483	483	483
4,850	4,900	488	488	488	488
4,900	4,950	493	493	493	493
4,950	5,000	498	498	498	498
5,000					
5,000	5,050	503	503	503	503
5,050	5,100	508	508	508	508
5,100	5,150	513	513	513	513
5,150	5,200	518	518	518	518
5,200	5,250	523	523	523	523
5,250	5,300	528	528	528	528
5,300	5,350	533	533	533	533
5,350	5,400	538	538	538	538
5,400	5,450	543	543	543	543
5,450	5,500	548	548	548	548
5,500	5,550	553	553	553	553
5,550	5,600	558	558	558	558
5,600	5,650	563	563	563	563
5,650	5,700	568	568	568	568
5,700	5,750	573	573	573	573
5,750	5,800	578	578	578	578
5,800	5,850	583	583	583	583
5,850	5,900	588	588	588	588
5,900	5,950	593	593	593	593
5,950	6,000	598	598	598	598

At least	But less than	Single	Married filing jointly *	Married filing separately	Head of a household
6,000					
6,000	6,050	603	603	603	603
6,050	6,100	608	608	608	608
6,100	6,150	613	613	613	613
6,150	6,200	618	618	618	618
6,200	6,250	623	623	623	623
6,250	6,300	628	628	628	628
6,300	6,350	633	633	633	633
6,350	6,400	638	638	638	638
6,400	6,450	643	643	643	643
6,450	6,500	648	648	648	648
6,500	6,550	653	653	653	653
6,550	6,600	658	658	658	658
6,600	6,650	663	663	663	663
6,650	6,700	668	668	668	668
6,700	6,750	673	673	673	673
6,750	6,800	678	678	678	678
6,800	6,850	683	683	683	683
6,850	6,900	688	688	688	688
6,900	6,950	693	693	693	693
6,950	7,000	698	698	698	698
7,000					
7,000	7,050	703	703	703	703
7,050	7,100	708	708	708	708
7,100	7,150	713	713	713	713
7,150	7,200	718	718	718	718
7,200	7,250	723	723	723	723
7,250	7,300	728	728	728	728
7,300	7,350	733	733	733	733
7,350	7,400	738	738	738	738
7,400	7,450	743	743	743	743
7,450	7,500	748	748	748	748
7,500	7,550	753	753	753	753
7,550	7,600	758	758	758	758
7,600	7,650	763	763	763	763
7,650	7,700	768	768	768	768
7,700	7,750	773	773	773	773
7,750	7,800	778	778	778	778
7,800	7,850	783	783	783	783
7,850	7,900	788	788	788	788
7,900	7,950	793	793	793	793
7,950	8,000	798	798	798	798
8,000					
8,000	8,050	803	803	803	803
8,050	8,100	808	808	808	808
8,100	8,150	813	813	813	813
8,150	8,200	818	818	818	818
8,200	8,250	823	823	823	823
8,250	8,300	828	828	828	828
8,300	8,350	833	833	833	833
8,350	8,400	838	838	838	838
8,400	8,450	843	843	843	843
8,450	8,500	848	848	848	848
8,500	8,550	853	853	853	853
8,550	8,600	858	858	858	858
8,600	8,650	863	863	863	863
8,650	8,700	868	868	868	868
8,700	8,750	873	873	873	873
8,750	8,800	878	878	878	878
8,800	8,850	883	883	883	883
8,850	8,900	888	888	888	888
8,900	8,950	893	893	893	893
8,950	9,000	900	898	900	898

At least	But less than	Single	Married filing jointly *	Married filing separately	Head of a household
9,000					
9,000	9,050	908	903	908	903
9,050	9,100	915	908	915	908
9,100	9,150	923	913	923	913
9,150	9,200	930	918	930	918
9,200	9,250	938	923	938	923
9,250	9,300	945	928	945	928
9,300	9,350	953	933	953	933
9,350	9,400	960	938	960	938
9,400	9,450	968	943	968	943
9,450	9,500	975	948	975	948
9,500	9,550	983	953	983	953
9,550	9,600	990	958	990	958
9,600	9,650	998	963	998	963
9,650	9,700	1,005	968	1,005	968
9,700	9,750	1,013	973	1,013	973
9,750	9,800	1,020	978	1,020	978
9,800	9,850	1,028	983	1,028	983
9,850	9,900	1,035	988	1,035	988
9,900	9,950	1,043	993	1,043	993
9,950	10,000	1,050	998	1,050	998
10,000					
10,000	10,050	1,058	1,003	1,058	1,003
10,050	10,100	1,065	1,008	1,065	1,008
10,100	10,150	1,073	1,013	1,073	1,013
10,150	10,200	1,080	1,018	1,080	1,018
10,200	10,250	1,088	1,023	1,088	1,023
10,250	10,300	1,095	1,028	1,095	1,028
10,300	10,350	1,103	1,033	1,103	1,033
10,350	10,400	1,110	1,038	1,110	1,038
10,400	10,450	1,118	1,043	1,118	1,043
10,450	10,500	1,125	1,048	1,125	1,048
10,500	10,550	1,133	1,053	1,133	1,053
10,550	10,600	1,140	1,058	1,140	1,058
10,600	10,650	1,148	1,063	1,148	1,063
10,650	10,700	1,155	1,068	1,155	1,068
10,700	10,750	1,163	1,073	1,163	1,073
10,750	10,800	1,170	1,078	1,170	1,078
10,800	10,850	1,178	1,083	1,178	1,083
10,850	10,900	1,185	1,088	1,185	1,088
10,900	10,950	1,193	1,093	1,193	1,093
10,950	11,000	1,200	1,098	1,200	1,098
11,000					
11,000	11,050	1,208	1,103	1,208	1,103
11,050	11,100	1,215	1,108	1,215	1,108
11,100	11,150	1,223	1,113	1,223	1,113
11,150	11,200	1,230	1,118	1,230	1,118
11,200	11,250	1,238	1,123	1,238	1,123
11,250	11,300	1,245	1,128	1,245	1,128
11,300	11,350	1,253	1,133	1,253	1,133
11,350	11,400	1,260	1,138	1,260	1,138
11,400	11,450	1,268	1,143	1,268	1,143
11,450	11,500	1,275	1,148	1,275	1,148
11,500	11,550	1,283	1,153	1,283	1,153
11,550	11,600	1,290	1,158	1,290	1,158
11,600	11,650	1,298	1,163	1,298	1,163
11,650	11,700	1,305	1,168	1,305	1,168
11,700	11,750	1,313	1,173	1,313	1,173
11,750	11,800	1,320	1,178	1,320	1,178
11,800	11,850	1,328	1,183	1,328	1,183
11,850	11,900	1,335	1,188	1,335	1,188
11,900	11,950	1,343	1,193	1,343	1,193
11,950	12,000	1,350	1,198	1,350	1,198

* This column must also be used by a qualifying widow(er).

NOTE: DRAFT AS OF SEPTEMBER 16, 2013.

(Continued)

2013 Tax Table—Continued

12,000

At least	But less than	Single	Married filing jointly *	Married filing separately	Head of a household
12,000	12,050	1,358	1,203	1,358	1,203
12,050	12,100	1,365	1,208	1,365	1,208
12,100	12,150	1,373	1,213	1,373	1,213
12,150	12,200	1,380	1,218	1,380	1,218
12,200	12,250	1,388	1,223	1,388	1,223
12,250	12,300	1,395	1,228	1,395	1,228
12,300	12,350	1,403	1,233	1,403	1,233
12,350	12,400	1,410	1,238	1,410	1,238
12,400	12,450	1,418	1,243	1,418	1,243
12,450	12,500	1,425	1,248	1,425	1,248
12,500	12,550	1,433	1,253	1,433	1,253
12,550	12,600	1,440	1,258	1,440	1,258
12,600	12,650	1,448	1,263	1,448	1,263
12,650	12,700	1,455	1,268	1,455	1,268
12,700	12,750	1,463	1,273	1,463	1,273
12,750	12,800	1,470	1,278	1,470	1,279
12,800	12,850	1,478	1,283	1,478	1,286
12,850	12,900	1,485	1,288	1,485	1,294
12,900	12,950	1,493	1,293	1,493	1,301
12,950	13,000	1,500	1,298	1,500	1,309

13,000

At least	But less than	Single	Married filing jointly *	Married filing separately	Head of a household
13,000	13,050	1,508	1,303	1,508	1,316
13,050	13,100	1,515	1,308	1,515	1,324
13,100	13,150	1,523	1,313	1,523	1,331
13,150	13,200	1,530	1,318	1,530	1,339
13,200	13,250	1,538	1,323	1,538	1,346
13,250	13,300	1,545	1,328	1,545	1,354
13,300	13,350	1,553	1,333	1,553	1,361
13,350	13,400	1,560	1,338	1,560	1,369
13,400	13,450	1,568	1,343	1,568	1,376
13,450	13,500	1,575	1,348	1,575	1,384
13,500	13,550	1,583	1,353	1,583	1,391
13,550	13,600	1,590	1,358	1,590	1,399
13,600	13,650	1,598	1,363	1,598	1,406
13,650	13,700	1,605	1,368	1,605	1,414
13,700	13,750	1,613	1,373	1,613	1,421
13,750	13,800	1,620	1,378	1,620	1,429
13,800	13,850	1,628	1,383	1,628	1,436
13,850	13,900	1,635	1,388	1,635	1,444
13,900	13,950	1,643	1,393	1,643	1,451
13,950	14,000	1,650	1,398	1,650	1,459

14,000

At least	But less than	Single	Married filing jointly *	Married filing separately	Head of a household
14,000	14,050	1,658	1,403	1,658	1,466
14,050	14,100	1,665	1,408	1,665	1,474
14,100	14,150	1,673	1,413	1,673	1,481
14,150	14,200	1,680	1,418	1,680	1,489
14,200	14,250	1,688	1,423	1,688	1,496
14,250	14,300	1,695	1,428	1,695	1,504
14,300	14,350	1,703	1,433	1,703	1,511
14,350	14,400	1,710	1,438	1,710	1,519
14,400	14,450	1,718	1,443	1,718	1,526
14,450	14,500	1,725	1,448	1,725	1,534
14,500	14,550	1,733	1,453	1,733	1,541
14,550	14,600	1,740	1,458	1,740	1,549
14,600	14,650	1,748	1,463	1,748	1,556
14,650	14,700	1,755	1,468	1,755	1,564
14,700	14,750	1,763	1,473	1,763	1,571
14,750	14,800	1,770	1,478	1,770	1,579
14,800	14,850	1,778	1,483	1,778	1,586
14,850	14,900	1,785	1,488	1,785	1,594
14,900	14,950	1,793	1,493	1,793	1,601
14,950	15,000	1,800	1,498	1,800	1,609

15,000

At least	But less than	Single	Married filing jointly *	Married filing separately	Head of a household
15,000	15,050	1,808	1,503	1,808	1,616
15,050	15,100	1,815	1,508	1,815	1,624
15,100	15,150	1,823	1,513	1,823	1,631
15,150	15,200	1,830	1,518	1,830	1,639
15,200	15,250	1,838	1,523	1,838	1,646
15,250	15,300	1,845	1,528	1,845	1,654
15,300	15,350	1,853	1,533	1,853	1,661
15,350	15,400	1,860	1,538	1,860	1,669
15,400	15,450	1,868	1,543	1,868	1,676
15,450	15,500	1,875	1,548	1,875	1,684
15,500	15,550	1,883	1,553	1,883	1,691
15,550	15,600	1,890	1,558	1,890	1,699
15,600	15,650	1,898	1,563	1,898	1,706
15,650	15,700	1,905	1,568	1,905	1,714
15,700	15,750	1,913	1,573	1,913	1,721
15,750	15,800	1,920	1,578	1,920	1,729
15,800	15,850	1,928	1,583	1,928	1,736
15,850	15,900	1,935	1,588	1,935	1,744
15,900	15,950	1,943	1,593	1,943	1,751
15,950	16,000	1,950	1,598	1,950	1,759

16,000

At least	But less than	Single	Married filing jointly *	Married filing separately	Head of a household
16,000	16,050	1,958	1,603	1,958	1,766
16,050	16,100	1,965	1,608	1,965	1,774
16,100	16,150	1,973	1,613	1,973	1,781
16,150	16,200	1,980	1,618	1,980	1,789
16,200	16,250	1,988	1,623	1,988	1,796
16,250	16,300	1,995	1,628	1,995	1,804
16,300	16,350	2,003	1,633	2,003	1,811
16,350	16,400	2,010	1,638	2,010	1,819
16,400	16,450	2,018	1,643	2,018	1,826
16,450	16,500	2,025	1,648	2,025	1,834
16,500	16,550	2,033	1,653	2,033	1,841
16,550	16,600	2,040	1,658	2,040	1,849
16,600	16,650	2,048	1,663	2,048	1,856
16,650	16,700	2,055	1,668	2,055	1,864
16,700	16,750	2,063	1,673	2,063	1,871
16,750	16,800	2,070	1,678	2,070	1,879
16,800	16,850	2,078	1,683	2,078	1,886
16,850	16,900	2,085	1,688	2,085	1,894
16,900	16,950	2,093	1,693	2,093	1,901
16,950	17,000	2,100	1,698	2,100	1,909

17,000

At least	But less than	Single	Married filing jointly *	Married filing separately	Head of a household
17,000	17,050	2,108	1,703	2,108	1,916
17,050	17,100	2,115	1,708	2,115	1,924
17,100	17,150	2,123	1,713	2,123	1,931
17,150	17,200	2,130	1,718	2,130	1,939
17,200	17,250	2,138	1,723	2,138	1,946
17,250	17,300	2,145	1,728	2,145	1,954
17,300	17,350	2,153	1,733	2,153	1,961
17,350	17,400	2,160	1,738	2,160	1,969
17,400	17,450	2,168	1,743	2,168	1,976
17,450	17,500	2,175	1,748	2,175	1,984
17,500	17,550	2,183	1,753	2,183	1,991
17,550	17,600	2,190	1,758	2,190	1,999
17,600	17,650	2,198	1,763	2,198	2,006
17,650	17,700	2,205	1,768	2,205	2,014
17,700	17,750	2,213	1,773	2,213	2,021
17,750	17,800	2,220	1,778	2,220	2,029
17,800	17,850	2,228	1,783	2,228	2,036
17,850	17,900	2,235	1,789	2,235	2,044
17,900	17,950	2,243	1,796	2,243	2,051
17,950	18,000	2,250	1,804	2,250	2,059

18,000

At least	But less than	Single	Married filing jointly *	Married filing separately	Head of a household
18,000	18,050	2,258	1,811	2,258	2,066
18,050	18,100	2,265	1,819	2,265	2,074
18,100	18,150	2,273	1,826	2,273	2,081
18,150	18,200	2,280	1,834	2,280	2,089
18,200	18,250	2,288	1,841	2,288	2,096
18,250	18,300	2,295	1,849	2,295	2,104
18,300	18,350	2,303	1,856	2,303	2,111
18,350	18,400	2,310	1,864	2,310	2,119
18,400	18,450	2,318	1,871	2,318	2,126
18,450	18,500	2,325	1,879	2,325	2,134
18,500	18,550	2,333	1,886	2,333	2,141
18,550	18,600	2,340	1,894	2,340	2,149
18,600	18,650	2,348	1,901	2,348	2,156
18,650	18,700	2,355	1,909	2,355	2,164
18,700	18,750	2,363	1,916	2,363	2,171
18,750	18,800	2,370	1,924	2,370	2,179
18,800	18,850	2,378	1,931	2,378	2,186
18,850	18,900	2,385	1,939	2,385	2,194
18,900	18,950	2,393	1,946	2,393	2,201
18,950	19,000	2,400	1,954	2,400	2,209

19,000

At least	But less than	Single	Married filing jointly *	Married filing separately	Head of a household
19,000	19,050	2,408	1,961	2,408	2,216
19,050	19,100	2,415	1,969	2,415	2,224
19,100	19,150	2,423	1,976	2,423	2,231
19,150	19,200	2,430	1,984	2,430	2,239
19,200	19,250	2,438	1,991	2,438	2,246
19,250	19,300	2,445	1,999	2,445	2,254
19,300	19,350	2,453	2,006	2,453	2,261
19,350	19,400	2,460	2,014	2,460	2,269
19,400	19,450	2,468	2,021	2,468	2,276
19,450	19,500	2,475	2,029	2,475	2,284
19,500	19,550	2,483	2,036	2,483	2,291
19,550	19,600	2,490	2,044	2,490	2,299
19,600	19,650	2,498	2,051	2,498	2,306
19,650	19,700	2,505	2,059	2,505	2,314
19,700	19,750	2,513	2,066	2,513	2,321
19,750	19,800	2,520	2,074	2,520	2,329
19,800	19,850	2,528	2,081	2,528	2,336
19,850	19,900	2,535	2,089	2,535	2,344
19,900	19,950	2,543	2,096	2,543	2,351
19,950	20,000	2,550	2,104	2,550	2,359

20,000

At least	But less than	Single	Married filing jointly *	Married filing separately	Head of a household
20,000	20,050	2,558	2,111	2,558	2,366
20,050	20,100	2,565	2,119	2,565	2,374
20,100	20,150	2,573	2,126	2,573	2,381
20,150	20,200	2,580	2,134	2,580	2,389
20,200	20,250	2,588	2,141	2,588	2,396
20,250	20,300	2,595	2,149	2,595	2,404
20,300	20,350	2,603	2,156	2,603	2,411
20,350	20,400	2,610	2,164	2,610	2,419
20,400	20,450	2,618	2,171	2,618	2,426
20,450	20,500	2,625	2,179	2,625	2,434
20,500	20,550	2,633	2,186	2,633	2,441
20,550	20,600	2,640	2,194	2,640	2,449
20,600	20,650	2,648	2,201	2,648	2,456
20,650	20,700	2,655	2,209	2,655	2,464
20,700	20,750	2,663	2,216	2,663	2,471
20,750	20,800	2,670	2,224	2,670	2,479
20,800	20,850	2,678	2,231	2,678	2,486
20,850	20,900	2,685	2,239	2,685	2,494
20,900	20,950	2,693	2,246	2,693	2,501
20,950	21,000	2,700	2,254	2,700	2,509

* This column must also be used by a qualifying widow(er).

(Continued)

NOTE: DRAFT AS OF SEPTEMBER 16, 2013.

2013 Tax Table—*Continued*

If line 43 (taxable income) is—		And you are—			
At least	But less than	Single	Married filing jointly *	Married filing separately	Head of a household
		Your tax is—			

21,000

At least	But less than	Single	Married filing jointly *	Married filing separately	Head of a household
21,000	21,050	2,708	2,261	2,708	2,516
21,050	21,100	2,715	2,269	2,715	2,524
21,100	21,150	2,723	2,276	2,723	2,531
21,150	21,200	2,730	2,284	2,730	2,539
21,200	21,250	2,738	2,291	2,738	2,546
21,250	21,300	2,745	2,299	2,745	2,554
21,300	21,350	2,753	2,306	2,753	2,561
21,350	21,400	2,760	2,314	2,760	2,569
21,400	21,450	2,768	2,321	2,768	2,576
21,450	21,500	2,775	2,329	2,775	2,584
21,500	21,550	2,783	2,336	2,783	2,591
21,550	21,600	2,790	2,344	2,790	2,599
21,600	21,650	2,798	2,351	2,798	2,606
21,650	21,700	2,805	2,359	2,805	2,614
21,700	21,750	2,813	2,366	2,813	2,621
21,750	21,800	2,820	2,374	2,820	2,629
21,800	21,850	2,828	2,381	2,828	2,636
21,850	21,900	2,835	2,389	2,835	2,644
21,900	21,950	2,843	2,396	2,843	2,651
21,950	22,000	2,850	2,404	2,850	2,659

22,000

At least	But less than	Single	Married filing jointly *	Married filing separately	Head of a household
22,000	22,050	2,858	2,411	2,858	2,666
22,050	22,100	2,865	2,419	2,865	2,674
22,100	22,150	2,873	2,426	2,873	2,681
22,150	22,200	2,880	2,434	2,880	2,689
22,200	22,250	2,888	2,441	2,888	2,696
22,250	22,300	2,895	2,449	2,895	2,704
22,300	22,350	2,903	2,456	2,903	2,711
22,350	22,400	2,910	2,464	2,910	2,719
22,400	22,450	2,918	2,471	2,918	2,726
22,450	22,500	2,925	2,479	2,925	2,734
22,500	22,550	2,933	2,486	2,933	2,741
22,550	22,600	2,940	2,494	2,940	2,749
22,600	22,650	2,948	2,501	2,948	2,756
22,650	22,700	2,955	2,509	2,955	2,764
22,700	22,750	2,963	2,516	2,963	2,771
22,750	22,800	2,970	2,524	2,970	2,779
22,800	22,850	2,978	2,531	2,978	2,786
22,850	22,900	2,985	2,539	2,985	2,794
22,900	22,950	2,993	2,546	2,993	2,801
22,950	23,000	3,000	2,554	3,000	2,809

23,000

At least	But less than	Single	Married filing jointly *	Married filing separately	Head of a household
23,000	23,050	3,008	2,561	3,008	2,816
23,050	23,100	3,015	2,569	3,015	2,824
23,100	23,150	3,023	2,576	3,023	2,831
23,150	23,200	3,030	2,584	3,030	2,839
23,200	23,250	3,038	2,591	3,038	2,846
23,250	23,300	3,045	2,599	3,045	2,854
23,300	23,350	3,053	2,606	3,053	2,861
23,350	23,400	3,060	2,614	3,060	2,869
23,400	23,450	3,068	2,621	3,068	2,876
23,450	23,500	3,075	2,629	3,075	2,884
23,500	23,550	3,083	2,636	3,083	2,891
23,550	23,600	3,090	2,644	3,090	2,899
23,600	23,650	3,098	2,651	3,098	2,906
23,650	23,700	3,105	2,659	3,105	2,914
23,700	23,750	3,113	2,666	3,113	2,921
23,750	23,800	3,120	2,674	3,120	2,929
23,800	23,850	3,128	2,681	3,128	2,936
23,850	23,900	3,135	2,689	3,135	2,944
23,900	23,950	3,143	2,696	3,143	2,951
23,950	24,000	3,150	2,704	3,150	2,959

24,000

At least	But less than	Single	Married filing jointly *	Married filing separately	Head of a household
24,000	24,050	3,158	2,711	3,158	2,966
24,050	24,100	3,165	2,719	3,165	2,974
24,100	24,150	3,173	2,726	3,173	2,981
24,150	24,200	3,180	2,734	3,180	2,989
24,200	24,250	3,188	2,741	3,188	2,996
24,250	24,300	3,195	2,749	3,195	3,004
24,300	24,350	3,203	2,756	3,203	3,011
24,350	24,400	3,210	2,764	3,210	3,019
24,400	24,450	3,218	2,771	3,218	3,026
24,450	24,500	3,225	2,779	3,225	3,034
24,500	24,550	3,233	2,786	3,233	3,041
24,550	24,600	3,240	2,794	3,240	3,049
24,600	24,650	3,248	2,801	3,248	3,056
24,650	24,700	3,255	2,809	3,255	3,064
24,700	24,750	3,263	2,816	3,263	3,071
24,750	24,800	3,270	2,824	3,270	3,079
24,800	24,850	3,278	2,831	3,278	3,086
24,850	24,900	3,285	2,839	3,285	3,094
24,900	24,950	3,293	2,846	3,293	3,101
24,950	25,000	3,300	2,854	3,300	3,109

25,000

At least	But less than	Single	Married filing jointly *	Married filing separately	Head of a household
25,000	25,050	3,308	2,861	3,308	3,116
25,050	25,100	3,315	2,869	3,315	3,124
25,100	25,150	3,323	2,876	3,323	3,131
25,150	25,200	3,330	2,884	3,330	3,139
25,200	25,250	3,338	2,891	3,338	3,146
25,250	25,300	3,345	2,899	3,345	3,154
25,300	25,350	3,353	2,906	3,353	3,161
25,350	25,400	3,360	2,914	3,360	3,169
25,400	25,450	3,368	2,921	3,368	3,176
25,450	25,500	3,375	2,929	3,375	3,184
25,500	25,550	3,383	2,936	3,383	3,191
25,550	25,600	3,390	2,944	3,390	3,199
25,600	25,650	3,398	2,951	3,398	3,206
25,650	25,700	3,405	2,959	3,405	3,214
25,700	25,750	3,413	2,966	3,413	3,221
25,750	25,800	3,420	2,974	3,420	3,229
25,800	25,850	3,428	2,981	3,428	3,236
25,850	25,900	3,435	2,989	3,435	3,244
25,900	25,950	3,443	2,996	3,443	3,251
25,950	26,000	3,450	3,004	3,450	3,259

26,000

At least	But less than	Single	Married filing jointly *	Married filing separately	Head of a household
26,000	26,050	3,458	3,011	3,458	3,266
26,050	26,100	3,465	3,019	3,465	3,274
26,100	26,150	3,473	3,026	3,473	3,281
26,150	26,200	3,480	3,034	3,480	3,289
26,200	26,250	3,488	3,041	3,488	3,296
26,250	26,300	3,495	3,049	3,495	3,304
26,300	26,350	3,503	3,056	3,503	3,311
26,350	26,400	3,510	3,064	3,510	3,319
26,400	26,450	3,518	3,071	3,518	3,326
26,450	26,500	3,525	3,079	3,525	3,334
26,500	26,550	3,533	3,086	3,533	3,341
26,550	26,600	3,540	3,094	3,540	3,349
26,600	26,650	3,548	3,101	3,548	3,356
26,650	26,700	3,555	3,109	3,555	3,364
26,700	26,750	3,563	3,116	3,563	3,371
26,750	26,800	3,570	3,124	3,570	3,379
26,800	26,850	3,578	3,131	3,578	3,386
26,850	26,900	3,585	3,139	3,585	3,394
26,900	26,950	3,593	3,146	3,593	3,401
26,950	27,000	3,600	3,154	3,600	3,409

27,000

At least	But less than	Single	Married filing jointly *	Married filing separately	Head of a household
27,000	27,050	3,608	3,161	3,608	3,416
27,050	27,100	3,615	3,169	3,615	3,424
27,100	27,150	3,623	3,176	3,623	3,431
27,150	27,200	3,630	3,184	3,630	3,439
27,200	27,250	3,638	3,191	3,638	3,446
27,250	27,300	3,645	3,199	3,645	3,454
27,300	27,350	3,653	3,206	3,653	3,461
27,350	27,400	3,660	3,214	3,660	3,469
27,400	27,450	3,668	3,221	3,668	3,476
27,450	27,500	3,675	3,229	3,675	3,484
27,500	27,550	3,683	3,236	3,683	3,491
27,550	27,600	3,690	3,244	3,690	3,499
27,600	27,650	3,698	3,251	3,698	3,506
27,650	27,700	3,705	3,259	3,705	3,514
27,700	27,750	3,713	3,266	3,713	3,521
27,750	27,800	3,720	3,274	3,720	3,529
27,800	27,850	3,728	3,281	3,728	3,536
27,850	27,900	3,735	3,289	3,735	3,544
27,900	27,950	3,743	3,296	3,743	3,551
27,950	28,000	3,750	3,304	3,750	3,559

28,000

At least	But less than	Single	Married filing jointly *	Married filing separately	Head of a household
28,000	28,050	3,758	3,311	3,758	3,566
28,050	28,100	3,765	3,319	3,765	3,574
28,100	28,150	3,773	3,326	3,773	3,581
28,150	28,200	3,780	3,334	3,780	3,589
28,200	28,250	3,788	3,341	3,788	3,596
28,250	28,300	3,795	3,349	3,795	3,604
28,300	28,350	3,803	3,356	3,803	3,611
28,350	28,400	3,810	3,364	3,810	3,619
28,400	28,450	3,818	3,371	3,818	3,626
28,450	28,500	3,825	3,379	3,825	3,634
28,500	28,550	3,833	3,386	3,833	3,641
28,550	28,600	3,840	3,394	3,840	3,649
28,600	28,650	3,848	3,401	3,848	3,656
28,650	28,700	3,855	3,409	3,855	3,664
28,700	28,750	3,863	3,416	3,863	3,671
28,750	28,800	3,870	3,424	3,870	3,679
28,800	28,850	3,878	3,431	3,878	3,686
28,850	28,900	3,885	3,439	3,885	3,694
28,900	28,950	3,893	3,446	3,893	3,701
28,950	29,000	3,900	3,454	3,900	3,709

29,000

At least	But less than	Single	Married filing jointly *	Married filing separately	Head of a household
29,000	29,050	3,908	3,461	3,908	3,716
29,050	29,100	3,915	3,469	3,915	3,724
29,100	29,150	3,923	3,476	3,923	3,731
29,150	29,200	3,930	3,484	3,930	3,739
29,200	29,250	3,938	3,491	3,938	3,746
29,250	29,300	3,945	3,499	3,945	3,754
29,300	29,350	3,953	3,506	3,953	3,761
29,350	29,400	3,960	3,514	3,960	3,769
29,400	29,450	3,968	3,521	3,968	3,776
29,450	29,500	3,975	3,529	3,975	3,784
29,500	29,550	3,983	3,536	3,983	3,791
29,550	29,600	3,990	3,544	3,990	3,799
29,600	29,650	3,998	3,551	3,998	3,806
29,650	29,700	4,005	3,559	4,005	3,814
29,700	29,750	4,013	3,566	4,013	3,821
29,750	29,800	4,020	3,574	4,020	3,829
29,800	29,850	4,028	3,581	4,028	3,836
29,850	29,900	4,035	3,589	4,035	3,844
29,900	29,950	4,043	3,596	4,043	3,851
29,950	30,000	4,050	3,604	4,050	3,859

* This column must also be used by a qualifying widow(er).

(Continued)

NOTE: DRAFT AS OF SEPTEMBER 16, 2013.

2013 Tax Table—*Continued*

If line 43 (taxable income) is— At least	But less than	And you are— Single	Married filing jointly *	Married filing separately	Head of a household
30,000				Your tax is—	
30,000	30,050	4,058	3,611	4,058	3,866
30,050	30,100	4,065	3,619	4,065	3,874
30,100	30,150	4,073	3,626	4,073	3,881
30,150	30,200	4,080	3,634	4,080	3,889
30,200	30,250	4,088	3,641	4,088	3,896
30,250	30,300	4,095	3,649	4,095	3,904
30,300	30,350	4,103	3,656	4,103	3,911
30,350	30,400	4,110	3,664	4,110	3,919
30,400	30,450	4,118	3,671	4,118	3,926
30,450	30,500	4,125	3,679	4,125	3,934
30,500	30,550	4,133	3,686	4,133	3,941
30,550	30,600	4,140	3,694	4,140	3,949
30,600	30,650	4,148	3,701	4,148	3,956
30,650	30,700	4,155	3,709	4,155	3,964
30,700	30,750	4,163	3,716	4,163	3,971
30,750	30,800	4,170	3,724	4,170	3,979
30,800	30,850	4,178	3,731	4,178	3,986
30,850	30,900	4,185	3,739	4,185	3,994
30,900	30,950	4,193	3,746	4,193	4,001
30,950	31,000	4,200	3,754	4,200	4,009
31,000					
31,000	31,050	4,208	3,761	4,208	4,016
31,050	31,100	4,215	3,769	4,215	4,024
31,100	31,150	4,223	3,776	4,223	4,031
31,150	31,200	4,230	3,784	4,230	4,039
31,200	31,250	4,238	3,791	4,238	4,046
31,250	31,300	4,245	3,799	4,245	4,054
31,300	31,350	4,253	3,806	4,253	4,061
31,350	31,400	4,260	3,814	4,260	4,069
31,400	31,450	4,268	3,821	4,268	4,076
31,450	31,500	4,275	3,829	4,275	4,084
31,500	31,550	4,283	3,836	4,283	4,091
31,550	31,600	4,290	3,844	4,290	4,099
31,600	31,650	4,298	3,851	4,298	4,106
31,650	31,700	4,305	3,859	4,305	4,114
31,700	31,750	4,313	3,866	4,313	4,121
31,750	31,800	4,320	3,874	4,320	4,129
31,800	31,850	4,328	3,881	4,328	4,136
31,850	31,900	4,335	3,889	4,335	4,144
31,900	31,950	4,343	3,896	4,343	4,151
31,950	32,000	4,350	3,904	4,350	4,159
32,000					
32,000	32,050	4,358	3,911	4,358	4,166
32,050	32,100	4,365	3,919	4,365	4,174
32,100	32,150	4,373	3,926	4,373	4,181
32,150	32,200	4,380	3,934	4,380	4,189
32,200	32,250	4,388	3,941	4,388	4,196
32,250	32,300	4,395	3,949	4,395	4,204
32,300	32,350	4,403	3,956	4,403	4,211
32,350	32,400	4,410	3,964	4,410	4,219
32,400	32,450	4,418	3,971	4,418	4,226
32,450	32,500	4,425	3,979	4,425	4,234
32,500	32,550	4,433	3,986	4,433	4,241
32,550	32,600	4,440	3,994	4,440	4,249
32,600	32,650	4,448	4,001	4,448	4,256
32,650	32,700	4,455	4,009	4,455	4,264
32,700	32,750	4,463	4,016	4,463	4,271
32,750	32,800	4,470	4,024	4,470	4,279
32,800	32,850	4,478	4,031	4,478	4,286
32,850	32,900	4,485	4,039	4,485	4,294
32,900	32,950	4,493	4,046	4,493	4,301
32,950	33,000	4,500	4,054	4,500	4,309

If line 43 (taxable income) is— At least	But less than	And you are— Single	Married filing jointly *	Married filing separately	Head of a household
33,000				Your tax is—	
33,000	33,050	4,508	4,061	4,508	4,316
33,050	33,100	4,515	4,069	4,515	4,324
33,100	33,150	4,523	4,076	4,523	4,331
33,150	33,200	4,530	4,084	4,530	4,339
33,200	33,250	4,538	4,091	4,538	4,346
33,250	33,300	4,545	4,099	4,545	4,354
33,300	33,350	4,553	4,106	4,553	4,361
33,350	33,400	4,560	4,114	4,560	4,369
33,400	33,450	4,568	4,121	4,568	4,376
33,450	33,500	4,575	4,129	4,575	4,384
33,500	33,550	4,583	4,136	4,583	4,391
33,550	33,600	4,590	4,144	4,590	4,399
33,600	33,650	4,598	4,151	4,598	4,406
33,650	33,700	4,605	4,159	4,605	4,414
33,700	33,750	4,613	4,166	4,613	4,421
33,750	33,800	4,620	4,174	4,620	4,429
33,800	33,850	4,628	4,181	4,628	4,436
33,850	33,900	4,635	4,189	4,635	4,444
33,900	33,950	4,643	4,196	4,643	4,451
33,950	34,000	4,650	4,204	4,650	4,459
34,000					
34,000	34,050	4,658	4,211	4,658	4,466
34,050	34,100	4,665	4,219	4,665	4,474
34,100	34,150	4,673	4,226	4,673	4,481
34,150	34,200	4,680	4,234	4,680	4,489
34,200	34,250	4,688	4,241	4,688	4,496
34,250	34,300	4,695	4,249	4,695	4,504
34,300	34,350	4,703	4,256	4,703	4,511
34,350	34,400	4,710	4,264	4,710	4,519
34,400	34,450	4,718	4,271	4,718	4,526
34,450	34,500	4,725	4,279	4,725	4,534
34,500	34,550	4,733	4,286	4,733	4,541
34,550	34,600	4,740	4,294	4,740	4,549
34,600	34,650	4,748	4,301	4,748	4,556
34,650	34,700	4,755	4,309	4,755	4,564
34,700	34,750	4,763	4,316	4,763	4,571
34,750	34,800	4,770	4,324	4,770	4,579
34,800	34,850	4,778	4,331	4,778	4,586
34,850	34,900	4,785	4,339	4,785	4,594
34,900	34,950	4,793	4,346	4,793	4,601
34,950	35,000	4,800	4,354	4,800	4,609
35,000					
35,000	35,050	4,808	4,361	4,808	4,616
35,050	35,100	4,815	4,369	4,815	4,624
35,100	35,150	4,823	4,376	4,823	4,631
35,150	35,200	4,830	4,384	4,830	4,639
35,200	35,250	4,838	4,391	4,838	4,646
35,250	35,300	4,845	4,399	4,845	4,654
35,300	35,350	4,853	4,406	4,853	4,661
35,350	35,400	4,860	4,414	4,860	4,669
35,400	35,450	4,868	4,421	4,868	4,676
35,450	35,500	4,875	4,429	4,875	4,684
35,500	35,550	4,883	4,436	4,883	4,691
35,550	35,600	4,890	4,444	4,890	4,699
35,600	35,650	4,898	4,451	4,898	4,706
35,650	35,700	4,905	4,459	4,905	4,714
35,700	35,750	4,913	4,466	4,913	4,721
35,750	35,800	4,920	4,474	4,920	4,729
35,800	35,850	4,928	4,481	4,928	4,736
35,850	35,900	4,935	4,489	4,935	4,744
35,900	35,950	4,943	4,496	4,943	4,751
35,950	36,000	4,950	4,504	4,950	4,759

If line 43 (taxable income) is— At least	But less than	And you are— Single	Married filing jointly *	Married filing separately	Head of a household
36,000				Your tax is—	
36,000	36,050	4,958	4,511	4,958	4,766
36,050	36,100	4,965	4,519	4,965	4,774
36,100	36,150	4,973	4,526	4,973	4,781
36,150	36,200	4,980	4,534	4,980	4,789
36,200	36,250	4,988	4,541	4,988	4,796
36,250	36,300	4,998	4,549	4,998	4,804
36,300	36,350	5,010	4,556	5,010	4,811
36,350	36,400	5,023	4,564	5,023	4,819
36,400	36,450	5,035	4,571	5,035	4,826
36,450	36,500	5,048	4,579	5,048	4,834
36,500	36,550	5,060	4,586	5,060	4,841
36,550	36,600	5,073	4,594	5,073	4,849
36,600	36,650	5,085	4,601	5,085	4,856
36,650	36,700	5,098	4,609	5,098	4,864
36,700	36,750	5,110	4,616	5,110	4,871
36,750	36,800	5,123	4,624	5,123	4,879
36,800	36,850	5,135	4,631	5,135	4,886
36,850	36,900	5,148	4,639	5,148	4,894
36,900	36,950	5,160	4,646	5,160	4,901
36,950	37,000	5,173	4,654	5,173	4,909
37,000					
37,000	37,050	5,185	4,661	5,185	4,916
37,050	37,100	5,198	4,669	5,198	4,924
37,100	37,150	5,210	4,676	5,210	4,931
37,150	37,200	5,223	4,684	5,223	4,939
37,200	37,250	5,235	4,691	5,235	4,946
37,250	37,300	5,248	4,699	5,248	4,954
37,300	37,350	5,260	4,706	5,260	4,961
37,350	37,400	5,273	4,714	5,273	4,969
37,400	37,450	5,285	4,721	5,285	4,976
37,450	37,500	5,298	4,729	5,298	4,984
37,500	37,550	5,310	4,736	5,310	4,991
37,550	37,600	5,323	4,744	5,323	4,999
37,600	37,650	5,335	4,751	5,335	5,006
37,650	37,700	5,348	4,759	5,348	5,014
37,700	37,750	5,360	4,766	5,360	5,021
37,750	37,800	5,373	4,774	5,373	5,029
37,800	37,850	5,385	4,781	5,385	5,036
37,850	37,900	5,398	4,789	5,398	5,044
37,900	37,950	5,410	4,796	5,410	5,051
37,950	38,000	5,423	4,804	5,423	5,059
38,000					
38,000	38,050	5,435	4,811	5,435	5,066
38,050	38,100	5,448	4,819	5,448	5,074
38,100	38,150	5,460	4,826	5,460	5,081
38,150	38,200	5,473	4,834	5,473	5,089
38,200	38,250	5,485	4,841	5,485	5,096
38,250	38,300	5,498	4,849	5,498	5,104
38,300	38,350	5,510	4,856	5,510	5,111
38,350	38,400	5,523	4,864	5,523	5,119
38,400	38,450	5,535	4,871	5,535	5,126
38,450	38,500	5,548	4,879	5,548	5,134
38,500	38,550	5,560	4,886	5,560	5,141
38,550	38,600	5,573	4,894	5,573	5,149
38,600	38,650	5,585	4,901	5,585	5,156
38,650	38,700	5,598	4,909	5,598	5,164
38,700	38,750	5,610	4,916	5,610	5,171
38,750	38,800	5,623	4,924	5,623	5,179
38,800	38,850	5,635	4,931	5,635	5,186
38,850	38,900	5,648	4,939	5,648	5,194
38,900	38,950	5,660	4,946	5,660	5,201
38,950	39,000	5,673	4,954	5,673	5,209

* This column must also be used by a qualifying widow(er).

(Continued)

NOTE: DRAFT AS OF SEPTEMBER 16, 2013.

2013 Tax Table—*Continued*

If line 43 (taxable income) is— At least	But less than	Single	Married filing jointly *	Married filing separately	Head of a household
39,000					
39,000	39,050	5,685	4,961	5,685	5,216
39,050	39,100	5,698	4,969	5,698	5,224
39,100	39,150	5,710	4,976	5,710	5,231
39,150	39,200	5,723	4,984	5,723	5,239
39,200	39,250	5,735	4,991	5,735	5,246
39,250	39,300	5,748	4,999	5,748	5,254
39,300	39,350	5,760	5,006	5,760	5,261
39,350	39,400	5,773	5,014	5,773	5,269
39,400	39,450	5,785	5,021	5,785	5,276
39,450	39,500	5,798	5,029	5,798	5,284
39,500	39,550	5,810	5,036	5,810	5,291
39,550	39,600	5,823	5,044	5,823	5,299
39,600	39,650	5,835	5,051	5,835	5,306
39,650	39,700	5,848	5,059	5,848	5,314
39,700	39,750	5,860	5,066	5,860	5,321
39,750	39,800	5,873	5,074	5,873	5,329
39,800	39,850	5,885	5,081	5,885	5,336
39,850	39,900	5,898	5,089	5,898	5,344
39,900	39,950	5,910	5,096	5,910	5,351
39,950	40,000	5,923	5,104	5,923	5,359
40,000					
40,000	40,050	5,935	5,111	5,935	5,366
40,050	40,100	5,948	5,119	5,948	5,374
40,100	40,150	5,960	5,126	5,960	5,381
40,150	40,200	5,973	5,134	5,973	5,389
40,200	40,250	5,985	5,141	5,985	5,396
40,250	40,300	5,998	5,149	5,998	5,404
40,300	40,350	6,010	5,156	6,010	5,411
40,350	40,400	6,023	5,164	6,023	5,419
40,400	40,450	6,035	5,171	6,035	5,426
40,450	40,500	6,048	5,179	6,048	5,434
40,500	40,550	6,060	5,186	6,060	5,441
40,550	40,600	6,073	5,194	6,073	5,449
40,600	40,650	6,085	5,201	6,085	5,456
40,650	40,700	6,098	5,209	6,098	5,464
40,700	40,750	6,110	5,216	6,110	5,471
40,750	40,800	6,123	5,224	6,123	5,479
40,800	40,850	6,135	5,231	6,135	5,486
40,850	40,900	6,148	5,239	6,148	5,494
40,900	40,950	6,160	5,246	6,160	5,501
40,950	41,000	6,173	5,254	6,173	5,509
41,000					
41,000	41,050	6,185	5,261	6,185	5,516
41,050	41,100	6,198	5,269	6,198	5,524
41,100	41,150	6,210	5,276	6,210	5,531
41,150	41,200	6,223	5,284	6,223	5,539
41,200	41,250	6,235	5,291	6,235	5,546
41,250	41,300	6,248	5,299	6,248	5,554
41,300	41,350	6,260	5,306	6,260	5,561
41,350	41,400	6,273	5,314	6,273	5,569
41,400	41,450	6,285	5,321	6,285	5,576
41,450	41,500	6,298	5,329	6,298	5,584
41,500	41,550	6,310	5,336	6,310	5,591
41,550	41,600	6,323	5,344	6,323	5,599
41,600	41,650	6,335	5,351	6,335	5,606
41,650	41,700	6,348	5,359	6,348	5,614
41,700	41,750	6,360	5,366	6,360	5,621
41,750	41,800	6,373	5,374	6,373	5,629
41,800	41,850	6,385	5,381	6,385	5,636
41,850	41,900	6,398	5,389	6,398	5,644
41,900	41,950	6,410	5,396	6,410	5,651
41,950	42,000	6,423	5,404	6,423	5,659

If line 43 (taxable income) is— At least	But less than	Single	Married filing jointly *	Married filing separately	Head of a household
42,000					
42,000	42,050	6,435	5,411	6,435	5,666
42,050	42,100	6,448	5,419	6,448	5,674
42,100	42,150	6,460	5,426	6,460	5,681
42,150	42,200	6,473	5,434	6,473	5,689
42,200	42,250	6,485	5,441	6,485	5,696
42,250	42,300	6,498	5,449	6,498	5,704
42,300	42,350	6,510	5,456	6,510	5,711
42,350	42,400	6,523	5,464	6,523	5,719
42,400	42,450	6,535	5,471	6,535	5,726
42,450	42,500	6,548	5,479	6,548	5,734
42,500	42,550	6,560	5,486	6,560	5,741
42,550	42,600	6,573	5,494	6,573	5,749
42,600	42,650	6,585	5,501	6,585	5,756
42,650	42,700	6,598	5,509	6,598	5,764
42,700	42,750	6,610	5,516	6,610	5,771
42,750	42,800	6,623	5,524	6,623	5,779
42,800	42,850	6,635	5,531	6,635	5,786
42,850	42,900	6,648	5,539	6,648	5,794
42,900	42,950	6,660	5,546	6,660	5,801
42,950	43,000	6,673	5,554	6,673	5,809
43,000					
43,000	43,050	6,685	5,561	6,685	5,816
43,050	43,100	6,698	5,569	6,698	5,824
43,100	43,150	6,710	5,576	6,710	5,831
43,150	43,200	6,723	5,584	6,723	5,839
43,200	43,250	6,735	5,591	6,735	5,846
43,250	43,300	6,748	5,599	6,748	5,854
43,300	43,350	6,760	5,606	6,760	5,861
43,350	43,400	6,773	5,614	6,773	5,869
43,400	43,450	6,785	5,621	6,785	5,876
43,450	43,500	6,798	5,629	6,798	5,884
43,500	43,550	6,810	5,636	6,810	5,891
43,550	43,600	6,823	5,644	6,823	5,899
43,600	43,650	6,835	5,651	6,835	5,906
43,650	43,700	6,848	5,659	6,848	5,914
43,700	43,750	6,860	5,666	6,860	5,921
43,750	43,800	6,873	5,674	6,873	5,929
43,800	43,850	6,885	5,681	6,885	5,936
43,850	43,900	6,898	5,689	6,898	5,944
43,900	43,950	6,910	5,696	6,910	5,951
43,950	44,000	6,923	5,704	6,923	5,959
44,000					
44,000	44,050	6,935	5,711	6,935	5,966
44,050	44,100	6,948	5,719	6,948	5,974
44,100	44,150	6,960	5,726	6,960	5,981
44,150	44,200	6,973	5,734	6,973	5,989
44,200	44,250	6,985	5,741	6,985	5,996
44,250	44,300	6,998	5,749	6,998	6,004
44,300	44,350	7,010	5,756	7,010	6,011
44,350	44,400	7,023	5,764	7,023	6,019
44,400	44,450	7,035	5,771	7,035	6,026
44,450	44,500	7,048	5,779	7,048	6,034
44,500	44,550	7,060	5,786	7,060	6,041
44,550	44,600	7,073	5,794	7,073	6,049
44,600	44,650	7,085	5,801	7,085	6,056
44,650	44,700	7,098	5,809	7,098	6,064
44,700	44,750	7,110	5,816	7,110	6,071
44,750	44,800	7,123	5,824	7,123	6,079
44,800	44,850	7,135	5,831	7,135	6,086
44,850	44,900	7,148	5,839	7,148	6,094
44,900	44,950	7,160	5,846	7,160	6,101
44,950	45,000	7,173	5,854	7,173	6,109

If line 43 (taxable income) is— At least	But less than	Single	Married filing jointly *	Married filing separately	Head of a household
45,000					
45,000	45,050	7,185	5,861	7,185	6,116
45,050	45,100	7,198	5,869	7,198	6,124
45,100	45,150	7,210	5,876	7,210	6,131
45,150	45,200	7,223	5,884	7,223	6,139
45,200	45,250	7,235	5,891	7,235	6,146
45,250	45,300	7,248	5,899	7,248	6,154
45,300	45,350	7,260	5,906	7,260	6,161
45,350	45,400	7,273	5,914	7,273	6,169
45,400	45,450	7,285	5,921	7,285	6,176
45,450	45,500	7,298	5,929	7,298	6,184
45,500	45,550	7,310	5,936	7,310	6,191
45,550	45,600	7,323	5,944	7,323	6,199
45,600	45,650	7,335	5,951	7,335	6,206
45,650	45,700	7,348	5,959	7,348	6,214
45,700	45,750	7,360	5,966	7,360	6,221
45,750	45,800	7,373	5,974	7,373	6,229
45,800	45,850	7,385	5,981	7,385	6,236
45,850	45,900	7,398	5,989	7,398	6,244
45,900	45,950	7,410	5,996	7,410	6,251
45,950	46,000	7,423	6,004	7,423	6,259
46,000					
46,000	46,050	7,435	6,011	7,435	6,266
46,050	46,100	7,448	6,019	7,448	6,274
46,100	46,150	7,460	6,026	7,460	6,281
46,150	46,200	7,473	6,034	7,473	6,289
46,200	46,250	7,485	6,041	7,485	6,296
46,250	46,300	7,498	6,049	7,498	6,304
46,300	46,350	7,510	6,056	7,510	6,311
46,350	46,400	7,523	6,064	7,523	6,319
46,400	46,450	7,535	6,071	7,535	6,326
46,450	46,500	7,548	6,079	7,548	6,334
46,500	46,550	7,560	6,086	7,560	6,341
46,550	46,600	7,573	6,094	7,573	6,349
46,600	46,650	7,585	6,101	7,585	6,356
46,650	46,700	7,598	6,109	7,598	6,364
46,700	46,750	7,610	6,116	7,610	6,371
46,750	46,800	7,623	6,124	7,623	6,379
46,800	46,850	7,635	6,131	7,635	6,386
46,850	46,900	7,648	6,139	7,648	6,394
46,900	46,950	7,660	6,146	7,660	6,401
46,950	47,000	7,673	6,154	7,673	6,409
47,000					
47,000	47,050	7,685	6,161	7,685	6,416
47,050	47,100	7,698	6,169	7,698	6,424
47,100	47,150	7,710	6,176	7,710	6,431
47,150	47,200	7,723	6,184	7,723	6,439
47,200	47,250	7,735	6,191	7,735	6,446
47,250	47,300	7,748	6,199	7,748	6,454
47,300	47,350	7,760	6,206	7,760	6,461
47,350	47,400	7,773	6,214	7,773	6,469
47,400	47,450	7,785	6,221	7,785	6,476
47,450	47,500	7,798	6,229	7,798	6,484
47,500	47,550	7,810	6,236	7,810	6,491
47,550	47,600	7,823	6,244	7,823	6,499
47,600	47,650	7,835	6,251	7,835	6,506
47,650	47,700	7,848	6,259	7,848	6,514
47,700	47,750	7,860	6,266	7,860	6,521
47,750	47,800	7,873	6,274	7,873	6,529
47,800	47,850	7,885	6,281	7,885	6,536
47,850	47,900	7,898	6,289	7,898	6,544
47,900	47,950	7,910	6,296	7,910	6,551
47,950	48,000	7,923	6,304	7,923	6,559

* This column must also be used by a qualifying widow(er).

(Continued)

NOTE: DRAFT AS OF SEPTEMBER 16, 2013.

2013 Tax Table—*Continued*

If line 43 (taxable income) is—		And you are—			
At least	But less than	Single	Married filing jointly *	Married filing separately	Head of a household
		Your tax is—			

48,000

At least	But less than	Single	MFJ *	MFS	HoH
48,000	48,050	7,935	6,311	7,935	6,566
48,050	48,100	7,948	6,319	7,948	6,574
48,100	48,150	7,960	6,326	7,960	6,581
48,150	48,200	7,973	6,334	7,973	6,589
48,200	48,250	7,985	6,341	7,985	6,596
48,250	48,300	7,998	6,349	7,998	6,604
48,300	48,350	8,010	6,356	8,010	6,611
48,350	48,400	8,023	6,364	8,023	6,619
48,400	48,450	8,035	6,371	8,035	6,626
48,450	48,500	8,048	6,379	8,048	6,634
48,500	48,550	8,060	6,386	8,060	6,641
48,550	48,600	8,073	6,394	8,073	6,649
48,600	48,650	8,085	6,401	8,085	6,659
48,650	48,700	8,098	6,409	8,098	6,671
48,700	48,750	8,110	6,416	8,110	6,684
48,750	48,800	8,123	6,424	8,123	6,696
48,800	48,850	8,135	6,431	8,135	6,709
48,850	48,900	8,148	6,439	8,148	6,721
48,900	48,950	8,160	6,446	8,160	6,734
48,950	49,000	8,173	6,454	8,173	6,746

49,000

At least	But less than	Single	MFJ *	MFS	HoH
49,000	49,050	8,185	6,461	8,185	6,759
49,050	49,100	8,198	6,469	8,198	6,771
49,100	49,150	8,210	6,476	8,210	6,784
49,150	49,200	8,223	6,484	8,223	6,796
49,200	49,250	8,235	6,491	8,235	6,809
49,250	49,300	8,248	6,499	8,248	6,821
49,300	49,350	8,260	6,506	8,260	6,834
49,350	49,400	8,273	6,514	8,273	6,846
49,400	49,450	8,285	6,521	8,285	6,859
49,450	49,500	8,298	6,529	8,298	6,871
49,500	49,550	8,310	6,536	8,310	6,884
49,550	49,600	8,323	6,544	8,323	6,896
49,600	49,650	8,335	6,551	8,335	6,909
49,650	49,700	8,348	6,559	8,348	6,921
49,700	49,750	8,360	6,566	8,360	6,934
49,750	49,800	8,373	6,574	8,373	6,946
49,800	49,850	8,385	6,581	8,385	6,959
49,850	49,900	8,398	6,589	8,398	6,971
49,900	49,950	8,410	6,596	8,410	6,984
49,950	50,000	8,423	6,604	8,423	6,996

50,000

At least	But less than	Single	MFJ *	MFS	HoH
50,000	50,050	8,435	6,611	8,435	7,009
50,050	50,100	8,448	6,619	8,448	7,021
50,100	50,150	8,460	6,626	8,460	7,034
50,150	50,200	8,473	6,634	8,473	7,046
50,200	50,250	8,485	6,641	8,485	7,059
50,250	50,300	8,498	6,649	8,498	7,071
50,300	50,350	8,510	6,656	8,510	7,084
50,350	50,400	8,523	6,664	8,523	7,096
50,400	50,450	8,535	6,671	8,535	7,109
50,450	50,500	8,548	6,679	8,548	7,121
50,500	50,550	8,560	6,686	8,560	7,134
50,550	50,600	8,573	6,694	8,573	7,146
50,600	50,650	8,585	6,701	8,585	7,159
50,650	50,700	8,598	6,709	8,598	7,171
50,700	50,750	8,610	6,716	8,610	7,184
50,750	50,800	8,623	6,724	8,623	7,196
50,800	50,850	8,635	6,731	8,635	7,209
50,850	50,900	8,648	6,739	8,648	7,221
50,900	50,950	8,660	6,746	8,660	7,234
50,950	51,000	8,673	6,754	8,673	7,246

51,000

At least	But less than	Single	MFJ *	MFS	HoH
51,000	51,050	8,685	6,761	8,685	7,259
51,050	51,100	8,698	6,769	8,698	7,271
51,100	51,150	8,710	6,776	8,710	7,284
51,150	51,200	8,723	6,784	8,723	7,296
51,200	51,250	8,735	6,791	8,735	7,309
51,250	51,300	8,748	6,799	8,748	7,321
51,300	51,350	8,760	6,806	8,760	7,334
51,350	51,400	8,773	6,814	8,773	7,346
51,400	51,450	8,785	6,821	8,785	7,359
51,450	51,500	8,798	6,829	8,798	7,371
51,500	51,550	8,810	6,836	8,810	7,384
51,550	51,600	8,823	6,844	8,823	7,396
51,600	51,650	8,835	6,851	8,835	7,409
51,650	51,700	8,848	6,859	8,848	7,421
51,700	51,750	8,860	6,866	8,860	7,434
51,750	51,800	8,873	6,874	8,873	7,446
51,800	51,850	8,885	6,881	8,885	7,459
51,850	51,900	8,898	6,889	8,898	7,471
51,900	51,950	8,910	6,896	8,910	7,484
51,950	52,000	8,923	6,904	8,923	7,496

52,000

At least	But less than	Single	MFJ *	MFS	HoH
52,000	52,050	8,935	6,911	8,935	7,509
52,050	52,100	8,948	6,919	8,948	7,521
52,100	52,150	8,960	6,926	8,960	7,534
52,150	52,200	8,973	6,934	8,973	7,546
52,200	52,250	8,985	6,941	8,985	7,559
52,250	52,300	8,998	6,949	8,998	7,571
52,300	52,350	9,010	6,956	9,010	7,584
52,350	52,400	9,023	6,964	9,023	7,596
52,400	52,450	9,035	6,971	9,035	7,609
52,450	52,500	9,048	6,979	9,048	7,621
52,500	52,550	9,060	6,986	9,060	7,634
52,550	52,600	9,073	6,994	9,073	7,646
52,600	52,650	9,085	7,001	9,085	7,659
52,650	52,700	9,098	7,009	9,098	7,671
52,700	52,750	9,110	7,016	9,110	7,684
52,750	52,800	9,123	7,024	9,123	7,696
52,800	52,850	9,135	7,031	9,135	7,709
52,850	52,900	9,148	7,039	9,148	7,721
52,900	52,950	9,160	7,046	9,160	7,734
52,950	53,000	9,173	7,054	9,173	7,746

53,000

At least	But less than	Single	MFJ *	MFS	HoH
53,000	53,050	9,185	7,061	9,185	7,759
53,050	53,100	9,198	7,069	9,198	7,771
53,100	53,150	9,210	7,076	9,210	7,784
53,150	53,200	9,223	7,084	9,223	7,796
53,200	53,250	9,235	7,091	9,235	7,809
53,250	53,300	9,248	7,099	9,248	7,821
53,300	53,350	9,260	7,106	9,260	7,834
53,350	53,400	9,273	7,114	9,273	7,846
53,400	53,450	9,285	7,121	9,285	7,859
53,450	53,500	9,298	7,129	9,298	7,871
53,500	53,550	9,310	7,136	9,310	7,884
53,550	53,600	9,323	7,144	9,323	7,896
53,600	53,650	9,335	7,151	9,335	7,909
53,650	53,700	9,348	7,159	9,348	7,921
53,700	53,750	9,360	7,166	9,360	7,934
53,750	53,800	9,373	7,174	9,373	7,946
53,800	53,850	9,385	7,181	9,385	7,959
53,850	53,900	9,398	7,189	9,398	7,971
53,900	53,950	9,410	7,196	9,410	7,984
53,950	54,000	9,423	7,204	9,423	7,996

54,000

At least	But less than	Single	MFJ *	MFS	HoH
54,000	54,050	9,435	7,211	9,435	8,009
54,050	54,100	9,448	7,219	9,448	8,021
54,100	54,150	9,460	7,226	9,460	8,034
54,150	54,200	9,473	7,234	9,473	8,046
54,200	54,250	9,485	7,241	9,485	8,059
54,250	54,300	9,498	7,249	9,498	8,071
54,300	54,350	9,510	7,256	9,510	8,084
54,350	54,400	9,523	7,264	9,523	8,096
54,400	54,450	9,535	7,271	9,535	8,109
54,450	54,500	9,548	7,279	9,548	8,121
54,500	54,550	9,560	7,286	9,560	8,134
54,550	54,600	9,573	7,294	9,573	8,146
54,600	54,650	9,585	7,301	9,585	8,159
54,650	54,700	9,598	7,309	9,598	8,171
54,700	54,750	9,610	7,316	9,610	8,184
54,750	54,800	9,623	7,324	9,623	8,196
54,800	54,850	9,635	7,331	9,635	8,209
54,850	54,900	9,648	7,339	9,648	8,221
54,900	54,950	9,660	7,346	9,660	8,234
54,950	55,000	9,673	7,354	9,673	8,246

55,000

At least	But less than	Single	MFJ *	MFS	HoH
55,000	55,050	9,685	7,361	9,685	8,259
55,050	55,100	9,698	7,369	9,698	8,271
55,100	55,150	9,710	7,376	9,710	8,284
55,150	55,200	9,723	7,384	9,723	8,296
55,200	55,250	9,735	7,391	9,735	8,309
55,250	55,300	9,748	7,399	9,748	8,321
55,300	55,350	9,760	7,406	9,760	8,334
55,350	55,400	9,773	7,414	9,773	8,346
55,400	55,450	9,785	7,421	9,785	8,359
55,450	55,500	9,798	7,429	9,798	8,371
55,500	55,550	9,810	7,436	9,810	8,384
55,550	55,600	9,823	7,444	9,823	8,396
55,600	55,650	9,835	7,451	9,835	8,409
55,650	55,700	9,848	7,459	9,848	8,421
55,700	55,750	9,860	7,466	9,860	8,434
55,750	55,800	9,873	7,474	9,873	8,446
55,800	55,850	9,885	7,481	9,885	8,459
55,850	55,900	9,898	7,489	9,898	8,471
55,900	55,950	9,910	7,496	9,910	8,484
55,950	56,000	9,923	7,504	9,923	8,496

56,000

At least	But less than	Single	MFJ *	MFS	HoH
56,000	56,050	9,935	7,511	9,935	8,509
56,050	56,100	9,948	7,519	9,948	8,521
56,100	56,150	9,960	7,526	9,960	8,534
56,150	56,200	9,973	7,534	9,973	8,546
56,200	56,250	9,985	7,541	9,985	8,559
56,250	56,300	9,998	7,549	9,998	8,571
56,300	56,350	10,010	7,556	10,010	8,584
56,350	56,400	10,023	7,564	10,023	8,596
56,400	56,450	10,035	7,571	10,035	8,609
56,450	56,500	10,048	7,579	10,048	8,621
56,500	56,550	10,060	7,586	10,060	8,634
56,550	56,600	10,073	7,594	10,073	8,646
56,600	56,650	10,085	7,601	10,085	8,659
56,650	56,700	10,098	7,609	10,098	8,671
56,700	56,750	10,110	7,616	10,110	8,684
56,750	56,800	10,123	7,624	10,123	8,696
56,800	56,850	10,135	7,631	10,135	8,709
56,850	56,900	10,148	7,639	10,148	8,721
56,900	56,950	10,160	7,646	10,160	8,734
56,950	57,000	10,173	7,654	10,173	8,746

* This column must also be used by a qualifying widow(er).

(Continued)

NOTE: DRAFT AS OF SEPTEMBER 16, 2013.

2013 Tax Table—*Continued*

If line 43 (taxable income) is— At least	But less than	And you are— Single	Married filing jointly *	Married filing separately	Head of a household
		Your tax is—			
57,000					
57,000	57,050	10,185	7,661	10,185	8,759
57,050	57,100	10,198	7,669	10,198	8,771
57,100	57,150	10,210	7,676	10,210	8,784
57,150	57,200	10,223	7,684	10,223	8,796
57,200	57,250	10,235	7,691	10,235	8,809
57,250	57,300	10,248	7,699	10,248	8,821
57,300	57,350	10,260	7,706	10,260	8,834
57,350	57,400	10,273	7,714	10,273	8,846
57,400	57,450	10,285	7,721	10,285	8,859
57,450	57,500	10,298	7,729	10,298	8,871
57,500	57,550	10,310	7,736	10,310	8,884
57,550	57,600	10,323	7,744	10,323	8,896
57,600	57,650	10,335	7,751	10,335	8,909
57,650	57,700	10,348	7,759	10,348	8,921
57,700	57,750	10,360	7,766	10,360	8,934
57,750	57,800	10,373	7,774	10,373	8,946
57,800	57,850	10,385	7,781	10,385	8,959
57,850	57,900	10,398	7,789	10,398	8,971
57,900	57,950	10,410	7,796	10,410	8,984
57,950	58,000	10,423	7,804	10,423	8,996
58,000					
58,000	58,050	10,435	7,811	10,435	9,009
58,050	58,100	10,448	7,819	10,448	9,021
58,100	58,150	10,460	7,826	10,460	9,034
58,150	58,200	10,473	7,834	10,473	9,046
58,200	58,250	10,485	7,841	10,485	9,059
58,250	58,300	10,498	7,849	10,498	9,071
58,300	58,350	10,510	7,856	10,510	9,084
58,350	58,400	10,523	7,864	10,523	9,096
58,400	58,450	10,535	7,871	10,535	9,109
58,450	58,500	10,548	7,879	10,548	9,121
58,500	58,550	10,560	7,886	10,560	9,134
58,550	58,600	10,573	7,894	10,573	9,146
58,600	58,650	10,585	7,901	10,585	9,159
58,650	58,700	10,598	7,909	10,598	9,171
58,700	58,750	10,610	7,916	10,610	9,184
58,750	58,800	10,623	7,924	10,623	9,196
58,800	58,850	10,635	7,931	10,635	9,209
58,850	58,900	10,648	7,939	10,648	9,221
58,900	58,950	10,660	7,946	10,660	9,234
58,950	59,000	10,673	7,954	10,673	9,246
59,000					
59,000	59,050	10,685	7,961	10,685	9,259
59,050	59,100	10,698	7,969	10,698	9,271
59,100	59,150	10,710	7,976	10,710	9,284
59,150	59,200	10,723	7,984	10,723	9,296
59,200	59,250	10,735	7,991	10,735	9,309
59,250	59,300	10,748	7,999	10,748	9,321
59,300	59,350	10,760	8,006	10,760	9,334
59,350	59,400	10,773	8,014	10,773	9,346
59,400	59,450	10,785	8,021	10,785	9,359
59,450	59,500	10,798	8,029	10,798	9,371
59,500	59,550	10,810	8,036	10,810	9,384
59,550	59,600	10,823	8,044	10,823	9,396
59,600	59,650	10,835	8,051	10,835	9,409
59,650	59,700	10,848	8,059	10,848	9,421
59,700	59,750	10,860	8,066	10,860	9,434
59,750	59,800	10,873	8,074	10,873	9,446
59,800	59,850	10,885	8,081	10,885	9,459
59,850	59,900	10,898	8,089	10,898	9,471
59,900	59,950	10,910	8,096	10,910	9,484
59,950	60,000	10,923	8,104	10,923	9,496

If line 43 (taxable income) is— At least	But less than	And you are— Single	Married filing jointly *	Married filing separately	Head of a household
		Your tax is—			
60,000					
60,000	60,050	10,935	8,111	10,935	9,509
60,050	60,100	10,948	8,119	10,948	9,521
60,100	60,150	10,960	8,126	10,960	9,534
60,150	60,200	10,973	8,134	10,973	9,546
60,200	60,250	10,985	8,141	10,985	9,559
60,250	60,300	10,998	8,149	10,998	9,571
60,300	60,350	11,010	8,156	11,010	9,584
60,350	60,400	11,023	8,164	11,023	9,596
60,400	60,450	11,035	8,171	11,035	9,609
60,450	60,500	11,048	8,179	11,048	9,621
60,500	60,550	11,060	8,186	11,060	9,634
60,550	60,600	11,073	8,194	11,073	9,646
60,600	60,650	11,085	8,201	11,085	9,659
60,650	60,700	11,098	8,209	11,098	9,671
60,700	60,750	11,110	8,216	11,110	9,684
60,750	60,800	11,123	8,224	11,123	9,696
60,800	60,850	11,135	8,231	11,135	9,709
60,850	60,900	11,148	8,239	11,148	9,721
60,900	60,950	11,160	8,246	11,160	9,734
60,950	61,000	11,173	8,254	11,173	9,746
61,000					
61,000	61,050	11,185	8,261	11,185	9,759
61,050	61,100	11,198	8,269	11,198	9,771
61,100	61,150	11,210	8,276	11,210	9,784
61,150	61,200	11,223	8,284	11,223	9,796
61,200	61,250	11,235	8,291	11,235	9,809
61,250	61,300	11,248	8,299	11,248	9,821
61,300	61,350	11,260	8,306	11,260	9,834
61,350	61,400	11,273	8,314	11,273	9,846
61,400	61,450	11,285	8,321	11,285	9,859
61,450	61,500	11,298	8,329	11,298	9,871
61,500	61,550	11,310	8,336	11,310	9,884
61,550	61,600	11,323	8,344	11,323	9,896
61,600	61,650	11,335	8,351	11,335	9,909
61,650	61,700	11,348	8,359	11,348	9,921
61,700	61,750	11,360	8,366	11,360	9,934
61,750	61,800	11,373	8,374	11,373	9,946
61,800	61,850	11,385	8,381	11,385	9,959
61,850	61,900	11,398	8,389	11,398	9,971
61,900	61,950	11,410	8,396	11,410	9,984
61,950	62,000	11,423	8,404	11,423	9,996
62,000					
62,000	62,050	11,435	8,411	11,435	10,009
62,050	62,100	11,448	8,419	11,448	10,021
62,100	62,150	11,460	8,426	11,460	10,034
62,150	62,200	11,473	8,434	11,473	10,046
62,200	62,250	11,485	8,441	11,485	10,059
62,250	62,300	11,498	8,449	11,498	10,071
62,300	62,350	11,510	8,456	11,510	10,084
62,350	62,400	11,523	8,464	11,523	10,096
62,400	62,450	11,535	8,471	11,535	10,109
62,450	62,500	11,548	8,479	11,548	10,121
62,500	62,550	11,560	8,486	11,560	10,134
62,550	62,600	11,573	8,494	11,573	10,146
62,600	62,650	11,585	8,501	11,585	10,159
62,650	62,700	11,598	8,509	11,598	10,171
62,700	62,750	11,610	8,516	11,610	10,184
62,750	62,800	11,623	8,524	11,623	10,196
62,800	62,850	11,635	8,531	11,635	10,209
62,850	62,900	11,648	8,539	11,648	10,221
62,900	62,950	11,660	8,546	11,660	10,234
62,950	63,000	11,673	8,554	11,673	10,246

If line 43 (taxable income) is— At least	But less than	And you are— Single	Married filing jointly *	Married filing separately	Head of a household
		Your tax is—			
63,000					
63,000	63,050	11,685	8,561	11,685	10,259
63,050	63,100	11,698	8,569	11,698	10,271
63,100	63,150	11,710	8,576	11,710	10,284
63,150	63,200	11,723	8,584	11,723	10,296
63,200	63,250	11,735	8,591	11,735	10,309
63,250	63,300	11,748	8,599	11,748	10,321
63,300	63,350	11,760	8,606	11,760	10,334
63,350	63,400	11,773	8,614	11,773	10,346
63,400	63,450	11,785	8,621	11,785	10,359
63,450	63,500	11,798	8,629	11,798	10,371
63,500	63,550	11,810	8,636	11,810	10,384
63,550	63,600	11,823	8,644	11,823	10,396
63,600	63,650	11,835	8,651	11,835	10,409
63,650	63,700	11,848	8,659	11,848	10,421
63,700	63,750	11,860	8,666	11,860	10,434
63,750	63,800	11,873	8,674	11,873	10,446
63,800	63,850	11,885	8,681	11,885	10,459
63,850	63,900	11,898	8,689	11,898	10,471
63,900	63,950	11,910	8,696	11,910	10,484
63,950	64,000	11,923	8,704	11,923	10,496
64,000					
64,000	64,050	11,935	8,711	11,935	10,509
64,050	64,100	11,948	8,719	11,948	10,521
64,100	64,150	11,960	8,726	11,960	10,534
64,150	64,200	11,973	8,734	11,973	10,546
64,200	64,250	11,985	8,741	11,985	10,559
64,250	64,300	11,998	8,749	11,998	10,571
64,300	64,350	12,010	8,756	12,010	10,584
64,350	64,400	12,023	8,764	12,023	10,596
64,400	64,450	12,035	8,771	12,035	10,609
64,450	64,500	12,048	8,779	12,048	10,621
64,500	64,550	12,060	8,786	12,060	10,634
64,550	64,600	12,073	8,794	12,073	10,646
64,600	64,650	12,085	8,801	12,085	10,659
64,650	64,700	12,098	8,809	12,098	10,671
64,700	64,750	12,110	8,816	12,110	10,684
64,750	64,800	12,123	8,824	12,123	10,696
64,800	64,850	12,135	8,831	12,135	10,709
64,850	64,900	12,148	8,839	12,148	10,721
64,900	64,950	12,160	8,846	12,160	10,734
64,950	65,000	12,173	8,854	12,173	10,746
65,000					
65,000	65,050	12,185	8,861	12,185	10,759
65,050	65,100	12,198	8,869	12,198	10,771
65,100	65,150	12,210	8,876	12,210	10,784
65,150	65,200	12,223	8,884	12,223	10,796
65,200	65,250	12,235	8,891	12,235	10,809
65,250	65,300	12,248	8,899	12,248	10,821
65,300	65,350	12,260	8,906	12,260	10,834
65,350	65,400	12,273	8,914	12,273	10,846
65,400	65,450	12,285	8,921	12,285	10,859
65,450	65,500	12,298	8,929	12,298	10,871
65,500	65,550	12,310	8,936	12,310	10,884
65,550	65,600	12,323	8,944	12,323	10,896
65,600	65,650	12,335	8,951	12,335	10,909
65,650	65,700	12,348	8,959	12,348	10,921
65,700	65,750	12,360	8,966	12,360	10,934
65,750	65,800	12,373	8,974	12,373	10,946
65,800	65,850	12,385	8,981	12,385	10,959
65,850	65,900	12,398	8,989	12,398	10,971
65,900	65,950	12,410	8,996	12,410	10,984
65,950	66,000	12,423	9,004	12,423	10,996

* This column must also be used by a qualifying widow(er).

NOTE: DRAFT AS OF SEPTEMBER 16, 2013.

(Continued)

2013 Tax Table—Continued

Header for all tables:

If line 43 (taxable income) is— At least	But less than	Single	Married filing jointly*	Married filing separately	Head of a household

Your tax is—

66,000

At least	But less than	Single	Married filing jointly*	Married filing separately	Head of a household
66,000	66,050	12,435	9,011	12,435	11,009
66,050	66,100	12,448	9,019	12,448	11,021
66,100	66,150	12,460	9,026	12,460	11,034
66,150	66,200	12,473	9,034	12,473	11,046
66,200	66,250	12,485	9,041	12,485	11,059
66,250	66,300	12,498	9,049	12,498	11,071
66,300	66,350	12,510	9,056	12,510	11,084
66,350	66,400	12,523	9,064	12,523	11,096
66,400	66,450	12,535	9,071	12,535	11,109
66,450	66,500	12,548	9,079	12,548	11,121
66,500	66,550	12,560	9,086	12,560	11,134
66,550	66,600	12,573	9,094	12,573	11,146
66,600	66,650	12,585	9,101	12,585	11,159
66,650	66,700	12,598	9,109	12,598	11,171
66,700	66,750	12,610	9,116	12,610	11,184
66,750	66,800	12,623	9,124	12,623	11,196
66,800	66,850	12,635	9,131	12,635	11,209
66,850	66,900	12,648	9,139	12,648	11,221
66,900	66,950	12,660	9,146	12,660	11,234
66,950	67,000	12,673	9,154	12,673	11,246

67,000

At least	But less than	Single	Married filing jointly*	Married filing separately	Head of a household
67,000	67,050	12,685	9,161	12,685	11,259
67,050	67,100	12,698	9,169	12,698	11,271
67,100	67,150	12,710	9,176	12,710	11,284
67,150	67,200	12,723	9,184	12,723	11,296
67,200	67,250	12,735	9,191	12,735	11,309
67,250	67,300	12,748	9,199	12,748	11,321
67,300	67,350	12,760	9,206	12,760	11,334
67,350	67,400	12,773	9,214	12,773	11,346
67,400	67,450	12,785	9,221	12,785	11,359
67,450	67,500	12,798	9,229	12,798	11,371
67,500	67,550	12,810	9,236	12,810	11,384
67,550	67,600	12,823	9,244	12,823	11,396
67,600	67,650	12,835	9,251	12,835	11,409
67,650	67,700	12,848	9,259	12,848	11,421
67,700	67,750	12,860	9,266	12,860	11,434
67,750	67,800	12,873	9,274	12,873	11,446
67,800	67,850	12,885	9,281	12,885	11,459
67,850	67,900	12,898	9,289	12,898	11,471
67,900	67,950	12,910	9,296	12,910	11,484
67,950	68,000	12,923	9,304	12,923	11,496

68,000

At least	But less than	Single	Married filing jointly*	Married filing separately	Head of a household
68,000	68,050	12,935	9,311	12,935	11,509
68,050	68,100	12,948	9,319	12,948	11,521
68,100	68,150	12,960	9,326	12,960	11,534
68,150	68,200	12,973	9,334	12,973	11,546
68,200	68,250	12,985	9,341	12,985	11,559
68,250	68,300	12,998	9,349	12,998	11,571
68,300	68,350	13,010	9,356	13,010	11,584
68,350	68,400	13,023	9,364	13,023	11,596
68,400	68,450	13,035	9,371	13,035	11,609
68,450	68,500	13,048	9,379	13,048	11,621
68,500	68,550	13,060	9,386	13,060	11,634
68,550	68,600	13,073	9,394	13,073	11,646
68,600	68,650	13,085	9,401	13,085	11,659
68,650	68,700	13,098	9,409	13,098	11,671
68,700	68,750	13,110	9,416	13,110	11,684
68,750	68,800	13,123	9,424	13,123	11,696
68,800	68,850	13,135	9,431	13,135	11,709
68,850	68,900	13,148	9,439	13,148	11,721
68,900	68,950	13,160	9,446	13,160	11,734
68,950	69,000	13,173	9,454	13,173	11,746

69,000

At least	But less than	Single	Married filing jointly*	Married filing separately	Head of a household
69,000	69,050	13,185	9,461	13,185	11,759
69,050	69,100	13,198	9,469	13,198	11,771
69,100	69,150	13,210	9,476	13,210	11,784
69,150	69,200	13,223	9,484	13,223	11,796
69,200	69,250	13,235	9,491	13,235	11,809
69,250	69,300	13,248	9,499	13,248	11,821
69,300	69,350	13,260	9,506	13,260	11,834
69,350	69,400	13,273	9,514	13,273	11,846
69,400	69,450	13,285	9,521	13,285	11,859
69,450	69,500	13,298	9,529	13,298	11,871
69,500	69,550	13,310	9,536	13,310	11,884
69,550	69,600	13,323	9,544	13,323	11,896
69,600	69,650	13,335	9,551	13,335	11,909
69,650	69,700	13,348	9,559	13,348	11,921
69,700	69,750	13,360	9,566	13,360	11,934
69,750	69,800	13,373	9,574	13,373	11,946
69,800	69,850	13,385	9,581	13,385	11,959
69,850	69,900	13,398	9,589	13,398	11,971
69,900	69,950	13,410	9,596	13,410	11,984
69,950	70,000	13,423	9,604	13,423	11,996

70,000

At least	But less than	Single	Married filing jointly*	Married filing separately	Head of a household
70,000	70,050	13,435	9,611	13,435	12,009
70,050	70,100	13,448	9,619	13,448	12,021
70,100	70,150	13,460	9,626	13,460	12,034
70,150	70,200	13,473	9,634	13,473	12,046
70,200	70,250	13,485	9,641	13,485	12,059
70,250	70,300	13,498	9,649	13,498	12,071
70,300	70,350	13,510	9,656	13,510	12,084
70,350	70,400	13,523	9,664	13,523	12,096
70,400	70,450	13,535	9,671	13,535	12,109
70,450	70,500	13,548	9,679	13,548	12,121
70,500	70,550	13,560	9,686	13,560	12,134
70,550	70,600	13,573	9,694	13,573	12,146
70,600	70,650	13,585	9,701	13,585	12,159
70,650	70,700	13,598	9,709	13,598	12,171
70,700	70,750	13,610	9,716	13,610	12,184
70,750	70,800	13,623	9,724	13,623	12,196
70,800	70,850	13,635	9,731	13,635	12,209
70,850	70,900	13,648	9,739	13,648	12,221
70,900	70,950	13,660	9,746	13,660	12,234
70,950	71,000	13,673	9,754	13,673	12,246

71,000

At least	But less than	Single	Married filing jointly*	Married filing separately	Head of a household
71,000	71,050	13,685	9,761	13,685	12,259
71,050	71,100	13,698	9,769	13,698	12,271
71,100	71,150	13,710	9,776	13,710	12,284
71,150	71,200	13,723	9,784	13,723	12,296
71,200	71,250	13,735	9,791	13,735	12,309
71,250	71,300	13,748	9,799	13,748	12,321
71,300	71,350	13,760	9,806	13,760	12,334
71,350	71,400	13,773	9,814	13,773	12,346
71,400	71,450	13,785	9,821	13,785	12,359
71,450	71,500	13,798	9,829	13,798	12,371
71,500	71,550	13,810	9,836	13,810	12,384
71,550	71,600	13,823	9,844	13,823	12,396
71,600	71,650	13,835	9,851	13,835	12,409
71,650	71,700	13,848	9,859	13,848	12,421
71,700	71,750	13,860	9,866	13,860	12,434
71,750	71,800	13,873	9,874	13,873	12,446
71,800	71,850	13,885	9,881	13,885	12,459
71,850	71,900	13,898	9,889	13,898	12,471
71,900	71,950	13,910	9,896	13,910	12,484
71,950	72,000	13,923	9,904	13,923	12,496

72,000

At least	But less than	Single	Married filing jointly*	Married filing separately	Head of a household
72,000	72,050	13,935	9,911	13,935	12,509
72,050	72,100	13,948	9,919	13,948	12,521
72,100	72,150	13,960	9,926	13,960	12,534
72,150	72,200	13,973	9,934	13,973	12,546
72,200	72,250	13,985	9,941	13,985	12,559
72,250	72,300	13,998	9,949	13,998	12,571
72,300	72,350	14,010	9,956	14,010	12,584
72,350	72,400	14,023	9,964	14,023	12,596
72,400	72,450	14,035	9,971	14,035	12,609
72,450	72,500	14,048	9,979	14,048	12,621
72,500	72,550	14,060	9,989	14,060	12,634
72,550	72,600	14,073	10,001	14,073	12,646
72,600	72,650	14,085	10,014	14,085	12,659
72,650	72,700	14,098	10,026	14,098	12,671
72,700	72,750	14,110	10,039	14,110	12,684
72,750	72,800	14,123	10,051	14,123	12,696
72,800	72,850	14,135	10,064	14,135	12,709
72,850	72,900	14,148	10,076	14,148	12,721
72,900	72,950	14,160	10,089	14,160	12,734
72,950	73,000	14,173	10,101	14,173	12,746

73,000

At least	But less than	Single	Married filing jointly*	Married filing separately	Head of a household
73,000	73,050	14,185	10,114	14,185	12,759
73,050	73,100	14,198	10,126	14,198	12,771
73,100	73,150	14,210	10,139	14,210	12,784
73,150	73,200	14,223	10,151	14,223	12,796
73,200	73,250	14,235	10,164	14,236	12,809
73,250	73,300	14,248	10,176	14,250	12,821
73,300	73,350	14,260	10,189	14,264	12,834
73,350	73,400	14,273	10,201	14,278	12,846
73,400	73,450	14,285	10,214	14,292	12,859
73,450	73,500	14,298	10,226	14,306	12,871
73,500	73,550	14,310	10,239	14,320	12,884
73,550	73,600	14,323	10,251	14,334	12,896
73,600	73,650	14,335	10,264	14,348	12,909
73,650	73,700	14,348	10,276	14,362	12,921
73,700	73,750	14,360	10,289	14,376	12,934
73,750	73,800	14,373	10,301	14,390	12,946
73,800	73,850	14,385	10,314	14,404	12,959
73,850	73,900	14,398	10,326	14,418	12,971
73,900	73,950	14,410	10,339	14,432	12,984
73,950	74,000	14,423	10,351	14,446	12,996

74,000

At least	But less than	Single	Married filing jointly*	Married filing separately	Head of a household
74,000	74,050	14,435	10,364	14,460	13,009
74,050	74,100	14,448	10,376	14,474	13,021
74,100	74,150	14,460	10,389	14,488	13,034
74,150	74,200	14,473	10,401	14,502	13,046
74,200	74,250	14,485	10,414	14,516	13,059
74,250	74,300	14,498	10,426	14,530	13,071
74,300	74,350	14,510	10,439	14,544	13,084
74,350	74,400	14,523	10,451	14,558	13,096
74,400	74,450	14,535	10,464	14,572	13,109
74,450	74,500	14,548	10,476	14,586	13,121
74,500	74,550	14,560	10,489	14,600	13,134
74,550	74,600	14,573	10,501	14,614	13,146
74,600	74,650	14,585	10,514	14,628	13,159
74,650	74,700	14,598	10,526	14,642	13,171
74,700	74,750	14,610	10,539	14,656	13,184
74,750	74,800	14,623	10,551	14,670	13,196
74,800	74,850	14,635	10,564	14,684	13,209
74,850	74,900	14,648	10,576	14,698	13,221
74,900	74,950	14,660	10,589	14,712	13,234
74,950	75,000	14,673	10,601	14,726	13,246

* This column must also be used by a qualifying widow(er).

(Continued)

NOTE: DRAFT AS OF SEPTEMBER 16, 2013.

2013 Tax Table—*Continued*

If line 43 (taxable income) is— At least	But less than	And you are— Single	Married filing jointly *	Married filing separately	Head of a household
		Your tax is—			
75,000					
75,000	75,050	14,685	10,614	14,740	13,259
75,050	75,100	14,698	10,626	14,754	13,271
75,100	75,150	14,710	10,639	14,768	13,284
75,150	75,200	14,723	10,651	14,782	13,296
75,200	75,250	14,735	10,664	14,796	13,309
75,250	75,300	14,748	10,676	14,810	13,321
75,300	75,350	14,760	10,689	14,824	13,334
75,350	75,400	14,773	10,701	14,838	13,346
75,400	75,450	14,785	10,714	14,852	13,359
75,450	75,500	14,798	10,726	14,866	13,371
75,500	75,550	14,810	10,739	14,880	13,384
75,550	75,600	14,823	10,751	14,894	13,396
75,600	75,650	14,835	10,764	14,908	13,409
75,650	75,700	14,848	10,776	14,922	13,421
75,700	75,750	14,860	10,789	14,936	13,434
75,750	75,800	14,873	10,801	14,950	13,446
75,800	75,850	14,885	10,814	14,964	13,459
75,850	75,900	14,898	10,826	14,978	13,471
75,900	75,950	14,910	10,839	14,992	13,484
75,950	76,000	14,923	10,851	15,006	13,496
76,000					
76,000	76,050	14,935	10,864	15,020	13,509
76,050	76,100	14,948	10,876	15,034	13,521
76,100	76,150	14,960	10,889	15,048	13,534
76,150	76,200	14,973	10,901	15,062	13,546
76,200	76,250	14,985	10,914	15,076	13,559
76,250	76,300	14,998	10,926	15,090	13,571
76,300	76,350	15,010	10,939	15,104	13,584
76,350	76,400	15,023	10,951	15,118	13,596
76,400	76,450	15,035	10,964	15,132	13,609
76,450	76,500	15,048	10,976	15,146	13,621
76,500	76,550	15,060	10,989	15,160	13,634
76,550	76,600	15,073	11,001	15,174	13,646
76,600	76,650	15,085	11,014	15,188	13,659
76,650	76,700	15,098	11,026	15,202	13,671
76,700	76,750	15,110	11,039	15,216	13,684
76,750	76,800	15,123	11,051	15,230	13,696
76,800	76,850	15,135	11,064	15,244	13,709
76,850	76,900	15,148	11,076	15,258	13,721
76,900	76,950	15,160	11,089	15,272	13,734
76,950	77,000	15,173	11,101	15,286	13,746
77,000					
77,000	77,050	15,185	11,114	15,300	13,759
77,050	77,100	15,198	11,126	15,314	13,771
77,100	77,150	15,210	11,139	15,328	13,784
77,150	77,200	15,223	11,151	15,342	13,796
77,200	77,250	15,235	11,164	15,356	13,809
77,250	77,300	15,248	11,176	15,370	13,821
77,300	77,350	15,260	11,189	15,384	13,834
77,350	77,400	15,273	11,201	15,398	13,846
77,400	77,450	15,285	11,214	15,412	13,859
77,450	77,500	15,298	11,226	15,426	13,871
77,500	77,550	15,310	11,239	15,440	13,884
77,550	77,600	15,323	11,251	15,454	13,896
77,600	77,650	15,335	11,264	15,468	13,909
77,650	77,700	15,348	11,276	15,482	13,921
77,700	77,750	15,360	11,289	15,496	13,934
77,750	77,800	15,373	11,301	15,510	13,946
77,800	77,850	15,385	11,314	15,524	13,959
77,850	77,900	15,398	11,326	15,538	13,971
77,900	77,950	15,410	11,339	15,552	13,984
77,950	78,000	15,423	11,351	15,566	13,996

If line 43 (taxable income) is— At least	But less than	And you are— Single	Married filing jointly *	Married filing separately	Head of a household
		Your tax is—			
78,000					
78,000	78,050	15,435	11,364	15,580	14,009
78,050	78,100	15,448	11,376	15,594	14,021
78,100	78,150	15,460	11,389	15,608	14,034
78,150	78,200	15,473	11,401	15,622	14,046
78,200	78,250	15,485	11,414	15,636	14,059
78,250	78,300	15,498	11,426	15,650	14,071
78,300	78,350	15,510	11,439	15,664	14,084
78,350	78,400	15,523	11,451	15,678	14,096
78,400	78,450	15,535	11,464	15,692	14,109
78,450	78,500	15,548	11,476	15,706	14,121
78,500	78,550	15,560	11,489	15,720	14,134
78,550	78,600	15,573	11,501	15,734	14,146
78,600	78,650	15,585	11,514	15,748	14,159
78,650	78,700	15,598	11,526	15,762	14,171
78,700	78,750	15,610	11,539	15,776	14,184
78,750	78,800	15,623	11,551	15,790	14,196
78,800	78,850	15,635	11,564	15,804	14,209
78,850	78,900	15,648	11,576	15,818	14,221
78,900	78,950	15,660	11,589	15,832	14,234
78,950	79,000	15,673	11,601	15,846	14,246
79,000					
79,000	79,050	15,685	11,614	15,860	14,259
79,050	79,100	15,698	11,626	15,874	14,271
79,100	79,150	15,710	11,639	15,888	14,284
79,150	79,200	15,723	11,651	15,902	14,296
79,200	79,250	15,735	11,664	15,916	14,309
79,250	79,300	15,748	11,676	15,930	14,321
79,300	79,350	15,760	11,689	15,944	14,334
79,350	79,400	15,773	11,701	15,958	14,346
79,400	79,450	15,785	11,714	15,972	14,359
79,450	79,500	15,798	11,726	15,986	14,371
79,500	79,550	15,810	11,739	16,000	14,384
79,550	79,600	15,823	11,751	16,014	14,396
79,600	79,650	15,835	11,764	16,028	14,409
79,650	79,700	15,848	11,776	16,042	14,421
79,700	79,750	15,860	11,789	16,056	14,434
79,750	79,800	15,873	11,801	16,070	14,446
79,800	79,850	15,885	11,814	16,084	14,459
79,850	79,900	15,898	11,826	16,098	14,471
79,900	79,950	15,910	11,839	16,112	14,484
79,950	80,000	15,923	11,851	16,126	14,496
80,000					
80,000	80,050	15,935	11,864	16,140	14,509
80,050	80,100	15,948	11,876	16,154	14,521
80,100	80,150	15,960	11,889	16,168	14,534
80,150	80,200	15,973	11,901	16,182	14,546
80,200	80,250	15,985	11,914	16,196	14,559
80,250	80,300	15,998	11,926	16,210	14,571
80,300	80,350	16,010	11,939	16,224	14,584
80,350	80,400	16,023	11,951	16,238	14,596
80,400	80,450	16,035	11,964	16,252	14,609
80,450	80,500	16,048	11,976	16,266	14,621
80,500	80,550	16,060	11,989	16,280	14,634
80,550	80,600	16,073	12,001	16,294	14,646
80,600	80,650	16,085	12,014	16,308	14,659
80,650	80,700	16,098	12,026	16,322	14,671
80,700	80,750	16,110	12,039	16,336	14,684
80,750	80,800	16,123	12,051	16,350	14,696
80,800	80,850	16,135	12,064	16,364	14,709
80,850	80,900	16,148	12,076	16,378	14,721
80,900	80,950	16,160	12,089	16,392	14,734
80,950	81,000	16,173	12,101	16,406	14,746

If line 43 (taxable income) is— At least	But less than	And you are— Single	Married filing jointly *	Married filing separately	Head of a household
		Your tax is—			
81,000					
81,000	81,050	16,185	12,114	16,420	14,759
81,050	81,100	16,198	12,126	16,434	14,771
81,100	81,150	16,210	12,139	16,448	14,784
81,150	81,200	16,223	12,151	16,462	14,796
81,200	81,250	16,235	12,164	16,476	14,809
81,250	81,300	16,248	12,176	16,490	14,821
81,300	81,350	16,260	12,189	16,504	14,834
81,350	81,400	16,273	12,201	16,518	14,846
81,400	81,450	16,285	12,214	16,532	14,859
81,450	81,500	16,298	12,226	16,546	14,871
81,500	81,550	16,310	12,239	16,560	14,884
81,550	81,600	16,323	12,251	16,574	14,896
81,600	81,650	16,335	12,264	16,588	14,909
81,650	81,700	16,348	12,276	16,602	14,921
81,700	81,750	16,360	12,289	16,616	14,934
81,750	81,800	16,373	12,301	16,630	14,946
81,800	81,850	16,385	12,314	16,644	14,959
81,850	81,900	16,398	12,326	16,658	14,971
81,900	81,950	16,410	12,339	16,672	14,984
81,950	82,000	16,423	12,351	16,686	14,996
82,000					
82,000	82,050	16,435	12,364	16,700	15,009
82,050	82,100	16,448	12,376	16,714	15,021
82,100	82,150	16,460	12,389	16,728	15,034
82,150	82,200	16,473	12,401	16,742	15,046
82,200	82,250	16,485	12,414	16,756	15,059
82,250	82,300	16,498	12,426	16,770	15,071
82,300	82,350	16,510	12,439	16,784	15,084
82,350	82,400	16,523	12,451	16,798	15,096
82,400	82,450	16,535	12,464	16,812	15,109
82,450	82,500	16,548	12,476	16,826	15,121
82,500	82,550	16,560	12,489	16,840	15,134
82,550	82,600	16,573	12,501	16,854	15,146
82,600	82,650	16,585	12,514	16,868	15,159
82,650	82,700	16,598	12,526	16,882	15,171
82,700	82,750	16,610	12,539	16,896	15,184
82,750	82,800	16,623	12,551	16,910	15,196
82,800	82,850	16,635	12,564	16,924	15,209
82,850	82,900	16,648	12,576	16,938	15,221
82,900	82,950	16,660	12,589	16,952	15,234
82,950	83,000	16,673	12,601	16,966	15,246
83,000					
83,000	83,050	16,685	12,614	16,980	15,259
83,050	83,100	16,698	12,626	16,994	15,271
83,100	83,150	16,710	12,639	17,008	15,284
83,150	83,200	16,723	12,651	17,022	15,296
83,200	83,250	16,735	12,664	17,036	15,309
83,250	83,300	16,748	12,676	17,050	15,321
83,300	83,350	16,760	12,689	17,064	15,334
83,350	83,400	16,773	12,701	17,078	15,346
83,400	83,450	16,785	12,714	17,092	15,359
83,450	83,500	16,798	12,726	17,106	15,371
83,500	83,550	16,810	12,739	17,120	15,384
83,550	83,600	16,823	12,751	17,134	15,396
83,600	83,650	16,835	12,764	17,148	15,409
83,650	83,700	16,848	12,776	17,162	15,421
83,700	83,750	16,860	12,789	17,176	15,434
83,750	83,800	16,873	12,801	17,190	15,446
83,800	83,850	16,885	12,814	17,204	15,459
83,850	83,900	16,898	12,826	17,218	15,471
83,900	83,950	16,910	12,839	17,232	15,484
83,950	84,000	16,923	12,851	17,246	15,496

* This column must also be used by a qualifying widow(er).

(Continued)

NOTE: DRAFT AS OF SEPTEMBER 16, 2013.

2013 Tax Table—Continued

If line 43 (taxable income) is—		And you are—			
At least	But less than	Single	Married filing jointly *	Married filing separately	Head of a household
		Your tax is—			

84,000

At least	But less than	Single	Married filing jointly	Married filing separately	Head of a household
84,000	84,050	16,935	12,864	17,260	15,509
84,050	84,100	16,948	12,876	17,274	15,521
84,100	84,150	16,960	12,889	17,288	15,534
84,150	84,200	16,973	12,901	17,302	15,546
84,200	84,250	16,985	12,914	17,316	15,559
84,250	84,300	16,998	12,926	17,330	15,571
84,300	84,350	17,010	12,939	17,344	15,584
84,350	84,400	17,023	12,951	17,358	15,596
84,400	84,450	17,035	12,964	17,372	15,609
84,450	84,500	17,048	12,976	17,386	15,621
84,500	84,550	17,060	12,989	17,400	15,634
84,550	84,600	17,073	13,001	17,414	15,646
84,600	84,650	17,085	13,014	17,428	15,659
84,650	84,700	17,098	13,026	17,442	15,671
84,700	84,750	17,110	13,039	17,456	15,684
84,750	84,800	17,123	13,051	17,470	15,696
84,800	84,850	17,135	13,064	17,484	15,709
84,850	84,900	17,148	13,076	17,498	15,721
84,900	84,950	17,160	13,089	17,512	15,734
84,950	85,000	17,173	13,101	17,526	15,746

85,000

At least	But less than	Single	Married filing jointly	Married filing separately	Head of a household
85,000	85,050	17,185	13,114	17,540	15,759
85,050	85,100	17,198	13,126	17,554	15,771
85,100	85,150	17,210	13,139	17,568	15,784
85,150	85,200	17,223	13,151	17,582	15,796
85,200	85,250	17,235	13,164	17,596	15,809
85,250	85,300	17,248	13,176	17,610	15,821
85,300	85,350	17,260	13,189	17,624	15,834
85,350	85,400	17,273	13,201	17,638	15,846
85,400	85,450	17,285	13,214	17,652	15,859
85,450	85,500	17,298	13,226	17,666	15,871
85,500	85,550	17,310	13,239	17,680	15,884
85,550	85,600	17,323	13,251	17,694	15,896
85,600	85,650	17,335	13,264	17,708	15,909
85,650	85,700	17,348	13,276	17,722	15,921
85,700	85,750	17,360	13,289	17,736	15,934
85,750	85,800	17,373	13,301	17,750	15,946
85,800	85,850	17,385	13,314	17,764	15,959
85,850	85,900	17,398	13,326	17,778	15,971
85,900	85,950	17,410	13,339	17,792	15,984
85,950	86,000	17,423	13,351	17,806	15,996

86,000

At least	But less than	Single	Married filing jointly	Married filing separately	Head of a household
86,000	86,050	17,435	13,364	17,820	16,009
86,050	86,100	17,448	13,376	17,834	16,021
86,100	86,150	17,460	13,389	17,848	16,034
86,150	86,200	17,473	13,401	17,862	16,046
86,200	86,250	17,485	13,414	17,876	16,059
86,250	86,300	17,498	13,426	17,890	16,071
86,300	86,350	17,510	13,439	17,904	16,084
86,350	86,400	17,523	13,451	17,918	16,096
86,400	86,450	17,535	13,464	17,932	16,109
86,450	86,500	17,548	13,476	17,946	16,121
86,500	86,550	17,560	13,489	17,960	16,134
86,550	86,600	17,573	13,501	17,974	16,146
86,600	86,650	17,585	13,514	17,988	16,159
86,650	86,700	17,598	13,526	18,002	16,171
86,700	86,750	17,610	13,539	18,016	16,184
86,750	86,800	17,623	13,551	18,030	16,196
86,800	86,850	17,635	13,564	18,044	16,209
86,850	86,900	17,648	13,576	18,058	16,221
86,900	86,950	17,660	13,589	18,072	16,234
86,950	87,000	17,673	13,601	18,086	16,246

87,000

At least	But less than	Single	Married filing jointly	Married filing separately	Head of a household
87,000	87,050	17,685	13,614	18,100	16,259
87,050	87,100	17,698	13,626	18,114	16,271
87,100	87,150	17,710	13,639	18,128	16,284
87,150	87,200	17,723	13,651	18,142	16,296
87,200	87,250	17,735	13,664	18,156	16,309
87,250	87,300	17,748	13,676	18,170	16,321
87,300	87,350	17,760	13,689	18,184	16,334
87,350	87,400	17,773	13,701	18,198	16,346
87,400	87,450	17,785	13,714	18,212	16,359
87,450	87,500	17,798	13,726	18,226	16,371
87,500	87,550	17,810	13,739	18,240	16,384
87,550	87,600	17,823	13,751	18,254	16,396
87,600	87,650	17,835	13,764	18,268	16,409
87,650	87,700	17,848	13,776	18,282	16,421
87,700	87,750	17,860	13,789	18,296	16,434
87,750	87,800	17,873	13,801	18,310	16,446
87,800	87,850	17,885	13,814	18,324	16,459
87,850	87,900	17,898	13,826	18,338	16,471
87,900	87,950	17,912	13,839	18,352	16,484
87,950	88,000	17,926	13,851	18,366	16,496

88,000

At least	But less than	Single	Married filing jointly	Married filing separately	Head of a household
88,000	88,050	17,940	13,864	18,380	16,509
88,050	88,100	17,954	13,876	18,394	16,521
88,100	88,150	17,968	13,889	18,408	16,534
88,150	88,200	17,982	13,901	18,422	16,546
88,200	88,250	17,996	13,914	18,436	16,559
88,250	88,300	18,010	13,926	18,450	16,571
88,300	88,350	18,024	13,939	18,464	16,584
88,350	88,400	18,038	13,951	18,478	16,596
88,400	88,450	18,052	13,964	18,492	16,609
88,450	88,500	18,066	13,976	18,506	16,621
88,500	88,550	18,080	13,989	18,520	16,634
88,550	88,600	18,094	14,001	18,534	16,646
88,600	88,650	18,108	14,014	18,548	16,659
88,650	88,700	18,122	14,026	18,562	16,671
88,700	88,750	18,136	14,039	18,576	16,684
88,750	88,800	18,150	14,051	18,590	16,696
88,800	88,850	18,164	14,064	18,604	16,709
88,850	88,900	18,178	14,076	18,618	16,721
88,900	88,950	18,192	14,089	18,632	16,734
88,950	89,000	18,206	14,101	18,646	16,746

89,000

At least	But less than	Single	Married filing jointly	Married filing separately	Head of a household
89,000	89,050	18,220	14,114	18,660	16,759
89,050	89,100	18,234	14,126	18,674	16,771
89,100	89,150	18,248	14,139	18,688	16,784
89,150	89,200	18,262	14,151	18,702	16,796
89,200	89,250	18,276	14,164	18,716	16,809
89,250	89,300	18,290	14,176	18,730	16,821
89,300	89,350	18,304	14,189	18,744	16,834
89,350	89,400	18,318	14,201	18,758	16,846
89,400	89,450	18,332	14,214	18,772	16,859
89,450	89,500	18,346	14,226	18,786	16,871
89,500	89,550	18,360	14,239	18,800	16,884
89,550	89,600	18,374	14,251	18,814	16,896
89,600	89,650	18,388	14,264	18,828	16,909
89,650	89,700	18,402	14,276	18,842	16,921
89,700	89,750	18,416	14,289	18,856	16,934
89,750	89,800	18,430	14,301	18,870	16,946
89,800	89,850	18,444	14,314	18,884	16,959
89,850	89,900	18,458	14,326	18,898	16,971
89,900	89,950	18,472	14,339	18,912	16,984
89,950	90,000	18,486	14,351	18,926	16,996

90,000

At least	But less than	Single	Married filing jointly	Married filing separately	Head of a household
90,000	90,050	18,500	14,364	18,940	17,009
90,050	90,100	18,514	14,376	18,954	17,021
90,100	90,150	18,528	14,389	18,968	17,034
90,150	90,200	18,542	14,401	18,982	17,046
90,200	90,250	18,556	14,414	18,996	17,059
90,250	90,300	18,570	14,426	19,010	17,071
90,300	90,350	18,584	14,439	19,024	17,084
90,350	90,400	18,598	14,451	19,038	17,096
90,400	90,450	18,612	14,464	19,052	17,109
90,450	90,500	18,626	14,476	19,066	17,121
90,500	90,550	18,640	14,489	19,080	17,134
90,550	90,600	18,654	14,501	19,094	17,146
90,600	90,650	18,668	14,514	19,108	17,159
90,650	90,700	18,682	14,526	19,122	17,171
90,700	90,750	18,696	14,539	19,136	17,184
90,750	90,800	18,710	14,551	19,150	17,196
90,800	90,850	18,724	14,564	19,164	17,209
90,850	90,900	18,738	14,576	19,178	17,221
90,900	90,950	18,752	14,589	19,192	17,234
90,950	91,000	18,766	14,601	19,206	17,246

91,000

At least	But less than	Single	Married filing jointly	Married filing separately	Head of a household
91,000	91,050	18,780	14,614	19,220	17,259
91,050	91,100	18,794	14,626	19,234	17,271
91,100	91,150	18,808	14,639	19,248	17,284
91,150	91,200	18,822	14,651	19,262	17,296
91,200	91,250	18,836	14,664	19,276	17,309
91,250	91,300	18,850	14,676	19,290	17,321
91,300	91,350	18,864	14,689	19,304	17,334
91,350	91,400	18,878	14,701	19,318	17,346
91,400	91,450	18,892	14,714	19,332	17,359
91,450	91,500	18,906	14,726	19,346	17,371
91,500	91,550	18,920	14,739	19,360	17,384
91,550	91,600	18,934	14,751	19,374	17,396
91,600	91,650	18,948	14,764	19,388	17,409
91,650	91,700	18,962	14,776	19,402	17,421
91,700	91,750	18,976	14,789	19,416	17,434
91,750	91,800	18,990	14,801	19,430	17,446
91,800	91,850	19,004	14,814	19,444	17,459
91,850	91,900	19,018	14,826	19,458	17,471
91,900	91,950	19,032	14,839	19,472	17,484
91,950	92,000	19,046	14,851	19,486	17,496

92,000

At least	But less than	Single	Married filing jointly	Married filing separately	Head of a household
92,000	92,050	19,060	14,864	19,500	17,509
92,050	92,100	19,074	14,876	19,514	17,521
92,100	92,150	19,088	14,889	19,528	17,534
92,150	92,200	19,102	14,901	19,542	17,546
92,200	92,250	19,116	14,914	19,556	17,559
92,250	92,300	19,130	14,926	19,570	17,571
92,300	92,350	19,144	14,939	19,584	17,584
92,350	92,400	19,158	14,951	19,598	17,596
92,400	92,450	19,172	14,964	19,612	17,609
92,450	92,500	19,186	14,976	19,626	17,621
92,500	92,550	19,200	14,989	19,640	17,634
92,550	92,600	19,214	15,001	19,654	17,646
92,600	92,650	19,228	15,014	19,668	17,659
92,650	92,700	19,242	15,026	19,682	17,671
92,700	92,750	19,256	15,039	19,696	17,684
92,750	92,800	19,270	15,051	19,710	17,696
92,800	92,850	19,284	15,064	19,724	17,709
92,850	92,900	19,298	15,076	19,738	17,721
92,900	92,950	19,312	15,089	19,752	17,734
92,950	93,000	19,326	15,101	19,766	17,746

* This column must also be used by a qualifying widow(er).

(Continued)

NOTE: DRAFT AS OF SEPTEMBER 16, 2013.

2013 Tax Table—*Continued*

93,000

If line 43 (taxable income) is—		And you are—			
At least	But less than	Single	Married filing jointly *	Married filing separately	Head of a house-hold
		Your tax is—			
93,000	93,050	19,340	15,114	19,780	17,759
93,050	93,100	19,354	15,126	19,794	17,771
93,100	93,150	19,368	15,139	19,808	17,784
93,150	93,200	19,382	15,151	19,822	17,796
93,200	93,250	19,396	15,164	19,836	17,809
93,250	93,300	19,410	15,176	19,850	17,821
93,300	93,350	19,424	15,189	19,864	17,834
93,350	93,400	19,438	15,201	19,878	17,846
93,400	93,450	19,452	15,214	19,892	17,859
93,450	93,500	19,466	15,226	19,906	17,871
93,500	93,550	19,480	15,239	19,920	17,884
93,550	93,600	19,494	15,251	19,934	17,896
93,600	93,650	19,508	15,264	19,948	17,909
93,650	93,700	19,522	15,276	19,962	17,921
93,700	93,750	19,536	15,289	19,976	17,934
93,750	93,800	19,550	15,301	19,990	17,946
93,800	93,850	19,564	15,314	20,004	17,959
93,850	93,900	19,578	15,326	20,018	17,971
93,900	93,950	19,592	15,339	20,032	17,984
93,950	94,000	19,606	15,351	20,046	17,996

94,000

At least	But less than	Single	Married filing jointly *	Married filing separately	Head of a house-hold
94,000	94,050	19,620	15,364	20,060	18,009
94,050	94,100	19,634	15,376	20,074	18,021
94,100	94,150	19,648	15,389	20,088	18,034
94,150	94,200	19,662	15,401	20,102	18,046
94,200	94,250	19,676	15,414	20,116	18,059
94,250	94,300	19,690	15,426	20,130	18,071
94,300	94,350	19,704	15,439	20,144	18,084
94,350	94,400	19,718	15,451	20,158	18,096
94,400	94,450	19,732	15,464	20,172	18,109
94,450	94,500	19,746	15,476	20,186	18,121
94,500	94,550	19,760	15,489	20,200	18,134
94,550	94,600	19,774	15,501	20,214	18,146
94,600	94,650	19,788	15,514	20,228	18,159
94,650	94,700	19,802	15,526	20,242	18,171
94,700	94,750	19,816	15,539	20,256	18,184
94,750	94,800	19,830	15,551	20,270	18,196
94,800	94,850	19,844	15,564	20,284	18,209
94,850	94,900	19,858	15,576	20,298	18,221
94,900	94,950	19,872	15,589	20,312	18,234
94,950	95,000	19,886	15,601	20,326	18,246

95,000

At least	But less than	Single	Married filing jointly *	Married filing separately	Head of a house-hold
95,000	95,050	19,900	15,614	20,340	18,259
95,050	95,100	19,914	15,626	20,354	18,271
95,100	95,150	19,928	15,639	20,368	18,284
95,150	95,200	19,942	15,651	20,382	18,296
95,200	95,250	19,956	15,664	20,396	18,309
95,250	95,300	19,970	15,676	20,410	18,321
95,300	95,350	19,984	15,689	20,424	18,334
95,350	95,400	19,998	15,701	20,438	18,346
95,400	95,450	20,012	15,714	20,452	18,359
95,450	95,500	20,026	15,726	20,466	18,371
95,500	95,550	20,040	15,739	20,480	18,384
95,550	95,600	20,054	15,751	20,494	18,396
95,600	95,650	20,068	15,764	20,508	18,409
95,650	95,700	20,082	15,776	20,522	18,421
95,700	95,750	20,096	15,789	20,536	18,434
95,750	95,800	20,110	15,801	20,550	18,446
95,800	95,850	20,124	15,814	20,564	18,459
95,850	95,900	20,138	15,826	20,578	18,471
95,900	95,950	20,152	15,839	20,592	18,484
95,950	96,000	20,166	15,851	20,606	18,496

96,000

If line 43 (taxable income) is—		And you are—			
At least	But less than	Single	Married filing jointly *	Married filing separately	Head of a house-hold
		Your tax is—			
96,000	96,050	20,180	15,864	20,620	18,509
96,050	96,100	20,194	15,876	20,634	18,521
96,100	96,150	20,208	15,889	20,648	18,534
96,150	96,200	20,222	15,901	20,662	18,546
96,200	96,250	20,236	15,914	20,676	18,559
96,250	96,300	20,250	15,926	20,690	18,571
96,300	96,350	20,264	15,939	20,704	18,584
96,350	96,400	20,278	15,951	20,718	18,596
96,400	96,450	20,292	15,964	20,732	18,609
96,450	96,500	20,306	15,976	20,746	18,621
96,500	96,550	20,320	15,989	20,760	18,634
96,550	96,600	20,334	16,001	20,774	18,646
96,600	96,650	20,348	16,014	20,788	18,659
96,650	96,700	20,362	16,026	20,802	18,671
96,700	96,750	20,376	16,039	20,816	18,684
96,750	96,800	20,390	16,051	20,830	18,696
96,800	96,850	20,404	16,064	20,844	18,709
96,850	96,900	20,418	16,076	20,858	18,721
96,900	96,950	20,432	16,089	20,872	18,734
96,950	97,000	20,446	16,101	20,886	18,746

97,000

At least	But less than	Single	Married filing jointly *	Married filing separately	Head of a house-hold
97,000	97,050	20,460	16,114	20,900	18,759
97,050	97,100	20,474	16,126	20,914	18,771
97,100	97,150	20,488	16,139	20,928	18,784
97,150	97,200	20,502	16,151	20,942	18,796
97,200	97,250	20,516	16,164	20,956	18,809
97,250	97,300	20,530	16,176	20,970	18,821
97,300	97,350	20,544	16,189	20,984	18,834
97,350	97,400	20,558	16,201	20,998	18,846
97,400	97,450	20,572	16,214	21,012	18,859
97,450	97,500	20,586	16,226	21,026	18,871
97,500	97,550	20,600	16,239	21,040	18,884
97,550	97,600	20,614	16,251	21,054	18,896
97,600	97,650	20,628	16,264	21,068	18,909
97,650	97,700	20,642	16,276	21,082	18,921
97,700	97,750	20,656	16,289	21,096	18,934
97,750	97,800	20,670	16,301	21,110	18,946
97,800	97,850	20,684	16,314	21,124	18,959
97,850	97,900	20,698	16,326	21,138	18,971
97,900	97,950	20,712	16,339	21,152	18,984
97,950	98,000	20,726	16,351	21,166	18,996

98,000

At least	But less than	Single	Married filing jointly *	Married filing separately	Head of a house-hold
98,000	98,050	20,740	16,364	21,180	19,009
98,050	98,100	20,754	16,376	21,194	19,021
98,100	98,150	20,768	16,389	21,208	19,034
98,150	98,200	20,782	16,401	21,222	19,046
98,200	98,250	20,796	16,414	21,236	19,059
98,250	98,300	20,810	16,426	21,250	19,071
98,300	98,350	20,824	16,439	21,264	19,084
98,350	98,400	20,838	16,451	21,278	19,096
98,400	98,450	20,852	16,464	21,292	19,109
98,450	98,500	20,866	16,476	21,306	19,121
98,500	98,550	20,880	16,489	21,320	19,134
98,550	98,600	20,894	16,501	21,334	19,146
98,600	98,650	20,908	16,514	21,348	19,159
98,650	98,700	20,922	16,526	21,362	19,171
98,700	98,750	20,936	16,539	21,376	19,184
98,750	98,800	20,950	16,551	21,390	19,196
98,800	98,850	20,964	16,564	21,404	19,209
98,850	98,900	20,978	16,576	21,418	19,221
98,900	98,950	20,992	16,589	21,432	19,234
98,950	99,000	21,006	16,601	21,446	19,246

99,000

If line 43 (taxable income) is—		And you are—			
At least	But less than	Single	Married filing jointly *	Married filing separately	Head of a house-hold
		Your tax is—			
99,000	99,050	21,020	16,614	21,460	19,259
99,050	99,100	21,034	16,626	21,474	19,271
99,100	99,150	21,048	16,639	21,488	19,284
99,150	99,200	21,062	16,651	21,502	19,296
99,200	99,250	21,076	16,664	21,516	19,309
99,250	99,300	21,090	16,676	21,530	19,321
99,300	99,350	21,104	16,689	21,544	19,334
99,350	99,400	21,118	16,701	21,558	19,346
99,400	99,450	21,132	16,714	21,572	19,359
99,450	99,500	21,146	16,726	21,586	19,371
99,500	99,550	21,160	16,739	21,600	19,384
99,550	99,600	21,174	16,751	21,614	19,396
99,600	99,650	21,188	16,764	21,628	19,409
99,650	99,700	21,202	16,776	21,642	19,421
99,700	99,750	21,216	16,789	21,656	19,434
99,750	99,800	21,230	16,801	21,670	19,446
99,800	99,850	21,244	16,814	21,684	19,459
99,850	99,900	21,258	16,826	21,698	19,471
99,900	99,950	21,272	16,839	21,712	19,484
99,950	100,000	21,286	16,851	21,726	19,496

$100,000 or over use the Tax Computation Worksheet

* This column must also be used by a qualifying widow(er).

NOTE: DRAFT AS OF SEPTEMBER 16, 2013.

¶ 1112 Earned Income Credit Table.

2013 Earned Income Credit (EIC) Table
Caution. This is **not** a tax table.

1. To find your credit, read down the "At least - But less than" columns and find the line that includes the amount you were told to look up from your EIC Worksheet.

2. Then, go to the column that includes your filing status and the number of qualifying children you have. Enter the credit from that column on your EIC Worksheet.

Example. If your filing status is single, you have one qualifying child, and the amount you are looking up from your EIC Worksheet is $2,455, you would enter $842.

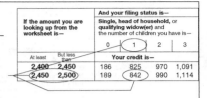

If the amount you are looking up from the worksheet is—		And your filing status is—			
		Single, head of household, or qualifying widow(er) and the number of children you have is—			
At least	But less than	0	1	2	3
		Your credit is—			
2,400	2,450	186	825	970	1,091
2,450	2,500	189	842	990	1,114

If the amount you are looking up from the worksheet is—		Single, head of household, or qualifying widow(er) and the number of children you have is—				Married filing jointly and the number of children you have is–			
		0	1	2	3	0	1	2	3
At least	But less than	Your credit is—				Your credit is–			
$1	$50	$2	$9	$10	$11	$2	$9	$10	$11
50	100	6	26	30	34	6	26	30	34
100	150	10	43	50	56	10	43	50	56
150	200	13	60	70	79	13	60	70	79
200	250	17	77	90	101	17	77	90	101
250	300	21	94	110	124	21	94	110	124
300	350	25	111	130	146	25	111	130	146
350	400	29	128	150	169	29	128	150	169
400	450	33	145	170	191	33	145	170	191
450	500	36	162	190	214	36	162	190	214
500	550	40	179	210	236	40	179	210	236
550	600	44	196	230	259	44	196	230	259
600	650	48	213	250	281	48	213	250	281
650	700	52	230	270	304	52	230	270	304
700	750	55	247	290	326	55	247	290	326
750	800	59	264	310	349	59	264	310	349
800	850	63	281	330	371	63	281	330	371
850	900	67	298	350	394	67	298	350	394
900	950	71	315	370	416	71	315	370	416
950	1,000	75	332	390	439	75	332	390	439
1,000	1,050	78	349	410	461	78	349	410	461
1,050	1,100	82	366	430	484	82	366	430	484
1,100	1,150	86	383	450	506	86	383	450	506
1,150	1,200	90	400	470	529	90	400	470	529
1,200	1,250	94	417	490	551	94	417	490	551
1,250	1,300	98	434	510	574	98	434	510	574
1,300	1,350	101	451	530	596	101	451	530	596
1,350	1,400	105	468	550	619	105	468	550	619
1,400	1,450	109	485	570	641	109	485	570	641
1,450	1,500	113	502	590	664	113	502	590	664
1,500	1,550	117	519	610	686	117	519	610	686
1,550	1,600	120	536	630	709	120	536	630	709
1,600	1,650	124	553	650	731	124	553	650	731
1,650	1,700	128	570	670	754	128	570	670	754
1,700	1,750	132	587	690	776	132	587	690	776
1,750	1,800	136	604	710	799	136	604	710	799
1,800	1,850	140	621	730	821	140	621	730	821
1,850	1,900	143	638	750	844	143	638	750	844
1,900	1,950	147	655	770	866	147	655	770	866
1,950	2,000	151	672	790	889	151	672	790	889
2,000	2,050	155	689	810	911	155	689	810	911
2,050	2,100	159	706	830	934	159	706	830	934
2,100	2,150	163	723	850	956	163	723	850	956
2,150	2,200	166	740	870	979	166	740	870	979
2,200	2,250	170	757	890	1,001	170	757	890	1,001
2,250	2,300	174	774	910	1,024	174	774	910	1,024
2,300	2,350	178	791	930	1,046	178	791	930	1,046
2,350	2,400	182	808	950	1,069	182	808	950	1,069
2,400	2,450	186	825	970	1,091	186	825	970	1,091
2,450	2,500	189	842	990	1,114	189	842	990	1,114

If the amount you are looking up from the worksheet is–		Single, head of household, or qualifying widow(er) and the number of children you have is–				Married filing jointly and the number of children you have is–			
		0	1	2	3	0	1	2	3
At least	But less than	Your credit is–				Your credit is–			
2,500	2,550	193	859	1,010	1,136	193	859	1,010	1,136
2,550	2,600	197	876	1,030	1,159	197	876	1,030	1,159
2,600	2,650	201	893	1,050	1,181	201	893	1,050	1,181
2,650	2,700	205	910	1,070	1,204	205	910	1,070	1,204
2,700	2,750	208	927	1,090	1,226	208	927	1,090	1,226
2,750	2,800	212	944	1,110	1,249	212	944	1,110	1,249
2,800	2,850	216	961	1,130	1,271	216	961	1,130	1,271
2,850	2,900	220	978	1,150	1,294	220	978	1,150	1,294
2,900	2,950	224	995	1,170	1,316	224	995	1,170	1,316
2,950	3,000	228	1,012	1,190	1,339	228	1,012	1,190	1,339
3,000	3,050	231	1,029	1,210	1,361	231	1,029	1,210	1,361
3,050	3,100	235	1,046	1,230	1,384	235	1,046	1,230	1,384
3,100	3,150	239	1,063	1,250	1,406	239	1,063	1,250	1,406
3,150	3,200	243	1,080	1,270	1,429	243	1,080	1,270	1,429
3,200	3,250	247	1,097	1,290	1,451	247	1,097	1,290	1,451
3,250	3,300	251	1,114	1,310	1,474	251	1,114	1,310	1,474
3,300	3,350	254	1,131	1,330	1,496	254	1,131	1,330	1,496
3,350	3,400	258	1,148	1,350	1,519	258	1,148	1,350	1,519
3,400	3,450	262	1,165	1,370	1,541	262	1,165	1,370	1,541
3,450	3,500	266	1,182	1,390	1,564	266	1,182	1,390	1,564
3,500	3,550	270	1,199	1,410	1,586	270	1,199	1,410	1,586
3,550	3,600	273	1,216	1,430	1,609	273	1,216	1,430	1,609
3,600	3,650	277	1,233	1,450	1,631	277	1,233	1,450	1,631
3,650	3,700	281	1,250	1,470	1,654	281	1,250	1,470	1,654
3,700	3,750	285	1,267	1,490	1,676	285	1,267	1,490	1,676
3,750	3,800	289	1,284	1,510	1,699	289	1,284	1,510	1,699
3,800	3,850	293	1,301	1,530	1,721	293	1,301	1,530	1,721
3,850	3,900	296	1,318	1,550	1,744	296	1,318	1,550	1,744
3,900	3,950	300	1,335	1,570	1,766	300	1,335	1,570	1,766
3,950	4,000	304	1,352	1,590	1,789	304	1,352	1,590	1,789
4,000	4,050	308	1,369	1,610	1,811	308	1,369	1,610	1,811
4,050	4,100	312	1,386	1,630	1,834	312	1,386	1,630	1,834
4,100	4,150	316	1,403	1,650	1,856	316	1,403	1,650	1,856
4,150	4,200	319	1,420	1,670	1,879	319	1,420	1,670	1,879
4,200	4,250	323	1,437	1,690	1,901	323	1,437	1,690	1,901
4,250	4,300	327	1,454	1,710	1,924	327	1,454	1,710	1,924
4,300	4,350	331	1,471	1,730	1,946	331	1,471	1,730	1,946
4,350	4,400	335	1,488	1,750	1,969	335	1,488	1,750	1,969
4,400	4,450	339	1,505	1,770	1,991	339	1,505	1,770	1,991
4,450	4,500	342	1,522	1,790	2,014	342	1,522	1,790	2,014
4,500	4,550	346	1,539	1,810	2,036	346	1,539	1,810	2,036
4,550	4,600	350	1,556	1,830	2,059	350	1,556	1,830	2,059
4,600	4,650	354	1,573	1,850	2,081	354	1,573	1,850	2,081
4,650	4,700	358	1,590	1,870	2,104	358	1,590	1,870	2,104
4,700	4,750	361	1,607	1,890	2,126	361	1,607	1,890	2,126
4,750	4,800	365	1,624	1,910	2,149	365	1,624	1,910	2,149
4,800	4,850	369	1,641	1,930	2,171	369	1,641	1,930	2,171
4,850	4,900	373	1,658	1,950	2,194	373	1,658	1,950	2,194
4,900	4,950	377	1,675	1,970	2,216	377	1,675	1,970	2,216
4,950	5,000	381	1,692	1,990	2,239	381	1,692	1,990	2,239

NOTE: DRAFT AS OF SEPTEMBER 16, 2013.

(Continued)

Earned Income Credit (EIC) Table - *Continued*   (**Caution.** This is **not** a tax table.)

If the amount you are looking up from the worksheet is–		Single, head of household, or qualifying widow(er) and the number of children you have is–				Married filing jointly and the number of children you have is–			
At least	But less than	0	1	2	3	0	1	2	3
		Your credit is–				Your credit is–			
5,000	5,050	384	1,709	2,010	2,261	384	1,709	2,010	2,261
5,050	5,100	388	1,726	2,030	2,284	388	1,726	2,030	2,284
5,100	5,150	392	1,743	2,050	2,306	392	1,743	2,050	2,306
5,150	5,200	396	1,760	2,070	2,329	396	1,760	2,070	2,329
5,200	5,250	400	1,777	2,090	2,351	400	1,777	2,090	2,351
5,250	5,300	404	1,794	2,110	2,374	404	1,794	2,110	2,374
5,300	5,350	407	1,811	2,130	2,396	407	1,811	2,130	2,396
5,350	5,400	411	1,828	2,150	2,419	411	1,828	2,150	2,419
5,400	5,450	415	1,845	2,170	2,441	415	1,845	2,170	2,441
5,450	5,500	419	1,862	2,190	2,464	419	1,862	2,190	2,464
5,500	5,550	423	1,879	2,210	2,486	423	1,879	2,210	2,486
5,550	5,600	426	1,896	2,230	2,509	426	1,896	2,230	2,509
5,600	5,650	430	1,913	2,250	2,531	430	1,913	2,250	2,531
5,650	5,700	434	1,930	2,270	2,554	434	1,930	2,270	2,554
5,700	5,750	438	1,947	2,290	2,576	438	1,947	2,290	2,576
5,750	5,800	442	1,964	2,310	2,599	442	1,964	2,310	2,599
5,800	5,850	446	1,981	2,330	2,621	446	1,981	2,330	2,621
5,850	5,900	449	1,998	2,350	2,644	449	1,998	2,350	2,644
5,900	5,950	453	2,015	2,370	2,666	453	2,015	2,370	2,666
5,950	6,000	457	2,032	2,390	2,689	457	2,032	2,390	2,689
6,000	6,050	461	2,049	2,410	2,711	461	2,049	2,410	2,711
6,050	6,100	465	2,066	2,430	2,734	465	2,066	2,430	2,734
6,100	6,150	469	2,083	2,450	2,756	469	2,083	2,450	2,756
6,150	6,200	472	2,100	2,470	2,779	472	2,100	2,470	2,779
6,200	6,250	476	2,117	2,490	2,801	476	2,117	2,490	2,801
6,250	6,300	480	2,134	2,510	2,824	480	2,134	2,510	2,824
6,300	6,350	484	2,151	2,530	2,846	484	2,151	2,530	2,846
6,350	6,400	487	2,168	2,550	2,869	487	2,168	2,550	2,869
6,400	6,450	487	2,185	2,570	2,891	487	2,185	2,570	2,891
6,450	6,500	487	2,202	2,590	2,914	487	2,202	2,590	2,914
6,500	6,550	487	2,219	2,610	2,936	487	2,219	2,610	2,936
6,550	6,600	487	2,236	2,630	2,959	487	2,236	2,630	2,959
6,600	6,650	487	2,253	2,650	2,981	487	2,253	2,650	2,981
6,650	6,700	487	2,270	2,670	3,004	487	2,270	2,670	3,004
6,700	6,750	487	2,287	2,690	3,026	487	2,287	2,690	3,026
6,750	6,800	487	2,304	2,710	3,049	487	2,304	2,710	3,049
6,800	6,850	487	2,321	2,730	3,071	487	2,321	2,730	3,071
6,850	6,900	487	2,338	2,750	3,094	487	2,338	2,750	3,094
6,900	6,950	487	2,355	2,770	3,116	487	2,355	2,770	3,116
6,950	7,000	487	2,372	2,790	3,139	487	2,372	2,790	3,139
7,000	7,050	487	2,389	2,810	3,161	487	2,389	2,810	3,161
7,050	7,100	487	2,406	2,830	3,184	487	2,406	2,830	3,184
7,100	7,150	487	2,423	2,850	3,206	487	2,423	2,850	3,206
7,150	7,200	487	2,440	2,870	3,229	487	2,440	2,870	3,229
7,200	7,250	487	2,457	2,890	3,251	487	2,457	2,890	3,251
7,250	7,300	487	2,474	2,910	3,274	487	2,474	2,910	3,274
7,300	7,350	487	2,491	2,930	3,296	487	2,491	2,930	3,296
7,350	7,400	487	2,508	2,950	3,319	487	2,508	2,950	3,319
7,400	7,450	487	2,525	2,970	3,341	487	2,525	2,970	3,341
7,450	7,500	487	2,542	2,990	3,364	487	2,542	2,990	3,364
7,500	7,550	487	2,559	3,010	3,386	487	2,559	3,010	3,386
7,550	7,600	487	2,576	3,030	3,409	487	2,576	3,030	3,409
7,600	7,650	487	2,593	3,050	3,431	487	2,593	3,050	3,431
7,650	7,700	487	2,610	3,070	3,454	487	2,610	3,070	3,454
7,700	7,750	487	2,627	3,090	3,476	487	2,627	3,090	3,476
7,750	7,800	487	2,644	3,110	3,499	487	2,644	3,110	3,499
7,800	7,850	487	2,661	3,130	3,521	487	2,661	3,130	3,521
7,850	7,900	487	2,678	3,150	3,544	487	2,678	3,150	3,544
7,900	7,950	487	2,695	3,170	3,566	487	2,695	3,170	3,566
7,950	8,000	487	2,712	3,190	3,589	487	2,712	3,190	3,589
8,000	8,050	483	2,729	3,210	3,611	487	2,729	3,210	3,611
8,050	8,100	479	2,746	3,230	3,634	487	2,746	3,230	3,634
8,100	8,150	475	2,763	3,250	3,656	487	2,763	3,250	3,656
8,150	8,200	472	2,780	3,270	3,679	487	2,780	3,270	3,679
8,200	8,250	468	2,797	3,290	3,701	487	2,797	3,290	3,701
8,250	8,300	464	2,814	3,310	3,724	487	2,814	3,310	3,724
8,300	8,350	460	2,831	3,330	3,746	487	2,831	3,330	3,746
8,350	8,400	456	2,848	3,350	3,769	487	2,848	3,350	3,769
8,400	8,450	452	2,865	3,370	3,791	487	2,865	3,370	3,791
8,450	8,500	449	2,882	3,390	3,814	487	2,882	3,390	3,814
8,500	8,550	445	2,899	3,410	3,836	487	2,899	3,410	3,836
8,550	8,600	441	2,916	3,430	3,859	487	2,916	3,430	3,859
8,600	8,650	437	2,933	3,450	3,881	487	2,933	3,450	3,881
8,650	8,700	433	2,950	3,470	3,904	487	2,950	3,470	3,904
8,700	8,750	429	2,967	3,490	3,926	487	2,967	3,490	3,926
8,750	8,800	426	2,984	3,510	3,949	487	2,984	3,510	3,949
8,800	8,850	422	3,001	3,530	3,971	487	3,001	3,530	3,971
8,850	8,900	418	3,018	3,550	3,994	487	3,018	3,550	3,994
8,900	8,950	414	3,035	3,570	4,016	487	3,035	3,570	4,016
8,950	9,000	410	3,052	3,590	4,039	487	3,052	3,590	4,039
9,000	9,050	407	3,069	3,610	4,061	487	3,069	3,610	4,061
9,050	9,100	403	3,086	3,630	4,084	487	3,086	3,630	4,084
9,100	9,150	399	3,103	3,650	4,106	487	3,103	3,650	4,106
9,150	9,200	395	3,120	3,670	4,129	487	3,120	3,670	4,129
9,200	9,250	391	3,137	3,690	4,151	487	3,137	3,690	4,151
9,250	9,300	387	3,154	3,710	4,174	487	3,154	3,710	4,174
9,300	9,350	384	3,171	3,730	4,196	487	3,171	3,730	4,196
9,350	9,400	380	3,188	3,750	4,219	487	3,188	3,750	4,219
9,400	9,450	376	3,205	3,770	4,241	487	3,205	3,770	4,241
9,450	9,500	372	3,222	3,790	4,264	487	3,222	3,790	4,264
9,500	9,550	368	3,239	3,810	4,286	487	3,239	3,810	4,286
9,550	9,600	365	3,250	3,830	4,309	487	3,250	3,830	4,309
9,600	9,650	361	3,250	3,850	4,331	487	3,250	3,850	4,331
9,650	9,700	357	3,250	3,870	4,354	487	3,250	3,870	4,354
9,700	9,750	353	3,250	3,890	4,376	487	3,250	3,890	4,376
9,750	9,800	349	3,250	3,910	4,399	487	3,250	3,910	4,399
9,800	9,850	345	3,250	3,930	4,421	487	3,250	3,930	4,421
9,850	9,900	342	3,250	3,950	4,444	487	3,250	3,950	4,444
9,900	9,950	338	3,250	3,970	4,466	487	3,250	3,970	4,466
9,950	10,000	334	3,250	3,990	4,489	487	3,250	3,990	4,489
10,000	10,050	330	3,250	4,010	4,511	487	3,250	4,010	4,511
10,050	10,100	326	3,250	4,030	4,534	487	3,250	4,030	4,534
10,100	10,150	322	3,250	4,050	4,556	487	3,250	4,050	4,556
10,150	10,200	319	3,250	4,070	4,579	487	3,250	4,070	4,579
10,200	10,250	315	3,250	4,090	4,601	487	3,250	4,090	4,601
10,250	10,300	311	3,250	4,110	4,624	487	3,250	4,110	4,624
10,300	10,350	307	3,250	4,130	4,646	487	3,250	4,130	4,646
10,350	10,400	303	3,250	4,150	4,669	487	3,250	4,150	4,669
10,400	10,450	299	3,250	4,170	4,691	487	3,250	4,170	4,691
10,450	10,500	296	3,250	4,190	4,714	487	3,250	4,190	4,714
10,500	10,550	292	3,250	4,210	4,736	487	3,250	4,210	4,736
10,550	10,600	288	3,250	4,230	4,759	487	3,250	4,230	4,759
10,600	10,650	284	3,250	4,250	4,781	487	3,250	4,250	4,781
10,650	10,700	280	3,250	4,270	4,804	487	3,250	4,270	4,804
10,700	10,750	277	3,250	4,290	4,826	487	3,250	4,290	4,826
10,750	10,800	273	3,250	4,310	4,849	487	3,250	4,310	4,849
10,800	10,850	269	3,250	4,330	4,871	487	3,250	4,330	4,871
10,850	10,900	265	3,250	4,350	4,894	487	3,250	4,350	4,894
10,900	10,950	261	3,250	4,370	4,916	487	3,250	4,370	4,916
10,950	11,000	257	3,250	4,390	4,939	487	3,250	4,390	4,939

NOTE: DRAFT AS OF SEPTEMBER 16, 2013.   *(Continued)*

Earned Income Credit (EIC) Table - *Continued*

(Caution. This is **not** a tax table.)

Income range 11,000 – 14,000

At least	But less than	Single, head of household, or qualifying widow(er) — 0	1	2	3	Married filing jointly — 0	1	2	3
11,000	11,050	254	3,250	4,410	4,961	487	3,250	4,410	4,961
11,050	11,100	250	3,250	4,430	4,984	487	3,250	4,430	4,984
11,100	11,150	246	3,250	4,450	5,006	487	3,250	4,450	5,006
11,150	11,200	242	3,250	4,470	5,029	487	3,250	4,470	5,029
11,200	11,250	238	3,250	4,490	5,051	487	3,250	4,490	5,051
11,250	11,300	234	3,250	4,510	5,074	487	3,250	4,510	5,074
11,300	11,350	231	3,250	4,530	5,096	487	3,250	4,530	5,096
11,350	11,400	227	3,250	4,550	5,119	487	3,250	4,550	5,119
11,400	11,450	223	3,250	4,570	5,141	487	3,250	4,570	5,141
11,450	11,500	219	3,250	4,590	5,164	487	3,250	4,590	5,164
11,500	11,550	215	3,250	4,610	5,186	487	3,250	4,610	5,186
11,550	11,600	212	3,250	4,630	5,209	487	3,250	4,630	5,209
11,600	11,650	208	3,250	4,650	5,231	487	3,250	4,650	5,231
11,650	11,700	204	3,250	4,670	5,254	487	3,250	4,670	5,254
11,700	11,750	200	3,250	4,690	5,276	487	3,250	4,690	5,276
11,750	11,800	196	3,250	4,710	5,299	487	3,250	4,710	5,299
11,800	11,850	192	3,250	4,730	5,321	487	3,250	4,730	5,321
11,850	11,900	189	3,250	4,750	5,344	487	3,250	4,750	5,344
11,900	11,950	185	3,250	4,770	5,366	487	3,250	4,770	5,366
11,950	12,000	181	3,250	4,790	5,389	487	3,250	4,790	5,389
12,000	12,050	177	3,250	4,810	5,411	487	3,250	4,810	5,411
12,050	12,100	173	3,250	4,830	5,434	487	3,250	4,830	5,434
12,100	12,150	169	3,250	4,850	5,456	487	3,250	4,850	5,456
12,150	12,200	166	3,250	4,870	5,479	487	3,250	4,870	5,479
12,200	12,250	162	3,250	4,890	5,501	487	3,250	4,890	5,501
12,250	12,300	158	3,250	4,910	5,524	487	3,250	4,910	5,524
12,300	12,350	154	3,250	4,930	5,546	487	3,250	4,930	5,546
12,350	12,400	150	3,250	4,950	5,569	487	3,250	4,950	5,569
12,400	12,450	146	3,250	4,970	5,591	487	3,250	4,970	5,591
12,450	12,500	143	3,250	4,990	5,614	487	3,250	4,990	5,614
12,500	12,550	139	3,250	5,010	5,636	487	3,250	5,010	5,636
12,550	12,600	135	3,250	5,030	5,659	487	3,250	5,030	5,659
12,600	12,650	131	3,250	5,050	5,681	487	3,250	5,050	5,681
12,650	12,700	127	3,250	5,070	5,704	487	3,250	5,070	5,704
12,700	12,750	124	3,250	5,090	5,726	487	3,250	5,090	5,726
12,750	12,800	120	3,250	5,110	5,749	487	3,250	5,110	5,749
12,800	12,850	116	3,250	5,130	5,771	487	3,250	5,130	5,771
12,850	12,900	112	3,250	5,150	5,794	487	3,250	5,150	5,794
12,900	12,950	108	3,250	5,170	5,816	487	3,250	5,170	5,816
12,950	13,000	104	3,250	5,190	5,839	487	3,250	5,190	5,839
13,000	13,050	101	3,250	5,210	5,861	487	3,250	5,210	5,861
13,050	13,100	97	3,250	5,230	5,884	487	3,250	5,230	5,884
13,100	13,150	93	3,250	5,250	5,906	487	3,250	5,250	5,906
13,150	13,200	89	3,250	5,270	5,929	487	3,250	5,270	5,929
13,200	13,250	85	3,250	5,290	5,951	487	3,250	5,290	5,951
13,250	13,300	81	3,250	5,310	5,974	487	3,250	5,310	5,974
13,300	13,350	78	3,250	5,330	5,996	487	3,250	5,330	5,996
13,350	13,400	74	3,250	5,350	6,019	482	3,250	5,350	6,019
13,400	13,450	70	3,250	5,372	6,044	479	3,250	5,372	6,044
13,450	13,500	66	3,250	5,372	6,044	475	3,250	5,372	6,044
13,500	13,550	62	3,250	5,372	6,044	471	3,250	5,372	6,044
13,550	13,600	59	3,250	5,372	6,044	467	3,250	5,372	6,044
13,600	13,650	55	3,250	5,372	6,044	463	3,250	5,372	6,044
13,650	13,700	51	3,250	5,372	6,044	459	3,250	5,372	6,044
13,700	13,750	47	3,250	5,372	6,044	456	3,250	5,372	6,044
13,750	13,800	43	3,250	5,372	6,044	452	3,250	5,372	6,044
13,800	13,850	39	3,250	5,372	6,044	448	3,250	5,372	6,044
13,850	13,900	36	3,250	5,372	6,044	444	3,250	5,372	6,044
13,900	13,950	32	3,250	5,372	6,044	440	3,250	5,372	6,044
13,950	14,000	28	3,250	5,372	6,044	436	3,250	5,372	6,044

Income range 14,000 – 17,000

At least	But less than	Single, head of household, or qualifying widow(er) — 0	1	2	3	Married filing jointly — 0	1	2	3
14,000	14,050	24	3,250	5,372	6,044	433	3,250	5,372	6,044
14,050	14,100	20	3,250	5,372	6,044	429	3,250	5,372	6,044
14,100	14,150	16	3,250	5,372	6,044	425	3,250	5,372	6,044
14,150	14,200	13	3,250	5,372	6,044	421	3,250	5,372	6,044
14,200	14,250	9	3,250	5,372	6,044	417	3,250	5,372	6,044
14,250	14,300	5	3,250	5,372	6,044	413	3,250	5,372	6,044
14,300	14,350	*	3,250	5,372	6,044	410	3,250	5,372	6,044
14,350	14,400	0	3,250	5,372	6,044	406	3,250	5,372	6,044
14,400	14,450	0	3,250	5,372	6,044	402	3,250	5,372	6,044
14,450	14,500	0	3,250	5,372	6,044	398	3,250	5,372	6,044
14,500	14,550	0	3,250	5,372	6,044	394	3,250	5,372	6,044
14,550	14,600	0	3,250	5,372	6,044	391	3,250	5,372	6,044
14,600	14,650	0	3,250	5,372	6,044	387	3,250	5,372	6,044
14,650	14,700	0	3,250	5,372	6,044	383	3,250	5,372	6,044
14,700	14,750	0	3,250	5,372	6,044	379	3,250	5,372	6,044
14,750	14,800	0	3,250	5,372	6,044	375	3,250	5,372	6,044
14,800	14,850	0	3,250	5,372	6,044	371	3,250	5,372	6,044
14,850	14,900	0	3,250	5,372	6,044	368	3,250	5,372	6,044
14,900	14,950	0	3,250	5,372	6,044	364	3,250	5,372	6,044
14,950	15,000	0	3,250	5,372	6,044	360	3,250	5,372	6,044
15,000	15,050	0	3,250	5,372	6,044	356	3,250	5,372	6,044
15,050	15,100	0	3,250	5,372	6,044	352	3,250	5,372	6,044
15,100	15,150	0	3,250	5,372	6,044	348	3,250	5,372	6,044
15,150	15,200	0	3,250	5,372	6,044	345	3,250	5,372	6,044
15,200	15,250	0	3,250	5,372	6,044	341	3,250	5,372	6,044
15,250	15,300	0	3,250	5,372	6,044	337	3,250	5,372	6,044
15,300	15,350	0	3,250	5,372	6,044	333	3,250	5,372	6,044
15,350	15,400	0	3,250	5,372	6,044	329	3,250	5,372	6,044
15,400	15,450	0	3,250	5,372	6,044	326	3,250	5,372	6,044
15,450	15,500	0	3,250	5,372	6,044	322	3,250	5,372	6,044
15,500	15,550	0	3,250	5,372	6,044	318	3,250	5,372	6,044
15,550	15,600	0	3,250	5,372	6,044	314	3,250	5,372	6,044
15,600	15,650	0	3,250	5,372	6,044	310	3,250	5,372	6,044
15,650	15,700	0	3,250	5,372	6,044	306	3,250	5,372	6,044
15,700	15,750	0	3,250	5,372	6,044	303	3,250	5,372	6,044
15,750	15,800	0	3,250	5,372	6,044	299	3,250	5,372	6,044
15,800	15,850	0	3,250	5,372	6,044	295	3,250	5,372	6,044
15,850	15,900	0	3,250	5,372	6,044	291	3,250	5,372	6,044
15,900	15,950	0	3,250	5,372	6,044	287	3,250	5,372	6,044
15,950	16,000	0	3,250	5,372	6,044	283	3,250	5,372	6,044
16,000	16,050	0	3,250	5,372	6,044	280	3,250	5,372	6,044
16,050	16,100	0	3,250	5,372	6,044	276	3,250	5,372	6,044
16,100	16,150	0	3,250	5,372	6,044	272	3,250	5,372	6,044
16,150	16,200	0	3,250	5,372	6,044	268	3,250	5,372	6,044
16,200	16,250	0	3,250	5,372	6,044	264	3,250	5,372	6,044
16,250	16,300	0	3,250	5,372	6,044	260	3,250	5,372	6,044
16,300	16,350	0	3,250	5,372	6,044	257	3,250	5,372	6,044
16,350	16,400	0	3,250	5,372	6,044	253	3,250	5,372	6,044
16,400	16,450	0	3,250	5,372	6,044	249	3,250	5,372	6,044
16,450	16,500	0	3,250	5,372	6,044	245	3,250	5,372	6,044
16,500	16,550	0	3,250	5,372	6,044	241	3,250	5,372	6,044
16,550	16,600	0	3,250	5,372	6,044	238	3,250	5,372	6,044
16,600	16,650	0	3,250	5,372	6,044	234	3,250	5,372	6,044
16,650	16,700	0	3,250	5,372	6,044	230	3,250	5,372	6,044
16,700	16,750	0	3,250	5,372	6,044	226	3,250	5,372	6,044
16,750	16,800	0	3,250	5,372	6,044	222	3,250	5,372	6,044
16,800	16,850	0	3,250	5,372	6,044	218	3,250	5,372	6,044
16,850	16,900	0	3,250	5,372	6,044	215	3,250	5,372	6,044
16,900	16,950	0	3,250	5,372	6,044	211	3,250	5,372	6,044
16,950	17,000	0	3,250	5,372	6,044	207	3,250	5,372	6,044

* If the amount you are looking up from the worksheet is at least $14,300 but less than $14,340, and you have no qualifying children, your credit is $2.
If the amount you are looking up from the worksheet is $14,340 or more, and you have no qualifying children, you cannot take the credit.

(Continued)

NOTE: DRAFT AS OF SEPTEMBER 16, 2013.

Earned Income Credit (EIC) Table - *Continued*   (**Caution.** This is **not** a tax table.)

If the amount you are looking up from the worksheet is–		Single, head of household, or qualifying widow(er) and the number of children you have is–				Married filing jointly and the number of children you have is–				If the amount you are looking up from the worksheet is–		Single, head of household, or qualifying widow(er) and the number of children you have is–				Married filing jointly and the number of children you have is–			
		0	1	2	3	0	1	2	3			0	1	2	3	0	1	2	3
At least	But less than	Your credit is–				Your credit is–				At least	But less than	Your credit is–				Your credit is–			
17,000	17,050	0	3,250	5,372	6,044	203	3,250	5,372	6,044	20,000	20,050	0	2,852	4,847	5,518	0	3,250	5,372	6,044
17,050	17,100	0	3,250	5,372	6,044	199	3,250	5,372	6,044	20,050	20,100	0	2,844	4,836	5,508	0	3,250	5,372	6,044
17,100	17,150	0	3,250	5,372	6,044	195	3,250	5,372	6,044	20,100	20,150	0	2,836	4,825	5,497	0	3,250	5,372	6,044
17,150	17,200	0	3,250	5,372	6,044	192	3,250	5,372	6,044	20,150	20,200	0	2,828	4,815	5,486	0	3,250	5,372	6,044
17,200	17,250	0	3,250	5,372	6,044	188	3,250	5,372	6,044	20,200	20,250	0	2,820	4,804	5,476	0	3,250	5,372	6,044
17,250	17,300	0	3,250	5,372	6,044	184	3,250	5,372	6,044	20,250	20,300	0	2,812	4,794	5,465	0	3,250	5,372	6,044
17,300	17,350	0	3,250	5,372	6,044	180	3,250	5,372	6,044	20,300	20,350	0	2,804	4,783	5,455	0	3,250	5,372	6,044
17,350	17,400	0	3,250	5,372	6,044	176	3,250	5,372	6,044	20,350	20,400	0	2,796	4,773	5,444	0	3,250	5,372	6,044
17,400	17,450	0	3,250	5,372	6,044	173	3,250	5,372	6,044	20,400	20,450	0	2,788	4,762	5,434	0	3,250	5,372	6,044
17,450	17,500	0	3,250	5,372	6,044	169	3,250	5,372	6,044	20,450	20,500	0	2,780	4,752	5,423	0	3,250	5,372	6,044
17,500	17,550	0	3,250	5,372	6,044	165	3,250	5,372	6,044	20,500	20,550	0	2,772	4,741	5,413	0	3,250	5,372	6,044
17,550	17,600	0	3,243	5,363	6,034	161	3,250	5,372	6,044	20,550	20,600	0	2,764	4,731	5,402	0	3,250	5,372	6,044
17,600	17,650	0	3,235	5,352	6,023	157	3,250	5,372	6,044	20,600	20,650	0	2,756	4,720	5,392	0	3,250	5,372	6,044
17,650	17,700	0	3,227	5,341	6,013	153	3,250	5,372	6,044	20,650	20,700	0	2,748	4,710	5,381	0	3,250	5,372	6,044
17,700	17,750	0	3,219	5,331	6,002	150	3,250	5,372	6,044	20,700	20,750	0	2,740	4,699	5,371	0	3,250	5,372	6,044
17,750	17,800	0	3,211	5,320	5,992	146	3,250	5,372	6,044	20,750	20,800	0	2,732	4,689	5,360	0	3,250	5,372	6,044
17,800	17,850	0	3,203	5,310	5,981	142	3,250	5,372	6,044	20,800	20,850	0	2,724	4,678	5,350	0	3,250	5,372	6,044
17,850	17,900	0	3,195	5,299	5,971	138	3,250	5,372	6,044	20,850	20,900	0	2,716	4,668	5,339	0	3,250	5,372	6,044
17,900	17,950	0	3,187	5,289	5,960	134	3,250	5,372	6,044	20,900	20,950	0	2,708	4,657	5,329	0	3,250	5,372	6,044
17,950	18,000	0	3,179	5,278	5,950	130	3,250	5,372	6,044	20,950	21,000	0	2,700	4,646	5,318	0	3,250	5,372	6,044
18,000	18,050	0	3,171	5,268	5,939	127	3,250	5,372	6,044	21,000	21,050	0	2,692	4,636	5,307	0	3,250	5,372	6,044
18,050	18,100	0	3,163	5,257	5,929	123	3,250	5,372	6,044	21,050	21,100	0	2,684	4,625	5,297	0	3,250	5,372	6,044
18,100	18,150	0	3,155	5,247	5,918	119	3,250	5,372	6,044	21,100	21,150	0	2,676	4,615	5,286	0	3,250	5,372	6,044
18,150	18,200	0	3,147	5,236	5,908	115	3,250	5,372	6,044	21,150	21,200	0	2,668	4,604	5,276	0	3,250	5,372	6,044
18,200	18,250	0	3,139	5,226	5,897	111	3,250	5,372	6,044	21,200	21,250	0	2,660	4,594	5,265	0	3,250	5,372	6,044
18,250	18,300	0	3,131	5,215	5,887	107	3,250	5,372	6,044	21,250	21,300	0	2,652	4,583	5,255	0	3,250	5,372	6,044
18,300	18,350	0	3,123	5,205	5,876	104	3,250	5,372	6,044	21,300	21,350	0	2,644	4,573	5,244	0	3,250	5,372	6,044
18,350	18,400	0	3,115	5,194	5,866	100	3,250	5,372	6,044	21,350	21,400	0	2,636	4,562	5,234	0	3,250	5,372	6,044
18,400	18,450	0	3,107	5,184	5,855	96	3,250	5,372	6,044	21,400	21,450	0	2,628	4,552	5,223	0	3,250	5,372	6,044
18,450	18,500	0	3,099	5,173	5,844	92	3,250	5,372	6,044	21,450	21,500	0	2,620	4,541	5,213	0	3,250	5,372	6,044
18,500	18,550	0	3,091	5,162	5,834	88	3,250	5,372	6,044	21,500	21,550	0	2,612	4,531	5,202	0	3,250	5,372	6,044
18,550	18,600	0	3,083	5,152	5,823	85	3,250	5,372	6,044	21,550	21,600	0	2,604	4,520	5,192	0	3,250	5,372	6,044
18,600	18,650	0	3,075	5,141	5,813	81	3,250	5,372	6,044	21,600	21,650	0	2,596	4,510	5,181	0	3,250	5,372	6,044
18,650	18,700	0	3,067	5,131	5,802	77	3,250	5,372	6,044	21,650	21,700	0	2,588	4,499	5,171	0	3,250	5,372	6,044
18,700	18,750	0	3,059	5,120	5,792	73	3,250	5,372	6,044	21,700	21,750	0	2,580	4,489	5,160	0	3,250	5,372	6,044
18,750	18,800	0	3,051	5,110	5,781	69	3,250	5,372	6,044	21,750	21,800	0	2,572	4,478	5,150	0	3,250	5,372	6,044
18,800	18,850	0	3,043	5,099	5,771	65	3,250	5,372	6,044	21,800	21,850	0	2,564	4,467	5,139	0	3,250	5,372	6,044
18,850	18,900	0	3,035	5,089	5,760	62	3,250	5,372	6,044	21,850	21,900	0	2,556	4,457	5,128	0	3,250	5,372	6,044
18,900	18,950	0	3,027	5,078	5,750	58	3,250	5,372	6,044	21,900	21,950	0	2,548	4,446	5,118	0	3,250	5,372	6,044
18,950	19,000	0	3,019	5,068	5,739	54	3,250	5,372	6,044	21,950	22,000	0	2,540	4,436	5,107	0	3,250	5,372	6,044
19,000	19,050	0	3,011	5,057	5,729	50	3,250	5,372	6,044	22,000	22,050	0	2,532	4,425	5,097	0	3,250	5,372	6,044
19,050	19,100	0	3,004	5,047	5,718	46	3,250	5,372	6,044	22,050	22,100	0	2,524	4,415	5,086	0	3,250	5,372	6,044
19,100	19,150	0	2,996	5,036	5,708	42	3,250	5,372	6,044	22,100	22,150	0	2,516	4,404	5,076	0	3,250	5,372	6,044
19,150	19,200	0	2,988	5,026	5,697	39	3,250	5,372	6,044	22,150	22,200	0	2,508	4,394	5,065	0	3,250	5,372	6,044
19,200	19,250	0	2,980	5,015	5,687	35	3,250	5,372	6,044	22,200	22,250	0	2,500	4,383	5,055	0	3,250	5,372	6,044
19,250	19,300	0	2,972	5,005	5,676	31	3,250	5,372	6,044	22,250	22,300	0	2,492	4,373	5,044	0	3,250	5,372	6,044
19,300	19,350	0	2,964	4,994	5,665	27	3,250	5,372	6,044	22,300	22,350	0	2,484	4,362	5,034	0	3,250	5,372	6,044
19,350	19,400	0	2,956	4,983	5,655	23	3,250	5,372	6,044	22,350	22,400	0	2,476	4,352	5,023	0	3,250	5,372	6,044
19,400	19,450	0	2,948	4,973	5,644	20	3,250	5,372	6,044	22,400	22,450	0	2,468	4,341	5,013	0	3,250	5,372	6,044
19,450	19,500	0	2,940	4,962	5,634	16	3,250	5,372	6,044	22,450	22,500	0	2,460	4,331	5,002	0	3,250	5,372	6,044
19,500	19,550	0	2,932	4,952	5,623	12	3,250	5,372	6,044	22,500	22,550	0	2,452	4,320	4,992	0	3,250	5,372	6,044
19,550	19,600	0	2,924	4,941	5,613	8	3,250	5,372	6,044	22,550	22,600	0	2,444	4,310	4,981	0	3,250	5,372	6,044
19,600	19,650	0	2,916	4,931	5,602	4	3,250	5,372	6,044	22,600	22,650	0	2,436	4,299	4,970	0	3,250	5,372	6,044
19,650	19,700	0	2,908	4,920	5,592	*	3,250	5,372	6,044	22,650	22,700	0	2,428	4,288	4,960	0	3,250	5,372	6,044
19,700	19,750	0	2,900	4,910	5,581	0	3,250	5,372	6,044	22,700	22,750	0	2,420	4,278	4,949	0	3,250	5,372	6,044
19,750	19,800	0	2,892	4,899	5,571	0	3,250	5,372	6,044	22,750	22,800	0	2,412	4,267	4,939	0	3,250	5,372	6,044
19,800	19,850	0	2,884	4,889	5,560	0	3,250	5,372	6,044	22,800	22,850	0	2,404	4,257	4,928	0	3,250	5,372	6,044
19,850	19,900	0	2,876	4,878	5,550	0	3,250	5,372	6,044	22,850	22,900	0	2,396	4,246	4,918	0	3,250	5,372	6,044
19,900	19,950	0	2,868	4,868	5,539	0	3,250	5,372	6,044	22,900	22,950	0	2,388	4,236	4,907	0	3,242	5,360	6,032
19,950	20,000	0	2,860	4,857	5,529	0	3,250	5,372	6,044	22,950	23,000	0	2,380	4,225	4,897	0	3,234	5,350	6,021

* If the amount you are looking up from the worksheet is at least $19,650 but less than $19,680, and you have no qualifying children, your credit is $1. If the amount you are looking up from the worksheet is $19,680 or more, and you have no qualifying children, you cannot take the credit.

(Continued)

NOTE: DRAFT AS OF SEPTEMBER 16, 2013.

Earned Income Credit (EIC) Table - *Continued*

(**Caution.** This is **not** a tax table.)

At least	But less than	Single, head of household, or qualifying widow(er) — 0	1	2	3	Married filing jointly — 0	1	2	3
23,000	23,050	0	2,372	4,215	4,886	0	3,226	5,339	6,011
23,050	23,100	0	2,364	4,204	4,876	0	3,218	5,329	6,000
23,100	23,150	0	2,356	4,194	4,865	0	3,210	5,318	5,990
23,150	23,200	0	2,348	4,183	4,855	0	3,202	5,308	5,979
23,200	23,250	0	2,340	4,173	4,844	0	3,194	5,297	5,969
23,250	23,300	0	2,332	4,162	4,834	0	3,186	5,287	5,958
23,300	23,350	0	2,324	4,152	4,823	0	3,178	5,276	5,948
23,350	23,400	0	2,316	4,141	4,813	0	3,170	5,266	5,937
23,400	23,450	0	2,308	4,131	4,802	0	3,162	5,255	5,927
23,450	23,500	0	2,300	4,120	4,791	0	3,154	5,245	5,916
23,500	23,550	0	2,292	4,109	4,781	0	3,146	5,234	5,906
23,550	23,600	0	2,284	4,099	4,770	0	3,138	5,224	5,895
23,600	23,650	0	2,276	4,088	4,760	0	3,130	5,213	5,884
23,650	23,700	0	2,268	4,078	4,749	0	3,122	5,202	5,874
23,700	23,750	0	2,260	4,067	4,739	0	3,114	5,192	5,863
23,750	23,800	0	2,252	4,057	4,728	0	3,106	5,181	5,853
23,800	23,850	0	2,244	4,046	4,718	0	3,098	5,171	5,842
23,850	23,900	0	2,236	4,036	4,707	0	3,090	5,160	5,832
23,900	23,950	0	2,228	4,025	4,697	0	3,082	5,150	5,821
23,950	24,000	0	2,220	4,015	4,686	0	3,074	5,139	5,811
24,000	24,050	0	2,212	4,004	4,676	0	3,066	5,129	5,800
24,050	24,100	0	2,205	3,994	4,665	0	3,058	5,118	5,790
24,100	24,150	0	2,197	3,983	4,655	0	3,050	5,108	5,779
24,150	24,200	0	2,189	3,973	4,644	0	3,042	5,097	5,769
24,200	24,250	0	2,181	3,962	4,634	0	3,034	5,087	5,758
24,250	24,300	0	2,173	3,952	4,623	0	3,026	5,076	5,748
24,300	24,350	0	2,165	3,941	4,612	0	3,018	5,066	5,737
24,350	24,400	0	2,157	3,930	4,602	0	3,010	5,055	5,727
24,400	24,450	0	2,149	3,920	4,591	0	3,002	5,045	5,716
24,450	24,500	0	2,141	3,909	4,581	0	2,994	5,034	5,705
24,500	24,550	0	2,133	3,899	4,570	0	2,986	5,023	5,695
24,550	24,600	0	2,125	3,888	4,560	0	2,978	5,013	5,684
24,600	24,650	0	2,117	3,878	4,549	0	2,970	5,002	5,674
24,650	24,700	0	2,109	3,867	4,539	0	2,962	4,992	5,663
24,700	24,750	0	2,101	3,857	4,528	0	2,954	4,981	5,653
24,750	24,800	0	2,093	3,846	4,518	0	2,946	4,971	5,642
24,800	24,850	0	2,085	3,836	4,507	0	2,938	4,960	5,632
24,850	24,900	0	2,077	3,825	4,497	0	2,930	4,950	5,621
24,900	24,950	0	2,069	3,815	4,486	0	2,922	4,939	5,611
24,950	25,000	0	2,061	3,804	4,476	0	2,914	4,929	5,600
25,000	25,050	0	2,053	3,794	4,465	0	2,906	4,918	5,590
25,050	25,100	0	2,045	3,783	4,455	0	2,898	4,908	5,579
25,100	25,150	0	2,037	3,772	4,444	0	2,890	4,897	5,569
25,150	25,200	0	2,029	3,762	4,433	0	2,882	4,887	5,558
25,200	25,250	0	2,021	3,751	4,423	0	2,874	4,876	5,548
25,250	25,300	0	2,013	3,741	4,412	0	2,866	4,866	5,537
25,300	25,350	0	2,005	3,730	4,402	0	2,858	4,855	5,526
25,350	25,400	0	1,997	3,720	4,391	0	2,850	4,844	5,516
25,400	25,450	0	1,989	3,709	4,381	0	2,842	4,834	5,505
25,450	25,500	0	1,981	3,699	4,370	0	2,834	4,823	5,495
25,500	25,550	0	1,973	3,688	4,360	0	2,826	4,813	5,484
25,550	25,600	0	1,965	3,678	4,349	0	2,818	4,802	5,474
25,600	25,650	0	1,957	3,667	4,339	0	2,810	4,792	5,463
25,650	25,700	0	1,949	3,657	4,328	0	2,802	4,781	5,453
25,700	25,750	0	1,941	3,646	4,318	0	2,794	4,771	5,442
25,750	25,800	0	1,933	3,636	4,307	0	2,786	4,760	5,432
25,800	25,850	0	1,925	3,625	4,297	0	2,778	4,750	5,421
25,850	25,900	0	1,917	3,615	4,286	0	2,770	4,739	5,411
25,900	25,950	0	1,909	3,604	4,276	0	2,762	4,729	5,400
25,950	26,000	0	1,901	3,593	4,265	0	2,754	4,718	5,390
26,000	26,050	0	1,893	3,583	4,254	0	2,746	4,708	5,379
26,050	26,100	0	1,885	3,572	4,244	0	2,738	4,697	5,369
26,100	26,150	0	1,877	3,562	4,233	0	2,730	4,686	5,358
26,150	26,200	0	1,869	3,551	4,223	0	2,722	4,676	5,347
26,200	26,250	0	1,861	3,541	4,212	0	2,714	4,665	5,337
26,250	26,300	0	1,853	3,530	4,202	0	2,706	4,655	5,326
26,300	26,350	0	1,845	3,520	4,191	0	2,698	4,644	5,316
26,350	26,400	0	1,837	3,509	4,181	0	2,690	4,634	5,305
26,400	26,450	0	1,829	3,499	4,170	0	2,682	4,623	5,295
26,450	26,500	0	1,821	3,488	4,160	0	2,674	4,613	5,284
26,500	26,550	0	1,813	3,478	4,149	0	2,666	4,602	5,274
26,550	26,600	0	1,805	3,467	4,139	0	2,658	4,592	5,263
26,600	26,650	0	1,797	3,457	4,128	0	2,650	4,581	5,253
26,650	26,700	0	1,789	3,446	4,118	0	2,642	4,571	5,242
26,700	26,750	0	1,781	3,436	4,107	0	2,634	4,560	5,232
26,750	26,800	0	1,773	3,425	4,097	0	2,626	4,550	5,221
26,800	26,850	0	1,765	3,414	4,086	0	2,618	4,539	5,211
26,850	26,900	0	1,757	3,404	4,075	0	2,610	4,529	5,200
26,900	26,950	0	1,749	3,393	4,065	0	2,602	4,518	5,190
26,950	27,000	0	1,741	3,383	4,054	0	2,594	4,507	5,179
27,000	27,050	0	1,733	3,372	4,044	0	2,586	4,497	5,168
27,050	27,100	0	1,725	3,362	4,033	0	2,578	4,486	5,158
27,100	27,150	0	1,717	3,351	4,023	0	2,570	4,476	5,147
27,150	27,200	0	1,709	3,341	4,012	0	2,562	4,465	5,137
27,200	27,250	0	1,701	3,330	4,002	0	2,554	4,455	5,126
27,250	27,300	0	1,693	3,320	3,991	0	2,546	4,444	5,116
27,300	27,350	0	1,685	3,309	3,981	0	2,538	4,434	5,105
27,350	27,400	0	1,677	3,299	3,970	0	2,531	4,423	5,095
27,400	27,450	0	1,669	3,288	3,960	0	2,523	4,413	5,084
27,450	27,500	0	1,661	3,278	3,949	0	2,515	4,402	5,074
27,500	27,550	0	1,653	3,267	3,939	0	2,507	4,392	5,063
27,550	27,600	0	1,645	3,257	3,928	0	2,499	4,381	5,053
27,600	27,650	0	1,637	3,246	3,917	0	2,491	4,371	5,042
27,650	27,700	0	1,629	3,235	3,907	0	2,483	4,360	5,032
27,700	27,750	0	1,621	3,225	3,896	0	2,475	4,350	5,021
27,750	27,800	0	1,613	3,214	3,886	0	2,467	4,339	5,011
27,800	27,850	0	1,605	3,204	3,875	0	2,459	4,328	5,000
27,850	27,900	0	1,597	3,193	3,865	0	2,451	4,318	4,989
27,900	27,950	0	1,589	3,183	3,854	0	2,443	4,307	4,979
27,950	28,000	0	1,581	3,172	3,844	0	2,435	4,297	4,968
28,000	28,050	0	1,573	3,162	3,833	0	2,427	4,286	4,958
28,050	28,100	0	1,565	3,151	3,823	0	2,419	4,276	4,947
28,100	28,150	0	1,557	3,141	3,812	0	2,411	4,265	4,937
28,150	28,200	0	1,549	3,130	3,802	0	2,403	4,255	4,926
28,200	28,250	0	1,541	3,120	3,791	0	2,395	4,244	4,916
28,250	28,300	0	1,533	3,109	3,781	0	2,387	4,234	4,905
28,300	28,350	0	1,525	3,099	3,770	0	2,379	4,223	4,895
28,350	28,400	0	1,517	3,088	3,760	0	2,371	4,213	4,884
28,400	28,450	0	1,509	3,078	3,749	0	2,363	4,202	4,874
28,450	28,500	0	1,501	3,067	3,738	0	2,355	4,192	4,863
28,500	28,550	0	1,493	3,056	3,728	0	2,347	4,181	4,853
28,550	28,600	0	1,485	3,046	3,717	0	2,339	4,171	4,842
28,600	28,650	0	1,477	3,035	3,707	0	2,331	4,160	4,831
28,650	28,700	0	1,469	3,025	3,696	0	2,323	4,149	4,821
28,700	28,750	0	1,461	3,014	3,686	0	2,315	4,139	4,810
28,750	28,800	0	1,453	3,004	3,675	0	2,307	4,128	4,800
28,800	28,850	0	1,445	2,993	3,665	0	2,299	4,118	4,789
28,850	28,900	0	1,437	2,983	3,654	0	2,291	4,107	4,779
28,900	28,950	0	1,429	2,972	3,644	0	2,283	4,097	4,768
28,950	29,000	0	1,421	2,962	3,633	0	2,275	4,086	4,758

NOTE: DRAFT AS OF SEPTEMBER 16, 2013.

(Continued)

Earned Income Credit (EIC) Table - *Continued*　　　　　　　　　　　**(Caution.** This is **not** a tax table.)

If the amount you are looking up from the worksheet is–		Single, head of household, or qualifying widow(er) and the number of children you have is–				Married filing jointly and the number of children you have is–			
At least	But less than	0	1	2	3	0	1	2	3
		Your credit is–				Your credit is–			
29,000	29,050	0	1,413	2,951	3,623	0	2,267	4,076	4,747
29,050	29,100	0	1,406	2,941	3,612	0	2,259	4,065	4,737
29,100	29,150	0	1,398	2,930	3,602	0	2,251	4,055	4,726
29,150	29,200	0	1,390	2,920	3,591	0	2,243	4,044	4,716
29,200	29,250	0	1,382	2,909	3,581	0	2,235	4,034	4,705
29,250	29,300	0	1,374	2,899	3,570	0	2,227	4,023	4,695
29,300	29,350	0	1,366	2,888	3,559	0	2,219	4,013	4,684
29,350	29,400	0	1,358	2,877	3,549	0	2,211	4,002	4,674
29,400	29,450	0	1,350	2,867	3,538	0	2,203	3,992	4,663
29,450	29,500	0	1,342	2,856	3,528	0	2,195	3,981	4,652
29,500	29,550	0	1,334	2,846	3,517	0	2,187	3,970	4,642
29,550	29,600	0	1,326	2,835	3,507	0	2,179	3,960	4,631
29,600	29,650	0	1,318	2,825	3,496	0	2,171	3,949	4,621
29,650	29,700	0	1,310	2,814	3,486	0	2,163	3,939	4,610
29,700	29,750	0	1,302	2,804	3,475	0	2,155	3,928	4,600
29,750	29,800	0	1,294	2,793	3,465	0	2,147	3,918	4,589
29,800	29,850	0	1,286	2,783	3,454	0	2,139	3,907	4,579
29,850	29,900	0	1,278	2,772	3,444	0	2,131	3,897	4,568
29,900	29,950	0	1,270	2,762	3,433	0	2,123	3,886	4,558
29,950	30,000	0	1,262	2,751	3,423	0	2,115	3,876	4,547
30,000	30,050	0	1,254	2,741	3,412	0	2,107	3,865	4,537
30,050	30,100	0	1,246	2,730	3,402	0	2,099	3,855	4,526
30,100	30,150	0	1,238	2,719	3,391	0	2,091	3,844	4,516
30,150	30,200	0	1,230	2,709	3,380	0	2,083	3,834	4,505
30,200	30,250	0	1,222	2,698	3,370	0	2,075	3,823	4,495
30,250	30,300	0	1,214	2,688	3,359	0	2,067	3,813	4,484
30,300	30,350	0	1,206	2,677	3,349	0	2,059	3,802	4,473
30,350	30,400	0	1,198	2,667	3,338	0	2,051	3,791	4,463
30,400	30,450	0	1,190	2,656	3,328	0	2,043	3,781	4,452
30,450	30,500	0	1,182	2,646	3,317	0	2,035	3,770	4,442
30,500	30,550	0	1,174	2,635	3,307	0	2,027	3,760	4,431
30,550	30,600	0	1,166	2,625	3,296	0	2,019	3,749	4,421
30,600	30,650	0	1,158	2,614	3,286	0	2,011	3,739	4,410
30,650	30,700	0	1,150	2,604	3,275	0	2,003	3,728	4,400
30,700	30,750	0	1,142	2,593	3,265	0	1,995	3,718	4,389
30,750	30,800	0	1,134	2,583	3,254	0	1,987	3,707	4,379
30,800	30,850	0	1,126	2,572	3,244	0	1,979	3,697	4,368
30,850	30,900	0	1,118	2,562	3,233	0	1,971	3,686	4,358
30,900	30,950	0	1,110	2,551	3,223	0	1,963	3,676	4,347
30,950	31,000	0	1,102	2,540	3,212	0	1,955	3,665	4,337
31,000	31,050	0	1,094	2,530	3,201	0	1,947	3,655	4,326
31,050	31,100	0	1,086	2,519	3,191	0	1,939	3,644	4,316
31,100	31,150	0	1,078	2,509	3,180	0	1,931	3,633	4,305
31,150	31,200	0	1,070	2,498	3,170	0	1,923	3,623	4,294
31,200	31,250	0	1,062	2,488	3,159	0	1,915	3,612	4,284
31,250	31,300	0	1,054	2,477	3,149	0	1,907	3,602	4,273
31,300	31,350	0	1,046	2,467	3,138	0	1,899	3,591	4,263
31,350	31,400	0	1,038	2,456	3,128	0	1,891	3,581	4,252
31,400	31,450	0	1,030	2,446	3,117	0	1,883	3,570	4,242
31,450	31,500	0	1,022	2,435	3,107	0	1,875	3,560	4,231
31,500	31,550	0	1,014	2,425	3,096	0	1,867	3,549	4,221
31,550	31,600	0	1,006	2,414	3,086	0	1,859	3,539	4,210
31,600	31,650	0	998	2,404	3,075	0	1,851	3,528	4,200
31,650	31,700	0	990	2,393	3,065	0	1,843	3,518	4,189
31,700	31,750	0	982	2,383	3,054	0	1,835	3,507	4,179
31,750	31,800	0	974	2,372	3,044	0	1,827	3,497	4,168
31,800	31,850	0	966	2,361	3,033	0	1,819	3,486	4,158
31,850	31,900	0	958	2,351	3,022	0	1,811	3,476	4,147
31,900	31,950	0	950	2,340	3,012	0	1,803	3,465	4,137
31,950	32,000	0	942	2,330	3,001	0	1,795	3,454	4,126
32,000	32,050	0	934	2,319	2,991	0	1,787	3,444	4,115
32,050	32,100	0	926	2,309	2,980	0	1,779	3,433	4,105
32,100	32,150	0	918	2,298	2,970	0	1,771	3,423	4,094
32,150	32,200	0	910	2,288	2,959	0	1,763	3,412	4,084
32,200	32,250	0	902	2,277	2,949	0	1,755	3,402	4,073
32,250	32,300	0	894	2,267	2,938	0	1,747	3,391	4,063
32,300	32,350	0	886	2,256	2,928	0	1,739	3,381	4,052
32,350	32,400	0	878	2,246	2,917	0	1,732	3,370	4,042
32,400	32,450	0	870	2,235	2,907	0	1,724	3,360	4,031
32,450	32,500	0	862	2,225	2,896	0	1,716	3,349	4,021
32,500	32,550	0	854	2,214	2,886	0	1,708	3,339	4,010
32,550	32,600	0	846	2,204	2,875	0	1,700	3,328	4,000
32,600	32,650	0	838	2,193	2,864	0	1,692	3,318	3,989
32,650	32,700	0	830	2,182	2,854	0	1,684	3,307	3,979
32,700	32,750	0	822	2,172	2,843	0	1,676	3,297	3,968
32,750	32,800	0	814	2,161	2,833	0	1,668	3,286	3,958
32,800	32,850	0	806	2,151	2,822	0	1,660	3,275	3,947
32,850	32,900	0	798	2,140	2,812	0	1,652	3,265	3,936
32,900	32,950	0	790	2,130	2,801	0	1,644	3,254	3,926
32,950	33,000	0	782	2,119	2,791	0	1,636	3,244	3,915
33,000	33,050	0	774	2,109	2,780	0	1,628	3,233	3,905
33,050	33,100	0	766	2,098	2,770	0	1,620	3,223	3,894
33,100	33,150	0	758	2,088	2,759	0	1,612	3,212	3,884
33,150	33,200	0	750	2,077	2,749	0	1,604	3,202	3,873
33,200	33,250	0	742	2,067	2,738	0	1,596	3,191	3,863
33,250	33,300	0	734	2,056	2,728	0	1,588	3,181	3,852
33,300	33,350	0	726	2,046	2,717	0	1,580	3,170	3,842
33,350	33,400	0	718	2,035	2,707	0	1,572	3,160	3,831
33,400	33,450	0	710	2,025	2,696	0	1,564	3,149	3,821
33,450	33,500	0	702	2,014	2,685	0	1,556	3,139	3,810
33,500	33,550	0	694	2,003	2,675	0	1,548	3,128	3,800
33,550	33,600	0	686	1,993	2,664	0	1,540	3,118	3,789
33,600	33,650	0	678	1,982	2,654	0	1,532	3,107	3,778
33,650	33,700	0	670	1,972	2,643	0	1,524	3,096	3,768
33,700	33,750	0	662	1,961	2,633	0	1,516	3,086	3,757
33,750	33,800	0	654	1,951	2,622	0	1,508	3,075	3,747
33,800	33,850	0	646	1,940	2,612	0	1,500	3,065	3,736
33,850	33,900	0	638	1,930	2,601	0	1,492	3,054	3,726
33,900	33,950	0	630	1,919	2,591	0	1,484	3,044	3,715
33,950	34,000	0	622	1,909	2,580	0	1,476	3,033	3,705
34,000	34,050	0	614	1,898	2,570	0	1,468	3,023	3,694
34,050	34,100	0	607	1,888	2,559	0	1,460	3,012	3,684
34,100	34,150	0	599	1,877	2,549	0	1,452	3,002	3,673
34,150	34,200	0	591	1,867	2,538	0	1,444	2,991	3,663
34,200	34,250	0	583	1,856	2,528	0	1,436	2,981	3,652
34,250	34,300	0	575	1,846	2,517	0	1,428	2,970	3,642
34,300	34,350	0	567	1,835	2,506	0	1,420	2,960	3,631
34,350	34,400	0	559	1,824	2,496	0	1,412	2,949	3,621
34,400	34,450	0	551	1,814	2,485	0	1,404	2,939	3,610
34,450	34,500	0	543	1,803	2,475	0	1,396	2,928	3,599
34,500	34,550	0	535	1,793	2,464	0	1,388	2,917	3,589
34,550	34,600	0	527	1,782	2,454	0	1,380	2,907	3,578
34,600	34,650	0	519	1,772	2,443	0	1,372	2,896	3,568
34,650	34,700	0	511	1,761	2,433	0	1,364	2,886	3,557
34,700	34,750	0	503	1,751	2,422	0	1,356	2,875	3,547
34,750	34,800	0	495	1,740	2,412	0	1,348	2,865	3,536
34,800	34,850	0	487	1,730	2,401	0	1,340	2,854	3,526
34,850	34,900	0	479	1,719	2,391	0	1,332	2,844	3,515
34,900	34,950	0	471	1,709	2,380	0	1,324	2,833	3,505
34,950	35,000	0	463	1,698	2,370	0	1,316	2,823	3,494

NOTE: DRAFT AS OF SEPTEMBER 16, 2013.　　　　　　　　*(Continued)*

Earned Income Credit (EIC) Table - Continued

(Caution. This is not a tax table.)

If the amount you are looking up from the worksheet is– At least	But less than	Single, HoH, or qualifying widow(er) — 0	1	2	3	Married filing jointly — 0	1	2	3	If the amount you are looking up from the worksheet is– At least	But less than	Single, HoH, or qualifying widow(er) — 0	1	2	3	Married filing jointly — 0	1	2	3
35,000	35,050	0	455	1,688	2,359	0	1,308	2,812	3,484	38,000	38,050	0	0	1,056	1,727	0	829	2,180	2,852
35,050	35,100	0	447	1,677	2,349	0	1,300	2,802	3,473	38,050	38,100	0	0	1,045	1,717	0	821	2,170	2,841
35,100	35,150	0	439	1,666	2,338	0	1,292	2,791	3,463	38,100	38,150	0	0	1,035	1,706	0	813	2,159	2,831
35,150	35,200	0	431	1,656	2,327	0	1,284	2,781	3,452	38,150	38,200	0	0	1,024	1,696	0	805	2,149	2,820
35,200	35,250	0	423	1,645	2,317	0	1,276	2,770	3,442	38,200	38,250	0	0	1,014	1,685	0	797	2,138	2,810
35,250	35,300	0	415	1,635	2,306	0	1,268	2,760	3,431	38,250	38,300	0	0	1,003	1,675	0	789	2,128	2,799
35,300	35,350	0	407	1,624	2,296	0	1,260	2,749	3,420	38,300	38,350	0	0	993	1,664	0	781	2,117	2,789
35,350	35,400	0	399	1,614	2,285	0	1,252	2,738	3,410	38,350	38,400	0	0	982	1,654	0	773	2,107	2,778
35,400	35,450	0	391	1,603	2,275	0	1,244	2,728	3,399	38,400	38,450	0	0	972	1,643	0	765	2,096	2,768
35,450	35,500	0	383	1,593	2,264	0	1,236	2,717	3,389	38,450	38,500	0	0	961	1,632	0	757	2,086	2,757
35,500	35,550	0	375	1,582	2,254	0	1,228	2,707	3,378	38,500	38,550	0	0	950	1,622	0	749	2,075	2,747
35,550	35,600	0	367	1,572	2,243	0	1,220	2,696	3,368	38,550	38,600	0	0	940	1,611	0	741	2,065	2,736
35,600	35,650	0	359	1,561	2,233	0	1,212	2,686	3,357	38,600	38,650	0	0	929	1,601	0	733	2,054	2,725
35,650	35,700	0	351	1,551	2,222	0	1,204	2,675	3,347	38,650	38,700	0	0	919	1,590	0	725	2,043	2,715
35,700	35,750	0	343	1,540	2,212	0	1,196	2,665	3,336	38,700	38,750	0	0	908	1,580	0	717	2,033	2,704
35,750	35,800	0	335	1,530	2,201	0	1,188	2,654	3,326	38,750	38,800	0	0	898	1,569	0	709	2,022	2,694
35,800	35,850	0	327	1,519	2,191	0	1,180	2,644	3,315	38,800	38,850	0	0	887	1,559	0	701	2,012	2,683
35,850	35,900	0	319	1,509	2,180	0	1,172	2,633	3,305	38,850	38,900	0	0	877	1,548	0	693	2,001	2,673
35,900	35,950	0	311	1,498	2,170	0	1,164	2,623	3,294	38,900	38,950	0	0	866	1,538	0	685	1,991	2,662
35,950	36,000	0	303	1,487	2,159	0	1,156	2,612	3,284	38,950	39,000	0	0	856	1,527	0	677	1,980	2,652
36,000	36,050	0	295	1,477	2,148	0	1,148	2,602	3,273	39,000	39,050	0	0	845	1,517	0	669	1,970	2,641
36,050	36,100	0	287	1,466	2,138	0	1,140	2,591	3,263	39,050	39,100	0	0	835	1,506	0	661	1,959	2,631
36,100	36,150	0	279	1,456	2,127	0	1,132	2,580	3,252	39,100	39,150	0	0	824	1,496	0	653	1,949	2,620
36,150	36,200	0	271	1,445	2,117	0	1,124	2,570	3,241	39,150	39,200	0	0	814	1,485	0	645	1,938	2,610
36,200	36,250	0	263	1,435	2,106	0	1,116	2,559	3,231	39,200	39,250	0	0	803	1,475	0	637	1,928	2,599
36,250	36,300	0	255	1,424	2,096	0	1,108	2,549	3,220	39,250	39,300	0	0	793	1,464	0	629	1,917	2,589
36,300	36,350	0	247	1,414	2,085	0	1,100	2,538	3,210	39,300	39,350	0	0	782	1,453	0	621	1,907	2,578
36,350	36,400	0	239	1,403	2,075	0	1,092	2,528	3,199	39,350	39,400	0	0	771	1,443	0	613	1,896	2,568
36,400	36,450	0	231	1,393	2,064	0	1,084	2,517	3,189	39,400	39,450	0	0	761	1,432	0	605	1,886	2,557
36,450	36,500	0	223	1,382	2,054	0	1,076	2,507	3,178	39,450	39,500	0	0	750	1,422	0	597	1,875	2,546
36,500	36,550	0	215	1,372	2,043	0	1,068	2,496	3,168	39,500	39,550	0	0	740	1,411	0	589	1,864	2,536
36,550	36,600	0	207	1,361	2,033	0	1,060	2,486	3,157	39,550	39,600	0	0	729	1,401	0	581	1,854	2,525
36,600	36,650	0	199	1,351	2,022	0	1,052	2,475	3,147	39,600	39,650	0	0	719	1,390	0	573	1,843	2,515
36,650	36,700	0	191	1,340	2,012	0	1,044	2,465	3,136	39,650	39,700	0	0	708	1,380	0	565	1,833	2,504
36,700	36,750	0	183	1,330	2,001	0	1,036	2,454	3,126	39,700	39,750	0	0	698	1,369	0	557	1,822	2,494
36,750	36,800	0	175	1,319	1,991	0	1,028	2,444	3,115	39,750	39,800	0	0	687	1,359	0	549	1,812	2,483
36,800	36,850	0	167	1,308	1,980	0	1,020	2,433	3,105	39,800	39,850	0	0	677	1,348	0	541	1,801	2,473
36,850	36,900	0	159	1,298	1,969	0	1,012	2,423	3,094	39,850	39,900	0	0	666	1,338	0	533	1,791	2,462
36,900	36,950	0	151	1,287	1,959	0	1,004	2,412	3,084	39,900	39,950	0	0	656	1,327	0	525	1,780	2,452
36,950	37,000	0	143	1,277	1,948	0	996	2,401	3,073	39,950	40,000	0	0	645	1,317	0	517	1,770	2,441
37,000	37,050	0	135	1,266	1,938	0	988	2,391	3,062	40,000	40,050	0	0	635	1,306	0	509	1,759	2,431
37,050	37,100	0	127	1,256	1,927	0	980	2,380	3,052	40,050	40,100	0	0	624	1,296	0	501	1,749	2,420
37,100	37,150	0	119	1,245	1,917	0	972	2,370	3,041	40,100	40,150	0	0	613	1,285	0	493	1,738	2,410
37,150	37,200	0	111	1,235	1,906	0	964	2,359	3,031	40,150	40,200	0	0	603	1,274	0	485	1,728	2,399
37,200	37,250	0	103	1,224	1,896	0	956	2,349	3,020	40,200	40,250	0	0	592	1,264	0	477	1,717	2,389
37,250	37,300	0	95	1,214	1,885	0	948	2,338	3,010	40,250	40,300	0	0	582	1,253	0	469	1,707	2,378
37,300	37,350	0	87	1,203	1,875	0	940	2,328	2,999	40,300	40,350	0	0	571	1,243	0	461	1,696	2,367
37,350	37,400	0	79	1,193	1,864	0	933	2,317	2,989	40,350	40,400	0	0	561	1,232	0	453	1,685	2,357
37,400	37,450	0	71	1,182	1,854	0	925	2,307	2,978	40,400	40,450	0	0	550	1,222	0	445	1,675	2,346
37,450	37,500	0	63	1,172	1,843	0	917	2,296	2,968	40,450	40,500	0	0	540	1,211	0	437	1,664	2,336
37,500	37,550	0	55	1,161	1,833	0	909	2,286	2,957	40,500	40,550	0	0	529	1,201	0	429	1,654	2,325
37,550	37,600	0	47	1,151	1,822	0	901	2,275	2,947	40,550	40,600	0	0	519	1,190	0	421	1,643	2,315
37,600	37,650	0	39	1,140	1,811	0	893	2,265	2,936	40,600	40,650	0	0	508	1,180	0	413	1,633	2,304
37,650	37,700	0	31	1,129	1,801	0	885	2,254	2,926	40,650	40,700	0	0	498	1,169	0	405	1,622	2,294
37,700	37,750	0	23	1,119	1,790	0	877	2,244	2,915	40,700	40,750	0	0	487	1,159	0	397	1,612	2,283
37,750	37,800	0	15	1,108	1,780	0	869	2,233	2,905	40,750	40,800	0	0	477	1,148	0	389	1,601	2,273
37,800	37,850	0	7	1,098	1,769	0	861	2,222	2,894	40,800	40,850	0	0	466	1,138	0	381	1,591	2,262
37,850	37,900	0	*	1,087	1,759	0	853	2,212	2,883	40,850	40,900	0	0	456	1,127	0	373	1,580	2,252
37,900	37,950	0	0	1,077	1,748	0	845	2,201	2,873	40,900	40,950	0	0	445	1,117	0	365	1,570	2,241
37,950	38,000	0	0	1,066	1,738	0	837	2,191	2,862	40,950	41,000	0	0	434	1,106	0	357	1,559	2,231

* If the amount you are looking up from the worksheet is at least $37,850 but less than $37,870, and you have one qualifying child, your credit is $2.
If the amount you are looking up from the worksheet is $37,870 or more, and you have one qualifying child, you cannot take the credit.

(Continued)

NOTE: DRAFT AS OF SEPTEMBER 16, 2013.

Earned Income Credit (EIC) Table - *Continued* (Caution. This is **not** a tax table.)

If the amount you are looking up from the worksheet is– At least	But less than	Single, head of household, or qualifying widow(er) — 0	1	2	3	Married filing jointly — 0	1	2	3
41,000	41,050	0	0	424	1,095	0	349	1,549	2,220
41,050	41,100	0	0	413	1,085	0	341	1,538	2,210
41,100	41,150	0	0	403	1,074	0	333	1,527	2,199
41,150	41,200	0	0	392	1,064	0	325	1,517	2,188
41,200	41,250	0	0	382	1,053	0	317	1,506	2,178
41,250	41,300	0	0	371	1,043	0	309	1,496	2,167
41,300	41,350	0	0	361	1,032	0	301	1,485	2,157
41,350	41,400	0	0	350	1,022	0	293	1,475	2,146
41,400	41,450	0	0	340	1,011	0	285	1,464	2,136
41,450	41,500	0	0	329	1,001	0	277	1,454	2,125
41,500	41,550	0	0	319	990	0	269	1,443	2,115
41,550	41,600	0	0	308	980	0	261	1,433	2,104
41,600	41,650	0	0	298	969	0	253	1,422	2,094
41,650	41,700	0	0	287	959	0	245	1,412	2,083
41,700	41,750	0	0	277	948	0	237	1,401	2,073
41,750	41,800	0	0	266	938	0	229	1,391	2,062
41,800	41,850	0	0	255	927	0	221	1,380	2,052
41,850	41,900	0	0	245	916	0	213	1,370	2,041
41,900	41,950	0	0	234	906	0	205	1,359	2,031
41,950	42,000	0	0	224	895	0	197	1,348	2,020
42,000	42,050	0	0	213	885	0	189	1,338	2,009
42,050	42,100	0	0	203	874	0	181	1,327	1,999
42,100	42,150	0	0	192	864	0	173	1,317	1,988
42,150	42,200	0	0	182	853	0	165	1,306	1,978
42,200	42,250	0	0	171	843	0	157	1,296	1,967
42,250	42,300	0	0	161	832	0	149	1,285	1,957
42,300	42,350	0	0	150	822	0	141	1,275	1,946
42,350	42,400	0	0	140	811	0	134	1,264	1,936
42,400	42,450	0	0	129	801	0	126	1,254	1,925
42,450	42,500	0	0	119	790	0	118	1,243	1,915
42,500	42,550	0	0	108	780	0	110	1,233	1,904
42,550	42,600	0	0	98	769	0	102	1,222	1,894
42,600	42,650	0	0	87	758	0	94	1,212	1,883
42,650	42,700	0	0	76	748	0	86	1,201	1,873
42,700	42,750	0	0	66	737	0	78	1,191	1,862
42,750	42,800	0	0	55	727	0	70	1,180	1,852
42,800	42,850	0	0	45	716	0	62	1,169	1,841
42,850	42,900	0	0	34	706	0	54	1,159	1,830
42,900	42,950	0	0	24	695	0	46	1,148	1,820
42,950	43,000	0	0	13	685	0	38	1,138	1,809
43,000	43,050	0	0	*	674	0	30	1,127	1,799
43,050	43,100	0	0	0	664	0	22	1,117	1,788
43,100	43,150	0	0	0	653	0	14	1,106	1,778
43,150	43,200	0	0	0	643	0	6	1,096	1,767
43,200	43,250	0	0	0	632	0	**	1,085	1,757
43,250	43,300	0	0	0	622	0	0	1,075	1,746
43,300	43,350	0	0	0	611	0	0	1,064	1,736
43,350	43,400	0	0	0	601	0	0	1,054	1,725
43,400	43,450	0	0	0	590	0	0	1,043	1,715
43,450	43,500	0	0	0	579	0	0	1,033	1,704

If the amount you are looking up from the worksheet is– At least	But less than	Single, head of household, or qualifying widow(er) — 0	1	2	3	Married filing jointly — 0	1	2	3
43,500	43,550	0	0	0	569	0	0	1,022	1,694
43,550	43,600	0	0	0	558	0	0	1,012	1,683
43,600	43,650	0	0	0	548	0	0	1,001	1,672
43,650	43,700	0	0	0	537	0	0	990	1,662
43,700	43,750	0	0	0	527	0	0	980	1,651
43,750	43,800	0	0	0	516	0	0	969	1,641
43,800	43,850	0	0	0	506	0	0	959	1,630
43,850	43,900	0	0	0	495	0	0	948	1,620
43,900	43,950	0	0	0	485	0	0	938	1,609
43,950	44,000	0	0	0	474	0	0	927	1,599
44,000	44,050	0	0	0	464	0	0	917	1,588
44,050	44,100	0	0	0	453	0	0	906	1,578
44,100	44,150	0	0	0	443	0	0	896	1,567
44,150	44,200	0	0	0	432	0	0	885	1,557
44,200	44,250	0	0	0	422	0	0	875	1,546
44,250	44,300	0	0	0	411	0	0	864	1,536
44,300	44,350	0	0	0	400	0	0	854	1,525
44,350	44,400	0	0	0	390	0	0	843	1,515
44,400	44,450	0	0	0	379	0	0	833	1,504
44,450	44,500	0	0	0	369	0	0	822	1,493
44,500	44,550	0	0	0	358	0	0	811	1,483
44,550	44,600	0	0	0	348	0	0	801	1,472
44,600	44,650	0	0	0	337	0	0	790	1,462
44,650	44,700	0	0	0	327	0	0	780	1,451
44,700	44,750	0	0	0	316	0	0	769	1,441
44,750	44,800	0	0	0	306	0	0	759	1,430
44,800	44,850	0	0	0	295	0	0	748	1,420
44,850	44,900	0	0	0	285	0	0	738	1,409
44,900	44,950	0	0	0	274	0	0	727	1,399
44,950	45,000	0	0	0	264	0	0	717	1,388
45,000	45,050	0	0	0	253	0	0	706	1,378
45,050	45,100	0	0	0	243	0	0	696	1,367
45,100	45,150	0	0	0	232	0	0	685	1,357
45,150	45,200	0	0	0	221	0	0	675	1,346
45,200	45,250	0	0	0	211	0	0	664	1,336
45,250	45,300	0	0	0	200	0	0	654	1,325
45,300	45,350	0	0	0	190	0	0	643	1,314
45,350	45,400	0	0	0	179	0	0	632	1,304
45,400	45,450	0	0	0	169	0	0	622	1,293
45,450	45,500	0	0	0	158	0	0	611	1,283
45,500	45,550	0	0	0	148	0	0	601	1,272
45,550	45,600	0	0	0	137	0	0	590	1,262
45,600	45,650	0	0	0	127	0	0	580	1,251
45,650	45,700	0	0	0	116	0	0	569	1,241
45,700	45,750	0	0	0	106	0	0	559	1,230
45,750	45,800	0	0	0	95	0	0	548	1,220
45,800	45,850	0	0	0	85	0	0	538	1,209
45,850	45,900	0	0	0	74	0	0	527	1,199
45,900	45,950	0	0	0	64	0	0	517	1,188
45,950	46,000	0	0	0	53	0	0	506	1,178

* If the amount you are looking up from the worksheet is at least $43,000 but less than $43,038, and you have two qualifying children, your credit is $4.
If the amount you are looking up from the worksheet is $43,038 or more, and you have two qualifying children, you cannot take the credit.
** If the amount you are looking up from the worksheet is at least $43,200 but less than $43,210, and you have one qualifying child, your credit is $1.
If the amount you are looking up from the worksheet is $43,210 or more, and you have one qualifying child, you cannot take the credit.

(Continued)

NOTE: DRAFT AS OF SEPTEMBER 16, 2013.

Earned Income Credit (EIC) Table - Continued

(Caution. This is **not** a tax table.)

If the amount you are looking up from the worksheet is—		Single, head of household, or qualifying widow(er) and the number of children you have is—				Married filing jointly and the number of children you have is—			
At least	But less than	0	1	2	3	0	1	2	3
		Your credit is—				Your credit is—			
46,000	46,050	0	0	0	42	0	0	496	1,167
46,050	46,100	0	0	0	32	0	0	485	1,157
46,100	46,150	0	0	0	21	0	0	474	1,146
46,150	46,200	0	0	0	11	0	0	464	1,135
46,200	46,250	0	0	0	*	0	0	453	1,125
46,250	46,300	0	0	0	0	0	0	443	1,114
46,300	46,350	0	0	0	0	0	0	432	1,104
46,350	46,400	0	0	0	0	0	0	422	1,093
46,400	46,450	0	0	0	0	0	0	411	1,083
46,450	46,500	0	0	0	0	0	0	401	1,072
46,500	46,550	0	0	0	0	0	0	390	1,062
46,550	46,600	0	0	0	0	0	0	380	1,051
46,600	46,650	0	0	0	0	0	0	369	1,041
46,650	46,700	0	0	0	0	0	0	359	1,030
46,700	46,750	0	0	0	0	0	0	348	1,020
46,750	46,800	0	0	0	0	0	0	338	1,009
46,800	46,850	0	0	0	0	0	0	327	999
46,850	46,900	0	0	0	0	0	0	317	988
46,900	46,950	0	0	0	0	0	0	306	978
46,950	47,000	0	0	0	0	0	0	295	967
47,000	47,050	0	0	0	0	0	0	285	956
47,050	47,100	0	0	0	0	0	0	274	946
47,100	47,150	0	0	0	0	0	0	264	935
47,150	47,200	0	0	0	0	0	0	253	925
47,200	47,250	0	0	0	0	0	0	243	914
47,250	47,300	0	0	0	0	0	0	232	904
47,300	47,350	0	0	0	0	0	0	222	893
47,350	47,400	0	0	0	0	0	0	211	883
47,400	47,450	0	0	0	0	0	0	201	872
47,450	47,500	0	0	0	0	0	0	190	862
47,500	47,550	0	0	0	0	0	0	180	851
47,550	47,600	0	0	0	0	0	0	169	841
47,600	47,650	0	0	0	0	0	0	159	830
47,650	47,700	0	0	0	0	0	0	148	820
47,700	47,750	0	0	0	0	0	0	138	809
47,750	47,800	0	0	0	0	0	0	127	799
47,800	47,850	0	0	0	0	0	0	116	788
47,850	47,900	0	0	0	0	0	0	106	777
47,900	47,950	0	0	0	0	0	0	95	767
47,950	48,000	0	0	0	0	0	0	85	756
48,000	48,050	0	0	0	0	0	0	74	746
48,050	48,100	0	0	0	0	0	0	64	735
48,100	48,150	0	0	0	0	0	0	53	725
48,150	48,200	0	0	0	0	0	0	43	714
48,200	48,250	0	0	0	0	0	0	32	704
48,250	48,300	0	0	0	0	0	0	22	693
48,300	48,350	0	0	0	0	0	0	11	683
48,350	48,400	0	0	0	0	0	0	**	672
48,400	48,450	0	0	0	0	0	0	0	662
48,450	48,500	0	0	0	0	0	0	0	651

If the amount you are looking up from the worksheet is—		Single, head of household, or qualifying widow(er) and the number of children you have is—				Married filing jointly and the number of children you have is—			
At least	But less than	0	1	2	3	0	1	2	3
		Your credit is—				Your credit is—			
48,500	48,550	0	0	0	0	0	0	0	641
48,550	48,600	0	0	0	0	0	0	0	630
48,600	48,650	0	0	0	0	0	0	0	619
48,650	48,700	0	0	0	0	0	0	0	609
48,700	48,750	0	0	0	0	0	0	0	598
48,750	48,800	0	0	0	0	0	0	0	588
48,800	48,850	0	0	0	0	0	0	0	577
48,850	48,900	0	0	0	0	0	0	0	567
48,900	48,950	0	0	0	0	0	0	0	556
48,950	49,000	0	0	0	0	0	0	0	546
49,000	49,050	0	0	0	0	0	0	0	535
49,050	49,100	0	0	0	0	0	0	0	525
49,100	49,150	0	0	0	0	0	0	0	514
49,150	49,200	0	0	0	0	0	0	0	504
49,200	49,250	0	0	0	0	0	0	0	493
49,250	49,300	0	0	0	0	0	0	0	483
49,300	49,350	0	0	0	0	0	0	0	472
49,350	49,400	0	0	0	0	0	0	0	462
49,400	49,450	0	0	0	0	0	0	0	451
49,450	49,500	0	0	0	0	0	0	0	440
49,500	49,550	0	0	0	0	0	0	0	430
49,550	49,600	0	0	0	0	0	0	0	419
49,600	49,650	0	0	0	0	0	0	0	409
49,650	49,700	0	0	0	0	0	0	0	398
49,700	49,750	0	0	0	0	0	0	0	388
49,750	49,800	0	0	0	0	0	0	0	377
49,800	49,850	0	0	0	0	0	0	0	367
49,850	49,900	0	0	0	0	0	0	0	356
49,900	49,950	0	0	0	0	0	0	0	346
49,950	50,000	0	0	0	0	0	0	0	335
50,000	50,050	0	0	0	0	0	0	0	325
50,050	50,100	0	0	0	0	0	0	0	314
50,100	50,150	0	0	0	0	0	0	0	304
50,150	50,200	0	0	0	0	0	0	0	293
50,200	50,250	0	0	0	0	0	0	0	283
50,250	50,300	0	0	0	0	0	0	0	272
50,300	50,350	0	0	0	0	0	0	0	261
50,350	50,400	0	0	0	0	0	0	0	251
50,400	50,450	0	0	0	0	0	0	0	240
50,450	50,500	0	0	0	0	0	0	0	230
50,500	50,550	0	0	0	0	0	0	0	219
50,550	50,600	0	0	0	0	0	0	0	209
50,600	50,650	0	0	0	0	0	0	0	198
50,650	50,700	0	0	0	0	0	0	0	188
50,700	50,750	0	0	0	0	0	0	0	177
50,750	50,800	0	0	0	0	0	0	0	167
50,800	50,850	0	0	0	0	0	0	0	156
50,850	50,900	0	0	0	0	0	0	0	146
50,900	50,950	0	0	0	0	0	0	0	135
50,950	51,000	0	0	0	0	0	0	0	125

* If the amount you are looking up from the worksheet is at least $46,200 but less than $46,227, and you have three qualifying children, your credit is $3.
If the amount you are looking up from the worksheet is $46,227 or more, and you have three qualifying children, you cannot take the credit.
** If the amount you are looking up from the worksheet is at least $48,350 but less than $48,378, and you have two qualifying children, your credit is $3.
If the amount you are looking up from the worksheet is $48,378 or more, and you have two qualifying children, you cannot take the credit.

(Continued)

NOTE: DRAFT AS OF SEPTEMBER 16, 2013.

Earned Income Credit (EIC) Table - *Continued*   (**Caution.** This is **not** a tax table.)

If the amount you are looking up from the worksheet is–		Single, head of household, or qualifying widow(er) and the number of children you have is–				Married filing jointly and the number of children you have is–			
		0	1	2	3	0	1	2	3
At least	But less than	Your credit is–				Your credit is–			
51,000	51,050	0	0	0	0	0	0	0	114
51,050	51,100	0	0	0	0	0	0	0	104
51,100	51,150	0	0	0	0	0	0	0	93
51,150	51,200	0	0	0	0	0	0	0	82
51,200	51,250	0	0	0	0	0	0	0	72
51,250	51,300	0	0	0	0	0	0	0	61
51,300	51,350	0	0	0	0	0	0	0	51
51,350	51,400	0	0	0	0	0	0	0	40
51,400	51,450	0	0	0	0	0	0	0	30
51,450	51,500	0	0	0	0	0	0	0	19
51,500	51,550	0	0	0	0	0	0	0	9
51,550	51,567	0	0	0	0	0	0	0	2

NOTE: DRAFT AS OF SEPTEMBER 16, 2013.

¶ 1113   Corporate income tax rates.

The rates for domestic corporations (other than qualified personal service corporations) are: (Code Sec. 11(b))[4]

Taxable income over—	But not over—	The tax is:	Of the amount over—
0	$ 50,000	15%	0
$ 50,000	75,000	$ 7,500 + 25%	$ 50,000
75,000	100,000	13,750 + 34%	75,000
100,000	335,000	22,250 + 39%	100,000
335,000	10,000,000	113,900 + 34%	335,000
10,000,000	15,000,000	3,400,000 + 35%	10,000,000
15,000,000	18,333,333	5,150,000 + 38%	15,000,000
18,333,333	—	35%	0

A qualified personal service corporation (as defined in Code Sec. 448(d)(2)) is taxed at a flat 35% of its taxable income. (Code Sec. 11(b)(2))[5]

Special taxes or rates on corporations include the alternative minimum tax, see ¶3200 *et seq.*; the accumulated earnings tax, see ¶3316; and the personal holding company tax, see ¶3320.

For tax rates on foreign corporations, see ¶4637 *et seq.*

¶ 1114   Gift and estate tax rates (unified rate schedule) for 2013.

The estate tax is imposed on the decedent's taxable estate (gross estate less deductions). For credits against the estate tax, see ¶5028 *et seq.* The gift tax is based on the cumulative value of current and prior gifts (after a specified exclusion) after specified deductions, see ¶5038 *et seq.* (Code Sec. 2001, Code Sec. 2501)[6]

For estates of decedents dying and gifts made in 2013 the unified rate schedule is as follows (Code Sec. 2001(c), Code Sec. 2502(a)(2)):

---

4. ¶D-1003; ¶114.01; TD ¶600,503
5. ¶D-1006; ¶114.02; TD ¶600,901

6. ¶s Q-8003 *et seq.*, R-7000 *et seq.*; ¶20,014 *et seq.*, ¶25,024 *et seq.* (Estate & Gift); TD ¶s 751,000 *et seq.*, 744,000 *et seq.*

Unified Rate Schedule for 2013

If the amount with respect to which the tentative tax to be computed is:	The tentative tax is:
Not over $10,000.	18% of such amount.
Over $10,000 but not over $20,000.	$1,800, plus 20% of the excess over $10,000.
Over $20,000 but not over $40,000.	$3,800, plus 22% of the excess over $20,000.
Over $40,000 but not over $60,000.	$8,200, plus 24% of the excess over $40,000.
Over $60,000 but not over $80,000.	$13,000, plus 26% of the excess over $60,000.
Over $80,000 but not over $100,000.	$18,200, plus 28% of the excess over $80,000.
Over $100,000 but not over $150,000.	$23,800, plus 30% of the excess over $100,000.
Over $150,000 but not over $250,000.	$38,800, plus 32% of the excess over $150,000.
Over $250,000 but not over $500,000.	$70,800, plus 34% of the excess over $250,000.
Over $500,000 but not over $750,000.	$155,800, plus 37% of the excess over $500,000.
Over $750,000 but not over $1,000,000.	$248,300, plus 39% of the excess over $750,000.
Over $1,000,000.	$345,800, plus 40% of the excess over $1,000,000.

The top estate and gift tax rate (and the GST tax rate) is 40% for 2013.

For the estate tax on non-income distributions from a qualified domestic trust for a surviving spouse who isn't a U.S. citizen, see ¶5026.

For the applicable exclusion amount and applicable credit amount, see ¶5028. For the credit against estate tax imposed on estates of nonresident aliens, see ¶5037.

¶ 1115   Excise tax rates (nonpenalty).

Here are selected "nonpenalty" excise tax rates. [7] For penalty-type excise taxes, see the entries under "Excise taxes" in the Topic Index.

Retail Excise Taxes

Trucks, trailers, etc.

- auto truck chassis and bodies (for vehicles weighing more than 33,000 lbs),

- truck trailer and semi-trailer chassis and bodies (for vehicles weighing more than 26,000 lbs)

- tractors used chiefly for highway transportation in combination with a trailer or semi-trailer (for tractors weighing more than 19,500 lbs and in combination with trailer or semi-trailer weighing more than 33,000 lbs)

- accessories sold with one of the above or installed within 6 months after one of the above is placed in service

12% of first retail sale amount. Tax scheduled to expire after 9/30/2016.

---

7. ¶s W-3100 *et seq.*, W-1500 *et seq.*, W-2000 *et seq.*; ¶s 40,009.05   *et seq.*, 40,609 *et seq.* (Excise)

Transportation Fuel Taxes

Gasoline other than aviation gasoline; gasohol	Through 9/30/2016, on removal at terminal: 18.4¢ per gal.; 4.3¢ per gal. thereafter
Aviation gasoline	Through 9/30/2015, on removal at terminal: 19.4¢ per gal.; 10/1/2015 through 9/30/2016: 4.4¢ per gal.; 4.3¢ per gal. thereafter
Diesel fuel[1]; diesohol	Through 9/30/2016, on removal at terminal or retail sale: 24.4¢ per gal.; 4.3¢ per gal. thereafter
• Diesel-water fuel emulsion	Through 9/30/2016, on removal at terminal: 19.8¢ per gal. After 9/30/2016, see diesel fuel rate above
• Dyed diesel fuel, other than for export	Through 9/30/2016, on removal at terminal or retail sale: .1¢ per gal.
Kerosene	Through 9/30/2016, on removal at terminal or retail sale, generally: 24.4¢ per gal.; thereafter, 4.3¢ per gal.
• Noncommercial aviation use—on removal directly into noncommercial aircraft's fuel tank	Through 9/30/2015: 21.9¢ per gal.; 10/1/2015-9/30/2016: 4.4¢ per gal.; 4.3¢ per gal. thereafter
• Commercial aviation use—on removal directly into commercial aircraft's fuel tank	Through 9/30/2016: 4.4¢ per gal.; 4.3¢ per gal. thereafter
• Retail sale for aviation use (where fuel not previously taxed)	Through 9/30/2016, for noncommercial aviation: 21.9¢ per gal.; for commercial aviation: 4.4¢ per gal. After 9/30/2016: 21.8¢ per gal. and 4.3¢ per gal., respectively
• Dyed kerosene, other than for export	Through 9/30/2016, on removal at terminal or retail sale: .1¢ per gal.
Alternative fuels	
• Special motor fuels (other than LPG and LNG)	Through 9/30/2016, on retail sale or use, for motor vehicle or motorboat use: 18.4¢ per gal.; After 9/30/2016: 4.3¢ per gal.
• Liquefied petroleum gas (LPG) (e.g., propane, butane)	18.3¢ per gal.
• Liquefied natural gas (LNG)	24.3¢ per gal.
• Liquid fuel (other than biomass (other than ethanol derived from coal, liquid hydrocarbons derived from biomass	Through 9/30/2016: 24.4¢ per gal.; 24.3¢ per gal. thereafter
• Partially exempt ethanol and methanol	Through 9/30/2016, for retail sale or use, of: partially exempt ethanol, 11.4¢ per gal.; partially exempt methanol, 9.25¢ per gal. After 9/30/2016, for partially exempt ethanol, 4.3¢ per gal.; for partially exempt methanol, 2.15¢ per gal.
Compressed natural gas (CNG)	18.3¢ per energy equivalent of a gal. of gasoline

Fuel used in commercial transportation on inland waterways	Through 9/30/2016, 20.1¢ per gal.; 20¢ per gal. thereafter
Fuel used in fractional ownership aircraft	Through 9/30/2021, 14.1¢ per gal. surtax.

Selected Manufacturers and Other Excise Taxes

Coal (except lignite)	
• From underground mines	Lower of $1.10 per ton or 4.4% of selling price
• From surface mines	Lower of 55¢ per ton or 4.4% of selling price
Tires (of type used in highway vehicles, wholly or in part made of rubber)	9.45¢ (4.725¢ for biasply or super single tires) for each 10 lbs. the tire's maximum rated load capacity exceeds 3,500 lbs. Tax scheduled to expire after 9/30/2016.
Sport fishing equipment	10% of mfrs. price of specified sport fishing equipment (up to max. of $10 on fishing rods and poles); 3% for electric outboard motors and fishing tackle boxes

Gas guzzling passenger autos, as follows:

If the fuel economy of the model type in which the automobile falls is:	*The tax is:*
At least 22.5	0
At least 21.5 but less than 22.5	$1,000
At least 20.5 but less than 21.5	1,300
At least 19.5 but less than 20.5	1,700
At least 18.5 but less than 19.5	2,100
At least 17.5 but less than 18.5	2,600
At least 16.5 but less than 17.5	3,000
At least 15.5 but less than 16.5	3,700
At least 14.5 but less than 15.5	4,500
At least 13.5 but less than 14.5	5,400
At least 12.5 but less than 13.5	6,400
Less than 12.5	7,700

Medical devices	2.3% of sales price
Indoor tanning	10% of amount paid for services.
Branded prescription drugs	Annual fee on "covered entities"
Health insurance policies and self-insured health plans	Annual fee, for policy or plan years before 10/1/2019
Health Insurance providers	Annual fee on "covered entities."

---

[1] Special rates apply to diesel fuel used in certain buses and trains.

¶ 1116   Applicable Federal Rates. ▆▆▆▆▆▆▆▆▆▆

The IRS tables below show the Applicable one-month Federal Rates (AFRs). The tables provide short-term (obligations not exceeding three years), mid-term (over three years but not over nine years) and long-term (over nine years) rates (in percentages) based on annual, semiannual, quarterly and monthly compounding assumptions.[8]

Applicable Federal Rate	Annual	Semi-annual	Quarterly	Monthly
November 2013				
Short-Term				
AFR	.27%	.27%	.27%	.27%
110% AFR	.30%	.30%	.30%	.30%
120% AFR	.32%	.32%	.32%	.32%
130% AFR	.35%	.35%	.35%	.35%
Mid-Term				
AFR	1.73%	1.72%	1.72%	1.71%
110% AFR	1.90%	1.89%	1.89%	1.88%
120% AFR	2.07%	2.06%	2.05%	2.05%
130% AFR	2.25%	2.24%	2.23%	2.23%
150% AFR	2.60%	2.58%	2.57%	2.57%
175% AFR	3.03%	3.01%	3.00%	2.99%
Long-Term				
AFR	3.37%	3.34%	3.33%	3.32%
110% AFR	3.70%	3.67%	3.65%	3.64%
120% AFR	4.05%	4.01%	3.99%	3.98%
130% AFR	4.39%	4.34%	4.32%	4.30%
October 2013				
Short-Term				
AFR	.32%	.32%	.32%	.32%
110% AFR	.35%	.35%	.35%	.35%
120% AFR	.38%	.38%	.38%	.38%
130% AFR	.42%	.42%	.42%	.42%
Mid-Term				
AFR	1.93%	1.92%	1.92%	1.91%
110% AFR	2.12%	2.11%	2.10%	2.10%
120% AFR	2.31%	2.30%	2.29%	2.29%
130% AFR	2.52%	2.50%	2.49%	2.49%
150% AFR	2.90%	2.88%	2.87%	2.86%
175% AFR	3.39%	3.36%	3.35%	3.34%
Long-Term				
AFR	3.50%	3.47%	3.46%	3.45%
110% AFR	3.86%	3.82%	3.80%	3.79%
120% AFR	4.20%	4.16%	4.14%	4.12%
130% AFR	4.56%	4.51%	4.48%	4.47%
September 2013				
Short-Term				
AFR	.25%	.25%	.25%	.25%
110% AFR	.28%	.28%	.28%	.28%
120% AFR	.30%	.30%	.30%	.30%
130% AFR	.33%	.33%	.33%	.33%
Mid-Term				
AFR	1.66%	1.65%	1.65%	1.64%
110% AFR	1.83%	1.82%	1.82%	1.81%
120% AFR	1.99%	1.98%	1.98%	1.97%
130% AFR	2.16%	2.15%	2.14%	2.14%
150% AFR	2.50%	2.48%	2.47%	2.47%
175% AFR	2.91%	2.89%	2.88%	2.87%
Long-Term				
AFR	3.28%	3.25%	3.24%	3.23%
110% AFR	3.61%	3.58%	3.56%	3.55%
120% AFR	3.94%	3.90%	3.88%	3.87%
130% AFR	4.27%	4.23%	4.21%	4.19%

Applicable Federal Rate	Annual	Semi-annual	Quarterly	Monthly
August 2013				
Short-Term				
AFR	.28%	.28%	.28%	.28%
110% AFR	.31%	.31%	.31%	.31%
120% AFR	.34%	.34%	.34%	.34%
130% AFR	.36%	.36%	.36%	.36%
Mid-Term				
AFR	1.63%	1.62%	1.62%	1.61%
110% AFR	1.79%	1.78%	1.78%	1.77%
120% AFR	1.95%	1.94%	1.94%	1.93%
130% AFR	2.12%	2.11%	2.10%	2.10%
150% AFR	2.44%	2.43%	2.42%	2.42%
175% AFR	2.86%	2.84%	2.83%	2.82%
Long-Term				
AFR	3.16%	3.14%	3.13%	3.12%
110% AFR	3.48%	3.45%	3.44%	3.43%
120% AFR	3.81%	3.77%	3.75%	3.74%
130% AFR	4.12%	4.08%	4.06%	4.05%
July 2013				
Short-Term				
AFR	.23%	.23%	.23%	.23%
110% AFR	.25%	.25%	.25%	.25%
120% AFR	.28%	.28%	.28%	.28%
130% AFR	.30%	.30%	.30%	.30%
Mid-Term				
AFR	1.22%	1.22%	1.22%	1.22%
110% AFR	1.34%	1.34%	1.34%	1.34%
120% AFR	1.47%	1.46%	1.46%	1.46%
130% AFR	1.60%	1.59%	1.59%	1.58%
150% AFR	1.84%	1.83%	1.83%	1.82%
175% AFR	2.15%	2.14%	2.13%	2.13%
Long-Term				
AFR	2.80%	2.78%	2.77%	2.76%
110% AFR	3.08%	3.06%	3.05%	3.04%
120% AFR	3.37%	3.34%	3.33%	3.32%
130% AFR	3.64%	3.61%	3.59%	3.58%
June 2013				
Short-Term				
AFR	.18%	.18%	.18%	.18%
110% AFR	.20%	.20%	.20%	.20%
120% AFR	.22%	.22%	.22%	.22%
130% AFR	.23%	.23%	.23%	.23%
Mid-Term				
AFR	.95%	.95%	.95%	.95%
110% AFR	1.05%	1.05%	1.05%	1.05%
120% AFR	1.14%	1.14%	1.14%	1.14%
130% AFR	1.24%	1.24%	1.24%	1.24%
150% AFR	1.44%	1.43%	1.43%	1.43%
175% AFR	1.67%	1.66%	1.66%	1.65%
Long-Term				
AFR	2.47%	2.45%	2.44%	2.44%
110% AFR	2.72%	2.70%	2.69%	2.68%
120% AFR	2.96%	2.94%	2.93%	2.92%
130% AFR	3.22%	3.19%	3.18%	3.17%

8.   ¶J-4192; ¶12,714.01; TD ¶153,030

May 2013

Applicable Federal Rate	Annual	Semi-annual	Quarterly	Monthly
Short-Term				
AFR	.20%	.20%	.20%	.20%
110% AFR	.22%	.22%	.22%	.22%
120% AFR	.24%	.24%	.24%	.24%
130% AFR	.26%	.26%	.26%	.26%
Mid-Term				
AFR	1.00%	1.00%	1.00%	1.00%
110% AFR	1.10%	1.10%	1.10%	1.10%
120% AFR	1.20%	1.20%	1.20%	1.20%
130% AFR	1.30%	1.30%	1.30%	1.30%
150% AFR	1.51%	1.50%	1.50%	1.50%
175% AFR	1.76%	1.75%	1.75%	1.74%
Long-Term				
AFR	2.60%	2.58%	2.57%	2.57%
110% AFR	2.86%	2.84%	2.83%	2.82%
120% AFR	3.12%	3.10%	3.09%	3.08%
130% AFR	3.38%	3.35%	3.34%	3.33%

February 2013

Applicable Federal Rate	Annual	Semi-annual	Quarterly	Monthly
Short-Term				
AFR	.21%	.21%	.21%	.21%
110% AFR	.23%	.23%	.23%	.23%
120% AFR	.25%	.25%	.25%	.25%
130% AFR	.27%	.27%	.27%	.27%
Mid-Term				
AFR	1.01%	1.01%	1.01%	1.01%
110% AFR	1.11%	1.11%	1.11%	1.11%
120% AFR	1.21%	1.21%	1.21%	1.21%
130% AFR	1.31%	1.31%	1.31%	1.31%
150% AFR	1.53%	1.52%	1.52%	1.52%
175% AFR	1.78%	1.77%	1.77%	1.76%
Long-Term				
AFR	2.52%	2.50%	2.49%	2.49%
110% AFR	2.77%	2.75%	2.74%	2.73%
120% AFR	3.02%	3.00%	2.99%	2.98%
130% AFR	3.28%	3.25%	3.24%	3.23%

April 2013

Applicable Federal Rate	Annual	Semi-annual	Quarterly	Monthly
Short-Term				
AFR	.22%	.22%	.22%	.22%
110% AFR	.24%	.24%	.24%	.24%
120% AFR	.26%	.26%	.26%	.26%
130% AFR	.29%	.29%	.29%	.29%
Mid-Term				
AFR	1.09%	1.09%	1.09%	1.09%
110% AFR	1.20%	1.20%	1.20%	1.20%
120% AFR	1.31%	1.31%	1.31%	1.31%
130% AFR	1.43%	1.42%	1.42%	1.42%
150% AFR	1.65%	1.64%	1.64%	1.63%
175% AFR	1.92%	1.91%	1.91%	1.90%
Long-Term				
AFR	2.70%	2.68%	2.67%	2.67%
110% AFR	2.97%	2.95%	2.94%	2.93%
120% AFR	3.25%	3.22%	3.21%	3.20%
130% AFR	3.51%	3.48%	3.46%	3.46%

January 2013

Applicable Federal Rate	Annual	Semi-annual	Quarterly	Monthly
Short-Term				
AFR	.21%	.21%	.21%	.21%
110% AFR	.23%	.23%	.23%	.23%
120% AFR	.25%	.25%	.25%	.25%
130% AFR	.27%	.27%	.27%	.27%
Mid-Term				
AFR	.87%	.87%	.87%	.87%
110% AFR	.96%	.96%	.96%	.96%
120% AFR	1.04%	1.04%	1.04%	1.04%
130% AFR	1.13%	1.13%	1.13%	1.13%
150% AFR	1.31%	1.31%	1.31%	1.31%
175% AFR	1.53%	1.52%	1.52%	1.52%
Long-Term				
AFR	2.31%	2.30%	2.29%	2.29%
110% AFR	2.55%	2.53%	2.52%	2.52%
120% AFR	2.78%	2.76%	2.75%	2.74%
130% AFR	3.01%	2.99%	2.98%	2.97%

March 2013

Applicable Federal Rate	Annual	Semi-annual	Quarterly	Monthly
Short-Term				
AFR	.22%	.22%	.22%	.22%
110% AFR	.24%	.24%	.24%	.24%
120% AFR	.26%	.26%	.26%	.26%
130% AFR	.29%	.29%	.29%	.29%
Mid-Term				
AFR	1.09%	1.09%	1.09%	1.09%
110% AFR	1.20%	1.20%	1.20%	1.20%
120% AFR	1.31%	1.31%	1.31%	1.31%
130% AFR	1.43%	1.42%	1.42%	1.42%
150% AFR	1.65%	1.64%	1.64%	1.63%
175% AFR	1.92%	1.91%	1.91%	1.90%
Long-Term				
AFR	2.66%	2.64%	2.63%	2.63%
110% AFR	2.92%	2.90%	2.89%	2.88%
120% AFR	3.20%	3.17%	3.16%	3.15%
130% AFR	3.46%	3.43%	3.42%	3.41%

December 2012

Applicable Federal Rate	Annual	Semi-annual	Quarterly	Monthly
Short-Term				
AFR	.24%	.24%	.24%	.24%
110% AFR	.26%	.26%	.26%	.26%
120% AFR	.29%	.29%	.29%	.29%
130% AFR	.31%	.31%	.31%	.31%
Mid-Term				
AFR	.95%	.95%	.95%	.95%
110% AFR	1.05%	1.05%	1.05%	1.05%
120% AFR	1.14%	1.14%	1.14%	1.14%
130% AFR	1.24%	1.24%	1.24%	1.24%
150% AFR	1.44%	1.43%	1.43%	1.43%
175% AFR	1.67%	1.66%	1.66%	1.65%
Long-Term				
AFR	2.40%	2.39%	2.38%	2.38%
110% AFR	2.65%	2.63%	2.62%	2.62%
120% AFR	2.89%	2.87%	2.86%	2.85%
130% AFR	3.13%	3.11%	3.10%	3.09%

¶ 1117 MACRS Tables.

Here are MACRS depreciation (cost recovery) tables.

The tables reproduced are the MACRS tables (general depreciation as well as alternative depreciation system (ADS)), plus the listed property tables used to determine income inclusion amounts by lessees of listed property other than automobiles. The depreciation amounts for automobiles under the luxury auto restrictions are carried at ¶1952; the income inclusion amounts for lessees of automobiles carried at ¶1118 are explained at ¶1957 *et seq.*

Under the general depreciation system (GDS) of MACRS, the table rates are based on: (1) the 200% declining balance method for 3-, 5-, 7-, and 10-year personal property; (2) the 150% declining balance method for 15- and 20-year personal property; and (3) the straight-line method for residential and nonresidential realty. Under the alternative depreciation system (ADS) of MACRS, the table rates for personal and real property are based on the straight-line method. The use of the tables is discussed in ¶1912. (IRS alternative minimum tax tables and the tables for straight line depreciation under the midquarter convention are not reproduced in this Handbook. For those tables, see the Appendix to Federal Tax Coordinator 2d Chapter L-7400.)

Table 1
General Depreciation System
Applicable Depreciation Method: 200 or 150 Percent
Declining Balance Switching to Straight Line
Applicable Recovery Periods: 3, 5, 7, 10, 15, 20 years
Applicable Convention: Half-year

If the Recovery Year is:	and the Recovery Period is:					
	3-year	5-year	7-year	10-year	15-year	20-year
			the Depreciation Rate is:			
1	33.33	20.00	14.29	10.00	5.00	3.750
2	44.45	32.00	24.49	18.00	9.50	7.219
3	14.81	19.20	17.49	14.40	8.55	6.677
4	7.41	11.52	12.49	11.52	7.70	6.177
5		11.52	8.93	9.22	6.93	5.713
6		5.76	8.92	7.37	6.23	5.285
7			8.93	6.55	5.90	4.888
8			4.46	6.55	5.90	4.522
9				6.56	5.91	4.462
10				6.55	5.90	4.461
11				3.28	5.91	4.462
12					5.90	4.461
13					5.91	4.462
14					5.90	4.461
15					5.91	4.462
16					2.95	4.461
17						4.462
18						4.461
19						4.462
20						4.461
21						2.231

Table 2

General Depreciation System
Applicable Depreciation Method: 200 or 150 Percent
Declining Balance Switching to Straight Line
Applicable Recovery Periods: 3, 5, 7, 10, 15, 20 years
Applicable Convention: Mid-quarter
(property placed in service in first quarter)

If the Recovery Year is:	and the Recovery Period is:					
	3-year	5-year	7-year	10-year	15-year	20-year
			the Depreciation Rate is:			
1	58.33	35.00	25.00	17.50	8.75	6.563
2	27.78	26.00	21.43	16.50	9.13	7.000
3	12.35	15.60	15.31	13.20	8.21	6.482
4	1.54	11.01	10.93	10.56	7.39	5.996
5		11.01	8.75	8.45	6.65	5.546
6		1.38	8.74	6.76	5.99	5.130
7			8.75	6.55	5.90	4.746
8			1.09	6.55	5.91	4.459
9				6.56	5.90	4.459
10				6.55	5.91	4.459
11				0.82	5.90	4.459
12					5.91	4.460
13					5.90	4.459
14					5.91	4.460
15					5.90	4.459
16					0.74	4.460
17						4.459
18						4.460
19						4.459
20						4.460
21						0.557

Table 3

General Depreciation System
Applicable Depreciation Method: 200 or 150 Percent
Declining Balance Switching to Straight Line
Applicable Recovery Periods: 3, 5, 7, 10, 15, 20 years
Applicable Convention: Mid-quarter
(property placed in service in second quarter)

If the Recovery Year is:	and the Recovery Period is:					
	3-year	5-year	7-year	10-year	15-year	20-year
			the Depreciation Rate is:			
1	41.67	25.00	17.85	12.50	6.25	4.688
2	38.89	30.00	23.47	17.50	9.38	7.148
3	14.14	18.00	16.76	14.00	8.44	6.612
4	5.30	11.37	11.97	11.20	7.59	6.116
5		11.37	8.87	8.96	6.83	5.658
6		4.26	8.87	7.17	6.15	5.233
7			8.87	6.55	5.91	4.841
8			3.33	6.55	5.90	4.478
9				6.56	5.91	4.463
10				6.55	5.90	4.463
11				2.46	5.91	4.463
12					5.90	4.463
13					5.91	4.463
14					5.90	4.463

Table 3

General Depreciation System
Applicable Depreciation Method: 200 or 150 Percent
Declining Balance Switching to Straight Line
Applicable Recovery Periods: 3, 5, 7, 10, 15, 20 years
Applicable Convention: Mid-quarter
(property placed in service in second quarter)
(continued)

	15-year	20-year
15	5.91	4.462
16	2.21	4.463
17		4.462
18		4.463
19		4.462
20		4.463
21		1.673

Table 4

General Depreciation System
Applicable Depreciation Method: 200 or 150 Percent
Declining Balance Switching to Straight Line
Applicable Recovery Periods: 3, 5, 7, 10, 15, 20 years
Applicable Convention: Mid-quarter
(property placed in service in third quarter)

If the Recovery Year is:	and the Recovery Period is:					
	3-year	5-year	7-year	10-year	15-year	20-year
			the Depreciation Rate is:			
1	25.00	15.00	10.71	7.50	3.75	2.813
2	50.00	34.00	25.51	18.50	9.63	7.289
3	16.67	20.40	18.22	14.80	8.66	6.742
4	8.33	12.24	13.02	11.84	7.80	6.237
5		11.30	9.30	9.47	7.02	5.769
6		7.06	8.85	7.58	6.31	5.336
7			8.86	6.55	5.90	4.936
8			5.53	6.55	5.90	4.566
9				6.56	5.91	4.460
10				6.55	5.90	4.460
11				4.10	5.91	4.460
12					5.90	4.460
13					5.91	4.461
14					5.90	4.460
15					5.91	4.461
16					3.69	4.460
17						4.461
18						4.460
19						4.461
20						4.460
21						2.788

Table 5

General Depreciation System
Applicable Depreciation Method: 200 or 150 Percent
Declining Balance Switching to Straight Line
Applicable Recovery Periods: 3, 5, 7, 10, 15, 20 years
Applicable Convention: Mid-quarter
(property placed in service in fourth quarter)

If the Recovery Year is:	and the Recovery Period is:					
	3-year	5-year	7-year	10-year	15-year	20-year
			the Depreciation Rate is:			
1	8.33	5.00	3.57	2.50	1.25	0.938
2	61.11	38.00	27.55	19.50	9.88	7.430
3	20.37	22.80	19.68	15.60	8.89	6.872
4	10.19	13.68	14.06	12.48	8.00	6.357
5		10.94	10.04	9.98	7.20	5.880
6		9.58	8.73	7.99	6.48	5.439
7			8.73	6.55	5.90	5.031
8			7.64	6.55	5.90	4.654
9				6.56	5.90	4.458
10				6.55	5.91	4.458
11				5.74	5.90	4.458
12					5.91	4.458
13					5.90	4.458
14					5.91	4.458
15					5.90	4.458
16					5.17	4.458
17						4.458
18						4.459
19						4.458
20						4.459
21						3.901

Table 6

General Depreciation System
Applicable Depreciation Method: Straight Line
Applicable Recovery Period: 27.5 years
Applicable Convention: Mid-month

If the Recovery Year is:	And the Month in the First Recovery Year the Property is Placed in Service is:											
	1	2	3	4	5	6	7	8	9	10	11	12
	the Depreciation Rate is:											
1	3.485	3.182	2.879	2.576	2.273	1.970	1.667	1.364	1.061	0.758	0.455	0.152
2-9	3.636	3.636	3.636	3.636	3.636	3.636	3.636	3.636	3.636	3.636	3.636	3.636
10	3.637	3.637	3.637	3.637	3.637	3.637	3.636	3.636	3.636	3.636	3.636	3.636
11	3.636	3.636	3.636	3.636	3.636	3.636	3.637	3.637	3.637	3.637	3.637	3.637
12	3.637	3.637	3.637	3.637	3.637	3.637	3.636	3.636	3.636	3.636	3.636	3.636
13	3.636	3.636	3.636	3.636	3.636	3.636	3.637	3.637	3.637	3.637	3.637	3.637
14	3.637	3.637	3.637	3.637	3.637	3.637	3.636	3.636	3.636	3.636	3.636	3.636
15	3.636	3.636	3.636	3.636	3.636	3.636	3.637	3.637	3.637	3.637	3.637	3.637
16	3.637	3.637	3.637	3.637	3.637	3.637	3.636	3.636	3.636	3.636	3.636	3.636
17	3.636	3.636	3.636	3.636	3.636	3.636	3.637	3.637	3.637	3.637	3.637	3.637
18	3.637	3.637	3.637	3.637	3.637	3.637	3.636	3.636	3.636	3.636	3.636	3.636
19	3.636	3.636	3.636	3.636	3.636	3.636	3.637	3.637	3.637	3.637	3.637	3.637
20	3.637	3.637	3.637	3.637	3.637	3.637	3.636	3.636	3.636	3.636	3.636	3.636
21	3.636	3.636	3.636	3.636	3.636	3.636	3.637	3.637	3.637	3.637	3.637	3.637
22	3.637	3.637	3.637	3.637	3.637	3.637	3.636	3.636	3.636	3.636	3.636	3.636
23	3.636	3.636	3.636	3.636	3.636	3.636	3.637	3.637	3.637	3.637	3.637	3.637
24	3.637	3.637	3.637	3.637	3.637	3.637	3.636	3.636	3.636	3.636	3.636	3.636
25	3.636	3.636	3.636	3.636	3.636	3.636	3.637	3.637	3.637	3.637	3.637	3.637
26	3.637	3.637	3.637	3.637	3.637	3.637	3.636	3.636	3.636	3.636	3.636	3.636
27	3.636	3.636	3.636	3.636	3.636	3.636	3.637	3.637	3.637	3.637	3.637	3.637
28	1.970	2.273	2.576	2.879	3.182	3.485	3.636	3.636	3.636	3.636	3.636	3.636
29	0.000	0.000	0.000	0.000	0.000	0.000	0.152	0.455	0.758	1.061	1.364	1.667

Table 7

General Depreciation System
Applicable Depreciation Method: Straight Line
Applicable Recovery Period: 31.5 years
Applicable Convention: Mid-month

And the Month in the First Recovery Year the Property is Placed in Service is:

If the Recovery Year is:	1	2	3	4	5	6	7	8	9	10	11	12
						the Depreciation Rate is:						
1	3.042	2.778	2.513	2.249	1.984	1.720	1.455	1.190	0.926	0.661	0.397	0.132
2-7	3.175	3.175	3.175	3.175	3.175	3.175	3.175	3.175	3.175	3.175	3.175	3.175
8	3.175	3.174	3.175	3.174	3.175	3.174	3.175	3.175	3.175	3.175	3.175	3.175
9	3.174	3.175	3.174	3.175	3.174	3.175	3.174	3.175	3.174	3.175	3.174	3.175
10	3.175	3.174	3.175	3.174	3.175	3.174	3.175	3.174	3.175	3.174	3.175	3.174
11	3.174	3.175	3.174	3.175	3.174	3.175	3.174	3.175	3.174	3.175	3.174	3.175
12	3.175	3.174	3.175	3.174	3.175	3.174	3.175	3.174	3.175	3.174	3.175	3.174
13	3.174	3.175	3.174	3.175	3.174	3.175	3.174	3.175	3.174	3.175	3.174	3.175
14	3.175	3.174	3.175	3.174	3.175	3.174	3.175	3.174	3.175	3.174	3.175	3.174
15	3.174	3.175	3.174	3.175	3.174	3.175	3.174	3.175	3.174	3.175	3.174	3.175
16	3.175	3.174	3.175	3.174	3.175	3.174	3.175	3.174	3.175	3.174	3.175	3.174
17	3.174	3.175	3.174	3.175	3.174	3.175	3.174	3.175	3.174	3.175	3.174	3.175
18	3.175	3.174	3.175	3.174	3.175	3.174	3.175	3.174	3.175	3.174	3.175	3.174
19	3.174	3.175	3.174	3.175	3.174	3.175	3.174	3.175	3.174	3.175	3.174	3.175
20	3.175	3.174	3.175	3.174	3.175	3.174	3.175	3.174	3.175	3.174	3.175	3.174
21	3.174	3.175	3.174	3.175	3.174	3.175	3.174	3.175	3.174	3.175	3.174	3.175
22	3.175	3.174	3.175	3.174	3.175	3.174	3.175	3.174	3.175	3.174	3.175	3.174
23	3.174	3.175	3.174	3.175	3.174	3.175	3.174	3.175	3.174	3.175	3.174	3.175
24	3.175	3.174	3.175	3.174	3.175	3.174	3.175	3.174	3.175	3.174	3.175	3.174
25	3.174	3.175	3.174	3.175	3.174	3.175	3.174	3.175	3.174	3.175	3.174	3.175
26	3.175	3.174	3.175	3.174	3.175	3.174	3.175	3.174	3.175	3.174	3.175	3.174
27	3.174	3.175	3.174	3.175	3.174	3.175	3.174	3.175	3.174	3.175	3.174	3.175
28	3.175	3.174	3.175	3.174	3.175	3.174	3.175	3.174	3.175	3.174	3.175	3.174
29	3.174	3.175	3.174	3.175	3.174	3.175	3.174	3.175	3.174	3.175	3.174	3.175
30	3.175	3.174	3.175	3.174	3.175	3.174	3.175	3.174	3.175	3.174	3.175	3.174
31	3.174	3.175	3.174	3.175	3.174	3.175	3.174	3.175	3.174	3.175	3.174	3.175
32	1.720	1.984	2.249	2.513	2.778	3.042	3.175	3.174	3.175	3.174	3.175	3.174
33	0.000	0.000	0.000	0.000	0.000	0.000	0.132	0.397	0.661	0.926	1.190	1.455

Table 7a

General Depreciation System
Applicable Depreciation Method: Straight Line
Applicable Recovery Period: 39 years
Applicable Convention: Mid-month

Month property placed in service

Year	1	2	3	4	5	6	7	8	9	10	11	12
1	2.461%	2.247%	2.033%	1.819%	1.605%	1.391%	1.177%	0.963%	0.749%	0.535%	0.321%	0.107%
2-39	2.564	2.564	2.564	2.564	2.564	2.564	2.564	2.564	2.564	2.564	2.564	2.564
40	0.107	0.321	0.535	0.749	0.963	1.177	1.391	1.605	1.819	2.033	2.247	2.461

Table 8

General and Alternative Depreciation Systems
Applicable Depreciation Method: Straight Line
Applicable Recovery Periods: 2.5-50 years
Applicable Convention: Half-year

If the Recovery Year is:	and the Recovery Period is:															
	2.5	3.0	3.5	4.0	4.5	5.0	5.5	6.0	6.5	7.0	7.5	8.0	8.5	9.0	9.5	10.0
	the Depreciation Rate is:															
1	20.00	16.67	14.29	12.50	11.11	10.00	9.09	8.33	7.69	7.14	6.67	6.25	5.88	5.56	5.26	5.00
2	40.00	33.33	28.57	25.00	22.22	20.00	18.18	16.67	15.39	14.29	13.33	12.50	11.77	11.11	10.53	10.00
3	40.00	33.33	28.57	25.00	22.22	20.00	18.18	16.67	15.38	14.29	13.33	12.50	11.76	11.11	10.53	10.00
4		16.67	28.57	25.00	22.23	20.00	18.18	16.67	15.39	14.28	13.33	12.50	11.76	11.11	10.53	10.00
5				12.50	22.22	20.00	18.19	16.66	15.38	14.29	13.34	12.50	11.76	11.11	10.52	10.00
6						10.00	18.18	16.67	15.39	14.28	13.33	12.50	11.77	11.11	10.53	10.00
7							8.33	15.38	14.29	13.34	12.50	11.76	11.11	10.52	10.00
8								7.14	13.33	12.50	11.76	11.11	10.53	10.00
9										6.25	11.76	11.11	10.52	10.00
10												5.56	10.53	10.00
11														5.00

If the Recovery Year is:	and the Recovery Period is:															
	10.5	11.0	11.5	12.0	12.5	13.0	13.5	14.0	14.5	15.0	15.5	16.0	16.5	17.0	17.5	18.0
	the Depreciation Rate is:															
1	4.76	4.55	4.35	4.17	4.00	3.85	3.70	3.57	3.45	3.33	3.23	3.13	3.03	2.94	2.86	2.78
2	9.52	9.09	8.70	8.33	8.00	7.69	7.41	7.14	6.90	6.67	6.45	6.25	6.06	5.88	5.71	5.56
3	9.52	9.09	8.70	8.33	8.00	7.69	7.41	7.14	6.90	6.67	6.45	6.25	6.06	5.88	5.71	5.56
4	9.53	9.09	8.69	8.33	8.00	7.69	7.41	7.14	6.90	6.67	6.45	6.25	6.06	5.88	5.71	5.55
5	9.52	9.09	8.70	8.33	8.00	7.69	7.41	7.14	6.90	6.67	6.45	6.25	6.06	5.88	5.72	5.56
6	9.53	9.09	8.69	8.33	8.00	7.69	7.41	7.14	6.89	6.67	6.45	6.25	6.06	5.88	5.71	5.55
7	9.52	9.09	8.70	8.34	8.00	7.69	7.41	7.14	6.90	6.67	6.45	6.25	6.06	5.88	5.72	5.56
8	9.53	9.09	8.69	8.33	8.00	7.69	7.41	7.15	6.89	6.66	6.45	6.25	6.06	5.88	5.71	5.56
9	9.52	9.09	8.70	8.34	8.00	7.69	7.41	7.14	6.90	6.67	6.45	6.25	6.06	5.88	5.72	5.55
10	9.53	9.09	8.69	8.33	8.00	7.70	7.40	7.15	6.89	6.66	6.45	6.25	6.06	5.88	5.71	5.55
11	9.52	9.09	8.70	8.34	8.00	7.69	7.41	7.14	6.90	6.67	6.45	6.25	6.06	5.89	5.72	5.56
12		4.55	8.69	8.33	8.00	7.70	7.40	7.15	6.89	6.66	6.45	6.25	6.06	5.88	5.71	5.55
13				4.17	8.00	7.69	7.41	7.14	6.90	6.66	6.45	6.25	6.06	5.88	5.72	5.56
14						3.85	7.40	7.15	6.89	6.66	6.45	6.25	6.06	5.88	5.72	5.55
15							3.57	7.15	6.90	6.67	6.45	6.25	6.06	5.88	5.72	5.56
16								3.57	6.90	6.67	6.46	6.25	6.06	5.88	5.71	5.55
17										3.33	6.46	6.25	6.07	5.89	5.72	5.56
18												3.12	6.07	2.94	5.71	5.55
19																2.78

Table 8

General and Alternative Depreciation Systems
Applicable Depreciation Method: Straight Line
Applicable Recovery Periods: 2.5-50 years
Applicable Convention: Half-year
(continued)

and the Recovery Period is:

If the Recovery Year is:	18.5	19.0	19.5	20.0	20.5	21.0	21.5	22.0	22.5	23.0	23.5	24.0	24.5	25.0	25.5	26.0
							the Depreciation Rate is:									
1	2.70	2.63	2.56	2.500	2.439	2.381	2.326	2.273	2.222	2.174	2.128	2.083	2.041	2.000	1.961	1.923
2	5.41	5.26	5.13	5.000	4.878	4.762	4.651	4.545	4.444	4.348	4.255	4.167	4.082	4.000	3.922	3.846
3	5.41	5.26	5.13	5.000	4.878	4.762	4.651	4.545	4.444	4.348	4.255	4.167	4.082	4.000	3.922	3.846
4	5.41	5.26	5.13	5.000	4.878	4.762	4.651	4.545	4.445	4.348	4.255	4.167	4.082	4.000	3.922	3.846
5	5.40	5.26	5.13	5.000	4.878	4.762	4.651	4.546	4.444	4.348	4.255	4.167	4.082	4.000	3.922	3.846
6	5.41	5.26	5.13	5.000	4.878	4.762	4.651	4.545	4.445	4.348	4.255	4.167	4.082	4.000	3.921	3.846
7	5.40	5.26	5.13	5.000	4.878	4.762	4.651	4.546	4.444	4.348	4.255	4.167	4.082	4.000	3.922	3.846
8	5.41	5.26	5.13	5.000	4.878	4.762	4.651	4.545	4.445	4.348	4.255	4.167	4.082	4.000	3.921	3.846
9	5.40	5.27	5.13	5.000	4.878	4.762	4.651	4.546	4.444	4.348	4.255	4.167	4.081	4.000	3.922	3.846
10	5.41	5.26	5.13	5.000	4.878	4.762	4.651	4.545	4.445	4.348	4.255	4.167	4.082	4.000	3.921	3.846
11	5.40	5.27	5.13	5.000	4.878	4.762	4.651	4.546	4.444	4.348	4.256	4.166	4.081	4.000	3.922	3.846
12	5.41	5.26	5.13	5.000	4.878	4.762	4.651	4.545	4.445	4.348	4.255	4.167	4.082	4.000	3.921	3.846
13	5.40	5.27	5.13	5.000	4.878	4.762	4.651	4.546	4.444	4.348	4.256	4.166	4.081	4.000	3.922	3.846
14	5.41	5.26	5.13	5.000	4.878	4.762	4.651	4.545	4.445	4.348	4.255	4.167	4.082	4.000	3.921	3.846
15	5.40	5.27	5.13	5.000	4.878	4.762	4.651	4.546	4.444	4.348	4.256	4.166	4.081	4.000	3.922	3.846
16	5.41	5.26	5.12	5.000	4.878	4.762	4.651	4.545	4.445	4.348	4.255	4.167	4.082	4.000	3.921	3.846
17	5.40	5.27	5.13	5.000	4.878	4.762	4.652	4.546	4.444	4.347	4.256	4.166	4.081	4.000	3.922	3.846
18	5.41	5.26	5.12	5.000	4.878	4.762	4.651	4.545	4.445	4.348	4.255	4.167	4.082	4.000	3.921	3.846
19	5.40	5.27	5.13	5.000	4.878	4.761	4.652	4.546	4.444	4.347	4.256	4.166	4.081	4.000	3.922	3.846
20		2.63	5.12	5.000	4.879	4.762	4.651	4.545	4.445	4.348	4.255	4.167	4.082	4.000	3.921	3.847
21				2.500	4.878	4.761	4.652	4.546	4.444	4.347	4.256	4.166	4.081	4.000	3.922	3.846
22						2.381	4.651	4.545	4.445	4.348	4.255	4.167	4.082	4.000	3.921	3.847
23								2.273	4.444	4.348	4.255	4.166	4.081	4.000	3.922	3.846
24										2.174	4.255	4.167	4.082	4.000	3.921	3.847
25												2.083	4.081	4.000	3.922	3.846
26														2.000	3.921	3.847
27																1.923

and the Recovery Period is:

If the Recovery Year is:	26.5	27.0	27.5	28.0	28.5	29.0	29.5	30.0	30.5	31.0	31.5	32.0	32.5	33.0	33.5	34.0
							the Depreciation Rate is:									
1	1.887	1.852	1.818	1.786	1.754	1.724	1.695	1.667	1.639	1.613	1.587	1.563	1.538	1.515	1.493	1.471
2-6	3.774	3.704	3.636	3.571	3.509	3.448	3.390	3.333	3.279	3.226	3.175	3.125	3.077	3.030	2.985	2.941
7	3.773	3.704	3.636	3.572	3.509	3.448	3.390	3.333	3.279	3.226	3.175	3.125	3.077	3.030	2.985	2.941
8	3.774	3.704	3.636	3.571	3.509	3.448	3.390	3.333	3.279	3.226	3.175	3.125	3.077	3.030	2.985	2.941
9	3.773	3.704	3.637	3.572	3.509	3.448	3.390	3.333	3.279	3.226	3.175	3.125	3.077	3.030	2.985	2.941
10	3.774	3.704	3.636	3.571	3.509	3.448	3.390	3.333	3.279	3.226	3.174	3.125	3.077	3.030	2.985	2.941
11	3.773	3.704	3.637	3.572	3.509	3.448	3.390	3.333	3.279	3.226	3.175	3.125	3.077	3.030	2.985	2.941
12	3.774	3.704	3.636	3.571	3.509	3.448	3.390	3.333	3.279	3.226	3.174	3.125	3.077	3.030	2.985	2.941
13	3.773	3.703	3.637	3.572	3.509	3.448	3.390	3.334	3.279	3.226	3.175	3.125	3.077	3.030	2.985	2.941
14	3.773	3.704	3.636	3.571	3.509	3.448	3.390	3.333	3.279	3.226	3.174	3.125	3.077	3.030	2.985	2.941
15	3.774	3.703	3.637	3.572	3.509	3.449	3.390	3.334	3.278	3.226	3.175	3.125	3.077	3.031	2.985	2.941
16	3.773	3.703	3.636	3.571	3.509	3.448	3.390	3.333	3.279	3.226	3.174	3.125	3.077	3.030	2.985	2.941
17	3.774	3.703	3.637	3.572	3.509	3.449	3.390	3.334	3.278	3.226	3.175	3.125	3.077	3.031	2.985	2.941
18	3.773	3.704	3.636	3.571	3.508	3.448	3.390	3.333	3.279	3.226	3.174	3.125	3.077	3.030	2.985	2.941
19	3.774	3.703	3.637	3.572	3.509	3.449	3.390	3.334	3.278	3.226	3.175	3.125	3.077	3.031	2.985	2.941
20	3.773	3.704	3.636	3.571	3.508	3.448	3.390	3.333	3.279	3.226	3.174	3.125	3.077	3.030	2.985	2.941
21	3.774	3.703	3.637	3.572	3.509	3.449	3.389	3.334	3.278	3.225	3.174	3.125	3.077	3.031	2.985	2.941
22	3.773	3.704	3.636	3.571	3.508	3.448	3.390	3.333	3.279	3.226	3.174	3.125	3.077	3.030	2.985	2.941
23	3.774	3.703	3.637	3.572	3.509	3.449	3.389	3.334	3.278	3.225	3.175	3.125	3.077	3.031	2.985	2.941
24	3.773	3.704	3.636	3.571	3.508	3.448	3.390	3.333	3.279	3.226	3.175	3.125	3.077	3.030	2.985	2.941
25	3.774	3.703	3.637	3.572	3.509	3.449	3.389	3.334	3.278	3.225	3.175	3.125	3.077	3.031	2.985	2.942
26	3.773	3.704	3.636	3.571	3.508	3.448	3.390	3.333	3.279	3.226	3.174	3.125	3.077	3.030	2.985	2.941
27	3.774	3.703	3.637	3.572	3.509	3.449	3.389	3.334	3.278	3.225	3.175	3.125	3.077	3.031	2.985	2.942
28		1.852	3.636	3.571	3.508	3.448	3.390	3.333	3.279	3.226	3.174	3.125	3.077	3.030	2.985	2.941
29			1.786	3.509	3.449	3.390	3.334	3.278	3.225	3.175	3.125	3.077	3.031	2.985	2.942	
30				1.724	3.390	3.333	3.279	3.226	3.174	3.125	3.077	3.030	2.985	2.941		
31					1.667	3.278	3.225	3.175	3.125	3.076	3.031	2.986	2.942			
32						1.613	3.174	3.125	3.077	3.030	2.985	2.941				
33							1.562	3.076	3.031	2.986	2.942					
34								1.515	2.985	2.941						
35									1.471							

Table 8

General and Alternative Depreciation Systems
Applicable Depreciation Method: Straight Line
Applicable Recovery Periods: 2.5-50 years
Applicable Convention: Half-year
(continued)

If the Recovery Year is:	and the Recovery Period is:															
	34.5	35.0	35.5	36.0	36.5	37.0	37.5	38.0	38.5	39.0	39.5	40.0	40.5	41.0	41.5	42.0
	the Depreciation Rate is:															
1	1.449	1.429	1.408	1.389	1.370	1.351	1.333	1.316	1.299	1.282	1.266	1.250	1.235	1.220	1.205	1.190
2	2.899	2.857	2.817	2.778	2.740	2.703	2.667	2.632	2.597	2.564	2.532	2.500	2.469	2.439	2.410	2.381
3	2.899	2.857	2.817	2.778	2.740	2.703	2.667	2.632	2.597	2.564	2.532	2.500	2.469	2.439	2.410	2.381
4	2.899	2.857	2.817	2.778	2.740	2.703	2.667	2.632	2.597	2.564	2.532	2.500	2.469	2.439	2.410	2.381
5	2.899	2.857	2.817	2.778	2.740	2.703	2.667	2.632	2.597	2.564	2.532	2.500	2.469	2.439	2.410	2.381
6	2.899	2.857	2.817	2.778	2.740	2.703	2.667	2.632	2.597	2.564	2.532	2.500	2.469	2.439	2.410	2.381
7	2.898	2.857	2.817	2.778	2.740	2.703	2.667	2.632	2.597	2.564	2.532	2.500	2.469	2.439	2.410	2.381
8	2.899	2.857	2.817	2.778	2.740	2.703	2.667	2.631	2.597	2.564	2.532	2.500	2.469	2.439	2.410	2.381
9	2.898	2.857	2.817	2.778	2.740	2.703	2.667	2.632	2.597	2.564	2.532	2.500	2.469	2.439	2.410	2.381
10	2.899	2.857	2.817	2.778	2.740	2.703	2.667	2.631	2.598	2.564	2.532	2.500	2.469	2.439	2.410	2.381
11	2.898	2.857	2.817	2.778	2.740	2.703	2.667	2.632	2.597	2.564	2.532	2.500	2.469	2.439	2.410	2.381
12	2.899	2.857	2.817	2.778	2.740	2.703	2.667	2.631	2.598	2.564	2.532	2.500	2.469	2.439	2.410	2.381
13	2.898	2.857	2.817	2.778	2.740	2.703	2.667	2.632	2.597	2.564	2.532	2.500	2.469	2.439	2.410	2.381
14	2.899	2.857	2.817	2.778	2.740	2.703	2.667	2.631	2.598	2.564	2.531	2.500	2.469	2.439	2.409	2.381
15	2.898	2.857	2.817	2.778	2.740	2.703	2.666	2.632	2.597	2.564	2.532	2.500	2.469	2.439	2.410	2.381
16	2.899	2.857	2.817	2.778	2.740	2.703	2.667	2.631	2.598	2.564	2.531	2.500	2.469	2.439	2.409	2.381
17	2.898	2.857	2.817	2.778	2.740	2.703	2.666	2.632	2.597	2.564	2.532	2.500	2.469	2.439	2.410	2.381
18	2.899	2.857	2.817	2.778	2.740	2.702	2.667	2.631	2.598	2.564	2.531	2.500	2.469	2.439	2.409	2.381
19	2.898	2.857	2.817	2.778	2.739	2.703	2.666	2.632	2.597	2.564	2.532	2.500	2.469	2.439	2.410	2.381
20	2.898	2.857	2.817	2.778	2.740	2.702	2.667	2.631	2.598	2.564	2.531	2.500	2.469	2.439	2.409	2.381
21	2.899	2.857	2.817	2.778	2.739	2.703	2.666	2.632	2.597	2.564	2.532	2.500	2.469	2.439	2.410	2.381
22	2.898	2.857	2.817	2.777	2.740	2.702	2.667	2.631	2.598	2.564	2.531	2.500	2.469	2.439	2.409	2.381
23	2.899	2.857	2.817	2.778	2.739	2.703	2.666	2.632	2.597	2.564	2.532	2.500	2.469	2.439	2.410	2.381
24	2.898	2.857	2.817	2.777	2.740	2.702	2.667	2.631	2.598	2.564	2.531	2.500	2.469	2.439	2.409	2.381
25	2.899	2.857	2.817	2.778	2.739	2.703	2.666	2.632	2.597	2.564	2.532	2.500	2.469	2.439	2.410	2.381
26	2.898	2.857	2.817	2.777	2.740	2.702	2.667	2.631	2.598	2.564	2.531	2.500	2.469	2.439	2.409	2.381
27	2.899	2.857	2.817	2.778	2.739	2.703	2.666	2.632	2.597	2.564	2.532	2.500	2.469	2.439	2.410	2.381
28	2.898	2.858	2.817	2.777	2.740	2.702	2.667	2.631	2.598	2.564	2.531	2.500	2.469	2.439	2.409	2.381
29	2.899	2.857	2.817	2.778	2.739	2.703	2.666	2.632	2.597	2.564	2.532	2.500	2.469	2.439	2.410	2.381
30	2.898	2.858	2.817	2.777	2.740	2.702	2.667	2.631	2.598	2.564	2.531	2.500	2.469	2.439	2.409	2.381
31	2.899	2.857	2.817	2.778	2.739	2.703	2.666	2.632	2.597	2.564	2.532	2.500	2.469	2.439	2.410	2.381
32	2.898	2.858	2.816	2.777	2.740	2.702	2.667	2.631	2.598	2.564	2.531	2.500	2.470	2.439	2.409	2.381
33	2.899	2.857	2.817	2.778	2.739	2.703	2.666	2.632	2.597	2.565	2.532	2.500	2.469	2.439	2.410	2.381
34	2.898	2.858	2.816	2.777	2.740	2.702	2.667	2.631	2.598	2.564	2.531	2.500	2.470	2.439	2.409	2.381
35	2.899	2.857	2.817	2.778	2.739	2.703	2.666	2.632	2.597	2.565	2.532	2.500	2.469	2.439	2.410	2.381
36		1.429	2.816	2.777	2.740	2.703	2.667	2.631	2.598	2.564	2.531	2.500	2.470	2.439	2.409	2.381
37				1.389	2.739	2.703	2.666	2.632	2.597	2.565	2.532	2.500	2.469	2.439	2.410	2.381
38						1.351	2.667	2.631	2.598	2.564	2.531	2.500	2.469	2.439	2.410	2.381
39								1.316	2.597	2.564	2.532	2.500	2.469	2.439	2.410	2.381
40										1.282	2.531	2.500	2.470	2.439	2.409	2.381
41												1.250	2.469	2.439	2.410	2.380
42														1.220	2.409	2.381
43																1.190

Table 8

General and Alternative Depreciation Systems
Applicable Depreciation Method: Straight Line
Applicable Recovery Periods: 2.5-50 years
Applicable Convention: Half-year
(continued)

and the Recovery Period is:

If the Recovery Year is:	42.5	43.0	43.5	44.0	44.5	45.0	45.5	46.0	46.5	47.0	47.5	48.0	48.5	49.0	49.5	50.0
									the Depreciation Rate is:							
1	1.176	1.163	1.149	1.136	1.124	1.111	1.099	1.087	1.075	1.064	1.053	1.042	1.031	1.020	1.010	1.000
2	2.353	2.326	2.299	2.273	2.247	2.222	2.198	2.174	2.151	2.128	2.105	2.083	2.062	2.041	2.020	2.000
3	2.353	2.326	2.299	2.273	2.247	2.222	2.198	2.174	2.151	2.128	2.105	2.083	2.062	2.041	2.020	2.000
4	2.353	2.326	2.299	2.273	2.247	2.222	2.198	2.174	2.151	2.128	2.105	2.083	2.062	2.041	2.020	2.000
5	2.353	2.326	2.299	2.273	2.247	2.222	2.198	2.174	2.151	2.128	2.105	2.083	2.062	2.041	2.020	2.000
6	2.353	2.326	2.299	2.273	2.247	2.222	2.198	2.174	2.151	2.128	2.105	2.083	2.062	2.041	2.020	2.000
7	2.353	2.326	2.299	2.273	2.247	2.222	2.198	2.174	2.150	2.128	2.105	2.083	2.062	2.041	2.020	2.000
8	2.353	2.326	2.299	2.273	2.247	2.222	2.198	2.174	2.151	2.128	2.105	2.083	2.062	2.041	2.020	2.000
9	2.353	2.325	2.299	2.273	2.247	2.222	2.198	2.174	2.150	2.128	2.105	2.083	2.062	2.041	2.020	2.000
10	2.353	2.326	2.299	2.273	2.247	2.222	2.198	2.174	2.151	2.128	2.105	2.083	2.062	2.041	2.020	2.000
11	2.353	2.325	2.299	2.273	2.247	2.222	2.198	2.174	2.150	2.128	2.105	2.083	2.062	2.041	2.020	2.000
12	2.353	2.326	2.299	2.273	2.247	2.222	2.198	2.174	2.151	2.128	2.105	2.083	2.062	2.041	2.020	2.000
13	2.353	2.325	2.299	2.273	2.247	2.222	2.198	2.174	2.150	2.128	2.105	2.083	2.062	2.041	2.020	2.000
14	2.353	2.326	2.299	2.273	2.247	2.222	2.198	2.174	2.151	2.128	2.105	2.083	2.062	2.041	2.020	2.000
15	2.353	2.325	2.299	2.273	2.247	2.222	2.198	2.174	2.150	2.128	2.105	2.083	2.062	2.041	2.020	2.000
16	2.353	2.326	2.299	2.273	2.247	2.222	2.198	2.174	2.151	2.128	2.105	2.083	2.062	2.041	2.020	2.000
17	2.353	2.325	2.299	2.273	2.247	2.222	2.198	2.174	2.150	2.128	2.105	2.083	2.062	2.041	2.020	2.000
18	2.353	2.326	2.299	2.273	2.247	2.222	2.198	2.174	2.151	2.128	2.105	2.083	2.062	2.041	2.020	2.000
19	2.353	2.325	2.299	2.273	2.247	2.222	2.198	2.174	2.150	2.127	2.105	2.084	2.062	2.041	2.020	2.000
20	2.353	2.326	2.299	2.273	2.247	2.222	2.198	2.174	2.151	2.128	2.105	2.083	2.062	2.041	2.020	2.000
21	2.353	2.325	2.299	2.273	2.247	2.222	2.198	2.174	2.150	2.127	2.105	2.084	2.062	2.041	2.020	2.000
22	2.353	2.326	2.299	2.273	2.247	2.222	2.198	2.174	2.151	2.128	2.105	2.083	2.062	2.041	2.020	2.000
23	2.353	2.325	2.299	2.272	2.247	2.222	2.198	2.174	2.150	2.127	2.105	2.084	2.062	2.041	2.020	2.000
24	2.353	2.326	2.299	2.273	2.247	2.222	2.198	2.174	2.151	2.128	2.105	2.083	2.062	2.041	2.020	2.000
25	2.353	2.325	2.299	2.272	2.247	2.222	2.198	2.174	2.150	2.127	2.105	2.084	2.062	2.041	2.020	2.000
26	2.353	2.326	2.299	2.273	2.247	2.222	2.198	2.174	2.151	2.128	2.106	2.083	2.062	2.041	2.020	2.000
27	2.353	2.325	2.299	2.272	2.247	2.223	2.198	2.174	2.150	2.127	2.105	2.084	2.062	2.041	2.020	2.000
28	2.353	2.326	2.299	2.273	2.247	2.222	2.198	2.174	2.151	2.128	2.106	2.083	2.062	2.041	2.020	2.000
29	2.353	2.325	2.299	2.272	2.247	2.223	2.198	2.174	2.150	2.127	2.105	2.084	2.062	2.041	2.020	2.000
30	2.353	2.326	2.299	2.273	2.248	2.222	2.197	2.174	2.151	2.128	2.106	2.083	2.062	2.041	2.020	2.000
31	2.353	2.325	2.299	2.272	2.247	2.223	2.198	2.174	2.150	2.127	2.105	2.084	2.062	2.041	2.021	2.000
32	2.353	2.326	2.299	2.273	2.248	2.222	2.197	2.174	2.151	2.128	2.106	2.083	2.062	2.041	2.020	2.000
33	2.353	2.325	2.298	2.272	2.247	2.223	2.198	2.174	2.150	2.127	2.105	2.084	2.062	2.041	2.021	2.000
34	2.353	2.326	2.299	2.273	2.248	2.222	2.197	2.174	2.151	2.128	2.106	2.083	2.062	2.040	2.020	2.000
35	2.353	2.325	2.298	2.272	2.247	2.223	2.198	2.174	2.150	2.127	2.105	2.084	2.062	2.041	2.021	2.000
36	2.353	2.326	2.299	2.273	2.248	2.222	2.197	2.174	2.151	2.128	2.106	2.083	2.062	2.040	2.020	2.000
37	2.353	2.325	2.298	2.272	2.247	2.223	2.198	2.174	2.150	2.127	2.105	2.084	2.061	2.041	2.021	2.000
38	2.353	2.326	2.299	2.273	2.248	2.222	2.197	2.174	2.151	2.128	2.106	2.083	2.062	2.040	2.020	2.000
39	2.353	2.325	2.298	2.272	2.247	2.223	2.198	2.174	2.150	2.127	2.105	2.084	2.061	2.041	2.021	2.000
40	2.353	2.326	2.299	2.273	2.248	2.222	2.197	2.173	2.151	2.128	2.106	2.083	2.062	2.040	2.020	2.000
41	2.352	2.325	2.298	2.272	2.247	2.223	2.198	2.174	2.150	2.127	2.105	2.084	2.061	2.041	2.021	2.000
42	2.353	2.326	2.299	2.273	2.248	2.222	2.197	2.173	2.151	2.128	2.106	2.083	2.062	2.040	2.020	2.000
43	2.352	2.325	2.298	2.272	2.247	2.223	2.198	2.174	2.150	2.127	2.105	2.084	2.061	2.041	2.021	2.000
44		1.163	2.299	2.273	2.248	2.222	2.197	2.173	2.151	2.128	2.106	2.083	2.062	2.040	2.020	2.000
45				1.136	2.247	2.223	2.198	2.174	2.150	2.127	2.105	2.084	2.061	2.041	2.021	2.000
46						1.111	2.197	2.173	2.151	2.128	2.106	2.083	2.062	2.040	2.020	2.000
47								1.087	2.150	2.127	2.105	2.084	2.061	2.041	2.021	2.000
48										1.064	2.106	2.083	2.062	2.040	2.020	2.000
49												1.042	2.061	2.041	2.021	2.000
50														1.020	2.020	2.000
51																1.000

Table 9
Alternative Depreciation System
Applicable Depreciation Method: Straight Line
Applicable Recovery Period: 40 years
Applicable Convention: Mid-month

And the Month in the First Recovery Year the Property is Placed in Service is:

If the Recovery Year is:	1	2	3	4	5	6	7	8	9	10	11	12
	the Depreciation Rate is:											
1	2.396	2.188	1.979	1.771	1.563	1.354	1.146	0.938	0.729	0.521	0.313	0.104
2 to 40	2.500	2.500	2.500	2.500	2.500	2.500	2.500	2.500	2.500	2.500	2.500	2.500
41	0.104	0.312	0.521	0.729	0.937	1.146	1.354	1.562	1.771	1.979	2.187	2.396

Table I
Leased MACRS Business Listed Property

Income Inclusion Amounts — Step (1) Computation Rates — for Business Listed Property (Except Autos) Leased After '86 (Reg §1.280F-7(b)(2)(i)(C))

First Taxable Year During Lease in Which Business Use Percentage is 50% or Less

Type of Property	1	2	3	4	5	6	7	8	9	10	11	12 & Later
Property with a Recovery Period of Less Than 7 Years under the Alternative Depreciation System (Such as Computers, Trucks and Airplanes)	0.0%	10.0%	22.0%	21.2%	12.7%	12.7%	12.7%	12.7%	12.7%	12.7%	12.7%	12.7%
Property with a 7- to 10-Year Recovery Period under the Alternative Depreciation System (Such as Recreation Property)	0.0%	9.3%	23.8%	31.3%	33.8%	32.7%	31.6%	30.5%	25.0%	15.0%	15.0%	15.0%
Property with Recovery Period of more Than 10 Years under the Alternative Depreciation System (Such as Certain Property with No Class Life)	0.0%	10.1%	26.3%	35.4%	39.6%	40.2%	40.8%	41.4%	37.5%	29.2%	20.8%	12.5%

Table II
Leased MACRS Business Listed Property

Income Inclusion Amounts — Step (2) Computation Rates — for
Business Listed Property (Except Autos) Leased After '86
(Reg §1.280F-7(b)(2)(i)(C))

First Taxable Year During Lease in Which Business Use Percentage is 50% or Less

Type of Property	1	2	3	4	5	6	7	8	9	10	11	12 & Later
Property with a Recovery Period of Less Than 7 Years under Alternative Depreciation System (Such as Computers, Trucks and Airplanes)	2.1%	−7.2%	−19.8%	−20.1%	−12.4%	−12.4%	−12.4%	−12.4%	−12.4%	−12.4%	−12.4%	−12.4%
Property with a 7- to 10-Year Recovery Period under the Alternative Depreciation System (Such as Recreation Property)	3.9%	−3.8%	−17.7%	−25.1%	−27.8%	−27.2%	−27.1%	−27.6%	−23.7%	−14.7%	−14.7%	−14.7%
Property with a Recovery Period of More Than 10 Years under the Alternative Depreciation System (Such as Certain Property with No Class Life)	6.6%	−1.6%	−16.9%	−25.6%	−29.9%	−31.1%	−32.8%	−35.1%	−33.3%	−26.7%	−19.7%	−12.2%

¶ 1118 Income Inclusion Amounts for Autos, Trucks and Vans. ▰▰▰▰

REV. PROC. 2013-21 TABLE 5

DOLLAR AMOUNTS FOR PASSENGER AUTOMOBILES (THAT ARE NOT TRUCKS OR VANS) WITH A LEASE TERM BEGINNING IN CALENDAR YEAR 2013

Fair Market Value of Passenger Automobile		Tax Year During Lease				
Over	Not Over	1st	2nd	3rd	4th	5th & later
$19,000	$19,500	2	4	6	7	8
19,500	20,000	2	5	6	9	9
20,000	20,500	2	5	8	9	11
20,500	21,000	3	6	8	10	12
21,000	21,500	3	6	10	11	13
21,500	22,000	3	7	10	13	14
22,000	23,000	4	8	11	14	16
23,000	24,000	4	9	14	16	18
24,000	25,000	5	10	15	18	21
25,000	26,000	5	12	16	21	23
26,000	27,000	6	12	19	23	25
27,000	28,000	6	14	20	25	28
28,000	29,000	7	15	22	27	30
29,000	30,000	7	16	24	29	33
30,000	31,000	8	17	26	31	35
31,000	32,000	8	19	27	33	38
32,000	33,000	9	20	29	35	40
33,000	34,000	10	21	31	37	43
34,000	35,000	10	22	33	39	45
35,000	36,000	11	23	35	41	48
36,000	37,000	11	25	36	43	50
37,000	38,000	12	26	38	45	53
38,000	39,000	12	27	40	47	55
39,000	40,000	13	28	42	49	58
40,000	41,000	13	29	44	52	59
41,000	42,000	14	30	45	54	63
42,000	43,000	14	32	47	56	64
43,000	44,000	15	33	48	59	67
44,000	45,000	15	34	51	60	69
45,000	46,000	16	35	52	63	72
46,000	47,000	17	36	54	65	74
47,000	48,000	17	38	55	67	77
48,000	49,000	18	39	57	69	79
49,000	50,000	18	40	59	71	82
50,000	51,000	19	41	61	73	84
51,000	52,000	19	42	63	75	87
52,000	53,000	20	43	65	77	89
53,000	54,000	20	45	66	79	92
54,000	55,000	21	46	68	81	94
55,000	56,000	21	47	70	84	96
56,000	57,000	22	48	72	85	99
57,000	58,000	22	50	73	88	101
58,000	59,000	23	51	75	90	103
59,000	60,000	24	52	76	92	106
60,000	62,000	24	54	79	95	110
62,000	64,000	25	56	83	99	115
64,000	66,000	27	58	87	103	120
66,000	68,000	28	60	90	108	125

Over	Not Over	1st	2nd	3rd	4th	5th & later
68,000	70,000	29	63	93	112	130
70,000	72,000	30	65	97	117	134
72,000	74,000	31	68	100	121	139
74,000	76,000	32	70	104	125	144
76,000	78,000	33	73	107	129	149
78,000	80,000	34	75	111	133	154
80,000	85,000	36	79	117	141	162
85,000	90,000	39	85	126	151	174
90,000	95,000	41	91	135	162	186
95,000	100,000	44	97	144	172	199
100,000	110,000	48	106	157	188	217
110,000	120,000	53	118	174	210	241
120,000	130,000	59	129	193	230	266
130,000	140,000	64	141	210	252	290
140,000	150,000	70	153	227	273	315
150,000	160,000	75	165	245	294	339
160,000	170,000	80	177	263	315	363
170,000	180,000	86	189	280	336	388
180,000	190,000	91	201	298	357	412
190,000	200,000	97	212	316	378	436
200,000	210,000	102	224	333	400	461
210,000	220,000	107	236	351	420	486
220,000	230,000	113	248	368	442	509
230,000	240,000	118	260	386	463	534
240,000	And up	124	272	403	484	558

REV. PROC. 2013-21 TABLE 6
DOLLAR AMOUNTS FOR TRUCKS AND VANS
WITH A LEASE TERM BEGINNING IN CALENDAR YEAR 2013

Fair Market Value of Truck or Van		Tax Year During Lease				
Over	Not Over	1st	2nd	3rd	4th	5th & later
19,000	19,500	1	3	4	5	6
19,500	20,000	2	3	5	6	7
20,000	20,500	2	4	6	7	8
20,500	21,000	2	5	7	8	9
21,000	21,500	2	5	8	9	11
21,500	22,000	3	6	8	10	12
22,000	23,000	3	7	10	11	14
23,000	24,000	4	8	11	14	16
24,000	25,000	4	9	14	16	18
25,000	26,000	5	10	15	18	21
26,000	27,000	5	12	17	20	23
27,000	28,000	6	13	18	23	25
28,000	29,000	6	14	20	25	28
29,000	30,000	7	15	22	27	30
30,000	31,000	7	16	24	29	33
31,000	32,000	8	17	26	31	35
32,000	33,000	8	19	27	33	38
33,000	34,000	9	20	29	35	41
34,000	35,000	10	21	31	37	43
35,000	36,000	10	22	33	39	46
36,000	37,000	11	23	35	41	48
37,000	38,000	11	25	36	43	51
38,000	39,000	12	26	38	45	53
39,000	40,000	12	27	40	48	55
40,000	41,000	13	28	42	49	58

41,000	42,000	13	29	44	52	60
42,000	43,000	14	30	46	54	62
43,000	44,000	14	32	47	56	65
44,000	45,000	15	33	48	59	67
45,000	46,000	15	34	51	60	70
46,000	47,000	16	35	52	63	72
47,000	48,000	17	36	54	65	74
48,000	49,000	17	38	55	67	77
49,000	50,000	18	39	57	69	79
50,000	51,000	18	40	59	71	82
51,000	52,000	19	41	61	73	84
52,000	53,000	19	42	63	75	87
53,000	54,000	20	43	65	77	89
54,000	55,000	20	45	66	80	91
55,000	56,000	21	46	68	81	94
56,000	57,000	21	47	70	84	96
57,000	58,000	22	48	72	86	98
58,000	59,000	22	50	73	88	101
59,000	60,000	23	51	75	90	103
60,000	62,000	24	52	78	93	108
62,000	64,000	25	55	81	97	113
64,000	66,000	26	57	85	101	118
66,000	68,000	27	60	88	106	122
68,000	70,000	28	62	92	110	127
70,000	72,000	29	64	96	114	132
72,000	74,000	30	67	99	118	137
74,000	76,000	31	69	103	122	142
76,000	78,000	32	72	105	127	147
78,000	80,000	34	73	110	131	151
80,000	85,000	35	78	116	138	160
85,000	90,000	38	84	124	149	172
90,000	95,000	41	90	133	160	184
95,000	100,000	44	95	142	171	196
100,000	110,000	48	104	156	186	214
110,000	120,000	53	116	173	207	240
120,000	130,000	58	128	191	228	264
130,000	140,000	64	140	208	249	288
140,000	150,000	69	152	226	270	313
150,000	160,000	75	164	243	292	336
160,000	170,000	80	176	261	312	361
170,000	180,000	85	188	278	334	386
180,000	190,000	91	199	296	355	410
190,000	200,000	96	211	314	376	434
200,000	210,000	101	223	332	397	459
210,000	220,000	107	235	349	418	483
220,000	230,000	112	247	367	439	507
230,000	240,000	118	259	384	460	532
240,000	And up	123	271	401	482	556

Chapter 2   Income—Taxable and Exempt

¶ 1200   Gross Income.

Gross income consists of all income, from all sources, such as compensation for services, business income, interest, rents, dividends and gains from the sale of property. Only items specifically exempt may be excluded.

Gross income also includes illegal gains and income derived from illegal or criminal activities (e.g., from embezzlement, kickbacks, extortion, fraudulent schemes, shareholder misappropriation, and drug dealing). (Reg § 1.61-14(a))[1]

Gross income is the starting point in determining tax liability and is broadly defined. (Code Sec. 61)[2]

¶ 1201   Assignment of income.

The person who earns and is entitled to receive income is taxed on it. He can't avoid tax on it by assigning it to another.[3] But if a taxpayer assigns or transfers income-producing *property* before the income is earned, the assignee will be taxed on the income.[4]

¶ 1202   Income from co-owned property—joint tenancies, etc.

In a tenancy in common (co-owners without survivorship), each co-owner is taxable on that part of the income attributable to his share.[5] Co-owners who are joint tenants (with survivorship) split income from their property according to their ownership interests.[6]

Similarly, any gain (or loss) from sale of jointly-owned property is divided among the co-owners unless the joint ownership was created to save taxes on the sale, in which case the original owner is taxed on the full amount of the gain.[7]

Co-owners who are husband and wife and file joint returns report their combined income, gains and losses from the jointly-owned property. If they file separately, the income, etc., from the property is split equally if they so share it under state law.[8]

¶ 1203   Community property and income.

Federal tax law recognizes the principle of community income in community property states (AZ, CA, ID, LA, NV, NM, TX, WA and WI) or countries, which treats half of community income and expenses as belonging to each spouse.[9] Community income is all the income from community property (including business property) and salaries, etc., for the services of either or both spouses. Income from separate property during marriage is community income only in ID, LA, TX and WI.[10] If one spouse acts as if he's solely entitled to the community income and fails to notify his spouse of the nature and amount of the income before the return due date (with extensions), IRS may deny him any community property benefit. (Code Sec. 66(b))[11]

While IRS has determined that registered domestic partners and those in civil unions aren't married for federal tax purposes, if state law extends full community property treatment to registered domestic partners, each partner must report one-half of the community property on his/her federal income tax return, whether received in the form of compensation

---

1. ¶J-1600 *et seq.*; ¶614.176; TD ¶197,500
2. ¶s J-1000 *et seq.*; ¶614; TD ¶101,000
3. ¶J-8151 *et seq.*; ¶s 614.185, 614.192; TD ¶201,001
4. ¶J-8172 *et seq.*; ¶s 614.192, 1024; TD ¶201,001
5. ¶J-8103; ¶614.202; TD ¶204,003
6. ¶s J-8101, J-8102; ¶614.202; TD ¶204,002

7. ¶J-8107; ¶614.202; TD ¶204,007
8. ¶J-8100 *et seq.*; ¶614.202; TD ¶204,005
9. ¶A-5001; ¶79,006.51; TD ¶573,501
10. ¶A-5008; TD ¶573,506
11. ¶A-5026; ¶664; TD ¶573,512

References beginning with a single letter are to paragraphs in RIA's Federal Tax Coordinator 2d and RIA's Analysis of Federal Taxes: Income. Those beginning with numbers are to paragraphs in RIA's United States Tax Reporter. Those beginning with TD are to paragraphs in RIA's Tax Desk.

for personal services or income from property. Thus, registered domestic partners in CA, NV, and WA, and same-sex spouses in CA must each report half the combined community income earned by the partners. A partner who has income that isn't community income must also report that separate income.[12]

Community property income for a calendar year is taxed to the spouse who earned it if in that year the couple lived apart for the entire year, filed separate returns *and* one or both spouses had earned income no part of which was transferred between them. (Code Sec. 66(a), Code Sec. 66(d)(1))[13]

A divorced individual who resided in a community property state was taxable on amounts he paid from his wages to his ex-spouse as ordered by a state court.[14]

Relief from separate return liability. A spouse who did not file a joint return for the tax year for which he seeks relief and omits from gross income his share of community income (¶1203) is relieved from tax liability on that omitted income if he establishes lack of knowledge or reason to know of the omitted item and, under all the facts and circumstances, it's inequitable to include the omitted item in his gross income ("traditional relief"). (Code Sec. 66(c); Reg § 1.66-4(a)(1))[15]

IRS may grant equitable relief to a separately-filing spouse from liability attributable to a community income item for which relief isn't available under the above provision ("equitable relief"). (Code Sec. 66(c); Reg § 1.66-4(b))

Traditional relief applies only to deficiencies arising out of items of omitted income but equitable relief includes relief for underpayments of tax or any deficiency, including those arising from disallowed deductions or credits. (Reg § 1.66-4(c))

A spouse requesting relief under the above provisions does so by filing Form 8857. (Reg § 1.66-4(j)(1))[16] For joint filers, see ¶4711.

¶ 1204   Claim of right.

Income received without restriction—income the taxpayer has dominion and control over—must be reported in the year received, even if there's a possibility it may have to be repaid in a later year.[17] For deduction in the repayment year, see ¶2860 *et seq.*

¶ 1205   The "tax benefit rule"—recoveries attributable to an earlier year's deduction or credit.

The recovery of an amount deducted or credited in an earlier tax year is included in a taxpayer's income in the current (recovery) year, except to the extent the deduction or credit *didn't* reduce federal income tax (or alternative minimum tax, but not the accumulated earnings or personal holding company "penalty" taxes (Code Sec. 111(d)(1))[18] imposed in the earlier year. (Code Sec. 111(a))[19]

Similarly, if there's a downward price adjustment (e.g., price reduction) during the tax year that affects an amount paid or incurred on which a credit (other than the investment credit or the foreign tax credit) was allowed in an earlier year, a taxpayer's tax for the adjustment year is increased by the amount of credit attributable to the adjustment, to the extent it reduced his tax in the earlier year. (Code Sec. 111(b))[20]

This "tax benefit rule" applies to recoveries of both itemized deductions (i.e., taxes, medical expenses and other items deductible on Form 1040, Schedule A) and non-itemized deductions

---

12. ¶A-5017
13. ¶A-5022; ¶664; TD ¶573,514
14. ¶A-5013; TD ¶573,513
15. ¶A-5029; ¶664; TD ¶573,609
16. ¶A-5034; ¶664; TD ¶573,613

17. ¶J-8001 *et seq.*; ¶4514.069 *et seq.*; TD ¶203,001
18. ¶J-5526, ¶J-5527; ¶1114; TD ¶181,004
19. ¶J-5500 *et seq.*; ¶1114 *et seq.*; TD ¶181,001
20. ¶J-5511; ¶1114.02; TD ¶181,001

(e.g., bad debts). The taxable amount is limited to the itemized deduction amount that reduced the tax in the earlier year. A taxpayer who recovers an amount he deducted in an earlier year as an itemized deduction is taxed on the *lesser* of the amount recovered, or the amount deducted on Schedule A. A taxpayer who wasn't required to itemize deductions in the earlier year is taxed on the *lesser* of his itemized deduction recoveries or the amount by which his itemized deductions exceeded the standard deduction.[21]

> **Illustration:** B's itemized deductions on his Year 1 return were $6,250. The standard deduction B could have claimed for that year was $5,150. In Year 2, B recovers $2,400 of his Year 1 itemized deductions. B must include $1,100 of the recoveries in his Year 2 income, since that's the smaller of his itemized deduction recoveries ($2,400) or the excess of his itemized deductions over the standard deduction ($6,250 – $5,150 = $1,100).[22]

If a taxpayer had negative taxable income for the year the items were deducted, the otherwise includable amount of the recovery is reduced by the negative amount.[23]

The tax benefit rule applies to state income taxes deducted in an earlier year where there's a refund or credit of taxes paid or the cancellation of taxes accrued.[24]

The increase of a carryover that hasn't expired as of the start of the tax year of the recovery (deduction) or adjustment (credit item) is treated as a reduction of tax imposed. (Code Sec. 111(c))[25]

The tax rates for the recovery (or adjustment) year are used to compute the tax on the portion that isn't excludible.[26] A recovery of amounts, e.g., bad debts, deducted in more than one tax year must be allocated pro rata between those years. (Reg § 1.111-1(a)(3))[27]

To claim any part of a recovery is tax-free, attach a schedule to the return showing the right to the exclusion. (Reg § 1.111-1(b)(1))[28]

¶ 1206 Miscellaneous taxable and exempt income.

Here are selected items not covered elsewhere in this Handbook, followed by whether they are includable in income (Taxable) or not (Excludable):

. . . Alaska Permanent Fund Dividend. Taxable.[29]

. . . Alcohol fuel credit. Taxable. (Code Sec. 87)[30]

. . . Car pool expenses reimbursed by fellow members. Excludable, unless received as part of a trade or business of transporting workers.[31] For exclusion as a qualified transportation fringe benefit, see ¶1247.

. . . Electronic health record incentive payments to health care professionals and hospitals for using patients electronic health records. Taxable.[32]

. . . Elderly in-home care payments by a state agency to caregiver to help elderly live at home instead of nursing home. Excludable, under so-called "general welfare exclusion". [33]

. . . Employer-provided death benefits of specified victims of terrorism and astronauts who die in the line of duty. Excludable. (Code Sec. 101(i)(1))[34]

. . . Energy conservation subsidies provided (directly or indirectly) by a public utility to customers for buying or installing "energy conservation measures" for dwelling units. Excludable. (Code Sec. 136)[35]

---

21. ¶J-5512; ¶1114.02; TD ¶181,020
22. ¶J-5512; ¶1114.02; TD ¶181,020
23. ¶J-5512; TD ¶181,020
24. ¶J-5701 *et seq.*; ¶1114; TD ¶183,001
25. ¶J-5524; ¶1114; TD ¶181,008
26. ¶J-5530; ¶1114.02; TD ¶181,030
27. ¶J-5603; ¶1114.02; TD ¶181,017
28. ¶J-5528; TD ¶181,003

29. ¶J-1493
30. ¶L-17505; ¶874
31. ¶J-1398; TD ¶196,003
32. ¶J-1430; TD ¶196,003
33. ¶J-1480A; TD ¶198,201
34. ¶C-9674; ¶1014.10; TD ¶579,624
35. ¶J-1401 *et seq.*; ¶1364; TD ¶198,510

. . . Executor's or administrator's fees or commissions that are waived. Excludable, if executor, etc., files a formal waiver within six months after appointment, or if his conduct amounts to an implied waiver.[36]

. . . Foster care payments by state or licensed/certified placement agency to individual foster care provider for caring for qualified foster individual (child or adult) in care provider's home (where provider resides). Excludable, if payments are not for the care of more than five individuals age 19 or older. "Difficulty-of-care payments." Excludable, if for ten or fewer individuals under age 19, and for five or fewer individuals age 19 or older. (Code Sec. 131)[37]

. . . Frequent flyer miles earned or received in connection with business travel. Excludable.[38]

. . . Grants to homeowners under a city program to preserve old neighborhoods. Taxable.[39]

. . . 25% of qualifying gain from conservation sales of qualifying mineral or geothermal interests. Excludable. (TRHCA § 403(c)(1)(Div. C, Title IV))[40]

. . . Insurance reimbursement for living expenses incurred due to the loss of use of (or government's denial of access to) principal residence (owned or rented) resulting from a fire, storm or other casualty. Excludable, to extent it covers additional living expenses (but balance of reimbursement is taxable). (Code Sec. 123; Reg § 1.123-1)[41]

. . . Use and occupancy insurance reimbursements for loss of profits if business is suspended. Taxable.[42]

. . . Leave donated and deposited in an employer-sponsored leave bank under a major disaster leave-sharing plan. Excludable, if plan treats payments made by the employer to leave recipients as wages.[43]

. . . Leave received under employer-sponsored leave-sharing plan which allows employees with a medical emergency to receive leave that other employees surrender or deposit into a leave bank. Taxable, as compensation.[44]

. . . Medical loss ratio rebate (whether received in cash or as a premium reduction). Excludable, if recipient didn't deduct premiums (either as an itemized or self-employed health insurance deduction). Taxable, if deducted, to extent of any tax benefit from the deduction.

. . . Medicare (Part A, Part B and Part D coverage gap ("donut hole") rebate). Excludable (except for Part B amounts attributable to medical deductions taken in an earlier year).[45]

. . . Mortgage assistance payments by a federal agency to a mortgagee on mortgagor's behalf, e.g., Pay-for-Performance Success Payments that reduce principal balance of taxpayer's home mortgage under Home Affordable Modification Program. Excludable, unless *not* made for the general welfare (e.g., interest reduction payments to mortgagee).[46]

. . . Property tax rebates. Taxable, to extent they exceed the property tax paid. Rebates received after the year of payment are subject to the tax benefit rule, see ¶1205. Rebates received in the year of payment reduce the amount of tax paid for that year. Where the tax was paid over two years, the rebate is apportioned over the two years.[47] However, state property tax credits are treated as a reduction in a taxpayer's property tax liability for the year the credit is claimed or for the year the credit is carried forward to.

. . . Rate reduction or nonrefundable credit provided by utility to customer for participation in energy conservation program. Excludable.[48]

. . . Rebates of part of purchase price to retail customers. Excludable, as an adjustment to the purchase price of acquiring the property.[49]

---

36. ¶J-1419; ¶4514.042; TD ¶198,511
37. ¶J-1500 *et seq.*; ¶s 1314.01, 1314.02; TD ¶196,501
38. ¶J-1393; TD ¶134,600
39. ¶J-1480
40. ¶I-8851; TD ¶229,901
41. ¶J-1311 *et seq.*; ¶1234; TD ¶195,501
42. ¶J-5830; ¶614.167; TD ¶182,019

43. ¶H-1013.1
44. ¶H-1013; TD ¶198,521
45. ¶J-1307; TD ¶194,506
46. ¶J-1489
47. ¶J-1394.1
48. ¶J-1431; TD ¶198,522
49. ¶J-1391; TD ¶196,005

. . . Relocation payments and similar government subsidies for moving expenses and actual direct losses of property because of displacement from personal residences, as a result of urban renewal projects. Excludable, to extent payments are made by government to compensate for (and are actually so used for) these expenses.[50] Taxable, to extent payments are made by nongovernmental landlords as part of co-op or condo conversion.[1]

. . . Restitution payments to human trafficking victims mandatorily awarded under 18 U.S.C. §1593. Excludable.[2]

. . . Security deposits received. If purpose is to guarantee performance of an obligation, not taxable where repayment is required if the obligation is performed. Taxable to the recipient when he becomes entitled to retain them because of a default.[3] If purpose is to protect taxpayer's interest in property and not to secure payment. Excludable.[4]

. . . Smart Grid Investment Grant made to a corporation. Excludable; corporation must properly reduce the basis of its property.[5]

. . . Subsidies received from Social Security by sponsors of qualified retiree prescription drug plans under the Medicare Prescription Drug Act of 2003 for certain covered retiree drug costs. Excludable.[6]

. . . Whistleblower's settlement under a Federal False Claims Act action against his former employer. Taxable.[7]

¶ 1207 Exclusion for qualified disaster relief or mitigation payments.

A qualified disaster relief payment isn't included in gross income. It also isn't earnings for self-employment tax purposes or wages for employment tax purposes. (Code Sec. 139) The exclusion doesn't apply to amounts received for the sale or disposition of property, but the involuntary conversion rules may apply to such amounts, see ¶2430.[8]

A qualified disaster relief payment is any amount (to the extent not compensated by insurance or otherwise) paid to or for the benefit of an individual:

(1) to reimburse or pay reasonable and necessary personal, family, living, or funeral expenses incurred as a result of a qualified disaster (defined below),

(2) to reimburse or pay reasonable and necessary expenses incurred to repair or rehabilitate a personal residence (including a rented residence) or repair or replace its contents to the extent that the need for the work results from a qualified disaster,

(3) by a person who provides or sells transportation as a common carrier because of the death or personal physical injuries arising from a qualified disaster, or

(4) if the amount is paid by a federal, state, or local government, or an agency or instrumentality of those governments, in connection with a qualified disaster in order to promote the general welfare (but not if payments are made to businesses or for income replacement or unemployment compensation).

A qualified disaster is a disaster which results from a terroristic or military action, a Federally declared disaster, a disaster resulting from an accident involving a common carrier, or from any other event, that is determined by IRS to be of a catastrophic nature, or for payments by a federal, state, or local government, or an agency or instrumentality of those governments, a disaster that is determined by the appropriate governmental authority (as determined by IRS) to warrant assistance from the governmental authority.[9]

Qualified disaster mitigation payments are excluded from gross income. (Code Sec. 139(g))

---

50. ¶J-1492; ¶614.006
1. ¶J-1492; TD ¶198,521
2. ¶J-1475A; TD ¶146,050A
3. ¶J-1371; ¶4514.166; TD ¶121,008
4. ¶G-2490; ¶4514.166; TD ¶121,008

5. ¶F-1914.1
6. ¶J-1480.2; ¶139A4
7. ¶J-1485.3; TD ¶198,210
8. ¶J-1296; ¶1394; TD ¶193,600
9. ¶J-1290 et seq.; TD ¶193,601

These include payments under the Flood Mitigation Assistance Program, Pre-Disaster Mitigation Program, and Hazard Mitigation Grant Program. The exclusion does not apply to amounts received for the sale or disposition of property, but the involuntary conversion rules may apply to such amounts, see ¶2430.[10]

¶ 1208 Compensation Income. ▀▀▀▀▀▀▀▀▀▀▀▀

All forms of compensation received for personal services are included in gross income.

¶ 1209 Compensation includible in gross income.

Gross income includes compensation for services including: wages, salaries, fees, tips (¶1211), salesperson's commissions (including on sales to self or family), percentage of profits paid as compensation, commissions on insurance premiums, bonuses (including Christmas bonuses, see ¶1212), termination or severance pay, golden parachute payments (excess golden parachute payments subject the recipient to a 20% excise tax (Code Sec. 4999(a)),[11] rewards, jury duty fees (Code Sec. 61(a)(1); Reg § 1.61-2(a)(1)),[12] and fringe benefits not excluded by statute (see ¶1228 *et seq.*). (Code Sec. 61(a)(1)) Vacation pay also is taxable.[13]

Pension or retirement allowances to employees (reported to recipients on Form 1099-R) generally are taxable to the recipient, see ¶4338 *et seq.* (Reg § 1.61-11(a))[14] For rules for certain military pensions, see ¶1284.

Amounts withheld from an employee's pay by his employer for income and social security taxes, savings bonds, union dues, etc., represent compensation constructively received by the employee and must be included in his income for the year in which withheld.[15] An employee is taxed on compensation even if his employer can't deduct all or part of the amount because it's "unreasonable." (¶1517). (Reg § 1.162-8)[16]

¶ 1210 Reporting compensation and self-employment income.

The amount of wages, salaries, tips, etc., that's includible in income (¶1209), which should be shown on a Form W-2 issued by the employer, is reported on Form 1040.[17]

Income (or loss) subject to self-employment tax (¶3140) from a business operated, or a profession practiced, as a sole proprietor is reported on Form 1040, Schedule C or C-EZ. If an individual operates more than one business as a sole proprietor, a separate Schedule C or C-EZ must be prepared for each business. An individual can't report his income on Schedule C or C-EZ if he earns it as an "employee." [18] For farm income, see ¶4501.

¶ 1211 Tips and similar payments.

Tips and similar payments for special services are income. (Reg § 1.61-2(a)(1)) A tip or gratuity is a payment made by a customer to one who serves him where the customer is entirely free to determine the amount of the payment, or to not make any payment. But a waiter may deduct the portion of tips that he turns over to assistants.[19] A tipped employee must maintain sufficient evidence to establish the amount of tip income he receives in a tax year. (Reg § 31.6053-4(a))[20] Service charges imposed by the employer on his customers (mandatory add-ons to food and drink bills) in lieu of tipping are part of the employee's wages (rather than a tip subject to tip reporting requirements).[21]

---

10. ¶J-1296; ¶1394; TD ¶193,600
11. ¶H-3003; ¶49,994; TD ¶132,504
12. ¶H-1001 *et seq.*; ¶614.007; TD ¶111,002
13. ¶s H-1001, H-1012; TD ¶130,505
14. ¶H-3245; ¶s 614.007, 4014; TD ¶141,000
15. ¶H-2152; TD ¶141,000

16. ¶H-1021; ¶614.014; TD ¶130,513
17. ¶H-1001.1; TD ¶102,002
18. ¶H-1001.1; TD ¶102,002
19. ¶s H-1009, H-4342; TD ¶131,006
20. ¶H-4343; ¶60,534; TD ¶131,003
21. ¶H-4341; ¶60,534; TD ¶532,009

For FICA purposes, IRS has extended the time for employers to comply with the proper treatment of service charges as wages to after Dec. 31, 2013.[22]

¶ 1212   Compensation distinguished from gift.

Although gifts are generally excluded from the recipient's gross income (¶1370), transfer by or for an employer to or for the benefit of an employee can't be excluded as a gift. (Code Sec. 102(c)(1)) Extraordinary transfers to the natural objects of an employer's bounty (e.g., an employee who is the employer's son) aren't transfers to or for the benefit of the employee if he can show the transfer wasn't made in recognition of his employment.[23] For de minimis fringe benefits, see ¶1246.

If, as a means of promoting goodwill, an employer makes a general distribution to employees of hams, turkeys or other merchandise of nominal value at Christmas or a comparable holiday, the value of the gifts isn't included in the employees' income. But if an employer distributes cash, gift certificates or similar items of readily convertible cash value, the value of the gifts is additional wages or salary, *regardless* of the value.[24]

¶ 1213   Below-market interest rate loans from employer.

An employee or independent contractor who receives a below-market (¶1306) compensation-related loan (except certain de minimis loans), recognizes compensation income equal to:

. . . on a compensation-related demand loan, the forgone interest (interest at the applicable federal rate (¶1116) over actual interest payable), and

. . . on any other compensation-related loan, the excess of the amount borrowed over the present value of all payments required to be made under the terms of the loan. (Code Sec. 7872(a)(1), Code Sec. 7872(b)(1))[25]

Certain employee-relocation loans are exempt from these rules. (Reg § 1.7872-5T(b)(6))[26]

¶ 1214   Vacation trips for salespersons; other noncash compensation.

If services rendered by the taxpayer are paid for in property or services rather than money, the fair market value (FMV) of the property or services must be included in income. For example, if a vacation trip is awarded to salespersons as a prize, the FMV of the trip is income. Where a price has been specified for the services being rendered, that price is considered the FMV of the property or services received if there's no evidence showing a different value. (Code Sec. 83; Reg § 1.61-2(d))[27]

¶ 1215   Notes receivable as compensation.

Notes and other evidences of indebtedness received in payment for services or in settlement of a claim for compensation are taxable as compensation in the amount of their fair market value when received. When a taxpayer receives as compensation a non-interest-bearing note regarded as good for its face value at maturity, he treats as income its fair discounted value computed at the prevailing rate. As note payments are received, he includes in income that portion of each payment representing the proportionate part of the discount originally taken on the entire note. (Reg § 1.61-2(d)(4))[28]

---

22. ¶H-4658; ¶60,534; TD ¶532,009
23. ¶H-1027.1 *et seq.*; ¶614.016, ¶1024; TD ¶132,010
24. ¶H-1033; ¶1324.06; TD ¶132,002
25. ¶s H-2002, H-2004; ¶78,724.14; TD ¶136,503

26. ¶H-2014; ¶78,724.20; TD ¶136,512
27. ¶H-2500 *et seq.*; ¶s 614.007, 614.027; TD ¶136,001
28. ¶H-2513; ¶614.034; TD ¶136,003

¶ 1216   Bargain purchase from employer.

If property, including stock, is transferred by an employer to an employee for less than its fair market value, the difference is compensation. (Code Sec. 83(a); Reg § 1.83-1(a))[29] For stock options, see ¶1219 *et seq.*

If an employee pays with a recourse note for stock acquired from his employer under a nonqualified stock option, and the employer later reduces the amount due on the note, the debt reduction is treated as compensation income.[30]

¶ 1217   Restricted stock or other property—Section 83 rules.

A person receiving a beneficial interest in stock or other property for his services has compensation income equal to the value of that property at the time of receipt. But if his interest in the property is subject to substantial risk of forfeiture (is "restricted") and can't be transferred free of that risk, then income is deferred until the interest in the property either: (1) is no longer subject to that risk, *or* (2) becomes transferable free of the risk, whichever occurs earlier. (Code Sec. 83)[31] For election not to defer income, see ¶1218.

But the employee (or other owner of the property) has income if he sells or disposes of the property before (1) or (2), above. (Code Sec. 83(a))[32]

The amount included in income (in the year in which (1) or (2) occurs) is the excess of: the fair market value of the property in that year (figured without regard to restrictions other than those that by their terms will never lapse), over the amount, if any, paid for the property. (Code Sec. 83(a))[33]

A substantial risk of forfeiture exists if a person's rights to full enjoyment of the property are conditioned, directly or indirectly, upon (a) the future performance (or refraining from performance) of substantial services by any individual, or (b) the occurrence of a condition related to the transfer's purpose, and the possibility of forfeiture is substantial if such condition isn't satisfied. (Code Sec. 83(c)(1); Reg § 1.83-3(c)(1)) Examples: a requirement that the property be returned to the employer if total earnings don't increase (Reg § 1.83-3(c)(2)),[34] and SEC restrictions, such as the "short swing" rule (insider must pay over profits if stock is sold within six months of receipt). (Code Sec. 83(c)(3))[35] The six-month period under the short swing rule is measured from the date a nonstatutory option to acquire the stock is granted, and not from the date of exercise.[36]

Under proposed regs, on which taxpayers may rely for property transferred after May 30, 2012, a substantial risk of forfeiture can only be established through (i) a service condition (see (a), above); or (ii) taking into account the likelihood that the forfeiture event will occur and be enforced, a condition related to the purpose of the transfer (see (b), above). Except as specifically provided in Code Sec. 83(c)(3) and its regs, transfer restrictions wouldn't create a substantial risk of forfeiture (including ones which carry the potential for forfeiture or disgorgement of some or all of the property, or other penalties). (Prop Reg. § 1.83-3(c)(1), ["Taxpayers may rely"])[37]

---

29. ¶H-2509; ¶614.030; TD ¶136,005
30. ¶H-2535
31. ¶H-2500, ¶H-2517 *et seq.*; ¶834; *et seq.*: TD ¶136,006
32. ¶H-2547 *et seq.*; ¶834.01; TD ¶136,006
33. ¶H-2532 *et seq.*; ¶834.01; TD ¶136,007

34. ¶H-2521; ¶834.02; TD ¶135,014
35. ¶H-2530, ¶H-2531; ¶834.02; TD ¶135,018
36. ¶H-2530
37. ¶H-2521; ¶834.02; TD ¶135,014

¶ 1218   Election not to defer income from restricted stock or other property.

An employee or other person who receives restricted stock or other property (¶1217) may elect to recognize the income immediately instead of deferring it. (Code Sec. 83(b)(1))[38]

The amount of compensation income included in the year the property is received is the excess of: the fair market value of the property at receipt (without regard to restrictions other than those that by their terms will never lapse), over the amount, if any, paid for the property. (Code Sec. 83(b)(1))[39]

recommendation: Elect if the income taxed at grant would be negligible. This defers tax on any post-grant appreciation until sale, makes it eligible for capital gain rates, and may eliminate additional income tax completely if the property is held until death.

If the stock or other property is forfeited after the election is made, the employee can't get a deduction or refund of tax previously paid on income reported. (Code Sec. 83(b)(1))[40] The employee will have capital loss at the time of forfeiture. (Reg § 1.83-2(a))[41]

Elect within 30 days after the property is transferred to the employee. (Code Sec. 83(b)(2)) To elect, file a statement (specified in the regs) with the IRS office where the person who performs the services files his return. Attach a copy of the statement to the return for the year the property was transferred. (Reg § 1.83-2(c))[42]

IRS will consent to a revocation if the election was filed under a mistake of fact in the underlying transaction and the revocation is requested within 60 days of discovering the mistake of fact. Request to revoke the election within the 30-day period for making the election will generally be granted.[43]

¶ 1219   Nonstatutory stock options.

An option—other than an option under an employee stock purchase plan (see ¶1220) or an incentive stock option (ISO, see ¶1221)—which is granted in connection with the performance of services, to buy stock at a bargain, results in compensation income to the employee (or independent contractor) grantee. (Code Sec. 83) If the option has a readily ascertainable fair market value (FMV) at grant, it's subject to the restricted property rules of Code Sec. 83 (¶1217 *et seq.*) when the option is granted. (Code Sec. 83; Reg § 1.83-7(a))[44]

An option "ordinarily" has a readily ascertainable FMV only if it (or a substantially identical option) is actively traded on an established market. If not so traded, it has value only if certain conditions specified in the regs exist. (Reg § 1.83-7(b))[45]

If the option doesn't have a readily ascertainable FMV when granted, the employee doesn't realize compensation until the optioned property is transferred at exercise. The amount of compensation is the FMV of the property at transfer less any amount paid for the property. (Reg § 1.83-7(a))[46] (For the employer's compensation deduction, see ¶1525.)

The above treatment for nonstatutory options without a readily ascertainable FMV doesn't apply where the option is transferred before exercise to a "related person." (Reg § 1.83-7(a))[47]

Under an exception, the exercise of an option is treated as the grant of another option, instead of a transfer of shares, where the amount paid for the exercise is a debt secured by the shares on which there is no personal liability. (Reg § 1.83-3(a)(2)) However, this exception doesn't apply simply because options are exercised through a margin loan, and income will be

38. ¶H-2540; ¶834.03; TD ¶135,016
39. ¶H-2541; ¶834.03; TD ¶135,016
40. ¶M-3503; ¶834.03; TD ¶135,016
41. ¶I-1020; ¶834.03; TD ¶135,016
42. ¶H-2542 *et seq.*; ¶834.03; TD ¶135,016

43. ¶H-2545
44. ¶s H-2853, H-2857; ¶s 834.07, 4214.03; TD ¶135,202
45. ¶H-2872; ¶834.07; TD ¶135,203
46. ¶H-2861; ¶834.07; TD ¶135,206
47. ¶H-2864.1; ¶834.07; TD ¶135,207

realized on the exercise of options without a readily ascertainable FMV.[48]

¶ 1220 Employee stock purchase plan (ESPP) options.

These are options issued to employees under an employer plan to buy stock in the employer. The employee pays no tax on the option or the stock until he disposes of the stock. If the option price at least equals the stock's fair market value (FMV) at grant, gain is capital gain. But gain is ordinary compensation income (to the extent of the spread between option price and FMV of stock when option is exercised) if the stock is sold within two years after the option was granted or within one year after its exercise. (Code Sec. 423(a), Code Sec. 423(c); Reg § 1.423-1, Reg § 1.423-2[49]

If the option price is less than 100% (but at least 85%) of the stock's FMV at grant, and the above holding period is met, the amount treated as ordinary income (rather than capital gain) is the *lesser* of: (1) the FMV of the stock when the option was granted, minus the option price, or (2) the excess of the FMV at the time of disposition or optionee's death over the amount paid for the share under the option. (Code Sec. 423(c); Reg § 1.423-2(k))[50]

An executive branch federal employee (or spouse or dependent child) who acquired stock through the exercise of an ESPP option (or ISO, see ¶1221) and sells the stock in order to comply with Code Sec. 1043 federal conflict-of-interest requirements is deemed to satisfy the Code Sec. 423(a)(1) (or Code Sec. 422(a)(1)) holding period requirement. (Code Sec. 421(d))

The plan must be nondiscriminatory, i.e., available to all employees (with certain exceptions). (Code Sec. 423(b)(4))[1]

¶ 1221 Incentive stock options (ISOs).

An ISO is granted to an employee by an employer corporation (or its parent or sub) to buy stock or ownership interests in one of those corporations (a term that takes in S corporations, foreign corporations, and limited liability companies treated as corporations for federal tax purposes). (Reg § 1.421-1(d)(3), Reg § 1.421-1(i)(1)) There are no regular income tax consequences when an ISO is granted or exercised; the employee has capital gain when the stock is sold at a gain. (Code Sec. 421(a))[2] To qualify, an ISO must meet various requirements. (Code Sec. 422(b))[3]

Stock acquired through the exercise of an ISO generally can't be disposed of within two years after the option is granted or one year after the stock is transferred to the employee. (Code Sec. 422(a)(1)) Also, for the entire time from the date an ISO is granted until three months (one year in case of total and permanent disability) before its exercise, the option holder must be an employee of the option grantor (or its parent or sub or certain successor corporations). (Code Sec. 422(a)(2), Code Sec. 422(c)(6))[4] For executive branch federal employee holding period rules, see ¶1220.

If there is a disqualifying disposition of a share of stock, Code Sec. 421 does not apply to the transfer of the share. Instead, the exercise of the option is governed by Code Sec. 83 and its regs. Thus, in the tax year in which the disqualifying disposition occurs, the individual recognizes compensation income (and gets a basis increase) equal to the FMV of the stock on the date the stock is transferred less the exercise price (determined without reduction for any brokerage fees or other disposition costs). (Reg § 1.421-2(b)) If the disqualifying disposition would trigger an allowable loss (e.g., not a sale to a related taxpayer), then the amount includible in the employee's income (and deductible by the employer, see ¶1525) as a result of

48. ¶H-2508.1; TD ¶135,012
49. ¶H-2952 *et seq.*; ¶4234.01; TD ¶136,101
50. ¶H-2953; ¶4234.01; TD ¶136,101
1. ¶H-2972; ¶4234.02; TD ¶136,103

2. ¶H-2750; ¶4224.01; TD ¶136,001
3. ¶H-2767; ¶4224.02; TD ¶136,004
4. ¶H-2795 *et seq.*; ¶4224.01; TD ¶136,006

that disqualifying disposition can't be more than the amount realized on the sale, minus the employee's adjusted basis in the stock. (Code Sec. 422(c)(2); Reg § 1.422-1(b)(2)(i))[5]

caution: For alternative minimum tax treatment, see ¶3209.

¶ 1222　Sale or cancellation of employment contract.

Proceeds from an employee's sale of rights under an employment contract to be performed are ordinary income. The same is true of amounts received from an employer in cancellation of an employment contract.[6]

¶ 1223　Members of Armed Forces.

The pay of Armed Forces members is taxable (Reg § 1.61-2(a)(1)), with exceptions:[7]

Gross income doesn't include any "qualified military benefit," which is any allowance or in-kind benefit (other than personal use of an automobile) received by a member or former member of the uniformed services of the U.S., or his dependent, and which was excludable from gross income on Sept. 9, '86 under any provision of law, reg or administrative practice (other than the Code) in effect on that date. (Code Sec. 134(b)) It includes any bonus payment made by a state or political subdivision to any member or former member of the U.S. uniformed services, or his dependent, because of his service in a combat zone. (Code Sec. 134(b)(6)) Excludable allowances include (within certain limitations): veteran's benefits (¶1224), medical benefits, disability benefits, dependent care assistance program benefits, professional education, moving and storage, group-term life insurance, survivor and retirement protection plan premiums, subsistence, uniform, housing, overseas cost-of-living, evacuation, family separation allowances, death gratuities, interment allowance, various travel allowances and dependent benefits.[8] Specifically, dislocation allowances, temporary lodging allowances and expenses and move-in housing allowances provided in connection with permanent changes of station are excludible from income. (Reg § 1.61-2(b)(2))[9] For treatment of retirement pay, see ¶1284. A "qualified military base realignment and closure" fringe benefit is excluded and isn't subject to FICA. This benefit is a payment (subject to a maximum allowance) received under the Homeowner's Assistance Program (HAP) (as in effect on 2/17/2009, for payments after that date). (Code Sec. 132(a)(8))[10]

The recipient of a tax-free military housing allowance isn't thereby prevented from deducting mortgage interest or real estate taxes on a personal residence. (Code Sec. 265(a)(6)(A))[11]

The Code also excludes combat-zone compensation (limited, for commissioned officers, to the maximum enlisted amount). (Code Sec. 112; Reg § 1.112-1) Areas designated as combat zones include: Pakistan; Tajikistan; Jordan; Uzbekistan; Kyrgyzstan; the Afghanistan area; Serbia/Montenegro; Albania; the Adriatic Sea; the Ionian Sea (north of the 39th parallel); the Persian Gulf area; the Red Sea; the Gulf of Oman; parts of the Arabian Sea; the Gulf of Aden; and the total land areas of Iraq, Kuwait, Saudi Arabia, Oman, Bahrain, Qatar, and the United Arab Emirates.[12]

For various deadline extensions for a member of the Armed Forces serving in a designated "combat zone," see ¶4719. For tax relief for military and civilian employees of the U.S. dying in combat or terrorist attacks, see ¶4715.

---

5. ¶H-2799; ¶4224.01; TD ¶136,008
6. ¶H-1048 *et seq.*; TD ¶182,009
7. ¶H-3101; ¶614.040; TD ¶138,001
8. ¶H-3102; ¶1344; TD ¶138,002

9. ¶H-3103; TD ¶138,003
10. ¶H-3104; ¶1324.11; TD ¶138,003.5
11. ¶K-9009; ¶2654
12. ¶H-3106 *et seq.*; ¶1124.01; TD ¶138,005

¶ 1224   VA and state benefits to veterans.

Benefits under any law, regulation, or practice in effect on Sept. 9, '86 and administered by the Department of Veterans' Affairs are excludable from the recipient's gross income, (Code Sec. 140(a)(3)) including interest earned on dividends left on deposit with the VA. It also includes amounts received under a VA administered work therapy program.[13] State bonuses to veterans for service rendered to the U.S. are also exempt.[14]

¶ 1225   Government employees' compensation.

Federal, state and municipal employees, including federal judges, are taxable on their salary, wages and other compensation the same as other employees.[15] Payments under the Civil Service Retirement System are taxed like annuities, see ¶1354 *et seq.*[16] For tax relief for military and civilian employees of the U.S. dying in combat or terrorist attacks, see ¶4715.

¶ 1226   Members of clergy.

Members of the clergy are taxable on the salaries and fees they receive, and on any offerings they receive for marriages, funerals, masses, etc., *but not* on offerings made to the religious institution. (Reg § 1.61-2(a))[17]

A current or retired member of the clergy who is a "minister of the gospel" [18] can exclude from gross income:

. . . the rental value of a home (parsonage allowance), including utilities, furnished to him as part of his compensation; (Code Sec. 107(1); Reg § 1.107-1(a)) or

. . . the rental allowance (parsonage allowance) paid to him as compensation, to the extent it's used in the year received to rent or provide a home(s) and to the extent it does not exceed the fair rental value of the home, including furnishings and appurtenances such as a garage, plus the cost of utilities. (Code Sec. 107(2)) The employer church or organization must designate the payment as a rental allowance before the payment is made. (Reg § 1.107-1(b))[19]

The rental allowance exclusion doesn't prevent a minister from deducting mortgage interest or real estate taxes on a personal residence. (Code Sec. 265(a)(6)(B))[20]

¶ 1227   Compensation of minors.

The income of a minor from compensation earned by him or received in respect of his services is income to him, even if received by the parent. (Code Sec. 73(a))[21]

observation: If the child is subject to the kiddie tax rules, the rate of tax on his unearned income may depend on the parent's tax rate, see ¶3135.

---

13. ¶H-3128; ¶614.041; TD ¶138,029
14. ¶H-3129; TD ¶138,030
15. ¶H-3130; ¶614.036; TD ¶138,031
16. ¶J-5052; ¶724.26; TD ¶141,006
17. ¶H-3151; ¶614.007; TD ¶138,501

18. ¶H-3163; ¶1074.02; TD ¶138,511
19. ¶H-3153 *et seq.*; ¶1074; TD ¶138,502 *et seq.*
20. ¶H-3160; ¶s 1074.03, 2654; TD ¶138,505
21. ¶H-3180; ¶734.01; TD ¶836,009

¶ 1228 Fringe Benefits. ▮▮▮▮▮▮▮▮▮▮▮▮▮▮▮▮▮▮▮▮

Fringe benefits received by an employee are taxable unless specifically excluded.

¶ 1229 Taxation of fringe benefits.

A fringe benefit provided to any person in connection with the performance of services is treated as compensation for those services. (Reg § 1.61-21(a)(3))[22] Unless it's specifically excluded (¶1242), the benefit is includible in the gross income of the person performing the services, even if it's furnished to someone else. (Code Sec. 61(a)(1); Reg § 1.61-21(a)(4))[23]

¶ 1230 Valuation of taxable fringe benefits—general rule.

An employee who is taxed on a fringe benefit (¶1229) must include in gross income the fair market value (FMV) of the benefit minus: (1) any payment for the benefit, and (2) any amount specifically excluded by a Code provision. (Reg § 1.61-21(b)(1))[24] The FMV of a fringe benefit generally is the amount that an individual would have to pay for the particular benefit in an arm's-length transaction. (Reg § 1.61-21(b)(2))[25]

Unless a special valuation rule (¶1232) applies, an employer-provided vehicle is valued at the comparable lease cost (¶1233) (Reg § 1.61-21(b)(4)),[26] and flights on an employer-provided aircraft at comparable charter or lease cost. (Reg § 1.61-21(b)(6), Reg § 1.61-21(b)(7))[27]

Chauffeur services are valued separately from vehicle availability, at comparable arm's-length transaction costs or by reference to the chauffeur's compensation (including any non-taxable lodging, see ¶1267). (Reg § 1.61-21(b)(5))[28]

¶ 1231 Transportation furnished because of unsafe conditions.

Transportation or reimbursement for such (e.g., cab fare) furnished by an employer under a written policy solely because of unsafe conditions for employee commuting is valued at $1.50 per one-way commute (i.e., from home to work, or work to home) for each qualifying employee. (Reg § 1.61-21(k)(3))[29]

¶ 1232 Special valuation rules for autos, other vehicles and airflights.

Special valuation rules may be used under certain circumstances for certain commonly provided fringe benefits (e.g., automobiles, noncommercial flights, commuting). (Reg § 1.61-21(b), Reg § 1.61-21(c)(1), Reg § 1.61-21(c)(3))[30] Where the special rules aren't used, either by choice or because they aren't permitted, or where they're improperly applied, the value of the fringe benefit must be determined under the general valuation principles at ¶1230. (Reg § 1.61-21(c)(5))[31]

An employee can't use a special valuation rule to value a fringe benefit unless the employer uses the same rule to value it. (Reg § 1.61-21(c)(2))[32]

¶ 1233 Annual lease value method for automobiles—use of IRS table.

To compute an auto's annual lease value, first determine fair market value (FMV) as of the first date it is made available to *any* employee for personal use. Under safe harbor rules, where the auto is bought at arm's length by the employer, the FMV is the cost, including

22. ¶H-1051; ¶614.027; TD ¶134,002
23. ¶H-1051, ¶H-1053; ¶614.027; TD ¶134,001; TD ¶134,002
24. ¶H-1055; ¶614.027; TD ¶134,003
25. ¶H-1056; ¶614.027; TD ¶134,003
26. ¶H-2232; ¶614.027; TD ¶134,502
27. ¶H-2302 *et seq.*; ¶614.027; TD ¶134,570

28. ¶H-2289 *et seq.*; ¶614.027
29. ¶H-2201 *et seq.*; TD ¶134,606
30. ¶H-1056, *et seq.*, ¶H-2200 *et seq.*, ¶H-2300 *et seq.*; ¶614.027; TD ¶134,500
31. ¶H-1057; ¶614.027; TD ¶134,502
32. ¶H-1060; ¶614.027; TD ¶134,555

sales tax, title fees and other purchase expenses. Where leased, it's the suggested retail price less 8%, the retail value as reported in a nationally recognized publication that regularly reports such values (Reg § 1.61-21(d)(5)), or the manufacturer's invoice price plus 4%.[33] Then, find the dollar range in column (1) of the table below that includes the auto's FMV. The corresponding amount in column (2) is its annual lease value. (Reg § 1.61-21(d)(2)(iii))

Automobile fair market value (1)	Annual lease value (2)	Automobile fair market value (1)	Annual lease value (2)
$0 to 999	$600	22,000 to 22,999	6,100
1,000 to 1,999	850	23,000 to 23,999	6,350
2,000 to 2,999	1,100	24,000 to 24,999	6,600
3,000 to 3,999	1,350	25,000 to 25,999	6,850
4,000 to 4,999	1,600	26,000 to 27,999	7,250
5,000 to 5,999	1,850	28,000 to 29,999	7,750
6,000 to 6,999	2,100	30,000 to 31,999	8,250
7,000 to 7,999	2,350	32,000 to 33,999	8,750
8,000 to 8,999	2,600	34,000 to 35,999	9,250
9,000 to 9,999	2,850	36,000 to 37,999	9,750
10,000 to 10,999	3,100	38,000 to 39,999	10,250
11,000 to 11,999	3,350	40,000 to 41,999	10,750
12,000 to 12,999	3,600	42,000 to 43,999	11,250
13,000 to 13,999	3,850	44,000 to 45,999	11,750
14,000 to 14,999	4,100	46,000 to 47,999	12,250
15,000 to 15,999	4,350	48,000 to 49,999	12,750
16,000 to 16,999	4,600	50,000 to 51,999	13,250
17,000 to 17,999	4,850	52,000 to 53,999	13,750
18,000 to 18,999	5,100	54,000 to 55,999	14,250
19,000 to 19,999	5,350	56,000 to 57,999	14,750
20,000 to 20,999	5,600	58,000 to 59,999	15,250
21,000 to 21,999	5,850		

For autos with a FMV in excess of $59,999, the annual lease value equals: $(.25 \times$ auto FMV$)$ + $500.[34]

⊗Illustration: On Jan. 1, of Year 1, X Co. provides a car worth $20,500 free to its employee E. None of the fringe benefit exclusions applies. The annual lease value (see chart above) is $5,600. This is the value of E's benefit for Year 1. E must include $5,600 in income.

This method takes into account the value of insuring and maintaining the auto, but not the value of fuel, which if provided in kind can be valued based on all facts and circumstances, or alternatively at $5\frac{1}{2}$¢ per mile for all miles driven (in the U.S., Canada or Mexico) by the employee. (Reg § 1.61-21(d)(3))[35]

The annual lease values computed above are determined on the basis of an assumed four-year lease term (beginning on the first date this method is used and ending on Dec. 31 of the following fourth full calendar year). The annual lease value for each next four-year period is determined on the basis of the FMV on the Jan. 1 after the preceding period, using the lease valuation table. (Reg § 1.61-21(d)(2)(iv))[36]

Subject to certain restrictions, an employer with a fleet of 20 or more autos may determine the annual lease value of each auto in the fleet as if its FMV were equal to the "fleet-average value." (Reg § 1.61-21(d)(5)) For 2013, this method can't be used for autos with a FMV

---

33. ¶H-2240; ¶614.027; TD ¶134,510
34. ¶s H-2238, H-2239; TD ¶134,508

35. ¶H-2253; ¶614.027; TD ¶134,521
36. ¶H-2246; ¶614.027; TD ¶134,516

¶ 1234 Chapter 2 / 2014 RIA FEDERAL TAX HANDBOOK

greater than $21,200 ($22,300 for trucks or vans).[37]

¶ 1234 Prorated annual lease value.

Where an employer-provided auto is continuously available to the employee for periods of 30 or more days, but less than an entire calendar year, the value of the availability of the auto is the prorated annual lease value, computed by multiplying the annual lease value (¶1234) by a fraction: the numerator is the number of days of availability, and the denominator is 365. (Reg § 1.61-21(d)(4))[38]

¶ 1235 Daily lease value.

Where an employer-provided auto is continuously available to the employee for at least one but less than 30 days, the value of the use of the auto is its daily lease value, calculated by multiplying the auto's annual lease value (¶1234) by a fraction: the numerator is four times the number of days of the auto's availability, and the denominator is 365. A 30-day period may be used even if availability is less than 30 days if this produces a lower valuation. (Reg § 1.61-21(d)(4))[39]

¶ 1236 Cents-per-mile valuation method.

Under this method, the value of an employer-provided auto equals the total number of miles the employee drove it for personal purposes in the tax year times the optional standard mileage rate (56.5¢ for 2013), see ¶1560.[40] This method takes into account the value of insuring and maintaining the vehicle, and the value of fuel provided by the employer. If fuel isn't provided, the cents-per-mile rate may be reduced by no more than 5.5¢ per mile. (Reg § 1.61-21(e)(3))[41] For 2013, the cents-per-mile method can't be used if the auto's fair market value, as of the date it's first made available to any employee for personal use, exceeds $16,000 for autos ($17,000 for a truck or van).[42]

¶ 1237 Commuting value method—$1.50 per one-way commute.

Under this method, the value of an employee's use of a vehicle, including an automobile, for commuting purposes only is computed as $1.50 per one-way commute (e.g., from home to work, or work to home). If there's more than one employee who commutes in a single vehicle, the commuting benefit is still $1.50 per one way commute for each employee. (Reg § 1.61-21(f)(3))[43] Various requirements must be satisfied. For example, the employee must be required to commute in the auto for bona-fide noncompensatory business reasons. The method can't be used for "control employees" (certain owner-employees, higher-paid employees, and directors) (Reg § 1.61-21(f)(1)), or to value the commuting use of any chauffeur-driven vehicle, except for the commuting use by the chauffeur. (Reg § 1.61-21(f)(2))[44]

¶ 1238 Employer-provided airflights.

Airflights provided by an employer for an employee's personal purposes are fringe benefits includible in the employee's gross income. (Reg § 1.61-21(a)(1))[45]

Special valuation methods are available to value noncommercial flights on employer-provided aircraft (¶1239 et seq.), and "space available" flights on commercial aircraft (¶1241). Use of a special method is optional. But if an employer uses either special rule, he must

37. ¶H-2260; ¶614.027; TD ¶134,527
38. ¶H-2243; ¶614.027; TD ¶134,513
39. ¶H-2245; ¶614.027; TD ¶134,515
40. ¶H-2268; ¶614.027; TD ¶134,536
41. ¶H-2277 et seq.; ¶614.027; TD ¶134,543

42. ¶H-2272; ¶614.027; TD ¶134,540
43. ¶H-2282; ¶614.027; TD ¶134,549
44. ¶H-2283; ¶614.027; TD ¶134,550
45. ¶H-2301; ¶614.027; TD ¶134,570

84

generally use it to value all flights taken by employees in a calendar year. (Reg § 1.61-21(g)(14)(i), Reg § 1.61-21(h)(5)(i))[46]

If an employee takes a trip on an employer-provided aircraft primarily for his employer's business which includes both personal flights and business flights, the value of the personal flights is a taxable fringe benefit. The value of the benefit equals the excess of the value of all the flights comprising the trip, over the value of the flights the employee would have taken had he travelled only for business. If the employee combines personal and business flights on a trip that's primarily personal, the amount includible is the value of the personal flights that would have been taken had there been only personal flights. The value of all these flights may be computed under the special valuation rules (¶1239 *et seq.*). (Reg § 1.61-21(g)(4))[47]

¶ 1239 SIFL formula for noncommercial flights.

Value is determined by multiplying the "base aircraft valuation formula" —also known as the Standard Industry Fair Level (SIFL) formula (cents-per-mile rates that are revised semi-annually)—in effect at the time of the flight by the "aircraft multiple" (based on the takeoff weight of the plane) and adding the applicable "terminal charge." (Reg § 1.61-21(g)(5))[48]

¶ 1240 "Seating capacity" (zero inclusion) rule for noncommercial flights.

The "seating capacity" rule is available for noncommercial flights on employer-provided aircraft where at least half of the aircraft's passenger seating capacity is occupied by employees whose flights are primarily for the employer's business (and whose flights are excludable as a working condition fringe, see ¶1245). In this situation, the includible value of the flight taken by the employee for personal purposes is zero. (Reg § 1.61-21(g)(12))[49]

¶ 1241 "Space-available" rule for commercial flights.

If an employer provides an employee (as specially defined at Reg § 1.132-1(b)(1)) with a flight on a commercial aircraft for the employee's personal purposes, the flight is a taxable fringe benefit whose value must be included in the employee's gross income (¶1238). If the flight is a "space-available flight" on a commercial airline, its value for certain current or former airline employees may be computed under a special rule: 25% of the actual carrier's highest unrestricted coach fare for the flight taken. (Reg § 1.61-21(h)(1))[50]

¶ 1242 Excludable fringe benefits.

A fringe benefit isn't included in gross income if it's excluded under a specific Code Section (see below) (Code Sec. 61(a)), or qualifies as one of the following: (Code Sec. 132(a))[1]

. . . no additional cost service (¶1243);

. . . qualified employee discount (¶1244);

. . . working condition fringe (¶1245);

. . . de minimis fringe (¶1246);

. . . qualified transportation fringe (¶1247);

. . . qualified moving expense reimbursement (¶1248);

. . . employer-provided retirement advice (¶1250).

For qualified military base realignment and closure fringe benefit, see ¶1223.

46. ¶H-2301 *et seq.*; ¶614.027; TD ¶134,570
47. ¶s H-2314, H-2315; ¶614.027
48. ¶H-2304, ¶H-2307 *et seq.*; ¶614.027; TD ¶134,570

49. ¶H-2319; ¶614.027; TD ¶134,570
50. ¶H-2337; ¶614.027; TD ¶134,570
1. ¶H-1051; ¶1324; TD ¶134,001

A fringe benefit that's expressly provided for in any other Code Section can't be excluded from gross income under the Code Sec. 132 rules, except as a de minimis fringe or as a qualified moving expense reimbursement. (Code Sec. 132(l))[2] Fringe benefits excluded under a specific Code Section include: holiday and other gifts of nominal value (¶1212); stock options (¶1219); clergy member's home ("parsonage allowance," ¶1226); employee achievement awards (¶1251); on-premises athletic facilities (¶1252); adoption assistance (¶1254); educational assistance (¶2215); medical care coverage, including accident and health insurance (¶1255 *et seq.*); group-term life insurance (¶1262); meals and lodging (¶1267); qualified campus lodging (¶1268); cafeteria (flexible benefit) plans (¶1269); dependent care assistance programs (¶1270); scholarships (¶2216); and cost of living allowances to certain U.S. government employees (¶4619).[3]

¶ 1243 No-additional-cost services.

No-additional-cost services are excluded from an employee's gross income (see ¶1242). (Code Sec. 132(a)(1))[4] These are services provided by an employer to an employee for personal use by the employee, his spouse or dependent children, if:

(1) the services are ordinarily offered for sale to nonemployee customers in the ordinary course of the line of business in which the employee works,

(2) the employer incurs no substantial additional cost (including foregone revenue) in providing the services to the employee—computed without regard to any amounts paid by the employee for the services (Code Sec. 132(b)),[5] and

(3) special nondiscrimination rules are satisfied. (Code Sec. 132(j)(1))[6]

No-additional-cost services include services that would remain unused if the employees didn't use them, e.g., hotel accommodations, transportation by air, train, bus, subway or cruise line, and telephone services. (Reg § 1.132-2(a)(2))[7]

¶ 1244 Qualified employee discounts.

A qualified employee discount is excluded from an employee's gross income (see ¶1242). (Code Sec. 132(a)(2))[8] This is an "employee discount" allowed with respect to "qualified property or services" provided by an employer to an employee, his spouse or dependent children, to the extent the discount doesn't exceed the limits described below. (Code Sec. 132(c)(1))[9]

An "employee discount" is the excess of: (a) the price at which property or services are offered by an employer for sale to nonemployee customers, over (b) the price at which the employer offers the same property or services to employees for use by those employees. (Code Sec. 132(c)(3))[10]

"Qualified property or services" means any property (other than real property, or personal property of a kind held for investment) or services that are offered for sale to nonemployee customers in the ordinary course of the employer's line of business in which the employee works. (Code Sec. 132(c)(4), Code Sec. 132(k))[11]

Limitations. The excludable amount of a qualified employee discount with respect to property is limited to the gross profit percentage of the price at which that property is offered by the employer to customers. (Code Sec. 132(c)(1)(A)) Gross profit percentage equals the aggregate sales price of the property sold by the employer to all customers, whether employees or

2. ¶H-1052; ¶1324; TD ¶134,001
3. ¶H-1052; ¶614.027; TD ¶134,018
4. ¶H-1871; ¶1324.03; TD ¶134,004
5. ¶H-1871; ¶1324.03; TD ¶134,004
6. ¶H-1930 *et seq.*; ¶1324.01; TD ¶134,007

7. ¶H-1872; ¶1324.03
8. ¶H-1901; ¶1324.04; TD ¶134,008
9. ¶H-1902; ¶1324.04; TD ¶134,009
10. ¶H-1904; ¶1324.04
11. ¶H-1903; ¶1324.04; TD ¶134,008

nonemployees (Reg § 1.132-3(c)(1)(i)), over the aggregate cost of the property (Code Sec. 132(c)(2)(A)(i)), divided by the aggregate sales price. (Code Sec. 132(c)(2)(A)(ii))[12]

The excludable amount for services is limited to 20% of the price at which the employer offers the service to nonemployee customers. (Code Sec. 132(c)(1)(B), Code Sec. 132(k))[13]

¶ 1245   Working condition fringes.

Working condition fringes are excluded from the employee's gross income (see ¶1242). (Code Sec. 132(a)(3))[14] A "working condition fringe" is any property or services provided to an employee by the employer to the extent the cost of the property or services would have been deductible by the employee under either Code Sec. 162 (as trade or business expenses) or Code Sec. 167 (as depreciation expenses) if the employee had paid for the property or services himself. (Code Sec. 132(d))[15] Examples are: employer-paid business travel and the use of employer-provided vehicles for business purposes.[16]

Certain benefits qualify as working condition fringes only if special requirements are satisfied. These include: the use of consumer goods manufactured for sale to nonemployee customers and provided to employees for product testing and evaluation outside the employer's work place (Reg § 1.132-5(n)(1));[17] the personal use of vehicles otherwise used in connection with the business of farming (Reg § 1.132-5(g));[18] job placement assistance;[19] employer-paid club dues (Reg § 1.132-5(s));[20] employer-paid expenses of a companion on a business trip (Reg § 1.132-5(t));[21] "qualified automobile demonstration use" by automobile salespersons (Code Sec. 132(j)(3); Reg § 1.132-5(o));[22] the use of employer-owned aircraft for business travel (Reg § 1.132-5(k));[23] certain forms of transportation and other employer-provided security measures provided because of bona fide business-oriented security concerns (Reg § 1.132-5(m));[24] the use of "qualified nonpersonal use vehicles" (Reg § 1.132-5(h));[25] and the use of a cell phone provided to an employee primarily for noncompensatory business reasons.[26]

If an employer provides the use of a vehicle and includes the entire amount in the employee's income (without excluding any working condition fringe benefit amount), the employee can deduct the value multiplied by the percentage of business use as a miscellaneous itemized deduction (subject to the 2% floor, see ¶3110). This deduction can't be computed under a cents-per-mile method. (Reg § 1.162-25(b))[27]

¶ 1246   De minimis fringe benefits.

De minimis fringe benefits are excluded from the recipient's gross income (see ¶1242). (Code Sec. 132(a)(4)) A de minimis fringe is any property or service whose value is so small that accounting for it is unreasonable or administratively impracticable, taking into account the frequency with which similar fringe benefits are provided by the employer to its employees. (Code Sec. 132(e)(1))

Examples of de minimis fringes include: occasional meals, supper money, or local transportation provided because of overtime work (Reg § 1.132-6(d)(2)); meals at employer-operated eating facilities (see below); transportation (e.g., taxi fare) where other available means of transportation are unsafe, in excess of value over $1.50 per each one-way commute (¶1231)

12. ¶H-1909; ¶1324.04; TD ¶134,009
13. ¶H-1914; ¶1324.04; TD ¶134,009
14. ¶H-1701; ¶1324.05; TD ¶134,010
15. ¶H-1701; ¶1324.05; TD ¶134,010
16. ¶H-1701; ¶1324.05; TD ¶134,012
17. ¶H-1712; ¶1324.05; TD ¶134,012
18. ¶H-2370; ¶1324.05; TD ¶134,012
19. ¶H-1711; ¶1324.05; TD ¶134,012
20. ¶H-2153.1; TD ¶136,529
21. ¶H-2153.2; TD ¶136,530
22. ¶H-2364; ¶1324.05; TD ¶134,568
23. ¶H-2351; ¶1324.05; TD ¶134,012
24. ¶H-2373 *et seq.*; ¶1324.05; TD ¶134,012
25. ¶H-2354; ¶1324.05; TD ¶134,012
26. ¶H-1707.2; ¶1324.05; TD ¶134,012
27. ¶s H-2363, L-1912; ¶s 1624.283, 2744.17; TD ¶293,019

(Reg § 1.132-6(d)(2)); occasional cocktail parties or picnics; traditional holiday gifts of property (not cash) with a low FMV; flowers, fruit, etc., provided under special circumstances, such as sickness or outstanding performance (Reg § 1.132-6(e)(1)); low-value clothing bearing employer's name, which must be worn by the employee; electronically filing the employee's income tax return (but not paying someone to prepare his return); and an employee's personal use of a cell phone provided by the employer primarily for noncompensatory business reasons.[28]

No qualified transportation fringe benefit (¶1247) (including amounts in excess of the dollar limit) may be excluded as a de minimis fringe benefit. (Code Sec. 132(f)(7))[29] However, partners, more-than-2% S corporation shareholders and independent contractors (but not employees) can exclude transit passes, tokens and fare cards if not in excess of $21 per month.[30]

Meals at employer-operated eating facilities are de minimis fringes if the facility's annual revenues normally equal or exceed its direct operating costs and certain nondiscrimination rules are met. Employees who are entitled (under the rules at ¶1267) to exclude the value of a meal provided at the facility are treated as having paid an amount for the meal equal to the direct operating costs of the facility attributable to the meal. (Code Sec. 132(e)(2); Reg § 1.132-7(a)(2), Reg § 1.132-7(c))[31] Direct operating costs are the costs of the food and beverages served and the labor for related services performed primarily on the facility's premises. (Reg § 1.132-7(b)(1))[32]

¶ 1247   Qualified transportation fringe benefits.

An employee (other than a self-employed person) may exclude from income qualified transportation fringe benefits up to specified dollar amounts (below). (Code Sec. 132(a)(5), Code Sec. 132(f)(5)) These benefits include:

(1) Transportation in a commuter highway vehicle (van pool), if in connection with travel between the employee's residence and place of employment. A commuter highway vehicle has a seating capacity of 6 adults (excluding the driver) for which 80% of the mileage must be reasonably expected to be for employee commuting and to be for trips where the vehicle is half full (excluding the driver).

(2) Transit passes for use on a mass transit facility (e.g., rail, bus or ferry) or a commuter highway vehicle.

(3) Qualified parking at or near the employer's business premises or a location from which the employee commutes to work by mass transit or hired commuter vehicle. Any parking at or near the employee's residence isn't qualified parking. (Code Sec. 132(f)(1), Code Sec. 132(f)(5); Reg § 1.132-9(b))

(4) Qualified bicycle commuting reimbursements, i.e., for any calendar year, any employer reimbursement during the 15-month period beginning with the first day of that calendar year for reasonable expenses incurred by the employee during that calendar year for the purchase of a bicycle and improvements, repair, or storage. The exclusion is limited to $20 per month a bicycle is regularly used for a substantial portion of the employee's commute. This benefit can't be used with commuter highway vehicle transportation, transit passes, or parking benefits. (Code Sec. 132(f)(5)(F))[33]

For 2013, an employee can exclude up to $245 a month of qualified parking, and $245 a month of for the combined value of transit passes and transportation in a commuter highway vehicle. For 2014, the exclusion is $250 for qualified parking, and $130 for the combined value of transit passes and transportation in a commuter highway vehicle. (Code

28. ¶H-1802 *et seq.*; ¶1324.06; TD ¶134,013
29. ¶H-2202; ¶1324.08; TD ¶134,596
30. ¶H-1806; TD ¶134,014
31. ¶H-1821; ¶1324.06; TD ¶131,510
32. ¶H-1823; ¶1324.06; TD ¶131,510
33. ¶H-2205; ¶1324.08; TD ¶134,016

Sec. 132(f)(2))[34]

✓observation: In prior years, the monthly exclusion for employer-provided transit and vanpooling benefits has been increased to equal that for parking.

✓observation: Cash reimbursements (but *not* cash advances) are excludable. But reimbursements for transit passes are excludable only where vouchers, etc. (which may be exchanged only for transit passes) aren't readily available for direct distribution by the employer to the employee. (Code Sec. 132(f)(3); Reg § 1.132-9(b))[35]

No amount is included in an employee's gross income solely because he may choose between any qualified transportation fringe and otherwise includible compensation. (Code Sec. 132(f)(4)) But if he chooses cash instead of a qualified transportation fringe, he will be taxed.[36] If he elects fringes rather than cash, he won't be taxed on any exchanged cash if requirements are met. (Reg § 1.132-9(b))[37]

The qualified transportation fringe exclusion doesn't apply to any arrangement that results in the reimbursement of an expense the employee hasn't actually incurred, e.g., where the employee is reimbursed for an item he paid for through a tax-free salary reduction.[38]

Partners, 2% S corporation shareholders and independent contractors can't exclude qualified transportation fringes. (Code Sec. 132(f)(5)(E))[39]

¶ 1248 Qualified moving expense reimbursement.

A taxpayer excludes from gross income any qualified moving expense reimbursement. (Code Sec. 132(a)(6))[40] A qualified moving expense reimbursement is any amount received (directly or indirectly) by the taxpayer from an employer as a payment of (or reimbursement for) moving expenses that would have been deductible had the taxpayer paid them directly (for employee's moving expense deduction, see ¶1646 *et seq.*). Expenses aren't excludable if the taxpayer actually deducted them in an earlier year. (Code Sec. 132(g))[41] Otherwise an employer's payment or reimbursement is income to the employee. (Code Sec. 82)[42] The employer reports moving expense reimbursements (but not qualifying payments to third parties or qualifying services furnished in kind) to the employee on Form W-2.[43]

¶ 1249 Reimbursement of employee in connection with sale of his home.

An employer's reimbursement for an employee's loss on sale of the employee's home is income to the employee.[44] However, if the employer buys the employee's home at its fair market value (FMV), the employee has no income other than gain on the sale. Where, as an alternative to reimbursing an employee for the loss, the employer buys the home for more than its FMV, that *excess* is taxable to the employee.[45]

¶ 1250 Employer-provided retirement advice.

Qualified retirement planning services are excluded from the income of the employee receiving the services. (Code Sec. 132(a)(7)) Qualified retirement planning services are any retirement planning services provided to an employee and his spouse by an employer maintaining a qualified employer plan (as defined in Code Sec. 219(g)(5)). (Code Sec. 132(m))[46]

34. ¶H-2217.1; ¶1324.08; TD ¶134,591
35. ¶H-2212, H-2216; ¶1324.08; TD ¶134,578
36. ¶H-2216.1; ¶1324.08; TD ¶134,016
37. ¶H-2216.1; ¶1324.08; TD ¶134,584 *et seq.*
38. ¶H-2216
39. ¶H-2206; ¶1324.08; TD ¶134,572
40. ¶H-1971; ¶1324.09; TD ¶136,541

41. ¶H-1971; ¶1324.09; TD ¶136,541
42. ¶H-4418; ¶824; TD ¶136,535
43. ¶S-3170; ¶60,514; TD ¶812,012
44. ¶s H-2161, H-2162; ¶824.01; TD ¶136,536
45. ¶H-2162; TD ¶136,536
46. ¶H-1980; ¶1324.10

¶ 1251   Employee achievement awards.

Employee achievement awards are excludable only to the extent the employer can deduct the cost of the award—generally limited to $400 for any one employee, or $1,600 for a "qualified plan award," see ¶1591. (Code Sec. 74(c)(2))[47]

¶ 1252   On-premises athletic facilities.

The value of an on-premises athletic facility provided by an employer is excluded from an employee's gross income. (Code Sec. 132(j)(4)(A))[48]

¶ 1253   Employer payment of employee's personal expenses.

Where an employer pays the debts or personal expenses of an employee, or reimburses the employee's payment, the employee must include the employer's payment or reimbursement in his (employee's) income.[49] For medical expenses, see ¶1255.

An employer's payment of an employee's income taxes (federal or state) or other taxes is income to the employee. Pyramiding of income, and of tax, results where the employer agrees to pay all the employee's tax. (Reg § 1.61-14)[50]

¶ 1254   Employer-provided adoption assistance.

An employee may exclude amounts paid or expenses incurred by his employer for qualified adoption expenses (¶2354) connected with the employee's adoption of a child, if the amounts are furnished under an adoption assistance program in existence (and known to the employee) before the expenses are incurred. For the adoption of a child with special needs, the exclusion applies regardless of whether the employee has qualified adoption expenses. (Code Sec. 137(a), Code Sec. 137(b), Code Sec. 137(f))[1]

For 2013, the excludable amount is phased out for taxpayers with adjusted gross income (AGI, as specially computed) over $194,580, adjusted for inflation annually, and is fully eliminated when AGI reaches $234,580. (Code Sec. 137(b)(2), Code Sec. 137(f)) For 2014, the phaseout begins at $197,880, and the exclusion is fully eliminated when AGI reaches $237,880. To compute the excluded employer-provided adoption benefits, use Form 8839.[2]

Amounts are excludable in the year in which the employer pays for qualified adoption expenses of an eligible child who is a U.S. citizen or resident when the adoption commenced. If the eligible child isn't a U.S. citizen or resident, the exclusion is available only for adoptions that become final, and only in the year that they are finalized. Where expenses of a foreign eligible child are paid in a year before the adoption becomes final, the employee includes the employer's assistance in income for that year, and claims the otherwise available exclusion in the year the adoption becomes final. A taxpayer may claim both an adoption expense credit (see ¶2354) and an exclusion for the adoption of an eligible child, but cannot claim a credit and an exclusion for the same expense.[3]

For 2013, the maximum exclusion for employer-provided adoption assistance is $12,970, per child (for both non-special needs and special needs adoptions). For 2014, the exclusion rises to $13,190. (Code Sec. 137(a)(2))

47. ¶L-2317 *et seq.*; ¶744.03; TD ¶132,007
48. ¶H-1951; ¶1324.07; TD ¶134,017
49. ¶H-2151; ¶s 614.007, 614.146; TD ¶136,527
50. ¶H-2157; ¶614.147; TD ¶198,506

1. ¶H-1450 et seq.; ¶1374; TD ¶133,600 *et seq.*
2. ¶H-1453; ¶1374; TD ¶133,603
3. ¶H-1451 *et seq.*; ¶1374; TD ¶133,602, TD ¶133,608

¶ 1255   Employee's medical expenses reimbursed or insured by employer.

An employee can exclude from gross income amounts received from his employer, directly or indirectly, as reimbursement for expenses for the medical care of himself, his spouse, and his dependents. The exclusion also applies to any child of an employee who hasn't attained age 27 as of the end of the year. (Code Sec. 105(b)) (These amounts are excludable even where a sole proprietor employer is the employee's spouse, and the amounts received are for the employer-spouse's medical care.)[4] However, reimbursement is includible in the employee's income to the extent it exceeds medical expenses or it's attributable to medical expense deductions he took in a previous year. (Code Sec. 105(b); Reg § 1.105-2)[5]

An employee also excludes the cost (i.e., premiums paid) of employer-provided *coverage* under an accident or health plan. (Code Sec. 106)[6] However, if the employer-provided policy, trust, etc., provides other benefits, only the portion of the employer contributions for the accident and health coverage is excludable. (Reg § 1.106-1)[7]

Where a plan allows reimbursements of a nonqualifying beneficiary's medical expense, no payment from the plan during the year to any person—including the employee, his spouse or dependents—is excluded from income.[8]

Insurance premiums paid for partners and more-than-2% S corporation shareholders (who are treated as partners) are not excludable.[9]

Highly compensated individuals (as defined in Code Sec. 105(h)(5)) who benefit from an employer's "self-insured" medical reimbursement plan that discriminates in their favor must include "excess reimbursements" (reimbursements for benefits not available to other plan participants) in income. (Code Sec. 105(h))[10]

¶ 1256   Employer contributions to Archer medical savings account (Archer MSA).

Small-employer contributions to an employee's Archer MSA are treated as excludable employer-provided coverage for medical expenses under an accident or health plan (¶1255) to the extent the amounts don't exceed the applicable statutory limits (see ¶1528). (Code Sec. 106(b)(1))[11] Generally, small employers are those that employed on average no more than 50 employees during either of the two preceding years. An employer that grows past the 50-employee limit in a succeeding year may continue MSA contributions until the year after the first year in which it has more than 200 employees. (Code Sec. 220(c)(4))[12] For treatment of Archer MSA distributions, see ¶1377. Employer Archer MSA contributions aren't excludable if made at the employee's election under a salary reduction arrangement under a cafeteria plan. (Code Sec. 125(f))

Employers that provide high deductible health plan coverage plus an MSA and make employer contributions must make available a comparable contribution on behalf of all employees with comparable coverage during the same period. A 35% penalty applies for noncompliance. (Code Sec. 4980E)[13]

For the cutoff date for Archer MSA contributions, see ¶1528.

---

4. ¶H-1110; TD ¶133,036
5. ¶H-1110 *et seq.*; ¶1054.01; TD ¶133,036
6. ¶H-1102; ¶1064; TD ¶133,032
7. ¶H-1106; ¶1064; TD ¶133,034
8. ¶H-1349.3

9. ¶H-1126; ¶1064; TD ¶133,026
10. ¶H-1138 *et seq.*; ¶1054.05; TD ¶133,013
11. ¶H-1101.1 et seq., ¶1064, TD ¶133,040
12. ¶s H-1333, H-1333.1; ¶2204.01; TD ¶288,102
13. ¶H-1336.3; ¶4980E4; TD ¶288,104

¶ 1257   Employer contributions to health savings accounts (HSAs).

Employer contributions to an HSA of the employee are treated as employer-provided coverage for medical expenses under an accident or health plan (¶1255) to the extent the amounts don't exceed the statutory limits (see ¶1529) applicable to the employee for the tax year, and are deductible by the employer in the year they are paid. (Code Sec. 106(d)(2)) Employer contributions to an HSA on behalf of an eligible individual are excludable from income.[14] The contributions must be reported on the employee's Form W-2, Box 12.[15] For HSA distributions, see ¶1378. However, where contributions exceed the limits and the employer doesn't recoup the amount, the excess must be included in the employee's income and reported on his Form W-2.[16]

There is no constructive receipt of income solely because the employee may choose between employer contributions to an HSA and to another health plan. (Code Sec. 106(d)(2)) Employer contributions to an HSA are excludable if made at the employee's election under a salary reduction arrangement in a cafeteria plan (see ¶1269). (Code Sec. 125(d)(2))

¶ 1258   Employer's payments for employee's loss of limb, disfigurement, etc.

Amounts received under an employer plan as payment for permanent loss or loss of use of a member or function of the body, or permanent disfigurement, of the employee, his spouse or his dependent are tax-free, but only if the payment is based on the nature of the injury without regard to the period the employee is absent from work. (Code Sec. 105(c))[17]

¶ 1259   Worker's compensation.

Amounts received under a worker's compensation act or similar law for personal injuries or sickness are excludable from the employee's (or survivor's) income. This rule doesn't apply to the extent payments are determined by reference to the employee's age or length of service or his prior contributions, even if his retirement is occasioned by occupational injury. (Reg § 1.104-1(b)) Worker's compensation is includible in income to the extent it's attributable to medical expense deductions taken in an earlier year. (Code Sec. 104(a)(1); Reg § 1.104-1(b))[18]

¶ 1260   Annuities paid to survivors of public safety officers killed in line of duty.

Survivor annuity benefits paid on account of the death of a public safety officer (including law enforcement officers, firefighters, rescue squad workers and ambulance crew members) killed in the line of duty are excluded if: (1) the annuity is provided under a governmental plan which meets the requirements of Code Sec. 401(a) to the officer's spouse, former spouse, or child; and (2) to the extent the annuity is attributable to the officer's service as a public safety officer. (Code Sec. 101(h)(1)) The exclusion doesn't apply under certain circumstances (e.g., if the death was caused by the officer's intentional misconduct). (Code Sec. 101(h)(2))[19]

¶ 1261   Employer-paid individual life insurance policies.

Premiums paid by an employer for policies on the life of an employee are taxable to the employee if the proceeds are payable to the employee's beneficiary (except for group-term insurance, see ¶1262) but not where the employer is the beneficiary. (Reg § 1.61-2(d)(2))[20]

---

14. ¶H-1101.5; ¶1064; TD ¶133,051
15. ¶S-3152; ¶60,514; TD ¶812,002
16. ¶H-1350.8D
17. ¶H-1201; ¶1054.02; TD ¶133,048

18. ¶H-1351; ¶1044.01; TD ¶133,049
19. ¶H-1650 *et seq.*; ¶1014.09; TD ¶141,090
20. ¶H-1501 *et seq.*; ¶614.031; TD ¶137,000

¶ 1262 Group-term life insurance premiums.

An employee isn't taxed on premiums paid by the employer on insurance covering the employee's life under a group-term life insurance policy, if the employee's total coverage under all such plans of all his employers doesn't exceed $50,000. If his total coverage does exceed $50,000, he's taxed on the "cost" (¶1263) of coverage over $50,000 minus the amount he paid. (Code Sec. 79(a))[21] For coverage of employee's spouse and dependents, see ¶1264.

An employee whose total coverage exceeds $50,000 for only part of the year includes the employer's payments for that part of the year coverage, even if his average coverage for the year is under this ceiling. (Code Sec. 79(a))[22]

A disabled terminated employee isn't taxable on group term coverage even if it exceeds $50,000. (Code Sec. 79(b)(1))[23]

Retired employees are generally treated the same as other employees. (Code Sec. 79(e))[24]

The exclusion doesn't apply to any insurance protection in excess of the maximum allowed by state law for employee group insurance. (Reg § 1.79-1(e))[25]

The exclusion is available to a key employee only if the plan doesn't discriminate in favor of key employees (at any time in the key employee's tax year) (Reg § 1.79-4T, Q&A-11) as to eligibility to participate and in the type and amount of benefits available. (Code Sec. 79(d))[26] If the plan is discriminatory, each key employee must include the *greater of* (a) the actual cost of the insurance (determined by apportioning the net premium allocable to the group-term coverage during the key employee's tax year among the covered employees (Reg § 1.79-4T, Q&A-6(b)), *or* (b) the cost determined from IRS's premium table. (Code Sec. 79(d)(1)(B))[27]

¶ 1263 "Cost" of taxable group-term insurance—IRS uniform premium table.

The employer must compute the "cost" of taxable group-term coverage (¶1262) and notify the employee on Form W-2 of the amount included in his income. The employee computes the cost only where he has two or more employers who provide him with coverage.

The cost of group-term life insurance is determined on the basis of uniform premiums (computed on the basis of five-year age brackets) prescribed by IRS. (Code Sec. 79(c)) The cost for each month of coverage is the number of thousands of dollars of coverage over $50,000 (to the nearest tenth) times the amount in IRS's table for the employee's attained age on the last day of the employee's tax year. (Reg § 1.79-3(d)(2))[28] Under the table, the cost per $1,000 of protection per month is 5¢ for under age 25; 6¢ for 25 through 29; 8¢ for 30 through 34; 9¢ for 35 through 39; 10¢ for 40 through 44; 15¢ for 45 through 49; 23¢ for 50 through 54; 43¢ for 55 through 59; 66¢ for 60 through 64; $1.27 for 65 through 69; and $2.06 for 70 and older.

If the employee contributes to the plan, all his contributions for the tax year are considered made for that part of his coverage over $50,000. (Code Sec. 79(a)(2))[29]

illustration: J, a 57-year-old employee, is provided with a $250,000 group-term life insurance policy by his employer for the year. For this coverage, J contributes 20¢ per $1,000 of coverage per month. The amount included in J's income for the $200,000 excess coverage ($250,000 – $50,000) is $432—the cost of the insurance above the excludable amount (43¢ monthly cost from the IRS table × 12 months × 200 [excess insurance]) less J's employee contribution (20¢ × 12 × 250 total insurance).

---

21. ¶H-1518; ¶794; TD ¶137,007
22. ¶H-1520; ¶794.01; TD ¶137,009
23. ¶H-1552; ¶794.03; TD ¶137,041
24. ¶s H-1555, H-1556; ¶794.06; TD ¶137,043
25. ¶H-1537

26. ¶H-1564; ¶794.05; TD ¶137,024
27. ¶H-1565; ¶794.05; TD ¶137,023; 137,025
28. ¶H-1521; ¶794.01; TD ¶137,010
29. ¶H-1522; ¶794.01; TD ¶137,011

¶ 1264   Group-term coverage of employee's spouse and dependents.

The cost (as determined at ¶1263) of group-term life insurance on the life of an individual other than an employee (e.g., the employee's spouse or dependent) provided in connection with the performance of services by the employee is includible in the employee's gross income. (Reg § 1.61-2(d)(2)(ii)(b)) If, however, the face amount of employer-provided group-term insurance payable on the death of an employee's spouse or dependent doesn't exceed $2,000, it's an excludable de minimis fringe (¶1246).[30]

¶ 1265   Group-permanent insurance premiums.

Group-permanent insurance premiums that an employer pays on an employee's life are included in the employee's income. Where a group term policy provides permanent benefits, the amount included in income for the permanent benefits is computed under a complex formula. (Reg § 1.79-1(d))[31]

¶ 1266   Split-dollar life insurance.

Under a "split-dollar" insurance arrangement, the employer pays part of the premium for a life insurance policy on the life of the employee (to the extent of the annual increase in cash surrender value) and the employee pays the rest. Out of the insurance proceeds, the employer gets either the cash surrender value or the amount it paid; the employee can designate the beneficiary of the balance.[32] For arrangements entered into (or materially modified) after Sept. 17, 2003, there are two mutually exclusive regimes for taxing split-dollar life insurance arrangements.

Under the economic benefit regime, the policy owner is treated as providing economic benefits to the non-owner (as valued in the regs). This regime governs the taxation of what are known as endorsement split-dollar arrangements (e.g., employer owns the policy and employee's rights are derived from the employer's endorsement in the contract of those rights to him). This regime automatically applies if the arrangement is (1) entered into in connection with the performance of services, and the employee or other service provider is not the contract owner, or (2) a gift situation, and the donee is not the contract owner. (Reg § 1.61-22)

Under the loan regime, the non-owner of the life insurance contract is treated as loaning premium payments to the contract owner. Unless specifically excepted, the loan regime applies to any split-dollar loan. The loan regime also governs what are known as collateral assignment split-dollar life insurance arrangements (e.g., employee owns the policy, which is used as collateral for employer's right to recover the premiums it pays). (Reg § 1.7872-15)

The employer (or donor in a gift arrangement) is treated as the owner of a split-dollar life insurance contract if the only economic benefit that the employee (or donee) has under the arrangement is current life insurance protection. (Reg § 1.61-22(c)(1))

Unless the non-owner's payments are made in consideration of economic benefits, then general income, employment, and gift tax principles apply to the arrangement. For example, if an employee/contract owner's repayment obligation to an employer were waived or cancelled, both parties have to account for the amount as compensation. (Reg § 1.61-22(b)(6))

In a split-dollar life insurance arrangement taxed under the economic benefit regime, the policy owner is treated as providing economic benefits to the non-owner, and those benefits have to be accounted for fully and consistently by both the owner and the non-owner. The

---

30. ¶H-1560 *et seq.*; ¶614.031, ¶1324.06; TD ¶137,044   32. ¶H-1601; ¶614.033; TD ¶137,030
31. ¶H-1545; ¶794.04; TD ¶137,016

value of the economic benefits, less any consideration paid by the non-owner, is treated as transferred from the owner to the non-owner. The tax consequences of that transfer depend on the relationship between the owner and the non-owner. Thus, depending on the circumstances, it might be treated as compensation, a dividend, or a gift. (Reg § 1.61-22(d)(1))

A payment made under a split-dollar life insurance arrangement is a split-dollar loan, and the policy owner and non-owner are treated, respectively, as borrower and lender, if: the payment is made directly or indirectly by the non-owner to the owner; the payment either is a loan under general tax law principles or if a reasonable person would expect the payment to be repaid in full to the non-owner; and repayment is to be made from, or secured by, the policy's death benefit or cash surrender value, or both. (Reg § 1.7872-15(a)(2))

Because split-dollar life insurance arrangements typically provide for deferred compensation, Code Sec. 409A (¶1275) generally applies. But Code Sec. 409A doesn't apply for earnings on amounts deferred under a split-dollar life insurance arrangement in tax years beginning before 2005 (unless the plan is materially modified after Oct. 3, 2004), including increases in the policy cash value—but not including increases attributable to continued services performed, compensation earned, or premium payments or other contributions made on or after 2005.[33]

For arrangements entered into before Sept. 18, 2003 and not materially modified on or after that date (unless rules similar to the above rules are relied on by taxpayers), an employee is taxed on the value of the insurance protection he receives, less any premium he paid; the taxable amount is determined under IRS's Table 2001 (carried in IRS Notice 2002–8), and *not* under the group-term table at ¶1263, plus cash dividends or other benefits received, reduced by any part of the premiums he paid. (But in some cases, an insurer's published gross premium rates for initial-issue standard-risk insurance can be used for policies issued by that insurer, or, for certain pre-Jan. 28, 2002 arrangements, the PS 58 rates may be used.) Insurance proceeds received by the employer and the employee's beneficiaries are tax-free.[34]

For split-dollar life insurance arrangements entered into before Jan. 28, 2002 under which an employer has made premium payments and has received, or is entitled to receive, full repayment of all of its payments, IRS won't assert that there has been a taxable transfer of property to a benefited person upon termination of the arrangement if, for all periods beginning on or after Jan.1, 2004, all payments by the employer from inception of the arrangement (less any repayments) are treated as loans for tax purposes, and the parties report the tax treatment consistently with this loan treatment. Any payments by the employer not previously treated as loans must be treated as loans entered into at the beginning of that first year in which the payments are treated as loans.[35]

¶ 1267   Meals and lodging furnished by or on behalf of employer.

Meals or lodging (including utilities) furnished to an employee and his family (spouse and dependents) is nontaxable to the employee if (Code Sec. 119):

(1) the meals and lodging are furnished by or on behalf of the employer for the convenience of the employer (e.g., meals supplied because eating places near work are scarce, or because employees must for valid business reasons remain on-premises until their shifts end) (Reg § 1.119-1(a)(2)), and

(2) (a) in the case of *meals,* they are furnished on the employer's business premises, or (b) in the case of *lodging,* the employee is required to accept the lodging as a condition of his employment (i.e., to properly perform his duties). (Reg § 1.119-1(b))[36] This means the employee's presence must be required from a business standpoint—e.g., ranches, hotels,

---

33. ¶H-3200.6; ¶409A4.01; TD ¶135,504.1
34. ¶H-1647.11 *et seq.*; ¶614.033; TD ¶137,031

35. ¶H-1647.10
36. ¶H-1751; ¶1194.01; TD ¶131,501

motels and resorts.[37] For faculty housing, see ¶1268.

The value (not the cost) of meals or lodging that fails to meet these tests generally is income to the employee. (Reg § 1.61-2(d)(3), Reg § 1.119-1(a)(1))[38] However, all meals furnished on the employer's business premises to its employees are treated as furnished for the employer's convenience—and so are excludable from the employees' income—if *more than half* of the employees to whom the meals are furnished on the premises are furnished the meals for the convenience of the employer. (Code Sec. 119(b)(4))[39]

observation: In other words, if the more-than-half test is met, all employees may exclude the value of meals provided on premises, even those who weren't supplied the meals for the convenience of the employer.

Cash allowances for meals are taxable.[40] If the employee can take either cash, or meals or lodging furnished in kind, the value of meals or lodging furnished is income. But occasional "supper money" paid to overtime employees is excludable as a de minimis fringe, see ¶1246.[41]

¶ 1268   Faculty housing—qualified campus lodging.

The value of qualified campus lodging furnished to an employee of an educational institution is excludable (with limits, below) from his gross income. (Code Sec. 119(d))[42]

Qualified campus lodging is lodging that isn't eligible for the exclusion at ¶1267, that's located on or near a campus of a tax-exempt educational institution (or a qualifying academic health center), and that's furnished by the institution to an employee, his spouse, and his dependents for use as a residence. (Code Sec. 119(d)(3), Code Sec. 119(d)(4))[43]

The exclusion isn't a total one. The employee must include the excess of: (1) the lesser of (a) 5% of the appraised value (as of the close of the tax year) of the qualified campus lodging, or (b) the average of the rentals paid by individuals other than employees or students for comparable lodging provided by the institution; over (2) the rent paid by the employee. (Code Sec. 119(d)(2))[44]

¶ 1269   Cafeteria plans (including flexible spending accounts).

No amount is included in the gross income of the participant in a cafeteria plan solely because, under the plan, the participant may choose among the benefits of the plan. (Code Sec. 125(a))[45] Cafeteria plans are generally the sole method of employers providing nontaxable benefits where employees can elect between taxable compensation and nontaxable benefits. (Prop Reg. § 1.125-1(b)(1) ["Taxpayers may rely"])

A "cafeteria plan" (also referred to as a flexible benefit plan) is a written plan under which participants (all employees) may choose their own "menu" of benefits consisting of "cash" and "qualified benefits." (Code Sec. 125(d))[46] For this purpose, cash means cash from current compensation (including salary reduction), payment for annual leave, sick leave, or other paid time off, severance pay, property, and certain after-tax employee contributions; distributions from qualified retirement plans are not cash. (Prop Reg. § 1.125-1(a)(2) ["Taxpayers may rely"]) A qualified benefit, which generally must be excludible from employees' gross income under a specific Code section—and must not defer compensation (with some exceptions) (Code Sec. 125(d)(2))—includes: group-term life insurance on an employee's life (up to the excludable $50,000 amount, see ¶1262); employer-provided accident and health plans (¶1255)

37. ¶H-1776; ¶1194.02; TD ¶131,511
38. ¶s H-1751, H-1785; ¶614.027, ¶1194 *et seq.*; TD ¶131,511
39. ¶H-1754; ¶1194.02
40. ¶H-1790; ¶1194.03; TD ¶131,506
41. ¶H-1791; ¶1324.06; TD ¶131,507

42. ¶H-1797; ¶1194.06; TD ¶131,525
43. ¶H-1799; ¶1194.06; TD ¶131,525
44. ¶H-1797; ¶1194.06; TD ¶131,525
45. ¶H-2401; ¶1254; TD ¶133,045
46. ¶H-2405; ¶1254.01; TD ¶133,042

(including health flexible spending arrangements (FSAs), and accidental death and dismemberment policies); a dependent care assistance program (¶1270); an adoption assistance program (¶1254); contributions to a Code Sec. 401(k) plan (¶4317); contributions to certain plans maintained by educational organizations, contributions to Health Savings Accounts (HSAs, see ¶1257); and long-term and short-term disability coverage. (Code Sec. 125(f); Prop Reg. § 1.125-1(a)(3) ["Taxpayers may rely"]) [47]

For tax years beginning after 2013, a qualified health plan purchased on the individual market through an Exchange isn't a qualified benefit for a cafeteria plan. However, a qualified health plan can be a qualified benefit if it's offered by a qualified employer (in plan years beginning before 2016, generally an employer with no more than 50 employees) offering the employee the opportunity to enroll in a qualified health plan through a health insurance Exchange in a group market. (Code Sec. 125(f)(3))[48]

In the case of a "highly compensated participant," the exclusion won't apply to any benefit attributable to a plan year for which the plan discriminates in favor of highly compensated participants as to contributions, benefits or eligibility to participate. (Code Sec. 125(b)(1))[49] An individual is a "highly compensated participant" if he is an officer or more-than-5% shareholder of the employer, a highly compensated employee or a spouse or dependent of such a person. (Code Sec. 125(e)(1))[50]

In the case of a key employee (defined in Code Sec. 416(i)(1)), the exclusion won't apply to any plan year if the qualified benefits provided to key employees under the plan exceed 25% of the total of such benefits provided for all employees under the plan. (Code Sec. 125(b)(2))[1]

FSAs. A cafeteria plan also can include one or more FSAs. An FSA is a benefit designed to reimburse employees for expenses incurred for certain qualified benefits, up to a maximum amount not substantially in excess of the salary reduction and employer flex-credits allocated for the benefit. The maximum amount of reimbursement reasonably available must be less than five times the value of the coverage. (Prop Reg. § 1.125-5(a) ["Taxpayers may rely"]) Employer flex-credits are non-elective contributions that an employer makes available for every employee eligible to participate in the cafeteria plan, to be used at the employee's election only for one or more qualified benefits (but not as cash or other taxable benefits). (Prop Reg. § 1.125-5(b) ["Taxpayers may rely"]) The three types of FSAs are dependent care assistance, adoption assistance and medical care reimbursements (health FSA).

A health FSA may be limited to a subset of permitted Code Sec. 213(d) medical expenses, or it may be an HSA compatible limited-purpose health FSA or post-deductible health FSA. (Prop Reg. § 1.125-5(m) ["Taxpayers may rely"]) A health FSA may not reimburse premiums for accident and health insurance or long-term care insurance. (Code Sec. 125(f)) For cafeteria plan years beginning after 2012, an employee can't contribute to a health FSA through salary reduction contributions in excess of $2,500 (adjusted for inflation after 2013) for the year. (Code Sec. 125(i)) The maximum remains at $2,500 for 2014. However, for a married couple, each person may contribute up to this maximum. The health FSA cap doesn't limit the amount permitted for reimbursement under other employer-provided coverage, such as an FSA for dependent care assistance.[2]

Use-it-or-lose-it rule. Unused cafeteria plan amounts left over at the end of a plan year generally have to be forfeited (use-it-or-lose-it rule). But a cafeteria plan can provide an optional grace period immediately following the end of each plan year, extending the period for incurring expenses for qualified benefits to the 15th day of the third month after the end of the plan year. It may apply to one or more qualified benefits but can't apply to paid time off or elective contributions to Code Sec. 401(k) plans. Benefits or contributions not used as of the

47. ¶H-2413 *et seq.*; ¶1254.01; TD ¶133,042
48. ¶H-2413.2 *et seq.*; ¶1254.01; TD ¶133,043.1
49. ¶H-2450; ¶1254.06; TD ¶133,045.

50. ¶H-2455; ¶1254.06
1. ¶H-2456; ¶1254.06; TD ¶133,045
2. ¶H-2461 *et seq.*; ¶1254.05; TD ¶133,044.1 *et seq.*

end of the grace period are forfeited. (Prop Reg. § 1.125-1(e)(1) ["Taxpayers may rely"]) [3] An exception to this rule, at the plan sponsor's option and in lieu of any grace period, allows employees to carry over up to $500 of unused amounts remaining at year-end in a health FSA (rather than forfeit it). A health FSA must be amended to adopt a carryover provision on or before the last day of the plan year from which amounts may be carried over and may be effective retroactively to the first day of that plan year; but for a plan year that begins in 2013 the plan may be amended at any time on or before the last day of the plan year that begins in 2014. (Notice 2013-71, 2013-47 IRB) Another exception allows FSAs to make distributions of all or part of unused health FSA benefits to military reservists who are called to active duty for a period exceeding 179 days (or an indefinite period). The distribution must be made during the period beginning with the call to active duty and ending on the last day of the coverage period of the FSA that includes the date of the call to active duty. (Code Sec. 125(h))

If a plan provides a grace period, unused salary reduction contributions to the health FSA that are carried over into the grace period will not count against the $2,500 limit for the later plan year.[4]

¶ 1270   Dependent care assistance payments—Form 2441.

Payments incurred by an employer for dependent care assistance under a written plan are excluded from an employee's gross income. (Code Sec. 129(a)(1))[5]

The amount an employee can exclude (computed on Form 2441 with Form 1040 or Form 1040A) can't exceed the employee's earned income (excluding employer dependent care assistance payments) or, for married employees, the earned income of the lower earning spouse. (Code Sec. 129(b))[6] The aggregate exclusion is further limited to $5,000 ($2,500 for a married individual filing separately). (Code Sec. 129(a)(2)(A)) Any excess is includible in the tax year the dependent care services are provided. (Code Sec. 129(a)(2)(B))[7]

Dependent care assistance is the payment for or provision of services that if paid for by the employee would be considered employment-related expenses under the child care credit rules (see ¶2351). (Code Sec. 129(e)(1))[8] For eligible dependents, see ¶2350. An employee includes a self-employed individual who can be covered under a self-employed retirement plan. An individual who owns the entire interest in an unincorporated trade or business is treated as his own employer. A partnership is treated as the employer of each partner who is eligible to be included in a self-employed retirement plan. (Code Sec. 129(e)(3), Code Sec. 129(e)(4))[9]

No amount is excludable unless the name, address and (except in the case of a tax-exempt service-provider) taxpayer identifying number (TIN) of the person providing the dependent care services are included on the employee's return. The employee can use Form W-10 to ask for this information from the service provider. Failure to provide this information is excused if the employee exercised due diligence in trying to do so. (Code Sec. 129(e)(9))[10]

The plan must satisfy specific nondiscrimination rules and certain other requirements. (Code Sec. 129(d))[11] If an otherwise qualified program fails to meet these requirements, the program will be a dependent care assistance program under which expenses are still excludable for nonhighly compensated employees. (Code Sec. 129(d)(1))[12]

For how excludable dependent care assistance affects the dependent care credit, see ¶2349.

3. ¶H-2417.1; TD ¶133,045.1
4. ¶H-2461.4 *et seq.*; ¶1254.05; TD ¶133,044.3
5. ¶H-1401; ¶1294 *et seq.*; TD ¶133,504
6. ¶H-1402; ¶1294; TD ¶133,505
7. ¶H-1402 *et seq.*; ¶1294; TD ¶133,503
8. ¶H-1419; ¶1294.02; TD ¶133,516
9. ¶H-1413 *et seq.*; ¶1294.02; TD ¶133,504
10. ¶H-1406 *et seq.*; ¶1294.03; TD ¶133,501
11. ¶H-1428 *et seq.*; ¶1294.01; TD ¶133,518
12. ¶H-1418; ¶1294.01; TD ¶133,515

¶ 1271   Time for Reporting Compensation. ▬▬▬▬▬▬▬▬▬▬▬▬▬▬▬▬▬▬

Compensation income is reported according to the recipient's accounting method, subject to constructive receipt, prepaid income and deferred income rules.

¶ 1272   Cash basis taxpayers.

Cash basis taxpayers report compensation for the tax year they actually receive it.[13]

Compensation paid by check is reported for the year the check is received, even if the check covers past or future services, or isn't cashed until the following year.[14]

Compensation income must be reported for the year it's constructively received (see ¶2822), even though it's not actually received until a later year. Income is constructively received for the year it's credited to the taxpayer's account, set apart for him, or otherwise made available so he can draw upon it at any time, or could have drawn upon it during the tax year if he had given notice of intention to withdraw. (Reg § 1.451-2(a))[15] For advances, see ¶1274.

¶ 1273   Accrual basis taxpayers.

Accrual basis taxpayers report compensation for the tax year in which it accrues. Compensation accrues when all events have occurred that fix the right to receive the income and its amount can be determined with reasonable accuracy. (Reg § 1.451-1(a))[16]

If the right to compensation for services or its amount can't be determined until the services are completed, the amount of compensation ordinarily isn't reported until the tax year the services are completed and the determination can be made. (Reg § 1.451-1(a))[17]

¶ 1274   Advances and drawing accounts.

A cash basis taxpayer who receives advances against commissions that haven't been earned reports the advances as income for the year they are received, if he isn't required to repay the amounts received in excess of commissions. If he must repay the excess drawings, those amounts aren't income until offset by a credit for commissions earned.[18]

¶ 1275   Deferred compensation plans.

All amounts deferred under a nonqualified deferred compensation (NQDC) plan for all tax years are currently includible in gross income to the extent not subject to a substantial risk of forfeiture and not previously included in gross income, unless the plan:

. . . meets specified distribution, acceleration of benefit, and election requirements; and

. . . is operated in accordance with these requirements. (Code Sec. 409A(a)(1)(A)(i))[19]

If a NQDC plan doesn't comply with the Code Sec. 409A rules, all amounts deferred under the plan for the tax year and all prior tax years, by any participant to whom the failure relates, are included in income for that year to the extent not subject to a substantial risk of forfeiture and not previously included in income. This amount is also subject to: (1) interest (at the underpayment rate plus one percentage point) on the tax underpayments that would have occurred had the amount been included in income for the tax year when first deferred, or if later, when not subject to a substantial risk of forfeiture; and (2) a penalty of 20% of the compensation required to be included in income. (Code Sec. 409A(a)(1)(B))

---

13. ¶H-3501; ¶s 614.023, 4514.003; TD ¶130,526
14. ¶H-3502; ¶s 614.023, 4514.004; TD ¶130,527
15. ¶H-3508; ¶4514.036; TD ¶130,531
16. ¶G-2471; ¶4514.011; TD ¶441,701

17. ¶H-3526; ¶4514.011; TD ¶441,702
18. ¶H-3515; ¶614.023; TD ¶130,518
19. ¶H-3200; ¶409A4.01; TD ¶135,508

For inclusion in income of deferred compensation from tax-indifferent corporations and partnerships, see ¶1277.

Compensation is subject to a substantial risk of forfeiture if entitlement to it is conditioned on a person's performance of substantial future services or the occurrence of a condition related to the compensation's purpose (e.g., an amount conditioned on involuntary separation from service without cause), and the possibility of forfeiture is substantial. An amount isn't subject to a substantial risk of forfeiture merely because the right to the amount is conditioned upon the refraining from performance of services, such as a noncompete clause. (Reg § 1.409A-1(d)(1))[20]

A NQDC plan is any plan that provides for the deferral of compensation, other than (1) a qualified employer plan (a qualified retirement plan, tax-deferred annuity, simplified employee pension, SIMPLE plan, qualified governmental excess benefit arrangement under Code Sec. 415(m), or eligible deferred compensation plan under Code Sec. 457(b)), and (2) any bona fide vacation leave, sick leave, compensatory time, disability pay, or death benefit plan. (Code Sec. 409A(d)) It also doesn't include annual bonuses, or other annual compensation amounts, paid within 2 ½ months after the later of a service recipient's or service provider's tax year. (Reg § 1.409A-1(b)(4))[21] IRS won't treat as subject to Code Sec. 409A common arrangements in which school teachers, who provide services during a ten-month school year, elect to be paid ratably over 12 months.[22]

Incentive stock options (ISOs) and options granted under an employee stock purchase plan (ESPP) aren't subject to Code Sec. 409A. Nonqualified stock options and stock appreciation rights (SARs) are similarly excepted if the exercise price may never be less than the fair market value (FMV) of the underlying stock when the option or right is granted, the number of shares subject to the option are fixed on the grant date, and there is no other deferral feature; in addition, the receipt, transfer or exercise of the stock option must be subject to tax under Code Sec. 83, and only the service recipient's stock may be delivered upon a SAR's exercise. (Reg § 1.409A-1(b)(5))[23]

The distribution requirement is met if a NQDC plan provides that compensation deferred under the plan cannot be distributed earlier than (1) the participant's separation from service; (2) the date the participant becomes disabled; (3) the participant's death; (4) a time specified, or a schedule fixed, under the plan as of the date of the deferral of the compensation (amounts payable on the occurrence of an event are not treated as payable at a specified time); (5) a change in the ownership or effective control of the corporation, or in the ownership of a substantial portion of the assets of the corporation; or (6) the occurrence of an unforeseeable emergency such as a severe financial hardship resulting from illness, casualty loss, etc. (Code Sec. 409A(a)(2); Reg § 1.409A-3(a))[24]

The acceleration of benefits requirement is met if a NQDC plan doesn't allow the acceleration of the time or schedule of any payment under the plan, except as provided in IRS regs. (Code Sec. 409A(a)(3)) Changes in the form of distribution that accelerate payments generally are subject to this rule. But payments made in accordance with plan provisions for acceleration in the event of a service provider's separation from service, death or disability, or in the event of a change in control do not violate these rules.[25] Nor do payments under a domestic relations order,[26] or to comply with a certificate of divestiture for a conflict-of-interest,[27] or de minimis nonelective payments to terminate a participant's entire interest in the plan (i.e., $17,500 or less for 2013 and 2014).[28] (Reg § 1.409A-3(j))

The election requirements are met if the plan provides that compensation for services

---

20. ¶H-3200.50; ¶409A4.01; TD ¶135,511
21. ¶H-3200.27; ¶409A4.01; TD ¶135,508.1
22. ¶H-3307.1
23. ¶H-3200.28 *et seq.*; ¶409A4.01; TD ¶135,520
24. ¶H-3200.56; ¶409A4.01; TD ¶135,514

25. ¶H-3200.66; ¶409A4.01; TD ¶135,513.1
26. ¶H-3200.67
27. ¶H-3200.68
28. ¶H-3200.69

performed during a tax year can be deferred at the participant's election only if the initial deferral election is made (1) not later than the close of the preceding tax year; or (2) at another time provided in IRS regs. For performance-based compensation (e.g., bonuses), based on services performed over a period of at least 12 months, the initial deferral election must be made no later than six months before the end of the period. The time and form of distributions have to be specified at the time of initial deferral. An election made after the initial election (a redeferral election) generally must not take effect until at least 12 months after the date on which the election is made and must require deferral for a period of not less than five years from the date on which payment would otherwise have been made. (Code Sec. 409A(a)(4))[29]

Relief provisions. Under IRS relief, if there is an unintentional operational failure to comply with specified Code Sec. 409A(a) requirements (e.g., incorrect amount treated as deferred compensation) that is corrected within the year, no amount is generally included in income under Code Sec. 409A(a). Relief is conditioned on timely filing and information reporting and taking commercially reasonable steps to avoid a recurrence of the failure. For other specified unintentional operational failures that aren't corrected in the same year, the amount included in income, and the resulting additional tax, is limited. A delay or acceleration in the payment of NQDC to comply with a Troubled Asset Relief Program (TARP) advisory opinion won't violate Code Sec. 409A. Neither will certain document failures.[30]

¶ 1276   Rabbi trusts and funding triggers.

Amounts deferred under nonqualified deferred compensation (NQDC) plans (¶1275) generally are not includible in income if the deferred compensation is payable from general corporate funds that are subject to the claims of general creditors. Arrangements known as "rabbi trusts" generally are irrevocable and don't permit the employer to use the assets for purposes other than payment of deferred compensation. However, the trust assets are subject to the claims of the employer's creditors in the case of insolvency or bankruptcy. Because of this feature, rabbi trusts are not considered to be funded and so compensation is deferred.

Assets directly or indirectly set aside in a trust for purposes of paying nonqualified deferred compensation are treated, for Code Sec. 83 purposes, as property transferred in connection with the performance of services (see ¶1217), whether or not the assets are available to satisfy claims of general creditors (1) at the time set aside, if the assets are located outside of the U.S.; or (2) at the time transferred, if the assets are later transferred outside of the U.S. (Code Sec. 409A(b)(1))

There is also a transfer of property, for Code Sec. 83 purposes, as of the earlier of (1) the date on which a NQDC plan first provides that assets will become restricted to the provision of benefits under the plan in connection with a change in the employer's financial health; or (2) the date on which assets are so restricted. (Code Sec. 409A(b)(2))[31]

Interest and a 20% penalty apply with regard to the off-shore rabbi trust and financial trigger rules.

¶ 1277   Deferred compensation from tax-indifferent corporations and partnerships.

For deferred amounts attributable to services performed after Dec. 31, 2008, any compensation that is deferred under a nonqualified deferred compensation (NQDC) plan of a non-qualified entity is includible in gross income when there is no substantial risk of forfeiture of the rights to the compensation. (Code Sec. 457A(a))[32] A person's rights to compensation are subject to a substantial risk of forfeiture only if those rights are conditioned on the future

29. ¶H-3200.72 *et seq.*; ¶409A4.01; TD ¶135,515
30. ¶H-3200.18 *et seq.*; ¶409A4.01; TD ¶135,507
31. ¶H-3233; ¶409A4.20; TD ¶135,507
32. ¶H-3401; ¶457A4; TD ¶135,801

performance of substantial services by any individual. (Code Sec. 457A(d)(1)) A nonqualified entity is: (1) any foreign corporation unless substantially all of its income is either effectively connected with the conduct of a trade or business in the U.S. or subject to a comprehensive foreign income tax; and (2) any partnership (either domestic or foreign), unless substantially all of its income is allocated to persons other than foreign persons for whom that income isn't subject to a comprehensive foreign income tax (as defined in Code Sec. 457A(d)(2)); or organizations that are exempt from U.S. income tax. (Code Sec. 457A(b))

A NQDC plan is generally one described in Code Sec. 409A(d) (see ¶1275), except that it includes any plan that provides a right to compensation based on the appreciation in value of a specified number of equity units of the service recipient (e.g., stock appreciation rights (SARs)). Compensation (other than that based on gain on an investment asset) isn't treated as deferred if the service provider receives payment not later than 12 months after the end of the service recipient's tax year during which the right to the payment of the compensation is no longer subject to a substantial risk of forfeiture. (Code Sec. 457A(d)(3)) For foreign corporations with income that is effectively connected with the conduct of a U.S. trade or business, Code Sec. 457A doesn't apply to compensation that the corporation could have deducted against its effectively connected income if it had been paid in cash on the date that it ceased to be subject to a substantial risk of forfeiture. (Code Sec. 457A(d)(4)) Code Sec. 457A doesn't apply to a NQDC plan if the compensation is: (a) payable to an employee of a domestic subsidiary of the entity and (b) reasonably expected to be deductible by that subsidiary under Code Sec. 404(a)(5) (¶1538) when it is includible in the employee's income.[33]

If an amount of compensation is not determinable when it is otherwise includible in income under Code Sec. 457A, it is taken into account when it becomes determinable, subject to an additional 20% tax and an interest charge at the Code Sec. 6621 underpayment rate plus one percentage point, from the tax year first deferred or, if later, the first tax year not subject to a substantial risk of forfeiture. (Code Sec. 457A(c)) An amount isn't determinable if, at the time it is no longer subject to a substantial risk of forfeiture, it varies depending on the satisfaction of an objective condition.[34]

To the extent provided in regs, if compensation is determined solely by reference to the amount of gain recognized on the disposition of an investment asset, that compensation is treated as subject to a substantial risk of forfeiture until the date of the disposition. An investment asset is any single asset, other than an investment fund or similar entity, that's acquired directly by an investment fund or similar entity for which neither the entity nor any person related participates in the active management of that asset (or if that asset is an interest in an entity, in the active management of the activities of the entity), and substantially all of any gain on the disposition of that asset (other than the NQDC) is allocated to investors in the entity. (Code Sec. 457A(d)(1))

Inclusion of pre-2009 amounts. For a deferred amount to which Code Sec. 457A doesn't apply solely because it's attributable to services performed before 2009, to the extent not includible in gross income in a tax year beginning before 2018, it is includible in the later of (1) the last tax year beginning before 2018; or (2) the tax year in which there is no substantial risk of forfeiture of the rights to the compensation. (Sec. 801(d)(2) of Division C, P.L. 110-343, 10/3/2008) Earnings on deferred amounts attributable to services performed before 2009, are subject to Code Sec. 457A only to the extent that the amounts to which the earnings relate are subject to Code Sec. 457A. (§801(d) EESA, DivC, PL 110-343, 10/3/2008)[35]

---

33. ¶H-3401; ¶457A4; TD ¶135,801   35. ¶H-3401; ¶457A4; TD ¶135,801
34. ¶H-3421; ¶457A4; TD ¶135,814.1

¶ 1278   Social Security, Unemployment and Certain Disability Payments. ▬▬▬▬▬

Social security benefits may be partly taxable. Unemployment benefits are fully taxable. Payments under military and government disability pensions may be excludible from income.

For voluntary withholding on social security and certain other federal payments, and on unemployment compensation payments, see ¶3009.

¶ 1279   Social security payments—the Tier I and Tier II taxes.

A taxpayer whose "provisional income" —i.e., modified adjusted gross income (modified AGI, see below) plus one half of the social security benefits (including Tier 1 Railroad Retirement benefits) received—for a tax year exceeds either of two threshold amounts is taxed on a portion of social security benefits received that year, as follows:

Tier I: If provisional income exceeds a "base amount," include in gross income the *lesser* of:

. . . 50% of the social security benefits received that year; (Code Sec. 86(a)(1)(A)) or

. . . 50% of the excess of provisional income over the "base amount." (Code Sec. 86(a)(1)(B))[36]

"Modified AGI" means AGI: (1) determined without regard to the social security benefits; the deduction for qualified education loan interest (¶2222); the deduction for higher education expenses; the exclusions for foreign earned income and housing costs (¶4612 *et seq.*), savings bond proceeds for education expenses (¶2220), employer-provided adoption assistance (¶1254), and income from sources within U.S. possessions and Puerto Rico, and (2) increased by the amount of tax-exempt interest received or accrued by taxpayer during the tax year. (Code Sec. 86(b)(2))[37]

The "base amount" is $32,000 for married individuals filing a joint return; zero for a married individual filing a separate return who doesn't live apart from his spouse for the entire tax year; and $25,000 for all other individuals (Code Sec. 86(c)(1)), such as those filing as single, head of household or qualifying widow(er).[38]

⟁*illustration:* G's modified AGI for the tax year consists of pension income of $15,000 and $3,000 of taxable interest and dividends. His social security benefit is $12,000. He's married and files a joint return. His wife has no income. The sum of their modified AGI ($18,000) plus one-half of his social security benefit ($6,000) is $24,000. This is less than their base amount ($32,000), so no part of his social security benefit is taxable.

Tier II: If provisional income exceeds an "adjusted base amount," include in gross income the *lesser* of:

. . . 85% of the social security benefits received that year; or

. . . the sum of: (a) the amount included under the above 50% rule or, if less, one-half of the difference between taxpayer's "adjusted base amount" and "base amount," plus (b) 85% of the excess of provisional income over the "adjusted base amount." (Code Sec. 86(a)(2))

The "adjusted base amount" is $44,000 for married individuals filing jointly; zero for a married individual filing separately who doesn't live apart from his spouse for the entire tax year); and $34,000 for all other individuals. (Code Sec. 86(c)(2))

⟁*caution:* Any spike in income, e.g., from the sale of stock or a mutual fund, or a retirement plan distribution, may subject a taxpayer to an unexpected tax on his social security

---

36. ¶J-1456; ¶864.04; TD ¶146,001
37. ¶J-1459; ¶864.02; TD ¶146,004

38. ¶J-1457; ¶864.03; TD ¶146,002

benefits, if the extra income causes him to exceed his base or adjusted base amount.

Benefits a taxpayer repays during a tax year reduce the benefits taxed that year, whether the repayment is for overpayments received that repayment year or any earlier year. (Code Sec. 86(d)(2)(A))[39]

If any portion of a lump-sum social security benefit received during a tax year is attributable to an earlier year, the taxpayer can elect (write "LSE" on the return) to include in gross income with respect to that portion, the sum of the increases in gross income that would have resulted had the portion been paid in the earlier year. (Code Sec. 86(e)(1))[40]

¶ 1280   Railroad Retirement Act benefits other than Tier 1 benefits.

Railroad Retirement Act benefits (other than Tier 1 benefits, see ¶1279) are treated as benefits provided under an employer plan that meets the requirements of Code Sec. 401(a) (a "qualified plan," see ¶4319 *et seq.*). (Code Sec. 72(r)(1), Code Sec. 72(r)(3)) Lump-sum termination (early retirement) payments have been held to be taxable under these rules.[41]

¶ 1281   Unemployment compensation.

Unemployment compensation (reported to recipients on Form 1099-G) is fully taxable. (Code Sec. 85(a)) Unemployment compensation includes any amount received under a law of the U.S. or a state that's in the nature of unemployment compensation. (Code Sec. 85(b)) It also includes disability benefits paid under federal or state law as a substitute for unemployment benefits to those who are ineligible for unemployment benefits because they're disabled.[42]

¶ 1282   Unemployment benefits paid by employers.

Unemployment benefits (not described at ¶1281) paid directly by an employer are includible in the employee's income. Amounts received by an employee from an employer under a "guaranteed annual wage plan" during periods of unemployment are taxable as wages. [43]

¶ 1283   Strike and lockout benefits.

Strike and lockout benefits paid to an employee by a union, from union dues, including both cash and the fair market value of goods received, are included in the employee's income unless the facts clearly show they're intended as a gift. To be excluded, at a minimum, the union must inquire into the recipient's personal needs and make payments accordingly.[44]

¶ 1284   Certain military and government disability pensions.

Eligible members of the armed forces of any country, the National Oceanic and Atmospheric Administration, or the Public Health Service, and individuals who receive a disability annuity under section 808 of the Foreign Service Act of 1980, exclude from gross income amounts received as pension, annuity or similar allowance for personal injuries or sickness resulting from active service. Those eligible are primarily individuals with combat-related injuries or sickness or entitled to disability compensation from the Department of Veterans Affairs. (Code Sec. 104(a)(4))[45] While armed forces retirement pay based on length of service is taxable, that pay is excludible to the extent it could be received as a disability pension.[46]

39. ¶J-1467; ¶864.05; TD ¶146,011
40. ¶J-1469; ¶864.08; TD ¶146,012
41. ¶J-1471; ¶724.26; TD ¶146,014
42. ¶H-3007 *et seq.*; ¶854.01; TD ¶132,506

43. ¶H-3005; ¶854.01; TD ¶132,501
44. ¶H-3009; TD ¶132,509
45. ¶H-3120; ¶s 614.041, 1044.04; TD ¶138,020
46. ¶H-3123; ¶s 614.040, 1044.04; TD ¶138,023

¶ 1285 Dividends. ▬▬▬▬▬▬▬▬▬▬▬

When a corporation distributes its earnings to its shareholders, the distribution is usually a dividend. If the dividend is "qualified" it is taxable at rates that apply to net capital gain; otherwise it is taxable as ordinary income. But not all corporate distributions are dividends. And some transactions that don't appear to be dividends may be taxed as constructive dividends.

For stock redemptions, see ¶3526 *et seq.* For liquidations, see ¶3574 *et seq.*

¶ 1286 How dividends are taxed to shareholders.

Dividends (defined at ¶1287) are taxable to the person who has the present, enforceable right to receive them, whether or not he's the owner of the underlying stock.[47] Dividends received by an agent are taxable to his principal.[48] If the stock is sold before a dividend is declared and paid, or between the declaration and record (or "ex dividend") dates, the dividends are taxed to the buyer. Dividends on stock sold on or after the record date are taxed to the seller. (Reg § 1.61-9(c))[49]

Dividends are taxable in the year received or unqualifiedly made subject to the shareholder's demand. This applies to both cash and accrual shareholders. Thus, if a corporation pays a dividend on Dec. 30 last year, and the shareholder receives the check on Jan. 2 this year, the shareholder reports it on this year's return. (Reg § 1.301-1(b))[50] For RIC (mutual fund) dividends, see ¶1298. For REIT dividends, see ¶1299.

Dividends are taxed to shareholders at the rates that apply to net capital gain if they constitute "qualified dividend income" (¶1288) paid to noncorporate shareholders (Code Sec. 1(h)(11)) and would otherwise be taxed at ordinary income rates to the extent of the distributing corporation's earnings and profits (E&P, ¶3522). (Code Sec. 301(c)(1)) Thus, for dividends received after 2012, the 15%/0% rates applies to taxpayers whose incomes fall below certain thresholds ($450,000 for joint filers and surviving spouses; $425,000 for heads of household; $400,000 for single filers; and $225,000 for married taxpayers filing separately), but taxpayers whose incomes exceed these thresholds are subject to a 20% rate (see ¶2604).

The part of a distribution in excess of E&P is treated as a tax-free return of capital and is applied against (reduces) the shareholder's basis in the stock. (Code Sec. 301(c)(2)) Any remaining excess (once basis is reduced to zero) is treated as payment for the stock, i.e., as capital gain if the stock is a capital asset in the shareholder's hands. (Code Sec. 301(c)(3))[1]

¶ 1287 Dividend defined.

A dividend is a distribution of property by a corporation to its shareholders with respect to its stock, out of accumulated or current earnings and profits (E&P, see ¶3522). (Code Sec. 316(a)) The distribution must be made in the ordinary course of the corporation's business, but it may be extraordinary in amount. (Reg § 1.316-1(a)(1))[2]

A dividend needn't be proportionate[3] and needn't be formally declared.[4]

"Property" includes money, securities and any other property (except the corporation's own stock or rights to that stock, see ¶1295). (Code Sec. 317(a)) Property also includes any economic benefit the corporation gives its shareholders, in whatever form (Reg § 1.317-1), e.g., paying their debts (see ¶1289).[5]

---

47. ¶J-2401; ¶3014.05; TD ¶172,013
48. ¶J-2405; ¶3014.05; TD ¶172,014
49. ¶J-2406; ¶3014.05; TD ¶172,021
50. ¶J-2451; ¶s 3014.07, 4514.036; TD ¶172,005
1. ¶J-2350 *et seq.*; ¶3014; TD ¶172,001

2. ¶J-2356; ¶3164 *et seq.*; TD ¶171,001
3. ¶J-2366; ¶3014; TD ¶171,001
4. ¶J-2360; ¶3014.01; TD ¶171,001
5. ¶s J-2357, J-2365; ¶s 3014.01, 3174; TD ¶171,002

¶ 1288   Qualified dividend income defined.

Qualified dividend income is dividend income received from domestic corporations and qualified foreign corporations—i.e., U.S. possession corporations and corporations eligible for benefits of a comprehensive income tax treaty with the U.S. that includes an exchange of information program (which can include controlled foreign corporation (CFC) dividends if not required to be included under Code Sec. 951(a)(1) (¶4622), but not passive foreign investment companies). (Code Sec. 1(h)(11)(B)(i)) Dividends paid by other foreign corporations also are qualified if paid on stock or American Depository Receipts (ADRs) readily tradable on an established U.S. securities market. (Code Sec. 1(h)(11)(C))

Qualified dividend income does not include: (1) dividends paid on stock unless the stock has been held for more than 60 days during the 121-day period beginning 60 days before the ex-dividend date (more than 90 days during the 181-day period beginning 90 days before the ex-dividend date for preferred stock dividends attributable to a period of more than 366 days) (Code Sec. 1(h)(11)(B)(iii)(I)); (2) dividends on stock to the extent that the taxpayer is under an obligation to make related payments with respect to positions in substantially similar or related property (Code Sec. 1(h)(11)(B)(iii)(II)); (3) any amount that the taxpayer elects to treat as investment income to support an investment interest deduction (Code Sec. 1(h)(11)(D)(i)) (see ¶1729; (4) dividends from corporations that for the distribution year or the preceding year are exempt from tax under Code Sec. 501 (see ¶4100) or Code Sec. 521 (exempt farmers' cooperatives, see ¶4206 *et seq.*) (Code Sec. 1(h)(11)(B)(ii)(I)); (5) dividends deductible under Code Sec. 591 by mutual savings banks (Code Sec. 1(h)(11)(B)(ii)(II)); and (6) dividends paid on employer securities owned by an employee stock ownership plan (ESOP), which are deductible under Code Sec. 404(k). (Code Sec. 1(h)(11)(B)(ii)(III))[6]

Qualified dividend income does not include payments in lieu of dividends (typically made to owners of stock that has been lent in connection with a short sale). However, if a payment in lieu of dividends is reported as dividend income on a Form 1099-DIV, the recipient may treat the payment for tax purposes as a dividend, and not as a payment in lieu of dividends, unless he knows, or has reason to know, of the actual character of the payment.[7]

If an individual, trust, or estate receives extraordinary dividends (within the meaning of Code Sec. 1059(c)) that are qualified dividend income, any loss on the dividend-paying stock is a long-term capital loss to the extent of the extraordinary dividends. (Code Sec. 1(h)(11)(D)(ii))[8]

For dividends from RICs, see ¶1298. For dividends from REITs, see ¶1299.

¶ 1289   Constructive or disguised dividends.

When a corporation pays excessive or unreasonably large amounts to a shareholder or a member of his family as salary (Reg § 1.162-7(b)(1)) or rent,[9] or for a purchase price,[10] the excess is a constructive dividend (assuming sufficient E&P, see ¶3522). Similarly, constructive dividends include a corporation's payments of a shareholder's debts[11] or personal expenses.[12] A dividend may also result without a direct payment to the shareholder, if the corporation makes a payment to a third party that's for the shareholder's benefit and made with respect to his stock.[13]

---

6. ¶I-5115; ¶14.085; TD ¶223,345
7. ¶I-5115.4; TD ¶223,349
8. ¶I-5104.1; ¶14.087; TD ¶223,307
9. ¶J-2726; ¶3014.09 *et seq.*; TD ¶175,052

10. ¶J-2730; ¶3014.11; TD ¶175,044
11. ¶J-2749; ¶3014.14; TD ¶175,038
12. ¶J-2757; ¶3014.13; TD ¶175,007
13. ¶J-2700 *et seq.*; ¶3014.14; TD ¶175,002

¶ 1290   Loan vs. dividend.

A shareholder may borrow money from the corporation with or without interest, and with or without security. If the agreement and the genuine intent (at withdrawal) is that the amount be repaid to the corporation, and there's persuasive evidence of both that intent *and* the shareholder's ability to carry it out, the amount received is treated as a loan (i.e., nontaxable), and not as a dividend[14] (unless a below-market interest rate is involved, see ¶1291).

¶ 1291   Dividends from below-market loans between corporation and shareholder.

For any below-market interest rate loan (¶1306) (directly or indirectly) between a corporation and a shareholder, the corporation/lender is treated as having paid a dividend, equal to the amount of the foregone interest, that's includible in the shareholder/borrower's income. De minimis ($10,000 or less) and certain other loans are excepted. (Code Sec. 7872(a))[15]

¶ 1292   Determining the amount of a dividend (cash and in-kind).

The amount of a dividend is the sum of the cash plus the fair market value (FMV), at distribution, of any other property received (Code Sec. 301(b)(1), Code Sec. 301(b)(3)), reduced (but not below zero) by the amount of any liability of the corporation that the shareholder assumes in connection with the distribution, or to which the property is subject. (Code Sec. 301(b)(2))[16] But the amount taxable as a dividend in kind can't exceed the distributing corporation's E&P (¶3522). (Reg § 1.316-1(a)(2))[17]

A dividend consisting of the corporation's obligations equals the FMV of the notes. (Reg § 1.301-1(d)) For stock dividends, see ¶1296.

These rules apply to both corporate (U.S. or foreign) and noncorporate shareholders[18] (but a corporate shareholder may get a dividends-received deduction, see ¶3306 *et seq.*), and to dividends from a foreign corporation to its U.S. corporate shareholder. (Code Sec. 301(b)(1))[19]

¶ 1293   Basis of distributed property to shareholder-distributee.

The basis to the shareholder (corporate or individual) for property received as a dividend (¶1287) is the property's fair market value at distribution (Code Sec. 301(d)), i.e., the amount treated as a dividend (see ¶1292), but without the reduction for liabilities.[20]

¶ 1294   Holding period for property received as a taxable dividend.

The shareholder's holding period for property received as a taxable dividend begins on the date of receipt (actual or constructive). (Code Sec. 1223(2))[21]

¶ 1295   Distributions of stock or rights to stock.

With certain exceptions (see ¶1296), a stock dividend—i.e., a corporation's distribution of its *own* stock, or rights (e.g., options or warrants) to buy its stock, that's made to shareholders with respect to their stock (i.e., not as compensation)—isn't taxable to the shareholder. (Code Sec. 305) But a corporation's distribution of stock, or rights to buy stock, in *another* corporation (even if affiliated) is a regular dividend in kind, taxed under the rules at ¶1286 *et seq.*[22]

---

14. ¶J-2707 *et seq.*; ¶3014.14; TD ¶175,014
15. ¶J-2721 *et seq.*; ¶78,724.16; TD ¶172,011
16. ¶J-2482; ¶3014.02; TD ¶173,503
17. ¶J-2361; ¶3164.01; TD ¶173,501
18. ¶J-2482; ¶s 3014, 3014.02

19. ¶3014.02
20. ¶P-5401; ¶3014.03; TD ¶217,501
21. ¶s I-8903, I-8918; TD ¶223,508
22. ¶J-2478; ¶3054.01; TD ¶174,009

Stock splits are treated as stock dividends if identical stock is distributed on stock held.[23]

For stock (rights) received in connection with corporate organizations, reorganizations or divisions, see ¶3554.

¶ 1296 Taxable stock (or rights) dividends.

Where a stock (or rights) dividend is taxable, the dividend amount is the fair market value (FMV) at distribution of the stock (rights), under the "regular" dividend-in-kind rules, see ¶1292.[24] Where the dividend is taxable because of a cash election, the "dividend" equals: (1) the cash received, for shareholders electing cash, and (2) the FMV of the stock (rights) at distribution, for those receiving stock (rights). (Reg § 1.305-1(b))[25]

These stock (or rights) dividends are *not* tax-free:

(1) A distribution in which *any* shareholder has the option to take cash or other property instead of the stock (or rights); (Code Sec. 305(b)(1); Reg § 1.305-2)[26]

(2) A "disproportionate" distribution that results in the receipt of property by some shareholders and, for others, an increase in their proportionate interests in the corporation's assets or earnings and profits; (Code Sec. 305(b)(2); Reg § 1.305-3)[27]

(3) A distribution that results in the receipt of preferred stock by some common shareholders and the receipt of common stock by others; (Code Sec. 305(b)(3); Reg § 1.305-4)[28]

(4) Any distributions on preferred stock, including a redemption premium treated as a distribution (for preferred stock issued after Oct. 9, '90, the premium is included as OID, see ¶1314 *et seq.*), *other than* an increase in the conversion ratio of convertible preferred stock made solely to take into account a stock dividend or stock split with respect to the stock into which the preferred is convertible; (Code Sec. 305(b)(4); Reg § 1.305-5)[29]

(5) Any distribution of convertible preferred stock unless IRS is satisfied it won't have the result in (2), above; (Code Sec. 305(b)(5); Reg § 1.305-6)[30]

(6) A constructive stock distribution, e.g., a change in conversion ratio or redemption price, or a redemption premium (difference between redemption price and issue price). (Code Sec. 305(c); Reg § 1.305-5(b), Reg § 1.305-7)[31]

¶ 1297 Cash for fractional shares.

Where a corporation's purpose in distributing cash (instead of scrip or fractional shares) in a distribution that otherwise qualifies as a nontaxable stock dividend (¶1295) is to save trouble, expense and inconvenience, and not to give any shareholder(s) an increased interest, the distribution is treated as if the fractional shares had been issued and then redeemed by the corporation. (Reg § 1.305-3(c)) The cash received is treated as an amount realized on the sale of a fractional share. Gain or loss is the cash received minus the basis of the share sold. (Reg § 1.305-3(c)(2))[32]

¶ 1298 Dividends from regulated investment companies (RICs, or mutual funds).

Ordinary dividends a RIC (¶4201) distributes to its shareholders generally are taxed to them just like other corporate dividends. (¶1286, ¶1292) (Code Sec. 852; Reg § 1.852-4(a))[33] However, if the amount of dividends eligible for qualified dividend income treatment (i.e., taxable at the capital gain rates) (¶1286) received by a RIC for a tax year is less than 95% of

---

23. ¶J-2501; ¶3054.02; TD ¶174,001
24. ¶J-2504, J-2506; ¶3054.02; TD ¶173,501
25. ¶J-2507; ¶3054.02; TD ¶174,006
26. ¶s J-2508 *et seq.*, J-2501; ¶3054.02; TD ¶174,017
27. ¶J-2510 *et seq.*; ¶3054.02; TD ¶174,020
28. ¶J-2515; ¶3054.02; TD ¶174,024

29. ¶J-2501, J-2516 *et seq.*; ¶3054.02; TD ¶174,025
30. ¶s J-2501, J-2526; ¶3054.02; TD ¶174,027
31. ¶J-2501, ¶J-2527 *et seq.*; ¶3054.02; TD ¶174,013
32. ¶J-2514; ¶3054.01; TD ¶174,014
33. ¶E-6150 *et seq.*; ¶8524.02; TD ¶172,005

its gross income (as specially computed), then only the amount of qualified dividend income received by the RIC for the tax year may be distributed to its shareholders as qualified dividend income. (Code Sec. 1(h)(11)(D)(iii), Code Sec. 854(b)(1)(B)) But capital gain dividends, which the RIC need not actually distribute, result in capital gain income (see ¶4201) (Code Sec. 852(b)(3)(D)),[34] and exempt-interest dividends are treated as tax-exempt interest (¶1331). (Code Sec. 852(b)(5)(B))[35] Capital gain dividends are not treated as qualified dividend income (¶1288). (Code Sec. 854(a)) The amount of RIC dividends that are qualifying dividend income must be reported to RIC shareholders within 60 days after the close of the RIC's tax year. (Code Sec. 854(b)(2))

A dividend the RIC pays after the close of its tax year generally is treated as received by the shareholder in the year actually paid, even if the RIC elects to treat it as paid in the preceding year (see ¶4203). (Code Sec. 855(b))[36] But dividends the RIC declares in Oct., Nov. or Dec. are treated as received by the shareholder on Dec. 31 if the RIC actually pays them during the following Jan. (Code Sec. 852(b)(7))[37]

caution: Since dividends paid in Jan. may have to be picked up in the preceding year's income, that year's Form 1099, and not the RIC's monthly statements, should be used to determine the dividends to report for that year.

A RIC can designate a dividend as a capital gain dividend and can make additional designations of its capital gain dividend distributions corresponding to the various maximum rates at which net capital gains may be taxed (¶2603). Limitations apply, e.g., the additional designation cannot exceed the maximum distributable amount in that class.[38]

Qualified dividend income is calculated without any reduction for expenses. In addition, where a RIC has several types of income that must be specially designated, the RIC may designate the maximum amount that may be designated in each category even if the aggregate of all the amounts so designated exceeds the total amount of the RIC's dividend distributions. Each shareholder may then apply these designations to the dividends he receives up to his share of these amounts, even though his designations differ from the designations applied by other shareholders.[39]

¶ 1299 Dividends from real estate investment trusts (REITs).

REITs (¶4202) distribute ordinary dividends and capital gain dividends which (as with RICs, see ¶1298) the beneficiaries or shareholders (investors) treat, respectively, as ordinary income (except there's no dividends-received deduction) (Code Sec. 857(c)) and capital gain. (Code Sec. 857(b)(3)(B))[40] The only REIT dividends that are eligible for qualified dividend income treatment (¶1286) are those that the REIT received as qualified dividend income, such as dividends paid to the REIT from a taxable REIT subsidiary. (Code Sec. 1(h)(11)(D)(iii), Code Sec. 857(c)(2)) For undistributed capital gains of REITs, see ¶4202. A deficiency dividend the REIT pays for any year is taxed to the shareholder in the year it's paid, not the year *for which* it's paid. (Reg § 1.860-2(a)(3)(i))[41] But any dividend declared by the REIT in Oct., Nov. or Dec. and payable to shareholders of record on a specified date in that month is considered received by the shareholder on Dec. 31 if the REIT actually pays it the next Jan. (Code Sec. 857(b)(8)(A))[42]

REITs are subject to the same capital gain designation rules as RICs (see ¶1298).[43]

---

34. ¶E-6152; ¶8524.02
35. ¶E-6160; ¶8524.02
36. ¶E-6201; ¶8554.01
37. ¶E-6202; ¶8554.01; TD ¶172,005
38. ¶E-6153.1; ¶8524.02; TD ¶173,000.1

39. ¶E-6163.1
40. ¶E-6616; ¶8574.02; TD ¶173,006
41. ¶E-6304; ¶8604
42. ¶E-6704; ¶8574.02; TD ¶172,005
43. ¶E-6617.1; ¶8574.02; TD ¶173,000.1

¶ 1300   Dividends to co-op patrons; patronage dividends.

Distributions made by a co-op (¶4206) on its stock or other proprietary interests are taxed under the "regular" dividend rules (see ¶1292), but the dividends-received deduction doesn't apply if the co-op is exempt. (Code Sec. 246(a)(1))[44]

Patronage dividends and per-unit retain allocations (¶4207) received in money are included in income by the patron in the year received. Qualified written notices of allocation and qualified per-unit retain certificates (¶4207) are included in income at their stated dollar amount when received. Other property (but not nonqualified allocations or nonqualified per-unit retain certificates) is included at its fair market value when received. (Code Sec. 1385)[45]

But the amount of any patronage dividend isn't included in income to the extent it is: (1) properly taken into account as an adjustment to basis of property, or (2) attributable to personal, living or family items. (Code Sec. 1385(b))[46]

¶ 1301   Interest Income.

Whatever the name given to the amounts or the form of the transaction, the receipt or accrual of interest is taxable as ordinary income, unless specifically exempt.

¶ 1302   Taxation of interest.

Unless specifically exempt, any interest received by or credited to a taxpayer is taxable as ordinary income. (Code Sec. 61(a)(4); Reg § 1.61-7(a))[47] The interest is taxable even if it's usurious unless applicable state law automatically converts the illegal portion into a payment of principal. (Reg § 1.61-7(a))[48]

¶ 1303   What is interest?

Interest is the price paid for the use of another's money or for the right to defer payment of money owed to another, regardless of the form of the transaction.[49] Interest generally includes the FMV of gifts or services received for opening or adding to accounts in financial institutions, but not if it's a de minimis premium (for a deposit of less than $5,000, the premium costs the bank $10 or less; for a deposit of $5,000 or more, it costs $20 or less).[50]

To be interest, generally a payment must be made with respect to a bona fide debt.[1] But other "interest" payments imposed by law, e.g., on judgments, tax refunds, installment sales, etc., are also interest.[2] And IRS may use the Code Sec. 482 allocation rules (¶2858) to "create" interest.[3]

¶ 1304   Interest on defaulted mortgage.

Amounts paid to a mortgagee as a result of the sale of property on foreclosure (or voluntary conveyance in lieu of foreclosure) of the mortgage, that represent accrued interest due on the mortgage, are taxable interest.[4] For mortgagee's gain or loss, see ¶1787.

For mortgage interest recipient's reporting requirements, see ¶4744.

---

44. ¶J-2608; ¶2434.04; TD ¶600,513
45. ¶J-2609 *et seq.*; ¶13,814.13; TD ¶171,042
46. ¶J-2612; ¶13,814.13
47. ¶J-2801; ¶614.067; TD ¶151,001
48. ¶J-2814; ¶614.068; TD ¶151,010
49. ¶J-2802 *et seq.*; TD ¶151,002

50. ¶J-2820; TD ¶811,513
1. ¶J-2803; ¶614.068; TD ¶151,003
2. ¶J-2834 *et seq.*; ¶614.068 *et seq.*; TD ¶151,030
3. ¶J-2817; ¶s 4824, 614.148;
4. ¶J-2819; ¶614.083

¶ 1305   "Points" and other loan-related fees.

Payments made to a bank or other lender to get a loan are interest, to the extent they are made for the use or forbearance of money rather than for services rendered. Thus, "points" (i.e., charges connected with mortgages that the borrower pays in addition to the stated interest) are interest, while commitment and service fees (for escrow, recording, credit inspection, appraisal) aren't.[5] For recipient's reporting requirements, see ¶4744.

¶ 1306   Below-market interest-rate loans.

The forgone interest on a "below-market" loan is taxed to the lender as interest income. (Code Sec. 7872)[6] A "below-market" loan is:

. . . *a demand loan* where interest is payable on the loan at a rate less than the applicable federal rate (AFR, see ¶1310), (Code Sec. 7872(e)(1)(A))[7] or

. . . *a term loan* where the amount loaned exceeds the present value of all payments due under the loan. (Code Sec. 7872(e)(1)(B))[8]

For a below-market demand loan, the "interest" for any period is the excess of: (1) the interest that would have been payable on the loan if it accrued annually at the AFR, over (2) any interest payable on the loan and properly allocable to the period. (Code Sec. 7872(e)(2)) For below-market term loans, the "interest" (treated as original issue discount (OID), see ¶1313 *et seq.*) is the excess of: (a) the amount loaned, over (b) the present value of all payments required to be made under the loan. (Code Sec. 7872(b)(2)(B))[9]

These rules don't apply to certain de minimis ($10,000 or less) loans (Code Sec. 7872(c)(2), Code Sec. 7872(c)(3)),[10] amounts treated as "unstated interest" (see ¶1307) (Code Sec. 7872(f)(8)),[11] or certain loans under a written continuing care contract to a qualified continuing care facility. (Code Sec. 7872(g))[12]

¶ 1307   Unstated (imputed) interest on deferred payment sales.

For certain deferred payment or installment sales (¶1308) where the sales contract fails to provide for interest at a minimum rate specified by the Code or by IRS, part of the payments received is treated as interest ("unstated interest") that's taxable to the seller despite any contrary intention of the parties. (Code Sec. 483)[13]

¶ 1308   Payments subject to unstated interest rules.

With certain exceptions (¶1312), the unstated interest rules (¶1307) apply to any payment where *all* the following requirements are met:

(1) The payment must be made on account of the sale or exchange of property.

(2) The payment must be part of the sales price under the contract.

(3) The "sales price" (determined at the time of sale) must be more than $3,000. "Sales price" includes the amount of any down payment, any liability encumbering the property and any amount treated as unstated interest under these rules, but not any *stated* interest payments.

(4) The payment must be due (under the contract) more than six months after the date of

5. ¶J-2818; ¶1634.005; TD ¶151,013
6. ¶J-2900; ¶78,724 *et seq.*; TD ¶151,504
7. ¶J-2939 *et seq.*; ¶78,724.04; TD ¶155,010
8. ¶J-2947 *et seq.*; ¶78,724.06; TD ¶155,015
9. ¶s J-2902, J-2904; ¶s 78,724.04, 78,724.06; TD ¶155,004
10. ¶J-2961; ¶78,724.12 *et seq.*; TD ¶155,027
11. ¶J-2918; ¶78,724.20; TD ¶155,021
12. ¶J-2988; ¶78,724.20; TD ¶155,056
13. ¶J-3750 *et seq.*; ¶4834; TD ¶152,001

the sale or exchange.

(5) At least one payment under the contract must be due more than one year after the date of the sale or exchange.

(6) There must be total unstated interest (¶1309) under the contract. (Code Sec. 483(c)(1), Code Sec. 483(d)(2); Reg § 1.483-1(b)(1))[14]

A debt instrument of the buyer given in exchange for property isn't itself treated as a payment. Rather, any payment due under the instrument is treated as due under the sales contract. (Code Sec. 483(c)(2))[15]

¶ 1309   What is "total unstated interest"?

There's "total unstated interest" under the contract (see ¶1308) if the sum of all payments (other than *stated* interest payments) due under it more than six months after the date of the sale or exchange exceeds the sum of: (1) the present value of all those payments, plus (2) the present value of all interest payments due under the contract (regardless of when due). The total unstated interest equals the excess, if any. (Code Sec. 483(b))[16]

The present value of a payment is determined as of the date of the sale, etc., using a "test" rate prescribed by IRS. This test rate, which depends on the type of property sold, is a discount rate equal to the then applicable federal rate (AFR, see ¶1310), compounded semiannually. (Code Sec. 483(b), Code Sec. 1274(b)(2))[17]

These discount rates are used to determine the amount of unstated interest the seller must report as interest income:

(1) For sales or exchanges of property (not described below), the discount rate may not exceed 9% compounded semiannually if the stated principal amount of the debt instrument doesn't exceed a specified amount, as adjusted for inflation ($5,468,200 for sales and exchanges in 2013). If the stated principal amount is over the specified amount, the discount rate is 100% of the AFR, compounded semiannually. (Code Sec. 483(b), Code Sec. 1274A(a))[18]

(2) For sales or exchanges of new investment credit property, the discount rate is 100% of the AFR, compounded semiannually. (Code Sec. 483(b))[19]

(3) For sales or exchanges where part of the sold property is leased back to the seller, the discount rate is 110% of the AFR, compounded semiannually. (Code Sec. 1274(e))[20]

(4) For sales, etc., of land between family members where the aggregate sales price for all land sales between those individuals in that calendar year isn't over $500,000, the discount rate can't exceed 6% compounded semiannually. (Code Sec. 483(e))[21]

¶ 1310   Applicable federal rate (AFR).

IRS issues monthly tables (reproduced at ¶1116 for the most recent 12 months available as we went to press) showing the AFRs to be used in determining whether there is unstated interest (¶1309) (or OID in some cases, see ¶1318) on a sale or exchange of property, and if there is, the amount of that unstated interest.[22] The rate to use on a particular sale or exchange depends on the term over which the payments are to be made. If the term is three years or less, use the short-term rate (from the tables). If it's more than three years but not more than nine years, use the mid-term rate. If it's more than nine years, use the long-term rate. (Code Sec. 1274(d)(1)(A))[23] The rate to use also depends on when the contract was made.

---

14. ¶J-3800 *et seq.*; ¶s 4834, 4834.01; TD ¶152,221
15. ¶J-3806; ¶4834.01; TD ¶152,226
16. ¶J-3814; ¶4834; TD ¶152,233
17. ¶J-3814 *et seq.*; ¶4834.01; TD ¶152,234
18. ¶J-3816 *et seq.*; ¶4834.01; TD ¶152,234

19. ¶J-3818; ¶4834.01; TD ¶152,234
20. ¶J-3819; ¶12,714.03; TD ¶152,234
21. ¶J-3820; ¶4834.01; TD ¶152,234
22. ¶J-4181 *et seq.*; ¶4834.01; TD ¶153,030
23. ¶J-4181; ¶4834.01; TD ¶153,030

(Code Sec. 1274(d)(2))[24]

¶ 1311 Allocating total unstated interest.

For any payment subject to the unstated interest rules (¶1307), that part of the total unstated interest under the contract (¶1309) which is properly allocable to that payment is treated as interest. This "interest" amount is determined in a manner consistent with the method used to compute the amount of currently includible OID (¶1321) (Code Sec. 483(a)) so that unstated interest income must be reported on an economic accrual basis.[25]

¶ 1312 Exceptions to unstated interest rules.

Even if all the requirements listed at ¶1308 are met, there's no unstated interest on:

(1) sales or exchanges where the sales price (¶1308) is $3,000 or less; (Code Sec. 483(d)(2))[26]

(2) any debt instrument (given in connection with a sale or exchange of property) whose issue price is figured under the OID rules (¶1313 *et seq.*); (Code Sec. 483(d)(1))[27]

(3) any amount received on the sale of patent rights described in Code Sec. 1235(a) that's contingent on the productivity, use or disposition of those rights; (Code Sec. 483(d)(4))[28]

(4) amounts received under certain annuity contracts;[29]

(5) lump-sum divorce payments and property settlements payable in installments;[30] and

(6) certain acquisitions of amortizable section 197 intangibles (¶1973). (Reg § 1.197-2(f)(3)(iv)(B)(3))[31]

(7) payments under options to buy or sell property (Reg § 1.483-1(c)(3)(v)).[32]

(8) assumptions of debt in connection with sales or exchanges and acquisitions of property subject to debt (Code Sec. 1274(c)(4)).[33]

(9) below-market interest rate loans (¶1306) (Code Sec. 7872(f)(8)).[34]

¶ 1313 Current inclusion of original issue discount (OID) as interest income.

If a debt instrument is acquired from an issuer for an amount less than what the issuer will have to pay the holder when the instrument matures, the difference is OID (see ¶1314). No matter which method of accounting the holder uses, he must report part of the OID as interest income in each tax year the debt instrument is held (¶1321), even though the OID won't be paid until maturity. (Code Sec. 1272)[35]

The OID current inclusion rules apply to all debt instruments issued with OID (Code Sec. 1272)[36] *other than:*

(1) Tax-exempt obligations (unless stripped). (Code Sec. 1272(a)(2)(A), Code Sec. 1286(d))

(2) U.S. savings bonds. (Code Sec. 1272(a)(2)(B))

(3) Short-term obligations (i.e., with a fixed maturity date not more than one year from the date of issue). (Code Sec. 1272(a)(2)(C))

(4) Debt instruments issued by natural persons before Mar. 2, '84. (Code Sec. 1272(a)(2)(D))

(5) Certain nonbusiness loans of $10,000 or less between natural persons. (Code

24. ¶J-4190 *et seq.*; ¶12,714.03; TD ¶153,030
25. ¶J-3951; ¶s 4834.01, 4464.01; TD ¶152,010
26. ¶J-3901; ¶4834.01; TD ¶152,005
27. ¶J-3902; ¶4834.01; TD ¶152,005
28. ¶J-3903; ¶4834.01; TD ¶152,005
29. ¶J-3905; ¶4834.01; TD ¶152,005
30. ¶J-3906; ¶4834.01; TD ¶152,005

31. ¶J-3903.1
32. ¶J-3904; ¶4834.01
33. ¶J-3909; ¶4834.01
34. ¶J-3910; ¶4834.01
35. ¶J-4000 *et seq.*; ¶12,714 *et seq.*; TD ¶153,001
36. ¶J-4051; ¶s 12,714, 12,714.01; TD ¶153,003

Sec. 1272(a)(2)(E))[37]

"Debt instruments" are bonds, debentures, notes, certificates or other instruments or contractual arrangements that are "indebtedness" under tax law principles, e.g., certificates of deposit or loans (Code Sec. 1275(a)(1); Reg § 1.1275-1(d)),[38] and REMIC interests and some similar instruments where payment may be accelerated. (Code Sec. 1272(a)(6)(C))[39] A debt instrument doesn't include a life annuity, or certain annuities issued by insurance companies. (Code Sec. 1275(a)(1)(B); Reg § 1.1275-1(j))[40]

A safe harbor accounting method (the proportional method) can be used in calculating OID accrual on a pool of credit card receivables.[41]

The OID current inclusion rules also apply to bonds, and preferred stock bought (after being stripped) after Apr. 30, '93. (Code Sec. 305(e), Code Sec. 1286(a))[42] The OID current inclusion rules don't apply to a holder who buys a debt instrument at a premium (Code Sec. 1272(c)(1))[43] (except as described at ¶1323).

¶ 1314 Original issue discount (OID) defined.

OID (see ¶1313) is the excess (if any) of: (1) a debt instrument's stated redemption price at maturity (¶1316) over (2) its issue price (¶1317). (Code Sec. 1273(a)(1))[44]

But the OID is treated as zero if that excess is less than: 0.25% of the stated redemption price at maturity, times the number of years to maturity. (Code Sec. 1273(a)(3)) In this case, all stated interest (including amounts that would otherwise be OID) is treated as "qualified stated interest" (¶1315). (Reg § 1.1273-1(d)(1))[45]

¶ 1315 "Qualified stated interest" defined.

"Qualified stated interest" is stated interest that's unconditionally payable in cash or property (other than the issuer's debt instruments), or will be constructively received under Code Sec. 451 (¶2822) at least annually at a single fixed rate. (Reg § 1.1273-1(c)(1))[46]

¶ 1316 Stated redemption price at maturity.

For OID (¶1314) purposes, an instrument's *stated redemption price at maturity* is usually its face value. It includes interest payable at maturity *but not* interest payable at a fixed rate at periodic intervals of a year or less during the entire term of the instrument (Code Sec. 1273(a)(2)), or "qualified stated interest" (¶1315). (Reg § 1.1273-1(b))[47]

¶ 1317 Issue price.

A debt instrument's issue price depends on whether it's issued for cash or property, and if issued for property, whether the instrument or property is publicly traded, as follows:

. . . For a *publicly offered debt instrument issued for money,* the issue price is the initial offering price to the public at which a substantial amount of the instruments is sold. (Code Sec. 1273(b)(1); Reg § 1.1232-3(b)(2)(i))[48]

. . . For a *privately offered debt instrument issued for money,* the issue price is the price paid by the first buyer of that instrument (Code Sec. 1273(b)(2)) or the first price at which a

37. ¶J-4060 *et seq.*; ¶12,714.01; TD ¶153,003
38. ¶s J-4054, J-4055; ¶12,714; TD ¶153,002
39. ¶J-4343; ¶12,714.01; TD ¶153,010
40. ¶J-4057; ¶12,714; TD ¶153,002
41. ¶J-4345.2
42. ¶J-4400 *et seq.*; ¶12,864; TD ¶153,501

43. ¶J-4005; ¶12714.01; TD ¶153,001
44. ¶J-4100 *et seq.*; ¶12,714; TD ¶153,004
45. ¶J-4102; ¶12,714.01; TD ¶153,004
46. ¶J-4112; TD ¶153,006
47. ¶J-4111; TD ¶153,005
48. ¶J-4130; TD ¶153,021

substantial amount of instruments in the issue is sold. (Reg § 1.1273-2(a)(1))[49]

. . . For a *debt instrument issued for property where there's public trading,* the issue price is the instrument's fair market value (FMV) as of the issue date, if it's publicly traded. If the instrument itself isn't publicly traded but is issued for property (i.e., stock or securities) that is, its issue price is the FMV of that property. (Code Sec. 1273(b)(3); Reg § 1.1232-3(b)(2)(iii), Reg § 1.1273-2(b)(1))[50]

. . . For a *nonpublicly traded debt instrument issued for nonpublicly traded property,* the issue price is its stated principal amount (total payments due under the instrument, less stated interest payments or payments designated as interest or points) if the instrument pays adequate stated interest (¶1318), or its imputed principal amount (¶1319) if it doesn't. (Code Sec. 1274(a); Reg § 1.1274-2(b)(1))[1] For exceptions, see ¶1320.

. . . For *Treasury securities,* the issue price is the average price of the securities sold (price sold at auction, if sold before Mar. 13, 2001). (Reg § 1.1275-2(d))[2]

. . . For a *debt instrument that provides for one or more contingent payments,* issued after Aug. 12, '96, the issue price is the lesser of the instrument's noncontingent principal payments, or the sum of the present values of the noncontingent payments. (Reg § 1.1274-2(g))[3]

. . . For a *tax-exempt obligation* issued after Aug. 12, '96, the issue price is (a) the greater of the obligation's FMV or its stated principal amount, or (b) for contingent obligations, its FMV. (Reg § 1.1274-2(j))[4]

The issue price of a debt instrument issued in a potentially abusive situation (e.g., a tax shelter) is the FMV of the property received in exchange for the instrument, reduced by the sum of the money plus the FMV of any property or rights (other than the instrument) that are given for the sale or exchange. (Reg § 1.1274-2(b)(3))[5]

¶ 1318   Adequate stated interest.

There's adequate stated interest for a debt instrument if the sum of the present values (using the discount rate at ¶1309) of all payments of principal and interest due under it equals or exceeds its stated principal amount (¶1317) (Code Sec. 1274(c)(2)), or if the instrument has a single fixed rate of interest that's paid or compounded at least annually and is at least equal to the test rate. (Reg § 1.1274-2(c))[6]

¶ 1319   Imputed principal amount.

The imputed principal amount is the sum of the present values of all payments of principal and interest due under a debt instrument, computed as of the date of the sale or exchange using the discount rates at ¶1309. (Code Sec. 1274(b)(2); Reg § 1.1274-2(c)(1))[7]

The imputed principal amount of a variable rate debt instrument that provides for stated interest at a qualified floating rate(s) generally is determined by assuming that the instrument provides for a fixed rate of interest for each accrual period to which a qualified floating rate applies. (Reg § 1.1274-2(f)(1)(i))[8]

In a potentially abusive situation (e.g., tax shelter), the imputed principal amount of an instrument received in exchange for property is the property's fair market value, adjusted for other considerations in the transaction. (Code Sec. 1274(b)(3)(A); Reg § 1.1274-3(a))[9]

49. ¶J-4138; TD ¶153,023
50. ¶J-4140; TD ¶153,024
1. ¶J-4151; ¶12,714.03; TD ¶153,025
2. ¶J-4131; TD ¶153,022
3. ¶J-4151.2; ¶12,714.037; TD ¶153,026
4. ¶J-4151.3, J-4151.4

5. ¶J-4151.5; TD ¶152,235
6. ¶J-4153 *et seq.*; ¶12,714.03; TD ¶153,027
7. ¶J-4154 *et seq.*; ¶12,714.03; TD ¶153,028
8. ¶J-4157
9. ¶J-4173 *et seq.*; ¶12,714.03; TD ¶153,029

¶ 1320 Exceptions to OID rules for nonpublicly traded debt instruments.

The issue price of a nonpublicly traded debt instrument issued for nonpublicly traded property is its stated redemption price at maturity (so there's no OID, see ¶1314), instead of the amount determined under the rules at ¶1317, in these cases: (Code Sec. 1273(b)(4))[10]

(1) sales or exchanges involving total payments of $250,000 or less; (Code Sec. 1274(c)(3)(C))

(2) sales or exchanges by an individual of his principal residence; (Code Sec. 1274(c)(3)(B))

(3) sales or exchanges of certain farms where the sales price cannot exceed $1,000,000; (Code Sec. 1274(c)(3)(A))

(4) certain sales of patents; (Code Sec. 1274(c)(3)(E))

(5) certain transfers of land between family members where the total price for all land sales between them for the year is not more than $500,000; (Code Sec. 1274(c)(3)(F))

(6) sales or exchanges where, in exchange for property, a nonaccrual method buyer (other than a dealer) issues a "cash method debt instrument" —i.e., a debt instrument whose principal amount doesn't exceed a specified amount ($3,905,900 for sales and exchanges in 2013), if the "regular" issue price rules otherwise would apply *and* buyer and seller jointly elect cash method treatment for the instrument; (Code Sec. 1274A(c))[11]

(7) sales or exchanges of personal use property (to the issuer) that evidence a below-market loan (¶1306); (Reg § 1.1274-1(b)(3)(i))[12]

(8) transactions involving "demand" below-market loans; (Reg § 1.1274-1(b)(3)(ii))[13] or

(9) transfers between spouses or incident to divorce. (Reg § 1.1274-1(b)(3)(iii))[14]

observation: Even if there's no OID, there may be unstated interest (see ¶1307).

¶ 1321 Determining amount of currently includible OID.

A holder of a debt instrument issued with OID (¶1314) who is required to include part of the OID in gross income currently must include in gross income for his tax year, an amount equal to the sum of the daily portions of the OID for each day he held the instrument during that year. (Code Sec. 1272(a)(1))[15] For accrual under the constant yield method, see ¶1322.

To determine the daily OID portion, allocate to each day in any "accrual period" (below) that day's ratable portion of the increase (during that period) in the instrument's adjusted issue price (below). This increase equals the excess of: (1) the adjusted issue price at the start of the accrual period times the yield to maturity (based on compounding at the end of each accrual period), over (2) the sum of the amounts payable as interest on the instrument during that accrual period. (Code Sec. 1272(a)(3))[16]

The adjusted issue price of a debt instrument at the start of any accrual period is the sum of its issue price (¶1317), plus all adjustments (i.e., OID inclusions) in that issue price for all earlier accrual periods. (Code Sec. 1272(a)(4))[17]

Accrual period generally means a six-month period (or shorter period from date of issuance) ending on a day in the calendar year corresponding to the debt instrument's maturity date, or a date six months before that date. (Code Sec. 1272(a)(5))[18]

For *inflation-indexed debt instruments,* OID is computed using the coupon bond method or

10. ¶J-4196; ¶12,714.03; TD ¶153,031
11. ¶J-4207
12. ¶J-4202; ¶12,714.03; TD ¶153,031
13. ¶J-4203; ¶12,714.03; TD ¶153,031
14. ¶J-4204; ¶12,714.03; TD ¶153,031

15. ¶J-4301; ¶12,714.01; TD ¶153,008
16. ¶J-4301; ¶12,714.01; TD ¶153,008
17. ¶J-4324; ¶12,714.01; TD ¶153,008
18. ¶J-4301; TD ¶153,008

the discount bond method (see ¶1333). (Reg § 1.1275-7(a))[19]

¶ 1322 Accrual of OID using constant yield method.

Under the constant yield method, the amount of OID includible in the holder's income for a tax year (¶1321) is determined as follows:

(1) Determine the instrument's yield to maturity. This is the discount rate that, when used to compute the present value of all payments under the instrument, produces an amount equal to the instrument's issue price. The yield must be constant over the instrument's term and must be calculated to at least two decimal places. (Reg § 1.1272-1(b)(1)(i))

(2) Determine the accrual period, which may be any length (based on any reasonable accounting convention), but can't exceed one year. Each scheduled payment must occur either on the first or last day of an accrual period. The simplest OID computation is where the accrual periods correspond to the intervals between payment dates set forth by the instrument. (Reg § 1.1272-1(b)(1)(ii))

(3) Determine the OID allocable to each accrual period. This is the instrument's adjusted issue price at the start of the accrual period, times the instrument's yield, less the "qualified stated interest" (¶1315) allocable to the period. (Reg § 1.1272-1(b)(1)(iii))

(4) Determine the daily portions of OID, by allocating to each day in an accrual period the ratable portion of the OID allocable to that period. The holder includes in income the daily portions of OID for each day in the tax year on which he held the instrument. (Reg § 1.1272-1(b)(1)(iv))[20]

The constant yield method may not be used for certain interests held by a REMIC, certain instruments with payments subject to acceleration or that provide for contingent payments, or certain variable rate instruments. (Reg § 1.1272-1(b)(2))[21]

¶ 1323 OID inclusion reduced where holder paid acquisition premium.

If the holder of a debt instrument bought it from someone other than the original issuer, paying an acquisition premium (i.e., an amount in excess of the original issue price plus all OID required to be included in the gross income of earlier holders), the holder's current OID inclusion (¶1321) is reduced. This is done by reducing each daily includible OID portion by this constant fraction: the acquisition premium, divided by the total OID (before reduction) allocable to the days after the purchase date and ending on the date of maturity. However, the reduction applies only to the OID inclusion and isn't taken into account in computing the instrument's adjusted issue price at the start of an accrual period. (Code Sec. 1272(a)(7))[22]

¶ 1324 Accrued market discount on disposition of "market discount bonds."

Gain on the disposition of a market discount bond (¶1326) is ordinary income to the extent of the accrued market discount on the bond (Code Sec. 1276(a)(1)) (unless the holder elects to include the discount currently, see ¶1327). This ordinary income is treated as interest income, with exceptions. (Code Sec. 1276(a)(4))[23] For partial principal payments, see ¶1325.

The accrued market discount interest is computed under a ratable accrual method or, at taxpayer's election, a constant interest rate method. (Code Sec. 1276(b))[24]

Dispositions by gift and transfers to controlled corporations also can result in interest income under this rule. (Code Sec. 1276(d)(1)(A))[25] If the disposition is other than by sale,

---

19. ¶J-4379 *et seq.*; ¶12,714.037; TD ¶153,043 *et seq.*
20. ¶J-4302; ¶12,714.01; TD ¶153,009
21. ¶J-4303; ¶12,714.01; TD ¶153,010
22. ¶J-4349; ¶12,714.01; TD ¶153,019

23. ¶J-4551; ¶12,764 *et seq.*; TD ¶154,001
24. ¶J-4560; ¶12,764.01; TD ¶154,004
25. ¶J-4570; ¶12,764.01; TD ¶154,007

exchange or involuntary conversion, the amount realized is equal to the bond's fair market value. (Code Sec. 1276(a)(2))[26]

Interest treatment applies even if the gain wouldn't otherwise be recognized. Regs may allow nonrecognition in certain nontaxable transactions. (Code Sec. 1276(a)(1), Code Sec. 1276(d)(1))[27]

¶ 1325　Accrued market discount when partial principal payments are made.

If the principal on a market discount bond (¶1326) (acquired after Oct. 22, '86) is paid in more than one installment, any partial principal payment is included as ordinary income to the extent of the accrued market discount on the bond (Code Sec. 1276(a)(3)(A))[28] (unless the holder elects to include the discount currently, see ¶1327).

Any amount that has been included in gross income under this rule reduces the amount of any accrued market discount that's included on any later disposition of (¶1324), or further partial principal payments on, the bond. (Code Sec. 1276(a)(3)(B))[29]

If bond principal can be paid in two or more payments, the accrued market discount is to be determined under regs. (Code Sec. 1276(b)(3))[30]

¶ 1326　What are market discount bonds.

Market discount bonds are any "bonds" having a market discount *other than* short-term obligations (one year or less), tax-exempt obligations bought before May 1, '93, U.S. savings bonds and certain installment obligations. (Code Sec. 1278(a)(1)(A), Code Sec. 1278(a)(1)(B))[31]

Market discount is the excess (if any) of the bond's stated redemption price at maturity (¶1316) over taxpayer's basis for the bond immediately after acquiring it. (Code Sec. 1278(a)(2))[32] The market discount is zero if it's less than 0.25% of the bond's stated redemption price at maturity times the number of years to maturity after the taxpayer acquires the bond. (Code Sec. 1278(a)(2)(C))[33]

Special rules determine the stated redemption price at maturity for this purpose if the bond was issued with original issue discount (OID). (Code Sec. 1278(a)(4))[34]

¶ 1327　Election to include accrued market discount in income currently.

Instead of including a bond's accrued market discount on disposition (¶1324) or partial payment of principal (¶1325), taxpayer may elect to include the discount as interest income for the tax years to which it is attributable, i.e., currently. Taxpayer may use either the ratable accrual method or the constant interest rate method. (Code Sec. 1278(b)(1))[35]

Elect by attaching to a timely filed income tax return, a statement that market discount has been included in gross income under Code Sec. 1278(b), describing the method used to determine the amount attributable to that tax year.[36]

¶ 1328　Acquisition discount on short-term obligations—mandatory accrual.

Certain holders (below) of short-term obligations (not more than one year) are currently taxed on their daily portions of the "acquisition discount" (for government obligations, or

---

26. ¶J-4551; ¶12,764.01; TD ¶154,001
27. ¶s J-4551, J-4569; ¶12,764.01; TD ¶154,007
28. ¶J-4566; ¶12,764.01; TD ¶154,006
29. ¶J-4567; ¶12,764.01; TD ¶154,006
30. ¶J-4568; TD ¶154,006
31. ¶s J-4552, J-4556; ¶12,764.01; TD ¶154,002

32. ¶J-4553; ¶12,764.01; TD ¶154,003
33. ¶J-4554; ¶12,764.01; TD ¶154,003
34. ¶J-4553; ¶12,764.01; TD ¶154,003
35. ¶J-4573; ¶12,764.02; TD ¶154,005
36. ¶J-4574; ¶12,764.02; TD ¶154,005

nongovernment obligations if the holder so elects) or original issue discount (for nongovernment obligations), for each day during the year that they hold the obligation. (Code Sec. 1281(a)(1), Code Sec. 1283(c)) Any other interest payable on the obligation also must be taken into account as it accrues. (Code Sec. 1281(a)(2))[37]

An obligation's "acquisition discount" is the excess of its stated redemption price at maturity (¶1316) over taxpayer's basis in it. (Code Sec. 1283(a)(2))[38]

The daily portion of the acquisition discount is computed using the ratable accrual method or, if taxpayer so elects, the constant interest method. (Code Sec. 1283(b))[39]

This mandatory accrual rule applies only to these holders of short-term obligations:

(1) Accrual basis taxpayers;

(2) Taxpayers who hold the obligations primarily for sale to customers in the ordinary course of their trade or business. (Code Sec. 1281(b)(1))[40] This doesn't include banks that make short-term loans to customers in the ordinary course of business;[41]

(3) Regulated investment companies (mutual funds, ¶4201) or common trust funds (¶4210);

(4) Taxpayers who identify the obligations as part of a Code Sec. 1256 hedging transaction;

(5) Taxpayers whose short-term obligations are stripped bonds or stripped coupons that taxpayer stripped. (Code Sec. 1281(b)(1))[42]

The mandatory accrual rule doesn't apply to the ordinary investor. [43]

Ⓡ*observation:* The mandatory accrual rule doesn't apply to a cash basis holder who isn't a dealer in these obligations and isn't subject to the Code Sec. 1256 hedging rules.

Special rules apply to obligations held by pass-through entities. (Code Sec. 1281(b)(2))[44]

¶ 1329   Interest on bonds sold between interest dates.

When fixed-interest bonds (not in default) are sold between interest dates, the amount the buyer pays that represents interest accrued as of the sale date is taxable interest to the seller. (Reg § 1.61-7(d)) Interest accrued after the sale date is taxable to the buyer on receipt.[45]

Bonds in default are usually traded "flat" (no part of the selling price is allocated between interest and principal). If there's accrued interest, the part of the selling price that represents interest accrued before the sale isn't taxable to the buyer until it exceeds the buyer's basis. [46]

¶ 1330   Interest credited to frozen deposits.

Interest credited to a frozen deposit (i.e., in a bankrupt or insolvent (actual or threatened) financial institution) during a calendar year, that's includible in the depositor's income for the year, can't exceed the sum of the net withdrawals during the year plus the amount withdrawable at the end of the year. (Code Sec. 451(g)(1))[47]

¶ 1331   Tax-exempt interest.

Interest on state and local bonds (i.e., obligations of a state, the District of Columbia, a U.S. possession, certain Indian tribal governments or any political subdivision of the foregoing) is exempt from federal income tax (Code Sec. 103(a), Code Sec. 103(c), Code Sec. 7871(a)(4))[48] (with certain exceptions, see ¶1332). For "educational expense" exclusion

37. ¶s J-4501, J-4506; ¶12,814; TD ¶153,801
38. ¶J-4501; ¶12,814.01; TD ¶153,803
39. ¶J-4500; ¶12,814.01; TD ¶153,804
40. ¶J-4502; ¶12,814; TD ¶153,802
41. ¶J-4501; TD ¶153,802
42. ¶J-4502; ¶12,814; TD ¶153,802

43. ¶J-4502
44. ¶J-4502; ¶12,814; TD ¶153,802
45. ¶J-2827; ¶614.080; TD ¶151,020
46. ¶J-2828 *et seq.*; ¶614.081; TD ¶151,021
47. ¶J-3711; ¶4514.185; TD ¶151,507
48. ¶J-3000; ¶1034; TD ¶158,001

for certain U.S. savings bonds, see ¶2220 *et seq.* For tax credit bonds, see ¶2366.

🅡**observation:** Even if interest isn't subject to federal income tax, it may have to be taken into account, e.g., in calculating the taxable portion of social security benefits (¶1279), for alternative minimum tax purposes for certain bonds (¶3208), in calculating earnings and profits (¶3525), and for certain other purposes.

🅡**caution:** There's also a bar against deducting interest on debt incurred or continued to buy or carry tax-exempt bonds (¶1723).

Every person required to file a return must report on it all tax-exempt interest received or accrued during the tax year. (Code Sec. 6012(d))[49]

¶ 1332 Taxable interest from private activity bonds, hedge bonds, arbitrage bonds.

Private activity bonds aren't eligible for the interest exemption described at ¶1331 unless the bond meets detailed requirements *and* is one of seven specified types of bonds (exempt facility, mortgage, veterans' mortgage, small issue, scholarship funding, redevelopment, or Code Sec. 501(c)(3) bonds). (Code Sec. 103(b)(1), Code Sec. 141(e))[50] Pre-Aug. 16, '86 industrial development bonds are subject to similar "qualification" rules. [1]

Hedge bonds (i.e., issued to "hedge" another bond) aren't exempt unless 85% of the bond's spendable proceeds (i.e., net of issuance expenses and certain reserves) are reasonably expected to be spent within specified periods, and at least 95% of the issuance costs (which can't be contingent) are paid within 180 days after issuance. (Code Sec. 149(g))[2]

Arbitrage bonds aren't exempt. (Code Sec. 103(b)(2)) This means a bond forming part of an issue any part of whose proceeds is reasonably expected to be used, directly or indirectly, to acquire (or refinance) nontemporary investments with a materially higher yield (more than $\frac{1}{8}$ of 1 percentage point) than the bond itself, unless a required rebate is paid. (Code Sec. 148(a), Code Sec. 148(f); Reg § 1.148-2(d)(2)) If an issuer enters a transaction for a principal purpose of getting a material financial advantage based on the difference between tax-exempt and taxable rates, IRS has discretion to clearly reflect the economic substance of the transaction. (Reg § 1.148-10(e)) An issuer can't avoid having a bond treated as an arbitrage bond by giving away the prohibited arbitrage bond profit, e.g., by buying investments at other than fair market value ("yield burning"). [3]

¶ 1333 Inflation-indexed debt instruments; Treasury Inflation-Indexed Securities.

There are two methods of accounting for stated interest and inflation adjustments on inflation-indexed debt instruments (issued after Jan. 1, '97). Inflation-indexed debt instruments are issued for cash, indexed for inflation and deflation using a general price or wage index, and are not otherwise contingent payment debt instruments. (Reg § 1.1275-7(c)(1), Reg § 1.1275-7(h)) These rules apply to Treasury Inflation-Indexed Securities (TIPS), but not certain debt instruments, e.g., U.S. savings bonds and bonds issued by qualified tuition programs. (Reg § 1.1275-7(b))[4]

(1) The coupon bond method is a simplified method that applies if (a) the debt instrument is issued at par, and (b) all stated interest on it is qualified stated interest (i.e., it's unconditionally payable in cash at least annually, see ¶1315). Under this method, the stated interest is taxable to the holder when received or accrued, in accordance with his accounting method. Any increase in the inflation-adjusted principal amount is treated as OID (¶1314) for the period in which it occurs. (Reg § 1.1275-7(d)) The coupon bond method applies to TIPS that

---

49. ¶J-3002; ¶60,124; TD ¶158,003
50. ¶s J-3000 *et seq.*, J-3100, J-3252 *et seq.*, J-3600; ¶1414 *et seq.*; TD ¶158,009
1. ¶s J-3153 *et seq.*, J-3227 *et seq.*, J-3251; ¶1034.01; TD ¶158,009
2. ¶J-3667 *et seq.*; ¶1494.06; TD ¶158,001
3. ¶J-3400 *et seq.*; ¶1484 *et seq.*; TD ¶158,001
4. ¶J-4056.1, J-4379.1 *et seq.*; ¶12,714.037; TD ¶153,043 *et seq.*

aren't stripped and to TIPS issued with more than a de minimis amount of premiums. (Reg § 1.1275-7(g)(2))[5]

⟲ *observation:* Assuming there's some inflation and principal continues to be adjusted upward, holders will have to include amounts not yet realized as interest income.

A decrease in a bond's inflation-indexed principal first reduces the interest income attributable to the interest payments for the year of the adjustment. If the decrease exceeds that income, the excess generally is an ordinary deduction to the extent taxpayer previously included interest from the bond in income. Any remaining decrease is carried forward to reduce interest income in future years. A taxpayer generally has a capital loss if he sells the bond, or it matures, before he has used all the decrease. (Reg § 1.1275-7(f)(1), Reg § 1.1275-7(d)(4))[6]

(2) The discount bond method is used if the instrument doesn't qualify for the coupon bond method (e.g., because it is issued at a discount). Under this method, taxpayers make current adjustments to their OID accruals to account for changes in the inflation-adjusted principal amount. If the daily portions for an accrual period are positive amounts, they are taken into account under Code Sec. 1272 by the holder (¶1313). If the daily portions are negative, they are taken into account under the rules for deflation adjustments described above. (Reg § 1.1275-7(e)) The discount bond method applies to TIPS that are stripped under the Treasury's STRIPS (Separate Trading of Registered Interest and Principal of Securities) program. (Reg § 1.1286-2)[7]

¶ 1334 Interest on U.S. savings bonds.

Interest on U.S. savings bonds now being issued is earned in three ways: On Series HH "face amount" bonds (not issued after Aug. 31, 2004), it's paid semiannually by check. On Series EE "discount" bonds, it's reflected as an increase in the bond's value over stated periods. On Series I inflation-indexed face amount bonds, it's credited monthly (at a fixed rate for the 30-year life of the bond and a semiannual variable inflation rate) and paid when the bond is cashed. The interest on these bonds (and on any unmatured or extended Series E and Series H bonds now outstanding) is fully taxable unless the exclusion at ¶2219 applies.[8]

Cash basis taxpayers report the interest on Series HH (or H) bonds in the year received.[9]

A cash basis owner of Series EE bonds (and outstanding Series E bonds) and Series I bonds may either: (1) defer reporting any interest (i.e., the bond's increase in value) until the year of final maturity, redemption, or other disposition, whichever is earlier, or (2) elect to report the annual increase in value in each year's return.[10]

Some Series E bonds can, at the owner's option, be held up to 30 years beyond their original maturity ("final maturity"). A cash basis owner who hasn't elected to report the interest on a Series E bond annually (under (2), above) must report all of the interest on the bond in the year in which the bond is redeemed or disposed of or, if earlier, the year in which it reaches "final maturity." (Code Sec. 454(a); Reg § 1.454-1(a)(1))[11]

⟲ *observation:* Series E bonds issued before Dec., '65 reach final maturity 40 years after their issue date. Series E bonds issued after Nov., '65, and before July, '80, and all Series EE bonds, reach final maturity 30 years after their issue dates. (Series E bonds were issued before July, '80, and stopped paying interest in June of 2011.) This means that any accrued interest on Series EE bonds issued in '82 was taxable in 2012. *Accrual basis taxpayers* include the interest on the above bonds as it accrues.[12]

---

5. ¶J-4379.1 *et seq.*; ¶12,714.037; TD ¶153,044
6. ¶J-4379.1 *et seq.*; ¶12,714.037; TD ¶153,044
7. ¶J-4379.5; ¶12,714.037; TD ¶153,045
8. ¶s J-3014, J-3719 *et seq.*; ¶4544.01; TD ¶156,001

9. ¶s J-3720, J-3721; ¶4544.01; TD ¶156,008
10. ¶J-3719; ¶4544 *et seq.*; TD ¶156,003
11. ¶s J-3721, J-3722; ¶4544 *et seq.*; TD ¶156,003
12. ¶J-3719 *et seq.*; ¶4544.01; TD ¶156,008

For the exclusion of income earned on qualified U.S. savings bonds by a payor of higher education expenses, see ¶2219 *et seq.*

¶ 1335   When to report interest income (other than OID).

Cash basis taxpayers report interest in the tax year it's actually or constructively received, regardless of when the interest is accrued on the debtor's books.[13] Generally, interest isn't constructively received if taxpayer's control of its receipt is subject to substantial limits or restrictions. (Reg § 1.451-2(a))[14] Thus, interest on a six-month certificate that isn't credited or made available before maturity without penalty isn't taxable until the certificate is redeemed or matures.[15]

Savings institution interest, or interest on life insurance dividends left to accumulate, is considered received when credited to the depositor's (policyholder's) account and subject to his withdrawal.[16]

Where a bank charges a penalty for premature withdrawals from a time savings account, the gross amount of interest paid or credited during the withdrawal year is reported as interest that year, even if the penalty partially or completely offsets the interest.[17] For deduction of forfeited interest, see ¶2168.

Matured interest coupons are constructively received in the year they mature unless it can be shown that there are no funds available for payment of the interest during the year.[18]

Accrual basis taxpayers report interest in the tax year in which the right to receive the interest becomes fixed, regardless of when it is received.[19] But if it appears reasonably certain the interest won't be paid because the debtor is insolvent, the creditor can delay reporting the interest until its collection appears reasonably certain.[20]

For cash and accrual taxpayers, there are special rules on when to include "interest" on below-market rate loans (¶1306), (Code Sec. 7872(a)(2), Code Sec. 7872(b)(2)(A))[21] "points" (¶1336), and unstated interest (¶1337).

 caution: These rules don't apply to debt issued with original issue discount (¶1313).

¶ 1336   When "points" are included in income.

"Points" (¶1305) in the form of discount are taken into account under the "principal-reduction method"—i.e., as stated principal payments on the loan are made. "Points" paid out of funds not from the lender are included on receipt.[22]

¶ 1337   When to report unstated interest income.

A cash method seller includes unstated interest allocated to a payment (¶1307) as interest income in the tax year the payment is received. An accrual method seller includes the unstated interest in the tax year the payment is due. (Reg § 1.483-2(a)(1)(ii))[23]

¶ 1338   Rents and Royalties. ▬▬▬▬▬▬▬

Rent is the payment for the use of real or tangible personal property. Royalties are payments for the use of certain rights, e.g., intangible rights such as patents. Both are includible in gross income.

---

13. ¶J-3703; ¶614.067; TD ¶151,501
14. ¶J-3706; ¶s 4514.036, 4514.053; TD ¶441,005
15. ¶J-3710; ¶4514.053; TD ¶151,015
16. ¶s J-3709, J-3717; ¶s 4514.036, 4514.053; TD ¶151,501
17. ¶J-2822; TD ¶151,501
18. ¶J-3715; ¶4514.053; TD ¶151,501
19. ¶J-3701; ¶4514.011; TD ¶151,502
20. ¶J-3702; ¶4514.023; TD ¶151,502
21. ¶J-3708; ¶78,724 *et seq.*; TD ¶155,000
22. ¶E-3004 *et seq.*; ¶4614.75; TD ¶151,503
23. ¶J-3758; ¶4834.01; TD ¶152,007

¶ 1339 Rents.

Rents are includible in gross income, whether paid in cash or property. (Code Sec. 61(a)(5); Reg § 1.61-1(a)) If paid in property, the property's fair market value (at receipt) is the amount taxed as rent.[24]

Rents are reported by cash basis taxpayers when received, and by accrual basis taxpayers when due unless they're considered uncollectible.[25] For advance rentals, see ¶1341.

¶ 1340 Bonuses; lease cancellation payments.

A bonus or extra payment by the tenant to the lessor or sublessor on the execution of the lease is taxable as rent to the lessor or sublessor.[26]

If the tenant pays the landlord for permission to cancel the lease, the payments are rent to the landlord (whether cash or accrual basis) in the year received. (Reg § 1.61-8(a)) Payments to the landlord for modifying a lease or consenting to a sublease are also considered rent.[27] Where the lessor pays the tenant to cancel the lease, see ¶1598.

¶ 1341 Advance rentals and security deposits.

An advance rental is currently taxable (Reg § 1.61-8(b)), even if it's refundable or can be applied against the purchase price.[28] But a security deposit (¶1206) isn't taxable rent.[29]

¶ 1342 Deferred rentals.

Where the rules on deferred payment leases over $250,000 apply (see ¶1600), the lessor has a "constant accrual" of rental income in the same way that rental expenses are deductible by the lessee. (Code Sec. 467)[30]

¶ 1343 Tenant's payment of landlord's expenses.

Where a tenant is required under the lease to pay interest, property taxes, mortgage principal, etc., thus satisfying the *landlord's* own payment obligation, the payments are treated as rent paid by the tenant to the landlord. (Reg § 1.61-8(c))[31]

¶ 1344 Tenant's improvements to the leased property; construction allowances from lessor.

Where a tenant erects a building or makes other improvements to leased property, the resulting increase in the property's value isn't income to the landlord either at the time the improvements are made or at the end of the lease term. (Code Sec. 109) But the landlord does have rental income if the improvements are made as rent substitutes.[32]

A lessee may exclude any amount received in cash (or as a rent reduction) from a lessor under a short-term lease (15 years or less) of retail space, that's for the purpose of the lessee's constructing or improving qualified long-term real property for use in the lessee's trade or business at the leased space. The construction allowance is excludible to the extent the lessee uses it for that purpose, within 8½ months after the end of the tax year it was received. Qualified long-term real property is nonresidential real property which is part of or otherwise

---

24. ¶J-2200 *et seq.*; ¶614.084 *et seq.*; TD ¶121,000
25. ¶J-2276; ¶s 4514.001, 4514.023; TD ¶121,002
26. ¶J-2278; TD ¶121,004
27. ¶J-2215 *et seq.*; ¶4514.022; TD ¶121,005
28. ¶J-2218; ¶4514.193; TD ¶121,003

29. ¶J-2277; ¶4514.194; TD ¶121,008
30. ¶L-6800 *et seq.*; ¶4674; TD ¶261,001
31. ¶J-2210 *et seq.*; ¶614.094; TD ¶121,007
32. ¶J-2250 *et seq.*; ¶1094.01 *et seq.*; TD ¶121,013

present at the retail space and reverts to the lessor at lease termination. The lessor treats any qualified long-term real property that's constructed or improved with an allowance excluded under these rules as its own nonresidential real property (¶1923). (Code Sec. 110; Reg § 1.110-1)[33]

¶ 1345   Royalties.

Royalties (payments received for the use of copyrights, patents, trademarks, secret processes and similar intangibles, and for the right to exploit mineral or other natural resources) are taxable as ordinary income (Code Sec. 61(a)(6)), regardless of the name given to them by the parties or the form of payment (e.g., lump sum or property such as stock).[34]

Royalties are included by cash basis taxpayers on receipt (actual or constructive), and by accrual basis taxpayers when their rights to them are fixed.[35]

¶ 1346   Life Insurance Proceeds.

Life insurance proceeds payable by reason of the insured's death are fully excludable or, if paid later than death under an interest option or in installments, partially excludable, from the recipient's gross income.

¶ 1347   How life insurance proceeds are taxed.

Amounts received under a "life insurance contract" that are paid by reason of the insured's death aren't included in the gross income of the recipient (i.e., beneficiary) (Code Sec. 101(a)) (unless the policy was transferred for value, see ¶1352). The exclusion applies to lump sum payments made at the time of the insured's death, and to amounts paid later to the extent the payment doesn't exceed the amount payable at death. (Reg § 1.101-1(a)(1))[36] For dividends and other lifetime payments, see ¶1350. For accelerated death benefits, see ¶1351.

For life insurance contracts that don't qualify, the exclusion is limited to the excess of the death benefits over the contract's net surrender value (i.e., value on surrender). (Code Sec. 7702(g)(2)) The net surrender value is treated as an annuity payment (¶1354 *et seq.*). Also, the owner of the contract is taxed (in the year it fails to qualify) on the income earned on it. This income equals the excess, for the year, of: (1) the sum of the net surrender value increase plus the cost of life insurance protection provided, over (2) premiums paid. (Code Sec. 7702(g)(1)(B))[37]

To qualify as a life insurance contract, a contract must be a life insurance (or endowment) contract under local law *and* satisfy either (a) a cash value accumulation test, or (b) a combined guideline premium requirement/cash value corridor test. (Code Sec. 101(f), Code Sec. 7702(a), Code Sec. 7702(h))[38] Pre-'85 contracts must entail risk shifting and risk distribution.[39]

¶ 1348   Life insurance proceeds paid in installments.

If the life insurance proceeds payable on the insured's death are paid in installments or for life, only part (below) of each payment is excluded. Any amount that exceeds the excluded portion is taxable when received. But if the amount of the total anticipated payments can't exceed the total amount payable at the insured's death, then each payment is fully excludable, whenever it's made. (Code Sec. 101(d)(1); Reg § 1.101-4(a)(1)(i))[40]

The excludable portion of each payment is: (1) the excludable amount held by the insurer

---

33. ¶J-2261 *et seq.*; ¶1104
34. ¶J-2300 *et seq.*; ¶614.084 *et seq.*; TD ¶122,001
35. ¶s J-2305, J-2306; ¶4514.001; TD ¶122,003
36. ¶J-4700 *et seq.*; ¶1014; TD ¶148,501
37. ¶J-4900 *et seq.*; ¶s 1014, 77,024.07; TD ¶148,504
38. ¶J-4800 *et seq.*; ¶s 1014, 77,024; TD ¶149,001
39. ¶J-4950 *et seq.*; ¶1014; TD ¶149,001
40. ¶J-4718; ¶1014.04; TD ¶148,505

with respect to the particular beneficiary, divided by (2) the number of payments to be made or, if payments are for life, the number of payments anticipated over the life expectancy of the beneficiary. This same prorated amount of each payment is excludable, regardless of how many payments are made (Reg § 1.101-4) (i.e., even if the beneficiary exceeds his anticipated life expectancy). The excludable amount is the present value to the beneficiary (as of the date of death) of the settlement.[41]

¶ 1349 Life insurance proceeds left at interest.

Where excludable life insurance proceeds are held by the insurer under an agreement to pay interest, the interest is taxable to the recipient, whether the interest option was chosen by the insured or by his beneficiaries or estate. No part of this interest may be excluded under the proration rules (¶1348). (Code Sec. 101(c); Reg § 1.101-3(a))[42]

¶ 1350 Proceeds paid before death of insured—loans, refunds, dividends, policy surrenders.

Payments made under life insurance or endowment contracts before the death of the insured (e.g., loans, refunds, dividends, and amounts received on surrender, redemption or maturity of a contract) generally are treated as amounts "not received" under an annuity contract (¶1366). (Code Sec. 72(a))[43] For accelerated death benefits received by terminally or chronically ill individuals, see ¶1351.

Thus, a transferee generally recognizes ordinary income in the amount received on the surrender of a life insurance policy (cash surrender value) less his adjusted basis in contract (aggregate premiums paid).[44]

¶ 1351 Accelerated death benefits—terminally or chronically ill insureds—viatical settlements.

Amounts received under a life insurance contract on the life of individuals who are certified terminally or chronically ill are excluded from gross income as amounts paid by reason of the death of an insured (¶1347). (Code Sec. 101(g)(1)) A similar exclusion applies to amounts received for the sale or assignment of any portion of a death benefit under a life insurance contract to a viatical settlement provider (one that regularly buys or takes assignments of life insurance contracts on the lives of the terminally ill and meets detailed standards) if the insured under the life insurance contract is either terminally or chronically ill. (Code Sec. 101(g)(2)(A))[45] In the case of chronically ill individuals, the exclusions apply only if detailed requirements are met. (Code Sec. 101(g)(3))[46]

¶ 1352 Death benefits exclusion where contract was transferred.

If a life insurance contract is transferred for valuable consideration, e.g., by sale, during the insured's lifetime, the transferee's exclusion for the life insurance proceeds he receives under the contract by reason of the insured's death (¶1347) is limited to the value of the consideration he paid for the contract, plus the net premiums and "other amounts" he paid later. (Code Sec. 101(a)(2))[47] For contracts issued after June 8, '97, "other amounts" includes interest paid or accrued by the transferee on debt with respect to a life insurance contract (or to an interest in one) that was transferred for valuable consideration, if the interest is disallowed under Code Sec. 264(a)(4) (see ¶1718). (Code Sec. 101(a)(2))

41. ¶J-4720; ¶1014.04; TD ¶148,505
42. ¶J-4717; ¶1014.03; TD ¶148,503
43. ¶J-5055 *et seq.*; ¶724 *et seq.*; TD ¶148,900 *et seq.*
44. ¶J-5058; TD ¶146,528

45. ¶J-4750 *et seq.*, ¶J-4818; ¶1014.015; TD ¶148,900 *et seq.*
46. ¶J-4754 *et seq.*; ¶1014.015; TD ¶148,905 *et seq.*
47. ¶J-4729; ¶1014.02; TD ¶148,528

Thus, IRS explained that a transferee generally recognizes income in the amount received over his adjusted basis in contract (i.e., aggregate premiums paid minus cost of insurance already provided). The cost of insurance is determined by the reduction in the contract's cash surrender value at the time of sale. Inside build-up immediately prior to sale (cash surrender value minus aggregate premiums paid) is ordinary income while any remaining amount is capital gain. On the sale of a term life contract with no cash surrender value, a transferee recognizes capital gain on the excess of the amount realized on the sale over his adjusted basis of contract, with the reduction for the cost of insurance that's been provided each month presumed to be equal to monthly premium paid.[48] For the sale or assignment of any portion of the death benefit to a viatical settlement provider, see ¶1351.

If only an interest in the contract is transferred, the limit applies only to the part of the proceeds attributable to the transferred interest.[49]

This limitation doesn't apply if:

... the transfer is to the insured, his partner, his partnership or a corporation in which he is a shareholder or officer; (Code Sec. 101(a)(2)(B)) or

... the transferee's basis for the contract (or interest) is determined in whole or in part by reference to the transferor's basis (Code Sec. 101(a)(2)(A))[50] as in a tax-free reorganization. (Reg § 1.101-1(b)(5), Ex 2)[1]

Where the transfer is gratuitous, i.e., a gift, the above limitation doesn't apply. The full death benefits exclusion is preserved. (Reg § 1.101-1(b)(2))[2]

¶ 1353   Employer-owned life insurance—Form 8925.

For contracts issued after Aug. 17, 2006 (except for tax-free Code Sec. 1035 exchanges), an employer in a trade or businesses treats proceeds payable to it from an employer-owned life insurance contract on an employee as income, excluding as a death benefit only the premiums and other amounts it paid for the contract. (Code Sec. 101(j)(1))[3] This rule doesn't apply for a contract for which notice and consent requirements are met, if:

(1) the insured was an individual who was an employee within 12 months of his death;

(2) at the time the contract was issued, the insured was a director; a "highly compensated employee," (i.e., a more-than-5% owner or employee who for the preceding year received in excess of $115,000 for 2013 and 2014) (¶4326); or a "highly compensated individual," i.e., one of the 5 highest paid officers, a shareholder owning more than 10%, or anyone else in the top 35% of employees ranked by pay;

(3) the amount is paid to: a family member of the insured (under Code Sec. 267(c)(4)), an individual who is a designated beneficiary under the contract (other than the policyholder), a trust established for either the family member's or beneficiary's benefit, or the insured's estate; or

(4) the amount is used to buy an equity (or partnership capital or profits) interest in the policyholder from the family member, beneficiary, trust or estate. (Code Sec. 101(j)(2)) It's intended that this amount be paid or used by the due date of the tax return for the policyholder's tax year in which the proceeds are received as a death benefit under the insurance contract, so that who is paid and what purchases are made with proceeds are known in the tax year in which the exception from the income inclusion rule is claimed.[4]

The notice and consent requirements are met if, before the issuance of the contract, the employee is notified (and consents) in writing to the employer insuring him with the employer

48. ¶J-5307; TD ¶146,624
49. ¶J-4731; ¶1014.02; TD ¶148,528
50. ¶J-4730; ¶1014.02; TD ¶148,528
1. ¶J-4742; ¶1014.02; TD ¶148,530

2. ¶J-4732; ¶1014.02; TD ¶148,529
3. ¶J-4744; ¶1014.11; TD ¶148,536
4. ¶J-4744; ¶1014.11; TD ¶148,536

as a beneficiary. The employee must be told the maximum face amount of the life insurance and if coverage continues after his termination. (Code Sec. 101(j)(4)) In guidance, IRS says it won't challenge an inadvertent notice and consent failure if: (1) the policyholder made a good faith effort to satisfy the requirements; and (2) the failure was inadvertent, and was discovered and corrected no later than the due date of the tax return for the tax year of the applicable policyholder in which the employer-owned life insurance contract was issued.[5]

Annual reporting (on Form 8925) and recordkeeping by policyholders that own one or more employer-owned life insurance contracts is also required. (Code Sec. 6039I; Reg § 1.6039I-1)

¶ 1354 Taxation of Annuity Payments.

Annuity payments consist generally of two parts: nontaxable return of investment (based on an exclusion ratio), and taxable interest. Other amounts (e.g., withdrawals, dividends) are taxable to the extent they exceed the contract's cost.

¶ 1355 How annuities are taxed.

Gross income includes any amount received "as an annuity" that's paid under an annuity, life insurance or endowment contract. (Code Sec. 72(a))[6] For exclusion under the "annuity rule," see ¶1356. For "nonannuity" payments under the contract (e.g., loans, dividends), see ¶1366. For private annuities, see ¶1369. For annuities paid to survivors of certain public safety officers, see ¶1260. For partial annuitization rule, see ¶1364.

¶ 1356 The annuity rule—"exclusion ratio" for amounts received "as an annuity."

If a payment under an annuity, life insurance or endowment contract is received "as an annuity" (i.e., a sum of money (or property) payable at regular intervals over a period of more than one full year from the starting date (¶1363) (Reg § 1.72-2(b)), all or part of it may be tax-free (for "natural person" holders, see ¶1357). The part of each "annuity" payment that represents return of investment (e.g., premiums paid) is excludable from the recipient's income until the entire investment is recovered. Excess receipts are fully taxable. (Code Sec. 72(b)(1); Reg § 1.72-4(a))[7]

The excludable portion is computed by multiplying each payment received by an "exclusion ratio," determined by dividing the investment in the contract (¶1361) by the contract's expected return (¶1362), as of the annuity starting date, and rounding to the nearest tenth. (Code Sec. 72(b); Reg § 1.72-4(a)) But the excludable portion of any payment can't exceed the amount of investment in the contract that is unrecovered immediately before the payment is received. (Code Sec. 72(b)(2))[8] (For employee annuities, see ¶1365.)

Once computed, the exclusion ratio is applied to each "annuity" payment received under the contract, until the total investment has been recovered tax-free. (Code Sec. 72(b); Reg § 1.72-4(a))[9] But the ratio must be recomputed if the contract is transferred for valuable consideration, matures, is surrendered, or is exchanged. (Reg § 1.72-4(a)(4))[10]

If there was no investment in the contract, all payments are taxable in full. If investment exceeds total expected return, all payments are tax-free. (Reg § 1.72-4(d))[11]

Where the annuitant's death causes the annuity payments (starting after Jan. 1, '86) to stop, the amount of any investment in the contract that the annuitant hasn't yet recovered tax-free may be deducted on his final income tax return. (Code Sec. 72(b)(3)(A))[12] For after-death distribution requirements, see ¶1358.

---

5. ¶J-4744; ¶1014.11; TD ¶148,536
6. ¶J-5001; ¶724 *et seq.*; TD ¶146,501
7. ¶J-5100 *et seq.*; ¶724; TD ¶146,541
8. ¶J-5105; ¶724.06; TD ¶146,545

9. ¶J-5104; ¶724.06; TD ¶146,545
10. ¶J-5106; ¶724.06; TD ¶146,547
11. ¶J-5104; ¶724.06; TD ¶146,545
12. ¶J-5109; ¶s 724, 724.06; TD ¶146,551

For annuities that started before '87, the exclusion ratio, once computed, applies to all payments no matter how long the annuitant lives (unless the contract is modified or exchanged). (Reg § 1.72-4(a))[13]

¶ 1357   Annuity rule exclusion available only to natural persons.

If an annuity contract is held by a person who isn't a natural person, the annuity rule (¶1356) doesn't apply. The income on the contract (for the holder's tax year) must be treated as ordinary income received or accrued by the holder during that year. (Code Sec. 72(u)(1))[14] A natural person doesn't include a trust or corporation. But holding by a trust, etc., *as agent* for a natural person is disregarded. (Code Sec. 72(u)(1))[15]

However, an *employer* that's the nominal owner (agent) of an annuity contract whose beneficial owners are (the employer's) employees is considered to hold the contract.[16]

The natural person rule *doesn't apply* to contracts: acquired by an estate by reason of the decedent's death; held by a qualified plan or IRA; that are "qualified funding assets" (¶1382); bought by an employer on termination of a qualified plan and held until all amounts under the contract are distributed to the employee (or his beneficiary) for whom the contract was bought; or that are immediate annuities. (Code Sec. 72(u)(3))[17]

¶ 1358   After-death distribution requirements for annuity contracts.

Payments under a contract aren't entitled to the partial exclusion under the annuity rule *unless* the contract provides that: (1) if any holder ("primary annuitant" for contracts not held by an individual) dies on or after the annuity starting date (¶1363) (and before the entire interest in the contract has been distributed), the balance will be distributed at least as rapidly as it was at the date of death, and (2) if any holder dies before the starting date, the entire interest must be distributed within five years of his death. (Code Sec. 72(s)(1))[18]

However, distributions that are payable to (or for) a designated beneficiary can be made for the beneficiary's life or a period not ending past his life expectancy. As long as the payments begin within one year of the holder's death, they'll be considered distributed on that starting date. (Code Sec. 72(s)(2)) A beneficiary who is the holder's surviving spouse will be considered the holder. (Code Sec. 72(s)(3))[19]

⊘*observation:* Treating the surviving spouse/beneficiary as the holder means that the after-death distribution provisions must be satisfied with respect to the *spouse's* death.

The after-death distribution rules *don't apply to:* contracts provided under qualified pension, profit-sharing, stock bonus or annuity plans; tax-sheltered annuities; individual retirement annuities (or contracts provided under IRAs); qualified funding assets (¶1382), regardless of any qualified assignment (Code Sec. 72(s)(5))[20] or contracts issued before Jan. 19, '85.[21]

¶ 1359   Variable annuities.

A variable annuity contract is one where the amount paid varies depending on investment experience, cost of living indexes, market fluctuations, etc. The excludable portion of each payment is computed by dividing the investment in the contract (¶1361) by the total number of anticipated payments. (Reg § 1.72-2(b)(3), Reg § 1.72-4(d)(3))[22]

The excludable amount stays the same regardless of changes in the amount received.

---

13. ¶J-5104; ¶724.06; TD ¶146,541
14. ¶s J-5005, J-5006; ¶724.25; TD ¶146,506
15. ¶J-5005; ¶724.25; TD ¶146,506
16. ¶J-5005; ¶724.25; TD ¶146,506
17. ¶J-5007; ¶724.25; TD ¶146,508

18. ¶s J-5014, J-5015; ¶724.01; TD ¶146,515
19. ¶J-5014; ¶724.01; TD ¶146,515
20. ¶J-5016; ¶724.01; TD ¶146,515
21. ¶J-5014; ¶724.01; TD ¶146,517
22. ¶J-5143; ¶724.08; TD ¶146,582

(Reg § 1.72-2(b)(3))[23] But if the amount received in a tax year is *less* than the excludable amount, taxpayer may elect (attach a specified statement to the return) to recompute the exclusion ratio for later years' payments. (Reg § 1.72-4(d)(3)(ii), Reg § 1.72-4(d)(3)(iv))[24]

¶ 1360   Joint and survivor annuity contracts.

Under a joint and survivor annuity contract, payments are made during the lives of two annuitants and, after the death of one, during the life of the survivor. A single exclusion ratio (¶1356), based on the aggregate expected return to both annuitants, is applied to the payments received by both annuitants. (Reg § 1.72-2(a)(2))[25]

¶ 1361   Investment in the contract.

For annuity rule purposes (¶1356), the "investment in the contract" is, in general, the net cost of the contract as of the annuity starting date (¶1363) or, if later, the date of the first contract payment. It equals the aggregate amount of premiums and other consideration paid (as of that date) for the contract, minus the aggregate amount previously received under the contract that was excluded from income. (Code Sec. 72(c)(1))[26] It must also be reduced to account for any refund feature. (Code Sec. 72(c)(2))[27] Separate computations may be required for pre-July '86 and post-June '86 investments. (Reg § 1.72-6(d))[28]

For an employee annuity, investment in the contract includes certain employer contributions that were taxable to the owner (employee). (Reg § 1.72-8(a))[29] Where the annuity began after Nov. 18, '96 (¶1365), or the safe-harbor method is elected for annuities beginning before Nov. 19, '96, no refund feature adjustment is required.[30]

For an employee annuity where the decedent died before Aug. 21, '96, the survivor-annuitant's investment in the contract also includes prior law's $5,000 death benefit exclusion, if applicable. (Reg § 1.72-8(b))[31]

¶ 1362   Expected return from the contract.

For annuity rule purposes (¶1356), the "expected return from the contract" is the total amount to be received (or estimated to be received) under the contract. It is computed as of the annuity starting date (¶1363) (Code Sec. 72(b)(1)) and doesn't take into account any amount for dividends or other payments *not* received as an annuity (¶1366). (Code Sec. 72(c)(3); Reg § 1.72-7(a))[32]

If the annuity is for a fixed term and doesn't depend on any life expectancy, the expected return is the amount of the payment specified for each period multiplied by the number of periods. (Reg § 1.72-5(c))[33]

If the annuity is payable for life or joint lives, the expected return is the amount of the *annual* payment multiplied by the number of years of life expectancy using IRS actuarial tables. (Code Sec. 72(c)(3)(A); Reg § 1.72-5(a))[34]

If the annuity is for an amount certain payable in periodic installments, the expected return is the total amount guaranteed. (Reg § 1.72-5(d))[35]

23. ¶J-5143; ¶724.08; TD ¶146,582
24. ¶J-5145; ¶724.08; TD ¶146,584
25. ¶J-5132 *et seq.*; ¶724.15; TD ¶146,572
26. ¶J-5113; ¶724.10; TD ¶141,033
27. ¶J-5122; ¶724.12; TD ¶141,038
28. ¶J-5117 *et seq.*; ¶724.10; TD ¶146,558
29. ¶H-11032 *et seq.*; ¶724.11; TD ¶141,034

30. ¶H-11047; ¶4024.02
31. ¶H-11037; ¶724.12; TD ¶141,034
32. ¶J-5124 *et seq.*; ¶724.14; TD ¶146,564
33. ¶J-5130; ¶724.14; TD ¶146,570
34. ¶J-5126 *et seq.*; ¶724.14; TD ¶146,564
35. ¶J-5131; ¶724.14; TD ¶146,571

¶ 1363   Annuity starting date.

The "annuity starting date" is the first day of the first period for which an amount is received *as an annuity* (¶1356) under the contract. This is the date the contractual obligation becomes fixed or, if later, the first day of the period (year, quarter, etc., depending on whether the payments are to be made annually, quarterly, etc.) that ends on the date of the first annuity payment. (Code Sec. 72(c)(4); Reg § 1.72-4(b)(1))[36] Special rules apply if the contract is transferred or exchanged. (Code Sec. 72(g)(3))[37]

¶ 1364   Partial annuitization of annuities.

Taxpayers may partially annuitize a nonqualified annuity, endowment, or life insurance contract. (Code Sec. 72(a)(2)) If any amount is received as an annuity for a period of 10 years or more, or during one or more lives, under any portion of an annuity, endowment, or life insurance contract:

(1) that portion will be treated as a separate contract for annuity taxation purposes;

(2) for purposes of applying Code Sec. 72(b) (calculation of the exclusion ratio for annuity distributions, ¶1356), Code Sec. 72(c) (investment in contract, expected return, and annuity starting date, ¶1361– ¶1363), and Code Sec. 72(e) (taxation of distributions from an annuity, endowment, or life insurance contract, that aren't received as an annuity, ¶1366), the investment in the contract is allocated pro rata between each portion of the contract from which amounts are received as an annuity, and the portion of the contract from which amounts are not received as an annuity, and

(3) a separate annuity starting date under Code Sec. 72(c)(4) (annuity starting date) is determined for each portion of the contract from which amounts are received as an annuity. (Code Sec. 72(a)(2))

Thus, holders of nonqualified annuities can elect to receive a portion of an annuity contract in the form of a stream of annuity payments, leaving the remainder of the contract to accumulate income on a tax-deferred basis.

The partial annuitization rule is not intended to change the rules for amounts received as an annuity (or as a lump sum) from Code Sec. 401(a) qualified plans, Code Sec. 403(a) annuity plans, Code Sec. 403(b) annuity plans, or individual retirement plans.

¶ 1365   Employee annuities—simplified method for computing nontaxable portion.

The nontaxable portion of amounts received as an annuity (¶1356) under a Code Sec. 401(a) qualified employee plan, a Code Sec. 403(a) qualified employee annuity or a Code Sec. 403(b) tax-sheltered annuity is computed under a simplified method, by dividing the investment in the contract (¶1361) as of the annuity starting date (¶1363) by a designated number of monthly payments. (Code Sec. 72(d)(1)(B))

For an annuity payable over the life of a single individual, the number of payments is 360 if the age of the annuitant on the annuity starting date is not more than 55; 310 payments if the age is more than 55 but not more than 60; 260 payments if more than 60 but not more than 65; 210 payments if more than 65 but not more than 70; and 160 payments if more than 70. (Code Sec. 72(d)(1)(B)(iii))[38]

For an annuity payable over the lives of more than one individual, the number of payments is 410 if the combined age of the annuitants on the annuity starting date is not more than 110; 360 payments if more than 110 but not more than 120; 310 payments if more than 120

---

36. ¶J-5110; ¶724.09; TD ¶141,019   38. ¶H-11012; ¶4024.02; TD ¶141,016
37. ¶J-5112; ¶724.09; TD ¶146,553

but not more than 130; 260 payments if more than 130 but not more than 140; and 210 payments if more than 140. (Code Sec. 72(d)(1)(B)(iv))[39]

Appropriate adjustments must be made if payments are not made on a monthly basis. (Code Sec. 72(d)(1)(F))[40]

The simplified method doesn't apply if the primary annuitant is 75 or older on the annuity starting date, unless there are fewer than 5 years of guaranteed payments under the annuity. (Code Sec. 72(d)(1)(E))[41]

A lump-sum payment received in connection with the start of annuity payments is taxable under Code Sec. 72(e) as if received before the annuity starting date (see ¶1366), and the investment in the contract is determined by taking into consideration the receipt of this lump-sum payment. (Code Sec. 72(d)(1)(D))[42]

For annuity starting dates before Jan. 1, '98 and after Nov. 18, '96, the designated number of payments is based on the age of the primary annuitant, and there is no separate table for annuities based on the life of more than one individual.[43]

For annuity starting dates before Nov. 19, '96, the regular annuity rules apply (¶1354 *et seq.*) unless the employee elects a simplified safe-harbor method.[44]

¶ 1366 Amounts "not" received as an annuity—cash withdrawals, dividends, etc.

Payments under life insurance, endowment and annuity contracts (other than modified endowment contracts, see ¶1368) that aren't "annuities" (e.g., cash withdrawals, loans, dividends, etc.) are fully taxable if received *on or after* the annuity starting date (¶1363). (Code Sec. 72(e)(2)(A), Code Sec. 72(e)(3)(A))[45]

"Nonannuity" amounts received *before* the annuity starting date are: (1) *not taxable,* to the extent that, as of the date of distribution, they don't exceed the cost of the contract (i.e., accumulated net premiums paid) and (2) *taxable,* to the extent allocable to income (i.e., excess of the contract's cash value over the owner's investment) at that time. (Code Sec. 72(e)(2)(B), Code Sec. 72(e)(3)(B))[46] (Veteran's insurance dividends are tax-free, regardless of cost.)[47]

caution: The pre-annuity starting date withdrawal may be subject to the premature distribution penalty (¶1367).

Receipts less than on insurance or endowment contract's cost don't give rise to a deductible loss.[48]

The contract's cost is reduced by the nontaxable amount of the dividend, etc., for purposes of computing the taxable portion of later payments. (Code Sec. 72(e)(6)(B))[49]

For these purposes, all contracts (other than immediate annuities or qualified plan annuities) issued by the same company (or its affiliates) to the same policyholder during any one calendar year are treated as a single contract. (Code Sec. 72(e)(11))[50]

¶ 1367 10% penalty on premature distributions from annuity contracts.

A penalty is imposed (except as noted below) on a person who receives any nonannuity distribution (¶1366) before the annuity starting date (¶1363) in the tax year the distribution is received. The penalty equals 10% of the taxable portion of the distribution. (Code

39. ¶H-11012; ¶4024.02; TD ¶141,016
40. ¶H-11012; ¶4024.02; TD ¶141,016
41. ¶H-11012; ¶4024.02; TD ¶141,016
42. ¶H-11012; ¶4024.02; TD ¶141,016
43. ¶H-11012; ¶4024.02; TD ¶141,016
44. ¶H-11012 *et seq.*; ¶724.07; TD ¶146,595

45. ¶J-5053; ¶724.17; TD ¶146,523
46. ¶724.17; TD ¶146,523
47. ¶J-5055; TD ¶146,525
48. ¶J-5308; TD ¶146,626
49. ¶J-5063; ¶724.10; TD ¶146,533
50. ¶J-5064; ¶724.17; TD ¶146,534

Sec. 72(q)(1))[1] Calculate and pay the penalty on Form 5329.[2]

This 10% penalty *doesn't apply* to any distribution:

(1) made on or after the date taxpayer (recipient) reaches age 59½;

(2) made on or after the death of the holder (or the primary annuitant, where the holder isn't an individual);

(3) attributable to recipient's total and indefinite disability;

(4) that's part of a series of substantially equal periodic payments (not less frequently than annually) made for the life (or life expectancy) of taxpayer or the joint lives (or joint life expectancies) of taxpayer and his designated beneficiary;

(5) made from a Code Sec. 401(a) qualified employee plan, a Code Sec. 403(a) qualified annuity plan, a Code Sec. 403(b) tax-sheltered annuity plan or a Code Sec. 818(a)(3) retirement plan for life insurance company employees (but for the separate penalty on premature distributions from these plans, see ¶4344);

(6) made from an individual retirement account or annuity (but for the separate penalty on premature distributions from these plans, see ¶4344);

(7) made under an annuity contract which is purchased by an employer on termination of a qualified plan (bonus, pension, profit-sharing or annuity) and which is held by the employer until the employee separates from service;

(8) under an immediate annuity;

(9) under a "qualified funding asset" (¶1382), regardless of any qualified assignment;

(10) to which the Code Sec. 72(t) tax on premature distributions from qualified plans applies (without regard to the Code Sec. 72(t)(2) exceptions), see ¶4344;

(11) allocable to pre-Aug. 14, '82 investment in the contract. (Code Sec. 72(q)(2))[3]

¶ 1368   Modified endowment contracts.

A modified endowment contract is a life insurance contract (entered into after June 20, '88) that fails to meet a "7-pay test" (or that is exchanged for such a contract). The test is failed if the accumulated amount paid under the contract during the first seven years exceeds the net level premiums that would have been paid as paid-up future benefits. (Code Sec. 7702A(a), Code Sec. 7702(b))[4]

Payments under a modified endowment contract that are received before the annuity starting date (¶1363) are includible in gross income to the extent allocable to income on the contract, as described at ¶1366. (Code Sec. 72(e)(10)(A)(i))[5] This applies to any amount received as a loan, or assigned or pledged on the value of the contract, unless the loan, etc., is made solely to cover burial expenses or prearranged funeral expenses where the maximum death benefit under the contract doesn't exceed $25,000. (Code Sec. 72(e)(10)(B)) However, taxpayer's investment in the contract (¶1361) is increased by the amount taxed to him (as a loan or assignment). (Code Sec. 72(e)(4)(A))[6]

Certain amounts received under a modified endowment contract that are includible in income are subject to a 10% penalty tax (Code Sec. 72(v)(1), Code Sec. 72(v)(2))[7] (use Form 5329).[8]

---

1. ¶J-5017; ¶724.21; TD ¶146,518
2. ¶S-2510; TD ¶146,519
3. ¶J-5018; ¶724.21; TD ¶146,520
4. ¶J-5066 *et seq.*; ¶s 724.17, 77,02A4; TD ¶146,536

5. ¶J-5065; ¶724.17; TD ¶146,535
6. ¶J-5063; ¶724.17; TD ¶146,529
7. ¶J-5076; ¶724.17; TD ¶146,540
8. ¶S-2510; TD ¶146,519

¶ 1369   Private annuities.

A private annuity generally involves the transfer of money or property to an individual or organization in exchange for the transferee's promise to make lifetime payments to the transferor. These transfers typically are made: to family members, controlled entities, or unrelated purchasers; to charitable organizations; and in settlement of a will contest.[9]

Transfer of an "unsecured" private annuity arrangement doesn't result in immediate taxable gain (or loss). Instead, any gain is reportable ratably over the lifetime of the transferor (i.e., annuitant). The gain equals the excess of the present value of the annuity (determined under regs) over the transferor's adjusted basis in the transferred property. Any loss may be disallowed if the arrangement is between related parties (¶2446 *et seq.*).[10]

If the arrangement is "secured" (i.e., the property transferred also is collateral for the payments), it's taxed (except for gift tax aspects) under the rules for commercial annuities, (¶1354 *et seq.*).[11] In applying those rules, the annuitant's basis in the property he transferred for the annuity is used as his investment in the contract.[12]

The value of annuities issued by charities is determined under IRS tables.[13]

¶ 1370   Gifts and Inheritances. ▮▮▮▮▮▮▮▮▮▮▮▮▮▮▮▮▮▮▮▮▮▮▮▮▮▮▮▮▮▮

Property received as a gift, bequest, devise or inheritance is exempt from income tax.

¶ 1371   Gifts and inheritances of property and income.

A gift of property isn't taxable to a recipient (Code Sec. 102; Reg § 1.102-1)[14] other than an employee, see ¶1212. For gifts of income, see ¶1371. For employee awards, see ¶1251. For gift tax, see ¶5038 *et seq.*

Gifts, devises, bequests, and inheritances (i.e., money and any property that pass on the death of a person by his will or under intestacy, including amounts received in settlement of a will contest) are excluded from gross income. (Code Sec. 102; Reg § 1.102-1)[15] For bequests of income, see ¶1371. For estate tax, see ¶5000 *et seq.*

The above exclusion applies only to the property transferred. Income from the property itself is taxable to the recipient, whether paid periodically or in a lump sum. (Code Sec. 102(b); Reg § 1.102-1(c))[16] For an exception for income paid or credited as a gift or bequest of specific property or money, see ¶3950.

¶ 1372   Prizes and Awards. ▮▮▮▮▮▮▮▮▮▮▮▮▮▮▮▮▮▮▮▮▮▮▮▮▮▮▮▮▮▮

Prizes and awards generally are taxable.

¶ 1373   Taxation of prizes and awards.

All prizes and awards (with exceptions for qualified scholarships, see ¶2216) are includible in gross income (Code Sec. 74(a); Reg § 1.74-1(b)) *unless:* the prize is primarily for religious, charitable, scientific, educational, artistic, literary, etc., achievement; the recipient was selected without any action on his part, and thus isn't required to render substantial future services; *and* it's transferred by the payor to a governmental unit or charity the recipient

---

9. ¶J-5252; ¶724.01; TD ¶146,601
10. ¶J-5256 *et seq.*; ¶724.05; TD ¶146,602
11. ¶J-5257; TD ¶146,606
12. ¶J-5254; ¶724.05; TD ¶146,603

13. ¶P-6615, ¶P-6674 *et seq.*; TD ¶146,612
14. ¶J-6000 *et seq.*; ¶1024; TD ¶178,001
15. ¶J-6000 *et seq.*; ¶1024.02; TD ¶178,010
16. ¶J-6004, ¶J-6005; ¶1024; TD ¶178,004

designated (Code Sec. 74(b))[17] before getting any benefit from it.[18] IRS specifies the requirements of the designation (including model language).[19] For employee awards, see ¶1251.

For a prize paid in property or services, the taxable amount is the prize's current fair market (resale) value. (Reg § 1.74-1(a)(2))[20]

Under the principle of constructive receipt (¶2822), the winner of a contest (e.g., a lottery, jackpot) who is given the option of receiving either a lump sum or an annuity has to include the value of the award in gross income, even if he or she takes the annuity. However, in the case of a cash basis individual, a "qualified prize option" (to choose either cash or an annuity not later than 60 days after becoming entitled to the prize) is disregarded in determining the tax year for which any portion of a "qualified prize" (one payable over at least 10 years and that meets other requirements) is included in income. (Code Sec. 451(h)) That is, the individual doesn't have to include the value of the prize in income immediately merely by having had the option to choose cash.[21]

¶ 1374   Accident and Health Insurance Benefits. ▬▬▬▬▬▬▬▬▬

Benefits received from accident and health insurance are excluded from gross income, unless the benefits compensate for medical expense deductions from an earlier year. Benefits from long-term care insurance policies are subject to special rules.

¶ 1375   Exclusion for benefits received through accident or health insurance.

Amounts received through accident or health insurance (or through an arrangement having the effect of accident or health insurance) for personal injuries or sickness are generally excluded from income, except to the extent attributable to medical expenses that were deducted in a previous year. This exclusion doesn't apply to amounts received by an employee to the extent the amounts are (1) attributable to employer contributions that weren't includible in the employee's gross income, or (2) are paid by the employer. (Code Sec. 104(a)(3))[22]

Where an employer-provided disability plan allows employees to elect annually to pay for coverage out of pre- or post-tax dollars, disability benefits paid to an employee who elected the post-tax option for the plan year in which he became disabled are excludable from gross income.[23]

¶ 1376   Exclusion for benefits from long-term care insurance—per diem limit.

Qualified long-term care insurance contracts (see ¶2145) issued after '96 are treated as accident and health insurance contracts. (Code Sec. 7702B(a)(1)) Pre-'97 contracts that met applicable state long-term care insurance requirements also qualify. (Reg § 1.7702B-2)[24] Amounts (other than policyholder dividends, as defined in Code Sec. 808 or premium refunds) received from such contracts are treated as amounts received for personal injury or sickness and as reimbursement for expenses actually incurred for medical care, and are excludable (see ¶1375), subject to a per diem limit, below.[25]

If the total of (1) the periodic payments received for any period under all qualified long-term care insurance contracts treated as made for qualified long-term care services for an insured and (2) the periodic payments received for the period which are treated under Code Sec. 101(g) (see ¶1351) as paid by reason of the death of the insured, exceeds the per diem limit for the period, the excess is includible in gross income. A payment isn't taken into account under (2) if the insured is a terminally ill individual at the time the payment is

---

17. ¶J-1201 *et seq.*; ¶744; TD ¶194,001
18. ¶J-1208; ¶744.01; TD ¶194,006
19. ¶J-1210; ¶744.01; TD ¶194,008
20. ¶J-1223; ¶744.04; TD ¶194,019
21. ¶G-2424.2; ¶4514.043; TD ¶441,012

22. ¶J-1301; ¶1044.03; TD ¶194,501
23. ¶H-1115 *et seq.*; ¶1044.03; TD ¶194,501
24. ¶K-2141.6; ¶77,02B4; TD ¶346,304
25. ¶J-1308; ¶7702B4.04; TD ¶194,507

received. (Code Sec. 7702B(d)(1))[26]

The per diem limit for any period is the excess (if any) of: (a) the greater of (i) $320 for 2013 ($330 for 2014), or the equivalent amount when payments are made on another periodic basis, or (ii) the costs incurred for qualified long-term care services provided for the insured for the period, over (b) the total payments received as reimbursement (by insurance or otherwise) for qualified long-term care services provided for the insured during the period. (Code Sec. 7702B(d)(2)) If payments exceed this limit, the excess is excludible only to the extent of actual costs incurred for long-term care services; amounts with respect to which no such actual costs are incurred are fully includible.[27]

¶ 1377 Exclusion for Archer medical savings account (MSA) distributions.

Distributions from an Archer MSA (see ¶1528 for limitations) are excludable from gross income if used exclusively to pay the qualified medical expenses of the individual (account holder) or his spouse or dependents. (Code Sec. 220(f)(1))[28] Otherwise, they are (1) included in gross income (Code Sec. 220(f)(2)) and (2) subject to an additional tax of 20% for distributions reported on Form 8853 unless made after the individual attains age 65, dies, or becomes disabled. (Code Sec. 220(f)(4))[29]

Qualified medical expenses are for medical care as defined under the medical expense deduction rules (see ¶2144), but only to the extent not reimbursed by insurance or otherwise. (Code Sec. 220(d)(2)(A)) Medicine or drugs are qualified medical expenses only if prescribed (whether or not over-the-counter) or if insulin. (Code Sec. 220(d)(2)(A)) Qualified medical expenses don't include insurance premiums other than premiums for qualified long-term care insurance (¶2145), health care continuation coverage (COBRA), and coverage while receiving unemployment compensation. (Code Sec. 220(d)(2)(B))[30]

In any year for which an MSA contribution is made, distributions from that MSA to pay medical expenses are included in gross income if, for the month in which the expense was incurred, the individual for whom the expense was incurred wasn't covered under a "high deductible health plan" or had ineligible coverage. (Code Sec. 220(d)(2)(C))[31]

¶ 1378 Exclusion for health savings account (HSA) distributions.

Distributions from an HSA (see ¶1529) that are used exclusively to pay the qualified medical expenses of an eligible individual (account holder) or his spouse or dependents are excludable from gross income. (Code Sec. 223(f)) For this purpose, an individual may qualify as a dependent without regard to whether he: (1) is subject to the general rule that a dependent of a taxpayer shall be treated as himself having no dependents; (2) is married and files a joint return; and (3) has gross income that exceeds an otherwise applicable gross income limitation. (Code Sec. 223(d)(2)(A))

Qualified medical expenses are expenses paid for medical care as defined under the medical expense deduction rules (see ¶2144), but only to the extent they're not reimbursed by insurance or otherwise. (Code Sec. 223(d)(2)) Medicine or drugs are qualified medical expenses only if prescribed (whether or not over-the-counter) or if insulin. (Code Sec. 223(d)(2)(A)) Qualified medical expenses, which must be incurred after the HSA is established, don't include insurance premiums other than premiums for qualified long-term care insurance (¶2145), health care continuation coverage (COBRA) (see ¶1531), and coverage while the eligible individual is receiving unemployment compensation. (Code Sec. 223(d)(2)(B))[32]

---

26. ¶J-1308; ¶7702B4.04; TD ¶194,507
27. ¶J-1308; ¶7702B4.04; TD ¶194,507
28. ¶H-1337 *et seq.*; ¶2204.01; TD ¶288,101 *et seq.*
29. ¶H-1338 *et seq.*; ¶2204.01; TD ¶288,101 *et seq.*

30. ¶H-1337.1 *et seq.*; ¶2204.01; TD ¶288,101 *et seq.*
31. ¶H-1337.2; ¶2204.01
32. ¶H-1350.1 *et seq.*; ¶2234; TD ¶289,103 *et seq.*

Distributions not used for qualified medical expenses are subject to tax, they also are subject to an additional 20% for distributions reported on Form 8853 unless made after the individual attains age 65, dies, or becomes disabled. (Code Sec. 223(f))[33]

Contributions for a year exceeding the deduction limit (see ¶1529) can be withdrawn tax-free if the distribution is: (1) completed by the extended tax return due date; and (2) accompanied by the net income (includible in the individual's income) attributable to the excess contribution. (Code Sec. 223(f)(3)(A))[34]

¶ 1379 Exclusion for benefits received through health reimbursement arrangements (HRAs).

Amounts received by an employee under an HRA are excluded from gross income as amounts received under an accident and health plan (¶1375). An HRA is a type of employee benefit plan reimbursing employees for medical expenses not covered by other forms of insurance. Medicine or drugs are qualified medical expenses only if prescribed (whether or not over-the-counter) or if insulin. (Code Sec. 106(f)) Benefits are paid up to a specific dollar amount from funds provided exclusively by the employer (and not through a salary reduction or otherwise under a cafeteria plan (¶1269)). Balances remaining in the employee's account at the end of a coverage period may be carried forward if the plan so provides. An HRA may use debit cards, credit cards, or other electronic media to support and document the tax-free reimbursement of an employee's claimed medical or dental expenses if proper safeguards and substantiation methods are used.[35]

¶ 1380 Damages. ▬▬▬▬▬▬▬▬▬▬▬

Compensatory damages received on account of personal physical injuries or personal physical sickness are tax-free (but punitive damages generally are not excludable).

¶ 1381 Nonbusiness damages—personal physical injury or sickness.

Damages other than punitive damages received (by suit or agreement, in a lump-sum or as periodic payments) as compensation for personal *physical* injury or personal *physical* sickness are excluded from income (Code Sec. 104(a)(2); Reg § 1.104-1) If an action has its origin in a physical injury or physical sickness, then all nonpunitive damages from that injury or sickness are excluded, whether or not the recipient is the injured party. Emotional distress is not considered a physical injury or physical sickness, but the exclusion does apply to damages received up to the amount paid for medical care attributable to emotional distress. (Code Sec. 104(a)) Thus, the exclusion doesn't apply to damages (other than for medical expenses attributable to emotional distress) based on a claim of employment discrimination or injury to reputation accompanied by a claim of emotional distress and does apply to nonpunitive damages received based on a claim of emotional distress, that are attributable to a physical injury or physical sickness.[36] The exclusion does not apply to "delay damages," i.e., damages awarded due to the delay in payment, which have been held to be in the nature of interest.[37]

Punitive damages generally are taxable, regardless of the nature of the claim. (Code Sec. 104(a)(2)) But under an exception, punitive damages received in connection with a physical injury or sickness are tax-free if received in a civil wrongful death action, and under applicable state law (as in effect on Sept. 13, '95, and without regard to later modification) which provides (or has been construed by a court to provide) that only punitive damages may be awarded in the action. (Code Sec. 104(c))[38]

Where a lump-sum award is specifically allocated by the parties between compensatory and

---

33. ¶H-1350.11 *et seq.*; ¶2234.01; TD ¶289,111 *et seq.*
34. ¶H-1350.10; ¶2234.04; TD ¶289,110
35. ¶H-1349 *et seq.*; TD ¶289,000
36. ¶J-5801; ¶1044.02; TD ¶182,001
37. ¶J-5817; ¶1044.02; TD ¶151,027
38. ¶J-5816.1 *et seq.*; TD ¶182,006

punitive damages, or between personal and business injury, that allocation generally controls. But if no allocation is made, the courts look to the nature of the claims (e.g., primary nature of the harm inflicted) and the payor's intent.[39]

¶ 1382 Amounts received for accepting assignment of personal injury liability.

Amounts received by an assignee (e.g., insurance company) for accepting assignment of a liability to make periodic payments as damages for personal injury or sickness (in a case involving *physical* injury or sickness), including a liability to pay workers' compensation, are excludable from the assignee's gross income, up to the aggregate cost of any "qualified funding asset" used to satisfy the liability. A "qualified funding asset" is a commercial annuity contract, or a U.S. obligation, having payment periods corresponding to those of the liability, which the assignee: (1) purchased within 60 days before or after the date of the assignment, and (2) uses to satisfy that liability. (Code Sec. 130(c))[40]

¶ 1383 Business damages.

Damages received for injury to business that represent compensation for lost profits (including business interruption insurance proceeds) are taxable as ordinary income. This applies to awards for breach of a contract of sale and for business slander. Amounts received for injury to capital (e.g., injury to good will, fraudulent stock sale) are tax-free to the extent of basis; any excess is capital gain.[41] Punitive damages (e.g., insiders' profits, treble damages under antitrust laws) are taxable. (Reg § 1.61-14(a))[42]

There is a special deduction for certain expired net operating losses that resulted from the same injury. (Code Sec. 186(d))[43]

¶ 1384 Attorney's fees payable out of judgment.

When a litigant's (taxpayer's) recovery —money judgment or settlement—constitutes income, the taxpayer must include in income the portion of the recovery paid to the attorney as a contingent fee (a fee that's paid to the attorney only in the case of a successful recovery; generally computed as a percentage of the recovery). In general, attorney's fees payable from the award are deductible only as a miscellaneous itemized deduction regardless of whether the fees are contingent or noncontingent.[44] However, certain attorney s fees related to qualifying civil rights suits and whistleblower awards are deductible from gross income; see ¶3108.

¶ 1385 Income Realized on Discharge or Cancellation of Indebtedness. ■■■■■■■■

Gross income includes income from discharge of indebtedness.

For information reporting by banks, etc., that discharge indebtedness, see ¶4746.

¶ 1386 Debtor has income on discharge of debt—COD income.

Reduction or cancellation of debt (recourse or nonrecourse) is income to the debtor. (Code Sec. 61(a)(12))[45] Cancellation of debt (COD) income thus can result where a creditor accepts less than full payment as a complete discharge of the debt, or where events or circumstances make its collection unlikely.[46] But if the debtor's payment of the liability would have given rise to a deduction, the debtor won't have income from the discharge. (Code Sec. 108(e)(2))[47]

---

39. ¶J-5810; ¶1044.02; TD ¶182,004
40. ¶J-5833 *et seq.*; ¶s 1304, 1304.01; TD ¶182,008
41. ¶J-5819 *et seq.*; ¶614.170 *et seq.*; TD ¶182,013
42. ¶J-5829; ¶614.168; TD ¶182,018
43. ¶K-8501 *et seq.*; ¶1864 *et seq.*

44. ¶J-8258; TD ¶201,086
45. ¶J-7001; ¶614.114; TD ¶186,001
46. ¶J-7001 *et seq.*; ¶614.114; TD ¶186,015
47. ¶J-7504; ¶1084.04; TD ¶188,003

¶ 1387   Cancellation of debt under student loan programs.

There is no income (COD income, see ¶1386) from the cancellation of all or part of certain government student loans (or certain loans made by tax-exempt educational organizations), or loans made by exempt educational organizations or other exempt organizations to refinance any student loan, if the debtor is required to perform public service work for a period of time in certain professions for any of a broad range of employers. (Code Sec. 108(f)(1))[48]

Nor does gross income include any amount received under: (a) Sec. 338B(g) of the Public Health Service Act (relating to the National Health Service Corps Loan Repayment Program); (b) a state program described in Sec. 338I of that Act; or (c) any State loan repayment or loan forgiveness program intended to provide for the increased availability of health care services in underserved or health professional shortage areas (as determined by the State). (Code Sec. 108(f)(4))[49]

¶ 1388   Discharge of indebtedness of solvent debtors outside bankruptcy.

Any discharge of indebtedness of a debtor, other than in a bankruptcy case (¶1390), or where the debtor is insolvent (¶1389), results in the current (i.e., year of discharge) recognition of income (COD income, see ¶1386) in the amount of the discharge (Reg § 1.61-12(a))[50] except for certain farm (¶1391) or real property (¶1392) indebtedness.

¶ 1389   Insolvent debtor outside bankruptcy—"insolvency exception"—Form 982.

If the indebtedness is discharged when the debtor is insolvent (but not in a bankruptcy case), the discharge is excluded from the debtor's gross income up to the amount of the insolvency. (Code Sec. 108(a)(1)(B), Code Sec. 108(a)(2)(A), Code Sec. 108(a)(3))[1]

The amount excluded under this "insolvency exception" must be applied to reduce the debtor's tax attributes such as loss or credit carryovers or basis in assets. (Credit carryovers are reduced 33⅓¢ per dollar of debt discharge amount; other tax attributes are reduced dollar for dollar.) (Code Sec. 108(b)(3)) (Use Form 982 to report the reduction of tax attributes.) Or the debtor can elect (on Form 982) to apply any or all of the excluded amount *first* to reduce his basis in *depreciable* assets (or real property held as inventory). (Code Sec. 108(b)(5)(A), Code Sec. 1017(b)(3); Reg § 1.108-4(b))[2]

Any balance of the discharged debt (excess over the amount the debtor is insolvent) is COD income, as for a wholly solvent debtor (¶1388). (Code Sec. 108(a)(2)(B), Code Sec. 108(a)(3))[3]

A debtor is insolvent for this purpose if, immediately before the debt is discharged, his liabilities exceed the fair market value of his assets. (Code Sec. 108(d)(3))[4]

If a reorganization or other transaction described in Code Sec. 381(a) ends a year in which the distributor or transferor corporation excludes COD income under Code Sec. 108(a), any tax attributes to which the acquiring corporation succeeds and the basis of property acquired by the acquiring corporation must reflect the reductions required by Code Sec. 108 and Code Sec. 1017. (Reg § 1.108-7(c), Reg § 1.1017-1(b)(4))

For partners and S corporations, see ¶1393.

---

48. ¶J-7508; ¶1084.04; TD ¶188,006
49. ¶J-7510.1; ¶1084.04; TD ¶188,008.1
50. ¶J-7001, ¶J-7200 *et seq.* ¶s 1084, 1084.01; TD ¶188,011
1. ¶J-7401; ¶1084.01; TD ¶188,011

2. ¶J-7404; ¶1084.02; TD ¶188,011
3. ¶J-7401; ¶1084.01; TD ¶188,014
4. ¶J-7403; ¶1084.01; TD ¶188,014

¶ 1390   Discharge of indebtedness of bankrupt debtor—Form 982.

No amount is included in a debtor's gross income by reason of a discharge of indebtedness in a bankruptcy case (Code Sec. 108(a)(1)(A)), even if the debtor is solvent after the discharge. (Code Sec. 108(a)(2))[5]

The amount of discharged debt that is excluded under this rule must be applied to reduce certain of the debtor's tax attributes (Code Sec. 108(b)(1)) (use Form 982) unless the debtor elects (on Form 982) to apply any or all of the excluded amount *first* to reduce his basis in depreciable assets (or real property held as inventory). (Code Sec. 108(b)(5)(A), Code Sec. 1017(b)(3); Reg § 1.1017-1(c))[6] For partners and S corporations, see ¶1393.

¶ 1391   Discharge of "qualified farm indebtedness" of solvent farmers.

A solvent taxpayer whose "qualified farm indebtedness" is discharged (outside bankruptcy) by certain unrelated lenders doesn't have COD income (see ¶1386), to the extent the discharge doesn't exceed the sum of his adjusted tax attributes plus the aggregate adjusted bases (as of the start of the year after discharge) of his business or income-producing property. (Code Sec. 108(a)(1)(C), Code Sec. 108(g)(1), Code Sec. 108(g)(3)) Any excess is COD income (but the insolvency (¶1389) or bankruptcy (¶1390) rules have precedence). (Code Sec. 108(a)(2))[7]

"Qualified farm indebtedness" is debt incurred directly in connection with taxpayer's farm business if at least 50% of taxpayer's total gross receipts for the three tax years preceding the tax year of the discharge is attributable to farming. (Code Sec. 108(g)(2))[8] For partners and S corporations, see ¶1393.

¶ 1392   Discharge of "qualified real property business indebtedness"—Form 982.

A solvent taxpayer other than a C corporation whose "qualified real property business indebtedness" (QRPBI) is discharged (outside bankruptcy) can elect to exclude the discharged amount from income, to the extent of the excess (if any) of (1) the outstanding principal amount of the QRPBI immediately before the discharge over (2) the fair market value (at discharge) of the property securing the QRPBI less the outstanding principal amount of any other QRPBI secured by the property at that time. (Code Sec. 108(a)(1)(D), Code Sec. 108(c)(2)(A), Code Sec. 108(c)(3)(C); Reg § 1.108-6(a))[9] The excluded amount must be applied (on Form 982) to reduce the basis of taxpayer's depreciable real property. (Code Sec. 108(c)(1)(A))[10]

QRPBI is indebtedness (other than qualified farm indebtedness, ¶1391) incurred or assumed by taxpayer in connection with real property used in a trade or business and secured by the real property (Code Sec. 108(c)(3)(A)) that:

. . . if incurred or assumed by the taxpayer after '92, is "qualified acquisition indebtedness" (Code Sec. 108(c)(3)(B))—i.e., indebtedness incurred or assumed to acquire, construct, reconstruct, or substantially improve the property (Code Sec. 108(c)(4)); *and*

. . . taxpayer elects to treat as "qualified real property business indebtedness" (Code Sec. 108(c)(3)(C))[11] on Form 982 attached to the return for the tax year of discharge. (Code Sec. 108(d)(9)(A); Reg § 1.108-5)[12]

---

5. ¶J-7402; ¶1084.01; TD ¶188,013

6. ¶J-7404; ¶1084.02; TD ¶188,016

7. ¶J-7405 *et seq.*; ¶1084.01; TD ¶188,018

8. ¶J-7406; ¶1084.01; TD ¶188,019

9. ¶J-7409; ¶1084.01; TD ¶188,022

10. ¶J-7411; ¶1084.01; TD ¶188,024

11. ¶J-7410; ¶1084.01; TD ¶188,023

12. ¶J-7412; ¶1084.01; TD ¶188,025

QRPBI also includes indebtedness incurred to refinance QRPBI, but only to the extent it doesn't exceed the amount of the indebtedness being refinanced. (Code Sec. 108(c)(3))[13]

¶ 1393   How COD income exclusions apply to partnership or S corporation debt.

For partnership debt, the insolvency (¶1389), bankruptcy (¶1390), qualified farm indebtedness (¶1391), and qualified real property indebtedness (¶1392) exclusions are applied at the partner level, not at the partnership level. (Code Sec. 108(d)(6)) In measuring a partner's insolvency for purposes of the insolvency exclusion, each partner treats as a liability an amount of the partnership's discharged excess nonrecourse debt (i.e., nonrecourse debt in excess of the fair market value of the property securing the debt) based on the allocation of cancellation of debt income to that partner under Code Sec. 704(b) (¶3725).[14] For an S corporation's debt, the exclusions are applied at the corporate level, not at the shareholder level. (Code Sec. 108(d)(7)(A))[15]

¶ 1394   Discounted purchase of debtor's own obligations.

When a debtor buys or otherwise acquires his own obligations for less than face value (i.e., at a discount), he usually realizes taxable income to the extent of the discount. (Reg § 1.61-12(a))[16] This also applies if a party related to the debtor acquires the debtor's indebtedness from an unrelated party. (Code Sec. 108(e)(4)(A); Reg § 1.108-2)[17]

A corporation that repurchases its own bonds (directly or indirectly) has cancellation of debt (COD) income (¶1386) to the extent of the excess of the adjusted issue price over the repurchase price. (Reg § 1.61-12(c)(2))[18]

For the debtor to be taxed, the obligation must require the unconditional payment of a fixed amount. If the obligation really represents an equity interest, a corporate debtor will be, in effect, acquiring its own stock and thus won't be taxed on the "discount." [19]

Debt instrument reacquired in 2009 and 2010. If the taxpayer elected, debt discharge income from the reacquisition of a discounted applicable debt instrument by the taxpayer or a related party after 2008 and before 2011 is deferred for up to five years, and then included in income ratably over five years. For reacquisitions in 2009, income is includible over the 5-year period beginning with the fifth tax year following the tax year in which it's reacquired; and for reacquisitions in 2010, beginning with the fourth tax year following the tax year in which it's reacquired. (Code Sec. 108(i)(1), Reg § 1.108(i)-0(a))[20]

¶ 1395   Satisfaction of debt with property or services (including "stock for debt").

If a debtor transfers property (other than debt) to, or performs services for, a creditor (or third party) in full satisfaction of the debt, and the property or services are worth the amount owed, there's no *cancellation* of the debt since it was actually paid. But a debtor who satisfies debt with services has taxable *compensation* equal to the debt. (Reg § 1.61-12(a))[21]

A debtor who transfers property (other than debt) in satisfaction of the debt has gain (or loss) to the extent the fair market value (FMV) of the property transferred exceeds (or is less than) his basis in it. The type of gain (or loss), or whether any loss is deductible, is determined under the regular sale or exchange rules (¶2400 *et seq.*). If the property transferred is worth less than the face amount of the debt, the difference is cancellation of debt (COD) income to the debtor.[22]

13. ¶J-7410; ¶1084.01; TD ¶188,023
14. ¶J-7415; ¶1084.03; TD ¶188,027
15. ¶J-7416; ¶1084.03; TD ¶188,028
16. ¶J-7011; ¶614.114; TD ¶186,020
17. ¶J-7016 *et seq.*; ¶1084.04; TD ¶186,024
18. ¶J-7204.1; ¶614.136; TD ¶186,003
19. ¶J-7007; TD ¶186,014
20. ¶J-7421; ¶1084.01; TD ¶188,032
21. ¶J-7040; ¶614.114; TD ¶186,033
22. ¶J-7206; ¶10,014.76; TD ¶221,401

If a debtor corporation transfers stock, or a debtor partnership transfers a capital or profits interest in that partnership, to a creditor in satisfaction of its recourse or nonrecourse debt, the corporation or partnership is treated as having satisfied the debt with an amount of money equal to the FMV of the stock or the interest. In the case of a partnership, Under a safe harbor, the FMV of the partnership interest in a debt-for-equity exchange will be its liquidation value. Any discharge of debt income recognized under this rule is included in the distributive shares of taxpayers that were partners in the partnership immediately before the discharge. (Code Sec. 108(e)(8), Reg § 1.108-8) So the debtor has taxable income to the extent the principal of the debt exceeds the value of the stock or interest.[23]

¶ 1396 Debt-for-debt exchanges.

A debtor may satisfy an outstanding "old" debt by issuing a "new" debt. The old debt is treated as having been satisfied with an amount of money equal to the issue price of the new debt. (Code Sec. 108(e)(10)(A)) The excess (if any) of the "old" adjusted issue price over the "new" issue price is COD income (¶1386) to the debtor.[24]

For this purpose, "issue price" is determined under the OID rules (¶1317). (Code Sec. 108(e)(10)(B)) However, if the Code Sec. 483 unstated interest rules (¶1307 *et seq.*) (rather than the OID rules) apply, the new debt's issue price is its stated redemption price at maturity (¶1316) less the unstated interest.[25]

¶ 1397 Home mortgage debt forgiveness before 2014—Form 982.

For indebtedness discharged before Jan. 1, 2014, gross income doesn't include any discharge of qualified principal residence indebtedness. (Code Sec. 108(a)(1)(E)) Qualified principal residence indebtedness is acquisition indebtedness under Code Sec. 163(h)(3)(B) with respect to the taxpayers's principal residence (see ¶1733), but with a $2 million limit ($1 million for married individuals filing separately). (Code Sec. 108(h)(2)) It includes indebtedness incurred in the acquisition, construction, or substantial improvement of a principal residence that is secured by the residence. It also includes refinancing of debt to the extent the amount doesn't exceed the amount of the refinanced indebtedness. "Principal residence" has the same meaning as under the homesale exclusion rules of Code Sec. 121 (see ¶2442). (Code Sec. 108(h)(5)) A taxpayer can have only one principal residence at any one time.[26]

The basis of the taxpayer's principal residence is reduced by the excluded amount, but not below zero. (Code Sec. 108(h)(1))[27]

If any loan is discharged, in whole or in part, and only part of the loan is qualified principal residence indebtedness, the mortgage forgiveness exclusion (claimed on Form 982) applies only to so much of the amount discharged as exceeds the amount of the loan (as determined immediately before the discharge) which is not qualified principal residence indebtedness. (Code Sec. 108(h)(4))

The exclusion doesn't apply to the discharge of a loan if the discharge is on account of services performed for the lender or any other factor not directly related to a decline in the value of the residence or to the taxpayer's financial condition.[28] The exclusion also doesn't apply to a taxpayer in a Title 11 bankruptcy (see ¶1390). (Code Sec. 108(h)(3)) An insolvent taxpayer (other than one in a Title 11 bankruptcy) can elect to have the mortgage forgiveness exclusion not apply and can instead rely on the Code Sec. 108(a)(1)(B) exclusion for insolvent taxpayers (see ¶1389). (Code Sec. 108(a)(2))[29]

---

23. ¶J-7015; ¶1084.04; TD ¶186,021
24. ¶J-7205; ¶1084.04; TD ¶186,004
25. ¶J-7205; ¶1084.04; TD ¶186,004
26. ¶J-7417; ¶1084.01; TD ¶188,029

27. ¶P-3006.2; ¶1084.01; TD ¶215,504.1
28. ¶J-7419; ¶1084.01; TD ¶188,031
29. ¶J-7420; ¶1084.01; TD ¶188,029

Chapter 3   Deductions—Expenses of a Business

¶ 1500   Start-Up Expenditures. ▬▬▬▬▬▬▬▬

Start-up expenditures must be capitalized, unless a taxpayer elects to expense up to $5,000 of the cost and amortize the balance over a 180-month period.

¶ 1501   Tax treatment of start-up expenditures.

Start-up expenditures must be amortized and can't be deducted unless the taxpayer elects (¶1502) to expense up to $5,000 of these costs with that amount reduced by the excess of total start-up expenditures over $50,000 in the tax year in which the trade or business begins. The remainder of the start-up expenditures may be amortized (deducted ratably) over a 180-month period. (Code Sec. 195(b)(1))[1]

Start-up expenditures are amounts paid or incurred in connection with:

. . . investigating the creation, acquisition, or establishment of an active trade or business, (Code Sec. 195(c)(1)(A)(i)) but not costs incurred after a taxpayer decides whether to enter a new business, and which new business it will enter or acquire;[2]

. . . creating an active trade or business (Code Sec. 195(c)(1)(A)(ii)); or

. . . any activity engaged in for profit and for the production of income before the day the active trade or business begins, in anticipation of that activity becoming an active trade or business. (Code Sec. 195(c)(1)(A)(iii))

The expenditure must be one that, if paid or incurred in connection with the operation of an existing active trade or business (in the same field as the taxpayer's new business), would be deductible for the year in which paid or incurred. (Code Sec. 195(c)(1)(B))[3]

Start-up expenses don't include any amounts deductible under Code Sec. 163(a) (i.e., as interest expenses); Code Sec. 164 (i.e., as taxes); or Code Sec. 174 (i.e., as research and experimental expenses). (Code Sec. 195(c)(1))[4]

¶ 1502   Election to expense/amortize start-up expenditures—Form 4562.

A taxpayer (1) is deemed to have elected to expense/amortize start-up costs under Code Sec. 195(b) (¶1501) for the tax year in which the active trade or business begins, but (2) may forgo the deemed election by clearly electing to capitalize start-up expenditures on a timely filed Federal income tax return (including extensions) for the tax year in which the active trade or business begins. The choice of expensing/amortizing or capitalizing start-up expenditures is irrevocable and applies to all start-up expenditures related to the active trade or business. (Reg § 1.195-1(b))

¶ 1503   Treatment of deferred start-up expenses on disposition of business.

If the trade or business is disposed of before the end of the amortization period, any deferred expenses not yet deducted may be deducted to the extent the disposition results in a loss under Code Sec. 165. (Code Sec. 195(b)(2))[5]

---

1. ¶L-5001; ¶1954; TD ¶301,001
2. ¶L-5013; ¶1954.01; TD ¶301,009
3. ¶L-5011; ¶s 1954, 1954.01; TD ¶301,012

4. ¶L-5011; ¶1954.01; TD ¶301,008
5. ¶L-5023; ¶1954.04; TD ¶301,015

References beginning with a single letter are to paragraphs in RIA's Federal Tax Coordinator 2d and RIA's Analysis of Federal Taxes: Income. Those beginning with numbers are to paragraphs in RIA's United States Tax Reporter. Those beginning with TD are to paragraphs in RIA's Tax Desk.

¶ 1504 Fruitless searches for new ventures.

A corporation that makes expenditures in fruitlessly searching for or investigating a new venture may deduct them as a loss when it abandons the effort.[6] A noncorporate taxpayer not engaged in the business of locating or promoting new ventures can't deduct expenditures made in fruitlessly searching for or investigating a new venture. However, once a taxpayer has focused on the acquisition of a specific business or investment, unsuccessful start-up expenses that are related to an attempt to acquire that business or investment are deductible as business or investment losses under Code Sec. 165 (¶1773).[7]

¶ 1505 Expanding an existing business.

A taxpayer can deduct expenditures made to expand an existing business. The taxpayer must show that the business contemplated and the one already conducted are closely related or "intramural," *and* that the expenditures are ordinary and necessary expenses of the business conducted when the expenses were incurred, and not capital expenditures.

Expansion costs must be capitalized if they provide the taxpayer with long-term benefits, or create separate and distinct assets, or relate to a change in the nature of the taxpayer's activities (e.g., wholesaler opening retail outlet).[8]

¶ 1506 Ordinary and Necessary Business Expenses.

Individuals, corporations and other taxpayers generally can deduct ordinary and necessary expenses paid or incurred during the tax year in carrying on any trade or business. Various limits (e.g., percentage limit on meal and entertainment deductions, see ¶1569) may apply.

¶ 1507 "Ordinary and necessary" requirement.

A deductible business expense must be both ordinary and necessary in relation to the taxpayer's industry. (Code Sec. 162(a))[9]

An expense is *ordinary* if it's customary or usual in the taxpayer's business.[10] But an unusual expense may be ordinary if it's reasonably related to the taxpayer's trade or business.[11] A *necessary* expense is one that's appropriate and helpful in developing and maintaining the taxpayer's business. It need not be essential or indispensable. Usually the taxpayer's judgment as to what's necessary will be accepted.[12] Expenditures are deductible as ordinary and necessary even if they are unwise.[13]

Some courts have held that to be deductible under Code Sec. 162, an expense must not only be ordinary and necessary, but also reasonable in amount and reasonable in relation to its purpose.[14] Some courts have held that depreciation deductions are not to be considered in assessing if business expenses are reasonable under Code Sec. 162.[15]

¶ 1508 Connection to taxpayer's trade or business.

To be deductible as a business expense, an item must be directly connected with or pertain to a trade or business carried on by the taxpayer. (Code Sec. 162(a); Reg § 1.162-1(a))[16]

Serving as an employee is a business (see ¶1631 for deduction limitations).[17] A trade or

6. ¶L-5019; ¶1954; TD ¶301,013
7. ¶L-5020; ¶1954; TD ¶301,014
8. ¶L-5101; ¶1624 *et seq.*; TD ¶301,016
9. ¶L-1200 *et seq.*; ¶1624.012; TD ¶255,512
10. ¶L-1201; ¶1624.012; TD ¶255,512
11. ¶s L-1201, L-1209; ¶1624.012; TD ¶255,512

12. ¶L-1201; ¶1624.012; TD ¶255,512
13. ¶L-1210; TD ¶255,522
14. ¶L-1202; ¶1624.013; TD ¶255,513
15. ¶L-1211
16. ¶L-1002; ¶1624; TD ¶256,001
17. ¶L-3900; ¶1624; TD ¶256,005

business need not be the taxpayer's principal occupation; a sideline can qualify.[18]

¶ 1509   Expense must benefit person claiming deduction.

A deductible expense must be an expense of *the taxpayer's* business. Expenses incurred on another's behalf aren't deductible.[19]

A corporation can't deduct payment of the personal expenses of its shareholders[20] or payment of the personal expenses of its officers and employees, except to the extent the payment represents reasonable compensation (¶1517) or is made for business reasons to provide benefits to employees in general.[21]

A corporate officer can't deduct an expenditure he makes to pay an expense of the corporation.[22]

If a taxpayer pays the debts or other obligations of another, the payment may sometimes qualify as a business expense.[23] Deductions have been allowed where such a payment is made for a good business reason, e.g., preserve sales-force morale and customer goodwill; reestablish or protect credit standing; avoid loss of business patronage, etc.[24]

¶ 1510   Right to deduction—*Cohan* rule.

Where a taxpayer's records or other proof aren't adequate to substantiate expense deductions, he may be allowed to deduct an estimated amount under the *Cohan* rule. But a court may allow a much smaller deduction than claimed, bearing heavily against a taxpayer whose inexactitude is of his own making.[25] The *Cohan* rule doesn't apply to travel or entertainment expenses, listed property, or business gifts, see ¶1579.

¶ 1511   Expenses of membership organizations.

Organizations that aren't exempt from tax under the rules discussed at ¶ 4100 *et seq.*, which are operated primarily to furnish services or goods to members, can deduct expenses of furnishing services, insurance, goods, or other items to members only to the extent of income derived during the year from members or transactions with members. (Code Sec. 277(a))[26] Any excess of expenses over income isn't deductible, but may be carried over to the following tax year. (Code Sec. 277(a))[27]

¶ 1512   Advertising and business promotion costs.

Advertising and business promotion costs relating to an existing business can be deducted currently, even though the business benefit they generate may extend over a period beyond the year they are incurred or paid.[28]

Production costs of a business catalog that will remain unchanged for several years must be capitalized according to IRS, but some courts disagree.[29] Display equipment (cabinets, signs, etc.) must be capitalized if it has a useful life beyond the tax year.[30] Package design costs (e.g., physical construction of a package containing a consumer product) do not have to be capitalized. (Reg § 1.263(a)-4(b)(3)(v))[31]

---

18. ¶L-1100 *et seq.*; ¶1624.002
19. ¶L-4400; ¶1624.104; TD ¶256,500
20. ¶L-1214; ¶1624.104; TD ¶256,517
21. ¶L-4414; ¶1624.205; TD ¶256,517
22. ¶L-4405; ¶1624.009; TD ¶256,505
23. ¶L-1214; ¶1624.104; TD ¶256,500
24. ¶L-1214 *et seq.*; ¶s 1624.015, 1624.026; TD ¶255,515

25. ¶L-4509 *et seq.*; ¶1624.014; TD ¶257,007
26. ¶L-4301; ¶2774; TD ¶307,724
27. ¶L-4301; ¶2774; TD ¶307,727
28. ¶L-2201; ¶1624.355; TD ¶300,500
29. ¶L-2205; ¶1624.355; TD ¶300,510
30. ¶L-2206; ¶1624.355; TD ¶300,511
31. ¶L-5629, ¶2634.18; TD ¶256,313

¶ 1513 Costs of determining or contesting tax liability.

Costs relating to tax matters that are ordinary and necessary in the course of the conduct of taxpayer's trade or business, including costs of tax advice, are deductible. The deduction applies to expenses incurred in: (1) preparing tax returns, (2) determining tax liability, (3) contesting tax liability, (4) securing tax counsel. (Code Sec. 62(a)(1); Reg § 1.62-1T(d)) This includes expenses incurred by an individual taxpayer in:[32]

• preparing that portion of the individual's tax return that relates to the taxpayer's business as sole proprietor,

• preparing schedules relating to income or loss from rentals or royalties, or farm income and expenses, and

• resolving asserted tax deficiencies relating to a business, to rental or royalty income, or to a farm.

For deduction of nonbusiness tax determination costs as miscellaneous itemized deductions subject to the 2%-of-AGI floor, see ¶3110. For deductibility of interest on taxes, see ¶1708.

¶ 1514 Other deductible costs of carrying on a trade or business.

These include:[33]

... cost of materials and supplies (see ¶1657 for timing of deduction);[34]

... annual license and regulatory fees;[35]

... amounts paid to cancel burdensome contracts;[36]

... cost of moving business equipment and machinery;[37]

... current membership fees (but not admission fees), dues (but for social club dues, see ¶1568) and assessments paid for business association, etc.;[38]

... restaurant's cost of smallware (glassware, flatware, etc.);[39]

... training costs; and[40]

... certain education expenses, see ¶2225 *et seq.*

¶ 1515 Compensation Deduction. ▬▬▬▬▬▬▬▬▬▬

Reasonable amounts that are paid or incurred in connection with a trade or business as compensation for personal services actually rendered are deductible, subject to a limit for top officers. Payments for fringe benefits are deductible as compensation, subject to some limits.

¶ 1516 Compensation paid for personal services.

Compensation (including severance pay)[41] paid or incurred for personal services rendered is deductible as a trade or business expense. (Code Sec. 162(a)(1)) Deductible compensation includes amounts paid to independent contractors, as well as employees.[42]

A parent can deduct reasonable wages he pays his unemancipated minor child for personal services actually rendered as a bona fide employee in the business.[43]

---

32. ¶L-3000 *et seq.*; ¶2124.14; TD ¶307,201
33. ¶L-4200 *et seq.*; ¶1624.404; TD ¶307,700 *et seq.*
34. ¶L-4207 *et seq.*; TD ¶307,718
35. ¶L-4216 *et seq.*; TD ¶307,717
36. ¶L-4213 *et seq.*; TD ¶307,714
37. ¶L-4209 *et seq.*; ¶1624.052; TD ¶307,711
38. ¶L-4231; ¶1624.061; TD ¶307,721
39. ¶L-4207.1; ¶1624.158
40. ¶L-4232.3; TD ¶256,201
41. ¶H-3600 *et seq.*; ¶1624.205; TD ¶276,000 *et seq.*
42. ¶H-3600 *et seq.*; ¶1624.205; TD ¶276,000
43. ¶H-3755; ¶1624.212; TD ¶276,045

For deductibility of amounts paid for fringe benefits, see ¶1524 *et seq.* For when compensation can be deducted, see ¶1537 *et seq.*

¶ 1517   Reasonableness of compensation.

Compensation is deductible only to the extent it's *reasonable*. Compensation paid to employee-shareholders also must be paid purely for services, or have a purely compensatory purpose, in order to be deductible. (Code Sec. 162(a)(1))[44] The question of reasonableness rarely arises unless the payments are made to a person "related" to the taxpayer —that is, to the members of an employer's family, or to stockholders of the employer, or to members of a stockholder's family.[45]

The unreasonable portion of compensation is nondeductible. If the recipient is a shareholder, the unreasonable portion may be treated as a dividend. (Reg § 1.162-7(b)(1))[46]

While reasonableness of compensation normally arises in determining whether a business is trying to deduct too high an amount of compensation, IRS finds the concept equally applicable to employment tax cases (e.g., where S corporation shareholder-employees pay themselves a low salary to reduce Medicare and Social Security taxes).[47]

¶ 1518   Factors determining reasonableness.

Reasonable compensation is the amount that would ordinarily be paid for like services by like enterprises under like circumstances. (Reg § 1.162-7(b)(3))[48] Other factors determining reasonableness include: (1) duties performed by the employee; (2) character and amount of responsibility; (3) amount of time required; (4) ability and achievements of the employee; (5) volume of business handled by the employee; (6) complexities of the business; (7) relationship of compensation to gross and net income of the business; (8) living conditions in locality; (9) compensation history of the employee; and (10) salary policy as to all employees.[49]

The Seventh Circuit applies a single independent-investor test in evaluating if a stockholder-employee's pay is reasonable (i.e., would an outside investor have paid the compensation amount based on performance). Other courts employ the independent-investor test in conjunction with an analysis of the above factors.[50]

The test of whether compensation is reasonable is normally applied to the compensation paid to the particular individual and not to the total compensation paid to a group of employees.[1] Services rendered in earlier years can be taken into account in determining the reasonableness of compensation paid during the current year.[2] Reasonableness of compensation for part-time services is determined under the usual reasonableness rules. Generally, salaries that are reasonable for an employee's full-time services aren't reasonable for his part-time services.[3]

¶ 1519   Deduction limit for compensation paid to top officers.

A publicly held corporation can't deduct applicable employee remuneration (defined below) in excess of $1 million per year paid to a covered employee (Code Sec. 162(m)(1))[4]; covered employees are the principal executive officer (or someone acting in that capacity) and the three highest paid officers (other than the principal executive officer or principal financial officer). (Code Sec. 162(m)(3); Reg § 1.162-27(c)(2))[5] The $1 million limit is reduced (but not below zero) by the amount, if any, paid to the executive but not deductible under the golden

44. ¶1624.229; TD ¶276,022
45. ¶s H-3725 *et seq.*, H-3752 *et seq.*; ¶1624.229; TD ¶276,044
46. ¶H-3607; ¶1624.268; TD ¶276,009
47. ¶H-4329
48. ¶H-3701; ¶1624.229; TD ¶276,023
49. ¶H-3706; ¶1624.229; TD ¶276,041

50. ¶H-3721; TD ¶276,027
1. ¶H-3705; ¶1624.229; TD ¶276,026
2. ¶H-3745; ¶1624.229; TD ¶276,062
3. ¶H-3715; ¶1624.229; TD ¶276,036
4. ¶H-3776; ¶1624.009; TD ¶276,001.1
5. ¶H-3780; ¶1624.009; TD ¶276,001.1

parachute rules (¶1535). (Code Sec. 162(m)(4)(F); Reg § 1.162-27(g))[6]

Applicable employee remuneration means a covered employee's aggregate remuneration for services performed (either during the deduction year or during another tax year) which would be deductible entirely for the tax year if the $1 million limit didn't apply. (Code Sec. 162(m)(4)(A)) But it doesn't include commissions generated directly by the executive's performance (Code Sec. 162(m)(4)(B); Reg § 1.162-27(d)), certain other performance-based compensation (Code Sec. 162(m)(4)(C); Reg § 1.162-27(e)), certain grandfathered contracts (Code Sec. 162(m)(4)(D)), qualified plan contributions and certain excludable employee fringe benefits. (Code Sec. 162(m)(4)(E); Reg § 1.162-27(c)(3)(ii))[7]

The above Code Sec. 162(m) deduction limit is reduced to $500,000 for remuneration paid by certain "applicable employers" to covered executives (generally, CEO, CFO, and the 3 highest paid other officers) by an employer that is a TARP recipient—i.e., it has received or will receive financial assistance under the Troubled Asset Relief Program established under §101, Div. A., PL 110-343, 10/3/2008. This limit applies to executive remuneration paid by a TARP recipient during the period in which any obligation arising from financial assistance provided under TARP remains outstanding. (Code Sec. 162(m)(5), §7001, PL 111-5, 2/17/2009)[8]

For services performed during a tax year in which an employer is a "covered health insurance provider" for any part of the tax year, the employer can't claim a compensation deduction for an "applicable individual" (officer, employee, director, or other worker or service provider such as a consultant) that is in excess of $500,000. A health insurance provider is a covered health insurance provider if at least 25% of its gross premium income from health business derives from health insurance plans that meet certain minimum requirements (Code Sec. 162(m)(6)) and those health insurance premiums received for providing minimum essential coverage are not less than 2% of the employer's gross revenues for that tax year. (Prop Reg. § 1.162-31(b)(4)(iii)(A) [Taxpayers may rely]) (Code Sec. 162(m)(6))[9]

The exceptions for performance-based compensation, commissions, or remuneration under existing binding contracts do not apply to remuneration paid by TARP recipients or covered health insurance providers. (Code Sec. 162(m)(5)(E), Code Sec. 162(m)(6)(D))

¶ 1520 Services rendered to another.

A taxpayer can't deduct payments for services rendered to someone other than the taxpayer—for example, payments by a shareholder to employees of the corporation for services to the corporation, or by a corporation to its officers for services to subsidiaries and related corporations, or by a corporation to employees of a sub. But salary paid by a parent corporation to its own executives for supervising the operations of a sub is deductible by the parent as an expense of the parent's business.[10]

¶ 1521 Payment of employee debts or expenses.

An employer's payment of an employee's debts or personal expenses is deductible by the employer as compensation paid (if reasonable, see ¶1517), just as if the employee had been paid directly and he had used the money to pay his debts or expenses.[11]

¶ 1522 Contingent compensation.

An employer can deduct contingent compensation, where it's freely bargained for between the employer and the individual before the services are rendered, and not influenced by any

---

6. ¶H-3809; ¶1624.009; TD ¶276,001.1
7. ¶H-3781 *et seq.*; ¶1624.009; TD ¶276,001.1
8. ¶H-3821; ¶1624.009; TD ¶276,001.1

9. ¶H-3810 *et seq.*; ¶1624.009; TD ¶276,501
10. ¶H-3613; ¶1624.104; TD ¶276,001
11. ¶H-4014; ¶1624.273; TD ¶136,527

consideration on the part of the employer other than that of securing the individual's services on fair and advantageous terms. This is so even though the arrangement results in higher compensation than would otherwise be allowed as a deduction. The reasonableness of the amount is determined by the circumstances at the date the contract for services is made, not when the contract is questioned. (Reg § 1.162-7(b)(2), Reg § 1.162-7(b)(3))[12]

¶ 1523   Payment in property other than cash.

The deduction for compensation paid in property, including a bargain sale and including restricted property, is the amount included in the income of the person who performed the services, to the extent the compensation is reasonable. (Code Sec. 83(h))[13] The "amount included" in income is the amount reported by the service provider on an original or amended return, or included in income as a result of an IRS audit. It includes excluded group-term life insurance and foreign income. (Reg § 1.83-6(a)(1))

Under a "deemed inclusion rule," however, a deduction may be taken by an employer (service recipient) if he timely complies with the applicable information reporting requirements. Thus, an employee is *deemed* to have included the property received in income, and a deduction can be claimed by the employer if he timely satisfies the Code Sec. 6041 or Code Sec. 6041A reporting requirements (Reg § 1.83-6(a)(2)), i.e., by timely reporting the transaction to the service provider and federal government on Form W-2 or Form 1099-MISC, whichever applies. If this rule isn't satisfied, an employer must demonstrate that the compensation amount deducted was actually included in the service provider's income.[14]

The deemed inclusion rule can be used where the service provider is a corporation by issuing Form 1099-MISC even though there would otherwise be a general reporting exemption for a service provider that's a corporation. (Reg § 1.83-6(a)(2))

If a transfer is less than $600 in any tax year (in which case the reporting requirements don't apply), or if the transfer is eligible for any other reporting exemption (applicable to a noncorporate service provider), no Form 1099 reporting is required in order for the service recipient to rely on the deemed inclusion rule.[15]

In addition, to be deductible a transfer can't be a capital expenditure, a deferred expense, or part of inventory. (Reg § 1.83-6(a)(4))[16]

If payment is in employer stock, no gain or loss results. (Code Sec. 1032)[17] If payment is in property other than the employer's stock, and the value of the property exceeds the employer's basis for the property, the excess is income to the employer (capital gain or ordinary income, depending on the character of the property used). (Reg § 1.83-6(b)) The employer has a loss deduction where the basis of the property exceeds its fair market value[18] (subject to related-taxpayer restrictions on losses).[19]

The deduction is allowed for the tax year of the employer in which, or with which, the employee's tax year ends. (Code Sec. 83(h))[20]

illustration: Corporation X, which is on a Sept. 30 fiscal year, pays calendar year employee J in stock on July 1, Year 1. J reports the income on his return for Year 1. X deducts the payment on its return for the year ending Sept. 30, Year 2, because that is X's tax year in which the tax year of J, in which the amounts are included in income, ends.

For restricted property, see ¶1217; for noncash fringe benefits, see ¶1524.

---

12. ¶H-3732; ¶1624.229; TD ¶276,053
13. ¶H-3650 *et seq.*; ¶s 834.04, 1624.273; TD ¶277,001
14. ¶H-3650 *et seq.*; ¶s 834.04, 1624.273, TD ¶277,003
15. ¶H-3654; ¶834.04; TD ¶277,003
16. ¶H-3650 *et seq.*; ¶s 834.04, 1624.273; TD ¶277,008

17. ¶H-3659; ¶10,324; TD ¶277,010
18. ¶H-3659; TD ¶277,010
19. ¶H-3659; TD ¶277,010
20. ¶H-3653; ¶834.04; TD ¶277,002

¶ 1524 Compensation paid as noncash fringe benefits.

If an employer furnishes a noncash fringe benefit to an employee as compensation, the employer may deduct only the costs it incurs in providing the property to its employees, not the property's value. The employer may claim a depreciation deduction if it owns the property or a deduction for leasing costs if it rents the property. (Reg § 1.162-25T(a))[21]

Furnishing property to an employee for his personal use is additional compensation to him and gives rise to a deduction by the employer. For example, the employer can deduct depreciation and maintenance expenses it pays on a car, house, etc., furnished for an employee's personal use and treated by the employer as compensation. (Code Sec. 274(e)(2))[22]

For deduction limits on entertainment expenses of officers, directors, and 10%-or-more owners, see ¶1572.

¶ 1525 Stock options.

An employer's deduction for a nonstatutory stock option is determined under the Code Sec. 83 payment-in-property rules at ¶1523 (and thus, the employer would deduct the amount the employee must include in income on exercise of the option, where the option has no readily ascertainable value at grant, see ¶1219).[23] The employer isn't allowed a compensation deduction for stock transferred under an incentive stock option or an employee stock purchase plan, unless the employee has income by reason of a disqualified (premature) disposition of the stock (¶1220 *et seq.*). (Code Sec. 421(a), Code Sec. 421(b))[24]

¶ 1526 Premiums on company-owned life insurance, endowment or annuity contracts.

A taxpayer can't deduct premiums on any life insurance policy, or endowment or annuity contract if it is directly or indirectly a beneficiary under the policy or contract. (Code Sec. 264(a)(1)) However, this rule doesn't apply to Code Sec. 72(s)(5) annuity contracts (certain qualified pension plans, retirement annuities, individual retirement annuities and qualified funding assets) or to any annuity contract to which Code Sec. 72(u) (annuity contracts held by other than natural persons) applies. (Code Sec. 264(b)(2)) Premiums are deductible as a noncash fringe benefit where only the insured employee or his beneficiaries will get the proceeds. For contracts issued before June 9, '97, the deduction disallowance only applies to premiums on the life of an officer, employee or any person financially interested in any trade or business carried on by the taxpayer if the taxpayer is directly or indirectly a beneficiary of any part of the policy.[25]

Premiums on group term life insurance are deductible (if the employer isn't directly or indirectly a beneficiary) even though the employee isn't taxed (¶1262) on group term coverage of $50,000 or less.[26]

For interest on business life insurance loans, see ¶1718.

¶ 1527 Health and accident insurance premiums and direct payment or reimbursement of medical expenses under a plan for employees.

The employer's payment of health and accident insurance premiums for employees and their families, or the employer's direct payment or reimbursement of actual expenses if under

---

21. ¶H-4002; ¶1624.283; TD ¶278,303
22. ¶s H-2150 *et seq.*, H-2160; ¶1624.283; TD ¶277,000 *et seq.*
23. ¶H-2883

24. ¶H-2960; ¶4214.01 *et seq.*; TD ¶136,102
25. ¶H-4031; ¶2644; TD ¶278,505
26. ¶H-4037; ¶s 614.031, 794; TD ¶278,507

a plan, is deductible. (Reg § 1.162-10(a))[27] Reimbursements are deductible even where the employee is the spouse of a sole proprietor, and the medical expenses incurred on behalf of the employee's family include those of the sole proprietor (as the employee's spouse).[28] IRS treats these amounts as additional compensation deductible by the employer to the extent that it, when added to other compensation, is reasonable.[29]

¶ 1528   Contributions to Archer medical savings account (MSA)—Form 8853.

Eligible small employers (see ¶1256), their employees, and self-employed individuals may deduct contributions to an Archer medical savings account (MSA). (Code Sec. 106, Code Sec. 220) An eligible self-employed claims deductions for MSAs above the line, to arrive at adjusted gross income. (Code Sec. 62(a)(16)) After 2007, no new contributions can be made to MSAs, except by or for individuals who previously had MSA contributions and employees who are employed by a participating employer. (Code Sec. 220(i))[30]

MSAs are available to employees covered under a high deductible health plan (HDHP) of a small employer (¶1256) and to self-employed individuals covered by a HDHP. An individual isn't eligible for an MSA if he's entitled to benefits under Medicare or covered under any other health plan, unless the other coverage is permitted insurance (e.g., insurance for a specified disease or illness, or fixed payment for hospitalization) or coverage for accidents, disability, dental care, vision care, or long-term care. For employees, contributions can be made by the employee or the employer, but not by both for the same year. An MSA is a tax-exempt entity but is subject to the tax on unrelated business income. (Code Sec. 220(c), Code Sec. 220(d))[31]

For 2013, an HDHP for MSA purposes is a health plan with an annual deductible of at least $2,150 and not more than $3,200 for individual coverage ($4,300 and not more than $6,450 for family coverage); in addition, the maximum out-of-pocket expenses can't exceed $4,300 for individual coverage ($7,850 for family coverage). For 2014, an HDHP for MSA purposes is a health plan with an annual deductible of at least $2,200 and not more than $3,250 for individual coverage ($4,350 and not more than $6,550 for family coverage); in addition, the maximum out-of-pocket expenses can't exceed $4,350 for individual coverage ($8,000 for family coverage). (Code Sec. 220(c)(2))[32]

The maximum annual contribution for individual coverage is 65% of the HDHP premium (75% for family coverage). The annual contribution limit is the sum of the limits determined separately for each month the individual is MSA-eligible. (Code Sec. 220(b)(1))[33] A self-employed's deduction for contributions to an MSA can't exceed his earned income from the trade or business that established the HDHP (Code Sec. 220(b)(4)(B)),[34] and an employee's contributions to an MSA can't exceed his compensation from the employer that set up the plan. (Code Sec. 220(b)(4)(A))[35] Contributions can be made until the unextended tax return due date. Excess contributions are subject to a 6% penalty tax (on Form 5329). (Code Sec. 4973(a)(2), Code Sec. 4973(d))[36]

For treatment of MSA distributions, see ¶1377.

¶ 1529   Contributions to health savings accounts (HSAs).

Eligible individuals may, subject to statutory limits, make deductible contributions to a health savings account (HSA). Other persons (e.g., family members) also may contribute on behalf of eligible individuals, as may employers (see ¶1257). (Code Sec. 106, Code Sec. 223) An

27. ¶s H-4071, H-4073; ¶1624.277; TD ¶278,901
28. ¶L-3510; TD ¶278,902
29. ¶L-3509; ¶1624.229; TD ¶278,901
30. ¶H-1326 *et seq.*; ¶2204 *et seq.*; TD ¶288,100 *et seq.*
31. ¶H-1331.1 *et seq.*, ¶H-1335.4; ¶2204.01; TD ¶288,108

32. ¶H-1332; ¶2204.01; TD ¶288,103
33. ¶s H-1335, H-1335.1; ¶2204.01; TD ¶288,101
34. ¶H-1335.3; ¶2204.01; TD ¶288,101
35. ¶H-1335.3; ¶2204.01; TD ¶288,101
36. ¶H-1336.1 *et seq.*; ¶2204.01; TD ¶288,101

account holder may deduct contributions to his HSA even if another (e.g., family member) makes the contributions. (Code Sec. 62(a)(19)) An HSA is a tax-exempt entity but is subject to the tax on unrelated business income. (Code Sec. 223(e)(1))

For tax-free HSA distributions for qualifying medical expenses see ¶1378.

Eligible individuals. These are individuals who are covered under a high deductible health plan (HDHP) (see below) and are not covered under any other health plan which is not a HDHP, unless the other coverage is permitted insurance (for worker's compensation, torts, ownership and use of property such as auto insurance, insurance for a specified disease or illness, or providing a fixed payment for hospitalization) or coverage for accidents, disability, dental care, vision care, or long-term care. (Code Sec. 223(c))[37] HSA contributions for an individual aren't deductible if he is claimed as a dependent by another taxpayer for the year. (Code Sec. 223(b)(6)) There's no deduction for an HSA contribution for any month an individual is eligible for and enrolled in Medicare. (Code Sec. 223(b)(7))

HDHP. For 2013 and 2014, a HDHP is a health plan with an annual deductible that is not less than $1,250 for individual coverage and $2,500 for family coverage. Maximum out-of-pocket expenses can't exceed $6,250 for individual coverage for 2013 ($6,350 for 2014) and $12,500 for family coverage for 2013 ($12,700 for 2014). (Code Sec. 223(c)(2))[38] However, an HDHP may have a zero preventive care deductible or a preventive care deductible below the minimum annual deductible. (Code Sec. 223(c)(2)(C)) Preventive care does not generally include any service or benefit intended to treat an existing illness, injury, or condition.

Other coverage. Health flexible spending accounts (FSAs, see ¶1269) and health reimbursement arrangements (HRAs, see ¶1379) are "other coverage" that will generally preclude HSA eligibility. However, exceptions apply for limited purpose FSAs and HRAs (those providing only certain benefits, e.g., dental and vision); suspended HRAs (where the employee elects to forgo reimbursements for the coverage period); FSAs and HRAs imposing annual deductibles, and HRAs providing benefits only after retirement. An otherwise eligible individual may be covered by an HRA which pays and reimburses expenses for (1) vision, dental and preventive care, and (2) premiums for coverage by an accident and health plan.[39] Coverage under a health FSA during the "grace period" (i.e., the period immediately following the end of a plan year during which unused benefits or contributions remaining may be paid or reimbursed to plan participants for qualified expenses) is disregarded coverage for HSA purposes if the balance in the health FSA at the end of the plan year is zero. (Code Sec. 223(c)(1)(B))

Limit on deductible contributions. The maximum annual HSA deductible contribution is the sum of the monthly contribution limits, based on eligibility and health plan coverage on the first day of the month. The monthly limit is 1/12 of the indexed amount for self-only coverage ($3,250 for 2013 and $3,300 for 2014) and for family coverage ($6,450 for 2013 and $6,550 for 2014). The maximum HSA contribution is increased by an additional catch-up contribution amount (computed on a monthly basis) for individuals age 55 or older as of the last day of the calendar year who are not enrolled in Medicare. The catch-up contribution amount is $1,000. There is no requirement that the individual have earnings. (Code Sec. 223(b))[40] Contributions for a year can be made until the account holder's tax return due date (without extensions) for that year. Excess contributions are subject to a 6% penalty tax (on Form 5329). (Code Sec. 4973(a)(5), Code Sec. 223(f)(3))[41] Maximum annual HSA contributions are reduced by Archer MSA (¶1528) contributions for that year. (Code Sec. 223(b)(4))

For computing the annual HSA contribution, a taxpayer who is an eligible individual in the last month of a tax year is "deemed eligible" during every month of that year. (Code Sec. 223(b)(8)) Thus, he can make contributions for months before he was enrolled in a

37. ¶H-1350.3 *et seq.*; ¶2204.01; TD ¶288,103
38. ¶H-1350.6; ¶2234.02; TD ¶289,106
39. ¶H-1350.4A

40. ¶H-1350, H-1350.7; ¶2234.02; TD ¶289,107
41. ¶H-1350.20; ¶49,734; TD ¶289,118

HDHP. But if he does not remain an eligible individual (except because of disability) during the testing period (from the last month of the tax year to the last day of the 12th month following that month), contributions for months in which he was "deemed eligible" are includible in gross income for the tax year of the first day during the testing period that the taxpayer is not an eligible individual and are subject to a 10% penalty tax. (Code Sec. 223(b)(8)(B))

HSA rollovers and carryover of HSA funds. Amounts in an HSA can be rolled over tax free from an HSA, or from an Archer MSA (¶1528) to an HSA. The rollover must be completed within 60 days after the date on which the account holder receives the amounts from the HSA or Archer MSA and is not taken into account in determining the annual contribution limits for the recipient HSA. Only one tax-free rollover into an HSA is permitted per one year period. (Code Sec. 223(f)(5), Code Sec. 220(f)(5))[42]

For one-time rollovers from IRAs, see ¶4364.

Comparability rule for employer contributions. In general, employer contributions to employee HSAs must be the same amount or the same percentage of the HDHP deductible for all employees with the same category of HDHP coverage (self-only, or family coverage, i.e., any coverage other than self-only). But employers may make larger HSA contributions for nonhighly compensated employees than for highly compensated employees (as defined in Code Sec. 414(q), see ¶4326). (Code Sec. 4980G(d)) Employers that provide self + 1, self + 2 and self + 3 family coverage apply the comparability rules separately to each category. The comparability rules apply separately to full time, part-time, and former employees (except for former employees under COBRA continuation coverage). An employer that fails the comparability rule is subject to a 35% penalty tax. The comparability rules do not apply to HSA contributions made through a cafeteria plan. Instead, the Code Sec. 125 discrimination rules apply. (Code Sec. 4980G; Reg § 54.4980G-1 - Reg § 54.4980G-5)

¶ 1530   Medicare Advantage Medical Savings Accounts.

Individuals eligible for Medicare can choose either the traditional Medicare program or a Medicare Advantage MSA, which is a medical savings account as defined in Code Sec. 220(d), (¶1528) but which is designated as a Medicare Advantage MSA by the individual account holder. (Code Sec. 138(b)(1)) A Medicare Advantage MSA is a tax-exempt trust (or a custodial account), similar to an IRA, created exclusively to pay qualified medical expenses of the account holder. The Health and Human Services Dept. makes contributions directly to the Medicare Advantage MSA designated by the account holder (the only other type of allowed contribution allowed is a trustee-to-trustee transfer from another Medicare Advantage MSA). Contributions and earnings on amounts held in a Medicare Advantage MSA aren't currently includible in income. (Code Sec. 138(a))

Distributions from a Medicare Advantage MSA for purposes other than qualified medical expenses of the account holder are included in income, and subject to a 50% penalty (except if made because of the account holder's disability or death). (Code Sec. 138(c)(2)) Distributions that are excludable from gross income can't be taken as a medical expense deduction. (Code Sec. 138(c)(1)) The 15% penalty on the amount includible in gross income for non-qualified distributions from regular Archer MSAs (¶1377) doesn't apply to any payment or distribution from a Medicare Advantage MSA. (Code Sec. 138(c)(2)(A))[43]

¶ 1531   Group-health plan continuation coverage (COBRA).

A group health plan of (or contributed to by) an employer must provide that each qualified beneficiary who would lose coverage under the plan because of a qualifying event may elect

---

42. ¶H-1350.9; ¶2234; TD ¶289,101   43. ¶H-1348; ¶1384; TD ¶288,500

continuation coverage under the plan within a specified at-least-60-day election period. (Code Sec. 4980B(f)(1))[44]

"Qualified beneficiaries" are the covered employee, his spouse or dependent child, a deceased employee's surviving spouse in certain cases, and a child born to or placed for adoption with the covered employee during the COBRA coverage period. (Code Sec. 4980B(g)(1))[45]

"Qualifying events" include: death of the covered employee; termination or reduction of hours of his employment; divorce or legal separation from the covered employee; cessation of a child's dependency; and the employee's entitlement to certain Medicare benefits. (Code Sec. 4980B(f)(3))[46]

Continuation coverage must be identical to coverage provided under the plan to similarly situated beneficiaries who haven't had a qualifying event. (Code Sec. 4980B(f)(2)(A))[47] Coverage for a qualified beneficiary must begin on the date of the qualifying event and end not earlier than: a statutory maximum period, the end of the plan, the failure to pay a premium, or the eligibility for group health plan coverage or Medicare.[48] Coverage of the cost of pediatric vaccines can't be reduced below the coverage provided by the plan as of May 1, '93. (Code Sec. 4980B(f)(1))[49]

Employers (or for a multiemployer plan, the plan) and certain responsible persons are liable for an excise tax (Code Sec. 4980B(e))[50] if, with certain exceptions, a group health plan fails to provide the above coverage. (Code Sec. 4980B(a))[1]

¶ 1532 Self-employed individual's health insurance deduction.

A self-employed individual (or a partner or a more-than-2%-shareholder of an S corporation) can deduct as a business expense 100% of the amount paid during the tax year for medical insurance on himself, spouse, dependents, and to any child of the taxpayer who has not attained age 27 as of the end of the year. (Code Sec. 162(l)(1)) Medicare premiums can be used in figuring the self-employed's deduction for health insurance costs.[2]

No deduction is allowed to the extent the deduction exceeds the individual's earned income as defined in Code Sec. 401(c) (net earnings from self-employment) derived from the trade or business for which the plan providing the coverage is established. (Code Sec. 162(l)(2)(A))[3] For purposes of applying the earned income limit to the deduction of a more-than-2% S corporation shareholder, that shareholder's wages from the S corporation are treated as his earned income. (Code Sec. 162(l)(5)(A))[4]

No deduction is available for any month in which the self-employed individual is eligible to participate in a subsidized health plan maintained by an employer of the taxpayer, the taxpayer's spouse, any dependent, or any child of the taxpayer who hasn't attained age 27 as of the end of the tax year. This test for eligibility is made for each calendar month. This rule is applied separately to (1) plans that provide coverage for qualified long-term care services (¶2144), or are qualified long-term care insurance contracts (¶2145) and (2) plans which don't include such coverage and aren't such contracts. (Code Sec. 162(l)(2)(B)) Thus, an individual eligible for employer-subsidized health insurance may still be able to deduct long-term care insurance premiums, so long as he isn't eligible for employer-subsidized long-term care insurance.[5]

44. ¶H-1250 *et seq.*; ¶49,80B4
45. ¶H-1266; ¶49,80B4
46. ¶H-1303; ¶49,80B4
47. ¶H-1272; ¶49,80B4
48. ¶H-1294; ¶49,80B4
49. ¶H-1250 *et seq.*; ¶49,80B4

50. ¶H-1316; ¶49,80B4
1. ¶H-1315; ¶49,80B4
2. ¶1624.403
3. ¶L-3510; ¶1624.403; TD ¶304,420
4. ¶L-3512; ¶1624.403; TD ¶304,421
5. ¶L-3510; ¶1624.403; TD ¶304,420

¶ 1533   Contributions to funded welfare benefit plans.

An employer's contribution to a "welfare benefit fund" is deductible only for the tax year paid, and only to the extent the contribution doesn't exceed the "qualified cost" of the plan for its tax year that relates to (ends with or within) the employer's tax year. (Code Sec. 419(a), Code Sec. 419(b))[6] Contributions for independent contractors are also subject to this rule. (Code Sec. 419(g))[7] The rule, however, doesn't apply to a ten-or-more employer plan if no employer (or related employer) normally contributes more than 10% of total contributions, unless the plan uses experience ratings to determine each employer's contribution. (Code Sec. 419A(f)(6); Reg § 1.419A(f)(6)-1(b)(1))[8]

A welfare benefit fund is a fund that is part of an employer's plan through which the employer provides welfare benefits to employees or their beneficiaries, but doesn't include amounts held under certain kinds of insurance contracts. (Code Sec. 419(e); Reg § 1.419A(f)(6)-1(b)(4))[9]

¶ 1534   Death benefits to employee's beneficiaries.

Payments to the widow or other beneficiaries of a deceased employee, i.e., continuing the decedent's salary for a reasonable period, are deductible by the employer to the extent they qualify as a business expense. A benefit paid as a gift based on the beneficiary's need doesn't qualify as a business expense. (Reg § 1.404(a)-12(b)(2))[10]

¶ 1535   "Golden parachute" payments.

No deduction is allowed for an excess parachute payment. (Code Sec. 280G)[11] An excess parachute payment is the amount by which a parachute payment (below) exceeds the base amount (below) allocated to it. (Code Sec. 280G(b)(1)) If there's only one parachute payment the entire base amount is allocated to it.[12]

A parachute payment is any payment in the nature of compensation to (or for the benefit of) a disqualified individual (described below) *if*:

(1) the payment is contingent on a change (a) in the ownership or effective control of the corporation, *or* (b) in the ownership of a substantial part of the corporation's assets, *and*

(2) the aggregate present value of all such contingent compensation payments equals, or exceeds, three times the base amount. (Code Sec. 280G(b))[13] This base amount is the average annualized compensation income includible in a disqualified individual's gross income in the five-tax-year period preceding the tax year in which the change of ownership or control of the corporation occurs. (Code Sec. 280G(b), Code Sec. 280G(d))[14]

A disqualified individual is one who is: (1) an employee, independent contractor, or other person specified in regs who performs personal services for a corporation, *and* (2) is an officer, shareholder or highly compensated individual. (Code Sec. 280G(c); Reg § 1.280G-1, Q&As 15 to 20)[15] Highly compensated individual means a member of the highest paid 1% of employees or, if less, the highest paid 250 employees. (Code Sec. 280G(c))[16]

A parachute payment doesn't include an amount that the taxpayer can establish, by clear and convincing evidence, is reasonable compensation for services to be rendered on, or after, the date of change in ownership or control. (Code Sec. 280G(b)(4)(A)) The amount of an excess

---

6. ¶s H-4101, H-4113 *et seq.*; ¶4194 *et seq.*; TD ¶278,001

7. ¶H-4104; ¶4194.01 *et seq.*

8. ¶H-4154; ¶419A4.02; TD ¶278,005

9. ¶H-4105 *et seq.*; ¶4194.02; TD ¶278,003

10. ¶H-4051 *et seq.*; ¶1624.277; TD ¶278,703

11. ¶H-3826; ¶280G4; TD ¶279,001

12. ¶H-3874; ¶280G4; TD ¶279,014

13. ¶H-3830; ¶280G4; TD ¶279,002

14. ¶H-3864; ¶280G4; TD ¶279,016

15. ¶H-3840; ¶280G4; TD ¶279,011

16. ¶H-3843; ¶280G4; TD ¶279,011

parachute payment can be reduced to the extent that the taxpayer can establish by clear and convincing evidence that the payment is reasonable compensation for personal services actually rendered before the date of change of ownership or control. (Code Sec. 280G(b)(4)(B))[17]

The parachute payment rules don't apply to a corporation (1) that was (immediately before the change in control or assets) a "small business corporation," without regard to whether it has a nonresident alien shareholder (¶3352) or (2) whose stock isn't readily tradeable if shareholder approval has been obtained. (Code Sec. 280G(b)(5)) A corporation that meets the requirements to elect to be treated as an S corporation, but does not elect S status, may nevertheless use the small business exemption. (Reg § 1.280G-1, Q&A 6(a)(1))[18]

Payments to or from a qualified pension or profit-sharing plan, Code Sec. 403(a) annuity, simplified employee pension or SIMPLE plan (¶4382 *et seq.*) aren't parachute payments. (Code Sec. 280G(b)(6); Reg § 1.280G-1, Q&A 8)[19]

¶ 1536 Compensation payments as capital outlays.

Payments otherwise designated as compensation may actually be payments for property. For example, where a partnership sells out to a corporation and the former partners agree to continue to work for the corporation, the salaries of the former partners may be in part payment for the transfer of their business. (Reg § 1.162-7(b)(1))[20]

¶ 1537 Year for deducting compensation.

An employer deducts compensation in the year allowed under its accounting method (¶2816 *et seq.*) with special rules for compensation in property and bargain sales (¶1214 *et seq.*), deferred compensation (¶1538), and contributions to employee benefit plans (¶4334).

If salary is paid or accrued in one year for services to be rendered in a later year, the deduction is allowed only over the period during which the services are rendered. This applies to both cash and accrual-basis employers.[21]

For limitations on accrual-basis taxpayers' deductions for compensation paid to related cash-basis taxpayers, see ¶2836.

¶ 1538 When to deduct deferred compensation.

An employer's contributions to a nonqualified deferred compensation plan are deductible in the tax year in which an amount attributable to the contribution is includible in the gross income of employees participating in the plan (Code Sec. 404(a)(5)), even if the employer is an accrual basis taxpayer.[22]

Benefits provided under a welfare benefit fund (Code Sec. 404(b)(2)(B)), and payments of bonuses or other amounts within 2½ months after the close of the tax year in which significant services required for payment have been performed (Reg § 1.404(b)-1T, 2(c)), aren't treated as deferred compensation.[23]

To determine if compensation is deferred compensation, and when deferred compensation is paid, no amount is treated as paid or received until it's actually received by the employee. (Code Sec. 404(a)(11))[24]

If the all events test (¶2832) and recurring item exception (¶2833) are otherwise met, an accrual basis taxpayer may treat its payroll tax liability as incurred in Year 1, regardless of whether the compensation to which the liability relates is deferred compensation deductible

---

17. ¶H-3876; ¶280G4; TD ¶279,019
18. ¶H-3835; ¶280G4; TD ¶279,006
19. ¶H-3839; ¶280G4; TD ¶279,010
20. ¶H-3604; ¶1624.205; TD ¶276,006

21. ¶H-3934; ¶1624.205; TD ¶279,520
22. ¶H-3677; ¶4044.16; TD ¶277,500
23. ¶s H-3673, H-3674; TD ¶277,503
24. ¶H-3674; ¶4044.16

under Code Sec. 404 in Year 2.[25]

¶ 1539   When to deduct bonuses paid to employees.

A cash basis employer deducts bonuses only for the year in which the bonuses are actually paid (¶1538).[26]

Bonuses by an accrual basis taxpayer are deductible in the tax year when all the events have occurred that establish the fact of liability to pay the bonus, the amount can be determined with reasonable accuracy, and economic performance has occurred for the liability (¶2833). (Reg § 1.461-1(a)(2)(i))[27]

To deduct a year-end bonus in the accrual year rather than the actual payment year an employer must pay the bonus within a brief period of time after the close of the employer's tax year. If an employer pays bonuses within 2 ½ months after the close of the tax year, then a deduction for the bonuses won't be subject to the deferred compensation rules (¶1538), which would bar the deduction until the bonus is included in the employee's income. (Reg § 1.404(b)-1T)[28] Payment after 2 ½ months is presumed to be deferred compensation, and that presumption can only be rebutted by showing that: (1) it was either administratively or economically impossible to avoid a later payment, and (2) as of the end of the employer's tax year, the impracticability was unforeseeable. (Reg § 1.404(b)-1T)[29]

For limitations on accrual-basis taxpayers' deductions for compensation paid to related cash-basis taxpayers, see ¶2836.

¶ 1540   When to deduct vacation pay.

Cash basis employers take a deduction when the vacation pay is paid (¶1538) in accordance with the general rules for cash basis employers.[30]

For an accrual basis employer, vacation pay earned during any tax year but not paid on or before 2 ½ months after the end of the tax year is deductible for the tax year of the employer in which it's paid. (Code Sec. 404(a)(5))[31]

¶ 1541   Travel Expenses. ■■■■■■■■■■■■■■■■■■■■■■■■

The costs of away-from-home business travel can qualify as deductible expenses.

¶ 1542   Deduction for away-from-home travel costs.

Ordinary and necessary expenses incurred while traveling "away from home" in pursuit of a trade or business are deductible. Those expenses include amounts (other than amounts that are lavish or extravagant) paid for meals (subject to a percentage limit, see ¶1569) and lodging. (Code Sec. 162(a)(2))[32]

A taxpayer isn't away from home unless he is away *overnight*, or at least long enough to require rest or sleep.[33] He need not be away from his tax home for an entire 24-hour day or throughout the hours from dusk to dawn if his relief from duty is long enough to get necessary sleep. A layover sufficient only for a short rest and to get a meal isn't "overnight." [34]

Deductible business travel expenses include baggage charges, air, rail and bus fares, cost of transporting sample cases or display materials, expenses for sample rooms, cost of maintaining or operating a car, house trailer or airplane, telephone expenses, laundry and dry cleaning costs, taxi fares, etc., from the airport or station to the hotel and back, from one customer

---

25. ¶H-3670; TD ¶279,504
26. ¶s H-3901, H-3916; ¶1624.218; TD ¶279,500
27. ¶H-3916; TD ¶279,503
28. ¶H-3919; TD ¶279,511
29. ¶H-3919; TD ¶279,512

30. ¶H-3922; ¶4614.01; TD ¶279,513
31. ¶H-3922; ¶4614.15; TD ¶279,513
32. ¶L-1701; ¶1624.114; TD ¶291,002
33. ¶L-1710; ¶1624.147
34. ¶L-1710; ¶1624.147

to another, transportation from where meals and lodging are obtained to the temporary work assignment, and reasonable tips for any of these expenses. (Reg § 1.162-2(a))[35] Travel expenses don't include expenses of the taxpayer's own entertainment. [36]

¶ 1543 Home defined for travel expense purposes.

A taxpayer's home for travel expense purposes is his "tax home" —his principal place of business, employment station, or post of duty, regardless of where his family lives.[37]

Where an individual has no principal place of business or employment but continually changes work locations (e.g., a traveling salesperson), his regular residence is his tax "home." [38] If such a taxpayer has no regular place of abode in a real and substantial sense, he has no "home" and can't deduct travel expenses. [39]

If a taxpayer regularly works at two or more separate locations, his tax home is the general area where his *principal* employment or business is, determined on the facts of the particular case. Important factors are: (1) time spent, (2) business activity, and (3) financial return. Income is the most significant factor.[40]

Costs of traveling to and from the minor place of employment, 50% of the cost of meals (but see ¶1569), and the cost of lodging at the minor post are deductible travel expenses.[41]

Certain state legislators may elect to treat their residence in their legislative district (instead of the state capitol) as their tax home. (Code Sec. 162(h), Reg § 1.162-24)[42]

¶ 1544 Temporary (one year or less) assignment away from home.

A temporary assignment away from home—an assignment whose termination can be foreseen within a fixed and reasonably short period—doesn't shift the "tax home." Therefore, a taxpayer may deduct the necessary traveling expenses in getting to his temporary assignment and also for the return trip to his tax home after the temporary assignment is completed, and his expenses for lodging and 50% of the cost of meals while he is in the place to which he is temporarily assigned.[43] If he returns home on his nonworking days, he may deduct his travel expenses to his home, but his travel expenses deduction is limited to the amount he would have spent to stay at his temporary location.[44]

A taxpayer isn't treated as being temporarily away from home if his period of employment exceeds one year (certain federal employees on crime investigations are exempt from this rule). (Code Sec. 162(a)) The one-year rule generally isn't triggered by short intermittent assignments that span more than one year.[45] Employment away from home at a single location for less than one year is treated as temporary, in the absence of facts and circumstances indicating otherwise. If employment away from home in a single location initially is realistically expected to last for one year or less, but later is realistically expected to exceed one year, then the employment will be treated as temporary (in the absence of facts and circumstances indicating otherwise) until the date that the taxpayer's realistic expectation changes (at which point the employment will no longer be "temporary"). [46]

¶ 1545 Indefinite assignment away from home.

An indefinite assignment away from home shifts the "tax home" and taxpayer can't deduct the expenses of travel, meals and lodging while in the location of the "indefinite"

---

35. ¶L-1705; ¶1624.114; TD ¶291,005
36. ¶L-1713; TD ¶291,007
37. ¶L-1801; ¶1624.125; TD ¶292,001
38. ¶L-1802; ¶1624.125; TD ¶292,002
39. ¶L-2025; ¶1624.125
40. ¶L-1807; ¶1624.141; TD ¶292,005

41. ¶s L-1805, L-2135; ¶1624.141; TD ¶292,005
42. ¶L-2026; ¶1624.141; TD ¶292,520
43. ¶s L-1810, L-2135; ¶1624.130; TD ¶292,009
44. ¶L-1813; TD ¶292,011
45. ¶L-1811; ¶1624.130
46. ¶L-1812; ¶1624.130; TD ¶292,009

assignment.[47] Employment is indefinite if it lasts for more than one year, or there is no realistic expectation that the employment will last for one year or less.[48]

¶ 1546   Meals and lodging when not away from home.

The cost of a taxpayer's meals not incurred in traveling away from home isn't deductible unless allowed under Code Sec. 162 (business expenses) or Code Sec. 212 (expenses for production of income). In general, lodging costs not incurred in traveling away from home aren't deductible unless allowed under Code Sec. 217. (Reg § 1.262-1(b)(5)) However, local lodging expenses (for lodging while not traveling away from home) may be deductible as a business expense (including a trade or business as an employee), if all the facts and circumstances so indicate. One factor is whether the taxpayer incurs the expense because of an employer-imposed bona fide condition or requirement of employment.

Under a safe harbor, local lodging expenses are ordinary and necessary business expenses if: (1) the lodging is necessary for the individual to participate fully in or be available for a bona fide business meeting, conference, training activity, or other business function; (2) the lodging is for a period not exceeding five calendar days and does not recur more frequently than once per calendar quarter; (3) if the individual is an employee, his employer requires him to remain at the activity or function overnight; and (4) the lodging is not lavish or extravagant under the circumstances and does not provide any significant element of personal pleasure, recreation, or benefit. (Prop Reg. § 1.162-31(b) [Taxpayers may rely])[49]

¶ 1547   U.S. travel for both business and pleasure.

Transportation costs to and from the destination are deductible only if the trip is related primarily to the taxpayer's business. Expenses at the destination allocable to the taxpayer's business are deductible even if the round-trip travel expenses are disallowed because the trip was primarily for pleasure.[50] If the trip is primarily for business, but the taxpayer extends his stay for personal reasons, makes side trips, or engages in other nonbusiness activities, he may deduct only the expenses, such as lodging and 50% of the cost of meals, that he would have incurred if the trip had been totally for business. But no allocation is required for travel costs to and from the business destination. (Reg § 1.162-2(b)(1))[1]

¶ 1548   Foreign travel for both business and pleasure.

If travel is primarily for pleasure, the rules at ¶1547 apply, so that only the amount directly allocable to business is deductible. But under special rules for foreign travel, even where travel is primarily for business, a portion of the transportation cost is nondeductible if the travel has a pleasure element. The nondeductible part is computed on a time ratio, usually in the proportion of nonbusiness days to all travel days.

This allocation and denial of deduction isn't made if: (1) travel is for one week or less; or (2) less than 25% of the time is spent on nonbusiness activity; or (3) the individual traveling had no substantial control over the arranging of the trip; or (4) a personal vacation wasn't a major consideration in making the trip. (Code Sec. 274(c); Reg § 1.162-2(b), Reg § 1.274-4(f)(5))[2] For foreign conventions, see ¶1549.

---

47. ¶L-1814; ¶1624.130; TD ¶292,012
48. ¶L-1811; ¶1624.130; TD ¶292,013
49. ¶L-1631; ¶1624.114; TD ¶290,601

50. ¶s L-1702, L-2135; ¶1624.119; TD ¶291,004
1. ¶L-1702; ¶1624.119; TD ¶291,004
2. ¶L-1726 *et seq.*; ¶2744.04; TD ¶291,507

¶ 1549 Convention expenses.

Travel expenses incurred in attending a domestic convention are subject to the regular business trip rules if attendance will benefit or advance the taxpayer's business or the employee's responsibilities as distinguished from serving some social, political, or other nonbusiness function. (Reg § 1.162-2(d))[3]

No business expense deduction is allowed for expenses allocable to a convention, seminar, or similar meeting held outside the North American area (defined below) unless the taxpayer establishes that the meeting is directly related to the active conduct of his trade or business, or to an activity relating to the production of income, and that after taking specified factors into account, it's as reasonable for the meeting to be held outside the North American area as within it. (Code Sec. 274(h)(1))

North American area means the U.S., its possessions, the Trust Territory of the Pacific Islands, Canada and Mexico. (Code Sec. 274(h)(3)(A)) U.S. possessions include Puerto Rico and the U.S. Virgin Islands.[4] "North American area" also includes Aruba, Antigua, Bahamas, Barbados, Barbuda, Bermuda, Costa Rica, Dominica, the Dominican Republic, Grenada, Guyana, Honduras, Jamaica, the Netherlands Antilles, Panama, Trinidad and Tobago.[5]

¶ 1550 Cruise ship convention—$2,000 deduction limit.

A deduction of up to $2,000 per individual per year is allowed for attending business conventions, etc., held aboard a cruise ship, but only if the ship is registered in the U.S. and all ports of call of the cruise ship are located in the U.S. or its possessions. (Code Sec. 274(h)(2)) A married couple filing a joint return can deduct $4,000 if each spent at least $2,000 for attending an otherwise deductible business-related cruise ship convention.[6] A taxpayer claiming the deduction must attach to his return two specified written substantiation statements (including one signed by the sponsor). (Code Sec. 274(h)(5))[7]

¶ 1551 Travel expense deduction for a companion.

No deduction is allowed (other than under Code Sec. 217, moving expenses) for travel expenses paid or incurred for a spouse, dependent, or other individual accompanying the taxpayer (or an officer or employee of the taxpayer) unless: (1) the spouse, etc., is an employee of the taxpayer; (2) the travel of the spouse, etc., is for a bona fide business purpose; and (3) the expenses would otherwise be deductible by the spouse, etc. (Code Sec. 274(m)(3))[8]

The limits on deductions for travel companions don't apply to a companion who (1) is a business associate (¶1562), (2) comes along for a bona-fide business purpose, and (3) could otherwise deduct the expense if he incurred it. (Reg § 1.274-2(g))

If a taxpayer is accompanied by a spouse on a business trip and the spouse's expenses aren't deductible, the deductible expense for transportation and lodging is the single rate cost of similar accommodations for the taxpayer. But the full rental for a car in which both spouses travel is deductible, since no part of the expense is attributable to the "extra" passenger.[9]

¶ 1552 Deduction for luxury water travel is limited.

The deduction allowed for travel by ocean liner, cruise ship, or other form of "luxury" water transportation is limited to twice the highest domestic per diem allowance of executive

3. ¶L-1716; ¶1624.119; TD ¶291,014
4. ¶s L-1744, L-1745; ¶2744.04; TD ¶291,515
5. ¶L-1746; ¶2744.04; TD ¶291,516
6. ¶L-1721; ¶2744.04; TD ¶291,018
7. ¶L-1722; ¶2744.04; TD ¶291,019
8. ¶L-1739; ¶2744.035; TD ¶291,023
9. ¶L-1740 *et seq.*; ¶1624.119

branch U.S. government employees (other than high-ranking executive personnel) multiplied by the number of days of luxury water travel. (Code Sec. 274(m)(1)(A)) If the cost includes separately stated amounts for meals and entertainment, these amounts must be reduced by 50% (¶1569). The per diem rule doesn't apply to expenses of a cruise-ship convention or seminar to which the rules at ¶1550 apply (Code Sec. 274(m)(1)(B)(i)), or to:

... expenses treated as compensation paid to an employee or otherwise included in the gross income of the recipient;

... reimbursed, accounted-for expenses of the taxpayer where the services are performed for someone else, and if performed for an employer, the reimbursement hasn't been treated as compensation;

... expenses for recreational or social activities primarily for the benefit of employees;

... services and facilities made available by the taxpayer to the general public; and

... services and facilities sold to customers. (Code Sec. 274(m)(1)(B)(ii))[10]

¶ 1553 Above-the-line deduction for overnight travel of reservists.

A member of the Armed Forces reserves who travels over 100 miles from home for an overnight stay connected with the performance of services (e.g., to attend meetings), can deduct travel expenses as an above-the-line adjustment to gross income. The amount deductible is limited to the regular federal per diem rate for lodging, meals, and incidental expenses, and the standard mileage rate for car expenses plus parking fees and tolls. (Code Sec. 62(a)(2)(E)) Expenses in excess of these limits, or for overnight travel not over 100 miles from home, are miscellaneous itemized deductions subject to the 2%-of-AGI floor (¶3110).[11]

¶ 1554 Transportation Expenses. ■■■■■■■■■■■■■■■■■■■■■■■■■■■■■■

Costs of local transportation (including the cost of operating and maintaining a car directly attributable to the conduct of a trade or business) can qualify as deductible expenses.

¶ 1555 Transportation expenses other than commuting expenses.

Transportation expenses (but not commuting expenses, see ¶1556) directly attributable to the conduct of the taxpayer's business are deductible even though he isn't away from home overnight. (Reg § 1.162-1(a)) These expenses (sometimes called local travel expenses) include air, train, bus and cab fares and costs of operating automobiles.[12] If a taxpayer works at two or more places each day, he can deduct the cost of getting from one to the other.[13]

¶ 1556 Expenses of daily transportation between home and work site.

Expenses of commuting between a taxpayer's residence and his regular business location, wherever situated, aren't deductible (Reg § 1.162-2(e), Reg § 1.162-2(f)).[14] But a taxpayer may deduct daily transportation expenses incurred in going between the taxpayer's residence and a temporary (¶1557) work location *outside* the metropolitan area where the taxpayer lives and normally works.[15]

Daily transportation expenses incurred in going between the taxpayer's residence and a temporary (¶1557) work location *within* the same metropolitan area is business transportation if: (1) the taxpayer has one or more regular work locations away from his residence; or (2) the taxpayer's residence is his principal place of business (¶1639 *et seq.*).[16]

---

10. ¶L-1708; ¶2744.05; TD ¶291,009
11. ¶A-2611.4; ¶624.02; TD ¶560,706.3
12. ¶L-1601; ¶1624.150; TD ¶290,501
13. ¶L-1602; ¶1624.153; TD ¶290,504

14. ¶L-1608 *et seq.*; ¶1624.151; TD ¶290,512
15. ¶L-1605; ¶1624.130; TD ¶290,506
16. ¶L-1605; ¶1624.151; TD ¶290,505

¶ 1557   One-year temporary workplace rule.

A work location is "temporary" for purposes of deducting daily transportation costs (¶1556) if employment at the location is realistically expected to last (and in fact does last) for one year or less. If the employment initially is realistically expected to last for one year or less, but at some later date it is realistically expected to exceed one year, that employment is temporary (absent facts and circumstances indicating otherwise) until the date that the taxpayer's realistic expectation changes, and is treated as not temporary after that date.

Where an assignment at a work location is expected to last for more than one year, but the taxpayer is realistically expected to be present at that location *for no more than 35 workdays (partial or complete)* during each of the calendar years in that period, the location is temporary for a calendar year in which he actually works there for no more than 35 partial or complete workdays.

illustration: A taxpayer who normally works in an office building works at an offsite location on an assignment lasting 36 months, but he is at the offsite location for only 30 days each year. The offsite location is "temporary," and his round-trip transportation costs between home and that location are deductible.[17]

¶ 1558   Automobile expenses.

The expenses of operating and maintaining a car used for business purposes, such as gasoline, oil, repairs, insurance, depreciation, interest to buy the car, taxes, licenses, garage rent, parking, fees, tolls, etc., are deductible.[18] If a taxpayer makes both personal and business use of his car, he must apportion his expenses between business (deductible) and personal (nondeductible) transportation.[19] Report business auto expenses on Form 2106 or Form 2106-EZ (employees) or on Form 1040, Schedule C or Form 1040, Schedule C-EZ (self-employeds).[20]

caution: An employee who uses a car for his job is subject to the 2%-of-AGI floor on deducting the *un*reimbursed auto expenses he incurs, see ¶3104, and can't deduct interest on a car loan (¶1715).

¶ 1559   Transporting tools to work.

A taxpayer may deduct only *additional* expenses incurred because of the need to transport tools, etc., to work *and* only if the additional expenses can be determined accurately. The deduction is only for that portion of the cost of transporting the tools, etc., that exceeds the cost of commuting *by the same mode of transportation* without the tools, etc.[21]

¶ 1560   Business standard mileage rate.

Taxpayers may use the optional business standard mileage rate in computing the deductible costs of operating passenger automobiles owned or leased by them (including vans and pickup or panel trucks) for business purposes.

A taxpayer who uses this method multiplies the number of business miles by 56.5¢ per mile for travel during 2013.[22]

A deduction using the standard mileage rate is in lieu of deducting operating and fixed costs. A taxpayer who uses the standard mileage rate forgoes deductions for depreciation (or

---

17. ¶L-1606; ¶1624.151; TD ¶290,507
18. ¶L-1902; ¶1624.150; TD ¶293,000
19. ¶L-1907; ¶1624.157; TD ¶293,014

20. ¶L-1901; ¶1624.157; TD ¶293,002
21. ¶L-1611; ¶1624.152; TD ¶290,515
22. ¶L-1903; ¶1624.157; TD ¶293,005

leasing costs), maintenance and repairs, tires, gasoline (including taxes), oil, insurance, and registration fees. But deductions for parking fees and tolls are still available.[23]

Use of the standard mileage rate isn't available for five or more autos that are used simultaneously, such as in fleet operations, nor is it available for a purchased car if the taxpayer previously depreciated it using any method other than the straight-line method, or if Code Sec. 179 expensing or additional first-year depreciation has been claimed. The standard mileage rate may generally be used for a leased auto only if the taxpayer uses this method (or a fixed and variable rate (FAVR) allowance, see ¶1575) for the entire lease period (including renewals).[24]

Rural mail carriers receiving qualified reimbursements (equipment maintenance allowance) don't report them in income even if they exceed the amount of their expenses. (Code Sec. 162(o)(1)) However, if the expenses exceed the amount of the qualified reimbursement, the mail carrier can take the excess into account in computing miscellaneous itemized deductions under Code Sec. 67. (Code Sec. 162(o)(2))[25]

A taxpayer may use the optional business standard mileage rate in substantiating reimbursed expenses paid by another.[26] For consequences if the reimbursement is made under an accountable plan, or under a nonaccountable plan, see ¶3104.

¶ 1561   Entertainment Expenses.

Costs incurred for entertainment must meet strict tests in order to be deductible. A 50% rule also limits otherwise-allowable deductions for meals and entertainment.

Entertainment expenses, except as limited by the rules in ¶1569 (percentage limit) and ¶1571 (other restrictions), are deductible if they are ordinary and necessary expenses of carrying on a trade or business. (Code Sec. 274(a), Code Sec. 274(e); Reg § 1.162-1(a)) Strict substantiation requirements must be met (¶1579). But no deduction is allowed unless the taxpayer can show that the entertainment expenses are: (1) "directly related" to the active conduct of a trade or business (¶1564), or (2) "associated with" the active conduct of a trade or business (¶1565), or (3) covered by one of the exceptions at ¶1566. (Code Sec. 274(a))[27]

"Entertainment" includes any activity generally considered to be entertainment, amusement or recreation. This covers entertaining guests at night clubs, theaters, sporting events, and at entertainment facilities such as yachts, country clubs, hunting lodges, etc. If the expense involves the use of an entertainment facility, see ¶1567. (Reg § 1.274-2(b)(1)) It doesn't include: supper money furnished to an employee working overtime, a hotel room maintained by an employer and furnished to employees while traveling on business, or an auto used for business even though used for commuting to and from work.[28]

Expenses of entertaining customers or clients at the taxpayer's home may be ordinary and necessary. But only the *extra* expense incurred because they are present is deductible. Failure to show a business purpose for entertaining bars a deduction.[29]

¶ 1562   Who may be entertained?

A "business associate" who may be entertained is a person with whom the taxpayer could reasonably expect to engage or deal with in the active conduct of his trade or business. Examples are customers, suppliers, clients, employees, agents, partners, or professional advisors, *whether established or prospective.* (Reg § 1.274-2(b)(2)(iii))[30] For spouses, see ¶1563.

---

23. ¶L-1905; ¶1624.157; TD ¶293,009
24. ¶L-1903 *et seq.*; ¶1624.157; TD ¶293,006
25. ¶L-1911; ¶1624.157; TD ¶293,018
26. ¶L-4715; ¶2744.17; TD ¶293,011

27. ¶L-2101; ¶2744.01; TD ¶294,001
28. ¶L-2102; TD ¶294,003
29. ¶L-2108 *et seq.*; ¶2744.01; TD ¶294,009
30. ¶L-2103; ¶2744.10; TD ¶294,007

¶ 1563 Entertainment expenses allocable to spouse.

A taxpayer can deduct the cost of entertaining taxpayer's spouse or the spouse of a business customer if taxpayer can show a clear business purpose rather than a personal or social purpose for incurring the expenses. For example, a customer's spouse may join the party for the entertainment because it's impracticable, under the circumstances, to entertain the customer without the spouse. And if the taxpayer's spouse joins the party because the customer's spouse is present, the cost of the entertainment allocable to the taxpayer's spouse is also deductible. (Reg § 1.274-2(d)(2), Reg § 1.274-2(d)(4))[31]

¶ 1564 "Directly related" test for deducting costs of entertainment.

Amounts paid for entertainment are deductible if they are directly related to the active conduct of the taxpayer's trade or business. This test is met if the entertainment: (1) involved an active discussion aimed at getting immediate revenue; (2) occurred in a clear business setting such as a hospitality room; or (3) must be reported as compensation for services performed by an individual other than an employee. (Reg § 1.274-2(c)(1))[32] Costs generally aren't "directly related" if entertainment occurs where there's little or no possibility of engaging in the active conduct of business, e.g., at night clubs, theaters, or sporting events, but they may be deductible under the "associated with" rule (¶1565). (Reg § 1.274-2(c)(7))[33]

¶ 1565 "Associated with" test for deducting costs of entertainment.

Entertainment expenses that fail the directly related test but are associated with the active conduct of the taxpayer's business are deductible if the entertainment directly precedes or follows a substantial and bona fide business discussion. (Reg § 1.274-2(d)(1))[34] An entertainment expense is generally associated with the active conduct of a taxpayer's business if he can show a clear business purpose in incurring the expenditure. (Reg § 1.274-2(d)(2))[35]

The portion of an otherwise deductible expense allocable to the spouse of a person who engaged in the discussion is ordinarily considered associated with the active conduct of the business (Reg § 1.274-2(d)(4)),[36] see ¶1563.

Whether a business discussion is substantial depends on all the facts of each case. The taxpayer must show that he or his representative actively engaged in a discussion, meeting, negotiation, or other bona fide business transaction (other than entertainment) in order to get a specific business benefit. The meeting doesn't have to be for any specific length of time, but the business discussion must be substantial in relation to the entertainment. Nor does more time have to be devoted to business than entertainment. (Reg § 1.274-2(d)(3)(i))[37]

¶ 1566 Expenses to which "directly related" and "associated" tests don't apply.

Certain ordinary and necessary entertainment expenses are deductible even if they aren't "directly related" to or "associated with" the active conduct of the taxpayer's trade or business. But they are subject to the strict substantiation requirements (¶1579) that apply to other entertainment expenses. The exceptions are:

(1) Food and beverages furnished on the taxpayer's business premises primarily for the taxpayer's employees.[38]

(2) The expense (other than club dues, see ¶1568) of providing recreational, social, or similar activities primarily for the benefit of the taxpayer's employees, other than highly-

---

31. ¶L-2104 *et seq.*; ¶2744.01; TD ¶294,008
32. ¶L-2112; ¶2744.01; TD ¶294,013
33. ¶L-2116; ¶2744.01; TD ¶294,017
34. ¶L-2118; ¶2744.01; TD ¶294,019

35. ¶L-2118; ¶2744.01; TD ¶294,020
36. ¶L-2104; ¶2744.01; TD ¶294,008
37. ¶L-2119; ¶2744.01; TD ¶294,020
38. ¶L-2122; ¶2744.01; TD ¶294,025

compensated employees (defined at ¶4326).[39]

(3) Goods, services, and the use of a facility, if treated as compensation and as wages by the employer for withholding tax purposes.[40]

(4) Expenses connected with meetings of directors, shareholders, employees or trade associations.[41]

(5) Cost of providing entertainment or recreational facilities to the general public as a means of advertising or promoting good will in the community.[42]

(6) Expense of providing entertainment, goods, and services, or use of facilities, that are sold to the public in a bona fide transaction for adequate and full consideration.[43]

(7) Reimbursed and substantiated expenses or allowances of employees where the employer hasn't treated the expenses as wages subject to withholding, and reimbursed, accounted-for entertainment expenses of self-employeds reimbursed or covered with an allowance by the client or customer. (Code Sec. 274(e); Reg § 1.274-2(f)(2)) In these situations, the "directly related" and "associated with" tests apply to the payor.   [44]

¶ 1567   Entertainment facilities.

No deduction is allowed for any expense paid or incurred for an entertainment facility used in conjunction with any activity that is generally considered to be entertainment, amusement or recreation. (Code Sec. 274(a)(1)(B))[45] Entertainment facilities include yachts, hunting lodges, fishing camps, swimming pools, tennis courts, and bowling alleys. Facilities also may include airplanes, automobiles, hotel suites, apartments, and houses located in recreational areas (e.g., beach cottages and ski lodges). However, a facility isn't an entertainment facility unless it's actually used at least in part for entertainment. Expenses of an automobile or an airplane used on business trips are allowed. (Reg § 1.274-2(e)(2))[46]

The following expenditures aren't subject to the entertainment facility rules and are subject to the regular rules that apply to these items:

. . . Interest, taxes, and casualty losses on entertainment facilities.

. . . Out-of-pocket expenses for such items as food and beverages, or expenses for catering furnished during entertainment at a facility.

. . . Actual business (as opposed to entertainment) use of a facility, such as using a plane or car for business transportation or chartering a yacht to an unrelated person. (Reg § 1.274-2(e)(3)(iii), Reg § 1.274-6)[47]

¶ 1568   Club dues.

Deductions are generally barred for the cost of membership in any club organized for business, pleasure, recreation or other social purpose (Code Sec. 274(a)(3)), such as country clubs, golf and athletic clubs, airline clubs, hotel clubs, and business luncheon clubs. (Reg § 1.274-2(a)(2)(iii)(a)) However, a deduction is allowed to the extent dues are treated as compensation income to an employee. (Reg § 1.132-5(s)) Dues for membership in professional and trade associations and civic or public service organizations (e.g., Rotary, Kiwanis) are deductible. (Reg § 1.274-2(a)(2)(iii)(b))[48]

---

39. ¶L-2125; ¶2744.01; TD ¶294,029
40. ¶L-2123; ¶2744.01; TD ¶294,026
41. ¶L-2129; ¶2744.01; TD ¶294,031
42. ¶L-2131; ¶2744.01; TD ¶294,033
43. ¶L-2132; ¶2744.01; TD ¶294,034

44. ¶L-2124; ¶2744.01; TD ¶294,028
45. ¶L-2149; ¶2744.02; TD ¶295,001
46. ¶L-2150; ¶2744.02; TD ¶295,002
47. ¶L-2152 *et seq.*; ¶2744.02; TD ¶295,004
48. ¶L-2181 *et seq.*; ¶2744.03; TD ¶295,201

¶ 1569   Meal and entertainment deduction limits—the 50% rule.

The amount of an otherwise allowable deduction for meal or entertainment expenses (including meals while on business travel status, ¶1541) is reduced by 50%. This reduction applies to any expense for food or beverages, and any item for entertainment, amusement, or recreation, or for a facility used for such an activity. (Code Sec. 274(n)(1))

The 50% limit doesn't apply to:

. . . Expenses treated as compensation paid to an employee or otherwise included in the gross income of the recipient of the meal or entertainment. (Code Sec. 274(n)(2)(A))

. . . Meals and entertainment expenses that are reimbursed. (Code Sec. 274(n)(2)(A)) Instead, the percentage limit applies to the person making the reimbursement.

. . . Traditional recreational expenses for employees (other than those who are highly compensated, see ¶4326). (Code Sec. 274(n)(2)(A))

. . . Services and facilities made available by the taxpayer to the general public. (Code Sec. 274(n)(2)(A))

. . . Expenses of goods, services, or use of facilities, sold by the taxpayer in a bona fide transaction (entertainment sold to customers). (Code Sec. 274(n)(2)(A))

. . . Food or beverage expenses that are excludable from the gross income of the recipient under the de minimis fringe benefit rules. (Code Sec. 274(n)(2)(B))

. . . An expense that is part of a package that includes a ticket to attend certain charitable sporting events. (Code Sec. 274(n)(2)(C)) The event must: (1) be organized for the primary purpose of benefiting a tax-exempt charitable organization, (2) contribute 100% of the net proceeds to the charity, and (3) use volunteers for substantially all work performed in carrying out the event. (Code Sec. 274(l)(1)(B))

. . . Food or beverage expenses of crews of certain drilling rigs and crews of certain commercial vessels (Code Sec. 274(n)(2)(E)), but not fishing vessels.[49]

Where an employee's deduction of unreimbursed employee business expenses is subject to the 2%-of-AGI floor discussed at ¶3110, the 50% limit is applied before the 2% floor.[50]

The deductible percentage of meals for certain transport workers (e.g., air transport employees, truck and bus drivers, railroad employees) while away from home during or incident to the period of duty subject to the hours of service limitations of the Dept. of Transportation is 80%. (Code Sec. 274(n)(3))[1]

¶ 1570   Limits on deductions for skyboxes.

Where a skybox or other private luxury box is leased for more than one sporting event, the amount allowable as a deduction for business-related entertainment use is limited to the face value of nonluxury box seat tickets for the seats in the box covered by the lease. (Code Sec. 274(l)(2)) This is reduced by 50% to determine the deduction. (Code Sec. 274(n))[2]

¶ 1571   Other restrictions on meal and entertainment deductions.

No deduction is allowed for any food or beverage expense unless—

(1) the expense isn't lavish or extravagant under the circumstances, and

(2) the taxpayer (or one of taxpayer's employees) is present when the food or beverages are furnished (Code Sec. 274(k)(1)), and

49. ¶L-2138 *et seq.*; ¶2744.01; TD ¶294,507 *et seq.*
50. ¶L-2135; ¶2744.01; TD ¶294,506

1. ¶L-2145.1; ¶2744.01
2. ¶L-2146 *et seq.*; ¶2744.01; TD ¶294,519

(3) the taxpayer establishes that the expenditure was directly related (¶1564) to the active conduct of taxpayer's business or, for an expenditure directly preceding or following a substantial and bona fide business discussion, was associated with the active conduct of the taxpayer's business (¶1565). (Code Sec. 274(a), Code Sec. 274(k))[3]

Neither the lavish or extravagant limit nor the presence test applies to any expense that is excepted from the percentage limit under ¶1569, above. (Code Sec. 274(k)(2))[4]

In determining the deduction for the cost of a ticket to an entertainment or recreation activity, the amount taken into account can't exceed the face value of the ticket (including any ticket tax). But the face value limit doesn't apply to a ticket to a charitable sporting event that's excepted from the percentage limit (¶1569). (Code Sec. 274(l)(1))[5]

¶ 1572 Deduction limit on entertainment expenses of officers, directors, and 10%-or-more owners.

For costs to provide entertainment-, amusement-, or recreation-related goods, services or facilities to "specified individuals" (e.g., an officer, director, or 10%-or-more owner of the entity, or a related entity) and their relatives or friends, an employer's deduction is limited to the amount of the costs which were treated by the employer as compensation on the employer's income tax return and as wages (or nonemployee compensation) to the qualified recipient. (Code Sec. 274(e)(2)(B), Code Sec. 274(e)(9); Reg § 1.274-9(b))[6]

Detailed rules apply for allocating plane costs between usage for entertainment of specified individuals and expenses for all other users (but in making this allocation, expenses of bona fide charters to third parties aren't counted).[7] Where a specified individual's flight includes a business segment and entertainment segment, the entertainment cost subject to the limit is the excess of the total cost of the flights over the cost of the flights that would have been taken without the entertainment segment or segments.[8] The deduction limit doesn't apply to business entertainment air travel or personal travel that can't be characterized as "entertainment" (e.g., flight to attend family member's funeral). (Reg § 1.274-10(b))[9]

¶ 1573 Expense Reimbursements.

An employee doesn't pay tax on an advance, reimbursement or other expense allowance received under an "accountable plan." The tax treatment of an advance or reimbursement to an independent contractor depends on whether he accounts to his principal for the expense.

An employee doesn't pay tax on an advance, reimbursement or other expense allowance received from his employer (or from a third party) under an "accountable plan." (Reg § 1.62-2(c)(4)) By contrast, an advance, etc., made under a "nonaccountable plan," is fully taxable to the employee and subject to FICA and income tax withholding. (Reg § 1.62-2(c)(5))[10]

An advance, etc., is treated as made under an "accountable plan" if:

(1) the employee receives the advance, etc., for a deductible business expense that he paid or incurred while performing services as an employee of his employer (¶1574),

(2) the employee must adequately account to his employer for the expense within a reasonable period of time (¶1575), and

(3) the employee must return any excess reimbursement or allowance within a reasonable period of time (¶1576).

---

3. ¶s L-2133 *et seq.*, L-2112, L-2118; ¶2744.01; TD ¶294,503 *et seq.*
4. ¶L-2134; ¶2744.12; TD ¶294,503 *et seq.*
5. ¶L-2145; ¶2744.01; TD ¶294,516
6. ¶L-2123; ¶2744.01; TD ¶294,026

7. ¶L-2123.2; TD ¶294,026.2
8. ¶L-2123.7
9. ¶L-2101.1; TD ¶294,001.1
10. ¶J-1050; TD ¶296,006.

An advance, etc., that doesn't satisfy all three conditions is treated as paid under a nonaccountable plan—it is taxed to the employee and is subject to FICA and income tax withholding. (Code Sec. 62(c); Reg § 1.62-2(c)(5))[11] An arrangement that recharacterizes taxable wages as nontaxable reimbursements or allowances (e.g., to provide a tool reimbursement for employees), won't satisfy the deductible business expense requirement (condition (1), above).[12] If an employee does not timely return advances or reimbursements in excess of those that are substantiated, only the excess is treated as made under a nonaccountable plan. (Reg § 1.62-2(c)(3)(ii))[13]

An arrangement that would in part be an accountable plan and in part be a nonaccountable plan if both parts were viewed separately is treated as two expense allowance arrangements—one an accountable plan, and the other a nonaccountable plan.[14] But the entire reimbursement for business-travel meals and incidental expenses (M&IE) is deemed paid under a nonaccountable plan if an employer routinely doesn't track expenses and doesn't require employees either to substantiate actual expenses or pay back amounts exceeding the deemed substantiated amount (¶1575).[15]

Reimbursement of employee expenses for reasonable employment-related cell phone usage is nontaxable in most instances.[16]

¶ 1574 Business connection requirement for employee business expenses.

An arrangement satisfies the "business connection" requirement if it provides advances, allowances (including per diem or mileage allowances, or allowances for meals and incidental expenses only), or reimbursements only for business expenses that are allowable as deductions, and that are paid or incurred by the employee in connection with performing services as an employee. (Reg § 1.62-2(d))[17] For example, a reimbursement for an employee's meal eaten while he was away from home overnight on employer business (¶1542) satisfies the business connection requirement, but a reimbursement for an employee's (non-business-entertainment) meal eaten during a non-overnight trip (¶1542) on employer business wouldn't satisfy the requirement. An advance, reimbursement or allowance that would be treated as made partially under a nonaccountable plan solely because the expense is subject to the 50% deduction limit for business meals and entertainment (¶1569) is treated as made under an accountable plan. (Reg § 1.62-2(h)(1))[18]

¶ 1575 Accounting to employer for expenses.

To the extent an employee business expense such as travel or entertainment isn't deductible unless the substantiation requirements of Code Sec. 274(d) are met (¶1579 *et seq.*), the employee must meet those requirements within a reasonable period of time (¶1576), i.e., submit to the payor information sufficient to substantiate the requisite elements of each expense or use.

For all other business expenses, sufficient information must be submitted to enable the one making the reimbursement to identify the specific nature of each expense and to conclude that the expense is attributable to the employer's business activities. (Reg § 1.62-2(e)(3))

For accounting via per diem allowances and other simplified methods, see ¶1581.

---

11. ¶S-3672
12. ¶L-4703.1A
13. ¶L-4703; TD ¶296,009
14. ¶L-4744; TD ¶296,007
15. ¶L-4704
16.
17. ¶L-4703.1; TD ¶561,009
18. ¶L-4703.1; TD ¶532,004

¶ 1576   Returning amounts in excess of expenses; when to substantiate.

Under an accountable plan, an employee must be required to return to the payor within a reasonable period of time any reimbursement in excess of substantiated business expenses. (Reg § 1.62-2(f)(1)) The definition of reasonable period of time depends on the facts and circumstances. However, under a safe-harbor rule, (1) an advance within 30 days of the time the employee has the expense, (2) an expense adequately accounted for within 60 days after it was paid or incurred, or (3) an amount returned to the employer within 120 days after the expense was paid or incurred will be treated as having occurred within a reasonable period of time. (Reg § 1.62-2(g)(2)(i)) If the employee is given a periodic statement (at least quarterly) that asks him to either return or adequately account for outstanding reimbursements and he complies within 120 days of the statement, the amount is adequately accounted for or returned within a reasonable period of time. (Reg § 1.62-2(g)(2))[19]

¶ 1577   Reporting reimbursed employee business expenses.

If an employee's expenses equal advances or reimbursements made under an accountable plan, he reports no income from the expenses and claims no deductions. However, if the employee's actual business expenses exceed nontaxable accountable-plan advances or reimbursements, and he wishes to deduct the excess, he can do so under the rules that follow for deductions under nonaccountable plan reimbursements.

An employee who pays for employment-related business expenses but receives a nonaccountable plan advance or reimbursement (e.g., he isn't required to account to the employer) reports the advance or reimbursement as income and claims otherwise allowable deductions on Form 2106 or Form 2106EZ, and on Form 1040, Schedule A as miscellaneous itemized deductions. The employee's meal and entertainment expenses are subject to the 50% limit (¶1569), and total miscellaneous itemized deductions are subject to the 2%-of-adjusted-gross-income limit (¶3110). The employee must be able to substantiate each element of his business expenditures. (Reg § 1.274-5T(f)(3))[20] For listed property, see ¶1584.

¶ 1578   Reimbursed expenses of a self-employed person.

Expenses of a self-employed person incurred on behalf of and reimbursed by a client or customer aren't included in the self-employed's gross income if the self-employed substantiates the expenses to his principal under the rules at ¶1579. But if he doesn't substantiate those reimbursed expenses to his principal, he must include the reimbursements in gross income and may deduct the expenses, subject to the usual limitations (e.g., 50% limit on business meals and entertainment), if he has kept the necessary records and receipts. (Reg § 1.274-5T(h)(1), Reg § 1.274-5T(h)(2))[21]

The client or customer must substantiate business travel or entertainment expenses (and is subject to the 50% limit) if a self-employed person accounts for those expenses to the client or customer and is reimbursed. However, if the self-employed person doesn't account for the expenses, the client or customer doesn't have to substantiate reimbursed expenses (and isn't subject to the 50% limit). (Reg § 1.274-5T(h)(2), Reg § 1.274-5T(h)(4))[22]

A self-employed person (or an employee) may adequately substantiate a meals and incidental expense to an initial payor that initially reimburses the expense, and the initial payor in connection with its performing services for a third party, may be reimbursed under a reimbursement or other expense allowance arrangement with the third party. Here, if the initial payor accounts to the third party in the same way that the self-employed (or employee)

---

19. ¶L-4746; TD ¶296,047
20. ¶L-4710; ¶2744.16; TD ¶296,012

21. ¶L-4757; ¶2744.16; TD ¶296,056
22. ¶L-4758; ¶2744.16; TD ¶296,057

accounted for the expenses to the initial payor, then the third party bears the expenses and is subject to the percentage limit (¶1569) on the expenses. (Prop Reg. § 1.274-2(f)(2), [Taxpayers may rely])[23]

¶ 1579 Substantiating T&E and "Listed Property" Expenses. ▄▄▄▄▄▄▄▄

In order to deduct travel and entertainment (T&E) expenses, each expense must be substantiated. With respect to listed property, certain elements of each expenditure or business use must be proved.

Taxpayers must substantiate each element of every T&E expense for which a deduction is claimed. (Code Sec. 274(d)(1), Code Sec. 274(d)(2), Code Sec. 274(d)(3)) The elements of away from home travel expenses are explained at ¶1580; entertainment expenses, at ¶1583; and business gifts, at ¶1592.

Taxpayers can't claim deductions or credits for "listed property" (¶1947), such as a passenger auto, unless they substantiate every element of each expenditure and use of the listed property (¶1584) for business or investment purposes. (Code Sec. 274(d)(4)) For depreciation of "listed property," see ¶1946 *et seq.*

Generally, proper substantiation requires "adequate records" (¶1585 *et seq.*), or a taxpayer statement supported by sufficient corroborating evidence (¶1587), plus documentary evidence where required (¶1586). (Code Sec. 274(d))[24] Approximations or estimates aren't sufficient. (Reg § 1.274-5T(a))[25] However, statistical sampling may be used in some cases to establish the amount of meal and entertainment expenses that isn't subject to the 50% limit (¶1569).[26] All elements of an expenditure or use must be proved. Failure to prove any one will bar the deduction. (Reg § 1.274-5T(c)(1))[27]

In the usual instance, an employee who substantiates expenses to the employer need not account for them to IRS. However, an employee who is "related" to his employer (certain close relatives of an individual employer, or a more than 10% shareholder of a corporate employer) may be asked by IRS to substantiate his expense accounts even though he has accounted to his employer. (Reg § 1.274-5T(f)(5)(ii))[28]

Simplified substantiation procedures apply to expenses of certain federal employees.[29]

¶ 1580 Proving travel and transportation expenses.

The taxpayer must prove all of the following elements by adequate records or by a sufficiently corroborated statement:

(1) The amount of each separate expenditure for traveling away from home, such as the cost of transportation or lodging. The daily cost of breakfast, lunch, and dinner and other incidental travel elements may be aggregated if they are set forth in reasonable categories, such as for meals, oil and gas, taxi fares, etc.

(2) The dates of the departure and return home for each trip, and the number of days spent on business away from home.

(3) The destinations or locality of the travel.

(4) The business reason for the travel or the nature of the business benefit derived or expected to be derived as a result of the travel. (Reg § 1.274-5T(b)(2))[30]

---

23. ¶L-2138.1
24. ¶L-4600 *et seq.*; ¶2744.10; TD ¶295,301
25. ¶L-4601; ¶2744.10; TD ¶295,301
26. ¶L-4641; ¶2744.10

27. ¶s L-4644, L-4608; ¶2744.10; TD ¶295,302
28. ¶L-4713; ¶2744.16; TD ¶296,014
29. ¶L-4700; ¶624.02
30. ¶L-4630; ¶2744.10; TD ¶295,324

169

Incidental travel expenses, e.g., tips, aren't subject to these rules. Where records are incomplete and documentary proof is unavailable, the taxpayer may establish the amount of incidental travel expenses by reasonable approximations. (Reg § 1.162-17(d)(3))[31]

¶ 1581   Substantiation by use of optional meal or incidental expenses allowance.

If a payor (i.e., the employer, its agent, or a third party) pays a per diem allowance in lieu of reimbursing actual expenses for lodging, meal and incidental expenses (M&IE) incurred or to be incurred by an employee for travel away from home, the amount of the expenses that is treated as substantiated for each calendar day (or part of that day) is the lesser of the per diem allowance or the appropriate IRS-approved maximums. An additional requirement is that the employee provides simplified substantiation (time, place and business purpose). Where these tests are met, the reimbursement is treated as made under an accountable plan—it isn't subject to income- or payroll-tax withholding and isn't reported on the employee's Form W-2. Receipts of expenses aren't required.[32]

Incidental expenses include fees and tips given to porters, hotel staff, etc.

An employee who is "related" to his employer (¶1579) *isn't* considered to have accounted to his employer for the full federal per diem allowances for lodging and M&IE, and must substantiate any deductions he claims, but he may use the meals-only per diem (¶1581) and the business standard mileage rate (¶1560).

The following simplified substantiation rules apply to per diems paid under an arrangement that otherwise qualifies as an accountable plan (¶1573):

. . . *Regular federal per diem allowance.* In general, the IRS-approved per-diem maximum is the GSA per-diem rate paid by the federal government to its workers on travel status. This rate varies from locality to locality.[33] For travel outside the continental U.S., a separate lodging expense rate and M&IE rate is available for each locality outside the continental U.S.[34]

. . . *Simplified (high-low) method for substantiating travel allowances.* A simplified method can be used for per diem amounts paid for lodging plus M&IE during travel within the continental U.S. If the regular federal per diem option (above) isn't used, for pre-Oct. 1 2013 travel, the payor may reimburse up to $242 for high-cost localities ($177 for lodging and $65 for M&IE) and $163 for other localities ($111 for lodging and $52 for M&IE); for post-Sept. 30, 2013 travel, the payor may reimburse up to $251 for high-cost localities ($186 for lodging and $65 for M&IE) and $170 for other localities ($118 for lodging and $52 for M&IE).[35]

. . . *Transportation industry per diem.* Employees or self-employeds whose work directly involves moving people or goods (e.g., by plane, bus, truck, ship) and regularly involves travel to different localities with different meal and incidental expense (M&IE) rates may, for 2013 and 2014 travel, treat $59 as the federal M&IE (meals and incidental expenses) rate for any locality in the continental U.S. and $65 as the M&IE rate for any locality outside the continental U.S. This method also can be used by payors of a per diem allowance only for M&IE away-from-home expenses to an employee in the transportation industry, if the payment qualifies as a regular meals-only allowance.[36]

. . . *Optional method for incidental expenses only.* Employees and self-employed individuals who don't pay or incur meal expenses for a calendar day (or partial day) of travel away from home for post-Sept. 30, 2013 travel may deduct $5 per day as incidental expenses for each away-from-home calendar (or partial) day.[37]

31. ¶L-4633; TD ¶295,326
32. ¶L-4717.1; ¶2744.18; TD ¶295,325
33. ¶L-4717; ¶2744.18; TD ¶296,019
34. ¶L-4713; TD ¶296,014

35. ¶L-4718; ¶2744.18; TD ¶296,020
36. ¶L-4721; ¶2744.17; TD ¶296,026
37. ¶L-4632.1; ¶2744.17; TD ¶295,325.1

An employee who is out of pocket for M&IE or is reimbursed under a nonaccountable plan may deduct an amount computed under this method only as an itemized deduction (subject to the percentage limit on meal and entertainment expenses, ¶1569, and then subject to the 2%-of-AGI floor on miscellaneous itemized deductions, ¶3110).

A self-employed individual deducts the amount in determining adjusted gross income. His deduction is subject to the percentage limit on meal and entertainment expenses (¶1569).[38]

¶ 1582 Substantiation by use of optional auto allowances.

The following simplified substantiation rules apply to allowances paid under an arrangement that otherwise qualifies as an accountable plan (¶1573):

. . . *Mileage allowance.* An employee who receives a fixed mileage allowance of not more than the optional business standard mileage rate (¶1560) to cover transportation expenses while traveling away from home or for transportation expenses is considered to have made an adequate accounting to his employer if the elements of time, place, and business purpose of the travel are substantiated. (Reg § 1.274-5T(f))[39]

. . . *Fixed and variable rate (FAVR) allowances for autos.* Where an employer provides a mileage allowance under a reimbursement or other expense allowance arrangement for an employee-owned or leased car, the substantiation requirement is satisfied (as to the amount of expense) if the employer reimburses in accordance with a FAVR allowance. A FAVR allowance is periodic fixed payments to cover fixed costs such as depreciation, coupled with periodic variable payments to cover operating costs such as gasoline. Among other things, a FAVR allowance may be paid only to an employee who substantiates at least 5,000 miles driven in connection with the performance of services as an employee, and at least five employees must be covered by the FAVR allowance.[40]

¶ 1583 Proving entertainment expenses.

For entertainment expenses, all these elements must be proved:

(1) The amount of each separate expenditure, except that incidental items like cab fares and telephone calls may be aggregated on a separate basis.

(2) The date the entertainment took place.

(3) The name (if any), address or location, and the type of entertainment, such as dinner or theater, if that information isn't clear from the location.

(4) The reason for entertaining, or the nature of the business benefit derived or expected to be derived, and the nature of any business discussion or activity that took place. If deducting entertainment "associated with" the active conduct of business (¶1565), the date, duration, place and nature of the business discussion, the persons entertained who participated in the business discussion, and the business reason for the entertainment or the nature of business benefit derived or expected to be derived as the result of entertaining.

(5) The occupation or other information about the person or persons entertained, including name, title or other designation, sufficient to establish his business relationship to the taxpayer. (Reg § 1.274-5T(b)(4), Reg § 1.274-5T(b)(3))[41]

¶ 1584 Substantiating costs of listed property.

For listed property (¶1579), all the relevant elements from the following list must be proved for each expenditure or business use of the property:

---

38. ¶L-4632; ¶2744.18; TD ¶294,502
39. ¶L-4715; ¶2744.18; TD ¶296,016
40. ¶L-4725 *et seq.*; ¶2744.18; TD ¶296,029
41. ¶L-4635; ¶2744.10; TD ¶295,327

(1) The amount and date of each separate expenditure (for example, the cost and date of acquisition or leasing, the cost and date of maintenance and repairs, etc.).

(2) The amount and date of each use of the item of listed property for business or investment, based on an appropriate measure (mileage for automobiles and other property used for transportation, time for other types of property, unless IRS approves an alternative method), and the total use of the item of listed property for the tax period.

(3) The business purpose for each expenditure or use with respect to the listed property. (Reg § 1.274-5T(b)(6))[42]

For optional business standard mileage rate, see ¶1560.

¶ 1585 Adequate records of T&E expenses and listed-property expenses.

Adequate records of travel and entertainment (T&E) expenses and of listed property (¶1579) expenditures and uses consist of a currently maintained account book, diary, log, statement of expenses, trip sheet, or similar record and, where necessary (¶1586), documentary evidence such as receipts and paid bills, which together are sufficient to establish each element of every expenditure or use that must be substantiated. Information reflected on a receipt need not be duplicated in an account book or other record so long as the account book or other record and the receipt complement each other in an orderly fashion. (Reg § 1.274-5T(c)(2)(i))[43] Both written and computer records are acceptable. (Reg § 1.274-5T(c)(2)(ii)(C)(2))[44]

Where the business purpose of an expenditure is evident from the surrounding facts and circumstances, a written explanation isn't required. (Reg § 1.274-5T(c)(2)(ii)(B))[45]

¶ 1586 Adequate documentary evidence to support lodging expenditures and other expenditures of $75 or more.

Documentary evidence, such as receipts or bills marked paid is required to support all expenditures for (1) lodging while away from home and (2) for any other expenses of $75 or more (except for transportation charges for which documentary evidence is not readily available). (Reg § 1.274-5(c)(2)(iii))[46]

Documentary evidence (original documents, faxes, e-mail printouts)[47] must disclose the amount, date, place, and essential character of the expenditure. For example, a hotel receipt is sufficient to support expenditures for business travel if it contains the name and location of the hotel, the date or dates taxpayer stayed there, and separate amounts for charges such as for lodging, meals, and telephone. A restaurant receipt is sufficient to support an expenditure for a business meal if it contains the name and location of the restaurant, the date and amount of the expenditure, and an indication that a charge (if any) is made for an item other than meals and beverages. A canceled check, together with a bill from the payee, ordinarily will establish the cost but may not alone show business purpose. (Reg § 1.274-5(c)(2)(iii))[48]

¶ 1587 Sufficiently corroborated statements used to substantiate expenses.

Taxpayers may substantiate the elements of their expenditures and uses not only by adequate records, but also by their own statements, written or oral, if those statements are supported by sufficient corroborating evidence. (Code Sec. 274(d))[49]

42. ¶L-4644; ¶2744.10; TD ¶295,333
43. ¶L-4616 *et seq.*; ¶2744.13; TD ¶295,311
44. ¶L-4616; ¶2744.13; TD ¶295,312
45. ¶L-4609; ¶2744.13; TD ¶295,307
46. ¶s L-4603, L-4619; ¶2744.13; TD ¶295,316
47. ¶L-4616; ¶2744.13; TD ¶295,316
48. ¶L-4619; ¶2744.13; TD ¶295,316
49. ¶L-4626 *et seq.*; ¶2744.14; TD ¶295,323

Corroborating evidence may be oral if from a disinterested, unrelated party who has knowledge of the expenditure or use in question. Written evidence has greater probative value, and its probative value increases if set down close to the time of the expenditure or use in question. (Reg § 1.274-5T(c)(1)) A taxpayer's written or oral statement must contain specific, detailed information about the element being substantiated, and the taxpayer must present other corroborative evidence sufficient to establish that element. (Reg § 1.274-5T(c)(3)(i))[50]

¶ 1588 Inadequate substantiation—remedies.

If a taxpayer hasn't fully substantiated a particular element of an expenditure or use, but does establish to IRS's satisfaction that he has substantially complied with the adequate records requirements, IRS may permit the taxpayer to establish the missing element by other evidence that it considers adequate. (Reg § 1.274-5T(c)(2)(v))

Where a taxpayer establishes that, by reason of "the inherent nature of the situation," he was unable to get either fully adequate records, or fully sufficient corroborating evidence in support of his own statement, he will be treated as satisfying the substantiation requirements if he presents other evidence that possesses the highest degree of probative value under the circumstances. (Reg § 1.274-5T(c)(4))[1]

Where a taxpayer establishes that he has maintained adequate records of an expenditure or use, but can't produce them because they have been lost through circumstances beyond his control (e.g., damage by fire, flood, etc.), he may prove his entitlement to a deduction by a reasonable reconstruction of the expenditure or use in question. (Reg § 1.274-5T(c)(5))[2] Destruction of records in marital disputes has been held to fall within this rule.[3]

¶ 1589 Business Gifts and Employee Awards. ▬▬▬▬▬▬

The costs of ordinary and necessary business gifts to individuals other than employees are deductible, subject to a $25 per-year per-person limit. Gifts to employees aren't deductible as gifts, but may be deductible as compensation. Certain noncash awards to employees are deductible.

¶ 1590 Business gifts.

The cost of ordinary and necessary business gifts may be deducted up to $25 a year to any one individual. Gift means any item excludable from gross income by the recipient under Code Sec. 102 (¶1212), but not excludable under any other income tax provision. (Code Sec. 274(b))[4] However, any item for general distribution having a cost of not more than $4 and on which the giver's name is clearly and permanently imprinted, and signs, display racks, or other promotional material donated to a retailer to be used on his business premises, aren't classified as gifts. (Code Sec. 274(b)(1); Reg § 1.274-3(b)(2))[5]

Since no amount transferred by or for an employer to or for the benefit of an employee is excludable as a gift (under Code Sec. 102) no such amount is deductible as a gift, though it may be deductible under other rules (e.g., as compensation).[6]

¶ 1591 Employee achievement awards.

An employer can deduct the cost of employee achievement awards (defined below). (Code Sec. 274(j)) The maximum deduction for awards made to one employee is $400 per year ($1,600 if the award is a qualified plan award, including the cost of awards that aren't

---

50. ¶L-4626; ¶2744.14; TD ¶295,323
1. ¶L-4628; ¶2744.15; TD ¶295,310
2. ¶L-4623; ¶2744.15; TD ¶295,320
3. ¶L-4624; TD ¶295,321

4. ¶L-2306; ¶2744.08; TD ¶303,005
5. ¶L-2306; ¶2744.08; TD ¶303,007
6. ¶H-4009; ¶1624.363; TD ¶278,309

qualified plan awards). (Code Sec. 274(j)(2)) The award must be given as part of a meaningful presentation under conditions and circumstances that don't create a likelihood that the payment is disguised compensation. (Code Sec. 274(j)(3))

An employee achievement award is an item of tangible personal property awarded to an employee because of length of service achievement, or safety achievement. (Code Sec. 274(j)(3))[7] Tangible personal property doesn't include cash or any gift certificate other than a nonnegotiable gift certificate conferring only the right to receive tangible personal property. (Reg § 1.274-3(b)(2)(iv))

A qualified plan award is an item awarded as part of a permanent, written, nondiscriminatory plan of the employer. (Code Sec. 274(j)(3)(B); Reg § 1.274-3(d))

A length-of-service award won't qualify for deduction under these rules if given during an employee's first five years of employment, or if a length-of-service award was given to the same employee during the same year or any of the earlier four years. (Code Sec. 274(j)(4)(B))

Safety achievement awards don't qualify if given to managerial, administrative, professional or clerical employees, or if such awards previously have been given to more than 10% of other employees during the year. (Code Sec. 274(j)(4)(C))[8]

No deduction is allowed for an employee achievement award (under the normal Code Sec. 162 ordinary and necessary rules or the Code Sec. 212 production of income rules) except under the above rules. (Code Sec. 274(j)(1))[9]

¶ 1592 Substantiating business gift expenses.

To substantiate business gift expenses adequate records or a sufficiently corroborated statement must show: (1) a description of the gift, (2) the taxpayer's cost, (3) when the gift was made, (4) the occupation of or other information about the gift's recipient, including his name, title, or other designation sufficient to establish his business relationship to the taxpayer, and (5) the reason for making the gift or the nature of business benefit derived or expected. (Reg § 1.274-5T(b)(5))[10]

¶ 1593 Rent Expense.

Rent is deductible if paid for the use of property used in the taxpayer's trade, business, or profession, or for the production of income.

Rent for the use of real or personal property in the taxpayer's trade, business, or profession, is deductible. (Code Sec. 162(a)(3)) But rent for personal-use property isn't. (Code Sec. 262(a); Reg § 1.262-1(b)(3))[11]

Besides normal cash rent payable periodically, rent includes a lump sum paid as advance rental, bonus, etc.; a percentage of the tenant's receipts or profits; the tenant's payment of the expenses of maintaining the rented property (taxes, insurance, etc.), and payment in property other than money (deductible to the extent of the property's fair market value).[12]

¶ 1594 Rent paid to related lessor.

Rentals paid between parties who are related either as members of a family or by stock ownership may not be deductible to the extent that they exceed the rent that would have been paid in an arm's-length transaction.

A corporation may deduct fair and reasonable rentals paid to corporate shareholders or

7. ¶L-2313; ¶2744.09; TD ¶303,012
8. ¶L-2315; ¶2744.09; TD ¶303,014
9. ¶L-2313 *et seq.*; ¶2744.09; TD ¶303,012

10. ¶L-4643; ¶2744.10; TD ¶295,332
11. ¶L-6604; ¶1624.285; TD ¶260,501
12. ¶L-6605 *et seq.*; ¶1624.285; TD ¶260,505

their relatives. But excessive rentals can be treated as nondeductible dividends.[13] Reasonable rental payments by a shareholder for use of corporate property are deductible.[14]

¶ 1595   Rent under leaseback arrangements.

A transfer by sale or gift coupled with a leaseback may be more advantageous than a mortgage loan and can create tax benefits for the transferor. Tax advantages (including rent deduction) of a sale and leaseback arrangement may be lost if IRS treats it as a mortgage loan, a tax-free exchange, or a sham transaction.[15]

A gift in trust with a leaseback of the property to the grantor will generally be upheld as a valid rental or royalty arrangement by the courts if: (1) the transfer is complete and irrevocable, (2) the trustee is independent, and (3) the rent is reasonable. Reasonableness of rent and the independence of the trustee are questions of fact.[16]

¶ 1596   Rent or purchase; lease with purchase options.

A payment is deductible as rent only if the taxpayer-lessee hasn't taken or isn't taking title to the property and has no equity interest in it. (Code Sec. 162(a)(3)) Thus, payments made under conditional sales contracts aren't deductible as rent.[17]

A lease that contains an option permitting the lessee to buy the property may be construed as a sale so that none of the payments is deductible as rent. Whether the lease is considered to be a sale depends essentially upon the intent of the parties, as shown in the agreement, read in light of the facts and circumstances existing at the time the agreement was made.[18] Important factors indicating sale instead of lease include nominal option price, excessive rent, designating part of the payment as interest, rental plus option price equal to the property's value plus interest, and application of rent payments to the lessee's equity in the property.[19]

¶ 1597   Lease acquisition costs.

Payments made by a lessee to get a business lease aren't currently deductible but must be amortized over the term of the lease. (Reg § 1.162-11(a)) This rule applies whether the tenant is on the cash or accrual basis and even though he has an option to buy the property.[20]

The term of the lease includes all renewal options (and any other period for which the parties reasonably expect the lease to be renewed) if less than 75% of the acquisition cost is attributable to the remaining lease period on the date of acquisition. In determining the term of the lease remaining on the date of acquisition, any period for which the lease may be renewed, extended or continued under an option exercisable by the lessee is not taken into account. (Code Sec. 178)[21]

¶ 1598   Lessor's costs.

Costs incurred by a lessor in leasing his property, or by a lessee in subletting, aren't currently deductible but must be amortized ratably over the term of the lease.[22] For tax treatment of construction allowances, see ¶1344.

The cost of MACRS improvements made by lessors are recoverable over the cost recovery period applicable to the leasehold improvements—regardless of the period of time the property is leased. (Code Sec. 168(i)(8))[23]

---

13. ¶L-6702; ¶1624.299; TD ¶260,522
14. ¶L-6710; ¶1624.299; TD ¶260,522
15. ¶L-6300 *et seq.*; ¶1624.299; TD ¶262,500
16. ¶L-6317; TD ¶262,510
17. ¶L-6209; ¶1624.284; TD ¶260,502
18. ¶L-6222 *et seq.*; ¶1624.305; TD ¶260,502

19. ¶L-6200 *et seq.*; ¶1624.305; TD ¶260,502
20. ¶L-6501; ¶1624.323; TD ¶261,501
21. ¶L-6504 *et seq.*; ¶1624.323; TD ¶261,504
22. ¶L-6401; ¶1624.081; TD ¶262,001
23. ¶L-6404; ¶1674.023; TD ¶262,004

A lessor's payments for cancellation of a lease must be amortized and deducted over the remaining term of the *cancelled* lease,[24] except that if the payment is made in order to enter a lease with a new tenant, the payment must be amortized over the term of the *new* lease.[25]

¶ 1599   Year of deduction for rent.

The tax year in which the rent is paid by a cash basis taxpayer or incurred by an accrual basis taxpayer is generally the proper year for deduction.[26] Advance rent paid by accrual basis taxpayers must be apportioned and deducted over the term of the lease or other rental period. For application of the 12-month rule to advance payments by cash basis taxpayers, see ¶1665. For deferred rental agreements, see ¶1600.[27]

¶ 1600   Deferred payments for the use of property or services.

Rent and interest attributable to a deferred rental agreement must be both reported and deducted as if both parties are accrual basis taxpayers. This rule applies to leases of over $250,000 that require either: (1) at least one payment for the use of property to be paid after the close of the calendar year following the calendar year of the use of the property, or (2) increases (or decreases) in the amounts to be paid as rent. (Code Sec. 467)[28]

For lessees, the deductible rental amount for the tax year is the sum of:

(1) rent deemed accrued by allocating rents in accordance with the rental agreement, taking into account the present value of rent to be paid after the close of the period, and

(2) interest for the year on amounts taken into account for earlier tax years (under (1), above), but which are as yet unpaid. (Code Sec. 467(b)(1))[29]

Present value and interest are computed using a rate equal to 110% of the applicable federal rate (¶1116). (Code Sec. 467(e)(4))[30]

If the agreement is silent as to rent allocation or the agreement is a disqualified leaseback or long-term agreement, then constant rental accrual applies. (Code Sec. 467(b)(2), Code Sec. 467(b)(3)) The constant rental amount is an amount paid as of the close of each lease period which would result in a total present value equal to the present value of the total payments required under the lease. (Code Sec. 467(e)(1))[31]

A rental agreement is a disqualified leaseback or long-term agreement if:

(1) it is part of a leaseback transaction to any person who had an interest in the leased property within two years before the leaseback (Code Sec. 467(e)(2)), or the term of the agreement exceeds 75% of a prescribed recovery period (Code Sec. 467(b)(4)), *and*

(2) a principal purpose of the increased rents provided in the agreement is tax avoidance. (Code Sec. 467(b)(4))[32]

An agreement isn't a disqualified leaseback or long-term agreement if it qualifies for any of the various safe harbors, including the uneven rent test, which is met if the rent allocated to each calendar year does not vary from the average rent allocated to all calendar years by more than 10%. (Reg § 1.467-3(c))

Under regs to be issued, similar rules will apply to certain deferred payments for services. (Code Sec. 467(g))[33]

---

24. ¶L-6405; ¶1624.081; TD ¶262,005
25. ¶L-6407; ¶1624.081; TD ¶262,006
26. ¶L-6616; ¶1624.285; TD ¶260,536
27. ¶L-6617; ¶s 1624.081, 1624.285; TD ¶260,537
28. ¶s L-6800, L-6801.13; ¶4674; TD ¶261,001

29. ¶L-6803; ¶4674; TD ¶261,035
30. ¶L-6804
31. ¶L-6805; ¶4674; TD ¶261,043
32. ¶L-6808; ¶4674; TD ¶261,050
33. ¶G-3451; ¶4674; TD ¶446,801

A reasonable rent holiday won't cause an agreement to be treated as a disqualified lease-back or long-term agreement. (Code Sec. 467(b)(5)) A rent holiday of 3 months or less at the beginning of the lease term is disregarded in determining if the rental agreement has increasing or decreasing rent. (Reg § 1.467-1(c)(2)(i)(B)) A lessor's granting of an 11.5 month zero rent period in a 25-year lease was held to be a reasonable rent holiday in an area where such inducements were needed to attract lessees.[34]

¶ 1601 Research and Experimental Expenditures.

Taxpayers can choose whether to immediately deduct or to capitalize research and experimental (R&E) expenditures. In some cases, they also have the option of writing off the expenditures over several years.

¶ 1602 Deduct or capitalize research & experimental expenditures.

Taxpayers can choose whether to immediately deduct or to capitalize research and experimental (R&E) expenditures. (Code Sec. 174(a)(1)) If the taxpayer adopts current expense treatment, he must use it for all qualifying expenses for the year he adopts it and for all later years, unless he gets IRS permission to switch. (Code Sec. 174(a)(3))[35]

For R&E expenditures that aren't chargeable to depreciable or depletable property, instead of current deduction or capitalizing, the taxpayer can elect (use Form 4562) to deduct the expenditures ratably over 60 months or longer, beginning with the month the taxpayer first realized benefits from the expenditures. (Code Sec. 174(b)(1); Reg § 1.174-4(b)(1))[36]

In general, expenditures that qualify as R&E costs are research and development costs in the experimental or laboratory sense. This includes all costs incident to the development or improvement of a product, including a pilot model, process, formula, invention, technique, patent or similar property. (Reg § 1.174-2(a)) The ultimate success, failure, sale, or other use of the research or property resulting from research or experimentation is not relevant to this definition. (Prop Reg. § 1.174-2(a)(1) [Taxpayers may rely])[37]

All taxpayers, including partners and S corporation shareholders, may elect to deduct all or any portion of these costs ratably over ten years. (Code Sec. 59(e)(1); Reg § 1.59-1)[38]

For limitations on deductions for R&E expenses that also qualify for the research credit or the orphan drug credit, see ¶ 2319 and ¶2328, respectively. For alternative minimum tax treatment of research and experimentation expenditures, see ¶ 3209.

¶ 1603 Legal and Accounting Expenses.

Legal expenses and accounting and related expenses may be deductible.

For expenses of determining or contesting tax liability, see ¶1513.

¶ 1604 Legal expenses.

Attorney's fees, court costs and other legal expenses can qualify as deductible business expenses. Legal expenses aren't deductible if they are either capital expenditures or a personal expense of the taxpayer. (Code Sec. 162, Code Sec. 262(a), Code Sec. 263)[39] Qualified legal expenses can include expenses incurred in litigation, for legal advice, and for the drafting of instruments,[40] but not to acquire, perfect or defend title to property. (Reg § 1.212-1(k))[41] A legal retainer must be capitalized if it is applied to legal expenses associated with the acquisition of a business.[42]

34. ¶L-6812; ¶4674; TD ¶261,053
35. ¶L-3117; ¶1744; TD ¶306,508
36. ¶L-3121 *et seq.*; ¶1744; TD ¶306,512
37. ¶L-3117; ¶1744; TD ¶306,505
38. ¶A-8194; ¶594; TD ¶695,503

39. ¶s L-2901, L-2969; ¶1624.040; TD ¶305,004
40. ¶L-2902; ¶1624.040; TD ¶305,004
41. ¶L-2908; ¶2634.01; TD ¶305,010
42. ¶L-2901.1; TD ¶305,002

¶ 1605   Accounting and related expenses.

Fees for bookkeeping and accounting work incurred in the operation of the taxpayer's business are deductible.[43]

¶ 1606   Insurance Premiums. ▬▬▬▬▬▬▬▬▬▬▬

Certain premiums that qualify as trade or business expenses, or as investment expenses, are deductible.

¶ 1607   Insurance premiums on nonlife policies.

Premiums for insurance against various types of risks, such as property damage, are generally deductible as business expenses (Code Sec. 162; Reg § 1.162-1(a)), but premiums on policies on taxpayer's residence, or for other personal use, aren't. (Code Sec. 262(a); Reg § 1.262-1(b))[44] Payments to an insurance company to assume capped costs certain to be incurred in the future isn't insurance for tax purposes.[45]

Self-insurance reserve funds aren't deductible even if taxpayer can't get business insurance coverage for certain business risks.[46] Neither are payments to "captive" insurance subsidiaries or other similar arrangements where there's no true risk-shifting.[47] But a limited deduction is allowed for certain payments made to a medical malpractice self-insurance pool.[48]

Premiums are nondeductible capital expenditures where paid for property insurance during construction. So are premiums for title insurance and for public liability and worker's compensation insurance paid in connection with the construction of a building.[49]

¶ 1608   Life insurance premiums.

Life insurance premiums aren't deductible if the taxpayer is directly or indirectly a beneficiary. (Code Sec. 264(a)(1); Reg § 1.264-1) See ¶1526. For example, the cost of a corporation's key person insurance isn't deductible.[50] Premiums paid by an individual for personal life insurance aren't deductible. (Reg § 1.262-1(b)(1))[1] For group-term premiums, see ¶1526.

¶ 1609   Time for deducting insurance premiums.

If a cash basis taxpayer pays an otherwise deductible premium for one year's coverage which applies in part to the following tax year, the entire premium is deductible in the year paid. But if premiums for several years are paid in advance, IRS and most courts require the premium to be amortized and deducted over the life of the policy, though one court has allowed a full deduction to a cash basis taxpayer in the year of payment where the taxpayer had consistently deducted premiums in the year of payment.[2]

For an accrual basis taxpayer, deductibility of an accrued liability for insurance expense is determined under the economic performance rules—that is, when the premium is paid. But where prepaid premiums cover more than one year, an accrual basis taxpayer must prorate the premium paid in advance over the life of the policy.[3]

For the "12-month rule" exception to capitalization of certain intangibles, see ¶1656.

43. ¶L-2959; TD ¶305,061
44. ¶L-3500 *et seq.*; ¶1624.032; TD ¶304,404
45. ¶L-3517
46. ¶L-3518; ¶1624.032; TD ¶304,423
47. ¶L-3520; ¶1624.032; TD ¶304,425
48. ¶L-3515; TD ¶304,413

49. ¶L-3530; TD ¶304,429
50. ¶L-3407; ¶2644; TD ¶304,006
1. ¶L-3401; ¶2644; TD ¶304,001
2. ¶L-3528; ¶1624.081; TD ¶441,410
3. ¶L-3526 *et seq.*; ¶1624.081; TD ¶304,430 *et seq.*

¶ 1610   Bribes, Kickbacks, Fines and Penalties. ▪▪▪▪▪▪▪▪▪▪▪▪▪▪▪▪▪▪▪▪▪

Certain illegal bribes, kickbacks, rebates and other payments aren't deductible. Nor are fines and penalties for violation of a law, including tax penalties.

Public policy isn't a ground for denying a deduction. Unless a payment is nondeductible by law, it's deductible if ordinary and necessary. (Reg § 1.162-1)[4]

¶ 1611   Bribes and other illegal payments.

No deduction is allowed for any illegal bribe, kickback or other illegal payment under any law of the U.S., or of a state (if the state law is generally enforced), that subjects the payor to a criminal penalty or the loss of license or privilege to engage in business, whether or not that penalty or loss of license actually occurs. A kickback includes a payment in consideration of the referral of a client, patient, or customer. (Code Sec. 162(c)(2))[5]

No deduction is allowed for any kickback, rebate, or bribe made by any provider of services, supplier, physician, or other person who furnishes Medicare or Medicaid items or services, if made in connection with the furnishing of such items or services or the making or receiving of such payments. A kickback includes a payment for the referral of a client, patient, or customer. For these payments, deduction is denied regardless of legality. (Code Sec. 162(c)(3))[6]

No business expense deduction is allowed for any illegal bribe or kickback made directly or indirectly to any federal, state, or local public official or employee. If the payment is to an official or an employee of a foreign government, no deduction is allowed if the payment violates the U.S. Foreign Corrupt Practices Act. (Code Sec. 162(c)(1))[7]

Business kickbacks, fee-splitting, etc., that aren't specifically disallowed are deductible if they qualify as ordinary and necessary.[8]

¶ 1612   Illegal businesses and drug trafficking.

The ordinary and necessary expenses incurred in operating an illegal business are deductible, even though payment of the expense and the acts performed by the employees of the business are illegal (e.g., a bookmaker's expenses).[9] But there's no deduction or credit for amounts paid or incurred in illegal drug trafficking (Code Sec. 280E), although gross receipts may be adjusted for cost of goods sold.[10]

¶ 1613   Fines and penalties.

No business expense deduction is allowed for fines or similar penalties paid to a government for the violation of any law. (Code Sec. 162(f))[11] For example, state law penalties on public school teachers for striking aren't deductible. Similarly, penalties paid for violating federal environmental protection laws aren't deductible.[12]

Also, penalties paid in connection with federal, state, and local taxes are generally not deductible—for example, penalties for negligence, delinquency, or fraud relating to federal taxes (Reg § 1.162-21(b)), and for failure to withhold federal payroll taxes.[13]

But, compensatory damages paid to a government do not constitute a fine or penalty. (Reg § 1.162-21(b)(2))

---

4. ¶L-2609; ¶1624.377; TD ¶304,804
5. ¶L-2606; ¶1624.384; TD ¶304,801
6. ¶L-2608; ¶1624.384; TD ¶304,807
7. ¶L-2601; ¶1624.384; TD ¶304,801
8. ¶L-2601; ¶1624.384; TD ¶304,804

9. ¶L-2631; ¶1624.382; TD ¶304,815
10. ¶L-2632; ¶280E4; TD ¶304,815
11. ¶L-2701 *et seq.*; ¶1624.388; TD ¶302,501
12. ¶L-2701; ¶1624.388; TD ¶302,501
13. ¶L-2709; ¶1624.388; TD ¶302,507

¶ 1614   Domestic Production Activities Deduction. ▰▰▰▰▰▰▰▰

Taxpayers are allowed a domestic production activities deduction (DPAD) under Code Sec. 199 equal to the specified percentage for the tax year of the taxpayer's qualified production activities income for the tax year, subject to certain limits.

¶ 1615   Deduction for manufacturing and production activities—Form 8903.

Taxpayers may claim a deduction on Form 8903 generally equal to 9% of the lesser of: (1) "qualified production activities income" (¶1616) for the tax year or (2) taxable income (modified adjusted gross income, for individuals) without regard to this deduction, for the tax year. (Code Sec. 199(a); Reg § 1.199-1(a))

The deduction as computed above is limited to 50% of the W-2 wages of the employer for the tax year. W-2 wages are the sum of the aggregate amounts that must be included on the employees' Forms W-2 under Code Sec. 6051(a)(3) (i.e., wages subject to withholding) and Code Sec. 6051(a)(8) (elective deferrals), that are made by the taxpayer during the calendar year that ends in the tax year. (Code Sec. 199(b); Reg § 1.199-1(a))[14] W-2 wages are the wages of employees including common-law employees and officers of a corporate employer which are properly included in a return filed with the Social Security Administration on or before the 60th day after the due date (including extensions) for that return. W-2 wages only include amounts that are properly allocable to domestic production gross receipts (DPGR) (¶1616). (Code Sec. 199(b)(2); Reg § 1.199-2(a)(1)) This allocation may be made using any reasonable method that satisfies IRS based on all facts and circumstances. Regs provide safe harbors for calculating W-2 wages. (Reg § 1.199-2(e)(2))[15]

The deduction is directly available to all taxpayers except pass-through entities (partnerships, S corporations, trusts and estates) and is available to owners of pass-through entities. (Code Sec. 199(d)) The deduction for partnerships and S corporations is determined at the partner or shareholder level. Partners or shareholders are treated as having W-2 wages equal to their allocable share of the entity's DPGR-related W-2 wages for the tax year. (Code Sec. 199(d)(1)(A); Reg § 1.199-5)

The otherwise allowable Code Sec. 199 deduction of a taxpayer with oil-related qualified production activities income is reduced by 3% of the least of (1) oil-related qualified production activities income for the tax year; (2) qualified production activities income for the tax year; or (3) taxable income (or for individuals, AGI), determined without regard to the domestic production activities deduction. (Code Sec. 199(d)(9)(A))

For treatment of the deduction for alternative minimum tax, see ¶3201.

¶ 1616   Qualified production activities income defined.

"Qualified production activities income" is equal to domestic production gross receipts (DPGR), reduced by the sum of: (1) the costs of goods sold that are allocable to the receipts; (2) other deductions, expenses, or losses that are allocable to these receipts; and (3) a ratable portion of other deductions, expenses, and losses that are not directly allocable to the receipts or to another class of income. (Code Sec. 199(c))[16]

DPGR is the taxpayer's gross receipts derived from:

   . . . any lease, rental, license, sale, exchange or other disposition of qualifying production property—i.e., tangible personal property, many types of computer software and certain sound recordings (Code Sec. 199(c)(5))[17] —that was manufactured, produced, grown or extracted by the taxpayer in whole or in significant part within the U.S. (Code

---

14. ¶L-4325; ¶1994; TD ¶307,800   16. ¶L-4367; ¶1994.084; TD ¶307,804
15. ¶L-4385.1; ¶1994.010; TD ¶307,803   17. ¶L-4352; ¶1994.064; TD ¶307,805

Sec. 199(c)(4)(A)(i)(I)),[18] Gross receipts from providing computer software to customers for their direct use while connected to the Internet may be treated as DPGR if certain conditions are met. (Reg § 1.199-3(i)(6)(iii))

. . . any lease, rental, license, sale, exchange or other disposition of qualified films produced by the taxpayer. (Code Sec. 199(c)(4)(A)(i)(II)) In general, the taxpayer's production of the qualified film must be substantial in nature, taking into account all the facts and circumstances. (Reg § 1.199-3(k)(6)) A qualified film (including any copyrights, trademarks, or other intangibles with respect to the film) is one for which 50% of the total compensation for production of the film is for services performed in the U.S. by actors, production personnel, directors and producers, and which does not depict certain sexually explicit conduct. (Code Sec. 199(c)(6))[19] A partner owning at least a 20% capital interest in the partnership is treated as having engaged directly in any film produced by the entity and a partnership is treated as having engaged directly in any film produced by any partner who owns at least a 20% capital interest in the entity (similar rules apply to S corporations). (Code Sec. 199(d)(1)(A)(iv))

. . . any sale, exchange or other disposition of electricity, natural gas, or potable water produced by the taxpayer in the U.S. (Code Sec. 199(c)(4)(A)(i)(III))

. . . construction of real property performed in the U.S. by a taxpayer engaged in the active conduct of a construction trade or business in the ordinary course of that trade or business (Code Sec. 199(c)(4)(A)(ii)),[20] including construction and substantial renovation of residential and commercial buildings and infrastructure. A taxpayer need not own the property being constructed, and more than one taxpayer may qualify for the same construction project.[21] Gross receipts from renting property that the taxpayer builds are not derived from construction and are not eligible for the deduction.[22] Generally, construction includes certain grading, demolition (including under Code Sec. 280B (¶1783)), clearing, excavating, and other activities that physically transform the land. (Reg § 1.199-3(m)(2)(iii), Reg § 1.199-3(m))

. . . engineering or architectural services with respect to the construction of real property in the U.S. performed in the U.S. by a taxpayer engaged in the active conduct of an engineering or architectural services trade or business in the ordinary course of that trade or business. (Code Sec. 199(c)(4)(A)(iii))[23]

Various de minimis rules are available for the computation of DPGR. (Reg § 1.199-1(d), Reg § 1.199-3)[24] Statistical sampling methods may be used if detailed conditions are met.[25] For a taxpayer's first eight tax years beginning after 2005, and before 2014, Puerto Rico is included in the term "U.S." in determining DPGR.

Qualifying production property is treated as manufactured, produced, grown or extracted in whole or in significant part within the U.S. if, based on all of the facts and circumstances, the manufacturing, production, etc., activity performed in the U.S. is substantial in nature, or, under a safe harbor, if the direct labor and overhead costs incurred by the taxpayer in the U.S. for the manufacture, production, growth, or extraction of the property are at least 20% of the taxpayer's (1) total cost for the property, or (2) in a transaction without cost of goods sold (e.g., a lease), unadjusted basis in the property. (Reg § 1.199-3(g)(3)(i))[26]

DPGR does not include gross receipts derived from:

. . . the sale of food or beverages prepared by the taxpayer at a retail establishment (Code Sec. 199(c)(4)(B)(i)), i.e., tangible property used in the trade or business of selling food or beverages to the public if retail (rather than wholesale) sales occur at the facility. A facility

18. ¶L-4327.1; ¶1994.036; TD ¶307,805
19. ¶L-4356; ¶1994.070; TD ¶307,805
20. ¶L-4340; ¶1994.036; TD ¶307,805
21. ¶L-4335; ¶1994.036; TD ¶307,805
22. ¶L-4350; ¶1994.036; TD ¶307,805

23. ¶L-4338; ¶1994.036; TD ¶307,805
24. ¶L-4338; ¶1994.034; TD ¶307,853
25. ¶L-4336.4; ¶1994.129; TD ¶307,821.1
26. ¶L-4330; ¶1994.036; TD ¶307,805

won't be treated as a retail establishment if less than 5% of total gross receipts for the tax year derived from the sale of food or beverages prepared at the facility are for retail sales. If a facility is a retail establishment, but food or beverages are prepared there and sold at wholesale, the taxpayer may allocate its gross receipts.[27]

... the transmission or distribution of electricity, natural gas, or potable water. (Code Sec. 199(c)(4)(B)(ii))[28]

... the lease, rental, license, sale, exchange, or other disposition of land. (Code Sec. 199(c)(4)(B)(iii))[29]

... property leased, licensed, or rented by the taxpayer for use by any related person (defined in Code Sec. 199(c)(7)(B)). (Code Sec. 199(c)(7)(A))[30]

In computing qualified production activities income, taxpayers may allocate cost of goods sold, and other expenses, deductions, etc., between DPGR and other gross receipts under any reasonable method. However, if the taxpayer has the necessary information readily available, and can do so without undue burden and expense, the taxpayer must make these allocations using a specific identification method under the regs. (Reg § 1.199-1(d)(2))[31]

¶ 1617   Miscellaneous Business Expenses.

Royalty payments, circulation costs, mine exploration and development costs, and other miscellaneous business costs are deductible subject to certain conditions and limits. A taxpayer may elect to capitalize some deductible expenses, and elect to deduct other expenses that are normally capitalized.

¶ 1618   Royalty payments.

Royalty payments made for the right to use patents, copyrights and similar rights are deductible.[32] Payments to acquire the property itself are capital expenditures.[33] One court has held that a manufacturer may currently deduct sales-based royalties paid under trademark licensing agreements, but IRS disagrees and says such royalties must be capitalized under Code Sec. 263A (¶1667).[34]

¶ 1619   Circulation costs.

Publishers of periodicals can deduct currently their expenditures to establish, maintain and increase circulation. (Code Sec. 173)[35] Or, instead, they may elect to capitalize those costs. (Reg § 1.173-1(c))[36] A taxpayer may elect (use Form 4562) to amortize circulation costs over three years beginning with the year the expenditure is made. (Code Sec. 59(e)(1); Reg § 1.59-1) For alternative minimum tax treatment of circulation costs, see ¶3210.

¶ 1620   Taxes, interest, and carrying charges—election to capitalize.

Some taxes and carrying charges that would normally be deducted currently or amortized may be capitalized if the taxpayer so elects.[37] For depreciable property, this has the effect of deferring the deduction to later years as depreciation. For nondepreciable property, such as unimproved real estate, the capitalized expenses increase basis and reduce gain (or increase loss) on a later sale of the property. (Code Sec. 266; Reg § 1.212-1(n), Reg § 1.266-1)[38]

---

27. ¶L-4330; ¶1994.036; TD ¶307,805
28. ¶L-4334; ¶1994.036; TD ¶307,805
29. ¶L-4350; ¶1994.074 *et seq.*; TD ¶307,805
30. ¶L-4346; ¶1994.038; TD ¶307,805
31. ¶L-4367.1; ¶1994.084; TD ¶307,804
32. ¶L-3201; ¶1624.284; TD ¶307,501
33. ¶L-3203; ¶1624.284; TD ¶307,505
34. ¶G-5494
35. ¶L-2213; ¶1734.01; TD ¶300,515
36. ¶L-2215 *et seq.*; ¶1734; TD ¶300,516
37. ¶L-5901; ¶2664; TD ¶256,221
38. ¶L-5901; ¶2664; TD ¶256,221

The capitalization election may be made:

. . . for taxes, mortgage interest (subject to the interest capitalization rules at ¶1669) and deductible carrying charges on unimproved and unproductive real property. (Reg § 1.266-1(b))[39]

. . . by a taxpayer engaged in the development of real estate or the construction of an improvement to real estate, for the following items relating to the project: loan interest; taxes measured by compensation paid to employees and taxes imposed on the purchase of materials, or on the storage, use, or other consumption of materials; and other necessary charges, including fire insurance premiums. (Reg § 1.266-1(b)(1))[40]

. . . for interest on a loan to finance the purchase, transportation, and installation of machinery and other assets, state and local taxes imposed on the taxpayer, transportation, storage, use or other consumption of the property, and state and local taxes, including sales and use taxes, and state and federal unemployment taxes, and the taxpayer's share of federal social security taxes on the wages of employees engaged in transportation and installation of the assets. (Reg § 1.266-1)[41]

¶ 1621 Architectural and transportation barrier removal expenses.

A taxpayer can elect to treat up to $15,000 of qualified architectural and transportation barrier removal expenses as a deduction rather than as a charge to capital account. (Code Sec. 190(a), Code Sec. 190(c)) To elect, claim the deduction as a separate item identified as such on the timely filed (including extension) return for the tax year for which the election is to apply. (Reg § 1.190-3(a))[42] For the credit for eligible access expenditures, see ¶2323.

¶ 1622 Serial contingent payments for franchises, trademarks, or trade names.

In the case of a transfer of a franchise, trademark or trade name, a deduction is allowed to the transferee for serial payments contingent on the productivity, use, or disposition of the franchise, trademark or trade name transferred. (Code Sec. 1253(d)(1))[43]

¶ 1623 Computer software.

The tax treatment of computer software depends on whether it is bought, licensed, or self-developed.

Purchased software. The cost of software bought by itself, rather than being bundled into hardware costs, is capitalized and amortized over 36 months using the straight-line method. This rule *doesn't* apply to any software that's a Code Sec. 197 intangible (see ¶1974). (Reg § 1.167(a)-14(b)(1))[44] However, the cost of software included or bundled, without being separately stated, in the cost of hardware is capitalized and depreciated as a part of the hardware cost. (Reg § 1.167(a)-14(b)(2))

Licensed software. The cost of software licensed for a specific period of time (unless properly chargeable to capital account) is deducted over that term, in the same way that a business tenant may under Reg § 1.162-11 deduct the cost of acquiring a leasehold over the lease term. (Reg § 1.167(a)-14(b)(2))[45] Rental payments for leased software are deducted just like any other rentals.[46]

Self-developed software. Costs of developing computer software (other than software that is a Code Sec. 197 intangible (¶1974)) can be either: (1) consistently expensed currently under

---

39. ¶L-5901; ¶2664; TD ¶256,223
40. ¶L-5904; ¶2664; TD ¶256,222
41. ¶s L-5901, L-5905; ¶2664; TD ¶256,224
42. ¶L-3151 *et seq.*; ¶1904 *et seq.*; TD ¶256,219

43. ¶I-8415 *et seq.*; ¶12534.01
44. ¶L-7935; ¶1674.033; TD ¶265,434
45. ¶L-5621; ¶1674.033; TD ¶265,434
46. ¶L-5615 *et seq.*; ¶1674.033; TD ¶265,434

Code Sec. 174(a), or (2) consistently treated as capital expenditures recoverable through deductions for ratable amortization over a period of 60 months from the date of completion of the development under Code Sec. 174(b) or over 36 months from the date the software is placed in service under Code Sec. 167(f)(1).[47] Costs of developing software may also qualify as research and experimental expenditures under Code Sec. 174 (see ¶1601).[48]

If costs for developing computer software that the taxpayer elected to treat as deferred expenses under Code Sec. 174(b) (¶1601) result in the development of property subject to depreciation, the 36-month amortization rule applies to the unrecovered costs. (Reg § 1.167(a)-14(b)(1))[49]

¶ 1624 Stock reacquisition expenses.

No deduction is allowed for any amount paid or incurred by a corporation in connection with the reacquisition of its stock (e.g., greenmail) or of the stock of any related person as specially defined in Code Sec. 465(b)(3)(C). Amounts deductible as interest under Code Sec. 163 or as dividends paid under Code Sec. 561 are among expenses not subject to this rule. (Code Sec. 162(k)) The no-deduction rule doesn't apply to deductions for amounts properly allocable to indebtedness (e.g., loan commitment fees) and amortized over the term of the indebtedness. (Code Sec. 162(k)(2)(A)(ii))[50]

¶ 1625 Co-op housing maintenance and lease expenses.

Cooperative housing maintenance and lease expenses are deductible if the cooperative unit is used in a trade or business or for the production of income. However, no deduction is allowed to the co-op stockholder for any payment to the co-op (in excess of the stockholder's share of taxes and interest) to the extent the payment is properly allocable to amounts chargeable to the co-op's capital account. The basis of the stockholder's stock is increased by the amount of any deduction disallowed under this rule. (Code Sec. 216(d))[1]

¶ 1626 Mine exploration costs.

Domestic mine exploration costs incurred before a mine has reached the development stage are nondeductible capital expenditures. However, taxpayers may elect to deduct mining exploration expenditures for minerals (other than oil and gas) that qualify for percentage depletion (Code Sec. 617).[2]

Deducted exploration costs are subject to recapture when the mine reaches the producing stage, when taxpayer receives a bonus or royalty, or when he disposes of all or part of the property, whichever happens first (except where IRS allows recapture to be postponed on disposition of a *part* interest). (Code Sec. 617(b)(1), Code Sec. 1254(a)(1); Reg § 1.1254-1(b))[3]

All taxpayers, including partners and S corporation shareholders, may elect (use Form 4562) to deduct all or any portion of their deductible mine exploration costs ratably over ten years. (Code Sec. 59(e); Reg § 1.59-1)[4]

Corporations' deductions for exploration costs are cut back 30% if they elect to write off the costs in the year they are incurred. (Code Sec. 291(b)(1)) The amount cut back is amortized over 60 months. (Code Sec. 291(b))[5]

47. ¶L-5616; ¶1674.033; TD ¶256,236
48. ¶L-5615; ¶1674.033; TD ¶256,234
49. ¶L-7935; ¶1674.033; TD ¶265,434
50. ¶s L-5305, L-5411; ¶1624.402; TD ¶301,033
1. ¶K-5900 *et seq.*; ¶2164.01; TD ¶213,014

2. ¶N-3103; ¶6174
3. ¶N-3601 *et seq.*; ¶6174.01
4. ¶N-3114; ¶594
5. ¶N-3104; ¶2914; TD ¶600,502

¶ 1627   Mine development costs.

A taxpayer who incurs expenditures to develop minerals other than oil or gas may: (1) deduct those expenditures in the year they were paid or incurred (Code Sec. 616(a));[6] (2) elect to treat them as deferred expenses and deduct them ratably as the units of produced minerals benefited by the expense are sold (Code Sec. 616(b); Reg § 1.616-2(a));[7] or (3) treat them as deferred expenses and elect (use Form 4562) to amortize them ratably over ten years. (Code Sec. 59(e); Reg § 1.59-1)[8]

Corporations' deductions for mine development costs are cut back 30% if the corporation elects to write off the costs in the year incurred. (Code Sec. 291(b)(1)(B)) The amount cut-back is amortized over 60 months. (Code Sec. 291(b))[9]

Deducted mine development costs are recaptured (on Form 4797) as ordinary income on disposition of the property. (Code Sec. 1254(a)(1); Reg § 1.1254-1(b))[10]

¶ 1628   Intangible oil and gas and geothermal well drilling and development costs.

Geological and geophysical costs incurred in exploring for oil and gas are capital expenditures.[11] Taxpayers, however, may capitalize, amortize (over 60 months) or expense the so-called intangible drilling and development costs (IDCs) of oil, gas and geothermal wells. (Code Sec. 59(e); Reg § 1.59-1; Code Sec. 263(c); Reg § 1.612-4, Reg § 1.612-5)[12] In general, such intangible costs include only those costs that in themselves don't have a salvage value, such as labor and fuel.[13] For alternative minimum tax treatment of IDCs, see ¶3208.

Deducted IDCs are recaptured (on Form 4797) as ordinary income on disposition of the oil or gas wells. (Code Sec. 1254(a)(1)(A); Reg § 1.1254-1(b))[14]

¶ 1629   Lobbying costs, influencing public on legislation.

Deductible business expenses don't include:

. . . Any amount paid or incurred (1) in influencing legislation; (2) in connection with participation in or intervention in any political campaign or any attempt to influence the general public with respect to elections, legislative matters, or referendums; or (3) in communicating directly with a covered executive branch official on official matters (Code Sec. 162(e)(1)).

. . . The portion of dues paid to a tax-exempt organization allocable to lobbying by the organization for which no deduction is allowed, if the organization informs taxpayer of the nondeductible portion. (Code Sec. 162(e)(3))

Taxpayers must allocate costs to legislative-branch lobbying and executive-branch lobbying in determining the nondeductible amount by consistently using a reasonable method. (Reg § 1.162-28(a)(1), Reg § 1.162-29(c)(2))[15]

In-house expenditures of $2,000 or less per year aren't subject to these rules. (Code Sec. 162(e)(5)(B)(i))

The disallowance concerning influencing legislation, above, doesn't apply to legislation of a local government. (Code Sec. 162(e)(2)(A))[16]

---

6. ¶N-3116; ¶6164; TD ¶213,512
7. ¶N-3123; ¶6164
8. ¶N-3124; ¶6164.04; TD ¶695,503
9. ¶N-3104; ¶2914
10. ¶N-3309 *et seq.*
11. ¶N-3201; ¶6124.001; TD ¶695,503

12. ¶N-3202 *et seq.*; ¶6124.008
13. ¶N-3206; ¶6124.009
14. ¶N-3406; ¶12,544 *et seq.*
15. ¶L-2400 *et seq.*; ¶1624.395; TD ¶306,000 *et seq.*
16. ¶L-2401 *et seq.*; ¶1624.395; TD ¶306,012

¶ 1630   Civil damages.

Civil damages paid under judgments and out-of-court settlements arising out of normal business operations are deductible as business expenses[17] if the litigation is directly connected with the taxpayer's business.[18]

No deduction is allowed for two-thirds of treble damage or settlement payments to private parties where the taxpayer (payor) in a criminal proceeding for violation of federal anti-trust law is convicted or pleads guilty or no contest. (Code Sec. 162(g); Reg § 1.162-22)[19]

¶ 1631   Employee Business Expenses.   ▮▮▮▮▮▮▮▮▮▮▮

Employees are engaged in the trade or business of being employees and thus can deduct certain employment-connected business expenses, such as travel expenses, union dues, work clothes, etc.

Unreimbursed employee business expenses are generally deductible only as miscellaneous itemized deductions subject to the 2%-of-AGI floor, see ¶3110. (Reg § 1.67-1T(a)(1)(i))[20] For unreimbursed moving expenses, see ¶1646 *et seq*. For travel expenses of reservists more than 100 miles from home, see ¶1553.

¶ 1632   Cost of seeking and securing employment.

An employee can deduct the expenses of seeking new employment in his same trade or business, whether or not he gets the new job. Any local transportation expenses and travel expenses away from home and costs such as printing and postage are deductible.

An employee can't deduct the cost of seeking employment in a different trade or business even if he gets the job. If an unemployed person is seeking a job and no substantial lack of continuity occurred between the time of the past employment and the seeking of the new employment, his trade or business is the services performed for his past employer. Where there's no continuity, or where a person looks for a job for the first time, the expenses aren't deductible, even if a job results.

If an individual travels to a destination where he both seeks new employment in his present trade or business and engages in personal activities, his round-trip travel expenses are deductible only if the trip is primarily related to seeking the new employment. Expenses allocable to seeking the job at the destination are deductible even if the travel expenses aren't.[21]

¶ 1633   Labor union dues, fees, and assessments.

Deduction has been permitted for dues, fines paid to remain in the union, strike funds, compulsory payments for unemployment benefits, and a mandatory service charge paid to a union by a nonmember. Deductions were denied for noncompulsory unemployment benefit fund payments, assessments for sick, accident, or death benefits, and other payments in exchange for valuable benefits.[22]

¶ 1634   Uniforms and special work clothes.

Deduction for the cost and maintenance of clothing is allowed if: (1) the employee's occupation is one that specifically requires special apparel or equipment as a condition of employment; and (2) the special apparel or equipment isn't adaptable to general or continued usage

---

17. ¶L-2500 *et seq*.; ¶1624.040; TD ¶303,500
18. ¶L-2502; ¶1624.040; TD ¶303,501
19. ¶L-2714; ¶1624.391; TD ¶303,511

20. ¶L-3900 *et seq*.; ¶1624.067; TD ¶561,603
21. ¶L-3850 *et seq*.; ¶1624.067; TD ¶351,503
22. ¶s L-3908, L-3910; ¶1624.067; TD ¶351,508

so as to take the place of ordinary clothing.

Thus, protective clothing, such as safety shoes, helmets, fishermen's boots, work gloves, oil clothes, etc., are deductible if required for the job. But work clothing and standard work shoes aren't deductible even if the worker's union requires them. [23]

¶ 1635   Other deductible employee expenses.

These include:

. . . membership dues in professional or business societies,[24]

. . . small tools and supplies,[25]

. . . salesman's briefcase used in business,[26]

. . . expenses incurred by a securities analyst for a stock brokerage firm in seeking to get new business for the employer and by so doing increase his own salary,[27]

. . . expenses of business use of home, see ¶1638 *et seq.*, and

. . . qualifying education expenses, see ¶2226.

¶ 1636   Deductions for expenses of professional individuals.

Individuals can deduct the expenses of their business or profession, such as supplies, rent, transportation, business, travel, telephone, etc., if they are self-employed. But a professional who is an employee may deduct only expenses allowed to employees.

Professionals, whether or not employees, can also deduct expenses peculiar to their professions such as dues to professional organizations, continuing professional education, subscriptions to professional journals, malpractice insurance and payments to assistants. The cost of professional books, furniture, instruments and equipment are deductible if their useful lives are short.[28] But expenses incurred by business or professional people to build up their reputations are capital expenditures to develop or enhance goodwill, unless the expenses can be tied directly to the production of added income.[29] The following material highlights the rules on deductions for professionals, etc.:

Accountants can't deduct costs of a CPA review course or the CPA exam. [30]

Lawyers have been allowed to deduct bar association dues, but not costs of securing admission to practice (including bar examination fees, expenses to be admitted to second state bar, travel) (Reg § 1.162-5, Reg § 1.212-1(f)) which must be amortized over taxpayer's remaining life expectancy. The cost of bar review courses can't be amortized.[31]

Doctors and dentists can't deduct costs of securing the right to practice, fees on their initial licensing, etc. (Reg § 1.212-1(f)[32] Fees paid to a hospital for staff privileges are amortizable over taxpayer's useful life, or the useful life of the hospital privilege if shorter.[33]

Teachers can deduct the cost of membership in professional societies, educational journals, and travel to teachers' conventions and similar events. Professors may deduct the costs of research, writing, or lecturing that the college or university expects, even though they receive no payment or extra compensation. Deductible costs may include travel and research costs.[34]

Costs of entering a profession or securing the right to practice are nondeductible. (Reg § 1.212-1(f))[35]

---

23. ¶L-3801; ¶1624.067; TD ¶351,001
24. ¶s L-3918, L-4100; ¶1624.195; TD ¶307,721
25. ¶L-3918; TD ¶351,517
26. ¶L-3918; TD ¶351,517
27. ¶L-4416
28. ¶L-4101
29. ¶L-4100 *et seq.*; ¶1624.191; TD ¶307,702

30. ¶L-3719; ¶1624.193; TD ¶302,019
31. ¶L-4102; ¶s 1624.193, 1624.195; TD ¶256,202
32. ¶s L-4100, L-4101; ¶1624.193; TD ¶307,702
33. ¶L-4107; TD ¶307,705
34. ¶L-4108; ¶s 1624.191, 1624.195; TD ¶302,035
35. ¶L-4101; ¶1624.193; TD ¶307,702

¶ 1637   Impairment-related work expenses.

Impairment-related work expenses are deductible (on Form 2106 or Form 2106-EZ). They are ordinary and necessary expenses, including attendant care services (e.g., a blind taxpayer's use of a reader) at the place of employment, to enable an individual who has a handicap to work. (Code Sec. 67(d)) Impairment-related work expenses are itemized deductions but aren't subject to the 2%-of-AGI floor. (Code Sec. 67(b)(6))[36]

¶ 1638   Residence Used in Part for Business—Home Office Deduction. ▄▄▄▄▄▄▄

Employees and self-employed individuals may take office-at-home deductions if tough tests are met.

The general rule is that no deduction is allowed for the business use of a dwelling unit that's also used by the taxpayer as a residence during the tax year. But exceptions, discussed below, allow deductions under certain circumstances. (Code Sec. 280A(a)) The disallowance rule applies to individuals, trusts, estates, partnerships, and S corporations. However, disallowance doesn't apply to any deduction allowable without regard to its connection with either a business or income-producing activity. (Code Sec. 280A(b)) For example, the deductions allowed under Code Sec. 163 for interest, Code Sec. 164 for certain taxes, and Code Sec. 165 for casualty losses may be claimed without regard to their connection with the taxpayer's trade or business or income-producing activities. In effect, this means that the disallowance applies only to otherwise deductible business expenses (Code Sec. 162) and depreciation.[37]

The home office deduction isn't allowed for expenses of an income-producing activity, unless the activity is a trade or business.[38]

Allowable home-office expenses are deducted on Form 1040, Schedule A (employees), Form 1040, Schedule C (most self-employed persons, who must also attach Form 8829), and Form 1040, Schedule F (farmers).

In situations in the following paragraphs, otherwise allowable business expenses are deductible (subject to the limits discussed at ¶1642 and ¶1643) even though they are incurred in connection with the business use of a portion of a taxpayer's residence. In addition, the cost of capital improvements made to the entire residence may be recovered through depreciation to the extent allocable to the portion of the residence used for the taxpayer's business.[39]

An employee gets a deduction (subject to the 2%-of-AGI floor on miscellaneous itemized deductions, see ¶3110) only if the exclusive business use of a portion of his residence is for the convenience of his employer. (Code Sec. 280A(c)(1))[40]

Charges (including taxes) for basic local telephone services for the first telephone line for any residence are treated as personal expenses. (Code Sec. 262(b))[41]

¶ 1639   Residence used as principal place of business.

Deduction is allowed to the extent allocable to a portion of a residence *used exclusively* and *on a regular basis* (¶1642) as the taxpayer's principal place of business for *any* trade or business of the taxpayer. (Code Sec. 280A(c)(1)(A))[42]

Following are the two ways to meet the principal place of business requirement:

(1) Under the statutory administrative/management activities test, the principal place of business test is met if a portion of the home is used for the administrative or management

---

36. ¶L-3906 *et seq.*; ¶674; TD ¶351,506
37. ¶L-1301 *et seq.*; ¶280A4 *et seq.*; TD ¶258,001 *et seq.*
38. ¶L-1305; ¶280A4.013; TD ¶258,002
39. ¶L-1306 *et seq.*; ¶280A4.04; TD ¶258,039

40. ¶L-1348 *et seq.*; ¶280A4.018; TD ¶258,021
41. ¶L-1307 *et seq.*; ¶2624; TD ¶258,035
42. ¶s L-1317, L-1324; ¶280A4.014; TD ¶s 258,005, 258,007

activities of any trade or business of the taxpayer, but only if there is no other fixed location where the taxpayer conducts substantial administrative or management activities of that trade or business. (Code Sec. 280A(c)(1)) Examples of administrative or management activities are: billing customers, clients or patients; keeping books and records; ordering supplies; setting up appointments; and forwarding orders or writing reports. A taxpayer's administrative or management activities at sites that aren't fixed locations of the business (e.g., car or hotel room), don't count. Moreover, if a taxpayer conducts some administrative or management activities at a fixed location of the business outside the home, he can still claim a home-office deduction as long as those activities aren't substantial (e.g., the taxpayer occasionally does minimal paperwork at another fixed location of the business). A taxpayer's eligibility to claim a home office deduction under the above rules won't be affected by the fact that he conducts substantial non-administrative or non-management business activities at a fixed location outside the home (e.g., meeting with, or providing services to, customers, clients, or patients at a fixed location outside of his home).[43]

illustration: Most of a self-employed plumber's time is spent at customers' homes and offices installing and repairing plumbing. His sole office is in his home and he uses it exclusively and regularly for the administrative or management details of his business (phoning customers, ordering supplies, and keeping his books). The plumber's home office qualifies as a principal place of business.

(2) Under the comparative analysis test, set forth in the Supreme Court's *Soliman* decision, the determination of a taxpayer's principal place of business requires a comparative analysis of: (1) the relative importance of the activities performed at each business location, and (2) the time spent at each place, i.e., time spent at the home compared with time spent in each of the other places where business activities occur. If the nature of the trade or profession requires the taxpayer to meet or confer with clients or patients or to deliver goods or services to a customer, the place where that contact occurs, particularly where that place is a facility with unique or special characteristics, is often important.[44]

¶ 1640 Residence used to meet clients.

Deduction is allowed to the extent allocable to a portion of a residence that's *used exclusively* and *on a regular basis* (¶1642) as a place of business (even if not a principal place of business) that is used by patients, clients, or customers in meeting or dealing with the taxpayer in the normal course of his trade or business. (Code Sec. 280A(c)(1)(B)) This permits a doctor, lawyer, sales rep, insurance agent, claims adjuster, etc., to deduct office-at-home expenses even though he operates his business or profession primarily from an office away from his residence. Telephone conversations alone aren't enough; patients, customers, etc., must be physically present for deductions to be claimed under this rule.[45]

¶ 1641 Specialized rules for business use of home.

A deduction is allowed:

* For costs allocable to a portion of a separate structure (e.g., artist's studio) not attached to the residence if it's used *exclusively* and *on a regular basis* (¶1642) in connection with the taxpayer's business. (Code Sec. 280A(c)(1)(C))[46]

---

43. ¶L-1335; ¶280A4.014; TD ¶258,009
44. ¶L-1330 *et seq.*; ¶280A4.014; TD ¶258,010

45. ¶L-1344 *et seq.*; ¶280A4.016; TD ¶258,019
46. ¶L-1347; ¶280A4.017; TD ¶258,020

- To the extent allocable to space in a residence that the taxpayer uses *on a regular basis* to store inventory and/or product samples in his business of selling products at retail or wholesale, if the residence is the sole fixed location of the trade or business. (Code Sec. 280A(c)(2))[47]

- If a residence is used regularly to provide day-care services for compensation to children, handicapped individuals, or persons 65 or over. If there is only part-time use of a portion of the residence, allocation must be made first on the basis of the proportion of total space used to furnish services and then on the basis of the amount of time that space is used for those services compared to the total time the space is available for all uses. The deduction is allowed only if the day-care services aren't primarily educational and comply with any applicable state licensing, certification, or approval requirements. (Code Sec. 280A(c)(4))[48]

¶ 1642 "Exclusive" use on a "regular" basis.

For purposes of the home-office rules (¶1638 *et seq.*), exclusive use means that the taxpayer must use a specific portion of a residence or detached structure for carrying on his business. For example, using a den to write legal briefs and prepare tax returns as well as for personal purposes doesn't meet the exclusive use test.[49] Part of a room used exclusively for business can qualify for the deduction, even though the room isn't divided.[50] Expenses attributable to the exclusive but incidental or occasional trade or business use of a portion of a dwelling unit aren't deductible because the space isn't used on a regular basis.[1]

¶ 1643 Gross income limit on home office deduction.

The deduction is limited to the activity's gross income reduced by all other deductible expenses that are allowable regardless of qualified use and by the business deductions that aren't allocable to the use of the home itself. (Code Sec. 280A(c)(5)(A), Code Sec. 280A(c)(5)(B)) Expenses disallowed solely because they exceed business income can be carried forward (Code Sec. 280A(c)(5)), subject to the gross income limitation in the later year.[2]

¶ 1644 Allocation of home office expenses.

Allocation of expenses and depreciation on a house is generally based on a comparison of space used for business and personal purposes. A safe harbor method ($5 per square foot, up to a maximum of 300 square feet) may be used as an alternative to the calculation, allocation, and substantiation of actual home office expenses.[3]

¶ 1645 Rental by employer of space in employee's home.

No home-office deduction is allowed for expenses attributable to the rental by an employee of all or part of his home to his employer if the employee uses the rented portion to perform services as an employee of the employer. (Code Sec. 280A(c)(6))[4]

¶ 1646 Moving Expenses. ▬▬▬▬▬▬▬▬▬▬▬▬▬▬▬

An employee or self-employed individual may deduct certain expenses of moving to a new home if the move results from a change in the individual's principal place of work and if distance and time (working at the new location) tests are met. Exceptions apply to members of the armed forces.

---

47. ¶L-1355 *et seq.*; ¶280A4.02; TD ¶258,023
48. ¶L-1359; ¶280A4.03; TD ¶258,024 *et seq.*
49. ¶L-1317 *et seq.*; ¶280A4.011; TD ¶258,005
50. ¶L-1317; ¶280A4; TD ¶258,005

1. ¶L-1324; ¶280A4.012; TD ¶258,007
2. ¶L-1365 *et seq.*; ¶280A4.060; TD ¶258,027
3. ¶L-1310 *et seq.*; ¶280A4.041; TD ¶258,041
4. ¶L-1354; ¶280A4.019; TD ¶258,003

¶ 1647 Claiming a moving expense deduction.

Form 3903 is filed by taxpayers, whether employed or self-employed, who claim moving expenses.[5] The deduction is ordinarily claimed on the return for the year in which the expenses were paid or incurred, see ¶1653. But in certain circumstances, taxpayers may elect to claim the deduction before satisfying the time tests, see ¶1650.

¶ 1648 Deductible above-the-line moving expenses.

An employee or self-employed individual who moves his residence because of a change in his principal place of work may deduct the reasonable expenses of (Code Sec. 217(b)(1)): (1) moving household goods and personal effects from the old residence to the new place of residence; and (2) traveling (including lodging but not meals) from the old residence to the new place of residence.[6]

If a taxpayer uses his auto to travel to the new home, he may deduct actual expenses (e.g., gas and oil) or, instead, 24¢ per mile for 2013.[7]

Moving expenses are "above-the-line" deductions; that is, they are deductible from gross income in arriving at adjusted gross income. (Code Sec. 62(a)(15))[8]

In the case of any individual other than the taxpayer, the expenses above are deductible only if the individual has both the former residence and the new residence as his principal place of abode and is a member of the taxpayer's household. (Code Sec. 217(b)(2))[9]

⟁/observation: There are no dollar limits on the amount of deductible moving expenses.

Moving expenses aren't deductible to the extent they are reimbursed by the employer and the reimbursements are excludable from the taxpayer's income (¶1248).

¶ 1649 50-mile distance test.

The new job site must be at least 50 miles farther from the taxpayer's old principal residence than was the old principal job site. If he didn't have a full-time job before the move, the new job site must be at least 50 miles from his old residence. (Code Sec. 217(c)(1))[10]

¶ 1650 39-week/78-week time tests.

A 39-week or 78-week test must be met: (Code Sec. 217(c)(2))

. . . 39-week test: An employee must be employed full-time in the general location of his new principal place of work for at least 39 weeks during the 12-month period immediately following his arrival in the new area. (Code Sec. 217(c)(2)(A))

. . . 78-week test: The taxpayer must be a "full time employee" or must "perform services as a self-employed individual on a full time basis" in the general location of his new principal place of work for at least 78 weeks during the 24-month period immediately following his arrival there. Thirty-nine of the 78 weeks must be during the 12-month period above. (Code Sec. 217(c)(2)(B))

Joint filers qualify for the deduction if either spouse satisfies the 39-week or 78-week test. But weeks worked by one spouse can't be added to weeks worked by the other. (Reg § 1.217-2(c)(4)(v), Reg § 1.217-1(c)(4))

---

5. ¶L-3601; TD ¶350,501
6. ¶L-3602 *et seq.*; ¶2174; TD ¶350,512
7. ¶L-3615; TD ¶350,515

8. ¶L-3602; ¶2174; TD ¶350,501
9. ¶L-3602; ¶2174; TD ¶350,502
10. ¶L-3619; ¶2174.01; TD ¶350,519

Failure to meet the 39- or 78-week test doesn't bar deduction if the failure was caused by: (1) death or disability, or (2) involuntary separation from employment (other than for willful misconduct), or re-transfer for the benefit of the employer *(not* initiated by the employee), after getting full-time employment in which the taxpayer could reasonably have been expected to meet the test. (Code Sec. 217(d)(1))[11]

¶ 1651   Foreign moves (from the U.S.).

Expenses of moving from the U.S. or its possessions to a new principal place of work outside the U.S. or its possessions include the reasonable expenses (no dollar ceiling) of moving household goods and personal effects to and from storage, and of storing these items while the new place of work is the taxpayer's principal place of work. (Code Sec. 217(h))[12]

Moving expenses aren't deductible to the extent allocable to exempt foreign-source earned income. In the absence of evidence to the contrary, reimbursement of expenses to move to a foreign country is attributed to future services to be performed at the new place of work. (Reg § 1.911-3(e)(5)(i))[13]

¶ 1652   Moving to U.S. not connected with employment.

Moving expense deductions under special rules are allowed for persons who worked abroad and move to the U.S. (or its possessions) on retirement, and for the spouse or dependent who moves to the U.S. following the death of a person who worked abroad. (Code Sec. 217(i))[14]

¶ 1653   When to deduct moving expenses.

A taxpayer may:

• deduct moving expenses in the year the expenses were paid or incurred even though the 39- or 78-week condition isn't satisfied before the due date for filing (including extensions) (Code Sec. 217(d)(2); Reg § 1.217-2(a)(2)), or

• wait until the applicable condition is satisfied; then file an amended return claiming the deduction for the tax year the moving expense was paid or incurred. (Reg § 1.217-2(d))[15]

¶ 1654   Moving expenses of members of the armed forces.

A move by an active duty member of the armed forces under a military order and incident to a permanent change of station can qualify for deduction regardless of the distance moved or the length of time worked at the new station. Cash reimbursements or allowances are excludable to the extent of moving and storage expenses actually paid or incurred, as are all in-kind moving and storage services provided by the military. This exclusion also applies to a spouse and dependents when they don't accompany an armed forces member and move to a location different from that *to* which he moves or different from that *from* which he moves. Where the military moves the member and family to or from separate locations and they incur unreimbursed expenses, their moves are treated as a single move to the member's new principal place of work. (Code Sec. 217(g)) No deduction is permitted for any moving or storage expense reimbursed by an excluded allowance. (Reg § 1.217-2(g)(6))[16]

¶ 1655   Deduction vs Capitalization of Tangible Property Costs. ▆▆▆▆▆▆▆▆

In general, repairs and maintenance are deductible currently, and materials and supplies are deductible either when used or consumed (if non-incidental), or when

---

11. ¶L-3620 *et seq.*; ¶2174.01; TD ¶350,520 *et seq.*
12. ¶L-3610; ¶2174.03; TD ¶350,533
13. ¶L-3635; ¶9114.11; TD ¶350,535

14. ¶L-3632; ¶L-3633; ¶2174.03; TD ¶350,533
15. ¶L-3637; ¶2174; TD ¶350,537
16. ¶L-3630; ¶2174.02; TD ¶350,530

paid (if incidental, and other conditions are met). Capitalized expenses generally can't be deducted except through depreciation, expensing, depletion, or amortization deductions.

¶ 1656 Deductible repairs and maintenance costs.

In general, amounts paid for repairs and maintenance to tangible property are currently deductible if they are not otherwise required to be capitalized. (Reg § 1.162-4(a)) Repair costs that don't directly benefit, and are not incurred because of, an improvement do not have to be capitalized, even if made at the same time as a capitalized improvement. (Reg § 1.263(a)-3(g)(1)(i))[17]

⚫*illustration:* A business may currently deduct as a repair the cost of replacing a truck's broken headlights and mending the driver's seat, even the work takes place when the truck is taken out of service to overhaul its engine (a capitalized expense).

For amounts paid or incurred in tax years that begin after Dec. 31, 2013 (Reg § 1.263(a)-3(r)(1)), taxpayers may elect to capitalize amounts paid for repair and maintenance consistent with their books and records. (Reg § 1.263(a)-3(n)(2)) For earlier years that begin after 2011, taxpayers can elect to apply either this reg or prior temporary or final regs. (Reg § 1.263(a)-3(r))

Regulated taxpayers (e.g., telecommunications companies) may use an optional simplified method to distinguish between repairs and capitalized costs. (Reg § 1.263(a)-3(m))

Routine maintenance safe harbors. Regs provide for a routine maintenance safe harbor for property other than buildings. (Reg § 1.263(a)-3(i)(1)(ii))

For tax years that begin after Dec. 31, 2013 (Reg § 1.263(a)-3(r)(1)), regs also provide for a routine maintenance safe harbor for buildings. (Reg § 1.263(a)-3(i)(1)(i)) For earlier years that begin after 2011, taxpayers can elect to apply either those regs or prior temporary or final regs. (Reg § 1.263(a)-3(r))

For both of these safe harbors, routine maintenance is treated as not improving the unit of property (UOP, see ¶1660) and therefore is currently deductible. (Reg § 1.263(a)-3(i)(1))

Expenses that are not treated as routine maintenance include amounts paid to return a UOP to its former ordinarily efficient operating condition, if the property has deteriorated to a state of disrepair and is no longer functional for its intended use. (Reg § 1.263(a)-3(i)(3))[18]

Effect of uniform capitalization rules. All of the above rules apply only to the extent they don't conflict with the uniform capitalization rules (¶1667 *et seq.*). (Reg § 1.263(a)-3(c)(1))

¶ 1657 When to deduct materials and supplies.

The costs of buying or producing *non-incidental* materials and supplies are deductible in the tax year in which they are used or consumed. But *incidental* materials and supplies that are carried on hand, and for which no record of consumption is kept or physical inventories at the beginning and end of the year are not taken, generally are deductible in the tax year in which they are paid for, if taxable income is clearly reflected. (Reg § 1.162-3(a))[19]

For tax years that begin after Dec. 31, 2013 (Reg § 1.162-3(j)(1)), "materials and supplies" means tangible property used or consumed in the taxpayer's business that is not inventory and that falls within *any* of the following categories:

(1) It is a component acquired to maintain, repair, or improve a unit of tangible property

---

17. ¶L-5601.6; ¶2634.16; TD ¶308,004
18. ¶L-5601.6; ¶2634.16; TD ¶308,004

19. ¶L-4702; ¶1624.158; TD ¶450,504

owned, leased, or serviced by the taxpayer and that is not acquired as part of any single unit of tangible property; or

(2) It consists of fuel, lubricants, water, and similar items that are reasonably expected to be consumed in 12 months or less, beginning when used in taxpayer's operations; or

(3) It is a unit of property (UOP, see ¶1660) with an economic useful life of 12 months or less, beginning when the property is used or consumed in the taxpayer's operations; or

(4) It is a UOP with an acquisition cost or production cost (as determined under Code Sec. 263A) of $200 or less (or other amount identified in published guidance); or

(5) It is identified in published IRS guidance as materials and supplies. (Reg § 1.162-3(c))[20]

For earlier years that begin after 2011, taxpayers can elect to apply either this reg or prior temporary or final regs. (Reg § 1.162-3(j))

For tax years that begin after Dec. 31, 2013 (Reg § 1.162-3(j)(1)), if a taxpayer elects to apply the de minimis safe harbor that is explained at ¶1660 to amounts paid for the production or acquisition of tangible property, then the taxpayer must, with limited exceptions, apply the de minimis safe harbor to amounts paid for all materials and supplies that meet the de minimis safe harbor requirements. (Reg § 1.162-3(f)) For earlier years that begin after 2011, taxpayers can elect to apply either this reg or prior temporary or final regs. (Reg § 1.263(a)-3(j))

⚠/caution: Materials and supplies may have to be capitalized under Code Sec. 263A (¶1667) to property produced or acquired for resale, and Code Sec. 471 (¶2864) may require certain materials and supplies to be included in inventory.

¶ 1658   Rotable, temporary and standby emergency spare parts.

Rotable and temporary spare parts. Rotable spare parts are materials and supplies (see ¶1657) acquired for installation on a unit of property (UOP, ¶1660), removable from that UOP, generally repaired or improved, and either reinstalled on the same or other property or stored for later installation. Temporary spare parts are materials and supplies that are used temporarily until a new or repaired part can be installed and then are removed and stored for later installation. (Reg § 1.162-3(c)(2))[21]

Rotable and temporary spare parts can be handled in one of four ways:

(1) Deduct the costs when the parts are disposed of. (Reg § 1.162-3(a)(1), Reg § 1.162-3(a)(3))

(2) Adopt an optional method for such costs. (Reg § 1.162-3(a)(3), Reg § 1.162-3(e))

(3) Deduct the costs under the elective *de minimis* rule explained at ¶1660. (Reg § 1.162-3(a)(3), Reg § 1.162-3(f)(1))

(4) Elect to capitalize and depreciate the costs. (Reg § 1.162-3(a)(3), Reg § 1.162-3(d))

Standby emergency spare parts. For tax years that begin after Dec. 31, 2013 (Reg § 1.162-3(j)(1)), standby emergency spare parts are materials and supplies (see ¶1657) that meet a list of 11 criteria including that they are: a) acquired when particular machinery or equipment is acquired (or later acquired and set aside for use in particular machinery or equipment); (b) set aside for use as replacements to avoid substantial operational time loss caused by emergencies due to particular machinery or equipment failure; and (c) located at or near the site of the installed related machinery or equipment so as to be readily available when needed. (Reg § 1.162-3(c)(3)) Options (1), (3) and (4) above are available for standby emergency spare parts. (Reg § 1.162-3(a)(1), Reg § 1.162-3(a)(3), Reg § 1.162-3(d))

For tax years that begin after Dec. 31, 2011 and before Jan. 1, 2014, taxpayers may apply

---

20. ¶G-2453; ¶1624.158   21. ¶G-2453.5; ¶1624.158

these standby emergency spare part rules or may apply either the applicable rules in the prior temporary regs or the applicable rules in the prior final regs. (Reg § 1.263(a)-3(j))

¶ 1659   General rules for capital expenditures.

A taxpayer must capitalize amounts paid: (a) for new buildings or for permanent improvements or betterments made to increase the value of any property or estate; or (b) for restoring property or in making good the exhaustion of the property for which an allowance (e.g., depreciation) is or has been made. (Code Sec. 263(a), Reg § 1.263(a)-1(a))

Examples of expenses that must be capitalized:

- An amount paid or incurred to facilitate the acquisition of a trade or business, a change in capital structure of a business entity, and certain other transactions. (Reg § 1.263(a)-1(d)) There's a rebuttable presumption that success-based fees (i.e., payments contingent on successfully closing a deal) facilitate the transaction. For success-based fees, taxpayers may elect to (a) allocate 70% to deductible fees paid in business acquisitions or reorganizations to activities that don't facilitate the transaction and deduct such fees currently; and (b) treat the remaining 30% as capitalized activities facilitating the transaction.[22]

- An amount paid to acquire or create interests in land, such as easements, life estates, mineral interests, timber rights, or zoning variances.

- An amount assessed and paid under an agreement between bondholders or shareholders of a corporation to be used in a reorganization of the entity or voluntary contributions by shareholders to the capital of the corporation for any corporate purpose. (Reg § 1.263(a)-1(d))[23]

For the Code Sec. 263A rules requiring direct and indirect costs to be capitalized to property produced by the taxpayer and to property acquired for resale, see ¶1666.

¶ 1660   Amounts paid to acquire or produce tangible property.

Unless the materials and supplies rule applies (see ¶1657) or the *de minimis* rule (discussed below) applies, a taxpayer must capitalize amounts paid to acquire or produce a unit of property (UOP), including leasehold improvement property, land and land improvements, buildings, machinery and equipment, and furniture and fixtures. The taxpayer also must capitalize costs for work (e.g., to make necessary repairs) performed before the date that the UOP is placed in service by the taxpayer. (Reg § 1.263(a)-2(d)(1))[24]

UOP defined. For purposes of the tangible property capitalization rules, the UOP for assets other than buildings generally consists of all the components that are functionally interdependent (i.e., where placing in service of one component is dependent on the placing in service of other component(s)). The UOP for a building generally is the building and its structural components. (Reg § 1.263(a)-3(e)(2)(i), Reg § 1.263(a)-3(e)(3)(i))[25]

Transaction costs. Amounts paid to facilitate the acquisition (or production) of real or personal property—i.e., paid in the process of investigating or otherwise pursuing the acquisition—must be capitalized and added to the basis of property acquired or produced. (Reg § 1.263(a)-2(f)(3)(i))[26]

✪ observation: Some facilitative expenses may qualify as amortizable start-up expenses under Code Sec. 195; see ¶1501.

Facilitative costs include "inherently facilitative" expenses made up of eleven categories.

---

22. ¶L-5762.1; ¶2634.80; TD ¶256,327
23. ¶L-5601; ¶2634; TD ¶256,201.1.
24. ¶L-5601.1; ¶2634.01; TD ¶256,201.2

25. ¶L-5601.12; ¶L-5601.13;¶2634.01
26. ¶L-5601.4; ¶2634.15

These include the costs of items such as shipping, moving or appraising property, application fees, sales and transfer taxes, finder's fees, and architectural, engineering, environmental or inspection services related to specific properties, brokers' fees, and services provided by a qualified intermediary in a Code Sec. 1031 exchange. (Reg § 1.263(a)-2(f)(2)(ii))[27]

Costs relating to the process of determining *whether* to acquire realty and *which* realty to acquire generally aren't facilitative expenses (and therefore may be currently deductible), unless they are "inherently facilitative" expenses (e.g., the cost of an engineering study or a broker's fee). (Reg § 1.263(a)-2(f)(2)(iii)) Employee compensation or overhead *doesn't* facilitate the acquisition of real or personal property (but, under Code Sec. 263A, may have to be capitalized to property produced by the taxpayer or acquired for resale). However, the taxpayer may elect to capitalize employee compensation or overhead expenses, or both, related to each acquisition. (Reg § 1.263(a)-2(f)(2)(iv)(B))

For commissions paid on the transfer of property, see ¶1662.

De minimis rules. The following rules apply to amounts paid in tax years that begin after Dec. 31, 2013. (Reg § 1.263(a)-1(h)(1)) For earlier years that begin after 2011, taxpayers can elect to apply either these rules or prior temporary or final regs. (Reg § 1.263(a)-1(h))

Amounts paid to acquire or produce a unit of tangible property, including materials and supplies (but not inventory or land) don't have to be capitalized if the taxpayer so elects and:

• the taxpayer has an applicable financial statement (AFS), such as one required to be filed with the Securities and Exchange Commission, or a certified audited financial statement accompanied by an independent CPA's report and used for credit or reporting purposes;

• the taxpayer has written accounting procedures in place at the beginning of the tax year for expensing amounts paid for such property if it costs less than a specified dollar amount or it has an economic useful life of 12 months or less;

• the taxpayer treats such amounts as expenses on its AFS in accordance with its written accounting procedures; and

• the amount paid for the property does not exceed $5,000 per invoice (or per item as substantiated by the invoice) or other amount as identified in published guidance in the Federal Register or in the Internal Revenue Bulletin. (Reg § 1.263(a)-1(f)(1)(i))[28]

A similar rule, but with a $500-per-item limit, applies to taxpayers that don't have an AFS. (Reg § 1.263(a)-1(f)(1)(ii))

If the taxpayer elects the de minimis safe harbor, that safe harbor must be applied to all eligible materials and supplies (other than rotable, temporary, and standby emergency spare parts subject to the election to capitalize, and rotable and temporary spare parts subject to the optional method of accounting for these parts, see ¶1658). (Reg § 1.263(a)-1(f)(1))

The cost of property to which the *de minimis* rule applies may be subject to capitalization under Code Sec. 263A if the amounts paid for tangible property comprise the direct or allocable indirect costs of other property produced by the taxpayer or property acquired for resale. (Reg § 1.263(a)-1(f)(3)(v))

¶ 1661　Amounts paid to improve tangible property.

An expense must be capitalized if it betters or improves a unit of property (UOP, ¶1660), restores it, or adapts it to a new and different use.

Capitalized betterment costs. For tax years that begin after Dec. 31, 2013 (Reg § 1.263(a)-3(r)(1)), capitalized betterment costs consist of amounts paid that:

---

27. ¶L-5601.12; ¶L-5601.13;¶2634.01　　　　　　28. ¶L-5601.5; ¶2634.01; TD ¶456,014.2

... ameliorate a material condition or defect that either existed prior to the taxpayer's acquisition of the UOP or arose during the production of the UOP, whether or not the taxpayer was aware of the condition or defect at the time of acquisition or production; or

... is for a material addition, including a physical enlargement, expansion, extension, or addition of a major component) to the UOP or a material increase in the capacity of the UOP; or

... is reasonably expected to materially increase the productivity, efficiency, strength, quality, or output of the UOP. (Reg § 1.263(a)-3(j)(1))[29]

For earlier years that begin after 2011, taxpayers can elect to apply either the above rule or prior temporary or final regs. (Reg § 1.263(a)-3(r))

Here are two examples of particular costs and whether they must be capitalized as betterments:

- Costs of cleaning up contamination caused by leaking of underground storage tanks installed by prior owner of property are capitalized. (Reg § 1.263(a)-3(j)(3), 1)
- Removal and replacement of asbestos installed by a taxpayer in a building before its health hazards were known don't result in a betterment. (Reg § 1.263(a)-3(j)(3), 2)

Capitalized restoration costs. Costs to restore a UOP are capitalized. An amount is treated as a restoration cost only if it:

(1) Replaces a component of a UOP where the taxpayer has (1) properly deducted a loss for that component (other than a casualty loss under Reg § 1.165-7) or (2) properly taken into account the adjusted basis of the component in realizing gain or loss resulting from the sale or exchange of the component;

Illustration: A taxpayer replaces inoperable components of a walk-in freezer, and either abandons the old components and claims a loss, or sells the old components and recognizes a loss. The cost of buying and installing the new components must be capitalized. (Reg § 1.263(a)-3(k)(7), Exs. 1 and 2)

(2) Repairs damage to a UOP for which the taxpayer is required to take a basis adjustment as a result of a casualty loss or casualty event under Code Sec. 165;

(3) Returns the UOP to its ordinarily efficient operating condition if the property has deteriorated to a state of disrepair and is no longer functional for its intended use;

(4) Results in the rebuilding of the UOP to a like-new condition after the end of its class life under Code Sec. 168 for alternative depreciation system (ADS) purposes; or

(5) Replaces a part or a combination of parts that comprise a major component or a substantial structural part of a UOP. (Reg § 1.263(a)-3(k)(1)) All the facts and circumstances are to be considered when determining if this condition is met. (Reg § 1.263(a)-3(k)(6)(i))[30]

Capitalized amounts to adapt property to a new or different use. A taxpayer must capitalize as an improvement an amount paid to adapt a unit of property to a new or different use. In general, a "new or different use" means a situation where the adaptation isn't consistent with the taxpayer's intended ordinary use of the property when he placed it in service. (Reg § 1.263(a)-3(l)(1)) For example, the cost of converting a company's manufacturing facility into a showroom facility must be capitalized. (Reg § 1.263(a)-3(l)(3), 1)[31]

Per-building safe harbor for qualifying small taxpayers. For amounts paid in tax years that begin after Dec. 31, 2013 (Reg § 1.263(a)-3(r)(1)), a safe harbor permits qualifying small taxpayers (those with $10 million or less average annual gross receipts in the three preceding

---

29. ¶L-5601.8; ¶2634.16
30. ¶L-5601.9; ¶2634.16

31. ¶L-5601.10; ¶2634.16

tax years (Reg § 1.263(a)-3(h)(3)(i))) to elect to currently deduct improvements made to an eligible building property (one with an unadjusted basis of $1 million or less (Reg § 1.263(a)-3(h)(4))). (Reg § 1.263(a)-3(h)(1)) This safe harbor election applies only if the total amount paid during the tax year for repairs, maintenance, improvements, and similar activities performed on the eligible building does not exceed the lesser of $10,000 or 2% of the building's unadjusted basis. (Reg § 1.263(a)-3(h)(1))

For earlier years that begin after 2011, taxpayers can elect to apply either the above rules or prior temporary or final regs. (Reg § 1.263(a)-3(r))

¶ 1662   Commissions paid on transfer of property.

Commissions paid for the *purchase* of real estate or other property aren't deductible as expenses but must be capitalized and added to the cost of the property, whether or not the taxpayer is engaged in the real estate business.[32]

Commissions paid for the *sale* of real estate or other property by a taxpayer who is not engaged in the real estate business must be capitalized but are not added to the property's basis and are not treated as an intangible. Instead, commissions are offset against the selling price to determine the gain or loss realized on a sale. If the seller is in the real estate business, commissions on property sales are deductible business expenses. (Reg § 1.263(a)-1(e))[33]

¶ 1663   Capitalization Rules for Intangible Assets. ■■■■■■■■■■■■■■■■■

Taxpayers generally must capitalize amounts paid to acquire or create intangible assets or facilitate the acquisition or creation of such assets.

¶ 1664   Capitalization rules for costs associated with intangible assets.

Taxpayers are required to capitalize amounts paid or incurred to (i) acquire or create an intangible asset, (ii) create or enhance a separate, distinct intangible asset, (iii) create or enhance a "future benefit" identified in published guidance as capitalizable, or (iv) "facilitate" the acquisition or creation of an intangible in (i) through (iii) (e.g., transaction costs). (Reg § 1.263(a)-4(b)(1)) Capitalizable costs cannot be deducted and are generally added to the basis of the intangible. (Reg § 1.263(a)-4) Compensation (including bonuses and commissions) and overhead costs do not facilitate the acquisition, creation or enhancement of an intangible asset. (Reg § 1.263(a)-4(e)(4)(i))[34] These rules do not affect the treatment of amounts specifically provided for in a Code Section other than Code Sec. 162 or Code Sec. 212 (e.g., Code Sec. 174 research expenses). (Reg § 1.263(a)-4(b)(4))

Ⓡ*observation:* Capitalized costs may be amortizable (e.g., payment to a departing employee for a 3-year noncompete covenant may be deducted ratably over the 3 years).

For the "12-month" and de minimis exceptions to these requirements, see ¶1665. For 15-year amortization of certain intangibles, see ¶1903.

¶ 1665   De minimis and 12-month rule exceptions to capitalization rules for intangibles.

The following are exceptions to the capitalization rules for intangibles discussed at ¶1663.

De minimis costs—i.e., costs that don't exceed $5,000—paid to another party to create, originate, enter into, renew, or renegotiate an agreement (Reg § 1.263(a)-4(d)(6)(v)), or paid in the process of investigating a transaction (Reg § 1.263(a)-4(e)(4)(iii)) don't have to be capitalized even if they facilitate a capital transaction and otherwise would be subject to the

---

32. ¶I-2536   34. ¶L-5751; ¶2634; TD ¶256,300
33. ¶I-2537; ¶2634.05; TD ¶222,023

capitalization rules. Payments made in the form of property are valued at fair market value at the time of payment. The de minimis rule applies on a transaction-by-transaction basis. If transaction costs (other than compensation and overhead) exceed $5,000, none of the costs are treated as de minimis. A pooling method may be used for de minimis transaction costs. Commissions paid to facilitate the acquisition of an intangible aren't treated as de minimis costs (and therefore must be capitalized).[35]

12-month rule. Capitalization is not required for amounts paid to create or facilitate the creation of any right or benefit that does not extend beyond the earlier of (1) 12 months after the first date on which the taxpayer realizes the right or benefit; or (2) the end of the tax year following the tax year in which the payment is made. (Reg § 1.263(a)-4(f)) Amounts paid to terminate an agreement before its expiration date create a benefit for the taxpayer that lasts for the unexpired term of the agreement immediately before the termination date. (Reg § 1.263(a)-4(f)(2)) The 12-month rule doesn't apply to amounts paid to create (or facilitate the creation of) financial interests or amortizable Code Sec. 197 intangibles or to amounts paid to create or enhance a right of indefinite duration. (Reg § 1.263(a)-4(f)(3), Reg § 1.263(a)-4(f)(4)) The 12-month rule does not affect the determination of whether a liability is incurred during the tax year, including the determination of whether economic performance has occurred. (Reg § 1.263(a)-4(f)(6))[36]

¶ 1666 Uniform Capitalization (UNICAP) Rules ▬▬▬▬▬▬▬▬▬▬▬▬▬▬

Under the Code Sec. 263A uniform capitalization (UNICAP) rules, a taxpayer must include in inventory costs the "allocable costs" of "property" that is inventory and capitalize the allocable costs of any other property.

¶ 1667 UNICAP rules—allocable costs of property.

Under the uniform capitalization (UNICAP) rules, a taxpayer must (1) include in inventory costs the "allocable costs" (defined below) of "property" (also defined below) that is inventory; (Code Sec. 263A(a)(1)(A)) and (2) capitalize the allocable costs of any other property that is subject to the UNICAP rules. (Code Sec. 263A(a)(2)(B)) The *allocable costs* are:

. . . the direct costs of the property (Code Sec. 263A(a)(2)(A));

. . . the indirect costs, to the extent of the property's proper share of that part (or all) of the costs allocable to that property. (Code Sec. 263A(a)(2)(B))

Allocable costs include all depreciation deductions for the taxpayer's assets, and interest, but only where the underlying debt was incurred or continued to finance certain produced property, see ¶1669. Taxes are allocable indirect costs. (Code Sec. 263A(a)(2)(B)) Environmental remediation costs incurred by a manufacturer (e.g., to clean land it contaminated with hazardous waste) must be included in inventory costs under these rules.[37]

Allocable costs don't include:

. . . selling, marketing, advertising and distribution expenses (Reg § 1.263A-1(e)(3)(iii)(A));

. . . any amounts allowable as a deduction under Code Sec. 174 for research and experimental expenditures (Code Sec. 263A(c)(2));

. . . any cost to the extent allowable as a deduction under Code Sec. 263(c) (intangible drilling and development costs), Code Sec. 616(a) (mining development expenses) or Code Sec. 617(a) (mining exploration expenses) (Code Sec. 263A(c)(3));

. . . any qualified creative expense incurred by a "writer," "photographer" or "artist" that would otherwise be deductible. Expenses related to printing photographic plates, motion picture films, video tapes or similar items aren't qualified creative expenses (Code

35. ¶L-5757.1, ¶L-5760.2; ¶2634; TD ¶256,317
36. ¶L-5760.5 *et seq.*; ¶2634; TD ¶256,320

37. ¶G-5500.1; ¶263A4 *et seq.*; TD ¶456,000 *et seq.*

Sec. 263A(h));

. . . "deductible service costs." (Reg § 1.263A-1(e)(3)(iii)(K))

Which property is subject to the UNICAP rules? Under the UNICAP rules, a taxpayer must include in inventory or capitalize the allocable costs for:

. . . real or tangible personal property (defined below) that the taxpayer *produced* (defined below) (Code Sec. 263A(b)(1));

. . . real or personal Code Sec. 1221(a)(1) property—inventory and property held primarily for sale to customers in the ordinary course of the taxpayer's trade or business—that the taxpayer acquired for resale. (Code Sec. 263A(b)(2)(A))

Tangible personal property includes a film, sound recording, video tape, book or similar property. (Code Sec. 263A(b))

A taxpayer "produces" tangible property if he constructs, builds, installs, manufactures, develops or improves it. (Code Sec. 263A(g)(1)) Where a taxpayer makes progress or advance payments to a contractor, the taxpayer is treated as producing any property the contractor produces for the taxpayer under the contract, to the extent of those payments (whether paid or incurred by the taxpayer under the contract or otherwise). (Code Sec. 263A(g)(2))

Property acquired for resale includes intangible as well as tangible property. Resellers must capitalize the acquisition cost of property acquired for resale, as well as certain indirect costs properly allocable to property acquired for resale. (Reg § 1.263A-1(e)) However, a reseller isn't required to capitalize handling and storage costs incurred at a retail sales facility. (Reg § 1.263A-3(c))

"Property" doesn't include (and so allocable costs don't have to be capitalized for):

. . . Any property produced by the taxpayer for use by the taxpayer other than in a trade or business or an activity conducted for profit. (Code Sec. 263A(c)(1))

. . . Any property produced by the taxpayer under a long-term contract (Code Sec. 263A(c)(4)) except for certain home construction contracts. (Code Sec. 460(e)(1))

. . . Timber and certain ornamental trees. (Code Sec. 263A(c)(5)(A))

. . . Personal property acquired for resale by certain taxpayers with average annual gross receipts of $10,000,000 or less. (Code Sec. 263A(b)(2)(B))[38]

Taxpayers who acquire and hold property for resale (such as retailers and wholesalers) may elect a simplified resale method to determine the additional costs properly allocable to the resale property. (Reg § 1.263A-3(d))[39] Qualifying motor vehicle dealerships may (1) treat certain sales facilities as retail sales facilities for purposes of Code Sec. 263A and/or (2) be treated as resellers without production activities for Code Sec. 263A purposes.[40]

For the application of the uniform capitalization rules to farmers and ranchers, see ¶4519.

¶ 1668   How to allocate costs to property under the UNICAP rules.

Allocable costs (¶1667) must be allocated to inventory or capitalized as follows:

. . . Direct labor costs are generally allocated by using a specific identification ("tracing") method (Reg § 1.263A-1(g)(2)), but any reasonable method may be used. (Reg § 1.263A-1(f)(4))

. . . Indirect costs should be allocated to particular production, resale, etc., activities using either a specific identification method, the standard cost method, or a method using burden rates, such as ratios based on direct costs, hours, or other items, or similar formulas, so long as the method employed reasonably allocates indirect costs among production, resale,

38. ¶G-5451 *et seq.*; ¶s 263A4 *et seq.*, 263A4.06 *et seq.*; TD ¶456,000

39. ¶G-5452 *et seq.*; ¶263A4.09; TD ¶456,011
40. ¶G-5526.1; ¶263A4.04

etc., activities. (Reg § 1.263A-1(g)(3)) Taxpayers may be able to use simplified methods such as the simplified production method (Reg § 1.263A-2) and the simplified resale method. (Reg § 1.263A-3)[41]

¶ 1669 Interest capitalization rules.

A taxpayer must capitalize interest he pays or incurs during a production period that is allocable to property he produces if that property (1) has a long useful life (it is real property or property with a class life of 20 years or more); (2) has an estimated production period exceeding two years; or (3) has an estimated production period exceeding one year and a cost exceeding $1,000,000. (Code Sec. 263A(f)(1); Reg § 1.263A-8(b)(1))[42]

The taxpayer must also capitalize any interest on debt allocable to an asset needed to produce the above property. (Code Sec. 263A(f)(3); Reg § 1.263A-8(a)(2)) A taxpayer must capitalize interest whether he produces the property for his own use or for sale.

The "production period" begins on the date production of the property begins and ends on the date it is ready to be placed in service or is ready to be held for sale. (Code Sec. 263A(f)(4)(B))[43]

Interest isn't capitalized for real or personal property acquired solely for resale.

A taxpayer doesn't capitalize interest allocable to property that's not subject to the capitalization rules, such as property produced under a long-term contract (see the discussion of this and other exceptions at ¶1667). (Reg § 1.263A-8(d)(2)(v)(A)) Thus, a taxpayer who produces property under a long term contract capitalizes interest only to the extent he doesn't report income under the percentage of completion method.[44]

Allocating interest to produced property. Interest is allocable to property a taxpayer produces if the taxpayer incurred or continued the underlying debt to finance the construction or production of the property.

A taxpayer is treated as having incurred or continued debt to finance the production of income: (1) where the debt can be specifically traced to production expenditures, and (2) where the debt can't be so traced, but where production or construction expenditures exceed the debt that is directly traceable. (Reg § 1.263A-9(a)(2))

The interest on the debt incurred or continued to finance production is allocated to the property produced as follows:[45]

(1) interest (other than qualified residence interest) on a debt that is directly attributable to production expenditures for the produced property is assigned to that property; (Code Sec. 263A(f)(2)(A)(i); Reg § 1.263A-9(a)(2)(i)(A)), and

(2) interest on any other debt is assigned to the produced property to the extent that the taxpayer's interest costs could have been reduced if production expenditures (not attributable to the debt in (1), above) had not been incurred (Code Sec. 263A(f)(2)(A)(ii); Reg § 1.263A-9(a)(2)(i)(B)) (that is, had the expenditures that were incurred for construction been used instead to repay the debt).

Except as provided in regs, a flow-through entity applies the interest allocation rules at the entity level and then, to the extent the entity has insufficient debt to support the production or construction expenditures, at the beneficiary level. (Code Sec. 263A(f)(2)(C))[46]

---

41. ¶G-5458; ¶263A4.06; TD ¶456,006
42. ¶L-5920; ¶263A4.11; TD ¶456,017 *et seq.*
43. ¶L-5932; ¶263A4.11; TD ¶456,023

44. ¶L-5918; ¶263A4.03; TD ¶456,017
45. ¶L-5926; ¶263A4.11; TD ¶456,021
46. ¶L-5928; TD ¶456,037

Chapter 4   Interest Expense—Taxes—Losses—Bad Debts

¶ 1700   Deduction for Interest. ▬▬▬▬▬▬▬▬▬▬▬▬▬▬▬▬▬▬

Generally, interest paid or accrued during the tax year is deductible whether or not it is incurred in a trade or business. To be deductible, the amount of interest must be definitely ascertainable, incurred with respect to a valid debt and actually paid or accrued during the tax year.

There is no deduction for personal interest (¶1715 *et seq.*). Interest deductions for investment interest (¶1726 *et seq.*); qualified residence interest (¶1730 *et seq.*); interest incurred in a passive activity (¶1810 *et seq.*); and qualified education loan interest (¶2222 *et seq.*) are subject to limitations.

¶ 1701   Interest is payment for the use or forbearance of money.

Interest is "the compensation allowed by law or fixed by the parties for use, or forbearance, or detention of money." This means that interest includes the amount paid for the use of money during the time agreed for a loan to run, and also for the detention of money after the agreed term of the loan has passed without repayment.[1]

¶ 1702   Mortgage interest.

Interest on a mortgage on real property (including a condominium or co-op, ¶1714) generally is deductible. (Reg § 1.163-1(b))[2] For "points," see ¶1703. For prepayment penalties and late payment charges, see ¶1705. For who deducts mortgage interest, see ¶1713.

🌀*caution:* Interest on a home mortgage must be "qualified residence interest" (¶1730 *et seq.*) to be deductible.

¶ 1703   "Points."

"Points" (loan origination fees, loan processing fees, loan discount fees, etc., that are a specified percentage of the amount borrowed) a borrower pays, out of his own funds, to a lender to get a loan are deductible as interest *only* if they are *solely* for the use or forbearance of money and not a charge for services. But points paid for services of the lender *in lieu of* specific service charges (e.g., a one-point charge for appraisal, etc.) aren't deductible as interest. Nor is a "commitment fee" charged for the lender's agreement to make a future loan. [3]

For when to deduct points, see ¶1745; home mortgage points, see ¶1746; and refinancing points, see ¶1747.

¶ 1704   Finance charges and credit card fees.

The amount of finance charges imposed on bank credit cards, revolving charge accounts, and similar credit arrangements is deductible as interest if based on the amount deferred and the length of the deferral (subject to the bar on personal interest deductions, see ¶1715). Similarly, credit card fees imposed for cash, check, or overdraft advances are deductible as interest, but only to the extent the payment isn't a service charge.[4]

---

1. ¶K-5020 *et seq.*; ¶1634; TD ¶311,501
2. ¶K-5043; ¶s 1634.050, 1634.052; TD ¶311,504

3. ¶K-5026; ¶1634.005; TD ¶311,506, 311,527
4. ¶K-5029, K-5031; ¶1634.050; TD ¶311,507

References beginning with a single letter are to paragraphs in RIA's Federal Tax Coordinator 2d and RIA's Analysis of Federal Taxes: Income. Those beginning with numbers are to paragraphs in RIA's United States Tax Reporter. Those beginning with TD are to paragraphs in RIA's Tax Desk.

202

¶ 1705   Prepayment penalties and late payment charges.

A penalty paid for prepaying a debt (including a mortgage) is deductible as interest as is a late payment charge (that isn't a service charge). [5]

¶ 1706   Interest and carrying charges on installment purchases and deferred tuition; 6% rule.

Interest on installment purchases that's separately stated or definitely determinable and provable is deductible as interest, subject to the rules for credit cards. see ¶1704. For deduction of "unstated interest," see ¶1707.

If carrying charges (including finance charges, service charges, etc.) on an installment purchase of personal property or educational services are *separately stated*, but the amount of *interest* included in the charges can't be ascertained, the installment payments are considered to include a 6% interest charge based on the average unpaid balance under the contract during the tax year. (Code Sec. 163(b); Reg § 1.163-2) [6]

¶ 1707   Unstated interest on deferred payment sales.

If property is sold in a deferred payment sale and the parties don't provide for an adequate interest charge on the deferred payments, part of each payment made by the buyer may be treated as "unstated interest" and may be deducted under certain rules. The amount of unstated interest attributed to the buyer is determined under the rules for determining the unstated interest that's taxed to the seller (¶1307 *et seq.*). (Code Sec. 483(a); Reg § 1.483-1) [7]

The unstated interest rules don't apply to (1) purchases of personal use property (Code Sec. 1275(b)(1)); or (2) payments made on account of an installment purchase of personal property where payments include separately stated carrying charges otherwise treated as interest (¶1706). (Code Sec. 483(d)(3)) [8]

¶ 1708   Interest on taxes.

Interest on delinquent tax payments may be deducted, to the extent it's otherwise deductible. [9] Thus, interest on sales, excise and similar taxes incurred in connection with a taxpayer's business or investment activities may be deducted. But interest paid by an individual (or a trust, S corporation or other pass-through entity) on income tax underpayments, or on debt used to pay those taxes, is nondeductible personal interest (¶1715). (Reg § 1.163-9T(b)(2)) Interest on an income tax deficiency arising from an unincorporated business is also nondeductible personal interest that can't be deducted as a business expense. [10]

No deduction is allowed for any interest paid or accrued on underpayments of tax where the underpayment is attributable to the portion of any reportable transaction understatement—generally, an understatement with respect to certain "listed" or "reportable" transactions that have a potential for tax avoidance or evasion. (Code Sec. 163(m)) [11]

¶ 1709   Corporate debt or equity; "thin" capitalization.

Corporations may favor heavy debt capitalization because interest paid on debt is deductible, while dividends paid on stock aren't. Also, repayment of a debt isn't taxable, while a stock redemption may be taxable to shareholders either as ordinary income or capital gain (¶3526 *et seq.*). [12]

5. ¶K-5032*et seq.*; ¶1634; TD ¶311,510 *et seq.*
6. ¶K-5151; ¶1634.050; TD ¶319,502
7. ¶K-5280 *et seq.*; ¶4834; TD ¶319,500 *et seq.*
8. ¶K-5281, K-5282; ¶4834.01; TD ¶319,501

9. ¶K-5048; ¶1634.013; TD ¶311,509
10. ¶K-5513; TD ¶314,002
11. ¶K-5506.1; ¶1634.013; TD ¶311,509.1
12. ¶K-5790 *et seq.*; ¶3854 *et seq.*; TD ¶313,501

The corporate issuer's characterization (at issuance) of a corporate instrument as stock or debt is binding on the issuer and all holders (unless the holder discloses inconsistent treatment on his return), but is not binding on IRS. (Code Sec. 385(c))[13] If IRS determines that a corporation's debt obligations should be treated as equity (stock), it will treat "interest" paid on the securities as nondeductible dividend income. For disallowed deductions for interest on corporate debt payable in the issuer's stock, see ¶1710.

A number of key factors are relevant in whether purported corporate debt will be treated as debt for federal tax purposes. No single factor is controlling. They include:

- the right to enforce payment of principal and interest and the source of payments;

- whether there is subordination to or preference over any indebtedness of the corporation;

- whether there is a high ratio of debt to equity;

- whether there is convertibility into the stock of the corporation; and

- the relationship between holdings of stock in the corporation and holdings of the interest in question.[14]

¶ 1710 No deduction for interest on corporate debt payable in issuer's stock.

No deduction is allowed for interest paid or accrued, or original issue discount (OID, ¶1751), on a disqualified debt instrument (Code Sec. 163(l)(1)).[15] A disqualified debt instrument is any corporate debt (or debt issued by a partnership to the extent of its corporate partners) that's payable in (1) equity (i.e., stock) of the issuer or a related party (under Code Sec. 267(b), see ¶2448, or Code Sec. 707(b), see ¶3731), or, (2) equity held by the issuer or any related party in any other person. (Code Sec. 163(l)(2), Code Sec. 163(l)(6))[16] But it doesn't include certain debt issued by dealers in securities. (Code Sec. 163(l)(5))[17]

A debt instrument is treated as payable in equity if (A) a substantial amount of the principal or interest is required to be paid or converted, or at the option of the issuer or a related party, is payable in, or convertible into, the equity, (B) a substantial amount of the principal or interest is required to be determined, or at the option of the issuer or a related party is determined, by reference to the value of the equity, or (C) the indebtedness is part of an arrangement which is reasonably expected to result in a transaction described in (A) or (B), such as in the case of certain issuances of a forward contract in connection with the issuance of debt, nonrecourse debt that is secured principally by stock, or certain debt instruments that are convertible at the holder's option when it is substantially certain that the right will be exercised.[18]

¶ 1711 Who may deduct interest?

With some exceptions (¶1712, ¶1713), a taxpayer's interest deduction is limited to interest he pays or accrues on his *own* indebtedness, and not for interest on debts of others.[19] But for joint obligors—i.e., persons who are jointly and severally liable for a debt—each obligor may deduct the amount of interest he actually pays on the debt.[20]

A person who is only secondarily liable for the debt, e.g., as endorser or guarantor, generally can't deduct interest on the debt. But under some circumstances, where the guarantor becomes primarily liable for the debt, he may be allowed to deduct the interest.[21]

---

13. ¶K-5791 *et seq.*; ¶3854.01; TD ¶313,501
14. ¶K-5801 *et seq.*; ¶1634.057; TD ¶313,501
15. ¶K-5507; ¶1634.059; TD ¶313,502
16. ¶K-5508; ¶1634.059; TD ¶313,502
17. ¶K-5509; ¶1634.059; TD ¶313,502.2

18. ¶K-5507 *et seq.*; ¶1634.059; TD ¶313,502
19. ¶K-5120 *et seq.*; ¶1634.015; TD ¶318,401
20. ¶K-5130; ¶1634.015; TD ¶318,405
21. ¶K-5133; ¶1664.450; TD ¶318,407

¶ 1712 Interest paid by another.

In certain cases, where a person other than taxpayer pays or accrues the interest on taxpayer's debt, the payments are treated as made by the taxpayer and he can deduct the interest. This occurs when the interest payor is acting (or is treated as acting) merely as the taxpayer's agent (e.g., where a tenant pays the interest on his landlord's mortgage), or where the taxpayer has given some consideration for the payor's payment.[22]

¶ 1713 Who deducts mortgage interest (and points).

A taxpayer who is personally liable for a mortgage debt may deduct the otherwise deductible mortgage interest (¶1702) (and points) he actually pays out of his own funds even if, when he makes the payments, he no longer owns the property subject to the mortgage (for points on seller-financed mortgages, see ¶1703; for co-ops, see ¶1714). But where a conveyance of mortgaged property would, under state law, automatically relieve the transferor of personal liability on the mortgage, he can't deduct the payments he makes after the transfer.[23]

A taxpayer who *isn't* personally liable for a mortgage debt may deduct the mortgage interest he actually pays *only* if he's the legal or equitable owner (solely or jointly with others) of the mortgaged property.[24] Home buyers whose occupancy of the residence gave them equitable (but not legal) title to it could deduct interest they paid on the builder's construction loan.[25]

Where the joint owners of mortgaged property are also jointly liable on the mortgage, each owner may deduct the mortgage interest he actually pays out of his own funds.[26]

caution: Mortgage interest that's deductible *solely* because it's "qualified residence interest" may be deducted *only* by the person who owns the property, see ¶1730.

¶ 1714 Cooperative housing corporation's (co-op's) mortgage payments.

Tenant-stockholders of co-ops deduct their share of the co-op's mortgage interest payments (subject to the "qualified residence interest" limits, see ¶1730). (Code Sec. 216)[27]

¶ 1715 No deduction for personal interest.

Noncorporate taxpayers can't deduct "personal interest." (Code Sec. 163(h)(1))[28] Personal interest is all interest *other than*: (1) interest properly allocable to trade or business debt (other than the trade or business of being an employee); (2) interest paid on qualified education loans (¶2222 *et seq.*); (3) qualified residence interest (¶1730 *et seq.*); (4) interest considered in computing income or loss from a passive activity (¶1810 *et seq.*); (5) investment interest (¶1728); and (6) interest on certain deferred estate tax payments. (Code Sec. 163(h)(2))[29]

¶ 1716 Net direct interest expense—market discount bonds.

A taxpayer's "net direct interest expense" with respect to any taxable market discount bond (¶1326) is deductible in a tax year only to the extent the expense exceeds the market discount allocable to the days during the year the bond was held by the taxpayer. (Code Sec. 1277(a); Code Sec. 1278(a)(1)(C))[30] For tax-exempt bonds, see ¶1723.

"Net direct interest expense" is any excess of: (1) interest paid or accrued on debt incurred

---

22. ¶K-5129; ¶1634.018; TD ¶318,409
23. ¶K-5135, ¶K-5136; TD ¶318,601
24. ¶K-5136; ¶1634.015; TD ¶318,602
25. ¶K-5136; TD ¶318,602
26. ¶K-5138; TD ¶318,604

27. ¶K-5140, K-5900*et seq.*; ¶2164.01; TD ¶314,511
28. ¶K-5510; ¶1634.054; TD ¶314,000
29. ¶K-5511; ¶1634.054; TD ¶314,001
30. ¶K-5341; ¶12,764.02; TD ¶316,501

or continued to buy or carry a market discount bond, over (2) interest (including OID, ¶1314) includible in income for the tax year with respect to the bond. (Code Sec. 1277(c))[31]

The disallowed interest expenses are deductible in the year the bond is disposed of (Code Sec. 1277(b)(2)(A)) or, earlier if the taxpayer so elects, to the extent that the taxpayer has net interest income from the bond. (Code Sec. 1277(b)(1))[32]

¶ 1717   Net direct interest expense—short-term government obligations.

The "net direct interest expense" (¶1716) with respect to a short-term government obligation is deductible in a tax year only to the extent the expense exceeds the total of: (1) the daily portions of the acquisition discount (i.e., the excess of the stated redemption price at maturity over the taxpayer's basis for the obligation) for each day during the year that the taxpayer held the obligation, plus (2) the amount of any other (stated) interest payable on the obligation that accrues during the tax year while the taxpayer held the obligation and that, because of the taxpayer's accounting method, wasn't included in his gross income. (Code Sec. 1282(a))[33]

Deduction of disallowed interest expense generally is deferred until (as with market discount bonds, see ¶1716) the taxpayer disposes of the obligation, or earlier if the taxpayer so elects. (Code Sec. 1282(c))[34]

¶ 1718   Interest on business life insurance, annuity or endowment contract loans.

In general, no deduction is allowed (for exception, see below) for any interest paid or accrued on any debt with respect to one or more life insurance policies owned by the taxpayer covering the life of any individual, or any annuity or endowment contract owned by the taxpayer covering any individual. (Code Sec. 264(a)(4))

For contracts issued before June 9, '97, the interest disallowance rule applies only if the covered individual is or was either an officer or employee of, or financially interested in, any trade or business currently or formerly carried on by the taxpayer. For policies purchased before June 21, '86, the disallowance rule generally didn't apply. [35]

A taxpayer *may* deduct a limited amount of interest (assuming it isn't barred by the rules at ¶1719 and ¶1720), subject to certain rate limitations, paid or accrued with respect to policies or contracts covering a "key person" (an officer or 20% owner) to the extent that the aggregate amount of the debt with respect to policies and contracts covering that person doesn't exceed $50,000. (Code Sec. 264(e)(1)) This exception applies only to a limited number of key persons (not more than the greater of: (1) 5 individuals, or (2) the lesser of 5% of total officers and employees, or 20 individuals). (Code Sec. 264(e)(3))[36]

¶ 1719   Single premium life insurance, endowment and annuity contracts.

No deduction is allowed for interest on debt incurred or continued to buy or carry single premium life insurance, endowment or annuity contracts. (Code Sec. 264(a)(2); Reg § 1.264-2) A contract is "single premium" if "substantially all" the premiums are paid within four years from the purchase date, or if an amount is deposited with the insurer for payment of a "substantial" number of future premiums on the contract. (Code Sec. 264(c))[37]

---

31. ¶K-5342; ¶12,764.02; TD ¶316,502
32. ¶K-5343; ¶12,764.02; TD ¶316,503
33. ¶K-5344; ¶12,814.02; TD ¶316,504
34. ¶K-5343; ¶12,814.02; TD ¶316,505

35. ¶K-5351; ¶2644; TD ¶316,801
36. ¶K-5352 *et seq.*; ¶2644; TD ¶316,802
37. ¶K-5570 *et seq.*; ¶2644; TD ¶317,200 *et seq.*

¶ 1720 "Plan of purchase" borrowing against life insurance contracts.

No deduction is allowed for interest on debt incurred or continued to buy or carry a life insurance, endowment or annuity contract under a plan of purchase (borrowing for more than 3 years is presumed to be a plan (Reg § 1.264-4(c)(1))) that contemplates the systematic direct or indirect borrowing of part or all of the increases in the contract's cash value from the insurer or another party (e.g., a bank). (Code Sec. 264(a)(3))[38]

There are exceptions to this rule, e.g., for borrowing incurred because of an unforeseen loss of income or substantial increase in financial obligations, or borrowing in connection with a taxpayer's trade or business. (Code Sec. 264(d); Reg § 1.264-4)[39]

¶ 1721 No deduction for interest allocable to unborrowed policy cash values ("inside buildup") on life insurance, annuity and endowment contracts.

Except as discussed below, no deduction is allowed to a taxpayer (other than a natural person) for interest expense that's allocable to unborrowed policy cash values (i.e., the cash surrender value of all life insurance, annuity, or endowment policies issued after June 8, '97, less loans on the policies). (Code Sec. 264(f))[40]

The portion of the interest expense that's allocable to unborrowed policy cash values is an amount that bears the same ratio to that interest expense as (1) average unborrowed policy cash values of life insurance policies, and annuity and endowment contracts, issued after June 8, '97, bears to (2) the sum of: (i) for assets that are life insurance policies or annuity or endowment contracts, the average unborrowed policy cash values of the policies and contracts; and (ii) for assets that aren't described in (i), the average adjusted bases (under Code Sec. 1016) of those assets. (Code Sec. 264(f)(2))[41]

The disallowance rule doesn't apply to any of the following:

(1) Any policy or contract owned by an entity engaged in a trade or business if the policy or contract covers only one individual and if that individual is (at the time first covered by the policy or contract) a 20% owner of the entity, or an individual (who isn't a 20% owner) who is an officer, director, or employee of the trade or business. (Code Sec. 264(f)(4)(A))[42]

(2) Any annuity contract to which Code Sec. 72(u) applies (i.e., annuity contracts subject to the natural-person-as-holder requirement, ¶1357). (Code Sec. 264(f)(4)(B))[43]

(3) Any policy or contract held by a natural person. But, if a trade or business is directly or indirectly the beneficiary, the policy or contract is treated as held by the trade or business and not by a natural person, but this doesn't apply to any trade or business carried on as a sole proprietorship, or to any trade or business of performing services as an employee. (Code Sec. 264(f)(5)(A))[44]

(4) Certain insurance companies. (Code Sec. 264(f)(8)(B))[45]

(5) Any policy or contract issued before June 9, '97.[46]

When a policy that qualifies under exception (1) is exchanged for a new policy in a tax-free Code Sec. 1035 exchange, the new policy must qualify on its own for the exception when it's received. Moreover, a policy or contract covering a 20% owner of an entity won't fail to meet the exception (1) test because the policy or contract covers the joint lives of the 20% owner and the owner's spouse.[47]

In applying the above rules, all members of a controlled group generally are treated as one

38. ¶K-5581*et seq.*; ¶2644; TD ¶317,500
39. ¶K-5584; ¶2644; TD ¶317,505
40. ¶K-5601; ¶2644.01; TD ¶317,601
41. ¶K-5604; ¶2644.01; TD ¶317,603
42. ¶K-5606; ¶2644.01; TD ¶317,605

43. ¶K-5606.1; ¶2644.01; TD ¶317,605
44. ¶K-5606.2; ¶2644.01; TD ¶317,605
45. ¶K-5606.3; ¶2644.01; TD ¶317,605
46. ¶K-5601; ¶2644.01; TD ¶317,601
47. ¶K-5606

taxpayer (Code Sec. 264(f)(8)(A));[48] in the case of partnerships and S corporations, the rules apply at the entity level. (Code Sec. 264(f)(5)(B))[49]

¶ 1722   Loans from qualified employer plans.

No deduction is allowed for interest on any loan from a qualified employer plan that isn't treated as a distribution, for the period: (1) on or after the first day the individual to whom the loan is made is a key employee (defined in Code Sec. 416(i)), or (2) during which the loan is secured by amounts attributable to elective deferrals under a Code Sec. 401(k) plan (¶4317) or a Code Sec. 403(b) annuity (¶4388 *et seq.*). (Code Sec. 72(p)(3))[50]

¶ 1723   Loans to buy or carry tax-exempt securities.

No deduction is allowed for interest on debt incurred or continued to buy or carry tax-exempt securities (e.g., state or local bonds, see ¶1331) (Code Sec. 265(a)(2)), or stock of a mutual fund (¶4201) distributing exempt interest. (Code Sec. 265(a)(4))[1]

¶ 1724   Registration-required obligations.

No deduction is allowed for interest on "registration-required obligations" (defined in Code Sec. 163(f)(2)) that aren't in registered form. (Code Sec. 163(f)(1))[2]

¶ 1725   Interest on corporate acquisition indebtedness.

The amount of a corporation's deductions for interest paid or accrued on indebtedness incurred to acquire the stock or assets of other corporations is limited. The maximum annual deduction for such interest is $5,000,000, less the amount of interest on certain acquisition indebtedness incurred after '67. Whether indebtedness is subject to this limitation is determined by tests for acquisition purpose, subordination, convertibility and debt-equity or interest coverage. (Code Sec. 279)[3]

¶ 1726   Investment Interest Deduction Limitations. ▬▬▬▬▬▬▬▬▬▬▬

Noncorporate taxpayers can deduct investment interest only to the extent of net investment income.

¶ 1727   Investment interest deductions of noncorporate taxpayers—Form 4952.

The amount of investment interest (¶1728) that may be deducted in any tax year by a noncorporate taxpayer generally is limited to the taxpayer's "net investment income" (¶1729) for the year. (Code Sec. 163(d)(1)) Form 4952 is used to compute the limitation.[4]

Interest that's disallowed because of this limit can be carried over and deducted in later years, subject to the later year's investment income limit. (Code Sec. 163(d)(2))[5]

¶ 1728   "Investment interest."

"Investment interest" is interest paid or accrued on indebtedness properly allocable to property held for investment. (Code Sec. 163(d)(3)(A))[6] The deduction limit on investment interest (¶1727) doesn't apply to interest expense that must be capitalized (e.g., construction interest), or that's disallowed under Code Sec. 265 (¶1723).[7]

Property held for investment is: (1) any property that produces income properly allocable to

---

48. ¶K-5602
49. ¶K-5603; ¶2644.01; TD ¶317,602
50. ¶K-5506, H-11065 *et seq.*; ¶724.23; TD ¶317,000
1. ¶K-5520 *et seq.*, ¶K-5546; ¶2654; TD ¶316,001
2. ¶K-5550 *et seq.*; ¶1634

3. ¶K-5405 *et seq.*; ¶1634, 2794
4. ¶K-5310 *et seq.*; ¶1634.053; TD ¶315,011
5. ¶K-5321; ¶1634.053 ; TD ¶315,021
6. ¶K-5312; ¶1634.053; TD ¶315,012
7. ¶K-5312; TD ¶315,012

portfolio income under the passive activity rules—e.g., interest, dividends (but stock is "held for investment" even if it doesn't pay dividends), royalties, annuities, see ¶1820; (Code Sec. 163(d)(5)(A)(i))[8], and (2) any interest in an activity involving a trade or business in which taxpayer doesn't materially participate, if that activity isn't "passive" under the passive activity rules (¶1822). (Code Sec. 163(d)(5)(A)(ii))[9]

Investment interest includes interest on a home mortgage (other than "qualified residence interest," see below) if its purpose is to acquire investment property.[10] It also includes any amount allowable as a deduction in connection with personal property used in a short sale. (Code Sec. 163(d)(3)(C))[11] Payments made in lieu of dividends by a short seller to a lender are subject to the investment interest limitations and are deductible only to the extent of net investment income. If the short sale is closed within 45 days, however, these "in lieu of dividend payments" are not deductible, but are added to the basis of the stock used to close the short sale. (Code Sec. 263(h))[12]

Investment interest *doesn't include* interest on funds borrowed in connection with a trade or business, or any interest that is: (1) taken into account in determining a taxpayer's income or loss from a passive activity, (2) qualified residence interest (¶1732) (Code Sec. 163(d)(3)(B)), or (3) properly allocable to a rental real estate activity in which, under the passive activity rules (¶1835), a taxpayer actively participates.[13]

¶ 1729 "Net investment income" defined—Form 4952.

A taxpayer's "net investment income" for a tax year is the excess of "investment income" over "investment expenses" for the year. (Code Sec. 163(d)(4)(A))[14] (For the definition of net investment interest for alternative minimum tax purposes, see ¶3209.)

"Investment income" is the sum of: (1) gross income (other than gain) from property held for investment (¶1728); (2) any excess of *net gain* attributable to the disposition of investment property over *net capital gain* determined by only taking into account gains and losses from these dispositions; (3) so much of taxpayer's *net capital gain* (or *net gain,* if less) described in (2), as he elects (on Form 4952) to include in investment income (for the effect of such an election on net capital gain, see ¶2604). Qualified dividend income (defined at ¶1288) is included in investment income only to the extent the taxpayer elects on Form 4952. (Code Sec. 163(d)(4)(B); Reg § 1.163(d)-1)[15]

"Investment expenses" are deductible expenses *other than interest* that are directly connected with the production of investment income (Code Sec. 163(d)(4)(C)), but limited to the amount allowed after the 2%-of-AGI floor (¶3110). Nonbusiness bad debts (¶1853) directly connected with the production of income are taken into account to the extent they are currently deductible.[16]

Investment income and expenses don't include any amounts taken into account in computing income or loss from a passive activity (¶1810 *et seq.*). (Code Sec. 163(d)(4)(D))[17]

¶ 1730 Qualified Residence Interest. ▬▬▬▬▬▬

A taxpayer may claim itemized deductions for "qualified residence interest" —i.e., interest on (1) up to $1,000,000 of acquisition debt and (2) up to $100,000 of home-equity debt. The debt must be secured by the taxpayer's "qualified residence."

8. ¶K-5322; ¶1634.053; TD ¶315,022
9. ¶K-5322; ¶1634.053; TD ¶315,018
10. ¶K-5313; TD ¶315,013
11. ¶K-5312; TD ¶315,012
12. ¶L-4224; TD ¶338,502

13. ¶K-5312 *et seq.*; ¶1634.053; TD ¶315,012
14. ¶K-5311; ¶1634.053; TD ¶315,015
15. ¶K-5315 *et seq.*; ¶1634.053; TD ¶315,015 *et seq.*
16. ¶K-5320; ¶1634.053; TD ¶315,020
17. ¶s K-5315, K-5320; ¶1634.053; TD ¶315,020

¶ 1731   Deduction of "qualified residence interest."

"Qualified residence interest" (¶1732) is not subject to the following limits and special rules:

- personal interest deduction bar (¶1715) (Code Sec. 163(h)(2)(D); Reg § 1.163-10T(b));

⊘*observation:* In other words, qualified residence interest is not subject to the prohibition on the deduction of personal interest, and may be deducted under the general rule allowing the deduction of interest, discussed at ¶1700 *et seq.*

- investment interest limitations (¶1728); (Code Sec. 163(d)(3)(B)(i); Reg § 1.163-10T(b))
- passive activity interest limitations (¶1815); (Code Sec. 469(j)(7); Reg § 1.163-10T(b))
- uniform capitalization rules (¶1667). (Reg § 1.163-10T(b))[18]

But qualified residence interest is subject to the interest bars and limits in connection with: single premium insurance (¶1719); tax-exempt income (¶1723); related-party transactions (¶2836); the "at-risk" rules (¶1803 *et seq.*); accrued market discount (¶1716); and straddle interest (¶2653 *et seq.*). (Reg § 1.163-10T(b))[19]

For how the interest allocation rules apply to qualified residence interest, see ¶1741.

⊘*caution:* For the treatment of residence interest for alternative minimum tax purposes, see ¶3209.

¶ 1732   What is "qualified residence interest"?

"Qualified residence interest" (see   ¶1731) is any interest paid or accrued during the tax year on acquisition indebtedness (¶1733) or home equity indebtedness (¶1734) with respect to any property that, at the time the interest is accrued, is the taxpayer's "qualified residence" (¶1735), but only to the extent the interest is paid or accrued while the debt is secured by the residence. (Code Sec. 163(h)(3)(A); Reg § 1.163-10T(j)(1)) For a cash basis taxpayer, it also includes certain "points" paid on debt incurred in connection with his principal residence. (Reg § 1.163-10T(j)(2)(i))[20] For treatment of certain mortgage insurance premiums as qualified residence interest, see ¶1736.

A debt may be part acquisition indebtedness (¶1733) and part home equity indebtedness (¶1734).[21]

¶ 1733   Acquisition indebtedness.

Acquisition indebtedness (interest on which is deductible qualified residence interest, see ¶1731) is debt that: (1) meets the dollar limitation described below; (2) is incurred in acquiring, constructing or substantially improving a taxpayer's "qualified residence" (¶1735) (or adjoining land) and (3) is secured by the residence. (Code Sec. 163(h)(3)(B)(i)) In general, acquisition debt must be an obligation of the taxpayer.[22] New debt a taxpayer incurs to refinance his acquisition indebtedness also qualifies, but only up to the amount of the refinanced debt. (Code Sec. 163(h)(3)(B)(i))[23] Debt is treated as incurred in acquiring, etc., a residence if the debt proceeds can be traced to payment of the costs of the acquisition, etc.[24]

The aggregate amount of debt that may be treated as acquisition indebtedness for any period can't exceed $1,000,000 ($500,000 for a married individual filing a separate return). (Code Sec. 163(h)(3)(B)(ii)) These dollar amounts are reduced (not below zero) by the aggregate amount of outstanding (including refinanced) "pre-Oct. 13, '87 indebtedness." (Code

---

18. ¶K-5473; ¶1634.052; TD ¶314,501
19. ¶K-5473 *et seq.*; TD ¶314,501
20. ¶K-5471; ¶1634.052; TD ¶314,502
21. ¶K-5491; TD ¶314,521

22. ¶K-5484; ¶1634.052; TD ¶314,515
23. ¶K-5488; ¶1634.052; TD ¶314,519
24. ¶K-5487; TD ¶318,001

Sec. 163(h)(3)(D)) IRS says that where a single property is owned by more than one taxpayer, each owner doesn't get his own $1,000,000 ceiling; rather a single acquisition debt ceiling applies to the property.[25] For where debt exceeds these limits, see ¶1741.

¶ 1734   Home equity indebtedness.

Home equity indebtedness (interest on which is deductible qualified residence interest, see ¶1731) is any debt (other than acquisition indebtedness, see ¶1733) secured by taxpayer's qualified residence (¶1735), to the extent the aggregate amount of the debt doesn't exceed the fair market value of the residence (as reduced by the amount of acquisition debt on the residence). (Code Sec. 163(h)(3)(C)(i)) Unlike acquisition debt (¶1733), home equity debt generally may be used for any purpose without affecting its deductibility, see ¶1741. The aggregate amount treated as home equity debt for any period may not exceed $100,000 ($50,000 for a married individual filing a separate return). (Code Sec. 163(h)(3)(C)(ii)) For debt that exceeds these limits, see ¶1741.[26]

¶ 1735   Qualified residence.

A qualified residence (¶1732) is: (1) taxpayer's principal residence (i.e., one that would qualify for exclusion of gain under Code Sec. 121 (¶2442) (Code Sec. 163(h)(4)(A)(i)(I)) and/or (2) any other residence (second residence) taxpayer properly elects to treat as qualified for the tax year, even if he didn't use it as a residence that year. But a second residence that taxpayer rents out to others during the year can't qualify unless he also uses it as a residence (i.e., uses it for personal purposes during the year for more than the greater of 14 days or 10% of the number of days it is rented out for a fair rental). (Code Sec. 163(h)(4)(A)(i)(II), Code Sec. 163(h)(4)(A)(iii); Reg § 1.163-10T(p)(3)(iii)) A taxpayer who has more than one residence that meets these tests may elect each year which to treat as the second (qualified) residence. (Code Sec. 163(h)(4)(A)(i); Reg § 1.163-10T(p)(3)(iv))[27]

A residence for this purpose includes a condominium or cooperative housing corporation (co-op). Any indebtedness secured by stock in a co-op is treated as secured by the house or apartment taxpayer is entitled to occupy. Even if local restrictions prohibit using the stock as security, it will be treated as securing the debt if taxpayer can show the debt was incurred to acquire the stock. (Code Sec. 163(h)(4)(B); Reg § 1.163-10T(p)(3))[28]

A time-share can also qualify if it satisfies the above tests for rental property. (Reg § 1.163-10T(p)(6))[29]

A residence under construction may be treated as a qualified residence for a period of up to 24 months, but only if it otherwise qualifies as of the time it's ready for occupancy. (Reg § 1.163-10T(p)(5))[30]

For married taxpayers filing jointly, the second residence may be owned and/or used by either spouse. For spouses filing separately, each may have only one qualified residence (unless the other spouse gives written consent otherwise). (Code Sec. 163(h)(4)(A))[31]

¶ 1736   Pre-2014 mortgage insurance premiums as qualified residence interest.

2014, premiums paid or accrued by a taxpayer during the tax year for qualified mortgage insurance in connection with acquisition indebtedness (¶1733) for a taxpayer's qualified residence are treated as qualified residence interest subject to a phase-out based on the taxpayer's adjusted gross income (AGI) (below). (Code Sec. 163(h)(3)(E)(i))[32]

observation: To be deductible under the above rule, premiums for qualified mortgage

---

25. ¶s K-5485, K-5489; ¶1634.052; TD ¶314,516
26. ¶K-5490; ¶1634.052; TD ¶314,520
27. ¶K-5474 *et seq.*; ¶1634.052; TD ¶314,504
28. ¶K-5481; ¶1634.052; TD ¶314,511

29. ¶K-5482; TD ¶314,512
30. ¶K-5483; TD ¶314,513
31. ¶K-5480; ¶1634.052; TD ¶314,510
32. ¶K-5493 *et seq.*; ¶1634.052; TD ¶314,519.1

insurance have to be paid or accrued in connection with acquisition indebtedness. But, since qualified mortgage insurance isn't a category of acquisition indebtedness, but rather a separate category of qualified residence interest, qualified mortgage insurance premiums aren't subject to the amount limitations on acquisition indebtedness, and don't affect the amount of indebtedness that could qualify as acquisition indebtedness under those limitations, see ¶1733.

Qualified mortgage insurance means mortgage insurance provided by the Veterans Administration (VA), the Federal Housing Administration (FHA), or the Rural Housing Administration (RHA), and private mortgage insurance, as defined by Sec. 2 of the Homeowners Protection Act of '98 (12 U.S.C. 4901), as in effect on Dec. 20, 2006. (Code Sec. 163(h)(4)(E)(ii))

Except for mortgage insurance provided by the VA or the RHA, premiums for qualified mortgage insurance that are properly allocable to periods after the end of the tax year (i.e., prepaid mortgage insurance) are generally treated as paid in the period to which they are allocated.[33]

But, no deduction is allowed for the unamortized balance of premiums that have been capitalized if the mortgage is satisfied before the end of its term. (Code Sec. 163(h)(4)(F))

An individual may allocate prepaid qualified mortgage insurance premiums that are treated as qualified residence interest under Code Sec. 163(h)(3)(E) over the shorter of (1) the stated term of the mortgage, or (2) a period of 84 months. (Reg § 1.163-11(a)(1))[34]

The rules treating qualified mortgage insurance premiums as deductible qualified residence interest apply only if the amounts: (1) are paid or accrued before Jan. 1, 2014; (2) aren't properly allocable to any period after Dec. 31, 2013; and (3) are paid or accrued with respect to a mortgage insurance contract issued after Dec. 31, 2006. (Code Sec. 163(h)(3)(E))

The amount of mortgage insurance premiums otherwise treated as qualified residence interest under the rule above must be reduced (but not below zero) by: (a) for taxpayers other than married persons filing separately, 10% of the amount of qualified mortgage insurance for each $1,000 (or fraction thereof) that the taxpayer's AGI for the tax year exceeds $100,000, and (b) for married persons filing separately, 10% of the amount of qualified mortgage insurance for each $500 (or fraction thereof) that the taxpayer's AGI for the tax year exceeds $50,000. (Code Sec. 163(h)(3)(E)(ii))[35]

¶ 1737   Allocation Rules for Interest and Debt. ■■■■■■■■■■■■■■

Debt proceeds may be used in ways that trigger more than one interest deduction limitation. To determine which limit applies (personal interest, ¶1715, investment interest, ¶1727, or passive activity interest, ¶1815), the interest and underlying debt must be properly allocated, generally by tracing the use of the borrowed money.

¶ 1738   Interest deduction limits require allocation of interest expense.

For certain taxpayers (¶1739), where the proceeds of a single debt are used for multiple purposes—e.g., to make investments *and* to buy "personal" items —the debt must be allocated among the various expenditures. (Reg § 1.163-8T)[36]

Interest expense is allocated the same way as the debt with respect to which the interest accrues, by tracing disbursements of the debt proceeds to specific expenditures. (Reg § 1.163-8T(a)(3), Reg § 1.163-8T(c)(1)) Except for qualified residence interest (¶1732), the nature of any property securing the debt isn't relevant. (Reg § 1.163-8T(c)(1))[37]

The interest, as allocated, is subject to the appropriate deduction limit, as follows:

---

33. ¶K-5493 *et seq.*; ¶1634.052; TD ¶314,519.1
34. ¶K-5493; ¶1634.052; TD ¶314,519.1
35. ¶K-5493.1; ¶1634.052; TD ¶314,519.1

36. ¶K-5231 *et seq.*; ¶1634.055; TD ¶318,001
37. ¶K-5231; ¶1634.055; TD ¶318,001

... Interest allocated to a passive activity expenditure (current or former) is subject to the passive activity limitations (¶1815).

... Interest allocated to an investment expenditure is subject to the investment interest limitations (¶1727).

... Interest allocated to a personal expenditure is treated as personal interest (i.e., it's not deductible, see ¶1715).

... Interest allocated to a trade or business expenditure is treated as trade or business interest (i.e., it's not subject to the personal or investment interest limits). (Code Sec. 469(l)(4); Reg § 1.163-8T(a)(4)(i))[38]

The interest expense allocation rules don't control the allocation of interest for any purpose other than those listed above.[39]

¶ 1739 Taxpayers who must allocate interest.

The interest expense allocation rules (¶1738) apply to all taxpayers *other than* widely-held C corporations. So, the rules apply to a pass-through entity (e.g., partnership or S corporation) that borrows money to make distributions to its owners (partners or shareholders), or whose debt is allocated to those distributions. Repayments of a pass-through entity's debt that is allocated partly to a distribution to its owners and partly to other expenditures are treated first as a repayment of the portion of the debt allocated to the distribution.[40]

¶ 1740 Time for allocation of debt and interest expense.

Debt is allocated to an expenditure for the period: (1) beginning on the date the proceeds of the debt are used or treated as used to make the expenditure, and (2) ending on the date the debt is repaid or reallocated (¶1742), whichever is earlier. (Reg § 1.163-8T(c)(2)(i))[41]

Generally, interest expense that accrues on a debt is allocated in the same manner as the debt is allocated from time to time, regardless of when the interest is actually paid. (Reg § 1.163-8T(c)(2)(ii)(A))[42]

¶ 1741 Qualified residence interest as "allocable" interest.

Qualified residence interest (¶1730 *et seq.*) is deductible without regard to how that interest expense or the underlying debt is allocated. (Reg § 1.163-8T(m)(3))[43]

But, where the debt exceeds the qualified residence interest limits (¶1733, ¶1734), allocation is required for the "excess." (Reg § 1.163-10T(e))[44]

¶ 1742 Reallocation of interest

Where the use of debt proceeds, or of assets bought with debt proceeds, changes, the interest on the debt must be reallocated to the new use. The interest so reallocated will be subject to any appropriate deduction limits (¶1738). (Reg § 1.163-8T(j)(1))[45]

¶ 1743 When Interest May Be Deducted.

The proper time for deducting interest is generally determined by the taxpayer's method of accounting. Special rules govern when mortgage "points," unstated interest and original issue discount (OID) must be deducted.

---

38. ¶K-5232; ¶1634.055; TD ¶318,000 *et seq.*
39. ¶K-5234; TD ¶318,002
40. ¶K-5259 *et seq.*; ¶1634.056; TD ¶318,033
41. ¶K-5233; ¶1634.055; TD ¶318,008

42. ¶K-5233; ¶1634.055; TD ¶318,008
43. ¶K-5238; ¶1634.055; TD ¶318,005
44. ¶K-5498 *et seq.*; TD ¶314,530
45. ¶K-5254 *et seq.*; ¶1634.055; TD ¶318,023

¶ 1744　Cash method taxpayer's interest deduction.

A cash method taxpayer may deduct interest only if it is actually *paid* during the tax year. (Code Sec. 163(a)) (For accrual taxpayers, see ¶1748.) The payment can be made with funds borrowed from another creditor, but not with funds borrowed from the same creditor, or by giving a note for the interest or adding the unpaid interest to principal.[46]

Contested interest (where the debtor claims he doesn't owe it) isn't deductible. But if a cash basis taxpayer transfers money or other property to provide for the satisfaction of the asserted (and otherwise deductible) interest, it's deductible in the year of the transfer. (Code Sec. 461(f))[47] For prepaid interest (including "points"), see ¶1745.

¶ 1745　Prepaid interest (including "points").

Interest that is prepaid, including "points" (except certain home mortgage points, see ¶1746), is deductible only in the tax year to which, and to the extent that, the interest is allocable—i.e., as it accrues. (Code Sec. 461(g)(1)) Cash method taxpayers thus generally deduct points ratably over the term of the loan (for refinancings, see ¶1747).[48]

A taxpayer who "pays" points by receiving discounted loan proceeds gets no current deduction (except certain mortgage points, ¶1746).[49] Instead, the discount is treated as original issue discount (OID), deductible by the borrower under the OID rules (¶1751). Discounts *not* subject to the OID rules may be deducted ratably as the underlying debt is repaid.[50]

If the mortgage ends early, e.g., because of a prepayment, refinancing, foreclosure or similar event, the taxpayer may deduct the remaining balance of points in the year it ends.[1]

¶ 1746　"Points" on a home mortgage—cash method taxpayer's deduction in year of payment.

A cash method taxpayer may (but doesn't have to) deduct points paid on indebtedness incurred in connection with the purchase or improvement of (and secured by) his principal residence, in the tax year of actual payment—i.e., in advance, not ratably (see ¶1745) (for refinancing, see ¶1747). The charging of points must reflect an established business practice in the geographical area where the loan is made, and the deduction allowed can't exceed the amount generally charged there. (Code Sec. 461(g)(2)) For loans used to improve the residence, the points must be paid with funds other than those borrowed from the lender or mortgage broker.[2]

For loans used to acquire the residence, cash basis taxpayers may currently deduct amounts that meet the above tests *and* are: (1) clearly designated (on Form HUD-1) as points incurred in connection with the debt (including "points" on VA and FHA loans) —i.e., they aren't paid in lieu of nondeductible amounts that are ordinarily stated separately, e.g., appraisal fees; (2) computed as a percentage of the stated principal amount of the debt; *and* (3) paid directly by taxpayer to the lender (or mortgage broker). Condition (3) is met where taxpayer provides, from funds that haven't been borrowed for this purpose as part of the overall transaction, an amount at least equal to what is required to be applied as points at closing (even if the amount so provided is used for down payments, escrow deposits, etc., actually paid at closing).[3]

Points paid by (or charged to) the seller in connection with a loan to the buyer (taxpayer) also are deductible by the buyer if he subtracts them from the purchase price in computing

---

46. ¶K-5170 *et seq.*; ¶s 1634.030, 1634.031; TD ¶318,700 *et seq.*
47. ¶G-2442 *et seq.*; ¶4614.56 *et seq.*; TD ¶319,004, 319,005
48. ¶K-5177; ¶s 1634.005, 1634.032, 4614.75; TD ¶318,707
49. ¶K-5178; ¶4614.75; TD ¶319,201

50. ¶K-5176; ¶4614.75; TD ¶318,706
1. ¶K-5183; TD ¶319,206
2. ¶K-5178 *et seq.*; ¶s 1634.005, 4614.75; TD ¶319,201
3. ¶K-5179; ¶4614.75; TD ¶319,202

the basis of the residence.[4]

¶ 1747 "Points" on refinancing.

Points paid to *refinance* an existing mortgage generally are deductible only ratably over the loan term (¶1745). But where the refinancing is incurred for home improvements, points paid from separate funds may be deducted currently.[5]

¶ 1748 Accrual method taxpayer's interest deduction.

Accrual method taxpayers deduct interest when all the events have occurred that fix the fact of the liability, the amount of the liability can be determined with reasonable accuracy, and economic performance (¶2832 *et seq.*) has occurred.[6] (For cash method, see ¶1744.)

The interest is deductible only in the year it accrues, without regard to when the (accrual basis) taxpayer pays it. For these purposes, interest (including prepaid interest) accrues ratably over the life of a loan. But interest that's contingent on events other than the creditor's demand for payment doesn't accrue until the contingency happens.[7]

Contested interest (where the debtor claims he doesn't owe it) isn't accrued or deductible. But if the accrual basis taxpayer transfers money or other property to provide for the satisfaction of the asserted interest, it's deductible in the year of the transfer. (Code Sec. 461(f))[8]

¶ 1749 Interest under the "Rule of 78s" method.

The Rule of 78's is a method of allocating interest on a loan among time periods during the term of the loan. The Rule of 78s method can't be used to compute interest. Interest so computed must be recomputed under an economic accrual method for federal income tax purposes.[9]

¶ 1750 When to deduct "unstated interest."

The unstated interest allocated to a payment in a deferred payment sale (¶1707) is deducted by cash method buyers in the year the payment is made, and by accrual method buyers in the year the payment is due.[10] But both cash and accrual taxpayers must use the cash method rules to deduct interest on cash method debt instruments (¶1320). (Code Sec. 1274A(c)(1)(B))[11]

¶ 1751 Original issue discount (OID).

The issuer of a debt instrument issued with OID (¶1313 *et seq.*) may (with some exceptions, ¶1753) deduct part of the OID (¶1752) in each tax year the instrument is outstanding, even though the OID isn't paid until maturity. (Code Sec. 163(e)(1); Reg § 1.163-3(a)(1), Reg § 1.163-4(a)(1)) This current deduction rule applies regardless of the method of accounting used by the issuer.[12] But a cash method obligor of a short-term obligation can only deduct OID (and other interest) when it is paid. (Code Sec. 163(e)(2)(C))[13]

An issuer may deduct OID only to the extent the issuer is primarily liable on the debt instrument. (Reg § 1.163-7(a))[14]

OID for this purpose has the same meaning as for purposes of requiring the holder to include OID in gross income currently (see ¶1314) *except*:

---

4. ¶K-5179; ¶4614.75; TD ¶318,606
5. ¶K-5180; ¶s 1634.005, 4614.75; TD ¶319,203
6. ¶K-5200 *et seq.*; ¶1634.035 *et seq.*; TD ¶319,000 *et seq.*
7. ¶s K-5200, K-5201; ¶s 1634.035, 1634.036; TD ¶319,001
8. ¶G-2643 *et seq.*; ¶4614.56 *et seq.*; TD ¶319,004, 319,005
9. ¶K-5153; ¶1634.030

10. ¶K-5283; ¶1634; TD ¶319,503
11. ¶K-5283; TD ¶319,503
12. ¶K-5700 *et seq.*; ¶1634.051; TD ¶319,701
13. ¶K-5712; ¶1634.032, 1634.051; TD ¶319,710
14. ¶K-5745; ¶1634.051; TD ¶319,714

. . . The de minimis exception doesn't apply. (Code Sec. 163(e)(2)(B))[15] But an issuer with de minimis OID may elect to deduct the OID at maturity. (Reg § 1.163-7(b)(2))[16]

. . . A nonpublicly traded debt instrument issued to a seller in exchange for personal use property isn't treated as issued with OID that the buyer (issuer) can deduct currently. (Code Sec. 1275(b)(1))[17]

In addition, the issuer can deduct as interest the repurchase premium (the excess of the price over the adjusted issue price) where the debt instrument is repurchased.[18]

¶ 1752   Amount of OID deductible currently.

The amount of OID the issuer of a debt instrument deducts currently (¶1751) is determined in the same way as the amount of OID the holder includes in gross income currently (using the constant yield method, see ¶1321), but without regard to (1) the reduction for any acquisition premium paid by the holder and (2) the treatment of stated interest as "qualified stated interest" where OID is de minimis. (Code Sec. 163(e)(2)(B); Reg § 1.163-7(a))[19]

¶ 1753   Limits on OID deduction for certain high yield OID obligations.

For certain applicable high yield discount obligations ("AHYDOs") (with yields at least five percentage points over the applicable federal rate for month of issue) issued after July 10, '89, a C corporation can't deduct (or otherwise take into account) any part of the OID until actually paid. In some cases, the deduction may be barred for all or part of the OID, depending on the obligation's yield, maturity date and amount of OID. However, these rules were suspended for certain obligations issued in a debt-for-debt exchange, including an exchange resulting from a significant modification of a debt instrument, after Dec. 31, 2009 and before Jan. 1, 2011. (Code Sec. 163(e)(5))[20]

¶ 1754   Deduction for Taxes. ■■■■■■■■■■■■■■■■■■■■■■■■■■■■■■■■■

Certain state, local, U.S. possessions and foreign taxes are deductible whether or not connected with a trade or business; so are some federal taxes, other than federal income taxes.

Only payments that are really taxes (regardless of what they are called) are deductible as taxes (see ¶1757). Taxes are charges imposed on persons or property by governmental authority to raise funds for the support of government or for public purposes. The mere fact that a levy is called a "tax" isn't conclusive. [21] Fees imposed primarily as charges for government services, e.g., fees for a driver's license or car inspection, or passport fees, aren't deductible as taxes.[22] Penalties paid to a government for violation of a law aren't taxes. (Code Sec. 162(f))[23]

¶ 1755   Which taxes are deductible?

Deductible *state, local and foreign taxes* are:

. . . state, local and foreign income, war profits and excess profits taxes;

. . . state, local and foreign real property taxes;

. . . state and local personal property taxes (¶1760); and

. . . other state, local and foreign taxes (e.g., occupational taxes) paid or accrued in business or for the production of income unless incurred in connection with an acquisition or disposition of property (e.g., sales taxes, see ¶1756). (Code Sec. 164(a)(1), Code Sec. 164(a)(3))[24]

---

15. ¶K-5727; ¶1634.051; TD ¶319,719
16. ¶K-5748; ¶1634.051; TD ¶319,725
17. ¶K-5724; TD ¶319,717
18. ¶K-5749; ¶1634.051; TD ¶319,744
19. ¶K-5745 *et seq.*; ¶1634.051; TD ¶319,725 *et seq.*

20. ¶K-5754; ¶K-5755.2; ¶1634.051
21. ¶K-4003; ¶1644; TD ¶326,011
22. ¶K-4003 *et seq.*; ¶1644; TD ¶326,011
23. ¶K-4009; ¶1644; TD ¶326,008
24. ¶K-4001; ¶1644.03; TD ¶326,008

For a deduction for state and local sales taxes instead of income taxes, before 2014, see ¶1756.

For state unemployment and disability taxes, see ¶1758.

These *federal taxes* are deductible as taxes:

- Federal (and state) generation-skipping transfer (GST) tax imposed on income distributions (¶5056 *et seq.*) (Code Sec. 164(a)(4), Code Sec. 164(b)(4));[25]
- Estate tax attributable to income in respect of a decedent (¶3972);
- 50% of the Code Sec. 1401 self-employment tax other than the additional 0.9% Medicare (HI) self-employment tax imposed beginning in 2013. (Code Sec. 164(f)(1))[26]

⚠️*caution:* For the deductibility of taxes for alternative minimum tax purposes, see ¶3209.

Taxes not included above (e.g., gasoline, diesel and other motor fuel taxes, Social Security (FICA) and unemployment (FUTA) taxes on employers, motor vehicle registration fees) aren't deductible as *taxes* (although some motor vehicle fees may qualify as personal property taxes), but may be deductible as *business expenses* or *expenses for the production of income* (¶1506 *et seq.*). (Reg § 1.164-2(f))[27]

For deduction of taxes by individuals who don't itemize, see ¶1757.

These taxes aren't deductible as taxes, expenses or otherwise:

(1) Federal income taxes, including amounts withheld from wages, interest, etc.

(2) Alternative minimum tax.

(3) Social Security (FICA) tax on employees, and Railroad Retirement tax on employees and employee representatives. (Code Sec. 275(a)(1); Reg § 1.164-2(a))

(4) Federal war profits and excess profits taxes. (Code Sec. 275(a)(2); Reg § 1.164-2(b))

(5) Estate, inheritance, legacy, succession and gift tax (other than GST). (Code Sec. 275(a)(3); Reg § 1.164-2(c))

(6) Income, war profits and excess profits taxes of any foreign country or U.S. possession if taxpayer takes the foreign tax credit for them (¶2367 *et seq.*). (Code Sec. 275(a)(4); Reg § 1.164-2(d)) But a deduction is allowed for any tax that isn't allowable as a foreign tax credit because of Code Sec. 901(j) (which denies the credit for taxes paid to certain foreign countries, see ¶2369) (Code Sec. 901(j)(3)), or because of Code Sec. 901(k) (relating to minimum holding period requirements for certain taxes, see ¶2374).

(7) Excise taxes imposed on: charities' excess expenditures to influence legislation; private foundations; qualified pension, etc., plans; certain investment entities (REITs and RICs); excess golden parachute payments; greenmail (Code Sec. 275(a)(6)) and charitable split-dollar insurance transactions (¶2115). (Code Sec. 170(f)(10)(F)(iv))[28]

¶ 1756 State and local sales taxes deductible instead of income tax before 2014—Form 1040.

For tax years beginning before 2014, taxpayers are allowed to elect (on Schedule A of Form 1040) to deduct state and local *general sales and use* taxes instead of state and local *income* taxes. With limited exceptions, a sales or use tax is general if imposed at one rate with respect to the retail sale of a broad range of classes of items. (Code Sec. 164(b)(5); Reg § 1.164-3)[29]

Electing taxpayers can deduct either:

(1) the amount of state and local general sales taxes paid, by accumulating receipts; or

25. ¶K-4403 *et seq.*; ¶1644.06; TD ¶326,004
26. ¶K-4401; ¶1644.07; TD ¶326,002
27. ¶K-4000, L-2350 *et seq.*; ¶1644; TD ¶327,001 *et seq.*
28. ¶L-2358; ¶1644; TD ¶327,003
29. ¶K-4510 *et seq.*; ¶1644.03; TD ¶326,019.1 *et seq.*

(2) the amount determined under IRS tables, plus the actual amount of sales taxes paid on motor vehicles, boats and other IRS-specified items (e.g., aircraft, homes). (Code Sec. 164(b)(5)(H))[30]

IRS publishes tables, as well as a worksheet for computing a taxpayer's state and local sales tax deduction on the basis of the tables. The tables provide an amount of sales taxes paid based on the taxpayer's state of residence, total available income, and number of exemptions. Taxpayers living in more than one state during the year must prorate the table amounts based on the number of days lived in each state. For married taxpayers (¶1762), use of the tables depends on whether they file jointly or separately, and whether they live in the same state.[31]

No foreign sales tax is deductible under the above rules. (Reg § 1.164-3(f)) The elective sales tax deduction doesn't apply to sales taxes paid on items used in a taxpayer's trade or business.[32]

State or local sales or use taxes paid or incurred in connection with the acquisition or disposition of property, and taxes on the transfer of property (e.g., securities, real estate), aren't deductible (the buyer treats them as part of the cost, the seller as a reduction in the amount realized). Other sales taxes are deductible only if paid or incurred in a trade or business or for the production of income. (Code Sec. 164(a))[33]

¶ 1757 Limitations on deduction for taxes if individual doesn't itemize–Form 1040.

An individual generally may deduct taxes only if he itemizes (on Schedule A of Form 1040). (Code Sec. 63(d))[34]

For an individual who doesn't itemize, the deduction is limited to the following taxes that are deductible "above the line" (i.e., from gross income in arriving at adjusted gross income, ¶3102): (1) taxes attributable to a trade or business (including taxes on real property) (Code Sec. 62(a)(1)), or to property held for the production of rents or royalties (Code Sec. 62(a)(4)), and (2) 50% of self-employment taxes. (Code Sec. 164(f))[35]

¶ 1758 State unemployment and disability taxes.

Employers' contributions to state unemployment insurance funds are deductible as taxes if the state so classifies them. Whether an employee's contributions to a state unemployment insurance fund or disability plan are deductible as taxes similarly is determined on a state-by-state basis.[36]

¶ 1759 Local benefit assessments.

Assessments that tend to increase the value of the assessed property (whether or not the value does increase) aren't deductible as taxes (but may be capitalized, see ¶1655 *et seq.*). But a deduction *is* allowed, to the extent the taxpayer shows the assessment is properly allocable to maintenance or interest charges. (Code Sec. 164(c)(1); Reg § 1.164-4(b)(1))[37]

¶ 1760 Personal property taxes.

Personal property taxes imposed by a state or local government are deductible. (Code Sec. 164(a)(2)) The tax must be imposed annually on personal property, on an ad valorem basis (i.e., based on the value of the personal property). (Code Sec. 164(b)(1))[38]

---

30. ¶K-4511; ¶1644.03; TD ¶326,019.2
31. ¶K-4511 *et seq.*; TD ¶326,019.2 *et seq.*
32. ¶K-4510 *et seq.*; ¶1644.03; TD ¶326,019.1 *et seq.*
33. ¶I-2502, K-4500, L-2352.1, P-1174.1; ¶1644.03, 1644.09; TD ¶326,006, 327,001

34. ¶A-2701; ¶634; TD ¶561,201
35. ¶L-2351; ¶624; TD ¶327,002
36. ¶K-4003 *et seq.*; ¶L-2353 *et seq.*; ¶1644.03; TD ¶327,006
37. ¶K-4600 *et seq.*; TD ¶326,020
38. ¶K-4502; ¶1644.03; TD ¶326,014

¶ 1761   Who deducts the tax?

Taxes generally are deductible only by the person on whom they are imposed. (Reg § 1.164-1(a))[39]

One who voluntarily pays a tax imposed on another isn't entitled to a deduction. So, a shareholder can't deduct his payment of the corporation's taxes, or vice versa.[40]

Property taxes are ordinarily imposed on, and so are deductible by, the property owner. (For the year of sale, see ¶1770.) A person who owns a beneficial interest in property may deduct property taxes he pays to protect that interest.[41]

Taxes on property that's leased are deductible by the landlord, even if it's the tenant who makes the payment (which the tenant treats as additional rent expense, see ¶1593). (Reg § 1.162-11(a)) But a tenant deducts taxes paid on improvements the tenant makes where the useful life of the improvements will terminate before the end of the lease.[42]

¶ 1762   Married couple's deduction of taxes.

Spouses filing joint federal returns may deduct on that return all deductible taxes paid by either spouse, whether or not they file joint *state* returns.[43]

If the spouses file separate federal and separate state returns, each spouse may deduct only the state income taxes imposed on and actually paid by that spouse. If a joint state return was filed, then for federal tax purposes, that joint state tax is prorated according to each spouse's gross income, but not to exceed the amount actually paid by the spouse.[44]

¶ 1763   Property taxes on co-owned property.

An individual's deduction for taxes on property he owns with other persons as tenants-in-common may be limited to his pro rata part of the taxes, i.e., the amount attributable to his interest, even if he pays *all* the taxes on the property. This pro rata share limit applies where the tenant is only assessed for his share, where he has a right to contribution from the other tenants, or where his share won't be subject to sale on their default.[45]

Tenants by the entirety (i.e., spouses) and joint tenants with right of survivorship are entitled to deduct in full the taxes they pay on the jointly-owned property.[46]

¶ 1764   Cooperative and condominium housing realty taxes.

Tenant-stockholders of cooperative housing corporations (co-ops) deduct their share of the co-op's real property taxes. (Code Sec. 216)[47] Condominium owners deduct the real property taxes on their individual interests.[48]

¶ 1765   When cash basis taxpayers deduct taxes.

A cash basis taxpayer's taxes are deductible for the tax year he pays them. State and local taxes withheld from the taxpayer's wages are deductible in the year they are withheld.[49] For accrual basis taxpayers, see ¶1767. For prepaid taxes, see ¶1766.

The tax is deductible in the year of payment even if the taxpayer contests the liability and seeks to recover the payment (¶1768).[50] For estimated tax payments, see ¶1766.

39. ¶K-4101 *et seq.*; ¶1644.01; TD ¶328,001
40. ¶K-4103, K-4114; ¶1644.01; TD ¶328,021
41. ¶K-4103; ¶1644.01; TD ¶328,002
42. ¶K-4104; TD ¶328,004
43. ¶s K-4105, K-4107; ¶1644.01; TD ¶328,011
44. ¶s K-4106, K-4108; ¶1644.01; TD ¶328,010

45. ¶K-4112; ¶1644.01; TD ¶328,017
46. ¶K-4112; ¶1644.01; TD ¶328,016
47. ¶K-5900 *et seq.*; ¶2164.01.
48. ¶K-4103; TD ¶328,002
49. ¶K-4201 *et seq.*; ¶1644.02; TD ¶329,001
50. ¶K-4201; ¶4614.56; TD ¶329,001

¶ 1766 Prepaid taxes and estimated tax payments.

A cash basis taxpayer may deduct an advance payment of tax in the year of payment as long as it's an actual good faith payment and not a mere deposit. But the advance payment of state taxes that are later refunded won't be deductible unless taxpayer had a reasonable basis, at the time of payment, for believing he owed the taxes.[1]

Deduction in the year of payment also is allowed for advance estimated tax payments made under a pay-as-you-go tax collection system.[2]

¶ 1767 When accrual basis taxpayers deduct taxes.

An accrual basis taxpayer deducts a tax liability in his tax year in which all events have occurred which determine that he is liable for the tax and fix the amount of that liability, and economic performance (¶2833) has occurred—i.e., the tax is paid. (Code Sec. 461(h); Reg § 1.461-1(a)(2), Reg § 1.461-4(g)(6))[3] (For cash basis taxpayers, see ¶1765.) For ratable accrual of real property taxes, see ¶1769. For construction period taxes, see ¶1656.

An accrual basis taxpayer who pays an additional State tax for prior years without protest or appeal must deduct that tax for federal tax purposes in the year the tax was originally due, and not when it is later assessed or paid.[4] For contested tax, see ¶1768.

¶ 1768 When to deduct contested tax.

An accrual basis taxpayer who contests (through an overt act of protest or suit) an assessment can't deduct the contested portion of the tax until the contest is ended and the amount determined.[5]

A taxpayer (cash or accrual) who, by transferring sufficient cash or property, pays the contested liability without giving up the contest may deduct the tax in the year of payment, if otherwise deductible in that (or an earlier) year. But the contest must have existed at the time of transfer. (Code Sec. 461(f))[6] But foreign or U.S. possession income, war profits and excess profits tax can't be deducted until the contest is finally determined. (Code Sec. 461(f))[7]

¶ 1769 Election by accrual method taxpayers to accrue realty taxes ratably—Form 3115.

An accrual basis taxpayer may elect to accrue real property taxes that relate to a definite period of time ratably over that period. (Code Sec. 461(c)(1); Reg § 1.461-1(c)(1))[8]

IRS consent isn't required for an election made for the first tax year taxpayer incurs real property taxes. The election must be made by the return due date (with extensions) for that first year. In all other cases, the election may be made at any time, but requires IRS consent. (Code Sec. 461(c)(2)) Application for IRS's consent must be made in writing (on Form 3115) within 90 days (or 180 days, if taxpayer applies for an automatic extension) after the start of the first tax year to which the election applies.[9] The election is binding unless IRS consents to its revocation. (Reg § 1.461-1(c)(4))[10]

¶ 1770 Apportionment of real property taxes between seller and buyer.

For both cash and accrual taxpayers (Code Sec. 164(d)(2)), the real property tax on property that's sold during the tax year is considered to be imposed:

1. ¶K-4203; ¶1644.02; TD ¶329,005
2. ¶K-4204; ¶1644.02; TD ¶329,006
3. ¶G-2673, K-4300 et seq.; ¶4614.75; TD ¶329,007
4. ¶K-4320; TD ¶329,015
5. ¶K-4319 et seq.; ¶4614.56; TD ¶329,017

6. ¶s G-2445, G-2645; ¶s 1644.02, 4614.56; TD ¶329,017
7. ¶K-4322; TD ¶329,019
8. ¶K-4327 et seq.; ¶s 1644.02, 4614.45; TD ¶329,025
9. ¶s K-4329, K-4330; ¶4614.45; TD ¶329,026
10. ¶K-4334; ¶4614.45; TD ¶329,028

...*on the seller* to the extent properly allocable to that part of the real property tax year (period to which the tax relates) ending on the day before the date of sale; and

...*on the buyer* to the extent properly allocable to that part of the real property tax year beginning on the date of sale. (Code Sec. 164(d)(1); Reg § 1.164-6)[11]

For when the seller or buyer deducts the sale year realty tax, see ¶1771. For where seller took an excessive deduction, see ¶1772.

¶ 1771 When seller or buyer deducts real property tax.

An *accrual basis* seller or buyer deducts his share of sale year realty tax (as apportioned, ¶1770) in his income tax year in which the accrual date (date of sale) falls. If an election to accrue realty taxes ratably (¶1769) is in effect for that year, his share of the tax is deductible in the year it accrues under the election. (Code Sec. 164(d)(2)(B); Reg § 1.164-6(d)(6))[12]

A *cash basis* seller or buyer deducts his portion of the sale year realty tax in the income tax year he pays it. But where the tax isn't payable until after the sale date, or where the buyer is liable for the tax under local law, the *seller* may, at his option, deduct the tax either in the year of sale (whether or not he actually paid it) or in the year of payment, if later. So, the seller can deduct a tax paid by the buyer. (Reg § 1.164-6(d)(1)(ii))[13]

¶ 1772 Excessive deduction of real property tax before sale.

If the seller (cash or accrual) deducted more than his share of realty taxes on property he sells in a later year, and that "excess" tax payment is allocable to and deductible by the buyer (¶1770), the seller is treated as receiving a recovery in the sale year. The seller must include this "recovery" in gross income for the sale year, to the extent he got a tax benefit (i.e., his excess deduction) in that earlier year (¶1205). (Reg § 1.164-6(d)(5))[14]

¶ 1773 Deduction for Losses.

Taxpayers may sustain a loss when their property is transferred, stolen, destroyed, confiscated, abandoned, taken by foreclosure or becomes worthless, and they receive less than adequate compensation for it. This loss may be deductible.

Subject to the limits discussed in the following paragraphs, the at-risk rules (¶1803 *et seq.*) and the passive loss rules (¶1810 *et seq.*), taxpayers may deduct losses they sustain that aren't compensated for by insurance or otherwise. (Code Sec. 165(a))[15]

For losses from a sale or exchange, see ¶ 2400 *et seq.*

¶ 1774 What is a deductible loss?

A deductible loss arises when a taxpayer loses or gives up money, property or rights, or when these items lose value as a result of an identifiable event. It must be shown that the taxpayer sustained a loss of a type that's deductible and that the loss was sustained in the tax year; the amount of the loss also must be shown.[16]

To be deductible, a loss must be evidenced by a closed and completed transaction fixed by identifiable events (Reg § 1.165-1(b)), such as a sale, exchange, foreclosure, stock redemption, casualty, theft, abandonment, governmental condemnation or seizure. Mere fluctuations in an asset's value don't result in deductible losses.[17]

---

11. ¶K-4117; ¶1644.01; TD ¶328,005
12. ¶s K-4129, K-4130; ¶1644.01; TD ¶329,024
13. ¶K-4124 *et seq.*; ¶1644.01; TD ¶329,004
14. ¶K-4131; TD ¶328,009

15. ¶M-1000; ¶1654; TD ¶360,501
16. ¶M-1000 *et seq.*; ¶1654.020 *et seq.*; TD ¶360,500 *et seq.*
17. ¶M-1101, M-1305 *et seq.*; ¶1654.020 *et seq.*; TD ¶361,001 *et seq.*

¶ 1775   How much loss is deductible?

The amount of a loss sustained on disposition of property is the adjusted basis of the property, minus the amount of any money and the fair market value of any property received in exchange. (Code Sec. 165(b); Reg § 1.165-1(c))[18] No loss is deductible to the extent the taxpayer was reimbursed or compensated for it. (¶1791, ¶1796) (Code Sec. 165(a))[19] No deduction is allowed to the extent that property has salvage value. (Reg § 1.165-1(c))[20] For limit on tax-exempt use losses, see ¶1782. For casualty and theft losses, see ¶1793 *et seq.* and ¶1799 *et seq.*

¶ 1776   Limits on losses of individuals.

Individuals may deduct losses only if they're from a trade or business (¶1777), a transaction entered into for profit (¶1778), a casualty (¶1793) or theft (¶1799). (Code Sec. 165(c))[21]

An individual's losses on personal transactions are deductible only if they qualify as casualty or theft losses. (Code Sec. 165(c)(3))[22] So, no loss deduction is allowed for a loss on taxpayer's residence or car (if used only for personal purposes) unless the loss is from casualty or theft. These rules also apply to losses of estates and trusts. (Code Sec. 165(c)(1)),[23][24]

Property that a taxpayer holds partly for personal use and partly for business or income-producing use is treated as two properties: one personal, one business (or income-producing). Loss on the personal part (except by casualty or theft) isn't deductible.[25]

¶ 1777   What is a trade or business?

A trade or business is a pursuit or occupation carried on for profit (¶1778), whether or not profit actually results. An isolated transaction isn't a business. A taxpayer may engage in one business, in more than one business, or in no business.[26]

¶ 1778   When a transaction is entered into for profit—Form 5213.

A transaction is entered into for profit if a taxpayer intends to receive income from it overall. For a transaction involving property, the taxpayer must intend to receive income from it or to profit from disposing of it.[27]

Profit must be the primary motive, not merely incidental. A loss deduction is possible where a secondary nonprofit motive exists, as long as the profit motive predominates.[28]

An activity is presumed to be engaged in for profit for a tax year if it shows a profit for any three or more out of five consecutive years ending in that tax year (or two out of seven years for breeding, showing or racing of horses). (Code Sec. 183(d); Reg § 1.183-1(c))[29] A taxpayer who hasn't engaged in an activity for more than five years (seven, for horse breeding, etc.) can elect (on Form 5213) to postpone the determination as to whether these presumptions apply until the close of the fourth tax year (sixth, for horse breeding, etc.) after the tax year taxpayer first engages in the activity. (Code Sec. 183(e); Reg § 12.9)[30]

Whether the activities of an S corporation are "engaged in for profit" is determined at the entity level as it is for partnerships. (Reg § 1.183-1(f))[31]

---

18. ¶M-1401; TD ¶363,001
19. ¶M-1408; ¶1654.304; TD ¶363,008
20. ¶M-1401; TD ¶363,001
21. ¶M-1510, M-1600, M-2100: ¶1654, 1654.060, 1654.300, 1650.350 *et seq.*; TD ¶421,000
22. ¶M-1500; ¶1654; TD ¶361,508
23. ¶M-1501; ¶s 1654, 1654.060 *et seq.*; TD ¶421,000
24. ¶M-1524, C-2215, C-7214; TD ¶361,508

25. ¶M-1420; ¶s 1654.061, 1654.430; TD ¶363,020
26. ¶L-1100 *et seq.*; ¶1654.060 *et seq.*; TD ¶256,001
27. ¶M-1510; ¶1654.062; TD ¶422,005
28. ¶M-1512; ¶1654.062; TD ¶422,024
29. ¶M-5818; ¶1834.02; TD ¶422,017
30. ¶M-5821; ¶1834.02; TD ¶422,020
31. ¶M-5802; TD ¶422,002

¶ 1779 Hobby (not-for-profit) losses.

For individuals, partnerships, estates, trusts and S corporations, deductions attributable to an activity not engaged in for profit (Code Sec. 183(a); Reg § 1.183-1(a))[32] are allowed only as follows:

(1) The amount of deductions otherwise allowable for the tax year without regard to whether the activity is engaged in for profit (e.g., home mortgage interest, state and local taxes, and casualty loss) (Code Sec. 183(b)(1); Reg § 1.183-1(b)(1)(i))—referred to as Category 1 deductions.

(2) Amounts allowable as deductions only if the activity were engaged in for profit, but only if the allowance *doesn't* result in a basis adjustment, *and only* to the extent the gross income from the activity exceeds the deductions in (1), above (Code Sec. 183(b)(2); Reg § 1.183-1(b)(1)(ii))—Category 2 deductions.

(3) Amounts allowable as deductions only if the activity were engaged in for profit, that if allowed *would* result in a basis adjustment (e.g., depreciation), *but only* to the extent the gross income from the activity exceeds deductions allowed or allowable under (1) and (2) (Code Sec. 183(b)(2); Reg § 1.183-1(b)(1)(iii))—Category 3 deductions.[33]

In other words, deductions attributable to the "not for profit" activity are allowed to the extent of income from it, or for the amount of related deductions allowable regardless of profit-seeking, *whichever is larger.*[34]

But, the deductions allowable under these rules are subject to the 2%-of-AGI floor (¶3110) on miscellaneous itemized deductions. (Reg § 1.67-1T(a)(1)(iv))[35]

¶ 1780 Vacation home expenses.

Where an individual, trust, estate, partnership or S corporation owns a vacation home or a dwelling unit (below) and uses it for both personal and rental purposes, deduction of expenses is limited, except for those expenses which are deductible without regard to business use of the property—e.g., mortgage interest, property taxes and casualty losses. (Code Sec. 280A)[36]

The owner's personal use of the home (or portion of it) for even one day in the tax year triggers these "vacation home" limits. (Code Sec. 280A(e)(1))[37]

For any tax year in which the owner uses the (rented) vacation home or other dwelling unit for personal purposes, or rents it out for less than a fair rental, the owner's deduction for maintenance, utilities, depreciation, etc., can't exceed the percentage of those total expenses for the year "attributable" to the rental period. (Code Sec. 280A(e)(1))[38] If a taxpayer who rents out a dwelling unit also uses it as a residence (see below), the deductions attributable to rental use are *further* limited to no more than the gross income derived from rental use for that year, *minus* the sum of (1) the deductions allocable to rental use that are allowable whether or not the unit (or portion of it) was used for rental (e.g., interest and taxes), and (2) deductions allocable to the business or rental activity but which aren't allocable to the use of the home itself. Excess rental expenses may be carried forward to later years. (Code Sec. 280A(c)(5))[39]

The proper ratio for allocating interest and taxes to the rental period is: (1) number of days for which the property is rented, to (2) number of days of total use (according to IRS, but not according to some courts: they would use "number of days in the year"). [40]

---

32. ¶M-5802; ¶1834 *et seq.*; TD ¶422,001
33. ¶M-5804 *et seq.*; ¶1834 ; TD ¶422,001 *et seq.*
34. ¶M-5804; ¶1834; TD ¶422,001
35. ¶A-2710; ¶674 ; TD ¶422,003
36. ¶M-6001; ¶280A4; TD ¶423,001

37. ¶M-6005; ¶280A4; TD ¶423,021
38. ¶M-6005, M-6028*et seq.*; ¶280A4.060, 280A4.072; TD ¶423,008, 423,021
39. ¶M-6018, M-6022; ¶280A4.060 *et seq.*; TD ¶423,023, 423,026
40. ¶M-6006; ¶280A4.065; TD ¶423,021

A home is used as a residence in any tax year in which the owner's use of the unit (or a portion of it) for personal purposes exceeds the longer of: (1) 14 days, or (2) 10% of the period of rental use. (Code Sec. 280A(d)(1))[41]

For purposes of applying the rules limiting rent-related deductions for a dwelling unit used as a residence, personal-use days don't include days the taxpayer used a dwelling unit as his principal residence (1) before or after a rental (or attempted rental) period of 12 or more consecutive months beginning or ending in the tax year, or (2) before a consecutive rental (or attempted rental) period of less than 12 months beginning in the tax year, at the end of which the residence is sold or exchanged. A fair rental rate must be charged. (Code Sec. 280A(d)(4))[42]

If a home is rented for less than 15 days a year, the owner can't deduct *any* of the rental expenses, but isn't taxed on any of the rental income. (Code Sec. 280A(g))[43]

¶ 1781 Worthless stock or securities.

A taxpayer may deduct a loss from worthlessness of stock or other securities (i.e., a bond, debenture, note, certificate or other evidence of indebtedness issued by a corporation or a government (or its political subdivision) with interest coupons or in registered form). (Code Sec. 165(g)(1))[44]

The taxpayer must show that the security had value at the end of the year preceding the deduction year and that an identifiable event caused a loss in the deduction year.[45]

The amount of the loss is, to extent not compensated for (e.g., by insurance), the security's adjusted basis for determining loss on sale (¶ 2474). (Code Sec. 165(b); Reg § 1.165-1(c))[46]

The deduction is a capital loss if the security is a capital asset to the taxpayer. (Code Sec. 165(g)(1)) Similarly, a loss from an abandoned security that is a capital asset is treated as a loss from the sale or exchange of a capital asset on the last day of the tax year. (Reg § 1.165-5(i))[47]

An ordinary loss deduction is allowed if the security is:

. . . not a capital asset (Reg § 1.165-5(b));

. . . Code Sec. 1244 stock (¶ 2644 *et seq.*); or

. . . for corporate taxpayers, stock in an "affiliated" corporation (at least 80%-owned by taxpayer), where more than 90% of the affiliate's gross receipts has been from sources other than passive income (e.g., royalties, dividends). (Code Sec. 165(g)(3))[48]

Certain losses by, or on stock of, small business investment companies also are ordinary losses. (Code Sec. 1242, Code Sec. 1243)[49]

Total worthlessness of the security is required for the deduction. No loss deduction is allowed for partial worthlessness or (except for dealers who inventory securities[50]) for mere decline in value. (Reg § 1.165-4, Reg § 1.165-5)[1]

A parent corporation can claim a worthless stock deduction: (i) on a merger of the sub into the parent; (ii) on a check-the-box election that changes the sub's classification from a corporation to a disregarded entity, where the sub's liabilities exceed the fair market value of its assets.[2]

No loss deduction is allowed on a shareholder's surrender of stock to the corporation,

41. ¶M-6024; ¶280A4.062, 280A4.064; TD ¶423,007
42. ¶M-6038; ¶280A4.067; TD ¶423,027
43. ¶M-6023; ¶280A4.064; TD ¶423,020
44. ¶M-3301; ¶1654.200 *et seq.*; TD ¶372,001
45. ¶M-3300 *et seq.*, ¶M-3400 *et seq.*; ¶1654.210; TD ¶372,010
46. ¶M-3305; ¶1654.205; TD ¶372,004
47. ¶M-3301; ¶1654.200; TD ¶372,001
48. ¶M-3310 *et seq.*; ¶1654.203; TD ¶372,021
49. ¶M-3308; ¶1654.203; TD ¶372,006
50. ¶G-5021; TD ¶228,718.1
1. ¶M-3304; ¶1654.200 *et seq.*; TD ¶372,009 *et seq.*
2. ¶M-3310

whether or not the surrender is pro rata. Instead, the shareholder's basis for stock surrendered is added to his basis for stock retained.[3]

¶ 1782 Limits on "tax-exempt use losses."

For leases entered into (and in the case of property treated as tax-exempt use property other than by reason of a lease, for property acquired) after Mar. 12, 2004,[4] a "tax-exempt use loss" for any tax year isn't allowed. (Code Sec. 470(a)) (For exceptions, see below.)[5]

A tax-exempt use loss is the amount by which the total deductions allocable to a "tax-exempt use property" exceed the total income from the property, for the tax year. (Code Sec. 470(c)(1)) Tax-exempt use property is Code Sec. 168(h) property (generally, property subject to leases, or certain other arrangements, involving governments, tax-exempts, or foreign persons or entities), with certain modifications. However, property that would be treated as tax-exempt use property solely by reason of Code Sec. 168(h)(6) (dealing with property owned by partnerships and pass-through entities) is excepted from being tax-exempt use property. (Code Sec. 470(c)(2))[6]

A tax-exempt use loss in excess of gross income may be carried forward to the next tax year, subject to that year's limit. (Code Sec. 470(b)) A special loss carryforward limit applies for "former tax-exempt use property." (Code Sec. 470(e)(1))[7]

If, during the tax year, a taxpayer disposes of its entire interest in tax-exempt use property (or former tax-exempt use property), rules similar to the Code Sec. 469(g) disallowed passive activity loss and credit rules (¶1838) apply. (Code Sec. 470(e)(2))[8]

The limit on "tax-exempt use losses" doesn't apply to any lease (an "excepted lease") which meets the requirements of Code Sec. 470(d).[9]

¶ 1783 Demolition losses.

Except as noted below, no deduction is allowed to the owner or lessee of a building for any loss on demolition of the building, or for any of the demolition expenses. (Code Sec. 280B(1)) The loss or expenses must be capitalized and added to the basis of the land. (Code Sec. 280B(2))[10] And the Tax Court held that a loss sustained before a building's demolition as a result of its abnormal retirement from a taxpayer's business because of a casualty to or an extraordinary obsolescence of the building isn't treated as sustained on account of the demolition.[11]

¶ 1784 Abandonment loss.

A loss deduction is allowed for loss of usefulness or for obsolescence of nondepreciable property, both tangible and intangible (e.g., land, a contract), *if*: (1) the loss is incurred in business or a transaction entered into for profit; (2) it arises from the sudden termination of usefulness in the business or transaction; *and* (3) the property is permanently discarded from use, or the business or transaction is discontinued. (Reg § 1.165-2) The taxpayer must be able to establish specifically which property has been abandoned.[12]

The loss is an ordinary loss not subject to capital loss limitations. (Reg § 1.165-2(b))[13] The loss can't exceed the adjusted basis of the property for determining loss on a disposition (¶ 2474). (Reg § 1.165-1(c))[14] For the loss on an abandoned security, see ¶1781.

For losses on mortgaged property, see ¶1787 and ¶1788.

3. ¶M-3501; TD ¶373,001
4. ¶L-6901; ¶4704; TD ¶261,202
5. ¶L-6901 *et seq.*; ¶4704; TD ¶261,201 *et seq.*
6. ¶L-6901 *et seq.*; ¶4704; TD ¶261,201 *et seq.*
7. ¶L-6902, ¶L-6903; ¶4704; TD ¶261,202; 261,203
8. ¶L-6904; ¶4704; TD ¶261,204

9. ¶L-6906 *et seq.*; ¶4704; TD ¶261,206 *et seq.*
10. ¶M-2200 *et seq.*; ¶s 1654.180, 280B4; TD ¶376,019
11. ¶M-2201; ¶s 1654.180, 280B4; TD ¶376,019
12. ¶M-2301; ¶1654.150 *et seq.*; TD ¶376,001
13. ¶M-2353; TD ¶376,005
14. ¶M-2351; TD ¶376,004

¶ 1785   Costs of unsuccessful investigation of proposed venture.

A corporation that pays or incurs expenses in *unsuccessfully* searching for or investigating a new venture may deduct those costs as a business loss, when it abandons the search or investigation (see ¶1504). But for a noncorporate taxpayer, these expenses are personal and nondeductible.[15] For expenses of a *successful* investigation, see ¶ 1500 *et seq.*

¶ 1786   Gambling losses.

A taxpayer may deduct gambling losses suffered in the tax year, but only to the extent of that year's gambling gains. (Code Sec. 165(d); Reg § 1.165-10) "Gains" include "comps" (complimentary goods and services taxpayer receives from a casino). Losses from one kind of gambling (e.g., horse bets) are deductible against gains from another kind (e.g., keno).[16] Individuals not engaged in the gambling business deduct gambling losses (to extent of gambling gains) only as miscellaneous itemized deductions (but not subject to the 2%-of-AGI floor),[17] and must report gambling gains even if they are exceeded by gambling losses.[18]

"Nonwagering" expenses of a gambling business aren't included in gambling losses. So, they aren't subject to the gambling income limitation of gambling losses to gambling gains, and are deductible business expenses under Code Sec. 162.[19]

¶ 1787   Mortgagee's loss (or gain) on mortgaged property.

The mortgagee (mortgage lender) treats a loss on mortgaged property as follows:

A loss on *compromise or settlement* of the debt of an insolvent debtor is treated as a bad debt (¶1848 *et seq.*).[20]

A lender to whom mortgaged or pledged property is surrendered has a bad debt deduction if the fair market value (FMV) of the property received is less than the debt. (The mortgagee has a gain if the FMV of the surrendered property is greater than the debt's basis.)[21] For where the surrender is a repossession by the seller, see ¶ 2467.

A loss on a *mortgage foreclosure* is treated as a bad debt (see ¶1848) equal to the sum of: (1) the excess of the debt's basis over the net proceeds from the property foreclosure; (2) accrued interest previously reported as income; plus (3) legal and other expenses. This is true whether the price is paid by the mortgagee (by applying the debt to the price) or someone else. (Reg § 1.166-6(a))[22]

A mortgagee that bids on the property at the foreclosure sale *also* realizes a loss to the extent the debt applied to the bid exceeds the property's FMV. He realizes a taxable gain to the extent FMV exceeds the amount of the debt so applied. FMV is assumed to equal the bid price, absent convincing proof to the contrary. (Reg § 1.166-6(b)(2))[23]

¶ 1788   Owner's loss on foreclosure, surrender or abandonment of mortgaged property.

The owner of mortgaged property, whether or not he's the mortgagor and whether or not he's personally liable for the mortgage debt, realizes a loss (occasionally a gain) on foreclosure of the mortgage or surrender of the property. The foreclosure (or surrender) is considered a sale or exchange.[24] The owner-borrower's gain or loss is the difference between adjusted basis of the transferred property and the amount realized. If the owner-borrower isn't personally

---

15. ¶L-5018 *et seq.*; TD ¶301,013
16. ¶M-6100 *et seq.*; ¶s 1654.500, 1654.501; TD ¶424,001
17. ¶M-6105; TD ¶424,003
18. ¶J-1651; TD ¶197,001
19. ¶M-6102.1; TD ¶424,001

20. ¶M-3709; ¶1664.350 *et seq.*; TD ¶371,021
21. ¶M-3710; ¶1664.353; TD ¶371,022
22. ¶M-3701; ¶1664.353 *et seq.*; TD ¶371,016
23. ¶M-3704; ¶1664.352; TD ¶371,019
24. ¶M-3801; ¶1654.451; TD ¶371,001

liable for repaying the debt secured by the transferred property, the amount realized includes the full amount of the debt canceled by the transfer. If the borrower is personally liable, the amount realized doesn't include any cancellation of debt income (¶1385) arising from the debt. But if the FMV of the property is less than the canceled debt, the amount realized includes canceled debt up to the FMV.[25]

Abandonment is generally treated as a sale or exchange.[26] For tax sales, see ¶1789.

¶ 1789 Loss on tax sale.

The tax treatment of an owner whose property is sold for delinquent taxes is similar to the tax treatment for foreclosure (¶1788). The tax sale is a sale or exchange.[27]

¶ 1790 When to deduct loss.

A loss is deductible only for the tax year it's sustained. (Code Sec. 165(a)) This is the year the loss occurs, as evidenced by closed and completed transactions and as fixed by identifiable events in that year. (Reg § 1.165-1(d))[28] For casualty or theft losses, see ¶1797 and ¶1801.

¶ 1791 Deducting reimbursable losses.

If taxpayer has a claim for reimbursement on which there's a reasonable prospect of recovery, that "reimbursable" loss can't be deducted until it's reasonably certain the reimbursement will or won't be made. This may be ascertained by, among other things, settlement, adjudication or abandonment of the claim. (Reg § 1.165-1(d)(2))[29]

¶ 1792 Casualty, Disaster, and Theft Losses. ▮▮▮▮▮▮▮▮▮▮▮▮▮▮

Losses from fire, storm, auto accident or other casualty, and losses from theft, are deductible, regardless of whether the loss is sustained in a business or for-profit transaction. An early deduction for disaster losses is available. An individual can elect to treat a loss on a frozen bank deposit as a casualty or theft loss.

¶ 1793 Casualty losses—Form 4684.

A deduction is allowed (report on Form 4684) for losses arising from a casualty (¶1794) where taxpayer actually sustains a loss *and* the loss is on *property*. (Code Sec. 165(c)(3)) The property must suffer physical damage and not just a decline in value, even if that decline results from being in or near an area where casualties have occurred and might occur again.[30] A co-op stockholder may be entitled to a casualty loss deduction for damage to the co-op's premises if the taxpayer has a sufficient property interest under state law.[31]

A taxpayer may deduct amounts paid for repairs and maintenance to tangible property only if the amounts paid are not otherwise required to be capitalized. (Reg § 1.162-4T(a))[32] Capitalized expenses generally are those that better or improve a unit of property, restore it, or adapt it to a new and different use. (Reg § 1.263(a)-3T)[33]

¶ 1794 "Casualty" defined.

A casualty is the complete or partial destruction of property resulting from an identifiable event of a sudden, unexpected or unusual nature such as a fire, storm, shipwreck, car crash, or similar event. Progressive deterioration from a steadily operating cause isn't a casualty.[34]

---

25. ¶M-3803; TD ¶371,001, 371,006
26. ¶M-3808; ¶1654.155; TD ¶371,003
27. ¶M-3806; ¶1654.155, 1654.451; TD ¶371,001
28. ¶M-1301; ¶s 1654.090, 1654.111; TD ¶362,001
29. ¶M-2136; ¶1654.304; TD ¶362,001

30. ¶M-1601, ¶M-2132; ¶1654.300 *et seq.*; TD ¶366,000; 366,001
31. ¶M-1606; TD ¶366,062
32. ¶L-6102; ¶1624.177; TD ¶308,004
33. ¶L-5601.6; ¶L-5601.8 ¶1624.177;TD ¶308,004
34. ¶M-1701; ¶1654.301; TD ¶366,008

¶ 1795   Amount of casualty loss—Form 4684.

The amount treated as a loss from a casualty depends on whether taxpayer held the property for personal or for business purposes, as follows:

For property held for personal use, the amount of the casualty loss is the *lesser* of: (1) the property's adjusted basis (i.e., its basis for determining loss on disposition, see ¶2474), or (2) its decline in value (i.e., its fair market value (FMV) immediately before the casualty *minus* its FMV immediately afterward). This applies whether the property is totally destroyed or merely damaged. (Reg § 1.165-7(b)) The loss is reduced for any salvage value, insurance or other compensation received (¶1796). (Reg § 1.165-1(c)(4))[35]

For property used in business or held for the production of income, the amount of the casualty loss is determined under the same rules as for personal-use property (above), except that if the property is *totally* destroyed, the amount of the loss is the property's adjusted basis in all cases. (Reg § 1.165-7(b)(1))[36]

The decline in a property's value should be ascertained by competent appraisal where possible.[37]

Costs of repairing, replacing, or cleaning up property after a casualty can be used to measure the amount of the loss (decline in value) if: the repair, etc., is necessary to restore the property to its pre-casualty condition; the amount spent isn't excessive; the repairs do no more than take care of the damage suffered; and the post-repair value is no greater than the pre-casualty value. (Reg § 1.165-7(a)(2))[38]

Except for individuals' casualty losses on personal-use property, the amount of a casualty loss, as determined above, is generally deductible in full. See ¶1774 *et seq.* A taxpayer may deduct a casualty loss on property not used in business or held for production of income only to the extent that: (1) the casualty loss exceeds $100 ("$100 floor"), and (2) all of taxpayer's casualty losses for the tax year exceed 10% of adjusted gross income (AGI) for the year ("10%-of-AGI limit") (Code Sec. 165(h))[39] as described below. For exceptions to the $100 floor and the 10%-of-AGI limit for losses incurred in a disaster, see below.

Corrosive drywall. IRS allows any individual who pays to repair damage to his personal residences or household appliances that results from corrosive drywall to apply a safe harbor formula to treat the costs of repairing the defective drywall as a casualty loss. A taxpayer claiming a casualty loss under the safe harbor must report the amount of the loss on Form 4684.[40]

$100 floor. Each personal-use property casualty is subject to a separate $100 floor to determine the extent it's deductible. But events closely related in origin give rise to a single casualty. Thus, one storm's damage to taxpayer's house and car is a single casualty, so only the total damage has to exceed $100 to be deductible. (Code Sec. 165(h)(1); Reg § 1.165-7(b)(4)(ii))[41] A single $100 floor applies where one casualty causes loss to joint filers, whether the loss is to property jointly or separately owned. But separate $100 floors apply to each spouse if they file separately, even if the property is jointly owned. (Code Sec. 165(h)(4)(B); Reg § 1.165-7(b)(4)(iii))[42]

10%-of-AGI floor. In addition to (and after applying) the $100 per casualty "floor" (above), personal-use property casualties are then subject to this other limit. If personal casualty losses for a tax year exceed personal casualty gains for that tax year, taxpayer may deduct those losses for that year, but only to the extent of the sum of:

(1) the amount of the personal casualty gains for the year, plus

---

35. ¶M-1801 *et seq.*; ¶1654.304; TD ¶368,001
36. ¶M-1802; ¶1654.304; TD ¶368,001
37. ¶M-1809; ¶1654.304; TD ¶368,008
38. ¶M-1815; ¶1654.304; TD ¶368,013

39. ¶M-1900 *et seq.*; ¶1654.304; TD ¶368,501
40. ¶M-1849; TD ¶368,517
41. ¶M-1901, ¶M-1902; ¶1654.304; TD ¶368,502; 368,503
42. ¶M-1904 *et seq.*; ¶1654.304; TD ¶368,506

(2) the amount by which (a) the excess of personal casualty losses over gains ((1) above), exceeds (b) 10% of taxpayer's AGI (¶3102) (computed without regard to casualty gains). (Code Sec. 165(h)(2)(A))[43]

In determining a taxpayer's personal casualty gains and losses, the amount of any recognized loss is subject to the $100 floor (see above) before netting. (Code Sec. 165(h)(1))[44]

If the personal casualty losses for a tax year exceed the personal casualty gains for that year, the deduction for personal casualty losses is allowable in computing AGI, to the extent of those gains. (Code Sec. 165(h)(4)(A))[45]

If the personal casualty gains for any tax year exceed the personal casualty losses for that year, all these gains and losses are treated as capital gains and losses (Code Sec. 165(h)(2)(B)) not subject to the 10% floor.[46]

Where property is held for both business (or profit) and personal purposes (e.g., a home office, ¶1638), these limits apply only to the personal part of the loss. (Reg § 1.165-7(b)(4)(iv))[47]

¶ 1796   Insurance or other compensation for casualty loss.

The casualty loss deduction isn't allowed to the extent the loss is compensated by insurance or otherwise (see ¶1795). (Code Sec. 165(a)) But, costs incurred in collecting the compensation reduce the recovery so as to increase the loss deduction.[48]

Where an individual's casualty and theft losses aren't attributable to a business or for-profit transaction, a loss covered by insurance is taken into account only if the taxpayer files a timely insurance claim. (Code Sec. 165(h)(5)(E)) But, this limit applies only to the extent the insurance policy would have provided reimbursement had the claim been filed.[49]

Compensation includes property insurance, damage recoveries, debt forgiveness, cash or property received from taxpayer's employer or from disaster relief agencies to rehabilitate the property (e.g., qualified disaster relief payments, see ¶1207), and condemnation awards. Compensation doesn't include disaster relief such as food, medical supplies, and other forms of assistance, unless they are replacements for lost or destroyed property. Nor does it include use and occupancy insurance reimbursements for lost business profits.[50]

A casualty loss to inventory is automatically reflected in cost of goods sold (¶2869). It isn't separately deducted as a loss unless adjustments are made to inventory.[1]

¶ 1797   When to deduct casualty losses.

A casualty loss is considered "sustained" (and deductible) only during the tax year the loss occurs, as fixed by identifiable events occurring in that year. (Code Sec. 165(a); Reg § 1.165-1(d)(1)) A loss may be sustained in the tax year even though repairs or replacements aren't made until a later year. And a loss may be sustained in a year *after* the casualty occurs, as when trees died a year after the year a blizzard damaged them.[2] For election to deduct disaster losses early, see ¶1798.

¶ 1798   Expensing of disaster losses and early deduction election for disaster losses.

A taxpayer may *elect* to deduct a disaster loss (defined below) for the tax year *before* the

---

43. ¶M-1907, M-1911; ¶1654.304; TD ¶368,508
44. ¶M-1911; ¶1654.304; TD ¶368,512
45. ¶M-1908; TD ¶368,508
46. ¶M-1910; ¶1654.304; TD ¶368,509
47. ¶M-1906, M-1908.1; ¶1654.304, 280A4.044; TD ¶368,507, 368,511

48. ¶M-1408, M-1421; ¶1654.304; TD ¶368,016, 363,019
49. ¶M-1914; ¶1654.304
50. ¶M-1411 *et seq.*; ¶1654.304; TD ¶363,011 *et seq.*
1. ¶M-1808; ¶s 1654.302, 4714.21; TD ¶368,007
2. ¶M-1610; ¶1654.111; TD ¶366,066

year the loss occurred, instead of for the year the loss occurred (¶1796). (Code Sec. 165(i))[3]

Individuals who incur a disaster loss with respect to nonbusiness property are subject to the regular $100 floor. (Code Sec. 165(i))[4]

A disaster loss is a loss that's attributable to a disaster occurring in a disaster area and attributable to a federally declared disaster. (Code Sec. 165(i)(1))[5] Also, the loss must be *otherwise* deductible as a loss. (Reg § 1.165-11(b)(3)) A taxpayer whose residence is located in a disaster area may deduct any loss attributable to the disaster as a casualty loss if the residence is rendered unsafe by the disaster, and he is ordered (within 120 days after the disaster designation) by the state or local government to demolish or relocate the residence. (Code Sec. 165(k))[6] A non-casualty loss may be a disaster loss if incurred in the course of a trade or business or profit-seeking transaction. For example, a farmer might deduct a loss from a drought disaster, even though loss from drought is ordinarily not deductible as a casualty loss.[7]

Generally, a taxpayer must make this election by filing a return, an amended return, or a refund claim on or before the later of (i) the due date of his income tax return (determined without regard to any filing extension) for the tax year in which the disaster actually occurred, or (ii) the due date of his tax return (determined with regard to any filing extension) for the immediately preceding tax year. The election is irrevocable 90 days after it is made. (Reg § 1.165-11(e))[8] A taxpayer, who sustained a loss attributable to Hurricane Sandy in 2012, is granted a postponement to Oct. 15, 2013 to make an election to take a deduction for the 2012 disaster loss. The loss must have occurred in a covered disaster area for Hurricane Sandy regardless of whether the taxpayer's principal residence or place of business was in one of the covered disaster areas.[9]

For involuntary conversion of a principal residence damaged in a Federally-declared disaster, see ¶2433.

¶ 1799　　Theft losses—Form 4684.

Theft losses (reported on Form 4684 are deductible under rules that closely follow those for casualty losses, including the $100/10%-of-AGI floors (¶1795 *et seq.*). (Code Sec. 165(a), Code Sec. 165(h)(1), Code Sec. 165(h)(2)) A theft is the unlawful taking and removing of money or property with the intent to deprive the owner of it, and includes larceny, robbery, embezzlement (Reg § 1.165-8(d)), burglary, extortion, kidnapping for ransom, blackmail and false representation.[10] For determining the amount of a theft loss, see ¶1800.

A theft loss deduction is not allowed for the decline in market value of stock purchased on the open market, where the decline is caused by the disclosure of accounting fraud or other illegal conduct on the part of officers or directors of the corporation that issued the stock.[11]

A taking by a person known to have a claim to the property (e.g., spouse, joint owner) isn't a theft unless there is evidence of criminal intent.[12]

Under a safe harbor, when certain conditions are met, taxpayers who have lost money in a Madoff-type Ponzi investment scheme can take a theft loss deduction for that loss.[13]

¶ 1800　　Amount of theft loss.

For theft of business or investment property, the *deductible loss* is the adjusted basis of the property minus insurance or other compensation received or recoverable (¶1796).

---

3. ¶M-2001; ¶1654.520; TD ¶369,002
4. ¶M-2009; ¶1654.304; TD ¶369,012
5. ¶M-2002; ¶1654.520; TD ¶369,001
6. ¶M-2010; ¶1654.302; TD ¶369,008
7. ¶M-2004; ¶1654.520; TD ¶369,009
8. ¶M-2011 *et seq.*; ¶1654.520; TD ¶369,003 *et seq.*

9. ¶M-2003, M-2012, TD ¶369,004, 570,306.1;
10. ¶M-2100 *et seq.*; ¶1654.351 *et seq.*; TD ¶367,001
11. ¶M-2111; ¶1654.351; TD ¶367,009
12. ¶M-2104; TD ¶367,003
13. ¶M-2145 *et seq.*; TD ¶367,042 ; ¶1654.390

(Reg § 1.165-8(c))[14]

For theft of personal-use property, the *loss* is: (1) the lesser of the property's fair market value (FMV) immediately before theft or its adjusted basis, reduced by (2) insurance or other compensation received or recoverable. (Reg § 1.165-8(c)) The $100/10%-of-AGI floors (¶1795) are then applied to determine the amount of the loss that is *deductible*. (Code Sec. 165(c)(3))[15]

If stolen personal-use property is recovered in the deduction year, the loss is the lesser of: (1) the property's adjusted basis, or (2) the decline in its FMV between theft and recovery. If it's recovered after the deduction year, the excess of the earlier deduction over the loss determined as above is included in income (under the tax benefit rule, see ¶1205) to the extent the earlier loss deduction decreased taxpayer's tax.[16]

¶ 1801 When to deduct theft loss.

A theft loss (¶1799) is deductible in the year the loss is *discovered*, regardless of when the theft actually occurred. (Code Sec. 165(e)) But the deduction is postponed to the extent the taxpayer, in the year of discovery, had a reimbursement claim on which there was a reasonable prospect of recovery. (Reg § 1.165-8(a))[17]

¶ 1802 Elections to treat frozen bank deposits as losses from casualty or from transaction entered into for profit—Form 4684.

If a "qualified individual" (other than the institution's officers, 1% owners, or those related to either)[18] has a loss on a deposit in a bankrupt or insolvent qualified financial institution, and that loss may be reasonably estimated, the loss may be treated, at the taxpayer's election: (1) as a casualty or theft loss (¶1793, ¶1799) instead of as a nonbusiness bad debt (¶1854) (Code Sec. 165(l)(1)),[19] or (2) as an ordinary loss incurred in a transaction entered into for profit, up to the first $20,000 of losses ($10,000 for marrieds filing separately). (Code Sec. 165(l)(5))[20]

The election to treat a loss on a deposit as a casualty loss is made on Form 4684. The losses that result from elections to treat the estimated loss on deposits as a casualty loss or as an ordinary loss from a for-profit transaction are treated as itemized deductions on the income tax return (including a timely filed amended return) for the tax year for which the taxpayer makes a reasonable estimate of the loss.[21]

¶ 1803 At-Risk Limitations.

For certain taxpayers, deductions from specified leveraged investment activities are limited to the aggregate amount the taxpayer-investor has "at risk."

¶ 1804 Taxpayers subject to "at-risk" rules.

The at-risk rules (¶1806) apply to: (1) individuals; (2) C corporations, but only if more than 50% in value of the corporation's stock is owned by not more than five individuals at any time during the last half of its tax year (Code Sec. 465(a)(1));[22] and (3) estates and trusts.[23] But even if the stock ownership test is met, the at-risk rules *don't apply* to:

. . . certain active businesses ("qualifying businesses") carried on by a qualified C corporation (i.e., *not* a personal holding company, or personal service corporation determined by substituting 5% for 10% in Code Sec. 269A(b)(2)), (Code Sec. 465(c)(7))[24] or

---

14. ¶M-2125; ¶1654.370; TD ¶367,023
15. ¶M-2126; ¶1654.370; TD ¶367,025
16. ¶M-2129; TD ¶367,027
17. ¶M-2132; ¶1654.380; TD ¶367,036
18. ¶M-1762; ¶1654.530; TD ¶366,073
19. ¶M-1761; ¶1654.530; TD ¶366,071

20. ¶M-1765, M-1766; ¶1654.530; TD ¶366,076, 366,077
21. ¶M-1771; ¶M-1772; ¶1654.530; TD ¶366,072
22. ¶M-4511, M-4515; ¶4654; TD ¶402,001
23. ¶M-4512; TD ¶402,002
24. ¶M-4516 *et seq.*; ¶4654; TD ¶402,006 *et seq.*

. . . the activity of equipment leasing. (Code Sec. 465(c)(4))[25]

observation: Even though the at-risk rules don't apply to pass-through entities such as S corporations and partnerships, they *do* apply to determine whether a person with an interest in any of those entities may deduct items of loss, etc., passed through.

¶ 1805   "At-risk" activities.

The at-risk rules (¶1806) apply to:

(A) certain specified activities: (1) holding, producing or distributing motion pictures or video tapes; (2) farming; (3) equipment leasing; (4) exploring for, or exploiting, oil and gas resources; or (5) exploring for, or exploiting, geothermal resources; (Code Sec. 465(c)(1)) and

(B) a "catch-all" group of activities engaged in by the taxpayer in carrying on a trade or business or in the production of income, other than those described in (A) above (e.g., real estate activities, see ¶1809). (Code Sec. 465(c)(3))[26]

In applying the at-risk rules to the specified activities, taxpayer's activity with respect to each property (e.g., each film in (1), above) is treated as a separate activity. (Code Sec. 465(c)(2)(A)) Activities in the "catch-all" group are treated as one activity ("aggregated") if either: (A) taxpayer actively participates in the management of the trade or business, or (B) the trade or business is carried on by a partnership or S corporation *and* 65% or more of the losses for the tax year are allocable to persons who actively participate in its management. (Code Sec. 465(c)(3)(B))[27]

¶ 1806   How the at-risk rules work—Form 6198.

For a taxpayer (¶1804) engaged in an at-risk activity (¶1805), any loss from the activity for the tax year is deductible in that year only to the extent that taxpayer is at risk (¶1807) with respect to the activity at the end of the year. (Code Sec. 465(a)) The losses so limited are the excess of the deductions allocable to the activity that otherwise would be allowed for the year, over the income (other than recapture, see ¶1808) received or accrued by taxpayer during the year from that same activity. (Code Sec. 465(d))[28]

Any loss thus disallowed is treated as allocable to the same activity in the next tax year, and may be deducted in the later year subject to that year's at-risk limit for the activity. (Code Sec. 465(a)(2)) So, a current year's "loss" may include "suspended" loss accounts from earlier years. (Code Sec. 465(d))[29]

caution: In addition to the at-risk rules, losses and credits from an activity may also be subject to the passive activity rules, discussed at ¶1810 *et seq.*

Form 6198 is used to compute the deductible loss from an at-risk activity.[30]

For the at-risk rules otherwise applicable to real property, see ¶1809.

¶ 1807   Amounts considered "at risk."

A taxpayer is considered at risk for an activity to the extent of:

(1) the amount of money and the adjusted basis of other property the taxpayer contributed to the activity (Code Sec. 465(b)(1)), plus

(2) amounts borrowed with respect to the activity to the extent the taxpayer is personally liable for the repayment of or has pledged property, other than property used in the activity, as security for the borrowed amount. The borrowings can't exceed the fair market

25. ¶M-4529; ¶4654; TD ¶403,009
26. ¶M-4521; ¶4654; TD ¶403,001
27. ¶M-4522 *et seq.*; ¶4654; TD ¶403,002

28. ¶M-4502; ¶4654; TD ¶401,001
29. ¶M-4502; ¶4564; TD ¶401,006
30. ¶M-4501; ¶4654; TD ¶401,001

value of the taxpayer's interest in the pledged property. No property is treated as security if it is directly or indirectly financed by indebtedness secured by property in (1), above. (Code Sec. 465(b)(1), Code Sec. 465(b)(2))[31]

Borrowed amounts "at risk" ((2) above) don't include borrowings from any person who has an interest in the activity other than as a creditor, or from a related person as specially defined. A corporation is at risk with respect to amounts it borrowed from a shareholder. (Code Sec. 465(b)(3))[32]

But amounts protected against loss by nonrecourse financing, guarantees, stop loss agreements, or other similar arrangements aren't at risk. (Code Sec. 465(b)(4))[33]

In determining the amount at risk for any tax year, the amount for that year is reduced by any losses allowed under these limitations in an earlier year. (Code Sec. 465(b)(5))[34]

¶ 1808 Recapture of losses where amount at risk is less than zero.

If a taxpayer's amount at risk (¶1807) is less than zero (e.g., by distributions to the taxpayer or by debt changing from recourse to nonrecourse), the taxpayer recognizes income to the extent of that negative amount. (Code Sec. 465(e)(1)(A)) But, the amount recaptured is limited to the excess of the losses previously allowed in that activity over any amounts previously recaptured. (Code Sec. 465(e)(2)) The amount added to income under this recapture rule is treated as a deduction allocable to the activity in the first succeeding year, and is allowed if and to the extent the taxpayer's at-risk basis is increased. (Code Sec. 465(e)(1)(B))[35]

¶ 1809 At-risk rules for real property.

A taxpayer engaged in the activity of holding real property is subject to the at-risk rules for losses on property placed in service after '86. The at-risk rules also apply to a taxpayer's losses from real estate attributable to an interest in a pass-through entity that is acquired after '86, regardless of when the entity acquired the real property.[36]

A taxpayer is considered at risk for his share of any "qualified nonrecourse financing" secured by the real property. (Code Sec. 465(b)(6); Reg § 1.465-27(b))[37]

¶ 1810 "Passive Activity" Losses and Credits. ▰▰▰▰▰▰▰▰

Losses from passive activities—activities in which the taxpayer doesn't materially participate, and most rental activities—may only be used to offset passive activity income (which doesn't include portfolio income); thus they can't be used to offset income from, for example, compensation, interest or dividends. Any losses that are unused in a tax year because of this rule are carried forward to the following year(s) until used, or until the taxpayer disposes of the interest in the activity (or substantially all of the activity) in a taxable transaction. Passive activity credits may be used only to offset tax on income from passive activities, with a carryover of any unused credits. But, individuals who actively participate in rental real estate activities may use up to $25,000 of losses from those activities to offset nonpassive income; and those activities are not automatically passive for real estate professionals.

caution: For passive activity losses for alternative minimum tax purposes, see ¶3210.

---

31. ¶M-4541 *et seq.*; ¶4654; TD ¶404,001, 404,008
32. ¶M-4557 *et seq.*; ¶4654; TD ¶404,017, 404,018
33. ¶M-4568 *et seq.*; ¶4654; TD ¶404,028
34. ¶M-4507; ¶4654; TD ¶401,007

35. ¶M-4509; ¶4654; TD ¶401,009
36. ¶M-4533; TD ¶403,013
37. ¶M-4534 *et seq.*; ¶4654; TD ¶403,014 *et seq.*

¶ 1811   Disallowance of passive activity losses and credits—Form 8582; Form 8582-CR; Form 8810.

A taxpayer subject to the passive activity rules (¶1812) may not deduct a passive activity loss (i.e., the excess of aggregate losses from passive activities over aggregate income from those activities, see ¶1814) (Code Sec. 469(a)(1)(A)) or use a passive activity credit (i.e, the excess of specified credits attributable to passive activities over the regular tax liability allocable to those activities) (Code Sec. 469(a)(1)(B)), except with respect to certain rental real estate activities (¶1832 *et seq.*). (Reg § 1.469-1T(a)(2))[38] For carryover of suspended losses and credits, see ¶1837. For deduction of suspended losses on disposition of the activity, see ¶1838.

A passive activity deduction disallowed for a tax year under these rules isn't taken into account as a deduction in computing taxable income (or self-employment income). (Reg § 1.469-1T(d)(3)) And a passive activity deduction that *is* allowed under these rules may still be disallowed under the Code Sec. 613A limit on percentage depletion of oil and gas wells, or the Code Sec. 1211 limit on capital losses. (Reg § 1.469-1(d)(2))[39]

Whether a loss is disallowed under these rules is determined *after* the application of the at-risk rules (¶1803 *et seq.*), and the interest deduction limitations (¶1726 *et seq.*), as well as other provisions measuring taxable income. (Reg § 1.469-2(d)(6), Reg § 1.469-1T(d))[40]

Where a taxpayer's disallowed passive activity losses are derived from more than one activity, a ratable portion of the loss (if any) from each passive activity, in general, is disallowed. (Reg § 1.469-1T(f)(2)(i))[41] Any loss so disallowed is then generally allocated ratably among all passive activity deductions (¶1815) from the activity for the year. (Reg § 1.469-1T(f)(2)(ii))[42] If all or any portion of a passive activity credit is disallowed, a ratable portion of each credit from each passive activity, in general, is disallowed. (Reg § 1.469-1T(f)(3)(i))[43]

The passive activity limits are calculated on Form 8582 (individuals, estates, and trusts), Form 8582-CR (credits for individuals, estates, and trusts), or Form 8810 (closely held corporations and personal service corporations).[44]

¶ 1812   Who is subject to the passive activity rules?

The passive activity limits (¶1811) apply to any individual, estate, trust (Code Sec. 469(a)(2)(A)) (other than a trust, or portion of a trust, which is a grantor trust) (Reg § 1.469-1T(b)(2)), personal service corporation (PSC) as specially defined (Code Sec. 469(a)(2)(C), Code Sec. 469(j)(2)) and closely held C corporation (except as described at ¶1814) as specially defined. (Code Sec. 469(a)(2)(B), Code Sec. 469(j)(1))[45] For pass-through entities, see ¶1813.

Spouses filing a joint return are treated as one taxpayer, with certain exceptions. (Reg § 1.469-1T(j)(1))[46]

The passive activity rules don't apply, except as regs may provide, to any corporation that isn't a PSC or a closely held corporation for the tax year. (Reg § 1.469-1T(g)(1))[47] But the rules *do* apply to any of the corporation's losses or credits that arose during a tax year when it *was* a PSC or closely held C corporation. (Code Sec. 469(f)(2))[48]

---

38. ¶M-4600 *et seq.*; ¶4694 *et seq.*; TD ¶411,001 *et seq.*
39. ¶M-4603; ¶4694.47; TD ¶411,002, 411,004
40. ¶M-4603 *et seq.*; ¶4694.30, 4694.31, 4694.47; TD ¶411,004 *et seq.*
41. ¶M-5501; ¶4694.40 ; TD ¶416,502
42. ¶M-5502; ¶4694.42; TD ¶416,503

43. ¶M-5604; ¶4694.44; TD ¶417,006
44. ¶M-5200; ¶4694, 4694.36; TD ¶411,001
45. ¶M-4700 *et seq.*; ¶4694; TD ¶411,500 *et seq.*
46. ¶M-4702; ¶4694.70; TD ¶411,502
47. ¶M-4705; ¶4694; TD ¶411,504
48. ¶M-4705; TD ¶411,504

¶ 1813   Pass-through entities subject to the passive activity rules.

Partnerships (unless publicly traded, see below) and S corporations aren't subject to the passive activity rules (¶1811). (Code Sec. 469(a)(2)) But the rules *do* apply to the losses and credits passed through to the partners and shareholders.[49]

The passive activity rules apply to publicly traded partnerships (PTPs, defined below) that aren't treated as corporations (¶3302). The rules are applied separately with respect to items attributable to each PTP (except in certain situations involving the low-income housing and rehabilitation credits). (Code Sec. 469(k)(1)) A partner's net passive income for a tax year from a PTP can't be offset by losses from other passive activities.[50]

A PTP is a partnership the interests of which are traded on an established securities market (national or local exchange, or an over-the-counter market) or are readily tradable on a secondary market (or the substantial equivalent). (Code Sec. 469(k)(2); Reg § 1.469-10(b))[1]

¶ 1814   Passive activity loss defined.

A passive activity loss for a tax year is the amount, if any, by which the aggregate losses from all passive activities (¶1822) for the tax year exceed the aggregate income from all passive activities for that year—i.e., the excess of "passive activity deductions" (¶1815) over "passive activity gross income" (¶1817) for the year. (Code Sec. 469(d)(1); Reg § 1.469-2T(b)(1))[2]

For a closely held C corporation, the passive activity loss is the excess of passive activity deductions over the sum of passive activity gross income *plus* the corporation's net active (but not portfolio) income for the tax year. (Code Sec. 469(e)(2)(A); Reg § 1.469-1T(g)(4))[3]

For how passive loss characterization affects other Code provisions, see ¶1811.

¶ 1815   What is a passive activity deduction?

A deduction is a "passive activity deduction" for a tax year only if it: (1) arises in connection with the conduct of an activity that is a passive activity for that year (¶1822), or (2) is carried over as a passive activity deduction from an earlier tax year (¶1837). (Reg § 1.469-2T(d)(1))[4]

The character of an item (as a passive activity deduction) allocated to the taxpayer by a partnership or S corporation is determined, in any case in which participation is relevant, by the taxpayer's participation in the activity that generated the item for the entity's tax year. (Reg § 1.469-2T(e))[5]

For when loss on the sale or other disposition of an interest in property is a passive activity deduction, see ¶1816.

Deductions in excess of a partner's (or shareholder's) basis, or in excess of the at-risk limits, aren't passive activity deductions for the tax year. (Reg § 1.469-2T(d)(6))[6]

¶ 1816   Loss on sale, exchange or other disposition as passive activity deduction.

Passive activity deductions (¶1815) include any loss recognized on the sale, exchange or other disposition of an interest in property used in an activity at the time of disposition, and any deduction allowed on account of the abandonment or worthlessness of the interest, *if and*

---

49. ¶s M-4709, M-5302; ¶4694.80; TD ¶411,508
50. ¶M-4710; ¶4694.85; TD ¶411,509
1. ¶M-4710; ¶4694.85; TD ¶411,510
2. ¶M-4601; ¶4694; TD ¶411,001

3. ¶M-5507 *et seq.*; ¶4694.36; TD ¶416,509
4. ¶M-5401; ¶4694.30; TD ¶416,001
5. ¶M-5402; ¶4694.80; TD ¶416,005
6. ¶M-4606; ¶4694.30; TD ¶411,007

only if the activity was a passive activity (¶1822) of the taxpayer for the tax year of disposition (or other event giving rise to the deduction). (Reg § 1.469-2T(d)(5)(i))[7]

If the interest in property disposed of was used in more than one activity during the 12-month period ending on the date of disposition, the amount realized from the disposition (as well as the adjusted basis of the interest) must be allocated among the activities (with a de minimis exception) on a basis that reasonably reflects those uses. (Reg § 1.469-2(d)(5)(iii), Reg § 1.469-2T(d)(5)(i), Reg § 1.469-2T(d)(5)(ii))[8]

Passive activity deductions don't include: (1) a loss from the disposition of property that produces portfolio income (¶1820) (Reg § 1.469-2T(d)(2)(iv)), or (2) a deduction for a disposition of an entire interest in a passive activity if, under the rules for those dispositions (¶1838), the deduction isn't treated as a passive activity deduction. (Reg § 1.469-2T(d)(2)(v))[9]

¶ 1817 Passive activity gross income.

Passive activity gross income is, in general, gross income from a passive activity (¶1822). (Reg § 1.469-2T(c)(1))[10] The character of a partner's or S corporation shareholder's allocable items of gross income as passive activity gross income is determined, in general, by reference to the partner's or shareholder's participation in the activity(ies) that generated the items for the entity's tax year. (Reg § 1.469-2T(e)(1))[11] For when gain on the disposition of a property interest is passive activity gross income, see ¶1818.

Passive activity gross income doesn't include portfolio income (¶1820), (Code Sec. 469(e)(1)(A)(i)(I); Reg § 1.469-2T(c)(3)(i)) compensation for personal services (as specially defined), (Code Sec. 469(e)(3); Reg § 1.469-2T(c)(4)), certain other income, (e.g., from intangible property) if a taxpayer's personal efforts contributed significantly to the property's creation; a tax refund; or reimbursement of a casualty or theft loss. (Code Sec. 469(c)(3)(B); Reg § 1.469-2(c)(6), Reg § 1.469-2(c)(7))[12]

¶ 1818 Gain on sale, exchange, or other disposition of interest in passive activity.

Gain recognized on the sale, exchange or other disposition of an interest in property generally is treated as passive activity gross income (¶1817) for the year the gain is recognized, if the activity in which the property was used was a passive activity (¶1822) for the year of disposition. (Reg § 1.469-2T(c)(2)(i)(A))[13] But gain from the disposition of an interest in property that is substantially appreciated (fair market value exceeds 120% of adjusted basis) is treated as not from a passive activity unless used in a passive activity for either 20% of the period taxpayer held the interest or the entire 24-month period ending on the date of disposition. (Reg § 1.469-2(c)(2)(iii))[14]

For disposition of an *entire* interest in (or substantially all of) a passive activity, see ¶1838.

¶ 1819 Disposition of interest in partnership or S corporation with passive activities.

Where there is a disposition of a partnership interest or S corporation stock, a ratable portion of the net gain (or loss) is treated as gain (or loss) from the disposition of an interest in each trade or business, rental, or investment activity in which the entity owns an interest. (Reg § 1.469-2T(e)(3)(ii)(A))[15] But, gain attributable to certain substantially appreciated property (¶1818) isn't passive activity gross income (¶1817) if that gain exceeds 10% of the gain allocated to the passive activity. (Reg § 1.469-2T(e)(3)(iii))[16]

7. ¶M-5406; ¶4694.32; TD ¶416,004
8. ¶M-5406; ¶4694.32; TD ¶416,004
9. ¶M-5421;¶4694.31; TD ¶416,018
10. ¶M-5301; ¶4694.21; TD ¶415,001
11. ¶M-5302; ¶4694.80; TD ¶415,019
12. ¶M-5325, ¶M-5332 *et seq.*; ¶4694.22; ¶4694.66; TD ¶415,022,

TD ¶415,028 *et seq.*
13. ¶M-5304; ¶4694.28; TD ¶415,002
14. ¶M-5306; ¶4694.28; TD ¶415,004
15. ¶M-5708;¶4694.82; TD ¶417,512
16. ¶M-5342; ¶4694.82; TD ¶415,045

¶ 1820 Portfolio income isn't passive activity income.

Portfolio income (treated as not passive activity gross income, see ¶1817) includes all gross income, *other than* income derived in the ordinary course of a trade or business attributable to:

... interest;

... dividends from a C corporation or an S corporation's accumulated earnings and profits;

... annuities;

... royalties;

... net income from publicly traded partnerships (¶1813);

... income (including dividends) from a regulated investment company (¶4201), real estate investment trust (¶4202), real estate mortgage investment conduit (¶4204), Code Sec. 1381(a) cooperative (¶4205), common trust fund (¶4210), controlled foreign corporation (¶4623) or qualified electing fund (¶4629);

... gain (loss) from the disposition of property that produces portfolio income;

... gain (loss) from the disposition of property held for investment (¶1728) (Code Sec. 469(e)(1)(A); Reg § 1.469-2T(c)(3)(i)); and

... income, gain or loss from investment of working capital.[17]

¶ 1821 Recharacterization of passive income as nonpassive income.

Income from the following passive activities *isn't* treated as income that is from passive activity: (i) income from: significant participation activities (in which the taxpayer participates for more than 100 hours during the tax year, but doesn't materially participate (defined at ¶1826 *et seq.*); (ii) income from rental of nondepreciable property; (iii) net interest income from an equity-financed lending activity or certain rental property; and (iv) certain royalty income. (Reg § 1.469-2T(f))[18]

¶ 1822 What is a passive activity?

A passive activity is any activity (¶1824) involving the conduct of any trade or business (¶1823) in which taxpayer doesn't materially participate (¶1826). (Code Sec. 469(c)(1))

For rental activities, see ¶1832.

¶ 1823 Trade or business activities under passive activity rules.

A trade or business that can be a passive activity (¶1822) includes any activity:

... in connection with a trade or business (under Code Sec. 162);

... with respect to which expenses are allowable as a deduction under Code Sec. 212 (for the production, etc., of income) (Code Sec. 469(c)(6));[19] and

... involving research or experimentation (under the Code Sec. 174 rules for deducting business-related research, etc., expenditures, see ¶1601). (Code Sec. 469(c)(5))[20]

For rules for grouping activities, see ¶1824.

Trade or business activities do not include rental activities (although rental activities generally are treated as passive activities, see ¶1832) or activities that are (under Reg § 1.469-1T(e)(3)(vi)(B)) incidental to an activity of holding property for investment.

---

17. ¶M-5325 *et seq.*; ¶4694.23 ; TD ¶415,023
18. ¶M-5335; ¶4694.25; TD ¶415,035

19. ¶M-4801 *et seq.*; ¶s 4694.01, 4694.02; TD ¶412,001 *et seq.*
20. ¶M-4802; ¶4694.02; TD ¶412,002

(Reg § 1.469-1(e)(2), Reg § 1.469-4(b)(1))[21]

¶ 1824 Rules for grouping "activities" for passive activity rules purposes.

A taxpayer may treat one or more trade or business activities (¶1823) or rental activities (¶1832) as a single activity if the activities are an appropriate economic unit for measuring gain or loss for Code Sec. 469 purposes (the "passive activity" rules) (Reg § 1.469-4(c)(1)) based on all the relevant facts and circumstances. (Reg § 1.469-4(c)(2))[22]

A rental activity (as defined in Reg § 1.469-1T(e)(3)) (Reg § 1.469-4(b)(2)) can't be grouped with a trade or business activity unless the activities being grouped together are an appropriate economic unit *and:*

... the rental activity is insubstantial in relation to the trade or business activity;

... the trade or business activity is insubstantial in relation to the rental activity; or

... each owner of the trade or business activity has the same proportionate ownership interest in the rental activity. In that case, the part of the rental activity that involves the rental of items of property for use in the trade or business may be grouped with the trade or business activity. (Reg § 1.469-4(d)(1))[23]

Real property rentals and personal property rentals (other than personal property rentals provided in connection with the real property, or vice versa) can't be grouped together. (Reg § 1.469-4(d)(2))[24]

Once the taxpayer has grouped activities, the taxpayer can't regroup them in later years. If a material change occurs that makes the original grouping clearly inappropriate, the taxpayer must regroup the activities. IRS may regroup activities to prevent tax avoidance. (Reg § 1.469-4(e), Reg § 1.469-4(f))[25] Taxpayers must report to IRS their groupings and regroupings of activities and the addition of specific activities within their existing groupings.[26]

In a year when there is a disposition of substantially all of an activity, taxpayer may under specified conditions treat the part disposed of as a separate activity. (Reg § 1.469-4(g))[27]

The passive activity grouping rules apply in determining whether a trade or business is a passive activity for purposes of 3.8% surtax on unearned income under Code Sec. 1411(c)(2) (¶1107). Proposed reliance regs allow taxpayers to regroup their activities for any tax year that begins during 2013, if Code Sec. 1411 would apply to taxpayers without regard to the effect of regrouping (i.e., they have net investment income and the applicable income threshold is met). A taxpayer may only regroup activities once, and any regrouping will apply to the tax year for which the regrouping is done and all later years. (Prop Reg. § 1.469-11(b)(3)(iv)) ["Taxpayers may rely"]

¶ 1825 Activities conducted through personal service corporations (PSCs), closely-held corporations, S corporations and partnerships for passive activity rule purposes.

For purposes of the passive activity rules (¶1810 *et seq.*), a taxpayer's activities include those conducted through PSCs, closely-held C corporations, S corporations, and partnerships. (Reg § 1.469-4(a))[28]

---

21. ¶M-4802; ¶4694.02; TD ¶412,002
22. ¶M-4803, M-4804; ¶4694.10; TD ¶412,003, 412,004
23. ¶M-4805; ¶4694.10; TD ¶412,005
24. ¶M-4806; ¶4694.10; TD ¶412,006

25. ¶M-4809; ¶4694.10; TD ¶412,013
26. ¶M-4808.1; TD ¶412,011
27. ¶M-5701.3; ¶4694.50; TD ¶412,001 *et seq.*
28. ¶M-4807.2; ¶4694.10; TD ¶412,009

¶ 1826   What is "material participation" under passive activity loss rules?

A taxpayer materially participates in an activity only if he's involved in the activity's operations on a regular, continuous and substantial basis (¶1827 *et seq.*). (Code Sec. 469(h)) A trust materially participates in an activity if a fiduciary, in his capacity as such, so participates.[29] A closely held C corporation or personal service corporation materially participates, in general, only if one or more of its shareholders who own more than 50% of its stock (by value) themselves materially participate. (Code Sec. 469(h)(4)(A))[30]

¶ 1827   Material participation by individuals under passive activity loss rules.

An individual materially participates in an activity for a tax year *if and only if* the individual meets at least *one* of the following tests:

(1) The individual participates (as defined at ¶1830) in the activity for more than 500 hours during the year. (Reg § 1.469-5T(a)(1))

(2) The individual's participation in the activity for the tax year is substantially all of the participation in the activity by all individuals (including nonowner individuals) for the year. (Reg § 1.469-5T(a)(2))

(3) The individual participates in the activity for more than 100 hours during the tax year and that isn't less than the participation in the activity of any other individual (including nonowners) for that year. (Reg § 1.469-5T(a)(3))

(4) The activity is a "significant participation activity" for the tax year, and the individual's aggregate participation in all significant participation activities that year exceeds 500 hours. A "significant participation activity" is a trade or business in which the individual significantly participates (for more than 100 hours), but in which he doesn't otherwise materially participate. (Reg § 1.469-5T(a)(4), Reg § 1.469-5T(c))

(5) The individual materially participated in the activity for any five tax years (consecutive or not) during the 10 immediately preceding tax years. (Reg § 1.469-5T(a)(5))

(6) The activity is a personal service activity, and the individual materially participated in the activity for any three tax years (consecutive or not) before the tax year. (Reg § 1.469-5T(a)(6), Reg § 1.469-5T(d))

(7) The individual meets a facts and circumstances test (¶1828). (Reg § 1.469-5T(a)(7))[31]

For participation by the individual's spouse, see ¶1831.

¶ 1828   Facts and circumstances test for material participation under passive activity loss rules.

For purposes of the passive activity loss rules, an individual materially participates (¶1827) in an activity if he participates on a regular, continuous and substantial basis during the year, based on all the facts and circumstances. (Reg § 1.469-5T(a)(7)) An individual who participates in the activity for 100 hours or less during the year doesn't meet this test. (Reg § 1.469-5T(b)(2)(iii))[32]

¶ 1829   Limited partner's material participation under passive activity loss rules.

For purposes of the passive activity loss rules, an individual limited partner is not treated as materially participating (¶1826) in any activity of a limited partnership with respect to his interest in that partnership (or to any gain or loss from the activity recognized on a sale or exchange of that interest) *unless* the individual would be treated as materially participating

---

29. ¶M-5005; TD ¶413,024.
30. ¶M-4901 *et seq.*, ¶M-5006; ¶4694.06; TD ¶413,002 *et seq.*

31. ¶M-4901 *et seq.*; ¶4694.06; TD ¶413,002 *et seq.*
32. ¶M-4912; ¶4694.06; TD ¶413,012

under the 500-hour, five-tax-years-out-of-ten, or three-year-personal-service-activity tests at ¶1827 (items (1), (5) or (6), respectively), if he weren't a limited partner. (Code Sec. 469(h)(2); Reg § 1.469-5T(e)(2))[33]

An individual's partnership interest *isn't* treated as a limited partnership interest if the individual is a general partner in the partnership at all times during the partnership's tax year ending with or within the individual's tax year. (Reg § 1.469-5T(e)(3)(ii))[34]

A member of a limited liability company (LLC) isn't treated as a limited partner under the above rule and may satisfy the material participation standard.[35]

¶ 1830   Participation defined under passive activity loss rules.

Any work done by an individual (without regard to the capacity in which he does the work) in connection with the activity, where the individual owns (directly or indirectly) an interest in the activity at the time the work is done, is treated as participation by that individual in the activity, except as otherwise provided. (Reg § 1.469-5(f)(1))[36]

Work not of a type customarily done by an owner isn't treated as participation if one of its principal purposes is to avoid the passive loss rules. (Reg § 1.469-5T(f)(2)(i))[37]

An individual's work as an investor is not participation unless the individual is directly involved in day-to-day management or operations. (Reg § 1.469-5T(f)(2)(ii))[38]

¶ 1831   Spouse's material participation under passive activity loss rules.

In determining whether a married taxpayer materially participates in an activity, the participation of taxpayer's spouse is taken into account (Code Sec. 469(h)(5)), without regard to whether the spouse owns an interest in the activity, or whether the spouses file a joint return for the year. (Reg § 1.469-5T(f)(3))[39]

¶ 1832   Rental activities as passive activities.

For purposes of the passive activity rules (¶1810 *et seq.*), all rental activities are treated as passive activities. (Code Sec. 469(c)(2)) However, this rule does not apply to individuals who actively participate in rental real estate activities (¶1833) and certain real estate professionals (¶1836).[40]

A rental activity is any activity where payments are principally for the use of tangible property (Code Sec. 469(j)(8)), without regard to whether a lease, service contract, or other arrangement is involved. (Reg § 1.469-1T(e)(3)(i)(B)) But, a rental activity doesn't include an activity involving the use of tangible property if:

(1) The average period the customer uses the property is 7 days or less (Reg § 1.469-1T(e)(3)(ii)(A)), or 30 days or less *and* the owner (or someone on the owner's behalf) provides significant personal services (as defined in the regs). (Reg § 1.469-1T(e)(3)(ii)(B))

(2) The owner (or someone on the owner's behalf) provides extraordinary personal services (as defined in the regs), without regard to the average period the customer uses the property. (Reg § 1.469-1T(e)(3)(ii)(C))

(3) The rental of the tangible property is incidental to a nonrental activity of the taxpayer (Reg § 1.469-1T(e)(3)(ii)(D)) (as measured by certain percentage and other tests). (Reg § 1.469-1T(e)(3)(vi))

(4) The taxpayer customarily makes the property available during defined business hours for nonexclusive use by various customers (e.g., a golf course). (Reg § 1.469-1T(e)(3)(ii)(E))

33. ¶M-5003 *et seq.*; ¶4694.06; TD ¶413,022
34. ¶M-5002.1; ¶4694.06; TD ¶413,022
35. ¶M-5002.2; ¶4694.06; TD ¶413,021
36. ¶M-4902; ¶4694.06; TD ¶413,002
37. ¶M-4903; ¶4694.06 ; TD ¶413,003
38. ¶M-4903; ¶4694.06; TD ¶413,003
39. ¶M-4902; ¶4694.06; TD ¶413,002
40. ¶M-5100 *et seq.*; ¶s 4694.01, 4694.60, 4694.63; TD ¶413,501

(5) The property is provided for use in a nonrental activity of a partnership, joint venture, or S corporation in which the taxpayer owns an interest, where the taxpayer provided the property in his capacity as owner of that interest (Reg § 1.469-1T(e)(3)(ii)(F)) (not as a renter of the property to the partnership, etc.).[41]

¶ 1833 Individuals' active participation rental real estate losses up to $25,000 may be used against nonpassive income.

A natural person who: (1) has at least a 10% interest in any rental real estate activity (¶1834), and (2) otherwise "actively participates" in that activity (¶1835), may offset up to $25,000 of nonpassive income with that portion of the passive activity loss, or of the deduction equivalent of the passive activity credit, attributable to that activity. (Code Sec. 469(i)(1), Code Sec. 469(i)(2), Code Sec. 469(j)(5))[42]

For a married person filing a separate return, the allowance is $12,500 if he lives apart from his spouse at all times during the tax year (Code Sec. 469(i)(5)(A)(i)), and zero if he does not live apart from his spouse at all times during the tax year. (Code Sec. 469(i)(5)(B))[43]

The $25,000 allowance ($12,500 for marrieds filing separately) is reduced (but not below zero) by 50% of the amount by which taxpayer's adjusted gross income (AGI) as specially computed exceeds (1) $100,000 ($50,000 for marrieds filing separately), or (2) $200,000 ($100,000 for marrieds filing separately) in the case of rehabilitation investment credits (¶2308). There's no AGI-based phaseout of the $25,000 ($12,500) offset for low-income housing credits (¶2320) or the commercial revitalization deduction (¶1972). (Code Sec. 469(i)(3), Code Sec. 469(i)(5))[44]

¶ 1834 Who is a 10%-or-more owner entitled to rental real estate allowance under passive activity loss rules?

An individual is a 10%-or-more owner (for the allowance at ¶1833) with respect to any interest in any rental real estate activity (¶1832) for any period only if *at all times* during that period (i.e., the tax year or shorter period the individual held the interest) his interest was at least 10% (by value) of all interests in that activity. The individual's interest includes any interest of his spouse. (Code Sec. 469(i)(6)(D))[45]

¶ 1835 What is "active participation" under passive activity loss rules?

Taxpayer must participate (¶1830) in an activity in a significant and bona fide sense to actively participate in it. Taxpayer participates if he makes management decisions, e.g., approves new tenants, decides on rental terms, approves capital or repair expenditures or arranges for others to provide services (such as repairs). He need not have regular, continuous and substantial involvement in operations. But, a merely formal and nominal participation in management, without a genuine exercise of independent discretion and judgment, is insufficient.[46] The active participation test is less stringent than the material participation requirement (¶1826). Active participation isn't required to take low-income housing (¶2320) or rehabilitation investment credits (¶2308), or the commercial revitalization deduction (¶1972). (Code Sec. 469(i)(6)(B))[47]

In determining whether taxpayer actively participates, the participation of taxpayer's spouse is taken into account. (Code Sec. 469(i)(6)(D))[48]

A taxpayer isn't treated as actively participating (except as regs may provide) with respect

---

41. ¶M-5101 *et seq.*; ¶4694.03; TD ¶413,502
42. ¶M-5131; ¶4694.60; TD ¶413,601
43. ¶M-5131; ¶4694.60; TD ¶413,601
44. ¶M-5142 *et seq.*; ¶4694.60; TD ¶413,612 *et seq.*

45. ¶M-5139; TD ¶413,609
46. ¶M-5138; ¶4694.60; TD ¶413,608
47. ¶M-5141; ¶4694.60; TD ¶413,611
48. ¶M-5138; ¶4694.70; TD ¶413,608

to any interest as a limited partner. (Code Sec. 469(i)(6)(C))[49]

¶ 1836 Rental real estate activities of real estate professionals not treated as automatically passive.

For any tax year in which the taxpayer is a "qualifying taxpayer" (usually known as a real estate professional), the rule treating all rental activities as passive activities (¶1832) doesn't apply to any rental real estate activity of the taxpayer. (Code Sec. 469(c)(7)(A)(i)) Instead, that activity is a passive activity unless the taxpayer materially participates (¶1826). (Reg § 1.469-9(e)(1))[50] Rental real estate activities do not include property used by customers for an average period of 7 days or less a year. Thus, a taxpayer who ran an inn where rooms were rented for an average of three days couldn't add the hours she spent running that business to the hours she spent on other real estate activities.[1]

⊘/observation: So, real estate professionals who materially participate in a rental real estate activity may use losses or credits from the activity to offset other, non-passive income.

A taxpayer qualifies as a real estate professional for a particular tax year if: (1) more than half of the personal services (see below) the taxpayer performs during that year are performed in real property trades or businesses (see below) in which the taxpayer materially participates (¶1826) (Code Sec. 469(c)(7)(B)(i)), and (2) the taxpayer performs more than 750 hours of services during that year in real property trades or businesses in which he materially participates. (Code Sec. 469(c)(7)(B)(ii))[2] A taxpayer's hours when he was "on call" to provide services to rental tenants couldn't be counted toward the 750-hour service performance requirement.[3]

A taxpayer who owns at least one interest in rental real estate and who meets the above tests is a real estate professional. (Reg § 1.469-9(b)(6))[4]

In determining whether a taxpayer is a real estate professional, each of his interests in rental real estate is treated as a separate activity, unless he elects (by filing a specified statement with his original income tax return) to treat all interests in rental real estate as one activity. (Code Sec. 469(c)(7)(A); Reg § 1.469-9(g))[5] The election is binding for the tax year it's made and for all future years in which the taxpayer qualifies. Taxpayers who qualify may make late elections.[6] Failure to elect in one year doesn't bar the election in a later year. (Reg § 1.469-9(g)(1)).[7]

Spouses filing a joint return qualify as real estate professionals only if one spouse separately satisfies the above tests (Code Sec. 469(c)(7)(B); Reg § 1.469-9(c)(4)), without regard to the other spouse's services.[8]

A closely-held C corporation qualifies as a real estate professional if more than 50% of its gross receipts for the tax year are derived from real property trades or businesses in which it materially participates. (Code Sec. 469(c)(7)(D)(i))[9]

A real property trade or business is any real property development, redevelopment, construction, reconstruction, acquisition, conversion, rental, operation, management, leasing or brokerage trade or business. (Code Sec. 469(c)(7)(C)) The determination of a taxpayer's real property trades or businesses is based on all relevant facts and circumstances. Once a taxpayer determines the real property trades or businesses in which personal services are provided, he can't redetermine them later unless the original determination was clearly erroneous or there has been a material change of facts and circumstances. (Reg § 1.469-9(d)(1))[10]

---

49. ¶M-5140; ¶4694.60; TD ¶413,610
50. ¶M-5161; ¶4694.63; TD ¶413,801
1. ¶M-5167; TD ¶413,503
2. ¶M-5168; ¶4694.63; TD ¶413,808
3. ¶M-5169; TD ¶413,809
4. ¶M-5168; ¶4694.63; TD ¶413,808

5. ¶M-5163 *et seq.*; ¶4694.63; TD ¶413,803, 413,804
6. ¶S-4827.2; ¶4694.63; TD ¶413,803
7. ¶M-5163; ¶4694.63; TD ¶413,803
8. ¶M-5171; ¶4694.63; TD ¶413,811
9. ¶M-5172; ¶4694.63; TD ¶413,812
10. ¶M-5175; ¶4694.63; TD ¶413,815

Personal services means any work performed by an individual in connection with a trade or business, but not as an investor. (Reg § 1.469-9(b)(4)) Services performed as an employee don't count, unless the individual is a more-than-5%-owner of the employer. (Code Sec. 469(c)(7)(D)(ii))[11]

¶ 1837   Carryover of suspended losses and credits.

Any deduction (or credit) from a passive activity (¶1822) that's disallowed under the passive loss rules (¶1810 *et seq.*) for a tax year is allocated among taxpayer's activities for the next tax year in a manner that reasonably reflects the extent each activity continues the business and rental operations that made up the loss activity. As so allocated, it is treated as a deduction (or credit) from that activity for that next year. (Code Sec. 469(b); Reg § 1.469-1(f)(4)(i))[12]

¶ 1838   Disposition of taxpayer's entire interest in passive activity or substantially all of passive activity.

If a taxpayer disposes of his entire interest in a passive activity (or former passive activity), and all gain or loss realized on the disposition is recognized, the excess of: (1) any loss from the activity for the tax year of disposition (including losses carried over from earlier years, ¶1837), over (2) any net income or gain for that year from all other passive activities (including loss carryovers), is treated as loss *not* from a passive activity. (Code Sec. 469(g)(1)(A)) Loss from the activity under (1) is computed by taking into account all income, gain, and loss, including gain and loss recognized on the disposition.[13]

A taxpayer that disposes of *substantially all* of an activity may be able to treat the part disposed of as a separate activity. (Reg § 1.469-4(g)(2))[14]

Where the disposition is by installment sale, the amount treated as a nonpassive loss is the portion of the losses from each tax year that bears the same ratio to all these losses as the gain recognized on the sale bears to the gross profit from the sale. (Code Sec. 469(g)(3))[15]

Special rules apply where a disposition is to a related party (Code Sec. 469(g)(1)(B)), where the interest in the activity is transferred by reason of death (Code Sec. 469(g)(2)), or where the disposition is by gift. (Code Sec. 469(j)(6))[16]

¶ 1839   Net Operating Losses (NOLs). ▬▬▬▬▬▬▬

An NOL sustained in one year may be used to reduce the taxable income for another year. It may be carried back to earlier years and yield tax refunds. If not exhausted in earlier years (or if taxpayer elects not to use the carryback), it may be carried forward to later years and reduce the tax for those years.

¶ 1840   Net operating loss (NOL) defined.

An NOL is the excess of business deductions (computed with certain modifications) over gross income in a particular tax year. A deduction is allowed for that loss, through an NOL carryback or carryover, in some other tax year(s) (see ¶1841) in which gross income exceeds business deductions. (Code Sec. 172(b))[17]

An NOL deduction is allowed to individuals, corporations (Code Sec. 172), estates and trusts (Code Sec. 642(d)) (and charitable organizations with respect to the unrelated business income tax. (Code Sec. 512(b)(6)))

---

11. ¶M-5169, M-5170 *et seq.*; ¶4694.63; TD ¶413,809, 413,810
12. ¶M-5504, ¶M-5604; ¶4694.45; TD ¶416,505, 417,006
13. ¶M-5701; ¶4694.50; TD ¶417,501
14. ¶s M-5701, M-5701.3; ¶4694.50; TD ¶417,504

15. ¶M-5701.2; ¶4694.50; TD ¶417,503
16. ¶M-5704 *et seq.*; ¶4694.50; TD ¶417,507 *et seq.*
17. ¶M-4001 *et seq.*; ¶1724; TD ¶354,001

An NOL deduction isn't allowed to partnerships (Code Sec. 703(a)(2)(D)), common trust funds (Code Sec. 584(g)) (but the deduction is allowed to the partners and beneficiaries), regulated investment companies (Code Sec. 852(b)(2)(B)), or S corporations (losses are passed through to shareholders). (Code Sec. 1366(a))[18]

¶ 1841   Net operating loss (NOL) carryover and carryback periods.

Except as noted below (or where a taxpayer elects to forgo a carryback, ¶1842), a NOL may be carried back two years and forward 20 years. (Code Sec. 172(b)(1)(A))[19] A decedent's NOL can be carried back, but not forward.[20] .

A three-year carryback period applies to the following:

. . . NOLs arising from property losses of individuals due to fire, storm, shipwreck, or other casualty, or from theft.

. . . For a small business, or a taxpayer engaged in the trade or business of farming, NOLs attributable to Federally declared disasters (¶1798). A small business is one whose average annual gross receipts (under Code Sec. 448(c)) are $5 million or less. (Code Sec. 172(b)(1)(F))[21]

At its election, a taxpayer may carry back an NOL for 2008 or 2009 for three, four, or five years. (Code Sec. 172(b)(1)(H))[22] The carryback period is five years for a certain "farming losses," see ¶4503.

A five-year carryback also applies for a qualified disaster loss and qualified Gulf Opportunity Zone loss (GO Zone loss). A qualified disaster loss is the sum of the losses allowable under Code Sec. 165 for the tax year attributable to a federally declared disaster occurring before Jan. 1, 2010 in a disaster area, and the NOL for the tax year. (Code Sec. 1400N(k))[23] A qualified GO Zone loss is equal to the lesser of: (1) the excess of: the taxpayer's NOL for the tax year, over the specified liability loss (SLL) for the tax year which qualifies for the 10-year SLL carryback period; or (2) the aggregate amount of specified deductions, to the extent they're taken into account in computing the NOL for the tax year.[24]

An NOL attributable to a SLL—i.e., a product liability loss and/or losses attributable to certain deferred statutory liabilities—may be carried back 10 years. (Code Sec. 172(b)(1)(C), Code Sec. 172(f)) The carry*forward* is the usual 20 years. (Code Sec. 172(b)(1)(A)(ii)) (The 10-year carryback isn't precluded by making the election at ¶1842 to forgo the carryback.) (Reg § 1.172-13(c)(4)) To carry back the loss under the regular two-year/20-year rules, taxpayer must so elect. (Code Sec. 172(f)(6))[25]

¶ 1842   Election to forgo net operating loss (NOL) carryback.

A taxpayer may elect not to use the carryback period (¶1841) and instead only carry over the NOL for the allowed *carryforward* period. Once the election is made for any tax year (on a statement attached to the return or amended return), it's irrevocable for that year. (Code Sec. 172(b)(3); Reg § 301.9100-12T(e)) (The election also applies to alternative minimum tax NOLs (ATNOLs, see ¶3212.)[26]

¶ 1843   How the net operating loss (NOL) deduction works.

Assume an NOL is sustained for a tax year beginning in 2013, and that the usual two-year carryback and 20-year carryover apply:

18. ¶M-4003; ¶1724.02; TD ¶354,003
19. ¶M-4300; ¶1724.31; TD ¶356,001
20. ¶M-4004; ¶1724.02; TD ¶354,004
21. ¶M-4307, M-4308; ¶1724.434, 1724.436; TD ¶356,010, 356,011
22. ¶M-4367 *et seq.*; ¶1724.315; TD ¶356,023 *et seq.*
23. ¶M-4350 *et seq.*; ¶14,00N4.06; TD ¶356,014 *et seq.*
24. ¶M-4351 *et seq.*; ¶14,00N4.06; TD ¶356,014 *et seq.*
25. ¶M-4331 *et seq.*; ¶1724.40; TD ¶356,033
26. ¶M-4304; ¶1724.33; TD ¶356,003

STEP (1). Compute the NOL. Note some deductions aren't allowed (¶1844 *et seq.*).

STEP (2). Find the earliest year to which this loss can be carried (here 2011).

STEP (3). Add this loss to all other NOLs carried to the year (2011), and deduct the total as an *NOL deduction*. Note that the 2013 loss is fully absorbed if 2011 taxable income (before NOL deduction) exceeds the sum of 2013 loss, plus pre-2013 losses, carried to 2011. File for refund if applicable.

STEP (4). To the extent the 2013 loss isn't deducted in 2011, it's carried to the next earliest year to which it may be carried (2012). Note that the amount carried to 2012 is reduced by "intervening years' modifications" (¶1847).

STEP (5). Repeat step (3)—that is, add the 2013 loss that may be carried to the next year (2012) to all other NOLs carried to that year, and deduct the total as an NOL deduction.

LATER STEPS. Repeat the process described in steps (3) and (4) for the first year after the loss year (2014 in our example) and then in order to each of the 19 following years or until the full amount of the NOL is absorbed, whichever happens first. If the loss is not absorbed by the 20th year succeeding the loss year, any further benefit is lost.[27]

¶ 1844 Computing the net operating loss (NOL) for noncorporate taxpayers.

A noncorporate taxpayer has an NOL in a tax year if allowable deductions exceed gross income. In determining excess deductions, NOL carryback or carryover deductions from other years, personal exemptions, exclusion of gain from qualified small business stock (¶2648), and the Code Sec. 199 deductions for domestic production activities (¶1614) are not allowed. Moreover, deductions for capital losses and nonbusiness deductions are only allowed to a limited extent. (Code Sec. 172(d); Reg § 1.172-3(a))[28]

¶ 1845 Computing the net operating loss (NOL) for corporate taxpayers.

A corporation's net operating loss (NOL) is figured by subtracting its deductions from its gross income, except that, in arriving at the NOL for the year: (1) NOL carrybacks and carryovers from other years aren't deducted; (2) the deduction for dividends received is taken without limiting it by a percentage of the corporation's taxable income; (3) the deduction for dividends paid on certain preferred stock of public utilities is computed without limiting it to the year's taxable income; and (4) the Code Sec. 199 deduction for domestic production activities (¶1614) isn't allowed. (Code Sec. 172(d); Reg § 1.172-2(a))[29]

¶ 1846 Amount of net operating loss (NOL) deduction.

The NOL deduction in any year is the sum of all NOL carrybacks and carryovers to that year. (Code Sec. 172(a))[30] For refunds based on NOL carrybacks, see ¶4850.

Where a husband and wife who make a joint return for the deduction year made a joint return for all other tax years involved in computing the NOL deduction, that deduction is computed on the basis of their joint NOLs and combined taxable incomes. (Reg § 1.172-7(c)) Special rules apply if they didn't make joint returns for all applicable years. (Reg § 1.172-7)[31]

🅡/caution: For limits on the NOL deduction for alternative minimum tax purposes, see ¶3212.

---

27. ¶M-4402; ¶1724.10; TD ¶354,002
28. ¶M-4109 *et seq.*; ¶1724.12; TD ¶355,008 *et seq.*
29. ¶M-4105 *et seq.*; ¶1724.11; TD ¶355,007

30. ¶M-4401; ¶1724.01; TD ¶354,001
31. ¶M-4405 *et seq.*; ¶1724.13; TD ¶354,006, 354,007

¶ 1847   Net operating loss (NOL) exceeds income in year to which carried; "intervening year."

If the NOL carried to an earlier tax year exceeds the taxable income for that year, modifications must be made in that year's taxable income, in computing the unused portion of the NOL that can be carried to the next year. These "intervening year modifications" apply only in computing NOL carryovers, and don't affect taxable income for other purposes. (Code Sec. 172(b)(2); Reg § 1.172-5)[32] Deductions for intervening years which are based on, or limited to, a percentage of adjusted gross income (AGI, ¶3102) or taxable income must be recomputed, based on AGI or taxable income as modified. (Reg § 1.172-5(a)(2)(ii))[33]

¶ 1848   Deduction for Bad Debts.

Bad debts are deductible whether or not connected with a taxpayer's business. A deduction is allowed for total worthlessness and, in some cases, for partial worthlessness.

Business bad debts are deductible as ordinary deductions. They are deductible if partially worthless as well as when wholly worthless. Nonbusiness bad debts are deducted only as short-term capital losses, and only when wholly worthless (¶1853).[34] An item can't be deductible both as a bad debt and as a loss. If it could be treated as either, it must be treated as a bad debt.[35]

But, a worthless debt that is evidenced by a security, and is owed by a corporation or a government, is a loss (see ¶1781), and not a bad debt, unless owed to a bank. (Code Sec. 165(g), Code Sec. 166(e), Code Sec. 582(a))[36]

¶ 1849   Bad debts of guarantors.

If a taxpayer makes a guarantee agreement in the course of his trade or business, he's entitled to a business bad debt deduction for any payment he makes as guarantor, of principal or interest. (Reg § 1.166-9(a))[37]

If a taxpayer makes a guarantee agreement in a transaction for profit (but not in the course of his business), and makes a payment of principal or interest, he's entitled to a nonbusiness bad debt deduction in the year his right of subrogation becomes totally worthless. (Reg § 1.166-9(b), Reg § 1.166-9(e)(2))[38] For general timing rules, see ¶1850.

¶ 1850   Time for deducting worthless debt.

A deduction is allowed for the tax year the debt becomes wholly worthless. (Code Sec. 166(a)(1))[39] (For *partial* worthlessness of *business* debts, see ¶1852.) Taxpayer must show the debt had value at the beginning of the year and no value at the end, and that the worthlessness occurred in the particular tax year claimed.[40] Worthlessness is a question of fact requiring consideration of all pertinent evidence, including the debtor's financial condition and the value of any security. (Reg § 1.166-2(a))[41]

¶ 1851   Amount of bad debt deduction.

The amount deductible for a wholly worthless debt (¶1850) is its adjusted basis for determining loss on a sale or exchange (¶2400 *et seq.*), regardless of its face value. (Code

---

32. ¶M-4202 *et seq.*; ¶1724, 1724.20 *et seq.*; TD ¶357,002 *et seq.*
33. ¶M-4207; ¶1724.20 *et seq.*; TD ¶357,007
34. ¶M-2801 *et seq.*, ¶M-2901 *et seq.*; ¶1664; TD ¶320,501 *et seq.*, TD ¶323,001 *et seq.*
35. ¶M-2503; ¶1654.040; TD ¶320,508
36. ¶s M-3301, M-3309; ¶1664.160; TD ¶320,501, 372,001

37. ¶M-3207; ¶1664.450; TD ¶324,007
38. ¶M-3210, M-3214; ¶1664.450; TD ¶324,011, 324,014
39. ¶M-2401; ¶1664; TD ¶320,501
40. ¶M-2701; ¶1664.220; TD ¶322,001
41. ¶M-2702; ¶1664.220; TD ¶322,002

Sec. 166(b); Reg § 1.166-1(d))[42] The adjustments used to figure adjusted basis are generally the debtor's payments on the debt. But a deduction allowed for a debt's partial worthlessness reduces the debt's basis to that extent, whether or not taxpayer got a tax benefit from the deduction.[43]

If the creditor (the taxpayer) has no basis in the debt, there is no deduction.[44] So there is no deduction for wages, rents, alimony, etc., that were never received, unless these items were included in income. (Reg § 1.166-1(e))[45] Where a taxpayer reports receivables at fair market value (FMV) rather than face, the deduction can't exceed FMV. (Reg § 1.166-1(d)(2))[46]

Where a taxpayer fails to prove a debt's exact basis, it may be estimated by a court if the taxpayer proves his right to *some* deduction.[47]

If a debt is compromised because of inability to pay the full amount, the taxpayer deducts the debt's adjusted basis minus any cash and the value of any property received. If the debt is compromised for some other reason, the taxpayer doesn't have a bad debt (but may have a loss).[48]

¶ 1852 Deduction for partially worthless business debts.

A deduction is allowed for partially worthless debts (Code Sec. 166(a)(2)) *only if*: (1) the debt is a business debt (see ¶1853); (2) IRS is satisfied that the specific debt is recoverable only in part; (3) the amount deducted was *charged off* on the books during the tax year; *and* (4) the debt is not evidenced by a security. (Code Sec. 166(d)(1), Code Sec. 166(e); Reg § 1.166-5(b))[49]

A taxpayer may charge-off and deduct a debt for partial worthlessness as the worthlessness occurs. Or he can defer charge-off and deduction to a later year when partial worthlessness is greater, thus deducting several years' partial worthlessness in one year. Or he can defer deduction until total worthlessness (but not beyond the year of total worthlessness. (Reg § 1.166-3(b))[50] For deducting "worthless securities" as losses, see ¶1781.

¶ 1853 Effect of classification as business or nonbusiness bad debt.

The need to determine whether a debt is a business or nonbusiness debt (¶1854) arises only for noncorporate taxpayers. A corporation's debts are always business debts. (Code Sec. 166(d))[1]

Business bad debts are fully deductible against income (Code Sec. 166(a)), while nonbusiness bad debts are short-term capital losses of limited deductibility. (Code Sec. 166(d)(1)(B))[2] Business and nonbusiness debts are deductible when wholly worthless (¶1850), but only business debts are deductible when partly worthless (¶1852). (Code Sec. 166(a), Code Sec. 166(d)(1)(A))[3]

¶ 1854 Business and nonbusiness debts defined.

A *business debt* is either: (1) a debt created or acquired in the course of the taxpayer's trade or business (whether or not it was related to that business when it became worthless, see ¶1850); or (2) a debt the loss from the worthlessness of which is incurred in the taxpayer's trade or business. This applies if the loss is proximately related to the taxpayer's business when the debt becomes worthless. A bad debt is proximately related to business if business is the dominant motivation for the debt. (Reg § 1.166-5(b))[4]

---

42. ¶M-2402; ¶1664.210; TD ¶320,502
43. ¶s M-2406, M-2407; TD ¶320,504
44. ¶M-2404; ¶1664.210; TD ¶320,502
45. ¶M-2506; ¶1664.210; TD ¶320,503
46. ¶M-2402; TD ¶320,502
47. ¶M-2405; TD ¶320,502
48. ¶M-2408; TD ¶320,504

49. ¶M-2801 *et seq.*; ¶1664.270 *et seq.*; TD ¶322,501 *et seq.*
50. ¶M-2801; ¶1664.271; TD ¶322,502
1. ¶M-2800; ¶s 1664, 1664.300; TD ¶323,001
2. ¶s M-2401, M-2901; ¶s 1664, 1664.300; TD ¶320,501
3. ¶s M-2401, M-2800; ¶s 1664.210, 1664.270, 1664.300; TD ¶322,501
4. ¶M-2902; ¶1664.301; TD ¶323,003

A *nonbusiness debt* is a debt other than a business debt. (Code Sec. 166(d)(2); Reg § 1.166-5(b))[5]

For effect of classification as business or nonbusiness bad debt to noncorporate taxpayers, see ¶1853.

¶ 1855 When a shareholders' loan or guarantee is treated as a business debt.

A shareholder in a corporation can't treat the corporation's business as his business even if he's the sole shareholder, or he devotes a lot of time and energy to a corporation's affairs. So, an individual shareholder's loan to his corporation isn't a business debt (¶1854) unless he shows the debt is related to his own business.[6] But a shareholder's loan to his corporation can be a business debt if the shareholder is in the business of promoting, financing, and selling corporations. He must be seeking more than a return on his investment, since investing isn't a business.[7]

If the shareholder is also an officer or other employee of the corporation, he may claim his loan, guarantee, or indemnity was made to protect his job (i.e., his business of being an employee). Business debt status is allowed if his dominant motive (not just a significant motive) for the loan, etc., was to protect his job. Which motive is dominant is determined by several factors, especially the amount of salary as compared to the amount of the investment. These principles also apply to a shareholder-employee who claims that his loan or guarantee for another corporation (e.g., his corporation's customer) was to protect his job.[8]

---

5. ¶M-2902; ¶1664.301; TD ¶323,003
6. ¶M-2904; ¶1664.303; TD ¶323,010

7. ¶M-2911; ¶1664.302; TD ¶323,006
8. ¶M-2914 *et seq.*; ¶1664.309; TD ¶323,011

Chapter 5   Depreciation, Amortization, Property Expensing and Depletion

¶ 1900   The Depreciation Allowance. ▮▮▮▮▮▮▮▮▮▮▮▮▮▮▮▮▮▮▮▮

Generally, a taxpayer that buys business or income-producing property (not held for sale) with a useful life of more than one year can't deduct its full cost as an expense for that year. However, the Code allows an annual deduction of a portion of the cost of the property. This deduction may be a deduction for depreciation, amortization or depletion (cost recovery deductions).

For most tangible property, a depreciation deduction is provided under the Modified Accelerated Cost Recovery System (MACRS) or under useful-life depreciation (see ¶1960). For the depreciation or amortization of most intangibles, see ¶1903, ¶1959, ¶1962 and ¶1973 *et seq.*

For certain property, in lieu of all or part of the cost recovery deductions otherwise permitted, all or part of the cost can be deducted in the year in which it is placed in service ("expensed"), see ¶1941 *et seq.*, ¶1964 *et seq.*

¶ 1901   Claiming the depreciation deduction—Form 4562.

Form 4562 is used to claim the deduction for depreciation. Individuals and other noncorporate taxpayers (including S corporations) don't have to complete or attach Form 4562 if (1) the only depreciation (or amortization) claimed is for assets (other than listed property, see ¶1947) placed in service before the tax year, (2) no Code Sec. 179 expense deduction is claimed, and (3) deductions are not claimed for a vehicle reported on a form other than Schedule C or C-EZ.[1] For how employees, self-employeds and farmers claim depreciation on a car or truck, see ¶1954.

Failure to take a depreciation deduction in one year doesn't allow a taxpayer to take a larger deduction in later years (Reg § 1.167(a)-10(a)) unless the taxpayer treats the failure as an impermissible method of accounting, correctable by filing a Form 3115 and otherwise following the procedures for changing to a permissible method of accounting in a later year. For changes in computing depreciation or amortization as changes in method of accounting, see ¶2839. An amended return can be used to correct depreciation if the error (1) is a mathematical or posting error, or (2) involves property for which the taxpayer has used the improper method for one tax year, but not two tax years in a row.[2]

¶ 1902   What property is depreciable?

Most items of tangible property (Reg § 1.167(a)-2), and certain intangibles (Reg § 1.167(a)-3) (as explained at ¶1903) are depreciable if they meet the following requirements:

(1) they are used in a trade or business, or held for the production of income. (Code Sec. 167(a))[3]

(2) they have an exhaustible useful life that can be determined with reasonable accuracy (Reg § 1.167(a)-1(a), Reg § 1.167(a)-1(b), Reg § 1.167(a)-2, Reg § 1.167(a)-3);[4] however, the mere fact that property diminishes in value doesn't mean that it's depreciable, if the decrease isn't the result of exhaustion, wear and tear, or obsolescence. (Reg § 1.167(a)-1(a))[5]

(3) they aren't inventory or stock in trade. (Reg § 1.167(a)-2) Thus, IRS ruled that property held primarily for sale isn't held depreciable even if it is sometimes rented to others before

---

1. ¶L-7501; ¶1674.001, ¶1684.025; TD ¶264,500
2. ¶G-2103, ¶G-2106.1, ¶G-2109, ¶G-2207.1; ¶4464.21, ¶4464.227, ¶4464.25; TD ¶442,402, TD ¶442,404, TD ¶442,407, TD ¶442,608

3. ¶L-7901; ¶1674.006; TD ¶265,401
4. ¶L-7901; ¶1674.006; TD ¶265,407
5. ¶L-7501; TD ¶264,501

References beginning with a single letter are to paragraphs in RIA's Federal Tax Coordinator 2d and RIA's Analysis of Federal Taxes: Income. Those beginning with numbers are to paragraphs in RIA's United States Tax Reporter. Those beginning with TD are to paragraphs in RIA's Tax Desk.

sale.[6]

Land (as distinct from buildings and other real property improvements) isn't depreciable.[7] However, a taxpayer holding a life estate or other term interest in land can amortize the cost of the interest over the term if (1) the interest is acquired by purchase, (2) the interest isn't created by the taxpayer's division of a larger interest and (3) the remainder interest isn't held by a person related to the taxpayer.[8]

Some courts have held that property can be depreciated under MACRS even if it doesn't have a determinable useful life, but IRS disagrees.[9]

Natural resources such as oil, gas, other minerals in the ground and timber qualify for *depletion* (¶1976 *et seq.*), not depreciation. (Reg § 1.167(a)-2)[10]

Property used solely for personal purposes isn't depreciable (Reg § 1.167(a)-2), but property used only partially for personal purposes is partially depreciable.[11]

¶ 1903   When intangible assets are depreciable.

An intangible asset is depreciable (but not under MACRS, see ¶1908) if it's used in a trade or business or production of income, has a limited, ascertainable useful life, and the taxpayer can show the cost of that asset. (Reg § 1.167(a)-3(a))

ⓡ/caution: Some intangibles (for example, goodwill) can be depreciated or amortized, even though they don't have a limited, ascertainable useful life. For how to depreciate or amortize most depreciable intangibles, see ¶1959, ¶1962 and ¶1973 *et seq.*

¶ 1904   Who is entitled to depreciation deductions?

Ordinarily the owner of depreciable property is the person entitled to deduct depreciation.[12] This is the person that has the benefits and burdens of ownership and not necessarily the owner of legal title.[13]

A *lessor* (landlord) deducts depreciation on property that is already on the leased premises when he leases out the property and on any improvements he constructs during the term of the lease. (Reg § 1.167(a)-4) But he can't deduct depreciation where the lease requires the lessee to replace property at the lessee's expense. In that case, the lessor suffers no "depreciable" loss, i.e., wear and tear, etc.[14] For the rules that apply to lessor-financed construction allowances on retail property, see ¶1344 and ¶1923.

A *lessee* (tenant) ordinarily depreciates the cost of improvements he makes,[15] see ¶1923, but the costs of acquiring a lease are amortizable, not depreciable, see ¶1597.

If a life tenancy is in depreciable property, the life tenant deducts depreciation as if he were the absolute owner of the property. (Code Sec. 167(d)) After the life tenant's death, the depreciation deduction, if any, is allowed to the remainderman. (Reg § 1.167(h)-1)[16]

Various rules limit the depreciation or amortization of life estates and other limited interests in non-depreciable property.[17]

A tenant-stockholder of a cooperative housing corporation who uses his proprietary lease in a trade or business or for the production of income, can, subject to an adjusted basis limitation and a carryover rule, depreciate the portion of the cost of his stock allocable to depreciable property. (Code Sec. 216(c))[18]

---

6. ¶L-7905; ¶1674.006; TD ¶265,401
7. ¶L-7901; ¶1674.006; TD ¶265,401
8. ¶L-7831 *et seq.*; ¶1674.120 ; ¶2734; TD ¶265,023 *et seq.*
9. ¶L-8201, ¶L-10901.1; TD ¶266,001, TD ¶268,103
10. ¶s L-7929, N-2250 *et seq.*; ¶6114 *et seq.*; TD ¶265,430
11. ¶L-7908; ¶1674.006; TD ¶265,409
12. ¶L-7802; ¶1674.002; TD ¶265,001

13. ¶L-7803 *et seq.*; ¶1674.002; TD ¶265,002
14. ¶L-7808, ¶L-7809; ¶1674.023; TD ¶265,007, TD ¶265,008
15. ¶L-7809; ¶1674.023; TD ¶267,020
16. ¶L-7830; ¶1674.117; TD ¶265,022
17. ¶L-7831 *et seq.*; ¶1674.120 *et seq.*, ¶2734; TD ¶265,023 *et seq.*
18. ¶K-5921 *et seq.*, ¶L-7828; ¶2164.01; TD ¶265,019

¶ 1905   When depreciation begins and ends.

Depreciation begins when an asset is placed in service (Reg § 1.167(a)-10(b)), i.e., when it's in a condition or state of readiness and availability for a specifically defined function.[19] Depreciation ends when the asset is retired from service, or its cost or other basis is fully recovered, or it's sold or otherwise disposed of, whichever occurs first. (Code Sec. 167, Code Sec. 168(d); Reg § 1.168(i)-8T(g); Prop Reg. § 1.168(i)-8;Reg § 1.167(a)-10(b), Reg § 1.167(b)-0(a)) For what transactions are treated as dispositions of MACRS assets, see ¶1906.

For MACRS property (¶1907 *et seq.*), the rules for the beginning and end of depreciation are subject to depreciation conventions (see ¶1927). For useful-life depreciable property (¶1960 *et seq.*), a proportionate part of a year's depreciation is allowed for the part of the year during which an asset is placed in service, but only if no depreciation convention is adopted for the asset. (Reg § 1.167(a)-10(b))

No depreciation deduction is allowed for MACRS property placed in service and disposed of in the same year. (Reg § 1.168(d)-1(b)(3)(ii))

¶ 1906   What transactions are dispositions of MACRS assets

Under temporary regs, for tax years beginning after Dec. 31, 2013 or, by election, after Dec. 31, 2011, a disposition of an asset depreciable under MACRS occurs when ownership of an asset is transferred or when the asset is permanently withdrawn from use either in the taxpayer's trade or business or in the production of income. A disposition includes the sale, exchange, retirement, physical abandonment, or destruction of an asset, the retirement of a building's structural component, and the transfer of an asset to a supplies, scrap, or similar account. (Reg § 1.168(i)-8T(b)(1))

However, under a proposed version of final regs on which taxpayer's can rely (see below for effective dates), a disposition would include the retirement or other disposition of a building structural component only in certain circumstances. Also, taxpayers would be allowed to elect to treat the disposition of an asset portion (such as a building structural component) as a disposition.

The proposed version of the final regs, if finalized, would be effective for tax years beginning after Dec. 31, 2013 or, by election, after Dec. 31, 2011. Taxpayers can rely on the proposed version of the final regs for tax years beginning in 2012 or 2013. Additionally, even after final regs become effective, taxpayers will be allowed to chose to apply the temporary regs (above) for tax years beginning in 2012 and 2013.[20]

¶ 1907   The Modified Accelerated Cost Recovery System (MACRS). ▪▪▪▪▪

MACRS depreciation is determined under one of two systems: (1) the general depreciation system (GDS) or (2) the alternative depreciation system (ADS), which is mandatory for some MACRS property (and elective for all other MACRS property, see ¶1930 *et seq.*). For "bonus depreciation," see ¶1933 *et seq.*

In both systems, the depreciation deduction is determined by applying the depreciation method (¶1925) to the depreciable basis (¶1922) of the property over the applicable recovery period (¶1924), and subject to the applicable placed-in-service conventions (¶1927).[21]

Subject to the exceptions discussed in ¶1908 (and the expensing and amortization rules discussed at ¶1941 *et seq.* and ¶1964 *et seq.*), most tangible depreciable property (as described at ¶1902) must be depreciated under MACRS. (Code Sec. 168(a))[22] For use of optional depreciation tables (reproduced at ¶1117), see ¶1912.

---

19. ¶L-7602; ¶1674.085; TD ¶264,506
20. ¶ L-10612; ¶1684.020; TD ¶269,602

21. ¶L-8100 *et seq.*; ¶1684 *et seq.*; TD ¶266,001
22. ¶L-8201; ¶1684; TD ¶266,008

¶ 1908   Property excluded from MACRS.

The following property isn't depreciable under MACRS: intangible property, see ¶1903 (Code Sec. 168(a)); property ineligible for MACRS under "anti-churning" rules; property which the taxpayer elects to depreciate under a method not expressed in a term of years, e.g., the income-forecast method (¶1959)); public utility property for which the taxpayer doesn't use the MACRS normalization method of accounting; motion picture films or video tapes, including videocassettes; and master sound recordings.[23] (Code Sec. 168(f))

¶ 1909   General asset accounts for MACRS property.

Taxpayers can elect to maintain one or more general asset accounts (GAAs) for eligible MACRS property. (Code Sec. 168(i)(4))[24] The election is made (on Form 4562) on a timely filed return (including extensions) for the tax year in which the assets are placed in service. (Reg § 1.168(i)-1(l)(2)) For partnerships and S corporations, the election is made at the entity level. (Reg § 1.168(i)-1T(l)(1))[25] The following are the rules applicable to GAAs under temporary regs for tax years beginning after Dec. 31, 2013, or, by election, after Dec. 31, 2011, except where, as noted below, different rules would apply under a proposed version of the final regs. The proposed version of the final regs, if finalized, would also be effective for tax years beginning after Dec. 31, 2013 or, by election, after Dec. 31, 2011. Taxpayers can rely on the proposed version of the final regs for tax years beginning in 2012 or 2013. Additionally, even after final regs become effective, taxpayers will be allowed to chose to apply the temporary regs for tax years beginning in 2012 and 2013.

Assets grouped in a GAA. Each GAA must include only assets with the same depreciation method, recovery period, and convention that are placed in service in the same tax year (and in the same calendar quarter if the asset is subject to the mid-quarter convention or in the same month for assets subject to the mid-month convention). The following must be grouped into separate GAAs: (1) Passenger autos subject to the luxury auto depreciation dollar limits (¶1951); (2) listed property (¶1947) other than passenger autos; (3) assets not eligible for "bonus depreciation" under any provision of the Code (¶1933, ¶1940) (including assets for which the taxpayer elected not to deduct the additional first-year depreciation); (4) assets eligible for bonus depreciation can only be grouped into a GAA with assets for which the taxpayer claimed the same percentage of bonus depreciation (30%, 50%, or 100%); (5) assets for which the depreciation for the placed-in-service year is not determined by using an optional depreciation table (¶1912); (6) certain mass assets subject to a rule allowing the taxpayer to identify which mass asset is disposed of or converted by way of a mortality dispersion table; and (7) certain assets subject to a shorter recovery period or a more accelerated depreciation method because of a change in the assets' use. (Reg § 1.168(i)-1T(c)(2))[26]

Mixed use property (i.e., used both for business or income producing use and personal use), and property bought and disposed of during the same tax year can't be in a GAA.[27] Additionally, special rules apply for assets generating foreign source income. (Reg § 1.168(i)-1T(c)(1))[28]

In general, after a taxpayer has elected to use a GAA, it depreciates the GAA as if it were a single asset rather than an account consisting of multiple assets. The depreciation allowance for the GAA must be recorded in a separate depreciation reserve account. (Reg § 1.168(i)-1T(d))[29]

Dispositions. A disposition from a GAA occurs when ownership of an asset is transferred or when the asset is permanently withdrawn from use either in the taxpayer's trade or business or in the production of income. A disposition includes the sale, exchange, retirement, physical abandonment, or destruction of an asset, the retirement of a building structural component,

---

23. ¶L-8201; ¶1684; TD ¶266,008
24. ¶L-8922 *et seq.*; ¶1684.07 *et seq.*; TD ¶266,215 *et seq.*
25. ¶L-8931; ¶1684.07
26. ¶L-8922A *et seq.*; ¶1684.07 *et seq.*

27. ¶L-8922; ¶1684.07
28. ¶ L-8922.1; ¶1684.07
29. ¶ L-8922.2; ¶1684.07

and the transfer of an asset to a supplies, scrap, or similar account. (Reg § 1.168(i)-1T(e)(1)) However, under proposed regs, on which taxpayers can rely (see above for effective dates), a disposition would include the retirement or other disposition of a building structural component only in certain circumstances. Also, in certain circumstances a disposition of an asset portion (such as a building structural component) would be treated as a disposition. (Prop Reg. § 1.168-1T(e)(1)) ["Taxpayers may rely"] [30]

Under the general rule for asset dispositions from a GAA:

(1) The asset that's disposed of is treated as having an adjusted basis of zero, so a loss can't be realized on the disposition.

(2) Any amount realized on the disposition is ordinary income to the extent that the sum of the GAA's unadjusted depreciable basis and any expensed cost for assets in the account exceeds any amounts previously recognized as ordinary income upon the disposition of other assets in the account. The recognition and character of any excess amount is determined under other applicable Code provisions (other than the recapture rules).

(3) The disposition does not affect how the GAA is depreciated. In other words, depreciation continues as if the disposed-of asset(s) were still in the GAA. (Reg § 1.168(i)-1T(e)(2)) [31]

Optional termination of GAA treatment for qualifying dispositions. A taxpayer can elect to terminate GAA treatment for a "qualifying disposition" of an asset. Recognition, amount, and character of gain or loss is determined under the rules generally applicable under the Code (rather than under the rules discussed immediately above), except that Code Sec. 1245/Code Sec. 1250 recapture is limited to the excess of the depreciation (and any expensing) allowed or allowable for the GAA, over any amounts previously recognized as ordinary income under the general GAA rules. Adjustments are made to the GAA and its depreciation reserve to reflect the removal of the asset. (Reg § 1.168(i)-1T(e)(3)(iii)) [32]

A qualifying disposition (1) is a disposition of less than all assets remaining in the GAA, (2) isn't a Code Sec. 168(i)(7)(B) "step in the shoes" transaction (¶1911), a Code Sec. 1031 like-kind exchange (¶2418) or a Code Sec. 1033 involuntary conversion (¶2430); (3) doesn't involve the technical termination of a partnership under Code Sec. 708(b)(1) (i.e., a termination because of a 50% transfer of interests, see ¶3782); and (4) isn't an abusive transaction. (Reg § 1.168(i)-1T(e)(3)(iii)(B)) However, under proposed regs, on which taxpayers can rely (see above for effective dates), a qualifying disposition would be one that does not involve all the assets, the last asset, or the remaining portion of the last asset, remaining in a general asset account and that is: (1) a direct result of a casualty or theft; (2) a deductible charitable contribution; (3) a direct result of a cessation, termination, or disposition of a business, manufacturing, or other income producing process, operation, facility, plant, or other unit (other than by transfer to a supplies, scrap, or similar account); or (4) a nonrecognition transaction, subject to the exceptions like those in the temporary regs' definition (e.g. like-kind exchange). (Prop Reg. § 1.168-1T(e)(3)(iii)(B)) ["Taxpayers may rely"] [33]

Optional termination of entire GAA. Generally, a taxpayer continues to recover the cost of a GAA over its normal recovery period even though all of its assets have been disposed of. Alternatively, a taxpayer can elect to end GAA treatment, and recover the GAA's adjusted depreciable basis, when it sells the remaining assets in a GAA. Recognition, amount, and character of gain or loss are determined as described above for qualifying dispositions. (Reg § 1.168(i)-1T(e)(3)(ii)) [34]

Mandatory termination. A GAA must be terminated when all of its remaining assets are transferred in a Code Sec. 168(i)(7)(B), Code Sec. 1031 or Code Sec. 1033 transaction. If not all GAA assets are transferred in any of those transactions, GAA treatment terminates only for transferred assets. Additionally, if the taxpayer disposes of an asset from a GAA in certain recapture transactions and abusive transactions, GAA treatment for that asset terminates.

30. ¶ L-8930; ¶1684.071
31. ¶ L-8924; ¶1684.071
32. ¶ L-8925; ¶1684.072

33. ¶ L-8930; ¶1684.072
34. ¶ L-8926; ¶1684.072

(Reg § 1.168(i)-1T(e)(3), Reg § 1.168(i)-1T(g))[35] A mandatory termination also takes place if there is a technical termination of a partnership. Reg § 1.168(i)-1T(e)(3)(vi))[36]

¶ 1910   Multiple asset accounts for MACRS property.

For tax years beginning after Dec. 31, 2013, or, by election, after Dec. 31, 2011, taxpayers can account for depreciation of MACRS assets using multiple-asset accounts (MAAs). In general, the only effects of accounting for MACRS assets in MAAs are that (1) annual calculations of depreciation are simplified and (2) instead of being permitted only the specific identification method to determine which asset, among similar assets, is being disposed of (and, thus, the unadjusted depreciable basis for the asset and the year of placement in service for the asset), a taxpayer can alternatively use (A) any other reasonable method to determine the basis of the disposed of asset, and (B) one of several methods prescribed by IRS to identify the asset and the year that it was placed in service. (Reg § 1.168(i)-7; Reg § 1.168(i)-8T; Prop Reg. § 1.168(i)-8)[37] For which transactions are treated as dispositions of MACRS assets, see ¶1906.

¶ 1911   "Step into the shoes" rule for certain carryover-basis property.

If property is acquired in certain nontaxable transfers (such as transactions described in Code Sec. 332 (¶3577), Code Sec. 351 (¶3510) or Code Sec. 361 (¶3562)) the transferee "steps into the shoes" of the transferor for the depreciation period and method of the transferred property. This applies to the extent that the transferee's basis in the property equals the transferor's adjusted basis. (Code Sec. 168(i)(7)(B), Code Sec. 168(i)(7)(C))[38] If the election was made, for estates of decedents dying in 2010, to not be subject to the estate tax and to apply modified carryover basis rules to property acquired from a decedent (¶2523), safe harbor guidance provides similar "step-in-the shoes" rules for the depreciable property covered by the election.[39]

¶ 1912   IRS optional MACRS rate tables.

Instead of making the MACRS computations described at ¶1907 and ¶1925 for either the general or alternate depreciation systems, a taxpayer can, with no notice to IRS, instead rely on tables provided by IRS (reproduced at ¶1117), subject to the following rules:

(1) All the tables' rates (accelerated or straight-line) are applied to the property's *unadjusted depreciable basis*. For that purpose, unadjusted depreciable basis is the basis for determining gain or loss, not reduced by prior depreciation, and reflecting reductions in basis for: (a) personal-use percentage of the asset for the tax year; (b) any portion of the asset that is expensed under Code Sec. 179 (¶1941); and (c) other initial basis adjustments—e.g., for the Code Sec. 44 disabled-access credit (¶2323), or, unless the taxpayer "elected out," for bonus depreciation ¶1933 *et seq.*). (Reg § 1.168(b)-1(a)(3))

(2) The taxpayer must use the tables to compute the annual depreciation allowances for the entire recovery period of the property. However, a taxpayer may not continue to use the tables if there are any adjustments to the basis of the property for reasons other than: (a) depreciation allowed or allowable, or (b) an addition or an improvement to such property that is subject to depreciation as a separate item of property.

(3) Use of the tables is denied for a short tax year and for later tax years with respect to MACRS personal property not fully depreciated by the end of the short tax year (¶1926).[40]

illustration: T bought an item of used 7-year property for $10,000, placed it in service on

---

35. ¶L-8925.1, L-8926.1, L-8926.2; ¶1684.072.
36. ¶L-8926.1A; ¶1684.072.
37. ¶L-8932 *et seq.*, ¶L-10614, L-10616; ¶1684.075, 1684.20; TD ¶269,600, 269,608

38. ¶L-10401; ¶1684.04; TD ¶266,508
39. ¶L-10402; ¶1684.04; TD ¶266,508
40. ¶L-8602, ¶L-8904 *et seq.*; ¶1684; TD ¶267,008

Aug. 11, Year 1, and used the item exclusively in his business. Also, T didn't expense the item under Code Sec. 179, and no other Code provisions requiring initial basis adjustments applied to the item. The unadjusted depreciable basis of the property is $10,000. The percentages for 7-year property using the 200% declining balance method and the half-year convention are found in Table 1, see ¶1117. The depreciation deduction each year of the recovery period is as follows:[41]

Year	Basis	Percentage	Deduction
1	$10,000	14.29%	$1,429
2	10,000	24.49%	2,449
3	10,000	17.49%	1,749
4	10,000	12.49%	1,249
5	10,000	8.93%	893
6	10,000	8.92%	892
7	10,000	8.93%	893
8	10,000	4.46%	446

¶ 1913   Determining the MACRS recovery class for an asset.

The assignment of MACRS property to a recovery class is generally made by reference to that property's class life as of Jan. 1, '86. (Code Sec. 168(i)(1)) The class life of many types of assets is carried in Rev Proc 87-56, 1987-2 CB 674. The assignment to a MACRS recovery class is determined as follows (Code Sec. 168(e)(1)):

MACRS Recovery Class	Property With a Class Life (in Years) of:
3-Year	4 or less
5-Year	More than 4 but less than 10
7-Year	10 or more but less than 16
10-Year	16 or more but less than 20
15-Year	20 or more but less than 25
20-Year	25 or more

Also, MACRS assigns certain property specific classes as follows (and as described at ¶1913 *et seq.*): certain water utility property is in the 25-year class; residential rental property is in the 27.5-year class; nonresidential real property placed in service before May 13, '93 is in the 31.5-year class; nonresidential real property placed in service after May 12, '93 is in the 39-year class; and any railroad grading and tunnel bore is in the 50-year class. (Code Sec. 168(c))[42]

¶ 1914   The three-year MACRS class.

This class includes:

... Depreciable personal property with a class life of four years or less (Code Sec. 168(e)(1)), such as: tractor units for use over-the-road; breeding hogs; special handling devices used in the manufacture of food and beverages; and special tools used in the manufacture of rubber products, finished plastic products, and motor vehicles.

... All racehorses placed in service after 2008 and before 2014, racehorses more than two years old when placed in service after 2013, and other horses more than 12 when placed in service. (Code Sec. 168(e)(3)(A))

caution: Check tax.thomsonreuters.com/federaltaxhandbookupdates to see if the above provision has been extended.

... Qualified rent-to-own (RTO) property (certain consumer durables held for rent). (Code Sec. 168(e)(3)(A)(iii), Code Sec. 168(i)(14))[43]

---

41. ¶L-8910
42. ¶L-8202; ¶1684; TD ¶266,202

43. ¶L-8204; ¶1684.01; TD ¶266,203

¶ 1915   The five-year MACRS class.

This class includes:

. . . Depreciable personal property with a class life of more than four years and less than ten years (Code Sec. 168(e)(1)), such as: information systems (computers); heavy general purpose trucks; trailers and trailer-mounted containers; breeding or dairy cattle; certain assets used in the drilling of oil and gas wells, construction, the manufacture of textile yarns, apparel, and other finished goods, and the cutting of timber. Also, IRS ruled that support vessels used in offshore oil and gas operations (whether or not used in connection with drilling) are five-year property.[44]

. . . Any automobiles or light-general purpose trucks (Code Sec. 168(e)(3)(B)(i));

. . . Semiconductor manufacturing equipment (Code Sec. 168(e)(3)(B)(ii)) in ADR class 36.0;

. . . Computer-based telephone central office switching equipment (Code Sec. 168(e)(3)(B)(iii));

. . . Qualified technological equipment (Code Sec. 168(e)(3)(B)(iv));

. . . Code Sec. 1245 property used in connection with research and experimentation (Code Sec. 168(e)(3)(B)(v));

. . . Gas station pump canopies (but not the concrete footings used to anchor the canopies);[45]

. . . Certain energy-related property. (Code Sec. 168(e)(3)(B)(vi), Code Sec. 48(a)(3)(A));

. . . Most farming equipment and machinery (other than grain bins, cotton ginning assets, fences, or other land improvements), the original use of which commenced with the taxpayer after Dec. 31, 2008, and which was placed in service before Jan. 1, 2010. (Code Sec. 168(e)(3)(B)(vii))[46]

. . . Consumer durable property (such as tangible personal property used in a home) subject to rent-to-own contracts if it isn't qualified rent-to-own property (see ¶1914).[47]

¶ 1916   The seven-year MACRS class.

This class includes:

. . . Property with a class life of 10 years or more, but less than 16 years (Code Sec. 168(e)(1)), such as: office furniture, fixtures, and equipment; machinery and equipment used in agriculture (including vineyard trellising); certain assets (except helicopters) used in air transport; certain assets used in exploration for and production of petroleum and natural gas products, the manufacture of wood products and furniture, and theme and amusement parks and recreation facilities (e.g., bowling alleys).

. . . Property that doesn't have a class life and isn't specifically assigned to any other MACRS class. (Code Sec. 168(e)(3)(C)(v)) Under this rule, the Tax Court held that street light assets of an electric utility are seven-year property.

. . . Any horse not assigned to the three-year class (see ¶1914).

. . . Railroad tracks. (Code Sec. 168(e)(3)(C)(i))[48]

. . . Motorsports entertainment complexes, as defined in Code Sec. 168(i)(15), placed in service before 2014. (Code Sec. 168(e)(3)(C)(ii), Code Sec. 168(i)(15))[49]

caution: Check tax.thomsonreuters.com/federaltaxhandbookupdates to see if the above provision has been extended.

. . . Alaska natural gas pipeline property placed in service after calendar year 2013, or treated, by election, as placed in service after 2013 if placed in service after 2004 and before

---

44. ¶L-8205; ¶1684.01; TD ¶266,205
45. ¶L-8205; TD ¶266,205
46. ¶L-8205; ¶1684.01; TD ¶266,205

47. ¶L-8205; ¶1684.01; TD ¶266,205
48. ¶L-8206; ¶1684.01; TD ¶266,206
49. ¶L-8206.3; ¶1684.01; TD ¶266,206

2014. (Code Sec. 168(e)(3)(C)(iii), Code Sec. 168(i)(16))[50]

RIA/*caution:* Check tax.thomsonreuters.com/federaltaxhandbookupdates to see if the above provision has been extended.

. . . "Natural gas gathering lines" the original use of which begins with the taxpayer. (Code Sec. 168(e)(3)(C)(iv)) There is no AMT depreciation adjustment (¶3207) for the entire recovery period of natural gas gathering lines. (Code Sec. 56(a)(1)(B))[1]

¶ 1917 The ten-year MACRS class.

This class includes:

. . . Property with a class life of 16 years or more but less than 20 (Code Sec. 168(e)(1)), such as: water transport equipment not used in marine construction; assets used in petroleum refining, manufacture of grain and grain mill products, sugar and sugar products, and vegetable oils and vegetable oil products.[2]

. . . A single purpose agricultural or horticultural structure (Code Sec. 168(e)(3)(D)(i)).

. . . Any tree or vine bearing fruit or nuts (Code Sec. 168(e)(3)(D)(ii)).

. . . Qualified smart electric meters or qualified smart electric grid systems placed in service after Oct. 3, 2008. (Code Sec. 168(e)(3)(D), Code Sec. 168(i)(18), Code Sec. 168(i)(19))[3]

¶ 1918 The 15-year MACRS class.

This class includes:

(1) Property with a class life of 20 years or more but less than 25 years (Code Sec. 168(e)(1)), such as: land improvements (e.g., sidewalks and roads) that aren't explicitly included in another class and aren't buildings or structural improvements; "modern" golf-course greens; assets such as service-station and car-wash buildings; and concrete footings used to anchor gas station pump canopies.

(2) Municipal wastewater treatment plants (Code Sec. 168(e)(3)(E)(i));

(3) Telephone distribution plants and comparable equipment used for two-way exchange of voice and data communications. (Code Sec. 168(e)(3)(E)(ii))

(4) Any Code Sec. 1250 property (generally, depreciable real property) which is a retail motor fuels outlet (many gas stations qualify). (Code Sec. 168(e)(3)(E)(iii))[4]

(5) Qualified leasehold improvement property, qualified restaurant property and qualified retail improvement property. With certain modifications, qualified leasehold improvement property is defined as it is for bonus first-year depreciation (¶1934) and must be placed in service before 2014. Qualified restaurant property is (1) a building improvement placed in service before 2014 if (a) the improvement is placed in service more than three years after the date the building was first placed in service and (b) more than 50% of the building's square footage is devoted to the preparation of, and seating for, on-premises consumption of prepared meals (the more-than-50% test) or (2) a building placed in service during calendar years after 2008 and before 2014 that passes the more-than-50% test. Qualified retail improvement property must be placed in service during calendar years after 2008 or before 2014 and includes certain interior improvements to retail space that are placed in service more than 3 years after the date the building was first placed in service and that meet other requirements. (Code Sec. 168(e)(3)(E), Code Sec. 168(e)(6), Code Sec. 168(e)(7), Code Sec. 168(e)(8))[5]

---

50. ¶L-8206.2; ¶1684.01
1. ¶L-8206.1; ¶1684.01; TD ¶266,206
2. ¶L-8207; ¶1684.01; TD ¶266,207
3. ¶L-8207; ¶1684.01; TD ¶266,207

4. ¶L-8208, ¶L-8804.1; ¶1684.02; TD ¶266,213
5. ¶L-8208.1, ¶L-8208.2; ¶L-8208.5; ¶1684.02; TD ¶266,208.1, TD ¶266,208.2

caution: Check tax.thomsonreuters.com/federaltaxhandbookupdates to see if the above provisions have been extended.

. . . Initial clearing and grading land improvements relating to gas utility property. (Code Sec. 168(e)(3)(E)(vi))[6]

. . . Certain new electrical transmission property (Code Sec. 168(e)(3)(E)(vii)), and

. . . Certain new "natural gas distribution lines" placed in service before Jan. 1, 2011. (Code Sec. 168(e)(3)(E)(viii))[7]

¶ 1919   The 20-year MACRS class.

This class includes property with a class life of 25 years or more (Code Sec. 168(e)(1)), such as farm buildings (other than single purpose agricultural or horticultural structures) and gas utility distribution facilities.[8]

¶ 1920   Residential and nonresidential buildings under MACRS.

A 27.5-year class is specifically assigned to residential rental property. (Code Sec. 168(c)) Residential real property is defined as a building or structure for which 80% or more of the gross rental income is from dwelling units. A dwelling unit is a house or apartment that provides living accommodations in a building or structure, but doesn't include a unit in a hotel, motel, or other establishment more than half of the units in which are used on a transient basis. (Code Sec. 168(e)(2)(A)).[9] In applying the 80% test, multiple structures that are on the same tract or parcel (or contiguous tracts or parcels) and operated as a single integrated unit are treated as a single building or structure. For example, an apartment building and a hotel were treated as a single building where located on the same tract and operated as a single integrated unit.[10] Otherwise-qualifying residential rental property can include manufactured homes, and, if permanently anchored, mobile homes. Also, housing in a senior citizens' community isn't barred from qualifying merely because services that include assisted living and nursing care are provided.[11]

A 39-year class life is specifically assigned to nonresidential real property (Code Sec. 168(c)), which is a classification that includes, generally, buildings or structures that aren't residential rental property. (Code Sec. 168(e)(2)(B)[12]

Elevators and escalators are treated as part of a building or structure. Assets that are viewed by IRS as buildings include floating casinos, if intended to remain permanently in place, and open-air parking garages.[13]

Whether an asset is part of a building or structure—and, thus, depreciated over a longer period than if it were treated as a separate asset—may depend on whether the asset would not have qualified as tangible personal property for purposes of prior law's investment tax credit.[14]

observation: Whether an asset is a structural component of a building and, therefore, depreciated over 27.5 years or 39 years (on a straight-line method, see ¶L-1925) or is, instead, personal property, and, thus, usually depreciated over 5 years (¶1915) or 7 years (¶1916) (usually on an accelerated method, see ¶1917), significantly changes the tax benefit that the taxpayer enjoys from depreciation of the asset. Thus, it is common for taxpayers to engage tax professionals, usually working with architects, builders or engineers, to produce "cost segregation studies" that, although not binding on IRS, substantiate (1) the taxpayer's treatment of some items of property associated with a building as structural components of a building and some items as belonging to various classes of personal property, and

6. ¶L-8208; ¶1684.01
7. ¶L-8208.3, ¶L-8208.4; ¶1684.01
8. ¶L-8209; ¶1684.01; TD ¶266,209
9. ¶L-8211; ¶1684.02; TD ¶266,211
10. ¶L-8211.1; ¶1684.02; TD ¶266,211.1

11. ¶L-8211; ¶1684.02; TD ¶266,211
12. ¶L-8210; ¶1684.02; TD ¶266,211
13. ¶L-8210; TD ¶266,211
14. ¶L-8210; TD ¶266,211

(2) the taxpayer's allocation of costs between the building components and personal property (and among the various classes of personal property).[15]

Nonresidential real property placed in service before May 13, '93, had a 31.5-year class.[16]

¶ 1921 Additions or improvements to real property.

The depreciation for any additions to, or improvement of, any real property (whether or not recovery property) is determined in the same manner as the depreciation deduction for the real property would be determined if the real property were placed in service at the same time as the addition or improvement. (Code Sec. 168(i)(6)(A))[17]

¶ 1922 Basis of recovery property for computing MACRS depreciation deductions.

If the taxpayer doesn't choose to apply the optional IRS depreciation tables (¶1912), MACRS depreciation deductions are computed on the property's adjusted basis (also referred to by IRS as the "unrecovered basis"), except that salvage value is considered to be zero, i.e., disregarded. (Code Sec. 168(b)(4)) This "unrecovered basis" is adjusted (i.e., ordinarily reduced) by depreciation previously allowed or allowable.[18] For the basis used if the optional IRS depreciation tables are applied, see ¶1912. For mixed-use property, see ¶1902.

¶ 1923 Depreciation of leasehold improvements by lessees or lessors.

Lessees are treated as any other owner-taxpayer for purposes of determining MACRS deductions for lessees' improvements subject to MACRS rules. Thus, a lessee's deductions for the property are determined without regard to the lease term. (Code Sec. 168(i)(8))

Where the lease ends or terminates before the end of the MACRS recovery period of the lessee's improvement, and the lessee doesn't retain the improvement, the lessee has a gain or loss for the remaining unrecovered basis of the property.[19]

⟨RIA⟩*observation:* A gain would arise if, for example, the tenant is paid to terminate the lease and the payment exceeds the basis of the leasehold improvements and lease acquisition costs, if any. For amortization of lease acquisition costs, see ¶1597.

A lessor is entitled to recover the cost of depreciable leasehold improvements that it makes. If such improvements are made for the lessee (e.g., to customize the space for the lessee) and are irrevocably disposed of or abandoned by the lessor at the termination of the lease by the lessee, then for purposes of determining gain or loss, the improvement is treated as disposed of by the lessor at that time. (Code Sec. 168(i)(8)(B))[20]

A lessor may advance construction funds to the lessee to help the lessee pay for retail leasehold improvements. If, under the rules explained at ¶1344, a lessee excludes the funds from income, the lessor treats the improvements as its own nonresidential real property, including for purposes of the disposition-of-improvements rule (see above). (Code Sec. 110(b))[21]

¶ 1924 MACRS depreciation periods.

For the 3-year, 5-year, 7-year, 10-year, 15-year and 20-year MACRS classes, the depreciation period is the same as the name of the class (e.g., 5 years for 5-year property). The depreciation period is 25 years for the water utility property class, 27.5 years for the residential rental property class, 39 years for the nonresidential real property class (but 31.5 years if the property is placed in service before May 13, '93) and 50 years for the railroad grading or tunnel bore class. (Code Sec. 168(c))[22]

15. ¶L-8210; TD ¶266,211
16. ¶L-8210.1; ¶1684.02; TD ¶266,211
17. ¶L-9105; TD ¶266,006
18. ¶L-8601; ¶1684; TD ¶266,003

19. ¶L-9106; ¶1684.02; TD ¶267,020
20. ¶L-9106; ¶1684.02; TD ¶267,020
21. ¶J-2265; ¶1104; TD ¶123,005
22. ¶L-8802; ¶s 1684.01, 1684.02; TD ¶267,004

Shorter depreciation periods applied for "qualified Indian reservation property" placed in service after '93 and before 2014. (Code Sec. 168(j))[23]

⟲/*caution:* Check tax.thomsonreuters.com/federaltaxhandbookupdates to see if the above provision has been extended.

Where the 150% declining balance method is elected for MACRS property eligible for the 200% declining balance method, the applicable recovery period is as follows (Code Sec. 168(b)(2)): for property placed in service before '99, the recovery period provided under the "Alternative Depreciation System" (ADS) discussed at ¶1930 *et seq.*; for property placed in service after '98, the regular MACRS recovery periods described above.[24]

¶ 1925   MACRS depreciation methods.

There are three depreciation methods used for MACRS property: the 200% and 150% declining balance methods with an appropriate switch to straight-line to maximize deductions, and the straight-line method. (Code Sec. 168(b)) Under the declining balance methods, the depreciation rate (in percentage terms) generally is determined by dividing the declining balance percentage (200% or 150%) by the applicable recovery period. For example, the 200% declining balance method applied to property with a 5-year recovery period results in a depreciation rate of 40% (i.e., 200% ÷ 5). This 40% rate remains constant for each tax year in which the 200% declining balance method is used.[25]

The 200% declining balance method can be used for MACRS property in the three-, five-, seven-, and ten-year recovery classes except for any property that must be depreciated on either of the methods discussed below. (Code Sec. 168(b)(1))

The 150% declining balance method is used for MACRS property (1) in the 15-year class (except for qualified leasehold improvements, qualified restaurant property, and qualified retail improvement property, see ¶1918), (2) the 20-year class (Code Sec. 168(b)(2)(A)), (3) unless described in Code Sec. 168(b)(3)) (below), any property used in a farming business (Code Sec. 168(b)(2)(B)) and qualified smart electric meters or qualified smart electric grid systems, (Code Sec. 168(b)(2)(C)), and, (4) if the taxpayer elects (as discussed below), any other property. (Code Sec. 168(b)(2)(D))

The straight-line method must be used for: residential rental property; nonresidential real property; qualified leasehold improvements; qualified restaurant property; qualified retail improvement property; any railroad grading or tunnel bore; any tree or vine bearing fruit or nuts; and water utility property. (Code Sec. 168(b)(3))[26]

For property not required to use the straight-line method, a taxpayer can elect (as discussed below) the straight-line method over the recovery period (¶1924) that applies to the property. (Code Sec. 168(b)(3))[27]

The elections discussed above to use the 150% declining balance method or the straight-line method are made on a class-by-class basis and are irrevocable. (Code Sec. 168(b)(5))

⟲/*observation:* Also, an alternative depreciation system election changes the depreciation method from accelerated to straight-line, see ¶1930 *et seq.*, as does an election to forego accelerated depreciation and bonus depreciation in exchange for the present allowance of certain otherwise-deferred tax credits, see ¶1933.

For computing depreciation under IRS optional MACRS rate tables, see ¶1912.

For the depreciation methods that must be used for alternative minimum tax purposes, see ¶3207 *et seq.*

---

23. ¶L-8806; ¶1684.01; TD ¶267,007
24. ¶L-8103; ¶1684.01; TD ¶267,017
25. ¶L-8902 *et seq.*; ¶1684.01; TD ¶266,004

26. ¶L-8917; ¶s 1684.01, 1684.02; TD ¶267,018
27. ¶L-8920 *et seq.*; ¶1684.01; TD ¶267,018

¶ 1926   Effect of short tax years on MACRS depreciation.

The depreciation allowance for MACRS personal property placed in service or disposed of in a short year can't be determined by using the IRS optional MACRS rate tables. The depreciation allowance for the short tax year is instead determined by: (1) multiplying the property's depreciable basis by the applicable depreciation rate, and (2) multiplying the product obtained in step (1) by a fraction, the numerator of which is the number of months (including fractions of months) the property is deemed in service during the short year under the applicable convention, and the denominator is 12.[28] The depreciation allowance for any tax year following the short tax year is determined by consistently using either the "allocation method" or the "simplified method" described in a revenue procedure. [29]

Rules are provided for how the half-year and mid-quarter conventions for MACRS personal property apply where property is placed in service or disposed of in a short tax year.[30]

When a taxpayer has a short tax year other than the first year in the recovery period, the MACRS depreciation allowance for that short year must account for the difference between recovery years and tax years.[31]

MACRS depreciation deductions for real property for the year it is placed in service, or disposed of, is based on the mid-month convention and on the number of months the property is in service, see ¶1927, regardless of the length of the taxpayer's tax year. [32]

¶ 1927   MACRS depreciation conventions.

The mid-month depreciation convention applies in determining MACRS depreciation deductions for the year that the following property is placed in service or disposed of: residential rental property and nonresidential real property discussed at ¶1920, railroad gradings and tunnel bores. Under this rule, property placed in service (or disposed of) during any month is treated as placed in service (or disposed of) at the mid-point of that month in computing MACRS depreciation deductions for the acquisition and disposition years. (Code Sec. 168(d)(2), Code Sec. 168(d)(4)(B))[33]

For all other MACRS property (referred to below as MACRS personal property), the half-year depreciation convention generally applies. It treats all MACRS personal property placed in service or disposed of during a tax year as placed in service or disposed of on the mid-point of that tax year. (Code Sec. 168(d)(1), Code Sec. 168(d)(4)(A))

Except as noted below, the mid-quarter convention applies to all MACRS personal property placed in service during a tax year if more than 40% of the total basis of all of that property placed in service during the year is placed in service during the year's last three months. (Code Sec. 168(d)(3))[34] Under the mid-quarter convention, property is treated as placed in service or disposed of on the mid-point of the applicable quarter. (Code Sec. 168(d)(4)(C))

When determining if the mid-quarter convention applies, the taxpayer excludes:

. . . That portion of the basis of property that is expensed under Code Sec. 179; see ¶1941. (Reg § 1.168(d)-1(b)(4)(i))

. . . Nonresidential real property, residential rental property, and any railroad grading or tunnel bore. (Code Sec. 168(d)(3)(B)(i))

. . . Property placed in service and disposed of in the same tax year. (Code Sec. 168(d)(3)(B)(ii))

. . . Property excluded from MACRS under Code Sec. 168(f) (Reg § 1.168(d)-1(b)(1)), such as films, videotapes and sound recordings.

---

28. ¶L-9002; ¶1684.01; TD ¶267,301
29. ¶L-9003 *et seq.*; ¶1684.01; TD ¶267,302
30. ¶L-8705, ¶L-8712; ¶1684.01; TD ¶266,705, TD ¶266,712
31. ¶L-9007; ¶1684.01; TD ¶267,301

32. ¶L-9104; ¶1684.01; TD ¶267,301
33. ¶L-8713; ¶1684.01, ¶1684.02; TD ¶266,713
34. ¶L-8103; ¶1684.01; TD ¶266,707

. . . The basis of a business car, if the taxpayer elects for the placed-in-service year to claim deductions using the standard mileage allowance method (¶1560).

. . . That portion of basis attributable to the personal-use portion of mixed-use assets (e.g., a self-employed's car used for both business and personal use). (Reg § 1.168(d)-1(b)(4)(iii))

¶ 1928   MACRS deductions for property after use change.

The following rules apply.[35]

Personal-use property converted to business or income-producing use (e.g., personal residence converted to rental property) is treated as placed in service on the conversion date, and is subject to the Code Sec. 168 depreciation method, recovery period, and placed-in-service convention applicable to the property beginning in the tax year of the conversion. The property's depreciable basis in the change year is the lesser of its fair market value or adjusted depreciable basis when it is converted. This rule doesn't apply when other rules (e.g., listed property rules under Code Sec. 280F(b)(2)(A)) prescribe the depreciation treatment for a change to business use. (Reg § 1.168(i)-4(b))

MACRS property converted from business or income-producing use to personal use generally is treated as a disposition, with depreciation for the conversion year computed by applying the applicable convention (¶1927). However, the conversion doesn't result in gain, loss, or depreciation recapture. (Reg § 1.168(i)-4(c))

For changes in the primary use of an asset after the after placed-in-service year, where the asset continues to be MACRS property in the taxpayer's hands (e.g., commercial property converted to residential rental property), MACRS depreciation for the change year is determined as though the change occurred on the first day of that year. (Reg § 1.168(i)-4(d)(2)(iii))

If a use-change results in:

. . . A shorter recovery period and/or a faster depreciation method, adjusted depreciable basis as of the beginning of the change year is depreciated over the shorter recovery period and/or by the faster method beginning with the year of change as though the property were first placed in service in that year. (Reg § 1.168(i)-4(d)(3)) Taxpayers may elect to continue to depreciate the property as though the change in use had not occurred. (Reg § 1.168(i)-4(d)(3)(ii))

. . . A longer recovery period and/or slower depreciation method, adjusted depreciable basis is depreciated over the longer recovery period and/or by the slower method beginning with the year of change as if the property had been originally placed in service with the longer recovery period and/or slower depreciation method. (Reg § 1.168(i)-4(d)(4))

Either miles or flight hours can be used to determine the primary use of an airplane for purposes of determining whether a change-in-use has occurred.[36]

Where use changes during placed-in-service year, the depreciation allowance generally is established by the primary use of the property during that tax year, determined in a consistently applied and reasonable manner. In determining whether property is used within or outside the U.S. during the placed-in-service year, the predominant use of the property governs. (Reg § 1.168(i)-4(e))

General asset accounts. A change in use doesn't cause or permit the revocation of a general asset account election (¶1909), but the property generally is removed from its existing general asset account and placed in a separate general asset account. (Reg § 1.168(i)-1T(h)(1), Reg § 1.168(i)-1T(h)(3))[37]

---

35. ¶L-8108, L-9122 *et seq.*, ¶L-9206.1; ¶1684.035; TD ¶266,010, 267,406.1, 267,451 *et seq.*

36. ¶L-9122; TD ¶266,010

37. ¶L-8108; TD ¶266,010

¶ 1929 Depreciating MACRS property acquired in a like-kind exchange or involuntary conversion.

MACRS property may be acquired (1) in exchange for MACRS property in a Code Sec. 1031 like-kind property exchange (¶2418 *et seq.*) or (2) to replace involuntarily converted MACRS property in a Code Sec. 1033 involuntary conversion (¶2430 *et seq.*). (Reg § 1.168(i)-6(c)(1)) The replacement property is for depreciation purposes divided into the depreciable exchanged basis (i.e., remaining basis of the relinquished property carried over to the replacement property), and the depreciable excess basis (i.e., additional consideration to acquire the replacement property). Where the properties share the same recovery class and depreciation method, the depreciable exchanged basis is written off over what's left of the relinquished property's recovery period; and the depreciable excess basis is in effect treated as a separate property with a recovery period that begins anew. (Reg § 1.168(i)-6(c)(3)(ii))[38]

> **illustration:** In 2011, ABX Corp. bought a used refrigerator truck (5-year MACRS property, ¶1915) for $100,000 and placed it in service that year. In 2013, ABX acquires a newer-model used truck in exchange for the truck bought in 2011 by trading in the truck bought in 2011 and paying $50,000 cash. ABX uses the optional rate tables (¶1912) to compute depreciation and is subject to the half-year convention (¶1927) in 2011 and 2013. ABC claimed $20,000 of depreciation in 2011 (20%), and $32,000 in 2012 (32%). For 2013, ABX may claim a depreciation deduction of $9,600 for the relinquished truck ($100,000 × .192 [recovery year 3 table percentage for 5-year property] × 6/12 [half-year convention applies]). The remaining depreciable basis of the relinquished truck (i.e., the depreciable exchanged basis) is $38,400 ($100,000 cost − $20,000 − $32,000 − $9,600), which is depreciated over 2013—2016 (what's left of the original recovery period). ABX's depreciable excess basis in the replacement truck is $50,000, the cash it pays to acquire it. Per the table percentages, the depreciation allowance for this excess basis is $10,000 for 2013 (20%), $16,000 for 2014 (32%), $9,600 for 2015 (19.2%), $5,760 for 2016 and 2017 (11.52%), and $2,880 (5.76%) for 2018.

If ABX's replacement truck were new instead of used, and it were eligible for bonus depreciation (see ¶1933 *et seq.*), ABX could claim a bonus depreciation allowance on both the remaining basis of the old truck and the cash paid to acquire the new truck. (Reg § 1.168(k)-1(f)(5)(iii)(A)) But if qualifying property is placed in service and disposed of in an exchange or involuntary conversion in the same tax year, the exchanged or involuntarily converted property isn't eligible for bonus depreciation. (Reg § 1.168(k)-1(f)(5)(iii)(B))[39]

Complex rules apply if the exchanged properties aren't depreciated with the same period and/or method. (Reg § 1.168(i)-6(c)(3)(iii), Reg § 1.168(i)-6(c)(4))[40]

Election out. A taxpayer may elect not to apply the above "split basis" approach to the exchanged properties, and, instead, treat the exchanged basis and excess basis, if any, in the replacement property as placed in service at the time of replacement and the adjusted depreciable basis of the relinquished MACRS property as being disposed of. (Reg § 1.168(i)-6(i))[41]

¶ 1930 The straight-line "alternative depreciation system" (ADS) of MACRS.

The alternative depreciation system (ADS) is a straight-line depreciation system, with generally longer depreciation periods than under the general depreciation system. (Code Sec. 168(g)(2)(C), Code Sec. 168(g)(3)(B)) ADS uses the same depreciation conventions as MACRS (Code Sec. 168(g)(2)(B)), see ¶1927, and like MACRS, disregards salvage value. (Code Sec. 168(g)(2)(A))

Depreciation deductions must be computed under ADS only for certain specified properties, see ¶1931. However, ADS must be used for all properties including properties depreciated

---

38. ¶L-10600 *et seq.*; TD ¶269,400 *et seq.*
39. ¶L-10602; ¶1684.048; TD ¶269,416

40. ¶L-10601.2A; TD ¶269,403
41. ¶L-10601.8; TD ¶269,413

under MACRS for purpose of computing earnings and profits of corporations (Code Sec. 312(k)(3)(A)). ADS also applies for purposes of computing the depreciation tax preference under the alternative minimum tax, under the rules explained at ¶3207.[42] ADS may be elected for all other properties—on a class by class basis for personal property and on an individual basis for residential rental and nonresidential real properties. (Code Sec. 168(g)(7)(A))

An ADS election is an irrevocable year-by-year election. (Code Sec. 168(g)(7)(B)) This election is in addition to the straight-line MACRS election (¶1925).

Property excluded from MACRS because a depreciation method not measured in term of years is elected (¶1908) is also excluded from ADS. (Code Sec. 168(f)(1))

¶ 1931   MACRS property required to be depreciated under ADS.

The following MACRS property must be depreciated under ADS:

. . . "Luxury" automobiles and other "listed" (i.e., mixed-use) property used 50% or more for personal purposes, see ¶1948. (Code Sec. 280F(b)(1))

. . . Properties used predominantly outside the U.S.[43] (Code Sec. 168(g)(1)(A)), except certain properties listed in the Code.[44] (Code Sec. 168(g)(4))

. . . Tax-exempt use property (generally, certain property leased to tax-exempt organizations, governmental units or foreign persons or entities, see Code Sec. 168(h)(3)).[45] (Code Sec. 168(g)(1)(B))

. . . Tax-exempt bond financed property.[46] (Code Sec. 168(g)(1)(C))

. . . Imported business equipment from countries that discriminate against U.S. goods from the date the equipment is placed on a restricted list by Presidential Executive Order. (Code Sec. 168(g)(6))[47]

. . . Pre-production costs of farming property excluded from the inventory-capitalization rule of Code Sec. 263A (discussed in ¶1667 *et seq.*).[48]

. . . Intermodal cargo containers not used predominantly in the direct transportation of property to or from the U.S.[49]

¶ 1932   ADS depreciation periods.

The prescribed ADS straight-line periods are:

. . . except as discussed below, the property's "class-life" (¶1913). (Code Sec. 168(g)(3)(B))

. . . four years—for qualified rent-to-own property (¶1914). (Code Sec. 168(g)(3)(B))[50]

. . . five years—for automobiles, light-purpose trucks (Code Sec. 168(g)(3)(D)) and qualified technological equipment.[1] (Code Sec. 168(g)(3)(C))

. . . 10 years—for most new farming equipment and machinery placed in service during calendar year 2009. (Code Sec. 168(g)(3)(B))

. . . 12 years—for personal property with no class life and not governed by any other rule discussed in this list. (Code Sec. 168(g)(2)(C))

. . . 14 years—new natural gas gathering lines (¶1916). (Code Sec. 168(g)(3)(B))

. . . 20 years—for any Code Sec. 1250 property (generally depreciable real property) which is a retail motor fuels outlet and initial clearing and grading land improvements relating to gas utility property (¶1918). (Code Sec. 168(g)(3)(B))

. . . 22 years—certain Alaska natural gas pipeline property (¶1916). (Code Sec. 168(g)(3)(B))

---

42. ¶A-8220; ¶s 564.01, 1684.03; TD ¶267,501
43. ¶L-9406; ¶s 280F4, 1684.03; TD ¶267,502
44. ¶L-9406; ¶1684.03; TD ¶267,504
45. ¶L-9600 *et seq.*; ¶s 1684.03, 1684.06; TD ¶267,502
46. ¶L-9500 *et seq.*; ¶1684.03; TD ¶267,502

47. ¶L-9405; ¶1684.03; TD ¶267,502
48. ¶L-9402; ¶s 263A4, 263A4.15, 1684.03; TD ¶267,502
49. ¶s L-9402, L-9407; TD ¶267,502
50. ¶L-9403; ¶1684; TD ¶267,503
1. ¶L-9403 *et seq.*; ¶1684.03; TD ¶267,503

. . . 30 years—certain new electrical transmission property (¶1918). (Code Sec. 168(g)(3)(B))

. . . 35 years—certain new natural gas distribution lines placed in service before Jan. 1, 2011 (¶1918). (Code Sec. 168(g)(3)(B))

. . . 39 years—qualified leasehold improvement property, qualified retail improvement property, and qualified restaurant property that meets the timing requirements for treatment as 15-year MACRS property (¶1918). (Code Sec. 168(g)(3)(B))

. . . 40 years—for nonresidential real property and for residential rental property other than low or moderate income housing qualifying for the 27.5-year period (Code Sec. 168(g)(2)(C)) and any Code Sec. 1245 real property with no class life. (Code Sec. 168(g)(3)(E))

Also, the ADS depreciation period is 5 years for semiconductor manufacturing equipment, 9.5 years for computer-based telephone central office switching equipment, 10 years for railroad tracks, 15 years for single-purpose agricultural or horticultural structures, 20 years for trees or vines bearing fruit or nuts, 24 years for a municipal wastewater treatment plant or for telephone distribution plant equipment and 50 years for railroad gradings, tunnel bores, or water utility property. (Code Sec. 168(g)(2)(C), Code Sec. 168(g)(3)(B))[2]

For "tax-exempt use property" (¶1931) subject to a lease, the above depreciation periods can't be less than 125% of the lease term. (Code Sec. 168(g)(1)(B), Code Sec. 168(g)(3)(A))[3]

¶ 1933   Bonus first-year depreciation allowances.

A bonus first-year depreciation allowance applies to "qualified property" (¶1934). The allowance, which is claimed in the first year that the property is placed in service by the taxpayer for use in its trade or business or for the production of income, is equal to the following percentage of the unadjusted depreciable basis (see ¶1912) of "qualified property" (¶1934):

. . . 50%, if acquired (¶1936) and placed in service: (1) after Dec. 31, 2007 and before Sept. 9, 2010; or (2) after Dec. 31, 2011 and before Jan. 1, 2014 (before Jan. 1, 2015 for property described in Code Sec. 168(k)(2)(B) and Code Sec. 168(k)(2)(C); i.e., certain aircraft and long-production-period property) (Code Sec. 168(k); Reg § 1.168(k)-1(d)(1)); and

⚫*caution:* Check tax.thomsonreuters.com/federaltaxhandbookupdates to see if the above provision has been extended.

. . . 100% if acquired (¶1936) and placed in service after Sept. 8, 2010 and before Jan. 1, 2012 (before Jan. 1, 2013 for property described in Code Sec. 168(k)(2)(B) and Code Sec. 168(k)(2)(C).

For specialized bonus depreciation provisions, as well as those relevant for property placed in service in earlier years, see ¶1940.

The adjusted basis of the property is reduced by the bonus depreciation before computing the amount otherwise allowable as a depreciation deduction for the tax year and any later tax year. (Code Sec. 168(k)(1)(B)) There is no AMT depreciation adjustment (¶3207) for the entire recovery period of qualified property. (Code Sec. 168(k)(2)(G); Reg § 1.168(k)-1(d)(2)(ii))[4]

¶ 1934   "Qualified property" eligible for the bonus first-year depreciation allowance.

"Qualified property" eligible for bonus first-year depreciation (¶1933) includes tangible property depreciated under MACRS with a recovery period of 20 years or less, "qualified

2. ¶L-9403; ¶1684.03; TD ¶267,503   4. ¶L-9310 *et seq.*; ¶1684.025 *et seq.*; TD ¶269,340 *et seq.*
3. ¶L-9602; ¶1684.06

leasehold improvement property" (i.e. certain interior improvements to nonresidential buildings), most computer software, and water utility property. (Code Sec. 168(k)(2)(A)(i))[5] In addition to being of a qualifying type, the property must meet original use (¶1935, timely acquisition (¶1936), and timely placed-in-service (¶1937) requirements. (Reg § 1.168(k)-1(b)(1))

Property is ineligible for a bonus first-year depreciation allowance if it must be depreciated under the alternative depreciation system, see ¶1931, ¶1948. (Code Sec. 168(k)(2)(D)) "Qualified retail improvement property," see ¶1918 (Code Sec. 168(e)(8)(D), Code Sec. 168(e)(3)(E)(ix)), and "qualified restaurant property," see ¶1918, are also ineligible (unless the property also satisfies the definition of qualified leasehold improvement property). (Code Sec. 168(e)(7)(B), Code Sec. 168(e)(7)(A)(i))[6]

¶ 1935 Original-use requirement for the bonus first-year depreciation allowance for "qualified property."

The original use of qualified property must begin with the taxpayer after Dec. 31, 2007 (after Sept. 8, 2010 for 100% bonus first year depreciation purposes). (Code Sec. 168(k)(2)(A)(ii), Code Sec. 168(k)(5))

"Original use" is the first use, whether or not that use is *by the taxpayer.* (Code Sec. 168(k)(2)(A)(ii); Reg § 1.168(k)-1(b)(3)(i)) New property first used by a taxpayer for personal use or as inventory and later used by the taxpayer in a trade or business meets the original-use requirement. (Reg § 1.168(k)-1(b)(3)(ii)) There are special rules for reconditioned or rebuilt property, sale-leasebacks, syndication transactions and fractional interests. (Code Sec. 168(k)(2)(E)(ii), Code Sec. 168(k)(2)(E)(iii); Reg § 1.168(k)-1(b)(3))

¶ 1936 Acquisition requirement for the bonus first-year depreciation allowance for "qualified property."

To be "qualified property" for purposes of the bonus first-year depreciation allowance (¶1933), otherwise eligible property must be:

(A) acquired by the taxpayer (1) for 50% bonus first-year depreciation purposes after Dec. 31, 2007, and before Jan. 1, 2014, and (2) for 100% bonus first-year depreciation purposes, after Sept. 8, 2010, and before Jan. 1, 2012, but only if no written binding contract for the acquisition was in effect before Jan. 1, 2008, or

(B) acquired by the taxpayer under a written binding contract which was entered into after Dec. 31, 2007, and before Jan. 1, 2014 (entered into after Sept. 8, 2010, and before Jan. 1, 2012, for 100% bonus first year depreciation purposes). (Code Sec. 168(k)(2)(A)(iii), Code Sec. 168(k)(5))

caution: Check tax.thomsonreuters.com/federaltaxhandbookupdates to see if the above provision has been extended.

Special rules apply to property that is treated as acquired by the taxpayer because it is manufactured, constructed or produced by or for the taxpayer. (Code Sec. 168(k)(2)(E); Reg § 1.168(k)-1(b)(4))[7] For example, manufacture, construction or production begins when physical work of a significant nature begins. Physical work doesn't include preliminary activities such as planning, designing, securing financing, exploring, or researching. Under a safe-harbor, physical work of a significant nature isn't considered to begin before the taxpayer incurs (in the case of an accrual basis taxpayer) or pays (in the case of a cash basis taxpayer) more than 10% of the total cost of the property, excluding the cost of the preliminary activities. For this purpose, capitalized interest is a cost of the property, and not a cost of preliminary activities.[8]

---

5. ¶L-9312; ¶1684.026; TD ¶269,342
6. ¶L-9313; ¶1684.026; TD ¶269,343

7. ¶L-9315 *et seq.*, ¶1684.025.1, 1684.026; TD ¶269,345 *et seq.*
8. ¶L-9315, L-9315B, ¶1684.026; TD ¶269,345, 269,345A

Also, other special rules apply to certain property purchased under a contract entered into by, or certain property manufactured, constructed or produced for or by, (1) users of the property and (2) persons related to the taxpayer or to users of the property. (Code Sec. 168(k)(2)(E)(iv); Reg § 1.168(k)-1(b)(4)(iv))[9]

¶ 1937 Placed-in-service requirement for the bonus first-year depreciation allowance for "qualified property."

To be "qualified property" for purposes of the 50% bonus first-year depreciation allowance (¶1933), otherwise eligible property generally must be placed in service by the taxpayer before Jan. 1, 2014 (Jan. 1, 2015 for certain aircraft and certain property with a long production period). (Code Sec. 168(k)(2)(A)(iv))

🅥 *caution:* Check tax.thomsonreuters.com/federaltaxhandbookupdates to see if the above provision has been extended.

For purposes of the 100% bonus first-year depreciation allowance, otherwise eligible property generally must be placed in service by the taxpayer before Jan. 1, 2012 (Jan. 1, 2013 for certain aircraft and certain property with a long production period). (Code Sec. 168(k)(5))[10]

Also, there are special rules for sale-leasebacks, syndication transactions and certain partnership terminations and non-recognition transactions. (Reg § 1.168(k)-1(b)(5))[11]

¶ 1938 Election not to claim bonus first-year depreciation allowance for "qualified property."

For "qualified property" eligible for bonus first-year depreciation (¶1933), a taxpayer may elect not to claim bonus first-year depreciation. This election-out may be made for any class of property for any tax year. (Code Sec. 168(k)(2)(D)(iii)) A taxpayer that elects to claim no bonus depreciation also loses its exemption (discussed at ¶1933) from AMT depreciation adjustments for the elected-for property. (Reg § 1.168(k)-1(e)(6))

Regs explain the time and manner of making the above elections. (Reg § 1.168(k)-1(e)(3)) An election-out can be revoked only with IRS consent, except that if the election was made on a timely filed return, the taxpayer can revoke the election by filing an amended return within 6 months of the original return's due date. (Reg § 1.168(k)-1(e)(7))

¶ 1939 Election to swap bonus and accelerated depreciation for certain credits— Form 8827.

For "eligible qualified property" (generally, "qualified property," see ¶1934) that is either (1) originally used and acquired after Mar. 31, 2008 and placed in service before Jan. 1, 2010 (Jan. 1, 2011 for certain long-production period property and certain aircraft) or (2) originally used and acquired after Dec. 31, 2010 and placed in service before Jan. 1, 2014 (Jan. 1, 2015 for certain long-production period property and certain aircraft), corporations can elect to forego bonus depreciation *and* accelerated depreciation (see ¶1925) in exchange for the present allowance, as refundable tax credits, of the following otherwise-deferred (under the rules at ¶2303) "pre-2006 credits:" (1) credits against regular tax for AMT paid (¶2365), to the extent the AMT is attributable to tax years before 2006, and, (2) only in applying the election to property that *isn't* "round 2 extension property" (defined below) or "round 3 extension property" (defined below), research credits (¶2319) from tax years beginning before 2006. Otherwise-applicable credit limits are increased by 20% of the difference between depreciation allowed for eligible qualified property if bonus depreciation is claimed less depreciation allowed if bonus depreciation isn't claimed. Cumulatively, the total increase in credit limitations can't exceed the lesser of $30 million or 6% of the pre-2006 credits. (Code Sec. 168(k)(4)).

9. ¶L-9315.2, ¶1684.026; TD ¶269,345.2
10. ¶L-9316 *et seq.*; ¶1684.027; TD ¶269,346 *et seq.*

11. ¶L-9316 *et seq.*; ¶1684.027; TD ¶269,346 *et seq.*

However, because the credit increase is calculated separately for (1) eligible qualified property that is not "extension property" (defined below), "round 2 extension property," or "round 3 extension property," (2) "extension property," (3) "round 2 extension property," and (4) "round 3 extension property" (Code Sec. 168(k)(4)(H)(i)(II); Code Sec. 168(k)(4)(I)(ii); Code Sec. 168(k)(4)(J)(ii)), the total allowance of refundable credits can be as much as $120 million.[12]

A corporation can choose to exclude from the election "extension property" (generally, eligible qualified property placed in service during 2009 (during 2010 for certain long-production period property and certain aircraft)) and/or "round 2 extension property" (generally, eligible qualified property placed in service during 2011 or 2012 (or 2013 for certain long-production period property and certain aircraft)) and/or "round 3 extension property" (generally, eligible qualified property placed in service during 2013 (or 2014 for certain long-production period property and certain aircraft)). (Code Sec. 168(k)(4)(H)(i)(I); Code Sec. 168(k)(4)(H)(iii); Code Sec. 168(k)(4)(I)(ii)(I); Code Sec. 168(k)(4)(I)(iv); Code Sec. 168(k)(4)(J)(ii)(I); Code Sec. 168(k)(4)(J)(iv)) The election can be made beginning with the first tax year ending after Mar. 31, 2008, ending after Dec. 31, 2008, ending after Dec. 31, 2010, or ending after Dec. 31, 2012. (Code Sec. 168(k)(4)(A); Code Sec. 168(k)(4)(H)(ii); Code Sec. 168(k)(4)(I)(iii); Code Sec. 168(k)(4)(J)(iii))[13]

Under Federal budgetary sequestration, for original or amended returns beginning on Aug. 13, 2013, the refundable credit with respect to pre-2006 AMT is reduced by 38%. After the Federal fiscal year ending Sept. 30, 2013, the rate of reduction, if any, is subject to Congressional action.[14]

caution: Check tax.thomsonreuters.com/federaltaxhandbookupdates for the future status of sequestration and to see if the provisions that allow a swap of bonus and accelerated depreciation for certain deferred credits have been extended.

¶ 1940   Other bonus first-year depreciation rules.

There are a number of specialized bonus depreciation allowance provisions, as well as bonus depreciation rules that applied for property placed in service in earlier years. Here is a summary:

• 50% bonus first-year depreciation applies for qualified second generation biofuel plant property placed in service after Jan. 2, 2013 and before Jan. 1, 2014. (Code Sec. 168(l))

caution: Check tax.thomsonreuters.com/federaltaxhandbookupdates to see if the above provision has been extended.

. . . 50% bonus first-year depreciation applies for qualified cellulosic biofuel plant property placed in service after Oct. 3, 2008 and before Jan. 3, 2013. (Code Sec. 168(l))

. . . 50% bonus first-year depreciation applied for qualified cellulosic biomass ethanol plant property purchased after Dec. 20, 2006 and placed in service before Oct. 4, 2008.[15]

. . . 50% bonus first-year depreciation applies for "qualified reuse and recycling property" that is purchased new by the taxpayer after Aug. 31, 2008 and that meets other detailed requirements. (Code Sec. 168(m))[16]

. . . 50% bonus depreciation applied for qualified property generally acquired and placed in service after May 5, 2003 and before Jan. 1, 2005, and 30% bonus depreciation applied for qualified property generally acquired after Sept. 10, 2001, and before May 6, 2003, and placed in service before Jan. 1, 2005.[17]

---

12. ¶L-15213 *et seq.*; ¶1684.0293; TD ¶380,511 *et seq.*
13. ¶L-15213 *et seq.*; ¶1684.0293; TD ¶380,511 *et seq.*
14. ¶L-15213; ¶1684.0293; TD ¶380,511
15. ¶L-9356; ¶1684.08; TD ¶696,514

16. ¶L-9361; ¶1684.09
17. ¶L-9311 *et seq.*, ¶L-9321 *et seq.*; ¶1684.025 *et seq.*; TD ¶269,340 *et seq.*, TD ¶269,351 *et seq.*

...30% bonus first-year depreciation applied for "qualified New York Liberty Zone property"—i.e., certain property used in the New York Liberty Zone (an area of southernmost Manhattan described in Code Sec. 1400L(h)), and, among other requirements, placed in service before Jan 1, 2007 (before Jan 1, 2010 for certain qualifying nonresidential real property and certain residential rental property).[18]

...50% bonus first-year depreciation applied for qualified Gulf Opportunity Zone (GO Zone) property. (Code Sec. 1400N(d)(1))[19] Such property had to meet detailed use requirements and generally had to be placed in service by the taxpayer before 2008 (before 2009 for nonresidential real property or residential rental property). But under an exception for specified GO Zone extension property—property in IRS-identified areas more-heavily-damaged by the 2005 hurricanes—nonresidential real property or residential rental property could be placed in service before 2012 and certain property in those buildings could be placed in service up to 90 days after the buildings are placed in service. (Code Sec. 1400N(d)(2)(A), (Code Sec. 1400N(d)(6))[20] Recapture rules applied similar to those under Code Sec. 179(d)(10), see ¶1945.

...50% bonus depreciation applied for "qualified disaster assistance property," a classification that had detailed requirements (Code Sec. 168(n)(1), Code Sec. 168(n)(2))[21]

¶ 1941   **Sec. 179 Expense Election—Form 4562.** ▬▬▬▬▬

Many taxpayers are eligible to deduct (in lieu of depreciation) the cost (subject to dollar limits) of most tangible personal property, and certain other property, used in the active conduct of a trade or business.

Taxpayers, except trusts, estates and certain noncorporate lessors (Code Sec. 179(d)(4), Code Sec. 179(d)(5)), can elect on Form 4562 to expense (deduct in lieu of depreciation) the cost (subject to the dollar limits discussed below) of "section 179 property" (see ¶1944). (Code Sec. 179(a), Code Sec. 179(b)(1))

The maximum amount that can be expensed for tax years beginning in 2012 and 2013 is $500,000. For tax years beginning after 2013, the maximum amount is $25,000. (Code Sec. 179(b)(1)) For special dollar limits for certain types of property, see ¶1942.

For tax years beginning in 2012 and 2013 the maximum annual expensing amount generally is reduced dollar-for-dollar by the amount of section 179 property placed in service during the tax year in excess of $2,000,000 (the investment ceiling). For tax years beginning after 2013, the investment ceiling is $200,000. (Code Sec. 179(b)(2)). For special investment ceiling rules for certain types of property, see ¶1942.

☑*caution:* Check tax.thomsonreuters.com/federaltaxhandbookupdates to see if the above provisions for tax years beginning in 2012 and 2013 have been extended.

The deduction amount is further limited to the amount of taxable income from any of taxpayer's active trades or businesses. Taxable income, for this purpose, is computed without regard to the cost of any qualified expense property, the deduction for one-half of self-employment tax, any net operating loss carryback or carryforward, and any deductions suspended under other Code sections (Code Sec. 179(b)(3); Reg § 1.179-2(c)(1)), e.g., the passive activity rules. Employees are considered to be engaged in the active conduct of the trade or business of their employment. (Reg § 1.179-2(c)(6)(iv))

An amount that can't be deducted because of the taxable income limit is carried over indefinitely until it can be deducted (Code Sec. 179(b)(3)(B)), except that amounts attributable to "qualified real property" (see ¶1944) can't be carried forward beyond tax years beginning in 2013 (and are instead included in the depreciable basis of the property under special rules). IRS provides special rules for determining what portion of expensing disallowed by the taxable income limit is attributable to qualified real property. (Code Sec. 179(f)(4))[22]

18. ¶L-9340 et seq.; ¶1400L4.05 et seq.; TD ¶267,700 et seq.
19. ¶L-9336 et seq.; ¶14,00N4.02 et seq.; TD ¶269,331 et seq.
20. ¶L-9337 et seq.; ¶14,00N4.021; TD ¶269,332 et seq.
21. ¶L-9365 et seq.; ¶1684.085 et seq.; TD ¶267,755 et seq.
22. ¶L-9900 et seq.; ¶1794 et seq.; TD ¶268,400 et seq.

Where an expense election deduction is allocated to a taxpayer from a partnership or an S corporation, the deduction limitation, the investment limitation, and the "taxable income" limitation are applied at both the partnership (or S corporation) level and the taxpayer level. (Code Sec. 179(d)(8); Reg § 1.179-2(c)) However, for purposes of the investment limitation, the cost of qualifying property that the partnership or S corporation placed in service isn't attributed and allocated to the partner or shareholder. (Reg § 1.179-2(b)(3))[23]

A controlled group is treated as a single taxpayer for purposes of the annual dollar limitation. (Code Sec. 179(d)(6); Reg § 1.179-2(b)(1)) However, the single-taxpayer rule doesn't apply to an S corporation.[24]

Married taxpayers filing jointly are treated as one taxpayer in applying the expense deduction limit. (Reg § 1.179-2(b)(5)) Married taxpayers filing separately may elect other than a 50-50 allocation of the expense deduction. Absent the election, the 50-50 allocation applies. (Code Sec. 179(b)(4); Reg § 1.179-2(b)(6))[25]

For tax years beginning before 2014, an expensing election or specification of property to be expensed can be revoked without IRS's consent, but, if revoked, can't be re-elected. (Code Sec. 179(c)(2)) A taxpayer can make or revoke an expensing election on an amended return filed within the time prescribed by law for filing an amended return for the tax year for which the election is made. (Reg § 1.179-5(c)(1)) A taxpayer that elected to expense only part of the cost basis of property for a particular tax year (or didn't make any expensing election) may file an amended return and expense any part of the cost basis of property that was not expensed under a prior Code Sec. 179 election. (Reg § 1.179-5(c)(2))[26]

caution: Check tax.thomsonreuters.com/federaltaxhandbookupdates to see if the above provision has been extended.

For a limit on the expensing election for SUVs, see ¶1943.

For prohibition of the expensing election for passenger autos and other "listed property" not predominantly used in business, see ¶1948.

For a dollar cap on the expensing election for passenger autos, see ¶1951.

¶ 1942 More generous expensing rules for special types of property.

The applicable maximum regular Code Sec. 179 expense election amount (described at ¶1941) is increased by $35,000 for "qualified zone property," placed in service, generally, before 2014, of an enterprise zone business. (Code Sec. 1397A(a)(1), Code Sec. 1400(a), Code Sec. 1400(f))[27] Only 50% of expensing-eligible enterprise zone property is taken into account before subtracting the applicable Code Sec. 179 phaseout amount (described at ¶1941). (Code Sec. 1397A(a)(2))[28] Recapture (¶1945) applies if the property ceases to qualify during its normal recovery period. (Code Sec. 1397A(b))[29] Qualified zone property must be used 85% or more in an empowerment zone (certain designated distressed areas) and meet other requirements. (Code Sec. 1397D(a)(1))[30]

caution: Check tax.thomsonreuters.com/federaltaxhandbookupdates to see if the above provision has been extended.

For property placed in service after Dec. 31, 2007 for disasters declared after Dec. 31, 2007, and occurring before Jan. 1, 2010, the maximum regular Code Sec. 179 expensing allowance (¶1941) is increased by the lesser of (1) $100,000, or (2) the cost of "qualified section 179 disaster assistance property" placed in service during the tax year (which, in some cases, can be as late as 2014). In addition, the regular phaseout level for the amount of expensing-eligible property placed in service during the year (¶1941) is increased by the lesser of (1)

23. ¶L-9909 *et seq.*; ¶1794.01; TD ¶268,414
24. ¶L-9908; ¶1794.01; TD ¶268,411
25. ¶L-9907; ¶1794.01; TD ¶268,412
26. ¶L-9933; ¶1794.04; TD ¶268,409
27. ¶L-9951, ¶J-3396.4; ¶1397A4; ¶14,004.01; TD ¶268,402

28. ¶L-9952; ¶1397A4; TD ¶268,413
29. ¶L-9964; ¶1397A4; TD ¶268,428
30. ¶L-9953, ¶L-9985; ¶1397A4, ¶14,00J4; TD ¶268,430,
    TD ¶268,701

$600,000, or (2) the cost of qualified section 179 disaster assistance property placed in service during the tax year. Recapture rules and rules that coordinate the increased expensing with certain other tax benefits apply. (Code Sec. 179(e))

¶ 1943 Restricted expensing deduction for heavy SUVs.

No more than $25,000 of the cost of a heavy SUV (sport utility vehicle) may be expensed under Code Sec. 179. (Code Sec. 179(b)(5)) The $25,000 expensing limit applies to any 4-wheeled vehicle which (1) is primarily designed (or can be used) to carry passengers on public streets, roads and highways (except for rail vehicles), and (2) has a GVWR (gross, or loaded, vehicle weight rating) of more than 6,000 pounds but not more than 14,000 pounds. (Code Sec. 179(b)(5)(B)(i))

observation: Amounts in excess of the $25,000 limit can be depreciated over the 5-year MACRS recovery period (¶1915) *without regard to* the depreciation dollar caps for luxury autos (¶1951), and are eligible for bonus first-year depreciation if the SUV is "qualified property" (see ¶1933).

A vehicle is *not* subject to the $25,000 expensing limit if it (1) is designed for more than nine individuals in seating rearward of the driver's seat; (2) is equipped with an open cargo area, or a covered box not readily accessible from the passenger compartment, of at least six feet in interior length; or (3) has an integral enclosure, fully enclosing the driver compartment and load carrying device, does not have seating rearward of the drivers seat, and has no body section protruding more than 30 inches ahead of the leading edge of the windshield. (Code Sec. 179(b)(5)(B)(ii))[31]

For prohibition of the expensing election for passenger autos and other "listed property" not predominantly used in business, see ¶1948.

For dollar caps on the expensing election for passenger autos, see ¶1951.

¶ 1944 Property eligible and ineligible for expense election.

Subject to the overall maximum dollar amount and investment ceiling discussed at ¶1941, property eligible for the expense election consists of the following assets, if "purchased" for use in the active trade or business of the taxpayer:

(1) tangible recovery property that's Code Sec. 1245 property (generally, most depreciable property other than buildings, thus including, for example, vineyards[32]),

(2) if placed in service in a tax year beginning before 2014, off-the-shelf computer software, (Code Sec. 179(d)(1)) and,

(3) if placed in service in a tax year beginning before 2014, up to $250,000 per year of qualified real property. (Code Sec. 179(f)(1), Code Sec. 179(f)(3)) Qualified real property is one of the following types of property (defined as discussed at ¶1918): (1) qualified leasehold improvement property, (2) qualified restaurant property or (3) qualified retail improvement property. (Code Sec. 179(f)(2))

caution: Check tax.thomsonreuters.com/federaltaxhandbookupdates to see if the above provisions concerning off-the-shelf computer software and qualified real property have been extended.

Code Sec. 179 property *does not include* property used in the production of income (Code Sec. 212 property), air conditioning and heating units, property used for lodging, property used outside the U.S., property used by certain tax-exempt organizations, property used by governmental units or foreign persons or entities. (Code Sec. 179(d)(1)) The election isn't available for the portion of the property's basis that's determined by reference to the basis of

31. ¶L-9907.2; ¶1794.015; TD ¶268,411.1   32. ¶L-9903, L-9922; TD ¶268,425

other property held at any time by the purchaser (e.g., trade-ins).[33]

Purchase is any acquisition of property *except* property (1) acquired from certain individuals or entities related to the taxpayer (or from a decedent) or (2) whose basis is determined by reference to the adjusted basis of the person from whom acquired (e.g., gifts).[34]

For prohibition of the expensing election for passenger autos and other "listed property" not predominantly used in business, see ¶1948.

¶ 1945   Recapture of amount expensed under Code Sec. 179—Form 4797.

Code Sec. 179 recapture is triggered when the business use of property placed in service in an earlier year is reduced to 50% or less during the recapture period.

The recapture period of the expense election is the entire recovery period of the qualifying Section 179 property. (Code Sec. 179(d)(10))

The recapture amount (report on Form 4797) equals the expense deduction taken minus the MACRS depreciation amount that would have been allowed on the expensed amount from the time the property was placed in service up to and including the year of recapture. (Reg § 1.179-1(e)(1))[35]

For the application of depreciation recapture to Code Sec. 179 expensing, including the allocation of recapture between Code Sec. 1245 and Code Sec. 1250 when qualified real property is disposed of, see ¶2692 *et seq.*

¶ 1946   "Luxury" Automobiles and "Listed Property." ▬▬▬▬▬▬▬▬▬▬▬

MACRS depreciation deductions and the Code Sec. 179 expense election are limited for "luxury" business autos and other "listed property." Lessees of such property are subject to special rules.

The following restrictions on depreciation (and the Code Sec. 179 expense election) apply to listed property (defined at ¶1947):

. . . Depreciation is under the straight-line method, and, generally, over longer recovery periods (and is ineligible for bonus depreciation, see ¶1934, and elective expensing, see ¶1941), if it is used no more than 50% for business, see ¶1948 *et seq.*

. . . Depreciation of passenger autos ("luxury autos") is subject to maximum ceiling limitations, see ¶1951.

. . . An employee may depreciate listed property only if its use is for the convenience of his employer and as a condition of employment, see ¶1955 *et seq.*

. . . A taxpayer who leases a "luxury" auto for business must add into income an "inclusion amount," see ¶1956 *et seq.*

. . . A taxpayer who leases listed property, other than a luxury auto, must take into income an "inclusion amount" when the property is no longer used more than 50% for business, see ¶1958.

. . . Specific recapture rules apply to listed property, see ¶2700.

. . . Strict substantiation rules apply to listed property expenses, see ¶1579 and ¶1584.

Lessors of listed property who are regularly engaged in the business of leasing that property aren't subject to the limitations applicable to owners for any listed property they lease or hold for leasing. (Code Sec. 280F(c)(1))[36]

---

33. ¶L-9903, L-9922; ¶1794.02; TD ¶268,424, 268,424.1
34. ¶L-9925; ¶1794.02; TD ¶268,427

35. ¶L-9935; ¶1794.03; TD ¶268,428
36. ¶L-10201; ¶280F4; TD ¶267,630

¶ 1947   "Listed property" defined.

"Listed property" consists of:

. . . passenger autos (defined as discussed at ¶1951);

. . . any other property used as a means of transportation (e.g., trucks, buses, trains, boats, airplanes), except for "qualified nonpersonal use vehicles" (defined below);

. . . any property of a type generally used for entertainment, recreation or amusement, including photographic, phonographic, communication and video recording equipment, except if that property is used either exclusively at the taxpayer's regular business establishment, or in connection with the taxpayer's principal trade or business;

. . . any computer or peripheral equipment except those owned or leased by the taxpayer, and used exclusively at the taxpayer's regular business establishment; and

. . . any other property specified by regs. (Code Sec. 280F(d)(4); Reg § 1.280F-6(b))[37]

For purposes of the above rules, "qualified nonpersonal use vehicles" (QNPUVs) are vehicles that by reason of their nature, aren't likely to be used more than a de minimis amount for personal purposes. (Code Sec. 274(i)); (Reg § 1.280F-6(f)). Regs list many types of QNPUVs, including, but not limited to, clearly marked police, fire, and public safety officer vehicles. (Reg § 1.274-5(k))[38]

¶ 1948   Depreciation and expensing restrictions for listed property used no more than 50% for business.

If, for the year listed property (¶1947) is placed in service, it is used 50% or less in a qualified business use (i.e., it isn't used predominantly on an annual basis in a qualified business use), the listed property: (1) doesn't qualify for the expense election (¶1941) (Reg § 1.280F-3T(c)(1)), (2) is depreciable only under straight-line and the "ADS" recovery periods (¶1932), and (3) is ineligible for the bonus first-year depreciation allowance (¶1933). (Code Sec. 168(k)(2)(D)(i), Code Sec. 280F(b)(1))[39]

🖉 observation: Under Code Sec. 280F(b)(1), if qualified business use for listed property starts out by being 50% or less of total use, the straight-line ADS deduction method is required for that property for that year and for all later years.

The actual deduction amount, however, is computed by using the "business/investment use" percentage (defined at ¶1950) and not by the qualified business use percentage. (Reg § 1.280F-6(d)(3)(i))[40]

The disallowed MACRS depreciation and Code Sec. 179 expense election deduction (if any) for the current and earlier years allocable to personal use is lost for all later years. (Code Sec. 280F(d)(2); Reg § 1.280F-4T(a)(1))[41]

If the more-than-50% requirement isn't met in a post-acquisition year (during the property's normal recovery period), the listed property becomes, retroactively to acquisition, straight-line ADS property. (Reg § 1.280F-3T(c)(2))[42] Depreciation previously taken in excess of straight-line (including amounts expensed, ¶1941, and bonus depreciation, ¶1933) is recaptured (on Form 4797). (Code Sec. 280F(b)(2)(A); Reg § 1.280F-3T(b)(2), Reg § 1.280F-3T(d)(2))[43]

---

37. ¶L-10002; ¶280F4; TD ¶267,616
38. ¶L-10002, ¶L-4658 *et seq.*; ¶280F4, ¶2744.10; TD ¶267,616, TD ¶295,346 *et seq.*
39. ¶L-10018; ¶280F4; TD ¶267,615
40. ¶L-10029; ¶280F4; TD ¶267,622
41. ¶L-10019; ¶280F4; TD ¶267,617
42. ¶L-10021; ¶280F4; TD ¶267,625
43. ¶s L-10021, L-10032; ¶280F4; TD ¶267,625

¶ 1949   "Qualified business use" for listed property defined.

For purposes of the depreciation and expensing restrictions discussed at ¶1948 and the income inclusion discussed at ¶1958, "qualified business use" generally is any use in a trade or business of the taxpayer. (Code Sec. 280F(d)(6)(B))[44]

The following are excluded from qualified business use:

(1) Code Sec. 212 production-of-income use. (Reg § 1.280F-6(d)(2))

(2) Leasing property to any 5% owner of the taxpayer or to any person related to the taxpayer.

(3) The use of listed property as compensation for services by a 5% owner or a related person.

(4) The use of listed property as compensation for services by any person other than a 5% owner or a related person, unless the provider of the property includes the value of the compensation in the recipient's gross income, properly reports it and, where necessary, treats it as wages subject to withholding. (Code Sec. 280F(d)(6)(C))[45]

The exclusion of items (2) through (4) doesn't apply to an aircraft if qualified business use, other than usage described in items (2) through (4), is at least 25% of the aircraft's total use. (Code Sec. 280F(d)(6)(C)(ii))

¶ 1950   "Business/investment use" for listed property defined.

"Business/investment use" (see ¶1948 and ¶1957) is the total of business use and investment use of any listed property for the tax year. For example, if an item of listed property is used 70% in a trade or business and 20% for the production of income, the taxpayer may claim, if the property otherwise qualifies, accelerated depreciation deductions (including the expense election deduction) based on 90% business/investment use. Business or investment use (with an exception concerning automobiles, see below) is determined under the normal rules of Code Sec. 162 and Code Sec. 212. (Reg § 1.280F-6(d)(3)(i), Reg § 1.280F-6(d)(5), Ex 2)[46]

The use of a taxpayer's automobile by another person (even if that other person is a 5% owner or a related person) is treated as business/investment use of the taxpayer if:

(1) its use is directly connected with the taxpayer's business,

(2) the value of that use is properly reported by the taxpayer as income to the other person, and where required, tax is withheld on that income, or

(3) the use of the taxpayer's automobile by that other person results in payment of fair market rent. (Reg § 1.280F-6(d)(3)(iv))

¶ 1951   Depreciation and expensing of business automobiles—"luxury" auto dollar caps.

Autos used in a trade or business normally are depreciated as 5-year MACRS property. (Code Sec. 168(b)(1), Code Sec. 168(e)(3)(B)) However, the deduction normally obtained for an auto by applying the MACRS 5-year property rules, the bonus depreciation allowance (¶1933), and the Code Sec. 179 expensing rules (¶1941), is limited by the so-called "luxury auto" dollar caps. (Code Sec. 280F(a)(1), Code Sec. 280F(d)(1)). The dollar caps are adjusted for inflation, based on the placed-in-service year. (Code Sec. 280F(d)(7))

The dollar caps apply to passenger autos, i.e., four-wheeled vehicles manufactured primarily for use on public streets, roads, and highways, and rated at an unloaded gross vehicle

---

44. ¶L-10025 *et seq.*; ¶280F4; TD ¶267,621   46. ¶L-10029; ¶280F4; TD ¶267,622
45. ¶s L-10025, L-10027; ¶280F4; TD ¶267,621

weight of 6,000 pounds or less. For a truck or van, the 6,000-pound test is applied to the truck's or van's gross (loaded) vehicle weight. (Code Sec. 280F(d)(5)(A); Reg § 1.280F-6(c)) Excepted from the dollar caps are ambulances or hearses used directly in a trade or business, taxis and other vehicles used directly in the trade or business of transporting people or property for pay, and trucks or vans specified by IRS regs. (Code Sec. 280F(d)(5)(B)) Thus, under regs, qualified nonpersonal use vehicles (discussed at ¶1947) are excepted. (Reg § 1.280F-6(c)(3)(iii), Reg § 1.280F-6(f))[47]

⟲observation: Sport-utility vehicles (SUVs) are trucks. Thus, SUVs rated at more than 6,000 pounds gross (loaded) vehicle weight are exempt from dollar caps because they fall outside of the Code Sec. 280F(d)(5) definition of a passenger auto.

For the restricted expensing deduction for heavy SUVs, see ¶1943. For the luxury-auto dollar cap amounts, see ¶1952 and ¶1953.

For qualified clean fuel vehicle property (certain property that enables cars to burn clean fuel) placed in service before 2006, the luxury auto dollar caps didn't apply. (Code Sec. 280F(a)(1)(C)(i), Code Sec. 179A(c)(1)(A), Code Sec. 179A(f))[48]

For purpose-built passenger vehicles (certain electric cars) placed in service before 2007, the luxury auto dollar caps were approximately tripled. (Code Sec. 280F(a)(1)(C)(ii))[49]

¶ 1952 Regular "luxury" auto depreciation and expensing dollar cap amounts.

The regular luxury auto dollar caps (i.e., limits on regular maximum depreciation and expensing allowances, see ¶1951) apply to passenger autos that are ineligible for bonus first-year depreciation (see ¶1934). For example, a passenger auto is ineligible if it was previously owned (see ¶1935) or if the taxpayer "elects out" of the bonus depreciation allowance under the rules explained at ¶1938. For the increased first-year cap that applies to passenger autos that are eligible for bonus first-year depreciation, see ¶1953.

The annual depreciation dollar caps for (1) autos, and (2) trucks or vans (passenger autos built on a truck chassis, including minivans and sport-utility vehicles (SUVs) built on a truck chassis) first placed in service in 2013, are subject to the luxury auto dollar limits, and used 100% for business are as follows:[50]

. . . for the placed-in-service year, $3,160 for autos, $3,360 for trucks and vans;

. . . for the second tax year, $5,100 for autos, $5,400 for trucks and vans;

. . . for the third tax year, $3,050 for autos and $3,250 for trucks and vans; and

. . . for each succeeding year, $1,875 for autos and $1,975 for trucks and vans.

⟲observation: For rented (i.e., leased) automobiles and other listed property, income "inclusion amounts" apply instead of the deduction limits, see ¶1956 *et seq.*

Where the "business/investment use percentage" (defined at ¶1950) is less than 100%, the caps are reduced proportionally to correspond to the taxpayer's business/investment use percentage. (Code Sec. 280F(a)(2))[1] Moreover, depreciation after the normal 5-year recovery period (actually six years because of the operation of the applicable convention) is based on unrecovered basis, i.e., adjusted basis determined as if the auto had been used 100% for business, so that the disallowed MACRS depreciation for the earlier years allocable to personal use is lost forever. (Code Sec. 280F(a)(1)(B), Code Sec. 280F(d)(8))

⟲illustration: In June of 2013 a calendar year taxpayer bought and placed in service a $20,000 previously owned passenger car. The car is used 100% for business for 2013 and 2014, and 80% for all later years. Here are the MACRS depreciation deductions for each of the first four tax years assuming that the taxpayer uses regular 200% declining balance

---

47. ¶L-10003; ¶280F4; TD ¶267,603
48. ¶L-10003.1; ¶179A4, ¶280F4; TD ¶267,604
49. ¶L-10004.1; ¶280F4; TD ¶267,602

50. ¶L-10004, ¶L-10004.4; ¶280F4; TD ¶267,601, TD ¶267,602.3
1. ¶L-10004; ¶280F4; TD ¶267,601

depreciation, doesn't make a Code Sec. 179 expense election for the car, and uses the half-year depreciation convention (¶1927) for 2013.

Year	MACRS Deductions
2013 (20% of $20,000 is $4,000 but limited to 100% of $3,160)	$ 3,160
2014 (32% of $20,000 is $6,400 but limited to 100% of $5,100)	5,100
2015 (19.20% of $20,000 is $3,840 but limited to 80% of $3,050)	2,440
2016 (11.52% of $20,000 is $2,304 but limited to 80% of $1,875)	1,500
Total 2013 through 2016 MACRS deductions	$12,200

If the vehicle purchased in the above illustration is a truck or van subject to the auto dollar limits, the dollar limits would be higher. For example, the deduction would be $3,360 for 2013 and $5,400 for 2014.

Where a vehicle isn't "predominantly used in a qualified business use" (as defined at ¶1949) only straight-line depreciation is available and neither the bonus first-year depreciation allowance nor the Code Sec. 179 expense election can be claimed for it, as explained at ¶1948.

A taxpayer that uses the IRS standard mileage allowance method (discussed at ¶1560) for a tax year isn't subject to the above limitations for that year.[2]

For vehicles placed in service in 2012, the dollar caps for cars were: for the 1st tax year, $3,160 for autos, $3,360 for trucks and vans; for the 2d tax year, $5,100 for autos, $5,300 for trucks and vans; for the 3rd tax year, $3,050 for autos and $3,150 for trucks and vans; and for each succeeding year, $1,875 for autos and $1,875 for trucks and vans.[3]

¶ 1953 Depreciation and expensing dollar cap for passenger autos eligible for bonus first-year depreciation.

For passenger autos that are eligible for either 50% or 100% bonus first-year depreciation (¶1933) (i.e., generally, new passenger autos acquired and placed in service after Dec. 31, 2007 and before Jan. 1, 2014, see ¶1934 *et seq.*), the regular first-year dollar cap on depreciation and Code Sec. 179 expensing is increased by $8,000. (Code Sec. 168(k)(2)(F))[4]

Vehicles eligible for 50% bonus depreciation. These are otherwise eligible new vehicles bought and placed in service after Dec. 31, 2007 and before Sept. 9, 2010, or after Dec. 31, 2011 and before Jan. 1, 2014 (see ¶1933), where the taxpayer does not elect out of bonus depreciation. Here, the depreciation deduction for years after the placed-in-service year is the lesser of (1) the depreciation that would be available if the Code Sec. 280F dollar caps didn't apply, or (2) the dollar cap for that later year.

illustration (1): On Jan. 10, 2013 a calendar-year business bought and placed in service a new $37,000 auto and uses it 100% for business. The auto is eligible for the 50% bonus depreciation allowance (¶1933) and the business does not elect out of the bonus depreciation allowance. It uses the optional MACRS rate tables (¶1912), does not expense any part of the auto's cost, and the half-year depreciation convention applies for 2013. The 2013 depreciation deduction for the auto is the lesser of: (1) $22,200, which is $18,500 of bonus depreciation [$37,000 × .50] + $3,700 of regular depreciation [($37,000 cost − $18,500 bonus depreciation) × .20 regular first year table allowance]; or (2) $11,160 ($3,160 regular first-year auto cap + $8,000). For 2014 assuming business use continues to be 100%, the depreciation deduction for the auto is $5,100, namely the lesser of: (1) $5,920 ([$37,000 − $18,500 presumed adjustment for 50% bonus depreciation] × .32 second year table percentage), or (2) $5,100 second-year cap.

caution: Check tax.thomsonreuters.com/federaltaxhandbookupdates to see if 50% bonus

---

2. ¶L-10013 *et seq.*; ¶280F4; TD ¶267,612   4. ¶L-10004.1A; ¶1684.0281,¶280F4; TD ¶267,602.2
3. ¶L-10004, ¶L-10004.4; ¶280F4; TD ¶267,601, TD ¶267,602.3,

depreciation has been extended.

Vehicles eligible for 100% bonus depreciation. These are otherwise eligible new vehicles bought and placed in service after Sept. 8, 2010, and before Jan. 1, 2012 (see ¶1933), where the taxpayer does not elect out of bonus depreciation. Because of the interaction between the Code Sec. 168(k)(5) 100% bonus depreciation rules and the Code Sec. 280F luxury auto rules, IRS says that unless an election is made (see below), if the unadjusted depreciable basis (i.e., basis for gain or loss before depreciation adjustments) of 100% bonus depreciation-eligible vehicles exceeds the first-year luxury auto limit, the excess amount is treated as a deductible expense in the first tax year succeeding the end of the normal 5-year (effectively 6-year) recovery period subject to an inflation-adjusted dollar cap (currently $1,775) applicable to all post-normal recovery period years.

> ✍*illustration (2):* For example, if a calendar-year taxpayer placed in service in 2011 a new $20,000 car that is eligible for bonus depreciation, the first-year depreciation deduction is limited to $11,060 ($3,060 regular dollar cap plus $8,000), there are no depreciation deductions for 2012 through 2016, and the "excess amount" of $8,940 ($20,000 – $11,060) is recovered beginning in tax year 2017, subject to the post-normal recovery period annual dollar cap (currently $1,775).

The above result is avoided if the taxpayer uses a deemed election procedure. Under this election, for most vehicles, the taxpayer calculates depreciation deductions for years after the placed-in-service year *as if* 50% bonus first-year depreciation applied instead of 100% bonus first-year depreciation. See illustration (1), above. Separate rules apply for lower-cost vehicles (namely those where the first-year depreciation deduction using a 50% deemed first-year depreciation allowance would be *less than* the luxury-auto dollar-limit for bonus-depreciation-eligible vehicles, e.g., for 2010 or 2011, $11,060 for autos. Essentially, the taxpayer would compute depreciation deductions for years after the placed in service year without reference to the depreciation tables, under an IRS-approved methodology.

The taxpayer makes the deemed election by adopting it to compute depreciation on its return for the first tax year following the vehicle's placed-in-service year.[5]

¶ 1954 Claiming auto depreciation (Form 2106, Form 2106-EZ, Form 4562, etc.).

Self-employeds and sole proprietors report their vehicle expenses on Form 1040, Schedule C (Form 1040, Schedule C-EZ for certain small businesses) or if they are farmers on Form 1040, Schedule F with Form 4562 attached. Employees deduct employee business expenses (including depreciation) on Form 2106. But if an employee is reimbursed for business related car expenses under an accountable plan (¶1573) and the expenses don't exceed the reimbursements, Form 2106 doesn't have to be filed. Form 2106-EZ can be used by an employee if (1) he isn't reimbursed by his employer for any expenses (amounts included in Box 1 of Form W-2 aren't considered reimbursements), and (2) if he claims vehicle expenses, he is using the standard mileage rate (and if he owns the vehicle, also used the standard mileage rate in the year the auto was first placed in service).[6] Otherwise, depreciation is reported on Form 4562, see ¶1901.

¶ 1955 Requirements for "listed property" deductions by employees.

Listed property that an individual owns and uses in connection with his employment is eligible for MACRS deductions only if the property is required for the convenience of the employer and as a condition of employment. "Convenience of the employer," and "condition of employment" are defined as used in determining the exclusion from gross income for lodging furnished to an employee, see ¶1267 *et seq.*

To satisfy the condition-of-employment requirement, the property must be required for the

---

5. ¶L-10004.1A; ¶280F4; TD ¶267,602.2   6. ¶L-10004; TD ¶267,601

employee to properly perform the duties of his or her employment. This requirement isn't satisfied merely by an employer's statement that the property is required as a condition of employment. (Code Sec. 280F(d)(3))[7]

A computer at home, even if used exclusively for the employer's work, is listed property if the taxpayer-employee doesn't qualify under the "office-at-home" requirements of Code Sec. 280A(c)(1), discussed in ¶1638 *et seq.*[8] If a home computer is listed property, the employee gets no depreciation or other deduction, unless he proves the computer is: (1) for the convenience of the employer, and (2) required as a condition of employment. (Reg § 1.280F-6(a))[9]

¶ 1956 Lessees' limitations on listed property.

Lessees of business autos and other listed property under leases of 30 days or more are subject to the MACRS limitations discussed in the preceding paragraphs, although indirectly. (Code Sec. 280F(c)(2), Code Sec. 280F(c)(3))[10]

Deductions for rental payments aren't limited. Instead, during every lease year, lessees of "luxury" autos must include in gross income an "inclusion amount," figured from IRS's tables, as discussed at ¶1957.

The "inclusion amount" for a business auto is based on the fair market value of the auto and the lessee's business/investment use. An amount must be included in the lessee's gross income for each year the auto is leased, whether or not it's used 100% for business/investment purposes. (Reg § 1.280F-5T(d), Reg § 1.280F-5T(e)) (Reg § 1.280F-5T(h)(2))[11]

For listed property other than business autos, there's no annual "inclusion amount." The lessee must, however, take an "inclusion amount" into income for the first year the property ceases to be used predominantly in a qualified business use (see ¶1958). (Reg § 1.280F-5T(f))[12]

¶ 1957 "Inclusion amount" for leased business autos, trucks, and vans.

For passenger autos, trucks, and vans that are subject to the luxury auto limits (¶1951) and are first leased in 2013 the inclusion amount (see ¶1956) for each tax year of the lease is computed as follows: (Reg § 1.280F-7(a)(2))[13]

(1) Find the line from the appropriate table at ¶1118, which includes the fair market value of the leased auto, truck or van.

(2) Prorate the dollar amount for the number of days in the lease term included in the tax year at issue.

(3) Multiply the prorated dollar amount by the "business/investment use" (see ¶1950) percentage for the auto, truck or van for that tax year. The resulting amount is the inclusion amount.

For the last tax year of the lease, the dollar amount for the preceding year is used.

illustration: On Apr. 1, 2013 a calendar year taxpayer leased and placed in service an auto (not a truck or van) with a FMV of $31,500. The lease is for three years and the business/investment use is 100% in each year. The taxpayer must include the following "inclusion amounts" (from Table at ¶1118) in gross income: for 2013, $6.01 ($8 inclusion amount × 275/365); for 2014, $19 (full inclusion amount); for 2015, $27 (full inclusion amount); and for 2016 $6.66 ($27 inclusion amount × 90/365). (Reg § 1.280F-7(a)(2)(i))

For vehicles first leased in 2013, there's no inclusion amount unless the fair market value

---

7. ¶L-10022; ¶280F4; TD ¶267,618
8. ¶L-10023; TD ¶267,619
9. ¶L-10023; ¶280F4; TD ¶267,619
10. ¶L-10200 *et seq.*; ¶280F4; TD ¶267,629

11. ¶L-10202, ¶L-10203; ¶280F4; TD ¶267,631, TD ¶267,632
12. ¶L-10205; ¶280F4; TD ¶267,631
13. ¶L-10204, ¶L-10204.2; ¶280F4; TD ¶267,632, TD ¶267,633

of the passenger auto, truck or van exceeds $19,000.

Income inclusion amounts for business autos leased before 2012 are carried in earlier editions of the RIA Federal Tax Handbook.

¶ 1958 Inclusion amount for MACRS leased listed property other than automobiles.

A lessee of listed property other than automobiles must include in gross income an inclusion amount in the first tax year in which the leased property isn't used predominantly—i.e., more than 50%—in a qualified business use, see ¶1949. (Reg § 1.280F-5T(f)(1))

The inclusion amount for MACRS listed property other than automobiles is the sum of the amount computed under Step (1) and Step (2), below. (Reg § 1.280F-7(b)(2))

STEP (1): Multiply the following three items: (a) the fair market value of the property, (b) the business/investment use of the property for the year that use is 50% or less, and (c) the applicable percentage from Table II reproduced at ¶1117. (Reg § 1.280F-7(b)(2)(i))

STEP (2): Multiply the following three items: (a) the fair market value of the property, (b) the average of the business/investment use for all tax years (in which the property is leased) that precede the year the business/investment use is 50% or less, and (c) the applicable percentage from Table I reproduced at ¶1117. (Reg § 1.280F-7(b)(2)(ii))

Special computation rules apply when a lease term for listed property begins within nine months of the end of the lessee's tax year, or when the lease term is less than one year. (Reg § 1.280F-5T(g))[14]

¶ 1959 Depreciation Deduction Under the Income Forecast Method. ▰▰▰▰▰▰▰

Depreciation deductions under the income forecast method are figured by multiplying the cost of the property (but only amounts that satisfy the Code Sec. 461(h) economic performance standard, ¶2833) less estimated salvage value, by a fraction, the numerator of which is the year's income generated by the property, and the denominator of which is all income earned before the close of the tenth tax year following the year in which the property was placed in service.

Under the income forecast method, the depreciation deduction for the tenth tax year after the tax year in which the property was placed in service is equal to the taxpayer's entire remaining basis in the property. (Code Sec. 167(g)(1)(C)) Taxpayers using the income forecast method pay (or receive) interest in recomputation years (generally in the third and tenth years after the property was placed in service, unless income earned by the property is within 10% of original estimates; use Form 8866 to compute) based on the recalculation of depreciation under a look-back method (but there's no look-back for property that had a cost basis of $100,000 or less). (Code Sec. 167(g))[15] (For 15-year amortization for films, sound recordings, video tapes, etc., see ¶1974.)

The income forecast method (or similar method) can be used only for: (1) Motion picture films, video tapes, and sound recordings; (2) copyrights; (3) books; (4) patents; and (5) any other property to be specified in regulations. The income forecast method (or similar method) can't be used to depreciate amortizable section 197 intangibles (see ¶1973). (Code Sec. 167(g)(6))[16]

Rules address the effect on the calculation of depreciation under the income forecast method of "participations and residuals" (costs that, by contract, vary with the amount of income earned from property). (Code Sec. 167(g)(5)(E), Code Sec. 167(g)(7))[17]

14. ¶L-10206 *et seq.*; ¶280F4; TD ¶267,634
15. ¶L-10704; ¶1674.100; TD ¶268,004
16. ¶L-10704A; ¶1674.100; TD ¶268,004
17. ¶L-10705, ¶L-10707, ¶L-10707.1, ¶L-10707.1A; ¶1674.100

¶ 1960   Depreciation Deduction Under the "Useful-Life" Rules. ▬▬▬

Property not depreciable under MACRS (¶1900, ¶1907 through ¶1908) or under ACRS (¶1900) (including, but not limited to, all depreciable property placed in service before '81) is usually depreciable under the useful-life rules. Under the useful-life rules, a depreciable asset is depreciated over the period during which a depreciable asset, or group of similar assets, may reasonably be expected to be useful to the taxpayer in his trade or business or in income production.[18] Under the useful-life rules, a permissible method of depreciation is either one that is (1) prescribed by Code Sec. 167, or, (2) where a method isn't prescribed by Code Sec. 167, a method that results in a reasonable allowance. (Code Sec. 167(a); Reg § 1.167(b)-0)[19] Useful-life property generally can't be depreciated below salvage value. (Reg § 1.167(a)-1(c), Reg § 1.167(b)-2(a))[20]

¶ 1961   Basis for depreciation.

Under the useful life rules (¶1960), the basis on which depreciation is taken is the adjusted basis under Code Sec. 1011 for the purpose of gain or loss on a sale or other disposition. (Code Sec. 167(c)(1)) For property acquired after Aug. 10, '93, if property is acquired subject to a lease, no portion of the adjusted basis can be allocated to the leasehold interest, and the entire adjusted basis is taken into account in determining any depreciation for the property subject to the lease. (Code Sec. 167(c)(2)) The no-allocation rule also applies to leases that terminate immediately after the acquisition.[21]

¶ 1962   Intangibles excluded from 15-year amortization.

For property acquired after Aug. 10, '93, certain property excluded from Code Sec. 197 (15-year amortization of many intangibles, see ¶1973 *et seq.*) is depreciated as follows:

(1) Computer software, in those situations in which it is excluded from 15-year amortization (see ¶1975), generally is depreciated using the straight-line method with a useful life of 36 months, beginning on the first day of the month that it is placed in service; see ¶1623 for exceptions. (Code Sec. 167(f)(1); Reg § 1.167(a)-14(b)(1))

(2) Rights to service debts secured by residential realty are depreciated using the straight-line method with a useful life of 108 months. (Code Sec. 167(f)(3); Reg § 1.167(a)-14(d)(1))

(3) Amortization of a right (other than one acquired as part of the purchase of a trade or business) to receive a fixed amount of tangible property or services under a contract or from a governmental unit is found by dividing its basis by a fraction (amount of tangible property or services received during the year divided by total amount of tangible property or services received or to be received). The cost or other basis of a right to receive an unspecified amount of tangible property or services over a fixed period is amortized ratably over the period of the right. The basis of a right to an unspecified amount over a fixed duration of less than 15 years is amortized over the term of the right. (Code Sec. 167(f)(2); Reg § 1.167(a)-14(c))

(4) If the purchase price of an interest in a patent or copyright (other than one acquired as part of a purchase of a trade or business) is payable at least annually either as a fixed amount per use or as a fixed percentage of revenue derived, the depreciation deduction is equal to the amount of the purchase price paid or incurred during the year. Otherwise, basis is depreciated either ratably over its remaining useful life or under the income forecast method (¶1959). (Code Sec. 167(f)(2); Reg § 1.167(a)-14(c)(4))

Effective for leases entered into after Mar. 12, 2004, the useful life of property described at items (1), (3) or (4) on the above list that, if it were tangible property, would be "tax-exempt

---

18. ¶L-11800 *et seq.*; ¶1674.040 *et seq.*; TD ¶268,122
19. ¶L-11901; ¶1674.100; TD ¶268,001
20. ¶L-11711; ¶1674.044; TD ¶268,123
21. ¶L-7911.1; ¶1784; TD ¶265,413

use property" (see ¶1931), can't be less than 125% of the lease term. (Code Sec. 167(f)(1)(C), Code Sec. 167(f)(2))[22]

Also, effective for intangible assets created on or after Dec. 31, 2003 (Reg § 1.167(a)-3(b)(4)), taxpayers may treat an intangible asset as having a useful life of 15 years unless:

. . . an amortization period or useful life for the intangible asset is specifically prescribed or prohibited by other rules (e.g., 15-year amortization under Code Sec. 197, see ¶1973);

. . . the intangible asset is described in Reg § 1.263(a)-4(c) (intangibles acquired from another person in a purchase or similar transaction) or Reg § 1.263(a)-4(d)(2) (relating to created financial interests);

. . . the useful life of the intangible asset can be estimated with reasonable accuracy; or

. . . the intangible asset is described in Reg § 1.263(a)-4(d)(8) (relating to certain benefits arising from the provision, production, or improvement of realty), in which case the taxpayer may treat the intangible asset as having a useful life equal to 25 years solely for purposes of Reg § 1.167(a)-3(a). (Reg § 1.167(a)-3(b)(1))

The above useful life safe harbor doesn't apply to amounts that must be capitalized by Reg § 1.263(a)-5 (amounts paid to facilitate an acquisition of a trade or business, a change in the capital structure of a business entity, and certain other transactions). (Reg § 1.167(a)-3(b)(2)) Under the safe harbor, the basis of the intangible (determined without regard to salvage value) is amortized ratably over 15 or 25 years beginning on the first day of the month in which the intangible asset is placed in service by the taxpayer. The intangible asset is not eligible for amortization in the month of disposition. (Reg § 1.167(a)-3(b)(3))[23]

¶ 1963 Specialized "useful-life" depreciation methods.

These include:

. . . operating day method used for equipment affected chiefly by wear and tear rather than obsolescence, such as rotary oil drills;[24]

. . . sinking fund method (Reg § 1.167(b)-4(a));[25]

. . . unit-of-production method used for property, the usefulness of which is closely related to its use in production or to a source of supply or similar factor. (Reg § 1.167(b)-0(b), Reg § 1.611-5(a), Reg § 1.611-5(b)(2))[26]

¶ 1964 Special Expensing and Amortization Provisions.

Instead of being subject to the ordinary depreciation or expensing rules, certain property is expensed or amortized as described below or at ¶1965 through ¶1975.

Research and experimental expenditures connected with a trade or business may be amortized over a 60-month period (¶1601). Also, start-up expenditures (¶1501), organization costs of a corporation (¶3520) and organization costs of a partnership (¶3707) may be amortized over a 180-month period. Bond premium (¶2169 *et seq.*) and lease acquisition costs are also amortized (¶1597).

Taxpayers can elect to expense 50% of the cost of qualified advanced mine safety equipment property placed in service after Dec. 20, 2006 and before 2014. (Code Sec. 179E)

🅁🄸🄰/caution: Check tax.thomsonreuters.com/federaltaxhandbookupdates to see if the above provision has been extended.

---

22. ¶L-7935, ¶L-8018, ¶L-8025, ¶L-8030; ¶1674.013, ¶1674.025, ¶1674.033; TD ¶265,434, TD ¶269,025, TD ¶269,026

23. ¶L-8001; ¶1674.013; TD ¶269,001

24. ¶L-10709; ¶1674.100; TD ¶268,015

25. ¶L-10711

26. ¶L-10702; ¶1674.100; TD ¶268,001

¶ 1965   Expensing election for costs of film and TV production.

For qualified film and television (TV) productions that commence before Jan. 1, 2014, taxpayers can elect to deduct production costs in the year the costs are incurred (i.e., to expense them) instead of capitalizing the costs and recovering them through depreciation allowances. (Code Sec. 181(a)(1)) Regs clarify which taxpayers are eligible for the election and the meaning of qualified production costs. (Reg § 1.181-1)[27] In general, expensing doesn't apply to the portion of the cost of any qualifying film or TV production that exceeds $15 million for each qualifying production. The limit is $20 million if production expenses are "significantly incurred" in areas (1) eligible for designation as a low-income community or (2) eligible for designation by the Delta Regional Authority (a federal-state partnership covering parts of certain states) as a low-income community or isolated area of distress. (Code Sec. 181(a)(2)(A))[28]

✔caution: Check tax.thomsonreuters.com/federaltaxhandbookupdates to see if the above provision has been extended.

A qualified film or TV production generally is any production of a motion picture or video tape if at least 75% of the total compensation expended on the production is "qualified compensation." Qualified compensation (but not participations and residuals, as defined by Code Sec. 167(g)(7)(B)) is compensation for services performed in the U.S. by actors, directors, producers, and other relevant production personnel. For property which is one or more episodes in a television series, only the first 44 episodes qualify. Sexually explicit productions, as defined by section 2257 of title 18 of the U.S. Code, don't qualify. (Code Sec. 181(d))[29]

Regs explain how and when to make the election. (Reg § 1.181-2) The election can be revoked only with prior consent of IRS. (Code Sec. 181(c)(2)) Substantial compliance with election requirements (i.e., making omissions that don't go to the substance or essence of the Code) is adequate to achieve a valid election.[30]

Recapture of the benefits of the expensing can apply if a production no longer qualify for expensing in tax years after the year for which the expensing election is made. (Reg § 1.181-4(a))[31]

¶ 1966   Expensing election for some refining costs.

Under Code Sec. 179C, refiners (even if they aren't small business refiners) can elect to expense 50% of the costs of "qualified refinery property" placed in service after Aug. 8, 2005. Among the requirements for "qualified refinery property" are that (1) the property be part of a qualified refinery (i.e., certain domestic refineries), (2) no written binding contract for construction of the property be in effect before June 15, 2005 and (3) the property be placed in service before either (a) Jan. 1, 2010, or (b) Jan. 1, 2014 and be either (i) subject to a written binding construction contract entered into before Jan. 1, 2010 or (ii) if self-constructed, be property the construction of which began before Jan. 1, 2010 and after June 14, 2005. The election can be revoked only with IRS consent.[32]

¶ 1967   Expensing for costs of making commercial buildings energy efficient.

Taxpayers may expense the cost of "energy efficient commercial building property" placed in service in calendar years 2006 through 2013. (Code Sec. 179D(a)) The deduction for any building for any tax year can't be more than the excess (if any) of (1) $1.80 × the square footage of the building over (2) the deductions allowed under Code Sec. 179D(a) for earlier years. (Code Sec. 179D(b))

---

27. ¶L-3140 *et seq.*; ¶1814 *et seq.*; TD ¶269,451 *et seq.*
28. ¶L-3144 *et seq.*; ¶1814.01; TD ¶269,453 *et seq.*
29. ¶L-3142 *et seq.*; ¶1814.07 *et seq.*; TD ¶269,452

30. ¶L-3146 *et seq.*; ¶1814.05, ¶1814.13; TD ¶269,455
31. ¶L-3147; ¶1814.15
32. ¶L-3156 *et seq.*; ¶179C4; TD ¶269,371 *et seq.*

✓ *caution:* Check tax.thomsonreuters.com/federaltaxhandbookupdates to see if the above provision has been extended.

"Energy efficient commercial building property" is property that is (1) depreciable or amortizable), (2) installed on or in a building located in the U.S. and (3) certified as being installed as part of a plan that will meet a 50% energy use reduction test described in Code Sec. 179D(c). In some situations in which the 50% test isn't satisfied, a partial deduction is permitted. (Code Sec. 179D(d)(1)) There is more than one way to qualify for a partial deduction, with maximum flexibility provided for property placed in service after Mar. 11, 2012.[33]

For property installed on government property, the person primarily responsible for designing the property is treated as the taxpayer. (Code Sec. 179D(d)(4))[34]

¶ 1968 Amortization elections for pollution control facilities.

A taxpayer may elect to amortize, over 60 months, part or all of the cost of new identifiable pollution control treatment facilities used in connection with a plant or other property in operation before '76. (Code Sec. 169(a), Code Sec. 169(d)) MACRS depreciation can be taken on any portion that doesn't qualify. (Code Sec. 169(g)) Also, a taxpayer may elect to amortize over an 84-month period *air* pollution control facilities used in connection with an electric generation plant or other property that is primarily coal fired. (Code Sec. 169(d)(5)) For both 60 month amortization and 84 month amortization, certain limits apply. (Code Sec. 169(f), Code Sec. 291(a)(4), Code Sec. 1363(b)(4))[35]

¶ 1969 Amortization election for expenses for creating or acquiring music.

For any tax year beginning after Dec. 31, 2005 and before Jan. 1, 2011, a taxpayer could elect to amortize over a 5-year period expenses that are both (1) paid or incurred to create or acquire a musical composition (including words), or a copyright to such property, and (2) otherwise properly capitalizable. The 5-year period began with the month in which the composition or copyright was placed in service. The election didn't apply to expenses that are Code Sec. 263A(h) qualified creative expenses (¶1667), subject to a specified simplified amortization procedure, amortizable section 197 intangibles (¶1974) or not otherwise allowable as a deduction. (Code Sec. 167(g)(8))[36]

¶ 1970 Expensing and amortization of reforestation expenditures—Form 4562.

Taxpayers other than trusts may elect to deduct up to $10,000 ($5,000 if married filing separately) of reforestation costs, and taxpayers (including estates and trusts) may elect to amortize the balance of reforestation costs over 84 months. (Code Sec. 194) Use Form 4562.

An individual needn't itemize to claim deductions under Code Sec. 194. (Code Sec. 62(a)(11))[37] Costs expensed or amortized under Code Sec. 194 are recaptured as ordinary income (to the extent of gain) if there's a disposition of the timber property within ten years. (Code Sec. 1245(a)(2)(C))[38]

Taxpayers making either election must create and maintain separate accounts for each qualified timber property. Any property subject to either election may not be included in any other timber account (e.g., a depletion block) for which depletion is allowed under Code Sec. 611 (¶1976 *et seq.*). And, at no time may an amortizable timber account become part of a depletable account for purposes of deduction under Code Sec. 165(a).[39]

IRS consent to revoke either election is granted only in rare and unusual circumstances.[40]

---

33. ¶L-3173; ¶179D4; TD ¶308,103
34. ¶L-3170 *et seq.*; ¶179D4; TD ¶308,100 *et seq.*
35. ¶L-12600 *et seq.*; ¶1694, ¶2914
36. ¶L-10707.19; ¶1674.027; TD ¶268,017

37. ¶A-2601, ¶N-6301; ¶624.04; TD ¶560,702
38. ¶N-3704; ¶12,454.03; TD ¶299,026
39. ¶N-6301, ¶N-6310; ¶1944; TD ¶272,001, TD ¶272,009
40. ¶N-6301; ¶1944; TD ¶272,001

¶ 1971   24-month amortization for certain oil or gas costs; 7-year amortization for major integrated oil companies.

Except for expenses of major integrated oil companies (see below), geological and geophysical ("G and G") expenses paid or incurred in connection with exploring or developing oil or gas within the U.S (as defined in Code Sec. 638) are amortized over the 24-month period beginning on the date that the expenses are paid or incurred. In calculating the amortization deductions, a half-year convention applies. (Code Sec. 167(h)(1), Code Sec. 167(h)(2))

⚫️✔️*observation:* Thus, 25% of the expenditures are deducted in the year paid or incurred (Year 1), 50% in Year 2, and 25% in Year 3.

"G and G" expenses of a major integrated oil company are amortizable over a 7-year period (a 5-year period for expenses paid or incurred after May 17, 2006 and before Dec. 20, 2007). (Code Sec. 167(h)(5))

Amortization continues over the full 24-month period (5- or 7-year period for a major integrated oil company) even if the underlying property is abandoned or retired. (Code Sec. 167(h)(4), Code Sec. 167(h)(5))[41]

¶ 1972   50% expensing or 120-month amortization for qualified commercial revitalization expenditures.

A taxpayer that placed into service a qualified revitalization building in a renewal community (communities designated as such by HUD) after 2001 but before 2010 could elect to write off qualified revitalization expenses by either (1) deducting *one-half* of qualified revitalization expenses for any qualified revitalization building for the tax year in which the building is placed in service or (2) amortizing *all* such expenses *over a 120-month period* beginning with the month in which the building is placed in service. (Code Sec. 1400I(a)) Eligible expenses per building couldn't exceed the lesser of $10,000,000, or the commercial revitalization expense amount allocated to the building by the commercial revitalization agency for the state in which the building is located. (Code Sec. 1400I(c)(2))[42]

¶ 1973   Amortization of Intangibles. ▬▬▬▬▬▬▬▬▬▬

The cost of most acquired intangible assets, including goodwill and going concern value, is amortized ratably over a 15-year period.

The cost of most acquired intangible assets, including goodwill and going concern value, is amortized ratably over a 15-year period. Specifically, taxpayers claim deductions on Form 4562 for "amortizable section 197 intangibles" (¶1974) by amortizing the adjusted basis (for purposes of determining gain) of that intangible ratably over a 15-year period beginning on the *later* of: the first day of the month in which the intangible is acquired, or, for property held in connection with the conduct of a trade or business or a production-of-income activity, the first day of the month in which the conduct of the trade or business or the activity begins. (Code Sec. 197(a); Reg § 1.197-2(f)(1)(i)))[43]

No loss deduction is permitted on the disposition of an amortizable section 197 intangible if the taxpayer retains one or more other intangibles acquired in the same transaction or series of related transactions along with the intangible disposed of. (Code Sec. 197(f)(1)(A)) On the disposition of the intangible, the bases of the other intangibles acquired in the same transaction or series of related transactions are increased, under a formula, by the amount of the loss barred. (Code Sec. 197(f)(1)(A)(ii))[44]

Anti-churning rules keep taxpayers from converting existing intangibles for which a depreciation or amortization deduction isn't allowable under prior law into amortizable section 197

---

41. ¶N-3201; ¶1674.126, TD ¶271,701   43. ¶L-7951; ¶1974; TD ¶269,002
42. ¶L-12701 *et seq.*; ¶14,0014, TD ¶269,301 *et seq.*   44. ¶L-7977; ¶1974; TD ¶269,015

intangibles. (Code Sec. 197(f)(9))[45]

Effective for leases entered into after Mar. 12, 2004, the amortization period of Code Sec. 197 property that, if it were tangible property, would be "tax-exempt use property" (see ¶1931), can't be less than 125% of the lease term. (Code Sec. 197(f)(10))[46]

If, after Aug. 8, 2005, more than one amortizable section 197 intangible is disposed of in one transaction, or a series of related transactions, all of the amortizable section 197 intangibles in the transaction (or transactions)—except for any amortizable section 197 intangible with an adjusted basis greater than its fair market value—are treated as a single asset for Code Sec. 1245 recapture purposes (see ¶2695). (Code Sec. 1245(b)(8))[47]

For depreciation of intangibles generally and of many intangibles that aren't section 197 intangibles, see ¶1903, ¶1959 and ¶1962.

For property acquired before Aug. 11, '93, (except for certain elections), the 15-year amortization provisions discussed above didn't apply.[48]

¶ 1974   Amortizable section 197 intangible.

An amortizable section 197 intangible is any section 197 intangible acquired (after Aug. 10, '93) and held in connection with the conduct of a trade or business or a Code Sec. 212 production-of-income activity. (Code Sec. 197(c)(1)) An acquisition may be made in the form of a stock acquisition or redemption.[49] Amortizable section 197 intangibles include:[50]

. . . goodwill (Code Sec. 197(d)(1)(A); Reg § 1.197-2(b)(1)),[1]

. . . going concern value (Code Sec. 197(d)(1)(B); Reg § 1.197-2(b)(2)),[2]

. . . workforce in place (Code Sec. 197(d)(1)(C)(i); Reg § 1.197-2(b)(3)),[3]

. . . business books and records, operating systems, or any other information base (including lists or other information with respect to current or prospective customers) (Code Sec. 197(d)(1)(C)(ii); Reg § 1.197-2(b)(4)),[4]

. . . any patent (but see the caution below), copyright (but see the caution below), process, design, pattern, know-how, format or similar item (Code Sec. 197(d)(1)(C)(iii); Reg § 1.197-2(b)(5)),[5]

. . . customer-based intangibles (Code Sec. 197(d)(1)(C)(iv); Reg § 1.197-2(b)(6)), including the deposit base and any similar asset of a financial institution. (Code Sec. 197(d)(2)(B)) Customer based intangibles are the composition of market, share, and any other value resulting from the future provision of goods or services out of relationships with customers (contractual or otherwise) in the ordinary course of business (Code Sec. 197(d)(2)(A)),[6]

. . . supplier-based intangibles. (Code Sec. 197(d)(1)(C)(v)) Supplier-based intangibles are the value resulting from the future acquisitions of goods or services out of relationships (contractual or otherwise) in the ordinary course of business with suppliers of goods or services to be used or sold by the taxpayer (Code Sec. 197(d)(3); Reg § 1.197-2(b)(7)),[7]

. . . government granted licenses, permits or other rights (but see the caution below) (Code Sec. 197(d)(1)(D); Reg § 1.197-2(b)(8));[8] and

. . . franchises, trademarks and trade names. (Code Sec. 197(d)(1)(F); Reg § 1.197-2(b)(10))[9]

✔️caution: Certain patents, copyrights, and government granted rights (above) qualify only if acquired with the acquisition of a business, see below.

---

45. ¶L-7983 *et seq.*; ¶1974; TD ¶269,010
46. ¶L-7951; ¶1974; TD ¶269,002
47. ¶I-10219.1; ¶12,454.05
48. ¶L-7951; ¶1974; TD ¶269,002
49. ¶L-7966; ¶1974; TD ¶269,002
50. ¶L-7952 *et seq.*; ¶1974; TD ¶269,002
1. ¶L-7953; ¶1974; TD ¶269,004
2. ¶L-7953; ¶1974; TD ¶269,004

3. ¶L-7954; ¶1974; TD ¶269,004
4. ¶L-7955; ¶1974; TD ¶269,004
5. ¶L-7957; ¶1974; TD ¶269,004
6. ¶L-7961; ¶1974; TD ¶269,004
7. ¶L-7964; ¶1974; TD ¶269,004
8. ¶L-7967; ¶1974; TD ¶269,004
9. ¶L-7968; ¶1974; TD ¶269,004

Section 197 intangibles also include any other item that is similar to workforce in place, information base, know-how, customer-based intangibles or supplier-based intangibles. (Code Sec. 197(d)(1)(C)(vi))[10]

The following intangibles are treated as section 197 intangibles only if acquired in connection with the acquisition of assets constituting a trade or business or a substantial portion thereof:[11]

. . . Computer software. (Code Sec. 197(e)(3))[12] (For the exclusion of "off-the-shelf" computer software from 15-year amortization, see ¶1975. For software developed by the taxpayer, see ¶1623.)

. . . Films, sound recordings, video tapes and books. (Code Sec. 197(e)(4)(A); Reg § 1.197-2(c)(4))

. . . Copyrights and patents. (Code Sec. 197(e)(4)(C))

. . . Rights to receive tangible property or services under a contract granted by the government. (Code Sec. 197(e)(4)(B))

. . . Contract rights and government grants if the right has a fixed duration of less than 15 years, or is fixed in amount and, without regard to Code Sec. 197 would be recoverable under a method similar to the unit of production method. (Code Sec. 197(e)(4)(D); Reg § 1.197-2(c)(13))[13]

Covenants not to compete or similar arrangements are section 197 intangibles if entered into in connection with the acquisition of an interest in a trade or business or a substantial portion thereof. (Code Sec. 197(d)(1)(E); Reg § 1.197-2(b)(9)) It has been held that a covenant not to compete agreed to by the seller in connection with an acquisition of an interest (e.g., stock) in a trade or business (as distinct from an acquisition of the trade or business's assets) isn't subject to the substantial portion requirement.[14]

¶ 1975   Intangibles excluded from section 197 intangibles.

The following are never treated as section 197 intangibles regardless of how acquired:[15]

. . . interests in corporations, partnerships, trusts and estates. (Code Sec. 197(e)(1)(A))

. . . computer software that's readily available for purchase by the general public, is subject to a non-exclusive license, and hasn't been substantially modified. (Code Sec. 197(e)(3)(A)) For 36-month straight line depreciation see ¶1962.

. . . futures, foreign currency contracts and notional principal contracts. (Code Sec. 197(e)(1)(B))

. . . land. (Code Sec. 197(e)(2)) But the right to use an American viticultural area (AVA) designation isn't an interest in land, and, thus, *is* a section 197 intangible as a government-granted license, permit or other right (see ¶1974).[16]

. . . leases of tangible property. (Code Sec. 197(e)(5)(A))

. . . debt instruments, except for deposit bases and similar items. (Code Sec. 197(e)(5)(B))

. . . mortgage servicing rights secured by residential real property. (Code Sec. 197(e)(6))

. . . sports franchises, if acquired before Oct. 23, 2004.[17]

. . . any fees for professional services or transaction costs incurred by parties to a transaction with respect to which any part of the gain or loss isn't recognized under the rules in Code Sec. 351 through Code Sec. 368 that govern corporate organizations and reorganizations. (Code Sec. 197(e)(7))

. . . accounts receivable. (Reg § 1.197-2(b)(6))

10. ¶L-7952; ¶1974; TD ¶269,004
11. ¶L-7952; ¶1974; TD ¶269,004
12. ¶L-7958.3; ¶1974; TD ¶269,014
13. ¶L-7967; ¶1974; TD ¶269,004

14. ¶L-7966; ¶1974; TD ¶269,004
15. ¶L-7952.1, L-7968 *et seq.*; ¶1974; TD ¶269,010
16. ¶L-7972; ¶1974
17. ¶L-7968.1; ¶1974; TD ¶269,010

Also, intangibles created by the taxpayer (or for the taxpayer by contract) aren't subject to 15-year amortization if they are (1) not (a) certain rights granted by a governmental unit, (b) covenants not to compete made in connection with acquisition of an interest in a trade or business, or (c) franchises, trademarks and trade names, and (2) not created in connection with a transaction (or a series of related transactions) that involves the acquisition of assets which constitute all, or a substantial portion of, a trade or business. (Code Sec. 197(c)(2); Reg § 1.197-2(d)(2)) Thus, the costs of creating, as opposed to acquiring, customer relationships aren't subject to 15-year amortization. The exclusion doesn't apply to self-created intangibles sold and repurchased in an unrelated transaction.[18]

¶ 1976 Depletion Deduction.

All exhaustible natural deposits and timber qualify for deduction of a reasonable allowance for depletion based on the taxpayer's cost or other basis of the resources — cost depletion. For mines and certain interests in oil or gas wells, the depletion deductions may be computed as a specified percentage of gross income if that is greater than cost depletion.

A taxpayer can claim percentage depletion on one property and cost depletion on another, or claim, on the same property, cost depletion for one year and percentage for another.[19]

Where the property is entitled to either cost or percentage depletion, the allowable deduction is the greater of the two. (Code Sec. 613)[20] Percentage depletion for oil and gas wells (except for gas from certain domestic geothermal deposits or geopressured brine) is limited to "independent producers and royalty owners," see ¶1979. The allowable deduction is never less than cost depletion. (Code Sec. 611, Code Sec. 612, Code Sec. 613) There's no official form for computing depletion, but Form T must be attached to the income tax return if a deduction for depletion of timber is taken.[21] The basis of the property must be reduced by the depletion deduction allowed or allowable, whichever is larger.[22]

A taxpayer may take a depletion deduction only if he owns an "economic interest" in the mineral deposit or the timber. (Reg § 1.611-1(b))[23]

¶ 1977 Cost depletion.

This deduction is based on the property's adjusted basis, the number of recoverable units of mineral at the beginning of the year and the number of units sold or for which payment is received during the year. (Reg § 1.611-2(a)) An elective safe harbor may be used to determine recoverable oil and gas reserves.[24] Taxpayer's total cost depletion deductions can't exceed his basis for the mineral property.[25]

Basis for cost depletion and gain or loss is its cost or other basis plus or minus basis adjustments. (Code Sec. 612) It doesn't include the basis of nonmineral property, such as amounts recoverable through depreciation, or the residual value of land and improvements at the end of operations. (Reg § 1.612-1(b)(1))[26] Additional basis adjustments also apply to natural resources. (Code Sec. 1016(a))

¶ 1978 Percentage depletion.

This is a specified percentage of the "gross income from the property" for the tax year. It can never exceed 50% (100% for oil and gas properties) of taxable income from the property before deducting depletion. (Code Sec. 613(a)) For this purpose, taxable income from the property is the excess of gross income from the property over the allowable deductions (exclusive of depletion) attributable to the mining processes (including mining transportation) on

18. ¶L-7975; ¶1974; TD ¶269,013
19. ¶N-2004, N-2250 *et seq.*; ¶6114; TD ¶270,501
20. ¶N-2004; ¶6114; TD ¶270,501
21. ¶N-3101 *et seq.*, ¶N-6107; ¶6114.027; TD ¶270,503
22. ¶N-3009; ¶6124.001; TD ¶214,000

23. ¶N-2055, ¶N-2056, ¶N-2058 *et seq.*; ¶6114 *et seq.*; TD ¶270,504, TD ¶270,506
24. ¶N-2255.2; TD ¶270,701
25. ¶N-2250 *et seq.*; ¶6114.020 *et seq.*; TD ¶270,701
26. ¶N-3000 *et seq.*; ¶s 6124, 6124.001; TD ¶270,703

which depletion is claimed. (Reg § 1.613-5(a))[27]

Percentage depletion, like cost depletion, reduces basis. But percentage depletion continues to be deductible as long as there is gross income from the property even after taxpayer's basis for the property has been reduced to zero. Cost depletion is to be used where higher than percentage depletion. (Code Sec. 613(a))[28]

A corporation's deductible depletion allowance for iron ore or coal (including lignite) is cut back by 20% of the otherwise allowable percentage depletion deduction in excess of the adjusted basis of the property at the close of the tax year (determined without regard to the depletion deduction for the tax year). (Code Sec. 291(a)(2))

The minerals listed below qualify for percentage depletion at the rates shown. (Code Sec. 613(b); Reg § 1.613-2(b))[29]

	Rate (%)
Oil and gas	(See ¶1979)
Sulphur and uranium	22
U.S. deposits of: anorthosite, clay, laterite, and nephelite syenite (to the extent that alumina and aluminum compounds are extracted therefrom), asbestos, bauxite, celestite, chromite, corundum, fluorspar, graphite, ilmenite, kyanite, mica, olivine, quartz crystals (radio grade), rutile, block steatite talc and zircon	22
U.S. deposits of ores of antimony, beryllium, bismuth, cadmium, cobalt, columbium, lead, lithium, manganese, mercury, molybdenum, nickel, platinum and platinum group metals, tantalum, thorium, tin, titanium, tungsten, vanadium and zinc	22
U.S. deposits of: gold, silver, copper, and iron ore and oil shale	15
Geothermal deposits in U.S. or its possessions	15
Metal mines that don't qualify for 22% or 15% rate, above	14
Rock asphalt and vermiculite	14
Ball clay, bentonite, china clay, sagger clay, and refractory clay exclusive of clay entitled to the 22% rate, above, or to 7½% or 5% rates	14
Asbestos (not entitled to 22% rate above), brucite, coal, lignite, perlite, sodium chloride and wollastonite	10
Natural gas from geopressurized brine from U.S. wells drilled after Sept. '78 and before '84	10
Clay and shale used or sold for use in the manufacture of sewer pipe or brick, and clay, shale, and slate used or sold for use as sintered or burned lightweight aggregates	7½
Clay used or sold for use, in the manufacture of drainage and roofing tile, flower pots and kindred products	5
Gravel, peat, pumice, sand, scoria, shale (other than shale entitled to 15% or 7½% rates, above) and stone (other than dimension and ornamental stone)	5
Bromine, calcium chloride and magnesium chloride (if from brine wells)	5

Other minerals: 14%, except generally 5% if used or sold as rip rap, ballast, road material, rubble, concrete aggregates or for similar purposes.

Natural resources that don't qualify for percentage depletion include timber (Reg § 1.611-1(a)), minerals from sea water and other inexhaustible sources. (Code Sec. 613(b)(7)) Coal or iron ore disposed of with a retained economic interest that qualifies for capital gain-ordinary

---

27. ¶N-2702; ¶6134.009 *et seq.*; TD ¶271,013   29. ¶N-2311; ¶s 2914, 6134 *et seq.*; TD ¶271,002
28. ¶N-2300 *et seq.*; ¶6114; TD ¶271,000 *et seq.*

loss treatment doesn't qualify for percentage depletion. (Reg § 1.611-1(b)(2))[30] For the treatment of percentage depletion for alternative minimum tax purposes, see ¶3208.

¶ 1979 Oil, gas and geothermal deposits percentage depletion.

Percentage depletion applies to oil and gas only in the following cases:[31]

• *Crude oil and natural gas production of independent producers and royalty owners.* 15% depletion is allowed a taxpayer who isn't a retailer or refiner for so much of his "average daily production" of domestic crude oil and domestic natural gas as doesn't exceed his "depletable oil quantity" or "depletable natural gas quantity." "Marginal production" may qualify for a higher percentage depletion rate (not to exceed 25%)[32] if the price of domestic crude oil is below $20 per barrel for the calendar year preceding the calendar year in which the tax year in question begins. (Code Sec. 613A(c)(6))

The maximum depletable amount is 1,000 barrels of oil or 6,000,000 cubic feet of gas per day. A taxpayer who has both crude oil and natural gas production allocates the maximum depletable amount between oil and gas at the rate of 6,000 cubic feet of gas per barrel of oil. Over-ceiling production isn't entitled to any depletion. (Code Sec. 613(d), Code Sec. 613A)

The deduction can't exceed 65% of the taxpayer's taxable income from all sources. (Code Sec. 613A(d)) Also, the deduction for any costs for which taxpayer claims the 15% enhanced oil recovery credit (¶2322) must be reduced by that credit amount. (Code Sec. 43(d)(1))

• *Production of natural heat from geothermal deposits and natural gas production from geopressured brine* located in the U.S. or its possession. (Code Sec. 613(e), Code Sec. 613A(b)(2))[33]

Percentage depletion isn't available with respect to any lease bonus, advance royalty or other amount payable without regard to production from any oil, gas or geothermal property. (Code Sec. 613(e)(3), Code Sec. 613A(d)(5))[34] The restriction on the use of percentage depletion applies only to oil and natural gas; other minerals from oil and gas wells can qualify.[35]

¶ 1980 Related and commonly controlled producers.

The depletable ceiling amounts applicable to oil or gas production of independent producers or royalty owners who are related or are under common control is allocated among them. Allocation is required among corporations that are part of a controlled group; corporations, trusts and estates owned by the same or related persons; and an individual and his spouse and minor children. (Code Sec. 613A(c)(8))[36]

¶ 1981 Aggregation and division of depletable property.

Cost or percentage depletion must be computed separately for each property. (Code Sec. 612, Code Sec. 613)[37] A "property" is each separate interest owned by the taxpayer in each separate tract or parcel of land. (Code Sec. 614(a)) "Interest" means economic interest. It includes working or operating interests, royalties, overriding royalties and net profits interests. It also includes production payments to the extent they aren't treated as loans. (Reg § 1.614-1(a)(2)) Separate properties may be aggregated and treated as a single property. (Code Sec. 614(b), Code Sec. 614(c), Code Sec. 614(e)) A single interest in a "mine" may be treated as two or more separate properties, at the taxpayer's election. (Code Sec. 614(c)(2); Reg § 1.614-3(b))

---

30. ¶N-2314; ¶s 6114.023, 6314.04; TD ¶271,003
31. ¶N-2400 *et seq.*; ¶613A4; TD ¶271,014
32. ¶N-2425; ¶613A4; TD ¶271,018
33. ¶N-2316; ¶s 6134.001, 613A4; TD ¶271,014

34. ¶N-2105 *et seq.*; ¶613A4.02; TD ¶271,010
35. ¶N-2400 *et seq.*; TD ¶271,014
36. ¶N-2420; ¶613A4; TD ¶271,026
37. ¶N-2901; ¶6114 *et seq.*; TD ¶271,027

Chapter 6 Charitable Contributions—Medical Expenses—Alimony—Other Nonbusiness Deductions

¶ 2100 Charitable Contribution Deduction. ▆▆▆▆▆▆▆

An individual who itemizes can deduct charitable contributions up to 50%, 30% or 20% of his adjusted gross income, depending on the type of property contributed and the type of donee. A corporation generally can deduct charitable contributions up to 10% of its taxable income. Amounts that exceed the ceilings can be carried forward for five years by both individuals and corporations. The deduction allowed for property contributions is usually the property's fair market value, but is reduced for gifts of certain types of property.

For individuals, charitable contributions are deductible only as an itemized deduction on Schedule A (Form 1040). (Reg § 1.170A-1(a))[1] For the charity's requirement to disclose the deductibility of contributions to it, see ¶4118.

¶ 2101 What is a deductible charitable contribution?

A deductible charitable contribution generally is one that:

. . . is to or for the use of a qualified charitable organization (¶2102) (Code Sec. 170(c));

. . . is paid within taxpayer's tax year, regardless of taxpayer's accounting method (¶2132) (except for certain accrual basis corporations, see ¶2133) (Code Sec. 170(a));

. . . is within the applicable statutory ceilings for individuals (¶2123 *et seq.*), and corporations (¶2131) (Code Sec. 170(b)); *and*

. . . meets certain substantiation requirements (¶2134 *et seq.*). (Reg § 1.170A-13)[2]

¶ 2102 Qualified charitable organizations.

A qualified charitable organization is one that fits into one of the specified categories *and* which IRS has ruled (or the donor establishes) is eligible to receive deductible contributions.[3] IRS Pub. No. 78, available on IRS's website, provides a cumulative list of charitable organizations within the meaning of Code Sec. 170(c), but isn't exhaustive.[4] Qualified charitable organizations include:

. . . a corporation, trust, community chest, fund or foundation (including a private foundation) that's organized *and* operated exclusively for charitable, religious, educational, scientific or literary purposes, or for the prevention of cruelty to children or animals, or to foster and conduct national or international amateur sports competition (but only if none of the activities involves providing athletic facilities or equipment); *and* that's organized or created in the U.S. or its possessions, or under their laws; *and* none of whose net earnings inures to the benefit of any private shareholder or individual. Corporate contributions to noncorporate donees must be used in the U.S. or its possessions. (Code Sec. 170(c)(2));[5] Additionally, contributions to disregarded single-member LLCs wholly owned and controlled by a U.S. charity are treated as made to the charity;[6]

. . . U.S. states or possessions, their political subdivisions, the U.S., and the District of Columbia, *but only* if the gift is exclusively for public purposes (Code Sec. 170(c)(1));[7]

. . . certain war veterans' organizations (Code Sec. 170(c)(3)),[8] certain domestic fraternal

---

1. ¶A-2701; ¶1704.01; TD ¶330,201
2. ¶K-2803; ¶1704 *et seq.*; TD ¶330,202
3. ¶K-2850 *et seq.*; ¶1704.20; TD ¶330,265
4. ¶K-2945; ¶1704.21; TD ¶330,279

5. ¶K-2862 *et seq.*; ¶1704.20 *et seq.*; TD ¶330,269
6. ¶K-2854
7. ¶K-2899; ¶1704.25; TD ¶330,274
8. ¶K-2915; ¶1704.27; TD ¶330,275

References beginning with a single letter are to paragraphs in RIA's Federal Tax Coordinator 2d and RIA's Analysis of Federal Taxes: Income. Those beginning with numbers are to paragraphs in RIA's United States Tax Reporter. Those beginning with TD are to paragraphs in RIA's Tax Desk.

290

societies, orders or associations (Code Sec. 170(c)(4)),[9] and certain nonprofit cemetery companies. (Code Sec. 170(c)(5)).[10]

¶ 2103 Charitable deductions barred for certain contributions.

No charitable deduction is allowed for the following types of contributions:

... To a charity that conducts lobbying activities on matters of direct financial interest to the donor's trade or business, if a principal purpose was to avoid income tax by getting a charitable deduction for expenses for which a business expense deduction would be disallowed (¶1629) had the donor conducted the activities directly. (Code Sec. 170(f)(9))[11]

... To an organization disqualified from tax exemption because a substantial part of its activities involves trying to influence legislation, or it participates in any political campaign (Reg § 1.170A-1(j)(5)), see ¶4102 *et seq.*[12]

... Made to or for an individual (except for certain students, see ¶2122), unless the individual is an agent for a qualified organization (¶2102).[13]

... By church members and earmarked for a specific individual, e.g., to cover the minister's medical expenses. The church must have control over the funds' use for the donation to be deductible.[14]

... To a charity to the extent the donor derives an economic benefit (for exception, see ¶2104). Thus, no charitable deduction is allowed for: tuition (or required "donation" of excess "tuition" payment), even for parochial school, [15] or a payment in connection with a person's admission to an old age or retirement home operated by a charity, to the extent allocable to care to be given (may be partly a *medical* expense, see ¶2146) or the privilege of being admitted.[16] But, contributions to state programs that entitled taxpayer to state tax credits were deductible.[17]

... Clothing and household items that aren't in good used condition or better (but deduction may be allowed if amount claimed for the item exceeds $500 and taxpayer includes a qualified appraisal with his return, see ¶2137). IRS may also deny a deduction for any contribution of clothing or a household item with minimal monetary value (e.g., used socks or undergarments). IRS says the price a buyer actually pays for a used item in a store such as a thrift shop is an indication of value, but dismissed as inaccurate "standard value listings" supplied by organizations like the Salvation Army. It also says valuation under a fixed formula or method (e.g., percentage of replacement cost), doesn't work well for used clothing. (Code Sec. 170(f)(16))[18]

¶ 2104 Fundraising events, entertainment, etc., for charity.

Where amounts are paid in connection with admission to fundraising events for charity (e.g., shows, lotteries, and athletic events), the receipt of tickets or other privileges raises a presumption that the payment isn't a gift. Taxpayer must show that a clearly identifiable part of the payment is a gift. Only the part made with the intention of making a gift *and* for which taxpayer receives no consideration qualifies as a contribution.[19] The charity must show (in its solicitation, tickets, receipts or other related documents) the value (or reasonable estimate) of the event, and how much of the contribution is deductible.[20] For an organization's fundraising disclosure requirements, see ¶4119 *et seq.*

However, the donor may deduct a contribution in full if the benefit is inconsequential or insubstantial. This applies if the charity informs patrons how much is deductible *and* any of these tests is met: (1) the fair market value (FMV) of all benefits received in connection with

9. ¶K-2921; ¶1704.26; TD ¶330,276
10. ¶K-2925; ¶1704.28; TD ¶330,277
11. ¶K-2804; ¶1624.395; TD ¶330,204
12. ¶K-2871; ¶1704.30; TD ¶332,269
13. ¶K-2953; ¶1704.20; TD ¶330,203
14. ¶K-2970; TD ¶330,203

15. ¶K-3110, K-3111; ¶1704.38; TD ¶330,242
16. ¶K-3047; ¶1704.38; TD ¶330,231
17. ¶K-3059
18. ¶K-3177.6; ¶1704.41; TD ¶337,617.4
19. ¶K-3089; ¶1704.38; TD ¶330,245
20. ¶K-3105; ¶1704.38; TD ¶330,257

the payment isn't more than 2% of the payment, or the following dollar figures: $102 for 2013 ($104 for 2014), if less; or (2) the payment is at least $51 for 2013 ($52 for 2014) and in connection with it the donor receives only token benefits (bookmarks, calendars, mugs, posters, tee shirts, etc.) generally costing no more than $10.20 for 2013 ($10.40 for 2014), or (3) the charity mails or otherwise distributes free, unordered items to patrons.[21]

A taxpayer may rely on either a contemporaneous written acknowledgment (for contributions of $250 or more, see ¶2136) or a written disclosure statement (for quid pro quo contributions of more than $75, see ¶4119) for the FMV of any goods or services he receives from the charity. Taxpayer can't treat an estimate as the FMV where he knows, or has reason to know, it's unreasonable. (Reg § 1.170A-1(h)(4))[22] Payment to a college or university where the donor receives a *right to buy* seating at an athletic event (even in a skybox) is 80% deductible. The ticket cost itself is nondeductible. (Code Sec. 170(l))[23] A taxpayer's failure to use the ticket, etc., doesn't increase the amount of the deduction.[24] Amounts paid for raffle tickets, to play bingo, etc., aren't contributions[25] (for deduction as a gambling loss, see ¶1786).

¶ 2105   Charitable contribution v. business expense.

Transfers to a charity that are directly related to a taxpayer's business and made with a "reasonable expectation of financial return commensurate with" the amount transferred may be deductible as business expenses. But no business expense deduction is allowed for the transfer if *any* part of it is deductible as a charitable contribution. (Reg § 1.162-15(a)(2))[26]

⊘*observation:* Business expense treatment may be preferable if the "contribution" would cause the taxpayer's total charitable contributions to exceed the charitable deduction ceiling (¶2123 *et seq.*). Also, some individual taxpayers would benefit more from reducing adjusted gross income (e.g., to avoid or minimize reductions in some otherwise available benefits) than from just reducing taxable income.

¶ 2106   Gift of property.

A gift of property to a qualified charitable donee (¶2102) is a contribution to the extent of the property's fair market value (FMV) at the time of the gift, whether or not it has appreciated (Reg § 1.170A-1(c)), except for gifts of ordinary income-type property (¶2107), and certain gifts of tangible personal property or capital gain property (¶2110).[27] For substantiation requirements, see ¶2134 *et seq.* The property's FMV is reduced for donor-placed restrictions on marketability or use (e.g., 3-year bar on transfer or license of donated patent).[28] No gain is realized on a contribution of appreciated property (for certain bargain sales, see ¶2112).[29]

⊘*observation:* Thus, taxpayer can deduct his basis in the property, plus his paper profit.

Taxpayer's charitable deduction for the gift can't exceed the property's FMV (at contribution), even if it's less than his basis.[30] Nor is taxpayer allowed a loss deduction on the difference between the property's basis and FMV.[31] Special rules apply to gifts of patents[32] and taxidermy property.[33] Where taxpayer arranged for his credit card rebate (1% of purchases) to be paid to charity, the rebate amounts weren't includible in taxpayer's gross income and were treated as charitable donations made by taxpayer.[34]

---

21. ¶K-3106; ¶1704.38; TD ¶330,262
22. ¶K-3087.2; ¶1704.38; TD ¶334,016
23. ¶K-3100; ¶1704.38; TD ¶330,256
24. ¶K-3094; TD ¶330,250
25. ¶K-3090; ¶1704.38; TD ¶330,246
26. ¶K-3068 *et seq.*; ¶1624.363; TD ¶334,700 *et seq.*
27. ¶K-3150 *et seq.*; ¶1704.40 *et seq.*; TD ¶331,601

28. ¶K-3151; TD ¶331,601
29. ¶K-3208 *et seq.*, ¶K-3179 *et seq.*; ¶1704.43; TD ¶331,679
30. ¶K-3151; ¶1704.41; TD ¶331,601
31. ¶M-1015; TD ¶331,679
32. ¶K-3177.1; ¶1704.42; TD ¶331,616.2
33. ¶K-3171.1
34. ¶K-3024.1; TD ¶330,208

¶ 2107 Gift of ordinary income-type appreciated property—deduction reduced.

For charitable gifts of ordinary income-type property (below), the amount contributed (property's fair market value (FMV), ¶2106) must be reduced by the amount which would have been recognized as gain other than long-term capital gain if the property had been sold by the donor for its then FMV. (Code Sec. 170(e)(1))[35] However, the reduction does not apply to any gain of a corporation that would not be treated as long-term capital gain under the rules of Code Sec. 291 discussed at ¶2697. For exceptions for certain gifts of C corporations, see ¶2108.

Ordinary income-type property is property which, if sold by taxpayer (donor) at its FMV on the date it was contributed, would have resulted in *some* amount of gain other than long-term capital gain. (Code Sec. 170(e)(1)) This includes: inventory or other property held for sale to customers; Code Sec. 306 stock (¶3535 *et seq.*); capital assets held for less than the long-term holding period as of the date contributed; property subject to depreciation, recapture, etc.; property used in taxpayer's trade or business; and art works, letters, memoranda, and similar property created by or for taxpayer. (Reg § 1.170A-4(b))[36]

For contributions before Jan. 1, 2014, taxpayers that aren't C corporations and donate "apparently wholesome food" inventory to eligible charities are entitled to the same enhanced deduction available to C corporations (¶2108), except that the deduction can't exceed 10% of net income as specially calculated. (Code Sec. 170(e)(3)(C)(i)(I))[37]

¶ 2108 Enhanced deductions for C corporation gifts for specified purposes.

A C corporation may claim an enhanced deduction equal to the lesser of (a) basis plus half of the property's appreciation, or (b) twice the property's basis, for:

(1) Contributions of inventory, property held primarily for sale to customers in the ordinary course of its trade or business, or depreciable real property used in its trade or business, if the contribution is to an exempt Code Sec. 501(c)(3) organization (see ¶4102) (other than certain private foundations) that uses the property solely for the care of the ill, the needy or infants, and meets other specified requirements. (Code Sec. 170(e)(3)(A))[38]

(2) Certain contributions of scientific equipment or apparatus constructed by taxpayer to a higher education institution or a tax-exempt organization (but not a private foundation) organized and operated primarily to conduct scientific research. (Code Sec. 170(e)(4))[39]

(3) Pre-2014 contributions of food inventory. It must be apparently wholesome food, i.e., meant for human consumption, and meet certain quality and labeling standards. (Code Sec. 170(e)(3)(C))[40]

¶ 2109 Property contribution where taxpayer realizes income on gift.

If a taxpayer realizes income (ordinary income or capital gain) on his gift of property, his charitable deduction isn't subject to the reduction described at ¶2107. Thus, he may deduct the full fair market value of donated installment obligations, obligations issued at a discount, or other receivables. (Reg § 1.170A-4(a))[41]

¶ 2110 Limits on contributions of tangible personal property; gifts to certain private foundations.

For certain gifts, the amount treated as contributed and deductible (subject to deduction ceilings, see ¶2123 *et seq.*) is the property's fair market value (FMV) *reduced* by the total

---

35. ¶K-3160 *et seq.*; ¶1704.42; TD ¶331,609
36. ¶K-3161; ¶1704.42; TD ¶331,610
37. ¶K-3201.1; ¶1704.42; TD ¶331,702
38. ¶K-3201 *et seq.*; ¶1704.42; TD ¶331,701 *et seq.*

39. ¶K-3221 *et seq.*; ¶1704.42; TD ¶331,721 *et seq.*
40. ¶K-3201.1; ¶1704.42; TD ¶331,702
41. ¶K-3178 *et seq.*; TD ¶331,618

amount of the gain that would have been long-term capital gain (determined without regard to Code Sec. 1221(b)(3), see ¶2622) if the property were sold for its then FMV. (Code Sec. 170(e)(1)(B))[42] The donor's deduction is thus limited to his basis for these contributions:

. . . tangible personal property that's unrelated to the donee's exempt function (e.g., art to a church that then sells it) (Code Sec. 170(e)(1)(B)(i)); and

. . . any capital gain property except for publicly traded stock (limited to aggregate contributions of not more than 10% of the value of a corporation's outstanding stock by a donor and his family) given to a private foundation that isn't an operating foundation or community foundation and that doesn't make timely qualifying distributions. (Code Sec. 170(e)(1)(B)(ii), Code Sec. 170(e)(5))[43]

For contributions of tangible personal property for which a FMV deduction is claimed, but which isn't used for exempt purposes, if the donee sells or disposes of tangible personal property with a claimed value of at least $5,000: (1) in the year of contribution, the deduction is limited to taxpayer's basis; or (2) after the year of contribution, but within the 3-year period beginning on the contribution date, the donor includes in income the amount of the claimed deduction in excess of his basis in the property. These rules don't apply if the organization makes a proper certification to IRS. A $10,000 penalty applies for fraudulent identifications of property (i.e., stating it's exempt-use property while knowing it was not intended for such use). (Code Sec. 170(e)(1)(B)(i)(II), Code Sec. 170(e)(7), Code Sec. 6720B)[44]

¶ 2111   Liabilities transferred as part of contribution.

The donor's charitable contribution must be reduced by any liability that's assumed (e.g., by the donee) in connection with the gift. (Reg § 1.170A-3(d)) Where the donor transfers property subject to a liability, the amount of that debt is treated as an amount realized for purposes of the bargain sale rules, see ¶2112 (but not for the rule at ¶2109).[45] A reduction also must be made for the prepayment of any interest on the liability attributable to any period after the contribution was made if the donor takes a deduction for interest expense on the same payment. (Code Sec. 170(f)(5))[46]

observation: A taxpayer who can't deduct the prepayment as interest, e.g., because it's personal interest, should be able to get a charitable deduction for that payment since the charity has the obligation to make the interest payment after the contribution.

¶ 2112   Bargain sale to charity.

A taxpayer who sells property to (or exchanges it with) a charity and receives less than its fair market value (FMV) may treat the "bargain" element as a charitable contribution. (Code Sec. 1011(b); Reg § 1.170A-4(c)(2)) In computing the deduction, the amount considered contributed (excess of FMV over selling price) must be reduced by the amount of any required adjustment for ordinary income-type appreciated property (¶2107) for the contribution portion. (Reg § 1.170A-4(c), Reg § 1.1011-2(a))[47]

But the donor generally also realizes taxable gain on the sale. His basis for measuring gain is only the portion of his total cost or other basis for the property that the bargain selling price (amount realized) bears to its FMV. (Code Sec. 1011(b); Reg § 1.1011-2) This is basis times the selling price, divided by FMV. (Reg § 1.170A-4(c)(2)(i))[48]

illustration: J owns long-term stock that cost $12,000 and is worth $20,000 when he sells it to charity for $12,000. A contribution deduction of $8,000 ($20,000 − $12,000) is allowable. J's basis for the stock is reduced to $7,200 ($12,000 cost × [$12,000 selling price ÷ $20,000 FMV]) which, applied against his $12,000 selling price, gives J a $4,800 taxable

---

42. ¶K-3160 *et seq.*; ¶1704.42; TD ¶331,609 *et seq.*
43. ¶K-3175 *et seq.*; ¶1704.42; TD ¶331,615
44. ¶K-3167 *et seq.*; ¶V-2704.1; ¶1704.42; TD ¶331,613 *et seq.*
45. ¶K-3155, K-3198; ¶1704.44; TD ¶331,605

46. ¶K-3157; ¶1704.44; TD ¶331,607
47. ¶K-3190; ¶1704.43; TD ¶331,690
48. ¶K-3194; ¶1704.43; TD ¶331,694

gain.

¶ 2113 Gift of stock to charity followed by redemption ("charitable bail-out").

Owners of closely held corporations may effectively withdraw earnings from their firms tax-free by making a charitable contribution of their corporate stock, which the corporation then redeems. As long as the charity isn't obligated to sell back the stock, the donor can claim a deduction, even if the redemption was preplanned.[49] But, a contribution of stock which is then redeemed from a private foundation may be subject to penalty excise taxes (¶4127).

¶ 2114 Contributions of partial interests in property.

For transfers in trust, a contribution of a partial interest in property (e.g., where the donor transfers only his right to use the property, or his income interest in it) qualifies for a charitable deduction if the interest is:

- a remainder interest transferred to a charitable remainder trust (CRT, ¶2116), or a pooled income fund (¶2117), (Code Sec. 170(f)(2)(A)); or

- an income interest in a charitable lead trust (¶2119). (Code Sec. 170(f)(2)(B))[50]

For transfers not in trust, no charitable deduction is allowed for a contribution of less than the donor's entire interest in the donated property, except to the extent the deduction would have been allowed had the transfer been in trust. (Code Sec. 170(f)(3)(A))[1] Thus, a taxpayer who gives a charity the *right to use* property (e.g., rent-free use of office space), while retaining the property itself, can't take a charitable deduction for the rental or other value of this right.[2] The bar on deductions for transfers not in trust doesn't apply to contributions of:

- A remainder interest in a personal residence or a farm. (Code Sec. 170(f)(3)(B)(i));[3]

- An undivided part of taxpayer's entire interest (even if partial) in property (Code Sec. 170(f)(3)(B)(ii)), such as a remainder or income interest.[4] No deduction is allowed for a contribution of an undivided part of a taxpayer's entire interest in tangible personal property unless, immediately before the contribution, all interests in the property are held by taxpayer or taxpayer and the donee. Additionally, the fair market value (FMV) of any additional contribution of a fractional interest in property is the lesser of: (1) its FMV at the time of the initial fractional contribution, or (2) its FMV at the time of the additional contribution. (Code Sec. 170(o)(1)(A), Code Sec. 170(o)(2)) The deduction is recaptured under certain circumstances. (Code Sec. 170(o)(3)(A), Code Sec. 2522(e)(2)(A));

- A partial interest in property where *all* of taxpayer's interests in the property are given to one or more charities (e.g., income interest to one charity and remainder interest to another charity). (Reg § 1.170A-6(a));[5]

- A partial interest in real property (including remainders and perpetual restrictions) exclusively for "conservation purposes," including a qualifying facade easement. (Code Sec. 170(f)(3)(B)(iii), Code Sec. 170(h)) A facade easement must satisfy a number of requirements, including that it preserve in perpetuity the building's entire exterior and prohibit any change inconsistent with its historical character. No deduction is allowed for a charitable donation of an interest in property which is subject to a mortgage unless the mortgagee subordinates its rights in the property to the right of the charitable donee to enforce the conservation purposes of the gift in perpetuity. (Reg § 1.170A-14(g)(2)) The perpetuity requirement is not met if other property can be substituted for the property originally transferred subject to the easement.[6]

49. ¶K-3186; TD ¶331,686
50. ¶K-3250 *et seq.*; ¶1704.46; TD ¶331,628 *et seq.*
1. ¶K-3440.1 *et seq.*; ¶1704.45; TD ¶331,620 *et seq.*
2. ¶K-3440.2; ¶1704.45; TD ¶331,626
3. ¶K-3440.4 *et seq.*; ¶1704.45; TD ¶331,619
4. ¶K-3451 *et seq.*; ¶1704.45; TD ¶331,621
5. ¶K-3473; ¶1704.45; TD ¶331,621
6. ¶K-3506 *et seq.*; ¶1704.47; TD ¶331,625

¶ 2115　"Personal benefit contract" transactions—Form 8870.

No charitable deduction is allowed for a transfer to or for the use of a charity if the charity directly or indirectly pays or paid any premium on any personal benefit contract (e.g., split-dollar life insurance, see ¶1266) for the transferor. Also, no deduction is allowed if there is an understanding or expectation that any person will directly or indirectly pay any premium on any such contract for the transferor. A charity must pay an excise tax (use Form 8870) if it or any such person pays such premiums. (Code Sec. 170(f)(10))[7]

¶ 2116　Charitable remainder trusts (CRTs)—CRATs and CRUTs.

A charitable remainder trust (CRT) is a trust formed to make current distributions to one or more noncharitable income beneficiaries and to pay the entire remainder to charity or use it for a charitable purpose, that's *either* a "charitable remainder annuity trust" (CRAT) or a "charitable remainder unitrust" (CRUT). (Code Sec. 664(d); Reg § 1.664-1)[8]

¶ 2117　Pooled income funds.

A pooled income fund is a trust formed to pay income to one or more noncharitable beneficiaries and the remainder to charity. It must be maintained by the donee charity (no donor or income beneficiary may be a trustee) and meet certain other requirements. (Code Sec. 642(c)(5); Reg § 1.642(c)-5)[9]

¶ 2118　Contributions to donor advised funds.

Donor advised funds (DAFs) are charitable accounts set up and sponsored by an organization to which donors contribute and provide advice on the account's distributions and investments, although the sponsoring organization must have final say on the actual distributions and investments. Contributions are deductible if: (1) the sponsoring organization isn't listed in Code Sec. 170(f)(18)(A) (e.g., a war veteran's organization or domestic fraternal lodge); and (2) the donor obtains contemporaneous written acknowledgment from the sponsoring organization certifying it has legal control over the contribution. (Code Sec. 170(f)(18)(A))[10]

¶ 2119　Contribution of income interest in trust—charitable lead trusts.

A charitable deduction is allowed for a contribution of an income interest in trust (remainder to a noncharity) *only* if: (1) the donor is taxable on the trust income, and (2) the donated income interest is either a "guaranteed annuity" or a "unitrust interest." (Code Sec. 170(f)(2)(B); Reg § 1.170A-6) This type of trust is a "charitable lead trust." [11]

¶ 2120　Services for charity and related deductible transportation expenses.

No deduction is allowed for the value of services a taxpayer renders to charity. (Reg § 1.170A-1(g))[12] However, taxpayer is allowed a deduction for his unreimbursed out-of-pocket expenses (for travel expenses, see ¶2121) necessarily incurred in performing services (other than lobbying) free for a charity. (Code Sec. 170(f)(6); Reg § 1.170A-1(g))[13]

A taxpayer who uses his car in performing these services may deduct 14¢ per mile as a contribution (Code Sec. 170(i)) or his actual (unreimbursed) expenses for gas and oil. Parking fees and tolls are deductible in either case, as are deductions otherwise allowable for interest or taxes connected with the car, but not depreciation, insurance, and repairs.[14]

---

7. ¶K-3661, K-3667; ¶1704.305; TD ¶331,622
8. ¶K-3261 *et seq.*, ¶K-3291 *et seq.*; ¶6644 *et seq.*;TD ¶331,629
9. ¶K-3363 *et seq.*; ¶s 1704.46, 6424.03; TD ¶331,632
10. ¶K-3987; ¶1704.285; TD ¶331,200

11. ¶K-3345 *et seq.*; ¶1704.46; TD ¶331,633
12. ¶K-3551; ¶1704.36; TD ¶332,301
13. ¶K-3601 *et seq.*; ¶1704.37; TD ¶332,301 *et seq.*
14. ¶K-3614 *et seq.*; ¶1704.37; TD ¶332,614 *et seq.*

¶ 2121   Charitable travel expenses.

No charitable deduction is allowed for taxpayer's travel expenses (including meals and lodging), whether or not reimbursed, while away from home, unless there is no significant element of personal pleasure, recreation or vacation in the travel. (Code Sec. 170(j)) Even then, deduction is limited to amounts necessarily incurred for meals and lodging while away from home overnight in rendering these services.[15]

¶ 2122   Maintaining student in taxpayer's home.

A charitable deduction is allowed to a taxpayer who, under a written agreement with a charity and without compensation, maintains a student in the 12th grade or lower (not his dependent or relative) in his home. (Code Sec. 170(g); Reg § 1.170A-2)[16] The contribution in any year is the amount so contributed, but not more than $50 times the number of full calendar months (15 days or more is a "month") during the year for which the individual was a member of taxpayer's household and a full-time student. (Code Sec. 170(g)(2); Reg § 1.170A-2(b))[17]

¶ 2123   Charitable deduction ceilings for individuals.

There's a ceiling on the amount an individual may deduct each year as a charitable contribution, based both on the type of property contributed and the type of charity to which the contribution is made. The ceilings (below) for any tax year are a percentage of taxpayer's "contribution base" (below) for the year, subject to an overall 50% ceiling for all charitable gifts. (Code Sec. 170(b)(1))[18] For carryover of excess contributions, see ¶2129.

If the contributions are all to "50% charities" (see ¶2124), the year's ceiling is 50% of taxpayer's contribution base for the year, except for contributions of appreciated capital gain property (¶2126). (Code Sec. 170(b)(1)(A))[19] If the contributions are all to "30% charities" (see ¶2125), or are "for the use" of *any* charities, the ceiling is 30% of taxpayer's contribution base (except for gifts of appreciated capital gain property, see ¶2128) or, if less, 50% of his contribution base minus his contributions to 50% charities. (Code Sec. 170(b)(1)(B))[20]

An individual's "contribution base" for a year is his adjusted gross income (¶3102) for the year, but without deducting any net operating loss carryback to that year. (Code Sec. 170(b)(1)(G))[21] For spouses filing joint returns, these ceilings apply to the couple's combined contributions and their combined contribution base. (Reg § 1.170A-8(a)(1))[22] See ¶4705 for who may file a joint return.

For qualified conservation contributions (i.e., contribution of a qualified real property interest to a qualified organization exclusively for conservation) made in tax years beginning before 2014, the 30% limit is 50% of the contribution base less all other contributions, and the carryforward period (¶2129) is 15 years.[23] For qualified farmers and ranchers (more than 50% of gross income from farming as defined at Code Sec. 2032A(e)(5)), this limit is 100% of the contribution base less all other contributions. For property in agriculture or livestock production to be eligible for the 100% limit, the qualified real property interest had to include a restriction that the property remain generally available for such production. (Code Sec. 170(b)(1)(E)).[24]

15. ¶K-3620 *et seq.*; ¶s 1704.37, 2744.01; TD ¶332,620 *et seq.*
16. ¶K-3650 *et seq.*; ¶1704.33; TD ¶332,650 *et seq.*
17. ¶K-3651; ¶1704.33; TD ¶332,651
18. ¶K-3670; ¶1704.05; TD ¶333,001
19. ¶K-3671; ¶1704.05; TD ¶333,004
20. ¶s K-3671, K-3674, K-3684 *et seq.*; ¶s 1704.05, 1704.10 *et seq.*;

TD ¶333,009
21. ¶K-3672; ¶1704.05; TD ¶333,002
22. ¶K-3673; ¶1704.06; TD ¶333,003
23. ¶K-3694.1, ¶K-3701.1; ¶1704.11; TD ¶333,021.1
24. ¶K-3694.2; ¶1704.11; TD ¶333,021.2

¶ 2124   50% charities.

For purposes of the deduction ceilings for individuals (¶2123), "50% charities" are (1) churches (or church conventions or associations); (2) tax-exempt educational organizations; (3) tax-exempt hospitals and certain medical research organizations; (4) certain organizations holding property for state and local colleges and universities; (5) a U.S. state or possession, or any political subdivision of any of these, or the U.S. or the District of Columbia, if the contribution is for exclusively public purposes; (6) organizations organized and operated exclusively for charitable, religious, educational, scientific or literary purposes, or for the prevention of cruelty to children or animals, or to foster national or international amateur sports competition if they normally get a substantial part of their support from the government or general public; (7) certain private foundations; and (8) certain membership organizations more than one-third of whose support comes from the public. (Code Sec. 170(b)(1)(A))[25]

¶ 2125   30% charities.

For purposes of the ceilings on an individual's charitable deduction (¶2123), "30% charities" are qualifying charitable organizations (¶2102) that aren't 50% charities (¶2124), e.g., war veterans' organizations, fraternal orders, cemetery companies, and certain private non-operating foundations. (Code Sec. 170(b)(1)(B);[26]

¶ 2126   Gifts of appreciated capital gain property to 50% charities—30% ceiling.

An individual's deduction ceiling in the tax year for gifts of certain appreciated capital gain property (below) to 50% charities is 30% of his contribution base (¶2123), unless he makes an election to reduce the amount of his contribution (in which case, the 50% ceiling applies, see ¶2127). (Code Sec. 170(b)(1)(C))[27] For ceiling on gifts to 30% charities, see ¶2128.

This rule applies to any capital asset which, if sold for fair market value at contribution, would have given rise to long-term capital gain, *other than* property subject to the reduction at ¶2110. (Code Sec. 170(b)(1)(C))[28]

¶ 2127   Individual's election of 50% ceiling for appreciated property contributions.

An individual donor whose gift of capital gain property to a 50% charity is otherwise subject to the 30% ceiling (¶2126) may elect the 50% ceiling for the gift, *but only* if he reduces the amount of his contribution (as described at ¶2107)—i.e., his contribution is limited to his basis in the property. (Code Sec. 170(b)(1)(C)(iii))[29]

recommendation: Elect where the appreciation is small (value of increased current deduction is greater than loss of eventual deduction of appreciation) or where the 30% limit will prevent deduction of the appreciation even over the carryover period (¶2129).

Once made, the election applies to all gifts of capital gain property (¶2126) to 50% charities made by the donor in the tax year. In computing carryovers to this year, contributions of this property in an earlier year for which the election was *not* made are reduced as if they were subject to the reduction when made. (Code Sec. 170(b)(1)(C)(iii); Reg § 1.170A-8(d)(2))[30] The election is made by attaching a statement specified in the regs, to the original income tax return for the election year. (Reg § 1.170A-8(d)(2)(iii))[31]

---

25. ¶K-3720 *et seq.*; ¶1704.08; TD ¶333,101
26. ¶K-3684 *et seq.*; ¶1704.10 *et seq.*; TD ¶333,010
27. ¶K-3686, K-3687; ¶1704.11; TD ¶333,013, 333,014
28. ¶K-3687; ¶1704.05; TD ¶333,014

29. ¶K-3689; ¶1704.11; TD ¶333,018
30. ¶K-3706; ¶1704.11; TD ¶333,314
31. ¶K-3690; TD ¶333,019

¶ 2128   Gifts of appreciated capital gain property to 30% charities—20% ceiling.

An individual's deduction ceiling for gifts of appreciated long-term capital gain property to 30% charities is 20% of his contribution base (¶2123) (and there's no election like the one for gifts to 50% charities, see ¶2127). (Code Sec. 170(b)(1)(D))[32]

¶ 2129   Carryover of excess charitable contributions by individuals.

If an individual's charitable gifts for a tax year exceed the percentage ceilings for the year (¶2123), the excess may generally be carried forward and deducted for up to five years (subject to the later year's ceiling). (Code Sec. 170(d)(1)) A statement must be filed with the return for the year the carryover is deducted. The carryforward is available even if the individual didn't itemize his deductions in the contribution year. (Reg § 1.170A-10(a)(2))[33]

Contributions are deductible in the following order, up to 50% of the contribution base:

(1) Contributions qualifying for the 50% charity limit (¶2124).

(2) Contributions qualifying for the 30% charity limit (¶2125) up to the lesser of:

. . . 30% of the contribution base, or

. . . (a) 50% of the contribution base minus (b) contributions to 50% limit organizations. For this purpose, (b) includes contributions of capital gain property subject to the 30% limit (¶2126).

(3) Contributions of capital gain property subject to the 30% limit (up to the lesser of 30% of the contribution base or 50% of the contribution base minus other contributions to 50% organizations).

(4) Contributions qualifying for the 20% limit (¶2128) up to the lesser of:

. . . 20% of the contribution base,

. . . 30% of the contribution base minus contributions subject to the 30% limit,

. . . 30% of the contribution base minus contributions of capital gain property subject to the special 30% limit, or

. . . 50% of the contribution base minus the total of contributions to 50% and 30% limit organizations. (Code Sec. 170(b)(1))[34]

Where charitable contributions in more than one limitation category are carried over, the ordering rules determine the deduction limits for each category of contribution. Starting with the first (50% limitation) category, the allowable deduction limit is determined. Current contributions in that category are deducted first. Next, within that category, amounts carried over are deducted, up to the limitation amount for the category. Then, the same process is applied to the next limitation category according to the ordering rules. (Reg § 1.170A-10(b), Reg § 1.170A-10(c)) If there are carryovers from two or more years in any category, the carryover from the earlier year is considered first.[35]

¶ 2130   Excess charitable contributions on decedent's final return.

If an individual dies, any charitable contribution that can't be used on the decedent's final return (under the normal ceilings, see ¶2123) is lost. (Reg § 1.170A-10(d)(4)(iii))[36]

---

32. ¶K-3694; ¶1704.11; TD ¶333,017
33. ¶K-3701 *et seq.*, ¶K-3711; ¶1704.13; TD ¶333,301, 333,310
34. ¶K-3701 *et seq.*; ¶s 1704.05, 1704.13; TD ¶333,302
35. ¶K-3701 *et seq.*; ¶1704.05; TD ¶333,307
36. ¶K-3710; ¶1704.13; TD ¶333,306

¶ 2131 Corporation's charitable deduction ceiling and carryover period.

A corporation's charitable deduction for a tax year can't exceed 10% of its taxable income for the year. Taxable income for this purpose is computed without deductions for charitable contributions or dividends received, net operating loss carrybacks or capital loss carrybacks to the year, (Code Sec. 170(b)(2); Reg § 1.170A-11(a))[37] or adjustments for excess inclusion income stemming from the corporation's residual interest in a REMIC (¶4204) under Code Sec. 860E.[38] To the extent contributions in any year exceed this limit, the excess can be carried forward and deducted for five years. (Code Sec. 170(d)(2))[39]

However, a corporation that is a qualified farmer or rancher may make a qualified conservation contribution before 2014 equal to 100% of its taxable income after taking into account other allowable charitable contributions. To be eligible, the corporation's stock can't be readily tradable on an established securities market at any time during the tax year the contribution is made. To be a qualified rancher or farmer, more than 50% of the corporation's gross income for the tax year must come from the trade or business of farming. A 15-year carryover is allowed. (Code Sec. 170(b)(2)(B)[40]

¶ 2132 When to deduct charitable contributions.

A charitable contribution is deductible in the tax year it's paid (subject to percentage ceilings, see ¶2123, ¶2131) (Code Sec. 170(a)), regardless of the donor's accounting method (except for accrual method corporations, see ¶2133) or when the gift was pledged. (Reg § 1.170A-1(a))[41] A contribution is "paid" when it's unconditionally delivered to the donee. A contribution by check that's delivered unconditionally is paid when delivered, if it clears in due course. If the check is mailed unconditionally and clears in due course, the contribution is paid when mailed. (Reg § 1.170A-1(b))[42] A contribution charged on a credit card is deductible by a cash basis donor in the year the charge is made, *not* in any later year when the credit card company is paid.[43]

¶ 2133 Corporate election to deduct post-year-end contribution.

An accrual method corporation whose board of directors has authorized a charitable contribution during the tax year may elect to deduct all or part of the contribution in that (authorization) year, if the contribution is paid by the 15th day of the third month following the close of the year. (Code Sec. 170(a)(2))[44] The election is made by reporting the contribution in the return and attaching a declaration signed by a principal officer, together with a copy of the directors' resolution authorizing the contribution. (Code Sec. 170(a)(2); Reg § 1.170A-11(b))[45]

¶ 2134 Specialized Rules for Claiming Charitable Contributions. ▄▄▄▄▄▄

Taxpayers (donors) must substantiate their charitable deductions, and supply appraisals and other information for certain property contributions. No charitable deduction is allowed for a contribution of $250 or more unless taxpayer substantiates it by a contemporaneous written acknowledgment from the donee. Special rules apply for contributions of cars, boats, and planes.

¶ 2135 Charitable contributions must be substantiated; donor's receipt.

A charitable deduction isn't allowed unless taxpayer can prove his right to it. (Code Sec. 170(a)(1))[46] For *donee's* information return requirement, see ¶4746.

---

37. ¶K-3830 *et seq.*; ¶1704.14; TD ¶333,022
38. ¶K-3832
39. ¶K-3833; ¶1704.14; TD ¶333,315
40. ¶K-3831.1 *et seq.*; ¶1704.14; TD ¶333,022.1
41. ¶K-3851; ¶1704.02; TD ¶333,701

42. ¶K-3858 *et seq.*; ¶1704.02; TD ¶333,706
43. ¶K-3861; ¶1704.02; TD ¶333,707
44. ¶K-3882 *et seq.*; ¶1704.03; TD ¶333,718
45. ¶K-3883; ¶1704.03; TD ¶333,718
46. ¶K-3901 *et seq.*; ¶1704.50, TD ¶334,001

For cash contributions, taxpayer must keep either a cancelled check, receipt or other reliable evidence. (Reg § 1.170A-13(a)(1))[47] A taxpayer can't deduct *any* contribution of a cash, check, or other monetary gift unless he maintains as a record of the contribution a bank record or a written communication from the donee organization showing its name, plus the date and amount of the contribution. (Code Sec. 170(f)(17)) For contributions of property (other than cash), taxpayer must have a receipt from the donee and keep records showing the donee's name and describing the gift. (Reg § 1.170A-13(b)(1))[48] For contributions made via payroll deductions, taxpayer must retain a pay stub, Form W-2, or other employer document showing the amount withheld for the purpose of payment to the donee, plus a pledge card or similar donee document showing the donee's name.[49] For contributions made through the Combined Federal Campaign or a similar program (e.g., United Way), the organization receiving the donation may be treated as the donee for substantiation purposes even if it distributes the funds to another organization. The written communication must contain the ultimate recipient's name.[50] Additional substantiation is required for: contributions of $250 or more (¶2136); noncash contributions exceeding $500 (¶2137); and contributions of cars, boats, and planes (¶2138).

¶ 2136 Substantiation requirement for contributions of $250 or more.

No charitable deduction is allowed for any (cash or property) contribution of $250 or more unless taxpayer substantiates it by a contemporaneous written acknowledgment (not just a cancelled check) from the donee (or its agent). (Code Sec. 170(f)(8)(A); Reg § 1.170A-13(f)(1))[1]

In general, the written acknowledgment must state: (1) the amount of cash and a description (but not the value) of any property other than cash contributed; (2) whether the donee provided any goods or services in consideration for the contribution, and if it did, a description and good-faith estimate of the value of those goods or services; and (3) if the goods or services consist entirely of intangible religious benefits (e.g., admission to a religious ceremony, but not religious school tuition or fees), a statement to that effect. (Code Sec. 170(f)(8)(B); Reg § 1.170A-13(f)(2)) Special requirements apply for gifts to a pooled income fund (¶2117). (Reg § 1.170A-13(f)(13))[2] The written acknowledgment requirement doesn't apply: (1) if the donee files a substantiating return (under regs to be issued) (Code Sec. 170(f)(8)(D));[3] or (2) to transfers to a charitable lead trust (¶2119), charitable remainder annuity trust or charitable remainder unitrust (¶2116). (Reg § 1.170A-13(f)(13))[4]

Goods or services that have insubstantial value (¶2104), and certain annual membership benefits the charity provides to taxpayer, taxpayer's employees, or the partners of a partnership donor in exchange for the contribution are disregarded in determining the $250 threshold. (Reg § 1.170A-13(f)(8)(i), Reg § 1.170A-13(f)(9)(i))[5] And, separate payments are generally treated as separate contributions. (Reg § 1.170A-13(f)(1))[6]

An employer's payment to a charity of $250 or more withheld from taxpayer's paycheck (the amount withheld from each single paycheck is treated as a separate contribution), may be substantiated by a combination of (1) a pay stub, Form W-2, or other employer-provided document showing the amount withheld for this purpose, and (2) a pledge card or other donee document which states it doesn't provide any consideration for the payroll contributions. (Reg § 1.170A-13(f)(11))[7]

47. ¶K-3919; ¶1704.50; TD ¶334,007
48. ¶s K-3926, K-3927; ¶1704.50; TD ¶334,011
49. ¶K-3939; TD ¶334,023.1D
50. ¶K-3941; TD ¶334,023
1. ¶K-3933; ¶1704.50; TD ¶334,015
2. ¶K-3933 *et seq.*; ¶1704.50; TD ¶334,015 *et seq.*

3. ¶K-3938
4. ¶K-3940.3; ¶1704.50
5. ¶K-3934; ¶1704.38; TD ¶334,016
6. ¶K-3934; ¶1704.50; TD ¶334,017
7. ¶K-3940; ¶1704.50; TD ¶334,020

¶ 2137   Proving noncash contributions exceeding $500—Form 8283.

For noncash contributions that are:

(1) more than $500 but not more than $5,000, the donor must attach to its return a description of the contributed property, on Form 8283. This requirement doesn't apply to a C corporation. (Code Sec. 170(f)(11)(B))

(2) more than $5,000 but not more than $500,000, the donor must obtain a "qualified appraisal" (one meeting specified IRS requirements) and attach to its return (using Form 8283) information about the property and appraisal (i.e., appraisal summary) as required by IRS. (Code Sec. 170(f)(11)(C))

(3) more than $500,000, the donor must attached a qualified appraisal (on Form 8283) to its return. (Code Sec. 170(f)(11)(D))

The requirements in (2) and (3), above, don't apply to: patents, copyrights, etc., as described in Code Sec. 170(e)(1)(B)(iii) (¶2106); property described in Code Sec. 1221(a)(1) (e.g., stock in trade, inventory); publicly traded securities; and "qualified vehicle donations" (¶2138). (Code Sec. 170(f)(11)(A)(ii)(I)) IRS will disallow a deduction if the above reporting requirements aren't met, unless the failure was due to reasonable cause. (Code Sec. 170(f)(11)(A))[8]

¶ 2138   Charitable contributions of cars, boats, and planes—Form 1098-C.

Special rules apply for contributions of motor vehicles, boats, and airplanes that aren't in taxpayer's inventory or held for sale in the ordinary course of his business ("qualified vehicle donations"), if the donation's claimed value exceeds $500. (Code Sec. 170(f)(12)) The donor's deduction can't exceed the gross proceeds from the charity's sale proceeds unless:

(1) there's a "significant intervening use" of the vehicle by the charity (actual, significant use to substantially further the charity's regularly conducted activities) before its sale;

(2) the charity materially improves the vehicle (significantly increases its value) before its sale (minor repairs or routine maintenance aren't enough); or

(3) the charity sells it at a price significantly below fair market value (FMV) (or gives it away) to a needy individual, in direct furtherance of its charitable purpose of relieving the poor and distressed or the underprivileged who need vehicles.

If (1), (2), or (3) applies, the donor may claim a deduction for the vehicle's FMV, using the "blue book" value for a similar vehicle (or private party sale amount, until regs are issued).

A deduction for donated vehicles whose claimed value exceeds $500 isn't allowed unless taxpayer substantiates the contribution by a contemporaneous written acknowledgment from the donee (on Form 1098-C). (Code Sec. 170(f)(12)(A)) It must:

. . . contain the donor's name and taxpayer identification number (TIN), the vehicle identification number (or similar number), and if exception (1), (2), or (3), above, applies, supporting details;

. . . indicate whether the donee provided goods or services in consideration of the vehicle (and, if so, describe them and estimate their value, or, if they consist solely of intangible religious benefits, a statement to that effect);

. . . generally be made within 30 days after the vehicle's sale (within 30 days of the contribution if exception (1), (2) or (3) applies); and

. . . if the charity sells the vehicle and none of the three above exceptions applies, state that the vehicle was sold in an arm's length transaction between unrelated parties, show the gross proceeds, and declare that the deductible amount can't exceed the gross proceeds.[9]

---

8. ¶K-3942 *et seq.*; ¶1704.50; TD ¶334,024 *et seq.*   9. ¶K-3948.1 *et seq.*; ¶1704.41; TD ¶334,028.1

¶ 2139 IRS "Statement of Value" for gifts of art appraised at $50,000 or more.

At taxpayer's request, IRS will issue a Statement of Value that taxpayer may rely on to substantiate the value of an item of art (paintings, sculpture, antique furniture, carpets, rare manuscripts, historical memorabilia, and similar objects) that has been appraised at $50,000 or more and transferred as a charitable gift. Taxpayer must request the statement before filing the return that first reports the gift, and must attach a copy of the statement (or of the request, if the statement hasn't been received yet) to that return.[10]

¶ 2140 Medical Expenses.

An individual who itemizes can deduct the amount by which certain unreimbursed medical and dental expenses paid during the year for himself, his spouse, and his dependents exceed 10% (7.5% if the individual or his spouse is over 65 before the end of the tax year) of his adjusted gross income (¶2141).

¶ 2141 How much is deductible—7.5%/10% of AGI floor.

The amount of medical expenses (¶2144) an individual can deduct (on Schedule A, Form 1040) in a tax year is the amount by which his unreimbursed payments for those expenses exceed 10% of his adjusted gross income (AGI, ¶3102) for the year. (There's no ceiling on the deduction.) (Code Sec. 213(a); Code Sec. 213(f)) But if the taxpayer or the taxpayer's spouse is 65 before the end of the tax year, the floor is 7.5% through 2016 regardless of whether they file joint or separate returns. The 10% floor applies to all taxpayers for tax years ending after 2016.[11] See ¶4705 for who is a spouse.

illustration: John, a single taxpayer, was born in '49. At the end of 2013, John will be age 64 and, thus, subject to the 10% floor for his 2013 tax year. For 2014 through 2016, John will be age 65 or over, and subject to the 7.5% floor. Starting in 2017, the 10% floor will once again apply to him.

observation: A change in the applicable floor can also occur as a result of marriage to, or divorce from, a spouse who is age 65 or over.

Any expense allowed as a Code Sec. 21 dependent care credit (¶2349), Code Sec. 35 credit for health insurance costs (¶2344), or Code Sec. 162(l) self-employed medical insurance deduction (¶1532) can't be treated as a medical expense. (Code Sec. 213(e), Code Sec. 35(g)(2), Code Sec. 162(l)(3))[12]

observation: The deduction is lost if medical expenses don't exceed the "floor."

For the percentage floor on deductible medical expenses for purposes of the alternative minimum tax, see ¶3209.

¶ 2142 Whose medical expenses may taxpayer deduct?

A taxpayer may deduct his own medical expenses, and those of his spouse (see ¶4705) and dependents if the status as spouse, etc., exists either when the medical care was rendered or when the expenses were paid. (Code Sec. 213(a); Reg § 1.213-1(e)(3)) For this purpose, "dependent" is defined in Code Sec. 152 (see ¶3119) and is determined without the gross income test for qualifying relatives, the rule that a joint return filer can't be a dependent, and the rule that a dependent is ineligible to have dependents. (Code Sec. 213(a); Reg § 1.213-1(a)(3)(i)) A child of divorced parents is considered a dependent of both if Code Sec. 152(e) applies (see ¶3126), so that each parent may deduct the medical expenses he or she pays for the child. (Code Sec. 213(d)(5))[13] An organ donor's medical expenses are deductible by the

---

10. ¶T-10080 *et seq.*; ¶1704.50; TD ¶526,012
11. ¶K-2002; ¶2134.14; TD ¶346,001

12. ¶K-2003; ¶s 2134, 2134.04; TD ¶346,002
13. ¶K-2300 *et seq.*; ¶s 2134.01, 2134.02; TD ¶346,011

payor, whether donor or recipient.[14]

¶ 2143 Decedent's medical expenses.

Expenses for a decedent's medical care that are paid out of his estate are treated as paid by him (and may be deducted) in the year incurred if: (1) they're paid within one year after his death, (2) they aren't deducted for federal estate tax purposes, and (3) a statement is filed with the income tax return (or amended return) showing that the expenses weren't allowed for estate tax purposes and that the estate tax deduction is waived. (Code Sec. 213(c))[15]

🅡🅘🅐*observation:* The choice of an income tax or estate tax deduction depends primarily on the extent to which the expense is deductible for income tax purposes, the decedent's top income tax rate, and the top effective estate tax rate.

¶ 2144 What kinds of medical expenses are deductible?

Deductible medical expenses are amounts paid for the diagnosis, mitigation, treatment, prevention of disease or for the purpose of affecting the body's structure or function (Code Sec. 213(d)(1)),[16] and the costs of nursing services (Reg § 1.213-1(e)(1)(ii))[17] (and related insurance payments, ¶2145, and transportation, ¶2148). The following costs are deductible:

... Eyeglasses, artificial teeth or limbs (Reg § 1.213-1(e)(1)(ii)), hearing aids, and similar items, as well as breast pumps and supplies that assist lactation.[18]

... Eye surgery to correct defective vision, including laser procedures (e.g., LASIK).[19]

... Discretionary medical procedures affecting the body's structure or function, including legal abortions and procedures to prevent or facilitate pregnancy (e.g., egg donor fees; but in vitro fertilization costs for a taxpayer who wasn't infertile weren't deductible).[20]

... Smoking cessation programs[21] and prescribed drugs designed to alleviate nicotine withdrawal, but not non-prescription nicotine gum and nicotine patches.[22]

... Attending a medical conference on a chronic disease suffered by an individual, his spouse (see ¶4705), or dependent (but not meal and lodging costs, ¶2149).[23]

... Legally procured prescription drugs (e.g., not aspirin) and insulin. (Code Sec. 213(b), Code Sec. 213(d)(3)) A controlled substance (such as marijuana) obtained for medical purposes, in violation of the federal Controlled Substances Act, isn't legally procured and is nondeductible, even if state law permits its doctor-prescribed use.[24]

... Weight-loss program for treatment of a specific disease (e.g., obesity, hypertension), but not the cost of diet food.[25]

... Diagnostic tests aiding in the detection of heart attack, diabetes, cancer, and other diseases (but not the collection and storage of DNA, absent a showing of how the DNA will be used for medical diagnosis). These include pregnancy tests, tests on healthy individuals, and tests taken not at the direction of a physician. Such a test will not fail to qualify due to high cost or if a less expensive alternative may be available.[26]

... Service animals used in mental health therapy.[27]

... Sex-change costs (except for breast augmentation undertaken to improve appearance).[28]

... Nonlicensed healthcare providers that provided physician-ordered assistance and supervision to a patient suffering from dementia.[29]

Expenses that aren't deductible as medical care include:

---

14. ¶K-2159; TD ¶346,008
15. ¶C-9556; ¶2134.03; TD ¶346,020
16. ¶K-2100 *et seq.*; ¶s 2134.04, 2134.08; TD ¶346,003
17. ¶K-2111; ¶2134.04; TD ¶346,506
18. ¶K-2162; ¶2134.04; TD ¶348,012
19. ¶K-2162
20. ¶K-2110; ¶2134.04; TD ¶346,505
21. ¶K-2117; ; TD ¶346,508

22. ¶K-2137; TD ¶346,505
23. ¶K-2161; TD ¶346,010
24. ¶K-2137; TD ¶347,003
25. ¶K-2116
26. ¶K-2105.1; TD ¶346,502.5
27. ¶K-2162
28. ¶K-2101, K-2109
29. ¶K-2122

... Expenses merely beneficial to the individual's general health. (Reg § 1.213-1(e)(1)(ii))[30]

... Costs of cosmetic surgery or similar procedure (e.g., teeth whitening), unless necessary to ameliorate a deformity arising from, or directly related to, a congenital abnormality, a personal injury resulting from an accident or trauma or a disfiguring disease (Code Sec. 213(d)(9))—e.g., breast reconstruction surgery after cancer mastectomy.[31]

... Payments for illegal operations or treatments. (Reg § 1.213-1(e)(1)(ii))[32]

Qualified long-term care services are treated as medical care (Code Sec. 213(d)(1)(C)) (unless provided by a relative who isn't a licensed professional, or by a related corporation or partnership. (Code Sec. 213(d)(11))) These services include necessary diagnostic, preventive, therapeutic, curing, treating, mitigating, and rehabilitative services, and maintenance or personal care services, which are required by a chronically ill individual and provided under a plan of care prescribed by a licensed health care practitioner. (Code Sec. 7702B(c)(1))[33]

¶ 2145 Accident and health insurance; Medicare.

The cost of insurance that's deductible as a medical expense is limited to amounts paid for insurance that covers *medical care* as defined at ¶2144. (Code Sec. 213(d)(1)(D))[34]

Amounts paid as *voluntary* premiums under Part B of Medicare (supplementary medical insurance benefits for the aged and disabled) are deductible as medical care, as are voluntary premiums under Medicare Part A (basic Medicare) (Code Sec. 213(d)(1)(D)), and Medicare Part D premiums, but not the *mandatory* employment or self-employment taxes paid for basic coverage under Medicare A. (Reg § 1.213-1(e)(4)(i)(a))[35] IRS has stated that all Medicare parts are insurance that constitutes medical care under Code Sec. 162(l) (see ¶1532).[36] For the business expense deduction for medical care insurance of sole proprietors, partners or 2%-or-more S corporation shareholders who pay Medicare premiums, see ¶1532.

When an insurance contract covers both medical care and other items (e.g., loss of income), no amount is treated as for medical care *unless:* the charge for medical insurance is separately stated, the amount treated as paid for medical insurance doesn't exceed the separately-stated charge, *and* the charge isn't unreasonably large in relation to the total premium for the contract. (Code Sec. 213(d)(6))[37]

Medical expenses include premiums paid for qualified long-term care (LTC) insurance, up to annual limits. For an individual whose attained age before the close of the tax year is:

... 40 or less, the limit is $360 for 2013 ($370 for 2014);

... more than 40, but not more than 50, the limit is $680 for 2013 ($700 for 2014);

... more than 50, but not more than 60, the limit is $1,360 for 2013 ($1,400 for 2014);

... more than 60, but not more than 70, the limit is $3,640 for 2013 ($3,720 for 2014); and

... more than 70, the limit is $4,550 for 2013 ($4,660 for 2014). (Code Sec. 213(d)(10))[38]

Qualified LTC insurance contracts must provide only coverage of qualified LTC services, must not pay or reimburse expenses to the extent the expenses are reimbursable under Medicare (or would be but for a deductible or coinsurance amount), must be guaranteed renewable, and must meet other detailed requirements. (Code Sec. 7702B(b))[39]

30. ¶K-2103; ¶2134.04; TD ¶346,004
31. ¶K-2109; ¶2134.04; TD ¶346,505
32. ¶K-2106; ¶2134.04; TD ¶346,503
33. ¶K-2122.1; ¶2134.075; TD ¶346,005
34. ¶K-2140 *et seq.*; ¶2134.08; TD ¶346,301
35. ¶K-2140; ¶2134.08; TD ¶346,301
36. ¶L-3510.2
37. ¶K-2141; ¶2134.08; TD ¶346,302
38. ¶K-2141.1; ¶2134.075; TD ¶346,303
39. ¶K-2141.2; ¶77,02B4; TD ¶346,304

¶ 2146   Deductible costs of care at hospitals and other institutions.

The cost of in-patient care (including meals and lodging, see ¶2149) furnished by a hospital is a deductible medical expense. (Reg § 1.213-1(e)(1)(v))[40] The cost of in-patient care (including meals and lodging) at a medical-care institution that *isn't* a hospital qualifies if the individual is there primarily for the availability of medical care (as defined at ¶2144), and the meals and lodging are a necessity incident to that care. If this test isn't met, only that part of the cost attributable to medical care qualifies. Medical care status depends on the patient's condition and the nature of the services he receives—not on the nature of the institution (e.g., federal, state, local or private). The deduction is allowed for:

. . . costs (including tuition, meals, and lodging) of a mentally or physically handicapped person at a special school (Reg § 1.213-1(e)(1)(v)), e.g., a school for children with learning disabilities like dyslexia. Costs allocable to medical care at a regular school qualify if the school supplies a cost breakdown;[41]

. . . costs of a nursing home or home for the aged. But if the person isn't there principally for medical reasons, only the cost of medical care qualifies. (Reg § 1.213-1(e)(1)(v))[42]

¶ 2147   "Medical" capital expenses for equipment or improvements.

Amounts incurred for elevators, swimming pools, and other permanent improvements to taxpayer's property (including capital expenditures to accommodate a residence to a physically handicapped individual) may be deductible medical expenses (¶2144) if the primary purpose is for the medical care of taxpayer, his spouse (see ¶4705), or dependents. But the medical deduction is limited to that part of the expenses that exceeds the amount by which the improvement increases the value of taxpayer's property. (Reg § 1.213-1(e)(1)(iii))[43]

illustration: On his doctor's advice, Joe installs an elevator in his two-story, single family home to avoid climbing stairs and to alleviate his heart condition. The cost of installing it is $15,000 and it decreases the value of Joe's home by $8,000 (because buyers don't want a single family home with an elevator). The full $15,000 is a medical expense.

Some expenses incurred by or for a physically handicapped individual to remove structural barriers in his residence to accommodate his physical condition (e.g., constructing access ramps, widening doorways, installing support bars) are presumed not to increase the value of the residence and may be deductible in full. (Reg § 1.213-1(e)(1)(iii))[44] Capital expenditures that are related only to the sick person and are detachable from the property aren't permanent improvements, so their full cost can be a medical expense (e.g., detachable inclinators and air conditioners). (Reg § 1.213-1(e)(1)(iii))[45] All the costs of operating or maintaining a medical capital asset are deductible, even if none or only a part of the cost of the asset itself qualifies. (Reg § 1.213-1(e)(1)(iii))[46]

¶ 2148   Transportation expenses for medical care.

The costs of transportation primarily for and essential to medical care (¶2144) qualify as medical expenses. (Code Sec. 213(d)(1)(B)) This includes food and lodging expense (¶2149) while en route to the place of medical treatment (Reg § 1.213-1(e)(1)(iv)), as well as taxi, train, plane, and bus fares and the cost of ambulance services.[47] Deductible medical expenses also include certain out-of-pocket car expenses, e.g., for gas, oil, parking fees, and tolls, but not depreciation, repair, insurance or maintenance. Instead of claiming the actual costs of gas and oil, a taxpayer who uses a car for qualified medical transportation may deduct a flat 24¢

---

40. ¶K-2142; ¶2134.04; TD ¶347,501
41. ¶K-2143 *et seq.*; ¶s 2134.10, 2134.11; TD ¶347,502
42. ¶K-2147; ¶2134.11; TD ¶347,504
43. ¶K-2180 *et seq.*; ¶2134.13; TD ¶348,009

44. ¶K-2181; ¶2134.13; TD ¶348,010
45. ¶K-2192; ¶s 2134.04, 2134.12; TD ¶348,012
46. ¶K-2182; ¶2134.13; TD ¶348,011
47. ¶K-2201; ¶s 2134.04, 2134.09; TD ¶348,501

a mile for expenses paid or incurred in 2013.[48] However, no medical expense deduction is permitted for the cost of commuting to and from work, even if taxpayer's illness or disability requires a special method of transportation.[49]

¶ 2149 "Away from home" expenses (meals and lodging)—$50 per night rule.

Expenses for meals and lodging away from home aren't medical expenses unless they're part of the cost of care in a hospital or other institution (¶2146) or medical travel (¶2148).[50] Taxpayer may deduct as a medical expense amounts paid for lodging (not food) while away from home, that's primarily for and essential to medical care in a hospital or equivalent, up to $50 per night for each individual. (Code Sec. 213(d)(2)) No deduction is allowed for lavish or extravagant lodging or where the travel has any significant element of personal pleasure, recreation or vacation. (Code Sec. 213(d)(2)(B))[1]

¶ 2150 When to deduct medical expenses; prepaid insurance.

Only medical expenses actually paid during the tax year are deductible. (Code Sec. 213(a)) Deduction is thus allowed for payments in the year even though the expenses were incurred in an earlier year. (Reg § 1.213-1(a)(1)) If the payment is made by credit card, the amount is deductible in the year the charge is made, regardless of when the credit card bill is paid.[2] Advance payment of anticipated medical expenses doesn't qualify for a current deduction unless there is a contractual obligation to pay in the current year.[3] Certain insurance premiums paid by a taxpayer who is under age 65 during the payment year, for medical care for himself, his spouse (see ¶4705), and dependents for the period *after* he reaches age 65, are deductible in the year paid. (Reg § 1.213-1(e)(4)(i)(b))[4]

¶ 2151 Medical expenses compensated for by insurance or otherwise.

Medical expenses aren't deductible if they have been compensated for by insurance or otherwise. (Code Sec. 213(a)) Taxpayer must reduce his medical expenses by amounts so compensated before applying the percentage of adjusted gross income floor (¶2141). But no reduction is required for amounts received as compensation for loss of earnings or as damages for personal injuries.[5] If reimbursements in a tax year exceed medical expenses in that year, no medical deduction is allowed.[6] Any part of the excess that's attributable to an employer's contribution is taxable; the rest is tax-free.[7] If a taxpayer is reimbursed for medical expenses in a year after he paid (and deducted) them, he must report the reimbursement as income to the extent attributable to the earlier deduction (Reg § 1.213-1(g))—i.e., to the extent he got a "tax benefit," see ¶1205.[8]

¶ 2152 Alimony or Separate Maintenance.

Payments of alimony or separate maintenance made under a divorce or separation instrument are deductible by the payor spouse and taxable to the payee spouse. Alimony must be paid in cash and must not continue beyond the death of the payee spouse. A payment that's fixed as child support isn't alimony.

¶ 2153 Tax treatment of alimony or separate maintenance payments.

Alimony or separate maintenance (¶2154) payments are taxable to the payee spouse in the year received (Code Sec. 71(a); Reg § 1.71-1(b)(5)), and are deductible by the payor spouse in the year paid, as a deduction from gross income. (Code Sec. 62(a)(10), Code Sec. 215(a))[9]

48. ¶K-2214 *et seq.*; ¶s 2134.04, 2134.09; TD ¶348,514 *et seq.*
49. ¶K-2202; ¶2134.09; TD ¶348,502
50. ¶K-2217; TD ¶348,517
1. ¶K-2218; ¶s 2134.04, 2134.09; TD ¶348,518
2. ¶K-2401; ¶2134.03; TD ¶346,016
3. ¶K-2403; ¶2134.03; TD ¶346,018

4. ¶K-2404; ¶2134.03; TD ¶346,019
5. ¶K-2601 *et seq.*; ¶s 2134.14, 2134.15; TD ¶346,021
6. ¶K-2605; TD ¶346,025
7. ¶H-1114; ¶2134.15; TD ¶133,012
8. ¶K-2604; ¶2134.15; TD ¶346,024
9. ¶J-1413, K-6001; ¶714 *et seq.*, ¶2154; TD ¶198,502, 341,001

Thus, the payor doesn't have to itemize to be allowed the deduction.[10] These rules don't apply if the spouses file a joint return with each other. (Code Sec. 71(e))[11] For a requirement that the spouses live apart, see ¶2156.

For who is a spouse, see ¶4705.

¶ 2154   Alimony requirements.

To qualify as alimony, a payment must be made in cash, under a divorce or separation instrument (¶2155). (Code Sec. 71(b)(1)) A transfer of property other than cash can't be alimony,[12] but cash payments can be designated as "nonalimony" (¶2160). There must be no requirement that payments continue beyond the death of the payee spouse (e.g., to the estate) or that any substitute payment (in cash or property) be made after the death of the payee spouse, i.e., the payments must end at the payee spouse's death. (Code Sec. 71(b)(1)(D)) If this rule isn't satisfied, *none* of the payments (even those made during the payee-spouse's life) are alimony. (Reg § 1.71-1T(b), Q&A-10) If it isn't clear from the divorce or separation agreement whether payments cease at the payee spouse's death, local law controls. A lump sum payment in lieu of future alimony payments makes the payments nondeductible.[13] See ¶2159 for the difference between alimony and child support payments.

¶ 2155   Payments must be under a divorce or separation instrument.

To be alimony, a payment must be made under a divorce or separation instrument (Code Sec. 71(b)(1)(A)), i.e., a (1) decree of divorce or separate maintenance or a written instrument issued incident to the decree, (2) written separation agreement, or (3) decree not described in (1) (e.g., a temporary support order). (Code Sec. 71(b)(2))[14] If made under a divorce or separate maintenance decree (or a written instrument incident to the decree), the payment must be made after the decree. (Reg § 1.71-1(b)(1)(i)) If made under a separation agreement, the payment must be made after execution of that agreement. (Reg § 1.71-1(b)(2))[15]

¶ 2156   Separate household requirement for alimony.

Spouses who are legally separated (but not divorced) under a divorce or separate maintenance decree must not live in the same household when the payment is made, or it won't be alimony (¶2154). (Code Sec. 71(b)(1)(C)) But if the spouses aren't legally separated, a payment under a written separation agreement or temporary support order may be alimony even if they are members of the same household. (Reg § 1.71-1T(b), Q&A 9)[16] The spouses aren't treated as members of the same household if one spouse is preparing to leave it, and does leave within one month after the payment.[17]

¶ 2157   "Alimony" payments to a third party.

Payments made in cash by the payor spouse to a third party on behalf of the payee spouse under the terms of the divorce or separation instrument can be alimony (¶2154). (Code Sec. 71(b)(1)(A)) Payments are on behalf of the payee spouse if they satisfy an obligation to that spouse. Thus, cash payments of the payee spouse's rent, mortgage, tax or tuition liabilities that the payor spouse makes as required by the instrument can qualify as alimony, as can payments made to a third party (e.g., a charity) at the payee spouse's written request, if the spouses intend them to be alimony.[18] But payments made to maintain property *owned by the payor spouse* but used by the payee spouse (including mortgage payments, realty taxes, and insurance premiums) *aren't* payments on behalf of the payee spouse (i.e., not alimony), even if made under the terms of the divorce or separation instrument. (Reg § 1.71-1T(b),

10. ¶A-2621, K-6002; ¶714.10, 2154 *et seq.*; TD ¶341,502, 560,720
11. ¶K-6001; ¶714.03; TD ¶341,501
12. ¶K-6005; ¶714.01; TD ¶341,505
13. ¶K-6036 *et seq.*; ¶714.01; TD ¶341,536 *et seq.*
14. ¶K-6013; ¶714.01; TD ¶341,513

15. ¶K-6018; ¶714.06; TD ¶341,518
16. ¶K-6035; ¶s 714.01, 714.06; TD ¶341,535
17. ¶K-6035; ¶714.01; TD ¶341,535
18. ¶K-6006; ¶714.01; TD ¶341,506

Q&A 8)[19] A payor spouse who is required by the divorce or separation instrument to pay the mortgage on a home he owns jointly with the payee spouse may deduct one-half of those payments as alimony, if they otherwise qualify (the rest may be deductible as qualified residence interest if paid on a qualified home, see ¶1730 *et seq.*).[20]

¶ 2158 Life insurance contracts as alimony.

Premiums that one spouse pays for insurance on his life as required by the divorce or separation instrument are alimony if the other (payee) spouse owns the policy.[21]

¶ 2159 Support payments for the payor's children aren't alimony.

A payment under a divorce or separation instrument that's "fixed" (or treated as fixed) as support for a child of the payor spouse *isn't* alimony. (Code Sec. 71(c)(1))[22] This applies if the instrument designates a specified amount of money or a part of a payment to be child support. The actual amount may fluctuate. (Reg § 1.71-1T(c), Q&A 16)[23] A part of a payment may be *treated* as fixed if the payment is to be reduced on the happening of a specified contingency relating to the child (Code Sec. 71(c)(2)), e.g., on the child's 18th birthday, or when he dies, marries or leaves school.[24] A payment may also be treated as fixed if it ends or is reduced at a time that can clearly be associated with the contingency. (Reg § 1.71-1T(c))[25] If a divorce or separation instrument provides specified amounts for alimony and child support, and the payor spouse pays the payee spouse less than the amount designated for child support, then the *entire* payment is child support; no part is alimony. (Code Sec. 71(c)(3))[26] However, if a fixed amount is paid for family support to a separated spouse, and there is no provision for reduction, e.g., when a child reaches a certain age or graduates from school, the entire amount may be treated as alimony.[27]

¶ 2160 Designating that payments aren't to be treated as alimony.

If a divorce or separation instrument designates a payment that would otherwise qualify as alimony as *not* to be treated as alimony (e.g., as a property settlement), the payment won't qualify as alimony. (Code Sec. 71(b)(1)(B); Reg § 1.71-1T, Q&A 8)[28]

¶ 2161 Alimony trusts.

A payor spouse can't deduct payments the payee spouse receives from an alimony trust which aren't includible in the payor's income under the Code Sec. 682 trust rules. (Code Sec. 215(d))[29] Under those rules, a wife who's divorced or legally separated, or separated under a written separation agreement, includes in her gross income her share of trust income that (without this rule) would be includible in her husband's income. This shifts the liability for tax on the income from the husband to the wife. But amounts payable for support of the husband's minor children are taxable to the husband. (Code Sec. 682(a))[30]

¶ 2162 Recapture rules—excess front-loading of alimony.

If there are "excess" alimony payments ("front-loading"), the payor spouse must "recapture" the "excess" by including it in his gross income for the third post-separation year (below) (Code Sec. 71(f)(1)(A)) (on Form 1040, line 11, cross out "received" and write "recapture").[31] The same amount is deducted by the payee spouse in computing adjusted gross income for *the payee's* third post-separation year (on Form 1040, line 31a; cross out "paid"

19. ¶K-6007; TD ¶341,507
20. ¶K-6008; TD ¶341,508
21. ¶K-6010; ¶714.01; TD ¶341,510
22. ¶K-6046; ¶714.02; TD ¶342,001
23. ¶K-6047; TD ¶342,002
24. ¶K-6049; ¶714.02; TD ¶342,004
25. ¶K-6049; ¶714.02; TD ¶342,004

26. ¶K-6048; ¶714.02; TD ¶342,003
27. ¶K-6047; TD ¶342,003
28. ¶K-6033; ¶714.01; TD ¶341,533
29. ¶K-6009; ¶2154.02; TD ¶341,509
30. ¶C-5432 *et seq.*; ¶6824; TD ¶657,039
31. ¶K-6043, K-6044; ¶714.03; TD ¶341,543, 341,544

and write "recapture"). (Code Sec. 71(f)(1)(B))[32] The "recapture" amount is the sum of:

(1) the excess of (a) the alimony or separate maintenance payments in the second post-separation year, over (b) the sum of the payments in the third year, plus $15,000; *plus*

(2) the excess of (a) the payments in the first post-separation year, over (b) the sum of the average of the payments in the second year (minus any excess payment in (1), above) and third year, plus $15,000. (Code Sec. 71(f))[33]

☑️*observation:* The payor spouse is, in effect, allowed to pay up to $15,000 of excess alimony in each of the first two post-separation years without recapturing the excess.

The first post-separation year is the first calendar year in which the payor spouse paid alimony, etc., to the payee spouse. The second and third post-separation years are the succeeding calendar years. (Code Sec. 71(f)(6))[34] There's no recapture if payments cease because either spouse dies or the payee spouse remarries before the close of the third post-separation year. Nor does recapture apply to temporary support payments or payments that fluctuate because of a continuing liability to pay, for at least three years, a fixed portion of income from business, property or services (including self-employment). (Code Sec. 71(f)(5))[35]

¶ 2163   "Nonbusiness" Expenses.

Individuals may deduct most ordinary and necessary expenses that, though not connected with their trade or business, are paid or incurred for the collection or production of income; the management, conservation or maintenance of property held for the production of income; or the determination, collection or refund of any tax.

But a *personal expense* or a *capital expenditure* for which deductions are barred can't be deducted as a nonbusiness expense. (Code Sec. 262(a), Code Sec. 263; Reg § 1.212-1(e))[36] For 2%-of-adjusted-gross-income floor on nonbusiness deductions, see ¶3110.

For nonbusiness expenses under the alternative minimum tax, see ¶3209.

¶ 2164   "Nonbusiness" (investment) expenses.

A taxpayer may deduct a wide variety of expenses related to his investments (not amounting to a business) if they are ordinary and necessary for the production or collection of income, or for the management, conservation or maintenance of property held for the production of income. (Code Sec. 212(1), Code Sec. 212(2))[37] Home office expenses allocable to "nonbusiness" investment activities aren't deductible (but this doesn't affect deductions for interest, taxes or casualty losses). (Code Sec. 280A)[38] Expenses of a convention, seminar, or similar meeting (e.g., day-trading courses) aren't deductible. (Code Sec. 274(h)(7))[39]

¶ 2165   Tax determination costs.

Individuals may deduct all the ordinary and necessary expenses incurred in connection with the determination, collection, or refund of any tax (for legal fees, see ¶2166). (Code Sec. 212(3)) This applies to income, estate, gift, property, and any other tax imposed by federal, state, municipal or foreign authorities. Included are the costs of: preparing tax returns, determining the extent of liability, contesting tax liability (including transferee liability[40]), getting tax counsel, protesting assessments, prosecuting refunds, compromising liability (Reg § 1.212-1(e)), a tax text used by an individual to prepare his own tax return,[41] tax advice[42] (including divorce and estate planning[43]), property appraisal to substantiate a

---

32. ¶K-6044; ¶714.03; TD ¶341,544
33. ¶K-6044; ¶714.03; TD ¶341,544
34. ¶K-6045; ¶714.03; TD ¶341,546
35. ¶K-6043; ¶714.03; TD ¶341,547
36. ¶s L-1400, L-1415, L-5601; ¶s 2124, 2624, 2634 ; TD ¶255,507, 256,201
37. ¶L-1401 *et seq.*; ¶2124 *et seq.*; TD ¶336,001
38. ¶L-1305; ¶280A4; TD ¶258,002
39. ¶L-1724; ¶s 2124.01, 2744.07; TD ¶291,021
40. ¶L-3015; TD ¶307,205
41. ¶L-3001 *et seq.*; ¶2124.14; TD ¶307,206
42. ¶L-3007; ¶2124.14; TD ¶307,210
43. ¶L-3010, L-3009; ¶2124.14; TD ¶307,208, 307,209

claimed deduction,[44] and contesting civil penalties, whether taxpayer is successful or not.[45]

¶ 2166 "Nonbusiness" legal expenses.

An individual may deduct nonbusiness legal fees, e.g., attorney's fees, court costs, etc., if incurred to produce income, preserve income-producing property, etc. (Reg § 1.212-1(k)),[46] as a miscellaneous itemized deduction (see ¶3110).[47] Nonbusiness legal expenses incurred to acquire, perfect, or defend title to property *aren't* deductible, unless allocable to collecting accrued rents on the property. (Reg § 1.212-1(k))[48] Legal expenses in connection with divorce, separation or a support decree are personal expenses that cannot be deducted by either spouse (Reg § 1.262-1(b)(7)),[49] *except that* (1) the part of legal fees attributable to the production or collection of taxable alimony is deductible by the payee spouse (Reg § 1.262-1),[50] and (2) taxpayer can deduct fees paid to his attorney for tax research and advice relating to a divorce and property settlement if the fee for the tax work is segregated, *but not* legal fees he pays to his spouse's attorney for tax advice given to the spouse.[1]

¶ 2167 Tax-exempt income expenses.

A taxpayer may not deduct costs incurred in the production of tax-exempt income (Code Sec. 265(a)(1))[2] (e.g., interest on indebtedness incurred or continued to buy or carry tax-exempt securities, see ¶1723). Expenses attributable to both taxable and tax-exempt income that can't be specifically identified must be prorated. (Reg § 1.265-1(c))[3]

¶ 2168 Premature withdrawal penalties.

An individual may deduct any interest or principal he forfeits to a bank or other financial institution as a penalty for premature withdrawal from a time savings account, certificate of deposit or similar deposit. The penalty is deductible from gross income in computing adjusted gross income (Code Sec. 62(a)(9)), see ¶3102.[4]

¶ 2169 Bond Premium Amortization.

Any premium on tax-exempt bonds must be amortized (Code Sec. 171(a)(2); Reg § 1.171-1(c)(1)), but premium on taxable bonds is amortized only if the holder so elects (see ¶2170). (Code Sec. 171(a)(1), Code Sec. 171(c); Reg § 1.171-1(c)(2)) The amortized amount reduces basis and, for taxable bonds, is treated as an offset to the interest received.[5]

"Bonds" include a bond, debenture, note, or certificate or other evidence of indebtedness. (Code Sec. 171(d); Reg § 1.171-1(b)) These rules don't apply to certain specified debt obligations. (Reg § 1.171-1(b)(2))[6] Bond premium generally arises when the stated interest rate on the bond is higher than its market yield when purchased. The premium is the excess of the holder's basis in the bond immediately after acquisition over the sum of all amounts payable on the bond after the acquisition date (other than payments of qualified stated interest, see ¶1315). (Reg § 1.171-1(d)(1))[7] Basis for this purpose is the holder's basis for determining loss on sale. (Code Sec. 171(b)(1)(A); Reg § 1.171-1(e)(1)(i))[8] If a convertible bond is purchased at a premium, any amount attributable to the conversion feature is excluded from amortizable bond premium. (Code Sec. 171(b)(1))[9] Regs provide special rules for variable rate debt instruments, inflation-indexed debt instruments, and bonds subject to contingencies. (Reg § 1.171-

---

44. ¶L-3005; TD ¶307,206
45. ¶L-3006; ¶2124.14; TD ¶307,206
46. ¶L-2902 *et seq.*; ¶2124.12; TD ¶305,005
47. ¶L-2903; ¶674
48. ¶L-2908 *et seq.*; ¶2124.12; TD ¶305,018
49. ¶L-2962; ¶s 2124.13, 2624; TD ¶305,064
50. ¶L-2965; ¶s 2124.13, 2624; TD ¶305,067
1. ¶L-3010; ¶2124.13; TD ¶307,208

2. ¶K-9000 *et seq.*; ¶2654; TD ¶653,017
3. ¶K-9002; ¶2654; TD ¶653,017
4. ¶A-2612; ¶624; TD ¶560,719
5. ¶K-5611; ¶s 1714.01, 10,164; TD ¶318,201
6. ¶K-5614; ¶1714.01; TD ¶318,204
7. ¶K-5616; ¶1714; TD ¶318,206
8. ¶K-5611; ¶1714.02; TD ¶318,201
9. ¶K-5622; ¶1714.035; TD ¶318,212

3)[10] For amortization of callable bonds, see ¶2171. For securities dealers, see ¶2173.

¶ 2170   Amortization deduction, basis reduction.

For *tax-exempt* bonds, no deduction is allowed for the amortizable bond premium for a tax year. (Code Sec. 171(a)(2))[11] The bond's basis is reduced by the amortizable bond premium barred as a deduction. (Code Sec. 1016(a)(5)); Reg § 1.1016-5(b)(3))[12] For *taxable* bonds, a taxpayer can elect (¶2172) to deduct amortizable bond premium (Code Sec. 171(a)(1)). The bond premium (computed under a constant-yield method based on yield to maturity (Code Sec. 171(b)(3)(A); Reg § 1.171-1(a)(1))) allocable to an accrual period is deducted as an offset to the qualified stated interest (¶1315) allocable to the period. (Code Sec. 171(e); Reg § 1.171-2(a)(1))[13] Basis is reduced by the offset amount. (Code Sec. 1016(a)(5))[14]

🅡 *observation:* If the holder of a taxable bond doesn't elect to amortize bond premium, the basis of the bond remains the original basis in the holder's hands for determining gain or loss on sale or redemption.

¶ 2171   Amortization of callable bonds.

The holder of a taxable bond generally amortizes bond premium by reference to the bond's stated maturity date (see ¶2170), even if the bond is likely to be called. (Code Sec. 171(b)(1)(B)(ii); Reg § 1.171-3(c)(4)(ii)(A), Reg § 1.171-3(e), Ex. 2)[15] The holder can deduct the unamortized bond premium of a called bond (excess of adjusted basis at start of the year over the greater of the amount (a) received on early redemption or (b) due on maturity). (Code Sec. 171(b)(2); Reg § 1.171-3(c)(5)(ii), Reg § 1.171-3(e), Ex. 2)[16]

¶ 2172   Election to amortize bond premium.

The election to amortize bond premium on taxable bonds (¶2169) is made by (a) offsetting interest income with bond premium in the holder's timely filed return for the first tax year to which the election applies, and (b) attaching an election statement to the return. (Code Sec. 171(c)(2); Reg § 1.171-4(a)(1)) IRS consent isn't needed. (Reg § 1.171-5(c)(1)) The election (unless revoked with IRS consent) is binding for the year made and later years, and applies to all taxable bonds (1) held by taxpayer at the beginning of the first tax year to which the election applies, and (2) those acquired after that year by taxpayer. (Code Sec. 171(c)(2); Reg § 1.171-4(b)) A holder who has elected to treat all interest on the bond as original issue discount (¶1314) is treated as having elected to amortize bond premium. (Reg § 1.171-4(a)(2))[17]

🅡 *recommendation:* The election provides a current interest income offset, which is preferable to a future capital loss deduction.

¶ 2173   Dealers in securities—bond premium amortization.

Taxable bonds that are stock in trade, held primarily for sale to customers, or includable in inventory if on hand at tax year-end aren't subject to the bond amortization rules (Code Sec. 171(d); Reg § 1.171-1(b)(2)(iv)), but tax-exempt bonds held primarily for sale to customers are. (Code Sec. 75(a))[18]

---

10. ¶K-5624 *et seq.*; ¶1714.036 *et seq.*; TD ¶318,214 *et seq.*
11. ¶K-5611; ¶1714; TD ¶318,201
12. ¶P-5043; ¶10,164; TD ¶216,026
13. ¶K-5611; ¶1714.03; TD ¶318,201
14. ¶P-5043; ¶10,164; TD ¶216,026
15. ¶K-5627; ¶1714.03; TD ¶318,217
16. ¶K-5628; ¶1714.03; TD ¶318,218
17. ¶K-5633; ¶1714.04; TD ¶318,223
18. ¶K-5651; ¶1714.01; ¶754; TD ¶318,251

Chapter 7   Education—Tax Credits, Exclusions, Deductions

¶ 2200   **Education—Tax Credits, Exclusions, Deductions.** ▬▬▬▬▬

There are a number of tax breaks designed specifically to help defray the costs of saving and paying for higher education, and one (the Coverdell education savings account, or CESA) that helps with pre-college costs as well.

There are three main categories of tax breaks for education:

(1) Tax credits, see ¶2201 *et seq.*,

(2) Exclusions, see ¶2205 *et seq.*, and

(3) Deductions, see ¶2222 *et seq.*

Other tax breaks. Pre-age-59½ distributions from traditional IRAs and Roth IRAs are excepted from the 10% premature distribution penalty tax to the extent they don't exceed qualified higher education expenses for the distribution year; see ¶4344 and ¶4357. Additionally, there's an unlimited gift-tax exclusion for gifts made on behalf of another individual directly to a qualifying educational organization; see ¶5047.

¶ 2201   **Tax Credits for Higher Education.** ▬▬▬▬▬

An individual taxpayer may claim an income tax credit for the American opportunity tax credit (AOTC; formerly called the Hope scholarship credit) in tax years beginning before 2018 (¶2202), and the Lifetime Learning credit (¶2203) for higher education expenses at accredited post-secondary educational institutions paid for themselves, their spouses, and their dependents. The AOTC is available for qualified expenses of the first four years of undergraduate education; and the Lifetime Learning credit is available for qualified expenses of any post-high school education at "eligible educational institutions." The AOTC can't be claimed along with the Lifetime Learning credit in the same tax year for expenses of any one student (see ¶2203), and the credits phase out for higher-income taxpayers (see ¶2202, ¶2203).

¶ 2202   **American opportunity tax credit (AOTC)—Form 8863.**

For tax years beginning before 2018, individuals may elect (on Form 8863, attached to an original or amended return filed by the limitations period for filing a claim for credit or refund for the year the credit is claimed) a personal, partially refundable AOTC equal to 100% of up to $2,000 of qualified higher education tuition and related expenses (¶2204) plus 25% of the next $2,000 of expenses paid for education furnished to an eligible student in an academic period. So, the maximum AOTC is $2,500 a year for *each* eligible student. (Code Sec. 25A(a)(1), Code Sec. 25A(i)(1))

For 2013 and 2014, the availability of the credit phases out ratably for taxpayers with modified AGI (MAGI, i.e., AGI increased by foreign, possessions, and Puerto Rico income exclusions) of $80,000 to $90,000 ($160,000 to $180,000 for joint filers). (Code Sec. 25A(i)(4))

Married taxpayers (¶4705) must file jointly to claim the credit. (Code Sec. 25A(g)(6)) The student's name and taxpayer identification number (TIN) must be included on the return of the taxpayer claiming the credit. (Code Sec. 25A(g)(1)) The AOTC (or Lifetime Learning credit, ¶2203) and tax-free Coverdell education savings account (CESA) distributions (¶2205) are allowed for the same student for the same year, as long as the credit isn't claimed for education expenses used to generate the tax-free CESA distribution. (Code Sec. 530(d)(2)(C)(i))

The AOTC may be elected for a student's expenses for four tax years, and only for students who haven't completed the first four years of post-secondary education as of the beginning of the tax year. (Code Sec. 25A(b)(2), Code Sec. 25A(i)(2); Reg § 1.25A-3(d)(1)(iii)) Additionally,

References beginning with a single letter are to paragraphs in RIA's Federal Tax Coordinator 2d and RIA's Analysis of Federal Taxes: Income. Those beginning with numbers are to paragraphs in RIA's United States Tax Reporter. Those beginning with TD are to paragraphs in RIA's Tax Desk.

313

for at least one academic period during the year, the student must be enrolled for at least half of the normal full-time workload for his course of study. (Code Sec. 25A(b)(3)(B); Reg § 1.25A-3(d)(1)(ii))

If a dependency deduction for an individual is allowed to another taxpayer, the dependent can't claim the AOTC, and qualified tuition and expenses paid by the dependent during the tax year are treated as paid by the taxpayer who is allowed the dependency deduction. (Code Sec. 25A(g)(3)) If a third party (not the taxpayer, spouse, or dependent) pays a student's qualified expenses directly to an educational institution, the student is treated as receiving the payment from the third party and, in turn, paying the expenses. If the student in such a case is claimed as a dependent on another's return, the expenses deemed to be paid by the student would be treated as expenses of the taxpayer claiming the student as a dependent. (Reg § 1.25A-5(a), Reg § 1.25A-5(b)) If a taxpayer is eligible to but doesn't claim a student as a dependent, only the student can claim the education credit for the student's qualified tuition and related expenses. (Reg § 1.25A-1(f))

> **observation:** It may pay for a parent not to claim the student as a dependent if (1) the parent can't claim education credits because of high modified AGI, and (2) the student pays or is deemed to pay the expense and has sufficient tax liability to claim the credit.

If qualified tuition and expenses are paid during one tax year for an academic period that begins during the first three months of the next tax year, the academic period is treated for AOTC purposes as beginning in the earlier year. (Code Sec. 25A(g)(4)) So, the credit is allowed only in the tax year in which the expenses are paid. (Reg § 1.25A-3(e)) Special rules apply for tuition refunds and excludable tuition assistance received after the tax year in which qualified tuition and related expenses are paid. (Reg § 1.25A-5(c), Reg § 1.25A-5(f)) An AOTC isn't allowed for a student convicted (as of the end of the tax year for which the credit is claimed) of a felony offense for possessing or distributing a controlled substance, or by a nonresident alien for any part of the tax year (unless treated as a resident alien under a Code Sec. 6013(g) or Code Sec. 6013(h) election). (Code Sec. 25A(b)(2)(D), Code Sec. 25A(g)(7))[1]

Subject to an exception, 40% of a taxpayer's otherwise allowable AOTC is refundable. No portion of the credit is refundable if the taxpayer claiming the credit is a child subject to the kiddie tax under Code Sec. 1(g) or a resident of a U.S. possessions (who instead claim the credit where they reside). (Code Sec. 25A(i)(5))

¶ 2203 Lifetime Learning credit—Form 8863.

Taxpayers may elect (on Form 8863) a Lifetime Learning credit equal to 20% of up to $10,000 of qualified tuition and related expenses paid (defined at ¶2204) during the tax year. The maximum credit is $2,000. (Code Sec. 25A(a)(2), Code Sec. 25A(c)(1))

Unlike the American opportunity tax credit (AOTC, ¶2202), which is available for the qualifying expenses of each qualifying student, the Lifetime Learning credit is available only per taxpayer. So, for example, a joint filing couple with two children could claim no more than a $2,000 Lifetime Learning credit, even if each family member is a qualifying student with qualifying expenses. For 2013, the credit is phased out ratably for taxpayers with modified AGI (MAGI) from $53,000 to $63,000 ($107,000 to $127,000 for marrieds filing jointly (¶4705)). For 2014, the credit is phased out ratably for taxpayers with MAGI from $54,000 to $64,000 ($108,000 to $129,000 for marrieds filing jointly).

The same treatment of expenses paid by dependent, adjustment for tax-free scholarships, etc., treatment of certain prepayments, denial of double benefit, denial of credit to marrieds not filing jointly, and nonresident alien bar that apply for AOTC purposes (¶2202) also apply to the Lifetime Learning credit. (Code Sec. 25A(d), Code Sec. 25A(e), Code Sec. 25A(f), Code Sec. 25A(g), Code Sec. 25A(h))

---

1. ¶A-4500 *et seq.*; ¶25A4; TD ¶568,923

Expenses for a student for whom an AOTC (¶2202) is allowed for the tax year don't qualify for the Lifetime Learning credit. (Code Sec. 25A(c)(2))[2]

¶ 2204 Qualified tuition and related expenses for education credit purposes.

"Qualified tuition and related expenses" for American opportunity tax credit (AOTC, ¶2202) and Lifetime Learning credit (¶2203) purposes means tuition and fees required for the enrollment or attendance of the taxpayer, his spouse, or tax dependent, at a post-secondary educational institution eligible to participate in the federal student loan program. For the AOTC, in tax years beginning before 2018, it also includes course materials.[3]

Room and board, insurance, transportation, or other similar personal, living, or family expenses don't qualify for the AOTC or Lifetime Learning credit, whether or not paid to an educational institution. Student activity fees and fees for course-related books, supplies, and equipment qualify for the AOTC, or Lifetime Learning credit only if they must be paid directly to the educational institution as a requirement for the enrollment or attendance of the student.(Code Sec. 25A(f); Reg § 1.25A-2(d)(2), Reg § 1.25A-2(d)(3))

The cost of any course of instruction at an eligible institution taken to acquire or improve job skills qualifies for the Lifetime Learning credit, but not the AOTC, even if it involves sports, games, hobbies, or is a noncredit course. (Code Sec. 25A(c)(2)(B); Reg § 1.25A-2(d)(5))

Qualified tuition and related expenses must be reduced by scholarship amounts excludable from income under Code Sec. 117 (¶2216), educational assistance under chapter 30 through 35 of title 38 U.S. Code or under chapter 1606 of title 10 U.S. Code, and other tax-free payments. But, qualified amounts aren't reduced by amounts paid by gift, bequest, devise, or inheritance. (Code Sec. 25A(g)(2)) No credit is allowed for any expense for which an income tax deduction is allowed. (Code Sec. 25A(g)(5)) Special rules apply for tuition refunds and excludable tuition assistance received after the tax year in which qualified tuition and related expenses are paid. (Reg § 1.25A-2(d)(2))

¶ 2205 Coverdell Education Savings Accounts (CESAs). ▬▬▬▬

Taxpayers can contribute up to $2,000 per year to Coverdell Education Savings Accounts (CESAs, formerly called education IRAs), for beneficiaries under age 18 and special needs beneficiaries of any age. The account is exempt from income tax, and distributions of earnings from CESAs are tax-free if used for qualified education expenses.

¶ 2206 Coverdell Education Savings Accounts (CESAs)—Forms 5305-E and 5305-EA.

A CESA is a trust (Form 5305-E) or custodial account (Form 5305-EA) created exclusively for the purpose of paying an individual beneficiary's qualified education expenses. (Code Sec. 530(b)(1), Code Sec. 530(g)) These accounts are exempt from tax except for the unrelated business income tax. (Code Sec. 530(a)) Allowable annual contributions to CESAs (¶2207) aren't deductible and aren't taxable when withdrawn, but distributions of earnings from CESAs for qualified education expenses are tax-free (¶2208).

CESAs can't invest in life insurance contracts, and, except for common trust or investment funds, trust assets can't be commingled. The account balance must be distributed to the beneficiary within 30 days after he turns age 30 (unless he has special needs), or, if sooner, to the beneficiary's estate within 30 days after the beneficiary's death (Code Sec. 530(b)(1), Code Sec. 530(d)(8)),[4] unless transferred to a family member's CESA (¶2208).

2. ¶A-4500 *et seq.*; ¶25A4; TD ¶568,933
3. ¶A-4474 *et seq.*; ¶25A4.07; TD ¶568,937
4. ¶A-4615; ¶5304; TD ¶147,215

¶ 2207   Contributions to Coverdell Education Savings Accounts (CESAs).

Annual contributions to CESAs for any beneficiary can't exceed $2,000, must be made in cash, and can't be made after the beneficiary turns age 18 (unless the beneficiary has special needs). (Code Sec. 530(b)(1)(A)) CESA contributions for a year may be made as late as the unextended tax return due date for that year. (Code Sec. 530(b)(4))[5]

If the contributor is an individual, the $2,000 limit phases out ratably between $95,000 and $110,000 ($190,000 and $220,000 for joint filers) of modified AGI (MAGI, i.e., AGI plus income excluded under Code Sec. 911, Code Sec. 931, and Code Sec. 933). (Code Sec. 530(c))[6]

observation: A corporation, without regard to any MAGI limits, may contribute to a CESA that has an employee's child as beneficiary. The contribution would, however, be taxed to the employee.

An individual who has received a military death gratuity or Servicemembers' Group Life Insurance (SGLI) payment can roll it over (contribute it) to one or more CESAs, without regard to the above annual contribution limit (Code Sec. 530(d)(9)(A)) or the AGI phase-out limit. The contribution must be made before the end of the one-year period beginning on the date on which the contributor received the payment. (Code Sec. 530(d)(9)(A)) The rule allowing only one rollover contribution to a CESA during any 12-month period (¶2208) doesn't apply to this rollover. (Code Sec. 530(d)(9)(B))[7]

Excess contributions are subject to a 6% excise tax in the contribution year and each year that an excess amount is in the account (report on Form 5329, Part V). But, the excise tax doesn't apply to rollover contributions, or contributions (with net earnings attributable to the excess contributions) returned before June 1 of the year following the contribution year. (Code Sec. 4973(e))[8]

For the gift tax treatment of CESAs, see ¶5047.

¶ 2208   Distributions from Coverdell Education Savings Accounts (CESAs).

A distribution from a CESA is included in the gross income of the distributee generally as provided under the annuity rules of Code Sec. 72. (Code Sec. 530(d)(1)) So, distributions consist of a pro-rata share of principal (recovered tax-free) and accumulated earnings (which *may* be excludable under the CESA rules). Distributions from a CESA are entirely excluded if qualified education expenses of the beneficiary equal or exceed total CESA distributions for the year. (Code Sec. 530(d)(2)(A))

Qualified education expenses include:

. . . higher education tuition, fees, books, and supplies, and, for half-time or greater students, certain room and board charges (Code Sec. 530(b)(2)(A));

. . . elementary and secondary (K through 12) public, private or religious school tuition and expenses, including tutoring, room and board, transportation, uniforms, and extended day programs (Code Sec. 530(b)(3)(B));

. . . special needs services for special needs beneficiaries enrolled in any of the above types of schools (Code Sec. 530(b)(2)(A), Code Sec. 530(b)(3)(B)); and

. . . contributions to a qualified tuition program (QTP, see ¶2209) on behalf of a designated beneficiary, (Code Sec. 530(b)(2)(B))[9] but in applying the Code Sec. 72 annuity rules to a CESA distribution that's contributed to a qualified tuition program (¶2210) for a designated beneficiary, any part of the contribution which isn't includible in gross income (because it doesn't exceed the beneficiary's qualified education expenses) won't result in an

---

5. ¶A-4606; ¶5304
6. ¶A-4604; ¶5304; TD ¶147,204
7. ¶A-4619.1; ¶5304.01; TD ¶147,219.1

8. ¶A-4607; ¶49,734; TD ¶147,207
9. ¶A-4610; ¶5304; TD ¶147,210

increase in the investment in the contract (Code Sec. 530(b)(2)(B)).

Qualified education expenses are reduced by the same tax-free scholarships and similar payments that reduce qualified tuition and related expenses for education credit purposes (¶2204) (Code Sec. 530(d)(2)(C)(i)(I)), and by the expenses taken into account in determining the education credit (¶2201).[10]

Distributions aren't taxed if rolled over within 60 days (but not more than once in a 12-month period) into a CESA for the same beneficiary or a member of the beneficiary's family (as defined at ¶2212) who is under age 30. (Code Sec. 530(d)(5), Code Sec. 530(d)(6))[11] A CESA transfer to a beneficiary's family member under a divorce decree or after the beneficiary's death also isn't taxable. (Code Sec. 530(d)(7))

If CESA distributions exceed qualified tuition expenses in a year, the excludable part of the distributions is the earnings portion of the distributions times a fraction having as its numerator the year's qualified education expenses and as its denominator the year's total distributions. (Code Sec. 530(d)(2)(B))[12] The balance of the earnings portion of the distribution is taxable. Any savings bond redemption proceeds transferred to a CESA in a tax-free transfer under Code Sec. 135 (see ¶2221) do *not* increase the investment in the contract in applying the Code Sec. 72 rules to the taxation of CESA distributions. (Code Sec. 135(c)(2)(C))

Any taxable amount also is subject to a 10% additional tax, but not: (1) if made on or after the beneficiary's death or disability, (2) to the extent the taxable amount doesn't exceed (a) the amount of a tax-free scholarship received by the beneficiary, or (b) the "advanced education costs" received by the beneficiary at a U.S. service academy (e.g., U.S. Military Academy), (3) if the distribution is taxable solely because of the rule (explained above) reducing the total amount of qualified education expenses by the expenses taken into account in determining the education credit for the year, or (4) if the tax is attributable to income on a contribution withdrawn (along with associated income) before June 1 of the year following the contribution year. (Code Sec. 530(d)(4))[13]

If aggregate distributions from CESAs and qualified tuition programs (¶2209) in a year exceed an individual's qualified education expenses, the expenses must be allocated among the distributions. (Code Sec. 530(d)(2)(C)) No deduction, credit, or exclusion is allowed under any other Code provision for an education expense taken into account in determining the CESA exclusion. (Code Sec. 530(d)(2)(C))[14]

¶ 2209 Qualified Tuition Programs (QTPs)—529 Plans. ▬▬▬▬

Distributions from a QTP (also known as a 529 plan) are excludable to the extent used to pay for qualified higher education expenses.

¶ 2210 Qualified tuition programs (QTPs).

A person can make nondeductible cash contributions to a QTP on behalf of a designated beneficiary. The earnings on the contributions build up tax-free and distributions from a QTP are excludable to the extent used to pay for qualified higher education expenses. A QTP is a tax-exempt program established and maintained by a state (including a state agency or instrumentality), or one or more eligible educational institutions (including private ones) under which a taxpayer may:

(1) buy tuition credits or certificates on behalf of a designated beneficiary (¶2212) which entitle the beneficiary to a waiver or payment of qualified higher education expenses (¶2211)—i.e., a prepaid educational services account, or

(2) make contributions to an account set up to meet the designated beneficiary's qualified

10. ¶A-4612; ¶5304; TD ¶147,212
11. ¶A-4619; ¶5304; TD ¶147,219
12. ¶A-4609; ¶5304; TD ¶147,209
13. ¶A-4618
14. ¶A-4609 *et seq.*; ¶5304 *et seq.*; TD ¶147,214

higher education expenses—i.e., an educational savings account. This option is available only for state (or state agency or instrumentality) programs. (Code Sec. 529(b)(1)(A); Prop Reg. § 1.529-2(c) ["Taxpayer may rely,"] [15]

observation: Prepaid educational services accounts allow credits or certificates to be purchased at the current tuition rate, even though they won't be used for some time.

A QTP must require all purchases or contributions to be made in cash (there's no dollar limit on contributions), provide separate accounting for each designated beneficiary, prohibit the contributor and designated beneficiary from directing, indirectly or directly, the investment of contributions or earnings (but a change in investment strategy is allowed once per calendar year), prohibit pledging an interest in the program as security, and provide adequate safeguards to prevent contributions in excess of amounts necessary for the beneficiary's qualified higher education expenses. (Code Sec. 529(b))[16] A QTP maintained by a private educational institution generally must get a ruling that it meets applicable requirements. (Code Sec. 529(b)(1))[17]

For the gift-tax treatment of contributions to a QTP, see ¶5047.

¶ 2211   Tax treatment of distributions from qualified tuition programs (QTPs).

Distributions from a QTP are includible in the distributee's income under the Code Sec. 72 annuity rules, to the extent not excluded under any other Code provision. (Code Sec. 529(c)(3)(A))[18]

In-kind distributions (e.g., tuition credits or waivers, payment vouchers) from state-sponsored QTPs aren't includible in gross income if the benefit, if paid for by the distributee, would have been a payment of a qualified higher education expense. (Code Sec. 529(c)(3)(B); Prop Reg. § 1.529-1(c), ["Taxpayer may rely,"]) [19]

Cash distributions are fully excludable if they don't exceed qualified higher education expenses, reduced by expenses for which in-kind distributions were received. If cash distributions exceed qualified expenses, the amount otherwise includible under the Code Sec. 72 annuity rules is reduced by the ratio of qualified expenses to distributions. (Code Sec. 529(c)(3)(B)(ii))[20]

Qualified higher education expenses for QTP purposes are: (1) tuition, fees, books, supplies, equipment required for the enrollment or attendance of a designated beneficiary (¶2212) at an eligible educational institution, and expenses for special needs services; and (2) room and board costs (subject to a limit) for students who are at least half-time. (Code Sec. 529(e)(3))[21]

For QTP exclusion purposes, total annual qualified higher education expenses are reduced by excludable scholarships or educational assistance received, and by any qualified higher education expenses taken into account in determining the American opportunity tax credit and Lifetime Learning credit (¶2201 *et seq.*) allowed to the taxpayer or any other person. (Code Sec. 529(c)(3)(B)(v))[22]

Distributions from a QTP aren't taxed if transferred (rolled over) within 60 days (but not more than once in 12 months) to another QTP for the same designated beneficiary or to a QTP for a member of the designated beneficiary's family (¶2212). (Code Sec. 529(c)(3)(C)(iii))[23] A change in the designated beneficiary isn't a distribution if the new beneficiary is a member of the old beneficiary's family; see ¶2212. (Code Sec. 529(c)(3)(C)(ii))[24]

A 10% additional tax applies to QTP distributions includible in gross income, in the same

15. ¶A-4727; ¶5294; TD ¶672,302
16. ¶A-4727; ¶5294; TD ¶672,302
17. ¶A-4729; ¶5294; TD ¶672,302
18. ¶A-4709 *et seq.*; ¶5294.02; TD ¶147,101 *et seq.*
19. ¶A-4709; ¶5294.02; TD ¶147,101

20. ¶A-4709; ¶5294.02; TD ¶147,101
21. ¶A-4711; ¶5294; TD ¶672,310
22. ¶A-4709; ¶5294.02; TD ¶147,101
23. ¶A-4721; ¶5294.02; TD ¶147,105
24. ¶A-4722; ¶5294.02; TD ¶147,107

way, and with the same exceptions, as for Coverdell education savings account (CESA) distributions (see ¶2208). (Code Sec. 529(c)(6))[25]

If total distributions from a QTP and from a CESA (see ¶2205 *et seq.*) exceed qualified higher education expenses otherwise taken into account under the QTP rules (after the above reductions), the taxpayer must allocate the expenses among the distributions for purposes of determining the QTP exclusion. (Code Sec. 529(c)(3)(B)(vi))[26]

¶ 2212 Designated beneficiary of a qualified tuition program (QTP).

The designated beneficiary of a QTP (¶2210) is:

(1) the individual so designated at the start of participation in the QTP; (Code Sec. 529(e)(1)(A))

(2) where beneficiaries are changed and the new one is a member of the same family (spouses, individuals meeting the relationship tests at ¶3119, spouses of these individuals, and first cousins of the beneficiary), the individual who is the new beneficiary; and (Code Sec. 529(e)(1)(B), Code Sec. 529(e)(2))

(3) in the case of an interest in a QTP purchased by a state or eligible educational institution as part of a scholarship program it operates, the individual receiving the interest as a scholarship. (Code Sec. 529(e)(1)(C))[27]

¶ 2213 Employer-Provided Educational Benefits; Scholarships and Fellowships. ▰▰▰

An employee may exclude the value of educational benefits provided by an employer if the benefit qualifies as a working condition fringe or is provided under an educational assistance program. Qualified tuition reductions for employees of educational institutions and qualifying scholarships and fellowships also are excludable.

¶ 2214 When education benefits are excluded as working condition fringes.

Employer-provided educational expenses are excludable from an employee's income as a working condition fringe benefit to the extent that if the employee paid for the benefit, the amount paid could have qualified as a deductible employee business expense. For the criteria that apply in determining if education is a deductible employee business expense, see ¶2226. (Reg § 1.132-1(f), Reg § 1.132-5(a)(2))[28] No business expense deduction is allowed for expenses incurred to meet minimum job qualifications, or qualify for a new trade or business.

¶ 2215 Exclusion for employer-provided educational assistance under a qualified program.

An employee may exclude educational assistance provided under an employer's qualified educational assistance program, up to an annual maximum of $5,250. (Code Sec. 127(a)(1)) The education received need not be job-related. (Code Sec. 127(a)(2))

Expenses paid by an employer for education or training provided to the employee that aren't excludable under this provision can only be excluded from income if they qualify as a working condition fringe benefit (¶2214). (Code Sec. 132(j)(8))

"Educational assistance" means the employer's payment for or provision of tuition, fees, books, supplies and equipment under an educational assistance program, including amounts for graduate-level courses. It doesn't include meals, lodging, transportation, or tools or supplies (other than textbooks) that may be retained after the course ends. (Code Sec. 127(c)(1); Reg § 1.127-2(c)(3))[29]

---

25. ¶A-4720; ¶5294.02; TD ¶147,109
26. ¶A-4716; ¶5294.02; TD ¶147,101
27. ¶A-4701; ¶5294; TD ¶672,309

28. ¶H-2052; ¶1324.05; TD ¶136,516
29. ¶H-2065; ¶1274.01; TD ¶136,525

Eligibility requirements can't discriminate in favor of "highly compensated employees" (see ¶4326). (Code Sec. 127(b)(2); Reg § 1.127-2(e)(1))[30] No deduction or credit can be taken by the employee for any amount excluded from income. (Code Sec. 127(c)(7))[31]

¶ 2216   Exclusion for qualifying scholarships and fellowships.

A scholarship or fellowship isn't taxable, to the extent it's a "qualified scholarship" granted to a degree candidate at an educational organization and isn't a stipend (¶2218). (Code Sec. 117(a), Code Sec. 117(c))[32] A "qualified scholarship" is any amount received as a scholarship and used for tuition and fees required for enrollment at an educational organization, and for required fees, books, supplies and equipment. (Code Sec. 117(b)(2))[33] An "educational organization" is one that normally maintains a regular faculty, curriculum and regularly enrolled student body in attendance. (Code Sec. 117(b)(2)(A))[34]

¶ 2217   Exclusion for qualified tuition reductions for school employees.

Qualified tuition reductions for employees of educational institutions are excluded from the recipient's gross income. (Code Sec. 117(d)) A "qualified tuition reduction" is the amount of tuition reduction provided to an employee of an educational organization for below-graduate-level education (not services, see ¶2218) at that or a similar institution, for the employee (whether active, retired, or disabled), or the employee's spouse or dependent children. (Code Sec. 117(d)(2)) But, a tuition reduction for a graduate student engaged in teaching or research can be tax-free. (Code Sec. 117(d)(5))[35]

A qualified tuition reduction provided with respect to a highly compensated employee (¶4326) is excludable only if it's available to all employees on a nondiscriminatory basis. (Code Sec. 117(d)(3))[36]

¶ 2218   Payments for teaching or research.

The exclusions for qualified scholarships (¶2216) and qualified tuition reductions (¶2217) don't apply to any amount received that represents payment for teaching, research or other services performed by the student as a condition for receiving the qualified benefit. (Code Sec. 117(c)(1))[37] This no-payment-for-services rule doesn't apply to amounts received under certain health professions scholarship programs (i.e., the National Health Service Corps (NHSC) Scholarship Program and the Armed Forces Health Professions Scholarship and Financial Assistance Program). (Code Sec. 117(c)(2)).[38]

¶ 2219   Higher Education Exclusion for Savings Bond Income.

Qualified U.S. savings bond income is excluded if redemption proceeds don't exceed qualified higher education expenses. The exclusion phases out at higher levels of modified adjusted gross income.

¶ 2220   Exclusion of savings bond income—Form 8815.

An individual who pays qualified higher education expenses (¶2221) during a tax year excludes from that year's gross income any amount of income from the redemption, that year, of any "qualified U.S. savings bond" (Series EE bond issued after '89, or Series I bond). (Code Sec. 135(a), Code Sec. 135(c)(1))[39] Use Form 8815 to compute the exclusion. Form 8818 (one per bond) may be used to keep a record of the redemptions.[40]

---

30. ¶H-2069; ¶1274.01; TD ¶136,526
31. ¶H-2064; ¶1274.01; TD ¶136,525
32. ¶J-1230; ¶1174.01; TD ¶193,501
33. ¶J-1232; ¶1174.01; TD ¶193,502
34. ¶J-1244; ¶1174.01; TD ¶193,507
35. ¶J-1252 *et seq.*; ¶1174.02; TD ¶193,512

36. ¶J-1255; ¶1174.02; TD ¶193,514
37. ¶J-1258; ¶1174.01; TD ¶193,517
38. ¶J-1258.1; ¶1174.05; TD ¶193,517
39. ¶J-3051; ¶1354 *et seq.*; TD ¶157,001
40. ¶J-3051; ¶1354.02; TD ¶157,001

If taxpayer's aggregate redemption proceeds (principal plus interest) for a tax year exceed the qualified higher education expenses paid that year, the excluded interest is limited to the otherwise excludable amount times this fraction: the qualified expenses paid that year, divided by the year's aggregate redemption proceeds. (Code Sec. 135(b)(1))[41]

Illustration: Taxpayer redeems $8,000 of qualified U.S. savings bonds ($4,000 interest, $4000 principal) and pays qualified higher education expenses of $6,000. The exclusion ratio is 75% ($6,000 ÷ $8,000), so $3,000 of the interest (75% × $4,000) (and the $4,000 principal) is excludable.[42]

The individual must have bought the bond(s) after having reached age 24 (Code Sec. 135(c)(1)(B)) and must be the sole owner (or joint owner with his spouse). The exclusion isn't available to the owner of a bond that was bought by another individual (other than a spouse). Nor is it available to a parent who buys the bonds and puts them in the name of a child or other dependent. But the owner may designate an individual (including a child) as the beneficiary for amounts payable at death without losing the exclusion.[43] A married individual (¶4705) must file a joint return to get the exclusion. (Code Sec. 135(d)(2))[44]

For 2013, the exclusion phases out for a taxpayer whose modified adjusted gross income (modified AGI, see below) for the year exceeds $74,700 ($112,050 on a joint return). For 2014, the phaseout amount is $76,000 ($113,950 on a joint return). The amount of the reduction in the exclusion (but not below zero) equals the amount otherwise excludable (*but for* this phaseout) times this fraction: the excess of modified AGI over the appropriate phaseout amount, divided by $15,000 ($30,000 for a joint return). (Code Sec. 135(b)(2)) So, the exclusion isn't available in 2013 when modified AGI reaches $89,700, or $142,050 for a joint return ($91,000, or $143,950 for a joint return for 2014).[45]

The exclusion generally applies only if the owner redeems the bonds, i.e., not if he transfers them to the educational institution (see ¶2221 for exceptions).[46]

Modified AGI is AGI determined without the Code Sec. 221 deduction for interest on a qualified education loan (¶2222), the Code Sec. 222 deduction for higher education expenses, the Code Sec. 199 U.S. production activities deduction (¶1614), the savings bond interest exclusion, itself, or the Code Sec. 911, Code Sec. 931, and Code Sec. 933 exclusions for income earned abroad or the Code Sec. 137 exclusion for employer-provided adoption assistance (¶1254). (Code Sec. 135(c)(4))[47]

¶ 2221   Qualified higher education expenses for savings bond exclusion.

For purposes of the savings bond exclusion (¶2220), qualified higher education expenses are tuition and fees required for the enrollment or attendance of taxpayer, taxpayer's spouse or any dependent for whom taxpayer is allowed a dependency exemption (¶3119) at an eligible educational institution, (Code Sec. 135(c)(2)(A)) e.g., most colleges, junior colleges, nursing schools and vocational schools. (Code Sec. 135(c)(3)) Expenses for any course or other education involving sports, games or hobbies, other than as part of a degree program, don't count. (Code Sec. 135(c)(2)(B))[48] The transfer of redemption proceeds to a qualified tuition program (QTP, ¶2209) or to a Coverdell education savings account (CESA, see ¶2207) for the taxpayer (or his spouse or dependent) also is a qualified higher education expense. (Code Sec. 135(c)(2)(C))[49]

Expenses otherwise taken into account must be reduced by amounts received for excludable qualified scholarships (¶2216), certain educational assistance allowances and other tax-exempt payments (other than gifts, bequests, devises or inheritances), and a payment, waiver, or reimbursement of qualified higher education expenses under a qualified tuition program.

41. ¶J-3052; ¶1354.02; TD ¶157,002
42. ¶J-3052; ¶1354.02; TD ¶157,002
43. ¶s J-3055, J-3056; ¶1354.01; TD ¶s 157,005, 157,006
44. ¶J-3051; ¶1354; TD ¶157,001
45. ¶J-3053; ¶1354.03; TD ¶157,003

46. ¶J-3051; ¶1354.02; TD ¶157,001
47. ¶J-3054; ¶1354.03; TD ¶157,004
48. ¶s J-3057, J-3061; ¶1354.02; TD ¶s 157,007, 157,011
49. ¶J-3059; ¶1354; TD ¶157,009

(Code Sec. 135(d)(1))[50] The amount of qualified higher education expenses also must be reduced by the amount of such expenses taken into account in figuring the exclusions for distributions from CESA (¶2214) and qualified tuition programs (¶2209), and by expenses taken into account in determining the education credits (¶2201) allowed to the taxpayer or any other person with respect to those expenses. This reduction is made before applying the rules reducing the excluded amount where redemption proceeds exceed higher education expenses and where taxpayer's modified AGI exceeds specified dollar amounts) (see ¶2220). (Code Sec. 135(d)(2))[1]

¶ 2222   Deduction for Interest Paid on Qualified Education Loans. ▬▬▬

Qualifying individuals may claim an above-the-line deduction for up to $2,500 of interest paid on a qualified higher education loan.

¶ 2223   Up to $2,500 of qualified education loan interest deductible above-the-line.

Student loan interest generally is treated as personal interest and thus isn't deductible. But, individuals may deduct a maximum of $2,500 annually for interest paid on qualified higher education loans. (Code Sec. 221)[2]

The deduction is claimed as an adjustment to gross income to arrive at adjusted gross income. (Code Sec. 62(a)(17))[3] There's no deduction for any amount for which a deduction is allowable under any other Code provision (e.g., home equity loan; see ¶1734). (Code Sec. 221(e)(1))[4]

For 2013, the deduction phases out ratably for taxpayers with modified AGI between $60,000 and $75,000 ($125,000 and $155,000 for joint returns). For 2014, the deduction phases out ratably for taxpayers with modified AGI between $65,000 and $80,000 ($130,000 and $160,000 for joint returns). (Code Sec. 221(b)(2)(B)) Modified AGI is AGI figured without regard to the deduction for qualified education loan interest, the deduction for qualified higher education expenses, the Code Sec. 199 U.S. production activities deduction (¶1614), and without regard to the exclusions for foreign, possession, and Puerto Rico income. (Code Sec. 221(b)(2)(C)(i))[5]

A person who is claimed as a dependent on another's return can't claim the education interest deduction. (Code Sec. 221(c))[6] The deduction may be claimed only by a person legally obligated to make the interest payments. (Reg § 1.221-1(b))[7] Married couples (¶4705) must file joint returns to take the deduction. (Code Sec. 221(e)(3))[8]

For information reporting requirements for interest payments received on qualified education loans, see ¶4746.

¶ 2224   Qualified education loan defined.

A qualified higher education loan is any debt incurred by the taxpayer solely to pay qualified higher education expenses that are: (1) incurred on behalf of the taxpayer, the taxpayer's spouse, or any dependent of the taxpayer as of the time the debt was incurred; (2) paid or incurred within a reasonable period of time before or after the debt is incurred; and (3) attributable to education furnished during a period when the recipient was an eligible student (as defined for the American opportunity tax credit purposes, i.e., at least a half-time student, see ¶2202). (Code Sec. 221(d)(1))

Revolving lines of credit generally aren't qualified education loans unless the borrower agreed to use the line of credit to pay only qualifying higher education expenses. A qualified

50. ¶J-3060; ¶1354.02; TD ¶157,010
1. ¶J-3060; ¶1354; TD ¶157,010
2. ¶K-5500 *et seq.*; ¶2214; TD ¶314,100 *et seq.*
3. ¶K-5501; ¶2214
4. ¶K-5503.2; ¶2214.02; TD ¶314,109

5. ¶K-5502; ¶2214.01; TD ¶314,106
6. ¶K-5503
7. ¶K-5501.1
8. ¶K-5501

education loan includes debt used to refinance debt that qualifies as a qualified education loan, but doesn't include certain debt owed to a related person or a loan under a qualified employer plan. (Code Sec. 221(e)(1))[9]

Qualified higher education expenses include tuition, fees, room and board, and related expenses, but must be reduced by the amount excluded by reason of such expenses under the rules for: employer-provided educational assistance benefits (¶2215), income from U.S. Savings Bonds used to pay higher education expenses (¶2219), Coverdell education savings accounts (CESAs) (¶2205), qualified tuition plans (¶2209), and scholarship or fellowship grants (¶2216). (Code Sec. 221(d)(2)) They also must be reduced by veterans' and armed forces' educational assistance allowances and any other educational assistance excludable from the student's gross income (other than as a gift, bequest, devise or inheritance). (Reg § 1.221-1(e)(2)(ii))[10]

¶ 2225 Education Expenses Related to Business or Employment. ▐▬▬▬▬▬▬▬▬▬▬▬▬

A taxpayer can deduct costs incurred to maintain or improve skills required in his business or employment, but not costs incurred to meet minimum requirements for a trade or profession or to qualify for a new trade or profession.

¶ 2226 When business- or employment-related expenses are deductible.

Education expenses are deductible if made by a taxpayer either to maintain or improve skills required in his business or employment or to meet the express requirements of his employer, or the requirements of law or regs, imposed as a condition to retaining his salary, status or employment. (Reg § 1.162-5)[11]

A lawyer who has actually practiced law may generally deduct the expenses of any further legal education on the grounds that it maintains or improves required skills even though the education qualifies him to practice as a specialist.[12] A non-lawyer employed in allied fields where a legal education is helpful or customary can't deduct legal education costs. (Reg § 1.162-5(b)(3))[13]

Deductions aren't allowed if the education:

. . . is needed to meet the minimum requirements for taxpayer's present or intended employment, trade, business or profession (Reg § 1.162-5(b)(2))[14] or

. . . is undertaken to fulfill general education aspirations or for other personal reasons,[15] or

. . . is part of a program of study that will lead to qualifying the individual in a new trade or business. (Reg § 1.162-5(b)(3)(i))[16]

Expenses that are otherwise deductible won't be disallowed because the course of studies leads to a degree. (Reg § 1.162-5(a))[17]

Self-employed taxpayers claim education deductions on Schedule C, C-EZ, or F of Form 1040; employees claim unreimbursed education expenses as miscellaneous itemized deductions on Schedule A, Form 1040.

¶ 2227 Travel and transportation expenses of education.

The expenses of travel as a form of education aren't deductible. (Code Sec. 274(m)(2))[18] But, travel expenses that are a necessary adjunct to other deductible education expenses may be deductible.[19]

---

9. ¶K-5504; ¶2214.02; TD ¶314,110
10. ¶K-5504.3
11. ¶L-3701; ¶1624.185; TD ¶302,001
12. ¶s L-3724, L-3722; ¶1624.185; TD ¶302,020
13. ¶L-3720 *et seq.*; TD ¶302,020 *et seq.*
14. ¶L-3713; ¶1624.185; TD ¶302,020

15. ¶L-3704; ¶1624.193; TD ¶302,001
16. ¶L-3715; ¶1624.185; TD ¶302,015
17. ¶L-3701; ¶1624.185; TD ¶302,001
18. ¶L-3734; ¶1624.185; TD ¶302,034
19. ¶L-3734; ¶1624.185; TD ¶302,034

Local transportation expenses for deductible education are deductible. These are expenses incurred in going directly from work to school, and, if the taxpayer is regularly employed and goes to school on a strictly temporary basis, the costs of returning from school to home, or the round-trip costs of going from home to school and back. In general, attendance at school is temporary if it's realistically expected to last (and does in fact last) for one year or less.[20]

Costs of seminar cruises or tours are disallowed if taken primarily for personal purposes even though part of the time is devoted to qualifying professional education.[21] Even if not for personal purposes, the deduction is limited under the rules at ¶1549 and ¶1550.

¶ 2228   Teachers' education expenses.

If the minimum teaching requirements have *already* been met, a teacher may deduct the expense of any education required to retain his or her position, salary or status, even if the education will qualify the teacher to teach a new or different subject. (Reg § 1.162-5) Costs of courses to renew a provisional teaching certificate, or that lead to a *permanent* certificate are deductible if necessary to continue teaching.[22] The cost of education to maintain or improve skills is deductible even if it leads to an advanced degree (Reg § 1.162-5(c)) or qualifies the teacher for a change of duties. (Reg § 1.162-5(b))[23] Education to meet minimum requirements isn't deductible. (Reg § 1.162-5(b)(2))[24]

¶ 2229   Limited above-the-line deduction for educator expenses before 2014.

For tax years beginning before 2014, an eligible educator—a grade K through 12 teacher, instructor, counselor, principal, or aide in a school for at least 900 hours during a school year (Code Sec. 62(d)(1))—can claim an "above the line deduction" (i.e., an adjustment to gross income to arrive at adjusted gross income) for up to $250 of trade or business expenses paid or incurred for books, supplies (other than nonathletic supplies for courses of instruction in health or physical education), computer equipment (including related software and services) and other equipment, and supplementary materials used in the classroom. (Code Sec. 62(a)(2)(D)) A deduction is allowed only to the extent the amount of expenses exceeds the amount excludable from income under Code Sec. 135 (education savings bonds), Code Sec. 529(c)(1) (qualified tuition programs), or Code Sec. 530(d)(2) (Coverdell education savings accounts). (Code Sec. 62(d)(2))[25]

caution: Check http://ria.thomson.com/federaltaxhandbook to see if this provision has been extended.

¶ 2230   Above-the-Line Deduction for Higher Education Expenses. ▬▬▬▬▬

For tax years beginning before 2014, eligible individuals can claim an above-the-line deduction for higher education expenses.

caution: Check http://ria.thomson.com/federaltaxhandbook to see if this provision has been extended.

¶ 2231   Above-the-line deduction for higher education expenses— Form 8917.

For tax years beginning before 2014, eligible individuals can deduct (on Form 8917) higher education expenses (¶2232)—i.e., "qualified tuition and related expenses" of the taxpayer, his spouse, or dependents—as an adjustment to gross income to arrive at adjusted gross income. (Code Sec. 222(a)) The higher education deduction can't exceed:

. . . $4,000 for taxpayers whose modified AGI for the tax year doesn't exceed $65,000 ($130,000 for a joint return);

---

20. ¶L-3730; ¶1624.185; TD ¶302,030
21. ¶L-3733; ¶2744.04; TD ¶302,033
22. ¶L-3703; ¶1624.185; TD ¶302,003

23. ¶L-3705; ¶1624.185; TD ¶302,025
24. ¶L-3714; ¶1624.185; TD ¶302,005
25. ¶A-2611.2; ¶624.02; TD ¶560.706.1

. . . $2,000 for taxpayers whose modified AGI exceeds $65,000 ($130,000 for a joint return), but doesn't exceed $80,000 ($160,000 for a joint return); and

. . . zero for other taxpayers. (Code Sec. 222(b)(2)(B))

caution: Check http://ria.thomson.com/federaltaxhandbook to see if this provision has been extended.

Modified AGI is AGI determined without regard to the higher education expense, the U.S. production activities deduction (¶1614) or the exclusions for foreign, possessions, and Puerto Rico income. (Code Sec. 222(b)(2))

The deduction for higher education expenses is allowed for any tax year only to the extent the qualified tuition and related expenses are for enrollment at a higher education institution during that year, except that the deduction is allowed for expenses paid during a tax year if the expenses are in connection with an academic term beginning during that year or during the first three months of the next year. (Code Sec. 222(d)(3))

The higher education expense deduction isn't allowed:

. . . unless the taxpayer includes on his tax return for the relevant year the name and taxpayer identification number (TIN) of the individual for whom the higher education expenses were paid, (Code Sec. 222(d)(2))

. . . for any expense for which a deduction is allowed to the taxpayer under any other provision of Chapter 1 of the Code, (Code Sec. 222(c)(1))

. . . for a tax year with respect to an individual's qualified tuition and related expenses if he or any other person elects to claim an American opportunity tax credit or Lifetime Learning credit (see ¶2201 *et seq.*) with respect to that individual for that year. (Code Sec. 222(c)(2)(A))

Higher education expense deductions can't be claimed by a taxpayer who: files separately for the tax year (Code Sec. 222(d)(4)); may be claimed as a dependent (¶3119) on another's return (Code Sec. 222(c)(3)); or is a nonresident alien for any part of the tax year, unless treated as a resident alien under a Code Sec. 6013(g) or Code Sec. 6013(h) election (to treat a spouse as a resident alien) by a U.S. citizen or resident with a nonresident alien spouse. (Code Sec. 222(d)(5))[26]

¶ 2232   Higher education expenses for the above-the-line deduction.

For purposes of the above-the line deduction for higher education expenses (¶2231), higher education expenses consist of qualified tuition and related expenses, defined the same way as for the American opportunity tax credit and Lifetime Learning Credit purposes (¶2201), but reduced by the amount of the expenses that are taken into account in determining amounts excluded under: Code Sec. 135 (interest on bonds used to pay for higher education expenses, ¶2219), Code Sec. 529(c)(1) (distributions from qualified tuition plans, but limited to the excludible earnings from such plans, ¶2209) and Code Sec. 530(d)(2) (full amount of distributions from CESAs, ¶2205). Qualified tuition and related expenses also are reduced by certain excludible scholarships and other payments. (Code Sec. 222(c)(2)(B), Code Sec. 222(d)(1))[27]

---

26. ¶A-4471; ¶2224; TD ¶352,001.

27. ¶A-4474; ¶2224

Chapter 8   Tax Credits

¶ 2300   **Tax Credits.** ▬▬

Tax credits are either business credits intended to provide special incentives for the achievement of certain economic objectives, or personal credits, which provide tax benefits to certain taxpayers (e.g., the elderly or disabled, etc.). The foreign tax credit, however, may apply to both business and nonbusiness taxpayers.

The three main categories of tax credits are:

(1) The business incentive credits, see ¶2301 et seq.

(2) The personal (refundable and nonrefundable) credits, see ¶2338 et seq.

(3) The foreign tax credit, see ¶2367 et seq.

For credit for alternative minimum tax (AMT), see ¶2365.

For tax credits attributable to certain "passive" activities, see ¶1810 et seq.

¶ 2301   **Business Incentive Credits.** ▬▬▬▬▬▬▬▬▬▬▬▬▬▬▬▬▬▬▬▬▬▬▬▬▬▬▬▬▬▬▬▬▬

Certain business incentive credits are combined into one general business credit (GBC) for purposes of determining each credit's allowance limitation for the tax year.

¶ 2302   **General business credit (GBC)—Form 3800.**

The GBC is made up of the:

. . . investment credit (Code Sec. 38(b)(1)) (¶2307 et seq.) (which includes the rehabilitation credit (¶2308), the energy credit (¶2311), the qualifying advanced coal and gasification project credits (¶2312), and the qualifying advanced energy project credit (¶2313);

. . . pre-2014 work opportunity credit (Code Sec. 38(b)(2)), see ¶2316 et seq.;

. . . pre-2014 cellulosic biofuel (second generation biofuel) production credit (Code Sec. 38(b)(3)), see ¶2318;

. . . pre-2014 research credit (Code Sec. 38(b)(4)), see ¶2319;

. . . low-income housing credit (Code Sec. 38(b)(5)), see ¶2320 et seq.;

. . . enhanced oil recovery (EOR) credit (Code Sec. 38(b)(6)), see ¶2322;

. . . disabled access credit (DAC) (Code Sec. 38(b)(7)), see ¶2323;

. . . renewable electricity production credit (Code Sec. 38(b)(8)), see ¶2324;

. . . pre-2014 empowerment zone employment credit (Code Sec. 38(b)(9)), see ¶2325;

. . . pre-2014 Indian employment credit (Code Sec. 38(b)(10)), see ¶2326;

. . . FICA tip credit (Code Sec. 38(b)(11)), see ¶2327;

. . . orphan drug credit (Code Sec. 38(b)(12)), see ¶2328;

. . . pre-2014 new markets credit (Code Sec. 38(b)(13)), see ¶2329;

. . . small employer pension plan startup credit (Code Sec. 38(b)(14)), see ¶2331;

. . . employer-provided child care credit (Code Sec. 38(b)(15)), see ¶2330;

. . . pre-2014 railroad track maintenance credit Code Sec. 38(b)(16), Code Sec. 45G);

. . . pre-2014 biodiesel fuel credit (Code Sec. 38(b)(17)), see ¶2333;

. . . marginal oil and gas well production credit (Code Sec. 38(b)(19), Code Sec. 45I);

. . . distilled spirits credit (Code Sec. 38(b)(20), Code Sec. 5011(a));

. . . advanced nuclear power facility production credit (Code Sec. 38(b)(21)), Code Sec. 45J(a)) for facilities placed in service before 2021;

. . . nonconventional source production credit (Code Sec. 38(b)(22)), see ¶2337;

. . . pre-2014 new energy efficient home credit (Code Sec. 38(b)(23)), see ¶2334;

References beginning with a single letter are to paragraphs in RIA's Federal Tax Coordinator 2d and RIA's Analysis of Federal Taxes: Income. Those beginning with numbers are to paragraphs in RIA's United States Tax Reporter. Those beginning with TD are to paragraphs in RIA's Tax Desk.

326

... pre-2014 energy efficient appliance credit (Code Sec. 38(b)(24)), see ¶2335;

... applicable portion (attributable to depreciable property) of the alternative motor vehicle credit (Code Sec. 38(b)(25)), see ¶2360;

... applicable portion (that attributable to depreciable property) of the alternative fuel vehicle refueling property credit (Code Sec. 38(b)(26)), see ¶2361;

... pre-2014 mine rescue training credit (Code Sec. 38(b)(31), Code Sec. 45N);

... pre-2014 differential wage payment credit (Code Sec. 38(b)(33)), see ¶2336;

... carbon dioxide sequestration credit (Code Sec. 38(b)(34)), see ¶2315;

... applicable portion (attributable to depreciable property) of the new qualified plug-in electric drive motor vehicles credit (including pre-2014 2- or 3-wheeled plug-in electric vehicle credit) (Code Sec. 38(b)(35)), see ¶2362; and

... small employer health insurance credit (Code Sec. 38(b)(36)), see ¶2332.

The credit for excise tax payments to the Trans-Alaska Pipeline Liability Fund (Code Sec. 4612(e)(1)), the pre-2010 renewal community employment credit (Code Sec. 1400H(a)), and the community development corporation credit for pre-July '99 contributions[1] aren't included in the above Code Sec. 38(b) list, but are also part of the current year business credit.

¶ 2303 Limitation on general business credits (GBCs) based on tax liability.

A GBC is allowed against income tax for a particular tax year equal to the sum of: (1) the business credit carry*forwards* carried to the tax year, (2) the *current year* GBC, plus (3) the business credit carry*backs* carried to the tax year. (Code Sec. 38(a))[2] For when bonus depreciation can be traded for deferred credits, see ¶1933.

The GBC allowed for any tax year (except for the empowerment zone employment credit, the New York Liberty Zone business employee credit, and "specified credits," see below) is limited to the excess of taxpayer's "net income tax" over the greater of: (1) the tentative minimum tax for the tax year, or (2) 25% of the amount of the taxpayer's "net regular tax" that exceeds $25,000. (Code Sec. 38(c)(1))[3] Spouses who file separate returns are each limited to $12,500 instead of $25,000, but if the taxpayer's spouse has no carryforward, carryback or current year GBC in the tax year that ends within or with the taxpayer's tax year, the taxpayer gets the full amount of $25,000. (Code Sec. 38(c)(6)(A))[4]

For estates and trusts, the $25,000 amount is reduced to an amount equal to $25,000 multiplied by a fraction (numerator is the estate's or trust's total income not allocated to beneficiaries, denominator is the estate's or trust's total income). (Code Sec. 38(c)(6)(D))[5]

Net income tax is the sum of the regular tax liability and the alternative minimum tax (AMT), ¶3200), reduced by the credits listed below. Net regular tax is the regular tax liability reduced by the sum of the following credits (Code Sec. 38(c)(1)): (1) household and dependent care credit (Code Sec. 21); (2) credit for the elderly and disabled (Code Sec. 22); (3) child tax credit (Code Sec. 24); (4) mortgage credit (Code Sec. 25); (5) American Opportunity (Hope) and Lifetime Learning credits (Code Sec. 25A); (6) saver's credit for elective deferrals and IRA contributions (Code Sec. 25B); (7) nonbusiness energy property credit (Code Sec. 25C); (8) residential energy efficient property (Code Sec. 25D); (9) foreign tax and possessions tax credit (for American Samoa) (Code Sec. 27, Code Sec. 936); (10) Puerto Rico economic activity credit (Code Sec. 30A); (11) alternative motor vehicle credit (Code Sec. 30B); (12) qualified alternative fuel vehicle refueling property credit (Code Sec. 30C); (13) D.C. homebuyer credit (Code Sec. 1400C); (14) new qualified plug-in electric drive motor vehicles credit (attributable to non-depreciable property); (Code Sec. 30D); and (15) qualified plug-in electric drive motor vehicles (QPEVs) (attributable to non-depreciable property) (Code Sec. 30(c)(2)(A)).[6]

1. ¶L-15650 *et seq.*; ¶384.01; TD ¶384,031
2. ¶L-15200; ¶384.01; ¶384.03; TD ¶380,500
3. ¶L-15202; ¶384.02; TD ¶380,502
4. ¶L-15204; ¶384.02; TD ¶380,505
5. ¶L-15207; ¶384.02; TD ¶380,507
6. ¶L-15202; ¶384.02, 384.03; TD ¶380,502

The empowerment zone employment credit (¶2325) is limited to the excess of the taxpayer's net income tax over the greater of: (1) 75% of its tentative minimum tax, or (2) 25% of so much of its net regular tax liability as exceeds $25,000. This limitation is reduced by the general credits (not including the empowerment zone employment credit, New York Liberty Zone business employee credit, eligible small business (ESB) credits, and other specified credits, see below) allowed for the tax year. (Code Sec. 38(c)(2)) The effect is that the empowerment zone employment credit may be used to offset up to 25% of a taxpayer's AMT.[7]

"Specified credits" may offset 100% of a taxpayer's AMT. (Code Sec. 38(c)(4)) Specified credits include: (Code Sec. 38(c)(4)(B)) (1) the alcohol fuel credit (¶2318); (2) the low-income housing credit for buildings placed in service after 2007 (¶2320); (3) credits determined under Code Sec. 45 (¶2324) to the extent attributable to electricity or refined coal produced at a facility which is originally placed in service after Oct. 22, 2004 and during the 4-year period beginning on the date the facility was originally placed in service; (4) the FICA tip credit (¶2327); (5) for tax years beginning after 2007 but before 2014, the Code Sec. 45G railroad maintenance credit; (6) the small employer health insurance credit (¶2332); (7) the rehabilitation investment credit for qualified rehabilitation expenditures properly taken into account after 2007 (¶2308); (8) the credits determined under Code Sec. 46 to the extent attributable to the energy credit under Code Sec. 48 (¶2311); and (9) the work opportunity tax credit (¶2316). Indian coal production credit during the 4-year period the property is first placed in service (¶2324)— is also a specified credit. (Code Sec. 45(e)(10))[8]

¶ 2304 Carryback or carryforward of general business credit (GBC)–Form 3800.

There's a one-year carryback (except for a 5-year carryback for the marginal well production credit under Code Sec. 39(a)(3)); and a 5-year carryback for eligible small business credits determined in the first tax year beginning in 2010 under Code Sec. 38(c)(5)) and a 20-year carryforward (on Form 3800). (Code Sec. 39(a), Code Sec. 39(a)(4)) No part of any unused current GBC attributable to a component credit may be carried back to tax years before the first tax year that the component credit was allowable. (Code Sec. 39(d))[9]

¶ 2305 Deduction for unused qualified business credits after the carryover period.

If any portion of a qualified business credit (investment credit, work opportunity credit (¶2316), alcohol fuels credit (¶2318), research credit (¶2319), enhanced oil recovery credit, empowerment zone employment credit (¶2325), FICA tip credit (¶2327), new markets tax credit (¶2329), small employer pension plan startup credit (¶2331), Indian employment credit (¶2326), biodiesel fuels credit (¶2333), pre-2010 low sulfur diesel fuel production credit, new energy efficient home credit (¶2334), and small employer health insurance credit (¶2332), (Code Sec. 196(c)) hasn't been allowed after the carryover period expires, the taxpayer can deduct the unused portion in the first tax year after the last tax year of the carryover period (or in the tax year of the taxpayer's death or cessation if earlier). (Code Sec. 196(a), Code Sec. 196(b)) But, for the investment tax credit (other than the rehabilitation credit), the deduction is 50% of the unused amount. (Code Sec. 196(d))[10]

¶ 2306 Ordering rules for the general business credits (GBCs).

The order in which the component credits of the GBC are used in a tax year or as a carryback or carryforward is determined on the basis of the order they are listed in Code Sec. 38(b) (¶2302) as of the close of the tax year in which the credit is used. (Code Sec. 38(d)(1)) The order in which the component credits of the business investment credit are used is determined on the basis of the order they are listed in Code Sec. 46 as of the close of the tax year in which the credit is used. (Code Sec. 38(d)(2))[11]

---

7. ¶L-15202.1; ¶384.02; TD ¶380,503
8. ¶L-15202.3; ¶384.02; TD ¶380,503.1
9. ¶L-15209; ¶384.01; ¶384.03; TD ¶380,509

10. ¶L-15212; ¶1964.01; TD ¶380,510
11. ¶L-15208; ¶384.01; TD ¶380,508

¶ 2307 The investment tax credits—Form 3468.

The Code Sec. 46 investment tax credit (claimed on Form 3468) consists of: (1) the rehabilitation investment credit (Code Sec. 47), see ¶2308 *et seq.*; (2) the energy credit (Code Sec. 48(a)), see ¶2311;[12] (3) the qualifying advanced coal project credit (Code Sec. 48A), see ¶2312;[13] (4) the qualifying gasification project credit; (Code Sec. 48B), see ¶2312;[14] and (5) the qualifying energy project credit (Code Sec. 48C), see ¶2313[15]

Property qualifying for the rehabilitation credit (depreciable or amortizable property) is treated as investment credit property. (Code Sec. 50(a)(5)) But certain otherwise qualified property is denied the applicable credit if it's property used:

... predominantly outside the U.S., except for property listed in Code Sec. 168(g)(4)—dealing with rolling stock, spacecraft, satellites, etc. (Code Sec. 50(b)(1))

... predominantly to furnish, or in connection with the furnishing of, permanent lodging, except for certain nonlodging commercial facilities, lodging facilities used by transients, certified historic structures, and energy property. (Code Sec. 50(b)(2))

... by certain tax-exempt organizations. (Code Sec. 50(b)(3)) If property is leased to a partnership or other pass-through entity, a proportionate share of the property is treated as leased to each tax-exempt entity partner (under the rules of Code Sec. 168(h)(5) and (6)) in determining whether any portion of the property is tax-exempt use property. (Code Sec. 50(b)(4))

... by the U.S. or other governmental units, except for short-lease property. (Code Sec. 50(b)(4))[16]

A *lessee* of new investment credit property can take the investment credit on the property if the lessor elects to pass it to him. (Code Sec. 50(d); Reg § 1.48-4) The election statement is described in the regs. (Reg § 1.48-4(f), Reg § 1.48-4(g)) The effect is to treat the lessee as having acquired the property for its FMV, but the lessor's basis is used instead when lessor and lessee are members of a controlled group. The lessee uses the same investment credit life for the property as the lessor.[17] But a lessor's election to pass the credit from property with an over 14-year ADR depreciation "class life" to his lessee results in only a partial transfer of the credit if the lease is for a period that is less than 80% of the property's "class life" and isn't a "net lease." (Reg § 1.48-4(a)(2))[18]

If there is a net decrease in the amount of nonqualified nonrecourse financing (under the *at-risk* rules, ¶1803 *et seq.*) as of the close of a tax year following that in which property was placed in service, the net decrease is treated as an increase in the credit base for the property. Thus, an increase in the taxpayer's at-risk amount for an investment credit property is additional qualified investment. (Code Sec. 49(a)(2))[19]

¶ 2308 Rehabilitation investment credits—Form 3468.

The rehabilitation credit (claimed on Form 3468) for a building is 10% (20% for a certified historic structure) of the qualified rehabilitation expenditure. (Code Sec. 47(a))[20]

A qualified rehabilitation expenditure is any amount charged to capital account and incurred in connection with the rehabilitation (including reconstruction, or an addition or improvement) of a qualified rehabilitated building (¶2309) that's depreciable under Code Sec. 168, and is nonresidential real property, residential rental property, or real property with a class life of more than 12.5 years. Expenditures for which straight-line depreciation

---

12. ¶L-16500; ¶s 474, 484; TD ¶381,400
13. ¶L-16450; ¶s 48A4; TD ¶381,400
14. ¶L-16470; ¶s 48B4; TD ¶381,401
15. ¶L-16461 *et seq.*; ¶48C4; TD ¶381,421 *et seq.*
16. ¶L-16501; ¶504.01; TD ¶381,401

17. ¶s L-16506, L-17010 *et seq.*; ¶484.10; TD ¶381,403
18. ¶L-17015; ¶484.10
19. ¶L-16505; ¶494; TD ¶381,402
20. ¶L-16103; ¶484.13; TD ¶381,503

isn't used are not qualified expenditures. (Code Sec. 47(c)(2))[21] If bonus first-year depreciation (¶1933) is claimed for the building, the credit may be claimed only if the taxpayer depreciates the remaining adjusted depreciable basis of rehabilitation expenses using the straight line method. (Reg § 1.168(k)-1(f)(10)), Reg § 1.1400L(b)-1(f)(9))[22]

Also excluded are expenditures in connection with the rehabilitation of a building that are allocable to that portion of the building that is (or that is reasonably expected to be) tax-exempt-use property. (Code Sec. 47(c)(2)(B)(v))[23]

In addition to owner-taxpayers of qualified property, the rehabilitation credits are available to lessees for qualified expenditures incurred by them, but only if, on the rehabilitation's completion date, the remaining term of the lease (without regard to renewal) is at least the recovery period under Code Sec. 168(c). (Code Sec. 47(c)(2)(B)(vi))[24]

¶ 2309   Which buildings qualify for the rehabilitation credit?

A "qualified rehabilitated building" is any building (and its structural components) that satisfies all of the following requirements:

(1) Except for certified historic structures, the building was first placed in service before '36. (Code Sec. 47(c)(1)(B))

(2) The building has been substantially rehabilitated. A substantial rehabilitation is one in which the qualified rehabilitation expenditures during the 24-month period selected by the taxpayer (as prescribed in regs) and ending with or within the year exceed the greater of: (a) $5,000; or (b) the adjusted basis of the building and its structural components as of the first day of the 24-month period, or of the holding period (without regard to reconstruction), whichever is later. (Code Sec. 47(c)(1)(C)(i)) Rehabilitation includes reconstruction. (Code Sec. 47(c)(1)(D))[25]

(3) The building was placed in service before the beginning of the rehabilitation.

(4) For any building other than a certified historic structure, the building retains in place (a) at least 75% of the external walls (including at least 50% as external walls), and (b) at least 75% of its internal structural framework.

(5) The building must be depreciable or amortizable. (Code Sec. 47(c)(1)(A))[26]

For any rehabilitation that may reasonably be expected to be completed in phases set forth in architectural plans and specifications completed before the rehabilitation begins, a 60-month (instead of 24-month) period applies. (Code Sec. 47(c)(1)(C)(ii))[27]

¶ 2310   Progress expenditure rehabilitation credit—Form 3468.

If any building being rehabilitated by or for the taxpayer has a normal rehabilitation period of 2 years or more, and it's reasonable to expect the building to be a qualified rehabilitated building (¶2309) in the taxpayer's hands when placed in service (Code Sec. 47(d)(2)), the taxpayer may irrevocably elect (on Form 3468) to account for qualified rehabilitation expenditures made for that property as follows:

(1) where it's reasonable to believe that more than half these expenditures will be made *directly* by the taxpayer, any qualified rehabilitation expenditure is taken into account for the tax year it's properly chargeable to capital account (i.e., includible in computing the property's basis), and

(2) where it's reasonable to believe that *no* more than half the qualified expenditure will be made directly by the taxpayer, any qualified rehabilitation expenditure is taken into account in the tax year it's paid. (Code Sec. 47(d)(1); Reg § 1.46-5(g)(1))[28]

---

21. ¶L-16102; ¶474; TD ¶381,502
22. ¶L-16102.1; ¶1684.025, ¶14,00L4.05; TD ¶381,502
23. ¶L-16115; ¶474; TD ¶381,516
24. ¶L-16102; ¶474; TD ¶381,501

25. ¶L-16106; ¶474; TD ¶381,506
26. ¶L-16101, L-16103; ¶474; TD ¶381,503
27. ¶L-16113; ¶474; TD ¶381,514
28. ¶L-16200; ¶474; TD ¶381,519

¶ 2311   Energy credit—Form 3468.

A taxpayer can claim (on Form 3468) the following energy credits (in each case, the percentage applies to the basis of eligible energy property placed in service during the year):

(1) 30% for qualified fuel cell property, (Code Sec. 48(a)(2)(A)(i)(I)) i.e., a fuel cell power plant with a nameplate capacity of at least 0.5 kilowatt (KW) of electricity using an electro-chemical process, and an electricity only generation efficiency of greater than 30%. The credit can't exceed an amount equal to $1,500 for each 0.5 KW of capacity. The credit isn't available after 2016. (Code Sec. 48(c))

(2) 30% for solar energy property, (Code Sec. 48(a)(2)(A)(i)(II)) i.e., equipment that uses solar energy to generate electricity, to heat or cool (or provide hot water for) a structure, or to provide solar process heat (but not for heating a swimming pool). (Code Sec. 48(a)(3)(A)(i)) The 30% credit is available only for periods ending before 2017. (Code Sec. 48(a)(2)(A)(i)(II)) After 2016, the credit will be 10%. (Code Sec. 48(a)(2)(A)(ii))

(3) 30% for solar energy to illuminate the inside of a structure using fiber optic distributed sunlight, for periods ending before 2017. (Code Sec. 48(a)(2)(A)(i)(III), Code Sec. 48(a)(3)(A)(ii))

(4) 10% for equipment used to produce, distribute, or use energy derived from a geothermal deposit. (Code Sec. 48(a)(2)(A)(ii), Code Sec. 48(a)(3)(A)(iii))

(5) 10% for qualified microturbine property, (Code Sec. 48(a)(2)(A)(ii), Code Sec. 48(a)(3)(A)(iv)) i.e., a stationary microturbine powerplant with a nameplate capacity of less than 2,000 KWs, and has an electricity only generation efficiency of not less than 26% at International Standard Organization conditions. The credit can't exceed $200 for each KW of the property's capacity and isn't available after 2016. (Code Sec. 48(c)(2))

(6) 10% for combined heat and power system property, (Code Sec. 48(a)(3)(A)(v)) i.e., property which uses the same energy source to simultaneously or sequentially produce electrical power, mechanical shaft power, or both (at least 20% of total useful energy), while generating steam or other forms of useful thermal energy, including heating or cooling applications (at least 20% of total useful energy); and has a greater than 60% energy efficiency percentage. The property must be placed in service before 2017. (Code Sec. 48(c)(3)(A))

(7) 30% for qualified small wind energy property, (Code Sec. 48(a)(3)(A)(vi)) i.e., property that uses a qualifying small wind turbine (with a nameplate capacity of not more than 100 KWs) to generate electricity. This doesn't include any property after 2016. (Code Sec. 48(c)(4))

(8) 10% for geothermal heat pump systems equipment, i.e. equipment that uses the ground or ground water as a thermal energy source to heat a structure or as a thermal energy sink to cool a structure, but only for a period ending before 2017. (Code Sec. 48(a)(3)(A)(vii))

No credit is allowed for property unless it's depreciable or amortizable; its construction, reconstruction or erection is completed by the taxpayer or, if acquired by the taxpayer, its original use begins with the taxpayer; and it meets the official quality and performance standards in effect at the time of acquisition. (Code Sec. 48(a)(3))[29] There is no reduction in basis for purposes of determining the energy credit if property is financed in whole or in part by subsidized financing or tax-exempt private activity bonds. (Code Sec. 48(a)(4))[30]

Taxpayers could have elected a nontaxable grant in lieu of the energy credit for property placed in service (a) during 2009, 2010, or 2011; or (b) after 2011 and before the credit termination date (generally, Jan. 1, 2017) but only if construction of the property began during 2009, 2010, or 2011. The basis of the property is reduced by 50% of the amount of the grant. (Code Sec. 48(d); ARRA § 1603 as amended by TRA §707)[31]

---

29. ¶L-16501; ¶484; TD ¶381,601
30. ¶L-16415; ¶484; TD ¶381,603

31. ¶L-16440; ¶484.02; TD ¶381,608

¶ 2312   Credits for qualifying advanced coal projects and gasification projects.

A credit can be claimed for investments in qualifying advanced coal projects. The credit is 20% of the qualified investment for the tax year in integrated gasification combined cycle projects, 15% of the qualified investment for the tax year in projects that use other advanced coal-based generation technologies; and 30% of the qualified investment for advanced coal-based generation technology projects. (Code Sec. 48A(a))[32] A separate investment credit can also be claimed for qualified investment in qualifying gasification projects. The credit is 20% or 30% of the qualified investment for the tax year. (Code Sec. 48B(a)) The Code Sec. 48B credit is not allowed for any qualified investment for which the Code Sec. 48A credit is allowed. (Code Sec. 48B(e))[33]

¶ 2313   New qualified advanced energy manufacturing project (QAEMP) credit.

A taxpayer can claim a 30% credit for investment in qualified property used in a QAEMP, (Code Sec. 48C) i.e., a project that re-equips, expands, or establishes a manufacturing facility for the production of property designed to: (1) be used to produce energy from the sun, wind, or geothermal deposits or other renewable resources; (2) manufacture fuel cells, microturbines, or an energy storage system for use with electric or hybrid-electric motor vehicles; (3) manufacture electric grids to support the transmission of intermittent sources of renewable energy, including storage of that energy; (4) manufacture equipment for use for carbon capture or sequestration; or (5) refine or blend renewable fuels (but not fossil fuels), to produce energy conservation technologies (including energy-conserving lighting technologies and smart grid technologies). It also includes a facility for the production of new qualified plug-in electric drive motor vehicles (¶2362); qualified plug-in electric vehicles (¶2362); components designed specifically for these vehicles; or other advanced energy property designed to reduce greenhouse gas emissions. (Code Sec. 48C(c)(1))[34] Qualified property must be depreciable (tangible) property used in a QAEMP (Code Sec. 48C(b)(1)) and doesn't include property designed to manufacture equipment for use in the refining or blending of any transportation fuel (other than renewable fuels). (Code Sec. 48C(c)(1)(B)) The property's basis is reduced by the amount of credit received.[35]

¶ 2314   Recapture of investment credits—Form 4255.

If investment credit property is disposed of or ceases to be investment credit property for the taxpayer before the end of the recapture period, the credit taken for all earlier years is recaptured on Form 4255 (i.e., added to the tax liability for the recapture year). (Code Sec. 50(a)(1)) The recapture percentage is 100% during the first full year after the property is placed in service. This percentage decreases by 20 percentage points every succeeding full year. There's no recapture after the fifth full year. (Code Sec. 50(a)(1)) Recapture applies only to credit used to reduce tax liability. If any part of it isn't used, carrybacks and carryovers of the credit must be appropriately adjusted. (Code Sec. 50(a)(3))

No recapture applies to a transfer by reason of death (Code Sec. 50(a)(4)(A)), a mere change in form of doing business (Code Sec. 50(a)(4)(B)), or a transfer between spouses or incident to divorce (under the rules of Code Sec. 1041(a)). (Code Sec. 50(a)(5)(B))[36]

Different recapture computation methods apply to progress expenditures credit (¶2310) depending on whether the recapture year occurs before or after the progress expenditure property is placed in service. (Code Sec. 50(a)(2))[37]

If the amount of nonqualified nonrecourse financing (¶1809) for at-risk property increases as of the close of the tax year, then the tax for the tax year is increased by the total decrease

---

32. ¶L-16450; ¶s 48A4; TD ¶381,413
33. ¶L-16470; ¶s 48B4; TD ¶381,414
34. ¶L-16463; ¶48C4; TD ¶381,423

35. ¶L-16461 *et seq.*; ¶48C4; TD ¶381,421 *et seq.*
36. ¶L-17301; ¶504.02; TD ¶381,405
37. ¶L-17314; ¶504.02; TD ¶381,407

in credits allowed in earlier tax years that would result if the credit base for the earlier credits had been reduced by the amount of the increase in the nonqualified nonrecourse financing. For purposes of computing recapture, the increase in nonqualified nonrecourse financing is treated as reducing the credit base and correspondingly reducing the qualified investment in the year the property was placed in service. (Code Sec. 49(b)(1)) The transfer of (or an agreement to transfer) any evidence of indebtedness won't be treated as an increase in nonqualified nonrecourse financing, if the transfer occurs (or the agreement is entered into) more than one year after the indebtedness was incurred. (Code Sec. 49(b)(2))[38]

If a taxpayer fails to pay the principal on a level payment nonqualified nonrecourse loan (¶1809) used for qualified energy property, the taxpayer is treated as increasing the amount of nonqualified nonrecourse financing to the extent of the recapture. (Code Sec. 49(b)(3))[39]

¶ 2315   Carbon dioxide sequestration credit—Form 8933.

A carbon dioxide sequestration credit is allowed for carbon dioxide captured. (Code Sec. 45Q) The credit for any tax year is an amount equal to the sum of: (1) $21.25 for 2013 (as adjusted for inflation) per metric ton of qualified carbon dioxide which is captured by the taxpayer at a qualified facility and disposed of by the taxpayer in secure geological storage; and (2) $10.63 for 2013 (as adjusted for inflation) per metric ton of qualified carbon dioxide which is captured by the taxpayer at a qualified facility and used by the taxpayer as a tertiary injectant in a qualified enhanced oil or natural gas recovery project. (Code Sec. 45Q(a)(2); Code Sec. 45Q(d)(7))

Qualified carbon dioxide is carbon dioxide captured from an industrial source that would otherwise be released into the atmosphere as industrial emission of greenhouse gas, and is measured at the source of capture and verified at the point of disposal or injection. (Code Sec. 45Q(b)(1))

To claim the credit (on Form 8933), a person must: (1) own an industrial facility at which carbon capture equipment is placed in service, (2) capture not less than 500,000 metric tons of qualified carbon dioxide there during the tax year, and (3) physically or contractually ensure that the qualified carbon dioxide is securely stored in a geologic formation.[40]

¶ 2316   Work opportunity tax credit (WOTC) before 2014—Forms 5884, 8850.

Generally, the WOTC allows employers who hire members of certain targeted groups before Jan. 1, 2014 to get a credit against income tax (use Form 5884) of 40% of first-year wages up to a maximum amount. The maximum amount of first -year wages is generally $6,000 per employee, but is $3,000 for qualified summer youth employees and various amounts for qualified veterans, see below. In some cases special rules apply. The credit percentage is 25% for employees who have completed at least 120 hours, but less than 400 hours of service for the employer. (Code Sec. 51(i))Where the employee is a long-term family assistance (LTFA) recipient, the WOTC is a percentage of first and second year wages, up to $10,000 per employee. (Code Sec. 51) LTFA recipients included an additional 50% of qualified-second year wages for a maximum credit of $9,000 [(.4 × $10,000) + (.5 × $10,000)]. (Code Sec. 51(e))[41]

⚠️*caution:* Check tax.thomsonreuters.com/federaltaxhandbookupdates to see if the above provision has been extended.

The amount of first-year wages taken into account in computing the WOTC for qualified veteran who begins work after Nov. 21, 2011 is:

(1) $6,000 for a veteran who is a member of a family receiving assistance under a food stamp program for at least three months, all or part of which is during the 12-month period

---

38. ¶L-17307; ¶494; TD ¶381,408
39. ¶L-16419; ¶494; TD ¶381,607

40. ¶L-18401 *et seq.*; ¶45Q4
41. ¶L-17775 *et seq.*; ¶514; TD ¶380,700

ending on the hiring date (maximum credit of $2,400 (.4 × $6,000));

(2) $12,000 for a veteran with a service-connected disability who has a hiring date that isn't more than one year after having been discharged or released from active duty (maximum credit of $4,800 (.4 × $12,000);

(3) $24,000 for a veteran with a service-connected disability who has aggregate periods of unemployment during the one-year period ending on the hiring date that equal or exceed six months (maximum credit of $9,600 (.4 × $24,000);

(4) $6,000 for a veteran who has aggregate periods of unemployment during the one-year period ending on the hiring date which equal or exceed four weeks, but less than six months (maximum credit of $2,400 (.4 × $6,000)); and

(5) $14,000 for a veteran who has aggregate periods of unemployment during the one-year period ending on the hiring date which equal or exceed six months ($5,600 (.4 × $14,000)). (Code Sec. 51(d)(3))

The targeted groups are: qualified IV-A recipients (qualified recipients of aid to families with dependent children or successor program); qualified ex-felons; designated community residents (i.e., the former "high-risk youths" targeted group but with the maximum age requirement raised and the residency requirement expanded to include rural renewal residents); vocational rehabilitation referrals; qualified summer youth employees; qualified supplemental nutrition assistance benefits recipients; qualified SSI recipients; long-term family assistance recipients, i.e., members of a family that receives or received assistance under a IV-A program for a minimum period of time; and certain unemployed veterans. (Code Sec. 51(d))[42]

The WOTC reduces the employer's wage deduction dollar-for-dollar. (Code Sec. 280C(a); Reg § 1.280C-1)[43] But the taxpayer can elect not to take the WOTC. (Code Sec. 51(j))[44]

Wages paid (1) for federally funded on-the-job training, (Code Sec. 51(c)(2)(A))[45] and (2) to an individual who performs the same or substantially similar services as those of employees participating in or affected by a strike or lockout at the employer's plant don't qualify for the credit. (Code Sec. 51(c)(3))[46] Creditable wages are reduced by any supplementation payments made to the employer for an employee under Social Security Act §482(e). (Code Sec. 51(c)(2)(B))[47]

Certification. To be eligible for the WOTC, a new employee must be certified as a member of a targeted group by a State Employment Security Agency (SESA). The employer can either get the certification by the day the prospective employee begins work or complete a pre-screening notice (use Form 8850) for the employee by the day he is offered employment, and submit it to the SESA (not to IRS) as part of a request for certification within 28 days after the employee begins work. A fast-tracked qualification process applies for certain qualified veterans. (Code Sec. 51(d)(13)) No WOTC is allowed for employees who are related to the employer or to certain owners of the employer. (Code Sec. 51(i))[48]

¶ 2317   Tax-exempt employers' payroll-tax credit for hiring qualified veterans— Form 5884-C.

A tax-exempt employer (one described in Code Sec. 501(c) and exempt from tax under Code Sec. 501(a)) may claim (on Form 5884-C) a credit for the work opportunity tax credit (WOTC, see ¶2316) it could claim for hiring qualified veterans if it were not tax-exempt (¶2316). The credit is allowed against the OASDI (Social Security) tax (¶3024). (Code Sec. 52(c)(2), Code Sec. 3111(e)) The credit, which can't exceed the OASDI tax otherwise payable for employment of all the tax-exempt's employees during the applicable employment period, is calculated as it

---

42. ¶L-17776 *et seq.*; ¶514; TD ¶380,701
43. ¶L-17780; ¶514; TD ¶380,703
44. ¶L-17781; ¶514; TD ¶380,704
45. ¶L-17784.2; ¶514; TD ¶380,707

46. ¶L-17783.3; ¶514; TD ¶380,707
47. ¶L-17783; ¶514
48. ¶L-17784.2; ¶514; TD ¶380,709

would be under Code Sec. 51, but with the following modifications:

. . . the general credit percentage of qualifying first-year wages is 26% (instead of 40%);

. . . the credit percentage of qualifying wages is 16.25% (instead of 25%) for a qualified veteran who has completed at least 120, but less than 400, hours of service for the employer; and

. . . the tax-exempt employer may only take into account wages paid to a qualified veteran for services in furtherance of the activities related to the purposes or function constituting the basis of the organization's exemption under Code Sec. 501. (Code Sec. 3111(e)(2), Code Sec. 3111(e)(3))

Any credit that exceeds the employer Social Security tax for the period the credit is claimed is carried forward.[49]

¶ 2318 Cellulosic biofuel (second generation biofuel) production credit before 2014—Form 6478.

An *alcohol fuels* credit (computed on Form 6478) is allowed for alcohol (other than that produced from petroleum, natural gas, coal or peat, or with a proof less than 150) (Code Sec. 40(d)(1)) used as a fuel. The cellulosic biofuel production credit is a component of the alcohol fuel credit. It applies to a sale or use after Dec. 31, 2008 and before Jan. 1, 2014. (Code Sec. 40(b)(6))[50] The other components of the alcohol fuel credit (the alcohol mixture credit; the alcohol credit; and the small ethanol producer credit) aren't available after Dec. 31, 2011. (Code Sec. 40(e)(1))

caution: Check tax.thomsonreuters.com/federaltaxhandbookupdates to see if the above provision has been extended.

The cellulosic biofuel producer credit is an income tax credit of $1.01 for each gallon of qualified cellulosic fuel production of the producer for the tax year. Qualified cellulosic biofuel production is any cellulosic biofuel produced by the taxpayer which is used or sold by the taxpayer to another person for use by that other person as a fuel in a trade or business; or for use in the production of a qualified cellulosic biofuel mixture in that person's trade or business (other than casual off-farm production); or is sold to the other person who sells the cellulosic biofuel at retail to another person and places the cellulosic biofuel in the fuel tank of that other person. No credit is allowed for fuels with significant water, sediment, or ash content, such as "black liquor."

For fuels sold or used before Jan. 3, 2013, cellulosic biofuel is any liquid fuel which is produced from any lignocellulosic or hemicellulosic matter that is available on a renewable or recurring basis, and meets the registration requirements for fuels and fuel additives established by the Environmental Protection Agency (EPA) under §211 of the Clean Air Act (42 USC 7545). For fuels sold or used after Jan. 2, 2013, cellulosic biofuel is any liquid fuel which is derived by, or from, qualified feedstocks (i.e., any lignocellulosic or hemicellulosic matter that is available on a renewable or recurring basis and any cultivated algae, cyanobacteria or lemna). (Code Sec. 40(b)(6))

The credit can't be carried over to any tax year beginning after the three-tax year period beginning with the tax year in which the credit ceases to apply. (Code Sec. 40(e)(2)) The fuel credit will be reduced to take into account excise tax exemptions. (Code Sec. 40(c))

A recapture tax of $1.01 per gallon is imposed on alcohol not used as fuel for one of the specified purposes and reported on Form 720.[1] (Code Sec. 40(d)(3)(C)) A taxpayer can elect out of the alcohol fuel credit (Code Sec. 40(f)(1)) by not taking the credit. (Reg § 301.9100-6T(e))[2] The credit doesn't apply to fuel produced outside the U.S. for use outside the U.S. (Code Sec. 40(d)(7))

---

49. ¶H-4687.8; ¶31,114; TD ¶541,002.2
50. ¶L-17516.1; ¶404.07; TD ¶382,213

1. ¶L-17507; TD ¶382,207
2. ¶L-17504; ¶404.04; TD ¶382,208

¶ 2319   Research credit before 2014—Form 6765.

For amounts paid or incurred before Jan. 1, 2014 (Code Sec. 41(h)(1)), the research credit (claimed on Form 6765) equals the sum of:

(1) 20% of the excess (if any) of the qualified research expenses (QREs) for the tax year over a base amount, (unless the taxpayer elects the alternative simplified research credit, which then replaces item (1)).

(2) The university basic research credit, i.e., 20% of the basic research payments determined under Code Sec. 41(e)(1)(A).

(3) 20% of the taxpayer's expenditures on qualified energy research undertaken by an energy research consortium. (Code Sec. 41(a))[3]

⚠️*caution:* Check tax.thomsonreuters.com/federaltaxhandbookupdates to see if the above provision has been extended.

The base amount is a fixed-base percentage of taxpayer's average annual gross receipts from a U.S. trade or business, net of returns and allowances, for the 4 tax years before the credit year, and can't be less than 50% of the year's QREs. (IRS says that a controlled group can only disregard a foreign sub's intercompany transfers related to research expenditures, not gross receipts, but a court has held to the contrary.) The fixed base percentage for a non-startup company is the percentage (not exceeding 16%) that taxpayer's total QREs are of total gross receipts for tax years beginning after '83 and before '89. (Code Sec. 41(c))[4]

Except when a taxpayer elects the alternative simplified research credit, described below, the Code assigns a fixed-base percentage of 3% in making the base amount computation for each of its first 5 tax years in which a "startup company" has QREs. (Code Sec. 41(c)(3)(B)(ii)(I)) For the second 5 tax years, the fixed-base percentage is a specified amount of the ratio or percentage—increased annually during this second 5-year period—determined by dividing QREs by gross receipts.[5]

To qualify for the research credit, research has to be conducted within the U.S. (including Puerto Rico and U.S. possessions). (Code Sec. 41(d), Code Sec. 41(f)) An expense has to:

(a) qualify as a research and experimental expenditure under Code Sec. 174;

(b) relate to research undertaken for the purpose of discovering information that is technological in nature and the application of which is intended to be useful in developing a new or improved business component of the taxpayer; and

(c) be for research in which substantially all of the activities are elements of a process of experimentation that relates to a new or improved function, performance, reliability or quality. (Code Sec. 41(d)(1); Reg § 1.41-4(a)(5))

Additional tests apply to research costs of software developed for the taxpayer's internal use. (Code Sec. 41(d)(4)(E)) Certain activities (e.g., marketing, surveys, duplication of existing business components, post-commercial-production activities) aren't qualified expenses. (Code Sec. 41(d)(4)) To pass test (b), above, research has to be intended to eliminate uncertainty about the development or improvement of a business component, and the process of experimentation has to fundamentally rely on principles of the physical or biological sciences, engineering, or computer science. A taxpayer can use existing technologies and rely on existing principles of these sciences. Courts generally have applied these tests strictly.[6] The issuance of certain patents is conclusive evidence that a taxpayer has discovered technological-in-nature information that is intended to eliminate uncertainty about the development or improvement of a business component. (Reg § 1.41-4(a)(3)(iii))

QREs are amounts the taxpayer paid or incurred during the tax year "in carrying on any

---

3. ¶L-15300 *et seq.*; ¶414 *et seq.*; TD ¶384,002   5. ¶L-15309 *et seq.*; ¶414 *et seq.*; TD ¶384,015
4. ¶L-15309.1   6. ¶L-15412

trade or business" (including certain start-up costs) of the taxpayer for: in-house research expenses, which consists of certain wages and supplies, and contract research expenses, i.e., 65% of amounts paid to certain nonemployees, and 100% of the taxpayer's expenditures to eligible small businesses, universities, and federal laboratories for qualified energy research. (Code Sec. 41(b); Reg § 1.41-2)[7]

For purposes of calculating the allowable research credit for persons that acquire the major portion of either a trade or business or a separate unit of a trade or business of another person, the amount of QREs paid or incurred by the acquiring person during the measurement period is increased by certain of the predecessor's expenses, and the acquiring person's gross receipts for the period is increased by certain of the predecessor's gross receipts. The measurement period is, for the tax year of the acquiring person for which the research credit is determined, any period of the acquiring person preceding the tax year which is taken into account for purposes of determining the credit for the year. (Code Sec. 41(f)(3)(A), Code Sec. 41(f)(3)(B))

The credit for each member of a controlled group is determined on a proportionate basis to its share of the aggregate of the QREs, basic research payments, and amounts paid or incurred to energy research consortiums, taken into account by the controlled group for purposes of the research credit. (Code Sec. 41(f)(1)(A)(ii)) A similar rule applies to members of a group of commonly controlled trades or businesses. (Code Sec. 41(f)(1)(B)(ii))

⊘observation: This rule means that it is not necessary to compute each member's stand-alone entity credits.

Any expense taken into account in computing the orphan drug credit (¶2328) for a tax year can't be taken into account in computing the credit. (Code Sec. 45C(c)(1)) But, any orphan drug expenses for any tax year which are QREs can be taken into account in determining base period research expenses in later tax years. (Code Sec. 45C(c)(2))[8]

No deduction is allowed for that portion of the otherwise deductible QREs or basic research expenses that equals the credit for the tax year. (Code Sec. 280C(c)(1)) If a taxpayer capitalizes rather than deducts expenses, the amount of the expenses capitalized during the year is reduced by the excess of the credit over the amount allowable (without regard to that disallowance) as a deduction for the tax year. (Code Sec. 280C(c)(2))[9] But a taxpayer can avoid the reduction for any tax year by claiming a reduced credit for the year. The election limits the taxpayer to a credit in the amount of the research credit before any reduction less the product of that credit amount times the maximum corporate tax rate. (Code Sec. 280C(c)(3))[10]

A taxpayer can elect an *alternative simplified research credit* equal to 14% of the excess of the QREs for the tax year over 50% of the average QREs for the three tax years preceding the tax year for which the credit is being determined. (Code Sec. 41(c)(5)(A), Reg § 1.41-9(a)) If a taxpayer has no QREs in any one of the three preceding tax years, the alternative simplified research credit is 6% of the QREs for the tax year for which the credit is being determined. (Code Sec. 41(c)(5)(B)) The election applies to the tax year for which it is made and all following tax years unless revoked with IRS's consent. It can't be made or revoked on an amended return. (Code Sec. 41(c)(5)(C); Reg § 1.41-9(b))[11]

The 20% *university basic research credit* component applies to 100% of cash expenditures by corporations (except S corporations, personal holding companies, or service organizations) for basic research over the sum of: (1) the minimum basic research amount, plus (2) the maintenance-of-effort amount. (Code Sec. 41(e); Reg § 1.41-7)[12] The minimum basic research amount (Code Sec. 41(e)(4); Reg § 1.41-7) is the greatest of: (1) 1% of the average amount paid for in-house and contract research expenses during the base period (the three tax years before the first tax year beginning after '83); (Code Sec. 41(e)(7)(B)) (2) the contract research expense for the base period; or (3) 50% of the basic research payments if the taxpayer wasn't

7. ¶L-15401 *et seq.*; ¶414.01; TD ¶384,008
8. ¶L-15621; ¶414.04
9. ¶L-3131; ¶280C4, ¶414.04; TD ¶306,508
10. ¶L-15308; ¶s 280C4, 414.04; TD ¶384,019
11. ¶L-15302.2; ¶414.0107; TD ¶384,003.1
12. ¶L-15501 *et seq.*; ¶s 414.01, 414.02; TD ¶384,018

in existence for a full year in the base period.[13] The maintenance-of-effort amount is: (a) the average charitable contribution to all educational institutions during the base period (see above) multiplied by the cost-of-living adjustment, *minus* (b) the charitable contributions to educational institutions for the year. (Code Sec. 41(e)(5)(A))[14]

¶ 2320   Low-income housing credit for qualified buildings—Forms 8609, 8586.

The low-income housing credit is allowed annually over a ten-year credit period beginning with the tax year the qualified building is placed in service, or, under an irrevocable election (on Form 8609), the next tax year. (Code Sec. 42(f)(1)) The credit period for an existing building can't begin before the first tax year of the tax period for rehabilitation expenses for the building. (Code Sec. 42(f)(5)(A))[15]

The credit equals the qualified building's qualified basis times the applicable percentage (see below) (Code Sec. 42(a)) prescribed by IRS for the month placed in service or elected in agreement with the housing credit agency. (Code Sec. 42(b)(2)(A)) The building owner can't claim a credit amount in excess of the allocation received from the state or housing credit agency for that year. (Reg § 1.42-1T(e)(1))[16]

IRS prescribes percentages that will yield, over a ten-year period, credit amounts that will have a present value equal to 70% of the qualified basis of new buildings (not federally subsidized) and 30% of the qualified basis of existing buildings and federally subsidized new buildings, see following table. For any new building that is placed in service by the taxpayer after July 30, 2008 with respect to housing credit dollar amount allocations made before Jan. 1, 2014, and that is not federally subsidized for the tax year, the applicable percentage won't be less than 9%. (Code Sec. 42(b))[17]

Month	Year	70% present value credit	30% present value credit
Nov.	2013	7.59%	3.25%
Oct.	2013	7.63%	3.27%
Sept.	2013	7.57%	3.24%
Aug.	2013	7.55%	3.24%
July	2013	7.46%	3.20%
June	2013	7.39%	3.17%
May	2013	7.41%	3.18%
Apr.	2013	7.43%	3.19%
Mar.	2013	7.43%	3.18%
Feb.	2013	7.40%	3.17%
Jan.	2013	7.36%	3.16%
Dec.	2012	7.38%	3.16%

caution: Check tax.thomsonreuters.com/federaltaxhandbookupdates to see if the above provision dealing with a 9% minimum applicable percentage for nonfederally subsidized buildings has been extended.

A credit for rehabilitation expenditures (treated as a separate building (Code Sec. 42(e)(1))) is allowed only if during any 24-month period they are the greater of: 10% of the building's adjusted basis or $3,000 per low-income unit. (Code Sec. 42(e)(3)(A))

To claim the credit, taxpayers must file Form 8586 for each tax year in the ten-year credit period. (Code Sec. 42(g)(4))[18] Form 8609 is filed once with the taxpayer's tax return.[19]

A qualified low-income building is a building that at all times during the "compliance period" of 15 tax years beginning with the first tax year of the credit period, is part of a qualified low-income housing project. (Code Sec. 42(c)(2), Code Sec. 42(i)(1), Code Sec. 42(g))

13. ¶s L-15508, L-15507; ¶414.02
14. ¶L-15509; ¶414.02
15. ¶L-15700 *et seq.*; ¶424.10, 424.55; TD ¶383,001
16. ¶L-15702; ¶424.10; TD ¶383,001
17. ¶L-15718; ¶424.10; TD ¶383,001
18. ¶S-3456; ¶424.50; TD ¶383,002
19. ¶S-3451; ¶424.50; TD ¶383,002

In addition, no credit is allowed unless an extended low income housing commitment (for an additional 15-year period) between the taxpayer and the housing credit agency is in effect at the end of the tax year. (Code Sec. 42(h)(6))[20]

¶ 2321   Recapture of low-income housing credit—Form 8611.

If, at the close of any year in the compliance period (¶2320), the building's qualified basis is less than it was at the close of the earlier tax year, the taxpayer's tax for the year is increased (Code Sec. 42(j)(1), Code Sec. 42(j)(4)(B)) by the sum of:

(1) the total decrease in taxpayer's general business credits for all earlier tax years that would have resulted if the accelerated portion of the credit (below) allowable for the earlier tax years wasn't allowed for all earlier tax years for the decrease in qualified basis, plus

(2) an amount of nondeductible interest on (1), above, computed at the rate charged for overpayment of tax, see ¶4853. (Code Sec. 42(j)(2))

The accelerated portion of the credit for the earlier tax years is the excess of the total credit allowed for the earlier tax years over the total credit that would have been allowable for those years if the total credit that would have been allowable for the entire compliance period were allowable ratably over 15 years. (Code Sec. 42(j)(3))[21]

The disposition of a building (or interest in it) won't result in an increase in tax from credit recapture if it's reasonably expected that the building will continue to be operated as a qualified low-income building for the remaining compliance period for that building. The otherwise applicable statute of limitations is extended until three years after IRS is notified (as specified in guidance) of noncompliance with the low-income housing tax credit rules. (Code Sec. 42(j)(6))[22]

¶ 2322   Enhanced oil recovery (EOR) credit.

The EOR credit for any tax year is 15% of the taxpayer's qualified EOR costs for the tax year. (Code Sec. 43(a)) These are amounts paid or incurred for: (1) qualifying tangible property that's depreciable or amortizable; (2) qualifying tertiary injectant acquisition and use costs that qualify for a deduction under Code Sec. 193; (3) qualifying intangible drilling and development costs (IDCs) that are eligible for the Code Sec. 263(c) expensing election; and (4) Alaska gas treatment plant construction costs. (Code Sec. 43(c)(1)) The credit is phased out as the average per barrel wellhead price of domestic crude oil (reference price) for the last calendar year that ended before the tax year in question exceeds $28 (adjusted for inflation). (Code Sec. 43(b)) Accordingly, the credit is phased out completely for 2013.[23]

¶ 2323   Disabled access credit (DAC)—Form 8826.

An "eligible small business" (ESB) may elect (on Form 8826) to apply against income tax a DAC of 50% of the amount of "eligible access expenditures" for the tax year that's over $250 and not more than $10,250. (Code Sec. 44(a))

observation: For any tax year, the credit can't exceed $5,000 [50% of ($10,250 – $250)].

For partnerships and S corporations, the limitation applies at the entity and the individual partner or shareholder levels. (Code Sec. 44(d)(3))

An ESB for any tax year is any person who either: (1) has gross receipts of $1 million or less for the past tax year, net of returns and allowances, or (2) employed 30 or less full-time employees in the past tax year; an employee who is employed at least 30 hours a week for 20 or more calendar weeks in the tax year is full-time. (Code Sec. 44(b), Code Sec. 44(d)(5))

Eligible access expenditures are amounts paid or incurred so a business can comply with

---

20. ¶L-15719 *et seq.*; ¶424.60; TD ¶383,004
21. ¶L-16050 *et seq.*; ¶424.85; TD ¶383,014

22. ¶L-16050 *et seq.*; ¶424.85; TD ¶383,014
23. ¶L-17615; ¶434.01; TD ¶384,050

the Americans With Disabilities Act of '90 (ADA, as in effect on Nov. 5, '90). (Code Sec. 44(c)(1)) These expenses include *only* expenses that are necessary to comply with ADA, that are paid or incurred: (1) for the purpose of removing architectural, communication, physical or transportation barriers in connection with any facility first placed in service before Nov. 6, '90, which prevent a business from being accessible to, or usable by, disabled individuals; (2) to provide qualified interpreters or other effective methods of making aurally delivered materials available to hearing impaired individuals; (3) to provide qualified readers, taped texts and other effective methods of making visually delivered materials available to visually impaired individuals; (4) to acquire or modify equipment or devices for disabled individuals; or (5) to provide other similar services, modifications, materials or equipment. (Code Sec. 44(c))[24] DAC didn't apply to software expenses to improve access to a business website.[25]

¶ 2324   Credit for producing electricity from renewable resources—Form 8835.

A renewable electricity production credit (claimed on Form 8835) is allowed for electricity produced by taxpayers from: (1) wind, (2) closed-loop biomass , (3) open-loop biomass , (4) geothermal energy, (5) municipal solid waste, (6) marine and hydrokinetic renewables (e.g., waves and tides); (7) qualified hydropower production, (8) small irrigation power and (9) solar power. (Code Sec. 45(c)) For facilities producing electricity from the resources in (1) through (7) (including landfill gas and trash facilities using municipal solid waste) to be qualified facilities, the facility's construction must begin before 2014. Qualified small irrigation power facilities had to be placed in service before Oct. 3, 2008. Qualified facilities for solar energy had to be placed in service before 2006. (Code Sec. 45(d))[26] The electricity production credit is generally available for a 10-year period beginning on the placed-in-service date of the qualifying facility for electricity produced during that period. (Code Sec. 45(a)(2)(A)) The 10-year credit period for a qualified hydropower facility begins on the date that the qualifying efficiency improvements or additions to capacity are placed in service. (Code Sec. 45(d)(9)(C))

For 2013, the credit is 2.3¢ per kilowatt hour (KWH). (Code Sec. 45(a)) But, for electricity produced and sold at any qualifying facility using open-loop biomass, small irrigation power, landfill gas, trash, or hydropower, marine or hydrokinetic the amount of the credit (before it's indexed for inflation for the calendar year), is reduced to 1.1¢ per KWH. (Code Sec. 45(b)(4)) The credit is allowed for qualified electricity sold to an unrelated person (Code Sec. 45(a)(2)(B))[27] and produced from U.S. (or U.S. possession) facilities (see above). The credit is allocated to a taxpayer in proportion to his ownership interest in the gross sales from the qualifying facility. (Code Sec. 45(e))[28]

The credit is proportionately phased out when the national average price of electricity produced from the applicable renewable resource exceeds a specified, inflation-adjusted threshold price per KWH. (Code Sec. 45(b)(1)) Accordingly, there is no phaseout for 2013.[29]

A credit applies for the domestic production of refined coal from a qualified facility placed in service after Oct. 22, 2004 and before 2012. (Code Sec. 45(c)(7), Code Sec. 45(d)(8)) The refined coal credit is equal to $6.590 for 2013 (as indexed for inflation) per ton of qualified refined coal and phases out as the market price of refined coal exceeds certain threshold levels. (Code Sec. 45(d)(8)) No phaseout applies for 2013.[30]

For Indian coal produced and sold before 2014, from a qualified facility placed in service before 2009, an inflation-adjusted Indian coal production credit is allowed ($2.308 per ton for 2013). (Code Sec. 45(e)(10))[31]

⚠ caution: Check tax.thomsonreuters.com/federaltaxhandbookupdates to see if the above provision has been extended.

---

24. ¶L-17900 *et seq.*; ¶444; TD ¶382,500 *et seq.*   28. ¶L-17755; ¶454; TD ¶384,055
25. ¶L-17902; TD ¶382,502   29. ¶L-17760 *et seq.*; ¶454; TD ¶384,056
26. ¶L-17751 *et seq.*; ¶454; TD ¶384,054   30. ¶L-17771.7B; ¶454.16; TD ¶384,054.1
27. ¶L-17754; ¶454; TD ¶384,054   31. ¶L-17771.8; ¶454.17; TD ¶384,054.1

340

Taxpayers can elect to have qualified property of certain qualified facilities treated as energy property eligible for a 30% investment credit under Code Sec. 48 (¶2311). These facilities are wind facilities placed in service in 2009 through 2014; and the other Code Sec. 45(d) facilities (other than refined or Indian coal facilities or solar facilities) placed in service in 2009 through 2014 that are otherwise eligible for the Code Sec. 45 credit, for which no such credit has been allowed. Qualified property is tangible property or other tangible property (not including a building or its structural components), but only if the property is used as an integral part of the qualified facility: for which depreciation (or amortization) is allowable; which is constructed, reconstructed, erected, or acquired by the taxpayer; and the original use of which begins with the taxpayer. (Code Sec. 48(a)(5)) The irrevocable election (on Form 3468) is made on a timely filed return (including extensions) for the tax year in which the facility is placed in service.[32]

No Code Sec. 45 credit is allowed for energy property for which a grant is made by the Treasury Secretary in lieu of the credit for property placed in service (a) during 2009, 2010, or 2011; or (b) after 2011 and before the credit termination date (generally, Jan. 1, 2017) but only if construction of the property began during 2009, 2010, or 2011. If the credit is allowed, recapture applies. The basis of the property is reduced by 50% of the amount of the grant. (Code Sec. 48(d), ARRA § 1603 as amended by TRA §707)[33]

¶ 2325 Empowerment zone employment credit before 2014—Form 8844.

Before 2014, employers can claim (on Form 8844) an empowerment zone employment credit for any tax year equal to 20% of the qualified zone wages paid or incurred during the calendar year that ended with or within that tax year. (Code Sec. 1396(a), Code Sec. 1400(d)) The amount of qualified zone wages (qualified wages paid to an employee who is a resident of certain designated distressed urban and rural areas and who performs substantially all employment services within the zone in the employer's trade or business) that are taken into account for each employee can't exceed $15,000 for a calendar year. (Code Sec. 1396(c)(2)) Thus, the credit can't exceed $3,000 per qualified employee.[34] Qualified zone wages don't include wages taken into account for the work opportunity tax credit (WOTC, ¶2314), and the $15,000 maximum amount above is reduced by the amount of wages taken into account for the WOTC. (Code Sec. 1396(c)(3))[35] The credit also reduces an employer's wage deduction for the year. (Code Sec. 280C(a))[36]

caution: Check tax.thomsonreuters.com/federaltaxhandbookupdates to see if the above provision has been extended.

¶ 2326 Indian employment credit before 2014—Form 8845.

For tax years beginning before Jan. 1, 2014 (Code Sec. 45A(f)),[37] the Indian employment credit (claimed on Form 8845) is 20% of the excess, if any, of the sum of qualified wages and qualified employee health insurance costs (not in excess of $20,000 per employee) paid or incurred (other than paid under salary reduction arrangements) to qualified employees (enrolled Indian tribe members and their spouses who meet certain requirements) during the tax year (Code Sec. 45A(a)(1), Code Sec. 45A(b)(2)) over the sum of these same costs paid or incurred in calendar year '93—determined as if the Indian employment credit had been in effect in '93. (Code Sec. 45A(a)(2); Code Sec. 45A(c)) Tax credits claimed for certain terminated employees are recaptured. (Code Sec. 45A(d)) Deductions for wages and health insurance costs are reduced by the credit. (Code Sec. 280C(a))

caution: Check tax.thomsonreuters.com/federaltaxhandbookupdates to see if the above provision has been extended.

---

32. ¶L-16401.1; ¶484.01; TD ¶381,601.1
33. ¶L-17773; ¶454.19; TD ¶384,058.1
34. ¶L-15630 *et seq.*; ¶13,964; TD ¶384,021

35. ¶L-15632; ¶13,964; TD ¶384,024
36. ¶L-15639.2; ¶13,964; TD ¶384,030
37. ¶L-15670 *et seq.*; ¶45A4; TD ¶384,039

¶ 2327   FICA tip credit—Form 8846.

A food and beverage establishment is allowed a credit (on Form 8846) for the amount of the employer's FICA tax obligation (7.65%) attributable to employee tips received for providing, delivering, or serving food or beverages (whether or not the tips are reported as required by Code Sec. 6053). However, no credit is given for tips used to meet the federal minimum wage rate. (Code Sec. 45B) Employers determine their Code Sec. 45B credit using the minimum wage in effect on Jan. 1, 2007 (Code Sec. 45B(b)(1)) (i.e., $5.15).[38] No deduction is allowed for any amount taken into account in determining the FICA tip credit. (Code Sec. 45B(c)) A taxpayer can elect out of the credit for any tax year. (Code Sec. 45B(d))[39]

¶ 2328   Qualified clinical testing expense ("orphan drug") credit—Form 8820.

A taxpayer that incurs qualified clinical testing expenses (QCTEs) for drugs for rare diseases may claim (on Form 8820) a credit equal to 50% of those expenses for the tax year. (Code Sec. 45C)[40] QCTEs are amounts which, with certain modifications, would qualify as qualified research expenses for the research credit (¶2319). (Code Sec. 45C(b)(1))

¶ 2329   New markets tax credit before 2014—Form 8874.

Before 2014, a "new markets tax credit" applies for qualified equity investments to acquire stock in a community development entity (CDE). Nationally, the maximum annual amount of qualifying equity investments is capped at $3.5 billion for 2010, 2011, 2012, and 2013; but no amount can be carried over to any calendar year after 2018. (Code Sec. 45D) A CDE is any domestic corporation or partnership (1) whose primary mission is serving or providing investment capital for low-income communities or low-income persons, (2) that maintains accountability to residents of low-income communities through representation on governing or advisory boards of the CDE, and (3) is certified by Treasury as an eligible CDE. A qualified equity investment is stock or a similar equity interest acquired directly from a CDE for cash. Substantially all (at least 85%, reduced to 75% for the final year of the 7-year credit period) of the cash has to be used by the CDE to make investments in, or loans to, qualified active businesses located in low-income communities or certain financial services to businesses and residents in low-income communities. A qualified equity investment made by an LLC (classified as a partnership) can include cash from a nonrecourse loan or a recourse loan to the LLC that the LLC invests as equity in a qualified CDE, where the loan is indebtedness for federal income tax purposes. (Code Sec. 45D; Reg § 1.45D-1(c)(5))[41]

caution: Check tax.thomsonreuters.com/federaltaxhandbookupdates to see if the above provision has been extended.

The new markets tax credit (claimed on Form 8874) is: (a) 5% for the year in which the equity interest is purchased from the CDE and for the first two anniversary dates after the purchase (for a total credit of 15%), *plus* (b) 6% on each anniversary date thereafter for the following 4 years (for a total of 24%).[42] The credit is recaptured if the entity fails to continue to be a CDE or the interest is redeemed within seven years, unless it is allowed to correct its failure, and does so. (Code Sec. 45D(g); Reg § 1.45D-1(e))[43]

¶ 2330   Credit for employer-provided child care—Form 8882.

A tax credit for 'employer-provided child care' (Code Sec. 45F(a)) is allowed for the sum of the following expenses (up to $150,000) for the tax year Code Sec. 45F(b)):[44]

---

38. ¶L-17860 *et seq.*; ¶45B4; TD ¶382,000 *et seq.*
39. ¶L-17860 *et seq.*; ¶45B4; TD ¶382,005
40. ¶L-15615 *et seq.*; ¶45C4
41. ¶L-17920 *et seq.*; ¶L-17924 ; ¶45D4 *et seq.*; TD ¶384,700 *et seq.*

42. ¶L-17922; ¶45D4; TD ¶384,702
43. ¶L-17928; ¶45D4.10; TD ¶384,713
44. ¶L-17872; ¶45F4; TD ¶382,102

(1) 25% of qualified child care expenses, which are expenses to buy, build, rehabilitate, or expand property to be used as part of an employer's qualified child care facility, for which a deduction for depreciation (or amortization) is allowable, and which isn't part of the taxpayer's (or an employee's) principal residence. Qualifying child care expenses also include operating costs of a taxpayer's qualified child care facility (including costs related to employee training, scholarship programs, and to providing increased compensation to employees with higher levels of child care training), and amounts paid under a contract with a qualified child care facility to provide child care services to the taxpayer's employees. (Code Sec. 45F(c)(1)(A)) Qualified child care expenses don't include expenses in excess of the FMV of the care. (Code Sec. 45F(c)(1)(B))

(2) 10% of qualified child care resource and referral expenses (i.e., amounts paid or incurred under a contract to provide child care resource and referral services to an employee).[45]

Generally, for purposes of (1), above, a qualified child care facility is one principally used to provide child care assistance, and which meets the requirements of the state or local government in which it is located, including its licensing as a child care facility. (Code Sec. 45F(c)(2)(A)) The facility must be open to the taxpayer's employees during the tax year, and, if it is the taxpayer's principal trade or business, at least 30% of its enrollees must be the dependents of the taxpayer's employees.[46]

The provision of child care resource and referral services or facilities can't discriminate in favor of highly compensated employees (within the meaning of Code Sec. 414(q)) (see ¶4326). (Code Sec. 45F(c)(2)(B), Code Sec. 45F(c)(3))[47]

A taxpayer claiming a Code Sec. 45F credit for acquiring, constructing, rehabilitating, or expanding a qualified child care facility must reduce its basis in the facility by the amount of the credit. (Code Sec. 45F(f)(1)(A))[48] No deduction or credit is allowed for any amount taken into account in determining Code Sec. 45F credit. (Code Sec. 45F(f)(2))[49]

Recapture rules apply for the first 10 years after the facility is placed in service. (Code Sec. 45F(d))[50]

For purposes of the credit, all persons treated as one employer under Code Sec. 52(a) or Code Sec. 52(b) are treated as one taxpayer. Regs are to address credit allocations between an estate or trust and its beneficiaries, and among partners of a partnership. (Code Sec. 45F(e))[12]

¶ 2331   Small employer pension plan startup credit—Form 8881.

Eligible small employers that adopt a new qualified defined benefit or defined contribution plan (including a Code Sec. 401(k) plan, SIMPLE plan, or SEP) may claim a credit. The credit equals 50% of administrative and retirement-related education expenses for the plan for each of the first three plan years, with a maximum credit of $500 for each year. The first credit year is the tax year that includes the date the plan becomes effective, or, electively, the preceding tax year. (Code Sec. 45E(a), Code Sec. 45E(b), Code Sec. 45E(d)(3))[3]

The pension plan startup credit is available only to businesses that did not employ, in the preceding year, more than 100 employees with compensation of at least $5,000. But, an employer isn't an eligible employer if, during the three-tax year period immediately preceding the first tax year for which the credit is otherwise allowable, it or any member of any controlled group including the employer (or any predecessor of either) established or maintained a qualified employer plan to which contributions were made, or benefits were accrued, for substantially the same employees that are in the qualified employer plan. (Code Sec. 45E(c)(2))[4] For purposes of Code Sec. 45E, all persons treated as a single employer under Code Sec. 52(a) or Code Sec. 52(b) or Code Sec. 414(m) or Code Sec. 414(o) are treated as one

45. ¶L-17870 *et seq.*; ¶45F4; TD ¶382,100 *et seq.*
46. ¶L-17874; ¶45F4; TD ¶382,104
47. ¶L-17875; ¶45F4; TD ¶382,105
48. ¶L-17876; ¶45F4; TD ¶382,106
49. ¶L-17877; ¶45F4; TD ¶382,107

50. ¶L-17878; ¶45F4.01; TD ¶382,108
1. ¶L-17879; TD ¶382,109
2. ¶L-17870; ¶45F4; TD ¶382,100
3. ¶L-15690 *et seq.*; ¶45E4; TD ¶384,060 *et seq.*
4. ¶L-15692; ¶45E4; TD ¶384,202

taxpayer. (Code Sec. 45E(e)(1))[5] To be eligible for the credit, the plan must cover at least one nonhighly compensated employee. If the credit is for the cost of a payroll-deduction IRA plan, it must be made available to all employees who have worked with the employer for at least three months. (Code Sec. 45E(d)(1))[6]

No deduction is allowed for that portion of the qualified startup costs paid or incurred for the tax year which is equal to the credit. (Code Sec. 45E(e)(2))[7] An eligible employer may elect not to have the credit apply for any tax year. (Code Sec. 45E(e)(3))[8]

¶ 2332   Small employer health insurance credit—Forms 8941; 990-T.

Subject to a phaseout (see below), an eligible small employer (ESE) may claim a credit (on Form 8941) equal to 35% in tax years beginning in 2010 to 2013 (i.e., the initial phase) of nonelective contributions for health insurance for its employees. This percentage increases to 50% in tax years beginning after 2013. (Code Sec. 45R)

An ESE is generally an employer with no more than 25 full-time equivalent employees (FTEs) employed during its tax year, and whose employees have average annual wages of no more than $50,000. (Code Sec. 45R(d)) However, the full credit is available only to an employer with 10 or fewer FTEs and whose employees have average annual full-time equivalent wages from the employer of not more than $25,000. (Code Sec. 45R(c)) Average annual wages may be computed in three ways (actual hours worked, days-worked equivalency, weeks-worked equivalency), and the same methods need not be applied for different classifications of employees, if the classifications are reasonable and consistently applied.

The FTEs of an ESE are determined by dividing the total hours of service (up to 2,080 hours of service determined by an employee's actual hours of service, a days-worked equivalency method, or a weeks-worked equivalency method) by 2,080. (Code Sec. 45R(d)) Average annual wages are determined by dividing (a) total wages (as defined for FICA purposes, without regard to the wage base limitation) paid to employees during the ESE's tax year by (b) the number of the FTEs for the year. The result is rounded down to the nearest $1,000 (if not otherwise a multiple of $1,000). (Code Sec. 45R(d)(3)(A), Code Sec. 45R(e)(4)) Aggregation rules apply in determining ESE status. (Code Sec. 45R(b))[9]

Self-employed individuals, including partners and sole proprietors, 2% S corporation shareholders, and 5% owners of the employer (within the meaning of Code Sec. 416(i)(1)(B)(i)): (1) aren't treated as employees; (2) their wages or hours are not counted in determining either the number of FTEs or the amount of average annual wages; and (3) premiums paid on their behalf are not counted in determining the credit. (Code Sec. 45R(e)) Similarly, an employee-spouse of any of the following isn't taken into account: (1) a more-than-2% S shareholder; (2) a more-than-5% owner of a business; (3) a partner owning more than a 5% interest in a partnership; and (4) a sole proprietor.

In the initial phase, an ESE has to contribute at least 50% of the cost of an employee's insurance premiums under a contribution arrangement.[10] An employer's self-insured plan, including a health reimbursement arrangement (HRA), health flexible spending arrangement (health FSA), health savings accounts (HSAs), or self-insured coverage provided through a multiemployer plan, isn't a health insurance plan for Code Sec. 45R purposes. The credit equals the lesser of the following two amounts multiplied by the percentage (described above):

(1) total nonelective contributions the ESE made on behalf of the FTEs during the tax year for qualifying health coverage. (Code Sec. 45R(b)) Qualifying health insurance for claiming the credit in the initial phase is health insurance coverage within the meaning of Code Sec. 9832(b)(1) (generally health insurance coverage bought from a state licensed insurance company). (Code Sec. 45R(g)(2))

---

5. ¶L-15699.1; TD ¶384,202
6. ¶L-15694; TD ¶384,202
7. ¶L-15698; ¶45E4; TD ¶384,208

8. ¶L-15699; ¶45E4; TD ¶384,209
9. ¶L-15682 *et seq.*; ¶45R4.02; TD ¶384,302
10. ¶L-15689.5 *et seq.*; ¶45R4.02; TD ¶384,302

(2) total nonelective contributions the ESE would have paid if each employee were enrolled in a plan with a premium equal to the average premium for the small group market in the state (or in an area in the state) in which the employer is offering health insurance coverage.[11] (Code Sec. 45R(b))

In tax years beginning after 2013, an ESE has to offer insurance through an exchange and an ESE can only claim the credit for two consecutive tax years. (Code Sec. 45R(d)(4); Code Sec. 45R(e)(2))

Generally, state tax credits and payments to an ESE do not reduce the credit, and state direct payments to an insurance company are treated as paid on an ESE's behalf. But, in no event can the amount of the credit exceed the amount of an ESE's net premium payments.[12]

Tax-exempt ESEs. The applicable percentage for an eligible small tax-exempt employer (tax-exempt ESE) is 25% for 2010 to 2013 and 35% after 2013. (However, for tax-exempt ESEs, the refundable portion of their claims is reduced by 8.7% due to the sequestration's automatic reduction that took place as of Mar. 1, 2013 and that applied until the end of the fiscal year (Sept. 30, 2013). For tax-exempt ESEs, the credit is a refundable tax credit (claimed on Form 990-T) limited to the amount of the employer's payroll taxes (income tax and Medicare tax withheld from employees' wages and the employer share of Medicare tax on employees' wages) during the calendar year in which the tax year begins. (Code Sec. 45R(b); Code Sec. 45R(f))

The credit reduces the ESE's Code Sec. 162 deduction. (Code Sec. 45R(e)(5))[13]

¶ 2333 Biodiesel fuel credit before 2014—Form 8864.

For fuels produced and sold or used before 2014 (Code Sec. 40A(g)), a taxpayer can claim a credit (on Form 8864) equal to the sum of: (1) a biodiesel mixture credit of $1 per gallon of biodiesel used in the production of a qualified biodiesel mixture; (2) a biodiesel credit of $1 per gallon of biodiesel, not in a mixture, used as a fuel in the taxpayer's trade or business, or sold at retail and placed in a vehicle fuel tank; and (3) for an eligible small agri-biodiesel producer, a small agri-biodiesel producer credit of 10¢ per gallon of agri-biodiesel, up to a 15,000,000 gallon maximum: (a) used by the producer or sold by the producer for use in the production of a qualified biodiesel mixture in a trade or business or as fuel in a trade or business, or (b) sold at retail and placed in a vehicle fuel tank by the producer or a person buying from the producer. (Code Sec. 40A(a), Code Sec. 40A(b))[14] The credit is inapplicable to fuel produced outside the U.S. for use outside the U.S. (Code Sec. 40A(d)(5)) Renewable diesel is treated like biodiesel. (Code Sec. 40A(f))[15]

caution: Check tax.thomsonreuters.com/federaltaxhandbookupdates to see if the above provision has been extended.

¶ 2334 New energy efficient home credit before 2014—Form 8908.

For homes acquired before 2014, eligible contractors (including manufacturers of manufactured homes) that construct new energy-efficient homes can qualify for a $2,000 or $1,000 credit (claimed on Form 8908) per qualifying home. (Code Sec. 45L(a), Code Sec. 45L(g))[16] A structure qualifies for the credit if it meets specific energy saving requirements under Code Sec. 45L(c), and its construction (which includes substantial reconstruction and rehabilitation) is substantially completed after Aug. 8, 2005. It has to be located in the U.S. (Code Sec. 45L(a), Code Sec. 45L(b)(2))[17] A property's basis is reduced by the amount of credit. (Code Sec. 45L(e))[18]

---

11. ¶L-15689.8A; ¶45R4.06
12. ¶L-15689.6B; ¶45R4.06
13. ¶L-15681; ¶45R4; TD ¶384,301
14. ¶L-17570; ¶40A4; TD ¶382,400

15. ¶L-17585; ¶40A4.05; TD ¶382,409
16. ¶L-17940; ¶45L4; TD ¶569,570
17. ¶L-17944; ¶45L4; TD ¶569,574
18. ¶L-17949.3; ¶45L4; TD ¶569,579.1

⚡*caution:* Check tax.thomsonreuters.com/federaltaxhandbookupdates to see if the above provision has been extended.

A home (including a manufactured one) qualifies for the $2,000 credit if it is certified to have a projected 50% reduction in the level of annual heating and cooling energy consumption, compared to comparable dwellings, and at least $1/5$ of the 50% reduction is from building envelope component improvements—insulation materials or systems specifically and primarily designed to reduce heat loss or gain, exterior windows (including skylights), doors, and any duct sealing and infiltration reduction measures. (Code Sec. 45L(a)(2), Code Sec. 45L(c))[19]

A manufactured home qualifies for a $1,000 credit if it is either (1) certified to have a projected 30% reduction in the level of annual heating and cooling energy consumption, compared to comparable dwellings, and its building envelope component improvements account for at least one-third of the 30% reduction, or (2) it meets the requirements under the Energy Star Labeled Homes program. (Code Sec. 45L(a)(2), Code Sec. 45L(c)(3))[20]

¶ 2335   Energy efficient appliance credit before 2014—Form 8909.

Manufacturers can qualify for a credit for producing energy efficient dishwashers, clothes washers, and refrigerators produced by the taxpayer during the calendar year before 2014 in the U.S. The credit (claimed on Form 8909) depended on the type of appliance and how much energy it saved. (Code Sec. 45M(b)) The aggregate credit amount allowed to a taxpayer for any tax year was $25 million less credit amounts allowed for all previous tax years beginning after 2010, with an exception for the refrigerator credit and the clothes washer credit. Also, the credit was subject to a gross receipts limitation (4% of a taxpayer's average annual gross receipts for the three previous tax years). (Code Sec. 45M(e))[21]

⚡*caution:* Check tax.thomsonreuters.com/federaltaxhandbookupdates to see if the above provision has been extended.

¶ 2336   Differential wage payment credit before 2014—Form 8932.

For payments made before 2014 (Code Sec. 45P(f)), eligible small business employers (ESBEs) that pay differential wages (i.e., payments for periods that employees are called to active duty with the U.S. uniformed services, see ¶3004) to a qualified employee can claim a credit (on Form 8932) equal to 20% of up to $20,000 of differential pay made to a qualified employee during the tax year. (Code Sec. 45P) A qualified employee is one who is an employee for the 91-day period immediately before the period for which any differential wage payment is made. (Code Sec. 45P(b)(2)) An ESBE is one that: (1) employs on average less than 50 employees on business days during the tax year; and (2) under a written plan, provides eligible differential wage payments to each of its qualified employees. Taxpayers under common control are aggregated when determining if a taxpayer is an ESBE. (Code Sec. 45P(b)(3))

⚡*caution:* Check tax.thomsonreuters.com/federaltaxhandbookupdates to see if the above provision has been extended.

The credit can't be claimed by a taxpayer that has failed to comply with the employment and reemployment rights of members of the uniformed services (as provided under Chapter 43 of Title 38 of the United States Code). (Code Sec. 45P(d)) No deduction can be taken for that part of compensation which is equal to the credit, and the amount of any otherwise allowable income tax credit for compensation paid to an employee has to be reduced by the differential wage payment credit allowed for the employee. (Code Sec. 280C(a))[22]

19. ¶L-17947; ¶45L4; TD ¶569,575
20. ¶L-17949; ¶45L4; TD ¶569,577
21. ¶L-17950; ¶45M4; TD ¶569,580
22. ¶L-15676; ¶45P4

¶ 2337 Alternate (nonconventional source) fuel production credit—Form 8907.

A credit of $3 (adjusted for inflation), multiplied by the barrel of oil equivalent (BOE) of certain qualified fuels, is allowed (claimed on Form 8907) for producing fuel from a nonconventional source. For 2012, there is a $3.58 credit (as indexed for inflation) per BOE allowed for coke and coke gas (other than that produced from petroleum based products) produced and sold after Dec. 31, 2005 at a facility placed in service before Jan. 1, '93 or after June 30, '98 and before Jan. 1, 2010. The credit for coke and coke gas isn't subject to a phaseout. The amount of credit-eligible coke produced can't exceed an average BOE of 4,000 barrels a day. (Code Sec. 45K(g))[23]

¶ 2338 Personal (Refundable and Nonrefundable) Credits. ▆▆▆▆▆▆▆▆▆▆

Taxpayers, whether or not in business, may qualify for one or more personal credits. Some credits are refundable—i.e., the excess of the credit over tax liability is refunded to the taxpayer, some are partly refundable, and some are nonrefundable.

The *refundable* credits are:

. . . Earned income credit (EIC), see ¶2339 *et seq.*;

. . . Pre-2014 health coverage tax credit for displaced workers and PBGC pensionees, see ¶2344;

. . . Post-2013 premium assistance credit, see ¶2345;

. . . Credit for income tax withheld, see ¶2346;

. . . Credit for excess social security tax withheld, see ¶2347;

. . . Child tax credit (partly refundable before 2018), see ¶2356;

. . . Alternative minimum tax (AMT) refundable credit for individuals, see ¶2365;

. . . American opportunity tax credit (AOTC) (partly refundable before 2018), see ¶2202;

. . . Credit for capital gain tax paid by a regulated investment company (RIC), see ¶4201; and

. . . Credit for excise tax on certain nontaxable uses of fuels. (Code Sec. 6420, Code Sec. 6421, Code Sec. 6427)

The *nonrefundable* credits are:

- Credit for the elderly and the permanently and totally disabled, see ¶2348;
- Credit for child and dependent care expenses, see ¶2349 *et seq.*;
- Credit for adoption expenses, see ¶2354;
- Child tax credit (but see above), see ¶2356;
- Credit for certain home mortgage interest, see ¶2357;
- AOTC credit (see above) and Lifetime Learning credit, see ¶2201 *et seq.*;
- Pre-2014 nonbusiness energy property credit, see ¶2358;
- Pre-2017 residential energy efficient property credit, see ¶2359;
- Alternative motor vehicle credit, see ¶2360;
- Pre-2014 credit for alternative fuel vehicle refueling property, see ¶2361;
- New qualified plug-in electric drive motor vehicles (NQPEDMV) credit, see ¶2362;
- Pre-2014 2- or 3-wheeled plug-in electric vehicle (QPEV) credit, see ¶2362;
- "Saver's" credit for elective deferrals and IRA contributions, see ¶2363;
- AMT credit, see ¶2365; and
- Credit for qualified tax credit bonds (QTCBs), see ¶2366.

---

23. ¶L-17706.1; ¶45K4; TD ¶396,001

For the limit on the combined amount of certain personal nonrefundable credits, see ¶2364.

For the treatment of a refund or advance payment of a refundable credit, see ¶4857.

¶ 2339   Earned income credit—overview—Schedule EIC.

An eligible individual (¶2341) is allowed an earned income credit (EIC) equal to the credit percentage of earned income (up to an "earned income amount") for the tax year. (Code Sec. 32(a)(1)) The EIC for a tax year (determined under IRS tables) can't be more than the excess (if any) of (1) the credit percentage of the earned income amount, over (2) the phaseout percentage of AGI (or earned income, if greater) over a phaseout amount. (Code Sec. 32(a)(2)) For 2013, these amounts are (phaseout amounts in table are for other than joint returns):[24]

Qualifying Children:	The Credit % is:	The Earned Income Amount is:	The Phaseout % is:	The Phaseout Amount is:
FOR 2013				
No qualifying children	7.65%	$ 6,370	7.65%	$ 7,970
1 qualifying child	34%	$ 9,560	15.98%	$17,530
2 qualifying children	40%	$13,430	21.06%	$17,530
3 or more qualifying children	45%	$13,430	21.06%	$17,530

The 2013 phaseout amounts for joint filers are $13,310 for no qualifying children, and $22,870 for one or more qualifying children.[25]

The maximum EIC for 2013 is $487 (no qualifying children), $3,250 (one qualifying child), $5,372 (two qualifying children), and $6,044 (three or more qualifying children).[26] It's completely phased out at the following amounts of earned income (or AGI, if greater):

. . . no qualifying children, $14,340 ($19,680 for joint filers),

. . . one qualifying child, $37,870 ($43,210 for joint filers), and

. . . two qualifying children, $43,038 ($48,378 for joint filers).

. . . three or more qualifying children, $46,227 ($51,567 for joint filers).[27]

Taxpayers claiming the credit must file Form 1040 or Form 1040A (or Form 1040EZ if no qualifying child) and attach Schedule EIC.[28] No EIC is allowed if the taxpayer has excess disqualified income, see ¶2342.

The EIC is refundable.[29]

No EIC is allowed for 10 years after a year in which the credit was claimed fraudulently (2 years for erroneously claimed credit due to reckless or intentional disregard of the rules). If the EIC is denied under deficiency procedures, including administrative procedures (but not mathematical or clerical errors), no credit is allowed for any later tax year unless the taxpayer provides information IRS requires to demonstrate eligibility (Code Sec. 32(k); Reg § 1.32-3(b)) (use Form 8862). (Reg § 1.32-3(c))[30] For due diligence requirements for return preparers, see ¶4888.

¶ 2340   Earned income defined for EIC purposes.

For tax years before 2018, earned income for EIC purposes includes wages, salaries, tips, and other employee compensation, but only if those amounts are includible in gross income for the tax year; plus net earnings from self-employment less the Code Sec. 164(f) deduction for half of self-employment tax (¶1755), for the year. (Code Sec. 32(c)(2)(A)) Taxpayers may elect to treat nontaxable combat pay (¶1223) as earned income. (Code Sec. 32(c)(2)(B)(vi))[31]

---

24. ¶A-4201 *et seq.*; ¶324 *et seq.*; TD ¶569,001 *et seq.*
25. ¶A-4202; ¶324.01; TD ¶569,002
26. ¶A-4201; ¶324.01; TD ¶569,001
27. ¶A-4202

28. ¶A-4201; ¶324.01; TD ¶569,001
29. ¶A-4201; ¶324.01; TD ¶569,001
30. ¶A-4205 *et seq.*; ¶324.02; TD ¶569,007
31. ¶A-4222 *et seq.*; ¶324.05; TD ¶569,023 *et seq.*

Earned income is reduced by any net loss in earnings from self-employment (Reg § 1.32-2(c)(2)) and *doesn't* include any amount received as a pension or an annuity (including social security or VA benefits), any amount subject to the 30% withholding tax on U.S. income (not connected with U.S. business) of nonresident alien individuals (Code Sec. 32(c)(2)(B)), unemployment or worker's compensation (Reg § 1.32-2(c)(2)), amounts earned while an inmate in a penal institution, or amounts received for "workfare" services to the extent subsidized by a state program. (Code Sec. 32(c)(2)(B)(iv)) Earned income is determined without regard to community property laws. (Code Sec. 32(c)(2))[32]

¶ 2341 Eligible individual defined for earned income credit (EIC) purposes.

An individual who has a "qualifying child" (¶2343) for the tax year is an eligible individual. (Code Sec. 32(c)(1)(A)(i)) An individual who doesn't have a qualifying child for the tax year is an eligible individual *if*:

... his principal place of abode is in the U.S. for more than half the tax year (U.S. Armed Forces personnel are considered to have a U.S. abode while they're stationed outside the U.S. on extended active duty (Code Sec. 32(c)(4))),

... either he or his spouse (if any) is older than 24 but younger than 65 before the end of the tax year, *and*

... he can't be claimed as another's dependent for a tax year beginning in the same calendar year as his tax year. (Code Sec. 32(c)(1)(A)(ii))[33]

An individual can't be an eligible individual for a tax year if he: is another's qualifying child (¶2343) (Code Sec. 32(c)(1)(B)); elects to exclude foreign earned income (¶4612) (Code Sec. 32(c)(1)(C)); or is a nonresident alien, unless he elects under Code Sec. 6013(g) or Code Sec. 6013(h) to be treated as a U.S. resident. (Code Sec. 32(c)(1)(D))[34]

Married individuals are eligible for only one EIC on their combined earned income and must file a joint return to claim the credit. (Code Sec. 32(d))[35]

Except for short-period returns due to an individual's death, only individuals filing a return for a full 12-month year can claim the credit. (Code Sec. 32(e))[36]

A person can't be an eligible individual unless he includes his (and his spouse's) taxpayer identification number (TIN, social security number, not an individual taxpayer identification number (ITIN) or adoption taxpayer identification number (ATIN)) and the name, age, and TIN (not ITIN or ATIN) of any qualifying child on the return for the tax year. (Code Sec. 32(m), Code Sec. 32(c)(1)(E), Code Sec. 32(c)(1)(F), Code Sec. 32(c)(3)(D))[37]

¶ 2342 No EIC where disqualified income is more than $3,300 in 2013.

A taxpayer with "disqualified income" over $3,300 in 2013 ($3,350 for 2014) can't claim the earned income credit (EIC). (Code Sec. 32(i)(1))[38] Disqualified income means:

(1) interest or dividends to the extent includible in gross income for the year (Code Sec. 32(i)(2)(A));

(2) tax-exempt interest (as defined for return disclosure rules) received or accrued in the year (Code Sec. 32(i)(2)(B));

(3) the excess (if any) of (a) gross income from nonbusiness rents or royalties, over (b) the sum of noninterest deductions clearly and directly allocable to that gross income plus properly allocable interest deductions (Code Sec. 32(i)(2)(C));

(4) capital gain net income for the year (but not gain treated as long-term capital gain under Code Sec. 1231(a)(1), ¶2684) (Code Sec. 32(i)(2)(D)); and

---

32. ¶A-4222 *et seq.*; ¶324.05; TD ¶569,023 *et seq.*
33. ¶A-4209, A-4217; ¶324.02; TD ¶569,009, 569,017
34. ¶A-4209; ¶324.02; TD ¶569,009
35. ¶A-4221; ¶324.02; TD ¶569,022

36. ¶A-4209; ¶324.02; TD ¶569,009
37. ¶A-4219; ¶324.02; TD ¶569,020
38. ¶A-4204; ¶324.02; TD ¶569,004

(5) the excess, if any, of total income from all passive activities for the year (without regard to amounts otherwise included in earned income, or other disqualified income) over total losses from all passive activities for the year (as so determined). (Code Sec. 32(i)(2)(E))[39]

¶ 2343   Qualifying child defined for earned income credit (EIC) purposes.

A "qualifying child" for EIC purposes means a qualifying child of the taxpayer, as defined for the dependency exemption in Code Sec. 152(c) (¶3120) but without the requirement that the child not have provided more than half his own support, and without regard to a custodial parent's release of the dependency exemption (¶3126). (Code Sec. 32(c)(3)(A))[40]

¶ 2344   Health coverage tax credit (HCTC) for health insurance costs of trade-displaced workers and PBGC pension recipients before 2014—Form 8885.

Before Jan. 1, 2014 (Code Sec. 35(b)(1)(B)), an "eligible individual" may claim (file Form 8885 with Form 1040) a refundable HCTC equal to 72.5% of the amount paid by the taxpayer for coverage of the taxpayer and qualifying family members (spouse and dependents (Code Sec. 35(d))) under qualified health insurance as defined in Code Sec. 35(e) (i.e., COBRA continuation coverage, VEBA coverage, and certain state-based coverage options) for eligible coverage months beginning in the tax year. (Code Sec. 35(a))[41] Qualifying family members may continue claiming the HCTC for up to 24 months after the eligible individual enrolls in Medicare, divorces, or dies. (Code Sec. 35(g)(9))[42]

Eligibility is determined on a monthly basis. An "eligible individual" is an (1) "eligible TAA recipient" as defined in Code Sec. 35(c)(2),[43] (2) "eligible alternative TAA recipient" as defined in Code Sec. 35(c)(3),[44] or (3) "eligible PBGC pension recipient" (i.e., an individual who has reached age 55 as of the first day of the month (but isn't entitled to Medicare), and is receiving a benefit for the month that is, in any part, paid by the Pension Benefit Guaranty Corporation (PBGC) under title IV of the Employee Retirement Income Security Act of '74, dealing with plan terminations (Code Sec. 35(c)(4))). (Code Sec. 32(c)(1))[45]

A month is an eligible coverage month if on the first day of the month the taxpayer is an "eligible individual," is covered by qualified health insurance for which he paid the premium, doesn't have other specified subsidized coverage (defined in Code Sec. 35(f)), and isn't imprisoned under federal, state, or local authority. (Code Sec. 35(b))[46]

Married taxpayers filing separate returns may claim the credit. For joint returns, the eligibility requirements are considered met for any month if one spouse meets them.[47]

An individual can't claim the HCTC if he can be claimed as a dependent on another's tax return. (Code Sec. 35(g)(4))[48]

IRS has an HCTC advance payment program for paying the credit in advance, directly to the insurer, for individuals for whom an HCTC cost eligibility certificate is in effect. Under certain conditions, IRS must also make one or more retroactive payments for qualifying individuals. (Code Sec. 7527)[49]

¶ 2345   Premium tax credit for health insurance purchased on Exchange after 2013.

For tax years ending after Dec. 31, 2013, individuals, whose household income is within certain income limits and who aren't eligible for other qualifying coverage or "affordable" employer-sponsored health insurance plans that provide "minimum value" are allowed a refundable premium tax credit (also know as a health care affordability tax credit or premium

---

39. ¶A-4205; ¶324.02; TD ¶569,005
40. ¶A-4210 *et seq.*; ¶324.02; TD ¶569,010 *et seq.*
41. ¶A-4231 *et seq.*; ¶354; TD ¶569,401 *et seq.*
42. ¶A-4235.3; ¶354; TD ¶569,404.1
43. ¶A-4232; ¶354; TD ¶569,402
44. ¶A-4233; ¶354; TD ¶569,402

45. ¶A-4234; ¶354; TD ¶569,402
46. ¶A-4231; ¶354; TD ¶569,401
47. ¶A-4231; ¶354; TD ¶569,401
48. ¶A-4231; ¶354; TD ¶569,401
49. ¶H-4870 *et seq.*; ¶75,274; TD ¶569,406

assistance credit) to subsidize the purchase of certain health insurance plans through a State-established American Health Benefit Exchange (Code Sec. 36B(a), Code Sec. 36B(c)(1)) or (as provided in regs) through federally-facilitated Exchanges. (Reg § 1.36B-1(k)) (Code Sec. 36B(c)(1)(C))[50]

An individual is eligible for the premium tax credit if he or she:

. . . purchases coverage through an Exchange;

. . . has household income (see below) that falls between 100% and 400% of the federal poverty line. (For 2013, for the 48 contiguous states, household income between $11,490 and $45,960 for one individual; $15,510 and $62,040 for a family of two; $23,550 and $94,200 for a family of four);

. . . isn't able to get "affordable coverage" through an eligible employer plan that provides "minimum value;"

. . . isn't actually enrolled in an employer-sponsored plan (regardless of minimum value or affordability);

. . . isn't eligible for coverage through a government program (such as Medicaid, Medicare, CHIP or TRICARE);

. . . files a joint return, if married; and

. . . isn't claimed as a dependent by another person. (Code Sec. 36B)

Household income is an individual's modified adjusted gross income plus that of every other individual in his family for whom he can properly claim a personal exemption deduction and who is required to file a federal income tax return. Modified adjusted gross income is the adjusted gross income on his federal income tax return plus any excluded foreign income, nontaxable Social Security benefits (including tier 1 railroad retirement benefits), and tax-exempt interest received or accrued during the tax year. It doesn't include Supplemental Security Income (SSI). (Code Sec. 36B(d)(2); Reg § 1.36B-1(e)(1))

An eligible employer-sponsored plan is "affordable" for related individuals for tax years beginning before Jan. 1, 2015 if the portion of the annual premium the employee must pay for self-only coverage doesn't exceed 9.5% of the taxpayer's household income with this percentage adjusted for inflation in plan years beginning in a calendar year after 2014. (Code Sec. 36B(c)(2)(C); Reg § 1.36B-2(c)(3)(v)) The affordability test applies only to the portion of the annual premiums for self-only coverage and doesn't include any additional cost for family coverage. The affordability of a plan that charges a higher initial premium for tobacco users will be determined based on the premium that is charged to non-tobacco users, or tobacco users who complete the related wellness program, such as attending smoking cessation classes. (Prop Reg. § 1.36B-2(c)(3)(v), "Taxpayer may rely" before 2015)

An employer-sponsored plan provides minimum value if the plan covers at least 60% of the expected total allowed costs for covered services. (Code Sec. 36B(c)(2)(C)(ii), Reg § 1.36B-2(c)(3)(vi)) Beginning in 2014, employers will provide employees with summary of benefits and coverage indicating whether the plan provides minimum value.

The credit against income tax and alternative minimum tax for the tax year equals the taxpayer's premium assistance amount determined under Code Sec. 36B(b)(2) (i.e., an applicable percentage, based on the taxpayer's income level relative to the poverty line) of the amounts paid for coverage under a qualified health plan for the year) for all of the taxpayer's coverage months (generally, months in which the taxpayer, his spouse or dependents, is covered by an Exchange-purchased qualified health plan). (Code Sec. 36B(b), Reg § 1.36B-3(a))[1]

The credit generally will be payable in advance by the Exchange directly to the insurer on the individual's behalf with the taxpayer reconciling the actual credit that he is due on a timely filed return. However, individuals will be allowed to elect to purchase health insurance

---

50. ¶A-4241 *et seq.*; ¶36B4.01 *et seq.*; TD ¶569,451 *et seq.*   1. ¶A-4244 *et seq.*; ¶36B4.01 *et seq.*; TD ¶569,459 *et seq.*

out-of-pocket and apply to IRS for the credit at the end of the tax year. If a taxpayer's credit amount exceeds the advance payments paid on his behalf, he may receive the excess as an income tax refund. If the advance payment exceeds his credit amount, he owes the excess as an additional tax liability (with certain inflation adjusted repayment limits applying). (Code Sec. 36B(f)(2), Reg § 1.36B-4(a)(3))[2]

¶ 2346   Credit for income tax withheld.

The recipient of wages, pensions, annuities, gambling winnings, etc., is allowed a credit for the amount of income tax withheld from those amounts in a calendar year, for the last tax year beginning in that calendar year. (Code Sec. 31(a); Reg § 1.31-1(a))[3] For amounts withheld under the backup withholding rules (¶3044 *et seq.*), the credit is allowed for the tax year in which the income is received. (Code Sec. 31(c))[4]

If spouses file separate returns, each must claim credit for the actual amount of tax withheld from his or her salary or wages. In a community property state, each spouse may claim a credit for half the tax withheld on community wages. (Code Sec. 31(a); Reg § 1.31-1(a))[5]

¶ 2347   Credit for excess social security tax withheld.

If more than the maximum social security tax (¶1108) is withheld from an employee's wages for a calendar year because he worked for two or more employers, the excess is a credit against income tax on the employee's return for the year. (Code Sec. 31(b)(1), Code Sec. 6413(c)(1); Reg § 1.31-2(a)(2), Reg § 31.6413(c)-1) If a husband and wife both work, the ceiling is applied separately to each. If more than the maximum was withheld by one employer, the employee can't claim the credit; the employer must refund the over-collection.[6]

¶ 2348   Credit for the elderly and permanently and totally disabled—Schedule R.

The credit is available to a "qualified individual"—i.e., one who: (1) is 65 or older at the end of the tax year, or (2) is under 65 at the end of the tax year, retired on permanent and total disability, received taxable disability income during the tax year, and hasn't reached mandatory retirement age on the first day of the tax year. (Code Sec. 22(b))[7]

Permanently and totally disabled means the individual is unable to engage in any substantial gainful activity because of a medically determinable physical or mental impairment that can be expected to result in death, or that has lasted or can be expected to last for a continuous period of at least 12 months. (Code Sec. 22(e)(3))[8] IRS requires a physician's statement (part of Schedule R of Form 1040 or Form 1040A) certifying the disability to be kept as part of taxpayer's records (but not filed). For joint returns, the statement is required for each spouse under 65 who is retired on permanent and total disability.[9]

Disability income is gross income from amounts received as (or in lieu of) wages while out of work due to a permanent and total disability. (Code Sec. 22(c)(2))[10]

Married individuals must file a joint return to claim the credit unless they qualify as married living apart, ¶3133. (Code Sec. 22(e)(1)) A nonresident alien isn't eligible for the credit (Code Sec. 22(f)), unless he has a U.S. spouse and elects under Code Sec. 6013(g) or Code Sec. 6013(h) to be treated as a U.S. resident. (Reg § 1.37-1(d))[11]

The credit is 15% of an "initial amount" (Step 1 below), reduced by amounts based on the taxpayer's AGI (Step 2) and on the taxpayer's income from tax-free pensions and annuities (Step 3) (for Form 1040 or Form 1040A, use Schedule R Form 1040, Schedule R, or Form 1040A, Schedule 3):

---

2. ¶A-4248 *et seq.*; ¶36B4.01; TD ¶569,478 *et seq.*
3. ¶A-4005 *et seq.*; ¶314.01; TD ¶568,502
4. ¶J-9009; ¶s 314.01, 34,064; TD ¶568,504
5. ¶A-4006; ¶314.01; TD ¶568,503
6. ¶A-4002; ¶314.02; TD ¶568,506

7. ¶A-4101; ¶224; TD ¶568,702
8. ¶A-4102; ¶224.02; TD ¶568,705
9. ¶A-4102; TD ¶568,706
10. ¶A-4103; ¶224.02; TD ¶568,708
11. ¶A-4101; TD ¶568,702

Step (1): The "initial amount" is:

. . . $5,000 for a single person, 65 or over;

. . . $5,000 for spouses filing jointly, one spouse is a qualified individual, 65 or over;

. . . $7,500 for spouses filing jointly, both spouses are qualified individuals, 65 or over;

. . . $3,750 for a married person, 65 or over, filing separately. (Code Sec. 22(c)(2)(A))

For *individuals under 65*, the "initial amount" is the *lesser* of the above initial amount, or:

• single persons/married filing separately: taxpayer's disability income for the year;

• joint returns, both spouses under 65 and disabled: spouses' combined disability incomes;

• joint returns, one spouse under 65 and disabled, other spouse 65 or older: sum of $5,000 plus disabled spouse's disability income;

• joint returns, both spouses under 65, one spouse disabled: disabled spouse's disability income. (Code Sec. 22(c)(2)(B))

Step (2): If AGI exceeds a threshold amount ($7,500 for single persons; $10,000 for joint returns; $5,000 for married filing separately), the "initial amount" must be reduced by one-half of the excess. (Code Sec. 22(d)) The reduction applies regardless of the taxpayer's age.

observation: Step (2) eliminates the credit for joint filers at AGI of $25,000 (both spouses 65 or over) or $20,000 (if one is), and for a single person at AGI of $17,500.

Step (3): The initial amount as adjusted under Step (2) must be further reduced by the sum of the amounts received by the individual (for a joint return, by either spouse) as a pension or annuity or as a disability benefit that's: (a) excluded from gross income and payable under title II of the Social Security Act, the Railroad Retirement Act of '74, or a law administered by the VA; or (b) excluded from gross income under any non-Code provision of law. (Code Sec. 22(c)(3)(A))[12] Social security benefits (¶1279) (Code Sec. 86(f)(1)) and worker's compensation that reduces such benefits (Code Sec. 22(c)(3)(B)) are received as a pension or annuity.[13]

¶ 2349 Credit for household and dependent care expenses.

The credit may be claimed by an individual who: (1) has one or more qualifying individuals (¶2350) and (2) incurs employment-related expenses (¶2351) enabling him to be gainfully employed. (Code Sec. 21(a)(1); Reg § 1.21-1(a))[14]

The credit is equal to 35% of employment-related expenses, for taxpayers with AGI of $15,000 or less. The percentage decreases by 1% for each $2,000 (or fraction) of AGI over $15,000, but not below 20%. (Code Sec. 21(a)(1), Code Sec. 21(a)(2); Reg § 1.21-1(a))[15]

The maximum amount of employment-related expenses that may be used to compute the credit is $3,000 for one qualifying individual, or $6,000 for two or more qualifying individuals. (Code Sec. 21(c); Reg § 1.21-2(a)(1)) These maximums must be reduced, dollar-for-dollar, by the total amount excludable from gross income under Code Sec. 129 (dependent care assistance exclusion, ¶1270). (Code Sec. 21(c); Reg § 1.21-2(a))[16]

An otherwise eligible taxpayer may claim the credit for a qualifying individual who lives him for more than half the year, even if he doesn't provide more than half the household maintenance costs. (Code Sec. 21(a); Reg § 1.21-1(b))[17]

12. ¶A-4105, A-4106; ¶224.02; TD ¶568,703, 568,704
13. ¶A-4107; ¶224.02; TD ¶568,709
14. ¶A-4301 *et seq.*; ¶214; TD ¶569,301 *et seq.*
15. ¶A-4301; ¶214; TD ¶569,301
16. ¶A-4302, A-4303; ¶214.04; TD ¶569,303
17. ¶A-4301; ¶214.03; TD ¶569,301

¶ 2350   Qualifying individual defined for the dependent care credit.

Qualifying individuals for a taxpayer's dependent care credit (¶2349) are:

. . . a taxpayer's under-age-13 dependent (as defined in Code Sec. 152(a)(1) for the dependency exemption, ¶3120) (Code Sec. 21(b)(1)(A), Reg § 1.21-1(b)(1));

. . . a taxpayer's dependent who is physically or mentally incapable of self care and who has the same principal place of abode as the taxpayer for more than half the tax year. For this purpose, "dependent" is defined in Code Sec. 152 (¶3119), but without the gross income test for qualifying relatives, the rule that a joint filer can't be a dependent, and the rule that a dependent can't have dependents (Code Sec. 21(b)(1)(B); Reg § 1.21-1(b)(1)); or

. . . the taxpayer's spouse, if the spouse is physically or mentally incapable of self care and has the same principal place of abode as the taxpayer for more than half the tax year. (Code Sec. 21(b)(1)(C); Reg § 1.21-1(b)(1))[18]

¶ 2351   Employment-related expenses for the dependent care credit.

Employment-related expenses qualifying for the credit are expenses for household services or for the care of qualifying individuals (¶2350) that are incurred to enable the taxpayer to be gainfully employed (for earned income limit, see ¶2352). Costs of a housekeeper, maid, baby-sitter, or cook ordinarily qualify. (Code Sec. 21(b)(2)(B); Reg § 1.21-1(d))[19]

Payments for services provided outside the taxpayer's household count only if incurred for a qualifying individual who either is a dependent under age 13, or regularly spends at least 8 hours each day in taxpayer's household. (Code Sec. 21(b)(2)(B); Reg § 1.21-1(e)(1))[20] Also, for services performed by a *dependent care center*, the center must comply with all applicable state or local laws and regulations. (Code Sec. 21(b)(2)(C); Reg § 1.21-1(e)(2))[21]

observation: The credit isn't available for expenses of full institutional care unless incurred for a dependent under age 13.

Payments to taxpayer's relatives or household members don't qualify if the person paid is: a dependent (under Code Sec. 151(c)) of the taxpayer or his spouse, a child of the taxpayer (under Code Sec. 152(f)(1)) under 19 at the end of the tax year, taxpayer's spouse, or the parent of taxpayer's child who's a qualifying individual. (Code Sec. 21(e)(6); Reg § 1.21-4(a))[22]

¶ 2352   Earned income limit on employment-related expenses.

The amount of employment-related expenses (¶2351) that may be taken into account can't exceed: (1) for an individual who isn't married at the end of the tax year, his earned income, or (2) for an individual who is married at the end of the tax year, the lesser of his, or his spouse's, earned income for the year (even if married for only part of the year). (Code Sec. 21(d)(1); Reg § 1.21-2(b))[23]

A spouse who is a full-time student or who is a qualifying individual because incapable of self-care is deemed to have earned income of $250 per month if there's one qualifying individual in the household, and $500 a month if there are two or more qualifying individuals. But this deemed earned income rule applies to only one spouse for any given month. (Code Sec. 21(d)(2); Reg § 1.21-2(b)(4))[24]

---

18. ¶A-4312; ¶214.02; TD ¶569,312
19. ¶A-4319 *et seq.*; ¶214.03; TD ¶569,319 *et seq.*
20. ¶A-4325; ¶214.03; TD ¶569,325
21. ¶A-4327; ¶214.03; TD ¶569,327
22. ¶A-4331; ¶214.01; TD ¶569,331
23. ¶A-4304, A-4305; ¶214.05; TD ¶569,304, 569,305
24. ¶A-4306; ¶214.06; TD ¶569,306

¶ 2353   Claiming the dependent care credit—Form 2441.

The credit is claimed on Form 2441.[25]

The credit is available to married couples only on a joint return. (Code Sec. 21(e)(2); Reg § 1.21-3(a))[26] A married individual living apart from his spouse may claim the credit on a separate return if he maintains a household for which he furnishes over half the maintenance costs for the tax year, the household is a qualifying individual's principal place of abode for more than half the tax year, and the other spouse is absent for the last six months of the tax year. (Code Sec. 21(e)(4), Reg § 1.21-3(b))[27]

Divorced or legally separated parents claim the credit for a child under who is under age 13 or physically or mentally incapable of self-care as follows: if the child receives more than half his support during the year from his parents, and is in the custody of one or both of the parents for more than half the calendar year, he's a qualifying individual for the parent having longer custody. That parent may claim the credit even if he can't claim the child as a dependent and even if he released the dependency exemption (¶3126) to the other parent. (Code Sec. 21(e)(5); Reg § 1.21-1(b)(5))[28]

The care provider's name, address, and taxpayer identification number (TIN) must be included on taxpayer's return. The TIN isn't required for tax-exempt care providers (write "tax-exempt" instead). (Code Sec. 21(e)(9)) The care provider should give this information and certify the TIN on Form W-10. If the care provider doesn't comply with a request, the taxpayer should furnish whatever information is available, and include a statement that the other required information was requested but wasn't given. (Code Sec. 21(e)(9))[29]

No credit is permitted for a qualifying individual unless his TIN is included on the return claiming the credit. (Code Sec. 21(e)(10))[30]

¶ 2354   Adoption expense credit rules—Form 8839.

An individual may claim a credit (use Form 8839 with Form 1040) for qualified adoption expenses (Code Sec. 23(a)(1)), which are reasonable and necessary adoption fees, court costs, attorney fees, and other expenses that are directly related to and the principal purpose of which is for the taxpayer's legal adoption of an eligible child (an individual under age 18, or physically or mentally incapable of self-care.) (Code Sec. 23(d)) The credit is a nonrefundable personal credit allowed against the income tax and alternative minimum tax. The total amount that may be taken as a credit for all tax years for the adoption of a child is $12,970 for 2013 ($13,190 for 2014). (Code Sec. 23(b)(1))[31]

For 2013, the credit begins to phase out for taxpayers with AGI (as specially modified) over $194,580 and is fully eliminated at $234,580 of modified AGI. For 2014, the phaseout amounts are $197,880 and $237,880, respectively. (Code Sec. 23(b)(2))[32]

If the expenses are paid or incurred before the tax year the adoption becomes final, the credit is allowed for the year after the year when they're paid or incurred. For expenses paid or incurred during or after the tax year the adoption becomes final, the credit is allowed for the year they're paid or incurred. (Code Sec. 23(a)(2))[33]

For an adoption of a child with special needs (defined in Code Sec. 23(d)(3)), the taxpayer is treated as having paid (in the tax year the adoption becomes final) the maximum credit amount regardless of actual expenses, i.e., as having paid the excess (if any) of $12,970 for 2013 ($13,190 for 2014) over the total qualified adoption expenses actually paid or incurred in

25. ¶A-4301; ¶214.08; TD ¶569,301
26. ¶A-4310; ¶214.07; TD ¶569,310
27. ¶A-4311; ¶214.07; TD ¶569,311
28. ¶A-4314; ¶214.07; TD ¶569,314
29. ¶A-4334; ¶214.09; TD ¶569,328

30. ¶A-4333; ¶214; TD ¶569,333
31. ¶A-4401, A-4407, A-4410; ¶234; TD ¶569,501, 569,507, 569,510
32. ¶A-4404; ¶234; TD ¶569,504
33. ¶A-4402; ¶234; TD ¶569,502

all tax years for the adoption. (Code Sec. 23(a)(3))[34]

The credit's not allowed for a foreign adoption unless it becomes final. Expenses paid or incurred in the tax year the adoption is finalized or in earlier years are allowed in the year finalized. Expenses paid or incurred after that year are taken into account when paid or incurred. (Code Sec. 23(e)) Taxpayers may treat certain adoptions as final if the competent authority enters a decree of adoption or a home state enters a decree of re-adoption. Under a safe harbor, IRS won't challenge another country's treatment of an adoption as final if it enters a final decree of adoption, or the Secretary of State issues a specified certificate.[35]

No adoption expense credit is allowed if a deduction or credit (or exclusion, ¶1254) is otherwise allowed, or government funds are received, for the expense. (Code Sec. 23(b)(3)).[36]

To get the credit, married individuals must file jointly (unless legally separated or living apart). (Code Sec. 23(f)(1))[37] The taxpayer's return must include (if known) the name, age and taxpayer identification number (TIN) of the child. (Code Sec. 23(f)(2))[38]

If the adoption expense credit exceeds the applicable limitation for the year, the excess is carried over to each of the next five years. The "applicable limitation" is the limitation imposed by Code Sec. 26(a) (¶2364) for the tax year, reduced by the nonrefundable personal credits (other than the adoption expense credit, the residential energy efficient property credit, and the D.C. first-time homebuyers credit) for the year. (Code Sec. 23(c)(1))[39]

¶ 2355   Child tax credit.

Under the child tax credit, individuals may claim (on Form 1040 or Form 1040A) a maximum $1,000 credit for each qualifying child (¶3120) the taxpayer can claim as a dependent. (Code Sec. 24(a))[40] The child must be under 17, and a U.S. citizen or resident alien. (Code Sec. 24(c))[41]

The amount of the allowable credit is reduced (not below zero) by $50 for each $1,000 (or fraction thereof) of modified AGI (AGI increased by excluded foreign, possession, and Puerto Rico income) above: $110,000 for joint filers, $75,000 for unmarried individuals, and $55,000 for marrieds filing separately. (Code Sec. 24(b))[42]

For refundability of excess, see ¶2356.

No child credit is allowed for a child for a tax year unless the taxpayer's return includes the child's name and taxpayer identification number (TIN). (Code Sec. 24(e))[43]

No credit is allowed for a short tax year unless due to taxpayer's death. (Code Sec. 24(f))[44]

For limits on combined amount of nonrefundable personal credits, see ¶2364.

¶ 2356   When child tax credit is refundable—Form 8812.

For tax years beginning before Jan. 1, 2018, the child tax credit is refundable, but only to the extent of the *greater of*: (1) 15% of taxable earned income above $3,000 for 2013 and 2014, or (2) for a taxpayer with three or more qualifying children, the excess of his social security taxes for the tax year over his earned income credit (¶2339) for the year. (Code Sec. 24(d)) IRS calls the amount of the child tax credit that's refundable (on Form 8812) the "additional child tax credit."[45]

Earned income is defined in Code Sec. 32 (¶2340), and includes amounts excluded from gross income under Code Sec. 112 (combat zone pay, see ¶1223). (Code Sec. 24(d)(1))[46]

---

34. ¶A-4401; ¶234; TD ¶569,501
35. ¶A-4402, A-4403; ¶234; TD ¶569,502; TD ¶569,503
36. ¶A-4409; ¶234; TD ¶569,509
37. ¶A-4412, A-4413; ¶234; TD ¶569,512, 569,513
38. ¶A-4414; ¶234; TD ¶569,514
39. ¶A-4406; ¶234; TD ¶569,506
40. ¶A-4051; ¶244; TD ¶569,101

41. ¶A-4053; ¶244; TD ¶569,103
42. ¶A-4052; ¶244; TD ¶569,102
43. ¶A-4059; ¶244; TD ¶569,109
44. ¶A-4051; ¶244; TD ¶569,101
45. ¶A-4055; ¶244.02; TD ¶569,105
46. ¶A-4055; ¶244.02; TD ¶569,105

¶ 2357 Credit for mortgage interest under QMCC program—Form 8396, Form 8828.

Under a state or local government qualified mortgage credit certificate (MCC) program, certificate holders claim a credit (on Form 8396) (Code Sec. 25) equal to the MCC rate multiplied by the interest paid or accrued by the taxpayer during the tax year on a mortgage. (Code Sec. 25(a)(1)) If the MCC rate exceeds 20%, the credit is limited to $2,000. (Code Sec. 25(a)(2)) A three-year carryover is allowed for certain excess amounts. (Code Sec. 25(e))[47] The credit is subject to recapture on Form 8828 if the taxpayer sells or otherwise disposes of any interest in the residence within nine years after the mortgage was provided. (Code Sec. 143(m))[48] If the credit exceeds the applicable limitation for the year, the excess is carried over to each of the next three years. The applicable limitation is the limitation imposed by Code Sec. 26(a) (¶2364) for the tax year, reduced by the nonrefundable personal credits (other than the MCC credit, the adoption expense credit, the residential energy efficient property credit, and the D.C. first-time homebuyers credit) for the year. (Code Sec. 25(e)(1))[49]

¶ 2358 Nonbusiness energy property credit before 2014—Form 5695.

For property placed in service before 2014, a taxpayer can claim (on Form 5695) a credit equal to 10% of the cost of: (1) qualified energy efficiency improvements, and (2) residential energy property expenditures. (Code Sec. 25C(a)) There is a lifetime credit limit of $500 (with no more than $200 due to windows and skylights) less the total credits allowed to the taxpayer for all earlier tax years ending after 2005. (Code Sec. 25C(b)) The expenses have to be for property originally placed in service by the taxpayer and made on or in connection with a dwelling unit located in the U.S. owned and used by taxpayer as his principal residence (under the Code Sec. 121 homesale exclusion) at the time of installation. (Code Sec. 25C(c), Code Sec. 25C(d))[50]

caution: Check tax.thomsonreuters.com/federaltaxhandbookupdates to see if the above provision has been extended.

Qualified energy efficiency improvements are energy efficient building envelope components, such as (a) insulation materials or systems specifically and primarily designed to reduce heat loss/gain, that meet criteria set by the International Energy Conservation Code (IECC); or (b) exterior windows, skylights or doors, or any metal roof with pigmented coating or asphalt roof with cooling granules specifically designed to reduce heat gain, installed on a dwelling unit that meet Energy Star program requirements. The component have to be expected to last for at least five years. (Code Sec. 25C(c)) This requirement is met if the manufacturer offers a two-year warranty to repair or replace at no extra charge.[1]

Residential energy property expenses are expenses for qualified energy property (including labor costs for onsite preparation, assembly, or original installation) that meet specific standards set out in Code Sec. 25C(d). The credit allowed for energy property expenditures can't exceed:

... $300 for any energy-efficient building property (electric heat pump water heater, electric heat pump; central air conditioner; natural gas, propane or oil water heater; or a stove burning biomass fuel to heat or provide hot water to a taxpayer's residence in the U.S.) that meets specific energy efficiency standards;

... $150 for a qualified natural gas, propane, or oil furnace; or qualified natural gas, propane, or oil hot water boiler; or

... $50 for an advanced main air circulating fan. (Code Sec. 25C(d))[2]

An expense will not fail to qualify just because it is made for two or more dwelling units;

---

47. ¶A-4008 *et seq.*; ¶254 *et seq.*; TD ¶568,507 *et seq.*
48. ¶I-4901 *et seq.*; ¶1434.02
49. ¶A-4010; ¶254.01; TD ¶380,502

50. ¶A-4751; ¶25C4; TD ¶569,551
1. ¶A-4754 *et seq.*; ¶25C4; TD ¶569,554 *et seq.*
2. ¶A-4759; ¶25C4; TD ¶569,558.1

the credit is computed separately for the expenses for each dwelling unit. (Code Sec. 25C(e)(2)(B))[3] If the credit is allowed for an expense for a property, the increase in the property's basis that would otherwise result is reduced by the credit allowed (¶2478). (Code Sec. 25C(f), Code Sec. 1016(a)(33))[4] No credit is allowed for expenditures made from subsidized energy financing. (Code Sec. 25C(e)(3))[5]

¶ 2359   Residential energy efficient property credit—Form 5695.

For property placed in service before 2017 (Code Sec. 25D(g)), an individual is allowed an annual credit (on Form 5695) for the purchase of residential energy efficient property equal to the sum of 30% of the amount paid for:

. . . qualified solar energy property (i.e., property that uses solar power to generate electricity in a home);

. . . qualified solar water heating property;

. . . qualified fuel cell property, up to a maximum $500 credit for each 0.5 kilowatt (kw) of capacity;

. . . qualified small wind energy property; and

. . . qualified geothermal heat pump property. (Code Sec. 25D(a), Code Sec. 25D(b)(1), Code Sec. 25D(d))[6]

The equipment must be installed in a dwelling unit that's located in the U.S. and used as the taxpayer's residence (Code Sec. 25D(d)), and can't be used to heat a swimming pool or hot tub. (Code Sec. 25D(e)(3)) For fuel cell expenses, the dwelling unit must be the taxpayer's principal residence (as defined in Code Sec. 121) (Code Sec. 25D(d)(3)), and special dollar limits apply for joint occupancy. (Code Sec. 25D(e)(4))[7]

Taxpayers can rely on an appropriate manufacturer's certification that a component meets energy requirements, unless IRS withdraws it before taxpayer's purchase.[8]

The credit covers installation and hardware costs. (Code Sec. 25D(e)(1)) An expense is treated as made when the original installation is completed, except an expense for the construction or reconstruction of a structure is treated as made when the taxpayer's original use of the constructed or reconstructed structure begins. (Code Sec. 25D(e)(8))[9] If the equipment is used less than 80% for nonbusiness purposes, only the expenses properly allocable to nonbusiness use are taken into account. (Code Sec. 25D(e)(7))[10]

For the limit on the combined amount of certain personal nonrefundable credits, see ¶2364.

If the credit is allowed for an expense for a property, the basis increase is reduced by the credit allowed (¶2478). (Code Sec. 25D(f), Code Sec. 1016(a)(34))[11]

For the Code Sec. 45L credit for manufacturers of energy-efficient residential homes, see ¶2334.

¶ 2360   Alternative motor vehicle credit—Form 8910.

Taxpayers can claim (on Form 8910) an alternative motor vehicle credit (AMVC) for qualifying vehicles placed in service during the tax year. (Code Sec. 30B(a)) The credit is allowed to the vehicle's owner (or lessor) (Code Sec. 30B(b)) or, for vehicles sold to and used by certain tax-exempt entities, the seller. (Code Sec. 30B(h)(6))[12]

observation: Although the alternative motor vehicle credit is made up of several component credits, the only one available in 2013 and later years is the new qualified fuel cell motor vehicle credit.

---

3. ¶A-4762; ¶25C4; TD ¶569,558.4
4. ¶A-4765; ¶25C4; TD ¶569,558.7
5. ¶A-4764; ¶25C4; TD ¶569,558.6
6. ¶A-4781, A-4782; ¶25D4; TD ¶569,561, 569,562
7. ¶A-4782, A-4785; ¶25D4; TD ¶569,562, 569,565

8. ¶A-4782.1; TD ¶569,562.1
9. ¶A-4783; ¶25D4; TD ¶569,563
10. ¶A-4784; ¶25D4; TD ¶569,564
11. ¶A-4788; ¶25D4; TD ¶569,568
12. ¶L-18021; ¶30B4; TD ¶397,101

Any part of the credit attributable to depreciable property is treated as part of the general business credit (¶2302). The remaining portion is a nonrefundable personal credit (Code Sec. 30B(g))[13] For limits on combined amount of nonrefundable personal credits, see ¶2364.

To qualify for the AMVC, a motor vehicle (defined in Code Sec. 30B(h)(1)) must comply with the applicable provisions of the Clean Air Act, and applicable motor vehicle safety provisions (Code Sec. 30B(h)(10)), and must be used predominantly in the U.S. (Code Sec. 30B(h)(7))[14]

No AMVC is allowable for any part of the cost taken into account under Code Sec. 179. (Code Sec. 30B(h)(7)) The vehicle's basis must be reduced by the AMCV allowed. (Code Sec. 30B(h)(4)) But a taxpayer may elect not to claim the AMVC for a vehicle. (Code Sec. 30B(h)(9))[15]

The new qualified fuel cell motor vehicle credit applies for the purchase of a fuel cell vehicle before 2015. It equals a base credit amount that depends upon the vehicle's weight class and, for passenger cars or light trucks (vehicles weighing 8,500 pounds or less), plus an amount that depends upon the vehicle's rated fuel economy compared to a base fuel economy. A qualifying fuel cell vehicle must be propelled by power derived from one or more cells that convert chemical energy directly into electricity by combining oxygen with hydrogen fuel stored on board the vehicle. (Code Sec. 30B(b))[16]

¶ 2361 Credit for alternative fuel vehicle refueling property before 2014 (before 2015 for hydrogen property)—Form 8911.

For property placed in service before 2014 (2015 for property relating to hydrogen) (Code Sec. 30C(g)), a taxpayer can claim (on Form 8911) a credit equal to 30% of the cost of qualified alternative fuel vehicle refueling (QAFVR) property placed in service by the taxpayer during the tax year, subject to the limits described below. Thus, for non-hydrogen property placed in service during 2013, a taxpayer can claim a credit equal to 30% of such costs, subject to the below limits. (Code Sec. 30C(a), Code Sec. 30C(e)(6)(A)(i))[17]

🅁🄸🄰*caution:* Check tax.thomsonreuters.com/federaltaxhandbookupdates to see if the above provision has been extended.

QAFVR property—i.e., certain property for the storage or dispensing of a clean-burning fuel or electricity into the fuel tank or battery of a motor vehicle—is defined in Code Sec. 179A(d) (dealing with clean-fuel vehicles and certain refueling property) but with certain modifications, e.g., property installed on property used as the taxpayer's principal residence (under Code Sec. 121) doesn't need to be depreciable. Property used outside the U.S. doesn't qualify. (Code Sec. 30C(c), Code Sec. 30C(e)(3))[18]

The maximum credit is $30,000 for depreciable QAFVR property and $1,000 for nonbusiness QAFVR property. (Code Sec. 30C(b), Code Sec. 30C(e)(6))[19]

Any portion of the QAFVR property credit attributable to depreciable property is treated as a part of the general business credit (¶2302). (Code Sec. 30C(d)(1)) The remaining portion, a personal credit, can't exceed the excess of (1) regular tax liability (defined in Code Sec. 26(b)) for the tax year reduced by the sum of allowable nonrefundable personal credits plus the foreign tax credit, over (2) tentative minimum tax for the tax year. (Code Sec. 30C(d)(2))[20]

No QAFVR property credit is allowable for the portion of the cost that's taken into account under Code Sec. 179 expensing. (Code Sec. 30C(e)(3))[21] Recapture rules apply. (Code Sec. 30C(e)(5))[22] The basis of the property must be reduced by the amount of the credit allowed. (Code Sec. 30C(e)(1), Code Sec. 1016(a)(36))[23] But a taxpayer may elect not to claim

13. ¶ L-18022;¶30B4; TD ¶397,102
14. ¶L-18021; ¶30B4; TD ¶397,101
15. ¶L-18023; ¶30B4; TD ¶397,103
16. ¶L-18024; ¶30B4.01; TD ¶397,104
17. ¶L-18041; ¶30C4; TD ¶397,201
18. ¶L-18049; ¶30C4.02; TD ¶397,203, 397,205

19. ¶L-18041, L-18046.1; ¶30C4; TD ¶397,201, 397,201.1
20. ¶L-18042; ¶30C4.01; TD ¶397,202
21. ¶L-18049; ¶30C4; TD ¶397,205
22. ¶L-18049; ¶30C4; TD ¶397,205
23. ¶L-18046.1; ¶30C4; TD ¶397,201.1

the credit. (Code Sec. 30C(e)(4))[24]

¶ 2362 Electric vehicle credits—Form 8936, Form 8834.

Two credits deal with electric vehicles:

New qualified plug-in electric drive motor vehicle credit. A taxpayer can claim (on Form 8936) a credit for each new qualified plug-in electric drive motor vehicle (NQPEDMV) placed in service during the tax year. (Code Sec. 30D(a))[25] For a conversion credit, see ¶2360.

To qualify for the credit, a vehicle must be treated as a motor vehicle for purposes of title II of the Clean Air Act; have a gross vehicle weight rating (GVWR) of less than 14,000 pounds; and be propelled to a significant extent by an electric motor that draws electricity from a battery that has a capacity of at least 4 kilowatt (kw) hours, and be capable of being recharged from an external source of electricity. (Code Sec. 30D(d)(1)) The taxpayer must be the original user of the vehicle (which must be used predominantly in the U.S. (Code Sec. 30D(f)(4)), and must have acquired it for use or lease and not for resale. (Code Sec. 30D(d)(1))[26] The vehicle must meet certain provisions of the Clean Air Act. (Code Sec. 30D(f)(7))

The amount of the NQPEDMV credit is the sum of: (1) $2,500; plus (2) for a vehicle that draws propulsion energy from a battery with not less than five kw hours of capacity, $417 for each kw hour of capacity in excess of 5 kw hours, but not in excess of $5,000. Thus, the maximum credit is $7,500, regardless of weight. (Code Sec. 30D(b))[27]

The credit (as computed above) phases out beginning in the second calendar quarter following that in which a manufacturer sells its 200,000th plug-in electric drive motor vehicle for use in the U.S. after 2009 (50% credit reduction in second and third quarter; 75% in fourth and fifth quarter; 0 credit allowed thereafter). (Code Sec. 30D(e))[28]

Any portion of the credit attributable to depreciable property is treated as part of the general business credit (¶2302). The remaining portion is a nonrefundable personal credit. (Code Sec. 30D(c)(1))[29] For limits on combined amount of nonrefundable personal credits, see ¶2364.

The vehicle's basis, and any other allowable deduction or credit, must be reduced by the amount of the NQPEDMV credit allowed. (Code Sec. 30D(f)(1), Code Sec. 30D(f)(2))[30] But a taxpayer may elect not to claim the credit. (Code Sec. 30D(f)(6))[31]

Qualified 2- or 3-wheeled plug-in electric vehicle credit before 2014. A taxpayer can claim (on Form 8834) a credit equal to 10% of the cost of each qualified plug-in electric vehicle (QPEV) placed in service during the tax year and acquired after Dec. 31, 2011, and before Jan. 1, 2014. The maximum credit for a vehicle is $2,500. (Code Sec. 30D(g)(1), Code Sec. 30D(g)(2))[32]

caution: Check tax.thomsonreuters.com/federaltaxhandbookupdates to see if the above provision has been extended.

A QPEV is an electric drive 2- or 3-wheeled vehicle (e.g., a motorcycle) if its original use begins with the taxpayer; it's acquired for use or lease; it's manufactured primarily for use on public streets, roads and highways (e.g., not golf courses); its GVWR is less than 14,000 pounds; it's capable of achieving a speed of at least 45 miles per hour; and it's propelled to a significant extent by an electric motor that draws electricity from a battery with a capacity of at least 2.5 kw hours and is capable of being recharged from an external source of electricity. It does not have to be a motor vehicle for purposes of title II of the Clean Air Act. (Code Sec. 30D(g)(3)[33]

24. ¶L-18048.1; ¶30C4; TD ¶397,204
25. ¶L-18031; ¶30D4; TD ¶397,131
26. ¶L-18032.3; ¶30D4.04; TD ¶s 397,134.1, 397,136
27. ¶L-18031.2; ¶30D4.015; TD ¶397,132.1
28. ¶L-18031.2; ¶30D4.02; TD ¶397,133.1
29. ¶L-18034, L-18034.1; ¶30D4.07; TD ¶397,132, 397,133
30. ¶L-18033.2, L-18033.3; ¶30D4.06; TD ¶397,140, 397,141
31. ¶L-18034.2; ¶30D4; TD ¶397,144
32. ¶L-18040; ¶30D4.08; TD ¶397,230
33. ¶L-18042; ¶30D4.08; TD ¶397,232

The rules that apply to NQPEDMVs (except as noted above) also apply to the credit for qualified 2- or 3-wheeled plug-in electric vehicles. (Code Sec. 30D(g)(1)(B))[34]

¶ 2363   "Saver's" credit for elective deferrals and IRA contributions—Form 8880.

An eligible lower-income taxpayer can claim a nonrefundable credit (use Form 8880 with Form 1040 or Form 1040A) for a percentage of up to $2,000 of his qualified retirement savings contributions—"the saver's credit." (Code Sec. 25B(a)) The applicable percentage (50%, 20%, or 10%) depends on filing status and AGI. For tax years beginning in 2013, the amounts (as adjusted for inflation) are: (Code Sec. 25B(b))

. . . Joint filers: $0 to $35,500, 50%; $35,500 to $38,500, 20%; and $38,500 to $59,000, 10% (no credit if AGI is above $59,000).

. . . Heads of households: $0 to $26,625, 50%; $26,625 to $28,875, 20%; and $28,875 to $44,250, 10% (no credit if AGI is above $44,250).

. . . All other filers: $0 to $17,750, 50%; $17,750 to $19,250, 20%; and $19,250 to $29,500, 10% (no credit if AGI is above $29,500).[35]

For tax years beginning in 2014, the amounts are:

. . . Joint filers: $0 to $36,000, 50%; $36,000 to $39,000, 20%; and $39,000 to $60,000, 10% (no credit if AGI is above $60,000).

. . . Heads of households: $0 to $27,000, 50%; $27,000 to $29,250, 20%; and $29,250 to $45,000, 10% (no credit if AGI is above $45,000).

. . . All other filers: $0 to $18,000, 50%; $18,000 to $19,500, 20%; and $19,500 to $30,000, 10% (no credit if AGI is above $30,000).

The taxpayer's AGI is determined without regard to the foreign, possessions, and Puerto Rico income exclusions. (Code Sec. 25B(e))

An individual is eligible for the credit if he has reached age 18 by the end of the tax year. But he isn't eligible if he's a full-time student or another claims him as a dependent for the tax year beginning in the calendar year his tax year begins. (Code Sec. 25B(c))[36]

The credit is available for elective contributions to a Code Sec. 401(k) plan (including a SIMPLE 401(k)), Code Sec. 403(b) annuity, Code Sec. 457 plan, SIMPLE IRA plan, or salary reduction SEP; contributions to a traditional or Roth IRA; and voluntary after-tax employee contributions to a qualified retirement plan or Code Sec. 403(b) annuity. (Code Sec. 25B(d)(1))[37] The credit is in addition to any otherwise applicable deduction or exclusion.[38][39]

The amount of any credit-eligible contribution is reduced (not below zero) by the distributions received by the individual (and by his spouse, for joint returns) from any of the above savings arrangements during a testing period to the extent they're either taxable or are Roth IRA distributions that aren't rolled over. The testing period consists of the tax year for which the credit is claimed, the two preceding tax years, and the period after the end of the tax year and before the due date (including extensions) for filing the taxpayer's return for that year. (Code Sec. 25B(d)(2)) Distributions listed in Code Sec. 25B(d)(2)(C), such as qualified plan loans not treated as distributions, don't reduce a credit-eligible contribution.[40]

For limits on the combined amount of nonrefundable personal credits, see ¶2364.

---

34. ¶L-18041; ¶30D4.08; TD ¶397,231
35. ¶A-4451; ¶25B4; TD ¶569,201
36. ¶A-4452; ¶25B4; TD ¶569,202
37. ¶A-4453; ¶25B4; TD ¶569,203

38. ¶A-4451
39. ¶A-4451; ¶25B4; TD ¶569,201
40. ¶A-4454; ¶25B4; TD ¶569,204

¶ 2364 Limit on combined amount of nonrefundable personal credits.

The total amount of nonrefundable personal credits (below) allowed for the tax year can't exceed the sum of: (1) the taxpayer's regular tax liability (below) for the tax year reduced by the foreign tax credit (¶2367), (Code Sec. 26(a)(1)) plus (2) the tax imposed by Code Sec. 55(a) (i.e., the alternative minimum tax [AMT]) for the year. (Code Sec. 26(a)(2)).[41]

❡*observation:* Thus, all of the otherwise allowable nonrefundable personal credits can be used to reduce AMT (as well as regular tax). Under this rule, the taxpayer can claim up to the amount of the sum of the regular tax and the AMT as nonrefundable personal credits.

❡*observation:* Allowing the nonrefundable personal credits to reduce AMT (as well as regular tax) benefits middle income individuals who: (a) have low taxable income (and thus a low regular tax), e.g., because of a large number of personal exemptions; (b) are subject to the AMT because personal exemptions (as well as the standard deduction and certain itemized deductions) generally aren't allowed in computing the AMT; and (c) have substantial nonrefundable personal credits such as the child tax credit.

The Code Sec. 26(a) limitation applies to the dependent care credit (¶2349); credit for the elderly and permanently and totally disabled (¶2348); adoption expense credit (¶2354); the child tax credit (¶2355); mortgage credit certificate (MCC) credit (¶2357); American Opportunity Tax Credit (AOTC) (¶2202) and Lifetime Learning credit (¶2203); saver's credit (¶2363); nonbusiness energy property credit (¶2359); residential energy efficient property (REEP) credit (¶2359); and the nonbusiness portions of: (a) the qualified plug-in electric vehicle (QPEV) credit (¶2362), (b) the alternative motor vehicle credit (AMVC), ¶2360), (c) the new qualified plug-in electric drive motor vehicles property (NQPEDMV) credit (¶2362), and (d) the pre-2012 first-time D.C. homebuyer credit.[42]

❡*observation:* The Code Sec. 26(a) limitation doesn't apply to the qualified alternative fuel vehicle (QAFV) refueling property credit. The separate tax liability limitation that applies to that credit doesn't allow the use of the nonbusiness portion of the credit (i.e., any portion that doesn't relate to depreciable property) as an offset against AMT, see ¶2361.

❡*observation:* The limitation under Code Sec. 26(a) is the starting point for determining the credit carryover for the adoption expense, MCC, AOTC, REEP, and D.C. first-time homebuyer credits.

Regular tax liability means the tax imposed by Chapter 1 *except for*: (Code Sec. 26(b))

(1) The AMT. (Code Sec. 55)

(2) Penalty taxes on certain premature distributions. (Code Sec. 72(m)(5)(B), Code Sec. 72(q), Code Sec. 72(t), Code Sec. 72(v))

(3) Tax on nonqualified withdrawals from capital construction funds. (Code Sec. 7518(g)(6))

(4) Accumulated earnings tax. (Code Sec. 531)

(5) Personal holding company tax. (Code Sec. 541)

(6) Certain recoveries of foreign expropriation losses. (Code Sec. 1351(d)(1))

(7) Tax on certain built-in gains of S corporations. (Code Sec. 1374)

(8) Tax imposed when passive investment income of an S corporation having Subchapter C earnings and profits exceeds 25% of gross receipts. (Code Sec. 1375)

(9) Tax on transfers of high-yield interest to disqualified holders of financial asset securitization trusts (FASITs). (Former Code Sec. 860K)

(10) The 30% tax on U.S. source income earned by nonresident aliens and foreign corporations. (Code Sec. 871(a), Code Sec. 881)

(11) The interest paid as additional income on tax deferred by installment sales of

---

41. ¶A-4901; ¶264; TD ¶569,601   42. ¶A-4902; ¶264; TD ¶569,602

timeshares and residential lots. (Code Sec. 453(l)(3), Code Sec. 453A(c))

(12) Recapture of federal subsidy from use of mortgage bonds and mortgage credit certificates. (Code Sec. 143(m))

(13) Tax on transfers of residual interests in a real estate mortgage investment conduit (REMIC) to a disqualified organization. (Code Sec. 860E(e))

(14) The branch profits tax. (Code Sec. 884)

(15) Additional tax on Archer MSA distributions and health savings account (HSA) distributions not used for medical expenses. (Code Sec. 220(f)(4), Code Sec. 223(f)(4))

(16) Additional tax on distributions from Coverdell education savings accounts not used for higher education expenses. (Code Sec. 530(d)(4))

(17) Penalty tax for certain distributions from Medicare Advantage MSA not used for qualified medical expenses. (Code Sec. 138(c)(2))

(18) Recapture of the first-time homebuyer credit. (Code Sec. 36(f))

(19) The 10% penalty taxes for failures to maintain high deductible health plan (HDHP) coverage, including: (i) the tax with respect to rollovers from flexible spending accounts and health reimbursement accounts into Health Savings Accounts (HSAs), (Code Sec. 106(e)(3)(A)(ii)) (ii) the tax with respect to contributions made to HSAs, (Code Sec. 223(b)(8)(B)(i)(II)), and (iii) the tax with respect to rollovers from IRAs to HSAs (Code Sec. 408(d)(9)(D)(i)(II))

(20) Additional tax on distributions from a Medicare Advantage MSA not used for qualified medical expenses, if a minimum balance is not maintained in the account (Code Sec. 138(c)(2))

(21) The 10% recapture tax imposed on a taxpayer who is required to recapture the charitable deduction he claimed for a gift of a fractional interest in tangible personal property (Code Sec. 170(o)(3)(B))

(22) The tax increase resulting from recapture of COBRA premium assistance.

(23) Interest and tax for violations of Code Sec. 409A nonqualified deferred compensation (NQDC) rules and tax on NQDC from certain tax-indifferent entities. (Code Sec. 409A(a)(1)(B), Code Sec. 409A(b), Code Sec. 457A(c)(1)(B)), (Code Sec. 26(b)(2))[43]

¶ 2365 Credit for alternative minimum tax (AMT)—Form 8801; Form 8827.

The minimum tax credit (MTC or AMT credit) is equal to (compute on Form 8801, Form 8827 for corporations) the adjusted net minimum tax (ANMT) the taxpayer paid in all earlier tax years for "deferral preferences" (for a corporation, also "exclusion preferences"), less the allowable MTCs for those years. (Code Sec. 53(a), Code Sec. 53(b)) The allowable credit for a tax year is limited (subject to the rule below for individuals and at ¶1933) to the excess of: (1) taxpayer's regular tax liability (¶2364) reduced by the sum of allowable nonrefundable credits, *over* (2) the tentative minimum tax (¶3201), for the year. (Code Sec. 53(c))[44]

For a small corporation exempt from AMT for a tax year (¶3205), the regular tax liability otherwise used in computing the year's credit limitation is reduced by 25% of the amount over $25,000. (Code Sec. 55(e)(5))[45]

A *noncorporate taxpayer's* ANMT for a tax year equals: (a) the AMT for the year, *less* (b) the amount of AMT that would have arisen if the only applicable AMT preferences and adjustments were "exclusion preferences." (Code Sec. 53(d)(1)(B))[46]

A *corporation's* ANMT for a tax year equals item (a), above. (Code Sec. 53(d)(1)(B))[47]

"Deferral preferences" are all the AMT preferences and adjustments except those for: (i) depletion, (ii) tax-exempt interest, (iii) itemized deductions of noncorporate taxpayers, (iv) the

43. ¶A-4905; ¶264, 264.01; TD ¶569,605
44. ¶A-8801; ¶534; TD ¶691,501
45. ¶A-8807; ¶534; TD ¶691,507
46. ¶A-8802; ¶534; TD ¶691,502
47. ¶A-8802; ¶534; TD ¶691,502

standard deduction, (v) personal exemptions, and (vi) the exclusion of gain from qualified small business stock. (Code Sec. 53(d)(1)(B)(ii)) "Exclusion preferences" are the AMT preferences/adjustments that aren't deferral preferences.[48]

Refundable AMT credit for individuals. For tax years beginning before 2013, if an individual has a "long-term unused MTC," his MTC for the year can't be less than the AMT refundable credit amount for the year (Code Sec. 53(e)(1)), and the "extra" amount so allowed is refundable. (Code Sec. 53(e)(4)) An individual's "long-term unused MTC" for a tax year is the portion of his MTC (determined under Code Sec. 53(b), above) attributable to ANMT for tax years before the third tax year immediately preceding the tax year. (Code Sec. 53(e)(3)(A)) For this purpose, credits are treated as allowed under Code Sec. 53(a) on a first-in, first-out (FIFO) basis. (Code Sec. 53(e)(3)(B))[49]

The AMT refundable credit for a tax year is the amount (not in excess of the long-term unused MTC for the year) equal to the greater of:

(1) 50% of the long-term unused MTC for the tax year, or

(2) the amount (if any) of the AMT refundable credit amount determined under Code Sec. 53(e) for the taxpayer's preceding tax year (but not including any increase under Code Sec. 53(f)(2), below). (Code Sec. 53(e)(2)) Thus, long-term unused MTCs may be claimed over a two-year period.[50]

¶ 2366   Qualified tax credit bonds.

Taxpayers holding qualified tax credit bonds (QTCBs) on specified "credit allowance dates" during the tax year are entitled to a nonrefundable credit (rather than interest payments) against regular income tax and alternative minimum tax (AMT) liability. The credit accrues quarterly and is includible in gross income as interest is paid on the bond. The amount of the credit is determined by multiplying the bond's credit rate by its face amount. The credit rate is determined by IRS and is a rate that allows the bonds to be issued without discount and interest cost to the issuer. A QTCB is a specified type of bond that is part of an issue that meets requirements relating to expenditures, reporting, arbitrage, maturity, and financial conflicts of interest. (Code Sec. 54A)[1] These bonds can be QTCBs:

. . . *Qualified forestry conservation bonds (QFCBs)* issued by qualified issuers (states and Code Sec. 501(c)(3) organizations) to finance qualified forestry conservation projects. (Code Sec. 54A(d)(1)(A), Code Sec. 54B)[2]

. . . *New clean renewable energy bonds (new CREBs)* issued for capital expenditures incurred by government bodies, public power providers, or cooperative electric companies to finance qualified renewable energy facilities. (Code Sec. 54A(d)(1)(B), Code Sec. 54C)[3]

. . . *Qualified energy conservation bonds (QECBs)* issued by a state or local government for qualified conservation purposes. (Code Sec. 54A(d)(1)(C), Code Sec. 54D)[4]

. . . *Qualified zone academy bonds (QZABs)* issued by a state or local government for repairing and renovating schools as well as for school equipment and teacher training. (Code Sec. 54A(d)(1)(D), Code Sec. 54E)[5]

. . . *Qualified school construction bonds (QSCBs)* issued by a state or local government for constructing, rehabilitating, or repairing a public school facility, or for acquiring land where a facility is to be constructed. (Code Sec. 54A(d)(1)(E); Code Sec. 54F)[6]

caution: No specific termination date is prescribed for the issuance of new CREBs, QECBs, QZABs, or QSCBs. But, a zero national bond volume limitation for QSCBs for years after 2010 means that the bonds can be issued after this date only if unused national

48. ¶A-8804; ¶534; TD ¶691,504
49. ¶A-8808, A-8811; ¶534.01; TD ¶691,508, 691,511
50. ¶A-8809; ¶534.01; TD ¶691,509
1. ¶L-15530 *et seq.*; ¶54A4; TD ¶568,521
2. ¶L-15550 *et seq.*; ¶54B4

3. ¶L-15560 *et seq.*; ¶54C4
4. ¶L-15570 *et seq.*; ¶54D4; TD ¶384,800
5. ¶L-15580 *et seq. et seq.*; ¶1397E4
6. ¶L-15590 *et seq.*; ¶54F4; TD ¶384,130

bond volume limitations from previous years can be carried forward.

Direct Pay Tax Credit Bonds. For new CREBs, QECBs, QZABs (but not QZABs issued under the 2011 national bond volume limitation), or QSCBs, the issuer may make an irrevocable election (on Form 8038-CP) for the bond to be treated as a "Direct Pay Tax Credit Bond" under Code Sec. 6431, entitling the issuer to receive a direct payment from IRS of an amount based on a market-determined interest rate, on the bond's interest payment dates. Special limits apply to new CREBs or QECBs. If the issuer elects the direct payment option, the holder can't claim any otherwise available QTCB credit for the bond, and is taxed on any bond interest paid to him. Any income tax deduction otherwise allowed to the issuer is reduced by the amount of the payment made under Code Sec. 6431 for the interest. (Code Sec. 6431(f))[7] (Due to the sequestration, a reduction applied to refundable credits under Code Sec. 6431 claimed on Form 8038-CP which results in a payment to the issuer on or after Mar. 1, 2013; the reduction applied until the end of the fiscal year (Sept. 30, 2013).

¶ 2367 Foreign Tax Credit. ▬▬▬▬▬▬▬▬

Most U.S. taxpayers who pay income taxes to foreign governments may deduct them for U.S. tax purposes or may credit them dollar-for-dollar against their U.S. tax liability on their worldwide income.

Taxpayers may elect to take a foreign tax credit against U.S. income tax for income tax paid to a foreign country or U.S. possession (or political subdivision thereof), or deduct them. (Code Sec. 901, Code Sec. 27, Code Sec. 164(a)(3); Reg § 1.901-1a))[8] Foreign income taxes may not, however, be deducted in the same year that a credit is claimed for any foreign income tax and excess eligible foreign taxes eligible for carryover cannot be claimed in a year in which a deduction for current foreign taxes is taken. The deduction of other foreign taxes doesn't effect the creditability of foreign income taxes. (Code Sec. 164(a), Code Sec. 275(a)(4), Code Sec. 904(c); Reg § 1.901-1(c), Reg § 1.901-1(h)(2))[9]

The credit for foreign taxes paid or accrued is allowed to U.S. citizens, domestic corporations, and electing possessions corporations for compulsory payments of taxes to foreign countries and U.S. possessions, (Code Sec. 901(b)(1), Code Sec. 901(g)) except to the extent attributable to income eligible for a dividends received deduction.[10] Aliens residing in the U.S. or residing in Puerto Rico during the entire tax year may credit taxes paid to foreign countries (Code Sec. 901(b)(3)). Nonresident aliens and foreign corporations can claim the credit for foreign or possessions tax only on certain income effectively connected with a U.S. business (¶4644).[11] (Code Sec. 901(b)(4), Code Sec. 906)

A U.S. person who is a member of a partnership, a beneficiary of an estate or trust or a shareholder of an electing regulated investment company (RIC) may credit his share of foreign tax paid or accrued by the partnership, estate, trust or RIC. (Code Sec. 901(b)(5), Code Sec. 853(a)) Tax credits of a partnership, however, must be allocated in accordance with the partners' interests in the partnership, or, in the case of special allocations, in accordance with the items to which the credit relates. Allocations to claim foreign tax credits that do not track associated income may be reallocated. (Reg § 1.704-1)[12] Taxes imposed on a trust or estate on distributions to a beneficiary, including taxes on trust income imposed on a settlor or other person would be treated as owner but for Code Sec. 672(f), are creditable. (Code Sec. 642(a), Code Sec. 665(d)(2)) On a joint return, the credit is based on total taxes paid by both spouses. (Reg § 1.902-1(e))[13] The Code Sec. 936 possessions tax credit has been generally phased out, but remains effective for American Samoa for the first eight tax years of a corporation beginning after Dec. 31, 2005 and before Jan. 1, 2014. (Act Sec. 119(a)(2), P.L. 109-432, 12/20/2006)[14]

🔷*caution:* Check tax.thomsonreuters.com/federaltaxhandbookupdates to see if the above

7. ¶L-15547 *et seq.*; ¶64,314.02; TD ¶568,521
8. ¶O-4002; ¶9014.04; TD ¶391,013
9. ¶O-4002; ¶K-4701; ¶2754; TD ¶326,025
10. ¶D-2226; TD ¶605,603

11. ¶O-4101, ¶O-4108; ¶O-1085;¶O-15111; ¶9014.01; TD ¶392,001
12. ¶B-2903.1 *et seq.*; ¶7044.07.
13. ¶O-4103; ¶O-4410; ¶9014 *et seq.*; TD ¶392,001 *et seq.*
14. ¶O-1500.1; ¶9314.06; TD ¶394,500.1

provision has been extended.

A foreign tax is only creditable by the taxpayer upon whom foreign law imposes legal liability for the tax, even if another person pays the tax. (Reg § 1.901-2(f)) In addition, foreign tax credits may be suspended when certain related persons account for the associated income in another tax period (known as a tax credit splitting event). IRS provides an exclusive list of arrangements that qualify as splitting events. (Code Sec. 909(d), Reg § 1.909-2T(b))[15]

¶ 2368   When and how to claim foreign tax credit—Form 1116; Form 1118.

The credit is claimed on Form 1116 by an individual, trust or estate, and on Form 1118 by a corporation. (Reg § 1.905-2(a)(1))[16] A cash basis taxpayer may elect to credit *all* qualified foreign taxes on an accrual basis, but the election is binding with respect to all taxes for that year, whenever paid. (Code Sec. 905(a); Reg § 1.905-1(a))[17]

¶ 2369   What taxes qualify for a foreign tax credit?

Income taxes, war profits taxes and excess profits taxes paid or accrued during the tax year to a foreign country or a U.S. possession qualify for the foreign tax credit. (Code Sec. 901) For example, the Supreme Court has ruled that the United Kingdom's windfall tax qualified for a credit as an excess profits tax. However, a tax conditioned on its eligibility for the credit (a soak up tax) or used by the foreign country to provide a subsidy doesn't qualify. A payment qualifies only if it is for a tax based on income or a so-called *in lieu* of tax. (Code Sec. 903) Taxes on wages, dividends, interest and royalties generally qualify. (Reg § 1.901-2)[18] In the case of certain elections and transactions that create additional asset basis for cost recovery in the U.S. (e.g., qualified stock purchases, acquisitions of partnership interests with a Code Sec. 754 election in place), a portion of the foreign income tax paid on the income or gain attributable to the underlying foreign assets is disqualified. (Code Sec. 901(m))[19]

Taxes imposed by and paid to blacklisted countries may not be credited, but may be taken as itemized deductions. (Code Sec. 901(j))[20] The credit is generally denied to international boycott participants (see ¶4632).

¶ 2370   Limitations on the foreign tax credit.

The total credit for foreign taxes for a year is limited to the amount of U.S. tax that would be imposed on the taxpayer's foreign source income (Code Sec. 904(a))[21] and separate calculations are required for different categories of income (see ¶2371).

For limits on combined amount of nonrefundable personal credits, see ¶2364.

An individual may elect an exemption from the limitation (by not filing the Form 1116) on *de minimis* amounts if he has $300 or less ($600 in the case of joint filers) of creditable foreign taxes and no foreign source income other than qualified passive income, so long as the amounts are shown on Form 1099 or other statement. However, there is no carryover of excess foreign taxes to or from a tax year for which the election is made. (Code Sec. 904(k)(2); Reg § 1.904(j)-1)[22]

A loss netting rule requires a taxpayer to reduce foreign source capital gain by U.S. capital losses (Code Sec. 904(b)(2) and (3); Reg § 1.904(b)-1(c) and (d), Reg § 1.904(b)-1(e)(1)) and the limitation is reduced to take into account any preferential rates for capital gain and qualifying dividends (¶1288). (Code Sec. 904(b)(2); Reg § 1.904(b)-1(c) and (d), Reg § 1.904(b)-1(e)(1)) In certain cases, noncorporate taxpayers may elect not to apply the adjustment for rate differentials. (Reg § 1.904(b)-1(b)(3), Reg § 1.904(b)-1(a)(1), Reg § 1.904(b)-1(f)(4))[23]

15. ¶O-4113 *et seq.*
16. ¶O-5501; ¶9054.02; TD ¶391,013
17. ¶O-5504; ¶9054.01; TD ¶391,014
18. ¶O-4200 *et seq.*; ¶9014.02; TD ¶391,005
19. ¶O-4211.1; ¶9014

20. ¶O-4007 *et seq.*;¶K-4701; ¶9014.07; TD ¶391,012
21. ¶O-4401*et seq.*; ¶9044.01; TD ¶393,001
22. ¶O-4413, ¶O-5500 *et seq.*; ¶9054.03
23. ¶O-4404 *et seq.*; ¶9044.01; TD ¶393,005

If foreign income taxes paid or accrued exceed the amount that may be credited for the tax year, the excess may be carried back 1 year and forward 10 years, using the current year's credits first. (Code Sec. 904(c)) Taxes are treated as carried over to the extent of any unused limitation in a year in which the taxpayer does not elect the credit. This generates no tax benefit, but the taxpayer may file an amended return within 10 years from the return due date for the year of the deduction to claim the foreign tax credit. (Reg § 1.904-2)[24] Special rules apply to carryovers of oil and gas extraction taxes. (Code Sec. 907(f))[25]

¶ 2371 Separate limitations on separate income categories.

The credit limitation is computed separately for two categories of income, i.e., the passive category income and the general category income, and in each case is the lesser of: (1) the amount of foreign taxes paid or accrued with respect to that category, or (2) the U.S. tax on the foreign income in that category. General limitation income includes high-taxed income that otherwise would be treated as passive. (Code Sec. 901(b), Code Sec. 904(a), Code Sec. 904(d)(2)(B)(iii), Reg § 1.904-4) Expenses are allocated and apportioned to gross foreign source income in each category to determine foreign source taxable income (TI) in each category. (Reg § 1.861-8 − 17) The maximum credit for each category is equal to the (total foreign source TI in the category ÷ total TI) × U.S. income tax rate.[26] Additional limitations apply to foreign taxes on foreign mineral income (Reg § 1.901-3(a))[27] and foreign oil and gas extraction income. (Code Sec. 907; Reg § 1.907(a)-1, Reg § 1.907(b)-1, Reg § 1.907(c)-1, Reg § 1.907(d)-1, Reg § 1.907(f)-1)[28]

Dividends, interest, rents, and royalties received from a CFC are characterized according to the source of the income to the CFC and are subject to separate limitations only to the extent that the limitations would apply to the CFC's income. Look through treatment extends to dividends from 10% − 50% U.S. owned foreign corporations (also called noncontrolled Section 902 corporations) (¶2374). Subpart F inclusions are subject to a separate limitation based on the character of the income triggering the inclusions. (Code Sec. 904(d)(3)); Reg § 1.904-4, Reg § 1.904-5)[29]

The credit is denied for foreign withholding tax if the underlying property wasn't held for a minimum holding period, or to the extent that the recipient is obligated to make related payments with respect to positions in substantially similar or related property. (Code Sec. 901(l)) This rule doesn't apply to foreign gross-basis withholding taxes on certain back-to-back licensing arrangements for intellectual property or copyrighted articles and arrangements for the retail distributions of copyrighted articles.[30]

For treatment of certain foreign source income as domestic income, see ¶2372.

¶ 2372 Foreign source losses: source rules and recapture.

Certain income derived from U.S. owned foreign corporations (in which U.S. persons hold at least 50% by vote or value) is recharacterized as U.S. source for purposes of the credit limitation (¶2370). Recharacterization applies to certain includible Subpart F income (¶4624) and income from a qualifying electing fund (QEF) (¶4629). It also applies to interest and dividends, unless less than 10% of the corporation's earnings and profits for the tax year are attributable to sources within the U.S. (Code Sec. 904(h))

A taxpayer may elect to treat income derived from a U.S. owned foreign corporation or from a branch or disregarded entity that would be foreign source under a treaty's source provision as foreign source income, in which case, the income is treated separately for purposes of the foreign tax credit limitation. (Code Sec. 904(h)(10); Code Sec. 904(d)(6))[31]

---

24. ¶O-4601 *et seq.*, ¶O-5109; ¶9044.02, ¶9074.04; TD ¶394,001
25. ¶O-5200 *et seq.*, ¶O-5109, ¶O-5230; ¶9044.02, ¶9074.04 ; TD ¶394,001
26. ¶O-4401, ¶O-11001 *et seq.*; ¶9044 *et seq.*; TD ¶393,001
27. ¶O-5100 *et seq.*; ¶9014.02; TD ¶393,006

28. ¶O-5200 *et seq.*
29. ¶O-4300 *et seq.*;¶9044.01;TD ¶393,006
30. ¶O-4011.1; ¶60,114; TD ¶817,002
31. ¶O-4368.1, ¶O-4501 *et seq.*, ¶O-4511; ¶9044.01

An overall foreign loss (OFL) is created whenever a taxpayer's foreign losses exceed foreign source income and offsets U.S. source income. OFLs must be recaptured in future tax years whenever there is net foreign source income. Recharacterized foreign source income reduces the credit limitation until the OFL is completely offset. If a foreign loss offsets income in a different limitation category, income in a later year will be recharacterized as income in that other category up to the amount of the offset. (Code Sec. 904(f)) Corporations track these amounts on Form 1118, Schedule J.[32] Special overall foreign loss recapture rules apply to certain disposition of stock of controlled foreign corporations (CFCs) (see ¶4623). (Code Sec. 904(f)(3)(D))

If a taxpayer has an overall domestic loss (ODL), that portion of U.S. source income in each later year equal to the lesser of (i) the full amount of the unrecharacterized loss not carried back, or (ii) 50% of U.S. source income for the later tax year, is recharacterized as foreign source. (Code Sec. 904(g); Reg § 1.904(g)-1)[33]

¶ 2373   Determining amount of foreign tax payments.

A cash-basis taxpayer uses the currency exchange rate in effect on a payment date. An accrual taxpayer translates foreign taxes at the average exchange rate for the year to which the taxes relate unless the taxes are paid more than two years after, or any time before, the tax year to which they relate, or if the taxes are denominated in an inflationary currency. A taxpayer may elect to use the spot rate for foreign taxes not paid in the taxpayer's functional currency. (Code Sec. 986(a)(1); Reg § 1.905-3T(b))[34]

¶ 2374   Credit for foreign tax paid or accrued by a foreign affiliate.

A U.S. corporate shareholder may also be entitled to deemed-paid credits for a portion of foreign taxes paid by a foreign subsidiary in which it holds at least 10% of the voting stock (1st tier corporation), including taxes on earnings distributed or included in gross income of a U.S. corporate shareholder under Subpart F. A deemed paid credit may also arise for taxes paid or accrued by a 2nd- through 6th-tier foreign corporation, except that foreign taxes deemed paid on Code Sec. 956 increased investments in U.S. property cannot exceed the amount that would be deemed-paid if the inclusion were distributed up the chain of foreign corporations to the U.S. shareholder in cash. (Code Sec. 902; Reg § 1.902-1)[35] The corporation claims a credit (subject to the general limitations, ¶2370) against dividend income from the affiliate, treating a portion of the foreign tax as dividend income. (Code Sec. 78, Code Sec. 902; Reg § 1.78-1(a))

There is a holding period requirement for crediting taxes on dividends and deemed paid taxes for stock (except in the case of securities dealers or brokers in the active conduct of a foreign securities dealer business); otherwise the credit is disallowed and neither the deduction disallowance (¶1755) nor the gross-up applies. (Code Sec. 901(k))

---

32. ¶O-4700 *et seq.*; ¶9044.01; TD ¶393,020 *et seq.*
33. ¶O-4720 *et seq.*; ¶9044.01; TD ¶393,022.1

34. ¶O-5300; ¶9864.01
35. ¶O-4904; ¶O-4800 *et seq.*; ¶9024.01; ¶9604.03

Chapter 9   Sales and Exchanges—Tax-Free Exchanges—Basis

¶ 2400   Gain or Loss on Sales or Exchanges. ▬▬▬▬▬▬▬▬

When a taxpayer sells or exchanges property at a price higher than his cost or tax basis, he realizes a gain. If he sells it at less than his basis, he realizes a loss. He doesn't realize gain or loss when property merely goes up or down in value.

¶ 2401   Computing gain or loss on a sale or exchange.

Taxpayers have gain to the extent the amount realized from a sale or exchange exceeds their adjusted basis (usually cost, increased for improvements and decreased for depreciation or amortization). If the adjusted basis of the property disposed of exceeds the amount realized, the difference is a loss. (Code Sec. 1001(a))[1]

🅁🄸🄰 *observation:* Whether gain or loss is recognized in the year of sale depends on whether it was realized in a taxable or tax-deferred transaction.

¶ 2402   Amount realized.

The amount realized on a sale or other disposition of property is the amount of money plus the fair market value (FMV) of any property received by the seller. (Code Sec. 1001(b))[2] Where the buyer of property assumes a debt of the seller, or pays one (e.g., pays seller's taxes or legal fees), the amount of the debt is added to the amount realized by the seller. (Reg § 1.1001-2(a))[3] FMV is the price at which the property would change hands between a willing buyer and a willing seller, neither being under any compulsion to buy or sell and both having reasonable knowledge of relevant facts. (Reg § 1.170A-1(c)(2), Reg § 1.412(c)(2)-1(c)(1), Reg § 1.1445-1(g)(7))[4]

If a taxpayer sells a capital asset, his selling expenses (such as brokers' commissions) ordinarily reduce the amount realized, thus reducing the gain or increasing the loss realized on the sale.[5]

For the effect of unstated interest on a deferred payment sale or installment sale of property, see ¶1307.

¶ 2403   Amount realized on sale of property subject to a debt.

If property is sold subject to a mortgage or other debt, the amount of the mortgage is included in the sales price whether or not the seller is personally liable on the mortgage debt. This is so whether or not the buyer assumes the mortgage.[6]

In determining the gain or loss on property, its fair market value is treated as being not less than the amount of the nonrecourse debt to which it's subject. (Code Sec. 7701(g))[7]

¶ 2404   Open sales.

When a seller receives payment in the form of a property right or obligation whose value depends on future events, if the seller can prove that the right or obligation has no ascertainable value, he reports gain only when the proceeds from the obligation exceed his basis, and loss is fixed only when further payments can't reasonably be expected.[8] For contingent payment sales and open sales under the installment sale rules, see ¶ 2455.

---

1. ¶I-2501; ¶10,014; TD ¶222,001
2. ¶I-2502; ¶10,014; TD ¶222,002
3. ¶I-2517; ¶10,014.03; TD ¶222,011
4. ¶P-6002; ¶10,114.25; TD ¶481,001

5. ¶I-2537; ¶10,014; TD ¶222,023
6. ¶I-2517; ¶10,014.03; TD ¶222,011
7. ¶I-2522; TD ¶222,019
8. ¶G-6567 *et seq.*; ¶4534.49; TD ¶467,015

References beginning with a single letter are to paragraphs in RIA's Federal Tax Coordinator 2d and RIA's Analysis of Federal Taxes: Income. Those beginning with numbers are to paragraphs in RIA's United States Tax Reporter. Those beginning with TD are to paragraphs in RIA's Tax Desk.

¶ 2405   Repossession of mortgaged real estate.

When real property is sold and the sale gives rise to a debt to the seller secured by the real property (a purchase-money mortgage or similar lien), and the seller later repossesses the property (through voluntary transfer or foreclosure) because of actual or imminent default by the buyer, then (1) no loss results to the seller from the repossession or reacquisition, nor does the mortgage debt become worthless; and (2) the seller's gain on repossession is limited to the money and the value of property (other than the repossessed property) received by the seller with respect to the original sale to the extent these amounts haven't already been reported as income. The resulting gain can't exceed the gain on the original sale. (Code Sec. 1038)[9]

If a homeseller's gain isn't recognized under the exclusion rules explained at ¶ 2442 and he repossesses the home and then resells it within one year after the date of the repossession, the above rules don't apply; the resale of the home is treated as part of the transaction constituting the original sale of the property. (Code Sec. 1038(e))[10]

observation: If the resale isn't made within one year, the regular repossession rules above apply.

¶ 2406   Personal property repossessed.

Gain or loss to the seller on repossession of personal property sold in a deferred payment transaction, not on the installment method, is the difference between the fair market value of the property when repossessed and the basis of the defaulted obligation, with that basis decreased by amounts paid on the note and increased for costs incurred in connection with the repossession. Gain or loss is reported in the year of repossession.[11]

¶ 2407   When cash basis taxpayers report gain or loss.

A cash basis seller reports gain on a sale or exchange in the year the sales proceeds are received, actually or constructively. A loss is reported in the year the transaction is completed by a fixed, identifiable event. (Code Sec. 451(a); Reg § 1.451-1(a))[12]

¶ 2408   When accrual basis taxpayers report gain or loss.

An accrual basis seller reports gain or loss in the year the sale is completed and an unqualified right to the purchase price arises—usually when title passes to the buyer.[13] For securities sales, see ¶2410.

¶ 2409   Delivery of deed or title in escrow.

Where both the deed (or other evidence of title) and the purchase price are placed in escrow pending examination and approval of the title by the buyer, a sale isn't completed (and gain or loss isn't realized) until the buyer signifies approval. Until then, the seller doesn't have an unqualified right to payment. Once the buyer approves title, the seller can't postpone reporting gain by directing the escrow agent to hold the payment.[14]

But if the deed is delivered in escrow as security for the performance of an unconditional obligation of the buyer (usually payment of the purchase price), the sale is completed when the deed is delivered and the buyer enters into possession of the property.[15]

9. ¶G-6851 *et seq.*; ¶10,384; TD ¶471,001
10. ¶G-6877 *et seq.*; ¶10,384; TD ¶471,013
11. ¶G-6801; TD ¶471,020
12. ¶I-2601; ¶4514.001; TD ¶222,401
13. ¶I-2602; ¶4464.07; TD ¶222,402
14. ¶I-1112; ¶4514.087; TD ¶220,608
15. ¶I-1124; ¶4514.101; TD ¶222,030

¶ 2410   Sales and exchanges of securities.

Gain or loss on the sale of securities arises when the seller has sold or committed himself to sell specific shares.[16] Gain or loss on the exchange of securities arises when the taxpayer acquires a right to specific securities.[17]

In stock exchange transactions, cash and accrual basis taxpayers realize gain or loss on the trade date, and not on the later settlement date.[18] For short sales, see ¶ 2639.

No gain or loss is recognized by owners of securities when they loan the securities in return for the agreement of the borrower to return identical securities, but the agreement must not reduce the transferor's risk of loss or opportunity for gain in the transferred securities. (Code Sec. 1058(a))[19]

Transactions structured to appear to be loans are sometimes found to be sales where they have the practical effect of sales, e.g., certain forward share and/or lending agreements where the taxpayer no longer has any substantial risk of loss.[20]

¶ 2411   Sales of load mutual funds with reinvestment right.

A load charge incurred in buying mutual fund shares is disregarded (in whole or in part) in computing gain or loss on the disposition of those shares within 90 days, if the buyer was given a reinvestment right under which shares in the same (or another) mutual fund could be bought at less than the usual load charge. The load charge is disregarded to the extent of the reduction in the load charge on the later purchase. (Code Sec. 852(f))[21]

¶ 2412   Significant modification of debt instrument treated as exchange.

A significant modification of a debt instrument results in an exchange of the original debt instrument for a modified instrument that differs materially either in kind or in extent. (Reg § 1.1001-3(b))[22]

> **observation:** The like-kind exchange rules (¶2418 *et seq.*) don't apply to exchanges of bonds, notes or other evidences of indebtedness. Exchanges of corporate bonds, but not of government bonds, may be tax-free under the reorganization provisions of the Code, but only to the extent the principal amount isn't increased. Thus, in most cases, an exchange (or modification, which is considered an exchange for tax purposes) results in the holder's recognizing gain or loss. For example, if a modification of a debt instrument results in a reduction of the debt, the debtor will have cancellation of debt income. (¶1385)

Examples of significant modifications in the terms of a debt instrument include:

. . . A change in the yield of a debt instrument, if the yield varies from the annual yield on the unmodified instrument (determined as of the date of the modification) by more than the greater of: 1/4 of 1% (25 basis points), or 5% of the annual yield of the unmodified instrument (.05 × annual yield). (Reg § 1.1001-3(e)(2)(ii))

. . . A modification that changes the timing of payments (including any resulting change in the amount of payments), if it results in the material deferral of scheduled payments. (Reg § 1.1001-3(e)(3)(i))

In some situations, a modification of a debt instrument may cause it to be recharacterized as an instrument or property right that is not debt, but a deterioration in the debtor's financial condition is not taken into account in making that determination unless there is a substitution of a new obligor or the addition or deletion of a co-obligor. (Reg § 1.1001-

---

16. ¶I-2615; TD ¶222,601;
17. ¶I-2616; TD ¶222,603
18. ¶I-2615.1; ¶4514.112; TD ¶222,602
19. ¶I-1311, I-3802; ¶10,584; TD ¶221,007

20. ¶I-3111 *et seq.*; TD ¶221,009.
21. ¶P-5038 *et seq.*; ¶8524.02; TD ¶216,021
22. ¶I-1050 *et seq.*; ¶10,014.83; TD ¶220,400 *et seq.*

3(f)(7)(ii))[23]

Qualifying taxpayers may elect to treat a substitution of certain publicly traded debt instruments for new ones as a realization event even if the substitution doesn't result in a significant modification of the terms of the old debt instrument, and therefore is not an exchange for tax purposes. Electing taxpayers do not recognize any realized gain or loss on the date of the substitution. Instead, gain or loss generally is taken into account as income or deductions over the term of the new debt instruments.[24]

¶ 2413 Nontaxable Exchanges.

A taxpayer doesn't recognize gain or loss on exchanges of common or preferred stock for other common or preferred stock of the same corporation. A corporation doesn't recognize gain or loss when it sells or exchanges its own stock for property or services. Certain U.S. obligations can be exchanged tax-free.

¶ 2414 Stock for stock of same corporation.

No gain or loss is recognized on the exchange of common stock for other common, or preferred stock for other preferred, of the same corporation. (Code Sec. 1036(a)) It's tax-free whether between a shareholder and the corporation or between two shareholders, and even if voting stock is exchanged for nonvoting stock. (Reg § 1.1036-1(a))[25]

Nonqualified preferred stock (¶3556) is treated as property other than stock for purposes of the rule allowing tax-deferred exchanges of preferred stock in the same corporation. (Code Sec. 1036(b))[26]

An exchange of common stock for preferred stock in the same corporation isn't tax-free. (Reg § 1.1036-1(a))[27] However, reorganization exchanges of stock for stock or stock and securities of the same or different corporations may be tax-free, see ¶3541 *et seq.*

¶ 2415 Corporation's sale or exchange of its own stock for property or services.

A corporation doesn't recognize gain or loss on the sale or exchange of its stock (including treasury stock) for money, other property or services. (Code Sec. 1032(a); Reg § 1.1032-1)[28] And it doesn't recognize gain or loss on the lapse of an option (warrant) to buy or sell its stock (including treasury stock). (Code Sec. 1032(a); Reg § 1.1032-3(d))[29]

¶ 2416 Tax-free exchanges of U.S. obligations.

IRS regs may provide for the tax-free exchange of one U.S. obligation (bond, note, etc.) for another. (Code Sec. 1037(a)) The Treasury designates the specific obligations it will exchange for the previously issued obligations without recognition of gain or loss.[30]

¶ 2417 Tax-free exchanges of insurance policies and annuities.

No gain or loss is recognized upon the exchange by the owner (or by a beneficiary on the death of the owner) of a life insurance contract for another or for an endowment or annuity contract, an endowment contract for an annuity or endowment contract providing for regular payments beginning at a date not later than the beginning date under the old contract, or an annuity contract for another. To qualify for tax-free exchange treatment, the insured or annuitant must remain the same. (Code Sec. 1035) The direct transfer of a part of funds from one annuity contract to another annuity contract qualifies as a nontaxable exchange under Code Sec. 1035 if certain conditions are met. Thus, the direct exchange of part of the cash

---

23. ¶I-1075.1; ¶10,014.83; TD ¶220,402
24. ¶I-1081.8; ¶10,014.83; TD ¶220,411
25. ¶I-3301; ¶10,364; TD ¶225,501
26. ¶I-3301.1; ¶10,364; TD ¶225,501

27. ¶I-3301; ¶10,364;TD ¶225,501
28. ¶I-3201, I-3208; ¶10,324; TD ¶233,401
29. ¶I-6517; ¶10,324; TD ¶252,010
30. ¶I-3400 *et seq.*; ¶10,374; TD ¶227,301

surrender value of an annuity contract for a new annuity contract issued by a second insurance company is tax-free even though the original annuity contract continued to exist.[31]

To the extent provided in regs, the rules allowing a tax-free exchange of insurance policies and annuities don't apply to any exchange having the effect of transferring property to a non-U.S. person. (Code Sec. 1035(c))[32]

No gain or loss is recognized on the exchange of a life insurance contract or an annuity contract for a qualified long-term care contract. (Code Sec. 1035(a))[33]

¶ 2418 "Like-Kind" (Code Sec. 1031) Exchanges. ▬▬▬▬▬▬▬

No gain or loss is recognized where business or investment property is exchanged solely for like-kind property. Whether property is business or investment property is determined by the taxpayer's intent at the time of the exchange. Multi-party exchanges may qualify. However, gain, but not loss, is recognized if boot (¶2421) is also received.

This nonrecognition provision doesn't apply to: stock in trade (inventory) and other property held primarily for sale; stocks, bonds, and notes; choices in action; interests in a partnership; certificates of trust or beneficial interest; or other securities or evidences of indebtedness or interest. (Code Sec. 1031(a))[34]

Nonrecognition under Code Sec. 1031 is mandatory if the conditions are met.[35]

Report a like-kind exchange on Form 8824. If gain is recognized on the exchange because money and/or non-like-kind property is received, also report the transaction on Form 8849 and Schedule D (Form 1040), Form 4797, or Form 6252 (whichever applies).[36]

¶ 2419 Like-kind defined.

"Like-kind" refers to the nature, character, or class of the property, not to its grade or quality. Thus, an exchange of real estate for real estate is an exchange of "like-kind" property. It doesn't matter where the real estate is located or whether it's improved or not, but foreign and U.S. real property can't be like-kind . (Code Sec. 1031(h)(1); Reg § 1.1031(a)-1(b))[37] State treatment of property as real or personal is not determinative for like-kind exchange purposes.

Personal property used predominantly in the U.S. and personal property used predominantly outside the U.S. aren't like-kind. (Code Sec. 1031(h)(2)(A)) In general, predominant use of relinquished property is determined based on the 2-year period that ends when the property is relinquished, and predominant use of the replacement property is determined based on the 2-year period beginning on the acquisition date. (Code Sec. 1031(h)(2)(B))[38]

Depreciable tangible personal property is exchanged for property of a "like kind" if it is exchanged for property of a like kind or like class. It is of a like class to other depreciable tangible personal property if the exchanged properties are either within the same General Asset Class or within the same Product Class. (Reg § 1.1031(a)-2(b)(1)) General asset classes are set forth by Revenue Procedure (Reg § 1.1031(a)-2(b)(2)); product classes are in Sectors 31, 32, and 33 (pertaining to manufacturing industries) of the North American Industry Classification System (NAICS) Manual. (Reg § 1.1031(a)-2(b)(3))[39]

Cars, light general-purpose trucks, crossovers, sport-utility vehicles (SUVs), minivans, and cargo vans are all like-kind, even if in different asset classes.[40]

No like classes are provided for nondepreciable or intangible personal property (e.g., a patent or copyright); an exchange of such property qualifies for nonrecognition only if the

31. ¶J-5302.1 *et seq.*; ¶10,354; TD ¶146,617 *et seq.*
32. ¶J-5306.1; ¶10,354; TD ¶146,623
33. ¶J-5301; ¶10,354; TD ¶146,616
34. ¶I-3050 *et seq.*; ¶10,314 *et seq.*; TD ¶223,601 *et seq.*
35. ¶I-3052; TD ¶223,603

36. ¶I-3051; TD ¶223,602
37. ¶I-3059; ¶10,314.02; TD ¶223,701
38. ¶I-3064.1; ¶10,314.04; TD ¶223,706
39. ¶I-3060 *et seq.*; ¶10,314.02; TD ¶223,703 *et seq.*
40. ¶I-3066; TD ¶223,708

exchanged properties are of a like kind. (Reg § 1.1031(a)-2(c)(1)) The goodwill or going concern value of a business can't be like-kind property. (Reg § 1.1031(a)-2(c)(2)) However, intangible assets such as trademarks, tradenames, mastheads, and customer-based intangibles, that can be valued separately and apart from goodwill, can qualify as like-kind property, as can emissions credits.[41]

While the exchange of a leasehold in real property for real property is generally not a like-kind exchange, under safe harbor rules, an exchange of real property for a 30-year leasehold on real property is a like-kind exchange. (Reg § 1.1031(a)-1(c))[42] Also, an undivided fractional interest in real property may qualify as like-kind replacement property for other real property.[43] Development rights that a corporation intended to acquire as replacement property were like-kind to a fee interest in relinquished property.[44]

Trade-ins are a common type of nontaxable exchange. Whether the taxpayer pays money or not, the trade-in is still a nontaxable exchange. (Reg § 1.1031(a)-1(c))[45]

IRS won't challenge whether a dwelling unit (e.g., a vacation home) qualifies as property held for productive use in a trade or business or for investment purposes if the unit (whether relinquished property or replacement property) meets certain ownership, rental, and personal use tests.[46]

¶ 2420   Multi-party (including deferred) nontaxable exchanges.

If a taxpayer wants to (or will only) exchange his property for like-kind property, but the party who wants taxpayer's property doesn't own the like-kind property, the taxpayer can still set up a nontaxable exchange if the other party acquires the like-kind property and taxpayer then exchanges his property for that like-kind property.

illustration: A holds Whiteacre for investment. He doesn't want to sell it if that would result in tax, but he would exchange it for Blackacre. B wants Whiteacre. C owns Blackacre and is willing to sell, but doesn't want Whiteacre. B buys Blackacre from C for cash. A transfers Whiteacre to B for Blackacre. The exchange is nontaxable to A.

The exchange is nontaxable (if the time limits at ¶2423 are met) even where the taxpayer transfers property in exchange for a written promise by the transferee to deliver like-kind property to the taxpayer in the future, i.e., a deferred or non-simultaneous exchange.

A multiparty nontaxable exchange can be set up by using a qualified intermediary (QI) (someone other than the taxpayer or a "disqualified person," e.g., taxpayer's agent) to facilitate the transaction. (Reg § 1.1031(k)-1(g)(4))[47] Reverse exchanges (replacement property is acquired before the relinquished property is transferred) may be implemented using qualified exchange accommodation arrangements under IRS-approved safe-harbor rules. However, the safe-harbor rules do not apply to replacement property owned by the taxpayer within the 180-day period ending on the date of transfer of ownership of the property to an exchange accommodation titleholder. IRS recognizes, however, that under case law, some reverse exchanges may still qualify even if they do not meet the safe-harbor requirements.[48]

Where property or cash is set aside in a qualified escrow account, qualified trust, or similar account ("exchange funds") pending completion of a deferred like-kind exchange, the exchange funds are generally treated as an exchange facilitator loan, i.e., a demand loan from the taxpayer to the exchange facilitator (i.e., the QI, transferee, escrow holder, trustee, or other party holding exchange funds for the taxpayer in the deferred exchange), and all items of income, deduction, and credit (including capital gains and losses) attributable to the exchange funds are taken into account by the exchange facilitator. (Reg § 1.468B-6(c)(1))[49] If all earnings attributable to the exchange funds are paid to the taxpayer under the terms of the

41. ¶I-3065; ¶I-3066; ¶10,314.02; TD ¶223,707
42. ¶I-3076; ¶10,314.03; TD ¶223,716
43. ¶I-3092.1; TD ¶224,003.1
44. ¶I-3073
45. ¶I-3057; ¶10,314.15; TD ¶223,708

46. ¶I-3083.2 *et seq.*; ¶10,314.01; TD ¶224,101
47. ¶I-3119, I-3120; ¶10,314.10; TD ¶224,230
48. ¶I-3095 *et seq.*; ¶10,314.10; TD ¶224,800 *et seq.*
49. ¶J-1379.1 *et seq.*; ¶468B4.2

agreement, then the taxpayer takes all items of income, deduction, and credit into account. (Reg § 1.468B-6(c)(2))[50]

¶ 2421   Taxing "boot" in otherwise nontaxable exchange.

If a taxpayer receives boot—money or any other property that doesn't qualify for nonrecognition of gain—in an otherwise nontaxable exchange of stock (¶2414), insurance policies (¶2417), like-kind property (¶2418), or U.S. obligations (¶2416), then gain to the taxpayer is recognized (is taxable) in an amount not exceeding the value of the boot received (Code Sec. 1031(b)), but loss to the taxpayer isn't recognized (isn't deductible) to any extent. (Code Sec. 1031(c))[1]

💡 illustration: Taxpayer exchanges business real estate worth $500,000 and having an adjusted basis of $200,000 for business real estate worth $400,000 plus $100,000 cash. His total gain is $300,000 ($400,000 + $100,000 − $200,000 basis), but the amount recognized is limited to the boot—$100,000. The tax on the remaining $200,000 gain is deferred because the transaction qualifies as a like-kind exchange.

Where the taxpayer gives money in the nontaxable exchange, no gain is recognized. But if the boot given is property other than money, gain or loss may be recognized. Thus, where stock that has depreciated in value is given in connection with a nontaxable exchange of real estate, loss on the stock is recognized to the extent the stock's adjusted basis exceeds its fair market value. (Reg § 1.1031(d)-1(e))[2]

¶ 2422   Assumption of liabilities.

Liabilities assumed are treated as a cash equivalent (boot). Whether a liability is "assumed" for this purpose is determined under Code Sec. 357(d) (see ¶3516). (Code Sec. 1031(d)) The taxpayer who assumes the liability is the one giving the boot, while the taxpayer whose liability is assumed *receives* the boot.[3] If each party assumes a liability of the other, only the net liability is boot given or received. (Reg § 1.1031(b)-1(c))

¶ 2423   Time limits on like-kind exchanges.

Like-kind treatment is barred if the property to be received is not identified (e.g., by being specified in the contract) on or before 45 days after the transfer, or isn't received within 180 days after the transfer or by the due date (with extensions) of the return for the year of transfer, if earlier. (Code Sec. 1031(a)(3))[4] There's no good faith exception to these deadlines,[5] but the deadlines may be extended for like-kind exchanges affected by disasters.[6] There is also a safe harbor method of reporting gain or loss for certain taxpayers who initiate deferred like-kind exchanges but fail to complete the exchange because a qualified intermediary defaults on its obligation to acquire and transfer replacement property to the taxpayer.[7]

¶ 2424   Related-party exchanges.

Where a taxpayer exchanges like-kind property with a related taxpayer under Code Sec. 267(b) (see ¶2448) or Code Sec. 707(b)(1) (see ¶3731) and, within two years of the date of the last transfer that was part of the exchange, either party disposes of the property received in the exchange, then gain or loss not recognized in the exchange is recognized on the date the later disposition occurs. A disposition includes indirect transfers. Exceptions are made for death, certain involuntary conversions, and non-tax-avoidance transactions. (Code Sec. 1031(f))[8] Form 8824 must be filed for the year of the exchange and also for the two years

---

50. ¶J-1379.1J *et seq.*; ¶468B4.2
1. ¶I-3160; ¶10,314.11; TD ¶225,001
2. ¶I-3163; ¶10,314.11; TD ¶225,001
3. ¶I-3165; ¶10,314.12; TD ¶225,005
4. ¶I-3099; ¶10,314.08; TD ¶224,209

5. ¶I-3101; TD ¶224,209
6. ¶S-8012; TD ¶904,003
7. ¶I-3120.2 *et seq.*; TD ¶224,244 *et seq.*
8. ¶I-3132 *et seq.*; ¶10,314.07; TD ¶224,701

following the exchange.[9]

A qualified intermediary (QI) (¶2420) can't be used to circumvent the limitations that would have applied to a direct exchange between related parties. For example, an exchange was part of a transaction to avoid the related party rules (and didn't qualify for nonrecognition treatment) where: (1) a taxpayer (T) transferred appreciated property to a QI, which (2) sold it to an unrelated party and used the proceeds to purchase like-kind property from a party related to T, then (3) transferred that property to T.[10]

¶ 2425 Exchanges of multiple properties.

These are exchanges in which more than one "exchange group" (see below) is created, or exchanges in which only one exchange group is created but there is more than one property being transferred or received within that exchange group. To compute gain, (1) separate the properties transferred into exchange groups, (2) offset all liabilities assumed by the taxpayer as part of the exchange by all liabilities of which the taxpayer is relieved as part of the exchange, with the excess liabilities assumed or relieved allocated among the exchange groups, and (3) apply the like-kind exchange rules separately to each exchange group to determine the amount of gain recognized in the exchange and the basis of the properties received in the exchange. (Reg § 1.1031(j)-1(a)(2)(i))[11]

Each "exchange group" consists of the properties transferred and received in the exchange, all of which are of a like kind or like class. (Reg § 1.1031(j)-1(b)(2)(i))[12]

¶ 2426 Rollover of Gain from Certain Sales. ▄▄▄▄▄▄▄▄▄▄▄▄▄

Eligible taxpayers may elect to roll over gain from (1) the sale of publicly traded securities tax-free into an investment in a Specialized Small Business Investment Company (SSBIC) (¶2427), (2) the sale of qualified empowerment zone assets (¶2428), and (3) the sale of qualified small business stock (¶2429), if certain holding period and reinvestment requirements are met.

¶ 2427 Rollover of securities sale gain into Specialized Small Business Investment Companies (SSBICs).

An individual and a C corporation may elect to limit the amount of capital gain they recognize on the sale of "publicly traded securities" (securities traded on an open market) to the excess of the amount realized on the sale, over (1) the cost of any common stock or partnership interest in an SSBIC bought during the 60-day period beginning on the sale date, reduced by (2) any part of that cost previously taken into account under this rule. (Code Sec. 1044(a), Code Sec. 1044(c)(1))[13] An SSBIC is any partnership or corporation licensed by the Small Business Administration under Sec. 301(d) of the Small Business Investment Act of '58 as in effect on May 13, '93. (Code Sec. 1044(c)(3))[14]

The gain an individual may roll over under the SSBIC rules for any tax year may not exceed the lesser of: $50,000, or $500,000 reduced by any gain excluded (rolled over) under this rule in all preceding years. (Code Sec. 1044(b)(1)) For married persons filing separately, the limits are $25,000 and $250,000, respectively. (Code Sec. 1044(b)(3))[15]

A C corporation's rollover for any tax year may not exceed the lesser of $250,000 or $1,000,000 reduced by any gain excluded under this rule in all preceding years. (Code Sec. 1044(b)(2)) This includes exclusions by members of the corporation's controlled group, or by its predecessor. (Code Sec. 1044(b)(4))[16]

Elect by reporting the entire gain from the sale of the publicly traded securities on Form

---

9. ¶I-3132; TD ¶224,701
10. ¶I-3137; TD ¶224,705
11. ¶I-3187 *et seq.*; ¶10,314.10; TD ¶225,402 *et seq.*
12. ¶I-3138 *et seq.*; ¶10,314.10; TD ¶225,408

13. ¶I-3791; ¶10,444; TD ¶225,503
14. ¶I-3794; ¶10,444; TD ¶225,503
15. ¶I-3792; ¶10,444; TD ¶225,504
16. ¶I-3793; ¶10,444; TD ¶225,504

8949 (for individuals) and Schedule D of the return (for C corporations) on or before the due date (including extensions) for the year the publicly traded securities are sold and by attaching a statement to the applicable form showing (1) how the nonrecognized gain was calculated; (2) the SSBIC in which common stock or a partnership interest was purchased and the date the stock or interest was purchased; and (3) the basis of the SSBIC stock or interest. (Reg § 1.1044(a)-1(b))[17]

For the effect of gain not recognized under the SSBIC rules upon taxpayer's basis in an SSBIC investment, see ¶2505.

¶ 2428 Election to roll over gain from qualified empowerment zone assets.

A taxpayer can elect to defer recognition of capital gain on the sale of a qualified empowerment zone asset held for more than one year where replacement empowerment zone assets are purchased within 60 days. (Code Sec. 1397B(a), Code Sec. 1391(d)(1)(A)(i)) DC Enterprise Zone assets aren't eligible for the tax-free rollover treatment. (Code Sec. 1397B(b)(1)(B))

The rollover rules do not apply to any gain treated as ordinary income or any gain attributable to real property, or an intangible asset, which is not an integral part of an enterprise zone business. (Code Sec. 1397B(b)(2))

If the rollover is elected, capital gain from the sale of a qualified empowerment zone asset is recognized only to the extent that the amount realized from the sale exceeds the cost of any qualified empowerment zone asset (with respect to the same zone as the asset sold) purchased during the 60-day period beginning on the sale date, reduced by any part of the cost previously taken into account under this rollover rule. (Code Sec. 1397B(a))

The basis of the replacement zone asset is reduced by gain not recognized on the rollover, but this rule doesn't apply for purposes of Code Sec. 1202 (exclusion for gain on the sale of small business stock; see ¶2648). (Code Sec. 1397B(b)(4))

The holding period of the replacement zone asset includes the holding period of the original zone asset, except that the replacement asset must actually be held for more than one year to qualify for another tax-free rollover. (Code Sec. 1223(13), Code Sec. 1397B(b)(5)(A))[18]

¶ 2429 Election to roll over capital gain from sale of qualified small business stock (QSBS).

Taxpayers other than corporations may elect to roll over capital gain from the sale of QSBS (¶2649) held for more than six months, so that gain is recognized only to the extent that the amount realized exceeds (1) the cost of QSBS bought during the 60-day period beginning on the sale date, reduced by (2) any part of the cost previously taken into account under the rule. (Code Sec. 1045(a))

Rules similar to those under Code Sec. 1202(g) (for determining which holders of interests in pass-through entities are eligible for the 50% exclusion of gain from the sale of QSBS, see ¶2648) apply to the rollover of gain from the sale of QSBS by a pass-through entity. (Code Sec. 1045(b)(5))[19]

The holding period of the replacement stock includes the holding period of the stock sold, but not for purposes of determining whether the 6-month holding period required for rollovers is met. To qualify as small business stock, the issuing corporation must meet an active business test during substantially all of the taxpayer's holding period for the stock. For purposes of the rollover provision, the replacement stock must meet this active business requirement for the 6-month period following the purchase. (Code Sec. 1045(b)(4))[20]

For adjustments to basis of the replacement QSBS, see ¶2506.

---

17. ¶I-3795; ¶10,444; TD ¶225,505
18. ¶I-3430 *et seq.*; ¶13,97B4; TD ¶227,350 *et seq.*

19. ¶I-9201; ¶10,454; TD ¶247,201
20. ¶I-9204; ¶10,454; TD ¶247,204

¶ 2430   Involuntary Conversions—Form 4797. ▬▬▬▬

No gain is recognized when property is compulsorily or involuntarily converted into property similar or related in service or use. Where property is involuntarily converted into money or into property that isn't similar or related in service or use, a taxpayer can avoid tax on any gain, if he so elects and he buys property that's similar or related in service or use or if he acquires control of a corporation that owns such property (or acquires the property within a specified time). The cost of the replacement property must be equal to or more than the net proceeds from the converted property. And the replacement must generally be made within two years after the close of the first tax year in which any part of the gain is realized. (Code Sec. 1033) A loss on an involuntary conversion is recognized or not recognized without regard to the involuntary conversion rules. (Reg § 1.1033(a)-1(a))[21] Individuals use Form 8949 to report gain or loss from an involuntary conversion. Form 4797 is used to report an involuntary conversion of assets used in a trade or business.[22]

¶ 2431   Nonrecognition of gain on involuntary conversions.

Where property is involuntarily converted into other property similar or related in service or use to the converted property, no gain is recognized. (Code Sec. 1033(a)(1)) However, where the taxpayer receives dissimilar property or cash when his property is involuntarily converted, he must buy "replacement" property (¶2438)[23] or 80% control of a corporation owning or acquiring replacement property within a specified time.[24] Gain is recognized only to the extent the amount realized on the conversion exceeds the cost of the replacement property. (Code Sec. 1033(a)(2)(A))[25]

If a principal residence is involuntarily converted and gain is excluded under Code Sec. 121 (¶2442), then the amount realized for purposes of the involuntary conversion provisions is the amount realized less the excluded gain. (Code Sec. 121(d)(5)(B))[26]

A business that realized gain from a state disaster relief grant to reimburse it for disaster-related damage to real and personal property may elect to defer the gain to the extent that an amount equal to the grant proceeds is used to timely purchase property similar or related in service or use to the destroyed or damaged property.[27]

¶ 2432   Involuntary conversion defined.

An involuntary conversion is the compulsory or involuntary conversion of taxpayer's property into similar property, dissimilar property or money as a result of the property's destruction, theft, seizure, requisition or condemnation (actual or threatened). (Code Sec. 1033(a))[28]

Involuntary conversions include the following: sales in actual or threatened condemnation (¶2435); certain sales (or the destruction) of livestock due to disease (Code Sec. 1033(d)); the sale or exchange of livestock (in excess of the number taxpayer would sell if he followed his usual business practices) solely on account of drought, flood, or other weather-related conditions (Code Sec. 1033(e)(1));[29] the sale or transfer of property to the federal government, a state or local government, or an Indian tribal government to implement hazard mitigation (Code Sec. 1033(k));[30] and the sale of publicly traded stock under a state escheat law.[31] However, payments for the temporary use of a taxpayer's property by the government where the taxpayer continues to own the property are treated as rental income and not payments in exchange for the property.[32]

---

21. ¶I-3701; ¶10,334; TD ¶229,701
22. ¶I-3773; ; TD ¶229,702
23. ¶I-3700 *et seq.*; ¶10,334 *et seq.*; TD ¶229,701
24. ¶I-3743; ¶10,334.23; TD ¶229,736
25. ¶I-3701; ¶10,334.31; TD ¶229,743
26. ¶I-4565; ¶1214.14; TD ¶225,745

27. ¶I-3702; TD ¶229,713
28. ¶I-3702; ¶10,334.01; TD ¶229,713
29. ¶N-1216 *et seq.*; ¶10,334.08; TD ¶229,713.1
30. ¶I-3716.1; ¶10,334.01; TD ¶193,606
31. ¶I-3712
32. ¶I-9021; TD ¶223,207

¶ 2433 Principal residence or contents converted as result of federally declared disaster.

If the taxpayer's principal residence, or any of its contents, is located in a disaster area and is compulsorily or involuntarily converted because of a "federally declared disaster," any gain resulting from the receipt of insurance proceeds for personal property that was part of the contents of the residence and wasn't "scheduled property" for insurance purposes isn't recognized, regardless of the use to which the taxpayer puts those proceeds. (Code Sec. 1033(h)(1))[33] "Federally declared disaster" and "disaster area" are defined in Code Sec. 165(h)(3)(C)(i). (Code Sec. 1033(h)(3)) Insurance proceeds received for the home or its "separately scheduled" contents are treated as received for a single item of property, and any property which is similar or related in service or use to the residence so converted (or its contents) is treated for purposes of the involuntary conversion rules as property similar or related in service or use to that single item of property.[34]

For the extended replacement period that applies, see ¶2441.

¶ 2434 Insurance that compensates for the loss of the right to use property.

Insurance proceeds that compensate for the loss of the right to use the property due to loss or destruction may qualify for nonrecognition as involuntary conversion proceeds, but the proceeds of a use and occupancy insurance contract that expressly insures against actual lost profits don't qualify and are treated as taxable income. (Reg § 1.1033(a)-2(c)(8))[35]

¶ 2435 Condemnations—actual or threatened.

A disposition under the threat or imminence of condemnation is treated as an involuntary conversion. (Code Sec. 1033(a)(2)(E)(ii))

Threat or imminence of condemnation exists (1) when taxpayer is informed, orally or in writing, by a representative of a governmental body or an authorized public official, that the body or official has decided to acquire the property, and taxpayer has reasonable grounds to believe that condemnation proceedings will be initiated if he doesn't voluntarily sell, or (2) where the taxpayer gets information as to a decision to acquire the property for public use through a report in the news media, if a representative of the governmental body or public official involved confirms the published report and taxpayer has reasonable grounds to believe that the necessary steps to condemn will be taken if he doesn't sell.[36] Sales to third parties (as distinguished from the condemning agency) also qualify as involuntary conversions if made under the threat or imminence of condemnation.[37]

¶ 2436 Amount of condemnation awards.

Condemnation proceeds cannot be greater than the amount specifically awarded for the requisitioned property. It may, however, be less if there are any legal or other expenses or special assessments which must be deducted. But sums withheld from the award to pay liens on the property don't reduce the amount realized.[38]

¶ 2437 Severance damages.

Where only part of the property is condemned, the owner may be paid severance damages as compensation for a loss of value in the part of the property retained. Severance damages may be paid, for example, because of impairment of access to the property retained. Payments

33. ¶I-3772.1 *et seq.*; ¶10,334.40; TD ¶229,750
34. ¶I-3772.2; ¶10,334.40; TD ¶229,750
35. ¶I-3724; ¶10,334.12; TD ¶229,749

36. ¶I-3703; ¶10,334.02; TD ¶229,713
37. ¶I-3706; TD ¶229,714
38. ¶I-3764; ¶10,334.31; TD ¶229,745

are considered severance damages only if specifically agreed to in the condemnation proceeding; otherwise, the entire award is considered made for the condemned property. Where severance damage proceeds are used to acquire replacement property, the taxpayer may elect nonrecognition under the involuntary conversion rules with respect to any gain from receipt of the severance damages.[39]

¶ 2438   Replacement property.

The replacement property must be similar or related in service or use to the property replaced. (Code Sec. 1033(a)(1)) "Similar or related in service or use" means the use of the replacement property must be substantially similar to the use of the replaced property.[40]

As an alternative to direct replacement of the converted property, the taxpayer may acquire control of a corporation owning property similar to that converted. (Code Sec. 1033(a)(2)(A)) Where this method is used, however, the special "like-kind" replacement rule for real property (¶2440) isn't available. The replacement property must qualify under the "similar use" rule. (Code Sec. 1033(g)(2))[41]

This test as applied to an owner-lessor of property looks to the use of the replacement property from the lessor's viewpoint, not the lessee's. If the replacement property involves similar business risks, management and landlord services, etc., it will qualify even though the lessee's use of the new property differs from the lessee's use of the old.[42]

Tangible property acquired and held for productive use in a trade or business is treated as similar or related in service or use to property that (a) was held for investment or for productive use on a trade or business (including inventory), and (b) was involuntarily converted as a result of a federally declared disaster. (Code Sec. 1033(h)(2))[43]

⚫️*illustration:* If a business loses its delivery truck in a federally declared disaster, it can avoid current tax on the gain realized by timely (¶2441) reinvesting the insurance proceeds in a production machine.

If, because of drought, flood, or other weather-related conditions or soil contamination or other environmental contamination, it is not feasible for the taxpayer to reinvest the proceeds from compulsorily or involuntarily converted livestock (¶2432) in property similar or related in use to the old livestock, he may reinvest the proceeds in other property used for farming purposes. In the case of soil contamination or other environmental contamination, "other property used for farming purposes" includes real property. (Code Sec. 1033(f))[44]

¶ 2439   Related-person exception to nonrecognition rule.

Nonrecognition treatment for gain in an involuntary conversion isn't permitted if a taxpayer described below acquires replacement property or stock from a related party (under Code Sec. 267(b) (¶2448), or Code Sec. 707(b)(1) (¶3731)):

. . . C corporations.

. . . A partnership if one or more C corporations own, directly or indirectly under Code Sec. 707(b)(3) (¶3733), more than 50% of the capital interest or the profits interest of the partnership at the time of the involuntary conversion.

. . . Any other taxpayer (including an individual) if, with respect to property which is involuntarily converted during the tax year, the aggregate realized gain on property on which there is realized gain exceeds $100,000. (Code Sec. 1033(i)(2))[45]

However, nonrecognition does apply to the extent the related party acquired the replacement property or stock from an unrelated party, within the period (¶2441) allowed for the

39. ¶I-3768 *et seq.*; ¶10,334.14; TD ¶229,747
40. ¶I-3725; ¶10,334.22; TD ¶229,727
41. ¶I-3743; ¶10,334.22; TD ¶229,736
42. ¶I-3730; TD ¶229,730

43. ¶I-3772.6; ¶10,334.2205; TD ¶229,752
44. ¶N-1220; ¶10,334.08; TD ¶229,713.1
45. ¶I-3733.1, I-3733.2; ¶10,334.221; TD ¶229,722

acquisition of replacement property or stock. (Code Sec. 1033(i)(1))[46]

In the case of a partnership (or S corporation), this denial of nonrecognition rule applies to a partnership (or S corporation) and to each partner (or S shareholder). Thus, the annual $100,000 limit applies to both the entity and each partner (or S shareholder).[47]

¶ 2440 Replacement of condemned real estate.

A replacement of condemned real estate held for productive business use or for rental or investment qualifies for nonrecognition treatment if the replacement property is property of a like-kind. (Code Sec. 1033(g)(1)) Determination of whether replacement property is of like-kind is made under the rules at ¶2418, rather than the "similar use" rule. For example, improved realty isn't similar in use to unimproved realty (Reg § 1.1033(a)-2(c)(9)(i)), but the two properties are of like-kind.[48]

The like-kind rule doesn't apply to real estate held primarily for sale (Code Sec. 1033(g)(1)) or where control of a corporation owning replacement property is acquired. (Code Sec. 1033(g)(2))[49]

¶ 2441 Replacement period.

Converted property must be replaced within a period:

(1) beginning with (a) the date the property was destroyed, stolen, condemned, etc., or (b) the date condemnation or requisition was first threatened or became imminent, whichever is earlier (Code Sec. 1033(a)(2)(B)), and

(2) ending (a) two years after the close of the first tax year in which any part of the gain is realized (three years in the case of condemnation or threat of condemnation of real property described at ¶2440; four years for principal residences converted due to federally declared disasters, see ¶2433), or (b) at a later date allowed by IRS upon application by the taxpayer. (Code Sec. 1033(a)(2)(B), Code Sec. 1033(g)(4), Code Sec. 1033(h)(1)(B)) A five-year replacement period applies to property involuntarily converted due to storms and tornados on after May 3, 2007 in the 24-county Kansas disaster area[50] and to property involuntarily converted by reason of a Midwestern disaster on or after the "applicable disaster date"[1] in the Midwestern disaster area.[2]

If a taxpayer sells livestock on account of drought, flood, or other weather-related conditions (see ¶2438) which result in the area being designated as eligible for assistance by the federal government, the replacement period is extended to four years. This four-year period may be extended further by IRS on a regional basis if the weather-related conditions continue for more than three years. (Code Sec. 1033(e)(2)) For persistent droughts, IRS has extended the replacement period until the end of taxpayers' first tax year ending after the first drought-free year (as specially defined) for applicable regions.[3]

¶ 2442 Exclusion of Gain on Principal Residence. ▬▬▬

A taxpayer can exclude from income up to $250,000 of gain ($500,000 for joint filers meeting certain conditions) from the sale of a home owned and used by the taxpayer as a principal residence for at least 2 of the 5 years before the sale. (Code Sec. 121(a))

The exclusion doesn't apply if, within the 2-year period ending on the sale date, the exclusion applied to another home sale by the taxpayer. (Code Sec. 121(b)(3))[4]

Married taxpayers filing jointly for the year of sale may exclude up to $500,000 of home-sale gain if (1) either spouse owned the home for at least 2 of the 5 years before the sale, (2)

46. ¶I-3733.1; ¶10,334.221; TD ¶229,722
47. ¶I-3733.2; ¶10,334.221; TD ¶229,723
48. ¶I-3727; ¶10,334.22 *et seq.*; TD ¶229,728
49. ¶I-3727; ¶10,334.22, 10,334.23; TD ¶229,728
50. ¶I-3772.9; ¶10,334.44; TD ¶229,754.3

1. ¶S-8567; ¶14,00R4.06; TD ¶570,462
2. ¶I-3772.10; ¶10,334.45; TD ¶229,754.4
3. ¶N-1216.2 *et seq.*; ¶10,334.08; TD ¶229,713.2 *et seq.*
4. ¶I-4520 *et seq.*; ¶1214; TD ¶225,700 *et seq.*

both spouses used the home as a principal residence for at least 2 of the 5 years before the sale, and (3) neither spouse is ineligible for the full exclusion because of the once-every-2-year limit. (Code Sec. 121(b)(2)(A))[5] A surviving spouse qualifies for the up-to-$500,000 exclusion if the sale occurs not later than 2 years after the other spouse's death, if the requirements for the $500,000 exclusion were met immediately before the spouse's death and the survivor hasn't remarried as of the date of the sale. (Code Sec. 121(b)(4))[6] See ¶4705 for who is a spouse and who is eligible to file a joint return.

For the excludable amount where married taxpayers aren't eligible for the full $500,000 exclusion, see ¶2444.

Gain from the sale or exchange of property that is attributable to periods of "nonqualified use" is not eligible for the exclusion. (Code Sec. 121(b)(4)(A) [sic Code Sec. 121(b)(5)(A)])[7]

"Nonqualified use" refers to any period after 2008 during which the property is not used as the principal residence of the taxpayer, or his spouse, or former spouse. (Code Sec. 121(b)(4)(C)(i) [sic Code Sec. 121(b)(5)(C)(i)])[8]

The gain allocated to periods of nonqualified use is the total amount of gain, multiplied by a fraction, the numerator of which is the aggregate periods of nonqualified use during the period the taxpayer owned the property, and the denominator of which is the period the taxpayer owned the property. (Code Sec. 121(b)(4)(B) [sic Code Sec. 121(b)(5)(B)])[9]

The exclusion also does not apply to gain attributable to post-May 6, '97 depreciation, and that gain is not taken into account in determining the amount of gain allocated to qualified use. (Code Sec. 121(b)(4)(D) [sic Code Sec. 121(b)(5)(D)])[10]

Exceptions to the definition of "period of nonqualified use" include (1) use occurring in the five-year testing period after the date the residence was last used as a principal residence, (2) temporary absence (not to exceed an aggregate period of two years), and (3) any period during which the taxpayer or his spouse is serving on qualified official extended duty (not to exceed an aggregate period of ten years), see ¶2445. (Code Sec. 121(b)(4)(C)(ii) [sic Code Sec. 121(b)(5)(C)(ii)])[11]

The exchange or involuntary conversion (destruction (but only if the residence is totally destroyed), as well as condemnation) of a principal residence is treated as a sale for purposes of the home-sale exclusion. (Code Sec. 121(d)(5)(A))[12]

The exclusion doesn't apply to gain attributable to post-May 6, '97 depreciation claimed for rental or business use of a principal residence. (Code Sec. 121(d)(6))[13]

If property is used for both residential and business (or investment) purposes, no allocation of gain is required if both the residential and non-residential portions of the property are within the same dwelling unit, but gain isn't excludable to the extent of any post-May 6, '97, depreciation. However, gain is allocated if the part of the home for which the use requirement isn't met is separate from the dwelling unit. (Reg § 1.121-1(e)(1))[14]

The exclusion isn't available to individuals subject to the expatriate tax rules (see ¶4653). (Code Sec. 121(e))[15]

For a taxpayer who acquired a home in a like-kind exchange (¶2418 *et seq.*) in which any gain wasn't recognized, or a donee of such a taxpayer, the exclusion doesn't apply for the 5-year period beginning with the date of the acquisition. (Code Sec. 121(d)(10))[16]

A taxpayer may elect not to apply the exclusion to the sale or exchange of a principal residence. (Code Sec. 121(f))[17]

---

5. ¶I-4536; ¶1214.02; TD ¶225,716
6. ¶I-4538.1; ¶1214.02; TD ¶225,718.1
7. ¶I-4568.1; ¶1214.07; TD ¶225,748.1
8. ¶I-4568.3; ¶1214.07; TD ¶225,748.3
9. ¶I-4568.2; ¶1214.07; TD ¶225,748.2
10. ¶I-4568.7; ¶1214.07; TD ¶225,748.7
11. ¶I-4568.4; ¶1214.07; TD ¶225,748.4

12. ¶I-4565; ¶1214.14; TD ¶225,745
13. ¶I-4568; ¶1214.06; TD ¶225,748
14. ¶I-4532 *et seq.*; ¶1214.06; TD ¶225,712 *et seq.*
15. ¶I-4569; ¶1214.18; TD ¶225,749
16. ¶I-4561.1; ¶1214.14; TD ¶225,741.1
17. ¶I-4570; ¶1214.20; TD ¶225,753

If home-sale gain is entirely excluded under Code Sec. 121, the transaction is not reported on the return at all. However, entries on Form 8949 are necessary if there is taxable gain on the home sale (e.g., realized gain exceeds the excludable amount).[18]

¶ 2443 Reduced exclusion for partially qualifying principal residence sales.

A reduced maximum exclusion may apply to taxpayers who sell their principal residence but (1) fail to qualify for the 2-out-of-5-year ownership and use rule, or (2) previously sold another home within the two-year period ending on the sale date of the current home in a transaction to which the exclusion applied (¶2442). If the taxpayer's failure to meet either rule occurs because he must sell the home due to a change of place of employment, health or, to the extent provided by regs, other unforeseen circumstances, then he may be entitled to a reduced maximum exclusion. Under these circumstances, the maximum gain that can be excluded is equal to the full $250,000 or $500,000 exclusion times a fraction having as its numerator the shorter of (a) aggregate periods of ownership and use of the home by the taxpayer as a principal residence during the 5 years ending on the sale date, or (b) the period of time after the last sale to which the exclusion applied, and before the date of the current sale, and having 2 years (or its equivalent in months) as its denominator. (Code Sec. 121(c))[19]

☯️ *Illustration:* Sara, a single taxpayer, sells her principal residence because she has a new job in another city. On the sale date, she has owned the home and used it as her principal residence for the last 18 months. She has never excluded gain from another home sale. Since Sara fails to meet the use and ownership requirements for the exclusion because of a change in place of employment, the amount of gain excluded by her can't exceed $187,500 ($250,000 times 1.5 years of ownership and use divided by 2 years). Thus, if Sara realized a gain of $50,000 on her home sale, all of it would be excludable.

The up-to-ten-year suspension for qualifying military services or Foreign Service members or intelligence community employees explained at ¶2445 may be elected to determine the amount of the reduced exclusion. (Code Sec. 121(d)(9)(A))[20]

To claim a reduced maximum exclusion, the sale or exchange must be made because of a change of place of employment, health, or unforeseen circumstances. If a safe harbor in the regs applies, a sale is deemed to be made by reason of a change in place of employment, health, or unforeseen circumstances. If a safe harbor does not apply, a sale or exchange is by reason of a change in place of employment, health, or unforeseen circumstances only if the primary reason for the sale or exchange is one of those reasons. (Reg § 1.121-3(b))[21]

A sale or exchange is because of a change in place of employment, if, in the case of a qualified individual (taxpayer, spouse (see ¶4705), co-owner of the residence, or a person whose principal place of abode is in the same household as the taxpayer), the primary reason for the sale or exchange is a change in the location of the individual's employment (including self-employment). Under a safe harbor, this condition is treated as met if (1) the new place of employment is at least 50 miles farther from the residence sold or exchanged than was the former place of employment (for the formerly unemployed, 50 miles between the new place of employment and the residence sold or exchanged), and (2) the change in place of employment occurs during the taxpayer's ownership and use of the home as his principal residence. (Reg § 1.121-3(c))[22]

The health condition is met if the primary reason for the sale is to (1) obtain, provide, or facilitate the diagnosis, cure, mitigation, or treatment of disease, illness, or injury of a qualified individual, or (2) obtain or provide medical or personal care for a qualified individual suffering from a disease, illness, or injury. A qualified individual includes those listed above under change of employment, plus (a) a parent, grandparent, stepmother, stepfather, child, grandchild, stepchild, adopted child, brother, sister, stepbrother, stepsister, half brother, half

18. ¶I-4521; ¶1214; TD ¶225,701
19. ¶I-4557; ¶1214.08; TD ¶225,737
20. ¶I-4563.1; ¶1214; TD ¶225,708.1

21. ¶I-4541; ¶1214.08; TD ¶225,721
22. ¶I-4542 *et seq.*; ¶1214.08; TD ¶225,722 *et seq.*

sister, mother-in-law, father-in-law, brother-in-law, sister-in-law, son-in-law, daughter-in-law, uncle, aunt, nephew, or niece even if they aren't his dependents; and (b) descendants of the taxpayer's grandparent (e.g., first cousins). A sale or exchange doesn't qualify for the health condition if it is merely beneficial to the general health or well-being of the individual. Under a safe harbor, the health condition is treated as met if a doctor recommends a change of residence for the health reasons listed above in (1) or (2). (Reg § 1.121-3(d); Reg § 1.121-3(f))[23]

observation: Qualified individuals in (a) and (b) above are defined in Reg § 1.121-3(f) by reference to paragraphs (1) through (8) of former Code Sec. 152(a). Presumably that reference still applies even though Code Sec. 152(a) now contains only two paragraphs.

A sale or exchange is caused by unforeseen circumstances if the primary reason for the sale or exchange is an event that the taxpayer could not reasonably have anticipated before purchasing and occupying the residence. A sale or exchange by reason of unforeseen circumstances (other than a circumstance covered by one of the safe harbors listed in regs, such as an involuntary conversion, or death of a qualified individual, or designated by IRS as an unforeseen circumstance in published guidance or in a ruling issued to a specific taxpayer) does not qualify for the reduced maximum exclusion if the primary reason for the sale or exchange is a preference for a different residence or an improvement in financial circumstances. (Reg § 1.121-3(e))[24]

¶ 2444   Amount excludable if married taxpayers ineligible for full exclusion.

If married taxpayers filing a joint return aren't eligible for the $500,000 maximum exclusion under the rules explained at ¶2442, the amount of the exclusion that they may claim is the sum of each spouse's (see ¶4705) maximum exclusion determined on a separate basis as if they had not been married. However, for purposes of this rule, each spouse is treated as owning the property during the period that either spouse owned the property. (Code Sec. 121(b)(2)(B))[25]

¶ 2445   Ownership and use tests to qualify for home-sale exclusion.

In general, the full home-sale exclusion applies only if the taxpayer owned the home and used it as a principal residence for at least 2 of the 5 years ending on the date that it is sold. (Code Sec. 121(a))

A taxpayer is treated as the owner and seller of the residence held by a trust during the period that he is treated as the owner of the trust or the part of the trust that includes the residence under the rules of Code Sec. 671 through Code Sec. 679 (grantors and others treated as substantial owners), see ¶3957 *et seq.* Similar treatment applies to certain single-owner entities where the entity is disregarded for federal tax purposes. (Reg § 1.121-1(c)(3))[26]

Each unmarried taxpayer who jointly owns a principal residence may be eligible to exclude from gross income up to $250,000 of gain that is attributable to that taxpayer's interest in the property. (Reg § 1.121-2(a)(2))[27]

Gain from the sale or exchange of partial interests (other than interests remaining after the sale or exchange of a remainder interest) in the taxpayer's principal residence is excludable if the interest sold or exchanged includes an interest in the dwelling unit. Only one maximum limitation amount of $250,000 ($500,000 for certain joint returns) applies to the combined sales or exchanges of partial interests. (Reg § 1.121-4(e))[28]

The bankruptcy estate of an individual in a chapter 7 or 11 bankruptcy case under title 11 of the United States Code succeeds to and takes into account his home-sale exclusion if the

23. ¶I-4545 *et seq.*; ¶1214.08; TD ¶225,725 *et seq.*
24. ¶I-4547 *et seq.*; ¶1214.08; TD ¶225,727 *et seq.*
25. ¶I-4537; ¶1214.02; TD ¶225,717

26. ¶I-4529 *et seq.*; ¶1214.12; TD ¶225,709 *et seq.*
27. ¶I-4535; ¶1214.02; TD ¶225,715
28. ¶I-4567; ¶1214.16; TD ¶225,747

individual otherwise satisfies the requirements. (Reg § 1.1398-3)[29]

Under the following circumstances, a taxpayer may "tack on" someone else's ownership and/or use period to his or her own ownership and/or use period.

. . . An unmarried individual whose spouse (see ¶4705) was deceased on the home-sale date may tack on the decedent's ownership and use period to his own ownership and use period. (Code Sec. 121(d)(2))[30]

. . . An individual who receives a home in a Code Sec. 1041(a) transaction (¶2447), such as a tax-free transfer from a spouse (or former spouse), may tack on the transferor's ownership period to his or her own ownership period. (Code Sec. 121(d)(3)(A))[31]

. . . An individual is treated as using a home as his or her principal residence during any period of ownership that the individual's spouse (see ¶4705) or former spouse is granted use of the property under a divorce or separation instrument. (Code Sec. 121(d)(3)(B))[32]

However, if a taxpayer voluntarily demolishes his principal residence and builds a new principal residence on the same land, the period he owned and used the demolished principal residence is not taken into account in determining whether he qualifies for the exclusion on the sale of the new principal residence.[33]

A relief provision applies to a taxpayer who becomes physically or mentally incapable of self-care and, during the 5-year period ending on the home's sale date, owns and uses the home as a principal residence for periods aggregating at least 1 year. Here, the taxpayer is treated as having used the home as a principal residence during any time in the 5-year period in which he owns the home and lives in a facility (including a nursing home) licensed by a state or political subdivision to care for someone in the taxpayer's condition. (Code Sec. 121(d)(7))[34] The up-to-ten-year suspension for qualifying military services, Foreign Services members, or employees of an intelligence community (discussed below) also may be elected for this relief provision. (Code Sec. 121(d)(9)(A))

A member of the uniformed services or the Foreign Service, an employee of the intelligence community for sales or exchanges after Dec. 20, 2006, and a Peace Corps Volunteer serving outside the U.S. for tax years beginning after 2007, can elect to suspend the 5-year period for measuring ownership and use during any period that he or his spouse (see ¶4705) is serving on extended duty at least 50 miles from the residence or while residing under orders in Government quarters. (Code Sec. 121(d)(9)(A), Code Sec. 121(d)(12)) The 5-year period can't be extended by more than 10 years. (Code Sec. 121(d)(9)(B))[35]

If an election out of the estate tax was made with respect to individuals dying in 2010, the home-sale exclusion will be extended to decedents' estates, heirs, and trusts that were qualified revocable trusts immediately before any such individual's death, so that they will be allowed to take into account the decedent's ownership and use of the home while alive. (Code Sec. 121(d)(11))[36]

¶ 2446   Sales and Exchanges Between Related Taxpayers. ▮▮▮▮▮▮▮▮▮

No gain or loss is recognized on a transfer of property between spouses (or former spouses incident to divorce). No deduction is allowed for any loss from the sale or exchange of property between specified related taxpayers. A loss from a transfer between members of the same controlled group is generally deferred until the property is transferred outside the group.

---

29. ¶C-9718.01; ¶13,984.01; TD ¶225,742
30. ¶I-4559; ¶1214.10; TD ¶225,739
31. ¶I-4558; ¶1214.10; TD ¶225,738
32. ¶I-4558; ¶1214.10; TD ¶225,738

33. ¶I-4527; TD ¶225,707
34. ¶I-4563; ¶1214.14; TD ¶225,743
35. ¶I-4528.1; ¶1214.14; TD ¶225,708.1
36. ¶I-4560; ¶1214.14; TD ¶225,740

¶ 2447   Gain or loss on transfer to spouse.

No gain or loss is recognized on a transfer of property to (or in trust for the benefit of) the transferor's spouse (see ¶4705), or to a former spouse incident to a divorce. (Code Sec. 1041(a))[37] Certain transfers to third parties on behalf of (i.e., in satisfaction of an obligation or liability of) the spouse or former spouse qualify for nonrecognition. (Reg § 1.1041-1T(c), Q&A-9)[38] However, the no-gain-or-loss rule doesn't apply to transfers in trust where liability exceeds basis (Code Sec. 1041(e)),[39] to transfers in trust of installment obligations (Code Sec. 453B(g)),[40] or where the transferee spouse is a nonresident alien. (Code Sec. 1041(d))[41]

A transfer of property is incident to divorce if it occurs within one year after the date the marriage ceases (Code Sec. 1041(c)(1)) or the transfer is related to the cessation of the marriage. (Code Sec. 1041(c)(2)) A transfer is related to the cessation if the transfer is under a divorce or separation instrument and the transfer occurs not more than six years after the date the marriage ceases. For later transfers, there's a presumption that the transfer isn't related to the cessation. (Reg § 1.1041-1T(b), Q&A-7)[42]

¶ 2448   Losses from sales and exchanges between related taxpayers.

No deduction is allowed for losses from sales or exchanges between certain related taxpayers. (Code Sec. 267(a)) The following are related taxpayers:

Members of the seller's family, but only brothers and sisters (whole or half blood), spouse (see ¶4705), ancestors, and lineal descendants. (Code Sec. 267(a), Code Sec. 267(b)(1), Code Sec. 267(c)(4))[43] In-laws aren't considered members of the seller's family. [44]

Controlled corporations. A taxpayer and his controlled corporation, and a fiduciary and a corporation controlled by the trust or grantor. "Control" is direct or indirect ownership of more than 50% in value of the outstanding stock. (Code Sec. 267(b)(2), Code Sec. 267(b)(8))[45]

Controlled group member. Corporations that are members of the same controlled group of corporations. (Code Sec. 267(b)(3))[46] Loss from a sale or exchange between members of a controlled group is deferred, as explained at ¶2450.

A corporation and a partnership, if the same persons own more than 50% in value of the outstanding stock of the corporation, and more than 50% of the capital interest, or the profits interest, in the partnership. (Code Sec. 267(b)(10))[47]

An S corporation and another S corporation, if the same persons own more than 50% in value of the outstanding stock of each corporation. (Code Sec. 267(b)(11))[48]

An S corporation and a C corporation, if the same persons own more than 50% in value of the outstanding stock of each corporation. (Code Sec. 267(b)(12))[49]

An estate and a beneficiary of that estate, except in the case of a sale or exchange in satisfaction of a pecuniary bequest. (Code Sec. 267(b)(13))[50]

Trustees, grantors, and beneficiaries, that is, the grantor and the fiduciary of a trust; the fiduciary and the beneficiary of a trust; the fiduciaries of two different trusts with the same grantor; a fiduciary of one trust and the beneficiary of another trust with the same grantor; and a trust fiduciary and a corporation more than 50% in value of the outstanding stock of which is owned directly or indirectly by or for the trust or its grantor. (Code Sec. 267(b)(4),

37. ¶I-3601, I-3609; ¶10,414; TD ¶228,201
38. ¶I-3604; ¶10,414; TD ¶228,205
39. ¶I-3605; ¶10,414; TD ¶228,206
40. ¶I-3606; ¶10,414; TD ¶228,207
41. ¶I-3608; ¶10,414
42. ¶I-3610; ¶10,414; TD ¶228,302
43. ¶I-3512; ¶2674.03, 2674.04; TD ¶227,905

44. ¶I-3515; ¶2674.03; TD ¶227,907
45. ¶I-3519; ¶2674.03; TD ¶227,908
46. ¶I-3522; ¶2674.05; TD ¶227,910
47. ¶I-3532; ¶s 2674.03, 2674.04; TD ¶227,921
48. ¶I-3531; ¶2674.03; TD ¶227,920
49. ¶I-3531; ¶2674.05; TD ¶227,920
50. ¶I-3533; ¶2674.03; TD ¶227,922

Code Sec. 267(b)(5), Code Sec. 267(b)(6), Code Sec. 267(b)(7), Code Sec. 267(b)(8))[1]

Exempt organizations. A person and an exempt organization controlled, directly or indirectly, by that person or the members of his family. (Code Sec. 267(b)(9))[2]

In applying the related taxpayer rules, ownership of stock is attributed to the taxpayer as follows:

(1) A stockholder is considered to own a proportionate share of the stock owned by the corporation.

(2) A partner is considered to own a proportionate share of the stock owned by the partnership.

(3) If an individual owns some stock in a corporation, he's considered the owner of stock owned by his partner.

(4) A beneficiary is considered to own a proportionate share of the stock owned by the trust or estate.

(5) An individual is considered to own stock owned by members of his family, as defined above, whether or not he's the actual owner of stock in the same corporation. (Code Sec. 267(c); Reg § 1.267(c)-1)[3]

¶ 2449 Later sale by related buyer.

A related buyer is allowed to reduce his gain on property he resells at a gain by the loss disallowed to his seller if these conditions are met: (1) a loss deduction was barred under the rules on related taxpayers (¶2448); (2) the resale or exchange is at a gain, and the property is either the property on which the loss was disallowed or property the basis of which is determined by reference to the basis of that property; and (3) the loss deduction on the original sale to the taxpayer wasn't barred under the wash sale rules (¶2461). (Code Sec. 267(d); Reg § 1.267(d)-1)[4]

Illustration: H sells to his wife, W, for $55,000, farmland with an adjusted basis for determining loss to him of $80,000. The loss of $25,000 is not allowable to H. W exchanges the farmland, held for investment purposes, with an unrelated individual for two city lots, also held for investment purposes. The basis of the city lots in the hands of W ($55,000) is a substituted basis determined by reference to the basis of the farmland. Later, W sells the city lots for $100,000. Although her realized gain is $45,000 ($100,000 minus $55,000), her recognized gain is only $20,000, the excess of the realized gain of $45,000 over the loss of $25,000 not allowable to H. (Reg § 1.267(d)-1(a)(4), Ex (4))

¶ 2450 Loss between members of controlled group.

With some exceptions, a loss from a transfer between members of the same controlled group is deferred (rather than denied). The loss is recognized when the property is transferred outside the group if the loss would be recognized under consolidated return principles. (Code Sec. 267(f)(2))[5]

For purposes of any Code section other than Code Sec. 267 which refers to a relationship which would result in a disallowance of losses under Code Sec. 267, deferral under Code Sec. 267(f)(2) is treated as a disallowance. (Code Sec. 267(f)(4); Reg § 1.267(f)-1)[6]

¶ 2451 Gain on sale of employer stock to ESOP or EWOC.

A taxpayer (but not a C corporation) or taxpayer's executor who sells qualified securities (certain common stock) to an employee stock ownership plan (ESOP) or eligible worker-owned

---

1. ¶I-3527; ¶2674.03; TD ¶227,917
2. ¶I-3530; ¶2674.03; TD ¶227,904
3. ¶I-3516; ¶2674.04; TD ¶227,913

4. ¶I-3541; ¶2674; TD ¶227,927
5. ¶s E-8250, I-3524 *et seq.*; ¶2674.05; TD ¶227,912
6. ¶I-3504.1; TD ¶227,903

cooperative (EWOC) that holds specified percentages of the securities, may elect nonrecognition of gain if the seller buys "qualified replacement property" (securities of another corporation that doesn't exceed certain passive income limits) within a specified period of time. The seller's gain is recognized only to the extent the proceeds of sale exceed his cost for the replacement property. Nonrecognition treatment applies only if the gain on the sale of the stock would otherwise have been long-term capital gain. (Code Sec. 1042)[7] However, with some exceptions (e.g., for gifts), gain not recognized on the sale to the ESOP is recognized on the disposition of the replacement property. (Code Sec. 1042(e))[8]

The deferral of gain under Code Sec. 1042 also applies to the sale of stock of a qualified refiner or processor to an eligible farmers' cooperative. (Code Sec. 1042(g)(1))

¶ 2452   Installment Sales and Other Deferred Payment Sales. ▬▬▬

Under the installment method, a nondealer (unless he elects out) reports gain on a sale as payments are received, instead of reporting all the gain in the year of sale.

For unstated interest on installment (and other deferred payment) sales, see ¶1307 *et seq.*

¶ 2453   Reporting gain under the installment sale rules—Form 6252.

The installment sale rules must be used to report gain on the disposition of non-dealer property where at least one payment is to be received after the close of the tax year in which the disposition occurs (Code Sec. 453(b)(1)) unless the taxpayer elects not to use the installment method (see ¶2456) or the transaction is one for which the installment method can't be used (see ¶2454).[9] The amount of a payment that's income to the taxpayer is that part of the installment payments received in the year that the gross profit realized or to be realized bears to the total contract price (the "gross profit ratio"). (Code Sec. 453(c); Reg § 15A.453-1(b)(2)(i))[10]

illustration: Taxpayer sells personal-use property for a gross profit of $20,000 at a contract price of $80,000. The gross profit ratio is 25% ($20,000 ÷ $80,000). Therefore, 25% of each payment collected on the sale (including the down payment) is gain and is included in gross income for the tax year it's collected. The ratio remains constant for all installment payments received on the sale.

Payments include:

(a) amounts actually received by the seller, e.g., cash, other property, foreign currency, marketable securities, or evidences of indebtedness of persons other than the buyer. (Reg § 15A.453-1(b)(3)(i))[11] Evidences of indebtedness of the buyer are treated as payment if they are payable on demand or readily tradable; (Code Sec. 453(f)(4))[12]

(b) the buyer's payments of the seller's selling expenses;[13] and

(c) the amount by which qualifying debt assumed or taken subject to by the buyer exceeds the seller's basis. (Reg § 15A.453-1(b)(3)(i))[14]

Gross profit is the selling price less the property's adjusted basis (as increased by selling expenses). (Reg § 15A.453-1(b)(2)(v))[15] The selling price is the gross selling price without reduction to reflect any existing mortgage or other encumbrance on the property (whether assumed or taken subject to by the buyer) and without reduction to reflect any selling expenses. Neither interest (whether stated or unstated) nor original issue discount is part of the selling price. (Reg § 15A.453-1(b)(2)(ii))

Gain recaptured under Code Sec. 1245 (¶2695) or Code Sec. 1250 (¶2696), including gain attributable to the Code Sec. 179 expense election (¶1941 *et seq.*), or so much of the unrealized

7. ¶H-12103 *et seq.*; ¶10,424
8. ¶H-12111; ¶10,424
9. ¶G-6000 *et seq.*; ¶4534.01; TD ¶461,000 *et seq.*
10. ¶G-6052 *et seq.*; ¶4534.21; TD ¶462,003
11. ¶G-6151 *et seq.*; ¶4534.22 *et seq.*; TD ¶462,501 *et seq.*
12. ¶G-6163; ¶4534.23; TD ¶462,509
13. ¶G-6151; TD ¶462,503
14. ¶G-6155; ¶4534.27; TD ¶462,504
15. ¶G-6053; ¶4534.21; TD ¶462,004

receivables under Code Sec. 751 (¶3756) as relates to Code Sec. 1245 or Code Sec. 1250, is fully taxed as ordinary income in the year of sale. Only gain that isn't recapture income is taken into account under the installment method. (Code Sec. 453(i))[16] The recaptured amount is added to the adjusted basis of the property for purposes of determining basis recovered and gain recognized from each installment.[17]

While gain on the sale of a partnership interest qualifies for installment reporting, gain attributable to inventories and unrealized receivables held by the partnership does not.[18]

The total contract price is the selling price, reduced by debt on the property that the buyer assumes (or takes subject to), but only to the extent of the seller's basis in the property. (Reg § 15A.453-1(b)(2)(iii))[19]

¶ 2454 Where installment method can't be used.

The installment method cannot be used by dealers in property, real or personal. (Code Sec. 453(b)(2))[20] However, the installment method may be used for:

- dispositions by farmers (not merchants) of any property used or produced in the trade or business of farming (Code Sec. 453(l)(2)(A)); and

- dispositions to an individual in the ordinary course of a taxpayer's trade or business of the following, but only if interest is paid on the tax deferred when the installment method is used: (Code Sec. 453(l)(2)(B))

. . . a timeshare right to use, or a timeshare right to an ownership interest in, residential real property for not more than six weeks per year, or a right to use specified campgrounds for recreational purposes (timeshare rights or ownership interests held by the spouse (see ¶4705), children, grandchildren or parents of an individual are treated as held by the individual), or

. . . any residential lots, but only if the taxpayer (or any related person) isn't to make any improvements with respect to the lots.[21]

The installment method can't be used for:

. . . sales of stock or securities traded on an established securities market (Code Sec. 453(k)(2)(A)), but it can be used for unregistered restricted stock sold in a private placement;[22]

. . . sales at a loss;[23]

. . . sales of depreciable property between persons related within the Code Sec. 1239(b) rules (¶2691), and between controlled partnerships as defined in Code Sec. 707(b)(1)(B) ¶3731 *et seq.*),[24] unless it's established to IRS's satisfaction that the sale didn't have as one of its principal purposes the avoidance of federal tax. (Code Sec. 453(g))[25]

¶ 2455 Contingent payment sales.

The installment method is used to report contingent payment sales (sales or other dispositions of property in a tax year in which the total selling price can't be determined at the close of that tax year), unless the taxpayer elects not to use the installment method. (Reg § 15A.453-1(c)(1)) In general, basis is allocated to payments received and to be received by treating the stated maximum selling price as the selling price. (Reg § 15A.453-1(c)(2)(i)) However, if:

. . . the maximum selling price can't be determined, but the maximum period over which

---

16. ¶G-6097 *et seq.*; ¶4534.05; TD ¶462,018
17. ¶G-6097; ¶4534.05; TD ¶462,018
18. ¶G-6010; ¶4534.05; TD ¶461,005
19. ¶G-6060; ¶4534.21; TD ¶462,013
20. ¶G-6601, G-6014.1; ¶4534.01, 4534.03; TD ¶466,001, 461,008

21. ¶G-6600 *et seq.*; ¶4534.01; TD ¶466,001 *et seq.*
22. ¶G-6016 *et seq.*; ¶4534.01; TD ¶461,012
23. ¶G-6015; ¶4534.01; TD ¶461,011
24. ¶G-6208; ¶4534.17; TD ¶463,503
25. ¶G-6201; ¶4534.17; TD ¶463,501

payments may be received is fixed, the seller's basis is allocated to the tax years in which payments may be received in equal annual increments. (Reg § 15A.453-1(c)(3)(i))

... the agreement neither specifies a maximum selling price nor limits payments to a fixed period, the transaction may be a sale or payments under the agreement may be rent or royalty income. If the transaction is a sale, basis (including selling expenses) generally is recovered in equal annual increments over a period of 15 years starting with the date of sale. (Reg § 15A.453-1(c)(4))[26]

A seller may (if IRS grants permission) use an alternative basis recovery method if it's able to demonstrate that applying the normal basis recovery rule would substantially and inappropriately defer recovery of basis and the alternative method would likely result in basis recovery at a rate at least twice as fast. (Reg § 15A.453-1(c)(7))[27]

¶ 2456   Electing out of the installment method.

An election not to have the installment method apply to a sale is made by reporting an amount realized equal to the selling price (including the full face amount of any installment obligation) on the tax return filed for the year the sale occurs. (Reg § 15A.453-1(d)(3)(i))[28]

The election out must be made on or before the due date (including extensions) for filing the return for the year of sale. (Code Sec. 453(d)(2))[29] A late election is allowed only if IRS concludes taxpayer had good cause for the failure to timely elect. (Reg § 15A.453-1(d)(3)(ii))[30]

An election out may be revoked only with IRS consent. (Code Sec. 453(d)(3))[31]

recommendation: Consider electing out of the installment method if the seller will be in a much higher tax bracket in post-sale years than in the sale year, or if he is selling a property with large suspended passive activity losses so these losses can be used immediately to offset nonpassive income (¶1838).

A taxpayer who elects not to report a deferred-payment sale on the installment method recognizes gain on the sale according to his method of accounting. The amount realized attributable to a debt instrument received is the debt instrument's issue price as determined under the OID rules discussed at ¶1317. (Reg § 1.1001-1(g))[32]

¶ 2457   Character of installment gain where depreciable realty is sold.

When depreciable real property is sold by a noncorporate taxpayer, the gain may be partially 25%-rate gain (unrecaptured section 1250 gain subject to a maximum tax of 25%, see ¶2605), and partially adjusted net capital gain (taxed at a lower rate, see ¶2604). If there are both types of gain, the 25%-rate gain is taken into account as payments are received before any adjusted net capital gain is included. (Reg § 1.453-12(a)) See ¶2600 *et seq.* for the taxation of capital gains.[33]

illustration: T sells depreciable real property for a total price of $150,000. He has a total gain of $30,000, $20,000 of which is 25%-rate gain, and $10,000 of which is adjusted net capital gain. The sales price is payable in five equal annual installments of $30,000, with the first installment due in the year of sale. T takes $6,000 of gain into account as each installment is paid. The entire gain of $6,000 on the receipt of the first three installments, and $2,000 of the gain on the receipt of the fourth installment, is taxed as 25%-rate gain. The remaining $4,000 of gain on the fourth installment and the entire $6,000 of gain on the fifth installment is taxed at the applicable rate for adjusted net capital gain.

Net Code Sec. 1231 gain that would otherwise be taxed as long-term capital gain, is taxed

26. ¶G-6250 *et seq.*; ¶4534.30; TD ¶463,000 *et seq.*
27. ¶G-6279, G-6280; ¶4534.30; TD ¶463,017
28. ¶G-6360; ¶4534.08; TD ¶461,503
29. ¶G-6352; ¶4534.08; TD ¶461,502
30. ¶G-6353; ¶4534.08; TD ¶461,502
31. ¶G-6362; ¶4534.08; TD ¶461,509
32. ¶G-6351, G-6550 *et seq.*; ¶4534.45 *et seq.*; TD ¶467,001
33. ¶G-6102; ¶4534.57; TD ¶462,023

as ordinary income to the extent of non-recaptured net Code Sec. 1231 losses for the preceding five years (¶2685). If net Code Sec. 1231 gain for a tax year consists of both 25%-rate gain and adjusted net capital gain, the 25%-rate gain is recharacterized as ordinary income first. This rule also applies to installment payments. (Reg § 1.453-12(d), Ex. 3)[34]

¶ 2458   Sale, exchange, or satisfaction of installment obligations.

For installment obligations satisfied at face value, gain or loss is computed under the general rules (¶2453) for computing income on the installment method.[35]

If an installment obligation is satisfied at other than face or is sold or exchanged, gain or loss is the difference between the basis of the obligation and the amount realized. If it's distributed, transmitted, or disposed of other than by sale or exchange, gain or loss is the difference between its basis and its fair market value (FMV) (Code Sec. 453B(a)),[36] except that if it's distributed in a complete liquidation of a subsidiary to which Code Sec. 337(a) applies (¶3577), no gain or loss is recognized. (Code Sec. 453B(d))[37] If there's a repossession by the seller of the personal property sold following the buyer's default (i.e., a disposition of the installment obligation by the seller),[38] the seller's gain or loss is: (1) the FMV of the property, plus anything received from the buyer in addition to the repossessed property; minus (2) the seller's basis in the installment obligation, plus any expense in connection with the repossession.[39] Transmission of an installment obligation at death doesn't result in gain or loss to the decedent. (Code Sec. 453B(c); Reg § 1.451-1(b)(2))[40]

A reduction of the purchase price, or a modification of an installment obligation by changing the payment terms (e.g., reducing the purchase price and interest rate, and deferring or increasing the payment dates) isn't a disposition of the installment obligation.[41]

The basis of an obligation is the excess of its face value over the amount equal to the income that would be returnable if the obligation were fully satisfied. (Code Sec. 453B(b))[42]

🅡🅘🅐 *observation:* This means the basis of the installment obligations is the adjusted basis of the property sold less the part of that basis allocated to any payment made at the time of sale.

¶ 2459   Sale to related person who then resells.

If a person disposes of property in an installment sale (first disposition) to a related person (see below) who then disposes of the property (second disposition) within two years of the first disposition, and before all payments are made on the first disposition, the amount the related person (the buyer in the first disposition) realizes as a result of the second disposition is treated as being received by the original seller at the time of the second disposition. (Code Sec. 453(e)(1), Code Sec. 453(e)(2))

The amount treated as received by the person making the first disposition because of the second disposition can't be more than:

. . . the lesser of the total amount realized on any second disposition of the property occurring in the tax year, or the total contract price for the first disposition; minus

. . . the sum of the aggregate amount of payments received with respect to the first disposition before the close of the tax year in which the second disposition occurs, and the aggregate amount treated as received with respect to the first disposition because of earlier dispositions of installment obligations by related persons. (Code Sec. 453(e)(3))[43]

For purposes of these rules, if the second disposition isn't a sale or exchange, the property's

---

34. ¶G-6105; ¶4534.58; TD ¶462,025
35. ¶G-6052; ¶4534.22; TD ¶465,002
36. ¶G-6454 *et seq.*; ¶453B4.05; TD ¶465,004
37. ¶G-6489; ¶453B4.11; TD ¶465,037
38. ¶G-6476; ¶453B4.07; TD ¶465,044

39. ¶G-6481; ¶453B4.07; TD ¶465,048
40. ¶G-6507; ¶453B4.13; TD ¶465,019;
41. ¶G-6486; TD ¶465,034
42. ¶G-6456; ¶453B4.07; TD ¶465,006
43. ¶G-6401 *et seq.*; ¶4534.18; TD ¶464,500 *et seq.*

fair market value is treated as the amount realized. (Code Sec. 453(e)(4))[44]

A "related person" is someone whose stock would be attributed to the initial seller under Code Sec. 318(a) (¶3534), other than under the option attribution rules, or a person who bears a relationship to the initial seller under Code Sec. 267(b) (¶2448) for purposes of the rules disallowing the deduction of losses on sales between related persons. (Code Sec. 453(f)(1))[45]

Exceptions exist for involuntary conversions, deaths, corporations' reacquisition of their own stock, and where IRS rules out tax avoidance. (Code Sec. 453(e)(6), Code Sec. 453(e)(7))[46]

The two-year period stops running when puts, options, or short sales, etc., are involved. (Code Sec. 453(e)(2)(B))[47] For marketable securities, there's no two-year limit. (Code Sec. 453(e)(2)(A))[48]

¶ 2460 Sales of certain property for more than $150,000—"pledge and interest" rule.

The following rules apply to an installment sale of "any" property (except personal use or farm property, and dealer sales of timeshares or residential lots) where the selling price is over $150,000: (Code Sec. 453A)[49]

(1) If an installment obligation from the sale plus all other installment obligations that arose from dispositions during the tax year and are still outstanding at the close of the tax year total over $5,000,000, the seller must pay, as additional tax, interest at the underpayment rate (¶4866) on the deferred tax attributable to those installment obligations.

(2) If an installment obligation from the sale becomes security for any indebtedness, the net proceeds of the indebtedness are treated as a payment of the obligation as of the later of the time the indebtedness becomes secured or the proceeds of the indebtedness are received by the seller. (Code Sec. 453A(d)(1)) Payment of indebtedness is treated as secured by an interest in an installment obligation to the extent that an arrangement allows the taxpayer to satisfy all or part of the debt with the installment obligation (i.e., gives him the *right* to repay the loan by transferring the installment note to his creditor). (Code Sec. 453A(d)(4))

¶ 2461 Wash Sales.

No loss deduction is allowed for any loss from any sale or other disposition of stock or securities (including contracts or options to acquire or sell stock or securities) if within a period beginning 30 days before and ending 30 days after the sale the taxpayer acquires, or has entered into a contract or option to acquire, substantially identical stock or securities.

¶ 2462 Wash sale loss disallowance rule.

Losses on the sale of (or on a contract or option to sell) stock or securities are not deductible if, within a period beginning 30 days before the date of the sale and ending 30 days after the date of the sale, the taxpayer acquires or has entered into a contract or option to acquire stock or securities that are substantially identical. (Code Sec. 1091(a); Reg § 1.1091-1(a))[50]

illustration: June 1: T buys 100 shares of Corp A stock for $15 per share. Dec. 1: T buys 100 shares of Corp A stock for $10 per share. Dec. 31: T sells the 100 shares of Corp A stock bought on June 1 for $10 per share realizing a $500 loss. No loss deduction is allowed because substantially identical stock was purchased within 30 days before the sale. The same result would occur if the second purchase had been made on the following Jan. 30.

---

44. ¶G-6403; ¶4534.18; TD ¶464,506
45. ¶G-6416; ¶4534.18; TD ¶464,503
46. ¶G-6411; ¶4534.18; TD ¶464,512
47. ¶G-6409; ¶4534.18; TD ¶464,510

48. ¶G-6408; ¶4534.18; TD ¶464,510
49. ¶G-6300 *et seq.*; ¶453A4; TD ¶464,001
50. ¶I-3901; ¶10,914; TD ¶227,001

caution: This rule can ensnare investors (e.g., investors in mutual funds) who participate in automatic dividend reinvestment plans since the automatic reinvestment of dividends within the prohibited period is a purchase of substantially identical securities.

Loss is also disallowed where the repurchase is made either by an individual retirement account (IRA) (¶4351) or by a Roth IRA (¶4368), established for the exclusive benefit of the original purchasing taxpayer or his beneficiaries.[1]

"Substantially identical securities" requires something less than precise correspondence. Stock or securities of different issuers or obligors are not substantially identical. Stock or securities of the same issuer are substantially identical if they are substantially the same in all important particulars.[2]

observation: It is often possible to recognize losses by selling a particular security and investing the proceeds in a similar but not substantially identical security (e.g., sell common stock in one drug company and buy stock in another drug company, or sell stock in one exchange-traded fund and buy stock in another exchange-traded fund that invests in the same types of securities).

The wash sale rule also disallows a loss on the closing of a short sale of stock or securities, or the sale, exchange, or termination of a securities futures contract to sell, if, within the period beginning 30 days before the date the short sale is closed and ending 30 days after that date: (1) substantially identical stock or securities are sold, or (2) another short sale of (or securities futures contracts to sell) substantially identical stock or securities is entered. (Code Sec. 1091(e))[3]

Special wash sale rules apply to residual interests in real estate mortgage investment conduits (REMICs) (Code Sec. 860F(d)),[4] and to tax straddles. (Reg § 1.1092(b)-1T, Reg § 1.1092(b)-5T)[5]

The wash sale rule doesn't apply to a dealer in stocks or securities if the loss is sustained in a transaction made in the ordinary course of that business. (Code Sec. 1091(a))[6]

For the basis of the acquired stock, see ¶2500. For the holding period of the acquired stock, see ¶2670.

¶ 2463 Basis of Property.

Basis is the amount of investment in property for tax purposes. It is the point of departure for determining gain or loss on the disposition of the property, for computing annual deductions for depreciation, amortization, depletion, casualty losses, bad debts, and losses from "at-risk" activities, and for many other tax computations. A taxpayer's basis for property acquired in a taxable exchange is usually its cost, subject to certain adjustments.

In general, basis for computing loss and gain is the same, whatever the transaction may be. But the basis for computing loss differs from the basis for computing gain for (1) property converted from personal use to business or income-producing use (¶2473), and (2) property acquired by gift (¶2508).

For determining basis in corporate transactions and in nontaxable exchanges, see ¶2482 *et seq.*

For basis of property acquired by gift, or from a decedent or a spouse (¶4705), see ¶2507 *et seq.*

---

1. ¶I-3906, P-5019; TD ¶227,014
2. ¶I-3914 *et seq.*; ¶10,914; TD ¶227,019
3. ¶I-3905; ¶10,914; TD ¶227,006
4. ¶I-3902, I-3903; ¶860A4; TD ¶227,011 *et seq.*
5. ¶I-7528; ¶10,924; TD ¶228,418
6. ¶I-3917; ¶10,914; TD ¶227,020

¶ 2464   Cost as basis.

The original basis for property is its cost to the taxpayer, except where otherwise specifically provided (Code Sec. 1012) (see ¶2496 *et seq.*) or where the transaction is not made at arm's length (see below). Cost is the amount paid in cash or other property, and liabilities incurred (¶2465). (Reg § 1.1012-1(a))[7] Payments made in connection with the acquisition of property, e.g., commissions and legal fees, are included in basis as part of the property's cost.[8]

IRS and most courts say that the cost basis of property received in an arm's-length taxable exchange is the fair market value (FMV) of the property *received* in the exchange, at the time of the exchange, unless the FMV of the property received cannot be determined with a fair degree of certainty. Then, the FMV of the property given up will be used as a way of valuing the property received. However, some courts say the cost basis of property received in an arm's-length taxable exchange is the FMV of the property given up, not the property received.[9]

When property isn't bought in an arm's-length deal, its basis is its FMV. This can occur in sham transactions, or where the buyer, for personal reasons, pays more than what the property is worth (e.g., to help out a friend).[10]

¶ 2465   Mortgages and other liabilities as part of basis.

Taxpayer's cost of property includes the amount of a mortgage or other liability assumed in connection with the purchase, plus the amount of any liabilities that the purchased property is subject to (whether or not the taxpayer assumes the liabilities).[11] Redeemable ground rents are treated as mortgages. (Code Sec. 1055)[12]

illustration: J buys a building by paying $20,000 cash and giving an $80,000 mortgage. J's basis is $100,000. It would also be $100,000 if instead J assumed an existing $80,000 mortgage. And it would be $100,000 if, in addition to paying $20,000 cash, J acquired the building subject to the mortgage without assuming it, or if J agreed to pay his seller's debt of $80,000.

Mortgages or other liabilities aren't part of the cost if they are contingent *and* there's a clear indication they might never have to be paid or that taxpayer doesn't intend to pay.[13]

¶ 2466   Effect of OID and unstated interest on basis.

If the original issue discount (OID) rules (¶1751 *et seq.*) or the unstated interest rules (¶1707), apply so that a part of a debt included in the buyer's cost for the property is treated as OID or unstated interest, the buyer's basis doesn't include the OID or unstated interest part. (Reg § 1.483-1(a)(2))[14]

¶ 2467   Basis of repossessed mortgaged real estate.

A seller's basis in repossessed property is equal to the adjusted basis of the mortgage debt (determined under Code Sec. 453 and Code Sec. 1011) to the seller (as of the date of repossession), *plus* the sum of: (1) the repossession gain, and (2) the amount of money and the fair market value of other property (other than the buyer's obligations) which the seller transfers in connection with the repossession.

If the mortgage debt isn't discharged on repossession, the seller's basis in the mortgage debt is zero. (Code Sec. 1038(c))[15]

7. ¶P-1119; ¶10,124 *et seq.*; TD ¶211,100
8. ¶P-1102; ¶10,124.03
9. ¶P-1114; ¶10,124.46; TD ¶211,106
10. ¶P-1108; ¶10,124.22; TD ¶211,104
11. ¶P-1104 *et seq.*; ¶10,124.04; TD ¶211,118

12. ¶P-1175; ¶10,554; TD ¶211,138
13. ¶P-1134; ¶10,124.04; TD ¶211,116
14. ¶s P-1138, P-1139; TD ¶211,120, 211,121
15. ¶G-6872 *et seq.*; ¶10,384; TD ¶471,009

¶ 2468 Satisfaction of debt or claim with property.

The cost basis of property received in whole or partial satisfaction of a debt or claim is the amount of the debt or claim satisfied, but not more than the property's fair market value.[16]

¶ 2469 Property acquired through exercise of options.

The basis of property acquired by exercising an option or warrant other than an option granted for services is (a) the basis of the option, plus (b) the option price.[17]

¶ 2470 Holder's basis in certain debt instruments acquired at a discount.

The holder's basis in a debt instrument issued with original issue discount (OID) is increased by the OID currently included in gross income under the rules discussed at ¶1313 *et seq.* (Code Sec. 1272(d)(2))[18] This rule also applies for inflation-indexed debt instruments (¶1333), whose basis must be reduced for deflation adjustments.[19]

Short-term debt instruments. If the holder includes the daily portions of acquisition discount (or OID) in gross income, that holder increases his basis in the debt instrument by the amount so included. (Code Sec. 1283(d)(1))[20]

Tax-exempt obligations issued with OID. A holder's basis is increased by the amount of OID that the holder would have had to include in gross income currently if the obligation had not been tax-exempt. (Code Sec. 1288(a)(2), Code Sec. 1288(b)(3))[21]

Market-discount bonds. Where an election is made to include accrued market discount in income currently (see ¶1327), the basis of the bond is increased by the amount of income so included. (Code Sec. 1278(b)(4))[22]

For determining cost of, and original basis in, property received in exchange for an OID debt instrument, see ¶2466.

¶ 2471 Cost of intangible assets.

The basis of goodwill, a patent, a copyright, or a covenant not to compete is the amount taxpayer paid for it.[23]

Where a patent is obtained from the government, the basis is the cost of development, such as research and experimental expenditures (but not if deducted currently), drawings, attorneys' and governmental fees, etc. The value of any time spent on an invention isn't part of an inventor's basis. The basis of a copyright acquired from the government is the cost of securing the copyright from the government, including the cost of producing the work covered by the copyright, but not including the value of the author's time.[24]

Accounts receivable in the hands of a cash basis taxpayer have a zero basis.[25]

¶ 2472 Basis allocation, including "applicable asset acquisitions."

If a single transaction involves a number of separate properties, the total cost is allocated to establish the cost of the individual properties. The total basis is allocated to each item in proportion to the fair market value (FMV) of each item at the time of acquisition.[26]

However, for an applicable asset acquisition (defined below), the residual method must be used to allocate the purchase price. Under the residual method, the purchase price is reduced

---

16. ¶P-1116; TD ¶211,107
17. ¶P-1165 *et seq.*; ¶10,124.13; TD ¶211,133
18. ¶P-5044; ¶12,714.01; TD ¶216,028
19. ¶P-5044.1
20. ¶P-5047; ¶12,814.01; TD ¶216,028
21. ¶P-5048; ¶12,884; TD ¶216,028

22. ¶J-4573 *et seq.*; ¶12,764.02; TD ¶154,005
23. ¶P-1178, P-1179, P-1180; ¶10,124.38; TD ¶212,513, 212,514
24. ¶P-1178; ¶1674.025; TD ¶211,111
25. ¶P-1121; TD ¶211,108
26. ¶P-1300 *et seq.*; ¶10,124.55; TD ¶212,500 *et seq.*

first by the amount of cash, demand deposits, and similar accounts. The amount remaining is allocated among the following assets in proportion to (but not in excess of) their FMV on the purchase date, in the following order: (1) certificates of deposit, U.S. Government securities, readily marketable stock or securities, foreign currency, and other items designated by IRS; (2) all assets other than those in the other categories; (3) all Code Sec. 197 intangibles (¶1974) except those in the nature of goodwill and going concern value; and (4) Code Sec. 197 intangibles in the nature of goodwill and going concern value.

The parties to an applicable asset acquisition may agree in writing to an allocation of consideration for, or a determination of the FMV of, any asset (including covenants not to compete) in the acquisition. The parties are bound by the allocation or valuation unless IRS determines that it's not appropriate. (Code Sec. 1060(a); Reg § 1.1060-1(c)(4), Reg § 1.1060-1(e))[27] A party to the agreement can challenge the terms of the agreement only by showing fraud, mistake, undue influence, etc.[28]

An applicable asset acquisition is any direct or indirect transfer of a group of assets that is a trade or business in the hands of either the seller or buyer if (except for certain like-kind exchanges) the buyer's basis in the transferred assets is determined wholly by reference to the buyer's consideration. (Code Sec. 1060(c); Reg § 1.1060-1(b)(1))[29]

The buyer and seller have to provide IRS with specified information about the assets (use Form 8594). (Code Sec. 1060(b); Reg § 1.1060-1(e)(1))[30]

¶ 2473 Personal use property converted to business use.

When a residence or other nonbusiness property is converted from personal use to business or income-producing use, for purposes of calculating losses or depreciation (but not for purposes of calculating gain), the basis for the property on the date of its conversion is the lower of its adjusted basis or fair market value on that date. This basis must thereafter be adjusted for depreciation, etc., after conversion. (Reg § 1.167(g)-1)[31]

¶ 2474 Adjusted basis.

Basis must be increased or decreased to reflect certain events, such as capital improvements or depreciation, whether the original basis was cost or something else.[32]

The basis of property is adjusted (increased) to include the amount of the capital expenditures with respect to the property. (Code Sec. 1016(a)(1))[33] A lessee's basis for his leasehold is increased by his capital expenditures.[34] However, a lessee's capital improvements don't increase or diminish the lessor's basis of the leased property. (Code Sec. 1019)[35]

Basis can be increased for items that are ordinarily deductible as expenses if the taxpayer has capitalized those items, e.g., taxes and carrying charges, see ¶1656.

For the requirement that brokers report on Form 1099-B information about a customer's basis (including information about organizational actions such as stock splits that would affect the basis) in stock and securities, see ¶4746.

For adjusted basis for alternative minimum tax purposes, see ¶3213.

¶ 2475 Contributions and returns of capital.

A stockholder's contribution of property to his corporation will increase his basis for his corporate stock.[36] A partner's contribution of cash to his partnership increases his basis in his partnership interest. See ¶3738 *et seq.*

---

27. ¶P-1400 *et seq.*; ¶10,604; TD ¶212,001 *et seq.*
28. ¶I-8612; TD ¶229,408
29. ¶P-1402 *et seq.*; ¶10,604; TD ¶212,002
30. ¶S-4301; ¶10,604; TD ¶212,012
31. ¶P-1908; ¶1674.037; TD ¶213,017

32. ¶P-1700 *et seq.*; ¶s 10,114, 10,164.01; TD ¶213,000 *et seq.*
33. ¶P-1801; ¶10,164.01; TD ¶213,501
34. ¶L-6510; ¶10,164;
35. ¶P-1809; ¶10,194; TD ¶213,504
36. ¶F-1916; ¶10,164.02; TD ¶232,312

Basis must be reduced for receipts representing a return of capital (Code Sec. 1016(a)(1); Reg § 1.1016-2(a)), such as damages taxpayer received for injury to property.[37]

¶ 2476 Depreciation, amortization, and other deductions.

Basis must be reduced for depreciation, cost recovery, amounts expensed under Code Sec. 179, amounts claimed under the Code Sec. 1400I commercial revitalization deduction, or amortization deductions with respect to the property. The amount of the reduction is the larger of (1) the amount of the depreciation, cost recovery, amortization, or depletion deductions *allowable* under the law, or (2) the amount that was actually *allowed* and resulted in a reduction of tax. (Code Sec. 1016(a)(2))[38]

Basis must also be reduced for the Code Sec. 179D energy efficient commercial building property deduction for property placed in service after 2005 and before 2014. (Code Sec. 1016(a)(31))[39]

Allowable depreciation (or cost recovery) is the amount the taxpayer was entitled to deduct under the law, whether or not he actually took more or less and whether or not a tax benefit results. Where a taxpayer didn't adopt a depreciation method under Code Sec. 167, the amount allowable is figured under the straight-line method. (Code Sec. 1016(a))[40]

The depreciation (or cost recovery) *allowed* is the amount claimed on a tax return and allowed by IRS.[41]

In the case of business autos for which the optional business standard mileage rate, see ¶1560, is used, depreciation is considered to have been allowed at a rate of 21¢ for 2008 and 2009, 23¢ for 2010, 22¢ for 2011, and 23¢ for 2012 and 2013.[42]

¶ 2477 Partial losses due to casualty or theft.

If property is partly lost or destroyed through casualty or theft, the basis is reduced by (1) the amount of insurance or other reimbursement received, and (2) the amount of deductible loss. But if a loss is *not* deductible under the rules discussed at ¶1792 *et seq.*, no basis reduction is required.

Expenditures with respect to such property, e.g., to remove debris and to restore the property to pre-casualty condition, increase the basis, unless they are deducted as repairs.[43]

¶ 2478 Basis of credit property reduced by certain credits allowed.

The basis of investment credit property (¶2307), for purposes of computing depreciation or cost recovery deductions and gain or loss, must be reduced by 100% of the amount of the credit for which the property qualifies. (Code Sec. 50(c)(1))[44] The basis of energy credit property (¶2311) must be reduced by 50% of the allowed credit. (Code Sec. 50(c)(3)(A))[45]

The basis of property also must be reduced for certain other credits, such as: the Code Sec. 25C nonbusiness energy property credit for property placed in service before 2008 or after 2008 and before 2014 (¶2358) (Code Sec. 1016(a)(33))[46]; the Code Sec. 25D residential energy efficient property credit for property placed in service before 2017 (¶2359) (Code Sec. 1016(a)(34))[47]; the Code Sec. 30B alternative motor vehicle credit (¶2360) (Code Sec. 1016(a)(35))[48]; the Code Sec. 30D credit for certain electric vehicles (¶2362) (Code Sec. 1016(a)(37))[49]; the Code Sec. 45F credit for employer-provided child care (¶2330) (Code Sec. 1016(a)(28))[50]; and the Code Sec. 45L energy efficient homes credit for homes acquired

37. ¶P-1821; ¶10,164.03; TD ¶213,515
38. ¶P-1901; ¶10,164.25; TD ¶214,001
39. ¶L-3176; ¶10,164; TD ¶308,106
40. ¶P-1902; ¶10,164.25; TD ¶214,002
41. ¶P-1903; ¶10,164.25; TD ¶214,003
42. ¶P-1909; ¶1624.157; TD ¶214,007
43. ¶P-1811; ¶1654.304; TD ¶213,503

44. ¶P-2000 *et seq.*; ¶504.03; TD ¶213,006
45. ¶P-2005; ¶504.03; TD ¶213,006
46. ¶P-1710.4; ¶10,164; TD ¶569,557
47. ¶P-1710.5; ¶10,164; TD ¶569,568
48. ¶L-18023; ¶10,164; TD ¶397,103
49. ¶P-1710.6; ¶10,164; TD ¶213,011.4
50. ¶P-1710.1; ¶10,164; TD ¶213,011.5

before 2014 (¶2334). (Code Sec. 1016(a)(32))[1]

¶ 2479 Recaptured tax credits.

Where certain tax credits are recaptured, a percentage of the recapture amount is added back to basis immediately before the event causing the recapture. The term "recapture amount" means any increase in tax (or adjustment in carrybacks or carryovers) due to the credit recapture provision. (Code Sec. 50(c)(2), Code Sec. 50(c)(3)(B))[2]

¶ 2480 Special lessor-lessee rule doesn't require basis-reduction adjustment.

A lessor of certain credit property who elects to pass the credit for the leased property to the lessee is not required to make the basis-reduction adjustment (¶2478). (Code Sec. 50(d)(5))[3]

¶ 2481 Basis in partnership or S corporation.

The basis of a partner's interest in a partnership or of a shareholder's stock in an S corporation is adjusted to reflect a partner's or shareholder's share of the required adjustments to the basis of partnership or S corporation property when credits are either allowed or recaptured. (Code Sec. 50(c)(5))[4]

¶ 2482 Property Acquired in Nontaxable Exchanges.

The basis of property received in a nontaxable exchange, depending on the type of transaction, generally will be the same as its basis in the hands of the transferor or will be the same as the basis of the property transferred by the recipient in the exchange. If gain is recognized in part on the transaction, the basis of the property received may have to be adjusted.

¶ 2483 Basis of property received by corporation in tax-free transfer.

The basis of property received by a controlled corporation in a tax-free transfer, whether upon the incorporation of the corporation or otherwise (see ¶3510 *et seq.*), is equal to the basis of the property in the transferor's hands increased by any gain recognized by the transferor on the transfer. (Code Sec. 362(a))[5]

The basis to a corporation of property acquired from a shareholder as a contribution to capital equals the basis of that property in the hands of the shareholder increased by the gain (if any) recognized by the shareholder on the transfer. (Code Sec. 362(a))[6]

For limitations on an increase in basis due to the assumption of a liability and/or a built-in loss, see ¶2485.

¶ 2484 Acquirer's basis in property received in reorganization.

The basis of property received by the acquiring corporation in a tax-free reorganization (¶3541), is the transferor's (target's) basis increased by any gain recognized to the target. However, if the property consists of stock or securities of the target, this rule applies only if the property was acquired in exchange for stock or securities of the acquirer or the acquirer's parent corporation. (Code Sec. 362(b))[7]

For when an acquirer must reduce basis in assets received in a tax-free reorganization if the transferor has cancellation of debt income in connection with the transfer, see ¶1389.

---

1. ¶P-1710.01; ¶10,164; TD ¶213,011.3
2. ¶P-2007; ¶504.03; TD ¶213,006
3. ¶P-2008; TD ¶213,007
4. ¶P-2009; TD ¶213,008

5. ¶F-1851; ¶3624.01; TD ¶232,001
6. ¶F-1851; ¶3624.05; TD ¶232,309
7. ¶F-4305; ¶3624.04; TD ¶233,501

For limitations on basis increase due to the assumption of a liability, see ¶2485.

¶ 2485 Limits on basis increase due to assumption of liability and/or built-in loss.

For purposes of the basis increase in the case of a tax-free transfer to a controlled corporation (¶2483) or in a reorganization exchange (¶2484), the property's basis can't be increased above its fair market value (FMV) on account of gain recognized by the transferor as a result of a liability assumed by the transferee. For this purpose, FMV is determined without regard to Code Sec. 7701(g) (which generally provides that a property's FMV is not less than the amount of nonrecourse debt to which it is subject). (Code Sec. 362(d)(1))[8]

Also, to prevent the importation of built-in losses, if property transferred was not taxable in the hands of the transferor but is taxable in the hands of the transferee corporation, and the total basis for the property in the hands of the transferee would otherwise (if not for this basis limitation rule) exceed its FMV, then the basis for each property in the hands of the transferee is its FMV. (Code Sec. 362(e)(1)) If this rule doesn't apply, a second carryover basis limitation rule (not limited to property as to which the transferor would not have recognized gain or loss) limits the total basis for property transferred by any transferor to its FMV. (Code Sec. 362(e)(2)) However, the transferor and transferee can jointly elect to reduce the basis of the stock received by the transferor instead of the basis of the assets transferred in the hands of the transferee. (Code Sec. 362(e)(2)(C)) IRS has prescribed how to make the election.[9]

¶ 2486 Target's basis in property received in reorganization.

The basis of property (other than stock and securities of another corporation that is a party to the reorganization, see ¶3555 *et seq.*) received under a plan of reorganization by the target equals the fair market value of the property. (Code Sec. 358(a)(2), Code Sec. 358(f))[10]

¶ 2487 Taxable acquisition of property by corporation for its stocks or bonds.

In cases other than tax-free contributions or reorganizations, the basis of property a corporation acquires in exchange for its stock is the fair market value of the stock at the time of the exchange.[11] The cost to a corporation of property it acquires in exchange for its bonds is the face amount of the bonds.[12] For bonds with original issue discount or unstated interest, see ¶2466.

¶ 2488 Basis of property to distributee shareholders or security holders.

For purposes of determining basis, property received by a distributee in connection with a transfer to a controlled corporation, a reorganization, or a corporate division (¶3510 *et seq.*) is classified as either nonrecognition property or other property. "Nonrecognition property" is property received without recognition of gain or loss to the recipient (stock in the transferee corporation in the case of a transfer to a controlled corporation, and stock or securities in the distributing corporation in tax-free reorganizations and corporate divisions). (Code Sec. 358(a)(1)) "Other property" is anything except "nonrecognition property" and money.

The basis of "nonrecognition property" is the same as the basis of the property given up in the exchange, except that this amount is (1) decreased by any money received, by the fair market value of any "other property" received, and by the loss, if any, recognized by the distributee on the exchange; and (2) increased by any part of the distribution that is treated as a dividend, and by any other gain recognized by the distributee on the exchange. (Code Sec. 358(a)(1))[13] The basis must be allocated among the nonrecognition property received in the transaction without recognition of gain or loss. (Reg § 1.358-2(a)(2))[14]

---

8. ¶F-1852; ¶3624.01; TD ¶232,002
9. ¶F-1871 *et seq.*; ¶3624.02, 3624.03; TD ¶232,001
10. ¶F-4304; ¶3584.02; TD ¶233,304
11. ¶P-1158; ¶10,124.47; TD ¶211,130

12. ¶P-1160; TD ¶211,130
13. ¶F-4034; ¶3584.02; TD ¶232,541 *et seq.*
14. ¶F-4036; ¶3584.03; TD ¶232,544

Where, as part of the consideration for the transfer of the distributee corporation's property to the acquirer, another party to the deal assumes a liability of the distributee, the assumption of that liability is treated as though it were money received by the distributee on the reorganization exchange (for basis purposes only). (Code Sec. 358(d)(1))[15]

✐observation: Thus, the basis of the nonrecognition property received by the distributee on the exchange is reduced by an amount equal to the liabilities assumed.

IRS may provide adjustments for divisive reorganization transactions (¶3559) among affiliated group members. (Code Sec. 358(g))

¶ 2489　Basis of other property received in tax-free transfer or reorganization.

The basis of property, other than stock or securities, received by a shareholder upon a tax-free transfer to a controlled corporation, a reorganization, or a corporate division (¶3510 *et seq.*) is its fair market value as of the date of the transaction. (Code Sec. 358(a)(2))[16]

¶ 2490　Basis of property received in complete liquidation of corporation.

If property is received in a complete liquidation and any gain or loss is recognized on the receipt of the property, its basis in the hands of the shareholder-distributee is its fair market value at the time of the distribution. (Code Sec. 334(a))[17]

¶ 2491　Basis after partnership incorporates.

If a partnership incorporates, the basis of the corporation in the partnership's property and the basis of the former partners in their stock in the corporation depends on the method used to incorporate.

If the partnership transfers all of its assets subject to its liabilities to a newly formed corporation in return for all its stock, then distributes the stock to the partners, the corporation's basis in the partnership's assets is equal to the partnership's basis in the assets before the transaction, and each partner's basis in the stock of the corporation is equal to the adjusted basis of that partner's interest in the partnership.

If the partnership distributes all of its assets subject to liabilities to the partners, who in turn transfer them to the new corporation for its stock, the corporation's basis in its assets is the same as the partners' basis in the assets prior to their contribution to the corporation, and the partners' basis in the stock of the corporation is the same as their basis in the assets distributed in liquidation reduced by liabilities assumed by the corporation.

If the partners transfer their interests in the partnership to the new corporation in exchange for its stock and the corporation then liquidates the partnership, the corporation's basis in its assets is equal to the partners' basis in their partnership interests before the transaction, and the partners' basis in their stock is equal to their basis in their partnership interests reduced by the liabilities assumed by the corporation.[18]

¶ 2492　Property received as a dividend.

The basis for property received as a dividend, including stock or stock rights received as a taxable stock dividend, is its fair market value on the date of distribution. (Code Sec. 301(d))[19]

¶ 2493　Basis allocation for nontaxable stock dividend.

If a shareholder gets a nontaxable dividend of stock or stock rights, the (adjusted) basis of the old stock (that is, of the stock on which the dividend was distributed) is allocated between

15. ¶F-4035; ¶3584.02; TD ¶232,543
16. ¶F-1804, F-4034, F-4304, F-5014; ¶3584.02; TD ¶231,912, 232,542, 233,304
17. ¶F-13119; ¶3344.01; TD ¶245,427
18. ¶s F-1011, F-1805; TD ¶231,015
19. ¶P-5400 *et seq.*; ¶3014.03; TD ¶217,501 *et seq.*

the old and new stock (or rights) in proportion to the fair market value (FMV) of each on the date of distribution. (Code Sec. 307(a)) Where only part of the stock dividend is nontaxable, the basis of the old stock is allocated between the old stock and that part of the new stock (or rights) which isn't taxable, in proportion to the FMV of each on the date of distribution. The date of distribution is, in both cases, the date on which the new stock (or the stock rights) was distributed, not the record date.[20]

⊘illustration: S bought one share of voting common for $45. The corporation distributed two new shares of voting common for each share held. This gave S three shares of voting common with a basis of $15 each. If he had owned two shares before the distribution, one purchased for $30 and the other for $45, he would have six shares: three with a basis of $10 each, and three with a basis of $15 each.

If the FMV of stock rights at the time of distribution is less than 15% of the FMV of the stock on which they were distributed, the basis for the rights received is zero unless the taxpayer elects to allocate basis to the rights. (Code Sec. 307(b)(1))[21]

¶ 2494 Basis of stock acquired through dividend reinvestment plans (DRPs).

If a corporation allows shareholders to receive dividends in either cash or stock, then, depending on the situation, the receipt of stock is treated either as the receipt of a taxable stock dividend, because the shareholder has the choice of receiving either cash or stock, or as the receipt of a cash dividend which the shareholder used to buy stock (in some cases, at a discount). If the transaction is treated as a stock dividend, the shareholder's basis is equal to the value of the shares received at the time of the receipt. On the other hand, if the transaction is treated as a cash dividend, the shareholder's basis in the shares is equal to the amount of cash he could have received.[22] The basis of stock acquired after 2010 in connection with a DRP, while held as part of the DRP, will be determined using one of the methods which can be used for determining the basis of stock in a mutual fund. (Code Sec. 1012(d)(1)) Thus, the average basis method for mutual fund shareholders (see ¶2498) also is available for shares of stock acquired after 2010 in connection with a DRP, but only if the shares are identical (i.e., have the same CUSIP number, or other acceptable security identifier number). (Reg § 1.1012-1(e)(1))[23]

¶ 2495 Effect of extraordinary dividends on corporate shareholder's basis.

If a corporation receives an extraordinary dividend with respect to a share of stock that it hasn't held for more than 2 years before the dividend announcement date, the basis of the stock is reduced (but not below zero) by the non-taxed part (i.e., the excess (if any) of: (a) the distribution amount over (b) the part of the dividend that is included in gross income, reduced by the amount of any dividend received deduction allowable under Code Sec. 243, Code Sec. 244, or Code Sec. 245). (Code Sec. 1059) Where a redemption is treated as an extraordinary dividend, the basis in the nonredeemed shares is also reduced if the redemption is part of a partial liquidation of the redeeming corporation, or isn't pro rata as to all shareholders, but not if the redemption wouldn't have been treated (in whole or in part) as a dividend if an option hadn't been taken into account under the Code Sec. 318(a)(4) option attribution rules or the Code Sec. 304(a) related-party stock purchase rules.[24]

¶ 2496 Identifying shares or bonds transferred.

Where taxpayer can adequately identify which shares of stock or which bonds are transferred, the basis used is the basis of that stock or those bonds (specific identification). Shares of stock or bonds are adequately identified where it can be shown that the shares or bonds

---

20. ¶P-5301; ¶3074.01 *et seq.*; TD ¶217,001
21. ¶P-5303; ¶3074.03; TD ¶217,002
22. ¶P-5402; TD ¶174,008

23. ¶P-5201.4; ¶10,124.7701; TD ¶218,001.4
24. ¶P-5100 *et seq.*; ¶10,594

that were delivered to the transferee are from a lot acquired on a certain date or for a certain price. (Reg § 1.1012-1(c)(1); Reg § 1.1012-1(c)(2); Reg § 1.1012-1(c)(6))[25]

If a number of lots were acquired and the ones sold can't be adequately identified, a first-in, first-out (FIFO) rule applies. If the earliest lot purchased or acquired is held in a stock certificate that represents multiple lots of stock, and the taxpayer does not adequately identify the lot from which the stock is sold or transferred, the stock sold or transferred is charged against the earliest lot included in the certificate. (Reg § 1.1012-1(c)(1)(i)) Where shares are held in more than one account, the FIFO rule applies only to the particular account from which the shares were transferred.[26]

¶ 2497   Adequate identification vs. wrong delivery.

In certain situations, if a taxpayer specifically identifies certain shares of stock or bonds as the ones to be transferred, and certain other conditions are met, these will be treated as the ones transferred even though some other lot is actually delivered. This rule applies (1) for sales of stock or bonds held by a broker or agent (Reg § 1.1012-1(c)(3)(i)), (2) where a single certificate represents different lots of stock (Reg § 1.1012-1(c)(3)(ii)), and (3) for certain transfers by a trustee, executor or administrator. (Reg § 1.1012-1(c)(4))[27]

¶ 2498   Methods for determining basis of mutual fund shares.

A taxpayer who sells mutual fund shares held by a custodian or agent in an account may elect to determine the basis of the shares sold by determining the average basis using the "single-category method." (Reg § 1.1012-1(e)(7)(i))) Generally, the single-category method groups in one category all shares regardless of holding period (but treats shares sold as sold on a first-in-first-out (FIFO) basis so that shares that qualify for long-term capital gain or loss treatment are treated as sold before shares that would get short-term treatment). A shareholder who doesn't elect the average-basis method must use the normal FIFO method for determining which shares were sold, see ¶2496.

Unless a single-account election is in effect, a taxpayer may not average together the basis of identical stock held in separate accounts that the taxpayer sells, exchanges, or otherwise disposes of. (Reg § 1.1012-1(e)(7)(i))[28]

¶ 2499   Determining basis for certain securities held in brokerage accounts.

In the case of a sale, exchange or other disposition on or after the "applicable date" (defined below), the broker reported basis in a "specified security" (defined below) is determined under the conventions prescribed in existing regulations and applied to each separate account, on an account-by-account basis. (Code Sec. 1012(c)(1)) Reported basis is computed using a first-in-first-out (FIFO) method, the specific-identification method, or the average-basis convention (Reg § 1.1012-1) (see ¶2496 and ¶2498).[29]

A "specified security" is stocks, notes, and other debt, certain commodity contracts and derivatives, and other securities deemed appropriate by the IRS. (Code Sec. 6045(g)(3)(B)) The applicable date is Jan. 1, 2012 for "average basis" stock, Jan. 1, 2011 for other stock, and Jan. 1, 2013 for other specified securities. (Code Sec. 6045(g)(3)(C))[30]

¶ 2500   Basis of stock acquired in wash sale.

Where a loss is disallowed under the wash sale rule (¶2461), the basis of the acquired stock takes account of the unrecognized loss in the following manner: (Code Sec. 1091(d))

(1) If the sales price is less than the repurchase price, the basis of the new stock is the basis

---

25. ¶P-5202 *et seq.*; ¶10,124.78; TD ¶218,002 *et seq.*
26. ¶P-5212 *et seq.*; ¶10,124.83; TD ¶218,011 *et seq.*
27. ¶P-5200 *et seq.*; ¶10,124.78; TD ¶218,002 *et seq.*

28. ¶P-5214 *et seq.*; ¶10,124.7801; TD ¶218,013 *et seq.*
29. ¶P-5201.1; ¶10,124.7701; TD ¶218,001.1
30. ¶P-5201.3; ¶60,454.08; TD ¶814,203 *et seq.*

of the stock sold plus the difference between the repurchase and the sales prices.

Illustration (1): T owns 100 shares of X company common which cost $100 per share. On May 1, T sells the 100 shares at $80 per share. On May 20, T buys 100 shares of X common at $90 per share. No loss is allowed on the May 1 sale. The basis of each share acquired May 20 is $110, i.e., the basis of the shares sold ($100) plus the $10 difference between the repurchase and sale prices ($90 – $80). (Reg § 1.1091-2(a))

(2) If the sales price is more than the repurchase price, the basis of the new stock is the basis of the stock sold minus the difference between the sale and the repurchase prices.[31]

Illustration (2): If, in the above illustration, the May 1 sale price had been $90 per share and the May 20 repurchase price was $80 per share, the basis of each share acquired May 20 would be $90, i.e., the basis of shares sold ($100) minus the difference between the sale and repurchase prices ($90 – $80). (Reg § 1.1091-2(a))

¶ 2501   Basis of properties after nontaxable exchange.

The basis of property received in a like-kind exchange and nontaxable exchanges of stock in the same corporation (¶2414), U.S. obligations (¶2416), and life insurance and annuity contracts (¶2417) where no part of the gain is recognized is the adjusted basis of the property traded away. (Code Sec. 1031(d))

If money is received as part of the exchange and some gain is recognized, basis in the property received is decreased by the money received and increased by the gain recognized. Reg § 1.1031(d)-1(b)) If money is paid, basis is increased by the amount paid. (Reg § 1.1031(d)-1(a))

In determining the basis, liabilities assumed by the other party are treated as money (boot) received by the taxpayer. (Reg § 1.1031(d)-2)

If other property (boot) is received and some gain is recognized, basis must be allocated (according to fair market value) to all the properties received. (Reg § 1.1031(d)-1(c))

If boot is given as part of the exchange, and gain or loss is recognized on transfer of the boot, the basis of the nonrecognition property received is the total basis of all the properties given, increased by any recognized gain on the boot, or decreased by any recognized loss on the boot. (Reg § 1.1031(d)-1(e))[32]

¶ 2502   Basis after exchange of multiple properties.

In an exchange of multiple properties qualifying for nonrecognition of gain or loss (see ¶2425), the aggregate basis of properties received in each of the "exchange groups" is allocated proportionately to each property in the group in accordance with its fair market value. (Reg § 1.1031(j)-1(c))[33]

¶ 2503   Basis of replacement property after involuntary conversion.

If property is involuntarily converted directly into similar property and gain on the conversion isn't recognized under Code Sec. 1033(a)(1) (¶2431), the basis of the property received is the basis of the converted property (1) decreased by the amount of any money received that wasn't spent in acquiring similar property, and (2) increased by the amount of gain recognized, or decreased by the amount of loss recognized. (Code Sec. 1033(b)(1)) Where the taxpayer's property is involuntarily converted into money or other property that isn't similar or related in use to the converted property and, within the prescribed period (¶2441), the taxpayer purchases other property that is similar or related in service or use to the converted property and elects not to recognize any part of the gain, the basis of the replacement

---

31. ¶P-5019; ¶10,914; TD ¶216,007

32. ¶I-3176 *et seq.*; ¶10,314.13; TD ¶225,200 *et seq.*

33. ¶I-3193; ¶10,314.14; TD ¶225,409

property is its cost, reduced by the amount of gain that isn't recognized. If more than one piece of property is bought as replacement, the basis (cost less nonrecognized gain) is allocated to each piece in proportion to its respective cost. (Code Sec. 1033(b)(2))[34] Where a taxpayer satisfies the replacement property requirement by buying a controlling stock interest in a corporation (¶2431), the corporation reduces its basis in its assets by the amount by which the taxpayer reduces its basis in the stock. (Code Sec. 1033(b)(3))[35]

¶ 2504　Basis of replacement for stock sold to ESOP or EWOC.

If the seller of qualified securities to an employee stock ownership plan (ESOP) or eligible worker-owned cooperative (EWOC) reinvests in qualified replacement property and elects gain nonrecognition (¶2451), basis is reduced by the gain not recognized. If more than one item of replacement property is bought, basis reduction is allocated among each such item (as the cost of that item bears to the cost of all items). (Code Sec. 1042(d))[36]

¶ 2505　Basis for SSBIC rollovers.

Any gain not recognized under the specialized small business investment company (SSBIC) rollover rules (¶2427) reduces taxpayer's basis in any SSBIC investment made during the 60-day rollover period. If taxpayer makes more than one SSBIC investment during this period, the bases of those other investments are reduced in the order they were acquired. (Code Sec. 1044(d))[37]

¶ 2506　Basis for QSBS rollovers.

Gain from the sale of qualified small business stock (QSBS) that isn't recognized because of the Code Sec. 1045(a) rollover election (see ¶2429) reduces (in the order acquired) the basis for determining gain or loss of any QSBS that's purchased by the taxpayer within the 60-day rollover period beginning on the sale date. (Code Sec. 1045(b)(3))[38]

¶ 2507　Property Acquired by Gift, from a Decedent, or from a Spouse. ▬▬▬

Special rules apply to determine the basis of property acquired by gift, from a decedent, or from a spouse (¶4705).

For the basis of property acquired by a gift or transfer in trust during the life of the transferor, see ¶2508 *et seq.*

For the basis of property acquired from a decedent, see ¶2512 *et seq.*

For basis of property acquired from a decedent dying in 2010 if an election out of being subject to estate tax was made, see ¶2523.

For the basis of property acquired from a spouse (or former spouse), see ¶2524.

¶ 2508　Basis of property acquired by gift or transfer in trust.

A donee's original or unadjusted basis (that is, the basis before adjustments made while the donee owned it) for property the donee acquires by gift is the same as the property's adjusted basis in the hands of the donor, or in the hands of the last preceding owner who didn't acquire the property by gift. But if the property's fair market value (FMV) at the date of the gift is lower than that adjusted basis, then the property's basis for determining *loss* is its FMV on that date. (Code Sec. 1015(a))[39]

Since two different methods determine basis of property acquired as a gift, it's possible that neither gain nor loss determined in reference to basis will be realized when the donee sells or

34. ¶P-1154; ¶10,334.33; TD ¶211,128
35. ¶P-1154.1; ¶10,334.231; TD ¶211,129
36. ¶H-12110; ¶10,424
37. ¶I-3791; ¶10,444; TD ¶225,503
38. ¶I-9206; ¶10,454; TD ¶247,208
39. ¶P-3103; ¶P-3104; ¶10,154.01; TD ¶215,002

exchanges the property. (Reg § 1.1015-1(a)(2))[40]

> ⟨RIA⟩*illustration:* Taxpayer acquires by gift income-producing property with an adjusted basis of $100,000 at the date of gift. The FMV on the date of gift is $90,000. Taxpayer later sells the property for $95,000. Taxpayer has neither gain nor loss since the basis for determining gain is $100,000 and the basis for determining loss is $90,000.

If a transfer in trust is made for consideration (whether full and adequate, or less), the basis is the same as it would be in the hands of the grantor, increased by the amount of gain or decreased by the amount of loss recognized to the grantor upon the transfer under the law applicable to the year in which the transfer was made. (Code Sec. 1015(b))[41]

For part sales and part gifts, see ¶2509.

¶ 2509 Basis after transfer that is part purchase, part gift.

Where a transfer of property is part purchase and part gift, the transferee's basis is the greater of cost or the transferor's adjusted basis for the property at the time of the transfer. However, for determining loss, the basis can't exceed the property's fair market value at the time of transfer. (Reg § 1.1015-4) In either event, basis is increased to the extent of any gift tax paid (¶2511).[42]

¶ 2510 Basis rules for donees of partial interests.

If two or more donees receive partial interests in the same property, the basis to each is his or her proportionate part of the donor's basis. To determine the part of total basis allowable to life tenants and remaindermen, see ¶2522. (Reg § 1.1015-1(b))[43]

¶ 2511 Increase in basis for gift tax paid.

If the property's fair market value at the date of the gift is greater than the donor's adjusted basis, the donee's basis (i.e., the donor's adjusted basis) is increased by the part of the gift tax paid that is attributable to the net appreciation in value of the gift. This part is determined by multiplying the gift tax paid by a fraction whose numerator is the net appreciation in value of the gift and whose denominator is the amount of the gift. (Code Sec. 1015(d)(6))

If a gift consists of more than one item of property, the gift tax paid with respect to each item is computed by allocating to each item a proportionate part of the gift tax paid with respect to the gift. If more than one gift was made during the calendar year, the total tax paid must be apportioned to each gift to determine the amount paid on each gift. (Code Sec. 1015(d)(2))

The gift tax paid on a husband-wife split gift is the sum of the taxes, computed separately, paid with respect to each half of the gift. (Code Sec. 1015(d)(3); Reg § 1.1015-5(b)(3))[44]

¶ 2512 Property acquired from a decedent.

The basis of property acquired from a decedent by inheritance, bequest, devise, etc. (see ¶2515), that hasn't been sold, exchanged, or otherwise disposed of before the decedent's death, is generally equal to its fair market value (FMV) at the date of the decedent's death. (Code Sec. 1014(a)(1)) However, if:

> (1) the fiduciary elects for estate tax purposes to value the decedent's gross estate at the alternate valuation date (¶5016), the basis of the property is its FMV at that date (Code Sec. 1014(a)(2));

---

40. ¶P-3105; TD ¶215,002
41. ¶P-3112; ¶10,154.16; TD ¶215,018
42. ¶P-1113; ¶10,154; TD ¶215,006

43. ¶P-3131; ¶10,154.06; TD ¶215,016
44. ¶P-3107 *et seq.*; ¶10,154.01; TD ¶215,004 *et seq.*

(2) the fiduciary elects for estate tax purposes the special use valuation method of valuing farm or other closely held business real property included in the decedent's gross estate (¶5017), the basis of the real property is its value determined for purposes of the special use valuation election (rather than its FMV). (Code Sec. 1014(a)(3))[45]

(3) land acquired at death is subject to a qualified conservation easement, it is excluded from the decedent's gross estate under the rules explained at ¶5016, and its basis (to the extent that it's subject to the easement) is the basis in the hands of the decedent. (Code Sec. 1014(a)(4))[46]

(4) the executor of the estate of a decedent who died in 2010 elected out of having the estate be subject to the estate tax, the modified carryover basis rules discussed at ¶2523 apply to determine the basis of property acquired from that decedent.

FMV on the date of the decedent's death (or the alternate valuation date, if applicable) doesn't apply to determine the basis of property:

. . . that's appreciated property reacquired by the donor within one year of transfer to the decedent, see ¶2514;

. . . included in the decedent's estate but disposed of by the taxpayer before the decedent's death, see ¶2516;

. . . that's stock in a domestic international sales corporation (DISC) or former DISC (Code Sec. 1014(d)), or of certain foreign entities; or

. . . that is a right to receive income in respect of a decedent (Code Sec. 1014(c)), see ¶3968.[47]

¶ 2513   When estate tax value is also income tax basis.

The fair market value (FMV) of property at the decedent's death or at the alternate valuation date as appraised for federal estate tax purposes (or, if no federal estate tax return is required to be filed, the FMV of the property appraised as of the date of death for purposes of state inheritance taxes) is considered also to be the FMV for purposes of determining the income tax basis of property acquired from a decedent. (Reg § 1.1014-3(a))[48] But the value for estate tax purposes is only presumptively correct for basis purposes. Except where facts have been misrepresented, neither taxpayer nor IRS is barred from using a value for basis purposes that differs from the value accepted for estate tax purposes. However, where a discount is allowed in valuing property (e.g., artwork) for estate tax purposes, full value generally will not be allowed in valuing the same property for income tax purposes.[49]

¶ 2514   Appreciated property reacquired by donor from decedent.

If: (1) appreciated property was acquired by the decedent by gift during the one-year period ending at death, and (2) that property is acquired from the decedent by (or passes from the decedent to) the donor of the property (or the donor's spouse (¶4705)), the basis of the property in the hands of the donor (or spouse) is the adjusted basis of the property in the decedent's hands immediately before his death. (Code Sec. 1014(e)(1))[50]

¶ 2515   When is property considered acquired from a decedent?

Property is acquired from a decedent if it is acquired by bequest, devise, or inheritance, or by the decedent's estate from the decedent. (Code Sec. 1014(b)(1))[1] Property acquired from a decedent includes certain pre-death transfers and other classes of property (¶2519 *et seq.*). Qualified terminable interest property (QTIP) includible in a surviving spouse's estate (¶5008) is treated as passing from that surviving spouse for purposes of determining the

---

45. ¶P-4001 *et seq.*; ¶s 10,144, 10,144.05; TD ¶215,501 *et seq.*
46. ¶P-4021.1; ¶10,144.055; TD ¶215,517
47. ¶P-4001 *et seq.*; ¶10,144.02; TD ¶215,514 *et seq.*
48. ¶P-4022; ¶10,144.03; TD ¶215,506

49. ¶s P-4023, P-4024; ¶10,144.03; TD ¶215,506
50. ¶P-4002; ¶10,144.02; TD ¶215,522
1. ¶P-4102; ¶10,144.01; TD ¶215,507

remaindermen's basis. (Code Sec. 1014(b)(10))[2] Property acquired from a decedent excludes:

. . . property the fiduciary acquires after the decedent's death, the basis of which to the fiduciary (or a distributee, if it's distributed) is its cost or other basis with appropriate adjustments. (Reg § 1.1014-3(c))[3]

. . . property bought from a decedent's estate. Its basis to the buyer is its cost or other basis with appropriate adjustments.[4]

. . . income in respect of a decedent (IRD, see ¶3968). (Code Sec. 1014(c)) Its basis is equal to the decedent's basis (if any).[5]

. . . property transferred by the executor, administrator or trustee to a beneficiary in discharge of a specific pecuniary bequest. The beneficiary's basis is the fair market value of the property on the date of the transfer. (Reg § 1.1014-4(a)(3))[6]

¶ 2516 Property acquired from decedent and included in decedent's gross estate.

Property is considered to have been acquired from a decedent if it was acquired from a decedent by reason of: death, form of ownership, or other conditions and the property is required to be included in determining the value of the decedent's gross estate whether or not an estate tax return is required or an estate tax is payable. Acquisitions covered by this rule include acquisitions as surviving joint tenant or tenant by the entirety (¶2517), acquisitions through exercise of a general power of appointment (¶2520), and gifts within three years of death (if includible in the gross estate for estate tax purposes, see ¶5002). (Reg § 1.1014-2(b))[7] If property is acquired before the death of the decedent, this basis must be reduced by the amount actually allowed to the taxpayer as deductions for depreciation, obsolescence, amortization, and depletion for the period before the decedent's death. (Code Sec. 1014(b)(9))[8] If property received as a gift (including a gift in trust) is disposed of by the donee before the donor's death, the property isn't treated as acquired from a decedent and the donee's basis is determined under the rules for gifts, see ¶2508. But property received in exchange for such gift property, or property acquired through reinvesting proceeds of sale of such gift property (or property acquired in further exchange or reinvestments), is treated as acquired from a decedent if it is properly includible in the decedent's gross estate. (Reg § 1.1014-3(d))[9]

¶ 2517 Tenants by the entirety and joint tenants.

Property that a person acquires as the surviving tenant by the entirety or as a surviving joint tenant is property acquired from a decedent to the extent the property is includible in the decedent's gross estate (¶5010 *et seq.*). The part of the property that's treated as acquired from the decedent gets a new basis under the rules discussed at ¶2512 *et seq.*[10] The reduction in basis for depreciation and similar deductions is required only for depreciation, etc., allowed to the surviving joint owner, whose new basis is at issue. (Code Sec. 1014(b)(9)) Local law applies to determine how depreciation is allocated to a husband and wife who file joint returns. (Reg § 1.1014-6(a)(2))[11]

¶ 2518 Community property.

Where a spouse (¶4705) dies owning community property and at least one-half of the entire community interest is includible in the deceased spouse's gross estate (whether or not an estate tax return is required or an estate tax is payable), the surviving spouse's interest is treated as property acquired from a decedent. (Code Sec. 1014(b)(6))[12]

2. ¶P-4104; ¶10,144.01; TD ¶215,507
3. ¶P-4054; ¶10,144.02; TD ¶215,511
4. ¶P-4118; TD ¶215,511
5. ¶P-4003; ¶10,144.02; TD ¶215,523
6. ¶P-4055; ¶10,124.07;TD ¶215,511
7. ¶P-4103; ¶10,144.01; TD ¶215,011

8. ¶P-4027; ¶10,144.01; TD ¶215,013
9. ¶P-3124; ¶10,144.02; TD ¶215,012
10. ¶P-4115; ¶10,144.01; TD ¶215,502
11. ¶P-4028 *et seq.*; ¶10,144.01; TD ¶215,502
12. ¶P-4112; ¶10,144.01; TD ¶215,510

⚫️❓observation: Under the above rule, the surviving spouse's share of the community property plus the decedent's share (included in the decedent's estate) is treated as property acquired from the decedent. Thus, both shares get a new basis.

¶ 2519 Inter vivos trust with power to revoke, alter, etc.

Property acquired from a decedent includes property that the decedent during his lifetime transferred in trust to pay the trust income to, or on the order of, the decedent, where the decedent also reserved to himself at all times before his death the right to make any change in the enjoyment of the trust through the exercise of a power to alter, amend, or terminate the trust (whether alone or with the consent of another not having an interest adverse to his). (Code Sec. 1014(b)(3))[13]

¶ 2520 General power to appoint property.

Property acquired from a decedent includes property passing without full and adequate consideration under a general power of appointment exercised by the decedent in his will. (Code Sec. 1014(b)(4))[14]

¶ 2521 Basis of postponed or contingent remainder interests.

Taxpayer's basis for property acquired from a decedent is determined on the date of the decedent's death under the rules at ¶2512 *et seq.*, whether or not, at the decedent's death, the taxpayer's interest was conditional or contingent, and whether or not the taxpayer can immediately possess and enjoy the property. (Reg § 1.1014-4(a)(2))[15]

⚫️❓observation: If an estate tax return is filed, and the alternate valuation date (¶2512) is elected, the value would be determined as of the alternate valuation date.

¶ 2522 Multiple interests in one property.

Where more than one person has an interest in property acquired from a decedent, the basis in the property is determined and adjusted without regard to the multiple interests. Therefore, a life tenant makes basis adjustments for depreciation as if he were the absolute owner. His basis adjustments are an adjustment in the hands of every person who receives an interest by reason of the decedent's death. (Reg § 1.1014-4(b))[16]

¶ 2523 Election out of the estate tax and into modified carryover basis rules for estates of decedents who died in 2010—Form 8939.

For estates of decedents who died in 2010, the executor or administrator (if none, a person in possession of any property of the decedent) could make an election under which (1) the estate tax didn't apply and (2) the modified carryover basis rules discussed below apply to property acquired from that decedent (instead of the new basis rules discussed at ¶2512 *et seq.*). For property subject to the election, basis upon sale is determined under the modified carryover basis rules even if the sale occurs after 2010.[17]

Under the election, the basis of property acquired from a decedent is generally the lower of the fair market value (FMV) on the date of the decedent's death or the adjusted basis of the property immediately before death. (Code Sec. 1022(a)) However, each estate receives $1.3 million of basis (but only $60,000 for estates of nonresident aliens) to be added to the carryover basis of any one or more of the assets held at death. (Code Sec. 1022(b)(2)(B), Code Sec. 1022(b)(3)) Also, an estate (other than that of a nonresident alien) received additional

---

13. ¶P-4109; ¶10,154.17; TD ¶215,508
14. ¶P-4110; ¶10,144.01; TD ¶215,509
15. ¶P-4018; TD ¶215,503

16. ¶P-4014 *et seq.*; ¶10,144.06; TD ¶215,505
17. ¶P-4060 *et seq.*; ¶R-1100 *et seq.*; ¶10,224 *et seq.*; TD ¶215,530 *et seq.*; TD ¶767,201 *et seq.*

basis equal to the sum of the decedent's unused capital loss and net operating loss carryforwards plus the amount of losses that would have been allowable under Code Sec. 165 if the property acquired from the decedent had been sold at FMV immediately before death. (Code Sec. 1022(b)(2)(C)) And, estates were allowed an additional $3 million of basis to be allocated to assets passing to a surviving spouse. (Code Sec. 1022(c)) However, no addition to basis may increase the new basis of any asset above its FMV on the date of death. (Code Sec. 1022(d)(2))

Safe harbor guidance is provided regarding the modified carryover basis rules, including, but not limited to, guidance concerning pre-death casualty losses, capital loss limitations, property sold or distributed before basis increase allocation, and the determination of FMV.[18]

Property acquired from the decedent includes property acquired by bequest, devise or inheritance, and from certain revocable and other trusts, as well as any other property passing because of death, if passed without consideration. (Code Sec. 1022(e)) Safe harbor guidance is provided regarding what property is acquired from a decedent.[19]

Property is eligible for basis increases only if owned by the decedent at death. In determining ownership, special rules apply to jointly held property, revocable trusts, powers of appointment and community property. (Code Sec. 1022(d)(1)(A), Code Sec. 1022(d)(1)(B)) Safe harbor guidance is provided regarding the ownership requirement.[20] The following otherwise-eligible property is excluded from basis increases: (1) property acquired by the decedent by gift, or other transfer for less than full consideration, within three years of death (except for certain property acquired from a spouse), (2) stock in certain special types of corporations, and (3) a right to receive income in respect of a decedent (see ¶3968). (Code Sec. 1022(d)(1)(C), Code Sec. 1022(d)(1)(D), Code Sec. 1022(f))[21]

For property for which the election was made, and that was acquired from the decedent or the decedent's estate, adjusted basis generally doesn't include liabilities in excess of basis. (Code Sec. 1022(g))[22]

¶ 2524   Basis of property transferred between spouses or incident to a divorce.

The transferee is treated as acquiring the property by gift; the transferee's basis in the property received is the transferor's adjusted basis in the property. (Code Sec. 1041(b)) This rule applies even where the transaction is a sale between the spouses (¶4705) or where the transferee-spouse pays the transferor-spouse (as required under the divorce settlement) for the transfer of title to the property to the transferee-spouse. (Reg § 1.1041-1T(a), Q&A-2) This carryover basis rule applies whether the adjusted basis of the transferred property is less than, equal to, or greater than its fair market value at the time of transfer and applies for purposes of determining loss as well as gain, upon later sale by the transferee. (Reg § 1.1041-1T(d), Q&A-11)[23] Exceptions apply to certain transfers in trust (where liabilities assumed by the trust exceed the transferor's adjusted basis) (Code Sec. 1041(e)), and to transfers of installment obligations into a trust (Code Sec. 453B(g)).[24] The transferor must, at the time of the transfer, give the transferee records sufficient to determine the adjusted basis and holding period of the property at the date of transfer. (Reg § 1.1041-1T(e), Q&A-14)[25]

18. ¶P-4062 *et seq.*; ¶P-4068; ¶10,224.02; TD ¶215,530.
19. ¶P-4061; ¶10,224.01; TD ¶215,531.
20. ¶P-4065; ¶10,224.04; TD ¶215,530.
21. ¶P-4066 *et seq.*, ¶P-4069; ¶10,224.05; TD ¶215,530.

22. ¶P-4071, ¶10,224.06; TD ¶215,530; TD ¶215,531.
23. ¶P-1146; ¶10,414; TD ¶211,124
24. ¶P-1147; ¶10,414; TD ¶211,125
25. ¶P-1153; ¶10,414; TD ¶211,127

Chapter 10   Capital Gains and Losses—Section 1231— Depreciation Recapture

¶ 2600   Capital Gains and Losses.

The tax treatment of capital gains and losses depends on whether the gains and losses are long-term or short-term and on whether the taxpayer is a corporation or not. For noncorporate taxpayers, the maximum tax rate on net long-term capital gains is lower than the top rate on ordinary income. The maximum tax rate on long-term capital gains depends on the type of capital asset sold, and the taxpayer's marginal tax rate (the top rate of tax on the person's ordinary income). The long-term capital gains of corporations, and the short-term gains of corporations and of noncorporate taxpayers, are taxable at the same rates as their ordinary income. The deduction for capital losses is limited, but unused capital losses of noncorporate taxpayers may be carried over indefinitely (¶2612) and unused capital losses of corporate taxpayers can generally be carried back for three years and carried over for five years, see ¶2615.

The main features of the income tax treatment of capital gains and losses are:

. . . Short-term capital gains and losses are netted, long-term capital gains and losses are netted, and then long- and short-term are netted with each other (¶2602 *et seq.*). Further netting may be required if a noncorporate taxpayer has capital losses as well as long-term capital gain subject to differing maximum rates of tax. (¶2609)

. . . A net capital gain (excess of net long-term capital gain over net short-term capital loss) of a noncorporate taxpayer is generally taxed more favorably than ordinary income. The maximum tax rate depends on whether the net capital gain is adjusted net capital gain (¶2603), unrecaptured section 1250 gain (¶2605), or collectibles gain (¶2607) or section 1202 gain (¶2608).

. . . Section 1231 nets gains and losses to arrive at a net of long-term capital gain or ordinary loss (¶2610 and ¶2684 *et seq.*).

. . . Recapture provisions restrict the possibility of converting ordinary income into capital gains via cost recovery or depreciation (¶2692 *et seq.*).

Capital gains and losses are the gains and losses from sales or exchanges (¶2676) of capital assets (¶2617). But capital gain treatment also applies to gains in certain transactions involving assets that aren't capital assets (such as depreciable property used in business, ¶2686).[1]

⬥*observation:* Not all losses (capital or ordinary) are deductible. An individual can only deduct losses incurred in business or transactions for profit, or resulting from a casualty or theft. Thus, a loss on a sale of a personal residence is a nondeductible capital loss.

For individuals. report capital gains and losses on Form 8949, and then carry the totals over to Schedule D (Form 1040) where the net short-term and long-term capital gain or loss in computed. For other taxpayers, report capital gains and losses on Schedule D of the applicable return (e.g., for estates and trusts, Form 1041). Taxpayers may report the total of their capital gains and losses transactions on the applicable schedule and provide details on attachments such as brokers' statements. Individuals whose only capital gains are capital gains distributions (other than unreported section 1250 gain or collectibles gain) reported on Form 1099-DIV do not have to file a Form 8949 or Schedule D. They enter capital gains on Form 1040 or 1040A and complete a capital gain tax worksheet in the instructions.

---

1. ¶I-5100 *et seq.*; ¶12,214 *et seq.*; TD ¶223,300 *et seq.*

References beginning with a single letter are to paragraphs in RIA's Federal Tax Coordinator 2d and RIA's Analysis of Federal Taxes: Income. Those beginning with numbers are to paragraphs in RIA's United States Tax Reporter. Those beginning with TD are to paragraphs in RIA's Tax Desk.

For the deduction when stock or securities become worthless, see ¶1781.

¶ 2601 Tax effect of capital asset sales and exchanges.

If a capital asset is held for not more than the short-term holding period (¶2667), the gain or loss from its sale or exchange is short-term. If held for more than the short-term holding period, gain or loss is long-term. (Code Sec. 1222)[2]

Short-term capital gains and losses are netted to get net short-term capital gain or net short-term capital loss. (Code Sec. 1222(5), Code Sec. 1222(6))

Long-term capital gains and losses are netted to get net long-term capital gain or net long-term capital loss. (Code Sec. 1222(7), Code Sec. 1222(8))

There's a further netting if one group shows a loss and the other a gain:

If there's a net short-term gain, it's taxable (both for noncorporate and corporate taxpayers) at the same rate as ordinary income.[3]

If capital losses exceed capital gains, see ¶2611 *et seq.* (noncorporate) or ¶2615 (corporate).

If net long-term capital gains exceed net short-term capital losses, the excess is net capital gain, taxed under the rules at ¶2603 to ¶2611 (individuals and other noncorporate taxpayers) or ¶2613 *et seq.* (corporate taxpayers). (Code Sec. 1222(11))

¶ 2602 Capital gain net income defined.

A taxpayer who has an excess of capital gains over capital losses (whether long-term or short-term) for the tax year, has "capital gain net income" (Code Sec. 1222(9)), which is included in gross income.[4]

¶ 2603 Noncorporate taxpayers' tax on net capital gain.

A noncorporate taxpayer's net capital gain is taxed as follows:

. . . For tax years beginning in 2013 or later, net capital gain that is adjusted net capital gain (¶2604) is taxed at a rate of (a) 20% if it would be taxed at a rate of 39.6% if it were ordinary income, (b) 15% if it would be taxed at a rate above 25% but below 39.6% if it were ordinary income, and (c) 0% (i.e., it would not be taxed) if it would be taxed at a rate below 25% if it were ordinary income. (Code Sec. 1(h)(1)(B), Code Sec. 1(h)(1)(C), Code Sec. 1(h)(1)(D)) See ¶1103 *et seq.* for the rates at which ordinary income of noncorporate taxpayers is taxed.

. . . The part of net capital gain attributable to unrecaptured section 1250 gain (¶2605) is taxed at a maximum rate of 25%. (Code Sec. 1(h)(1)(E))

. . . Net capital gain attributable to collectibles gain (¶2607) and section 1202 gain (¶2608) is taxed at a maximum rate of 28%. (Code Sec. 1(h)(1)(F), Code Sec. 1(h)(4))[5]

Sellers of interests in S corporations, partnerships, and trusts held for more than one year recognize collectibles gain if the entity owns such appreciated assets at the time of sale. (Code Sec. 1(h)(5)(B)) Regs explain how to figure the seller's deemed collectibles gain and his residual long-term gain or loss and use the same approach for sales of interests in various entities. (Reg § 1.1(h)-1) See ¶3765 for the regs' approach in the context of sales of partnership interests, which also may cause a partner to recognize unrecaptured section 1250 gain. However, sales of interests in S corporations and trusts don't trigger unrecaptured section 1250 gain—only collectibles gain and residual long-term capital gain or loss.[6]

2. ¶s I-5103, I-5102; ¶s 12,224.01, 12,224.02; TD ¶223,501
3. ¶s I-5111, I-5116; ¶12,224.01; TD ¶223,326
4. ¶I-5106; ¶12,224.03; TD ¶223,309

5. ¶I-5110; ¶14.08; TD ¶223,312
6. ¶I-5110.14; ¶14.08; TD ¶223,324

For the 3.8% surtax that will apply in tax years beginning in 2013 or later on net investment income (including capital gains) of noncorporate taxpayers whose modified adjusted gross income is over specified thresholds, see ¶1107.

For netting rules where a noncorporate taxpayer has capital losses, see ¶2609.

¶ 2604　Adjusted net capital gain defined.

Adjusted net capital gain is net capital gain (¶2601) determined without taking qualified dividend income (see ¶1288) into account less the amount that the taxpayer takes into account as investment income under Code Sec. 163(d)(4)(B)(iii) (see ¶1729), reduced (but not below zero) by the sum of:

. . . unrecaptured section 1250 gain (¶2605), and

. . . 28% rate gain (as defined at ¶2606), and increased by

the amount of qualified dividend income. (Code Sec. 1(h)(3))[7]

observation: Effectively, adjusted net capital gain is the sum of that part of a taxpayer's net capital gain that is eligible to be taxed at a maximum rate below 25% (see ¶2603), plus the amount of qualified dividend income.

¶ 2605　Noncorporate taxpayer's unrecaptured section 1250 gain taxed at a maximum rate of 25%.

Unrecaptured section 1250 gain, taxed at a maximum rate of 25%, is the excess (if any) of:

(1) the amount of long-term capital gain (¶2601) which is not otherwise treated as ordinary income, and which would be treated as ordinary income if Code Sec. 1250(b)(1) recapture applied to all depreciation (rather than only to depreciation in excess of straight line), and the applicable percentage under Code Sec. 1250(a) (¶2696) were 100%, over

(2) the excess (if any) of the amount of losses taken into account in computing 28% rate gain (¶2606) over the amount of gains taken into account in computing 28% rate gain. (Code Sec. 1(h)(6))[8]

The amount in (1), above, from sales exchanges and conversions described in Code Sec. 1231(a)(3)(A) (i.e., section 1231 gain, see ¶2684) for any tax year can't exceed the net section 1231 gain (see ¶2685) for that tax year. (Code Sec. 1(h)(6)(B))

observation: Under MACRS, real property must be depreciated using the straight-line method (¶1925). Thus, any gain on the sale or exchange of such property that's attributable to depreciation will be unrecaptured section 1250 gain if held for more than one year.

illustration: Y, an individual, sells nonresidential real property on Aug. 15 for $200,000, realizing a gain of $50,000. This is Y's only transaction involving a capital asset for the year. Y held the property for more than one year. He depreciated the property using MACRS, and claimed $25,000 of depreciation during his ownership. There is no depreciation recapture under Code Sec. 1250(b)(1) because Y didn't claim accelerated depreciation. However, $25,000 of Y's gain, representing depreciation deductions claimed by Y, is unrecaptured section 1250 gain.

For how to handle unrecaptured section 1250 gain where a sale of real property is reported on the installment method, see ¶2457.

For how unrecaptured section 1250 gain can arise on sale of a partnership interest, see ¶3765.

7. ¶I-5110.10; ¶14.08; TD ¶223,319.4　　　　8. ¶I-5110.8; ¶14.08; TD ¶223,319.2

¶ 2606   Noncorporate taxpayer's 28% rate gain.

The term 28% rate gain means the sum of collectibles (¶2607) gain and losses and section 1202 gain (¶2608), less the sum of collectibles loss, the net short-term capital loss for the tax year, and the long-term capital loss carryover to the tax year. (Code Sec. 1(h)(4))[9]

> **observation:** As a result of the way 28% rate gain is defined, a long-term capital loss carryover from an earlier tax year will always be used first to offset 28% rate gain, see ¶2609.

¶ 2607   Noncorporate taxpayer's collectibles gain or loss.

Collectibles gain or loss is gain or loss from the sale or exchange of a collectible which is a capital asset held for more than one year, but only to the extent such gain or loss is taken into account in computing gross income. (Code Sec. 1(h)(5)) Any work of art, rug or antique, metal or gem, stamp or coin, alcoholic beverage, or any other tangible personal property specified by IRS for this purpose is a collectible.[10]

For how collectibles gain can arise on the sale of interests in a partnership, S corporation, or trust, see ¶2603.

¶ 2608   Noncorporate taxpayers' section 1202 gain.

Section 1202 gain is the excess of (1) the gain that would be excluded from gross income on the sale of certain qualified small business stock under Code Sec. 1202, if the percentage limitations of Code Sec. 1202(a) (see ¶2648) didn't apply, over (2) the gain actually excluded under Code Sec. 1202. (Code Sec. 1(h)(7))[11]

> **observation:** If 50% of the gain on the disposition of qualifying small business stock is excluded from gross income, the 50% includible in gross income is taxed at a maximum rate of 28% (since it's excluded from adjusted net capital gain). This makes the maximum effective rate on the total gain from the sale of qualified small business stock 14%.

See ¶3209 for AMT treatment of section 1202 gain.

¶ 2609   Netting rules where taxpayer has capital losses.

The following netting and ordering rules apply where the taxpayer has capital losses:

(1) Short-term capital losses are applied first to reduce short-term capital gains, if any. If there's a net short-term capital loss, it first reduces any net long-term gain from the 28% group, then gain from the 25% group, and finally reduces adjusted net capital gain.

(2) Long-term capital losses are handled as follows:

. . . A net loss from the 28% group (including long-term capital loss carryovers from prior years) is used first to reduce gain from the 25% group, then to reduce adjusted net capital gain.

. . . A net loss from a group in which net gain would be treated as adjusted net capital gain is used first to reduce net gain from the 28% group, then to reduce gain from the 25% group.[12]

> **illustration:** T, in the highest tax bracket, has a loss of $40,000 from the sale of stock. T has collectibles gain of $25,000 and unrecaptured section 1250 gain of $25,000. T's net

9. ¶I-5110.11; ¶14.08; TD ¶223,321
10. ¶I-5110.12; ¶14.08; TD ¶223,322
11. ¶I-5110.13; ¶14.08; TD ¶223,323
12. ¶I-5107; ¶14.08; TD ¶223,310

capital gain is $10,000 (total gain of $50,000 less $40,000 loss). T's loss from the sale of stock completely offsets the collectibles gain of $25,000, and $15,000 of the unrecaptured section 1250 gain of $25,000, leaving him with unrecaptured section 1250 gain of $10,000.

¶ 2610 Noncorporate taxpayer's nonrecaptured net section 1231 losses.

If any Section 1231 gain is treated as ordinary income under Code Sec. 1231(c) (relating to Section 1231 gain being treated as ordinary income to the extent of nonrecaptured Section 1231 losses, see ¶2685), the amount to be treated as ordinary income is allocated first to any net section 1231 gain in the 28% group, then to any section 1231 gain in the 25% group, and then to any net section 1231 gain in the 0%/15%/20% group.[13]

¶ 2611 Capital losses of noncorporate taxpayers.

A noncorporate taxpayer may deduct capital losses only to the extent of capital gains plus (if the losses exceed the gains) the lower of:

(1) $3,000 ($1,500 for married individuals filing separate returns), or

(2) the excess of the losses over the gains. (Code Sec. 1211(b))[14]

🄡illustration: B has a short-term capital loss of $100 and a long-term capital loss of $3,600 for his tax year. His total capital loss for the tax year is $3,700. This capital loss is deductible from ordinary income up to a maximum of $3,000. See ¶2612 for carrying over the excess capital loss.

A noncorporate taxpayer's capital losses for a tax year consist of the capital losses sustained during the year plus the total of all capital losses sustained in other years that are carried to that tax year (¶2612). (Code Sec. 1212(b); Reg § 1.1211-1(b)(1))[15]

¶ 2612 Noncorporate capital loss carryovers.

If an individual, trust or estate sustains a net capital loss that exceeds the maximum deductible in the current year (¶2611), the excess is carried forward to later years indefinitely until it's absorbed. (Code Sec. 1212(b)) Carry*backs* aren't allowed.[16] A decedent's unused capital loss is lost; it can't be carried over.[17] However, for estates of decedents who died in 2010 that elected to have zero estate tax and modified carryover basis, a decedent's unused capital losses could be used to increase the estate's basis in his capital assets, see ¶2523.

The capital loss keeps its original character as long- or short-term when carried over. For purposes of determining the amount of excess long-term or short-term capital loss that is carried over, short-term capital loss is applied first to offset ordinary income, and long-term capital loss is applied only to the extent that the amount that can be offset exceeds the total short-term capital loss for the year (including any short-term capital loss carried over from an earlier year). (Code Sec. 1212(b))[18]

¶ 2613 Capital gains of corporate taxpayers.

Corporate taxpayers must include capital gains in full in gross income but only to the extent that they exceed capital losses.[19]

---

13. ¶I-9003.1
14. ¶I-5112; ¶12,114; TD ¶223,327
15. ¶I-5113; ¶12,124 *et seq.*; TD ¶223,337
16. ¶I-5122; ¶12,124.01; TD ¶223,336

17. ¶I-5133; TD ¶223,344
18. ¶I-5123; ¶12,124.01; TD ¶223,337
19. ¶I-5116; ¶12,114; TD ¶223,331

¶ 2614   Corporation's alternative tax on capital gains.

A corporation with an excess of net long-term capital gain over net short-term capital loss ("net capital gain") (Code Sec. 1222(11)) pays an alternative tax instead of the regular corporate tax if the alternative tax is smaller. The alternative tax applies a tax rate of 35% to the corporation's net capital gain, but only if the top regular corporate tax rate for the year (see ¶1113) is higher than 35% (determined without regard to the additional tax on (1) the corporation's taxable income over $100,000, and (2) the corporation's taxable income over $15,000,000). (Code Sec. 1201(a))[20]

☉⃝observation: Thus, the above alternative tax doesn't apply for 2013 or 2014 since the top corporate rate for those years is 35%.

¶ 2615   Corporation's capital losses.

Corporations may deduct capital losses only to the extent of their capital gains. Excess capital losses can't be deducted from a corporation's ordinary income. (Code Sec. 1211(a))[21]

A corporation's capital losses in excess of its capital gains for the current year are carried back three years, but only to the extent the loss isn't attributable to a foreign expropriation capital loss and to the extent that the carryback doesn't increase or produce a net operating loss for the tax year to which it's carried back. (Code Sec. 1212(a)(1)(A)) A net capital loss can't be carried back to a tax year in which the corporation is either a regulated investment company (RIC) or a real estate investment trust (REIT). (Code Sec. 1212(a)(4))

The carryforward period is five years (ten years for foreign expropriation capital losses, and there is no limit on how long a RIC may carry forward capital losses). (Code Sec. 1212(a)(1)(B);Code Sec. 1212(a)(1)(C); Code Sec. 1212(a)(3))[22]

A capital loss carryback or carryover is treated as a short-term capital loss whether or not it was short-term when sustained (Code Sec. 1212(a)(1)) except that the capital losses of a RIC retain their character as short-term or long-term when carried over. (Code Sec. 1212(a)(3)(A)) A carryover from one year can't be included in computing a new net capital loss for another year. (Code Sec. 1222(10))[23]

¶ 2616   Assets to Which Capital Gain and Loss Rules Apply. ▬▬▬▬▬▬▬▬▬

The capital gain or loss rules apply to assets that are capital in nature. An asset's character depends upon what it is and what use it has in the taxpayer's hands.

¶ 2617   Capital assets defined.

Capital assets include all assets held by the taxpayer except:

(1) Stock in trade of the taxpayer or other property of a kind that would properly be included in the inventory of the taxpayer if on hand at the close of the tax year.

(2) Property held by the taxpayer primarily for sale to customers in the ordinary course of his trade or business.

(3) Accounts or notes receivable acquired in the ordinary course of a trade or business for services rendered or from the sale of any properties described in (1) or (2), above.

(4) Depreciable property, amortizable Code Sec. 197 intangibles, and real property used in the taxpayer's trade or business.

(5) Certain copyrights, literary, artistic, or musical works (unless, for musical works or

20. ¶I-5117; ¶12,014; TD ¶223,332
21. ¶I-5121; ¶12,114; TD ¶223,335

22. ¶I-5125 *et seq.*; ¶12,124.04; TD ¶223,339
23. ¶I-5125 ; ¶12,124.04; TD ¶223,341

copyrights in them, the election discussed at ¶2622 is made), and certain letters, memoranda, or similar property, see ¶2622.

(6) U.S. government publications (e.g., Congressional Record) received from the government without charge or below the price sold to the public, in the hands of the recipient and carryover-basis transferees.

(7) Commodities derivative financial instruments held by a commodities derivatives dealer (except for certain instruments not connected to the dealing activity).

(8) Any hedging transaction (e.g., to manage risk of price changes or currency fluctuations) clearly identified as such before the close of the day on which it was acquired, originated, or entered.

(9) Supplies of a type regularly used or consumed by the taxpayer in the ordinary course of the taxpayer's trade or business. (Code Sec. 1221(a))[24]

Property held for personal use is a capital asset, as is property used for the production of income. (Reg § 1.1221-1(b)) Examples of capital assets include stock and securities held for investment,[25] including tax-exempt bonds[26] (discussed at ¶2636). A payment received in exchange for the right to ordinary income (e.g., the right to receive future lottery payments) is not a capital asset.[27]

If the election is made, for estates of decedents who died in 2010, to not be subject to the estate tax and to apply modified carryover basis rules to property acquired from a decedent (¶2523), the property generally retains the same character in the hands of the estate or other recipient as it had in the hands of the decedent.[28]

¶ 2618   Hedging transactions.

The term capital asset doesn't include property that's part of a hedging transaction. (Reg § 1.1221-2(a)) A hedging transaction is a transaction that a taxpayer enters into in the normal course of the taxpayer's trade or business, primarily to reduce the risk of price changes or currency fluctuations with respect to ordinary property, or to reduce the risk of interest rate or price changes or currency fluctuations with respect to borrowings or ordinary obligations. (Reg § 1.1221-2(b)(1)) Property is ordinary property if its sale or exchange by the taxpayer couldn't produce capital gain or loss regardless of the holding period. An obligation is an ordinary obligation if performance or termination of the obligation by the taxpayer could not produce capital gain or loss. (Reg § 1.1221-2(c)(2))[29] Thus, hedging in corn futures (to stabilize the cost of corn inventory) as an integral part of a taxpayer's inventory-purchase system produces ordinary income and loss.[30]

A taxpayer must identify a transaction (including recycling an existing hedge) as a hedging transaction before the close of the day he enters it. (Reg § 1.1221-2(f)(1))[31]

The accounting method used for a hedging transaction must clearly reflect income and reasonably match the timing of the transaction with the timing of the item(s) being hedged. Special rules detail the accounting methods for various transactions. (Reg § 1.446-4)[32]

¶ 2619   Options to buy or sell.

Gain or loss from the sale or exchange of a noncompensatory option to buy or sell property is considered a gain or loss from the sale or exchange of a capital asset if the optioned property is (or would be if acquired) a capital asset in the taxpayer's hands. (Code

24. ¶I-6001; ¶12,214; TD ¶249,001
25. ¶I-6201; ¶12,214.21; TD ¶250,001
26. ¶I-7801
27. ¶I-6824.1; TD ¶223,014
28. ¶I-5004.1; TD ¶223,007.1

29. ¶I-6231 *et seq.*; ¶12,214.80; TD ¶250,006
30. ¶I-6268; TD ¶250,009
31. ¶I-6250; ¶12,214.80; TD ¶250,007
32. ¶G-2519 *et seq.*; ¶4464.01; TD ¶447,501 *et seq.*

Sec. 1234(a)(1); Reg § 1.1234-1(a))[33] If the holder of an option incurs a loss because he fails to exercise the option, the option is considered to have been sold or exchanged on the date it expires. (Code Sec. 1234(a)(2); Reg § 1.1234-1(b))[34]

A dealer in options is considered a dealer in the property subject to the option, and any gain or loss received from sale or exchange of the option is ordinary. (Reg § 1.1234-1(d))[35]

¶ 2620   "Put" and "call" options; straddles.

There are no tax consequences to the buyer or writer of an option until the option is exercised, otherwise closed out, or lapses. The holder treats the premium paid as a nondeductible capital expenditure at the time of payment. The premium isn't included in income of the writer at the time of receipt.[36] The premium received by the writer for granting a "put" or "call" option that's not exercised ("lapses"), so that the writer simply keeps the money, is generally treated as ordinary income, and gain or loss to the writer on repurchase of an option ("closing transaction") is also generally ordinary. (Reg § 1.1234-1(b)) However, gain or loss to a nondealer from a lapse or closing transaction involving options in stocks, securities, commodities or commodity futures is treated as short-term capital gain or loss. (Code Sec. 1234(b); Reg § 1.1234-3)[37]

Where a put is exercised, the premium received by the writer for granting the option is deducted from the option price for the property in determining the net basis to the writer of the property purchased. The holder deducts the premium from the amount received from the writer, in computing the gain or loss realized on the sale. Where a call is exercised, the premium received by the writer (i.e., seller) for granting the option is added to the sale proceeds received. This is included in the holder's (buyer's) basis for the property.[38]

illustration: A bought a 180-day put from B for $5,000 that gave A the right to sell 1,000 shares of stock to B for $50,000. The stock originally cost A $25,000. The put was timely exercised. A has a gain of $20,000 on the sale ($50,000, less $30,000 ($5,000 paid for put and $25,000 original cost of stock). B's basis in the stock is $45,000 ($50,000 paid to A on the exercise of the put, less $5,000 received by B from A for the put).

When the put or call is bought from the original holder (or his assignee), the buyer is treated as a holder, and the amount paid by him to the original holder is likewise treated as a premium. However, the original holder is not treated as a writer, and must include that premium in his amount realized upon disposition of the option, see ¶2619.[39]

observation: Thus, if a holder (other than a dealer) of a put or call option on publicly traded stock closes out a position by selling the option on an exchange, the gain or loss is a capital gain or loss.

A "straddle" option combines a put and a call. (Reg § 1.1234-3(b)(4))[40] The allocation of a premium received for a straddle or multiple option between or among the component options is made on the basis of the relative market value of the component options at the time of their issuance or on any other reasonable and consistently applied basis which is acceptable to IRS. (Reg § 1.1234-3(e))[41]

¶ 2621   Patents.

If an individual inventor or his financial backer transfers (other than by gift, inheritance or devise) all substantial rights to a patent, or an undivided interest (e.g., a half, a third) in

---

33. ¶I-6504; ¶12,344; TD ¶252,002
34. ¶I-6510; ¶12,344; TD ¶252,003
35. ¶I-6509; ¶12,344.03; TD ¶252,002
36. ¶s I-6521, I-6522; ¶12,344 *et seq.* TD ¶252,001, 252,005
37. ¶I-6515; ¶12,344 *et seq.*; TD ¶252,006

38. ¶s I-6530, I-6531; ¶s 12,344.03, 12,344.04; TD ¶252,008, 252,009
39. ¶I-6523; ¶s 12,344.03, 12,344.04; TD ¶252,002
40. ¶I-6526; ¶12,344.06
41. ¶I-6528

those rights, the transfer is considered a sale or exchange of a long-term capital asset even though the transferor hasn't held the patent property for the period required for long-term treatment (see ¶2667), and even though the payments to the seller are: (1) made periodically during the buyer's use of the property, or (2) contingent on the productivity, use or disposition of the buyer's rights in the property (i.e., are like royalties). (Code Sec. 1235(a))[42]

It's not necessary that the patent or patent application be in existence at the time of that transfer for long-term capital gain treatment to apply. (Reg § 1.1235-2(a))[43]

This treatment doesn't apply to a transfer by the inventor's employer. (Code Sec. 1235(b)(2)(A))[44] Nor does it apply to transfers made (directly or indirectly) to or by certain persons related to the inventor. (Code Sec. 1235(b)(2)(B); Reg § 1.1235-2(f))[45]

Transferors that don't qualify for this special long-term capital gain treatment nevertheless qualify for capital gain or loss treatment if they can establish that the patent is a capital asset or a Section 1231 asset. (Reg § 1.1235-1(b))[46]

The long-term capital gain rule doesn't apply unless all substantial rights (or an undivided interest in those rights) are transferred. (Reg § 1.1235-2(b))[47]

¶ 2622   Copyrights, literary, musical, artistic composition, etc.

Copyrights, literary, artistic, and (except as noted below) musical compositions, etc., aren't capital assets or Section 1231 assets if the taxpayer is either (1) the author or creator of property through his own personal efforts, or (2) the donee of the author or creator, or one who otherwise has a basis for the property determined in whole or in part by reference to the basis in the hands of that donor.

A letter, memorandum or similar property prepared or produced for a taxpayer isn't a capital asset to him (or his donee or other carryover-basis transferee). (Code Sec. 1221(a)(3))[48]

However, if a taxpayer inherits property from a decedent who died in 2010, and in whose hands the property was not a capital asset under the rules described above, an election to have zero estate tax apply will not prevent the property from being treated as a capital asset in the taxpayer's hands merely because the taxpayer's basis for figuring gain from a sale or exchange is determined in whole or in part by reference to the decedent's basis in the property under the modified-carryover-basis-at-death rules of Code Sec. 1022 (¶2523). (Code Sec. 1221(a)(3)(C))[49]

A taxpayer may elect to treat a sale or exchange of musical compositions or copyrights in musical works created by the taxpayer's personal efforts (or having a basis determined by reference to the basis in the hands of a taxpayer whose personal efforts created them) as the sale or exchange of a capital asset. (Code Sec. 1221(b)(3)) A taxpayer must make the election on Schedule D, Capital Gains and Losses, of the appropriate tax return (or in the case of an individual taxpayer on Form 8949) on or before the due date (including extensions) of his return for the tax year of the sale or exchange. (Reg § 1.1221-3(b)) The election is revocable with IRS consent. IRS automatically grants taxpayers a 6-month extension from the due date of the taxpayer's income tax return (excluding extensions) to revoke an election, if the taxpayer timely filed his income tax return and, within the 6-month extension period, files an amended return that treats the sale or exchange as the sale or exchange of property that is not a capital asset. (Reg § 1.1221-3(c))[50]

---

42. ¶I-8301; ¶12,354; TD ¶229,101
43. ¶I-8307
44. ¶I-8322; ¶12,354.04; TD ¶229,102
45. ¶s I-8301, I-8325; ¶12,354.06; TD ¶229,112
46. ¶I-6700; ¶12,354.01; TD ¶229,101

47. ¶I-8301; ¶12,354.09; TD ¶229,106
48. ¶I-6601 *et seq.*; ¶12,214.08; TD ¶252,501
49. ¶I-6601.2; ¶12,214.45
50. ¶I-6601; ¶12,214.45; TD ¶252,501

¶ 2623 Real property.

Real property held primarily for sale in the ordinary course of the taxpayer's trade or business doesn't qualify as a capital asset. Whether particular real estate sold is a capital asset is decided on a case by case basis taking into consideration many factors including the number and taxpayer's frequency of sales, subdividing and promotional activities.[1]

¶ 2624 Five-year land subdivision rule for taxpayers other than C corporations.

A taxpayer other than a C corporation (e.g., an individual, trust, estate or S corporation) won't be treated as holding land primarily for sale to customers merely because the taxpayer subdivided a tract of land into lots or parcels and engaged in advertising, promotion, selling activities or the use of sales agents in selling lots in the subdivision, if the taxpayer:

... hasn't previously held any part of the same land primarily for sale to customers in the ordinary course of business, and, in the year of sale doesn't hold any other real estate for sale to customers;

... doesn't (while he holds the land or as part of a contract of sale with the buyer) make "substantial improvements" on the land that substantially increase the value of the lot sold (except, if elected, improvements needed to make marketable land that has been held for ten years or more); and

... either has owned the land for five years or more, or acquired it by inheritance or devise. (Code Sec. 1237(a); Reg § 1.1237-1(a)(2), Reg § 1.1237-1(a)(5), Reg § 1.1237-1(b)(1))[2]

However, if more than five lots or parcels in the same tract are sold or exchanged, gain from any sale or exchange (which occurs in or after the tax year in which the sixth lot or parcel is sold or exchanged) of any lot or parcel covered by the above 5-year rule will be treated as ordinary income to the extent of 5% of the selling price. (Code Sec. 1237(b)(1); Reg § 1.1237-1(e)(2))[3]

illustration: A divides a tract covered by the 5-year rule into six parcels. If he sells all six parcels in Year 1, 5% of the gain from the sale of each parcel will be treated as ordinary income. However, if he doesn't sell the sixth parcel until Year 2, only 5% of the gain from the sale of that parcel will be treated as ordinary income.

The sale or exchange of qualifying subdivided land that's business property can result in an ordinary loss, see ¶2684. (Reg § 1.1237-1(f))[4]

¶ 2625 Sale of a sole proprietorship.

When a sole proprietorship is sold, there isn't a sale of just one asset (the business). Rather, there's a sale of the individual assets that comprise the business. Thus, gain or loss on some assets will be ordinary while on others it will be capital.[5]

¶ 2626 Allocation of selling price on sale of business.

If assets of a going business are sold, the selling price must be allocated among the assets (including goodwill) for purposes of determining gain or loss (and the type of gain or loss, e.g., capital gain or ordinary income) separately for each. Allocation is made under the rules for determining the buyer's basis in each of them, see ¶2472.[6]

---

1. ¶I-6300 *et seq.*; ¶12,214.31; TD ¶250,502
2. ¶I-6400 *et seq.*; ¶12,374.01; TD ¶251,501
3. ¶I-6420; ¶12,374.05; TD ¶251,502

4. ¶I-6424; ¶12,374.07; TD ¶251,512
5. ¶I-8501; ¶12,214.53; TD ¶229,401
6. ¶I-8506 *et seq.*; ¶12,214.51; TD ¶212,000

¶ 2627   Goodwill and covenants not to compete.

Goodwill is a capital asset, unless it is treated as an amortizable section 197 intangible under the rules explained at ¶1973 *et seq*. To the extent that the Code Sec. 197 rules don't apply, proceeds from the sale of a business that are allocable (¶2626) to goodwill are taxed under the capital gain and loss rules,[7] and payments for a covenant not to compete that is severable from the sale of goodwill results in ordinary income.[8]

¶ 2628   Investments by dealer in securities.

A securities dealer who buys securities for resale to customers may also hold securities purchased as investments for the dealer's own account. But gain from the sale or exchange of those securities won't be capital gain unless (1) the security is clearly identified in the dealer's records as a security held for investment on the day it is acquired, and (2) the security is not held by the dealer primarily for sale to customers in the ordinary course of a trade or business at any time after the acquisition date. (Code Sec. 1236(a))[9]

A loss is a capital loss if the security has ever been clearly identified in the dealer's records as held for investment, even though held primarily for sale at the time of its disposition. (Code Sec. 1236(b); Reg § 1.1236-1(b))[10]

¶ 2629   Franchise, trademark or trade name transfers.

The transfer of a franchise, trademark or trade name isn't a sale or exchange of a capital asset if the transferor retains any significant power, right or continuing interest (such as the right to terminate at will, prescribe standards of quality or require the transferee to sell only the transferor's products). (Code Sec. 1253(a), Code Sec. 1253(b)(2))[11] In any case, ordinary income treatment applies to payments received by a transferor that are contingent on production, use, or disposition of a franchise, trademark or trade name. (Code Sec. 1253(c))[12]

For deduction of these payments, see ¶1622; for amortization of payments made for the transfer of a franchise, trademark, or trade name, see ¶1974.

¶ 2630   Life estates, term of years, etc.

A life tenant, a tenant for a term of years, or an income beneficiary of a trust is generally entitled to capital gain on the sale of that interest.[13] However, where the interest was acquired by gift, from a decedent, by a transfer in trust, or by a transfer from a spouse (or a former spouse incident to divorce), that part of the basis that's determined under the Code rules for those types of acquisitions (e.g., fair market value basis where acquired from a decedent dying before or after 2010 (or in 2010 if election to have zero estate tax apply is not made), see ¶2512) isn't taken into account in computing gain or loss on the sale or exchange of the interest, unless the entire interest in the underlying property is transferred in the same transaction. See ¶4705 for who is a spouse. (Code Sec. 1001(e); Reg § 1.1001-1(f))[14]

¶ 2631   Small business investment company (SBIC) stock.

Losses from the sale, exchange or worthlessness of SBIC (¶4205) stock are deductible by a shareholder as an ordinary loss attributable to the shareholder's business. (Code Sec. 1242; Reg § 1.1242-1) Gains on the sale or exchange of SBIC stock are capital gains.[15]

---

7. ¶I-8601; ¶12,214.55; TD ¶229,501
8. ¶I-8603; ¶12,214.56; TD ¶229,502
9. ¶I-6209; ¶12,364.01; TD ¶250,004
10. ¶I-6215; ¶12,364.01
11. ¶s I-8401; ¶12,534 *et seq.*; TD ¶229,301

12. ¶I-8412; ¶12,534.01; TD ¶229,306
13. ¶I-7014; ¶12,214.66
14. ¶P-3129; ¶10,144.07; TD ¶215,015
15. ¶I-9543; ¶12,424 *et seq.*; TD ¶355,011, TD ¶372,006

¶ 2632   Regulated investment company (RIC) stock.

A loss realized on the sale or exchange of stock in a RIC is a long-term capital loss to the extent of any long-term capital gain realized via a distribution made with respect to the stock, if the taxpayer held the stock for six months or less. Also, the loss of a shareholder who receives an exempt-interest dividend on stock which is held for six months or less is disallowed to the extent of the exempt interest dividend received by the shareholder. Rules for periodic liquidations differ. (Code Sec. 852(b)(4))[16]

¶ 2633   Sale or exchange of debt instruments issued with original issue discount (OID).

If a debt instrument is issued with OID (¶1314) and, if at the time of original issue there was an intention to call the debt instrument before maturity, any gain realized on the sale or exchange of the instrument is treated as ordinary income to the extent the gain doesn't exceed the OID reduced by the part of the OID previously included in the income of any holder. For purposes of this rule, any part of the OID that would have been included in the income of the holder had there been no acquisition premium is treated as if it had been included. (Code Sec. 1271(a)(2)(A))

The above rule doesn't apply to tax-exempt obligations or to the sale or exchange by a holder who purchased the debt instrument at a premium. (Code Sec. 1271(a)(2)(B))[17]

¶ 2634   Sale or exchange of short-term government obligations.

On the sale or exchange of any short-term government obligation, any gain realized that doesn't exceed an amount equal to the ratable share of the acquisition discount is treated as ordinary income (Code Sec. 1271(a)(3)(A)) unless the seller was required to include the acquisition discount in gross income currently under the rules at ¶1328. (Code Sec. 1283(d)(3))[18]

¶ 2635   Sale or exchange of short-term nongovernment obligations.

On the sale or exchange of any short-term nongovernment obligation, any gain realized that doesn't exceed an amount equal to the ratable share of original issue discount (OID) is treated as ordinary income (Code Sec. 1271(a)(4)(A)), unless the seller was required to include the acquisition discount in gross income currently under the rules at ¶1328. (Code Sec. 1283(d)(3))[19]

¶ 2636   Sale or exchange of tax-exempt bonds.

The sale or exchange of tax-exempt obligations is a taxable event, even if the interest on the bonds is exempt. The seller has gain to the extent that the amount realized exceeds his adjusted basis (¶2474) in the bonds. The seller's basis for this purpose means the price he paid, whether or not he bought the bonds at a discount. However, the holder of a tax-exempt bond issued with original issue discount (OID) can increase his adjusted basis in the bond by the amount of OID accrued during the period the bond is held. If the bond is bought at a premium over face value, the holder must reduce his adjusted basis in the bond by the amount by which the premium is amortized under the rules discussed at ¶2169.[20]

---

17. ¶I-8001; ¶12,714; TD ¶227,601
18. ¶I-8004; ¶12,714.05; TD ¶227,602

19. ¶I-8005; ¶12,714.05; ¶12,814; TD ¶227,603
20. ¶I-4001 *et seq.*; TD ¶227,401 *et seq.*

¶ 2637   Constructive Sales of Appreciated Financial Positions. ▆▆▆▆▆▆

The constructive sale rules restrict a taxpayer's ability to defer recognition of gain on appreciated property he owns even though he locks in his gain and limits risk of loss through the use of "short sales against the box" and similar transactions. In general, the taxpayer is treated as constructively selling property he owns if he borrows and sells the same or substantially identical property.

A taxpayer must recognize gain upon entering into a constructive sale of any appreciated financial position in stock, a partnership interest, or certain debt instruments. (Code Sec. 1259) In general, an appreciated financial position is any position with respect to any stock, debt instrument, or partnership interest if there would be gain if the position were sold, assigned, or otherwise terminated at its fair market value. (Code Sec. 1259(b)(1)) Except as provided at ¶2638, a constructive sale of an appreciated position occurs when the taxpayer (or a related person):

(1) enters into a short sale of the same or substantially identical property,

(2) enters into an offsetting notional principal contract with respect to the same or substantially identical property,

(3) enters into a futures or forward contract to deliver the same or substantially identical property,

(4) in the case of an appreciated financial position that's a short sale or a contract described in (2) or (3) above with respect to any property, acquires the same or substantially identical property, or

(5) to the extent provided in regs, enters into one or more other transactions (or acquires one or more positions) that have substantially the same effect as a transaction described in (1), (2), (3), or (4) above. (Code Sec. 1259(c)(1))[21]

Persons are "related" with respect to a transaction if their relationship is described in Code Sec. 267(b) (¶2448) or Code Sec. 707(b) (¶3731), and the transaction is entered into with a view toward avoiding the purposes of the constructive sale rules. (Code Sec. 1259(c)(4))[22]

The constructive sale rules don't apply to a short sale of stock that the seller borrows if he doesn't hold substantially identical property at the time of the sale. However, if he acquires the same stock that he borrowed and sold, and has a gain, the constructive sale rules apply on the acquisition date even if the acquired stock isn't delivered to the lender.[23]

As a result of a constructive sale,

. . . the taxpayer recognizes gain as if the position were sold, assigned, or otherwise terminated at its FMV value on the constructive sale date (Code Sec. 1259(a)(1)), and

. . . for purposes of applying the Code for periods after the constructive sale, (1) an appropriate adjustment is made in the amount of gain or loss later realized on the position for the gain taken into account because of the constructive sale rule, and (2) a new holding period for the position begins as if the taxpayer had acquired the position on the date of the constructive sale. (Code Sec. 1259(a)(2))[24]

✏️*illustration:* On May 1, 2013, S bought 100 shares of ABC stock for $10,000. On Sept. 3, 2013, S sold short 100 shares of ABC stock for $16,000. He made no other transactions involving ABC stock for the rest of 2013 and the first 30 days of 2014. S's short sale is treated as a constructive sale of an appreciated financial position because a sale of the ABC stock on the date of the short sale would have resulted in a gain. S recognizes a $6,000 short-term capital gain from the constructive sale and he has a new holding period in his

---

21. ¶I-7732; ¶12,594; TD ¶228,602
22. ¶I-7733; ¶12,594; TD ¶228,603

23. ¶I-7732; ¶12,594; TD ¶228,602
24. ¶I-7731; ¶12,594; TD ¶228,601

ABC stock that begins on Sept. 3, 2013.

The term "appreciated financial position" does *not* include (1) certain positions with respect to nonconvertible debt if certain specified conditions with respect to principal and interest are met (Code Sec. 1259(b)(2)(A)); (2) any hedge with respect to a position described in (1), above (Code Sec. 1259(b)(2)(B)); and (3) any position which is marked to market under any Code section or the regs under that Code section. (Code Sec. 1259(b)(2)(C))[25]

¶ 2638   Exceptions to constructive sale rules.

A taxpayer is not treated as having made a constructive sale solely because the taxpayer enters a contract for the sale of any stock, debt instrument, or partnership interest which isn't a marketable security if the contract settles within one year after the date the contract is entered. (Code Sec. 1259(c)(2))[26] In addition, any transaction which would otherwise cause a constructive sale during the tax year is disregarded if:

(1) it's closed on or before the 30th day after the close of the tax year it was entered,

(2) the taxpayer holds the appreciated financial position to which the transaction relates (e.g., the stock where the transaction is a short sale) throughout the 60-day period beginning on the date the transaction is closed, and

(3) at no time during that 60-day period is the taxpayer's risk of loss reduced with respect to the position (applying the principles of Code Sec. 246(c)(4), relating to suspension of the holding period where the risk of loss is diminished for purposes of the dividends received deduction, see ¶3312). (Code Sec. 1259(c)(3)(A))[27]

observation: If a taxpayer meets the above requirements, a "short sale against the box" is not a constructive sale as long as he remains at risk with respect to the appreciated financial position for sixty days after the closing.

¶ 2639   Short Sales. ■■■■■■■■■■■■■■■■■■■■■■■■■■■■■■■■■■■■■■

In a short sale, an investor sells a security for delivery in the future. The short seller may meet his obligation to deliver by buying the security on the delivery ("closing") date. If the security has declined in value by the time he closes or covers the sale, he has a gain equal to the price at which he sold minus his cost; if the value has increased, his purchase price is higher than the sale price, and the short seller has a loss. The nature of the gain or loss on a short sale depends upon the nature of the property used to close the short transaction.

If the property used to close the short sale is a capital asset in the hands of the short seller, the gain or loss on the transaction is capital gain or loss. (Code Sec. 1233(a); Reg § 1.1233-1(a)(1))[28] Where the property used to close the short sale is a capital asset, the period the taxpayer held the property determines whether the gain or loss is long or short term, unless the limits at ¶2640 *et seq.* apply. (Reg § 1.1233-1(a)(3))[29]

caution: Entering into certain short sales may result in a taxpayer recognizing gain under the constructive sale rules (¶2637 *et seq.*).

Entering into a securities futures contract (¶2661) to sell is treated as a short sale and the settlement of the contract is treated as the closing of the short sale for determining whether gain or loss is long- or short-term and for the holding period rules at ¶2670. (Code Sec. 1233(e)(2)(E))[30]

For the effect of the wash sale rules on short sales, see ¶2462.

---

25. ¶I-7739 *et seq.*; ¶12,594; TD ¶228,609 *et seq.*

26. ¶I-7736; ¶12,594; TD ¶228,606

27. ¶I-7737; ¶12,594; TD ¶228,607

28. ¶I-7704; ¶12,334.01; TD ¶228,901

29. ¶I-7708; ¶12,334.01; TD ¶228,905

30. ¶I-7712.2; ¶12,334.09; TD ¶228,911.1

¶ 2640   Capital gain limits on short sales.

Capital gain realized in a short sale is short-term, regardless of the actual holding period, where the seller either: (1) as of the date of the short sale, has owned for not more than one year (determined without regard to the effect of the short sale on the holding period, see ¶2670) property that's "substantially identical" (¶2462) to that which he used to close the sale, or (2) after the short sale and on or before its closing, he acquires substantially identical property. (Code Sec. 1233(b); Reg § 1.1233-1(c)(2)) This doesn't apply to any capital gain on property in excess of the amount of substantially identical property. This keeps the taxpayer from turning what would normally be a short-term capital gain into a long-term capital gain.[31]

The above rule applies only to stocks, securities and commodity futures. (Code Sec. 1233(e)(2)(A))[32]

¶ 2641   Capital loss limits on short sales.

If property "substantially identical" (¶2462) to that sold short was held by the taxpayer for more than one year as of the sale date, any loss on closing of the short sale is long-term capital loss, regardless of how long he held the property used to close the sale. (Code Sec. 1233(d)) This doesn't apply to any capital loss on property used to close the short sale in excess of the amount of substantially identical property. (Code Sec. 1233(e)(1))[33] This rule applies only to stocks, securities and commodity futures. (Code Sec. 1233(e)(2)(A))[34]

¶ 2642   Commodity futures and hedging transactions.

Commodity transactions are generally subject to the same rules for short sales as stocks and securities. A commodity future is a contract to buy some fixed amount of a commodity at a future date at a fixed price. Gain or loss from the short sale of a commodity future is capital gain or loss if the future used to close the short sale is a capital asset to the taxpayer. However, the short sale rules don't apply where the sale of the commodity future is a bona fide hedging transaction, see ¶2660. (Code Sec. 1233(g); Reg § 1.1233-1(b))[35] A transaction is a bona fide hedging transaction if the commodity future purchased is directly related to the taxpayer's business, e.g., flour millers buying and selling wheat futures.[36]

¶ 2643   Gain recognition required when property sold short becomes worthless.

If a taxpayer enters into a short sale of property, and that property becomes substantially worthless, the taxpayer recognizes gain in the same manner as if the short sale were closed when the property becomes substantially worthless. (Code Sec. 1233(h)(1))[37] To the extent provided in regs, this rule will also apply for any option with respect to property, any offsetting notional principal contract with respect to property, any futures or forward contract to deliver any property, and any other similar transaction. (Code Sec. 1233(h)(1))[38]

Where property becomes substantially worthless during a tax year and any short sale of the property remains open at that time, then the statutory period for the assessment of any deficiency attributable to any part of the gain on the transaction doesn't expire before the earlier of: (1) the date which is three years after the date IRS is notified by the taxpayer (in a manner that IRS may prescribe by regs) of the substantial worthlessness of the property, or (2) the date which is six years after the date the return for the tax year during which the

---

31. ¶I-7710; ¶12,334.03; TD ¶228,907   35. ¶I-7724; ¶12,334.14; TD ¶228,901
32. ¶I-7709; ¶12,334.03; TD ¶228,905   36. ¶I-7724; ¶12,334.12
33. ¶I-7714; TD ¶228,913   37. ¶I-7707.1; ¶12,334.02; TD ¶228,917
34. ¶I-7709; ¶12,334.03; TD ¶228,905   38. ¶I-2616.1; ¶12,334.02

position became substantially worthless is filed. In addition, the deficiency may be assessed before the expiration of the assessment period described above in spite of any other law or rule of law which would otherwise prevent the assessment. (Code Sec. 1233(h)(2))[39]

¶ 2644 Section 1244 ("Small Business Corporation") Stock.

Loss on the sale, exchange or worthlessness of Section 1244 stock is deductible, within limits, as an ordinary loss, even though gain on the stock is capital gain. This ordinary deduction is available only to an individual to whom the stock was issued by a small business corporation, or an individual who was a partner in a partnership at the time the stock was issued to a partnership by a small business corporation. Transferees of these original purchasers don't qualify. (Code Sec. 1244(a); Reg § 1.1244(a)-1(b)(2))[40]

The aggregate amount of the ordinary loss is limited to $50,000 on separate returns and $100,000 on joint returns each year. Spouses may deduct the $100,000 maximum in a joint return even if only one spouse owned the stock. See ¶4705 for who may file a joint return. (Code Sec. 1244(b))[41]

A loss on qualifying Section 1244 stock is deductible as an ordinary loss attributable to the shareholder's business. As such, the loss is deductible in full from gross income and may give rise to a net operating loss. Losses exceeding the limits must be treated as regular capital losses. (Code Sec. 1244(d)(3))[42]

¶ 2645 Qualifying for Section 1244 ordinary loss treatment.

To qualify as Section 1244 stock, all of the following tests must be met: (Code Sec. 1244(c))[43]

. . . The stock must be stock of a domestic corporation. It may be common or preferred, voting or nonvoting. (Reg § 1.1244(c)-1(b))[44]

. . . The stock must have been issued for money or property (other than stock and securities). But stock issued for the cancellation of corporate debt (not evidenced by a security or issued for services) does qualify. Stock issued for services rendered or to be rendered to, or for the benefit of, the issuing corporation, does not qualify. (Reg § 1.1244(c)-1(d)(1))[45]

. . . The issuing corporation must have shown that over 50% of its aggregate gross receipts within the five most recent tax years ending before the date of the loss were derived from sources other than rents, royalties, dividends, interest, annuities, and sales or exchanges of stock or securities.[46]

. . . The stock had to be issued by a domestic "small business" corporation (¶2647).[47]

¶ 2646 How to claim the Section 1244 ordinary loss—Form 4797.

Claim the ordinary loss on Form 4797 (attached to Form 1040). No information statement is required to be filed with the return but records must be maintained to establish a loss and whether the stock qualifies as Section 1244 stock. (Reg § 1.1244(e)-1(b))[48]

¶ 2647 Small business corporation (SBC) defined.

A corporation is an SBC if at the time the stock is issued its capital receipts don't exceed $1,000,000. (Special designation rules must be met for stock issued in a year capital receipts

39. ¶T-4221.2; ¶12,334.02; TD ¶228,917
40. ¶I-9503; ¶12,444.02; TD ¶247,354
41. ¶I-9505; ¶12,444.01; TD ¶247,359
42. ¶I-9502; ¶12,444; TD ¶247,353
43. ¶I-9508 *et seq.*; ¶12,444.03; TD ¶247,302

44. ¶I-9508 *et seq.*; ¶12,444.03; TD ¶247,302 *et seq.*
45. ¶I-9511, I-9512; ¶12,444.03; TD ¶247,309 *et seq.*
46. ¶I-9524 *et seq.*; ¶12,444.03; TD ¶247,336
47. ¶I-9517; ¶12444.03; TD ¶247,325 *et seq.*
48. ¶I-9537, I-9538; ¶12,444.05; TD ¶247,363, 247,365

do exceed $1,000,000.)[49] Capital receipts means the aggregate amount of money and other property received by the corporation for stock, as a contribution to capital, and as paid-in surplus. This includes amounts received for the Section 1244 stock and for all stock issued previously. (Code Sec. 1244(c)(3)(A))[50]

¶ 2648   Exclusion of Gain from Qualified Small Business Stock (QSBS). ███████

Under the rules described below, a taxpayer (other than a corporation) may exclude all (or, in some cases, part) of the gain realized on the disposition of QSBS (¶2649) held for more than five years. (Code Sec. 1202(a)(1))

For QSBS acquired after Sep. 27, 2010 and before 2014, noncorporate taxpayers may exclude all of the gain on the disposition of QSBS stock. For QSBS acquired after Feb. 17, 2009 and before Sep. 28, 2010, noncorporate taxpayers can exclude 75% of any gain realized on the disposition of QSBS. For QSBS acquired after 2013 or before Feb. 18, 2009, noncorporate taxpayers may exclude 50% of the gain on the disposition of QSBS. (Code Sec. 1202(a))[1]

The acquisition date is the first day on which the stock was held by the taxpayer determined after the application of the holding period rules provided in Code Sec. 1223 permitting the tacking of holding periods for substituted basis property, see ¶2674. (Code Sec. 1202(a)(3); Code Sec. 1202(a)(4))

The exclusion is 60%, rather than 50%, for periods that the 75% or 100% exclusion doesn't apply, for gain on the sale of empowerment zone stock (but not District of Columbia Enterprise Zone stock) acquired after Dec. 21, 2000, held for more than five years, and not attributable to periods after 2016. The empowerment zone stock must be in a corporation that qualifies as an enterprise zone business under Code Sec. 1397C(b) during substantially all of the taxpayer's holding period. (Code Sec. 1202(a)(2))[2]

However, a taxpayer (or a related party) who takes an offsetting short position before the required five-year holding period is completed cannot exclude gain from the disposition of QSBS. (Code Sec. 1202(j))[3]

For each corporation in which the taxpayer invests, the total amount of gain eligible for the partial exclusion for a tax year may not exceed the greater of:

... $10,000,000 ($5,000,000 for marrieds filing separately) (Code Sec. 1202(b)(1)(A), Code Sec. 1202(b)(3)(A)) reduced by taxpayer's total gain on dispositions of the corporation's stock that he took into account in earlier years. (Code Sec. 1202(b)(1)(A)) The amount of eligible gain is allocated equally between spouses who file jointly (see ¶4705), to apply this limit to later years (Code Sec. 1202(b)(3)(B)); or

... ten times the aggregate adjusted bases of any of the corporation's QSBS that taxpayer disposed of during the year. (Code Sec. 1202(b)(1)(B)) For this purpose, the adjusted basis of any stock doesn't include any additions to basis after the date it was originally issued (Code Sec. 1202(b)(1)), or any reductions for SSBIC rollovers (¶2505). (Code Sec. 1044(d))[4]

The exclusion is denied where the corporation redeems stock from the taxpayer or a related person during certain periods, or buys its own stock in excess of certain amounts during specified periods. (Code Sec. 1202(c)(3))[5]

Additional rules apply where passthrough entities hold the stock. (Code Sec. 1202(g))[6]

For the rollover of gain from QSBS to other QSBS, see ¶2429.

For alternative minimum tax treatment of the exclusion, see ¶3209.

49. ¶I-9518 et seq.; ¶12,444.04; TD ¶247,326
50. ¶I-9518; ¶12,444.04; TD ¶247,327
1. ¶I-9100 et seq.; ¶12,024; TD ¶246,600 et seq.
2. ¶I-9100.1C; ¶12,024; TD ¶246,602

3. ¶I-9115; ¶12,024.03; TD ¶246,610
4. ¶I-9112 et seq.; ¶12,024.01; TD ¶246,603 et seq.
5. ¶I-9102; ¶12,024; TD ¶246,637
6. ¶I-9116; ¶12,024.03; TD ¶246,612

¶ 2649   Qualified small business stock (QSBS) defined.

QSBS is any stock (but not an option to acquire stock) in a C corporation which is originally issued after Aug. 10, '93 if:

. . . as of the date of issuance, the corporation is a qualified small business. (Code Sec. 1202(c)(1)(A)) This means a domestic C corporation whose total gross assets (treating all members of the same parent-subsidiary controlled group as one corporation) at all times after Aug. 10, '93 and before the issuance, and immediately after the issuance (taking into account amounts received in the issuance), don't exceed $50,000,000, and that meets certain reporting requirements (Code Sec. 1202(d));

. . . the taxpayer claiming the exclusion acquired the stock at its original issuance for money or other property (not stock) or as compensation for services provided to the corporation (other than services performed as an underwriter) (Code Sec. 1202(c)(1)(B)); *and*

. . . during substantially all of taxpayer's holding period for the stock, the corporation is a C corporation (other than certain excluded corporations) *and* meets an active business test. (Code Sec. 1202(c)(2)(A), Code Sec. 1202(e)) An SSBIC (¶2427) meets the active business test.[7]

¶ 2650   Tax-Free Capital Gains for Investment in Renewal Communities and DC Zone Assets.

Taxpayers will be able to exclude all capital gains realized from the sale of certain qualifying community renewal or DC Zone assets held for more than 5 years.

¶ 2651   Tax-free capital gains from sale of qualifying community renewal assets held for more than 5 years.

Taxpayers will be able to exclude 100% of their "qualified capital gain" recognized on the sale or exchange of a "qualified community asset" if the asset is (1) acquired after 2001 and before 2010 and (2) held for more than 5 years. (Code Sec. 1400F(a), Code Sec. 1400F(b)(2)(A)(i), Code Sec. 1400F(b)(3)(A), Code Sec. 1400F(b)(4)(A)(i))

"Qualified capital gain" is gain recognized on the sale or exchange of a capital asset, or property used in a trade or business, as defined in Code Sec. 1231(b), see ¶2686. (Code Sec. 1400F(c)(1)) It doesn't include (1) any gain attributable to periods before 2002 or after 2014 (Code Sec. 1400F(c)(2)), (2) gain recaptured under Code Sec. 1245 (¶2695) or under Code Sec. 1250 (¶2696) (including gain that would be recaptured if Code Sec. 1250 applied to all depreciation rather than just to additional depreciation) (Code Sec. 1400F(c)(3), Code Sec. 1400B(e)(3)), (3) gain attributable to real property, or an intangible asset, that isn't integral to a "renewal community business" (as defined in Code Sec. 1400G) (Code Sec. 1400F(c)(3), Code Sec. 1400B(e)(4)), and (4) gain attributable in whole or in part to certain related-party transactions. (Code Sec. 1400F(c)(3), Code Sec. 1400B(e)(5))

A "qualified community asset" is qualifying stock in a U.S. corporation (defined in Code Sec. 1400F(b)(2)), a qualifying capital or a profits interest in a U.S. partnership (defined in Code Sec. 1400F(b)(3)), or qualifying community business property (defined in Code Sec. 1400F(b)(4)).

Special rules apply for subsequent holders of qualifying property, and where qualifying community assets cease to qualify as a renewal community business (or property ceases to be used in such a business) after the 5-year period beginning after the date the taxpayer acquired the assets. (Code Sec. 1400F(d))[8]

---

7. ¶I-9101 *et seq.*; ¶12,024.02; TD ¶246,639 *et seq.*   8. ¶I-8801 *et seq.*; ¶14,00F4; TD ¶229,952 *et seq.*

¶ 2652   Tax-free gain from the sale or exchange of qualifying DC Zone assets.

Gross income doesn't include qualified capital gain from the sale or exchange of any DC Zone asset held for more than five years. Qualified capital gain is any gain recognized on the sale or exchange of: a capital asset, or property used in the trade or business. (Code Sec. 1400B(a), Code Sec. 1400B(e)(1))

Qualified capital gain does *not* include any gain (1) attributable to periods before '98 or after 2014 (Code Sec. 1400B(e)(2)), (2) which would be treated as ordinary income under the recapture rules of Code Sec. 1245 (¶2695) or Code Sec. 1250 (¶2696) if Code Sec. 1250 applied to all depreciation rather than the additional depreciation (Code Sec. 1400B(e)(3)), (3) which is attributable to real property, or an intangible asset, that is not an integral part of a DC Zone business (Code Sec. 1400B(e)(4)), or (4) which is attributable, directly or indirectly, in whole or in part, to a transaction with a related person (under Code Sec. 267(b) (¶2448) or Code Sec. 707(b)(1)) (¶3732)). (Code Sec. 1400B(e)(5))

In general, a DC Zone asset is qualifying DC Zone business stock, DC Zone partnership interests, and DC Zone business property, acquired before 2012. (Code Sec. 1400B(b)(1))[9]

¶ 2653   Tax Straddles and Section 1256 Contracts. ■■■■■■■■■■■■■■■■■■■■■■

Losses on certain unregulated straddles are deferred, to the extent taxpayer has an offsetting unrecognized gain. Related interest and carrying charges must be capitalized. Regulated futures contracts are subject to the "mark-to-market" rule which treats the unrealized capital gain (or loss) from the contract for the year as 60% long-term and 40% short-term. Hedging transactions are excepted from these rules.

There are a number of rules provided to restrict tax avoidance opportunities in commodity futures straddles and to curb certain tax shelters involving tax straddles.[10]

Under the constructive sale rules (¶2637), a taxpayer must recognize gain (but not loss) upon entering into a constructive sale of any appreciated financial position in stock, a partnership interest, or certain debt instruments. (Code Sec. 1259). The constructive sale rules generally are intended to apply to transactions that are identified as hedging or straddle transactions under other Code provisions such as Code Sec. 1092(a)(2) (dealing with a special rule for straddles that are identified as straddles at the close of a tax year), Code Sec. 1092(b)(2) (dealing with regs with respect to identified mixed straddles, ¶2658), Code Sec. 1092(e) (dealing with an exception for hedging transactions), and Code Sec. 1256(e) (dealing with the nonapplication of the mark-to-market rules to hedging transactions, ¶2660).[11]

The interest and carrying charges properly allocable to personal property that is part of a straddle aren't deductible, but must be charged to the capital account of the property for which they were paid or incurred. (Code Sec. 263(g)(1)) However this requirement doesn't apply to any identified hedging transactions (¶2660). (Code Sec. 263(g)(3))[12]

¶ 2654   Straddle defined.

A straddle is "offsetting positions" with respect to personal property. (Code Sec. 1092(c)(1)) A "position" is an interest, including a futures or forward contract or option, in personal property. (Code Sec. 1092(d)(2)) In general, personal property does not include stock (but it does include stock options and contracts to buy stock). (Code Sec. 1092(d)(3)(A)) However, stock is included in the definition of personal property for straddle purposes if (1) the stock is part of a straddle in which at least one of the offsetting positions is either an option to buy or sell the stock or substantially identical stock or securities, or a position on substantially

---

9. ¶I-8750 *et seq.*; ¶14,00B4; TD ¶246,550 *et seq.*
10. ¶I-7500 *et seq.*; ¶10,924; TD ¶228,401

11. ¶I-7746
12. ¶L-5985; ¶2634; TD ¶228,715

similar or related property (other than stock); or (2) the stock is in a corporation formed or availed of to take positions in personal property that offset positions taken by any shareholder. (Code Sec. 1092(d)(3)(B))

A taxpayer holds "offsetting positions" if he has reduced his risk of loss from holding the property by holding one (or more) other positions, whether or not the items of personal property involved in the different positions are the same kind. (Code Sec. 1092(c)(2)(A))[13]

An obligation under a debt instrument may be a position in personal property that is part of a straddle. (Reg § 1.1092(d)-1T(d))

¶ 2655 Recognition of losses postponed on certain nonregulated futures straddles (loss deferral rule).

Loss deductions on nonregulated straddles, that is, those straddle positions not on the "mark-to-market" system (see ¶2656), are limited to the amount by which the losses exceed "unrecognized gains" on any offsetting straddle positions. Losses in excess of the limitation (deferred losses) are carried forward to the next year and are subject to the deferral rules in that year. (Code Sec. 1092(a)(1))[14]

¶ 2656 Regulated futures contracts, etc. (Section 1256 contracts), under "mark-to-market" system.

Taxpayers must report (on Form 6781) gains and losses from regulated futures contracts and other "Section 1256 contracts" (¶2657) on an annual basis under the "mark-to-market" rule. All Section 1256 contracts must be marked to market at year end. Each Section 1256 contract held by a taxpayer is treated as if it were sold for fair market value on the last business day of the year. (Code Sec. 1256(a)(1)) If a taxpayer holds Section 1256 contracts at the beginning of a tax year, any gain or loss later realized on the contracts must be adjusted to reflect any gain or loss taken into account with respect to the contracts in an earlier year. (Code Sec. 1256(a)(2))

Any capital gain or loss on a Section 1256 futures contract that is marked-to-market is treated as if 40% of the gain or loss is short-term capital gain or loss, and as if 60% of the gain or loss is long-term capital gain or loss. (Code Sec. 1256(a)(3))[15]

The wash sale rules (¶2462) don't apply to losses taken into account when a Section 1256 contract is marked to market. (Code Sec. 1256(f)(5))[16]

¶ 2657 Section 1256 contracts defined.

Section 1256 contracts include: regulated futures contracts, foreign currency contracts, nonequity options, dealer equity options, and dealer securities futures contracts (¶2663). (Code Sec. 1256(b))[17] For a partnership that's a qualified fund, Section 1256 contracts include bank forward contracts, foreign currency futures contracts, and similar instruments prescribed by IRS regs. (Code Sec. 988(c)(1)(E)(iv)(I))[18] However, a foreign currency call option isn't a foreign currency transaction that is treated as a Section 1256 contract. [19]

Section 1256 contracts do not include any securities futures contract, or option on a securities futures contract, unless the contract or option is a dealer securities futures contract, or any interest rate swap, currency swap, basis swap, interest rate cap, interest rate floor, commodity swap, equity swap, equity index swap, credit default swap, or similar agreement. (Code Sec. 1256(b)(2))[20]

---

13. ¶I-7503 *et seq.*; ¶10,924; TD ¶228,406
14. ¶I-7501; ¶10,924; TD ¶228,403
15. ¶I-7602, ¶I-7603.3; ¶12,564 *et seq.*; TD ¶228,700 *et seq.*
16. ¶I-7602; ¶12,564.02; TD ¶228,701

17. ¶I-7604; ¶12,564.01; TD ¶228,704
18. ¶I-7607; ¶9884.01
19. ¶I-7611
20. ¶I-7604; ¶12,564.01

¶ 2658   Election for mixed straddles.

If straddles are composed of at least one position in a Section 1256 contract (¶2657) and one or more positions in interests in property that aren't Section 1256 contracts, a taxpayer may elect on Form 6781 to exclude all positions in the mixed straddle (including Section 1256 contracts) from the mark-to-market rules, in which case they will be subject to the loss deferral, wash sale, and short sale rules, and the straddle won't be a mixed straddle. (Code Sec. 1256(d))[21] If that election isn't made, so that the straddle is a mixed straddle, a taxpayer may elect to offset gains and losses in the mixed straddle by either separately identifying the positions of the mixed straddle or establishing a mixed straddle account. (Reg § 1.1092(b)-4T)[22]

For all identified mixed straddles established after Aug. 1, 2013, unrealized gain or loss on a position held before establishing an identified mixed straddle is taken into account at the time, and has the character, provided by the Code provisions that would apply if the identified mixed straddle had not been established. (Reg § 1.1092(b)-6T(a))[23]

¶ 2659   Carryback election for losses from Section 1256 contracts—Form 6781.

Taxpayers other than corporations, estates or trusts can elect to carry net Section 1256 losses back 3 years and apply them against net Section 1256 gains for the period. The carryback is available only if, after netting Section 1256 contracts and other positions subject to the mark-to-market rule with capital gains and losses from other sources, there is a net capital loss for the tax year which, but for the election, would be a capital loss in the succeeding year. The lesser of that net capital loss or the net loss resulting from the application of the mark-to-market rules is the net Section 1256 loss which may be carried back. Capital losses carried back must be treated as if 40% of the losses are short-term capital losses and 60% are long-term capital losses. The losses must be absorbed in the earliest year to which they may be carried back. Any remainder is then carried forward to the next year. The losses may be applied in the carryback year against the lesser of net Section 1256 contracts gain or capital gain net income for that year. (Code Sec. 1212(c))

Capital losses that are carried forward, to the extent they were determined under the mark-to-market rule, continue to be treated as losses from Section 1256 contracts in the year to which they are carried. (Code Sec. 1212(c)(6))[24]

¶ 2660   Hedging transactions not covered by the mark-to-market rules.

The "mark-to-market" rules don't apply to "hedging transactions" as defined in Code Sec. 1256(e)(2). (Code Sec. 1256(e)(1))[25]

¶ 2661   Securities Futures Contracts. ▇▇▇▇▇▇▇▇▇▇▇▇▇▇▇▇▇▇▇▇

Gain or loss from a securities futures contract generally has the same character as gain or loss from transactions in the underlying security. A dealer securities futures contract is treated as a section 1256 contract.

¶ 2662   Gain or loss from nondealer securities futures contracts.

Gain or loss on the sale, exchange, or termination of a securities futures contract (as defined in Code Sec. 1234B(c)) generally has the same character as gain or loss from transactions in the underlying security. (Code Sec. 1234B(a)(1)) For example, if the underlying asset

21. ¶I-7616; ¶12,564.03; TD ¶228,714
22. ¶I-7571 *et seq.*; ¶10,924
23. ¶I-7570; ¶10,924

24. ¶I-7606; ¶12,124.02; TD ¶228,706
25. ¶I-7620; ¶12,564.05; TD ¶228,715

would be a capital asset in the hands of the taxpayer, gain or loss from the sale of the contract is capital gain or loss. This rule does not apply to securities futures contracts that are not capital assets because they are Code Sec. 1221(a)(1) inventory assets, are identified as Code Sec. 1221(a)(7) hedging transactions, or any income derived in connection with a contract which would otherwise not be capital gain. (Code Sec. 1234B(a)(2))[26]

Except as provided in regs to Code Sec. 1092(b) or Code Sec. 1234B, or in Code Sec. 1233, capital gain or loss from the sale, exchange, or termination of a securities futures contract to sell property is treated as short-term capital gain or loss. (Code Sec. 1234B(b))

If the security to which a securities futures contract (that is not a Code Sec. 1256 contract (see ¶2663)) relates is acquired in satisfaction of that contract, the taxpayer's holding period for the security includes the period for which the taxpayer held the contract if the contract was a capital asset in the taxpayer's hands. (Code Sec. 1223(14))[27]

¶ 2663 Dealer securities futures contracts are section 1256 contracts.

Dealer securities futures contracts are treated as Code Sec. 1256 contracts (¶2656). (Code Sec. 1256(b)(1)(E)) A dealer securities futures contract is any securities futures contract (see ¶2662) and any option to enter into such a contract that (1) is entered into by the dealer (or, in the case of an option, is purchased or granted by the dealer) in the normal course of his activity of dealing in such contracts or options, as the case may be, and (2) is traded on a qualified board or exchange. (Code Sec. 1256(g)(9)(A))[28]

¶ 2664 Conversion and Constructive Ownership Transactions. ▬▬▬▬▬▬

Capital gain on the disposition of property that was part of a conversion transaction (i.e., functionally equivalent to a loan) is treated as ordinary income. Certain gains from derivative contracts (constructive ownership transactions) with respect to financial assets are recharacterized as ordinary income.

¶ 2665 Gain recharacterized on conversion transactions similar to loans.

Gain recognized on the disposition or other termination of any position held as part of a conversion transaction (defined below), that would otherwise be treated as capital gain, is treated as ordinary income, to the extent it doesn't exceed the applicable imputed income amount. (Code Sec. 1258(a))[29] The applicable imputed income amount equals the excess of (1) taxpayer's net investment in the transaction multiplied by 120% of (a) the applicable federal rate (¶1116), compounded semiannually, for the period covered by the transaction, if the transaction has a definite term, or of (b) the federal short-term rates (compounded daily) in effect under Code Sec. 6621(b) for the period of the conversion transaction, if the term of the transaction is indefinite, over (2) the amount already so treated with respect to the same transaction. (Code Sec. 1258(b), Code Sec. 1258(d)(2))[30]

When a taxpayer disposes or terminates all positions of an identified (as part of the same transaction, on taxpayer's books and records) netting transaction within a 14-day period in a single tax year, all gains and losses on those positions realized within that period are netted to determine the amount of gain treated as ordinary income. (Reg § 1.1258-1(b))[31]

A conversion transaction is any transaction where substantially all of taxpayer's expected net return is attributable to the time value of his net investment, and which is:

... the holding of any property (whether or not actively traded) and substantially contemporaneous making of a contract to sell that or substantially identical property at a price

---

26. ¶I-6280 *et seq.*; ¶12,34B4; TD ¶250,200 *et seq.*
27. ¶I-8924.1; ¶12,234.27; TD ¶223,521
28. ¶I-7615.1; ¶12,564.01; TD ¶228,712

29. ¶I-8200 *et seq.*; ¶12,584; TD ¶227,801
30. ¶I-8208; ¶12,584; TD ¶227,806
31. ¶I-8209.1 *et seq.*; ¶12,584; TD ¶227,802

determined in accordance with the contract (Code Sec. 1258(c)(2)(A));

. . . a straddle (¶2654) of actively traded personal property (Code Sec. 1258(c)(2)(B));

. . . any other transaction that is marketed or sold as producing capital gains, and substantially all of the expected return from that transaction is attributable to the time value of the taxpayer's net investment in the transaction (Code Sec. 1258(c)(2)(C)); or

. . . any other transaction specified in regs to be issued. (Code Sec. 1258(c)(2)(D))[32]

Conversion transactions don't include transactions of options dealers and commodities traders in the normal course of their trade or business. (Code Sec. 1258(d)(5)(A))[33]

¶ 2666   Certain long-term capital gains from constructive ownership transactions are recharacterized as ordinary income.

The amount of long-term capital gain a taxpayer can recognize from certain derivative contracts (constructive ownership transactions (defined in Code Sec. 1260(d))) with respect to certain financial assets is limited, and an interest charge is imposed on the tax underpayment for each year that the constructive ownership transaction was open. (Code Sec. 1260) If a taxpayer has gain from a constructive ownership transaction with respect to any financial asset and that gain would otherwise be treated as a long-term capital gain, then (1) the gain is treated as ordinary income to the extent it exceeds the net underlying long-term capital gain, and (2) to the extent gain is treated as long-term capital gain, the determination of the capital gain rate (or rates) applicable to the gain under Code Sec. 1(h) (i.e., the individual capital gains rates) is determined on the basis of the respective rate (or rates) that would have applied to the net underlying long-term capital gain. (Code Sec. 1260(a))[34]

¶ 2667   Holding Period.

The length of time that a capital asset is held before its sale or exchange determines whether the proceeds from the sale or exchange are taxable as long-term capital gain or loss or as short-term capital gain or loss.

The length of time an asset is held is also crucial in qualifying for Section 1231 (capital gain/ordinary loss) treatment, see ¶2686.

Holding a capital asset for the short-term holding period (one year or less) results in short-term capital gain or loss on the sale or exchange of that asset. (Code Sec. 1222(1), Code Sec. 1222(2)) Holding a capital asset for the long-term holding period (more than one year) results in long-term capital gain or loss on the sale or exchange of that asset. (Code Sec. 1222(3), Code Sec. 1222(4))[35]

The long-term holding period is more than six months for futures transactions in any commodity subject to the rules of a board of trade or commodity exchange. (Code Sec. 1222)[36]

¶ 2668   How to measure the holding period.

The holding period is computed in terms of calendar months, not days.[37] It begins on the day after the day of acquisition and ends on the day of sale, exchange or other disposition. Thus, the taxpayer excludes the day of acquisition but includes the date of disposition.[38]

illustration: A capital asset is acquired on Feb. 15. To meet the long-term holding period, it must be held until Feb. 16 of the following year. To meet the more-than-six-month long-term holding period for a commodity future (¶2667), it must be held until Aug. 16 of

---

32. ¶I-8205; ¶12,584; TD ¶227,805
33. ¶I-8210 *et seq.*; ¶12,584
34. ¶I-8251; ¶12,604; TD ¶229,551
35. ¶I-8901; ¶12,234; TD ¶223,501

36. ¶I-8971; ¶12,234.27; TD ¶223,550
37. ¶I-8904; ¶12,234.01; TD ¶223,504
38. ¶s I-8904, I-8906; ¶12,234.01; TD ¶223,502

the year in which it was bought. If the asset were acquired on Jan. 31, it would have to be held until Feb. 1 of the following year to meet the more-than-one-year holding period, or until Aug. 1 of the year in which it was bought to meet the more-than-six-month period.

¶ 2669 Holding period of partnership interest.

A partner doesn't have a divided holding period in his partnership interest unless he acquired parts of it at different times or in exchange for property transferred at the same time but resulting in different holding periods. (Reg § 1.1223-3(a)) The holding period of a part of a partnership interest is determined based on a fraction equal to the fair market value (FMV) of the part of the partnership interest received in the transaction to which the holding period relates over the FMV of the entire partnership interest (determined immediately after the transaction). (Reg § 1.1223-3(b))[39]

illustration: A contributes $50,000 and a nondepreciable capital asset that he's held for two years to a partnership for a 50% interest in it. His basis in the capital asset is $50,000, and its FMV is $100,000. After the exchange, A's basis in his interest in the partnership is $100,000, and the FMV of the interest is $150,000. A's holding period in one-third of the interest received for cash begins on the day after the contribution. Under Code Sec. 1223(1), A has a two-year holding period in two-thirds of the interest received in the partnership for the capital asset.

¶ 2670 Holding period for stocks and securities.

The holding period for stocks and securities acquired by purchase, whether on a registered securities exchange or in the "over-the-counter" market, is determined by reference to the "trade date" on which the stock or security is acquired and the "trade date" on which it is sold. The "settlement dates" aren't considered. [40]

The holding period for stock or securities acquired from a corporation by the exercise of rights begins on, and includes, the day the rights are exercised. (Code Sec. 1223(5); Reg § 1.1223-1(f))[41]

The holding period for property "substantially identical" to that sold short in a transaction to which the rule at ¶2640 applies is considered to begin on the day the short sale is closed or, if earlier, on the date the property is sold, given away or otherwise disposed of. (Code Sec. 1233(b)(2); Reg § 1.1233-1(c)(2))[42]

The holding period for stock, stock rights or other property received as a taxable dividend begins on the date the distribution is actually or constructively received.[43] If the distribution is tax-free, the holding period for the stock, etc., includes the period that the underlying stock was held. (Code Sec. 1223(4); Reg § 1.1223-1(e))[44]

The holding period for restricted stock (or property) begins after it is substantially vested, unless an election (¶1218) is made to include the property in income in the year of transfer, in which case it begins just after the transfer. (Code Sec. 83(f); Reg § 1.83-4(a))[45]

Where the loss on a sale of stock or securities is disallowed under the "wash sale" rules (¶2461), the holding period for the new similar stock includes the holding period for the old stock that was sold. (Code Sec. 1223(3))[46]

The holding period for U.S. Treasury bonds and notes is measured from the acquisition date; for those sold at auction, this is the date the Treasury gives notice of acceptance to

---

39. ¶I-8934.1; ¶12,234.29; TD ¶223,556
40. ¶I-8914 *et seq.*; ¶12,234.07; TD ¶223,513
41. ¶I-8924; ¶12,234.25; TD ¶223,520
42. ¶I-7720; ¶12,334.03; TD ¶228,919

43. ¶I-8918; ¶12,234.25; TD ¶223,517
44. ¶I-8921; ¶3054.02; TD ¶223,518
45. ¶I-8916; ¶834 *et seq.*; TD ¶223,515
46. ¶I-8929; ¶12,234.25; TD ¶223,525

bidders; for those sold in a subscription offering at a specified interest rate, it's the date the buyer submits an offer.[47]

If an individual elects to roll over gain from qualified small business stock (QSBS) by way of the timely acquisition of other QSBS stock (¶2429), the holding period for the acquired QSBS stock includes the holding period for the sold QSBS stock. (Code Sec. 1223(13))[48]

¶ 2671   Property acquired through options.

The holding period for property acquired through the exercise of an option begins the day after the option is exercised.[49]

¶ 2672   Holding period for property inherited from a decedent.

The holding period of property acquired from a decedent starts with the date of death.[50] However, property acquired from a decedent which is sold within the short-term capital gain holding period after the decedent's death is considered to be held for the *long*-term capital gain holding period if the person selling the property has a basis that is determined under Code Sec. 1014 (by reference to the property's fair market value on the date of death or alternate valuation date). (Code Sec. 1223(9))[1]

The long-term holding period is also met where special use valuation property (¶5017) is acquired by a "qualified heir" from the decedent's estate, and is sold within the short-term holding period to another "qualified heir." (Code Sec. 1223(10))[2]

The holding period of the surviving spouse's share of community property that vested at the time of the acquisition by the community (as opposed to the share inherited from the deceased spouse) starts from the date of acquisition. See ¶4705 for who is treated as a spouse.[3]

If an election out of the estate tax is made for the estate of a decedent who died in 2010, the transfer of property to the estate or other recipient is treated as made by gift for purposes of determining the holding period, so that the decedent's holding period is tacked on for purposes of determining how long the property was held (¶2673).[4]

¶ 2673   Holding period for gifts.

The holding period for property acquired by gift includes the donor's holding period if the property has the same basis for gain or loss (see ¶2463 *et seq.*) in whole or in part in the hands of the donee as it would have in the donor's hands. (Code Sec. 1223(2); Reg § 1.1223-1(b)) But if the property is sold by the donee at a loss based on its market value on the date of the gift (and not the donor's basis), the holding period starts from the date of the gift.[5]

¶ 2674   Tax-free exchange property.

The holding period for property received in a partially or wholly tax-free exchange (¶2413), includes the holding period for the property surrendered. This "tacking on" applies where the new property has the same basis, in whole or in part, as the old property (Code Sec. 1223(1)), e.g., like-kind exchanges, tax-free stock distributions (¶2670), involuntary conversions (¶2675), or incorporations and tax-free corporate reorganizations (¶3510 *et seq.*).[6]

---

47. ¶I-8915; TD ¶223,514
48. ¶I-9207; ¶12,234.24; TD ¶247,211
49. ¶I-8949; ¶12,234.10; TD ¶223,542
50. ¶I-8944; ¶12,234.21; TD ¶223,537
1. ¶I-8942; ¶12,234.21; TD ¶223,535

2. ¶I-8943; ¶12,234.21; TD ¶223,536
3. ¶I-8945; ¶12,234.21; TD ¶223,538
4. ¶I-8942.1; ¶10,224.07; TD ¶223,535.1
5. ¶I-8966; ¶12,234.22; TD ¶223,511
6. ¶I-8960 *et seq.*; ¶12,234.18; TD ¶223,507

¶ 2675　Replacements for property lost or damaged in an involuntary conversion.

The holding period of the original property is tacked on to that of property acquired to replace property lost or damaged in an involuntary conversion (¶2430 *et seq.*), where gain isn't recognized.[7]

¶ 2676　Sales and Exchanges.

Unless a transaction involving a capital asset is treated as a sale or exchange, any resulting gain or loss doesn't qualify as capital gain or loss.

A sale is a transfer of property for an amount of money or a money equivalent that is fixed or determinable. An exchange is a transfer of property for property other than money or a cash equivalent. (Reg § 1.1002-1(d))[8]

To qualify as a sale or exchange, the transaction must be complete, and bona fide in all respects. If it's real in substance as well as form, it qualifies as a sale or exchange even though it was designed to reduce taxes.[9] However, it may be treated as a sham for tax purposes if (a) there is no business motive for the transaction other than getting tax benefits, and (b) the transaction has no economic substance. (Code Sec. 7701(o))[10]

Where shareholders deal with their corporation, or family members sell or exchange property among themselves, IRS scrutinizes the deal closely. If a sale or exchange is a sham, IRS can disallow any of the sought-after tax benefits.[11]

¶ 2677　Gain or loss from certain terminations treated as capital gain or loss.

Gain or loss attributable to the cancellation, lapse, expiration, or other termination of the following is treated as gain or loss from the sale of a capital asset:

(1) A right or obligation (other than a securities futures contract under Code Sec. 1234B) with respect to property which is (or on acquisition would be) a capital asset in the hands of the taxpayer (Code Sec. 1234A(1)), or

(2) A section 1256 contract (¶2657) not described in (1) above which is a capital asset in the hands of the taxpayer. (Code Sec. 1234A(2))

These rules don't apply to the retirement of any debt instrument (whether or not through a trust or other participation arrangement). (Code Sec. 1234A)[12]

¶ 2678　Retirement of debt instruments.

In general, amounts received by a holder on retirement of a debt instrument are treated as received in exchange for the debt instrument. (Code Sec. 1271(a)(1))[13]

observation: To the extent that an instrument issued with original issue discount (OID) (¶1313) is retired at face value before maturity, part of the amount received on the retirement will be treated as OID.

¶ 2679　Payment of debt with property as a sale.

A debtor realizes gain or loss when he transfers property to his creditor in complete or partial satisfaction of his debt. The transfer is treated as a sale or exchange of the property by the debtor. Gain or loss is the difference between the amount of debt satisfied and the basis of

---

7. ¶I-8963; ¶12,234.18; TD ¶223,507
8. ¶I-1002, I-1104; ¶12,224.07; TD ¶220,201
9. ¶I-1212 *et seq.*; ¶12,224.07; TD ¶220,600 *et seq.*
10. ¶M-5901

11. ¶I-1201 *et seq.*; TD ¶220,801
12. ¶I-7619; ¶12,34A4; TD ¶221,208
13. ¶I-1901; ¶12,714; TD ¶221,501

the transferred property.[14]

¶ 2680 Cancellation of lease or distribution agreement as sale or exchange.

Amounts received by a lessee or tenant for the cancellation of a lease, or by a distributor of goods for the cancellation of a distributorship agreement, are considered amounts received *in exchange* for the lease or agreement. (Code Sec. 1241)[15] Thus, Section 1231 treatment (¶2684) is available for gain or loss from the cancellation of a business lease or distributorship held long-term. If the lease was for the tenant's home, a gain would be taxed as a capital gain, but any loss wouldn't be deductible.[16]

¶ 2681 Convertible bonds.

No gain or loss is realized upon the conversion of bonds into stock of the *same* corporation under a conversion privilege set forth in the terms of the bond.[17]

¶ 2682 Sale with leaseback, reservations or restrictions.

The fact that a sale of property is accompanied by a leaseback doesn't bar recognizing the sale as closed for tax purposes.[18] However, a leaseback of realty (including renewal options) extending for 30 years or more may be considered an exchange of like-kind property on which gain or loss isn't recognized.[19] A sale restricting the buyer's use of the property may be recognized as a completed sale, as where stock is sold subject to security-device restrictions,[20] but if the rights retained are significant enough, the seller may be considered as selling only a partial interest or as granting a license to use.[21]

¶ 2683 Part gift, part sale; conditional gifts.

If an owner combines a gift with a sale (e.g., to a family member), gain is realized to the extent the price received exceeds the owner's adjusted basis. However, no loss is recognized if the amount received is less than the owner's basis. (Reg § 1.1001-1(e))[22]

If a donor gives appreciated property to a donee on condition the donee pay the donor's gift tax, there's a sale by the donor for the amount of the gift tax. To the extent the gift tax paid by the donee exceeds the donor's basis, the donor has income.[23]

¶ 2684 Capital Gain—Ordinary Loss Rule.

Under Code Sec. 1231, if there's a net gain for the tax year from (1) sales and exchanges of property used in a trade or business, and (2) involuntary or compulsory conversions of certain assets used in the trade or business or held in connection with a trade or business or a transaction entered for profit, it's treated as long-term capital gain. A net loss is treated as an ordinary loss.

¶ 2685 Applying the Section 1231 rules—Form 4797.

If the recognized gains are greater than the recognized losses on sales, exchanges and involuntary conversions of Section 1231 assets, the net amount is treated as a long-term capital gain, except as discussed below. But, if those losses are greater than those gains, the net amount is treated as an ordinary loss. (Code Sec. 1231(a); Reg § 1.1231-1(b))[24] Section

14. ¶I-1501 *et seq.*; ¶10,014.76; TD ¶221,401
15. ¶I-1400 *et seq.*; ¶12,414; TD ¶221,201
16. ¶M-1500; ¶12,414
17. ¶I-1909; ¶10,014.42; TD ¶221,505
18. ¶I-1122; TD ¶220,620
19. ¶I-3077; TD ¶223,717
20. ¶I-1125
21. ¶I-1602 *et seq.*
22. ¶I-1006; ¶10,014.06; TD ¶220,205
23. ¶I-1007; TD ¶222,411
24. ¶I-9001; ¶12,314; TD ¶223,201

1231 gains and losses are reported and netted on Form 4797.

A net Section 1231 gain is treated as ordinary income to the extent of nonrecaptured net Section 1231 losses. (Code Sec. 1231(c)(1))

A nonrecaptured net Section 1231 loss is the net Section 1231 loss for the five most recent preceding tax years that hasn't been offset by a net Section 1231 gain in an intervening tax year. (Code Sec. 1231(c)(2)) Net Section 1231 gain means the excess of the Section 1231 gains over the Section 1231 losses. Net Section 1231 loss means the excess of the Section 1231 losses over the Section 1231 gains. (Code Sec. 1231(c)(3), Code Sec. 1231(c)(4))[25]

illustration: X Corp., a calendar year taxpayer, had a net Section 1231 loss of $1,000,000 in 2009 that was offset against ordinary income. X Corp. had no net Section 1231 gain in 2010, 2011, or 2012, but has a net Section 1231 gain of $1,400,000 (consisting of a $2,000,000 gain on condemnation of land, and a $600,000 loss on the sale of machinery) in 2013. $1,000,000 of the net Section 1231 gain for 2013 is treated as ordinary income, and the remaining $400,000 is treated as long-term capital gain.

If the recognized losses from involuntary conversions arising from fire, storm, shipwreck or other casualty, or from theft, exceed the recognized gain, they aren't included in the Section 1231 computations. (Code Sec. 1231(a)(4)(C), Code Sec. 1231(c)(5))[26]

observation: This means that losses from such involuntary conversions will be treated as ordinary losses, but will not reduce the amount of net Section 1231 gains realized from other transactions eligible for capital gain treatment. However, if there is a net gain from such involuntary conversions, that net gain will be eligible for Section 1231 treatment.

Capital gain treatment under Section 1231 is also barred to the extent that the depreciation recapture rules apply, see ¶2692 *et seq.*

¶ 2686   Section 1231 assets defined.

Section 1231 assets are certain assets used in taxpayer's trade or business that were held for more than one year at the time of disposition. Except as explained below, these assets include depreciable tangible and intangible personal property, and real property, whether or not depreciable. They include timber, certain livestock (other than poultry), and unharvested crops that are transferred with land. (Code Sec. 1231(b))

They don't include: (1) inventory, (2) property held primarily for sale to customers in the ordinary course of the taxpayer's business, (3) copyrights, artistic, literary, or musical compositions (unless, for musical compositions or copyrights in them, the election discussed at ¶2622 is made), letters or memoranda, or similar property, in the hands of the creator or other taxpayer described in Code Sec. 1221(a)(3), and (4) U.S. government publications obtained without charge or below the price sold to the general public. (Code Sec. 1231(b)(1); Reg § 1.1231-1(c))[27]

Property held for rent usually is treated as property used in business, but IRS (with the support of some, but not all, courts) denies this status where rental activity is slight.[28]

If, for estates of decedents who died in 2010, the election is made to have the estate not be subject to the estate tax and to apply modified carryover basis rules to property acquired from a decedent (¶2523), safe harbor guidance applies to the question of whether the property continues to be a Section 1231 asset in the hands of the estate or other recipient.[29]

25. ¶I-9003; ¶12,314.15; TD ¶223,205
26. ¶I-9004; ¶s 12,314.09, 12,314.15; TD ¶223,206
27. ¶I-9007 *et seq.*; ¶12,314 *et seq.*; TD ¶223,208 *et seq.*

28. ¶I-9013; ¶12,314.02 *et seq.*; TD ¶223,213
29. ¶I-5004.1; ¶10,224; TD ¶223,007.1

¶ 2687　Timber cutting treated as sale or exchange—Form T.

A taxpayer who owned timber, or had a contract right to cut it, for more than one year before it was cut, may elect to treat the cutting as a sale or exchange qualifying for Section 1231 capital gain-ordinary loss treatment. Taxpayers who elect must file Form T with their returns unless they only have an occasional sale of timber. Once made, the election can be revoked only with IRS's consent unless it was made for a tax year ending before Oct. 23, 2004, in which case it can be revoked for any later tax year without IRS's consent. (Code Sec. 631(a); Code Sec. 1231(b)(2); ; Reg § 1.631-1)[30]

¶ 2688　Timber, coal or U.S. iron ore sold with a retained economic interest.

A disposition of timber, coal or U.S. iron ore held more than 1 year qualifies for Section 1231 treatment if disposed of under a contract in which the taxpayer retains an economic interest. (Code Sec. 631(b), Code Sec. 631(c), Code Sec. 1231(b)(2); Reg § 1.631-2(a)(1), Reg § 1.631-3(a)(1))[31] For sales of timber, Section 1231 treatment also applies if the owner makes an outright sale of the timber even if no economic interest is retained. (Code Sec. 631(b))[32]

When the disposition qualifies for Section 1231 treatment, no cost depletion deduction (¶1977) is allowed. (Reg § 1.611-1(b)(2)) And, for dispositions of coal and iron ore, no percentage depletion deduction is allowed if the maximum tax rate for the year on net capital gain is less than the maximum rate for ordinary income. (Code Sec. 631(c); Reg § 1.611-1(b)(2))[33]

¶ 2689　Advance payments for timber, coal or domestic iron ore.

Advance or minimum royalty payments or other amounts received or accrued before cutting of timber or before the mining of coal or iron ore (disposed of with a retained economic interest) are treated as realized from a sale subject to Section 1231 if the contract of disposal provides that they are to be applied as payment for timber cut later or coal or iron ore mined later. (Reg § 1.631-2(d)(1), Reg § 1.631-3(c)(1)) But if the right to cut or to mine ends or is abandoned before the timber, coal or iron ore that has been paid for is cut or mined, the advance payments for them are ordinary income. (Reg § 1.631-2(d)(2), Reg § 1.631-3(c)(2))

If the taxpayer elects to treat the date of payment as the date of disposal of timber (Code Sec. 631(b); Reg § 1.631-2(b)(1)), Section 1231 applies only if the timber is held for the required period at the time of the advance payment. (Reg § 1.631-2(c)(2)) If the election isn't made, the required holding period is measured as of the time it's cut. (Reg § 1.631-2(d)(1))[34] This election is made by attaching a specified statement to the return (filed not later than the due date, including extensions) for the year payment is received. (Reg § 1.631-2(c))[35]

¶ 2690　Sale of Depreciable Property to Related Parties. ▬▬▬▬▬▬

Any recognized gain on the sale or exchange of depreciable property is ordinary income if it's made directly or indirectly between related persons.

¶ 2691　Capital gain bar on sales or exchanges of depreciable property.

In a direct or indirect sale or exchange of property between related persons, any gain recognized is treated as ordinary income if that property is, in the hands of the transferee, subject to the Code Sec. 167 allowance for depreciation, or is an amortizable Code Sec. 197 intangible asset. (Code Sec. 197(f)(7), Code Sec. 1239(a)) It also applies to property that would

---

30. ¶N-6201 *et seq.*; ¶6314 *et seq.*; TD ¶271,603 *et seq.*
31. ¶N-7001 *et seq.*; ¶6314; TD ¶223,608
32. ¶N-7001; ¶6314

33. ¶N-7021; ¶6114.013; TD ¶271,605
34. ¶N-7025 *et seq.*; ¶6314 *et seq.*
35. ¶N-7026

be subject to depreciation except that the buyer has elected amortization instead of depreciation (Reg § 1.1239-1(a)), and to patent applications. (Code Sec. 1239(e))[36]

Related persons are:

(1) a person and all entities that are controlled entities with respect to that person (see below) (Code Sec. 1239(b)(1));

(2) a taxpayer and any trust in which the taxpayer or his spouse (see ¶4705) is a beneficiary (unless the interest is a remote contingent interest) (Code Sec. 1239(b)(2));

(3) an executor of an estate and a beneficiary of the estate (except in the case of a sale or exchange in satisfaction of a pecuniary bequest) (Code Sec. 1239(b)(3));

(4) an employer and any person related to the employer (within the meaning of (1) through (3) above) (Code Sec. 1239(d)(1)); and

(5) a welfare benefit fund controlled directly or indirectly by anyone in (4), above (Code Sec. 1239(d)(2)).[37]

A controlled entity ((l), above) means, with respect to any person:

. . . a corporation more than 50% of the value of the stock of which is owned (directly or indirectly) by or for the person (Code Sec. 1239(c)(1)(A)),

. . . a partnership more than 50% of the capital interest or profits interest in which is owned (directly or indirectly) by or for the person (Code Sec. 1239(c)(1)(B)), or

. . . any entity that is a related person to the person under Code Sec. 267(b)(3) (controlled group of corporations), Code Sec. 267(b)(10) (certain related corporations and partnerships), Code Sec. 267(b)(11) (S corporations controlled by the same person), or Code Sec. 267(b)(12) (S corporations and C corporations controlled by the same person). (Code Sec. 1239(c)(1)(C))

And, under Code Sec. 267(c), there is attribution for stock owned by children, grandchildren, ancestors and siblings, as well as by the spouse (see ¶4705). (Code Sec. 1239(c)(2))[38]

¶ 2692   Depreciation Recapture.

Two provisions restrict the possibility of converting ordinary income into capital gains by use of depreciation or amortization deductions.

One applies to personal property that is Section 1245 property (¶2693); the other, to real property that is Section 1250 property (¶2694). (Code Sec. 1245(a)(3), Code Sec. 1250(c)) Recapture applies only to the extent of gain on a sale or other "disposition" (¶2699) of property. (Code Sec. 1245(a)(1), Code Sec. 1250(a)) Compute recapture on Form 4797.

¶ 2693   What is Section 1245 property?

Section 1245 property includes:

(1) all MACRS property other than residential real property (27.5-year class) and nonresidential real property (39-year class; 31.5-year class if placed in service before May 13, '93);

(2) all ACRS property other than 19-year, 18-year or 15-year real property: (a) that is residential rental property, (b) that is foreign-held realty, (c) with respect to which an optional (straight-line) cost recovery period was elected, or (d) that includes any one of certain categories of subsidized low-income rental housing;

(3) other property subject to the depreciation rules of Code Sec. 167 or the amortization rules of Code Sec. 197 (¶1974) that's personal property, certain real property (not including buildings) and real property to the extent of certain amortization (or Code Sec. 179) deductions taken.[39]

---

36. ¶I-8702; ¶12,394; TD ¶229,601
37. ¶I-8703 *et seq.*; ¶12,394; TD ¶229,602

38. ¶I-8708; ¶12,394; TD ¶229,605
39. ¶I-10101 *et seq.*; ¶12,454.01; TD ¶223,105

Section 1245 property includes property, other than a building or its structural components, used as an integral part of manufacturing, production or extraction, or for furnishing transportation, communication or other public utility services, and research or storage facilities used in connection with any of these activities. It also includes single purpose agricultural or horticultural structures, and storage facilities (except buildings and their structural components) used in distributing petroleum or any primary product of petroleum. (Code Sec. 1245(a)(3); Reg § 1.1245-3))[40]

Property for which a qualified disaster expense would have been capitalized but for the rules of Code Sec. 198A (¶1783) is treated as Section 1245 property for purposes of depreciation recapture. (Code Sec. 198A(d)) (Code Sec. 1245(a)(3); Reg § 1.1245-3(b))[41]

¶ 2694   What is Section 1250 property?

All real property subject to depreciation that isn't Section 1245 property is Section 1250 property. (Code Sec. 1250(c)) Thus, Section 1250 property includes:

(1) MACRS residential real property (in the 27.5-year class) and nonresidential real property (in the 39-year class; 31.5-year class if placed in service before May 13, '93).

(2) The types of ACRS real property that aren't Section 1245 property, see ¶2693.

(3) The following real property placed in service before '81: (a) depreciable intangible real property, such as a leasehold interest in land, (b) all depreciable buildings and their structural components, and (c) other depreciable real property excluded from the definition of Section 1245 property (¶2693). (Reg § 1.1250-1(e)(3))[42]

¶ 2695   Recapture rules for Section 1245 property.

A gain on the disposition (¶2699) of Section 1245 property is treated as ordinary income to the extent of depreciation or amortization allowed or allowable on the property. (Code Sec. 1245(a))[43] The following deductions are treated as amortization for purposes of the Section 1245 recapture rules: the expense deduction under Code Sec. 179 (¶1941 *et seq.*); the deduction for clean fuel vehicles placed in service before 2006 under Code Sec. 179A; the deductions for refining costs under Code Sec. 179B and Code Sec. 179C (¶1966); the deduction for the cost of energy efficient commercial buildings under Code Sec. 179D (¶1967); the deduction for the costs incurred before 2010 of qualified film and TV productions under Code Sec. 181 (¶1965); qualified architectural and transportation barrier removal expenses under Code Sec. 190 (¶1621); and reforestation expenses under Code Sec. 194 (¶1970). (Code Sec. 1245(a)(2)(C))[44]

The environmental remediation expensing deduction (¶1661) (Code Sec. 198(e)),[45] the commercial revitalization deduction (¶1972) (Code Sec. 1400I(f)(2)),[46] and the amortization of a Section 197 intangible (¶1974) (Code Sec. 197(f)(7)) also are subject to recapture under Code Sec. 1245.[47]

The amount of gain treated as ordinary income on the disposition is limited to the lower of:

(1) the recomputed basis of the property minus the adjusted basis of the property. (Code Sec. 1245(a)(1)(A)) Recomputed basis is the adjusted basis of the property increased by the recapturable depreciation and amortization deductions reflected in the adjusted basis (Code Sec. 1245(a)(2)); or

(2) in the case of a sale, exchange or involuntary conversion, the amount realized minus the adjusted basis of the property; or in the case of any other disposition, the fair market

40. ¶I-10101; ¶12,454.01; TD ¶223,105
41. ¶L-5816; ¶198A4.01
42. ¶I-10112 *et seq.*; ¶12,504.01; TD ¶223,109
43. ¶I-10200 *et seq.*; ¶12,454; TD ¶223,102

44. ¶I-10204; ¶12,454.05; TD ¶223,103
45. ¶L-6150.3; ¶1984
46. ¶L-12709; ¶14,00I4; TD ¶269,308
47. ¶L-7981.2; ¶1974; TD ¶223,103

value of the property minus the adjusted basis of the property. (Code Sec. 1245(a)(1)(B))[48]

If a taxpayer disposes of more than one amortizable Code Sec. 197 intangible (¶1974) in a transaction or a series of related transactions, all of the amortizable intangibles are treated as one Code Sec. 1245 property for purposes of the recapture rules. However, this rule does not apply to any such intangible if its adjusted basis exceeds its fair market value. (Code Sec. 1245(b)(8))[49]

A taxpayer who disposes of qualified real property (¶1944) for which a Code Sec. 179 election has been made (¶1941 *et seq.*) may use any reasonable allocation method to determine the part of the gain that is attributable to Code Sec. 1245 property, i.e., to the part of the unadjusted basis of the property that was reduced by the Code Sec. 179 expense deduction. The remaining unadjusted basis of the property is allocated to Code Sec. 1250 property, see ¶2596.

If the election is made, for estates of decedents who died in 2010, to not be subject to the estate tax and to apply modified carryover basis rules to property acquired from a decedent (¶2523), safe harbor guidance applies to the question of whether the property continues to be subject to recapture in the hands of the estate or other recipient.[50]

¶ 2696 Recapture rules for Section 1250 property.

Part or all of the gain on the sale or other disposition (¶2699) of Section 1250 property may be treated as ordinary income. (Code Sec. 1250(a))[1] But where property was held more than one year, there's no depreciation recapture if it was depreciated via straight line. (Code Sec. 1250(b)) Thus, Section 1250 recapture doesn't apply to residential rental or nonresidential real property depreciated under MACRS, see ¶1920. For Section 1250 property held more than one year, the amount of gain treated as ordinary income is the lower of (1) the "applicable percentage" of the part of the "additional depreciation" (see below) attributable to periods after '75, or (2) in the case of a sale, exchange or involuntary conversion, the excess of the amount realized over the adjusted basis, or in the case of any other disposition, the fair market value of the property over its adjusted basis. (Code Sec. 1250(a)(1))[2]

Special rules apply to determine the amount to be recaptured as ordinary income for (a) additional depreciation attributable to periods after '69 and before '76 to determine the amount to be recaptured as ordinary income (Code Sec. 1250(a)(2)), and (b) additional depreciation attributable to periods before '70. (Code Sec. 1250(a)(3))[3]

Additional depreciation is the excess of actual post-'63 depreciation deductions over the amount that would have resulted during the same period had the straight-line method been used for the entire period the property was held. (Code Sec. 1250(b)(1), Code Sec. 1250(b)(3))[4] For additional amounts for corporations, see ¶2697.

The applicable percentage differs depending upon various factors, including whether the property is nonresidential real property, residential real property or low income housing.[5]

For the allocation between Code Sec. 1245 and Code Sec. 1250 of recapture income on the sale of qualified real property (¶1944) for which the Code Sec. 179 election (¶1941 *et seq.*) was made, see ¶2695.

If the election is made, for estates of decedents who died in 2010, to not be subject to the estate tax and to apply modified carryover basis rules to property acquired from a decedent (¶2523), safe harbor guidance applies to the determination of the applicable percentage for the property, and the question of whether the property continues to be subject to recapture in

---

48. ¶I-10200; ¶12,454.05; TD ¶223,102
49. ¶I-10219.1; ¶12,454.05; TD ¶223,106.1
50. ¶I-5004.1; ¶10,224; TD ¶223,007.1
1. ¶I-10400 *et seq.*; ¶12,504; TD ¶223,107

2. ¶I-10400 *et seq.*; ¶12,504.06; TD ¶223,110
3. ¶I-10402; ¶12,504.06; TD ¶223,110
4. ¶I-10403; ¶12,504.06; TD ¶223,110
5. ¶I-10417 *et seq.*; ¶12,504.06; TD ¶223,111

the hands of the estate or other recipient.[6]

For the tax treatment of a noncorporate taxpayer's unrecaptured Code Sec. 1250 gain, see ¶2605.

¶ 2697   Additional 20% recapture on disposition of realty by corporations.

For sales or other dispositions (of both residential and nonresidential property), 20% of the amount by which the gain recapturable if Section 1245 rules applied exceeds the gain recaptured under Section 1250 is treated as ordinary income (to the extent of gain) to a corporation. (Code Sec. 291(a))[7] This rule applies to an S corporation only if it was formerly a C corporation for any of the three immediately preceding tax years. (Code Sec. 1363(b)(4))[8]

¶ 2698   Treatment of basis reduction for investment credit.

In determining the recapturable amount, the reduction of basis for the investment credit is treated as a deduction allowed for depreciation. (Code Sec. 50(c)(4)(A))[9] However, this basis reduction is disregarded in computing straight-line depreciation for purposes of determining "additional depreciation" subject to recapture for Section 1250 property. (Code Sec. 50(c)(4)(B))[10]

¶ 2699   Transactions and events that trigger or escape depreciation recapture.

The following is a list of transactions and events that either trigger or escape depreciation recapture:

* A sale in a sale and leaseback transaction, a sale under a conditional sales contract, and a transfer of title back to the seller, creditor, or new purchaser upon foreclosure of a security interest trigger recapture. But, a transfer of legal title to a creditor upon creation of a security interest, or to a debtor upon termination of a security interest, escapes recapture. (Reg § 1.1245-1(a)(3), Reg § 1.1250-1(a)(2)(i))

* For trade-ins, exchanges and involuntary conversions, Section 1245 depreciation is not recaptured unless gain is recognized or non-Section 1245 property is acquired (Code Sec. 1245(b)(4); Reg § 1.1245-4(d)); and Section 1250 depreciation is not recaptured except where gain is recognized, stock is bought to acquire control of a corporation owning replacement property, or non-Section 1250 property is acquired. (Code Sec. 1250(d)(4); Reg § 1.1250-3(d))

* Conversion to personal use (except for Code Sec. 179 property, see ¶1945) doesn't trigger recapture, but a later sale will.

* Termination or disposition of a lease where depreciation was taken by the lessee (or sublessee) generally triggers recapture. (Reg § 1.1245-2(a)(3)(i))

* Incorporation of a business doesn't trigger recapture, except to the extent that gain is otherwise recognized. (Code Sec. 1245(b)(3), Code Sec. 1250(d)(3); Reg § 1.1245-4(c), Reg § 1.1250-3(c))

* Corporate distributions in kind (including liquidating distributions) generally trigger recapture, except in a tax-free complete liquidation of a subsidiary with carryover basis, where recapture is triggered upon disposition by the parent-transferee. (Code Sec. 1245(b)(3), Code Sec. 1250(d)(3); Reg § 1.1245-4(c), Reg § 1.1250-3(c))

* Corporate split-ups and reorganizations generally don't trigger recapture, except to the extent that gain is otherwise recognized on transfer of the property. (Code Sec. 1245(b)(3), Code Sec. 1250(d)(3); Reg § 1.1245-4(c), Reg § 1.1250-3(c))

---

6. ¶I-5004.1; ¶10,224; TD ¶223,007.1
7. ¶I-10422 *et seq.*; ¶2914; TD ¶223,108
8. ¶I-10422; ¶2914, 13634.01; TD ¶614,503,

9. ¶I-10204; TD ¶223,103
10. ¶I-10507

- S corporation elections or termination of S status don't trigger recapture.
- Sale of a partnership interest triggers recapture. Contributions to a partnership generally don't trigger recapture, but may if property is subject to a liability. (Code Sec. 1245(a), Code Sec. 1245(b)(3), Code Sec. 1250(a), Code Sec. 1250(d)(3); Reg § 1.1245-4(c), Reg § 1.1250-3(c))
- Gifts generally don't trigger recapture, but recapturable depreciation is carried over to donee. (Code Sec. 1245(b)(1), Code Sec. 1250(d)(1); Reg § 1.1245-4(a), Reg § 1.1250-3(a))
- For transfers by reason of death, recapturable depreciation is neither triggered nor carried over (except as provided under the Code Sec. 691 rules (income in respect of a decedent), and where the modified carryover basis rules apply for an estate of a decedent who died in 2010 that elected out of the estate tax, see ¶2523). (Code Sec. 1245(b)(2), Code Sec. 1250(d)(2); Reg § 1.1245-4(b), Reg § 1.1250-3(b))[11]
- When a trust or estate realizes gain from the distribution of depreciable property in satisfaction of a fixed-dollar bequest, or when it realizes gain or loss from a distribution in kind, recapture is triggered. (Reg § 1.1245-4(b), Reg § 1.1250-3(b))[12]

For the effect of depreciation recapture on installment sales, see ¶2453.

¶ 2700 Special recapture rules for listed property.

A reduction of business use of listed property (¶1946 *et seq.*) from more-than-50% to 50% or less triggers recapture of excess depreciation previously taken. (Code Sec. 280F(b)(2)(A)) "Excess depreciation" means depreciation allowable for years before the first year in which the property wasn't predominantly used in a qualified business use, over the amount of depreciation which would have been allowable for those years if the property hadn't been predominantly used in a qualified business (¶1948 *et seq.*) for the year it was acquired and if there had been no Section 179 expense election for the property. (Code Sec. 280F(b)(2)(B))[13]

---

11. ¶I-10002, I-10301 *et seq.*; ¶s 12,454.03, 12,504.01; TD ¶223,114   13. ¶L-10032; ¶280F4; TD ¶267,625
12. ¶C-7154; ¶s 12,454.03, 12,504.01; TD ¶223,114

Chapter 11   Tax Accounting—Inventories

¶ 2800   Accounting Periods.

Each taxpayer must compute taxable income and file a return on the basis of an accounting period called a tax year. An S corporation generally has to use a calendar year as its tax year unless it specially elects to use a fiscal year. So does a personal service corporation. A partnership generally has to use a "majority interest tax year" unless it makes the fiscal year election.

¶ 2801   Tax year.

Taxpayers must compute their taxable income on the basis of their tax year. (Code Sec. 441(a); Reg § 1.441-1(a)) "Tax year" is the taxpayer's annual accounting period (the annual period on the basis of which the taxpayer regularly computes his income in keeping his books) (Code Sec. 441(c)), but only if that's the calendar year or a fiscal year. (Code Sec. 441(b)(1))[1]

The calendar year is the 12-month period ending on Dec. 31. (Code Sec. 441(d)) A taxpayer must use the calendar year if the taxpayer keeps no books (unless it gets IRS consent to use a fiscal year (Reg § 1.441-1(c)(2)), or has no annual accounting period, or has an annual accounting period that doesn't qualify as a fiscal year (Code Sec. 441(b)(2), Code Sec. 441(g)), or if the taxpayer hasn't established a fiscal year. (Reg § 1.441-1(b)(1)(iv))[2]

A fiscal year is any 12-month period ending on the last day of a month other than December, or the 52-53 week tax year described at ¶2802. (Code Sec. 441(e))[3]

If a return is properly made for a period of less than 12 months (see ¶2804), the tax year is the short tax year for which the return is made. (Code Sec. 441(b)(3))[4]

Certain taxpayers must use a required tax year. (Code Sec. 441(f)(3), Code Sec. 441(f)(4); Reg § 1.441-1(b)(2))

¶ 2802   Tax year of 52-53 weeks.

A 52-53 week tax year varies from 52 to 53 weeks and always ends on the same day of the week. The day chosen must be either the day of the week that last occurs in a calendar month or the day that falls nearest to the end of the calendar month (in which case the last day of the tax year may fall in the next month). (Code Sec. 441(f)(1); Reg § 1.441-2(a)(1)) A taxpayer may elect a 52-53 week tax year if it otherwise satisfies Code Sec. 441 and its regs. (Reg § 1.441-2(a)(3))[5]

Wherever the applicability of any provision of the Code, or filing date, is expressed in terms of tax years beginning, including, or ending with reference to a specified date that's the first or last day of the month, the actual opening and closing dates of 52-53 week years are disregarded. The year is considered to begin on the first day of the calendar month beginning nearest to the first day of that tax year, and to end on the last day of the calendar month ending nearest to the last day of that tax year. (Code Sec. 441(f)(2)(A))[6]

If a pass-through entity or a pass-through owner, or both, use a 52-53-week tax year and the tax years of both end with reference to the same calendar month, then, for purposes of determining the tax year in which pass-through items are taken into account by its owner, the owner's tax is deemed to end on the last day of the pass-through's tax year. (Reg § 1.441-2(e)(1)) Similarly, if the tax year of a personal service corporation (PSC) and an employee-

---

1. ¶G-1000 et seq.; ¶4414; TD ¶431,001
2. ¶s G-1001, G-1003; ¶4414; TD ¶431,001
3. ¶G-1004; ¶4414; TD ¶431,006

4. ¶s G-1001; ¶4414; TD ¶431,001
5. ¶G-1101; ¶4414; TD ¶432,501
6. ¶G-1103; ¶4414; TD ¶432,503

References beginning with a single letter are to paragraphs in RIA's Federal Tax Coordinator 2d and RIA's Analysis of Federal Taxes: Income. Those beginning with numbers are to paragraphs in RIA's United States Tax Reporter. Those beginning with TD are to paragraphs in RIA's Tax Desk.

owner end with reference to the same calendar month, then for purposes of determining the tax year in which an employee-owner takes into account items that are deductible by the PSC and includible in the income of the employee-owner, the employee-owner's tax year is deemed to end on the last day of the PSC's tax year. (Reg § 1.441-2(e)(2))

¶ 2803 Establishing a tax year.

A new taxpayer generally may adopt any tax year that satisfies Code Sec. 441 and its regs, without IRS approval, by filing its first federal income tax return using that tax year. (Reg § 1.441-1(c)(1)) However, a newly formed partnership, S corporation, or personal service corporation that wants to adopt a tax year other than its required tax year, a tax year elected under Code Sec. 444 (¶2813), or a 52-53 week tax year (¶2802) that ends with reference to its required tax year or one elected under Code Sec. 444 must establish a business purpose and get IRS approval. (Reg § 1.441-1(c)(2)) Use Form 1128 following IRS procedures.[7]

If taxpayer's "annual accounting period" (¶2801), as established by the basis on which taxpayer keeps his books, is the calendar year or a fiscal year, his tax year is that annual accounting period. (Code Sec. 441(b)(1), Code Sec. 441(c)) Otherwise, the taxpayer must use the calendar year as his tax year. (Code Sec. 441(b)(2), Code Sec. 441(g))[8]

A new taxpayer using a 52-53 week tax year (¶2802) must file a statement (specified in the regs) with the return for its first 52-53 week tax year. (Reg § 1.441-2(b)(1)(ii))[9]

¶ 2804 Short tax years.

A taxpayer must use a tax "year" of less than 12 months if: (1) the taxpayer isn't in existence for what would otherwise be his full tax year (Code Sec. 443(a)(2));[10] or (2) the taxpayer properly changes his annual accounting period (¶2814). (Code Sec. 443(a)(1))[11] But if the short year arises because of the taxpayer's death, his last return may be filed and the tax paid as if he had lived to the end of his last tax year. (Reg § 1.443-1(a)(2))[12]

For filing requirements for short years, see ¶ 4716 and ¶ 4724.

¶ 2805 Computing tax for a short year.

If the short year results from a change of the taxpayer's annual accounting period, the short period's taxable income must be annualized. (Code Sec. 443(b))

Under the general method of annualization, gross income for the short period (less allowable deductions for the short period and, for individuals, the ratable amount of personal exemptions) is multiplied by 12 (months) and divided by the number of months in the short period. The result is the annualized taxable income on which the tentative tax is computed. The tax due is arrived at by multiplying the tentative tax by the number of months in the short period and dividing by 12. (Code Sec. 443(b)(1); Reg § 1.443-1(b)(1)(i))[13] Special annualization rules apply to the alternative minimum tax. (Code Sec. 443(d))[14]

There are exceptions to the annualization requirements for self-employment tax, accumulated earnings tax, personal holding company tax, undistributed foreign personal holding company income and income of regulated investment companies.[15]

The net operating loss (NOL) deduction can reduce actual income for the short period before computing short period income on an annual basis. Therefore, if the NOL deduction wipes out short period actual income there would be nothing to annualize and therefore no short period taxable income.[16]

---

7. ¶4414; TD ¶432,001
8. ¶G-1051; ¶4414; TD ¶432,001
9. ¶s G-1054, G-1753; ¶4414; TD ¶432,004
10. ¶G-1153; ¶4434; TD ¶431,011
11. ¶G-1155; ¶4434; TD ¶431,011

12. ¶G-1154; ¶4434; TD ¶431,011
13. ¶G-1166; ¶4434; TD ¶431,012
14. ¶A-8119; ¶4434; TD ¶691,018
15. ¶G-1163; ¶4434
16. ¶G-1166; ¶4434; TD ¶431,012

The income is *not* annualized if the short year is caused by the taxpayer not being in existence for a full tax year. (Code Sec. 443(b)) In this case, tax is computed as if the short period were a full year, and individuals need not prorate their personal exemptions. (Reg § 1.443-1(a)(2))[17]

If a taxpayer changes to or from a 52-53 week year, income for the short period must be annualized, with this exception: if the short period is 359 days or more, it is treated as a full tax year, while if it is six days or less it is added to the following tax year. (Reg § 1.443-1(b)(1)(ii))[18]

¶ 2806   Optional look-back method of computing tax for the short period.

The annualizing method at ¶2805 may create a tax hardship for taxpayers who have a disproportionately large amount of taxable income in the short period. To avoid this, taxpayers may use an optional method that computes the tax for the full 12 months starting at the beginning of the short year and prorates the tax according to the amount of income earned in the short period. (Code Sec. 443(b)(2))

The optional method is available only on a claim for credit or refund, filed no later than the due date (including extensions) of taxpayer's return for the first tax year that ends on or after the day that is 12 months after the first day of the short period. (Reg § 1.443-1(b)(2)(v)(a))[19]

¶ 2807   Tax year of sole proprietorship.

A sole proprietorship must use the same tax year as the proprietor. Thus, a calendar year employee who later operates as a sole proprietorship must use the calendar year for the proprietorship unless he gets IRS consent to use a fiscal year.[20]

¶ 2808   Tax years of trusts and estates.

Trusts must use the calendar year, except for trusts exempt from tax under Code Sec. 501(a), wholly charitable trusts described in Code Sec. 4947(a)(1) (Code Sec. 644)[21] and grantor trusts.[22] Estates may adopt either a calendar year or a fiscal year.[23]

¶ 2809   Tax years of foreign sales corporations and DISCs.

Foreign Sales Corporations (FSCs) and Domestic International Sales Corporations (DISCs) must use the tax year of the shareholder (or group of shareholders with the same 12-month tax year) with the highest percentage of voting power. (Code Sec. 441(h)(1))[24]

¶ 2810   Tax year of S corporation.

An S corporation (unless it makes the election at ¶2813, or elects a 52-53 week tax year (¶2802) ending with reference to its required year) must have a "required year," i.e., a calendar year or any other accounting year for which it shows a business purpose satisfactory to IRS; use Form 2553. (Code Sec. 1378; Reg § 1.441-1(b)(2)(i)(L), Reg § 1.441-1(b)(2)(ii)(B), Reg § 1.1378-1(a))[25]

¶ 2811   Tax year of personal service corporation (PSC).

The tax year of a PSC (¶3329) must be a calendar year unless the corporation makes the election at ¶2813, elects a 52-53 week tax year ending with reference to the calendar year or

17. ¶G-1162; ¶4434; TD ¶431,012
18. ¶G-1108; ¶4434
19. ¶G-1170 *et seq.*; ¶4434; TD ¶431,013
20. ¶G-1062; ¶4414; TD ¶432,006
21. ¶G-1400; ¶6454; TD ¶651,009

22. ¶G-1401; ¶6454; TD ¶651,009
23. ¶C-7008; ¶4414; TD ¶661,008
24. ¶O-2041; ¶4414
25. ¶G-1250; ¶13,784; TD ¶433,201

the year elected under the rules at ¶2813, or can satisfy IRS that there's a business purpose for a different tax year. (Code Sec. 441(i)(1); Reg § 1.441-1(b)(2)(i)(B), Reg § 1.441-3(a))[26]

A PSC is, as defined under the rules permitting IRS to reallocate PSC income and deductions (¶2859), any corporation whose principal activity is the performance of personal services that are substantially performed by employee-owners. But for this purpose PSC doesn't include S corporations, and the term "owner-employee" includes all employees with *any* stock ownership in the corporation. In determining ownership, attribution from a corporation (under Code Sec. 318(a)(2)(C)) is applied if *any* stock is owned by the shareholder in that corporation. (Code Sec. 441(i)(2))[27] Certain independent contractors who own stock in the corporation and perform personal services for or on behalf of it are treated as employees. (Reg § 1.441-3(g)(2))[28]

The performance of personal services is considered the corporation's principal activity if the corporation's compensation cost for a testing period for activities that are considered the performance of personal services exceeds 50% of its total compensation cost for the period. (Reg § 1.441-3(e)(1)) The testing period is the preceding tax year (or, for a corporation's first tax year, the period beginning the first day of the first tax year and ending the last day of that tax year or, if earlier, the last day of the calendar year in which that tax year began). (Reg § 1.441-3(c)(2)) Personal services are substantially performed by employee-owners if during the testing period more than 20% of the corporation's compensation cost (excluding qualified plan or SEP contributions) attributable to the performance of personal services is attributable to personal services performed by employee-owners. (Reg § 1.441-3(f), Reg § 1.441-3(e)(2)(ii))[29]

¶ 2812 Tax year of partnership—"majority interest tax year."

Unless the partnership makes the election at ¶2813, or can satisfy IRS that there's a business purpose for a different tax year (Code Sec. 706(b)(1)(C)),[30] a partnership must adopt:

(1) the "majority interest tax year" (Code Sec. 706(b)(1)(B)(i))—the tax year of one or more of the partners having an aggregate interest in partnership profits and capital of more than 50% on each testing day (the first day of the partnership's tax year as otherwise determined, or days prescribed by IRS) (Code Sec. 706(b)(4)(A));

(2) the tax year of all its principal (5%-or-more) partners, if there's no majority interest tax year (Code Sec. 706(b)(1)(B)(ii));

(3) the "least-aggregate-deferral" year, if there's no majority interest tax year and the principal partners don't have the same tax year. (Code Sec. 706(b)(1)(B)(iii); Reg § 1.706-1(b)(2)(i)(C))[31]

A partnership may have a tax year other than its required year if it makes an election under Code Sec. 444 (¶2813), elects to use a 52-53-week tax year (¶2802) that ends with reference to its required year or a tax year elected under Code Sec. 444, or establishes a business purpose for it and gets IRS approval. (Reg § 1.706-1(b)(2)(ii))

A partnership that's required to change to a majority-interest tax year isn't required to change to another tax year for either of the two tax years following the year of change. (Code Sec. 706(b)(4)(B))[32]

A partnership tax year ends as dictated by the accounting period selected or required, except that it closes earlier: (1) for a partner who sells his entire interest or whose interest is completely liquidated (Code Sec. 706(c); (Reg § 1.706-1(c)(2)(i)), and (2) with respect to all its partners on the date the partnership terminates for tax purposes. (Reg § 1.706-1(c)(1))[33]

26. ¶G-1300; ¶4414; TD ¶433,401
27. ¶G-1302; ¶4414; TD ¶433,403
28. ¶G-1306; ¶4414
29. ¶G-1303; ¶4414

30. ¶G-1200 *et seq.*; ¶7064.01; TD ¶433,002
31. ¶G-1200 *et seq.*; ¶7064.01; TD ¶433,001
32. ¶G-1201; ¶7064.01
33. ¶G-1224, G-1225; ¶7064.02; TD ¶433,024

¶ 2813 Section 444 election of tax year other than required tax year—Form 8716; Form 8752; Form 1120, Schedule H.

An S corporation, personal service corporation (PSC), or partnership may elect (on Form 8716) to have a tax year other than the required tax year (Code Sec. 444(a)), but only if the deferral period (number of months between beginning of elected fiscal tax year and following Dec. 31) for the tax year elected isn't longer than three months. (Code Sec. 444(b)(1); Reg § 1.444-1T(b))[34]

A partnership or S corporation that elects has to make a "required payment" (report on Form 8752) that approximates the tax the partners or S corporation shareholders would have paid on short-period income if the election hadn't been made. (Code Sec. 7519; Reg § 1.444-3T)[35]

A PSC that elects a fiscal tax year but doesn't make required minimum distributions to its employee-owners before the end of the calendar year must postpone part or all of its corresponding deduction to its next fiscal tax year. (Code Sec. 280H) To figure the required minimum distribution and maximum deductible amount, use Form 1120, Schedule H.[36]

¶ 2814 How to change accounting periods—Form 1128.

A taxpayer must get prior IRS approval to change accounting periods unless the change is authorized by the Code or one of those listed at ¶2815. (Reg § 1.441-1(e), Reg § 1.442-1(a))[37]

IRS will approve a request for a change in tax years only if the taxpayer establishes a substantial business purpose for the change,[38] and agrees to any terms, conditions or adjustments required to effect the change, including any that IRS feels are necessary to avoid a substantial distortion of the taxpayer's income as a result of the change. (Reg § 1.442-1(b)(1))[39]

To request IRS approval, file Form 1128 within the time and in the manner as provided in IRS administrative procedures. (Reg § 1.442-1(b)(1), Reg § 1.442-1(b)(3))[40] Fiscal year individuals must follow an exclusive procedure to change to a calendar year.[41]

If a taxpayer changed its annual accounting period within 48 months before the last month of the requested tax year, a copy of the application for the previous change, the ruling letter, and any other related correspondence from IRS, must be attached to the application.[42]

Limitations apply to the carryback of certain net operating losses (NOLs) and capital losses generated in the short period necessary to effect a change of tax year.[43]

¶ 2815 "No prior approval needed" changes of accounting period.

A taxpayer that has adopted a tax year generally must continue to use it unless it obtains IRS approval to change or is otherwise authorized to change without the IRS approval under the Code (e.g., Code Sec. 444, ¶2813) or regs. (Reg § 1.442-1(a))[44] A taxpayer may change his annual accounting period without IRS approval, or with "automatic" IRS approval, where the taxpayer:

. . . changes to a 52-53 week tax year that ends with reference to the same calendar month as the month ending his previous tax year (Reg § 1.441-2(b)(2));[45]

. . . is an individual who marries a person with a different tax year (Reg § 1.442-1(d)(1));[46]

34. ¶G-1500 *et seq.*; ¶4444; TD ¶434,003
35. ¶s G-1500, G-1550; ¶75,194; TD ¶434,012
36. ¶G-1600; ¶280H4; TD ¶434,014
37. ¶G-1800; ¶4424; TD ¶435,000
38. ¶G-1803 *et seq.*; ¶4424; TD ¶435,015
39. ¶G-1812 *et seq.*; ¶4424
40. ¶G-1701.1; ¶4424; TD ¶435,002

41. ¶G-1726; ¶4424; TD ¶436,001
42. ¶G-1882
43. ¶G-1827 *et seq.*; ¶4424; TD ¶439,027
44. ¶G-1701; ¶s 4424, 7064.01; TD ¶435,001
45. ¶G-1101; ¶4414; TD ¶432,501
46. ¶G-1708; ¶4424; TD ¶435,013

. . . is an individual with a fiscal year tax year who changes to a calendar year tax year;[47]

. . . is a partnership changing its tax year to meet the tests described at ¶2812;[48]

. . . is a C corporation that meets certain tests;[49]

. . . is an S corporation changing its tax year to meet the tests described at ¶2810;[50]

. . . is a personal service corporation changing to a calendar year or a 52-53 week tax year ending with reference to a calendar year; (Reg § 1.441-3(b)(2))[1]

. . . is a subsidiary corporation required to change its tax year to that of members of its affiliated group that file a consolidated return. (Reg § 1.442-1(c))

¶ 2816 Accounting Methods.

Methods of tax accounting are the methods and systems by which taxpayers determine the amount of their income, gains, losses, deductions and credits, as well as the time when those items must be realized and recognized. Various methods of tax accounting are permissible, but each must be used consistently, and each must clearly reflect income.

¶ 2817 Establishing a method of accounting.

Because a taxpayer's book accounting method determines his accounting method, a taxpayer establishes a tax accounting method by setting up books, keeping accounts, and preparing income tax returns under any of the permissible methods. The method first used in accounting for business income and deductions in connection with each trade or business, as evidenced in the taxpayer's income tax return in which the income or deductions are first reported, must be followed consistently after that. (Reg § 1.446-1(d)(1))[2] The requirement to maintain books and records can be met by using certain electronic storage systems.[3]

A taxpayer may use one method of accounting to keep personal books and another to keep the books for his trade or business. But the two must be strictly separated. (Reg § 1.446-1(c)(1)(iv)(b))

A taxpayer whose only income is wages doesn't have to keep formal books in order to establish an accounting method, but may establish a method of accounting by means of tax returns (or copies) or other records. (Reg § 1.446-1(b)(2))[4]

A new taxpayer may adopt a method of accounting in connection with filing the first income tax return. An existing taxpayer entering into a business that's separate and distinct from any trade or business that the taxpayer previously carried on may adopt a method of accounting for the separate and distinct business in connection with filing the first tax return reporting income from the business. (Reg § 1.446-1(e)(1))[5]

Use of different accounting methods isn't permitted if there's a creation or shifting of profits or losses between the taxpayer's various trades or businesses (e.g., by using inventory adjustments, sales, purchases or expenses, and this results in a distortion of the taxpayer's income). (Reg § 1.446-1(d)(3))[6]

Taxpayers may use any combination of the cash, accrual, and specifically permitted special methods of accounting if the combination clearly reflects income and is consistently used. (Reg § 1.446-1(c)(1)(iv))[7]

47. ¶G-1725; ¶4424; TD ¶436,001
48. ¶G-1222; ¶4424; TD ¶433,020
49. ¶G-1800 *et seq.*; ¶4424; TD ¶435,008
50. ¶G-1250.1; ¶13,784; TD ¶433,201
1. ¶G-1301; ¶4424; TD ¶433,402
2. ¶G-2051; ¶4464.01; TD ¶440,518

3. ¶G-2019; ¶60,014; TD ¶440,509 *et seq.*
4. ¶G-2051; TD ¶440,518
5. ¶G-2051; ¶4464.01; TD ¶440,518
6. ¶G-2052; ¶4464.01; TD ¶440,803
7. ¶G-2003; ¶4464.09; TD ¶440,802

¶ 2818   Limits on choice of accounting methods.

The accrual method is mandatory for purchases and sales (unless IRS consents to a change) where inventories must be used. (Reg § 1.446-1(c)(2)(i)) Inventories must be used where the production, purchase or sale of merchandise is an income-producing factor. (Reg § 1.446-1(a)(4)(i))[8] However, exceptions apply for certain small businesses:

- *$1 million or less average gross receipts.* Taxpayers (other than tax shelters) with 3-year average annual gross receipts of $1 million or less do not have to account for inventories or use an accrual method of accounting. Instead they may treat merchandise inventory in the same way that cash method taxpayers must treat material or supplies that are not incidental (under Reg § 1.162-3). Generally, a taxpayer has average annual gross receipts of $1 million or less if for each earlier tax year, its (or its predecessor's) average annual gross receipts for the 3-tax-year period ending with the applicable prior tax year does not exceed $1 million (using the method of accounting actually used for federal tax purposes).[9]

- *More than $1 million but not more than $10 million average gross receipts.* Qualifying small businesses with 3-year average annual gross receipts of more than $1 million but not more than $10 million that are not prohibited from using the cash method under Code Sec. 448 (see below) and otherwise would have to keep inventories and use accrual accounting may, instead, use the cash method for an eligible trade or business. Generally, a taxpayer has average annual gross receipts of $10 million or less if, for each prior tax year ending after Dec. 30, 2000, its average annual gross receipts for the 3-tax-year period ending with the applicable prior tax year does not exceed $10 million. Qualifying small businesses that may use the cash method for all of their trades and businesses are: (1) businesses whose principal business activity for the immediately preceding tax year is other than mining, manufacturing, wholesale trade, retail trade, or information industries; (2) service providers, including those providing property incident to those services; and (3) fabricators or modifiers of tangible personal property on demand in accordance with customer design or specifications.[10]

C corporations (other than qualified personal service corporations), and partnerships with a C corporation (other than a qualified personal service corporation) as a partner, with average annual gross receipts of more than $5 million for any prior 3-tax-year period (or the period of its existence, if less) can't use the cash method. Tax shelters can't use the cash method in any event. (Code Sec. 448(a))[11] The limitation on the cash method doesn't apply to farming businesses (except tax shelters) (Code Sec. 448(b)(1)), but for special farm accounting rules, see ¶4505 *et seq.*[12] For purposes of these restrictions, an accounting method that records some but not all items on the cash method (i.e., a hybrid method) is treated as the cash method of accounting. (Reg § 1.448-1T(a)(4))[13] Tax-exempt trusts are treated as C corporations with respect to unrelated trade or business income. (Code Sec. 448(d)(6))[14]

¶ 2819   The Cash Method of Accounting. ▪▪▪▪▪▪▪▪▪▪▪▪▪▪

Under the cash method, gross income includes cash or property actually or constructively received during the tax year. Deductions are usually taken in the year cash or property is actually paid or transferred. It doesn't matter when the income was earned, or when the expense was incurred.

---

8. ¶G-5000; ¶4464.07; TD ¶440,827
9. ¶G-5005A, ¶G-5005.3; ¶4714.10; TD ¶450,508
10. ¶G-5005.4; ¶4714.15
11. ¶G-2054; ¶4484; TD ¶440,806

12. ¶G-2057; ¶s 614.053, 4474; TD ¶440,814
13. ¶G-2054; ¶4484; TD ¶440,806
14. ¶G-2055; ¶4484; TD ¶440,806

¶ 2820   Cash basis accounting.

Under the cash basis method of accounting, income is reported when cash or property is actually or constructively received (¶2822), and deductions are taken in the year cash or property is paid or transferred.[15]

For income a taxpayer receives under a claim of right, see ¶1204. For restrictions on use of the cash method by certain taxpayers, see ¶2818; for exceptions to those restrictions for small businesses, see ¶2818.

¶ 2821   When is a check income?

A check issued by a solvent payor is income when received by a cash basis payee, unless there's a restriction on the payee's right to cash the check.[16] Receipt of a check by an agent is considered receipt by the principal.[17]

¶ 2822   Constructive receipt of income.

Income not actually received is constructively received and reportable if it's within the taxpayer's control. Cash basis taxpayers must report money unconditionally subject to their demand as income, even if they haven't received it.[18] There's no constructive receipt if the amount is available only on surrender of a valuable right,[19] or if there are substantial limits on the right to receive it. (Reg § 1.451-2(a))[20]

¶ 2823   Timing of deductions under the cash method.

Cash method taxpayers generally take deductions (if otherwise allowable) in the year the items are paid. (Reg § 1.461-1(a)(1))[21] There's no constructive payment doctrine.[22]

Where an expense (e.g., rent or an insurance premium) relates to a period covering more than 12 months, IRS and most courts agree that the deduction must be spread over the period to which the expense applies.[23] For an exception for points paid on a home mortgage, see ¶1746. For deduction of prepaid taxes, see ¶1766.

A check is payment when delivered, not when cashed, if it's honored when it's first presented for payment.[24]

¶ 2824   The Accrual Method of Accounting. ▮▮▮▮▮▮▮▮▮▮▮▮▮▮▮▮

Under the accrual method, income is reported in the tax year in which the right to the income becomes fixed and the amount of the income can be determined with reasonable accuracy. Deductions are claimed in the period in which all events have occurred that determine the fact of the liability and the amount of the liability can be determined with reasonable accuracy.

¶ 2825   Accrual basis accounting.

Income accrues and must be reported in the year all events have occurred that determine taxpayer's right to receive it (¶2832), and the amount can be determined with reasonable accuracy (Reg § 1.451-1(a)), even if it's received in a later year. That is, the right to receive the income must not be contingent on a future event; the amount must be reasonably suscep-tible of accurate estimate; and there must be a reasonable expectation that it will be received

---

15. ¶G-2410 *et seq.*; ¶s 4464.05, 4514.003; TD ¶441,001
16. ¶G-2415; ¶s 4514.003, 4514.004; TD ¶441,003
17. ¶G-2419; TD ¶441,002
18. ¶G-2424; ¶4514.036 ; TD ¶441,005
19. ¶G-2426; ¶4514.036; TD ¶441,007
20. ¶G-2425; ¶4514.036; TD ¶441,006
21. ¶G-2436 *et seq.*; ¶4614.01; TD ¶441,401
22. ¶G-2443; TD ¶441,409
23. ¶L-3526 *et seq.*, ¶L-6616 *et seq.*; ¶1624.081; TD ¶441,410
24. ¶G-2438; ¶4614.02; TD ¶441,404

in due course.[25]

Accrual basis taxpayers do not need to accrue income from the performance of services that, based on their experience, will not be collected if, among other things, interest isn't charged on the debt and there is no penalty for late payment. This "nonaccrual experience method" is available only for: (1) amounts owing for services in the fields of health, law, engineering, architecture, accounting, actuarial science, performing arts, or consulting, or (2) other services, if the taxpayer's three-year average annual gross receipts doesn't exceed $5 million. Uncollectible amounts may be determined using specified safe-harbor methods. (Code Sec. 448(d)(5)) A taxpayer's nonaccrual experience method must be tested against actual experience unless he has adopted one of the five safe harbor methods in the regs (Reg § 1.448-2(d)) or a book safe harbor provided in IRS guidance.[26]

¶ 2826   Contingent rights to income.

Where the right to income is contingent on a future event, an accrual basis taxpayer doesn't have to recognize the income until that event occurs.[27]

Advance payments to a retailer under which it agreed to purchase specified amounts from its supplier were held by a court to be income on receipt. But another court found similar cash advances by a wholesaler to a retailer in exchange for a volume purchase commitment not includible on receipt; they were contingent on the purchases being made. Generally adopting the latter approach, IRS allows taxpayers to adopt an advance trade discount method of accounting in which advance trade discounts aren't recognized as income on receipt by accrual method taxpayers with inventories, but instead are taken into account in the amount and manner that the taxpayer accounts for the discount in its financial statements.[28]

Where litigation is involved and liability to the taxpayer is admitted, the income must be recognized if the taxpayer can accurately estimate the amount of recovery.[29] But if liability isn't admitted, the income accrues when the litigation is concluded or settlement reached, whichever is earlier.[30] An offer in compromise is income when the dispute is settled or the offer is unconditionally accepted.[31]

¶ 2827   Income accrual for disputed liability for goods.

If an accrual method taxpayer overbills a customer due to clerical error and the customer discovers the error and, in the following year, disputes its liability, gross income accrues in the year of sale for the correct amount. An accrual method taxpayer does not accrue income in the year of sale if, during that year, the customer disputes its liability because incorrect goods were shipped. However, income does accrue in the year of sale if excess quantities of goods are shipped and the customer agrees to pay for them.[32]

¶ 2828   Dealers' reserves.

Dealers commonly discount customers' notes with a finance company that keeps a portion of the amount due the dealer as security against possible default by the customer. A dealer that uses the accrual method must include the full amount of the discount price, undiminished by the portion retained by the finance company—the "dealer reserve," in income as soon as the notes are sold to the finance company. This is so even if the dealer assigned the notes to the finance company "without recourse." [33]

25. ¶G-2471; ¶4514.012 ; TD ¶441,701
26. ¶G-2501 *et seq.*; ¶4514.023 *et seq.*; TD ¶441,707
27. ¶s G-2484, G-2485; ¶s 4514.011, 4514.012; TD ¶441,703
28. ¶G-2483
29. ¶G-2506; ¶s 4514.021, 4514.055; TD ¶441,704
30. ¶G-2506; ¶4514.055; TD ¶441,704
31. ¶s G-2506, G-2507; ¶4514.058
32. ¶G-2511.1
33. ¶G-2513; ¶4514.017; TD ¶441,702

¶ 2829 Deferral method for certain advance payments.

Under the deferral method of accounting for advance payments, accrual basis taxpayers can defer to the next succeeding tax year the inclusion in gross income of specified advance payments to the extent the advance payments are not recognized in revenues (or, in certain cases, are not earned) in the tax year of receipt. Except for certain short tax years of less than 93 days, deferral to a tax year later than the next succeeding tax year isn't allowed. Alternately, taxpayer, under the full inclusion method of accounting for advance payments, can include the full amount of advance payments in gross income in the tax year of receipt, whether or not the taxpayer earns the full amount of advance payments in that tax year.[34]

An advance payment is eligible for the deferral method if:

(A) including the payment in income for the tax year of receipt generally is a permitted method of accounting for tax purposes (without regard to the revenue procedure authorizing the deferral method));

(B) taxpayer recognizes the payment (partially or completely) in revenues in its applicable financial statement for a later tax year (or, if doesn't have one, it earns the payment, partially or completely, in a later tax year); and

(C) the payment is for: services; sale of goods (other than goods for which the taxpayer uses the deferral method of Reg § 1.451-5(b)(1)(ii), see ¶2830); use (including by license or lease) of intellectual property; occupancy or use of property ancillary to the provision of services; sale, lease, or license of computer software; guaranty or warranty contracts ancillary to the preceding items; subscriptions (other than those for which an election under Code Sec. 455 is in effect), whether or not provided in a tangible or intangible format; organization membership (other than those for which an election under Code Sec. 456 is in effect); or any combination of the preceding items.

✪illustration: Accrual method, calendar year C Corp sells and repairs TVs. On July 1, 2013, C receives an advance payment for a 2-year contract under which it will repair or replace broken parts in a customer's TV. In its applicable financial statement, C recognizes $1/4$ of the payment in revenues for 2013, $1/2$ in revenues for 2014, and $1/4$ in revenues for 2015. Under the deferral method, C includes $1/4$ of the payment in gross income for 2013 and the remaining $3/4$ of the payment in gross income for 2014.

✪observation: Given the deferral possibilities outlined above, cash-basis service providers who bill in advance should consider switching to the accrual method. The benefits of deferring reporting a portion of cash receipts for one year (on an ongoing basis, if applicable), should be compared with the costs and effort of making the accounting method change.

Payments ineligible for the deferral method include rent (unless it's for the use of intellectual property, occupancy or use of property ancillary to the provision of services, or software) and payments for financial instruments (e.g., debt instruments, letters of credit). (Rev Proc 2004-34, 2004-1 CB 991, as modified)[35]

¶ 2830 Advance payments received for merchandise or construction.

Advance merchandise payments and advance payments under long-term construction contracts are reported by accrual method taxpayers when the income is properly accruable under their method of accounting.[36] But that method must be used for all tax reporting and for credit purposes. (Reg § 1.451-5(b))[37]

An accrual basis taxpayer or a taxpayer using one of the long-term contract methods (¶2848 *et seq.*) can defer reporting an advance payment received under an agreement for the sale or

---

34. ¶G-2548; ¶4514.191; TD ¶441,712
35. ¶G-2548; ¶4514.191; TD ¶441,712

36. ¶G-2592 *et seq.*; ¶s 4514.121, 4514.191 ; TD ¶441,715
37. ¶G-2595; TD ¶441,715

other disposition in a future tax year of goods held primarily for sale to customers, or for the building, installing, constructing or manufacturing of items, where the work isn't completed in the year the advance payment is received. (Reg § 1.451-5(a)(1)) Deferral also applies to advance payments for services to be performed under the agreement as an integral part of the above activities, and for gift certificates. (Reg § 1.451-5(a)(2))[38] Amounts due and payable under the contract are treated as advance payments received. (Reg § 1.451-5(a))[39]

There's a limited deferral for certain inventoriable goods. Where a payment for goods is received several years before they are delivered, taxpayer can postpone reporting the advance payments for one year past the year total advance payments first equal or exceed the anticipated cost of the goods. Thereafter, all prepayments received are reported and actual or expected costs deducted. (Reg § 1.451-5(c))[40] A taxpayer who defers reporting advance payments for merchandise must attach an annual information schedule to its tax return for each year. (Reg § 1.451-5(d))[41]

Use Form 3115 (¶2840) to get IRS consent to switch to deferral. (Reg § 1.451-5(e))[42]

¶ 2831   Advance payments or security deposits.

Amounts received as security aren't taxable until used. A deposit that guarantees the customer's payment of amounts owed to the creditor isn't a deposit but an advance payment includible in income (unless deferred, see ¶2829 and ¶2830), while a deposit securing someone's property is a true security deposit and not an advance payment.[43]

¶ 2832   Timing of expense deductions—all-events test.

Expenses are deductible under the accrual method in the period in which: (1) all events have occurred that determine the fact of the liability; (2) the amount of the liability can be determined with reasonable accuracy; and (3) economic performance (¶2833) has occurred. (Code Sec. 461(h)(4); Reg § 1.461-1(a)(2)) The fact of a liability—generally, the earlier of the event fixing the liability (e.g., the required performance) or when payment is due—isn't established by executing a contract for services to be provided in the future. A reasonable estimate of the liability must be accrued for the tax year in which it was incurred. If there is a difference between the estimate and the amount finally determined, the difference must be added to or deducted from income when the final determination is made. For bonuses that are payable to a group of employees that can't revert back to the employer, IRS has ruled that the fact of the liability can be shown, even though the employer doesn't know the identity of any particular bonus recipient or the amount payable to that individual recipient until after the end of the tax year.[44]

IRS held that a manufacturer's contractual liability to pay certain trade promotion rebates to customers became fixed and determinable under the all events test in the year that the underlying goods were purchased; the later filing of a rebate claim was a mere formality that didn't delay accrual of the liabilities. But an automobile company couldn't deduct its anticipated warranty costs under the accrual method based on estimates; until a claim had been filed under the warranty, liability for it remained contingent.[45]

Where the accrual doesn't involve a current expense, but results in the creation of an asset having a useful life extending substantially beyond the end of the tax year, the deduction must be taken as depreciation, amortization or similar deduction. (Reg § 1.461-1(a)(2))[46]

An accrual basis taxpayer may deduct a properly accrued expense, regardless of whether he has actually paid that expense.[47]

38. ¶s G-2592, G-2594; TD ¶441,715
39. ¶G-2599; ¶4514.121; TD ¶441,715
40. ¶G-2596; ¶4514.166; TD ¶441,717
41. ¶G-2597; TD ¶441,718
42. ¶G-2598; TD ¶441,719

43. ¶J-1435 *et seq.*; ¶s 4514.193, 4514.194; TD ¶441,711
44. ¶G-2620 *et seq.*; ¶4614.15; TD ¶442,000
45. ¶G-2620 *et seq.*; ¶4614.15; TD ¶442,000
46. ¶G-2620; ¶4614.15; TD ¶442,001
47. ¶G-2620; ¶4614.15; TD ¶442,000

¶ 2833 Economic performance.

Accrual basis taxpayers won't be considered to have met the all-events test (¶2832), until economic performance has occurred. (Code Sec. 461(h))[48] Economic performance occurs when the property or service to which the accrual relates is actually provided or used. (Code Sec. 461(h)(2))[49] Thus, economic performance for a liability to pay compensation generally occurs as the employee renders his services. For a liability to pay tax, it generally occurs as the tax is paid to the taxing authority (an exception applies under Code Sec. 461(h) for accelerated taxes); payment for this purpose includes payments of estimated income tax. (Reg § 1.461-4(g)(6)(i)) For a liability to pay a rebate, refund, or similar payment to another person (including a price reduction for future goods or services), economic performance occurs as payment is made to the person to which the liability is owed. (Reg § 1.461-4(g)(3))

Exceptions. A taxpayer is allowed to treat property or services as provided when he pays for them, but only if he can reasonably expect the property or services to be provided by the other person within 3 ½ months after the payment is made. (Reg § 1.461-4(d)(6)(ii))[50]

In addition, certain "recurring" expenditures may be treated as incurred in the year the all-events test is otherwise met, even though economic performance doesn't occur until the following year. This applies if:

(1) economic performance occurs on or before the date taxpayer files a timely (including extensions) return for the tax year the expense is accrued or, if shorter, 8 ½ months after the close of that year; and

(2) the item is recurring and taxpayer consistently treats items of that kind as incurred in the tax year the all-events test (not including the economic performance test) is met; and

(3) the item is either not a material item or its accrual in the year before economic performance results in a more proper match against income than would be achieved by accruing it in the year of economic performance. IRS ruled that the recurring item exception didn't apply to expenses of a lease and service contract with a maintenance company (to clean and repair leased property) because they were material items and early accrual didn't result in a more proper match against income. (Code Sec. 461(h)(3)(A); Reg § 1.461-5(b))[1]

The recurring item exception is allowed for payroll taxes on compensation and, under a safe harbor, for bonuses and vacation pay.[2] A taxpayer can adopt the recurring item exception as part of its method of accounting for any type of income for the first tax year that type of item is incurred. (Reg § 1.461-5(d)(1)) Tax shelters can't use the recurring item exception. (Code Sec. 461(i)(1); Reg § 1.461-5(c))[3] The 3 ½ month rule, as well as the 8 ½ month recurring item exception, apply only to property or services completely provided within that period; a prorated deduction isn't allowed where all services to be performed aren't provided within that period.[4]

¶ 2834 Accruing contested liability.

An otherwise deductible expense isn't allowable, as long as the taxpayer denies and contests the liability, until the contest is resolved by agreement or final court decision.[5] However, a deduction is allowed in the year of transfer (payment) where:

(1) the taxpayer contests an asserted liability;

(2) the taxpayer transfers money or other property to satisfy the liability;

(3) the contest with respect to the asserted liability exists after the transfer; and

(4) but for the contest, a deduction would be allowed for the tax year of the transfer (or an

---

48. ¶G-2653; ¶4614.15; TD ¶442,012
49. ¶G-2656; ¶4614.15; TD ¶442,013
50. ¶G-2656; ¶4614.15; TD ¶442,014
1. ¶G-2686; ¶4614.15; TD ¶442,035

2. ¶K-4302.1; ¶4614.17; TD ¶442,606
3. ¶G-2458; ¶4614.15; TD ¶442,035
4. ¶G-2656
5. ¶G-2643; ¶s 4614.56, 4614.59; TD ¶442,006

earlier year). (Code Sec. 461(f)) The contest need not involve court proceedings.[6]

Except as provided under Code Sec. 468B (¶2835), economic performance does not occur when a taxpayer transfers money or property to a trust, escrow account, or court to provide for the satisfaction of a contested workers compensation, tort, or a liability that arises out of a breach of contract or violation of law and requires a payment or a series of payments to another person unless the trust, escrow account, or court is the claimant, or the taxpayer's payment discharges the taxpayer's liability to the claimant. (Reg § 1.461-2(e)(2)(ii))[7]

¶ 2835 Accrual basis taxpayer's payments for tort liabilities.

If the liability of a taxpayer requires a payment to another person that arises out of a tort, "economic performance" (¶2833) occurs as the payments are made. (Code Sec. 461(h)(2)(C))[8] A qualified payment to a court-ordered or designated settlement fund that extinguishes a taxpayer's tort liability is economic performance for the liability as the payment is made. The present or future claims against the taxpayer must arise out of personal injury, death or property damage. (Code Sec. 468B)[9]

¶ 2836 Accrual basis taxpayer's payables to related cash basis taxpayer.

An accrual basis taxpayer can deduct expenses and interest owed to a related cash basis person only when payment is made and the amount involved is includible in the gross income of the cash basis payee. (Code Sec. 267(a)(2)) That is, an accrual basis taxpayer is treated as on the cash method for purposes of deducting amounts owed to a related cash basis person.[10]

The rule applies in general to all deductible expenses if the timing of the deduction depends on the taxpayer's method of accounting or on electing to expense the item. But it doesn't apply to defer the deduction of otherwise deductible original issue discount or below-market loan interest. (Reg § 1.267(a)-2T(b), Q&A-2) Nor does it apply to defer the deduction of otherwise deductible depreciation or amortization, except as to amounts owed to a related person for interest, rent, or for the performance or nonperformance of services (which amount the payor capitalized or treated as a deferred expense). (Reg § 1.267(a)-2T(b), Q&A-4)[11]

The above rule, barring an accrual method corporation from deducting unpaid accrued interest on a loan made to the company from its cash-basis owner, continues to apply after the loan is sold by the owner to an unrelated third-party. Interest that accrued in years before the sale cannot be deducted by the corporation until the unrelated party includes it in income. However, interest that accrues in the year of the sale can be deducted before it is paid.[12]

¶ 2837 Changes of Accounting Methods. ▬▬▬▬▬▬▬

Usually, taxpayers may change their methods of accounting only with IRS consent, and only on IRS-imposed terms. However, automatic consent is available in certain circumstances where IRS-prescribed procedures are followed.

¶ 2838 IRS permission to change method of accounting.

Generally, once a taxpayer has adopted an accounting method, he must continue to use it until: IRS requires him to change the method; or he requests, and gets, IRS permission to change. (Code Sec. 446(e); Reg § 1.446-1(e)(2)) This is so even if the taxpayer has been using an incorrect method, or a method that doesn't clearly reflect income.[13] Taxpayers can't, without IRS consent, retroactively change from an erroneous to a permissible accounting method by filing amended returns, even if the time for amending the return for the first year

---

6. ¶G-2645; ¶s 4614.56, 4614.59; TD ¶442,007
7. ¶G-2645; ¶4614.56; TD ¶442,007
8. ¶G-2736; ¶4614.15; TD ¶442,019
9. ¶G-2788 *et seq.*; ¶468B4; TD ¶442,025

10. ¶G-2700 *et seq.*; ¶2674; TD ¶442,027
11. ¶G-2701 *et seq.*; ¶2674; TD ¶442,028
12. ¶G-2701
13. ¶G-2201; ¶4464; TD ¶442,601

in which the erroneous method was used hasn't expired. [14]

Taxpayers under examination[15] or before an appeals office[16] or federal court[17] may request prospective accounting method changes in certain circumstances.

For automatic consent procedures for certain accounting method changes, see ¶2845.

For changes to inventory methods, see ¶2881.

¶ 2839 What is a change in accounting method?

A change in accounting method is a change of the taxpayer's overall method of accounting or a change in the treatment of a material item of income or expense. Changes in overall methods of accounting include changes:

. . . from the cash to accrual basis, or vice-versa;

. . . from the long-term contract method to the cash or accrual method, or vice-versa;

. . . from one basis of inventory valuation to another;

. . . to or from a specialized basis, e.g., the crop basis. (Reg § 1.446-1(e)(2)(ii))[18]

A material item is any item that involves the proper time for the inclusion of the item in income or the taking of a deduction. It doesn't include corrections of mathematical or posting errors, or errors in computing tax liability. (Reg § 1.446-1(e)(2)(ii))[19] For example, IRS has privately ruled that a taxpayer's correction of an error by recharacterizing its activity as a passive activity (¶1810) wasn't an accounting method change. [20]

Depreciation changes that aren't accounting method changes include: adjustments in the useful life of a depreciable or amortizable asset for which depreciation is determined under Code Sec. 167 (other than under current (or former) Code Sec. 168, Code Sec. 1400I, and Code Sec. 1400L); changes in computing depreciation or amortization allowances in the tax year in which the use of an asset changes in the hands of the same taxpayer; changes in depreciation caused by certain revocations of elections and late elections; and changes in the placed-in service date. (Reg § 1.446-1(e)(2)(ii), Reg § 1.167(e)-1(a)(2))

However, most changes in computing depreciation (or amortization) are treated as accounting method changes. Changes that are accounting method changes include changes: in depreciation or amortization methods, recovery periods or conventions, e.g., half-year to midquarter (but a switch from 200% or 150% declining balance to straight line is allowable without IRS's consent in the first tax year in which it produces a higher allowance); from regular MACRS to the alternative depreciation system; in claiming bonus first-year depreciation without electing; from treating property as nondepreciable or nonamortizable to depreciable or amortizable (or vice versa); and from depreciating or amortizing an item to deducting it as an expense (or vice versa). (Reg § 1.167(e)-1(a)(1), Reg § 1.446-1(e)(2)(ii))[21]

¶ 2840 Applying for a change in accounting method—Form 3115.

An application for change generally must be filed with IRS on the latest version of Form 3115 by the end of the tax year of the change. (Reg § 1.446-1(e)(3)(i))[22] However, automatic consent accounting method change requests (¶2845), may be made on Form 3115:

(1) with a timely filed (including extensions) original income tax return for the change year (file a copy with the IRS National Office), or

(2) within six months of the original tax return due date (excluding extensions) for the change year, if the taxpayer (a) timely filed (including extensions) its return for the change

---

14. ¶G-2201; ¶s 4464.21, 4464.22; TD ¶442,601
15. ¶G-2237; ¶4464.22; TD ¶442,605
16. ¶G-2256.1; ¶4464.22; TD ¶442,605
17. ¶G-2257.1; ¶4464.22; TD ¶442,605
18. ¶G-2103; ¶4464.21; ¶4464.24; TD ¶442,403

19. ¶G-2104; ¶4464.24; TD ¶442,404
20. ¶G-2109.1
21. ¶G-2106.1; ¶4464.25; TD ¶442,407
22. ¶G-2225; ¶4464.22; TD ¶442,601

year; (b) files an amended return within the six-month extension period; (c) attaches the original Form 3115 to the amended return; (d) files a copy with the national office at the same time or sooner; and (e) writes "FILED PURSUANT TO Reg § 301.9100-2" at the top of the application.[23]

Extensions won't be granted except in unusual and compelling circumstances. The taxpayer must include all information required by the form, and state that he agrees to the conditions set by IRS and will take into account any required adjustments (¶2841).[24]

¶ 2841   Adjustments required on change—Code Sec. 481(a) adjustments.

In any year in which taxpayer uses a different tax accounting method from the method used in the preceding year, Code Sec. 481(a) adjustments must be made to prevent items of income or expense from being duplicated or entirely omitted. (Reg § 1.446-1(e)(3)(i))[25] The adjustments must take into account inventories, accounts receivable, accounts payable, and any other necessary items. (Reg § 1.481-1(b))[26] The adjustments can be positive (increasing taxable income), or negative (decreasing taxable income). (Reg § 1.481-1(c))[27]

¶ 2842   When Code Sec. 481(a) adjustments are taken into account.

Except as noted below or where the Code or another federal statute provides otherwise, the Code Sec. 481(a) adjustment required as a result of an accounting method change (¶2841) must be taken into account in the year of change—i.e., the first tax year in which the taxpayer's method of accounting is different from that used in the previous tax year. (Code Sec. 481(a); Reg § 1.481-1(a)(1)) This applies to both positive and negative adjustments. (Reg § 1.481-1(c))[28]

Instead of taking the Code Sec. 481(a) adjustment into account in the year of change, taxpayer may take it into account over an appropriate period agreed to (in writing) by IRS. (Code Sec. 481(c); Reg § 1.481-4(a), Reg § 1.481-4(b)) The adjustment must be taken into account ratably over the years included in the adjustment inclusion period (¶2843).[29]

¶ 2843   Adjustment inclusion periods prescribed by IRS—four-year/one-year rules.

The Code Sec. 481(a) adjustment period for voluntary accounting method changes, including automatic consent changes (¶2845), is one tax year for negative adjustments and four tax years for positive adjustments beginning with the year of change.[30] However, taxpayers may elect to account for a positive adjustment in the year of change if it's less than $25,000. Cooperatives generally must take the adjustment into account for the year of change. Taxpayers that terminate their existence or cease to engage in a trade or business must take any remaining balance into account in the year of the cessation or termination. Except for last-in-first-out (LIFO) discontinuance, acceleration of a Code Sec. 481(a) adjustment isn't required on conversion from C to S corporation status, or vice versa.[31]

If an accounting method issue (an issue regarding whether the taxpayer's accounting treatment of an item is proper, but only if changing the taxpayer's treatment of that item could constitute a change in accounting method) results from an examination, any resulting positive Code Sec. 481(a) adjustment is made in the earliest tax year under examination, with a one-year Code Sec. 481(a) adjustment period.[32]

Situations with a different "adjustment inclusion period" are explained at the place in this Handbook where the item subject to the accounting rule is discussed.

---

23. ¶G-2203.9; ¶4464.225
24. ¶G-2220 *et seq.*; ¶4464.22
25. ¶G-2215; ¶4464.21; TD ¶443,301
26. ¶G-2290 *et seq.*; ¶4814; TD ¶443,301
27. ¶G-2304; ¶4814; TD ¶443,302

28. ¶G-2360; ¶4814; TD ¶440,817
29. ¶G-2309; ¶4814; TD ¶443,304
30. ¶G-2311; ¶4814; TD ¶443,303
31. ¶G-2308; ¶4814; TD ¶443,303
32. ¶G-2308; ¶4464.21; TD ¶442,555

¶ 2844 Relief for high-impact adjustments.

Where Code Sec. 481(a) adjustments increase taxable income of the change-over year by more than $3,000, the taxpayer can compute his tax for that year using whichever of these two methods produces the lower tax:

(1) *Three-year allocation*—The tax that would have resulted if one-third of the increase had been included in taxable income in each of the two preceding years and in the change-over year. (Code Sec. 481(b)(1); Reg § 1.481-2(a))

(2) *Allocation of specific years under new method of accounting*—Where the taxpayer establishes his taxable income under the new method of accounting for one or more tax years consecutively preceding the year of change (in which the old method was actually used), the tax is reduced to the amount that would have been paid if:

(a) the tax for the preceding years was figured under the new method, and

(b) the then-remaining adjustments were allocated to the change-over year. (Code Sec. 481(b)(2); Reg § 1.481-2(b))[33]

In making the above computations, the entire Code Sec. 481(a) adjustment required as a result of the accounting method change is taken into account. (Reg § 1.481-1(d))[34]

¶ 2845 Automatic consent procedures for certain accounting method changes.

IRS provides automatic procedures for obtaining IRS consent to make some accounting method changes. Guidance on these are contained in *Rev Proc 2011-14,* 2011-4 IRB 330, which for changes within its scope is the exclusive means of obtaining an accounting method change.[35] Some of the more commonly applicable "automatic consent" items are those involving: permissible to permissible accounting method for depreciation; uniform capitalization methods of small resellers; cash or hybrid method to accrual method; series E or EE U.S. savings bonds; timing of incurring liabilities for employee compensation, workers' compensation, and payroll taxes; change from last-in-first-out (LIFO); retail safe harbor method (and certain other methods) for estimating inventory shrinkage; and capitalizing costs incurred in acquiring or creating intangible assets. IRS has announced that it will provide procedures for automatic consent to changes in accounting procedures under the recent repair/capitalization regs under Code Sec. 162 and Code Sec. 263 for tax years beginning after 2011. (TD 9636, 919/2013) There are generally no user fees for automatic-consent accounting method change requests.[36] For applying for an automatic consent accounting method change, see ¶2840.

¶ 2846 Reserves for Expenses. ▄▄▄▄▄▄▄▄▄▄▄▄▄▄▄▄▄▄▄▄▄▄▄▄▄▄▄▄▄

Taxpayers often maintain accounting reserves for various future liabilities. Generally, no deduction is allowed for additions to these reserves.

¶ 2847 Reserves for estimated expenses and contingent liabilities.

Deduction or exclusion from income isn't allowed for additions to reserves for estimated expenses or contingent liabilities, even if reserves are required by state law or by contract, unless the reserve is expressly authorized by the Code (e.g., depreciation)[37] or is a reserve for trading stamps or coupons (Reg § 1.451-4(a))[38] or for container deposits. However, the use of this method for container deposits applies only where the containers are leased or loaned (*not* sold). Thus, no reserve is permitted for refundable deposits on empty beverage containers under states' environmental and conservation laws. The deposits are includible in income

---

33. ¶G-2401; ¶4814; TD ¶443,304
34. ¶G-2401; ¶4814; TD ¶443,304
35. ¶G-2203 *et seq.*; ¶4464; TD ¶442,606 *et seq.*

36. ¶G-2203.13
37. ¶s G-2733, G-2737; ¶4514.017; TD ¶442,036
38. ¶G-2742; ¶s 4514.161, 4514.163; TD ¶442,037

when received and refunds are deductible when paid.[39]

¶ 2848   Long-Term Contracts. ▬▬▬▬▬▬

Long-term contracts generally must be accounted for by the percentage-of-completion method. For how to account for long-term contracts for alternative minimum tax purposes, see ¶3208.

¶ 2849   Accounting for long-term contracts.

Taxpayers must account for long-term contracts (except for certain home and other real property construction contracts, see ¶2850) under the percentage-of-completion method (¶2852), subject to an election to use a modified percentage-of-completion method ("10% method," see ¶2853). (Code Sec. 460)[40]

A long-term contract is any contract for the manufacture, building, installation, or construction of property, if not completed in the tax year in which entered into. (Code Sec. 460(f)(1); Reg § 1.460-1(b)(1)) Whether the taxpayer reasonably expected that the contract would be completed within the tax year is not relevant.[41] But a manufacturing contract isn't long-term unless it involves manufacture of a unique item (of a type not normally included in inventory), or an item that normally requires more than 12 months to complete.[42] (Code Sec. 460(f)(2))

¶ 2850   Exception for small construction contracts.

Home construction contracts (specially defined) aren't limited to the percentage-of-completion method. Nor are any other real property construction contracts if originally estimated to be completed within two years of the contract start date, and if the taxpayer's average annual gross receipts for the three previous tax years don't exceed $10 million (including receipts of certain related businesses). (Code Sec. 460(e); Reg § 1.460-3(b)) Regs provide reporting methods for exempt contracts. (Reg § 1.460-4(c))[43]

¶ 2851   Allocation of costs to long-term contracts.

All costs that directly benefit, or are incurred by reason of, a long-term contract (including research and experimental costs) must be allocated to the contract in the same manner as costs were allocated to extended-period long-term contracts entered into before Mar. 1, '86, under Code Sec. 451 and former Reg. § 1.451-3(d) except that past service pension costs must be allocated to the contract. Also, in the case of a cost-plus contract or a federal long-term contract or subcontract, any other costs (e.g., general and administrative expenses) must be allocated to the contract if identified by the taxpayer (or a related person) as being attributable to it under the contract, or under federal, state, or local law or regulation. (Code Sec. 460(c)(1), Code Sec. 460(c)(2))[44] Interest costs are allocated to long-term contracts in a way that's similar to the way interest costs are allocated under the uniform capitalization rules (Code Sec. 263A(f)) (¶1667) that apply to property produced by a taxpayer. (Code Sec. 460(c)(3); Reg § 1.460-5(b)(2)(v))[45]

The allocation rules don't apply to any expenses for unsuccessful bids and proposals; marketing, selling, and advertising expenses; or independent research and development (IR&D) expenses. IR&D expenses don't include expenses directly attributable to a long-term contract in existence when the expenses are incurred, or expenses under an agreement to perform research and development. (Code Sec. 460(c)(4), Code Sec. 460(c)(5))[46] Costs of a guaranty, warranty, or maintenance agreement aren't treated as part of a long-term contract.

---

39. ¶G-2740; TD ¶442,039
40. ¶s G-3100, G-3229; ¶4514.125; TD ¶445,001
41. ¶G-3103; ¶4604; TD ¶445,027
42. ¶s G-3102, G-3106; ¶4604; TD ¶445,029

43. ¶G-3209; ¶4604; TD ¶445,033
44. ¶G-3143 *et seq.*; ¶s 4514.132, 4604; TD ¶445,016
45. ¶G-3150; ¶s 4514.132, 4604; TD ¶445,019
46. ¶G-3154 *et seq.*; ¶4604; TD ¶445,021

(Reg § 1.460-1(d)(2))

Alternatively, a taxpayer may elect to use the simplified cost-to-cost allocation method, under which a contract's completion factor is determined based upon only direct material costs; direct labor costs; and depreciation, amortization, and cost recovery allowances on equipment and facilities directly used to manufacture or construct the subject matter of the contract. Material or labor costs associated with a subcontractor's activities must be allocated to the contract. A taxpayer electing this method must use it to apply the look-back method (¶2854) and to determine alternative minimum taxable income. Elect the simplified cost-to-cost method for all long-term contracts entered into during the tax year by using it on the original federal income tax return for the election year. The election isn't available if the percentage-of-completion method (¶2852) is not used for all long-term contracts or if the 10% method (¶2853) is used. (Code Sec. 460(b)(3)(A); Reg § 1.460-5(c))[47]

Home construction contracts and real property construction contracts not subject to long-term contract accounting restrictions (¶2849) are exempt from the above cost allocation rules other than the interest allocation rules. (Code Sec. 460(e))[48]

¶ 2852 Percentage-of-completion method.

Under this method, a long-term contract's percentage of completion must be determined by comparing costs allocated to the contract and incurred before the close of the tax year, with estimated total contract costs. (Code Sec. 460(b)(1)(A)) For qualified property placed in service after 2009 and before 2011 (before 2012 for certain property with a long production period) or after 2012 and before 2014 (before 2015 for certain property with a long production period), bonus depreciation (¶1933) isn't taken into account in applying the percentage of completion method. (Code Sec. 460(c)(6)) Events that occur after the end of the tax year that are reasonably subject to estimate as of the last day of the tax year are taken into account.[49]

Gross income recognized in a particular year under the percentage-of-completion method equals total revenue expected from the contract times the cumulative percentage of the contract completed as of the end of the tax year, less the total cumulative amount of contract revenue required to be included in gross income in all preceding tax years. (This can result in a deductible loss for a year if total estimated contract costs increase.) (Reg § 1.460-4(b)(2))[50]

If the total contract price has not been included in gross income by the completion year, the taxpayer must include the remaining portion of the total contract price in gross income for the following tax year. (Reg § 1.460-4(b)(3))

When the contract is completed (or, for amounts received or accrued after completion, when those amounts are received or accrued), the taxpayer must either pay or is entitled to receive interest computed under the look-back method discussed at ¶2854. (Code Sec. 460(b)(1)(B))[1]

¶ 2853 Modified percentage-of-completion method—"the 10% method."

For purposes of the percentage-of-completion method (¶2852), a taxpayer may elect not to recognize income under the contract and not to take into account any costs allocable to the long-term contract for any tax year if, as of the end of the tax year, less than 10% of the estimated total contract costs have been incurred. (Code Sec. 460(b)(5)) Elect by using the 10% method for all long-term contracts entered into during the tax year on the original federal income tax return for the election year. If elected, the method is used to apply the look-back method (¶2854) and to determine alternative minimum taxable income. It can't be used if the simplified cost-to-cost method (¶2851) is used. (Reg § 1.460-4(b)(6)(ii))[2]

---

47. ¶G-3138; ¶4604; TD ¶445,023
48. ¶G-3209 *et seq.*; ¶4604; TD ¶445,033
49. ¶G-3143; ¶4604; TD ¶445,002

50. ¶G-3126 *et seq.*; ¶4604; TD ¶445,002
1. ¶G-3156; ¶4604; TD ¶445,044
2. ¶G-3229 *et seq.*; ¶4604; TD ¶445,088

¶ 2854 Look-back method for interest on tax—Form 8697.

In the tax year a long-term contract (with exceptions, below) is completed, the taxpayer must compare the amount of taxes paid in previous years under the percentage method with the tax that would have been owed if actual, rather than anticipated, costs and contract price had been used to compute gross income. Interest at the "adjusted overpayment rate" (overpayment rate (¶4853) for the calendar quarter in which the "interest accrual period" begins) for any "interest accrual period" (period beginning the day after the return due date, without extensions, and ending on the return due date of the following tax year) is owed by or payable to the taxpayer (use Form 8697) if there is, respectively, an underpayment or overpayment for any tax year. (Code Sec. 460(b)(2), Code Sec. 460(b)(7))[3] For pass-through entities, see ¶2855.

Taxpayers may elect (for all contracts completed in the election year and all future years, revocable only with IRS consent) not to apply the look-back method if at the close of each contract year before the tax year in which the look-back method would otherwise have to be applied, the cumulative taxable income (or loss) under the contract (using estimated contract price and costs) is within 10% of the cumulative look-back income or loss under the contract. (Code Sec. 460(b)(6)) Elect by attaching a statement to a timely filed (including extensions) original return for the election year. (Reg § 1.460-6(j))[4]

The look-back method doesn't apply to any contract whose gross price (at completion) doesn't exceed the lesser of $1,000,000 or 1% of taxpayer's average annual gross receipts for the three tax years preceding the tax year the contract was completed if the contract is completed within two years of its start date. (Code Sec. 460(b)(3)(B))[5] Nor does it apply to home construction contracts or others described at ¶2850. (Reg § 1.460-6(b)(2))[6]

¶ 2855 Simplified look-back marginal-impact method for pass-through entities.

For partnerships, S corporations and trusts (that aren't 50% or more held directly or indirectly by five or fewer persons), a simplified look-back marginal-impact method is applied at the entity level if substantially all the income from the contract is U.S.-source. The amount of taxes treated as overpaid or underpaid under a contract in any year is found by multiplying the amount of contract income over- or under-reported for the year by the top marginal tax rate applicable for the year. (Code Sec. 460(b)(4); Reg § 1.460-6(d)(1))[7] Individuals, C corporations and owners of closely-held pass-through entities may elect to use this method. Also, widely-held pass-through entities may use it for foreign contracts. (Reg § 1.460-6(d)(4))[8]

¶ 2856 Long-term contract following mid-contract change.

The tax treatment following a mid-contract change in taxpayer of a long-term contract depends on whether the change is a "constructive completion transaction" or a "step-in-the-shoes transaction." In a constructive completion transaction, the old taxpayer is treated as completing the contract and the new taxpayer as entering into a new contract on the transaction date. This approach applies to any transaction not subject to the step-in-the-shoes approach. (Reg § 1.460-4(k)(2)) In general, with a step-in-the-shoes transaction, the old taxpayer's obligation to account for the contract terminates on the transaction date and is assumed by the new taxpayer. The new taxpayer assumes the old taxpayer's methods of accounting for the contract, with both the contract price and allocable contract costs based on amounts taken into account by both parties. Special rules apply to the treatment of certain partnership transactions. (Reg § 1.460-4(k), Reg § 1.460-6(g))[9]

---

3. ¶G-3161 *et seq.*; ¶4604; TD ¶445,054
4. ¶G-3203.1; ¶4604; TD ¶445,049
5. ¶G-3158; ¶4604; TD ¶445,050 *et seq.*
6. ¶G-3159; TD ¶445,051

7. ¶G-3195 *et seq.*; ¶4604; TD ¶445,074
8. ¶G-3201; ¶4604; TD ¶445,074
9. ¶G-3246; ¶4604.04

¶ 2857 Reconstruction of Income by IRS.

Where taxpayer's records are inadequate, IRS can reconstruct taxpayer's income by whatever method will in its opinion most clearly reflect income.

The methods most often used are:

The net worth method. Here, IRS attempts to establish an opening net worth or total value of the taxpayer's assets at the beginning of a given year. It then proves increases in the taxpayer's net worth for each later year during the period under examination and calculates the difference between the adjusted net values of the taxpayer's assets at the beginning and end of each of the years involved. The taxpayer's nondeductible expenditures, including living expenses, are added to these increases. If the resulting figure for any year is substantially greater than the taxable income reported by the taxpayer for that year, IRS treats the excess as unreported taxable income.[10]

Bank deposit method. The bank deposit method assumes that all deposits represent income unless the taxpayer can show otherwise.[11]

Percentage markup method. IRS determines taxpayer's net income by applying certain percentages, e.g., gross profit to sales, or net income to gross income, or net income to sales, derived from other taxpayers in the same kind of business.[12]

¶ 2858 Reallocations of Income by IRS.

IRS is authorized (under Code Sec. 482) to distribute, apportion, or allocate gross income, deductions, credits or allowances among two or more organizations, trades, or businesses owned or controlled by the same interests in order to prevent tax evasion or to reflect the true taxable income of any of those entities. A similar rule also allows IRS to reallocate tax items (under Code Sec. 269A) for a personal service corporation.

IRS can reallocate income under Code Sec. 482 regardless of the entities' *motives* for shifting it, and can reallocate even if the shift was unintentional. (Reg § 1.482-1(c))[13]

If an allocation is made for a transaction between controlled taxpayers, IRS will also take into account the effect of any other non-arm's length transaction between the same controlled taxpayers in the same tax year which will result in a setoff against the original allocation. (Reg § 1.482-1(g)(4)(i)) Procedures have been issued for notifying IRS of a proposed setoff.[14]

The tax treatment of services transactions ensures that valuable intangibles cannot be transferred outside the U.S. for less than arm's length consideration, and update guidance on the transfer pricing methods to determine the arm's-length price in services transactions. (Reg § 1.482-9)[15]

Under advance pricing agreements (APAs) with IRS, taxpayers can prospectively determine and apply transfer pricing methodologies to international transactions by related foreign or domestic taxpayers (and resolve other related issues).[16]

¶ 2859 Reallocation of personal service corporation (PSC) income.

To prevent tax avoidance or evasion or to clearly reflect income, IRS may allocate all income, deductions, credits, exclusions and other allowances between a PSC and its employee-owner who owns more than 10% of the PSC stock (on any day in the tax year) if: substantially all of its services are performed by or for one other corporation, partnership, or entity (including related parties) and are availed of principally to avoid federal income tax by securing for

---

10. ¶G-2912; ¶s 4464.41, 4464.42; TD ¶444,010
11. ¶G-2941; ¶s 4464.41, 4464.67; TD ¶444,027
12. ¶G-2948; ¶s 4464.41, 4464.76; TD ¶444,031
13. ¶G-4018; ¶4824

14. ¶G-4108; ¶4824.08
15. ¶G-4200; ¶G-4500; ¶4824.04, ¶4824.06
16. ¶G-4700 *et seq.*; ¶4824.07

any employee-owner significant tax benefits that he wouldn't otherwise have. (Code Sec. 269A(a))[17] A PSC is one whose principal activity is the performance of personal services, substantially all of which are performed by employee-owners for one other corporation, partnership, or entity (including related parties). The Code Sec. 318 attribution rules apply for purposes of the 10% test, except that for purposes of applying the Code Sec. 318(a)(2)(C) rules, attribution is triggered by 5% rather than 50% stock ownership. (Code Sec. 269A(b)(2))[18]

¶ 2860   Previously Reported Income Repayments.

Taxpayers who must repay amounts they previously reported as income may deduct the repayments in the year the repayments are made. If the amount repaid exceeds $3,000, the taxpayer may recover the tax paid on that amount in the year he reported it, if that gives him the greater tax benefit.

¶ 2861   Deducting the repayment of previously reported income.

A taxpayer who must repay previously-reported income is entitled to deduct the amount repaid.[19] For relief where the repayment exceeds $3,000, see ¶2862.

For a cash basis taxpayer, the year of the deduction, and accordingly the year that the special computation might be available, is the year the income previously reported was repaid. If the taxpayer reported the income as constructively received, the year of deduction is the year he had to relinquish his claim to the income. (Reg § 1.1341-1(e))[20]

For an accrual basis taxpayer, the year of deduction is the year liability for repayment becomes fixed. Where the taxpayer received the income reported, the year of deduction is the year it's finally established the taxpayer had no unrestricted right to it. (Reg § 1.1341-1(e))[21]

¶ 2862   Repayments that exceed $3,000.

If the amount of the deduction allowed for a tax year (¶2861) with respect to an item reported as income in an earlier tax year is more than $3,000, and:

... that item was included in gross income in the earlier year because it appeared that the taxpayer had an unrestricted right to it then; and

... the deduction is allowed because it was shown after the close of the earlier year that taxpayer did *not* have an unrestricted right to all or part of that item,

then the tax for the year in which the deduction is allowed is the lesser of:

(1) the tax for that year computed with the deduction, or

(2) the tax for that year computed *without the deduction,* minus the decrease in tax for the earlier year that would result solely from excluding the deductible repayment. (Code Sec. 1341(a))

This relief for repayments exceeding $3,000 doesn't apply:

... where repayment is required because of a liability that arose later, as distinguished from absence of an unrestricted right to the income previously reported;[22]

... where an item was originally included in gross income by reason of the sale or other disposition of stock-in-trade, or other property includible in inventory if on hand at close of the earlier tax year, or property held primarily for sale to customers in the ordinary course of business—i.e., it doesn't apply to sales returns and allowances and similar items (Code Sec. 1341(b)(2); Reg § 1.1341-1(f));

17. ¶G-4751; ¶269A4
18. ¶G-4766; ¶269A4
19. ¶G-3001; ¶13,414; TD ¶203,015
20. ¶G-3027; ¶13,414.01; TD ¶444,520
21. ¶G-3028; ¶13,414.01; TD ¶444,520
22. ¶G-2308; ¶13,414; TD ¶444,511

. . . to deductions attributable to bad debts or to legal fees and other expenses incurred in contesting the repayment of income previously included. (Reg § 1.1341-1(g), Reg § 1.1341-1(h))[23]

¶ 2863 Inventories.

Where producing, buying or selling merchandise is an income-producing factor, inventories are needed to determine the correct cost of goods sold.

Inventories serve to allocate the expense of buying merchandise to the year in which that merchandise is sold.[24]

Inventories must be used whenever IRS finds their use is needed to clearly determine a taxpayer's income. (Code Sec. 471) Generally, this is the case where the "production, purchase or sale of merchandise" is an income-producing factor. (Reg § 1.471-1)[25] A taxpayer that must use inventories also must use the accrual method of accounting for its purchases and sales. (Reg § 1.446-1)[26] However, IRS has excepted non-tax-shelters with average annual gross receipts of $1 million or less from having to account for inventories and certain taxpayers with not more than $10 million average annual gross receipts, see ¶2818. Also, pending the release of further guidance, IRS will not assert that construction contractors must maintain inventory accounts for the supplies used in their businesses.[27]

caution: Under the uniform inventory inclusion and capitalization rules (¶1667 *et seq.*), certain direct and indirect costs are either included in inventory or capitalized.

¶ 2864 What goods are included in inventory?

Inventories include all merchandise that is held for sale in the ordinary course of business or that is to become a physical part of merchandise intended for sale. Inventories generally cover finished or partly finished goods as well as raw materials and supplies acquired for sale or that will physically become a part of merchandise intended for sale. For items to be included in inventory, taxpayer must have title. (Reg § 1.471-1)[28] Prescription drugs and similar items administered by healthcare providers are not merchandise.[29]

Merchandise shipped on approval or sold on sample is kept in the seller's inventory until its acceptance. Consigned goods or goods in the hands of others for processing (e.g., dyeing) and returnable in kind are kept in the consignor's inventory. A seller's inventory includes goods he has contracted to sell but not yet segregated and applied to the contract, while a buyer's inventory includes merchandise in transit to him or that for other reasons hasn't been reduced to possession but to which he has title. But a buyer does *not* include in inventory goods ordered for future delivery.[30]

Containers that are to be *sold* with the merchandise they contain should be included in the seller's inventory, regardless of whether they are returnable. If the containers are merely leased or loaned with a deposit received to guarantee the return, they aren't included in inventory since they aren't part of the merchandise held for sale. In that case they can be inventoried at cost the same as supplies, considered as fixed assets and depreciated, or, if they have a useful life of less than a year, currently deducted.[31]

¶ 2865 Valuing inventory.

The two most commonly recognized bases of valuing inventories are: (1) cost, and (2) cost or market, whichever is lower. (Reg § 1.471-2(c))[32] Farmers may use other valuation methods, see ¶4513 *et seq.* For inventories of dealers in securities, see ¶2879.

---

23. ¶s G-3032, G-3034, G-3035; ¶13,414.01; TD ¶444,523
24. ¶G-5000 *et seq.*; ¶4714; TD ¶450,500
25. ¶G-5001; ¶4714; TD ¶450,501
26. ¶G-2089; ¶4464.07; TD ¶450,506
27. ¶G-5001

28. ¶G-5006 *et seq.*; ¶4714; TD ¶450,509 *et seq.*
29. ¶G-5001
30. ¶G-5009; ¶4714; TD ¶450,517
31. ¶G-5010; ¶4714; TD ¶450,513
32. ¶G-5101; ¶s 4714.21, 4714.41, 4714.51; TD ¶451,001

Consistency from year to year in whatever inventory procedure is adopted is of first importance. (Reg § 1.471-2(b))[33]

¶ 2866   Valuation of unsalable, slow-moving and traded-in goods.

Any goods in inventory that are unsalable at normal prices or in the normal way because of damage, imperfections, style changes, etc., can at the taxpayer's option be written down — that is, valued at selling prices less direct costs of disposition, whether the cost or the lower of cost or market method is used. If the goods consist of raw materials or partly finished goods held for use or consumption, they must be valued upon a reasonable basis, considering the usability and condition of the goods, but in no case at less than scrap value. (Reg § 1.471-2(c))[34] Selling price means the actual price at which goods are offered for sale during a period ending not later than 30 days after the date of inventory. (Reg § 1.472-2(c))[35]

Normal but slow-moving inventory (i.e., goods in excess of current demand) can't be written down based on arbitrary cut-off time periods.[36]

¶ 2867   Prohibited valuation methods and practices.

The following aren't permitted:

(1) Deducting from inventory a reserve for price changes or an estimated depreciation in the value of inventory (but for permissible estimates of inventory shrinkage, see ¶2868).

(2) Valuing work in process, or other parts of the inventory, at a nominal price or at less than its proper value.

(3) Omitting portions of the stock on hand.

(4) Using a constant price or nominal value for so-called normal quantity of material or goods in stock.

(5) Segregating indirect production costs into fixed and variable classifications and allocating only the variable costs to the cost of goods produced while treating fixed costs as currently deductible (the "direct cost" method).

(6) Treating all or substantially all indirect production costs (whether classified as fixed or variable) as currently deductible (the "prime cost" method). (Reg § 1.471-2(f))[37]

¶ 2868   Estimates of inventory shrinkage.

A method of determining inventories doesn't fail to clearly reflect income solely because it uses estimates of inventory shrinkage that are confirmed by a physical count only after the last day of the tax year if the taxpayer: (1) normally does a physical count at each location on a regular and consistent basis, and (2) makes proper adjustments to inventories and to its estimating methods if estimates are greater or less than actual shrinkage. (Code Sec. 471(b)) Use the automatic consent procedure (¶2845), with some modifications, to change to the retail safe harbor method of estimating inventory shrinkage (using a historical ratio of shrinkage-to-sales to estimate shrinkage occurring between the last physical inventory and the end of the tax year), or to a method that clearly reflects income other than the retail safe harbor method if the method being changed from didn't estimate inventory shrinkage.[38]

¶ 2869   What is cost?

The cost of goods on hand at the start of an accounting period is the amount at which they were valued in the closing inventory of the period before. (Reg § 1.471-3(a))[39]

---

33. ¶G-5002; ¶4714.21; TD ¶450,502
34. ¶G-5159; ¶4714.35; TD ¶451,510
35. ¶G-5161; ¶4714.35; TD ¶451,511
36. ¶G-5164; TD ¶451,514

37. ¶G-5124; ¶4714.21; TD ¶451,020
38. ¶G-5120.1; ¶4714.38; TD ¶451,014
39. ¶G-5102; ¶4714.41; TD ¶451,002

The cost of the goods purchased ordinarily is the invoice price reduced by trade or other discounts. Strictly cash discounts approximating a fair interest rate may be deducted at the option of the taxpayer if the method is consistently followed. (Reg § 1.471-3(b))[40] To this net invoice price should be added transportation or other necessary charges incurred in acquiring possession of the goods. (Reg § 1.471-3(b))[41]

The costs of goods produced by the taxpayer include, in addition to the opening inventory, cost of raw materials and supplies entering into or consumed in manufacture, regular and overtime direct labor costs, and the indirect costs required to be included under the "full absorption" method. (Reg § 1.471-3(c))[42]

For the uniform capitalization rules for including costs in inventory, see ¶1667 *et seq.*

¶ 2870 Valuing inventory using the lower of cost or market method.

Under this method, market value on the inventory date is compared with the cost of each item. The lower of the two is the inventory value of the item. Total inventory is the aggregate of the inventory values so computed for each item in the inventory. It is *not* the lower of the total cost or total market value of all items. (Reg § 1.471-4(c))[43]

¶ 2871 Market value defined.

Market value normally means the current bid price prevailing at the inventory date for the particular merchandise in the volume usually purchased by the taxpayer. Market price is applied to: (1) goods purchased and on hand, and (2) the basic elements of cost (materials, labor and overhead) of goods in process of manufacture and of finished goods on hand. (Reg § 1.471-4(a))[44]

Market price may not be applied to goods on hand or in process if the merchandise is covered by a firm sales contract at fixed prices (i.e., not legally subject to cancellation by either buyer or seller). If, under the contract, the taxpayer is protected against actual loss, the goods must be inventoried at cost with no deduction for inventory decline. (Reg § 1.471-4(a)) Moreover, goods covered by firm sales contracts at the end of the year must be valued at cost even though the contracts are cancelled after the close of the year at the customer's request.[45] If the contract gives the seller an almost certain loss, IRS says the seller isn't allowed to write the inventory down but must value it at cost, thus taking the loss when actually realized (Reg § 1.471-4(a)), but some courts disagree.[46]

A taxpayer may write down inventory below market if, in the regular course of business, he has offered the merchandise for sale at below-market prices. (Reg § 1.471-4(b))

If no market exists, or if quotations are nominal because of an inactive market, the taxpayer must use whatever evidence of a fair market price at the date or dates nearest his inventory date as may be available, e.g., specific purchases and sales made by the taxpayer or others in reasonable volume and in good faith, or compensation paid for cancellation of contracts for purchase commitments. (Reg § 1.471-4(b))[47]

¶ 2872 Inventory cost identification methods.

Under the specific identification method, goods are matched with their invoices (less appropriate discounts) to find the cost of each item.[48]

Where it isn't possible or practicable to identify each item of inventory with its cost, an

---

40. ¶G-5107, G-5108; ¶4714.41; TD ¶451,003
41. ¶G-5103, G-5110; ¶4714.41; TD ¶451,006
42. ¶s G-5102 *et seq.*, G-5402; ¶4714.41
43. ¶G-5150; ¶4714.51; TD ¶451,501
44. ¶G-5151; ¶4714.51; TD ¶451,502

45. ¶G-5154 *et seq.*; ¶4714.51; TD ¶451,505
46. ¶G-5154 *et seq.*; ¶4714.51; TD ¶451,503
47. ¶G-5157; ¶4714.51; TD ¶451,508
48. ¶s G-5121, G-5265; ¶4714.41; TD ¶452,020

assumption must be made to determine which items were sold and which remain in inventory. Although only two methods of costing intermingled merchandise are specifically approved (the "first-in, first-out" (FIFO) and the "last-in, first-out" (LIFO) methods,   ¶2873), any method that comes within the best accounting practice of the particular business and clearly reflects income is acceptable. Two permissible cost identification methods are averaging the cost of each type or grade of goods in the inventory (¶2875), and mainly relying on the taxpayer's accounting records to arrive at the correct inventory value (¶2877). The base stock method (the assumption that a certain portion of inventory will be maintained from year to year and therefore need not be revalued) isn't permitted.[49]

The inventory price index computation (IPIC) method, under which inventory price indexes are computed with reference to consumer or producer price indexes published by the U.S. Bureau of Labor Statistics (BLS) (Code Sec. 472(f); Reg § 1.472-8(e)(3)), is intended to simplify the use of the dollar-value LIFO method (¶2875).[50]

¶ 2873   FIFO (first-in, first-out) and LIFO (last-in, first-out) methods.

Under the FIFO method, the cost of goods that are so intermingled they cannot be identified with specific invoices is considered to be the cost of goods most recently purchased or produced. (Reg § 1.471-2(d))[1]

Under the LIFO method of inventory valuation, the most recently purchased merchandise is treated as the first sold. (Code Sec. 472(b)(1))[2] LIFO may generally be used only where inventory is valued at cost. (Reg § 1.472-2(b))[3] If a taxpayer had written down inventory to a lower market value, the difference between that value and cost must be restored to income ratably over a three-year period (beginning with the year of the election to LIFO). (Code Sec. 472(d))[4]

In order to use LIFO for tax purposes, the enterprise must also use LIFO in its reports to partners, stockholders, etc., and for credit purposes. (Code Sec. 472(c))[5]

Qualifying heavy equipment dealers using LIFO or FIFO may, like auto dealers, use replacement cost to determine the cost of their heavy parts inventory under safe harbor rules.[6]

¶ 2874   Electing last-in, first-out (LIFO)—Form 970.

File Form 970 (or other acceptable statement) with the return for the tax year as of the close of which LIFO is first to be used (Reg § 1.472-3)[7] or re-elected in the fifth or later tax year after changing from LIFO (otherwise IRS permission is needed for the change, see ¶2838 *et seq.*) Once made, the election applies to all later years unless IRS grants permission to change. (Reg § 1.472-5)[8] Automatic consent procedures (¶2845) apply to adoption of certain specialized LIFO methods and to changes from LIFO.

¶ 2875   Dollar-value last-in, first-out (LIFO) and simplified dollar-value LIFO.

Under this method, a taxpayer who deals in a large variety of products may value inventory by the use of the dollar value rather than natural units. The assumption is that items in the inventory are homogeneous. The taxpayer is therefore required to break up the inventory into a series of "pools" —the natural business unit pool or multiple pools. (Reg § 1.472-8)[9] Any taxpayer electing to use the dollar-value LIFO method can elect to compute an inventory price index in accordance with the Inventory Price Index Computation method (Reg § 1.472-8(e)(3)(ii), see ¶2872.

---

49. ¶G-5125 *et seq.*; ¶4714.41
50. ¶G-5253; ¶4724; TD ¶452,055
1. ¶G-5121; ¶4714.41; TD ¶451,017
2. ¶G-5200; ¶4724; TD ¶452,001
3. ¶G-5212; ¶4724; TD ¶452,001
4. ¶G-5208; ¶4724; TD ¶452,009

5. ¶G-5307; ¶4724; TD ¶452,076
6. ¶G-5248.4
7. ¶G-5202; ¶4724; TD ¶452,003
8. ¶G-5201; ¶4724; TD ¶452,002
9. ¶G-5245 *et seq.*; ¶4724; TD ¶452,046

An eligible small business may elect to use a simplified dollar-value method of pricing inventories for purposes of the LIFO method. Under this method, the cost of each grade of goods is averaged. (Code Sec. 474(a)) An eligible small business is a taxpayer whose average annual gross receipts don't exceed $5 million for the three-tax-year period ending immediately before the tax year. (Code Sec. 474(c))[10]

¶ 2876 Retailers' inventory.

Retailers can value each item of merchandise in stock at the end of the year at its retail selling price, but adjusted to approximate cost by eliminating the average percent of markup. (Reg § 1.471-8(a))[11] This retail inventory method may be used in conjunction with FIFO and specific identification methods, as well as LIFO (¶2873), if the taxpayer adjusts his selling price for both markups and markdowns. (Reg § 1.471-8(g))[12] Price change adjustments are determined by reference generally to U.S. Bureau of Labor Statistics price indexes. (Reg § 1.472-1(k))[13]

¶ 2877 Book (perpetual) inventory method.

Under this method, inventory accounts are charged with the actual cost of goods purchased or produced, and credited with the cost of goods used, transferred or sold. The net amount is considered to be the cost of the goods on hand, if the balances shown on the books are adjusted at reasonable intervals to conform to physical inventories. (Reg § 1.471-2(d))[14]

¶ 2878 Miners' and manufacturers' inventory.

Miners and manufacturers who use a single process or uniform series of processes, and derive a product of two or more kinds, sizes or grades with a unit cost substantially alike, may allocate a share of total cost to each kind, size or grade as a basis for pricing inventories. (Reg § 1.471-7)[15]

¶ 2879 Securities and commodities dealers' inventories—mark-to-market rules.

Any security that's inventory in the hands of a securities dealer must be included in inventory at its fair market value. (Code Sec. 475(a)(1)) In the case of a non-inventory security that's held at the close of a tax year, the dealer must recognize gain or loss as if the security were sold for its fair market value on the last business day of that year, and any gain or loss must be taken into account for that tax year, generally as ordinary income or loss. (Code Sec. 475(a)(2), Code Sec. 475(d)(3))[16] A "security" doesn't include any security held for investment, certain other securities, and hedges of those securities (but only if the hedge is clearly identified as a hedge in the dealer's records before the close of the business day on which it was acquired, originated or entered into). (Code Sec. 475(b))[17] A security also doesn't include nonfinancial customer paper arising from the sale of nonfinancial goods or services by sellers or providers of those goods or services which are held by them (or related parties) at all times since issue. (Code Sec. 475(c)(4))[18] Commodities dealers may elect (under interim procedures[19]) to apply the mark-to-market rules to commodities held by them in the same way that the rules apply to securities held by securities dealers. (Code Sec. 475(e)(1)) Once made, the election may be revoked only with IRS consent. (Code Sec. 475(e)(3))[20] Where the Code Sec. 475 rules don't apply, a securities dealer inventories securities at: (1) cost, (2) lower of cost or market, or (3) market value. (Reg § 1.471-5)[21]

---

10. ¶G-5302 *et seq.*; ¶4744; TD ¶452,070
11. ¶G-5351; ¶4724.06; TD ¶453,001
12. ¶G-5357; ¶4724.06; TD ¶453,006
13. ¶G-5362; ¶4724.06; TD ¶453,011
14. ¶G-5119; ¶4714.21; TD ¶451,013
15. ¶G-5020; ¶4714.85; TD ¶450,520

16. ¶I-7652; ¶4754
17. ¶I-7657 *et seq.*; ¶4754
18. ¶I-7657.1; ¶4754
19. ¶I-7669; ¶4754.02
20. ¶I-7667 *et seq.*; ¶4754.01
21. ¶G-5021; ¶s 4754, 4714.67

A dealer is one who regularly buys and sells securities to customers (or enters into or terminates positions in securities with customers) in the ordinary course of business. (Code Sec. 475(c)(1))[22] If one's sole business is trading in securities he's not a dealer[23] (but for the mark-to-market election by traders, see ¶2880).

¶ 2880   Mark-to-market election for securities and commodities traders.

A person engaged in the trade or business of securities trader or commodities trader may elect (under interim procedures[24]) to have the following mark-to-market rules apply to the trade or business: (1) gain or loss is recognized on any security (or commodity) held in connection with the trade or business at the close of any tax year as if the security (or commodity) were sold for its fair market value on the last business day of the tax year, and (2) gain or loss is taken into account for the tax year (Code Sec. 475(f)(1)(A), Code Sec. 475(f)(2)) as ordinary income or loss. Once made, the election may be revoked only with IRS consent. (Code Sec. 475(f)(3)) These elective mark-to-market rules don't apply to securities or commodities that have no connection to the electing person's trading activities if they are clearly identified as such before the close of the day acquired. (Code Sec. 475(f)(1)(B)) Securities and commodities subject to this election aren't subject to the constructive sale rules of Code Sec. 1259 (¶2637). (Code Sec. 475(f)(1)(C))[25]

¶ 2881   Changing inventory method—Form 3115.

A change in the method of valuing inventory, with the exception of a change to LIFO (¶2874) and to certain specialized LIFO methods (¶2845), requires IRS approval. This includes adoption of either: (1) cost, or (2) cost or market, whichever is lower, where the taxpayer has been on a different basis, and changes to and from the various methods of determining inventory costs. Use Form 3115, under the rules at ¶2840. (Reg § 1.446-1(e))[26] An automatic consent procedure also applies for certain taxpayers changing *from* LIFO (¶2845).[27]

---

22. ¶G-5023; ¶4754
23. ¶I-7656.1; ¶4754
24. ¶I-7675; ¶4754.02

25. ¶I-7670 *et seq.*; ¶4754.01
26. ¶G-2101 *et seq.*, ¶G-5201 *et seq.*; ¶4464.21; TD ¶451,022
27. ¶G-5217 *et seq.*; ¶s 263A4.10, 4464.21, 4724; TD ¶452,018

Chapter 12   Withholding Tax on Wages and Other Income Payments

¶ 3000   Withholding on Wages.

Employers must withhold income tax from wages paid to employees, but not from amounts paid to independent contractors. "Wages" includes most forms of taxable compensation. Employees are entitled to minimum, and sometimes additional, withholding exemptions or allowances. Withheld tax must be paid through electronic funds transfers.

For withholding on certain federal payments (e.g., social security payments), see ¶3009. For other nonpayroll withholding, see ¶3031. For withholding from U.S. source amounts paid to nonresident aliens and foreign corporations, see ¶4662.

¶ 3001   Withholding by employers.

Employers must withhold. (Code Sec. 3402(a)(1); Reg § 31.3402(a)-1(b))[1] An employer is any person or organization for whom an individual performs any service as an employee. (Code Sec. 3401(d)) An employer includes any person paying wages to a former employee, (Reg § 31.3401(d)-1(b)) and includes tax-exempt organizations. (Reg § 31.3401(d)-1(d))[2] Employers who outsource some or all of their payroll responsibilities remain liable for all taxes, penalties and interest due.[3]

If the actual employer doesn't have control over the payment of wages, the person who does have control must withhold. (Code Sec. 3401(d)(1)) A lender, surety or other person is personally liable for the employee income tax required to be withheld if he: (1) directly pays wages to another's employees (Code Sec. 3505(a)), or (2) supplies funds specifically for the payment of the wages of another's employees knowing the employer can't or doesn't intend to pay payroll taxes. In the case of (2), liability is limited to 25% of the amount supplied (inclusive of interest). (Code Sec. 3505(b); Reg § 31.3505-1(b))

A disregarded single-owner entity is treated as a separate entity (i.e., as a corporation) for purposes of employment taxes and related reporting requirements. (Reg § 1.1361-4(a)(7), Reg § 301.7701-2(c)(2)) An owner of a disregarded entity treated as a sole proprietorship is subject to self-employment taxes. (Reg § 301.7701-2(c)(2))[4]

If a person pays wages on behalf of a nonresident employer not engaged in trade or business in the U.S., that person must withhold. (Code Sec. 3401(d)(2))[5]

¶ 3002   Employees defined.

Every individual who performs services subject to the will and control of an employer, both as to what is to be done and how it's to be done, is an employee for withholding purposes. It doesn't matter that the employee has considerable discretion and freedom of action, so long as the employer has the *legal right* to control both the method and the result of the services. (Reg § 31.3401(c)-1(b)) For how IRS determines whether a worker is an employee or independent contractor, see ¶3003.

It doesn't matter that the employee is designated a partner, agent or independent contractor, or how payments are measured or paid or what they're called. (Reg § 31.3401(c)-1(e))[6]

No distinction is made between classes of employees. Managers and other supervisory

1. ¶H-4222; ¶34,024; TD ¶531,001
2. ¶H-4226; ¶34,014.60; TD ¶534,001
3. ¶V-1664
4. ¶H-4223; TD ¶534,002
5. ¶s H-4229, H-4236, H-4374; ¶34,014.60; TD ¶532,038
6. ¶H-4251; ¶34,014.37; TD ¶535,001

References beginning with a single letter are to paragraphs in RIA's Federal Tax Coordinator 2d and RIA's Analysis of Federal Taxes: Income. Those beginning with numbers are to paragraphs in RIA's United States Tax Reporter. Those beginning with TD are to paragraphs in RIA's Tax Desk.

personnel are employees. An officer of a corporation is an employee (Code Sec. 3401(c)), but a director in his capacity as director isn't an employee. (Reg § 31.3401(c)-1(f))[7]

Persons in business for themselves aren't employees. For example, self-employed physicians, lawyers, dentists, veterinarians, construction contractors and others who offer their services to the public aren't employees. (Reg § 31.3401(c)-1(c))[8]

Qualified real estate agents and direct sellers are treated as independent contractors. (Code Sec. 3508(a))[9]

Statutory employees, such as certain drivers, life insurance salespersons, home workers, and other salespersons, who are treated as employees for FICA purposes (Code Sec. 3121(d)(3)) but aren't common law employees, aren't employees for income tax purposes.[10]

 observation: A person not treated as an employee for income tax purposes can't be covered under employee plans, e.g., medical reimbursement and group-term life insurance plans.

If payment is made for services rendered and the payor isn't sure whether the payee is an employee or independent contractor, the payor may get an IRS ruling by filing Form SS-8. (Reg § 31.3401(d)-1(d))[11] Adverse rulings can be reviewed by the Tax Court (Code Sec. 7436) after IRS sends an adverse notice of determination.[12]

Employees who have been misclassified as independent contractors by an employer use Form 8919 to figure and report the employee's share of uncollected Social Security and Medicare taxes due on their compensation. The worker performing the services must meet one of several criteria supporting his belief that he's an employee, e.g., receipt of an SS-8 determination letter.[13]

¶ 3003   How IRS determines employee or independent contractor status.

To determine whether a worker is an independent contractor or an employee, IRS examines the relationship between the worker and the business, and considers all evidence of control and independence. The facts that provide this evidence fall into the following three categories:

(1) *Behavioral control* covers facts that show whether the business has a right to direct and control how the work is done through instructions, training, or other means. Employees are generally given instructions on when and where to work, what tools to use, where to purchase supplies, what order to follow, etc.

(2) *Financial control* covers facts that show whether the business has a right to control the financial and business aspects of the worker's job. This includes the extent to which the worker has unreimbursed business expenses; the extent of his investment in the facilities being used; the extent to which he makes his services available to the relevant market; how he's paid; and the extent to which he can realize a profit or incur a loss.

(3) *Type of relationship* includes written contracts describing the relationship the parties intended to create; the extent to which the worker is available to perform services for other, similar businesses; whether the business provides the worker with employee-type benefits, such as insurance, a pension plan, vacation pay, or sick pay; the permanency of the relationship; and the extent to which services performed by the worker are a key aspect of the company's regular business.

---

7. ¶H-4252; ¶s 34,014.39, 34,014.40; TD ¶535,003
8. ¶H-4258; ¶34,014.47, 34,014.48, 34,014.50, 34,014.61; TD ¶535,001
9. ¶H-4283; ¶34,014.37; TD ¶535,032

10. ¶H-4300; ¶624.03; TD ¶542,007
11. ¶H-4282; ¶34,014.37; TD ¶535,008
12. ¶U-2143; ¶74,364; TD ¶806,067
13. ¶S-1709.1; TD ¶570,208.1

IRS's three-category approach essentially distills the 20-factor test IRS had used to determine whether a worker was an employee or an independent contractor.[14]

A consultant can simultaneously be an employee and an independent contractor when working on two projects for the same company. IRS will separately examine the relationship between the worker and the business for each performance of services.[15]

In certain cases in which a taxpayer has a reasonable basis for treating an individual as a non-employee (e.g., judicial precedent, IRS ruling, past audit allowance), a special statutory rule (section 530 of the '78 Revenue Act) may allow non-employee treatment regardless of the above factors.[16]

IRS has a voluntary compliance program that allows employers to prospectively reclassify—as employees—those workers they have erroneously treated as independent contractors. The program features settlement terms and provides audit relief for previous years. Eligible taxpayers apply by filing Form 8952, at least 60 days before they want to begin treating the workers as employees.[17]

¶ 3004 Wages subject to withholding.

"Wages" cover all types of employee compensation, including salaries, fees, bonuses, commissions and fringe benefits. It's immaterial whether payments are based on the hour, day, week, month, year or on a piecework or percentage plan, or whether they're called wages, salaries, fees, etc. (Code Sec. 3401(a); Reg § 31.3401(a)-1(a)(2), Reg § 31.3401(a)-1(a)(3))[18] Bonuses received for signing employment contracts are wages, as are payments received for canceling employment contracts.[19] Wages also include amounts includible in an employee's gross income for failure to comply with the Code Sec. 409A deferred compensation rules (¶1275). (Code Sec. 3401(a)) For withholding purposes they are treated as paid in the year they are includable in gross income.[20]

Noncash wages are the fair market value of the goods, lodging, meals or other consideration given for services. (Reg § 31.3401(a)-1(a)(4))[21]

Vacation allowances[22] and back pay, including retroactive wage increases, are wages. (Reg § 31.3401(a)-1(b)(3))[23] An appellate court has ruled that an age discrimination settlement payment received by a taxpayer was wages.[24] The Supreme Court has agreed to resolve a circuit split on whether severance pay is subject to FICA tax.[25] Amounts received as "front pay" are wages subject to withholding, according to IRS, but some courts have disagreed. Front pay is an amount paid to an individual for pay he would have received after a settlement date or court award but for the employer's wrongful conduct and the circumstances— e.g., extreme animosity between the parties—that make it impractical to place the employee in the position.[26] IRS isn't bound by the settlement allocation of payments under a class action lawsuit and can instead convert portions of a settlement allocated to penalty and interest payments into wages subject to employment taxes.[27]

Supplemental unemployment compensation benefits are treated as wages for income tax purposes (Code Sec. 3402(o)(1)(A), Code Sec. 3402(o)(2)),[28] but they aren't subject to FICA if certain conditions are met.[29] Differential wage payments are also wages for income tax purposes and are treated as supplemental wage payments (¶3011). These are payments to employees for periods that they are called to active duty with the U.S. uniformed services (for

14. ¶H-4259; TD ¶535,009
15. ¶H-4258.1; TD ¶535,001
16. ¶H-4303 *et seq.*; ¶34,014.375; TD ¶537,003
17. ¶H-4282.1; TD ¶535,008.1
18. ¶H-4326; ¶34,014.01, 34,014.02, 34,014.09; TD ¶532,001
19. ¶H-4360.2, ¶H-4361.1
20. ¶H-4326, ¶H-4333.1; ¶34,014.025; TD ¶532,046
21. ¶H-4327; ¶34,014.09; TD ¶532,001

22. ¶H-4364; ¶34,014.04; TD ¶532,029
23. ¶H-4355; ¶34,014.09; TD ¶532,024
24. ¶H-4355
25. ¶H-4664; TD ¶544,021
26. ¶H-4360.1
27. ¶J-5810
28. ¶H-4351
29. ¶H-4664

more than 30 days) that represent all or part of the wages that they would otherwise received from the employer. (Code Sec. 3401(h)) They aren't subject to FICA and FUTA withholding.[30]

Withholding is computed on gross wages before any deductions by the employer for social security tax, pensions, union dues, insurance, etc. (Reg § 31.3401(a)-1(b)(5))[31]

Employers are required to withhold an additional 0.9% Medicare tax on wages (see ¶1108), and are liable for the tax that it fails to withhold from wages or collect from the employee. The obligation applies only to wages in excess of $200,000 that the employee receives from the employer. An employer isn't required to notify an employee when it begins withholding the additional tax, and should begin withholding in the pay period in which it pays wages to the employee exceeding the $200,000 threshold and not earlier. If the $200,000 threshold is exceeded, the additional tax must be withheld even if the employee ultimately won't owe the tax because the taxpayer and spouse file a joint return and won't meet the $250,000 threshold for joint filers. The employer disregards any wages paid to the employee by another employer. Wages paid by two or more employers aren't combined to reach the threshold unless the payor is a common paymaster. IRS provides FAQs explaining employers' withholding obligations.[32]

¶ 3005   Tips.

Wages includes tips. (Code Sec. 3401(f)) But, withholding isn't required on cash tips of less than $20 a month received by an employee, or for tips paid in any medium other than cash (such as passes, tickets or other goods or commodities). (Code Sec. 3401(a)(16); Reg § 31.3401(a)(16)-1) But, if cash tips amount to $20 or more in a month, none of the cash tips are exempt. The $20 test is applied separately with respect to cash tips received by the employee for his services to each employer. (Reg § 31.3401(a)(16)-1)[33] (For the business tax credit for employer FICA tax paid on tips for food and beverage service, see ¶2327.)

¶ 3006   Exempt "wages"—fringes, reimbursed expenses, domestic service, etc.

The following aren't wages subject to income tax withholding:

. . . Fringe benefits, if it's reasonable to believe that the employee will be able to exclude them from income as a qualified scholarship, a no-additional-cost service, a qualified employee discount, a working condition fringe, a de minimis fringe, a qualified transportation fringe, a qualified moving expense reimbursement, an on-premises athletic facility, or an employee achievement award. (Code Sec. 3401(a)(19))[34] (For the employer's election not to withhold on a vehicle fringe benefit, see ¶3007.)

. . . Amounts specifically advanced or reimbursed to employees for traveling or other ordinary and necessary expenses incurred or reasonably expected to be incurred in the employer's business. But they must be either paid separately, or specifically identified if combined with wages in a single payment. (Reg § 31.3401(a)-4(a)) If a reimbursement or other expense allowance arrangement meets the requirements of Code Sec. 62(c) (¶3104, i.e., an "accountable plan"), payments that don't exceed the substantiated expenses aren't wages and aren't subject to withholding. Payments that aren't substantiated within a reasonable period of time or are in excess of substantiated expenses are wages and subject to withholding. Per diem or mileage allowances at a rate in excess of the deemed substantiated amount are subject to withholding. If the arrangement doesn't meet the Code Sec. 62(c) requirements (i.e., a "nonaccountable plan"), all amounts paid are wages and subject to withholding. (Reg § 31.3401(a)-4(a), Reg § 31.3401(a)-4(b), Reg § 1.62-2(h)(1), Reg § 1.62-2(h)(2))[35]

30. ¶H-4372; ¶34,014.11; TD ¶532,036
31. ¶H-4331; TD ¶532,001
32. ¶H-4701.1; ¶31,114; TD ¶546,001

33. ¶H-4341; ¶34,014.31; TD ¶532,011
34. ¶H-4400 *et seq.*; ¶s 34,014.09, 34,024; TD ¶533,001
35. ¶H-4340; ¶34,014.03; TD ¶532,004

... Moving expense reimbursements, if a corresponding deduction is allowable under the normal Code Sec. 217 rules, see ¶1646, (determined without regard to the Code Sec. 274(n) percentage limit on meal expenses). (Code Sec. 3401(a)(15))[36]

... Tips, under the circumstances at ¶3005.

... Benefits paid by a labor union to workers unemployed because of a strike or lockout.[37]

... Payments for agricultural labor except if during the year: (1) cash payments to an employee are $150 or more, or (2) the employer pays all such employees $2,500 or more (unless the employee is a hand harvest laborer who is paid on a customary basis, commutes daily to the farm from his permanent residence and was employed in agriculture less than 13 weeks during the prior year). (Code Sec. 3401(a)(2), Code Sec. 3121(a)(8))[38]

... Payments for domestic service in a private home, local college club, or fraternity or sorority chapter. (Code Sec. 3401(a)(3))[39]

... Certain payments for services by a U.S. citizen for an employer outside the U.S. (Code Sec. 3401(a)(8)(A)(i))[40]

... Premiums paid by an employer for group term insurance on an employee's life. (Code Sec. 3401(a)(14))[41]

... Payments to or on behalf of an employee or his beneficiary to or from a qualified plan (except payments for services rendered by an employee of the plan) (Code Sec. 3401(a)(12)(A)); to or under a qualified annuity plan (Code Sec. 3401(a)(12)(B)); under a SIMPLE retirement account (Code Sec. 3401(a)(12)(D)); to or under a governmental section 457 plan (Code Sec. 3401(a)(12)(E)); or, if it's reasonable to believe the employee will be entitled to exclude the payment, for contributions to a simplified employee pension for an employee. (Code Sec. 3401(a)(12)(C))[42]

... Payments made under educational assistance or dependent care programs if it's reasonable to believe that the employee can exclude them. (Code Sec. 3401(a)(18))[43]

... Payment of deceased employee's accrued wages to his estate or beneficiaries.[44]

... Combat zone compensation excludible under Code Sec. 112. (Code Sec. 3401(a)(1))[45]

... Employer contributions to medical savings accounts. (Code Sec. 3401(a)(21), Code Sec. 3401(a)(22))[46]

... Qualified adoption expenses paid under an employer's adoption assistance program.[47]

... Disqualifying dispositions of stock acquired through the exercise of an incentive stock option or an option under an employee stock purchase plan (ESPP) (Code Sec. 421(b)) or with respect to any amount treated as compensation as a result of the ESPP discount option rule which treats a part of the gain on a disposition of stock acquired through the exercise of an option under an ESPP as compensation income if the option price at which the stock was acquired was between 85% and 100% of its fair market value at the time the option was granted. (Code Sec. 423(c))[48]

¶ 3007 Employer's election not to withhold on vehicle fringe benefit.

Employers may elect not to withhold on an employee's use of an employer-provided vehicle where that use is wages to the employee. The employer must notify the employee of the election and include the amount of the benefit on a timely furnished Form W-2. (Code Sec. 3402(s))[49]

---

36. ¶H-4418; ¶34,014.30; TD ¶533,014
37. ¶H-4354; ¶34,014.10; TD ¶532,023
38. ¶H-4426; ¶34,014.18; TD ¶536,023
39. ¶H-4450 *et seq.*; ¶34,014.19; TD ¶536,006
40. ¶s H-4442, H-4443; ¶34,014.23; TD ¶536,013
41. ¶H-1518 *et seq.*, ¶H-4400 *et seq.*; ¶34,014.29
42. ¶H-10500 *et seq.*; ¶34,014.27; TD ¶553,237

43. ¶H-4401; ¶34,014.05; TD ¶533,001
44. ¶H-4350; ¶34,014.07; TD ¶532,019
45. ¶H-4447; ¶34,014.17; TD ¶536,004
46. ¶H-4326; ¶34,014.67; TD ¶533,001
47. ¶H-4401; TD ¶533,001
48. ¶H-4448.2; TD ¶532,035.1
49. ¶s H-4411, H-4412; ¶34,024.27; TD ¶533,010

¶ 3008   Withholding on sick pay—Form W-4S.

If the recipient of sick pay that isn't wages requests the payor (on Form W-4S) to withhold a specified amount of at least $20 from each payment, the payor must withhold that amount. (Code Sec. 3402(o)(1)(C); Reg § 31.3402(o)-3(b)) An employee doesn't have to request withholding if his employer makes the sick payments since employers are required to withhold income tax from sick pay.[50]

¶ 3009   Voluntary withholding agreements—Form W-4 and Form W-4V.

Household, and other employees who aren't subject to income tax withholding may elect to have tax withheld, if their employers agree. (Code Sec. 3402(p)) Other employees can also have their withholding increased voluntarily. (Code Sec. 3402(i))

The rules generally applicable to mandatory withholding, including withholding rates and tables, apply to the voluntary withholding. An employee requests voluntary withholding by filing a Form W-4 with his employer—unless he wants the voluntary withholding to apply for a *limited period of time*. In that case, he must also give the employer a statement that includes the date the voluntary withholding is to terminate.

A voluntary withholding agreement may be terminated by the employer or employee by giving advance notice to the other in accordance with the regs. (Reg § 31.3402(p)-1)[1]

A taxpayer can request voluntary withholding at a rate of 7%, 10%, 15%, or 25% on certain federal payments, including Social Security benefits, crop disaster payments, and Commodity Credit Corporation loans (Code Sec. 3402(p)(1)), and at a 10% rate on unemployment compensation payments (¶1281). (Code Sec. 3402(p)(2)) Use Form W-4V.[2]

¶ 3010   Fringe benefits.

Fringe benefits must be treated as paid at least annually. Except for transfers of either personal property of a kind normally held for investment or real property (which must be reported when they are actually paid), an employer may elect to treat fringe benefits as paid quarterly, semiannually, annually, or on another basis. An employer may also treat a fringe benefit as paid in installments, even if the entire benefit is paid at one time. Benefits provided in a calendar year must be treated as paid by Dec. 31 of that year.[3]

Employers may treat fringe benefits as part of regular wages for the payroll period and compute withholding on the total, or instead withhold 20% of the value of the benefit from regular wages. (Reg § 31.3501(a)-1T, Q&A-10) Any noncash fringe benefit provided in a calendar quarter may be treated as provided on the last day of that quarter. (Reg § 31.3501(a)-1T, Q&A-1)[4]

For when withholding isn't required on a presumptively tax-free fringe benefit, see ¶3006. For the election to not withhold on the value of a vehicle fringe benefit provided to the employee, see ¶3007.

¶ 3011   Supplemental wage payments.

Withholding on bonuses, commissions, overtime pay or other supplemental wages paid:

. . . *with regular wages*, should be determined as if the total supplemental and regular wages were a single payment for the regular payroll period; (Reg § 31.3402(g)-1(a))

50. ¶H-4337; ¶H-4481 *et seq.*; ¶34,024.25; TD ¶532,015
1. ¶H-4477 *et seq.*; ¶34,024.19; TD ¶538,049 *et seq.*
2. ¶H-4483 *et seq.*; ¶34,024.25; TD ¶538,053 *et seq.*

3. ¶H-4403; ¶34,024; TD ¶533,002 *et seq.*
4. ¶H-4404 *et seq.*; ¶s 34,024, 34,024.27; TD ¶533,003

. . . at a different time, can be determined by adding the supplemental wages either to the regular wages for the current payroll period or to the last preceding payroll period within the same calendar year; (Reg § 31.3402(g)-1(a))

. . . where tax has been withheld on regular wages, generally can be determined by using a flat rate of not less than 25% without allowance for exemptions and without reference to any regular wage payment. (Reg § 31.3402(g)-1(a)) Where tax has been withheld on regular wages (during the calendar year of the payment or the preceding one), withholding generally can be determined (at the employer's option) by using a flat rate of 25% without allowance for exemptions and without reference to any regular wage payment, if the supplemental wages are either paid at a different time than the regular wages or are separately stated on the employer's payroll records. (Reg § 31.3402(g)-1(a))[5]

But, for supplemental wage payments totalling more than $1 million for a calendar year, the withholding rate is increased to the maximum tax rate under Code Sec. 1 (i.e., 39.6%).[6]

The employer has the option of treating either the entire supplemental payment or just that which brings the total payment over $1 million as subject to this mandatory withholding. (Reg § 31.3402(g)-1(a)(4)(iv))[7]

Where tax isn't withheld from regular wages for employees who receive both regular wages and supplemental wages (e.g., tips), the flat supplemental withholding rate can't be used; the tips are added to the current or preceding regular wage payment and withholding is computed at the regular graduated rates.[8] A payment qualifies as supplemental wages even if no regular wages have been paid to the employee.

Extra pay for working during a vacation period is treated as a supplemental wage payment. (Reg § 31.3402(g)-1(c))[9] Employers have the option to treat tips and overtime pay as either regular or supplemental wages. (Reg § 31.3402(g)-1(a))[10]

IRS provides guidance on withholding on supplemental wages in a variety of situations.[11] An employee can't ask an employer to withhold additional amounts, other than those required to be withheld, from supplemental wages, with respect to the mandatory and optional flat rate methods of withholding. But, an employee has some control over withholding if the aggregate procedure is used.[12]

¶ 3012 Computing the amount withheld—percentage and wage bracket methods.

There are two principal systems of withholding: (1) the percentage or exact method, and (2) the wage bracket method. IRS provides tables to use for each.[13] Whichever method is used, the employer applies the withholding allowances and marital status indicated by the employee, see ¶3014 *et seq.* For variations of these two methods, see ¶3013.

If an employer fails to withhold income tax and the employee's portion of FICA taxes because the employer failed to treat the payee as an employee, for prior years the withholding rate is generally reduced to 1.5% of wages for income tax withholding, and only 20% of the regular amount to be withheld for FICA will generally have to be withheld. Certain exceptions apply. (Code Sec. 3509)[14]

¶ 3013 Alternative withholding methods.

IRS also authorizes withholding on the basis of: (1) annualized wages, (2) cumulative wages, (3) part-year employment, (4) average estimated wages, and (5) any other method that

---

5. ¶s H-4531, H-4539, H-4544.1; ¶34,024.13; TD ¶538,516
6. ¶H-4542; ¶34,024.13; TD ¶538,519
7. ¶H-4538.3 *et seq.*; ¶34,024.13; TD ¶538,520
8. ¶H-4538.4
9. ¶H-4538.5; ¶34,024.13; TD ¶538,514

10. ¶H-4538.3 *et seq.*; ¶34,024.13; TD ¶538,503
11. ¶H-4540
12. ¶H-4539; TD ¶538,516
13. ¶H-4493 *et seq.*; ¶34,024.02 *et seq.*; TD ¶538,004 *et seq.*
14. ¶H-4225; ¶35,094; TD ¶531,004

results in substantially the same amount of withholding as the percentage method. (Methods (2) and (3) are at the employee's request.) (Code Sec. 3402(h))[15]

¶ 3014   Employee's withholding allowance certificate—Form W-4.

An employer should ask each new employee to fill out a Form W-4 withholding allowance certificate before employment begins. (Code Sec. 3402(f)(2)(A)) Employers must take into account the marital status and exemptions and allowances of each employee on the basis of that Form W-4. A certificate filed by a new employee is effective on the first payment of wages. (Code Sec. 3402(f)(3)) If an employee fails to furnish a certificate, the employer must withhold tax as if the employee were a single person with no withholding exemptions or allowances. (Code Sec. 3401(e); Reg § 31.3402(f)(2)-1(e))[16]

An employer can establish a system for its employees to file Form W-4 electronically. (Reg § 31.3402(f)(5)-1(c))[17]

¶ 3015   Withholding exemptions.

An employee is allowed: (1) a regular exemption for himself, unless he's claimed as another's dependent; (2) a regular exemption for his spouse, unless the spouse is employed and claims a regular exemption; (3) an exemption for each dependent he may claim on his tax return; (Code Sec. 3402(f)(1); Reg § 31.3402(f)(1)-1)[18] and (4) additional withholding allowances, ¶3016.

A taxpayer working for more than one employer must allocate his allowances on separate Forms W-4 filed with each employer. (Code Sec. 3402(f)(7); Reg § 31.3402(m)-1(f)(2))[19]

The withholding exemption allowance is the same amount as allowed for a personal exemption, ¶3115. (Code Sec. 3402(a)(2))[20]

¶ 3016   Additional withholding allowances.

Employees may claim (on Form W-4) additional withholding allowances for: estimated tax credits like those shown on Form 1040; and estimated itemized deductions and other deductions including the additional standard deduction for the aged and blind, but only if his spouse doesn't have in effect a Form W-4 claiming the same allowances. (Code Sec. 3402(m); Reg § 31.3402(m)-1)[21]

caution: A taxpayer who has too little tax withheld because he has claimed too many withholding allowances may have to pay a penalty for underpayment of estimated tax, see ¶3163.

An additional withholding allowance (called a "standard deduction allowance") can be claimed by an employee who is single and has only one job. Even if an employee is married (¶4705) and his spouse is also employed, or even if he has two or more jobs, he can claim the special withholding allowance if his and his spouse's combined wages is $1,500 or less. (Code Sec. 3402(f)(1)(E); Reg § 31.3402(f)(1)-1(e))[22]

¶ 3017   Employees with no tax liability.

Employees with no tax liability can be exempt from income tax withholding. To qualify, the employee certifies on Form W-4 to his employer that he expects to have no federal income tax liability for the current year, *and* he had no federal income tax liability in the preceding year.

15. ¶H-4492; ¶34,024.18; TD ¶538,006 *et seq.*
16. ¶H-4516; ¶34,024.09 *et seq.*; TD ¶538,031
17. ¶H-4523.1; ¶34,024.11; TD ¶538,038
18. ¶H-4505; ¶34,024.10; TD ¶538,020

19. ¶H-4516; ¶34,024.10; TD ¶538,024
20. ¶H-4492; ¶34,024.10; TD ¶538,020
21. ¶H-4518 *et seq.*; ¶34,024.23; TD ¶538,026
22. ¶H-4506; ¶34,024.10; TD ¶538,021

(Code Sec. 3402(n); Reg § 31.3402(n)-1)[23]

An employee who can be claimed as a dependent on someone else's tax return (whether or not actually claimed) can't claim exemption from withholding for 2013 or 2014 if his income exceeds $1,000 and includes more than $350 of unearned income, such as interest and dividends. Special calculations must be made by an employee who is 65 or older and/or blind.[24]

¶ 3018   Amending withholding certificate.

The employee *must* amend his Form W-4, reducing the number of allowances, within ten days: (Code Sec. 3402(f)(2)(B); Reg § 31.3402(f)(2)-1(b))

. . . when the spouse he has been claiming is divorced or legally separated from him, or claims her own allowance on a separate W-4;

. . . when he loses the right to exemption for a claimed dependent;

. . . when he loses the right to the number of withholding allowances he has claimed.[25] The employer must give effect to an amended W-4 no later than the beginning of the first payroll period ending (or the first payment of wages made without regard to a payroll period) on or after the 30th day after the day the amended W-4 is furnished. (Code Sec. 3402(f)(3)(B)(i))[26]

An amended Form W-4 must be filed by Dec. 1 if the number of allowances is expected to *decrease* for next year. If the change resulting in the decrease occurs in Dec., the amended Form must be furnished within ten days of the date of the change. The number of allowances drops if a spouse or dependent died during the year or an individual will no longer qualify as a dependent.[27]

If the number of allowances is expected to increase next year, the employee can amend his W-4 by Dec. 1. If the change arises in Dec., the amended W-4 may be filed on or after the date of the change. (Code Sec. 3402(f)(2)(C); Reg § 31.3402(f)(2)-1(c)) This W-4 doesn't take effect and isn't to be made effective with respect to any payment of wages in the calendar year it's furnished. (Code Sec. 3402(f)(3)(B)(iii))[28]

¶ 3019   Employer withholding tax return—Forms 941 and 944.

Every employer (except household employers, see ¶3029) must file with IRS a quarterly return reporting withheld income taxes on Form 941. (Reg § 31.6011(a)-1, Reg § 31.6011(a)-4) Employers must submit copies of W-4S to IRS only when directed to do so by written notice or as directed in published guidance. (Reg § 31.3402(f)(2)-1(g)(1)) Where a serious underwithholding problem is found to exist for a particular employee, IRS will notify the employer to withhold income tax from that employee at a more appropriate rate (i.e., issue a "lock-in letter"). (Reg § 31.3402(f)(2)-1(g)(2))[29]

In certain cases (e.g., for taxpayers who must separately account, see ¶3025) IRS can require monthly wage withholding returns. (Reg § 31.6011(a)-5(a)(1))[30]

Form 941 must be filed by Apr. 30, July 31, Oct. 31 and Jan. 31 for the calendar quarters ending Mar. 31, June 30, Sept. 30 and Dec. 31, respectively, unless monthly filing is required. But the returns may be filed ten days later if timely deposits in full payment of the tax are made. (Reg § 31.6071(a)-1(a))[31] Form 941 reflects the 0.9% Medicare surtax that first applies in 2013 (¶1108).[32]

---

23. ¶H-4519; ¶34,024.24; TD ¶538,033.1
24. ¶H-4519; ¶34,024.24; TD ¶538,033.1
25. ¶H-4524; ¶34,024.11; TD ¶538,040
26. ¶H-4526; ¶34,024.11; TD ¶538,041.1
27. ¶H-4525; ¶34,024.11; TD ¶538,041

28. ¶H-4532; ¶34,024.11; TD ¶538,041
29. ¶S-2603; ¶s 34,034, 35,014.002; TD ¶557,001
30. ¶S-2604; ¶60,114.011; TD ¶557,004
31. ¶S-4918; ¶60,114.011; TD ¶557,002
32. ¶H-4687; TD ¶541,002

Form 941, Schedule D, can be used to explain reporting discrepancies after (1) statutory mergers and consolidations, and (2) acquisitions satisfying the requirements for predecessor-successor status.[33]

Employers with annual employment tax liabilities of $1,000 or less who have received written notification from IRS that they qualify for the program can file Form 944 annually, if they choose, instead of Form 941. (Reg § 31.6011(a)-4(a)(4)(i))[34] Employers that request to participate in the Form 944 program must receive notice to file Form 944 before they may file. Once notice is received, they must file Form 944 for each year and can't file Form 941 until they are notified that their filing requirement has been changed to Forms 941 either because they contacted IRS to request that their filing requirement be changed to Form 941 or they no longer qualify for the Form 944 program. (Reg § 31.6011(a)-1(a)(5))[35]

For nonpayroll withholding (backup withholding, withholding for pension, annuities, and gambling winnings, etc.), see ¶3031.

¶ 3020   Errors in withholding and payment of tax.

Where underwithholding of FICA and income tax is ascertained before the return is filed, the employer must report and pay the correct amount of tax by the due date of the return. (Reg § 31.6151-1, Reg § 31.6205-1(b)(1), Reg § 31.6205-1(c)(1))[36]

Rules are provided for making corrections (in some cases on an interest-free basis) after the return is filed.[37] Form 941-X is used to correct errors in a previously filed Form 941.[38]

Adjustment of same-sex spouses' employment taxes. Under optional, special administrative procedures, employers can correct overpayments of employment taxes as to certain benefits paid to same-sex spouses—i.e., employer-provided health coverage and fringe benefits that were provided to a same-sex spouse and are excludable from income under Code Sec. 106, Code Sec. 117(d), Code Sec. 119, Code Sec. 129, or Code Sec. 132 based on an individual's marital status (see ¶4705). After repaying or reimbursing the employees, employers may use the fourth quarter 2013 Form 941 to correct overpayments of employment taxes for the first three quarters of 2013. Alternatively, employers may file one Form 941-X for the fourth quarter of 2013 to correct the overpayments of FICA taxes for all quarters of 2013.

For overpayments of FICA taxes for years before 2013, employers can make a claim or adjustment for all four calendar quarters of a calendar year on one Form 941-X filed for the fourth quarter of the year if the limitations period on refunds hasn't expired and, in the case of adjustments, the limitations period will not expire within 90 days of filing the adjusted return. (Notice 2013-61, 2013-42 IRB)

¶ 3021   Wage and tax statement—Form W-2.

Along with other information, Form W-2 includes the amount of wages paid by the employer to the employee and the taxes withheld from the wages during the calendar year. (Code Sec. 6051(a)) An employer must show the value of the employee's health insurance coverage sponsored by the employer (Code Sec. 6051(a)(14)). The aggregate cost of employer-sponsored coverage must be reported on Form W-2, with an exception for small employers (defined as those that were required to file less than 250 Forms W-2 for the preceding calendar year).[39]

An employer in business must give each employee copies of Form W-2, on or before Jan. 31 of the year after the calendar year for which the wages were paid. If an employee leaves the

33. ¶S-3195.1
34. ¶S-4918; ¶60,114.011; TD ¶557,002
35. ¶S-4918.3; ¶60,114.011
36. ¶S-5525; ¶35,014.005; TD ¶559,516

37. ¶S-5526; ¶35,014.005; TD ¶559,516
38. ¶S-5533; ¶35,014.007; TD ¶557,003.
39. ¶S-3152; ¶S-3312; ¶60,514; TD ¶812,002

job before the end of the calendar year and isn't expected to return within the calendar year, Form W-2 must be given to him not later than 30 days after the employer receives a written request for it from the employee, if that 30-day period ends before Jan. 31. (Code Sec. 6051; Reg § 31.6051-1(d))[40]

¶ 3022 Nonreceipt of Form W-2 by employee—Form 4852.

If an employee doesn't receive a Form W-2, he should ask his employer for it. If the employer doesn't provide the form, the taxpayer should telephone IRS toll-free at the number listed in the income tax return instructions; IRS will ask the employer to send a copy or duplicate form. If the employee hasn't received a Form W-2 in time to file his tax return, he should file a return estimating wages and the income tax withheld on Form 4852.[41]

¶ 3023 Earned income credit notice to employees with no tax withheld—Notice 797.

An employer must notify any employee who hasn't had any tax withheld from his wages (other than an employee who certifies, see ¶3017, that he has no tax liability) that the employee may be eligible for a refund because of the earned income credit (¶2339 *et seq.*). IRS Notice 797 or a written statement containing an exact reproduction of the wording in Notice 797 must be used and furnished within one week of the date the employee should receive a timely Form W-2 or, if none is required, before Feb. 8th of the following calendar year. (Reg § 31.6051-1(h))[42]

¶ 3024 Payroll taxes.

The Federal Insurance Contributions Act (FICA) imposes two taxes, the Old Age, Survivors and Disability Insurance (OASDI) tax and the Medicare Hospital Insurance (HI) tax. These taxes are imposed on employers for wages paid with respect to employment and on employees for wages received with respect to employment. The OASDI tax rate is 6.2% on wages up to an annually-adjusted "wage base" (see ¶1108).[43]

The HI tax rate generally is 1.45% on all wages, regardless of amount. But, an additional 0.9% HI tax applies to certain high wage earners; see ¶1108.

For the credit against OASDI tax for hiring qualified veterans after Nov. 21, 2011 that a tax-exempt employer can claim (for the work opportunity tax credit that it could otherwise claim if it weren't tax-exempt), see ¶2316.

¶ 3025 Separate accounting for employment tax.

IRS can require an employer who fails to collect, account for, deposit, etc., income or related employment taxes or make timely deposits or file returns to make deposits in a special trust account. (Code Sec. 7512; Reg § 301.7512-1(b))[44]

¶ 3026 Deposit of employment taxes.

An employer is either a monthly or semi-weekly depositor. (Reg § 31.6302-1(a))

An employer is a monthly depositor for the entire calendar year if the aggregate amount of employment taxes reported for the lookback period (i.e., the 12-month period ended the preceding June 30) is $50,000 or less. (Reg § 31.6302-1(b)(2)(i), Reg § 31.6302-1(b)(4)) These employers must deposit taxes on or before the 15th day of the following month.

40. ¶S-4930; ¶60,514
41. ¶S-3193; TD ¶812,025
42. ¶H-4851 *et seq.*; ¶s 324.04, 60,514; TD ¶569,027

43. ¶H-4687; ¶35,014.07; TD ¶541,002
44. ¶S-5541 *et seq.*; ¶75,124; TD ¶531,002

(Reg § 31.6302-1(c)(1))[45]

An employer is a semi-weekly depositor for the entire calendar year if the aggregate amount of employment taxes reported for the lookback period (i.e., the 12-month period ended the preceding June 30) exceeds $50,000. (Reg § 31.6302-1(b)(3), Reg § 31.6302-1(b)(4)) The employer must deposit taxes on or before the following dates. (Reg § 31.6302-1(c)(2))[46]

If the wage payment date is:

. . . Wednesday, Thursday, and/or Friday, the deposit date is on or before the following Wednesday.

. . . Saturday, Sunday, Monday, and/or Tuesday, the deposit date is on or before the following Friday.

If a return period (quarterly or annual) ends during a semi-weekly period, the employer must designate on his deposit coupon the proper return period for which the deposits relates (the period in which the payment is made). If the return period ends during a semi-weekly period during which the employer has two or more payment dates, two deposit obligations may exist. (Reg § 31.6302-1(c)(2)(ii))[47]

Notwithstanding the above rules, under the "one-day rule," if on any day an employer has $100,000 or more of employment taxes accumulated, these taxes must be deposited by the close of the next banking day. (Reg § 31.6302-1(c)(3)) The day after a monthly depositor becomes subject to the one-day rule it becomes a semi-weekly depositor for the remainder of that calendar year and for the following calendar year. (Reg § 31.6302-1(b)(2)(ii))[48]

If a tax deposit day isn't a banking day, deposits are timely if made on the next day that is a banking day. (Reg § 31.6302-1(c)(4)) In addition, if one of the three weekdays following the close of a semi-weekly period is a bank holiday, the employer has an extra banking day to deposit taxes. (Reg § 31.6302-1(c)(2)(iii))[49]

Deposits are considered timely if mailed (postmarked, or date marked by a designated delivery service, see ¶4754) at least two days before the due date if the deposit is actually received by the bank. (Code Sec. 7502(e)) But a deposit of $20,000 or more by a person who is required to make a deposit more than once a month must be actually received by the due date. (Code Sec. 7502(e)(3))[50]

Taxpayers must deposit taxes by electronic funds transfer (¶3028).

¶ 3027 Deposit safe harbor and de minimis rules.

Under the single deposit safe harbor, an employer will be considered to have satisfied his deposit obligations if:

(1) the amount of any shortfall (the excess of the amount required to be deposited over the amount deposited for the applicable period—monthly, semi-weekly or daily) doesn't exceed the greater of $100 or 2% of the amount of employment taxes required to be deposited (Reg § 31.6302-1(f)(1)(i), Reg § 31.6302-1(f)(2)), and

(2) the employer deposits the shortfall on or before the shortfall make-up date. (Reg § 31.6302-1(f)(1)(ii)) For a monthly depositor, this is no later than the due date for the quarterly return. For a semi-weekly or a one-day depositor, this is on or before the first Wednesday or Friday (whichever is earlier) falling on or after the 15th day of the month following the month the deposit was required to be made. (Reg § 31.6302-1(f)(3))[1]

An employer with accumulated employment taxes of less than $2,500 for a return period

---

45. ¶S-5503; ¶63,014; TD ¶559,503
46. ¶S-5506; ¶63,014; TD ¶559,504
47. ¶S-5507; ¶63,014; TD ¶559,505
48. ¶S-5510; ¶63,014; TD ¶559,507

49. ¶S-5512; ¶63,014; TD ¶559,508
50. ¶T-10777 *et seq.*; ¶63,014, 75,024
1. ¶S-5513 *et seq.*; ¶63,014; TD ¶559,509

(quarterly or annual) doesn't have to make deposits and can instead remit his full liability with a timely filed return for the period. (Reg § 31.6302-1(f)(4))[2]

¶ 3028 Tax deposits by electronic funds transfer (EFT).

Unless exempted, all of the following are required to be deposited via EFT: FICA and FUTA taxes and withheld income taxes; corporate income and estimated taxes; unrelated business income taxes of tax-exempt organizations; private foundation excise taxes; taxes withheld on nonresident aliens and foreign corporations; estimated taxes on certain trusts; railroad retirement taxes; nonpayroll taxes, including backup withholding; and certain excise taxes. (Code Sec. 6302(h); Reg § 31.6302-1(h)(2)(iii))[3]

A taxpayer required to deposit by EFT must use the Electronic Federal Tax Payment System (EFTPS) to make federal tax deposits.[4] Taxpayers must enroll in EFTPS before they can make EFT deposits. Enroll on-line at www.eftps.gov.[5]

Federal income taxes (including estimated taxes) (Reg § 1.6302-4), estate (Reg § 20.6302-1) and gift taxes (Reg § 25.6302-1), and various excise taxes (Reg § 40.6302(a)-1) may be made voluntarily by EFT.[6]

A taxpayer required to deposit taxes by EFT that (without reasonable cause) deposits by other means is subject to the Code Sec. 6656 failure to deposit penalty.[7]

¶ 3029 Payment of Domestic Service Employment Tax ("Nanny Tax"). ▬▬▬

Domestic service employment taxes (income tax, FICA, and FUTA) can be paid in a lump sum when the employer's income tax return is filed.

¶ 3030 "Nanny tax"—Form 1040, Schedule H.

Employers of domestic service employees must file annual returns of domestic service employment taxes on a calendar-year basis (Code Sec. 3510(a)(1)) on or before the 15th day of the fourth month following the close of the employer's tax year. (Code Sec. 3510(a)(2)) Household employers report withheld income and FICA tax for their household employees on their individual income tax return (Form 1040, Schedule H) and need employer identification numbers (EINs, apply on Form SS-4).[8]

Annual Form 940 (FUTA) doesn't have to be filed for domestic employees. There is no requirement to make deposits of domestic service employment taxes, or to pay installments of these taxes under Code Sec. 6157 (Code Sec. 3510(a)(3)), dealing with quarterly payment of FUTA tax.

"Domestic service employment taxes" are: (1) any FICA and FUTA taxes on remuneration paid for domestic service in a private home of the employer (for dollar threshold see below), and (2) and any income tax on these payments that's withheld under the Code Sec. 3402(p) voluntary withholding agreement rules (¶3009) (for the otherwise applicable exemption from income tax withholding on domestic service employment, see ¶3006). (Code Sec. 3510(c))[9]

Domestic service is service of a household nature performed in and about the private home of the person for whom the services are performed. (Reg § 31.3121(a)(7)-1(a), Reg § 31.3401(a)(3)-1(a))[10]

Noncash payments for domestic services in an employer's private home are excluded from FICA wages. Cash remuneration paid by an employer for domestic service in the employer's

2. ¶S-5516; ¶63,014; TD ¶559,510
3. ¶S-5620 *et seq.*; ¶63,014; TD ¶559,850 *et seq.*
4. ¶S-5621; TD ¶559,857
5. ¶S-5630; TD ¶559,857
6. ¶S-5629; TD ¶559,863 *et seq.*

7. ¶V-1658; TD ¶559,853
8. ¶S-2608; ¶35,104; TD ¶557,007
9. ¶S-2608.3; ¶35,104
10. ¶H-4654; TD ¶536,006

private home isn't FICA wages if the cash remuneration paid during the year is less than the "applicable dollar threshold" —$1,800 in 2013, and $1,900 in 2014. (Code Sec. 3121(a)(7), Code Sec. 3121(x))[11]

✐ observation: The dollar threshold applies separately to each domestic employee. So, for example, if an employer pays $1,800 each to a babysitter and a housekeeper in 2013, no FICA tax is due for either.

Domestic service performed in the private home of the employer in any year by an individual under the age of 18 during any portion of the year is excepted from employment for FICA if the service isn't the principal occupation of the employee. (Code Sec. 3121(b)(21))[12]

Form W-2. An employer must furnish Form W-2 to household employees whose wages are subject to Social Security taxes even if they aren't subject to income tax withholding. (Reg § 31.6051-1(b)(1)) Use a Form W-3 transmittal to file even one Form W-2.[13]

¶ 3031 Nonpayroll Withheld Taxes. ▬▬▬▬▬

Income tax on gambling winnings, payments subject to backup withholding, retirement plan payments, IRAs, annuities and certain other deferred compensation are withheld under "nonpayroll withheld taxes" rules.

The employment tax deposit rules of ¶3026 *et seq.* apply to determine the time and manner of making deposits of nonpayroll withheld taxes. (Reg § 31.6302-4(a))[14] Whether a taxpayer is a monthly or a semi-weekly depositor for a calendar year is based on an annual determination and generally depends on the aggregate amount of nonpayroll withheld taxes reported by the taxpayer for the "lookback period" —i.e., the second calendar year preceding the current calendar year. So, the lookback period for calendar year 2014 is calendar year 2012. A new taxpayer is treated as having nonpayroll withheld taxes of zero for any calendar year in which the taxpayer didn't exist. (Reg § 31.6302-4(c)(2)(iv))[15]

A taxpayer is a monthly depositor of nonpayroll withheld taxes for a calendar year if the amount of nonpayroll withheld taxes accumulated in the lookback period is $50,000 or less. A taxpayer ceases to be a monthly depositor of nonpayroll withheld taxes on the first day after the taxpayer is subject to the "one-day rule" (¶3026) with respect to nonpayroll withheld taxes. At that time, the taxpayer immediately becomes a semi-weekly depositor of nonpayroll withheld taxes for the remainder of the calendar year and the succeeding calendar year. (Reg § 31.6302-4(c)(2)(ii))

A taxpayer is a semi-weekly depositor of nonpayroll withheld taxes for a calendar year if the amount of nonpayroll withheld taxes accumulated in the lookback period exceeds $50,000. (Reg § 31.6302-4(c)(2)(iii))

Nonpayroll withheld taxes are income taxes withheld from: gambling winnings (¶3033) (Reg § 31.6302-4(b)(1)); retirement pay for services in the Armed Forces under Code Sec. 3402 (Reg § 31.6302-4(b)(2); retirement plan payments, IRAs, annuities and certain other deferred compensation (¶3034) (Reg § 31.6302-4(b)(3)); and under the backup withholding rules (¶3044). (Reg § 31.6302-4(b)(5))[16]

For the requirement that some taxpayers deposit nonpayroll withheld taxes by electronic funds transfer (EFT), see ¶3028.

¶ 3032 Annual nonpayroll tax return—Form 945.

Taxpayers who withhold income tax from nonpayroll payments must report the withholding annually on Form 945. The return must be filed on or before Jan. 31 following the

---

11. ¶H-4653 *et seq.*; ¶35,104; TD ¶544,009
12. ¶H-4611.1; TD ¶543,031
13. ¶S-3159; TD ¶812,004

14. ¶S-5582 *et seq.*; ¶63,014
15. ¶S-5585; ¶63,014; TD ¶559,005
16. ¶S-5581; ¶63,014

calendar year. But, if timely deposits of tax have been made, the return may be filed by Feb. 10. (Reg § 31.6071(a)-1(a)(1))[17]

¶ 3033 Withholding on gambling winnings—Form W-2G and Form 5754.

Payors must withhold 25% on proceeds of more than $5,000 (Code Sec. 3402(q)(1)) from:

(1) a wagering transaction in a parimutuel pool with respect to horse races, dog races or jai alai if the amount of the proceeds is at least 300 times as large as the amount wagered; (Code Sec. 3402(q)(3)(C)(ii))

(2) a wager placed in a state-conducted lottery; (Code Sec. 3402(q)(3)(B))

(3) a sweepstakes, wagering pool or lottery (other than a state-conducted lottery); (Code Sec. 3402(q)(3)(C)(i)) or

(4) all other wagering transactions if the amount of the proceeds is at least 300 times as large as the amount wagered. (Code Sec. 3402(q)(3)(A))[18]

"Proceeds" means amount received from the wager reduced by the amount of the wager. (Code Sec. 3402(q)(4)(A))[19] Amounts paid with respect to identical wagers are treated as paid with respect to a single wager. (Reg § 31.3402(q)-1(c)(1)(ii))[20]

A person who receives gambling winnings subject to withholding must provide certain information on Form W-2G or Form 5754 and give it to the payor. (Code Sec. 3402(q)(6); Reg § 31.3402(q)-1(e))[21]

The above withholding rules don't apply to slot machines, keno and bingo winnings. (Code Sec. 3402(q)(5)) But, backup withholding (¶3044) may apply.[22] A payor must file a Form W-2G for every person the payor pays $1,200 or more in winnings from slot machines or bingo, or $1,500 or more from Keno (after deducting the cost of the winning Keno game). (Reg § 7.6041-1)[23]

Casinos and other sponsors of poker tournaments must report tournament winnings of more than $5,000. Sponsors who comply with the reporting requirement won't need to withhold. But, if the reporting requirement isn't met, IRS will enforce it and also require the sponsor to pay any tax that should have been withheld.[24]

Withholding on Indian casino profits. Withholding equal to a payment's proportionate share of annualized tax is required under tables provided by IRS (Reg § 31.3402(r)-1(a)(2)) on payments to Indian tribal members from the net revenue of most gambling activities of the tribe. (Code Sec. 3402(r))[25]

¶ 3034 Pension, Annuity and Other Withholding. ▬▬▬▬▬▬

Withholding of 20% is required on any designated distribution that's an eligible rollover distribution, unless there's a direct trustee-to-trustee transfer. Withholding is required on periodic and lump-sum payments from certain employee plans and certain annuities. But, certain recipients may elect not to have tax withheld.

¶ 3035 Mandatory 20% withholding on eligible rollover distributions.

Unless a distributee elects to have the distribution paid directly to an eligible retirement plan under the Code Sec. 401(a)(31)(A) trustee-to-trustee rules (¶4319), a payor must withhold 20% of any designated distribution that's an "eligible rollover distribution" as defined

---

17. ¶S-2609.1 *et seq.*, S-4918; TD ¶559,000 *et seq.*
18. ¶J-8603; ¶34,024.26; TD ¶554,001 *et seq.*
19. ¶J-8606 *et seq.*; ¶34,024.26; TD ¶554,002
20. ¶J-8610; ¶34,024.26; TD ¶554,006
21. ¶J-8614; ¶34,024.26; TD ¶554,010

22. ¶J-8604; ¶34,024.26; TD ¶554,002
23. ¶S-3697; ¶60,414; TD ¶816,025
24. ¶J-8603; ¶34,024.26; TD ¶554,002
25. ¶J-8617; ¶34,024.261; TD ¶554,013

by Code Sec. 402(f)(2)(A). The Code Sec. 3405(a) and Code Sec. 3405(b) elective withholding rules (¶3036 *et seq.*) don't apply to an eligible rollover distribution. (Code Sec. 3405(c); Reg § 31.3405(c)-1, Q&A-1)[26]

An eligible rollover distribution (reported by the payor on Form 1099-R) (Reg § 31.3405(c)-1, Q&A-16) is any distribution to an employee from a qualified trust (not from an IRA, SEP, or SIMPLE plan) *other than:*

... a required distribution under Code Sec. 401(a)(9);

... any distribution that's one of a series of substantially equal periodic payments made (a) not less frequently than annually for the life (or life expectancy) of the employee (or joint lives or expectancies of the employee and his designated beneficiary), or (b) for a specified period of ten years or more; or

... a hardship distribution from a 401(k) or 403(b) plan. (Code Sec. 3405(c)(3), Code Sec. 402(c)(4), Code Sec. 402(f)(2)(A), Code Sec. 403(b)(8)(B); Reg § 1.402(c)-2, Q&A-3)[27]

No withholding is required if the total distribution paid to the distributee under the plan within one tax year is expected to be less than $200. (Reg § 31.3405(c)-1, Q&A-14)[28]

¶ 3036   Required withholding for designated distributions.

Withholding is required for designated distributions (Code Sec. 3405(d)(1)),[29] but the recipient generally may elect out (¶3038) unless the distribution is an eligible rollover distribution (¶3035). Designated distributions are periodic as well as nonperiodic (including lump-sum) payments from pension, profit sharing, stock bonus or other employer deferred compensation plans, as well as from IRAs (other than Roth IRAs) and commercial annuities, whether or not the contract was purchased under an employer's plan for employees. (Code Sec. 3405(e)) Annuity payments and other distributions under a state or local government deferred compensation plan, other than a Code Sec. 457 plan, including the Civil Service Retirement System are subject to income tax withholding as well. (Reg § 35.3405-1T, Q&A-22 and 23)[30]

The payor of a designated distribution must withhold and is liable for the payment of the tax (unless the payee elects out). But, in the case of a qualified pension, profit sharing, stock bonus, annuity, or 457 governmental plan, the plan administrator has the responsibility, unless he directs the payor to withhold and provides the payor with the information set out in the regs. In that case, the responsibility reverts to the payor. (Code Sec. 3405(d); Reg § 35.3405-1T, Q&A E-3)[31]

¶ 3037   Withholding from periodic payments.

Tax must be withheld in accordance with a recipient's withholding certificate or, if none, by treating the payee as a married individual (¶4705) claiming three withholding exemptions (Code Sec. 3405(a)(4))[32] even if the payor is aware the payee is single. (Reg § 35.3405-1T, Q&A B-4) The amount to be withheld is calculated separately from any amounts that actually are wages to the payee for the same period. (Reg § 35.3405-1T, Q&A B-1)

¶ 3038   Election out of withholding on periodic payments—Form W-4P.

A recipient of periodic payments (except for certain U.S. citizens and expatriates living abroad, see ¶3042) may elect not to have any tax withheld. The election remains in effect until revoked. (Code Sec. 3405(a)(2))[33] Elect (or revoke) on Form W-4P.[34]

---

26. ¶J-8577 *et seq.*; ¶34,054; TD ¶553,244 *et seq.*
27. ¶J-8586; ¶4024.04; TD ¶553,246
28. ¶s J-8584; ¶4014.22; TD ¶553,247
29. ¶J-8501 *et seq.*; ¶34,054; TD ¶553,204
30. ¶J-8504 *et seq.*; ¶34,054; TD ¶553,203

31. ¶J-8518 *et seq.*; ¶34,054; TD ¶553,205
32. ¶J-8525; ¶34,054; TD ¶553,220
33. ¶J-8526; ¶34,054; TD ¶553,221
34. ¶J-8528; ¶34,054; TD ¶553,221

If the recipient doesn't furnish his taxpayer identification number (TIN) to the payor or if IRS has notified the payor that the TIN furnished is incorrect, an election out of withholding isn't effective. (Code Sec. 3405(e)(12))[35]

For periodic payments that are "eligible rollover distributions," see ¶3035.

¶ 3039 Withholding from nonperiodic distributions.

The payor of any nonperiodic distribution that isn't an eligible rollover distribution subject to 20% mandatory withholding (¶3035) must withhold an amount equal to 10% of that distribution (Code Sec. 3405(b)(1)),[36] unless the recipient elects out of withholding (¶3040).

¶ 3040 Electing out of withholding on nonperiodic distributions—Form W-4P.

A payee (except for recipients of eligible rollover distributions (¶3035), and certain U.S. citizens and expatriates living abroad (¶3042)) may elect exemption from withholding for any nonperiodic distribution. The election is made on Form W-4P on a distribution-by-distribution basis. (Code Sec. 3405(b)(2))[37]

If the recipient doesn't furnish his taxpayer identification number (TIN) to the payor or if IRS has notified the payor that the TIN furnished is incorrect, an election out of withholding isn't effective. (Code Sec. 3405(e)(12))[38]

¶ 3041 Payor must notify payee of right to elect to have no tax withheld.

For periodic payments, the notice to make, renew, or revoke the election out of withholding is required no earlier than six months before and no later than the date of the first payment. For nonperiodic payments, the notice should be given not earlier than six months before the distribution and not later than the time that will give the payee reasonable time to elect out. (Code Sec. 3405(e)(10)(B); Reg § 35.3405-1T, Q&A D-4 and D-9)[39] The notice must state that withholding will apply unless the payee elects otherwise, and if he elects no withholding, estimated tax may apply. A sample statement is in the regs. (Reg § 35.3405-1T, Q&A D-21 and D-25)[40]

¶ 3042 Electing out of withholding where payment is delivered outside the U.S.

An election out of withholding can't be made for any periodic or nonperiodic payment that is to be delivered outside the U.S. and its possessions (Code Sec. 3405(e)(13)(A)) *unless* the recipient certifies to the payor that the recipient is neither a U.S. citizen, a resident alien, nor a nonresident alien who in the last 10 years has lost his U.S. citizenship in order to avoid U.S. taxes and is therefore subject to Code Sec. 877. (Code Sec. 3405(e)(13)(B))[41]

¶ 3043 Backup Withholding. ▄▄▄▄▄▄▄▄▄▄▄

A payor of any reportable payment must withhold a specified percentage of the payment.

¶ 3044 When backup withholding is required.

A payor of any reportable payment (¶3045) must withhold 28% of the payment if:

(1) The payee has failed to furnish his taxpayer identification number (TIN) to the payor (Code Sec. 3406(a)(1)(A)) or furnishes an "obviously incorrect number," (Code

---

35. ¶J-8513; TD ¶553,212
36. ¶J-8533; ¶34,054; TD ¶553,227
37. ¶J-8539; ¶34,054; TD ¶553,230
38. ¶J-8513; ¶34,054; TD ¶553,212

39. ¶J-8528 *et seq.*, ¶J-8539 *et seq.*; ¶34,054; TD ¶553,223
40. ¶J-8541, J-8543; ¶34,054; TD ¶553,223
41. ¶J-8554; ¶34,054

Sec. 3406(h)(1)) i.e., one without nine digits or which includes letters of the alphabet. (Reg § 31.3406(h)-1(b))

(2) IRS or a broker has notified (the "B-notice") the payor that the TIN furnished by the payee is incorrect. (Code Sec. 3406(a)(1), Code Sec. 3406(d)(2))

(3) There has been a notified payee underreporting with respect to interest and dividends. (Code Sec. 3406(a)(1)(C))

(4) The payee has failed to make the exemption certification (on Form W-9) with respect to interest and dividends. (Code Sec. 3406(a)(1)(D))[42]

Backup withholding doesn't apply to any payment made to an organization exempt from tax under Code Sec. 501(a) (with certain exceptions); the U.S., a state, the District of Columbia, a U.S. possession, or their political subdivisions; a foreign government or its political subdivisions; an international organization; any wholly-owned agency or instrumentality of any of the above political entities; or any other person specified in regs. (Code Sec. 3406(g)(1)) Payments to a fiduciary or nominee account, or to an exempt recipient (Reg § 31.3406(d)-5(b)), aren't subject to backup withholding.[43]

¶ 3045 Reportable payments.

Reportable payments include most payments for which information returns are required, such as an interest or dividend payment. (Code Sec. 3406(b)(1))[44] Original issue discount (OID) is treated as a payment of interest for backup withholding purposes, but the amount withheld is limited to the cash paid. (Reg § 31.3406(b)(2)-2(a))[45] Code Sec. 6050W reportable payment transactions (¶4746) are subject to backup withholding.[46]

Reportable payments are treated as if they were wages. Amounts deducted and withheld are treated as if they were deducted and withheld from wages. (Code Sec. 3406(h)(10))[47]

¶ 3046 How to stop backup withholding.

A payee can stop backup withholding once it has started by showing that there was no underreporting, correcting any underreporting, showing that backup withholding will cause undue hardship and that it's unlikely he will underreport again, or showing that a bona fide dispute exists as to whether there has been any underreporting. (Reg § 35a.3406-2(g)(1), Reg § 31.3406(c)-1(g)) If IRS determines that backup withholding should stop, it will give the payee a written certification to that effect and notify payors and brokers to stop withholding. (Reg § 35a.3406-2(h)(1), Reg § 35a.3406-2(d)(1), Reg § 31.3406(c)-1(g)(1))

Withholding must stop as of the close of the day before the "stop date" (generally 30 days after receipt of the stop notice from IRS or a copy of the certification IRS gave the payee, whichever is earlier). (Code Sec. 3406(e)(5)) The payor may elect to shorten or eliminate the 30-day period. (Code Sec. 3406(e)(5)(C); Reg § 35a.3406-2(e)(2)(iii), Reg § 31.3406(c)-1(e)(2)(i)(B)).[48]

---

42. ¶J-9001; ¶34,064; TD ¶554,501
43. ¶J-9109; ¶34,064; TD ¶554,502
44. ¶J-9101; ¶34,064; TD ¶554,503
45. ¶J-9111; ¶34,064

46. ¶J-9126.2; ¶34,064.01; TD ¶554,503
47. ¶J-9009; TD ¶554,501
48. ¶J-9607; ¶34,064; TD ¶554,513

Chapter 13 Individual's Tax Computation—Kiddie Tax— Self-Employment Tax—3.8% Surtax—Estimated Tax

¶ 3100 How Income Tax on Individuals Is Computed. ▬▬▬▬▬▬

An individual's annual income tax liability on taxable income is computed using either the tax rate schedules or (if taxable income is less than $100,000) the tax tables, see ¶1101 *et seq.* This tax liability may be increased by other taxes, e.g., self-employment tax or alternative minimum tax, and is reduced by certain credits.

For taxation of unearned income of children subject to the kiddie tax, see ¶3135 *et seq.*

For the threshold amounts of gross income that must be reached before a tax return must be filed, see ¶4701.

¶ 3101 Steps in computing taxable income.

An individual taxpayer first computes gross income—generally all income from all sources (Code Sec. 61), see ¶1200 *et seq.*

From gross income, taxpayer subtracts the deductions specified at ¶3102 to reach adjusted gross income (AGI). (Code Sec. 62)

Finally, taxpayers who itemize reduce AGI by allowable deductions and personal exemptions (¶3115) (Code Sec. 63(a)), see ¶3109 *et seq.* Nonitemizers reduce AGI by the standard deduction (¶3112) and personal exemptions. (Code Sec. 63(b))[1]

¶ 3102 Deductions taken "above the line" to reach adjusted gross income (AGI).

Subtract the following deductions from gross income to reach AGI: (Code Sec. 62)[2]

... Trade or business expenses (¶1508) (other than unreimbursed employee business expenses, see ¶3104). For business-related deductions of "statutory employees," see ¶3103.

... Self-employed medical insurance premiums, ¶1532.

... Moving expenses, ¶1646 *et seq.*

... One-half of self-employment tax (¶1755), *other than* the additional 0.9% self-employment tax, ¶1108.

... Amortization or expensing of reforestation expenditures, ¶1970.

... Amounts forfeited on premature withdrawal of savings accounts or deposits, ¶2168.

... Alimony and separate maintenance payments, ¶2152 *et seq.*

... Employee expenses that are reimbursed by the employer or a third party, ¶3104.

... Employee business expenses of certain performing artists (¶3105) and of state and local government officials compensated on a fee basis, ¶3106.

... Jury duty pay remitted to an employer, ¶3107.

... Contributions to tax-favored retirement plans for the self-employed, ¶4327.

... Contributions to individual retirement accounts (IRAs) or annuities, ¶4351.

... The "total taxable amount" of a retirement plan lump-sum distribution with respect to a participant born before '36, to the extent included in recipient's gross income, ¶4339.

... Deductions for property held for production of rents or royalties. (Code Sec. 62(a)(4))

... Depreciation and depletion deductions of a life tenant or an income beneficiary of a trust, or of an heir, legatee or devisee of an estate, ¶3927.

---

1. ¶A-2500 *et seq.*; ¶634; TD ¶560,500 *et seq.*   2. ¶A-2601; ¶624; TD ¶560,702

References beginning with a single letter are to paragraphs in RIA's Federal Tax Coordinator 2d and RIA's Analysis of Federal Taxes: Income. Those beginning with numbers are to paragraphs in RIA's United States Tax Reporter. Those beginning with TD are to paragraphs in RIA's Tax Desk.

489

. . . Losses from the sale or exchange of property, ¶2400.

. . . Repayments of supplemental unemployment compensation. (Code Sec. 62(a)(12))

. . . Certain foreign housing costs of individuals having income earned abroad, ¶4614.

. . . Contributions to an Archer medical savings account (Archer MSA, see ¶1528).

. . . Contributions to a health savings account (HSA, see ¶1529).

. . . Deduction for interest on qualified education loans, ¶2222 *et seq.*

. . . Pre-2014 deduction for certain higher education expenses, ¶2230.

. . . Pre-2014 deduction of up to $250 of qualifying expenses of educators, ¶2229.

. . . Certain unreimbursed travel expenses of National Guard and Reserve members, ¶1553.

. . . Attorney fees and court costs of civil rights suits and whistleblower awards, ¶3108.

. . . Domestic production activities deductions, ¶1614.

¶ 3103   Business-related expenses of "statutory employees."

For purposes of computing adjusted gross income, the allowable deductions attributable to the services rendered by a statutory employee (drivers, life insurance salespersons, home workers and other salespersons meeting certain conditions) are treated as trade or business expenses (deductible on Schedule C, rather than as itemized deductions).[3]

¶ 3104   Reimbursed and unreimbursed employee expenses.

In computing adjusted gross income (AGI), an employee can deduct from gross income employee expenses for which he is reimbursed by the employer, its agent, or third party (for whom he performs services as an employee of the employer) under an express agreement for reimbursement or other expense allowance under an accountable plan. (But there's no normal "deduction," since the reimbursement is excluded from the employee's gross income —i.e., no deduction for the expense to the extent there's no inclusion of the reimbursement.) (Code Sec. 62(a)(2)(A); Reg § 1.62-2(c)(4))[4] The expense must be otherwise allowable as a deduction (i.e., not a personal expense).[5]

If the reimbursement is for less than the total expenses paid or incurred by the employee, the unreimbursed expenses are deductible from *adjusted* gross income (not gross income), as an itemized deduction, subject to, for example, the 2%-of-AGI floor (¶3110), and the percentage limit on meal and entertainment expenses (¶1569). (Reg § 1.62-1T(e)(3))[6]

A reimbursement or other expense allowance arrangement under an accountable plan is one that meets tests for (1) business connection, (2) substantiation, and (3) return of amounts in excess of expenses. (Reg § 1.62-2(c)(2)) See ¶1573 *et seq.* for details.

A payor can have more than one arrangement as to one employee. (Reg § 1.62-2(c)(1))[7]

For an above-the-line deduction for expenses of educators, see ¶2229.

¶ 3105   Expenses of certain performing artists—Form 2106.

Expenses of certain performing artists are deductible (use Form 2106 or Form 2106-EZ) in arriving at adjusted gross income (AGI) (despite the disallowance of unreimbursed employee business expenses as above-the-line deductions). (Code Sec. 62(a)(2)(B)) To qualify, the taxpayer must have earned at least $200 as a performing artist from each of at least two employers during the tax year. (Code Sec. 62(b)(1)(A), Code Sec. 62(b)(2)) Also, the allowable expenses must exceed 10% of gross income from the services, and AGI for the year (before deducting these expenses) can't exceed $16,000. (Code Sec. 62(b)(1)(B), Code Sec. 62(b)(1)(C)) A married performing artist who lives with his spouse at any time during the year must file a

---

3. ¶A-2603; ¶624.03; TD ¶560,704
4. ¶A-2604; ¶624.02; TD ¶561,001
5. ¶A-2602; ¶624.02; TD ¶561,001

6. ¶A-2605; ¶624.02; TD ¶561,003
7. ¶L-4703.2; TD ¶561,006

joint return to deduct these expenses to reach AGI. (Code Sec. 62(b)(3)(A)) The two-employer requirement and 10%-of-gross-income test are applied separately to each spouse, but the $16,000 test is applied to their combined income. (Code Sec. 62(b)(3)(B))[8]

¶ 3106 Business expenses of state and local officials paid on a fee basis.

Employee business expenses relating to service as an official of a state or local government (or a political subdivision thereof) are deductible in computing AGI, if the official is compensated on a fee basis. (Code Sec. 62(a)(2)(C))[9]

¶ 3107 Jury duty pay remitted to an employer.

An individual may deduct jury pay from gross income if the individual is required to remit any of the jury pay to his employer in exchange for compensation for the period the individual was performing jury duty. (Code Sec. 62(a)(13))[10]

¶ 3108 Attorney fees & court costs of civil rights suits and whistleblower awards.

Any deduction allowable under Chapter 1 for attorney fees and court costs paid by, or on behalf of, the taxpayer in connection with the following is deductible from gross income:

. . . an action involving a claim (1) of unlawful discrimination (defined in Code Sec. 62(e)), (2) of a violation of subchapter III of chapter 37 of title 31, United States Code (Claims Against the U.S. Government), or (3) made under Sec. 1862(b)(3)(A) of the Social Security Act (42 U.S.C. 1395y(b)(3)(A)) (private cause of action under the Medicare Secondary Payer statute), but only up to the amount includible in taxpayer's gross income for the tax year on account of the judgment or settlement. (Code Sec. 62(a)(20))[11]

. . . any Code Sec. 7623(b) whistleblower award, but only up to the amount includible in taxpayer's gross income for the tax year on account of the award. (Code Sec. 62(a)(21))[12]

¶ 3109 Itemized deductions.

Itemized deductions are all the allowable Chapter 1 deductions *other than* the deductions taken from gross income to reach adjusted gross income (AGI) (¶3102) and the deductions for personal exemptions. (Code Sec. 63(d))[13]

caution: For itemized deductions under the alternative minimum tax, see ¶3209.

¶ 3110 Miscellaneous itemized deductions—2%-of-AGI floor.

Miscellaneous itemized deductions are allowed only to the extent that they, in the aggregate, exceed 2% of adjusted gross income (AGI). (Code Sec. 67(a))[14] To the extent any other limit or restriction is placed on a miscellaneous itemized deduction, that other limit applies before the 2% floor. For example, the 2% floor is applied after the percentage limit for business meals and entertainment (¶1569). (Reg § 1.67-1T(a)(2))[15]

observation: Miscellaneous itemized deductions that don't exceed 2% of AGI are lost. There's no carryover.

Miscellaneous itemized deductions are itemized deductions *other than* deductions for medical expenses; taxes; interest; charitable contributions; casualty and theft losses; gambling losses (non-professional gamblers); impairment-related work expenses; estate tax on income in respect of a decedent; personal property used in a short sale; restored amounts held under

---

8. ¶A-2611; ¶624.02; TD ¶560,705
9. ¶A-2611.1; ¶624.02; TD ¶560,706
10. ¶A-2623; ¶624.04; TD ¶560,723
11. ¶A-2628; ¶624.04; TD ¶560,715.2

12. ¶A-2629; ¶624.04; TD ¶560,702
13. ¶A-2700 *et seq.*; ¶634; TD ¶561,201
14. ¶A-2711 *et seq.*; ¶674; TD ¶561,601
15. ¶A-2711; ¶674; TD ¶561,601

claim of right; annuity payments ending before investment is recovered; amortizable bond premium; tenant-stockholder share of co-op housing corp expenses. (Code Sec. 67(b))[16]

Miscellaneous itemized deductions *include* unreimbursed employee business expenses, including union and professional dues and home office expenses; expenses related to investment income or property, e.g., investment counsel or advisory fees; allowable losses from traditional IRAs (¶4357) or Roth IRAs (¶4373); tax return preparation costs and related expenses, including credit/debit card convenience fees charged for paying federal individual income taxes (for deduction of tax determination costs as business expenses, see ¶1513); tax counsel fees, and appraisal fees, e.g., to determine the amount of a casualty loss; and hobby expenses to the extent of hobby income. (Reg § 1.67-1T(a)(1))[17]

If an expense relates to both a trade or business activity (not subject to the 2% floor) and a production of income or tax preparation activity (subject to the 2% floor) the taxpayer must allocate it between the activities on a reasonable basis. (Reg § 1.67-1T(c))[18]

¶ 3111 2% floor applied to partnerships, S corporations, and other pass-through entities.

A partner or S corporation shareholder must take into account separately his distributive or pro rata share of the partnership's or S corporation's miscellaneous itemized deductions. Similarly, the 2% floor applies to the grantor (or other person treated as the owner) of a grantor trust with respect to items treated as miscellaneous itemized deductions of the grantor (or other owner). (Reg § 1.67-2T(b)(1))[19] Similar rules apply to affected investors in common trust funds (Reg § 1.67-2T(d)(1)(ii)),[20] nonpublicly offered regulated investment companies (RICs), (Reg § 1.67-2T(e)(1)(ii))[21] and REMICs. (Reg § 1.67-3T(b)(1))[22]

The above rules don't apply to publicly offered RICs (Code Sec. 67(c)(2)), cooperatives, and REITs. (Code Sec. 67(c)(3))[23] For estates and trusts, see ¶3921.

¶ 3112 Standard deduction.

The standard deduction is the sum of the basic standard deduction, and the additional standard deduction, as adjusted each year for inflation. (Code Sec. 63(c)(1))[24] Here are the basic standard deduction amounts:[25]

Basic Standard Deduction

Filing Status	2013	2014
Joint filers and surviving spouses	$12,200	$12,400
Heads of household	8,950	9,100
Singles	6,100	6,200
Marrieds filing separately	6,100	6,200

For 2013, the basic standard deduction of individuals who can be claimed as dependents by another taxpayer can't exceed the greater of (a) $1,000 or (b) $350 plus the individual's earned income. For 2014, the amount for (a) is $1,000, and the amount for (b) is $350. But the basic standard deduction can't be more than the regular basic standard deduction amount shown above ($6,100 for 2013; $6,200 for 2014). (Code Sec. 63(c)(5))[26]

The standard deduction is zero for: a married individual filing separately whose spouse itemizes deductions; a nonresident alien individual; and an individual filing a short-year return due to an accounting period change. (Code Sec. 63(c)(6))[27]

16. ¶A-2721 *et seq.*; ¶674; TD ¶561,603
17. ¶A-2722 *et seq.*; ¶674; TD ¶561,603
18. ¶A-2725, A-2726 *et seq.*; ¶674; TD ¶561,603
19. ¶A-2715; ¶674; TD ¶561,610
20. ¶A-2716; ¶674; TD ¶561,611
21. ¶A-2717; ¶674; TD ¶561,612

22. ¶A-2713; ¶674; TD ¶561,608
23. ¶A-2713; ¶674; TD ¶561,601
24. ¶A-2801; ¶634; TD ¶562,001
25. ¶A-2803; ¶634; TD ¶562,003
26. ¶A-2804; ¶634; TD ¶562,003
27. ¶A-2802; ¶634; TD ¶562,002

Elderly and blind taxpayers get additional standard deductions. (Code Sec. 63(c)(3)) A tax-payer who is 65 before the end of his tax year, or blind at the end of his tax year, is entitled to an additional standard deduction. Here are the additional standard deduction amounts: (Code Sec. 63(f)(1), Code Sec. 63(f)(2), Code Sec. 63(f)(3), Code Sec. 63(c)(4))[28]

Additional Standard Deduction

Filing Status	2013	2014
Marrieds and surviving spouses	$1,200	$1,200
Heads of household	1,500	1,550
Singles	1,500	1,550

One who's elderly *and* blind gets each additional standard deduction. (Code Sec. 63(c)(3))[29]

A married individual who files a separate return can claim a spouse's additional standard deduction if the spouse has no gross income and isn't the dependent of another taxpayer. (Code Sec. 63(f)(1)(B), Code Sec. 63(f)(2)(B), Code Sec. 151(b))[30]

An individual claiming an additional standard deduction for blindness who isn't totally blind must get (and keep, but not file) a certification from an eye doctor or registered optome-trist. If the eye condition will never improve, the statement should state this.[31]

On a decedent's final return, the fiduciary may claim the full amount of the appropriate standard deduction regardless of the date of death.[32]

caution: For the standard deduction under the alternative minimum tax, see ¶3209.

¶ 3113 Election to itemize deductions in computing taxable income.

No itemized deductions are allowed unless an election to itemize is made on the return. (Code Sec. 63(e)(1), Code Sec. 63(e)(2)) A taxpayer who elected to itemize and wants to switch to the standard deduction, or vice versa, can. But the change isn't allowed unless his sepa-rately filing spouse makes a consistent change, and both spouses consent in writing to assess-ment of any deficiency resulting from the change. (Code Sec. 63(e)(3); Reg § 1.63-1)[33]

¶ 3114 Reduction in itemized deductions—3%/80% rule.

If an individual's adjusted gross income (AGI) exceeds the "applicable amount" (see be-low), certain otherwise allowable itemized deductions are reduced (the "Pease limitation") by the lesser of:

(1) 3% of the excess of AGI over the applicable amount, or

(2) 80% of the itemized deductions otherwise allowable for the tax year. (Code Sec. 68(a))[34]

The reduction is determined after the application of any other limits on the allowance of an itemized deduction (Code Sec. 68(d))[35] and doesn't apply to the deductions for medical ex-penses, investment interest, nonbusiness casualty and theft losses, and gambling losses. (Code Sec. 68(c))[36]

For 2013, the applicable amount is $300,000 for a joint filer or a surviving spouse ($305,050 for 2014), $275,000 for a head of household ($279,650 for 2014), $250,000 for a single individ-ual who isn't a surviving spouse ($254,200 for 2014), and $150,000 (i.e., 50% of the joint return amount) for marrieds filing separately ($152,525 for 2014). (Code Sec. 68(b)(1))[37]

28. ¶A-2806, A-2807; ¶634; TD ¶562,004, 562,005
29. ¶A-2806; ¶634; TD ¶562,004
30. ¶A-2806; TD ¶562,004
31. ¶A-2808; TD ¶562,006
32. ¶C-9603; ¶60,124.04; TD ¶579,507

33. ¶A-2702; ¶634; TD ¶561,202
34. ¶A-2731; ¶684; TD ¶561,801
35. ¶A-2731; ¶684; TD ¶561,803
36. ¶A-2731; ¶684; TD ¶561,801
37. ¶A-2731; ¶684; TD ¶561,801

¶ 3115   Deduction for personal exemptions.

Each taxpayer may be entitled to an exemption for himself and his spouse (¶3118), and may qualify for an additional exemption for each dependent (¶3119 *et seq.*).

The exemption amount is $3,900 for 2013 ($3,950 for 2014). (Code Sec. 151(d))[38]

But an individual (e.g., a child) who can be claimed as a dependent by another (e.g., the child's parent) can't claim a personal exemption for himself. (Code Sec. 151(d)(2))[39]

caution: The child can't claim a personal exemption even if the parent doesn't take the dependency exemption.

The personal exemption phase-out rules (¶3117) don't apply in determining whether a deduction for a personal exemption is available to another taxpayer. (Code Sec. 150(d)(3)(D))[40]

Resident aliens can claim exemptions under the same rules as U.S. citizens. (Code Sec. 6013(g); Reg § 1.6013-1(b))[41]

caution: For personal exemptions under the alternative minimum tax, see ¶3209.

No exemption is allowed for any individual unless his taxpayer identification number (TIN) is included on the return claiming the exemption. (Code Sec. 151(e))[42]

¶ 3116   Effect of death on personal exemptions.

The deduction for personal exemptions on a decedent's final return isn't reduced or pro-rated because the return is for a short year. (Reg § 1.443-1(a)(2)) However, if the decedent could be claimed as a dependent by another taxpayer (e.g., a parent), the decedent's personal exemption isn't allowed on the final return.[43]

If one spouse dies during the tax year, the survivor can claim the deceased spouse's exemption on a joint return, unless the survivor remarries in that year.[44] A surviving spouse who has no gross income for the calendar year his spouse died can be claimed as an exemption on the decedent's final separate return.[45]

¶ 3117   Phase-out of personal exemptions.

The personal exemption amount of a taxpayer whose adjusted gross income (AGI) exceeds a specified threshold amount (described below), is reduced (personal exemption phaseout, or "PEP") by an "applicable percentage." (Code Sec. 151(d)(3)(A) This applicable percentage is 2% for each $2,500 (or fraction thereof) by which the AGI of a taxpayer (other than a married taxpayer filing separately) exceeds the threshold amount for that taxpayer. For married taxpayers filing separately, the applicable percentage is 2% for each $1,250 (or fraction of that amount) by which the taxpayer's AGI exceeds the threshold amount. The applicable percentage can't exceed 100%. (Code Sec. 151(d)(3)(B))[46]

The personal exemption phases out for taxpayers with the following AGI amounts:

. . . for joint filers and surviving spouses, the phaseout begins to apply at $300,000 for 2013 ($305,050 for 2014) and is completed at $422,500 for 2013 ($427,550 for 2014);

. . . for heads of household, the phaseout begins to apply at $275,000 for 2013 ($279,650 for 2014) and is completed at $397,500 for 2013 ($402,150 for 2014);

. . . for single filers (other than surviving spouses and heads of household), the phaseout begins to apply at $250,000 for 2013 ($254,200 for 2014) and is completed at $372,500 for

38. ¶A-3500.1; ¶1514; TD ¶562,201
39. ¶A-3501, A-3502; ¶1514; TD ¶562,203, 564,401
40. ¶A-3500 *et seq.*; ¶1514; TD ¶564,401
41. ¶A-3507; ¶1514; TD ¶562,205
42. ¶A-3501.1, A-3603; ¶s 1514; 61,094; TD ¶562,404

43. ¶C-9602; ¶4434; TD ¶579,508
44. ¶A-3504; ¶1514.01; TD ¶562,204
45. ¶A-3504; ¶1514.01; TD ¶562,204
46. ¶A-3502, ¶1514; TD ¶564,401

2013 ($376,700 for 2014);

. . . for marrieds filing separately, the phaseout begins to apply at $150,000 for 2013 ($152,525 for 2014) and is completed at $211,250 for 2013 ($213,775 for 2014).[47]

¶ 3118 Exemptions for spouse.

If a married couple files a joint return, each spouse is allowed one personal exemption, whether or not a spouse has gross income or is a dependent of another taxpayer (but the *other* taxpayer will be denied an exemption, see ¶3119). (Reg § 1.151-1(b))[48]

illustration: A son and his wife file a joint return, but the son's mother supports him for the entire tax year while he's in college. The son (and his wife) can claim a personal exemption for himself. But even if all other dependency tests are met, the mother can't claim a dependency exemption for the son.

On a separate return, a taxpayer may claim an exemption for a spouse only if, for the calendar year in which the taxpayer's tax year begins, the spouse has no gross income *and* isn't the dependent of another. (Code Sec. 151(b))[49]

observation: If the son's wife (above) filed a separate return, she couldn't claim an exemption for her husband, since he's a dependent of his mother.

¶ 3119 Exemption for dependents.

A taxpayer is entitled to a deduction equal to the exemption amount (¶3115) for each person who qualifies as his "dependent" for the tax year. (Code Sec. 151(c))[50]

A person qualifies as a taxpayer's dependent if he is the taxpayer's qualifying child (¶3120) or qualifying relative (¶3122). (Code Sec. 152(a))[1] But an individual who is a taxpayer's dependent for a tax year is treated as having no dependents for his tax year beginning in the calendar year when the taxpayer's tax year begins. (Code Sec. 152(b)(1))[2] Also, an individual can't be a taxpayer's dependent if he has made a joint return with his spouse for the tax year beginning in the calendar year when the taxpayer's tax year begins. (Code Sec. 152(b)(2))[3]

A dependent must be a U.S. citizen, national, or resident, or a resident of a contiguous country (i.e., Canada or Mexico) at some time in the calendar year in which the taxpayer's tax year begins. (Code Sec. 152(b)(3)(A))[4] But a nonresident alien child who is legally adopted by the taxpayer (or lawfully placed with taxpayer for legal adoption by him) can be the taxpayer's dependent if he has the same principal place of abode as taxpayer and is a member of taxpayer's household for the entire tax year, and taxpayer is a U.S. citizen or national. (Code Sec. 152(b)(3))[5]

¶ 3120 Qualifying child.

A taxpayer's "qualifying child" (¶3119) for a tax year is an individual who: (1) bears a relationship to the taxpayer specified below; (2) has the same principal place of abode as the taxpayer for more than half the tax year; (3) hasn't reached a specified age (see below); and (4) hasn't provided over half his own support for the calendar year in which the taxpayer's tax year begins. (Code Sec. 152(c)(1), Code Sec. 152(c)(2))[6] For tie-breaking rules, see ¶3121.

The following relationships of an individual to the taxpayer meet requirement (1), above:

. . . a child (defined below) of the taxpayer, or a child's descendant (Code Sec. 152(c)(2)(A)), or

47. ¶A-3502; ¶1514; TD ¶564,401
48. ¶A-3501; ¶1514.01; TD ¶562,203
49. ¶A-3501; ¶1514.01; TD ¶562,203
50. ¶A-3601; ¶1524; TD ¶562,401
1. ¶A-3601; ¶1524; TD ¶562,401

2. ¶A-3626; ¶1524; TD ¶562,431
3. ¶A-3622; ¶1524; TD ¶562,427
4. ¶A-3623; ¶1524; TD ¶562,428
5. ¶A-3624; ¶1524; TD ¶562,429
6. ¶A-3605.2; ¶1524; TD ¶562,408

. . . a brother, sister, stepbrother, stepsister, half-brother, or half-sister of the taxpayer or a descendant of these relatives. (Code Sec. 152(c)(2)(B), Code Sec. 152(f)(4))[7]

For this purpose, the term "child" means an individual who is:

• a son, daughter, stepson, or stepdaughter of the taxpayer (Code Sec. 152(f)(1)(A)(i)), or

• an eligible foster child of the taxpayer (Code Sec. 152(f)(1)(A)(ii)), i.e., an individual who is placed with the taxpayer by an authorized placement agency or by judgment, decree, or other order of any court of competent jurisdiction. (Code Sec. 152(f)(1)(C))

For this purpose, a registered domestic partner is the stepparent of his partner's child if so treated under the law of the state in which the partners reside.[8]

In determining if an individual is taxpayer's son, daughter, stepson, stepdaughter, brother, or sister, one who's legally adopted by an individual, or lawfully placed with one for legal adoption by him, is treated as a child of that individual by blood. (Code Sec. 152(f)(1)(B))[9]

An individual meets the age requirement in (3), above, if he:

. . . is younger than the taxpayer and hasn't reached age 19 as of the end of the calendar year in which the taxpayer's tax year begins;

. . . is younger than the taxpayer and is a student who hasn't reached age 24 as of the end of that calendar year (Code Sec. 152(c)(3)(A)); or

. . . is permanently and totally disabled, as defined in Code Sec. 22(e)(3) (¶2348), at any time during that calendar year. (Code Sec. 152(c)(3)(B))[10]

🅁ⓘobservation: If a child of the taxpayer doesn't meet the definition of a "qualifying child," for example, because he doesn't meet the age test, he may still qualify as a dependent under the "qualifying relative" test, ¶3122.

An individual who is married and files a joint return (unless the return is filed only to claim a refund) for the tax year beginning in the calendar year in which the taxpayer's tax year begins can't be a qualifying child. (Code Sec. 152(c)(1)(E))[11]

¶ 3121   Tie-breaking rules where two or more taxpayers claim a qualifying child.

If an individual may be claimed as a qualifying child by two or more taxpayers for a tax year beginning in the same calendar year, the following tie-breaking rules apply (generally uniformly to all provisions relying on the same definition, according to IRS):

(1) If two or more taxpayers may claim an individual as a qualifying child for a tax year beginning in the same calendar year, the individual is treated as the qualifying child of the taxpayer who is: (a) a parent of the individual, or (b) if item (a) doesn't apply, the taxpayer with the highest adjusted gross income (AGI) for that tax year. (Code Sec. 152(c)(4)(A))

(2) If the parents don't file a joint return together, the child is treated as the qualifying child of: (a) the parent with whom the child resided for the longest period of time during the tax year, or (b) if the child resided with both parents for the same amount of time during the tax year, the parent with the highest AGI. (Code Sec. 152(c)(4)(B)) The same rule applies where a child is a qualifying child of both parents who are registered domestic partners.

(3) If an individual's parents may claim him as a qualifying child but no parent does, another taxpayer may claim him as a qualifying child, but only if that taxpayer's AGI is higher than the highest AGI of any parent of the individual. (Code Sec. 152(c)(4)(C))[12]

---

7. ¶A-3605.3; ¶1524; TD ¶562,409
8. ¶A-3605.3; ¶1524; TD ¶562,409
9. ¶A-3612; ¶1524; TD ¶562,420

10. ¶A-3605.4; ¶1524; TD ¶562,410
11. ¶A-3605.2; ¶1524; TD ¶562,408
12. ¶A-3605.5; ¶1524; TD ¶562,411

¶ 3122 Qualifying relative.

A "qualifying relative" (¶3119) for a tax year is an individual:

(1) who bears a specified relationship to the taxpayer (see below);

(2) whose gross income for the calendar year in which that tax year begins is less than the exemption amount (¶3115);

(3) with respect to whom taxpayer provides over half his support (¶3124) for the calendar year in which that tax year begins (for multiple support agreements, see ¶3123); and

(4) who isn't a qualifying child (¶3120) of that taxpayer or of any other taxpayer for any tax year that begins in the calendar year in which that tax year begins. (Code Sec. 152(d)(1)) Under an administrative exception, an individual is not a qualifying child of any other taxpayer if the individual's parent (or other person with respect to whom the individual is defined as a qualifying child) isn't required by Code Sec. 6012 to file an income tax return and (i) does not file one, or (ii) files one solely to get a refund of withheld tax.[13]

A registered domestic partner can be a dependent of his partner if the requirements of Code Sec. 151 and Code Sec. 152 are met. Registered domestic partners who live in community property states are unlikely to meet the requirements of (2) and (3) above.[14]

The following relationships of an individual to the taxpayer meet the relationship test (item (1), above): a child or a descendant of a child, including foster and adopted children who qualify under the rules in ¶3120; a brother, sister, half-brother, half-sister, stepbrother, or stepsister; the father or mother, or an ancestor of either; stepfather or stepmother; a nephew or niece; an uncle or aunt; a son-in-law, daughter-in-law, father-in-law, mother-in-law, brother-in-law, or sister-in-law; and an individual (other than one who, at any time in the tax year, was the taxpayer's spouse, determined without regard to Code Sec. 7703) whose principal place of abode is the taxpayer's home and who is a member of the taxpayer's household, for the taxpayer's tax year. (Code Sec. 152(d)(2), Code Sec. 152(f)(4))[15]

¶ 3123 Multiple support agreement—Form 2120.

For purposes of the support test for qualifying relatives (¶3122), over one-half of an individual's support for a calendar year is treated as received from the taxpayer if:

(1) no one person contributed over half of that support;

(2) over half of that support was received from 2 or more persons each of whom, but for the fact that he alone didn't contribute over half of that support, would have been entitled to claim the individual as a dependent for a tax year beginning in that calendar year;

(3) the taxpayer contributed over 10% of that support; *and*

(4) each person described in (2), other than the taxpayer, who contributed over 10% of that support agrees not to claim the individual as a dependent for that year, by giving the taxpayer a signed statement to that effect (waiver declaration). The waiver(s) needn't be filed with IRS, but must be kept in the taxpayer's records. A Form 2120 showing that the taxpayer has waivers from the other eligible persons, with their names, addresses and social security numbers, must be attached to Form 1040 or Form 1040A. (Code Sec. 152(d)(3); Reg § 1.152-3(c))[16]

¶ 3124 "Support" defined.

Support includes:[17]

. . . food, school lunches, toilet articles and haircuts;

---

13. ¶A-3605.6; ¶1524; TD ¶562,412
14. ¶A-3608.1; ¶1524; TD ¶562,412
15. ¶A-3606; ¶1524; TD ¶562,413

16. ¶A-3731; ¶1524; TD ¶563,801
17. ¶A-3711 *et seq.*; ¶1524.06; TD ¶563,302 *et seq.*

. . . clothing;

. . . recreation, including toys, summer camp, horseback riding, entertainment, vacations;

. . . medical and dental care, including premiums on accident and health insurance;

. . . child care expenses, even though a credit is also allowed for these expenses;

. . . allowances, gifts;

. . . son's or daughter's wedding costs;

. . . lodging—when furnished in kind, it's measured by its fair market value rather than actual cost (Reg § 1.152-1(a)(2));[18]

. . . education—these costs include board, uniforms at military schools, and tuition, even where free schooling is available. Scholarship payments received by a dependent are treated as support furnished by someone other than the taxpayer. However, scholarships aren't counted in determining if the taxpayer furnished more than half the dependent's support if the dependent is the taxpayer's child (including stepchild, foster child, or child adopted or placed for adoption) who's a full-time student at an educational institution. (Code Sec. 152(f)(5), Reg § 1.152-1(c))[19]

Social security benefits received by a child and used for his support are considered provided by the child. (Reg § 1.152-1(a)(2)(ii))[20]

Armed Forces dependency allotments—the amount contributed by the government *and* the amount withheld from the pay of the member of the Armed Forces are treated as contributed by the member.[21]

¶ 3125 Allocating support of several contributors to several dependents.

Where more than one member of a household contributes towards expenses that are equally applicable to all members of the household, the contributors are presumed (absent contrary evidence) to have pooled their contributions towards the support of all members. The total contributed is divided equally among the members as amounts paid for their support, unless there is proof of how much was actually spent for particular members.[22]

¶ 3126 Release of dependency exemption by custodial parent—Form 8332.

A child is treated as being the "qualifying child" (¶3120) or "qualifying relative" (¶3122) of the noncustodial parent for a calendar year if:

(1) the child receives over half of his support during the calendar year from his parents;

(2) the child's parents: (a) are divorced or legally separated under a decree of divorce or separate maintenance; (b) are separated under a written separation agreement; or (c) live apart at all times during the last six months of the calendar year, whether or not they are or were married;

(3) the child is in the custody of one or both parents for over half the calendar year;

(4) the custodial parent releases his claim to the exemption for the child by signing a written declaration (on Form 8332) stating that he won't claim that child as a dependent for the tax year beginning in that calendar year, *and*

(5) the noncustodial parent attaches that written declaration to the noncustodial parent's return for the tax year beginning during that calendar year. (Code Sec. 152(e)(1), Code Sec. 152(e)(2); Reg § 1.152-4(b))[23]

The custodial parent is the parent with whom the child resides for the greater number of nights during the calendar year. (Code Sec. 152(e)(4)(A); Reg § 1.152-4(d))[24]

18. ¶A-3701, A-3714 *et seq.*; ¶1524.09; TD ¶563,309
19. ¶A-3721; ¶1524.07; TD ¶563,316
20. ¶A-3712; TD ¶563,306
21. ¶A-3711; ¶1524.09; TD ¶563,305
22. ¶A-3708; TD ¶563,325
23. ¶A-3851; ¶1524.10; TD ¶564,051
24. ¶A-3853; ¶1524.10; TD ¶564,053

The above rules apply despite: the Code Sec. 152(c)(1)(B) requirement that a qualifying child have the same principal place of abode as the taxpayer for more than half the year, ¶3120; the Code Sec. 152(c)(4) tie-breaking rules, ¶3121; or the Code Sec. 152(d)(1)(C) support test for qualifying relatives, ¶3122. (Code Sec. 152(e)(1); Reg § 1.152-4(a))[25]

In certain cases, IRS will treat a child of parents who are divorced, separated, or living apart as the dependent of both parents for purposes of Code Sec. 105(b) (employer-provided medical expense reimbursements, ¶1256), Code Sec. 132(h)(2)(B) (excludable fringe benefits, ¶1243), Code Sec. 213(d)(5) (deductible medical expenses, ¶2142), Code Sec. 220(d)(2) (Archer Medical Savings Accounts (MSAs), ¶1528), and Code Sec. 223(d)(2) (Health Saving Accounts (HSAs), ¶1529) when the custodial parent hasn't released the claim to the exemption for the child under Code Sec. 152(e)(2).[26]

The above rules don't apply where, under the Code Sec. 152(d)(3) rules for multiple support agreements (¶3123), more than half the child's support is treated as having been received from a taxpayer. (Code Sec. 152(e)(5))[27]

For purposes of these rules, if a parent remarries, support of a child received from this remarried parent's spouse is treated as received from the parent. (Code Sec. 152(e)(6))[28]

¶ 3127 Dependents of married couples.

On a joint return, the married couple can claim exemptions for all persons who are dependents of either or both spouses. On a separate return, however, a spouse can claim exemptions only for his own dependents.[29]

If a husband and wife in a community property state file separate returns, they can divide the total of their exemptions for dependents between them, but they can't divide an exemption for any one dependent.[30]

¶ 3128 Effect of birth, death, and divorce on exemption for dependent.

If a taxpayer's child is born alive at any time during the year, and the dependency tests (¶3119) are met, the taxpayer is allowed a full exemption for the child.[31]

If a dependent died during the year, and the dependency tests were met for the part of the year he lived, the taxpayer can claim a full exemption for him.[32]

In determining relationships qualifying for a dependency exemption (¶3120, ¶3122), death or divorce doesn't end relationships established by marriage. Thus, the relationship of son-in-law and father-in-law survives the spouse's death. (Reg § 1.152-2(d))[33]

¶ 3129 Tax status of kidnapped children.

Solely for the purposes listed below, a taxpayer's child who is presumed by law enforcement authorities to have been kidnapped by a non-family member, and who had, for the tax year in which the kidnapping occurred, the same principal place of abode as the taxpayer for more than half of the portion of that year before the kidnapping date, is treated as meeting the requirement that a qualifying child (¶3120) have the same principal place of abode as the taxpayer for more than half the tax year for all tax years ending during the period that the individual is kidnapped. (Code Sec. 152(f)(6)(A)) This rule applies for purposes of the dependency deduction; the child tax credit; surviving spouse or a head of a household status; and the earned income credit. (Code Sec. 152(f)(6)(B)) Comparable treatment applies to certain qualifying relatives (¶3122). (Code Sec. 152(f)(6)(C))[34]

---

25. ¶A-3851; ¶1524.10; TD ¶564,051
26. ¶A-3860; ¶1524.10; TD ¶564,051
27. ¶A-3851; ¶1524.10; TD ¶564,051
28. ¶A-3851; ¶1524.10; TD ¶564,051
29. ¶A-3607; ¶1524.03

30. ¶A-3605.1; TD ¶562,407
31. ¶A-3602; ¶1524.03; TD ¶562,403
32. ¶A-3602; ¶1524.03; TD ¶562,403
33. ¶A-3607; ¶1524.03; TD ¶562,414
34. ¶A-3601.1; ¶1514.02; TD ¶562,402

¶ 3130   Tax rate schedules for individuals.

There's a tax rate schedule for:

(1) Single persons (not married at year's end), including certain marrieds living apart (¶3133), see ¶1102. These rates are more favorable than those for marrieds filing separate returns, but less favorable than head of household and (generally) joint return rates.

(2) Married couples filing joint returns, and certain widows and widowers who qualify as "surviving spouses" (¶3132), see ¶1103. These are often the most favorable rates.

(3) Heads of household, see ¶1105—more favorable rates than those for single persons.

(4) Married persons filing separately, see ¶1104—least favorable rates. (Code Sec. 1)[35]

There are 7 tax brackets at rates of 10%, 15%, 25%, 28%, 33%, 35% and 39.6% (Code Sec. 1)[36]

¶ 3131   Tax tables.

IRS has prepared tax tables, based on the tax rates. (Code Sec. 3(a)(1))[37] The draft 2013 table for Form 1040, Form 1040A or Form 1040EZ filers with taxable income less than $100,000 is reproduced at ¶1111. However, the tables aren't used by those who file a short period return because they changed their accounting period. (Code Sec. 3(b)(1))[38]

¶ 3132   When surviving spouse (qualifying widow/er) gets lower joint return rates.

A surviving spouse (qualifying widow/er) whose spouse died during either of the surviving spouse's two tax years immediately preceding the tax year (Code Sec. 2(a)(1)) is taxed at joint return rates (Code Sec. 1(a)(2)) if the surviving spouse:

. . . hasn't remarried at any time before the end of the tax year (Code Sec. 2(a)(2)(A)),

. . . "maintains" (pays over 50% of the costs of) a household as his home that's the "principal place of abode" of a dependent (a) who is taxpayer's son or daughter (including adopted children, but not foster children), stepson, or stepdaughter, and (b) for whom taxpayer is entitled to a dependency deduction for the tax year (Code Sec. 2(a)(1)), and

. . . could file a joint return with the deceased for the year of death. (Code Sec. 2(a)(2)(B))[39]

✐ *observation:* The surviving spouse rules *don't* apply for the year the spouse died. For when a joint return can be filed (and joint return rates used) in such year, see ¶4705 and ¶4708.

A special rule applies for spouses of individuals in "missing status" as a result of "combat zone" or "qualified hazardous duty area" service. If an MIA or POW is officially determined to be dead, and so is removed from the missing status rolls, surviving spouse status doesn't depend on the actual date of death. The relevant date is the date of the official determination, or, if earlier, two years after the date of official termination of combat activities in that zone. If a later actual death is established, that date will control. (Code Sec. 2(a)(3))[40]

¶ 3133   Certain married individuals living apart treated as unmarried.

A married taxpayer is considered single for tax purposes if the taxpayer meets all of the following tests (Code Sec. 7703(b); Reg § 1.7703-1(b)):

(1) Files a separate return.

(2) Maintains as his home a household that for more than half the tax year is the principal

---

35. ¶A-1101 *et seq.*; ¶14.08; TD ¶560,504
36. ¶A-1102; ¶14.08; TD ¶568,201
37. ¶A-1100; ¶34 *et seq.*; TD ¶568,251
38. ¶A-1181; ¶34.02; TD ¶568,251
39. ¶A-1700 *et seq.*; ¶24.02; TD ¶567,002
40. ¶A-1703; ¶24.02; TD ¶567,003

place of abode of a child (defined in Code Sec. 152(f)(1), ¶3120) for whom he's entitled to a dependency deduction for the year, or would be so entitled if the taxpayer hadn't released the exemption to the noncustodial parent (¶3126). (Code Sec. 7703(b)(1))

(3) Furnishes over half the cost of maintaining the household. (Code Sec. 7703(b)(2))

(4) During the last six months of the tax year, his spouse isn't a member of his household. (Code Sec. 7703(b)(3))[41]

⬥observation: Individuals treated as unmarried under this "abandoned spouse" rule can use the single or head of household rates.

Either or both spouses can qualify as "unmarried" by meeting the tests. If only one spouse qualifies, the other spouse must use married-filing-separately rates.[42]

A taxpayer who doesn't meet the above rules is considered married even though living apart from his spouse, unless legally separated under a decree of divorce or separate maintenance. (Reg § 1.7703-1(a))[43]

¶ 3134   Head of household status.

To qualify as a head of household for a tax year, a taxpayer must: (1) be unmarried (or treated as unmarried, ¶3133) at the end of the year; (2) not be a surviving spouse; (3) not be a nonresident alien at any time that year; *and* (4) maintain a household:

(a) that's his home, and for more than half of the tax year, the principal place of abode of (i) the taxpayer's qualifying child (below) or (ii) an individual for whom the taxpayer may claim a dependency deduction. (Code Sec. 2(b)(1)(A)), or

(b) (not necessarily his own) that for the tax year is the principal place of abode for either the taxpayer's father or mother, if the taxpayer is entitled to a dependency deduction for that parent. (Code Sec. 2(b)(1)(B))[44]

A qualifying child for this purpose is defined in Code Sec. 152(c) (¶3120), but without regard to Code Sec. 152(e) (custodial parent's release of exemption, ¶3126). But a taxpayer isn't eligible for head of household status if the child is married at the end of taxpayer's tax year and isn't taxpayer's dependent because he filed a joint return and/or isn't a U.S. citizen or resident. (Code Sec. 2(b)(1)(A)(i))[45] If registered domestic partners who reside in a community property state pay all the costs of maintaining a household from community funds, each partner has incurred half the cost, and neither can qualify. But if one partner pays more than half by contributing separate funds, that partner can qualify.[46]

¶ 3135   Tax on Unearned Income of Children—Kiddie Tax. ▰▰▰▰▰

Under the "kiddie tax" rules, certain children (¶3136) are taxed at their parents' highest tax rate on the child's unearned income over $2,000 for 2013 and 2014, if that tax is higher than what the child would otherwise pay on it. The parents can, if certain conditions are met, elect to include the child's gross income on their own return.

¶ 3136   Child subject to kiddie tax.

A child is subject to the kiddie tax if: (1) the child either (a) is under age 18 at the end of the tax year, or (b) is age 18, or 19-23 if a full-time student, at the end of the tax year *and* his earned income doesn't exceed one-half of his support; (2) either parent is alive at the end of the tax year; (3) the child doesn't file a joint return for the tax year; *and* (4) the child's unearned income is more than $2,000 for 2013 and 2014. (Code Sec. 1(g)(2))[47]

---

41. ¶A-1610 *et seq.*; ¶77,034.01; TD ¶566,511
42. ¶A-1502; ¶14.01; TD ¶566,002
43. ¶A-1611; ¶77,034.01; TD ¶566,511
44. ¶A-1401.1 *et seq.*; ¶24.03; TD ¶565,501.1 *et seq.*

45. ¶A-1406 *et seq.*; ¶24.03; TD ¶565,506 *et seq.*
46. ¶A-1416 *et seq.*; TD ¶565,517 *et seq.*
47. ¶A-1301; ¶14.09; TD ¶568,301

¶ 3137   Computing the kiddie tax—Form 8615.

A child subject to the kiddie tax (¶3136) pays a tax (computed on Form 8615, attached to the child's Form 1040 or 1040A) equal to the *greater* of:

(1) the sum of (a) the tax that would be imposed if the child's taxable income for the tax year were reduced by the child's net unearned income (¶3138), plus (b) the child's share of the allocable parental tax (below) (Code Sec. 1(g)(1)(B)), or

(2) the tax imposed on the child without regard to (1), above (Code Sec. 1(g)(1)(A))—i.e., the tax imposed on the child as a single person.[48]

The "child's share" of the allocable parental tax ((1), above) equals the amount that bears the same ratio to the total allocable parental tax (below) as the child's net unearned income bears to the total net unearned income of all children of that parent to whom these rules apply. (Code Sec. 1(g)(3)(B); Reg § 1.1(i)-1T, Q&A5)[49]

The "allocable parental tax" is the excess of: (1) the tax that would be imposed on the parent's taxable income if that income included the net unearned income of all that parent's children subject to these rules, over (2) the tax imposed on the parent without regard to these rules. (Code Sec. 1(g)(3)(A); Reg § 1.1(i)-1T, Q&A4)[50]

Parents of a child subject to the kiddie tax must give the child their taxpayer identification number (TIN) so it can be included on the child's return. (Code Sec. 1(g)(6))[1] If a child can't get the required information from his parent, he (or his legal representative) may request the necessary information from IRS. (Code Sec. 6103(e)(1)(A)(iii); Reg § 1.1(i)-1T, Q&A22)[2]

☑*caution:* For the child's alternative minimum tax, see ¶3204.

¶ 3138   "Net unearned income" for kiddie tax purposes.

"Net unearned income" is the portion of the child's "AGI not attributable to earned income" (i.e., investment income), reduced by the sum of the following amounts (Code Sec. 1(g)(4)(A); Reg § 1.1(i)-1T, Q&A6):

(1) the amount in effect for the tax year under Code Sec. 63(c)(5)(A) (Code Sec. 1(g)(4)(A)(ii)(I); Reg § 1.1(i)-1T, Q&A6), relating to one component of the standard deduction for a child who can be claimed as a dependent—i.e., $1,000 for 2013 and 2014 (¶3112);

(2) the greater of (a) the amount in (1), or (b) the amount of the itemized deductions directly connected with the production of the unearned income if the child itemizes deductions (Code Sec. 1(g)(4)(A)(ii)(II); Reg § 1.1(i)-1T, Q&A6);

(3) adjustments to income attributable to the unearned income, such as the penalty on early withdrawal of savings.[3]

But a child's net unearned income can't exceed his taxable income. (Code Sec. 1(g)(4)(B))[4]

Thus, for 2013, the child's first $1,000 of unearned income (first $1,000 for 2014) isn't taxed at all, the next $1,000 of unearned income (next $1,000 for 2014) is taxed at the child's tax rate, and the child's "excess" unearned income is taxed at the parent's marginal rate. [5]

Earned income means earned income as defined in Code Sec. 911(d)(2)—i.e., income attributable to wages, salaries, or other amounts received as compensation for personal services. (Code Sec. 1(g)(4)(A)(i); Reg § 1.1(i)-1T, Q&A6) Distributions from certain qualified disability trusts are treated as earned income. (Code Sec. 1(g)(4)(C))) But the taxable part of social security or pension benefits paid to the child are unearned income. (Reg § 1.1(i)-1T, Q&A9)

48. ¶A-1301 *et seq.*; ¶14.09; TD ¶568,301
49. ¶A-1310; ¶14.09; TD ¶568,310
50. ¶A-1311; ¶14.09; TD ¶568,311
1. ¶S-1544; ¶14.09; TD ¶568,303

2. ¶S-6403; ¶61,034.04; TD ¶568,303
3. ¶A-1305; ¶14.09; TD ¶568,305
4. ¶A-1305; ¶14.09; TD ¶568,305
5. ¶A-1304 *et seq.*; ¶14.09; TD ¶568,305

Unearned income also includes taxable interest, dividends, capital gains (including capital gain distributions), rents, royalties, etc.[6]

¶ 3139 Parents' election to be taxed on child's unearned income—Form 8814.

A parent can irrevocably elect (on Form 8814) to include in the parent's gross income for the tax year, the child's gross income in excess of $2,000 for 2013 and 2014. (Code Sec. 1(g)(7)(B)(i); Reg § 301.9100-8(a)(4)(i)) The child is then treated as having no gross income for the year and isn't required to file a return. (Code Sec. 1(g)(7)(A))[7]

The election applies only if the child's gross income is only from interest, dividends, and capital gain distribution; it's more than $1,000 and less than $10,000 for 2013 and 2014; the child made no estimated tax payments for, and didn't apply any overpayments to, the year; and backup withholding didn't apply. (Code Sec. 1(g)(7)(A))[8]

The electing parent's tax equals the sum of: (1) the tax on the parent's taxable income after taking into account the child's gross income over $2,000 for 2013 and 2014, plus (2) 10% of the lesser of (a) $1,000 for 2013 and 2014 or (b) the excess of the child's income over $1,000 for 2013 and 2014. (Code Sec. 1(g)(7)(B)(ii))[9] Any interest income that is a tax preference item of the child is treated as that of the electing parent. (Code Sec. 1(g)(7)(B)(iii))[10]

illustration: S, age 6, receives $5,000 in interest income in 2013. The requirements for making the election to report his income on his parents' return are satisfied, and his parents make the election. So they include $3,000 of S's gross income on their tax return ($5,000 gross income, minus $2,000 (2 × $1,000)). They also must pay an additional tax of $100 (i.e., 10% of the lesser of (a) $1,000, or (b) $4,000 ($5,000 – $1,000)). Assuming a 25% tax bracket applies to the parents, the added tax under the election would be $850, i.e., $750 (25% × $3,000) + $100.

caution: The election could increase total family taxes, because the income picked up from the child could lower various tax breaks of the parent that are geared to AGI.

¶ 3140 Self-Employment Tax.

Self-employed persons pay social security and Medicare taxes as part of their income tax. This self-employment (SE) tax is based on net earnings from self-employment, not on taxable income.

¶ 3141 Self-employment tax imposed—Schedule SE.

The self-employment (SE) tax consists of: (1) a social security (OASDI) tax, and (2) a Medicare (hospital insurance) tax. These taxes are imposed (compute on Form 1040, Schedule SE) on self-employment income (¶3142). (Code Sec. 1401(a), Code Sec. 1401(b)).[11] For contribution bases and rates for the SE tax, including the 0.9% additional Medicare self-employment tax, see ¶1109. For who is subject to the SE tax, see ¶3146.

¶ 3142 Self-employment (SE) income subject to SE tax.

SE income consists of net earnings from self-employment (¶3143). But in computing an individual's SE tax (¶3141), the maximum amount of SE income subject to OASDI tax for a tax year (whether 12 months or less) is the contribution base (¶1109) for the calendar year in which the tax year begins, minus the amount of any wages received by the individual in the same tax year. If net earnings from self-employment are less than $400 ($100 for a church employee (Code Sec. 1402(j)(2)(B))), SE income for that year is zero. (Code Sec. 1402(b); Reg § 1.1402(b)-1)[12]

6. ¶A-1301.1, A-1307; ¶14.09; TD ¶568,301.1, 568,307
7. ¶A-1326; ¶14.11; TD ¶568,401
8. ¶A-1327; ¶14.11; TD ¶568,402
9. ¶A-1330; ¶14.11; TD ¶568,405

10. ¶A-1331; ¶14.11; TD ¶568,406
11. ¶A-6001; ¶14,024; TD ¶575,501
12. ¶A-6031 *et seq.*; ¶14,024.02; TD ¶576,001 *et seq.*

observation: Since a 7.65% deduction (¶3143) is allowed from net profits (i.e., net earnings from self-employment before that deduction), an individual can have actual net profits of up to $433.13 (92.35% of $433.13 = $400) without triggering SE tax.

A mitigation provision can come into play where wages were erroneously reported as self-employment income or vice versa. (Code Sec. 6521)[13]

¶ 3143   Net earnings from self-employment.

This is gross income, under the individual's income tax accounting method, from a trade or business carried on by him, less allowable deductions for that business, plus his distributive share of partnership taxable income (whether or not distributed) or loss from a partnership of which he's a member. (Code Sec. 1402(a); Reg § 1.1402(a)-1)[14]

A deduction is allowed for an amount equal to 7.65% of his net earnings from self-employment for the tax year (determined without this deduction). This deduction is computed without regard to the 0.9% additional Medicare self-employment tax (see ¶1109). (Code Sec. 1402(a)(12))[15]

An individual with more than one business must combine the net earnings from each to determine self-employment income. The gains and loss from the businesses are netted, so a loss in one reduces a gain in another. (Reg § 1.1402(a)-2(c))[16] If an individual has a part-time business and a regular job as an employee, only the income from the part-time business is included in determining net earnings.[17]

In computing net earnings from self-employment, the following deductions *aren't* allowed:

. . . deduction for personal exemptions (Code Sec. 1402(a)(7));

. . . deduction for half of SE taxes (Code Sec. 1402(a)(12));

. . . deduction for net operating losses (Code Sec. 1402(a)(4));

. . . domestic production activities deduction (Code Sec. 1402(a)(16));

. . . nonbusiness deductions;[18]

Net earnings from self-employment *don't include*:

• certain income received by a retired partner under a written plan of the partnership (Code Sec. 1402(a)(10));[19]

• dividends or interest on investments (Code Sec. 1402(a)(2));[20]

• gains (or losses) from disposition of a capital asset or other property that's not inventory or held for sale to customers (Code Sec. 1402(a)(3));[21] but options and commodities dealers must include gains and losses derived from dealing or trading in options and regulated futures subject to mark-to-market rules in SE net earnings (Code Sec. 1402(i));[22]

• gain or loss of a securities or commodities trader that is treated as ordinary solely by reason of the election of mark-to-market treatment (Code Sec. 475(f)(1)(D));[23]

• qualified disaster relief (or mitigation) payments (Code Sec. 139(d));[24]

• rents from real estate (and personal property leased with it) held for investment. (Code Sec. 1402(a)(1)) But rents are included in net earnings if received by real estate dealers in the normal course of business (Reg § 1.1402(a)-4(a)),[25] or if the rent is for living quarters where *services* (e.g., maid service) are also rendered primarily for the occupant's convenience (Reg § 1.1402(a)-4(c)(2)), such as in hotels, boarding houses, tourist camps or homes, parking lots, warehouses and storage garages;[26]

13. ¶T-3634; ¶14,024.18, 65,214.01; TD ¶836,007
14. ¶A-6100 *et seq.*; ¶14,024.07; TD ¶576,012
15. ¶A-6114; ¶14,024; TD ¶576,025
16. ¶A-6103; ¶14,024; TD ¶576,011
17. ¶A-6103; ¶14,024; TD ¶576,036
18. ¶A-6113; ¶14,024; TD ¶576,023
19. ¶A-6166; ¶14,024.16; TD ¶576,211

20. ¶A-6108; ¶14,024.05; TD ¶576,021
21. ¶A-6109; ¶14,024.06; TD ¶576,022
22. ¶A-6112; ¶14,024.06; TD ¶576,017
23. ¶A-6112.1; ¶4754.01; TD ¶576,017
24. ¶A-6105; ¶1394; TD ¶576,018
25. ¶A-6105, A-6106; ¶14,024.04; TD ¶576,018
26. ¶A-6107; ¶14,024.04; TD ¶576,020

- rents paid in crop shares unless paid under an arrangement where the landowner (or tenant) materially participates in crop production or controls and directs the farming operation and pays the farmer at a fixed rate as his employee (Reg § 1.1402(a)-4(b));[27]
- certain termination payments received by former insurance salesmen (Code Sec. 1402(k));[28]
- a shareholder's share of an S corporation's income (whether distributed or not) or loss. [29]

A passive activity loss that's disallowed for income tax purposes isn't taken into account in computing net earnings from self-employment. (Reg § 1.469-1T(d)(3))[30]

Holding public office isn't an SE trade or business, except for certain state or local officials paid solely on a fee basis (¶3146). (Code Sec. 1402(c)(1))[31]

¶ 3144 Partner's self-employment tax.

A partner's net earnings from self-employment are, generally, his distributive share of the partnership's taxable income arising out of the trade or business of the partnership plus his guaranteed payments. (Code Sec. 1402(a); Reg § 1.1402(a)-1(a)(2), Reg § 1.1402(a)-1(b))[32]

The distributive share of any item of income or loss of a limited partner is excluded. But this exclusion doesn't apply to guaranteed payments to that partner for services actually rendered to or on behalf of the partnership, to the extent the payments are shown to be remuneration for those services. (Code Sec. 1402(a)(13))[33]

¶ 3145 Married couple's self-employment (SE) tax.

SE tax is computed on the separate self-employment income of each spouse, whether or not they file joint returns. But the spouses are jointly and severally liable for SE tax due on a joint return. (Code Sec. 6017; Reg § 1.6017-1(b))[34]

¶ 3146 Who is subject to self-employment (SE) tax?

The SE tax is a tax on self-employed individuals (U.S. citizens and resident aliens). (Code Sec. 1401, Code Sec. 1402(b)) Income earned as an employee isn't subject to SE tax (Code Sec. 1402(c)(2)),[35] with these exceptions:

. . . Members of the clergy, see ¶3147.

. . . Persons 18 or older employed to sell magazines and newspapers to the public at a fixed price, whose pay is the excess of the fixed price over their cost. (Code Sec. 1402(c)(2)(A))[36]

. . . U.S. citizens employed by a foreign government, its wholly owned instrumentality, or an international organization (e.g., the U.N.). (Code Sec. 1402(c)(2)(C))[37]

. . . Fishing boat crewmen who work on a boat that normally has fewer than 10 crew members and who get no fixed remuneration other than a share of the catch and certain small cash payments. (Code Sec. 1402(c)(2)(F))[38]

. . . Sharecroppers whose earnings depend on production.[39]

. . . State or local government officials whose pay is *solely* fees, unless the services are covered by social security under a federal-state agreement. (Code Sec. 1402(c)(2)(E))[40]

Statutory employees (¶3103) don't pay SE tax (they pay FICA instead) even if treated as self-employed for income tax purposes. (Code Sec. 1402(d), Code Sec. 3121(d)(3))[41]

27. ¶A-6202 *et seq.*; ¶14,024.04; TD ¶576,018
28. ¶A-6032.1; ¶14,024.155; TD ¶576,009
29. ¶A-6084; TD ¶576,037
30. ¶M-4603; ¶4694.47; TD ¶411,002
31. ¶A-6095; ¶14,024.13; TD ¶576,051
32. ¶A-6150 *et seq.*; ¶14,024.16; TD ¶576,200 *et seq.*
33. ¶A-6157; ¶14,024.16; TD ¶576,207
34. ¶S-1812; ¶60,174; TD ¶570,607

35. ¶A-6092; ¶14,024.09; TD ¶576,049
36. ¶A-6087.1; ¶14,024.09; TD ¶576,049
37. ¶A-6097; ¶14,024.09; TD ¶576,053
38. ¶A-6090; ¶14,024.14; TD ¶576,047
39. ¶A-6202; ¶14,024.04; TD ¶576,066
40. ¶A-6092; ¶14,024.13; TD ¶576,051
41. ¶A-6093; ¶14,024.09; TD ¶576,050

Members of certain religious sects who are conscientiously opposed to social security and file a benefits exemption (on Form 4029) are exempt from SE tax. (Code Sec. 1402(g); Reg § 1.1402(h)-1)[42]

¶ 3147   Members of the clergy.

Members of the clergy, members of religious orders, and Christian Science practitioners are subject to self-employment tax on services performed in the exercise of their ministry (Code Sec. 1402(c)(4), Code Sec. 1402(c)(5)) *unless* they have taken a vow of poverty (Code Sec. 1402(c))[43] or irrevocably elect (on Form 4361) *not* to be covered. (Code Sec. 1402(e))[44]

¶ 3148   Farmers' self-employment (SE) tax.

Self-employed persons must pay SE tax on the income from their farming operations. (Code Sec. 1402(a)) Conservation reserve program (CRP) payments are treated as includible farm income unless received by an individual who is getting social security retirement or disability payments. (Code Sec. 1402(a)(1)) Since a farmer has an optional method of computing SE tax on farm income (¶3149), he may have to distinguish farm income from other self-employment income. Farm income comes from an operation on a farm in which more than half the time is devoted to farming activities. (Reg § 1.1402(a)-13)[45]

¶ 3149   Optional methods for computing self-employment earnings.

The optional method—referred to as the "nonfarm optional method" for nonfarming businesses and the "farm optional method" for farming businesses—is as follows: For 2013, if an individual's gross income from the business is not more than $6,960, he may elect to treat 66⅔% of that gross income as his SE net earnings from the business. If it's more than $6,960 for 2013 ($7,200 for 2014) and his net profits from the business are less than $5,024 for that year ($5,198 for 2014), he may elect to treat $4,640 ($4,800 for 2014) as SE net earnings from the business. But if net profits are $5,024 for 2013 ($5,198 for 2014), he must use the net profits. (Code Sec. 1402(a), Code Sec. 1402(l); Reg § 1.1402(a)-15(a)(1))[46]

The optional nonfarm method may be used for 2013 only if: net profits from the nonfarming business are less than $5,024 ($5,198 for 2014) *and* less than 72.189% of gross nonfarm income, SE net earnings were at least $400 in 2 of the prior 3 years, *and* taxpayer has used this method for fewer than 5 years (consecutive or not). (Code Sec. 1402(a), Code Sec. 1402(h))[47]

An individual may use the optional farm method for 2013 if gross farm income is not more than $6,960 ($7,200 for 2014), or net farm profits are less than $5,024 ($5,198 for 2014). (Code Sec. 1402(a), Code Sec. 1402(h))[48]

An individual with both farm and nonfarm incomes may use both methods (if otherwise allowed): the farm optional method for the farm income and the nonfarm optional method for the nonfarm income. For 2013, if both methods are used, the combined total SE net earnings can't be more than $4,640 ($4,800 for 2014). (Code Sec. 1402(a); Reg § 1.1402(a)-15)[49]

Elect the optional method by computing (on Schedule SE, Form 1040) SE net earnings under that method. The election may be made or revoked after the return is filed, on an amended return. (Code Sec. 1402(a); Reg § 1.1402(a)-16)[50]

42. ¶A-6327 *et seq.*; ¶14,024.15; TD ¶576,092
43. ¶A-6301; ¶14,024.10; TD ¶576,075
44. ¶A-6321; ¶14,024.10; TD ¶576,085
45. ¶A-6201 *et seq.*; ¶614.051; TD ¶576,064
46. ¶A-6117; ¶14,024.20; TD ¶576,028

47. ¶A-6121; ¶14,024.20; TD ¶576,028
48. ¶A-6122; ¶14,024.20; TD ¶576,030
49. ¶A-6119; ¶14,024.20; TD ¶576,032
50. ¶A-6125; ¶14,024.20; TD ¶576,029, 576,031

¶ 3150   3.8% Surtax on Unearned Income. ▨

For tax years beginning after 2012, certain unearned income of individuals, trusts, and estates is subject to a 3.8% surtax (i.e., it's payable on top of any other tax payable on that income).

¶ 3151   Calculating the 3.8% surtax on unearned income—Form 8960.

For individuals, the post-2012 surtax on unearned income (also called the unearned income Medicare contribution tax or the net investment income tax) is 3.8% of the lesser of:

(1) net investment income (NII, ¶3152); or

(2) the excess of modified adjusted gross income (MAGI) over an unindexed threshold amount ($250,000 for joint filers or surviving spouses, $125,000 for a married individual filing a separate return, and $200,000 in any other case). (Code Sec. 1411(a)(1), Code Sec. 1411(b))[1]

illustration (1): For 2013, a single taxpayer who has NII of $15,000 and wages of $180,000, won't pay the surtax because his MAGI ($195,000) doesn't exceed his threshold amount ($200,000).

illustration (2): For 2013, a single taxpayer who has NII of $90,000 and wages of $180,000 will pay a surtax equal to 3.8% of the lesser of (1) $90,000 NII, or (2) the $70,000 amount by which his $270,000 MAGI exceeds his threshold amount of $200,000. The surtax is $2,660 ($70,000 × 3.8%).

MAGI is adjusted gross income (AGI) plus any amount excluded as foreign earned income under Code Sec. 911(a)(1) (net of the deductions and exclusions disallowed with respect to the foreign earned income). (Code Sec. 1411(d))

For an estate or trust, the surtax is 3.8% of the lesser of (1) undistributed NII or (2) the excess of adjusted gross income (AGI, as defined in Code Sec. 67(e)) over the dollar amount at which the highest income tax bracket applicable to an estate or trust begins (see ¶1106). (Code Sec. 1411(a)(2))[2]

¶ 3152   What is net investment income (NII)?

For 3.8% surtax purposes, NII is investment income less deductions properly allocable to NII. Investment income is:

... gross income from interest, dividends, annuities, royalties, and rents, unless derived in the ordinary course of a trade or business to which the 3.8% surtax *doesn't* apply,

... other gross income derived from a trade or business to which the 3.8% surtax *does* apply, and

... net gain (to the extent taken into account in computing taxable income) attributable to the disposition of property other than property held in a trade or business to which the 3.8% surtax *doesn't* apply. (Code Sec. 1411(c))[3]

The 3.8% surtax applies to a trade or business only if it is a Code Sec. 469 passive activity of the taxpayer or a trade or business of trading in Code Sec. 475(e)(2) financial instruments or commodities. (Code Sec. 1411(c)(2), Prop Reg. § 1.1411-5, "Taxpayers may rely.")

Gain or loss from a disposition of an interest in a partnership (¶3765) or S corporation (¶3367) is taken into account by the partner or shareholder as NII only to the extent of the net gain or loss that the transferor would take into account if the entity had sold all its

---

1. ¶A-6361 *et seq.*; ¶14,114.01 *et seq.*; TD ¶576,301
2. ¶C-5801; ¶C-9581; ¶14,114.02; TD ¶579,201; ¶651,301

3. ¶A-6363 ; ¶14,114.01 ; TD ¶576,302

property for fair market value immediately before the disposition. (Code Sec. 1411(c)(4), Prop Reg. § 1.1411-7, "Taxpayers may rely.")

Deductions properly allocable to NII. Such deductions include: investment interest expense; investment advisory and brokerage fees; expenses related to rental and royalty income; and state and local income taxes. Deductions subject to the 2% floor beneath miscellaneous itemized deductions (Code Sec. 67, ¶3110) or the overall limit on itemized deductions (Code Sec. 68, ¶3114) are allowed in determining NII only to the extent permitted by the floor or limit (with Code Sec. 67 applied first). Deductions don't include losses allowed under Code Sec. 165; such losses are deductible only in determining net gain, and only to the extent of gains. (Prop Reg. § 1.1411-4, "Taxpayers may rely.")

Items excluded from NII. Investment income for surtax purposes does not include any amount subject to the self-employment tax (¶1109), amounts distributed from retirement plans (¶4357), or tax-exempt income (¶1206). (Code Sec. 1411(b)(5), Code Sec. 1411(b)(6)) Income from sources such as Social Security benefits, unemployment compensation, or alimony also is excluded.

☑caution: Although income from sources such as self-employment and taxable distributions from retirement plans are excluded from NII, they *are* included in the taxpayer's MAGI for surtax calculation purposes (see ¶3150).

The surtax does *not* apply to active businesses conducted by a sole proprietor, partnership, or S corporation (but income or gain on working capital isn't treated as derived from a trade or business and thus is subject to the surtax). (Code Sec. 1411(c)(3), (Prop Reg. § 1.1411-6(a), "Taxpayers may rely.") [4]

¶ 3153   Who is subject to the 3.8% surtax.

The 3.8% surtax applies to individuals, trusts, and estates. (Code Sec. 1411(a)) A bankruptcy estate in which the debtor is an individual is treated as a married taxpayer filing a separate return. (Prop Reg. § 1.1441-3(d), "Taxpayers may rely.")

The 3.8% surtax under Code Sec. 1411 does not apply to: nonresident aliens (special rules apply to nonresident aliens married to U.S. citizens or residents); bona fide residents of a U.S. territory (but the surtax does apply if the individual is required to file U.S. income tax return after application of Code Sec. 931, Code Sec. 932, Code Sec. 933 or Code Sec. 935); trusts, all the unexpired interests in which are devoted to charitable purposes described in Code Sec. 170(c)(2)(B); trusts exempt from tax under Code Sec. 501; charitable remainder trusts (CRTs) exempt from tax under Code Sec. 664 (¶2116); or "grantor trusts" (but the income and deductions of the trusts are taken into account in determining the owners' NII). (Code Sec. 1411(e)) (Prop Reg. § 1.1411-2, Prop Reg. § 1.1411-3, "Taxpayers may rely.") Electing small business trusts (ESBTs, ¶3354) and CRTs are subject to special rules. (Prop Reg. § 1.1411-3(c), "Taxpayers may rely.") [5]

¶ 3154   Individual Estimated Tax. ▬▬▬▬▬▬▬▬▬▬▬▬▬▬▬▬▬▬▬▬▬▬

An individual must make four quarterly installment payments of estimated tax based on the amount of his "required annual payment" to avoid an underpayment penalty. The required annual payment is the lower of 90% of the tax shown on the current year return or 100% (110%, for high income individuals) of the tax shown on the prior year return. There's no penalty if the tax shown on the return (after withholding) is less than $1,000, or if other specified exceptions or waivers apply.

To avoid the penalty, an individual must: (1) pay each "required installment" (¶3157) by its due date (¶3160), (2) meet an exception (¶3164), *or* (3) get a waiver (¶3165).[6]

---

4. ¶A-6372 ; ¶14,114.01 ; TD ¶576,304   6. ¶S-5200 *et seq.*; ¶66,544 *et seq.*; TD ¶571,300
5. ¶C-5802 ; ¶14,114.01 ; TD ¶561,302

> 🅡 ✓*caution:* The 3.8% surtax on "unearned income" (¶1107) isn't subject to withholding, so individuals who are subject to that tax should increase either their withholding or their estimated tax payments.

¶ 3155 How to pay estimated tax—Form 1040-ES.

Make estimated tax payments by check or money order using payment-voucher Form 1040-ES (Form 1040-ES (NR) for nonresident aliens); by phone or online using a credit (MasterCard, VISA, American Express, or Discover) or debit card: call 1-888-729-1040 or 1-800-272-9829, or go to www.PAY1040.com, www.officialpayments.com, or www.payUSAtax.com; by EFTPS using the Internet or phone; or by EFW if filing electronically. (Reg § 301.6311-2)[7]

Estimated tax liability is computed as the expected taxes on expected taxable income for the year, minus the tax withheld (or to be withheld) from the year's wages and the expected tax credits (Code Sec. 6654(f), Code Sec. 6654(g); Reg § 1.6654-5(a)), taking into account the taxes, credits, and other amounts listed in Reg § 1.6654-1(a)(4). (Reg § 1.6654-5(b))[8]

¶ 3156 Married individuals' estimated tax.

A married person determines estimated tax liability based on his separate income. Spouses making joint estimated tax payments apply the rules on a joint basis. Joint estimated tax payments don't affect the choice of joint or separate income tax returns.[9] Joint payments can be apportioned between the spouses' separate returns. (Reg § 1.6654-2(e)(5))[10]

¶ 3157 Amount of required installment.

Unless the annualized income method (¶3158) is used, the amount of each required installment is 25% of the "required annual payment." For most individuals, the required annual payment is the lower of: (1) 90% of the tax shown on the current year's return (or, if no return is filed, 90% of the current year tax), or (2) 100% of the tax shown on the previous year's return, if that tax year was a 12-month year and the taxpayer filed a return (even a late one) for that year. (Code Sec. 6654(d)(1))[11]

Different rules apply to high income individuals. If an individual's previous year's return showed adjusted gross income exceeding $150,000 ($75,000 for marrieds filing separately), the required annual payment is the lower of (1), above, or 110% of the tax shown on the previous year's return. (Code Sec. 6654(d)(1)(C))[12]

¶ 3158 Annualized income method.

For any installment for which the taxpayer establishes that the "annualized income installment" (below) is less than the required installment determined under the rules at ¶3157, the annualized income installment becomes the required installment. (Code Sec. 6654(d)(2)(A)(i)) The annualized income installment is the excess (if any) of:

(1) an amount equal to the "applicable percentage" (below) of the annualized tax (computed by placing taxable income, alternative minimum taxable income (AMTI), and adjusted self-employment income (below) on an annualized basis) for the months in the tax year ending before the due date for the installment, over

(2) the sum of any earlier required installments for the tax year. (Code Sec. 6654(d)(2)(B))[13]

The applicable percentages are 22.5%, 45%, 67.5% and 90%, respectively, for the first, second, third and fourth required installments. (Code Sec. 6654(d)(2)(C)(ii))[14]

---

7. ¶S-5253; ¶63,114; TD ¶571,341
8. ¶S-5201; ¶66,544.01; TD ¶571,301
9. ¶S-5254; ¶66,544.01; TD ¶571,347
10. ¶S-5255; ¶66,544.01; TD ¶571,347

11. ¶S-5204; ¶66,544.03; TD ¶571,304
12. ¶S-5204.1; ¶66,544.03; TD ¶571,305
13. ¶S-5219 *et seq.*; ¶66,544.04; TD ¶571,312 *et seq.*
14. ¶S-5235; ¶66,544.04; TD ¶571,330

Adjusted self-employment income means self-employment income (¶3142) except that wages for calendar months ending before the installment due date must be annualized as in (1), above. (Code Sec. 6654(d)(2)(C)(iii))[15]

If, for an installment, the annualized income installment is the required installment because it's less than the installment determined under the rules at ¶3157, the excess must be recaptured—i.e, added to the next required installment that isn't an annualized income installment. (Code Sec. 6654(d)(2)(A)(ii))[16]

¶ 3159   Withholding as payment of estimated tax.

Any withholding is treated as a payment of estimated tax. An equal part of the withheld tax is considered paid on each installment date unless the individual establishes the dates the amounts were actually withheld. (Code Sec. 6654(g)(1))[17]

recommendation: An individual who underpays an early required installment can avoid or reduce the underpayment penalty by increasing withholding for the rest of the year.

¶ 3160   Time for paying installments.

Calendar year individuals (not farmers and fishermen (¶3161) or nonresident aliens (¶3162)) must pay estimated taxes in four installments, due Apr. 15, June 15, Sept. 15 of the current year, and Jan. 15 of the next year. (Code Sec. 6654(c)) But an individual who first has income subject to the tax after Mar. 31 makes the first payment by the due date for the period in which he has the income.[18] The last installment, ordinarily due on Jan. 15, needn't be paid if the individual files his return and pays the tax shown on it by Jan. 31. (Code Sec. 6654(h))[19]

For fiscal year taxpayers, the due dates are the 15th day of the 4th, 6th, and 9th month of the fiscal year and the 15th day of the first month of the next tax year. (Code Sec. 6654(k))[20]

¶ 3161   Farmers and fishermen.

A farmer or fisherman doesn't have to pay estimated tax for a year if he files his return and pays the tax shown on it by Mar. 1 of the next year. Otherwise, he must make one estimated tax payment for the year, due Jan. 15 of the next year.[21] The required installment calculation (¶3157) uses 66^2/$_3$% (not 90%) of the current year tax. (Code Sec. 6654(i)(1))[22]

An individual is a farmer or fisherman if at least 66^2/$_3$% of his gross income for the current or preceding tax year is from farming or fishing. (Code Sec. 6654(i)(2))[23]

¶ 3162   Nonresident aliens—Form 1040-ES (NR).

Nonresident aliens required to file U.S. income tax returns (¶4657) must pay three required installments for the year, due on June 15, Sept. 15, and Jan. 15 of the next year. (Code Sec. 6654(j)(2))[24] The required installments (compute on Form 1040-ES(NR)) are 50%, 25%, and 25%, respectively, of the required annual payment (¶3157). (Code Sec. 6654(j)(3)(A)) The applicable percentages under the annualized income method (¶3158) are 45%, 67.5%, and 90%, respectively. (Code Sec. 6654(j)(3)(B))[25]

---

15. ¶S-5225; ¶66,544.04; TD ¶571,318
16. ¶S-5229; ¶66,544.04; TD ¶571,324
17. ¶S-5248; ¶66,544.02; TD ¶571,342
18. ¶S-5241, S-5242; ¶66,544.02; TD ¶571,335, 571,336
19. ¶S-5268; ¶66,544.02; TD ¶571,362
20. ¶S-5243; ¶66,544.02; TD ¶571,337

21. ¶S-5247; ¶66,544.06; TD ¶571,340
22. ¶S-5237; ¶66,544.06; TD ¶571,332
23. ¶S-5238; ¶66,544.06; TD ¶571,332
24. ¶S-5246; ¶66,544.07
25. ¶S-5236; ¶66,544.07

¶ 3163　Penalty for underpayment of estimated tax—Form 2210, Form 2210F.

The penalty for underpayment equals the product of the interest rate (using simple interest) (Code Sec. 6622(b)) on deficiencies (¶4866), times the amount of the underpayment (below), for the period of the underpayment (below). (Code Sec. 6654(a))[26]

The *amount of the underpayment* is the excess of the "required installment" (¶3157) over any amount paid on or before the due date of the installment. (Code Sec. 6654(b)(1))[27] It's adjusted to reflect the number of days the underpayment is outstanding.[28]

The *period of underpayment* runs from that due date to the earlier of: (1) Apr. 15 following the end of the tax year, or (2) the date the underpayment is paid. (Code Sec. 6654(b)(2)) For these purposes, a payment is credited against unpaid installments in the order the installments are required to be paid. (Code Sec. 6654(b)(3))[29]

Form 2210 (Form 2210F for farmers and fishermen) may be used to compute the penalty,[30] or IRS will compute it and send a bill.[31] For exceptions, see ¶3164. For waivers, see ¶3165.

¶ 3164　Exceptions to underpayment penalty.

The underpayment penalty (¶3163) doesn't apply:

(1) if the tax shown on the return (or the tax due if no return is filed) is less than $1,000 after reduction for withholding tax paid (Code Sec. 6654(e)(1)),[32] or

(2) if the individual was a U.S. citizen or resident for the entire preceding tax year, he had no tax liability for that year, and that year was a 12-month year (Code Sec. 6654(e)(2)),[33] or

(3) for the 4th installment, if the individual (not a farmer or fisherman, ¶3161) files his return by the end of the 1st month after the tax year (Jan. 31 for calendar year taxpayers), and pays in full the tax computed on the return (Code Sec. 6654(h)),[34] or

(4) in certain cases while a Title 11 bankruptcy case is pending. (Code Sec. 6658(a))[35]

¶ 3165　Waiver of penalty.

The underpayment penalty (¶3163) may be waived by IRS if:

(1) failure to pay was due to casualty, disaster, or other unusual circumstances where penalty would be inequitable or against good conscience (Code Sec. 6654(e)(3)(A)),[36] or

(2) underpayment was due to reasonable cause (not willful neglect), and the taxpayer retired (after reaching age 62) or became disabled during the year for which the payments in question were required or in the preceding tax year. (Code Sec. 6654(e)(3)(B))[37]

---

26. ¶S-5260; ¶66,544.02; TD ¶571,353
27. ¶S-5261, S-5262; ¶66,544.02; TD ¶571,355, 571,356
28. ¶S-5260; ¶66,544.02; TD ¶571,353
29. ¶S-5263; ¶66,544.02; TD ¶571,357
30. ¶S-5265; TD ¶571,359
31. ¶S-5260; TD ¶571,353

32. ¶S-5266; TD ¶571,360
33. ¶S-5267; ¶66,544.05; TD ¶571,361
34. ¶S-5268; ¶66,544.02; TD ¶571,362
35. ¶V-7378; ¶66,584; TD ¶571,363
36. ¶S-5270; ¶66,544.05; TD ¶571,364
37. ¶S-5271.5; ¶66,544.05; TD ¶571,365

Chapter 14   Alternative Minimum Tax

¶ 3200   Alternative Minimum Tax.

The alternative minimum tax (AMT) equals the excess (if any) of the tentative minimum tax over the regular tax.

The AMT was designed to prevent a taxpayer from avoiding all tax liability by using exclusions, deductions, and credits. It's paid only if and to the extent it exceeds the taxpayer's regular tax. (Code Sec. 55(a)) Taxpayers who are subject to the regular tax generally are subject to the AMT. (Code Sec. 55(a), Code Sec. 55(b)) Thus, partnerships (Code Sec. 701) and S corporations (Code Sec. 1363(a)) aren't subject to AMT, but their partners and shareholders are. Foreign corporations are subject only as to taxable income effectively connected with conduct of a U.S. trade or business. (Code Sec. 882(a)(1))[1] For a "small corporation" exemption, see ¶3205.

For the AMT credit (against regular tax), see ¶2365.

For the AMT refundable credit available to individuals, see ¶2365.

¶ 3201   Computing the AMT—Form 6251; Form 4626.

The alternative minimum tax (AMT) equals the excess (if any) of the tentative minimum tax (see below) for the tax year, over the regular tax (see below) for the tax year. (Code Sec. 55(a)) AMT is computed on Form 6251 for individuals, Schedule I of Form 1041 for fiduciaries (estates and trusts), or Form 4626 for C corporations.[2]

For a noncorporate taxpayer (other than a married person filing separately), the tentative minimum tax for the tax year equals 26% of the "taxable excess" (defined below) that doesn't exceed $175,000 (as adjusted for inflation, i.e., for 2013, $179,500, and for 2014, $182,500), plus 28% of the taxable excess above $175,000 (as adjusted for inflation, above), reduced by the AMT foreign tax credit (AMTFTC, ¶3214) for the year. (Code Sec. 55(b)(1)(A)(i); Code Sec. 55(d)(4)(B)(i)) For marrieds filing separately, the amount used to compute tentative minimum tax is 50% of the amount used for marrieds filing jointly. (Code Sec. 55(b)(1)(A)(iii)) Tentative minimum tax on net capital gain and qualified dividend income is computed using the long-term capital gain rates that apply for regular tax purposes (Code Sec. 55(b)(3)), see ¶2603. "Taxable excess" is the excess of alternative minimum taxable income (AMTI, ¶3202) for the tax year over the "exemption amount" (¶3203). (Code Sec. 55(b)(1)(A)(ii))[3]

For a corporation (other than a small corporation, ¶3205), the tentative minimum tax (Code Sec. 55(b)(1)) for the tax year is 20% of AMTI for the year in excess of the exemption amount, reduced by the AMTFTC for the year. (Code Sec. 55(b)(1)(B))[4]

The regular tax is the regular tax liability used for determining the limitation on various nonrefundable credits (¶2364), reduced by the regular (i.e., not the AMT) foreign tax credit (¶2367) and the possessions tax credit, and without including any investment credit recapture (¶2314), low-income housing credit recapture (¶2321), or Code Sec. 45(e)(11)(C) income tax increase for cooperatives from electricity production credits passed through to patrons. (Code Sec. 55(c)(1))[5]

In computing regular tax liability for AMT purposes, income averaging for farmers and fishermen is not taken into account. (Code Sec. 55(c)(2))[6]

observation: This means that the "regular tax" used to determine if the farmer or

---

1. ¶A-8130 *et seq.*; ¶554; TD ¶691,000 *et seq.*
2. ¶A-8101; ¶554.01; TD ¶691,001
3. ¶A-8101, ¶A-8102; ¶554.01; TD ¶691,001, TD ¶691,002

4. ¶A-8103; ¶554.01; TD ¶691,003
5. ¶A-8105; ¶554.01; TD ¶691,005
6. ¶A-8105; ¶554.01; TD ¶691,005

References beginning with a single letter are to paragraphs in RIA's Federal Tax Coordinator 2d and RIA's Analysis of Federal Taxes: Income. Those beginning with numbers are to paragraphs in RIA's United States Tax Reporter. Those beginning with TD are to paragraphs in RIA's Tax Desk.

fisherman is subject to AMT is computed as if income averaging had not been used. Thus, the use of three-year income averaging does not trigger or increase AMT liability.

The Code Sec. 291 "cutback" rules generally apply before the AMT rules. (Code Sec. 59(f))[7]

¶ 3202   Alternative minimum taxable income (AMTI).

AMTI is taxable income, with various "adjustments," plus tax preferences, see ¶3206 *et seq.* (Code Sec. 55(b)(2))[8] The alternative minimum tax (AMT) can apply if a taxpayer has only adjustments. A taxpayer without preferences must still compute AMTI with the adjustments.[9]

All Code provisions that apply in determining regular taxable income also apply in determining AMTI. (Reg § 1.55-1(a)) For example, the limitations on the use of capital losses by noncorporate (¶2611, ¶2612) and corporate (¶2615) taxpayers also apply for AMTI purposes.[10]

A noncorporate taxpayer's net capital gain and qualified dividend income are included in AMTI, but taxed as long-term capital gains, see ¶3201.[11]

The at-risk rules (¶1803), and the partnership (¶3735) and S corporation (¶3369) loss limitation rules, are applied with the AMT adjustments and preferences. (Code Sec. 59(h))[12]

In taking the Code Sec. 199 domestic production activity deduction (¶1614) into account for AMTI purposes: (1) qualified production activities income (¶1616) is determined without any adjustments under Code Sec. 56 – Code Sec. 59; and (2) for a corporation, the taxable income limit (¶1615) on the deduction is applied by substituting "AMTI" for "taxable income." (Code Sec. 199(d)(6); Reg § 1.199-8(d))[13]

If a taxpayer's regular tax is determined by reference to an amount other than taxable income (e.g., unrelated business taxable income of an exempt organization, ¶4122), that amount is treated as taxable income in determining AMTI. (Code Sec. 55(b)(2))[14]

There are rules for the apportionment of items that are treated differently for AMT purposes among holders of interests in regulated investment companies (RICs), real estate investment trusts (REITs), and common trust funds. (Code Sec. 59(d))[15]

¶ 3203   Alternative minimum tax (AMT) exemption amount.

The exempt portion of an individual's alternative minimum taxable income (AMTI, ¶3202)—the AMT exemption amount, as adjusted for inflation—is:

... *Married individuals filing jointly and surviving spouses:* for 2013: $80,800, less 25% of AMTI exceeding $153,900 (zero exemption when AMTI is $477,100); for 2014: $82,100, less 25% of AMTI exceeding $156,500;

... *Unmarried individuals:* for 2013: $51,900, less 25% of AMTI exceeding $115,400 (zero exemption when AMTI is $323,000); for 2014: $52,800, less 25% of AMTI exceeding $117,300; (but for a child subject to the kiddie tax, see ¶3204) and

... *Married individuals filing separately:* for 2013: $40,400 (i.e., 50% of the joint return amount), less 25% of AMTI exceeding $76,950 (i.e., 50% of the phase-out amount for joint returns) (zero exemption when AMTI is $238,550); for 2014: $41,050, less 25% of AMTI exceeding $78,250. (Code Sec. 55(d)(1), Code Sec. 55(d)(3)) But AMTI is increased by the lesser of $40,400 ($41,050 for 2014) or 25% of the excess of AMTI (without this exemption reduction) over $238,550 (for 2014, over the amount at which the exemption is zero). (Code

7. ¶A-8103.3; ¶594
8. ¶A-8101; ¶554.01; TD ¶691,001
9. ¶A-8109; TD ¶691,008
10. ¶A-8108; ¶554.01; TD ¶691,007
11. ¶A-8102; TD ¶691,001

12. ¶A-8115 *et seq.*; ¶594; TD ¶691,014 *et seq.*
13. ¶A-8103.2; ¶1994.130; TD ¶691,003.2
14. ¶A-8107; ¶554.01; TD ¶691,006
15. ¶A-8111; ¶594; TD ¶691,010

Sec. 55(d))[16]

The inflation adjustment to the above amounts for a calendar year is made using the consumer price index (CPI) computation in Code Sec. 1(f)(3) by substituting calendar year 2011 for 1992. (Code Sec. 55(d)(4)(A); Code Sec. 55(d)(4)(B)(ii); Code Sec. 55(d)(4)(B)(iii))[17]

For estates and trusts, the AMT exemption amount for tax years beginning in 2013 is $23,100 ($23,500 for 2014) less 25% of AMTI exceeding $76,950 (for 2014, $78,250), for 2013, zero exemption when AMTI is $169,350. The exemption amount for trusts and estates is adjusted for inflation. (Code Sec. 55(d)(4)(B)(ii))[18]

For corporations, the AMT exemption amount is $40,000, less 25% of AMTI exceeding $150,000 (zero exemption when AMTI is $310,000).[19] For "small corporations," see ¶3205.

In no case can the AMT exemption amount be less than zero. (Code Sec. 55(d))[20]

¶ 3204   AMT exemption amount of a child subject to the kiddie tax.

The AMT exemption amount for a child subject to the kiddie tax (¶3136) can't exceed the child's earned income (under Code Sec. 911(d)(2)) for the tax year plus $7,150 for 2013 ($7,250 for 2014). (Code Sec. 59(j)) But this exemption amount can't be more than the child's regular AMT exemption, i.e., the unmarried individual's $51,900 (before a phaseout) exemption amount for 2013 ($52,800 for 2014). (¶3203).[21]

¶ 3205   AMT exemption for "small corporations."

A corporation's tentative minimum tax (¶3201) is zero (making the corporation exempt from AMT) for a tax year if its average annual gross receipts (determined by applying Code Sec. 448(c)(2) and Code Sec. 448(c)(3), ¶2818) (Code Sec. 55(e)(1)(D)) for all three-tax-year periods beginning after '93 and ending before the tax year don't exceed $7,500,000. (Code Sec. 55(e)(1)(A)) Substitute $5,000,000 for $7,500,000 for the first three-tax-year period (or portion thereof) taken into account under the test. (Code Sec. 55(e)(1)(B))[22]

Notwithstanding the above tests, a corporation is exempt from AMT for its first tax year (Code Sec. 55(e)(1)(C)) unless it fails the gross receipts test because its gross receipts are aggregated with an existing corporation's (under Code Sec. 448(c)(2)) or it's treated as having a predecessor corporation (under Code Sec. 448(c)(3)(D)).[23]

A corporation that has been exempt from AMT and that ceases to meet the gross receipts test becomes subject to AMT prospectively from the first day of the first tax year for which the gross receipts test isn't met, except that the Code Sec. 56(g)(4)(A) ACE depreciation adjustment (¶3211) doesn't apply. (Code Sec. 55(e)(2)) However, prospective-only application doesn't apply to certain items carried over in Code Sec. 381 transactions (¶3564) or to other property with a basis carried over from a transferor. (Code Sec. 55(e)(3))[24]

For a limitation on the AMT credit for corporations exempt from AMT, see ¶2364.

¶ 3206   AMT adjustments and preferences.

Adjustments differ from preferences, in computing alternative minimum taxable income (AMTI, ¶3202). Adjustments involve *substituting* AMT treatment of an item for the regular tax treatment. Preferences involve *adding* the difference between the AMT treatment and the regular tax treatment. Some (but not all) adjustments can be negative amounts—i.e., they

16. ¶A-8162; ¶554.01; TD ¶691,302
17. ¶A-8162; ¶554.01; TD ¶691,302
18. ¶A-8164; ¶554.01; TD ¶691,304
19. ¶A-8161; ¶554.01; TD ¶691,301
20. ¶A-8161 *et seq.*; ¶554.01; TD ¶691,301 *et seq.*

21. ¶A-8163; ¶594; TD ¶691,303
22. ¶A-8141, ¶A-8142; ¶554; TD ¶691,201
23. ¶A-8141; ¶554; TD ¶691,201
24. ¶A-8143; ¶554; TD ¶691,201, TD ¶691,202

may result in AMTI that's less than taxable income. Preferences can't be negative amounts. [25]

A taxpayer can avoid preference/adjustment treatment for certain costs by electing amortization (use Form 4562), rather than a current deduction. (Code Sec. 59(e); Reg § 1.59-1)[26]

¶ 3207 Depreciation adjustment.

Except as provided below, the following rules apply to all taxpayers subject to the AMT, for depreciable property placed in service after '86 (and after July 31, '86 and before '87, for which the taxpayer elected to have the MACRS rules, ¶1907 *et seq.*, apply):

(1) For property placed in service before '99, AMT depreciation for Code Sec. 1250 property (¶2694) and property depreciated under the straight-line method for regular tax purposes is computed using the Alternative Depreciation System (ADS, ¶1930). For property subject to accelerated depreciation for regular tax purposes, AMT depreciation is computed using ADS recovery periods and the 150% declining balance method (switching to straight-line in the year that method yields a higher allowance).

(2) For property placed in service after '98, AMT depreciation is computed using the 150% declining balance method (switching to straight-line in the year that method yields a higher allowance), except straight-line is used for Code Sec. 1250 property and other property for which straight-line is used for regular tax purposes. (Code Sec. 56(a)(1)(A), Code Sec. 56(a)(1)(C)(ii)) The recovery period is the same as for regular tax purposes.[27]

The AMT adjustment (i.e., the amount to be added or subtracted in computing alternative minimum taxable income (¶3202)) generated by the above calculations is determined by subtracting the amount of AMT depreciation for all property covered by the above rule from the MACRS depreciation for that property.[28]

The above rules don't apply to: (a) certain property to which the MACRS rules don't apply; (b) natural gas gathering lines placed in service after Apr. 11, 2005 (Code Sec. 56(a)(1)(B), Code Sec. 56(a)(1)(C));[29] (c) qualified property under Code Sec. 168(m) (qualified reuse and recycling property, ¶1940) or Code Sec. 168(n) (qualified disaster assistance property, ¶1940) (Code Sec. 168(m)(2)(D), Code Sec. 168(n)(2)(D));[30] (d) for bonus first-year depreciation—qualified property under Code Sec. 168(k) (¶1940), under Code Sec. 1400L(b) (qualified New York Liberty Zone property, ¶1940), under Code Sec. 1400N(d) (GO Zone property, ¶1940), or under Code Sec. 168(l) (qualified cellulosic biomass ethanol plant property, ¶1933); (Code Sec. 168(k)(2)(G), Code Sec. 1400L(b)(2)(E), Code Sec. 1400N(d)(4), Code Sec. 168(l)(6));[31] and (e) qualified Indian reservation property placed in service after '93. (Code Sec. 168(j)(4))[32]

¶ 3208 Other AMT preferences and adjustments applicable to all taxpayers.

(1) Tax-exempt interest on certain private activity bonds (not certain housing bonds or bonds issued in 2009 or 2010), less related expenses that aren't deductible for regular tax purposes, is a preference item. (Code Sec. 57(a)(5))[33]

(2) Except for independent oil and gas producers and royalty owners, the excess of percentage depletion (¶1978) over the property's adjusted basis (disregarding the current year's depletion) at the end of the year is a preference item. (Code Sec. 57(a)(1))[34]

(3) Excess intangible drilling costs (IDCs) are a preference. This is the excess of the allowable Code Sec. 263(c) IDC deduction for the tax year for oil, gas, and geothermal wells (¶1628),

25. ¶A-8191; ¶564, ¶574; TD ¶695,501
26. ¶A-8194 *et seq.*; ¶594; TD ¶695,503
27. ¶A-8220; ¶564.01; TD ¶696,514
28. ¶A-8220; ¶564.01; TD ¶696,513
29. ¶A-8221 *et seq.*; ¶564.01; TD ¶695,513 *et seq.*
30. ¶A-8221 *et seq.*; ¶1684.029, ¶1400L4.07, ¶1684.08;

TD ¶696,514
31. ¶A-8221 *et seq.*; ¶1400L4.07, ¶1684.08; TD ¶696,514
32. ¶L-8806; ¶1684.01
33. ¶A-8201, ¶574; TD ¶696,501, TD ¶696,501.1
34. ¶A-8233; ¶574; TD ¶696,527

over the amount that would have been allowable had the costs been capitalized and amortized ratably over 120 months. For integrated oil companies, the preference equals this excess, reduced by 65% of the net income received from all oil, gas, and geothermal properties. For other taxpayers, the preference applies only to the extent that, had it applied fully, it would have increased alternative minimum taxable income (AMTI, ¶3202) by more than 40% of the AMTI for the tax year (without the IDC preference or the alternative tax NOL deduction, ¶3212). Compute the preference separately for oil and gas properties, and for geothermal properties. (Code Sec. 57(a)(2), Code Sec. 57(b), Code Sec. 59(e)(6))[35]

(4) The deduction for amortization of pollution control facilities (under Code Sec. 169, ¶1968) (adjustment) is computed for AMT purposes without the Code Sec. 291(a)(4) 20% cutback that applies for regular tax purposes. For facilities placed in service after '86 and before '99, the AMT deduction is the amount allowable under the Alternative Depreciation System (ADS, ¶1930). For facilities placed in service after '98, the AMT deduction is determined under Code Sec. 168 using straight-line depreciation. (Code Sec. 56(a)(5))[36]

(5) Mine exploration and development costs are adjusted. The AMT deduction is the amount that results from capitalizing the costs allowed under Code Sec. 616(a) or Code Sec. 617(a) for the tax year without the Code Sec. 291(b)(1) 30% cutback (¶1626, ¶1627), and amortizing them ratably over 10 years. (Code Sec. 56(a)(2)(A), Code Sec. 59(e)(6))[37]

(6) For long-term contracts (except home construction contracts) (adjustment), AMTI is computed using the percentage-of-completion method of accounting (¶2852). For small construction contracts (under Code Sec. 460(e)(1), ¶2850), use the Code Sec. 460(b)(3) simplified cost allocation method (¶2855) to find the percentage of contract completed. (Code Sec. 56(a)(3); Reg § 1.460-4(f))[38]

(7) The alcohol fuel credit amount that's included in gross income (¶1206) isn't included in AMTI (adjustment). (Code Sec. 56(a)(7))[39]

¶ 3209   AMT preferences and adjustments for noncorporate taxpayers only.

(1) *Itemized deductions adjustment.* Itemized deductions for AMT purposes are computed the same as for regular tax purposes, *except:*

(a) Medical expenses are deductible only to the extent they exceed 10% of the taxpayer's adjusted gross income (AGI), even for taxpayers aged 65 and over and their spouses (for whom a 7.5%-of-AGI floor otherwise applies for 2013–2016 for regular tax purposes), ¶2141. (Code Sec. 56(b)(1)(B))[40]

(b) Property, income, and state and local general sales taxes generally aren't deductible if not allowed in computing AGI (¶1757). (Code Sec. 56(b)(1)(A)(ii))[41]

(c) Qualified housing interest (rather than qualified residence interest [QRI]) is deductible. (Code Sec. 56(b)(1)(C), Code Sec. 56(e)) Thus, home equity indebtedness isn't allowed for AMT purposes unless it's used to buy, build, or substantially improve the taxpayer's principal residence or one other qualified residence.[42]

(d) Net investment income (the limit on deduction of investment interest) is generally computed the same as for regular tax (¶1729), but excluding qualified housing interest (not QRI) and taking into account AMT adjustments and preferences. Tax-exempt bond interest that's an AMT preference (¶3208) is included. (Code Sec. 56(b)(1)(C))[43]

(e) Miscellaneous itemized deductions (¶3110) aren't allowed. (Code Sec. 56(b)(1)(A)(i))[44]

35. ¶A-8238 *et seq.*; ¶574; TD ¶696,532 *et seq.*
36. ¶A-8237; ¶564.01; TD ¶696,531
37. ¶A-8235; ¶564.01; TD ¶696,529
38. ¶A-8202 *et seq.*; ¶564.01; TD ¶696,502 *et seq.*
39. ¶A-8247; ¶564.01; TD ¶696,540

40. ¶A-8307; ¶564.02; TD ¶697,007
41. ¶A-8308; ¶564.02; TD ¶697,008
42. ¶A-8310 *et seq.*; ¶564.02; TD ¶697,010 *et seq.*
43. ¶A-8313; ¶564.02; TD ¶697,013
44. ¶A-8314; ¶564.02; TD ¶697,014

(f) The Code Sec. 68 3%/80% reduction in itemized deductions (¶3114) doesn't apply to the computation of the AMT. (Code Sec. 56(b)(1)(F))[45]

(2) *Standard deduction and personal exemptions adjustments.* The standard deduction (¶3112) and the deduction for personal exemptions (including those of trusts and estates) (¶3115) *aren't* allowed. (Code Sec. 56(b)(1)(E))[46]

(3) *State, etc., tax recoveries adjustment.* If an itemized deduction for state, etc., taxes paid is permitted for regular tax purposes but denied for AMT purposes ((1)(b), above), and any portion of that tax is refunded, the refund isn't included in AMTI. (Code Sec. 56(b)(1)(D))[47]

(4) *Research and experimental (R&E) expenditures adjustment.* The deduction allowed is the amount that results from capitalizing Code Sec. 174(a) R&E expenditures (¶1602) and amortizing them on a straight-line basis over 10 years. (Code Sec. 56(b)(2)(A)(ii), Code Sec. 59(e)(6)) This doesn't apply to expenses incurred in an activity in which the taxpayer materially participates under Code Sec. 469(h) (¶1826). (Code Sec. 56(b)(2)(D))[48]

(5) *Incentive stock option (ISO) adjustment.* The Code Sec. 83 restricted property rules (¶1217) (not the favorable Code Sec. 421 rules that apply for regular tax purposes, ¶1221) apply in determining AMTI, unless the stock is acquired and disposed of in the same tax year. (Code Sec. 56(b)(3))[49] The amount included in AMTI (but not regular income) equals the excess of the stock's fair market value (FMV) on the exercise date over the exercise (strike) price. This applies to vested stock, and to nonvested stock for which the taxpayer makes a Code Sec. 83(b) election (¶1218).[50] But certain underpayments of tax (and interest or penalty) attributable to pre-2008 ISO adjustments are abated. (Code Sec. 53(f)(1))[1]

(6) *Qualified small business stock (QSBS) exclusion preference.* With respect to gain on the disposition of QSBS that is partly excluded from gross income (¶2648 *et seq.*), 7% is treated as an AMT preference. (Code Sec. 57(a)(7)) But for QSBS to which the 100% exclusion applies, the excluded portion of the gain isn't treated as an AMT preference item. (Code Sec. 1202(a)(4)(C))[2]

¶ 3210 Preferences and adjustments applicable to all noncorporate taxpayers and to certain corporations.

(1) *Farm losses.* No loss is permitted from any "tax shelter farm activity" of a noncorporate taxpayer or personal service corporation, except to the extent the taxpayer is insolvent at the end of the tax year. A tax shelter farm activity is (a) a farming syndicate (under Code Sec. 464(c), ¶4511), or (b) any other "passive activity" (¶1822) consisting of farming unless the taxpayer materially participates in it. (Code Sec. 58(a), Code Sec. 58(c)(1))[3]

(2) *Passive losses.* The rules limiting the regular tax deduction of losses from passive activities (¶1810 *et seq.*) apply for AMT purposes *except that:*

. . . AMT preferences and adjustments are taken into account;

. . . qualified housing interest (¶3209) (rather than qualified residence interest) is omitted from the passive loss calculation (Code Sec. 58(b)); and

. . . the amount of losses disallowed under the regular tax limitation is reduced by the amount, if any, by which the taxpayer is insolvent at year end. (Code Sec. 58(c)(1))[4]

(3) *Circulation expenditures.* Under an adjustment only for individuals and personal holding companies, the AMT circulation expenditures deduction is the amount that results from

---

45. ¶A-8306; ¶564.02; TD ¶697,006
46. ¶A-8305, ¶A-8315; ¶564.02; TD ¶697,005, TD ¶697,015
47. ¶A-8309; ¶564.02; TD ¶697,009
48. ¶A-8316; ¶564.02; TD ¶697,016
49. ¶A-8302, ¶A-8303; ¶564.02; TD ¶697,002

50. ¶A-8302, ¶H-2508.2; TD ¶697,002, TD ¶697,003
1. ¶A-8302; ¶64,044; TD ¶842,038
2. ¶A-8304 *et seq.*; ¶574; TD ¶697,004, TD ¶697,004.1
3. ¶A-8242; ¶584; TD ¶699,001
4. ¶A-8244; ¶584; TD ¶699,003

capitalizing the costs and amortizing them over three years (¶1619). (Code Sec. 56(b)(2))[5]

¶ 3211 Earnings and profits (E&P) adjustments applicable only to corporations.

A corporations's alternative minimum taxable income (AMTI, ¶3202) is *increased* by 75% of the excess of its adjusted current earnings (ACE, defined below) over its pre-adjustment AMTI (i.e., AMTI before this adjustment or the alternative tax net operating loss deduction [ATNOLD, ¶3212]). (Code Sec. 56(c)(1), Code Sec. 56(g)(1)) If pre-adjustment AMTI exceeds the ACE amount, AMTI is *reduced* by 75% of the difference, but this reduction is limited to the total amount of AMTI increases under this rule in earlier years. (Code Sec. 56(g)(2)) The ACE adjustment doesn't apply to S corporations, regulated investment companies, real estate investment trusts, or real estate mortgage investment conduits. (Code Sec. 56(g)(6))[6]

ACE equals pre-adjustment AMTI plus those items (and related deductions) that, although included in E&P as computed for Subchapter C purposes, never enter into the calculation of regular income or AMTI. But interest on certain tax-exempt housing bonds or bonds issued in 2009 or 2010, certain cancellation of debt income (¶1386), and the "inside buildup" on life insurance contracts (¶1721), aren't included. No deduction is allowed for items that won't ever be deductible for E&P purposes. But an adjusted dividends received deduction (¶3306) and the Code Sec. 199 production activities deduction (¶1614) are allowed. There are additional adjustments, such as: requiring a special depreciation method for property placed in service before '94, including "excess" percentage depletion deductions (¶3208) taken for mines placed in service before '90, disallowing the installment method, and certain E&P adjustments. Also, in computing ACE, the adjusted basis of property to which an ACE adjustment applies generally takes that adjustment into account. (Code Sec. 56(g)(3), Code Sec. 56(g)(4), Code Sec. 56(g)(5); Reg § 1.56(g)-1)[7]

Special adjustments apply for Blue Cross, Blue Shield and similar organizations (Code Sec. 56(c)(3))[8] and for merchant marine capital construction funds. (Code Sec. 56(c)(2))[9]

¶ 3212 Alternative tax net operating loss deduction.

For AMT purposes, an alternative tax net operating loss deduction (ATNOLD or ATNOL deduction) is allowed instead of the regular tax net operating loss (NOL) deduction (RNOLD, see ¶1839 *et seq.*). (Code Sec. 56(a)(4))[10]

In general, the ATNOLD is the same as the RNOLD *except that:*

(1) the amount of the ATNOLD is limited to 90% of alternative minimum taxable income (AMTI, ¶3202) determined without regard to the ATNOLD and the Code Sec. 199 production activities deduction (¶1614). But the 90%-of-AMTI limitation doesn't apply to carrybacks and carryovers of amounts attributable to: 2008 or 2009 NOLs for which an extended carryback period was elected under Code Sec. 172(b)(1)(H) (¶1841), pre-2010 qualified disaster losses, or certain other disaster losses such as qualified GO Zone losses (¶1841) (Code Sec. 56(d)(1)(A), Code Sec. 56(d)(3), Code Sec. 1400N(k)(1)(B)), which can offset up to 100% of AMTI;[11] and

(2) the ATNOL is determined with AMT adjustments and reduced by AMT preferences (but only to the extent the preference increased the NOL for the year). (Code Sec. 56(d)(2))[12]

An election to forgo the regular NOL carryback period (¶1842) also applies for ATNOLD purposes. (The election must be made for regular tax purposes to get it for AMT purposes.)[13]

5. ¶A-8245; ¶564.02; TD ¶699,004
6. ¶A-8401 *et seq.*; ¶564.03; TD ¶698,001 *et seq.*
7. ¶A-8404 *et seq.*; ¶564.03; TD ¶698,004 *et seq.*
8. ¶A-8197; ¶564.03
9. ¶A-8198; ¶564.03

10. ¶A-8210 *et seq.*; ¶564.01; TD ¶696,000 *et seq.*
11. ¶A-8212, ¶A-8213; ¶564.01; TD ¶696,508, TD ¶696,509
12. ¶A-8211; ¶564.01; TD ¶696,503
13. ¶A-8216; ¶564.01; TD ¶696,006

The difference between the regular tax basis and AMT basis (¶3213) of stock acquired under an incentive stock option (ISO) isn't an adjustment and doesn't result in an ATNOL. [14]

¶ 3213 Different AMT adjusted basis for some property.

For AMT purposes, the adjusted bases of the following types of property are computed by taking into consideration the AMT preference or adjustment listed below with the property:

(1) Depreciable property subject to the Code Sec. 56(a)(1) depreciation adjustment (¶3207).

(2) Property subject to the Code Sec. 56(b)(2) adjustment for circulation or research and experimental expenditures (¶3209, ¶3210) paid or incurred after '86.

(3) Property subject to the Code Sec. 56(a)(2) adjustment for mine exploration or development expenditures (¶3208) paid or incurred after '86.

(4) Pollution control facilities subject to the Code Sec. 56(a)(5) adjustment (¶3208), if placed in service after '86. (Code Sec. 56(a)(6))

(5) Stock acquired under an incentive stock option (ISO) (¶3209). Generally, the basis of the stock is determined under the Code Sec. 83 rules rather than the Code Sec. 421 rules. (Code Sec. 56(b)(3)) Thus, the taxpayer gets a cost basis in the ISO stock for regular tax purposes, and a fair market value basis in the stock for AMT purposes (¶1221).[15]

¶ 3214 AMT foreign tax credit (AMTFTC).

The AMTFTC is available to both corporate and noncorporate taxpayers. (Code Sec. 55(b)(1)(A)(i), Code Sec. 55(b)(1)(B)(ii))[16]

The AMTFTC is computed the same as the regular foreign tax credit (¶2367), except that in applying the Code Sec. 904 limitation on the amount of the credit: (1) alternative minimum taxable income (AMTI, ¶3202) is substituted for taxable income (but see below); (2) the "pre-credit tentative minimum tax" is substituted for "the tax against which the foreign tax credit is taken"; (3) items included in AMTI by reason of the ACE adjustment (¶3211) are sourced on an item-by-item basis; and (4) the AMT rate (¶3201) is used in determining "high-taxed" income. (Code Sec. 59(a)(1), Code Sec. 59(a)(2); Reg § 1.904-4(k))[17]

If a taxpayer so elects for the first tax year for which he claims an AMTFTC (Code Sec. 59(a)(3)(B)(i)), the AMTFTC limitation is figured in a simplified way, based on the proportion that regular taxable income from sources outside the U.S. (but not in excess of the taxpayer's entire AMTI) bears to the entire AMTI for the tax year. (Code Sec. 59(a)(3)(A)) Letting taxpayers use foreign source regular taxable income to compute the limitation eliminates the need to reallocate and reapportion every deduction.[18] Once made, the election applies to all tax years and can be revoked only with IRS consent. (Code Sec. 59(a)(3)(B)(ii))[19]

14. ¶A-8211; TD ¶696,507
15. ¶A-8193; ¶564.01 *et seq.*; TD ¶695,502
16. ¶A-8181;¶594; TD ¶691,401

17. ¶A-8181; ¶594; TD ¶691,401
18. ¶A-8183; ¶594; TD ¶691,403
19. ¶A-8183; ¶594; TD ¶691,403

Chapter 15 Corporations—Accumulated Earnings Tax— Personal Holding Companies—Consolidated Returns—Estimated Tax—S Corporations

¶ 3300 Taxation of Corporations.

A corporation is an entity distinct from its shareholders. How a corporation is taxed depends on whether it is a C corporation or an S corporation.

¶ 3301 What is a corporation for tax purposes—Form 8832?

Under regs that set forth a "check-the-box" system of classifying entities for federal tax purposes, the following business entities are mandatorily classified as corporations:

. . . A business entity organized under a federal or state statute, or under a statute of a federally recognized Indian tribe, if the statute describes or refers to the entity as incorporated or as a corporation, body corporate, or body politic.

. . . An association as determined under Reg § 301.7701-3.

. . . A business entity organized under a state statute, if the statute describes or refers to the entity as a joint-stock company or joint-stock association.

. . . An insurance company.

. . . A state-chartered business entity conducting banking activities, if any of its deposits are insured under the Federal Deposit Insurance Act.

. . . A business entity wholly owned by a state or any of its political subdivisions.

. . . A business entity that's taxable as a corporation under a provision of the Code other than Code Sec. 7701(a)(3), such as a publicly traded partnership (see ¶3302).

. . . Certain foreign business entities ("per se" corporations) (Reg § 301.7701-2(b)(8)) and business entities formed under the laws of U.S. territories and possessions. (Reg § 301.7701-2(b))[1]

Under the "check-the-box" regs, if a joint undertaking is an entity separate from its owners for federal tax purposes, the entity is a business entity and not a trust, and the business entity is an "eligible entity" (i.e., not mandatorily classified as a corporation), it may elect its classification for federal tax purposes. An eligible entity with at least two members may elect to be classified as a partnership or as an association (i.e., a corporation). An eligible entity with a single owner may elect to be classified as an association or to be disregarded as an entity separate from its owner.[2] An eligible entity that wishes to elect a classification other than its default classification, or any eligible entity that wishes to change its classification, does so by filing Form 8832 with the IRS Center designated on the form.[3]

An entity organized in more than one jurisdiction is treated as a corporation for federal tax purposes if it is so treated in any of those jurisdictions. (Reg § 301.7701-2(b)(9))[4]

¶ 3302 Publicly traded partnerships (PTPs) as corporations.

A PTP is taxable as a corporation, see ¶3303. (Code Sec. 7704(a))[5] A partnership is a PTP if interests in the partnership either: (1) are traded on an established securities market (including a national exchange, a regional or local exchange, certain foreign exchanges, and an interdealer quotation system), or (2) are readily tradable on a secondary market or its substantial equivalent. (Code Sec. 7704(b); Reg § 1.7704-1)[6]

---

1. ¶D-1101 et seq.; ¶77,014.14; TD ¶600,202
2. ¶D-1151; ¶77,014.15; TD ¶580,501
3. ¶D-1158; ¶77,014.15; TD ¶580,511

4. ¶D-1101.1; ¶77,014.13; TD ¶600,202
5. ¶D-1321; ¶77,044; TD ¶600,300
6. ¶D-1343; ¶77,044.03; TD ¶600,302

References beginning with a single letter are to paragraphs in RIA's Federal Tax Coordinator 2d and RIA's Analysis of Federal Taxes: Income. Those beginning with numbers are to paragraphs in RIA's United States Tax Reporter. Those beginning with TD are to paragraphs in RIA's Tax Desk.

However, a PTP won't be treated as a corporation if at least 90% of its gross income for the tax year is specified passive-type income, and certain other requirements are met. (Code Sec. 7704(c))[7]

¶ 3303 How C Corporations Are Taxed.

C corporations generally are subject to tax at graduated rates on their taxable income. The benefits of the graduated rates phase out after taxable income reaches a specified amount.

For the rates at which a C corporation's income is taxed, and for the amount at which the graduated rates are phased out, see ¶1113. For limits on the use of graduated rates and other tax benefits by members of a controlled group of corporations, see ¶3337.

C corporations that are qualified personal service corporations (PSCs, see ¶3329) are taxed at a flat 35% rate. (Code Sec. 11(b)(2))[8]

Some C corporations are also subject to an alternative minimum tax (¶3200 *et seq.*).

For penalty taxes imposed on corporations with unreasonable earnings accumulations, see ¶3316 *et seq.*

For personal holding company tax, see ¶3320 *et seq.*

For taxation of corporations making certain outbound transfers, see ¶3588.

¶ 3304 C corporation's taxable income.

A C corporation's taxable income equals its gross income less the deductions allowed by the Code. (Code Sec. 63)[9] Generally, a C corporation's gross income doesn't include contributions to its capital. (Code Sec. 118) IRS has provided a number of safe harbors for treating certain types of grants as capital contributions. For a C corporation's gain or loss from distributing property to its shareholders, see ¶3538.

¶ 3305 Computing a C corporation's tax.

A C corporation's tax is computed by applying the Code Sec. 11 rates in effect for its tax year (¶1113) to its taxable income (¶3304) for that year, and then subtracting any available tax credits (¶2300 *et seq.*).[10]

Special rules apply for computing the tax for years that straddle a rate change (Code Sec. 15(a))[11] and for short tax years, see ¶2805.

¶ 3306 Dividends-Received Deduction.

Corporate shareholders are allowed a deduction for dividends received.

¶ 3307 Deduction for dividends from domestic corporations—70%, 80%, and 100% deductions.

Subject to specific disallowances, reductions, and limitations (¶3311 *et seq.*), a C corporation may deduct 70% of the dividends received or accrued from domestic corporations. (Code Sec. 243(a)(1))[12] The deduction is 80% for dividends received or accrued from a corporation at least 20% of the stock of which (not counting preferred stock described in Code Sec. 1504(a)(4)) is owned, by vote and value, by the corporate shareholder. (Code Sec. 243(c))[13]

Members of an affiliated group (as specially defined) that file separate returns may deduct 100% of the dividends received from other group members if certain requirements are met.

7. ¶D-1363 *et seq.*; ¶77,044; TD ¶600,303
8. ¶D-1006; ¶s 114.01, 114.02; TD ¶600,901
9. ¶D-1001; ¶634; TD ¶600,501
10. ¶D-1001 *et seq.*; ¶114.01; TD ¶600,501

11. ¶D-1009 *et seq.*; ¶154.01; TD ¶600,506
12. ¶D-2201; ¶2434.01; TD ¶600,509
13. ¶D-2205 *et seq.*; ¶2434.01; TD ¶600,509

(Code Sec. 243(a)(3), Code Sec. 243(b))[14]

For a small business investment company's dividends-received deduction, see ¶4205.

The deduction applies to taxable dividends (¶1285 *et seq.*) (Code Sec. 243(a)), "boot" dividends (¶3556), consent dividends (¶3334)[15] and the "dividend equivalent" portion of high yield original issue discount (OID) obligations (¶1753). (Code Sec. 163(e)(5)(B))[16] For dividends that aren't deductible, see ¶3315.

¶ 3308   Dividends from regulated investment companies (RICs).

A corporate shareholder that receives a properly designated dividend (other than capital gain or exempt-interest dividends) from a RIC is eligible for the dividends-received deduction (DRD) to the extent the RIC would have been allowed to deduct the amount as a DRD if it were taxed as a regular corporation. (Code Sec. 243(d)(2), Code Sec. 854(b)(4))[17]

¶ 3309   Dividends on certain public utility preferred stock.

Dividends received from a public utility are eligible for the dividends-received deduction, but the deduction is reduced if the utility was entitled to a dividends-*paid* deduction (¶3330) for those dividends. (Code Sec. 244(a))[18]

¶ 3310   Dividends from foreign corporations and possession corporations.

A U.S. corporation that owns at least 10% (by vote and value) of the stock of a foreign corporation (other than a foreign passive investment company) may deduct the applicable percentage (70% or 80%, see ¶3307) of the U.S.-source portion of the dividends it receives from that foreign corporation. (Code Sec. 245(a)(1), Code Sec. 245(a)(2))[19]

The U.S.-source portion of any dividend is the amount that bears the same ratio to the dividend that the payor's post-'86 undistributed U.S. earnings bears to its total post-'86 undistributed earnings. (Code Sec. 245(a)(3), Code Sec. 245(a)(4), Code Sec. 245(a)(5))[20] Special rules apply for dividends paid out of pre-'87 earnings.[21]

A 100% dividends-received deduction is allowed (instead of the above percentages) if all the foreign corporation's gross income is effectively connected with its U.S. business in the year the dividends are earned, and all its outstanding stock is owned by the U.S. payee both in that year and in the payee's tax year in which the dividends are received. (Code Sec. 245(b))[22]

For domestic international sales corporation (DISC) dividends, see ¶3315.

¶ 3311   Taxable income limit on dividends-received deduction (DRD).

In the case of dividends that are subject to the 70% or 80% (but not the 100%) rule (¶3307), the DRD may not exceed 70% or 80% of the corporation's taxable income. Net operating loss (NOL) deductions, capital loss carrybacks, and the DRD itself are not taken into account when computing taxable income for this limitation. (Code Sec. 246(b)(1)) A corporation is not subject to this limitation where it has an NOL for the tax year. (Code Sec. 246(b)(2))[23]

If a taxpayer receives both 80% and 70% dividends, this limitation is applied in two stages. First, the 80% deduction for dividends from 20%−owned corporations is restricted to 80% of taxable income. Second, for dividends qualifying for the 70% deduction, the limitation is 70% of the taxable income reduced by dividends from 20% or greater owned corporations. (Code

---

14. ¶D-2223 *et seq.*; ¶2434.01; TD ¶600,509
15. ¶D-2209 *et seq.*; ¶2434.01; TD ¶602,019
16. ¶D-2221; ¶1634.051; TD ¶600,512
17. ¶D-2216, ¶E-6163; ¶8524.02; TD ¶600,512
18. ¶D-2222; ¶2434.02; TD ¶600,512

19. ¶D-2244; ¶2434.03; TD ¶600,509
20. ¶s D-2244, D-2246; ¶2434.03
21. ¶D-2246; ¶2434.03
22. ¶D-2247; ¶2434.03; TD ¶600,509
23. ¶s D-2251, D-2252; ¶2434.04; TD ¶600,518

Sec. 246(b)(3))[24] For this purpose, taxable income is computed without regard to the deductions for capital loss carrybacks, NOLs, dividends received, and income attributable to domestic production activities (¶1616), and without any basis reduction for extraordinary dividends (¶2495). (Code Sec. 246(b)(1))[25]

¶ 3312 Holding period requirements.

No dividends-received deduction (DRD) is allowed for any dividend on any share of stock that's held by the taxpayer for 45 days or less during the 91-day period beginning on the date that is 45 days before the date on which the stock becomes ex-dividend (i.e., the latest purchase date for collecting a dividend) with respect to the dividend (90 days or less out of the relevant 181-day period for any preferred stock with respect to which the taxpayer gets dividends that are attributable to a period or periods aggregating in excess of 366 days). (Code Sec. 246(c)) In other words, a DRD is allowed only if the taxpayer's holding period for the dividend paying stock is satisfied over a period immediately before or immediately after the taxpayer becomes entitled to receive the dividend.[26]

In determining how long the shareholder has held the stock, the day of disposition but not the day of acquisition is taken into account. (Code Sec. 246(c)(3)(A))[27]

The shareholder's holding period for the stock is reduced for any period during which he:

(1) has an option to sell, is under a contractual obligation to sell, has made (and not closed) a short sale of, or is the grantor of an option to buy, substantially identical stock or securities (as defined under the "wash sale" rules, see ¶2461). (Code Sec. 246(c)(4)(A), Code Sec. 246(c)(4)(B); Reg § 1.246-3(c)(2))[28]

(2) has diminished the risk of loss by holding one or more other positions with respect to substantially similar or related property (i.e., the fair market values (FMVs) of the stock and the property primarily reflect a single firm or enterprise, and changes in the stock's FMV are reasonably expected to approximate (directly or indirectly) changes in the property's FMV), where changes in the FMVs of the stock and the positions are reasonably expected to vary inversely. (Code Sec. 246(c)(4)(C); Reg § 1.246-5)[29]

¶ 3313 No dividends-received deduction (DRD) where shareholder is obligated to make certain payments.

A corporate shareholder gets no DRD for any dividends received on any stock acquired after July 18, '84 to the extent the shareholder is under an obligation (by a short sale or otherwise) to make related payments with respect to positions in substantially similar or related property (as defined at ¶3312). (Code Sec. 246(c)(1)(B))[30]

¶ 3314 Deduction reduced for dividends on debt-financed portfolio stock.

The 70% and 80% dividends-received deduction (but not the 100% deduction) (¶3307) is reduced for dividends on debt-financed portfolio stock with a holding period that began after July 18, '84. As reduced, the applicable percentage for deducting these dividends equals: (1) 70% (80% for dividends from 20%-owned corporations), multiplied by (2) 100% minus the "average indebtedness percentage." (Code Sec. 246A(a), Code Sec. 246A(b)) The reduction for any dividend may not exceed the interest deduction (including short sale expense) allocable to that dividend. (Code Sec. 246A(e))[31]

---

24. ¶D-2253; ¶2434.04; TD ¶600,518
25. ¶D-2251; ¶2434.04; TD ¶600,518
26. ¶D-2263; ¶2434.04; TD ¶600,516
27. ¶D-2263; ¶2434.04

28. ¶s D-2264, D-2266; ¶2434.04; TD ¶600,517
29. ¶D-2268 *et seq.*; ¶2434.04; TD ¶600,517
30. ¶D-2261; ¶2434.04; TD ¶600,515
31. ¶D-2255; ¶2434.05; TD ¶600,520

¶ 3315   Dividends from certain corporations aren't deductible.

No dividends-received deduction is allowed for dividends from:

. . . a corporation that's exempt from tax as a charitable organization under Code Sec. 501 or as a farmer's cooperative under Code Sec. 521. (Code Sec. 246(a)(1))[32]

. . . a domestic international sales corporation (DISC; ¶4621) or former DISC to the extent paid out of accumulated DISC income or previously taxed income, or amounts considered distributed in the year of qualification as a DISC. (Code Sec. 246(d))[33]

. . . a real estate investment trust (REIT). (Code Sec. 243(d)(3))[34]

. . . a mutual savings bank, savings and loan associations and other banks allowed a deduction under Code Sec. 591. (Code Sec. 243(d)(1))[35] However, certain dividends from federal home loan banks qualify to the extent set out in a specific formula. (Code Sec. 246(a)(2))[36]

¶ 3316   Accumulated Earnings Tax. ▰▰▰▰▰▰▰▰▰

With limited exceptions (see below), every corporation that accumulates earnings and profits, rather than distributes them, in order to avoid the imposition of income tax on its shareholders (¶3317) is subject to an annual accumulated earnings (penalty) tax equal to 20% of its "accumulated taxable income" for the year (¶3318). The tax is in addition to the regular corporate tax.

The tax generally applies to all corporations, regardless of the number of shareholders and regardless of whether the corporation is widely held.[37] It also applies to foreign corporations on their U.S.-source income if *any* of their shareholders is subject to U.S. income tax on distributions. (Reg § 1.532-1(c))[38]

Personal holding companies (¶3320), tax-exempt corporations, passive foreign investment companies, and S corporations are specifically exempt from the accumulated earnings tax. (Code Sec. 532(b), Code Sec. 1363(a))

¶ 3317   "Reasonable needs" of the business.

For purposes of the accumulated earnings tax (¶3316), a corporation that accumulates earnings and profits (E&P) beyond the reasonable needs of its business is considered to have done so to avoid tax on its shareholders *unless* it proves otherwise by the preponderance of the evidence. (Code Sec. 533(a))[39]

An accumulation is in excess of the reasonable needs of a business if it exceeds the amount that a prudent business person would consider appropriate for the present purposes of the business and for its reasonably anticipated future needs. (Code Sec. 537; Reg § 1.537-1(a), Reg § 1.537-1(b)(1))[40] The reasonable needs of a corporation's business include the Code Sec. 303 death tax redemption needs of the business (Code Sec. 537(a)(2)[41] and the excess business holdings redemption needs of the business. (Code Sec. 537(a)(3))[42]

Corporations facing an accumulated earnings tax may use a formula to compute the amount reasonably needed for working capital to test their liability for the penalty. The Tax Court in *Bardahl Manufacturing Corp* held that necessary working capital should be determined by: (1) calculating a corporation's operating cycle percentage (the period of time, expressed as a percent of a year, needed to convert cash to inventory, inventory to sales and accounts receivable, and accounts receivable to cash), and then (2) multiplying that percentage by the corporation's total operating expenses for the year.[43]

32. ¶D-2213; ¶2434.04; TD ¶600,513
33. ¶D-2212; ¶2434.04; TD ¶600,513
34. ¶D-2215; ¶2434.01; TD ¶600,513
35. ¶D-2211; ¶2434.01; TD ¶600,513
36. ¶s D-2214, D-2219; ¶2434.04; TD ¶600,512
37. ¶D-2602; ¶5324; TD ¶601,002

38. ¶D-2607; ¶5324; TD ¶601,003
39. ¶D-2704; ¶s 5324.01, 5374; TD ¶601,014
40. ¶D-2779, D-2783, D-2792; ¶s 5314, 5374; TD ¶601,019
41. ¶D-2828;¶5374; TD ¶601,030
42. ¶D-2830; ¶5374; TD ¶601,030
43. ¶D-2848; ¶5374; TD ¶601,032

A corporation with a history of paying dividends isn't likely to be hit with the penalty.[44]

¶ 3318 Accumulated taxable income.

For purposes of computing the accumulated earnings tax (¶3316), a corporation's accumulated taxable income is its taxable income, adjusted as described below, *minus:* (1) the dividends-paid deduction (¶3330), and (2) the accumulated earnings credit (¶3319). (Code Sec. 535(a))[45]

The corporation's taxable income is *reduced* by:

. . . federal income and excess profits taxes accrued during the tax year (not the accumulated earnings tax or the personal holding company tax) (Code Sec. 535(b)(1));

. . . taxes of foreign countries and U.S. possessions accrued or deemed paid by a domestic corporation and included in the foreign tax credit (¶2367 *et seq.*) (Code Sec. 535(b)(1));[46]

. . . charitable contributions in excess of the deduction ceiling (¶2131) (Code Sec. 535(b)(2));[47]

. . . net capital gains (less attributable taxes). (Code Sec. 535(b)(6)(A)) A mere holding or investment company deducts net *short*-term capital gain (less attributable taxes) to the extent it doesn't exceed capital loss carryover to the year (Code Sec. 535(b)(8)(B)); other corporations must reduce their net capital gain deduction by net capital losses from any earlier year (Code Sec. 535(b)(7)(A), Code Sec. 535(b)(8)(B));[48] and

. . . net capital losses. (Code Sec. 535(b)(5)(A)) A mere holding or investment company gets no net capital loss deduction (Code Sec. 535(b)(8)(A)); any other corporation must reduce its net capital loss deduction by the lesser of: (1) its nonrecaptured capital gain deduction, or (2) its accumulated E&P as of the close of the preceding tax year. (Code Sec. 535(b)(5))[49]

Taxable income is *increased* by:

. . . special corporate deductions (e.g., for dividends received (¶3306 *et seq.*), but not for organizational expenditures) (Code Sec. 535(b)(3));

. . . net operating loss deduction (¶1839 *et seq.*) (Code Sec. 535(b)(4)); and

. . . capital loss carryback or carryover (¶2615). (Code Sec. 535(b)(7)(B))[50]

¶ 3319 Accumulated earnings credit.

For purposes of computing accumulated taxable income (¶3318), for corporations other than a mere holding or investment company, the accumulated earnings credit equals the *greater* of:

(1) $250,000 ($150,000 for a corporation whose principal function is the performance of health, legal, engineering, accounting, or certain other services) *plus* dividends paid during the first 2½ months of the tax year *minus* accumulated earnings and profits (E&P) at the end of the preceding tax year (Code Sec. 535(c)(2), Code Sec. 535(c)(4)); or

(2) an amount equal to that part of the E&P for the tax year that is retained for the reasonable needs of the business (i.e., the amount in excess of the dividends-paid deduction (¶3331, Code Sec. 535(c)(4))), *minus* the net capital gain deduction, if any, allowed in adjusting the corporation's taxable income (¶3318). (Code Sec. 535(c)(1))[1]

A mere holding or investment company's accumulated earnings credit is the amount, if any, by which $250,000 plus dividends paid in the first 2½ months of the tax year exceeds accumulated E&P at the close of the preceding year. (Code Sec. 535(c)(3), Code Sec. 535(c)(4))[2]

44. ¶D-2715; ¶5374; TD ¶601,016
45. ¶D-2901; ¶5354.01; TD ¶601,009
46. ¶D-2913; ¶5354.01; TD ¶601,009
47. ¶D-2906; ¶5354.01; TD ¶601,009
48. ¶D-2908; ¶5354.01; TD ¶601,009
49. ¶D-2911; ¶5354.01; TD ¶601,009
50. ¶D-2907; ¶5354.01; TD ¶601,009
1. ¶D-2915; ¶5354.01; TD ¶601,012
2. ¶D-2915; ¶5354.01; TD ¶601,013

🅡🅘🅐*observation:* Such companies get no credit for reasonable needs.

¶ 3320   Personal Holding Company (PHC) Tax. ▬▬▬▬▬▬

For any year in which a corporation is a PHC, it is liable for an additional 20% penalty tax on its undistributed PHC income (¶3321), reported on Form 1120, Schedule PH. (Reg § 1.6012-2(b))[3] With exceptions (¶3322), a corporation is a PHC for the tax year if the following "PHC tests" are met: (i) it is closely held (i.e., at any time during the last half of the year, more than 50% of the value of its outstanding stock is owned, directly or indirectly, by not more than five individuals, see ¶3323); and (ii) at least 60% of the adjusted gross income of which is "PHC income." [4]

The foreign tax credit isn't allowed against the PHC tax. (Reg § 1.545-2(a)(3))[5]

¶ 3321   Undistributed personal holding company (PHC) income subject to the PHC penalty tax.

A corporation's undistributed PHC income that is subject to the PHC penalty tax (¶3320) is its taxable income (Code Sec. 545(a)),[6] adjusted as described below.

. . . The following amounts are *subtracted* from taxable income:

. . . Federal income tax accrued during the year, and U.S. possession and foreign income taxes not deductible in computing taxable income. (Code Sec. 545(b)(1))[7]

. . . Excess charitable contributions, i.e., amounts over the *corporate* ceiling up to the amount allowed under the *individual* ceiling (¶2123 *et seq.*). (Code Sec. 545(b)(2))[8]

. . . Net capital gain (i.e., excess of net long-term capital gain over net short-term capital loss), minus income taxes attributable to that excess. (Code Sec. 545(b)(5))[9]

. . . The preceding tax year's net operating loss (NOL) carryforward. (Code Sec. 545(b)(4))[10]

. . . The dividends-paid deduction (¶3330 *et seq.*). (Code Sec. 545(a))[11]

. . . The following amounts are *added* to taxable income:

. . . Special corporate deductions. (¶3306 *et seq.*). (Code Sec. 545(b)(3))[12]

. . . NOL deduction. (Code Sec. 545(b)(4))[13]

. . . Expenses and depreciation exceeding income from property (unless income was highest obtainable). (Code Sec. 545(b)(6))[14]

¶ 3322   Corporations exempt from personal holding company (PHC) classification.

The following entities are excluded from the definition of PHCs subject to the PHC penalty tax (¶3320):

. . . S corporations (¶3350 *et seq.*); (Code Sec. 1363(a))

. . . tax-exempt corporations; (Code Sec. 542(c)(1))

. . . banks or domestic building and loan associations; (Code Sec. 542(c)(2))

. . . life insurance companies; (Code Sec. 542(c)(3))

. . . surety companies; (Code Sec. 542(c)(4))

. . . certain active lending or finance companies; (Code Sec. 542(c)(6), Code Sec. 542(d))

---

3. ¶D-3601; ¶5454.02; TD ¶609,805
4. ¶D-3203; ¶5424; TD ¶601,502
5. ¶D-3619; ¶9014
6. ¶D-3603; ¶5454; TD ¶601,516
7. ¶D-3606; ¶5454; TD ¶601,516
8. ¶D-3609; ¶5454; TD ¶601,516

9. ¶D-3610; ¶5454; TD ¶601,516
10. ¶D-3614; ¶5454; TD ¶601,516
11. ¶D-3800; ¶5454; TD ¶601,516
12. ¶D-3613; ¶5454; TD ¶601,516
13. ¶D-3614; ¶5454; TD ¶601,516
14. ¶D-3615; ¶5454; TD ¶601,516

... small business investment companies (¶2631), if no shareholders own, directly or indirectly, a 5%-or-more interest in a small business concern to which the investment company provides funds; (Code Sec. 542(c)(7))

... corporations subject to the jurisdiction of a court in a bankruptcy case or in a receivership, foreclosure or similar proceeding in a federal or state court, if the proceedings aren't primarily to avoid the PHC tax; (Code Sec. 542(c)(8)) and

... foreign corporations. (Code Sec. 542(c)(5))[15]

¶ 3323   Determining stock ownership.

For purposes of determining liability for the personal holding company (PHC) penalty tax (¶3320), an individual is the owner of any stock he owns directly or indirectly (Code Sec. 542(a)(2)), or constructively under these rules:

(1) Stock owned by or for a corporation, partnership, estate or trust is considered owned proportionately by its shareholders, partners or beneficiaries. (Code Sec. 544(a)(1))[16]

(2) Stock owned by or for an individual's family or partner is considered owned by the individual. An individual's family includes only his brothers and sisters (whether by the whole or half blood), spouse, ancestors and lineal descendants. (Code Sec. 544(a)(2))[17]

(3) If any person has an option to acquire stock, the stock subject to the option is considered owned by that person. An option to acquire the option, and each one of a series of these options, is considered an option to acquire the stock. (Code Sec. 544(a)(3))[18]

Stock that may be considered owned by an individual under either rule (2) or rule (3) is considered owned by him under rule (3). (Code Sec. 544(a)(6))[19]

Rules (2) and (3) apply only if the result is to make the corporation a PHC or to make income PHC income (¶3325). (Code Sec. 544(a)(4))[20]

Stock *constructively* owned by a person under rule (1) or rule (3) is considered *actually* owned by that person for purposes of again applying rule (1), or applying rule (2), to make *another* person the *constructive* owner of the same stock. (Code Sec. 544(a)(5))[21]

Only outstanding stock (i.e., not Treasury stock) is counted. (Reg § 1.542-3(b))[22] Outstanding securities convertible into stock are considered outstanding stock *but only if* converting them would make the corporation a PHC or the income PHC income (except where there are differing conversion dates). (Code Sec. 544(b))[23]

¶ 3324   Adjusted ordinary gross income used in personal holding company (PHC) tests.

For purposes of determining liability for the PHC penalty tax (¶3320), *adjusted ordinary gross income* is ordinary gross income (below) minus certain interest income, with these adjustments: for each of the separate categories of rents, mineral, oil and gas royalties, working interests in an oil or gas well and property produced by the taxpayer, gross income from the category is reduced (but not below zero) by certain expenses allocated to each category. (Code Sec. 543(b)(2))[24]

Ordinary gross income is gross income minus all gains from the sale or other disposition of capital assets and Code Sec. 1231(b) assets. (Code Sec. 543(b)(1))[25]

---

15. ¶D-3301; ¶5424.02; TD ¶601,503
16. ¶D-3406; ¶5444.01; TD ¶601,512
17. ¶D-3408; ¶5444.01; TD ¶601,512
18. ¶D-3410; ¶5444.01; TD ¶601,512
19. ¶D-3411; ¶5444.01 *et seq.*; TD ¶601,512
20. ¶s D-3408, D-3410; ¶5444.01; TD ¶601,512

21. ¶D-3411; ¶5444.01; TD ¶601,512
22. ¶D-3402; ¶5424.04; TD ¶601,510
23. ¶D-3412; ¶5444.01 *et seq.*; TD ¶601,513
24. ¶D-3506; ¶5424.03; TD ¶601,504
25. ¶D-3505; ¶5424.03; TD ¶601,504

¶ 3325   Personal holding company (PHC) income used in PHC tests.

For purposes of determining liability for the PHC penalty tax (¶3320), PHC income is the portion of adjusted ordinary gross income (¶3324) that consists of: dividends; interest; annuities; rents (¶3326); mineral, oil and gas royalties; copyright, patent, etc., royalties (but not certain "active business computer software royalties"); produced film rents; compensation for more-than-25% shareholder's use of corporate property (¶3327); amounts received under personal service contracts (¶3328); and amounts received from estates and trusts. (Code Sec. 543(a))[26]

¶ 3326   Rents.

The adjusted income from rents is personal holding company (PHC) income (¶3325) for purposes of determining liability for the PHC penalty tax (¶3320), unless: (1) it is 50% or more of adjusted ordinary gross income (¶3324); *and* (2) certain other *undistributed* PHC income, as specially defined, is 10% or less of ordinary gross income (¶3324). This "specially defined" PHC income *includes* copyright royalties and adjusted income from mineral, oil and gas royalties but *excludes* rents and compensation for a 25%-or-more shareholder's use of corporate property. The 10% test is met if the total of (a) dividends paid during the tax year, plus (b) late-paid dividends (¶3332), plus (c) consent dividends (¶3334), equals or exceeds the amount, if any, by which "PHC income" exceeds 10% of ordinary gross income. (Code Sec. 543(a)(2))[27]

Rents are compensation (however designated) for the use of, or the right to use, property (Code Sec. 543(a)(1)(A), Code Sec. 543(b)(3)), *except* for: compensation for a shareholder's use of corporate property that is PHC income (¶3327), copyright royalties, produced film rents, or compensation for the right to use any tangible personal property manufactured or produced by the corporation, if during the tax year it's engaged in substantial manufacturing or production of property of the same type. (Code Sec. 543(b)(3))[28]

¶ 3327   Compensation for use of corporate property by a 25%-or-more shareholder.

Amounts received by the corporation from a shareholder as compensation for the use of, or right to use, tangible property of the corporation are included in the corporation's personal holding company (PHC) income (¶3325) for purposes of determining liability for the PHC penalty tax (¶3320), if, during the tax year, 25% or more in value of the corporation's outstanding stock is owned by or for an individual entitled to use that property (directly or through a sublease). (Code Sec. 543(a)(6)(A)) But this doesn't apply if the corporation's PHC income (as specially defined, see ¶3326) doesn't exceed 10% of its ordinary gross income (¶3324).

¶ 3328   Receipts under personal service contract.

For purposes of determining liability for the personal holding company (PHC) penalty tax (¶3320), PHC income (¶3325) includes amounts received under a contract pursuant to which the corporation furnishes personal services, and amounts received from the sale or other disposition of the contract, if:

(1) some person other than the corporation has the right to designate (by name or description) the individual who performs the services, or if the individual who is to perform the services is so designated in the contract, *and*

(2) at some time during the tax year, 25% or more in value of the corporation's outstanding stock is owned, directly or indirectly, by or for that individual. (Code Sec. 543(a)(7);

---

26. ¶D-3507; ¶5434; TD ¶601,505   28. ¶D-3524; ¶s 5434.06, 5434.07, 5434.09; TD ¶601,506
27. ¶D-3522; ¶5434.07; TD ¶601,506

Reg § 1.543-1(b)(8)(i))[29]

¶ 3329   Qualified Personal Service Corporations (PSCs). ▬▬▬▬▬

Qualified PSCs are subject to special rules, e.g., they are subject to a flat 35% tax rate and are required to use the cash method for accounting purposes. A corporation is a qualified PSC if it meets two tests:

(1) Substantially all of its activities involve the performance of services in the fields of health, law, engineering, architecture, accounting, actuarial science, performing arts, or consulting. "Substantially all" means that 95% or more of the time spent by the corporation's employees, serving in their capacity as employees, is devoted to performing such services. Brokerage services, including commission-based financial services, are excepted from consulting services.

(2) Substantially all (95% or more) of the stock by value (not including treasury shares) is held directly or indirectly by: employees performing the services or retired employees who had performed such services; or the estates of such employees, or any other person who, during the two-year period starting with the date that such an employee died, acquired that individual's stock because his death. (Code Sec. 448(d)(2); Reg § 1.448-1T(e)(4))[30]

For the tax rate applicable to qualified PSCs, see ¶3303. For the rules on allowable accounting methods, see ¶2818. For the tax year of PSCs, see ¶2811.

¶ 3330   Dividend Distributions to Cut Special Taxes on Corporations. ▬▬▬▬

A deduction for dividends paid is allowed in computing the accumulated earnings penalty tax (¶3316) and personal holding company (PHC) penalty tax (¶3320), and in determining a corporation's qualification as a regulated investment company (¶4201) or real estate investment trust (¶4202). A deduction is also allowed in some cases for undistributed amounts shareholders consent to report as dividends.

Depending on the entity involved, the dividends-paid deduction may consist of:

(1) dividends paid during the tax year (¶3331),

(2) "late paid" dividends (¶3332),

(3) liquidating dividends (¶3333),

(4) consent dividends (¶3334),

(5) dividend carryover—only for PHCs (¶3335), and

(6) deficiency dividends (¶3336)—only for PHCs. (Code Sec. 561 *et seq.*; Reg § 1.561-1)[31]

¶ 3331   Dividends paid during the tax year.

The dividends-paid deduction includes dividends (¶1287) paid and actually received by the shareholder during the tax year. (Code Sec. 561(a)(1); Reg § 1.561-2(a)(1))[32]

No deduction is allowed if the dividend is preferential, i.e., it must be pro rata. (Code Sec. 562(c); Reg § 1.562-2(a))[33]

The amount of "dividends" paid is the amount by which the distribution reduces the corporation's earnings and profits (E&P). (Code Sec. 316(a), Code Sec. 562(a))[34]

A personal holding company's (PHC's, ¶3320 *et seq.*) dividends-paid deduction may equal its undistributed PHC income, even if this exceeds its E&P. (Code Sec. 316(b)(2), Code Sec. 562(a))[35]

---

29. ¶D-3531; ¶5434.05; TD ¶601,515
30. ¶G-2058 *et seq.*; ¶4484; TD ¶440,809
31. ¶D-3800; ¶5614; TD ¶602,000 *et seq.*
32. ¶D-3810; ¶5614.01

33. ¶D-3819 *et seq.*; ¶5624.06; TD ¶602,003
34. ¶D-3807; ¶3164, 5614, 5624; TD ¶602,004
35. ¶D-3807; ¶s 3164.03, 5614; TD ¶602,005

¶ 3332   Deduction for "late paid" dividends.

A corporation may treat dividends paid after the close of the tax year but within the first 2½ months of the next year as paid on the last day of the earlier year for purposes of the accumulated earnings tax (¶3316 *et seq.*) and, if elected (on the earlier year return), personal holding company (PHC) tax (¶3320 *et seq.*). (Code Sec. 563(a), Code Sec. 563(b))[36]

¶ 3333   Liquidating distributions.

Corporations (including mutual funds and real estate investment trusts) other than personal holding companies (PHCs) may include liquidating distributions in their dividends-paid deduction, to the extent the distribution is properly chargeable to earnings and profits (E&P). (Code Sec. 562(b)(1)(A))[37] Where there's a deficit in E&P at the start of the tax year of distribution, no dividends-paid deduction is allowed if current E&P for that year doesn't exceed the deficit. (Reg § 1.562-1(b)(1))[38] A liquidation for this purpose includes a redemption of stock to which Code Sec. 302 applies (¶3526 *et seq.*), other than a redemption by a mere investment or holding company. (Code Sec. 562(b)(1))[39]

If a *complete* liquidation of a corporation other than a PHC occurs within 24 months after the plan of liquidation is adopted, any distribution under the plan within the 24-month period is treated as a dividend for this purpose, to the extent of the corporation's E&P for the tax year of the distribution, computed without regard to capital losses. (Code Sec. 562(b)(1)(B)) Thus, the dividends-paid deduction is allowed for the amount of the distribution up to current E&P, even if there's an E&P deficit at the start of the year. (Reg § 1.562-1(b)(1))[40]

For PHCs only, distributions made within 24 months after the plan of liquidation is adopted qualify for the dividends-paid deduction.[41] Distributions (in this period) to *corporate* shareholders qualify to the extent the undistributed PHC income for the tax year of the distribution is allocable to corporate shareholders. (Code Sec. 562(b)(2))[42] Distributions to *noncorporate* shareholders qualify if the corporation designates the amount distributed as a dividend and notifies the shareholders that it must be reported as a dividend. (Code Sec. 316(b)(2)(B), Code Sec. 562(b)(2))[43]

¶ 3334   Consent dividends—Form 972 and Form 973.

A corporation may claim a dividends-paid deduction for amounts with respect to "consent" stock (below) it doesn't actually pay out as dividends, if those who are shareholders on the last day of its tax year consent (on Form 972) to report these hypothetical amounts as dividend income on their tax returns. (Code Sec. 565(a); Reg § 1.565-1(a), Reg § 1.565-1(b))[44]

This amount is treated for all tax purposes as if it had been distributed in money to the consenting shareholder on the last day of the corporation's tax year, and contributed to the corporation's capital by the shareholder on the same day. (Code Sec. 565(c))[45]

Consent stock includes common stock, and preferred stock with unlimited participation rights. (Code Sec. 565(c); Reg § 1.565-6(a)(1))[46]

The corporation must file the Form 972 duly executed by each consenting shareholder, and a return on Form 973, with its income tax return not later than the due date (with extensions) of the return. (Reg § 1.565-1(b)(3))

36. ¶D-3825 *et seq.*; ¶5634; TD ¶602,007
37. ¶D-3828; ¶5624.02; TD ¶602,010
38. ¶D-3835; ¶5624.02; TD ¶602,013
39. ¶D-3829; ¶s 5624.02, 5624.05; TD ¶602,010
40. ¶D-3836; ¶5624.02; TD ¶602,014
41. ¶D-3837; ¶s 3164.03, 5624.02; TD ¶602,015

42. ¶D-3844 *et seq.*; ¶5624.02; TD ¶602,018
43. ¶D-3838 *et seq.*; ¶s 3164.03, 5624.02; TD ¶602,016
44. ¶s D-3851, D-3854, D-3861; ¶5654; TD ¶602,019
45. ¶D-3853; ¶5654; TD ¶602,021
46. ¶s D-3859, D-3861; ¶5654; TD ¶602,024

¶ 3335 Dividend carryover for personal holding companies (PHCs).

A PHC may increase its dividends-paid deduction for the tax year by the excess of: (1) dividends paid in the two preceding tax years, over (2) its undistributed PHC income for those years. (Code Sec. 564; Reg § 1.564-1)[47]

¶ 3336 Personal holding company (PHC) deficiency dividend deduction—Form 976.

If a corporation is "determined" (i.e., by a final court decision, closing agreement, or signed agreement with IRS relating to PHC tax liability, Code Sec. 547(c))[48] to be liable for a deficiency in PHC tax (¶3320 *et seq.*) for any tax year, it may reduce or eliminate the deficiency (or get a refund of part or all of any deficiency paid) by making a "deficiency dividend" distribution and then claiming a deduction (on Form 976) for it. This deduction is allowed only for purposes of determining the *PHC tax* for that year (but not any interest, additional amounts or assessable penalties computed with respect to the PHC tax). (Code Sec. 547(a))[49]

The deduction isn't allowed if the determination finds that any part of the deficiency is due to fraud or willful failure to file a timely income tax return. (Code Sec. 547(g))[50]

¶ 3337 Limitation on Tax Benefits for Members of "Controlled Groups." ▬▬▬

If two or more corporations constitute a controlled group of corporations (below), the corporate tax rate schedule (¶1113) is applied to the group as one, and the group is allowed only one credit and exemption in computing the accumulated earnings (¶3319) and alternative minimum taxes (¶3203).[1] However, under final regs, a group member that incurs a loss for a tax year may not apply that loss to reduce the amount of the combined taxable income (or combined alternative minimum taxable income) of the controlled group for purposes of determining the amount of the additional tax or the reduction in the exemption amount. (Reg § 1.1561-2(a)(2)(ii)(A), Reg § 1.1561-2(b)(1))

A controlled group of corporations is a group of two or more corporations connected through stock ownership and may consist of a parent-subsidiary group, a brother-sister group, or a combined group (a combined parent-subsidiary/brother-sister group).

A *parent-subsidiary controlled group* consists of one or more chains of corporations connected through stock ownership with a common parent where:

. . . the common parent owns stock having at least 80% of the total combined voting power of all classes of stock entitled to vote, or at least 80% of the total value of shares of all classes of stock, of at least one other corporation in the chain; *and*

. . . at least 80% of the stock (combined voting power or value) of each corporation in the chain (other than the parent) is owned by one or more of the other corporations in the chain. (Code Sec. 1563(a)(1); Reg § 1.1563-1(a)(2))[2]

A *brother-sister controlled group* consists of two or more corporations if (a) more than 50% of the total combined voting power of all classes of stock, or (b) more than 50% of the value of all shares of stock, of each corporation is owned by five or fewer persons who are individuals, estates, or trusts, taking into account the stock ownership of each person only to the extent the stock ownership is identical for each corporation. (Code Sec. 1563(a)(2), Code Sec. 1563(f)(5); Reg § 1.1563-1(a)(3))[3]

Specific constructive ownership rules apply in determining whether these stock ownership

---

47. ¶D-3869; ¶5644; TD ¶602,030
48. ¶D-3705; ¶5474; TD ¶601,517
49. ¶s D-3703, D-3716; ¶5474; TD ¶601,519
50. ¶D-3719; ¶5474; TD ¶601,517

1. ¶E-10301; ¶15,614; TD ¶607,301; TD ¶607,401 *et seq.*
2. ¶E-10601; ¶15,634; TD ¶607,501
3. ¶E-10613; ¶15,634; TD ¶607,509

tests are met. (Code Sec. 1563(d))[4]

¶ 3338 **Consolidated Returns by Affiliated Groups.** ▬▬▬▬▬▬

An affiliated group (defined at ¶3339) can elect to file a single consolidated return instead of each group member filing a separate return.

Any affiliated group of one or more chains of "includible" corporations (¶3339) connected through the requisite stock ownership with a common parent may file a consolidated return in place of separate returns by each member. (Code Sec. 1501—Code Sec. 1505)[5] Generally, once this election to file a consolidated return is made, the group must continue to file a consolidated return. (Reg § 1.1502-75(a)(2))[6]

Tax saving considerations usually determine whether to file a consolidated return. Advantages of consolidated returns include:

. . . operating losses of one group member offset operating profits of other members.[7]

. . . capital losses of one group member offset capital gains of other members.[8]

. . . deferral of income on intercompany distributions.[9]

. . . group's ability to use of foreign taxes paid by a member in excess of its limitation on foreign tax credits.[10]

. . . the 70% or 80% dividends-received deduction for dividends received from unrelated corporations, that may not be fully usable on a separate return basis because of the income limitation rule, may be fully used in a consolidated return. (¶3307)[11]

Regs prescribe detailed rules for treating items of income, gain, deduction and loss of members from intercompany transactions. The rules are designed to clearly reflect the group's taxable income (and tax liability) as a whole by preventing intercompany transactions from creating, accelerating, avoiding, or deferring consolidated taxable income or consolidated tax liability. (Reg § 1.1502-13)[12]

¶ 3339 **"Affiliated group" defined.**

In order to qualify as an affiliated group:

(1) the common parent must directly own at least 80% of the total voting power and 80% of the total value of the stock in at least one other "includible" corporation; *and*

(2) one or more of the other includible corporations must directly own at least 80% of the stock (by vote or value) in each of the remaining includible corporations (i.e., not the parent). (Code Sec. 1504(a))[13]

All corporations connected through these stock ownership requirements are "includible" corporations *except*:

. . . tax-exempt organizations;

. . . life insurance companies, except (under certain conditions) where two or more insurance companies are themselves an affiliated group;

. . . regulated investment companies (i.e., mutual funds) and real estate investment trusts (REITs, ¶4201 *et seq.*);

. . . foreign corporations, except for certain Mexican or Canadian subs of a U.S. parent;

. . . corporations that have a Code Sec. 936 election (possessions tax credit) in effect for the tax year;

. . . domestic international sales corporations (DISCs, ¶4621);

---

4. ¶E-10700 *et seq.*; ¶15,634; TD ¶607,702 *et seq.*
5. ¶E-7500 *et seq.*; ¶15,014; TD ¶603,601
6. ¶E-10000; ¶15,024.16; TD ¶606,801
7. ¶E-7503; ¶15,024; TD ¶603,203
8. ¶E-7503; ¶15,024; TD ¶603,203

9. ¶E-9050 *et seq.*; ¶15,024; TD ¶603,203
10. ¶E-9050 *et seq.*; ¶15,024; TD ¶603,203
11. ¶E-8905; ¶2434.01; TD ¶605,604
12. ¶E-8250 *et seq.*; ¶15,024; TD ¶604,500 *et seq.*
13. ¶E-7601; ¶s 15,024.16, 15,024.17; TD ¶603,300

... S corporations. (Code Sec. 1504(b), Code Sec. 1504(c))[14]

¶ 3340 Forms for consolidated reporting—Form 851, Form 1120, and Form 1122.

A consolidated return is made by the common parent on Form 1120 with an attached Form 851 (affiliation schedule), and a Form 1122 (consent) signed by each subsidiary unless a consolidated return was filed (or required) for the preceding tax year. (Reg § 1.1502-75(b), Reg § 1.1502-75(h))[15] If a group member fails to file Form 1122, IRS can nonetheless treat that member as having joined in the making of a consolidated return if the facts and circumstances warrant such treatment. (Reg § 1.1502-75(b)(2))

¶ 3341 Consolidated groups—unified loss rules.

When a member of a consolidated group claims a loss on the disposition or worthlessness of a share of another member's stock, the unified loss rules determine what portion of that loss is allowable. The unified loss rules apply when a consolidated group member transfers stock of a subsidiary (S), and after taking into account all applicable rules, the share is a loss share (i.e., its basis exceeds its value). In such a case: (1) the members' basis in the transferred S stock is redetermined to reduce any disparity between the members' bases in the S stock; (2) if the transferred share is still a loss share, the transferor members' basis in the transferred loss share is reduced; and (3) if the transferred share is still a loss share, attributes of S and of its lower-tier subsidiaries are reduced. Thus, the selling group is now entitled to claim its stock loss, but the departing member must reduce its tax attributes immediately after it leaves the group, thereby precluding that member (or the consolidated group it joins) from enjoying a second tax benefit. (Reg § 1.1502-36) The unified loss rules apply to "transfers" or worthlessness events on or after Sept. 17, 2008, except that the former loss disallowance rules will apply if there is a "binding contract" that was in effect before Sept. 17, 2008 and at all times thereafter. (Reg § 1.337(d)-2).[16] Different rules applied with respect to the deduction of losses on the disposition of subsidiary stock before Sept. 17, 2008.[17]

Special anti-avoidance rules under Reg § 1.1502-35 bar the circumvention of the basis redetermination and loss suspension rules,[18] including rules that prevent groups from avoiding the loss suspension rule by "reimporting" losses to the group. (Reg § 1.1502-35(g)(3))[19]

Special rules apply when assets are distributed to multiple group members from a liquidating member in a Code Sec. 332 liquidation. (Reg § 1.1502-80)[20]

¶ 3342 Dual Consolidated Losses. ▬▬▬▬▬▬▬▬▬▬▬▬▬▬▬

A corporation that is subject to tax on its worldwide income in the U.S. and a foreign jurisdiction (e.g. a company incorporated in the U.S. but managed and controlled in another country) is referred to as a "dual resident corporation" (DRC). If a DRC is a resident of a foreign country that permits its losses to offset the income of other commonly controlled foreign corporate residents, then the DRC could use a single loss to offset both foreign and U.S. taxable income.[21] The use of a dual consolidated loss to offset the income of a domestic affiliate is permitted only if the loss does not offset the income of a foreign corporation under foreign law. (Reg § 1.1503(d)-8)[22]

¶ 3343 Corporate Estimated Tax. ▬▬▬▬▬▬▬▬▬▬▬▬▬▬▬

Corporations owing $500 or more in income tax for the tax year must make estimated tax payments, or be subject to a penalty. (Code Sec. 6655(f))

14. ¶E-7646; ¶s 15,024, 15,024.17; TD ¶603,301
15. ¶E-7754 *et seq.*; ¶15,024.16; TD ¶603,603
16. ¶E-8574 *et seq.*; ¶3374.025.
17. ¶E-8640*et seq.*; ¶3374.025; TD ¶605,251
18. ¶E-8566; ¶3374.025

19. ¶E-8569; ¶3374.025
20. ¶E-7552.2 ; ¶15,024.03
21. ¶E-9200 *et seq.*; ¶15,024.005; TD ¶606,008
22. ¶E-9201 *et seq.*; ¶15,024.005

For quick refund where a corporation pays *too much* in estimated tax, see ¶4851.

¶ 3344   The required annual payment.

A corporation must make installment payments (¶3346) of its "required annual payment," which equals the *lesser* of:

(1) 100% of the tax shown on its return for the year (or if no return is filed, 100% of its tax for that year); or

(2) 100% of the tax shown on its return for the preceding tax year (except as noted below). (Code Sec. 6655(d)(1)(B))[23]

A corporation's required annual payment can't be based on the preceding year's tax if:

. . . it didn't file a return for the preceding tax year showing a liability for tax (Code Sec. 6655(d)(1)) (a return showing zero tax, e.g., because of a net operating loss (NOL), isn't a return showing a liability for tax);

. . . the preceding tax year was less than 12 months (Code Sec. 6655(d)(1)); or

. . . it's a "large corporation." (Code Sec. 6655(d)(2)(A)) However, a large corporation may use its last year's tax to determine the amount of its first required installment for any tax year, but it must recapture any resulting reduction in that first installment, by increasing its next required installment by the amount of the reduction. (Code Sec. 6655(d)(2)(B))[24]

A corporation is "large" in any tax year if it (or any predecessor corporation) had taxable income of $1,000,000 or more for any of the three immediately preceding tax years. For this purpose, taxable income doesn't include carryback or carryover of NOLs or capital losses. Special rules apply to controlled groups. (Code Sec. 6655(g)(2))[25]

¶ 3345   What is "tax" for estimated tax purposes?

A corporation's "tax" for estimated tax purposes is the excess of: (1) the sum of its regular corporate (income) tax, the alternative minimum tax, and (for foreign corporations) the tax on gross transportation income (¶4651), over (2) the sum of its tax credits. (Code Sec. 6655(g)(1))[26]

For S corporations, regular corporate taxes also include: built-in gains tax (¶3362) or tax on net capital gains for certain S corporations (¶3361), tax on excess passive income (¶3365), and tax on recapture of pre-S election investment credit (Code Sec. 6655(g)(4)(A)), but not the last-in, first-out (LIFO) recapture tax (¶3364).[27]

Special rules apply for foreign corporations, insurance companies and tax-exempt organizations (for unrelated business income tax). (Code Sec. 6655(g)(1), Code Sec. 6655(g)(3))[28]

¶ 3346   "Required installments" of corporate estimated tax—Form 8109.

Generally, a corporation pays its estimated tax electronically, if required (see ¶3028), otherwise with Form 8109 in four equal "required installments" of its "required annual payment" (¶3344).[29] (Code Sec. 6655(c)(1), Code Sec. 6655(d)(1)(A)) For a calendar year corporation, the installments are due as follows: first, Apr. 15; second, June 15; third, Sept. 15; fourth, Dec. 15, assuming that those days do not fall on a Saturday, Sunday, or legal holiday. (Code Sec. 6655(c)(2)) For a fiscal year corporation, they are due on the 15th day of the corresponding months of the tax year (Code Sec. 6655(i)(1)) (i.e., the fourth, sixth, ninth and twelfth months).[30]

---

23. ¶s S-5327, S-5328; ¶66,554; TD ¶609,216 *et seq.*
24. ¶S-5328 *et seq.*; ¶66,554; TD ¶609,218
25. ¶S-5331 *et seq.*; ¶66,554; TD ¶609,221
26. ¶S-5322; ¶66,554; TD ¶609,205

27. ¶S-5401; ¶66,554; TD ¶628,501
28. ¶S-5321 *et seq.*, S-5421; ¶66,554
29. ¶T-10796; ¶75,034; TD ¶570,240
30. ¶S-5324.1; ¶66,554; TD ¶609,201

For lower installments in certain situations, see ¶3347 and ¶3348.

¶ 3347 Use of lower "annualized income installment" as required installment— Form 8842.

A corporation may use an "annualized income installment" as its estimated tax installment, if that's less than the "required installment" (¶3346). (Code Sec. 6655(e)(1)(A))[31]

The annualized income installment is the excess (if any) of: (1) the applicable percentage of the full year's tax computed by placing on an annualized basis (as provided by regs) the taxable income, alternative minimum taxable income (AMTI), and modified AMTI for the months to which the installment applies, *over* (2) the sum of any earlier required installments for the tax year. (Code Sec. 6655(e)(2)(A), Code Sec. 6655(e)(2)(B); Reg § 1.6655-2)[32]

Alternatively, a corporation may elect on Form 8842, by the due date of the first installment (Reg § 1.6655(e)-1(b)), to determine its annualized income based on its income for *either:* (1) the first two months (first installment), first four months (second), first seven months (third) and first ten months (fourth); *or* (2) the first three months (first), first five months (second), first eight months (third), and first eleven months (fourth). (Code Sec. 6655(e)(2)(C))[33]

Any reduction in an installment resulting from using the annualization method must be made up (recaptured) by increasing the amount of the next required installment that *isn't* determined under the annualization method by the amount of the reduction. (Code Sec. 6655(e)(1)(B))[34]

¶ 3348 Use of lower "adjusted seasonal installment" as required installment.

A corporation may use an "adjusted seasonal installment" as its estimated tax installment if it's less than the required installment (¶3346) or the annualized income installment (Code Sec. 6655(e)(1)(A)), but only if the corporation's "base period percentage" (below) for any six consecutive months of the tax year is at least 70%. (Code Sec. 6655(e)(3)(B); Reg § 1.6655-3)[35]

A corporation computes its adjusted seasonal installment by: (1) computing the taxable income for all months during the tax year before the filing month (i.e., the month the installment is required to be paid), (2) dividing this amount by the base period percentage for those preceding months, (3) determining the tax on the result, (4) multiplying that tax by the base period percentage for the filing month and all preceding months in the tax year (Code Sec. 6655(e)(3)(C), Code Sec. 6655(e)(3)(D)(ii)), and subtracting the aggregate of all earlier required installments. (Code Sec. 6655(e)(3)(A); Reg § 1.6655-3(c))[36]

The "base period percentage" for any specific period of months is the average percent that the corporation's taxable income for the corresponding months in each of the three preceding tax years bears to its taxable income for those three years. (Code Sec. 6655(e)(3)(D)(i); Reg § 1.6655-3(d))[37]

Any reduction in an installment resulting from the adjusted seasonal method must be made up (recaptured), by increasing the amount of the next required installment that *isn't* determined under the adjusted seasonal method by the amount of the reduction. (Code Sec. 6655(e)(1)(B))[38]

¶ 3349 Penalty for failure to pay estimated tax—Form 2220.

A corporation that underpays its estimated tax must add to its income tax an amount equal to the underpayment interest rate (¶4866) times the amount of the underpayment, for

---

31. ¶S-5326; ¶66,554; TD ¶609,216
32. ¶S-5338 *et seq.*; ¶66,554; TD ¶609,223
33. ¶S-5342 *et seq.*; ¶66,554; TD ¶609,226
34. ¶S-5347; ¶66,554; TD ¶609,232

35. ¶S-5344; ¶66,554; TD ¶609,233
36. ¶S-5345 *et seq.*; ¶66,554; TD ¶609,234
37. ¶S-5346; ¶66,554; TD ¶609,235
38. ¶S-5348; ¶66,554; TD ¶609,236

the period of the underpayment. (Code Sec. 6655(a)) Compute on Form 2220.[39]

The amount of the underpayment is the excess of the required installment (¶3346) over the amount (if any) of the installment paid on or before its due date. (Code Sec. 6655(b)(1))[40]

The period of the underpayment runs from the due date for the installment to the earlier of: (1) the 15th day of the third month after the close of the tax year, or (2) with respect to any portion of the underpayment, the date the portion is paid. (Code Sec. 6655(b)(2)) For this purpose, a payment of estimated tax is credited against unpaid required installments in the order those installments were due. (Code Sec. 6655(b)(3))[41]

No estimated tax penalty is imposed for any tax year if the tax shown on the return for that year (or if no return is filed, the tax liability) is less than $500. (Code Sec. 6655(f))[42] Nor is the penalty imposed for a period in which the failure to pay the required installment(s) results from a pending Title 11 bankruptcy case. (Code Sec. 6658(a))[43]

¶ 3350　S Corporations.

An eligible corporation may elect to be taxed as an S corporation which, with limited exceptions, isn't taxed at the corporate level. Instead, its items of income, loss, deduction and credit are passed through to, and taken into account by, its shareholders in computing their individual tax liabilities.

¶ 3351　S election eligibility.

An S corporation is a corporation for which an election to be taxed under Subchapter S of the Code is in effect. (Code Sec. 1361(a)(1))[44] Only a small business corporation may elect to be an S corporation. (Code Sec. 1362(a)(1)) A corporation (or an unincorporated entity that's taxable as a corporation) qualifies as a small business corporation if:[45]

(1) It is a domestic corporation (created under the law of the U.S. or of any state). (Code Sec. 1361(b)(1))[46]

(2) It is not *ineligible*. (Code Sec. 1361(b)(1); Reg § 1.1361-1(d))

A corporation is ineligible if it is:

. . . a financial institution that uses a reserve method of accounting for bad debts,

. . . taxable as an insurance company (with certain exceptions),

. . . a domestic international sales corporation (DISC) or former DISC (¶4621) (Code Sec. 1361(b)(2)), or

. . . a taxable mortgage pool. (Reg § 301.7701(i)-4(c)(1))[47]

(3) It doesn't have more than 100 shareholders, see ¶3353. (Code Sec. 1361(b)(1)(A); Reg § 1.1361-1(e))[48]

(4) All shareholders are individuals, decedents' estates, bankruptcy estates, trusts described at ¶3354, or tax-exempt Code Sec. 501(c)(3) charitable organizations (Code Sec. 1361(b)(1)(B); Reg § 1.1361-1(f)), except that an otherwise eligible S corporation can be wholly owned by another S corporation, see ¶3352. A partnership can hold S corporation stock as a nominee for an eligible shareholder. (Reg § 1.1361-1(e)(1))[49] With a very limited exception for certain banks that are S corporations, Individual Retirement Accounts (including one designated as a Roth IRA) may not be shareholders in an S corporation. (Reg § 1.1361-1(h)(1)(vii), Reg § 1.1361-1(h)(3)(i)(G))

39. ¶S-5358; ¶66,554; TD ¶609,208
40. ¶S-5359; ¶66,554; TD ¶609,209
41. ¶S-5324; ¶66,554; TD ¶609,210
42. ¶S-5359; ¶66,554; TD ¶609,213
43. ¶V-7378; TD ¶571,363
44. ¶D-1421; ¶13,614 *et seq.*; TD ¶611,001

45. ¶D-1431; ¶13,614; TD ¶611,001
46. ¶D-1432; ¶13,614.01; TD ¶611,001
47. ¶D-1434 *et seq.*; ¶ 77,014.32; TD ¶611,002
48. ¶D-1441; ¶13,614.02; TD ¶611,003
49. ¶D-1445; ¶13,614.03; TD ¶611,005

(5) No shareholder is a nonresident alien (Code Sec. 1361(b)(1)(C)), or married to a nonresident alien who has a current ownership interest in his stock under local law (unless the spouses elect under Code Sec. 6013(g) to be taxed as U.S. residents (¶3115)). (Reg § 1.1361-1(g)(1))[50]

(6) It has only one class of stock, see ¶3355. (Code Sec. 1361(b)(1)(D); Reg § 1.1361-1(b)(1))[1]

¶ 3352 S corporation subsidiaries—Form 8869.

S corporations may have 80%-or-more owned C ("regular") corporation subsidiaries and wholly-owned S corporation subsidiaries. (Code Sec. 1361(b))

A C corporation subsidiary is treated as a separate taxpayer. If it operates profitably, it pays tax on its income. If it operates at a loss, it cannot pass the loss through to the S corporation. A C corporation subsidiary may file a consolidated return with other C corporations with which it is affiliated. The S corporation cannot be included in this return (¶3339).

An S corporation cannot have a corporate shareholder. (Code Sec. 1361(b)(1)(B); Reg § 1.1361-1(f)) This rule ordinarily prevents a subsidiary from being an S corporation. However, an S corporation can have an S corporation subsidiary if it owns 100% of the subsidiary's stock, the sub is not an ineligible corporation, and the S corporation parent elects (on Form 8869)[2] to treat the subsidiary as a qualified subchapter S subsidiary (QSub). (Code Sec. 1361(b)(3)(B); Reg § 1.1361-2, Reg § 1.1361-3)[3]

A QSub isn't treated as a separate corporation for federal tax purposes; rather, its assets, liabilities, and items of income, deduction, and credit are treated as those of the parent S corporation. (Code Sec. 1361(b)(3)(A); Reg § 1.1361-4)[4] However, except to the extent otherwise provided by IRS, QSubs are treated as separate entities for purposes of making information returns. (Code Sec. 1361(b)(3)(E))[5]

If a QSub loses its qualification, it is treated as if it sold an undivided interest in its assets (based on a percentage of the stock sold) and transferred the remaining assets to itself in a tax-free incorporation. Thus, if an S corporation sells 21% of the stock of its QSub to an unrelated party, it will recognize 21% of the gain on the QSub's assets. (Code Sec. 1361(b)(3)(C); Reg § 1.1361-5)[6] If QSub status terminates, the corporation or its successor may not elect QSub status or S corporation status before its fifth year beginning after the first tax year for which the termination was effective, without IRS consent. (Code Sec. 1361(b)(3)(D); Reg § 1.1361-5(c))[7] IRS may waive inadvertent or invalid QSub elections and terminations of elections. (Code Sec. 1362(f))[8] For late election relief, see ¶3358.

A QSub uses the parent S corporation's employee identification number (EIN). If the election terminates, the sub must get an EIN; but if the entity either had an EIN before becoming a QSub or got an EIN while it was a QSub, it must use that EIN. (Reg § 301.6109-1(i))[9] However, where an S corporation undergoes a type F reorganization in which the operating S corporation becomes a QSub of a new holding corporation, the holding company must obtain a new EIN and the existing S corporation (now the QSub) must retain its EIN.[10]

¶ 3353 Number of shareholders.

In applying the 100-shareholder limit (¶3351), everyone who owns stock is counted separately, even if the stock is owned jointly with someone else (e.g., joint tenant, tenant in common), except as follows:

(1) A husband and wife (and their estates) are treated as one shareholder, no matter how

50. ¶D-1457; ¶13,614.03; TD ¶611,001
1. ¶D-1496; ¶13,614.04; TD ¶611,043
2. ¶D-1539; ¶13,614.05; TD ¶611,006
3. ¶D-1540; ¶13,614.05; TD ¶611,006
4. ¶D-1531; ¶13,614.05; TD ¶611,006
5. ¶D-1532; ¶13,614.05; TD ¶611,007

6. ¶D-1536; ¶13,614.05; TD ¶611,006
7. ¶D-1538; ¶13,614.05; TD ¶611,006
8. ¶D-1564.1; ¶13,624.03; TD ¶623,018
9. ¶D-1532; ¶13,614.05; TD ¶611,007
10. ¶D-1532; ¶13,614.05; TD ¶611,010

the stock is held (separately, jointly, etc.). (Code Sec. 1361(c)(1)(A)(i); Reg § 1.1361-1(e)(2))[11]

(2)   Where stock is owned by a grantor trust and also by the grantor directly, they are treated as one shareholder.[12]

(3)   All members of a family and their estates are treated as one shareholder. Family members include the common ancestor, lineal descendants of the common ancestor, and the spouses (or former spouses) of the lineal descendants or common ancestor. But, an individual isn't considered a common ancestor if, on the applicable date, the individual was more than six generations removed from the youngest generation of shareholders who would (but for this limitation) be family members. For this purpose, a spouse (or former spouse) is treated as being of the same generation as the individual to which such spouse is (or was) married. Adopted children are treated as children if they are (i) legally adopted, (ii) lawfully placed with an individual for legal adoption, or (iii) eligible foster children (defined under Code Sec. 152(f)(1)(C), ¶3120). (Code Sec. 1361(c)(1)) The applicable date is the latest of: the date the S election was made; the earliest date that a family member holds stock in the S corporation; or Oct. 22, 2004. (Code Sec. 1361(c)(1)(B)(ii))[13]

Each potential current beneficiary (i.e., one who may receive a discretionary distribution of income or principal during the relevant period) of an electing small business trust (¶3354) is treated as a shareholder in applying the limit. The trust is treated as the shareholder for periods when there's no potential current beneficiary. (Code Sec. 1361(c)(2)(B)(v); Reg § 1.1361-1(m)(4)) However, unexercised powers of appointment are not taken into account in determining potential current beneficiaries. In addition, a person who first becomes a potential current beneficiary during the one-year period ending with the date of the trust's disposition of all of its stock in an S corporation isn't a potential current beneficiary of that corporation. (Code Sec. 1361(e)(2))[14]

¶ 3354   Trusts as shareholders.

Only the following trusts may be S corporation shareholders:

(1) Grantor trusts—domestic trusts that are treated as being owned by an individual ("grantor") who is a U.S. citizen or resident, during the period the trust holds the S corporation stock. The grantor, not the trust, is treated as the shareholder. (Code Sec. 1361(c)(2); Reg § 1.1361-1(h)) But after the grantor dies, the trust may continue as the shareholder for two years. (Code Sec. 1361(c)(2)(A)(ii))[15]

(2) Code Sec. 678 trusts—where a person other than the grantor is treated as the substantial owner of the trust, during the period the trust holds the S corporation stock. The deemed owner, who must be a U.S. citizen or resident, is treated as the shareholder. (Code Sec. 1361(c)(2); Reg § 1.1361-1(h))[16]

(3) Voting trusts, but each beneficiary is counted as a separate shareholder. (Code Sec. 1361(c)(2); Reg § 1.1361-1(h))[17]

(4) Testamentary trusts, for two years beginning with the day when stock was transferred to the trust under the testator's will. (Code Sec. 1361(c)(2)(A)(iii); Reg § 1.1361-1(h)(1)(iv))[18]

(5) "Qualified Subchapter S trusts" (QSSTs), if the beneficiary elects (on Form 2553, in certain circumstances) to be treated as the owner of the trust so that it is eligible to hold the S stock (as in (1), above), and is treated as the shareholder. (Code Sec. 1361(d); Reg § 1.1361-1(j)) For purposes of applying the passive activity loss rules (¶1810 *et seq.*) and the at-risk rules (¶1803 *et seq.*) to a beneficiary of a QSST, a disposition of S corporation stock by a QSST is treated as a disposition by that beneficiary. (Code Sec. 1361(d)(1)(C))[19] For late election relief, see ¶3358.

11. ¶D-1447; ¶s 13,614.02, 13,614.03; TD ¶611,003
12. ¶D-1461; ¶s 13,614.02, 13,614.03; TD ¶611,003
13. ¶D-1447.1; ¶13,614.02; TD ¶611,003.1
14. ¶D-1484 *et seq.*; ¶13,614.03; TD ¶611,037
15. ¶s D-1460, D-1461; ¶13,614.03; TD ¶611,018

16. ¶D-1461; ¶13,614.03; TD ¶611,018
17. ¶D-1492; ¶13,614.03; TD ¶611,017
18. ¶D-1491; ¶13,614.03; TD ¶611,017
19. ¶D-1465 *et seq.*; ¶13,614.03; TD ¶611,020 *et seq.*

A QSST can be converted to an electing small business trust (ESBT) if certain conditions are met.[20]

(6) ESBTs—these trusts are subject to fewer restrictions than QSSTs but carry a heavy tax cost, see ¶3910. (Code Sec. 1361(c)(2)(A)(v), Code Sec. 1361(e); Reg § 1.1361-1(m)) To elect, the trustee must sign and file a specified statement with the service center with which the corporation files its income tax return. In the case of a newly electing S corporation, the trustee can attach the ESBT's consent to the Form 2553.[21] An ESBT can be converted to a QSST if certain conditions are met.[22] For late election relief, see ¶3358.

(7) Tax-exempt Code Sec. 401(a) qualified plan trusts. (Code Sec. 1361(c)(6))[23]

¶ 3355 One class of stock.

A corporation is treated as having only one class of stock (¶3351) if:

... all outstanding shares of its stock confer identical rights to distribution and liquidation proceeds, based on certain governing provisions (i.e., corporate charter, by-laws, state law, etc.) (Reg § 1.1361-1(l)(1), Reg § 1.1361-1(l)(2)(i)); and

... it hasn't issued any instrument or obligation or entered into any arrangement that's treated as a second class of stock. (Reg § 1.1361-1(l)(4))[24]

The one-class-of-stock rule isn't violated *solely* because of differences in voting rights. Thus, voting and nonvoting common can be issued. (Code Sec. 1361(c)(4))[25]

Buy-sell agreements among shareholders, redemption agreements and agreements restricting the transferability of stock generally won't violate the one-class-of-stock rule *unless:* (1) a principal purpose of the agreement is to circumvent the rule, and (2) it establishes a purchase price for the stock that's significantly above or below its fair market value (FMV). (Reg § 1.1361-1(l)(2)(iii))[26]

A call option, warrant or similar instrument is, with certain exceptions, treated as a second class of stock if it's substantially certain to be exercised and has a strike price substantially below the stock's FMV on the date it's issued, transferred to an ineligible shareholder, or materially modified. (Reg § 1.1361-1(l)(4)(iii)(A))[27]

Straight debt isn't treated as a second class of stock if specified safe harbor rules are met. (Code Sec. 1361(c)(5)(A), Code Sec. 1361(c)(5)(B))[28] However, any instrument, obligation or arrangement is, with certain exceptions, treated as a second class of stock if: (1) it constitutes equity or otherwise results in the holder being treated as the owner of stock under general tax law, and (2) its principal purpose is to circumvent these rules. (Reg § 1.1361-1(l)(4))[29] Restricted bank director stock is not taken into account for the one class of stock requirement. (Code Sec. 1361(f)(1))[30]

¶ 3356 How to elect S corporation status—Form 2553.

The S election is made by the corporation (Code Sec. 1362(a)(1)) by filing a Form 2553 signed by its authorized officer, with the required shareholder consents (¶3357) (and IRS user fee), at the IRS Service Center designated on the form. (Reg § 1.1362-6(a)(2))[31]

An S election for a tax year may be made during the preceding tax year, or by the 15th day of the third month of the tax year for which it's to be effective. (Code Sec. 1362(b)(1)) If this first tax year is less than two months and 15 days, the election must be made no later than

---

20. ¶D-1489; ¶13,614.03; TD ¶611,041
21. ¶D-1482; ¶13,614.03; TD ¶611,034
22. ¶D-1490; ¶13,614.03; TD ¶611,042
23. ¶D-1493; ¶13,614.03
24. ¶D-1496 *et seq.*; ¶13,614.04; TD ¶611,043
25. ¶D-1499; ¶13,614.04; TD ¶611,043

26. ¶D-1507 *et seq.*; ¶13,614.04; TD ¶611,045
27. ¶D-1523; ¶13,614.04; TD ¶611,046
28. ¶D-1517; ¶13,614.04; TD ¶611,046
29. ¶D-1512 *et seq.*; ¶13,614.04; TD ¶611,046
30. ¶D-1444.1; ¶13,614.02
31. ¶D-1552; ¶T-10004; ¶s 13,624, 13,624.01; TD ¶612,001

two months and 15 days after the first day of that year. (Code Sec. 1362(b)(4))[32]

An S election will be effective retroactively to the first day of a tax year *only if:*

. . . on all days in the tax year before the day the election is made, the corporation would have been eligible to elect (Code Sec. 1362(b)(2)(B)(i)), *and*

. . . all persons who were shareholders at any time during the tax year before the day of the election, but who aren't shareholders on that date, consent (along with persons who *are* shareholders, see ¶3357). (Code Sec. 1362(b)(2)(B)(ii))[33]

If either of the above conditions isn't met, the election is treated as made for the next tax year. (Code Sec. 1362(b)(2))[34]

A partnership that converts to a corporation under check-the-box rules (¶3301) or a state law conversion statute may make an S election effective for the corporation's first tax year.[35]

IRS may waive invalid elections (e.g., because of an inadvertent failure to get all the necessary consents, ¶3357, or to qualify to elect S status). (Code Sec. 1362(f))[36] For late election relief, see ¶3358.

¶ 3357   Shareholder consents.

All shareholders owning stock in the corporation on the day it elects S status must consent to the election. (Code Sec. 1362(a)(2); Reg § 1.1362-6(b)(2)(i))[37] The consents may be given on Form 2553 (¶3356), or on separate statements attached to the Form 2553. (Reg § 1.1362-6(b))[38]

A shareholder's failure to file a timely consent won't invalidate an otherwise valid timely filed election if consents are filed within an extended period of time as granted by IRS, and IRS is satisfied that: (1) there was reasonable cause for the failure; (2) the extension was requested within a reasonable time; and (3) its interests won't be jeopardized by treating the election as valid. (Reg § 1.1362-6(b)(3)(iii)(A))[39] Special rules apply for requests for automatic relief when a community property spouse fails to timely consent to an S corporation election.[40]

¶ 3358   Relief for late S corporation and related elections.

Generally effective for requests pending with IRS on Sept. 3, 2013 and those received thereafter, IRS has provided exclusive simplified methods for taxpayers to request relief for late S corporation elections, electing small business trust (ESBT) elections, qualified Subchapter S trust (QSST) elections, qualified Subchapter S subsidiary (QSub) elections, and late corporate classification elections under Reg § 301.7701-3(c)(1)(v)(C) which the taxpayer intended to take effect on the same date that an S corporation election for the entity was to take effect. (Rev Proc 2013-30) If certain requirements are met, a taxpayer can obtain relief without having to obtain a private letter ruling (PLR). However, if the taxpayer doesn't qualify for the simplified method in Rev Proc 2013-30, the taxpayer may still seek relief through a PLR. In considering the taxpayer's PLR request, IRS has the authority to treat an election as timely made if it determines, among other things, that there was reasonable cause for the failure to timely elect.[41]

¶ 3359   "Taxable income" of an S corporation.

An S corporation's taxable income is computed in the same manner as an individual's taxable income *except that*: (Code Sec. 1363(b))[42]

---

32. ¶s D-1565, D-1568; ¶13,624.01; TD ¶612,008, 612,011
33. ¶D-1566; ¶13,624.01; TD ¶612,009
34. ¶D-1566; ¶13,624.01; TD ¶612,009
35. ¶D-1456; TD ¶580,512
36. ¶D-1564.1; ¶13,614.03; TD ¶612,006
37. ¶D-1554; ¶13,624.01; TD ¶612,002

38. ¶D-1555; ¶13,624.01; TD ¶612,001
39. ¶D-1564.2; ¶13,624.03; TD ¶612,004
40. ¶D-1572.3; ¶13,624.03; TD ¶612,016; TD ¶612,006.5
41. ¶D-1572.1 *et seq.*; ¶13,624.03; TD ¶612,014 *et seq.*
42. ¶D-1591; ¶13,634.01; TD ¶614,501

(1) Items of income (including tax-exempt interest), loss, deduction or credit must be separately stated if their separate treatment by a shareholder could affect his tax liability. (Code Sec. 1363(b)(1))

(2) The corporation can't take the following deductions allowed to individuals: personal exemptions; foreign taxes; charitable contributions; net operating loss (NOL) deduction; additional itemized deductions; and oil and gas depletion. (Code Sec. 1363(b)(2))

(3) A deduction is allowed for the amortization of the corporation's organizational expenditures under Code Sec. 248 (¶3520). (Code Sec. 1363(b)(3))[43]

(4) The Code Sec. 291 rules that reduce certain corporate tax benefits apply to an S corporation (or any predecessor) that was a C corporation for any of the three immediately preceding tax years. (Code Sec. 1363(b)(4))[44]

Except as otherwise provided in the Code, or to the extent inconsistent with the Subchapter S rules, the Subchapter C rules (transfers to related corporations, redemptions, reorganizations, liquidations, etc., see ¶3510 *et seq.*) apply to an S corporation and its shareholders. (Code Sec. 1371(a))[45] But there are these modifications:

. . . With respect to liquidating distributions, no gain or loss is recognized on distributions of installment obligations where the shareholders' receipt of them (as part of a 12-month complete liquidation) isn't treated as payment for their stock by reason of Code Sec. 453(h)(1). (Code Sec. 453B(h)(1))[46]

. . . Except for the organizational expenditures deduction (above), Code provisions governing the computation of taxable income which apply only to corporations (e.g., dividends-received deduction, ¶3306) don't apply to S corporations. (Code Sec. 1363(b))[47]

. . . Limitations on the amount allowed for: (1) expensing certain depreciable assets (Code Sec. 179(d)(8)), and (2) writing off reforestation expenses (Code Sec. 194(b)(2)(B)) are determined at both the corporate and shareholder level.[48]

. . . Generally, an item (e.g., an NOL) cannot be carried over from a year the corporation was a C corporation to a year the corporation was an S corporation (except in computing the built-in gains tax, see ¶3362). (Code Sec. 1371(b)(1))[49]

¶ 3360 Deductions for fringe benefits—Form W2.

In applying the Code's fringe benefit rules, an S corporation is treated as a partnership and its more-than-2% shareholders are treated as partners. (Code Sec. 1372) Fringe benefits furnished by an S corporation to its more-than-2% shareholder-employees are treated like partnership guaranteed payments[50] and reported on Form W-2.[1]

⚫️*observation:* An S corporation is entitled to deduct the cost of fringe benefits for its more-than-2% shareholder-employees who are required to include the value of those benefits in income.

¶ 3361 Taxation of S corporations.

An S corporation is generally exempt from federal income taxes. (Code Sec. 1363(a))[2] Instead, the corporation's income is passed through, and taxed, to its shareholders (¶3367). But some S corporations may be subject to corporate-level taxes on recognized built-in gains (¶3362); excess net passive income (¶3365); last-in, first-out (LIFO) recapture (¶3364); capital gains attributable to certain substituted basis property, if the S election was made before '87;[3]

43. ¶D-1594; ¶13,634.01; TD ¶614,501
44. ¶D-1595; ¶13,634.01; TD ¶614,503
45. ¶D-1602; ¶13,714; TD ¶614,511
46. ¶s D-1600, D-1601; ¶453B4.11; TD ¶614,509
47. ¶D-1595; ¶13,634.01; TD ¶614,503
48. ¶D-1596; ¶1794.01; TD ¶614,504

49. ¶D-1603; ¶13,714.01; TD ¶614,510
50. ¶D-1621; ¶13,724; TD ¶614,505
1. ¶S-3178; TD ¶812,019
2. ¶D-1641; ¶13,634; TD ¶615,001
3. ¶D-1674 *et seq.*; ¶13,744.02; TD ¶615,002

and recapture of investment credit.[4] For an S corporation's liability to make estimated tax payments, see ¶3343 *et seq.*

¶ 3362   Built-in gains tax—Form 1120S, Schedule D.

An S corporation is subject to a corporate-level built-in gains tax in any tax year beginning in the recognition period (below) in which it has a "net recognized built-in gain" (¶3363). (Code Sec. 1374(a)) But the tax is imposed only on S corporations that were formerly C corporations. (Code Sec. 1374(c)(1))[5]

In addition, the built-in gains tax may be imposed where an S corporation acquires property and its basis in the property is determined by reference to the basis that the property had in the hands of a C corporation. (Code Sec. 1374(d)(8)(A); Reg § 1.1374-1(e))[6]

The built-in gains tax (computed on Form 1120S, Schedule D) equals the highest corporate rate (¶1113) times the net recognized built-in gain. (Code Sec. 1374(b)(1))[7]

In this computation, net recognized built-in gains are taken into account only to the extent of the excess of the net *unrealized* built-in gain over net recognized built-in gains for earlier tax years in the recognition period. (Code Sec. 1374(c)(2); Reg § 1.1374-2(a))[8] Net unrealized built-in gain means the excess (if any) of: (1) the fair market value of the S corporation's assets (including inventory) over (2) the aggregate adjusted basis of the assets, at the start of its first tax year as an S corporation ("S tax year"). (Code Sec. 1374(d)(1))[9]

The recognition period is generally the ten-year period beginning on the first day of the corporation's first S tax year. However, for S corporation tax years beginning in 2011, 2012, and 2013, the recognition period is reduced to five years. (Code Sec. 1374(d)(7))[10]

The built-in gains tax applies to transactions occurring after Dec. 26, '94, regardless of the date of the S corporation's election. (Reg § 1.1374-8(a))[11]

Regs prevent gain or loss from being counted twice for the built-in gains tax when a C corporation converting to S status owns stock in a subsidiary that's later liquidated. (Reg § 1.1374-3)[12]

¶ 3363   Net recognized built-in gain defined.

The *net recognized built-in gain* for any tax year in the recognition period (¶3362) is the *lesser of:* (1) the amount that would be the S corporation's taxable income for that year if only recognized built-in gains (below) and recognized built-in losses are taken into account, or (2) the taxable income for that year determined without taking into account net operating loss (NOL) carryovers or special corporate deductions, e.g., for dividends received. (Code Sec. 1374(d)(2)(A))[13] However, if (1) is more than (2), the excess is treated as recognized built-in gain in the next tax year, but only if the S election was made after Mar. 31, '88. (Code Sec. 1374(d)(2)(B); Reg § 1.1374-2(c))[14]

Recognized built-in gain means any gain recognized (and certain related amounts taken into account) during the recognition period on the disposition of any asset held on the first day of the corporation's first S tax year (¶3362), but only to the extent the gain doesn't exceed the excess (if any) of the asset's fair market value over its adjusted basis, on that first day. (Code Sec. 1374(d)(3); Reg § 1.1374-4)[15]

4. ¶s D-1640, D-1685; ¶13,714.03; TD ¶615,029
5. ¶D-1643; ¶13,744.01; TD ¶615,002
6. ¶D-1650; ¶13,744.01; TD ¶615,002
7. ¶D-1657; ¶13,744.01; TD ¶615,004
8. ¶D-1657; ¶13,744.01; TD ¶615,003
9. ¶D-1658; ¶13,744.01; TD ¶615,015

10. ¶D-1655; ¶13,744.01; TD ¶615,014
11. ¶D-1666; ¶13,744.03; TD ¶615,020
12. ¶D-1650.1; ¶13,744.01
13. ¶D-1644; ¶13,744.01; TD ¶615,003
14. ¶D-1645; ¶13,744.01; TD ¶615,005
15. ¶D-1646 *et seq.*; ¶13,744.01; TD ¶615,007

Special rules apply to determine an S corporation's recognized built-in gain on the disposition of transferred-basis and exchanged-basis property acquired after it became an S corporation. (Code Sec. 1374(d)(8); Reg § 1.1374-8)[16]

¶ 3364 Last-in, first-out (LIFO) recapture amount.

A C corporation that maintained its inventory using the LIFO method for its last tax year before the S corporation election is effective must include a "LIFO recapture amount" in its income for that last C corporation year. (Code Sec. 1363(d)(1))[17] In addition, a C corporation that transfers LIFO inventory to an S corporation must include a LIFO recapture amount in income the year of the transfer. (Reg § 1.1363-2(a))[18]

The "LIFO recapture amount" is the excess (if any) of the inventory amount under FIFO (first-in, first-out) over the inventory amount under LIFO, at the close of the last C corporation tax year. (Code Sec. 1363(d)(3))[19]

Any resulting increase in tax is payable in four equal installments over four tax years. The first installment must be paid on or before the due date (without regard to extensions) for the tax return for the last year for which the corporation was a C corporation. The other three installments must be paid on or before the due date for the corporation's return for the three succeeding tax years. (Code Sec. 1363(d)(2))[20]

A C corporation holding LIFO inventory indirectly through a partnership must recognize a lookthrough LIFO recapture amount if it either elects to be an S corporation or transfers its partnership interest to an S corporation in a nonrecognition transaction. (Reg § 1.1363-2(b))[21]

¶ 3365 Tax on excess net passive income.

A corporate-level tax is imposed on an S corporation's "excess net passive income" (below) for any tax year in which it has: (1) accumulated earnings and profits (i.e., E&P from a year it was taxed as a C corporation) at the close of the tax year, and (2) passive investment income (¶3366) that exceeds 25% of gross receipts (¶3366). This tax is imposed at the highest regular corporate rate (¶1113) (Code Sec. 1375(a)),[22] but IRS can waive the tax if the S corporation shows that its determination of no year-end C corporation E&P was made in good faith, and that within a reasonable time after it was determined otherwise, those E&P were distributed. (Code Sec. 1375(d))[23]

Net passive income is passive investment income reduced by deductions directly connected with the production of that income. (Code Sec. 1375(b)(2)) A deduction item that is attributable partly to passive investment income and partly to other income is allocated on a reasonable basis. (Reg § 1.1375-1(b)(3)(ii))[24] But passive investment income may not be reduced by the net operating loss (NOL) deduction or any of the special corporate deductions (e.g., for dividends received). (Code Sec. 1375(b)(2))[25]

Excess net passive income means that amount that bears the same ratio to the total net passive income for the year as: (1) the amount by which the passive investment income for the tax year exceeds 25% of gross receipts for the year ("excess passive investment income"), bears to (2) the total passive investment income for the tax year. However, an S corporation's excess net passive income for the year can't exceed its taxable income for the year computed as though it were a C corporation but without any NOL deduction or any of the special corporate deductions described above. (Code Sec. 1375(b)(1))[26]

---

16. ¶D-1650 *et seq.*; ¶13,744.01; TD ¶615,011, 615,012
17. ¶D-1581; ¶13,634.02; TD ¶613,001
18. ¶D-1583; ¶13,634.02; TD ¶613,003
19. ¶D-1582; ¶13,634.02; TD ¶613,002
20. ¶D-1585; ¶13,634.02; TD ¶613,007
21. ¶D-1582.1; ¶13,634.02

22. ¶D-1690 *et seq.*; ¶13,754; TD ¶615,021
23. ¶D-1696; ¶13,754.01; TD ¶615,026
24. ¶D-1693 *et seq.*; TD ¶615,023
25. ¶D-1693; ¶13,754; TD ¶615,023
26. ¶D-1692; ¶13,754; TD ¶615,025

¶ 3366   "Passive investment income" and "gross receipts" defined.

For purposes of the tax on excess net passive income (¶3365) and involuntary terminations (¶3376), passive investment income means gross receipts derived from royalties, rents, dividends, interest, annuities, and, for tax years beginning before May 26, 2007, (to the extent of gains) sales or exchanges of stock or securities. (Code Sec. 1362(d)(3)(C), Code Sec. 1375(b)(3))[27]

However, in the case of a bank, a bank holding company, a financial holding company, or a depository institution holding company, passive investment income does not include (1) interest income earned by the bank or company or (2) dividends on assets that must be held by the bank or company. (Code Sec. 1362(d)(3)(C)(v)(I))[28]

Gross receipts are the total amount received or accrued under the S corporation's accounting method before reduction for returns, allowances, cost, or deductions. But gross receipts don't include amounts received in nontaxable sales or exchanges except to the extent gain is recognized by the corporation. (Code Sec. 1362(d)(3), Code Sec. 1375(b)(3))[29]

Special rules apply to determine gross receipts from the sale of capital assets.[30]

¶ 3367   Taxation of S corporation's shareholders.

An S corporation's income is taxed directly to its shareholders by allocating the corporation's items of income, loss, deduction and credit for each day in its tax year pro rata among the persons who were shareholders on that day. (Code Sec. 1366(a)(1); Reg § 1.1366-1(a); Code Sec. 1377(a)(1))[31]

Items of income, loss, deduction and credit are separately allocated to each shareholder whenever separate treatment could affect the tax liability of a shareholder. (Code Sec. 1366(a)(1)(A); Reg § 1.1366-1(a)) Under regs, the following S corporation items must be taken into account separately:

. . . The combined net amount of gains and losses from sales or exchanges of capital assets grouped by applicable holding periods, Code Sec. 1(h) tax rates, and by any other classification that may be relevant in determining the shareholder's tax liability.

. . . The combined net amount of gains and losses from sales or exchanges of Code Sec. 1231 property grouped by applicable holding periods, Code Sec. 1(h) tax rates, and by any other classification that may be relevant in determining the shareholder's tax liability.

. . . The charitable contributions, grouped by the Code Sec. 170(b) percentage limitations (see ¶2123 *et seq.*), paid by the corporation within its tax year.

. . . The foreign taxes paid (or accrued) by the corporation.

. . . Each of separate items involved in determining credits, except credits for certain uses of gasoline and special fuels.

. . . Each of these separate items: Code Sec. 165(d) gains and losses from wagering transactions; Code Sec. 175 soil and water conservation expenditures; Code Sec. 179 expense election deductions; Code Sec. 213 medical, dental, etc., additional itemized deductions for individuals under Code Sec. 212 *et seq.*; and any other deductions subject to the Code Sec. 67 or Code Sec. 68 limitations on itemized deductions.

. . . Any of the corporation's items of portfolio income or loss, and related expenses, as defined in the regulations under Code Sec. 469.

. . . The corporation's tax-exempt income.

. . . The corporation's alternative minimum tax adjustments described in Code Sec. 56, and

---

27. ¶D-1713 *et seq.*; ¶s 13,624.02, 13,754; TD ¶615,022
28. ¶D-1737.1; ¶13,624.02
29. ¶s D-1702, D-1703; ¶13,624.02; TD ¶615,022

30. ¶D-1701 *et seq.*; ¶13,624; TD ¶615,503
31. ¶D-1761 *et seq.*; ¶13,664; TD ¶614,701

Code Sec. 58 and tax preference items described in Code Sec. 57; and

. . . Any item identified in IRS guidance (including forms and instructions) as an item required to be separately stated. (Reg § 1.1366-1(a)(2))[32]

The character of any item in the shareholder's hands is determined as if the item had been realized directly from the source from which the corporation realized it, or incurred in the same manner as incurred by the corporation. (Code Sec. 1366(b); Reg § 1.1366-1(b))[33]

A shareholder's share of an S corporation's items is taken into account in his tax year that includes the last day of the corporation's tax year (¶2810). (Code Sec. 1366(a)(1); Reg § 1.1366-1(a)(1))[34]

When shareholders perform services for an S corporation but don't draw a salary, any dividends paid to the shareholders in lieu of reasonable compensation for these services are treated as wages subject to employment taxes. Even where an S corporation pays a salary to shareholders for services together with dividends, IRS can recharacterize all or part of the dividends as additional compensation subject to employment taxes.[35]

If a shareholder sells all of his S corporation stock during the corporation's tax year and all affected shareholders (all terminating shareholders and their transferees) consent (by attaching a specified statement to Form 1120S for the tax year during which the shareholder's interest is terminated), the corporation's tax year can be split into two tax years, the first of which ends on the date the seller's interest is terminated. Items will be allocated between those tax years according to its normal method of accounting. (Code Sec. 1377(a)(2); Reg § 1.1377-1(b))[36] This also applies where the S corporation elects to terminate its tax year because of a "qualifying disposition." (Reg § 1.1368-1(g))[37]

Any gain or loss from a shareholder's disposition of an interest in an S corporation is taken into account by the shareholder as net investment income for purposes of the 3.8% surtax on unearned income (¶3150 *et seq.*) *only* to the extent that of the net gain or loss that the transferor would take into account if the entity had sold all its property for fair market value immediately before the disposition. (Code Sec. 1411(c)(4))

If a shareholder dies (or a trust terminates) before the end of an S corporation tax year, his (or its) pro rata part of the corporation's items is reported on his (its) final return. (Code Sec. 1366(a)(1))[38]

¶ 3368 Amount passed through to shareholders reduced for corporate-level taxes.

The amount of any corporate-level built-in gains tax (¶3362) that's imposed on an S corporation is treated as a loss sustained by the corporation during the tax year. The character of the loss is determined by allocating it proportionately among the recognized built-in gains giving rise to the tax. (Code Sec. 1366(f)(2); Reg § 1.1366-4(b)) If a corporate-level tax is imposed on an S corporation's excess net passive income (¶3365), each item of passive investment income that's passed through to a shareholder is reduced by a pro rata part of that tax. (Code Sec. 1366(f)(3); Reg § 1.1366-4(c))[39]

¶ 3369 Shareholders' deductions and losses limited to basis.

All deductions and losses of an S corporation (e.g., capital losses and net operating losses) are passed through to and (except as otherwise limited by the Code) deductible by shareholders. However, a shareholder may deduct his pro rata share of these passed-through items only to the extent of his adjusted basis (¶3371) in his S corporation stock, determined by taking into account the increases in basis for his share of the S corporation income during the

32. ¶D-1765; ¶13,664; TD ¶614,701
33. ¶D-1762; ¶13,664; TD ¶614,703
34. ¶D-1764; ¶13,774; TD ¶614,702
35. ¶H-4329; TD ¶532,002

36. ¶D-1769; ¶13,774; TD ¶614,707
37. ¶D-1771; ¶13,684.09; TD ¶614,711
38. ¶D-1774; ¶13,664; TD ¶614,715
39. ¶D-1767; ¶13,664.02; TD ¶614,705

year, and the decreases in basis for nondividend distributions for the year, plus any debt owed to him by the corporation. A shareholder gets no basis increase for debts of the corporation that he guaranties. (Code Sec. 1366(d)(1); Reg § 1.1366-2)[40]

Any deduction or loss that can't be deducted (for lack of basis) is suspended and may be carried over to be used whenever the shareholder has basis to apply against all or part of the amount the shareholder carried over. One Court of Appeals has held that if a shareholder fails to claim a suspended loss deduction when able to do so, the shareholder doesn't get a corresponding reduction in basis. The disallowed loss is personal to the shareholder and cannot be transferred, except for in certain post-2004 tax-free transfers to a spouse or former spouse incident to divorce (¶2447). (Code Sec. 1366(d)(2); Reg § 1.1366-2(a)(2))[41] Special rules apply where the S corporation is in bankruptcy or is insolvent. (Code Sec. 108(d)(7)(B))[42]

If an S corporation's stock, or the debt it owes to a shareholder, becomes worthless in any tax year of the corporation or shareholder, the corporate items for that year will be taken into account by the shareholders and the adjustments to basis of stock or debt will be made, before the worthlessness is taken into account. (Code Sec. 1367(b)(3))[43]

¶ 3370 Consistent treatment on shareholder's return and S corporation's return— Form 8082.

A shareholder must on his own return treat a Subchapter S item in a manner that is consistent with the treatment of that item on the corporation's return (Form 1120S). A shareholder that treats a Subchapter S item differently must notify IRS of the inconsistency (Code Sec. 6037) on Form 8082.[44]

¶ 3371 Shareholder's basis in S corporation's stock or debt.

A shareholder's basis in the stock of an S corporation is *increased* by his share of the corporation's income items that are passed through to him—i.e., its separately and non-separately computed income items (including tax-exempt income) and the excess of the deduction for depletion over the basis of depletable property. (Code Sec. 1367(a)(1); Reg § 1.1367-1(b)) Debt discharge income of an S corporation that is excluded from its income is not income to a shareholder and does not increase shareholder basis in the S corporation's stock.[45] Basis in stock is *decreased* (but not below zero) by: the shareholder's share of the corporation's items of deduction, loss and nondeductible expenses (except those chargeable to the capital account); the shareholder's depletion deduction for oil and gas property; and distributions to the shareholder that aren't taxable as dividends. (Code Sec. 1367(a)(2); Reg § 1.1367-1(c))[46]

In any tax year of an S corporation when the total of the amount of items (other than distributions) that reduce a shareholder's basis in stock exceeds the amount that would reduce that basis to zero, the balance is applied to reduce the basis (but not below zero) of any shareholder debt in the S corporation. (Code Sec. 1367(b)(2)(A); Reg § 1.1367-2(b))[47]

If the shareholder's basis in S corporation debt in any tax year is reduced below his original basis in it, that basis must be increased to (but not above) its original amount, before the shareholder's basis in *stock* is increased. (Code Sec. 1367(b)(2)(B); Reg § 1.1367-2(b))[48] For purposes of the basis adjustment rules, shareholder advances aggregating less than $25,000 and not evidenced by separate written instruments and repayments on the advances are treated as a single indebtedness. (Reg § 1.1367-2(a)(2))[49]

40. ¶D-1775; ¶13,664; TD ¶614,716
41. ¶D-1785; ¶13,664; TD ¶614,718
42. ¶D-1786; ¶1084.03; TD ¶614,718
43. ¶D-1789; ¶13,674; TD ¶614,722
44. ¶D-1801; ¶60,374; TD ¶614,724

45. ¶D-1863; ¶13,674; TD ¶617,001
46. ¶D-1865; ¶13,674; TD ¶617,001
47. ¶D-1877; ¶13,674; TD ¶617,007
48. ¶D-1881; ¶13,674; TD ¶617,009
49. ¶D-1878;¶13,674.10; TD ¶617,007

¶ 3372   Tax treatment of S corporation distributions.

The amount of a distribution from an S corporation to a shareholder equals the amount of cash distributed plus the fair market value (at distribution) of any other property distributed. (Code Sec. 301(c), Code Sec. 1368(a))[50]

If an S corporation has no accumulated earnings and profits (E&P), the amount distributed reduces the shareholder's basis in his stock (¶3371). If the amount exceeds basis, the excess is treated as payment in exchange for stock, i.e., as capital gain. (Code Sec. 1368(b)(2))[1]

If IRS finds that the salary paid to an S corporation shareholder-employee is unreasonably low, it may reclassify dividend payments made to the shareholder as salary.[2]

If an S corporation has accumulated E&P, its distributions are treated as follows:[3]

(1) The portion of the distribution that doesn't exceed the accumulated adjustments account (AAA, see ¶3374) is taxed the same as a distribution from an S corporation with no accumulated E&P (above). If more than one distribution is made in a tax year, and the total amount distributed exceeds the amount in the AAA at the end of that year, the balance in that account is allocated among the distributions in proportion to the size of each distribution. (Code Sec. 1368(c)(1))[4]

(2) The portion of the distribution that remains after applying (1) is treated as a dividend to the extent it doesn't exceed the S corporation's accumulated E&P. (Code Sec. 1368(c)(2))

(3) Any portion of the distribution remaining after applying (2) is treated the same as a distribution by an S corporation with no accumulated E&P. (Code Sec. 1368(c)(3))[5]

The tax effects of an S corporation's distributions to shareholders with respect to stock are determined only after taking into account:

(i) adjustments that increase the basis of the shareholder's stock and

(ii) adjustments to the AAA, other than for distributions to shareholders and without regard to any net negative adjustments, for the S corporation's tax year. (Code Sec. 1368(d); Reg § 1.1368-1(e)(2))[6]

observation: The effect of taking the basis increases, but not the decreases, into account is that the shareholder may receive more nontaxable distributions, at the cost of a decrease in the amount of loss that he may deduct.

An S corporation may elect, with the consent of all affected shareholders (i.e., those to whom distributions are made), to treat distributions as made out of accumulated E&P *before* being made out of the AAA. (Code Sec. 1368(e)(3); Reg § 1.1368-1(f)(2))[7]

¶ 3373   S corporation's earnings and profits (E&P).

An S corporation, unlike a C corporation, generally does not generate E&P.[8] Any E&P carried over from prior C corporation years, or acquired from a C corporation in a reorganization, remain unadjusted while the corporation retains S status, except: (Code Sec. 1371(c)(1))

. . . E&P are reduced to reflect distributions that are taxable to the shareholders as dividends. (Code Sec. 1371(c)(3))

. . . E&P are adjusted (up or down) to reflect the effect of redemptions, liquidations, tax-free reorganizations and corporate divisions. (Code Sec. 1371(c)(2))

. . . E&P are reduced to reflect any tax paid by an S corporation because of the recapture of

50. ¶D-1813; ¶13,684; TD ¶616,501
1. ¶D-1815; ¶s 13,684, 13,684.07; TD ¶616,502
2. ¶H-4329; TD ¶532,002
3. ¶s D-1817, D-1816; ¶13,684.01; TD ¶616,502
4. ¶D-1816, D-1819; ¶13,684.01; TD ¶616,502

5. ¶s D-1817, D-1816; ¶13,684.01; TD ¶616,502
6. ¶D-1818
7. ¶D-1835; ¶13,684.03; TD ¶616,509
8. ¶D-1631; ¶13,684.01 *et seq.*; TD ¶616,507

a pre-S election investment credit. (Code Sec. 1371(d)(3))[9]

... E&P are adjusted for LIFO recapture tax. (¶3364) (Code Sec. 1363(d)(5))[10]

For purposes of determining the S corporation's accumulated E&P, all pre–'86 S corporation generated E&P has been eliminated for tax years beginning after May 25, 2007.[11]

¶ 3374 Accumulated adjustments account (AAA).

The AAA is a corporate account consisting of the corporation's income that was previously taxed to its shareholders and not distributed. An S corporation's AAA[12] is increased each tax year by:

(1) Separately computed items of income (other than income that is exempt from tax).

(2) Nonseparately computed income.

(3) The excess of deductions for depletion over the basis of property subject to depletion. (Code Sec. 1368(e)(1); Reg § 1.1368-2(a)(2))[13]

The AAA is decreased each tax year by:

(a) Items of separately computed loss and deduction.

(b) Nonseparately computed loss.

(c) Nondeductible expenses (other than expenses chargeable to capital account) unless related to tax-exempt income.

(d) The amount of the shareholder's deduction for depletion under Code Sec. 611 with respect to oil and gas wells.

(e) Distributions from an S corporation that has no E&P and distributions that are made out of the AAA.

(f) The amount that was treated as paid out of the AAA on redemptions that were treated as payments in exchange for stock under Code Sec. 302(a) or Code Sec. 303(a). This equals the amount in the account before the redemption multiplied by a fraction, the numerator of which is the number of redeemed shares and the denominator of which is the total number of outstanding shares before the redemption. (Code Sec. 1368(e)(1); Reg § 1.1368-2(a)(3))[14]

Special ordering rules apply with regard to the above mentioned increases and decreases. (Reg § 1.1368-2(a)(5))[15]

Where there is a net negative adjustment for the tax year, any net loss for the year is disregarded in adjusting the AAA for purposes of distributions made during the tax year. (Code Sec. 1368(e)(1)(C))[16]

The balance in an S corporation's AAA at the end of a tax year may be reduced below zero if the items that reduce the AAA exceed the sum of the AAA plus the items that increase the AAA (items (1) – (3), above). (Code Sec. 1368(e)(1)(A)) Income in a later year will cause the AAA to become positive only after the negative balance has been restored. (Reg § 1.1368-3)[17]

The AAA isn't to be adjusted (i.e., reduced) for federal taxes attributable to any tax year when the S corporation was a C corporation. (Code Sec. 1368(e)(1))[18]

If distributions made during the year exceed the AAA at the close of the tax year, then the AAA is allocated pro rata among the distributions (Code Sec. 1368(c); Reg § 1.1368-2(b)(1))[19]

Special rules apply to distributions after the S election is terminated. (Code Sec. 1371(e))[20]

---

9. ¶D-1633; ¶13,714.03; TD ¶616,507
10. ¶D-1581; TD ¶616,507
11. ¶D-1632; ¶13,684.07
12. ¶D-1823; ¶13,684.02; TD ¶616,506
13. ¶D-1824; ¶13,684.02; TD ¶616,506
14. ¶D-1825, D-1827; ¶13,684.02; TD ¶616,506

15. ¶D-1829; ¶13,684.02; TD ¶616,506
16. ¶D-1826.1; TD ¶616,506
17. ¶D-1830; ¶13,684.02; TD ¶616,506
18. ¶D-1823; ¶13,684.02; TD ¶616,506
19. ¶D-1819; ¶13,684.02; TD ¶616,505
20. ¶D-1846 *et seq.*; ¶13,714.04; TD ¶616,516

¶ 3375   Voluntary revocation of the S election; rescission.

A corporation's S election may be revoked with the consent of holders of a majority of the corporation's issued and outstanding stock (including non-voting stock). (Code Sec. 1362(d)(1); Reg § 1.1362-2(a)(1))[21]

If no effective date is specified, a revocation is effective for the tax year in which made, if made by the 15th day of the third month of that year. Otherwise, it will be effective as of the first day of the next tax year. (Code Sec. 1362(d)(1)(C))[22] However, if the revocation specifies that it is to be effective on a date that is on or after the date it's made, it will be effective on that date even if it causes the corporation's tax year to be split. (Code Sec. 1362(d)(1)(D))[23]

A corporation may *rescind* the revocation at any time before it becomes effective. A rescission may be made only with the consent of each person who consented to the revocation and of each person who became a shareholder during the period from the day after the date the revocation was made through the date the rescission is made. (Reg § 1.1362-2(a)(4))[24]

¶ 3376   Involuntary termination of S election.

A corporation's S election is terminated if either:

(1) The corporation ceases to meet any of the S corporation eligibility requirements discussed at ¶3351. (Code Sec. 1362(d)(2)(A)) The termination is effective as of the day the eligibility requirement is no longer met (Code Sec. 1362(d)(2)(B));[25] or

(2) The S corporation's passive investment income (¶3366) exceeds 25% of its gross receipts for three consecutive tax years and at the end of each of those years, the corporation had accumulated earnings and profits (E&P, ¶3365). The termination is effective as of the first day of the first tax year beginning after the third of these years. (Code Sec. 1362(d)(3)(A))[26]

IRS can waive inadvertent terminations or invalid elections if certain conditions are met. (Code Sec. 1362(f)) Regs explain how to request relief. (Reg § 1.1362-4(c))[27] QSubs are eligible for the same relief (as discussed above) for an inadvertently invalid QSub election or inadvertent termination. (Reg § 1.1362-4)

Filing a voluntary bankruptcy petition does not terminate an S corporation election.[28]

¶ 3377   When new S election can be made after termination or revocation.

After a revocation or termination of its S election, a corporation must wait five years before making a new S election unless IRS consents to an earlier election. (Code Sec. 1362(g))[29]

---

21. ¶D-1901; ¶13,624.02; TD ¶623,001
22. ¶D-1903; ¶13,624.02; TD ¶623,003
23. ¶D-1905; ¶13,624.02; TD ¶623,003
24. ¶D-1907 *et seq.*; ¶13,624.02; TD ¶623,005
25. ¶D-1911; ¶13,624.02; TD ¶623,006

26. ¶D-1914; ¶13,624.02; TD ¶623,008
27. ¶D-1928; ¶13,624.03; TD ¶623,018
28. ¶D-1911
29. ¶s D-1951, D-1953; ¶13,624.02; TD ¶623,023

Chapter 16   Corporate Transactions—
Organization—Distributions—Reorganization—
Acquisitions—Liquidations

¶ 3510   Incorporations and Transfers to Controlled Corporations—Code Sec. 351.   ▬▬

Incorporating a business or transferring property to a controlled corporation can be partly or wholly tax-free if technical requirements are satisfied. But an intentional failure to satisfy the requirements may not result in the recognition of gain or loss in every case.[1]

No gain or loss is recognized if property (¶3511) is transferred to a corporation solely in exchange for stock (¶3512) of that corporation, if, immediately after the transfer, the transferor or transferors are in control (¶3513) of the corporation. (Code Sec. 351(a))[2]

For exceptions, see ¶3517 and ¶3518.

For transfers to foreign corporations, see ¶3588.

For basis of property received in the exchange, see ¶2482 *et seq.*

¶ 3511   Property.

Property that may be transferred tax-free under Code Sec. 351 includes cash, tangible property and intangible personal property, e.g., stock, partnership interests, patent rights, and working interests in oil and gas properties.[3]

Property doesn't include: (i) services to the transferee corporation (Code Sec. 351(d)(1));[4] (ii) transferee corporation debt not evidenced by a security (Code Sec. 351(d)(2));[5] or (iii) unpaid interest on transferee corporation debt accrued during the transferor's holding period for the debt. (Code Sec. 351(d)(3))[6]

¶ 3512   Stock.

Property must be transferred *solely in exchange for stock*, which does not include (1) stock rights, options or warrants (Reg § 1.351-1(a)), or (2) nonqualified preferred stock. (Code Sec. 351(g)) (¶3556)[7]

Shares in an association, joint stock company or insurance company are treated as stock. (Code Sec. 7701(a)(7))[8] A transferee can be treated as receiving stock even if no stock certificate is issued.[9]

¶ 3513   Control.

Control means at least 80% of the transferee's combined voting power and at least 80% of all other classes of the transferee's stock, see ¶3553. (Code Sec. 368(c))[10] The transferor group must hold at least 80% of the voting power immediately after the transfer; but not every transferor must hold voting stock.[11]

---

1. ¶F-1014; TD ¶231,014
2. ¶F-1001; ¶3514.01; TD ¶231,001
3. ¶F-1101 *et seq.*; ¶3514.03; TD ¶231,004
4. ¶F-1104; ¶3514.03; TD ¶231,004
5. ¶F-1102; TD ¶231,004
6. ¶F-1103; TD ¶231,004

7. ¶F-1004; ¶3514.04; TD ¶231,005
8. ¶F-1004; ¶3514.04; TD ¶231,005
9. ¶F-1004 *et seq.*; ¶3514.05; TD ¶231,005
10. ¶s F-1200 *et seq.*, F-5501 *et seq.*; ¶3514.05; TD ¶231,701
11. ¶F-1202; TD ¶231,702

¶ 3514   Gain on receipt of cash or property ("boot").

If transferors receive *boot* (see ¶3556) as well as stock in an otherwise qualifying Code Sec. 351 transfer, nonrecognition is limited and the transferor (i) recognizes gain up to the amount or fair market value of the boot, and (ii) does not recognize any losses. (Code Sec. 351(b))[12]

¶ 3515   Assumption of liabilities.

When a corporation assumes liabilities (¶3516) in connection with an otherwise tax-free exchange, the transfer is still tax-free (Code Sec. 357(a))[13] subject to the following exceptions.

- *Tax avoidance rule.* If the principal purpose for the assumption of liabilities is tax avoidance or isn't a bona fide business purpose, the full amount of *all assumed liabilities are treated as cash received by the transferor* (even those assumed for nontax avoidance or valid business purposes) and taxed as boot (¶3514). (Code Sec. 357(b)(1))[14]

- *Excess liabilities rule.* If the total liabilities assumed exceed the transferor's adjusted basis in the transferred property, gain is recognized to the extent of the excess. (Code Sec. 357(c)(1))[15]

Where both anti-abuse rules apply, tax avoidance takes precedence and all liabilities are treated as boot. (Code Sec. 357(c)(2)(A))[16]

The excess liabilities rule does not apply to any liability that (i) would give rise to a deduction when paid by the transferor, or (ii) would be a liquidating payment to a partner described in Code Sec. 736(a), see ¶3769. (Code Sec. 357(c)(3)(A))[17]

The excess liabilities rule applies to transfers in a divisive Type D reorganization under Code Sec. 361.[18] It does not apply, however, to acquisitive reorganizations in which the transferor corporation goes out of existence (and cannot benefit from the transferee's assumption of liabilities), i.e., Code Sec. 351 transfers that also qualify as either (1) a Type A or Type C reorganization, or (2) a nondivisive Type D or Type G reorganization that meets the requirements of Code Sec. 354(b)(1) (discussed at ¶3544 *et seq.*).[19]

The amount of a liability assumed in a Code Sec. 351 exchange reduces the transferor's basis in the stock received, regardless of whether the transferor recognizes any gain or loss on the exchange. (Code Sec. 358(a), Code Sec. 358(d)(1)) However, the transferor's basis in the stock will not be reduced by the assumption of any liability described in Code Sec. 357(c)(3) that would have been deductible by the transferor had it not been assumed. (Code Sec. 358(d)(2))[20]

If a transferor's basis in stock received in a Code Sec. 351 exchange exceeds the fair market value (FMV) of the stock, the basis is reduced (but not below FMV) by the amount of any liability that (i) is assumed in exchange for the stock, and (ii) did not otherwise reduce the transferor's basis in the stock by reason of the assumption. However, basis is not reduced if (1) the trade or business with which the liability is associated is transferred as part of the exchange to the person assuming the liability, or (2) substantially all of the assets with which the liability is associated are transferred as part of the exchange to the person assuming the liability. (Code Sec. 358(h); Reg § 1.358-5)[21]

---

12. ¶F-1501; ¶3514.10; TD ¶231,302
13. ¶F-1509; ¶3574.01; TD ¶231,501
14. ¶F-1511 *et seq.*; ¶3574.02; TD ¶231,504
15. ¶F-1515 *et seq.*; ¶3574.03; TD ¶231,507
16. ¶F-1519; TD ¶231,510

17. ¶F-1521; ¶3574; TD ¶231,512
18. ¶F-4203; TD ¶233,010
19. ¶F-4204; TD ¶235,008
20. ¶F-1803; ¶F-1521; ¶3584.04; TD ¶232,543; TD ¶233,302
21. ¶F-1803.1; TD ¶231,905

¶ 3516   When a liability is treated as assumed.

Except as provided in regs,

(1) A recourse liability is treated as having been assumed by the transferee if, based on all facts and circumstances, the transferee has agreed to and is expected to satisfy it, regardless of whether the transferor has been relieved of the liability. (Code Sec. 357(d)(1)(A))

(2) A nonrecourse liability is treated as having been assumed by the transferee of any asset subject to the liability, except that the amount so treated is reduced by the lesser of:

(i) the amount of the liability that the owner of other, untransferred assets subject to the same liability, has agreed with the transferee to, and is expected to, satisfy, or

(ii) the FMV of other, untransferred assets, determined without regard to Code Sec. 7701(g) (providing generally that the FMV of property subject to nonrecourse debt is not less than the debt). (Code Sec. 357(d)(2))[22]

✪/observation: If the owner of untransferred assets securing nonrecourse debt doesn't agree to pay any of it, the amount of the liability treated as assumed by the transferee isn't reduced at all, in which case liabilities may exceed basis and trigger gain recognition.

For the limit on basis increase for assumption of liabilities, see ¶2485.

¶ 3517   Transfers to investment companies (swap funds).

Gain or loss is recognized on the transfer of property to an investment company in exchange for its stock when the transfer diversifies a transferor's interests (Reg § 1.351-1(c)(5)),[23] except where each transferor transfers a portfolio of already diversified assets. (Reg § 1.351-1(c)(6))[24] Gain or loss is also recognized when a transfer to an investment company results in the transferred property being held by a regulated investment company (RIC), a real estate investment trust (REIT), or a corporation more than 80% of the value of whose total investment assets are marketable securities, interests in mutual funds or REITs, or stocks and securities (including specified types of property, such as money, that are treated as stocks or securities under Code Sec. 351(e)(1)).[25] (Reg § 1.351-1(c)(1))[26]

¶ 3518   Transfer of debtor's property in a bankruptcy or similar proceeding.

The Code Sec. 351 nonrecognition rule does not apply to transfers in a bankruptcy, receivership, foreclosure or similar proceeding (including agency receivership proceedings involving banks). Gain or loss is recognized to the extent the stock received by the debtor in exchange for assets is used to satisfy the debtor's indebtedness. (Code Sec. 351(e)(2))[27]

¶ 3519   Gain or loss to corporation on issuance of stock.

A corporation does not recognize gain or loss on the exchange of its stock (including treasury stock) for property or money. (Code Sec. 1032(a))[28] Similarly, no gain or loss is recognized in otherwise taxable transactions where a corporation acquires stock directly or indirectly from the issuing corporation in what otherwise would be a transferred basis transaction and immediately transfers the stock to acquire money or other property (including services), and no party receiving the issuing corporation stock receives a substituted basis in the stock of the issuing corporation. (Reg § 1.1032-3(b), Reg § 1.1032-3(c))[29] For stock issued

22. ¶F-1509.2; ¶3574.01; TD ¶231,502
23. ¶F-1307; ¶3514.06; TD ¶232,103
24. ¶F-1307.1; ¶3514.06; TD ¶232,103
25. ¶F-1303; ¶3514.06; TD ¶232,101

26. ¶F-1302; ¶3514.06; TD ¶232,102
27. ¶F-1308; ¶3514.07; TD ¶231,018
28. ¶I-3201; ¶10,324; TD ¶233,401
29. ¶I-3213; ¶10,324

to a creditor in satisfaction of a corporation's debt, see ¶1395.

¶ 3520 Deductibility of costs of organizing a corporation.

A corporation is deemed to have made an election to deduct up to $5,000 of its organizational expenditures in the tax year in which it begins business. (Reg § 1.248-1(c)) The $5,000 amount is reduced (but not below zero) by the amount, if any, by which its organizational expenditures exceed $50,000. Remaining organizational expenditures are deductible ratably over the 180-month period beginning with the month in which it begins business. (Code Sec. 248(a))[30]

A corporation may irrevocably forgo the deemed election by clearly electing to capitalize *all* organizational expenditures on a timely filed Federal income tax return (including extensions) for the tax year in which it begins business. (Reg § 1.248-1(c))

Qualifying expenses include outlays for legal services, incorporation fees, temporary directors' fees and organizational meeting costs. Costs relating to capital structure, e.g., of issuing stock, can't be deducted or otherwise recovered. (Code Sec. 248(b); Reg § 1.248-1(b))[31]

¶ 3521 Corporate Distributions; Earnings and Profits (E&P). ▬▬▬▬

A distribution of property (i.e., money, securities, and any other property except stock of the distributing corporation) by a corporation to its shareholders is taxable to the shareholders as a dividend to the extent it is made out of current or accumulated E&P (¶1285 *et seq.*).[32] The amount of a distribution is reduced by an associated liability only if it is assumed by the shareholder within the meaning of Code Sec. 357(d). (¶3516) (Reg § 1.301-1(g))[33]

¶ 3522 Earnings and profits (E&P).

A distribution of money or other property by a corporation to its shareholders is treated as a dividend and is taxable as ordinary income to the extent it is made out of current and accumulated E&P (¶1285 *et seq.*). The portion of the distribution in excess of E&P is treated as a return of capital to the extent of the shareholder's basis in the stock of the distributing corporation (his cost or net capital investment). (Code Sec. 301(c)) The remainder of the distribution, if any, is generally taxed as capital gain.[34]

For tax treatment of the distributing corporation, see ¶3538 *et seq.*

For increases in E&P for alternative minimum tax purposes, see ¶3211.

¶ 3523 How distributions affect earnings and profits (E&P).

With certain exceptions discussed below, distributions of property by a corporation with respect to its stock reduce E&P by the following amounts:

(1) The amount of money distributed. (Code Sec. 312(a)(1))[35]

(2) The principal (face) amount of the corporation's obligations (i.e., its own notes, bonds, etc.) distributed without original issue discount (OID). (¶1313 *et seq.*) (Code Sec. 312(a)(2))[36]

(3) The aggregate issue price of the corporation's obligations distributed with OID. (Code Sec. 312(a)(2))[37]

(4) The adjusted basis of other distributed property (Code Sec. 312(a)(3), Code Sec. 312(b))[38] as determined for purposes of computing E&P. (Code Sec. 312(b)(1))[39]

30. ¶L-5202 ; TD ¶301,023
31. ¶L-5204; ¶2484; TD ¶301,026
32. ¶J-2351; ¶3014.01
33. ¶J-2352.1; ¶3014.02; TD ¶172,002
34. ¶J-2352 *et seq.*; ¶3014; TD ¶172,001

35. ¶F-10502; ¶3124.02; TD ¶171,008
36. ¶F-10503; ¶3124.02; TD ¶171,008
37. ¶F-10504; ¶3124.02; TD ¶171,008
38. ¶F-10505; ¶3124.02; TD ¶171,008
39. ¶F-10505; ¶s 3124.02, 3124.04; TD ¶171,008

E&P is *not* reduced in the case of the following types of distributions.

(1) Distributions of appreciated property (other than the corporation's own obligations) increase E&P to the extent of any gain realized (fair market value (FMV) over adjusted basis) by the distributing corporation on the distribution. (Code Sec. 312(b)(1))[40] This decreases the reduction to E&P for the distribution of property by the amount of any liability assumed by the shareholder in connection with the distribution or to which the distributed property is subject. (Code Sec. 312(c); Reg § 1.312-3)[41]

(2) Redemption distributions that are treated as payment in exchange for stock (¶3526) reduce E&P by an amount not in excess of the ratable share of the distributing corporation's E&P attributable to the redeemed stock. (Code Sec. 312(n)(7))[42]

(3) Reorganizations and other tax-free distributions don't reduce E&P if the distributee does not recognize any gain. (Code Sec. 312(d)(1)(A); Reg § 1.312-11(b), Reg § 1.312-11(c))[43]

(4) Tax-free distributions of a corporation's own stock (stock dividends under Code Sec. 305(a)) don't reduce E&P. (Code Sec. 312(d)(1)(B); Reg § 1.312-1(d)) If a distribution of stock is *taxable* to the shareholders (see ¶1296), E&P is reduced by the FMV of the taxable portion of the stock or rights. (Reg § 1.312-1(d))[44]

(5) Distributions to 20% corporate shareholders may require adjustments to E&P solely for purposes of determining the distributee's income and stock basis. (Code Sec. 301(e))[45]

Basis can be different for E&P and taxable income (TI) purposes because the corporation may use different depreciation or cost recovery methods for computing E&P and TI. (¶3524).[46]

¶ 3524 Effect of depreciation on earnings and profits (E&P).

Depreciation deductions for E&P purposes are often lower than the corresponding deductions for computing taxable income. (¶1900 *et seq.*) For modified accelerated cost recovery system (MACRS) property (other than property expensed under Code Sec. 179 and Code Sec. 179A), the E&P deduction is computed under the alternative depreciation system (ADS), even if a different system is used in computing taxable income. (Code Sec. 312(k)(3)(A))[47] For ACRS property placed in service before '87, the E&P deduction is computed by using the straight-line method over the regular or alternative ACRS recovery periods, which may be longer than those used in computing taxable income.[48] The E&P deduction for depreciable property placed in service before '81 is computed by using the straight-line or similar method (e.g., units of production), even if an accelerated method is used in computing taxable income.[49] For expensed property, i.e., Code Sec. 179 and Code Sec. 179A property, the cost is deducted from E&P ratably over five tax years. (Code Sec. 312(k)(3)(B))[50]

observation: The additional first-year depreciation deduction under Code Sec. 168(k) (¶1933 *et seq.*) is not allowed for purposes of computing E&P.

¶ 3525 Other adjustments to earnings and profits (E&P).

Other common adjustments are made to E&P to reflect economic gain or loss.

. . . Circulation expenses must be capitalized and treated as part of the basis of the asset to which they relate, even if they are deducted currently in computing taxable income (TI). (Code Sec. 312(n)(3))[1]

---

40. ¶F-10506; ¶3124.02; TD ¶171,011
41. ¶F-10508; ¶3124.02; TD ¶171,011
42. ¶F-10701; ¶3124.07; TD ¶171,034
43. ¶F-10801; ¶3124.02; TD ¶171,034
44. ¶F-10509 *et seq.*; ¶3124.02; TD ¶171,015
45. ¶F-10601 *et seq.*; ¶3014; TD ¶171,008

46. ¶F-10300 *et seq.*; ¶3124.01 *et seq.*; TD ¶171,008
47. ¶F-10303; ¶3124.04; TD ¶171,022
48. ¶F-10307; ¶3124.04; TD ¶171,022
49. ¶F-10309; ¶3124.04; TD ¶171,022
50. ¶F-10304; ¶3124.04; TD ¶171,023
1. ¶F-10206; ¶3124.07; TD ¶171,019

... Completed contract method of accounting can't be used for E&P purposes. The percentage of completion method must be used instead. (Code Sec. 312(n)(6))[2]

... Construction period carrying charges (interest, property taxes, etc.) must be capitalized as part of the assets to which they are allocable. (Code Sec. 312(n)(1)(A)) The capitalized amounts must be written off for E&P purposes, as is the asset itself.[3]

... Depletion is taken into account on a *cost,* not percentage, basis. (Reg § 1.312-6(c)(1))[4]

... Estimated tax payments by a cash method taxpayer reduce E&P in the year paid.[5]

... Exempt income (e.g., state or local bond interest) increases E&P. (Reg § 1.312-6(b))[6]

... Installment sales are accounted for without regard to the installment method, i.e., principal amounts must be treated as received in the year of sale. (Code Sec. 312(n)(5))[7]

... Intangible drilling and development costs that are deductible when paid or incurred for TI purposes (other than costs incurred in connection with a nonproductive well) must be capitalized and deducted ratably over a 60-month period. (Code Sec. 312(n)(2)(A))[8]

... Income tax liabilities reduce E&P as of the close of the tax year, for an accrual basis corporation, and according to some courts, a cash basis corporation. (IRS and other courts say a cash basis corporation reduces E&P only when the tax is *paid.*)[9]

... Life insurance proceeds increase E&P if the corporation is the beneficiary, even if not includible in TI.[10]

... LIFO (last-in, first-out) recapture amount increases and decreases at the close of each tax year increase or decrease E&P by the same amount. (Code Sec. 312(n)(4))[11]

... Losses that are recognized but not allowed as a deduction decrease E&P by the disallowed amount.[12]

... Mineral exploration and development costs that are deductible for taxable income purposes must be capitalized and deducted ratably over a 120-month period. (Code Sec. 312(n)(2)(B))[13]

... Loss carryovers and carrybacks don't reduce E&P of the year to which they are carried and reductions of loss carryovers do not increase E&P in a later carryover year.[14]

... Organizational expenses must be capitalized and treated as part of the basis of the asset to which they relate, even if they are amortized in computing TI (as described at ¶3520). (Code Sec. 312(n)(3))[15]

... Premiums paid for life insurance on corporate officers reduce E&P, even if they are not deductible in computing TI.[16]

¶ 3526 Stock Redemptions.

The acquisition by a corporation of its own stock from a shareholder in exchange for cash or property is treated as a taxable dividend distribution to the shareholder (¶1285 *et seq.*) unless the redemption qualifies for sale or exchange treatment, in which case it is treated as a sale or exchange for which capital gain treatment is allowed (if the stock is a capital asset in the hands of the taxpayer) whether or not the stock acquired is cancelled, retired, or held as treasury stock. (Code Sec. 317(b))[17] A redemption will be treated as a sale or exchange of stock if it qualifies under any of the following exceptions:

(1) The redemption is *substantially disproportionate.* (¶3527)

(2) The distribution is in *complete redemption* of a shareholder's interest. (¶3528)

2. ¶F-10008; ¶3124.07; TD ¶171,021
3. ¶F-10208; ¶3124.07; TD ¶171,025
4. ¶F-10314; ¶3124.04; TD ¶171,024
5. ¶F-10224; ¶3124.03; TD ¶171,009
6. ¶F-10101; ¶s 3124.01, 3124.07; TD ¶171,012
7. ¶F-10405; ¶3124.07; TD ¶171,021
8. ¶F-10221; ¶3124.07; TD ¶171,026
9. ¶F-10223, F-10225; ¶3124.03; TD ¶171,009
10. ¶F-10102; ¶3124.07; TD ¶171,012
11. ¶F-10212; ¶3124.07; TD ¶171,021
12. ¶F-10403; ¶3124.05
13. ¶F-10220; ¶3124.07; TD ¶171,026
14. ¶F-10012; ¶3124.03; TD ¶171,032
15. ¶F-10204; ¶3124.07; TD ¶171,028
16. ¶F-10234; TD ¶175,042
17. ¶F-11001; ¶3174.01; TD ¶241,002

(3) The redemption is *not essentially equivalent to a dividend.* (¶3530)

(4) The redemption is in partial liquidation of a noncorporate shareholder. (¶3531)

(5) The distribution is in redemption of a decedent's stock to pay death taxes. (¶3532) (Code Sec. 302(a))[18]

For constructive ownership rules applicable to redemptions, see ¶3534.

¶ 3527   Substantially disproportionate redemptions.

A redemption is *substantially disproportionate* if it satisfies both of the following tests:

(1) *80% test.* Immediately after the redemption, the ratio of the shareholder's voting stock to the corporation's total outstanding voting stock is less than 80% of that ratio immediately before the redemption. The same 80% test must also be met with regard to the corporation's *common stock,* voting and nonvoting, based on the fair market value (FMV) of the aggregate shares of each class of common stock. (Code Sec. 302(b)(2)(C))

(2) *50% test.* Immediately after the redemption, the shareholder owns less than 50%, by vote, of the corporation's total voting stock. (Code Sec. 302(b)(2)(B))[19]

A redemption solely of nonvoting stock doesn't qualify as substantially disproportionate. However, if voting stock is redeemed at the same time in a redemption that qualifies as substantially disproportionate, the redemption of the nonvoting stock (other than Section 306 stock, see ¶3535 *et seq.*) will also be substantially disproportionate. (Reg § 1.302-3(a))[20]

¶ 3528   Complete redemptions—termination of a shareholder's interest in the corporation.

To qualify as a complete redemption, all stock in the corporation that is owned, or treated as owned under the constructive ownership rules (¶3534) (unless waived (¶3529)) by the shareholder must be redeemed. (Code Sec. 302(b)(3)) Accordingly, if a shareholder owns both common and preferred stock, the redemption of all the shares of only one class of stock will not qualify as a complete redemption.[21]

A redemption on the installment basis can qualify as a complete redemption if the corporation and the shareholder are bound by a purchase agreement to complete the redemption by a certain date and for a maximum price.[22]

¶ 3529   Family attribution rules waived on complete terminations.

An individual who receives a distribution that is otherwise in complete redemption of all the stock he actually owns will not be treated as constructively owning the stock owned by a spouse, child, grandchild or parent if:

(1) He has no personal financial interest in the corporation (prohibited interest), other than as a creditor, immediately after the redemption;

(2) He no longer serves as director, officer or employee;

(3) He doesn't acquire any prohibited interest (except by inheritance) or position within ten years after the redemption;

(4) He didn't acquire any of the redeemed stock from close family members, and didn't transfer any stock to them, within ten years before the redemption, except acquisitions or transfers not principally motivated by tax avoidance; *and*

18. ¶F-11101 *et seq.*; ¶3024.02; TD ¶241,001
19. ¶F-11203 *et seq.*; ¶3024.04; TD ¶242,000 *et seq.*
20. ¶F-11212; ¶3024.04; TD ¶242,014
21. ¶F-11301 *et seq.*; ¶3024.05; TD ¶241,201
22. ¶F-11307; ¶3024.05; TD ¶241,211

556

(5) He attaches a separate statement (in duplicate) to his income tax return for the redemption year stating that he hasn't acquired any new prohibited interest (except by inheritance) and that he will notify the district director within 30 days after acquiring any new interest. (Code Sec. 302(c)(2); Reg § 1.302-4)[23]

Waiver of family attribution allows an individual to completely redeem his interest without all related persons redeeming their stock and applies only for purposes of determining that a distribution is a complete redemption. Accordingly, there is no need for the waiver if the redemption would otherwise qualify as payment in exchange for stock. (Code Sec. 302(b)(5))[24]

A partnership, estate, trust or corporation (entity) can waive family attribution if the partner, beneficiary or shareholder (related person) owns stock solely as a function of the family constructive ownership rules. Such ownership is not reattributed to the entity if both the entity and the related person satisfy the conditions for a waiver and agree to be jointly and severally liable for any tax deficiency resulting from any acquisition of an interest within the ten-year period. (Code Sec. 302(c)(2)(C))[25]

¶ 3530   Redemptions not essentially equivalent to a dividend.

A redemption is not essentially equivalent to a dividend if it results in a meaningful reduction in the redeemed shareholder's proportionate interest in the distributing corporation, without regard to how it affects the distributing corporation. (Reg § 1.302-2(b))[26]

A redemption of a sole shareholder and a pro rata redemption do not reduce a shareholders' proportionate interest in the distributing corporation and cannot be essentially equivalent to a dividend.[27]

A redemption from a shareholder with over 50% of the voting power usually results in a meaningful reduction if that shareholder's voting power is reduced to 50% or less.[28]

A redemption of voting stock from a substantial minority shareholder results in a meaningful reduction if, after the redemption, the number of shareholders the redeemed shareholder must act in concert with to control the corporation is increased.[29]

A redemption of voting stock from a low percentage minority shareholder is usually treated as a meaningful reduction so long as there is some reduction in proportionate interest.[30]

Redemptions of nonvoting preferred stock from shareholders who own no common stock and no voting stock always results in a meaningful reduction in interest.[31]

The constructive ownership rules (¶3534) apply in determining the redeemed shareholder's stock ownership before and after the redemption (Code Sec. 302(c)(1)), even if no stock is actually owned after the redemption.[32]

¶ 3531   Redemptions in partial liquidation of a noncorporate shareholder.

A partial liquidating distribution in redemption of stock of a noncorporate shareholder is treated as a sale or exchange even if it is made pro rata. A redemption distribution is treated as made in partial liquidation, even if it is pro rata, if it is (1) made with respect to a noncorporate shareholder, (2) not essentially equivalent to a dividend (as determined at the corporate level), and (3) made under a plan within the tax year in which the plan is adopted or the next tax year. (Code Sec. 302(b)(4), Code Sec. 302(e)(1))[33] Partial liquidations are meant to include cases involving the genuine contraction of a corporate business. (Reg § 1.346-1(a))[34]

---

23. ¶F-11313 *et seq.*; ¶3024.05; TD ¶241,401*et seq.*
24. ¶F-11311; ¶3024.05; TD ¶241,405
25. ¶F-11314; ¶3024.05; TD ¶241,403
26. ¶F-11402; ¶3024.03; TD ¶242,201
27. ¶F-11407; ¶3024.03; TD ¶242,208
28. ¶F-11418; ¶3024.03; TD ¶242,225

29. ¶F-11424; ¶3024.03
30. ¶F-11425; ¶3024.03; TD ¶242,213
31. ¶F-11429 *et seq.*; ¶3024.03; TD ¶242,218
32. ¶F-11410 *et seq.*; ¶3024.03; TD ¶242,009
33. ¶F-11500 *et seq.*; ¶3024.06; TD ¶242,604
34. ¶F-11509; ¶3024.06; TD ¶242,614

If a corporation is engaged in two or more active trades or businesses for five years or more, a distribution in partial liquidation won't be essentially equivalent to a dividend if the corporation terminates one of the businesses, distributes all of the assets of the discontinued business (or its sales proceeds), and continues to operate the second business. (Code Sec. 302(e)(2), Code Sec. 302(e)(3))[35]

¶ 3532   Redemption of decedent's stock to pay death taxes.

Distributions in redemption of stock included in a decedent's gross estate for federal estate tax purposes are treated as payment for stock up to the sum of: (1) all death taxes (federal and state), including interest, and (2) funeral and administration expenses allowable as federal estate tax deductions (Code Sec. 303(a)),[36] *but only if*:

(1) The value of the redeeming corporation's stock included in the estate exceeds 35% of the decedent's adjusted gross estate; (Code Sec. 303(b)(2)(A)) (Code Sec. 303(b)(2)(B))[37]

(2) The redemption distribution takes place after the decedent's death and within three years and 90 days after the estate tax return is filed (or due, if filed early), or, in some cases, later specified dates (Code Sec. 303(b)(1));[38] and

(3) The redeemed shareholder bears the burden of the taxes or expenses. (Code Sec. 303(b)(3))[39]

¶ 3533   Stock sales between related corporations.

If shareholders control two corporations and sell stock of one controlled corporation (Issuer) to the other (Acquirer) in return for cash or other property, the sale is treated as a stock redemption. If the Acquirer is a brother corporation of the Issuer, the sale is treated as a redemption by the Acquirer. If the Issuer is a parent of the Acquirer, the sale is treated as a redemption by the Issuer. (Code Sec. 304(a)(1), Code Sec. 304(a)(2))[40] The resulting redemption is treated as payment in exchange for stock (and not as a dividend) if it qualifies under one of the exceptions listed at ¶3526. (Code Sec. 304(a))[41]

If the sale is treated as a dividend, the amount taxable to the shareholder is determined as if it were distributed *first* by the Acquirer to the extent of its earnings and profits (E&P), and *then* by the Issuer to the extent of its E&P. (Code Sec. 304(b)(2))[42] The parties to transactions subject to Code Sec. 304 entered into with a principal purpose of avoiding its application to certain corporations, however, may be recast for purposes of determining the dividend amount. (Reg § 1.304-4)[43] In the case of a *foreign* Acquirer, (a) the amount of E&P that can support a deemed dividend is limited to E&P attributable to stock of a U.S. shareholder accumulated while Acquirer was a controlled foreign corporation (CFC) (¶4622 *et seq.*) and (b) its E&P is not taken into account if more that 50% of the consequent dividend would *neither* be subject to U.S. tax for the year of the dividend, *nor* includible in the E&P of a CFC. (Code Sec. 304(b)(5))[44]

If a deemed distribution from a stock sale between brother-sister corporations is treated as a dividend, (1) the stock that was sold is deemed to have been transferred by Issuer to Acquirer for stock of Issuer in a tax-free transfer to a controlled corporation, and (2) Acquirer is deemed to have redeemed the stock that is treated as having been issued to it in the constructive transfer, preventing Issuer from using the dividends-received deduction to shelter any part of the deemed distribution. (Code Sec. 304(a)(1))[45]

---

35. ¶F-11516 *et seq.*; ¶3024.06; TD ¶242,608
36. ¶F-11600 *et seq.*; ¶3034.01; TD ¶243,001
37. ¶F-11605 *et seq.*; ¶3034.01; TD ¶243,013 *et seq.*
38. ¶F-11613; ¶3034.01; TD ¶243,018
39. ¶F-11617; ¶3034.01; TD ¶243,009
40. ¶F-11701 *et seq.*; ¶3044 *et seq.*; TD ¶243,301 *et seq.*

41. ¶F-11704; ¶s 3044.02, 3044.03; TD ¶243,301
42. ¶F-11706; ¶3044.03TD ¶243,305
43. ¶F-11707; ¶3044.05; TD ¶243,305
44. ¶F-11719.2; ¶F-11719.3; ¶3044.04
45. ¶F-11716; ¶3044.03; TD ¶243,311

A corporation is a parent if it controls another corporation. (Code Sec. 304(a)(2)) A brother-sister relationship exists where the same person or persons controls each of two corporations. (Code Sec. 304(a)(1)) Control means ownership of stock possessing at least 50% of the total combined voting power of all classes of the voting stock, or at least 50% of the total value of all classes of stock. (Code Sec. 304(c)(1))[46] Constructive ownership rules similar to those at ¶3534 apply with modifications. (Code Sec. 304(c)(3)(A))[47]

The parent-subsidiary redemption rules apply even if, as a result of the constructive ownership rules, a brother-sister relationship also exists.[48]

¶ 3534 Constructive ownership.

For purposes of the stock redemption rules, a person is treated as owning not only his own direct holdings, but also those of certain closely related taxpayers: (Code Sec. 302(c))

... An individual is considered as owning stock owned, directly or indirectly, by his spouse (unless divorced or legally separated), children (including adopted children), grandchildren and parents. (Code Sec. 318(a)(1))[49]

... Stock owned by or for an S corporation, partnership or estate is considered as owned proportionately by its shareholders, partners, or beneficiaries. (Code Sec. 318(a)(2)(A), Code Sec. 318(a)(5)(E)) Stock owned by or for an S corporation shareholder, partner or estate beneficiary is attributed in full to the S corporation, partnership or estate. (Code Sec. 318(a)(3)(A), Code Sec. 318(a)(5)(E))[50]

... Stock owned by or for a trust is considered owned by its beneficiaries in proportion to their actuarial interest in the trust. (Code Sec. 318(a)(2)(B)(i)) Stock owned by or for a trust beneficiary is attributed in full to the trust unless the beneficiary's interest in the trust is a remote contingent interest. (Code Sec. 318(a)(3)(B)(i))[1]

... A 50%-or-more shareholder in a C corporation is considered as owning his proportionate share of stock in other corporations owned by the C corporation. (Code Sec. 318(a)(2)(C)) A C corporation is considered as owning all the stock (except its own) owned by its 50%-or-more shareholder. (Code Sec. 318(a)(3)(C))[2]

... The holder of an option to buy stock is treated as the owner of the stock covered by the option. (Code Sec. 318(a)(4)) This includes an option that isn't exercisable until after the lapse of a fixed time.[3]

Stock constructively owned is considered to be actually owned for purposes of further attribution (Code Sec. 318(a)(5)(A))[4] *except* as follows (where so-called double or sidewise attribution is prohibited):

... Stock constructively owned by a person under the family attribution rules won't be attributed further to make another family member the constructive owner of that stock. (Code Sec. 318(a)(5)(B))[5]

illustration: If a father and son each own 50 shares in a corporation, each is treated as owning all 100 shares. But the father's constructive ownership of the son's shares can't be further attributed from the father to his daughter.

... Stock constructively owned by a partnership, estate, trust or corporation can't be further attributed from the partnership, etc., to make another (partner, heir, beneficiary or shareholder) the constructive owner of that stock. (Code Sec. 318(a)(5)(C))[6]

---

46. ¶F-11711; ¶3044.01; TD ¶243,307
47. ¶F-11720 *et seq.*; ¶3044.01; TD ¶243,323
48. ¶F-11723; ¶3044.04; TD ¶243,321
49. ¶F-11803 *et seq.*; ¶3184.02; TD ¶243,627
50. ¶F-11812 *et seq.*; ¶3184.03; TD ¶243,615 *et seq.*
1. ¶F-11827 *et seq.*; ¶3184.04; TD ¶243,618

2. ¶F-11808 *et seq.*; ¶3184.05; TD ¶243,614
3. ¶F-11834 *et seq.*; ¶3184.06; TD ¶243,632
4. ¶F-11805
5. ¶F-11804; ¶3184.07; TD ¶243,629
6. ¶s F-11811, F-11814, F-11824, F-11832; ¶3184.07; TD ¶243,623 *et seq.*

¶ 3535   Section 306 Stock. ▆▆▆▆▆▆▆▆▆▆▆▆▆▆▆▆▆▆▆▆▆▆▆▆▆▆▆

Code Sec. 306 prohibits capital gain treatment on the disposition of certain preferred stock received either as a nontaxable stock dividend or in certain substituted basis transactions when ordinary income treatment would have applied if cash had been distributed instead. Exemptions apply to dispositions that do not ordinarily bail out a corporation's earnings and profits.

¶ 3536   Dispositions of Section 306 stock.

Proceeds from a redemption of Section 306 stock (defined at ¶3537) are treated as a current distribution of property subject to the regular Code Sec. 301 dividend rules (see ¶1285 *et seq.*). (Code Sec. 306(a)(2))[7]

If Section 306 stock is sold or otherwise disposed of in a transaction other than a redemption, the entire amount realized is treated as ordinary income to the extent the fair market value on the distribution date would have been a dividend had the corporation distributed cash instead of stock. Ordinary income treatment is thus limited to the corporation's E&P at the time of the distribution rather than the sale. (Code Sec. 306(a)(1)(A))[8]

Gain is recognized to the extent the amount received exceeds the sum of the amount treated as ordinary income plus the adjusted basis of the stock. (Code Sec. 306(a)(1)(B))[9] Loss is not recognized. (Code Sec. 306(a)(1)(C))[10] The ordinary income is treated as qualified dividend income for individuals and other noncorporate taxpayers (¶1288) and may be taxable as net capital gain. (¶2604) (Code Sec. 306(a)(1)(D))[11]

An amount realized on the disposition of Section 306 stock will not be treated as a dividend in the case of:

... A complete disposition of the shareholder's interest in the corporation, including stock attributed under the Code Sec. 318(a) constructive ownership rules. (Code Sec. 306(b)(1)(A))

... A redemption (i) of all of a shareholder's Section 306 stock terminating the shareholder's corporate ownership, or (ii) from a noncorporate shareholder in partial liquidation of the corporation. (Code Sec. 306(b)(1)(B)).

... A redemption in a complete liquidation of the corporation. (Code Sec. 306(b)(2))

... A transaction in which gain or loss is not recognized on the disposition of the Code Sec. 306 stock (in which case the stock retains the Section 306 taint in the transferee's hands). (Code Sec. 306(b)(3))

... A transaction, if the issuance and/or subsequent disposition of the stock was not pursuant to a plan having one of its principal purposes the avoidance of federal income tax. (Code Sec. 306(b)(4))[12]

¶ 3537   Stock treated as Section 306 stock.

Section 306 stock includes:

(1) Stock received as a stock dividend, other than common stock issued with respect to common stock, if any part was not taxable on its receipt, usually preferred stock distributed on common stock. (Code Sec. 306(c)(1)(A))[13]

(2) Stock other than common stock received in a reorganization, spin-off, split-up or split-off, to the extent that (a) the transaction was substantially the same as the receipt of a stock dividend, or (b) the stock was received in exchange for Section 306 stock. (Code

---

7. ¶F-12106; ¶3064.02; TD ¶244,406
8. ¶s F-12103, F-12101; ¶3064.02; TD ¶244,401
9. ¶F-12103; ¶3064.02; TD ¶244,402
10. ¶F-12103; ¶3064.02; TD ¶244,403

11. ¶F-12101; ¶3064.02; TD ¶244,401
12. ¶F-12108 *et seq.*; ¶3064.02; TD ¶244,413
13. ¶F-12122; ¶3064.01; TD ¶244,408

Sec. 306(c)(1)(B))[14]

(3) Stock (unless described in (2) above) whose basis is determined by reference to the basis of Section 306 stock. (Code Sec. 306(c)(1)(C))[15]

(4) Preferred stock (but not nonqualified preferred stock (see ¶3556)) received in a Code Sec. 351 transfer (except for certain bank transfers), provided that if cash had been distributed instead, part of the cash would have been a dividend under the related corporation redemption rules (¶3531). (Code Sec. 306(c)(3)(A))[16]

Section 306 stock does not include any stock of any class which, at the time of distribution, would not in any part have been a dividend if cash had been distributed instead because there were no earnings and profits. (Code Sec. 306(c)(2))[17]

¶ 3538   Nonliquidating Property Distributions.

A corporation recognizes taxable gain when it makes a nonliquidating distribution (e.g., redemption, dividend) of appreciated property (other than its own obligations) to its shareholders as if the property had been sold, at the time of the distribution, to the distributee for its then fair market value. (Code Sec. 311(b)(1))[18]

A corporation recognizes no loss on a nonliquidating distribution of property. (Code Sec. 311(a)(2))[19] IRS is authorized to issue regs to prevent circumvention of the partial liquidation provision. (Code Sec. 346(b))[20]

For how nonliquidating distributions affect earnings and profits (E&P), see ¶3523.

¶ 3539   Distribution of property subject to a liability.

If a corporation's nonliquidating distribution consists of property subject to liabilities in excess of basis, or if a shareholder assumes liabilities of the distributor corporation in connection with the distribution, then in computing the corporation's gain on the distribution (¶3538), the property's fair market value (FMV) is treated as not less than the amount of the liabilities. (Code Sec. 311(b)(2))[21] If the liability is unsecured, it is allocated among all the distributed assets (including any asset that secures another liability) according to the assets' relative FMVs.[22]

¶ 3540   Distributions of stock or stock rights.

Except for distributions of appreciated property, a corporation doesn't recognize gain or loss on distributions (not in complete liquidation) of its own stock or of rights to acquire its own stock. (Code Sec. 311(a)(1))[23]

¶ 3541   Corporate Reorganizations.

If one corporation transfers property to another corporation solely in exchange for stock or securities of the other corporation and the exchange is made pursuant to a plan of reorganization, neither will recognize gain or loss on the exchange, provided the transaction complies with strict statutory and regulatory requirements.

¶ 3542   Conditions common to all reorganizations.

The following definitions and requirements apply to all reorganization types, with exceptions noted. Failure to meet any requirement may disqualify a reorganization and result in

---

14. ¶F-12124 *et seq.*; ¶3064.01; TD ¶244,408
15. ¶F-12128; ¶3064.01; TD ¶244,408
16. ¶F-12123; ¶3064.01; TD ¶244,408
17. ¶F-12132; ¶3064.01; TD ¶244,411
18. ¶F-14004 *et seq.*; ¶3114.01; TD ¶244,203

19. ¶F-14002; ¶3114.01; TD ¶244,209
20. ¶F-14607; ¶3114.01, ¶3024.06, ¶3464.02
21. ¶s F-14005, F-14402; ¶3114.01; TD ¶244,204
22. ¶F-14006; ¶3114.01; TD ¶244,206
23. ¶F-14002; ¶3114; TD ¶244,209

gain recognition and/or dividend treatment.[24]

Plan of reorganization. An exchange must be pursuant to plan of reorganization. (Code Sec. 354(a)(1); Reg § 1.368-2(c), Reg § 1.368-2(g))[25] The plan must be adopted by each party to the reorganization (see below) and each party must include a statement on its return pursuant to regs. (Reg § 1.368-2(c))[26]

Party to a reorganization. A corporation whose stock or securities are exchanged must be a party to the reorganization for nonrecognition treatment to apply. (Code Sec. 354(a)(1))[27] This includes any corporation resulting from a reorganization and, in the case of an acquisition by one corporation of the stock or properties of another, both corporations. The parent of the acquiring corporation in a Type B, C, or G reorganization is a party to the reorganization if its stock is the consideration for the acquisition of assets or stock. A parent of the surviving corporation in a statutory merger is a party to the reorganization if its stock is used as consideration and the transaction qualifies as a Type A reorganization under Code Sec. 368(a)(2)(D) or Code Sec. 368(a)(2)(E). If assets or stock received in a Type A, B, C, or G reorganization are dropped down under Code Sec. 368(a)(2)(C), the corporation controlling the transferee is a party to the reorganization. (Code Sec. 368(b)) (Reg § 1.368-2(f))[28]

Continuity of interest. The regulatory continuity of proprietary interest doctrine incorporates the judicial requirement that the former target shareholders retain a significant equity participation in the target corporation after the reorganization. A proprietary interest in the target is sufficiently preserved if (1) it is exchanged for a proprietary interest in the issuing corporation, (2) it is exchanged by the acquiring corporation for a direct interest in the target corporation enterprise, or (3) it otherwise continues as a proprietary interest in the target corporation. (Reg § 1.368-1(e))[29]

Continuity of business enterprise. An acquiring corporation must either (1) continue the target's historic business (generally, its most recent business unless the most recent business was entered under the plan of reorganization), or (2) use a significant portion of the target's historic business assets in a business. (Reg § 1.368-1(d)(1), Reg § 1.368-1(d)(2)) The business may be conducted by, or the assets held through, one or more members of the acquiring corporation's qualified group, i.e., one or more chains of corporations connected through stock ownership, if the acquiring corporation has 80% control of at least one of them and each of the other corporations is controlled by one of the other corporations). (Reg § 1.368-1(d)(4)(ii))[30]

Business purpose. A transaction that is structured as a reorganization but has no business purpose is not in the nature of a reorganization and is not treated as such.[31]

The continuity of interest and continuity of business enterprise requirements do not apply to (i) recapitalizations involving a single corporation (Type E reorganizations, ¶3548)[32] or (ii) change-in-identity reorganizations (Type F reorganizations, ¶3549). (Reg § 1.368-1(b))[33]

¶ 3543   Reorganizations involving investment companies.

If two or more investment companies are parties to a transaction, the transaction cannot qualify as a nonrecognition reorganization with respect to either company or the holders of its stock and securities (Code Sec. 368(a)(2)(F)(ii)),[34] unless it was a regulated investment company,[35] real estate investment trust,[36] or a corporation that meets specific diversified investment company requirements. (Code Sec. 368(a)(2)(F)(i))[37]

---

24. ¶F-3500 *et seq.*; ¶3684; TD ¶232,508
25. ¶s F-4009; ¶3684.09; TD ¶232,509
26. ¶F-4118; ¶3684.09
27. ¶F-4013 *et seq.*; ¶3684.08; TD ¶232,501
28. ¶F-4013; ¶3684.08; TD ¶232,517
29. ¶s F-3501, F-3600 *et seq.*; ¶3684.10; TD ¶236,202
30. ¶F-3701 *et seq.*; ¶3684.11; TD ¶236,401

31. ¶F-3800 *et seq.*; ¶3684.12, ¶79,006.07; TD ¶236,500 *et seq.*
32. ¶F-3626; ¶3684.05; TD ¶236,221
33. ¶F-3107; ¶3684.06; TD ¶236,408
34. ¶F-2103; ¶3684.14
35. ¶E-6001; ¶8514
36. ¶E-6500; ¶8564
37. ¶F-2101 *et seq.*; ¶3684.14

¶ 3544   Type A: Merger or consolidation.

A Type A reorganization is a merger or consolidation effected under statutory law (including foreign laws). (Code Sec. 368(a)(1)(A); Reg § 1.368-2(b)(1)(ii))[38] The merger of a disregarded entity into a corporation doesn't qualify as a tax-free statutory merger or consolidation, although the merger of a corporation into a disregarded entity may qualify. (Reg § 1.368-2)[39]

¶ 3545   Type B: Acquisition of stock in exchange for stock.

A Type B reorganization is the acquisition by one corporation of stock in a second (target) corporation in exchange *solely for voting stock* of the acquiring corporation (or voting stock of its parent in the case of a triangular Type B reorganization (¶3551)), if the acquiring corporation is in *control* (¶3553) of the target immediately after the exchange. (Code Sec. 368(a)(1)(B)) An acquiring corporation that transfers property other than voting stock in connection with a Type B reorganization plan doesn't violate the *solely for voting stock* requirement as long as the target's *stock* is acquired solely for voting stock.[40]

¶ 3546   Type C: Acquisition of a target's assets for stock.

A Type C reorganization is the acquisition by one corporation of *substantially all* of the properties of a target corporation in exchange for voting stock of the acquiring corporation (or the stock of its parent in the case of a triangular C reorganization (¶3551)). Except as noted below, liabilities assumed by the acquiring corporation are disregarded. (Code Sec. 368(a)(1)(C))[41]

There is no definition of *substantially all* of a target's properties or rules on what portion of the assets the target can safely retain.[42] However, for purposes of a favorable IRS ruling, the target must transfer at least 90% of the fair market value (FMV) of the net assets and at least 70% of the FMV of the gross assets that it held immediately before the transfer.[43]

A transaction won't qualify as a C reorganization unless the target, under the plan of reorganization, liquidates and distributes to its shareholders all stock, securities and other property received under the plan, as well as its other properties. IRS may waive this distribution requirement under certain conditions. (Code Sec. 368(a)(2)(G))[44]

To satisfy the *solely for voting stock* requirement, at least 80% of the FMV of property received must be acquired solely for voting stock. The remainder of the property may be acquired for cash or other property. If any cash or other property is transferred, liabilities assumed with respect to acquired properties are treated as cash. (Code Sec. 368(a)(2)(B))[45] Preexisting ownership by an acquiring corporation of a portion of the target's stock does not, in and of itself, prevent the solely for voting stock requirement from being satisfied. (Reg § 1.368-2(d)(4))[46]

¶ 3547   Type D: Transfer of assets to subsidiary.

A Type D reorganization is the transfer by one corporation of all or part of its assets to a second corporation, if, immediately after the transfer, the transferor and/or its shareholders are in control (¶3553) of the transferee corporation *and* the transferor satisfies a distribution requirement by:

... distributing all of the assets (including stock and securities) of the transferee to its

38. ¶F-2201 *et seq.*; ¶3684.01; TD ¶234,100
39. ¶F-2201.2 *et seq.*; ¶3684.01
40. ¶F-2500 *et seq.*; ¶3684.02; TD ¶234,601 *et seq.*
41. ¶F-2600 *et seq.*; ¶3684.03; TD ¶235,001
42. ¶F-2618; ¶3684.03; TD ¶235,018

43. ¶F-2618, F-2620; ¶3684.03; TD ¶235,020
44. ¶F-2629; ¶3684.03; TD ¶235,025
45. ¶F-2613; ¶3684.03; TD ¶235,014
46. ¶F-2617; ¶3684.03; TD ¶235,017

shareholders under a plan of reorganization as a part of the transferor's liquidation (*acquisitive* or *nondivisive* D); or

... distributing the stock and securities of the transferee in a tax-free spin-off, split-off or split-up (corporate separation, or *divisive* D (¶3559 *et seq.*). (Code Sec. 368(a)(1)(D))[47]

The distribution requirements of Code Sec. 368(a)(1)(D) and Code Sec. 354(b)(1)(B) are deemed satisfied even if no stock is actually distributed in cases where the same person or persons own(s) directly or indirectly all of the stock of the transferor and transferee corporations in the same proportions. Except in certain related party triangular reorganizations, if fair market value (FMV) is paid for the assets, the transferee is deemed to issue a nominal share of stock to the transferor, which is deemed further distributed as necessary to reflect actual ownership. (Reg § 1.368-2(l)(2))[48]

An acquiring corporation's transfer of target corporation assets to a controlled subsidiary as part of a plan of reorganization may not disqualify an otherwise qualifying D reorganization. (Reg § 1.368-2(k))[49]

A Type D reorganization may also qualify as a Type C, in which case it will be treated only as a Type D. (Code Sec. 368(a)(2)(A))[50]

¶ 3548   Type E: Recapitalization.

A Type E reorganization is a recapitalization (Code Sec. 368(a)(1)(E)) or change in the capital structure of a single corporation. A recapitalization may be achieved through an exchange of stock for stock, bonds for bonds, stock for bonds, or bonds for stock. Recapitalizations include:

... An issuance of preferred stock in discharge of outstanding bonds;

... An exchange of one class of common for another class of common, or preferred for common (provided that new preferred is not Section 306 stock (¶3534)), or vice-versa;

... An exchange of old bonds for new bonds with a different face value, interest rate, etc.;

... Changes in stock or securities effected by a change in the corporate charter. (Reg § 1.368-2(e))[1]

¶ 3549   Type F: Change in Identity.

A Type F reorganization is limited to a change in identity, form or place of organization *of one corporation* (Code Sec. 368(a)(1)(F)), but may include a reincorporation as part of a plan that includes a public stock offering, a merger, or a C reorganization.[2]

¶ 3550   Type G: Bankruptcy.

A Type G reorganization is the transfer by a corporation of all or part of its assets to another corporation (including a bridge bank) under a court-approved reorganization plan in a Title 11 or similar case (e.g., bankruptcy, receivership, or foreclosure), but only if stock or securities of the corporation to which the assets are transferred are distributed in a transaction that qualifies under Code Sec. 354, Code Sec. 355, or Code Sec. 356. (Code Sec. 368(a)(1)(G), Code Sec. 368(a)(3)(A))[3] The acquirer can use parent stock to acquire the debtor corporation in a triangular Type G reorganization. (Code Sec. 368(a)(2)(D))[4]

---

47. ¶s F-2004, F-2700 *et seq.*; ¶3684.04; TD ¶237,000
48. ¶F-2708 *et seq.*; ¶3684.041;
49. ¶F-2702.1
50. ¶s F-2004, F-2700 *et seq.*; ¶3684.04; TD ¶237,000

1. ¶F-3000 *et seq.*; ¶3684.05; TD ¶235,601
2. ¶F-3100 *et seq.*; ¶3684.06; TD ¶235,801
3. ¶F-3200 *et seq.*; ¶3684.07; TD ¶236,001
4. ¶F-3207; ¶3684.07; TD ¶236,007

¶ 3551 Triangular reorganizations.

Tax-free treatment applies to the following triangular reorganizations in which the acquirer's parent is a party to the transaction:

(1) *Forward triangular merger.* Where the acquirer uses parent stock to acquire *substantially all* of the target's assets (¶3546), the transaction is a forward triangular merger. If certain requirements are met, a forward triangular merger qualifies as a Type A reorganization. (Code Sec. 368(a)(2)(D))[5]

(2) *Triangular C reorganization.* Where the acquiring corporation acquires substantially all the assets of the target corporation solely in exchange for all or a part of the voting stock of the acquirer's parent, the transaction qualifies as a triangular Type C reorganization.[6] The acquiring corporation can distribute to its parent (i.e., have its parent assume) a substantial portion of the target's liabilities that it assumed without disqualifying the Type C reorganization. (Reg § 1.368-2(k)(1)(i))[7] A triangular reorganization qualifies for Type B treatment if acquirer acquires target stock solely in exchange for parent stock.[8]

(3) *Reverse triangular merger.* If the acquiring corporation acquires enough of target's stock for control and then merges into the target with the target surviving, the transaction is a reverse triangular merger. (Code Sec. 368(a)(2)(E))[9] A reverse triangular merger is tax-free despite a later sale of half of the target's operating assets.[10] If certain requirements are met, a reverse triangular merger may qualify as a Type A or Type B reorganization. (Reg § 1.368-2(k)(1)(ii))[11]

¶ 3552 Transfer of property acquired in a reorganization.

An otherwise tax-free reorganization is not disqualified by one or more later (or successive) transfers of assets or stock, provided that (i) there is continuity of business enterprise (¶3542), (ii) target's corporate existence is not terminated in connection with the drop-down, and (iii) the drop-down does not cause the target to cease to be a member of the qualified group. (Reg § 1.368-2(k))[12]

¶ 3553 Control defined.

For purposes of the rules for reorganizations (other than nondivisive Type Ds), *control* is the ownership of: (i) stock possessing at least 80% of the total combined voting power of all voting stock, and (ii) at least 80% of the total number of shares of each class of nonvoting stock. (Code Sec. 368(c))[13] For nondivisive Type Ds, *control* is defined under the related corporation redemption rules (i.e., 50%, rather than 80%, ownership, see ¶3533). (Code Sec. 368(a)(2)(H)(i))[14]

If the corporate division requirements of Code Sec. 355 (¶3560) are satisfied, control isn't affected by later transfers by shareholders of the distributed controlled corporation stock or by the issuance by the corporation whose stock was distributed of additional stock. (Code Sec. 368(a)(2)(H)(ii))[15]

¶ 3554 How shareholders are taxed in a reorganization.

If, under a plan of reorganization, the holder of stock or securities receives only stock in a corporation that's a party to the reorganization, the recipient recognizes no gain or loss.

5. ¶F-2301 *et seq.*; ¶3684.01; TD ¶234,200
6. ¶F-2650; TD ¶235,028
7. ¶F-2651 *et seq.*; ¶3684.08; TD ¶235,028
8. ¶F-2551; ¶3684.08; TD ¶234,614
9. ¶F-2401 *et seq.*; ¶3684.01; TD ¶234,400
10. ¶F-2413

11. ¶F-2400; ¶3684.01; TD ¶234,401
12. ¶F-2308, ¶F-3251; ¶3684.135; TD ¶234,209, TD ¶234,414, TD ¶235,027
13. ¶F-4502, ¶F-5500 *et seq.*; ¶3684.13; TD ¶236,701
14. ¶F-2702; ¶3684.13; TD ¶235,404
15. ¶F-4502; ¶3684.13; TD ¶237,003

Nonrecognition also applies when securities of a corporate party to the reorganization are received in exchange for other securities, if the principal (face) amount of the securities received isn't more than the face amount given up. (Code Sec. 354(a)(1))[16] Nonqualified preferred stock (¶3556) received for stock that isn't nonqualified preferred stock is not treated as stock or securities for these purposes unless it's received in a recapitalization (¶3548) of a family-owned corporation. (Code Sec. 354(a)(2)(C))[17] Stock rights (except to acquire nonqualified preferred stock (¶3556)) (Reg § 1.356-6(a)(2))[18] not received as part of a family corporation recapitalization (¶3548) (Reg § 1.356-6(b)(1)) are treated as securities with no principal amount. (Reg § 1.354-1(e), Reg § 1.355-1(c))[19] For the treatment of nonqualified preferred stock and excess securities as boot, see ¶3556.

Type D and Type G reorganizations are not tax-free unless (i) the transferee corporation receives substantially all of the transferor's assets, and (ii) the stock, securities and other property received by the transferor, as well as its remaining assets, are distributed by the transferor under the reorganization plan. (Code Sec. 354(b))[20]

If nonrecognition would apply but for the fact that property other than stock or securities (i.e., boot (¶3556)) is also received in the exchange, gain is recognized up to the sum of the boot received. (Code Sec. 356(a)(1))[21] Gain recognized in a reorganization with boot is treated as a dividend if the exchange has the effect of a distribution (see ¶3526). The gain is treated as ordinary income to the extent of the taxpayer's ratable share of the accumulated earnings and profits (E&P) of the distributing corporation, and the balance is treated as gain from the sale or exchange of property. (Code Sec. 356(a)(2))[22]

For basis of property received in the exchange, see ¶2488.

¶ 3555   How the corporate parties are taxed in a reorganization.

No gain or loss is recognized by a corporation that is a party to a reorganization (¶3542) and that exchanges property solely for stock or securities of another corporation that is also a party to that reorganization. (Code Sec. 361(a))[23] If the corporation receives other property or money (boot, see ¶3556) in addition to stock or securities, then if the corporation distributes all of the boot, it doesn't recognize gain on the exchange (but may recognize gain on the distribution of appreciated property, see below). However, if the corporation does not distribute any part of the boot, gain is recognized on the exchange, but only to the extent of the undistributed boot. (Code Sec. 361(b))[24]

Gain or loss isn't recognized on the distribution of *qualified property* received under the plan of reorganization. Qualified property is stock (or the right to acquire stock) in the distributing corporation, and stock or obligations of another party to the reorganization that are received in the reorganization exchange. Gain (but not loss) is recognized on the distribution of property that isn't qualified property. (Code Sec. 361(c))[25]

For acquirer's basis in property received in the exchange, see ¶2484. For target's basis, see ¶2486.

¶ 3556   Boot.

Boot is money or the fair market value (FMV) of property other than stock or securities of a party to the reorganization (¶3542) that's received by the target in exchange for its property, or by target shareholders in exchange for their stock, under the plan of reorganization.[26] Nonqualified preferred stock received for stock other than nonqualified preferred stock is boot

---

16. ¶F-4001, F-4022; ¶s 3544.01, 3544.03; TD ¶232,501
17. ¶F-4001, F-4001.1; ¶s 3544.01, 3544.03; TD ¶232,501
18. ¶F-4012.1; TD ¶232,515
19. ¶F-4012; ¶3544.06; TD ¶232,514
20. ¶s F-2701, F-3205; ¶3544.02; TD ¶235,401
21. ¶F-4017; ¶3564.02; TD ¶232,529

22. ¶F-4017; ¶3564.02; TD ¶232,533
23. ¶F-4100 *et seq.*; ¶3614.01; TD ¶233,001
24. ¶F-4106 *et seq.*; ¶3614.01; TD ¶233,003
25. ¶F-4108 *et seq.*; ¶3614.03; TD ¶233,007
26. ¶F-4017; ¶3564.01; TD ¶231,305

unless received in a recapitalization of a family-owned corporation. (Code Sec. 356(e))[27] Non-qualified preferred stock is generally preferred stock that the issuer is required to redeem, or is more likely than not to redeem, or preferred stock with a dividend rate that varies with changes in interest rates or other similar indices. (Code Sec. 351(g)(2))[28] For the effect of liabilities on characterization of property as boot, see ¶3557.

Securities in corporations not parties to the reorganization are always boot and gain is taxable to the extent of the securities' FMV. In the case of securities in corporations that are parties to the reorganization, only the excess face amount of securities received over the face amount of securities surrendered is boot. If no securities are surrendered, the FMV of any securities received is boot. (Code Sec. 354(a)(2), Code Sec. 356(d)) A stock right treated as a security having no principal amount (¶3554) isn't boot whether or not securities are surrendered in the exchange. (Reg § 1.356-3(b))[29]

¶ 3557 Assumption and transfer of liabilities.

Where a party to a reorganization (¶3542) exchanges property for stock or securities in a corporation and the corporation assumes the transferor's liabilities, the assumed liabilities are not treated as boot (¶3556) for the purpose of *recognizing* gain. (Code Sec. 357(a))[30] However, if the principal purpose for the assumption of the liabilities is tax avoidance, or is something other than a bona fide business purpose, *all the liabilities assumed* are treated as cash (i.e., boot) for purposes of both computing *and* recognizing gain. (Code Sec. 357(b))[31]

If, in the case of a Type D reorganization (¶3547) in which stock or securities of the transferee corporation are distributed in a qualifying tax-free separation under Code Sec. 355 (¶3559), the sum of the liabilities assumed exceeds the total adjusted basis of the property transferred, the excess is taxed as a gain from the sale or exchange of property (capital gain or ordinary, depending on the character of the property in the hands of the transferor). (Code Sec. 357(c))[32]

For what constitutes assumption of a liability, see ¶3516.

¶ 3558 Deductibility of reorganization costs.

Generally, expenses incurred in connection with a corporate reorganization, including borrowing costs, are capital expenditures (¶1655) and not deductible business expenses. If a proposed reorganization is abandoned, the costs are deductible in the year of abandonment.[33]

IRS has provided a safe harbor allowing taxpayers to allocate 70% of the success-based fees paid in business acquisitions or reorganizations to activities that don't facilitate the transaction and deduct such fees currently. The remaining 30% is treated as going to activities that facilitate the transaction and must be capitalized.[34]

¶ 3559 Spin-Offs, Split-Offs and Split-Ups.

A corporate division may be accomplished on a tax-free basis in the form of a (1) *spin-off*, i.e., a pro rata distribution of a controlled corporation's stock to the distributing corporation's shareholders without requiring the shareholders to surrender any of their distributing corporation stock; (2) *split-off*, i.e., a pro rata or non pro rata distribution of a controlled corporation's stock to one or more of the distributing corporation's shareholders in exchange for stock held in the distributing corporation; or (3) *split-up*, i.e., a transfer of all the businesses of a distributing corporation to

27. ¶F-4001.1; ¶3564.01; TD ¶231,305
28. ¶F-1530; ¶3514.13; TD ¶231,306
29. ¶F-4021 *et seq.*; ¶3564.01; TD ¶238,006
30. ¶F-4201; ¶3574.01; TD ¶231,501

31. ¶F-4202; ¶3574.02; TD ¶231,504
32. ¶F-4203; ¶3574.03; TD ¶233,203
33. ¶L-5401, ¶L-5416; ¶2484; TD ¶301,047, TD ¶301,037
34. ¶L-5762.1A, TD ¶256,327.1

controlled corporations followed by a distribution of the stock of the controlled corporations to the distributing corporation's shareholders and the liquidation of the distributing corporation. The distribution of controlled corporation stock to the distributing corporation's shareholders can be pro rata or non pro rata.[35]

¶ 3560   Requirements for a tax-free spin-off, split-off or split-up.

The following requirements for nonrecognition apply to spin-offs, split-offs, or split-ups.

(1) The distributing corporation (P) must distribute to its shareholders "with respect to" their stock, or to its security holders in exchange for their securities, solely stock or securities in a corporation (S) that it "controls" (¶3553) immediately before the distribution. (Code Sec. 355(a)(1)) Although "control" is generally defined in terms of stock ownership, IRS has privately ruled that a membership interest can satisfy Code Sec. 355(a)(1)(A)'s requirement that the distribution be made to a shareholder "with respect to" its stock. Nonqualified preferred stock (¶3514) received in exchange for other than nonqualified preferred stock is not treated as stock or securities for this purpose. (Code Sec. 355(a)(3)(D))[36]

(2) The transaction must not be used principally as a device for distributing earnings and profits (E&P) of either P or S. (Code Sec. 355(a)(1)(B)) The regs identify "device factors" (the presence of which are evidence of a device) and nondevice factors, and certain distributions that aren't ordinarily considered to have been used principally as a device even though device factors are present. (Reg § 1.355-2(d))[37]

(3) There must be continuity of interest (¶3542), i.e., P's pre-distribution shareholders must end up with an amount of stock that establishes a continuity of interest in both P and S, though not necessarily proportionately (see (6), below). (Reg § 1.355-2(c)(1))[38]

(4) Both P and S (or each controlled subsidiary) must be engaged in the active conduct of a trade or business immediately after the distribution. (Code Sec. 355(b)(1)(A)) A corporation satisfies the active conduct of a trade or business test if and only if it is engaged in the active conduct of a trade or business (Code Sec. 355(b)(2)(A)) with all members of the corporation's separate affiliated group being treated as one corporation. (Code Sec. 355(b)(3)(A))[39] The trades or businesses must have been actively conducted throughout the five-year period ending on the date S's stock is distributed. (Code Sec. 355(b)(2)(B))[40]

(5) The active trade or business (see 4 above) must not have been acquired during the five-year period ending on the date S's stock is distributed in a transaction in which gain or loss was recognized. (Code Sec. 355(b)(2)(C))[41]

(6) A distribution doesn't qualify as a tax-free Code Sec. 355 division if immediately after the transaction (including any series of related transactions) (1) either the distributing or controlled corporation is a disqualified investment corporation,[42] and (2) any person that did not hold 50% or more by vote or value in the disqualified investment corporation immediately before the transaction holds a 50% or greater interest (voting or value). (Code Sec. 355(g))[43]

(7) P must distribute either all its stock or securities in S, or at least an amount of S stock that's treated as "control" (¶3553). The distributions don't have to be pro rata or under a plan of reorganization. However, if P retains *any* stock or securities in S, tax avoidance must not be a principal purpose for the retention. (Code Sec. 355(a)(1)(D), Code Sec. 355(a)(2))[44]

In addition, one or more corporate business purposes must support the transaction for

35. ¶F-4600 *et seq.*; ¶3554.01; TD ¶237,001
36. ¶F-4608; ¶3544.01; TD ¶237,002
37. ¶F-4701 *et seq.*; ¶3554.01; TD ¶237,201
38. ¶F-4613; ¶3554.03; TD ¶237,014
39. ¶F-4802 *et seq.*; ¶3554.02; TD ¶237,426.1

40. ¶F-4819; ¶3554.02; TD ¶237,403
41. ¶F-4826 *et seq.*; ¶3554.02; TD ¶237,409
42. ¶F-5403; ¶3554.035
43. ¶F-5401; ¶3554.035; TD ¶237,004.1
44. ¶F-4602 *et seq.*; ¶3544.01; TD ¶237,007

nonrecognition treatment to apply. (Reg § 1.355-2(b))[45] IRS established guidelines for whether a corporate business purpose exists.[46]

¶ 3561 Boot taxed to shareholders in Sec. 355 transactions.

The receipt of boot in an otherwise tax-free spin-off, split-off or split-up (¶3560) may trigger shareholder tax. Boot includes cash and the fair market value of:

... Any property (including stock warrants, short-term notes, etc.) *except* (and subject to the limitations below) stock or securities (other than nonqualified preferred stock (¶3556) (Code Sec. 356(e)) in the spun-off corporation (S) (Code Sec. 356(a));

... Any excess in the face amount of securities of S received over the face amount of securities in distributing corporation (P) which are surrendered. (Code Sec. 355(a)(3)(A), Code Sec. 356(d)(2)(C)) Stock rights are treated as securities having no principal amounts. (Reg § 1.355-1(c))

... Stock in S that P acquired in a partially or wholly taxable transaction during the five-year period preceding the distribution. (Code Sec. 355(a)(3)(B))[47]

Boot received in a spin-off (where no stock or securities of P are surrendered) is treated like a Code Sec. 301 dividend (¶1286). (Code Sec. 356(b))[48]

Boot received in a split-off or split-up (where stock or securities of P are surrendered) is taxable to the recipient to the extent gain is recognized, but not in excess of the value of the boot received. (Code Sec. 356(a)(1)) If, however, the exchange "has the effect of the distribution of a dividend," it is treated as a dividend to the extent of the taxpayer's ratable share of accumulated earnings and profits. The remainder, if any, of the recognized gain is generally treated as capital gain. (Code Sec. 356(a)(2))[49] In determining whether boot has the effect of a dividend, the transaction is treated as though the shareholder had retained the P stock which he actually surrendered in exchange for S stock, and had received the boot in exchange for an amount of P stock with a value equal to the amount of the boot; the redemption rules (¶3526 *et seq.*) are then applied to determine whether the boot is treated as a dividend.[50]

No loss is recognized, whether or not boot is received. (Code Sec. 355(a), Code Sec. 356(c))[1]

For shareholders' basis in property received, see ¶2488.

¶ 3562 How distributing corporation is taxed.

No gain or loss is generally recognized by a distributing corporation (P) on its distribution of stock or securities of a corporation it controls (S) in a tax-free corporate separation (Code Sec. 355(c)(1), Code Sec. 361), with the following exceptions.

(1) The distribution is *disqualified* (as defined below), in which case P recognizes gain (but not loss) as if the property were sold for its fair market value (FMV). If the distributee assumes a liability to which the property was subject, the property's FMV will be no less than the assumed liability. (Code Sec. 355(c)(2), Code Sec. 355(d)(1) *et seq.*)[2]

(2) Pursuant to *a plan or series of related transactions*, there is an acquisition (direct or indirect) of an interest greater than or equal to 50% in either S or P following the distribution, in which case P generally must recognize gain as if it had sold the stock or securities of S to the distributee for FMV immediately before the distribution. (Code Sec. 355(e)) Regulations discuss factors for and against a finding of a plan or a series of related transactions and describe nine safe harbors to avoid gain recognition. (Reg § 1.355-7)[3]

---

45. ¶F-4900 *et seq.*; ¶3554.03; TD ¶237,701
46. ¶F-4902 *et seq.*; ¶3554.03; TD ¶237,702
47. ¶F-5003 *et seq.*; ¶s 3554.01, 3564.02; TD ¶238,004 *et seq.*
48. ¶F-5000 *et seq.*; ¶3564.02; TD ¶238,004
49. ¶F-5000 *et seq.*; ¶3564.02; TD ¶238,003

50. ¶F-4026; ¶3564.02; TD ¶232,534
1. ¶F-5000 *et seq.*; ¶3564.02; TD ¶238,204
2. ¶F-5201 *et seq.*; ¶s 3554.01, 3554.04; TD ¶238,205
3. ¶F-5301; ¶s 3554 *et seq.*

Tax-free division treatment isn't available for distributions from one affiliated group member to another except as provided in regulations if it is part of a plan under which any person acquires (directly or indirectly) an interest greater than or equal to 50% in either P or S, determined after application of Code Sec. 355(e). (Code Sec. 355(f))[4]

A distribution is disqualified (unless it doesn't violate the purpose of Code Sec. 355(d) (Reg § 1.355-6(c)(4)(i))) if (1) immediately after the distribution, any shareholder (or any two or more shareholders acting under a plan (Reg § 1.355-6(b)(3))) holds (actually or constructively) at least 50% of the stock of P or S, and (2) that stock was purchased (or acquired) within the immediately preceding five-year period, or was received as a distribution on P stock purchased (or acquired) during that period. (Code Sec. 355(c), Code Sec. 355(d))[5]

Changes in proportionate ownership attributable solely to fluctuations in the relative FMV of different classes of stock are generally not considered in determining stock ownership under Code Sec. 382. (Code Sec. 382(l)(3)(C)) In interim guidance, IRS indicated that it won't challenge a reasonable application of either a full value methodology or the hold constant principle (including certain HCP alternative methodologies) that is applied consistently.[6]

¶ 3563   Carryovers of Tax Items.

A corporation that acquires the assets of another corporation in certain tax-free reorganizations or liquidations also succeeds to and takes into account numerous tax items of the transferor (predecessor) corporation.

A predecessor's tax items are carried over to the successor corporation in a:

... Type A, C or F reorganization;

... Type D or G reorganization, but only if the transferor transfers substantially all its assets to the acquiring corporation and then (in effect) completely liquidates; or

... Complete liquidation of an 80% subsidiary. (Code Sec. 381(a))[7]

The carryover rules do not generally apply to divisive reorganizations, but items may be carried over under general principles of corporate succession. (Reg § 1.381(a)-1(b))[8]

¶ 3564   Tax attributes that are carried over.

When the Code's carryover provisions apply, the acquiring corporation succeeds to and takes into account the following tax items of the transferor (Code Sec. 381(c)): accounting method; amortization of bond discount or premium; capital loss carryovers; charitable contributions carryover; depreciation allowance and method; earnings and profits (E&P); employee benefit plan contributions; general business credit; installment method; inventory method; involuntary conversions; minimum tax credit; mining development and exploration expenses; net operating loss carryovers; percentage depletion on extraction of ores or minerals from waste or residue of earlier mining; personal holding company (PHC) deficiency dividend; PHC dividend carryover; real estate investment trust (REIT) or regulated investment company (RIC, or mutual fund) deficiency dividend; tax benefit items; items under Subchapter U (dealing with enterprise zones), as prescribed by regs.[9]

IRS has also privately ruled that, despite the lack of specific authority on the issue, the transferee in a Code Sec. 351 drop-down transaction followed by a Type D reorganization succeeded to the transferor's Code Sec. 59(e) election.[10]

Tax attributes to which an acquiring corporation succeeds, including the basis of property acquired, must reflect reductions for cancellation of debt. (Reg § 1.108-7(c))[11]

---

4. ¶F-4630 *et seq.*; TD ¶237,004
5. ¶F-5202 *et seq.*; ¶3554.04; TD ¶238,404
6. ¶F-7505.1
7. ¶F-7000 *et seq.*; ¶3814.01; TD ¶240,100

8. ¶F-7005; ¶F-7013; ¶3814.01; TD ¶240,100
9. ¶F-7012, F-7098, F-7099; ¶3814.02; TD ¶240,101
10. ¶A-8194; ¶594; TD ¶269,003
11. ¶J-7404.2; ¶1084.02; TD ¶188,016.1

¶ 3565   Tax Avoidance Acquisition Bar to Tax Benefits.

Under Code Sec. 269, any deduction, credit or other allowance may be disallowed where, for the principal purpose of tax avoidance:

... Any person or persons acquire, directly or indirectly, stock having at least 50% of the total combined voting power of all classes of a corporation's voting stock, or at least 50% of the total value of all classes of its stock; or

... Any corporation acquires, directly or indirectly, property of another corporation not controlled, directly or indirectly, by the acquirer (or its shareholders) immediately before the acquisition, if the acquirer takes a carryover basis in the property. (Code Sec. 269(a))[12]

IRS may also disallow tax attributes where a target that a corporation acquired in a qualified stock purchase (¶3583) *without* making a Code Sec. 338 election (¶3581) is liquidated primarily for tax avoidance or evasion, under a plan of liquidation adopted within two years after the acquisition date. (Code Sec. 269(b))[13]

¶ 3566   Limits on Use of Built-in Gains of One Corporation to Offset Losses of Another.

When one corporation is acquired by another corporation, there are limits on the extent to which built-in gains of one of the corporations (gain corporation) can be used to offset the other corporation's pre-acquisition losses. Specifically, if a corporation acquires directly (or through one or more other corporations) control of another corporation, or acquires the assets of another corporation in a Type A, C, or D reorganization, and either corporation is a gain corporation, then any income of either corporation attributable to recognized built-in gain within a five-year period beginning on the date of the ownership change (¶3571) can't be offset by any pre-acquisition loss of the other corporation. (Code Sec. 384(a))[14] Control means stock ownership that satisfies the requirements at ¶3338. (Code Sec. 384(c)(5))[15]

Similar rules limit the use of any excess credit or net capital loss. (Code Sec. 384(d))[16]

The above offset prohibition doesn't apply to any pre-acquisition loss of any corporation if that corporation and the gain corporation were members of the same controlled group at all times during the five-year period ending on the acquisition date (or shorter period of either corporation's existence). (Code Sec. 384(b))[17]

¶ 3567   Trafficking in Net Operating Losses (NOLs) and Other Carryovers—Code Sec. 382 Limitation.

If an ownership change occurs with respect to a loss corporation, that corporation's taxable income for any post-change year can be offset by pre-change losses only to the extent of a certain percent of the value of the corporation at the time of the change. Similar rules limit the use of capital loss carryovers and carryovers of certain credits.

¶ 3568   The Code Sec. 382 limitation on loss carryovers after an ownership change.

A *loss corporation* is entitled to use a net operating loss (NOL) carryover or has an NOL for the tax year in which an ownership change (¶3571) occurs (Code Sec. 382(k)(1))[18] and may offset taxable income for any tax year ending after the ownership change by pre-change loss carryforwards only to the extent of the Section 382 limitation for that year. (Code Sec. 382(a))[19] The Section 382 limitation for any post-change year is equal to the value of the

---

12. ¶F-7900 *et seq.*; ¶2694; TD ¶240,702
13. ¶F-7923 *et seq.*; ¶2694; TD ¶240,703
14. ¶s F-7851, F-7852; ¶3844; TD ¶240,801
15. ¶F-7853; ¶3844.01; TD ¶240,813

16. ¶F-7875 *et seq.*; ¶3844.04; TD ¶240,806
17. ¶F-7860 *et seq.*; ¶3844.01; TD ¶240,804
18. ¶F-7203; ¶3824.01
19. ¶F-7201; ¶3824.01; TD ¶240,302

loss corporation immediately before the ownership change multiplied by the long-term tax-exempt rate (¶3569). (Code Sec. 382(b)(1))[20] Value for Code Sec. 382 purposes is determined under special rules. (Code Sec. 382(e)(1), Code Sec. 382(e)(2), Code Sec. 382(l)(1)(A), Code Sec. 382(l)(4))[21]

If a loss corporation has net unrealized built-in gain on the change date in excess of a defined amount, the Section 382 limitation may be increased by recognized built-in gains on an asset within the five-year period starting on the date of the ownership change, but only if the asset was held immediately before the change date and only to the extent of the excess of the asset's fair market value over its adjusted basis on that date. Pre-paid income is not treated as built-in gain. The limitation may also be increased by certain recognized Code Sec. 338 gains. (Code Sec. 382(h)(1), Code Sec. 382(h)(6))[22] The disallowed portion of a recognized built-in loss can be carried forward like an NOL subject to the Section 382 limitation in later years as if it were a pre-change NOL. IRS guidance describes two alternative safe harbors to determine built-in income and deduction items after an ownership change.[23]

Special rules apply to determine the amount (and applicability) of the Section 382 limitation for the tax year in which the ownership change occurs. (Code Sec. 382(b)(3))[24] The Section 382 limitation doesn't apply if the old loss corporation is under the jurisdiction of a court in a bankruptcy, receivership, foreclosure, or similar proceeding (unless it elects not to have this exception apply). (Code Sec. 382(l)(5); Reg § 1.382-9(i))[25] Special rules apply for consolidated (Reg § 1.1502-90 to Reg § 1.1502-96, and Reg § 1.1502-98 to Reg § 1.1502-99) and controlled groups (Reg § 1.382-8), and for successive ownership changes. (Reg § 1.382-5(d))

¶ 3569 Long-term tax-exempt rate.

The long-term tax-exempt rate is the highest of the adjusted federal long-term rates for any month in the three-calendar month period ending with the month in which the ownership change occurs. (Code Sec. 382(f))[26] The long-term tax-exempt rate for ownership changes in:[27]

... Nov. 2013 is 3.50%
... Oct. 2013 is 3.50%
... Sept. 2013 is 3.28%
... Aug. 2013 is 3.16%
... July 2013 is 2.80%
... June 2013 is 2.70%
... May 2013 is 2.70%
... Apr. 2013 is 2.77%
... Mar. 2013 is 2.77%
... Feb. 2013 is 2.83%
... Jan. 2013 is 2.84%
... Dec. 2012 is 2.87%

¶ 3570 Pre-change losses and credits subject to Section 382 limitation.

The Section 382 limitation (¶3568) applies to (1) any net operating losses (NOLs) of the old loss corporation that are carried forward to the tax year ending with the ownership change or in which the change date occurs; (2) any NOL of the old loss corporation for the tax year in which the ownership change occurs to the extent the loss is allocable to the period in that

20. ¶F-7251; ¶3824.12; TD ¶240,314
21. ¶F-7301 *et seq.*; ¶3824.12; TD ¶240,315
22. ¶F-7340*et seq.*; ¶3824.25; TD ¶240,319 *et seq.*
23. ¶F-7340 *et seq.*; ¶3824.25; TD ¶240,321
24. ¶F-7255 *et seq.*; ¶3824.12; TD ¶240,323
25. ¶F-7700 *et seq.*; ¶3824.26; TD ¶240,325
26. ¶F-7336; ¶3824.12; TD ¶240,316
27. ¶F-7336; ¶3824.12; TD ¶240,316

year on or before the change date; (3) any recognized built-in loss for any tax year if a part of that tax year is in the recognition period (¶3568); (4) any pre-change capital loss (below); and (5) any pre-change credits (below). (Code Sec. 382(d)(1); Reg § 1.382-2(a)(2))[28] Pre-change capital losses are losses described in (1)–(3), but with respect to capital losses. (Reg § 1.383-1(c)(2))[29] Pre-change credits are excess foreign taxes under Code Sec. 904(c), unused Code Sec. 38 business credits, and the available Code Sec. 53 minimum tax credit, to the extent attributable to periods ending on or before the change date. (Reg § 1.383-1(c)(3))[30]

¶ 3571   Ownership change defined.

There is an ownership change if, immediately after any owner shift involving a 5% shareholder or an equity structure shift, the stock of the loss corporation owned by one or more 5% shareholders has increased by more the 50 percentage points over these shareholders' lowest percent ownership at any time during a three-year testing period. (Code Sec. 382(g)(1))[31]

A 5% shareholder is any person holding 5% or more by value of the stock of the corporation at any time during the testing period. (Code Sec. 382(h)(7)) The percent of stock owned is determined on the basis of value, and nonvoting preferred stock is generally not taken into account. (Code Sec. 382(k)(6))[32] Certain nonstock interests may be treated as stock. (Reg § 1.382-2T(f)(18)(iii))[33] Special aggregation rules apply to treat groups of shareholders as single shareholders. (Reg § 1.382-2T)[34]

¶ 3572   Limitations on credit and capital loss carryforwards—Section 383 limitation.

Code Sec. 383 provides limitations on the use of unused general business credits, unused minimum tax credits, excess foreign taxes and net capital losses similar to the limits on net operating loss carryovers. If an ownership change occurs in a loss corporation, the Section 382 limitation (¶3568) for a post-change year applies to limit the amount of taxable income and regular tax liability that may be offset, respectively, by pre-change capital losses and pre-change credits (¶3570) of the new loss corporation. (Code Sec. 383; Reg § 1.383-1(b))[35]

¶ 3573   Order of loss absorption for Section 382 limitation.

A loss corporation must absorb its Section 382 limitation in the following order for each post-change year: (1) pre-change losses that are built-in capital losses recognized during that year, (2) pre-change losses that are capital loss carryovers, (3) pre-change losses that are built-in ordinary losses recognized during that year, (4) pre-change losses that are net operating loss carryovers, (5) pre-change credits for excess foreign taxes carried forward under Code Sec. 904(c), (6) pre-change credits that are unused general business credits carried over under Code Sec. 39, and (7) pre-change credits that are unused minimum tax credits under Code Sec. 53. (Reg § 1.383-1(d)(2))[36]

The losses absorb the Section 382 limitation on a dollar-for-dollar basis, but the credits must be converted to a "deduction equivalent" for this purpose. (Reg § 1.383-1(e)(2))[37]

¶ 3574   Corporate Liquidations.

If a corporation distributes its assets to its shareholders in complete liquidation, the shareholders generally recognize capital gain or loss on the receipt of the distributions. A corporation generally recognizes taxable gain or loss on the distribution or sale of property in liquidation.

---

28. ¶F-7363; ¶s 3824, 3824.01, 3824.25
29. ¶F-7386; ¶3834.01; TD ¶240,329
30. ¶F-7408; ¶3834.01; TD ¶240,330
31. ¶F-7441; ¶3824.02; TD ¶240,303
32. ¶F-7505 *et seq.*; ¶s 3824.01, 3824.10; TD ¶240,303

33. ¶F-7603; ¶3824.10; TD ¶240,312
34. ¶F-7500 *et seq.*; ¶3824.15
35. ¶F-7400 *et seq.*, ¶E-8953.1; ¶3834.01; TD ¶240,328
36. ¶F-7360, F-7405; ¶3834.01; TD ¶240,331
37. ¶F-7361, F-7404; ¶3834.01; TD ¶240,331

¶ 3575   Shareholder's tax on liquidating distributions.

Amounts received by a shareholder in a distribution in complete liquidation of a corporation are treated as payment in exchange for the stock (i.e., capital gain or loss). (Code Sec. 331(a))[38] Gain or loss is the total amount distributed minus the shareholder's basis in his stock. (Reg § 1.331-1(b)) The amount of the distribution is the sum of the cash plus the fair market value of any other property (reduced by any liability assumed) received by the shareholder in exchange for his stock. (Code Sec. 1001(b))[39]

A shareholder who receives a series of distributions in complete liquidation of a corporation reports gain only after the cost or other basis of all of his stock has been recovered.[40]

For basis of property received in the distribution, see ¶2490.

¶ 3576   How corporations are taxed on liquidation.

A liquidating corporation recognizes taxable gain or loss on distributions of property as if the property had been sold to the distributee for its fair market value (FMV). (Code Sec. 336(a)) If the distributed property is subject to a liability, or if any shareholder assumes a liability of the liquidating corporation in connection with the distribution, the property's FMV is treated as not less than the amount of the liability. (Code Sec. 336(b))[41]

Exceptions apply for gain or loss on liquidating distributions made (i) by an 80%-owned subsidiary to its parent (¶3577), and (ii) in connection with tax-free reorganizations (¶3553, ¶3560). (Code Sec. 336(c))[42]

¶ 3577   Liquidation of 80% subsidiaries.

When a parent corporation completely liquidates its 80%-owned subsidiary, the *parent* (as shareholder) doesn't recognize gain or loss on the liquidating distributions (Code Sec. 332(a)), whether *cash* or other property is distributed,[43] if: (i) the parent owns at least 80% of the subsidiary stock by vote and value on the date the plan of liquidation is adopted and until the final liquidating distribution is received (Code Sec. 332(b)(1));[44] (ii) the distributions are made under a plan of *complete* liquidation, and in complete redemption of all of the subsidiary's stock (Code Sec. 332(b)(2), Code Sec. 332(b)(3));[45] and (iii) the distributions are made within one taxable year of the subsidiary, or within three years from the close of the taxable year during which the first of the series of distributions under the plan of liquidation is made. (Code Sec. 332(b); Reg § 1.332-4(a))[46]

If the 80% subsidiary liquidation qualifies for nonrecognition treatment, the parent takes a carryover basis in the distributed assets. (Code Sec. 334(b)(1))[47] Special rules apply to subsidiary liquidations when the subsidiary is indebted to its parent. (Reg § 1.332-7)[48]

Where a distribution from a regulated investment company (RIC) or a real estate investment trust (REIT) qualifies as a distribution in complete liquidation of the RIC or REIT under Code Sec. 332(b),[49] the corporation receiving the distribution is required to include in income as a dividend from the RIC or REIT an amount equal to the dividends-paid deduction allowable to the RIC or REIT by reason of the distribution.[50] (Code Sec. 332(c))

Minority shareholders of a subsidiary must generally recognize gain or loss under the regular liquidation rules (¶3575). (Reg § 1.332-5)[1]

---

38. ¶F-13101; ¶3314.01; TD ¶245,401
39. ¶F-13108; ¶3314.01; TD ¶245,402
40. ¶F-13112; ¶3314.01; TD ¶245,406
41. ¶F-14401 *et seq.*; ¶3364.01; TD ¶245,201 *et seq.*
42. ¶F-14401 *et seq.*; ¶3364.01; TD ¶233,011
43. ¶F-13200 *et seq.*; ¶3324; TD ¶245,701
44. ¶F-13202 *et seq.*; ¶3324.01; TD ¶245,703

45. ¶F-13207 *et seq.*; ¶3324.01; TD ¶245,714
46. ¶F-13209; ¶3324.01; TD ¶245,712
47. ¶F-13227 *et seq.*; ¶3344.01; TD ¶245,733
48. ¶F-13216 *et seq.*; TD ¶245,737
49. ¶F-13201; ¶3324.02; TD ¶245,701
50. ¶D-3800 *et seq.*, ¶D-3828
1. ¶F-13223; ¶3324.01; TD ¶245,738

¶ 3578 How 80% subsidiary is taxed on liquidating distributions.

A sub doesn't recognize any gain or loss on liquidating distributions to its 80% distributee-parent, but it does recognize gain (but not loss) on distributions to minority shareholders. (Code Sec. 336(d)(3), Code Sec. 337(a))[2] However, if property of a C corporation becomes the property of a regulated investment company (RIC) or real estate investment trust (REIT) by the qualification of that C corporation as a RIC or REIT or by the transfer of assets of that C corporation to a RIC or REIT, then the RIC or REIT will be subject to tax on the net built-in gain on the converted property under Code Sec. 1374 (¶3362) unless the C corporation elects to recognize gain and loss as if it sold the converted property to an unrelated party at its fair market value (deemed sale election). (Reg § 1.337(d)-7(c)(1)) An exception is provided in proposed regs (Prop Reg. § 1.337(d)-7 [taxpayers may rely]) for a transfer of property by a C corporation to a RIC or REIT to the extent that the transfer qualifies for nonrecognition treatment under Code Sec. 1031 (¶2418) or Code Sec. 1033 (¶2430). In these types of transactions, the C corporation's basis in the property it receives is derived from its basis in the transferred property and thus already reflects the built-in gain.

¶ 3579 Taxation of asset transfer to exempt entity or change to exempt entity status.

A corporation must recognize gain or loss on the transfer of its assets to a tax-exempt entity and on a change of its status to tax-exempt, subject to exceptions. (Reg § 1.337(d)-4)[3]

¶ 3580 Deductibility of costs of corporate dissolution and liquidation.

Filing fees, attorney's and accountant's fees and other expenditures, including payments for tax advice, incurred in connection with the complete liquidation and dissolution of a corporation are generally deductible in full by the dissolved corporation.[4]

¶ 3581 Code Sec. 338 Election to Treat a Stock Purchase as an Asset Purchase. ▬▬▬

A corporate acquirer that makes a qualified stock purchase (¶3583) of the stock of another corporation (target) may be able to get a stepped-up basis for the target's assets by making a Code Sec. 338 election to treat the stock purchase as an asset purchase.

🅡ⓘⓐ*observation:* The Code Sec. 338 election can best be used where the target has losses to offset gains, owns predominantly depreciated property, or will benefit from stepped-up basis through deductions for depreciation or amortization.

🅡ⓘⓐ*caution:* If a Code Sec. 338 election is made, the target may have to recognize gain from the "sale" of its assets (see ¶3582), and if the seller's basis in the target stock is less than the stock's fair market value, the seller must recognize gain on the sale of the stock.

For the consistency requirement, see ¶3584. For how and when to make the election, see ¶3585. For an election where target is a member of a consolidated group, see ¶3586.

¶ 3582 Effect of Code Sec. 338 election.

If a Code Sec. 338 election is made, the target is treated (for tax purposes only) as two corporations: an old target and a new target. The old target is treated as if it sold its assets as of the close of the acquisition date for their fair market value (FMV) (i.e., the "aggregate deemed sale price") in a single transaction. (Code Sec. 338(a)(1); Reg § 1.338-4(a))[5]

---

2. ¶F-14504; ¶3364; ¶3374.01; TD ¶246,201; TD ¶246,204
3. ¶F-14609 *et seq.*; ¶3374.03

4. ¶L-5500 *et seq.*; ¶2484; TD ¶301,048
5. ¶s F-8301, F-8302; ¶3384.05; TD ¶239,018

The new target is treated as though it had purchased all of the assets of the old target as of the beginning of the day after the acquisition date (Code Sec. 338(a)(2)), for an amount equal to the sum of: the grossed-up basis of the acquiring corporation's recently purchased stock, the basis of the acquiring corporation's nonrecently purchased stock, the target's liabilities, and other relevant items. This sum (as adjusted) is the target's "adjusted grossed-up basis" for the assets. (Code Sec. 338(b)(1), Code Sec. 338(b)(2); Reg § 1.338-5(b)(1))[6]

The acquirer may step up its basis in the target's assets by making a "gain recognition election" (on Form 8023, see ¶3585). (Code Sec. 338(b)(3); Reg § 1.338-5(d)(3))[7] Regs specify how basis is allocated among the target's assets. (Code Sec. 338(b)(5); Reg § 1.338-6)[8]

¶ 3583   "Qualified stock purchase" (QSP) requirement.

The Code Sec. 338 election may be made only if the acquiring corporation makes a QSP of the target. (Code Sec. 338(a))[9] A QSP occurs when one corporation's (acquiring) purchase, in one or more transactions during a 12-month acquisition period, of another (target) corporation's stock, if the shares so purchased have at least 80% of the target's total combined voting power and at least 80% of the value of all the target's stock. (Code Sec. 338(d)(3))[10]

¶ 3584   Consistency as to purchases from target or target affiliate.

The Code provides that purchases by a purchasing corporation with respect to a target or a target affiliate must be treated consistently (all as stock purchases or all as asset purchases) if made within a consistency period (defined below). (Code Sec. 338(e), Code Sec. 338(f)) But under the regs, the consistency rules apply only where gain on the sale of an asset (or stock in the case a Code Sec. 338(h)(10) election applies) (¶3586) results in a step-up in the seller's basis in the target's stock under the consolidated return regs. Instead of resulting in a deemed election, the rules require the acquiring corporation to take a carryover basis in the acquired stock. (Reg § 1.338-5(a))[11]

🛈 observation: A corporation recognizes gain on a sale in liquidation of the corporation. The consistency rules are limited to specific situations where the gain on the appreciated assets of the corporation isn't fully taxed.

The consistency period includes: (1) the one-year period before the beginning of the 12-month acquisition period, (2) that part of the acquisition period up to and including the acquisition date (i.e., the date on which the last purchase of stock needed to complete a qualified stock purchase is made) and (3) the one-year period beginning on the day after the acquisition date. (Code Sec. 338(h)(4)(A))[12]

¶ 3585   Making the Code Sec. 338 election—Form 8023.

The acquirer makes the Code Sec. 338 election on Form 8023 on or before the 15th day of the ninth month beginning after the month of the acquisition. (Code Sec. 338(g)(1))[13] Once made, the election is irrevocable. (Code Sec. 338(g)(3))[14]

¶ 3586   Election by selling consolidated group to recognize gain or loss on deemed sale of target's assets—Code Sec. 338(h)(10) election.

In the case of a qualified stock purchase (¶3583) of the stock of a member of a selling consolidated return group (selling group), the acquiring corporation and the selling group can

---

6. ¶F-8601 *et seq.*; ¶3384.09; TD ¶239,021
7. ¶F-8511; ¶3384.09; TD ¶239,023
8. ¶F-8601; ¶3384.10; TD ¶212,004.1
9. ¶F-8101; ¶3384; TD ¶239,013
10. ¶F-8101; ¶3384.02; TD ¶239,002

11. ¶F-8201 *et seq.*; ¶3384.11; TD ¶239,015
12. ¶F-8917; ¶3384.11; TD ¶239,017
13. ¶F-8701 *et seq.*; ¶3384.01; TD ¶239,027
14. ¶F-8706; ¶3384.01; TD ¶239,027

jointly elect (on Form 8023 (¶3585)) to have the selling group recognize (and report) gain or loss as though the target sold all of its assets in a single taxable transaction while still a member of the selling group. (Code Sec. 338(h)(10); Reg § 1.338(h)(10)-1(c))[15]

A Code Sec. 338(h)(10) election results in the following tax consequences:

. . . No gain or loss will be recognized by the selling group on the actual sale of target stock in a qualified stock purchase.

. . . The target is treated as if, at the close of the acquisition date but after the deemed sale, it had distributed all of its assets in complete liquidation under Code Sec. 331 (¶3576), or under the 80% subsidiary liquidation rules (¶3577).

. . . If the acquirer owns nonrecently purchased target stock, it is deemed to have made a "gain recognition election" with respect to that stock.

. . . The acquirer's adjusted gross-up basis in the target is determined under the rules described at ¶3582, with adjustments. (Reg § 1.338(h)(10)-1(d))[16]

¶ 3587 Code. Sec. 336(e) election to treat stock sales as asset transfers.

If a domestic corporation sells, exchanges, or distributes (or any combination thereof) stock of another domestic corporation amounting to 80% ownership (by vote and value) within a 12-month period, a Code Sec. 336(e) election can be made to treat the stock sale as an asset sale. The deemed asset sale follows the model of an election under Code Sec. 338(h)(10) (¶3586) for a qualified stock purchase (¶3583), with the result that gain is not recognized on the stock sale.[17]

¶ 3588 Transfers to Foreign Corporations—Code Sec. 367 Transfers. ■■■■■■

Transfers of property to foreign corporations (outbound transfers) that would otherwise be tax-free under Code Sec. 351 or under the reorganization or liquidation provisions are treated as transfers to non-corporate transferees for purposes of determining the extent to which gain is recognized on the transfer, unless an exception applies. (Code Sec. 367(c), Code Sec. 367(a)(1))[18]

Active foreign business exception. Subject to certain exceptions (below), assets may be transferred for use in a transferee's active conduct of a trade or business located outside of the U.S. on a nonrecognition basis if transferor complies with reporting requirements under Code Sec. 6038B. (Code Sec. 367(a)(3)(A); Reg § 1.367(a)-2T(a))[19]

However, this exception doesn't apply to transfers of certain "tainted assets," e.g., inventory, installment obligations and accounts receivable, foreign currency, intangibles, depreciation recapture and leased property, and these transfers are therefore subject to gain recognition. (Code Sec. 367(d); Reg § 1.367(a)-5T)[20] In addition, the exception doesn't apply to gain realized on the transfer of assets of a foreign branch of a U.S. person to a foreign corporation in a Code Sec. 367 exchange. In this case, gain is recognized to the extent necessary to recapture previously deducted losses. (Code Sec. 367(a)(3)(C); Reg § 1.367(a)-6T)[21] Therefore, a transferor with an overall foreign loss for foreign tax credit limitation purposes may be forced to recognize gain on the incorporation of a branch (with previously deducted losses).

Exceptions for certain stock transfers. The transfer of foreign corporation stock or securities by a U.S. person to another foreign corporation is not taxable under Code Sec. 367(a) if (i) the U.S. person owns less than 5% of the vote and value of the transferee stock immediately after the transfer, or (ii) the U.S. person enters into a gain recognition agreement ("GRA," see below) with respect to the transferred stock or securities. (Code Sec. 367(a)(2); Reg § 1.367(a)-

15. ¶F-8820 *et seq.*; ¶3384.075; TD ¶239,031
16. ¶F-8800 *et seq.*; ¶s 3384.075, 3384.09; TD ¶239,031
17. ¶E-10801; ¶3364.02; TD ¶607,901
18. ¶F-6000 *et seq.*; ¶3674.01

19. ¶F-6101; ¶3674.02
20. ¶F-6119 *et seq.*; ¶3674.03
21. ¶F-6129 *et seq.*; ¶3674.02

3(b)(1))[22] The transfer of foreign corporation stock as part of a Type E recapitalization qualifies for nonrecognition. (Reg § 1.367(a)-3(a))[23]

In addition, the transfer of U.S. stock or securities to a foreign corporation is not taxable under Code Sec. 367(a) if (i) U.S. transferors receive 50% or less of the vote and value of the transferee stock in the transaction, (ii) U.S. persons who are officers or directors of the U.S. target or 5% transferee shareholders do not own more than 50% of the transferee stock, (iii) either the U.S. transferor is not a 5% transferee shareholder, or, if the U.S. transferor is a 5% transferee shareholder, it enters into a GRA, and (iv) the transferee has been actively engaged in business for at least three years. (Reg § 1.367(a)-3(c))[24]

The above exceptions for transfers of assets used in a foreign trade or business and foreign stock do not generally apply to Code Sec. 361(a) and Code Sec. 361(b) outbound transfers incident to a reorganization. (Code Sec. 367(a)(5))[25] However, regs contain an elective exception under which, if five or fewer domestic corporations are in Code Sec. 368(c) control (¶3553) of the transferor corporation and subject to basis adjustment regs, the exceptions may apply to *asset* reorganizations under Code Sec. 361(a) or Code Sec. 361(b). (Reg § 1.367(a)-7)[26]

Qualification under some exceptions may require a GRA under which the U.S. transferor generally agrees to include in income any gain not recognized on the original transfer of stock or securities to the foreign corporation if the foreign transferee disposes of the stock or securities within five years. Certain nonrecognition transactions, however, are not triggering events when certain requirements are satisfied. (Reg § 1.367(a)-8)[27] The amount of gain recognized under a GRA when a disposition or other event requires recognition under more than one GRA is determined under an ordering rule. (Reg § 1.367(a)-8(c)(1)(ii))[28]

Outbound distributions of subsidiary stock under Code Sec. 355 are generally treated as exchanges and result in recognition of gain (but not loss) unless the distribution is made to a qualified U.S. person, i.e., a domestic corporation or a U.S. citizen or resident. (Code Sec. 367(e)(1); Reg § 1.367(e)-1)[29] Outbound parent-subsidiary liquidation distributions generally result in recognition of both gain and loss to the liquidating subsidiary. (Code Sec. 367(e)(2); Reg § 1.367(e)-2)[30] Code Sec. 381 applies to the carryover of certain tax attributes from the domestic corporation to the distributee foreign corporation (Reg § 1.367(e)-2(b)(3)(iii))[31]

---

22. ¶F-6202 *et seq.*; ¶3674.02
23. ¶F-6201; ¶3674.02
24. ¶F-6209 *et seq.*; ¶3674.02
25. ¶F-6207; ¶3674.02
26. ¶F-6239 *et seq.*; ¶3674.02

27. ¶F-6300 *et seq.*; ¶3674.02
28. ¶F-6300 *et seq.*; ¶3674.02
29. ¶F-6801; ¶3674.01
30. ¶F-6801 *et seq.*; ¶3374.01
31. ¶F-6912

Chapter 17 Partnerships

¶ 3700 Partnerships.

For tax purposes, a partnership is a business entity that has elected, or defaulted to, partnership classification under "check-the-box" entity classification regs.

¶ 3701 Partnership defined.

A "partnership" includes a syndicate, group, pool, joint venture or other unincorporated organization through, or by means of which, any business, financial operation or venture is carried on if it isn't, within the meaning of the Code, a corporation, trust or estate. (Code Sec. 761(a))[1] Under the "check-the-box" entity classification regs, a partnership is a business entity, with two or more members, that isn't mandatorily classified as a corporation, and that has elected, or defaulted, to partnership tax status. (Reg § 301.7701-2(c))[2] Under default provisions, unless a domestic eligible entity elects otherwise, it's a partnership if it has two or more members. (Reg § 301.7701-3(b)(1)(i))[3] In general, an eligible entity that wishes to elect a classification other than its default classification, or that wishes to change its classification, does so by filing Form 8832. (Reg § 301.7701-3(c)(1)(i))[4] A partnership that changes to an association is deemed to contribute all of its assets and liabilities to the association in exchange for stock in it. Then, the partnership is deemed to liquidate by distributing the stock to its partners. (Reg § 301.7701-3(g)(1)(i))[5] An eligible entity classified as a partnership becomes disregarded as an entity separate from its owner when the entity's membership is reduced to one member. (Reg § 301.7701-3(f)(2))[6]

A qualified joint venture conducted by a husband and wife who file a joint return for the tax year is not treated as a partnership for tax purposes if the spouses so elect. (Code Sec. 761(f)(1)) IRS has stated that a qualified joint venture includes only businesses owned and operated by spouses as co-owners, and not in the name of a state law entity (including a partnership or limited liability company).[7]

For tax years of a partnership, see ¶2812.

For partnership tax returns (including Schedule K-1 (Form 1065)), see ¶4731.

¶ 3702 Electing large partnerships.

Simplified flow-through reporting (Form 1065-B) applies for an electing large partnership, i.e., a partnership with at least 100 partners in the prior tax year that elects simplified reporting under Code Sec. 771 through Code Sec. 777. (Code Sec. 775(a)(1))[8] These rules differ from the regular rules for tax partners (¶3715 et seq.), in that, for example, fewer partnership items pass through to partners (Code Sec. 772)[9] and limitations on deductions and credits generally are applied at the partnership level. (Code Sec. 773)[10]

¶ 3703 Limited liability companies (LLCs).

LLCs are a creation of state law. LLCs are owned (and in some cases managed) by members who aren't personally liable for the LLC's debts or obligations.[11]

Under the "check-the-box" entity classification rules (¶3701), if an LLC isn't mandatorily classified as a corporation, it's an "eligible entity" that may elect (on Form 8832) to be

---

1. ¶B-1000 et seq.; ¶7614.01, 7614.03; TD ¶580,101
2. ¶D-1151; ¶77,014.15; TD ¶580,501
3. ¶D-1152; ¶77,014.15; TD ¶580,521
4. ¶D-1158; ¶77,014.15; TD ¶580,511
5. ¶D-1170; ¶77,014.155; TD ¶580,517
6. ¶D-1171; ¶77,014.165; TD ¶580,505

7. ¶B-1222; ¶7614.02
8. ¶B-4401 et seq.; ¶7754; TD ¶594,101
9. ¶B-4402 et seq.; ¶7724; TD ¶594,112
10. ¶B-4410 et seq.; ¶7734; TD ¶594,109
11. ¶D-1150 et seq.; TD ¶582,500

References beginning with a single letter are to paragraphs in RIA's Federal Tax Coordinator 2d and RIA's Analysis of Federal Taxes: Income. Those beginning with numbers are to paragraphs in RIA's United States Tax Reporter. Those beginning with TD are to paragraphs in RIA's Tax Desk.

579

classified for tax purposes either as a partnership or as a corporation (Reg § 301.7701-2(c)), except that a single member LLC that doesn't elect to be a corporation is treated as not having any entity status, i.e., it can't be treated as a partnership. (Reg § 301.7701-2(a), Reg § 301.7701-2(c)(2)(i))[12]

observation: If an LLC is characterized as a partnership for federal tax purposes, the LLC form will offer the flow-through of tax attributes, as well as limited liability. Pass-through of tax attributes and limited liability are also available to S corporations, but S corporations are subject to many restrictions (see ¶3351) that don't apply to LLCs.

¶ 3704   Family partnerships.

If capital isn't a material income-producing factor, a family member is recognized as a partner only if he contributes substantial services.[13]

If capital is a material income-producing factor in the enterprise, a valid family partnership may be created by gift of a capital interest. (Code Sec. 704(e)(1))[14]

The donee-partner's distributive share of partnership income is included in his gross income subject to two limitations:

. . . It must be determined after allowance of reasonable compensation for services rendered to the partnership by the donor.

. . . The donee's share attributable to donated capital must not be proportionately greater than the donor's share attributable to his capital. (Code Sec. 704(e)(2))[15]

A capital interest purchased from a partner by the partner's spouse, ancestor, lineal descendant or any trust for the primary benefit of such persons is considered to be a gift of the partnership interest by the seller to the buyer. (Code Sec. 704(e)(3))[16]

A donee or purchaser of a capital interest in a family partnership isn't recognized as a partner unless the transfer to him is bona fide. (Reg § 1.704-1(e)(1)(iii))[17]

A minor child generally won't be recognized as a partner unless either: (1) the child is shown to be competent (despite legal disability under state law) to manage his or her own property, or (2) control of the child's interest is exercised by a fiduciary for the child's sole benefit, subject to any required judicial supervision. (Reg § 1.704-1(e)(2)(viii))[18]

¶ 3705   Election to be excluded from partnership rules.

Certain unincorporated organizations can elect to be excluded from the partnership rules, i.e., exempt from Subchapter K of the Code (or only some of those provisions under a partial exclusion election). The election is available only if the income of each separate member of the partnership can be adequately determined without computation of partnership taxable income. (Code Sec. 761(a); Reg § 1.761-2(a)(1))[19] The election is available for:

. . . "Investing partnerships" whose members own property as co-owners, reserve the right separately to dispose of their share of property, and aren't engaged in the active conduct of a business. (Reg § 1.761-2(a)(2))[20]

. . . "Operating agreement groups" under which a number of co-owners engage in the joint production, extraction or use of property, but not for the purpose of selling services or property produced or extracted. (Reg § 1.761-2(a)(3))[21]

. . . Syndications formed for a short period by dealers in securities to underwrite, sell or

---

12. ¶D-1167; ¶77,014.15
13. ¶B-3422; ¶7044.17; TD ¶588,713
14. ¶B-3402; ¶7044.14; TD ¶588,702
15. ¶B-3423; ¶7044.12; TD ¶588,714
16. ¶B-3426; ¶7044.11; TD ¶588,702

17. ¶B-3408; ¶7044.15; TD ¶588,706
18. ¶B-3416; ¶7044.15; TD ¶588,708
19. ¶B-1200 *et seq.*; ¶7614.02; TD ¶581,006
20. ¶B-1207; ¶7614.02; TD ¶581,012
21. ¶B-1208; ¶7614.02; TD ¶581,013

distribute an issue of securities. (Code Sec. 761(a)(3))[22]

¶ 3706 Partnerships vs. other forms of doing business.

Partnerships are "pass-through entities" —that is, their income is subject to tax only once, at the partner level. They share this characteristic with S corporations, but not C corporations (whose income is taxed twice, at the corporate and again at the shareholder levels). Partnerships also offer these advantages over S corporations:

. . . There are no limitations on who may be a partner, or on how many persons may be partners, unlike an S corporation, which is subject to limitations on who may be a shareholder and on how many shareholders the corporation may have, see ¶3351.

. . . There is far greater flexibility in allocating the enterprise's profits, losses and credits (by means of special allocations, see ¶3724 *et seq.*) among partners of a partnership than among shareholders of an S corporation, see ¶3367.

. . . A partner's basis in his partnership interest, unlike a shareholder's basis in S corporation shares, includes the partner's share of partnership liabilities, see ¶3759 *et seq.*

¶ 3707 Organization and syndication fees.

No deduction is allowed to a partnership or to any partner for any amounts paid or incurred to organize a partnership or to promote the sale of, or to sell, an interest in that partnership, except as described below. (Code Sec. 709(a))[23]

A partnership may elect to deduct in the tax year it begins business up to $5,000 of its organization expenses. The $5,000 amount is reduced (but not below zero) by the amount, if any, by which the total of the organization expenses exceeds $50,000. Organization expenses in excess of the amount deductible in the year the partnership begins business are deductible ratably over the 180-month period beginning with the month in which it begins business. If a partnership is liquidated before the end of the 180-month period, any organization expenses not yet deducted may be deducted as a loss. (Code Sec. 709(b)(1))

A taxpayer (1) is deemed to have elected to expense/amortize organizational costs under Code Sec. 248 for the tax year in which the business begins, but (2) may forgo the deemed election by clearly electing to capitalize organizational expenditures on a timely filed Federal income tax return (including extensions) for the tax year in which the business begins. The choice of expensing/amortizing or capitalizing organizational expenditures is irrevocable and applies to all such expenditures. (Reg § 1.709-1(b)(2))

Syndication expenses aren't amortizable and must be capitalized. They are expenses connected with the marketing of interests in the partnership. (Reg § 1.709-2(b)) Syndication expenses can't be deducted as a loss when the partnership is liquidated (Reg § 1.709-1(b)(3)) or the syndication effort is abandoned.[24]

For an election to deduct start-up costs, see ¶1501.

¶ 3708 Partnership anti-abuse rules.

If a partnership is formed or used in connection with a transaction with a principal purpose of substantially reducing the present value of the partners' total tax liability in a manner that is inconsistent with the intent of subchapter K, IRS may recast the transaction as appropriate to achieve a tax result that is consistent with the intent of subchapter K.[25] These anti-abuse rules apply only with respect to federal income taxes. (Reg § 1.701-2(h))[26]

IRS also may treat a partnership as an aggregate of its partners, in whole or in part (except

22. ¶B-1215; ¶7614.02
23. ¶B-1301; ¶7094; TD ¶581,201
24. ¶B-1306; ¶7094.04; TD ¶581,207

25. ¶B-1251; ¶7014; TD ¶580,107
26. ¶B-1250 *et seq.*; ¶7014; TD ¶580,107

as described below), as appropriate in order to carry out the purpose of any provision of the Code or regs. (Reg § 1.701-2(e)(1)) But IRS may not treat a partnership as an aggregate to the extent that:

(1) a Code or reg provision prescribes the treatment of a partnership (in whole or in part) as an entity; and

(2) that treatment and the ultimate tax results, taking into account all the relevant facts and circumstances, are clearly contemplated by that provision. (Reg § 1.701-2(e)(2))[27]

¶ 3709   Treatment of Contributions to a Partnership. ■■■■■■■■

Contributions from a partner to a partnership are generally tax-free.

¶ 3710   Contributions to a partnership.

Whether contributions to a partnership's capital are made on formation of the partnership or later, no gain or loss is ordinarily recognized to the partners or the partnership. (Code Sec. 721; Reg § 1.721-1) However, this rule doesn't apply where a partner acts in his individual capacity (vs. as a partner) in a transaction with the partnership (¶3729); a partner contributes property to a partnership and the partnership assumes a liability of the partner, with the resulting decrease in the partner's liabilities being treated as a distribution of money to the contributing partner (¶3744); disguised sales;[28] or in the situations listed at ¶3711 *et seq.*[29] Also, IRS has regulatory authority (1) to provide for gain recognition in cases where the gain would otherwise be transferred to foreign partners (Code Sec. 721(c)) and (2) to treat intangibles transferred to a foreign partnership as sold. (Code Sec. 721(d)) Depreciation recapture isn't triggered (Code Sec. 1245(b)(3), Code Sec. 1245(b)(6), Code Sec. 1250(d)(3)),[30] and investment credit isn't recaptured, as long as the transfer is a mere change in the form of conducting the business of the contributing partner. (Reg § 1.47-3(f)(6), Ex (5))[31]

For gain or loss on the distribution of contributed built-in gain or loss property, see ¶3752.

¶ 3711   Exchange fund partnerships.

Gain is recognized where a transfer of appreciated stocks, securities or other property is made to a partnership that would be treated as an investment company under Code Sec. 351 were the partnership a corporation. (Code Sec. 721(b)) The partnership is treated as an investment company if, after the exchange, over 80% of the value of its assets (excluding cash and nonconvertible debt) are held for investment and are readily marketable stocks or securities (or interests in real estate investment trusts or regulated investment companies).

¶ 3712   Contribution of services.

Where a taxpayer receives a capital interest in a partnership in exchange for services, that interest is taxable compensation income to him. When the income must be recognized depends on the facts and circumstances, including whether there are any restrictions on the taxpayer's right to withdraw from the partnership or otherwise dispose of the partnership interest. (Reg § 1.721-1(b)(1))[32]

Where a taxpayer receives a profits interest in a partnership (even if substantially unvested) in exchange for services, IRS won't treat the transaction as giving rise to compensation income, unless: (1) the profits interest relates to a substantially certain and predictable stream of income from partnership assets; (2) the partner disposes of the profits interest within two years; or (3) the profits interest is a limited partnership interest in a publicly traded partnership. Cases hold that no income is includible where the profit interest has only

27. ¶B-1255; ¶7014; TD ¶580,109
28. ¶B-2100; ¶7074.02; TD ¶585,000
29. ¶B-1401; ¶7214; TD ¶581,401

30. ¶s I-10311, I-10503; ¶7214.01; TD ¶223,114
31. ¶L-17418; ¶474.03; TD ¶381,409
32. ¶B-1407 *et seq.*; ¶7214.01; TD ¶581,406

speculative value.[33]

¶ 3713 Partnership's basis in property contributed to it.

Property received by a partnership from a contributing partner takes the same basis in the partnership's hands as it had in the contributing partner's hands at the time of the contribution (increased by any gain recognized if the partnership is an "investment company partnership," see ¶3711). (Code Sec. 723; Reg § 1.723-1)[34]

¶ 3714 Partnership's holding period for contributed property.

A partnership's holding period for property contributed to it includes the contributing partner's holding period. (Code Sec. 1223(2); Reg § 1.723-1)[35]

¶ 3715 Partnership Income and Deductions. ▮▮▮▮▮▮▮▮▮▮▮▮▮▮▮▮

A partnership is essentially a conduit which passes through to each partner his share of income and deductions generated by the partnership.

¶ 3716 Partners taxed on partnership income.

The partners, not the partnership, are taxed on the partnership's income. (Code Sec. 701) The partnership only files an information return (Form 1065, see ¶4731) showing each partner's distributive share of the partnership income, gains, losses, etc. Each partner includes his share of these items on his own return. (Code Sec. 702)[36]

¶ 3717 Partnership taxable income.

Partnership taxable income is computed the same as an individual's, except the following deductions aren't allowed:

... standard deduction (Code Sec. 63(c)(6)(D));

... personal exemptions;

... charitable contributions;

... nonbusiness expenses, medical expenses, alimony, retirement savings under Code Sec. 219, and taxes and interest paid to cooperative housing corporations;

... capital loss carryovers;

... net operating loss deduction;

... taxes paid to a foreign country or U.S. possession that can be taken as a credit or as a deduction (income and similar taxes);

... oil and gas well depletion. (Code Sec. 703(a)(2); Reg § 1.703-1(a)(2))[37]

¶ 3718 "Separately stated" items of income and deductions.

Partnerships are required to "state separately" —that is, to compute as separate items— certain classes of income and deductions. These are then directly "passed through" to the partnership's partners, who take them into account for tax purposes by including their distributive share of each of the classes as separate items on their tax returns. (Code Sec. 702(a))

Key items that must be separately stated are:

... charitable contributions;

... dividends for which a dividends-received deduction is allowed to C corporations, or

---

33. ¶B-1408; ¶7214.01; TD ¶581,407
34. ¶B-1418; ¶7234.01; TD ¶581,411
35. ¶B-1419; ¶7234.01; TD ¶581,412

36. ¶B-1900 *et seq.*; ¶7014; TD ¶584,000 *et seq.*
37. ¶B-1901; ¶7034.01; TD ¶584,001

qualified dividend income eligible for long-term capital gains treatment by noncorporate taxpayers;

. . . foreign and U.S. possession taxes eligible for the foreign tax credit;

. . . income, gains and losses from the sale or exchange of unrealized receivables and substantially appreciated inventory;

. . . income, gain, loss, deduction or credit items that are specially allocated under the partnership agreement;

. . . intangible drilling and development expenses;

. . . long-term capital gains and losses (including separately reporting 28% rate gain and unrecaptured section 1250 gain, see ¶2605 *et seq.*);

. . . mining explorations expenditures;

. . . nonbusiness production of income expenses;

. . . recoveries of tax benefit items;

. . . Code Sec. 1231 gains and losses;

. . . short-term capital gains and losses;

. . . soil and water conservation expenses.

Partnerships must also separately state—and partners must separately take into account their distributive share of—any partnership item, if separately stating that item would result in a tax liability for any partner different from that partner's tax liability if the item weren't separately stated. (Reg § 1.702-1(a)(8))[38]

¶ 3719   Items not required to be separately stated.

After determining which of its items of income, gains, losses, deductions and credits must be separately stated, a partnership computes its taxable income or loss based on items that don't have to be separately stated. The partnership's partners, in computing their income tax liabilities, take into account their distributive shares of the partnership's nonseparately stated income or loss, as well as their distributive shares of each separately stated item. (Code Sec. 702(a)(8); Reg § 1.702-1(a)(9))[39]

¶ 3720   Character of partnership income.

Each item passed through to the partners and separately stated on their returns has the same character as if realized or incurred directly by the partnership. (Code Sec. 702(b); Reg § 1.702-1(b))[40]

¶ 3721   Consistent treatment on partner's and partnership's return— Form 8082.

A partner must, on his own return, treat a partnership item in a manner that's consistent with the treatment of that item on the partnership's return. (Code Sec. 6222(a)) A partner that treats a partnership item differently must notify IRS of the inconsistency on Form 8082. (Code Sec. 6222(b))[41]

The above consistency rule doesn't apply to certain small partnerships that aren't covered by the unified audit and review procedures for partnerships (¶4841). (Code Sec. 6231(a)(1)(B))[42]

---

38. ¶B-1903; ¶7024.01; TD ¶584,003
39. ¶B-1904; ¶7024.01; TD ¶584,004
40. ¶B-1905; ¶7024.02; TD ¶584,005

41. ¶B-1801; ¶62,214; TD ¶584,010
42. ¶T-2104; ¶62,214.10

¶ 3722   When partnership income is reported by the partners.

Each partner reports his distributive share of the partnership income, deductions and other items (including guaranteed salary and interest payments) for a partnership tax year on his individual return for his tax year within or with which the partnership tax year (discussed at ¶2812) ends. (Code Sec. 706(a); Reg § 1.706-1(a))[43]

If two partnership tax years end within a partner's individual tax year, he must report in that year his share of the partnership income for both partnership years.[44]

¶ 3723   Elections.

Elections affecting partnership taxable income must be made by the partnership except for certain elections involving discharge of indebtedness, foreign tax credits, mining exploration costs, and the election by nonresident alien individuals and foreign corporations regarding income from U.S. real property, which must be made by each partner for himself.[45]

¶ 3724   Partnership Allocations. ▬▬▬▬▬▬▬▬▬▬▬▬▬▬▬▬▬▬

A partner's distributive share of income, gain, loss, deduction or credit is controlled by the partnership agreement, unless there is no partnership agreement or the allocation in the agreement has no substantial economic effect; then, the allocation is made in accordance with the partner's interest in the partnership.

¶ 3725   Allocation rules.

A partnership's allocations (the partners' distributive shares) of partnership income, gains, losses, deductions and credits are normally determined by the partnership agreement. (Code Sec. 704(a)) If, however, the partnership agreement fails to make such allocations, they must be determined in accord with the partners' interests in the partnership. (Code Sec. 704(b)(1)) If the partnership agreement does make allocations of partnership items, these will be respected for tax purposes if:

. . . they have substantial economic effect, see ¶3726; or

. . . they are in accord with the partners' interests in the partnership; or

. . . they are treated as being in accord with the partners' interests in the partnership. (Code Sec. 704(b); Reg § 1.704-1(b)(1))[46]

Special allocation rules apply to: built-in gain and loss property (¶3752); tax preferences associated with pre-'87 cost recovery property;[47] income, gains, losses, etc., with respect to property whose book value differs from its adjusted basis;[48] tax credits and credit recapture amounts;[49] creditable foreign taxes;[50] "excess percentage depletion;" [1] the basis of partnership oil and gas properties;[2] recapture income under Code Sec. 1245 and Code Sec. 1250;[3] and allocations attributable to the partnership's nonrecourse debt.[4]

Retroactive allocations—that is, allocations that give particular partners shares of partnership items of income, expense, etc., that were paid or accrued before these partners joined the partnership—aren't permitted. (Code Sec. 706(d)(1))[5]

Except to the extent provided in regs to be issued, if there is a change in any partner's interest during any partnership tax year, each partner's share of any "allocable cash basis

---

43. ¶B-1701; ¶7064; TD ¶584,008
44. ¶B-1701; TD ¶584,008
45. ¶B-1907; ¶7034.02; TD ¶584,007
46. ¶B-2401; ¶7044; TD ¶586,101
47. ¶B-2901
48. ¶B-2902; ¶7044.07; TD ¶586,101
49. ¶B-2903; ¶7044.07; TD ¶586,101

50. ¶B-2903.1; ¶7044.07
1. ¶B-2904; ¶7044.07; TD ¶586,101
2. ¶B-2905; ¶7044.07; TD ¶586,101
3. ¶B-2906 *et seq.*; ¶7044.07; TD ¶587,405
4. ¶B-3001; ¶7044.08; TD ¶587,600
5. ¶B-3201; ¶7064.02; TD ¶588,501

item" is determined by assigning the appropriate portion of the item to each day in the period to which the item is attributable. (Code Sec. 706(d)(2))

If a part of any allocable cash basis item is attributable to a period preceding the partnership tax year, it will be assigned to the first day of the tax year. (Code Sec. 706(d)(2)(C)) Any amount which would be allocated under that procedure to a person who is not a partner on the first day of the partnership's tax year is capitalized by the partnership and added to the basis of the partnership assets in accordance with the basis allocation rules of Code Sec. 755. (Code Sec. 706(d)(2)(D)) Similarly, a part of an item attributable to a period following the tax year is to be assigned to the last day of the tax year. (Code Sec. 706(d)(2)(C))

¶ 3726 Determining whether an allocation has substantial economic effect.

An allocation of partnership income, gain, loss, deduction or credit among partners has substantial economic effect if it passes a two-part test applied as of the end of the partnership year to which the allocation relates.

First, the allocation must have economic effect. (Reg § 1.704-1(b)(2)(i)) This means that it must be consistent with the underlying economic arrangement of the partners. An allocation will be treated as having economic effect only if throughout the full term of the partnership, the partnership agreement states:

(1) the partners' capital accounts are to be determined and maintained according to rules set forth in the regs (see ¶3727);

(2) when the partnership liquidates, or a partner's interest is liquidated, liquidating distributions are to be made according to the partners' positive capital account balances; and

(3) a partner with a deficit balance in his capital account after the liquidation of his partnership interest is unconditionally obligated to restore the amount of the deficit to the partnership. (Reg § 1.704-1(b)(2)(ii))[6]

Second, the economic effect of the allocation must be substantial. (Reg § 1.704-1(b)(2)(i)) The economic effect of an allocation is substantial if there's a reasonable possibility that it will affect substantially the dollar amounts to be received by the partners from the partnership, independent of the tax consequences. (Reg § 1.704-1(b)(2)(iii))[7]

observation: Generally speaking, the economic effect test is designed to ensure that partnership allocations of income and gain ultimately correspond to real distributions of money and property, and that allocations of deductions, losses and credits ultimately correspond to the partners' actual liabilities for partnership expenses and losses. The substantiality test is designed to ensure that the economic effects of an allocation don't arise principally from the tax character of the allocated item—for example, from the fact that an income item is tax-exempt or foreign-sourced, or that a loss is from the sale of partnership property used in its trade or business.

Final regs provide for how to test whether the economic effect of an allocation is substantial where partners are look-through entities (e.g., partnerships, S corps, trusts or estates), or members of a consolidated group. The tax consequences that result from the interaction of an allocation with the tax attributes of any person that is an owner (or for a trust or estate, the beneficiary) of an interest in the partner must be taken into account. (Reg § 1.704-1(b)(2)(iii)(d)(1))[8]

---

6. ¶B-2503 *et seq.*; ¶7044.03; TD ¶586,503
7. ¶B-2700 *et seq.*; ¶7044.02; TD ¶586,519

8. ¶B-2702; ¶7044.05; TD ¶586,520

¶ 3727 Partner capital account rules.

For partner capital accounts to be determined and maintained properly for purposes of the economic effect rules (see ¶3726), each partner's account must be increased by cash contributed by the partner (including cash treated as contributed when the partner assumes partnership liabilities), and by the fair market value of property contributed by the partner (net of liabilities secured by the property). The account must also be increased by the partner's allocable share of partnership income and gain, including tax-exempt income, book income (not tax income) for property whose book value differs from basis, and unrealized income with respect to accounts receivable and certain other accrued but unpaid items.

Each account must be decreased by cash distributed to the partner (including cash treated as distributed when the partnership assumes partner liabilities), and by the fair market value of property distributed to the partner (net of liabilities secured by the property). The account must also be decreased by the partner's allocable share of partnership expenditures that are neither deductible nor capitalizable, and partnership loss and deduction, including book (not tax) loss for property whose book value differs from basis, and unrealized deductions for accounts payable and certain other accrued but unpaid items.

Capital account adjustments may also be required when partnership property is revalued or distributed, and on the transfer of a partnership interest. For example, partnership property may be revalued (and capital accounts adjusted) if property is contributed by, or distributed to, a partner in exchange for a partnership interest. Revaluation is also allowed where a partnership interest is granted as payment for services.

An adjustment may also be required if an optional basis adjustment election is in effect (see ¶3775) and property is distributed or an interest is transferred. (Reg § 1.704-1(b)(2)(iv))[9]

¶ 3728 Partner's Dealings with Partnership. ▄▄▄▄▄▄▄▄▄▄▄▄▄▄

Partners may deal with their partnerships in other than their capacity as partners. "Guaranteed payments" to partners are generally treated as made to nonpartners. Certain sales between partners and their partnerships establish the character of any gain, and require the deferral of loss.

¶ 3729 "Separate entity" transactions between partner and partnership.

If a partner provides services for or transfers property to his partnership, he may be treated as dealing with the partnership either as a member or as an outsider. If there's a related allocation and distribution of partnership income (direct or indirect), and the transaction on the whole is properly characterized as a sale or exchange between a partnership and an outsider, it will be treated in that way for tax purposes. (Code Sec. 707(a)(2)(A), Code Sec. 707(a)(2)(B))[10] Contribution and distribution transactions that occur within two years of one another are generally presumed to cause a sale unless the facts and circumstances clearly establish otherwise. (Reg § 1.707-3(c)(1))

¶ 3730 Guaranteed payments.

Guaranteed payments are payments to a partner for services or capital *without regard to partnership income.*[11] Guaranteed payments for a partner's services or capital are treated like salary payments to employees or interest payments to creditors, not like partnership distributions. (Code Sec. 707(c); Reg § 1.707-1(c))[12]

For a guaranteed payment to be deductible as a business expense by the partnership, it must meet the business expense tests as if the payment had been made to a person who

---

9. ¶B-2600 *et seq.*; ¶7044.04; TD ¶587,000
10. ¶B-2000 *et seq.*; ¶7074.01; TD ¶584,501

11. ¶B-2005; ¶7074.04; TD ¶584,505
12. ¶B-2006 *et seq.*; ¶7074.04; TD ¶584,505

wasn't a member of the partnership. (Code Sec. 707(c))[13] In determining whether a partnership can deduct or must capitalize a guaranteed payment, the regular capital expenditure rules apply. (Code Sec. 707(c))[14]

When a partnership makes a guaranteed payment using property other than cash, it is treated as a sale or exchange of that property by the partnership on which gain is recognized, and not a partnership distribution treated as discussed at ¶3743.[15]

¶ 3731   Losses on sales and exchanges with controlled partnership.

No deduction is allowed for losses from sales or exchanges between:

. . . a partnership and a person owning, directly or indirectly, over 50% of the capital interest, or profits interest, in the partnership; or

. . . two partnerships in which the same persons own over 50% of the capital or profits interests.

For constructive ownership rules, see ¶3733.

If property on which a loss was disallowed under the above rule is later sold by the transferee at a gain, the gain is taxable only to the extent it exceeds the loss previously disallowed. (Code Sec. 707(b)(1); Reg § 1.707-1(b)(1))[16]

¶ 3732   Gain on sale or exchange with controlled partnership.

The character of the property in the hands of the transferee, immediately after the transfer, determines the character of a *gain to the transferor* on a direct or indirect sale or exchange of property between:

. . . a partnership and a person owning, directly or indirectly, over 50% of the capital interest, or profits interest, in the partnership; or

. . . two partnerships in which the same persons own, directly or indirectly, more than 50% of the capital interest or profits interest in each.(Code Sec. 707(b)(2); Reg § 1.707-1(b)(2))[17]

Thus, if the property is a noncapital asset in the hands of the transferee, the transferor will have ordinary income on the sale. (Code Sec. 707(b)(2); Reg § 1.707-1(b)(2))[18]

For constructive ownership rules, see ¶3733.

¶ 3733   Constructive ownership of partnership interests.

In determining the percentage of ownership of partnership interests for purposes of ¶3731 and ¶3732, the constructive ownership rules for stock under Code Sec. 267(c) (¶2448) apply (substituting "capital or profits interest" for "stock"), except that a partner isn't considered as owning the interest of his partners (unless they are relatives, etc.). (Code Sec. 707(b)(3))[19]

¶ 3734   Limitations on a Partner's Deductible Loss. ■■■■■■■■■■■■

A partner's deduction for partnership losses may not exceed the basis of his interest in the partnership. However, partners (although not partnerships) are allowed loss carrybacks and carryovers.

13. ¶B-2001; ¶7074.04; TD ¶584,505
14. ¶B-2009; ¶7074.04; TD ¶584,507
15. ¶B-2009.1
16. ¶B-2016; ¶7074.03; TD ¶584,514

17. ¶B-2017; ¶7074.03; TD ¶584,515
18. ¶B-2017; ¶7074.03; TD ¶584,515
19. ¶B-2018; ¶7074.03; TD ¶584,516

¶ 3735 Limitation on partner's share of partnership loss.

A partner can deduct his distributive share of partnership *losses* only up to the amount of the adjusted basis of his interest in the partnership (¶3738 *et seq.*) at the end of the partnership's loss year. (Code Sec. 704(d))

Where a partnership has more than one class of losses (e.g., capital losses, Code Sec. 1231 losses, and operating losses) in the same year and a partner's total share of those losses exceeds the adjusted basis of his partnership interest, the limitation is allocated proportionately to each type of loss. (Reg § 1.704-1(d))

Excess losses disallowed to a partner in any year are carried over, and are deductible by him at the end of the partnership year in which the adjusted basis of the partner's interest at the end of the year exceeds zero (before reduction by that year's loss). (Reg § 1.704-1(d)(4))[20]

For limits on a partner's loss under the at-risk rules, see ¶1804 *et seq.*, and under the passive activity rules, see ¶1813 *et seq.*, ¶1819, and ¶1829.

¶ 3736 Basis adjustments made before applying loss limitations.

In determining whether a partner's deductible share of partnership loss exceeds (and is thus limited by) his basis in his partnership interest (¶3735), the basis adjustments described at ¶3740 are made first. (Reg § 1.704-1(d)(2))[21]

¶ 3737 Loss carrybacks and carryovers.

A carryover or carryback of net operating losses isn't allowed to a partnership, but a partner may carry back or carry over his share of the partnership's net business loss for any year to the extent it can't be used by that partner in the year it's passed through to him. (Code Sec. 702)[22]

¶ 3738 Basis of Partnership Interest. ■■■■■■■■■■■■■

A partner's basis for his interest in a partnership ("outside basis") depends on how he acquired it. It may be the amount of cash he contributed to the partnership, the adjusted basis of the property he contributed, or the amount he paid to purchase it.

¶ 3739 Initial basis of partnership interest.

A partner's interest acquired by a tax-free contribution of money or property to the partnership has a basis equal to the amount of money plus the partner's adjusted basis for the property when contributed. (Code Sec. 722)[23] If the contributed property is subject to indebtedness or if liabilities of the partner are assumed by the partnership, the basis of the contributing partner's interest is reduced by the portion of the indebtedness assumed by the other partners. (Reg § 1.722-1)[24]

A partner's capital interest acquired for services has a basis equal to the value of the capital interest acquired. (Reg § 1.722-1)[25]

A partner's interest acquired by purchase or inheritance has a basis determined under the general basis rules (¶2463 *et seq.*). (Code Sec. 742; Reg § 1.742-1)[26]

A partner may have a divided holding period in his partnership interest, see ¶2669. (Reg § 1.1223-3)[27]

---

20. ¶B-3500 *et seq.*; ¶7044.10; TD ¶589,001 *et seq.*
21. ¶B-3501 *et seq.*; ¶7044.10; TD ¶589,001
22. ¶B-3508; ¶7024.01; TD ¶589,007
23. ¶B-1502; ¶7224.01; TD ¶581,418

24. ¶B-1506; ¶7224.01; TD ¶581,422
25. ¶B-1502; ¶7224.02; TD ¶581,418
26. ¶B-1501; ¶7424.01; TD ¶581,415
27. ¶I-8934.1; ¶12,234.29; TD ¶223,556

¶ 3740　Adjustments to basis of partner's interest.

The basis of a partner's interest is increased:

... by further contributions (but not by his own personal note given to the partnership);[28]

... by the cost of additional interests purchased or inherited (¶3739) (Code Sec. 742);

... by any increase in his share of partnership liabilities since the increase is treated as a contribution of money to the partnership, see ¶3760;[29]

... by his distributive share of partnership income, including tax-exempt income and any excess of net long-term capital gains over losses (Code Sec. 705(a)(1));

... by his distributive share of the excess of percentage depletion deductions over the basis of the depletable property. (Code Sec. 705(a)(1))[30]

The basis of a partner's interest is reduced (but not below zero) by:

... the adjusted basis allocable to any part of his interest sold or otherwise transferred;[31]

... the amount of money and the adjusted basis of partnership property distributed to him in nonliquidating distributions (Code Sec. 705(a)(2), Code Sec. 733);[32]

... by any decrease in his share of partnership liabilities since the decrease is treated as a distribution of money by the partnership, see ¶3760;

... his distributive share of partnership losses (including capital losses) *and* nondeductible expenditures not chargeable to the capital account (Code Sec. 705(a); Reg § 1.705-1(a)) (for the partner's distributive share of losses in excess of his adjusted basis, see ¶3735);

... his percentage depletion deduction for partnership oil and gas property to the extent the deduction doesn't exceed his allocated proportionate share of the property's basis. (Code Sec. 705(a)(3))[33]

Regs prevent the acceleration or duplication of losses through a partnership's assumption of obligations that are not treated as resulting in a deemed cash contribution or distribution by or to the partner under the rules discussed at ¶3759. These obligations are called "Reg § 1.752-7 liabilities." Where such a liability is assumed by a partnership from a partner in a property contribution by a partner to a partnership in exchange for a partnership interest (a Code Sec. 721(a) contribution), the liability is treated as having a built-in loss (see ¶3752) equal to the amount of the liability as of the date of the partnership's assumption of the liability. (Reg § 1.752-7)[34]

Regs prevent inappropriate increases or decreases in the basis of a corporate partner's interest in a partnership resulting from the partnership's disposition of the corporate partner's stock. (Reg § 1.705-2)[35]

¶ 3741　Alternative adjusted basis computation.

The adjusted basis of a partner's interest may be determined under a "short-cut" method by reference to what would be his proportionate share of the adjusted basis of the partnership property upon a termination of the partnership (Code Sec. 705(b)) where: (1) it isn't practicable to use the regular rule, or (2) IRS is satisfied the result under the alternative method won't vary substantially from that under the regular rule. (Reg § 1.705-1(b))[36]

¶ 3742　Distributions to a Partner. ▮▮▮▮▮▮▮▮▮▮▮▮▮▮▮▮▮▮▮▮▮▮▮

A partnership generally doesn't recognize gain or loss on a distribution to a partner,

---

28. ¶B-1504; ¶7054.01; TD ¶581,418
29. ¶B-1506; ¶7524; TD ¶581,422
30. ¶B-1507; ¶7054.01; TD ¶581,423
31. ¶B-3805
32. ¶B-1505; ¶7334.01; TD ¶581,423

33. ¶B-1507; ¶7054.02; TD ¶581,423
34. ¶B-1506.1; ¶7524.04; TD ¶581,422.2
35. ¶B-1504.1; ¶7054.03
36. ¶B-1514; ¶7054.04; TD ¶581,428

but the partner often will recognize gain or loss.

¶ 3743   Partnership's gain or loss on distribution.

No gain or loss is recognized to a partnership on a current or liquidating distribution to a partner of money or other property, except where a disproportionate distribution is treated as a sale by the partnership, see ¶3755. (Code Sec. 731(b))[37]

¶ 3744   Partner's gain or loss on receipt of distribution.

Gain or loss isn't recognized to a partner on receipt of a current or liquidating distribution from a partnership, except as follows:

. . . Gain is recognized to the extent that *money* (defined to include marketable securities, see ¶3745) distributed exceeds the adjusted basis of the partner's interest in the partnership immediately before the distribution. (Code Sec. 731(a))[38] This is treated as a gain from sale or exchange of the partner's interest. (Reg § 1.731-1(a)(3))[39] A reduction in a partner's liabilities (due either to the partnership's assumption of them or a reduction in the partner's share of partnership liabilities) is treated as a money distribution. (Code Sec. 752(b))[40]

. . . Loss is recognized to the extent the adjusted basis of the partner's interest exceeds the sum of any money, and the basis to the distributee of any unrealized receivables and inventories received if the distribution is in liquidation of the partner's interest in the partnership *and* no other property is distributed. This is treated as a loss from sale or exchange of the partner's interest in the partnership. (Code Sec. 731(a))[41]

If gain or loss is recognized under one of the above rules, the partnership may elect to, or may have to, adjust the basis of its assets, as explained at ¶3775 *et seq.*

The above rules on recognition of a partner's gains and losses don't apply to (Code Sec. 731(c); Reg § 1.731-1(c)):[42]

. . . disproportionate distributions treated as sales or exchanges of property, see ¶3755;

. . . liquidation payments made to a retiring partner or to a deceased partner's successor in interest treated as a share of income or as guaranteed payments, see ¶3769;

. . . recognition of precontribution gain under Code Sec. 737, see ¶3752.

¶ 3745   Distribution of marketable securities treated as cash.

Subject to exceptions, a distribution of marketable securities (stock and other equity instruments, evidences of indebtedness, precious metals commodities, options, forward or futures contracts, notional principal contracts and derivatives) is treated as a distribution of money. They are taken into account at their fair market value (FMV) as of the date of the distribution. (Code Sec. 731(c); Reg § 1.731-2)

Gain is recognized by a distributee partner to the extent that the cash and the FMV of the marketable securities exceed the basis of the partner's interest in the partnership. But where a partner realizes a loss on a distribution of marketable securities, the loss isn't recognized. These rules are applied after the application of the rules that treat a shift in the partners' interests in accounts receivables and substantially appreciated inventory as a sale. (Code Sec. 731(a))[43]

The amount of marketable securities taken into account under the above rule is reduced (but not below zero) by the excess (if any) of:

37. ¶B-3601; ¶7314.01; TD ¶589,501
38. ¶B-3602; ¶7314.01; TD ¶589,502
39. ¶B-3602; ¶7314.01; TD ¶589,502
40. ¶B-3608; ¶7524.01; TD ¶582,002

41. ¶B-3603; ¶7314.01; TD ¶589,508
42. ¶B-3605; ¶7314.01; TD ¶589,510
43. ¶B-3602.1 *et seq.*; ¶7314.01; TD ¶588,035

(1) the partner's distributive share of the net gain that would be recognized if all marketable securities of the same class and issuer as the distributed securities held by the partnership were sold (immediately before the transaction to which the distribution relates) by the partnership for FMV, over

(2) the partner's distributive share of the net gain attributable to the marketable securities of the same class and issuer as the distributed securities held by the partnership immediately after the transaction, determined using the FMV described in (1) above. (Code Sec. 731(c)(3)(B))

All marketable securities held by the partnership are treated as marketable securities of the same class and issuer as the distributed securities. (Reg § 1.731-2(b))[44]

¶ 3746   Partner's holding period.

A partner's holding period for property distributed to him in kind includes the period the partnership held the property. (Code Sec. 735(b)) If contributed to the partnership by a partner, the recipient partner's holding period also includes the period that the property was held by the contributing partner before contribution. (Reg § 1.735-1(b))[45]

¶ 3747   Character of certain contributed property.

When a partner contributes what was an unrealized receivable in his hands to a partnership, the partnership's gain or loss on disposition of the item will still be ordinary income or loss. (Code Sec. 724(a)) The same rule applies to contributed inventory, but in this case, ordinary income or loss will result only if the assets are disposed of by the partnership within five years of the contribution. (Code Sec. 724(b))[46]

If a partner contributes a capital asset with a basis higher than its fair market value, and the partnership disposes of it within five years of the contribution, the partnership's loss will be capital to the extent of the basis/value variance at contribution. (Code Sec. 724(c))[47]

If any of the above property is disposed of by the partnership in a nontaxable disposition, the above rules apply to the substituted basis property that results. (Code Sec. 724(d)(3))[48]

¶ 3748   Partner's basis for property received in nonliquidating distributions.

The basis to a partner of property distributed to him, in kind, other than in liquidation of his partnership interest, is the same as the property's adjusted basis to the partnership immediately before the distribution. But the basis of the property to the partner may not exceed the adjusted basis of his interest in the partnership reduced by any money distributed to him in the same transaction. (Code Sec. 732(a); Reg § 1.732-1(a))[49]

¶ 3749   Partner's basis for property distributed in liquidation.

A partner's basis for property distributed in liquidation of his partnership interest is the same as the adjusted basis for his partnership interest reduced by any money distributed to him in the same transaction. However, the partner's basis in inventory and unrealized receivables cannot exceed the basis the partnership had in such items. (Code Sec. 732(b), Code Sec. 732(c); Reg § 1.732-1(b))[50]

---

45. ¶B-3706; ¶7354.02; TD ¶589,523
46. ¶B-1420; ¶7244; TD ¶581,413
47. ¶B-1421; ¶7244; TD ¶581,414

48. ¶B-1422; ¶7244.01; TD ¶581,415
49. ¶B-3701; ¶7324.01; TD ¶589,518
50. ¶B-3702; ¶7324.01; TD ¶589,519

¶ 3750   Basis adjustments to assets of corporation whose stock is distributed to corporate partner.

A corporate partner that receives a distribution of stock in another corporation ("distributed corporation") must, subject to limitations and exceptions, reduce the basis of the distributed corporation's assets if:

. . . the corporate partner "controls" (by 80% vote and value) the distributed corporation immediately after the distribution or at any time thereafter, and

. . . the partnership's adjusted basis in the stock of the distributed corporation immediately before the distribution exceeded the corporate partner's adjusted basis in such stock immediately after the distribution. (Code Sec. 732(f)(1))[1]

The basis reduction equals the excess described above and is applied to the property held by the distributed corporation following the distribution, if the corporate partner then has control of the distributed corporation. (Code Sec. 732(f)(1))[2]

The basis reduction cannot exceed the lesser of:

(A) the amount by which (i) the sum of the aggregate adjusted bases of the property and the amount of money of the distributed corporation exceeds (ii) the corporate partner's adjusted basis in the stock of the distributed corporation, or

(B) the adjusted basis of any property of the distributed corporation (determined before the reduction). (Code Sec. 732(f)(3))[3]

If, in applying the basis-reduction rule, the amount by which basis is to be reduced exceeds the aggregate adjusted bases of the property of the distributed corporation, then the excess is recognized by the corporate partner as long-term capital gain and increases its basis in the stock of the distributed corporation. (Code Sec. 732(f)(4))[4]

¶ 3751   Allocation of basis to distributed property when limited by basis of partner's interest.

In a current distribution in which the partner's basis in his partnership interest is less than the partnership's basis in the property distributed and in a liquidating distribution, the partner's basis in his partnership interest (reduced by any money received) must be allocated among the distributed property in the following manner:

(1) First, to any unrealized receivables and inventory items in an amount equal to the adjusted basis of each such property to the partnership. (Code Sec. 732(c)(1)(A)(i)) If the basis to be allocated is less than the sum of the adjusted bases of these properties in the hands of the partnership, a basis decrease is applied as described below. (Code Sec. 732(c)(1)(A)(ii); Reg § 1.732-1(c)(1)(i))

(2) To the extent any basis isn't allocated under (1), basis is allocated to other distributed properties. This allocation is made by assigning to each property its adjusted basis in the hands of the partnership (Code Sec. 732(c)(1)(B)(i); Reg § 1.732-1(c)(1)(ii)) and then increasing or decreasing the basis to the extent any increase or decrease in basis is required in order for the adjusted bases of the other distributed properties to equal the remaining basis under the rules described below. (Code Sec. 732(c)(1)(B)(ii); Reg § 1.732-1(c)(1)(ii))

Any basis *increase* is allocated (i) first to properties with unrealized appreciation in proportion to their respective amounts of unrealized appreciation before such increase to the extent of each property's unrealized appreciation (Code Sec. 732(c)(2)(A); Reg § 1.732-1(c)(2)(ii)) and (ii) to the extent the required increase isn't allocated under (i), in proportion to the respective

1. ¶B-3704; ¶7324.03
2. ¶B-3704; ¶7324.03
3. ¶B-3704.1; ¶7324.03
4. ¶B-3704.2; ¶7324.03

fair market values of the properties. (Code Sec. 732(c)(2)(B); Reg § 1.732-1(c)(2)(ii))

Any basis *decrease* is allocated (a) first to properties with unrealized depreciation in proportion to their respective amounts of unrealized appreciation before such decrease to the extent of each property's unrealized depreciation (Code Sec. 732(c)(3)(A); Reg § 1.732-1(c)(2)(i)) and (b) to the extent the required decrease isn't allocated under (a), in proportion to the respective bases of the properties (as adjusted under (a)). (Code Sec. 732(c)(3)(B); Reg § 1.732-1(c)(2)(i))[5]

¶ 3752 Built-in gain or loss property—seven-year rule.

If the basis of property contributed to a partnership by a partner is different from the property's fair market value (FMV) at the time of contribution (i.e., there is built-in gain or loss), then the following rules apply:

If the partnership distributes the contributed property to a partner or partners *other than the contributing partner* within seven years of the contribution, then the distributed property is treated as sold by the partnership for its FMV at the time of the distribution, and the contributing partner must recognize any gain or loss from this constructive sale in an amount equal to the amount of gain or loss that would have been allocated to him if the property had actually been sold. (Code Sec. 704(c)(1)(B); Reg § 1.704-4(a)(5), Ex (1))[6]

Where property is distributed to the partner *who contributed the property,* the partner will recognize as gain the lesser of (a) the excess of the FMV of the property over the adjusted basis of the partner's interest in the partnership immediately before the distribution (reduced, but not below zero, by any money also received, where money is defined to include marketable securities, see ¶3745), or (b) the partner's net precontribution gain, i.e., the gain that would have been recognized by the distributee partner under the rules discussed, above, if all property held by the partnership immediately before the distribution that had been contributed to it by the distributee partner within seven years of the distribution, was distributed to another partner. (Code Sec. 737(a), Code Sec. 737(b))[7] Distributions of property previously contributed by the distributee partner aren't taken into account for purposes of determining (a) and (b), above. (Code Sec. 737(d)(1))[8]

Special rules apply if the partnership distributes to the contributing partner property that's of "like kind" to the contributed property (within the meaning of Code Sec. 1031, see ¶2418) to limit recognition of gain by the contributing partner. (Code Sec. 704(c)(2))[9]

The rules requiring gain recognition on distributions described above do not apply when a partnership transfers all of its assets and liabilities to a partnership in exchange for an interest in the transferee partnership, and distributes the interest to its partners in liquidation as part of the same plan (a merger). With respect to a later distribution of "built-in gain" property that was transferred, the seven-year period begins when the property was originally contributed to the transferor partnership, and not from the date of the transfer to the transferee partnership. However, the merger is considered a contribution of assets, so a new seven-year period begins but only with respect to the appreciation in value that occurred while the property was held by the transferor partnership.[10]

Income, gain, loss and deductions with respect to property which was contributed to the partnership after Mar. 31, '84 are to be shared among the partners so as to take into account the difference between the property's FMV and its basis at the time of the contribution. (Code Sec. 704(c)(1)(A)) Built-in gain or loss must be allocated using a reasonable method, i.e., the traditional method following the ceiling rule or with curative allocations, the remedial allocation method or another method appropriate to the circumstances. (Reg § 1.704-3(a)(1)) Under anti-abuse rules, an allocation isn't reasonable if made with a view to shifting the tax consequences of built-in gain or loss among partners (including indirect partners), in a way that

---

5. ¶B-3703; ¶7324.01; TD ¶589,521
6. ¶B-3125; ¶7044.09; TD ¶588,019
7. ¶B-3171 *et seq.*; ¶7374; TD ¶588,031

8. ¶B-3178; ¶7374.03; TD ¶588,037
9. ¶B-3151 *et seq.*; ¶7044.09; TD ¶588,025
10. ¶B-3157; ¶7044.097; TD ¶588,024

substantially reduces the present value of the partners' aggregate tax liability. (Reg § 1.704-3(a)(10)) With respect to property contributed before Apr. 1, '84, a similar special allocation applies only if the partnership agreement so provides.[11]

If any property contributed to a partnership after Oct. 22, 2004 has a built-in loss, then:

... the built-in loss is taken into account only in determining the amount of items allocated to the contributing partner, and

... except as provided in regs, in determining the amount of items allocated to other partners, the basis of the contributed property in the hands of the partnership is treated as being equal to its FMV at the time of the contribution. (Code Sec. 704(c)(1)(C))

If a partnership makes an installment sale of built-in gain or loss property, the installment obligation it receives is treated as built-in gain or loss property. (Reg § 1.704-3(a)(8)(ii))[12]

¶ 3753 Character of unrealized receivables and inventory to a distributee-partner.

Gain or loss on disposition of unrealized receivables and inventory by a distributee-partner is:

... in the case of *unrealized receivables*, ordinary gain or loss; (Code Sec. 735(a)(1))

... in the case of *inventory items* (whether or not substantially appreciated) sold or exchanged within five years from the date of the distribution, ordinary gain or loss. (Code Sec. 735(a)(2)) If disposed of after five years from the date of distribution, the character of the gain or loss depends upon the character of the item in the partner's hands on the date of disposition. (Reg § 1.735-1(a)(2))[13]

¶ 3754 Disproportionate Distributions.

Disproportionate distributions of partnership property that include "unrealized receivables" (including recapturable deductions, certain transfers of franchises, trademarks or trade names, see ¶3756) and "substantially appreciated inventory" (see ¶3757) (collectively, "hot assets") may trigger ordinary income, gain or loss to both the partnership and its partners.

¶ 3755 Disproportionate distributions defined.

A disproportionate distribution of partnership assets to a partner is treated as a sale or exchange that may result in recognition of gain or loss to the partner and the partnership. The rule applies to all distributions, both liquidating and nonliquidating, except for: (1) a distribution of contributed property to the same partner who contributed it; and (2) liquidation payments to a retiring or deceased partner that are treated as ordinary income under the rules at ¶3769. (Code Sec. 751(b))[14]

A distribution is "disproportionate" if a partner receives more than his proportionate share of "hot assets" (see ¶3754) and less of his proportionate share of other property (including money), or vice versa.

In such a case, a partner, in effect, sells or exchanges part or all of his share in property of one category for property of the other category, see ¶3758. The general rules on partnership distributions apply to the balance of the distribution not treated as a sale or exchange. (Reg § 1.751-1(b))[15]

The partners may agree as to which particular assets in one category shall be considered to have been sold or exchanged for particular assets in the other category. Absent such an agreement, a proportionate part of each asset relinquished in one category will be considered

---

11. ¶B-3103 *et seq.*; ¶7044.09; TD ¶588,001
12. ¶B-3100; ¶7044.09; TD ¶588,014
13. ¶B-3705; ¶7354.01; TD ¶589,522

14. ¶B-3905 *et seq.*; ¶7514.01; TD ¶591,003
15. ¶B-3910 *et seq.*; ¶7514.01; TD ¶591,006

to have been sold or exchanged for excess assets received in the other. (Reg § 1.751-1(g))[16]

¶ 3756   "Unrealized receivables."

Unrealized receivables include any contractual or other rights to payment for:

... goods delivered, or to be delivered, to the extent the proceeds would be treated as amounts received from sale or exchange of noncapital assets;

... services rendered, or to be rendered.

Such receivables are included only to the extent not previously includible in income under the method of accounting used by the partnership. (Code Sec. 751(c))[17]

Unrealized receivables also include (other than for payments to retiring partners or deceased partners under Code Sec. 736, see ¶3769): (Code Sec. 751(c))

... depreciation recapturable under Code Sec. 1245 and Code Sec. 1250;

... mine exploration deductions recapturable under Code Sec. 617;

... soil and water conservation deductions recapturable under Code Sec. 1252;

... recapturable deductions for oil, gas or certain geothermal well intangible costs under Code Sec. 1254;

... understated rental income under a Code Sec. 467 rental agrement;[18]

... domestic international sales corporation stock;

... stock in certain foreign corporations as described in Code Sec. 1248 (¶4625);[19]

... market discount bonds, to the extent they would give rise to ordinary income if sold by the partnership (¶1326);

... short term obligations as defined in Code Sec. 1283 (¶1328);[20]

... franchises, trademarks or trade names whose transfer is treated as a sale of a noncapital asset under Code Sec. 1253.[21]

¶ 3757   "Inventory items" and "substantially appreciated" inventory items.

Inventory items include property properly includible in inventory and property held primarily for sale to customers in the ordinary course of business (Code Sec. 751(d)(1)), as well as:

... any other property that would produce ordinary income on sale or exchange by the partnership (Code Sec. 751(d)(2)), including accounts receivable for goods or services and unrealized receivables as described at ¶3756 (Reg § 1.751-1(d)(2)(ii));

... any other property held by the partnership that would be inventory items, as defined above, if held by the selling or distributee-partner. (Code Sec. 751(d)(3)) However, this rule doesn't apply to property actually distributed to a partner. (Reg § 1.751-1(d)(2)(iii))[22]

Inventory items are "substantially appreciated" in value if the fair market value of *all* such items (including unrealized receivables) exceeds 120% of their adjusted basis to the partnership. (Code Sec. 751(b)(3)(A)) The 120% limit is computed by excluding any item acquired principally to avoid meeting it. (Code Sec. 751(b)(3)(B))

If the test is met on the basis of all inventory items, a distribution of any inventory item is a distribution of a substantially appreciated one, even though the particular item may not have appreciated at all. If the test isn't met on the basis of all items, no distribution of an inventory item is a distribution of a substantially appreciated item. (Reg § 1.751-1(d)(1))[23]

---

16. ¶B-3902 *et seq.*; ¶7514.01; TD ¶591,006
17. ¶B-3914; ¶7514.02; TD ¶591,010
18. ¶B-3916; ¶7514.02; TD ¶591,012
19. ¶B-3918; ¶7514.02; TD ¶591,011

20. ¶B-3920; ¶7514.02; TD ¶591,013
21. ¶B-3919; ¶7514.02; TD ¶591,014
22. ¶B-3921; ¶7514.02; TD ¶591,015
23. ¶B-3922; ¶7514.02; TD ¶591,016

¶ 3758   Gain or loss on disproportionate distribution.

If a distributee-partner receives *more* than his share of unrealized receivables and substantially appreciated inventory items and *less* than his share of other property (including money), he is considered to have sold or exchanged the portion of his share of the other property that he relinquished for the excess unrealized receivables and substantially appreciated inventory items he received. (Reg § 1.751-1(b)(2)(i), Reg § 1.751-1(b)(2)(iii))

The partnership (as constituted after the distribution) is considered to have sold or exchanged the excess other property distributed to the partner for the unrealized receivables and substantially appreciated inventory items he relinquished. (Reg § 1.751-1(b)(2)(i), Reg § 1.751-1(b)(2)(ii))[24]

Rules analogous to those described above apply where the distributee partner receives a disproportionate distribution of *less* than his share of unrealized receivables and substantially appreciated inventory items and *more* than his share of other property (including money). (Reg § 1.751-1(b)(3))[25]

¶ 3759   Liabilities of Partnerships and Partners. ▪▪▪▪▪▪▪▪

Changes in partners' shares of partnership liabilities are treated as cash contributions to, or distributions by, the partnership. Partners' shares of partnership liabilities depend on whether the liability is recourse or nonrecourse.

¶ 3760   Partnership liabilities.

If a partner's share of the partnership liabilities increases, or if he assumes any partnership liabilities, it's treated as a contribution of money from the partner to the partnership. (Code Sec. 752(a); Reg § 1.752-1(b))[26]

If a partner's share of the partnership liabilities decreases, or if the partnership assumes any of his liabilities, it's treated as a distribution of money to the partner. (Code Sec. 752(b); Reg § 1.752-1(c))[27]

An unassumed liability to which property is subject is considered a liability of the owner of the property (e.g., the partnership) to the extent of its fair market value. (Code Sec. 752(c))[28]

For these purposes and for determining "Reg § 1.752-7 liabilities" (see ¶3740), a liability is any fixed or contingent obligation to make payment without regard to whether the obligation is otherwise taken into account for tax purposes. Obligations include, but are not limited to, debt obligations, environmental obligations, tort obligations, contract obligations, pension obligations, obligations under a short sale, and obligations under derivative financial instruments such as options, forward contracts, and futures contracts. (Reg § 1.752-1(a)(4)(ii))[29]

¶ 3761   Share of recourse liabilities.

A partnership debt is a recourse liability to the extent that any partner bears the economic risk of loss for the liability.[30] A partner's share of a recourse liability is the part of the economic risk of loss for the liability the partner bears. (Reg § 1.752-1(a)(1))[31]

Generally, a partner bears the economic risk of loss for a partnership liability to the extent that he (or a related person) would be obligated to pay the creditor or contribute to the partnership (and wouldn't be entitled to reimbursement) in the case of a constructive liquidation. (Reg § 1.752-2(b)(1))[32] However, IRS may disregard a partner's purported obligation to

---

24. ¶B-3910 *et seq.*; ¶7514.01; TD ¶591,003
25. ¶B-3911; ¶7514.01; TD ¶591,008
26. ¶B-1601; ¶7524.01; TD ¶582,004
27. ¶B-1602; ¶7524.01; TD ¶582,004
28. ¶B-1608; ¶7524.01; TD ¶582,007

29. ¶B-1607; ¶7524.01.
30. ¶B-1651; ¶7524.03; TD ¶582,012
31. ¶B-1653 *et seq.*; ¶7524.03; TD ¶582,011
32. ¶B-1654 *et seq.*; ¶7524.03; TD ¶582,013

make a payment under an anti-abuse rule. (Reg § 1.752-2(j))

¶ 3762   Share of nonrecourse liabilities.

If no partner bears the economic risk of loss for a partnership liability (e.g., unassumed mortgages), the liability is nonrecourse. (Reg § 1.752-1(a)(2)) Nonrecourse liabilities of a partnership are first allocated among all the partners to reflect their shares of:

. . . "partnership minimum gain" (gain on the disposition of property subject to a nonrecourse liability that exceeds its adjusted basis); and

. . . the gain that would be allocated to the partners under Code Sec. 704(c), or under similar principles in connection with a revaluation of partnership property, if, in a taxable transaction, the partnership disposed of all property subject to a nonrecourse liability in satisfaction of those liabilities and for no other consideration.

Any excess is allocated among the partners in proportion to their interests in partnership profits. The partnership agreement may specify the partners' profit interests as long as those interests are reasonably consistent with allocations (which have substantial economic effect) of some significant item of partnership income or gain among the partners. Alternatively, the excess may be allocated in accordance with the manner in which it's expected that the deductions attributable to the nonrecourse debt will be allocated. In addition, the excess may be allocated based on the excess gain attributable to the property securing the liability. (Reg § 1.752-3(a))[33]

¶ 3763   Transfer and Liquidation of Partnership Interest. ■■■■■■

The transfer or liquidation of a partnership interest, while generally resulting in capital gain or loss, is subject to special rules that may turn part of the gain or loss from capital to ordinary.

¶ 3764   Liquidation vs. sale of partner's interest.

Withdrawal of a partner from a partnership ordinarily may be accomplished either by a retiring partner's sale or liquidation of his interest in the partnership.

Where a partner's interest is liquidated, payments are taxable to that partner as guaranteed payments or income distributions to the extent they exceed the value of his interest in the partnership property (¶3768 *et seq.*).[34]

Where a partner *sells* his interest, payments to him that exceed his basis for his interest are capital gain except to the extent of payments for unrealized receivables and inventory items (¶3765 *et seq.*). (Code Sec. 741; Reg § 1.741-1)[35]

¶ 3765   Sale or exchange of partnership interest.

If a partner sells or exchanges all or a part of his interest in the partnership after holding it for more than one year, he may recognize ordinary income, collectibles gain (¶2607), section 1250 gain, or residual long-term capital gain or loss. (Reg § 1.1(h)-1(a)) He recognizes ordinary income (¶3766) to the extent his gain is attributable to unrealized receivables (¶3756) and inventory (¶3757). (Code Sec. 741, Code Sec. 751(a), Code Sec. 751(c))[36]

The capital gain or loss is the difference between:

. . . the amount realized *reduced* by the portion attributable to unrealized receivables and inventory; and

. . . the transferor-partner's adjusted basis for the partnership interest transferred *reduced*

---

33. ¶B-1670; ¶7524.03; TD ¶582,017
34. ¶B-3811, B-4102; ¶7364.01; TD ¶590,507
35. ¶B-3801 *et seq.*; ¶7414.01; TD ¶590,501
36. ¶B-3850 *et seq.*; ¶7414.01; TD ¶590,600 *et seq.*

by the portion attributable to unrealized receivables and inventory. (Reg § 1.741-1(a))[37]

Any gain or loss from a partner's disposition of an interest in a partnership is taken into account by the partner as net investment income for purposes of the 3.8% surtax on unearned income (¶3150 *et seq.*) *only* to the extent that of the net gain or loss that the transferor would take into account if the entity had sold all its property for fair market value immediately before the disposition. (Code Sec. 1411(c)(4))

The seller's collectibles gain is the amount that would be allocated to him if the partnership had sold all of its collectibles for fair market value in a fully taxable transaction immediately before the sale of the interest in the entity. (Reg § 1.1(h)-1(b)(2)(ii)) The seller must take into account under Code Sec. 1(h)(6)(A)(i) in determining his unrecaptured section 1250 gain (¶2605) the amount of "section 1250 capital gain" that would be allocated to him if the partnership had sold all of its section 1250 property in a fully taxable transaction immediately before the transfer of the partnership interest. (Reg § 1.1(h)-1(b)(3)(ii)) The amount of residual long-term capital gain or loss recognized by a selling partner is the amount of long-term capital gain or loss that the partner would recognize under Code Sec. 741 (as explained above) minus (1) the collectibles gain allocable to the sold interest, and (2) the section 1250 gain allocable to the sold interest. (Reg § 1.1(h)-1(c))

¶ 3766   Ordinary gain or loss.

To the extent that money or property received by a partner in exchange for all or part of his partnership interest is attributable to his share of partnership unrealized receivables or inventory items—collectively Code Sec. 751 property—the gain or loss is ordinary income or loss. (Code Sec. 751(a))

The income or loss realized by a partner upon the sale or exchange of its interest in Code Sec. 751 property is the amount of income or loss from Code Sec. 751 property (including any remedial allocations) that would have been allocated to the partner (to the extent attributable to the partnership interest sold or exchanged) if the partnership had sold all of its property in a fully taxable transaction for cash in an amount equal to the fair market value (FMV) of such property (taking into account the Code Sec. 7701(g) rule that the FMV must be not less than the amount of the nonrecourse debt to which the property is subject) immediately before the partner's transfer of the interest in the partnership. Gain or loss attributable to Code Sec. 751 property is ordinary. The difference between the amount of capital gain or loss that the partner would realize absent Code Sec. 751 and the amount of ordinary income or loss is capital gain or loss on the sale of its partnership interest. (Reg § 1.751-1(a)(2))[38]

The basis for unrealized receivables includes all attributable costs or expenses paid or accrued but not previously taken into account under the partnership's method of accounting. (Reg § 1.751-1(c)(2)) The basis of any potential gain from the following property (treated as unrealized receivables) is zero: (1) mining exploration expenditures recapture under Code Sec. 617; (2) gain from stock of a domestic international sales corporation (DISC) or a former DISC under Code Sec. 995(c); (3) depreciation recapture under Code Sec. 1245 and Code Sec. 1250; (4) gain from stock of a controlled foreign corporation under Code Sec. 1248(a); (5) gain from disposition of farm land under Code Sec. 1252(a)(1); (6) gain from transfers of franchises, trademarks, or trade names under Code Sec. 1253(a); or (7) oil, gas, or geothermal wells intangible drilling and development cost recapture under Code Sec. 1254. (Reg § 1.751-1(c)(5))[39]

37. ¶s B-3802, B-3901; ¶7414.01; TD ¶590,501
38. ¶B-3901; ¶7514.01; TD ¶591,001

39. ¶B-3903; ¶7514.02; TD ¶591,002

¶ 3767   Sale of partnership business vs. sale of partnership assets.

Where *all* of the old partners sell out, whether the transaction is a sale of the partnership interests or a sale of the partnership assets generally depends on whether what was actually transferred was a going business or simply assets.[40]

¶ 3768   Payments After Partner's Death or Retirement. ▬▬▬▬▬▬

When a partner either retires or dies and payments are made in liquidation of his partnership interest, the payments are broken down into several categories, which are treated as ordinary income or capital gains.

¶ 3769   Liquidation payments to retiring or deceased partners.

These payments may be for the partner's interest in the fair market value of the partnership assets, his interest in unrealized receivables, or payments under an agreement akin to mutual insurance. These amounts have to be separately considered.[41]

Liquidation payments received by a retiring partner, a partner expelled from a partnership or by a deceased partner's successor in interest are treated as distributions taxable under the rules for regular distributions discussed at ¶3744 if they are for the partner's interest in partnership property, see ¶3770. (Code Sec. 736(b)(1))[42] Payments for *substantially appreciated* inventory (¶3757) may result in ordinary income under the rules governing disproportionate distributions (see ¶3758). (Reg § 1.736-1(b)(1))

Liquidation payments that aren't in exchange for partnership property are treated either as distributive shares of partnership income (if the amount is determined with regard to partnership income), or as guaranteed payments (if the amount is determined without regard to partnership income). (Code Sec. 736(a); Reg § 1.736-1(a)(3))[43]

¶ 3770   Payment for interest in partnership property.

Payments for partnership property don't include payments to a retiring or deceased general partner in a partnership in which capital isn't a material income-producing factor for (i) unrealized receivables (which for this purpose includes only accounts receivable and unbilled amounts) or (ii) goodwill (unless the partnership agreement provides for payment with respect to goodwill). (Code Sec. 736(b)(2), Code Sec. 736(b)(3))[44]

¶ 3771   Allocation of payments between income and property.

The allocation problem comes up where payments are made over two or more years. Retirement or death payments must be allocated between the portion received in exchange for partnership property and the balance, received in the form of guaranteed payments or as a distributive share of partnership income. This allocation may be made in any manner in which the remaining partners and the withdrawing partner (or a deceased partner's successor in interest) agree. However, the *total* allocated to property must not exceed the fair market value of the property at the date of death or retirement. (Reg § 1.736-1(b)(5)(iii))

In the absence of an allocation agreement, payments will be apportioned between income and property as follows:

. . . Payments that aren't fixed in amount are first treated as made in exchange for the partner's interest in partnership property to the extent of the value of that interest. Additional amounts are ordinary income. (Reg § 1.736-1(b)(5)(ii))

---

40. ¶B-3809; TD ¶590,508
41. ¶B-4102 *et seq.*; ¶7364.01; TD ¶592,000 *et seq.*
42. ¶B-4103; ¶7364.02; TD ¶592,001

43. ¶B-4106; ¶7364.03; TD ¶592,005
44. ¶B-4104; ¶7364.02; TD ¶592,004

... Payments fixed in amount and to be received over a fixed number of years are apportioned year by year in accordance with the overall ratio of property payments to total payments. (Reg § 1.736-1(b)(5)(i))[45]

A payment for goodwill is treated as a payment made in exchange for partnership property where payment for goodwill is provided by the partnership agreement. (Reg § 1.736-1(b)(3))[46]

¶ 3772 Withdrawing partner's share of final year's income.

A retiring partner must pick up his distributive share of the partnership income for the partnership year in which he retires. His share of the partnership income for the year is allocable to him only for the portion of the year he was a member of the partnership. (Reg § 1.736-1(a)(4))[47]

¶ 3773 Income of deceased partner.

The tax year of a partnership closes with respect to a deceased partner on the date of his death. Thus, partnership items for the short partnership tax year that closes on the partner's death are included in his final return. (Code Sec. 706(c)(2))[48]

¶ 3774 Continuation of retiring or deceased partner's partner status.

A retiring partner or a deceased partner's successor in interest who receives retirement or death payments is regarded as a partner until his entire interest in the partnership is liquidated. Thus, even a two-person partnership isn't terminated until the retiring or deceased partner's interest is liquidated. (Reg § 1.708-1(b)(1)(i), Reg § 1.736-1(a)(6))[49]

¶ 3775 Special Basis Adjustments to Partnership Property. ▬▬▬▬▬▬

A partnership's basis in its assets ("inside basis") is unaffected by partnership distributions and transfers of partnership interests unless the partnership makes a special basis election. Under certain circumstances, the transferee of a partnership interest may elect to adjust the basis of property distributed to him as if the partnership had made the special basis election.

¶ 3776 Post-transfer adjustments to basis.

A transfer of a partnership interest by reason of a sale or exchange or the death of a partner causes a basis adjustment of the partnership's property if a basis adjustment election under Code Sec. 754 is in effect, or if the partnership has a substantial built-in loss immediately after the transfer. (Code Sec. 743(a)) A partnership is treated as having a substantial built-in loss if the partnership's adjusted basis in the partnership property is more than $250,000 more than the fair market value of that property. (Code Sec. 743(d)(1)) IRS has issued procedures for complying with the basis adjustments required in the case of substantial built-in losses.[50]

However, a contribution of cash or property to the partnership does not cause a basis adjustment to the partnership's property, regardless of whether a basis adjustment election is in effect. (Reg § 1.743-1(a))[1] If the election is in effect, the partnership's basis in its property with respect to the transferee partner is increased by any excess of the partner's basis in his interest over his share of the basis of partnership property (or decreased if his basis in his interest is lower). (Reg § 1.743-1(b))[2] Regs provide rules for allocating the basis adjustment

45. ¶s B-4109, B-4110; ¶7364.01; TD ¶592,007
46. ¶B-4105; ¶7364.02; TD ¶592,004
47. ¶B-4107; ¶7064.02; TD ¶592,006
48. ¶B-4202; ¶7064.02; TD ¶592,502

49. ¶B-4112; ¶7084.03; TD ¶592,010
50. ¶B-4008; ¶7434; TD ¶591,511
1. ¶B-4010; ¶7434; TD ¶591,512
2. ¶B-4007 *et seq.*; ¶7434; TD ¶591,500 *et seq.*

among the partnership's assets. (Reg § 1.755-1)[3]

¶ 3777 Post-distribution adjustments to basis of undistributed property.

The basis of partnership property is not adjusted when the partnership makes a distribution to a partner unless a basis adjustment election under Code Sec. 754 is in effect, or the partnership has a "substantial basis reduction" with respect to the distribution. (Code Sec. 734(a)) A substantial basis reduction exists where the sum of (i) the amount of the partner's loss on the distribution, and (ii) the basis increase to the distributed properties, is over $250,000. (Code Sec. 734(d))[4] If an adjustment is made on a partnership distribution, the partnership's basis in its retained property (1) is increased by the amount of gain recognized by the distributee partner on the distribution, and the amount by which the basis of the distributed property in the hands of the partnership before the distribution exceeds the basis of the property in the hands of the distributee partner (Code Sec. 734(b)(1)), and (2) is decreased by the amount of loss recognized by the distributee partner on the distribution and the amount by which the basis of the distributed property in the hands of the distributee partner exceeds the basis the partnership had in the property before the distribution. (Code Sec. 734(b)(2)(B))[5] Regs provide rules for allocating the basis adjustment among the partnership's assets. (Reg § 1.755-1)[6]

However, in allocating any basis reduction in partnership property under Code Sec. 734(b) as a result of a distribution, no allocation may be made to stock in a corporation that is a partner in the partnership, or to the stock of any person related to the corporation, and any amount not allocable to stock is allocated to other partnership property. Where the reduction that must be allocated to other partnership property exceeds the aggregate adjusted basis of the other partnership property immediately before the required allocation, gain is recognized by the partnership to the extent of the excess. (Code Sec. 755(c))[7]

Where the basis of a partnership's recovery property is increased as a result of a distribution of property by the partnership, the increased portion of the basis is taken into account for depreciation purposes as if it were newly purchased recovery property placed in service when the distribution or transfer occurs. Any applicable recovery period and method may be used to determine the recovery (depreciation) deduction for the increased portion of the basis. However, no change is allowed in determining the recovery (depreciation) deduction for the portion of the basis of recovery property for which there is no increase. (Reg § 1.734-1(e)(1))[8]

Where the basis adjustment requires a decrease in the basis of partnership recovery property, the basis decrease must be accounted for over the remaining recovery period of the property beginning with the recovery period in which the basis is decreased. (Reg § 1.734-1(e)(2))[9]

¶ 3778 Partner's basis adjustments.

Where a partnership interest is transferred and the partnership later distributes property, but hasn't made the election described at ¶3776, the transferee-partner may elect to have the basis of the property distributed to him adjusted as if the partnership had made the election. The election to make the adjustment applies only for purposes of determining the basis of distributed property (other than money) in the partner's hands. It doesn't enable the partner to amend prior income tax returns to recompute income based on an adjusted basis. (Code Sec. 732(d)) Accordingly, in computing the adjustment, no deduction is made for any depletion or depreciation of that portion of the basis of partnership property which arises from the basis adjustment, since no depletion or depreciation on the basis adjustment for the period before the distribution is allowed or allowable unless the partnership had an election in effect.

---

3. ¶B-4050 *et seq.*; ¶7554; TD ¶591,526 *et seq.*
4. ¶B-4002.1; ¶7344; TD ¶591,504
5. ¶B-4002; ¶7344.01; TD ¶591,504
6. ¶B-4021 *et seq.*; ¶7554; TD ¶591,532

7. ¶B-4054.1; ¶7554
8. ¶B-4007; ¶7344.01; TD ¶591,509
9. ¶B-4007; ¶7344.01; TD ¶591,509

(Reg § 1.732-1(d)(1)(iv))[10]

The transferee-partner may make this election only with respect to property (other than money) distributed to him within two years after he acquired his interest by transfer. (Code Sec. 732(d))[11]

The adjustment is *required* (without regard to the two-year limit) if, at the time the transferee-partner acquired the transferred partnership interest, all three of the following conditions existed:

(1) The fair market value of all partnership property (other than money) exceeded 110% of its adjusted basis to the partnership.

(2) Allocation of basis under Code Sec. 732(c) (general rule for allocation of basis of distributed properties) upon a liquidation of his interest immediately after the transfer of the interest would have resulted in a shift of basis from property not subject to depreciation, depletion or amortization to property that is so subject.

(3) The post-transfer adjustment would change the basis to the transferee-partner of the property actually distributed. (Code Sec. 732(d); Reg § 1.732-1(d)(4))[12]

¶ 3779 Basis of unrealized receivables and inventory items distributed to a partner.

If unrealized receivables or inventory items are distributed to a *transferee partner* who has a special basis adjustment for those assets under either the post-transfer adjustment rule (¶3776) or the distributed property adjustment rule (¶3777), the partnership's adjusted basis, immediately before distribution, of any unrealized receivables or inventory items distributed to such a partner takes into account the following portions of the post-transfer or distributed property basis adjustments that the distributee partner has for those assets:

. . . The entire amount of the post-transfer or distributed property basis adjustments *if* the distributee-partner receives his entire share of the fair market value of the unrealized receivables or inventory items of the partnership.

. . . The same proportion of the post-transfer or distributed property basis adjustments as the value of the unrealized receivables or inventory items distributed to him bears to his entire share of the total value of all those items of the partnership, *if* the distributee-partner gets less than his entire share of those items. (Reg § 1.732-2(c))[13]

¶ 3780 Electing basis adjustments.

The election to adjust the basis of the partnership assets on a distribution, sale, or transfer of a partnership interest (¶3776, ¶3777) is made by the partnership filing a statement of election with the partnership return for the tax year during which the transfer of interest or the distribution of property occurs. (Code Sec. 754; Reg § 1.754-1(b)) Once made, the election applies to all current and future distributions and transfers until revoked. (Code Sec. 754; Reg § 1.754-1(a))[14]

A transferee-partner who wishes to make the distributed property adjustment (¶3778) must elect as follows:

. . . If the distribution includes any depreciable, depletable, or amortizable property, elect with the return for the distribution year.

. . . If it doesn't include any such property, elect not later than the first tax year in which the basis of any of the distributed property is pertinent in determining the transferee-partner's tax. (Reg § 1.732-1(d)(2), Reg § 1.732-1(d)(3))[15]

---

10. ¶B-4029; ¶7324.01; TD ¶591,537
11. ¶B-4029; ¶7324.01; TD ¶591,537
12. ¶B-4033; ¶7324.01; TD ¶591,540

13. ¶B-4018; TD ¶591,520
14. ¶B-4023 *et seq.*; ¶7544 *et seq.*; TD ¶591,501
15. ¶B-4031; ¶7324.01; TD ¶591,538

¶ 3781   Terminations. ▌

A partnership ordinarily terminates only on discontinuance of operations as a partnership, or on sale or exchange of 50% or more of the total interests in the partnership.

¶ 3782   Termination of partnership.

A partnership terminates for tax purposes (whether or not it has terminated under applicable local law) when:

. . . it stops doing business as a partnership, or

. . . 50% or more of the total interest in partnership capital and profits changes hands by sale or exchange (or by distribution, unless excepted by regs) within 12 consecutive months. (Code Sec. 708, Code Sec. 761(e); Reg § 1.708-1(b)(1))[16] There has been such a change if a corporation transfers its 50% or more interest in a partnership to a new or different corporation in connection with a tax-free corporate reorganization.[17]

As a result of this sale or exchange, the partnership is deemed to transfer all of its assets and liabilities to a new partnership in exchange for an interest in the new partnership, and immediately after that, the terminated partnership is deemed to distribute interests in the new partnership to the purchasing partner and the remaining partners in liquidation of the terminated partnership, either for the continuation of the business of the new partnership or for its dissolution and winding up. (Reg § 1.708-1(b)(4))[18]

The sale may be made to an existing partner or an outsider. It may be made by one or more persons. A gift, bequest, or inheritance or liquidation of a partnership interest doesn't count; nor does a contribution of property to a partnership in exchange for a partnership interest, even if this produces a 50% or more change. (Reg § 1.708-1(b)(2))[19]

¶ 3783   Split-up of partnership.

If a partnership splits up into two or more partnerships, each resulting partnership is considered a continuation of the old partnership as long as the members of the resulting partnership had more than a 50% interest in the capital and profits of the old partnership. A resulting partnership whose members had an interest of only 50% or less in the old partnership is treated as a new partnership.

If the members of none of the resulting partnerships had more than a 50% interest in the old partnership, the old partnership is considered terminated as of the date of the division, and all the resulting partnerships are treated as new partnerships. (Code Sec. 708(b)(2)(B); Reg § 1.708-1(d)(2))[20]

Any members of the original partnership who do not become members of a resulting partnership that is treated as a continuation of the original partnership are considered to have had their partnership interests liquidated as of the date of the division. (Reg § 1.708-1(d)(1))

For divisions, the resulting partnership that is treated as the divided partnership must file a return for the tax year of the partnership that has been divided and must retain the employer identification number (EIN) of the prior partnership. All other resulting partnerships that are regarded as continuing and new partnerships must file separate returns for the tax year beginning on the day after the date of the division with new EINs for each partnership. (Reg § 1.708-1(d)(2))

---

16. ¶B-4301; ¶7084; TD ¶594,001
17. ¶B-4303; ¶7084.05; TD ¶594,004
18. ¶B-4305; ¶7084; TD ¶594,006
19. ¶B-4303; ¶7084.02; TD ¶594,004
20. ¶B-4308; ¶7084.06; TD ¶594,009

Chapter 18   Trusts—Estates—Decedents

¶ 3900   Trust and Estate Income Tax Rules. ▮▮▮▮▮▮▮▮▮▮

Trusts and estates are generally treated as separate taxpayers and, with some important qualifications, are taxed in the same way as individuals.

¶ 3901   Taxation of trusts and estates—Form 1041.

Trust and estate income is normally taxed to the fiduciary (that is, to the trust or estate itself), if retained by the trust, or to the beneficiary, if distributed. Thus, if the fiduciary passes on income to the beneficiary, the trust or estate deducts the distributed income which then becomes taxable to the beneficiary. A special yardstick called "distributable net income" (DNI) (see ¶3935 and ¶3937) is used to limit both the amount deducted by the trust or estate as a distribution and the amount taxed to the beneficiary. (Code Sec. 643, Code Sec. 651, Code Sec. 652, Code Sec. 661, Code Sec. 662)[1]

The income that's passed on to the beneficiary has the same tax attributes in the beneficiary's hands as when received by the fiduciary, see ¶3946.

Trusts and estates compute their tax under a tightly-compressed, five-bracket tax rate schedule (¶1106) that quickly reaches the top marginal rate. (Code Sec. 1(e))[2] Trusts and estates can't use the tax tables to figure their tax. (Code Sec. 3(b)(2))

Ⓡcaution: For treatment of trusts and estates for AMT purposes, see ¶3200 *et seq.*

A foreign trust or estate is taxed as if it were a nonresident alien individual who isn't present in the U.S. at any time, see ¶4637 *et seq.*, subject to special rules for trusts. (Code Sec. 641(b))[3]

For income tax returns of trusts and estates (Form 1041), see ¶4732 *et seq.* Beneficiaries must report items consistently with the entity's return or notify IRS (on Form 8082) of the inconsistency. (Code Sec. 6034A(c)).[4]

For the 3.8% surtax on a trust's or estate's unearned income, see ¶3956

For the tax years of trusts and estates, see ¶2808.

Optional Form 1041-V, Payment Voucher is used to include information about the taxpayer's remittance of the balance due on Form 1041. IRS encourages its use if payment is made by check or money order.

¶ 3902   Election to treat revocable trust as part of estate—Form 8855.

An election can be made to have an individual's revocable trust treated as part of his estate for income tax purposes. (Code Sec. 645) If there is an executor, the trustee and the executor make the election by filing Form 8855. If there is no executor, the trustee makes the election by filing Form 8855. (Reg § 1.645-1(c))[5]

¶ 3903   Estimated tax payments by trusts and estates—Form 1041-ES.

Trusts and certain estates must make estimated income tax payments (using Form 1041-ES and vouchers) under rules similar to those that apply to individuals, with certain adjustments. (Code Sec. 6654(l)(1))[6] Trusts and estates generally have 45 days to compute their

---

1. ¶C-2600 *et seq.*, ¶C-7000 *et seq.*; ¶6414; TD ¶s 651,001, 661,001
2. ¶s C-1003 *et seq.*, C-7002 *et seq.*; ¶6414; TD ¶s 651,003, 661,003
3. ¶C-1014 *et seq.*, ¶O-10118; ¶6414; TD ¶665,501
4. ¶s C-3081, C-9081; ¶60,34A4; TD ¶665,029, TD ¶655,500
5. ¶C-1021 *et seq.*; ¶6454; TD ¶661,002
6. ¶S-5300 *et seq.*; ¶66,544.08; TD ¶658,501

References beginning with a single letter are to paragraphs in RIA's Federal Tax Coordinator 2d and RIA's Analysis of Federal Taxes: Income. Those beginning with numbers are to paragraphs in RIA's United States Tax Reporter. Those beginning with TD are to paragraphs in RIA's Tax Desk.

estimated tax payments under the annualization rules. (Code Sec. 6654(l)(4))[7]

Estates and grantor trusts that receive the residue of a probate estate are exempt from making estimated tax payments for their first two tax years after the date of decedent's death. (Code Sec. 6654(l)(2))[8] Charitable trusts subject to tax under Code Sec. 511 are subject to corporate, not individual estimated taxes. (Code Sec. 6654(l)(3), Code Sec. 6655(g)(3))[9]

Where an electing small business trust election (see ¶3910) is effective on a date other than the first day of the trust's tax year, the trust is considered one trust for estimated tax purposes. (Reg § 1.1361-1(m)(3)(v))[10]

¶ 3904   Estimated tax payments for trusts and estates with short year.

A trust or estate with a short tax year must pay estimated tax installments on or before the 15th day of the 4th, 6th and 9th month of such tax year, and the 15th day of the first month of the following year. For a short tax year in which the trust or estate terminates, installments due before the last day of the short year must be paid, and a final installment must be paid by the 15th day of the first month following the month the short year ends.[11]

¶ 3905   Election to treat estimated tax payments as paid by beneficiary—Form 1041-T.

A trustee may elect (on Form 1041-T) to treat any part of the trust's estimated tax payments as paid by a beneficiary. Any amount so treated is considered paid or credited to the beneficiary on the last day of the trust's tax year and is considered an estimated tax payment made by the beneficiary on Jan. 15, following the trust's tax year. (Code Sec. 643(g)(1))[12]

This election is available to an estate for a tax year reasonably expected to be its last tax year. (Code Sec. 643(g)(3))

Elect on or before the *65th day* after the tax year. (Code Sec. 643(g)(2)) Attach Form 1041-T to Form 1041 only if the election is made with Form 1041. Otherwise, file Form 1041-T separately. The election is irrevocable. (Reg § 301.9100-8(a)(4))[13]

RIA *observation:* The income tax return of a trust or estate is due 3 ½ months after the close of its tax year, see ¶4732. Thus the election must be made before the return due date.

¶ 3906   Trust's termination.

When a trust terminates, it ends as a separate tax entity and no longer reports gross income or claims the deductions, credits, etc. (Reg § 1.641(b)-3(d))

Though the duration of a trust may depend on the occurrence of a particular event under the trust instrument, e.g., the life beneficiary reaching a specified age, for tax purposes the trust will nevertheless continue for a reasonable period beyond this time to allow for the orderly completion of administration. (Reg § 1.641(b)-3(b))[14]

For unused deductions allowed to a beneficiary on a trust's termination, see ¶3951.

¶ 3907   Estate's termination.

An estate's status as a separate taxpayer exists only during the period of administration or settlement of the estate. (Code Sec. 641(a)(3)) This is the period actually required to perform

7. ¶S-5304; ¶6434.08; TD ¶658,506
8. ¶s S-5302, S-5203; ¶66,544.08; TD ¶s 658,502, 666,002
9. ¶s S-5301, S-5420; ¶66,554; TD ¶658,500
10. ¶S-5301

11. ¶S-5311; ¶6434.08; TD ¶658,503
12. ¶S-5309; ¶66,544.08; TD ¶654,022
13. ¶S-5310; ¶6434.08; TD ¶658,510
14. ¶C-1012; ¶6414.07; TD ¶651,011

the ordinary duties of administration, such as collecting assets and paying legacies and debts.[15] If estate administration is unduly prolonged, IRS considers the estate terminated for tax purposes after expiration of a reasonable period for performance by the executor of all the duties of administration. (Reg § 1.641(b)-3(a))[16]

For unused deductions allowed to a beneficiary on an estate's termination, see ¶3951.

¶ 3908 Trust taxed as business entity.

The fact that any organization is technically cast in the trust form won't change the real character of the organization if the organization is more properly classified as a business entity under Reg § 301.7701-2. (Reg § 301.7701-4(b))[17]

¶ 3909 Liquidating trusts.

Liquidating trusts are ordinary trusts if their primary purpose is to liquidate the assets transferred to them. They are corporations if liquidation is only an incidental or ultimate intention and the primary objective is to continue normal business operations for an indefinite time. (Reg § 301.7701-4(d))[18]

¶ 3910 Electing small business trusts (ESBTs) for holding S stock.

ESBTs may hold stock of an S corporation. For the portion of an ESBT consisting of S stock, the normal pass-through rules don't apply; instead, the trust is taxed at a flat rate of 39.6% on its taxable ordinary income as specially computed and its capital gains are taxed at the preferential rates that apply for individuals. Interest paid or accrued on debt incurred to acquire S stock is taken into account in determining the income of the S portion of an ESBT. (Code Sec. 641(c)) A grantor trust may elect to be an ESBT and if it does, the trust consists of a grantor portion, an S portion, and a non-S portion. The items of income, deduction, and credit attributable to the grantor portion are taxed to the deemed owner of that portion. The S portion is taxed under the special rules of Code Sec. 641(c), while the non-S portion is subject to the normal trust rules. (Reg § 1.641(c)-1)[19]

¶ 3911 Environmental remediation trusts.

An environmental remediation trust is treated as a grantor trust. Each contributor is taxed on the portion of the trust relating to his contributions. (Reg § 301.7701-4(e))[20]

¶ 3912 Funeral trusts—Form 1041-QFT.

A trustee of a qualified funeral trust may elect simplified tax treatment for the trust on Form 1041-QFT, if it would otherwise be treated as a grantor trust. (Code Sec. 685)[21]

¶ 3913 Multiple trusts.

If a grantor creates multiple trusts, each trust is treated as a separate taxpayer. Separate trusts may be created even though there is only one trust instrument and only one trustee.[22]

Two or more trusts are treated as one if: (1) the trusts have substantially the same grantor or grantors and substantially the same primary beneficiary or beneficiaries, and (2) a principal purpose of the trusts is avoidance of federal income tax. (Code Sec. 643(f)) However, if a

15. ¶C-7010; ¶6414.03; TD ¶661,010
16. ¶C-7011 *et seq.*; ¶6414.03; TD ¶661,010
17. ¶C-5003; ¶77,014.13; TD ¶651,025
18. ¶C-5015; ¶77,014.17; TD ¶651,027

19. ¶C-5700 *et seq.*; ¶6414.08; TD ¶657,500 *et seq.*
20. ¶C-5035.1; ¶77,014.12; TD ¶657,005
21. ¶C-1013.1; ¶6854; TD ¶657,018
22. ¶C-5150 *et seq.*; ¶6434.07; TD ¶651,034

trust was irrevocable on Mar. 1, '84, this consolidation rule applies only to that portion of the trust attributable to contributions to corpus after Mar. 1, '84.[23]

¶ 3914　Charitable remainder annuity trust and charitable remainder unitrust.

These types of trusts (¶2116) are not subject to income tax. However, if they have unrelated business taxable income (UBTI), they must pay an excise tax equal to 100% of the UBTI. (Code Sec. 664(c); Reg § 1.664-1(a)(1))[24]

¶ 3915　Pooled income fund (PIF).

A PIF formed to pay income to noncharitable beneficiaries and the remainder to charity (¶2117) generally is taxed under the trust rules[25] even if it isn't a trust under local law. (Reg § 1.642(c)-5(a)(2))[26] However, a PIF is allowed a charitable deduction for long-term capital gain that is, under the terms of its governing instrument, permanently set aside for charitable purposes during the tax year. (Code Sec. 642(c)(3); Reg § 1.642(c)-2(c)) No amount of net long-term capital gain will be considered "permanently set aside for charitable purposes" if, under the terms of the PIF's governing instrument and applicable local law, the trustee has the power, whether or not exercised, to satisfy the income beneficiaries' right to income by the payment of either (1) an amount equal to a fixed percentage of the fair market value of the PIF's assets, whether determined annually or averaged on a multiple year basis; or (2) any amount that takes into account unrealized appreciation in the value of the PIF's assets. (Reg § 1.642(c)-2(c))[27]

¶ 3916　Gross income of trusts and estates.

What would be gross income in the hands of an individual is gross income when received by a trust or estate. (Reg § 1.641(a)-2)[28]

Gross income includes income accumulated or held for future distribution under the terms of a will or trust, income that's currently distributable, income received by a decedent's estate during administration or settlement, and income that, in the fiduciary's discretion, may be either accumulated or distributed. (Code Sec. 641(a))[29]

¶ 3917　Income from real estate passing directly to heirs.

Where under local law, real property is subject to an estate's administration, the income from it is that of the estate for the period that the estate is under administration.[30]

Where state law vests legal title to decedent's real estate upon his death directly in his heirs, devisees, or other beneficiaries, income from it is taxed to the beneficiaries and not the estate. (Reg § 1.661(a)-2(e))[31]

¶ 3918　Gain or loss on distribution of property in kind.

Gain or loss is realized by a trust or estate (or the other beneficiaries) by reason of a distribution of property in kind if the distribution is in satisfaction of a right to receive a specific dollar amount, specific property other than that distributed, or income, if income is required to be distributed currently. In addition, gain or loss is realized if the trustee or executor makes the Code Sec. 643(e) election to recognize gain or loss. (Reg § 1.661(a)-2(f))[32]

23. ¶C-5154; ¶6434.07; TD ¶651,034
24. ¶C-5039; ¶6644; TD ¶651,030
25. ¶s C-2312, C-2316; TD ¶651,031
26. ¶C-5040; TD ¶651,031
27. ¶C-2316; ¶6424.03
28. ¶s C-2100 *et seq.*, C-7100 *et seq.*; ¶6414; TD ¶s 652,001,

662,001
29. ¶s C-2101, C-7101; ¶6414 *et seq.*; TD ¶s 652,001, 662,001
30. ¶C-7105; TD ¶662,009
31. ¶C-7109; TD ¶662,009
32. ¶s C-2151, C-7151; ¶6614.01; TD ¶s 652,006, 662,018

Trusts and estates may not deduct a loss on property to which a Code Sec. 643(e)(3) election applies because of the rule barring losses on sales between related parties. See ¶2448.

¶ 3919 Estate income from community property.

If a decedent dies leaving community property, the income from one-half of the property is taxable to the estate and the income from the other half is taxable to the surviving spouse.[33]

¶ 3920 Deductions and credits of trusts and estates.

Deductions and credits of trusts and estates are basically those allowed to individuals except for the special deduction rules discussed in the following paragraphs. (Code Sec. 641(b); Reg § 1.641(b)-1)[34]

¶ 3921 Two percent floor on miscellaneous itemized deductions.

For purposes of this floor (see ¶3110), the adjusted gross income of a trust or estate is computed the same as for an individual, except the deductions for: (1) costs paid or incurred in connection with the administration of the trust or estate (¶3922) that wouldn't have been incurred if the property weren't held in the trust or estate; (2) the trust's or estate's personal exemptions (¶3928); and (3) distribution deductions (¶3934 and ¶3936), are allowed as deductions in arriving at adjusted gross income. (Code Sec. 67(e)) Thus, these expenses aren't subject to the floor. The Supreme Court has held that investment advisory fees paid by a trust are subject to the floor if the investment advisor doesn't charge the trust more than it would charge an individual. However, until final regs are issued, nongrantor trusts and estates don't have to "unbundle" a fiduciary fee into components that are subject to the deduction limit and those that aren't. Thus, until regs are issued, they can deduct the full amount of a bundled fiduciary fee without regard to the 2% floor.

Amounts that wouldn't be allowable as miscellaneous itemized deductions if paid directly by an individual can't be indirectly deducted through grantor trusts. (Code Sec. 67(c); Reg § 1.67-2T(g)(1), Reg § 1.67-2T(g)(2))

¶ 3922 Administration expenses.

Reasonable amounts paid or incurred by the fiduciary of an estate or trust on account of administration expenses, including fiduciaries' fees and litigation expenses, that are ordinary and necessary in the performance of duties of administration are deductible. (Reg § 1.212-1(i)) Deductible items include commissions and legal fees, whether allocable to corpus or income.[35] For the election to deduct these expenses against income or estate tax, see ¶3925.

¶ 3923 Interest deduction.

An estate or trust may deduct interest to the same extent as an individual, see ¶1700 *et seq.* Thus, an estate or trust is subject to the bar on the deduction of "personal" interest. But otherwise deductible interest on deferred estate tax on a closely held business interest or a reversionary interest (see ¶5036) isn't subject to this limit (Code Sec. 163(h)), except that for estates of individuals dying after '97 (and, if elected, of individuals dying before '98), interest on deferred estate tax on a closely held business interest isn't deductible. (Code Sec. 163(k))[36]

---

33. ¶C-7108; ¶6414.06; TD ¶662,008
34. ¶s C-2200 *et seq.*, C-7200 *et seq.*; ¶6414; TD ¶s 651,001, 661,001

35. ¶s C-2217, C-7215; ¶s 2124.09, 6424; TD ¶s 653,016, 663,014
36. ¶K-5513; ¶s 1634.013, 1634.054; TD ¶663,010

¶ 3924   Expenses of exempt income.

No deduction may be taken for *any* expenses allocable to tax-exempt income. (Code Sec. 265; Reg § 1.212-1(i))[37]

¶ 3925   Election to take either income tax or estate tax deduction.

Administration expenses, including commissions and other selling expenses, and casualty and theft losses during administration may be taken either: (1) as a deduction (or as an offset against the sales price of property in determining gain or loss) in computing the estate's taxable income for *income tax* purposes, or (2) as a deduction in computing the decedent's taxable estate for *estate tax* purposes, but not both. (Code Sec. 642(g)) To take the income tax deduction, the executor should file in duplicate (a) a statement that the amount involved hasn't already been taken as a deduction for federal estate tax purposes, and (b) a waiver of the right to take it as an estate tax deduction. (Reg § 1.642(g)-1)[38]

Some items or portion of an item can be deducted for income tax purposes if the statement and waiver are filed, while a similar item or different portion of the same item can be taken for estate tax purposes. (Reg § 1.642(g)-2)[39]

Similar rules apply for purposes of the GST tax. (Code Sec. 642(g))[40]

¶ 3926   Deductions that can be claimed for both income and estate tax purposes.

The rule barring deductions for *both* income tax and estate tax purposes (¶3925) doesn't apply to obligations of the decedent for interest, taxes and expenses that are allowable as deductions in respect of a decedent as explained at ¶3971 (Reg § 1.642(g)-2), or items that qualify for deduction on the estate tax return as claims against the estate.[41]

¶ 3927   Depreciation and depletion.

Depreciation and depletion deductions of trust or estate property must be apportioned.

For a *trust*, these deductions are generally apportioned between the beneficiaries and the trustee on the basis of the trust income allocable to each. (Code Sec. 167(d), Code Sec. 611(b)(3), Code Sec. 642(e))[42] But if the trustee is required or permitted by the trust instrument or local law to maintain a reserve for the deduction, the deduction belongs to the trust to the extent that income is actually set aside for the reserve. Apart from this, the regs bar any deduction by the trust or a beneficiary that exceeds the trust's or beneficiary's allocable share of trust income. (Reg § 1.167(h)-1(b), Reg § 1.611-1(c)(4))[43]

For an *estate*, the deductions are apportioned between the estate and the beneficiaries on the basis of the estate income allocable to each, regardless of the terms of the will. (Code Sec. 167(d), Code Sec. 611(b)(4))[44]

¶ 3928   Personal exemption.

An estate is entitled to a deduction for a personal exemption of $600. (Code Sec. 642(b))[45]

A trust that's required to distribute all of its income currently has a $300 exemption (even for a year in which it makes a corpus distribution or a charitable contribution). A qualified disability trust is allowed a personal exemption amount equal to the individual personal

---

37. ¶s C-2217, C-2219, C-7217; ¶2654; TD ¶s 653,016, 663,014
38. ¶C-7226 *et seq.*; ¶6424.07; TD ¶s 663,025, 776,082
39. ¶C-7232; ¶6424.07; TD ¶663,025, 776,082
40. ¶C-7227; ¶6424.07; TD ¶663,026
41. ¶s C-7234, C-7235; ¶6914.04; TD ¶663,033, TD ¶776,082

42. ¶C-2222 *et seq.*; ¶6424.06; TD ¶s 653,019, 663,019
43. ¶C-2214, C-2224; ¶6424.06; TD ¶653,019
44. ¶C-7220; ¶s 1674.119, 6424.06; TD ¶663,019
45. ¶C-7207; ¶6424.01; TD ¶663,006

exemption. (see ¶3115) All other trusts deduct $100. (Code Sec. 642(b); Reg § 1.642(b)-1)[46]

¶ 3929   Standard deduction.

The standard deduction of a trust or estate is zero. (Code Sec. 63(c)(6)(D))[47]

¶ 3930   Net operating loss (NOL).

Trusts and estates are entitled to the NOL deduction. (Code Sec. 642(d)) In computing the NOL, the charitable deduction and the deduction for distributions are disregarded. (Reg § 1.642(d)-1)[48]

¶ 3931   Charitable contributions—Form 1041-A.

An estate or trust may deduct any amount of gross income, without limitation, that, under the terms of the governing instrument is *paid* during the tax year for a charitable purpose. (Code Sec. 642(c)(1); Reg § 1.642(c)-1(a)) A provision in a governing instrument or local law that specifically provides the source from which amounts are to be paid, permanently set aside, or used for a purpose specified in Code Sec. 642(c), must have economic effect independent of income tax consequences in order to be respected for Federal tax purposes. (Reg § 1.642(c)-3(b)(2), Reg § 1.643(a)-5(b)) A contribution made out of income accumulated in earlier years is deductible, but only if no deduction was allowed for any previous year for the amount currently contributed. However, for a donation of property purchased from income in a prior year, the entity may claim a charitable deduction only for the property's adjusted basis and not its higher fair market value.[49] These deductions aren't subject to the 2% floor on miscellaneous itemized deductions, see ¶3110. (Code Sec. 67(b)(4)) File Form 1041-A for a trust that claims a charitable deduction under Code Sec. 642(c). Use Form 8868 for an extension, see ¶4124.

Estates are allowed to deduct any amount of gross income, without limit, which under the terms of the governing instrument is, during the tax year, permanently *set aside* for a charitable purpose. (Code Sec. 642(c)(2); Reg § 1.642(c)-2(a), Reg § 1.642(c)-2(b))[50] *Trusts* are denied the set-aside deduction, except for pooled income funds. (Code Sec. 642(c)(2), Code Sec. 642(c)(3); Reg § 1.642(c)-2(b), Reg § 1.642(c)-2(c))[1]

Contributions made out of tax-exempt income, such as state or municipal bond interest, aren't deductible. (Reg § 1.642(c)-3(b), Reg § 1.643(a)-5(b))[2]

¶ 3932   Election to accelerate charitable deduction.

A trust or estate can elect to treat a contribution actually paid in one tax year as paid in the preceding tax year. The election must be made not later than the due date (including extensions) of the income tax return for the tax year *following the tax year* to which the deductions are pushed back. (Code Sec. 642(c)(1))[3] Elect by attaching a statement to the return or amended return for the year to which the deductions are pushed back. (Reg § 1.642(c)-1(b))[4]

---

46. ¶C-2206; ¶6424.01; TD ¶653,004
47. ¶s C-2204, C-7205; ¶634; TD ¶s 653,003, 663,004
48. ¶s C-2226, C-7222; ¶6424.05; TD ¶s 653,022, 663,021
49. ¶s C-2301 *et seq.*, C-7301 *et seq.*; ¶6424.02; TD ¶s 653,023, 663,036

50. ¶C-7311; ¶6424.02; TD ¶663,036
1. ¶C-2312 *et seq.*; ¶6424.03; TD ¶653,031
2. ¶s C-2308, C-7308; ¶6424.02; TD ¶s 653,029, 663,042
3. ¶s C-2303, C-7304; ¶6424.02; TD ¶s 653,026, 663,039
4. ¶s C-2305, C-7305; ¶6424.02; TD ¶s 653,027, 663,039

¶ 3933 Deduction for distributions to beneficiaries of trusts and estates.

Distributions to beneficiaries are deductible up to the "distributable net income" (DNI) of the trust or estate for the tax year. (Code Sec. 651(b), Code Sec. 661(a))[5] The distribution deduction of a trust depends on whether the trust is a simple trust or a complex trust.

A "simple" trust (¶3934) is one that makes no distribution other than of current income and the terms of which require all of its income to be distributed currently and do not provide for charitable or similar contributions. A "complex" trust (¶3936) permits accumulation of income or charitable contributions or distributes principal.

A trust may shift its character from simple to complex and vice versa. (Reg § 1.651(a)-1, Reg § 1.661(a)-1)[6]

¶ 3934 Distributions deduction of a simple trust.

This deduction for a simple trust is the amount of its income for the tax year that's required to be distributed currently, up to the ceiling of its distributable net income (DNI) for the year (¶3935). (Code Sec. 651(b)) Tax-exempt income is excluded both from accounting income and DNI in figuring the deduction. (Reg § 1.651(b)-1)[7]

¶ 3935 Distributable net income (DNI) of a simple trust.

The starting point is *taxable* income, i.e., gross income minus deductions. These adjustments are then made to taxable income:

(1) Add back the deduction for personal exemption and any deduction for distributions. (Code Sec. 643(a)(1), Code Sec. 643(a)(2); Reg § 1.643(a)-1, Reg § 1.643(a)-2)

(2) Subtract any extraordinary dividends (in cash or property) and taxable stock dividends that the trustee doesn't pay or credit because he determines they are allocable to principal. (Code Sec. 643(a)(4); Reg § 1.643(a)-4)

(3) Subtract any capital gains that are allocated to principal and aren't paid, credited or required to be distributed during the tax year. Add back any capital losses, except to the extent they are taken into account in computing capital gains that are paid, credited or required to be distributed during the tax year. Add back any gain excluded under Code Sec. 1202 on the sale of qualified small business stock. (Code Sec. 643(a)(3); Reg § 1.643(a)-3(b))[8]

Gains from the sale or exchange of capital assets are included in DNI to the extent they are allocated to: (i) income; (ii) corpus, but treated consistently by the fiduciary on the trust's books, records, and tax returns as part of a distribution to a beneficiary; or (iii) corpus, but actually distributed to the beneficiary or used by the fiduciary in determining the amount that is distributed or required to be distributed to a beneficiary. (Reg § 1.643(a)-3(b))[9]

¶ 3936 Distributions deduction of a complex trust or estate.

A complex trust or estate deducts, up to its distributable net income (DNI) ceiling for the year (¶3937), the sum of:

(1) any income for the tax year required to be distributed currently (¶3938); and

(2) any other amounts, whether income or principal, properly paid or credited or required to be distributed for that tax year (¶3939). (Code Sec. 661(a); Reg § 1.661(a)-2(a))[10]

---

5. ¶s C-2501, C-8001; ¶6514; TD ¶s 654,001, 664,001
6. ¶C-2501; ¶6514.01; TD ¶654,030
7. ¶C-2603 *et seq.*; ¶6514.01; TD ¶654,013

8. ¶C-2606 *et seq.*; ¶6434.01; TD ¶654,032
9. ¶C-2608; ¶6434.01; TD ¶654,034
10. ¶s C-2701, C-8101; ¶6614.01; TD ¶s 654,037, 664,001

No distributions deduction may be taken for any portion of DNI that represents an item, such as tax-exempt interest, that isn't included in the gross income of the trust or estate. (Code Sec. 661(c); Reg § 1.661(c)-1) Unless the instrument or local law requires another allocation, the distribution is considered to contain the same proportion of tax-exempt items entering into DNI as the total tax-exempt income bears to total DNI. (Code Sec. 661(b); Reg § 1.661(b)-1)[11]

¶ 3937 Distributable net income (DNI) for a complex trust or estate.

The DNI of a complex trust or an estate is its taxable income with these adjustments:

(1) No deduction for distributions or personal exemption is allowed. (Code Sec. 643(a)(1))

(2) Capital gains are excluded unless: allocated to income; allocated to corpus, but treated consistently by the fiduciary as part of a distribution to a beneficiary; allocated to corpus but actually distributed to the beneficiary or used by the fiduciary in determining the amount that is distributed or required to be distributed to a beneficiary; or allowed as a charitable deduction. Capital losses are excluded except to the extent they enter into a determination of any capital gains paid, credited or required to be distributed to a beneficiary during the tax year. Add back any gain excluded under Code Sec. 1202 on the sale of qualified small business stock. (Code Sec. 643(a)(3); Reg § 1.643(a)-3(b))

(3) Tax-exempt interest, reduced by allocable, nondeductible expenses, is *included* except to the extent allocable to the charitable deduction. (Code Sec. 643(a)(5); Reg § 1.643(a)-5)[12]

¶ 3938 "Income required to be distributed currently."

Income required to be distributed currently means accounting income of the trust or estate determined under the trust instrument or will and applicable local law. It doesn't include items of gross income that the fiduciary allocates to corpus. (Code Sec. 643(b))

An allocation of amounts between income and principal under applicable local law will be respected if local law provides for a reasonable apportionment between the income and remainder beneficiaries of the total return of the trust for the year, including ordinary and tax-exempt income, capital gains, and appreciation. (Reg § 1.643(b)-1)

A distribution required to be made out of income or corpus, such as an annuity, is considered to be out of currently distributable income to the extent it's paid out of income for the tax year. (Code Sec. 661(a)(1); Reg § 1.661(a)-2(b))

Currently distributable income is deductible for the tax year of the trust or estate in which it is received even though, as a matter of practical necessity, it isn't distributed until after the end of that year. (Reg § 1.651(a)-2(a), Reg § 1.651(a)-2(b))[13]

¶ 3939 "Other amounts properly paid or credited or required to be distributed."

Other amounts properly paid or credited or required to be distributed must be actually distributed or at least made available on demand by the beneficiary. Even though designated by the fiduciary as a payment of *principal* of the trust or estate, a distribution actually paid or made available is deductible by the fiduciary as a distribution of "other amounts." It isn't necessary that the distribution actually be made out of income. (Code Sec. 661(a); Reg § 1.661(a)-2(c))[14] An amount that a trust has elected to treat as an estimated tax payment by a beneficiary (¶3905) is a deductible distribution. (Code Sec. 643(g))[15]

11. ¶s C-2707, C-8107; TD ¶s 654,043, 664,036.
12. ¶s C-2702 *et seq.*, C-8102 *et seq.*; ¶6434.01; TD ¶s 654,038, 664,030
13. ¶s C-2504 *et seq.*, C-8003 *et seq.*; ¶s 6434.03, 6514.01, 6624.01;

TD ¶s 654,003, 664,003
14. ¶s C-2524 *et seq.*, C-8014 *et seq.*; ¶s 6614.01, 6624.01; TD ¶s 654,018, 664,013
15. ¶C-2530; ¶6434.08; TD ¶654,022

¶ 3940   Deduction for distribution of property in kind.

Distributions of property in kind qualify for deduction as other amounts paid. (Reg § 1.661(a)-2(c)) If the trust or estate elects to recognize gain or loss (¶3918), the property distributed is taken into account at its fair market value for purposes of the distribution deduction. If the election isn't made, the property is taken into account only to the extent of the lesser of the basis of the property in the hands of the beneficiary (¶3949) or the fair market value of the property. (Code Sec. 643(e)(2), Code Sec. 643(e)(3))[16]

¶ 3941   Family support allowances—"widow's allowance."

Family support allowances (for a decedent's widow or dependent) paid by an estate under a court order or decree, or under local law, are treated as distributions deductible by the estate, subject to the regular distributable net income (DNI) deduction ceiling. (Reg § 1.661(a)-2(e), Reg § 1.662(a)-2(c))[17]

¶ 3942   Nondeductible distributions.

No *distributions* deduction is allowed for:

. . . distributions to charity (Reg § 1.663(a)-2);[18]

. . . the value of any interest in real estate, title to which passes directly from decedent to his heirs and devisees (Reg § 1.661(a)-2(e));[19]

. . . a gift or bequest of specific property or of a specific sum of money that is paid or credited all at once or in not more than three installments—an amount that can be paid only from income isn't considered a gift or bequest of a specific sum of money and is therefore includible in the distributions deduction (Code Sec. 663(a)(1));[20]

. . . any amount reported as a distribution in an earlier year's return because it was credited or required to be distributed in the earlier year (Code Sec. 663(a)(3); Reg § 1.663(a)-3);[21]

. . . any amount paid or credited within the first 65 days of the current year which the fiduciary elected to treat as paid or credited in the preceding year, see ¶3943.

¶ 3943   Election to deduct "late paid" distributions—the "65-day rule."

The fiduciary of a complex trust and the executor of an estate can elect, by checking a box on Form 1041, to treat an amount properly paid or credited within the first 65 days of any tax year of the entity as paid or credited on the last day of the preceding tax year. (Code Sec. 663(b))[22] This gives the trustee or executor time to determine income earned by the trust for the year, and the opportunity to deduct distributions of that income on the return for the year earned.

The amount to which the election applies can't exceed the greater of: (1) the entity's accounting income for the year for which the election is made, or (2) its distributable net income (DNI) for that year, in each case reduced by any amounts paid, credited, or required to be distributed in that year other than amounts considered paid or credited in a preceding tax year by reason of the "65-day" rule. (Reg § 1.663(b)-1(a))[23]

16. ¶s C-2525, C-8015; ¶6434.05; TD ¶s 654,019, 664,014
17. ¶C-8011; ¶6614.01; TD ¶664,011
18. ¶s C-2533, C-8026; ¶6614.01; TD ¶654,027, 664,025
19. ¶C-8027; TD ¶664,026
20. ¶s C-2531 *et seq.*, C-8022 *et seq.*; ¶6614.01; TD ¶654,024,

664,021
21. ¶s C-2534, C-8028; ¶6614.01; TD ¶s 654,028, 664,027
22. ¶C-2713, ¶C-8113; ¶6634.03; TD ¶654,052, TD ¶664,047
23. ¶C-2713, ¶C-8113; ¶6634.03; TD ¶654,052

¶ 3944 Amount taxed to beneficiary of a simple trust.

The beneficiary of a simple trust is generally taxed on the *lower* of these two items:

(1) the amount of trust income for the tax year of the trust required to be distributed to the beneficiary currently whether distributed or not; or

(2) the beneficiary's proportionate share of the trust's DNI. (Code Sec. 652(a); Reg § 1.652(a)-1)

Distributable net income (DNI) is computed as explained at ¶3935, except that for this purpose it includes tax-exempt interest minus allocable deductions. (Code Sec. 643(a)(5)) Tax-exempt income items, however, aren't taxable to the beneficiary because of the character rule explained at ¶3946. Income from sources outside the U.S. is included for foreign trusts. (Code Sec. 643(a)(6))[24]

¶ 3945 Amount taxed to beneficiary of a complex trust or estate.

The beneficiary of a complex trust or of an estate includes in gross income the sum of the following amounts, subject to the distributable net income (DNI) ceiling (see below) and the elimination of tax-exempt items under the character rule (¶3946):

(1) income required to be distributed to him currently (though not actually distributed), which includes an annuity or other amount required to be paid out of income or corpus, to the extent it is paid out of income for the tax year; and

(2) all other amounts (whether from income or principal) properly paid, credited or required to be distributed to him for the tax year (Code Sec. 662(a))[25] including income from property distributed in-kind, see ¶3949. (Reg § 1.662(a)-3(b))

A beneficiary of a complex trust or an estate need not report as income more than his share of DNI, so that the total amount of income reported by all beneficiaries cannot exceed the total DNI of the trust or estate for the tax year. For this purpose, the beneficiaries are divided into two groups or "tiers:"

(1) The first tier is composed of beneficiaries entitled to income distributions currently, that is "income required to be distributed currently."

(2) The second tier is composed of beneficiaries receiving or entitled to receive other "noncurrent" distributions. (Code Sec. 662(a); Reg § 1.662(a)-3(c))[26]

First-tier beneficiaries report, in the aggregate, the amount of their current distributions, up to the amount of DNI for the tax year of the trust or estate, computed as explained at ¶3937 without any charitable deduction. Thus, if the total of first-tier distributions is equal to or less than DNI (without charitable deduction), each first-tier beneficiary reports his full share of the distributions. (Code Sec. 662(a)(1))[27]

But if the total of first-tier distributions exceeds DNI (without charitable deduction) each beneficiary reports an amount equal to his pro rata share of DNI (without charitable deduction). (Code Sec. 662(a)(1); Reg § 1.662(a)-2(b))[28]

Second-tier beneficiaries report, in the aggregate, the amount of their second-tier distributions up to the DNI of the trust or estate as reduced for first-tier distributions of current income. For this purpose, DNI is computed *with* allowance of any charitable deduction.

24. ¶C-3001; ¶s 6524, 6524.02, 6434.01; TD ¶655,001
25. ¶s C-3006 *et seq.*, C-9001 *et seq.*; ¶6624; TD ¶s 655,006, 665,001
26. ¶s C-3010, C-9006; ¶6624; TD ¶s 655,009, 665,005
27. ¶s C-3011 *et seq.*, C-9007 *et seq.*; ¶6624; TD ¶s 655,010, 665,006
28. ¶s C-3011, C-9008; ¶6624; TD ¶s 655,011, 665,007

If the total of second-tier distributions equals or is less than the ceiling (DNI as reduced for first-tier distributions), each second-tier beneficiary reports his or her full share of the second-tier distributions. But, if the total of second-tier distributions exceeds the ceiling, each second-tier beneficiary reports only his pro rata share of the ceiling amount. (Code Sec. 662(a)(2); Reg § 1.662(a)-3(c))[29]

¶ 3946   Character of trust's and estate's income in beneficiary's hands.

For simple trusts, complex trusts and estates, the amounts taxable to the beneficiaries have the same character (e.g., as tax-exempt income) in the hands of the beneficiaries as the amounts had when received by the trust or estate. (Code Sec. 652(b), Code Sec. 662(b); Reg § 1.652(b)-1, Reg § 1.662(b)-1)[30]

Unless the instrument specifically allocates different classes of income to different beneficiaries, amounts distributed are treated as consisting of the same proportion of each class of items entering into the computation of distributable net income (DNI) as the total of each class bears to the total DNI of the trust or estate. (Code Sec. 652(b), Code Sec. 662(b); Reg § 1.652(b)-1, Reg § 1.662(b)-1)[31]

Deductions that enter into the computation of DNI are allocated among the classes as follows:

. . . Deductions *directly* attributable to a particular class of income (interest, rents, dividends, capital gains, etc.) are allocated to that class.

. . . If deductions *directly* attributable to a class of income exceed that class, the excess may be allocated to any other class (including capital gains) included in DNI in the manner shown below for deductions not directly attributable, except that excess deductions directly attributable to tax-exempt income cannot be used to reduce any other class of income.

. . . Deductions not directly attributable to a specific class of income can be allocated to any item of income (including capital gains) included in DNI, but a part must be allocated proportionately to tax-exempt income. Examples of these "neutral" deductions are trustees' commissions (both income and corpus), and state income and personal property taxes. (Reg § 1.652(b)-3)[32]

A *charitable deduction* by an estate or complex trust is allocated just before the other deductions. Allocation follows the terms of the instrument or local law, or if these are silent, the charitable deduction is allocated to each class of income items in the proportion that the total of each class bears to the total of all classes. (Reg § 1.643(a)-5(b), Reg § 1.662(b)-2)[33]

¶ 3947   Beneficiaries' separate shares treated separately.

If a complex trust or an estate accumulates income for one beneficiary and distributes principal to another beneficiary, the normal tax rules would impose a tax burden on the recipient of principal since he in effect must pay tax on income accumulated for the other beneficiary. To prevent this, the "separate share rule" treats substantially separate and independent shares of different beneficiaries of a single trust or estate as though each share represented a separate trust or estate. This applies *only* in computing distributable net income (DNI) as a ceiling on the amount deductible by the trust or estate and taxable to the beneficiaries (Code Sec. 663(c); Reg § 1.663(c)-1(b)), and is mandatory. (Reg § 1.663(c)-1(d))[34] Code Sec. 663(c), Reg § 1.663(c)-1(a))[35] A surviving spouse's elective share is a separate

---

29. ¶s C-3013, C-9009; ¶6624; TD ¶s 655,012, 665,008
30. ¶s C-3002, C-3016, C-9012; ¶s 6524.03, 6624.03; TD ¶s 655,002, 655,015, 665,011
31. ¶s C-3003, C-3016, C-9012; ¶s 6524.02, 6624.02; TD ¶s 655,005, 655,015, 665,011

32. ¶s C-3004, C-3017, C-9013; ¶s 6524, 6524.02, 6624.02; TD ¶s 655,005, 655,016, 665,012
33. ¶s C-3018, C-9015; ¶6624; TD ¶655,017, 665,014
34. ¶C-2711 *et seq.*; ¶6634.01; TD ¶654,047
35. ¶C-8111; ¶6634.01; TD ¶664,040

share,[36] as is a pecuniary formula bequest unless it's not entitled to income or to share in appreciation or depreciation and can paid or credited in more than three installments. (Reg § 1.663(c)-4(b))[37]

¶ 3948   When a beneficiary is taxed.

Amounts required to be distributed currently are taxed to the beneficiary when they are required to be distributed even though not actually distributed. Other distributions are taxed to a beneficiary when they are made or credited, or required to be made. (Code Sec. 652(a), Code Sec. 662(a); Reg § 1.662(a)-3(a))[38]

If a beneficiary's tax year is different from that of the estate or trust, the beneficiary includes his share of the trust or estate income in his return for the tax year in which the tax year of the trust or estate ends. (Code Sec. 652(c), Code Sec. 662(c))[39]

Upon termination of an estate, a beneficiary must include in his calendar year return income received from the estate during both the estate's fiscal year and final short year where both years end within his calendar year.[40]

Where the 65-day rule is elected (¶3943), the beneficiary is considered as receiving the distribution in his tax year that includes the close of the trust's or estate's tax year in which the distribution is considered made. (Reg § 1.663(b)-1(a)(2)(ii))[41]

¶ 3949   Distributions in kind includible in a beneficiary's income.

For property distributed in kind, the amount taken into account under Code Sec. 662(a)(2) (¶3945) for purposes of determining the amount includible in the beneficiary's income and for purposes of determining his basis in the property depends on whether the estate or trust elected to recognize gain or loss on the distribution (see ¶3918).

If the estate or trust elects, the property is taken into account at its fair market value. (Code Sec. 643(e)(3))

If the estate or trust doesn't elect, the property is taken into account only to the extent of the lesser of: (1) the fair market value of the property, or (2) its basis in the hands of the beneficiary. (Code Sec. 643(e)(2))[42]

The beneficiary's basis for property distributed in kind is the adjusted basis of the property in the hands of the estate or trust immediately before the distribution, adjusted for any gain or loss recognized by the estate or trust on the distribution. (Code Sec. 643(e)(1))[43]

¶ 3950   Nontaxable gifts and bequests.

A beneficiary isn't taxable on any amount paid or credited as a gift or bequest of specific property or of a specific sum of money, and that is paid or credited all at once or in not more than three installments. (Code Sec. 663(a)(1))[44]

¶ 3951   Beneficiaries' deductions on estate or trust termination.

Beneficiaries who succeed to property of a trust or estate on its termination can deduct as a miscellaneous itemized deduction the unused deductions in excess of gross income for the last

36. ¶C-8112.1; ¶6634.01; TD ¶664,042
37. ¶C-8112.2; ¶6634.01; TD ¶664,043
38. ¶s C-3025, C-9017; ¶s 6524.01, 6624.01; TD ¶s 655,020, 665,016
39. ¶s C-3026, C-9018; ¶s 6524.04, 6624.04; TD ¶s 655,021, 665,017

40. ¶C-9018; TD ¶665,017
41. ¶C-3028, ¶C-9019; ¶6634.03; TD ¶655,020
42. ¶s C-3009, C-9004; ¶6434.05; TD ¶s 655,008, 665,003
43. ¶s C-3009, C-9004; ¶6614.01; TD ¶s 655,008, 665,003
44. ¶s C-2531, C-8022; ¶6634.02; TD ¶s 654,024, 664,021

tax year of the trust or estate, other than the personal exemption and charitable contributions. The deduction is allowed only for the beneficiary's tax year in which the trust or estate terminates. It is taken into account in computing the beneficiary's items of tax preference. (Code Sec. 642(h); Reg § 1.642(h)-2(a)) Estate beneficiaries who wouldn't receive any of the estate's property under a settlement agreement dealing with the decedent's unpaid income taxes, couldn't claim the estate's unused capital loss carryovers because they weren't "beneficiaries succeeding to the property of the estate."[45]

¶ 3952   Taxation of beneficiaries of charitable remainder trusts (CRTs).

Amounts paid to an income beneficiary of a CRT retain the character they had in the hands of the trust, with this qualification: each payment is treated as consisting of (1) ordinary income, to the extent of the trust's ordinary income for that year and undistributed ordinary income for earlier years, (2) capital gain, to the extent of capital gain for that year and undistributed capital gain (determined on a cumulative net basis) for earlier years, (3) other income (e.g., tax-exempt interest), to the extent of that income for that year and undistributed amounts for earlier years, and (4) trust corpus. (Code Sec. 664(a), Code Sec. 664(b); Reg § 1.664-1(d)(1)) Within categories (1) and (2), items are assigned to different classes to reflect rate differences (e.g., qualified dividends and different capital gain classes). (Reg § 1.664-1(d)(1)(i)(b))[46]

¶ 3953   Distribution of accumulated trust income—"throwback" rules.

The "throwback rules" tax beneficiaries on distributions of income accumulated by the trust before the year of distribution, as though the income had been distributed currently to the beneficiaries in the years received by the trust. (Reg § 1.665(a)-0A(a)(1))[47]

The throwback rules apply to foreign trusts, domestic trusts previously treated as foreign trusts (except as provided in regs), and domestic trusts created before Mar. 1, '84, that would be treated as multiple trusts under Code Sec. 643(f). (Code Sec. 665(c))

The throwback rules generally apply only to complex trusts. Estates aren't subject to the throwback rules. (Code Sec. 666; Reg § 1.665(a)-0A(d))[48]

The fiduciary of a trust subject to the throwback rules must complete Schedule J (Form 1041) and attach it to the trust's return.[49]

¶ 3954   Distributions exempt from the throwback rules.

These distributions are exempt from the throwback rules:

• Distributions of income accumulated before birth of beneficiary or before beneficiary reaches age 21. But this exclusion doesn't apply to distributions from a foreign trust or to certain distributions from multiple trusts. (Code Sec. 665(b))[50]

• Distributions not exceeding accounting income. (Code Sec. 665(b))[1]

¶ 3955   Beneficiary's tax under throwback rules—Form 4970.

The beneficiary includes in his income for the current year:

. . . the amount of the accumulation distribution considered distributed; and

. . . the trust's income tax considered distributed. (Code Sec. 667(a), Code Sec. 666(b))[2]

---

45. ¶s C-3033 *et seq.*, C-9053 *et seq.*; ¶6434.04; TD ¶s 655,025, 665,022
46. ¶C-3051; ¶6644.01; TD ¶655,030
47. ¶C-4001; ¶6664; TD ¶656,001
48. ¶C-4002; ¶6664; TD ¶656,002

49. ¶C-4001; ¶6664; TD ¶656,001
50. ¶C-4007; ¶6664; TD ¶656,005
1. ¶C-4008; ¶6664; TD ¶656,005
2. ¶C-4101; ¶6664; TD ¶656,008

The beneficiary's total tax liability for the current year is:

(1) a partial tax on the beneficiary's taxable income *reduced* by the total amounts considered distributed to the beneficiary under the throwback rules; *plus*

(2) a partial tax on the amounts considered distributed under the throwback rules (Code Sec. 667(a)); *plus*

(3) in the case of a foreign trust, a special nondeductible interest charge. (Code Sec. 667(b))[3]

The beneficiary's partial tax under (2) is computed (on Form 4970) under a special "shortcut" method and is then reduced by any estate tax or generation-skipping transfer tax attributable to the partial tax. (Code Sec. 667(b)(6))[4]

¶ 3956   3.8% surtax on "unearned income" of estate or trust—Form 8960.

For tax years beginning after Dec. 31, 2012, certain unearned income of individuals (¶3153), estates, and trusts is subject to a surtax on "unearned income" (i.e., it's payable on top of any other tax payable on that income). For an estate or trust, the surtax is 3.8% of the lesser of (1) undistributed net investment income (¶3152) or the excess of adjusted gross income (as defined in Code Sec. 67(e), see ¶3921) over the dollar amount at which the highest income tax bracket applicable to an estate or trust begins. (Code Sec. 1411(a)(2)) The tax does not apply to trusts all the unexpired interests in which are devoted to charitable purposes; trusts exempt from tax under Code Sec. 501; or charitable remainder trusts exempt from tax under Code Sec. 664. (Code Sec. 1411(e)) Proposed reliance regs clarify many aspects of the 3.8% surtax including issues unique to estates and trusts. The 3.8% tax is computed on Form 8960 and reflected on and paid with Form 1041.[5]

¶ 3957   Grantor or others taxed as owner of trust—grantor trust rules.

A trust grantor or another person with power over a trust or its property may be taxed on its income as the "owner" of the trust. These grantor trust rules are discussed at   ¶3958 *et seq.*[6] These rules don't apply to charitable remainder trusts or pooled income funds. (Reg § 1.671-1(d)[7] These rules generally apply only to the extent they result in amounts being currently taken into account in computing the income of a U.S. citizen, resident or domestic corporation. (Code Sec. 672(f); Reg § 1.672(f)-1, Reg § 1.672(f)-2, Reg § 1.672(f)-3)

> **🅡observation:** Thus, the grantor trust rules generally don't apply where they would treat a foreign person as owner of the trust. This ensures that either the U.S. or the foreign jurisdiction taxes the trust income.

For this purpose, a grantor includes any person who creates a trust, or directly or indirectly makes a gratuitous transfer of property, including cash, to a trust. (Reg § 1.671-2(e))[8]

These rules may be applicable to the entire trust or, where appropriate, to only a specific portion of a trust. (Reg § 1.671-3(a))[9] If a grantor or other person is considered to be the owner of the *entire* trust, he computes his own personal income tax by taking into account all trust income, deductions and credits, as though the trust didn't exist. (Reg § 1.671-3(a)(1)) But, where a grantor is treated as owner solely because of his interest in trust *income,* he takes into account only his share of trust items that would be reported by a current income beneficiary. (Reg § 1.671-3(c))[10]

For purposes of taxing the grantor as the owner of a trust, the grantor is treated as holding any power or interest held by any individual who was the spouse of the grantor at the time of

---

3. ¶C-4101; ¶6664; TD ¶656,009
4. ¶C-4100 *et seq.*; ¶6664; TD ¶656,009
5. ¶C-5800; ¶C-9850; ¶14,114.02; TD ¶579,201
6. ¶C-5200 *et seq.*; ¶6714; TD ¶657,000

7. ¶C-5216; ¶6714; TD ¶655,030
8. ¶C-5201; ¶6714; TD ¶657,001
9. ¶C-5207 *et seq.*; ¶6714; TD ¶657,013
10. ¶C-5209 *et seq.*; ¶6714; TD ¶657,012

the creation of the power or the interest, or who became the spouse of the grantor after the creation, but only for periods after the individual became the spouse. (Code Sec. 672(e)(1)) This rule applies only to transfers in trust made after Mar. 1, '86.[11]

A "defective grantor trust" is a trust intentionally structured so that the grantor, rather than the trust or its beneficiaries, will be taxed on the trust's income without the trust being included in the grantor's estate. A defective grantor trust can lower income taxes where the grantor is in a lower bracket than the beneficiary or some income would be accumulated in the trust and taxed at the highly compressed trust tax brackets. The grantor's payment of income tax on trust income taxed to him is not a gift to the beneficiaries. If a defective grantor trust or applicable state law requires the trustee to reimburse the grantor for the income tax on trust income, the full value of the trust property will be included in the grantor's gross estate for trusts created after Oct. 3, 2004.[12]

¶ 3958   Power to revoke.

If the grantor of a trust reserves the power to take back title to the trust funds for himself, he is considered the owner of the trust, whether or not he actually exercises that power. (Code Sec. 671, Code Sec. 676) The power to get back the trust funds may be a power to revoke, terminate, alter or amend, or to appoint. (Reg § 1.676(a)-1)

The grantor is taxed if he can exercise the power alone, if it can be exercised only by another who is regarded as a *nonadverse* party, or if it can be exercised by both the grantor and a nonadverse party together. (Code Sec. 676(a))[13] The grantor is not taxed if the power can be exercised only by or with consent of an adverse party. (Code Sec. 672(a), Code Sec. 676(a); Reg § 1.676(a)-1)[14]

An "adverse party" is any person with a substantial beneficial interest in the trust (including a general power of appointment over trust property) which would be adversely affected by the exercise or non-exercise of his power with regards to the trust. (Code Sec. 672(a)) A beneficiary is ordinarily an adverse party. (Reg § 1.672(a)-1(b)) A "nonadverse party" has either no beneficial interest, or one that is not substantial, or one which would not be adversely affected by the exercise of his power with regard to the trust. (Code Sec. 672(b); Reg § 1.672(b)-1)[15]

¶ 3959   Income for grantor, spouse or dependent.

The grantor of a trust is treated as its owner and taxed on its income, if the trust income is:

... distributed actually or constructively to the grantor or his spouse;

... held or accumulated for future distribution to the grantor or his spouse; or

... applied to pay premiums on life insurance policies taken out on the life of the grantor or his spouse (and not irrevocably payable to charities). (Code Sec. 677(a))

The income isn't taxable to the grantor if the application of the income to any of these purposes requires the approval of an adverse party (¶3958). (Reg § 1.677(a)-1(b))[16]

If trust income is *actually* used to support a beneficiary (other than the grantor's spouse) whom the grantor is legally obligated to support, such as his minor children, the grantor is taxable on that income. But the mere fact that trust income *may* be so used doesn't make him taxable, unless the use is discretionary with the grantor as an *individual* (not trustee). (Reg § 1.677(b)-1(d), Reg § 1.677(b)-1(e), Reg § 1.677(b)-1(f))[17]

11. ¶C-5204 *et seq.*; ¶6724.02; TD ¶657,009
12. ¶C-5200; ¶6714
13. ¶C-5301; ¶6764; TD ¶657,025
14. ¶C-5303; ¶6764; TD ¶657,025

15. ¶C-5312 *et seq.*; ¶6724.01; TD ¶657,027
16. ¶C-5401; ¶6774.01; TD ¶657,029
17. ¶C-5423; ¶6774.04; TD ¶657,033

¶ 3960   Reversionary interests.

For transfers in trust made after Mar. 1, '86, the grantor of a trust is generally taxable as the owner on its income if he has a reversionary interest in the corpus or income and, as of the inception of the trust, the value of that interest is more than 5% of the value of the trust. (Code Sec. 673(a)) The value of the reversionary interest must be determined by assuming the maximum exercise of discretion in favor of the grantor. (Code Sec. 673(c))

Any postponement of the date specified for the reacquisition of possession or enjoyment of the reversionary interest is treated as a new transfer in trust starting with the date the postponement is effective and terminating with the date prescribed by the postponement. However, income for any period isn't included in income of the grantor by reason of this rule if it wouldn't be includible in the absence of the postponement. (Code Sec. 673(d))

The grantor isn't treated as the owner where the reversionary interest takes effect on the death before age 21 of a beneficiary who (1) is a lineal descendant of the grantor, and (2) holds all present interests in the trust. (Code Sec. 673(b))[18]

¶ 3961   Power to control beneficial enjoyment (including "sprinkling" and "spray" powers).

Trust income is generally taxable to the grantor as the owner of the trust property if the beneficial enjoyment of trust corpus or income is subject to a power of disposition that may be exercised by him personally, or by a nonadverse party (¶3958), or both, and requires no consent or approval of an adverse party (¶3958). (Code Sec. 674)[19]

Similarly, the grantor will be taxed if he retains certain administrative powers, such as borrowing powers and dealing with the trust for less than full consideration. (Code Sec. 675)[20]

But certain relatively broad powers to shift benefits may be given to "independent" trustees without causing the grantor to be treated as owner. These so called "sprinkling" and "spray" powers permit the trustee to distribute, apportion or accumulate income, or to pay out corpus to or among beneficiaries (Code Sec. 674(c)), but not to add beneficiaries except to include after-born or after-adopted children. These powers vested solely in trustees won't cause the grantor to be taxed as the owner of the trust if the grantor isn't eligible as a trustee or co-trustee and no more than half the trustees vested with the power are related or subordinate parties subservient to the grantor's wishes. (Code Sec. 674(c), Code Sec. 674(d); Reg § 1.674(d)-2(b))

Also, a power to distribute, apportion or accumulate income won't subject the grantor to tax if he and his spouse (living with him) are ineligible to exercise the power as trustee or co-trustee and the power is limited by a reasonably definite external standard set forth in the trust instrument. (Code Sec. 674(d); Reg § 1.674(d)-1)[21]

¶ 3962   Person other than the grantor as owner (including "Crummey" powers).

A trustee, beneficiary, or some other person may be taxable on the income as the owner, if that person:

. . . has a power exercisable solely by himself to vest the corpus, or income from it, in himself; or

. . . has previously modified or released such a power and afterward retains control which would make the grantor taxable under the rules discussed at ¶3957 *et seq.* (Code Sec. 678)[22]

---

18. ¶C-5450 *et seq.*; ¶6734.01; TD ¶657,041
19. ¶C-5531; ¶6744; TD ¶657,000
20. ¶C-5551 *et seq.*; ¶6754; TD ¶657,057

21. ¶C-5542 *et seq.*; ¶6744; TD ¶657,055
22. ¶C-5571; ¶6784; TD ¶657,058

A holder of a "Crummey" power (see ¶5046) is treated as owner under the above rule.[23]

¶ 3963   Foreign trust grantors or other transferors—Form 3520, Form 3520-A.

If a U.S. person (e.g., a grantor) makes a transfer to a foreign trust with a U.S. beneficiary, the income of the trust (including foreign source income) will be taxed currently to the transferor as the owner of the trust. (Code Sec. 679(a)(1); Reg § 1.679-1) This rule doesn't apply where the transfer is: (a) by reason of death, (b) for fair market value, or (c) to a foreign employee benefit or charitable trust. (Code Sec. 679(a); Reg § 1.679-4)

A trust is treated as having a U.S. beneficiary for a tax year unless (1) under the terms of the trust, no part of the trust's income or corpus may be paid or accumulated during the tax year to or for the benefit of a U.S. person, and (2) if the trust is terminated at any time during the tax year, no part of the income or corpus could be paid to or for the benefit of a U.S. person. Effective Mar. 18, 2010, an amount is treated as accumulated for the benefit of a U.S. person even if the U.S. person's interest in the trust is contingent on a future event. (Code Sec. 679(c)(1))

Also effective Mar. 18, 2010:

. . . If a U.S. person directly or indirectly transfers property to a foreign trust, there is a rebuttable presumption that the trust has a U.S. beneficiary unless the U.S. person submits information as required by IRS and demonstrates to its satisfaction that requirements (1) and (2) in the above paragraph are met. (Code Sec. 679(d))

. . . If any person has the discretion to make a distribution from the trust to, or for the benefit of, any person, the trust is treated as having a U.S. beneficiary unless: (i) the trust terms specifically identify the class of persons to whom the distributions may be made; and (ii) none of those persons is a U.S. person during the tax year. (Code Sec. 679(c)(4))

. . . If any U.S. person who directly or indirectly transfers property to the trust is directly or indirectly involved in any agreement or understanding that may result in the income or corpus of the trust being paid or accumulated to or for the benefit of a U.S. person, that agreement or understanding is treated as a term of the trust. (Code Sec. 679(c)(5))

. . . For purposes of determining whether a foreign trust has a U.S. beneficiary, a loan of cash or marketable securities (or the use of any other trust property) directly or indirectly to or by any U.S. person (whether or not the U.S. person is a beneficiary under the terms of the trust) is treated as paid or accumulated for the benefit of a U.S. person, unless the U.S. person repays the loan at a market rate of interest (or pays the fair market value of the use of the property) within a reasonable period of time. (Code Sec. 679(c)(6))

The changes to the Code which became effective on Mar. 18, 2010 are meant to be consistent with already-existing regs on when a foreign trust that received property from a U.S. transferor is treated as having a U.S. beneficiary. (Reg § 1.679-2)[24]

The above rules also apply to (1) certain foreign persons who transfer property to a foreign trust and later become a U.S. person (Code Sec. 679(a)(4); Reg § 1.679-5(a)) and (2) to a U.S. person who transferred property to a domestic trust that becomes a foreign trust during the transferor's life. (Code Sec. 679(a)(5); Reg § 1.679-6(b))[25]

A foreign trust with a U.S. owner must file Form 3520-A to satisfy information reporting requirements. (Code Sec. 6048(b)(1))[26]

For tax years beginning after Mar. 18, 2010, a U.S. person who is treated as an owner of any portion of a foreign trust must provide information as IRS may require with respect to the trust. (Code Sec. 6048(b)(1))

---

23. ¶C-5574; ¶6784
24. ¶C-5600 *et seq.*; ¶6794; TD ¶657,060

25. ¶s C-5603.1, C-5603.2; ¶6794; TD ¶657,062
26. ¶S-3645; ¶60,484; TD ¶659,024

¶ 3964   Beneficiary treated as grantor to the extent of gifts to foreign grantor.

Where a foreign person would ordinarily be treated as the owner of any portion of a trust, *and* the trust has a beneficiary who is a U.S. person, the beneficiary generally is treated as the grantor of that portion to the extent the beneficiary has after Nov. 5, '90, made transfers by gift (directly or indirectly) to the foreign grantor. Gifts which are excluded from the calculation of gift tax under Code Sec. 2503(b) (generally, annual gifts of present interests of up to $14,000 for 2013 and 2014; see ¶5046) aren't included. (Code Sec. 672(f)(5); Reg § 1.672(f)-5) This rule applies even if the beneficiary wasn't a U.S. person at the time of the transfer.[27]

¶ 3965   Decedent's Income and Deductions. ▮▮▮▮▮▮▮▮▮▮▮▮

A decedent's last tax year ends on his death. A cash basis decedent's final return includes only the income he actually or constructively received before he died. An accrual basis decedent's return includes income and deductions properly accruable at death (but not solely by reason of death). Post-death income and deductions "in respect of a decedent" must be reported by decedent's estate or others who acquire his rights or obligations.

¶ 3966   Income includible and deductions taken on decedent's last return.

The last tax year of a decedent ends with the day of his death. (Reg § 1.451-1(b))[28]

For a *cash basis* decedent, include only the income received, actually or constructively, up to the end of the day of death (Code Sec. 691(a); Reg § 1.451-1(b)(1), Reg § 1.691(a)-1(b)), and deduct expenses only to the extent paid before death (except for the special deduction for the unrecovered investment in an annuity contract, see ¶3967, and certain medical expenses paid within one year after death, see ¶2143).[29]

For an *accrual basis* decedent, include income and deductions computed on the accrual method. But an amount of income or deduction accrued *solely* by reason of death isn't includible on the final return. (Code Sec. 451(b), Code Sec. 461(b))[30]

¶ 3967   Deduction for unrecovered investment in annuity contract.

A decedent's unrecovered investment in an annuity contract is an itemized deduction (*not* subject to the 2%-of-AGI floor) (Code Sec. 67(b)(10)) for the decedent's last tax year, if the annuity payments cease by reason of his death. (Code Sec. 72(b)(3)(A))[31]

¶ 3968   Income in respect of a decedent (IRD, after-death income).

Income in respect of a decedent (IRD) covers income (including capital gain) which a decedent had a right to receive but that: (1) wasn't actually or constructively received by a cash basis decedent, or (2) wasn't accrued by an accrual basis decedent. IRD includes insurance renewal commissions, a monthly pension paid to deceased employee's widow, taxable distributions from a qualified employee plan or IRA, a death benefit under a deferred annuity contract, partnership income of a deceased partner (Reg § 1.742-1) and S corporation income of a deceased shareholder. (Code Sec. 1367(b)(4))[32]

27. ¶C-5218.31; ¶6724.03; TD ¶657,059
28. ¶C-9601; ¶6914; TD ¶579,501
29. ¶s C-9556, C-9605; ¶6914; TD ¶579,503

30. ¶s C-9606, C-9608; ¶6914.03; TD ¶579,504
31. ¶C-9608; ¶674; TD ¶579,506
32. ¶C-9505 *et seq.*; ¶s 6914, 6914.03; TD ¶578,505

¶ 3969   Installment obligations, including self-cancelling installment notes (SCINs).

Uncollected installment obligations held by the decedent and disposed of at his death are income in respect of a decedent (Code Sec. 453B(c); Reg § 1.691(a)-5(a)) and not reported on the decedent's final return. (Code Sec. 691(a)(4)) The amount of the income in respect of a decedent is the excess of the face amount of the obligation over its basis in the hands of the decedent. (Code Sec. 453B(b), Code Sec. 691(a)(4)) On collecting the face amount, the executor, beneficiary or other recipient includes in gross income the same proportion of the payment that would have been reported by the decedent if he had lived and received the payment. (Reg § 1.691(a)-5(a))

If the executor or beneficiary transfers the installment obligation, the amount included in gross income for the tax year of the transfer is the fair market value of the obligation at the time of the transfer plus any excess of sales proceeds over fair market value (if it's sold) minus an amount equal to the basis of the obligation in the hands of the decedent (adjusted to reflect the receipt of any installment payments since the decedent's death). (Code Sec. 691(a)(4); Reg § 1.691(a)-5(b))

If the installment obligation is transferred to the obligor or is cancelled by the executor, any previously unreported gain from the installment sale will be recognized by the seller's estate. (Code Sec. 691(a)(5)) The result is the same where payments due on an installment note are extinguished at the holder's death under a provision contained in the sales agreement and installment note, i.e., a "death-terminating" installment note or self-cancelling installment note (SCIN).[33]

¶ 3970   Who is taxed on income in respect of a decedent?

A decedent's income in respect of a decedent (IRD) not includible on his last return must be reported, for the tax year when received, by:

. . . the decedent's estate, if it acquired the right to receive the item of income from the decedent;

. . . the person who, by reason of the decedent's death, acquires the right to the income whenever this right isn't acquired by the decedent's estate from the decedent; or

. . . the person who acquires the right from the decedent by bequest, devise or inheritance, if the amount is received after distribution by the decedent's estate of the right to the income. (Code Sec. 691(a)(1))[34]

The character of IRD is the same as it would have been in the hands of the decedent, if he had lived and received the income. (Code Sec. 691(a)(3); Reg § 1.691(a)-3(a))[35]

¶ 3971   Decedent's deductions and credits available to estate or beneficiaries.

Deductions for a decedent's business expenses, expenses for the production of income, interest, taxes, depletion and the credit for foreign taxes are available to the decedent's estate if the estate is liable for the obligation giving rise to the deduction or credit and it isn't allowable in the decedent's final (or any previous) return. If not available to the estate, the deduction or credit may be taken by the person who acquires an interest in the decedent's property from the decedent by reason of the decedent's death, or by bequest, devise or inheritance, subject to the obligation. (Code Sec. 691(b))[36]

---

33. ¶C-9528; ¶6914; TD ¶578,528
34. ¶C-9501; ¶6914; TD ¶578,501

35. ¶C-9506; ¶6914.05; TD ¶578,506
36. ¶C-9551; ¶6914.04; TD ¶579,001

¶ 3972 Deduction for estate tax attributable to income in respect of a decedent.

The decedent's right to income in respect of a decedent (IRD) is frequently included in his gross estate for federal estate and GST tax purposes although it's taxed as income to the recipient. As a relief, the recipient of the IRD can deduct the estate and GST tax attributable to inclusion of the right to income in the gross estate. (Code Sec. 691(c)(1); Reg § 1.691(c)-1(a)) This relief is available to an individual only if he itemizes his deductions but the deduction isn't subject to the 2%-of-AGI floor. (Code Sec. 67(b)(8))[37]

If IRD includes capital gains or qualified dividends, the Code in effect treats the deduction as an offset against the capital gains or qualified dividends. For purposes of computing (1) the Code Sec. 1211 limitation on capital losses, (2) the maximum tax on a noncorporate taxpayer's capital gains or qualified dividends under Code Sec. 1(h), (3) the alternative tax on a corporation's capital gains, and (4) the full or partial exclusion of gain realized on the disposition of qualified small business stock, the amount of any gain taken into account that is treated as IRD must be reduced (but not below zero) by the amount of the allowable deduction for estate tax attributable to that gain. (Code Sec. 691(c)(4))[38]

Annuity payments received by the surviving annuitant of a joint and survivor annuity are IRD of the deceased annuitant to the extent that the payments are includible in gross income of the survivor. The portion of the estate tax attributable to the survivor's annuity is allowable as a deduction to the survivor over his life expectancy (determined under IRS tables). (Code Sec. 691(d); Reg § 1.691(d)-1(c))[39]

¶ 3973 Bankruptcy Estate for Bankrupt Individual. ▬▬▬▬▬▬

The bankruptcy estate of an individual is treated as a separate taxable entity for income tax purposes, subject to special rules.

¶ 3974 Bankruptcy estate as separate taxable entity.

The separate entity rules apply if a bankruptcy case involving an *individual* debtor (not a corporation or partnership) is brought under Chapter 7 (relating to liquidations) or Chapter 11 (reorganizations) of Title 11 of the U.S. Code. (Code Sec. 1398(a))[40]

For income tax returns of bankruptcy estates (Form 1040 and Form 1041), see ¶4736.

¶ 3975 Debtor's election to close tax year.

An individual debtor can elect to close his tax year as of the day before the date the bankruptcy case commences. (Code Sec. 1398(d)(2)(A), Code Sec. 1398(d)(3)) If the election is made, the debtor's tax year that otherwise would include the commencement date is divided into two "short" tax years. The first year ends on the day before the commencement date; the second begins on the commencement date. (Code Sec. 1398(d)(2)(A))[41]

¶ 3976 Taxation of bankruptcy estate.

The gross income of the bankruptcy estate of an individual consists of: (1) any gross income of the individual debtor (other than any amount received or accrued as income by the debtor before the commencement of the case), that under the substantive law of bankruptcy (Title 11 of the U.S. Code), is property of the bankruptcy estate, and (2) the gross income of the estate beginning on and after the date the case commenced. (Code Sec. 1398(e)(1))[42]

---

37. ¶C-9557 *et seq.*; ¶674; TD ¶579,007
38. ¶C-9563; ¶6914.07; TD ¶579,012
39. ¶C-9569; ¶6914.07; TD ¶579,018

40. ¶C-9701; ¶13,984; TD ¶578,001
41. ¶C-9802 *et seq.*; ¶13,984.05; TD ¶577,504
42. ¶C-9711; ¶13,984.01; TD ¶578,004

Except as otherwise provided, the taxable income of the bankruptcy estate is computed the same as in the case of an individual. (Code Sec. 1398(c)(1))[43] The estate is allowed a personal exemption deduction equal to that of an individual (two exemptions for married debtors jointly filing for bankruptcy)[44] and the same standard deduction as married individuals filing separately. (Code Sec. 1398(c)(3)) The tax rate schedule applicable to the estate is the same as for married individuals filing separate returns. (Code Sec. 1398(c)(2))[45]

The estate succeeds to various income tax attributes of the debtor (including certain carryovers and unused passive activity and at-risk losses). (Code Sec. 1398(g); Reg § 1.1398-1, Reg § 1.1398-2)[46]

¶ 3977 Deduction of business and administrative expenses.

An amount paid or incurred by the bankruptcy estate is deductible or creditable by the estate to the same extent that the item would be by the debtor had the debtor remained in the same trades, businesses or activities after the case commenced as before and had the debtor paid or incurred the amount. (Code Sec. 1398(e)(3))[47]

The estate can deduct: (1) any administrative expense allowed under 11 U.S. Sec. 503 (11 USCS 503), and (2) any court fees and costs assessed against the estate under Chapter 123 of Title 28 of the U.S. Code. (Code Sec. 1398(h)(1))[48]

¶ 3978 Carrybacks and carryovers.

Any deduction for administrative and related expenses not used in the current year can be carried back by the estate three years and carried forward seven years (Code Sec. 1398(h)(2)), but only to a tax year of the *estate,* not of the debtor. (Code Sec. 1398(h)(2)(D))

The administrative expense carrybacks and carryovers that may be carried to a particular tax year are "stacked" after the net operating loss deductions (allowed by Code Sec. 172) are computed for the particular year. (Code Sec. 1398(h)(2)(C))[49]

If the bankruptcy estate itself incurs a net operating loss (apart from losses passing to the estate from the individual debtor), the bankruptcy estate can carry back its net operating losses not only to earlier tax years of the estate, but also to tax years of the debtor before the year in which the case commenced. (Code Sec. 1398(j)(2)(A))[50]

¶ 3979 Tax attributes on termination of estate.

On termination of the bankruptcy estate, the debtor succeeds to various tax attributes of the estate (including certain carryovers). (Code Sec. 1398(i))[1] However, the Tax Court has held that a debtor (taxpayer) wasn't allowed to succeed to net operating loss (NOL) carryovers of a terminated bankruptcy estate where the estate, with the bankruptcy court's approval, had entered into a compromise of the estate's tax liabilities with IRS which expressly stated that there was no NOL carryover from the estate to the taxpayer.[2]

---

43. ¶C-9708; ¶13,984.01; TD ¶578,009
44. ¶C-9709; ¶13,984.01; TD ¶578,011
45. ¶C-9707; ¶13,984.01; TD ¶578,012
46. ¶C-9718; ¶13,984.02; TD ¶578,015
47. ¶C-9714; ¶13,984.01; TD ¶578,005

48. ¶C-9715; ¶13,984.01; TD ¶578,006
49. ¶C-9720; ¶s 1724.05, 13,984.01; TD ¶578,007
50. ¶C-9721; ¶s 1724.05, 13,984.01; TD ¶578,013
1. ¶C-9812; ¶13,984.02; TD ¶577,512
2. ¶C-9812; TD ¶577,512

Chapter 19 Exempt Organizations

¶ 4100   Tax-Exempt Organizations.

Certain nonprofit organizations are exempt from federal income taxation, but they may be taxable on income from unrelated businesses they conduct.

Exempt organizations include:

... U.S. corporate instrumentalities organized under an Act of Congress (Code Sec. 501(c)(1));[1]

... corporations exclusively holding title to property, and collecting and remitting the income from it (less expenses) to an exempt organization (Code Sec. 501(c)(2));[2]

... religious, charitable, scientific, literary and educational organizations, organizations testing for public safety, organizations that foster national or international amateur sports competition, those organized and operated for preventing cruelty to children or animals (¶4102) (Code Sec. 501(c)(3)), qualified charitable risk pools, (Code Sec. 501(n)) cooperative hospital (Code Sec. 501(e)) and educational organization, service organizations; (Code Sec. 501(f))[3]

... religious and apostolic organizations (¶4105);

... nonprofit civic organizations operated exclusively for social welfare, and local employees' associations whose net earnings are used solely for charitable, educational or recreational purposes (Code Sec. 501(c)(4));[4]

... labor, agricultural or horticultural organizations (Code Sec. 501(c)(5), Code Sec. 501(g));[5]

... chambers of commerce, business leagues, real estate boards, boards of trade or professional football leagues not organized for profit or private benefit (Code Sec. 501(c)(6));[6]

... social clubs organized for pleasure, recreation and other nonprofitable purposes (¶4107) (Code Sec. 501(c)(7)) and fraternal beneficiary societies, orders or associations operating under the lodge system and providing life, sick, accident or other benefits to members and their dependents (Code Sec. 501(c)(8));[7]

... domestic fraternal societies operating under the lodge system that don't provide payment of benefits, if their net earnings are devoted exclusively to religious, charitable, etc., and fraternal purposes (Code Sec. 501(c)(10));[8]

... voluntary employees' beneficiary associations providing benefit payments to members and their dependents (Code Sec. 501(c)(9));[9]

... local teachers' retirement fund associations (Code Sec. 501(c)(11));[10]

... certain local benevolent life insurance associations, mutual ditch or irrigation companies, mutual or cooperative telephone companies or like organizations, (Code Sec. 501(c)(12));[11]

... nonprofit cemetery companies and burial corporations (Code Sec. 501(c)(13));[12]

... credit unions and certain entities organized before Sept. 1, '57 to provide reserve funds and insure shares or deposits in building and loan associations, cooperative banks or mutual savings banks (Code Sec. 501(c)(14));[13]

... certain nonlife insurance companies (Code Sec. 501(c)(15));[14]

... farmers' cooperatives that are crop financing corporations (Code Sec. 501(c)(16));[15]

... supplemental unemployment benefit plans (SUBs) (Code Sec. 501(c)(17));[16]

1. ¶D-6301; ¶5014.03
2. ¶D-5801; ¶5014.04; TD ¶672,542
3. ¶D-4100 et seq.; ¶5014.04; TD ¶670,500 et seq.
4. ¶D-5100 et seq.; ¶5014.13; TD ¶672,501
5. ¶D-4600 et seq.; ¶5014.14; TD ¶672,508
6. ¶D-4800 et seq.; ¶5014.15; TD ¶671,501
7. ¶D-4300 et seq.; ¶5014.17; TD ¶671,007
8. ¶D-4304; ¶5014.19; TD ¶671,010

9. ¶D-4400 et seq.; ¶5014.18; TD ¶672,001
10. ¶D-5500 et seq.; ¶5014.20
11. ¶D-6100 et seq.; ¶5014.21
12. ¶D-6000 et seq.; ¶5014.22
13. ¶D-4900 et seq.; ¶5014.23
14. ¶D-5900 et seq.; ¶5014.24
15. ¶E-1041 et seq.; ¶5014.25
16. ¶D-4500; ¶5014.26

References beginning with a single letter are to paragraphs in RIA's Federal Tax Coordinator 2d and RIA's Analysis of Federal Taxes: Income. Those beginning with numbers are to paragraphs in RIA's United States Tax Reporter. Those beginning with TD are to paragraphs in RIA's Tax Desk.

. . . certain domestic veterans' organizations (Code Sec. 501(c)(19));[17]

. . . qualified employee benefit trusts (¶4319);

. . . trusts established by the Pension Benefit Guaranty Corporation (PBGC) in connection with a terminated plan (Code Sec. 501(c)(24));[18]

. . . pooled real estate investment funds of exempt organizations (Code Sec. 501(c)(25));[19]

. . . certain trusts created before June 25, '59, to pay benefits under a pension plan funded only by employee contributions (Code Sec. 501(c)(18));[20] black lung benefit trusts (Code Sec. 501(c)(21)); and[21] state sponsored workmen's compensation reinsurance organizations established before June 1, '96 (Code Sec. 501(c)(27)(A));[22]

. . . organizations (including mutual insurance companies) providing worker's compensation (Code Sec. 501(c)(27)(B))[23] ;

. . . state sponsored high-risk health coverage organizations (Code Sec. 501(c)(26));[24] and

. . . qualified tuition programs. (Code Sec. 529)[25]

IRS may suspend the tax-exempt status of an organization designated or identified as a terrorist organization. (Code Sec. 501(p))[26]

For private foundations, see ¶4125 *et seq.*

¶ 4101   Feeder organizations.

An organization operated for the primary purpose of carrying on a business for profit (not just holding title to property) is taxable on all its income, even if all its profits are payable to exempt organizations. (Code Sec. 502(a); Reg § 1.502-1(a))[27]

But this type of "feeder" organization is exempt if it's controlled by and furnishes its services *solely* to: a single exempt organization, an exempt parent organization and its exempt subs, or exempt subs having a common parent. (Reg § 1.502-1(b))[28]

¶ 4102   Religious, charitable, educational and similar organizations.

A corporation, community chest, fund, foundation, or other organization is exempt if:

. . . it's both organized *and* operated exclusively for: religious, charitable, scientific, literary or educational (including certain child care) purposes; public safety testing; prevention of cruelty to children or animals; or fostering national or international amateur sports competition (even if it has local or regional membership); (Code Sec. 501(c)(3); Reg § 1.501(c)(3)-1(a))

. . . no part of its net earnings inures to benefit any private shareholder or individual; *and*

. . . no substantial part of its activities consists of carrying on propaganda or otherwise attempting to influence legislation, i.e., lobbying (subject to an election, see ¶4103), or intervening in any political campaign for or against any candidate (Code Sec. 501(c)(3))[29] — i.e., it can't be an "action" organization. (Reg § 1.501(c)(3)-1(c)(3)) IRS guidance shows examples of prohibited and permissible political activities of tax-exempts.[30] (For excise tax on these expenditures, see ¶4104.)

Special qualification requirements apply to any Code Sec. 501(c)(3) organization that operates at least one hospital facility. (Code Sec. 501(r),[31] Code Sec. 6033(b))

For the "private foundation" presumption, see ¶4125.

---

17. ¶D-5200 *et seq.*; ¶5014.28; TD ¶672,022
18. ¶D-5303
19. ¶D-5850 *et seq.*; ¶5014.32; TD ¶672,546
20. ¶D-5400 *et seq.*; ¶5014.27
21. ¶D-6200 *et seq.*; ¶5014.30
22. ¶5014.40
23. ¶D-6346
24. ¶D-6320; ¶5014.39

25. ¶A-4701; ¶5294
26. ¶D-4001A; ¶5014.44
27. ¶D-7101; ¶5024
28. ¶D-7103; ¶5024.01
29. ¶D-4101; ¶5014.05; TD ¶670,601
30. ¶D-6401; TD ¶677,001
31. ¶D-4141.1

¶ 4103　Lobbying expenditures election for Code Sec. 501(c)(3) organizations— Form 5768.

Certain Code Sec. 501(c)(3) organizations (other than church-related ones or private foundations) may elect (on Form 5768) to make limited lobbying expenditures without losing their exempt status. (Code Sec. 501(h))[32] The election is effective for all tax years that end after it's made, and that begin before it's revoked. (Code Sec. 501(h)(6))[33]

An electing charity's permissible lobbying expenditures for any tax year can't exceed ("general limit") the *lesser of:* (1) $1,000,000, or (2) the sum of 20% of the first $500,000 it paid or incurred for exempt purposes (including related administrative costs) for the year, plus 15% of the second $500,000, plus 10% of the third $500,000, plus 5% of any additional such expenditures. (Code Sec. 4911(c)(2); Reg § 56.4911-1(c)(1)) Also, only 25% of this lobbying amount may go to influencing legislation ("grass roots expenditures"). (Code Sec. 4911(c)(4); Reg § 56.4911-1(c)(2))[34] Charities must keep records of these expenditures (and show them on their annual returns, see ¶4124). (Reg § 56.4911-6)[35]

In any tax year an electing charity's lobbying expenditures exceed either the general or the grass roots limit, a 25% excise tax is imposed on that excess. If both limits are exceeded, the tax is imposed on the greater excess. (Code Sec. 4911(a), Code Sec. 4911(b))[36] Pay the tax on Form 4720. Use Form 8868 for an extension (¶4124).[37]

Also, an electing charity can lose its tax exemption if its lobbying expenditures over a four-year period exceed 150% of either limit. (Code Sec. 501(h)(1), Code Sec. 501(h)(2))[38] For the excise tax that applies if that happens, see ¶4104.

¶ 4104　Excise tax on Code Sec. 501(c)(3) organizations' political and lobbying expenditures—Form 4720.

A Code Sec. 501(c)(3) organization is subject to a two-tier excise tax on its *political expenditures.* An initial tax of 10% of the expenditure is imposed on the organization, and an initial 2.5% tax (up to $5,000 per expenditure) is imposed on any organization manager who willfully and without reasonable cause agreed to the expenditure. (Code Sec. 4955(a), Code Sec. 4955(c)(2); Reg § 53.4955-1(b))[39] Use Form 4720 to report these taxes, and Form 8868 for an extension. (¶4124)[40] Additional taxes are imposed on both the organization (100%) and management (50%, up to $10,000 per expenditure) if the expenditure isn't corrected within a reasonable time. (Code Sec. 4955(b), Code Sec. 4955(c)(2))[41]

A Code Sec. 501(c)(3) organization (other than charities making the lobbying expense election (¶4103), private foundations and church-related organizations) whose *lobbying expenditures* for a tax year cause it to lose its tax exemption is subject to a 5% tax on those disqualifying amounts. The 5% tax also is imposed on any organization manager who agreed to the expenditure knowing that disqualification could result. (Code Sec. 4912)[4243]

IRS may also seek to enjoin a Code Sec. 501(c)(3) organization from engaging in flagrant political activities. (Code Sec. 7409(a); Reg § 301.7409-1(a))[44]

¶ 4105　Religious or apostolic associations.

Even if an organization carries on business activities so that it can't be exempt under Code Sec. 501(c)(3) (as *exclusively* for exempt purposes), it still can be exempt as a *religious or*

32. ¶D-6500 *et seq.*, ¶D-6571; ¶5014.12, ¶60,334; TD ¶677,020 *et seq.*
33. ¶D-6501; ¶5014.12; TD ¶677,023
34. ¶D-6507 *et seq.*; ¶49,114; TD ¶677,027
35. ¶D-6571; TD ¶677,028
36. ¶D-6532 *et seq.*; ¶5014.12, 49,114; TD ¶677,047
37. ¶S-2512; TD ¶688,030

38. ¶D-6572 *et seq.*; ¶5014.12; TD ¶677,042
39. ¶D-6421 *et seq.*; ¶49,554; TD ¶677,005
40. ¶S-2512; TD ¶688,029
41. ¶D-6421 *et seq.*; ¶49,554; TD ¶677,005
42. ¶D-6417 *et seq.*; ¶49,124; TD ¶677,017
43. ¶S-2512; TD ¶688,030
44. ¶V-2713; ¶74,094

apostolic association. The organization may thus be exempt if it has a common or community treasury, and if its income (whether or not distributed) is taxed pro rata to its members, as a dividend received, for the organization's tax year ending with or within the member's tax year. (Code Sec. 501(d); Reg § 1.501(d)-1)[45]

❧observation: Exemption under Code Sec. 501(c)(3) is preferable because it means that contributions to the organization also may be deductible (¶2102).

¶ 4106   Civic leagues for social welfare.

A civic league is exempt if it isn't organized or operated for profit; it is operated exclusively for the promotion of social welfare; no part of its net earnings inures to the benefit of any private shareholder or individual; (Code Sec. 501(c)(4)) and no substantial part of its activities consists of providing commercial-type insurance. (Code Sec. 501(m)(1))[46]

¶ 4107   Social clubs.

For a social club to be exempt, it must be organized and operated substantially for pleasure, recreation or other nonprofit purposes, its governing instruments or written policies can't provide for discrimination based on color, race or religion, and no part of its earnings may benefit any private shareholder. (Code Sec. 501(c)(7))[47]

Up to 35% of a social club's gross receipts (including investment income) may be from sources outside of its membership. Within this 35%, not more than 15% of gross receipts may be from the general public's (i.e., not members or their guests) use of the club's facilities or services.[48]

If the club fails the 35% or 15% tests (and a facts and circumstances test) in any tax year, all of its income, even amounts (reduced by allocable costs) received from members, is subject to tax in that year. (Code Sec. 277)[49]

¶ 4108   Nondiscrimination requirements for voluntary employees' beneficiary associations (VEBAs) and supplemental unemployment benefit trusts (SUBs).

A VEBA or SUB won't be exempt unless it satisfies nondiscrimination rules similar to those applicable to qualified employee benefit plans (¶4325). (Code Sec. 501(c)(17)(A), Code Sec. 505(a)(1), Code Sec. 505(b)(1))[50]

¶ 4109   Political organizations—Form 1120-POL; Form 990; Form 8871; Form 8872; Form 8453-X.

A political organization is a party, committee, association, fund (including certain newsletter funds) or other organization (whether or not incorporated) that's organized and operated primarily to accept contributions and/or make expenditures for an "exempt function," e.g., influencing or attempting to influence the selection, nomination, election or appointment of any individual to public office. (Code Sec. 527(e)(1), Code Sec. 527(e)(2), Code Sec. 527(g))[1] Subject to exceptions, political organizations must (1) give notice of status electronically (use Form 8871 and Form 8453-X), (2) provide periodic reports of contributions and expenditures, electronically in some cases (use Form 8872), and (3) file annual returns. Although generally tax-exempt (Code Sec. 527(a)), a political organization is taxed, at the *highest* corporate rate, on income (minus connected expenses) that isn't from its exempt function. (Code Sec. 527(b)(1), Code Sec. 527(c))[2] A political organization, whether or not tax-exempt, that has more than $100 of taxable income must file an annual income tax return on Form 1120-POL.

45. ¶D-5601; ¶5014.33   49. ¶D-4206; ¶5014.16; TD ¶671,001
46. ¶D-5100 *et seq.*; ¶5014.13; TD ¶672,501   50. ¶s D-4418, D-4501, D-6351; ¶5054; TD ¶672,011
47. ¶D-4201; ¶5014.16; TD ¶671,001   1. ¶s D-5002, D-5021; ¶5274; TD ¶672,513
48. ¶D-4206; ¶5014.16; TD ¶671,004   2. ¶D-5008; ¶5274; TD ¶672,518

(Code Sec. 6012(a)(6)) Only tax-exempt political organizations may have to file annual information returns. Subject to exceptions, a tax-exempt political organization (other than a qualified state or local political organization) with $25,000 or more of annual gross receipts must file Form 990. Qualified state or local political organizations must file Form 990 (see ¶4124) if they have annual gross receipts of $100,000 or more. (Code Sec. 6033(g)(1)) IRS has provided a safe harbor for establishing that a political organization's failure to report certain contributor information on Form 8872 was due to reasonable cause and not due to willful neglect.[3]

IRS has a website for political organizations to electronically file documents and allow public access and searches for contributions and expenditures.

¶ 4110 Homeowners' associations—Form 1120-H.

Associations for the management of residential real estate and condominiums and timeshare associations (but not cooperative housing corporations) that meet an organization and operation test and an income test may elect (by filing Form 1120-H) to be treated as exempt organizations. (Code Sec. 528(a), Code Sec. 528(c))[4] Electing associations are taxed at a 30% (32% for timeshare associations) rate on income other than amounts received as dues, fees or assessments from members. (Code Sec. 528(b))[5] This taxable income must be reported on Form 1120-H.[6]

¶ 4111 Loss of exemption for exempt employee trusts engaging in prohibited transactions.

Some employee trusts (including church and governmental plans) will lose or be denied their exemption from income tax (and are subject to an excise tax, see ¶4347) if they engage in "prohibited transactions." (Code Sec. 503(a)(1))[7]

A *prohibited transaction* occurs if a trust engages in an activity with its creator, a substantial contributor or person related to either, in which it:

(1) lends any part of its income or corpus without receiving adequate security and a reasonable rate of interest;

(2) pays any compensation in excess of a reasonable allowance for personal services actually rendered;

(3) makes any part of its services available on a preferential basis;

(4) makes any substantial purchase of securities or any other property for more than adequate consideration;

(5) sells any substantial part of its securities or any other property for less than adequate consideration; or

(6) engages in any other transaction that results in a substantial diversion of its income or corpus. (Code Sec. 503(b))[8]

¶ 4112 Excise tax on excess benefit transactions by disqualified persons and organization managers—Form 4720.

Penalty excise taxes are imposed on disqualified persons and organization managers who benefit from an excess benefit transaction with a Code Sec. 501(c)(3) or Code Sec. 501(c)(4) organization (other than a private foundation), or that was such an organization at any time within five years before the transaction. (Code Sec. 4958(a); Reg § 53.4958-1) An excess benefit transaction is one in which the exempt organization provides a benefit directly or indirectly to or for the use of a disqualified person (any person in a position to exercise substantial influence over the organization at any time during the five years before the

3. ¶S-1921; ¶5274; TD ¶672,518
4. ¶D-5701 *et seq.*; ¶5284; TD ¶672,531 *et seq.*
5. ¶D-5712; ¶5284; TD ¶672,539
6. ¶S-1922; ¶5284; TD ¶609,812
7. ¶D-6700 *et seq.*; ¶5034.01
8. ¶D-6702 *et seq.*; ¶5034.02

transaction (Code Sec. 4958(f); Reg § 53.4958-4), or certain related parties, that exceeds the value of the consideration, including services, received in exchange. (Code Sec. 4958(c))[9]

The disqualified person is liable for a tax of 25% of the excess benefit (200% if the transaction is not corrected by the time a deficiency notice is mailed or the tax is assessed). (Code Sec. 4958(a)(1), Code Sec. 4958(b); Reg § 53.4958-1)[10] An organization manager (officer, director, trustee, etc.) who knowingly participates in an excess benefit transaction is liable for a tax of the lesser of 10% or $20,000. (Code Sec. 4958(a)(2), Code Sec. 4958(d)(2))[11] Distributions from a donor advised fund to a donor, donor advisor, or related person are automatically treated as excess benefit transactions. (Code Sec. 4958(c)(2)) Excess benefit transactions of Code Sec. 509(a)(3) supporting organizations are determined under special rules. (Code Sec. 4958(c)(3))[12] IRS may abate the first-tier taxes for reasonable cause. (Code Sec. 4962(b))[13] Persons liable for excess benefit transaction excise taxes report them on Form 4720. (Reg § 53.6071-1(f)) Use Form 8868 for an extension (¶4124).

¶ 4113 Excise tax on entities that are parties to prohibited tax shelter transactions, and on entity managers who knowingly approve prohibited tax shelter transactions.

Excise taxes are imposed on (1) certain tax-exempt entities that are parties to "prohibited tax shelter transactions" (Code Sec. 4965(a)(1)) and (2) "entity managers" of tax-exempt entities who approve the entity as a party (or otherwise cause the entity to be a party) to a prohibited tax shelter transaction and know or have reason to know that the transaction is a prohibited tax shelter transaction. (Code Sec. 4965(a)(2)) IRS has issued regs under Code Sec. 4965 that define "party" and address other aspects of the above taxes. (Reg § 53.4965-1 through Reg § 53.4965-9)[14]

¶ 4114 Tax-exempt entities must disclose participation in prohibited tax shelter transactions to IRS or face penalties—Form 8886-T.

Every tax-exempt entity described in Code Sec. 4965(c) that is a party to a prohibited tax shelter transaction (¶4113) must disclose to IRS (on Form 8886-T): (a) that the entity is a party to the prohibited tax shelter transaction; and (b) the identity of any other party to the transaction which is known to such tax-exempt entity. (Code Sec. 6033(a)(2))[15] The penalty for failing to comply is $100 for each day during which such failure continues, not to exceed $50,000 with respect to any one disclosure. IRS may make a written demand on any entity or manager subject to the penalty for nondisclosure, specifying a reasonable future date by which the required disclosure must be filed. Failure to comply with the demand is subject to an additional penalty of $100 for each day after the expiration of the time specified in the demand during which such failure continues, not to exceed $10,000 with respect to any one disclosure. (Code Sec. 6652(c)(3)(B)(ii))[16] For non-plan entities, these penalties are imposed on the tax-exempt entity. For plan entities, they are imposed on the entity manager of the tax-exempt entity.

Any taxable party to a prohibited tax shelter transaction must disclose by statement to any tax-exempt entity that is a party to the transaction that it's a prohibited tax shelter transaction. (Code Sec. 6011(g))[17]

---

9. ¶D-6650 *et seq.*; ¶49,584; TD ¶676,500
10. ¶D-6652; ¶49,584
11. ¶D-6653; ¶49,584
12. ¶D-6654; ¶49,584
13. ¶D-6652; ¶49,624

14. ¶D-8301; ¶49,654
15. ¶S-2895; ¶60,334
16. ¶V-2538; ¶66,524.01
17. ¶S-4433; ¶60,114.023

¶ 4115 Donee organization must acknowledge and report qualified vehicle donations—Form 1098-C.

An organization that receives a charitable contribution of a "qualified vehicle" (¶2138) must provide the donor with a contemporaneous written acknowledgment of the contribution if the claimed value is more than $500, and report the information to IRS (use Form 1098-C) or face a penalty, which also applies for furnishing a false or fraudulent acknowledgment. It also must indicate whether the donee provided any goods or services in consideration for the vehicle, and, if so, a description and good faith estimate of their value, or, if they consist solely of intangible religious benefits, a statement to that effect. (Code Sec. 170(f)(12)(B))[18]

¶ 4116 Application for exemption—advance rulings—Form 1023; Form 1024.

An organization must apply in writing (on Form 1023 for Code Sec. 501(c)(3) organizations, Form 1024 for most others, and with the appropriate user fee with for an IRS ruling or determination that it's exempt from federal income tax. (Reg § 1.501(a)-1(a)(2)) A parent organization's exemption doesn't cover its subsidiary. [19] But organizations under the general control of a central organization may apply on a group basis.[20] When applying for tax-exempt status, sponsoring organizations must notify IRS of any donor advised fund they maintain or intend to maintain. (Code Sec. 508(f))[21]

¶ 4117 Modification or revocation of exemption.

IRS may modify or revoke rulings and determination letters that granted exempt status to an organization (e.g., for failure to comply with exemption requirements, or prohibited transactions, see ¶4111). (Reg § 601.201(n)(6)) The revocation may be retroactive, in which case deficiencies and penalties may be imposed for open years.[22]

¶ 4118 Disclosure of nondeductibility of contributions.

Certain exempt organizations that aren't eligible to receive deductible contributions must expressly state that fact (in a conspicuous and easily recognizable format) in every fundraising solicitation. (Code Sec. 6113)[23]

¶ 4119 Disclosure requirement for quid pro quo contributions.

Certain charities that are eligible to receive deductible contributions must, in connection with soliciting or receiving a quid pro quo contribution in excess of $75, inform the donor in writing that his charitable deduction is limited to the excess of his contribution over the value of the goods or services provided by the charity (with a good faith estimate, made by using any reasonable method in good faith, of the value of those goods and services). (Code Sec. 6115; Reg § 1.6115-1)[24]

¶ 4120 Disclosure of annual return and exemption application—Form 990; Form 990-PF; Form 990-T; Form 4720.

A Code Sec. 501(c) or Code Sec. 501(d) organization must make a copy of its annual returns (Form 990) for the last three years and its exempt status application and supporting documents available for inspection during business hours, but religious or apostolic organizations don't have to make K-1s available. (Code Sec. 6104(a), Code Sec. 6104(b), Code Sec. 6104(d); Reg § 301.6104(a)-1)[25] The organization must provide a copy of the application without

18. ¶K-3948.2; ¶67,204; TD ¶861,084
19. ¶T-10450 *et seq.*; ¶5014.01; TD ¶670,502
20. ¶T-10481; ¶5014.01
21. ¶T-10462.1; ¶5074; TD ¶331,204

22. ¶s T-10485, T-10486
23. ¶D-4004 *et seq.*; ¶61,134; TD ¶673,001
24. ¶K-3126 *et seq.*; ¶61,154; TD ¶s 330,257, 330,259
25. ¶S-6601 *et seq.*; ¶61,044

charge, except reasonable reproduction and mailing costs, to any individual who requests it. Copies must be provided within 30 days, for written requests, or immediately for in-person requests. (Code Sec. 6104(d)(1)) Requests don't have to be honored if the information has been made widely available or if the request is determined by IRS to be part of a harassment campaign. (Code Sec. 6104(d)(4); Reg § 301.6104(d)-3, Reg § 301.6104(d)-3)[26] These requirements apply to annual information returns (Form 990-PF and Form 4720) of private foundations, which also must disclose names and addresses of contributors. (Reg § 301.6104(d)-1(b)(4)(ii))[27] Returns of certain political organizations (¶4109) also are subject to disclosure requirements. (Code Sec. 6104(a), Code Sec. 6104(b), Code Sec. 6104(d))[28] Code Sec. 501(c)(3) organizations (¶4102) must make available for public inspection copies of their annual unrelated business income tax (UBIT) returns (Form 990-T) for the three-year period following the filing of the return. (Code Sec. 6104(d)(1)(A)(ii)) IRS has issued interim guidance on meeting this requirement pending the issuance of regs.[29]

More specifically, an organization's completed Form 990, Form 990-EZ, and Form 990-T, are available for public inspection as required by Code Sec. 6104. Schedule B (Form 990, 990-EZ, or 990-PF), Schedule of Contributors is available for public inspection for section 527 organizations filing Form 990 or 990-EZ. For other organizations that file Form 990 or 990-EZ, parts of Schedule B (990, 990-EZ, or 990-PF) may be open to public inspection.[30]

¶ 4121   Unrelated business income tax (UBIT)—Form 990-T.

Exempt organizations (other than U.S. corporate instrumentalities and certain other exempt organizations) are subject to a tax on income (¶4122) from any unrelated business (defined below); the "unrelated business income tax" (UBIT). (Code Sec. 511(a), Code Sec. 512(a), Code Sec. 512(b)(12); Reg § 1.511-2(a)(1))[31] Form 990-T is used to report and pay the tax. (Reg § 1.6012-2(e), Reg § 1.6012-3(a)(5))[32] Imposition of this tax doesn't affect the organization's exempt status. (Code Sec. 501(b), Code Sec. 511)[33]

An unrelated business is a trade or business (i.e., carried on for the production of income, whether or not profit results) regularly carried on (including seasonally) by the organization, that isn't substantially related (aside from providing funds) to the exercise or performance of its exempt purpose or function. (Code Sec. 513(a), Code Sec. 513(c); Reg § 1.513-1)[34] An unrelated trade or business doesn't include the activity of soliciting and receiving qualified sponsorship payments (payments from a person engaged in a trade or business with respect to which the person won't get any substantial return benefit other than the use or acknowledgment of the donor's name or logo as part of a sponsored event or certain goods or services that have an insubstantial value). (Code Sec. 513(i); Reg § 1.513-4)[35] Regs provide guidance on whether a tour activity is an unrelated business. (Reg § 1.513-7)[36] Debt management plan services are an unrelated trade or business, if the organization is *not* a tax-exempt credit counseling organization. (Code Sec. 513(j))[37]

For exempt SUBs, qualified employee pension, etc., trusts, and nonexempt trusts, *any* business it regularly carries on is "unrelated." (Code Sec. 513(b))[38]

But an unrelated business doesn't include an activity where substantially all the work is performed for the organization without compensation, e.g., by volunteers. (Code Sec. 513(a)(1))[39]

The rules on assessment, collection, and penalties applicable to income tax, including estimated tax and foreign tax credit, apply. (Code Sec. 515, Code Sec. 6655(g)(3)(A); Reg § 1.511-3(a)) The corporate tax rates and filing dates apply if the organization is a corporation, and

---

26. ¶61,044
27. ¶S-6603; ¶61,044
28. ¶S-6642 *et seq.*; ¶61,044
29. ¶S-6603; ¶61,044
30. ¶S-6601 *et seq.*; ¶61,044
31. ¶D-6800 *et seq.*; ¶5114 *et seq.*; TD ¶681,000 *et seq.*
32. ¶S-2101; ¶5114; TD ¶688,501

33. ¶D-6801; ¶5114
34. ¶D-6804 *et seq.*; ¶5134.01; TD ¶681,019
35. ¶D-6819 *et seq.*; ¶5134.02; TD ¶681,026
36. ¶D-6829.1; ¶5134.03
37. ¶D-6848; ¶5134
38. ¶D-6807; ¶5134; TD ¶681,034
39. ¶D-6836; ¶5134; TD ¶681,028

those for trusts if it's a charitable trust. (Code Sec. 511(a), Code Sec. 511(b))[40]

Tax-exempt organizations must make estimated tax payments on their unrelated business taxable income. (Code Sec. 6655(g)(3))[41]

¶ 4122 Unrelated business taxable income (UBTI) defined.

UBTI is the gross income derived from any unrelated trade or business (¶4121), less directly connected allowable deductions, but with certain exceptions (below), additions and limitations (Code Sec. 512(a), Code Sec. 512(b)), including a specific deduction of $1,000. (Code Sec. 512(b)(12))[42]

Social clubs, VEBAs, SUBs and veterans organizations are allowed special exclusions. (Code Sec. 512(a)(3))[43] A charitable organization's income or gain from ownership of S corporation stock is UBTI. (Code Sec. 512(e))[44]

Dividends (except certain insurance income received from a controlled foreign corporation (Code Sec. 512(b)(17))), interest, rents, royalties, annuities, payments with respect to securities loans, loan commitment fees, and gains or losses from property dispositions are excluded from UBTI, as are gains or losses from the lapse or termination of options to buy or sell securities or real property, or from the forfeiture of good-faith deposits to buy, sell, or lease real property in connection with the organization's investment activities, (Code Sec. 512(b))[45] and annual dues of up to $155 for 2013 ($158 for 2014) per member received by agricultural or horticultural organizations. (Code Sec. 512(d))[46]

But to the extent the dividends, etc., are attributable to property acquired through debt financing ("debt-financed property," see ¶4123), they *are* included in UBTI. The includible portion (computed separately for each property) equals a percentage (not over 100%) of the dividends, etc., derived from the property during the tax year, based on the ratio of: (1) the average acquisition indebtedness, to (2) the average adjusted basis of debt-financed property, for the year. (Code Sec. 514(a)(1))[47] This same percentage also is used to compute the allowable deductions for that property (other than capital loss carryovers or depreciation). (Code Sec. 514(a)(2), Code Sec. 514(a)(3))[48]

¶ 4123 Property acquired through debt financing—"debt-financed property."

Debt-financed property, with certain exceptions, is any property held to produce income (including gains from its disposition, as well as rents, dividends and other recurring income) (Code Sec. 514(b); Reg § 1.514(b)-1(a)), with respect to which there's an acquisition indebtedness at any time during the tax year. Securities purchased on margin by a tax-exempt trust that donated money to a university were held to be debt-financed property. As a result, income from the sale of the securities was subject to the unrelated business income tax.[49]

"Acquisition indebtedness" for any property generally means: (1) the unpaid amount of indebtedness incurred by the organization in acquiring or improving the property; and (2) indebtedness incurred at other times which *but for* the acquisition or improvement wouldn't have been incurred (if incurred after the acquisition, etc., the debt must have been reasonably foreseeable at that time). (Code Sec. 514(c))[50]

Any mortgage or other lien on the acquired property is considered incurred in that acquisition, whether or not it's assumed by the organization. (Code Sec. 514(c)(2)(A))[1]

---

40. ¶D-6928 *et seq.*; TD ¶681,002
41. ¶S-5421; ¶66,554; TD ¶689,001
42. ¶D-6900 *et seq.*; ¶5124; TD ¶681,004
43. ¶D-6929 *et seq.*; ¶5124; TD ¶681,034
44. ¶D-6916.1; TD ¶681,012
45. ¶D-6901 *et seq.*; ¶5124; TD ¶681,006

46. ¶D-6847; ¶5124; TD ¶681,033
47. ¶D-6901 *et seq.*; ¶5144; TD ¶682,001 *et seq.*
48. ¶s D-7007, D-7010; ¶5144; TD ¶682,001
49. ¶D-7012 *et seq.*; ¶5144; TD ¶682,003
50. ¶D-7040 *et seq.*; ¶5144; TD ¶682,005
1. ¶D-7043; ¶5144; TD ¶682,007

¶ 4124   Exempt organization returns—Form 990; Form 8868.

In general, every organization that's exempt from tax, or whose exemption application is pending, must file an annual information return (Form 990 series) and keep the records and make sworn statements as required by IRS. (Code Sec. 6033; Reg § 1.6033-2)[2] Code Sec. 509(a)(3) supporting organizations must file annual information returns (Code Sec. 509(a)(3)) containing specific information (Code Sec. 6033(l))[3] Certain exempt organizations that acquire interests in life insurance contracts must file an information return or face a penalty. (Code Sec. 6050V, Code Sec. 6724(d)(1)(B)(xiv), Code Sec. 6721(e)(2)(D))[4] For private foundations, see ¶4131.

The return must show the organization's total lobbying and political expenditures for the year (Code Sec. 6033(b)(8)), (except political expenditures of nonpolitical organizations taxed under Code Sec. 527(f) (Code Sec. 6033(e)(1)(B)(iii)))[5] and the total amount of dues and similar receipts to which the expenditures are allocable. There are exceptions for Code Sec. 501(c)(3) organizations' in-house expenditures not exceeding $2,000 (Code Sec. 6033(e)(1))[6] and certain nondeductible dues.[7]

Form 990 includes a core form to be completed by all organizations, and schedules to be completed depending on an organization's type and activities. IRS has released Publication 4839, and has posted numerous materials on its web site to help tax-exempt organizations in filing Form 990.

IRS allows an exempt organization (other than a private foundation or Code Sec. 509(a)(3) supporting organization) whose annual gross receipts aren't normally in excess of $50,000 to electronically file the simpler Form 990-N (the e-Postcard) instead of Form 990. There's no monetary penalty for failure to file Form 990-N (Code Sec. 6652(c)(1)(E)), but a failure to file for 3 years will result in revocation of exempt status (see below).[8]

Information returns of parent tax-exempt organizations must include information about transactions with controlled entities. (Code Sec. 6033(h))[9]

Sponsoring organizations must disclose information about donor advised funds on information returns. (Code Sec. 6033(k))

Form 990 must be for the organization's annual accounting period or, if it has none, the calendar year. (Reg § 1.6033-2(b)) It must be filed on or before the 15th day of the fifth full calendar month after the close of the annual accounting period. (Reg § 1.6033-2(e))[10]

An exempt organization required to file a return on Form 990 (except for Form 990-C), Form 1041-A, Form 4720, Form 5227, or Form 8870 may obtain an automatic three-month filing extension by filing on or before the return due date a Form 8868 showing the full amount properly estimated as tax, and remitting the full amount of properly estimated unpaid tax. (Reg § 1.6081-9(a))

An exempt organization that fails to file the required information return or notice for three consecutive years will automatically lose its exempt status and must reapply to be recognized as an exempt organization. IRS will publish and maintain a list of organizations whose status has been so revoked (Code Sec. 6033(j))[11]

Most exempt organizations must file an information return (with Form 990) on liquidation, dissolution, termination or contraction if it was exempt for any of its last five years. (Code Sec. 6043(b))[12]

Tax-exempt organizations must electronically file their Forms 990, if they have $10 million

2. ¶S-2801 *et seq.*; ¶60,334; TD ¶688,001
3. ¶S-2823.1
4. ¶S-2896; ¶60,50V4
5. ¶S-2853; ¶60,334; TD ¶688,016
6. ¶s S-2858.1, S-2858.2; ¶60,334
7. ¶S-2858.3; ¶60,334

8. ¶S-2802; ¶66,524
9. ¶S-2862.2
10. ¶S-4928; ¶60,334; TD ¶688,003
11. ¶S-2802; ¶60,334
12. ¶S-2883; ¶60,334

or more in total assets and file 250 or more returns a year. In addition, private foundations and charitable trusts must e-file Forms 990-PF, regardless of their asset size, if they file at least 250 returns. (Reg § 301.6033-4)[13] For other information return requirements, see ¶4746.

IRS Publication 4779 provides important information on the steps that must be taken when an exempt organization is merged or terminated including the return to be filed to inform IRS, the date by which it must be filed, information that must be disclosed on the return, required attachments to the return, and other items.

¶ 4125   Private Foundations and Donor Advised Funds. ▬▬▬▬▬

Private foundations are generally exempt from income tax, but are subject to excise taxes, notification requirements and other restrictions.

A private foundation is any domestic or foreign religious, scientific, charitable, etc., organization described in Code Sec. 501(c)(3) (¶4102) *other than* organizations that:

(1) are "50% charities" (¶2124), except operating foundations and membership organizations (Code Sec. 509(a)(1));[14]

(2) meet detailed public support tests (Code Sec. 509(a)(2), Code Sec. 509(d));[15]

(3) operate exclusively for the benefit of one or more of the above organizations (as Type I, Type II, or Type III supporting organizations) and aren't controlled by disqualified persons (¶4127, other than foundation managers) (Code Sec. 509(a)(3));[16]

(4) are organized and operated exclusively for testing for public safety. (Code Sec. 509(a)(4))[17]

Strict accountability requirements apply to qualify as a Type III supporting organization (Code Sec. 509(f)(1), Reg § 1.509(a)-4(f)(5), Reg § 1.509(a)-4(i));[18] and Type I and Type II supporting organizations lose their status as non-private foundations if they accept gifts from prohibited persons. (Code Sec. 509(f)(2)(A))[19]

A Code Sec. 501(c)(3) organization (other than a church or an organization whose annual gross receipts don't exceed $5,000) is presumed to be a private foundation unless it notifies IRS to the contrary (Code Sec. 508(b), Code Sec. 508(c))[20] on Form 1023 within 15 months from the end of the month it was organized. (Reg § 1.508-1(b)(2))[21]

IRS has established a specific procedure for organizations classified as supporting organizations under Code Sec. 509(a)(3) that wish to seek reclassification under Code Sec. 509(a)(1) or Code Sec. 509(a)(2).[22]

A revenue procedure provides guidance to grantor determinations of public charity status under Code Sec. 509(a)(1), Code Sec. 509(a)(2) or Code Sec. 509(a)(3), for purposes of the excise taxes imposed on grants to certain supporting organizations under Code Sec. 4942 (¶4127), Code Sec. 4945 (¶4127), and Code Sec. 4966 (¶4129).

¶ 4126   Taxable trusts and foreign organizations subject to private foundation rules—Form 1041-A; Form 5227.

Certain charitable trusts and split interest trusts, and foreign organizations meeting the private foundation definition (¶4125), may be subject to the private foundation excise taxes (¶4127) and rules on prohibited acts, but not the notification requirements. (Code Sec. 4947, Code Sec. 4948) File Form 1041-A for a split interest trust. Use Form 8868 for an extension, see ¶4124. Use Form 5227 to report the financial activities of a split-interest trust and to determine if it is treated as a private foundation and is subject to excise tax. Use Form 8868

---

13. ¶S-2822.2; ¶60,334; TD ¶688,001
14. ¶D-7203; ¶5074; TD ¶683,506
15. ¶s D-7204, D-7207, D-7209; ¶5074; TD ¶683,507
16. ¶D-7212 *et seq.*; ¶5074; TD ¶683,508
17. ¶D-7202; ¶5074; TD ¶670,632

18. ¶D-7211; ¶D-7213.0 *et seq.*;¶5074; ¶5074.01
19. ¶D-7211; ¶5074
20. ¶s D-7216, D-7217; ¶5074; TD ¶683,503
21. ¶T-10464; ¶5074; TD ¶683,503
22. ¶T-10492

for an extension, see ¶4124.[23]

¶ 4127   Excise taxes on private foundations—Form 990-PF; Form 4720.

Private foundations may be subject to the following excise taxes.

Net investment income. An *exempt* private foundation is liable for an excise tax of 2% on its net investment income for the tax year. (Code Sec. 4940(a); Reg § 53.4940-1)[24] The tax is reduced to 1% if the foundation makes certain charitable distributions (Code Sec. 4940(e))[25] and is eliminated altogether for certain operating foundations. (Code Sec. 4940(d))[26] For a *taxable* foundation, the excise tax equals the amount (if any) by which: (1) the sum of 2% of its net investment income (computed as if it were exempt) plus the unrelated business income tax (¶4122) that would have been imposed on it had it been exempt, *exceeds* (2) the income tax actually imposed on it for the tax year. (Code Sec. 4940(b))[27] Report the tax on Form 990-PF. (Reg § 53.6011-1(d))[28]

Self-dealing. An excise tax is imposed when a disqualified person (substantial contributors, foundation managers, and specified owners, family members and related entities of these, as well as government officials) (Code Sec. 4946(a)(1)) engages in any of certain acts of self-dealing with a private foundation.[29]

For *each* act of self-dealing (Code Sec. 4941(a), Code Sec. 4941(b)),[30] the disqualified person (except a foundation manager) is subject to an initial tax of 10% on the amount (not exceeding the amount he actually benefits) involved (Code Sec. 4941(a)(1); Reg § 53.4941(a)-1(a))[31] and a 200% additional tax if the self-dealing isn't timely corrected. (Code Sec. 4941(b)(1))[32] Any foundation manager who knowingly participates in the act is subject to an initial 5% tax. (Code Sec. 4941(a)(2))[33] and, if he refuses to agree with all or part of the correction, an additional 50% tax. (Code Sec. 4941(b)(2))[34] Managers may be jointly and severally liable, but their maximum liability for any one act is $20,000 in initial tax and $20,000 in additional tax. (Code Sec. 4941(c))[35] Report the initial taxes on Form 4720. (Reg § 53.6011-1(b)) Use Form 8868 for an extension, see ¶4124.[36]

Failure to distribute income. A foundation (other than an operating foundation) that fails to distribute its income for a tax year by the end of the *next* year is subject to an initial tax equal to 30% of the income (based on a minimum investment return) (Code Sec. 4942(a); Reg § 53.4942(a)-1(a)), which IRS may abate for reasonable cause (Code Sec. 4962(a))[37] and a 100% additional tax if the foundation fails to distribute the income by the date the initial tax is assessed or IRS issues a 90-day letter for it. (Code Sec. 4942(b))[38] Distributions by nonoperating private foundations to certain supporting organizations are not qualifying distributions. (Code Sec. 4942(g)(4))[39] Report the initial taxes on Form 4720. (Reg § 53.6011-1(b)) Use Form 8868 for an extension, see ¶4124.[40]

Excess business holdings. A foundation that has any excess business holdings is subject to an initial tax (which IRS may abate for reasonable cause) equal to 10% of those excess holdings, based on their value on the day during the tax year when those holdings were the greatest. (Code Sec. 4943(a), Code Sec. 4962)[41] If the foundation fails to timely correct its holdings, an additional 200% tax is imposed. (Code Sec. 4943(b))[42] The excess business holding tax applies to donor advised funds (Code Sec. 4943(e))[43] and the excess business holdings rules apply to certain supporting organizations. (Code Sec. 4943(f))[44] Report the initial taxes

---

23. ¶s D-7300 *et seq.*, D-7400 *et seq.*; ¶s 49,474, 49,484; TD ¶688,009
24. ¶D-7501; ¶49,404; TD ¶684,001
25. ¶D-7503; ¶49,404; TD ¶684,006
26. ¶D-7504; ¶49,404; TD ¶684,009
27. ¶D-7506; ¶49,404.
28. ¶S-2511; ¶60,334; TD ¶684,001
29. ¶D-7600 *et seq.*; ¶s 49,414; 49,464; TD ¶684,500
30. ¶s D-7606, D-7608; ¶49,414.02; TD ¶684,500
31. ¶D-7601; ¶49,414.02; TD ¶684,501
32. ¶D-7602; ¶49,414.02; TD ¶684,503
33. ¶D-7602; ¶49,414.02; TD ¶688,038

34. ¶D-7602; ¶49,414.02; TD ¶684,505
35. ¶s D-7603, D-7604; ¶49,414.02; TD ¶684,506
36. ¶S-2511; TD ¶684,504
37. ¶s D-7701, D-8201; ¶s 49,424, 49,614; TD ¶685,001
38. ¶s D-7701, D-7706; ¶49,424.01; TD ¶685,002
39. ¶D-7711; ¶49,424.03
40. ¶S-2511; TD ¶685,001
41. ¶s D-7800 *et seq.*, D-8201; ¶s 49,434, 49,614; TD ¶685,509
42. ¶D-7801; ¶49,434; TD ¶685,509
43. ¶D-7801; ¶49,434
44. ¶D-7800 *et seq.*; ¶49,434

on Form 4720. (Reg § 53.6011-1(b)) Use Form 8868 for an extension, see ¶4124.[45]

Investments that jeopardize a foundation's charitable purpose. An excise tax is imposed if a foundation makes investments that jeopardize its charitable purpose. An initial tax of 10% of the amount invested is imposed on the foundation *and* on any foundation manager who knowingly participated in the investment. (Code Sec. 4944(a))[46] Additional taxes are imposed on the foundation (25%) if the investment is not timely removed from jeopardy (Code Sec. 4944(b)(1))[47] and on any manager (5%) who refuses to agree to removing the investment from jeopardy. (Code Sec. 4944(b)(2))[48] Foundation managers may be jointly and severally liable for these taxes, but the initial tax on management with respect to any one investment is limited to $10,000, and the additional tax to $20,000. (Code Sec. 4944(d))[49] The initial taxes are reported on Form 4720. (Reg § 53.6011-1(b)) Use Form 8868 for an extension, see ¶4124.[50]

Propaganda, legislative activities and other taxable expenditures. An excise tax is imposed for engaging in propaganda or legislative activities or for making other taxable expenditures. An initial tax equal to 20% of the amount of the taxable expenditure is imposed on the foundation, and a 5% initial tax is imposed on any foundation manager who willfully agreed to the expenditure. (Code Sec. 4945(a))[1] An additional tax is imposed on the foundation (100%) if the expenditure isn't timely corrected, and on any foundation manager (50%) who refuses to agree to part or all of the correction. (Code Sec. 4945(b))[2] Foundation managers may be jointly and severally liable, but the maximum tax that may be imposed on them for any one taxable expenditure is $10,000 of initial tax and $20,000 of additional tax. (Code Sec. 4945(c)) These taxes don't apply if the political expenditures tax (¶4104) applies. (Code Sec. 4955(e))[3] Report the initial taxes on Form 4720. (Reg § 53.6011-1(b)) Use Form 8868 for an extension, see ¶4124.[4]

¶ 4128 Termination of private foundation status; termination tax—Form 990-PF.

Except as otherwise provided below, an organization's status as a private foundation may terminate only if either: (1) the organization notifies IRS of its intent to terminate, or (2) the organization is guilty of willful repeated acts or omissions or of a willful and flagrant act or omission resulting in liability for any of the excise taxes on private foundations (see ¶4127), and IRS notifies the organization that it's liable for tax on termination of its status as a private foundation. (Code Sec. 507(a))[5]

The organization must pay a tax (use Form 990-PF, see ¶4131) on termination of its private foundation status. Unless abated by IRS, the tax equals the lesser of: (1) the aggregate tax benefit (as adequately substantiated by the foundation) resulting from its Code Sec. 501(c)(3) status, or (2) the value of its net assets. (Code Sec. 507(c), Code Sec. 507(g))[6]

Where there's no willful repeated acts or omissions or willful and flagrant acts or omissions resulting in private foundation excise tax liability, a private foundation's status may be terminated without imposition of the tax on termination, if: (a) it distributes all its net assets to one or more public charities that have been in existence as such for at least 60 calendar months before the distribution (IRS guidance illustrates termination under this rule); or (b) it notifies IRS of its intent to terminate, and the organization becomes a public charity for a continuous 60-month period. (Code Sec. 507(b))[7]

45. ¶S-2511; TD ¶685,509
46. ¶s D-7901, D-7903; ¶s 49,444, 49,614; TD ¶685,503
47. ¶D-7905; ¶49,444; TD ¶685,505
48. ¶D-7906; ¶49,444; TD ¶685,507
49. ¶D-7907; ¶49,444; TD ¶685,508
50. ¶S-2511; TD ¶685,501
1. ¶D-8001; ¶s 49,454, 49,614; TD ¶685,018

2. ¶D-8001; ¶49,454.02; TD ¶685,019
3. ¶D-8003; ¶49,554; TD ¶685,017
4. ¶S-2511; ¶s 60,114.04, 60,334; TD ¶685,017
5. ¶s D-7220, D-7222; ¶5074; TD ¶683,509
6. ¶D-7228; ¶5074
7. ¶D-7223; ¶5074

¶ 4129   Excise tax on taxable distributions from donor advised funds—Form 4720.

If a taxable distribution is made from a donor advised fund (see below):

(1) a tax equal to 20% of the amount distributed is imposed and must be paid by the donor advised fund's sponsoring organization (Code Sec. 4966(a)(1)); and

(2) a tax equal to 5% of the amount distributed is imposed if any fund manager agreed to the making of a distribution knowing that it was a taxable distribution. The tax must be paid by any fund manager who agreed to the making of the distribution. (Code Sec. 4966(a)(2))[8]

The maximum amount of tax imposed by item (2) as to any one taxable distribution is $10,000. (Code Sec. 4966(b)(2))[9]

Subject to exceptions, a *donor advised fund* is a fund or account which is:

(1) separately identified by reference to contributions of a donor or donors,

(2) owned and controlled by a sponsoring organization, and

(3) as to which a donor (or any person appointed or designated by the donor) has, or reasonably expects to have, advisory privileges as to the distribution or investment of amounts held in the fund or account by reason of the donor's status as a donor. (Code Sec. 4966(d)(2))[10]

¶ 4130   Excise taxes imposed on prohibited benefits received by a donor, donor advisor or related person from a donor advised fund—Form 4720.

If a distribution from a donor advised fund (¶4129) results in a donor, donor advisor, or a related person ("Subsection (d) person." as set forth in Code Sec. 4967(d)) receiving directly or indirectly a more than incidental benefit as a result of the distribution:

(1) A tax equal to 125% of the amount of the benefit is imposed on the advice of any Subsection (d) person to have a sponsoring organization make the distribution. The tax must be paid by the Subsection (d) person who advises that a distribution be made or who receives a benefit as a result of the distribution. (Code Sec. 4967(a)(1))

(2) A tax equal to 10% of the amount of the benefit is imposed on the agreement of any fund manager to the making of the distribution knowing that the distribution would confer a benefit described at item (1) (above). This tax must be paid by the fund manager who agreed to the making of the distribution. (Code Sec. 4967(a)(2)) However, the maximum amount of tax imposed on a fund manager as to any distribution is $10,000. (Code Sec. 4967(c)(2))[11]

Tax is not imposed as to any distribution as to which tax has been imposed under the Code Sec. 4958 excess benefit transaction rules, ¶4112. (Code Sec. 4967(b))

¶ 4131   Annual return of private foundations—Form 990-PF.

A private foundation must file an annual information return on Form 990-PF (Reg § 1.6033-2(a)(2)(i)) on or before the fifteenth day of the fifth month following the close of the tax year. (Reg § 1.6033-2(e))[12] For return disclosure requirements, see ¶4120. Certain private foundations must file returns electronically. (Reg § 301.6033-4)

8. ¶D-8152 *et seq.*; ¶49,664
9. ¶D-8152; ¶49,664
10. ¶D-8155; ¶49,664.02; TD ¶331,201

11. ¶D-8160 *et seq.*; ¶49,674
12. ¶s S-2801, S-4928; ¶60,334; TD ¶688,021

Chapter 20 RICs (Mutual Funds), REITs, REMICs, Banks and Other Special Corporations

¶ 4200 Special Corporations and Other Entities. ▬▬▬▬▬▬▬▬

Regulated investment companies (mutual funds), real estate investment trusts, real estate mortgage investment conduits, and certain other entities get special tax treatment.

¶ 4201 Regulated investment companies (RICs)—mutual funds.

If it makes certain distributions, a RIC (mutual fund) is taxed only on: (1) the undistributed portion of its ordinary net income, at the regular corporate rates; and (2) the undistributed portion of its net long-term capital gains, at the corporate capital gains rate. (Code Sec. 852(b))[1] The RIC isn't taxed on the amounts it distributes to shareholders, thus allowing it to pass through ordinary income, net capital gains, qualified dividend income eligible for capital gain treatment (see ¶1288), dividend income eligible for the corporate dividends-received deduction, and certain other items to them (see ¶1298) without any tax at the RIC level (if requirements are met). (Code Sec. 852(b))[2] For "late-paid" and year-end dividends, see ¶4203.

The RIC's *undistributed* capital gains may also be designated (on Form 2439) and passed through to the shareholders (but the RIC pays tax (on Form 2438) on the retained gains). The effects of designation are that the shareholders: (1) include their shares of the undistributed capital gains in income, (2) get a credit or refund for their shares of the tax the RIC paid on these amounts (so that only one tax is paid), and (3) get a basis step-up in their shares equal to the difference between the amount of the includible capital gains from the dividend and the tax the shareholder is deemed to have paid with respect to those shares. (Code Sec. 852(b)(3)(D))[3]

A RIC is a domestic corporation that at all times in the tax year is registered with the SEC as a management company or unit investment trust, has an election in effect to be treated as a business development company under the '40 Investment Company Act, or is a mutual or common trust fund other than an "investment company" under that Act. (Code Sec. 851(a))[4] It must also meet gross income, (Code Sec. 851(b)(2))[5] diversification, (Code Sec. 851(b)(3))[6] and E&P tests, (Code Sec. 852(a)(2))[7] make certain distributions (Code Sec. 852(a)(1))[8] *and* elect on its return (Form 1120-RIC) to be taxed as a RIC. (Code Sec. 851(b)(1))[9]

¶ 4202 Real estate investment trusts (REITs).

REITs are generally taxed only on amounts not distributed to their shareholders or beneficiaries, as follows: (1) at *regular* corporate rates on undistributed earnings and profits and net capital gains, and (2) at the *highest* corporate rate on net income from foreclosure property. (Code Sec. 857(b))[10] A REIT may pass through the character of its capital gains and qualified dividend income eligible for capital gain treatment (see ¶1288) to its shareholders, see ¶1299. In addition, a REIT's *undistributed* capital gains may be passed through to the shareholders (on Form 2439). The REIT pays tax on the retained gains (on Form 2438) and the shareholders: (1) include their shares of the undistributed capital gains in income, (2) get a credit or refund for their shares of the tax the REIT paid on these amounts (so that only one tax is paid), and (3) get a basis step-up in their shares equal to the difference between the amount of the includible capital gains from the dividend and the tax the shareholder is deemed to

---

1. ¶E-6100 *et seq.*; ¶8524.10
2. ¶E-6150; ¶8524.02
3. ¶E-6155; ¶8524.02; TD ¶173,001
4. ¶E-6001 *et seq.*; ¶8514
5. ¶E-6004; ¶8514.02
6. ¶s E-6012, E-6015; ¶8514.04
7. ¶E-6020; ¶8524.01
8. ¶E-6101; ¶8524.01
9. ¶E-6002; ¶8514.01
10. ¶E-6600 *et seq.*; ¶8574.01

References beginning with a single letter are to paragraphs in RIA's Federal Tax Coordinator 2d and RIA's Analysis of Federal Taxes: Income. Those beginning with numbers are to paragraphs in RIA's United States Tax Reporter. Those beginning with TD are to paragraphs in RIA's Tax Desk.

have paid with respect to those shares. (Code Sec. 857(b)(3)(D))[11] For "late-paid" and year-end dividends, see ¶4203.

The REIT must be a calendar-year (Code Sec. 859) corporation, trust or association that meets certain requirements as to the source of income, earnings and profits, type of its investments, nature of its activities, and its relationships with financially interested parties (Code Sec. 856(a)), and certain recordkeeping and distribution requirements. (Code Sec. 857(a)) And it must elect on its return (Form 1120-REIT) to be a REIT. (Code Sec. 856(c)(1); Reg § 1.856-2(b))[12]

observation: REITs are designed to do for real estate investors what mutual funds (RICs, see ¶4201) do for investors in securities—i.e., pool resources and get a return on capital without paying a corporate tax on the gain.

¶ 4203   RIC (mutual fund) and REIT dividends paid after close of tax year; year-end dividends.

A regulated investment company (RIC, ¶4201) or real estate investment trust (REIT, ¶4202) may elect to treat all or part of any dividend paid after the end of a tax year ("late-paid dividends") as paid during the year, if the dividend is declared and paid within the required statutory periods. (Code Sec. 855(a), Code Sec. 858(a))[13]

A dividend declared by a RIC or REIT in October, November or December of any calendar year, that's payable to shareholders of record on a specified date in one of those months, is considered to have been paid on Dec. 31 if the dividend is actually paid during January of the following calendar year. (Code Sec. 852(b)(7), Code Sec. 857(b)(9))[14]

For shareholders' tax on these dividends, see ¶1298 (RICs) and ¶1299 (REITs).

¶ 4204   Real estate mortgage investment conduits (REMICs).

REMICs are fixed mortgage pools with multiple classes ("regular" and "residual" (Code Sec. 860G(a)(1), Code Sec. 860G(a)(2); Reg § 1.860G-1)) of investment interests, that have elected REMIC status (on Form 1066). (Code Sec. 860D; Reg § 1.860D-1)[15] REMICs, which are treated as partnerships for procedural purposes (Code Sec. 860F(e))[16] generally aren't taxable. (Code Sec. 860A(a))[17] The REMIC's income is allocated to, and taken into account by, the holders of its interests. (Code Sec. 860A(b)) REMICs report on Form 1066.[18]

Although not subject to federal income tax, a REMIC is subject to penalty taxes on: income from foreclosure property (Code Sec. 860G(c)), contributions after the start-up date (Code Sec. 860G(d)), and prohibited transactions (Code Sec. 860F(a)), and an excise tax (reported on Form 8831) on certain transfers of residual interests. (Code Sec. 860E(e))[19]

¶ 4205   Small business investment companies (SBICs).

SBICs are licensed and operated under the Small Business Investment Act of '58.[20] They are subject to these special tax rules:

. . . Loss on stock received through the conversion of convertible debentures originally acquired for long-term equity capital supplied to small business concerns is a fully deductible ordinary loss. (Code Sec. 1243)[21]

. . . An SBIC's gain or loss on sale of bonds, debentures, etc., (regardless of issuer) is ordinary gain or loss. (Code Sec. 582(c); Reg § 1.582-1(d))[22]

---

11. ¶E-6617.1; ¶8574.02
12. ¶s E-6501, E-6623; ¶8564.02
13. ¶s E-6201, E-6701; ¶s 8554, 8584
14. ¶s E-6202, E-6704; ¶s 8554.01, 8574.02; TD ¶172,005
15. ¶s E-6901, E-6903; ¶860A4
16. ¶E-6927; ¶860A4
17. ¶E-6917; ¶860A4

18. ¶E-7000 *et seq.*; ¶s 860A4.01, 860A4.02
19. ¶E-6920 *et seq.*; ¶E-7106; ¶s 860A4.05, 860A4.06, 860A4.07; TD ¶162,010
20. ¶I-9541; ¶12,424
21. ¶I-9542; ¶12,424; TD ¶372,006
22. ¶I-9544

... Dividends the SBIC receives from taxable domestic corporations are 100% deductible. (Code Sec. 243(a)(2))[23]

... An SBIC is exempt from personal holding company tax (¶3320 *et seq.*), unless at any time in the tax year any shareholder of the SBIC owns, directly or indirectly, a 5%-or-more interest in the companies financed by the SBIC. (Code Sec. 542(c)(7))[24]

¶ 4206   Cooperatives (co-ops).

A cooperative is an entity in which the same persons are both owners and customers. Although some co-ops are *classified* as "exempt," most co-ops are taxed like any ordinary business corporation, and at the regular corporate rates, but with a specific deduction for patronage dividends, see ¶4207. (Code Sec. 1382(b)) "Exempt" farmers' co-ops also may deduct certain nonpatronage distributions. (Code Sec. 1382(c))[25]

¶ 4207   Patronage dividends and per-unit retain allocations.

Both "exempt" farmers' co-ops and nonexempt co-ops exclude (deduct) from their income amounts paid as patronage dividends or per-unit retain allocations. (Code Sec. 1381(a), Code Sec. 1382(b))[26] For deduction of nonpatronage dividends, see ¶4208. For how the patrons or shareholders treat these amounts, see ¶1300.

A patronage dividend represents distributions of net earnings among the cooperators and other patrons on the basis of each person's patronage. (Code Sec. 1388(a))[27] It may be paid in money, a certificate of indebtedness, or other property, including a qualified written notice of allocation.[28]

A per-unit retain allocation is an allocation by a co-op to a patron with respect to products marketed for him. (Code Sec. 1388(f))[29]

A written notice of allocation must disclose the dollar amount allocated to the patron and the portion that is a patronage dividend. (Code Sec. 1388(b); Reg § 1.1388-1(b))[30]

¶ 4208   Nonpatronage distributions deductible by exempt co-ops.

In addition to patronage distributions (¶4207), an "exempt" farmers' co-op may also deduct: dividends paid during the tax year on its capital stock and on any other evidence of proprietary interest in the co-op, (Code Sec. 1382(c)(1); Reg § 1.1382-3(b)) distributions to patrons on a patronage basis out of earnings from nonpatronage sources, (Code Sec. 1382(c)(2)(A); Reg § 1.1382-3(c), Reg § 1.1382-3(c)(3)) and payments in redemption of nonqualified written notices of allocation issued to patrons on a patronage basis with respect to earnings from nonpatronage sources. (Code Sec. 1382(c)(2)(B); Reg § 1.1382-3(d))[31]

¶ 4209   Taxation of banks and other financial institutions.

Banks are generally taxed like regular corporations (Reg § 1.581-1), except that:[32]

Gains and losses from sales or exchanges of bonds, debentures, notes or certificates or other evidences of indebtedness (including any regular or residual interest in a REMIC, see ¶4204) are treated as ordinary gains and losses. (Code Sec. 582(c)(1)) Sales of stock and securities are subject to the regular wash sale provisions, see ¶2461.[33]

Interest paid or credited on deposits or CDs is deductible (special rules apply to frozen deposits).[34] But no deduction is allowed for any portion of interest expense that's allocable (comparing the bank's adjusted bases in taxable and exempt investments) to investment in

23. ¶D-2243; ¶12,424
24. ¶D-3311; ¶5424.02; TD ¶601,503
25. ¶E-1100 *et seq.*; ¶13,814.01
26. ¶E-1100 *et seq.*; ¶13,814.01
27. ¶E-1104; ¶13,814.05
28. ¶E-1120; ¶13,814.01

29. ¶E-1126; ¶13,814.14
30. ¶E-1123; ¶13,814.02
31. ¶s E-1140, E-1141, E-1142; ¶13,814.01
32. ¶E-3000 *et seq.*, ¶E-3300 *et seq.*; ¶5814
33. ¶E-3022 *et seq.*; ¶5824
34. ¶E-3105; ¶5914

tax-exempts. (Code Sec. 265(b)(1), Code Sec. 265(b)(2))[35] However, interest allocable to tax-exempts acquired (or treated as acquired) before Aug. 8, '86, is 80% deductible (100% deductible if acquired before '83). (Code Sec. 291(a)(3), Code Sec. 291(e)(1)(B))[36]

Bad debts. Banks generally must treat bad debts (e.g., losses on loans) by taking a specific deduction ("charge-off") for the debt but non-large banks can choose to deduct additions to bad debt reserves. (Code Sec. 585(a))[37] Banks using reserves must use the experience method to compute the additions. Under this method, the additions can't bring the reserve above the bank's loans outstanding at year-end, times a six-year moving average percentage (ratio of total bad debts to total outstanding loans). (Code Sec. 585(b))[38]

Losses a bank incurs on account of its deposits in other banks must be specifically deducted, whether or not it uses the reserve method for other bad debts.[39]

Worthless securities. A bad debt deduction is allowed to banks for total or partial worthlessness (¶1781) of debts evidenced by securities. (Code Sec. 582(a)) Under the charge-off method, a bank's debt is conclusively presumed to be worthless where the charge-off is made under specific orders or in conformance with established policies, of federal or state supervisory authorities, or is in accordance with a properly made "conformity" election. (Reg § 1.166-2(d))[40]

Mutual savings banks or stock associations, savings and loan associations, building and loan associations, and cooperative banks are subject to special tax rules.[41] Gain or loss from the sale or exchange of any qualifying Fannie Mae and Freddie Mac preferred stock by any applicable financial institution (those referred to in Code Sec. 582(c) or financial institution holding companies) is treated as ordinary income or loss. (§ 301 of Division A, P.L. 110-343, 10/3/2008)[42]

¶ 4210 Common trust funds.

A common trust fund isn't subject to tax (Code Sec. 584(b)) but must file a return (on Form 1065) and pass through its income or loss and other items attributable to each participant. (Reg § 1.6032-1)[43] A common trust fund is a fund maintained by a bank or trust company exclusively to collectively invest and reinvest moneys that it, in its capacity as a trustee, executor, administrator, guardian or custodian, contributes to the fund. (Code Sec. 584(a))[44]

¶ 4211 Taxation of insurance companies.

Life insurance companies are taxed, at the regular corporate rates, on their "life insurance company taxable income" (LICTI). (Code Sec. 801(a)(1))[45] LICTI is life insurance company gross income minus general deductions and, if applicable, the small life insurance company deduction. (Code Sec. 803(a), Code Sec. 804)[46] Gain from the redemption at maturity of certain market discount bonds is taxed under a special rule.[47]

A corporation (whether stock, mutual, or mutual benefit) is taxed as a life insurance company if: (1) it's an insurance company, (2) it's engaged in the business of issuing life insurance and annuity contracts, and (3) it meets a reserve test. (Code Sec. 816(a))[48]

Nonlife insurance companies (stock and mutual) are taxed like corporations generally (¶3303 *et seq.*), with certain deductions peculiar to insurance. Gross income is investment and underwriting income, and gain or loss from property dispositions. (Code Sec. 831, Code Sec. 832)[49] Certain small nonlife insurance companies may elect to be taxed only on investment income, (Code Sec. 831(b))[50] and others may be exempt. (Code Sec. 501(c)(15))[1]

35. ¶E-3108; ¶2654
36. ¶s E-3111, E-3124; ¶2914
37. ¶E-3201, ¶E-3224
38. ¶E-3227; ¶5854
39. ¶E-3139
40. ¶E-3201 *et seq.*; ¶5824
41. ¶E-3300 *et seq.*; ¶5814
42. ¶E-3022.1 *et seq.*; ¶5854
43. ¶s E-3600 *et seq.*, S-4105; ¶s 5844, 60,324

44. ¶E-3600 *et seq.*; ¶5844
45. ¶E-4801; ¶8014
46. ¶E-4801 *et seq.*; ¶s 8034, 8044
47. ¶E-4819
48. ¶E-5401; ¶8164
49. ¶E-5500 *et seq.*; ¶8324.01
50. ¶E-5503; ¶8314
1. ¶D-5901

Chapter 21 Pension and Profit-Sharing Plans—401(k) Plans—Roth 401(k) Plans—IRAs—Roth IRAs— SEPs—SIMPLE Plans

¶ 4310 Employee Benefit Plans.

Qualified pension, profit-sharing and stock bonus plans offer substantial tax benefits to sponsor-employers and their employees.

The principal tax advantages are:

. . . the employer gets an immediate deduction for contributions under the plan (Code Sec. 404);[1]

. . . the income earned by funds while held under the plan is tax-exempt (Code Sec. 501(a));[2]

. . . the employee isn't taxed on his share of the fund until amounts are distributed to him (usually after retirement), ¶4338 et seq., (Code Sec. 402; Reg § 1.402(a)-1);[3]

. . . qualifying "lump-sum" distributions for those born before '36 can get favorable tax treatment, ¶4339, (Code Sec. 402(d));[4]

. . . amounts transferred in a direct trustee-to-trustee transfer are excluded from income (¶4359) (Code Sec. 402(e)(6)) and eligible rollover distributions can be rolled over tax-free to eligible retirement plans (¶4359) (Code Sec. 402(c)(1));[5]

. . . tax is deferred on qualifying distributions of appreciated employer stock until the stock is sold, see ¶4340. (Code Sec. 402(e)(4))[6]

For the small-employer retirement plan start-up tax credit, see ¶2331.

¶ 4311 Pension plans.

A qualified pension plan provides systematically for the payment of definitely determinable benefits to employees (and their beneficiaries) after retirement over a period of years, usually for life.[7] Retirement benefits are generally measured by such factors as years of the employee's service and compensation received. (Reg § 1.401-1(b)(1)(i))[8] Benefits under a defined benefit plan are "definitely determinable" if they are determined actuarially, on a basis that precludes employer discretion. (Code Sec. 401(a)(25))[9] A money-purchase plan—contributions geared to a fixed formula (e.g., 10% of compensation), rather than to profits—is a pension plan if the plan "designates" its intent to be a money purchase pension plan. (Code Sec. 401(a)(27)(B); Reg § 1.401-1(b)(1)(i))[10]

Defined benefit plans also include so-called "hybrid plans," such as cash balance plans, which resemble defined contribution plans in that they determine an employee's benefit by reference to the employee's "cash balance" or other hypothetical account. Each employee's hypothetical account is the sum of the hypothetical pay credit allocations for earlier plan years, plus subsequent interest adjustments through normal retirement age. Under another type of hybrid plan called a pension equity plan (PEP), benefits typically are described as a percentage of the participant's final average pay, with the percentage determined on the basis of points received for each year of service.

For "applicable defined benefit plans" (i.e., cash balance, pension equity, and other hybrid plans; also called "statutory hybrid plans"), a safe harbor provides that the plans won't be treated as violating the Code and ERISA's age discrimination rules so long as a participant's

1. ¶H-10000 et seq.; ¶4014; TD ¶280,101
2. ¶H-10500 et seq.; ¶4014; TD ¶280,101
3. ¶H-11006 et seq.; ¶4014; TD ¶280,101
4. ¶H-11200 et seq.; ¶4014; TD ¶280,101
5. ¶H-8250 et seq.; ¶s 4014.27, 4024.04; TD ¶280,101
6. ¶H-11500 et seq.; ¶s 4014, 4024.02; TD ¶280,101
7. ¶H-5328; ¶4014.02; TD ¶280,105
8. ¶H-5328; ¶4014.02; TD ¶280,102
9. ¶H-5328; ¶4014.10; TD ¶280,102
10. ¶s H-5205, H-5337; ¶4014.02; TD ¶280,107

References beginning with a single letter are to paragraphs in RIA's Federal Tax Coordinator 2d and RIA's Analysis of Federal Taxes: Income. Those beginning with numbers are to paragraphs in RIA's United States Tax Reporter. Those beginning with TD are to paragraphs in RIA's Tax Desk.

accrued plan benefit is equal to (or greater than) that of any similarly situated, younger individual who is (or could be) a plan participant. (Code Sec. 411(b)(5))[11]

An applicable defined benefit plan also fails to meet the age discrimination rules unless it provides that the interest credit rate (or an equivalent amount) for any plan year does not exceed a "market rate of return." A plan is not treated as failing to meet the "market rate of return" requirement merely because it provides for a reasonable minimum guaranteed rate of return, or a rate of return equal to the greater of a fixed or variable rate of return. (Code Sec. 411(b)(5))[12]

IRS has issued guidance on how hybrid defined benefit plans can satisfy these age discrimination rules. (Reg § 1.411(b)(5)-1)[13]

¶ 4312   Profit-sharing and stock bonus plans.

A qualified profit-sharing plan must have a definite, predetermined formula for allocating contributions made under the plan among the participants, and for distributing the funds accumulated under the plan only after a fixed number of years, the attainment of a stated age or upon the occurrence of some event (such as disability, retirement, death or severance of employment). (Reg § 1.401-1(b)(1)(ii))[14]

Contributions can be made to a qualified profit-sharing plan whether or not the employer has current or accumulated profits, and whether or not the employer is a tax-exempt organization. (Code Sec. 401(a)(27)(A))[15]

A qualified stock bonus plan provides benefits in the form of the employer-corporation's own stock. Stock bonus plans must generally satisfy the qualification requirements that apply to profit sharing plans, plus some additional requirements.[16]

¶ 4313   Paid time off (PTO) plans.

A plan may allow contributions of an employee's unused PTO, under the employer's PTO plan, as long as certain requirements are satisfied. A "PTO plan" refers to a sick and vacation leave plan under which a participant may take paid leave without regard to whether the leave is due to illness or incapacity. If certain nondiscrimination and contribution requirements are met, then a participant does not include in gross income (i) plan contributions of the dollar equivalent of unused PTO until distributed to the participant, as provided under the rules for taxing plan contributions; and (ii) amounts paid for the dollar equivalent of unused PTO that's not contributed to the plan until the tax year in which the amount is paid to the participant.[17]

¶ 4314   Employee stock ownership plans (ESOPs).

An ESOP is a qualified defined contribution plan that is either a stock bonus plan, or a combination stock bonus and money purchase plan, that invests primarily in employer securities (Code Sec. 4975(e)(7)), and is formally designated as an ESOP.[18]

To ensure that S corporation ESOPs benefit a broad range of employees, restrictions apply under Code Sec. 409(p) that generally prohibit the accrual or allocation of S corp. stock to certain disqualified persons in an ESOP where 10% owners hold 50% or more of the interests in the S corp. (Code Sec. 409(p); Reg § 1.409(p)-1)[19]

Dividends on employer securities that are distributed from an ESOP under Code Sec. 404(k) must be reported on a Form 1099-R that does not report any other distributions, rather than on Form 1099-DIV.[20]

11. ¶H-7239.2 *et seq.*; ¶4114.33; TD ¶286,020
12. ¶H-7239.2 *et seq.*; ¶4114.33; TD ¶286,020
13. ¶H-7239.4 *et seq.*; ¶4114.3303 *et seq.*
14. ¶H-5337 *et seq.*; ¶4014.03; TD ¶280,109
15. ¶H-5337; ¶4014.03; TD ¶280,109
16. ¶H-5209; ¶4014.04; TD ¶280,111
17. ¶H-8980; H-8980.1
18. ¶H-9300 *et seq.*; ¶49,754; TD ¶280,112
19. ¶H-5337; ¶4014.03; TD ¶280,109
20. ¶S-3419.1

¶ 4315   Annuity plans.

The tax advantages of a qualified plan can be obtained without a trust by using contributions to buy retirement annuities directly from an insurance company. (Code Sec. 403(a)(1), Code Sec. 404(a)(2))[21] For Code Sec. 403(b) "tax-sheltered annuities" for employees of tax-exempt organizations and public schools, see ¶4388 *et seq.*

¶ 4316   "Thrift" and "savings" plans.

A thrift plan is in the nature of a profit-sharing plan and provides for the contribution by the participants of a specified percentage (the same for all participants) of their salaries. This employee contribution is then matched by the employer, either dollar for dollar or in some other specified manner, out of profits.[22]

A savings plan permits employees to make voluntary employee contributions which aren't limited to any specific percentage of compensation.[23]

These plans may allow withdrawal of the voluntary employee contributions (plus earnings) before retirement or termination. However, these contributions are subject to nondiscrimination testing, see ¶4317.[24]

¶ 4317   401(k) plans—elective deferral.

Cash or deferred arrangements (CODAs), popularly known as "401(k)" plans (from Code Sec. 401(k)), allow an employee to choose whether the employer should pay a certain amount directly to the employee in cash, or should instead pay that amount on the employee's behalf to a qualified trust under a profit-sharing plan, a stock bonus plan, a pre-ERISA money purchase plan, or a rural cooperative defined contribution pension plan. (Code Sec. 401(k))[25] For salary-reduction arrangements similar to 401(k) plans under SIMPLE retirement plans, SEPs established before '97, and tax-sheltered annuities, see ¶4382, ¶4381, and ¶4388.

For 2013 and 2014, an employee may elect to defer a maximum of $17,500 on a pre-tax basis under a 401(k) plan, SEP, or Code Sec. 403(b) tax-sheltered annuity (¶4388). (Code Sec. 402(g)(1), Code Sec. 402(g)(5))[26] Individuals who attain age 50 by the end of the plan year may make (if their plan permits (Reg § 1.414(v)-1(a))) additional pre-tax "catch-up" contributions of up to $5,500 for 2013 and 2014. (Code Sec. 414(v)(2)(B)(i), Code Sec. 414(v)(2)(C)) The maximum catch-up amounts apply to all qualified plans, tax sheltered annuity plans, SEPs and SIMPLE plans of an employer on an aggregated basis, as if all plans were a single plan. (Code Sec. 414(v)(2)(D))[27]

If all the requirements are met, any amount set aside under the CODA is not taxed to the employee currently but instead is taxed at the time of distribution. However, elective deferrals and designated Roth contributions (¶4375) are included in wages for purposes of social security and Medicare taxes. (Code Sec. 3121(v)(1)(A))[28]

Excess deferrals are included in the employee's gross income. (Code Sec. 402(g)(1)(A); Reg § 1.402(g)-1(d)(1)) They will be taxed again on distribution unless distributed to the employee in a corrective (nontaxable) distribution during the tax year or by the Apr. 15th following the close of the employee's tax year. (Code Sec. 402(g)(2)(C); Reg § 1.402(g)-1(e)(8))[29]

A 401(k) plan must meet all the normal tax qualification rules (¶4319), including the nondiscrimination rules (¶4325), and, in addition, all of the following requirements:

(1) amounts must not be distributable except by reason of (a) retirement, death, disability

---

21. ¶H-5212 *et seq.*; ¶4034; TD ¶280,113
22. ¶H-5214; TD ¶280,114
23. ¶H-5215; TD ¶280,114
24. ¶H-5313; TD ¶280,114
25. ¶H-8975 *et seq.*; ¶4014.17; TD ¶280,116

26. ¶H-9151; ¶4024; TD ¶284,025
27. ¶H-9246; ¶4144.26; TD ¶284,116
28. ¶H-4624; TD ¶544,002
29. ¶H-9155 *et seq.*; ¶s 4014.176, 4154.015; TD ¶284,024 *et seq.*

or other separation from employment, including certain transfers in connection with the sale of a business, (b) hardship (see below) or attainment of age 59½ (for profit-sharing or stock bonus plans), (c) in a lump sum on termination of the plan, or (d) in a lump sum, on the employer's disposition of (i) substantially all of its trade or business assets, or (ii) a subsidiary (Code Sec. 401(k)(2)(B))[30] (for loans from 401(k) plans, see ¶4343);

(2) employer contributions made under the employee's election must be nonforfeitable at all times (Code Sec. 401(k)(2)(C));[31]

(3) a covered employee must be able to elect to have the employer make plan contributions on the employee's behalf or make the payment directly to the employee in cash (Code Sec. 401(k)(2)(A))[32] (automatic contributions are permitted for employees who don't affirmatively elect to receive cash, see below);[33]

(4) elective deferrals under the plan (as aggregated with all other plans, etc., of the employer) must be prohibited from exceeding the above indexed dollar limits;[34] and

(5) special nondiscrimination rules that require the plan to satisfy one of two "actual deferral percentage (ADP) tests," so highly compensated employees can't elect to defer a disproportionately higher amount of their salary, must be met. (Code Sec. 401(k)(3)(A))[35] Similar requirements—actual contribution percentage (ACP) tests—apply to limit employer matching or employee contributions made on behalf of highly compensated employees. (Code Sec. 401(m))[36]

A 401(k) plan is treated as meeting these requirements if it's a "SIMPLE" plan (¶4382) that meets specified matching or nonelective contribution tests and other requirements. (Code Sec. 401(k)(11))[37]

An alternative nondiscrimination safe harbor based on employer matching or nonelective contributions also is available. (Code Sec. 401(k)(12))[38] A 401(k) plan providing for safe harbor matching contributions won't be treated as failing to satisfy the ADP or ACP tests for a plan year where the employer sponsoring the plan reduces or suspends safe harbor nonelective contributions during the plan year because of a substantial business hardship. (Prop Reg. § 1.401(k)-3, Prop Reg. § 1.401(m)-3 ["Taxpayers may rely"]) [39]

Similar rules apply to employer and matching contributions under Code Sec. 401(m). (Code Sec. 401(m)(3))[40]

A nondiscrimination safe harbor applies for automatic enrollment 401(k) programs (called qualified automatic contribution arrangements, or "QACAs") that meet certain contribution, vesting, and withdrawal requirements. (Code Sec. 401(k)(13)(A))

Similar rules apply for 403(b) plans, see ¶4388.

A 401(k) plan can include a qualified Roth contribution program; see ¶4375.

An in-service distribution on account of hardship may only be made if the employee has "an immediate heavy financial need" and the distribution is "necessary to meet such need." But a distribution may be considered for hardship only to the extent that, as shown by the employee, the need can't be relieved by certain alternate sources, e.g., loans, insurance. (Reg § 1.401(k)-1(d)(2))[41]

401(k) plans may permit hardship distributions for the medical, tuition, funeral etc. expenses of a named plan beneficiary, or of a person who has an unconditional right to all or a part of the participant's account balance on the participant's death. [42]

Hardship distributions are not rollover-eligible, see ¶4359.

---

30. ¶H-9201 *et seq.*; ¶4014.17
31. ¶H-8975.12; ¶4014.17; TD ¶284,003
32. ¶H-8975.12; ¶4014.17; TD ¶284,003
33. ¶H-9053.1I; TD ¶284,007
34. ¶s H-9150, H-9159; ¶4014.17; TD ¶284,003
35. ¶H-6579 *et seq.*; ¶4014.17; TD ¶284,003
36. ¶H-6555 *et seq.*; ¶4014.212; TD ¶284,042

37. ¶H-9087; ¶4014.1735; TD ¶284,022
38. ¶H-9053.1; ¶4014.21; TD ¶284,003
39. ¶H-9053.1D *et seq.*; ¶4014.178; TD ¶284,010
40. ¶H-9050 *et seq.*; ¶4014.176; *et seq.* TD ¶284,042
41. ¶H-9211 *et seq.*; ¶4014.17
42. ¶H-9211 *et seq.*; ¶4014.17

For the small-employer retirement plan start-up tax credit, see ¶2331. For the saver's credit for lower-income taxpayers' elective contributions to 401(k) plans, see ¶2363.

¶ 4318 Defined contribution and defined benefit plans.

Certain rules governing employee benefit plans specifically apply either to "defined contribution plans" or to "defined benefit plans."

A "defined contribution plan" provides for individual accounts for participants and for benefits based on those accounts. (Code Sec. 414(i)) Included are money purchase pension plans, profit-sharing plans and stock bonus plans.

A "defined benefit plan" is a pension plan other than a defined contribution plan. (Code Sec. 414(j)) It provides for the payments of definitely determinable benefits to the employee over a period of years, usually for life, after retirement. (Reg § 1.401-1(b)(1)(i))[43]

Employers with 500 or fewer employees may establish a combined defined benefit-401(k) plan (a "DB(k) plan"). (Code Sec. 414(x)(2))[44]

¶ 4319 Qualification requirements for a qualified employee plan.

The chief requirements for tax qualification of an employee benefit plan and tax-exempt trust are:

(1) The plan must be a definite written program[45] that's communicated to the employees. (Reg § 1.401-1(a)(2))[46]

(2) The plan must be established by the employer for the *exclusive* benefit of the employees or their beneficiaries. (Code Sec. 401(a)(1))[47]

(3) The plan must generally provide that benefits can't be assigned, except for transfers under a qualified domestic relations order (QDRO) and judgments or settlements for certain ERISA crimes and violations. (Code Sec. 401(a)(13); Reg § 1.401(a)-13(g)(2))[48]

(4) The plan must meet special tests based on coverage and eligibility of employees to participate (¶4323).

(5) The plan must not discriminate in favor of highly compensated employees with respect to contributions or benefits (¶4325).

(6) The plan must be properly funded (¶4330), and must meet certain vesting requirements (¶4322).

(7) Under a defined benefit plan, forfeitures must not be applied to increase the benefits of the employees. (Code Sec. 401(a)(8))[49]

(8) A pension plan (and certain other plans) must in general pay a married participant's benefits in the form of a qualified joint and survivor annuity (QJSA), unless the participant elects otherwise (with written spousal consent). The monthly survivor benefit must be at least 50% of the joint benefit. (Code Sec. 417(b))[50] Plans that offer a QJSA must offer, as an option, a joint and survivor benefit that provides at least a 75% survivor benefit. (Code Sec. 417(a)(1)(A), Code Sec. 417(g)) Plans subject to the QJSA requirements must provide, to a participant who waives the QJSA, the chance to elect a qualified optional survivor annuity (QOSA), and must provide a written explanation to participants of the QOSA's terms and conditions. (Code Sec. 417(a)(1)(A)(ii))[1]

(9) In the event of a merger or consolidation with, or transfer of assets or liabilities to, any other plan, each participant must be entitled to a termination benefit after the merger, etc., at least equal to his pre-merger termination benefit. (Code Sec. 401(a)(12))[2]

(10) The plan may not provide for contributions or benefits that exceed specified overall

43. ¶H-5200 *et seq.*; ¶s 4014.02, 4014.03; TD ¶280,100
44. ¶H-9252; ¶4144.27
45. ¶H-5301; ¶4014.05; TD ¶286,001
46. ¶H-5303; ¶4014.05
47. ¶H-5304; ¶4014.09; TD ¶286,001

48. ¶H-8200 *et seq.*; ¶4014.14
49. ¶H-7502; ¶4014.11; TD ¶286,032
50. ¶H-8611; ¶4174.02
1. ¶H-8623.1 *et seq.*; ¶4174.02; ¶4174.035
2. ¶H-8800 *et seq.*; ¶4014.07

limitations (Code Sec. 401(a)(16))[3] (¶4328).

(11) The plan must provide that benefit payments begin (unless otherwise elected) no later than the 60th day after the plan year in which occurs the latest of: (a) the date the participant reaches age 65 (or earlier retirement age), (b) the 10th anniversary of the employee's participation in the plan, or (c) the date the participant terminates service. (Code Sec. 401(a)(14); Reg § 1.401(a)-14(a))[4]

Qualified pension plans may allow employees age 62 or older to receive in-service distributions (i.e. receive plan benefits before retirement). (Code Sec. 401(a)(36); Reg § 1.401(a)-1(b)(1)(i))[5]

(12) The plan must provide certain required minimum distribution rules (Code Sec. 401(a)(9) (¶4345).

(13) A pension plan can't allow withdrawal of employer contributions before termination of employment, or of the plan.[6] But employer contributions accumulated in a profit-sharing plan may be distributed after a fixed number of years (not less than two years). (Reg § 1.401-1(b)(1)(ii))[7] A profit-sharing plan may also permit withdrawal of employer contributions for hardship[8] or by participants with at least 60 months of participation.[9]

(14) Every plan must provide that a distributee of an eligible rollover distribution may elect to have the distribution transferred directly to an eligible retirement plan (¶4359). (Code Sec. 401(a)(31)(A); Reg § 1.401(a)(31)-1)[10] Plans also must adhere to certain involuntary cash-out rollover rules (see ¶4359). (Code Sec. 401(a)(31)(B))

(15) The plan can't reduce plan benefits (including death or disability) to account for post-separation social security benefit increases. (Code Sec. 401(a)(15))[11]

(16) A plan may take into account only the first $255,000 for 2013 ($260,000 for 2014) of each employee's annual compensation. (Code Sec. 401(a)(17))[12]

(17) Defined benefit plans other than government plans must meet minimum participation requirements (¶4323) (Code Sec. 401(a)(26)) in addition to the coverage and eligibility requirements (¶4324).[13]

(18) If a plan member elects to have an eligible rollover distribution paid directly to a specified eligible retirement plan, the plan must make the distribution in the form of direct trustee-to-trustee transfer. (Code Sec. 401(a)(31))[14]

(19) A qualified trust that's a retirement plan must provide that the survivors of a participant who dies while performing qualified military service are entitled to any additional benefits (other than benefit accruals relating to the period of qualified military service) under the plan as if the participant had resumed and then terminated employment on account of his death. (Code Sec. 401(a)(37))[15]

For the cash-out requirements under the minimum survivor annuity rules, which allow participant accounts of $5,000 or less to be distributed, the present value of plan benefits is calculated using the "applicable mortality table" and the "applicable interest rate." (Code Sec. 417(e)(3)) The "applicable interest rate" is the adjusted first, second, and third segment rates for the month before the distribution date (or as IRS regs prescribe).[16] The "applicable mortality table" is a mortality table, modified as appropriate by IRS, based on the mortality table specified for the plan year.[17]

---

3. ¶H-5901 et seq.; ¶4154; TD ¶282,001
4. ¶H-8271; ¶4014.15; TD ¶286,034
5. ¶H-8273.2; ¶4014.141
6. ¶H-5310; TD ¶286,003
7. ¶H-5346; TD ¶280,109
8. ¶H-5348
9. ¶H-5346
10. ¶H-8250 et seq.; TD ¶144,037
11. ¶H-5311; ¶4014.22; TD ¶286,022
12. ¶H-5919; ¶4014.18; TD ¶280,505
13. ¶H-5700 et seq.; ¶4014.25; TD ¶286,007
14. ¶H-8251; ¶4014.27
15. ¶H-9963 et seq.; ¶4014.28TD ¶286,040
16. ¶H-8705.1; ¶4174.06
17. ¶H-8704; ¶4174.06

¶ 4320 Distributions pursuant to domestic relations orders.

The rules prohibiting the assignment or alienation of qualified plan benefits do not apply to the creation, assignment, or recognition of a right to any benefit payable with respect to a participant under a domestic relations order that is determined to be a "qualified domestic relations order" (i.e., a "QDRO"). (Code Sec. 401(a)(13)(B)) A domestic relations order is any judgment, decree, or order (including approval of a property settlement agreement) that: (i) relates to the provision of child support, alimony payments, or marital property rights to a spouse, former spouse, child, or other dependent of the participant, and (ii) is made under a state domestic relations law (including a community property law). (Code Sec. 414(p)(1))[18]

The term "QDRO," which (i) provides an exception to the anti-alienation rules, and (ii) may place the responsibility for the taxation of plan distributions on an alternate payee who is a spouse or former spouse of a plan participant, means a "domestic relations order" (see above) that: (1) creates or recognizes the existence of an alternate payee's right, or assigns to an alternate payee (see below) the right, to receive all or a portion of a plan participant's benefits payable under a plan, (2) clearly specifies certain facts, such as the amount or percentage of, and manner that, the participant's benefits are to be paid to the alternate payee, and (3) does not alter the amount or form of benefit. (Code Sec. 414(p)(1)(A), Code Sec. 414(p)(2), Code Sec. 414(p)(3))[19]

For purposes of the rules on QDROs, an "alternate payee" includes any spouse, former spouse, child, or other dependent of a participant who is recognized by a qualified domestic relations order as having a right to receive all, or a portion of, the benefits payable under a plan with respect to the participant. (Code Sec. 414(p)(8))[20]

A spouse (or former spouse) who has a right to receive all or a part of a distribution under a QDRO as an alternate payee, is treated as the distributee of any distribution received under the QDRO. However, a distribution to a participant's non-spouse dependent (who also may be an alternate payee) is taxed to the participant. (Code Sec. 402(e)(1)(A)) Similar rules apply to distributions from Code Sec. 457 plans. (Code Sec. 414(p)(12))[21]

Lump-sum distributions made to alternate payees who are spouses (or ex-spouses) of participants are eligible for preferential tax treatment (see ¶4339) so long as the distributions would qualify for the preferential tax treatment if made to the participant. Further, any amounts paid or distributed under a qualified plan to an alternate payee who is the spouse (or former spouse) of the participant under a QDRO may be rolled over (see ¶4359 *et seq.*) as if the alternate payee were the participant. Thus, a QDRO distribution made to an employee's spouse (or former spouse) as an alternate payee is an eligible rollover distribution. (Code Sec. 402(e)(1)(B))[22]

In the case of a distribution made to the spouse (or former spouse) of the plan participant as alternate payee under a QDRO, net employee contributions (together with other amounts treated as the participant's investment in the contract) are apportioned between the participant and the alternate payee. The apportionment is made pro rata, on the basis of the present value of all benefits of the participant under the plan and the present value of all benefits of the alternate payee under the plan (as alternate payee with respect to the participant under a QDRO). (Code Sec. 72(m)(10))[23]

observation: Under IRS guidance, the QDRO rules may now apply to same-sex married couples; see ¶4705.

18. ¶H-8207; ¶H-8208; ¶4144.20; TD ¶141,004
19. ¶H-8209; ¶4144.20;TD ¶141,005
20. ¶H-8209.1; ¶4364.08; TD ¶141,005
21. ¶H-11008; ¶4364.08; TD ¶141,005
22. ¶H-11439; TD ¶144,022
23. ¶H-11049; TD ¶141,040

¶ 4321   Incidental benefits.

Life or accident and health insurance features that are incidental to the primary benefit of a qualified plan, may be included to a limited extent. (Reg § 1.401-1(b)(1)(i), Reg § 1.401-1(b)(1)(ii))[24]

¶ 4322   Vesting of benefits.

Plans must provide that a participant's right to his accrued benefit (defined below) vests at certain rates during the years of his employment. Benefits derived from employee contributions must be 100% vested at all times. (Code Sec. 411(a); Reg § 1.411(a)-1(a)(2)) Benefits derived from employer contributions must become nonforfeitable when the employee reaches normal retirement age (defined below). (Code Sec. 411(a)) A defined benefit plan also must meet one of two alternative minimum vesting standards for vesting in benefits derived from employer contributions before normal retirement age: (1) a five-year cliff schedule requiring full vesting after five years of service, or (2) a three-to-seven year graded schedule requiring 20% vesting after three years of service and 20% additional vesting in each of the following years. (Code Sec. 411(a)(2); Reg § 1.411(a)-3T) For a defined contribution plan, slightly faster vesting (three-year cliff or two-to-six year graded) applies to all employer contributions (non-elective employer contributions as well as matching contributions). (Code Sec. 411(a)(2)(B))[25]

The accelerated three-year cliff or two-to-six year graded vesting schedule applies to *all* employer contributions in a defined contribution plan (non-elective employer contributions as well as matching contributions). (Code Sec. 411(a)(2)(B))[26]

For hybrid defined benefit plans (¶4311), IRS regs provide guidance on the accelerated three-year vesting for employer contributions. (Reg § 1.411(a)(13)-1(c))[27]

Accrued benefit means the participant's annual benefit (or its actuarial equivalent) starting at normal retirement age (defined benefit plans) or the balance in the participant's account (defined contribution plans). (Code Sec. 411(a)(7)(A))[28]

Normal retirement age is the earlier of the time a participant attains normal retirement age under the plan or the later of: (1) the time the participant reaches age 65, or (2) the 5th anniversary of the individual's participation in the plan. (Code Sec. 411(a)(8))[29]

IRS regs allow plans to set normal retirement age lower than age 65, so long as this age isn't earlier than the earliest age that is reasonably representative of the typical age for the industry in which the covered workforce is employed. The regs establish age 62 (coinciding with the rule allowing in-service distributions to employees age 62 or older, see ¶4319) as a safe harbor for this requirement. (Reg § 1.401(a)-1(b)(2))[30]

¶ 4323   Coverage and eligibility requirements.

A qualified plan other than a government plan must meet special tests designed to ensure adequate coverage of rank and file employees and avoid discrimination.

The plan must, on at least one day in each quarter of its tax year, either: (1) benefit 70% of the employees who aren't "highly compensated" (¶4326), (2) benefit a percentage of nonhighly compensated employees that is at least 70% of the highly compensated benefiting, or (3) meet a test under which the average benefit for the nonhighly compensated is at least 70% of the average benefit for the highly compensated. (Code Sec. 410(b)(1)) This "average benefits test" also requires that the plan benefit employees under a nondiscriminatory classification. (Code Sec. 410(b)(2))[31] However, a plan maintained by an employer that has no

24. ¶H-8104 *et seq.*; ¶4014.13; TD ¶280,105
25. ¶H-7400 *et seq.*; ¶s 4114, 4114.01; TD ¶286,028
26. ¶H-7410 ; ¶4114.01
27. ¶H-7239.22; ¶4114.3320

28. ¶H-7200 *et seq.*; ¶4114.06; TD ¶286,020
29. ¶H-7404; ¶4114.08; TD ¶286,027
30. ¶H-7404; ¶4114.08; TD ¶286,027
31. ¶H-5410 *et seq.*; ¶s 4104.11, 4104.12; TD ¶286,006

employees other than highly compensated employees for a year is treated as meeting the coverage requirement for the year. (Code Sec. 410(b)(6)(F))[32]

A qualified plan can't require as a condition of participation that any employee complete a period of service extending beyond the later of the date he: (1) reaches age 21, or (2) completes one year of service (or two years, if the plan provides full and immediate vesting for all participants). (Code Sec. 410(a)(1)(A), Code Sec. 410(a)(1)(B)(i))[33]

¶ 4324 Minimum participation requirement—the 50-employee/40% test.

A defined benefit plan other than a governmental plan isn't qualified unless, on each day of the plan year, the plan benefits at least the lesser of (a) 50 employees of the employer, or (b) the greater of 40% of employees, or 2 employees (or 1 employee if there is only 1 employee). (Code Sec. 401(a)(26)(A))[34] Instead of meeting the test on each day of the plan year, compliance on a single representative "snapshot" day during the year is sufficient. (Reg § 1.401(a)(26)-7(b))[35]

¶ 4325 Contributions or benefits must be nondiscriminatory.

Contributions or benefits under a plan other than a governmental plan must not discriminate in favor of "highly compensated employees", see ¶4326. (Code Sec. 401(a)(4))[36] To comply, a plan must satisfy three requirements: (1) either the contributions or benefits under the plan must be nondiscriminatory in amount, (2) the plan's optional forms of benefit, ancillary benefits (e.g., disability benefits), and other rights and features (e.g., plan loans and investment alternatives) must be made available to employees in a nondiscriminatory manner, and (3) the effect of the plan under certain plan amendments, grants of past service credit, and plan terminations must be nondiscriminatory. (Reg § 1.401(a)(4)-1(b))[37] Defined benefit plans can be cross-tested for discrimination on the basis of equivalent employer contributions to profit-sharing plans, and vice versa. (Reg § 1.401(a)(4)-8) "Catch-up" elective deferrals by older employees (¶4317) are not subject to nondiscrimination requirements, above, but all eligible employees must have the opportunity to make these "catch-up" contributions (the "universal availability" requirement). (Code Sec. 414(v)(3)(B))[38]

¶ 4326 Who is a highly compensated employee.

A highly compensated employee is an employee who (1) was a 5% owner at any time during the determination year or the preceding year, or (2) for the preceding year, received more than $115,000 for 2013 and 2014 in compensation from the employer and, if the employer elects, also was in the "top-paid group" (top 20%) of employees for that year. (Code Sec. 414(q))[39]

¶ 4327 Plans covering self-employed persons (Keogh plans).

A person who is a "self-employed individual," i.e., derives "earned income" from a business or profession that he owns or conducts, or who has earned income from a partnership in which he is a partner, or has other self-employment income (such as director's fees), can establish and be covered by a qualified retirement plan (sometimes called a Keogh plan). (Code Sec. 401(c)(1))[40] Earned income for this purpose consists essentially of earnings attributable to personal services, whether from a sole proprietorship, partnership or other unincorporated venture, derived from the trade or business with respect to which the plan is established. (Code Sec. 401(c)(2), Code Sec. 401(d))[41]

---

32. ¶H-5410; ¶4104.12
33. ¶s H-5804, H-5807 *et seq.*; ¶4104.02; TD ¶286,008
34. ¶H-5701 *et seq.*; ¶4014.25; TD ¶286,007
35. ¶H-5704; ¶4014.25
36. ¶H-6100 *et seq.*; ¶4014.19; TD ¶286,010

37. ¶H-6350 *et seq.*; ¶4014.19; TD ¶286,010
38. ¶H-9247.1; ¶4144.26; TD ¶284,119
39. ¶H-6702; ¶s 4144.21, 4154.015; TD ¶286,012
40. ¶s H-5218, H-9500 *et seq.*; ¶4014.24; TD ¶284,500 *et seq.*
41. ¶H-9512 *et seq.*; ¶4014.24; TD ¶284,522

¶ 4328   Overall limitations on plan contributions and benefits.

A plan can't be qualified if it provides for contributions or benefits that exceed the overall limitations described below.

Benefits under a defined benefit plan will disqualify the plan if the "annual benefit" for each participant beginning at age 65 exceeds the lesser of: (1) $205,000 for 2013 ($210,000 for 2014), but actuarially reduced if benefit begins before age 62, and increased if the benefit begins after age 65), or (2) 100% of the participant's average compensation for his three high consecutive years of active plan participation. (Code Sec. 415(b); Reg § 1.415(b)-1(a)(1))[42] The maximum dollar benefit is reduced if the employee has less than ten years of plan participation when retirement benefits begin. (Code Sec. 415(b)(5)) This reduction doesn't apply to pro rata benefit increases under a terminating plan if there is no discrimination in favor of highly compensated employees. (Code Sec. 4980(d)(4)(C))[43] Neither the dollar nor the percentage limitation applies if the annual benefit payable under a defined benefit plan doesn't exceed $10,000 and the employer has never had a defined contribution plan in which the employee participated. (Code Sec. 415(b)(4))[44]

Annual additions under a defined contribution plan may not exceed the lesser of: (1) $51,000 for 2013 ($52,000 for 2014), or (2) 100% of the participant's compensation. (Code Sec. 415(c)(1)) Annual additions include employer contributions, employee contributions other than qualified cost-of-living contributions to a defined benefit plan (Code Sec. 415(k)(2)(A)), and employee forfeitures. (Code Sec. 415(c); Reg § 1.415(c)-1(a)(1))[45]

Mandatory employee contributions that are made to a defined benefit plan are treated as contributions made to a defined contribution plan, and are therefore subject to the Code Sec. 415(c) contribution limit. An individual medical account that is part of a pension or annuity plan under Code Sec. 401(h), and an account established to provide post-retirement medical benefits or life insurance for a key employee under Code Sec. 419A(d)(1), are treated as defined contribution plans, so that contributions to these accounts are also subject to the Code Sec. 415(c) limit.[46]

Special rules apply the limits to certain ESOPs. (Code Sec. 415(c)(6); Reg § 1.415(c)-1(f))[47]

Benefits provided to alternate payees under any qualified domestic relations order (QDRO) relating to a participant's benefits must be aggregated with benefits provided to the participant from all defined benefit and defined contribution plans in applying the Code Sec. 415 limitations.[48]

¶ 4329   Additional qualification requirements for "top-heavy" plans.

A "top-heavy" plan is one that primarily favors officers, shareholders, partners and other key employees. If more than 60% of the accrued benefits in a defined benefit plan, or more than 60% of the aggregate of the account balances in a defined contribution plan, are for "key employees," the plan is top-heavy and must meet additional requirements for minimum vesting, and minimum benefits or contributions for non-key employees, in determining contributions or benefits. (Code Sec. 416(a))[49] SIMPLE retirement plans (¶4382) and Code Sec. 401(k) plans that meet safe-harbor nondiscrimination requirements, aren't subject to the top-heavy rules. (Code Sec. 416(g)(4)(G), Code Sec. 416(g)(4)(H))[50]

Vesting requirements. For any plan year for which a plan is a top-heavy plan, an employee's rights to accrued benefits must be 100% vested after three years of service or, at the employer's option, 20% vested after two years' service and 20% in each of the following years

---

42. ¶H-5950; ¶4154.02; TD ¶287,002
43. ¶H-5962; ¶4154.02
44. ¶H-5965; ¶4154.02; TD ¶282,002
45. ¶H-6000 *et seq.*; ¶4154.06; TD ¶287,003
46. ¶H-6000 *et seq.*; ¶4154.06; TD ¶287,003

47. ¶H-6016; ¶4154.09
48. ¶s H-5950, H-6000, H-8217 *et seq.*; ¶4154.02
49. ¶H-8000 *et seq.*; ¶4164; TD ¶286,002
50. ¶H-8001 *et seq.*; ¶4164.02; TD ¶286,002

(100% vested after six years of service). (Code Sec. 416(b))[1]

Minimum benefits or contributions. A top-heavy defined benefit plan must provide a minimum annual retirement benefit, not integrated with social security, for each non-key employee equal to the lesser of: (1) 2% of the participant's average compensation for years in the testing period multiplied by his years of service with the employer, or (2) 20% of his average compensation in the years in the testing period. (Code Sec. 416(c)(1))[2]

In a defined contribution plan, the employer must contribute for each non-key employee not less than 3% of that employee's compensation (including employer matching contributions). (Code Sec. 416(c)(2))[3]

¶ 4330   Minimum funding requirements.

To qualify for tax advantages, defined benefit plans and money purchase plans (including target benefit plans) must meet minimum funding standards. To the extent the minimum funding standard is not met, the employer must pay nondeductible taxes on the amount of the deficiency until the deficiency is eliminated.

A plan is treated as satisfying the minimum funding standard for a plan year if:

(1)   for a single-employer defined benefit plan, the employer makes contributions to, or under, the plan for the plan year which, in total, are not less than the minimum required contribution for the plan year;

(2)   for a single-employer money purchase plan, the employer makes contributions to, or under, the plan for the plan year, which are required under the plan's terms; and

(3)   for a multiemployer plan, the employers make contributions to, or under, the plan, for any plan year which, in the aggregate, are sufficient to ensure that the plan does not have an accumulated funding deficiency as of the end of the plan year. (Code Sec. 412(a)(2))[4]

For single-employer defined benefit plans, the minimum required contribution generally depends on whether the value of plan assets covers the plan's "funding target," which is the present value of all benefits accrued, earned, or otherwise allocated to years of service before the first day of the plan year. (Code Sec. 430(d)(1); Reg § 1.430(d)-1(b)(2))[5]

If the value of plan assets (less any prefunding balance or funding standard carryover balance) is less than the funding target, the minimum required contribution is the sum of the plan's target normal cost and the shortfall and waiver amortization charges for the plan year. (Code Sec. 430(a)(1); Reg § 1.430(d)-1(b)(2)) If the value of plan assets (less any prefunding balance or funding standard carryover balance) equals or exceeds the funding target, the minimum required contribution is the plan's target normal cost for the plan year reduced (but not below zero) by the amount of the excess. (Code Sec. 430(a)(2); Reg § 1.430(d)-1(b)(2))

A plan's target normal cost is the present value of the benefits that are expected to accrue or to be earned during the plan year, plus any plan-related expenses expected to be paid from plan assets, and less any mandatory employee contributions expected to be made during the plan year. (Code Sec. 430(b)(1)(A); Reg § 1.430(d)-1(b)(1))[6]

To determine a plan's target normal cost and funding target, plan liabilities are calculated by discounting future payments to present value using required interest rates based on corporate bonds. Plans must discount future liabilities using three different interest rates (segment rates), depending on the length of time until the liabilities must be paid. A short-term interest (segment) rate is used to calculate the present value of liabilities that will come due within 5 years. A midterm interest (segment) rate is used for liabilities that will come due in 5 to 15 years, and a long-term interest (segment) rate is applied to liabilities that will come due in more than 15 years. These rates are derived from a "yield curve" of investment-

---

1. ¶H-7423; ¶4164.04; TD ¶286,030
2. ¶H-8025; ¶4164.05; TD ¶286,025
3. ¶H-8032; ¶4164.06; TD ¶286,026

4. ¶H-7601; ¶4124.20
5. ¶H-7752.1; ¶4304
6. ¶H-7751.1; ¶4304.01

grade corporate bonds averaged over the most recent 24 months (i.e., the interest rates are "smoothed" over a 24-month period).

Effective generally for plan years beginning after Dec. 31, 2011, if the rates determined under the regular rules are outside of a specified range of the average of the segment rates for the preceding 25-year period (so-called 25-year smoothing), the segment rate is adjusted. The average segment rate is the average of the segment rates determined under the regular rules for the 25-year period ending September 30 of the calendar year preceding the calendar year in which the plan year begins. (Code Sec. 430(h)(2)(C)(iv))[7]

Typically, a plan will have a funding shortfall for a plan year if its funding target for the year exceeds the value of the plan's assets. The shortfall amortization base for a plan year is (1) the plan's funding shortfall, less (2) the present value, determined using one of several permissible rates, of the total of the shortfall amortization installments that have been determined for the current plan year and any succeeding plan years. The total of these installments is referred to as the shortfall amortization charge.[8]

Plans in "at risk status" (generally, plans that are less than 80% funded) must use additional actuarial assumptions to determine their funding target and target normal cost. (Code Sec. 430(i); Reg § 1.430(i)-1)[9]

Finally, underfunded defined benefit plans must also satisfy funding-based limits on the accrual and payment of benefits, such as plant shutdown benefits, plan amendments that increase liabilities for benefits, the payment of accelerated benefit distributions, etc. (Code Sec. 436; Reg § 1.436-1)[10]

¶ 4331   Returning veteran's pension rights.

An employee who returns to a civilian employer following qualified military service is entitled to restoration of certain qualified plan benefits that would have accrued but for the absence due to military service. Qualified military service of a reemployed person must not be treated as a break in service, and must be considered service with the employer for purposes of determining the nonforfeitability and the accrual of the individual's benefits. (Code Sec. 414(u)(8)(B))[11] "Make-up" contributions in excess of the usual contribution and deduction limits for the year made, and suspension of plan loan repayment during uniformed service do not cause loss of a plan's qualified status. (Code Sec. 414(u)(1); Code Sec. 414(u)(4))[12] Plans must permit returning employees to make additional elective deferrals and employee contributions, and must make matching contributions that would have been required had the deferral been made during the period of military service. (Code Sec. 414(u)(2)(A)) Report make-up contributions on Form W-2 or a separate statement identifying the type of plan, years involved, and amounts.[13]

For retirement plans that are subject to Code Sec. 414(u): (1) an individual receiving a differential wage payment (¶3004) has to be treated as an employee of the employer making the payment; (2) the differential wage payment has to be treated as compensation; and (3) the plan won't be treated as failing to meet certain nondiscrimination requirements by reason of any contribution or benefit that is based on the differential wage payment (but other nondiscrimination requirements apply). (Code Sec. 414(u)(12)(A)) Despite (1), an individual is treated as having been severed from employment during any period he is performing service in the uniformed services for purposes of the limitation on in-service distributions for: elective deferrals under a Code Sec. 401(k) plan; amounts attributable to a salary reduction agreement under a Code Sec. 403(b) tax-sheltered annuity; amounts contributed to a Code Sec. 403(b)(7) custodial account; and amounts deferred under a Code Sec. 457(b) eligible deferred compensation plan. (Code Sec. 414(u)(12)(B))

7. ¶H-7751.2A; ¶4304.011
8. ¶H-7751.3; ¶H-7751.2; ¶4304.01
9. ¶H-7759.1 *et seq.*; ¶4304.01*et seq.*
10. ¶H-7730.5 *et seq.*; ¶4364.04*et seq.*

11. ¶H-9951; TD ¶286,040
12. ¶H-9952 *et seq.*; TD ¶286,041 *et seq.*
13. ¶H-9956; TD ¶286,041

Death benefits. Qualified retirement plans, including Code Sec. 403(b) tax-deferred annuities and Code Sec. 457(b) plans, must provide that, where a plan participant dies while performing qualified military service, the participant's survivors are entitled to any additional benefits (other than benefit accruals relating to the period of qualified military service) that would have been provided under the plan had the participant resumed employment and then terminated employment on account of death. The types of additional benefits subject to this requirement include accelerated vesting, ancillary life insurance benefits, and other survivor's benefits provided under a plan that are contingent on a participant's termination of employment on account of death. However, benefit accruals for the period of qualified military service are excepted from these additional benefits. Thus, benefit accruals (whether benefit accruals under a defined benefit plan or contributions under a defined contribution plan) are not required to be imputed for the period of qualified military service in determining death benefits that are based on a deceased participant's accrued benefit.[14]

¶ 4332 How to get IRS approval of plan—Form 5300; Form 5307.

Although advance IRS approval isn't required, it's desirable and customary to seek it by requesting a determination letter on special forms issued by IRS (e.g., Form 5300).[15]

Master and prototype plans. Instead of establishing a plan on its own, an employer may adopt (use Form 5307) a qualified plan using an IRS-approved master or prototype plan prepared and sponsored by trade or professional associations, banks, insurance companies or regulated investment companies (mutual funds).[16] IRS has a five-year remedial amendment cycle for issuing determination letters for individually designed plans, and a six-year amendment/approval cycle for pre-approved plans.[17]

For the small-employer retirement plan start-up tax credit, see ¶2331.

¶ 4333 Employee contributions and employer matching contributions.

A plan may require an employee to contribute to the plan, as a condition to participation, or it may permit such contributions, if no discrimination results.[18]

Employee contributions and employer matching contributions under defined contribution plans (and those under a defined benefit plan treated as made under a defined contribution plan) must meet a nondiscrimination test that restricts the extent to which the actual contribution percentage (ACP) of eligible highly compensated employees can exceed the ACP for all other eligible employees. (Code Sec. 401(m), Code Sec. 414(k)(2)) The current year ACP for highly compensated employees is compared to the previous year's, or, electively, the current year's ACP for other employees. (Code Sec. 401(m)(2)) The ACP test can be satisfied using a safe-harbor. (Code Sec. 401(m)(11))[19] "SIMPLE" plans (¶4382) are deemed to satisfy the ACP test. (Code Sec. 401(m)(10))[20]

Defined contribution plans generally must allow participants to immediately diversify any employee contributions or elective deferrals invested in employer securities into at least 3 other investment options. For employer contributions, other than elective deferrals, invested in employer securities, the same diversification rights must be given to participants with at least 3 years of service, or each beneficiary of such participants or deceased participants. (Code Sec. 401(a)(35)) A plan is not treated as holding employer securities to which the diversification rules apply if the securities are held by either a registered investment company or a regulated pooled investment vehicle. (Code Sec. 401(a)(35)(H)(i)(I))[21]

Individuals with diversification rights must be offered the opportunity to divest the employer securities and reinvest in another investment at least quarterly.[22]

---

14. ¶H-9963*et seq.*; TD ¶286,040
15. ¶T-10500 *et seq.*; ¶4014.01
16. ¶T-10631; ¶4014.01
17. ¶H-8760 *et seq.*
18. ¶H-6556.1 *et seq.*; ¶4014.21

19. ¶H-6565; ¶4014.21
20. ¶H-6565; ¶4014.21
21. ¶4014.12
22. ¶H-8071; ¶4014.12

An ESOP won't lose its exemption from the application of the diversification rules just because it receives rollover contributions of amounts from another plan that are held in a separate account. The exemption continues to apply even if those amounts were attributable to contributions that were subject to Code Sec. 401(k) or Code Sec. 401(m) in the other plan.[23]

¶ 4334 Ceiling on deductions for contributions to pension and annuity plans.

Subject to applicable limits (see following) an employer can deduct its timely paid (¶4337) contributions to a qualified plan. (Code Sec. 404(a); Reg § 1.404(a)-1(b))[24] However, the plan to which the contribution is made must be in existence by the end of the employer's tax year.[25]

The employer may choose one of three alternative special ceilings on annual deductions for contributions to a pension or annuity plan, to get the largest deduction:[26]

(1) The "level cost" ceiling permits a deduction equal to an amount necessary to provide for all participating employees the remaining unfunded cost of their past and current service credits, distributed as a level amount (or level percentage of compensation) over the entire future remaining service of each employee. If the remaining unfunded cost with respect to any three individuals is more than 50% of the total remaining unfunded cost, the unfunded cost attributable to those three must be distributed over at least five tax years. (Code Sec. 404(a)(1)(A)(ii))

(2) The "normal cost" ceiling permits the employer to deduct contributions equal to (a) the "normal cost" (cost of credits for current services determined as though past service credits had been properly funded), plus (b) an amount necessary to amortize the cost of past service or supplementary or annuity credits provided by the plan in equal annual payments (until fully amortized) over ten years. (Code Sec. 404(a)(1)(A)(iii))

(3) If the minimum funding standard (¶4330) exceeds the "level cost" or "normal cost" ceiling applicable to the plan, the employer can deduct the amount necessary to satisfy the minimum funding standard. (Code Sec. 404(a)(1)(A)(i))

The single-employer defined benefit plan contribution deduction limit for any tax year is the greater of:

(i) the excess (if any) of (A) the sum of: the plan's funding target, the plan's target normal cost, and a cushion amount for a plan year, over (B) the value of plan assets (determined under Code Sec. 430(g)(3)) as of the valuation date for the plan year (Code Sec. 404(o)(2)(A)); over

(ii) the minimum required contribution for the plan year. (Code Sec. 404(o))[27]

The multiemployer defined benefit plan contribution deduction limit is the excess (if any) of:

(a) 140% of the plan's current liability (as determined under Code Sec. 431(c)(6)(C)); over

(b) the value of the plan's assets (as determined under Code Sec. 431(c)(2)). (Code Sec. 404(a)(1)(D))[28]

The maximum annual deduction under the above ceilings, however, cannot generally exceed the full funding limitation for the year (Code Sec. 404(a)(1)(A)).[29] Money purchase and target benefit plans also are subject to the 25%-of-compensation deduction limit that applies to profit-sharing plans (¶4335). (Code Sec. 404(a)(3)(A)(v))[30]

Contributions in excess of the amount deductible (except contributions to SIMPLE plans (¶4382) for household workers (Code Sec. 4972(c)(6))) are subject to a nondeductible 10%

23. ¶H-8072; ¶4014.12
24. ¶H-10001; ¶4044.01; TD ¶280,500
25. ¶H-10021; ¶4044.02; TD ¶280,518
26. ¶H-10102 *et seq.*; ¶4044.04; TD ¶281,006

27. ¶H-10106; ¶4044.02
28. ¶H-10112; ¶4044.02
29. ¶H-10105 *et seq.*; ¶4044.04; TD ¶281,006
30. ¶H-10102; ¶4044.07; TD ¶281,006

excise tax in certain cases (Code Sec. 4972), but may be carried over and deducted in later years, subject to the above limitations. (Code Sec. 404(a)(1)(E))[31]

¶ 4335 Ceiling on deductions for contributions to profit-sharing and stock bonus plans.

The special ceiling on deductions for contributions under a profit-sharing, stock-bonus, or "SIMPLE" plan is 25% of the aggregate compensation (exclusive of qualified plan contributions) paid or accrued during the tax year for all employees participating in the plan. (Code Sec. 404(a)(3)(A); Code Sec. 404(m)(1); Reg § 1.404(a)-9(c)) Contributions in excess of this limit may be carried over and deducted in a later year to the extent that contributions for that later year are below the applicable percentage limit for that year. (Code Sec. 404(a)(3)(A)(ii))[32]

The percentage of compensation limit on deductible contributions to a stock bonus or profit-sharing plan for a self-employed individual (Keogh plan) is 25% of "earned income," which is 25% of net earnings from self-employment less the self-employment tax deduction and deductible qualified plan contributions. (Code Sec. 404(a)(8)(B))[33]

Elective deferrals (¶4317) are not subject to the deduction limits for stock bonus and profit sharing plans, combination defined contribution and defined benefit plans, or ESOPs. (Code Sec. 404(n))[34] Compensation includes elective deferral amounts, amounts deferred to a cafeteria plan, and certain pre-disability compensation. (Code Sec. 404(a)(12))[35]

¶ 4336 Deduction ceiling for combinations of qualified plans.

If there is a mixture of one or more defined contribution plans and one or more defined benefit plans, or any combination of two or more pension trusts, annuity plans, and stock bonus or profit-sharing trusts, an overall limit on deductible contributions applies. Under this limitation, the total amount deductible for *all* plans is the greater of: (1) 25% of the compensation (exclusive of qualified plan contributions) paid or accrued during the tax year to the beneficiaries of the various trusts or plans, or (2) the total contributions to the trusts or plans to the extent those contributions don't exceed the amount necessary to satisfy the Code Sec. 412 minimum funding standards. The amount necessary to satisfy the Code Sec. 412 minimum funding standard must not be less than the plan's funding shortfall under Code Sec. 430. (Code Sec. 404(a)(7)(A))

The 25% limit does not apply if the only amounts contributed to the defined compensation plan are elective deferrals. (Code Sec. 404(a)(7)(C)(ii))[36] Further, the combined plan limit applies only to employer contributions to one or more defined contribution plans to the extent the contributions exceed 6% of the compensation otherwise paid or accrued to plan beneficiaries during the tax year.[37]

In determining the limit on deductions where there is a combination of one or more defined benefit and one or more defined contribution plans, any defined benefit plan guaranteed by the PBGC is not taken into account. (Code Sec. 404(a)(7)(C)(iv))

¶ 4337 Timely payment requirement.

A contribution actually must be paid to the trust or under the plan to be deductible. (Code Sec. 404(a))[38] However, payments (including those made to "SIMPLE" plans (¶4382) (Code Sec. 404(m)(2)(B)), made after the end of a year are considered paid on the last day of the year if paid by the employer no later than the due date of its tax return (including extensions).

31. ¶H-10125 *et seq.*; ¶4044.04; TD ¶280,500
32. ¶H-10202; ¶4044.06; TD ¶281,302
33. ¶H-10204; ¶4044.08; TD ¶281,305
34. ¶H-10202; ¶4044.08; TD ¶281,302

35. ¶H-10203; ¶4044.08; TD ¶281,303
36. ¶H-10120 *et seq.*; ¶4044.09; TD ¶281,014
37. ¶H-10120
38. ¶H-10010; ¶4044.01; TD ¶280,506

(Code Sec. 404(a)(6))[39] This applies to both cash and accrual employers, even if other accrual requirements are not met. (Reg § 1.404(a)-1(c))[40]

¶ 4338 How employees are taxed.

Apart from certain "lump-sum" payments qualifying for the preferential tax treatment (¶4339 *et seq.*), and "rollovers" (¶4359), distributions from a qualified plan (reported to recipients on Form 1099-R) generally are taxed to the employee under the annuity rules (¶1354 *et seq.*) in the year distributed or otherwise made available to the employee. (Code Sec. 402(a); Reg § 1.402(a)-1(a)) Thus, the excess of the distribution (cash or fair market value of property) over the amount of any after-tax plan contributions made by the employee, is ordinary income. (Code Sec. 402; Reg § 1.402(a)-1(a)(1)(i))[41]

Certain early (¶4344) distributions are subject to penalty.

¶ 4339 Preferential treatment for certain lump-sum distributions.

Distributions from a qualified plan to an employee or his beneficiaries, that are lump-sum distributions, are taxable as ordinary income, subject to special elections for pre-'74 capital gain treatment and/or ten-year forward averaging for those born before '36.

A lump-sum distribution eligible for preferential tax treatment is a distribution or payment from an exempt trust or annuity within one tax year of the recipient of the balance to the credit of the participant (excluding amounts payable to an alternate payee under a qualified domestic relations order (QDRO; see ¶4320), which separately can qualify for lump-sum treatment to the alternate payee): (1) on account of an employee's (other than a self-employed's) separation from service; or (2) after attaining age 59½ (regardless of his separation from service); or (3) on account of his death; or (4) on account of his disability. (Code Sec. 402(e)(4)(D))[42]

¶ 4340 Lump-sum distributions of securities of employer corporation.

If a lump-sum distribution consists in part of securities of the employer, the net unrealized appreciation in value of the securities while held by the trust is not taxed to the recipient at the time of distribution. But the same amount also is excluded from the recipient's basis in the securities, so that it's taken into account for tax purposes if and when the securities are later disposed of in a taxable transaction. The distributee, however, has the right to elect, on the tax return on which a distribution is required to be included, to have this rule not apply, i.e., to include any net unrealized appreciation in income. (Code Sec. 402(e)(4)(B); Reg § 1.402(a)-1(b)(1))[43] Net unrealized appreciation that isn't included in income at the time of distribution is long-term capital gain when it's realized in a later taxable transaction. (Reg § 1.402(a)-1(b)(1)(i))[44]

¶ 4341 Tax on current payments for life insurance protection.

The cost of current life insurance protection under a life insurance contract purchased with employer contributions to a qualified plan (or earnings thereon) is income to the insured employee for the tax year of purchase, where the benefits are payable to him or his beneficiaries. (Code Sec. 72(m)(3); Reg § 1.72-16(b)) The taxable amount is generally determined under IRS's "Table 2001," carried at IRS Notice 2002-8. [45]

39. ¶H-10016; ¶4044.01; TD ¶280,513
40. ¶H-10017; ¶4044.01; TD ¶280,513
41. ¶H-11006 *et seq.*; ¶4024; TD ¶141,002
42. ¶H-11200 *et seq.*; ¶4024.03; TD ¶142,001

43. ¶s H-11501, H-11503; ¶4024.02; TD ¶142,058
44. ¶H-11510; TD ¶142,063
45. ¶H-10507 *et seq.*; ¶724.24; TD ¶141,081

¶ 4342 Tax on failure to notify participants of benefit-accrual reduction.

Defined benefit plans and individual account plans subject to minimum funding standards are subject to an excise tax of $100 per day per participant, subject to an overall dollar limit, for failure to provide written notice to any participant, employee organization, or alternate payee under a qualified domestic relations order within a reasonable time when the plan is amended to provide for a significant reduction in the rate of future benefit accrual. (Code Sec. 4980F(a); Reg § 54.4980F-1)[46] Plans with fewer than 100 participants or that offer participants the option to choose between a new benefit formula and the old one may be able to use a simplified notice form or be exempted by IRS from the notice requirements. (Code Sec. 4980F(e)(2)(A))[47]

¶ 4343 Loans from qualified plans.

A loan from a qualified plan isn't treated as a taxable distribution to the plan participant only if it must be repaid within five years (except for certain home loans), and doesn't exceed the *lesser* of: (1) $50,000, or (2) the greater of (a) $\frac{1}{2}$ of the present value of the employee's nonforfeitable accrued benefit under the plan, or (b) $10,000. If a plan loan (when added to the employee's outstanding balance of all other plan loans at the time the loan is made and the highest outstanding loan balance during the year before the loan was made) exceeds these limits, the excess is treated (and taxed) as a plan distribution (¶4338). The entire amount of a plan loan that isn't required to be repaid within five years (except for certain home loans) is treated as a plan distribution. (Code Sec. 72(p))[48] The outstanding balance of a plan loan is treated as distributed if the borrower fails to make a scheduled loan repayment installment before any allowable grace period expires. (Reg § 1.72(p)-1, Q&A 10(b))[49] Loan repayment following a deemed distribution increases the participant's investment in the contract (basis). (Reg § 1.72(p)-1, Q&A 21)[50]

A plan loan must be amortized in substantially level payments, at least quarterly, over its term. (Code Sec. 72(p)(2)(C))[1] The level amortization requirement doesn't apply while the employee is on leave without pay for up to one year. (Reg § 1.72(p)-1, Q&A 9)[2]

¶ 4344 Penalty for early withdrawals—Form 5329.

Early withdrawals from a qualified retirement plan, SIMPLE plan, or IRA result in an additional tax (reported on Form 5329) equal to 10% of the amounts withdrawn that are includible in gross income. (Code Sec. 72(t)(1)) The additional tax applies to all withdrawals unless specifically excepted. Exceptions include distributions (i) made on or after age 59$\frac{1}{2}$; (ii) made to a beneficiary or estate on or after death; (iii) attributable to disability; (iv) from a qualified plan after an employee's separation from service in or after the year in which he attains age 55 (this rule does not apply to IRAs); (v) not in excess of the amount allowable as a medical expense deduction for the year, whether or not the distributee itemizes; (vi) that are part of a series of substantially equal periodic (annual or more frequent) payments (made after separation from service if from a qualified plan) for the life (or life expectancy) of the employee or the joint lives (or joint life expectancies) of the employee and his beneficiary; (vii) from an IRA not exceeding amounts paid for medical insurance by IRA owners who have received unemployment compensation for at least 12 weeks (or could have except for being self-employed); (viii) from an IRA for qualified higher education expenses; (ix) from an IRA for qualified "first-home" purchases, subject to $10,000 lifetime cap; (x) from a qualified plan to an alternate payee under a qualified domestic relations order (QDRO ¶4320; this rule does not apply to IRAs); (xi) made on account of an IRS tax levy, and (xii) from a phased or

46. ¶H-7374
47. ¶H-7368
48. ¶H-11067 *et seq.*; ¶724.23; TD ¶141,049 *et seq.*
49. ¶H-11070; ¶724.23; TD ¶141,049

50. ¶724.23; TD ¶141,049
1. ¶H-11068; ¶724.23; TD ¶141,054
2. ¶H-11068.1; ¶724.23; TD ¶141,067

composite retirement annuity under the Federal Phased Retirement Program. (Code Sec. 72(t)(2), Code Sec. 72(t)(3))[3]

For transfers of an IRA to a spouse (or former spouse) under a divorce or separation instrument, see ¶4357.

Taxpayers who used the annuitization or amortization methods to compute substantially equal payments can make a one-time switch to the required minimum distribution method, which generally requires smaller annual distributions, without triggering the 10% penalty.[4]

The additional tax is 25%, rather than 10% on amounts received from a SIMPLE retirement account (¶4382) during the employee's first two years of participation. (Code Sec. 72(t)(6))[5]

The tax applies to certain involuntary cash-outs and deemed distributions. It doesn't apply to amounts distributed from unfunded deferred compensation plans of tax-exempt employers or state and local government employees, i.e., Code Sec. 457 plans.[6]

The 10% early withdrawal tax does not apply to distributions from a governmental defined benefit pension plan to a qualified public safety employee (e.g., firefighter or policeman) who separates from service after age 50. (Code Sec. 72(t)(10))

The 10% additional tax also does not apply to any "qualified reservist distribution" made to individuals ordered or called to active duty for more than 179 days (or an indefinite period) after Sept. 11, 2001. (Code Sec. 72(t)(2)(G)(i))[7] Recipients of such distributions may, at any time during the two-year period beginning on the day after the end of the active duty period, make contributions to their IRAs in an aggregate amount not to exceed the amount of the distribution (i.e., they may make "pay back" contributions). The regular IRA dollar contribution limits don't apply to "pay back" contributions, but these contributions aren't deductible. (Code Sec. 72(t)(2)(G)(i))[8]

¶ 4345   Required minimum distributions.

A qualified plan must provide that the employee's entire interest will be distributed, starting Apr. 1 of the calendar year following the later of the year in which he: (a) reaches age 70 $\frac{1}{2}$ or (b) retires (except for 5% owners), no later than over (i) his life, (ii) his life and the life of a designated beneficiary, (iii) a period of not more than his life expectancy, or (iv) a period of not more than his life expectancy and that of a designated beneficiary. (Code Sec. 401(a)(9)(A), Code Sec. 401(a)(9)(C)) (Similar rules apply to IRAs, see ¶4357.) A qualified plan may provide that the required beginning date for all employees (including non-5% owners) is Apr. 1 of the calendar year following the calendar year in which the employee attained age 70$\frac{1}{2}$.[9]

Where distributions to a participant have begun, but he dies before his entire interest has been distributed, his remaining interest must be distributed at least as rapidly as under the method of distribution in effect at the date of his death. (Code Sec. 401(a)(9)(B)(i)) Where he dies before receiving any required plan distributions, his entire interest must be distributed within five years after his death, except where the employee's interest: (1) is distributed over the life of a designated beneficiary (or over a period not extending beyond the life expectancy of the beneficiary) and the distributions begin no later than one year after the date of the employee's death (Code Sec. 401(a)(9)(B)(ii), Code Sec. 401(a)(9)(B)(iii)), or (2) is distributed over the life of the surviving spouse (or over a period not extending beyond his life expectancy), and the distributions begin no later than the date on which the employee would have reached age 70$\frac{1}{2}$. If the surviving spouse dies before payments must begin, then the 5-year rule applies as if the surviving spouse were the employee. (Code Sec. 401(a)(9)(B)(iv))

3. ¶H-11100 *et seq.*; ¶724.22; TD ¶145,501
4. ¶H-11107
5. ¶H-12377; TD ¶282,815
6. ¶H-11101; ¶724.22

7. ¶H-11116; ¶724.22; TD ¶145,513.1
8. ¶H-11116.1; TD ¶145,513.2
9. ¶H-8275.1 *et seq.*; ¶4014.15; TD ¶144,300

If the 5-year payout rule applies to an account with respect to any decedent, the 5-year period is determined without regard to calendar year 2009, for which RMDs were not required. (Code Sec. 401(a)(9)(H)(ii)(II)) For example, for an account with respect to an individual who died in 2007, the five year period ends in 2013 instead of 2012. (Committee Report)

Failure to make the required distributions is subject to an excise tax (report on Form 5329) equal to 50% of the minimum amount that should have been distributed over the amount actually distributed. (Code Sec. 4974(a))[10]

Lifetime distributions. The RMD for each year is found by dividing the account balance as of the end of the preceding year by the age-based factor from the table in Reg § 1.401(a)(9)-9, Q&A 2. Portions of this table are excerpted below (the full table goes to age 115).

Uniform Lifetime Table

Employee's Age	Distribution Period	Employee's Age	Distribution Period
70	27.4	83	16.3
71	26.5	84	15.5
72	25.6	85	14.8
73	24.7	86	14.1
74	23.8	87	13.4
75	22.9	88	12.7
76	22.0	89	12.0
77	21.2	90	11.4
78	20.3	91	10.8
79	19.5	92	10.2
80	18.7	93	9.6
81	17.9	94	9.1
82	17.1	95	8.6

This table is used for lifetime distributions of the account owner regardless of the identity of the beneficiary or age differential between account owner and designated beneficiary, unless the account owner's spouse is the sole beneficiary and is more than 10 years younger than the account owner, in which case the distribution period may be measured by the joint life and last survivor life expectancy of the employee and spouse, using the life expectancies in the joint and last survivor table of Reg § 1.401(a)(9)-9, Q&A 3.[11]

✔️*observation:* Under IRS guidance, the RMD rules may now apply to same-sex couples; see ¶4705.

Determination of designated beneficiary. The account owner's designated beneficiary is determined based on the beneficiaries designated as of the account owner's date of death who remain beneficiaries on Sept. 30 of the year following the year of the account owner's death. Any beneficiary eliminated by distribution of the benefit or through disclaimer (or otherwise) during the period between the account owner's death and Sept. 30 of the year following the year of death is disregarded in determining the designated beneficiary for purposes of calculating RMDs. (Reg § 1.401(a)(9)-4, Q&A 4(a)) Except for certain trusts (see below), only an individual may be a designated beneficiary for purposes of the RMD rules. (Reg § 1.401(a)(9)-4, Q&A 3)[12]

Trusts as beneficiaries. An underlying beneficiary of a trust may be treated as the account owner's designated beneficiary for RMD purposes when the trust is named as the beneficiary of a retirement plan or IRA, if certain requirements are met (e.g., documentation of the underlying beneficiaries of the trust must be provided timely to the plan administrator, and beneficiaries of the trust can be identified). (Reg § 1.401(a)(9)-4, Q&A 6(b), Reg § 1.401(a)(9)-4, Q&A 5)[13]

---

10. ¶H-8500 *et seq.*; ¶49,744; TD ¶145,515
11. ¶H-8279; ¶4014.153

12. ¶H-8278; ¶4014.153
13. ¶H-8278.4; ¶4014.153

Post-death distributions. For non-annuity-type payouts after the death of the account owner:

... If the account has a designated beneficiary, and the account owner died before his required beginning date (generally, April 1 following the year in which the account owner attains age 70 1/2), the remaining account balance may be paid out over the remaining life expectancy of the beneficiary, using the life expectancy of the beneficiary in the Single Life Table of Reg § 1.401(a)(9)-9, Q&A 1.

... If the account has a designated beneficiary, and the account owner died after the date he was required to begin receiving distributions, the remaining account balance may be paid out over the longer of the remaining life expectancy of the beneficiary or the remaining life expectancy of the account owner. In either instance, the life expectancy for post-death RMDs is determined using the Single Life Table of Reg § 1.401(a)(9)-9, Q&A 1.

... If the account does not have a designated beneficiary: (1) If the account owner dies after his required beginning date (generally, April 1 following the year in which the IRA owner attains age 70-1/2), the remaining balance is paid out over the remaining life expectancy of the account owner, using the Single Life Table of Reg § 1.401(a)(9)-9, Q&A 1. (2) If the account owner dies before his required beginning date, the account balance must be paid out no later than 5 years after the year of the owner's death. (Reg § 1.401(a)(9)-3, Q&A 1, Reg § 1.401(a)(9)-5, Q&A 5)[14]

The 50% excise tax on failures to make RMDs is waived during the first five years after the year of the account owner's death before the required beginning date if the entire benefit is distributed by the end of the fifth year following the year of death. (Reg § 54.4974-2, Q&A 4)

Annuity type distributions. Separate rules apply to annuity type required distributions, namely defined-benefit (i.e., pension) plan RMDs, as well as annuity contracts purchased from firms such as insurance companies to make RMDs from other qualified plans and IRAs. (Reg § 1.401(a)(9)-6) Under these rules, distributions of an employee's entire interest must be paid in the form of periodic annuity payments for the employee's or beneficiary's life (or the joint lives of the employee and beneficiary) or over a comparable period certain. The payments must be nonincreasing or only increase as provided in the regs. (Reg § 1.401(a)(9)-6, Q&A 1)[15]

¶ 4346   Excise tax on employer reversions—Form 5330.

An "employer reversion" from a qualified plan (except for certain exempt employers and government plans) is, in addition to being includible in the employer's gross income, also subject to a 50% excise tax (20% in certain cases). (Code Sec. 4980(a), Code Sec. 4980(b), Code Sec. 4980(c)(1), Code Sec. 4980(d)) Pay with Form 5330 filed no later than the last day of the month following the month in which the reversion occurred.[16]

¶ 4347   Excise tax on prohibited transactions—Form 5330.

An excise tax is imposed on a disqualified person who takes part in a prohibited transaction with a qualified plan, IRA, or medical savings account. The tax (report on Form 5330 each year for each transaction (Reg § 54.6011-1(b))) is 15% of the amount involved in the prohibited transaction for each tax year (or part of the year) in the taxable period. And if the prohibited transaction isn't timely corrected, the disqualified person must pay an additional tax of 100% of the amount involved. (Code Sec. 4975(a), Code Sec. 4975(b))[17] Neither level of tax is imposed on a fiduciary acting only as such. (Code Sec. 4975(a))[18]

Providing investment advice through an "eligible investment advice arrangement" to participants and beneficiaries of a defined contribution plan who direct the investment of their

---

14. ¶H-8279.8; ¶4014.153
15. ¶H-8280; ¶4014.153
16. ¶H-8900 *et seq.*; ¶49,804; TD ¶286,004

17. ¶H-12510; TD ¶287,501
18. ¶H-12514 *et seq.*; ¶49,754; TD ¶287,501

accounts under the plan and to beneficiaries of IRAs (as well as HSAs, Archer MSAs, and Coverdell education savings accounts) is exempt from the prohibited transaction rules. (Code Sec. 4975(d)(17))[19]

Other transactions also are exempt from the prohibited transaction rules, including certain transactions between plans and service providers, for adequate consideration (Code Sec. 4975(d)(20)), certain cross trades of securities between a plan and a party in interest (Code Sec. 4975(d)(22)), and certain otherwise prohibited transactions involving the sale or exchange of securities and commodities between the plan and a party in interest that are corrected within 14 days (Code Sec. 4975(d)(23)).

¶ 4348 Transfers to health benefits and applicable life insurance accounts before 2022.

Before Jan. 1, 2022, excess pension assets may be transferred to a retiree health benefit account without the transfer being treated as either a prohibited transaction or a reversion to the employer if certain conditions are met. For such transfers made after July 6, 2012, transfers of excess pension assets may also be made to buy retiree group-term life insurance (an "applicable life insurance account"). (Code Sec. 420(a))[20]

Single-employer plans can use excess pension assets to fund future retiree health or life insurance benefits by making qualified future transfers to retiree health benefit accounts or applicable life insurance accounts, if certain minimum cost requirements are maintained. Similar rules apply to "collectively bargained transfers" to fund collectively bargained retiree health liabilities or life insurance benefits. A qualified future transfer or collectively bargained transfer must meet the requirements applicable to qualified transfers, with certain modifications to the requirements, one of which is the minimum cost requirement. (Code Sec. 420(f))

For qualified future transfers, the minimum cost requirement is satisfied if, during the transfer period and the four subsequent years, the annual average amount of employer costs is not less than applicable employer cost determined for the transfer. For collectively bargained transfers, the minimum cost requirement is satisfied if each collectively bargained group health plan or group-term life insurance plan provides that the collectively bargained employer cost for each tax year in the collectively bargained cost maintenance period is not less than the amount specified by the collective bargaining agreement.

Qualified transfers may satisfy the minimum cost requirement by satisfying the minimum cost requirement that applies to a collectively bargained transfer. (Code Sec. 420(c)(3)(A))[21]

Multiemployer plans may transfer excess pension assets to retiree health accounts. (Code Sec. 420(a); Code Sec. 420(e)(5)) The funding rules for defined benefit plans (see ¶4330) are integrated into the rules on the transfer of excess pension assets to retiree health accounts. (Code Sec. 420(e)(2), Code Sec. 420(e)(4)) Further, any assets transferred in a qualified transfer to a retiree health account or applicable life insurance account will not be treated as assets in the plan for purpose of the minimum contribution rules. (Code Sec. 430(l))[22]

Generally, only group-term life insurance not in excess of $50,000 may be purchased with excess pension assets, because such insurance coverage may be provided through a retiree life insurance account only to the extent that the coverage is not includible in the retiree's gross income.[23]

¶ 4349 Distributions from governmental retirement plans for health and long-term care insurance for public safety officers.

Public safety officers may exclude from income governmental retirement plan distributions

---

19. ¶H-12558.1; ¶49,754.01
20. ¶H-8163; ¶4204
21. ¶H-8173; ¶4204.01

22. ¶H-8164; ¶4304.01
23. ¶H-8167; ¶4204

that don't exceed accident, health or long-term care insurance premiums for themselves, their spouses, and dependents, if the distributions are paid directly to insurers. The exclusion is limited to $3,000 per year. (Code Sec. 402(l), Code Sec. 403(a), Code Sec. 403(b), Code Sec. 457(a))[24] The accident or health plan receiving the payments of qualified health insurance premiums may be a self-insured plan.[25]

¶ 4350   Plans that fail to qualify or that lose qualified status.

The following rules apply to a plan that fails to qualify or loses its qualified status:

Contributions to the trust by an employer are included in the gross income of the employee. (Code Sec. 402(b)) The employee must report the value of his interest in the employer's contributions the first time his interest isn't subject to substantial risk of forfeiture, or is transferable free of such risk, whichever occurs first. (Reg § 1.402(b)-1)[26]

An employer's contributions are deductible in the tax year in which an amount attributable to the contribution is includible in the gross income of employees participating in the plan (Code Sec. 404(a)(5)), even if the employer is an accrual basis taxpayer.[27]

The amount actually distributed or made available to the employee or other distributee (beneficiary, etc.) is taxable in the year distributed or made available under the regular annuity rules (¶1354 *et seq.*), with a minor exception for distribution of trust income before the annuity is to begin. (Code Sec. 402(b)(2))[28]

Premiums paid by an employer for an annuity contract not purchased under a qualified annuity plan (¶4315), are included in the employee's gross income. Amounts actually paid or made available to any employee-beneficiary under the nonqualified annuity contract are taxed under regular annuity rules. (Code Sec. 403(c))[29]

¶ 4351   Retirement Savings Plans for Individuals (IRAs). ▬▬▬▬▬▬▬

Employees and self-employed individuals who aren't active participants in an employer-maintained retirement plan can set aside and deduct up to $5,500 for 2013 and 2014, for contributions to an individual retirement account (IRA), or for the purchase of individual retirement annuities or endowment contracts. An individual who is an active participant in an employer plan (or whose spouse is) can't make deductible IRA contributions unless his adjusted gross income is below specified levels (¶4352).

An individual retirement account (IRA) is a trust (or custodial account) created or organized in the U.S. with a written governing instrument.[30] The assets of the account must be invested in a trusteed or custodial account with a bank, savings and loan association, credit union or other qualified person. (Code Sec. 408(a)(2))[31]

IRAs may be set up by employers for employees and by unions for members if these employer- and association-sponsored IRAs separately account for the interest of each participant (or his spouse). (Code Sec. 408(c); Reg § 1.408-2(c))[32] Qualified retirement plans, tax-sheltered annuities, and government retirement plans may allow employees to make voluntary contributions to separate IRA or Roth IRA accounts or annuities. (Code Sec. 408(q))[33]

Individuals who turn age 50 before the close of the tax year may increase the maximum permitted annual contribution by $1,000; a "catch-up" contribution. (Code Sec. 219(b)(5)(B))[34]

Except for rollover contributions (¶4359) the maximum amount that may be contributed to IRAs for any individual for the 2013 and 2014 tax years is $6,500 ($5,500 + $1,000 catch-up contribution). (Code Sec. 408(a)(1), Code Sec. 408(b)(4), Code Sec. 219(b)(1)(A), Code

24. ¶H-11089; ¶4024.02; TD ¶141,090.1
25. ¶H-11091
26. ¶H-3200 *et seq.*; ¶4024.01; TD ¶135,532
27. ¶H-3677 *et seq.*; ¶4044.16; TD ¶277,506
28. ¶H-3246; ¶4024.01; TD ¶135,532
29. ¶H-3249; ¶4034.05; TD ¶135,532

30. ¶H-12201; ¶4084.02; TD ¶283,041
31. ¶H-12202 *et seq.*; ¶4084.02
32. ¶s H-12212, H-12213; ¶4084.02; TD ¶283,045
33. ¶H-12280; ¶4084.07
34. ¶H-12215; ¶2194.01; TD ¶283,001

Sec. 219(b)(5)(A), Code Sec. 219(b)(5)(D))[35]

IRA funds can't be used to buy life insurance. (Code Sec. 408(a)(3))[36] IRA contributions may not be invested in "collectibles" (except for certain coins and bullion), the acquisition of which is treated as an includible distribution (and possibly subject to early distribution penalties). (Code Sec. 408(m))[37]

Individual retirement annuities are nontransferable flexible premium annuity or endowment contracts issued by an insurance company. (Code Sec. 408(b))[38]

No tax is paid on income earned on contributions until the retirement savings are distributed or retirement bonds are cashed, at which time the distributions or retirement bond proceeds are taxable (Code Sec. 408(d)(1))[39] though the tax-free "rollover" provisions (¶4359) may apply. Rules penalize excess contributions, early (before age 59½) distributions (¶4344), and certain distributions deferred beyond age 70½ (¶4357).

For deductible contributions, see ¶4352; for nondeductible contributions to traditional IRAs, see ¶4354.

For Roth IRAs, see ¶4367 *et seq*. For the saver's credit for lower-income taxpayers' contributions to IRAs, see ¶2368.

¶ 4352 Deduction for IRA.

An individual who isn't an active participant in certain employer-sponsored retirement plans, and whose spouse isn't an active participant, can deduct, for a tax year, cash contributions to an IRA for that year, up to the lesser of: (1) $5,500 for 2013 and 2014, plus a catch-up contribution, if eligible, see ¶4351, or (2) 100% of the compensation that's includible in his gross income for that year. (Code Sec. 219(b)(1))[40] For spousal IRAs, see ¶4355.

If the individual (or his spouse) is an active plan participant (for any part of a plan year in his tax year), and has adjusted gross income (AGI) that exceeds an "applicable dollar limit," the IRA deduction limit is reduced (but not below zero) by an amount (rounded to the next lowest multiple of $10) that bears the same ratio to the dollar limit on the deduction that his (and his spouse's if a joint return is filed) AGI (determined without regard to the IRA deduction and with certain other modifications), minus the applicable dollar limit, bears to $10,000 ($20,000 for joint return filers, except for non-active plan participants whose spouses are active plan participants). (Code Sec. 219(g)(1), Code Sec. 219(g)(2), Code Sec. 219(g)(3)(A), Code Sec. 219(g)(7)(B)) But the maximum IRA deduction can't be reduced below $200 unless the applicable dollar limit is reduced to zero. (Code Sec. 219(g)(2)(B))[41] The applicable dollar limit is higher than the usual limit for an individual who is not an active participant in an employer plan during any part of the year, but whose spouse is an active plan participant. The higher limit does not apply to the active-participant spouse. (Code Sec. 219(g)(7))[42] The income limits for deductible contributions for active participants in an employer sponsored plan and non-active participants whose spouses are active participants (but not for marrieds filing separately) are indexed for inflation.

For 2013, for joint filers, the deduction phaseout begins at modified adjusted gross income (AGI) of $95,000 and is fully phased-out at modified AGI of $115,000 ($96,000 to $116,000 for 2014). For 2013, for single filers, or heads of households, the deduction phaseout begins at modified AGI of $59,000 and is fully phased-out at modified AGI of $69,000 ($60,000 to $70,000 for 2014). For marrieds filing separately, the deduction phaseout begins at modified AGI of zero, and is fully phased-out at modified AGI of $10,000. Finally, for a non-active participant whose spouse is an active participant, the deduction phaseout for 2013 begins at modified AGI of $178,000 and is fully phased-out at modified AGI of $188,000 ($181,000 to $191,000 for 2014).

35. ¶H-12215; ¶2194.01; TD ¶283,001
36. ¶H-12201; ¶4084.02
37. ¶H-12259; ¶4084.03; TD ¶143,012
38. ¶H-12208 *et seq*.; ¶4084.02; TD ¶283,042

39. ¶H-12253; ¶4084.03; TD ¶143,003
40. ¶H-12215; ¶2194; TD ¶283,001
41. ¶H-12217; ¶2194.02; TD ¶283,002
42. ¶H-12217.2; ¶2194.02; TD ¶283,002*et seq*.

Spouses who file separate returns and live apart at all times during the year aren't treated as married for purposes of the IRA deduction phase-out. (Code Sec. 219(g)(4))[43]

"Compensation" means wages, salaries, commissions, tips, bonuses, professional fees and other amounts received for personal services. It doesn't include earnings from property, such as interest, rents and dividends, or pension and annuity payments or other deferred compensation. Only compensation includible in gross income is used. (Code Sec. 219(f)(1))[44] Compensation includes taxable alimony paid under a decree of divorce or separate maintenance. Compensation also includes any differential wage payments (¶3004). (Code Sec. 219(f)(1))[45]

The amount shown on Form W-2 as "Wages, tips, other compensation," less any amount shown as distributions from nonqualified plans can be used as "safe harbor" compensation. [46]

The "compensation" of a self-employed individual includes net earnings from self-employment reduced by any allowable deduction for contributions on his behalf to a tax-qualified plan, e.g., a Keogh plan. (Code Sec. 219(f)(1))[47] A self-employed individual's net earnings from self-employment are also reduced by the deduction allowed for one-half of the self-employment tax (¶1755). (Code Sec. 219(f)(1), Code Sec. 401(c)(2)(A)(vi))[48]

Combat pay excluded under Code Sec. 112 (¶1223) is treated as if it were includible compensation for IRA purposes. (Code Sec. 219(f)(7))[49]

No deduction is allowed for contributions for the benefit of an individual for the tax year he attains age 70½ or any later year. (Code Sec. 219(d)(1))[50]

The IRA must be established no later than the due date (*not* including extensions) of the taxpayer's income tax return for the year the deduction is claimed. To be deductible for the preceding tax year, the contribution also must be made by that date. (Code Sec. 219(f)(3))[1]

No part of a premium (under an IRA endowment policy) that's used to buy life insurance is deductible. (Code Sec. 219(d)(3))[2]

No deduction is permitted for a rollover contribution (¶4359) (Code Sec. 219(d)(2))[3] or for any contribution to an "inherited" IRA — one acquired by other than the surviving spouse as a result of the death of the employee-participant. (Code Sec. 219(d)(4))[4]

¶ 4353   Active participant defined.

An individual who (or whose spouse) is an active participant in a qualified pension, profit-sharing, stock bonus or annuity plan, government plan, tax-sheltered annuity plan, SEP, SIMPLE retirement plan, or certain other trusts can't make deductible IRA contributions unless his adjusted gross income falls with the dollar limits at ¶4352. (Code Sec. 219(g))[5]

An individual is an active participant for any tax year in which he's eligible to participate in a defined benefit plan, or any year in which employer or employee contributions or forfeitures are added to his account in a defined contribution plan.[6]

¶ 4354   Nondeductible IRA contributions—Form 8606.

An active participant in a qualified plan who may not be eligible to make deductible contributions either in whole or in part to an IRA (see ¶4353), can make (use Form 8606) designated nondeductible contributions (DNCs) to an IRA for a tax year (Code Sec. 408(o)(2)(C)(i)) up to the due date (*without* extensions) for the taxpayer's income tax return for that year. (Code Sec. 408(o)(3))[7]

---

43. ¶H-12217; ¶2194.02; TD ¶283,002
44. ¶H-12226; ¶2194.01; TD ¶283,012
45. ¶H-12232; ¶2194.01; TD ¶283,018
46. ¶H-12226; TD ¶283,012
47. ¶H-12226; TD ¶283,012
48. ¶s H-9514, H-12228; TD ¶284,523
49. ¶H-12215.1 *et seq.*; TD ¶283,018.1
50. ¶H-12234; ¶2194.01; TD ¶283,020

1. ¶H-12233; ¶2194.01; TD ¶283,019
2. ¶H-12236; ¶2194.01; TD ¶283,022
3. ¶H-12235; TD ¶283,021
4. ¶H-12237; ¶2194.01; TD ¶283,023
5. ¶H-12217 *et seq.*; ¶2194.02; TD ¶283,006
6. ¶H-12220 *et seq.*; ¶2194.02; TD ¶283,007
7. ¶s H-12238, H-12240; ¶4084.01; TD ¶283,024

The amount of any DNCs made in any tax year on behalf of an individual is limited to the excess of: (1) the lesser of $5,500 in 2013 and 2014, plus an additional $1,000 for those 50 and over, see ¶4351, or 100% of compensation (including the higher-earning spouse's compensation (¶4355)), over (2) the amount allowable as a deduction for IRA contributions by active participants. (Code Sec. 408(o)(2)(B)(i))[8]

A taxpayer can elect to treat an otherwise deductible contribution as a DNC, thereby increasing, to that extent, his DNC limit for that year. (Code Sec. 408(o)(2)(B)(ii))[9]

DNCs and deductible contributions may be made to the same IRA.[10]

¶ 4355 Special IRA deduction rules for married taxpayers.

Married taxpayers can each make deductible contributions to separate IRAs, subject to the deduction phase-out rules at ¶4352 that apply if either or both are active participants in an employer retirement plan for any part of the tax year.[11]

An individual who files a joint return and has less taxable compensation than his spouse may contribute to a spousal IRA and deduct the lesser of (1) $5,500 in 2013 and 2014, plus an additional $1,000 for those 50 and over, see ¶4351, or (2) the sum of (a) that individual's includible compensation for the tax year, plus (b) the includible compensation of the individual's spouse reduced by the sum of the spouse's allowable IRA deduction, designated nondeductible IRA contribution, and Roth IRA contribution for that tax year. (Code Sec. 219(c))[12]

⊘*observation:* Under IRS guidance, the IRA deduction rules that apply for married taxpayers may now apply to same-sex couples; see ¶4705.

¶ 4356 Penalties for excess contributions—Form 5329.

An individual who contributes more to an IRA than he is entitled to deduct must pay (use Form 5329) a 6% excise tax on the excess *every year*. The tax for any particular year, however, can't exceed 6% of the value of the IRA (as of the close of the tax year). (Code Sec. 4973(a))

An excess contribution to an IRA is the sum of: (1) the excess of the amount contributed for the tax year (*other than* a contribution to a Roth IRA or a rollover contribution), over the amount allowable as a deduction for the contribution, plus (2) any excess contribution for the preceding tax year, *reduced by* the sum of taxable distributions for the tax year, distributions for the tax year of excess contributions after the due date of the return, and the excess (if any) of the maximum amount allowable as a deduction for the tax year, over the amount contributed to the IRA for the tax year (without regard to any deduction for a preceding year's excess contribution), *including* the amount contributed to a Roth IRA. (Code Sec. 4973(b))[13]

There's no 6% penalty for the year of the contribution (or any other year) if the taxpayer is allowed no IRA deduction for the excess *and* withdraws the excess (together with any net income earned on it) by the due date for filing his income tax return for the year the excess contribution was made. (Code Sec. 4973(b))[14]

For tax on excess contributions to Roth IRAs, see ¶4369.

¶ 4357 Distributions from IRAs and individual retirement annuities.

Payouts from an IRA can be made without penalty once the participant attains age 59½ (or earlier in the case of death, disability, annuitized payments, certain medical-related distributions, higher education expenses, certain first-time homebuyer expenses, and IRS levies, see ¶4344). These distributions can be made in a lump-sum or in installments and are taxable as ordinary income under the annuity rules (see ¶1354 *et seq.*), when received, except that

---

8. ¶H-12239; ¶4084.01; TD ¶283,025
9. ¶H-12240; ¶4084.01; TD ¶283,027
10. ¶H-12238; ¶4084.01; TD ¶283,024
11. ¶H-12217; ¶2194.02; TD ¶283,002

12. ¶s H-12230, H-12231; ¶2194.01; TD ¶s 283,016, 283,017
13. ¶H-12242 *et seq.*; ¶49,734; TD ¶283,030
14. ¶H-12247 *et seq.*; ¶49,734; TD ¶283,031 *et seq.*

distributions are tax-free if reinvested (i.e., "rolled over," see ¶4359 *et seq.*) within 60 days into that or another IRA. (Code Sec. 408(d)(3)(A))[15] (If not reinvested, the distribution is taxable in the year received, not the year in which the 60-day rollover period ends.)[16] A distribution from a SIMPLE retirement plan (¶4382) can't be rolled over tax-free except to another SIMPLE plan during the employee's first two years of participation in the plan. (Code Sec. 408(d)(3)(G))

caution: Although an IRA account can be used as a source for an interest-free "loan" (of up to 60 days), this can be done only once in a one-year period, see ¶4360.

Amounts distributed from an IRA are included in gross income under the Code Sec. 72 annuity rules. (Code Sec. 408(d)(1)) In applying the annuity rules, all IRAs (other than Roth IRAs) are treated as one contract, all distributions made during any tax year are treated as one distribution, and the value of the contract, income on the contract, and investment in it are determined at the end of the calendar year in which the tax year begins. (Code Sec. 408(d)(2))[17] Part of an individual's withdrawal from an IRA is excludible if he previously made nondeductible IRA contributions. The excludible part is (the amount withdrawn × [aggregate nondeductible IRA contributions ÷ aggregate balance on the last day of the tax year of all IRAs of the individual]). For purposes of the calculation, IRAs include all of the taxpayer's traditional IRAs, SEPs and SIMPLE IRAs.[18]

For tax years beginning after 2009 and before Jan. 1, 2014, up to $100,000 of taxable IRS distributions from a traditional IRA (or Roth IRA, see ¶4368) may be excluded from a taxpayer's income each year if the distribution is made: (1) directly by the IRA trustee to a Code Sec. 170(b)(1)(A) charity, other than a Code Sec. 509(a)(3) organization (see ¶4125) or a Code Sec. 4966(d)(2) donor advised fund (see ¶4129); and (2) on or after the date the IRA owner attains age 70½. (Code Sec. 408(d)(8)(F))

observation: Thus, taxpayers may arrange to have up to $100,000 in required minimum distributions (RMDs, see ¶4345) transferred directly to a charity, without first having to include the $100,000 in income.

Special rules applied to RMDs made after Nov. 30, 2012, and before Jan. 1, 2013 (i.e., during Dec. 2012) and after Dec. 31, 2012, and before Feb. 1, 2013 (i.e., during Jan. 2013) that allowed these distributions to be treated as tax-free qualified charitable distributions for 2012, if the IRA owner so elected in accordance with prescribed IRS guidance. (2012 Taxpayer Relief Act §208(b)(2))

A loss in an individual's traditional IRA is recognized only when *all* amounts have been distributed from *all* of the individual's traditional IRAs, and the amounts distributed are less than the individual's unrecovered basis (total nondeductible contributions) in his traditional IRAs.[19] For how to claim the loss, see ¶3110. For losses from Roth IRAs, see ¶4373.

Distributions from an IRA are reported on Form 1099-R. Distribution recipients who at any time made nondeductible contributions to a IRA (¶4354), must file Form 8606.

The transfer of an interest in an IRA (but not the distribution of funds from an IRA) to a spouse under a divorce or separation instrument isn't taxable (the transferred IRA is treated as the spouse's). (Code Sec. 408(d)(6))[20] Roth IRAs (¶4367 *et seq.*) are treated separately. (Code Sec. 408A(d)(4))

For the tax on early distributions from an IRA, see ¶4344.

Distribution of a participant's entire interest in his IRA (other than a Roth IRA, see ¶4373) must be made under rules similar to the Code Sec. 401(a)(9) required distribution rules for qualified plans (¶4345), (Code Sec. 408(a)(6), Code Sec. 408(b)(3)) except that required distributions from an IRA can't be deferred beyond age 70-½ due to the account owner's not being

---

15. ¶H-12253; ¶4084.03; TD ¶143,003
16. ¶s H-11460, H-12253; ¶4084.03; TD ¶144,034
17. ¶H-12253; ¶4084.03; TD ¶143,003

18. ¶H-12253; ¶4084.03; TD ¶143,003
19. ¶H-12255; TD ¶143,005
20. ¶H-12261; ¶4084.03; TD ¶143,013

retired (Code Sec. 401(a)(9)(C)(ii)(II), see ¶4319). While the required minimum distribution must be separately calculated for each IRA an individual has, the amounts may then be totalled, and the total distribution taken from any one or more of the individual's IRAs. Failure to make the required distributions results in a nondeductible excise tax payable (on Form 5329) by the recipient. The tax is 50% of the excess of the minimum amount that should have been distributed over the amount actually distributed. (Code Sec. 4974(a))[21] IRS can waive the 50% tax if the shortfall in the amount distributed is due to "reasonable error" and reasonable corrective steps are taken. (Code Sec. 4974(d))[22]

¶ 4358   Exemption of IRA from tax.

Income earned by an IRA is tax-exempt until distribution. This tax exemption doesn't apply to the unrelated business income tax, see ¶4121. Engaging in a prohibited transaction causes loss of the exemption. (Code Sec. 408(e))[23] Certain nominal gifts, free banking services, and free group term life insurance offered by banks for opening and contributing to an IRA are exempted from the prohibited transaction rules.[24]

If the owner of an individual retirement annuity borrows any money under, or by use of, the annuity contract, the contract stops being an individual retirement annuity as of the first day of the tax year, and the owner must include in income for that year an amount equal to the fair market value of the contract on the first day of the year. (Code Sec. 408(e)(3))[25] If the individual for whom an IRA is established uses the account or any portion of it as security for a loan, that portion is treated as distributed to that individual. (Code Sec. 408(e)(4))[26]

¶ 4359   Tax-free rollovers from qualified plans.

A tax-free rollover from a qualified plan is any portion of the balance of an employee's credit in a qualified trust paid to the employee in an "eligible rollover distribution," any portion of which the employee then transfers to an "eligible retirement plan." (Code Sec. 402(c)(1))[27] A distribution must be rolled over within 60 days after receipt to be tax-free, but IRS may waive the 60-day rollover period for equitable reasons, including cases of casualty, disaster, or other events beyond an individual's control (Code Sec. 402(c)(3), Code Sec. 408(d)(3); Reg § 301.7508A-1(c)(1)) such as bank error, if certain conditions are met.[28]

An "eligible rollover distribution" is any distribution to an employee of all or any portion of the balance to the credit of the employee in a qualified trust. (Code Sec. 402(c)(4)) An "eligible rollover distribution" does *not* include:

(1) any distribution that's one of a series of substantially equal periodic payments made (at least annually) for (a) the life (or life expectancy) of the employee, or the joint lives (or joint life expectancies) of the employee and the employee's designated beneficiary, or (b) a specified period of ten years or more (Code Sec. 402(c)(4)(A));

(2) any distribution to the extent it is a required distribution under Code Sec. 401(a)(9); (Code Sec. 402(c)(4)(B); Reg § 1.402(c)-2) and

(3) any hardship distribution. (Code Sec. 402(c)(4)(C), Code Sec. 403(b)(8)(B))[29]

caution: An eligible rollover distribution from a qualified plan is subject to 20% withholding, unless there is a direct trustee-to-trustee transfer, see ¶3035.

Amounts transferred in a direct trustee-to-trustee transfer (¶4319) are excludable from income for the tax year of the transfer. (Code Sec. 402(e)(6))[30]

---

21. ¶H-8501; ¶49,744; TD ¶145,515
22. ¶H-8508; ¶49,744
23. ¶H-12214; ¶4084.03; TD ¶283,044
24. ¶H-12530
25. ¶H-12251; ¶4084.03

26. ¶H-12252; ¶4084.03
27. ¶H-11402; ¶4024.04; TD ¶144,001
28. ¶H-11452; ¶H-11452.2; ¶4024.04; TD ¶144,034
29. ¶H-11406; ¶4024.04; TD ¶144,006
30. ¶H-11403; ¶4024.04; TD ¶144,003

Certain payments can't be rolled over, e.g., corrective distributions of excess 401(k) contributions, loans treated as deemed distributions, and dividends paid on employer securities. (Reg § 1.402(c)-2, Q&A 4) However, where a plan loan offset amount is treated as a default, it is an eligible rollover distribution that may be rolled over tax–free to an IRA. (Reg § 1.402(c)-2, Q&A 9)[31]

An "eligible retirement plan" is: (1) an individual retirement account (not a Roth IRA), (2) an individual retirement annuity (other than an endowment contract), (3) a qualified trust, (4) an annuity plan, (5) a Code Sec. 403(b) annuity, and (6) a governmental section 457 plan. If any portion of an eligible rollover distribution is attributable to payments or distributions from a designated Roth account (see ¶4375), then an eligible retirement plan with respect to that portion includes only (a) another designated Roth account, and (b) a Roth IRA. (Code Sec. 402(c)(8)(B))[32]

If noncash property (e.g., securities) is distributed, the employee can sell the property and roll over the proceeds. There's no gain or loss recognized on the sale if the full proceeds are rolled over. (Code Sec. 402(c)(6)(A))[33] If cash is distributed, it must be recontributed as cash.[34]

Plan administrators must inform recipients of potential rollovers in writing ("a section 402(f) notice") of the applicable rollover rules, no less than 30 days, and no more than 90 days before making an eligible rollover distribution (but the 30-day time period may be waived by a participant in certain cases, and a summary notice procedure also is available). (Code Sec. 402(f); Reg § 1.402(c)-2, Q&A 2, Reg § 1.402(f)-1, Q&A 2(b)) IRS has provided a model safe harbor explanation of this notice.[35]

Where a participant with a small accrued benefit (a nonforfeitable accrued benefit whose present value is $5,000 or less) is terminating his employment with the company sponsoring the plan, the plan may provide for the distribution of the employee's benefit without his consent, or the consent of his spouse (a "mandatory distribution" or an "involuntary cash-out distribution"). Such mandatory distributions must follow the automatic rollover rules. Under these rules, plans with mandatory distribution provisions must transfer the amount of the distribution to an IRA of a designated trustee or issuer where:

. . . the distribution of a nonforfeitable accrued benefit is more than $1,000, but no more than $5,000; and

. . . the plan participant (or beneficiary) receiving the distribution does not elect to have the distribution paid directly to another qualified plan or IRA (a direct rollover), and does not elect to receive the distribution himself. (Code Sec. 401(a)(31)(B))[36]

The plan administrator must also notify the distributee in writing, either separately or as part of the section 402(f) notice (see above), that the distribution may be transferred without cost or penalty to another IRA.[37]

For rollovers of after-tax contributions, see ¶4362.

¶ 4360　Other types of rollovers.

Permissible types of tax-free 60-day rollovers, besides those covered at ¶4359, include:

. . . Rollovers from one type of IRA (individual retirement account or individual retirement annuity) to the same or another type. But these rollovers may be made no more than once in a one-year period. (Code Sec. 408(d)(3))[38] Qualified rollovers from an IRA to a Roth IRA are disregarded for purposes of the one-year rule. (Code Sec. 408A(e)) However, a distribution from a SIMPLE retirement plan (¶4382) can't be rolled over tax-free except to another SIMPLE plan during the employee's first two years of participation in the plan. (Code Sec. 408(d)(3)(G))

31. ¶H-11415; ¶4014.27; TD ¶144,018
32. ¶H-11440; ¶4024.04; TD ¶144,023
33. ¶H-11448; ¶4024.04; TD ¶144,028
34. ¶H-11402; TD ¶144,001

35. ¶H-11458; ¶4024.04; TD ¶144,053
36. ¶H-8251.3; ¶4014.27; TD ¶144,037.1
37. ¶H-8251.6; TD ¶144,053
38. ¶H-11460 *et seq.*; ¶4084.03; TD ¶144,055

672

... From one type of IRA (individual retirement account or individual retirement annuity) to an eligible retirement plan (¶4359) (limited to amount which would otherwise be included in gross income). (Code Sec. 408(d)(3)(A)(ii))

... Eligible rollover distributions from a Code Sec. 403(b) plan to an eligible retirement plan (¶4359) and from an eligible retirement plan to a Code Sec. 403(b) plan. (Code Sec. 402(c)(8)(B), Code Sec. 403(b)(8)(A)(ii))

... Eligible rollover distributions from a Code Sec. 457 plan to an eligible retirement plan (¶4359) and from an eligible retirement plan to a Code Sec. 457 plan. (Code Sec. 402(c)(8)(B), Code Sec. 457(e)(16))

For taxable rollovers to Roth IRAs, see ¶4363.

¶ 4361 Partial rollovers.

When an employee elects to roll over less than his entire distribution:

(1) the portion not rolled over is taxed under the regular rules for taxing ordinary income. Ten-year forward averaging and/or capital gains treatment, where applicable, for lump-sum distributions (¶4339) don't apply if any part of the lump-sum distribution is rolled over; (Code Sec. 402(c)(1), Code Sec. 402(d)(4)(K), before amended by Sec. 1401(a), P.L. 104-188, 8/20/96)

(2) the basis recovery rules of Code Sec. 72(e) apply to a distribution that's rolled over under Code Sec. 402(c); and

(3) any net unrealized appreciation in employer securities attributable to nondeductible employee contributions is subject to tax immediately.[39]

¶ 4362 Rollovers of after-tax contributions.

Generally, only otherwise taxable amounts of an eligible rollover distribution may be rolled over. However, the "nontaxable" portion of a eligible rollover distribution (attributable to after-tax employee contributions) may be rolled over to the extent that the "taxable" portion is rolled over to (1) an IRA, or (2) to a defined contribution plan or tax-sheltered Code Sec. 403(b) annuity that will account separately for the taxable and nontaxable portions. In such a case, the amount transferred is treated as consisting first of the portion of the distribution that would be includible in income were it not for the rollover. (Code Sec. 402(c)(2))[40]

¶ 4363 Qualified plan to Roth IRA rollovers.

Distributions from qualified retirement plans, tax-sheltered Code Sec. 403(b) annuities, and governmental Code Sec. 457 plans may be rolled over directly into a Roth IRA, generally subject to the usual rules that apply to rollovers from a traditional IRA into a Roth IRA (see ¶4371). For example, a rollover from a qualified retirement plan into a Roth IRA is includible in gross income (except to the extent it represents a return of after-tax contributions), and the 10% early distribution tax does not apply. (Code Sec. 408A(e)) A rollover from a qualified plan, etc., to a Roth IRA doesn't count for purposes of the one-rollover-per-year rule.[41] The rollover also can be made through a distribution from the plan that's then contributed (rolled over) to the Roth IRA within 60 days. In either case, the amount rolled over must be an eligible rollover distribution.

For the tax treatment of amounts rolled into a Roth IRA from an eligible retirement plan that are later distributed within 5 years, see ¶4374.

---

39. ¶H-11405 *et seq.*; ¶4024.04; TD ¶144,005
40. ¶H-11406.1; ¶4024.04; TD ¶144,007

41. ¶H-11463; ¶408A4; TD ¶283,318

¶ 4364   One-time IRA to HSA rollovers.

Taxpayers may make a one-time-only tax-free rollover, via direct trustee-to-trustee-transfer, from an IRA to a Health Savings Account (HSA) (¶1529). (Code Sec. 408(d)(9)) The rollover amount is nondeductible and is limited to the otherwise maximum deductible HSA contribution amount, computed on the basis of the type of coverage under the taxpayer's high deductible health plan (HDHP) at the time of the contribution. The rollover reduces the otherwise allowable HSA contribution amount.

Generally, only one rollover may be made during a taxpayer's lifetime, but if one is made during a month in which he has self-only coverage as of the first day of the month, an additional rollover may be made during a subsequent month within the tax year in which he has family coverage. (Code Sec. 408(d)(9)(C)(ii))

If a taxpayer does not remain an eligible individual (except because of death or disability) during the testing period (begins with the month of the contribution and ends on the last day of the 12th month following that month), the amount of the IRA distribution that would otherwise have been includible is taxed to him and is subject to a 10% penalty tax. The amount is includible in income for the tax year of the first day during the testing period that the taxpayer is not an eligible individual. (Code Sec. 408(d)(9)(D))[42]

A qualified HSA funding distribution may be made from a traditional IRA or a Roth IRA, but not from an ongoing SIMPLE IRA or SEP IRA. Further, a qualified HSA funding distribution must not exceed the IRA or Roth IRA account owner's maximum annual HSA contribution.[43]

¶ 4365   Surviving spouse's rollover of distribution from decedent.

A surviving-spouse beneficiary may elect to treat the entire beneficiary interest in the decedent's IRA as the spouse-beneficiary's own IRA if he or she is the sole beneficiary of the IRA and has an unlimited right to withdraw amounts from it. However, this requirement is not satisfied if a trust is named beneficiary of the IRA even if the spouse is sole beneficiary of the trust. (Reg § 1.408-8, Q&A 5(a)) The election is made by the surviving spouse redesignating the account as an account in her name as IRA owner rather than as beneficiary. Alternatively, a surviving spouse is deemed to have made the election if, at any time, either of the following occurs: (1) any amount required to be distributed to the surviving spouse as beneficiary is not timely distributed, or (2) any additional amount is contributed to the IRA. (Reg § 1.408-8, Q&A 5(b)) If the election is made, the surviving spouse is considered the IRA owner for all purposes under the Code. (Reg § 1.408-8, Q&A 5(c))[44]

A surviving spouse may also roll a distribution from a qualified plan, annuity, or IRA over to any other qualified plan, annuity, or IRA in which the surviving spouse participates that accepts rollover contributions. (Code Sec. 402(c)(9), Code Sec. 408(d)(3)(C))[45]

observation: Under IRS guidance, the surviving-spouse rollover rules may now apply to same-sex couples; see ¶4705.

¶ 4366   Rollover by beneficiary other than surviving spouse.

Distributions from qualified plans, tax-sheltered annuities (¶4388 *et seq.*), and Code Sec. 457 government plans may be rolled over (in a direct trustee–to–trustee transfer, see ¶4319) to a non-spouse beneficiary's IRA that's established for the purpose of receiving the distribution. This "recipient IRA" is treated as an inherited IRA, and so is subject to the required minimum distribution (RMD) rules that apply to inherited IRAs of nonspouse beneficiaries (¶4345). To the extent provided by IRS, the change applies to benefits payable to a

---

42. ¶H-12253.1A; ¶4084.03; TD ¶143,003.1A
43. ¶H-12253.1B; ¶4084.03; TD ¶143,003.1B

44. ¶H-12264.7; TD ¶143,024
45. ¶H-11467 *et seq.*; ¶4084.03; TD ¶144,065

trust maintained for a designated beneficiary to the same extent it applies to the beneficiary. (Code Sec. 402(c)(11), Code Sec. 403(a)(4)(B), Code Sec. 457(e)(16)(B))[46]

¶ 4367 Roth IRAs. ▆▆▆▆▆▆

Taxpayers can make nondeductible contributions to Roth IRAs. Qualified distributions from Roth IRAs are tax-free and penalty-free. Roth IRAs aren't subject to the post-age 70-$\frac{1}{2}$ lifetime required distribution rules. Traditional IRAs can be rolled over penalty-free (but not tax-free) into Roth IRAs.

¶ 4368 Roth IRAs—overview.

A Roth IRA is an IRA that is designated as a Roth IRA when it's established (Code Sec. 408A(b)); it's treated as a traditional IRA (¶4351 *et seq.*) except to the extent that special rules apply to it. (Code Sec. 408A(a)) Contributions to a Roth IRA aren't deductible (Code Sec. 408A(c)(1)), and are limited based on modified adjusted gross income (¶4369). Qualified distributions from a Roth IRA aren't included in income (Code Sec. 408A(d)(1)) and other distributions are treated as a return of investment to the extent of contributions to Roth IRAs (¶4373). (Code Sec. 408A(d)(4)) Rollovers from traditional IRAs to Roth IRAs are taxable, but not subject to the 10% early distribution penalty tax. (Code Sec. 408A(d)(3))[47] (Reg § 1.408A-3, Reg § 1.408A-4, Reg § 1.408A-5)

Use Form 5305-R, Form 5305-RA, and Form 5305-RB to set up Roth trust, custodial, and annuity accounts, respectively, with financial institutions.

¶ 4369 Contributions to Roth IRAs.

An individual can make annual nondeductible contributions to a Roth IRA in amounts up to $5,500 for 2013 and 2014, plus an additional $1,000 for those 50 and older, or 100% of compensation, if less, reduced by the amount of contributions for the tax year made to all other IRAs (Code Sec. 408A(c)(1), Code Sec. 408A(c)(2)) but not reduced by contributions to a SEP (¶4377) or SIMPLE plan (¶4382) (Code Sec. 408A(f)(2); Reg § 1.408A-3, Q&A 3(c))[48] The allowable contribution phases out ratably (in $10 increments) over the following levels of modified adjusted gross income (AGI):

- For joint filers, $178,000 to $188,000 for 2013 ($181,000 to $191,000 for 2014);
- For married persons filing separately, $0 to $10,000 for 2013 and 2014; and
- For single taxpayers and heads of household, $112,000 to $127,000 for 2013 ($114,000 to $129,000 for 2014).

However, a $200 contribution may be made if the phase-out lowers the contribution limit to under $200 but more than $0. (Code Sec. 408A(c)(3)(A), Code Sec. 408A(c)(3)(B); Reg § 1.408A-3, Q&A 3(b))

AGI for purposes of the Roth IRA contribution phaseout is defined as it is for traditional IRA purposes (¶4352), except that it does not include income resulting from the conversion from a traditional IRA to a Roth IRA (¶4371). (Code Sec. 408A(c)(3)(B)(i); Reg § 1.408A-3, Q&A 5)[49]

⊘*observation:* The modified AGI-based contribution limits for Roth IRAs apply whether or not the taxpayer is a participant in a qualified retirement plan.

Roth IRA contributions for a year must be made by the unextended tax return due date for the contribution year. (Code Sec. 408A(c)(7); Reg § 1.408A-3, Q&A 2(b))[50] Unlike traditional IRAs, contributions are permitted after age 70½. (Code Sec. 408A(c)(4))[1] For rollover contributions, see ¶4371.

46. ¶H-11437; ¶H-11438; TD ¶144,020; TD ¶144,021
47. ¶H-12290 *et seq.*; ¶408A4; TD ¶283,300 *et seq.*
48. ¶H-12290.7; ¶408A4; TD ¶283,306 *et seq.*

49. ¶H-12290.9; ¶408A4; TD ¶283,310
50. ¶H-12290.14; ¶408A4; TD ¶283,315
1. ¶H-12290.13; ¶408A4; TD ¶283,314

A 6% excise tax is imposed each year on excess contributions to an IRA (¶4356). Similar rules apply to a Roth IRA. (Code Sec. 4973(f))[2]

Any contribution distributed from a Roth IRA before the due date of the individual's tax return is treated as an amount not contributed. (Code Sec. 4973(f))[3]

For the saver's credit for lower-income taxpayers' contributions to Roth IRAs, see ¶2363.

A recipient of a military death gratuity or Servicemembers' Group Life Insurance (SGLI) proceeds can contribute the amounts received (reduced by any amounts contributed to a Coverdell education savings account, ¶2207) to a Roth IRA as qualified rollover contributions. The requirement that only one tax-free rollover contribution can be made to a Roth IRA during any one-year period (¶4360) doesn't apply. The rollover has to be made within one year of receipt of a payment. (Code Sec. 408A(e)(2))[4]

¶ 4370   Recharacterizing (changing the nature of) IRA contributions.

A taxpayer may elect to recharacterize an IRA contribution, that is, treat a contribution to one type of IRA (Roth IRA or traditional IRA) as made to a different type of IRA. (Code Sec. 408A(d)(6); Reg § 1.408A-5)

🅡/observation: The recharacterization election allows a contribution to a traditional IRA to be treated as made to a Roth IRA, or a contribution to a Roth IRA to be treated as made to a traditional IRA. It also allows a taxpayer to "reverse" a traditional-IRA-to-Roth IRA conversion (¶4371), in other words, treat the conversion as if it had never been made.

To make the recharacterization election:

. . . The taxpayer must notify the trustees of the first (distributing) and second (receiving) IRAs of his election to recharacterize a contribution (regular or conversion), i.e., that he is electing for tax purposes to treat the contribution as having been made to the second IRA, instead of the first IRA. The taxpayer must provide the trustees with specified information (including the type and amount of the contribution being recharacterized) sufficient to effect the recharacterization transfer.

. . . The contribution (regular or conversion) originally made to first IRA, plus net income (if any) allocable to the contribution (Reg § 1.408A-10, Reg § 1.408A-5, Q&A 2(c)), must be transferred from the first IRA to the second IRA via a trustee-to-trustee transfer.

. . . The trustee-to-trustee transfer must be made on a timely basis. (Reg § 1.408A-5, Q&A-6)[5]

An IRA contribution for a tax year may be recharacterized as late as six months after the unextended due date for filing the return for that year. (Reg § 301.9100-2(b))[6]

A recharacterization election cannot be revoked after the transfer. (Reg § 1.408A-5, Q&A 6(b))

The contribution that is being recharacterized is treated as having been originally contributed to the second IRA on the same date and (in the case of a regular contribution) for the same tax year that the contribution was made to the first IRA. (Reg § 1.408A-5, Q&A 3)

🅡/caution: For the limit on *reconversion* to a Roth IRA following a recharacterization from a Roth IRA to a traditional IRA, see ¶4372.

¶ 4371   Conversions of traditional IRAs to Roth IRAs—Form 8606.

Taxpayers, including marrieds filing separately, may convert amounts in a traditional IRA to amounts in a Roth IRA without regard to their modified adjusted gross income (AGI) or

---

2. ¶H-12242.1; ¶49,734; TD ¶283,032
3. ¶H-12242.1; ¶49,734; TD ¶283,032
4. ¶H-12290.19A

5. ¶H-12290.22; ¶408A4; TD ¶283,328
6. ¶H-12290.23A; TD ¶283,331

filing status.[7] The conversion may be done in one of three ways:

(1) Rollover to a Roth IRA of a distribution from a traditional IRA within 60 days of the distribution.

(2) Trustee-to-trustee transfer from the trustee of the traditional IRA to the trustee of the Roth IRA.

(3) Transfer of an amount in a traditional IRA to a Roth IRA maintained by the same trustee. (Code Sec. 408A(d)(3)(C); Reg § 1.408A-4, Q&A 1(b))

Amounts from a SEP-IRA (¶4378) or a SIMPLE IRA (¶4357) also may be converted to a Roth IRA, but a conversion from a SIMPLE IRA may be made only after the 2-year period beginning on the date on which the taxpayer first participated in any SIMPLE IRA maintained by the taxpayer's employer. (Reg § 1.408A-4, Q&A 4)

The conversion is subject to tax (report on Form 8606) as if it were distributed from the traditional IRA and not recontributed to another IRA (¶4357) (Code Sec. 408A(d)(3)(A)(i)), but isn't subject to the 10% early distribution tax. (Code Sec. 408A(d)(3)(A)(ii); Reg § 1.408A-4, Q&A 7)[8]

When a traditional individual retirement annuity is converted to a Roth IRA, the amount treated as distributed is the FMV of the annuity contract on the date it is converted. Similarly, when a traditional IRA holding an annuity contract as an account asset is converted to a Roth IRA, the amount that is treated as distributed with respect to the annuity contract is the FMV of the annuity contract on the date the annuity contract is converted (i.e., distributed or treated as distributed from the traditional IRA). (Reg § 1.408A-4, Q&A 14(a))[9]

¶ 4372 Reconversion to Roth IRA.

A person who has converted an amount from a traditional IRA to a Roth IRA (¶4371) may not only transfer the amount back to a traditional IRA in a recharacterization (¶4370), but may later reconvert that amount from a traditional IRA to a Roth IRA, and, under certain circumstances, have his resulting income fixed at the time of the reconversion.

An IRA owner who converts an amount from a traditional IRA to a Roth IRA and then transfers that amount back to a traditional IRA by way of a recharacterization can't reconvert that amount from the traditional IRA to another Roth IRA before the beginning of the tax year following the tax year in which the amount was converted to a Roth IRA or, if later, the end of the 30-day period beginning on the day on which the IRA owner transfers the amount from the Roth IRA back to a traditional IRA by way of a recharacterization. This timing rule applies regardless of whether the recharacterization occurs during the tax year in which the amount was converted to a Roth IRA or the following tax year. (Reg § 1.408A-5, Q&A 9(a)(1))

🅡 *observation:* This restriction prevents a taxpayer from recharacterizing a Roth IRA as a traditional IRA if the market value of the IRA has been substantially reduced, e.g., because of a sharp decline in the market value of stocks held in the IRA, and then immediately reconverting to a Roth IRA to take advantage of the lower market value in determining the income to be reported from the conversion.

A reconversion made before the later of the beginning of the next tax year or the end of the 30-day period that begins on the day of the recharacterization is treated as a failed conversion, subject to correction through a recharacterization back to a traditional IRA. A failed conversion results in a distribution from the traditional IRA that's subject to tax (and possibly penalty tax) followed by a regular contribution to the Roth IRA. To the extent it exceeds the annual contribution limit, the amount treated as a regular contribution to the Roth IRA is treated as an excess contribution subject to the excise tax under Code Sec. 4973.

---

7. ¶H-12290.16A; ¶408A4; TD ¶283,317.1
8. ¶H-12290.20; ¶408A4; TD ¶283,326 *et seq.*

9. ¶H-12290.20A; ¶408A4.

(Reg § 1.408A-4, Q&A 3(b), Reg § 1.408A-4, Q&A 1(d), Reg § 1.408A-5, Q&A 9(a)(1)) For purposes of the reconversion timing rules, above, a failed conversion resulting from not having satisfied the statutory requirements is treated as a conversion in determining when an IRA owner may make a reconversion. (Reg § 1.408A-5, Q&A 9(a)(2))[10]

¶ 4373   Distributions from Roth IRAs—Form 8606.

Qualified distributions. Qualified distributions from Roth IRAs aren't included in income. (Code Sec. 408A(d)(1)) These are distributions made after the five-tax-year period beginning with the first tax year for which the taxpayer or the taxpayer's spouse made a contribution to a Roth IRA established for the taxpayer, including a qualified rollover contribution from an IRA other than a Roth IRA (Code Sec. 408A(d)(2)(B)), and that are made:

(1) on or after attaining age 59½,

(2) at or after death (to a beneficiary or estate),

(3) on account of disability, or

(4) for a first-time home purchase expense under Code Sec. 72(t)(2)(F). (Code Sec. 408A(d)(2)(A), Code Sec. 408A(d)(5); Reg § 1.408A-6, Q&A 1)[11]

The five-year period for qualified distributions isn't recalculated when a Roth IRA owner dies. The five-year period for a beneficiary's inherited Roth IRA is determined independently of the period for any other Roth IRA that the beneficiary may have, except that the 5-year period for a spousal beneficiary with both an inherited Roth IRA and his own Roth IRA ends with the earlier of the five-year periods. (Reg § 1.408A-5, Q&A 7)

Corrective distributions made by the return due date, plus extensions, for the tax year of the contribution aren't qualified distributions. (Code Sec. 408A(d)(2)(C); Reg § 1.408A-6, Q&A 2)[12]

Nonqualified distributions. Distributions that aren't qualified distributions are treated as made first from contributions to all of an individual's Roth IRAs and are nontaxable to that extent; distributions in excess of contributions are taxable. (Code Sec. 408A(d)(4))[13]

Order of distributions. Distributions are treated as made from contributions to the Roth IRA to the extent that the distribution, when added to all previous distributions from the Roth IRA, doesn't exceed the total amount of all contributions. (Code Sec. 408A(d)(4)(B)(i)) Contributions are treated as withdrawn in the following order: first, contributions other than qualified rollover contributions (i.e., qualified conversions, see ¶4371); second, qualified rollover contributions (on a FIFO basis); third, a distribution allocable to a qualified rollover contribution is allocated first to the part of the contribution required to be included in gross income. (Code Sec. 408A(d)(4)(B)(ii); Reg § 1.408A-6, Q&A 8)[14] All of a taxpayer's Roth IRAs are treated as a single Roth IRA. (Code Sec. 408A(d)(4)(A), Code Sec. 408(d)(2))

If the taxpayer withdraws all amounts from all of his Roth IRAs, a loss is recognized if the amounts distributed are less than his unrecovered basis (regular and conversion contributions).[15] For how to claim the loss, see ¶3110.

Report Roth IRA distributions on Form 8606, Part III.

Roth IRAs aren't subject to the required minimum distribution rules of Code Sec. 401(a)(9)(A) or the incidental benefit requirements of Code Sec. 401(a) (¶4345). Instead, after the Roth IRA owner's death, the distribution rules in Reg § 1.408-8 apply as though the Roth IRA owner died before his required beginning date. Thus, the entire Roth IRA must generally be distributed within five years of the owner's death unless it is distributed over the life expectancy of a designated beneficiary, and distributions commence prior to the end of the calendar year following the year of the owner's death. Where the sole beneficiary of a Roth

---

10. ¶H-12290.15 *et seq.*; ¶408A4; TD ¶283,321 *et seq.*
11. ¶H-12290.28; ¶408A4; TD ¶283,337
12. ¶H-12290.30; ¶408A4; TD ¶283,338

13. ¶H-12290.34; ¶408A4; TD ¶283,342
14. ¶H-12290.35; ¶408A4; TD ¶283,343
15. ¶H-12255; TD ¶143,005

IRA is the Roth IRA owner's surviving spouse, the spouse may delay distributions until the Roth IRA owner would have reached age 70½, or may treat the Roth IRA as his or her own. (Reg § 1.408A-6, Q&A 14(b)) (Code Sec. 408A(c)(5))[16]

⊕observation: Under IRS guidance, the rules governing distributions from a Roth IRA to a surviving spouse may now apply to same-sex couples; see ¶4705.

For the 10% early distribution penalty tax, see ¶4374. For distributions from designated Roth accounts, see ¶4375.

¶ 4374   10% early distribution tax on Roth IRA distributions.

As with other IRAs (¶4344) the Code Sec. 72(t) 10% early withdrawal tax applies to the portion of an early withdrawal that is includible in income. In addition, however, a distribution from a Roth IRA is subject to the early withdrawal tax as if it *were* includible in income, if that distribution (or any portion of it): (1) is allocable (under rules at ¶4373) to a "qualified rollover contribution;" and (2) is made within the five-tax year period beginning with the tax year for which the contribution was made. However, the 10% tax applies only to the extent that the amount of the qualified rollover contribution was includible in income. (Code Sec. 408A(d)(3)(F))[17]

¶ 4375   Designated Roth (Roth 401(k)) Accounts. ▬▬▬▬▬▬▬▬

An employer's Code Sec. 401(k) plan, or Code Sec. 403(b) annuity (¶4388) may include a qualified Roth contribution program (i.e., a "Roth 401(k)") that allows participants to elect to have all or part of their elective deferrals treated as Roth contributions—that is to make "designated Roth contributions." (Code Sec. 402A) Designated Roth contributions, which are currently includible in income, aren't subject to the AGI-based phaseouts for regular Roth IRA contributions (¶4369). Qualified distributions are excludable from income. (Code Sec. 402A(d))[18]

Designated Roth contributions. These are elective contributions under a 401(k) plan that are:

(1) designated irrevocably by the employee when he makes the cash or deferred arrangement (CODA) election as designated Roth contributions;

(2) treated by the employer as includible in the employee's income when he would have received the contribution in cash had he not made the CODA election (e.g., by treating the contributions as wages subject to applicable withholding requirements); and

(3) maintained by the plan in a separate account. (Code Sec. 402A(b)(2); Reg § 1.401(k)-1(f)(1), Reg § 1.401(k)-1(f)(2))[19]

A 401(k) plan can't provide for designated Roth contributions unless it also offers pre-tax elective contributions. (Reg § 1.401(k)-1(f)(1)(i))[20]

A designated Roth contribution must satisfy the requirements that apply to elective contributions made under a qualified CODA (i.e., a 401(k) plan), such as the nonforfeitability and distribution restrictions for elective contributions, and the Code Sec. 401(k) ADP (actual deferral percentage) test); see ¶4317. (Reg § 1.401(k)-1(f)(3))[21]

Governmental section 457 plans may also provide designated Roth accounts. (Code Sec. 402A(e)(1)(C))[22]

In-plan Roth rollovers. Employers may amend their Roth 401(k), 403(b), or 457 plans to allow participants to transfer an eligible rollover distribution (ERD) to their designated Roth account in the plan. (Code Sec. 402A(c)(4)) An ERD is a distribution (1) from a non-designated

---

16. ¶H-12290.42; ¶408A4; TD ¶283,351
17. ¶H-12290.38; ¶408A4; TD ¶283,346
18. ¶H-12295.1 *et seq.*; ¶402A4; TD ¶283,400 *et seq.*
19. ¶H-12295.5

20. ¶H-12295.5
21. ¶H-12295.3
22. ¶H-12295.2

Roth account in the same plan, (2) because of an event that triggers an ERD from the plan; and (3) otherwise meets the rollover requirements. However, for transfers of amounts not otherwise distributable that are made after 2012, a plan will not be treated as violating the distribution restrictions of (i) Code Sec. 401(k)(2)(B)(i), (ii) Code Sec. 403(b)(7)(A)(i), (iii) Code Sec. 403(b)(11), (iv) Code Sec. 457(d)(1)(A), or (v) 5 USC §8433, solely because of the transfer. (Code Sec. 402A(c)(4)(E))

Thus, for transfers to designated Roth accounts after 2012, IRS timing restrictions on distributions—such as age or severance from employment—need not be met.[23]

The participant must include in gross income the amount that would be includible in gross income if it were not part of a qualified rollover distribution. (Code Sec. 402A(c)(4)(A)(i))[24]

Any distribution from an applicable retirement plan (other than from a designated Roth account) that is contributed in a qualified rollover contribution to the designated Roth account, is not taken into account as a designated Roth contribution. (Code Sec. 402A(c)(4)(C))[25]

Distributions from designated Roths. A qualified distribution from a designated Roth is excluded from income if it meets the requirements for qualified distributions from Roth IRAs (¶4373), with the following differences:

. . . A distribution for a first-time home purchase isn't excluded. (Code Sec. 402A(d)(2)(A)[26]

. . . The five-year period necessary for a distribution to be excluded begins on the first day of the employee's tax year for which he first had designated Roth contributions made to the plan. If a direct rollover is made from a designated Roth account under another plan, the five-year period begins on the first day for which the employee first had designated Roth contributions made to the other plan, if earlier. (Reg § 1.402A-1, Q&A 4)[27]

. . . Designated Roth accounts are subject to the lifetime required minimum distribution (RMD) rules of Code Sec. 401(a)(9)(A) and Code Sec. 401(a)(9)(B) (¶4345). (Reg § 1.401(k)-1(f)(4)(i)) By contrast, a regular Roth IRA is not subject to the Code Sec. 401(a)(9)(A) lifetime RMD rules (¶4373).

A distribution from a designated Roth account that is not a qualified distribution is taxable to the distributee under the Code Sec. 72 rules, *not* under the regular Roth IRA ordering rules (¶4373). (Reg § 1.402A-1, Q&A 3)

¶ 4376   Deemed IRAs.

Qualified plans, Code Sec. 403(b) annuities (¶4388), and governmental Code Sec. 457 plans may include a deemed IRA, which is a separate account or annuity in a qualified employer plan to which plan participants may make voluntary IRA or Roth IRA contributions.

The qualified plan must elect to allow employees to make voluntary employee contributions (designated as such by the employees) to a separate account or annuity (meeting the requirements for a traditional IRA or Roth IRA) established under the plan. However, the general requirement that IRA assets not be commingled does not apply to deemed IRAs. (Code Sec. 408(q))[28]

SEPs (see ¶4377) and SIMPLE IRAs (¶4382) cannot be used as deemed IRAs. (Reg § 1.408(q)-1(b))[29]

Contributions to a deemed IRA are treated as contributions to an IRA, and not as contributions to the qualified employer plan. Thus, a deemed IRA contribution is in addition to the $17,500 maximum amount for 2013 and 2014 that can be contributed to a 401(k) plan (excluding catch-up contributions). (Code Sec. 408(q)(1))

23. ¶H-12295.5E
24. ¶H-12295.5K
25. ¶H-12295.5A
26. ¶H-12295.6A

27. ¶H-12295.6B *et seq.*
28. ¶H-12280; ¶4084.07; TD ¶283,080
29. ¶H-12280; ¶4084.07; TD ¶283,080

The ceilings on modified adjusted gross income that limit a taxpayer's ability to make Roth IRA contributions (¶4369) or deductible contributions to a regular IRA (¶4352) also apply to voluntary contributions to a deemed IRA. (Code Sec. 408(q)(1)(B); Reg § 1.408(q)-1(f)(4))[30]

A deemed IRA isn't subject to the rules that apply to the qualified employer plan, so contributions to a deemed IRA are not taken into account in applying those rules to any other contributions under the plan. Thus, deemed IRA contributions don't count against the 100% of income or dollar limit on annual additions to defined contribution plans. (Reg § 1.408(q)-1(c))

¶ 4377   Simplified Employee Pensions (SEPs). ▄▄▄▄▄▄▄▄

An employer can make deductible contributions on behalf of its employees to a simplified employee pension (SEP). These deductible employer contributions are excluded from the gross income of the employee.

¶ 4378   Simplified employee pension (SEP) defined.

A SEP is an individual retirement account or individual retirement annuity (IRA, see ¶4351), established by an employer by filing Form 5305-SEP, in which:

(1) The employer contributions are made only under a definite written allocation formula that is executed within the time for making a deductible contribution (¶4379)[31] that specifies (a) the requirements that an employee must satisfy to share in an allocation, and (b) how the allocated amount is computed. (Code Sec. 408(k)(5))[32]

(2) Employer contributions for a year must be made to each SEP of each employee who has reached age 21, performed service for the employer during at least three of the immediately preceding five years and has received at least $550 in compensation for 2013 and 2014. (Code Sec. 408(k)(2))[33]

(3) The employer contributions don't discriminate in favor of highly compensated employees. (Code Sec. 408(k)(3)(A))[34]

(4) The employer contributions aren't conditional on the retention in the plan of any portion of the amounts contributed. (Code Sec. 408(k)(4))[35]

(5) The employer doesn't restrict employee withdrawals. (Code Sec. 408(k)(4)(B))[36]

(6) Elective deferrals made by each highly compensated employee under a salary reduction arrangement may not exceed the average of the deferral percentage of all other eligible employees multiplied by 1.25. (Code Sec. 408(k)(6)(A)(iii))[37]

Employer contributions are discriminatory unless they bear a uniform relationship to the first $255,000 for 2013 ($260,000 for 2014) of the compensation (including self-employed income) of each employee maintaining the SEP. (Code Sec. 408(k)(3)(C))[38]

Employees covered by a collective bargaining agreement and nonresident aliens may be excluded from participation in the plan and from the discrimination test under certain conditions. (Code Sec. 408(k)(3)(B))[39]

Maximum allowable contributions made by an employer to a SEP on behalf of an employee for any year cannot exceed the lesser of: (1) 25% of compensation (limited by the annual compensation limit, see ¶4319) from the employer includible in the employee's gross income for the year (determined without regard to the employer's contributions to the SEP), or (2) the dollar limitation for defined contribution plans ($51,000 for 2013 and $52,000 for 2014, see ¶4328). (Special calculations are needed for self-employeds, like those for Keogh plans, see ¶4327.) Employee elective deferrals to a SEP (¶4381) do not count towards the limit. Where

30. ¶H-12284; TD ¶283,084
31. ¶H-12303; ¶4084.05; TD ¶282,306
32. ¶H-12310; ¶4084.05; TD ¶282,306
33. ¶H-12305; ¶4084.05; TD ¶282,302
34. ¶H-12306; ¶4084.05; TD ¶282,303

35. ¶H-12309; ¶4084.05; TD ¶282,305
36. ¶H-12309; ¶4084.05; TD ¶282,305
37. ¶H-12321; ¶4084.05; TD ¶282,315
38. ¶H-12307; ¶4084.05; TD ¶282,304
39. ¶H-12306; TD ¶282,303

the SEP is integrated with social security, the dollar limitation in (2) is reduced by the amount taken into account above the integration level, in the case of a highly compensated employee. (Code Sec. 402(h)(2))[40]

¶ 4379   Employer's deduction for contributions to a SEP.

A contribution by an employer to a SEP is deductible for a tax year if made on account of that year and not later than the time prescribed for filing the return for that year plus extensions.[41] The deduction can't exceed 25% of the compensation paid to the employees during the calendar year, up to the defined contribution plan limit (¶4328). Contributions that exceed this limit can be carried over to, and deducted in, succeeding tax years in order of time. (Code Sec. 404(h))[42]

An employer may elect to use either the calendar year or, subject to such terms and conditions as IRS may prescribe, its own tax year as the computation period for purposes of determining contributions to a SEP. (Code Sec. 408(k)(7)) If the calendar year is used, contributions made for a year are deductible for the employer's tax year with which or within which the calendar year ends. If the employer's "regular" tax year is used, contributions are deductible for that tax year. For purposes of deductibility, contributions are treated as if they were made for a tax year if the contributions are made on account of the tax year and are made not later than the time prescribed by law for filing the return for the tax year, plus extensions. (Code Sec. 404(h)(1)(A), Code Sec. 404(h)(1)(B))[43] Special rules apply where the employer also contributes to other plans. (Code Sec. 404(h)(2), Code Sec. 404(h)(3))[44]

¶ 4380   Employee's treatment of SEP contributions and withdrawals.

Contributions made to a SEP by an employer on behalf of an employee are excluded from the employee's gross income, up to the deduction limits at ¶4379. (Code Sec. 402(h)(1)) Contributions in excess of those limits are taxed to the employee in the year made. (Code Sec. 402(h)(2))[45] Payments made from the SEP are taxed to the recipient under the IRA rules (¶4357). (Code Sec. 402(h)(3))[46]

¶ 4381   Salary reduction SEPs (SARSEPs).

Employers can no longer establish salary reduction SEPs. However, a SEP that's maintained by an employer (except for tax-exempt or governmental employers) with no more than 25 employees at any time during the year before a particular tax year may include a salary reduction arrangement with the SEP for that year, if the plan as in effect on Dec. 31, '96 had a salary reduction arrangement. Not less than 50% of the participating employees must be able to elect to have the employer either make contributions to the SEP on his behalf or pay him cash. The amount of the elective deferrals for any year must satisfy the CODA deferral limits, including catch-up contributions for those age 50 and over (¶4317). Also, the SEP must provide for distribution of excess contributions. (Code Sec. 408(k)(6))[47]

For the saver's credit for lower-income taxpayers' elective contributions to SEPs, see ¶2363.

¶ 4382   "SIMPLE" Retirement Plans. ■■

An employer with 100 or fewer employees that doesn't have a qualified plan can establish a "SIMPLE" (savings incentive match plan for employees) retirement plan, without having to meet most requirements for qualified plans.

---

40. ¶s H-12308, H-12311; ¶4084.05; TD ¶282,307
41. ¶H-12312 *et seq.*; ¶4084.05; TD ¶282,311
42. ¶H-12315; ¶4044.08; TD ¶282,309
43. ¶H-12317; ¶4044.08; TD ¶282,311

44. ¶H-12318 *et seq.*; ¶4084.05; TD ¶282,312
45. ¶H-12311; ¶4084.05; TD ¶282,307
46. ¶H-12319.3; TD ¶143,001
47. ¶H-12321; ¶4084.05; TD ¶282,314

¶ 4383   Employers eligible to adopt SIMPLE retirement plans.

A "SIMPLE retirement plan" can be adopted (use Form 5305-SIMPLE, Form 5304-SIM-PLE if there is no designated financial institution, or Form 5305-SA for a SIMPLE individual retirement custodial account) by an employer with 100 or fewer employees who received at least $5,000 of compensation from the employer for the preceding year (Code Sec. 408(p)(2)(C)(i)(I)) that doesn't have another employer-sponsored retirement plan (including a SEP or annuity plan), except for a collectively bargained plan covering employees ineligible to participate in the SIMPLE plan, to which contributions were made or benefits accrued for the year. (Code Sec. 408(p)(2)(D))[48] "Employee" includes a self-employed individual. (Code Sec. 408(p)(6)(B)) A qualifying employer that maintains a SIMPLE plan but later fails to qualify may continue to maintain the plan for two years after its last year of eligibility, subject to certain restrictions for acquisitions, dispositions and similar transactions. (Code Sec. 408(p)(2)(C)(i)(II), Code Sec. 408(p)(10))[49]

¶ 4384   "Qualified salary reduction arrangements" under SIMPLE plans.

Employees designate contributions to be made to a SIMPLE plan under a "qualified salary reduction arrangement." This is a written arrangement under which an employee may elect to have the employer make elective employer contributions (expressed as a percentage of compensation, or, if the employer permits, a specific dollar amount) to a SIMPLE retirement account on behalf of the employee, or to the employee directly in cash. The amount that an employee may elect for any year can't exceed $12,000 for 2013 and 2014. (Code Sec. 408(p)(2)(A)(i), Code Sec. 408(p)(2)(A)(ii), Code Sec. 408(p)(2)(E))[50] SIMPLE 401(k) or SIMPLE IRA participants who are age 50 or over by the end of the plan year may make additional catch-up contributions of up to $2,500 for 2013 and 2014. (Code Sec. 414(v)(2)(B)(ii), Code Sec. 414(v)(2)(C))[1]

For the saver's credit for lower-income taxpayers' elective contributions to SIMPLE plans, see ¶2363.

The employer must make either:

(1) a matching contribution equal to the amount the employee contributes, up to 3% (Code Sec. 408(p)(2)(C)(ii)(I)) of the employee's compensation for the year, or, electively, as little as 1% in no more than two out of the previous five years, if the employer timely notifies the employees of the lower percentage (Code Sec. 408(p)(2)(C)(ii)(II))[2] ; or

(2) a nonelective contribution of 2% of compensation for each employee eligible to participate who has at least $5,000 of compensation from the employer for the year. (Code Sec. 408(p)(2)(B)(i))[3]

No other contributions may be made. (Code Sec. 408(p)(2)(A)(iv), Code Sec. 408(p)(8)) Elective employer contributions must be made no later than 30 days after the month for which the contributions are to be made. (Code Sec. 408(p)(5)(A)(i)) Matching contributions and nonelective contributions must be made by the deductible contribution due date for the year. (Code Sec. 408(p)(5)(A)(ii))[4]

"Compensation" is wages for income tax withholding purposes plus the amount of the employee's elective deferrals (Code Sec. 408(p)(6)(A)(i)) (for a self-employed person, net self-employment earnings (under Code Sec. 1402(a)) without regard to the SIMPLE retirement plan provisions. (Code Sec. 408(p)(6)(A)(ii)) For purposes of determining contributions to a SIMPLE plan, the definition of compensation includes wages paid to domestic workers, even though those amounts are not subject to income tax withholding. (Code Sec. 408(p)(6)(A)(i))

---

48. ¶H-12351; ¶4084.06; TD ¶282,801
49. ¶H-12352.1; ¶4084.06; TD ¶282,801
50. ¶H-12357; ¶4084.06; TD ¶282,803
1. ¶H-9244.1; ¶4144.26; TD ¶284,114

2. ¶H-12359; ¶4084.06
3. ¶H-12360; ¶4084.06
4. ¶H-12364; ¶4084.06; TD ¶282,809

The compensation taken into account for purposes of determining the amount of the 2% nonelective contribution can't exceed the limit on compensation (under Code Sec. 401(a)(17), see ¶4319) that may be taken into account for the year. (Code Sec. 408(p)(2)(B)(ii))[5]

¶ 4385   SIMPLE retirement account defined.

A "SIMPLE retirement account" into which employer contributions under a SIMPLE retirement plan are made), is an individual retirement account or annuity (Code Sec. 408(p)(1)) for which the only contributions allowed are contributions under a "qualified salary reduction arrangement" and that meets certain vesting, participation and administrative requirements (Code Sec. 408(p)(1)(A)). Employees' rights to all SIMPLE account contributions must be nonforfeitable. (Code Sec. 408(p)(3)) All employees (except those who can be excluded from a qualified plan (Code Sec. 408(p)(4)(B)) who received at least $5,000 in compensation from the employer during any two preceding years (Code Sec. 408(p)(4)(A)(i)), and are reasonably expected to receive at least $5,000 in compensation during the current year (Code Sec. 408(p)(4)(A)(ii)) must be eligible either to elect to make a salary reduction contribution or receive nonelective contributions. (Code Sec. 408(p)(4)(A))[6]

¶ 4386   Contributions to SIMPLE retirement accounts.

Employer contributions to SIMPLE accounts are deductible in the employer's tax year with which (or within which) the calendar year for which the contributions were made ends. (Code Sec. 404(m)(1); Code Sec. 404(m)(2)(A)) Contributions are treated as made for the tax year if they are made (a) on account of that year, and (b) not later than the time for filing that year's tax return (including extensions). (Code Sec. 404(m)(2)(B))[7]

✪/observation: "Employer contributions" include elective contributions, matching contributions, and nonelective contributions.

Contributions to simplified employee pensions are excluded from the employee's income similar to the rules for SEPs under Code Sec. 402(h)(1) (¶4380). Employees aren't entitled to a deduction for employer contributions made on their behalf to a SIMPLE retirement account. (Code Sec. 219(b)(4)) Any elective contributions under a SIMPLE retirement plan are included in the sum of elective deferrals, subject to an annual limit on the amount that can be excluded from income. (Code Sec. 402(g)(3)(D))[8] Matching contributions on behalf of self-employed persons aren't treated as employer elective contributions for this purpose. (Code Sec. 408(p)(9))[9]

✪/observation: Thus, matching SIMPLE contributions for a self-employed person don't count toward the annual limit on elective deferrals (¶4317).

SIMPLE plans may also incorporate an automatic enrollment arrangement (ACA), which permits an employer to make contributions to an employee's SIMPLE IRA without the employee having made an affirmative election to participate in the plan.[10]

¶ 4387   SIMPLE retirement account distributions.

Rules similar to those for distributions from simplified employee pensions (SEPs), apply to SIMPLE retirement accounts. (Code Sec. 402(k)) Thus, they are taxed under the rules relating to IRAs in the year of distribution. (Code Sec. 402(h)(3))[11] For tax-free rollovers of SIMPLE retirement account distributions, see ¶4357.[12] For early withdrawal penalties for SIMPLE account distributions, see ¶4344.[13]

---

5. ¶H-12358; ¶4084.06
6. ¶H-12361; ¶4084.06; TD ¶282,807
7. ¶H-12372; ¶4084.06; TD ¶282,811
8. ¶H-12373; TD ¶282,813
9. ¶H-12357; ¶4084.06

10. ¶H-12365.1
11. ¶H-12374; ¶4084.06; TD ¶282,814
12. ¶H-12375; TD ¶282,816
13. ¶H-12377; TD ¶282,815

¶ 4388   Tax-Sheltered 403(b) Annuities. ■■■■■■■

Employees of tax-exempt educational, charitable, religious, etc., organizations, or public schools get special tax advantages from annuities bought for them by the exempt employers.

Tax-sheltered annuities offer benefits similar to those under a qualified employee plan. The tax isn't imposed when the annuity is bought, but is deferred until payments are received. (Code Sec. 403(b); Reg § 1.403(b)-1)[14] These annuities may be bought only for common law employees of certain exempt educational, charitable, religious, etc., employers, and by or for certain self-employed ministers. (Code Sec. 403(b)(1)(A))[15] The annuity must be nonforfeitable (except for failure to pay premiums) and nontransferable. (Code Sec. 403(b)(1)(C); Reg § 1.401-9(b)(3))[16] Certain elective deferral limits must be met if the annuity is part of a salary reduction arrangement (¶4390). (Code Sec. 403(b)(1)(E))[17] Also, except for annuities bought by church employers, certain nondiscrimination tests must be met. (Code Sec. 403(b)(1)(D), Code Sec. 403(b)(12))[18] Tax-sheltered annuities are treated as defined contribution plans for purposes of the contribution limits (¶4328).[19]

¶ 4389   How tax-sheltered annuity arrangements work.

Employees of a qualifying employer can get a prescribed amount of their compensation in the form of a tax-sheltered annuity. The employee pays no immediate tax on the amount the employer pays for the annuity, but is taxed under the regular annuity rules (¶1354 *et seq.*) when the annuity payments are made. (Code Sec. 403(b)(1))[20]

The tax deferral is denied for distributions attributable to contributions made under a salary reduction agreement (¶4390), unless the annuity provides that payments may be paid only: (1) when the employee attains age 59½, separates from employment, dies, or becomes disabled, or (2) in the case of hardship. (Code Sec. 403(b)(11)) (The early distribution penalty applies, ¶4344). (Code Sec. 72(t)) The contract may not provide for the distribution of any income attributable to such contributions in the case of hardship. (Code Sec. 403(b)(11))[21] Tax-sheltered annuities are subject to the loan rules at ¶4343. (Code Sec. 72(p)(4)(A))[22]

For rollovers to and from Code Sec. 403(b) plans, see ¶4359 and ¶4360.

¶ 4390   Tax-sheltered annuity salary-reduction agreements.

An employee of a qualifying employer can agree to reduce his salary or forego an increase as a means of contributing to a 403(b) plan. The rules that apply to cash or deferred arrangements under Code Sec. 401(k) (¶4317) determine how often a salary reduction may be entered into, the compensation to which the agreement applies, and the ability to revoke the agreement.[23]

All of the employer's employees (except those covered by a CODA or an eligible Code Sec. 457 plan for tax-exempt and governmental employers) must get a chance to elect to have the employer contribute more than $200 under the salary reduction agreement, on a nondiscriminatory basis, if *any* employee may so elect. (Code Sec. 403(b)(12)(A))[24] The employee's elective deferrals for a year can't exceed the CODA limits, including catch-up contributions for those age 50 or over (¶4317). (Code Sec. 403(b)(1)(E); Reg § 1.403(b)-4(c))[25]

A 403(b) plan can include a qualified Roth contribution program (see ¶4375).

The term "salary reduction agreement" includes a plan or arrangement whereby a payment will be made if the employee:

---

14. ¶H-12450 *et seq.*; ¶4034.04; TD ¶135,506
15. ¶H-12452, H-12453; ¶4034.04
16. ¶H-12454; ¶4034.04
17. ¶H-12454 *et seq.*; ¶4034.04
18. ¶H-12464; ¶4034.04
19. ¶H-12454 *et seq.*; ¶4034.04; TD ¶284,029

20. ¶H-12451
21. ¶H-12479; ¶4034.04
22. ¶H-11066; ¶724.23
23. ¶H-12465; ¶4034.04
24. ¶H-12465; ¶4034.04
25. ¶H-12454; ¶4034.04

... elects to reduce compensation pursuant to a cash or deferred election as defined at Reg § 1.401(k)-1(a)(3);

... elects to reduce compensation pursuant to a one-time irrevocable election made at or before the time of initial eligibility to participate in the plan or arrangement (or pursuant to a similar arrangement involving a one-time irrevocable election); or

... agrees as a condition of employment (whether the condition is set by statute, contract, or otherwise) to make a contribution that reduces the employee's compensation. (Reg § 31.3121(a)(5)-2(a))[26]

For the saver's credit for lower-income taxpayers' contributions to 403(b) annuities, see ¶2363.

¶ 4391 Tax-sheltered annuity contribution limit.

If a qualifying employer buys a tax-sheltered annuity for an employee and the employee's rights are nonforfeitable, the premium paid is not taxable to the employee at that time, up to the applicable limit for a defined contribution plan under Code Sec. 415 (¶4328). (Code Sec. 403(b)(1), Code Sec. 415(c)(1), Code Sec. 415(k)(4); Reg § 1.403(b)-3(b)(3))[27]

Special limits apply for contributions by church plans. (Code Sec. 415(c)(7))

¶ 4392 "Includible compensation" and "years of service."

"Includible compensation" means the amount of compensation received by the employee from the qualified employer that is includible in his gross income (without regard to the exclusion for certain foreign source earned income) for the most recent period ending not later than the close of the employee's tax year that can be counted as one "year of service" and which precedes the tax year by no more than five years. Amounts contributed by the employer for tax-sheltered annuities are not included. Elective deferrals and any amount contributed or deferred by the employer at the employee's election that is excluded from income under Code Sec. 125 or Code Sec. 457 are included. (Code Sec. 403(b)(3))[28]

"Includible compensation" doesn't include any compensation *earned* when the employer wasn't a qualified employer. But it's immaterial whether the employer was qualified when the compensation is actually *received* by the employee.[29]

Similar rules apply to compensation received from "eligible employers." (Reg § 1.403(b)-2(b)(11)

The employee's "years of service," which can't be less than one, includes one year for each full year he was a full-time employee of the organization buying the annuity for him, plus a fraction of each year, as prescribed by regs, for each full year he was a part-time employee, or for each part of a year he was a full or part-time employee. (Code Sec. 403(b)(4))[30])

An employee's years of service equals the aggregate of the annual work periods during which he is employed by the eligible employer. (Reg § 1.403(b)-4(c))

---

26. ¶H-4650; TD ¶544,018
27. ¶H-12467; ¶4034.04
28. ¶H-12468; ¶4034.04

29. ¶H-12468; ¶4034.04
30. ¶H-12469 *et seq.*; ¶4034.04

Chapter 22   Farmers

¶ 4500   Farmers.

Farmers get tax breaks not generally available to others: three-year income averaging, a generally longer net operating loss (NOL) carryback period, favorable accounting and inventory methods, income deferrals, capital gain-ordinary loss treatment, and the deduction of items normally capitalized.

¶ 4501   Farmers' income and expenses—Schedule F (Form 1040).

A farmer's gross income includes cash and the fair market value of goods received ("barter income") from crops, produce, poultry and livestock. (Reg § 1.61-4(c)) The value of produce consumed by the farmer and his family isn't included, but expenses incurred in raising that produce can't be deducted.[1]

Farmers may deduct the ordinary and necessary expenses of operating a farm for profit—e.g., rent, labor, feed (¶4515), fertilizer (¶4516). (Reg § 1.162-12(a))[2] For required capitalization of certain expenses, see ¶4519. Where farming isn't engaged in for profit, see ¶1779.

¶ 4502   Three-year averaging for farming or fishing income—Schedule J.

An individual (including a partner in a partnership and a shareholder of an S corporation, but not including an estate or trust) engaged in a farming or fishing business may elect three-year averaging of "elected farm income" (below) for regular income tax (but not for employment tax) purposes. If the election is made, the tax for the year is equal to the sum of (1) the tax computed on taxable income reduced by elected farm or fishing income, and (2) the increase in tax that would result if taxable income for the three prior tax years were increased by an amount equal to one-third of the elected farm or fishing income. Any adjustment under this provision for any tax year is taken into account in applying this provision for any later tax year. (Code Sec. 1301(a), Code Sec. 1301(b)(3); Reg § 1.1301-1(b)) Taxable income for prior years can be less than zero, but in that case any amount that may provide a benefit in another tax year (such as an NOL) is added back in determining base year taxable income. (Reg § 1.1301-1(d)(2))[3]

Elect by filing Form 1040, Schedule J with a return for the election year (including a late or amended return if the time for filing for a credit or refund has not expired). An individual may change or revoke a previous election, if the period of limitation on filing a claim for credit or refund has not expired for the election year. (Reg § 1.1301-1(c))

"Elected farm income" means the amount of taxable income for the tax year attributable to any farming or fishing business that's specified in the election to average farm or fishing income (Code Sec. 1301(b)(1)(A); Reg § 1.1301-1(e)(2)) including farm wages paid to an S shareholder (Reg § 1.1301-1(e)(1)), income of fishing-boat crew members compensated by a share of the boat's catch or a share of the catch proceeds (Reg § 1.1301-1(b)(3)) and certain crop-share income. (Reg § 1.1301-1(b)(2)) Gain from the sale or other disposition of property (other than land) regularly used by the taxpayer in a farming or fishing business for a substantial period is treated as attributable to that farming business. (Code Sec. 1301(b)(1)(B); Reg § 1.1301-1(e)(1)(ii)(A))[4] A landlord is engaged in a farming business for farm averaging purposes for rental income based on a share of production (not fixed rent) from a tenant's farming business determined under a written agreement entered into before the tenant begins significant activities on the land. Similar rules apply to fishing-boat lessors

---

1. ¶N-1151; ¶1624.340; TD ¶116,001
2. ¶N-1301; ¶1624.340; TD ¶297,501

3. ¶N-1515 *et seq.*; TD ¶119,001 *et seq.*
4. ¶N-1515 *et seq.*; TD ¶119,004

References beginning with a single letter are to paragraphs in RIA's Federal Tax Coordinator 2d and RIA's Analysis of Federal Taxes: Income. Those beginning with numbers are to paragraphs in RIA's United States Tax Reporter. Those beginning with TD are to paragraphs in RIA's Tax Desk.

who share in the catch. (Reg § 1.1301-1(e)(2)) Tobacco quota payments don't qualify for income averaging.[5]

Electing income averaging does not cause the taxpayer's AMT to increase because regular tax liability for determining the AMT is computed as though the election had not been made, see ¶3201.

¶ 4503   Three- or five-year NOL carryback.

Although net operating losses (NOLs) generally may be carried back only two years, a taxpayer engaged in the business of farming gets a three-year carryback for NOLs (other than those that qualify for the five-year carryback, below) attributable to federally declared disasters (Code Sec. 172(b)(1)(F)(ii)(III))[6] , see ¶1841. And "farming losses" (any NOL attributable to the income and deductions of a farming business, but not in excess of the taxpayer's NOL for the year; qualified disaster losses aren't included) may be carried back five years (Code Sec. 172(b)(1)(G)) (and forward for the regular 20-year period).[7] Farmers may elect (by the due date, including extensions, for the loss year, or, if a timely return was filed, on an amended return within six months of the original return due date) not to have the five-year carryback apply, in which case the regular NOL rules apply (¶1841); once made, the election is irrevocable for that year. (Code Sec. 172(i)(3))[8]

¶ 4504   Limitation on deduction of farm losses.

The farming loss of a taxpayer, other than a C corporation, is limited for any tax year in which any applicable subsidies are received. The loss is limited to the greater of (a) $300,000 ($150,000 for a married person filing separately), or (b) the taxpayer's total net farm income for the prior five tax years. Applicable subsidies are (1) any direct or counter-cyclical payments under title I of the Food, Conservation, and Energy Act of 2008 (or any payment elected in lieu of any such payment), or (2) any Commodity Credit Corporation (CCC) loan. (Code Sec. 461(j))[9] For partnerships and S corporations, the limit is applied at the partner or shareholder level. (Code Sec. 461(j)(5))

Total net farm income is an aggregation of all income and loss from farming businesses for the prior five tax years. Any loss that is disallowed under this rule in a particular year is carried forward to the next tax year and treated as a deduction attributable to farming businesses in that year. Farming losses due to fire, storm, or other casualty, or disease or drought, are disregarded for purposes of calculating the limitation. (Code Sec. 461(j))

¶ 4505   Farmers' accounting methods.

Farmers (unless listed at ¶4510) may use the cash method (¶4506), the accrual method (¶4509), the crop method (¶4512), or a "hybrid" method combining any of these methods if it clearly reflects income (¶2817). (Reg § 1.61-4, Reg § 1.446-1(c), Reg § 1.471-6(a))[10]

While most taxpayers who produce, buy or sell merchandise must use inventories (and therefore the accrual method, see ¶2863), farmers may choose not to, except to the extent they are subject to the uniform capitalization rules (¶4519). (Reg § 1.471-6(a))[11] But a farmer who does use inventories must use the accrual method at least for purchases and sales.[12] However, IRS has excepted the following from having to account for inventories or use an accrual method of accounting: (1) any business with average annual gross receipts of $1 million or less; and (2) taxpayers whose principal business activity is not mining, manufacturing, wholesale trade, retail trade, or information industries, for all of their trades or businesses, if

5. ¶N-1501 *et seq.*; ¶13,014; TD ¶119,004
6. ¶M-4308; ¶1724.436; TD ¶356,011
7. ¶M-4301; ¶1724.437; TD ¶356,011
8. ¶M-4313; ¶1724.437; TD ¶356,013

9. ¶N-1331; ¶4614.78; TD ¶297,701
10. ¶N-1010 *et seq.*; ¶s 614.053, 4464.09; TD ¶118,001
11. ¶N-1100 *et seq.*; ¶4714.73; TD ¶118,002
12. ¶N-1017; TD ¶118,009

average annual gross receipts are $10 million ($5 million for C corporations) or less, see ¶2818.

¶ 4506 Cash method farmers.

Cash method farmers include income in the year actually or constructively received, whichever is earlier (¶2819). Gross income includes receipts of: (1) proceeds from sales of *raised* livestock or produce; (2) profits from the sale of any *purchased* property, including livestock, (3) breeding fees, (4) fees from renting teams, machinery or land, (5) taxable subsidy and conservation payments, (6) crop insurance proceeds, and (7) all other gross income. (Reg § 1.61-4(a))[13] For deferral of insurance proceeds and forced livestock sales, see ¶4508.

Expenses are ordinarily deductible in the year paid (other than the cost of animals and plants bought for resale, see ¶4507). (Reg § 1.61-4(a))[14] For feed expenses, see ¶4515, and for pre-paid expenses, see ¶4517. An option to accelerate the receipt of any payment under a production flexibility contract that is payable under the FAIR Act of 1996 as in effect on Dec. 17, '99 won't accelerate the recognition of income unless the option is exercised. (Sec. 525 of P.L. 106-170) The constructive receipt rules also don't apply to options to receive payments under the Farm Security and Rural Investment Act of 2002.[15]

¶ 4507 Cash method farmer's deduction of costs of purchased animals and plants—election to deduct in year bought or year sold.

Cash method farmers generally deduct the costs of animals and plants bought for resale only in the year the animals or plants are disposed of. (Reg § 1.61-4(a)) But for these animals and plants, a farmer may elect to deduct the costs either for the year they are purchased or for the year they are sold, if the method chosen clearly reflects income:

. . . baby chicks and pullets bought for raising and resale;

. . . hens bought for commercial egg production;

. . . seeds and young plants (other than Christmas trees and timber) bought for further development and cultivation before sale. (Reg § 1.162-12)[16]

The farmer makes the election by deducting the cost for the first year in which he buys the items. Once the farmer elects this option—which is a method of accounting—he must use it consistently until IRS consents to a change (¶2838).[17]

¶ 4508 One-year deferral elections for cash method farmers—"disaster" receipts.

A cash method farmer can elect to defer reporting certain insurance proceeds and federal disaster payments (including payments under Title II (but not Title I) of the '88 Disaster Assistance Act) until the tax year after the year of the destruction or damage to, or inability to plant, the crops, if he shows that under his practice, the income from the crops would be reported in a later year. To elect, check box in Part I on Schedule F and attach a statement to the return (or amended return) for the year payments are received. (Code Sec. 451(d); Reg § 1.451-6)[18]

One-year deferral also may be elected for income from livestock sold on account of a drought, flood or other weather-related condition so severe the sale had to take place in an earlier year than normal. Elect on a statement attached to the return for the sale year. (Code Sec. 451(e)(1); Reg § 1.451-7(g)) However, if the period for buying replacement property for such livestock under the involuntary conversion rules is extended to four years from the end

---

13. ¶N-1013; ¶614.054; TD ¶118,002
14. ¶614.054; TD ¶297,500
15. ¶N-1152.1; ¶4514.039

16. ¶s N-1021, N-1022; TD ¶118,007
17. ¶N-1022; TD ¶118,007
18. ¶N-1024 *et seq.*; ¶s 614.054, 4514.171; TD ¶118,005

of the year of sale (see ¶2438), the election of one-year deferral is valid if made during that replacement period. (Code Sec. 451(e)(3))[19] (For involuntary conversions, see ¶2432.)

¶ 4509   Accrual method farmers.

Accrual farmers include farm income for the year earned, regardless of when payment is received, and deduct farm expenses for the year the "all events test" is met (¶2824 *et seq.*). Inventories must be used (¶4513). (Code Sec. 461(h); Reg § 1.61-4(b), Reg § 1.446-1(c))[20]

An accrual farmer's gross income for a tax year is the sum of: (1) the sales price of all livestock and other products held for sale that are sold during the year, (2) the inventory value of the livestock, etc. (i.e., the proceeds from the disposition of livestock, etc., during the year, plus the inventory value of livestock, etc., not sold at the end of the year, reduced by the inventory value of livestock, etc., on hand at the start of the year, and by the cost of any livestock, etc., bought during the year and included in inventory), (3) miscellaneous farm receipts, e.g., fees from breeding, (4) all subsidy and conservation payments includible that year, plus (5) gross income from all other sources. Crop shares are included in the year they are reduced to money or its equivalent. (Reg § 1.61-4(b))[21]

¶ 4510   When accrual accounting is mandatory for farmers.

Corporations (except as noted below) and any partnership in which a corporation is a partner must use the accrual method of accounting to compute their taxable income from farming (as must tax shelters, which include farm syndicates, see ¶4511). Raisers and harvesters of nut and fruit trees are covered by this rule, but nurseries, sod farms and raisers and harvesters of other types of trees aren't. (Code Sec. 447(a))[22]

The mandatory accrual rule doesn't apply to:

(1) S corporations. (Code Sec. 447(c)(1))

(2) A "family corporation" (family members own at least 50% of (a) the total combined voting power of all voting stock, and (b) the total number of shares of all other classes of stock) other than one whose gross receipts exceed $25 million for any tax year. (Code Sec. 447(c)(2), Code Sec. 447(d)(2))[23] Two- or three-family corporations must meet special ownership tests, and must have been engaged in farming since Oct. 4, '76. (Code Sec. 447(h))[24]

(3) A corporation whose gross receipts (or any predecessor's) don't exceed $1 million for any tax year. (Code Sec. 447(c)(2), Code Sec. 447(d)(1))[25]

(4) Certain corporations (and partnerships having a corporate partner) engaged in growing sugar cane, any plant with a pre-productive period of two years or less, or, if an (irrevocable) election made for the first tax year beginning after '86 is in effect, any other plant (other than any citrus or almond tree). And, for all ten tax years ending with the first tax year beginning after '75, the corporation (or partnership) must have used an "annual accrual method" of accounting for the trade or business. (Code Sec. 447(g))[26]

¶ 4511   Tax shelters and farming syndicates.

All tax shelters, including farming syndicates, must use the accrual method. (Code Sec. 448(a)(3))[27] For pre-paid expenses, see ¶4517. For uniform capitalization rules, see ¶4519. For tax shelter losses for AMT purposes, see ¶3210.

19. ¶N-1031 *et seq.*; ¶4514.176; TD ¶118,003
20. ¶N-1017; ¶4614.15; TD ¶118,009
21. ¶N-1014, N-1017; ¶614.051; TD ¶118,009
22. ¶N-1036 *et seq.*; ¶4474; TD ¶118,012
23. ¶s N-1036, N-1040; ¶4474; TD ¶118,012

24. ¶N-1056; ¶4474; TD ¶118,013
25. ¶N-1036; ¶4474; TD ¶118,012
26. ¶N-1049; ¶4474; TD ¶118,012
27. ¶G-2456; ¶4484; TD ¶118,001

690

A farming syndicate is any partnership (or other noncorporate enterprise) or S corporation engaged in the business of farming if:

... at any time, interests in the partnership, etc., have been offered for sale in an offering required to be registered with any federal or state agency having authority to regulate the offering of securities for sale; or

... more than 35% of the losses during any periods are allocable to limited partners or limited entrepreneurs (Code Sec. 464(c)); or

... it's a tax shelter. (Code Sec. 461(i)(3), Code Sec. 461(i)(4))[28]

¶ 4512 Crop method.

A farmer may, with IRS consent, use the crop method to report income from crops (other than timber) for which the process of planting, harvesting and sale isn't completed within the same tax year. (Reg § 1.61-4(c))[29] Under this method, all expenses of the crop (including expenses of seed or young plants) are charged, and all crop receipts are credited, to a crop account. Profit (or loss) is realized and included in income (or loss deducted) only in the year the crop is harvested and disposed of. (Reg § 1.61-4(c), Reg § 1.162-12(a))[30]

¶ 4513 Farmers' inventories.

A farmer using inventories (¶4514) *must* inventory:

... all livestock and poultry, raised or purchased, held primarily for sale (Reg § 1.61-4(b));

... all harvested and purchased farm products held for sale, feed, or seed, such as grain, hay ensilage, concentrates, cotton, tobacco;

... supplies, unless only small amounts are on hand;

... if in the hatchery business, eggs in incubation and growing and pre-market chickens. (Inventories *may* be used for hens primarily held for egg production which are also held for sale after their egg-producing life.)[31]

Livestock held for dairy, breeding, sporting or draft purposes may be inventoried at the taxpayer's election. But raised livestock must be inventoried by farmers using the unit-livestock-price method. (Reg § 1.61-4(b), Reg § 1.471-6(f))[32]

¶ 4514 Inventory valuation methods for farmers.

Methods that farmers use to value inventory include:

... *Cost method* (¶2869). (Reg § 1.471-3)[33]

... *Lower-of-cost-or-market method* (¶2870). (Reg § 1.471-4)[34]

... *Farm price method.* Each item, raised or purchased, is valued at its market price less estimated direct cost of disposition. A farmer using this method must use it for all his inventory, but may use the unit-livestock-price method for livestock. (Reg § 1.471-6(d))[35]

... *Unit-livestock-price method.* Livestock is reasonably classified according to kind and age. A standard unit price is used for each animal within a class. Unit prices must reflect costs capitalized under the uniform capitalization rules, see ¶4519. Once established, the accounting methods used to determine unit prices and to classify animals must be consistently applied in all future tax years. Users of this method must annually reevaluate their unit prices and adjust them to reflect increases or decreases in the costs of raising livestock.

28. ¶G-2456 *et seq.*; ¶4644; TD ¶442,023
29. ¶N-1018 *et seq.*; ¶614.056; TD ¶118,010
30. ¶N-1019; ¶614.056; TD ¶118,010
31. ¶N-1102; ¶614.057; TD ¶298,001
32. ¶s N-1109, N-1113; ¶s 614.057, 4714.73; TD ¶298,001
33. ¶N-1106; ¶s 614.057, 4714.41, 4714.73; TD ¶298,003
34. ¶N-1107; ¶s 614.057, 4714.51; TD ¶298,004
35. ¶N-1112; ¶s 614.057, 4714.73; TD ¶298,005

IRS consent isn't required for these adjustments; however it is required for other changes in classification or unit prices. (Reg § 1.471-6(f))[36]

¶ 4515 Feed.

The cost of feed is a deductible business expense. (Reg § 1.162-12(a))[37] A cash method farmer may deduct in the year paid, the cost of feed his livestock will consume that year. Payments for feed to be used in the next tax year ("pre-paid feed") aren't deductible until the year of consumption, except the farmer may deduct pre-paid feed expenses in the payment year if: (1) the payment represents a purchase and not a deposit, (2) the advance payment is for a business purpose and not merely for tax avoidance, *and* (3) deduction in the payment year doesn't materially distort income.[38] For pre-paid farm expenses generally, see ¶4517.

¶ 4516 Fertilizer.

The cost of acquiring fertilizer, lime, marl, and other materials used to enrich, neutralize, or condition farmland, and the costs of applying them, are deductible in the year the costs are paid or incurred if the benefit doesn't last beyond one year. If the benefit lasts substantially more than a year the costs generally are capitalized but the farmer may elect to deduct them in the year paid or incurred (Code Sec. 180(a))[39] by deducting them on his return for that year. (Code Sec. 180(c); Reg § 1.180-2)[40] The election to deduct isn't allowable for costs of preparing land not previously used for farming by the taxpayer or his tenant. (Code Sec. 180(b); Reg § 1.180-1(b))[41]

If fertilizer expenses are capitalized, the taxpayer may deduct a portion of the capitalized amounts for each year the benefits last. The portion deducted each year need not be the same if benefits are clearly greater in the early years.[42]

¶ 4517 Pre-paid farm expenses.

A cash method taxpayer's current deduction for pre-paid farm expenses (e.g., for seed, fertilizer, and similar farm supplies that won't be used until a later tax year) is limited to one-half of his other deductible farming expenses for the year (for a special rule for feed, see ¶4515). The "excess" part (i.e., over that one-half amount) isn't deductible until the year the supplies are used. (Code Sec. 464(f)(1), Code Sec. 464(f)(2))[43] This rule also applies to farming syndicates (required to use the accrual method, see ¶4511). (Code Sec. 464(a))[44]

But this limit *doesn't apply* if the taxpayer's (or a family member's) principal home (within the meaning of Code Sec. 121, see ¶2442) is a farm or his principal business is farming, if: (1) for the three preceding tax years, his total pre-paid farm expenses are less than 50% of his total other deductible farm expenses, or (2) for the current year, his pre-paid farm expenses are more than 50% of his other farm expenses because of a change in business operations attributable to extraordinary circumstances. (Code Sec. 464(f)(3))[45]

¶ 4518 Pre-productive period expenses.

The taxpayer has the option to either deduct or capitalize certain costs of developing and operating his farm and crops (e.g., taxes, interest, upkeep) during its pre-productive period (Reg § 1.162-12(a))[46] (subject to the uniform capitalization rules, see ¶4519). But he can't

36. ¶N-1113; ¶s 614.057, 4714.73; TD ¶298,006
37. ¶N-1311; ¶1624.340; TD ¶297,514
38. ¶N-1312; ¶1624.340; TD ¶297,515
39. ¶N-1306; ¶1804; TD ¶297,510
40. ¶N-1307; TD ¶297,511
41. ¶N-1306; TD ¶297,510

42. ¶N-1306; TD ¶297,510
43. ¶N-1319 *et seq.*; ¶4644; TD ¶297,519
44. ¶N-1319 *et seq.*; ¶4644; TD ¶297,519
45. ¶N-1319; ¶4644; TD ¶297,520
46. ¶N-1302; ¶1624.349; TD ¶298,009

deduct any capital expenditures.[47] The pre-productive period begins when the farmer first acquires the seed or plant, and ends when the plant produces marketable quantities or is reasonably expected to be sold or otherwise disposed of. (Code Sec. 263A(e)(3))[48]

¶ 4519 Application of uniform capitalization rules to farmers and ranchers.

Farmers and ranchers are subject to the uniform capitalization rules for taxpayers generally (¶1667) with respect to the production, growing, or raising of property that:

. . . is produced by a farmer required to use the accrual method (¶4510), (Code Sec. 263A(a), Code Sec. 263A(d)(1); Reg § 1.263A-4(a), Reg § 1.263A-4(b)) or

. . . has a pre-productive period (¶4518), of more than two years. (Code Sec. 263A(d)(1)(A)(ii))

For taxpayers not required to use the accrual method, the uniform capitalization rules *don't apply* to costs related to any animal, or plant with a pre-productive period of two years or less, which is produced by a taxpayer in a farming business. (Code Sec. 263A(d)(1)(A); Reg § 1.263A-4(a)(2))[49] The preproductive period is the period before the first marketable crop or yield, for plants that have more than one crop or yield (e.g., the orange tree); the period before a crop or yield is disposed of, for the crop or yield of a plant that will have more than one crop or yield (e.g., the orange); or, for any other plant, the period before it is disposed of. (Reg § 1.263A-4(b)(2)) IRS has published a noninclusive list of plants with preproductive periods in excess of 2 years.[50]

For exception for replanting because of casualties, see ¶4520. For election out of the uniform capitalization rules, see ¶4521.

¶ 4520 Exception to uniform capitalization rules for replanting because of casualty.

The uniform capitalization rules (¶4519) don't apply to costs incurred for the replanting, cultivation, maintenance and development of plants bearing an edible crop for human consumption (including citrus or almond) that were lost or damaged (while in the taxpayer's hands) by freezing temperatures, disease, drought, pests, or casualty (replanting costs). (Code Sec. 263A(d)(2)(A); Reg § 1.263A-4(e)(1), Reg § 1.263A-4(e)(4))[1]

This casualty exception generally applies to the costs of the person owning ("owner") the plants at the time of the loss or damage. But costs paid or incurred by another person (payor) in any tax year also may qualify if in that year: (1) the owner has a more-than-50% equity interest in the plants, and (2) the payor owns any of the remaining equity interest in them *and* materially participates in their planting, maintenance, cultivation or development. (Code Sec. 263A(d)(2)(B); Reg § 1.263A-4(e)(2))[2]

¶ 4521 Farmers' election to have uniform capitalization rules not apply.

Except as noted below, a farmer may elect to have the uniform capitalization rules at ¶4519 *not* apply to any plant produced in his farm business (Code Sec. 263A(d)(3)(A)), so he may currently deduct all otherwise deductible preproductive costs.[3]

If the taxpayer or any related person (as specially defined) makes the election, he must use Code Sec. 168(g)(2) alternative (i.e., straight-line) depreciation for all his property used predominantly in the farming business that was placed in service in any tax year during

47. ¶N-1303; ¶1624.349; TD ¶298,009
48. ¶N-1074; TD ¶298,009
49. ¶N-1071 et seq.; ¶263A4; TD ¶298,011
50. ¶N-1071.1; ¶263A4.15

1. ¶N-1081; ¶1624.339; TD ¶298,014
2. ¶N-1082; ¶263A4; TD ¶298,014
3. ¶N-1084; ¶263A4; TD ¶298,015

which the election is in effect (Code Sec. 263A(e)(2)(A); Reg § 1.263A-4(d)(4)(ii)) and follow other requirements in the regs. (Reg § 1.263A-4(d)(4))[4]

If the election is made, any plant with respect to which amounts would have been capitalized *but for* the election is treated as Code Sec. 1245 property (if it's not otherwise Code Sec. 1245 property). (Code Sec. 263A(e)(1)(A)(i); Reg § 1.263A-4(d)(4)(i)) Deductible amounts that *but for* the election would have been capitalized are treated as depreciation deductions for Code Sec. 1245 purposes (Code Sec. 263A(e)(1)(A)(ii), Code Sec. 263A(e)(1)(B)) so that they are recaptured as ordinary income when the product is disposed of, see ¶2695.[5]

The election can't be made for any item attributable to the planting, maintenance or development of any citrus or almond grove (or part of a grove) that's incurred before the close of the fourth tax year beginning with the tax year the trees were planted. For this purpose, the portion of a grove planted in one tax year must be treated separately from the portion planted in another tax year. (Code Sec. 263A(d)(3)(C); Reg § 1.263A-4(d)(2))[6]

Elect out of UNICAP by not applying the rules of Code Sec. 263A to determine the capitalized costs of plants produced in a farming business and by applying the rules of Reg § 1.263A-4(d)(4) on the original return for the first tax year capitalization of Code Sec. 263A costs is required. For partnerships or S corporations, the election is made by the partner, shareholder, or member. (Code Sec. 263A(d)(3)(D); Reg § 1.263A-4(d)(3)(i)) A taxpayer that does not make the automatic election described above must get IRS consent (¶2838) to change accounting methods. (Reg § 1.263A-4(d)(3)(ii))[7] The election can't be made by a corporation, partnership, or tax shelter that is required to use the accrual method of accounting, see ¶4510 and ¶4511. (Code Sec. 263A(d)(3)(B))[8]

¶ 4522　Soil and water conservation and erosion prevention costs.

Farmers may deduct currently, as business expenses, certain outlays for soil and water conservation or erosion prevention that are incurred to maintain the farm and preserve its normal productivity, and not to increase its value or convert it to a new use. Costs that result in the acquisition of depreciable property must be capitalized.[9]

A farmer may elect to deduct certain nondepreciable expenditures for conservation, etc., with respect to land he uses for farming (Code Sec. 175(a)) if the expenditures are consistent with a federal or state approved conservation plan. (Code Sec. 175(c)(3))[10] Qualifying expenditures include (1) costs of: treating or moving earth (e.g., leveling, terracing or restoring fertility); constructing and protecting diversion channels, drainage ditches, earthen dams; eradicating brush; planting windbreaks; producing vegetation primarily to conserve soil or water, or prevent soil erosion and (2) expenses paid or incurred for endangered species recovery, including site-specific management actions under the Endangered Species Act of '73. (Code Sec. 175(c); Reg § 1.175-2(a), Reg § 1.175-2(b)(2)) Costs of draining or filling wetlands or for center pivot irrigation systems don't qualify. (Code Sec. 175(c)(3)(B)) Nor does the election apply to depreciable assets. (Reg § 1.175-1)[11]

The amount of conservation, etc., expenses a farmer may deduct in any tax year under this election can't exceed 25% of his gross income from farming for the year. Any excess may be carried over to and deducted in the next tax year (subject to that year's 25% ceiling). (Code Sec. 175(b); Reg § 1.175-5(b))[12]

Elect by deducting the expenses on the return for the first tax year they are incurred. (Reg § 1.175-6(a))[13] IRS consent is needed to elect for a year other than that first year. (Code

4. ¶N-1090; ¶263A4; TD ¶298,015
5. ¶N-1093; ¶263A4; TD ¶298,015
6. ¶N-1089; ¶263A4; TD ¶298,015
7. ¶N-1087; ¶263A4; TD ¶298,016
8. ¶N-1085; ¶263A4; TD ¶298,015

9. ¶N-1401; ¶1754; TD ¶299,001
10. ¶N-1402; ¶1754.02; TD ¶299,002
11. ¶s N-1406, N-1407; ¶1754.02; TD ¶299,002
12. ¶N-1415; ¶1754.02; TD ¶299,015
13. ¶N-1420; TD ¶299,020

Sec. 175(d)(2))[14] Once the election is made, a farmer must continue to deduct all qualifying expenditures (subject to the 25% ceiling) unless IRS consents to a change. (Code Sec. 175(e))[15]

A farmer must recapture as ordinary income (use Form 4797) part of the conservation, etc., expenses if the farm land is disposed of after being held for less than 10 years. (Code Sec. 1252)[16]

¶ 4523 Depreciation for farm property—Form 4562.

A farmer may take depreciation deductions (on Form 4562) on property used in a farming business (Code Sec. 168(b)(2)(B)), including: buildings (except his dwelling); farm machinery; other physical property (not including land); orchards (trees and vines bearing fruits or nuts); and draft, breeding, sporting or dairy livestock (unless inventoried). (Reg § 1.167(a)-6(b))[17]

Farm property generally is depreciated under MACRS using the 150% declining balance method, but straight line applies to nonresidential real property, trees or vines bearing fruits or nuts. (Code Sec. 168(b)(1)(B), Code Sec. 168(b)(2)(B), Code Sec. 168(b)(3)(A), Code Sec. 168(b)(3)(B))[18]

The cost of *purchased* dairy, etc., livestock may be recovered under MACRS. The cost of *raised* livestock may be either deducted (but costs so deducted can't be included in depreciable basis) (Reg § 1.61-4(a), Reg § 1.162-12(a)) or capitalized as the taxpayer chooses.[19] But accrual method farmers using inventories can't depreciate any purchased dairy, etc., livestock that's inventoried. (Reg § 1.167(a)-6)[20]

¶ 4524 Unharvested crop sold with land.

Gain or loss on an unharvested crop sold, exchanged, or compulsorily or involuntarily converted with the underlying land qualifies under the capital gain-ordinary loss rule of Code Sec. 1231 (¶2684 *et seq.*), if: (1) the land was used in the taxpayer's trade or business and was held for the long-term capital gain holding period (¶2667), *and* (2) the land and crops are sold at the same time and to the same person. (Code Sec. 1231(b)(4)) It doesn't matter how long the *crops* were held, or their state of maturity. (Reg § 1.1231-1(f))[21]

¶ 4525 Dispositions of converted wetlands or highly erodible croplands.

Gain on the disposition of land used for farming that is converted wetland or highly erodible cropland is ordinary income. Loss is long-term capital loss. (Code Sec. 1257)[22]

¶ 4526 Dispositions of breeding, dairy, sporting, draft livestock.

Gains and losses from the sale, exchange, or involuntary conversion of animals held for draft, breeding, dairy, or sporting purposes qualify for capital gain-ordinary loss treatment under Code Sec. 1231 (¶2684 *et seq.*) as follows:

. . . cattle and horses held for 24 months or more from the date of acquisition;

. . . other livestock (except poultry) held for 12 months or more from the date of acquisition. (Code Sec. 1231(a), Code Sec. 1231(b)(3); Reg § 1.1231-2(a))[23]

Inventorying the livestock doesn't preclude Code Sec. 1231 treatment if the animal is held for the required purposes and relevant period and not for sale to customers.[24]

---

14. ¶N-1421; ¶1754; TD ¶299,021
15. ¶N-1422; TD ¶299,022
16. ¶N-1423; ¶12,524; TD ¶299,023
17. ¶N-1304; ¶1674.035; TD ¶298,501
18. ¶L-8912; ¶1684.01; TD ¶267,014
19. ¶s N-1020, N-1350 *et seq.*; ¶1624.339; TD ¶298,501

20. ¶N-1351; ¶1674.035; TD ¶298,501
21. ¶N-1206; ¶12,314.13; TD ¶117,012
22. ¶N-1431 *et seq.*; ¶12,574; TD ¶299,031
23. ¶s N-1209, N-1223; ¶s 12,314, 12,314.12; TD ¶117,001
24. ¶N-1209; TD ¶117,001

¶ 4527   Like-kind exchange of livestock.

The trading of livestock may qualify as a tax-free like-kind exchange (¶2418 *et seq.*) if the exchanged animals are the same sex. (Code Sec. 1031(e); Reg § 1.1031(e)-1)[25]

¶ 4528   Special farm payments.

Conservation programs. Unless the taxpayer elects out (Code Sec. 126(c)), gross income doesn't include the excludable part of payments received under certain cost-sharing conservation programs specified in Code Sec. 126(a)(1) to Code Sec. 126(a)(10). (Code Sec. 126(b))[26] Part or all of the cost-share payments made under the Forest Health Protection Program may qualify for the Code Sec. 126 exclusion.

Pledge of crops to secure CCC loan. Farmers who pledge part or all of their production to secure a Commodity Credit Corporation (CCC) loan can make a special election to treat the loan proceeds as income in the year received and obtain a basis in the commodity for the amount reported as income. Thus, instead of a loan, the money advanced to the farmer may be treated as the sales price of the commodity pledged for the loan. Elect by reporting the CCC loan proceeds as income on Schedule F, Form 1040 for the year the loan is received and attaching a statement to the return showing the details of the CCC loan.[27]

Payments under the Tobacco Transition Payment Program. Eligible tobacco quota holders may receive total payments of $7 per pound of quota in 10 equal annual payments in fiscal years 2005 through 2014 in exchange for the termination of tobacco marketing quotas and related price support. Payments are proceeds from a sale of the owner's tobacco quota and may be reported on the installment method under Code Sec. 453 or deferred under the like-kind exchange rules of Code Sec. 1031 (if the owner otherwise qualifies).[28]

---

25. ¶N-1215; ¶10,314.04; TD ¶117,002
26. ¶N-1181; ¶1264; TD ¶116,002

27. ¶N-1164; ¶774.03; TD ¶221,008
28. ¶N-1152.5

Chapter 23   Foreign Income—Foreign Taxpayers—Foreign Currency Transactions

¶ 4610   Foreign Income of U.S. Taxpayers.

U.S. taxpayers—U.S. citizens, U.S. residents, U.S. (domestic) corporations and other taxable U.S. entities—ordinarily are fully taxable on their income from outside the U.S., subject to special exemptions and other special treatment for particular taxpayers and particular kinds and sources of income. Nonresident aliens, foreign corporations and other foreign entities, however, are taxed only on their income that is effectively connected with a U.S. trade or business, and certain passive income derived from U.S. sources. Nonresidents who give up U.S. citizenship or terminate long-term U.S. residency are subject to special expatriation tax rules.

¶ 4611   Foreign income of U.S. citizens.

U.S. citizens (Reg § 1.1-1(c)), whether they reside in the U.S. or abroad, are generally subject to U.S. income tax on their income from sources within and without the U.S. (Reg § 1.1-1(b)), with exemptions for foreign earned income and housing costs (¶4612 et seq.), income from U.S. possessions (¶4618), and certain allowances for U.S. government employees (¶4619).[1]

For the foreign tax credit, see ¶2367 et seq. For when a foreign corporation's *undistributed* income is taxed to its U.S. shareholders, see ¶4622, ¶4629, and ¶4630. For the taxation of a resident alien's income, see ¶4633 et seq.

¶ 4612   Partial exclusion for foreign earned income.

For any tax year in which an individual is a qualified individual (¶4615), he may elect (¶4617) to exclude from gross income his foreign earned income up to the inflation-adjusted exclusion amount. (Code Sec. 911(a)(1), Code Sec. 911(b)(2))[2] For a *separate* exclusion for foreign housing costs, see ¶4613. For limitations applicable to both the foreign earned income and foreign housing costs exclusions, see ¶4616.

An individual's foreign earned income is his earned income from foreign sources attributable to services he performed during the period he was a qualified individual, with certain exceptions. (Code Sec. 911(b)(1))[3] Earned income means wages and other amounts received as compensation (i.e., not as a distribution of profits) for personal services actually rendered, including the fair market value of compensation paid with property (Code Sec. 911(d)(2)(A); Reg § 1.911-3(b)(1)) and, where both personal services and capital are material income-producing factors in the taxpayer's noncorporate business, a reasonable allowance (up to 30% of his share of the net profits) as compensation for personal services. (Code Sec. 911(d)(2)(B))[4]

An individual's foreign earned income exclusion amount for a tax year can't exceed his foreign earned income for the year, as computed on a daily basis at an annual rate of $97,600 for 2013, as indexed for inflation ($99,200 in 2014). (Code Sec. 911(b)(2)(A), Code Sec. 911(b)(2)(D))[5]

For married couples where both spouses are qualified individuals, each chooses whether to elect the exclusion. (Reg § 1.911-5(a)(1)) The amount of the exclusion is computed separately for each spouse based on the income attributable to that spouse's services. If the spouses file separate returns, each may exclude the amount of his foreign earned income attributable to his services, subject to the ceilings. If the spouses file a joint return, the sum of those separate

---

1. ¶O-1000 et seq.; TD ¶190,500 et seq.
2. ¶O-1100; ¶9114 et seq.; TD ¶191,000 et seq.
3. ¶O-1140; TD ¶191,024 et seq.

4. ¶O-1117; TD ¶191,019
5. ¶O-1102; ¶9114.12; TD ¶191,004

References beginning with a single letter are to paragraphs in RIA's Federal Tax Coordinator 2d and RIA's Analysis of Federal Taxes: Income. Those beginning with numbers are to paragraphs in RIA's United States Tax Reporter. Those beginning with TD are to paragraphs in RIA's Tax Desk.

amounts may be excluded. (Reg § 1.911-5(a)(2))[6]

¶ 4613   Partial exclusion for foreign housing costs.

A qualified individual (¶4615) may elect (¶4617) to exclude from gross income his housing cost amount. (Code Sec. 911(a)(2))[7] For deduction of nonemployer-provided housing expenses, see ¶4614. For limitations applicable to both the foreign earned income and foreign housing costs exclusions, see ¶4616.

A qualified individual who elects the housing costs exclusion may not claim less than the full amount of the allowable exclusion. (Reg § 1.911-4(d)(1))[8]

The housing cost amount is the excess of: (1) the individual's housing expenses for the year (but not exceeding an amount that is equal to 30% of the taxpayer's foreign earned income exclusion (computed on a daily basis) (¶4612) multiplied by the number of qualifying days in the tax year, over (2) 16% of the taxpayer's foreign earned income exclusion (computed on a daily basis) multiplied by the number of qualifying days in the tax year. (Code Sec. 911(c)) Housing expenses are those reasonable expenses paid or incurred during the tax year by or on behalf of an individual for housing for the individual (and, if they reside with him, for his spouse and dependents) in a foreign country. (Code Sec. 911(c)(3)(A)) The 30% limit may be adjusted for high-cost areas. (Code Sec. 911(c)(2)(B))[9]

Illustration: Thus, the maximum amount of the foreign housing cost exclusion is $13,664 for 2013 ($97,600 × 30%) − ($97,600 × 16%). For 2014, it's $13,888 ($99,200 × 30%) − ($99,200 × 16%).

For married couples where both spouses are qualified individuals, each chooses whether to elect the exclusion. (Reg § 1.911-5(a)(1)) The housing cost amount attributable to employer provided amounts is determined separately for each spouse. (Reg § 1.911-5(a)(3)(iii)) Where spouses reside together and file a joint return, they may compute their exclusion separately or jointly. If they reside together and file separate returns, they must make separate computations, but they may allocate the housing expenses between them. (Reg § 1.911-5(a)(3)(i)) Where spouses reside apart, they both may exclude (or deduct) their respective housing cost amounts if their tax homes (¶4615) aren't within reasonable commuting distance of each other and neither spouse's residence is within a reasonable commuting distance of the other spouse's tax home. If the spouses' tax homes or residences *are* within reasonable commuting distance, only one spouse may exclude (or deduct) his housing cost amount. (Reg § 1.911-5(a)(3)(ii))[10]

¶ 4614   Deduction for foreign housing expenses not provided by employer.

A qualified individual (¶4615) may deduct foreign housing expenses that aren't attributable to employer-provided amounts. (Code Sec. 911(c)(4)(A)) The deduction is limited to the individual's foreign earned income for the tax year which isn't otherwise excluded from gross income under either the foreign earned income (¶4612) or foreign housing costs (¶4613) exclusions. (Code Sec. 911(c)(4)(B)) Any unused housing expenses may be carried over and deducted in the next tax year, subject to that year's limits. (Code Sec. 911(c)(4)(C))[11]

¶ 4615   Who qualifies for the foreign earned income/housing costs exclusions?

A taxpayer qualifies for the foreign earned income (¶4612) and housing costs (¶4613) exclusions for a tax year if his "tax home" (below) is in a foreign country *and* he is either:

... a U.S. citizen who can establish that he has been a bona fide *resident* of one or more foreign countries for an uninterrupted period which includes the entire tax year; (Code

6. ¶O-1115; ¶9114.09; TD ¶191,006
7. ¶O-1160 *et seq.*; ¶9114.02; TD ¶191,028 *et seq.*
8. ¶O-1168; TD ¶191,001

9. ¶O-1166; ¶9114.02; TD ¶191,028
10. ¶s O-1174, O-1175; ¶9114.09; TD ¶191,031, TD ¶191,032
11. ¶O-1171, ¶O-1173; TD ¶191,030

Sec. 911(d)(1)(A))[12] or

... a U.S. citizen or resident who, during any period of 12 consecutive months, is *present* in one or more foreign countries during at least 330 full days. (Code Sec. 911(d)(1)(B))[13]

An individual's "tax home" is his home for purposes of deducting away-from-home travel expenses (¶1543). He has no tax home in a foreign country for any period his abode is in the U.S. (Code Sec. 911(d)(3)) But the fact that an individual is temporarily present in the U.S. or maintains a U.S. dwelling (even if used by his spouse or dependents) doesn't necessarily mean his abode is in the U.S. (Reg § 1.911-2(b))[14] For married couples, qualification is determined separately. Reg § 1.911-5(a)(1)

¶ 4616 Additional limitations on foreign earned income and foreign housing costs exclusions.

Where an individual is entitled to the foreign earned income exclusion (¶4612) and foreign housing costs exclusion (¶4613) and/or deduction (¶4614) for a tax year, the total of the foreign earned income exclusion and the housing cost amount excluded or deducted from income may not exceed the individual's foreign earned income (¶4612) for the year. (Code Sec. 911(d)(7))[15]

observation: Thus, the foreign earned income exclusion is limited to the lesser of (1) the taxpayer's foreign earned income for the year less the amount excluded for housing costs, and (2) the foreign income exclusion amount.

A "stacking rule" limits the benefits of the earned income and housing costs exclusions by adding back the excluded amounts to taxable income solely for purposes of determining the applicable marginal tax rate. Special rules apply where the net capital gain exceeds the individual's taxable income for a tax year. (Code Sec. 911(f))[16]

No deduction, exclusion or credit, including any credit or deduction for foreign or possessions taxes (¶2367 *et seq.*), is allowable to the extent the deduction, etc., is allocable to or chargeable against foreign income excluded from gross income under the foreign earned income (¶4612) or housing costs (¶4613) exclusions. (Code Sec. 911(d)(6))[17]

¶ 4617 Electing foreign earned income and housing costs exclusions— Form 2555 and Form 2555-EZ.

The foreign earned income (¶4612) and housing costs (¶4613) exclusions won't apply unless elected. (Code Sec. 911(a)) Once either exclusion is elected for a year, it's effective for that year and all later years, unless revoked. (Code Sec. 911(e)) If an election is revoked, the taxpayer cannot, without IRS's consent, again elect the same exclusion until the sixth tax year after the tax year for which the revocation was made. (Reg § 1.911-7(b)(1)) Each exclusion must be elected separately, on Form 2555 attached to the taxpayer's return for the first tax year it is to apply. (Reg § 1.911-7(a)(1)) (Form 2555-EZ may be used if only the foreign earned income exclusion is claimed and certain other conditions are met).[18]

¶ 4618 Exemption for certain U.S. possessions income—Form 4563.

An individual (regardless of citizenship) who is a bona fide resident of American Samoa for the entire tax year is exempt from U.S. tax on his income (except for amounts earned as an employee of the U.S.) from sources within, or effectively connected with his conduct of a trade or business within American Samoa, Guam, or the Commonwealth of the Northern Mariana

---

12. ¶O-1250 *et seq.*; ¶9114.04; TD ¶191,504
13. ¶O-1300 *et seq.*; ¶9114.05; TD ¶191,501
14. ¶O-1202, ¶O-1203; ¶9114.03
15. ¶O-1102 , ¶O-1168, ¶O-1171; ¶9114.01; TD ¶191,004

16. ¶O-1101.1; ¶9114; TD ¶191,001.1
17. ¶O-1112; ¶9114.11; TD ¶191,002
18. ¶O-1350 *et seq.*; ¶9114.13; TD ¶191,036 *et seq.*

Islands (CNMI). (Code Sec. 931(a), Code Sec. 931(d); Reg § 1.931-1(a)) Form 4563 is used to claim the exemption. An individual who is a bona fide resident of Guam or CNMI for the entire tax year must file a return only with the possession and is not subject to U.S. tax. (Former Code Sec. 935; Reg § 1.935-1) Special rules apply to determine if a person is a bona fide possessions resident and if income is possessions source income. (Code Sec. 937; Reg § 1.937-1, Reg § 1.937-2)[19]

An individual (regardless of citizenship) who is a bona fide resident of Puerto Rico for the entire tax year is exempt from U.S. tax on income from Puerto Rican sources, *except* amounts received for services performed for the U.S. government. But no deductions (other than for personal exemptions) or credits are allowed (i.e., from *taxable* non-Puerto Rican source income) for items attributable to the excluded amounts. (Code Sec. 933(1)) A U.S. citizen who gives up Puerto Rican residence after being a bona fide resident there for at least two years may exclude from gross income for the year of change in residence any income from Puerto Rican sources attributable to the period before the change (including amounts received *after* that year), to the extent allowed above. (Code Sec. 933(2); Reg § 1.933-1)[20]

An individual who is a *bona fide Virgin Islands (VI) resident* for the entire tax year (or files a joint return with such a person) files a VI return and pays VI tax on his worldwide income for that year. If the individual properly files and reports all his income from all sources on a VI tax return and pays the VI tax, he is not subject to tax in the U.S. (Code Sec. 932(c); Reg § 1.932-1) For a joint return, resident status is based on the residence of the spouse with the greater adjusted gross income (AGI) for the year, without regard to community property laws. (Code Sec. 932(d))[21]

A U.S. citizen or resident who derives income from the VI but is *not a bona fide VI resident* for the entire tax year must file two identical returns, one with the U.S. and one with the VI. (Code Sec. 932(a)) The individual is taxed in the VI on the proportion of his AGI from VI sources, and the VI tax (if any) is credited (¶2367 *et seq.*) against his total U.S. tax liability. (Code Sec. 932(b); Reg § 1.932-1)[22]

¶ 4619   Exemption for certain U.S. government employees' allowances.

Certain allowances are exempt from tax. These include (a) cost-of-living allowances received by U.S. government civilian officers and employees stationed outside the continental U.S. (except Alaska) (Code Sec. 912(2)),[23] (b) amounts received as allowances or otherwise (but not amounts received as post differentials) under: Chapter 9 of Title I of the '80 Foreign Service Act; Section 4 of the '49 Central Intelligence Agency Act; Title II of the Overseas Differentials and Allowances Act; or Subsection (e) or (f) of the first section of, or Section 22 of, the '46 Administrative Expenses Act (Code Sec. 912(1)),[24] and (c) allowances to a Peace Corps volunteer or volunteer leader and members of his family under Section 5 or 6 of the Peace Corps Act, *except:* termination payments, leave allowances, allowances to members of the family of a volunteer leader who is training in the U.S., and the part of an allowance designated as basic compensation. (Code Sec. 912(3))[25]

¶ 4620   U.S. beneficiaries of foreign trusts.

A U.S. beneficiary is taxed on a foreign trust's foreign- and U.S.-source income at the time it becomes distributable. (Code Sec. 643(a)(6), Code Sec. 652(a))[26] Distributions to the U.S. beneficiary of accumulated trust income are subject to the trust throwback rules (¶3953 *et seq.*)[27] and a nondeductible interest charge. (Code Sec. 668)[28]

---

19. ¶O-1085 *et seq.*, ¶O-10987 *et seq.*, ¶O-1402 *et seq.*, ¶O-1432 *et seq.*; ¶9314 *et seq.*
20. ¶O-1450 *et seq.*; ¶9314.04
21. ¶O-1472 *et seq.*; ¶9314.05
22. ¶O-1471; ¶9314.05
23. ¶H-3133; TD ¶138,034

24. ¶H-3135; TD ¶138,036
25. ¶H-3136; ¶9124.02; TD ¶138,037
26. ¶C-3021; TD ¶655,001 *et seq.*
27. ¶C-4003; ¶s 6664, 6684; TD ¶656,002
28. ¶C-4107 *et seq.*; ¶6684; TD ¶656,009

If the trust makes a loan (or permits the use of trust property without being paid fair market value for such use within a reasonable time) to a U.S. beneficiary, U.S grantor or related party, the loan (or use) is generally treated as a distribution. A subsequent repayment of the loan (or return of property) is disregarded for tax purposes. (Code Sec. 643(i))[29]

¶ 4621 Domestic corporations—taxation of U.S. and foreign income.

A domestic corporation is generally subject to U.S. tax on its income from both foreign and U.S. sources. (Code Sec. 11, Code Sec. 61(a), Code Sec. 63(a)) A domestic corporation is one created or organized in, or under the laws of, the U.S. or any state. (Code Sec. 7701(a)(4)) A domestic corporation's taxable income may include undistributed amounts if, for example, it is a shareholder in a controlled foreign corporation (¶4622) or in certain types of passive foreign investment companies. (¶4629, ¶4630)

A qualifying domestic corporation which elects (on Form 4876-A) to be a small interest-charge DISC (domestic international sales corporation) can defer income attributable to $10 million or less of qualified export receipts subject to an interest charge on its shareholders. (Code Sec. 991 *et seq.*)[30]

¶ 4622 Tax on U.S. Shareholders of controlled foreign corporations (CFCs)—Form 5471.

If a foreign corporation is a CFC (¶4623) for an uninterrupted period of 30 days or more during its tax year, every person who is a "U.S. Shareholder" (¶4623) of the CFC at any time that year, and who owns stock in the CFC on the last day of its tax year, must include in his gross income:

... his pro rata share of the foreign corporation's "Subpart F income" (¶4624) for that year; (Code Sec. 951(a)(1)(A)(i))[31]

... his pro rata share of previously excluded income withdrawn during the year from investment in less developed countries, as determined under rules in effect before the enactment of the Tax Reduction Act of '75; (Code Sec. 951(a)(1)(A)(ii))[32]

... his pro rata share of previously excluded Subpart F income withdrawn from foreign base company shipping operations for that year; (Code Sec. 951(a)(1)(A)(iii))[33] and

... his pro rata share of the increase during the tax year in earnings invested in U.S. property (to the extent not included as Subpart F income). (Code Sec. 951(a)(1)(B)) The share of this increase is the lesser of (1) the U.S. Shareholder's pro rata share of the average amount of U.S. property (calculated by basis) held (directly or indirectly) by the CFC as of the close of each quarter of the tax year, less that portion of the CFC's earnings and profits attributable to amounts included previously in that shareholder's gross income under this rule or under any of the other CFC rules, and (2) the U.S. Shareholder's pro rata share of the CFC's applicable earnings. (Code Sec. 951(a)(1)(B), Code Sec. 956)[34]

The U.S. Shareholder must report theses amounts on Form 5471. (Code Sec. 6038(a)(4))[35]

¶ 4623 Controlled foreign corporation (CFC) and U.S. Shareholder defined.

A CFC is a foreign corporation more than 50% (25%, for certain insurance companies) of whose stock *by vote or value* is, on any day in the corporation's tax year, owned (directly, indirectly, or constructively) by "U.S. Shareholders." (Code Sec. 957(a), Code Sec. 957(b)) A "U.S. Shareholder" is a U.S. person (i.e., a U.S. citizen or resident, or a U.S. corporation, partnership, estate or trust), that owns (directly, indirectly or constructively) 10% or more of

29. ¶C-4107.1; ¶6434.10; TD ¶656,002
30. ¶O-2020 *et seq.*; ¶9914 *et seq.*
31. ¶O-2401, O-2407; ¶9514.01
32. ¶9514.01

33. ¶O-2401, O-2740 *et seq.*; ¶9514.01, 9554, 9554.01
34. ¶O-2760 *et seq.*; ¶9564.01
35. ¶O-2781, S-3586.1; ¶9514.01

the corporation's voting stock. (Code Sec. 951(b))[36]

¶ 4624   What is Subpart F income?

A controlled foreign corporation's (CFC's) Subpart F income consists of:

(1) Insurance income. (Code Sec. 952(a)(1), Code Sec. 953)[37]

(2) Foreign base company income (FBCI) (Code Sec. 952(a)(2), Code Sec. 954; Reg § 1.954-1), which is

(a) Foreign personal holding company income (FPHCI). This includes investment income such as dividends, interest, rents, royalties and annuities; gains from certain property and commodities transactions; certain personal services income; and certain other passive type income. Exceptions apply for certain income received from related parties or as part of an active business. For tax years of foreign corporations beginning before Jan. 1, 2014, and tax years of U.S. Shareholders with or within which such tax years of foreign corporations end, interest, rent, and royalties received or accrued from a CFC which is a related person will not be treated as FPHCI to the extent attributable or properly allocable to income of the related person which is not subpart F income or treated as effectively connected with a U.S. trade or business if deductions for those amounts don't create a deficit which reduces the subpart F income of the related CFC payor or another CFC. (Code Sec. 954(c); Reg § 1.954-2)[38]

(b) Foreign base company sales, services, and oil-related income. (Code Sec. 954(d), Code Sec. 954(e), Code Sec. 954(g); Reg § 1.954-3, Reg § 1.954-4, Reg § 1.954-8)[39]

(3) Income from operations in compliance with an unsanctioned international boycott. (Code Sec. 952(a)(3))[40]

(4) The amount of any illegal (under the U.S. Foreign Corrupt Practices Act) payment made (directly or indirectly) by or for the CFC to a government official, employee or agent in fact. (Code Sec. 952(a)(4))[41]

(5) Income (reduced by allocable deductions and taxes) from a foreign country during any period that Code Sec. 901(j) (which denies any credit for taxes paid to certain foreign countries, see ¶2369) applies to that country. (Code Sec. 952(a)(5))[42]

For tax years of foreign corporations beginning before 2014 (and for tax years of U.S. Shareholders with or within which any such tax year of the foreign corporation ends), exceptions apply for certain income derived in the active conduct of a banking, financing, or similar business, or in the conduct of an insurance business. (Code Sec. 953(e)(10), Code Sec. 954(h)(9))[43]

In any tax year where the sum of the CFC's FBCI and insurance income exceeds 70% of its gross income, *all* of the CFC's gross income is includible in its subpart F income. However, in any tax year where this sum is less than 5% of the CFC's gross income or $1,000,000 (whichever is less), *none* of the CFC's income is FBCI or insurance income. (Code Sec. 954(b)(3); Reg § 1.954-1(b)) In addition, any item of FBCI or insurance income that is subject to an effective rate of foreign tax which is greater than 90% of the maximum U.S. corporate rate may, at the election of the CFC's controlling U.S. Shareholders, be excluded from Subpart F income. (Code Sec. 954(b)(4); Reg § 1.954-1(d))[44]

36. ¶O-2302 *et seq.*; ¶9514.01, 9574
37. ¶O-2500 *et seq.*; ¶9534.01
38. ¶O-2530 *et seq.*; ¶9544.02
39. ¶O-2620 *et seq.*; ¶9544.03, ¶9544.035, ¶9544.05
40. ¶O-2731; ¶9524.02
41. ¶O-2732; ¶9524.03
42. ¶O-2733; ¶9524.04
43. ¶O-2508 *et seq.*, ¶O-2584 *et seq.*
44. ¶O-2670 *et seq.*; ¶9544.01

¶ 4625   Disposition of controlled foreign corporation (CFC) stock.

Gain from the sale or exchange of stock in a foreign corporation is taxable as ordinary dividend income *if*:

... the selling or exchanging shareholder is a U.S. person; *and*

... that shareholder was a "U.S. Shareholder" (¶4623) of the corporation at some time during the five-year period ending on the date of the sale or exchange; *and*

... at some point during that five-year period, the foreign corporation was a CFC (¶4623) at the same moment as the shareholder was a U.S. Shareholder. (Code Sec. 1248(a))[45]

A sale or exchange includes a redemption of stock under Code Sec. 302(a) (¶3526 *et seq.*), a liquidation under Code Sec. 331(a) (¶3575), as well as amounts treated as gain from a sale of exchange under Code Sec. 301(c)(3). (Reg § 1.1248-1(b))[46]

Dividend treatment generally applies to a sale or exchange of stock in a foreign corporation only if gain is recognized in whole or in part upon the sale or exchange. (Reg § 1.1248-1(c))[47]

Dividend treatment may also apply to certain distributions by, and dispositions of, a *domestic* corporation, e.g., where such corporation was formed or availed of principally for holding (directly or indirectly) stock of one or more foreign corporations. (Code Sec. 1248(e), Code Sec. 1248(f))[48]

Dividend treatment under this provision doesn't apply to Code Sec. 303 redemptions or amounts treated under other Code provisions as dividends, ordinary income, or short-term capital gains. (Code Sec. 1248(g))[49]

There is a ceiling on the tax on the amount treated as a dividend for an individual shareholder who has held the stock for the long-term holding period (¶2667). (Code Sec. 1248(b))[50]

¶ 4626   Sales of patents, etc., to a foreign corporation.

A U.S. citizen or resident, or a domestic partnership, corporation, trust or estate, that sells (or exchanges) a patent, invention, formula or process, or similar property right to a foreign corporation in which the seller owns (directly, indirectly or constructively) stock with over 50% of the combined voting power of all classes of stock must treat as *ordinary income* any gain recognized on that sale (or exchange). (Code Sec. 1249)[1]

¶ 4627   Passive foreign investment company (PFIC) defined.

A PFIC is any foreign corporation if: (1) at least 75% of its gross income for its tax year is passive, or (2) at least 50% of the assets it held during the year produce passive income or are held for the production of passive income. (Code Sec. 1297(a)) The 50% test is based on the adjusted basis of the corporation's assets if the corporation (i) isn't publicly traded, and (ii) is a controlled foreign corporation or elects to use the basis test. The 50% test is based on the value of the corporation's assets if the corporation (i) is publicly traded for the tax year or (ii) the basis test isn't applicable. (Code Sec. 1297(e))[2]

The taxation of a PFIC's U.S. shareholder depends on whether such shareholder has not made any election (¶4628), has made a qualifying electing fund (QEF) election (¶4629), or has made a mark-to-market election (¶4630) with respect to his interest.

---

45. ¶O-2801; ¶12,484
46. ¶O-2801; ¶12,484
47. ¶O-2803; ¶12,484.01
48. ¶O-2804 through ¶O-2805

49. ¶O-2803; ¶12,484.01
50. ¶O-2811; ¶12,484.04
1. ¶O-2900 *et seq.*; ¶12,494
2. ¶O-2201 *et seq.*; ¶12,974

¶ 4628　Non-electing U.S. shareholders in a passive foreign investment company (PFIC)—Form 8621.

A U.S. shareholder in a PFIC (¶4627) that has not made a qualifying electing fund (¶4629) or mark-to-market (¶4630) election can defer the U.S. tax with respect to that investment until he disposes of the PFIC stock or receives an "excess distribution." At that time, the shareholder must pay U.S. tax, plus interest based on the value of the tax deferral, at ordinary income rates, and report the amounts on Form 8621. The excess distribution and gain amounts are allocated ratably to each day of the taxpayer's holding period. (Code Sec. 1291(a)(1), Code Sec. 1291(a)(2))[3]

An "excess distribution" is a current year distribution received by a shareholder on PFIC stock, to the extent the distribution exceeds its ratable portion of 125% of the average amount received with respect to the stock during the three preceding years (or, if shorter, the shareholder's holding period prior to the tax year). (Code Sec. 1291(b))[4] Portions of distributions that aren't "excess distributions" are taxed under the normal rules for corporate distributions, see ¶1285 *et seq.*[5]

IRS has the authority to promulgate regs requiring the recognition of gain under these rules for a transfer of stock on which gain wouldn't otherwise be recognized. (Code Sec. 1291(f))[6]

A PFIC shareholder may claim both direct and indirect ("deemed") foreign tax credits (¶2367 *et seq.*) with respect to these dispositions and distributions. (Code Sec. 1291(g))[7]

A corporation is not treated as a PFIC with respect to a shareholder during the period such shareholder is a U.S. Shareholder (¶4623) of a controlled foreign corporation (¶4623). However, this exclusion does not apply if that corporation was previously a PFIC with respect to that shareholder and no QEF election (¶4629) was made. (Code Sec. 1297(d))[8]

Each U.S. shareholder of a PFIC may be required to file an annual report containing information as IRS may require. (Code Sec. 1298(f))[9]

¶ 4629　Electing qualified electing fund (QEF) treatment for passive foreign investment company (PFIC) stock—Form 8621.

A PFIC (¶4627) is treated as a QEF with respect to a particular shareholder if he so elects and the PFIC complies with the requirements for determining its ordinary earnings and net capital gain and otherwise carrying out the purposes of the election. (Code Sec. 1295)[10]

A U.S. investor in a PFIC makes the QEF election by attaching a completed Form 8621 to his timely filed income tax return (original or amended, by the due date (as extended) for the original return) for that year, reflecting the information provided by the PFIC in its annual information statement. (Code Sec. 1295(b)(2); Reg § 1.1295-1(e), Reg § 1.1295-1(f)(1))[11]

If the election is made, the shareholder's U.S. tax on disposition of the stock or receipt of an excess distribution won't be increased by the otherwise applicable interest charge (¶4628). (Code Sec. 1291(d)(1))[12] But the electing shareholder must currently include in income his share of the PFIC's earnings and profits (with appropriate basis adjustments for amounts not distributed and previously taxed distributions). The fund's ordinary income and net capital gain are passed through to the shareholder as ordinary income and long-term capital gain. (Code Sec. 1293) A 10% corporate shareholder is allowed a foreign tax credit on its share of

3. ¶O-2200 *et seq.*; ¶12,914.01
4. ¶O-2227; ¶12,914.01
5. ¶O-2225
6. ¶O-2238; ¶12,914.01
7. ¶O-2246 *et seq.*; ¶12,914.01

8. ¶O-2250; ¶12,974
9. ¶O-2258; ¶12,984
10. ¶O-2260 *et seq.*; ¶12,954
11. ¶O-2270; ¶12,954, ¶12,954.01
12. ¶O-2261; ¶12,954

the PFIC's earnings. (Code Sec. 1293(f))[13]

The controlled foreign corporation (CFC) rules override the QEF rules as to a U.S. Shareholder of a CFC (¶4623). Thus, amounts that can be included in gross income under the CFC rules (¶4622) are not included under the QEF rules. (Code Sec. 951(c))[14]

¶ 4630 Electing mark-to-market treatment for passive foreign investment company (PFIC) stock—Form 8621.

A U.S. shareholder of a PFIC may make a mark-to-market election with respect to marketable PFIC stock and avoid the otherwise applicable PFIC rules described at ¶4628. (Code Sec. 1296, Code Sec. 1291(d))[15]

The election is made by filing Form 8621 with an annual original or amended return filed before the return due date (including extensions). Indirect shareholders may also make the election which is specifically applicable to their entire PFIC interest. Special rules apply where the shareholder is a controlled foreign corporation. (Reg § 1.1296-1(b), Reg § 1.1296-1(h)(1))[16]

If the election is made, the shareholder includes in income each year an amount equal to the excess, if any, of the fair market value (FMV) of the PFIC stock as of the close of the tax year over the shareholder's adjusted basis in the stock. Conversely, the shareholder is allowed a deduction for the lesser of (i) the excess, if any, of the adjusted basis of the PFIC stock over its FMV as of the close of the tax year, and (ii) the "unreversed inclusions" with respect to the PFIC stock, i.e., the excess, if any, of the mark-to-market gains previously included by the shareholder (including any amount which were included under Code Sec. 1291 under an election year coordination rule), over the mark-to-market losses previously allowed as deductions. All amounts so included in income or deducted, as well as any gain or loss on the actual sale or disposition of the PFIC stock, are treated as ordinary income or loss. (Code Sec. 1296)[17]

¶ 4631 Recognition of gain on transfers to certain foreign estates or trusts.

Except as provided in regs, gain is recognized upon a transfer of appreciated property by a U.S. person to a foreign estate or trust to the extent its fair market value (FMV) exceeds its basis in the hands of the transferor. (Code Sec. 684) Regs except transfers to foreign grantor trusts, exempt charitable trusts, certain transfers by reason of death of the U.S. transferor, transfers to unrelated foreign trusts for FMV, and transfers of stock by a domestic corporation to a foreign trust if the domestic corporation doesn't recognize gain on the transfer under Code Sec. 1032. (Reg § 1.684-3) In addition, gain is not recognized upon a distribution to a trust on an interest held by the trust in a corporation, partnership, investment trust, liquidating trust, or environmental remediation trust. (Reg § 1.684-3(f))

If a U.S. person transfers property to a domestic trust and that trust becomes a foreign trust and neither trust is treated as owned by any person under the grantor trust rules, the domestic trust is deemed to have transferred all of its assets to a foreign trust, and must immediately recognize gain unless one of the above exceptions applies at that time. (Reg § 1.684-4)

For gain recognition on transfers to a foreign corporation, see ¶3588. For gain recognition on transfers to foreign partnerships, see ¶3710.[18]

¶ 4632 Tax sanctions for international boycott activities— Form 5713.

Participation in or cooperation with an international boycott can result in: (1) reduction of the allowable foreign tax credit (¶2367 *et seq.*); (Code Sec. 908) (2) reduced deferral under the

13. ¶O-2261; ¶12,934
14. ¶O-2266; ¶9514.03
15. ¶O-2290 *et seq.*; ¶12,964

16. ¶O-2217.7; ¶12,964
17. ¶O-2290 *et seq.*; ¶12,964
18. ¶C-1020 etseq.; ¶6844; TD ¶658,009

domestic international sales corporation (DISC) rules (¶4621); (Code Sec. 995(b)(1)(F)) and (3) a controlled foreign corporation's (CFC's) undistributed earnings being currently taxed to its U.S. shareholders (¶4624). (Code Sec. 952(a)(3)) Taxpayers must report (on Form 5713) boycott operations and requests to participate or cooperate. (Code Sec. 999)[19]

¶ 4633   Resident Aliens Taxed as U.S. Persons. ■■■■■■■■■■■■■■■■■■■■■■■■■■■

A resident alien individual generally is subject to U.S. tax in the same manner as a U.S. citizen.

¶ 4634   Resident aliens as U.S. persons.

Resident aliens are taxed like U.S. citizens on their U.S. and foreign source income with certain minor exceptions. (Reg § 1.871-1(a))[20] An alien individual is treated as a U.S. resident for any calendar year in which he (1) meets a lawful permanent residence ("green card") test, (2) meets a "substantial presence" test (¶4635), or (3) makes the "first year election" (¶4636). (Code Sec. 7701(b)(1)(A))[21] For nonresident aliens, see ¶4637 *et seq.*

¶ 4635   Substantial presence test—Form 8843, Form 8840.

Subject to certain exceptions, an individual meets the substantial presence test (i.e., is a U.S. resident) for any calendar (current) year if:

(1) he is present in the U.S. on at least 31 days during the year, *and*

(2) the sum of the number of days he was present in the U.S. during the current year and the two preceding calendar years, when multiplied by the applicable multiplier (1 for the current year, $1/3$ for the first preceding year, and $1/6$ for the second preceding year), is at least 183. (Code Sec. 7701(b)(3)(A))[22]

An individual isn't present in the U.S. on any day on which he's exempt (e.g., foreign official, teacher), or his medical condition prevents him from leaving the U.S. (Code Sec. 7701(b)(3)(D), Code Sec. 7701(b)(5)) File Form 8843 to claim the exemption. (Reg § 301.7701(b)-8(b)(2)(i))[23]

An individual who otherwise meets the substantial presence test can avoid being treated as a U.S. resident that year if he: (1) is present in the U.S. on fewer than 183 days during the year, and (2) files a "closer connection statement" on Form 8840 which establishes that for the year, he has a tax home (¶1543) in a foreign country to which he has a closer connection than to the U.S. (Code Sec. 7701(b)(3)(B); Reg § 301.7701(b)-8(b)(1)(i)) If the individual is required to file Form 1040 or 1040NR, the statement must be attached to the return for the relevant tax year. An individual who doesn't have to file a return should send the form to the IRS center in Philadelphia, PA, by the due date (including extensions) for filing an income tax return for the calendar year for which the statement applies. (Reg § 301.7701(b)-8(c))[24]

¶ 4636   "First year" election to be taxed as a U.S. resident.

A qualifying alien who arrives in the U.S. too late in a calendar year to meet the substantial presence test (¶4635) may elect (on a statement attached to the return) to be taxed as a U.S. resident for part of that first (election) year if he meets the substantial presence test in the next calendar year. (Code Sec. 7701(b)(4); Reg § 301.7701(b)-4(c)(3))[25] For the joint return election where one spouse is a nonresident alien, see ¶4706.

---

19. ¶O-3500 *et seq.*; ¶9994.01
20. ¶O-1008; TD ¶190,502
21. ¶O-1051; ¶8714; TD ¶190,509
22. ¶O-1057; ¶8714; TD ¶190,510

23. ¶s O-1062, O-1080; ¶8714; TD ¶190,515 *et seq.*
24. ¶s O-1063, O-1081; ¶8714; TD ¶190,516
25. ¶O-1051, ¶O-1072 *et seq.*; ¶8714; TD ¶190,529

¶ 4637 Taxation of Nonresident Aliens and Foreign Corporations. ▰▰▰▰

A nonresident alien or foreign corporation (¶4638) is generally only taxed on (i) investment income from U.S. sources (at a 30% or lower treaty rate) and (ii) if engaged in a U.S. trade or business, net income effectively connected with that business (at regular U.S. rates). The latter is subject to modification by treaty, which usually conditions U.S. taxation on the presence of a permanent establishment (or sometimes, a fixed base).[26]

A foreign taxpayer also may be subject to the accumulated earnings tax (¶3316 *et seq.*), a branch profits tax (¶4647), a transportation tax (¶4651), and/or the alternative minimum tax (¶3200 *et seq.*).

¶ 4638 Nonresident alien individuals and foreign corporations.

A *nonresident alien individual* is an individual who isn't a U.S. citizen or resident. (Code Sec. 7701(b)(1)(B)) Aliens who are bona fide residents of Puerto Rico, Guam, American Samoa, or the Commonwealth of the Northern Mariana Islands (CNMI) for the entire tax year are generally taxed like resident aliens, except for their income from those possessions (see ¶4618). (Code Sec. 876)[27]

A *foreign corporation* is one that's created or organized outside the U.S. or under any law other than that of the U.S., a state, or the District of Columbia. (Code Sec. 7701(a)(4), Code Sec. 7701(a)(5), Code Sec. 7701(a)(9))[28]

A corporation created or organized in or under the law of American Samoa or the Virgin Islands isn't treated as foreign for any tax year if: (1) at all times that year, less than 25% by value of its stock is owned (directly or indirectly) by foreign persons; (2) at least 65% of its gross income for the last three tax years (or shorter period of existence) is shown to IRS's satisfaction to be effectively connected with a trade or business in either the possession or the U.S.; *and* (3) no substantial part of its income is used (directly or indirectly) to satisfy obligations to persons who are not bona fide residents of that possession or the U.S. (Code Sec. 881(b)(1); Reg § 1.881-5(c)) A corporation formed in Guam or the CNMI is treated as foreign if: (a) at all times during the tax year, less than 25% by value of its stock is owned (directly or indirectly) by foreign persons; and (b) at least 20% of its gross income is shown to IRS's satisfaction to have been derived from sources within the possession for the three-year period ending with the close of the preceding tax year of the corporation (or for such part of the period it was in existence). (Reg § 1.881-5(d))[29]

¶ 4639 Tax treaties—Form 8833.

Tax treaties typically exempt or reduce U.S. tax on certain business, compensation and investment income. (Code Sec. 894(a))[30] IRS Publication 515 lists the treaty countries and the benefits available for the residents of each country.[31] With limited exceptions, a taxpayer who takes a return position that a treaty overrules or otherwise modifies, and reduces any tax incurred at any time, must disclose that return position on Form 8833 attached to the return. (Code Sec. 6114(a); Reg § 301.6114-1)[32]

¶ 4640 Is income from U.S. or foreign sources?

Specific rules are used to determine the source of the following types of income:

Interest—generally, where the debtor is located. (Code Sec. 861(a)(1), Code Sec. 862(a)(1))[33]

---

26. ¶O-10100 *et seq.*, ¶O-10300 *et seq.*; ¶s 8714.01, 8814
27. ¶s O-1010, O-1086; ¶s 8714, 8764, 9314; TD ¶630,110
28. ¶O-10360; ¶8814.01; TD ¶632,005
29. ¶O-10361; ¶s 8814.01, 8814.02; TD ¶632,005.1

30. ¶O-15000 *et seq.*; ¶8944; TD ¶630,107
31. ¶O-12029; ¶8944; TD ¶192,010
32. ¶O-15010 *et seq.*; ¶61,144; TD ¶192,006
33. ¶O-10906; ¶8614.01; TD ¶633,002

Dividends—generally, where the corporation is incorporated. However, dividends received from a foreign corporation are treated in part as from U.S. sources if 25% or more of the corporation's gross income was effectively connected with the conduct of a U.S. business for the three-year period (or shorter period of its existence) ending with the close of its tax year preceding the declaration of the dividends. (Code Sec. 861(a)(2), Code Sec. 862(a)(2))[34] Dividend equivalents, including substitute dividends, payments made under specified notional contract, and other similar payments, are treated as U.S.-source dividends. (Code Sec. 871(m))[35]

Compensation—generally, where the services were performed, except in the case of nonresident aliens temporarily present in the U.S. (Code Sec. 861(a)(3), Code Sec. 862(a)(3); Reg § 1.861-4)[36]

Rents and royalties—where the property is located or used. (Code Sec. 861(a)(4), Code Sec. 862(a)(4))[37]

Sales of personal property—where the seller resides. (Code Sec. 865(a)) Special rules apply to the sale of depreciable and intangible property (Code Sec. 865(c), Code Sec. 865(d)), and to inventory. (Code Sec. 865(b)) Income from the sale of any personal property (other than inventory sold for use or disposition outside the U.S.) that's attributable to a nonresident's U.S. office is U.S.-source income. (Code Sec. 865(e)(2)) Sales of certain property by a U.S. resident through a foreign office is generally foreign-source, but only if at least a 10% foreign tax is paid on it. (Code Sec. 865(e)(1), Code Sec. 865(g))[38]

Sales of real property or natural resources—location of the property or resource. (Code Sec. 861(a)(5), Code Sec. 862(a)(8))[39]

Guarantees—amounts received directly or indirectly are from U.S. sources if paid by: (1) a noncorporate U.S. resident or a U.S. corporation for the provision of a guarantee of the resident or corporation; or (2) any foreign person for the provision of a guarantee if the payment is connected with income that is effectively connected, or treated as effectively connected, with the conduct of a U.S. trade or business. (Code Sec. 861(a)(9))[40]

Transportation income from transportation that either begins or ends in the U.S. is half foreign- and half U.S.-source. (Code Sec. 863(c)(2)(A))[41]

International communications income of a U.S. person is half foreign- and half U.S.-source. (Code Sec. 863(e)(1)(A)) A foreign person's international communications income is foreign-source, except where it is attributable to an office or fixed place of business in the U.S. (Code Sec. 863(e)(1)(B))[42]

Space and ocean activity income of a U.S. person is U.S.-source (while that of a foreign person is foreign-source). (Code Sec. 863(d)(1))[43]

Insurance income from insuring U.S. risks is U.S.-source. (Code Sec. 861(a)(7))[44]

¶ 4641   Allocating deductions between U.S.- and foreign-source income.

Deductions other than interest (and certain other deductions not considered definitely related to any gross income) are allocated or apportioned based on the factual relationship of deductions to gross income. (Reg § 1.861-8(a)(2))[45] Interest is attributed on the basis of the taxpayer's assets or under another permitted method. (Reg § 1.861-9T)[46]

---

34. ¶O-10928; ¶8614.09 *et seq.*; TD ¶633,003
35. ¶O-10930B; ¶8714.02
36. ¶O-10931.1, O-10934; ¶8614.15 *et seq.*; TD ¶633,004
37. ¶O-10936; ¶8614.22; TD ¶633,005
38. ¶O-10948; ¶8654 *et seq.*; TD ¶633,011 *et seq.*
39. ¶O-10945, O-10946; ¶8614.24; TD ¶633,009
40. ¶O-10923; ¶8614.14

41. ¶O-10941; ¶8634.03; TD ¶633,023
42. ¶O-10984; ¶8634.03; TD ¶633,023
43. ¶O-10976; ¶8634.04; TD ¶633,021
44. ¶O-10985; ¶8614.27
45. ¶O-11000 *et seq.*; ¶8614.29
46. ¶O-11100 *et seq.*; ¶8614.29

¶ 4642 U.S.-source investment income not effectively connected with a U.S. business—30% tax.

Nonresident aliens and foreign corporations are taxed at a flat 30% (or lower treaty rate) on the following types of income, if U.S.-source and not "effectively connected" with a U.S. business:

... Interest (other than described below), but not original issue discount (OID) amounts, dividends (other than described below), rents, salaries, wages, premiums, annuities, compensations, remunerations, emoluments and other fixed or determinable annual or periodical gains, profits and income ("FDAP"). (Code Sec. 871(a)(1)(A), Code Sec. 881(a)(1))

... Payments on bonds with OID, and amounts received on their disposition, that are ordinary income under the OID rules (¶1313 *et seq.*). (Code Sec. 871(a)(1)(C), Code Sec. 881(a)(3))

... Amounts includible in income of residual real estate mortgage investment conduit (REMIC) interest holders. (Code Sec. 860G(b)(1)) Special rules apply for this type of income, including rules regarding allocations by partnerships that hold residual REMIC interests. (Reg § 1.860G-3)

... 85% of Social Security benefits paid to nonresident aliens. (Code Sec. 871(a)(3))

... Gains on sale or exchange of patents, copyrights and the like, where payments are contingent on productivity, etc. (Code Sec. 871(a)(1)(D), Code Sec. 881(a)(4))

... Gains from the disposal, with a retained economic interest, of timber, coal, or iron ore. (Code Sec. 871(a)(1)(B), Code Sec. 881(a)(2))

... Only in the case of a nonresident alien present in the U.S. for 183 days or more during the tax year, the excess of U.S.-source gains over losses from sales or exchanges of capital assets. Non-"effectively connected" long- and short-term capital gains (except as listed above) aren't taxed to foreign corporations. (Code Sec. 871(a)(2))[47]

The following types of income are exempt from the 30% tax otherwise applicable under the rules above:

... certain dividends including (i) dividends paid by a foreign corporation with a minimum of 25% effectively connected income, (Code Sec. 871(i)(2)(D)) (ii) dividends paid by an existing 80/20 company, (Code Sec. 871(i)(2)(B)(i)) and (iii) interest-related regulated investment company (RIC) dividends that would not be subject to withholding and short-term capital gains for tax years beginning before 2014. (Code Sec. 871(k), Code Sec. 881(e))[48]

... certain interest including (i) portfolio interest, (Code Sec. 871(h), Code Sec. 882(c)) (ii) interest earned on bank account deposits, (Code Sec. 871(i)(2)(A) and (iii) interest paid by an existing 80/20 company. (Code Sec. 871(i)(2)(B)(ii))[49]

... gambling winnings from blackjack, baccarat, craps, roulette or big six wheel, except to the extent provided in regs. (Code Sec. 871(j))

No deductions are allowed against this income. The 30% tax is on the *gross* amount. (Code Sec. 873, Code Sec. 882(c))[50]

¶ 4643 Election for investment income from U.S. real property.

A nonresident alien or foreign corporation may elect to treat certain income from U.S. real property held for investment as effectively connected with the conduct of a U.S. business (¶4644). (Code Sec. 871(d), Code Sec. 882(d)) The electing foreign taxpayer is taxed at regular U.S. rates (not 30%) on net rather than gross income, and can take depreciation deductions,

---

47. ¶O-10201 *et seq.*; ¶s 8714.02, 8814.02; TD ¶630,100*et seq.*,TD ¶632,001 *et seq.*
48. ¶O-10228, O-10230.1; ¶8714.05; TD ¶630,129 *et seq.*
49. ¶O-10204, O-10220, O-10912.1; ¶8714.05; TD ¶630,119, 630,120 *et seq.*
50. ¶O-10641, O-10648; ¶s 8734, 8814.02; TD ¶641,004

etc.[1] Elect on a statement attached to the income tax return for the election year. (Reg § 1.871-10(d)(1)(ii))[2]

¶ 4644   When is income "effectively connected" with a U.S. business?

A foreign corporation or nonresident alien engaged in a U.S. business (¶4645) at any time in the tax year is taxed at regular U.S. rates on taxable income "effectively connected" with that business—i.e., the gross income effectively connected with the U.S. business, less allowable deductions (¶4646). (Code Sec. 871(b), Code Sec. 882(a))[3]

All *U.S.-source* income, gain, or loss (other than fixed or determinable annual or periodical (FDAP) income and capital gains and losses) derived by a nonresident alien or foreign corporation engaged in a U.S. business any time in the tax year is treated as effectively connected, whether it is or not. U.S.-source FDAP income, and capital gains and losses are treated as effectively connected if they satisfy one of two tests. (Code Sec. 864(c)(2), Code Sec. 864(c)(3))[4]

Foreign-source income treated as "effectively connected" is limited to the items below and only to the extent the item is attributable to an office or other fixed place of business in the U.S.:

. . . Rents, royalties and gains on intangible personal property derived from an active licensing business.

. . . Dividends, interest, or guarantee fees derived from an active banking, financing or trading business.

. . . Certain inventory sales attributable to a U.S. sales office.

. . . Items that are economically similar to the above items on this list.

. . . Foreign source income of a foreign insurance company attributable to its U.S. business. (Code Sec. 864(c)(4))[5]

¶ 4645   What is "engaging in a U.S. business"?

The performance of personal services in the U.S. constitutes engaging in a U.S. trade or business *unless* the performer of services is a nonresident alien individual (i) whose compensation for those services is $3,000 or less, (ii) who is in the U.S. for 90 days or less, *and* (iii) who works for a foreign person not engaged in business in the U.S., or foreign office of a U.S. person. (Code Sec. 864(b)(1)) A limited exclusion from income is available for compensation received for services as an employee of a foreign government or international organization. (Code Sec. 893)[6]

The trading of securities and commodities through a resident broker, commission agent, custodian, or other independent agent does not constitute engaging in a trade or business so long as the taxpayer does not have a U.S. office through which the trading transactions are effected. The trading of securities and commodities for one's own account is not engaging in a U.S. trade or business, however effected. These two exceptions apply to certain commodity trading as well. (Code Sec. 864(b)(2))[7]

If a partnership, estate or trust is engaged in a U.S. business, the entity's foreign partners or beneficiaries are considered so engaged. (Code Sec. 875)[8]

Special rules apply to foreign students and trainees. (Code Sec. 871(c))[9]

1. ¶O-10615; ¶8714.04; TD ¶642,016
2. ¶O-10619; TD ¶642,016
3. ¶O-10600 *et seq.*; ¶8644.02 *et seq.*; TD ¶642,000 *et seq.*
4. ¶O-10604 *et seq.*; ¶8644.03; TD ¶642,006 *et seq.*
5. ¶O-10622; ¶8644.04; TD ¶642,011

6. ¶O-10502, O-11829; ¶8644.01, ¶8934; TD ¶630,114, TD ¶647,000 *et seq.*
7. ¶O-10510; ¶8644.01; TD ¶641,515 *et seq.*
8. ¶O-10504; ¶8754
9. ¶O-10503; ¶8714.03; TD ¶641,507 *et seq.*

¶ 4646 Deductions and credits of foreign corporations and nonresident aliens.

Foreign corporations and nonresident aliens generally may take deductions only to the extent related (under regs) to "effectively connected" income (¶4644). (Code Sec. 873(a), Code Sec. 882(c)(1)(A)) Regs provide rules for how interest deductions are allocated to effectively connected income in the case of foreign corporations. (Reg § 1.882-5)[10] However the following deductions are allowed, whether or not related to that income: charitable contributions; and for nonresident aliens, nonbusiness casualty and theft losses, and personal exemptions (limited). (Code Sec. 873(b), Code Sec. 882(c)(1)(B))[11]

Credits also generally are allowable only if attributable to "effectively connected" income, with certain exceptions (e.g., for taxes withheld at source, earned income credit). (Code Sec. 874(a), Code Sec. 882(c)(2))[12]

Generally, a return (¶4656 *et seq.*) must be filed in order to get the benefit of an otherwise allowable deduction or credit. (Code Sec. 874(a), Code Sec. 882(c)(2))[13] The regs require the return be timely filed. However, IRS may waive the deadlines in certain cases. (Reg § 1.874-1(b)(2), Reg § 1.882-4(a)(3)(ii))[14]

¶ 4647 Branch profits tax on foreign corporations.

A foreign corporation engaged in a U.S. trade or business through a branch office in the tax year is liable for a branch profits tax (in addition to regular income tax) equal to 30% of the year's "dividend equivalent amount." (Code Sec. 884(a)) The "dividend equivalent amount" is the corporation's effectively connected earnings and profits (E&P), *reduced* (not below zero) by any increase for the year in its U.S. net equity (i.e., amounts reinvested in the U.S. business), and *increased* (within limits) by any decrease for the year in its U.S. net equity. (Code Sec. 884(b))[15]

If a foreign corporation is subject to the branch profits tax for any tax year (whether any branch profits tax is actually due), income tax withholding (¶4662 *et seq.*) isn't required on any dividends it pays out of its E&P for that year. (Code Sec. 884(e)(3))[16]

⬥/observation: The branch profits tax is the counterpart of the withholding tax on dividends paid by a U.S. subsidiary to its foreign parent (¶4642).

The branch profits tax isn't imposed on a foreign corporation for the year it completely terminates its U.S. trade or business, except where there is a corporate liquidation or reorganization, or a Code Sec. 351 incorporation. The corporation must waive the statute of limitations for the year (on Form 8848 attached to the income tax return). (Reg § 1.884-2)[17]

The branch profits tax may be reduced or eliminated by treaty, but only if the taxpayer is a "qualified resident" of the treaty country. (Code Sec. 884(e))[18]

¶ 4648 Branch-level interest tax.

If a foreign corporation is engaged in a U.S. trade or business or has gross income treated as "effectively connected" income, interest paid by the corporation's U.S. trade or business (i.e., its U.S. branch) is treated as if it were paid by a U.S. (subsidiary) corporation and is therefore subject to the 30% tax (¶4642). (Code Sec. 884(f)(1)(A)) If the interest allocable to the branch exceeds the interest actually paid by the branch, the difference is treated as interest paid by a U.S. subsidiary to its foreign parent also subject to the 30% tax. (Code Sec. 884(f)(1)(B)) The branch-level interest tax may be reduced or eliminated by treaty, but

10. ¶O-10641, ¶O-10648, ¶O-10649; ¶8734, 8824, 8824.01; TD ¶641,004, TD ¶641,010
11. ¶O-10243, O-10648; ¶8734, 8824; TD ¶641,004
12. ¶s O-10643, O-10675; ¶8824; TD ¶641,006, 641,011
13. ¶s O-10644, O-10676; ¶8824; TD ¶641,007, 641,012
14. ¶O-10645.1, O-10676.1
15. ¶O-11300 *et seq.*; ¶8844
16. ¶O-11454; ¶8844
17. ¶O-11356 *et seq.*; ¶8844
18. ¶O-11348; ¶8844

only if the taxpayer is a "qualified resident" of the treaty country. (Code Sec. 884(f)(3))[19]

¶ 4649   Dispositions of U.S. real property—Foreign Investment in Real Property Tax Act (FIRPTA) rules.

A gain or loss of a nonresident alien or foreign corporation from the disposition of a U.S. real property interest (USRPI) is treated as effectively connected with a U.S. trade or business. (Code Sec. 897(a)(1))[20] For related reporting and withholding requirements, see ¶4661 and ¶4671, respectively.

A USRPI includes: (1) an interest in real property located in the U.S. or the Virgin Islands, and (2) any interest (other than solely as a creditor) in any U.S. corporation unless it's shown *not* to have been a U.S. real property holding corporation (USRPHC) during the five-year period ending on the date of disposition. (Code Sec. 897(c)(1)(A))[21] A USRPI does *not* include an interest in a domestically controlled qualified investment entity (i.e., a real estate investment trust (REIT) or, only through Dec. 31, 2013, a regulated investment company (RIC) that would be a USRPHC under certain circumstances). (Code Sec. 897(h)(2), Code Sec. 897(h)(4)(A))[22] Special rules apply to foreign taxpayers who receive distributions from RICs and REITs. (Code Sec. 897(h))[23]

Foreign taxpayers that hold USRPIs indirectly (through their interest in a corporation, partnership, estate or trust) are subject to U.S. tax on any gain attributable to the entity's USRPIs upon the disposition of their interest in the entity. (Code Sec. 897(g))[24]

¶ 4650   Election by foreign corporation to be treated as a U.S. corporation for purposes of the Foreign Investment in Real Property Tax Act (FIRPTA) rules.

A foreign corporation protected by treaty (with respect to U.S. real property interests (USRPIs)) may elect to be treated as a U.S. corporation for purposes of the FIRPTA rules (¶4649), including reporting and withholding (¶4661 and ¶4671) (Code Sec. 897(i)), if the corporation: (i) will thereafter qualify as a U.S. real property holding corporation (¶4649) (Reg § 1.897-8T(b)); (ii) holds a USRPI at the time of the election; and (iii) submits an election statement in proper form. (Reg § 1.897-3(b))[25]

¶ 4651   4% tax on transportation income.

A 4% tax is imposed on the U.S.-source gross transportation income of foreign corporations and nonresident aliens. (Code Sec. 887) Income subject to this 4% gross-basis tax isn't subject to the 30% tax (¶4642) or the regular U.S. tax on "effectively connected" income (¶4644). (Code Sec. 887(c))[26]

¶ 4652   Excise tax on foreign procurement payments.

A 2% excise tax applies to specified Federal procurement payments to foreign persons. Specified Federal procurement payments are payments made under a contract with the U.S. for the provision of goods manufactured or produced, or services provided, in any country which is not a party to an international procurement agreement with the U.S. The excise tax is enforced by withholding. (Code Sec. 5000C)[27]

19. ¶O-11376; ¶8844
20. ¶O-10700 *et seq.*; ¶8974 *et seq.*; TD ¶643,001 *et seq.*
21. ¶O-10735 *et seq.*; ¶8974; TD ¶643,016 *et seq.*
22. ¶O-10753; ¶8974; TD ¶643,016
23. ¶O-10734; ¶8974.02; TD ¶643,015

24. ¶O-10733; ¶8974; TD ¶643,014
25. ¶O-10810 *et seq.*; ¶8974.01; TD ¶643,029
26. ¶O-11501 *et seq.*; ¶8874; TD ¶644,501 *et seq.*
27. ¶O-13351; ¶50,000C4

¶ 4653 Giving up U.S. citizenship or terminating long-term residency (expatriation) — Form 8854.

Under a mark-to-market deemed sale rule, property of certain "covered expatriates" (see below) who expatriate after June 16, 2008 is treated as sold on the day before the expatriation date for fair market value (FMV). (Code Sec. 877A)[28]

The gain from the deemed sale is taken into account at that time without regard to other Code provisions, and any loss generally is taken into account to the extent otherwise provided in the Code, except that the wash sale rules of Code Sec. 1091 don't apply. (Code Sec. 877A(a)(2)) However, any net gain on the deemed sale is taxed only to the extent it exceeds an inflation adjusted amount that is $668,000 in 2013 ($680,000 in 2014). (Code Sec. 877A(a)(3))[29] Subsequent gains or losses that are realized are adjusted for the gains and losses taken into account under the deemed sale rules, without regard to this exemption. (Code Sec. 877A(a)(2))

While the mark-to-market tax applies to most types of property interests held on the date of citizenship relinquishment or residency termination, deferred compensation items, interests in nongrantor trusts, and specified tax deferred accounts are excepted from the tax but are subject to special rules. (Code Sec. 877A(c))[30]

Covered expatriates. are U.S. citizens who relinquish citizenship and long-term residents who terminate U.S. residency, if they meet one of the following tests: (Code Sec. 877A(g)(1)(A))

(1) the individual's average annual net income tax for the period of five tax years ending before the date of the loss of U.S. citizenship was greater than an inflation adjusted amount that is $155,000 for losses of citizenship in 2013 ($157,000 for 2014);

(2) the individual's net worth as of that date was $2,000,000 or more; or

(3) the individual: (i) fails to certify under penalty of perjury that he has met the requirements of the Code for the five preceding tax years, or (ii) fails to submit evidence of his compliance as IRS may require. (Code Sec. 877(a)(2)) The certification is made on Form 8854.

However, neither the average annual net income tax nor the net worth tests are treated as met if (1) an individual who was born as a dual citizen of the U.S. and another country on the expatriation date continues to be a citizen of, and is taxed as a resident of, the other country, and has been a U.S. resident (under the substantial presence test) for not more than 10 tax years during the 15 tax-year period ending with the tax year in which the expatriation date occurs; *or* (2) an individual gives up his U.S. citizenship before becoming 18 ½ years old and was a U.S. resident for not more than 10 tax years before the relinquishment date. (Code Sec. 877A(g)(1)(B))[31]

Election to defer tax on expatriation. An individual may irrevocably elect, on a property-by-property basis, to defer payment of the mark-to-market tax imposed on the deemed sale of property. Interest is charged for the period the tax is deferred. The deferred tax generally is due when the return is due for the tax year in which the property is disposed of. (Code Sec. 877A(b))[32]

¶ 4654 Giving up U.S. citizenship or terminating long-term residency before June 17, 2008.

A nonresident alien individual who lost U.S. citizenship within the 10-year period immediately preceding the close of the tax year, was subject to alternative expatriate income tax

---

28. ¶O-11650 *et seq.*; ¶877A4; TD ¶645,000 *et seq.*
29. ¶O-11652; ¶877A4; TD ¶645,002
30. ¶O-11654; ¶877A4; TD ¶645,004 *et seq.*

31. ¶O-11659; ¶877A4; TD ¶645,009
32. ¶O-11653; ¶877A4; TD ¶645,003

graduated rates for the year (if this alternative tax, after reducing it for the payment of foreign taxes, was greater than the ordinary tax on nonresident aliens to which he would be subject, and if the individual met certain other requirements). (Code Sec. 877) Individuals would continue to be taxed as U.S. citizens or residents if they satisfied a substantial presence test. (Code Sec. 877(g)(1))

An annual statement on Form 8854 is required.[33]

¶ 4655   Corporate and partnership expatriations (inversions).

The below rules apply where (i) a foreign corporation directly or indirectly acquires substantially all of the properties held by a domestic corporation or substantially all of the properties constituting a trade or business of a domestic partnership, (ii) the former owners of the domestic entity receive interests in the successor entity as part of the transfer, and (iii) the entity (including certain related parties) does not have substantial business activities in the country in which the successor entity is organized. (Code Sec. 7874)

. . . The successor entity is treated as a domestic entity if the former owners own 80% or more of the interests. (Code Sec. 7874(b))

. . . The taxable income of the expatriated entity cannot be less than the gain on the expatriation transaction (including certain post-expatriation transactions with related entities) if the former owners own 60% or more of the interests. (Code Sec. 7874(a), Code Sec. 7874(d)) The offset of tax on this gain against losses or credits is limited. (Code Sec. 7874(e))[34]

¶ 4656   Returns Relating to Foreign Taxpayers.

U.S. income tax returns must be filed by nonresident alien individuals and foreign corporations engaged in a U.S. business. Information returns are required for certain foreign transactions.

¶ 4657   Return of nonresident alien individual—Forms 1040NR and 1040NR-EZ.

A nonresident alien individual must file a U.S. tax return (Form 1040NR, or, for certain nonresident aliens with no dependents, Form 1040NR-EZ) for any tax year he was engaged in business in the U.S. (¶4645) or deemed to be so engaged, even if (i) he has no income effectively connected to such business (¶4644) or other U.S.-source income, or (ii) his income is tax-exempt (by treaty or otherwise). (Reg § 1.6012-1(b)(1)) However, if the individual is at no time during the year engaged in a U.S. trade or business, he is not required to file a return if his tax liability is fully satisfied by withholding. (Reg § 1.6012-1(b)(2))[35] In general, the individual won't get the benefit of otherwise allowable deductions and credits if he does not file a true and accurate return. (Code Sec. 874(a); Reg § 1.874-1(a))[36]

Form 1040NR and Form 1040NR-EZ are due by the 15th day of the sixth month (i.e., June 15), or fourth month (April 15) if the alien had wages subject to wage withholding, after the close of the tax year. (Reg § 1.6072-1(c))[37]

¶ 4658   Departing alien "sailing permits"— Form 1040C, Form 2063.

An alien (resident or nonresident) leaving the U.S. generally must get a "certificate of [tax] compliance" ("sailing permit"), except for most tourists, students, and foreign government personnel. (Code Sec. 6851(d)(1); Reg § 1.6851-2(a)(2)) The alien files either Form 1040C (if he has income subject to U.S. tax) or Form 2063 (if he has no such income) in order to receive the permit. (Reg § 1.6851-2(b))[38]

---

33. ¶O-11701 *et seq.*; ¶8774; TD ¶644,701 *et seq.*
34. ¶F-5700 *et seq.*; ¶78,744 *et seq.*; TD ¶236,900 *et seq.*
35. ¶S-1750 *et seq.*; ¶60,124.02; TD ¶630,104

36. ¶O-10644; ¶8744; TD ¶641,007
37. ¶S-4703; ¶60,724
38. ¶S-1760 *et seq.*; ¶68,514.04

¶ 4659 Return of foreign corporation—Form 1120F.

A foreign corporation must file a U.S. income tax return (Form 1120F) if it was engaged in business in the U.S. (¶4645) during the tax year (or deemed to be so engaged), even if (i) the corporation has no income effectively connected to such business (¶4644) or other U.S.-source income, or (ii) its income is tax-exempt (by treaty or otherwise). However, if the foreign corporation has no gross income for the tax year, it is not required to complete the return schedules. (Reg § 1.6012-2(g))[39] In general, the foreign corporation won't get the benefit of otherwise allowable deductions and credits if it does not file a true and accurate return. (Code Sec. 882(c)(2))[40]

A foreign corporation must file the return on or before the 15th day of the third month (sixth month if it has no U.S. office or place of business) following the close of the tax year. (Code Sec. 6072(b), Code Sec. 6072(c))[41]

¶ 4660 Return of foreign partnership—Form 1065.

A foreign partnership isn't required to file a partnership return (Form 1065), unless it has gross income that is (or is treated as) effectively connected with the conduct of a trade or business within the U.S. (ECI) or has gross income (including gains) derived from sources within the U.S. (U.S.-source income). (Code Sec. 6031(e)) A foreign partnership, other than a withholding foreign partnership, that has $20,000 or less of U.S.-source income and has no ECI during its tax year need not file a partnership return if, at no time during the partnership tax year, 1% or more of any item of partnership income, gain, loss, deduction, or credit is allocable in the aggregate to direct U.S. partners. The U.S. partners must directly report their shares of the allocable items of partnership income, gain, loss, deduction, and credit. (Reg § 1.6031(a)-1(b)(2))

A foreign partnership (other than a withholding foreign partnership) for which one or more withholding agents file the required Form 1042 and Form 1042-S and pay the associated withholding tax, and that has U.S.-source income but no ECI and no U.S. partners, is not required to file a partnership return. If such partnership does have U.S. partners, it must file a partnership return, but it need only file Schedules K-1 for its direct U.S.partners and for its passthrough partners through which U.S. partners hold an interest in the foreign partnership. (Reg § 1.6031(a)-1(b)(3))[42]

¶ 4661 Information returns—Form 5471; Form 5472; Form 926; Form 8865.

A U.S. person who controls a foreign corporation for at least 30 consecutive days in his tax year must furnish IRS with certain information concerning the foreign corporation on Form 5471. (Code Sec. 6038; Reg § 1.6038-2(a)) "Control" means more than 50% ownership (by total vote or total value) of the corporation's stock. (Code Sec. 6038(e)(2))[43] Similarly, a U.S. partner that controls a foreign partnership must also furnish IRS with information on Form 8865. (Code Sec. 6038) A person controls a partnership if the person owns, directly or indirectly, more than a 50% interest in the partnership. (Code Sec. 6038(e)(3))[44]

The organization or reorganization of, or acquisition of stock in, a foreign corporation must be reported (on Form 5471) by certain U.S. persons. (Code Sec. 6046)[45] The acquisition, disposition or substantial change in size of an interest in a foreign partnership must be reported (on Form 8865) by a U.S. person if he holds a 10% or greater interest in the partnership either before or after the event. (Code Sec. 6046A)[46]

If a U.S. corporation is at least 25% owned by a single foreign person, or if a foreign

39. ¶S-1910; ¶60,124.03; TD ¶609,808
40. ¶O-10676; ¶8824;TD ¶641,012
41. ¶S-4704; ¶60,724
42. ¶S-2717.1 *et seq.*; ¶60,314.01

43. ¶S-3586 *et seq.*; ¶60,384; TD ¶815,503
44. ¶S-3585 *et seq.*; ¶60,384; TD ¶815,503
45. ¶S-3602 *et seq.*; ¶60,464; TD ¶815,501
46. ¶S-3643 *et seq.*; ¶60,46A4;TD ¶815,507

corporation is engaged in a U.S. trade or business, it must maintain records and furnish IRS with certain information (on Form 5472) concerning specified transactions with related parties in that year. (Code Sec. 6038A(a), Code Sec. 6038C)[47]

Each U.S. person (i) transferring property to a foreign corporation (or a partnership under certain conditions) in specified tax-free exchanges, or (ii) distributing property in complete liquidation to a non-U.S. person, must report the transfer to IRS (on Form 926 for corporations, Form 8865 for partnerships). (Code Sec. 6038B)[48]

To the extent provided in regs, foreign investors in U.S. real property must report their direct ownership interests to IRS. (Code Sec. 6039C)[49]

¶ 4662   Tax Withholding on Payments to Foreign Taxpayers.

Several withholding regimes enforce the imposition of tax on foreign taxpayers. These include (i) withholding at a 30% (or lower) rate on the gross amount of certain U.S. source fixed and determinable income items ("FDAP withholding"), (ii) wage withholding, (iii) withholding on effectively connected income of foreign partners in a partnership, (iv) withholding on the disposition of U.S. real property interests, and (v) the new FATCA regime.

¶ 4663   Which foreigners are subject to FDAP withholding?

Nonresident alien individuals and foreign partnerships are subject to withholding at the source on their U.S.-source fixed and determinable income items ("FDAP" income, ¶4667) (Code Sec. 1441(a)), as are foreign corporations (Code Sec. 1442(a)), foreign trusts, foreign estates, foreign branches of U.S. persons that furnish intermediary withholding certificates (but only for withholding purposes), and any other person that is not a U.S. person. (Reg § 1.1441-1(c)(2)) However, an alien individual who made an election to be treated as a resident of the U.S. is nevertheless treated as a nonresident alien individual for withholding purposes. (Reg § 1.1441-1(c)(3)(ii)) A corporation organized in the Virgin Islands, American Samoa, Guam, or the Commonwealth of the Northern Mariana Islands is not a foreign corporation for withholding purposes if certain tests are met. (Code Sec. 1442(c))[50]

¶ 4664   Who has FDAP withholding responsibility (who is the withholding agent)?

Any person having the control, receipt, custody, disposal, or payment of specified items of income ("FDAP" income, ¶4667) (a "withholding agent") must deduct and withhold U.S. income tax from those items, to the extent they are gross income from U.S. sources of foreigners subject to withholding (¶4663). The amount of tax to be deducted and withheld on an item is generally 30% unless a reduced rate applies by treaty, or because the item is a scholarship or fellowship, or the item is specified compensation that's exempt from such withholding. (Code Sec. 1441(a)) Regs explain how to claim reduced withholding under a treaty. (Reg § 1.1441-6)[1]

A withholding agent must withhold the 30% tax on any withholdable payment unless it can reliably associate the payment with documentation that the payment can be treated as made to a U.S. payee, or a foreign beneficial owner entitled to a reduced rate (see ¶4666). However, the withholding agent need not withhold where the foreign person assumes responsibility for withholding on the payment as a (1) qualified intermediary (QI); (2) U.S. branch of a foreign person (or U.S. possessions financial institution treated as one); or (3) withholding foreign partnership or authorized foreign agent. (Reg § 1.1441-1(b)(1))[2] A withholding agent generally determines if a payee is a U.S. or foreign person on the basis of a withholding certificate (Form W-8), Form 8233 (indicating foreign status of the payee or beneficial owner), or a Form

47. ¶S-3485 *et seq.*, ¶S-3510 *et seq.*; ¶60,38A4, 60,38C4; TD ¶815,504
48. ¶S-3629 *et seq.*; ¶60,38B4; TD ¶815,506
49. ¶S-3481 *et seq.*; ¶60,39C4; TD ¶815,508
50. ¶O-11922 *et seq.*; ¶14,414 *et seq.*
1. ¶O-11900 *et seq.*; ¶14,414 *et seq.*; TD ¶634,001*et seq.*
2. ¶O-11914; ¶14,414

W-9 (indicating U.S. status of the payee). (Reg § 1.1441-1(b)(2))[3]

Withholding by QI. A QI is typically a foreign financial institution that enters into an agreement with IRS under which it acts as an agent with a withholding obligation with respect to its account holders. (Reg § 1.1441-1(e)(5)) A QI is subject to the withholding and reporting provisions applicable to withholding agents and payors under the Code Sec. 1441 *et seq.* withholding, information reporting, and the backup and other withholding rules, except to the extent provided under the agreement. The QI is not required to assume primary withholding responsibility. (Reg § 1.1441-1(e)(5)(iii))[4]

Foreign trusts and partnerships may similarly enter into agreements with IRS under which they may act as withholding agents. (Reg § 1.1441-5(c)(2), Reg § 1.1441-5(e)(5)(v))[5]

Withholding by domestic partnership. A U.S. partnership must withhold when any distributions (including guaranteed payments) that include amounts subject to FDAP withholding (¶4667) are made. To the extent a foreign partner's distributive share of income subject to withholding has not been distributed to the foreign partner, the partnership must withhold on the partner's distributive share of the income on the earlier of the date the Form K-1 is mailed or otherwise furnished to the partner, or the due date for furnishing the Form K-1. Withholding on the later distribution of that amount is not required. (Reg § 1.1441-5(b)(2))[6]

¶ 4665 Reporting FDAP withholding—Form 1042, Form 1042-S.

Form 1042 is an annual income tax return filed by a withholding agent to report tax withheld and deposited by such agent which was reported on information returns (on Form 1042-S, see below) for the preceding year. It must be filed with IRS on or before Mar. 15 of the succeeding year, even if no tax was required to be withheld during a given year. (Reg § 1.1461-1(b)(1))

A withholding agent (other than an individual who is not acting in the course of a trade or business with respect to a payment) must also make an information return on Form 1042-S for each foreign recipient of an amount subject to Code Sec. 1441 withholding (as well as amounts subject to FATCA withholding, see ¶4672) paid during the preceding year, as well as for any amount actually withheld upon, whether or not withholding was in fact required. One copy of each Form 1042-S must be filed with IRS on or before Mar. 15 of the succeeding year, one copy must be furnished to the payee on or before Mar. 15 of the succeeding year, and one copy must be retained by the withholding agent. (Reg § 1.1461-1(c)(1))[7]

¶ 4666 Documenting right to withholding exemption or reduction—Forms W-9, W-8, 8233.

Exemption based on U.S. status of beneficial owner or payee. Absent actual knowledge or reason to know otherwise, a withholding agent (¶4664) may treat a payee as a U.S. person if (i) the payee is required to furnish a Form W-9 and furnishes it under the backup withholding rules, and it includes the payee's taxpayer identification number (TIN) or (ii) the payee is not required to furnish the Form W-9 but provides the withholding agent with a Form W-9 (or a substitute form) that contains the payee's name, address, and TIN. The form must be signed under penalties of perjury. (Reg § 1.1441-1(d)) A withholding agent that makes a payment to an intermediary, flow-through entity, or U.S. branch may treat the payment as made to a U.S. payee to the extent that, prior to the payment, the withholding agent can reliably associate the payment with: (a) a Form W-9 attached to a valid intermediary, flow-through, or U.S. branch withholding certificate; or (b) a Form W-8 that evidences an agreement to treat a U.S. branch as a U.S. person. (Reg § 1.1441-1(d)(4))[8]

Exemption based on income being effectively connected. Absent actual knowledge or reason

---

3. ¶O-11926
4. ¶O-12700 *et seq.*; ¶14,414.01
5. ¶O-12005.8 *et seq.*, ¶O-12013 *et seq.*; ¶14,414 *et seq.*

6. ¶O-12010; ¶14,414.07
7. ¶S-3471 *et seq.*; ¶14,414
8. ¶O-11963

to know otherwise, a withholding agent may rely on a claim of exemption from withholding for income effectively connected with a U.S. trade or business if, prior to the payment to the foreign person, the withholding agent can reliably associate the payment with a Form W-8ECI which is valid only if, in addition to other applicable requirements, it includes the TIN and represents, under penalties of perjury, that the amounts for which the certificate is furnished are effectively connected with the conduct of a trade or business in the U.S. and includable in the beneficial owner's gross income for the tax year. (Reg § 1.1441-4(a)(2)(i))[9]

Exemption or reduced rate based on treaty. Absent actual knowledge or reason to know otherwise, a withholding agent may rely on a claim that a beneficial owner is entitled to a reduced rate of withholding on income other than compensation based upon an income tax treaty if, prior to the payment, the withholding agent can reliably associate the payment with a Form W-8BEN that includes the beneficial owner's TIN (with certain exceptions), a representation that the beneficial owner derives the income under Code Sec. 894 and the regs thereunder (if required), a representation that the beneficial owner meets the limitation on benefits provisions of the treaty (if any), as well as certain other representations and certifications. (Reg § 1.1441-6(b)(1))[10] In the case of compensation income, the form used is Form 8233 (or an acceptable substitute or such other form as the IRS may prescribe) containing the required information. (Reg § 1.1441-4(b)(2)(ii))[11]

¶ 4667   What income items are subject to and exempt from FDAP withholding?

The gross amounts of the following items of income *from U.S. sources* are subject to withholding:

. . . Interest (other than original issue discount (OID) and certain portfolio and bank account interest), dividends, rent, salary, wages, premiums, annuities, compensations, remunerations and emoluments, as well as other fixed or determinable annual or periodical (FDAP) gains, profits and income. (Code Sec. 1441(b))

. . . OID upon the sale or exchange, or payment of the obligation. (Code Sec. 1441(b))

. . . Gains from the disposal of timber, coal, or domestic iron ore with retained economic interests. (Code Sec. 1441(b))

. . . Contingent gains from the sale or exchange of patents and other intangibles, and all gains on the sale of patents before Oct. 5, '66. (Code Sec. 1441(b))

. . . Social Security benefits paid to nonresident aliens, but only to the extent of 85% of those benefits. (Code Sec. 1441(g))

. . . Amounts includible in the gross income of the holder of a residual interest in a real estate mortgage investment conduit (REMIC). (Code Sec. 860G(b)(1))[12]

Items exempt from withholding include (but are not limited to):

. . . Income (other than compensation for personal services) which is effectively connected with the conduct of a U.S. business and taxed at regular U.S. tax rates. (Code Sec. 1441(c)(1))

. . . Portfolio interest, substitute interest payments, certain kinds of deposit interest, interest and OID on short-term obligations. (Code Sec. 1441(c); Reg § 1.1441-1(b)(4)).

. . . Non-U.S. source income. (Reg § 1.1441-1(b)(4)(v))

. . . Compensation for personal services of a nonresident alien individual if such compensation is effectively connected with the conduct of a trade or business within the U.S. *and* meets the requirements described at ¶4668. (Code Sec. 1441(c)(4))

. . . Regulated investment company (RIC) dividends that are paid out of interest that would not be subject to withholding, and certain short-term capital gains. (Code Sec. 1441(c)(12))[13]

9. ¶O-11968; TD ¶634,021
10. ¶O-12032; ¶14,414.025
11. ¶O-12047 *et seq.*; ¶14,414.06; TD ¶634,006 *et seq.*

12. ¶O-11901 *et seq.*; ¶14,414; TD ¶634,001
13. ¶O-11901 *et seq.*; ¶14,414.02

¶ 4668   When is compensation exempt from withholding?

Withholding is generally applicable to all forms of U.S.-source salaries, compensation, remuneration, etc. received by a nonresident alien individual. (Code Sec. 1441(b)) However, withholding doesn't apply if the compensation:

(1) is subject to the "wages" withholding regime under Code Sec. 3402 (see ¶4669);

(2) would be subject to the Code Sec. 3402 regime, except that it is specifically exempted from wages by Code Sec. 3401(a), with certain exceptions;

(3) is for services performed by Canadian or Mexican residents who enter or leave the U.S. at frequent intervals;

(4) is exempt from tax by law or treaty (see ¶4666 for documentation);

(5) is paid as a commission or rebate by a ship supplier under certain circumstances; or

(6) is exempt from withholding under Code Sec. 3402 due to the Code Sec. 3402(e) "all-or-nothing rule," if the employee and employer enter into a voluntary nonwage withholding agreement. (Code Sec. 1441(c)(4); Reg § 1.1441-4(b)(1))[14]

¶ 4669   Graduated wage withholding on compensation for personal services of a nonresident alien individual.

Compensation paid for personal services performed by a nonresident alien individual which meets the definition of "wages" (¶3004) and which is effectively connected with a U.S. trade or business, is subject to regular graduated income tax withholding with certain adjustments under Code Sec. 3402. (Reg § 31.3401(a)(6)-1(a))[15]

The following aren't wages subject to the wage withholding regime:

(1) Wages paid for services performed outside the U.S. by a nonresident alien individual other than a resident of Puerto Rico. (Reg § 31.3401(a)(6)-1(b))

(2) Remuneration paid to Canadian and Mexican residents who enter or leave the U.S. at frequent intervals and are engaged in transportation service or in service on international projects. (Reg § 31.3401(a)(6)-1(c))

(3) Wages paid (i) to Puerto Rican residents for services performed in Puerto Rico for an employer other than the U.S. government, (ii) for services performed outside the U.S., but not in Puerto Rico, by a Puerto Rican resident for an employer other than the U.S. government if the individual does not expect to be a Puerto Rican resident during the entire tax year, or (iii) for services performed outside the U.S. by a nonresident alien individual who is a resident of Puerto Rico as an employee of the U.S. government, if the individual does not expect to be a Puerto Rican resident during the entire tax year. (Reg § 31.3401(a)(6)-1(d))

(4) Wages exempt from tax by law or treaty. (Reg § 31.3401(a)(6)-1(f))[16]

⊙*observation:* Although compensation paid to self-employed individuals would generally not meet the definition of wages for purposes of the above, and so would not be subject to these withholding provisions, such amounts *would* be subject to withholding under the FDAP provisions (¶4662 *et seq.*) unless one of the FDAP withholding exceptions (¶4667) applied.

¶ 4670   Withholding by partnerships with respect to foreign partners— Form 8813, Form 8804, Form 8805.

A partnership must pay a withholding tax if it has "effectively connected taxable income"

---

14. ¶O-11991; ¶14,414.06
15. ¶H-4436,¶O-11988 *et seq.*; ¶34,014.22; TD ¶634,023
16. ¶O-11989 *et seq.*; ¶34,014.22; TD ¶634,023

for the tax year (whether or not the income is distributed), any part of which is allocable to a foreign partner. (Code Sec. 1446(a)) Unless the partner can show that the tax should be lower, the partnership must withhold at the highest rate of U.S. (corporate or individual, as applicable) tax to which the foreign partner would be subject on that allocable income. (Code Sec. 1446(b); Reg § 1.1446-3, Reg § 1.1446-6) The partnership must determine the status of its partners based on the Form W-8 or Form W-9 filed by the partners. In the absence of documentation of a partner's status, the partnership must follow the presumptions in the regs. (Reg § 1.1446-1) Special rules apply to publicly traded partnerships and tiered partnerships. (Reg § 1.1446-4, Reg § 1.1446-5)[17]

The partnership must pay the withheld amount in installments together with a Form 8813. The partnership must report the partnership's total withholding liability for its year on Form 8804 and notify each foreign partner of his share thereof on Form 8805. (Reg § 1.1446-3)[18]

¶ 4671   U.S. real property dispositions—Form 8288, Form 8288-A.

U.S. tax must generally be withheld by at the rate of 10% on the amount realized when a foreign person disposes of a U.S. real property interest (USRPI) (¶4649). (Code Sec. 1445(a)) The amount realized is the sum of cash received (not including any stated or unstated interest or original issue discount), the fair market value of any other property received, and any liability assumed by the transferee (e.g., buyer) or to which the USRPI was subject. (Reg § 1.1445-1(g)(5))[19]

Withholding at the 10% rate is also required on certain dispositions of partnership interests or beneficial interests in a trust or estate where the partnership, estate, or trust directly or indirectly owns a USRPI. (Code Sec. 1445(e)(5); Reg § 1.1445-11T(b))[20] Withholding on certain distributions of USRPIs to a foreign partner or beneficiary by a partnership, trust, or estate in a taxable transaction will also be required once implementing regs are issued. (Code Sec. 1445(e)(4); Reg § 1.1445-11T(c))[21]

The withholding obligation is generally imposed on the transferee of the USRPI, who must report (on Form 8288 and Form 8288-A) and pay over to IRS the amounts withheld by the 20th day after transfer. (Reg § 1.1445-1(c), Reg § 1.1445-1(d))[22]

Withholding is not required where the transferor gives the transferee (or a qualified substitute) (i) a sworn "nonforeign affidavit" which includes his U.S. taxpayer identification number (Code Sec. 1445(b)(2), Code Sec. 1445(b)(9)), or (ii) a sworn "non-USRPHC affidavit" stating the interest in not a USRPI (Code Sec. 1445(b)(3)), *unless* the transferee knows the relevant affidavit is false. (Code Sec. 1445(b)(7)) Withholding also does not apply if the USRPI is acquired by the transferee as his residence, and the amount realized doesn't exceed $300,000. (Code Sec. 1445(b)(5)) A transferee may also be able to obtain a qualifying statement that the transferor is exempt from withholding because he has reached an agreement with IRS concerning the payment of the underlying tax on any gain to be recognized or because no underlying tax is due. (Code Sec. 1445(b)(4))[23]

¶ 4672   Withholdable payments to foreign financial institutions (FFIs) and other foreign entities under the Foreign Account Tax Compliance Act (FATCA) — Form 8966, Form 1042, Form 1042-S.

In order to induce reporting on specified foreign accounts owned by specified U.S. persons or by U.S.-owned foreign entities, a 30% withholding tax is imposed on (i) certain payments to FFIs that do not agree to report the required information to IRS regarding their U.S. accounts, and (ii) certain payments to certain nonfinancial foreign entities (NFFEs) that do not

17. ¶O-12100 *et seq.*; ¶14,464; TD ¶634,030
18. ¶S-2718 *et seq.*; TD ¶634,031
19. ¶O-13001 *et seq.*; ¶14,454 *et seq.*; TD ¶644,000 *et seq.*
20. ¶O-13037; ¶14,454.02; TD ¶644,020

21. ¶O-13038; ¶14,454.02
22. ¶S-5662; ¶14,454; TD ¶644,006
23. ¶O-13010 *et seq.*; ¶14,454; TD ¶644,007, TD ¶644,010

provide information on their substantial U.S. owners to the withholding agent. (Code Sec. 1471 through Code Sec. 1474)[24]

Payment to FFIs. A withholding agent must withhold a tax equal to 30% of any withholdable payment (see below) made to a FFI unless the FFI: (i) enters into an FFI agreement with IRS under which it assumes specific compliance obligations (a "participating" FFI) including withholding on "passthru" payments (which are withholdable payments and foreign passthru payments) to recalcitrant account holders and nonparticipating FFIs, and reporting certain information on Form 8966; (ii) is treated as complying with certain of the compliance obligations and other reporting requirements (a "deemed-compliant" FFI); or (iii) satisfies the compliance obligations, but elects to be withheld upon rather than to withhold ("nonparticipating" FFIs), in which case withholding is required to the extent allocable to the recalcitrant account holders. A "financial institution" is any entity that: (i) accepts deposits in the ordinary course of a banking or similar business; (ii) holds financial assets for the account of others as a substantial part of its business; (iii) engages primarily in the business of investing, reinvesting, or trading in securities, partnership interests, or commodities, or any interest in them; (iv) is an insurance company that makes payments with respect to cash value insurance or annuities; and/or (v) is a holding company or treasury center related to certain functions. Certain exceptions apply. (Code Sec. 1471; Reg § 1.1471-2(a), Reg § 1.1471-5(e))[25]

Payments to nonfinancial foreign entities. A withholding agent must withhold a tax equal to 30% of any withholdable payment (see below) made to a nonfinancial foreign entity if the beneficial owner of the payment is any nonfinancial foreign entity, unless (i) the payee or the beneficial owner provides the withholding agent with either a certification that the foreign entity does not have a substantial U.S. owner or the name, address and taxpayer identification number (TIN) of each substantial U.S. owner, and (ii) certain reporting requirements are met. Withholding does not apply to "excepted NFFEs," which include certain publicly traded corporations and active NFFEs. (Code Sec. 1472; Reg § 1.1472-1)[26]

Withholdable payments. Withholdable payments re non-effectively connected (1) U.S. source "FDAP" type income (interest, dividends, etc) and (2) gross proceeds from the sale or other disposition of property that can produce interest and dividend income. (Code Sec. 1473(1); Reg § 1.1473-1(a))

Reporting requirements. Every withholding agent must file an income tax return on Form 1042 showing the aggregate amount of reportable amounts under FATCA and the tax withheld for the preceding calendar year by the withholding agent (in addition to the amounts subject to FDAP withholding, see ¶4665). The withholding agent must file an information return on Form 1042-S to report the amounts paid to a recipient (who receives a copy of the form) during the preceding calendar year. (Reg § 1.1474-1(c), Reg § 1.1474-1(d))[27]

Implementation Dates. Withholding under the FATCA regime begins on July 1, 2014, for U.S. source FDAP income, and on Jan. 1, 2017, for offshore U.S. source income, gross proceeds and foreign passthru payments. Payments on certain obligations outstanding on July 1, 2014 (grandfathered obligations) are exempt. Payments on certain preexisting obligations are also temporarily exempt.[28]

¶ 4673 Individuals must file disclosure statement for specified foreign financial assets with return—Form 8938.

Individuals with an interest in a "specified foreign financial asset" during the tax year must attach a disclosure statement (Form 8938) to their income tax return for any year in which the aggregate value of all such assets is greater than $50,000 or a specified higher threshold. (Code Sec. 6038D(a); Reg § 1.6038D-2T(a)) In addition, IRS may require disclosure

---

24. ¶O-13070 *et seq.*; ¶14,714 *et seq.*
25. ¶O-13072; ¶14,714.1 *et seq.*
26. ¶O-13072, O-13094; ¶14,724, 14,724.1

27. ¶S-3471.1 *et seq.*; ¶14,744
28. ¶O-13071 *et seq.*; ¶14,714.1 *et seq.*

for any domestic entity formed or availed of for purposes of holding, directly or indirectly, specified foreign financial assets. (Code Sec. 6038D(f))

"Specified foreign financial assets" are: (1) depository or custodial accounts at foreign financial institutions, and (2) to the extent not held in an account at a financial institution, (a) stocks or securities issued by foreign persons, (b) any other financial instrument or contract held for investment that is issued by or has a counterparty that is not a U.S. person, and (c) any interest in a foreign entity. (Code Sec. 6038D(b); Reg § 1.6038D-3T)

Individuals who fail to make the required disclosures are subject to a penalty of $10,000, with additional penalties for continued noncompliance, up to a $50,000 maximum penalty. (Code Sec. 6038D(d); Reg § 1.6038D-8T) The penalty is subject to a reasonable cause exception. (Code Sec. 6038D(g)) For assessment purposes, if an individual with an interest in one or more financial assets doesn't provide sufficient information to determine the value of the assets, the aggregate value is presumed to exceed $50,000 (or any higher threshold amount prescribed by IRS). (Code Sec. 6038D(e))

There are exceptions from the reporting requirements to avoid duplicative reporting requirements and for bona fide residents of a U.S. possession. (Reg § 1.6038D-7T) IRS may prescribe additional exceptions by regs or other guidance. (Code Sec. 6038D(h))[29]

¶ 4674   Foreign Currency Rules. ▬▬▬▬▬▬▬▬▬▬▬▬▬▬▬▬▬▬▬

Transactions involving foreign currency must be expressed in U.S. dollars for U.S. tax purposes.

¶ 4675   Functional currency.

U.S. taxpayers are required to make all federal income tax determinations in their "functional currency." (Code Sec. 985(a))[30] A U.S. taxpayer's functional currency is generally the U.S. dollar (Code Sec. 985(b)(1)(A)), unless it has a "qualified business unit" (QBU) that uses the currency of the economic environment in which a significant part of its activities are conducted and which is used to keep its books and records. (Code Sec. 985(b)(1)(B)). A QBU may elect to use the U.S. dollar instead if it meets certain requirements. (Code Sec. 985(b)(3))[31]

A QBU is any separate and clearly identified unit (or activity) of a trade or business of a taxpayer which maintains separate books and records. (Code Sec. 989(a)) A corporation is a QBU and a partnership, trust or estate is a QBU of a partner or beneficiary. An individual is not a QBU. (Reg § 1.989(a)-1(b)(2)(i))[32] If a U.S. taxpayer has one or more QBUs with non-dollar functional currencies, profits and losses are computed separately for each unit in its functional currency, and are then translated into dollars at the appropriate exchange rate. (Code Sec. 987)[33]

¶ 4676   Foreign currency gains and losses; section 988 transactions.

Foreign currency gain or loss attributable to a "section 988 transaction" must generally be computed separately for each transaction and treated as ordinary income or expense, as the case may be. (Code Sec. 988(a)(1)(A)) However, a taxpayer may elect to treat the foreign currency gain or loss attributable to certain forward contracts, futures contracts, or option as capital gain or loss. (Code Sec. 988(a)(1)(B))[34] A "section 988 transaction" is (i) the acquisition of a debt instrument or becoming the obligor under a debt instrument, (ii) the accruing (or otherwise taking into account) of an item of expense or gross income or receipts which is to be paid or received after the accrual date, or (iii) the entering into or acquiring of a forward contract, futures contract, option, or similar financial instrument, if the amount the taxpayer

29. ¶S-3650.1 *et seq.*; ¶60,38D4; TD ¶815,516   32. ¶G-6912
30. ¶G-6900 *et seq.*; ¶9854 *et seq.*   33. ¶G-6978; ¶9874
31. ¶G-6901; ¶9854   34. ¶G-7001, G-7024

is entitled to receive, or is required to pay, by reason of such transaction is either: (1) denominated in terms of a nonfunctional currency; or (2) determined by reference to the value of one or more nonfunctional currencies. (Code Sec. 988(c)(1))[35]

The source of currency gains and losses is determined by reference to the residence of the taxpayer or qualified business unit (QBU) on whose books the relevant asset, liability, or item of income or expense is properly reflected. A special source rule applies for certain related party loans. (Code Sec. 988(a)(3))[36]

Two or more separate transactions may be integrated into a single "section 988 hedging transaction" which is taxed in accordance with its economic substance. (Code Sec. 988(d); Reg § 1.988-5)[37]

The Code Sec. 988 rules do not apply to a personal transaction (any transaction entered into by an individual unless the expenses properly allocable to it qualify as deductible business or investment expenses) unless the gain that would otherwise be recognized exceeds $200. An individual recognizes no gain from the fluctuations in exchange rates upon the disposition of foreign currency in a personal transaction. (Code Sec. 988(e))[38]

¶ 4677 Reporting Gifts from Foreign Persons.

U.S. persons must report certain gifts from foreign persons.

¶ 4678 Reporting foreign gifts—Form 3520.

If the value of the aggregate foreign gifts received by a U.S. person (other than an exempt Code Sec. 501(c) organization) exceeds a specified threshold amount (below), the U.S. person must report (on Form 3520) each foreign gift to IRS. (Code Sec. 6039F(a)) "Foreign gifts" include any amounts received from a non-U.S. person that the recipient treats as a gift or bequest. The term doesn't include any qualified tuition or medical payments made on behalf of a U.S. person or any distribution from a foreign trust that was properly disclosed under Code Sec. 6048(c)). (Code Sec. 6039F(b))

For gifts from a nonresident alien or foreign estate, reporting of gifts over $5,000 is required only if the aggregate amount of gifts from that person exceeds $100,000 during the tax year. For gifts from foreign corporations and foreign partnerships, the reporting threshold amount is an inflation-adjusted aggregate amount of gifts of $15,102 for tax years beginning in 2013. For gifts made in 2014, the reporting threshold is $15,358.[39]

---

35. ¶G-6988 *et seq.*; ¶9884 *et seq.*
36. ¶G-7029; ¶9884.01
37. ¶G-7037; ¶9884.02

38. ¶G-7047, ¶G-7048; ¶9884.01
39. ¶S-3649.1 *et seq.*; ¶60,39F4; TD ¶746,002

Chapter 24   Returns and Payment of Tax

¶ 4700   Returns and Payment of Tax. ▪▪▪▪▪▪▪▪▪

An individual taxpayer must file an income tax return if his gross income equals or exceeds a specified amount. Married taxpayers may file a joint return. Corporations, trusts and estates must also file income tax returns. A partnership files an information return of income. Payors and others must file information returns to report specified payments, sales, etc. Times, places and methods of paying tax are specified.

¶ 4701   Who must file individual income tax returns?

An income tax return must be filed by every individual U.S. citizen and resident alien (including an alien who is a bona fide resident of Puerto Rico during the entire tax year) (Reg § 1.1-1(b), Reg § 1.6012-1(a)(1)) and nonresident or dual-status alien married to a U.S. citizen or resident at year-end who elects to be treated as a resident alien (Reg § 1.6013-6(a))[1] who has gross income (including excluded homesale gain and foreign earned income (Code Sec. 6012(c)) that equals or exceeds the following amounts:

	2013	2014
(1) Single (Code Sec. 6012(a)(1)(A)(i))	$10,000	$10,150
—65-or-over (Code Sec. 6012(a)(1)(B))	11,500	11,700
(2) Married filing joint return (Code Sec. 6012(a)(1)(A)(iv))	20,000	20,300
—one 65-or-over (Code Sec. 6012(a)(1)(B))	21,200	21,500
—both 65-or-over (Code Sec. 6012(a)(1)(B))	22,400	22,700
(3) Married filing separate return (Code Sec. 6012(a)(1)(A))	3,900	3,950
(4) Head of Household (Code Sec. 6012(a)(1)(A)(ii))	12,850	13,050
—65-or-over (Code Sec. 6012(a)(1)(B))	14,350	14,600
(5) Surviving spouse (Code Sec. 6012(a)(1)(A)(iii))	16,100	16,350
—65-or-over (Code Sec. 6012(a)(1)(B))	17,300	17,550

If an individual can be claimed as a dependent, that individual/dependent must file a return if (a) his unearned income exceeds $1,000 for 2013 ($1,000 for 2014), plus any additional standard deduction (¶3112), or (b) his total gross income is more than the standard deduction (¶3112). (Code Sec. 6012(a)(1)(C)(i))[2] A married dependent whose spouse files a separate return and itemizes deductions must file if he has gross income of $5 or more.[3] But, no return is required for a child where the parent elects (¶3139) to include the child's income on the parent's return. For 2013, the election is available if the child's income exceeds $1,000 ($1,000 for 2014) and is less than $10,000 ($10,000 for 2014). (Code Sec. 1(g)(7)(A))[4]

The filing threshold in (2), above, applies only if the spouses, at the end of the tax year, had the same household as their home (Code Sec. 6012(a)(1)(A)(iv)) and no other taxpayer could claim an exemption for either spouse. (Code Sec. 6012(a)(1)(A))

Individuals who file a short year return due to an accounting period change must file if gross income received during the short year equals or exceeds $3,900 for 2013 ($3,950 for 2014), prorated in the ratio that the short year's months bear to 12. (Reg § 1.6012-1(a)(2)(v))[5]

---

1. ¶S-1701; ¶60,124.02; TD ¶570,201
2. ¶S-1705; ¶60,124; TD ¶570,204
3. ¶S-1705; TD ¶570,204
4. ¶S-1704.1; ¶14.11; TD ¶568,400
5. ¶S-1707; ¶60,124; TD ¶570,206

References beginning with a single letter are to paragraphs in RIA's Federal Tax Coordinator 2d and RIA's Analysis of Federal Taxes: Income. Those beginning with numbers are to paragraphs in RIA's United States Tax Reporter. Those beginning with TD are to paragraphs in RIA's Tax Desk.

The following may have to file an income tax return even though they have gross income below the levels listed above: individuals received tips from which social security tax wasn't withheld;[6] individuals owing AMT;[7] employees who receive more than $108.28 of wages from a church or church-controlled organization that is exempt from payroll taxes;[8] individuals receiving income from U.S. possessions;[9] nonresident aliens (NRAs)[10] but not NRAs who earn less than the personal exemption;[11] individuals who change their citizenship or country of residence during the year;[12] individuals who must pay a tax with respect to an IRA or other tax-favored account (if filing only for this reason, use Form 5329 by itself);[13] individuals who owe uncollected payroll tax on group-term life insurance;[14] individuals who owe recapture tax on certain credits;[15] and certain self-employed individuals (¶4713).

The individual filing thresholds for a decedent's final return aren't reduced or prorated. [16]

Returns for minors and others who are incapable of filing their own returns should be filed for them by their guardians or fiduciaries. A minor may make his own return. (Reg § 1.6012-3(b)(3))[17] For the election to claim a child's income on a parent's return, see ¶3139.

¶ 4702   Individual income tax returns—Forms 1040, 1040A, and 1040EZ.

U.S. citizens and residents use Form 1040 (Reg § 1.6012-1(a)(6)), Form 1040A (Reg § 1.6012-1(a)(7)(i)), or Form 1040EZ. Form 1040A may be used by a taxpayer in any filing status who: (1) has income only from wages, salaries, tips, interest, ordinary dividends, capital gain distributions, taxable scholarships and fellowship grants, pensions, annuities, IRAs, unemployment compensation, taxable social security and railroad retirement benefits, and AK Permanent Fund dividends; (2), can only claim certain adjustments to gross income (deductions for educator expenses, IRA contributions, student loan interest, and tuition and fees); (3) doesn't itemize deductions; (4) has taxable income less than $100,000; and (5) has only certain tax credits. Form 1040A may be used even if the taxpayer owes AMT.[18]

Single or married filing jointly taxpayers under 65 who aren't blind can use Form 1040EZ if they claim no dependents, have income only from wages, salaries, tips, taxable scholarships or fellowships, unemployment compensation, AK Permanent Fund dividends, and interest (of $1,500 or less), no adjustments to gross income, no itemized deductions, taxable income of less than $100,000 and no tax credits other than the earned income credit (EIC).[19]

¶ 4703   E-filing individual returns.

Tax preparers can e-file current year returns (Form 1040, Form 1040A and Form 1040EZ) (but not after Oct. 15 even with a filing extension) and Form 4868 automatic filing extensions for individual taxpayers,[20] including returns that show a balance due.[21] But, e-filing isn't allowed for returns for years other than the current tax year, amended returns, fiscal year returns, or in certain other situations.[22]

An electronic return may be a composite return consisting of electronically transmitted data and of paper documents (filed later) that can't be electronically transmitted, or it may be completely paperless.[23] There are procedures for accepting digital or electronic signatures. (Code Sec. 6061(b))[24] All taxpayers who e-file their returns have to use electronic signatures

---

6. ¶S-1709; ¶60,124; TD ¶570,203
7. ¶S-1716; ¶60,124; TD ¶570,215
8. ¶S-1718; ¶60,124; TD ¶570,217
9. ¶S-1704.3; ¶60,124.02; TD ¶570,207
10. ¶S-1750 *et seq.*; ¶60,124.02
11. ¶S-1755
12. ¶S-1758
13. ¶S-1708.1; ¶60,124; TD ¶570,203
14. ¶S-1708.1; ¶60,124; TD ¶570,208
15. ¶S-1708.1; ¶60,124; TD ¶570,203

16. ¶C-9602, ¶C-9603; ¶60,124.04; TD ¶579,501
17. ¶S-1704.1; ¶s 60,124, 60,124.04; TD ¶570,211
18. ¶S-1715; ¶60,114.01; TD ¶570,214
19. ¶S-1715; ¶60,114.01; TD ¶570,214
20. ¶S-1601; ¶60,114.08; TD ¶572,010
21. ¶S-1617; ¶60,114.08; TD ¶572,029
22. ¶S-1604; TD ¶572,009
23. ¶S-1601.2 *et seq.*; ¶S-1601.4; ¶60,114.08; TD ¶572,005
24. ¶S-4518; ¶60,614

under 1 of 2 methods: either a self-select Personal Identification Number (PIN) or a practitioner PIN. Practitioner PINs require the use of Form 8879, which is retained by the practitioner.[25] For submitting payments, see ¶4720.

¶ 4704   Spouses—joint or separate returns.

Married persons (including married same-sex couples, see ¶4705) can choose to file a joint return (reporting their combined taxable income) (Code Sec. 6013(a))[26] or a separate return. (Code Sec. 1(d))[27]

Neither a return prepared and executed by IRS nor a Form 870 waiver is a valid election to file a joint return.[28]

observation: Filing separately may save taxes due to the floors on some deductions (e.g., medical expenses, miscellaneous itemized deductions, casualty losses). Each floor is measured against AGI, so if either spouse has high amounts of these expenses, measuring them against a separate AGI can produce a larger deduction than if measured against joint AGI. But, any advantages may be offset by many restrictive rules for separate filers.

Separate returns. Each spouse is liable only for his own tax and penalties.[29]

Joint returns. Except as noted at ¶4709 to ¶4711, each spouse is jointly and severally liable for the full amount of the tax, penalties (other than civil fraud (¶4882)), and interest arising out of their joint return, regardless of the amount of his separate taxable income. (Code Sec. 6013(d)(3)) Only the spouse committing fraud can be subjected to fraud penalties.[30]

¶ 4705   Married defined for joint return purposes.

To file a joint return (¶4704), individuals must be legally married as of the *end* of the tax year. (Code Sec. 6013(d))[31] If the spouses filed a joint return during their "marriage" and later get an annulment, they must refile as separate unmarried persons.[32]

After Sept. 16, 2013, the terms "spouse," "husband and wife," "husband," and "wife" include an individual married to a person of the same sex if the individuals are lawfully married under state law, and the term "marriage" includes a marriage between same sex individuals. IRS recognizes a marriage of same-sex individuals that was validly entered into under the law of the state in which it was performed ("state of celebration"), even if the married couple is domiciled in a state that does not recognize same-sex marriage. Marriage does not include a registered domestic partnership, civil union, or other similar formal relationship recognized under state law that is not denominated as a marriage. This guidance is based on *Windsor* (Supreme Court decision striking down federal prohibitions on the recognition of same-sex marriages, see ¶5021).[33]

For tax year 2013 and going forward, same-sex spouses generally must file using a married filing separately or jointly filing status. Same-sex spouses generally may, but are not required to, file amended returns for earlier open tax years.

¶ 4706   Qualifying for joint returns.

Spouses may file a joint return even if only one has income (Code Sec. 6013(a))[34] and even if they have different accounting *methods.*

A joint return *can't* be filed if: (a) *either spouse was a nonresident alien* (NRA) at any time during the tax year (Code Sec. 6013(a)(1)),[35] but where 1 spouse is an NRA for the entire year

---

25. ¶S-1617.3
26. ¶S-1801; ¶60,134 *et seq.*; TD ¶570,601
27. ¶A-1502; ¶14.01; TD ¶566,002
28. ¶S-1827
29. ¶V-8504; TD ¶570,903
30. ¶V-8502; ¶s 60,134.05, 66,534.11; TD ¶570,901

31. ¶S-1803; ¶60,134.03; TD ¶570,602
32. ¶A-1609; ¶60,134.03; TD ¶566,509
33. ¶A-1603; ¶K-2141.5; TD ¶566,503
34. ¶S-1801; ¶60,134; TD ¶570,601
35. ¶S-1802; ¶60,134; TD ¶570,601

(Code Sec. 6013(g)) or where an NRA spouse becomes a U.S. resident during the tax year (Code Sec. 6013(h)), spouses can file jointly if they agree to subject their worldwide income to U.S. tax;[36] or (b) *the spouses have different tax years,* except when 1 spouse dies, see ¶4708.

¶ 4707 Changing from joint to separate returns and vice versa.

Once a joint return has been filed, spouses may revoke it by filing separate returns up until the return's due date. After the due date, they can't switch. (Reg § 1.6013-1(a))[37]

observation: A couple may file jointly in 1 year and separately in another.

A married couple who filed separate returns may switch to a joint return after the due date if: (a) the joint return is filed within 3 years from the original due date (without extension), and (b) neither spouse has, with respect to his previously filed separate return, petitioned the Tax Court, filed a suit for refund, or entered into a closing agreement or final compromise. (Code Sec. 6013(b); Reg § 1.6013-2(b))[38]

¶ 4708 Joint return for year spouse(s) dies.

A joint return may be filed for spouses where their tax years start on the same day and end on different days because of the death of either or both (unless the surviving spouse (SS) remarries before the end of his tax year). The joint return must for the tax year of each. (Code Sec. 6013(a)(2))[39] For when to file, see ¶4716.

recommendation: File a joint return to get the benefits of the joint return rates, and to use up decedent's (DS's) net operating loss, capital loss, charitable contribution carryforwards, or other expiring deductions or credits, if SS has income or can generate income before the end of SS's tax year.

SS may file the joint return if: DS hasn't already filed a return for the tax year; an executor wasn't appointed when the joint return is made; and an executor hasn't been appointed before the due date (with extensions) for filing SS's return. (Code Sec. 6013(a)(3))[40]

observation: The return for the year before the year of death also is subject to these rules if DS died before filing a return for that year.

If an executor or administrator is appointed by the filing due date, SS *can't* file a joint return for DS. Only the fiduciary can act for DS, so both the fiduciary and SS must sign the joint return. Even if SS properly filed a joint return (because no fiduciary had been appointed by the due date), the fiduciary may disaffirm (revoke) the joint return by filing a *separate* return for DS within 1 year after the due date (including extensions). Any "joint" return improperly filed by SS or disaffirmed by the fiduciary is treated as SS's *separate* return. (Code Sec. 6013(a)(3))[41] For when SS can use joint return *rates,* see ¶3132.

¶ 4709 Elective relief from joint tax liability (innocent spouse rule)—Form 8857.

Unless an exception (¶4712) applies, an individual who has filed a joint return may elect relief from joint and several liability (¶4704) under innocent spouse rules. (Code Sec. 6015(a)(1)) An individual is relieved of liability for tax, interest, penalties, etc. for a tax year to the extent the liability is due to an understatement if: (a) a joint return was filed for the tax year; (b) there's an understatement of tax on the return due to the other spouse's erroneous items; (c) the individual shows that, in signing the return, he didn't know or had no reason to know of the understatement; (d) under the facts and circumstances, it would be inequitable to hold the individual liable for the deficiency; and (e) the individual elects the benefits of the innocent spouse rules, by filing Form 8857 (separately from the tax return)

36. ¶A-1800 *et seq.*; ¶60,134.01; TD ¶567,501
37. ¶S-1831; ¶60,134.01; TD ¶570,622
38. ¶S-1829; ¶60,134.01; TD ¶570,620

39. ¶S-1805; ¶60,134; TD ¶570,603
40. ¶S-1806; ¶60,134; TD ¶570,604
41. ¶S-1806; ¶60,134; TD ¶570,605

and the required attached statement, no later than 2 years after IRS has begun collection activities against the individual. (Code Sec. 6015(b)(1))[42]

> **©✓observation:** Innocent spouse relief isn't available for unpaid liabilities that were properly reported on a joint return, because in that situation there's no understatement of tax. However, equitable relief (¶4711) may be available.

A spouse who knew or had reason to know of the understatement, but shows that he didn't know or have reason to know of its *extent*, can be relieved of liability to the extent of the understatement of which he didn't know or have reason to know. (Code Sec. 6015(b)(2))[43]

Special innocent spouse relief applies to a spouse of a partner in a partnership subject to unified partnership audit procedures (¶4840).

Any determination of innocent spouse relief is made without regard to the operation of community property laws. (Reg § 1.6015-1(f)(1))[44] For a spouse's separate liability election, see ¶4710.

Upon receipt of a request for relief (¶4710; ¶4711), IRS must send a notice to the nonrequesting spouse's last known address informing that spouse of the requesting spouse's claim for relief. (Reg § 1.6015-6(a)(1)) The nonrequesting spouse may file a protest and receive an IRS appeals conference regarding a determination. IRS's procedures protect domestic abuse victims who fear retaliation for applying for innocent spouse relief.[45] The nonrequesting spouse may also intervene to support the requesting spouse's innocent spouse claim.[46]

¶ 4710   Separate liability ("allocation of liability") election—Form 8857.

An individual who files a joint return and meets the eligibility requirements can elect to limit his liability for a deficiency. The separate liability election may be made in addition to the innocent spouse election (¶4709). (Code Sec. 6015(a)(2))[47] This relief is available only for unpaid liabilities from understatements; refunds aren't allowed. (Reg § 1.6015-3(c)(1))[48]

An individual can elect only if, when the election is filed, he's no longer married to, or is legally separated from, the spouse with whom the joint return was filed, or wasn't a member of the same household as that spouse at any time during the previous 12-month period. If IRS shows that assets were transferred between spouses in a fraudulent scheme joined in by both spouses, a separate liability election by either spouse is invalid. (Code Sec. 6015(c)(3)(A))[49]

To elect, file Form 8857 (separately from the return) with specified attachments no later than 2 years after IRS begins collection activity against the electing spouse. (Code Sec. 6015(c)(3)(B); Reg § 1.6015-5)[50] For equitable claims, see ¶4711.

Except as provided below, an electing spouse's liability for a deficiency that IRS assesses won't exceed the portion of the deficiency properly allocable to that spouse. (Code Sec. 6015(c)(1), Code Sec. 6015(d)(3)(A))[1] The liability is generally allocated between the spouses in proportion to the net items taken into account in determining the deficiency as if separate returns were filed. (Code Sec. 6015(d)(1))[2] But, the limitation on an electing spouse's tax liability is increased by the value of property transferred to that spouse by the nonelecting spouse principally to avoid tax, which is rebuttably presumed (except for divorce or separate maintenance transfers) to be the case for transfers made anytime after 1 year before the first letter of proposed deficiency is sent. (Code Sec. 6015(c)(4))[3] Also, except where a joint return was signed under duress, the election doesn't apply to the extent that IRS has evidence that the electing spouse had *actual* knowledge of an item giving rise to all or part of a deficiency

---

42. ¶V-8506 *et seq.*; ¶60,154.01; TD ¶570,904
43. ¶V-8516; ¶60,154.01; TD ¶570,905
44. ¶V-8511
45. ¶V-8550
46. ¶U-2152
47. ¶V-8533; ¶60,154.02; TD ¶570,933

48. ¶T-5513
49. ¶V-8534; ¶60,154.02; TD ¶570,934
50. ¶V-8536; ¶60,154.02; TD ¶570,936
1. ¶V-8537; ¶60,154.02; TD ¶570,941
2. ¶V-8539; ¶60,154.02; TD ¶570,939
3. ¶V-8538; ¶60,154.02; TD ¶570,938

allocable to the other spouse. (Code Sec. 6015(c)(3)(C))[4]

¶ 4711 Equitable relief for spouses—Form 8857.

If under all the facts and circumstances it's inequitable to hold a spouse liable for any portion of any unpaid tax or deficiency, and relief isn't available under the innocent spouse (¶4709) or separate liability election (¶4710) rules, IRS may relieve that spouse of liability for that unpaid tax or deficiency (Code Sec. 6015(f); Reg § 1.6015-4) and in limited cases may issue a refund. To request equitable relief, file Form 8857 (separately from the tax return) with specified attached statement. (Reg § 1.6015-5(a))

For relief requests filed after Sept. 15, 2013 or for requests pending on Sept. 15, 2013, these threshold conditions must be met for equitable relief:

(1) The requesting spouse filed a joint return for the tax year for which relief is sought.

(2) Relief isn't available under Code Sec. 6015(b) or Code Sec. 6015(c).

(3) The relief claim must be timely filed. Requests must be made before the collection statute expiration date (CSED) under Code Sec. 6502 or within the limitations period on credits or refunds in Code Sec. 6511.

(4) No assets were transferred between the spouses as part of a fraudulent scheme.

(5) The nonrequesting spouse didn't transfer disqualified assets to the requesting spouse. If there were transfers, relief is limited to the extent the liability exceeds the assets' value.

(6) The requesting spouse didn't knowingly file a fraudulent joint return.

(7) The liability is attributable (in full or partially) to an item of the nonrequesting spouse or an underpayment from the nonrequesting spouse's income.[5]

IRS will make a streamlined determination where a requesting spouse establishes that the requesting spouse: (a) is no longer married to the nonrequesting spouse; (b) would suffer economic hardship if relief isn't granted; and (c) did not know or have reason to know of the understatement or deficiency. If a requesting spouse doesn't qualify for a streamlined determination, IRS considers these factors (a nonexclusive list): marital status; economic hardship (based on federal poverty guidelines) if relief isn't granted; knowledge or reason to know of the item giving rise to the understatement or underpayment; abuse by the nonrequesting spouse; whether either spouse had a legal obligation to pay the liability; whether the requesting spouse significantly benefitted; whether the requesting spouse has made a good faith effort to comply with the tax law in tax years after the year for which the request is made; and whether the requesting spouse was in poor physical or mental health.[6]

If the nonrequesting spouse abused the requesting spouse or maintained control over the household finances by restricting the requesting spouse's access to financial information, IRS may: (i) consider certain threshold conditions and the conditions for streamlined determinations met, or (ii) weigh certain factors in favor of relief.

The Tax Court reviews denied claims under a de novo standard.[7]

¶ 4712 Exceptions to innocent spouse relief.

Innocent spouse relief (¶4709, ¶4710, ¶4711) isn't available: (1) for liabilities other than income taxes, (e.g. "nanny" taxes, see ¶3030), that are reported on a joint federal income tax return (Reg § 1.6015-1(a)(3));[8] (2) for a tax year for which the spouse seeking relief has entered into an offer in compromise or a closing agreement with IRS that disposes of the liability (Reg § 1.6015-1(c));[9] or (3) if a spouse transferred assets to the other spouse as part of a fraudulent scheme to defraud IRS or another third party. (Reg § 1.6015-1(d))[10]

---

4. ¶V-8549; ¶60,154.02; TD ¶570,949
5. ¶V-8553; ¶V-8554.11; ¶V-8550.1; ¶60,154.04; TD ¶570,928
6. ¶V-8554; ¶60,154.04; TD ¶570,954
7. ¶V-8554; ¶60,154.04; TD ¶570,954

8. ¶V-8501; ¶60,154
9. ¶V-8506.1A; ¶60,154
10. ¶V-8506.1A; ¶60,154; TD ¶570,935

¶ 4713   Self-employed individuals' tax returns—Form 1040 and Schedule SE.

Individuals (except nonresident aliens) who have $400 or more net earnings from self-employment (¶3143) have to file Form 1040 (including Form 1040, Schedule SE) even if the individual's gross income is less than the filing thresholds (¶4701). (Code Sec. 6017) Report self-employment tax (¶3140) on Form 1040.[11]

¶ 4714   Decedent's final return.

A final income tax return must be filed for a deceased person who would be required to file if alive, for the part of the year up to the date of death. A decedent's final return is filed by the person entrusted with his property (e.g., the estate's executor). (Code Sec. 6012(b)(1))[12] For refunds, see ¶4847.[13] For a surviving spouse's joint return, see ¶4708. For personal exemption and standard deduction on a decedent's final return, see ¶3116 and ¶3112.[14] For due date, see ¶4716. For the income and deductions reportable on the return, see ¶3965.

🅡 recommendation: Even though a final return may not otherwise be required, file one to claim any refund due for tax withheld from salary or for estimated tax paid.

¶ 4715   U.S. military and civilian employees dying in combat/terrorist attacks.

If a military or civilian employee of the U.S. dies as a result of wounds or injury sustained in a terrorist or military action, income tax won't apply for the year of death and any earlier year beginning with the last year ending before the year in which the wounds or injury were sustained. (Code Sec. 692(c)(1)) IRS has outlined procedures for determining whether a terrorist or military action has occurred. Refund of withheld or estimated taxes may be claimed by filing Form 1040, or, on an amended return (Form 1040X). On joint returns, the tax liability is allocated between the deceased and surviving spouses.[15]

¶ 4716   When and where to file individual returns.

Income tax returns (including self-employment tax returns and a decedent's final return) of U.S. citizens and resident aliens must be filed by the 15th day of the 4th month following the end of the tax year (Apr. 15 for calendar year taxpayers) at the address specified on the form or in the instructions. (Code Sec. 6072(a); Reg § 1.6072-1(a)(1), Reg § 1.6072-1(b))[16] For a nonresident alien's return, see ¶4657.

A "short period return" must be filed by the 15th day of the 4th month following the end of the short period. (Reg § 1.6071-1(b))[17]

¶ 4717   Extensions of time for filing individual returns—Form 4868.

File Form 4868 to get an automatic 6-month filing extension (until Oct. 15 for a calendar year taxpayer). (Reg § 1.6081-4)[18] The form must show the full amount properly estimated as tax for the year but it doesn't have to include payment of the balance of the tax estimated to be due. (Reg § 1.6081-4(b))[19] Failure to include the balance due won't affect the extension, but interest and penalties apply.[20] Extension requests may be e-filed.[21] For payment extensions, see ¶4721. IRS can terminate extensions on 10 days' notice. (Reg § 1.6081-4(d))[22]

Extensions can't exceed 6 months unless the taxpayer is abroad. (Code Sec. 6081(a))[23]

---

11. ¶S-1717; ¶14,024; ¶60,174TD ¶570,216
12. ¶C-9601, S-2003; ¶60,124.04; TD ¶570,212, TD ¶579,501
13. ¶T-5710; ¶60,124.04; TD ¶802,039
14. ¶C-9602 *et seq.*; TD ¶579,507
15. ¶C-9660; ¶6924; TD ¶579,601
16. ¶S-4701 *et seq.*; ¶S-5100 *et seq.*; ¶60,724; ¶60,914; TD ¶570,219 *et seq.*; TD ¶570,225

17. ¶S-4701; ¶60,724; TD ¶570,219
18. ¶S-5011; ¶60,814.03; TD ¶570,301
19. ¶S-5013; ¶60,814.03; TD ¶570,301
20. ¶s S-5010, S-5011; ¶60,814.03; TD ¶570,301
21. ¶S-1606; ¶60,814.03; TD ¶570,301
22. ¶S-5009; ¶60,814.03; TD ¶570,301
23. ¶S-5003; ¶60,814.01; TD ¶570,302

¶ 4718   Extension for citizen or resident with non-U.S. tax home—Forms 4868, 2350.

A U.S. citizen or resident whose tax home and abode is outside the U.S. and Puerto Rico (Reg § 1.6081-5(a)(5)) and a U.S. citizen or resident in military or naval service on duty outside the U.S. and Puerto Rico (Reg § 1.6081-5(a)(6)) get automatic extensions until the 15th day of the sixth month after the end of the tax year. A statement must be attached to the return which shows that the taxpayer qualified for the extension. (Reg § 1.6081-5(b)) The automatic 6-month extension for individuals (¶4717) runs concurrently with the 2-month extension of time to file. (Reg § 1.6081-4(a))

🅡🅘🅐*Illustration:* On Apr. 15, T, a U.S. citizen using the calendar year, has a tax home outside the U.S. and Puerto Rico. T's tax return and tax payment are due on June 15. If T files Form 4868 by June 15 and pays any estimated unpaid tax, T has until Oct. 15 to file.

U.S. citizens or resident aliens who expect to qualify for the foreign earned income exclusion (¶4612) (and owe no tax), but not until more than 2 months after the regular return due date, should file extension request Form 2350 by that due date. (Reg § 1.911-7(c)(2))[24]

¶ 4719   Combat zone, declared disaster, terrorist or military action extensions.

Individuals serving in the U.S. armed forces in a Presidentially-designated area as a "combat zone" (¶1223) or in a 10 USC §101(a)(13) "contingency operation" can suspend the period of time to perform various tax actions (e.g., tax return filing). (Code Sec. 7508) The suspension also applies to individuals serving in support of the Armed Forces in a combat zone, or acting under the Armed Forces' direction. These individuals are allowed extra time to perform tax acts (e.g., filing of a return, or filing a refund claim, etc.) and the period is extended for the determination and assessment of their federal tax liability. (Code Sec. 7508(a)(1)) The suspension includes (1) any period of continuous hospitalization as a result of injury received while serving in the combat zone, and (2) time in missing in action status plus a 180-day period after the termination of service or hospitalization.[25]

IRS may allow taxpayers affected by a Code Sec. 165(h)(3)(C)(i) "federally-declared" disaster or a Code Sec. 692(c)(2) terrorist or military action to extend for up to 1 year (1) the timely performance of acts under Code Sec. 7508(a)(1) (including filing a return); (2) the amount of any interest, penalty, additional amount, or addition to tax due for periods after the disaster date; and (3) the amount of any tax credit or refund.[26] (Code Sec. 7508A) IRS has specified acts subject to postponement,[27] (Reg § 301.7508A-1) including disasters occurring in 2013.[28]

On notice to IRS, the collection of income tax of a servicemember falling due before or during his military service is deferred up to 180 days after termination of the taxpayer's service (or his release from it), if his ability to pay the tax is materially affected by the military service. No interest or penalty will accrue for this deferment period because of the nonpayment of any deferred amount. Also, the running of the statute of limitations against the collection of any deferred amount, by seizure or otherwise, is suspended for the period of service plus 270 days.[29] For tax relief for military and civilian employees of the U.S. dying in combat or terrorist attacks, see ¶4715.

¶ 4720   Payment of taxes due—Form 1040-V.

The tax is due on the original due date for filing the return despite any extensions of time for *filing* the return. (Code Sec. 6151(a); Reg § 1.6151-1(a))[30] If IRS computes the tax, the tax

---

24. ¶S-5020; ¶9114.13; TD ¶570,305
25. ¶S-8007; ¶75,084; TD ¶138,018
26. ¶S-8502; ¶75,08A4; TD ¶868,531 *et seq.*
27. ¶S-8012; ¶75,08A4; TD ¶570,306

28. ¶S-8501.16; TD ¶570,317.7
29. ¶S-8001; ¶63,014.04; TD ¶904,001
30. ¶S-5451; ¶61,514; TD ¶570,226

due date is the later of the thirtieth day after the date IRS mails the tax bill or the tax return due date. (Reg § 1.6151-1(b))[31] The automatic filing extension for taxpayers with a tax home and abode, or in military service, outside the U.S. (¶4718), also extends the time for payment. (Reg § 1.6081-5(a))[32] For treatment of extension requests without full payment, see ¶4717.

Taxpayers with a balance due on a return use Form 1040-V to make their payments, make a credit card payment by phone or by Internet, or make a payment using the electronic federal tax payment system (EFTPS).[33] Make tax payments by check or money order payable to the U.S. Treasury. Receipt of the check is payment, if the check is honored. IRS will accept personal checks or money orders drawn on any U.S. financial institution if the check or money order is payable in U.S. currency at par. Express, telegraphic, and similar money orders are also acceptable. (Reg § 301.6311-1)[34]

Taxes (including interest and penalties) can be paid by any commercially acceptable means that IRS deems appropriate by regs, including approved credit or debit cards as provided in IRS forms, etc. (Code Sec. 6311(a), Code Sec. 6311(d)(1); Reg § 301.6311-2) Taxpayers can: (1) authorize IRS to debit a bank account for the unpaid balance, or (2) make credit or debit card payments through tax software, by phone, or online. IRS doesn't set or collect any fees for credit or debit card payments, but convenience fees may be charged by these service providers: Official Payments Corp. (888-872-9829; OfficialPayments.com/fed; 866-964-2552; ChoicePay.com/fed); Link2Gov Corp. (888-729-1040; Pay1040.com; Businesstaxpayment.com); and WorldPay US, Inc (PayUSAtax.com; 888-972-9829). All filers (paper or electronic) may use this system to charge taxes to credit or debit cards. The option to pay taxes by credit or debit card also applies to payments with automatic extensions and to estimated tax payments. Taxpayers who charge a payment with an automatic extension request or who charge an estimated tax payment do not need to file the respective paper Form 4868 or Form 1040-ES.[35]

Tax payment by credit or debit card is deemed made when the issuer properly authorizes the transaction, provided payment is actually received by IRS in the ordinary course of business and isn't returned due to error resolution processing. (Reg § 301.6311-2(b))[36]

Where quarterly estimated tax payments (¶3154) aren't necessary, payments are generally made with the individual's return (¶4716).[37]

¶ 4721   Extension of time for paying individual income tax—Form 1127.

Apply on Form 1127 for a reasonable extension of time (not to exceed 6 months, unless taxpayer is abroad) to pay the tax. (Code Sec. 6161(a)(1)) File by the due date for payment of the tax. (Reg § 1.6161-1(c)) IRS grants extensions, generally within 30 days, only on a satisfactory showing that payment on the due date will result in undue hardship (more than an inconvenience), e.g., that taxpayer would have to sell property at a great financial sacrifice (i.e., below fair market value) to pay the tax. (Reg § 1.6161-1(b))[38]

¶ 4722   Installment payments of individual income tax—Forms 9465, 433-A, 433-F.

To request an installment agreement, attach Form 9465 to the front of a balance-due return. A fee of $105 (proposed to increase to $120 after 2013) ($52 if directly debited from a bank account; $43 for some low-income taxpayers), (Reg § 300.1(b)),[39] interest, and a late-payment penalty apply, see ¶4874.

IRS must enter into an installment agreement (guaranteed installment agreement) requested by an *individual* whose aggregate tax liability (without interest, penalties, additions

---

31. ¶S-5454; ¶61,514
32. ¶S-5064; ¶60,814
33. ¶S-5454.1
34. ¶S-5752; ¶63,114; TD ¶559,802
35. ¶S-5756.1A *et seq.*, ¶S-1629.1; ¶63,114; TD ¶559,803

36. ¶S-5756.4
37. ¶S-5200 *et seq.*
38. ¶S-5851; ¶61,614; TD ¶570,305
39. ¶T-10021; ¶61,594; TD ¶901,006

to tax, and additional amounts) isn't more than $10,000; and who (or whose spouse for joint return liability) hasn't failed to file or to pay income tax, or entered into another installment agreement, during any of the preceding 5 tax years, if IRS determines that the taxpayer is financially unable to pay the liability in full when due (and the taxpayer submits information that IRS may require to make this determination). The agreement must require full payment within 3 years, and the taxpayer must agree to comply with all Code provisions while it's in effect. (Code Sec. 6159(c); Reg § 301.6159-1(c)) IRS grants streamlined installment agreement requests to taxpayers who agree to pay a balance due of $50,000 or less within a 6-year period, without requiring a collection manager's approval. Taxpayers seeking installment agreements exceeding $50,000 have to supply IRS with Form 433-A or Form 433-F.[40]

IRS may (but isn't required to, except as noted above) enter into an installment agreement if it determines that the agreement will facilitate full or partial collection of the tax. (Code Sec. 6159(a); Reg § 301.6159-1(a)) IRS may disregard frivolous submissions of installment payment applications. (Code Sec. 7122(f))[41]

An individual who had an automatic 6-month extension of time to file without paying the tax estimated to be due (¶4717), but can't pay by the extended due date, should use Form 9465 to arrange an installment agreement.[42]

¶ 4723 Amended income tax returns—Form 1040X.

Amended income tax returns (on Form 1040X) may be filed to claim a refund (¶4849) after an original return has been filed if the period of limitations is open. (Reg § 301.6402-3(a)(2))[43] Amended returns can't be e-filed.[44]

¶ 4724 Corporate returns.

Every corporation that is subject to income tax, and that's in existence during any portion of a tax year, must file an income tax return for that year (or portion), regardless of the amount of its gross income or whether it has taxable income. (Code Sec. 6012(a)(2); Reg § 1.6012-2(a))[45] A corporation that has merely received a charter doesn't have to file if it furnishes a statement to IRS that it hasn't perfected its organization, transacted any business, or received income from any source. (Reg § 1.6012-2(a)(2))[46]

After a corporation ceases business and dissolves, retaining no assets, it must file a return for that part of the year during which it was in existence. But retention of even a small amount of cash keeps the corporation alive for filing purposes until the cash is distributed or paid. (Reg § 1.6012-2(a)(2))[47] A receiver, bankruptcy trustee, etc. that has control and custody of all (or substantially all) of a corporation's business or property must make the return in the same manner as the corporation would. (Code Sec. 6012(b)(3))[48]

If a corporation fails to file a required return, IRS may make its return. (Code Sec. 6020)[49]

¶ 4725 Who signs corporate returns.

The return and all related documents requiring a signature on behalf of a corporation, must be signed by the president, vice-president, treasurer, assistant treasurer, chief accounting officer (controller) or any other officer duly authorized to sign. If a return is made for the corporation by a trustee, receiver or assignee, that fiduciary must sign. (Code Sec. 6062)[50]

40. ¶V-5010 *et seq.*; ¶61,594; TD ¶901,006 *et seq.*
41. ¶V-5010; ¶61,594; TD ¶901,006
42. ¶s S-5020, V-5010 *et seq.*; ¶61,594; TD ¶570,227
43. ¶S-5151.5; ¶s 60,114.01, 64,024.15; TD ¶805,006
44. ¶S-1604; TD ¶572,011
45. ¶s S-1900, S-1901, S-1908; ¶60,124.03; TD ¶609,801

46. ¶S-1908; ¶60,124.03; TD ¶609,801
47. ¶S-1909; ¶60,124.03; TD ¶609,803
48. ¶S-2014; ¶60,124.04; TD ¶803,056
49. ¶S-1004; ¶60,204; TD ¶570,104
50. ¶S-4508; ¶60,614; TD ¶609,801.1

¶ 4726   Corporate income tax forms—Form 1120.

Most domestic corporations file Form 1120 as their income tax return. (Reg § 1.6012-2(a)) Form 1120, Schedule PH must be attached if the corporation is a personal holding company (¶3320 *et seq.*). (Reg § 1.6012-2(b))[1] (For foreign corporation returns, see ¶4659.)

A regulated investment company (mutual fund) uses Form 1120-RIC,[2] a real estate investment trust, Form 1120-REIT,[3] a political organization, Form 1120-POL, a homeowners association, Form 1120-H,[4] and a designated settlement fund, Form 1120-SF.[5] Insurance companies use Form 1120L (life) or Form 1120-PC (property and casualty).[6]

An S corporation uses Form 1120S, which must show information on actual and constructive distributions to shareholders. (Code Sec. 6037(a); Reg § 1.6012-2(h)) The corporation must, by the date it files the return, furnish this information to anyone who was a shareholder during the tax year. (Code Sec. 6037(b))[7]

Small corporations (less than $250,000 in gross receipts and less than $250,000 in assets) don't have to complete Schedules L, M-1, and M-2 of Form 1120; or Schedules L and M-1 of Form 1120S.[8] Large corporations (reporting total assets of $10 million or more on Form 1120, Schedule L) and large partnerships (¶4731) must file the more detailed Schedule M-3 instead of M-1. On the M-3, research and development costs have to be separately stated but no supporting attachment is required. M-3 filers must file Schedule B reporting information about allocations, transfers of interest, cost sharing arrangements, and changes in methods of accounting. For tax years ending Dec. 31, 2014 and later, corporations and partnerships with at least $10 million but less than $50 million in total assets at year end can file Schedule M-1 in place of Schedule M-3, Parts II and III. Those taxpayers have to file Schedule M-3, Part I. Corporations and partnerships filing Forms 1120, 1120-C, 1120-F, 1120S, 1065, and 1065B with $10 million to $50 million in total assets will not be required to file Form 1120, Schedule B, Form 1065, Schedule C, or Form 8916-A.[9]

Corporations (filing Form 1120), insurance companies (filing Form 1120L or Form 1120PC), and foreign corporations (filing Form 1120F) with both uncertain tax positions and at least $100 million of assets have to file Schedule UTP if they or a related party issued audited financial statements. (Reg § 1.6012-2(a)(4)) Schedule UTP requires a concise description of each uncertain *federal* tax position for which the taxpayer or a related entity recorded a reserve on financial statements (or which no reserve was recorded because of an expectation to litigate). The description shouldn't exceed a few sentences; but, it must contain relevant facts affecting the tax treatment of the position and information that reasonably can be expected to apprise IRS of the tax position's identity and nature. Tax positions are ranked by size (i.e., the amount of the reserve) but the size of a tax position isn't reported. Positions have to be designated as major tax positions if the reserve for that position exceeds 10% of the reserves for all tax positions reported. Tax positions taken *before 2010* do not have to be reported. The requirement to report the tax position exists even if IRS identifies the tax position for examination before the recording of the reserve. A separate Form 8275 need not be filed to avoid accuracy-related penalties with respect to the tax position other than a reportable transaction. Schedule UTP is phased in over 5 years, the $100 million asset threshold is reduced to $50 million in 2012 and to $10 million in 2014. IRS has announced rules under which it will seek workpapers that document the completion of Schedule UTP.[10]

If the corporation deducts: (a) the cost of goods sold, it must file Form 1125-A and (b) officer compensation and has $500,000 of receipts, it must file Form 1125-E.[11] A corporation uses

1. ¶s S-1902, S-1903; ¶60,124.03; TD ¶609,801
2. ¶S-1920; ¶8514.09
3. ¶S-1919; ¶8564.10
4. ¶S-1921, ¶S-1922; ¶5284, ¶60,124; TD ¶609,811, TD ¶609,812
5. ¶S-1925; ¶468B4
6. ¶S-1904; ¶60,124.03; ¶8314

7. ¶s S-1905, S-1906; ¶60,374; TD ¶628,002
8. ¶S-1902; TD ¶609,806
9. ¶S-1902.1; TD ¶609,801
10. ¶S-4462.1; TD ¶816,030
11. ¶S-1902; TD ¶609,801

Form 8822-B to notify IRS of a new business address or location.

E-filing. A corporation that files at least 250 returns of any kind in the aggregate, including information returns, during the calendar year ending with or within its tax year must e-file its income tax return (i.e., the Form 1120 and Form 1120S series) if it has assets of $10 million or more. Exemptions apply for forms that can't be e-filed and where IRS waives the requirement for undue hardship. A corporation can request a written request for a waiver. All members of a controlled group must e-file if the controlled group in the aggregate files at least 250 returns (including information returns). Failure to e-file when required to do so is deemed to be a failure to file a return. (Reg § 301.6011-5) IRS allows a filer 10 calendar days from the date of first transmission to perfect a rejected e-file return for resubmission. For returns that can't be accepted for processing electronically, the filer generally has 10 days to file a paper return.[12]

¶ 4727 When and where to file corporate income tax returns.

Domestic corporations (including RICs, REITs, and S corporations) must file their returns by the 15th day of the 3rd month after the end of the tax year (Mar. 15 for a calendar year corporation). (Code Sec. 6072(b); Reg § 1.6037-1(b))[13] For extensions, see ¶4728.

"Short period" returns must be filed by the 15th day of the 3rd month after the end of the short period. A dissolved corporation must file its final return by the 15th day of the 3rd month after the dissolution date.[14]

File as directed on the form's instructions. (Code Sec. 6091(b)(2)(A); Reg § 1.6091-2(c)) Hand-carried returns may be filed with any person assigned the responsibility to receive hand-carried returns in the local IRS office (i.e., the office in which the corporation has its principal place of business). (Code Sec. 6091(b)(4); Reg § 1.6091-2(d)(2))[15]

¶ 4728 Extensions for filing corporate returns—Form 7004.

Automatic six-month extensions—Form 7004. A corporation (including an S corporation, an affiliated group planning to file a consolidated return (¶3338), and a foreign corporation with a U.S. office) can get an automatic 6-month extension by filing Form 7004 that shows its estimated tax liability by the original due date. (Reg § 1.6081-3)[16] But this won't extend the time for *paying* the tax, see ¶4729. (Reg § 1.6081-3(c))[17] IRS can terminate an extension on 10 days' notice. (Code Sec. 6081(b); Reg § 1.6081-3(d))[18]

Blanket extensions. A domestic corporation that transacts business and keeps its records outside the U.S. or Puerto Rico, or whose principal income is from sources within U.S. possessions, and a resident foreign corporation, may file its return up to the 15th day of the sixth month after the end of the tax year. A statement setting forth the qualifying facts must be attached to the return. (Reg § 1.6081-5(a)(2), Reg § 1.6081-5(a)(4), Reg § 1.6081-5(b))[19]

¶ 4729 Payment of corporate tax; extensions—Forms 1127, 1138.

Pay in full by the due date (without extension) for filing the return (¶4727). (Code Sec. 6151(a))[20] For corporate estimated tax, see ¶3343 *et seq.*

Six-month extension for undue hardship—Form 1127. An extension (up to 6 months) for making a payment of corporate income tax may be granted by IRS at the taxpayer's request (on Form 1127) by the payment due date on a showing of undue hardship (¶4721). Late applications won't be considered. (Code Sec. 6161(a); Reg § 1.6161-1)[21]

---

12. ¶S-1941; ¶60,114.022TD ¶609,801.2
13. ¶S-4704; ¶s 60,374, 60,724
14. ¶S-4710; ¶60,724
15. ¶S-5104; ¶60,914
16. ¶S-5027 *et seq.*; ¶60,814.02; TD ¶609,802

17. ¶S-5027; ¶60,814.02; TD ¶609,802
18. ¶S-5009; ¶60,814.02
19. ¶S-5064; ¶60,814.01
20. ¶S-5451; ¶61,514
21. ¶S-5850 *et seq.*; ¶61,614; TD ¶659,018

Loss carryback expected—Form 1138. A corporation that expects a net operating loss in a current year can get an extension for paying the *preceding* year's tax based on the expected carryback (Code Sec. 6164(a)), by filing Form 1138. (Reg § 1.6164-1) The extension expires the last day of the month for filing the current year return or, if an application for a tentative carryback refund (Form 1139, see ¶4850) is filed before that date, on the date IRS sends notice that the refund is allowed or disallowed. (Code Sec. 6164(d))[22]

¶ 4730   Tax deposits.

Unless an exemption applies, a corporation must make electronic deposits of all depository taxes using the Electronic Federal Tax Payment System (EFTPS). (Reg § 31.6302-1(h)(2)(iii)) For how taxpayers make tax deposits by Automated Clearing House (ACH) payments or by telephone, see ¶3028. Also, if corporations are unwilling or unable to use EFTPS, it can arrange for a tax professional, financial institution, payroll service, etc. to make a deposit on its behalf using a master account. It can also arrange for its financial institution to initiate a same-day tax wire payment on its behalf.[23]

Corporations must make their income and estimated tax payments by depositing them by the return due date (¶4727) (Code Sec. 6302; Reg § 1.6302-1(a))[24] and report the deposits on the return.[25] For de minimis rule that applies to deposits of employment taxes, see ¶3027.

¶ 4731   Partnership income tax return—Form 1065, Schedule K-1; Form 7004.

Partnerships (except foreign partnerships with no or de minimis U.S. source gross income and no gross income effectively connected with a U.S. trade or business) (Reg § 1.6031(a)-1(b)) must file Form 1065 (Form 1065-B for electing large partnerships) to report its income and deductions. (Code Sec. 6031(a), Code Sec. 6031(e); Reg § 1.6031(a)-1(a))[26] Certain tax-exempt bond partnerships are exempt from filing.[27] (Reg § 1.6031(a)-1(a)(3)(ii)) A foreign partnership that is otherwise exempt from filing must file a return to make an election, (Reg § 1.6031(a)-1(b)) and a foreign or domestic partnership must file to elect out of the Code's partnership rules. (Reg § 1.6031(a)-1(c))

A partnership needn't file a partnership return for any period before it has taxable income or incurs deductible expenses. (Reg § 1.6031(a)-1(a)(3))[28] Nor does it file if it doesn't have any gross income that is effectively connected with the conduct of a U.S. trade or business, or any U.S. source gross income. (Reg § 1.6031(a)-1(b)(1))[29]

Form 1065 is due on the 15th day of the 4th month after the end of the partnership's tax year (Apr. 15 for a calendar year partnership). (Code Sec. 6072(a))[30] For an automatic 5-month extension of time for filing a partnership return, use Form 7004. An extension doesn't extend the time for filing a partner's return. (Reg § 1.6081-2)[31]

Every partnership required to file a return must furnish (by the extended return due date) Form 1065, Schedule K-1, containing information from the return to every person who was a partner (or who held a partnership interest as a nominee for another person) at any time during the partnership's tax year. Form 1065, Schedule K-1 must indicate whether a partner contributed built-in gain or loss property during the tax year. An "electing large partnership" (¶3702) must provide the information by Mar. 15th following the end of its tax year. (Code Sec. 6031(b); Reg § 1.6031(b)-1T(a))[32] (The nominee must in turn give the information it gets to the other person (Code Sec. 6031(c)(2); Reg § 1.6031(c)-1T(h)) and furnish the partnership with specified information about that person.) (Code Sec. 6031(c)(1); Reg § 1.6031(c)-1T(a))[33]

22. ¶S-5865 *et seq.*; ¶61,644; TD ¶804,016 *et seq.*
23. ¶S-5623; ¶S-5628; ¶63,014; TD ¶559,853
24. ¶s S-5601, S-5604, S-5607; ¶63,014; TD ¶609,202
25. ¶S-5601
26. ¶S-2701; ¶60,314; TD ¶596,001
27. ¶S-2708
28. ¶S-2701; ¶60,314; TD ¶596,001
29. ¶S-2717.1; ¶60,314
30. ¶S-4923; ¶60,724; TD ¶596,016
31. ¶S-5030; ¶60,814; TD ¶596,017
32. ¶S-2710; ¶60,314; TD ¶596,008
33. ¶S-2740; ¶60,314; TD ¶596,014

If a partnership deducts the cost of goods sold, it must file Form 1125-A.[34] For large partnerships that have to file Schedule M-3, see ¶4727.

E-filing. Partnerships with more than 100 partners must e-file Form 1065 and Form 1065, Schedule K-1, unless IRS excludes them from e-filing. Hardship waivers are available. (Reg § 301.6011-3)[35] Partnerships can furnish Form 1065, Schedule K-1 electronically to partners if the recipient affirmatively consents to that format.[36]

¶ 4732 Income tax returns of trusts and estates—Forms 1041, K-1, 7004, etc.

Trusts (¶4733) and estates (¶4734) must file income tax and information returns.[37]

If there are *joint* fiduciaries, a return by one will suffice if he states in the return that he has sufficient knowledge of the facts to make the return and that it is true to the best of his knowledge and belief. (Reg § 1.6012-3(c))[38]

A fiduciary who prepares the trust's or estate's return must furnish to beneficiaries (or their nominees) receiving distributions, or to whom an income item is allocated, a Form 1041, Schedule K-1 or a substitute containing the same information. This must be furnished on or before a return is filed, and a copy must be filed with Form 1041. (Code Sec. 6034A(a)) If a nominee is given the information, he must furnish it to his beneficiary, and he must furnish to the estate or trust specified information about the beneficiary. (Code Sec. 6034A(b))[39]

Income tax returns that must be filed by estates and domestic trusts, and foreign trusts having a U.S. office or place of business are due by the 15th day of the 4th month following the end of the tax year. (Reg § 1.6072-1(a)(1)) Foreign trusts and estates of nonresident aliens that don't have an office or place of business in the U.S. must file by the 15th day of the sixth month following the end of the tax year. (Reg § 1.6072-1(c))[40]

Trusts (¶4733) and estates (¶4734) get an automatic 5-month extension to file Form 1041 by filing Form 7004 showing the full amount properly estimated as tax by the trust's return due date. The automatic extension doesn't extend the beneficiary's return due date. (Reg § 1.6081-6)[41] IRS can terminate the automatic extension on 10 days' notice. (Reg § 1.6081-6(e))[42] For *payment* extensions, see ¶4721.

¶ 4733 Income tax returns of trusts—Forms 1041; 1041-A.

A trustee files Form 1041 if the trust isn't tax-exempt and if the trust has: (a) any taxable income for the year; (b) gross income of $600 or more; or (c) any beneficiary who is a nonresident alien. (Code Sec. 6012(a)(4), Code Sec. 6012(a)(5))[43]

Trust income taxable to the grantor or other "owner" is reported on a separate attachment to Form 1041, except that alternative reporting methods are available. The alternatives available depend on whether the trust is treated as owned by 1 grantor, or by 2 or more grantors (which in the latter case may require a trustee to provide Form 1099 and a statement showing trust income items, deductions and credits). (Reg § 1.671-4(b))[44]

Split-interest trusts file Form 1041-A even if they must currently distribute all net income. (Code Sec. 6034(a))[45]

¶ 4734 Income tax returns of estates—Form 1041.

The executor or administrator must file Form 1041 if gross income for the estate's tax year is $600 or more (Code Sec. 6012(a)(3)) *or* if any beneficiary is a nonresident alien. (Code

34. ¶S-2701; TD ¶596,001
35. ¶S-1350 *et seq.*; ¶60,114.065; TD ¶596,025
36. ¶S-2710.1; TD ¶596,008.1
37. ¶s S-2004, S-2007; ¶60,124.04; TD ¶659,000
38. ¶S-2002; ¶60,124.04; TD ¶659,001
39. ¶s S-2019, S-2020; ¶60,34A4; TD ¶659,011

40. ¶S-4707; ¶60,724; TD ¶667,002, TD ¶659,013
41. ¶S-5032; ¶60,814.05; TD ¶659,014; TD ¶667,004
42. ¶S-5009; ¶60,814.05
43. ¶S-2007; ¶60,124.04; TD ¶659,003
44. ¶S-2009 *et seq.*; ¶6714; TD ¶659,004
45. ¶S-2806; ¶60,344

Sec. 6012(a); Reg § 1.6012-3(a)(1)(iii))[46] A fiduciary doesn't have to file a copy of the will for income tax purposes unless IRS *requests* a copy. (Reg § 1.6012-3(a)(2))[47]

The executor who probates the entire will (in the state the decedent was domiciled) files Form 1041 reporting all the income. Any out-of-state (i.e., ancillary) executor *also* files a Form 1041, but it shows only the gross income received by the ancillary fiduciary and the deductions attributable to that income. (Reg § 1.6012-3(a)(3))[48]

¶ 4735   Extension for making elections.

Two automatic extensions are available for taxpayer elections, if the taxpayer takes corrective action within the extension period:

(1) An automatic *12-month extension* for certain regulatory elections specified in Reg § 301.9100-2(a)(2). The more widely applicable ones are: the election to use a tax year other than the required tax year (¶2813); the election to use the LIFO inventory method (¶2874); and the election to adjust basis on partnership transfers and distributions (¶3780). The extension is available regardless of whether the taxpayer timely filed its return for the year the election should have been made. (Reg § 301.9100-2(a)(1))[49]

(2) An automatic *6-month extension* for regulatory elections and statutory elections which are required to be made by the due date of the return or the due date of the return *including extensions,* for taxpayers who timely filed the return for the year in which the election should have been made. (Reg § 301.9100-2(b))[50]

Nonautomatic extensions of time are available for regulatory elections that don't qualify for an automatic extension, if the taxpayer shows IRS that he acted reasonably and in good faith, and that granting relief won't prejudice IRS's interests. (Reg § 301.9100-3(a)) A request for a nonautomatic extension is generally a request for a letter ruling, and is submitted under those procedures, with the applicable user fee. (Reg § 301.9100-3(e)(5))[1]

The grant of an extension of time to make an election isn't a determination that the taxpayer is otherwise eligible to make the election. (Reg § 301.9100-1(a))[2]

¶ 4736   Income tax returns of individual bankruptcy estates—Forms 1041, 7004.

The debtor-in-possession or trustee, if one is appointed, for a bankruptcy estate for an individual under Chapter 7 or 11 must file an income tax return (Form 1041) if the estate's gross income equals at least the sum of the exemption amount plus the basic standard deduction for unmarried taxpayers who weren't surviving spouses or heads of household. (Code Sec. 6012(a)(8)) This amount is $10,000 for 2013 ($10,150 for 2014).[3] File Form 7004 for an automatic 6-month extension. (Reg § 1.6081-6(a)(2))[4]

¶ 4737   Information returns—Form 1099, etc. and filing dates.

Taxpayers report certain of their activities with third parties on information returns and statements. These are filed with IRS and in some cases furnished to third parties.[5] For e-filing, see ¶4753. Payors (including nominees, see ¶4738) report their payments for a calendar year by filing an appropriate Form 1099 (or permitted substitute form) for payee (with a Form 1096 transmittal statement) after Sept. 30 of the calendar year of the payment (but not before the payor's final payments for the year) and by the next Feb. 28. (Reg § 1.6042-2(c), Reg § 1.6044-2(d), Reg § 1.6049-1(c))[6] However, returns filed electronically aren't due until Mar. 31 after the end of the calendar year to which they relate. (Code Sec. 6071(b);

---

46. ¶S-2004; ¶60,124.04; TD ¶667,001
47. ¶S-2006; ¶60,124.04; TD ¶667,009
48. ¶S-2005; ¶60,124.04; TD ¶667,008
49. ¶S-4819; ¶78,054.02
50. ¶S-4821; ¶78,054.02
1. ¶S-4823; ¶78,054.02

2. ¶S-4815.1; ¶78,054.02
3. ¶C-9700 *et seq.*, S-2016; ¶60,124; TD ¶578,021
4. ¶S-5032; ¶60,814.05
5. ¶s S-2900 *et seq.*, S-4930; TD ¶811,000
6. ¶S-4930; ¶s 60,424, 60,494; TD ¶811,003

Reg § 31.6071(a)-1(a)(3)(i))[7] For extensions, see ¶4747. For payee statements, see ¶4742.

¶ 4738 Nominees and middleman information returns—Form 1099.

If reportable interest or dividends are paid to any person who, as middleman or nominee, then pays them over to the actual (or beneficial) owner, the original payor (corporation, bank, etc.) must file an information return (Form 1099) with respect to the nominee, who must file another Form 1099 with respect to the actual or beneficial owner. (Code Sec. 6042(a)(1)(B), Code Sec. 6049(a)(2); Reg § 1.6042-2(a)(1)(iii), Reg § 1.6049-4(b)(3))[8]

A nominee is a payee who isn't the actual owner of the dividend or interest, but who would be required to furnish his TIN (¶4752) to the payor for inclusion on the *payor's* return. Nominees include banks, etc., and, for dividends, dealers and brokers. (Reg § 1.6042-2(a)(2), Reg § 1.6049-1(a)(2))[9] Special reporting rules apply to payments to joint payees (Reg § 1.6041-1(c)); and payments on behalf of another. (Reg § 1.6041-1(e))

¶ 4739 Dividend reporting—Forms 1099-DIV, 5452, 1099-PATR.

A payor (including nominees, see ¶4738) must file a Form 1099-DIV for each person to whom it pays "reportable" dividends aggregating $10 or more during the calendar year. (Code Sec. 6042(a), Reg § 1.6042-2(a)(1)) Dividends qualifying for preferential tax rates must be differentiated from nonqualified dividends.[10] For payee statements, see ¶4742.

Reportable dividends are corporate "dividends" (¶1285 *et seq.*) and substitute dividends (e.g., payments in lieu of dividends that brokers pay on short sales). (Code Sec. 6042(b)(1))[11] Nontaxable dividends are reported on Form 5452.[12]

Cooperatives (¶4206) report *patronage dividends* aggregating $10 or more to any payee in a calendar year on Form 1099-PATR. (Code Sec. 6044(a)(1); Reg § 1.6044-2(b))[13]

¶ 4740 Interest reporting—Forms 1099-INT; 1042-S.

Every person (including nominees, see ¶4738) who pays $10 or more of reportable interest to any person (except certain payees) in a calendar year must report the payments (Code Sec. 6049(a)(1), Code Sec. 6049(d)) on Form 1099-INT.[14] For payee statements, see ¶4742.

Reportable interest is interest on: (a) obligations issued publicly or in registered form (other than a short-term obligation held by a corporation), (b) deposits with banks or brokers, and (c) amounts held by insurance or investment companies. (Code Sec. 6049(b)(1))[15] Reportable interest also includes original issue discount (¶4741); amounts includible in gross income with respect to regular real estate mortgage investment conduits interests (¶4204) (Code Sec. 6049(d)(6)(A)(i), Code Sec. 6049(d)(7)(A));[16] and interest paid on tax-exempt bonds. But interest on obligations issued by a natural person isn't "reportable." (Code Sec. 6049(b)(2))[17]

A payor reports on Form 1042-S interest aggregating $10 or more that is paid to a nonresident alien individual (NRA) on deposits maintained at U.S. offices of financial institutions if the NRA resides in a country with which the U.S. has in effect an information exchange agreement. A payor can elect to report all interest paid to all NRAs. (Reg § 1.6049-4(b)(5), Reg § 1.6049-8)[18]

---

7. ¶S-1305; ¶S-4930; ¶60,414.06
8. ¶S-2904 *et seq.*; ¶s 60,424, 60,494; TD ¶811,007
9. ¶s S-2904 *et seq.*, S-3003 *et seq.*; ¶s 60,424, 60,494; TD ¶811,008
10. ¶S-2901; ¶60,424; TD ¶811,001
11. ¶S-2910, ¶S-3724; ¶60,424; TD ¶811,010
12. ¶S-2914; ¶60,424; TD ¶811,012

13. ¶S-2951; ¶60,444; TD ¶811,021
14. ¶S-3001 *et seq.*; ¶60,494; TD ¶811,501
15. ¶S-3011 *et seq.*, ¶S-3023 *et seq.*; ¶60,494; TD ¶811,512
16. ¶s S-3073, S-3087; ¶60,494; TD ¶811,537.
17. ¶s S-3040, S-3042; ¶60,494; TD ¶811,523
18. ¶S-3012.1; ¶60,494.05; TD ¶811,517

¶ 4741   Reporting original issue discount (OID)—Forms 1099-OID, 8281.

Original issue discount (OID) of $10 or more on any obligation must be reported by the issuer (or nominee, see ¶4738) as a payment of interest. (Code Sec. 6049(d)(6)) Form 1099-OID is used to report the OID and any interest actually paid on the obligation.[19] In addition, Form 8281 must be filed by certain issuers of publicly-offered debt instruments having OID within 30 days after issuance. (Code Sec. 1275(c)(2); Reg § 1.1275-3(c))[20]

✐*observation:* The one-time reporting requirement on Form 8281 is in addition to the annual information reporting on Form 1099-OID.

For covered securities acquired after Dec. 31, 2013, if a broker is required to file a statement for a debt instrument (statements to recipients of interest payments and holders of obligations for attributed OID), the broker generally must report any bond premium (as defined in Reg § 1.171-1(d), see ¶2169) or acquisition premium (as defined in Reg § 1.1272-2(b)(3), see ¶2633) for the calendar year. (Reg § 1.6049-9T)[21]

¶ 4742   Payee statements—Form 1099.

Payors of reportable dividends (and payments in lieu of dividends) and interest (including OID) must furnish payees with specified written statements of the amount reported to IRS (i.e., Copy B of Form 1099 sent to IRS). This generally must be done, either in person or in a "statement mailing," by Jan. 31 of the year following the calendar year for which the payor's Form 1099 was required. (Reg § 1.6042-4(d)(1), Reg § 1.6044-5(b), Reg § 1.6049-3(c)(1)) However, if payees consent, Form 1099 statements may be furnished electronically.[22]

¶ 4743   Business payments of $600 or more—Form 1099-MISC.

With limited exceptions, every person, corporate or otherwise, engaged in a trade or business who, in the course of that business, makes payments aggregating $600 or more to another person (e.g., an independent contractor) in a calendar year must file Form 1099-MISC setting forth the payee's name and address and the amount paid, and furnish a statement to the payee. Reportable payments are: rent, salaries, wages, premiums, annuities, compensations, remunerations, emoluments, prizes or awards (that aren't for services rendered), or other fixed or determinable gains, profits and income. (Code Sec. 6041; Reg § 1.6041-1)[23] This rule doesn't apply to transactions covered by other information return rules (e.g., dividends, see ¶4739), or most payments to corporations. (Reg § 1.6041-3)[24] IRS has issued guidance on how reporting applies to payments made with credit or debit cards.[25]

¶ 4744   Mortgage interest (and points) received—Form 1098.

A person ("interest recipient") who receives interest, or reimburses interest overpayments, aggregating $600 or more for a calendar year on a mortgage must report (on Form 1098) those receipts or reimbursements, even if the interest is received on behalf of another. This applies to any person (including cooperative housing corporations) who, in the course of his trade or business (except governmental recipients), receives interest on a mortgage secured all or in part by real property, where the payor of record is an individual. (Code Sec. 6050H; Reg § 1.6050H-1, Reg § 1.6050H-2(a))[26] The return must also include any points received in the year that were paid directly by the buyer (including certain points paid by or charged to the seller). (Code Sec. 6050H(b)(2)(C); Reg § 1.6050H-1(f))[27] For calendar years 2011-2015, HUD and state housing finance authorities (State HFAs) can report payments made to or on

---

19. ¶s S-3073, S-3074; ¶60,494; TD ¶811,530
20. ¶S-3080 *et seq.*; ¶12,714.06; TD ¶811,536
21. ¶S-3078.1; ¶60,494.01; TD ¶811,533.5
22. ¶S-2927 *et seq.*; ¶s 60,424, 60,444, 60,494; TD ¶811,015
23. ¶S-3655 *et seq.*; ¶S-3658¶s 60,414, 60,414.06; TD ¶814,001;

TD ¶814,002
24. ¶S-3676; ¶60,414.06; TD ¶814,001
25. ¶S-3656.1, J-9325; ¶34,064
26. ¶S-3901 *et seq.*; ¶60,50H4; TD ¶814,054
27. ¶S-3907 *et seq.*; TD ¶814,065

behalf of financially distressed homeowners under programs such as Emergency Homeowners' Loan Program (EHLP) or similar programs designed by State HFAs on Form 1098-MA or on a statement containing the required information.[28]

¶ 4745   Reporting qualified residence interest on seller-provided financing.

A return on which taxpayer claims a deduction for qualified residence interest (¶1730) on seller-provided financing must show the name, address and TIN of the person (the seller) to whom the interest is paid or accrued on Form 1040, Schedule A. Any person who receives or accrues interest from seller-provided financing must include on Form 1040, Schedule B for the tax year in which the interest is so received or accrued the name, address and TIN of the person liable for the interest. (Code Sec. 6109(h))[29]

¶ 4746   Other information returns.

. . .*Abandonment or foreclosure of property held as security* for a business loan must be reported by the lender on Form 1099-A (Code Sec. 6050J; Reg § 1.6050J-1T) (unless related to a discharge of debt reported on Form 1099-C, below).[30]

. . .*Accelerated death benefits* paid to any individual must be reported by the payor (Code Sec. 6050Q) on Form 1099-LTC.[31]

. . .*Acquiring corporation in taxable acquisition* must file information returns with IRS and furnish statements to shareholders if a shareholder of the acquired corporation recognizes gain or loss in whole or in part due to the acquisition. (Code Sec. 6043A(a))[32]

. . .*Alcohol and biodiesel fuel tax benefits, Code Sec. 34 credit for farming, off-highway and certain other nontaxable uses of fuel*—information return required by persons claiming alcohol or biodiesel fuel tax benefits or a Code Sec. 34 credit, providing information on the benefits or credit. (Code Sec. 4104(a))[33]

. . .*Attorney's fees* paid in the course of a trade or business that aren't reportable as wages or under Code Sec. 6041 (¶4743) (or would have to be reported under Code Sec. 6041 but for the $600 limitation), whether or not the services are performed for the payor (Code Sec. 6045(f); Reg § 1.6045-5) and whether or not the attorney is the exclusive payee, on Form 1099-MISC. (Reg § 1.6045-5)[34]

. . .*Applicable large employers* required to offer their full-time employees and their dependents the opportunity to enroll in minimum essential coverage (MEC, ¶4896) under an eligible employer-sponsored plan and *offering employers* (those offering MEC to employees and paying any portion of the coverage, but only if the required employer contribution of any employee exceeds 8% of the employee's wages) have to report insurance coverage for periods beginning after 2014. (Code Sec. 6056)[35]

. . .*Banks and online payment networks* (payment settlement entities (PSEs) or third party settlement organizations (TPSOs)) have to report credit card sales to IRS and participating payees on Form 1099-K. TPSOs have to report payments made in settlement of third party network transactions only if the amount to be reported exceeds $20,000 and the aggregate number of transactions exceeds 200 for any payee within a calendar year. (Code Sec. 6050W; Reg § 1.6050W-1) In late 2014, IRS will notify payors of incorrect name and TIN combinations reported on Form 1099-K for calendar year 2013 payments.[36]

. . .*Barter exchanges* through which at least 100 exchanges of property or services are made in the calendar year are reported on Form 1099-B. (Code Sec. 6045; Reg § 1.6045-1(e))[37]

28. ¶V-1810.4 *et seq.*; TD ¶861,060.1
29. ¶S-1524 *et seq.*; ¶61,094
30. ¶S-4200 *et seq.*; ¶60,50J4; TD ¶816,001
31. ¶S-3440; ¶60,50Q4
32. ¶S-4317; ¶6043A4; TD ¶815,010

33. ¶S-4466; ¶41,044
34. ¶S-3851; ¶60,454.06; TD ¶814,087
35. ¶S-3331; ¶60,564; TD ¶816,301
36. ¶S-3699.18; ¶60,50W4; TD ¶814,088
37. ¶S-3700 *et seq.*; ¶60,454; TD ¶814,037

. . . *Brokers* must report each sale of securities, commodities, and forwards or futures contracts the broker effects for its customers, on Form 1099-B. (Code Sec. 6045; Reg § 1.6045-1(c), Reg § 1.6045-2)[38] For certain less complex debt instruments and options granted or acquired after 2013, brokers have to report information relating to the lapse of, or a closing transaction with respect to, an option on certain securities. More complex debt instruments (e.g., variable rate or contingent payment debt instruments) and options will be subject to reporting if acquired after 2015. Certain short-term debt instruments are exempt from reporting. Unless a customer notifies broker of an election, brokers use default assumptions in reporting basis. (Code Sec. 6045(h); Reg § 1.6045-1(n))[39] Brokers also must report customer's adjusted basis (determined under Reg § 1.6045-1(n)(6)) and character of gain or loss for sales of "covered securities" (as defined in Code Sec. 6045(g)(3) and Reg § 1.6045-1(a)(15); in general, corporate stock acquired after 2010 or mutual fund shares or shares in a dividend reinvestment program acquired after 2011). Brokers can treat all securities as covered securities to simplify reporting. (Code Sec. 6045(g); Reg § 1.6045-1(d)(6))[40] Also, brokers that transfer covered securities to other brokers have to provide statements to other brokers starting in 2014 (for less complex debt instruments) and in 2016 (for more complex debt instruments). (Code Sec. 6045A; Reg § 1.6045A-1)[41]

. . . *Cash of more than $10,000,* including certain cash equivalents (e.g., cashier's checks, foreign currency) received in connection with a trade or business must be reported by the recipient (Code Sec. 6050I(a), Code Sec. 6050I(d); Reg § 1.6050I-1(a)(1), Reg § 1.6050I-1(c)(1)) within 15 days after receipt. Use Form 8300 (Reg § 1.6050I-1(e)), except that banks file Form 4789 and casinos, under special rules (Reg § 1.6050I-1(d)(2)), file Form 8362 (certain Nevada casinos file Form 8852) to report cash from gaming activities.[42] Special rules apply for cash installment payments. (Reg § 1.6050I-1(b))[43]

. . . *Change in control or recapitalization of a corporation* generally must be reported on Form 8806 showing the parties to the transaction, the fees involved, the changes in capital structure and any other information IRS requires. (Code Sec. 6043(c); Reg § 1.6043-4)[44]

. . . *Charitable organization required to acknowledge gift of auto, plane, or boat* (¶2138) must provide the information required on Form 1098-C to IRS. (Code Sec. 170(f)(12)(D))[45]

. . . *Charitable property disposition* by the donee within 3 years of contribution must be reported on Form 8282 by the charity, if the deduction claimed for the property exceeds $5,000 (but disposition of items appraised for $500 or less doesn't have to be reported). (Code Sec. 6050L; Reg § 1.6050L-1)[46]

. . . *Commodity Credit Corporation (CCC)* must report market gain associated with the repayment of a CCC loan, regardless of whether the taxpayer repays the loan with cash or uses CCC certificates in repayment of the loan, on Form 1099-G. (Code Sec. 6039J)[47]

. . . *Direct sales of consumer goods* of $5,000 or more to any 1 buyer in a calendar year must be reported by the seller (Code Sec. 6041A) on Form 1099-MISC.[48]

. . . *Discharge of debt (including student loans) by banks, and certain other financial entities and organizations that have a significant lending trade or business* of $600 or more must be reported to IRS, on Form 1099-C. (Code Sec. 6050P; Reg § 1.6050P-1, Reg § 1.6050P-2)[49]

. . . *Donee of qualified intellectual property* (¶2106) must file annual information return (Form 8899) of net income from property for each specified tax year of the donee. (Code Sec. 6050L(b)(1); Reg § 1.6050L-2)[50]

. . . *Education-related payments* received (or billed) by higher education institutions for qualified tuition and related expenses; qualified tuition refunds (Form 1098-T) (Reg § 1.6050S-1); and interest of $600 or more received from an individual for a calendar

---

38. ¶S-3700 *et seq.*; ¶60,454; TD ¶814,023
39. ¶S-3747; ¶S-3748; ¶60,454.08; TD ¶814,207
40. ¶S-3741 *et seq.*; ¶60,454.08; TD ¶814,201
41. ¶S-3761 *et seq.*; ¶60,45A4; TD ¶814,301
42. ¶S-4000 *et seq.*; ¶60,50I4 *et seq.*; TD ¶814,074
43. ¶S-4019 *et seq.*; ¶60,50I4.02; TD ¶814,084
44. ¶S-4308; ¶60,434; TD ¶815,006

45. ¶K-3948.1; ¶S-2872.1
46. ¶S-2873; ¶60,50L4; TD ¶688,033
47. ¶N-1171.1; ¶60,39J4
48. ¶S-3677; ¶60,41A4; TD ¶814,020
49. ¶S-4251 *et seq.*; ¶60,50P4; TD ¶816,008
50. ¶S-2882.1; ¶60,50L4; TD ¶688,042

year on an educational loan (Form 1098-E) are reported. (Code Sec. 6050S; Reg § 1.6050S-3)[1] For educational loans, lenders report amounts (in addition to all other interest paid) attributable to capitalized interest and loan origination fees.[2] Certain statements to students and borrowers may be provided electronically. (Reg § 1.6050S-2(a)(1), Reg § 1.6050S-4(a))[3]

...*Education savings distributions* (certain) from Coverdell ESAs[4] and qualified tuition programs or 529 plans are reported on Form 1099-Q.[5]

...*Employer-owned life insurance contracts* issued after Aug. 17, 2006, must be reported on Form 8925 by applicable policyholders. (Code Sec. 6039I; Reg § 1.6039I-1)[6]

...*Fishing boat operators* report crew payments on Form 1099-MISC. (Code Sec. 6050A; Reg § 1.6050A-1)[7]

...*Fish purchased for resale* for cash are reported on Form 1099-MISC for each seller by persons engaged in the trade or business of purchasing fish for resale. (Code Sec. 6050R)[8]

...*Foreign financial accounts* are reported on Form TD F 90-22.1 (FBAR) by any person with a financial interest in or signature authority over the account, if the aggregate value of these accounts exceeds $10,000 at any time during the calendar year. FBAR is due by June 30 of the year following the year that the account holder meets the $10,000 threshold. Certain employees or officers of a covered entity or controlled person that have signature authority over, but no financial interest in, a foreign account have until June 30, *2014* to file the FBARs for calendar year 2012 and earlier years.[9]

...*Individual holders of any interest in specified foreign financial assets* have to attach the information required on Form 8938 to their income tax returns if the aggregate value of those assets exceed $50,000 ($100,000 for certain married individuals) or a higher amount prescribed by IRS. (Code Sec. 6038D; Reg § 1.6038D-1T; Reg § 1.6038D-2T)[10]

...*Insurers* (including employers who self-insure) that provide minimal essential coverage (MEC, ¶4896) to any individual during a calendar year must report certain health insurance coverage information for coverage provided after 2014. (Code Sec. 6055)[11]

...*IRA (and Roth IRA) contributions and withdrawals* must be reported by the IRA trustees or issuer (Code Sec. 408(i), Code Sec. 408A(d)(3)(D)), on Form 5498.[12] The trustee also must report on Form 5498 that a minimum distribution is required (but not the amount) for a calendar year. (Reg § 1.408-8, Q&10)[13] For required distributions, additional information must be provided to the IRA owner by Jan. 31 of the required distribution year.[14]

...*Issuers* of specified securities (i.e., stocks, bonds, commodity contracts, etc.) report organizational actions (e.g., stock splits, mergers, acquisitions, etc.) that affect basis on Form 8937. It is due within 45 days of the action or, if earlier, by Jan. 15 of the next calendar year. But, the issuer can post the return on its primary public website in a readily accessible format by the due date (instead of filing a return). Actions relating to more complex debt instruments don't have to be reported until 2016. (Code Sec. 6045B; Reg § 1.6045B-1)[15]

...*Liquidating corporations* report the adoption of the plan of liquidation on Form 966,[16] and liquidating distributions (Code Sec. 6043(a)) on Form 1099-DIV.[17]

...*Long-term care payments* made under a long-term care insurance contract to any individual must be reported by the payor (Code Sec. 6050Q) on Form 1099-LTC.[18]

...*Medical savings account and health savings account contributions and distributions*

1. ¶S-3430 *et seq.*; ¶60,50S4; TD ¶816,500 *et seq.*
2. ¶S-3436; ¶60,50S4.01
3. ¶S-1370; ¶60,50S4.01
4. ¶S-3428
5. ¶S-3422
6. ¶S-3246; ¶60,39I4
7. ¶S-3695; ¶60,50A4; TD ¶816,024
8. ¶S-3695.1; ¶60,50R4
9. ¶S-3650; ¶60,114.06

10. ¶S-3650.1; ¶60,38D4TD ¶815,516
11. ¶S-3321; ¶60,554; TD ¶812,313
12. ¶S-3391; ¶4084.04; TD ¶813,032
13. ¶S-3392.1; ¶4084.04; TD ¶813,033.1
14. ¶S-3392.2; ¶4084.04; TD ¶813,033.1
15. ¶S-3781; ¶60,45B4; TD ¶814,401
16. ¶S-4314; ¶60,434; TD ¶815,009
17. ¶S-4315; ¶60,434; TD ¶815,009
18. ¶S-3440; ¶60,50Q4

must be reported by the trustee on Form 5498-SA and Form 1099-SA. (Code Sec. 220(h))[19]

. . . *Mortgage credit certificate* (MCC) information is reported (on Form 8329) by each person who makes a "certified indebtedness" loan under an MCC program. (Reg § 1.25-8T(a))[20] Each state or political subdivision with MCC programs reports (on Form 8330) the amount of MCCs issued each quarter. (Code Sec. 25(g); Reg § 1.25-4T)[21]

. . . *Mortgage insurance premiums* aggregating $600 or more for any calendar year must be reported on Form 1098 by any person who, in the course of a trade or business, received the premiums. (Code Sec. 6050H(h)(1), Reg § 1.6050H-3T)[22]

. . . *Outbound Code Sec. 355 distributions* (¶3559) and outbound Code Sec. 332 corporate liquidations (Reg § 1.6038B-1(e))[23] are reported on Form 926.[24]

. . . *Parent tax-exempt organizations* that are controlling organizations (Code Sec. 512(b)(3)) report transactions with controlled entities on Form 990-T. (Code Sec. 6033(h))[25]

. . . *Partnership interest sales or exchanges* due to unrealized receivables, inventory, collectibles, or Code Sec. 1250 gain are reported by partnerships on Form 8308. (Code Sec. 6050K; Reg § 1.1(h)-1(e), Reg § 1.6050K-1(a)(1))[26] The partnership doesn't have to file until it's notified of the exchange (Code Sec. 6050K(c)(2)), i.e., when it receives written notification required from the transferor, or has knowledge of it. (Reg § 1.6050K-1)[27]

. . . *Pension, profit-sharing plans* file annual return/report forms in the Form 5500 series (Code Sec. 6058(a)),[28] file Form 5310A to notify IRS of a merger, consolidation or division of the plan, (Code Sec. 6057(b)(4))[29] and make returns and reports of designated Roth contributions. (Code Sec. 6047(f))[30] Form 8955-SSA is used to report information about separated participants with deferred vested benefits.[31] A short Form 5500-SF may be filed by plans: covering fewer than 100 participants at the beginning of the plan year; not holding employer securities; investing 100% in certain secure, easy to value assets; eligible for a waiver under DOL annual examination and report rules; and not multiemployer plans.[32] Certain 1-participant plan with total assets of $250,000 or less are exempt from filing the annual return. If a 1-participant plan must file a return, it can file a paper Form 5500-EZ (or Form 5500-SF filed electronically).[33] All other annual reports—including any statements and schedules—are filed electronically with DOL using EFAST2.[34] Use Form 5558 to request extensions for filing Form 5500 and Form 8955-SSA.[35]

. . . *Political organizations* except for certain state and local committees under Code Sec. 527 must file an initial notice of status (Form 8871) (Code Sec. 527(i)),[36] and periodic reports of contributions and expenditures (Form 8872) (Code Sec. 527(j)(2)), which can be filed online at www.irs.gov/polorgs with an IRS-supplied user ID and password.[37]

. . . *Real estate* reporting persons (as specially defined) must report real estate transactions on Form 1099-S, including the sale of a condominium unit or stock in a cooperative housing unit. For a residential transactions, the return includes any portion of real property tax treated as imposed on the buyer. Reporting isn't required for sales of principal residences for $250,000 or less ($500,000 or less for married sellers) (regs can permit higher amounts) if the reporting person receives specified written assurances (on IRS's certification form) from the seller by Jan. 31 following the year of sale. (Code Sec. 6045(e); Reg § 1.6045-4)[38] Reportable real estate transactions also include sales or exchanges of standing timber for lump-sum payments. (Reg § 1.6045-4(b)(2)(i)(E), Reg § 1.6045-4(s))[39]

. . . *Refunds of state and local income tax* of $10 or more must be reported by the state or

---

19. ¶H-1328.1; ¶2204.02; TD ¶288,105
20. ¶S-4206; ¶254.02; TD ¶816,011
21. ¶S-4207; ¶254.02; TD ¶816,012
22. ¶S-3923; ¶60,50H4; TD ¶814,074.1
23. ¶S-3640.1; ¶S-3640.1A
24. ¶S-3630; ¶60,38B4
25. ¶S-2862.2; ¶60,334
26. ¶S-2725 *et seq.*; ¶60,50K4; TD ¶591,019
27. ¶S-2734 *et seq.*; ¶60,50K4; TD ¶591,022
28. ¶S-3351; ¶s 4014.01, 60,584; TD ¶813,001
29. ¶s S-3383, S-3384; ¶s 4014.01, 60,574; TD ¶813,028

30. ¶S-3400.1
31. ¶S-3369
32. ¶S-3355.1
33. ¶S-3357; TD ¶813,010
34. ¶S-3351
35. ¶S-5057¶60,814.11TD ¶813,017
36. ¶S-2858.7
37. ¶S-2858.9
38. ¶S-3800 *et seq.*; ¶60,454.04; TD ¶814,040 *et seq.*
39. ¶S-3813; ¶60,454.04; TD ¶814,045

local tax authority/payor on Form 1099-G. (Code Sec. 6050E; Reg § 1.6050E-1)[40]

. . . *Royalty payments* of $10 or more per year per payee (including nominees) must be reported unless the payee is a corporation, exempt organization or government (Code Sec. 6050N), on Form 1099-MISC. Where a publisher pays royalties to an author's agent and the agent subtracts his commission and expenses, both parties report the gross royalties on Form 1099-MISC, unreduced by the subtracted amounts.[41]

. . . *Stock transfers under incentive stock options and employee stock purchase plans* are reported by corporations on Form 3921 and Form 3922. (Code Sec. 6039(a); Reg § 1.6039-1)[42]

. . . *Sick pay* (nonwage) paid by a third party to an employee must be reported by the third party to the employee's employer. (Code Sec. 6051(f)(1); Reg § 31.6051-3(a))[43]

. . . *Simplified employee pension (SEP) contributions* must be reported by the SEP trustee or issuer of a SEP endowment contract (Code Sec. 408(l)) on Form 5498.[44]

. . . *Sponsoring organizations* (defined in Code Sec. 4966(d)(1), ¶4129), on their annual information returns (Form 990-T), must include information relating to donor advised funds (DAFs, ¶4125) owned by an organization at the end of the tax year. (Code Sec. 6033(k))[45]

. . . *Supporting organizations* (Code Sec. 509(a)(3)) must file annual information returns listing supported organizations, the type of supporting organization, certify that the organization that it isn't controlled by 1 or more disqualified persons. (Code Sec. 6033(l))[46]

. . . *Tips* must be reported by employees to employers on Form 4070. (Code Sec. 6053(a); Reg § 31.6053-1(b)(2))[47] Large food and beverage establishments (more than 10 employees on a typical business day) must report to IRS (on Form 8027) and to employees, tips reported by the employees to the employer plus the excess (as specially allocated) of 8% of the establishment's gross receipts (as specially defined) over the amount of tips thus reported by the employees. The 8% can be reduced to not below 2%, on application to IRS. (Code Sec. 6053(c)(3); Reg § 31.6053-3)[48] An employer doesn't have to report tips that aren't reported to the employer until it receives a Code Sec. 3121(q) Notice and Demand. Then, the employer reports them on its next Form 941.[49]

. . . *Unemployment insurance benefit* payments of $10 or more must be reported by the payor on Form 1099-G. (Code Sec. 6050B; Reg § 1.6050B-1)[50]

¶ 4747 Extension of time for information returns—Form 8809.

Use Form 8809 to request a 30-day extension to file the following forms: W-2 series, 1042-S, 1098 series, 1099 series, 5498 series, and 8027. Approval is automatic for 30-day extension requests (no signature or explanation needed). Detailed explanation and signature are required for requests beyond the original 30-day extension. (Reg § 1.6081-8(d))[1] Automatic extension is also available to file Social Security Administration's copy of Forms W-2 and W-3. (Reg § 31.6081(a)-1) Make a written application (don't use Form 8809) to request an extension of up to 30 days for furnishing the payee statement, see ¶4742.[2]

¶ 4748 Material advisors must disclose reportable transactions and maintain lists—Forms 8918, 13976.

Each material advisor with respect to any reportable transaction (under Code Sec. 6707A(c), ¶4891) files Form 8918 setting out: information identifying and describing a transaction and its expected tax benefits, and any other information that IRS requests. (Code

---

40. ¶S-3690; ¶60,50E4; TD ¶816,020
41. ¶S-3684 *et seq.*; ¶60,50N4; TD ¶816,016
42. ¶S-3206.1 *et seq.*; ¶60,394; TD ¶812,015.1 *et seq.*
43. ¶S-3173; ¶60,514; TD ¶812,013
44. ¶S-3399 *et seq.*; ¶4084.05; TD ¶813,035
45. ¶S-2862.3; ¶60,334
46. ¶S-2823.1; ¶60,334

47. ¶H-4344; ¶60,534; TD ¶532,011
48. ¶S-3250 *et seq.*; ¶S-3303; ¶60,534; TD ¶812,054
49. ¶H-4714.1; TD ¶546,007.1
50. ¶S-3694; ¶60,50B4; TD ¶816,023
1. ¶S-5049; ¶60,814.07
2. ¶s S-5041, S-5042; ¶60,814.07; TD ¶811,015

Sec. 6111(a); Reg § 301.6111-3(a)) It is due by the last day of the month following the calendar quarter in which a person becomes a material adviser.[3] For penalties, see ¶4893.

A material advisor is any person who provides any material aid, assistance, or advice with respect to organizing, managing, promoting, selling, implementing, insuring, or carrying out any reportable transaction, and who directly or indirectly derives gross income in excess of a threshold amount (or such other amount prescribed by IRS) for that assistance or advice. (Code Sec. 6111(b)(1)(A); Reg § 301.6111-3(b)) A person becomes a material adviser when (1) he makes a tax statement, (2) he receives (or expects to receive) the minimum fees, and (3) the transaction is entered into by the taxpayer.[4]

The threshold amount is $50,000 for a reportable transaction substantially all of the tax benefits from which are provided to natural persons, and $250,000 in any other case. (Code Sec. 6111(b)(1)(B); Reg § 301.6111-3(b)(3))

Each material advisor must maintain a list with respect to any reportable transaction. The list must identify each person for whom the advisor acted as a material advisor for the transaction and contain any other information as IRS regs may require. The list may (but is not required to) be kept on Form 13976. (Code Sec. 6112(a); Reg § 301.6112-1)[5]

¶ 4749 Participation in confidential tax avoidance transactions—Form 8886.

Taxpayers must disclose (on Form 8886 due with an original or amended return reporting participation) their participation in "reportable transactions," by attaching an information statement to their income tax returns, including: (a) listed transactions (i.e., transactions that have been specifically identified by IRS as tax avoidance transactions such as "sale in/lease-out" (SILO) or "lease-in-lease-out" (LILO) transactions, certain offsetting currency transactions solely used to import losses but not gains); (b) confidential transactions offered under conditions of confidentiality and for which the taxpayer has paid an advisor a minimum fee; (c) transactions with contractual protection; (d) loss transactions resulting in a taxpayer claiming a tax loss exceeding specified amounts; and (e) transactions of interest (i.e., transactions that are the same or substantially similar to transactions identified by IRS). (Reg § 1.6011-4) Transactions of interest include certain charitable contributions of real property interests ("successor member interests") that involve inflated valuations, "toggling" grantor trust transactions where grantor trusts are purportedly terminated and recreated to generate large losses, certain sales of interests in charitable remainder trusts that result in the grantor or other non-charitable recipient receiving the value of the trust while claiming to recognize little or no taxable gain, and certain transaction involving blocker partnerships to avoid the inclusion of income of lower-tier controlled foreign corporations.[6]

A copy of Form 8886 must be sent to the IRS Office of Tax Shelter Analysis (OTSA). For penalties, see ¶4891. Taxpayers also must disclose participation in listed transactions involving estate tax (Reg § 20.6011-4), gift tax (Reg § 25.6011-4), employment tax (Reg § 31.6011-4), excise tax related to private foundations and certain other tax exempts (Reg § 53.6011-4), excise taxes relating to qualified pension and other plans under Code Sec. 4971 through Code Sec. 4980F (Reg § 54.6011-4), and excise taxes relating to public charities. (Reg § 56.6011-4) Confidential corporate tax shelters also are subject to the tax shelter registration rules of Code Sec. 6111. Affected transactions are listed transactions and other tax-structured transactions as specially defined. (Reg § 301.6111-2)[7]

¶ 4750 Preparer's duty in preparation of returns.

A tax return preparer (¶4751) must:

. . . *sign the return* as prescribed by IRS in forms, instructions, etc. (Code Sec. 6695(b)) If the

---

3. ¶S-4401, ¶S-4413; ¶61,114; TD ¶817,005
4. ¶S-4403; ¶61,114; TD ¶817,003
5. ¶S-4414; ¶61,124

6. ¶S-4429; ¶61,114
7. ¶S-4434; ¶61,114; TD ¶817,002

return isn't signed electronically, he must sign a completed return before it is presented to a taxpayer for signature. If the preparer is unavailable for signature, another preparer must review the entire return and sign it. (Reg § 1.6695-1(b)(1)) Preparers may sign original or amended returns, or extension requests, as a return preparer with a stamp, mechanical device, or computer software program. The method used must contain either a facsimile of the preparer's signature or his printed name.[8]

... enter a preparer tax ID number (PTIN). (Code Sec. 6109(a)(4)) All compensated preparers (including those who already have PTINs) must register on the on-line registration system (on the Tax Professionals page at irs.gov) or submit a paper Form W-12 (4 to 6 weeks of response time). Preparers must renew PTINs annually and pay the associated user fee ($64.25 for 2013) after Oct. 15 and before Jan. 1. Preparers who aren't CPAs (or LPAs in certain states as listed on irs.gov), attorneys, or enrolled agents have to satisfy competency testing and continuing education requirements to obtain a PTIN, unless they are: (1) nonsigning preparers (¶4751) working under proper supervision (e.g., of an attorney, CPA, etc.) and meeting certain other conditions; (2) signing preparers (¶4751) of non-Form-1040 returns only; or (3) a registered tax return preparer (RTRP) who meets competency testing (test can be scheduled online via a PTIN account or by calling 855-IRS-TEST), continuing education courses (10 hours of federal tax law, 3 hours federal tax law changes, 2 hours of ethics annually) from an IRS-approved continuing education provider, and ethical standards. RTRPs also have to pass a background check (that may include fingerprinting) and a tax compliance check. But, a district court enjoined IRS from enforcing the RTRP requirements. Thus, pending appeal, tax return preparers don't have to complete competency testing or secure continuing education. The court's ruling didn't affect the regulatory practice requirements for CPAs, attorneys, enrolled agents, enrolled retirement plan agents, or enrolled actuaries, or the PTIN requirements.(Reg § 1.6109-2)[9] An enrolled retirement plan agent (ERPA) needs a PTIN if, for compensation, he prepares, or assists in the preparation of, all or substantially all of any tax return or claim for refund that is not an exempt form (e.g., Form 5300 and Form 5500 are exempt forms).[10]

... enter an address where the return was prepared on any return he prepares; if there's a partnership or employment arrangement between 2 or more preparers, the identifying number of the partnership or employer must also appear on the return or claim for refund. The identifying number of a preparer (whether an individual, corporation, or partnership) who employs or engages 1 or more persons to prepare returns or refund claims is that preparer's employer identification number (EIN). (Reg § 1.6109-2(a))[11]

... furnish the taxpayer with a completed copy of any tax return no later than when the return is presented for signature. (Code Sec. 6107(a)) The same rule applies to a return prepared for a nontaxable entity (i.e., partnership or S corporation). (Reg § 1.6107-1(a))[12]

... retain for 3 years a completed copy of each return or a list of the name and TIN of each taxpayer for whom a return was prepared (Code Sec. 6107(b));[13]

... retain a record of the name, TIN, and principal place of work of each income tax return preparer employed or engaged by the preparer/employer during each July 1 through June 30 period. (Reg § 1.6060-1(a)(1))[14]

... e-file individual income tax returns (and estate and trust returns), unless the preparer neither files nor reasonably expects to file 10 or more individual income tax returns in a calendar year. (Code Sec. 6011(e); Reg § 301.6011-7) E-filing is mandatory for preparers anticipating filing 11 or more federal individual or trust tax returns. Firms have to compute the number of returns in the aggregate that they reasonably expect to file as a firm. Clients can independently choose to file paper returns. Preparers should document each client's choice to file a paper return and keep a copy of the signed statement on file. Use

8. ¶S-4603; ¶S-4604; ¶66,954; TD ¶867,010
9. ¶S-1522; ¶61,094; TD ¶867,012
10. ¶S-1522.1; TD ¶867,012
11. ¶S-1523; ¶61,094; TD ¶867,012

12. ¶S-1102; ¶61,074; TD ¶867,015
13. ¶V-2675; ¶61,074; TD ¶867,014
14. ¶V-2676; ¶60,604; TD ¶867,013

Form 8944 to request hardship waivers from e-filing requirement.[15]

¶ 4751   Tax return preparer defined.

A tax return preparer is any person, including a partnership or corporation, who, in return for compensation, prepares, or employs or engages another to prepare, all or a substantial portion of any tax return or refund claim under the Internal Revenue Code. (Code Sec. 7701(a)(36)(A)) A *signing* tax return preparer is the individual tax return preparer who has the primary responsibility for the overall substantive accuracy of the preparation of the return or refund claim. (Reg § 301.7701-15(b)(1))

A *nonsigning* tax return preparer is any tax return preparer who is not a signing tax return preparer but who prepares all or a substantial portion of a return or claim for refund for events that have occurred at the time the advice is rendered. Time spent on advice that is given after events have occurred that represents less than 5% of the individual's aggregate time with respect to the position giving rise to the understatement is not taken into account. Examples of nonsigning tax return preparers are preparers who provide advice to a taxpayer or another preparer when that advice leads to a position or entry that is a substantial portion of the return. (Reg § 301.7701-15(b)(2)(i))[16]

A person may also be a "preparer" of a related return if an entry on a return he actually prepared (e.g., partnership or S corporation return) is directly reflected on the related return (e.g., partner's or shareholder's return), and the entry is a substantial portion of the related return. (Reg § 301.7701-15(b)(3)(iii))[17]

A portion of a return prepared by a nonsigning tax return preparer won't be "substantial" if, aggregating all schedules, etc., he prepared, that portion involves amounts of gross income, deductions, or amounts on which credits are based that are: (1) less than $10,000, or (2) less than $400,000 *and* less than 20% of the gross income (adjusted gross income, for individuals) as shown on the return. (Reg § 301.7701-15(b)(3)(ii)(A))[18]

A tax consultant is a "preparer" even though he may do no more than review a return already prepared by the taxpayer.[19] A person is a "preparer" if he supplies enough information and advice so that completion of a return is a mere mechanical or clerical matter (Reg § 301.7701-15(c))[20] but not if he merely furnishes typing, reproducing or other mechanical assistance with respect to preparing a return. (Code Sec. 7701(a)(36)(B)(i); Reg § 301.7701-15(f)(1)(viii)) A person who provides a computerized return preparation service is a preparer if his computer programs provide substantive tax determinations, but not if his services are limited to mechanical calculations and processing.[21]

¶ 4752   Taxpayer identification number (TIN)—Forms SS-5; W-7.

Any person who files a return, statement, or other document must include his own TIN (Code Sec. 6109(a)(1))[22] and the TIN of any other person, as required by the form or instructions to the form. (Code Sec. 6109(a)(3); Reg § 301.6109-1(c))[23] Thus, an alimony payor's return must include the payee's TIN. (Use Form W-9 to request another person's TIN.)[24] A child to whom the kiddie tax rules, ¶3135 *et seq.*, apply for any tax year must provide his parent's TIN on his (child's) tax return for that year. (Code Sec. 1(g)(6))[25]

Social security numbers (SSNs) are used to identify most individuals, sole proprietors not otherwise required to use employer identification numbers (EINs), and grantor trusts. (Code Sec. 6109(d); Reg § 301.6109-1(a))[26] To get an SSN, file Form SS-5 with the Social Security

15. ¶S-1601; ¶60,114.075; TD ¶572,002
16. ¶S-1107; ¶77,014.24; TD ¶867,002
17. ¶S-1117; TD ¶867,002
18. ¶S-1116; TD ¶867,006
19. ¶S-1109; TD ¶867,004
20. ¶S-1109; ¶61,074; TD ¶867,004

21. ¶S-1110; ¶61,075; TD ¶867,005
22. ¶S-1502; ¶61,094; TD ¶570,106
23. ¶S-1531; ¶61,094; TD ¶861,050
24. ¶S-1535; ¶2154.03; TD ¶861,050
25. ¶S-1544
26. ¶S-1505; ¶61,094; TD ¶570,106

Administration. (Reg § 301.6109-1(d)(1))[27] Information return filers can use a truncated TIN (TTIN) on paper payee statements (e.g., Form 1098, Form 1099, and Form 5498). (Prop Reg. § 301.6109-4 ["Taxpayers may rely"]) [28]

Aliens who aren't eligible for SSNs use IRS individual taxpayer identification numbers (ITINs) requested on Form W-7. (Reg § 301.6109-1(a))[29] Prospective adoptive parents who have had a child placed in their household by an authorized placement agency may apply (use Form W-7A) for a temporary (2-year) adoption taxpayer identification number (ATIN) for the child (unless the child is an alien eligible to get an ITIN) to satisfy filing requirements (but not for earned income credit purposes (¶2339)). (Reg § 301.6109-3)[30]

Other entities use EINs. (Reg § 301.6109-1(a)) Taxpayers can request an EIN instantly through http://www.irs.gov by entering the required information or by phone, mail, or fax. Persons issued an EIN must provide IRS with any updated application information that IRS requires. (Reg § 301.6109-1(d))[31] All employers (corporations, partnerships or sole proprietors) must get and use EINs for reporting employment and excise taxes.[32] Large food and beverage establishments use an identifying number for tip reporting. (Reg § 31.6053-3(a)(5))[33]

Buildings that have been or will be allocated a low-income housing credit must be assigned a building identification number (BIN) by the applicable state housing credit agency.[34]

Foreign transferors of U.S. real property interests (and transferees where applicable) must provide their TINs on withholding tax returns, applications for withholding certificates, etc. Foreign persons must have TINs for placement on any return, statement, or other document required by the regs under Code Sec. 897 or Code Sec. 1445. (Reg § 301.6109-1(b)(2)(vi))[35]

¶ 4753   Magnetic media and electronic filing—Form 4419.

Certain information returns *must* be filed on magnetic media. (Code Sec. 6011(e)(2)(A))[36] There are exceptions for certain low-volume filers (fewer than 250 returns), but partnerships with more than 100 partners (counting any person who is a partner at any time during its tax year) must file on magnetic media. (Reg § 301.6011-3)[37] E-filing satisfies the magnetic media requirement. Hardship waivers (request on Form 8508) are available. (Code Sec. 6011(e)(2)(B))[38] All annual reports—including any statements and schedules—for employee benefit plans must be filed electronically under the EFAST2 program (¶4746).[39]

The 250−or−more−return rule doesn't apply to any return filed by a financial institution for tax for which the institution is liable as a withholding agent under Code Sec. 1461 or Code Sec. 1474(a)). (Code Sec. 6011(e)(4))[40]

Submit Form 4419 at least 30 days before the return due date to apply to transmit information returns electronically/magnetically.[41] The due dates for filing paper information returns with IRS also apply to magnetic media filings, but not to e-filing. For magnetic media, Form 1098, forms in the Form 1099 series, and Form W-2G must be submitted to IRS postmarked by Feb. 28. For e-filing, however, the due date for information returns is Mar. 31.[42] A transmittal statement on Form 4804 must accompany magnetic media; Form 4804 isn't required for e-filers.[43]

Authorized IRS e-file providers include their e-filing identification numbers (EFINs) with all electronic return data transmitted to IRS.[44]

27. ¶S-1581; ¶61,094; TD ¶570,106
28. ¶S-1501A; TD ¶570,106.1
29. ¶S-1508.1; ¶61,094; TD ¶570,106
30. ¶S-1504.6 *et seq.*; ¶61,094.01; TD ¶570,110
31. ¶S-1582 *et seq.*; ¶61,094; TD ¶659,009
32. ¶S-1505; ¶61,094
33. ¶S-3289; TD ¶812,039
34. ¶S-1521; ¶424.70
35. ¶S-1508

36. ¶S-1301; ¶60,114.07; TD ¶861,061
37. ¶S-1350; ¶60,114.065; TD ¶596,025
38. ¶S-1314; ¶60,114.07
39. ¶S-3351; ¶S-3353
40. ¶S-1302; ¶60,114.07; TD ¶861,061
41. ¶S-1311
42. ¶S-1305; TD ¶861,062
43. ¶S-1308; TD ¶861,062
44. ¶S-1611; TD ¶572,019

Individuals and organizations with 25 or more trucks, tractors or other heavy vehicles used on highways have to file excise tax Form 2290 electronically.[45]

¶ 4754 Timely mailing as timely filing and paying.

A return, claim, statement, document or payment (except a tax deposit) that must be filed or made by a certain date generally is considered timely filed or made if it has a timely postmark. (Code Sec. 7502(c)(1))[46] This also applies to claims for credit or refund made on a late-filed original return but doesn't apply to an amended return showing additional tax. (Reg § 301.7502-1(f))[47] For the timely mailing rule to apply, the return, etc., must be: (1) deposited in the U.S. mail in a properly addressed envelope or wrapper with sufficient postage; (Code Sec. 7502(a)(2)(B)) (2) postmarked by the prescribed filing or payment date (Code Sec. 7502(a)(2)(A)) (returns postmarked after the due date are considered filed when received by IRS); and (3) actually delivered by U.S. mail to the proper place. (Code Sec. 7502(a)(1))A Tax Court petition mailed in a foreign country was timely even though it lacked a U.S. postmark where it was shown by the U.S. mail tracking system to have entered the U.S. domestic mail service within the required time period.[48] Some courts permit delivery to be proven by a common-law "mailbox rule" (i.e., when mail is properly addressed and deposited in the U.S. mail, with prepaid postage, there is a rebuttable presumption that the addressee received it in the ordinary course of the mail).[49]

The timely-mailing rule applies to private delivery services (PDSs) such as: *DHL* Same Day Service; *FedEx* Priority Overnight, FedEx Standard Overnight, FedEx 2Day, FedEx International Priority, and FedEx International First; *UPS* Next Day Air, UPS Next Day Air Saver, UPS 2nd Day Air, UPS 2nd Day Air A.M., UPS Worldwide Express Plus, and UPS Worldwide Express. (Code Sec. 7502(f); Reg § 301.7502-1(c)(3))[50]

The postmark stamp date on the mailing envelope overrides the postmark stamp date on a Certificate of Mailing (P.S. Form 3817).[1] If a private postage meter is used, the postmark isn't enough. The document must actually be received by the proper office or officer not later than the time the postmark indicates it ordinarily would be received. If it is actually received later, taxpayer can prove timely mailing only by showing: (1) that the document was deposited in the mail before the last collection that was postmarked (by the U.S. Post Office) on the last day for filing; and (2) that the delay in receiving the document was due to delay in transmission of the mail; and (3) the cause of the delay. (Reg § 301.7502-1(c)(1)(iii)(B))[2]

An e-filed tax return (¶4703) isn't considered filed until IRS acknowledges the electronic portion of the return as accepted and a signature has been received either electronically or on Form 8453 (used to transmit paper schedules or forms that can't be e-filed).[3]

¶ 4755 Effect of registered or certified mail.

The date of registration is considered to be the postmark date, (Code Sec. 7502(c)(1)(B)) and registration is prima facie evidence the return, etc., was delivered to the agency, officer or office to which addressed. (Code Sec. 7502(c)(1)(A))[4] The U.S. postmark date on the sender's receipt is treated as the postmark date of a document sent by certified mail (Reg § 301.7502-1(c)(2)), and proof that a properly postmarked certified mail sender's receipt was properly issued and that the envelope or wrapper was properly addressed is prima facie evidence that the document was properly delivered. (Reg § 301.7502-1(e)(2))[5]

---

45. ¶W-6456
46. ¶T-10751; ¶75,024; TD ¶570,237
47. ¶T-10752.1; ¶75,024
48. ¶T-10751 *et seq.*; ¶75,024; TD ¶570,237
49. ¶T-10774 *et seq.*
50. ¶T-10781; ¶75,024; TD ¶570,238

1. ¶T-10762
2. ¶T-10763; TD ¶570,237
3. ¶S-1609, ¶S-1617.3; ¶60,114.08; TD ¶572,018
4. ¶T-10762.3; ¶75,024; TD ¶570,237
5. ¶T-10776.1; TD ¶570,237

¶ 4756　Due date on Saturday, Sunday or holiday.

If a due date falls on Saturday, Sunday or legal holiday, there is an automatic extension of time to the next succeeding day that isn't a Saturday, Sunday or legal holiday. The rule applies to *all acts* required to be performed under the Code both by the *taxpayer* and IRS. "Legal holiday" includes: (1) the legal holidays throughout the state or possession where the office at which the act to be performed is located even if not a legal holiday in the state or possession where the taxpayer resides, and (2) all legal holidays in the District of Columbia (D.C.) (Code Sec. 7503), i.e.: New Year's Day (Jan. 1); Inauguration Day (Jan. 20, every fourth year); Martin Luther King, Jr.'s birthday (3rd Mon. in Jan.); President's Day (3rd Mon. in Feb.); Emancipation Day (Apr. 16); Memorial Day (last Mon. in May); Independence Day (July 4); Labor Day (first Mon. in Sept.); Columbus Day (second Mon. in Oct.); Veterans Day (Nov. 11); Thanksgiving Day (4th Thurs. in Nov.); and Christmas Day (Dec. 25). If a holiday in D.C. falls on Sunday, the next day is a holiday in D.C. When a legal holiday in D.C. (other than Inauguration Day) falls on a Saturday, it's treated as falling on the preceding Friday.[6]

¶ 4757　How to get a copy of a tax return— Forms 4506, 4506T, 4506T-EZ.

Use Form 4506.[7] IRS charges $57 for each return requested. Use Form 4506-T to request free tax return transcripts, tax account transcripts, W-2 information, 1099 information, verification of non-filing, or a record of account.[8] For a free Form 1040 series tax return transcript, use Form 4506T-EZ or IRS's telephone automated system to order. Transcripts requested under the automated system can't be mailed to a third party.

---

6. ¶T-10790 *et seq.*; ¶75,034; TD ¶570,240

7. ¶S-6407; ¶s 61,034, 61,034.09

8. ¶S-6409; ¶61,034

Chapter 25   Deficiencies—Refunds—Penalties

¶ 4800   **Tax Audits, Deficiencies and Assessments.** ▬▬▬▬▬▬▬▬▬▬

IRS makes certain preliminary cursory checks of every return filed; it selects returns for audit based on various criteria. Once IRS finishes an audit, a taxpayer has various alternatives it can pursue to resolve any disputed items.

¶ 4801   **Mathematical, etc., check of returns.**

IRS checks every return for math errors and computes tax using figures on the return. If the taxpayer made a computational error resulting in a tax underpayment, IRS sends a corrected computation and a notice and demand for payment of any balance due (which doesn't entitle the taxpayer to go to Tax Court) (Code Sec. 6213(b)(1)) or reduces any refund. (Reg § 601.105(a)) Failure to include a correct taxpayer identification number (TIN) on the return, as required under Code Sec. 21 (child care credit), Code Sec. 24 (child credit), Code Sec. 25A (higher education credit), Code Sec. 32 (earned income credit (EIC)), and Code Sec. 151 (personal exemptions), is treated as a math or clerical error and assessed accordingly. If an EIC is claimed on net earnings from self-employment, failure to pay the proper amount of self-employment tax is treated as a math error. So is failing to provide IRS with certain information after improperly claiming an EIC. (Code Sec. 6213(g)(2)(K)) IRS may treat an EIC claim on a noncustodial parent's return as a math error. (Code Sec. 6213(g)(2)(M))[1]

Adjustments to make an S corporation shareholder's return consistent with the corporation's return are treated as resulting from math or clerical error. (Code Sec. 6037(c)(3))[2] Similar rules apply when estate and trust beneficiaries file returns inconsistent with the entity's. (Code Sec. 6034A(c)(3))[3] A taxpayer's federal income and estate tax returns may also be checked against his state or foreign tax returns.[4]

¶ 4802   **Check against information returns.**

IRS compares the taxpayers' income tax returns against information returns, such as wage, interest and dividend statements, under a document matching program (Information Returns Program). If there is a mismatch, IRS sends the taxpayer a computer-generated notice (CP-2000), which must describe the basis for, and identify, any amounts of taxes, additions, interest or penalties claimed to be due. (Code Sec. 7522) The notice, which isn't a demand for payment, can be challenged by the taxpayer, who has the burden of proof. IRS also matches information filed by pass-through entities (partnerships, S corporations, and trusts) to what the partners, shareholders, and beneficiaries report on their own returns.[5]

¶ 4803   **Returns selected for examination.**

IRS selects returns for examination, e.g., based on discrepancy with information returns (¶4802), the filing of frivolous returns, random sampling (National Research Program (NRP)), etc. IRS's computerized "discriminant function" (DIF) technique ranks and selects returns having the greatest audit potential. In fiscal year 2012, IRS audited 1.0% of all individual returns that were filed in the previous year.[6]

---

1. ¶T-3628; ¶62,134.02; TD ¶836,017
2. ¶D-1801; ¶60,374; TD ¶614,724
3. ¶C-3081; ¶C-9081; ¶60,34A4; TD ¶655,501, 665,029
4. ¶T-1001; TD ¶821,001
5. ¶s T-1003, T-1004; ¶75,224; TD ¶821,003
6. ¶T-1023, T-1060 *et seq.*; TD ¶821,004

References beginning with a single letter are to paragraphs in RIA's Federal Tax Coordinator 2d and RIA's Analysis of Federal Taxes: Income. Those beginning with numbers are to paragraphs in RIA's United States Tax Reporter. Those beginning with TD are to paragraphs in RIA's Tax Desk.

¶ 4804 Individual taxpayers' average deductions.

2011 Average Deductions Claimed Based on Adjusted Gross Income
Adjusted Gross Income in Thousands of Dollars

AGI	$0-15	$15-30	$30-50	$50-100	$100-200	$200-250	$250 & UP
Medical	8,351	7,838	6,943	7,376	10,003	16,814	34,797
Taxes Paid	3,137	3,249	3,988	6,235	10,853	18,083	47,616
State & local tax*	733	1,017	1,663	3,216	6,324	11,622	37,357
Income taxes only	1,104	1,231	1,907	3,656	7,105	13,016	43,488
Gen. sales tax only	559	791	1,097	1,514	2,125	3,212	4,119
Contributions	1,443	2,127	2,287	2,881	3,890	5,703	18,490
Interest	7,414	7,346	7,436	8,768	11,266	15,217	20,685
Total itemized	15,014	15,092	15,422	19,311	26,832	38,814	88,058

* State and local taxes are the total of both income taxes and general sales taxes.

observation: RIA computed these averages from IRS's latest available statistics.

¶ 4805 Settlement initiatives.

IRS periodically offers qualifying taxpayers who have participated in various tax shelters or who have otherwise taken tax positions that IRS considers abusive an opportunity to settle on terms that are more favorable than could result if the parties litigated.[7] IRS will consider voluntary taxpayer disclosures in determining whether cases will be criminally prosecuted. Early in 2012, IRS announced the reopening of its voluntary disclosure program which is set to remain open for an indefinite period until otherwise announced. A streamlined compliance procedure became available Sept. 1, 2012, for nonresident taxpayers who owe little or no back taxes and seek to catch up with filing.[8]

¶ 4806 Types of examinations (audits); time and place.

IRS fixes the time and method of examination, which must be reasonable under the circumstances. (Code Sec. 7605(a); Reg § 301.7605-1(a)) Depending on the amounts and sources of income and the nature of the taxpayer's business, an examination may be at: (1) an IRS office, with the taxpayer bringing (office audit) or mailing (correspondence audit) his records (Reg § 601.105(b)(2)(ii)), or (2) the office of the taxpayer (or his representative) (field audit). (Reg § 601.105(b)(3))[9]

IRS generally won't conduct the audit at the taxpayer's place of business if the business is so small that doing so essentially requires him to close the business.[10] The taxpayer may ask to have the audit transferred, e.g., to where his books and records are kept. IRS also may initiate a transfer, but the taxpayer may ask to keep the original site. (Reg § 301.7605-1(e), Reg § 301.7605-1(g))[11] Restrictions apply to IRS's use of financial status or economic reality examination techniques (so-called "lifestyle" audits). (Code Sec. 7602(e))[12]

---

7. ¶M-5977
8. ¶V-1813.5 *et seq.*
9. ¶T-1090 *et seq.*; ¶76,054; TD ¶821,011

10. ¶T-1094; ¶76,054; TD ¶821,011
11. ¶T-1102; TD ¶821,015
12. ¶T-1076; ¶76,024; TD ¶821,010

¶ 4807 Taxpayer's rights in an examination.

Before or at an initial in-person interview (other than criminal investigations), IRS must give the taxpayer an explanation (written or oral) of the audit process (and assessment and collection) and his rights under that process. (Code Sec. 7521(b)(1))[13] A taxpayer has the right to: be represented by an advisor (¶4808); make certain audio (but generally not videotape) recordings of meetings (on advance notice) with the IRS agent (Code Sec. 7521(a)(1)); claim additional deductions not claimed on the return; ask that a particular technical question raised in the examination be referred to IRS's National Office for technical advice; not be subjected to unnecessary examinations (¶4810); and claim constitutional rights if questioned about possible criminal violations.[14]

¶ 4808 Who can represent the taxpayer?

The taxpayer's representative may be an attorney, CPA, enrolled agent, enrolled actuary or any other person permitted (under Circular 230, Reg § 10.3) to represent taxpayers before IRS, who isn't disbarred or suspended from practice before IRS, and who has a written power of attorney (on Form 2848) executed by the taxpayer. Absent a summons, IRS can't require the taxpayer to accompany the representative. (Code Sec. 7521(c))[15] If, during an interview, the taxpayer clearly states a desire to consult with a representative, IRS must suspend the interview for that purpose. (Code Sec. 7521(b)(2))[16]

Where legal advice of any kind is sought from a professional legal adviser in that capacity, the communications relating to that purpose, made in confidence by the client, are protected from disclosure by himself or the adviser unless he waives the protection.[17] The work product privilege protects written statements, private memoranda and personal recollections, prepared or formed by an adverse party's counsel in the course of his legal duties, that aren't protected by the attorney-client privilege. The First Circuit held it doesn't protect tax accrual workpapers.[18] An attorney-client privilege of communications applies for other federally authorized tax practitioners with respect to tax advice (except for tax shelters) in any noncriminal tax matter or proceeding. (Code Sec. 7525)[19] An individual can check a box on his return to authorize IRS to communicate with his paid preparer (¶4751) about math error notices and the status of a refund or payment, but must sign a power of attorney for representation on examination matters, underreported income, appeals and collections notices.[20]

¶ 4809 IRS's power to summon persons and records.

IRS can issue a summons for a taxpayer's testimony and records (Code Sec. 7602(a)) for a legitimate purpose, if IRS doesn't make unreasonable demands.[21] The summons (Form 2039) must describe with reasonable certainty the records sought (Code Sec. 7603), and set the examination time—not less than ten days from summons date. (Code Sec. 7605(a))[22] If the taxpayer intentionally disregards the summons, IRS can apply to the district court (or U.S. Commissioner) for an order directing compliance. (Code Sec. 7604(b))[23]

IRS may issue a summons ("third-party summons") to a person other than the taxpayer (e.g., his employer, or a "third-party recordkeeper," such as his bank) for testimony and records bearing on its examination of the taxpayer. (Certain communications (see ¶4808) are privileged.) Subject to exceptions, within three days of the service of a summons on a third party, but no later than the 23rd day before the day fixed in the summons as the day when

---

13. ¶T-1122 *et seq.*; ¶75,214; TD ¶821,016
14. ¶s T-1120 *et seq.*, T-1129 *et seq.*; ¶76,024.10; TD ¶821,017
15. ¶s T-1124, T-1127; ¶75,214; TD ¶821,018
16. ¶T-1127; ¶75,214; TD ¶821,017
17. ¶T-1314
18. ¶T-1330

19. ¶T-1334; ¶75,254; TD ¶822,011
20. ¶S-6405.3
21. ¶T-1201, T-1212; ¶76,024; TD ¶822,001
22. ¶T-1354; ¶76,024.04; TD ¶822,002
23. ¶T-1357; ¶76,044; TD ¶822,012

the records are to be examined, IRS must send by registered or certified mail a notice of the summons, including a copy of the summons, and an explanation of the taxpayer's right to institute a suit to quash the summons. (Code Sec. 7609(a)(1); Reg § 301.7609-1) If the taxpayer intervenes in a proceeding to enforce a third-party summons, the running of the assessment period for the taxpayer is suspended for the period during which a proceeding, and any appeal, as to the enforcement of the summons is pending. (Code Sec. 7609(e)(1); Reg § 301.7609-5(b)) IRS generally can't contact any third parties without providing reasonable notice in advance to the taxpayer. (Code Sec. 7602(c)(1); Reg § 301.7602-2(d))[24] With some exceptions, IRS may not issue, or begin any action to enforce, any summons to produce or analyze any tax-related computer software source code. (Code Sec. 7612)[25] A summons can't be issued (or enforced) against a person for whom a Justice Department referral is in effect (i.e., criminal tax prosecution is recommended). (Code Sec. 7602(d))[26]

¶ 4810 One examination rule—unnecessary examinations.

Unnecessary examinations are barred. IRS may make only one inspection of a taxpayer's books and records for each tax year unless the taxpayer requests otherwise, or IRS notifies him *in writing* that an additional inspection is necessary (Code Sec. 7605(b)), or IRS suspects fraud.[27] Re-examination also is permitted if the taxpayer doesn't file a timely Tax Court petition after receiving a 90-day letter (¶4824) for the year.[28]

¶ 4811 National Taxpayer Advocate (NTA)—Taxpayer Assistance Orders (TAOs).

The Office of the Taxpayer Advocate is headed by the NTA, who reports directly to the Commissioner. (Code Sec. 7803(c)(1)) Its functions are to assist taxpayers in resolving problems with IRS, identify areas where taxpayers have problems dealing with IRS, propose changes in IRS administrative practices to mitigate these identified problems, and identify potential legislative changes that may do so. (Code Sec. 7803(c)(2)(A)) The NTA is responsible for appointing local taxpayer advocates. (Code Sec. 7803(c)(2)(D)) On taxpayer's application to the Office of the Taxpayer Advocate, the NTA can issue a TAO if it determines that the taxpayer is suffering (or will suffer) significant hardship because of IRS's administration of the tax laws. (Code Sec. 7811(a)(1)) The taxpayer's application is made in the manner prescribed in the regs. (Reg § 301.7811-1(b))[29]

¶ 4812 User fees for IRS rulings or determinations.

IRS charges taxpayers a separate user fee for each request for a ruling, closing agreement, installment agreement or similar service. (Code Sec. 7528(a))[30]

¶ 4813 Proposed deficiencies—revenue agent's report (RAR).

An IRS examiner may propose adjustments to a taxpayer's return before *determining* a deficiency (¶4823), (which generally doesn't exist until IRS issues a statutory notice of deficiency—"90-day letter," see ¶4824).[31] The agent will discuss the proposed adjustments with the taxpayer to settle the case informally. The taxpayer can agree to the adjustments or argue they should be modified ("unagreed" case) before the examiner submits his RAR. Once the RAR is submitted, the taxpayer can discuss and settle the case only in an Appeals Office conference (¶4816).[32]

In an unagreed field audit case, the agent prepares a report explaining the proposed

---

24. ¶T-1250 *et seq.*; ¶76,094; TD ¶822,013
25. ¶T-1290; ¶76,124; TD ¶822,200
26. ¶s T-1205, T-1206; ¶76,024; TD ¶822,004
27. ¶76,024.09
28. ¶T-1425 *et seq.*; ¶76,024.10; TD ¶822,022

29. ¶T-10205 *et seq.*; ¶78,114 *et seq.*; TD ¶821,024
30. ¶T-10000 *et seq.*; ¶75,284
31. ¶T-1550 *et seq.*; TD ¶823,502
32. ¶T-1550 *et seq.*; TD ¶824,001

adjustments. After review by the district review staff, the RAR is sent to the taxpayer with a transmittal letter ("30-day letter," see ¶4814). (Reg § 601.105(c)(2)(i))[33] In an office audit, the taxpayer will usually be informed of the examiner's findings and given an opportunity to agree at the end of the interview. If he doesn't agree, he may request an immediate meeting with an appeals officer. If the taxpayer doesn't request an immediate conference, or it isn't practicable, the RAR (and 30-day letter) will be mailed to him. (Reg § 601.105(c)(1)(ii))[34]

¶ 4814   The 30-day letter.

The examiner's report that IRS sends, along with a transmittal ("30-day letter") to a taxpayer who rejects the examiner's findings from a field or office audit, must show the basis for and amount of any proposed adjustments. (Code Sec. 7522(a), Code Sec. 7522(b)(3)) The letter also explains appeal procedures and asks a taxpayer to indicate within 30 days whether he will: accept the findings and sign a waiver of restrictions on assessment (Form 870, which allows IRS to collect the deficiency without issuing a 90-day letter (¶4824), and limits the taxpayer's appeal to a claim or suit for refund (no Tax Court petition)); request an Appeals Office conference (¶4816); or do nothing and IRS will send a 90-day letter. (Reg § 601.105(d)(1)) IRS must include an explanation of the entire process from examination through collection as to a proposed deficiency with any first letter of proposed deficiency that allows the taxpayer an opportunity for administrative review in the IRS Office of Appeals.[35]

¶ 4815   Early referral to Appeals.

Any taxpayer may request early referral of one or more unresolved issues, from either the examination or collection division, to the IRS Office of Appeals. (Code Sec. 7123(a))[36]

¶ 4816   Appeals Office conference.

The taxpayer can get an Appeals Office conference by sending a written request (in response to a 30-day letter, see ¶4814) and any required protest (¶4817) to IRS.[37] The Appeals Office proceedings are informal and testimony isn't under oath, although the taxpayer may be asked to submit affidavits. (Reg § 601.106(c))[38] An Appeals Office conference still is available to a taxpayer even after IRS has issued a 90-day letter (¶4824), e.g., where the taxpayer ignored the 30-day letter or where the assessment period was about to expire (or the taxpayer requested the 90-day letter). If the taxpayer then files a Tax Court petition (income, estate or gift tax case) or pays the additional tax assessed, he can get an Appeals conference. (Reg § 601.106(a)(1))[39]

¶ 4817   Protest.

An oral request is enough to get Appeals consideration in all office or correspondence audit cases. In a field audit case, a written protest is: *required* if the total amount of the proposed increase in tax (including penalties), proposed overassessment or claimed refund, or compromise offer exceeds $10,000 for any tax period; *optional* (but a statement of issues is required) if that total amount is between $2,500 and $10,000; and *not required* if it is less than $2,500. (Reg § 601.106(a)(1)(iii)(a))[40] The 30-day letter (¶4814) contains instructions for the protest (Reg § 601.105(d)(2)) and spells out the required information.[41]

33. ¶T-1601; TD ¶823,502
34. ¶T-1604 *et seq.*; TD ¶823,505 *et seq.*
35. ¶T-1601 *et seq.*; TD ¶823,503
36. ¶T-1709; ¶71,234; TD ¶824,001
37. ¶T-1711; TD ¶824,002

38. ¶T-1720
39. ¶s T-1710, T-1900 *et seq.*
40. ¶T-1713; TD ¶824,008
41. ¶T-1717; TD ¶824,009

¶ 4818 Appeals Office settlement authority; nonbinding mediation and arbitration.

The Appeals Office has authority to settle all factual and legal issues raised by the examiner's report (RAR, see ¶4813) or the taxpayer's protest (¶4817) (Reg § 601.106(f)(2))[42] as long as the case isn't docketed in the Tax Court. (Reg § 601.106(a)(2))[43] If no settlement is reached, IRS will prepare a 90-day letter (¶4824).[44] Under procedures prescribed by IRS, either the taxpayer or IRS Office of Appeals can request nonbinding mediation on any issue that is still unresolved after the conclusion of appeals procedures, or unsuccessful attempts to enter into a closing agreement or a compromise. (Code Sec. 7123(b)(1))[45] In addition, a taxpayer and IRS can jointly request binding arbitration of factual issues unresolved after the conclusion of appeals procedures, or unsuccessful attempts to enter into a closing agreement or a compromise. (Code Sec. 7123(b)(2))[46]

¶ 4819 Execution of Appeals Office settlement—Form 870, Form 890.

If the taxpayer accepts IRS's position in full, with no concessions, he signs a Form 870 (Form 890, in gift, estate or generation-skipping transfer tax cases), waiving restrictions on assessment (¶4830). (Reg § 601.106(d)(2))[47] For concessions, see ¶4820.

¶ 4820 Settlement with concessions—Form 870-AD, Form 890-AD.

If the Appeals Office makes any concessions, a Form 870-AD (Form 890-AD, in estate tax cases) is executed stating that: the settlement is subject to acceptance by IRS; on acceptance, it won't be reopened by IRS absent fraud, malfeasance, concealment or misrepresentation of a material fact, an important mathematical mistake, or an excessive tentative net operating loss (NOL) carryback; *and* the taxpayer waives his right to file a claim for refund (other than from an NOL carryback) for any years covered by the agreement.[48]

¶ 4821 Final closing agreements—Form 866, Form 906.

The taxpayer and IRS may conclusively settle a tax dispute by entering into a final agreement to close either a tax year that has ended (use Form 866) (Code Sec. 7121(a); Reg § 301.7121-1(b)(2), Reg § 601.202(a)(2))[49] or a *specific transaction,* past or future (use Form 906). (Reg § 601.202(b))[50] The agreement is irrevocable (except for fraud, malfeasance or misrepresentation of a material fact) and binds *both* parties. (Code Sec. 7121(b))[1]

¶ 4822 Offer in compromise—Form 656, Form 433-A, Form 433-B.

Civil or criminal tax cases can be compromised by IRS, after assessment, before referral to the Department of Justice (after referral, compromise can be only by the Attorney General). (Code Sec. 7122(a))[2] IRS may compromise tax liabilities on any of these grounds: (1) doubt as to collectibility, (2) doubt as to liability, (3) to promote effective tax administration because either (a) collection of the full amount would cause economic hardship for the taxpayer, or (b) compelling public policy or equity considerations justify compromise. (Reg § 301.7122-1(b)) To make an offer, file Form 656 (which has a box allowing a taxpayer to designate someone to assist while IRS is processing the offer) and, except for offers based solely on doubt as to liability, Form 433-A (individuals) or Form 433-B (businesses) (sole proprietors file must file both of the latter forms) and pay the $150 processing fee that has applied since 2003.

42. ¶T-1721; TD ¶824,003
43. ¶T-1725; TD ¶824,003
44. ¶T-1732; TD ¶824,003
45. ¶T-1733; ¶71,234; TD ¶824,003.1
46. ¶T-1756
47. ¶T-1731; TD ¶824,005

48. ¶T-3401 *et seq.*; ¶62,134.03; TD ¶824,006
49. ¶T-9500; ¶71,214.02; TD ¶841,011
50. ¶T-9521; ¶71,214.02 *et seq.*; TD ¶841,012
1. ¶T-9507; ¶s 71,214.07, 71,214.08; TD ¶841,005
2. ¶T-9600; T-9649; ¶71,224 *et seq.*; TD ¶842,001

(Reg § 301.7122-1(d)(1))[3] IRS may disregard frivolous offer submissions. (Code Sec. 7122(g))[4]

¶ 4823 Deficiency defined.

A deficiency is the amount by which a taxpayer's correct tax liability is more than the excess of: (1) the tax shown on the return (math or clerical errors corrected), plus (2) the amounts previously assessed (or collected without assessment) as a deficiency, over (3) the amount of any rebates (credits, refunds, or other repayments). (Code Sec. 6211(a), Code Sec. 6213(b)) The correct tax and the tax shown on the return are computed without regard to credits for estimated taxes and taxes withheld under Code Sec. 31 (i.e., on wages, including excess social security withholdings, and back-up withholding). (Code Sec. 6211(b)(1)) In determining a deficiency, any excess of certain specified credits over the tax imposed by subtitle A (without taking into account those credits) and any excess of those credits shown by the taxpayer on the return over the amount shown as tax on the return (without taking into account those credits) is taken into account as a negative amount of tax. The specified credits are the additional child tax credit under Code Sec. 24(d), the education credit allowable by reason of Code Sec. 25A(i)(5), the Code Sec. 34 gasoline and special fuel tax credit, the earned income credit, the Code Sec. 35 health coverage credit, the first-time homebuyer credit applicable to certain pre-May 2010 contracts, the Code Sec. 53(e) AMT refundable credit, the Code Sec. 168(k)(4) credit in lieu of depreciation, and the Code Sec. 6431 credit for certain bond issuers. (Code Sec. 6211(b)(4)) If no return was filed, or if a return doesn't show any tax, the deficiency equals the entire amount of the correct tax. Additional taxes reported on an amended return filed after its due date are treated as "tax shown" ((1) above), not deficiencies. (Reg § 301.6211-1(a))[5] If a taxpayer elects to have IRS compute the tax, IRS's computation of tax imposed is the "tax shown" on the return. (Code Sec. 6211(b)(3))[6] Where a joint return deficiency is challenged by only one spouse, the deficiency for that spouse is reduced by any tax collected from the other spouse.[7]

¶ 4824 Notice of deficiency—"90-day letter."

A statutory notice of deficiency ("90-day letter") tells a taxpayer that IRS has determined a deficiency (in income, estate or gift tax, or excise tax on private foundations or pension plans). This is the only notice IRS will issue for that determination.[8] It must describe the basis for and identify the amounts (if any) of tax, interest, additional amounts, additions to tax and assessable penalties (for exceptions, see ¶4826) (Code Sec. 7522(a)),[9] and be sent by certified or registered mail to the taxpayer at his last known address.[10] After receiving the letter, the taxpayer can: pay the deficiency, not pay and seek to rescind it, pay and file a refund claim (¶4849), take no action (let tax be assessed) and then file a compromise offer (¶4822), or file a Tax Court petition (¶4859).[11]

All 90-day letters must include the date determined by IRS as the last day on which the taxpayer may file a petition with the Tax Court, ¶4859. (Code Sec. 6213(a)) But the Tax Court says that failure to include the date doesn't necessarily invalidate the letter.[12] Notices must include information about interest (Code Sec. 6631) and penalties (Code Sec. 6751).[13]

¶ 4825 Time for making assessments.

Unless the taxpayer and IRS sign a closing agreement (¶4821), or the taxpayer voluntarily pays the deficiency or signs a Form 870 (¶4814), or IRS determines collection is in jeopardy

---

3. ¶T-10024; ¶71,224.03; TD ¶842,012
4. ¶T-9612; ¶71,224.03; TD ¶842,012
5. ¶T-1501; ¶62,114; TD ¶822,501
6. ¶T-1506; ¶62,114.01; TD ¶822,501
7. ¶T-1507; TD ¶822,501
8. ¶T-2701; ¶62,124; TD ¶831,001

9. ¶T-2714; ¶75,224; TD ¶831,004
10. ¶T-2801; ¶62,124; TD ¶831,007; 831,008
11. ¶T-2738; TD ¶831,009
12. ¶T-2912.1; ¶62,134.1
13. ¶T-2714.1, ¶T-2714.2; ¶67,514, ¶66,314

(¶4828), or in the case of court ordered restitution (¶4827), IRS can't assess deficiencies in income, estate, and gift taxes, and the excise taxes on private foundations and qualified pension, etc., plans until after the taxpayer has had an opportunity to make a Tax Court appeal. (Code Sec. 6213(a))[14]

¶ 4826 Assessment of interest and penalties.

Interest may be assessed when the underlying tax is collectible. (Code Sec. 6601(g))[15] For income, estate, gift and certain excise taxes, the negligence and fraud penalties are assessed like deficiencies (¶4825). So are the delinquency penalties (¶4873, ¶4874), but only if attributable to a deficiency and not if measured by the tax shown on the return. The penalty for estimated tax underpayments (¶3349) is assessed as a deficiency only if no return is filed. (Code Sec. 6665(b); Reg § 301.6659-1(c))[16] The normal assessment and collection rules don't apply to the penalties for promoting an abusive tax shelter (¶4889) or for aiding and abetting a tax understatement (¶4885). A taxpayer may delay collection of these penalties by paying at least 15% of the penalty and filing a claim for refund of it, within 30 days of notice and demand for payment. If IRS denies the claim, the taxpayer has 30 days to sue for refund in a district court (where IRS may counterclaim for the unpaid penalty amount). The normal procedures also don't apply to the penalty for filing a frivolous return (¶4898). (Code Sec. 6703(b), Code Sec. 6703(c))[17]

¶ 4827 Assessment of restitution payments.

IRS can assess and collect restitution for unpaid taxes owed by defendants in criminal tax cases as if it were a tax. (Code Sec. 6201(a)(4))[18] Court-ordered restitution can be assessed, or a court proceeding for the amount can be begun without assessment, at any time. (Code Sec. 6501(c)(11))[19] Because amounts of tax liability ordered pursuant to a restitution order are not subject to the deficiency procedures described at ¶4824, taxpayers may not challenge an assessment of restitution in any proceeding including before the Tax Court. (Code Sec. 6201(a)(4)(C))

IRS may not collect criminal restitution and a civil tax liability for the same period because that would be impermissible double collection. Any payments made to satisfy the restitution-based assessment must also be applied by IRS to satisfy the civil tax liability for the same tax period.[20]

¶ 4828 Jeopardy assessment and termination of a tax year.

If IRS believes assessment or collection of a deficiency will be jeopardized by delay, it can immediately assess the deficiency (plus interest and penalties) and demand payment. (Code Sec. 6861(a); Reg § 301.6861-1(a)) But, within 60 days after the assessment, IRS must issue the taxpayer a 90-day letter (¶4824) if it hasn't already done so. (Code Sec. 6861(b))[21] IRS Chief Counsel must pre-approve jeopardy assessments. (Code Sec. 7429(a)(1)(A))[22] IRS can presume the collection of income tax is in jeopardy if an individual who has physical possession of more than $10,000 in cash or cash equivalents denies ownership of it and doesn't claim it belongs to another identifiable person who acknowledges ownership. (Code Sec. 6867(a), Code Sec. 6867(d); Reg § 301.6867-1(f)(2), Reg § 301.6867-1(f)(3)) The entire amount of the cash is presumed to represent income of the possessor for the year and is taxable at the highest individual tax rate. (Code Sec. 6867(b)) The possessor is treated as the taxpayer for assessment and collection purposes (unless the true owner comes forward), but

---

14. ¶T-3602; ¶62,134; TD ¶836,002
15. ¶T-3646; ¶66,014.01; TD ¶836,011
16. ¶T-3638 *et seq.*; ¶66,654; TD ¶836,012
17. ¶V-5650; ¶67,034
18. ¶T-3639; ¶62,014; TD ¶836,003

19. ¶T-4172; ¶65,014.149
20. ¶T-3639; ¶62,014; TD ¶836,003
21. ¶T-3700 *et seq.*; ¶68,614 *et seq.*; TD ¶837,002
22. ¶T-3733.1; ¶74,294

not for purposes of administrative or judicial review of the assessment. (Code Sec. 6867(b), Code Sec. 6867(c); Reg § 301.6867-1(c), Reg § 301.6867-1(d), Reg § 301.6867-1(f)(4))[23]

IRS can also terminate a tax year and demand immediate payment of income taxes for the current and preceding year, if it finds that a taxpayer plans to leave (or remove his property from) the U.S. quickly, conceal himself or his property in the U.S., or do any other act that would prejudice the collection of those taxes ("termination assessment"). Within 60 days after the due date (with extensions) of the taxpayer's return for the full tax year or, if later, the date the return is actually filed, IRS must issue a 90-day letter to the taxpayer for the full year. (Code Sec. 6851(a), Code Sec. 6852(a))[24] There are procedures for administrative and judicial review of jeopardy and termination assessments (Code Sec. 7429)[25] and for stay of collection. (Code Sec. 6863)[26]

✪observation: A jeopardy assessment is used only where IRS makes its determination *after* the end of the tax year to which it relates. In a termination assessment, the determination is made *before* the related tax year ends or *before* the due date to file a return and pay the tax.

¶ 4829   Assessments in bankruptcy or receivership proceedings.

IRS may make an immediate assessment of any deficiency in income, estate and gift taxes, and certain excise taxes, whether or not a notice of deficiency (90-day letter, see ¶4824) has been issued in these situations: (1) on the debtor's estate in a case under Title 11 of the U.S. Code (bankruptcy cases); (2) on the debtor, but only if liability for the tax becomes res judicata under a determination in a Title 11 case; or (3) on the appointment of a receiver for the taxpayer in any receivership proceeding. (Code Sec. 6871(a), Code Sec. 6871(b))[27]

¶ 4830   General three-year statute of limitations on assessments.

Generally (for exceptions, see ¶4832, ¶4835), all taxes must be assessed: (1) within three years after the date the return was filed (below), or (2) if the tax is payable by stamp, within three years after the date any part of the tax was paid. (Code Sec. 6501(a))[28] A return filed before the deadline is considered filed on the due date. (Code Sec. 6501(b)(1))[29] But a return of tax withheld (from wages or at source) for any period ending with or within a calendar year is, if filed before Apr. 15 of the next calendar year, considered filed *on* Apr. 15. (Code Sec. 6501(b)(2); Reg § 301.6501(b)-1(b))[30] The assessment period for a late-filed return starts on the day after actual filing, whether the lateness is due to taxpayer's delinquency, or a filing extension granted by IRS. (Code Sec. 6501(a))[31] If within 60 days before the limitations period expires, IRS receives an amended return that shows an increase in tax liability, IRS has 60 days from the receipt to assess the additional tax. (Code Sec. 6501(c)(7))[32]

The assessment period for items of a partnership, S corporation, trust or estate that are passed through to and reported by the partners, shareholders or beneficiaries, is based on their returns (not the partnership's, etc.), as specifically codified in Code Sec. 6501(a).[33] Subject to exceptions and special rules, the period for assessing tax attributable to a partnership item (or affected item), for a partnership tax year won't expire before the date that is three years after the later of: (1) the date the partnership return was filed, or (2) the last day for filing the return for that year (without regard to extensions). (Code Sec. 6229(a)) Courts have held that this special rule cannot shorten the general limitation period.[34]

If a taxpayer makes (or revokes) an election to have the alcohol fuel credit, enhanced oil

23. ¶T-3726 *et seq.*; ¶68,674; TD ¶837,006
24. ¶T-3717 *et seq.*; ¶68,514
25. ¶T-3735 *et seq.*; ¶74,294; TD ¶837,009
26. ¶T-3757 *et seq.*; ¶68,634 *et seq.*; TD ¶903,002
27. ¶T-3802; ¶68,714; TD ¶837,007
28. ¶T-4001; ¶65,014; TD ¶838,001

29. ¶T-4002; ¶65,014.09; TD ¶838,002
30. ¶T-4010; ¶65,014.09; TD ¶838,002
31. ¶T-4003; ¶s 65,014.01, 65,014.02; TD ¶838,002
32. ¶T-4209.1; ¶65,014.28; TD ¶838,030
33. ¶T-4020 *et seq.*; ¶65,014.04; TD ¶838,003; 838,005; 838,006
34. ¶T-4018; ¶62,294; TD ¶838,003

recovery credit, employer social security credit for taxes paid on employee tips, work opportunity credit, the qualified plug-in electric drive motor vehicle credit, the alternative motor vehicle credit, the qualified alternative fuel vehicle refueling (QAFVR) property credit, the credit for production of low sulfur diesel fuel, or the "orphan drug" credit apply for a tax year, the assessment period for a deficiency due to the election (or revocation) won't expire until one year after IRS is notified of the election or revocation. (Code Sec. 6501(m))[35]

¶ 4831 Expiration of the limitations period as a bar to assessment.

A taxpayer who claims that the assessment of a tax is barred by the expiration of the limitations period (¶4830) must raise the issue and has the burden of proof.[36]

¶ 4832 Six-year assessment period.

Over-25% omissions. The assessment period is six years for income tax (or estate, gift or excise tax) returns that omit from gross income (or gross estate, total gifts made in the return period, or excise tax) more than 25% of the gross income (or gross estate, total gifts or excise tax) that is reported. In applying these tests, capital gains and losses aren't netted; only gains are taken into account. These "omissions" don't include amounts for which adequate information is given on the return or attached statements. For this purpose, gross income, as it relates to a trade or business, means the total of the amounts received or accrued from the sale of goods or services, without reduction for the cost of those goods or services. (Code Sec. 6501(e)) The Supreme Court held that an overstatement of basis is not an omission of gross income for this purpose.[37]

Personal holding company tax on a personal holding company (PHC) that didn't file a PHC schedule with its income tax return may be assessed within six years after the income tax return was filed. (Code Sec. 6501(f))[38]

Understatements due to foreign financial assets. A 6-year limitations period applies for assessment of tax on understatements of income attributable to foreign financial assets. This limitations period applies if there is an omission of gross income in excess of $5,000, and the omitted gross income is attributable to an asset for which information reports are required under Code Sec. 6038D (¶4673), applied without regard to the dollar threshold and certain exceptions. (Code Sec. 6501(e)(1)(A))[39] The extended limitations period rule for foreign financial asset omissions is also applicable where a partnership omits such foreign financial assets. (Code Sec. 6229(c)(2))[40]

Both the special definition of gross income for a trade or business and the rule treating adequately disclosed items on the return (or attachment) as not omitted (see over-25% omissions above) also apply for foreign financial asset omissions. (Code Sec. 6501(e)(1)(B))

¶ 4833 Assessment period for carrybacks to and carryovers from closed years.

A deficiency attributable to a taxpayer's carryback of a net operating loss (NOL), capital loss, or business credit may be assessed at any time before expiration of the period applicable to the year the loss was sustained or the credit earned. (Code Sec. 6501(h), Code Sec. 6501(j))[41] A deficiency attributable to a foreign tax credit carryback may be assessed up to one year after the credit year's assessment period expires. (Code Sec. 6501(i))[42] Where a credit carryback results from the carryback of an NOL, capital loss or other credit carryback from a later year, a deficiency for the carryback year can be assessed at any time before the

35. ¶T-4014.1; ¶65,014
36. ¶T-4030; ¶65,014.01; TD ¶838,007
37. ¶T-4201 *et seq.*; ¶65,014.15; TD ¶838,016
38. ¶T-4218; ¶65,014.29; TD ¶838,026

39. ¶T-4210.1; ¶65,014.155
40. ¶T-4215; ¶62,214.08
41. ¶T-4034; ¶65,014.28; TD ¶838,008
42. ¶T-4042; ¶65,014.28; TD ¶838,009

expiration of the period for the later year. (Code Sec. 6501(j))[43]

¶ 4834   Assessment period for unreported listed transactions.

If a taxpayer fails to include on any return or statement for any tax year any information with respect to a listed transaction (as defined at ¶4891) that's required under Code Sec. 6011, the time for assessment of any tax as to that transaction won't expire before one year after the earlier of: (1) the date the required information is furnished to IRS, or (2) the date a material advisor meets the Code Sec. 6112 list-maintenance requirements as to a request by IRS under Code Sec. 6112(b) relating to the transaction with respect to the taxpayer. (Code Sec. 6501(c)(10))[44] Taxpayers can rely on proposed regs or previously issued guidance to start the one-year period above. (Prop Reg. § 301.6501(c)-1, [Taxpayers may rely])

¶ 4835   When the assessment period remains open.

The assessment period is open indefinitely where a taxpayer:

. . . fails to file a required return (Code Sec. 6501(c)(3)), but the assessment period starts to run if a trust or partnership return is filed by a taxpayer later held to be a corporation (Code Sec. 6501(g)(1)) or an exempt organization return is filed by an organization later held to be taxable (Code Sec. 6501(g)(2));[45]

. . . files a false or fraudulent income, gift or estate tax return with intent to evade tax. (Code Sec. 6501(c)(1)) The Tax Court has held that an income tax preparer's fraudulent intent can keep a taxpayer's fraudulent income tax return open indefinitely under this rule, even if the taxpayer had no intent to evade taxes.[46] Filing a later amended, nonfraudulent return won't start the running of the normal three-year assessment period;[47]

. . . willfully attempts in any manner to defeat and evade taxes (Code Sec. 6501(c)(2));[48]

. . . fails to pay any part of a tax required to be paid by stamp (Code Sec. 6501(a); Reg § 301.6501(a)-1);[49]

. . . for gift tax, fails to show or adequately disclose (1) any gift of property (or increase in taxable gifts) whose value is determined under the special valuation rules or (2) any post-Aug. 5, '97 gift. (Code Sec. 6501(c)(9); Reg § 301.6501(c)-1(e), Reg § 301.6501(c)-1(f))[50] Filing an amended return with required information will get the limitation period running for a prior gift that wasn't adequately disclosed.[1]

. . . is subject to the tax for termination of private foundation status, see ¶4128.[2]

IRS says that a responsible person liable for the trust fund recovery penalty is subject to an unlimited assessment period where the employer has committed fraud, willfully attempted to evade tax, or failed to file an employment tax return.[3] The penalties for promoting abusive tax shelters, or for aiding and abetting an understatement, can be assessed at any time,[4] as can the penalty (but not the tax) imposed on a return preparer for willful tax understatements,[5] and certain restitution in criminal tax cases (¶4827).[6]

For information required under certain provisions, the assessment period for tax as to any tax return, event or period to which the information relates won't expire before the date that is 3 years after the information is given to IRS. The provisions include Code Sec. 1295(b), Code Sec. 1298(f), Code Sec. 6038, Code Sec. 6038A, Code Sec. 6038B, Code Sec. 6038D, Code Sec. 6046, Code Sec. 6046A, and Code Sec. 6048. If a failure is due to reasonable cause and

43. ¶T-4039; ¶65,014.28; TD ¶838,009
44. ¶T-4163; ¶65,014.147; TD ¶838,055
45. ¶T-4101 *et seq.*; ¶s 65,014.05, 65,014.06, 65,014.14; TD ¶838,012 *et seq.*
46. ¶T-4127; ¶65,014.13; TD ¶838,014
47. ¶T-4209; ¶65,014.04; TD ¶838,014
48. ¶T-4141; ¶65,014.13; TD ¶838,015
49. ¶T-4122; TD ¶838,001

50. ¶T-4147; ¶65,014.28; TD ¶838,022
1. ¶T-4162
2. ¶T-4143
3. ¶T-4029.1
4. ¶s T-4125, T-4126; ¶67,034; TD ¶838,027
5. ¶T-4145; ¶66,964; TD ¶838,011
6. ¶T-4172; ¶65,014.149

not willful neglect, the above suspension rule applies only to items related to that failure. (Code Sec. 6501(c)(8))[7]

¶ 4836 Voluntary extension of the assessment period—Form 872.

At any time *before* expiration of the assessment period (¶4830), a taxpayer and IRS can agree in writing (usually on one of the Form 872 series) to extend the assessment period (except for estate taxes). They can also enter into successive agreements further extending the period. (Code Sec. 6501(c)(4))[8]

observation: Form 872 is generally referred to by IRS as a *"consent."* Tax practitioners sometimes refer to it as a *"waiver,"* which technically means a Form 870, ¶4819.

Restricted consent. A restricted consent postpones the close of the tax year with respect to an unsettled issue. It is used where some issues are resolved, but settlement of others must await the establishment of an IRS position through a court decision, etc., or where other equally meritorious circumstances exist.[9]

Indefinite consent—Form 872-A. A taxpayer whose case is before the Appeals Office (¶4816) can execute Form 872-A, which is an indefinite extension.[10] It expires 90 days after: (1) Appeals receives notice (on Form 872-T) of the taxpayer's desire to terminate the extension, (2) IRS mails Form 872-T to the taxpayer, or (3) IRS mails a 90-day letter.[11]

IRS must notify the taxpayer of his right to refuse to extend the assessment limitations period, or to limit the extension to particular issues or a particular time period, on each occasion the taxpayer is requested to provide consent. (Code Sec. 6501(c)(4)(B))[12]

¶ 4837 Suspension of the assessment period.

A 90-day letter (¶4824) suspends the assessment period. It stops running on the date IRS mails the letter, and doesn't resume until 60 days after: (1) the 90-day period (150 days if the letter is addressed to a person outside the U.S.) if no petition is filed, or (2) the Tax Court's decision becomes final if a petition is filed. (Code Sec. 6503(a))[13] A taxpayer's application for a Taxpayer Assistance Order (¶4811) also suspends the assessment period, up to the date the National Taxpayer Advocate makes a decision. (Code Sec. 7811(d))[14]

IRS's mailing of a notice of adjustment suspends the statute of limitations on the making of assessments for the longer of (1) the period during which IRS is prohibited from making the assessment, or (2) if a proceeding in respect of the notice of adjustment is placed on the docket of the Tax Court, until the decision of the Tax Court becomes final, and for 60 more days. (Code Sec. 6234(e)(2))[15] The assessment period is suspended in Tax Court employment tax determinations. (Code Sec. 7436(d)(1))[16]

For returns of corporations being examined under the coordinated examination program or a successor program, the issuance of a "designated summons" or a related summons also suspends the assessment period, pending final resolution of its enforcement. (Code Sec. 6503(j); Reg § 301.6503(j)-1)[17]

¶ 4838 Request for prompt assessment—Form 4810.

The normal three-year assessment period can be cut to 18 months *at the taxpayer's request* (use Form 4810) for an income tax return of a decedent or an estate, or for a return of a

---

7. ¶T-4146; ¶65,014.28
8. ¶T-4400 *et seq.*; ¶65,014.17 *et seq.*; TD ¶838,034
9. ¶T-4445; TD ¶838,034
10. ¶T-4402; TD ¶838,036
11. ¶T-4457 *et seq.*; TD ¶838,036
12. ¶T-4403; ¶65,014; TD ¶838,035

13. ¶T-4300 *et seq.*; ¶65,034.01; TD ¶838,043
14. ¶T-4325; ¶78,114.01; TD ¶838,045
15. ¶T-3554; ¶62,344
16. ¶T-4301.2; ¶74,364
17. ¶T-4333 *et seq.*; ¶65,034.04; TD ¶838,046

dissolved or dissolving corporation. (Code Sec. 6501(d))[18]

¶ 4839   Statutory (mitigation) and judicial relief for barred years.

Generally, after the period for assessment or refund has run, IRS can't make an assessment and a taxpayer can't get a refund. But an otherwise closed year may be reopened under the Code's "mitigation" provisions under certain circumstances. (Code Sec. 1311, Code Sec. 1312, Code Sec. 1313)[19] Relief from the limitation periods may be available in the district court or Court of Federal Claims if the statutory mitigation conditions aren't met, under equitable recoupment (closed year's overpayment or underpayment used to offset open year's deficiency or refund, see ¶4859 for Tax Court's authority to do this),[20] estoppel,[21] or election.[22]

¶ 4840   Unified Audit and Review for Partnerships. ▆▆▆▆▆▆▆▆▆▆▆

IRS generally can't adjust partnership items on a partner's return except by a unified entity-level proceeding (i.e., a "TEFRA proceeding," as enacted by the Tax Equity and Fiscal Responsibility Act). A decision in the unified proceeding binds all partners and permits IRS to make the necessary corresponding adjustments on their individual returns. Simplified procedures apply for electing large partnerships.

¶ 4841   Unified audit and review procedure for partnerships and partners.

The tax treatment of any partnership item (¶4842), and the applicability of any penalty, addition to tax or additional amount which relates to an adjustment to a partnership item, is generally determined at the partnership level, in one unified proceeding. This applies at both the administrative and judicial levels. (Code Sec. 6221; Reg § 301.6221-1(c)) Partnership level determinations include all the legal and factual determinations that underlie the determination of any penalty, addition to tax, or additional amount (other than partner level defenses). (Reg § 301.6221-1(c))[23] No assessment of a deficiency attributable to any partnership item may be made before the end of the 150th day after IRS issues a notice of final partnership administrative adjustment (FPAA, see ¶4844) to the tax matters partner (TMP, see ¶4843) or, if the TMP files a Tax Court petition in that 150-day period, before the Tax Court decision becomes final. (Code Sec. 6225(a))[24] However, IRS can make an earlier assessment in certain abusive tax shelter situations. (Reg § 301.6231(c)-1)[25]

These rules generally apply to any partnership (except certain small partnerships, see ¶4845) required to file a partnership return (Form 1065), and to any entity that, for the year it filed a partnership return, either wasn't a partnership or didn't exist for the full year. (Code Sec. 6231(a)(1), Code Sec. 6233; Reg § 301.6233-1)[26] A real estate mortgage investment conduit (¶4204) is treated as a partnership for these purposes. (Code Sec. 860F(e))[27] Special consistency and audit rules apply for electing large partnerships (¶3702) and their partners. (Code Sec. 6240 through Code Sec. 6255)[28] IRS may rely on the partnership return in deciding whether unified audit rules apply. (Code Sec. 6231(g))[29] Unified proceedings usually begin when IRS notifies the partnership that its return has been selected for audit. Or the TMP may file (use Form 8082) a request for an administrative adjustment for the partnership. The request is treated as a substituted return (correcting errors) or a claim for refund. (Code Sec. 6227(a))[30] Special deficiency procedures apply to a partner's "oversheltered return" (one that shows no taxable income and a net loss from a partnership). (Code Sec. 6234)[31]

18. ¶T-4500 *et seq.*; ¶65,014.16; TD ¶838,032
19. ¶T-5000 *et seq.*; ¶13,134; TD ¶823,507
20. ¶T-5200 *et seq.*; ¶65,144; TD ¶444,531
21. ¶T-5300 *et seq.*; ¶74,338.400
22. ¶T-5400 *et seq.*; ¶74,338.424
23. ¶T-2100 *et seq.*; ¶62,214; TD ¶825,001
24. ¶T-4015; ¶62,254; TD ¶838,003

25. ¶T-6517; ¶62,214; TD ¶804,012
26. ¶T-2103; ¶62,214.11; TD ¶825,002
27. ¶E-6927; ¶860A4
28. ¶T-2300 *et seq.*; ¶62,404; TD ¶825,501 *et seq.*
29. ¶T-2108.1; ¶62,214.10; TD ¶825,007
30. ¶T-2201; ¶62,214.06; TD ¶825,201
31. ¶T-3551 *et seq.*; ¶62,344

¶ 4842   What are "partnership items"?

A "partnership item" is any item that must be taken into account for the partnership's tax year, to the extent regs provide the item is more appropriately determined at the partnership level than at the partner level (Code Sec. 6231(a)(3)), including: items of income, gain, loss, deduction or credit; expenditures not deductible in computing taxable income (e.g., charitable contributions); any partner's tax preference items; tax-exempt income; partnership liabilities; amounts needed to enable the partnership or the partners to compute the investment credit (or recapture), at-risk amounts or depletion; and items relating to contributions to or distributions from the partnership, and transactions between a partner and the partnership (e.g., guaranteed payments). (Reg § 301.6231(a)(3)-1(a))[32] In some contexts, courts have held that amounts at risk were not partnership items.[33]

¶ 4843   Tax matters partner (TMP).

The TMP acts on behalf of the partners in unified partnership proceedings. The TMP is: (a) the general partner the partnership designates as such on its return (Form 1065) (Form 1066, for a real estate mortgage investment conduit (Reg § 1.860F-4(d))); or (b) if no designation is made, the general partner with the largest profits interest in the partnership at the end of the tax year. (Code Sec. 6231(a)(7)) IRS may select a general partner (or limited partner, if no general partner is eligible) (Reg § 301.6231(a)(7)-1(p)) as TMP if no designation is made under (a), above, and it is impracticable (under regs) (Reg § 301.6231(a)(7)-1(o)) to use (b). (Code Sec. 6231(a)(7); Reg § 301.6231(a)(7)-1(n))[34] The other partners generally must receive notice from the TMP of both IRS's and the TMP's actions. (Code Sec. 6223(g); Reg § 301.6223(g)-1)[35]

¶ 4844   Final partnership administrative adjustment (FPAA).

If after auditing the partnership IRS concludes that adjustments to the return are needed, it will issue a FPAA, which must be sent to the tax matters partner (TMP) and to "notice partners" IRS knows are eligible to receive notice. (Code Sec. 6223(a))[36] The TMP has 90 days from when the FPAA was mailed to file a petition for judicial review of it. (Code Sec. 6226(a)) If the TMP doesn't file in that time, any notice partner can file the partnership petition within the next 60 days. (Code Sec. 6226(b)(1)) Detailed procedures govern the conduct of the partnership-level proceeding (Code Sec. 6224; Reg § 301.6224(a)-1, Reg § 301.6224(c)-3),[37] assessments (Code Sec. 6225, Code Sec. 6229), judicial review of FPAAs (Code Sec. 6226, Code Sec. 6228; Reg § 301.6226(f)-1), and other matters.[38]

¶ 4845   Exception for certain small partnerships.

The unified audit rules at ¶4841 *et seq.* don't apply to a "small" partnership (unless it elects them under procedures set forth by regs). (Reg § 301.6231(a)(1)-1(b)(2)) A partnership is "small" for a tax year if it has ten or fewer partners, each of whom is an individual (other than a nonresident alien), a C corporation, or an estate of a deceased partner. (Code Sec. 6231(a)(1)(B)(i); Reg § 301.6231(a)(1)-1(a)(1), Reg § 301.6231(a)(1)-1(a)(3))[39]

¶ 4846   Refunds; Tax Litigation. ▰▰▰▰▰▰▰▰▰▰▰▰▰▰▰▰▰▰▰▰▰▰▰

A taxpayer can recover an overpayment as a credit or a refund by properly filing a claim and, if the claim is denied, bringing suit. A taxpayer who has been issued a 90-

---

32. ¶T-2110; ¶62,214; TD ¶825,009
33. ¶T-2111
34. ¶T-2121; TD ¶825,023
35. ¶T-2151; TD ¶825,056

36. ¶T-2215 *et seq.*; TD ¶825,217
37. ¶T-2156 *et seq.*; ¶62,214; TD ¶825,055
38. ¶T-2215 *et seq.*; TD ¶825,224
39. ¶T-2104, T-2109; ¶62,214.10; TD ¶825,003, 825,008

day letter can go to Tax Court without first paying the disputed tax.

¶ 4847   Overpayments—recovery by refund or credit.

An overpayment is the excess of the amount paid (or withheld) as tax over the taxpayer's correct tax liability. It includes the part of a correct tax paid after the applicable assessment period has run. (Code Sec. 6401)[40] An overpayment can be recovered as a refund or credit, generally only by the taxpayer who paid the tax. But IRS may first credit the overpayment (including interest) against *any* of the taxpayer's past due tax liability (including interest, additions, penalties). (Code Sec. 6402(a); Reg § 301.6402-3(a)(5))[41] For offset against nontax debts, see ¶4848. Electronic filers may elect (on Form 8453) to have their refunds deposited directly into their bank accounts. Paper filers elect direct deposit by filling in the appropriate blanks on the "Refund" lines of Form 1040. In either case, use Form 8888 to direct deposit a refund into two or three accounts including IRAs.[42] A refund may be claimed for a deceased taxpayer. Attach Form 1310 (not needed for surviving spouse filing jointly with decedent) to the decedent's final return (¶4714).[43]

¶ 4848   Overpayments applied to child support and other nontax debts.

If a state notifies the Treasury that a taxpayer owes any child support payments, it must first apply the taxpayer's overpayment (including earned income amounts) to those past-due obligations, before making any refund or credit. (Code Sec. 6402(c))[44] If a federal agency notifies the Treasury of any past-due, legally enforceable nontax debt a taxpayer owes the agency, IRS must apply the balance (i.e., after the child support offset) of the taxpayer's overpayment to that nontax debt. (Code Sec. 6402(d))[45] After these reductions, refunds can be reduced by state income tax debts, (Code Sec. 6402(e))[46] or reduced to recover debts to states for certain overpayments of unemployment compensation. (Code Sec. 6402(f))[47]

¶ 4849   Refund claim.

To get a refund, a taxpayer must file a timely (¶4854) written claim. For income, gift and federal unemployment taxes, a separate claim must be made for each tax year or period. (Reg § 301.6402-2(a), Reg § 301.6402-2(d))[48] Official forms are:

. . . Form 1040X (amended U.S. individual income tax return). (Use Form 1040, Form 1040A, or Form 1040-EZ *only* for refund of overwithheld taxes or excess estimated taxes.) (Reg § 301.6402-3(a)(2), Reg § 301.6402-4)

. . . Form 1120 or Form 1120X (original or amended corporate income tax return). (Reg § 301.6402-3(a)(3))

. . . Amended returns for taxpayers who filed a form other than Form 1040, Form 1040A, Form 1040-EZ or Form 1120 (e.g., a return for an estate or trust). (Reg § 301.6402-3(a)(4))

. . . Form 843 for refunds of non-income taxes (Reg § 601.105(e)(1)), except excise taxes reported on Form 720, Form 730, or Form 2290. Form 720X and Form 8849 are used for excise tax refund claims.[49]

IRS must explain disallowances of refund claims (Code Sec. 6402(l)) and it now notifies taxpayers whose refunds have been frozen under its questionable refund program.[50]

40. ¶T-5500 *et seq.*; ¶64,014; TD ¶801,006
41. ¶T-5600 *et seq.*, T-5700 *et seq.*; ¶64,024; TD ¶803,012
42. ¶T-5610 *et seq.*; TD ¶802,011; TD ¶802,012
43. ¶T-5710; TD ¶802,039
44. ¶T-6013 *et seq.*; ¶64,024.26; TD ¶803,022
45. ¶T-6023 *et seq.*; ¶64,024.23; TD ¶803,026

46. ¶T-6038; ¶64,024; TD ¶803,030
47. ¶T-6045.1; TD ¶803,012.1
48. ¶T-6702; ¶s 64,024, 64,024.08; TD ¶805,002
49. ¶T-6707 *et seq.*; ¶64,024; TD ¶805,004 *et seq.*
50. ¶T-5618.1; ¶64,024.33; TD ¶802,018

¶ 4850   Quick refund for carrybacks and claim of right—Form 1045; Form 1139.

A taxpayer who reports a carryback of a capital loss, net operating loss (NOL), business credit, or capital loss from a Code Sec. 1256 contract under Code Sec. 1212(c) on his return can quickly recover a refund based on the carryback by filing Form 1045 (individuals) or Form 1139 (corporations) *on or after* the date the return for the loss or credit year is filed, and within 12 months after the end of the tax year *from which* the carryback is made. (Code Sec. 6411(a); Reg § 1.6411-1(b)(1))[1] This procedure also applies to overpayments attributable to a "claim of right" adjustment (¶2862), where the amount of repayment in any one year exceeds $3,000. (Code Sec. 6411(d))[2] IRS has 90 days from the later of the date the claim is filed or the last day of the month the loss year return is due (with extensions), to make any credit or refund. (Code Sec. 6411(b); Reg § 1.6411-3)[3] IRS's determination is tentative. If the claim is rejected, the taxpayer can't sue but must first file a standard refund claim. (Code Sec. 6411(b); Reg § 1.6411-3(c)) Even if IRS grants the refund, it can later examine the loss year return and the refund application. IRS may assess any part of the refund it finds excessive, without issuing a 90-day letter. (Code Sec. 6213(b)(3))[4]

¶ 4851   Quick refunds of corporate estimated tax overpayments—Form 4466.

A corporation that overpaid estimated tax (¶3343 *et seq.*) can get a refund within 45 days after filing Form 4466. (Code Sec. 6425(b)(1), Code Sec. 6425(b)(2); Reg § 1.6425-1(b)) The form must be filed *after* the corporation's tax year ends and *on or before* the 15th day of the third month after the year ends (or before the corporation first files its income tax return for that year, if earlier). (Code Sec. 6425(a)(1); Reg § 1.6425-1(c)(1)) The corporation's estimated tax overpayment must be at least 10% of its revised expected annual tax, *and* at least $500. (Code Sec. 6425(b)(3)) If a refund is excessive, an addition to tax equal to the underpayment interest rate (¶4866), times the excessive amount is imposed. (Code Sec. 6655(h))[5]

¶ 4852   Protective refund claims.

A protective refund claim is a regular refund claim (see ¶4849) filed merely to keep a particular claim alive. It's generally used where IRS has a settled view adverse to a taxpayer on an issue being litigated by other taxpayers. A protective refund claim is usually filed just before the refund claim period expires. It will keep the taxpayer's claim alive (i.e., protect his right to sue) for the additional period from the date of filing to the date of rejection plus the refund suit period.[6]

¶ 4853   Interest on overpayments.

Interest on overpayments is allowed. (Code Sec. 6611(a)) The interest (compounded daily) runs from the date of the overpayment (below) to a date not more than 30 days before the refund is made (or to the (unextended) return due date for the amount against which the overpayment is credited). (Code Sec. 6611(b))[7] But no interest is payable on a refund arising from an original income, employment, excise, estate or gift tax return made within 45 days after the later of the return due date (without extensions) or the date it was filed. (Code Sec. 6611(e)(1); Reg § 301.6611-1(j))[8] If a refund arising from an amended return or refund claim is issued within 45 days, no interest is payable for that up-to-45 day period. (Code Sec. 6611(e)(2))[9] For refunds or credits arising from an adjustment initiated by IRS, the interest period is reduced by 45 days. (Code Sec. 6611(e)(3))[10] The grace period during which

1. ¶T-6501 *et seq.*; ¶64,114; TD ¶804,001
2. ¶T-6522; ¶64,114; TD ¶804,015
3. ¶T-6509; ¶64,114; TD ¶804,007
4. ¶T-3633; ¶62,134.02; TD ¶836,002
5. ¶T-6600 *et seq.*; ¶s 64,254, 66,554; TD ¶804,500 *et seq.*

6. ¶T-6742; ¶64,024.17; TD ¶805,033
7. ¶s T-8008, T-8031, T-8034; ¶66,114; TD ¶807,006
8. ¶T-8024; ¶66,114; TD ¶807,012
9. ¶T-8027; ¶66,114; TD ¶807,015
10. ¶T-8028; ¶66,114; TD ¶807,016

the government isn't required to pay interest on overpayments is increased from 45 days to 180 days for overpayments resulting from excess amounts deducted and withheld under chapter 3 of the Code (Code Sec. 1441 through Code Sec. 1464 (withholding on nonresident aliens and foreign corporations)) or chapter 4 of the Code (Code Sec. 1471 through Code Sec. 1474). (Code Sec. 6611(e)) With respect to returns filed after the due date (with extensions), no interest is payable for the period preceding the actual filing date. (Code Sec. 6611(b)(3))[11] And, no interest is payable on an estate's overpayment unless it shows that the interest (and refund) won't escheat to the state. (Code Sec. 6408)[12] IRS also won't pay interest when it refunds a conditional or advance payment of taxes.[13]

The overpayment rate for corporations except C corporations with large overpayments is the short-term AFR plus 2 percentage points. But, the overpayment rate for individuals is the short-term AFR plus 3 percentage points (same as the underpayment rate, see ¶4866). (Code Sec. 6621(a)(1))[14] For the period from Oct. 1, 2011 to Dec. 31, 2013, the overpayment rate for corporations is 2%.[15] For C corporations, the rate is reduced to the short-term AFR plus 0.5 percentage points, to the extent the overpayment for any period exceeds $10,000. (Code Sec. 6621(a)(1))[16] For the period from Oct. 1, 2011 to Dec. 31, 2013, this rate is 0.5%.[17]

A deposit that is returned to a taxpayer is treated as a payment of tax for any period to the extent (and only to the extent) attributable to a disputable tax for that period. (Code Sec. 6603(d)(1)) However, the interest on the return of such a deposit is payable only at the short-term AFR rate compounded daily. (Code Sec. 6603(d)(4))[18] The overpayment date for taxes withheld or paid as estimated taxes is the unextended due date of the return. (Code Sec. 6513(b))[19] Overpayments resulting from the carryback of an NOL, net capital loss, business credit, or foreign tax credit, are considered not to have been made before the "filing date" for the tax year in which the loss or credit arose or the foreign tax was in fact paid or accrued. (Code Sec. 6611(f))[20] Similarly, where a business credit carryback is attributable to an NOL, etc., carryback from a later year, the overpayment is considered not to have been made before the filing date for that later year. (Code Sec. 6611(f)(3))[21]

¶ 4854   Deadline for refund claims.

A claim for credit or refund of a tax paid by *return* must be filed within the later of: (1) three years from the date the return was timely or untimely filed (or the due date if filed earlier), or (2) two years from the date the tax was paid. If the required return wasn't filed, the claim must be filed within two years from when the tax was paid. (Code Sec. 6511(a))[22] A refund claim filed on a Form 1040X after the limitations period expired was allowed where it was found to be amendment to an original timely claim, rather than an untimely new claim. For the prohibited transaction excise tax (¶4347), the relevant return is the plan's annual Form 5500, not Form 5330 on which the tax is reported.[23] A remittance accompanying an automatic filing extension is a tax payment for this purpose.[24]

However, a longer refund claim period applies in these cases:

. . . If a taxpayer and IRS execute one of the Form 872 series extending the assessment period (see ¶4836), the claim can be filed within six months after the expiration of the extended assessment period. (Code Sec. 6511(c)(1))[25]

. . . For an overpayment resulting from carryback of an NOL, net capital loss, or business credit, the period expires three years after the time the return is due (including extensions) for the year the loss or credit arose, not the year to which it's carried back. The Federal

---

11. ¶T-8008; ¶66,114; TD ¶807,006
12. ¶s T-8063, T-8065; ¶64,084; TD ¶807,044
13. ¶T-8046
14. ¶T-8002; ¶66,214; TD ¶807,002
15. ¶T-8003.1; ¶66,214; TD ¶807,003
16. ¶T-8002.1; ¶66,214; TD ¶807,003
17. ¶T-8003.2; ¶66,214
18. ¶S-5804.3; ¶66,034.01; TD ¶807,006.1

19. ¶T-7530; ¶s 66,114, 65,134; TD ¶806,026
20. ¶T-8049 *et seq.*; ¶66,114; TD ¶807,034
21. ¶T-8051; ¶66,114; TD ¶807,035
22. ¶T-7501 *et seq.*; ¶65,114; TD ¶806,001
23. ¶T-7524; ¶65,114.04; TD ¶806,022
24. ¶S-5801.8; TD ¶806,031
25. ¶T-7574; ¶65,114.09; TD ¶806,068

Circuit has held that this exception does not apply to a year to which a net capital loss is carried over. (Code Sec. 6511(d)(2), Code Sec. 6511(d)(4))[26] If the overpayment is attributable to a carryback from a later year, the period expires three years after the time for filing the return (including extensions) for that later year. (Code Sec. 6511(d)(4))[27]

. . . For an overpayment resulting from the payment or accrual of foreign taxes for which a foreign tax credit is allowed, the claim period is ten years. (Code Sec. 6511(d)(3))[28]

. . . For an overpayment resulting from a bad debt or from worthless securities, the claim period is seven years. (Code Sec. 6511(d)(1))[29]

. . . For self-employment tax claims attributable to Tax Court employment status proceedings, the claim period is two years after the calendar year in which the Tax Court determination becomes final. (Code Sec. 6511(d)(7))[30]

. . . For credit or refund claims filed after June 17, 2008 for retired military personnel who receive disability determinations from the Dept. of Veterans Affairs (VA), the refund claim filing period is extended for one year after the date of a disability determination from the VA (if later than the time allowed under the general refund limitations period). (This would apply to cases where an individual receives includible retirement benefits that are later retroactively determined to have been service-connected disability benefits excludable from income.) But, the extended time period doesn't apply for any tax year beginning more than five years before the date of the disability determination. (Code Sec. 6511(d)(8))[31]

Also, under certain circumstances, the limitations period is suspended during any period an individual is unable to manage his financial affairs by reason of his medically-determinable physical or mental impairment. (Code Sec. 6511(h))[32]

¶ 4855 Refund suit period.

A taxpayer *must* file a refund claim with IRS before starting a suit for refund (or credit). (Code Sec. 7422(a))[33] The refund suit can't be started *before* six months from filing the claim (unless IRS acts on the claim in that period), or *after* two years from the date IRS mails a notice of disallowance. (Code Sec. 6532(a)(1)) The taxpayer can waive (on Form 2297) issuance of this notice and the two-year period will start on the date the waiver is filed. (Code Sec. 6532(a)(3)) Also, the taxpayer and IRS can execute a Form 907 extending the two-year period. (Code Sec. 6532(a)(2))[34]

¶ 4856 Limits on amount of refund or credit.

If a claim is filed within three years from the time the return was filed, the refund or credit is limited to the portion of tax paid during the three years (plus the period of any filing extension) immediately preceding the filing of the claim. (Code Sec. 6511(b)(2)(A))[35] If the claim wasn't filed within the three-year period, the refund or credit is limited to the portion of the tax paid during the two years immediately preceding the filing of the claim. (Code Sec. 6511(b)(2)(B)) This two-year limitation also applies if a claim, but no return, was filed. (Reg § 301.6511(b)-1(b)(1)(iii))[36] Where no claim is filed and a refund or credit is allowed within three years from the time the return was filed, the refund or credit is limited to the portion of the tax paid during the three years immediately before the allowance. If the refund or credit is not allowed within that three-year period, it's limited to the portion of the tax paid during the two years immediately before the allowance. (Code Sec. 6511(b)(2)(C))[37] The Tax Court cannot refund taxes that a non-filer paid more than two years before a deficiency notice

26. ¶T-7554; ¶s 65,114.11, 65,114.13; TD ¶806,050
27. ¶T-7563; ¶65,114.13; TD ¶806,058
28. ¶T-7569; ¶65,114.12; TD ¶806,063
29. ¶T-7552; ¶65,114.10; TD ¶806,049
30. ¶T-7573.1; ¶65,114.155; TD ¶806,067
31. ¶T-7573.2; ¶65,114.16; TD ¶806,076

32. ¶T-7506; ¶65,114.04; TD ¶806,008
33. ¶T-6701; ¶74,224; TD ¶808,006
34. ¶T-9034; ¶65,324.01; TD ¶808,023
35. ¶T-7537; ¶65,114.07; TD ¶806,037
36. ¶s T-7546, T-7547; ¶65,114.07
37. ¶T-7548; ¶65,114.07; TD ¶806,045

was mailed. (Code Sec. 6512(b)(3))[38] For purposes of determining the amount of an individual taxpayer's refund or credit under these rules, the refund claim periods described above are suspended during any period when the individual is unable to manage his financial affairs (see ¶4854). (Code Sec. 6511(h))[39]

¶ 4857 Refunds of refundable credits.

Any refund or advance payment of a refundable credit made to an individual under the Code isn't taken into account as income, and isn't taken into account as resources for a period of 12 months from receipt, in determining the eligibility of the recipient or any other individual for benefits or assistance, or the amount or extent of benefits or assistance, under any federal program or any state or local program financed in whole or part with federal funds. (Code Sec. 6409)

¶ 4858 Tax litigation.

A taxpayer may go to:

. . . the Tax Court to set aside a deficiency determined by IRS (¶4859) (Code Sec. 6214(a));[40]

. . . a U.S. district court or the U.S. Court of Federal Claims to recover an overpayment of taxes (after filing a refund claim) (Code Sec. 6532(a));[41]

. . . a U.S. district court or the U.S. Court of Federal Claims to determine the correct amount of (or for a refund of) the estate's estate tax liability, even if it wasn't fully paid due to a Code Sec. 6166 election. (Code Sec. 7422(j)(1))[42]

. . . the Tax Court, the district court for the DC Circuit, or the U.S. Court of Federal Claims for a declaratory judgment on the tax status of a charity or foundation (Code Sec. 7428(a));[43]

. . . the Tax Court for a declaratory judgment on retirement plan qualification (Code Sec. 7476(a)),[44] eligibility for deferral of estate tax on a closely held business interest (Code Sec. 7479),[45] or the value of certain gifts made. (Code Sec. 7477; Reg § 301.7477-1);[46]

. . . the Tax Court for review of IRS's failure to abate interest (Code Sec. 6404(g));[47]

. . . the Tax Court for a worker classification determination in certain cases. (Code Sec. 7436)[48]

. . . a U.S. district court to enjoin IRS from assessing and collecting a tax in certain cases (¶4910), or to get damages for IRS's unauthorized collection activities or failure to release a lien. (Code Sec. 7432, Code Sec. 7433)[49]

. . . a bankruptcy court to sue for up to $1 million in damages for willful IRS violations of automatic stay or discharge in bankruptcy. (Code Sec. 7433(e))[50]

For taxpayers other than certain large partnerships, corporations, and trusts, IRS has the burden of proof in any court proceeding with respect to any factual issue relevant to ascertaining a taxpayer's liability for any tax imposed by subtitle A or B of the Code, e.g., income and self-employment, gift, estate, and generation-skipping transfer taxes, if the taxpayer: introduces credible evidence with respect to the issue; has complied with the substantiation requirements; has maintained all required records; and has cooperated with reasonable IRS requests. (Code Sec. 7491(a))[1] IRS has the burden of production (i.e., to come forward initially with evidence) in any court proceeding with respect to the liability of any individual for any penalty imposed by the Code. (Code Sec. 7491(c))[2] The Supreme Court has declined to review

38. ¶T-7578
39. ¶T-7506; ¶65,114.04; TD ¶806,008
40. ¶U-2100 *et seq.*; ¶62,144, ¶74,414
41. ¶s U-4000 *et seq.*, U-6000 *et seq.*; ¶74,224; TD ¶802,019
42. ¶T-9007.1; ¶74,224; TD ¶808,004
43. ¶s U-3800 *et seq.*, U-4116, U-6005; ¶74,284
44. ¶U-3700 *et seq.*; ¶74,764
45. ¶U-3851 *et seq.*;¶74,217.02

46. ¶U-3880;¶74,217.02;¶74,774
47. ¶U-2129.1; ¶64,044
48. ¶U-2143; ¶74,364; TD ¶806,067
49. ¶s V-5801, V-6113; ¶s 74,324, 74,334; TD ¶903,010
50. ¶V-5820 *et seq.*; ¶74,334;TD ¶903,011
1. ¶U-1351; ¶74,914 ;TD ¶444,041
2. ¶U-1331; ¶74,914; TD ¶444,041

a Second Circuit decision holding that a shift of the burden of proof to IRS didn't require the Tax Court to adopt the estate's valuation method.

¶ 4859 The Tax Court.

To get Tax Court review of a deficiency, a taxpayer must file a petition with the Tax Court at Washington, D.C., in response to a 90-day letter (see ¶4824) from IRS, within 90 days (150 days if the letter is addressed to a person outside the U.S.) after the letter is mailed (i.e., postmarked). A petition is treated as timely if it's filed with the Tax Court on or before the last date specified by IRS in the 90-day letter for filing it. (Code Sec. 6213(a))[3]

The Tax Court's jurisdiction generally is limited to the review (without a jury) of deficiencies asserted by IRS (and not paid when the 90-day letter is issued). It can order payment of a refund if it determines the taxpayer overpaid. (Code Sec. 6512(b)) But it can't grant equitable relief. The Tax Court has jurisdiction to order a refund of any amount collected while IRS was prohibited from collecting a deficiency by levy or court proceeding but only if a timely petition for a redetermination of the deficiency has been filed and only with respect to the deficiency at issue. (Code Sec. 6213(a))[4] The Tax Court has jurisdiction, which the Supreme Court has held is exclusive, to review IRS's failure to abate interest to taxpayers within certain net worth limits who bring an action within 180 days of IRS's final adverse determination, and to order abatement if IRS abused its discretion. (Code Sec. 6404(h))[5] It can also determine worker classification in certain cases and, according to it, the correct amount of employment taxes that relate to such determinations. (Code Sec. 7436)[6] It has jurisdiction to determine innocent spouse relief when a deficiency has been issued and the taxpayer elects regular or separate innocent spouse relief or requests equitable relief, but it can't rule on the timeliness of an assessment in reviewing a denial of innocent spouse relief. (Code Sec. 6015(e)) The Tax Court has held that it could adjudicate a taxpayer's claim for spousal relief even though her former spouse intervened and later filed for bankruptcy, triggering an automatic stay.[7] The Tax Court generally is barred from determining whether the tax for any period not before it has been overpaid or underpaid. However, it may apply the doctrine of equitable recoupment, even though, according to the Tax Court, it lacks subject matter jurisdiction over the type of tax to which the equitable recoupment claim is directed. (Code Sec. 6214(b))[8] The Tax Court has exclusive jurisdiction over appeals of Collection Due Process hearings (¶4905).

¶ 4860 Settlement after Tax Court petition is filed.

IRS District Counsel will refer all docketed Tax Court cases to the Appeals Office for consideration of settlement (unless Appeals issued the deficiency notice, in which case there will be no referral if there is little likelihood that all or part of the case can be settled in a reasonable period of time). Counsel and Appeals can agree otherwise, work together, or transfer the case back and forth to promote efficient disposition of the case. The taxpayer-petitioner and/or his representative will be notified as to who has the case and the settlement authority.[9] If the taxpayer and IRS agree on a settlement, they enter into a written agreement stipulating the amount of any deficiency or overpayment. This stipulation is filed with the Tax Court which will enter a decision in accordance with it. (Reg § 601.106(d)(3)(i))[10]

¶ 4861 Small tax claims in Tax Court.

Special informal procedures apply, at a taxpayer's election and with the Tax Court's concurrence, to any Tax Court case where neither the amount (including any additions to tax, additional amounts and penalties) of the deficiency disputed nor of any claimed overpayment

---

3. ¶U-2300 *et seq.*; ¶62,134 *et seq.*
4. ¶U-2134.1; ¶s 65,124, 74,424; TD ¶806,072
5. ¶U-2129.1; ¶64,044
6. ¶U-2143; ¶74,364
7. ¶U-2148
8. ¶U-2138; ¶62,144.02
9. ¶T-1902 *et seq.*; TD ¶832,003
10. ¶T-1909; TD ¶832,004

exceeds $50,000 (the Tax Court has held that the limit includes tax, interest and penalties and applies to the total owed for all years in a single proceeding). The taxpayer thus gets the Court's decision faster and more easily, but gives up the right to appeal. (Code Sec. 7463)[11]

¶ 4862   Appeals from Tax Court, district court and U.S. Court of Federal Claims.

Decisions of the Tax Court and U.S. district courts are appealable to the U.S. Court of Appeals.[12] The appeal is made generally in the circuit where the taxpayer's legal residence (for appeals from Tax Court)[13] or the trial court (for appeals from district courts) is located.[14] U.S. Court of Federal Claims decisions may be appealed to the Court of Appeals for the Federal Circuit.[15] Appeals from U.S. Courts of Appeals are to the U.S. Supreme Court.[16]

¶ 4863   Recovery of attorneys' fees and costs.

Taxpayers whose net worth doesn't exceed specified limits, who meet other requirements, and who prevail against the U.S. in court (or at the administrative level) may be awarded reasonable litigation and administrative costs (including the costs of recovering the award). (Code Sec. 7430) The limit on attorney fee recoveries is $190 per hour. (Code Sec. 7430(c)(1)) To avoid an award of fees, IRS must show its position was substantially justified. (Code Sec. 7430(c)(4)(B)) Administrative costs can be awarded from the date IRS sends the "30-day letter." (Code Sec. 7430(c)(2)) IRS losses on similar issues in other circuits are taken into account in determining whether its position was substantially justified (Code Sec. 7430(c)(4)(B)(iii)), and costs can be awarded where IRS rejects a taxpayer's offer and later gets a judgment not exceeding the offer. (Code Sec. 7430(c)(4)(E)(i); Reg § 301.7430-7)[17]

¶ 4864   Interest and Penalties. ▬▬▬▬▬▬▬▬▬▬▬

Interest is charged on underpayments of tax. Various civil and criminal penalties are imposed on taxpayers (and/or return preparers) who violate the tax law.

¶ 4865   Interest on underpayments.

Interest is generally payable whenever any tax or civil penalty isn't paid when due (Code Sec. 6601(a)), even if the taxpayer has been granted an extension of time to pay the tax. (Code Sec. 6601(b)(1); Reg § 301.6601-1(a)) There's no interest on late payments of estimated tax (Code Sec. 6601(h)) (but for comparable penalty computations, see ¶3163 (individuals) and ¶3349 (corporations)) or unemployment tax. (Code Sec. 6601(i))[18] Interest is payable on an erroneous refund or credit. (Code Sec. 6602)[19]

¶ 4866   Interest rate on underpayments.

The rate of interest on tax underpayments and penalties is keyed to the short-term applicable federal rate (AFR) for the first month of the previous calendar quarter (Code Sec. 6621(a)(2)), and is compounded daily.[20] For the period from Oct. 1, 2011 to Dec. 31, 2013, the interest rate on underpayments is 3%.[21] If a C corporation's tax underpayment for any tax period exceeds $100,000, a higher interest rate applies for the period after the 30th day after a notice (or proposed notice) of deficiency. For the period from Oct. 1, 2011 to Dec. 31, 2013, this rate is 5%. (Code Sec. 6621(c)(3); Reg § 301.6621-3)[22] A net interest rate of zero applies to equivalent amounts of underpayments and overpayments. (Code Sec. 6621(d)) Taxpayers request interest netting on Form 843.[23]

---

11. ¶U-3600 *et seq.*; ¶74,536.1704
12. ¶s U-3417, U-5000 *et seq.*; ¶s 74,336.12, 74,824
13. ¶U-5202; ¶74,824
14. ¶U-5401
15. ¶U-6001; ¶74,336.10
16. ¶s U-5700 *et seq.*, U-7000 *et seq.*; ¶74,336.15
17. ¶U-1240 *et seq.*; ¶74,304

18. ¶V-1000 *et seq.*; ¶66,014; TD ¶852,001
19. ¶T-9108; ¶66,024; TD ¶852,008
20. ¶s V-1101, V-1104; ¶66,214; TD ¶851,001
21. ¶V-1102; ¶66,214; TD ¶851,001
22. ¶V-1106 *et seq.*; ¶66,214; TD ¶851,005
23. ¶V-1301.1; ¶66,014; TD ¶851,008

¶ 4867   Interest accrual period.

Interest on unpaid tax liabilities runs from the last day prescribed by the Code for payment (disregarding extensions or any installment payment agreement) (Code Sec. 6601(b)(1)), to the date paid. (Code Sec. 6601(a)) However, where the tax is paid within 21 days after notice and demand (10 business days if the amount is $100,000 or more), interest stops on the date of the notice and demand. (Code Sec. 6601(e)(3))[24] (For payments to stop interest, see ¶4868.) Also, where a taxpayer consents to immediate assessment (by signing one of the Form 870 waiver of assessment series, see ¶4819) and IRS doesn't make notice and demand for payment within 30 days of the filing of that consent, interest stops running during the period beginning immediately after that 30th day and ending with the date of the notice and demand. (Code Sec. 6601(c))[25]

Interest on civil penalties runs from the date of notice and demand if not paid within 21 days after that date (10 business days for amounts of $100,000 or more). (Code Sec. 6601(e)(2)(A)) But for the penalties for failure to file, valuation misstatement (income tax) or understatement (estate or gift tax), substantial understatement, negligence, and (except for returns due (without extension) before '89) fraud, the interest period begins on the *return* due date (with extensions). In either case, the interest stops on the date the penalty is paid. (Code Sec. 6601(e)(2)(B))[26]

¶ 4868   Deposits to prepay and/or stop the running of interest.

A cash deposit made in conformity with IRS rules may be used to pay income, gift, estate, or generation-skipping tax or certain excise taxes that have not yet been assessed at the time of the deposit. (Code Sec. 6603(a)) The amount of the deposit that is later used by IRS to pay tax is treated as a tax payment at the time of the deposit, for purposes of determining whether the taxpayer owes interest on an underpayment of tax. (Code Sec. 6603(b)) Interest may be allowed on the return of all or part of such a deposit, see ¶4853.[27]

¶ 4869   How other year's tax payments affect interest.

Interest on a deficiency isn't eliminated when the deficiency is eliminated by a net operating loss (NOL), net capital loss or business credit carryback (or a foreign tax credit carryback arising in a tax year beginning after Aug. 5, '97). It accrues from its original due date to the filing date for the tax year in which the carryback arose (or, with respect to any portion of a credit carryback attributable to a carryback from a later year, to the filing date for that later year). (Code Sec. 6601(d))[28]

An underpayment of tax in one year may be paid by crediting against it an overpayment of tax in another year. (Code Sec. 6402(a)) No interest accrues on any portion of the underpayment so paid for any period after the return due date (*without* extension) for the overpayment year or, if later, when the offsetting return is filed. This rule doesn't apply to the extent the zero rate (¶4866) applies. (Code Sec. 6601(f))[29] When a taxpayer elects to apply an overpayment to the following year's estimated taxes, the overpayment will be applied to unpaid installments of estimated tax due on or after the date(s) the overpayment arose, in the order in which they are required to be paid to avoid an estimated tax penalty. IRS will assess interest on a later determined deficiency for the overpayment year only from the date(s) that the overpayment is applied to the following year's estimated taxes.[30]

---

24. ¶V-1200 *et seq.*, ¶V-1300; ¶66,014.02; TD ¶853,001
25. ¶V-1307; ¶66,014.02; TD ¶853,002
26. ¶V-1225; ¶66,014.02; TD ¶853,018
27. ¶S-5804 *et seq.*; ¶66,034; TD ¶853,009 *et seq.*

28. ¶V-1302; ¶66,014.03; TD ¶853,015
29. ¶V-1301; ¶66,014.03
30. ¶V-1210; TD ¶853,013

¶ 4870   Abatement of interest, penalties and additions to tax—Form 843.

IRS has discretion to abate any interest that was assessed because of a deficiency attributable to any unreasonable error or delay by an IRS employee acting in his official capacity when performing a managerial or ministerial act, or that is due on a notice of deficiency to the extent any error or delay in payment is attributable to an IRS employee being erroneous or dilatory in performing a managerial or ministerial act, but only if no significant aspect of the error or delay can be attributed to the taxpayer involved. (Code Sec. 6404(e)(1); Reg § 301.6404-2)[31] IRS must abate any portion of any penalty or addition to tax attributable to erroneous written advice (as specifically defined) (Reg § 301.6404-3(c)(1)) furnished to a taxpayer by an IRS employee acting in an official capacity in response to a specific written request. The taxpayer must have reasonably relied on the advice (Code Sec. 6404(f)(1), Code Sec. 6404(f)(2)(A)), and the portion of the penalty or addition to tax must not have resulted from his failure to provide adequate or accurate information. (Code Sec. 6404(f)(2)(B))[32] Make the abatement request on Form 843 (as annotated and with certain attachments as required by the regs). (Reg § 301.6404-3(d))[33] For taxpayers affected by a federally declared disaster or a terroristic or military action, IRS may postpone the deadlines for performing various tax acts for a period of up to one year. The postponement period may be disregarded in determining the amount of interest due for periods after the disaster date. (Code Sec. 7508A(a)(2))[34]

¶ 4871   Interest and penalty suspension for failing to notify individual of liability.

Subject to exceptions (including a gross misstatement such as a substantial omission of items to which the six-year statute of limitation applies (see ¶4832), a gross valuation misstatement (see ¶4880), undisclosed reportable transactions, and listed transactions (see ¶4891)), the imposition of interest and penalties with respect to any failure relating to a timely filed individual income tax return must be suspended if, before the end of the 36-month period beginning on the date the return is filed or, if later, the date it's due (without extensions), IRS fails to provide a notice to the taxpayer specifically stating the taxpayer's liability and the basis for the liability. The suspension period begins on the day after the end of the 36-month period and ends on the date that's 21 days after IRS provides the notice. Where a taxpayer files an amended return (or other written document) showing additional tax liability, the 36-month period for IRS to issue the required notice of liability (and avoid interest or penalty suspension) is restarted. (Code Sec. 6404(g); Reg § 301.6404-4)[35]

¶ 4872   When reasonable cause excuses civil penalties.

Certain civil penalties won't be imposed if the taxpayer's failure to perform the required act was due to reasonable cause—e.g., reliance on tax expert or IRS advice, irregularities in mail delivery, death or serious illness, unavoidable absence, casualty, disaster. Generally, a taxpayer who challenges IRS's imposition of a civil penalty has the burden of showing that his failure was due to reasonable cause and not willful neglect.[36]

No accuracy-related (¶4875 *et seq.*) or fraud (¶4882) penalty applies as to any portion of an underpayment for which the taxpayer shows reasonable cause and that he acted in good faith. (Code Sec. 6664(c)(1); Reg § 1.6664-4) A taxpayer's failure to disclose a reportable transaction (¶4749) is a strong indication of failure to act in good faith. (Reg § 1.6664-4(d))[37]

The reasonable cause exception generally doesn't apply to an underpayment attributable to a substantial or gross valuation overstatement as to charitable deduction property. But, this

31. ¶T-3951 *et seq.*; ¶64,044; TD ¶837,601
32. ¶T-3908 *et seq.*; ¶64,044; TD ¶837,504
33. ¶T-3914 *et seq.*; ¶64,044; TD ¶837,510
34. ¶T-3973; ¶75,08A4; TD ¶837,623

35. ¶V-1401, ¶V-1601.2; ¶64,044; TD ¶s 837,509, 852,006
36. ¶V-1776 *et seq.*, ¶V-2750 *et seq.*; ¶66,644; TD ¶868,500 *et seq.*
37. ¶V-2060; TD ¶863,001

bar doesn't apply to a substantial valuation overstatement if the claimed value of the property was based on a qualified appraisal made by a qualified appraiser, and the taxpayer made a good faith investigation of the value of the contributed property. (Code Sec. 6664(c)(2))[38]

¶ 4873 Failure to file income, estate or gift tax returns when due.

The penalty is 5% of the amount of tax required to be shown on the return (less any earlier payments and credits) for the first month (Code Sec. 6651(b)(1)), plus an additional 5% for each month (or fraction of a month) the failure continues without reasonable cause (¶4872), but not more than 25%. (Code Sec. 6651(a)(1))[39] There's a minimum penalty for failure to file any income tax return within 60 days of the due date (including extensions), except if due to reasonable cause and not willful neglect. This minimum penalty is the lesser of $135 or the amount of tax required to be shown on the return. (Code Sec. 6651(a))[40] The failure-to-file penalty (5%) is reduced (but not below the above minimum) by the amount of any failure-to-pay penalty (1/2%, see ¶4874) for that month. (Code Sec. 6651(c)(1)) The 25% ceiling is applied to each penalty before making this reduction.[41] If the failure to file is fraudulent, the penalty is increased to 15% per month (or fraction), up to a 75% cap. (Code Sec. 6651(f))[42]

¶ 4874 Failure to pay tax.

A penalty is imposed on a taxpayer who, without reasonable cause (¶4872) fails to pay the tax shown on a return or an assessed deficiency of that tax by the prescribed date. The penalty is 1/2% of tax shown (or assessed) for each month (or fraction of a month) that it isn't paid (but not more than 25%). (Code Sec. 6651(a)(2), Code Sec. 6651(a)(3))[43] A substitute return prepared by IRS is a return. (Code Sec. 6651(g)(2); Reg § 301.6020-1(b)(3))[44] The penalty is increased to 1% per month or fraction (up to 25% penalty maximum) if the tax isn't paid within ten days after IRS serves notice of levy. (Code Sec. 6651(d))[45] The penalty is reduced to 1/4% per month for individuals paying in installments. (Code Sec. 6651(h))[46] An individual who gets an automatic extension of time for *filing* is subject to the penalty (absent reasonable cause) if any additional payment due with the extended return *either*: (1) exceeds 10% of the total shown on Form 1040, *or* (2) isn't paid by the extended filing date. (Reg § 301.6651-1(c)(3))[47]

¶ 4875 Accuracy-related penalty.

An "accuracy-related" civil penalty applies if any portion of an understatement of tax on a tax return is due (absent reasonable cause, see ¶4872) to: negligence (¶4876), substantial income tax valuation misstatements (¶4877), income tax understatements (¶4878), estate or gift tax valuation understatements (¶4880), pension liability overstatements (¶4881), disallowance of benefits due to lack of economic substance (¶4895), or undisclosed foreign financial asset understatements (¶4879). (Code Sec. 6662(a), Code Sec. 6662(b), Code Sec. 6664(c)(1); Reg § 1.6662-2(a))[48] The accuracy-related penalty doesn't apply to any portion of an underpayment for which the fraud penalty (¶4882) is imposed or to the portion of any underpayment which is attributable to a reportable transaction understatement on which the Code Sec. 6662A reportable transaction understatement penalty is imposed, except: (i) for purposes of determining whether an underpayment is substantial or (ii) where the 40% gross valuation misstatement penalty applies. (Code Sec. 6662(b))[49] Also, it only applies if a return is filed by the taxpayer (not by IRS). (Code Sec. 6664(b); Reg § 1.6662-2(a))[50]

---

38. ¶V-2237; ¶66,644; TD ¶863,001
39. ¶V-1750 *et seq.*; ¶66,514.01; TD ¶861,001
40. ¶V-1752; ¶66,514.01; TD ¶861,001
41. ¶V-1791; ¶66,514.01; TD ¶861,001
42. ¶V-1753; ¶66,514.01;TD ¶861,004
43. ¶V-1671 *et seq.*; ¶66,514.01; TD ¶862,501
44. ¶V-1685; ¶60,204; TD ¶862,515

45. ¶V-1683; ¶66,514.01; TD ¶862,513
46. ¶V-1684; ¶66,514; TD ¶862,514
47. ¶V-1681; ¶66,514; TD ¶66,514.06
48. ¶V-2000 *et seq.*; ¶66,624; TD ¶863,000
49. ¶V-2002; ¶66,624; TD ¶865,004
50. ¶V-2051; ¶66,624; TD ¶863,001

¶ 4876   Negligence.

The "accuracy-related" penalty is imposed if any part of an underpayment of tax is due either to negligence or to disregard of rules or regs but without intent to defraud. The penalty is 20% of the portion of the underpayment attributable to the negligence, etc. (Code Sec. 6662(a), Code Sec. 6662(b)(1)) For rules common to all accuracy-related penalties, see ¶4875. "Negligence" includes any failure to make a reasonable attempt to comply with the law or to exercise ordinary and reasonable care in preparing a tax return, as well as failure to keep adequate books and records or to substantiate items properly. "Disregard" includes any careless, reckless or intentional disregard. (Code Sec. 6662(c); Reg § 1.6662-3(b))[1] The penalties are not imposed for a position with respect to an item (other than a reportable transaction) that is contrary to a revenue ruling or a notice (other than a proposed rulemaking) published in the IRB, if the position has a realistic possibility of being sustained on its merits. (Reg § 1.6662-3(a)) The penalty for disregard of rules or regs isn't imposed where a position is contrary to a rule or reg if the position is disclosed and has a reasonable basis, the taxpayer keeps adequate books and records and substantiates items properly; and, in the case of a position contrary to a reg, the position represents a good faith challenge to the reg. (Reg § 1.6662-3(c), Reg § 1.6662-7(c))[2]

¶ 4877   Misstating value or basis of property on income tax return.

The accuracy-related penalty is imposed on a taxpayer who makes any of these "substantial valuation misstatements": (Code Sec. 6662(b)(3))

. . . any value (or adjusted basis) claimed on an income tax return that is 150% or more of the correct figure (Code Sec. 6662(e)(1)(A));

. . . Code Sec. 482 transfer price adjustments where the price for any property (or its use) or services on an income tax return is 200% or more, or 50% or less, of the correct figure—transactional penalty (Code Sec. 6662(e)(1)(B)(i); Reg § 1.6662-6(b));

. . . a net increase in taxable income for a tax year (without regard to carryovers) resulting from all Code Sec. 482 adjustments in the transfer price of any property (or its use) or services, that (with certain adjustments) exceeds the lesser of $5 million or 10% of the taxpayer's gross receipts—net adjustment penalty. (Code Sec. 6662(e)(1)(B)(ii), Code Sec. 6662(e)(3); Reg § 1.6662-6(c))[3]

The penalty equals 20% of the portion of any income tax underpayment that results from the misstatement (except to the extent the fraud penalty is imposed) (Code Sec. 6662(a), Code Sec. 6662(b))—40% if the misstatement is gross (the above 200%, 150%, 50% and $5 million/10% figures are, respectively, 400%, 200%, 25% or $20 million/20%, or the correct value or basis is zero). (Code Sec. 6662(h); Reg § 1.6662-5(g))[4] The penalty doesn't apply unless the amount of the underpayment for the tax year attributable to all these misstatements for the year exceeds $5,000 ($10,000 for corporations other than S corporations or personal holding companies). (Code Sec. 6662(e)(2))[5] Reasonable cause (¶4872) excuses the penalty. There's no disclosure exception. (Code Sec. 6664(c)(1); Reg § 1.6662-5(a))[6] Strict appraisal requirements apply to overvalued charitable gifts. (Code Sec. 6664(c)(3))[7]

¶ 4878   Penalty on substantial understatements of income tax.

The 20% accuracy-related penalty is imposed on any portion of an underpayment of tax that (absent reasonable cause, see ¶4872) is attributable to any substantial understatement

---

1. ¶V-2105; ¶66,624.01; TD ¶863,005.5
2. ¶V-2106 *et seq.*; ¶66,624.02; TD ¶863,005.7
3. ¶V-2200 *et seq.*; ¶66,624; TD ¶863,010
4. ¶V-2206 *et seq.*; ¶66,624; TD ¶863,010

5. ¶V-2205; ¶66,624; TD ¶863,010
6. ¶V-2234; ¶66,644; TD ¶863,001
7. ¶V-2237; ¶66,644; TD ¶863,011

of income tax, self-employment tax (¶3140 *et seq.*), (Code Sec. 6662(a), Code Sec. 6662(b)(1); Reg § 1.6662-4(b)(3))[8] or unrelated business income tax (¶4121).[9] For rules common to all accuracy-related penalties, see ¶4875. For corporate taxpayers (other than S corporations and personal holding companies), an understatement is substantial if the amount of the understatement exceeds the lesser of (1) 10% of the tax required to be shown on the return for that tax year (or $10,000 if that is greater), or (2) $10 million. For other taxpayers, an understatement is substantial if it exceeds the greater of $5,000 or 10% of the tax required to be shown on the return. (Code Sec. 6662(d)(1); Reg § 1.6662-4(b)(1))[10] An understatement is the excess of (a) the tax amount required to be shown on the return, over (b) the tax amount that's shown (or withheld) reduced by any rebate. (Code Sec. 6662(d)(2)(A); Reg § 1.6662-4(b)(2), Reg § 1.6662-4(b)(3))[11] The understatement is reduced to the extent attributable to any item (other than tax shelter items, see below) for which:

... there is or was substantial authority for how the taxpayer treated it (Code Sec. 6662(d)(2)(B)(i)), or

... the relevant facts affecting the item's tax treatment are adequately disclosed either on the return (IRS each year lists which items on the return qualify) or on a Form 8275 (Form 8275-R if the taxpayer's position is contrary to a reg) attached to the return *and* there's a reasonable basis (¶4876) for the taxpayer's treatment of the item. (Code Sec. 6662(d)(2)(B)(ii); Reg § 1.6662-4(f)) A corporation doesn't have a reasonable basis for its tax treatment of an item attributable to a multi-party financing transaction if the treatment doesn't clearly reflect its income. (Code Sec. 6662(d)(2))[12]

"Substantial authority" exists for the tax treatment of an item (only if the weight of the authorities supporting the treatment is substantial in relation to the weight of authorities supporting contrary positions. (Reg § 1.6662-4(d)(3)(i))[13]

¶ 4879 Penalty on undisclosed foreign financial assets understatement.

A 40% penalty is imposed on any understatement attributable to an undisclosed foreign financial asset. (Code Sec. 6662(j)(3)) The term "undisclosed foreign financial asset" includes all assets subject to information reporting requirements under Code Sec. 6038 (return of U.S. person who controls a foreign corporation or partnership), Code Sec. 6038B (return of U.S. person making "outbound" transfers to foreign entities), Code Sec. 6038D (self-reporting required for "specified foreign financial assets"), Code Sec. 6046A (return of U.S. person who acquires, disposes of, or has substantial changes in, foreign partnership interests), or Code Sec. 6048 (information reporting as to foreign trusts) for which the required information wasn't provided by the taxpayer as required under the applicable reporting provisions. (Code Sec. 6662(j)(2)) An understatement is attributable to an undisclosed foreign financial asset if it is attributable to any transaction involving the asset. (Code Sec. 6662(j)(1))[14]

¶ 4880 Penalty for understating value of property on gift or estate tax return.

If the value of any property claimed on any gift or estate tax return is 65% or less of the correct value, the 20% accuracy-related penalty (¶4875) is imposed on an underpayment of tax that's attributable to that understatement. (Code Sec. 6662(a), Code Sec. 6662(b)(5), Code Sec. 6662(g)(1)) The penalty is increased to 40% for gross misstatements—i.e., the claimed value is 40% or less of the correct figure. (Code Sec. 6662(h)(1), Code Sec. 6662(h)(2)(C))[15] The

---

8. ¶V-2150 *et seq.*; ¶66,624.03; TD ¶863,014
9. ¶V-2151; TD ¶863,014
10. ¶V-2159; ¶66,624.03; TD ¶863,014
11. ¶V-2154; ¶66,624.03; TD ¶863,015
12. ¶s V-2154, V-2167 *et seq.*; ¶66,624.04; TD ¶863,015

13. ¶V-2161, ¶V-2163; ¶66,624.04; TD ¶863,016
14. ¶V-2276; ¶66,624.13; TD ¶863,021
15. ¶s V-2251, V-2252; ¶66,624 (Estate & Gift), ¶66,624.10; TD ¶863,013

penalty applies only if the portion of the underpayment attributable to all these undervaluations for the tax period exceeds $5,000. (Code Sec. 6662(g)(2))[16]

¶ 4881   Overstatement of pension liabilities.

A taxpayer who (absent reasonable cause, see ¶4872) substantially overstates pension liabilities for a tax year is subject to the accuracy-related penalty (¶4875) if the overstatement results in an income tax underpayment of $1,000 or more. (Code Sec. 6662(a), Code Sec. 6662(b)(4), Code Sec. 6662(f)(2))[17] The penalty equals 20% of the underpayment (40% for "gross" overstatements). (Code Sec. 6662(a), Code Sec. 6662(h)(1))[18] Pension liabilities are substantially overstated if the actuarial determination of the liabilities taken into account in computing the contribution deduction (¶4334) is at least 200% of the correct amount. (Code Sec. 6662(f)(1)) The overstatement is "gross" if it's 400% or more of the correct figure. (Code Sec. 6662(h)(2)(B))[19]

¶ 4882   Fraud.

Fraudulent underpayment of tax required to be shown on a return results in a civil penalty of 75% of the portion of the underpayment attributable to fraud. (Code Sec. 6663(a))[20] The fraud penalty can be imposed only if a return is filed (not by IRS). (Code Sec. 6664(b))[21] It won't be imposed where the taxpayer shows reasonable cause (¶4872) for the underpayment, and that he acted in good faith. (Code Sec. 6664(c)(1))[22] Imposition of the fraud penalty on any part of an underpayment precludes imposition of any of the accuracy-related penalties (¶4875) on that same part. (Code Sec. 6662(b))[23] If IRS establishes that any part of an underpayment is attributable to fraud, the entire underpayment is treated as attributable to fraud, except for any part the taxpayer establishes (by a preponderance of the evidence) isn't so attributable. (Code Sec. 6663(b))[24]

¶ 4883   Trust fund recovery penalty for responsible persons.

Willful failure to collect or account for and pay over a tax or willful attempt to evade or defeat a tax, by a "responsible person" required to collect, account for, and pay over the tax carries a civil "trust fund recovery penalty" equal to 100% of the total tax evaded or not accounted for and paid over. (Code Sec. 6672) IRS can't assess the penalty without notifying a responsible person of its intent to do so at least 60 days before making notice and demand for the penalty (unless collection is in jeopardy). (Code Sec. 6672(b)) A "responsible person" is an officer or employee of the corporation, or a partner or employee of a partnership, who is under a duty to perform the act at issue. (Code Sec. 6671(b))[25] A responsible person also includes any person who is connected or associated with an employer in such a manner that he has the power to see that the taxes are paid.[26] Unpaid volunteer board members of exempt organizations who aren't involved in day-to-day financial activities and don't know about the penalized failure are exempt from the penalty, unless that results in no one being liable for it. (Code Sec. 6672(e))[27] IRS must disclose, at the written request of a responsible person, the names of other responsible persons and the collection activities related to them. (Code Sec. 6103(e)(9))[28] Responsible persons who pay more than their proportionate share of tax have the right to recover the excess from other responsible persons. (Code Sec. 6672(d))[29]

16. ¶V-2251; ¶66,624 (Estate & Gift), ¶66,624.10; TD ¶863,013
17. ¶V-2260 *et seq.*; ¶66,624.09; TD ¶863,012
18. ¶V-2262; ¶66,624.09; TD ¶863,012
19. ¶V-2263; ¶s 66,624, 66,624.09; TD ¶863,012
20. ¶V-2300 *et seq.*; ¶s 66,634, 66,534; TD ¶865,001
21. ¶V-2051; ¶66,634; TD ¶865,001
22. ¶V-2060; ¶66,644; TD ¶865,001

23. ¶V-2002; ¶66,624; TD ¶865,004
24. ¶V-2302; ¶66,634; TD ¶865,001
25. ¶V-1700 *et seq.*; ¶66,724; TD ¶864,001
26. ¶V-1704; ¶66,724
27. ¶V-1703.1; TD ¶864,009
28. ¶S-6313.1; TD ¶864,024
29. ¶V-1730; TD ¶864,024

¶ 4884 Penalty for filing erroneous refund claim.

If a claim for refund or credit of income tax (other than one relating to the earned income credit) is made for an "excessive amount," the person making the claim is liable for a penalty equal to 20% of the excessive amount. (Code Sec. 6676(a)) An "excessive amount" is the amount by which the claimed refund or credit exceeds the allowable amount. (Code Sec. 6676(b)) The penalty doesn't apply if it is shown that the claim for the excessive amount has a reasonable basis. (Code Sec. 6676(a)) But the reasonable basis exception doesn't apply to transactions that lack economic substance (¶4895). (Code Sec. 6676(c)) The penalty doesn't apply to any portion of the excessive amount that's subject to an accuracy-related penalty imposed under Code Sec. 6662 (¶4875) or Code Sec. 6662A (¶4892) or a fraud penalty under Code Sec. 6663 (¶4882). (Code Sec. 6676(c))[30]

¶ 4885 Penalty for aiding and abetting understatement of tax liability.

A penalty of $1,000 ($10,000 for a corporation) (Code Sec. 6701(b))[31] is imposed on any person who aids or assists, procures or advises with respect to the preparation or presentation of any portion of a return, affidavit, claim or other document connected with any matter arising under the internal revenue laws, and who knows (or has reason to believe) that the portion will be used in connection with any material matter arising under those laws, and knows that an understatement of another person's tax would result from that use (Code Sec. 6701(a)) even if there is no actual understatement.[32] The penalty applies whether or not the taxpayer knew of or gave consent to the understatement. (Code Sec. 6701(d))[33] The term "advises" includes the actions of lawyers and accountants who counsel a particular course of action[34] and appraisers who falsely or fraudulently overstate the value of property in a qualified appraisal (of property for which a charitable contribution is claimed, see ¶2137). (Reg § 1.170A-13(c)(3)(iii))[35]

observation: Unlike the return preparer penalties, which apply only to "paid" preparers (¶4886), the aiding and abetting penalty applies regardless of whether a fee is charged.

¶ 4886 Return preparer understatement penalties.

If a tax return preparer prepares a return or refund claim for which any part of a tax liability understatement is due to an "unreasonable position" and the preparer knew or should have known of the position, the preparer must pay a penalty for each return or claim equal to the greater of $1,000 or 50% of the income derived (or to be derived) by the preparer with respect to the return or claim. (Code Sec. 6694(a)(1)) In the case of a position with respect to a reportable transaction (to which Code Sec. 6662A applies, ¶4892) or a tax shelter, a position is unreasonable if it wasn't reasonable to believe that the position would more likely than not be sustained on its merits. In other cases, a position is unreasonable if (1) there wasn't substantial authority for it or (2) for a position that was disclosed in the return or in a statement attached to the return (under Code Sec. 6662(d)(2)(B)(ii)(I)), there was no reasonable basis for it. (Code Sec. 6694(a)(2); Reg § 1.6694-2(a)(1)) However, there's no penalty if it is shown that there was reasonable cause for the understatement and the preparer acted in good faith. (Code Sec. 6694(a)(3); Reg § 1.6694-2(e))

"Tax return preparer" means any person who is a tax return preparer under the rules at

---

30. ¶V-2291; ¶66,764; TD ¶866,101
31. ¶V-2352; ¶67,104; TD ¶867,030
32. ¶V-2351 *et seq.*; ¶67,014; TD ¶867,027

33. ¶V-2354; ¶67,014; TD ¶867,027
34. ¶V-2353; ¶67,014; TD ¶867,027
35. ¶V-2351; TD ¶867,032

¶4751. An individual is a tax return preparer subject to the penalty if he is primarily responsible for the position on the return or claim for refund giving rise to an understatement. There is only one individual within a firm who is primarily responsible for each position on the return or claim for refund giving rise to an understatement. If there is a signing tax return preparer under the rules at ¶4751, he will generally be considered the person primarily responsible for the positions on the return or claim for refund giving rise to an understatement, unless, based on credible information from any source, it's concluded that the signing tax return preparer isn't primarily responsible for the position. (Reg § 1.6694-1(b))[36]

A tax return preparer who prepares a return or refund claim for which any part of a tax liability understatement is due to "willful or reckless conduct" must pay a penalty for each return or claim equal to the greater of (1) $5,000; or (2) 50% of the income derived (or to be derived) by the tax return preparer for preparing the return or claim. (Code Sec. 6694(b); Reg § 1.6694-3(a)) "Willful or reckless conduct" is conduct by the tax return preparer which is a willful attempt to understate the tax liability on the return or claim, or a reckless or intentional disregard of rules or regulations. (Code Sec. 6694(b)(2); Reg § 1.6694-3(b), Reg § 1.6694-3(c)) A penalty payable by a person due to willful or reckless conduct in connection with a return or refund claim is reduced by the penalty paid by that person due to an unreasonable position. (Code Sec. 6694(b)(3); Reg § 1.6694-3(f))[37]

IRS has provided lists of the documents covered by the above penalties.[38]

¶ 4887 Penalty for valuation misstatements attributable to incorrect appraisals.

A penalty is imposed on any person who: (A) prepares a property appraisal and knows, or reasonably should have known, that the appraisal would be used in connection with a return or a refund claim, and (B) the claimed property value on the return or refund claim that is based on the appraisal results in a substantial valuation misstatement under Code Sec. 6662(e), a gross valuation misstatement under Code Sec. 6662(h) (¶4877), or a substantial estate or gift tax valuation understatement under Code Sec. 6662(g). (Code Sec. 6695A(a))[39]

¶ 4888 Other penalties on tax return preparers.

A tax return preparer who fails to perform the duties described at ¶4750 is subject to these civil penalties (up to a maximum $25,000 per calendar year for any single type of failure):

. . . $50 for each failure to sign a return as required. (Code Sec. 6695(b))[40]

. . . $50 for each failure to show his taxpayer ID number or preparer tax identification number (PTIN) as required. (Code Sec. 6695(e))[41]

. . . $50 for each failure to furnish completed copy of return to the taxpayer. (Code Sec. 6695(a))[42]

. . . $50 for each failure to retain a copy of a prepared return or to include it on a list of prepared returns. (Code Sec. 6695(c))[43]

. . . $50 for each failure to retain and make available a record of the preparers employed or engaged, plus $50 for each failure to include a required item in the record required to be retained and made available. (Code Sec. 6695(e))[44]

. . . $500 (with no annual maximum) for each check with respect to taxes issued to a taxpayer that the preparer endorses or otherwise negotiates, except where the preparer is a bank and deposits the check to the taxpayer's account in the bank. (Code Sec. 6695(f))[45]

36. ¶V-2632 *et seq.*; ¶66,944; TD ¶867,002
37. ¶V-2630; ¶66,944
38. ¶V-2631.3; ¶66,944
39. ¶V-2691; ¶66,95A4; TD ¶867,201
40. ¶V-2673; ¶66,954; TD ¶867,016
41. ¶V-2677; ¶66,954; TD ¶867,016
42. ¶V-2674; ¶66,954; TD ¶867,016
43. ¶V-2675; ¶66,954; TD ¶867,016
44. ¶V-2676; ¶66,954; TD ¶867,016
45. ¶V-2671; ¶66,954; TD ¶867,018

. . . $500 for each failure to follow regulatory due diligence requirements in claiming the earned income credit (EIC). To avoid the penalty, Form 8867 must be submitted with the return or refund claim claiming the EIC. (Code Sec. 6695(g); Reg § 1.6695-2)[46]

Improper disclosure or use of information by return preparers is subject to a civil penalty of $250 for each improper disclosure or use ($10,000 maximum per calendar year), (Code Sec. 6713(a))[47] as well as a criminal penalty. (Code Sec. 7216)[48] Regs provide exceptions to these penalties (Reg § 301.7216-1(a), Reg § 301.7216-2)[49] and additional exceptions where the taxpayer consents.

IRS may get a district court to enjoin a preparer from engaging in specific misconduct, but only if an injunction is appropriate to prevent recurrence of the misconduct. If the court finds that the preparer has continually or repeatedly engaged in this misconduct and an injunction isn't sufficient to prevent the preparer's interference with proper tax administration, it can enjoin him from practicing. (Code Sec. 7407(b))[50]

¶ 4889 Abusive tax shelters and conduct.

A person who promotes an abusive tax shelter is subject to a penalty equal to the lesser of $1,000 or 100% of the gross income derived or to be derived from the activity. However, if an activity on which the penalty is imposed involves a false or fraudulent statement, the penalty equals 50% of the gross income derived or to be derived by that person from the activity. (Code Sec. 6700(a))[1] IRS may seek an injunction to stop any action or failure to take action:

(1) that is subject to penalty under Code Sec. 6700, Code Sec. 6701 (aiding or abetting an understatement, see ¶4885), Code Sec. 6707 (failure to furnish information regarding reportable transactions, see ¶4893), and Code Sec. 6708 (failure to provide list of advisees with respect to reportable transactions, see ¶4890) or

(2) in violation of any requirement imposed by regs issued under Section 330 of Title 31 of the U.S. Code (rules regulating the practice of taxpayer representatives before the Department of the Treasury), i.e., the Circular 230 rules. (Code Sec. 7408)[2]

¶ 4890 Penalty for failure to provide reportable transaction advisee list.

Any person required under Code Sec. 6112 to maintain a list of advisees with respect to reportable transactions (see ¶4748) who fails to make that list available to IRS on its written request within 20 business days after the date of the request is liable for a $10,000 per day penalty for each day of that failure after the 20th day. This penalty isn't imposed, however, for any day that the failure to provide the list is due to reasonable cause. In certain circumstances, IRS has the discretion to extend the 20-day production period. (Prop Reg. § 301.6708-1 ["Taxpayers may rely"]) (Code Sec. 6708(a))[3]

¶ 4891 Penalty imposed for failure to report reportable transactions.

A penalty is imposed on any person who fails to include on any return or statement any information that's required to be disclosed under Code Sec. 6011 (see ¶4749) with respect to a reportable transaction. (Code Sec. 6707A(a); Reg § 301.6707A-1(a)) The penalty is 75% of the decrease in tax shown on the return resulting from the transaction (or which would have resulted if the transaction were respected) subject to a maximum of $10,000 for natural persons and $50,000 for others (increased to $100,000 and $200,000 respectively if a listed transaction is involved). The minimum penalty per transaction is $5,000 for natural persons

---

46. ¶V-2677.1; ¶S-1106.1; ¶66,954.01; TD ¶867,017
47. ¶V-2678; ¶67,134; TD ¶867,035
48. ¶V-3308; ¶72,164; TD ¶871,010
49. ¶V-2678; ¶V-3309 *et seq.*; ¶72,164; TD ¶871,010

50. ¶V-2679 *et seq.*; ¶74,074; TD ¶867,033
1. ¶V-2403; ¶67,004
2. ¶V-2451; ¶74,084
3. ¶V-2503; ¶67,084

and $10,000 for others. (Code Sec. 6707A(b)) The status of transactions as reportable transactions and listed transactions is determined under regs under Code Sec. 6011. (Code Sec. 6707A(c); Reg § 1.6011-4(b))

IRS can rescind all or a portion of a Code Sec. 6707A penalty if (a) the violation relates to a reportable transaction that isn't a listed transaction and (b) rescission would promote compliance with the Code and effective tax administration. (Code Sec. 6707A(d)) The rescission also applies to any penalty on a material advisor under Code Sec. 6707 (¶4893). (Code Sec. 6707(c)) Regs list factors considered in determining whether to grant rescission requests. (Reg § 301.6707A-1(d)) IRS procedures establish how to request rescission.[4]

¶ 4892   Penalty for understatements regarding reportable transactions.

A 20% accuracy-related penalty applies for reportable transaction understatements. (Code Sec. 6662A(a)) The penalty is 30% for any portion of any reportable transaction understatement for which specified disclosure rules are not met. (Code Sec. 6662A(c)) A reportable transaction understatement is the sum of (1) the amount of the increase (if any) in taxable income resulting from a difference between (a) the proper tax treatment of an item subject to the penalty rules and (b) the taxpayer's treatment of the item (on the taxpayer's tax return), multiplied by the highest noncorporate rate (or corporate tax rate, in the case of a corporation), and (2) the amount of the decrease (if any) in the total amount of income tax credits which results from a difference between (a) the taxpayer's treatment of an item subject to the penalty rules (on the taxpayer's tax return) and (b) the proper tax treatment of the item. (Code Sec. 6662A(b)(1)) The penalty doesn't apply to any part of an understatement on which the 40% penalty for transactions that lack economic substance (¶4895) is imposed. (Code Sec. 6662A(e)(2)(B))[5] For this purpose, any reduction in the excess of deductions allowed in the tax year over gross income for the year, and any reduction in the amount of capital losses which would (without regard to the capital loss carryover rules) be allowed for the year, is treated as an increase in taxable income. (Code Sec. 6662A(b)(1))

An item is subject to the penalty rules if the item is attributable to any listed transaction and any reportable transaction (other than a listed transaction) if a significant purpose of the transaction is federal income tax avoidance or evasion. (Code Sec. 6662A(b)(2)(B)) Listed and reportable transactions are defined under the Code Sec. 6707A penalty rules for reportable transactions for which disclosure is required (see ¶4891) (Code Sec. 6662A(d)) A limited reasonable cause exception applies if certain disclosure, substantial authority and reasonable belief requirements are met. (Code Sec. 6662A(d))[6] But this exception doesn't apply to any part of a reportable transaction understatement which is attributable to a transaction that lacks economic substance under Code Sec. 7701(o) or fails to meet the requirements of any similar rule of law (¶4895). (Code Sec. 6664(d)(2))[7]

¶ 4893   Material advisor's penalty for not reporting reportable transactions.

A material advisor who fails to file a timely information return required under Code Sec. 6111(a) (¶4748), or who files a false or incomplete information return, for a reportable transaction (including a listed transaction) is subject to a penalty of $50,000 for each failure. But, if the failure relates to a listed transaction, the penalty increases to the greater of: (1) $200,000, or (2) 50% of the gross income received by the advisor that is attributable to aid, assistance, or advice provided for the listed transaction before the date the advisor files an information return including the transaction. If the reporting failure for a listed transaction is due to an intentional failure or act, the 50% of gross income penalty amount (item 2 above) is increased to 75% of gross income. (Code Sec. 6707(a), Code Sec. 6707(b)) Reportable and

---

4. ¶V-2531 *et seq.*; ¶67,07A4; TD ¶866,501
5. ¶V-2281; ¶66,62A4; TD ¶868,101

6. ¶V-2284; ¶66,62A4; TD ¶868,104
7. ¶V-2284; ¶66,644.01

listed transactions are defined under Code Sec. 6707A(c) (see ¶4891). (Code Sec. 6707(d))[8]

¶ 4894 Penalties for tax-exempts acting as tax shelter accommodation parties.

Certain tax-exempt entities are subject to penalties for participating in a prohibited tax-shelter transaction as accommodation parties, see ¶4113. An exempt organization that participates in a reportable transaction (including a listed transaction) in order to reduce its own liability is also subject to disclosure rules. (Code Sec. 6033(a)(2), Code Sec. 6652(c)(3))[9]

¶ 4895 Penalty for transaction lacking economic substance.

A 20% penalty applies to an underpayment attributable to any disallowance of claimed tax benefits by reason of a transaction lacking economic substance (as defined in Code Sec. 7701(o), see below), or failing to meet the requirements of any similar rule of law. (Code Sec. 6662(b)(6)) The penalty rate is increased to 40% if the taxpayer doesn't adequately disclose the relevant facts affecting the tax treatment in the return or a statement attached to the return. (Code Sec. 6662(i)(1)) An amended return or supplement to a return is not taken into account if filed after the taxpayer has been contacted for audit or such other date as IRS specifies. (Code Sec. 6662(i)(3)) No reasonable cause and good faith exception applies. (Code Sec. 6664(c)(2)) This provision doesn't apply to personal transactions of individuals, only to transactions entered into in connection with a trade or business or an activity engaged in for the production of income. (Code Sec. 7701(o)(5)(B)) The penalty also doesn't apply to any portion of an underpayment on which a fraud penalty is imposed (¶4882).[10]

Economic substance. A transaction is treated as having economic substance only if (apart from Federal income tax effects): (1) the transaction changes in a meaningful way the taxpayer's economic position, and (2) the taxpayer has a substantial purpose for entering into the transaction. (Code Sec. 7701(o)(1)) Any State or local income tax effect which is related to a Federal income tax effect is treated in the same manner as a Federal income tax effect. (Code Sec. 7701(o)(3)) A taxpayer may rely on factors other than profit potential to show that a transaction results in a meaningful change in the taxpayer's economic position or that the taxpayer has a substantial non-Federal-income-tax purpose for entering the transaction. Code Sec. 7701(o) doesn't require or establish a minimum return that will meet the profit potential test. But, if a taxpayer relies on profit potential, the present value of the reasonably expected pre-tax profit must be substantial in relation to the present value of the expected net tax benefits that would be allowed if the transaction were respected ("the pre-tax profit to tax benefit ratio test"). (Code Sec. 7701(o)(2)(A)) Fees and other transaction expenses are considered as expenses in determining pre-tax profit. (Code Sec. 7701(o)(2)(B)) The economic substance doctrine is defined as the common law doctrine under which tax benefits under subtitle A with respect to a transaction aren't allowed if the transaction doesn't have economic substance or lacks a business purpose. (Code Sec. 7701(o)(5)(A)) IRS will continue to rely on relevant case law under the common-law economic substance doctrine in applying the two-prong conjunctive test at items (1) and (2) above.[11]

¶ 4896 Post-2013 health care penalties.

For periods beginning after Dec. 31, 2014, an applicable large employer (generally, one with at least 50 full-time employees or a combination of full-time and part-time employees that equals at least 50) must pay an "assessable payment," also called an "employer shared responsibility payment," if any full-time employee is certified to the employer as having purchased health insurance through a state exchange with respect to which a tax credit or cost-sharing reduction is allowed or paid to the employee, if the employer either (1) doesn't

---

8. ¶V-2500; ¶67,074
9. ¶V-2538; ¶66,524.01

10. ¶V-2271; ¶66,624.12; TD ¶868,201
11. ¶M-5901; ¶77,014.35; TD ¶422,301

offer health care coverage for its full-time employees, or (2) offers minimum essential coverage that is unaffordable, or does not provide minimum value. (Code Sec. 4980H) Proposed regs on which taxpayers may rely provide three safe harbors under which affordability may be determined by reference to W-2 wages, rate of pay or the federal poverty line. (Prop Reg. § 54.4980H-5(e), ["Taxpayers may rely"]) Proposed rules are also provided for determining status as a large employer (Code Sec. 4980H(c)(2)(A); Prop Reg. § 54.4980H-2, ["Taxpayers may rely"]), determining full-time employees (Code Sec. 4980H(c)(4); Prop Reg. § 54.4980H-3, ["Taxpayers may rely"]), and determining assessable payments. (Code Sec. 4980H(a); Prop Reg. § 54.4980H-4, ["Taxpayers may rely"] *et seq.*) While no employer shared responsibility payments will be assessed for 2014, IRS encourages employers and other affected entities to voluntarily comply with the information reporting provisions (¶4897) and to maintain or expand health coverage in 2014.[12]

For each month beginning after Dec. 31, 2013, nonexempt U.S. citizens and legal residents must maintain "minimum essential health coverage" for themselves and dependent family members or pay a shared responsibility penalty with their federal tax return. (Code Sec. 5000A)[13] This requirement is commonly referred to as the "individual mandate." Minimum essential coverage includes government-sponsored programs, eligible employer-sponsored plans, plans in the individual market, certain grandfathered group health plans, and other specified coverage. (Code Sec. 5000A(f)(1); Reg § 1.5000A-2) The amount of the penalty is generally the sum of "monthly penalty amounts" for all months in the tax year in which any nonexempt individual for whom the taxpayer is liable did not have minimum essential coverage. (Code Sec. 5000A(c)) The monthly penalty amounts, in turn, are computed based on either a flat dollar amount ($95 for 2014, $325 for 2015, and $695 for 2016) or a percentage (1% for tax years beginning in 2014, 2% for tax years beginning in 2015, and 2.5% for tax years beginning after 2015) of the amount by which the taxpayer's household income exceeds the filing threshold.

For tax years beginning after Dec. 31, 2017, a 40% nondeductible excise tax will be levied on insurance companies and plan administrators for employer-sponsored health coverage to the extent that annual premiums exceed $10,200 for single coverage and $27,500 for family coverage. (Code Sec. 4980I) An additional threshold amount of $1,650 for single coverage and $3,450 for family coverage will apply for retired individuals age 55 and older and for plans that cover employees engaged in high risk professions.[14]

¶ 4897   Information return penalties.

A payor who, without reasonable cause, fails to timely file a required information return (¶4737 *et seq.*) in the required manner (e.g., on magnetic media), or fails to include all of the information required to be shown on the return, or includes incorrect information, is subject to a $100 penalty for each return, up to a $1,500,000 calendar year maximum ($500,000 if the payor's gross receipts for the year don't exceed $5 million). (Code Sec. 6721(a), Code Sec. 6721(d)(1)(A), Code Sec. 6724(a)) The penalty and maximum are reduced to $30 per return ($250,000 maximum—$75,000 if gross receipts test is met) if corrected within 30 days from the required filing date, (Code Sec. 6721(b)(1), Code Sec. 6721(d)(1)(B)) or to $60 per return ($500,000 maximum—$200,000 if gross receipts test is met) if corrected on or before Aug. 1 of the calendar year of the required filing date. (Code Sec. 6721(b)(2), Code Sec. 6721(d)(1)(C))[15] A payor who, without reasonable cause, fails to timely furnish a payee statement to the person prescribed, fails to include all of the required information on the statement, or includes incorrect information, is subject to a penalty of $100 for each such statement, up to a $1,500,000 calendar year maximum, subject to reductions for correction within specified periods. (Code Sec. 6722(a), Code Sec. 6722(b), Code Sec. 6724(a))[16] However,

---

12. ¶H-1170 *et seq.*; ¶49,80H4
13. ¶A-6401 *et seq.*; ¶50,000A4 *et seq.*; TD ¶576,150 *et seq.*
14. ¶H-1226 *et seq.*; ¶49,80I4; TD ¶133,101

15. ¶V-1803 *et seq.*; ¶s 67,214, 67,244.01; TD ¶861,053 *et seq.*
16. ¶V-1814 *et seq.*; ¶s 67,224, 67,244.01; TD ¶861,066 *et seq.*

subject to exceptions, the above penalties are increased *with no calendar year maximum* if the failure is due to intentional disregard. (Code Sec. 6721(e), Code Sec. 6722(e))[17]

The penalties won't apply to a de minimis number of information returns that don't include all the required information, or that include incorrect information, if the failure is corrected by Aug. 1 of the calendar year in which the required filing date occurs. This exception for any calendar year is limited to ten information returns or, if greater, 1/2% of the total number of such returns the payor is required to file that year (Code Sec. 6721(c)), and doesn't apply to returns that aren't due on Feb. 28 or Mar. 15. (Reg § 301.6721-1(d)(4))[18] Also, no penalty will be imposed solely by reason of any failure to comply with the rules requiring filing on magnetic media (¶4753) except (1) to the extent the failure is with respect to more than 250 returns or (2) in the case of a partnership having more than 100 partners, to the extent the failure occurs with respect to more than 100 information returns. (Code Sec. 6724(c); Reg § 301.6721-1(a)(2)(ii)) But, failures by financial institutions to file returns described in Code Sec. 6011(e)(4) (¶4753) on magnetic media can trigger a penalty without regard to the number of returns involved. (Code Sec. 6724(c))[19]

The penalties described above apply to information returns required under:

. . . Code Sec. 110(d) (qualified lease construction allowances for short-term leases).

. . . Code Sec. 264(f)(5)(A)(iv) (natural-person-as-holder exception to the disallowance of the deduction of interest buildup on certain life insurance and annuity contracts).

. . . Code Sec. 338(h)(10)(C) (relating to elective recognition of gain or loss).

. . . Code Sec. 408(i) (individual retirement accounts (IRAs) or annuities).

. . . Code Sec. 1060(b) or Code Sec. 1060(e) (information required of transferors and transferees with respect to applicable asset acquisitions).

. . . Code Sec. 4101(d) (relating to fuels taxes).

. . . Code Sec. 6039(a) (transfers of stock from exercises of incentive stock options and certain purchases from employee stock purchase plans).

. . . Code Sec. 6041(a) (payments of $600 or more).

. . . Code Sec. 6041(b) (collection of foreign items).

. . . Code Sec. 6041A(a) (payments by recipients of services) or Code Sec. 6041A(b) (returns of direct sellers).

. . . Code Sec. 6042(a)(1) (corporate dividends).

. . . Code Sec. 6043A(a) (taxable mergers and acquisitions).

. . . Code Sec. 6044(a)(1) (patronage dividends).

. . . Code Sec. 6045(a) (transactions, including realty transactions, reportable by brokers).

. . . Code Sec. 6045(d) (certain "substitute payments" made to brokers on behalf of customers in connection with short sales).

. . . Code Sec. 6045B(a) (organizational actions affecting the basis of a "specified security").

. . . Code Sec. 6047(d) (employers, plan administrators, etc.).

. . . Code Sec. 6049(a)(1) (payments of interest).

. . . Code Sec. 6050A(a) (payments made by certain fishing boat operators).

. . . Code Sec. 6050H(a) (payments of $600 or more in a calendar year of mortgage interest that is received in the course of a trade or business).

. . . Code Sec. 6050H(h)(1) (mortgage insurance premiums of $600 or more in a calendar year).

. . . Code Sec. 6050I(a) (receipts of more than $10,000 in cash in one transaction (or two or more related transactions) that are received in the course of a trade or business).

17. ¶s V-1811 *et seq.*, V-1816 *et seq.*; ¶s 67,214, 67,224; TD ¶861,063

18. ¶V-1809; ¶67,214; TD ¶861,059

19. ¶V-1810; ¶67,214; TD ¶861,060

. . . Code Sec. 6050I(g)(1) (receipt of more than $10,000 in cash by court clerks as bail).

. . . Code Sec. 6050J(a) (foreclosures and abandonments of property held as security for business loans).

. . . Code Sec. 6050K(a) (certain exchanges of partnership interests).

. . . Code Sec. 6050L(a) (certain dispositions of donated property).

. . . Code Sec. 6050N(a) (payments of royalties).

. . . Code Sec. 6050P(a) (discharges of debt by certain financial and government entities).

. . . Code Sec. 6050Q (relating to certain long-term care benefits).

. . . Code Sec. 6050R (cash payments by purchasers of fish for resale).

. . . Code Sec. 6050S (payments for qualified tuition and related expenses and deductible payments of interest on qualified education loans).

. . . Code Sec. 6050T (credit for health insurance costs of eligible individuals).

. . . Code Sec. 6050U (for charges or payments for qualified long-term care insurance contracts, under combined arrangements).

. . . Code Sec. 6050V (applicable insurance contracts in which certain exempt organizations hold interests).

. . . Code Sec. 6050W (for returns relating to payment card transactions and third party network transactions; penalty relief is available for good faith incorrect information reported for 2012 and 2013 payments on returns filed in 2013 and 2014).

. . . Code Sec. 6051(d) (tax withheld).

. . . Code Sec. 6052(a) (wages paid in the form of group-term life insurance).

. . . Code Sec. 6053(c)(1) (certain tips from "large food or beverage establishments").

. . . Code Sec. 6055 (minimum health coverage for calendar years beginning after Dec. 31, 2014).

. . . Code Sec. 6056 (health care coverage by applicable large employers for periods beginning after Dec. 31, 2014). (Code Sec. 6724(d)(1))[20]

¶ 4898   Other civil penalties relating to information reporting and other items.

Other civil penalties are provided for:

. . . failure of group health plans to satisfy detailed requirements, such as portability, prohibitions on denying coverage based on certain factors, guaranteed renewability of coverage, and coverage of preventive services. (Code Sec. 4980D.[21]

. . . failure to file information returns for dividend payments under $10 (Code Sec. 6652(a));

. . . failure to file actuarial report of pension plan (¶4746) (Code Sec. 6652(e));[22]

. . . failure to file annual return for a pension plan (¶4746) (Code Sec. 6652(e));[23]

. . . failure to file annual return for an exempt organization or private foundation (¶4124) (Code Sec. 6652(c));[24]

. . . failure by split-interest trust to file an information return (Code Sec. 6652(c)(2)(C));[25]

. . . failure by an exempt organization to report excise tax on personal benefit contracts (Code Sec. 170(f)(10)(F)(iii));

. . . failure by any person, under a duty to comply with Code Sec. 6104(d) requirements relating to public inspection of, and provision of copies of, exempt organization annual returns or exempt status application materials (Code Sec. 6652(c)(1)(C), Code Sec. 6652(c)(1)(D));[26]

---

20. ¶V-1804; ¶67,214; TD ¶861,054
21. ¶H-1325.34, ¶49,80D4
22. ¶V-1971; ¶66,924
23. ¶V-1971; TD ¶861,037

24. ¶V-2714; ¶66,524; TD ¶861,032
25. ¶V-2717; ¶66,524; TD ¶861,032
26. ¶V-2718; ¶s 66,524, 66,854; TD ¶861,032

. . . failure to file fringe benefit plan return (Code Sec. 6652(e));[27]

. . . failure to provide a written explanation to the recipient of a qualified rollover distribution (Code Sec. 6652(i));[28]

. . . failure to file report on deductible employee contributions (Code Sec. 6652(g));[29]

. . . failure to file notification of change of status of pension plan (Code Sec. 6652(d)(2));[30]

. . . failure to file registration statement of pension plan (¶4746) (Code Sec. 6652(d)(1)),[31] or to give a plan participant a statement of the information in the statement (Code Sec. 6690);[32]

. . . failure to file individual retirement account, simple retirement account reports, Archer MSA, HSA, CESA, and qualified tuition program, reports (Code Sec. 6693);[33]

. . . overstatement reported on return by IRA participant of the amount of designated nondeductible contributions (Code Sec. 6693(b));[34]

. . . failure to keep records for reporting on pension, annuity, etc., payments subject to withholding (Code Sec. 6704(a));[35]

. . . failure to notify recipients of plan distributions of their option to elect out of withholding (Code Sec. 6652(i));

. . . failure by a corporation that issues qualified small business stock to make prescribed reports to IRS (Code Sec. 6652(k));[36]

. . . failure to file certain returns for foreign corporations, partnerships (Code Sec. 6679),[37] and trusts (Code Sec. 6677);[38]

. . . failure to file information returns in connection with foreign corporations and partnerships (¶4661) (Code Sec. 6038(b), Code Sec. 6038(c), Code Sec. 6038A(d), Code Sec. 6038B(c), Code Sec. 6038C(c));[39]

. . . failure to include tax information with passport or green card applications (Code Sec. 6039E(c));[40]

. . . failure to keep records, furnish information, or file domestic international sales corporation (DISC) returns (¶4621) (Code Sec. 6686);[41]

. . . failure to keep records, furnish information or file returns for a foreign sales corporation (FSC) or former FSC (Code Sec. 6686);[42]

. . . failure to meet FIRPTA reporting requirements (Code Sec. 6652(f));[43]

. . . failure to file notice of redetermination of certain foreign taxes (Code Sec. 6689);[44]

. . . failure to withhold tax on U.S. income of certain foreign persons (Code Sec. 1463);[45]

. . . failure to disclose a treaty-based position taken on a return that overrules or otherwise modifies the tax law (¶4639) (Code Sec. 6712);[46]

. . . failure by individual who loses U.S. citizenship or terminates U.S. residency (¶4654) to file expatriate information statement (Code Sec. 6039G(d));

. . . failure by an exempt organization to disclose that information it is offering to sell or soliciting money for is available free from the federal government (Code Sec. 6711);[47]

. . . failure by an exempt organization to disclose that fund-raising solicitations are nondeductible as charitable contributions (¶4119) (Code Sec. 6710);[48]

27. ¶V-1973
28. ¶V-1984; ¶66,524; TD ¶861,037
29. ¶V-1980
30. ¶V-1971; ¶66,524; TD ¶861,037
31. ¶V-1971; TD ¶861,037
32. ¶V-1972; ¶66,904
33. ¶V-1974 *et seq.*; ¶66,934; TD ¶861,037
34. ¶V-1981; ¶66,934; TD ¶861,037
35. ¶V-1986; ¶67,044; TD ¶868,006
36. ¶V-1843
37. ¶V-1903; ¶66,794; TD ¶861,045

38. ¶V-1901; ¶66,774; TD ¶861,046
39. ¶V-1903; V-1931; V-1951; V-1961 *et seq.*; TD ¶861,043 *et seq.*
40. ¶V-1910 ; TD ¶816,027
41. ¶V-1912; ¶66,864
42. ¶V-1912; ¶66,864
43. ¶V-1909; TD ¶861,049
44. ¶V-1983; ¶66,894; TD ¶861,049
45. ¶O-11911; ¶14,614.01
46. ¶V-1908; ¶67,124; TD ¶868,011
47. ¶V-2705; ¶67,114; TD ¶861,032
48. ¶V-2701; ¶67,104; TD ¶861,032

. . . failure by an exempt organization to make the required disclosure for quid pro quo contributions of $75 or more (¶4119) (Code Sec. 6714);[49]

. . . willful failure to make available for inspection or provide copies of, a return or application for exemption of certain exempt organizations (Code Sec. 6685);[50]

. . . any repeated or willful and flagrant act or failure to act by any person who becomes liable for any excise tax on a private foundation by reason of the act or failure to act (Code Sec. 6684);[1]

. . . making a negligent or fraudulent misstatement in connection with the issuance of a mortgage credit certificate or failing to file the required report (¶4746) (Code Sec. 6709);[2]

. . . failure to file a partnership return (¶4731) exposes the partnership to a penalty of $195 per month per partner (Code Sec. 6698);[3]

. . . failure to file an S corporation return exposes the S corporation to a penalty of $195 per month per shareholder (Code Sec. 6699);[4]

. . . failure to file returns with respect to qualified rental housing projects (Code Sec. 42(l)(2), Code Sec. 6652(j));[5]

. . . failure to deposit taxes (an IRS procedure explains how IRS applies deposits in determining the penalty when there is a shortfall) (Code Sec. 6656(a))[6] (including deposits required to be made by electronic funds transfer (EFT, see ¶3028);[7]

. . . use of any commercially acceptable instrument to pay taxes, if the amount isn't duly paid (Code Sec. 6657);[8]

. . . failure to pay stamp taxes (Code Sec. 6653);[9]

. . . claiming excessive gasoline tax rebates (Code Sec. 6675);[10]

. . . filing a frivolous income tax return or submitting a position identified as frivolous on IRS's list of frivolous positions (Code Sec. 6702);[11]

. . . use of Tax Court primarily for delay or where taxpayer's position is frivolous or groundless, he hasn't exhausted administrative remedies or he has instituted a frivolous or groundless claim for damages against the U.S. (Code Sec. 6673);[12]

. . . failure to supply taxpayer identification numbers (Reg § 301.6723-1(a));[13]

. . . failure to report tips (¶4746) (Code Sec. 6652(b));[14]

. . . failure by broker to provide back-up withholding notice (Code Sec. 6705);[15]

. . . failure to file information return for change in control or recapitalization of corporation (¶4746) (Code Sec. 6652(l));[16]

. . . making a false statement that results in reduced amounts of withholding (Code Sec. 6682),[17] or relates to the applicability of backup withholding. (Code Sec. 6682)[18]

¶ 4899 Damages for filing fraudulent information return.

A person who is the subject of a fraudulent Code Sec. 6724(d)(1)(A) information return may sue the filer for damages of the greater of (1) $5,000, or (2) actual damages plus costs, and, in the court's discretion, reasonable attorney's fees. The court must specify the correct amount, if any, that should have been reported on the return. (Code Sec. 7434)[19]

---

49. ¶V-2703; ¶67,144; TD ¶861,032
50. ¶V-2718; ¶66,854
1. ¶V-2721; ¶66,844; TD ¶868,005
2. ¶V-1998; ¶67,094; TD ¶861,040
3. ¶V-1762 *et seq.*; ¶66,984; TD ¶861,041
4. ¶V-1763.1; ¶66,994; TD ¶861,042.1
5. ¶V-1996; ¶66,524; TD ¶861,039
6. ¶V-1652; ¶66,564; TD ¶862,001
7. ¶V-1658
8. ¶V-1687; ¶66,574; TD ¶868,001
9. ¶V-2722; ¶66,530.40

10. ¶V-2726; ¶66,754 ; TD ¶868,012
11. ¶V-2551; ¶V-2571;¶67,024; TD ¶866,001
12. ¶V-2601 *et seq.*; ¶66,734; TD ¶836,014
13. ¶V-1821 *et seq.*; ¶67,234; TD ¶861,050
14. ¶V-1745; ¶66,524; TD ¶861,038
15. ¶V-1842; ¶67,054; TD ¶861,079
16. ¶V-1845; ¶66,524; TD ¶861,031.2
17. ¶V-1741; ¶66,824; TD ¶868,002
18. ¶V-1743; ¶66,824; TD ¶868,004
19. ¶S-4470 *et seq.*; TD ¶810,501

¶ 4900   Criminal tax evasion.

Tax evasion is a felony punishable by a fine of up to $100,000 ($500,000 for a corporation) and/or up to five years' imprisonment, plus costs of prosecution. The elements of the crime are willfulness, an attempt to evade tax and additional tax due. (Code Sec. 7201)[20]

¶ 4901   Other criminal penalties.

Any person who willfully aids or assists in, or procures, counsels or advises the preparation or presentation of a materially false or fraudulent return, affidavit, claim or other document, is subject to a criminal penalty of up to $100,000 ($500,000 for a corporation) and/or up to three years' imprisonment, plus costs of prosecution. (Code Sec. 7206(2))[21] Other criminal penalties (fines and/or imprisonment) are imposed for willful failure to: (1) file a return (Code Sec. 7203);[22] (2) pay a tax (Code Sec. 7203);[23] (3) collect or pay over a tax as required (Code Sec. 7202);[24] (4) keep proper records (Code Sec. 7203);[25] (5) supply tax information (Code Sec. 7203);[26] or (6) furnish a W-2 to employees in the manner, at the time or with the information required, or willful filing of a false or fraudulent W-2. (Code Sec. 7204)[27] Criminal penalties are also imposed for: willful filing of a false or fraudulent return (Code Sec. 7207);[28] failure to obey a summons (Code Sec. 7210);[29] and various other offenses relating to returns, statements, stamp taxes, etc.[30]

¶ 4902   Tax Collection. ▰▰▰▰▰▰▰▰▰▰▰▰▰▰▰

IRS has broad tax collection powers, including seizure and sale of a taxpayer's property (levy and distraint) and liens.

¶ 4903   Collection procedures.

Within 60 days after a tax has been assessed, IRS must send the taxpayer a notice of the amount assessed and a demand for payment, before it can start administrative collection proceedings. (Code Sec. 6303(a), Code Sec. 6331(a))[31] The taxpayer usually gets at least ten days from a date stated in the notice and demand to pay the tax, unless IRS finds that collection is in jeopardy. (Code Sec. 6331(a); Reg § 301.6331-1(a)(3))[32] Taxpayers suffering undue hardship can get an extension of time for paying the assessed taxes. For installment agreements, see ¶4904.[33] IRS must send delinquent taxpayers a written notice of the amount of the delinquency at least annually. (Code Sec. 7524)[34] IRS may pay rewards to informers (whistleblowers) for information on tax law violations.[35]

¶ 4904   Agreements for installment payments of tax—Form 9465.

IRS may enter into a written agreement with a taxpayer for that taxpayer to satisfy liability for *any tax* in installment payments. (Code Sec. 6159(a); Reg § 301.6159-1(a))[36] An individual who owes $10,000 or less and meets other conditions can force IRS to enter into an installment agreement. (Code Sec. 6159(c))[37] A taxpayer uses Form 9465 (attached to his balance due return) to request an installment agreement.[38] IRS may require the taxpayer to agree to certain terms and conditions. (Reg § 301.6159-1(b)(1))[39] Individuals can also apply

20. ¶V-4100 *et seq.*; ¶72,014; TD ¶871,001
21. ¶V-3113; ¶72,064; TD ¶871,009
22. ¶V-3002; ¶72,034; TD ¶871,015
23. ¶V-3001; ¶72,034; TD ¶871,015
24. ¶V-3017; ¶72,024; TD ¶871,008
25. ¶V-3007; ¶72,034; TD ¶871,015
26. ¶V-3008; ¶72,034; TD ¶871,013
27. ¶V-3013; ¶72,044
28. ¶V-3122; TD ¶871,013
29. ¶V-3503; ¶72,104; TD ¶871,014

30. ¶V-3500 *et seq.*; TD ¶871,014
31. ¶s V-5003, V-5004; ¶s 63,014.03, 63,314.01; TD ¶901,013
32. ¶V-5007; ¶63,314.01; TD ¶901,014
33. ¶V-5009; TD ¶901,015
34. ¶V-5009.2; TD ¶901,002
35. ¶T-1030; ¶76,234; TD ¶821,500
36. ¶V-5010; ¶61,594; TD ¶901,006
37. ¶V-5012; ¶61,594; TD ¶901,007
38. ¶V-5010; ¶61,594; TD ¶901,006
39. ¶V-5011; ¶61,594; TD ¶901,006

online by completing an Online Payment Agreement on IRS's website. A user fee is imposed for entering into, or restructuring or reinstating, an installment agreement. (Reg § 300.0, Reg § 300.1, Reg § 300.2)[40] See ¶4722.

♥observation: Submit the fee with the first installment payment, not with the Form 9465 request. A reminder notice (Form 521) sent to the taxpayer will reflect this.

The agreement remains in effect for its term unless the taxpayer fails to comply with it. (Code Sec. 6159(b)(2); Reg § 301.6159-1(c)(3)) However, IRS may modify or terminate the agreement under certain circumstances after 30 days' notice to the taxpayer. (Code Sec. 6159(b); Reg § 301.6159-1(e)(4))[41]

¶ 4905   Seizure and sale of a delinquent taxpayer's property—levy and distraint.

IRS has power to collect taxes by levy and distraint. This means it may seize any property (unless it's exempt) of a delinquent taxpayer (whether held by the taxpayer or someone else), sell it, and apply the proceeds to pay the unpaid taxes.[42] The property seized may be real, personal, tangible, or intangible, including receivables, evidences of debt, securities (Code Sec. 6331(a)) and, to the extent they exceed a specified amount, present and future wages. (Reg § 301.6331-2(c)) There are exemptions for certain kinds of income (Code Sec. 6334(d)) and property (e.g., clothing, tools) (Code Sec. 6334(a)), and a complete exemption for a taxpayer's principal residence unless a judge or magistrate approves the levy in writing. (Code Sec. 6334(a)(13)(B)) There also is an exemption for real property used as a residence by a taxpayer, or any nonrental real property of the taxpayer used by any other individual as a residence, if the amount of the levy is $5,000 or less (Code Sec. 6334(a)(13)(A)), as well as an exemption for tangible personal property or real property (other than real property which is rented) used in a trade or business of an individual taxpayer, unless collection is in jeopardy, or the levy is approved in writing by authorized IRS personnel. (Code Sec. 6334(a)(13)(B)) Levy is prohibited where an installment agreement is pending or in effect. (Code Sec. 6331(k); Reg § 301.6331-4) Levy also is barred for unpaid divisible taxes (provided a portion of the taxes is paid and other conditions are met). (Code Sec. 6331(i)) Regs enumerate exemptions. (Reg § 301.6334-1)[43] IRS must give the taxpayer 30 days' advance written notice before it can levy on any of his property, except where collection is in jeopardy. (Code Sec. 6331(d))[44]

Subject to exceptions, IRS may not levy against a person's property or right to property unless it gives the person a notification in writing of his right to, and the opportunity for, a pre-levy Collection Due Process hearing with IRS (a CDP hearing). (Code Sec. 6330(a)(1); Reg § 301.6330-1(a)(1)) The exceptions relate to jeopardy levies, levies to collect from state tax refunds, federal contractor levies, and persons subject to employment tax levies who made a previous recent hearing request as to unpaid employment taxes. (Code Sec. 6330(f)) The notice—the Collection Due Process Hearing Notice (CDP Notice)—must be given at least 30 days before the day of the first levy with respect to the unpaid tax for the tax period. (Code Sec. 6330(a)(2)) A person who receives a CDP Notice may request a hearing (use Form 12153) with the IRS Office of Appeals within the 30-day period beginning on the day after the date of the CDP Notice. (Code Sec. 6330(b)(1); Reg § 301.6330-1(b)(1), Reg § 301.6330-1(c)(1)) A person who requests a CDP hearing can, within 30 days of the date it was made, appeal the determination reached at the hearing. (Code Sec. 6330(d); Reg § 301.6330-1(f)) The Tax Court has sole jurisdiction over all CDP appeals. (Code Sec. 6330(d)(1)) IRS can disregard frivolous requests for a hearing before a levy is made. (Code Sec. 6330(g))[45]

A penalty (plus costs and interest) applies if the person fails or refuses to surrender the property. (Code Sec. 6332(d))[46] If IRS is unable to sell the seized property for the minimum

---

40. ¶T-10020 *et seq.*; ¶61,594; TD ¶901,006
41. ¶V-5014 *et seq.*; ¶61,594; TD ¶901,006
42. ¶V-5100 *et seq.*; ¶63,314; TD ¶902,001
43. ¶V-5200 *et seq.*; ¶s 63,314.03, 63,314.05; TD ¶902,231
44. ¶V-5253 *et seq.*; ¶63,314.01; TD ¶902,505
45. ¶V-5271-*et seq.*; ¶63,304; TD ¶902,505*et seq.*
46. ¶V-5116; ¶63,314.04

price it establishes, it can return the property to the taxpayer and add the cost of the unsuccessful sale to the unpaid tax liability. (Code Sec. 6335(e)(1)(D))[47]

Salary and wages and certain other payments are subject to continuous levy. (Code Sec. 6331(e); Code Sec. 6331(h)(1))[48]

¶ 4906 Wrongful seizures.

If IRS wrongfully levies on property, it may, on written request, return the specific property seized (or the proceeds from its sale) or the amount of money levied on (Code Sec. 6343(b)), with interest (Code Sec. 6343(c)). IRS may also return (without interest) property, including money deposited in the Treasury, that has been levied on if IRS determines that: (1) the levy was premature or otherwise not in accordance with its administrative procedures (Code Sec. 6343(d)(2)(A)); (2) the taxpayer has agreed to pay off the underlying tax liability in installments, unless the agreement provides otherwise (Code Sec. 6343(d)(2)(B)); (3) the return of the property will make collection of the underlying tax liability easier (Code Sec. 6343(d)(2)(C)); or (4) the return of the property is in the taxpayer's best interests, as determined by the National Taxpayer Advocate (¶4811), and IRS, and the taxpayer or the National Taxpayer Advocate consent. (Code Sec. 6343(d)(2)(D); Reg § 301.6343-3)[49]

¶ 4907 Third-party remedies for wrongful IRS seizures.

If IRS wrongfully seizes property of a person other than the taxpayer, the third party may sue for its return (or the sale proceeds, if it has been sold) (Code Sec. 7426), but must start the suit within nine months of the levy. (Code Sec. 6532(c)(1)) The Supreme Court held that Code Sec. 7426(a)(1) is the exclusive remedy for third-party levy claims.[50] The third party may also recover damages (subject to limits, see ¶4908) if the action results in a finding that any IRS officer or employee recklessly, intentionally, or negligently disregarded any Code or reg provision. (Code Sec. 7426(h)) Regs spell out procedures for claiming damages. (Reg § 301.7426-2)[1] The owner (or his heirs, etc.) of any realty sold to satisfy a tax liability can redeem the property at any time within 180 days after the sale. (Code Sec. 6337(b)(1))[2]

¶ 4908 Damages for unauthorized IRS collection actions.

If any IRS officer or employee recklessly, intentionally or negligently disregards a Code or reg section in connection with collection of tax, the taxpayer may bring a civil suit for damages against the U.S. in a district court. Damages are limited to the lesser of (1) $1 million ($100,000 for negligence) or (2) the actual, direct economic damages thus sustained plus the costs of the action. (Code Sec. 7433(h); Reg § 301.7433-1)[3] A taxpayer may petition a bankruptcy court for damages (subject to the above limits) if, in connection with any collection of tax, an IRS officer or employee willfully violates any provision of 11 USC 362 (relating to the automatic stay arising when a debtor files for bankruptcy) or 11 USC 524 (relating to the effect of a bankruptcy discharge, which operates as an injunction against commencement or continuation of actions to collect a discharged debt as a personal liability of the debtor). (Code Sec. 7433(e); Reg § 301.7433-2)[4]

¶ 4909 Collection period.

IRS must generally start distraint or court proceedings within ten years after assessment (Code Sec. 6502(a)). But if no return is filed, a collection suit may be brought at any time,

47. ¶V-5437; ¶63,354.01
48. ¶V-5214, ¶V-5216; ¶63,314.01; TD ¶902,214, TD ¶902,216
49. ¶V-5136, ¶V-5137; TD ¶902,005; TD ¶903,008
50. ¶V-5120, ¶V-5126; ¶s 65,324.04, 74,264; TD ¶903,007

1. ¶V-5135; ¶74,264; TD ¶903,007
2. ¶V-5424; ¶63,354.03; TD ¶903,007
3. ¶V-5800 *et seq.*; ¶74,334; TD ¶903,010
4. ¶V-5820; ¶74,334; TD ¶903,011

without assessment. (Code Sec. 6501(c)(3))[5] The collection period may be extended in connection with installment agreements, (Code Sec. 6502(a); Reg § 301.6502-1)[6] or suspended under various circumstances. (Code Sec. 6330(e)(1); Reg § 301.6330-1(g))[7]

¶ 4910 Injunctions against tax collection.

Injunctions against collection of taxes are generally barred. But exceptions apply during the period allowed to file a Tax Court petition or, where a petition has been filed, before the Tax Court's decision becomes final, and where an individual other than the taxpayer sues to recover property wrongfully seized and in other cases. (Code Sec. 7421(a))[8]

¶ 4911 Federal tax liens.

Federal tax liens are claims against a taxpayer's property for payment of delinquent taxes (including any interest, additional amounts, additions to tax, assessable penalties, or accrued costs).[9] There are various federal tax liens, including:

. . . general tax lien, which applies to all property, both real and personal, tangible and intangible including a tenancy by the entirety and an heir's interest in an estate even though he later attempts to disclaim it (Code Sec. 6321; Reg § 301.6321-1);[10]

. . . gift tax lien (Code Sec. 6324(b); Reg § 301.6324-1(b));[11]

. . . estate tax lien (Code Sec. 6324(a); Reg § 301.6324-1(a));[12]

. . . special lien for deferred estate tax attributable to a farm or other closely held business (Code Sec. 6324A; Reg § 20.6324A-1, Reg § 301.6324A-1);[13]

. . . special lien for recapture of estate tax attributable to special use valuation of a farm or closely held business (Code Sec. 6324B; Reg § 20.6324B-1);[14]

. . . generation-skipping transfer tax lien. (Code Sec. 2661; Reg § 26.2662-1(f))[15]

IRS must give written notice of its filing of a notice of lien (NFTL), to the person whose property is to be subject to the lien, not more than five days after it files the notice of lien (Code Sec. 6320(a); Reg § 301.6320-1(a))[16] IRS must hold a Collection Due Process hearing with respect to the filing if the taxpayer timely requests one (use Form 12153). (Code Sec. 6320(b)(1); Reg § 301.6320-1(b)) But IRS can disregard frivolous requests for a hearing before a lien is filed. (Code Sec. 6320(c))[17] Regs explain how a request for a withdrawal of a federal tax lien is made. (Reg § 301.6323(j)-1)[18]

¶ 4912 Priority of tax liens.

Priority of tax liens is governed by federal, not state, law.[19] The general rule is that a lien first in time is first in right.[20] But a tax lien is subordinated to certain later liens that arise before notice of the tax lien (Form 668) is filed. This protects judgment lien creditors, mechanic's lienors, and certain qualifying purchasers and holders of security interests. (Code Sec. 6323(a); Reg § 301.6323(a)-1)[21] Another exception protects certain interests arising even after the notice of the tax lien was filed, e.g., attorney's liens and certain security interests. (Code Sec. 6323(b); Reg § 301.6323(b)-1)[22]

The special gift and estate tax liens don't have to be filed to be superior to claims arising after the special lien arises. But certain later purchasers and creditors are protected. (Code

5. ¶V-5600 *et seq.*; ¶65,024; TD ¶901,025
6. ¶V-5604 *et seq.*; ¶65,024; TD ¶901,027
7. ¶V-5277; ¶63,304; TD ¶902,527
8. ¶V-5701; ¶74,214
9. ¶V-5900 *et seq.*; TD ¶911,000 *et seq.*
10. ¶V-5902 *et seq.*; ¶63,214 ; TD ¶911,023
11. ¶V-6042; ¶63,244 (Estate & Gift); TD ¶911,026
12. ¶V-6044; ¶63,244 (Estate & Gift); TD ¶911,027
13. ¶V-6046; ¶63,24A4 (Estate & Gift); TD ¶911,029

14. ¶V-6051; ¶63,24B4 (Estate & Gift); TD ¶911,031
15. ¶V-6053; TD ¶911,033
16. ¶V-6001; ¶63,204; TD ¶911,002
17. ¶V-6005; ¶63,204; TD ¶911,006
18. ¶V-6134; ¶63,234.18
19. ¶V-6324; ¶63,234; TD ¶913,001
20. ¶V-6301; ¶63,214.04; TD ¶913,001
21. ¶V-6400 *et seq.*; ¶63,234; TD ¶913,002
22. ¶V-6426; ¶63,234; TD ¶913,003

Sec. 6324A(d)(3), Code Sec. 6324B(c)(1))[23]

IRS may withdraw a notice of lien if it was filed prematurely or otherwise not in accordance with its administrative procedures, and for certain other reasons. (Code Sec. 6323(j)(1)) At the taxpayer's request, IRS must make reasonable efforts to notify credit reporting agencies and creditors specified by the taxpayer of the withdrawal of the notice. (Code Sec. 6323(j)(2))[24]

¶ 4913 Taxes in bankruptcy or receivership proceedings.

A receiver in a receivership proceeding must give IRS notice of the receivership. (Code Sec. 6036) (Use Form 56) But a bankruptcy trustee, debtor-in-possession, or other like fiduciary in a bankruptcy proceeding needn't give notice (Reg § 301.6036-1(a)(1)(i)), because notice under the Bankruptcy Rules is sufficient.[25] The filing of a federal bankruptcy petition (but not the start of a state receivership proceeding) automatically stays any tax proceedings against the taxpayer-debtor.[26] The running of the assessment period is suspended from the date a bankruptcy or receivership proceeding is instituted until 30 days after IRS has received notice of the proceeding, but the suspension may not exceed two years. (Code Sec. 6872; Reg § 301.6872-1)[27]

Although a taxpayer's bankruptcy triggers an immediate assessment (¶4829) collection of the tax is stayed while the taxpayer-debtor's assets are under the control of a court in bankruptcy or receivership proceedings.[28] There is no general bar to discharge of taxes in bankruptcy, but there are broad rules barring discharge of taxes in certain circumstances.[29]

¶ 4914 Transferee's liability for transferor's unpaid taxes.

A transferee is liable for a taxpayer-transferor's unpaid taxes (and interest and penalties) where: (1) the transfer is void or voidable under rules of equity,[30] (2) transferee liability is imposed by statute,[31] or (3) transferee liability arises under contract.[32] Transferees include a donee, heir, legatee, devisee or distributee of a decedent's estate, a shareholder of a dissolved corporation, the assignee or donee of an insolvent person, certain fiduciaries, a successor in a tax-free corporate reorganization, and various other classes of distributees. (Code Sec. 6901(h); Reg § 301.6901-1(b))[33] IRS must assess the (first) transferee within one year after the limitations period against the transferor has run. (Code Sec. 6901(c)(1))[34]

¶ 4915 Early discharge of executor's personal liability.

An executor or administrator can be discharged from personal liability for estate tax as early as nine months after the estate tax return is due (or filed, if later) if he makes a written request to IRS to determine the estate tax liability, and any tax determined to be due is paid (or a bond is posted if the payment period was extended). (Code Sec. 2204(a))[35] A trustee or other fiduciary can get a similar discharge. (Code Sec. 2204(b))[36] An executor or administrator can also request (on Form 5495) early discharge from personal liability for a decedent's income and gift taxes. (Code Sec. 6905(a))[37]

---

23. ¶s V-6455, V-6456; ¶63,244; TD ¶911,028
24. ¶V-6134; TD ¶911,021.1
25. ¶S-4103; ¶60,364; TD ¶817,504
26. ¶U-1220; ¶68,714
27. ¶T-4323.1; ¶68,724; TD ¶838,050
28. ¶V-7301 *et seq.*; ¶68,714; TD ¶838,050
29. ¶V-7360 *et seq.*; ¶68,734.01
30. ¶s V-9100 *et seq.*, V-9200 *et seq.*; ¶69,014

31. ¶V-9300 *et seq.*; ¶69,014
32. ¶V-9400 *et seq.*; ¶69,014.02
33. ¶V-9001; ¶69,014.01
34. ¶V-9801; ¶69,014.10
35. ¶s T-4511, T-4512; ¶22,044
36. ¶T-4513; ¶22,044
37. ¶T-4518; ¶69,054

Chapter 26 Estate, Gift and Generation-Skipping Transfer Taxes

¶ 5000 Estate Tax.

The federal estate tax is imposed on the transfer of an individual's property at death and on other transfers considered to be the equivalent of transfers at death. The tax is imposed on the "taxable estate," which is the value of the total property transferred or considered transferred at death (the "gross estate"), reduced by various deductions. The tax is computed under a unified rate schedule under which lifetime taxable gifts and transfers at death are taxed on a cumulative basis.

For decedents dying and gifts made in 2013 and 2014, the maximum estate, gift and generation-skipping transfer (GST) tax rate is 40%. (Code Sec. 2001(c)). The basic exclusion amount for gifts and estates, and the exemption amount for GSTs, is $5,250,000 for 2013 ($5,340,000 for 2014) (¶5028).

In determining the tax on estates of individuals who at death were citizens or residents of the U.S., the entire estate is considered. (Code Sec. 2033; Reg § 20.0-2(b)(1))[1] For nonresident aliens, see ¶5037.

The paragraphs that follow explain how the estate tax is computed, what items are within reach of the tax, valuation issues, allowable deductions, credits against the tax, and other items.

¶ 5001 Property owned by the decedent.

The gross estate of a decedent, who was a U.S. citizen or resident at the time of his death, includes the value of all property in which the decedent had an interest at the time of his death, to the extent of the interest beneficially owned by the decedent. (Code Sec. 2033; Reg § 20.2033-1(a))[2]

The gross estate of a nonresident alien includes property "situated in the U.S." (see ¶5037).

¶ 5002 Gifts within three years of death—Form 706, Schedule G.

An individual who transferred an interest in, or relinquished a power over, any property within three years of death must include the value of the property in his gross estate (on Form 706, Schedule G) to the extent it would have been included in his gross estate under Code Sec. 2036 (transfers with retained life estate, etc., ¶5004), Code Sec. 2037 (transfers taking effect at death, ¶5006), Code Sec. 2038 (revocable transfers, ¶5007), or Code Sec. 2042 (life insurance proceeds, ¶5014), if the interest or relinquished power had been retained. (Code Sec. 2035(a))[3] This rule doesn't apply to any bona fide sale for full and adequate consideration. (Code Sec. 2035(d))

¶ 5003 Gift tax "gross-up"—Form 706, Schedule G.

Gift tax paid by the decedent, his estate or his donees on gifts made by decedent or his spouse including, according to the Ninth Circuit and Tax Court, deemed gifts under Code Sec. 2519 (¶5048) within three years of decedent's death, is included in his gross estate (on Form 706, Schedule G). But, gift tax paid by the spouse on the spouse's share of decedent's gifts under the gift-splitting rules isn't included. (Code Sec. 2035(b))[4] The gift tax gross-up rule does not apply to the payment of a gift tax by a nonresident alien within three years of

---

1. ¶R-1010 *et seq.*, ¶R-2000 *et seq.*; ¶20,314 *et seq.*, ¶20,334 *et seq.*; TD ¶761,001
2. ¶R-2001; ¶20,334; TD ¶761,001

3. ¶R-2201 *et seq.*; ¶20,354; TD ¶763,001
4. ¶s R-2210, R-2211; ¶20,354; TD ¶763,010

References beginning with a single letter are to paragraphs in RIA's Federal Tax Coordinator 2d and RIA's Analysis of Federal Taxes: Income. Those beginning with numbers are to paragraphs in RIA's United States Tax Reporter. Those beginning with TD are to paragraphs in RIA's Tax Desk.

death.[5]

¶ 5004 Retained life estate—Form 706, Schedule G.

A decedent's gross estate includes transfers under which he retained the possession or enjoyment of, or the right to the income from, the transferred property (on Form 706, Schedule G). (Code Sec. 2036(a)(1); Reg § 20.2036-1)[6]

The decedent's gross estate also includes transfers where he retained the right to designate the person(s) to possess or enjoy the transferred property or its income. (Code Sec. 2036(a)(2))[7]

These rules don't apply to any bona fide sale for full and adequate consideration. (Code Sec. 2036(a))

A decedent who transfers property during life to a trust and retains the right to an annuity, unitrust, or other income payment from, or retains the use of an asset in, the trust has retained the right to income from all or a specific portion of the property transferred. The includible amount is that portion of the trust corpus, valued as of the decedent's death (or the alternate valuation date, if applicable) necessary to yield that annual payment (or use) applying the appropriate Code Sec. 7520 interest rate in effect on the date of death (or alternate valuation date). The regs also provide guidance on the portion of trust property includible in the grantor's gross estate where the grantor has retained a "graduated retained interest." (Reg § 20.2036-1(c)(2))[8]

Under IRS guidance, the corpus of an irrevocable trust that a grantor created during life is not includible in his gross estate under Code Sec. 2036 on account of the grantor having retained the power, exercisable in a nonfiduciary capacity, to acquire property held by the trust by substituting other property of equivalent value.[9]

IRS has had mixed results in getting assets transferred to family limited partnerships (FLPs) included in the transferor's gross estate under Code Sec. 2036. In a 2010 case, the Tax Court held that timberland and an interest in a FLP holding timberland, which the decedent had transferred to another FLP, were not includible in the decedent's gross estate because the decedent had a legitimate and significant nontax reason (the desire to preserve the family timber business) for making the transfers. In a 2012 case, the Tax Court held that real estate transferred to a FLP did not have to be included in the transferor's gross estate because the transfer was a bona fide sale for an adequate and full consideration in money or money's worth. Also, the Fifth Circuit determined that a decedent capitalized a FLP before her death, notwithstanding that she hadn't completed certain documents, resulting in a huge refund to the estate, which initially reported the assets to be owned outright.

But in 2011, the Tax Court held that real estate transferred from a revocable trust to a FLP was includible in the trust grantor's gross estate. Also, the Ninth Circuit affirmed a Tax Court decision holding that transfers of a largely untraded portfolio of marketable securities to FLPs were not bona fide sales because the decedent did not have a legitimate and significant nontax reason for making the transfers, so the securities were includible in her gross estate.[10]

¶ 5005 Retention of voting rights in stock of a controlled corporation—Form 706, Schedule G.

Retention of voting rights in stock of a controlled corporation is a retention of the enjoyment of the transferred stock. The value of the transferred stock is included in the decedent's gross estate (on Form 706, Schedule G). (Code Sec. 2036(b))[11]

---

5. ¶R-8006
6. ¶R-2400 *et seq.*; ¶20,364; TD ¶764,001
7. ¶R-2450; ¶20,364; TD ¶764,002
8. ¶R-2408.1; ¶20,364

9. ¶R-2454.1
10. ¶R-2421.1
11. ¶R-2436; ¶20,364; TD ¶764,032

¶ 5006   Transfers taking effect at death—Form 706, Schedule G.

If a decedent transfers property during his lifetime, but the transferee can't possess or enjoy the property except by surviving the decedent, and the decedent retained a significant reversionary interest (exceeding 5% of the value of the transferred property immediately before the decedent's death), then the property is includible in decedent's gross estate (on Form 706, Schedule G). This rule doesn't apply to bona fide sales for full and adequate consideration. (Code Sec. 2037)[12]

¶ 5007   Revocable transfers—Form 706, Schedule G.

The decedent's gross estate includes (on Form 706, Schedule G) his lifetime transfers if the enjoyment of the transferred property was subject at his death to any change through the exercise by him of a power to *alter, amend, revoke or terminate*. This includes any power affecting the time or manner of enjoyment of property or its income. (Code Sec. 2038(a)(1)) This rule doesn't apply to any bona fide sale for full and adequate consideration.[13]

Includible revocable transfers include savings bank (Totten) trusts that are revocable in form,[14] and custodial accounts where the donor is custodian.[15]

Under IRS guidance, corpus of an irrevocable trust that a grantor created during life is not includible in his gross estate under Code Sec. 2038 on account of the grantor having retained the power, exercisable in a nonfiduciary capacity, to acquire property held by the trust by substituting other property of equivalent value.[16]

¶ 5008   Qualified terminable interest property (QTIP).

Qualified terminable interest property (QTIP) for which the estate tax (¶5023) or gift tax (¶5048) marital deduction was elected is includible in the estate of the donee spouse at its then fair market value unless the donee disposed of any part of the qualifying income interest for life. (Code Sec. 2044) The property is treated as passing from the surviving spouse. (Code Sec. 2044(c)) Where a predeceased spouse's estate made an unnecessary QTIP election that did not reduce its estate tax liability, steps may be taken so that the unneeded election will be treated as null and void for federal estate, gift, and GST tax purposes. As a result, the property won't have to be included in the survivor's estate.[17]

The surviving spouse's executor may recover the estate taxes caused by the inclusion from the persons to whom the property passes at the surviving spouse's death, unless the surviving spouse's will specifically indicates an intent to waive the right of recovery. (Code Sec. 2207A(a))[18]

¶ 5009   Powers of appointment—Form 706, Schedule H.

If the decedent possessed a general power of appointment (created after Oct. 21, '42) at the time of his death, the property subject to the power is included in his gross estate (on Form 706, Schedule H). (Code Sec. 2041(a))[19] A "general" power is one exercisable in favor of the decedent, his estate, his creditors, or the creditors of his estate. (Code Sec. 2041(b)(1))[20]

¶ 5010   Jointly-held property—Form 706, Schedule E.

Joint ownership acquired through gift, bequest, devise, or inheritance from another. The decedent's fractional share of the property is included in the gross estate (on Form 706,

---

12. ¶R-2500 *et seq.*; ¶20,374; TD ¶765,000
13. ¶R-2600 *et seq.*; ¶20,384; TD ¶765,501
14. ¶R-2621; TD ¶765,520
15. ¶R-2620; ¶20,384.03; TD ¶765,519
16. ¶R-2612.1

17. ¶R-2900 *et seq.*; ¶20,444; TD ¶777,032
18. ¶R-6439 *et seq.*; ¶s 20,444, 20,564.08, 22,07A4, 25,194; TD ¶778,135
19. ¶R-3000 *et seq.*; ¶20,414; TD ¶767,301
20. ¶R-3006; ¶20,414; TD ¶767,319

Schedule E). (Reg § 20.2040-1(a)(1))[21]

Joint ownership created by co-owners. Except for husband-wife tenancies (¶5011), the *entire* value of the property is included in the co-owner's gross estate except the part, if any, attributable to the consideration in money or money's worth furnished by the other joint owner(s). Consideration furnished by the surviving joint owner(s) doesn't include money or property acquired from the decedent for less than full and adequate consideration in money or money's worth. (Reg § 20.2040-1(a)(2))[22]

Tenancy in common. Only the value of decedent's undivided share of the property is included in his gross estate.[23]

¶ 5011 Spouses' jointly-held property—Form 706, Schedule E.

If an interest in property created after '76 is held by a decedent and his spouse as tenants by the entireties or as joint tenants with right of survivorship (if the decedent and his spouse are the only joint tenants), one-half of the value of the jointly-owned interest will be included in the estate of the decedent spouse regardless of which spouse furnished the original consideration (on Form 706, Schedule E). (Code Sec. 2040(b)) Where the surviving spouse isn't a U.S. citizen, this rule applies only if the property passes in a qualified domestic trust (QDOT, ¶5026). (Code Sec. 2056(d)(1)(B), Code Sec. 2056(d)(2))[24]

Thus, the survivor gets a new basis for one-half of the property, see ¶2517.

¶ 5012 Community property.

The value of the interest in community property vested in the decedent by state law—ordinarily, half of the community property—is included in the decedent spouse's estate.[25]

¶ 5013 Annuities—Form 706, Schedule I.

The value of an annuity or other payment receivable by a beneficiary is included in the decedent's gross estate (on Form 706, Schedule I) if, under the contract or agreement, either:

(1) an annuity or other payment was payable to decedent, either alone or with another person(s), for decedent's life or for any period not ascertainable without reference to his death or for any period that doesn't in fact end before his death; or

(2) the decedent possessed, for one of the periods in (1), above, the right to receive such an annuity or other payment, either alone or with another. (Code Sec. 2039(a))

The amount included is an amount proportionate to the part of the purchase price contributed by the decedent. Contributions made by an employer are considered made by the employee if made by reason of his employment. (Code Sec. 2039(b))[26]

¶ 5014 Life insurance—Form 706, Schedule D.

Proceeds of insurance on the decedent's life receivable by the executor or administrator, or payable to the decedent's estate, are includible in his gross estate (on Form 706, Schedule D). (Code Sec. 2042(1)) The estate needn't be specifically named as the beneficiary. (Reg § 20.2042-1(b)(1))[27]

Proceeds of insurance on the decedent's life not receivable by or for the benefit of the estate are includible if the decedent possessed at his death or transferred within 3 years of death any incidents of ownership in the policy, exercisable either alone or with any other person. (Code Sec. 2042(2)) "Incidents of ownership" include the power to change the beneficiary, to

21. ¶s R-2705, R-2709; ¶20,404; TD ¶766,005
22. ¶R-2700 *et seq.*; ¶20,404; TD ¶766,005
23. ¶R-2707; ¶20,334.15; TD ¶766,006
24. ¶R-2724 *et seq.*; ¶20,404; TD ¶766,019 *et seq.*

25. ¶R-2800 *et seq.*; ¶s 20,334.16, 20,334.17; TD ¶766,022
26. ¶R-4401 *et seq.*; ¶20,394; TD ¶768,054
27. ¶R-4002 *et seq.*; ¶20,424.01; TD ¶768,002

revoke an assignment, to pledge the policy for a loan, etc. (Reg § 20.2042-1(c)(2)), and certain reversionary interests. (Reg § 20.2042-1(c)(3)) Under IRS guidance, an individual's retention of the power, exercisable in a nonfiduciary capacity, to acquire an insurance policy on his life held by a trust he created by substituting other assets of equivalent value won't cause the value of the policy to be includible in his gross estate.[28]

¶ 5015 Group term life insurance—Form 706, Schedule D.

An employee can prevent inclusion in his estate (under the rule at ¶5014, on Form 706, Schedule D) of the proceeds of group term life insurance furnished by his employer by transferring the insurance before his death, if:

(1) the group policy and applicable state law permit the employee to make an absolute assignment of all his incidents of ownership, and

(2) the employee irrevocably assigns all policy rights.[29]

¶ 5016 Value of property included in the gross estate.

The value of property included in the gross estate is the fair market value (FMV) of the property at the date of the decedent's death (or at the alternate valuation date, see below). (Code Sec. 2031; Reg § 20.2031-1)[30]

Regs provide rules for valuing specific types of properties including: stocks and bonds (Reg § 20.2031-2); business interests (Reg § 20.2031-3); notes (Reg § 20.2031-4); household and personal effects (Reg § 20.2031-6); and life insurance and annuity contracts. (Reg § 20.2031-8) IRS concedes that, in determining the value of stock in a closely-held corporation, there is no legal prohibition against a discount for built-in capital gains tax liabilities. However, IRS may still challenge the applicability and amount of the discount, based on the circumstances of each case.[31]

An executor may elect (on Form 706, Schedule U) to exclude from the gross estate up to 40% of the value of land subject to a qualified conservation easement meeting certain requirements and subject to a dollar cap of $500,000. (Code Sec. 2031(c))[32]

The FMV of annuities (other than commercial annuities), life estates, term of years, remainders, and reversions is determined under IRS tables, which include an interest rate component and, if applicable, a mortality component. The interest rate component changes monthly and this can affect planning strategies (e.g., lower interest rates favor private annuities and GRATs, ¶5054).

The annuity tables typically are used to value lottery winnings and structured settlement payments.[33]

The executor can elect (irrevocably, on Form 706) to use an alternate valuation date rather than the decedent's date of death to value the property included in the gross estate. This alternate date is generally six months after decedent's death or earlier date of sale or distribution. (Code Sec. 2032(a))[34] Alternate valuation can be elected only if its use decreases both the value of the gross estate and the combined estate and GST tax liability. (Code Sec. 2032(c); Reg § 20.2032-1(b)(1))[35]

observation: The executor can't elect in order to step up the basis of assets that increase in value after death (for example, where there would otherwise be no estate tax cost to the increased valuation because the marital deduction eliminates any tax).

IRS says that alternate valuation cannot be used to achieve a discount for restrictions

---

28. ¶R-4006 *et seq.*; ¶20,424; TD ¶768,008
29. ¶R-4033; TD ¶768,032
30. ¶R-1006; ¶20,314; TD ¶751,005
31. ¶P-6366.2

32. ¶R-4700 *et seq.*; ¶20,314.13; TD ¶773,400
33. ¶P-6679.1
34. ¶R-5002; ¶20,324; TD ¶773,001
35. ¶R-5001; ¶20,324; TD ¶773,001

placed on stock in a post-death reorganization.[36]

¶ 5017 Special-use valuation of farm or other business real property—Form 706, Schedule A-1.

If certain conditions are met, an executor may elect (irrevocably, on Form 706, Schedule A-1) to value qualified real property used for farming purposes or in a trade or business on the basis of the property's value for its actual use, rather than on its highest and best use. The total decrease in the value of all real property under this election may not exceed $1,070,000 for individuals dying in 2013 ($1,090,000 for individuals dying in 2014). (Code Sec. 2032A)[37]

One condition for electing special use valuation is that at least 25% of the adjusted value of the gross estate must consist of the adjusted value of real property which meets certain requirements. Under Reg § 20.2032A-8(a)(2), special use valuation may be elected for less than all of an estate's qualified real property, if the partial election covers sufficient property to satisfy the threshold requirements of at least 25% of the adjusted value of the gross estate. But a district court has held that this reg is invalid to the extent that it bars a partial special use valuation election covering less than 25% of the adjusted value of the gross estate.[38]

The resulting estate tax savings from special use valuation may be recaptured (use Form 706-A) under certain conditions. (Code Sec. 2032A(c))[39]

¶ 5018 Computing the taxable estate.

To get the taxable estate, deduct the following from the gross estate (¶5000):[40]

... Funeral expenses. (Code Sec. 2053(a)(1))

... Administration expenses, such as executors' and administrators' commissions, attorneys', accountants' and appraisers' fees, and court costs. (Code Sec. 2053(a)(2); Reg § 20.2053-3)

... Claims against the estate, including property taxes accrued before the decedent's death, unpaid income and gift taxes, and medical expenses of the decedent paid by his estate after his death (to the extent not claimed as an income tax deduction, see ¶2143). (Code Sec. 2053(a)(3); Reg § 20.2053-6)

... Transfers in satisfaction of claims by the decedent's former spouse. (Code Sec. 2043(b)(2))

... Indebtedness on property if the total value of the property is included in the gross estate. (Code Sec. 2053(a)(4))

... Casualty and theft losses. (Code Sec. 2054)

... Transfers to charitable and similar organizations (Code Sec. 2055), see ¶5020.

... Transfers to surviving spouse (marital deduction) (Code Sec. 2056), see ¶5021.

... State death taxes (Code Sec. 2058), see ¶5027.

For an item to be deductible as a debt, claim, or expense, it must also be allowable by the jurisdiction under which the estate is being administered. (Code Sec. 2053(a))[41] Post-death events are taken into account in determining the deductible amount of a claim or other expense under Code Sec. 2053, and deductions generally are limited to amounts actually paid by the estate in satisfaction of deductible claims and expenses. Exceptions apply for claims against the estate with respect to which there is an asset or claim includible in the gross estate that is substantially related to the claim against the estate, and for claims against the

---

36. ¶R-5022.1
37. ¶R-5200 *et seq.*; ¶20,32A4; TD ¶771,001
38. ¶R-5256; TD ¶771,038
39. ¶R-5301; ¶20,32A4; TD ¶771,053

40. ¶R-5400 *et seq.*; ¶s 20,514, 20,534, 20,544, 20,554, 20,564; TD ¶776,001
41. ¶R-5404; ¶20,534 *et seq.*; TD ¶776,003

estate that, collectively, do not exceed $500,000 (not including those deductible as ascertainable amounts). However, in each case, the amount of the deduction is subject to adjustment to reflect post-death events. (Reg § 20.2053-1, Reg § 20.2053-4)

A new Schedule PC–Protective Claim for Refund has been added to Form 706. By filing Schedule PC, taxpayers can preserve their right to a refund of estate taxes paid when a claim or expense which is the subject of unresolved controversy at the time of filing the return later becomes deductible.[42]

¶ 5019   Income v. estate tax deduction.

Many estate administration expenses can qualify as an estate tax deduction on the estate tax return and as an income tax deduction, or an offset against the sales price of property in determining gain or loss, on the estate's income tax return. But the estate is entitled to an income tax deduction or offset only if an estate tax deduction for the item is waived. (Code Sec. 642(g))[43] For the election to take an income tax or estate tax deduction, see ¶3925.

¶ 5020   Deductions for charitable bequests—Form 706, Schedule O.

Deductions are allowed (on Form 706, Schedule O) for the value of property included in the gross estate and transferred by decedent during life or by will to or for the use of the U.S., any state, political subdivision thereof, or the District of Columbia, and to various types of charitable organizations (Code Sec. 2055(a)), including foreign ones.[44]

Strict requirements apply where the charitable bequest is of an income interest or a remainder interest. (Code Sec. 2055(e))[45]

¶ 5021   Marital deduction—Form 706, Schedule M.

A marital deduction is allowed (on Form 706, Schedule M) for the value of all property included in the gross estate that passes to the decedent's surviving spouse in a manner qualifying for the deduction. (Code Sec. 2056(a)) The Supreme Court has held that Section 3 of the Defense of Marriage Act (which provided that "spouse" was a person of the opposite sex as a husband or wife) is unconstitutional (see ¶4705), and has allowed a marital deduction for property left to a decedent's same-sex spouse.[46]

The Tax Court has held that property brought back into the gross estate under Code Sec. 2036, see ¶5004, did not pass to the surviving spouse and thus did not qualify for the marital deduction.[47] For terminable interests, see ¶5022. For where the surviving spouse isn't a U.S. citizen, see ¶5026.

¶ 5022   Terminable interests and the marital deduction—Form 706, Schedule M.

With certain exceptions (see, e.g., ¶5023), a terminable interest doesn't qualify for the marital deduction (on Form 706, Schedule M) if another interest in the same property passed from the decedent to some other person for less than adequate and full consideration in money or money's worth, and by reason of its passing that other person or his heirs may enjoy part of the property after the termination of the surviving spouse's interest. (Code Sec. 2056(b)(1); Reg § 20.2056(b)-1(c)) A terminable interest is one that will terminate or fail after a certain period of time, the happening of some contingency, or the failure of some event to occur. (Reg § 20.2056(b)-1(b))[48]

---

42. ¶R-5403; TD ¶776,002
43. ¶R-5507; ¶20,534; TD ¶776,082
44. ¶R-5700 *et seq.*; ¶20,424; TD ¶777,000
45. ¶R-5735 *et seq.*; ¶s 20,554, 20,554.14, 20,554.16; TD ¶777,035

46. ¶R-6005; TD ¶778,001
47. ¶R-6000 *et seq.*; ¶20,564; TD ¶778,001
48. ¶R-6300 *et seq.*; ¶20,564; TD ¶778,049

¶ 5023 Qualified terminable interest property (QTIP) election—Form 706, Schedule M.

Property in which a spouse is given only a life estate may qualify for the marital deduction as an exception to the terminable interest rule (¶5022) if the executor elects (by listing the property on Form 706, Schedule M and deducting its value) to have all or part of the property so qualify and the surviving spouse has a "qualifying income interest for life." A surviving spouse has such an interest if:

(1) the surviving spouse is entitled for life to all the income from the property, payable at least annually, or the spouse has a usufruct interest for life in the property; and

(2) no person (including the spouse) has a power to appoint any part of the property to any person other than the surviving spouse during the surviving spouse's life. (Code Sec. 2056(b)(7))[49]

A surviving spouse's interest can meet the "all income" requirement if the spouse is entitled to income as determined by applicable local law that provides for a reasonable apportionment between the income and remainder beneficiaries of the trust's total return. (Reg § 20.2056(b)-5(f)(1), Reg § 20.2056(b)-7(d)(2))[50]

QTIP treatment isn't defeated merely because the spouse's income interest is contingent on the executor making a QTIP election. (Reg § 20.2056(b)-7(d)(3))[1]

An annuity, including one arising under community property law, where only the surviving spouse has the right to receive payments before the death of that surviving spouse, is a qualifying income interest for life, and the QTIP election is treated as made with respect to that interest unless the executor otherwise elects. (Code Sec. 2056(b)(7)(C))[2]

Certain individual retirement accounts (IRAs) qualify. (Reg § 20.2056(b)-7(h), Ex 10)[3]

Partial QTIP elections that relate to a fractional or percentage share of the property are allowed. (Reg § 20.2056(b)-7(b)(2))[4] Protective QTIP elections are possible. (Reg § 20.2056(b)-7(c))[5]

For inclusion of the QTIP in the surviving spouse's estate, see ¶5008.

¶ 5024 Effect of death taxes on amount of marital deduction.

Federal estate or other death taxes payable out of the marital share reduce the amount of the bequest that qualifies for the marital deduction. (Code Sec. 2056(b)(4)(A))

The surviving spouse's interest can be completely absolved from the burden of the tax by a provision in decedent's will that is effective under local law. In such a case, death taxes won't affect the amount of the deduction.[6]

¶ 5025 Effect of administration expenses on amount of marital deduction.

The marital deduction is reduced by estate transmission expenses paid from the marital share (Reg § 20.2056(b)-4(d)(2)), but not by estate management expenses attributable to and paid from the marital share unless those expenses are deducted on the estate tax return under Code Sec. 2053. (Reg § 20.2056(b)-4(d)(3)) The marital deduction is reduced to the extent estate management expenses are paid from the marital share and are attributable to other property. (Reg § 20.2056(b)-4(d)(4)) Estate transmission expenses are expenses that wouldn't have been incurred but for the necessity of collecting the decedent's assets, paying

49. ¶R-6393; ¶20,564.08; TD ¶778,100
50. ¶R-6355
1. ¶R-6400; ¶20,564.08; TD ¶778,115
2. ¶R-6413 *et seq.*; ¶20,564.08; TD ¶778,125

3. ¶R-6421; TD ¶778,129
4. ¶R-6431; ¶20,564.08; TD ¶778,106
5. ¶R-6430; TD ¶778,105
6. ¶R-6612 *et seq.*; ¶20,564.17; TD ¶778,145

his debts and death taxes, and distributing his property. They include any administration expense that is not a management expense. (Reg § 20.2056(b)-4(d)(1)(ii)) Management expenses are those incurred in connection with the investment of estate assets or with their preservation or maintenance during a reasonable period of administration. (Reg § 20.2056(b)-4(d)(1)(i))[7]

¶ 5026   Marital deduction where surviving spouse isn't a U.S. citizen—qualified domestic trust (QDOT) requirement.

No marital deduction is allowed if the surviving spouse isn't a U.S. citizen (Code Sec. 2056(d)(1)(A); Reg § 20.2056A-1(a)), unless the property passes (or is treated as passing) to the spouse in a QDOT (Code Sec. 2056(d)(2))—a trust that satisfies certain requirements (Code Sec. 2056A; Reg § 20.2056A-2)—or the spouse timely becomes a citizen. (Code Sec. 2056(d)(4); Reg § 20.2056A-1(b))[8]

An estate tax is imposed (use Form 706-QDT) on any distribution (other than an income or a hardship distribution (Reg § 20.2056A-5(c))) from the trust before the date of the surviving spouse's death and on the value of the property remaining in the trust on the date of death of the surviving spouse (Code Sec. 2056A(b)(1)) (or the date the trust ceases to qualify). (Code Sec. 2056A(b)(3))[9]

¶ 5027   Deduction for state death taxes.

The value of the taxable estate is determined by deducting from the gross estate any estate, inheritance, legacy, or succession taxes actually paid to any state or the District of Columbia for any property included in the gross estate, but not including any taxes paid for the estate of a person other than the decedent. (Code Sec. 2058)[10]

¶ 5028   Applicable exclusion amount and applicable credit amount.

For decedents dying in 2013 and 2014, the applicable exclusion amount equals the decedent's basic exclusion and, in the case of a surviving spouse, the deceased spousal unused exclusion (DSUE) amount (see ¶5029), if any. (Code Sec. 2010(c)(2))

For decedents dying in 2013, the basic exclusion amount is $5,250,000 ($5,340,000 for decedents dying in 2014). The basic exclusion amount is adjusted annually for inflation (Code Sec. 2010(c)(3)).

The applicable credit amount equals the amount of the tentative tax that would be owed under the rate schedule set forth at ¶1114 on an amount equal to the applicable exclusion amount. (Code Sec. 2010(c)(1)) For 2013, the applicable credit amount is $2,045,800, which is the tax that would otherwise be imposed on $5,250,000. For 2014, the applicable credit amount is $2,081,800, which is the tax that would otherwise be imposed on $5,340,000.

The credit is reduced by 20% of the amount of the pre-'77 $30,000 gift tax exemption allowed for gifts made before '77 and after Sept. 8, '76. (Code Sec. 2010(b))[11]

¶ 5029   Deceased spousal unused exclusion (DSUE) amount allows "portability" of unused part of exclusion of first spouse to die—Form 706.

For a surviving spouse of a deceased spouse, the DSUE amount, used in computing the unified credit against estate tax, see ¶5028, is the lesser of (1) the basic exclusion amount (see ¶5028), or (2) the excess of (a) the applicable exclusion amount of the last deceased spouse of the surviving spouse (below), over (b) the amount on which the tentative tax on the estate of

---

7. ¶R-6608; ¶20,564.05; TD ¶778,142
8. ¶R-6201 *et seq.*; ¶s 20,564, 20,56A4; TD ¶778,027
9. ¶R-7081 *et seq.*; ¶20,56A4.02; TD ¶781,501

10. ¶R-6901; ¶20,584; TD ¶779,001
11. ¶R-7103; ¶20,104; TD ¶781,803

the deceased spouse is determined. (Code Sec. 2010(c)(4))[12]

The 2012 Taxpayer Relief Act replaced "basic exclusion amount" with "applicable exclusion amount" (see (a), above) to correct what was thought to have been a drafting error in the 2010 Tax Relief Act.

A DSUE amount may not be taken into account by a surviving spouse unless the executor of the estate of the deceased spouse files an estate tax return on which the amount is computed, and makes an election on the return that the amount may be taken into account by the surviving spouse. The election, once made, is irrevocable. No election may be made if the estate tax return of the deceased spouse is filed after the due date (including extensions) for filing the return. (Code Sec. 2010(c)(5)(A))[13]

The only action required to elect portability of the DSUE amount, if any, is to file a timely and complete Form 706. Executors of estates who are not required to file Form 706 but who are filing to elect portability of the DSUE amount to the surviving spouse aren't required to report the value of certain property eligible for the marital deduction or the charitable deduction, but the value of those assets must be estimated and included in the total value of the gross estate. Taxpayers can opt out of electing to transfer any DSUE amount to a surviving spouse by checking the box on Section A of Part 6 of Form 706. (Reg § 20.2010-2T(a))[14]

If the executor of the decedent's estate elects transfer or portability of the DSUE amount, the surviving spouse can apply the DSUE amount received from the estate of his or her last deceased spouse (see below) against any tax liability arising from subsequent lifetime gifts (by completing Schedule C of Form 709) and transfers at death. (Code Sec. 2010(c)(4), Reg § 20.2010-3T)[15]

¶ 5030   Credit for tax on prior transfers—Form 706, Schedule Q.

Credit is allowed (on Form 706, Schedule Q) against the estate tax for federal estate tax paid by the estate of another decedent (the transferor) on the transfer of property to the present decedent from that transferor where the transferor died within ten years before, or within two years after, the present decedent's death. (Code Sec. 2013)[16]

Where a transferor decedent was denied a marital deduction because the surviving spouse wasn't a U.S. citizen or where the estate tax on qualified domestic trust distributions applied (see ¶5026), the surviving spouse decedent is allowed a credit for the estate tax paid by the transferor decedent, or by the trust, without regard to when the transferor decedent died. (Code Sec. 2056(d)(3))[17]

¶ 5031   Credit for gift taxes paid on pre-'77 gifts.

Credit for gift taxes paid on pre-'77 gifts is allowed against the estate tax where gifts were made by a decedent before '77 of property included in his gross estate. (Code Sec. 2012(a))[18]

¶ 5032   Credit for foreign death taxes—Form 706, Schedule P.

Credit is allowed (on Form 706, Schedule P), subject to certain limits, against the estate tax for estate, inheritance, legacy, or succession taxes actually paid to any foreign country or U.S. possession. (Code Sec. 2014)[19]

---

12. ¶R-7107 *et seq.*; ¶20,104.01; TD ¶781,807
13. ¶R-7110; ¶20,104.01; TD ¶781,810
14. ¶R-7111; ¶20,104.01; TD ¶781,812
15. ¶R-7109; ¶20,104.01; TD ¶781,809

16. ¶R-7300 *et seq.*; ¶20,134; TD ¶782,500 *et seq.*
17. ¶R-7301; ¶20,564; TD ¶782,515
18. ¶R-7501; ¶20,124; TD ¶783,001
19. ¶R-7400 *et seq.*; ¶20,144; TD ¶782,801

¶ 5033   Computation of estate tax—Form 706.

First, compute a tentative tax under the unified rate schedule at ¶1114 (which applies a maximum tax rate of 40% for 2013 and 2014) on the total of: (1) the amount of the taxable estate (¶5018), and (2) the total amount of adjusted taxable gifts made by the decedent after '76 that aren't includible in his gross estate. (Code Sec. 2001(b)(1)) Then reduce this amount by the amount of gift tax payable on the decedent's post-'76 gifts to get the gross estate tax payable (before credits). The gift tax payable is the gift tax that would have been paid if the rates in effect at the time of the decedent's death had applied, and not the amount actually paid based on the rates in effect at the time of the gift. (Code Sec. 2001(b)(2); Code Sec. 2001(g))

The net estate tax payable is the gross estate tax minus the unified credit and allowable credits for gift taxes on pre-'77 gifts, estate taxes on earlier transfers, and foreign death taxes (¶5028 *et seq.*). (Code Sec. 2010, Code Sec. 2011, Code Sec. 2012, Code Sec. 2013, Code Sec. 2014)[20]

The estate of a "qualified decedent" who was an armed forces member, victim of terrorism, or an astronaut who died in the line of duty, is entitled to compute its estate tax liability under a special estate tax rate schedule containing lower rates. (Code Sec. 2201)[21]

¶ 5034   Return requirements—Form 706.

An executor must file an estate tax return Form 706 if the decedent's gross estate at death exceeds the basic exclusion amount ($5,250,000 for estates of individuals dying in 2013; $5,340,000 for estates of individuals dying in 2014), see ¶5028). This dollar amount is reduced by certain gifts made by the decedent. (Code Sec. 6018(a)(1), Code Sec. 6018(a)(3))[22]

¶ 5035   When to file estate tax return.

Generally, file within nine months after the date of death. (Code Sec. 6075(a))[23]

IRS will grant an automatic 6-month extension to file Form 706 and may grant a 6-month discretionary filing extension (1) for estates that didn't seek an automatic extension, (2) to file Form 706-NA for the estates of nonresident alien, and (3) to file specialized estate tax forms for various recapture estate taxes (e.g., Form 706-A for recapture of special use valuation). (use Form 4768 for all extensions). An executor who is abroad can request a longer discretionary extension. (Reg § 20.6081-1)[24]

The Ninth Circuit has ruled that an executor's reliance on the estate accountant's incorrect assessment of the extension period, which caused a delay in filing the estate tax return, was not reasonable.[25]

¶ 5036   When to pay tax.

The estate tax must be paid at the time for filing the return (see ¶5035). Filing extensions don't extend the time for payment (Reg § 20.6151-1),[26] but extensions of time to pay can be granted (use Form 4768) for reasonable cause. (Code Sec. 6161(a)(1))[27]

Special extensions (elected on Form 706) are available where a future interest is included in the estate (Code Sec. 6163)[28] or where the estate consists largely of a closely-held business. (Code Sec. 6166)[29]

---

20. ¶R-7001 *et seq.*; ¶20,014.02; TD ¶780,501
21. ¶R-7011; ¶22,014; TD ¶780,510
22. ¶S-2300 *et seq.*; ¶60,184; TD ¶751,015
23. ¶S-4902; ¶60,754; TD ¶783,508
24. ¶S-5035.1; ¶60,814; TD ¶783,509

25. ¶V-1778; TD ¶868,507
26. ¶S-5851; ¶61,514; TD ¶783,513
27. ¶S-5900 *et seq.*; ¶61,614; TD ¶783,514
28. ¶S-5910; ¶61,634; TD ¶782,807
29. ¶S-6000 *et seq.*; ¶61,664; TD ¶784,001

The estate tax on distributions made from qualified domestic trusts (QDOTs, see ¶5026), before the surviving spouse's death is due on Apr. 15 of the year following the calendar year the taxable event occurs. (Code Sec. 2056A(b)(5))[30]

¶ 5037   Estates of nonresident aliens—Form 706-NA.

Decedents who were neither U.S. citizens nor U.S. residents are taxed only on the transfer of property situated within the U.S. (on Form 706-NA). With that exception, the make-up of the gross estate is the same as that for a U.S. citizen or resident. (Code Sec. 2103)

The same rate schedule that applies to the estates of U.S. citizens (¶1114) applies to the estates of nonresident aliens. (Code Sec. 2101(b))

A marital deduction is allowed under the principles of the regular marital deduction rules (¶5021 *et seq.*), with respect to U.S. property. (Code Sec. 2106(a)(3)) Other deductions are also allowed, within limits. (Code Sec. 2106)

A unified credit of $13,000 is allowed against the estate tax of nonresident aliens, with an alternative credit computation for estates of certain residents of U.S. possessions (Code Sec. 2102(b)(1), Code Sec. 2102(b)(2)), and to the extent required under certain treaty obligations of the U.S. (Code Sec. 2102(b)(3)(A)) The $13,000 is reduced by any gift tax unified credit allowed. (Code Sec. 2102(b)(3)(B))

Credits are also allowed for estate tax on prior transfers and gift tax on certain pre-'77 gifts. (Code Sec. 2102(b)(5))[31]

An estate tax return on Form 706-NA must be filed for the estate of every nonresident not a U.S. citizen if the value of the part of the estate in the U.S. exceeds $60,000 (Code Sec. 6018(a)(2)), reduced by: (1) the amount of adjusted taxable gifts made by the decedent after '76, and (2) the amount of any pre-'77 specific exemption allowed for gifts made by the decedent after Sept. 8, '76. (Code Sec. 6018(a)(3))[32] The time for filing the return is the same as for U.S. citizens or residents, see ¶5035.

Expatriates and former long-term residents who gave up citizenship or terminated residency before June 17, 2008. A tougher expatriate estate tax is imposed on the transfer of a taxable estate of a decedent nonresident non-U.S. citizen who dies during the 10-year period that he is subject to the expatriate alternative tax described at ¶4659. (Code Sec. 2107(a))[33]

Expatriates and former long-term residents who gave up citizenship or terminated residency after June 16, 2008. A special transfer tax (the Code Sec. 2801 tax) is imposed on any U.S. citizen or resident who receives any "covered gift or bequest" from a "covered expatriate," see ¶4654. (Code Sec. 2801(a)) The tax applies to any covered gift or bequest valued in excess of the annual exclusion amount in effect for gift tax purposes in the year of the transfer. (Code Sec. 2801(c)) The amount of the Code Sec. 2801 tax is determined by multiplying the value of the covered gift or bequest by the greater of (i) the highest estate tax rate listed in the Code Sec. 2001(c) rate table in effect on the date the transferee receives the covered gift or bequest, or (ii) the highest gift tax rate listed in the Code Sec. 2502(a) rate table in effect on that date. (Code Sec. 2801(a))[34]

¶ 5038   Gift Tax. ▬▬▬▬▬▬▬▬

For gifts made and decedents dying in 2013 and 2014, the gift tax is integrated with the estate tax under a "unified" rate schedule that imposes a single tax on transfers during life and at death (see ¶5000) which effectively imposes no tax on gifts unless the total amount of taxable gifts for the year and all prior years exceeds $5,250,000 for 2013 ($5,340,000 for 2014).

---

30. ¶R-7085 *et seq.*; ¶20,56A4.02; TD ¶781,506
31. ¶R-8000 *et seq.*; ¶21,014.02; TD ¶786,000 *et seq.*
32. ¶S-2302; ¶60,184; TD ¶783,504

33. ¶R-8033; ¶21,074
34. ¶R-8100; ¶28,014

The tax is imposed on the transfer, not on the property transferred. It applies even though the property transferred may be exempt from income or other taxes. (Code Sec. 2501(a); Reg § 25.2501-1, Reg § 25.2511-1(a), Reg § 25.2511-2)[35]

The paragraphs that follow explain who must pay the gift tax, what a gift is, allowable exclusions and deductions, credits against the tax, how the tax is computed, and other items.

¶ 5039 Who must pay gift tax?

The gift tax must be paid by the person (the donor) who makes the gift. (Code Sec. 2501(a); Reg § 25.2511-2(f)) It applies only to donors who are individuals (Reg § 25.2501-1(b)), but a gift by a corporation may be treated as a gift by the shareholders. (Reg § 25.2511-1(h)(1))[36]

If the donor fails to pay the tax when due, the donee is also liable for the tax to the extent of the value of his gift. (Code Sec. 6324(b); Reg § 25.2502-2, Reg § 301.6324-1(b)) A district court held that donees were liable for interest assessed under Code Sec. 6601 and Code Sec. 6621 on their separate personal liabilities created by Code Sec. 6324(b) as a result of the failure of the estate of the donor to pay the gift taxes assessed against it for gifts made by the decedent before he died.[37]

These rules apply to a U.S. citizen or resident no matter where the gift property (tangible or intangible) is situated. (Code Sec. 2501(a); Reg § 25.2501-1(a), Reg § 25.2511-3(a))[38]

A nonresident who's not a U.S. citizen is subject to gift tax only if the gift property is real estate or tangible personal property and is situated in the U.S. at the time of the gift. (Code Sec. 2501(a), Code Sec. 2511(a); Reg § 25.2511-1(b), Reg § 25.2511-3(a)) A nonresident generally isn't subject to tax on a gift of intangible property. (Code Sec. 2501(a)(2))

For a special transfer tax for recipients of gifts and bequests from expatriates and former long-term residents who gave up citizenship or terminated residency after June 16, 2008, see ¶5037.

¶ 5040 What is a gift?

All transactions whereby property or property rights are gratuitously bestowed on another are gifts. (Reg § 25.2511-1(c))

A gift isn't complete until the donor parts with dominion or control over the transferred property or property interest. He must be left without power to change the disposition of the property either for his own benefit or for that of others. (Reg § 25.2511-2(b))[39]

A transfer of property (such as a winning lottery ticket, as occurred in one case) to a corporation for less than adequate consideration represents gifts to the other individual shareholders of the corporation to the extent of their proportionate interests. (Reg § 25.2511-1(h)(1))

There's no gift tax on a transfer to a political organization. (Code Sec. 2501(a)(4))[40]

¶ 5041 Below-market loans.

If a below-market (or interest-free) loan is a "gift loan" (that is, a below-market loan where the forgoing of interest is in the nature of a gift), it's treated as: (1) a loan to the borrower/donee in exchange for an interest-paying note, and (2) a gift to the borrower of the funds to pay the interest. The amount of the gift equals:

... the forgone interest—excess of interest payable at the applicable federal rate (AFR, ¶1116) over actual interest payable—if the loan is a demand loan; or

35. ¶Q-1000 *et seq.*; ¶s 25,009, 25,014; TD ¶701,002
36. ¶s Q-1000 *et seq.*, Q-2400 *et seq.*; ¶s 25,014, 25,114; TD ¶714,000
37. ¶V-9301; ¶63,244; TD ¶702,001
38. ¶Q-1016; ¶25,014, 25,114; TD ¶703,002
39. ¶Q-3004; ¶25,114.01; TD ¶711,005
40. ¶Q-3201; ¶25,014; TD ¶716,015

. . . the excess of the amount loaned over the present value (using a discount rate equal to the AFR) of all payments required under the terms of the loan, if the gift loan is a term loan. (Code Sec. 7872)[41]

For demand loans, the gift is treated as made on the last day of the calendar year. (Code Sec. 7872(a)) For term loans, the gift is treated as made on the date the loan was made. (Code Sec. 7872(b))[42]

These rules don't apply to certain gift loans between individuals that don't exceed $10,000. (Code Sec. 7872(c)(2))[43]

If the outstanding balance of a gift loan made between individuals is $100,000 or less, the amount of interest treated as retransferred by the borrower to the lender each year doesn't exceed the borrower's net investment income for that year. If the net investment income is $1,000 or less, the amount treated as retransferred is zero. (Code Sec. 7872(d)(1))[44]

¶ 5042 Joint ownership of property.

A gift may result where property is placed in joint ownership with someone other than a spouse or where joint ownership with someone other than a spouse ends.[45]

If an individual with his own funds buys property and has the title conveyed to himself and others as joint tenants, with rights of survivorship, but which rights may be defeated by any joint tenant severing his interest, there is an immediate gift to the other joint tenants of equal shares of the property. (Reg § 25.2511-1(h)(5))[46]

An individual doesn't make a gift when he opens a joint bank account with his own funds for himself and another but can regain the entire fund without the other's consent. A gift is made only when the other person withdraws money for his own benefit. (Reg § 25.2511-1(h)(4)) Similar rules apply for joint brokerage accounts and U.S. savings bonds.[47]

¶ 5043 Qualified disclaimers.

A qualified disclaimer (an irrevocable and unqualified refusal to accept ownership, made in writing by a specified deadline) with respect to any interest in property has the effect of treating that interest, for gift (and estate and generation-skipping transfer tax) purposes, as if it had never been transferred to the disclaimant. (Code Sec. 2518) And the disclaimant isn't treated as having made a gift to the person to whom the interest passes by reason of the disclaimer. (Reg § 25.2518-1(b))[48]

¶ 5044 Amount of the gift.

The amount of the gift is the money given or, if property is given, the property's value as of the date of the gift. (Code Sec. 2512(a))[49]

Various court decisions have found gift-adjustment or savings clauses to be void as against public policy. However, the Tax Court held that individuals transferred gifts of a specified dollar value of membership units in a limited liability company (LLC) to their children and grandchildren, rejecting IRS's contentions that the gifts were of fixed percentage interests in the LLC and void as against public policy. This was so even though the interests received by the donees, when expressed as a percentage of units in the LLC, were lowered as a result of an IRS audit increasing the value of a unit in the LLC.[50]

The market value of annuities (other than commercial annuities), unitrust interests, life

41. ¶Q-2150 *et seq.*; ¶78,724; TD ¶155,001 *et seq.*
42. ¶Q-2150; ¶78,724; TD ¶155,003
43. ¶Q-2165; ¶78,724; TD ¶155,027
44. ¶J-2905; ¶78,724; TD ¶155,005
45. ¶Q-2900 *et seq.*; ¶25,114; TD ¶714,501

46. ¶Q-2906; ¶25,114; TD ¶714,507
47. ¶Q-2921 *et seq.*; TD ¶714,519
48. ¶Q-2350 *et seq.*; ¶25,184; TD ¶713,012
49. ¶Q-1200; ¶25,124; TD ¶741,000
50. ¶Q-1982; TD ¶711,023

estates, term of years, remainders, and reversions transferred by gift is determined by use of standard or special Code Sec. 7520 actuarial factors. (Reg § 25.2512-5(a), Reg § 25.7520-1(a)) These factors are derived by using the appropriate Code Sec. 7520 interest rate[1] and, if applicable, the mortality component for the valuation date of the interest that's being valued. These factors appear in IRS issued tables. (Reg § 25.2512-5(d)(1))[2]

¶ 5045 Taxable gifts.

Taxable gifts are the gifts made during the calendar year after the annual exclusion (¶5046), and reduced by allowable deductions (¶5048, ¶5049). (Code Sec. 2503(a), Code Sec. 2503(b))[3]

¶ 5046 Annual exclusion.

For 2013 and 2014, the first $14,000 of gifts of a present interest made by a donor *to each donee* is excluded from the amount of the donor's taxable gifts. (Code Sec. 2503(b))[4] For 2013, the first $143,000 ($145,000 for 2014) of gifts made by a donor to a spouse who isn't a U.S. citizen is excluded. (Code Sec. 2523(i)(2))[5]

No annual exclusion is allowed for gifts of future interests (Code Sec. 2503(b); Reg § 25.2503-2), e.g., reversions or remainders. (Reg § 25.2503-3)[6] Gifts of interests in (i) a limited liability company and (ii) a limited partnership (LP) didn't qualify for gift tax annual exclusions because restrictions in the operating or partnership agreement prevented the transferred interests from qualifying as present interests. Gifts of LP interests in which the donees did not receive unrestricted and noncontingent rights to immediate use, possession or enjoyment of the LP interests themselves nonetheless qualified as present interests because the donees received such rights in the income from the LP interests.[7]

A "Crummey" power (in general, a trust beneficiary's noncumulative right to withdraw a specified amount of trust principal within a limited period) makes a transfer to the trust a gift of a present interest, but not if the Crummey power is unenforceable in a state court.[8]

A transfer for the benefit of a *minor* isn't considered a gift of a future interest if the property and its income:

(1) may be expended by or for the benefit of the minor before he reaches 21, and

(2) any balance not so expended *will pass to the minor* when he reaches 21, or if he dies before 21 will go either to his *estate* or as he may appoint under a general power of appointment. (Code Sec. 2503(c); Reg § 25.2503-4(a))[9]

Gifts to minors made through custodians designated under Uniform Acts for gifts or transfers to minors qualify for the annual exclusion.[10]

¶ 5047 Educational or medical payment exclusion.

The gift tax doesn't apply to amounts paid by one individual:

(1) on behalf of another individual directly to a qualifying educational organization as tuition for that other individual. (Code Sec. 2503(e); Reg § 25.2503-6(b)(2))

(2) on behalf of another individual directly to a provider of medical care as payment for that medical care. (Code Sec. 2503(e); Reg § 25.2503-6(b)(3)) Payments for medical insurance qualify for this exclusion. (Reg § 25.2503-6(b)(3))

These exclusions are available in addition to the annual gift tax exclusion (¶5046).

---

1. ¶P-6619
2. ¶P-6615; ¶25,124; TD ¶521,501
3. ¶Q-1000; ¶25,034; TD ¶744,008
4. ¶Q-5000 *et seq.*; ¶25,034; TD ¶731,002
5. ¶Q-5003; ¶25,034; TD ¶731,003

6. ¶Q-5100 *et seq.*; ¶25,034; TD ¶731,008
7. ¶Q-5104.1
8. ¶Q-5112; ¶25,034; TD ¶731,022
9. ¶Q-5201 *et seq.*; ¶25,034; TD ¶732,001
10. ¶Q-5212; ¶25,034; TD ¶732,014

(Reg § 25.2503-6(a))[11] No gift tax return is required. (Code Sec. 6019)[12]

Contributions to qualified tuition programs (QTPs, ¶2209 *et seq.*) and Coverdell Education Savings Accounts (CESAs, ¶2205 *et seq.*) don't qualify for the Code Sec. 2503(e) tuition exclusion but, instead, are treated as present gifts that can qualify for the gift tax annual exclusion including by electively spreading contributions in a single year over a five-year period. A contributor isn't subject to gift tax on distributions from QTPs and CESAs. (Code Sec. 529(c), Code Sec. 530(d)(3)) A transfer by reason of a change in the designated beneficiary under a QTP, or a rollover to the account of a new beneficiary, is subject to gift and generation-skipping transfer taxes unless the new beneficiary is: (1) assigned to the same generation as, or a higher generation than, the old beneficiary; and (2) a member of the old beneficiary's family. (Code Sec. 529(c)(5)(B))

¶ 5048 Marital deduction.

A marital deduction is allowed for the value of all qualifying gifts made by one spouse to the other if the donee spouse is a U.S. citizen (with some exceptions) and the gift isn't a nondeductible "terminable interest." (Code Sec. 2523)[13]

Qualified terminable interest property (QTIP) qualifies for the deduction if the donee spouse receives income payments for life and no person has a power to appoint any part of the property to anyone other than the donee spouse during that spouse's life. (Code Sec. 2523(f))[14]

For an increased exclusion for transfers to noncitizen spouses, see ¶5046.

If an estate (¶5023) or gift tax QTIP marital deduction is taken, the QTIP property is included in the spouse's estate on her death (¶5008). However, transfer tax is accelerated if the spouse makes a gift of her income interest. Under Code Sec. 2519, if a spouse makes a gift of any portion of her qualifying income interest in the QTIP trust, she is deemed to make a transfer of the entire value of the remainder.[15]

¶ 5049 Charitable gifts.

Charitable gifts and certain similar gifts are deducted in arriving at taxable gifts for the calendar year. (Code Sec. 2522)[16] The Fifth and Ninth Circuits have upheld the use of defined value formula clauses to limit the gift tax liability resulting from transfers of hard-to-value assets (e.g., closely-held stock or family limited partnership interests), by reallocating the transferred assets among charitable and noncharitable donees when the value of the assets is increased on audit of the gift tax return.[17]

¶ 5050 Credit against gift tax.

For gifts made in 2013, there is a credit against the gift tax of $2,045,800. This is the amount that exempts $5,250,000 (the basic exclusion amount for 2013, see ¶5028) from gift tax. For gifts made in 2014, there is a credit against the gift tax of $2,081,800 (the amount that exempts the $5,340,000 basic exclusion amount for 2014 from gift tax).

The credit against tax on gifts in a calendar year is reduced by the sum of all amounts allowable as a credit in preceding calendar periods. In determining this reduction, the gift tax rates that are in effect for the calendar year of the gift (instead of the rates in effect for the preceding calendar periods) are used in determining the amounts allowable as a credit for all preceding calendar periods. (Code Sec. 2505)[18] The instructions to Form 709 contain a worksheet that is used to determine the amount of the unified credit used for post-'76 gifts, where prior gifts total more than $500,000.

11. ¶Q-5250 *et seq.*; ¶25,034; TD ¶732,501
12. ¶S-2201; ¶25,014; TD ¶746,001
13. ¶Q-6100 *et seq.*; ¶25,234; TD ¶734,001
14. ¶Q-6300 *et seq.*; ¶25,234; TD ¶736,001
15. ¶Q-6315; ¶25,194; TD ¶764,007
16. ¶Q-6000 *et seq.*; ¶25,224; TD ¶733,001
17. ¶Q-1983.2
18. ¶Q-8005; ¶25,054; TD ¶744,004

¶ 5051   How to compute gift tax if no gifts made before current year.

If a person has *not* made any taxable gifts (in excess of annual exclusions and deductions and the pre-'77 specific lifetime exemption) before the calendar year for which the tax is being computed, the gift tax is computed as follows:[19]

(1) Determine the aggregate value of the total gifts made during the calendar year for which the tax is being computed. If the donor is married, and he and his wife have consented to split their gifts to third parties, only half of the gifts he made to third parties plus half of the gifts, if any, she made to third parties are included in computing his total gifts. (A separate gift tax computation is made for the wife, and the other half of the husband's gifts to third parties plus the other half of the wife's gifts to third parties are included in computing the wife's total gifts.)

(2) Deduct from the amount in (1), above, any amounts qualifying for the year's annual exclusion (¶5046).

(3) From the excess of (1) over (2), above, subtract the amount of charitable (¶5049) and marital (¶5048) gifts.

(4) Compute a gift tax on the excess of (1) over the sum of (2) and (3); for gifts made during 2013 or 2014, use the rate schedule at ¶1114.

(5) Subtract from the gift tax computed in (4) the allowable unified credit.

¶ 5052   Cumulative computation where gifts were made before current year.

Previous taxable gifts affect the amount of gift tax imposed on gifts made in the current year. These taxable gifts are taken into account whether they were made before '77 or after '76. (Code Sec. 2502) In general, the gift tax (before unified credit) is the excess of: (1) a tentative tax computed under the unified rate schedules on the aggregate sum of taxable gifts for the current calendar year for which the tax is being computed *and* taxable gifts (made after June 6, '32) for all preceding years, over (2) a tentative tax (determined on the basis of the gift tax rates in effect for the current year, see ¶5050) on the aggregate sum of the taxable gifts for all of the years preceding the current calendar year for which the tax is being computed. (Code Sec. 2502(a)) The gift tax payable is the excess of the tentative tax in (1) over the tentative tax in (2), reduced by the unified credit allowable.[20]

¶ 5053   Split gifts to third parties by married donors.

A husband and wife may consent to have their gifts to others treated as if made one-half by each (Code Sec. 2513(a); Reg § 25.2513-1) if:

. . . both spouses are U.S. citizens or residents on the date of the gift (Code Sec. 2513(a));

. . . both spouses consent (on Form 709) to have all gifts made to others in the calendar year treated as split gifts (Code Sec. 2513(a), Code Sec. 2513(b), Code Sec. 2513(c); Reg § 25.2513-1(b)(5)); and

. . . the consenting spouses are married to each other on the date of the gift and don't remarry during the remainder of the calendar year. (Code Sec. 2513(a))[21]

Each spouse is liable, jointly and severally, for the *entire* gift tax for the period in which he or she consents to split gifts. (Code Sec. 2513(d); Reg § 25.2513-4)[22]

Gifts of community property to a third party are generally considered to have been made one half by each spouse.[23]

---

19. ¶Q-8010 *et seq.*; ¶25,009; TD ¶744,008
20. ¶Q-8011; ¶25,024; TD ¶744,008
21. ¶Q-7000 *et seq.*; ¶25,134; TD ¶743,001

22. ¶V-8505 *et seq.*; ¶25,134; TD ¶746,007
23. ¶Q-2929 *et seq.*; ¶25,134.01; TD ¶743,001

¶ 5054   Gift tax on "estate freeze" transfers (Chapter 14 rules).

For gift tax valuation purposes, certain interests retained by the transferor after a transfer to a family member are disregarded. These Chapter 14 (of the Code) rules apply to:[24]

. . . transfers of interests in corporations and partnerships;

. . . transfers of interests in trusts (other than certain trusts known as GRATs, GRUTs, and qualified personal residence trusts, see below);

. . . buy-sell agreements and options; and

. . . lapsing rights.

An individual can save transfer tax by setting up a GRAT (grantor retained annuity trust). The individual retains an annuity interest for a specified term at the expiration of which the trust property goes to a child or other individual named at the outset. Gift tax is payable but only on the present value of the remainder interest.

A GRIT (grantor retained income trust) is like a GRAT, except that the grantor retains an income interest instead of an annuity interest. Code Sec. 2702 generally treats the grantor as making a gift of the full value of the property. However, the value of the gift of the remainder is determined under the valuation tables where the trust is funded with a personal residence of the grantor or the remainder goes to someone falling outside of the definition of a family member.

A GRUT is a grantor retained unitrust.

¶ 5055   Gift tax returns—Form 709.

Any individual who makes gifts to any one donee during a calendar year which aren't fully excluded under the annual exclusion (see ¶5046) must file a gift tax return (Form 709). A return must be filed even if no tax is payable. (Reg § 25.6019-1(f)) But, no return is required to report a qualified transfer for educational or medical costs (¶5047), most charitable transfers, or a transfer that qualifies for the marital deduction (¶5048) (Code Sec. 6019), except that a return must be filed to make a QTIP (¶5048) election. (Reg § 25.6019-1(a))[25] The return is due on Apr. 15 of the year following the year the gifts were made. (Code Sec. 6075) A different rule applies if the donor has died.[26] An extension for filing the income tax return automatically extends the time for filing the gift tax return for the same calendar year. (Code Sec. 6075(b)(2)) Use Form 8892 to request an extension of time to file Form 709 when not applying for an extension to file an income tax return or to make a payment of gift (or GST) tax when applying for an extension of time to file Form 709. (Reg § 25.6081-1)[27]

¶ 5056   Generation-Skipping Transfer (GST) Tax. ■■■■■■■■■■■■■■■■■

A GST tax is imposed on transfers outright or in trust to beneficiaries more than one generation below the transferor's generation at a rate equal to the maximum gift and estate tax rate, which for 2013 and 2014, is 40% (Code Sec. 2001(c)) multiplied by the "inclusion ratio." (Code Sec. 2641)[28]

¶ 5057   Transfers subject to tax.

The generation-skipping transfer (GST) tax is imposed on every GST. (Code Sec. 2601)

The GST tax generally applies to GSTs made after Oct. 22, '86. (Tax Reform Act of '86 (TRA '86) § 1431(a)) However, it doesn't apply to any GST from a trust that was irrevocable on Sept. 25, '85. The exception doesn't apply to a transfer made out of corpus added to the

---

24. ¶Q-3350; ¶s 27,014, 27,024, 27,034, 27,044; TD ¶721,002
25. ¶S-2200 *et seq.*; ¶s 25,014, 60,194; TD ¶746,001
26. ¶S-4901; ¶60,754; TD ¶746,009
27. ¶S-5035; ¶s 60,754, 60,814; TD ¶746,010
28. ¶R-9575; ¶26,414; TD ¶791,003

trust after Sept. 25, '85. (TRA '86 § 1433(b)(2)(A))

A GST is any one of three taxable events: (1) a *taxable termination* of an interest in a trust if, after the termination, all interests in the trust are held by or for the benefit of persons two or more generations below that of the transferor (trustee pays the GST tax on taxable terminations on Form 706GS(T)), (2) a *taxable distribution* of income or principal from a trust to or for the benefit of a person two or more generations below that of the transferor (transferee pays the tax on Form 706GS(D), the trustee must file Form 706GS(D-1)), and (3) a *direct skip,* which is a transfer of an interest in property to or for the benefit of a person two or more generations below that of the transferor (transferor pays tax with Form 709 for lifetime direct skips, executor pays with Form 706 and attached Form 706, Schedule R or Form 706, Schedule R-1, for direct skips occurring at death). (Code Sec. 2611(a), Code Sec. 2612) (Use Form 8892 to request an extension of time to file Form 709 when not applying for an extension to file an income tax return or to make a payment of GST tax when applying for an extension of time to file Form 709.) In determining whether there is a GST, a special rule "steps up" the generation of an individual (or the descendants of an individual) with a deceased parent that's a descendant of the transferor's parent. (Code Sec. 2651(e)(1); Reg § 26.2651-1)[29]

¶ 5058   Exemptions from tax.

Every individual is allowed an exemption equal to the estate tax basic exclusion ($5,250,000 for 2013; $5,340,000 for 2014, see ¶5028), which may be allocated to any property transferred. (Code Sec. 2631) Married couples may treat transfers as made one-half by each spouse, in effect giving them a combined $10,500,000 exemption for transfers in 2013 ($10,680,000 in 2014). (Code Sec. 2652(a)(2))[30] Once a transfer is designated as exempt, all later appreciation in the value of the exempt property is also exempt.[31] The tax doesn't apply to lifetime transfers (except for certain transfers in trust) that are exempt from gift tax because of the annual exclusion (¶5046) or the exclusion for certain tuition and medical expense payments (¶5047). (Code Sec. 2642(c)(3)) For lifetime transfers, the available GST exemption is automatically allocated to a direct skip under Code Sec. 2632(b), and to indirect skips made after Dec. 31, 2000 under Code Sec. 2632(c), unless the individual elects out of the automatic allocation under Code Sec. 2632(b)(3) and Code Sec. 2632(c)(5), respectively. The automatic allocation under Code Sec. 2632(c) also applies to an indirect skip occurring upon the post-2000 termination of an estate tax inclusion period. (Code Sec. 2632(c)(4)) Regs provide details about these elections. (Reg § 26.2632-1)[32]

¶ 5059   Computation of GST tax—Form 706, Schedule R.

The amount of GST tax imposed on any GST is the "taxable amount" multiplied by the "applicable rate." (Code Sec. 2602) The calculation of the GST tax is made on Form 706, Schedule R.

The "taxable amount" is the value of the property subject to GST tax and depends on what type of GST is involved (see ¶5057).[33]

The "applicable rate" is the product of the maximum federal estate tax rate (40% for 2013 and 2014) and the "inclusion ratio," which is determined according to the amount of the GST exemption allocated to the trust (or allocated to the property transferred in the skip in cases of a direct skip).[34]

29. ¶R-9500 *et seq.*; ¶26,014, 26,114, 26,124; TD ¶791,001 *et seq.*
30. ¶R-9551; ¶s 26,014, 26,314; TD ¶791,004
31. ¶R-9557; ¶26,324; TD ¶791,004
32. ¶R-9501 *et seq.*; ¶26,424; TD ¶791,001
33. ¶R-9571 *et seq.*; ¶26,014; TD ¶791,003
34. ¶R-9575*et seq.*; ¶26,014; TD ¶791,003

INDEX

References are to paragraph [¶] numbers.

A

Abandonment
. loss
    generally 1784
. . deductible loss 1773; 1774
. . mortgaged property 1788
. reorganizations 3558
. reporting of, for secured property 4746
. U.S. citizenship *See "Expatriation"*
Abatement of interest
    generally 4870
. failure to abate 4858; 4859
Abortion, as medical expense 2144
Above-the-line deductions (adjustments to income)
    generally 3102
. alimony paid 2153
. Archer medical savings accounts (MSAs) 1528
. education expenses . . . . 2230 et seq.
. IRA contributions 4351; 4352
. military reservists, overnight travel expenses 1553
. moving expenses 1648
. performing artists, expenses of 3105
. self-employed health insurance 1532
. student loan interest . . . . 2222 et seq.
. taxes 1757
. teachers' classroom expenses 2229
Abusive tax shelters, penalties 4826; 4835; 4889
Accelerated depreciation *See "Depreciation"*
Accident and health insurance plans *See "Health and accident insurance plans"*
Accountants
. audits by IRS, representing taxpayer at 4808
. expenses of 1636
. fees for 1603; 1605; 5018
Accounting income 3938
Accounting methods
    generally . . . . 2816 et seq.
. accrual method *See "Accrual basis"*
. advance trade discount method 2826
. carryover by successor corporation 3564
. cash method *See "Cash basis"*
. changes of
    generally . . . . 2837 et seq.
. . adjustments required . . . . 2841 et seq.
. . allocations, relief for high-impact adjustments 2844
. . application for 2840
. . automatic consent procedure 2840; 2845
. . definition 2839
. . depreciation, accounting for 1901; 2839
. . four-year/one-year rule, adjustment inclusion periods 2843
. . inventories 2868; 2881
. . IRS permission to change 2838
. . Sec. 481(a) adjustments . . . . 2841 et seq.

Accounting methods — Cont'd
. establishing method 2817
. farmers . . . . 4505 et seq.
. hybrid methods 2818
. limits on choice of 2818
. long-term contracts . . . . 2848 et seq.
. nonaccrual experience method 2825
. records to substantiate 2817
Accounting period *See also "Taxable year"*
    generally . . . . 2800 et seq.
. change of 2805; 2814; 2815
Accounting reserves, deductibility 2846; 2847
Accounts receivable
. amortization 1975
. capital assets 2617
. intangible assets 2471
Accrual basis
    generally . . . . 2824 et seq.
. advance payments . . . . 2829 et seq.
. all-events test 2832
. charitable contributions, 2 1/2 month rule 2133
. compensation for personal services
. . time for deduction . . . . 1537 et seq.
. . time to report 1273
. contested liability 2834
. contingent rights to income 2826
. dealers' reserves 2828
. decedents 3966
. discounts on purchases 2869
. disputed liability for goods, income accrual for 2827
. economic performance 2833
. farmers . . . . 4509 et seq.
. gain or loss on sale or exchange 2408
. interest income, time to report 1335; 1337
. interest paid, time to deduct 1748; 1750
. payments to related cash basis taxpayer 2836
. payroll tax liability 1538
. prepaid insurance 1609
. previously reported income, repayments of, time for deduction of repayment 2861
. real property tax
. . apportioned between buyer and seller 1770
. . election to accrue ratably 1769
. . time for deduction 1771
. recurring item exception 2833
. rental income, time to report 1339
. royalties 1345
. security deposits 2831
. small taxpayer exceptions 2818
. taxes, accrual of
. . contested tax 1768
. . deduction, time for . . . . 1767 et seq.
. . realty taxes . . . . 1769 et seq.
. tort liabilities 2835
Accrued market discount . . . . 1324 et seq.
Accumulated adjustments account 3372; 3374
Accumulated earnings tax
    generally 3316

Accumulated earnings tax — Cont'd
. avoidance of tax, accumulations for purposes of 3317
. credit, accumulated earnings 3319; 3337
. dividends-paid deduction .... 3330 et seq.
. reasonable needs of business, accumulations for 3317
.. credit for 3319
.. operating cycle formula (Bardahl) 3317
. taxable income 3318
Accumulation distribution .... 3953 et seq.
ACE (adjusted current earnings) 3211
Achievement awards, employee
. deduction of 1591
. gross income exclusion 1251
. withholding on 3006
Acquisition indebtedness
. corporate, interest on 1725
. exempt organizations 4123
. home mortgage indebtedness 1736
.. discharge of 1397
. qualified residence interest 1733
Acquisitions, corporate
. *generally* .... 3541 et seq.
. basis 2484
. built-in gains, limit on use to offset losses ... 3566; 3568
. capital expenditures 1659
. carryover of tax attributes to which acquiring corporation succeeds 3563; 3564
. COD income exclusion, effect on tax attributes and basis of acquiring corporation 1389
. information returns 4746
. net operating losses .... 3567 et seq.
. Sec. 269 tax avoidance acquisitions 3565
Acquisitions of property
. capital expenditures 1660; 1663; 1664
Active participation
. at-risk activities 1805
. passive losses, rental real estate 1833; 1835
Actual use valuation of real property *See "Special use valuation"*
Additional standard deduction 3112
Adjusted basis *See "Basis"*
Adjusted current earnings (ACE) 3211
Adjusted gross income (AGI)
. casualty losses, limitations on 1795
. computation .... 3102 et seq.
. estates and trusts 3921
. medical expense deduction 2141
. modified adjusted gross income, Social Security payments, test for taxability of 1279
. personal holding companies .... 3324 et seq.
Administration expenses
. bankruptcy estate 3977
. estates and trusts 3922; 3925; 5018; 5019
. marital deduction, effect on 5025
Adoption
. credit for adoption expenses 2354
. dependent, adopted child as
.. personal exemptions 3119; 3120; 3124
. identification number for children in process of 4752
Adoption assistance programs for employees
. *generally* 1254
. cafeteria plans 1269
. withholding on 3006
Advance payments
. advance trade discount method 2826

Advance payments — Cont'd
. against commissions 1274
. deferral method of accounting 2829
. employee business expenses .... 1573 et seq.
. health insurance costs credit 2344
. insurance premiums 1609
. interest on deficiencies, deposits to prepay and/or stop running of interest 4868
. medical expenses 2150
. merchandise, for 2830
. premium tax credit 2345
. rents and royalties 1341; 1599
. security deposits 2831
. timber, coal, iron ore 2689
Advance pricing agreements (APAs) 2858
Adverse party (trust rules)
. beneficial enjoyment, power to control 3961
. inter vivos trusts 2519
. power to revoke 3958
Advertising, deductions 1512
Affiliated corporations
. consolidated returns 3338
. definition of affiliated group 3339
. distributions 3562
. dividends received deduction 3307
. stock transactions between 3533
Agent
. charitable contribution to individual acting as 2103
. check received by 2821
. dividends, taxation 1286
Aggregation
. depletable property 1981
. Section 1245 property, recapture rules 1973; 2695
Agricultural labor 3006
Agricultural organizations 4100; 4122
Agricultural products, depreciation of assets used in production of 1916; 1917
Aiding and abetting tax understatement, penalty for 4826; 4885
Aircraft
. charitable contributions 2138; 4115
. depreciation 1916; 1928; 1933; 1937; 1939; 1949
. entertainment facilities 1567; 1572
. fringe benefit, use of as
.. *generally* 1245
.. special valuation rules .... 1232; 1238 et seq.
Alaska Permanent Fund dividends 1206
Alcohol fuel credit
. generally 2318
. alternative minimum tax 3208
. cellulosic biofuel production 2318
. gross income 1206
. information returns 4746
Alimony
. *generally* .... 2152 et seq.
. adjusted gross income, computation 3102
. child support distinguished from 2159
. deduction for payor .... 2152 et seq.
. divorce or separation instrument, payment under 2155
. ID number of payee 4752
. IRA, compensation for purposes of 4352
. legal expenses associated with, deductibility 2166
. life insurance contracts as 2158
. payments not treated as 2160
. recapture rules 2162
. requirements for treatment as 2154

Alimony — Cont'd
. separate household requirement 2156
. third party payments 2157
. trusts 2161
All-events test 2832
Allocations
. basis
.. generally 2472
.. multiple properties 2502; 2511
.. partnerships 3751
. change of accounting methods, relief for
   high-impact adjustments 2844
. deductions, between U.S. and foreign
   source income 4641
. depletion deduction 1980
. employer-provided child care credit 2330
. generation-skipping transfer tax exemp-
   tions 5058
. home office expenses 1641; 1644
. interest . . . . 1737 et seq.
. long-term contracts, allocation of costs 2851
. partnership income, loss, etc. . . . . 3724 et seq.
. personal service corporations 2859
. real property tax apportioned between buy-
   er and seller 1770
. Section 482 rules 2858
. selling price, of 2626
. support payments 3125
. tax liability, joint returns, separate liability
   election 4710
. uniform capitalization rules, allocable costs . . . . 1666 et seq.
Alternate fuel production credit 2337
Alternate valuation date 2513; 2521;
                                                                      5016
Alternative minimum tax
. generally . . . . 3200 et seq.
. adjustments and preferences . . . . 3206 et seq.
.. all taxpayers 3208
.. alternative tax net operating loss deduc-
   tion (ATNOLD) 3212
.. basis adjustments 3213
.. corporations 3210; 3211
.. depreciation 1933; 3207
.. noncorporate taxpayers 3209; 3210
. alternative minimum taxable income (AMTI) 3202; 3211
. computation of, generally 3201
. credits 2303
.. adoption expense credit 2354
.. child tax credit 2355
.. election to swap bonus and accelerated
   depreciation for certain credits 1939
.. foreign tax credit 3214
.. nonrefundable credits, effect on 2364
.. premium tax credit 2345
.. tax credit bonds 2366
. exemption amounts
.. generally 3203
.. child subject to kiddie tax 3204
.. small corporation exemption 3205
. minimum tax credit 2365; 3337
. regular tax liability for purposes of 3201; 3202
. taxes, deductibility of 1755
. tentative minimum tax 3201
Alternative tax
. corporate capital gains 2614
**Amateur sports competition, organiza-
   tions fostering** 4100; 4102
. charitable contributions 2102; 2124
Ambulances
. depreciation 1951
. medical expense 2148

Amended returns
.. generally 4723
. depreciation 1901; 1938
. electronic filing 4703
. foreign tax credit 2370
. notice of tax liability, limitation period for
   providing 4871
. refund claims 4849; 4853;
                                                                      4854
. same-sex spouses 4705
. Section 179 expensing election 1941
. withholding certificate 3018
. withholding, correction of errors in 3020
American opportunity tax credit
. generally . . . . 2201 et seq.
. qualified tuition and related expenses for 2204
American Samoa
. foreign corporation treatment 4638
. possessions tax credit 2367
. residence in, U.S. tax and 4618
Amortization
. basis reduction for 2476
. bond discount 3564
. bond premium . . . . 2169 et seq.
. capital expenditures 1655; 1664
. circulation costs 1619
. commercial revitalization expenses 1972
. computer software 1623
. election 3206
. 15-year, intangibles . . . . 1973 et seq.
.. exclusions 1962
. government contracts, right to receive prop-
   erty or services under 1962
. intangible drilling and development costs 1628
. lease cost or improvements 1597; 1602
. mine development and exploration costs . . . 1626; 1627
. music, expenses of creating or acquiring 1969
. oil and gas costs 1971
. organizational expenditures
.. generally 1964
.. deemed election 3520
.. earnings and profits adjustments 3525
.. partnerships 3707
.. S corporations 3359
. plan loans 4343
. pollution control facilities 1968; 3208
. reforestation expenditures 1970; 3102
. research and experimental expenditures 1601; 1602;
                                                                      1964
. Section 197 intangibles 1973; 1974
.. excluded items 1975
. special provisions . . . . 1964 et seq.
. sports franchises 1975
. start-up expenses . . . . 1500 et seq.;
                                                                      1964
. work force in place 1974
AMT See "Alternative minimum tax"
Annualization of income
. generally 2805
. estimated tax 3158; 3347
**Annual lease value method and table (for
   valuing autos)** 1233; 1234
Annuities and annuity contracts
. generally . . . . 1354 et seq.
. after-death distribution requirements 1358
. amounts "not" received as annuity 1366
. "annuity rule" . . . . 1356 et seq.
. death benefits paid as 1260
. employee 1361; 1365
. estate tax, inclusion in gross estate 5013; 5016
. exclusion ratio . . . . 1356 et seq.
. "expected return" 1362

Annuities and annuity contracts — Cont'd
. gift tax valuation 5044
. holder of contract 1357
. individual retirement annuities, distributions
   from 4357
. interest deductions . . . . 1718 et seq.
. investment in the contract 1361; 1364
. joint and survivor 1260; 1360;
                                          3972; 4319;
                                             5023
. modified endowment contracts 1368
. natural person as holder of contract 1357
. nonqualified plans 4350
. partial annuitization of annuities 1364
. premature distributions, penalties 1367
. private 1369
. qualified employee plans
   generally 4315
. . distributions taxed under annuity rule 4338
. . employer deduction 4334
. . nontaxable portion, computation . . . . 1365 et seq.
. . premature distributions 1367
. "secured" annuities 1369
. separate contract treatment, partial annui-
   tization of annuities 1364
. starting date 1363; 1364
. tax-free exchange 2417
. trusts 2116; 2119;
                                         2136; 5054
. unrecovered investment in 3967
. unrelated business taxable income 4122
. "unsecured" private annuities 1369
. variable 1359
. withholding on . . . . 3034 et seq.
Anti-churning rules 1908; 1973
Appellate division conference . . . . 4816 et seq.
Appliances, household
. credit for energy efficient 2335
Applicable asset acquisition 2472
Applicable federal rate
. below-market interest rate loans 5041
. leases and rentals 1600
. overpayments of tax, interest on 4853
. table of 1115
. underpayments of tax, interest on 4866
. unstated interest 1310
Appraisals of property
. casualties 1795; 3110
. charitable gifts 2137; 4877
. . overstatement of value 4872
. . "Statement of Value" for gifts of art 2139
. cost of 2165; 5018
. false or fraudulent 4885
. penalty for valuation misstatements 4887
Appreciated property
. charitable contribution of . . . . 2107; 2128 et
                                            seq.
. corporate distribution of
   generally 3538
. . earnings and profits, effect on 3523
. financial positions, constructive sale of 2637; 2638
. gift of 2683
. partnership distributions 3757
. passive activity, disposition of as 1819
. reacquisition by donor, basis 2514
Arbitrage bonds 1332
Arbitration of tax disputes 4818
Archer medical savings account (MSA)
. contributions to
. . adjusted gross income computation 3102
. . deductibility 1528
. distributions from, exclusion for 1377

Archer medical savings account (MSA) — Cont'd
. employer contributions to 1256
. Medicare Advantage Medical Savings Ac-
   counts 1530
Architectural barriers, removal expenses 1621; 2147;
                                          2323; 2695
Armed forces *See also "Reservists"*
. combat zone compensation, exempt wages 3006
. Coverdell ESAs, rollover of military death
   gratuity or Service Members' Group
   Life Insurance payments to 2207
. dependency exemption, effect of depen-
   dency allotments on 3124
. differential wage payment credit 2336
. disability pension, exclusion for 1284
. dying in combat or terrorist attacks
. . death benefits under qualified retirement
    plans 4331
. . estate tax computation 5033
. . Roth IRA contributions 4369
. . tax relief 4715
. earned income credit 2340; 2341
. exclusions and allowances 1223
. extensions of time 4718; 4719
. "missing status" spouse 3132
. moving expenses 1654
. principal residence, exclusion of gain on
   sale 2443; 2445
. veterans' benefits 1224
Art, charitable contributions 2139
Artists
. creative, expenses of 1641; 1667
. performing, expenses of 3105
Assessments
. bankruptcy proceedings 4829; 4913
. bar to, expiration of limitation period 4831
. "designated summons," issuance of 4837
. extension of assessment period 4854
. immediate 4867
. local benefit, for 1759
. mathematical error on return 4801
. open assessment period 4835
. period, assessment . . . . 4832 et seq.
. prompt assessment, request for 4838
. restitution payments 4827
. statute of limitations on . . . . 4830 et seq.
. suspension of assessment period 4837
. time for making 4825
. unrelated business income tax 4121
. unreported listed transactions 4834
. voluntary extension of assessment period 4836
Assets
. capital and noncapital . . . . 2616 et seq.
. in reorganizations *See "Reorganizations"*
. stock sales treated as transfers of, Section
   336(e) election 3587
Assignment
. benefits of qualified plans 4319
. income, of 1201
. personal injury liability, of 1382
Assistance orders, taxpayer 4811
Associations, shares in 3512
Assumption of liabilities
. basis 2465; 2485;
                                             2488
. charitable contributions, in connection with 2111
. controlled corporations, transfers to 3515; 3516
. corporate distributions
   generally 3539
. . earnings and profits, effect on 3523
. dividends, determination of amount 1292
. exempt organizations 4123

Assumption of liabilities — Cont'd
. like-kind exchanges 2422
. liquidations 3576
. mortgages 2465
. partnerships 3740; 3760
. reorganizations
    generally 3557
. . Type C 3546
. shareholders 3521
. unstated interest, exception to rules 1312
Astronauts dying in line of duty
. employer-provided death benefits 1206
. special estate tax rate 5033
"At risk" limitations
    generally . . . . 1803 et seq.
. activities "at risk" 1805
. alternative minimum tax 3202
. amounts considered "at risk" 1807
. business investment credit 2307
. real property, rules for 1809
. recapture of previously allowed losses 1808
. taxpayers subject to rules 1804
Attorneys
. audit by IRS, representing taxpayer 4808
. expenses of
. . bar association membership 1636
. . home-office deduction 1640
. . professional expenses 1636
. fees for
. . administration expenses, taxable estate 5018
. . business expense, as 1603; 1604
. . civil rights suits and whistleblower
        awards, deduction of fees in connec-
        tion with 3108
. . dissolution or liquidation of corporation 3580
. . information returns 4746
. . nonbusiness legal expenses 2166
. . payable out of judgment 1384
. . recovery of 4863
Audits (by IRS)
    generally . . . . 4800 et seq.
. partnerships and partners
. . administrative adjustment request (AAR) 4841
. . final partnership administrative adjust-
        ment (FPAA) 4844
. . small partnerships 4845
. . unified audit and review procedure for . . . . . 4840 et seq.
. protest, instructions for 4817
. representation, taxpayer 4808
. selection of returns for 4803
. settlement initiatives 4805
. summons of persons and records 4809
. taxpayer's rights 4807
. types of audits, time and place 4806
Authors, expenses of 1667
Automobile dealers, capitalization rules 1667
Automobiles
. alternative motor vehicle credit 2360
. annual lease value 1233
. cents-per-mile valuation method 1236
. charitable contributions 2138; 4115
. commuting value method 1237
. daily lease value 1235
. depreciation
. . ADS depreciation period 1932
. . bonus first-year depreciation 1953
. . business standard mileage rate 1560
. . charitable use mileage rate 2120
. . "luxury" automobiles . . . . 1946 et seq.
. . MACRS depreciation 1915
. entertainment facilities 1567
. expenses, deductibility 1558; 1560

Automobiles — Cont'd
. fringe benefit, as
. . valuation rules . . . . 1232 et seq.
. . withholding on 3007
. . working condition fringes 1245
. losses on 1776
. luxury (listed property) . . . . 1946 et seq.
. mileage or per diem allowances 1560; 1582;
                                                          1648; 2120;
                                                                  2148
. prorated annual lease value 1234
. reporting auto expenses 1558
. salesperson, qualified demonstration auto
        used by, exempt wages 1245

B

Backpay awards 3004
Backup withholding
    generally 3031; 3043
. conditions requiring 3044
. credit for tax withheld 2346
. payee's request to stop 3046
. reportable payments 3045
Bad debts
. banks 4209
. business debts
. . defined 1854
. . shareholder loans or guarantees as 1855
. charge-off 1852
. deduction
    generally . . . . 1848 et seq.
. . amount of deduction 1851
. . business debt . . . . 1852 et seq.
. . guarantees by shareholders 1855
. . guarantors, bad debts of 1849
. . nonbusiness debt 1853
. . partially worthless debts 1852
. . shareholders' loans 1855
. . short-term capital losses 1848
. . worthless debts . . . . 1850 et seq.;
                                                                  4209
. guarantees 1855
. guarantor's, endorser's and indemnitor's
        losses 1849
. losses distinguished 1848
. mortgaged property 1787
. nonbusiness debts
. . classification as 1853
. . defined 1854
. refund claim period for overpayment result-
        ing from 4854
. reserve method, banks 4209
Bank deposits
. frozen *See "Frozen deposits"*
. premature withdrawal of 2168; 3102
. reconstruction of income by use of 2857
Bankruptcy and receivership *See also "In-*
        solvency"
. assessments, immediate 4829
. collection of tax, automatic stay 4858; 4908
. corporations, classification as personal
        holding companies 3322
. debtors, bankrupt 1390
. estates and trusts . . . . 3973 et seq.
. . income tax returns of bankruptcy estates 4736
. principal residence, exclusion of gain on 2445
. proceedings, taxation in 4913
. S corporations 3369; 3376
. transfers of debt for property in bankruptcy 3518
. Type G reorganization 3550; 3554
. underpayment penalty, exception to 3164

Banks and trust companies
. generally . . . . 4209 et seq.
. dividends from 3315
. information returns 4746
. personal holding companies, classification
   as 3322
. S corporations, passive investment income . . . 3366
Bargain purchases and sales
. charity, sale to 2112
. compensation for personal services paid in
   property 1523
. employee, sale by employer to 1216
Barter 4746
Basic standard deduction 3112
Basis
. generally . . . . 2463 et seq.
. acquiring corporation, to 2484
. adjustments to
  . generally 2472; 2474
  . alternative minimum tax 3213
  . decedent dying in 2010, property ac-
    quired from 2523
  . depreciation, amortization, and depletion . . . 2476
  . partnerships
    generally . . . . 3740; 3775 et
            seq.
  . . . alternative method for partner's interest . . . 3741
. allocations
  . generally 2472
  . multiple properties 2502
  . partnerships 3751
. amortization 2170; 2476
. amount of debt included in 2466
. applicable asset acquisitions 2472
. appreciated property reacquired by donor . . . 2514
. assumption of liabilities 2485; 2488
. bad debt deduction 1851
. beneficiary's, in property from estate or
   trust 3949
. bonds
  . amortization of premium 2170
  . identification of 2496; 2497
  . property acquired in exchange for 2487
. business use, personal use property converted to 2473
. capital contributions 2475; 2483
. carryover basis rules for decedents dying in
   2010 . . . . 1911; 2523
. casualty losses 2477
. community property 2518
. contingent remainder interests 2521
. contributed property, partnerships . . . . . 3713 et seq.
. contributing partner's interest in partnership . . . 3739
. corporate liquidations 2490; 3575;
                                    3577
. corporate transactions, property acquired in . . . 2482 et seq.
. cost as 2464; 2471
. debt
  . satisfied by transfer of property 2468
  . S corporation shareholders 3371
. decedent, property acquired from . . . . . . 2512 et seq.
. defined 2463
. depreciation 1961; 2476
. distributed property 1293
. distributee shareholders, basis of property
   to 2488
. dividends . . . . 2492 et seq.
. divorce, transfers incident to 2524
. energy property credit 2478
. fair market value as basis 2489
  . decedent, property acquired from 2512
  . estate tax value also income tax basis 2513

Basis — Cont'd
. fair market value as basis — Cont'd
  . property acquired by gift or in trust 2508
. gifts and transfers in trust
  . generally . . . . 2507 et seq.
  . gift tax, increase in basis 2511
  . partial interests, donees of 2510
  . part purchase, part gift 2509
. identification of stocks or bonds 2496; 2497
. incorporation by partnerships 2491
. installment obligations 2458
. intangible assets, cost of 2471
. inter vivos trusts 2519
. inventories . . . . 2865 et seq.
. investment credit, reductions for 2478
. involuntary conversion, replacement prop-
   erty in 2503
. joint tenants 2517
. leasehold 2474
. lessor-lessee rule 2480
. liabilities as part of basis 2465
. like-kind exchanges 2501
. mortgage foreclosure property 2467
. mortgages as part of basis 2465
. multiple interests in one property 2522
. multiple properties, exchange of 2502
. nonrecognition property 2488
. nontaxable exchanges, property acquired
   in . . . . 2482 et seq.
. options, exercise of 2469
. original issue discount 2466; 2470
. partial interests, donees of 2510
. partnerships
  . adjustments to basis . . . . 3775 et seq.
  . contributed property . . . . 3713 et seq.
  . "inside" basis 3775
  . liquidating distributions, partner's basis in . . . 3749
  . nonliquidating distributions, partner's ba-
    sis in 3748
  . "outside" basis 3738
  . partner's interest 2481; 2491;
                            3738 et seq.
  . stock distributions to corporate partner,
    basis adjustments in connection with 3750
. postponed interests 2521
. powers of appointment 2520
. qualified small business stock rollovers 2506
. real property
  . demolition losses 1783
  . redeemable ground rents 2465
  . repossessions, mortgaged real estate 2467
. recaptured tax credits 2479
. replacement property . . . . 2503 et seq.
. sale or other disposition of property . . . . . 2463 et seq.
. S corporations 2481
. Section 338 election, stock purchase treat-
   ed as asset purchase 3582; 3584
. securities
  . determining 2499
  . holders, basis of property to 2488
. specialized small business company (SS-
   BIC) investments 2505
. spouses, transfer between 2524
. stock
  . assumption of liabilities 3515
  . dividends
    generally . . . . 2492 et seq.
   . extraordinary 2495
   . reinvestment plans, stock acquired
    through 2494
  . eligible worker owned cooperative
    (EWOC), replacement for stock sold to . . . 2504

Basis — Cont'd
. stock — Cont'd
.. employee stock ownership plan (ESOP),
    replacement for stock sold to 2504
.. identification of 2496; 2497
.. mutual fund shares 2498
.. property acquired in exchange for 2487
.. reorganizations . . . . 2484 et seq.
.. rights 2492; 2493
.. S corporation 2481; 3369;
                                                3371
.. unified loss rules 3341
.. wash sale, acquired in 2500
. tenants by the entirety 2517
. theft losses 2477
. trust, transfers in 2508
. unstated interest 2466

Below-market loans
. dividend, treatment as 1291
. employment related 1213
. foregone interest 1291
. gift loan 5041
. interest 1306; 2836
. unstated interest, exception to rules 1312

Beneficiaries *See also "Estates and trusts"*
. continuation coverage (COBRA) 1531
. deductions in respect of decedent 3971
. depreciation and depletion 3927
. determination of designated, minimum dis-
    tribution rules 4345
. employee death benefits . . . . 1260 et seq.
. income in respect of decedent 3970
. qualified tuition programs, designated ben-
    eficiary 2212

Benevolent life insurance associations 4100
Bequests and devises
. basis of property 2512
. capital asset property 2622
. exclusion from gross income . . . . 1370 et seq.
. expatriates, transfer tax on bequests re-
    ceived from 5037
. holding period 2672
. nontaxable gifts and bequests 3950

Betterment costs, capital expenditures 1661
Bicycle commuting expenses 1247
Biodiesel fuel credit 4746
Blacklisted countries, credit for taxes paid
    to 2369
Black lung benefit trusts 4100
Blind, additional standard deduction 3016; 3112
Blue Cross, Blue Shield and similar or-
    ganizations 3211
Boards of trade 4100
Boats, charitable contributions 2138; 4115
Bonds
. amortization of premium or discount . . . . . 2169 et seq.
. convertible, gain or loss on exercising 2681
. exclusion of income on U.S. savings bonds
    used to pay for higher education . . . . 2219 et seq.
. exempt
.. capital assets 2617
.. depreciation of property financed by 1931
.. market discount 1326
.. sale or exchange of 2636
.. state and local bonds 1331
. identification, determination of basis 2496; 2497
. market discount . . . . 1324 et seq.
. repurchase of below issue price 1394
. savings bonds, U.S . . . . 1334 et seq.
. sold between interest dates 1329
. taxable interest . . . . 1332 et seq.
. tax credit bonds, credit for holders of 2366

Bonds — Cont'd
. U.S., tax-free exchanges of 2416
. worthless 1781
Bonuses
. employee 1209
. lessors or sublessors 1340
. time for deduction 1538; 1539;
                                                  2832
. veterans, to, from states 1224
. withholding on 3004; 3011
Boot
. amount of, taxation up to 3554; 3555
. assumption of liabilities 3515; 3557
. controlled corporations, transfers to 3514; 3515
. defined 3556
. like-kind exchanges 2421; 2422;
                                                2501
. spin-offs, split-offs and split-ups 3561
. Type C reorganizations 3546
Bottle deposits 2847
Boycott, international 2369; 4624;
                                                4632
Branch-level interest tax 4648
Branch profits tax 4647
Breeding livestock 4526
Bribes
    generally . . . . 1610 et seq.
. government officials or employees 1611
. Medicare and Medicaid, under 1611
. Subpart F income 4624
Brokers, reporting by 4741; 4746;
                                                4898
Brother-sister corporations 3337; 3533
Buildings
. building identification number (BIN) 4752
. capitalization of expenses 1660; 1661
. demolition losses 1783
. depreciation
.. dispositions of MACRS assets 1906
.. farm buildings 1919
.. residential and nonresidential properties 1920; 1940
. energy efficient commercial building prop-
    erty
.. deduction 2476
.. expensing election 1967
.. recapture rules for Sec. 1245 property 2695
. facade easements, contribution of 2114
. low-income housing credit 2320
. qualified commercial revitalization ex-
    penses 1972
. rehabilitation investment credits . . . . 2308 et seq.
Built-in gains, losses
. acquisitions, corporate 3566; 3568;
                                                3570
. basis increase due to assumption of built-in
    loss 2485
. 80% subsidiary liquidations 3578
. partnerships
.. property contributions 3752
.. transfers of partnership interests 3776
. S corporations 3362; 3363;
                                                3368
Bundled fees, estates and trusts 3921
Burden of proof 4858; 4872
Burial corporation 4100
Business connection requirement
. ordinary and necessary expenses 1508
. reimbursed expenses 1574
Business credits . . . . 2301 et seq.
Business damages 1383
Business, generally *See "Trade or busi-*
    ness"

Business gifts . . . . 1589 et seq.
Business leagues 4100
Business meetings, entertainment ex-
  penses 1566
Business property
. capital gain-ordinary loss rule . . . . 2684 et seq.
. casualty losses 1795
. converted to or from personal use 1928
. depreciation 1902; 1903;
                               1906; 1909
. listed property, "business/investment" use
  for 1950
. materials and supplies 1657
. repairs and maintenance 1656
. special use valuation 5017
Business use of home . . . . 1638 et seq.

C

Cafeteria plans 1269
Calendar year *See "Taxable year"*
Callable bonds, amortization of premium 2171
"Call" or "put" options, capital gains and
  losses 2620
Canadians, withholding on services per-
  formed by 4668; 4669
Cancellation of debt *See "Discharge of in-
debtedness"*
Cancellation of leases and distributor-
  ships 1340; 2680
Capital assets
  generally . . . . 2616 et seq.
. charitable contributions . . . . 2126 et seq.
. defined
  generally 2617
. . hedging transactions 2618
. exclusions 2617
. holding period . . . . 2667 et seq.
. sale or exchange transactions . . . . 2676 et seq.
. Section 1231 assets . . . . 2684 et seq.
Capital contributions
. basis of property 2475; 2483
. capitalization of expenses 1659
. income, computation 3304
. partnerships 3710
Capital expenditures
  generally . . . . 1655 et seq.
. acquiring or producing property 1660
. acquisitions, corporate 1659
. adaptation of property to new or different
  use 1661
. advertising and business promotion 1512
. allocating costs to property . . . . 1666 et seq.
. amortization 1655
. architectural barrier removal expenses 1621
. basis, adjustments 2474
. betterment costs 1661
. carrying charges 1620
. circulation expenses 1619
. commissions 1662
. compensation payments 1536
. computer software costs 1623
. deductibility 1655
. de minimis rule 1660
. demolition expenses 1783
. depreciation 1655
. disallowance of deductions . . . . 1626; 1655 et
                               seq.
. election to capitalize or deduct . . . . 1617; 1626 et
                               seq.
. environmental cleanup costs 1661; 1667
. examples of 1659

Capital expenditures — Cont'd
. expansion of business 1505
. expensing 1655
. facilitative costs 1660
. improvement project, real estate 1620; 1659
. insurance premiums 1607
. intangible assets, costs associated with . . . . . . 1663 et seq.
. . de minimis and 12-month rule exceptions 1665
. interest 1620; 1667;
                               1669
. material and supplies 1657
. medical care purposes 2147
. mine exploration costs 1626
. natural resources, deductible . . . . 1626 et seq.
. organization expenses 3520; 3707
. reorganizations 1659; 3558
. repairs and maintenance 1656
. research and experimental expenses 1601; 1602
. restoration costs 1661
. royalty payments 1618
. spare parts, rotable and temporary 1658
. start-up expenses 1500; 1502
. taxes 1620; 1667
. transportation barrier removal expenses 1621
. uniform capitalization rules . . . . 1666 et seq.;
                              4519 et seq.
. unimproved and unproductive real estate 1620
. unit of property, defined 1660
Capital gain dividends 1298; 1299
Capital gain-ordinary loss rule
  generally . . . . 2684 et seq.
. livestock 4526
. non-recaptured net Sec. 1231 losses 2610
. unharvested crops sold with land 4524
Capital gains and losses *See also "Capital
  gain-ordinary loss rule"*
  generally . . . . 2600 et seq.
. adjusted net capital gain, defined 2604
. alternative tax computation 2614; 3201;
                              3202
. appreciated financial positions 2637; 2638
. artistic compositions 2622
. bad debt deduction, short-term capital
  losses 1848
. business property, sale, exchange or invol-
  untary conversion . . . . 2684 et seq.
. business, sale of 2626
. capital assets
  generally . . . . 2616 et seq.
. . sales and exchanges, effect of 2601
. capital gain net income 2602
. capital loss deductions 2611; 2615
. carrybacks and carryovers
  generally 2615
. corporate acquisitions 3564; 3570;
                              3572
. . long-term capital loss 2606
. . noncorporate taxpayers 2612
. . quick refund for carrybacks 4850
. . Sec. 1256 contract losses 2659
. collectibles gain 2603; 2606;
                              2607
. computation of tax 2609
. conversion and constructive ownership
  transactions . . . . 2664 et seq.
. copyrights 2622
. corporations
  generally . . . . 2600; 2613 et
                              seq.
. . alternative tax computation 2614
. . capital loss deductions 2615
. . distributions 3522

Capital gains and losses *See also "Capital gain-ordinary loss rule"* — **Cont'd**
. corporations — Cont'd
. . personal holding companies 3321
. . real estate investment trusts 4202
. . regulated investment companies 4201
. . worthless securities 1781
. covenant not to compete 2627
. decedents, capital losses of 2612
. deferring gain, short sales . . . . 2639 et seq.
. defined 2600
. distributable net income of complex trust or
      estate 3937
. dividends 1285; 1286
. effectively-connected income 4644
. employee stock purchase plan options 1220
. empowerment zone assets, qualified 2428
. exempt obligations 2636
. farmers and farming 4525
. foreign currency 4676
. foreign tax credit 2370
. franchise transfers 2629
. goodwill 2627
. hedging transactions 2618
. holding period . . . . 2667 et seq.
. incentive stock options 1221
. income in respect of decedent 3972
. individuals . . . . 2600 et seq.
. life estate 2630
. literary compositions 2622
. lump-sum distributions 4339
. mark-to-market rule 2653
. musical compositions 2622
. net capital gains, computation of . . . . 2603 et seq.
. net capital loss, refund of overpayment re-
      sulting from carryback of 4854
. netting rules 2601; 2609
. noncompetition agreement 2627
. noncorporate (individual) taxpayers . . . . 2600 et seq.
. nonresident aliens 4642
. options 2619; 2620
. original issue discount . . . . 2633 et seq.
. partnerships
. . dispositions of contributed property 3747
. . sale or exchange of interest 3765
. . separately stated items 3718
. patents sold or exchanged 2621
. pooled income funds, set aside of
      long-term capital gain for charity 3915
. real property
      generally 2624
. . installment sales 2457
. . subdivided for sale 2623
. regulated investment companies (RICs)
      generally 4201
. . stock of, sale or exchange 2632
. related persons, sales between 2690; 2691
. renewal community and D.C. zone assets . . . . 2650 et seq.
. Section 1202 gain 2606; 2608
. Section 1250 gain, unrecaptured 2603; 2605
. Section 1256 contracts 2653; 2656
. securities
. . futures contracts 2662
. . investments by dealers 2628
. . worthless 1781
. short sales
      generally . . . . 2639 et seq.
. . futures, commodity 2642
. . hedging transactions 2642
. . limits 2640; 2641
. . worthless property 2643
. short-term obligations

Capital gains and losses *See also "Capital gain-ordinary loss rule"* — **Cont'd**
. short-term obligations — Cont'd
      generally . . . . 2634 et seq.
. . government obligations 2634
. . nongovernment obligations 2635
. small business investment company (SBIC)
      stock 2631
. sole proprietorship, sale of 2625
. spouses, capital losses 2611
. termination of rights or obligations 2677
. term interests 2630
. timber . . . . 2687 et seq.
. trademark or trade name, transfers 2629
Carbon dioxide sequestration credit 2315
Car pools 1206; 1247
Carrybacks and carryovers
. acquiring corporations 3563; 3564
. adoption expense credit 2354
. at-risk losses, disallowed 1806
. bankruptcy estate, by 3978
. built-in loss (unused, unrecognized under
      Sec. 382) 3570
. business expense deduction 1511
. capital gains and losses *See "Capital gains*
      and losses"
. charitable contributions . . . . 2129 et seq.
. closed years 4833
. credits . . . . 2304 et seq.
. depreciation deduction 1904
. dividends, personal holding companies 3335
. foreign housing expenses 4614
. foreign tax credit 2370
. general business credit . . . . 2304 et seq.
. home office deduction in excess of gross
      income limitation 1643
. investment interest in excess of deductible
      limits 1727
. limitation on carryovers . . . . 3567 et seq.
. losses
. . earnings and profits 3525
. . tax-exempt use losses 1782
. net operating loss *See "Net operating loss"*
. partnership losses in excess of partner's
      basis . . . . 3735 et seq.
. passive activity losses and credits 1815; 1837
. pension and profit-sharing plans, employer
      deduction for 4335; 4379
. quick refunds 4850
. reorganization, tax-free 3563
. S corporations
. . C corporation, from 3359
. . losses in excess of basis, by sharehold-
      ers 3369
. Section 179 expense election 1941
. Section 1256 contract losses 2659
. soil and water conservation expenses 4522
. straddle losses 2655
. successors 3563; 3979
. tentative carryback 4849
Carrying charges
. election to capitalize 1620
. installment purchases 1706
Cars *See "Automobiles"*
Cash
. alimony requirements 2154
. contributions of 2135; 2136
. dividends 1297
. marketable securities distributions, treated
      as cash distributions 3745
. possession of, unexplained 4828
. Section 351 transfers 3511

Cash — Cont'd
. transactions, reporting of 4746
Cash balance plans 4311
Cash basis
    generally . . . . 2819 et seq.
. advances against commissions 1274
. checks as income 2821
. checks as payments 2823
. compensation
. . reporting of 1272; 1274
. . when deductible . . . . 1537 et seq.
. constructive receipt 2822; 2823
. decedents 3966
. deductions 2823
. farmers . . . . 4506 et seq.
. foreign tax credit 2368
. gain or loss on sale or exchange 2407
. interest income, time to report 1335; 1337
. interest, time for deduction . . . . 1744 et seq.
. prepaid insurance 1609
. previously reported income, repayments of,
    time for deduction of repayment 2861
. real property tax
. . apportioned between buyer and seller 1770
. . time for deduction 1771
. rental income, time to report 1339
. restrictions on 2818
. royalties 1345
. taxes, time for deduction . . . . 1765 et seq.
Cash withdrawals, amounts not received
    as annuity 1366
Casualty losses
. basis adjustment 2477
. buildings 1783
. business property 2685
. crops 4520
. deductions
    generally . . . . 1792 et seq.;
                                 3114
. . amount of loss 1795
. . appraisal fees 3110
. . compensation 1796
. . definition of "casualty" 1794
. . definition of deductible loss 1774
. . frozen bank deposits 1802
. . individuals 1776
. . insurance 1796
. . limitation on 1795
. . time to deduct 1797
. entertainment facilities 1567
. estate tax 5018
. estimated tax penalty, waiver of, because
    of 3165
. insurance reimbursement for living ex-
    penses 1206
. net operating losses 1841
. nonresident aliens 4646
. of records (substantiation rules) 1588
Catch-up contributions
. 401(k) plans, 403(b) annuities, SEPs, and
    Sec. 457 plans 4317
. health savings accounts 1529
. IRAs 4351
. nondiscrimination rules 4325
. Roth IRAs 4369
. SIMPLE plans 4384
Cell phones
. expense reimbursements 1573
. fringe benefits 1245; 1246
Cellulosic biofuel production credit 2318
Cemeteries
. charitable organizations 2102; 2125

Cemeteries — Cont'd
. exempt organizations 4100
Cents-per-mile valuation method 1236
Certificates of deposit, taxability
. interest 1335
. premature withdrawal of, penalty, deduct-
    ibility 2168
Certified mailing of returns 4755
CFC *See "Controlled foreign corporations*
    (CFCs)"
Chambers of commerce 4100
Chapter 14 rules 5054
Charge account, interest on 1704
"Charitable bail-out" 2113
Charitable bequests, deduction for 5020; 5049
Charitable contributions
    generally . . . . 2100 et seq.
. accrual corporations, year of deduction
    election 2133
. annuity trusts 2116; 2136
. appraisals 2137; 2139;
                                   4877
. appreciated property . . . . 2107; 2126 et
                                   seq.
. artworks, "Statement of Value" 2139
. bargain sales as 2112
. benefit to contributor 2103; 2104;
                                   2115
. business expenses vs. 2105
. capital gain property . . . . 2110; 2126 et
                                   seq.
. care of the ill, needy, or infants 2108
. carryover of deduction . . . . 2129 et seq.
. cars, boats and planes 2138; 4115
. ceiling on deduction . . . . 2100; 2123 et
                                   seq.
. charitable remainder trust 3914
. conservation purposes of charity 2114; 2123;
                                   2131
. contribution base 2123
. corporations 2108; 2131;
                               2133; 3564
. decedent's final return 2130
. deductions
    generally . . . . 2100 et seq.
. . ineligible contributions 2103
. . when deductible 2132; 2133
. definition of deductible charitable contribu-
    tion 2101
. donor advised funds 2118
. entertainment 2104
. estates and trusts . . . . 3931 et seq.
. facade easements 2114
. farm, charitable remainder in 2114
. 50% charities, generally . . . . 2124 et seq.
. foreign corporations 4646
. fund raising affairs 2104
. gift tax 5049
. income interest in trust . . . . 2114 et seq.
. income realized on contribution 2109
. individuals, benefit of 2103
. information returns 4746
. interest expense 2111
. inventories 2108
. IRA distributions 4357
. lead trusts 2119
. liabilities transferred as part of contribution 2111
. limitations on deduction . . . . 2110; 2123 et
                                   seq.
. mortgaged property 2114
. noncash contributions, substantiation 2137
. nondeductible 4118

Charitable contributions — Cont'd
. ordinary income property 2107
. out-of-pocket expenses 2120
. partial interest in property 2114
. partnerships 3717; 3718
. patents 2106
. payroll deduction, made through 2135; 2136
. percentage limitation . . . . 2123 et seq.
. personal holding companies 3321
. personal residence, charitable remainder in 2114
. pooled income fund 2114; 2117;
                                                                   2136; 3915
. private foundations 2110
. property, of . . . . 2100; 2106 et
                                                                              seq.
. qualified organizations 2102
. quid pro quo contributions 4119
. receipts 2135
. reduction of deduction 2107; 2111
. remainder interests . . . . 2114 et seq.
. repurchase, gift of stock followed by 2113
. sales of contributed property 2110; 2138
. scientific property 2108
. services performed for charity 2120
. split-dollar insurance 2115
. stock, redemption or repurchase following
    gift of 2113
. student in home as 2122
. substantiation . . . . 2134 et seq.
. . vehicle donations, donee acknowledg-
    ment 2138; 4115
. tangible personal property 2110
. 30% charities 2125; 2128
. time for deducting 2132
. trade or business, property held primarily
    for sale 2108
. transactions of interest, reporting require-
    ments 4749
. travel expenses 2121
. trusts 2114; 2116;
                                                                            2119; 2136;
                                                                            3931 et seq.
. 20% limitation 2128
. $250 or more, substantiation requirements . . 2134 et seq.
. undivided portion of entire interest 2114
. unitrust 2116; 2119;
                                                                          2136; 3914
. use of property 2114
. valuation . . . . 2104 et seq.
. valuation overstatement, penalties 4872
. written acknowledgment of 2136
Charitable lead trusts 2119; 2136
Charitable organizations *See "Exempt or-
    ganizations"*
Charitable remainder trusts 3952
. annuity trusts 2116; 2136;
                                                                            3914
. unitrusts 2116; 2136;
                                                                          3914

**Chauffeur services, valuation of fringe
    benefits** 1230
Checks
. cash method deductions 2823
. charitable contributions paid by 2132
. income, check as 2821
. tax paid with 4720
**Check-the-box system of entity classifica-
    tion**
. corporations 3301
. partnerships . . . . 3700 et seq.
Child and dependent care credit *See also
    "Employer-provided child care credit"*

Child and dependent care credit *See also "Employer-provided
child care credit"* **— Cont'd**
    generally . . . . 2349 et seq.
. earned income limitation 2352
. employment-related expenses 2351; 2352
. qualifying individuals 2350
. relatives, payments to 2351
Children *See also "Minors"*
. alternative minimum tax 3204
. child tax credit *See "Child tax credit"*
. credit for care of *See "Child and dependent
    care credit"*
. earned income credit . . . . 2339 et seq.
. exemption for 3119
. . birth of child 3128
. . qualifying child 3120
. . . of two or more taxpayers 3121
. . . release of exemption by custodial parent 3126
. kiddie tax *See "Kiddie tax"*
. kidnapped children as dependents 3129
. self-employed health insurance deduction
    for child under age 27 1532
. students *See "Students"*
. support, child 2159; 4848
. wages paid to, deductibility 1516
Child tax credit
    generally 2355
. kidnapped children 3129
. refundable (additional) credit 2356
**Chronically ill individuals, death benefits,
    acceleration of** 1351
Churches
. charitable contributions 2124
. employees
. . filing requirements 4701
. . self-employment tax 3142
. . tax-sheltered annuities . . . . 4388 et seq.
. exemption 4100
Circuit courts of appeal 4862
Circulation expenses 1619; 3210;
                                                                         3213; 3525
Citizenship
. expatriation *See "Expatriation"*
Civic associations, exemption 4100; 4106
Civil damages, deduction for payment of 1630
Claim of right, income received under
    generally 1204
. deduction for repayment of
    generally . . . . 2860 et seq.
. . quick refund 4850
Claims
. against the estate, estate tax deduction 5018
. refund . . . . 4849 et seq.
Claims Court 4858; 4862
Clean renewable energy bonds (CREBs) 2366
Clergy
. charitable contributions to 2103
. income 1226
. self-employment tax 3147
. tax-sheltered annuities 4388
Clinical testing expense credit 2328
**"Closed-loop biomass," electricity pro-
    duction, credit for** 2324
Closely-held corporations
. passive activity loss rules 1811; 1814;
                                                                              1825
. stock valuation 5016
Closing agreements 4812; 4821
Clothing
. charitable contributions 2103
. deductibility of as employee business ex-
    pense 1634

Clothing — Cont'd
. de minimis fringe benefits 1246
. support, as part of 3124
Club memberships
. business and professional associations 1635; 1636
. social clubs *See "Social clubs"*
Coal
. advance payments 2689
. capital gains and losses 2688; 2689
. credit for qualifying advanced coal projects 2312
. electricity production from renewable re-
   sources, credit for 2324
. percentage depletion 1978
. pollution control facilities, amortization elec-
   tion 1968
. source of income 4642
COBRA *See "Continuation coverage (CO-*
   BRA)"
CODAs (cash or deferred arrangements)
   See "401(k) plans"
Cohan rule 1510
Coke and coke gas, alternate fuel produc-
   tion credit 2337
Collectibles, capital gains and losses 2603; 2606;
                                         2607
Collection of tax
   generally . . . . 4902 et seq.
. annual notice of amount of delinquency 4903
. Appeals Office, early referral to 4815
. combat zone service, extensions of time 4719
. costs in connection with, deductibility 2165
. injunction 4910
. limitation period 4909
. unauthorized collection actions 4858; 4908
. unrelated business income tax 4121
Colleges and universities, charitable con-
   tributions 2124
Combat zone
   generally 1223
. extensions of time for taxpayers serving in 4719
. tax relief for military and civilian employees
   dying in combat 4715
Commercial revitalization deduction 2476
Commissions
. advances against 1274
. capital expenditures 1662
. executors 1206; 3922
. gross income 1209
. withholding tax 3004; 3011
Commodities dealers and traders
. engaging in U.S. business 4645
. mark-to-market rules 2879; 2880;
                                         3143
Commodity contracts 2499
Commodity Credit Corporation (CCC)
   loans
. crops pledged to secure loans from 4528
. information returns 4746
Commodity futures
   generally 2642
. capital gains and losses 2618
. holding period 2667
. short sales rules 2642
. tax straddles . . . . 2653 et seq.
Common trust funds
   generally 4210
. acquisition discount, accrual of 1328
. alternative minimum tax 3202
. net operating losses 1840
. portfolio income 1820

Communications income 4640
Community development entities (CDEs),
   new markets tax credit 2329
Community property
. decedent, acquired from 2518
. dependency exemption 3127
. estate's income from 3919
. gifts 5053
. gross estate inclusion 5012
. holding period 2672
. income from 1203
. . estate's income 3919
. . relief for separate return liability attributa-
   ble to 1203
. innocent spouse rule 4709
. withholding on wages, credit for 2346
Commuting
. commuting value method 1237
. expenses 1231; 1247;
                                       1556; 1559
. highway vehicle, qualified transportation
   fringe benefits 1247
Company-owned life insurance (COLI)
. interest deduction 1721
. premiums on 1526
Compensation for personal services
   generally . . . . 1208 et seq.
. accrual basis taxpayer 1273
. advances 3006
. another person than taxpayer, services ren-
   dered to 1520
. armed forces, exclusions for members of 1223
. bargain purchases 1216; 1523
. bonuses as 1539
. business expenses . . . . 1515 et seq.
. capital outlays, as 1536
. cash basis taxpayers 1272; 1274
. clergy 1226
. club dues 1568
. contingent 1522
. credits for
. . differential wage payment credit for em-
   ployers 2336
. . empowerment zone employment credit 2325
. . Indian employment credit 2326
. . work opportunity credit 2316; 2317
. death benefits 1534
. debt payments
. . employee, payment by employer 1521
. . services performed by debtor 1395
. deductibility . . . . 1515 et seq.
. . manufacturing and production activities 1615
. . $1,000,000 limitation 1519
. deferred compensation *See "Deferred com-*
   pensation"
. dividend, as 1289; 1517
. employee stock purchase plan options 1220
. employment contract, sale or cancellation
   of 1222
. entertainment provided to officers, direc-
   tors, etc 1572
. exempt wages 3006
. expenses paid by employer 1521
. film and TV production, expensing election
   for 1965
. fringe benefits *See "Fringe benefits"*
. gifts
. . business gifts 1589; 1590
. . distinguished from compensation 1212
. "golden parachute" payments 1535
. government employees 1225

Compensation for personal services — Cont'd
. government employees — Cont'd
.. allowances for employees stationed
    outside the U.S. 4619
. gross income . . . . 1208 et seq.
. health insurance providers, limitation on de-
    duction 1519
. incentive stock options 1221
. individual retirement accounts, defined for
    purposes of 4352
. information returns . . . . 3021 et seq.
. Keogh plans, for purposes of 4327
. loans 1213
. minors 1227; 1516
. noncash compensation 1214
. nonresident aliens 4668; 4669
. nonstatutory stock options 1219
. notes 1215
. officers of corporations, compensation de-
    duction limit 1519
. partnership interest as 3712
. part-time services 1518
. prior year's services, reasonableness de-
    termined by 1518
. property, in 1523; 1524
. purchase price or compensation 1536
. reasonable compensation
    generally . . . . 1517 et seq.
.. clear and convincing evidence 1535
.. factors determining 1518
.. property other than cash, payment in 1523
. related taxpayers, payments to 1517
. reporting 1210
. restricted stock or other property for em-
    ployees . . . . 1217 et seq.
. sick pay 3008; 4746
. source rules 4640
. statements for payees 4743
. stock 1523; 1525
. strike and lockout benefits 3006
. tax-sheltered annuities 4392
. time for deducting . . . . 1537 et seq.
. time for reporting . . . . 1271 et seq.
. tips 1211; 3005
. vacation pay 1540
. veterans' benefits 1224
. welfare benefit funds 1533
. withholding on . . . . 3000 et seq.;
                                4662; 4668;
                                         4669
. workers' compensation 1259
Completed-contract accounting 3525
Complex trusts
. beneficiary, amount taxed to 3945
. character of income 3946
. defined 3933
. distributable net income 3936; 3937
. distribution deductions 3936
. throwback rules . . . . 3953 et seq.
Compromises with IRS 4822
Computers *See also "Software, computer"*
. home computer, depreciation and Section
    179 expense election 1955
. MACRS depreciation 1915; 1947
. semiconductor manufacturing equipment,
    depreciation 1932
Condemnation
    generally . . . . 2435 et seq.
. awards, amount realized 2436
. involuntary conversion, defined 2432
. losses, deductibility 1774
. replacement property 2440; 2441

Condemnation — Cont'd
. severance damages 2437
Condition of employment
. listed property depreciation deduction 1955
. meals and lodging furnished as 1267
Condominiums
. homeowners' associations 4110
. principal residence, as 1735
. real estate taxes 1764
Conferences, medical conferences, ex-
    penses of attending 2144
Conflict of interest
. stock options sold by federal employees to
    meet conflict of interest requirements 1220
Consent dividends 3334
Consents
. assessment period, extension of 4836
. employer-owned life insurance 1353
. S corporation shareholders 3357
Conservation *See also "Recycling"*
. energy conservation
.. qualified energy conservation bond credit 2366
.. subsidy, rate reduction or credit from utili-
    ty 1206
. farmers, special payments to 4528
. forestry conservation bonds, qualified 2366
. land subject to qualified conservation ease-
    ment 2512; 5016
. qualified conservation contributions 2123; 2131
. real property, charitable contribution for
    conservation purposes 2114
. soil and water conservation expenses
    generally 4522
.. partnerships 3718; 3756
.. special farm payments 4528
Consistency rules (Sec. 338 election) 3584
Consolidated returns
. affiliated group . . . . 3338 et seq.
. dual consolidated losses 3342
. forms for filing 3340
. intercompany transactions 3338
. Sec. 338 election 3586
. unified loss rules 3341
Consolidation of corporations 3544
Construction
. advance payments for 2830
. allowances from lessor 1344
. capital expenditures 1620; 1659
. contractors
.. inventories of 2863
.. new energy efficient home credit 2334
. depreciation of assets used in 1915
. domestic production activities, deduction
    for 1616
. insurance premiums for property during, as
    capital expenditure 1607
. long-term contracts . . . . 2849 et seq.
. qualified school construction bonds, credit
    for 2366
Construction period carrying charges,
    capitalization 3525
Constructive dividends . . . . 1289 et seq.
Constructive ownership
. attribution rules 3534
. characterization of income from construc-
    tive ownership transactions 2664; 2666
. controlled groups 3337
. ownership change 3571
. partnership interests 3733
. personal holding companies 3323
. redemption of stock rules 3530; 3533;
                                       3534

Constructive ownership — Cont'd
. related taxpayers 2448
Constructive receipt
. cash basis taxpayers . . . . 2820 et seq.
. . compensation 1272
. checks 2821; 2823
. dividends . . . . 1289 et seq.
. income 2822
. interest 1335
. prizes and awards 1373
Constructive sales
. appreciated financial positions 2637; 2638
. hedging or straddle transactions 2653
Consultants 3003
Containers
. deposits on 2847
. inventories 2864
Contested liability
. accrual of 2834
. taxes 1765; 1768
Contingent compensation 1522
Contingent debt instruments 1317
Contingent payment sales 2455
Continuation coverage (COBRA) 1531
Continuity of business enterprise 3542
Continuity of interest 3542; 3560
Contracts
. cancellation of 1222; 1514;
                                          2677
. government
. . amortization of right to receive property or
    services under 1962; 1974
. . excise tax on foreign procurement pay-
    ments 4652
. long-term, accounting . . . . 2848 et seq.
. personal service, personal holding compa-
    ny income 3328
Contributions
. capital, to *See "Capital contributions"*
. charitable *See "Charitable contributions"*
Controlled corporations
. basis 2488; 2489
. capital gain bar on sales of depreciable
    property 2691
. control defined
. . for purposes of Sec. 351 transfers 3513
. . for reorganizations 3553
. depletion 1980
. foreign *See "Controlled foreign corpora-*
    tions (CFCs)"
. limitation on tax benefits 3337
. losses from sales to or from 2448; 2450
. reallocation of income and deductions of 2858
. research credit 2319
. spin-offs, split-offs and split-ups 3560
. stock sales
. . between corporations 3533
. . Section 336(e) election to treat as asset
    transfers 3587
. tax-free exchange, requirements for 3510
. transfers to . . . . 3510 et seq.
. voting rights, estate tax 5005
Controlled entities, information returns 4124; 4746
Controlled foreign corporations (CFCs)
    See also "Subpart F income"
. boycott activities 4632
. defined 4623
. dividends 1288
. foreign tax credit 2374
. income received from, foreign tax credit
    separate limitation rules 2371
. information returns 4661

Controlled foreign corporations (CFCs) *See also "Subpart F income"* **— Cont'd**
. loss recapture rules 2372
. passive activity loss rules 1820
. passive foreign investment companies,
    50% test 4627
. sales to 4626
. stock; sale, exchange or redemption of 4625
. U.S. shareholders . . . . 4622 et seq.
Convenience of employer test
. listed property MACRS deductions 1955
. meals and lodging 1267
Conventions, expenses of attending
    generally 1549
. cruise ships 1550
. foreign conventions 1549
. luxury water travel 1552
. nonbusiness expenses 2164
. professional organizations 1636
Conversion transactions, gain on 2664; 2665
Convertible securities
. amortization of bond premium 2169
. exchanges 2414; 2681
Cooperatives
    generally . . . . 4206 et seq.
. apartment
. . casualty losses 1793
. . depreciation deduction 1904
. . maintenance and leases, business ex-
    penses 1625
. . mortgage interest payments, deduction 1714
. . qualified residence interest 1735
. . real estate taxes 1764
. farmers *See "Farmers' cooperatives"*
. nonpatronage distributions 4208
. patronage dividends 1300; 4207
. per-unit retain allocations 4207
. worker-owned (EWOC) 2451; 2504
Copyrights
. amortization 1974
. basis 2471
. business expenses 1618
. capital assets, as 2622
. depreciation 1959; 1962
. royalties . . . . 1345; 3325 et
                                                seq.
Corporations
    generally . . . . 3300 et seq.
. accounting methods 2818
. accumulated earnings tax . . . . 3316 et seq.
. acquisition indebtedness *See "Acquisition*
    indebtedness"
. alternative minimum tax . . . . 3201 et seq.
. . exemption amount 3203
. . minimum tax credit 2365
. at-risk rules 1804
. capital gains and losses 2600; 2601;
                                     2613 et seq.
. carryovers on corporate acquisitions 3563; 3564
. C corporations
. . dividends-received deduction 3307
. . income tax . . . . 3303 et seq.
. change to exempt status 3579
. charitable contributions . . . . 2100 et seq.;
                                    2108; 2131;
                                    2133; 3564
. check-the-box system of entity classifica-
    tion 3301
. consolidated returns . . . . 3338 et seq.
. contributions to capital 2483
. defined 3301
. depreciation

Corporations — Cont'd
. depreciation — Cont'd
. . election to swap bonus depreciation for
    certain credits 1939
. . recapture 2697
. dissolution costs 3580
. distributions
    generally . . . . 1285 et seq.
. . corporate partners, stock distributions to 3750
. . earnings and profits . . . . 3521 et seq.
. . liabilities in excess of basis, subject to 3539
. . liquidating . . . . 3574 et seq.
. . nonliquidating . . . . 3538 et seq.
. . stock or stock rights 3540
. dividends-received deduction . . . . 3306 et seq.
. estimated tax
    generally 3343
. . "adjusted seasonal installment" 3348
. . "annualized income installment" 3347
. . earnings and profits, effect of payments
    on 3525
. . quick refund of 4851
. . required annual payment 3344
. . required installments 3346
. . "tax" defined 3345
. . underpayment penalty 3349
. expatriations (inversions) 4655
. farming 4510
. foreign See "Foreign corporations"
. foreign income 4610; 4621
. foreign tax credit 2367; 2368
. income tax
    generally . . . . 3300 et seq.
. . C corporations . . . . 3303 et seq.
. . deposit of payments 4730
. . due dates for payments 4729
. . extensions of time for payments 4729
. . rates of tax 1113
. . returns . . . . 4724 et seq.
. interest deduction 1739
. liquidation . . . . 2490; 3574 et
                                                        seq.; 4746
. merger or consolidation 3544
. net operating loss See "Net operating loss"
. new business address or location 4726
. organization costs, deductibility 3520
. overpayments, interest on 4853
. partnerships, publicly traded 3302
. passive activity loss rules 1812
. personal holding company tax . . . . 3320 et seq.
. personal service See "Personal service cor-
    porations"
. rates of tax . . . . 2614; 3303 et
                                                             seq.
. reorganizations
    generally . . . . 3541 et seq.
. . basis in property received in . . . . 2484 et seq.
. returns
    generally 4724
. . forms 4726
. . place for filing 4727
. . signatures 4725
. . time for filing 4727
. . . extensions of time 4728
. S corporations See "S corporations"
. shareholders
. . constructive ownership rules 3534
. small business See "Small business corpo-
    rations"
. stock transfers
. . to corporate partner 3750
. . foreign 3588; 4631

Corporations — Cont'd
. substantial understatement of tax, penalty
    for 4878
. taxable income 3304
. tax avoidance acquisitions, Section 269
    rules 3565
. tax, computation of 3305
. tentative carryback adjustments 4729
. termination 4724
. thin capitalization 1709
. transfers to . . . . 3510 et seq.
. transfers to exempt entities 3579
. underpayments, interest on 4866
Corrosive drywall 1795
Cosmetic surgery 2144
Cost depletion, mineral property 1977
Cost of goods sold
. deduction for, returns 4726; 4731
. domestic production activities deduction 1616
. inventories
    generally 2863
. . definition of cost 2869
. . valuation of inventory 2865
Coupons, discount 2847
Covenant not to compete See "Noncompe-
    tition agreement"
**Coverdell education savings accounts
    (CESAs)**
    generally 2205
. contributions to 2207
. . gift tax on 5047
. distributions from 2208; 4746
. penalty for failure to report 4898
. qualified education expenses for purposes
    of 2208
. trust or custodial accounts, forms 2206
Credit cards
. business payments of $600 or more 4743
. charitable contributions paid by 2132
. interest 1704
. medical expenses paid by 2150
. OID accrual on pool of receivables 1313
. rebates, charitable contributions of 2106
. reporting of credit card sales 4746
. tax payments made with 3155; 4720
Credits See also "Energy credits"
    generally . . . . 2300 et seq.
. accumulated earnings tax 3319
. adoption expenses 2354
. American opportunity tax credit . . . . 2201 et seq.
. amount of, limitation on 4856
. basis of property reduced by credits 2478
. bonds, credit for holders of tax credit bonds 2366
. business . . . . 2301 et seq.
. carryovers . . . . 2304 et seq.
. child care . . . . 2349 et seq.
. . employer-provided child care credit 2330
. child tax credit . . . . 2355 et seq.
. deficiency due to election of, assessment
    period 4830
. differential wage payment credit for em-
    ployers 2336
. disabled access credit 2323
. disabled, permanently and totally 2348
. earned income See "Earned income credit"
. education expenses . . . . 2200 et seq.
. elderly, for 2348
. election to swap bonus and accelerated de-
    preciation for certain credits 1939
. elective deferrals, credit for 2363
. empowerment zone employment credit 2325
. erroneous, interest on 4865

Credits *See also "Energy credits"* — **Cont'd**
. estates and trusts 3920
. estate tax
. . foreign death taxes 5032
. . gift tax 5031
. . prior transfers, credit for tax on 5030
. federal unemployment tax (FUTA) 1110
. foreign corporations 4646
. foreign tax *See "Foreign tax credit"*
. general business credit . . . . 2302 et seq.
. gift tax 5050
. health insurance
. . costs of trade-displaced workers and
. . . . PBGC pension recipients 2344
. . premium tax credit 2345
. . small employer health insurance credit 2332
. household and dependent care credit . . . . . . 2349 et seq.
. Indian employment credit 2326
. investment credit . . . . 2305 et seq.
. IRA contributions, credit for 2363
. Lifetime Learning credit 2201; 2203;
. . . . 2204
. limitations on 2303; 2364;
. . . . 2370; 2371
. low-income housing credit 2320; 2321
. minimum tax credit 2365; 3573
. mortgage credit 2357
. new markets tax credit 2329
. nonrefundable 2338; 2364
. nonresident aliens 4646
. nontax debts, applied to 4848
. ordering rules 2306
. orphan drug credit 2328
. overpayments, generally 4869
. passive activity credits . . . . 1810 et seq.
. personal credits . . . . 2338 et seq.;
. . . . 2364
. qualified clinical testing expense credit 2328
. recaptured tax credits, basis 2479
. refundable credits . . . . 2338 et seq.;
. . . . 4857
. rehabilitation credit . . . . 2308 et seq.
. research credit 2319
. small employer pension plan startup credit 2331
. Social Security credit for employee tips 2327
. tax credit bonds, credit for holders of 2366
. unused qualified business credits, deduc-
. . . . tion of 2305
. withheld tax on wages
. . generally 2346
. . Social Security tax, excess withholding 2347
. work opportunity credit 2316; 2317
Credit unions 4100
Criminal penalties
. generally 4901
. restitution payments 4827
. tax evasion 4900
Crop method of accounting 4512
Cruises
. conventions on cruise ships, deductibility 1550
. education expenses 2227
Crummey power 3962; 5046
Custodial accounts 2206; 4368;
. . . . 4383; 5007;
. . . . 5046

D

Daily lease value (automobiles) 1235
Damages
. business damages 1383
. compensatory damages, deductibility 1613

Damages — **Cont'd**
. deduction for payment of 1630
. fraudulent information returns, for filing 4899
. nonbusiness 1381
. personal injuries or sickness
. . compensation for 2151
. . exclusion from gross income . . . . 1380 et seq.
. suit against IRS for 4907; 4908
Day care facility, home-office deduction 1641
Dealers
. installment sales by 2454
. reserves, accrual basis 2828
. securities dealers
. . generally 2628
. . amortization 2173
. . futures contracts 2663
. . mark-to-market rules 2879
Death benefits
. generally . . . . 1260 et seq.
. acceleration of, chronically or terminally ill 1351
. acceleration of, for chronically or terminally
. . ill 4746
. annuities
. . investment in the contract 1361
. . survivors of public safety officers killed in
. . . line of duty 1260
. astronauts dying in line of duty, exclusion
. . . from gross income 1206
. employee's beneficiaries 1534
. employer-owned life insurance 1353
. life insurance proceeds . . . . 1346 et seq.
. qualified retirement plan participants dying
. . . during military service 4331
. terrorism victims, exclusion from gross in-
. . . come 1206
Debit cards
. business payments of $600 or more 4743
. tax payments 3155; 4720
Debt-financed property, UBTI 4123
Debt instruments
. adequate stated interest 1318
. amortization 1975
. basis in 2470; 2499;
. . . . 3371
. corporate debt payable in issuer's stock,
. . . interest deduction 1710
. imputed principal amount of 1319
. inflation-indexed . . . . 1321; 1333 et
. . . . seq.
. issue price 1317
. modification of instrument treated as ex-
. . . change 2412
. nonpublicly traded, exception to OID rules 1320
. original issue discount (OID) . . . . 1313 et seq.;
. . . . 1751 et seq.
. retirement 2678
Debts *See also "Bad debts"*
. allocation rules . . . . 1737 et seq.
. assets taken for 2679
. . bankruptcy or foreclosure 3518
. assumption of *See "Assumption of liabili-
. . ties"*
. debt-for-debt exchanges 1396
. discharge or cancellation of *See "Discharge
. . of indebtedness"*
. employee's, paid by employer 1253; 1509;
. . . . 1521
. equity vs. 1709
. nonrecourse *See "Nonrecourse debt"*
. property transfer to discharge 2468; 2679
. service rights to, depreciation 1962
. stock-for-debt exchanges 1395

Debts *See also "Bad debts"* — **Cont'd**
. stockholder's, paid by corporation 1289
Decedent
. annuities and annuity contracts
. . after-death distribution requirements 1358
. . unrecovered investment in annuity con-
     tract 3967
. capital losses of 2612
. deductions in respect of . . . . 3926; 3965 et
                                                              seq.
. exemptions of 3116; 3128
. income in respect of 2513; 2516;
                                                      3965 et seq.
. individual retirement account of 4352; 4365;
                                                      4366; 4373
. installment obligations, income from 3969
. medical expenses of 2143
. military and U.S. civilian employees dying
     in combat or terrorist attacks, tax relief 4715
. partner
. . income included in final return 3773
. . liquidating payments from partnership . . . . 3768 et seq.
. pre-death transfers 2516
. principal residence, exclusion of gain on
     sale 2445
. property acquired from
. . appreciated property reacquired by donor 2514
. . basis of 1911; 2507;
                                                      2512 et seq.
. . carryover basis rules for decedents dying
     in 2010 2523
. . community property 2518
. . contingent remainder interests 2521
. . estate tax value also income tax basis 2513
. . gross estate of decedent, inclusion in 2516
. . holding period of 2672
. . inter vivos trusts 2519
. . joint tenants 2517
. . multiple interests in one property 2522
. . passive activity interest 1838
. . postponed interests 2521
. . powers of appointment 2520
. . tenants by the entirety 2517
. . time property considered acquired from 2515
. returns for
     generally 4714
. . assessment of tax, prompt 4838
. . charitable contribution carryover 2130
. . executors and administrators 4714; 4915
. . filing threshold 4701
. . income and deductions . . . . 3965 et seq.
. . joint 4708
. . personal exemption 3116
. . refund claim, overpaid taxes 4847
. . standard deduction 3112
. stock owned by, redemption of 3532
. withholding on accrued wages of 3006
Declaratory judgments 4858
Declining-balance depreciation *See "De-
  preciation"*
Deductions *See also individual listing of
  specific item*
. individual taxpayer average deductions 4804
Deemed IRAs 4376
Deferred compensation
. credit for elective deferrals 2363
. deducting, time for 1538; 1539
. rabbi trusts 1276
. reporting 1275
. restricted stock . . . . 1217 et seq.
. substantial risk of forfeiture 1217; 1275

Deferred compensation — **Cont'd**
. tax-indifferent corporations and partner-
     ships, from 1277
. withholding 3031
Deferred payment sales . . . . 2452 et seq.
. repossessions 2406
. unstated interest on . . . . 1307 et seq.;
                                                              1707
Deferred rental agreements 1342; 1600
Deficiencies
. defined 4823
. interest on . . . . 4864 et seq.
. notice of tax deficiency, 90-day letter *See
     "90-day letter"*
. proposed 4814
. revenue agent's report (RAR) 4813
. Tax Court review 4859
Deficiency dividends 1299; 3336
**Defined benefit and defined contribution
  plans** 4311; 4318;
                                                      4324; 4328 et
                                                              seq.
Delinquent returns 4873
Delinquent tax payments, interest 1708
Demand loans, below-market loans 1306
De minimis fringe benefits 1246; 1569
Demolition
. losses 1783
Dental expenses *See "Medical and dental
  expenses"*
Dependent care assistance programs
     generally 1270
. armed forces 1223
. cafeteria plans 1269
. withholding, exemption 3006
Dependents
. age test 3120
. birth of 3128
. credit for care of *See "Child and dependent
     care credit"*
. death of 3128
. divorced or separated parents, children of 3126
. earned income credit 2341
. education credits . . . . 2202 et seq.
. education expenses, deduction 2231
. exemptions . . . . 3015; 3119 et
                                                              seq.
. group-term life insurance coverage of 1264
. health coverage tax credit for
     trade-displaced workers and PBGC
     pension recipients 2344
. health savings accounts (HSAs) 1378
. income tax returns 4701
. kidnapped children 3129
. medical expenses of 1255; 2142
. multiple support agreement 3123
. personal exemptions . . . . 3115 et seq.
. qualifying child 3120
. relationship test . . . . 3120 et seq.
. relatives, qualifying 3122
. release of deduction by custodial parent 3126
. standard deduction 3112
. student loan interest deduction 2223
. students 3120
. support of . . . . 3123 et seq.
. . alimony as 2159
. . legal obligation 3959
. two or more taxpayers, qualifying child of 3121
. withholding 3017
Depletion
     generally . . . . 1976 et seq.
. alternative minimum tax preference 3208; 3211

Depletion — Cont'd
. basis adjustment for 2476
. capital expenditures 1655
. earnings and profits, adjustments to 3525
. estates and trusts 3927
. percentage depletion . . . . 1978 et seq.
. research and experimental expenses 1602

Deposit of tax payments
. corporations 4730
. electronic funds transfer 3028
. employment tax
. . electronic funds transfer 3028
. . safe harbor and de minimis rules 3027
. . time for deposit 3026
. interest on overpayments
. . deposit rules for purposes of 4853
. interest on underpayments
. . deposits to stop running of 4868
. nonpayroll withheld taxes 3031
. penalties 4898

Deposits
. container 2847
. security 1206; 2831

Depreciation
        generally . . . . 1900 et seq.
. accounting methods
. . carryover of method by acquiring corpora-
        tion 3564
. . change of 2839; 2845
. ACRS (accelerated cost recovery system)
. . effect on earnings and profits 3524
. ADS (alternative depreciation system)
        generally . . . . 1907; 1930 et
                                                            seq.
. . effect on earnings and profits 3524
. . property depreciated under 1921
. . straight-line recovery period 1925; 1930;
                                                        1932; 1948
. . tables 1116
. alternative minimum tax 3207; 3211;
                                                            3213
. automobiles 1558; 1560;
                                                        1946 et seq.
. basis
        generally 1922; 1961;
                                                            2476
. . bonus first-year depreciation 1933
. . carryover basis property 1911
. . property acquired from decedent 2517
. bonus first-year depreciation allowance
        generally 1933
. . automobiles 1953
. . biofuel plant property 1940
. . date of acquisition requirement 1936
. . disaster assistance property, qualified 1940
. . election not to claim or to claim at re-
        duced rate . . . . 1938 et seq.
. . election to swap bonus and accelerated
        depreciation for certain credits 1939
. . excluded property 1934
. . 50% (instead of 100%) bonus deprecia-
        tion allowance 1933
. . Gulf Opportunity Zone property 1940
. . New York Liberty Zone property 1940
. . original-use requirement 1935
. . placed-in-service requirement . . . . 1937 et seq.
. . qualified disaster assistance property 1942
. . qualified property . . . . 1934 et seq.
. . qualified reuse and recycling property 1940
. . reconditioned or rebuilt property 1935
. . self-constructed property 1936
. buildings 1920

Depreciation — Cont'd
. capital expenditures 1655
. carryovers 1904
. claiming deduction 1901
. . automobiles 1954
. computer software 1623; 1934;
                                                            1962
. copyrights 1959; 1962
. declining balance method 1925; 4523
. depreciable property 1902
. . as capital assets 2617
. . capital gain bar on sales between related
        persons 2690; 2691
. depreciation conventions . . . . 1905 et seq.
. earnings and profits, effect on 3524
. estates and trusts 3927
. failure to deduct 1901
. farming property 4523
. GDS (general depreciation system) 1116; 1907
. income forecast method 1959
. Indian reservation property 1924
. intangible assets 1903; 1962
. inventory 1902
. leased property 1598; 1904
. life tenant, deductions of 3102
. livestock 1914; 1915;
                                                            4523
. MACRS (modified ACRS)
        generally . . . . 1900; 1907 et
                                                            seq.
. . additions to property 1921
. . agricultural products, assets used in pro-
        duction of 1917
. . agricultural structures 1917; 1932
. . air transport, assets used in 1916
. . allocation method 1926
. . amusement parks and recreational facili-
        ties 1916
. . anti-churning rules 1908
. . automobiles
        generally 1915; 1932
. . business . . . . 1117; 1951 et
                                                            seq.
. . luxury . . . . 1931; 1946 et
                                                            seq.
. . basis of recovery property 1922
. . buildings, residential and nonresidential 1920; 1927
. . business property converted to or from
        personal use 1928
. . cargo containers, intermodal 1931
. . cattle 1915
. . change in use of property 1928
. . classes (recovery) . . . . 1913 et seq.
. . computers 1915; 1955
. . condition of employment requirement for
        listed property 1955
. . construction, assets used in 1915
. . consumer durable property subject to
        rent-to-own contracts 1914; 1915;
                                                            1932
. . declining balance methods 1925
. . depreciation conventions . . . . 1905 et seq.
. . earnings and profits, effect on 3524
. . electrical transmission property 1917; 1918;
                                                        1925; 1932
. . equipment or fixtures 1916
. . excluded property 1908
. . exempt bonds, property financed by 1931
. . farming property 1915; 1919;
                                                        1932; 4523
. . 15-year property 1918
. . 5-year property 1915

Depreciation — Cont'd
. MACRS (modified ACRS) — Cont'd
.. furniture 1916
.. general asset accounts 1909; 1928
.. golf course greens 1918
.. half-year convention 1926; 1927
.. horses 1914; 1916
.. horticultural structures 1917; 1932
.. imports from restricted countries 1931
.. improvements to real property 1918; 1921;
                                                               1932
.. inclusion amounts
... leased automobiles 1117; 1956;
                                                               1957
... leased listed property other than auto-
       mobiles 1958
.. Indian reservation property 1924
.. intangible property, ineligible for MACRS 1908
.. involuntary conversion, property acquired
       in 1929
.. leased automobiles 1117; 1956;
                                                               1957
.. leasehold improvements 1918; 1923;
                                                          1932; 1934
.. like-kind exchange, property acquired in 1929
.. listed property
       generally . . . . 1946 et seq.
... business/investment use defined 1950
... computers, home 1955
... condition of employment requirement 1955
... 50% qualified business use 1948
... leased property . . . . 1956 et seq.
... qualified business use 1949
... requirements 1931; 1955
.. low-income housing 1932
.. luxury automobiles . . . . 1931; 1946 et
                                                               seq.
.. machinery and equipment 1914
.. methods of depreciation 1925
.. mid-month convention 1927
.. mid-quarter convention 1926; 1927
.. motion picture films 1908; 1927
.. motorsports entertainment complexes 1916
.. multiple asset accounts 1910
.. oil and gas
... drilling, assets used in 1915
... exploration, assets used in 1916
... pipelines 1916; 1918;
                                                               1932
... refining, assets used in 1917
.. optional rate tables 1912
.. part business/part personal use property 1927
.. periods, recovery 1924; 1932
.. personal property . . . . 1926 et seq.
.. pollution control facilities 1968
.. pre-production costs of farming 1931
.. public utility property 1908; 1919;
                                                               1924
.. qualified business use 1949
.. qualified technological equipment 1915; 1932
.. railroad tracks 1916; 1924;
                                                          1925; 1927;
                                                               1932
.. real property . . . . 1918 et seq.
... deductions in short tax years 1926
.. restaurant property 1918; 1925;
                                                          1932; 1934
.. retail improvement property 1918; 1925;
                                                          1932; 1934
.. sale or disposition of property 1905; 1906;
                                                          1909; 1910
.. Section 1245 property 2693

Depreciation — Cont'd
. MACRS (modified ACRS) — Cont'd
.. Section 1250 property 1918; 1932;
                                                               2694
.. service stations and car washes 1915; 1918;
                                                               1932
.. 7-year property 1916
.. short tax year . . . . 1926 et seq.
.. simplified method 1926
.. smart electric meters and grids 1917
.. sound recordings 1908; 1927
.. straight-line method
       generally 1925
... alternative depreciation system (ADS) 1930
.. straight-line periods 1932
.. tables 1116
.. tax-exempt use property 1931
.. telephone distribution plants 1918
.. telephone equipment 1915; 1932
.. 10-year property 1917
.. textiles, assets used in manufacture of 1915
.. 31.5-year property 1920
.. 39-year property 1920
.. 3-year property 1914
.. timber, assets used in cutting of 1915
.. trucks 1915; 1932
.. tunnel bores 1924; 1925;
                                                               1927
.. 20-year property 1919
.. 27.5-year property 1920
.. video tapes 1908; 1927
.. vines, fruit or nut bearing 1917; 1925;
                                                               1932
.. wastewater treatment plants 1918
.. water transport equipment 1917
.. water utility property 1924; 1925
. mileage, on the basis of, for autos 2476
. motion picture films 1927; 1959
. natural resources 1902
. operating day method 1963
. party entitled to deduction 1904
. patents 1959; 1962
. period of depreciation 1905
. personal holding companies 3321
. personal use property . . . . 1902; 1926 et
                                                               seq.
. qualifying property 1902
. real property . . . . 1902; 1918 et
                                                               seq.
.. character of installment gain where de-
       preciable realty sold 2457
. recapture of
       generally . . . . 2692 et seq.
.. bonus first-year depreciation 1940
.. "dispositions" triggering 2699
.. film and TV production costs, expensing
       of 1965
.. investment credit, basis reduction for 2698
.. listed property 1948
.. special rules for 2700
.. partnerships 3710
.. realty disposed of by corporations, addi-
       tional 20% recapture 2697
.. Section 179 expense election 2695
.. Section 1231 assets, effect on 2685
.. Section 1245 property 2695
.. Section 1250 property 2696
. research and experimental expenses 1602
. Section 1245 property 1932; 1944
.. defined 2693
.. recapture . . . . 2692 et seq.
. Section 1250 property

Depreciation — Cont'd
. Section 1250 property — Cont'd
  generally 1932
. . alternative minimum tax 3207
. . defined 2694
. . recapture . . . . 2692 et seq.
. . unrecaptured Sec. 1250 gain 2605
. sinking fund method 1963
. sound recordings 1908; 1927;
                                    1959
. straight-line method
  generally 1925
. . alternative depreciation system (ADS) 1930; 1948
. . farming property 4523
. tables, MACRS 1912
. . luxury automobiles 1952
. unit of production method 1963
. use change, following 1928
. useful life of asset
  generally . . . . 1900 et seq.;
                                  1960; 1963
. . intangibles excluded from 15-year amorti-
    zation 1962
. video tapes 1908; 1927;
                                  1959
. water utility property 1924; 1925;
                            1932; 1934
. wear, tear, exhaustion, or obsolescence of
    property, significance of 1902
. year of sale or disposition 1905
Designated settlement fund 2835; 4726
Determination letters
. exempt status 4116
. . modification or revocation of 4117
. pension and profit-sharing plans 4332
**Diagnostic tests, medical expense deduc-
tion** 2144
Diesel fuel
. biodiesel fuel credit 2333
Differential pay
. as compensation
. . for purposes of IRA contribution rules 4352
. . for retirement plan purposes 4331
. credit for eligible small business employers 2336
Directors
. entertainment provided to treated as com-
    pensation 1572
. fees 3520
Direct pay tax credit bonds 2366
Direct sales, information returns 4746
Disability *See also "Handicapped"*
. benefits
. . accident or health insurance, received
      through 1375
. . cafeteria plans 1269
. . government and military pensions 1278; 1284
. . limb, loss of 1258
. . state plan, deduction for contributions to . . . 1758
. . unemployment compensation 1281
. permanent and total, credit for 2348
. refund claims, limitation period 4854
. work opportunity credit, disabled veterans 2316
Disabled access credit 2323
Disaster assistance property
. alternative minimum tax depreciation ad-
    justment 3207
. bonus first-year depreciation allowance for
    qualified property 1940
. Section 179 expensing election, increased 1942
Disaster losses
. early deduction 1792; 1798
. federally declared disaster

Disaster losses — Cont'd
. federally declared disaster — Cont'd
  generally 1798
. . net operating losses 1841
. . principal residence 2433
. . replacement period 2441
. . trade or business property 2438
. net operating losses
. . carryback and carryover 3212
. . federally declared disaster 1841
Disaster relief
. abatement of interest 4870
. extensions of time for taxpayers affected by
    federally declared disaster 4719
. farmers 4508
. like-kind exchanges, time limits on 2423
. mitigation payments, exclusion for 1207
. qualified disaster relief payments
. . defined 1207
. . exclusion for 1207
. reasonable cause exception to penalties 4872
. self-employment tax 3143
. state grants, corporation's election to defer
    gain on proceeds used to purchase
    similar property 2431
. waiver of penalties 3165
DISC *See "Domestic international sales corporations"*
Discharge of indebtedness
. bankrupt debtors 1390
. debt-for-debt exchanges 1396
. discounted purchase of debtor's own obli-
    gations 1394
. home mortgage debt 1397
. income from . . . . 1385 et seq.;
                                     1788
. information returns 4746
. insolvent debtors 1389
. partnerships 1393; 3723
. property, satisfaction of debt with 1395; 2468;
                                     2679
. qualified real property business indebted-
    ness,
. . income from discharge of excluded from
      gross income 1392
. S corporations 1393
. services, satisfaction of debt with 1395
. solvent debtors 1388; 1391
. student loans 1387
Disclaimers, qualified 5043
Disclosure
. charitable contributions, deductibility 4118; 4119
. confidential tax avoidance transactions,
    participation in 4749
. exempt organizations 4120
. specified foreign financial assets 4673
. tax return preparers, improper disclosure
    by 4888
. tax shelter prohibited transactions 4114
Discount coupons 2847
Discounts, employee 1244
Discrimination
. age discrimination
. . in retirement plans 4311
. . withholding on settlement payments 3004
. job discrimination damages 1381
. legal fees in connection with, deduction for 3108
Disproportionate distributions
. partnerships
  generally . . . . 3754 et seq.
. . gain or loss on 3758
. . inventory items 3757

Disproportionate distributions — Cont'd
. partnerships — Cont'd
. . sales and exchanges as disproportionate
    distributions 3755
. . unrealized receivables 3754
. stock or rights 1296
Disqualifying dispositions 1221; 1525
Disregarded entities
. employment taxes 3001
. mergers 3544
Dissolution of corporation *See "Liquida-*
    tions"
Distributable net income (DNI) . . . . 3933 et seq.
Distributions
. corporations *See also "Dividends"*
    generally . . . . 1285 et seq.
. . earnings and profits . . . . 3521 et seq.
. . liquidating . . . . 3333; 3574 et
                                                                  seq.
. . nonliquidating . . . . 3538 et seq.
. . redemptions of stock . . . . 3526 et seq.
. . S corporations 3372
. . Section 306 stock . . . . 3535 et seq.
. . separations, corporate 3562
. . spin-off, split-off or split-up 3560
. . stock or stock rights 3540
. donor advised funds 4129; 4130
. employee stock ownership plans (ESOPs) 4314
. estate or trust . . . . 3918; 3933 et
                                                                   seq.
. individual retirement accounts (IRAs)
    generally 4357
. . Roth IRAs 4373; 4374
. nonqualified deferred compensation plans 1275
. partnerships
    generally . . . . 3742 et seq.
. . basis . . . . 3777 et seq.
. . disproportionate distributions . . . . 3754 et seq.
. . foreign partners, withholding on distribu-
    tions to 4670
. . termination of partnership 3782
. qualified retirement plans . . . . 4338 et seq.
Distributorship, canceling 2680
District courts 4858; 4862
District of Columbia
. qualifying DC zone assets, capital gain ex-
    clusion 2650; 2652
Dividends
. alternative minimum tax 3201; 3202
. amount of, determination of 1292; 1296
. amounts not received as annuity 1366
. basis of property received as . . . . 1293; 2492 et
                                                                   seq.
. below-market loans 1291
. CFC stock disposition as 4625
. compensation as 1517
. consent 3334
. constructive or disguised . . . . 1289 et seq.
. cooperatives, patronage dividends 1300
. debt treated as equity, payments on 1709
. deficiency 3336
. definition 1287
. effectively connected income 4644
. exempt-interest dividends, loss on 2632
. extraordinary dividends 1288; 2495;
                                                                  3935
. foreign corporations 4647
. foreign tax credit . . . . 2370 et seq.
. fractional shares, cash for 1297
. holding period for property received 1294
. income, as . . . . 1285 et seq.

Dividends — Cont'd
. information returns 4738; 4739;
                                                                  4898
. life insurance, on 1350
. loans vs. 1290
. nondeductible 3315
. partnerships 3718
. passive investment income test for bank S
    corporations 3366
. patronage dividends *See Patronage divi-*
    dends
. payee statements 4742
. payments in lieu of 1288
. persons taxable 1286
. portfolio income 1820
. preferred stock 1296
. property distributions . . . . 1287; 1292 et
                                                                   seq.
. qualified dividend income, defined 1288
. real estate investment trusts (REITs) 1299; 4203
. redemptions 3533
. . not essentially equivalent to dividend 3530
. regulated investment companies (RICs) 1298; 4203
. reinvestment plans
. . basis of stock acquired through 2494
. . wash sale loss disallowance rule 2462
. rent as 1594
. S corporations 3367
. Sec. 306 stock . . . . 3535 et seq.
. self-employment tax 3143
. source of (U.S. or foreign) 4640
. stock or rights . . . . 1295 et seq.
. . basis . . . . 2492 et seq.
. . earnings and profits, effect on 3523
. . Sec. 306 stock . . . . 3535 et seq.
. taxable . . . . 1285 et seq.
. tax year considered paid 1298; 1299
. time dividends become taxable 1286
. unrelated business income of exempt or-
    ganizations 4122
. U.S. source income not effectively connect-
    ed with U.S. business 4642
. withholding 4667
. . backup withholding 3044
. . back-up withholding 3045
Dividends-paid deduction . . . . 1845; 3330 et
                                                                  seq.

Dividends-received deduction
    generally . . . . 3306 et seq.
. alternative minimum tax 3211
. consolidated returns 3338
. holding period . . . . 3312 et seq.
. net operating losses, computation 1845
. portfolio stock 3314
. small business investment companies 4205
Divorce *See also "Alimony"*
. dependent care credit 2353
. dependents
. . effect on dependent status 3128
. . exemptions 3126
. . medical expense deduction 2142
. legal fees for, deductibility 2166
. lump-sum payments 1312
. separate liability election 4710
. transfers incident to
    generally 2447
. . basis 2524
. . IRA interests 4357
. . original issue discount 1320
. withholding allowances, effect on 3018

DNI (Distributable net income) . . . . 3933 et seq.
Doctors and dentists *See also "Medical and*
dental expenses"
. expenses incurred by 1636; 1640
. student loan programs, cancellation of debt
under 1387
Dollar-value LIFO 2875
Domestic international sales corporations
. boycott 4632
. consolidated returns, includible corpora-
tions 3339
. dividends from 3315
. interest charge DISC 4621
. penalties related to 4898
. S corporations, as 3351
. taxable year 2809
Domestic partners
. community property 1203
. dependency exemptions . . . . 3120 et seq.
. head of household status 3134
Domestic production activities deduction . . . . 1614 et seq.
Domestic service 3006; 3029;
3030
Domestic violence
. equitable relief for spouses 4711
Donations *See "Charitable contributions"*
Donor advised funds (DAFs)
. *generally* 2118; 4125
. excess benefit transactions 4112
. exempt status, application for 4116
. information returns 4124; 4746
. prohibited benefits received by donor, advi-
sor or related person 4130
. taxable distributions, excise tax on 4129
Drilling and development costs 1627; 1628
Drought
. disaster losses 1798; 4508
. involuntary conversions 2432
. livestock sold because of 2432; 2438;
2441; 4508
. replanting costs incurred because of 4520
Drugs
. illegal, trafficking in 1612
. . education credits, effect on 2202
. . income from 1200
. . medical expenses, as 2144
. . qualified medical expenses, only pre-
scribed drugs as . . . . 1377 et seq.
. Social Security subsidies received by spon-
sors of qualified retiree prescription
drug plans 1206
Dual citizenship, expatriation rules 4653; 4654
Dual resident corporations 3342
Due dates of returns *See "Returns"*
Dues, business expense
. clubs 1568
. deductible costs 1514
. labor unions 1633
. miscellaneous itemized deductions 3110
. professional societies 1635; 1636
Dwelling unit
. depreciation 1920
. like-kind exchanges 2419
. nonbusiness energy property credit 2358
. residential energy efficient property credit 2359

E

Early distributions, penalties 4344; 4374
. exceptions 4344
Earned income
. child care credit, limitation 2352

Earned income — **Cont'd**
. dependent care assistance payments, limi-
tation 1270
. earned income credit 2340
. foreign 2372; 3006;
4612 et seq.
. self-employed, of
. . IRAs 4352
. . Keogh plans 4327
Earned income credit
. *generally* . . . . 2339 et seq.
. combat pay as earned income, election to
treat 2340
. definition of earned income 2340
. disqualified income 2342
. eligible individual defined 2341
. notice 3023
. qualifying child
. . defined 2343
. . eligible individual with 2341
. . kidnapped child as 3129
. return preparers, due diligence 4888
. tables 1112
Earnings and profits
. accumulation of, tax on *See "Accumulated*
earnings tax"
. adjustments to . . . . 3523 et seq.
. alternative minimum tax preference 3211
. carryovers, acquiring corporations 3564
. depreciation, effect of 3524
. distributions from . . . . 3521 et seq.
. distributions in excess of 1286
. real estate investment trusts 4202
. redemptions through related corporations 3533
. reorganization or liquidation 3564
. S corporations 3373
. spin-offs, split-offs and split-ups 3560
Economic interest
. depletion allowance for 1976; 1981
. timber, coal or iron ore sold with retained
interest 2688
Economic performance, accrual basis 2833
Economic substance
. penalty for transactions lacking 4895
Educational organizations 2216
. charitable contributions 2102; 2124
. . scientific property 2108
. qualified school construction bonds, credit
for 2366
. qualified zone academy bonds, credit for 2366
. tax exemption 4100; 4102
. tax-sheltered annuities . . . . 4388 et seq.
Education expenses *See also "Tuition"*
. above-the-line deduction . . . . 2230 et seq.
. American opportunity tax credit . . . . 2201 et seq.
. armed forces members 1223
. business or employment, related to 2225; 2226
. Coverdell education savings accounts (ES-
As) . . . . 2205 et seq.
. deductions . . . . 2200 et seq.
. employer's education assistance program 2213
. . educational assistance defined 2215
. . exclusion as working condition fringe 2214
. . exclusion under qualified program 2215
. . tuition reduction for school employees 2217
. exclusions . . . . 2200 et seq.
. information returns 4746
. Lifetime Learning credit 2201; 2203;
2204
. professionals 1636
. qualified education expenses defined

Education expenses *See also "Tuition"* — **Cont'd**
. qualified education expenses defined — Cont'd
. . for Coverdell education savings accounts
      (ESAs) 2208
. . for education credits 2204
. . for expense deduction purposes 2231; 2232
. . for qualified tuition programs 2211
. . for savings bond exclusion 2221
. qualified education loans
. . deduction for interest paid on . . . . 2222 et seq.
. . defined 2224
. qualified tuition programs (Sec. 529 plans) . . . . 2209 et seq.
. savings bond interest exclusion for qualified
      higher education expenses . . . . 2219 et seq.
. seminar cruises or tours, costs of 2227
. support, as 3124
. tax credits . . . . 2200 et seq.
. teachers, deduction for 2228
. travel and transportation expenses 2227
Educators *See "Teachers"*
EE bonds 1334
Effectively connected income
      generally . . . . 4644 et seq.
. withholding 4662; 4666;
                                                     4667; 4669

Elderly
. additional standard deduction 3016; 3112
. catch-up contributions to pension, etc.
      plans 1529; 4317;
                                                     4351; 4369;
                                                     4384
. credit for 2348
. estimated tax penalty, waiver of 3165
. in-home care payments by state agency,
      exclusion from income 1206
. medical expense deduction 2141
. withholding 3017
Elections
. advance payments, to defer 2830
. alcohol fuel credit, to not take 2318
. alternate valuation date, to use for estate
      tax 5016
. alternative depreciation system (ADS) 1930
. annuities, variable, to recompute excluda-
      ble amount 1359
. architectural and transportation barrier re-
      moval expenses, to deduct 1621
. bank deposit loss, to treat as casualty loss
      or ordinary loss 1802
. basis
. . mutual fund shares 2498
. . partnership property . . . . 3776 et seq.
. . "split basis" approach for relinquished
      and replacement properties 1929
. bond discount, accrued market, to include
      in income currently 1327
. bond premium amortization 2172
. bonus first-year depreciation allowance
. . automobiles 1953
. . election out . . . . 1938 et seq.
. . swapped for certain credits 1939
. capital asset treatment for musical compo-
      sitions or copyrights 2622
. capitalize, to
. . business expenses 1617
. . carrying charges 1620
. . circulation expenses 1619
. . election to not capitalize 1660
. . intangible costs, oil and gas wells 1628
. . repairs and maintenance 1656
. charitable contributions

Elections — **Cont'd**
. charitable contributions — Cont'd
. . accrual corporations, year of deduction
      for 2133
. . appreciated capital gain property, to have
      50% ceiling apply 2127
. child's unearned income, to include on par-
      ent's return 3139
. conservation easement, land subject to,
      partial exclusion from gross estate 5016
. consolidated returns, to file 3338
. deferral of compensation 1275
. depletion 1981
. disabled access credit 2323
. disaster losses 1798
. dividends
. . RIC and REIT dividends paid after close
      of tax year 4203
. estates and trusts
. . trusts and estates, below
. estate tax
. . deceased spousal unused exclusion
      amount 5029
. . out of, decedents dying in 2010 2523
. . special use valuation 5017
. expatriation, deferral of tax on 4653
. expensing *See "Expensing elections";*
      "Section 179 expense election"
. extensions of time for making 4735
. farmers
. . disaster payments, deferral of reporting 4508
. . fertilizer costs 4516
. . income averaging 4502
. . loan proceeds treated as income where
      crops pledged as security 4528
. . net operating loss, three- or five-year car-
      ryback 4503
. . plant or livestock costs 4507; 4521
. . soil and water conservation expenses, to
      deduct currently 4522
. fiscal year, to use 2813
. foreign corporations, to be U.S. corpora-
      tions 4650
. foreign currency
. . functional, to use dollar as 4675
. . gain or loss on certain contracts, to treat
      as capital gain or loss 4676
. foreign earned income exclusion 4617
. foreign housing cost exclusion 4613; 4617
. foreign tax credit . . . . 2367 et seq.
. fringe benefits, vehicles, to not withhold on . . . 3007
. individual retirement accounts (IRAs), sur-
      viving spouse 4365
. installment method, out of 2456
. inventory (LIFO) 2874
. investment credit, to pass through to lessee . . . 2307
. itemizing deductions 3113
. long-term contracts
. . accounting methods, generally 2849
. . look-back method, not to apply 2854
. . modified percentage-of-completion (10%)
      method 2853
. . simplified cost-to-cost method 2851
. low-income housing credit, to begin credit
      period in year after building is placed in
      service 2320
. lump-sum distributions 4339
. MACRS (modified accelerated cost recov-
      ery system)
. . dispositions of assets 1906
. . general asset and vintage accounts 1909
. . straight-line method 1925

References are to paragraph [¶] numbers.

Elections — Cont'd
. marital deduction for QTIP property 5023
. market discount, accrued, to include in in-
　　come 1327
. mark-to-market rules
. . PFIC stock 4630
. . securities and commodities traders 2880
. mine development costs 1627
. mine exploration costs 1626
. mixed straddle account, to establish 2658
. music, amortization of expenses to create
　　or acquire 1969
. net operating loss
. . carryback, to forego 1842; 3212
. . three-, four-, or five-year carryback 1841
. organization costs, deduction of 3520; 3707
. partnerships
. . audit procedures, unified, small partner-
　　　ship to be covered by 4845
. . basis . . . . 3776 et seq.
. . fiscal year, to use 2812
. . not to be taxed as 3705
. . organization expenses, to amortize 3707
. . taxable income, elections affecting 3723
. personal holding companies, late-paid divi-
　　dends, to deduct 3332
. plug-in electric vehicle credit, election out 2362
. pollution control facilities, amortization of 1968
. property tax, to accrue ratably 1769
. publicly traded debt instruments, recogni-
　　tion of gain or loss on exchange 2412
. qualified electing fund, PFIC treatment 4629
. qualified real property business indebted-
　　ness, treatment of indebtedness as 1392
. qualified residence, second home treated
　　as 1735
. real estate (U.S.) income, to treat as effec-
　　tively connected 4643
. real property interests, treatment of multiple
　　properties as single interest for pur-
　　poses of passive activity loss rules 1836
. research and experimental expenditures
. . capitalization or current deduction 1601; 1602
. . credit for, reduction of 2319
. resident aliens' "first year" election to be
　　taxed as U.S. resident 4636
. restricted stock, to not defer income 1218
. rights, stock (warrants), to allocate basis to 2493
. rollover of gain
　　generally 2426
. . qualified empowerment zone assets 2428
. . qualified small business stock 2429
. . specialized small business investment
　　　companies, into 2427
. S corporations
. . distributions from, to treat as made out of
　　　accumulated earnings and profits 3372
. . election to be treated as
　　generally 3356
. . . relief for late or nonexistent election 3358
. . . revocation or termination of election . . . . . . 3375 et seq.
. . . shareholder consents 3357
. . fiscal year, to use 2813
. . qualified Subchapter S trust, by benefici-
　　　ary of to be treated as shareholder 3354
. Sec. 1256 contract losses, to carry back 2659
. Section 179 expense election See "Section
　　179 expense election"
. self-employment tax
. . clergy or members of religious sects, to
　　　not be covered by 3146; 3147
. . optional methods of computing 3149

Elections — Cont'd
. separate liability of spouses 4710
. small employer pension plan startup credit,
　　to not apply 2331
. Social Security benefits, lump-sum, to treat
　　as received in earlier years 1279
. start-up expenses, to amortize . . . . 1500 et seq.
. state and local sales tax, election to deduct
　　in lieu of state income tax 1756
. stock purchase as asset purchase . . . . 3581 et seq.
. stock sales as asset transfers 3587
. straddles, mixed, to exclude from
　　mark-to-market rules 2658
. Tax Court, to have small claims procedures
　　apply 4861
. tax year of debtor, to close 3975
. timber cutting, to treat as sale or exchange 2687
. trusts and estates
. . administration expenses, to deduct for in-
　　　come tax 3925
. . charitable contributions, to accelerate 3932
. . estimated tax payments, to treat excess
　　　as paid by beneficiary 3905
. . property distributions, to recognize gain
　　　or loss on 3918
. . revocable trust treated as part of estate 3902
. . 65-day rule for late-paid distributions 3943
. withholding
. . pensions, from, election out of . . . . 3038 et seq.
. . vehicle fringe benefits, to not withhold on 3007
**Electricity, production from renewable re-
　　sources** 2324
Electric vehicles
. advanced energy manufacturing project
　　credit 2313
. alternative motor vehicle credit 2360
. plug-in elective vehicle credits 2362
**Electronic Federal Tax Payment System
　　(EFTPS)** 3028; 3155;
　　　　　　　　　　　　　　　　　　　　　　　　 4720; 4730
Electronic filing of tax returns
　　generally 4703
. corporations 4726
. exempt organizations 4124
. Form W-4 3014
. fringe benefit, as 1246
. information returns 4737; 4746;
　　　　　　　　　　　　　　　　　　　　　　　　　　　　4753
. partnerships 4731
. payee statements 4742
. penalties 4897
. political organizations 4109
. refunds 4847
. return preparers 4750
. timely filing 4754
Electronic funds transfer, tax deposits by 3028; 4730
Electronic records
. incentive payments for electronic health
　　records 1206
Elevators, medical expense deduction 2147
Eligible rollover distributions See "Roll-
　　overs of pension, etc., distributions"
Eligible small business credits
　　generally 2304
. disabled access credit 2323
**Eligible worker owned cooperative
　　(EWOC)**
. basis of replacement for stock sold to 2504
. sales of employer stock to 2451
Embezzlement
. income from 1200
. as theft 1799

Employee achievement awards
. deductibility 1591
. exempt wages, as 3006
. gross income exclusion 1251
Employee benefit plans
. electronic filing 4753
. nonqualifying 4350
Employee business expenses
        generally . . . . 1508; 1631 et
                                       seq.
. adjusted gross income computation . . . . 3102 et seq.
. automobiles 1954
. away-from-home travel . . . . 1541 et seq.
. education expenses 2225; 2226
. home office deduction 1638
. impairment-related work expenses 1637
. job-hunting 1632
. labor union dues, fees, and assessments . . . 1633
. moving expenses . . . . 1646 et seq.
. professionals 1635; 1636
. reimbursements of expenses . . . . 1573 et seq.;
                                        3104
. related employers and employees, reim-
     bursed expenses 1579
. statutory employees 3103
. substantiation requirements 1575; 1576
. teachers
. . classroom expenses 2229
. . education expenses 2228
. tools and supplies 1635
. uniforms and special work clothes 1634
. unreimbursed, deduction for 3110
Employees
. bargain purchases from employer 1216
. below market interest rate loans 1213
. benefit associations 4100
. classification of 3003; 4858;
                                        4859
. definition for withholding on wages 3002
. fringe benefits *See "Fringe benefits"*
. government (U.S.) *See "Government offi-
     cials and employees"*
. highly compensated *See "Highly compen-
     sated employees"*
. IRS determination of status 3003
. residence of, employer's rental of space in 1645
. statutory employees *See "Statutory em-
     ployees"*
. withholding on wages . . . . 3000 et seq.
Employee stock ownership plan (ESOP)
. basis of replacement for stock sold to 2504
. defined 4314
. diversification rules, exemption from 4333
. dividends on employer securities owned by . . 1288
. gain on sale of employer stock to 2451
. limitations on contributions and benefits 4328
. related taxpayers, transactions between 2451
Employee stock purchase plan 1220; 4746
Employer identification number (EIN) 3030; 3352;
                                        4752
Employer-owned life insurance 1353
Employer-provided child care credit 2330
Employer reversions 4346
**Employers, defined for purposes of with-
     holding on wages** 3001
**Employment-related expenses, child and
     dependent care credit** 2351; 2352
Employment taxes *See also
     "Self-employment tax"*
. accrual basis taxpayers, time for deduction 1538
. deposit of
        generally . . . . 3026 et seq.

Employment taxes *See also "Self-employment tax"* — **Cont'd**
. deposit of — Cont'd
. . de minimis rules 3027
. . electronic funds transfer 3028
. . safe harbor rules 3027
. domestic servants 3029; 3030
. separate accounting 3025
. statement required to be furnished to em-
     ployee
        generally 3021
. . nonreceipt of statement 3022
. unemployment *See "Unemployment tax"*
Empowerment zones *See also "Enterprise
     zones"*
. employment credit 2303; 2325
. exclusion of gain on sale of empowerment
     zone stock 2648
. qualified zone academy bonds, credit for 2366
. rollover of gain on qualified zone assets 2428
Endowment contracts *See "Life insurance
     and endowment contracts"*
Energy conservation bonds, qualified 2366
Energy credits
        generally 2311
. advanced coal and gasification projects,
     qualifying 2312
. advanced energy manufacturing project
     credit 2313
. alcohol fuel credit 1206; 3208
. alternate fuel production credit 2337
. alternative fuel vehicle refueling property . . . 2361
. alternative motor vehicle credit 2360
. appliances, credit for energy efficient 2335
. basis of energy credit property 2478
. biodiesel fuel credit 2333
. carbon dioxide sequestration credit 2315
. cellulosic biofuel production credit 2318
. clean renewable energy bond credit 2366
. coal projects, qualifying advanced 2312
. conservation, for 1206
. electricity production from renewable re-
     sources 2324
. enhanced oil recovery credit 2322
. gasification projects, qualifying 2312
. grant in lieu of credit 2311; 2324
. new energy efficient home credit 2334
. nonbusiness energy property credit 2358
. nonconventional fuel credit 2337
. oil recovery credit 2322
. plug-in electric vehicle credits 2362
. residential energy efficient property credit . . . 2359
**Energy efficient commercial building
     property**
. deduction 2476
. expensing election 1967
. recapture rules for Sec. 1245 property 2695
Energy property *See also "Energy efficient
     commercial building property"; "Solar
     energy property or equipment"*
. advanced energy manufacturing project
     credit 2313
. biofuel plant property, depreciation 1940
. cellulosic ethanol plant property, deprecia-
     tion 3207
. smart electric meters or grid systems
        generally 1206
. . advanced energy manufacturing project
     credit 2313
. . depreciation 1917; 1925
Enhanced oil recovery credit 2322
Enterprise zones
. carryovers, corporate acquisitions 3564

Enterprise zones — Cont'd
. qualified zone academy bonds, credit for 2366
. Section 179 expense amount, qualified
        zone property 1942
Entertainment expenses *See also "Meals
        and lodging"; "Travel expenses"*
. adequate contemporary records 1585
. "associated with" entertainment 1565; 1566;
                                                                1583
. business associates 1562
. business connection requirement 1574
. business meetings 1566
. as charitable contribution 2104
. club dues 1568
. corroborated oral or written statements
        substantiating expenses 1587
. deductibility
        generally . . . . 1561 et seq.
. . officers and directors, entertainment pro-
        vided to 1572
. . percentage limitations . . . . 1569 et seq.
. definition of "entertainment" 1561
. directly related entertainment 1564; 1566
. documentary evidence of 1586
. exceptions to rules for 1566
. facilities, use of 1566; 1567
. inadequate substantiation, remedies for 1588
. officers, directors and 10% owners 1572
. parties who may be entertained 1562
. percentage limitation, deductible expenses . . . 1561; 1569 et
                                                                seq.
. reporting and substantiation
        generally . . . . 1561 et seq.
. . proof of entertainment expense 1583
. . recordkeeping . . . . 1585 et seq.
. . restrictions . . . . 1569 et seq.
. skyboxes 1570
. spouse 1563
. swimming pools 1567
. tennis courts 1567
. tickets . . . . 1561; 1569 et
                                                                seq.
Environmental remediation
. cleanup costs 1661; 1667
Environmental remediation trusts 3911
Equipment *See "Machinery and equipment"*
Equitable relief, liability of spouses 1203; 4711;
                                                                4859
Equity vs. debt 1709
Erosion
. highly erodible croplands, disposition of 4525
. prevention 4522
Erroneous returns
. mathematical or clerical errors, assess-
        ments 4801
Escheat
. involuntary conversion, as 2432
Escrow payments 2409
. like-kind exchanges 2420
ESOP *See "Employee stock ownership plan
        (ESOP)"*
Estates and trusts
        generally . . . . 3900 et seq.
. administration expenses 3922; 3925
. alimony trusts 2161
. alternative minimum tax 3201
. . exemption amount 3203
. at-risk rules 1804
. bankruptcy and receivership . . . . 3973 et seq.;
                                                                4736
. beneficiaries

Estates and trusts — Cont'd
. beneficiaries — Cont'd
        generally . . . . 3933; 3944 et
                                                                seq.
. . charitable remainder trusts 3952
. . consistency requirements 3901
. . depreciation and depletion 3927
. . different year, beneficiary with 3948
. . estimated tax, election to treat as paid by
        beneficiary 3905
. . foreign trusts 4620
. . grantor of foreign trust, treated as 3964
. . information returns 4732
. . minimum distribution rules, trusts as ben-
        eficiaries 4345
. . nonresident aliens 4645
. . related taxpayers 2448
. . separate share rule 3947
. . stock attribution rules 3534
. . taxation of, generally . . . . 3901; 3948 et
                                                                seq.
. . termination of estate or trust, deductions
        upon 3951
. . throwback rules 3953; 3955
. . withholding 4671
. business entity, taxed as 3908
. capital gains and losses 2600; 3952
. character of amounts distributed 3946
. charitable contribution deduction . . . . 3931 et seq.
. charitable lead trusts 2119
. charitable remainder annuity trusts 2116; 3914
. charitable remainder trusts 3952
. charitable remainder unitrusts 2116; 3914
. charitable trusts 4124; 4126
. collectibles gain on sale or exchange of
        interest 2603
. community property 3919
. complex trusts
. . beneficiary, amount taxed to 3945
. . character of income 3946
. . distributable net income (DNI) 3936; 3937
. . distribution deductions 3936
. . distributions, generally 3945
. . throwback rules . . . . 3953 et seq.
. computation of tax . . . . 3901 et seq.
. credits
        generally 3920
. . general business credit 2303
. Crummey power 5046
. deductions . . . . 3920 et seq.
. distributable net income (DNI) . . . . 3933 et seq.
. distributions
. . beneficiary's basis 3949
. . complex trusts 3936; 3937;
                                                                3945
. . currently distributable income 3938
. . deduction . . . . 3933 et seq.
. . gain or loss on 3918
. . in-kind distributions 3940; 3949
. . nonqualifying 3942
. . principal, deduction for 3939
. . requirements 3938; 3939
. . simple trusts 3934; 3935;
                                                                3944
. . 65-day rule for late-paid distributions 3943; 3948
. . support of decedent's widow or depen-
        dents 3941
. . tax-exempt income 3934
. domestic production activities, deduction
        for 1615
. environmental remediation trusts 3911
. estimated taxes . . . . 3903 et seq.

Estates and trusts — Cont'd
. family support allowance 3941
. first-tier beneficiaries, distributable net in-
    come (DNI) 3945
. foreign tax credit 2367; 2368
. foreign trusts *See "Foreign trusts"*
. funeral trusts 3912
. gift and leaseback 1595
. grantor trusts *See "Grantor trusts"*
. income
    generally 3916
. . benefit of grantor, for 3959
. . community property, from 3919
. . rates of tax 1106
. . real estate passing directly to heirs 3917
. . in respect of decedent 3970
. . tax exempt income 3924
. information returns 4898
. in-kind distributions 3918; 3940;
                                          3949
. interest deductions 3923
. liquidating trusts 3909
. losses 1776
. medical expenses of decedent paid by es-
    tate 2143
. Medicare surtax on unearned income . . . . . . 1107; 3150 et
                                          seq.
. minors, trusts for 5046
. miscellaneous itemized deductions, 2%
    floor on 3921
. multiple trusts 3913
. net investment income tax 3956
. net operating losses 1840; 3930
. nontaxable gifts and bequests 3950
. passive activity losses 1811; 1812
. personal exemptions 3928
. personal holding company income received
    from 3325
. pooled income funds 2117; 3915
. qualified disability trusts 3928
. qualified dividend income 1288
. qualified domestic trusts 5026
. qualified Subchapter S trusts 3354
. real estate, income from 3917
. residence, exclusion of gain on sale 2445
. retained rights or powers in trusts, gross
    estate inclusion 5004; 5007
. returns . . . . 4732 et seq.
. reversionary interests 3960
. revocable 3958
. . election to treat revocable trust as part of
    estate 3902
. S corporations, as shareholders of 3353; 3354
. separate share rule 3947
. short year
. . estimated tax payments 3904
. . taxation of beneficiary 3948
. simple trusts
. . beneficiary, amount taxed to 3944
. . character of income 3946
. . distributable net income, computation of . . 3935
. . distributions 3934; 3944
. . 65-day rule 3943; 3948
. split-interest trusts 4126
. standard deduction 3929
. support allowance 3941
. taxable year 2808
. tax tables 1106
. termination
    generally 3906; 3907
. . bankruptcy and receivership 3979
. . beneficiaries' deductions 3951

Estates and trusts — Cont'd
. throwback rules . . . . 3953 et seq.
. transfers in trust
. . basis of 2508
. . charitable contributions *See "Charitable
    contributions"*
. . "estate freeze" (Chapter 14 rules) 5054
. . generation-skipping transfer tax . . . . 5056 et seq.
Estate tax
    generally 5000
. alternate valuation date 5016
. annuities 5013
. charitable bequests 5020
. claims against the estate 5018
. community property 5012
. computation of 5018; 5033
. credit amount 5028
. deductibility 1755
. . income tax, against 3972
. deductions in computing
    generally . . . . 5018 et seq.
. . double deductions 3926
. . income tax vs estate tax deduction 3925; 5019
. . state death taxes 5027
. deferred
    generally 4858
. . interest on 1715; 3923
. deposit by electronic funds transfer 3028
. election out of, decedents dying in 2010 2523
. exclusion amount 5000; 5028;
                                          5029
. executor's personal liability for, early dis-
    charge of 4915
. expatriation rule 5037
. foreign death taxes, credit for 5032
. gifts, lifetime, within 3 years of death 5002
. gift tax, credit for 5031; 5033;
                                          5037
. gross estate, valuation of property 5016
. income tax basis, estate tax value also 2513
. jointly held property . . . . 5010 et seq.
. liens 4911; 4912
. life insurance proceeds 5014; 5015
. marital deduction . . . . 5021 et seq.
. noncitizen spouse 5026
. nonresident aliens 5037
. payment of, generally 5036
. powers of appointment 5009
. prior transfers, credit for tax on 5030; 5037
. property owned by decedent 5001
. qualified domestic trust (QDOT), estate tax
    on 5026; 5036
. qualified terminable interest property
    (QTIP) 5008; 5023
. rates 1114; 5000;
                                          5033
. redemption of stock to pay 3532
. retained life estate 5004
. returns . . . . 5034 et seq.
. . failure to file 4873
. . time for filing 5035
. . understatement of property value, penalty . . 4880
. revocable transfers 5007
. special use valuation 5017
. state death taxes, deduction for 5027
. surviving spouse . . . . 5021 et seq.
. . portability of unused exclusion 5029
. taxable estate 5018
. terminable interest . . . . 5022 et seq.
. three years of death, gifts within 5002
. transfers taking effect at death 5006
. unified credit 5037

Estate tax — Cont'd
. voting rights, stock of controlled corporation 5005
Estimated expenses
. Cohan rule 1510
. reserves 2846; 2847
Estimated tax
. corporations
. . generally 3343
. . "adjusted seasonal installment" 3348
. . "annualized income installment" 3347
. . earnings and profits, effect of payments
. . . . on 3525
. . quick refund of 4851
. . required annual payment 3344
. . required installments 3346
. . "tax" defined 3345
. . underpayment penalty 3349
. deposit by electronic funds transfer 3028
. individuals
. . generally 3154
. . amount of required installment 3157
. . annualized income method 3158
. . computation 3155
. . farmers and fishermen 3161; 3163
. . nonresident aliens 3162
. . payment 4720
. . . withholding as 3159
. . spouses 3156
. . time for paying installments . . . . 3160 et seq.
. . underpayment penalty
. . . generally 3163
. . . exceptions to 3164
. . . waiver of 3165
. interest on 4865
. payments . . . . 1766; 3154 et
. . . . seq.; 4720
. trusts and estates . . . . 3903 et seq.
. unrelated business income 4121
Evasion of tax *See "Tax avoidance and eva-*
sion"
Examination of tax returns, etc. *See also*
"Audits (by IRS)"
. generally . . . . 4800 et seq.
. Appeals Office, early referral to 4815
. information returns, check against 4802
. mathematical check 4801
. one-examination rule 4810
. selection of returns 4803
. type of examinations, time and place 4806
. unnecessary examinations 4810
Excess benefit transactions, exempt or-
ganizations 4112
Excess business holdings, private foun-
dations 4127
Excess distributions
. passive foreign investment companies
. . (PFICs) 4628
Excess profits tax
. deductibility 1755
. foreign tax credit 2369
Excess receipts, annuities and annuity
contracts 1356
Exchange fund partnerships 3711
Exchanges of property *See also "Sales or*
exchanges"
. basis 2463
. cancellation of lease or distributor's agree-
. . ment 2680
. convertible securities 2681
. debt-for-debt exchanges 1396
. gain or loss . . . . 2400 et seq.
. held for productive use or investment . . . . 2418 et seq.

Exchanges of property *See also "Sales or exchanges"*
— Cont'd
. like-kind exchanges . . . . 2418 et seq.
. . . . *See also*
"Like-kind ex-
changes"
. related taxpayers . . . . 2446 et seq.
. stock
. . bonds of same corporation 2681
. . debt, exchanged for 1395
. . other property or money, for . . . . 2415; 3510 et
. . . . seq.
. . stock of same corporation 2414
. tax-free exchanges . . . . 2413 et seq.
. U.S. obligations 2416
Excise taxes
. continuation coverage, failure to provide 1531
. deductibility 1755
. deposit by electronic funds transfer 3028
. education savings accounts, excess contri-
. . butions 2207
. exempt organizations
. . donor advised funds 4129; 4130
. . excess benefit transactions 4112
. . political or lobbying expenditures 4103; 4104
. . premiums paid on personal benefit con-
. . . tracts 2115
. . private foundations 4125; 4127
. foreign procurement payments, on 4652
. fuel taxes, credits 2318
. golden parachute payments 1209
. health insurance providers 4896
. health savings account distributions not
. . used for qualified medical expenses 1378
. highway vehicles, electronic filing 4753
. individual retirement accounts
. . excess contributions 4356; 4369
. . minimum distributions 4357
. medical savings account distributions not
. . used for qualified medical expenses 1377
. pension and profit-sharing plans *See "Pen-*
sion and profit-sharing plans"
. private foundations, termination of 4128
. refunds 4854
. tax shelter prohibited transactions 4113
. . disclosure to escape tax 4114
Exclusion ratio, annuities, investment in
contract . . . . 1356 et seq.
Exclusions *See specific items*
Executors and administrators *See also "Fi-*
duciaries"
. commissions and fees 1206; 5018
. decedent's return 4714; 4915
. returns by 5034
Exempt corporations
. accumulated earnings tax 3316
. cooperatives . . . . 4206 et seq.
. dividends 1288
. personal holding companies, classification
. . as 3322
. small employer health insurance credit 2332
Exempt income *See "Tax-exempt income"*
Exemptions *See specific items*
Exempt obligations
. amortization of bond premium 2169; 2170;
. . . . 2173
. capital gains and losses 2636
. issue price 1317
Exempt organizations
. generally . . . . 4100 et seq.
. application for exemption 4116
. . disclosure of 4120

Exempt organizations — Cont'd
. backup withholding 3044
. change to exempt entity status 3579
. feeder organizations 4101
. information returns 4746
. . disclosure of 4120
. . penalties 4898
. investment tax credit 2307
. leases to, tax-exempt use losses 1782
. lobbying expenses . . . . 4102 et seq.
. prohibited transactions . . . . 4111 et seq.
. related taxpayers, sales and exchanges be-
    tween 2448
. returns 4124
. tax-sheltered annuities . . . . 4388 et seq.
. tax shelter transactions, exempts acting as
    accommodation parties in 4894
. transfers to 3579
. unrelated business income of *See "Unrelat-*
    ed business income"
. work opportunity credit 2317

Expansion of existing business, start-up
    expenses 1505

Expatriation
    generally 4610
. alternative expatriate income tax 4654
. corporate and partnership expatriations (in-
    versions) 4655
. estate tax 5037
. mark-to-market deemed sale rule, expatria-
    tions after June 16, 2008 4653
. reporting requirements 4898

"Expected return," annuity contract 1362

Expenses *See specific items*

Expensing elections *See also "Section 179*
    expense election"
. commercial revitalization expenses 1972
. computer software development costs 1623
. disaster losses 1798
. film and TV production costs 1965
. reforestation expenses 1970
. special provisions . . . . 1964 et seq.
. start-up expenses . . . . 1500 et seq.

Exploration costs
. amortization 1971
. earnings and profits, effect on 3525
. mines 1626
. uniform capitalization rules 1667

Extension of time *See also "Returns"*
. assessment period, voluntary extension of 4836
. for making elections 1798; 4735

Extraordinary dividends
. basis 2495
. qualified dividend income 1288
. simple trusts 3935

F

Faculty housing 1268

Family
. allowance, support 3941
. dependency exemption, qualifying relative
    for purposes of 3122
. "estate freeze" transfers 5054
. sales and exchanges between 2448
. stock redemption, attribution rules 3534
. . waiver of 3529
. travel expenses 1551

Family partnerships 3704; 5004

Farmers and farming
    generally . . . . 4500 et seq.

Farmers and farming — Cont'd
. accounting methods . . . . 2818; 4505 et
                                   seq.
. accrual basis . . . . 4509 et seq.
. actual use valuation of farm property 5017
. at-risk rules 1805
. capital expenditures . . . . 4519 et seq.
. cash basis taxpayers . . . . 4506 et seq.
. casualty losses 4520
. charitable remainder in farm 2114
. conservation reserve program (CRP) pay-
    ments 3148
. corporations 4510
. crop method of accounting 4512
. crops
. . highly erodible croplands, disposition of 4525
. . pledged to secure CCC loans 4528
. . unharvested crop sold with land 4524
. depreciation 4523
. . automobiles 1954
. . buildings 1919
. . equipment 1915; 1916;
                                     1932
. disaster payments to 4508
. estimated tax 3161
. feed, cost of 4515
. fertilizer costs 4516
. home office deduction 1638
. hybrid accounting methods 4505
. income and expenses . . . . 4501 et seq.
. income averaging . . . . 3201 et seq.
. indebtedness of, discharge of 1391
. installment sales 2454
. inventories . . . . 4505; 4513 et
                                   seq.
. like-kind exchanges 4527
. livestock
. . depreciation 4523
. . dispositions 4526
. . inventories 4513; 4514
. . like-kind exchanges 4527
. . purchase price 4507
. . sale of 2441; 4508
. losses, limitation on 4504
. net operating losses 1841; 4503
. partnerships 4510
. plants
. . accrual accounting 4510
. . depreciation 4523
. . pre-productive period expenses 4510; 4519
. . purchase price 4507
. . replanting costs 4520
. . uniform capitalization rules, election to
      not apply 4521
. prepaid expenses 4517
. pre-productive period expenses
    generally . . . . 4518 et seq.
. . depreciation 1931
. qualified conservation contributions 2123; 2131
. self-employment tax . . . . 3148 et seq.
. soil and water conservation expenses 4522
. special farm payments to 4528
. syndicates 4511
. tax preference items 3210
. uniform capitalization rules . . . . 4519 et seq.
. vehicles used in
. . claiming expense deductions 1954
. . fringe benefits 1245
. wetlands, disposition of converted 4525

Farmers' cooperatives
    generally . . . . 4100; 4206 et
                                     seq.

Farmers' cooperatives — Cont'd
. dividends-received deduction 3315
. stock of qualified refiner or processor sold
    to 2451
**Federal home loan banks, divi-
    dends-received deduction** 3315
Federal payments
. special farm payments 4528
. voluntary withholding on 3009
Feed, cost of 4515
Feeder organizations 4101
Fees
. accountants 1603; 1605;
                                                        5018
. clergy 1226
. installment payment requests 4722
. IRS rulings or determinations, user fees 4812
. legal *See "Attorneys"; "Legal expenses"*
. professional services, amortization 1975
. returns, copies of 4757
. split fees 1611
. trustees 3922
. union 1633
Fellowships *See "Scholarships and fellow-
    ships"*
**Fertility treatments, medical expense de-
    duction** 2144
Fertilizer costs 4516
FICA *See "Medicare"; "Social security tax"*
Fiduciaries
. fees of estates and trusts 3921
. related taxpayers, transactions between 2448
. returns
. . corporate returns 4725
. . decedents 4708
. . information returns 4746
. . for minors and incompetents 4701
. . trusts and estates . . . . 4732 et seq.
. transferee liability 4914
Field audit 4806
15-year amortization of intangibles . . . . 1973 et seq.
52-53 week tax year
    generally 2802
. change to or from 2805
. establishing tax year 2803
. passthrough entities 2802
Filing returns *See "Electronic filing of tax
    returns"; "Returns"*
Films *See "Motion picture films"*
Finance charges 1704
. installment purchases 1706
Financial institutions
    generally 4209
. electronic filing of returns 4753
. gifts or services received from for opening
    or adding to accounts 1303
. penalties 4897
. personal holding companies, classification
    as 3322
. S corporations, as 3351
. . passive investment income 3366
. withholdable payments to foreign financial
    institutions 4672
**Financial positions, appreciated, con-
    structive sales** 2637; 2638
Fines, deductibility of 1610; 1613
Firefighters
. early withdrawals from qualified plans 4344
. killed in line of duty, annuities paid to survi-
    vors 1260
. retirement plan distributions for health and
    long-term care insurance 4349

Fiscal year *See "Taxable year"*
Fishermen
. estimated tax 3161
. income averaging 3201; 4502
. self-employment tax 3146
**Fishing boat operators, information re-
    turns** 4746
Fixed and determinable periodic income . . . . 4662 et seq.
Fixtures
. capital expenditures 1660
. depreciation 1916
Flexible spending accounts 1269
Food *See also "Meals and lodging"; "Restau-
    rants"*
. charitable contributions of 2107; 2108
Foreclosure
. losses, deductibility 1773; 1787;
                                                        1788
. mortgage interest 1304
. reporting of, for secured property 4746
. transfer of debtor's property in 3518
Foreign base company income (FBCI) 4624
Foreign corporations *See also "Controlled
    foreign corporations (CFCs)"*
    generally . . . . 4637 et seq.
. accumulated earnings tax 3316
. alternative minimum tax 3200
. branch-level interest tax 4648
. branch profits tax 4647
. consolidated returns, includible corpora-
    tions 3339
. credits 4646
. deductions 4646
. deferred compensation from 1277
. defined 4638
. dividend income, qualified 1288
. dividends-received deduction 3310
. domestic corporations succeeded by (inver-
    sions) 4655
. effectively connected income . . . . 4610; 4644 et
                                                        seq.
. election to be treated as U.S. corporation 4650
. engaging in U.S. business defined 4645
. foreign tax credit 2367
. personal holding companies, classification
    as 3322
. real estate (U.S.) income, treatment as ef-
    fectively connected 4643
. related party sales 3533
. returns 4656; 4659;
                                                        4661; 4726;
                                                        4728; 4898
. Section 367 rule 3588
. transfers to 3588; 4661
. transportation income 4651
. U.S. persons . . . . 4622 et seq.;
                                                        4661
. U.S. real property interest (USRPI)
. . dispositions of 4649
. . election to be treated as U.S. corporation 4650
. U.S.-source income not effectively connect-
    ed with U.S. business 4642
. withholding of tax at source 4663
Foreign currency
    generally . . . . 4674 et seq.
. contracts, amortization 1975
. foreign tax payments 2373
. functional currency 4675
. personal transactions 4676
. Section 988 transactions 4676
. translating into dollars 4675

Foreign entities
. leases to, tax-exempt use losses 1782
. withholdable payments to 4672
Foreign expropriation losses 2615
Foreign financial accounts
. information returns 4746
. . withholding to enforce reporting require-
    ments 4672
Foreign financial assets
. disclosure statement for specified foreign
    financial assets 4673
. penalty on undisclosed foreign financial as-
    set understatements 4879
. understatements due to, assessment peri-
    od 4832
Foreign gifts 4677; 4678
Foreign governments
. employees
. . certificate of tax compliance 4658
. . limited income exclusion 4645
. . self-employment tax 3146
. payments to, backup withholding 3044
Foreign housing costs
. adjusted gross income computation 3102
. exclusion . . . . 4613 et seq.
Foreign income
    generally . . . . 4610 et seq.
. compensation, as 1523
. domestic corporations 4621
. earned income exclusion . . . . 4612 et seq.
. estates and trusts 4620
. foreign housing costs . . . . 4613 et seq.
. government employees 4619
. U.S. citizens 4611
. U.S. possessions . . . . 4618 et seq.
Foreign Investment in Real Property Tax
    Act (FIRPTA) 4650
Foreign personal holding company
    (FPHC)
. classification as PHC 3322
. Subpart F income, defined 4624
Foreign sales corporation (FSC)
. penalties, civil 4898
. taxable year 2809
Foreign source income
. deductions allocated between U.S. source
    and 4641
. effectively connected income 4644
. resident aliens 4634
. as U.S. income 2372
Foreign tax credit
    generally . . . . 2367 et seq.
. alternative minimum tax 3214
. amount of foreign tax payments 2373
. boycott 4632
. foreign affiliate, taxes paid or accrued by 2374
. limitations on . . . . 2370 et seq.
. partnerships 3718; 3723
. personal holding company tax 3320
. qualifying taxes 2369
. separate limitations on separate income
    categories 2371
Foreign taxes
. deductibility 1754; 1755
. deduction vs credit 2367
Foreign trusts
    generally 3963; 3964
. grantors 3963; 3964
. returns 4732
. throwback rules
    generally . . . . 3953 et seq.
. . related party, loans to 4620

Foreign trusts — **Cont'd**
. transfers to 3963; 4631
. U.S. beneficiaries 3963; 4620
. withholding 4663; 4664
Forest Health Protection Program (FHPP) 4528
Forestry conservation bonds, qualified 2366
Forgiveness of debt *See "Discharge of in-*
    debtedness"
Forms
. 433-A 4722; 4822
. 433-B 4822
. 433-F 4722
. 656 4822
. 668 4912
. 706 . . . . 5016; 5029;
    5033 et seq.
. . Schedule A-1 5017
. . Schedule D 5014; 5015
. . Schedule E 5010; 5011
. . Schedule G . . . . 5002 et seq.
. . Schedule H 5009
. . Schedule I 5013
. . Schedule M . . . . 5021 et seq.
. . Schedule O 5020
. . Schedule P 5032
. . Schedule PC 5018
. . Schedule Q 5030
. . Schedule R 5057; 5059
. . Schedule R-1 5057
. . Schedule U 5016
. 706-A 5017; 5035
. 706GS(D) 5057
. 706GS(D-1) 5057
. 706GS(T) 5057
. 706-NA 5035; 5037
. 706-QDT 5026
. 709 . . . . 5050; 5053;
    5055; 5057
. 720 . . . . 2318; 4849
. 720X 4849
. 730 4849
. 843 . . . . 4866; 4870
. 851 3340
. 866 4821
. 870 . . . . 4704; 4814;
    4819; 4825
. 870-AD 4820
. 872 4836
. 872-A 4836
. 872-T 4836
. 890 4819
. 890-AD 4820
. 906 4821
. 907 4855
. 926 . . . . 4661; 4746
. 940 3030
. 941 . . . . 3019; 4746
. . Schedule D 3019
. 941-X 3020
. 944 3019
. 945 3032
. 966 4746
. 970 2874
. 972 3334
. 973 3334
. 976 3336
. 982 . . . . 1389; 1390;
    1392; 1397
. 990 . . . . 4109; 4120;
    4124
. . Schedule B 4120
. 990-EZ 4120

Forms — Cont'd

. 990-N	4124
. 990-PF	4120; 4124; 4127; 4128; 4131
. 990-T	2332; 4120; 4121; 4746
. 1023	4116; 4125
. 1024	4116
. 1040	105; 1210; 1270; 2162; 2355; 3016; 3131; 4702; 4703; 4713; 4715; 4757
. . Schedule A	1205; 1577; 1638; 1756; 1757; 2100; 2141
. . Schedule C	1210; 1558; 1638; 1954; 3103
. . Schedule C-EZ	1210
. . Schedule D	2418; 2427; 2600
. . Schedule EIC	2339
. . Schedule F	1638; 1954; 4501; 4508
. . Schedule H	3030
. . Schedule J	4502
. . Schedule R	2348
. . Schedule SE	3141; 3149; 4713
. 1040A	1270; 2355; 3131; 4702; 4703
. . Schedule 3	2348
. . Schedule EIC	2339
. 1040C	4658
. 1040-ES	3155; 4720
. 1040-ES(NR)	3155; 3162
. 1040EZ	3131; 4702; 4703
. 1040NR	4657
. 1040NR-EZ	4657
. 1040-V	4720
. 1040X	4723
. 1041	3901; 3943; 4732 et seq.
. . Schedule D	2600
. . Schedule I	3201
. . Schedule J	3953
. . Schedule K-1	4732
. 1041-A	3931; 4126; 4733
. 1041-ES	3903
. 1041-QFT	3912
. 1041-T	3905
. 1041-V	3901
. 1042	4660; 4665; 4672
. 1042-S	4660; 4665; 4672; 4740
. 1045	4850
. 1065	3716; 4210; 4660; 4726; 4731; 4843
. . Schedule C	4726
. . Schedule K-1	4660; 4731
. 1065-B	3702; 4726; 4731
. 1066	4204

Forms — Cont'd

. 1098	4744; 4746; 4753
. 1098-C	2138; 4115; 4746
. 1098-E	4746
. 1098-MA	4744
. 1098-T	4746
. 1099	1298; 2370; 4733; 4737; 4738; 4742; 4753; 4757
. 1099-A	4746
. 1099-B	4746
. 1099-C	4746
. 1099-DIV	1288; 4739
. 1099-G	1281; 4746
. 1099-INT	4740
. 1099-K	4746
. 1099-LTC	4746
. 1099-MISC	4743; 4746
. 1099-OID	4741
. 1099-PATR	4739
. 1099-Q	4746
. 1099-R	1209; 3035; 4314; 4338; 4357
. 1099-S	4746
. 1099-SA	4746
. 1116	2368; 2370
. 1118	2368
. . Schedule J	2372
. 1120	3340; 4726
. . Schedule B	4726
. . Schedule H	2813
. . Schedule L	4726
. . Schedule M-1	4726
. . Schedule M-3	4726
. . Schedule PH	3320; 4726
. . Schedule UTP	4726
. 1120-C	4726
. 1120F	4659; 4726
. 1120-H	4110; 4726
. 1120L	4726
. 1120-PC	4726
. 1120-POL	4109; 4726
. 1120-REIT	4202; 4726
. 1120-RIC	4201; 4726
. 1120S	3367; 3370; 4726
. . Schedule D	3362
. 1120-SF	4726
. 1120X	4849
. 1122	3340
. 1125-A	4726; 4731
. 1125-E	4726
. 1127	4721; 4729
. 1128	2814
. 1138	4729
. 1139	4850
. 1310	4847
. 2039	4809
. 2063	4658
. 2106	1558; 1577; 1637; 1954; 3105
. 2106-EZ	1558; 1577; 1637; 1954; 3105
. 2120	3123
. 2210	3163
. 2210F	3163

References are to paragraph [¶] numbers.

Forms — Cont'd

2220	3349
2290	4753; 4849
2297	4855
2350	4718
2438	4201; 4202
2439	4201; 4202
2441	1270; 2353
2553	2810; 3354; 3356; 3357
2555	4617
2555-EZ	4617
2848	4808
3115	1769; 1901; 2830; 2840; 2881
3468	2307; 2308; 2310; 2311
3520	3963; 4678
3520-A	3963
3800	2302; 2304
3817	4754
3903	1647
3921	4746
3922	4746
4029	3146
4070	4746
4255	2314
4361	3147
4419	4753
4466	4851
4506	4757
4506T	4757
4506T-EZ	4757
4562	1502; 1602; 1619; 1626; 1627; 1901; 1909; 1941; 1954; 1970; 1973; 3206; 4523
4563	4618
4626	3201
4684	1793; 1795; 1799; 1802
4720	4103; 4104; 4112; 4120; 4124; 4127; 4129; 4130
4768	5035; 5036
4789	4746
4797	1627; 1628; 1945; 1948; 2418; 2430; 2646; 2685; 2692; 4522
4804	4753
4852	3022
4868	4703; 4717; 4718; 4720
4876-A	4621
4952	1727; 1729
4970	3955
5213	1778
5227	4124; 4126
5300	4332
5304-SIMPLE	4383
5305-E	2206
5305-EA	2206
5305-R	4368
5305-RA	4368
5305-RB	4368

Forms — Cont'd

5305-SA	4383
5305-SEP	4378
5305-SIMPLE	4383
5307	4332
5310A	4746
5329	1367; 1368; 1528; 2207; 4344; 4345; 4356; 4357; 4701
5330	4346; 4347
5452	4739
5471	4622; 4661
5472	4661
5495	4915
5498	4746
5498-SA	4746
5500	4746
5500-SF	4746
5558	4746
5695	2358; 2359
5713	4632
5754	3033
5768	4103
5884	2316
5884-C	2317
6198	1806
6251	3201
6252	2418; 2453
6478	2318
6765	2319
6781	2656; 2658 et seq.; 2659
7004	4728; 4731; 4732; 4736
8023	3582; 3585; 3586
8027	4746
8038-CP	2366
8082	3370; 3721; 3901
8109	3346
8233	4664; 4666
8275	4726; 4878
8281	4741
8282	4746
8283	2137
8288	4671
8288-A	4671
8300	4746
8308	4746
8329	4746
8330	4746
8332	3126
8362	4746
8396	2357
8453	4754
8453-X	4109
8508	4753
8582	1811
8582-CR	1811
8586	2320
8594	2472
8606	4354; 4357; 4371; 4373
8609	2320
8611	2321
8615	3137
8621	4628; 4629; 4630
8697	2854

References are to paragraph [¶] numbers.

Forms — Cont'd

8716	2813
8752	2813
8801	2365
8804	4670
8805	4670
8806	4746
8809	4747
8810	1811
8812	2356
8813	4670
8814	3139
8815	2220
8818	2220
8819	4675
8820	2328
8822-B	4726
8824	2418; 2424
8826	2323
8827	1939; 2365
8828	2357
8829	1638
8831	4204
8832	3301; 3701; 3703
8833	4639
8834	2362
8835	2324
8839	1254; 2354
8840	4635
8842	3347
8843	4635
8844	2325
8845	2326
8846	2327
8848	4647
8849	2418; 2442; 2600; 4849
8850	2316
8852	4746
8853	1377; 1378; 1528
8854	4653; 4654
8855	3902
8857	1203; 4709 et seq.
8862	2339
8863	2202; 2203
8864	2333
8865	4661
8866	1959
8867	4888
8868	4112; 4124
8869	3352
8870	2115; 4124
8871	4109; 4746
8872	4109; 4746
8874	2329
8879	4703
8880	2363
8881	2331
8882	2330
8885	2344
8886	4749
8886-T	4114
8888	4847
8892	5055; 5057
8899	4746
8903	1615
8907	2337
8908	2334
8909	2335

Forms — Cont'd

8910	2360
8911	2361
8916-A	4726
8917	2231
8918	4748
8919	3002
8925	1353; 4746
8932	2336
8933	2315
8936	2362
8937	4746
8938	4673
8939	2523
8941	2332
8944	4750
8949	2427; 2430; 2622
8952	3003
8955-SSA	4746
8960	3151; 3956
8966	4672
9465	4722; 4904
13976	4748
HUD-1	1746
SS-5	4752
SS-8	3002
T (timber)	1976; 2687
TDF 90-22.1	4746
W-2	1248; 1257; 1263; 1615; 2135; 2136; 3007; 3021; 3022; 3030; 3360; 4757; 4901
W-2G	3033; 4753
W-3	3030
W-4	3009; 3014 et seq.
W-4P	3038; 3040
W-4S	3008; 3019
W-4V	3009
W-7	4752
W-7A	4752
W-8	4664; 4666; 4670
W-8BEN	4666
W-8ECI	4666
W-9	3044; 4664; 4666; 4670; 4752
W-10	1270; 2353
W-12	4750

Foster children
. dependents, exemption for — 3120
. payments received for care of — 1206

401(k) plans
generally — 4317
. annual amount that can be deferred — 4317
. catch-up contributions — 4317
. combined defined benefit-401(k) plans — 4318
. contributions — 4317
. hardship distributions from — 4317
. loans from — 1722
. qualified automatic contribution arrangements (QACAs) — 4317
. requirements — 4317
. Roth 401(k) accounts — 4375
. saver's credit for contributions to — 2363
. SIMPLE retirement plans *See "SIMPLE retirement plans"*

Franchise
. amortization 1974; 1975
. business expenses 1622
. capital asset, as 2629
Fraternal organizations
. contributions to 2102; 2125
. tax exemption 4100
Fraud
. criminal penalties 4901
. income from 1200
. information returns, damages for filing 4899
. personal holding companies 3336
. returns 4835
. underpayment 4882
Fringe benefits
       generally . . . . 1228 et seq.
. achievement awards 1251; 1591;
                                                             3006
. adoption assistance 1254
. airflights . . . . 1232; 1238 et
                                                              seq.
. athletic facilities, on-premises 1252; 3006
. automobiles . . . . 1232 et seq.
. cafeteria plans 1269
. company-owned life insurance (COLI) 1526
. compensation paid as . . . . 1229; 1524 et
                                                              seq.
. death benefits . . . . 1260 et seq.
. de minimis 1246
. dependent care assistance 1270
. discounts, qualified employee 1244
. educational benefits . . . . 2213 et seq.
. expenses of employee paid by employer 1253
. gross income
. . exclusions from . . . . 1242 et seq.
. . inclusions in . . . . 1209; 1228 et
                                                              seq.
. health and accident insurance . . . . 1527 et seq.
. life insurance . . . . 1261 et seq.
. loss of limb or disfigurement, employer's
       payment for 1258
. meals and lodging 1246; 1267;
                                                             1268
. medical expenses, direct payment or reim-
       bursement of . . . . 1255; 1527 et
                                                              seq.
. medical savings accounts 1256
. moving expense reimbursements 1248; 3006
. no-additional-cost services 1243
. noncash . . . . 1524 et seq.
. residence, employer reimbursement of em-
       ployee's loss on sale or exchange 1249
. retirement advice, employer-provided 1250
. S corporations, deductibility by 3360
. transportation, qualified 1247
. valuation of . . . . 1230 et seq.
. welfare benefit plans 1533
. withholding 3004; 3006;
                                                             3010
. workers' compensation 1259
. working condition fringes 1245; 2214
Front pay, withholding 3004
Frozen deposits
. casualty loss, treatment as 1792; 1802
. interest credited to 1330
FSC *See "Foreign sales corporation (FSC)"*
Fuel
. alcohol fuel credit 2318; 4746
. alternative fuel vehicle refueling property,
       credit for 2361
. biodiesel fuel credit 2333; 4746
. clean fuel vehicles 1951; 2695

Fuel — Cont'd
. excise taxes 1755
. production credit 2337
Fuel cell property
. credit for 2311
. . advanced energy manufacturing project
       credit 2313
. . alternative motor vehicle credit 2360
. . residential energy efficient property credit 2359
Functional currency 4675
Fundraising
. charitable fundraising and entertainment 2104; 4118
. disclosure
. . civil penalties 4898
. . exempt organizations 4118
Funeral expenses 3532; 5018
. pre-need funeral trust 3912
FUTA *See "Unemployment tax"*
Future interests 5036; 5046
Futures, commodity *See "Commodity fu-*
       tures"
Futures contracts
. amortization 1975
. inventory, goods included in 2864
. security futures . . . . 2661 et seq.

G

Gain or loss *See also "Capital gains and*
       losses"; "Losses"
. basis for computation of . . . . 2463 et seq.
. built-in *See "Built-in gains, losses"*
. cancellation of lease or distributor's agree-
       ment 2680
. controlled group 2450
. conversion and constructive ownership
       transactions . . . . 2664 et seq.
. convertible securities 2681
. corporate distributions 3562
. estate or trust distributions 3918
. foreign currency transactions 4676
. foreign entities, transfers to 4631
. involuntary conversions . . . . 2430 et seq.
. liquidations . . . . 3574 et seq.
. nonliquidating distributions . . . . 3538 et seq.
. partnerships
. . contributed property, disposition of 3747
. . controlled partnership, sales and ex-
       changes with 3731; 3732
. . disproportionate distributions 3758
. . distributions by . . . . 3743 et seq.
. . transfer or liquidation of interest . . . . 3763 et seq.
. . unrealized receivables and inventory,
       character to distributee-partner 3753
. patent sold to foreign corporation 4626
. property
. . held for productive use or investment 2418
. . mortgaged property 1787; 1788
. . partners' contributions 3710
. . real, subdivided for sale 2624
. recognition . . . . 2400 et seq.
. . transfers to foreign corporations 3588
. related taxpayers, transactions between . . . . 2446 et seq.
. sales or exchanges . . . . 2400 et seq.
                                                      See also "Sales
                                                      or exchanges"
. . small business investment companies 4205
. securities futures contracts . . . . 2661 et seq.
. stock 2414; 2415;
                                                             4625
. unascertainable value of proceeds 2404

Gambling
. information returns 4746
. losses, deductibility of 1786; 3114
. "nonwagering" expenses of a gambling
    business 1786
. U.S. source income not effectively connect-
    ed with U.S. business 4642
. withholding on winnings from 3031; 3033
Gasoline stations, depreciation 1915; 1918;
                                                                    1932
General business credit . . . . 2302 et seq.
                                *See also en-
                                tries for individ-
                                ual credits*

Generation-skipping transfer tax
    generally . . . . 5056 et seq.
. computation 5059
. deductibility 1755
. exemption 5058
. income tax deduction for 3972
. liens 4911
. returns 5057
. transfers subject to 5057
Geothermal wells
. advanced energy manufacturing project
    credit 2313
. alternative minimum tax 3208
. at-risk rules 1805
. electricity production from renewable re-
    sources, credit for 2324
. energy credit 2311
. intangible drilling costs 1628
. percentage depletion 1979
Gifts
. appreciated property, of 2683
. basis of property received as . . . . 2507 et seq.
. business expenses . . . . 1589 et seq.
. certificates 1591; 2830
. charitable, etc . . . . 2100 et seq.
. compensation distinguished 1212
. defined 5040
. employee, to
    generally 1212; 1589;
                                                        1590
. . beneficiaries of deceased employee 1534
. . de minimis fringe benefits 1246
. expatriates, transfer tax on gifts received
    from 5037
. from financial institutions, in exchange for
    opening or adding to accounts 1303
. foreign, reporting 4677; 4678
. holding period 2673
. holiday gifts 1246
. leaseback 1595
. part purchase/part gift, basis of 2509
. passive activity interest 1838
. property and income from property . . . . . 1370 et seq.
. sale, combined with 2683
. strike benefits as 1283
. three years of death, within 5002; 5003
. trusts, with leaseback 1595
Gift tax
    generally . . . . 5038 et seq.
. annual exclusion 5046
. assessment period, failure to disclose gift
    of property 4835
. basis, increase for tax paid 2511
. below-market loans 5041
. charitable gifts 5049
. computation
. . gifts made before current year 5052
. . no gifts made before current year 5051

Gift tax — Cont'd
. credit 5050
. Crummey power 5046
. deductibility 1755
. deposit by electronic funds transfer 3028
. disclaimers, qualified 5043
. donee, payment by 2683
. educational payment exclusion 5047
. "estate freeze" transfers 5054
. "gross up" of 5003
. jointly-owned property 5042
. liens 4911; 4912
. marital deduction 5048
. medical payment exclusion 5047
. person responsible for 5039
. private annuities 1369
. rates 1114
. returns 5055
. . failure to file 4873
. . understatement of property value, penalty 4880
. split gifts to third parties by married donors . . . 5051; 5053
. taxable gifts 5045
. unified credit 5038
. valuation 5044
. . Chapter 14 rules 5054
Going concern
. amortization of going concern value 1973; 1974
Golden parachute payments
. deductibility 1535
. excise taxes on 1755
. gross income 1209
Goodwill
. amortization 1973; 1974
. capital asset, as 2627
. cost of 2471
. partnerships 3770; 3771
Governmental plans
. early withdrawals from 4344
. health and long-term care insurance, distri-
    butions for 4349
Governmental units
. contributions to 2102
. leases to, tax-exempt use property 1782
Government employees *See "Government
    officials and employees"*
Government obligations
. exchanges, tax-free 2416
. holding period 2670
. savings bonds . . . . 1334 et seq.
. short-term obligations
. . net direct interest expense 1717
. . sale or exchange, capital gains and
    losses 2634
. tax-exempt interest 1331; 1723
. Treasury Inflation-Indexed Securities 1333
Government officials and employees
. bribes 1611
. business expenses 1579; 3106
. civilian employees dying in combat or ter-
    rorist attacks, tax relief 4715
. compensation
    generally 1225
. . allowances for employees stationed
    outside the U.S. 4619
. employee stock purchase plan options 1220
. travel expenses 1543
. . luxury water travel 1552
**Government publications as capital as-
    sets** 2617
Grantor trusts
    generally . . . . 3957 et seq.
. beneficial enjoyment 3961

References are to paragraph [¶] numbers.

Grantor trusts — Cont'd
. estate freeze (Chapter 14 rules) 5054
. foreign trusts 3963; 3964
. income for grantor 3959
. owner other than grantor 3962
. returns 4733
. revoke, power to 3958
. S corporation shareholders 3353; 3354
. taxpayer identification numbers 4752
. transactions of interest, disclosure 4749
Greenmail
. deductibility of excise taxes on 1755
. reacquisition of stock 1624
Gross estate . . . . 2516; 5001 et
                                                                  seq.
Gross income
    generally . . . . 1200 et seq.
. adjusted gross income *See "Adjusted gross*
    income (AGI)"
. annuities 1355
. bankruptcy estate 3976
. claim of right doctrine 1204
. community property 1203
. compensation for personal services . . . . 1208 et seq.
. disaster relief payments, exclusion for 1207
. discharge of indebtedness . . . . 1385 et seq.
. exempt income 1206
. farmers 4501
. fringe benefits
    generally . . . . 1228 et seq.
. . exclusions from . . . . 1242 et seq.
. health reimbursement arrangement (HRA),
    amounts excluded from 1379
. IRA distributions 4357
. omissions from 4832
. passive activity . . . . 1817 et seq.
. tax benefit rule 1205
. trusts and estates 3916
Gross receipts
. AMT exemption for small corporations 3205
. domestic production gross receipts 1616
Gross up of gift tax 5003
Ground rent, redeemable
. basis, as part of 2465
Group health plans
. continuation coverage *See "Continuation*
    coverage (COBRA)"
. penalties 4898
Group life insurance
. permanent life insurance 1265
. term insurance
. . armed forces members 1223
. . cafeteria plans 1269
. . compensation, as 1523
. . exempt wages 3006
. . gross estate, inclusion in 5015
. . IRS uniform premium table 1263
. . premiums . . . . 1262 et seq.
. . retiree insurance, excess pension assets
    used to fund 4348
. . spouse and dependents, coverage of 1264
Guam
. foreign corporation treatment 4638
. residence in, U.S. tax and 4618
Guaranteed payments to partners 3730; 3771
Guarantees 1711; 1849;
                                                            1855; 4640
Guardians, returns filed by 4701
Gulf Opportunity Zone
. bonus first-year depreciation 1940; 3207
. net operating losses, carryback and carry-
    over 1841; 3212

H

Handicapped
. architectural barriers, expenses of remov-
    ing 1621; 2147
. day care for, use of residence as 1641
. disabled access credit 2323
. employee, employer payments to 1258
. estimated tax penalty, waiver of 3165
. group term insurance coverage 1262
. impairment-related work expenses 1637
. medical expense deduction 2146; 2147
Hardship
. backup withholding 3046
. corporate tax payments 4729
. distributions
. . 401(k) plans 4317
. . tax-sheltered annuities 4389
. electronic filing waiver 4750; 4753
. extensions of time 4903
. Taxpayer Assistance Order (TAO) 4811
Hazard mitigation
. property transferred to federal, state or Indi-
    an tribal government to implement 2432
Head of household
. child qualifying taxpayer for status as 3134
. . kidnapped child 3129
. filing threshold 4701
. itemized deductions 3114
. personal exemptions 3117
. qualification as 3134
. spouses living apart 3133
. standard deduction 3112
. tax tables 1105
Health and accident insurance plans
. Archer medical savings account (MSA) *See*
    "Archer medical savings account
    (MSA)"
. assignment of personal injury liability,
    amounts received for accepting 1382
. benefits, exclusion for . . . . 1374 et seq.
. continuation coverage 1531
. employer-provided 1255
. . cafeteria plans 1269
. . continuation coverage 1531
. . excise tax on high-cost coverage 4896
. . exclusions 1375
. . information reporting 3021; 4746
. . loss of limb, disfigurement, etc 1258
. . penalty on larger employers not offering
    affordable coverage 4896
. . pension and profit-sharing plans 4321
. . premium tax credit for individuals not eli-
    gible for affordable coverage 2345
. . small employer health insurance credit 2332
. fringe benefits . . . . 1527 et seq.
. governmental plan distributions for, public
    safety officers 4349
. health savings accounts *See "Health sav-*
    ings accounts (HSAs)"
. information returns 4746
. medical expense, as 2145; 2150
. penalty for individuals not carrying insur-
    ance 4896
. premium tax credit 2345
. refundable credit, insurance costs of dis-
    placed workers and PBGC pension re-
    cipients 2344
. retiree health accounts, excess plan assets
    to fund 4348
. self-employed individuals 1532

Health insurance providers
. compensation deduction limitation 1519
. excise tax 4896
Health reimbursement arrangements (HRAs)
. exclusion for benefits received through 1379
Health savings accounts (HSAs)
. contributions to 1529
. . adjusted gross income computation 3102
. . cafeteria plan benefits 1269
. . employer contributions 1257; 1529
. distributions from, exclusion for 1378
. eligibility to participate in 1529
. information returns 4746
. rollovers 1529; 4364
Hedging transactions
. *generally* 2642; 2660
. acquisition discount, accrual of 1328
. capital assets 2617; 2618
. defined 2618
. "mark-to-market" rules 2660
HH bonds 1334
Higher education expenses *See "Education expenses"*
High income individuals
. estimated tax installments 3157
Highly compensated employees
. cafeteria plans 1269
. defined 1535; 4326
. education assistance programs 2215
. employer-provided child care credit 2330
. entertainment expenses 1566
. life insurance 1353
. medical expense reimbursements 1255
. pension and profit-sharing plans 4326
. qualified tuition reductions 2217
. simplified employee pensions (SEPs) 4378
High-risk individuals, health coverage, state-sponsored organizations 4100
Historic structures, investment credit 2308
Hobby losses and expenses 1779; 3110
Holding companies, accumulated earnings tax 3319
Holding period
. *generally* . . . . 2667 et seq.
. computation of 2668
. decedent, property acquired from 2672
. dividends
. . property received as 1294
. . qualified dividend income 1288
. dividends-received deduction . . . . 3312 et seq.
. foreign tax credit 2371
. gifts 2673
. partnership interest 2669
. partnership property
. . contributed 3714
. . distributed 3746
. principal residence, exclusion of gain on
  sale 2445
. qualified small business stock 2670
. renewal community and D.C. zone assets . . . . 2650 et seq.
. replacement property . . . . 2427 et seq.; 2675
. tacking rules 2672
. tax-free exchange property 2674
Holidays
. due dates on 4756
. gifts for 1246
Home *See "Housing"; "Residence"; "Tax home"*
Home construction contracts, small construction contracts 2850

Home equity indebtedness
. alternative minimum tax 3209
. qualified residence interest 1734
Home mortgage interest *See "Qualified residence interest"*
Home office deduction
. *generally* 1638
. allocation of expenses 1644
. clients, meeting place for 1640
. day-care center, residence used as 1641
. deductible expenses 1638
. employer rental of space in employee's
  home 1645
. "exclusive" use on "regular" basis 1642
. gross income limitation on 1643
. inventory, storage at residence of 1641
. investment expenses 2164
. miscellaneous itemized deductions 3110
. principal place of business requirement 1639
. product samples, storage at residence of 1641
. separate structure not attached to resi-
  dence 1641
Homeowner's Assistance Program
. military base realignment and closure fringe
  benefits 1223
Homeowners' associations 4110; 4726
Home sale exclusion . . . . 2442 et seq.
Hope Scholarship credit *See "American opportunity tax credit"*
Horses, depreciation 1914; 1916
Horticultural organizations 4100; 4122
Horticultural structures, depreciation 1917; 1932
Hospitalization insurance *See "Health and accident insurance plans"*
Hospitals
. charitable contributions 2124
. electronic health record incentive payments
  to 1206
. medical expense deduction 2146
. tax exempt 4100; 4122
"Hot assets" 3754; 3755
Household and dependent care credit *See "Child and dependent care credit"*
Household employees
. withholding tax 3006; 3029; 3030
. . voluntary withholding agreements 3009
Household goods
. charitable contributions 2103
. principal residence converted as result of
  federally declared disaster 2433
Housing
. allowance, armed forces 1223
. employer, furnished by 1267; 1268
. foreign, exclusion . . . . 4613 et seq.
**Human trafficking victims, restitution pay-
ments** 1206
Hurricane Sandy 1798
Husbands and wives *See "Spouses"*
Hybrid methods of accounting 2818
Hydrogen
. credit for alternative fuel vehicle refueling
  property 2361
Hydropower resources
. credit for electricity production from renew-
  able resources 2324

I

I bonds 1334
Identifying numbers *See "Taxpayer identifi-
cation number (TIN)"*

Illegal payments . . . . 1200; 1610 et
                                                                    seq.
Improvements
. basis of property, adjustments 2474
. capital expenditures . . . . 1620; 1659 et
                                                                    seq.
. depreciation of
. . eligibility for deduction 1904
. . land improvements 1918; 1934
. . leasehold improvement property *See*
      "Leasehold improvement property"
. . MACRS 1921; 1923
. leased property 1344; 1598
. for medical purposes 2147
Imputed interest *See "Unstated (imputed)*
      interest"
Incentive stock options 1221; 3209;
                                                              3212; 4746
Incidents of ownership 5014; 5015
Inclusion amounts
. leased MACRS business automobiles 1117; 1956;
                                                                   1957
. listed property other than automobiles 1116; 1958
Income *See also "Gross income"*
. assignment of 1201
. charitable contribution, realized on 2109
. contingent rights to 2826
. foreign . . . . 4610 et seq.
. gifts and bequests of 1371
. partnerships . . . . 3715 et seq.
. previously reported, repayments of . . . . 2860 et seq.
. qualified production activities income de-
    fined 1616
. reallocation of by IRS 2858; 2859
. reconstruction by IRS 2857
Income averaging
. farmers and fishermen 3201; 4502
. lump-sum distributions 4339
Income forecast method of depreciation . . . 1959
Income in respect of decedent (IRD)
      generally 2513; 2516;
                                                              3968 et seq.
. beneficiaries 3970
. deduction for estate tax attributable to 3972
. partner, deceased 3773
Incompetent persons, returns for 4701
Incorporation
      generally . . . . 3510 et seq.
. costs, deductibility 3520
. partnerships, basis of property 2491
Independent contractors *See also*
      "Self-employed persons"
. compensation, deductibility 1516
. defined 3002
. IRS determination of status 3003
. reimbursed expenses 1573
. self-employment tax . . . . 3140 et seq.
. withholding . . . . 3000 et seq.
Indian employment credit 2326
Indian reservation property
. alternative minimum tax 3207
. casino profits, withholding on 3033
. coal, renewable electricity production credit 2324
. depreciation 1924
Individual retirement accounts (IRAs)
      generally . . . . 4351 et seq.
. active participant defined 4353
. after-tax contributions, rollovers of 4362
. contributions to . . . . 3102; 4351 et
                                                              seq.; 4369 et
                                                                    seq.
. . annual contribution limit 4351

Individual retirement accounts (IRAs) — Cont'd
. contributions to — Cont'd
. . catch-up contributions 4351
. . credit for 2363
. . deemed IRAs 4376
. conversion to Roth IRA
      generally 4371
. . changing nature of (recharacterizing) con-
      tributions 4370
. . reconversions 4372
. decedents 4365; 4366;
                                                                    4373
. deduction for
      generally 4352
. . married taxpayers, special rule for 4355
. deemed IRAs 4376
. distributions 4357
. . early withdrawals 4344
. . rollovers . . . . 4359 et seq.
. . Roth IRAs 4373; 4374
. education expenses, premature distribu-
      tions for 2200
. eligible retirement plan, defined 4359
. eligible rollover distributions
. . qualified plans, tax-free rollovers 4359
. . trustee-to-trustee transfers 4359
. excess contributions 4356; 4369
. excise taxes
. . contributions, excess 4356; 4369
. . minimum distributions 4357
. . prohibited transactions 4347
. exemption from tax 4358
. information returns 4746
. losses from, itemized deductions 3110
. marital deduction, estate tax 5023
. nondeductible contributions . . . . 4354; 4367 et
                                                                    seq.
. partial rollovers 4361
. penalty for failure to report 4898
. qualified terminable interest property 5023
. recharacterizing contributions to 4370
. rollovers . . . . 4359 et seq.
. Roth IRAs . . . . 4367 et seq.
. spouses 4355; 4365
. surviving spouses 4365
. types of rollovers 4360
. wash sales 2462
Industrial development bonds *See "Private*
      activity bonds"
Inflation-indexed bonds . . . . 1333 et seq.
Information returns *See also "Forms" (for*
      numerical finding list)
      generally . . . . 4737 et seq.
. business payments of $600 or more 4743
. controlled foreign corporations 4661
. electronic filing of 4753; 4897
. exempt organizations
. . annual returns 4124
. . disclosure of 4120
. expatriates 4654
. extension of time to file 4747
. foreign partnerships 4661
. fraudulent, damages for filing 4899
. income tax return checked against 4802
. interest or dividends . . . . 4738 et seq.
. nominees *See "Nominees, information re-*
      turns"
. passive foreign investment companies 4628
. payee statements . . . . 4742 et seq.
. . penalties 4897
. . taxpayer identification numbers 4752

Information returns *See also "Forms" (for numerical finding list)* — Cont'd
. penalties 4893; 4897; 4898
. withholding 4665
Inheritances *See "Bequests and devises"*
Injunction
. collection of tax 4910
. promoters of abusive tax shelters 4889
In-kind distributions
. dividends 1292; 1296
. estates and trusts 3918; 3940; 3949
Innocent spouse relief . . . . 4709 et seq.
. exceptions to 4712
. Tax Court jurisdiction 4859
Inside build-up on life insurance 1721; 3211
Insolvency
. alternative minimum tax, effect on 3210
. discharge of indebtedness of insolvent
    debtor 1389; 1397
Installment obligations
. foreign corporations, transfers to 3588
. income in respect of decedent 3969
. sale, exchange, or satisfaction of 2458
Installment payments
. life insurance proceeds 1348
. tax payments 4906
. . agreement for installment payments 4722; 4904
. . application fee 4722; 4812
. . estimated tax of corporations . . . . 3344; 3346 et seq.
. . estimated tax of individuals . . . . 3154; 3157 et seq.
. . failure to pay, penalty 4874
. . income tax of individuals 4722
Installment purchases 1706
Installment sales
    generally . . . . 2452 et seq.
. character of gain 2457
. contingent payment sales 2455
. disallowed use 2454
. earnings and profits 3525
. election out of installment method 2456
. passive activities, of 1838
. payments 2453
. "pledge and interest" rule, sale of property
    for more than $150,000 2460
. reporting gain under 2453
. self-canceling installment notes (SCINs) 3969
. unstated interest on . . . . 1307 et seq.; 1707
Institutional care as medical expense 2146
Insurance *See also "Health and accident insurance plans"; "Life insurance and endowment contracts"; "Long-term care insurance"*
. casualty losses 1796
. financed . . . . 1718 et seq.
. premiums *See "Insurance premiums"*
. proceeds *See "Insurance proceeds"*
. self insurance 1607
. Subpart F income 4624
. underwriting, source of income 4640
Insurance companies
. captive 1607
. effectively connected income 4644
. life 4211
. mutual, other than life 4100; 4211
. other than life or mutual 4211
. returns
    generally 4726

Insurance companies — Cont'd
. returns — Cont'd
. . consolidated 3339
. S corporations, as 3351
. stock 3512
Insurance premiums *See also "Life insurance and endowment contracts"*
. advance or prepaid, deduction of 1609
. alimony 2157; 2158
. capital expenditures, as 1607
. construction of building, property insurance 1607
. earnings and profits 3525
. health and accident insurance 1527
. . premium tax credit 2345
. . self-employed individuals 1532; 3102
. investment expenses . . . . 1606 et seq.
. loan, paid by, deductibility of interest . . . . . 1718 et seq.
. malpractice insurance 1607; 1636
. medical expense, deductibility 2145; 2150
. mortgage insurance 1736; 4746
. public liability 1607
. time for deduction 1609
. title insurance 1607
. trade or business expenses, as . . . . 1526; 1527; 1606 et seq.
Insurance proceeds
. disaster losses; federally declared disasters, principal residence damaged by 2433
. earnings and profits 3525
. involuntary conversions 2434
. life insurance
    generally . . . . 1346 et seq.
. . accelerated benefits, chronically or terminally ill 1351
. . consideration, contract transferred for 1352
. . death benefits exclusion . . . . 1346 et seq.
. . employer-owned insurance 1353
. . estate tax . . . . 5014 et seq.
. . installment payments 1348
. . interest, proceeds left at 1349
. . prior to death of insured, proceeds paid 1350
. . split-dollar 1266
. . surrender, redemption or maturity of contract 1350
. . transferred contracts 1352
. medical expenses reimbursed 2151
. use and occupancy insurance 1206
Intangible assets
. basis of 2471
. capital assets, as 1618; 2622; 2629
. capitalization rules . . . . 1663 et seq.
. . de minimis and 12-month rule exceptions 1665
. depreciation 1903; 1908; 1962
. 15-year amortization . . . . 1973 et seq.
. . exclusions 1962
. like-kind exchanges 2419
. sales or exchanges 4667
. Section 351 transfers 3511
Intangible drilling and development costs
. alternative minimum tax 3208
. business expenses 1628
. earnings and profits, adjustment to 3525
. partnership items of income and deductions 3718
Intercompany transactions 3338
Interest
    generally . . . . 1301 et seq.
. abatement of 4858; 4859; 4870
. acquisition indebtedness
. . corporate 1725

Interest — Cont'd

. acquisition indebtedness — Cont'd
.. qualified residence acquisition indebted-
    ness 1733
. adequate stated interest 1318
. allocation rules
   generally .... 1737 et seq.
.. deduction limits 1738
.. produced property 1669
.. qualified residence interest 1741
.. reallocation 1742
.. "rule of 78s" 1749
.. taxpayers who must allocate 1739
.. time for allocation 1740
.. unstated (imputed) interest 1311
. applicable federal rate 1115; 1310;
    4866
. automobile loans 1558
. below market *See "Below-market loans"*
. bonds .... 1313 et seq.
.. tax credit bonds 2366
. capitalization of 1620; 1667;
    1669
. charitable deductions, effect on 2111
. deductible
   generally .... 1700 et seq.
.. accrual method taxpayers, time for de-
    duction 1748
.. acquisition indebtedness 1725
.. allocation rules .... 1737 et seq.
.. another person, interest paid by 1712
.. cash method taxpayers .... 1744 et seq.
.. cooperative housing corporations 1714
.. education loans .... 2222 et seq.
.. eligibility for deduction .... 1711 et seq.
.. entertainment facilities 1567
.. exempt income expenses 3924; 4209
.. finance charges 1704
.. forbearance or use of money 1701
.. home equity debt 1734
.. installment purchases 1706
.. investment interest .... 1726 et seq.
.. late payment charges 1705
.. market discount bonds 1716
.. mortgage interest 1702; 1713;
    1714
.. original issue discount .... 1751 et seq.
.. "points" paid on mortgage 1703
.. prepaid interest 1745
.. prepayment penalties 1705
.. qualified residence interest .... 1730 et seq.
.. "rule of 78s" 1749
.. short-term government obligations 1717
.. taxes, interest on 1708
.. thin capitalization 1709
.. time for deduction .... 1743 et seq.
.. unstated interest 1707; 1750
. deficiencies .... 4864 et seq.
. definition of interest
   generally 1303
.. qualified residence interest 1732
. effectively connected income 4644
. exempt *See "Tax-exempt income"*
. forbearance or use of money 1701
. foreign tax credit 2371
. frozen deposits, on 1330
. government bonds .... 1331; 1333 et
    seq.
. imputed *See "Unstated (imputed) interest"*
. information returns .... 4738; 4740 et
    seq.
. installment purchases 1706

Interest — Cont'd

. investment, deduction of .... 1726 et seq.
. limitations on deductions 1716; 1717;
    1726 et seq.
. long-term tax-exempt rate 3569
. look-back (long-term contracts) method,
   under 2854
. mortgage *See also '"Points" paid on mort-*
   gage"
   generally 1304; 1702
.. capitalization of 1620
.. cooperative housing corporations 1714
.. credit for 2357
.. investment interest 1728
.. jointly owned property 1713
.. liability for debt 1713
.. qualified residence interest .... 1730 et seq.
.. reporting requirements 4744
. mortgage insurance premium 1736
. net investment income
.. alternative minimum tax 3209
.. defined 1729; 3152
.. Medicare surtax on unearned income *See*
   "Net investment income tax"
.. private foundations 4127
. netting of 4866
. nondeductible
.. annuity contracts .... 1718 et seq.
.. corporate debt payable in issuer's stock 1710
.. endowment contracts .... 1718 et seq.
.. exempt securities 1723
.. life insurance loans .... 1718 et seq.
.. personal interest 1715
.. qualified employer plans, loans from 1722
.. registration-required obligations 1724
. original issue discount .... 1313 et seq.
. overpayments, on 4853
. paid
.. deduction for .... 1700 et seq.
.. estates and trusts 3923
.. insurance premiums, on loan to pay ..... 1718 et seq.
.. premature withdrawal penalty 2168; 3102
.. statements for payees 4742
.. time for deduction .... 1743 et seq.
. penalties, on .... 4865 et seq.
. pension plans, on loans from 1722
. personal holding company income received
   from 3325
. personal interest limit 1715
. "points" paid on mortgage *See '"Points"*
   paid on mortgage"
. portfolio income 1820
. prepaid 1745
. production period 1669
. qualified residence interest .... 1730 et seq.
. qualified stated interest 1315
. refunds, on 4865
. residence, qualified .... 1730 et seq.
. savings bonds, U.S .... 1334 et seq.
.. higher education expenses, exclusion for
   income used to pay .... 2219 et seq.
. source (U.S. or foreign) 4640; 4641
. stock, sale or exchange
.. loan to buy mutual fund stock 1723
. suspension, IRS failure to notify taxpayer of
   liability 4871
. taxes, on, generally 1708
. time for reporting income from .... 1335 et seq.
. underpayments, on
   generally .... 4864 et seq.
.. abatement 4870
.. accrual period 4867

Interest — Cont'd
. underpayments, on — Cont'd
. . assessment 4826
. . deposits to prepay and/or stop running of
      interest 4868
. . errors in withholding and payment of tax 3020
. . other year's tax payments 4869
. . rate of interest 4866
. unrelated business taxable income 4122
. unstated (imputed) interest . . . . 1307 et seq.;
                                                          1707
. U.S. source income not effectively connect-
      ed with U.S. business 4642
. withholding
. . backup withholding 3044; 3045
. . foreign taxpayers 4667
Internal Revenue Service
. Appeals Office . . . . 4815 et seq.
. audits by . . . . 4800 et seq.
. National Taxpayer Advocate 4811
. user fees for rulings or determinations 4812
International organizations
. employees, limited income exclusion 4645
. payments to, backup withholding 3044
Inter vivos trusts, basis of property ac-
      quired from decedent 2519
Inventories
      generally . . . . 2863 et seq.
. accounting methods 2818; 2845
. . change of method 2868; 2881
. . small taxpayer exceptions 2818
. appreciated, partnerships . . . . 3754 et seq.
. book inventory 2877
. capital assets 2617
. charitable contribution of 2107; 2108
. commodities dealers and traders,
      mark-to-market rules 2879; 2880
. farmers . . . . 4505; 4513 et
                                                          seq.
. FIFO (first-in, first-out)
      generally 2873
. . stock, identification of shares 2496; 2498;
                                                          2499
. foreign corporations, transfers to 3588
. futures contracts 2864
. goods included 2864
. identification methods . . . . 2872 et seq.
. inventory price index computation (IPIC)
      method 2872; 2875
. LIFO (last-in, first-out)
      generally . . . . 2873 et seq.
. . earnings and profits adjustment 3525
. . recapture 3364
. lower of cost or market valuations 2870; 4514
. market value defined 2871
. materials and supplies 1657
. miners and manufacturers 2878
. partnerships
. . basis adjustments 3779
. . distributions 3757
. . . substantially appreciated inventory . . . . 3754 et seq.
. . gain or loss on 3753; 3766
. . information returns 4746
. retailers 2876
. sales, effectively connected income 4644
. securities dealers and traders,
      mark-to-market rules 2879; 2880
. shrinkage estimates 2868
. storage in residence of 1641
. uniform capitalization rules . . . . 1666 et seq.
. valuation . . . . 2865 et seq.
. . prohibited methods 2867

Inventory price index computation (IPIC)
      method 2872
. dollar value LIFO 2875
Inversions, corporate and partnership 4655
Investment companies
. accumulated earnings tax 3319
. diversification, portfolios already diversified 3517
. exchange fund partnerships 3711
. passive foreign investment companies . . . . 4628 et seq.
. reorganizations 3543; 3560
. swap funds 3517
Investment credit
      generally . . . . 2307 et seq.
. basis of credit property, effect of credit on 2478
. basis reduction for, treatment of 2698
. deduction of unused credits 2305
. ordering rules 2306
. property qualifying for 2307
. recapture 2314
. rehabilitation investment credit . . . . 2308 et seq.
. renewable electricity production credit 2324
Investment in annuity contract . . . . 1356 et seq.
Investment interest . . . . 1726 et seq.;
                                                          3114
Investments
. advice provided through qualified plans,
      prohibited transactions 4347
. conversion and constructive ownership
      transactions . . . . 2664 et seq.
. dividend reinvestment plans, basis of stock
      acquired through 2494
. employer securities, qualified plan invest-
      ments in 4333
. expenses in connection with 1606; 2164;
                                                          3110
. foreign investment in U.S. real estate 4649; 4650;
                                                     4661; 4671
Involuntary conversions
      generally . . . . 2430 et seq.
. carryovers 3564
. condemnation . . . . 2435 et seq.
. defined 2432
. depreciation of property acquired in 1929
. disaster losses 2433
. insurance compensation 2434
. livestock 4526
. replacement property . . . . 2431; 2438 et
                                                          seq.
. . basis 2503
. . holding period of 2675
. . Section 1231 transactions, as . . . . 2684 et seq.
IRA (individual retirement account) *See*
      "Individual retirement accounts (IRAs)"
Iron ore
. advance payments 2689
. capital gains and losses 2688
. depletion 1978
. source of income 4642
IRS *See "Internal Revenue Service"*
ISOs *See "Incentive stock options"*
Itemized deductions
. alternative minimum tax purposes 3209
. charitable contributions 2100
. defined 3109
. election to itemize 3113
. impairment-related work expenses 1637
. investment in annuity contract 3967
. medical expenses . . . . 2140 et seq.
. miscellaneous itemized deductions *See*
      "Miscellaneous itemized deductions"
. reduction in-3%/80% rule 3114
. tax benefit rule 1205

Itemized deductions — Cont'd
. taxes 1757
Itinerant worker, travel expenses 1543

J

Jeopardy assessments 4828
Job-hunting expenses 1632
. assistance programs 1245
Joint and survivor annuities
. after-death income 3972
. exclusion ratio 1360
. public safety officers killed in line of duty 1260
. qualified employee plans 4319
. qualified terminable interest property 5023
Joint ownership
. decedent, basis of property acquired from 2517
. deductibility of taxes 1763
. estate tax . . . . 5010 et seq.
. gift tax 5042
. income from 1202
. residence 2445
. spouses' jointly-held property 5011
. survivorship rights 1763
Joint returns
    generally . . . . 4704 et seq.
. adoption expense credit 2354
. alimony 2153
. alternative minimum tax exemption amount 3203
. change to or from separate returns 4707
. death of spouse, year of 4708
. deficiencies 4823
. equitable relief from liability 4711
. filing threshold 4701
. innocent spouse rule 4709
. itemized deductions 3114
. liability for tax, interest and penalties 4704
. married defined for purposes of 4705
. moving expenses 1650
. net operating loss deduction 1846
. passive activity losses 1812
. performing artists 3105
. personal exemptions 3117; 3118;
                                                    3127
. qualified residence interest 1735
. qualifying for 4706
. self-employment tax 3145
. separate liability election 4710
. standard deduction 3112
. surviving spouse 3132
. tax tables 1103
Joint tenancy *See "Joint ownership"*
Joint ventures 3701
Judgment
. attorney's fees payable out of 1384
Jury duty
. gross income 1209
. remittance of pay to employer, deduction
    for 3102; 3107

K

Kansas disaster area
. replacement period for involuntary conver-
    sions 2441
Keogh plans 4327
Key employees
. cafeteria plans 1269
. life insurance premiums 1608
. . group-term life insurance 1262
. . interest incurred with respect to, deduct-
    ibility 1718

Key employees — Cont'd
. loans from plans 1722
. top-heavy plans 4329
Kickbacks
    generally . . . . 1610 et seq.
. government officials or employees 1611
. income from 1200
. Medicare and Medicaid, under 1611
Kiddie tax
    generally . . . . 3135 et seq.
. allocable parental tax 3137
. alternative minimum tax 3204
. child subject to 3136
. computation 3137
. identification numbers 4752
. net unearned income 3138
. parent's election to claim child's unearned
    income 3139; 4701
Know-how, amortization 1974

L

Labor unions
. dues, fees, and assessments 1633
. tax exemption 4100
Land
. amortization 1975
. capital expenditures 1659; 1660
. depreciation 1902
. . improvements 1918
. qualified conservation easements 2512; 5016
. sales or exchanges 1320
. . growing crops, sold with 4524
. wetlands or highly erodible croplands, dis-
    position of 4525
"Large" corporation
. estimated tax 3344
. income tax returns 4726
Last-in-first-out (LIFO) method *See "Inven-
    tories"*
Lavish expenses 1542; 1552;
                                                1570; 1571;
                                                2149
Lawyers *See "Attorneys"*
Leasebacks
. gift and leaseback 1595
. rental agreement as disqualified leaseback 1600
. rent expense 1595
. sale and leaseback 1595; 2682
Leasehold improvement property
. basis 2474
. capitalization of expenses 1660
. depreciation 1918; 1923;
                                                1925; 1932;
                                                1934
. Section 179 expense election 1944
Leases *See also "Lessor and lessee"*
. amortization 1975
. . acquisition expenses 1597
. . Section 197 property 1973
. at-risk rules 1804; 1805
. automobiles
. . inclusion amount for leased luxury autos 1117; 1956;
                                                1957
. . standard mileage rate allowance 1560
. . valuation rules . . . . 1233 et seq.
. bonuses 1340
. cancellation 1340; 1598;
                                                2680
. cooperative housing lease expenses 1625
. depreciation 1904
. . intangibles leases 1962

Leases *See also "Lessor and lessee"* — **Cont'd**
. depreciation — Cont'd
. . qualified leasehold improvement property
    See "Leasehold improvement property"
. listed property 1946; 1956; 1958
. . inclusion amounts 1116
. purchase options 1596
. rental income . . . . 1339 et seq.
. rent expense . . . . 1593 et seq.
. sale or lease 1596
. tax-exempt use property
. . depreciation 1932
. . losses on 1782
Leaves, employer-sponsored
    leave-sharing plan 1206
Legal expenses *See also "Attorneys"*
    generally 1603; 1604
. condemnation awards 2436
. court costs in connection with civil rights
    suits and whistleblower awards, deduc-
    tion of 3108
. nonbusiness legal expenses 2166
. payable out of judgment 1384
Legislation
. influencing public concerning 1629; 4102
Lessor and lessee
. basis-reduction adjustment 2480
. bonuses 1340
. construction allowances from lessor 1344
. depreciation 1904
. . listed property 1956
. expenses of lessor paid by lessee 1343
. improvements by 1344; 1598; 1923
. investment credit 2307; 2308
. rents *See "Rent"*
. subletting, amortization of incurred costs 1598
. taxes of lessor paid by lessee 1761
Levy for taxes
. seizure and sale of property 4905
Liability for tax
. costs of determining or contesting 1513; 2165
. fiduciaries . . . . 4913 et seq.
. gift tax 5039
. IRS failure to provide notice of
. . suspension of interest and penalties 4871
. partners 3716; 3719
. spouses 1203; 4704
. . innocent spouse relief . . . . 4709 et seq.
. transferee 4914
Liberty Zone *See "New York Liberty Zone"*
Licenses
. fees, deductibility 1514; 1623
. government granted, amortization 1974; 1975
Liens
    generally 4911
. notice of, withdrawal 4912
. priority 4912
Life estates
. allocation of basis 2522
. capital asset, as 2630
. depreciation allowance 1904
. gift to spouse 5048
. marital deduction 5023
. retained right to govern enjoyment 5004
. valuation 5016; 5044
Life insurance and endowment contracts
. alimony payments, premiums as 2158
. deduction of premiums 1608
. . company-owned life insurance 1526
. definition of life insurance contract 1347

Life insurance and endowment contracts — **Cont'd**
. employer-owned insurance 1353; 4746
. estate tax . . . . 5014 et seq.; 5015
. fringe benefits, exempt income . . . . 1261 et seq.
. group-term insurance *See "Group life insur-
    ance"*
. information returns 4124; 4746
. interest
. . deductions
. . . business life insurance loans 1718
. . . inside buildup 1721
. . . "plan of purchase" borrowing against
      life insurance 1720
. . . single premium life insurance 1719
. income, reporting 1335
. key person insurance 1608; 1718
. modified endowment contracts 1368
. "plan of purchase" borrowing against life
    insurance 1720
. premiums paid by employer . . . . 1261 et seq.
. proceeds . . . . 1346 et seq.
. qualified plan, purchased with employer
    contributions to 4341
. single premium life insurance 1719
. split-dollar plans 1266
. . charitable contributions 2115
. tables and charts 1263
. tax-free exchanges 2417
. transfers for consideration 1352
Life insurance companies, personal hold-
    ing companies, classification as 3322
Life tenant, depreciation deductions 3102
Lifetime Learning credit 2201; 2203
. qualified tuition and related expenses for 2204
LIFO (last-in, first-out) method *See "Inven-
    tories"*
Like-kind exchanges
    generally . . . . 2418 et seq.
. assumption of liabilities 2422
. basis of property 2501
. boot 2421; 2422
. deferred 2420
. defined 2419
. depreciation of property acquired in 1929
. exchange funds 2420
. farms and farmers 4527
. leasebacks 2682
. multi-party nontaxable exchanges 2420
. multiple properties 2425
. related party exchanges 2424
. replacement property, condemned real es-
    tate 2440
. "reverse" or "forward" exchange 2420
. time limitations 2423
Limited liability companies (LLCs) 2102; 3703; 5044; 5046
Liquidating trusts 3909
Liquidations
    generally . . . . 3574 et seq.
. basis of property received
    generally 2490; 3575; 3577
. . partnerships 3749
. carryovers of acquiring corporation 3563
. costs of 3580
. 80% subsidiaries 3577; 3578
. gain or loss . . . . 3574 et seq.
. information returns 4124; 4746
. liquidating dividends . . . . 3333; 3574 et seq.
. parent and subsidiaries 3577; 3578

Liquidations — Cont'd
. partial liquidation of noncorporate share-
    holder 3531
. partnership interest . . . . 3768 et seq.
. returns by corporations 4727; 4746
. shareholder's tax on distributions 3575
. subsidiaries 3577; 3578
. taxation of corporation 3576
Listed property
. adequate records 1585
. ADS depreciation 1931
. defined 1947
. inclusion amounts for leased property . . 1116
. MACRS depreciation deductions, limita-
    tions . . . . 1946 et seq.
. recapture rules 2700
. substantiating expenses . . . . 1579; 1584 et
                               seq.
Listed transactions
. assessment of tax on unreported 4834
. disclosure 4749
. failure to report, penalty for 4891
. . material advisors 4893
. . suspension of 4871
. understatements regarding, penalty for . 4892
Livestock
. accrual method farmers 4509
. depreciation 1914; 1915;
                               4523
. inventories 4513; 4514
. like-kind exchanges 4527
. purchase price 4507
. sale/involuntary conversion 2432; 2438;
                               2441; 4508;
                               4526
Loans
. at-risk rules, borrowed amounts 1807
. below-market interest rate *See "Be-*
   low-market loans"
. Commodity Credit Corporation (CCC)
    loans, crops pledged to secure 4528
. costs of 1620
. dividends distinguished from 1290
. gift 5041
. life insurance
   generally 1350
. . interest deduction . . . . 1718 et seq.
. qualified employer plans, loans from
   generally 4343
. . interest deduction 1722
. of securities, recognition of gain or loss . 2410
. shareholder, to corporation 1855
. student loans . . . . 1387; 2222 et
                               seq.
Lobbying expenses
. business expenses 1629
. charitable organizations 2103
. exempt organizations . . . . 4102 et seq.
. information returns 4124
Local benefit assessments 1759
Long-term capital gains and losses . . . 2600 et seq.;
                               2609; 2667;
                             2672
Long-term care insurance
. benefits
   generally 1374
. . exclusion, per diem limit 1376
. . information returns 4746
. premiums
. . governmental plan distributions for, public
    safety officers 4349
. . as medical expense 2145

Long-term care insurance — Cont'd
. self-employed individuals 1532
. tax-free exchanges 2417
Long-term care services, medical ex-
   pense, as 2144
Long-term contracts
. accounting methods
   generally . . . . 2848 et seq.
. . accrual method, construction contracts . 2830
. allocation of costs 2851
. alternative minimum tax 3208
. "constructive completion transaction" . . 2856
. defined 2849
. home construction contracts 2850
. look-back method 2854
. mid-contract change, following 2856
. percentage of completion method
   generally . . . . 2848 et seq.
. . modified 2853
. simplified look-back marginal-impact
    method 2855
. "step-in-the-shoes" transaction 2856
Look-back method
. long-term contracts 2854
. tax computation 2806
Loss corporations . . . . 3568 et seq.
Losses
. abandonment 1773; 1774;
                             1784; 1788
. amount deductible 1775
. at-risk limitations . . . . 1803 et seq.
. bad debts distinguished 1848
. bank deposits, frozen 1792; 1802
. capital 2611; 2612;
                             2615
. casualty losses *See "Casualty losses"*
. condemnation 1774
. controlled groups 3337
. corporations
. . dual consolidated losses 3342
. . limitation on capital losses 2615
. . nonliquidating distributions of property . 3538
. . proposed venture, unsuccessful investi-
    gation of 1785
. . related taxpayers, transactions between . 2448; 2450
. . small business investment company . . 1781; 4205
. deductibility . . . . 1773 et seq.
. demolition 1783
. disaster *See "Disaster losses"*
. drought *See "Drought"*
. earnings and profits 3525
. farm 3210; 4503
. . limitations on 4504
. foreclosure 1773; 1774;
                             1787; 1788
. foreign 2372
. gambling losses 1786
. hobby losses 1779
. individual retirement accounts (IRAs) . . 3110; 4357
. individuals
   generally . . . . 1776 et seq.
. . small business stock 2644
. limitation on deduction . . . . 1776 et seq.
. mortgaged property 1787; 1788
. operating *See "Net operating loss"*
. overall domestic loss, recharacterization as
    foreign source 2372
. passive activity, limits . . . . 1810 et seq.
                    See also "Pas-
                    sive activity
                    loss rules"
. profit, transactions for 1778

Losses — Cont'd
. proposed venture, unsuccessful investiga-
  tion of 1785
. reimbursement claim 1791
. related parties, sales or exchanges be-
  tween 2448
. S corporations 3369
. securities 1781; 4209
. seizure of property 1774
. stock
. . intercompany transactions 3341
. . redemptions 1774
. . small business . . . . 1781; 2644 et
  seq.; 4205
. . wash sales 2462
. . worthless 1781
. straddles . . . . 2653 et seq.
. tax-exempt use property 1782
. tax sales 1789
. theft losses *See "Theft losses"*
. time to deduct 1790
. trade or business . . . . 1776 et seq.
. vacation homes, owner's expenses 1780
. worthless stock or securities 1781
Lottery payments
. constructive receipt of award 1373
. right to receive future, as capital asset 2617
. withholding 3033
**Low-income communities, new markets
  tax credit** 2329
Low-income housing credit 2321
  generally 2320
. building identification number 4752
Low-income housing, depreciation
. ADS depreciation periods 1932
Lump-sum payments *See also "Pension
  and profit-sharing plans"*
. alimony 2154
Luxury automobiles
. MACRS depreciation limitations
  generally . . . . 1931; 1946 et
  seq.
. . inclusion amounts 1117; 1956;
  1957
Luxury water travel 1552

M

Machinery and equipment
. capital expenditure, cost as 1620; 1660
. depreciation
. . farm 1915; 4523
. . MACRS 1914; 1916
. installation charges 1620
. standby emergency spare parts 1658
MACRS *See "Depreciation"*
Magnetic media filing 4753; 4897
Mail and mailing
. filing, mailing as 4754; 4755
. 90-day letter 4824
. rural mail carriers, automobile expenses of 1560
Majority interest taxable year 2812
Malpractice insurance premiums 1607; 1636
Manufacturers
. advanced energy manufacturing project
  credit 2313
. bonus first-year depreciation allowance 1936
. domestic production activities, deduction
  for . . . . 1614 et seq.
. inventories 2878
Marginal well production credit
. carryback and carryover 2304

Marital deduction
. estate tax
  generally . . . . 5021 et seq.
. . administration expenses, effect of 5025
. . death taxes, effect of 5024
. . election for QTIP property 5008; 5023
. . noncitizen spouse 5026
. . nonresident aliens 5037
. . terminable interests 5022
. gift tax 5048
Market discount bonds
  generally . . . . 1324 et seq.
. definitions 1326
. election to include in income currently 1327
. holder's basis 2470
. net direct interest expense 1716
. partial principal payment made 1325
. partnerships, unrealized receivables 3756
Mark-to-market rules
  generally . . . . 2653 et seq.
. dealers in securities and commodities 2879
. deemed sale rule, terminating U.S. citizen-
  ship or residency after June 16, 2008 4653
. mixed straddles, elections for 2658
. PFIC stock 4630
. self-employment, net earnings from 3143
. traders in securities and commodities 2880
Married couples *See "Spouses"*
**Mass transit, qualified transportation
  fringe benefits** 1246; 1247
Material participation
. farmers and farming
. . alternative minimum tax, farm losses 3210
. . replanting costs 4520
. investment interest 1728
. net earnings from self employment, crop
  shares 3143
. passive activity losses
  generally . . . . 1826 et seq.
. . facts and circumstances test 1828
. . individuals, material participation by 1827
. . limited partners 1829
. . participation defined 1830
. . real property business 1836
. . spouses 1831
Materials and supplies 1514; 1635;
  1636; 1657;
  1658; 2617
Meals and lodging
. business connection requirement 1574
. campus lodging 1268
. cash, option of employee to take 1267
. charitable expense, as 2121
. condition of employment, lodging as 1267
. deductibility 1569; 1571
. documentary evidence of 1586
. education expenses 2204
. employer, furnished by 1246; 1267;
  1268; 1561;
  1566
. foreign housing . . . . 4613 et seq.
. lavish expenses 1571
. medical expense, as 2146; 2148;
  2149
. moving expenses 1648
. optional meal allowance 1581
. percentage limitations 1569
. per diem allowance 1581
. reporting and substantiation . . . . 1580 et seq.
. restrictions 1569; 1571
. support, as 3124
. travel expenses . . . . 1542 et seq.

Meals and lodging — Cont'd
. when not away from home 1546
Mediation of tax disputes 4818
**Medicaid; kickbacks, rebates, and bribes
    under** 1611
Medical and dental expenses
    generally . . . . 2140 et seq.
. AGI-based floor
    generally 2141
. . alternative minimum tax 3209
. Archer medical savings account distribu-
    tions for, exclusion from gross income 1377
. armed forces, allowances for 1223
. capital expenditures for purposes of 2147
. decedent's expenses 2143
. deduction, generally 3114
. dependents 2142
. employer's payment of 1527
. estate tax deduction 5018
. generation-skipping transfer tax 5058
. gift tax exclusion, amounts paid on behalf
    of another 5047
. health insurance
    generally 2145
. . employer-provided . . . . 1527 et seq.
. . self-employed persons 1532
. health reimbursement arrangements, exclu-
    sion for benefits received under 1379
. health savings account distributions for, ex-
    clusion from gross income 1378
. institutional care 2146
. long-term care insurance contract 2145
. meals and lodging 2149
. reimbursement 1255; 1527;
    2151
. support, as 3124
. time for deduction 2150
. transportation expenses 2148
. types of deductible expenses 2144
Medical emergencies, leaves of absence 1206
Medical research organizations
. charitable contributions 2124
Medical savings account (MSA) *See also
    "Archer medical savings account
    (MSA)"*
. exempt wages 3006
. information returns 4746
. Medicare Advantage Medical Savings Ac-
    counts 1530
. penalty for failure to report 4898
. prohibited transactions 4347
Medicare
. kickbacks, rebates, and bribes under 1611
. medical expense deduction 2145
. Medicare Advantage Medical Savings Ac-
    counts 1530
. Parts A, B and D, as income 1206
. Secondary Payer statute, suits in connec-
    tion with
. . deduction of legal expenses 3108
. surtax on *See "Net investment income tax"*
Medicare tax
. Hospital Insurance (HI) tax 3024
. rates of tax 1108; 3024
. unearned income of higher-income individ-
    uals, Medicare surtax on . . . . 1107; 3150 et
    seq.
. withholding 3004
Membership organizations
. charitable contributions 2124
. dues 1514; 1568;
    1635; 1636

Membership organizations — Cont'd
. expenses of, deduction 1511
Merger or consolidation 3544
. employer withholding 3019
Mexicans
. services performed by, withholding 4668; 4669
Microturbine property
. advanced energy manufacturing project
    credit 2313
. energy credit 2311
Midwestern disaster area
. replacement period for involuntary conver-
    sions 2441
Mileage allowances
. basis reduction 2476
. business standard rate 1560
. cents-per-mile valuation method 1236
. charitable expense, as 2120
. medical travel 2148
. optional auto allowances 1582
Military *See "Armed forces"*
Mines and mining
. capital expenditures 1626
. coal, capital gains treatment 2688; 2689
. depletion . . . . 1976 et seq.;
    3211
. development costs 1627; 1667;
    3208; 3564
. exploration expenditures
    generally 1626
. . alternative minimum tax 3213
. . capitalization 1667
. . carryovers 3564
. . partnerships 3718; 3723;
    3756
. . recapture of exploration costs in produc-
    tion stage 1626
. foreign tax credit 2371
. inventory valuation, allocated cost basis 2878
. iron ore, capital gains treatment 2688; 2689
. mineral interests, capital expenditures 1659
. safety equipment property 1964
Minimum tax credit 2365; 3564;
    3573
Minors
. compensation 1227; 1516
. expatriation rules 4653
. generation-skipping transfer tax . . . . 5056 et seq.
. gifts to 5046
. kiddie tax *See "Kiddie tax"*
. returns for 4701
. throwback rules 3954
Miscellaneous itemized deductions
. adjusted gross income, 2% of AGI floor 3110; 3111
. alternative minimum tax 3209
. annuity contract, unrecovered investment in 3967
. business expenses 1631
. estates and trusts 3921
. gambling losses 1786
. legal expenses 2166
. nonbusiness expenses . . . . 2163 et seq.
. not-for-profit activities 1779
. partnerships 3111
. passthrough entities 3111
. S corporations 3111
Misstatement of value 4871; 4877;
    4887
Mitigation of statute of limitations 4839
**Modified accelerated cost recovery sys-
    tem (MACRS)** *See "Depreciation"*

Modified endowment contracts 1368
Money purchase plans 4311; 4314;
. . . . 4317; 4330
Mortgage insurance premiums 1736; 4746
Mortgages
. alimony, payment as 2157
. assistance payments 1206
. charitable contribution of mortgaged prop-
. . erty 2114
. credit 2357; 4746;
. . . . 4898
. foreclosures of 1787; 1788;
. . . . 2405
. information returns 4746
. interest *See "Interest"; "Qualified residence
. . interest"*
. points *See "'Points" paid on mortgage"*
. prepayment penalty 1705
. REMICs 4204
. on residence, debt forgiveness 1397
. servicing rights, amortization 1975
Motion picture films
. amortization 1974
. at-risk rules 1805
. capitalization of costs 1667
. depreciation 1908; 1927;
. . . . 1959
. domestic production activities, deduction
. . for 1616
. election to expense production costs 1965
. . recapture rules 2695
Moving expenses
. . *generally* . . . . 1646 et seq.
. above-the-line-expenses 1648; 3102
. armed forces 1654
. distance test 1649
. equipment and machinery 1514
. foreign moves 1651
. reimbursement of
. . allowances for, armed forces members 1223
. . qualified moving expense reimbursement 1248
. . withholding on 3006
. relocation allowances and loans 1206; 1213
. self-employed persons 1646
. 78-week test 1650
. 39-week test 1650
. time for deduction 1647; 1653
. United States, moves to 1652
Multiple corporations . . . . 3337 et seq.
**Multiple support agreements, personal ex-
. emptions** 3123
Multiple trusts 3913
Music
. amortization of expenses to create or ac-
. . quire 1969
Mutual insurance companies 4100

N

Nanny tax 3029; 3030
National Guard
. travel expenses 3102
**National Health Service Corps Loan Re-
. payment Program** 1387
Native Americans *See "Indian employment
. credit"; "Indian reservation property"*
Natural resources
. capital expenditures 1626; 1628
. depletion deduction . . . . 1976 et seq.
. depreciation 1902
. royalties 1345
. sales and exchanges 4667

Natural resources — Cont'd
. source of income 4640
Negligence
. damages against IRS for 4907; 4908
. penalty 4876
Net earnings from self-employment 3143
Net investment income tax . . . . 1107; 3150 et
. . . . seq.; 3765;
. . . . 3768
. calculating 3151
. estates and trusts 3956
. estimated tax payments 3154
. net investment income 3152
. passive activities 1824
. S corporation shareholders 3367
. who is subject to 3153
Net operating loss
. . *generally* . . . . 1839 et seq.
. acquiring corporation 3564
. alternative minimum tax (ATNOLD) 3212
. bankruptcy estate 3978
. carrybacks and carryovers
. . *generally* . . . . 1839 et seq.
. . bankruptcy estate 3979
. . built-in loss (unused, unrecognized under
. . . Sec. 382) 3570
. . credit carryforwards, limitations on 3572
. . election to forego carryback 1842; 3212
. . extension of time for payment of tax, ex-
. . . pected NOL carryback 4729
. . farmers 4503
. . intervening year modifications 1847
. . ownership change defined 3571
. . partnership, of 3737
. . refunds 4850; 4853
. . Section 382 limitations . . . . 3567 et seq.
. . successor corporation's use of 3564
. . tentative carryback 4729
. change in ownership . . . . 3567 et seq.
. common trust funds 1840
. computation
. . *generally* 1843
. . corporate taxpayers 1845
. . noncorporate taxpayers 1844
. deduction 1843; 1846
. defined 1840
. dividends-received deduction, effect on 3311
. estates and trusts 1840; 3930
. partnerships 1840; 3717;
. . . . 3737
. personal holding companies 3321
. self-employment tax 3143
. specified liability losses 1841
Net worth
. expatriation rules 4653
. method of determining income 2857
New markets tax credit 2329
New York Liberty Zone
. qualified zone property, bonus first year de-
. . preciation allowance 1940; 3207
90-day letter 4813; 4824;
. . . . 4836; 4859
**No-additional-cost services, excludable
. fringe benefits, as** 1243
Nominees, information returns
. . *generally* 4738
. partnerships 4731
. trusts and estates 4732
Nonbusiness expenses . . . . 2163 et seq.
Non-cash compensation 1214; 3004
Noncompetition agreement
. amortization 1974; 1975

Noncompetition agreement — Cont'd
. basis of 2471; 2472
. capital asset, as 2627
Nonconventional fuel credit 2337
Nondiscrimination rules
. cafeteria plans 1269
. employer-provided child care credit 2330
. employer-provided educational assistance 2215
. 401(k) plans 4317
. group-term life insurance 1262
. health savings accounts (HSAs) 1529
. paid time off (PTO) plans 4313
. pension and profit-sharing plans 4311; 4319;
4325 et seq.
. simplified employee pensions (SEPs) 4378
. small employer pension plan startup credit 2331
. supplemental unemployment benefit plans
(SUBs) 4108
. tax-exempt organizations 4108
. tax-sheltered annuities 4388
. tuition reductions 2217
. voluntary employee beneficiary associa-
tions (VEBAs) 4108
Nonpayroll taxes, withholding . . . . 3031 et seq.
Nonprofit organizations . . . . 4100 et seq.
**Nonqualified deferred compensation
plans** 1275
. funding triggers 1276
. from tax-indifferent entities 1277
Nonrecognition of gain or loss . . . . . . 2400; 2413 et
seq.
Nonrecourse debt
. allocation rules 3725
. assumption of liabilities 3516
. at-risk rules 1807
. credit, allowance for 2307
. partnerships 3725; 3762
. sale of property subject to debt 2403
Nonrefundable personal credits 2338
. foreign tax credit, effect on 2370
. limit on amount of 2364
. offset alternative minimum tax 2364
Nonresident aliens
generally . . . . 4637 et seq.
. compensation for personal services 4668; 4669
. credits 4646
. deductions 4646
. defined 4638
. dependency exemption 3119
. education credits 2202; 2203
. education expenses, deduction 2231
. effectively connected income . . . . 4610; 4644 et
seq.
. engaging in U.S. business defined 4645
. estate tax
.. generally 5037
.. expatriation rule 5037
.. marital deduction 5026
.. returns 5035
. estimated tax 3155; 3162
. expatriates See "Expatriation"
. foreign tax credit 2367
. gift tax 5039
. interest payments 4740
. net investment income tax 3153
. real estate (U.S.) income, treated as effectively connected 4643
. returns . . . . 4656 et seq.;
4701
.. joint returns, nonresident alien spouse 4706
. sailing permits 4658
. S corporation shareholders 3351

Nonresident aliens — Cont'd
. settlement initiatives 4805
. spouse, transfers to 2447
. standard deduction 3112
. taxpayer identification numbers 4752
. transportation income 4651
. U.S. real property interest (USRPI), dispositions of 4649; 4671
. U.S.-source income not effectively connect-
ed with U.S. business 4642
. withholding of tax . . . . 4663 et seq.
Nonstatutory stock options 1219
North American area, travel expenses 1549
Northern Mariana Islands
. foreign corporation treatment 4638
. residence in, U.S. tax and 4618
"Not-for-profit" activities, losses on 1779
Notice
. adjustments, effect on assessment period 4837
. benefit-accrual reduction 4342
. delinquency, annual notice of amount of 4903
. earned income credit 3023
. employer-owned life insurance 1353
. levy for taxes 4905
. liability for tax, IRS failure to provide
.. suspension of interest and penalties 4871
. lien for taxes 4911
.. withdrawal of 4912
. rollover distributions 4359
. statutory notice of deficiency, 90-day letter
See "90-day letter"
. third-party summons 4809
. withholding, election out of 3041
Notional principal contracts, amortization 1975
Nursing home care 2103; 2146
. principal residence ownership and use
tests, effect on 2445

O

Obsolescence of property 1783; 1784;
1902
Ocean activity, source of income 4640
Offer in compromise 2826
Office-at-home See "Home office deduction"
Office audit 4806
Officers of corporations
. business expenses 1509
. compensation deduction limit 1519
. employees, as, for withholding purposes 3002
. entertainment provided to treated as compensation 1572
. life insurance 1608; 3525
. loans to corporation by 1855
OID See "Original issue discount"
Oil and gas
. amortization of exploration and develop-
ment costs 1971
. at-risk rules 1805
. depletion . . . . 1976 et seq.
. depreciation
.. drilling, assets used in 1915; 1963
.. exploration, assets used in 1916
.. pipelines 1916; 1918;
1932
.. refining, assets used in 1917
. enhanced oil recovery credit 2322
. foreign tax credit 2371
. intangible drilling and development costs
generally 1628; 3525
.. alternative minimum tax 3208

Oil and gas — Cont'd
. nonconventional source fuel production
     credit 2337
. percentage depletion 1979; 1980
. personal holding company income . . . . 3324 et seq.
. qualified production activities income,
     oil-related 1615
. qualifying gasification projects, credit for 2312
. refiners, expensing election for refining
     costs 1966
Online payment networks, reporting by 4746
"Open" sales 2404
Operating agreement groups, partner-
     ships 3705
Options *See also "Stock options"*
. basis 2469
. capital gains and losses 2619; 2620
. holding period 2671
. lease with purchase options 1596
. wash sale rules 2462
Ordinary and necessary business ex-
     penses, deduction . . . . 1506 et seq.
Organizational expenditures
. amortization 1964
. corporations 3520
. earnings and profits adjustments 3525
. partnerships 3707
. S corporations 3359
Original issue discount
. acquisition premium paid by holder 1323; 4741
. back-up withholding 3045
. constant yield method 1322
. currently includible OID, determination of
     amount of . . . . 1321 et seq.
. debt instruments
     generally . . . . 1313 et seq.
. . amount of OID deductible currently 1752
. . applicable high yield obligations, limits on
     deduction 1753
. . basis in 2466; 2470
. . corporate debt payable in issuer's stock 1710
. . retirement of 2678
. . sales or exchanges of . . . . 2633 et seq.
. deductibility . . . . 1743; 1751 et
                           seq.
. defined 1314
. interest income, inclusion as . . . . 1313 et seq.
. reporting requirements 4741
. short-term obligations 1328
. stated redemption price at maturity 1316
. tax-exempt bonds 2636
. withholding 4667
Orphan drug credit 2328
Outbound transfers 3588; 4746
Overall foreign losses (OFLs) 2372
Overpayments
. interest on 4853
. refunds *See "Refunds"*

P

Paid time off (PTO) plans 4313
PALs *See "Passive activity loss rules"*
Parachute payments *See "Golden para-*
     chute payments"
Parent-sub controlled groups 3337; 3533
Parking
. fees 1558; 1560;
                              2120; 2148
. qualified transportation fringe benefits 1247

Parsonage rental allowance 1226
Participation
. active participation *See "Active participa-*
     tion"
. material participation *See "Material partici-*
     pation"
. significant participation activities 1821
Partnerships
     generally . . . . 3700 et seq.
. accounting methods 2818
. allocations
     generally . . . . 3724 et seq.
. . change in partnership interests 3725
. . liabilities 3762
. . retirement or death payments 3771
. . substantial economic effect, determina-
     tion of 3726
. alternative minimum tax 3200; 3202
. anti-abuse rules 3708; 3761
. assessments, limitation period on 4830
. assets, sale of vs. sale of partnership busi-
     ness 3767
. at-risk rules 1805
. audit of, unified audit and review . . . . 4709; 4840 et
                              seq.
. basis
     generally . . . . 2481; 3775 et
                              seq.
. . adjustments to basis of partnership prop-
     erty . . . . 3775 et seq.
. . adjustments to basis of partner's interest 3740; 3741;
                              3751
. . alternative adjusted basis computation 3741
. . contributed property . . . . 3713 et seq.
. . incorporation, basis after 2491
. . "inside" basis 3775
. . liquidating distributions, partner's basis of
     property received in 3749
. . loss limitations, basis adjustments made
     before applying 3736
. . nonliquidating distributions, partner's ba-
     sis of property received in 3748
. . "outside" basis 3738
. . partnership interest . . . . 3738 et seq.
. . stock distributions to corporate partner,
     basis adjustments in connection with 3750
. capital accounts of partners 3727
. capital contributions 3710
. contributions to
     generally . . . . 3709 et seq.
. . built-in gain or loss property 3752
. . character of contributed property 3747
. controlled partnership, sales and ex-
     changes with 3731; 3732
. deceased partner, payments in respect of . . . . 3768 et seq.
. deductions of
     generally . . . . 3715 et seq.
. . separately stated items 3718
. deferred compensation from 1277
. defined 3701
. distributions
     generally . . . . 3742 et seq.
. . basis adjustments . . . . 3777 et seq.
. . basis, allocation of 3751
. . built-in gain or loss property 3752
. . disproportionate . . . . 3754 et seq.
. . gain or loss . . . . 3743 et seq.
. . holding period 3746
. . liquidations 3749
. . marketable securities 3745
. . nonliquidating 3748

Partnerships — Cont'd
. distributions — Cont'd
. . stock distributions to corporate partner,
    basis adjustments in connection with 3750
. . termination of partnership 3782
. domestic production activities, deduction
    for 1615
. electing large partnerships 3702; 4731
. electronic filing requirement 4731
. exchange fund partnerships 3711
. exclusion from rules, election 3705
. expatriations (inversions) 4655
. family partnerships 3704; 5004
. farming 4510
. final year's income
. . deceased partner 3773
. . retired partner 3772
. foreign partnerships
. . domestic partnerships succeeded by (in-
    versions) 4655
. . returns 4660; 4661;
    4731
. . withholding 4663; 4664;
    4671
. foreign partners, withholding on 4662; 4664;
    4670
. foreign tax credit 2367
. gifts of interests in 5046
. guaranteed payments 3730; 3769;
    3771
. holding period
. . contributed property 3714
. . interest in partnership 2669
. income of . . . . 3715 et seq.
. incorporation, basis of property after 2491
. information returns 4746; 4753;
    4897
. interest in
. . amortization 1975
. . appreciated financial positions, construc-
    tive sales 2637; 2638
. . basis . . . . 3738 et seq.
. . changes in, effect on allocation of part-
    nership items 3725
. . constructive ownership 3733
. . dispositions, withholding on 4671
. . foreign partnership, acquisition or disposi-
    tion of interest 4661
. . holding period 2669
. . like-kind treatment of partnership inter-
    ests 2418
. . liquidation . . . . 3768 et seq.
. . transfer in satisfaction of debt 1395
. . transfer or liquidation of . . . . 3763 et seq.
. inventory items
. . basis adjustments 3779
. . distributions 3757
. . gain or loss on 3753; 3766
. liabilities of partnerships and partners
    generally . . . . 3759 et seq.
. . assumption of 3740; 3760
. . nonrecourse liabilities 3762
. . recourse liabilities 3761
. limited liability companies (LLCs) 3703
. liquidation
. . distributions 3749
. . interest in partnership . . . . 3763 et seq.
. . retired partners or successors in interest,
    payments to 3769; 3774
. . sale of partner's interest, liquidation vs. 3764
. losses
    generally . . . . 3734 et seq.

Partnerships — Cont'd
. losses — Cont'd
. . basis adjustments 3736
. . distributions . . . . 3743 et seq.
. . net operating loss 1840; 3717
. . partners' share of partnership loss . . . . . . 3735 et seq.
. . Section 1244 stock 2644
. miscellaneous itemized deductions 3111
. net operating loss 1840; 3717
. . carrybacks and carryovers 3737
. nonliquidating distributions 3748
. nonrecourse liabilities 3762
. organization costs 3707
. partners
. . aggregate of its partners, partnership
    treated as 3708
. . allocation of basis 3751
. . alternative minimum tax 3200
. . basis in partnership 2481; 3778
. . capital accounts 3727
. . character of partnership income to 3720
. . consistent treatment of items on returns 3721
. . constructive ownership of interests 3534; 3733
. . controlled partnership, sales and ex-
    changes with 3731; 3732
. . dealings with partnership . . . . 3728 et seq.
. . discharge of indebtedness 1393
. . distributions to . . . . 3742 et seq.
. . distributive share of income, gain, loss,
    etc . . . . 3724 et seq.
. . guaranteed payments 3730
. . liability for tax 3716; 3719
. . nonresident aliens 4645
. . passive activity gross income 1817
. . passive activity loss rules 1829
. . reporting of partnership income 3722
. . self-employment tax 3143; 3144
. . "separate entity" transactions 3729
. . share of partnership liabilities . . . . 3759 et seq.
. . share of partnership loss . . . . 3735 et seq.
. . tax matters partner 4843
. passive activity limits 1815; 1819;
    1825
. payments for interest in . . . . 3768 et seq.
. property
. . contributions of . . . . 3709 et seq.
. . payment for interest in 3770
. publicly traded 3302
. recourse liabilities 3761
. replacement property 2439
. required payments 2813
. retired partner, payments to . . . . 3768 et seq.
. returns 3783; 4275;
    4660; 4731;
    4898
. sale or exchange of partnership interest
    generally . . . . 3765 et seq.
. . assets, sale of vs. sale of partnership
    business 3767
. . collectibles gain 2603
. . installment reporting 2453
. . liquidation vs. sale of partner's interest 3764
. . ordinary gain or loss 3766
. . unrealized receivables or inventory 3766
. S corporations, comparison with 3706
. Section 179 expense election 1941
. separately stated items of income and de-
    ductions . . . . 3718 et seq.
. services, contribution of 3712
. split-ups 3783
. spousal partnership 3701
. substantial economic effect of allocations 3726

Partnerships — Cont'd
. taxable income 3717
. . elections affecting 3723
. taxable year of 2812; 2813;
                                          2815
. terminations . . . . 3781 et seq.
. transactions between partner and partner-
     ship 3729
. transfer or liquidation of partnership interest . . . . 3763 et seq.
. . post-transfer adjustments to basis 3776
. unified audit and review
. . administrative adjustment request (AAR) 4841
. . final partnership administrative adjust-
     ment (FPAA) 4844
. . innocent spouse relief 4709
. . "partnership items" 4842
. . small partnership exception 4845
. . tax matters partner 4843
. unrealized receivables
     generally 3756; 3766
. . basis of 3779
. . contributed property 3747
. . disproportionate distributions . . . . 3754 et seq.
. . gain or loss on disposition 3753
. . partner's gain or loss on receipt of distri-
     bution 3744
. . payments for 3770
. . retired partners or successors in interest,
     payments to 3769; 3770
. withholding on distributions, foreign part-
     ners, effectively connected income 4670

Passive activity loss rules
     generally . . . . 1810 et seq.
. alternative minimum tax, rules for 3210
. carryovers of suspended losses and credits 1837
. closely-held corporations 1825
. deduction, defined 1815
. definition of passive activity 1822
. definition of passive activity loss 1814
. disallowance of passive activity losses and
     credits 1811
. dispositions
. . entire interest in or substantially all of
     passive activity 1838
. . gain on 1818
. . loss on 1816
. . partnership or S corporation interest 1819
. gross income from passive activity 1817
. grouping of activities 1824
. material participation in activity
     generally . . . . 1826 et seq.
. . facts and circumstances test 1828
. . individuals, material participation by 1827
. . limited partners 1829
. . participation defined 1830
. . real property business 1836
. . spouses 1831
. partnerships
. . activities conducted through 1825
. . disposition of interest in 1819
. passthrough entities 1813
. personal service corporations 1825
. portfolio income 1820
. publicly traded partnerships 1813
. recharacterization of passive income as
     nonpassive income 1821
. rental activities . . . . 1832 et seq.
. rental real estate
     generally . . . . 1833 et seq.
. . active participation 1833; 1835

Passive activity loss rules — Cont'd
. rental real estate — Cont'd
. . exception from automatic passive treat-
     ment for activities of real estate profes-
     sionals 1836
. . 10%-or-more owner 1834
. . $25,000 allowance 1833; 1834
. sales and exchanges
. . gain on 1818
. . loss on 1816
. S corporations
. . activities conducted through 1825
. . disposition of interest in 1819
. self-employment tax 3143
. significant participation passive activity
     (SPPA) 1821
. taxpayers subject to rules 1812
. trade or business activities under 1823

Passive foreign investment companies
     (PFICs)
. accumulated earnings tax 3316
. defined 4627
. 50% test 4627
. mark-to-market rules 4630
. non-electing U.S. shareholders 4628
. qualified electing funds 4629
. 10% U.S. shareholder 4629

Passive income *See also "Passive activity*
     loss rules"
. foreign tax credit 2371
. S corporations . . . . 3365 et seq.;
                                          3376

Passthrough entities
. acquisition discount, accrual of 1328
. at-risk rules 1804; 1809
. domestic production activities, deduction
     for 1615
. interest allocation rules 1739
. investment credits 2307
. miscellaneous itemized deductions 3111
. passive activity losses 1813
. rollover of gain from qualified small busi-
     ness stock 2429
. simplified look-back marginal-impact
     method 2855

Patents
. amortization 1974
. basis 2471
. business expenses 1618
. capital assets, as 2621
. charitable contributions 2106
. depreciation 1959; 1962
. royalties 1345
. sales or exchanges 1312; 1320;
                                      2621; 4626;
                                        4642; 4667

Patronage dividends
. cooperatives 1300; 4207
. reporting 4739

Payment of tax *See also "Deposit of tax*
     payments"
. advance payments 1766
. compromise offers 4822
. convenience fees for debit and credit card
     payments 3110
. employer, by, for employee 1253
. errors in 3020
. estate tax, time for payment 5036
. estimated tax . . . . 3154 et seq.
. extensions of time
. . corporate income tax 4729
. . estate tax 5036

Payment of tax *See also "Deposit of tax payments"* — **Cont'd**
. extensions of time — Cont'd
. . hardship 4903
. . individual income tax 4720; 4721
. failure to pay
. . assessment period 4835
. . penalty 4874
. income tax
. . corporations . . . . 3343 et seq.
. . deadline for payment 4720
. . electronic filing 4720
. . estimated tax . . . . 3343 et seq.
. . extensions of time 4720; 4721
. . forms . . . . 4720 et seq.
. . individuals . . . . 4720 et seq.
. . installment payments 4722
. installment payments *See "Installment pay-*
      ments"
. notice and demand 4903
. tax calendar for 2014 1000
. timely mailing as timely payment 4754
. underpayment *See "Underpayment"*
Penalties
    generally . . . . 4864 et seq.
. abatement of 4870
. abusive tax shelters 4826; 4835;
                                                          4889
. accumulated earnings of corporations, tax
      on . . . . 3316 et seq.
. accuracy-related penalty . . . . 4875 et seq.
. advice, tax; false or fraudulent 4901
. aiding and abetting 4826; 4835;
                                                          4885
. annuity contracts, early distributions from 1367
. appraisals, valuation misstatements attribu-
      table to incorrect 4887
. assessment of 4826; 4835
. charitable contributions, failure to substanti-
      ate 4115
. criminal 4827; 4900;
                                                          4901
. deductibility of 1613
. . bribes and kickbacks 1610
. . premature withdrawal from savings de-
      posits 2168; 3102
. deposit of taxes, failure to make 3028; 4898
. early distributions 4344; 4374
. economic substance, transactions lacking 4895
. estimated tax, underpayment of . . . . 3154; 3163 et
                                                    seq.; 3349
. excess benefit transactions 4112
. excess contributions
. . Archer medical savings accounts 1528
. . health savings accounts (HSAs) 1529
. . Roth IRAs 4369
. excess distributions
. . Medicare Advantage Medical Savings Ac-
      counts 1530
. file, failure to 4873; 4893;
                                                          4897
. foreign financial asset understatement 4879
. fraud
. . criminal penalties 4901
. . underpayment 4882
. frivolous returns 4826; 4898
. health insurance coverage
. . individuals not carrying 4896
. . larger employers not offering affordable 4896
. identification numbers, failure to furnish 4888; 4898
. information returns 4893; 4897;
                                                          4898
. interest on . . . . 4865 et seq.

Penalties — **Cont'd**
. joint returns 4704
. modified endowment contracts 1368
. negligence 4876
. pay, failure to 4874
. pension and profit-sharing plans
. . failure to supply notice of benefit-accrual
      reduction 4342
. . overstatement of pension liabilities 4881
. personal holding company tax . . . . 3320 et seq.
. prepayment penalties 1705
. real estate mortgage investment conduits 4204
. reasonable cause excuse 4872
. records, failure to keep 4898
. refund claims, erroneous 4884
. reportable transactions
. . advisee lists, failure to maintain 4890
. . failure to report 4891
. . . material advisors 4893
. . understatements regarding 4892
. return preparers, on *See "Tax return*
      preparers"
. specified foreign financial assets, failure to
      disclose 4673
. suspension, IRS failure to notify taxpayer of
      liability 4871
. tax shelters 4889
. . prohibited transactions 4113; 4114
. . tax-exempts acting as accommodation
      parties 4894
. trust fund recovery penalty 4883
. understatement
. . accuracy-related penalty 4875
. . aiding and abetting 4885
. . assessment 4835
. . foreign financial assets 4879
. . interest on . . . . 4865 et seq.
. . property on estate or gift tax return 4880
. . reportable transactions 4892
. . return preparer, by 4886
. . substantial 4878
. unrelated business income tax 4121
. valuation
. . misstatements 4871; 4877
. . . attributable to incorrect appraisals 4887
. . understatement . . . . 4878 et seq.
Pension and profit-sharing plans
    generally . . . . 4310 et seq.
. active participant defined 4353
. age discrimination 4311
. annuity plans . . . . 1365 et seq.
. approval by IRS of 4332
. benefits
. . incidental 4321
. . limitations 4328
. . nondiscrimination rules 4325
. . notice of benefit-accrual reduction 4342
. . top-heavy plans 4329
. cash balance plans 4311
. cash or deferred (CODA) plans 4317
. combination of qualified plans 4336
. combined defined benefit-401(k) plans 4318
. compensation taken into account 4319
. contributions
. . employee contributions 4333
. . . catch-up contributions 4317; 4351;
                                                          4384
. . . trusts created to pay benefits under
      plan funded only by, pre- '59 4100
. . limitations 4328
. . matching contributions by employer . . . . 4333 et seq.
. . minimum funding requirements 4330

Pension and profit-sharing plans — Cont'd
. contributions — Cont'd
.. nondiscrimination requirement 4325
.. qualification requirements for plan 4319
.. timely payment requirement 4337
.. top-heavy plans 4329
. coverage and eligibility requirements 4323
. death benefits for participants dying during
    military service 4331
. deduction ceilings . . . . 4334 et seq.
. defined benefit and contribution plans 4311; 4318;
                                                          4324; 4328 et
                                                                   seq.
. delivery of payment outside U.S., withhold-
    ing on 3042
. determination letters 4332
. disability pension 1278; 1284
. discrimination prohibition 4325; 4378
. distributions
.. annuity type distributions 4338; 4345
.. domestic relations orders, pursuant to 4320
.. early withdrawals 4344
.. loans treated as 4343
.. minimum distribution rules 4345
.. post-death distributions 4345
.. required beginning date 4319
.. small accrued benefit, mandatory distribu-
    tion on termination of employment 4359
.. taxation of employees . . . . 4338 et seq.
.. withholding on . . . . 3034 et seq.
. early withdrawals 4344
. elective deferrals
.. ceiling on deductions and contributions 4335
.. CODAs 4317
.. credit for 2363
. eligibility requirements 4323
. eligible rollover distributions
    generally . . . . 4359 et seq.
.. trustee-to-trustee transfers 4310; 4359
.. withholding on 3035
. employer deductions . . . . 4334 et seq.
. employer reversions 4346
. excess contribution carryover 4334; 4379
. excise taxes
.. contributions, excess 4334; 4356;
                                                              4369
.. disqualified persons 4347
.. distributions
... early withdrawals 4344
... minimum 4345; 4357
.. prohibited transactions 4347
.. reversions, employer 4346
. funding 4330
. governmental plans
.. early withdrawals from 4344
.. health and long-term care insurance, dis-
    tributions for 4349
. gross income 1209
. health benefit and applicable life insurance
    accounts, transfer of excess pension
    assets to 4348
. highly compensated employees 4326
. hybrid plans 4311
. incidental benefits 4321
. individual retirement accounts (IRAs) . . . . 4351 et seq.
. information returns 4746; 4898
. insurance benefits 4341
. Keogh plans 4327; 4335
. life insurance premiums paid from plan
    contributions 4341
. limitations on contributions and benefits 4328
. loans from qualified plans 1722; 4343

Pension and profit-sharing plans — Cont'd
. lump-sum distributions
    generally . . . . 4310; 4338 et
                                                                   seq.
.. eligible rollover distributions 4310
.. preferential treatment 4339
.. securities of employer corporation 4340
.. ten-year averaging 4339
.. total taxable amount, deduction from
    gross income 3102
. master and prototype plans, IRS-approved 4332
. matching contributions by employer . . . . 4333 et seq.
. minimum participation requirements 4324
. nondiscrimination rules . . . . 4325 et seq.
. nonperiodic distributions 3039; 3040
. nonqualifying plans 4350
. participation 4324
. pension equity plans (PEPs) 4311
. pension liabilities, overstatement of, penalty
    for 4881
. periodic payments, withholding 3037; 3038
. premature distributions 1367
. profit-sharing plans, generally 4312; 4335
. prohibited transactions 4347
. qualification requirements 4319; 4329
. qualified domestic relations order, distribu-
    tions pursuant to 4320
. qualified plan trusts as S corporation share-
    holders 3354
. reversion to employer 4346
. rollovers . . . . 4359 et seq.
. savings plans 4316
. securities of employer corporation,
    lump-sum distributions 4340
. simplified employee pensions (SEPs) . . . . 4377 et seq.
. small employer pension plan startup credit 2331
. stock bonus plans 4312; 4318;
                                                              4335
. taxability of distributions . . . . 4338 et seq.
. thrift plans 4316
. timely payment requirement for contribu-
    tions 4337
. top-heavy plans 4329
. trustee-to-trustee transfers, eligible rollover
    distributions 4310
. underfunded plans 4330
. vesting of benefits 4322; 4329
. veterans, returning 4331
. voluntary employee contributions 4333
. withholding 3006; 3031;
                                                          3034 et seq.

**Pension Benefit Guaranty Corporation
    (PBGC)**
. refundable health insurance credit for
    PBGC pension recipients 2344
. trusts established by 4100
Percentage depletion See "Depletion"
**Percentage markup method for recon-
    structing income** 2857
Percentage method, withholding 3012
Percentage of completion method
. earnings and profits 3525
. long-term contracts . . . . 2848 et seq.
. modified 2853
Per diem allowances
. luxury water travel 1552
. meals and lodging 1581
Personal exemptions
    generally . . . . 3115 et seq.
. alternative minimum tax 3209
. bankruptcy estate 3976
. decedents 3116

Personal exemptions — Cont'd
. dependents, for . . . . 3119 et seq.
. estates and trusts 3928
. net operating loss computation 1844
. nonresident aliens 4646
. partnerships 3717
. phase-out 3117
. self-employment tax 3143
. spouse, exemption for 3118

Personal holding companies (PHCs)
. accumulated earnings tax 3316
. adjusted ordinary gross income test . . . . . 3324 et seq.
. deficiency dividends 3564
. dividends-paid deduction . . . . 3330 et seq.
. exemptions from classification as 3322
. misstatement penalty, applicability 4878
. penalty tax on undistributed income . . . . . . 3320 et seq.
. requirements for classification as
. . adjusted ordinary gross income test . . . . . 3324 et seq.
. . stock ownership 3323
. . returns 4726
. six-year assessment period 4832
. small business investment companies, ex-
     emption from PHC tax 4205
. stock ownership, determination of 3323
. undistributed income subject to PHC penal-
     ty tax 3321

Personal injury damages . . . . 1380 et seq.

Personal interest 1708; 1715;
                                                                3923

Personal property
. business use, converted to or from 1928; 2473
. casualty losses 1795
. charitable contributions of tangible personal
     property 2110
. depreciation . . . . 1902; 1926 et
                                                                seq.
. . part business/part personal use 1927
. like-kind exchanges 2419
. repossessions 2406
. taxes, deductibility 1760
. theft loss 1800

Personal service corporations
. defined 2811
. passive activity rules 1811; 1812;
                                                                1825
. qualified personal service corporations 3329
. rate of tax applicable to 1113
. reallocation (by IRS) of income and deduc-
     tions 2859
. tax year of 2811; 2813;
                                                                2815

Phase-out rule
. adoption assistance, employer-provided 1254
. adoption expense credit 2354
. alternative fuel production credit 2337
. child tax credit 2355
. Coverdell ESA contributions 2207
. dependent care credit 2349
. earned income credit 2339
. education credit 2202; 2203
. education loan interest deduction 2223
. elderly or disabled, credit for 2348
. electricity production from renewable re-
     sources, credit for 2324
. enhanced oil recovery credit 2322
. IRA deductions 4352
. personal exemptions 3117
. plug-in electric vehicle credit 2362
. Roth IRA contributions 4369
. savings bond income, higher education ex-
     clusion for 2220

Phase-out rule — Cont'd
. small employer health insurance credit 2332

Plug-in electric vehicle credits 2362

"Points" paid on mortgage
. cash basis taxpayers, deduction for . . . . 1745 et seq.
. deductibility 1713; 1743;
                                                                1745 et seq.
. defined 1305; 1703
. home mortgage 1746
. inclusion in income 1336
. information returns 4744
. refinancing 1747

Police officers
. early withdrawals from qualified plans 4344
. killed in line of duty, survivor annuities 1260
. retirement plan distributions for health and
     long-term care insurance 4349

Political contributions 4104; 5040
. information returns 4124

Political organizations 4120
. returns 4109; 4726;
                                                                4746

Pollution control facilities
. alternative minimum tax 3208; 3213
. amortization 1968

**Pooled income funds, charitable contribu-
     tions** 2114; 2117;
                                                                2136; 3915

Portfolio income *See "Passive activity loss
     rules"*

Possession corporations
. dividend income, qualified 1288
. dividends-received deduction 3310
. foreign tax credit 2367
. returns, time for filing 4728
. withholding 4663

Postmarks, timely mailing as timely filing 4754; 4755

Power of attorney 4808

Powers of appointment
. decedent, basis of property acquired from 2520
. estate tax 5009
. qualified terminable interest property
     (QTIP) 5023
. revocable transfers 5007

Preferred stock
. dividends 1296; 3309
. Fannie Mae and Freddie Mac, sale or ex-
     change by financial institution 4209
. nonqualified, exchanges of 2414; 3512;
                                                                3554; 3556
. Section 306 stock 3537
. spin-ff, split-off, or split-up 3560

Premature distributions, penalties 1367; 2200

**Premature withdrawal penalty (from sav-
     ings account)** 2168; 3102

Prepaid expenses
. farm expenses 4517
. . livestock feed 4515
. insurance premiums 1609
. rent 1599
. taxes 1766

Preparers of tax returns *See "Tax return
     preparers"*

Preproductive period expenses . . . . 4518 et seq.

Presidentially-declared disasters *See "Dis-
     aster losses"*

**Prevention of cruelty to children or ani-
     mals, organizations for**
. charitable contributions 2102; 2124
. tax exemption 4100; 4102

**Previously reported income, repayments
     of**

Previously reported income, repayments of — Cont'd
. *generally* . . . . 2860 et seq.
. exceeding $3,000 2862
. time for deduction of repayment 2861
Private activity bonds
. alternative minimum tax 3208
. interest 1332
. investment credit, effect on 2311
Private annuities 1369
Private foundations
. *generally* . . . . 4125 et seq.
. charitable contributions 2102; 2110;
                                 2124; 2125
. disclosure requirements 4120
. excise taxes 4127
. information returns 4124
. penalties 4898
. returns 4131
. taxes, deductibility 1755
. termination of status 4128
. trusts and foreign organizations subject to
     rules 4126
Privileged communications 4808
Prizes and awards
. compensation, as 1214
. constructive receipt of 1373
. employee achievement awards 1251; 1591;
                                        3006
. gross income, inclusion in . . . . 1372 et seq.
. information returns 4743
. property or services, prizes paid in 1373
. withholding 3006
Production, domestic, deduction for . . . . . . 1614 et seq.
. adjusted gross income computation 3102
. alternative minimum tax 3202; 3211
. net operating losses 1844; 1845
. self-employment tax 3143
Product liability losses 1841
Profit-sharing plans *See "Pension and prof-*
     it-sharing plans"
Progress expenditure credits 2310
Prohibited transactions
. excise tax on 4130; 4347
. exempt organizations . . . . 4111 et seq.
. exempt transactions 4347
. tax shelters 4113
. . disclosure of 4114
Promotion costs, business expenses 1512; 1566
Propaganda, private foundations 4127
Property
. basis . . . . 2463 et seq.
. charitable contributions of . . . . 2100; 2106 et
                                         seq.
. commissions paid upon transfer of 1662
. compensation paid in 1523; 1524
. controlled corporation, transfer to . . . . 3510 et seq.
. debt satisfied by transfer of 1395; 2468;
                                         2679
. defined, Section 351 transfers 3511
. depreciable 1902
. distributions of
. . corporation, by . . . . 3521 et seq.;
                               3533; 3538 et
                                         seq.
. . estates and trusts, by 3940; 3949
. . partnerships, by . . . . 3742 et seq.
. dividends . . . . 1287; 1292 et
                                         seq.
. domestic production activities deduction,
     qualifying production property for 1616
. investment credit property, defined 2307
. personal property *See "Personal property"*

Property — Cont'd
. prize paid in 1373
. qualified terminable interest *See "Qualified*
     terminable interest property (QTIP)"
. real property *See "Real estate"*
. reorganization, transfer of property ac-
     quired in 3552
. rights or obligations with respect to 2677; 3313
. taxes . . . . 1755; 1760 et
                                 seq.; 3209
. . rebates or credits 1206
. uniform capitalization rules . . . . 1666 et seq.
. wear, tear, exhaustion, or obsolescence of,
     depreciation and 1902
Protective refund claim 4852
Protest (Appellate Division conference) 4817
Provisional income, Social Security pay-
     ments 1279
PTO (paid time off) plans 4313
Public assistance recipients
. work opportunity credit 2316
Public Health Service Act 1387
Publicly traded partnerships
. corporations, as 3302
. limited partnership interest, profits interest
     in 3712
. passive activity loss rules 1813; 1820
. withholding with respect to foreign partners 4670
Publicly traded securities
. exchanges of, election to recognize gain or
     loss on 2412
. issue price 1317
. rollover of gain into specialized small busi-
     ness investment companies 2427
Public schools, tax-sheltered annuities . . . . 4388 et seq.
Public utilities
. depreciation of property 1908; 1919
. . gas utility property 1932
. . street light assets of electric utility 1916
. . water utility property 1924; 1925;
                                 1932; 1934
. net operating losses 1845
. preferred stock dividends 3309
Puerto Rico, residence in
. U.S. tax and 4618
. withholding 4669
Punitive damages . . . . 1380 et seq.
"Put" or "call" options, capital gains and
     losses 2620

Q

QTIP *See "Qualified terminable interest prop-*
     erty (QTIP)"
Qualified 2- or 3-wheeled plug-in electric
     vehicle credit 2362
Qualified advanced energy manufacturing
     project credit 2313
Qualified alternative fuel vehicle refueling
     (QAFVR) property 2361
Qualified business units (QBUs) 4675; 4676
Qualified campus lodging 1268
Qualified clean fuel vehicles, depreciation 1951
Qualified clinical testing expense credit 2328
Qualified commercial revitalization ex-
     penditures 1972
Qualified conservation contributions 2123; 2131
Qualified disaster, defined 1207
Qualified disclaimer, gift tax 5043
Qualified dividend income 1285; 1286;
                                 1288; 1298;
                                 1299

Qualified domestic relations order 4320; 4328;
4342
Qualified domestic trust (QDOT) 5026; 5036
Qualified electing fund (QEF) 1820; 2372;
4629
Qualified employee discounts 1244
Qualified funding assets 1367
Qualified housing interest 3209; 3210
Qualified nonrecourse financing, "at risk"
  limitations 1809
Qualified personal residence trust 5054
Qualified personal service corporations 3329
Qualified plan award 1591
Qualified plans *See "Pension and prof-*
  it-sharing plans"
Qualified prize options 1373
Qualified production activities income . . . 1615; 1616
Qualified real property business indebted-
  ness 1392
Qualified renewal community assets 2650; 2651
Qualified replacement property, ESOPs 2451
Qualified residence 1735
Qualified residence interest
. acquisition indebtedness 1733
. . mortgage insurance premiums paid or in-
    curred for 1736
. allocation 1741
. alternative minimum tax 3209; 3210
. deduction . . . . 1702; 1730 et
seq.
. defined 1732
. definition of qualified residence 1735
. home equity indebtedness 1734
. home mortgage debt forgiveness 1397
Qualified salary reduction arrangements,
  SIMPLE retirement plans
    generally 4384
. SIMPLE retirement account defined 4385
Qualified S corporation subsidiaries
  (QSubs) 3352
Qualified securities, sales to ESOP or
  EWOC 2451
Qualified small business stock (QSBS)
. defined 2649
. exclusion of gain on disposition
    generally 2648
. . AMT preference item 3209
. . NOL deduction, effect on 1844
. . Section 1202 gain, taxation of 2608
. information reports, failure to make 4898
. rollover of gain
    generally 2429
. . basis for 2506
. . holding period 2670
Qualified stated interest 1315
Qualified stock purchase 3583
Qualified Subchapter S trusts 3354; 3358
Qualified terminable interest property
  (QTIP) 2516; 5048
. income interest for life 5023
. surviving spouse's estate 5008
Qualified transportation fringe benefits 1247
Qualified tuition programs (QTPs)
    generally 2209
. beneficiary, change in 5047
. contributions to 2210
. designated beneficiary 2212
. distributions from 2211; 4746
. exempt organizations 4100
. gift tax on contributions 5047
. penalty for failure to report 4898

Quick refunds 4850
Quid pro quo contributions, disclosure re-
  quirements 4119

R

Rabbi trust 1276
Railroad Retirement Act payments 1279; 1280
Railroad retirement tax
. deposit by electronic funds transfer 3028
Ranchers, uniform capitalization rules 4519
Rates of tax *See "Tax rates"*
Reacquisition of stock, deductibility of ex-
  penses 1624
Real estate
. additions to, depreciation 1921
. at-risk rules 1809
. boards 4100
. brokers, reporting requirements 4746
. buildings *See "Buildings"*
. business property 2440; 2686
. buyer and seller, apportionment of tax be-
    tween 1770
. . excessive deduction of tax before sale 1772
. . time for deduction 1771
. capital asset, as 2617; 2623;
2624
. carrying charges 1620
. commissions paid upon transfer of property 1662
. condemnation of 2440
. construction contracts . . . . 2849 et seq.
. dealers in 2623; 2624
. decedent, owned by 5017
. depreciation
. . depreciable property 1902
. . installment sales of depreciable realty 2457
. . MACRS depreciation . . . . 1918 et seq.
. . recapture 2697
. . Section 1245 property 2693
. . short tax years 1926
. estate income from real estate passing di-
    rectly to heirs 3917
. exchanges of
. . farm land 4524
. . like-kind exchanges 2419
. foreign-held, depreciation 2693
. foreign investment in 4649; 4650;
4661; 4671
. ground rents 2465
. improvements
. . capital expenditures 1659
. . depreciation 1921
. installment sales of 2457
. investment income from U.S. real property,
    election to treat as effectively connect-
    ed 4643
. investment interest, rental real estate 1728
. mortgages on *See "Mortgages"*
. passive activity loss rules
    generally . . . . 1833 et seq.
. . material participation in real property bus-
    iness 1836
. qualified real property business indebted-
    ness, income from discharge of 1392
. rental real estate
. . depreciation 1924
. . investment interest 1728
. . passive activity loss rules . . . . 1833 et seq.
. repossession of 2405; 2467
. residential *See "Residence"*
. Section 179 expense election 1941; 1944
. source of income 4640

Real estate — Cont'd
. subdivided for sale 2623; 2624
. taxes, deduction . . . . 1764; 1769 et
     seq.
. unrelated business taxable income 4122
Real estate investment trust (REIT)
     generally 4200; 4202
. alternative minimum tax 3202
. consolidated return, inclusion in 3339
. dividends from 1299; 3577;
     4203
. dividends-paid deduction 3330
. dividends-received deduction 3315
. portfolio income 1820
. reorganizations 3543
. returns 4726; 4727
. swap funds 3517
. U.S. real property interests, dispositions of 4649
**Real estate mortgage investment conduit
    (REMIC)** 1820; 4200;
     4204
. interest holders
. . U.S.-source income not effectively con-
     nected with U.S. business 4642
. . withholding 4667
. tax matters partner 4843
. wash sales 2462
Reasonable cause 4872
Reasonable compensation . . . . 1517 et seq.
Rebates
. manufacturers, time for deduction 2832
. Medicare and Medicaid, under 1611
. of purchase price, exclusion from income 1206
. of taxes, inclusion in gross income 1206
Recapitalization
. costs 1659
. defined 3548
. foreign stock transfers 3588
. information returns 4746
Recapture
. alcohol fuel credit 2318
. alimony payments 2162
. alternative fuel vehicle refueling property
     credit 2361
. at-risk losses previously taken 1808
. basis, addition to for recaptured credits 2479
. conservation expenses 4522
. depreciation *See "Depreciation"*
. employer-provided child care credit 2330
. estate tax
. . returns 5035
. . savings from special use valuation 5017
. estimated tax (corporate), of reduction in 3347; 3348
. foreign losses 2372
. Indian employment credit 2326
. intangible drilling and development costs
     deducted 1628
. investment credit 2314
. LIFO inventories
. . earnings and profits adjustment 3525
. . S corporations 3364
. low-income housing credit 2321
. mine exploration and development costs 1626; 1627
. mortgage interest credit 2357
. new markets tax credit 2329
. plant costs expensed 4521
. reforestation expenses 1970
. Section 179 expense election 1942; 1945;
     2695
. Section 1250 property 2696

Receiver 4725; 4913
Receivership proceedings *See "Bankruptcy
    and receivership"*
Recognition of gain or loss . . . . 2400 et seq.
Records
. accounting methods, to substantiate 2817
. adequacy 4876
. amortization 1974
. audit by IRS 4809
. charitable contributions . . . . 2134 et seq.
. penalty for failure to keep 4898; 4901
. securities dealers, stock held as investment 2628
. travel, entertainment, and gift expenses,
     substantiation of . . . . 1585 et seq.
Recoveries
. attorneys' fees and costs 4863
. damages
. . business 1383
. . nonbusiness 1381
. real property taxes 1772
. tax benefit rule 1205
Recovery periods *See "Depreciation"*
Recycling
. "qualified reuse and recycling property," de-
     preciation 1940; 3207
Redeemable ground rent 2465
Redemption of stock
     generally . . . . 3526 et seq.
. charitable gift followed by 2113
. complete redemptions 3528; 3529
. constructive ownership rules 3534
. controlled foreign corporations 4625
. death taxes, for payment of 3532
. decedent's stock 3532
. dividends, redemptions not essentially
     equivalent to 3530
. earnings and profits, effect on 3523
. family attribution rules 3529
. liquidations, partial 3531
. losses, deductibility 1774
. related corporations, sales between as re-
     demptions 3533
. Section 306 stock 3536
. substantially disproportionate redemptions 3527
Reforestation
. expenses
. . amortization 1970; 3102
. . writing off 3359
. recapture rules for Section 1245 property 2695
Refunds
. amended returns 4723
. amount of refund, limitations 4856
. beverage container deposits 2847
. child support, applied to 4848
. child tax credit, refundable 2356
. claims . . . . 4849 et seq.
. . erroneous claims, penalty 4884
. credits, refundable 4857
. decedents 4714; 4715
. direct deposit of 4847
. electronically filed returns 4847
. erroneous, interest on 4865
. estate tax, protective claims 5018
. interest on overpayments 4853
. limitation period . . . . 4854 et seq.
. military and civilian U.S. employees dying
     in combat or terrorist attacks 4715
. nontax debts, applied to 4848
. offset for other tax liabilities 4847
. overpayments, generally . . . . 4846 et seq.
. protective refund claim 4852
. quick refunds 4850

Refunds — Cont'd
. state tax refunds 4746
. suit for 4855; 4856
. tax benefit rule 1205
. Tax Court jurisdiction 4859
Registered mailing of return 4755
Registration of obligations 1724
Regulated investment companies (RICs)
. *generally* 4200; 4201
. acquisition discount, accrual of 1328
. alternative minimum tax 3202
. consolidated returns, inclusion in 3339
. dividends 1298; 3577;
. . . . 4203; 4667
. dividends-paid deduction 3330
. dividends-received deduction 3308
. foreign tax credit 2367
. income tax returns 4726
. net operating loss 1840
. portfolio income 1820
. reorganizations 3543
. returns 4727
. stock of, sale or exchange
. . basis 2411; 2498
. . capital gains and losses 2632
. . swap funds 3517
. U.S. real property interests, dispositions of 4649
Rehabilitation credit . . . . 2308 et seq.
Reimbursed expenses
. accounted for (or not) by employee 1578
. artist, performing 3105
. documentary evidence of 1586
. employees 3104
. . accountable plans . . . . 1573 et seq.
. . automobile expenses 1582; 1954
. . business connection requirement 1574
. . nonaccountable plans . . . . 1573 et seq.
. . personal expenses of 1253
. . related to employer 1579
. . reporting requirement 1577
. . substantiating reimbursement 1573; 1575
. entertainment expenses 1566; 1569;
. . . . 1583
. excess of expenses over reimbursements 3104
. excess reimbursements over expenses
. . *generally* . . . . 1573 et seq.
. . reasonable time requirement for return of 1576
. living expenses, for loss of residence due
. . to casualty 1206
. losses 1791; 1796
. medical expenses 1255; 1379;
. . . . 1527; 2151
. mileage allowances 1560
. moving expenses 1248
. qualified transportation fringe benefits 1247
. sale of home 1249
. self-employed person 1578
. stockholders, over 10 percent 1579
REIT *See "Real estate investment trust*
. *(REIT)"*
Related taxpayers *See also "Family"*
. accrued expenses payable to 2836
. compensation for personal services 1517; 2351
. defined 2448
. dividends, constructive or disguised 1289
. expenses accrued but unpaid 2836
. foreign corporation transactions with relat-
. . ed parties 4661
. reallocations of income and deductions
. . *generally* 2858
. . personal service corporations 2859
. rent expense 1594

Related taxpayers *See also "Family"* **— Cont'd**
. replacement property acquired from 2439
. sales and exchanges between
. . *generally* . . . . 2446 et seq.
. . capital assets 2676
. . controlled corporations 2448; 2450;
. . . . 2691
. . controlled partnerships 3731; 3732
. . depreciable property, gain on sale of 2690; 2691
. . eligible worker owned cooperative
. . . (EWOC) 2451
. . employee stock ownership plan (ESOP) 2451
. . grantors 2448
. . installment method 2454
. . later sale by related buyer 2449; 2459
. . like-kind exchanges 2424
. . losses 2448
. . passive activity interests 1838
. . spouses 2447
. . stock redemptions 3533
Religious and apostolic associations
. disclosure 4120
. tax exemption 4100; 4102;
. . . . 4105
Relocation payments
. *generally* 1206
. loans 1213
Remainder interests
. charitable contributions . . . . 2114 et seq.
. decedent, basis of property acquired from,
. . contingent remainder interests 2521
. estate tax valuation 5016
. gift tax annual exclusion 5046
. gift tax valuation 5044
Renewal communities
. commercial revitalization expenditures, ex-
. . pensing or amortization election 1972
. qualified renewal community assets, capital
. . gain exclusion 2650; 2651
Rent
. advance payments 1599
. alimony payments 2157
. allowances, to clergy 1226
. bonuses 1340
. deferred 1342; 1600
. defined 1338
. dividend, as 1594
. effectively connected income 4644
. expenses of landlord paid by tenant 1343
. foreign tax credit 2371
. ground, redeemable 2465
. home office deduction 1645
. improvements to property by tenant 1344
. information returns 4743
. paid . . . . 1593 et seq.
. partnerships, unrealized receivables 3756
. personal holding company income, as 3326
. property held for production of 2686; 3102
. received . . . . 1339 et seq.
. security deposits 1341
. self-employment earnings, as 3143
. software, for lease of 1623
. source rules 4640
. time for reporting income 1339
. unrelated business taxable income 4122
Rental activity, passive activity rules 1821; 1824;
. . . . 1832 et seq.
Rent expense
. *generally* . . . . 1593 et seq.
. advance payments 1599
. amortization of lease costs or improve-
. . ments 1597; 1598

Rent expense — Cont'd
. deferred payments for use of property or
　　services 1600
. improvements to leased property by lessor 1598
. leaseback arrangements 1595
. leases
. . acquisition costs of 1597
. . cancellation of 1598
. . purchase options with 1596
. lessor's costs 1598
. personal-use property, rent for 1593
. purchase or rent 1596
. related lessor, rent to 1594
. trade or business, rent for use of property
　　in . . . . 1593 et seq.
. year of deduction for rent 1599
Rent-to-own property, depreciation 1914; 1915;
　　　　　　　　　　　　　　　　　　　　　　　　　1932
Reorganizations
　　generally . . . . 3541 et seq.
. assumption of liabilities 3515; 3557
. basis of property received in
　　generally . . . . 2484 et seq.
. . acquirer's basis 2484
. . assumption of liabilities, effect of 2485
. . distributee shareholders, basis of proper-
　　ty to 2488
. . fair market value as basis 2489
. . security holders, basis of property to 2488
. . stocks or bonds, acquisition of property
　　for 2487
. . target's basis 2486
. boot 3556
. business purpose 3542; 3560
. capital expenditures 1659
. carryovers in 3563; 3564
. continuity of business 3542
. continuity of interest 3542
. control, defined 3553
. corporate parties, taxation of 3555
. costs of, deductibility 3558
. earnings and profits, effect on 3523
. exempt entity status, change to 3579
. foreign corporations 3588; 4661
. investment companies 3543
. parties to 3542
. plan 3542
. requirements 3542
. reverse triangular 3551
. Section 306 stock 3537
. shareholders, taxation of 3554
. spin-offs, split-offs, split-ups . . . . 3559 et seq.
. transfer of property acquired in 3552
. triangular 3551
. Type A: merger or consolidation 3544
. . triangular 3551
. Type B: stock for stock 3545
. . triangular 3551
. Type C: assets for stock 3546
. . triangular 3551
. Type D: transfer of assets to subsidiary 3547; 3553;
　　　　　　　　　　　　　　　　　　　　　　　　　3554; 3557;
　　　　　　　　　　　　　　　　　　　　　　　　　3564
. Type E: recapitalization 3548
. Type F: change in identity, form, or place 3549
. Type G: bankruptcy 3550; 3554
Repairs
. accounting methods 2845
. capital expenditures 1656
. casualty loss 1793; 1795

Repayment of previously reported income . . . . 2860 et seq.
Replacement property
. basis . . . . 2503 et seq.
. ESOPs 2451
. holding period 2670; 2675
. involuntary conversion . . . . 2430 et seq.
. . basis 2503
. period for replacement 2441
Reportable transactions
. advisee lists
. . material advisers, reporting requirements 4748
. . penalty for failure to maintain 4890
. confidential tax avoidance transactions 4749
. failure to report, penalty for 4891
. . material advisors 4893
. . suspension of 4871
. material advisers, reporting requirements 4748
. penalties . . . . 4890 et seq.
. understatements regarding, penalty for 4892
Repossessions
. personal property 2406
. real estate 2405; 2467
Required minimum distributions 4345
**"Required payments," partnerships and S
　　corporations** 2813
Research and experimental expenses
. alternative minimum tax 3209; 3213
. alternative simplified research credit 2319
. amortization 1964
. computer software 1623
. credit for 2319
. . election to swap bonus and accelerated
　　depreciation for certain credits 1939
. current expense method, election of 1601; 1602
. deduction for
. . capitalization or deduction, election 1601; 1602
. . reduction of for credit taken 2319
. depletion 1602
. depreciation of property used in connection
　　with 1602; 1915
. passive activity loss rules 1823
. professors 1636
. university basic research credit 2319
Resellers
. uniform capitalization rules 1667
Reserves
. accounting reserves, additions to 2846; 2847
. contingent liabilities, for 2847
. self-insurance reserve funds 1607
Reservists
. differential wage payments from employers,
　　withholding on 3004
. early withdrawals from qualified plans 4344
. health flexible spending account benefits 1269
. travel expenses 1553; 3102
Residence
. business use . . . . 1638 et seq.
. casualty loss 1798
. charitable remainder in personal residence 2114
. credit for new energy efficient homes 2334
. depreciation 1920; 1925;
　　　　　　　　　　　　　　　　　　　　　　　　　1927; 1940;
　　　　　　　　　　　　　　　　　　　　　　　　　2693
. disaster losses, federally declared disasters 2433
. displacement from, payment for 1206
. entertainment expenses incurred at 1561
. exclusion of gain on sale . . . . 2442 et seq.
. . health, sale due to change in 2443
. . ownership and use test, qualifying for ex-
　　clusion 2445
. . . periods of nonqualified use 2442

Residence — Cont'd
. exclusion of gain on sale — Cont'd
. . place of employment, sale due to change
     in 2443
. . reduced exclusion, partially qualifying
     sales 2443; 2444
. . spouses . . . . 2442; 2444 et
                                                                seq.
. . "unforeseen circumstance," sale due to . . . 2443
. insurance on 1607
. interest, qualified . . . . 1730 et seq.
. involuntary conversion . . . . 2431 et seq.
. loss on, deductibility 1776
. military members, special rules for 2443; 2445
. nonbusiness energy property credit 2358
. office-at-home . . . . 1638 et seq.
. principal residence
. . exclusion of gain . . . . 2442 et seq.
. . home mortgage indebtedness, discharge
     of 1397
. qualified campus lodging as 1268
. qualified personal residence trust 5054
. rental 1645; 1780
. . depreciation 1920; 1925;
                                                           1932; 1940
. residential energy efficient property credit 2359
. sales or exchanges
. . employer reimbursement of employee's
     loss on 1249
. . exclusion of gain . . . . 2442 et seq.
. . information returns 4746
. . original issue discount rules, applicability . . . 1320
. . repossession by seller 2405
. vacation home 1780
Resident aliens
. dependency exemption for 3119
. election to be taxed as U.S. resident 4636
. foreign income 4610
. foreign tax credit 2367
. gift tax 5039
. personal exemptions 3115
. returns and payment of tax 4701; 4716;
                                                               4718
. self-employment tax 3146
. substantial presence test 4635
. terminating long-term residency See "Expa-
     triation"
. U.S. persons, taxed as . . . . 4633 et seq.
Restaurants
. depreciation of restaurant property 1918; 1925;
                                                           1932; 1934
. receipts from sale of food or beverages at
     retail establishments, domestic produc-
     tion activities deduction 1616
. Section 179 election for restaurant property . . . 1944
. smallware, deductible expenses of 1514
Restitution payments
. assessment of court ordered 4827
. human trafficking victims 1206
Restoration costs, capital expenditures 1661
Restricted stock for employees . . . . 1217 et seq.
Retiree health accounts 4348
Retirement age 4322
Retirement of assets 1906; 1909
Retirement pay 1223; 3031
**Retirement planning services, excludable
   fringe benefits** 1250
Retirement plans See "Pension and prof-
   it-sharing plans"
Return preparers See "Tax return
   preparers"

Returns See also "Forms" (for numerical
   finding list)
. amended 4723
. certified mailing of 4755
. copies
. . preparer's duty to furnish taxpayer 4750
. . requesting from IRS 4757
. corporate
     generally . . . . 4724 et seq.
. . consolidated . . . . 3338 et seq.
. . foreign corporations 4659; 4661
. . uncertain tax positions on 4726
. cost of preparing 1253; 2165
. decedents . . . . 3965 et seq.
. departing aliens 4658
. disclosure of, exempt organizations 4120
. electronic filing of 4703; 4737;
                                                                4754
. estate tax . . . . 5034 et seq.
. examination of by IRS . . . . 4800 et seq.
. exempt organizations 4124; 4131
. extension of time to file
. . bankruptcy estate 4736
. . combat zone, taxpayers serving in 4719
. . corporate tax returns 4728
. . disaster victims 4719
. . electronic filing of application 4703; 4717
. . estate income tax returns 4732
. . estate tax returns 5035
. . exempt organizations 4124
. . generation-skipping transfer tax 5057
. . gift tax returns 5055
. . individual returns . . . . 4717 et seq.
. . information returns 4747
. . partnership returns 4731
. . trust income tax returns 4732
. failure to file 4873; 4897;
                                                                4901
. foreign corporations 4656; 4659;
                                                                4661
. foreign partnerships 4660
. fraudulent 4835; 4901
. frivolous, penalty for filing 4826; 4898
. gift tax 5055
. homeowners' associations 4726
. income tax
     generally 4700
. . bankruptcy estate 4736
. . copies of 4757
. . corporations
     generally . . . . 4724 et seq.
. . . deposit of tax payments 4730
. . . due dates for payment 4729
. . . extension of time for filing 4728
. . . extension of time for payment 4729
. . . foreign 4659
. . . signatures 4725
. . . time and place for filing 4727
. . decedents 4708; 4714;
                                                                4715
. . estates and trusts
     generally . . . . 4732 et seq.
. . . bankruptcy estate 4736
. . . extension of time to file 4732
. . . forms to use 4733
. . . will, copies of 4734
. . . failure to file 4873
. . . fiduciary . . . . 4732 et seq.
. . . foreign corporations 4659
. . . fractional year (short year) 4716; 4727
. . . household employers 3030
. . . income tax return preparers 4750

Returns *See also "Forms" (for numerical finding list)* — **Cont'd**
. income tax — Cont'd
.. incompetents, returns for 4701
.. individual
 generally . . . . 4700 et seq.
... abroad, residing 4718
... aliens . . . . 4656 et seq.
... amended returns 4723
... decedents 4714
... electronic filing 4703
... extensions of time for filing . . . . 4717 et seq.
... forms for filing 4702
... incompetent individuals 4701
... minors 4701
... parties who must file 4701
... payment of tax . . . . 4720 et seq.
... spouses . . . . 4704 et seq.
... time and place for filing . . . . 4716 et seq.
... what's new for 2013 105
.. joint *See "Joint returns"*
.. mailing as filing 4754; 4755
.. minimum income amounts for return filing 4701
.. minors 4701
.. partnerships
 generally 4731
... extension of time to file 4731
... foreign 4660
.. political organizations 4109
.. self-employment tax 4713
.. spouses . . . . 4704 et seq.
.. tax home 4718
.. taxpayer identification number (TIN) 4750
.. who must file 4701
. information *See "Information returns"*
. joint *See "Joint returns"*
. life insurance companies 4726
. nonresident aliens . . . . 4656 et seq.
. partnerships 3783; 4661;
            4731; 4898
. political organizations 4109; 4726
. preparation costs, deduction 3110
. preparers *See "Tax return preparers"*
. private delivery service, use of 4754
. private foundations 4131
. real estate investment trusts 4726; 4727
. registered mailing of 4755
. regulated investment companies 4726; 4727
. Saturday, Sunday and holiday filing dates 4756
. S corporations . . . . 3370; 4726 et
            seq.; 4898
. self-employment tax 4713
. short period 4716; 4727
. signing
.. corporations, for 4725
.. electronic filing 4703
.. preparer 4750; 4886;
            4888
. taxpayer identification number (TIN) 4750
. time for filing
.. calendar of due dates 1000
.. corporations 4727
.. electronic filing 4753
.. employment tax returns 3019
.. estate tax 5035
.. foreign corporations 4659
.. gift tax 5055
.. individuals . . . . 4716 et seq.
.. information returns
 generally 4737
... W-2 3021
.. mailing 4754; 4755
.. nonpayroll tax returns 3032

Returns *See also "Forms" (for numerical finding list)* — **Cont'd**
. time for filing — Cont'd
.. nonresident aliens 4657
.. partnerships 4731
.. Saturday, Sunday or holiday due date 4756
.. statute of limitations on assessments 4830
. transcripts of, request for 4757
. withholding 3019
**Revitalization expenditures, qualified, ex-
 pensing or amortization election for** 1972
Revocable transfers 5007
Revocable trusts 3958
. election to treat as part of estate 3902
Revolving charge accounts 1704
Rights, stock
. allocation of basis 2493
. definition of stock 3512
. disproportionate distributions 1296
. distributions . . . . 1295 et seq.;
            3523; 3540
. dividend, property received as 2492; 2493
. reorganization exchanges 3554
. valuation 1296
Rollover of gain
 generally . . . . 2426 et seq.
. qualified empowerment zone assets 2428
. qualified small business stock 2429; 2506;
            2670
. specialized small business investment
 companies, into 2427; 2506
Rollovers of pension, etc., distributions
 generally . . . . 4319; 4359 et
            seq.
. after-tax contributions 4362
. beneficiary other than surviving spouse 4366
. Coverdell ESAs 2207; 2208
. eligible rollover distributions
.. defined 4359
.. designated Roth accounts 4375
.. qualified plans, tax-free rollovers 4359
.. trustee-to-trustee transfers
 generally 4310
... exclusion for direct transfers 4359
... withholding 3035
. hardship distributions 3035
. health savings accounts (HSAs) 1529
. one-time IRA rollover to 4364
. partial rollovers 4361
. qualified tuition programs 2211
. Roth IRAs 4363; 4368;
            4369; 4371;
            4375
. surviving spouse 4365
. types of rollovers 4360
Roth IRAs
 generally 4367; 4368
. contributions to 4369
.. changing nature of (recharacterizing) 4370
.. designated Roth contributions 4375
.. excess, penalty for 4369
. conversion from traditional IRA to
 generally 4371
.. changing nature of (recharacterizing) contributions 4370
.. reconversions 4372
. designated Roth (Roth 401(k)) accounts 4375
. distributions 4368
 generally 4373
.. designated Roth accounts 4375
. early distributions tax 4374
. information returns 4746
. losses from, itemized deductions 3110

Roth IRAs — Cont'd

. qualified plan rollovers to 4363

Royalties

. business expenses 1618
. capital gains and losses 2689
. defined 1338
. depletion 1981
. effectively connected income 4644
. income from 1345; 1820; 1821
. . foreign tax credit 2371
. . holding companies . . . . 3324 et seq.
. information returns 4746
. property held for production of 3102
. source of income 4640
. unrelated business taxable income 4122

Rulings

. employee or contractor, status as 3002
. exempt status
. . application for 4116
. . modification or revocation of 4117
. S corporation status 3358
. user fees for 4812

Rural mail carriers 1560

S

Safe harbors

. accrual basis accounting 2825
. capitalization 1660; 1661
. casualty losses 1795
. cost depletion, minerals 1977
. distributions, corporate 3562
. employment tax, deposit of taxes 3027
. 401(k) plans, contributions to 4317
. grants treated as capital contributions 3304
. home office expenses 1644
. like-kind exchanges 2423
. local lodging expenses 1546
. materials and supplies 1657
. original issue discount 1313
. plan age discrimination rules 4311
. principal residence, exclusion of gain on
    sale 2443
. reimbursements in excess of expenses 1576
. reorganization costs 3558
. repairs and maintenance 1656
. theft losses, Madoff-style schemes, losses
    from 1799
. useful life of asset 1962

Sailing permit 4658

Salary reduction agreements

. flexible spending accounts 1269
. simplified employee pensions 4381
. tax-sheltered annuities 4390

Sale and leaseback 1595; 1935; 1937; 2682

Sales and use taxes

. alternative minimum tax deductions 3209
. state taxes, deductibility 1756

Sales or exchanges

. abandonment, as 1788
. amount realized . . . . 2402 et seq.
. appreciated financial positions 2637; 2638
. bargain *See "Bargain purchases and sales"*
. bonds
. . interest dates, sold between 1329
. . stock of same company for 2681
. . tax-exempt 2636
. business property . . . . 2684 et seq.
. capital assets
    generally . . . . 2676 et seq.

Sales or exchanges — Cont'd

. capital assets — Cont'd

. . convertible bonds 2681
. . distributorships, cancellation as sale or
      exchange 2680
. . gain or loss . . . . 2600 et seq.; 3935
. . gift, sale combined with 2683
. . leasebacks 2682
. . leases, cancellation as sale or exchange . . . 2680
. . payment with property as sale 2679
. . related taxpayers 2676
. . retirement of debt instruments 2678
. computing amount of gain or loss . . . . 2401 et seq.
. contingent payment sales 2455
. contributed property 2110; 2138
. controlled foreign corporation, sales to 4626
. conversion and constructive ownership
    transactions . . . . 2664 et seq.
. debt, paying with property 2679
. deemed sale rules, terminating U.S. citizen-
    ship or residency after June 16, 2008 4653
. deferred payment sales, unstated (imputed)
    interest . . . . 1307 et seq.; 1707
. depreciable property
. . dispositions of MACRS assets 1906; 1909; 1910
. . related taxpayers, capital gain bar 2690; 2691
. employment contracts 1222
. fair market value (FMV) 2402
. foreclosures as 1788
. foreign entity, to 4631
. gain or loss, treatment of
    generally . . . . 2400 et seq.
. . accrual basis taxpayers 2408
. . adjusted gross income computation 3102
. . amount realized . . . . 2402 et seq.
. . banks and financial institutions 4209
. . cash basis taxpayers 2407
. . computation of amount . . . . 2401 et seq.
. . controlled corporation stock 4625
. . D.C. Zone assets 2652
. . debt instruments, significant modification . . . 2412
. . deductible losses 1774
. . deed, delivery in escrow 2409
. . foreign corporations, sales to 4626
. . installment sales . . . . 2452 et seq.
. . like-kind exchanges . . . . 2418 et seq.
. . load mutual funds, sale of shares in 2411
. . open sales 2404
. . partnership interest . . . . 3764 et seq.
. . passive activities, gain on 1818
. . related taxpayers, sales and exchanges
      between . . . . 2446 et seq.
. . repossessions 2405; 2406
. . residence, sale of . . . . 2442 et seq.
. . rollovers . . . . 2426 et seq.
. . Section 306 stock 3535; 3536
. . securities transactions 2410
. . tax-free exchanges not solely in kind 2421
. . timber cutting as sale or exchange 2687
. . title, delivery in escrow 2409
. . U.S. obligations, exchanges 2416
. . wash sales, stock and securities 2462
. installment obligations 2458
. installment sales *See "Installment sales"*
. involuntary conversions *See "Involuntary
    conversions"*
. like-kind exchanges *See "Like-kind ex-
    changes"*
. livestock 4526

Sales or exchanges — Cont'd
. options to buy or sell 2619; 2620
. partnerships
. . controlled, to or with 3731; 3732
. . disproportionate distributions as 3755
. . interest in partnership . . . . 3764 et seq.
. passive activity rules 1818
. patents 2621; 4626
. property . . . . 2400 et seq.
. real estate 4649
. . deduction of realty taxes . . . . 1770 et seq.
. related taxpayers, between . . . . 2446 et seq.
. . depreciable property 2690; 2691
. . stock redemptions 3533
. residences
. . exclusion of gain . . . . 2442 et seq.
. . information returns 4746
. source of income 4640
. stock *See "Stock"*
. tax-free exchanges *See "Tax-free exchanges"*
. unharvested crop sold with land 4524
. unrelated business income 4122
. wash sales *See "Wash sales"*
Salvage value
. inventory scrap value 2866
. loss deduction, limit on 1775
Same-sex spouses *See "Spouses"*
SARSEPs *See "Simplified employee pensions (SEPs)"*
Saturdays, Sundays and holidays
. deposit of employment taxes 3026
. due dates on 4756
Saver's credit 2363
Savings accounts
. frozen *See "Frozen deposits"*
. penalty for premature withdrawal from 2168; 3102
Savings bonds, interest . . . . 1334 et seq.
. higher education expenses, exclusion for
. . income used to pay . . . . 2219 et seq.
Scholarships and fellowships
. education expenses reduced by amount of 2204
. employer-provided educational expenses 2213
. exclusion for qualifying 2216
. exempt wages 3006
. support, as 3124
. withholding 4664
Scientific organizations
. contributions to 2108
. tax exemption 4100; 4102
S corporations
. *generally* . . . . 3350 et seq.
. accumulated adjustments account 3374
. accumulated earnings tax 3316
. alternative minimum tax 3200; 3202
. at-risk rules 1805
. built-in gains tax 3362; 3368
. . net recognized built-in gain 3363
. collectibles gain on sale or exchange 2603
. consolidated returns, includible corporations 3338
. corporate level, taxes paid at 3368
. depreciation recapture 2697
. discharge of indebtedness 1393
. distributions 3372
. domestic production activities deduction 1615
. earnings and profits . . . . 3372 et seq.
. election . . . . 3350 et seq.
. . revocation or termination of election . . . . 3375 et seq.
. eligibility . . . . 3351 et seq.
. employee stock ownership plans (ESOPs) 4314
. estimated tax 3345

S corporations — Cont'd
. excess net passive income . . . . 3365 et seq.
. farming 4510
. fringe benefits 3360
. "golden parachute" payments 1535
. gross receipts defined 3366
. LIFO recapture 3364
. losses . . . . 1778 et seq.
. miscellaneous itemized deductions 3111
. net operating losses 1840
. one class of stock 3355
. partnership, contrast with 3706
. passive activity loss rules 1812; 1815;
. . . . 1819; 1825
. passive income . . . . 3365 et seq.;
. . . . 3376
. personal holding companies, classification
. . as 3322
. related taxpayers, transactions between 2448
. required payments 2813
. returns . . . . 4726 et seq.;
. . . . 4898
. . consistent treatment on returns 3370
. revocation or termination of election . . . . 3375 et seq.
. . involuntary termination 3376
. . time new election can be made 3377
. Section 179 expense election 1941
. shareholders
. . alternative minimum tax 3200
. . basis of shareholder in stock or debt 3371
. . . adjustments 2481
. . consents 3357
. . consistent treatment on return 3370
. . constructive ownership rules 3534
. . eligibility requirements 3351
. . losses in excess of basis 3369
. . number of 3353
. . passive activity gross income 1817
. . self-employment tax, shareholder's share
. . . of income 3143
. . taxation of 3350; 3361;
. . . . 3367 et seq.
. . termination of interest 3367
. . trusts as 3354; 3910
. small business trusts for holding S stock,
. . election of 3354; 3910
. subsidiaries 3352
. taxable income 3359
. taxation . . . . 3361 et seq.
. tax year 2810; 2813;
. . . . 2815; 3356;
. . . . 3367

Section 38 property *See "Investment credit"*
Section 179 expense election
. *generally* . . . . 1941 et seq.
. automobiles, business . . . . 1946 et seq.
. basis reduction for 2476
. commercial buildings, cost of making energy efficient 1967
. disaster assistance property, increased expensing election 1942
. earnings and profits, effect on 3524
. eligible property 1944
. enterprise zone property 1942
. excluded property 1944
. limitations on . . . . 1941 et seq.
. listed property other than automobiles . . . . . 1946 et seq.
. . business/investment use 1950
. . qualified business use 1949
. purchase of property for use in trade or
. . business 1944
. recapture 1945; 2695

Section 179 expense election — Cont'd
. refining costs 1966
. retail improvement property 1944
. revocation 1941
. S corporations 3359
. Section 1245 property, recapture 2695
. sport utility vehicles (SUVs) 1943
Section 197 intangibles
. amortization 1973; 1974
. computer software 1623
. excluded items 1962; 1975
Section 269 tax avoidance acquisitions . . . 3565
Section 306 stock . . . . 3535 et seq.
. stock treated as 3537
Section 336(e) election 3587
Section 338 election . . . . 3581 et seq.
. consistency rules 3584
. consolidated group 3586
. Form 8023 3585
. "qualified stock purchase" requirement 3583
Section 351 transfers . . . . 3510 et seq.
Section 367 transactions 3588
Section 382 limitation
    generally . . . . 3567 et seq.
. order of loss absorption of 3573
Section 401(k) plans *See "401(k) plans"*
Section 403(b) annuities 4317; 4360;
                                                  4388 et seq.
Section 482 transfer pricing 2858; 4877
Section 501(c) organizations
    generally 4100
. disclosure 4120
. lobbying expenditures 4103; 4104
. qualification requirements for organization
    operating hospital facility 4102
Section 529 plans *See "Qualified tuition pro-
    grams (QTPs)"*
Section 988 transactions 4676
Section 1031 like-kind exchanges *See
    "Like-kind exchanges"*
**Section 1231 (capital gain-ordinary loss)
    transactions**
    generally . . . . 2684 et seq.
. application of rules 2685
. assets, defined 2686
. coal 2688; 2689
. iron ore 2688; 2689
. livestock sales 4526
. non-recaptured net Section 1231 losses . . . 2610
. timber . . . . 2687 et seq.
. unharvested crops sold with land 4524
Section 1244 stock . . . . 2644 et seq.
Section 1245 property *See "Depreciation"*
Section 1250 property *See "Depreciation"*
Section 1256 contracts
    generally . . . . 2653; 2656 et
                                                          seq.
. carryback of losses
. . election 2659
. . quick refund for 4850
. defined 2657
. mark-to-market system, under 2656
. mixed straddles, election for 2658
. securities futures . . . . 2661 et seq.
. termination 2677
Securities transactions
. appreciated financial positions, constructive
    sales 2637; 2638
. basis
. . bonds 2470
. . determination 2499

Securities transactions — Cont'd
. basis — Cont'd
. . nontaxable stock dividends 2493
. . stock and securities . . . . 2494 et seq.
. bonds
. . amortization of premium . . . . 2169 et seq.
. . as bad debts 1848
. . discounted purchase of debtor's own obli-
    gations 1394
. . holder's basis in 2470
. . loss on worthless 1781
. . market discount . . . . 1324 et seq.
. . modification of debt instruments 2412
. . original issue discount . . . . 1313 et seq.
. . tax-exempt 1331
. . Treasury Inflation-Indexed Securities 1333
. commodities transactions
. . defined 2642
. . holding period 2667
. . mark-to-market rules 2879; 2880
. conversion and constructive ownership
    transactions . . . . 2664 et seq.
. dealers, securities 2628
. . bond premium amortization 2173
. . mark-to-market rules 2879
. dividend reinvestment plans 2462; 2494
. employer securities
. . lump-sum distributions of 4340
. . qualified plan investments in 4333
. engaging in U.S. business 4645
. futures transactions . . . . 2642; 2656 et
                                                          seq.
. . gains and losses . . . . 2661 et seq.
. . mark-to-market rules 2656
. hedging transactions *See "Hedging trans-
    actions"*
. holding period 2667; 2670
. identification of stocks and bonds 2496; 2497
. information returns 4746
. installment sales 2454
. like-kind exchanges 2418
. market discount bonds . . . . 1324 et seq.
. . holder's basis 2470
. mark-to-market rules . . . . 2656 et seq.
. . dealers in securities and commodities 2879
. . traders in securities and commodities 2880
. options, sale or exchange of 2619
. original issue discount . . . . 1313 et seq.
. partnerships 3745
. "puts" and "calls" 2620
. regulated futures contracts . . . . 2656 et seq.
. reporting requirements
. . broker reporting (Form 1099-B) 4746
. . dividends (Form 1099-DIV) 4739
. . Section 1256 contracts . . . . 2656 et seq.
. short sales . . . . 2639 et seq.
. . holding period 2670
. stock and securities
. . distribution of rights to . . . . 1295 et seq.
. . dividends on . . . . 1285 et seq.
. . gain or loss on sale 2410
. . holding period 2670
. . loss on worthless 1781
. . "substantially identical" stock 2462
. straddles . . . . 2620; 2653 et
                                                          seq.
. traders, securities, mark-to-market rules 2880; 3143
. wash sales 2461; 2462
. . basis 2500
. . holding period 2670
. worthless stock or securities 1781

References are to paragraph [¶] numbers.

Security
. crops pledged to secure Commodity Credit
    Corporation loans 4528
. deposits 1206; 1341;
    2831
. employer-provided security measures, as
    fringe benefit 1245
Seizure of property
    generally 4905
. involuntary conversion, defined 2432
. losses, deductibility 1774
. wrongful seizures 4906
.. third-party remedies 4907
Self-dealing 4127
Self-employed pension plans
    generally 4327
. contributions ceiling 4335
. individual retirement account (IRA) plans . . . . 4351 et seq.
Self-employed persons *See also "Independent contractors"*
. Archer medical savings account contributions 1528
. automobile expenses 1558
. home office deduction 1638
. meal and entertainment expenses, limit 1581
. medical insurance expense deduction 1532; 3102
. moving expenses 1646
. professional business expenses 1636
. reimbursed expenses of 1566; 1578
. retirement plans 3102
. sale of business 2625
. self-employment tax on *See "Self-employment tax"*
. taxable year 2807
. vehicles, business use, claiming expense
    deductions 1954
. withholding 4669
Self-employment tax
    generally . . . . 3140 et seq.
. adjusted gross income computation 3102
. clergy 3147
. components of 3141
. computation of 3149
. deductibility 1755; 1757
. deductions from 3143
. farmers . . . . 3148 et seq.
. income subject to 3142
. net earnings from self employment 3143
. optional methods of computing 3149
.. farmers 3149
. partners' net earnings 3144
. rates 1109
. refunds 4854
. returns 1210; 4713
. spouses 3145
. taxpayers subject to . . . . 3146 et seq.
Self-insurance 1255; 1607
Separate maintenance *See "Alimony"*
Separate returns
    generally 4704
. alternative minimum tax 3201
.. exemption amount 3203
. change to or from joint returns 4707
. controlled groups 3338
. dependents, exemptions for 3127
. election to itemize deductions 3113
. exemption for spouse 3118
. filing threshold 4701
. itemized deductions 3114
. personal exemptions 3117
. same-sex spouses 4705
. spouses' liability for tax and penalties 1203; 4704

Separate returns — Cont'd
. standard deduction 3112
. tax tables 1104
Separate share rule (trusts and estates) 3947
SEPs *See "Simplified employee pensions (SEPs)"*
Service charges 1211
Service organizations, tax exempt 4100
Services, satisfaction of debt with 1395
Settlement of tax disputes
. Appeals Division . . . . 4818 et seq.
. IRS initiatives 4805
. Tax Court petition, after filing of 4860
7-pay test, modified endowment contracts 1368
Severance damages 2437
Severance pay 1209; 3004
Sham transactions 2676
Sharecrop rentals 3143; 3146
Shareholders *See "Stockholders"*
Short period returns 4701; 4716;
    4727
. child tax credit 2355
. standard deduction 3112
Short sales
    generally . . . . 2639 et seq.
. capital gains and losses, limits on 2640; 2641
. dividends-received deduction, effect on 3313
. futures, commodity 2642
. hedging transactions 2642
. investment interest 1728
. securities futures contract, entering into to
    sell 2639
. worthless property 2643
Short taxable year *See "Taxable year"*
Short-term capital gains and losses . . . . 1848; 2600 et
    seq.; 2609
Short-term obligations
. acquisition discount 1328
. capital gains and losses
    generally . . . . 2634 et seq.
.. government obligations 2634
.. nongovernment obligations 2635
Sick pay
. information returns 4746
. PTO (paid time off) plans 4313
. withholding from wages 3008
. workers' compensation 1259
SIMPLE retirement plans
    generally . . . . 4382 et seq.
. catch-up contributions 4317; 4384
. early withdrawals 4344
. employee, defined 4383
. employers' eligibility 4383
. qualified salary reduction arrangements
    generally 4384
.. compensation, defined 4384
.. simple retirement account defined 4385
. rollovers 4360
. Roth IRA, conversion to 4371
. SIMPLE retirement account
.. contributions to 4386
.. defined 4385
.. distributions 4387
Simple trusts
. beneficiary, amount taxed to 3944
. character of income 3946
. defined 3933
. distributable net income, computation of 3935
. distribution deductions 3934
Simplified employee pensions (SEPs)
    generally . . . . 4377 et seq.
. catch-up contributions 4317

Simplified employee pensions (SEPs) — Cont'd
. employer contributions 4378
. . deduction for 4379
. employee treatment 4380
. information returns 4746
. salary reduction SEPs 4381
. withdrawals 4380
Single taxpayers
. alternative minimum tax exemption amount 3203
. income tax returns 4701
. itemized deductions 3114
. personal exemptions 3117
. spouses living apart treated as 3133
. standard deduction 3112
. tax tables 1102
Small business corporations
. alternative minimum tax 3205
. defined 2647
. "golden parachute" payments 1535
. investment companies *See "Small business
      investment companies (SBICs)"*
. qualified small business stock *See "Quali-
      fied small business stock"*
. refining costs, expensing election 1966
. returns 4726
. Section 1244 (SBC) stock
      generally . . . . 2644 et seq.
. . defined 2645
. . definition of small business corporation 2647
. . ordinary loss treatment 2645
. . . claim for, Form 4797 2646
. . stock losses . . . . 2644 et seq.
**Small business investment companies
      (SBICs)**
      generally 4205
. personal holding companies
. . classification as 3322
. . exemption from PHC tax 4205
. specialized small business investment
      companies *See "Specialized small bus-
      iness investment companies (SSBICs)"*
. stock
. . capital gains and losses 2631
. . losses 1781; 4205
. worthless stock or securities 1781
Small business trusts
. estimated taxes 3903
. late election relief 3358
. S corporation shareholders 3354; 3910
Small employers
. Archer medical savings accounts (MSA) 1528
. differential wage payment credit 2336
. health insurance credit 2332
. pension plan startup credit 2331
Soak up tax 2369
Social clubs
. membership costs 1568
. tax exemption 4100; 4107
. unrelated business income 4122
Social security benefits
. disabled 2348
. elderly 2348
. source of income not effectively connected
      with U.S 4642
. support, as 3124
. taxation of 1278; 1279
. withholding 3009; 4667
Social Security numbers *See "Taxpayer
      identification number (TIN)"*
Social security tax
. capitalization of 1620
. credit for employee tips 2327

Social security tax — Cont'd
. deductibility 1755
. deposit by electronic funds transfer 3028
. employees misclassified as independent
      contractors 3002
. errors in withholding and paying 3020
. excess withholding 2347
. household employees 3029; 3030
. Old Age, Survivors and Disability Insurance
      (OASDI) tax 3024
. rates of tax 1108; 3024
Social welfare organizations, exemption 4106
Software, computer
. amortization 1623; 1962;
                                                            1974; 1975
. bonus first-year depreciation 1934
. deductibility of costs 1623; 1962
. development costs 1623
. disabled access credit for 2323
. domestic production activities deduction 1616
. research credit 2319
. Section 179 expense election 1944
. summons for 4809
Soil and water conservation expenses
. farmers 4522
. partnerships 3756
. . items of income and deductions 3718
**Solar energy property or equipment, cred-
      it for**
      generally 2311; 2324
. advanced energy manufacturing project
      credit 2313
. residential energy efficient property credit 2359
Sole proprietorships *See also
      "Self-employed persons"*
. identification numbers 4752
. sale of, capital gains and losses 2625
. taxable year 2807
. vehicles, business use, claiming expense
      deductions 1954
Sound recordings
. amortization 1974
. capitalization of costs 1667
. depreciation 1908; 1927;
                                                                  1959
Source-of-income rules 2372; 4640
Spare parts, rotable and temporary 1658
**Specialized small business investment
      companies (SSBICs)**
. rollover of gain from sales of publicly traded
      securities into 2427
. . basis of 2505
Special use valuation
. decedent, property acquired from 2512; 2513;
                                                                  2672
. farm or business real property 5017
. lien for taxes 4911
Specified foreign financial assets, defined . . . 4673
Spin-offs, split-offs and split-ups 3547
. boot, receipt of 3561
. defined 3559
. partnerships 3783
. taxation of distributing corporation 3562
. taxation of shareholders 3561
. tax-free, requirements for 3560
Split-dollar life insurance
. charitable contributions 2115
. economic benefit regime 1266
. excise taxes, deductibility 1755
. loan regime 1266
Split-interest trusts
. private foundation rules 4126

Split-interest trusts — Cont'd
. returns 4733
Sporting events *See "Entertainment ex-*
    penses"
Sport utility vehicles (SUVs)
. heavy SUVs
. . exemption from luxury auto depreciation
    rules 1951
. . Section 179 limits on 1943
. luxury auto depreciation rules 1952
Spousal remainder trust 3959
Spouses
. alimony *See "Alimony"*
. alternative minimum tax exemption amount 3203
. capital losses 2611
. community property *See "Community prop-*
   erty"
. credit for tax withheld 2346
. dependent care credit 2350; 2352;
                                       2353
. dependents of 3127
. earned income credit 2341
. elderly or disabled, credit for 2348
. entertainment expenses of 1563
. estimated tax 3156
. foreign earned income exclusion 4612; 4615
. foreign housing cost exclusion 4613; 4615
. general business credit 2303
. generation-skipping transfer tax 5058
. gifts and transfers in trust, basis 2507
. grantor trust rules 3959
. group term life insurance coverage 1264
. individual retirement accounts (IRAs) 4352; 4355;
                                       4365
. joint ownership
. . estate tax 5011
. . income from 1202
. joint returns *See "Joint returns"*
. joint ventures 3701
. liability for tax 1203; 4704
. living apart 2353; 3133;
                                       4711
. marital deduction
. . estate tax . . . . 5021 et seq.
. . gift tax 5048
. net operating losses 1846
. noncitizen spouse, estate tax 5026
. overwithholding adjustments, same-sex
    spouses 3020
. passive activity losses, participation in ac-
   tivity . . . . 1831 et seq.
. personal exemptions 3118
. residence 1735; 2442;
                                   2444 et seq.
. returns . . . . 4704 et seq.
. Section 179 expense election 1941
. Section 1244 stock loss limits 2644
. self-employment tax 3145
. separate returns *See "Separate returns"*
. state tax deductions 1762
. third party, gifts to 5051; 5053
. transfers between 2447
. . basis 2524
. travel expenses 1551
. withholding 3015; 3016
Stamp taxes 4898; 4901
Standard deduction
    generally 3112
. alternative minimum tax 3209
. estates
    generally 3929
. . bankruptcy estates 3976

Standard deduction — Cont'd
. trusts 3929
. withholding allowance for 3016
Standard mileage rate 1560; 2120
Start-up expenses
    generally . . . . 1500 et seq.
. amortization . . . . 1500 et seq.;
                                   1964
. deduction . . . . 1503 et seq.
. defined 1501
. disposition of business 1503
. election to amortize 1502
. expansion of existing business 1505
. fruitless searches 1504
State and local governments
. officials
. . expenses of 3106
. . self-employment tax 3146
. tax credit bonds issued by, credit for hold-
    ers of 2366
State and local taxes
. capitalization 1620
. deductibility . . . . 1754 et seq.
. . death taxes 5027
. . sales tax vs income tax deduction 1756
. offset of federal tax refunds 4848
. penalties, deductibility 1613
. refunds of
. . alternative minimum tax 3209
. . information returns 4746
. . tax benefit rule 1205
. spouses 1762
Statute of limitations
. assessments
    generally . . . . 4830 et seq.
. . mitigation of statute on 4839
. collection of tax 4909
. like-kind exchanges 2423
. refund claims . . . . 4854 et seq.
Statutory employees 3002
. business-related expenses 3103
. self-employment tax 3146
Statutory merger 3544
Step-in-the-shoes transactions
. carry-over basis property 1911
. long-term contracts 2856
Stock *See also "Preferred stock"*
. basis
. . distributions to corporate partner, basis
    adjustments in connection with 3750
. . ESOP or EWOC, replacement for stock
    sold to 2504
. . identification of shares transferred 2496; 2497
. . S corporation shareholders 3369; 3371
. capital assets, as . . . . 2617 et seq.
. capital stock 2415
. "charitable bail-out" 2113
. closely-held corporations 5016
. compensation paid in 1523
. convertible, gain or loss on exercising 2681
. debt, exchange for 1395; 1710
. defined, transfers to corporation 3512
. distributions of by corporation 3540; 3560
. dividends *See "Dividends"*
. foreign corporation 3588; 4630
. holding period 2670
. installment sales 2454
. issuance of 3519
. options *See "Stock options"*
. personal holding companies 3323
. qualified small business stock *See "Quali-*
    fied small business stock (QSBS)"

Stock *See also "Preferred stock"* — **Cont'd**
. reacquisition expenses 1624
. redemption *See "Redemption of stock"*
. regulated investment company 2632
. reorganization exchanges . . . . 3545 et seq.
. repurchases by corporation . . . . 3526 et seq.
. restricted . . . . 1217 et seq.
. rights *See "Rights, stock"*
. sales or exchanges
. . consolidated returns 3341
. . controlled foreign corporations 4625
. . disposition by corporation of its own stock 2415; 3519
. . dividends, to whom taxed 1286
. . identification 2496; 2497
. . redemptions 3526; 3531;
                                                            3533
. . Section 306 stock 3535; 3536
. . Section 336(e) election to treat as asset
        transfers 3587
. . small business investment company
        (SBIC) 1781
. . small business stock . . . . 2644 et seq.
. . stock of same company, for 2414
. . tax-free exchanges . . . . 2413 et seq.
. S corporations 3355
. Sec. 306 . . . . 3535 et seq.
. Sec. 1244 . . . . 2644 et seq.
. small business investment companies
        (SBICs) 2631; 4205
. specialized small business investment
        companies (SSBICs) 2505
. theft losses 1799
. warrants 3512
. wash sales 2500
. worthless *See "Worthless stock or securi-
        ties"*
Stock bonus plans 4312; 4314;
                                                            4318; 4335

**Stock exchange, sale of stock on, time for
        reporting** 2410
Stockholders
. compensation of shareholder-employee 1517
. controlled foreign corporations . . . . 4622 et seq.
. distributions to, effect on earnings and prof-
        its 3523
. dividends, constructive or disguised 1289
. entertainment expenses in connection with 1566
. expenses of paid by corporation 1509
. family attribution rule waived on complete
        redemptions 3529
. gifts to and by 5039; 5040
. liquidation, gain on 3575
. loans to corporation 1855
. losses 1781
. partial liquidation of interest 3531
. passive foreign investment company . . . . 4628 et seq.
. reorganization, taxation in 3554
. S corporations . . . . 3351 et seq.
. Section 355 transaction, taxation in 3561
. termination of interest 3528; 3529
. transactions with corporation 2448
. use of corporate property 3327
Stock options
. compensation deduction 1525
. constructive ownership through 3323; 3534
. definition of stock 3512
. employee stock purchase plan options 1220
. incentive stock options 1221; 3209;
                                                            3213
. nonqualified deferred compensation 1275
. nonstatutory options 1219
. personal holding companies 3323

Stock options — **Cont'd**
. "put" or "call" options 2620
. withholding 3006
**Stock purchase as asset purchase (Sec-
        tion 338 election)** . . . . 3581 et seq.
Stock purchase plan 1220
Stock splits 1295; 2493
Stolen property . . . . 1799 et seq.
Strikes
. benefits 1283; 3006
. penalties 1613
**Stripped bonds or coupons, acquisition
        discount, accrual of** 1328
Students
. alien 4658
. dependency exemption, qualifying child for
        purposes of 3120
. dependent care credit, earned income limit 2352
. kiddie tax 3136
. qualified tuition reductions for employees of
        educational institutions 2217
. support of, charitable contributions 2122
. teaching or research, payments for 2218
Students loans, interest on . . . . 2222 et seq.;
                                                            4746

Subchapter S corporations *See "S corpo-
        rations"*
Subdividing land 2623; 2624
Subpart F income *See also "Controlled for-
        eign corporations (CFCs)"*
. defined 4624
. foreign tax credit 2371; 2372;
                                                            2374
Subsidiaries
. liquidations 3577; 3578
. transfer of assets to 3547
. worthless stock or securities 1781
Subsidies
. received by sponsors of qualified retiree
        prescription drug plans 1206
**Substantial authority for position taken on
        return** 4878
Substantially justified position of IRS 4863
Substantial presence test, aliens 4635; 4654
Substantiation
. business gifts 1592
. entertainment expenses
        generally . . . . 1561 et seq.
. . adequate records 1585
. . corroborated statements used to substan-
        tiate expenses 1587
. . loss of records 1588
. listed property expenses . . . . 1579; 1584 et
                                                            seq.
. meals, expenses of . . . . 1578; 1580 et
                                                            seq.
. medical expenses 1379
. travel expenses . . . . 1575; 1580 et
                                                            seq.
Summons on examination 4809
**Supplemental unemployment benefit
        plans (SUBs)**
        generally 4100
. nondiscrimination requirements 4108
. unrelated business income 4121
**Supplemental unemployment compensa-
        tion benefits, wages, treated as** 3004
Supplemental wages, withholding on 3011
Supporting organizations
        generally 4125
. information returns 4124; 4746

Support of dependents
. alimony, as 2159
. allocating support of several contributors to
    several dependents 3125
. child support 2159
. defined 3124
. legal obligation 3959
. multiple support agreement 3123
. overpayments applied to 4848
Surviving spouse
. alternative minimum tax exemption amount 3203
. annuities 1358
. deceased spousal unused exclusion
    amount 5029
. employer's payments to 1534
. estate tax
. . credit for prior transfers 5030
. . portability of unused exclusion 5029
. filing threshold 4701
. individual retirement accounts 4365
. inherited property 2672
. itemized deductions 3114
. joint returns 3132; 4708
. kidnapped child qualifying taxpayer for sta-
    tus as 3129
. marital deduction, estate tax . . . . 5021 et seq.
. personal exemptions 3117
. principal residence, exclusion of gain on
    sale 2442
. qualified terminable interest property 5008; 5023
. rollovers of pensions, etc 4365
. standard deduction 3112
. tax tables 1103
Suspended losses
. "at-risk" rules 1806
. passive activity losses 1837
SUVs *See "Sport utility vehicles (SUVs)"*
"Swap funds" 3517
Syndicates
. farming 4511
. partnership rules, exclusion 3705
Syndication fees 3707

T

Tables and charts
. applicable federal rates 1115; 1310
. automobile annual lease values 1233
. deductions, individual taxpayer average de-
    ductions 4804
. depreciation tables 1116
. . luxury autos 1952
. . optional MACRS rates 1912
. earned income credit 1112; 2339
. filing thresholds 4701
. inclusion amount
. . leased business automobiles 1117
. . leased non-auto listed property 1116
. income tax rates
. . corporate 1113
. . individuals . . . . 1101 et seq.;
                                   1111 et seq.
. . trusts and estates 1106
. life insurance
. . group-term cost 1263
. . IRS Table 2001 1266
. long-term tax-exempt rate 3569
. low-income housing credit applicable per-
    centages 2320
. minimum required distributions 4345
. percentage depletion 1978
. standard deduction 3112

Tables and charts — Cont'd
. tax calendar, 2014 due dates 1000
. tax tables, generally . . . . 1100 et seq.;
                                            3131
. valuation of annuities, life estates, term in-
    terests, remainders and reversions 5016; 5044
Taxable estate
. computation 5000; 5018
. nonresident aliens 5037
Taxable income
    generally 1206
. accumulated earnings tax 3318
. computation . . . . 3100 et seq.
. corporations 3304
. dividends-received deduction, limitation on 3311
. foreign, for foreign tax credit purposes 2371
. individuals . . . . 3100 et seq.
. insurance companies 4211
. partnerships 3717
. percentage depletion purposes, defined for 1978
. PHC income subject to penalty tax 3321
. real estate investment trusts 4202
. regulated investment companies 4201
. resident aliens . . . . 4633 et seq.
. S corporations 3359
Taxable year
    generally . . . . 2800 et seq.
. alternative minimum tax 2805
. calendar of due dates 1000
. change of 2814; 2815
. defined 2801
. DISCs 2809
. establishment of 2803
. estates and trusts 2808
. 52-53 week tax year 2802; 2805
. fiscal year 2800
. foreign sales corporations 2809
. partnerships 2812; 2813
. personal service corporations 2802; 2811;
                                            2813
. S corporations 2810; 2813;
                                     3356; 3367
. self-employed persons 2807
. short
    generally . . . . 2804 et seq.
. . corporation 4727
. . debtor, bankrupt 3975
. . depreciation for . . . . 1926 et seq.
. . estate, of 3948
. . estimated tax payments 3904
. . individual 3112; 4701;
                                           4716
. . partnerships 3773
. . standard deduction 3112
. . tax tables 3131
. . trust 3948
. termination of 3965; 3975;
                                           4828
Tax advice
. corporate dissolution or liquidation, deduc-
    tion of fees 3580
. false or fraudulent 4901
. return preparers 1253
Tax avoidance and evasion
. accumulated earnings penalty tax 3317
. assessment period, effect on 4835
. criminal penalties 4900
. economic substance, transactions lacking 4895
. expatriation rules 5037
. participation in confidential tax avoidance
    transactions, reporting 4749

Tax avoidance and evasion — Cont'd
. reallocation of income and deductions by
    IRS 2858; 2859
. Section 269 tax avoidance acquisitions 3565
Tax benefit rule, gross income 1205
Tax conventions *See "Treaties"*
Tax Court
    generally . . . . 4858 et seq.
. jurisdiction 4859
. penalties for using Court for delay 4898
. small tax claims in 4861
Taxes *See also specific type of tax*
. deductible . . . . 1754 et seq.
. interest on 1708
Tax-exempt income
    generally 1206
. armed forces 1223
. bequests and devises . . . . 1370 et seq.
. deductions allocable to
. . banks and trust companies 4209
. . complex trusts 3936; 3937
. . estates and trusts, generally 3924
. . foreign income 4616
. . nonbusiness expenses 2167
. . Puerto Rican residents 4618
. . simple trusts 3934; 3944
. earnings and profits, effect on 3525
. foreign-source income, moving expenses
    allocable to 1651
. gifts as . . . . 1370 et seq.
. interest
. . alternative minimum tax 3211
. . original issue discount 1313
. . regulated investment companies, divi-
    dends 1298
. . Social Security payments, effect of
    tax-exempt interest on taxability of 1279
. . state and local bonds 1331
. life insurance proceeds . . . . 1346 et seq.
. treaties, under 4639
Tax-exempt organizations *See "Exempt or-
    ganizations"*
Tax-exempt rate, long-term 3569
Tax-exempt use property
. depreciation 1932
. limitations on losses 1782
Tax-free exchanges
    generally . . . . 2320 et seq.
. basis of property acquired in . . . . 2482 et seq.;
                                                        2501
. . depreciable property 1911
. controlled corporations . . . . 3510 et seq.
. disposition by corporation of its own stock 2415
. government obligations 2416
. holding period 2674
. insurance policies 2417
. like-kind exchanges *See "Like-kind ex-
    changes"*
. livestock 4527
. reorganizations . . . . 3541 et seq.
. stock
. . Section 336(e) election to treat as asset
    transfers 3587
. . for stock of same corporation 2414
Tax home
. abroad, extension of time to file 4718
. foreign earned income/housing cost exclu-
    sion 4615
. travel expense purposes . . . . 1543 et seq.
Taxicabs
. depreciation 1951
. fare, de minimis fringe benefits 1246

Taxicabs — Cont'd
. transportation expenses 1555
Taxidermy property 2106
Tax liens *See "Liens"*
Tax litigation . . . . 4858 et seq.
Tax matters partner 4843
Taxpayer Advocate, National 4811
Taxpayer assistance order (TAO) 4811; 4837
Taxpayer identification number (TIN)
    generally 4752
. adoption expense credit 2354
. application for SSN 4752
. backup withholding, missing or incorrect
    TIN 3044
. child tax credit 2355
. dependent care credit 2353
. earned income credit 2341
. foreign person filing U.S. returns, Social
    Security numbers, inability to obtain 4752
. kiddie tax 3137
. nonperiodic distributions, election out of
    withholding 3040
. periodic payments, election out of withhold-
    ing 3038
. personal exemptions 3115
. return preparers 4750; 4753;
                                                        4888
Taxpayer rights, audits 4807
Tax preferences . . . . 3206 et seq.
Tax rates
. alternative minimum tax . . . . 3201 et seq.
. built-in gains tax 3362
. capital gains . . . . 2600 et seq.
. cash, unexplained, on 4828
. corporate 1113; 2614;
                                                        3303 et seq.
. estates and trusts 1106; 3901
. estate tax 1114; 5000;
                                                        5033; 5037
. generation-skipping transfer tax 5056
. gift tax 1114
. head of household 1105
. homeowners associations 4110
. individual income tax 1101; 1111;
                                                        3130 et seq.
. joint returns 1103
. minors (kiddie tax) 3135
. personal holding company tax 3320
. schedules 3130
. self-employment tax 1109
. separate returns 1104
. single individuals 1102
. Social Security and Medicare taxes 1108; 3024
. spouses living apart 3133
. surviving spouse 1103; 3132
. tables . . . . 1100 et seq.
. unemployment tax 1110
. U.S.-source income not effectively connect-
    ed with U.S. business 4642
. withholding, voluntary 3009
Tax return preparers
. advice by 1253
. copies of returns, furnishing, retaining 4750; 4888
. defined 4751
. disclosure of return information by 4888
. due diligence requirements, earned income
    credit 4888
. electronic filing of returns by 4703; 4750
. endorsing taxpayer's refund check 4888
. fees for return preparation, deductibility . . . 1513; 2165
. identification number of 4750; 4888
. IRS communication with 4808

References are to paragraph [¶] numbers.

Tax return preparers — Cont'd
. penalties on 4886
.. assessment 4835
.. criminal 4901
. preparers, list of, failure to maintain 4888
. registered tax return preparer (RTRP) requirements 4750
. signing returns 4750; 4886;
                                  4888
. suspension from practice 4888
. understatement of taxpayer's liability by 4835; 4886
. unreasonable position 4886
. willful or reckless conduct 4886
Tax returns *See "Forms"; "Returns"*
Tax sale losses 1789
Tax-sheltered annuities
   generally .... 4317; 4388 et
                                   seq.
. contribution limit 4391
. designated Roth (Roth 401(k)) accounts 4375
. distributions 4389
. "includible compensation," defined 4392
. salary-reduction agreements 4390
. "year of service," defined 4392
Tax shelters
. abusive *See "Abusive tax shelters"*
. cash method, use of by 2818
. confidential corporate tax shelters 4749
. economic performance 2833
. farming syndicates 3210; 4511
. prohibited transactions, excise tax 4113
.. disclosure to escape tax 4114
. settlement initiatives 4805
. tax-exempts acting as accommodation parties in, penalties 4894
Tax straddles
   generally .... 2653 et seq.
. conversion transactions 2665
. defined 2654
. loss deferral rule 2655
. mixed straddles, election for 2658
. nonregulated futures straddles 2655
. put or call options 2620
Tax tables .... 1100 et seq.
Teachers
. classroom expenses 2229
. education expenses 2228
. election to be paid ratably over 12 months,
   not subject to deferred compensation
   rules 1275
. professional societies, membership 1636
. retirement fund associations 4100
. strikes, penalties 1613
. students, teaching payments for 2218
Telephone
. distribution plants, depreciation 1918
. equipment, depreciation 1915; 1932
. expenses 1636; 1638
. tax payment by 3155
Telephone company, mutual 4100
Television
. election to expense production costs 1965
Tenancy by entirety, or in common *See*
   "Joint ownership"
Tentative minimum tax 2365; 3201
Tentative refund claim 4849; 4850
Terminable interest, marital deduction
   See "Qualified terminable interest prop-
   erty (QTIP)"
Terminally ill individuals, death benefits,
   acceleration of 1351

Termination assessment 4828
Term interests
. capital assets, as 2630
. estate tax valuation 5016
. gift of 2510
. gift tax valuation 5044
Terrorism
. disaster relief payments, exclusion from
     gross income 1207
. estate tax, special rate schedule for terror-
     ism victims 5033
. extensions of time for taxpayers affected by 4719
. military and U.S. civilian employees dying
     in combat or terrorist attacks, income
     tax relief 4715
. organization designated or identified as ter-
     rorist, suspension of exempt status 4100
Testing period
. partnership tax year determinations 2812
. personal service corporation definition 2811
. Section 382 limitation rules 3571
Theft losses
   generally 1799
. amount of 1800
. basis adjustment 2477
. deductibility .... 1773 et seq.;
                      1792; 1799 et
                      seq.; 3114
. estate, taxable 5018
. frozen bank deposits 1802
. involuntary conversions 2432
. net operating losses 1841
. nonresident aliens 4646
. time to deduct 1801
Thermal energy
. credit for combined heat and power system
   property 2311
Third parties
. alimony payments to 2157
. education expenses paid by 2202
. reimbursements by 1578
. summons, examination of returns 4809
. wrongful seizures, remedies for 4907
30-day letter .... 4814 et seq.
Throwback rules
   generally .... 3953 et seq.
. beneficiaries or grantors 3955
.. loans to 4620
. minors, distributions to 3954
Timber
. advance payments 2689
. amortization 1970
. capital expenditures 1659
. capital gain-ordinary loss (Section 1231)
   transactions .... 2687 et seq.
. depletion deduction 1976; 1978
. depreciation of assets used in cutting of 1915
. sales or exchanges 4667; 4746
. source of income 4642
Timeshares 1735; 2454;
                              4110
TIN *See "Taxpayer identification number*
   (TIN)"
Tips
. compensation, as 1211
. reporting with respect to
.. identification numbers 4752
.. information returns 4746
.. penalty for failure to report 4898
. Social Security credit for employee tips 2327
. substantiation, as incidental transportation
     expenses 1580

Tips — Cont'd
. withholding on 3005; 3011
Tobacco Transition Payment Program 4528
Tools 1559; 1635; 1914
Top-heavy plans 4329
Totten trust 5007
Trade discounts 2869
Trade-ins 2419
Trademarks and trade names
. amortization 1974; 1975
. business expenses 1622
. capital assets, as 2629
. like-kind exchanges 2419
. royalties 1345
Trade or business
. active conduct requirement
. . spin-ff, split-off, or split-up 3560
. bad debt deduction . . . . 1852 et seq.
. cash transactions exceeding $10,000 4746
. compensation for personal services in con-
     nection with . . . . 1515 et seq.
. defined 1777
. employees engaged in, expenses of . . . . 1631 et seq.
. entertainment expenses in connection with . . . . 1561 et seq.
. illegal, deductibility of expenses 1612
. insurance premiums as expenses of . . . . 1606 et seq.
. legal and accounting expenses . . . . 1603 et seq.
. losses . . . . 1776 et seq.
. miscellaneous expenses in connection with . . . . 1617 et seq.
. ordinary and necessary business expenses . . . . 1506 et seq.
. passive activity loss rules
. . activities in connection with trade or busi-
      ness 1823
. . definition of passive activity 1822
. . grouping activities 1824
. . portfolio income 1820
. payments of $600 or more 4743
. property held primarily for sale, charitable
     contributions 2107; 2108
. rent expense in connection with . . . . 1593 et seq.
. research and experimental expenses in
     connection with 1601; 1602
. sale of, capital gains and losses . . . . 2625 et seq.
. Section 179 expense election . . . . 1941 et seq.
. taxes, deductibility . . . . 1754 et seq.
. . interest on taxes 1708
. transportation expenses in connection with . . . . 1554 et seq.
. travel expenses in connection with . . . . 1541 et seq.
. trusts taxed as 3908
. unrelated . . . . 4121 et seq.
Training costs 1514
Transferees 4914
Transfer pricing 2858; 4877
Transfers
. commissions paid on 1662
. to controlled corporations . . . . 3510 et seq.
. to exempt entities 3579
. to foreign corporations 3588; 4661
. franchises, trademarks, or trade names 1622
. to health benefit accounts 4348
. taking effect at death 5006
Transportation *See also "Travel expenses"*
. automobile expenses 1558; 1560
. barriers, expense of removing 1621; 2695
. business expenses . . . . 1554 et seq.
. commuting 1231; 1556; 1559
. deductibility . . . . 1547; 1554 et seq.
. de minimis fringe benefits 1246
. education, expenses of 2204; 2227

Transportation *See also "Travel expenses"* — **Cont'd**
. expenses other than commuting 1555
. listed property 1584
. medical expense, as 2148
. mileage allowance 1560; 2120
. qualified transportation fringe benefits 1247
. services to charitable organizations 2120
. source of income 4640
. substantiating expenses 1580
. temporary work location 1557
. tools, transporting 1559
. unsafe conditions, furnished because of 1231
. U.S.-source income from 4651
Transportation industry
. meal expenses 1569; 1581
Transportation property, depreciation 1947
Travel expenses *See also "Transportation"*
. adequate records 1585
. away-from-home expenses . . . . 1541 et seq.
. business combined with pleasure . . . . 1547 et seq.
. charitable travel 2121
. companion 1551
. conventions . . . . 1549 et seq.
. cruise ship conventions 1550
. deductibility . . . . 1541 et seq.
. documentary evidence of 1586
. education, expenses of 2227
. foreign travel 1548; 1549
. home defined for purposes of 1543
. inadequate substantiation, remedies for 1588
. incidental expenses, deductions for 1581
. indefinite assignment away from home 1545
. job-hunting 1632
. lavish 1552; 2149
. luxury water transportation 1552
. medical expenses, as 2149
. military reservists 1553; 3102
. moving expenses 1648
. National Guard and reserve members 3102
. optional meal allowance 1581
. "overnight" trip away from home 1542
. . military reservists 1553
. per diem rule
. luxury water travel 1552
. . meals and lodging 1581
. pleasure combined with business . . . . 1547 et seq.
. professors 1636
. rental cars 1551
. spouse 1551
. substantiating expenses . . . . 1575; 1580 et
                                            seq.
. tax home . . . . 1543 et seq.
. temporary assignment away from home 1544
Treasury bonds
. inflation-indexed
. . Series I 1334
. . Treasury Inflation-Indexed Securities 1333
. issue price 1317
Treasury stock 2415; 3519
Treaties
     generally 4637; 4639
. branch-level interest tax 4648
. branch profits tax 4647
. penalties, civil 4898
. return positions, treaty-based 4639
. source of income rules 2372
. withholding exemption or reduction 4664; 4666; 4668
Trees, fruit or nut bearing
. accrual accounting 4510
. depreciation 1917; 1925; 1932; 4523

Troubled assets relief program (TARP)
. nonqualified deferred compensation, accel-
    eration in payment of 1275
. officer compensation deduction limit for
    companies whose troubled assets are
    acquired under 1519
Trucks and trailers
. alternative motor vehicle credit 2360
. annual lease value 1233
. cents-per-mile valuation method 1236
. depreciation 1915; 1932;
                                                1951 et seq.
. "inclusion amount" for leased MACRS
    trucks and vans 1117; 1957
. standard mileage rate 1560
Trustees *See "Fiduciaries"*
Trustee-to-trustee transfers
. eligible rollover distributions
. . exclusion for direct transfers 4310
. . qualified retirement plans 4359
. individual retirement accounts
. . changing nature of IRA contributions 4370
. . conversions to Roth IRAs 4371
. . one-time rollover to health savings ac-
    count (HSA) 4364
. withholding 3034; 3035
**Trust fund recovery penalty, responsible
    person** 4835; 4883
Trusts *See "Estates and trusts"*
Tuition
. above-the-line deduction for . . . . 2230 et seq.
. alimony, as 2157
. American opportunity tax credit 2202
. charitable contribution, as 2103
. Coverdell education savings accounts (ES-
    As) . . . . 2205 et seq.
. generation-skipping transfer tax 5058
. gift tax, applicability of 5047
. information returns 4746
. installment payments, interest on 1706
. Lifetime Learning credit 2203
. medical expense, as 2146
. qualified reduction of, employees of educa-
    tional institutions 2217
. qualified tuition and related expenses 2204
. qualified tuition programs *See "Qualified tu-
    ition programs (QTPs)"*
. support, as 3124

                            U

Underpayment
. economic substance, attributable to trans-
    actions lacking 4895
. employment taxes 3020
. estimated tax . . . . 3154; 3163 et
                                                        seq.
. interest on . . . . 1708; 4864 et
                                                        seq.
. penalty . . . . 3163 et seq.;
                                                4881; 4882;
                                                        4895
Understatement of tax
. aiding and abetting 4885
. foreign financial asset understatement 4879
. innocent spouse relief . . . . 4709 et seq.
. penalties *See "Penalties"*
. return preparer, by 4835; 4886
. substantial authority for tax treatment of
    item 4878
. substantial understatement 4878

Unearned income
. Medicare surtax on *See "Net investment
    income tax"*
. of minor . . . . 3135 et seq.
Unemployment compensation benefits
. employer, paid by 1282
. information returns 4746
. overpayments of 4848
. repayment of 3102
. taxability 1278; 1281;
                                                        1282
. withholding, voluntary 3009
Unemployment tax 1758; 3028;
                                                3029; 3030
. capitalization 1620
. credit for employers 1110
. deductibility 1755
. FUTA tax rate 1110
Unified audit procedures, partnerships . . . . 4840 et seq.
Unified credit
. estate tax 5033
. gift tax . . . . 5038; 5050 et
                                                        seq.
. nonresident aliens 5037
**Uniform acts for gifts or transfers to mi-
    nors** 5046
Uniform capitalization rules . . . . 1666 et seq.;
                                                4519 et seq.
Uniforms 1223; 1634
Unions, strike and lockout benefits 1283
Unitrust, charitable contribution 2116; 2119;
                                                2136; 3914
University basic research credit 2319
Unrelated business income
. charitable remainder trusts 3914
. exempt organizations
    generally 4121
. . debt-financed property 4123
. . defined 4122
Unstated (imputed) interest
. allocation 1311
. applicable federal rate 1310
. basis, inclusion in 2466
. deferred payment sales . . . . 1307 et seq.;
                                                        1707
. exceptions to rules 1312
. payments subject to rules 1308
. time for deduction 1743; 1750
. time for reporting 1337
. total unstated interest, defined 1309
U.S. Claims Court 4858; 4862
Useful life, depreciation . . . . 1900 et seq.;
                                                1960; 1963
Use of property
. adaptation to new or different use 1661
. charitable contribution of 2114
. MACRS depreciation, change in property
    use 1928
. residence, exclusion of gain on sale 2445
U.S. Foreign Corrupt Practices Act 4624
U.S. possessions
. charitable contributions 2124
. defined for purposes of travel expense de-
    ductions 1549
. foreign tax credit 2369
. income from . . . . 4618 et seq.;
                                                        4701
. net investment income tax 3153
**U.S. real property holding corporation
    (USRPHC)** 4649; 4650;
                                                        4671

**U.S. real property interest (USRPI), dispo-
sitions of**
  generally 3723; 4649;
                                            4671; 4752
. withholding 4662
U.S. source income
. corporations 4621
. deductions allocated between foreign in-
  come and 4641
. effectively connected income 4644
. foreign income treated as 2372
. nonresident aliens and corporations . . . . . 4637 et seq.
. not effectively connected with U.S. busi-
  ness 4642
. withholding 4667

V

Vacation
. home, expenses 1780
. pay
. . as compensation
    generally 1209; 1269
. . . withholding 3004; 3011
. . when deductible 1540
. PTO (paid time off) plans 4313
. trip
. . charitable deduction for 2121
. . medical expense deduction for 2149
. . prize, as 1214
. . travel expenses 1547; 1548
Valuation
. airplane flights, employer provided . . . . 1238 et seq.
. . personal and business flights included in
    trip 1238
. . seating capacity rule, noncommercial
    flights 1240
. . SIFL formula for noncommercial flights 1239
. . space available rule, commercial flights 1241
. alternate date, estate tax
    generally 5016
. . basis of property valued at 2512
. automobile, employer-provided
. . annual lease value table 1233
. . cents-per-mile method 1236
. . commuting value method 1237
. . daily lease value 1235
. . prorated annual lease value 1234
. . special valuation rules . . . . 1232 et seq.
. charitable contributions of property . . . . 2106 et seq.
. dividends 1292; 1296
. fringe benefits, generally . . . . 1230 et seq.
. gifts 5044; 5049;
                                              5051
. gross estate 5016
. inventories . . . . 2865 et seq.
. . farmers 4514
. misstatement of valuation, penalty 4877; 4887
. . undervaluation . . . . 4878 et seq.
. restricted stock 1217; 1218
. special use, estate tax 2513; 2672;
                                       4911; 5017
. stock options . . . . 1219 et seq.
Vehicles
. alternative fuel vehicle refueling property,
    credit for 2361
. alternative motor vehicle credit 2360
. charitable contributions 2138; 4115
. clean fuel vehicles 1951; 2695
. like-kind exchanges 2419
. plug-in electric vehicle credits 2362
. qualified fuel cell motor vehicle credit 2360

Vehicles — Cont'd
. qualified nonpersonal use vehicles
    (QNPUVs) 1947
. sport utility vehicles (SUVs) *See "Sport utili-
    ty vehicles (SUVs)"*
Vesting of benefits 4322; 4329
Veterans
. benefits 1224
. . disability benefits, refund claim period for
    overpayment resulting from 4854
. organizations
. . charitable 2102; 2125;
                                          4100
. . unrelated business taxable income 4122
. pension rights of returning veterans 4331
. work opportunity credit 2316; 2317
Video tapes and cassettes
. amortization 1974
. capitalization of costs 1667
. depreciation 1908; 1927;
                                          1959
Virgin Islands
. foreign corporation treatment 4638
. taxation of income from 4618
**Voluntary employees' beneficiary as-
    sociations (VEBAs)**
. exemption 4100
. nondiscrimination requirements 4108
. unrelated business income 4122
Volunteer firefighters *See "Firefighters"*

W

Wage bracket withholding 3012
Wagering *See "Gambling"*
Wages *See "Compensation for personal ser-
    vices"*
War profits tax 1755; 2369
Warrants, stock 3512
Wash sales
  generally 2461
. holding period for stock or securities, effect
    on 2670
. loss disallowance rule 2462
. stock acquired in 2500
Welfare benefit plans 1533; 1538
Wetlands 4522; 4525
Whistleblower awards
  generally 1206; 4903
. legal expenses in connection with 3108
Widows and widowers *See "Surviving
    spouse"*
Wind power
. advanced energy manufacturing project
    credit 2313
. credit for small wind energy property 2311
. renewable electricity production credit 2324
. residential energy efficient property credit . . . 2359
Withholding
  generally . . . . 3000 et seq.
. agent . . . . 4664 et seq.
. allowances 3014; 3016;
                                          3018
. backup . . . . 2346; 3043 et
                                          seq.
. certificate, Form W-4 . . . . 3014; 3018
. credit against tax for 2346; 2347
. deposit of taxes by electronic funds transfer 3028
. employer defined for 3001
. errors in 3020
. estimated tax, as 3159

Withholding — Cont'd
. exemptions 3006; 3015;
               3017; 4666 et
               seq.
. foreign entities, payments to 4672
. foreign tax credit 2371
. foreign taxpayers . . . . 4662 et seq.
. fringe benefits 3006; 3007;
               3010
. gambling winnings 3033
. gross income, withheld amounts included in 1209
. information returns 4665
. methods 3012; 3013
. nonpayroll taxes . . . . 3031 et seq.
. nonresident aliens . . . . 4663 et seq.
. partnership distributions to foreign partners 4670
. penalties with respect to 4898
. pensions, annuities and other deferred in-
      come, on
      generally . . . . 3034 et seq.
. . designated distributions 3036
. . election out of withholding . . . . 3038 et seq.
. . eligible rollover distributions 3035
. . nonperiodic distributions 3039; 3040
. . payment delivered outside U.S 3042
. . periodic payments 3035; 3037;
               3038
. qualified intermediary 4664
. rate, failure to treat payee as employee 3012
. refund of overpayments 4853
. returns 3019
. same-sex spouses 3020

Withholding — Cont'd
. sick pay 3008
. Social Security tax, excess withholding 2347
. source, at, nonresident aliens and foreign
      corporations 4663
. supplemental wage payments 3011
. tip income 3005
. U.S. real property dispositions 4671
. voluntary withholding agreements 3009; 4668
. wages, on . . . . 3000 et seq.
Wives and husbands *See "Spouses"*
Workers' compensation
      generally 1259; 1607
. assignment of liability for, amounts re-
      ceived for accepting 1382
Workers' compensation reinsurance or-
      ganizations 4100
Working capital
. accumulated earnings 3317
. portfolio income 1820
Work opportunity tax credit 2316; 2317
Work product privilege 4808
Worthless debts *See "Bad debts"*
Worthless stock or securities 1781; 2643;
               2644; 3341;
               3369; 4209;
               4854

Y

Yacht, entertainment expenses 1561; 1567

NOTES

NOTES

NOTES

NOTES

NOTES

HIGHLIGHTS
What's New on the Form 1040
Tax Calendar
Quick Reference Card

1   INCOME TAX RATES AND TABLES
FICA/FUTA, Depreciation Tables

2   INCOME
Taxable and Exempt, Compensation

3   DEDUCTIONS
    • Business Expenses

4   • Interest, Taxes, Losses,
Bad Debts

5   • Depreciation, Expensing,
Amortization of Intangibles

6   • Charitable Contributions,
Medical Expenses, Alimony

7   EDUCATION
Credits, Exclusions, Deductions

8   TAX CREDITS
Business, Personal, Foreign

9   SALES AND EXCHANGES
Tax-free Exchanges, Basis,
Installment Sales

10   CAPITAL GAINS AND LOSSES

11   TAX ACCOUNTING
Inventories

12   WITHHOLDING

13   INDIVIDUAL'S TAX COMPUTATION
Kiddie Tax, Self-Employment Tax,
Estimated Tax

14   ALTERNATIVE MINIMUM TAX

15   CORPORATIONS
Tax Computation, Estimated Tax,
S Corporations

16   CORPORATE TRANSACTIONS
Organization, Reorganizations,
Acquisitions, Liquidations

17   PARTNERSHIPS

18   TRUSTS-ESTATES-DECEDENTS

19   EXEMPT ORGANIZATIONS

20   BANKS
RICs, REITs, Other Special Corporations

21   RETIREMENT PLANS
401(k) Plans, IRAs, Roth IRAs, SEPs,
SIMPLE plans

22   FARMERS

23   FOREIGN INCOME-FOREIGN
TAXPAYERS

24   RETURNS AND PAYMENT OF TAX
Tax Return Preparers, Information Returns

25   DEFICIENCIES-REFUNDS-PENALTIES

26   ESTATE AND GIFT TAXES
Generation-Skipping Transfer Tax

27   INDEX

MARGIN INDEX
To use, bend book in half and follow margin index to page with black edge marker.

The left index column refers to the left bank of markers; the right index column
to the right bank of markers.